NEW VENTURE CREATION

A GUIDE TO ENTREPRENEURSHIP

The Irwin Series in Management and The Behavioral Sciences
L. L. Cummings and E. Kirby Warren *Consulting Editors*

NEW VENTURE CREATION

SECOND EDITION

A GUIDE TO ENTREPRENEURSHIP

Jeffry A. Timmons, A.B., M.B.A., D.B.A.
Professor of Entrepreneurial
  Studies and Management
Babson College
Babson Park, Massachusetts

—with—

Leonard E. Smollen, B.S., M.S.
Executive Vice President
Venture Founders Corporation
Waltham, Massachusetts

Alexander L. M. Dingee, Jr., B.S.
President
Venture Founders Corporation
Waltham, Massachusetts

1985

RICHARD D. IRWIN, INC.
Homewood, Illinois   60430

ISBN 0-256-03476-1

Library of Congress Catalog Card No. 85–060245

Printed in the United States of America

1 2 3 4 5 6 7 8 9 0 ML 2 1 0 9 8 7 6 5

Dedication

To Paul T. and Edith Y. Babson and their son, Donald, whose unprecedented generosity and support created the Paul T. Babson Professorship in Entrepreneurial Studies, which made this second edition possible. Entrepreneurs, investors, and entrepreneurship educators, researchers, and students share a debt of gratitude for their pioneering efforts and contributions to the rebirth of entrepreneurship in America.

Foreword

The creation of new business ventures is vital both to our society and to the many individuals who will attempt to create them. For society, recent experience has shown that new ventures are the primary source of new employment opportunities. New ventures are the fountains of innovation. They are the most efficient mechanisms for trial and error strategic experimentation with new concepts and technologies. They may well be the grease that prevents the friction created by social, technological, and economic change from destroying our society. For the individual, new ventures have been the mechanism for upward economic mobility. Even if dreams of wealth and achievement have not been fulfilled, many individuals have found in new venture creation a mechanism for gaining control over their own lives. Through new ventures they have achieved the satisfaction of self-fulfillment.

This book, *New Venture Creation,* has taken on an awesome task. It is designed to help you, the reader, understand the phenomenon of entrepreneurship as it applies to you. Entrepreneurship in this sense is not simply the question of whether you are prepared to launch your own new venture. This book treats entrepreneurship as the meeting of an opportunity, an individual, and the environment. The book is designed to help you assess each of these elements and to study the fit among them. You will understand this combination better as you work to develop your business plan and to prepare its implementation.

The book is not theoretical. It is based on the experience of the authors as investors, venture founders, and teachers. New cases, concepts, and sections have been added to this second edition to reflect both changes in the environment and the emergence of new tools, new sources of information, and new research findings. You cannot approach the book casually. It will demand thought, careful analysis, and even multiple iterations if you are to get the most from it.

The key to successful entrepreneurship is understanding opportunity. Most business failures arise from two sources: the opportunity is not real, or the means required to pursue it are not available. The first section of the book helps you to understand how to find, to analyze, and to pursue an opportunity. It helps with that difficult process of generating new business ideas. You are then led to examine the way in which ideas can be screened in order to see whether they might really be opportunities. This section is outward looking. It recognizes that no product, service, or technology will be the basis of a successful entrepreneurial venture unless it meets the test of the market. You must find customers and create a sustainable competitive niche. The good entrepreneur knows that the goal is to find a place in which his or her skills give an unfair advantage.

The second major section shifts the focus to the most difficult and personal area—yourself. The founders are of critical importance to every venture. Self-knowledge is critical to success. This section looks at some modern research findings that go well beyond the search for the "entrepreneurial personality." The state of the art shows that entrepreneurs are both born and made. Practical suggestions are made that will enable you to learn more about how successful entrepreneurs think, feel, and act. The section explores what you will need to know and when you may need to know it. It helps you to develop your own Management Competency Inventory so that you can thoughtfully examine the fit of your own skills with the opportunity that you are considering pursuing.

The section goes beyond your individual hopes, needs, and desires. Experience has shown that teams are most likely to succeed. Not necessarily teams of equals, but teams with balanced skills and attributes. This section helps you to think about the development of the team by looking at the important issues of member choice, climate creation, and the problems of sharing the possible success. You will get practical advice about the rewards and pitfalls that are common in the building of teams for entrepreneurship.

The individual entrepreneur is faced with another set of critical personal choices. These have to do with family relationships and ethical dilemmas. These two issues are often key to the success or failure of the entrepreneur. The great pressures that may build in these areas can ultimately determine success or failure. Some examples and practical guidelines from experience are given.

The section ends with a series of assessment exercises. These are designed to help you to better your understanding of yourself, your partners, and the developmental path that you have chosen.

The third section examines the environment for entrepreneurship. This environment is the major source of the resources that will be available to you as an entrepreneur. Use of other people's resources will be critical: their skills, knowledge, energy, and money. This section helps you to develop the attitude necessary in the process of acquiring the use of other people's resources. It then helps you to develop the business plan that is so vital both to plan what resources you need when and also to help in raising them. Considerable attention is paid to how a business plan can most easily and effectively be prepared. Guidelines and exercises will help you along your way to the development of a business plan that will work as both a planning and a selling document.

The financing of your venture is treated as a separate section in the organization of the book. You are led through the sources of capital and the nature of their preferred investments. First, you will be helped to assess what kind of capital you need: equity, debt, or grant. Based on your needs, guidelines are given to help you approach traditional venture sources, lenders, and other investors in an efficient and effective manner.

If you take advantage of the advice that you have been given and the analysis that you have done, you may actually get a venture under way. The final two chapters will help you to prepare for the inevitable problems that follow start-up and to think about your harvest strategy as part of the initial business plan. No book can list all of the problems that you might eventually run into. This section simply gives some helpful rules for addressing some of the most common ones. Generic responses to problems are examined, and simple strategies for success are outlined. The consequences of different options are explored. The practical examples of successful entrepreneurs are studied.

Using This Book

This book is not designed for skimming. It is rich with examples, samples, and exercises for the mind and for the pencil. As you focus on starting a venture, you will get the most out of it if you devote the time and concentration necessary to try the exercises, to study the cases, and to apply your "learning by doing" toward the realization of your entrepreneurial dream.

This book is unlike many books that are designed simply to motivate you toward entrepreneurship. Instead, it is designed to help you to discover or, for many, to reinforce the notion that entrepreneurship can unleash enormous personal energy and creativity. It then helps you to increase the tools, know-how, and resources that you have already accumulated and to direct your energy toward attaining your entrepreneurial aspirations. It is a guidepost for a journey that is both difficult and rewarding. It will show you many of the signposts that have been planted in the hard ground by others who have gone before. Its rules and guidance can save you time and money and prevent many time-consuming errors. It cannot accomplish its goals unless you personally meet the challenges that it sets forth.

Remember, where entrepreneurship is concerned: "Today is the first day of the rest of your life."

Howard H. Stevenson
Sarofim-Rock Professor of Business Administration
Harvard University
Graduate School of Business Administration
Boston, Massachusetts

Preface

New Venture Creation—its models, methods, and illustrations—is built on knowledge and experience gained from working with real entrepreneurs launching real companies. The first edition, written in 1975–76, contained what were then state-of-the-art concepts and guidelines that the authors had developed and used in their own venture capital firm. Now, ten years later, the revised edition incorporates our cumulative learning curves and scar tissues gained through helping more entrepreneurs launch more companies. We have applied and refined our approaches to venture capital investment and business development, not only in this country, but also in Canada, the United Kingdom, and Sweden.

In addition, we have included a wealth of new information drawn from the venture capital industry and from the research of scholars in academia and government. Finally, our knowledge base has been enriched by the many students who have used our text in the classroom and then gone forth to start their own businesses. The consensus of real-world entrepreneurs and investors about the first edition was: It works! The second edition, the authors believe, will work even more effectively.

0.1.1 Eight Times Greater Number of Entrepreneurs among Former Students since 1973

One relevant question is: What has occurred among college students and MBAs who took our New Venture Creation courses and utilized the first edition? If you are a student using the book with aspirations to start a company of your own, you will be interested in the track records of some of our former students who used the first edition. To get our answers, we conducted a modest follow-up survey of former students and compared their venture creation activity with that of a matched random sample of their business school contemporaries (the "control group").[1]

Of course, no direct causal connection can be inferred between completion of a course and subsequent entrepreneurial activity. To establish such a connection, an immense number of variables would have to be sorted out, and a considerable amount of time and money would be necessary to do so. And we would certainly expect a large self-selection bias among the entrepreneurially inclined students who opted for such a course in the first place. Also, it would have been nice to have long-term performance data on the firms they own: What has been their level of attainment?

Though comparative figures are hard to come by, the results of the survey are worth noting.

Nearly 40 percent of the students at Northeastern University graduating be-

[1] Jeffry A. Timmons, "A Survey of Entrepreneurship Alumni of Northeastern University, 1973–81," unpublished paper, June 1982.

tween 1973 and 1981 who took at least two courses covering the core topics in *New Venture Creation* were active owners of their own companies by 1981.[2] This is nearly eight times the rate at which the other NU business school graduates in our survey became entrepreneurs. In this 1981 follow-up research to learn what became of graduates, we found that 40 percent was a significantly greater proportion than that of the random sample of other students. Only 5 percent of the sample of other business school graduates started their own firms during this same period. Not surprisingly, the general curriculum of at least this business school appears to neither attract nor produce entrepreneurs. Yet, quite the opposite seems to be true among the graduates of our courses, judging by this quite limited sample. We do not think that this was an accident. Nor do we argue that the courses were the sole factor influencing the results.

How might these figures compare with the figures for other groups? Again, while we are aware of no directly comparable data, we offer the following:

> Among the adult working population in the United States, about one person in eight is self-employed.
>
> Among the MBA class of 1977 at Harvard Business School, a group roughly contemporary with our NU sample, about 11 percent claimed to be self-employed. Most would argue that young people don't attend HBS to become entrepreneurs, yet about 25–30 percent of its graduates end up as heads or principals in their own companies.
>
> Babson College (Wellesley, Massachusetts), a business school with an entrepreneurial heritage and reputation, has found that about 25 percent of its graduates are self-employed CEOs or principals in a smaller firm.

We do not pretend that these are matched samples, or that our book and the courses made the sole difference in the substantially greater entrepreneurial activity among the NU graduates in our classes. Yet, the 40 percent figure should give you heart.

0.1.2 A Few "Real-World" Experiences

To illustrate the variety of situations in which entrepreneurs have used our approach successfully, we have chosen a few examples both in this country and abroad.

> Venture Founders Corporation, a venture capital firm that we founded in 1970 to help develop and invest in start-up and early stage companies, has been the means through which we have tested, refined, and applied our approach to launching and building growth ventures. One measure of our success is the confidence that investors have placed in us: a series of investment pools now totaling nearly $50 million.

Some of the ventures that we have helped include:

> A Massachusetts entrepreneur with a proven innovation for replacing the wave soldering method with printed circuit boards. With some consultation and a small infusion of capital this entrepreneur built his firm to nearly $7 million in sales. In mid-1984 the firm was purchased for $15 million.

---

[2]These two courses were New Venture Creation and Opportunity Analysis and Risk Capital, both of which were developed and taught by Professor Timmons.

A Canadian husband and wife team manufacturing private label diapers and sanitary napkins. In 1977 their sales were $130,000, with a net loss of $30,000. With a fully developed business plan and assistance in raising capital they are projecting sales of $47 million in 1985.

In these and other successful instances we have first recognized strong entrepreneurs and then worked with them to develop strong business plans.

A gratifying spin-off of our approach has been:

Kentucky Highlands Investment Corporation in London, Kentucky. In 1972 KHIC was the first client with which we worked to find, screen, and invest in start-up and early stage ventures with high potential. In rural America, working against odds in an economic environment that few entrepreneurs would relish (let alone investors with a Silicon Valley mind-set), we faced a great challenge. Today KHIC is one of the most successful Community Development Corporations in the country.

In 1974 our track record helped convince Scottish and English institutional investors to back our English subsidiary, Venture Founders, Limited, the first U.S. venture capital firm to operate in the United Kingdom. Interestingly, we found that our first challenge was not to raise capital but rather to explain the American method of venture capital investment to a culture accustomed to thinking of venture capital as just another type of debt investment—including annual interest fees and minimum management assistance. The discovery that our firm would be a partner as well as a lender brought us much attention in the European financial community and, judging from the three pools that we have raised to date, totaling nearly $50 million, a degree of investor confidence as well. Our investments have included:

One of the first firms to offer a product to enable word processors made by different manufacturers to communicate with one another. In a short time sales had reached several million pounds, and the company now has entered the U.S. market.

Finally, in Sweden, SVETAB and a sister firm, Investkontakt AB, have adopted our methods to build their own venture capital firm. Since 1980 they have raised nearly $20 million, and they now have over three dozen companies in their portfolio. Over 40 venture capital firms have been launched in Sweden since 1980.

Of particular note is the fact that our activities have spanned a range of technologies—high, low, and no—and businesses whose output includes both products and services.

0.1.3 Research and Collaboration

In addition to working directly with entrepreneurs, the authors have collaborated with organizations both here and abroad to develop programs to foster new venture creation. In the course of preparing and conducting venture capital seminars in the United States, Sweden, Australia, the United Kingdom, Canada, and the Philippines, the authors have worked with such groups as the publishers of *Venture Capital Journal,* government departments and banks in Sweden, the Ministry of Industry and the Department of Science and Technology in Australia, the World Bank, and universities in each sponsoring country.

Additional research on venture capital, the commercialization of technology, and the development of higher-potential ventures and their implications for national policy has been made possible by such sponsors as the National Science Foundation.

0.1.4   If It Works, Keep Going...

We have been gratified and encouraged by the results that have been obtained from this book and by the favorable response that we have had to it. We do not believe that there will ever be the perfect book for all entrepreneurs and for all ventures. Nor do we believe that it will ever be possible to enclose such a book under one cover. But we are reasonably confident now, based on responses both from real-world entrepreneurs and from teachers and students of entrepreneurship, that this book addresses the vital issues that you need to consider: the founder(s), the opportunity, and the needed resources. It contains the substance about these driving forces behind new venture creation that you need to assess for yourself, to digest, and to apply. We know of no better way to "get the odds in your favor" and thereby become an exception to the failure rate. The book does so in a way that is understandable, practical, and informative. And, most important, we believe that the approach has proven itself in the real world.

0.2   APPROACH AND CONTENT

The approach and content of this book, as explained above, are rooted both in real-world application and in several years of refinement in classrooms and new venture workshops. The approach is based on three important notions: first, the individual can make an enormous difference in the success of a venture; second, pattern recognition of opportunities and critical issues can be developed; and third, learning-by-doing and involvement are superior to conventional lecture and learning-by-rote methods of education. No doubt about it: there is no substitute for the real thing—actually starting a company. But short of that, it is possible to expose students to many of the vital issues, to provide them with role models and case examples, and to immerse them in the development of a business plan, thereby compressing key learning experiences.

There are lots of ways to do this, of course. Certainly, many of the more subtle and "gut level" aspects of deciding to launch, and then actually launching, a venture can only be appreciated by doing the real thing. Other important aspects—such as being able to tell the difference between a good idea and a good opportunity and being able to gauge whether you have the relevant experience and commitment to take the plunge now—can be gained through a course on new ventures, which often includes involvement in all the presteps for starting a business, and occasionally even results in a start-up. And there is a substantial body of knowledge that entrepreneurs need to acquire if they are to get the odds in their favor, prior to taking and while taking the start-up plunge, including knowing where to look for ideas, knowing how to determine the difference between an idea and an opportunity, knowing what the risks and trade-offs are, knowing how to assess and shape a personal entrepreneurial strategy, knowing how to determine whether you need a team and how to shape one, knowing how to use microcomputers, knowing that cash flow is king, knowing how to identify the minimal resources necessary, knowing how to develop a business plan, knowing where to raise capital and how to get it, knowing how to value and finance the venture, and knowing how to prepare for a harvest.

The design and flow of the book are aimed at creating knowledge, skills, awareness, and involvement in the process and critical aspects of creating a new venture and then making it grow.[3] Ideally, having a solid idea for a business that you actually want to start, or be a part of, is the most constructive project for such a course. Each chapter will come alive with direct application to your proposed venture, culminating in the development of a business plan. What follows is an overview of how each chapter builds this learning-by-doing and pattern recognition process.

Chapter 1, "The Entrepreneurial Process," is an overview chapter introducing the framework and foundation for the book. It examines the role of three driving forces behind entrepreneurial success: the lead entrepreneur and team, the opportunity, and the required resources. It shows why these are the essential ingredients sought by entrepreneurs, venture capitalists, and others. The Mountain Ventures, Inc. (A) case describes two young entrepreneurs who are considering leaving their current jobs to start a new venture.

Part I of the book focuses on the opportunity.

Chapter 2 discusses new venture ideas and where they can be found. An "idea generation" assignment will help you to identify your own personal criteria for an idea that can be a serious opportunity for you. Numerous sources, including the latest computer networks and databanks, are noted. The chapter concludes with the Beantown Seafoods (A) case, an actual student business plan for a start-up idea.

Chapter 3 develops some tools and criteria for evaluating and screening ideas. Entrepreneurs are rarely lacking in ideas—they have dozens of them. The hard part is recognizing the difference between a good idea and a good opportunity: the former are limitless; the latter are a select few. Evaluating an idea and shaping it into an opportunity are part of the entrepreneurial craft.

The Venture Opportunity Screening Guide in Chapter 4 is a new tool to help you focus on the opportunity and the marketplace so that you can increase the chances that your idea is also a sound opportunity. This guide should be xeroxed and completed as early as possible. It will often help you to spot fatal flaws in your ideas and to find a new opportunity before you are locked into "just another idea" bound for nowhere. It will also help you to decide whether it is worth the effort to develop a complete business plan for your idea.

Part II focuses on the lead entrepreneur and the founders; *you* can make an enormous difference.

Chapter 5, "The Entrepreneurial Mind," discusses new knowledge about entrepreneurs: who the entrepreneurs are—and who they are not; what the difference is between a job and a high-potential venture; myths and realities about the entrepreneur; how entrepreneurs are born and made better; and the acquirable

[3]At Babson College this real experience is encouraged by the annual competition for the Philip Charm Entrepreneur Prize, created by Mr. Leslie Charm, '64, in honor of his father. This $4,000 prize is awarded to the student or group of students presenting the business plan judged to have the best promise for implementation. The judges are outside entrepreneurs, venture capitalists, and other practitioners. It is hard to imagine a more suitable climax to the experience of preparing a business plan than the opportunity to put it into action.

and learnable attributes and philosophies of successful entrepreneurs. The chapter also discusses the "nonentrepreneurial mind": what to look out for in partners and presidents, whether you work with them or for them or you invest in them.

"The Entrepreneurial Manager" is the focus of Chapter 6. It addresses both the distinctions and the overlaps between the entrepreneurial and the administrative domains. What do entrepreneurial managers need to know to start, to survive, and to grow? What competencies are needed? What is different about managing rapid growth? And what about corporate entrepreneurial management? The chapter includes the Management Competency Inventory, which will aid you in assessing these issues and competencies.

"The New Venture Team," the subject of Chapter 7, is necessary in order to build a higher-potential business. Over half of the teams formed end in divorce in the first five years, their conflicts usually crippling or destroying the venture. What are the issues you need to consider, what are the traps, how will ownership be divided, and how can these matters be addressed—in advance and along the way? The chapter provides examples, a framework, and an exercise to help you sort out these complex subjects.

Chapter 8 addresses "The Family Venture," a special case of the team. All the complexities of a nonfamily team become compounded when family members or relatives are involved. The chapter concludes with the Beantown Seafoods (B) case, which examines some of the father-son and family issues in a growing venture.

According to a recent study, 72 percent of the company presidents attending Harvard's Smaller Company Management Program said that ethics had a definite place in the curriculum of business schools.[4] "Personal Ethics and the Entrepreneur," Chapter 9, gives this vital topic only a portion of the attention that its importance warrants.

Chapter 10, "Shaping a Personal Entrepreneurial Strategy," provides a completely integrated self-assessment and goal-setting framework. The chapter will enable you to address many of the important questions you may have about "taking the plunge." It will result in your shaping a personal strategy for acquiring the know-how, experience, and apprenticeship that are needed to get the odds of success on your side.

"Necessary Resources: Recognizing, Locating, and Controlling Them" are the core issues of the four chapters in Part III.

Chapter 11 examines how successful entrepreneurs approach resources and use other people's resources. Such entrepreneurs focus on minimizing, controlling, and using resources rather than just on owning them. The process of selecting and managing outside professionals is also examined.

Chapter 12 discusses the microcomputer, the "entrepreneurial tool for the 80s." Why the revolution in the use of the microcomputer is occurring, why the spreadsheet is queen, and how the microcomputer can help entrepreneurs are among the key issues that we examine in this chapter. Applications software is discussed, along with specific steps for getting started and cautions and pitfalls that you should be alert to. We describe how you can use the spreadsheet—if you aren't already doing so—to model your start-up.

[4] Jeffry A. Timmons and Howard H. Stevenson, "Entrepreneurship Education in the 80's," presented at the 75th Anniversary Entrepreneurship Symposium, Harvard Business School, Boston, 1983.

Chapter 13 discusses what a business plan is, why you should prepare one—even if you aren't seeking outside capital—and how to go about it. The Rapidrill Business Plan case at the end of the chapter presents an actual plan for analysis and discussion.

Chapter 14 presents a revised and enhanced "Business Plan Guide" as a tool for shaping a highly professional business plan.

"Financing Entrepreneurial Ventures" is the theme of Part IV.

Chapter 15 is a comprehensive discussion and summary of all the sources of capital available to entrepreneurs, including debt and equity and private and governmental sources. Summary tables and specific criteria show the latest developments in venture financing. Also included are recent changes in the securities laws that affect private placements and partnerships. Venture capital is discussed in detail.

Chapter 16 discusses at length how to obtain capital from venture capital firms, informal capital sources, banks, and other commercial lenders. The chapter also discusses the valuation of the venture, the negotiation and structuring of the deal, and the investment agreement. The Genetics Labs case is an actual start-up that provides a framework for determining the valuation and actually negotiating the investment share price with classmates.

Part V deals with "Life after Start-Up."

Chapter 17, "Entrepreneurs in Action: Some Examples," describes the anatomy of the iterative process by which entrepreneurs gain their "apprenticeship" and eventually achieve success.

Chapter 18, "The Harvest and Beyond," discusses why a harvest goal is important for entrepreneurs, the harvest options, how to craft a harvest strategy, and some of the issues beyond achieving a harvest, including this unavoidable reality: You can't take it with you.

The appendixes include a discussion of the legal documentation of a venture capital investment agreement, the legal process by which such an agreement is reached, sample term sheets, stock restriction and vesting agreements, and the Robert Morris Associates database.

The book concludes with an annotated bibliography of publications, both for general reference and for specific sources of information.

0.3 ABOUT THE AUTHORS

Collectively, the authors now represent over 40 years of experience in conceiving, launching, and building their own venture capital firm and working with entrepreneurs in dozens of emerging growth companies across a wide range of technologies and businesses. They have taught courses in New Venture Creation and Business Plan Development to students and entrepreneurs across the country. They have participated in international venture capital seminars. They have conducted research on venture capital, the commercialization of technology, and high technology and job creation. In short, they are attuned to every aspect of the latest developments in new venture creation.

Jeffry A. Timmons
Leonard E. Smollen
Alexander L. M. Dingee, Jr.

Acknowledgments

The original book, and now its revision, is a cumulative effort, reflecting the encouragement, thinking, and achievements of many associates, entrepreneurs and venture capitalists, former teachers and students, current students, colleagues, and friends.

Much of the materials and concepts in this book stems from the doctoral dissertation research of Jeffry A. Timmons at the Harvard Business School. Another major source of information has been his ongoing work with his cofounders and associates at Venture Founders Corporation to devise new ways to find, evaluate, fund, and grow high-potential ventures—with real-world applications in the United States, Canada, the United Kingdom, and Sweden. A third source of knowledge and feedback has been Professor Timmons' course development work, first with the new venture courses at Northeastern University and then with the new venture development and financing courses at Babson College.

Our early interest in pursuing this area of effort and eventually in sharing the results of our work can be credited to many. We were especially inspired and encouraged by Paul R. Lawrence, Arthur N. Turner, and David McClelland of Harvard University; George H. Litwin, formerly of the Harvard Business School; and Richard C. Whitely and John Humphrey of the Forum Corporation.

In addition to those who were so helpful to the development of the first edition, numerous others have lent their intellectual capital and experience to the development of the revised edition.

Above all, we wish to thank Nancy B. Tieken for her tremendous, tireless efforts in assisting us with the revision. Without her cheerful and diligent help as an editor, reviser, rewriter, and researcher the project could not have been completed. These efforts were made possible by the generous support of the Paul T. Babson Chair, endowed by the Babson family. Our wide support and encouragement at Babson began at the top with President William Dill and Vice President Melvyn Copen and included help from Deans Bayer and Deneault and Professors Kassarjian, Cohen, and Hornaday. Connie Stumpf and her word-processing crew could not have been more professional in getting the manuscript completed. We are most appreciative.

The shaping and crafting of the revision were also influenced by numerous exchanges of ideas and experiences between Jeffry Timmons and his colleagues and good friends Sarofim-Rock Professor Howard H. Stevenson and entrepreneur and lecturer John Van Slyke, both at the Harvard Business School.

Over a hundred researchers have contributed to the Babson Entrepreneurship Research Conferences, begun in 1981 by Professor Karl Vesper, while serving as Paul T. Babson Professor. This rich body of knowledge has added to our thinking and provided a source of data totally unavailable for the first edition. We are especially mindful of the work of Professors Block, Boyd, Brockhaus, Brown, Bruno and Tyebjee, Bygrave, Churchill, Cooper, Feigen, Gasse, Hoy, Hutt, Kirchoff, Knight, MacMillan, Miner, Mitton, Roberts, Ronstadt, Sexton, Shapero, Smith, Tarpley, Vesper, and Wetzel.

Our practical knowledge and earlier research of the venture capital industry have been enhanced by the publications and work of our friends and colleagues Stanley E. Pratt and Norman D. Fast, founders of Venture Economics and publishers of *Venture Capital Journal,* Wellesley Hills, Massachusetts.

In Sweden the founding management teams of Investkontakt AB and SVE-TAB were wonderful hosts and co-workers and made innumerable innovations in applying our earlier concepts and approaches to their venture capital and business development activities. These teams include Hakan Raihle, Morgan Olsson, Ingvar Svenson, Gunnar Olofgors, Lars Bostrom, Per Wahlstrom, and their staffs.

Further fine-tuning occurred when these concepts and approaches were applied in the United Kingdom. Contributing to this effort were Brian Haslett, Jack Peterson, Jack Hayes, and Paul Croke of Venture Founders and Charles Cox and Rob Ashmeade of VF in the United Kingdom. Professor Chris Harling of Cranfield Business School was an extraordinary co-worker in this effort.

Mr. Joel R. Pitlor has spent hundreds of hours with us in working with start-up entrepreneurs around the United States. His boundless insight and creativity in our efforts to be more effective in working with start-up and growth-minded entrepreneurs have been, and continue to be, invaluable.

If we listed all of the entrepreneurs and venture capitalists whose experience and insight have touched us over the years, the list would be lengthy indeed. We are most appreciative of them all, and we especially want to thank Doug Kahn, Brian Dwyer, Joe Frye, John Bray, J. C. Egnew, John Moore, Art Beisang, Ken DaFoe, Fred Alper, Karl Baumgartner, Don Spigarelli, Bill Egan, Harry Healer, Dan Gregory, Arthur Little, Jim Morgan, Bill Congleton, Earl Linehan, Allan Harle, Colin Chapman, Ken Fisher, Bill Poduska, Bill Foster, Richard Testa, Burt McMurtry, Brent Rider, Howard Head, and Paul Kelley.

Jeffry Timmons' work with his good friend and colleague David Gumpert of *Harvard Business Review* on articles and two other books helped to make the writing of this revision easier.

We are most appreciative to Richard J. Testa of Testa, Hurwitz and Thibeault, Boston, for contributing his excellent article, "The Legal Process of Venture Capital Investment," reproduced as Appendix II from *Pratt's Guide to Venture Capital Sources,* 8th edition.

We are also grateful to Robert Morris Associates of Philadelphia for permission to use its "Annual Statement Studies" (Appendix I).

Without the help, encouragement, and know-how of Jeffry Timmons' dear friend and microcomputer guru Michael Harde this project could not have been completed. More important, he opened our eyes to the power, potential, and occasional pain of microcomputing, for which we are most grateful. We would also like to thank copy editor Eugene Zucker for his careful and professional job.

Finally, we are perhaps most indebted to the real-world entrepreneurs and the MBA and undergraduate students at Babson College who responded to earlier versions of the revision and whose critiques and suggestions have been invaluable in finalizing its content.

J.A.T.
L.E.S.
A.L.M.D.

Contents

The Entrepreneurial Process: What Is It, and What Drives It?

1

Who can be an entrepreneur?
Anyone who wants to experience the deep, dark canyons of uncertainty and ambiguity; and who wants to walk the breathtaking highlands of success. But I caution, do not plan to walk the latter until you have experienced the former.[1]

1.1 WHAT IS ENTREPRENEURSHIP?

1.1.1 Visionary, Creative, and Committed

Entrepreneurship is the ability to create and build something from practically nothing: fundamentally it is a human, creative act. It is finding personal energy by initiating and building an enterprise or organization, rather than by just watching, analyzing, or describing one. Making such a personal statement about your vision requires a willingness to take calculated risks—both personal and financial—and then to do everything possible to put the odds in your favor, thereby reducing the chances of failure. Entrepreneurship is the ability to build a "founding team" to complement your own skills and talents. It is the knack for sensing an opportunity where others see chaos, contradiction, and confusion. It is possessing the know-how to find, marshal, and control resources (often owned by others) and to make sure you don't run out of money when you need it most.

Entrepreneurs work very hard, driven by an intense commitment and determined perseverence. They see the cup half full rather than half empty. They strive for integrity. They burn with the competitive desire to excel and win. They use failure as a tool for learning, and eschew perfection in favor of effectiveness. They have enough confidence in themselves to believe that they can personally make an enormous difference in the final outcome of their ventures, and their lives.

1.1.2 Who Can Be an Entrepreneur?

Judging the extraordinary variety of people, opportunities, and strategies that characterize the approximately 14 million businesses in this country, literally anyone can give entrepreneurship a try. Not only have many people tried but some of them have succeeded beyond what anyone could possibly have imagined

---

[1]From an interview with his father, an entrepreneur, by Gian Perotti, Babson College, Class of 1984.

beforehand.[2] And if an entrepreneur fails, no other country in the world has laws, institutions, and social norms that are more forgiving and that provide more of a learning curve and a second or third chance.

Yet, while anyone can try to start a business, relatively few can grow one to beyond $1 million in sales. According to government data, only about 1 in 30 of those 14 million businesses had sales in 1980 of over $1 million. Starting a venture and growing and harvesting it successfully are not the same. In that respect, we are reminded of the comment by George Bernard Shaw, taken from a slightly different context: "Any darned fool can start a love affair, but it takes a real genius to end one successfully."

1.1.3   Not a Spectator Sport

New venture creation is decidedly not a spectator sport. Rather, it is akin to surgery and athletics: its winning strategies require intense, active, and creative involvement. It is a sport of challenge, uncertainty, calculated risk taking and risk minimizing. It parallels other activities with similar demands and unknowns. Take, for instance, the unknowns, and urgency to act, faced by Chuck Yeager, the legendary first X–2 test pilot at the outer edge of "the performance envelope."[3]

In the thin air at the edge of space, where the stars and the moon came out at noon, in an atmosphere so thin that the ordinary laws of aerodynamics no longer applied and a plane could skid into a flat spin like a cereal bowl on a waxed Formica counter and then start tumbling, end over end like a brick. . .you had to be "afraid to panic." In the skids, the tumbles, the spins there was only one thing you could let yourself think about: What do I do next?

The successful entrepreneurial act can also remind you of the improvisation and resourcefulness of the broken-field runner, or of the blitz of the downhill ski racer, speeding like a projectile, always at the precipice of disaster, but just as close to victory. The balance shifts to victory if your talents and abilities exceed the competition, and if your nanosecond judgments and mental calculations result in actions that keep you pointed toward victory. And as with a downhill racer, disaster for an entrepreneur can also pounce with unexpected suddenness—just ask Adam Osborne.

Some have likened the uncanny talents of successful entrepreneurs for combining and blending people with diverse skills and personalities—so that the whole is greater than the sum of the parts—to the mastery and balancing of the symphony conductor. Or to the adroitness under stress and pressure of the skillful juggler, who keeps many balls in the air at once and recovers quickly from the slightest miscue.

No doubt about it: all of these acts are artistic and creative. Their outcomes all tend to be either highly rewarding successes or painful and visible failures. And common to all of them is that stark urgency: What do I do next?

1.1.4   Nearly Anyone Can Start a Business, but. . .

There is a lot in common between these demanding activities and the challenges, rewards, excitement, and pain that entrepreneurs face. Fortunately, judg-

---

[2]We include only nonfarm businesses in the 14 million figure.
[3]Tom Wolfe, *The Right Stuff* (New York: Bantam Books, 1980), pp. 51–52.

ing the more than 14 million businesses in our country, there is plenty of room out there for new ventures. While being a genius certainly helps and has sometimes resulted in spectacular successes, you do not have to be one to create your own successful business. Far from it; in fact, nearly anyone can start a business in America. While the rigors of doing so may favor the young—Nolan Bushnell asserts that "if you are not a millionaire or bankrupt by the time you are 30, you are not really trying!"—age is apparently no barrier to entry, with Colonel Sanders the leading inspiration. But realizing a capital gain from a business you create is decidedly more difficult than starting a business.

1.1.5 Creating and Building New Ventures

This book, then, is about the creation of new ventures: the entrepreneurs who launch and build them, the forces that drive the entrepreneurial process, and the practicalities necessary to get the odds of success in your favor.

Who creates and builds new ventures? What does this take in the way of experience, skills, know-how, and other attributes? What are the critical issues and trade-offs to be resolved? What do entrepreneurs need to know? Can you find enough customers for your new idea before you run out of cash? How can it be financed? What does it take to put together a business plan that you can implement? What analytical techniques and concepts are most useful? What are the problems and pitfalls that court failure, and how can they be avoided?

Further, the book deals, not just with getting started, but with how to grow successfully and to conclude with a successful harvest. After all, many entrepreneurs caution from hard-won experience that attaining a capital gain and an enhanced track record is the truly hard part.

1.2 THE PROBLEM OF SURVIVAL

No doubt about it: the odds of survival are definitely not in favor of the vast majority of new businesses in the country. While the government, researchers, and "business mortality statisticians" may not agree on what the precise failure and survival figures are, they do agree that failure is the rule, not the exception. No one really knows the exact numbers, and considerable debate continues about them.

For one thing, it is not easy to define and identify failures. It has been said that "success has a thousand sires, but failure is an orphan." That is true of small business failures as well. They are often very difficult to locate. And, complicating efforts to keep track of these numbers is the fact that reliable statistics and databases just aren't available. Success, on the other hand, is quite visible to all. That's one of the more positive things about profitability as a measure: at least you can keep a reasonably good score.

Despite the problems of new businesses, an unprecedented number have been formed in the United States in the past few years. Many believe that the total number of new businesses exceeds half a million each year.[4]

[4]*The State of Small Business: A Report of the President, Transmitted to the Congress, March 1983* (Washington, D.C.: SBA, 1983).

1.2.1 High Failure Rates

What happens to these new ventures? The birth and death watchers agree that the picture is rather bleak. The failure and bankruptcy rates continue at high levels. For every three new businesses formed, two close their doors.[5] Some types of businesses seem to face worse odds than others. Retail trade, construction, and service businesses, for instance, account for just 3 of the 21 categories reported by Dun & Bradstreet, yet they accounted for 70 percent of all failures and bankruptcies in 1980.[6]

What is worse, smaller firms—employing fewer than 100 persons—suffer the most. In 1981 and 1982 approximately 99 percent of all the businesses filing for bankruptcy were such firms.[7]

Take a look at Exhibit 1.1, for instance, which attempts to summarize the overall picture. The odds shown in the exhibit are supported by other recent studies as well.[8] For instance, it has been reported that over 53 percent of all business failures and bankruptcies occur in the first 5 years of a new firm's life, nearly 30 percent in years 6 through 10; and the remaining 20 percent for firms in existence more than 10 years.[9] Can anyone argue that the odds are generally in favor of the entrepreneur?

Exhibit 1.1
Overall New Business Failure Rates

By the End of:	Percentage that Fail
1st year	40%
2d year	60
10th year	90

Sources: Commerce Department; SBA; Dun & Bradstreet.

To make matters worse, most people perceive the failure rates as being much higher. Time and again, when we have asked for estimates of the failure rates in seminars, workshops, and classes, the answers have been more pessimistic than the actual rates summarized here. And these answers have come from people who were self-proclaimed entrepreneurs. If such people are pessimistic about their chances of succeeding in a new venture, what does that say about the population at large? And since, as most informed persons would agree, actions are governed, more often than not, by perceptions rather than facts, this dismal perception of failure can be a serious obstacle to aspiring entrepreneurs.

That's not to say that all of the failures need to be eliminated. A certain level of failure is part of the "creative self-destruction" described by Joseph Schumpeter. It is part of the dynamics of innovation and economic renewal. It is also part of the learning process inherent in gaining an entrepreneurial apprenticeship. The failure of a single venture does not mean the failure of a venture career.

[5]Ibid., p. 248.

[6]Dun & Bradstreet, Business Economics Division, *The Business Failure Record, 1980* (New York, 1982).

[7]*State of Small Business,* pp. 156–57.

[8]The most complete summary of these studies is reported by Albert N. Shapero and Joseph Giglierano, "Exits and Entries: A Study in Yellow Pages Journalism," in *Frontiers of Entrepreneurship Research: 1982,* ed. K. Vesper (Babson Park, Mass.: Babson College, 1982), pp. 113–41.

[9]*Business Failure Record, 1980,* p. 10.

1.2.2 $1 Million Sales Threshold

Since the publication of the first edition of this book, some very significant new studies profiling the dynamics of new company formation have emerged. The thrust of their important messages was that a very disproportionate share—probably 70 percent or more—of the net new jobs in our country comes from new and growing firms.[10] But what is less well known has significant implications for would-be entrepreneurs.

A useful "threshold concept" emerges from these studies if we interpret their data in terms of start-up dynamics and size. There appears to be a minimum threshold size for new firms—at least 10 employees, and 20 is even better—that is closely linked to both survival odds and the promise of expansion. Roughly translated into total sales, the findings from several studies suggest that this threshold begins at a minimum of around $500,000. (Obviously, any estimates based on sales per employee vary considerably from industry to industry. A useful rule of thumb used here is $50,000 to $60,000 of sales per employee annually.)

The message is clear: the survival odds and signs of prosperity—namely significant job creation—improve even further once the $1 million in sales level has been attained. So if you are thinking about creating a new venture with the survival odds in your favor, think big enough. Thinking small may stack the deck against you. Much below half a million in sales after a few years in the business tends to mean that you are fragile and vulnerable to competition, or it may mean that you have not focused on real opportunities. It may also mean that you don't want to. You may have personal values and lifestyle goals that conflict with the level of commitment necessary to grow a substantial venture. But this may be a rationalization, when you simply are not able enough. Exhibit 1.2 indicates that

Exhibit 1.2
One-Year Survival Rates by Firm Size

Firm Size (employees)	Survival Percent
0–9	77.8%
10–19	85.5
20–99	95.3
100–249	95.2
250+	100.0

Source: Michael B. Teitz et al., "Small Business and Employment Growth in California," Working Paper No. 348, University of California at Berkeley, March 1981, p. 42.

the one-year survival rates jump from 77.8 percent for firms with up to 9 employees to 95.3 percent for firms with 20–99 employees. The same trend occurs for the four-year survival odds shown in Exhibit 1.3. In the D&B study the survival rate was 37.4 percent for firms with 19 or fewer employees, but it jumped to 53.6 percent for firms with 20–49 employees.

All of this may be well and good for the macroeconomic philosopher or broad-

[10]See David L. Birch and Susan MacCracken, "Corporation Evolution: A Micro-Based Analysis," prepared for the SBA by MIT (Washington, D.C.: January 1981); Michael B. Teitz et al., "Small Business and Employment Growth in California," Working Paper No. 348, University of California at Berkeley, March 1981; and Catherine Armington and Marjorie Odle, "Small Business—How Many Jobs?" *Brookings Review,* Washington, D.C., Winter 1982, pp. 14–17.

Exhibit 1.3
Four-Year Survival Rates by Firm Size

Firm Size (employees)	D&B Study (1969–1976)	California Study (1976–1980)
0–19	37.4%	49.9%
20–49	53.6	66.9
50–99	55.7	66.9
100–499	67.7	70.0

Sources: David L. Birch, *MIT Studies, 1979–80;* and Michael B. Teitz et al., "Small Business and Employment Growth in California," Working Paper No. 348, University of California at Berkeley, March 1981, table 5, p. 22.

brush policymaker. But what about you? What about the lone, aspiring entrepreneur who wants to succeed, not fail? Who wants to innovate and renew, rather than degenerate and collapse? Are there any exceptions to this failure rule?

1.3 EXCEPTIONS TO THE FAILURE RULE

Fortunately, the record of new business failure has a notable pattern of exceptions to these national averages: just the opposite results characterize the failure record for entrepreneurs who are able to attract start-up financing from private venture capital companies. Instead of the 70–90 percent *failure* rate that characterizes all types of new firms, these growth-minded new ventures enjoy a *survival* rate nearly that high. And their records of successes, especially in a "great bull market" such as that of 1982 and 1983, are often quite spectacular.[11]

Earlier studies[12] have been confirmed by more recent studies and by our own experiences. Roberts reported a 20 percent failure rate; Taylor found a 35 percent failure rate among 279 California high-tech start-ups; and Faucett reported an 18 percent loss rate among 14 venture capital firms.[13] In the portfolio of an experienced and professional venture capital firm, typically total losses of the original investment will result for about 15–20 percent of the companies. It is unusual for a loss rate to exceed 30–35 percent or for it to fall below 10 percent.

For example, a recent study by the leading industry observers analyzed 218 investments made by five prominent venture capital firms during the 1970s. These observers found that 14.7 percent of the 218 investments resulted in complete losses and that another 24.8 percent resulted in partial losses. Thus, roughly 50 percent resulted in losses. Offsetting this much lower than average failure pattern were the spectacular successes. Of the 218 investments, 3.8 percent returned at least 10 times the original investment in the 10-year period and another 8.3 percent returned 5 to 10 times the original investment, all after taxes. This translates into about 25 percent compounded return on investment after taxes.[14] A 1980 study by other researchers showed a 17 percent failure rate (Huntsman and Hoban).

[11] *Time*, "Making a Mint Overnight," January 23, 1984, pp. 44–54.

[12] J. A. Timmons et al., *New Venture Creation* (Homewood, Ill.: Richard D. Irwin, 1977), pp. 10–11.

[13] E. B. Roberts, "How to Succeed in a New Technology Enterprise," *Technology Review* 2, no. 2 (1970); C. Taylor, "Starting-Up in the High Technology Industries in California," commissioned by the Wells Fargo Investment Company, 1969; R. B. Faucett, "The Management of Venture Capital Investment Companies," Sloan School master's thesis, MIT, 1971; and R. B. Faucett, "Venture Capital: Fact and Myth," Foothill Group, 1972.

[14] T. Dehudy, N. D. Fast, and S. E. Pratt, *Venture Economics* (Wellesley Hills, Mass.: Venture Economics, 1981).

Finally, an analysis of the venture capital investments made by our own firm, Ventures Founders Corporation, and its English subsidiary shows a total loss rate of 15–25 percent of the dollars and pounds invested. Associates in Sweden have had a similar experience, with a failure rate of around 10 percent. All of these are relatively new funds, so it is too early to judge real performance.

1.3.1 Why Is This So?

What is going on here? What do these talented entrepreneurs and their venture capital backers do differently? What is accounting for this exceptional record? Are there some lessons here for aspiring entrepreneurs? The professional venture capital investors have had a unique approach to doing their business. But we have noticed that quite successful entrepreneurs, who grow multimillion-dollar firms, often from scratch and sometimes with little money, also understand that entrepreneurial achievement is driven by people who search for and shape superior opportunities.

1.3.2 Not Just the Domain of Venture Capitalists

Granted, there are almost as many different approaches, philosophies, and nuances to the art of new venture creation as there are venture capital companies and entrepreneurs. Yet, time and again, some central themes rise to the surface. And these themes are not the monopoly of entrepreneurs backed by venture capital. Take, for instance, Tony and Susan Harnett. Tony came to this country from his native Ireland as a young high school dropout. He had a lot of ambition and was in search of opportunity. In 1976 Tony and his wife bought a natural foods store in Brookline, Massachusetts, with annual sales of a meager $110,000 per year. By paying a lot of attention to the critical driving forces that venture capitalists seem to concentrate on, they built Bread & Circus into a multistore venture whose sales in 1984 exceeded $16 million. And they did this without having to raise a dime of venture capital.

Such real-world experiences, in turn, suggest some fundamental insights and understandings regarding what drives the entrepreneurial process. What are the crucial ingredients to which successful entrepreneurs pay enormous attention? What can we learn from their collective experiences that can help focus our own efforts?

1.4 WHAT DRIVES THE ENTREPRENEURIAL PROCESS? A MATTER OF FIT

There are many successful entrepreneurs, and they have achieved their successes in many ways. Any unidimensional model that attempts to distill the common basis for their collective successes—such as a single psychological profile or characteristic, or a single idea or technology—can tell only part of the story.

Instead, we are suggesting a framework, illustrated in Exhibit 1.4, that isolates the three primary driving forces behind successful new venture creation—the founders, the opportunity, and the necessary resources. Experience shows that these elements can actually be assessed and influenced, in order to improve the chances of succeeding. The key, we have found, is a careful and realistic assessment of these driving forces: of your strengths and weaknesses, of the opportunity, and of what is needed for successful implementation and eventual harvesting. It is much

Exhibit 1.4
New Venture Creation: The Driving Forces

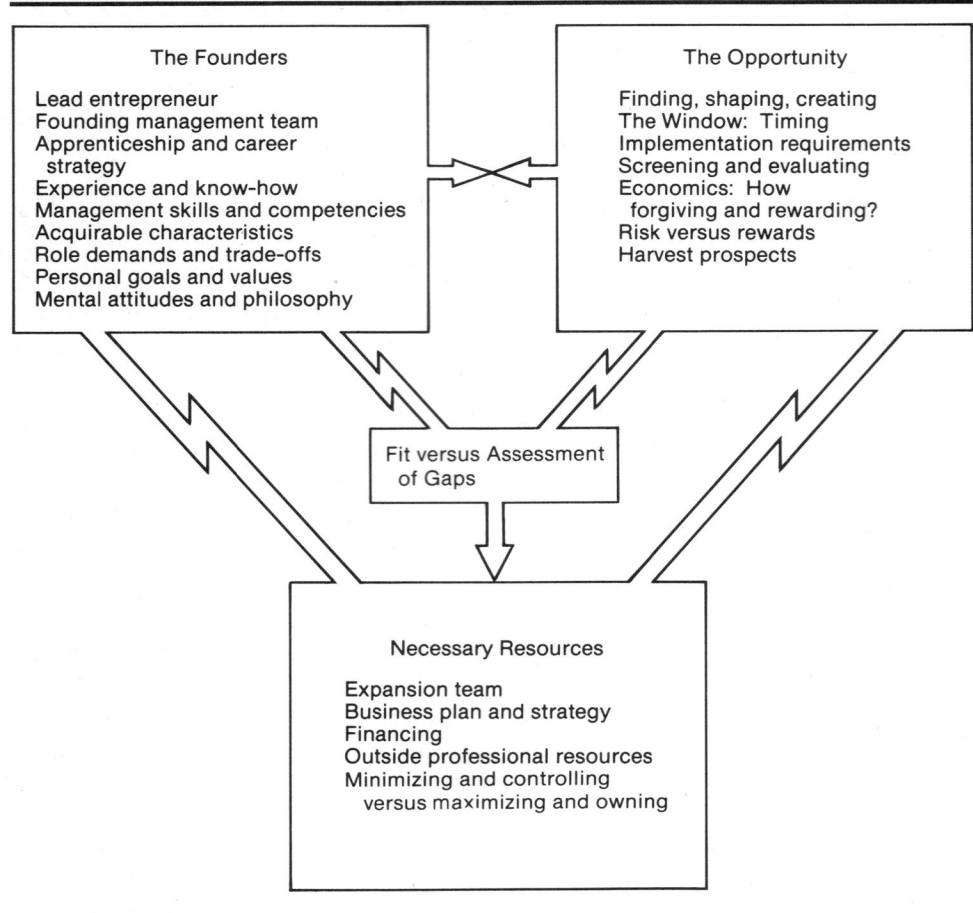

more a trial and error, iterative process of finding out what it takes, what "gaps" you face as the venture unfolds, and how to shape a good "fit." Not surprisingly, this process seems to work well for a lot of innovative undertakings. After all, before attaching a motor-driven propeller to their airplane, the Wright brothers flew over a thousand glider flights in their trial and error efforts to find out what worked.

1.5   THE FOUNDERS

1.5.1   The Team Concept

Ask the venture capitalists, and they will make it plain and simple. What are the three most important success factors? (1) The lead entrepreneur and the quality of the team. (2) The lead entrepreneur and the quality of the team. (3) The lead entrepreneur and the quality of the team. Several studies have confirmed this view widely held by practitioners, including a recent study of the 50 most active U.S. venture capital firms.[15]

[15]J. A. Timmons and D. E. Gumpert, "Discard Many Old Rules for Raising Venture Capital," *Harvard Business Review,* January–February 1982.

According to recent research, the same principle seems to hold true for high-technology companies formed in this country since 1967. Even in the most highly innovative technological ventures, where you would expect the elegance of the technology and the idea to have a special importance, just the opposite was shown to be true. Of course, you cannot win the high-tech game without innovative technology and good products, but venture capitalists who are among the most active and prominent investors in the country still insist that they place the greatest weight and emphasis on the quality and proven track record of the management team.[16]

A good example is the philosophy of T. A. Associates, a Boston-based firm. It is one of the largest and most successful venture capital firms, with over $500 million under management at this writing and investments in over 80 emerging companies, including such winners as Biogen, Continental Cablevision, Federal Express, and Tandon. Its strong preference for high-quality management is stated this way:

The management team must have quality, depth, and maturity. It must be experienced in the industry in which the company competes. The top manager should have had prior profit center responsibility. Management must possess intimate knowledge of the market for its products and have a well-thought-out strategy for the penetration of this market. The strength of the management team is the most important consideration in the investment decision.

1.5.2 "Apprenticeship" and Career Strategy Notion

Our treatment of the lead entrepreneur and, as appropriate, the management team has several dimensions. For one thing, there is the underlying notion of "an apprenticeship" with paths for preparation, entry strategies, and planning and managing the whole process in order to gain the relevant business experience needed. Most of the successful entrepreneurs we have known do not leave this to accident or osmosis. Increasingly, there is evidence from research about the career paths of entrepreneurs and the self-employed suggesting that success is linked to thoughtful preparation and planning before taking the plunge.[17] We will examine who does it and why; what it takes to succeed; what risks, rewards, and trade-offs are worth considering; and what strategies work.

1.5.3 Role Models

There is no more powerful teacher than a good example. Seeing what has been and can be done cleanly and simply points the way and plants the seed of what is possible. No wonder, then, that numerous studies show a strong connection between the presence of role models and the emergence of entrepreneurs. These studies also dispel the notion that entrepreneurs are "born, not made." For instance, one recent study showed that more than half of the new business starters had parents who owned a business.[18] The authors summed it up this way:

[16]J. A. Timmons, N. D. Fast, S. E. Pratt, and W. D. Bygrave, "Venture Capital Investing in Highly Innovative Technological Ventures," published by Venture Economics, March 1984, for the National Science Foundation.

[17]See Robert Ronstadt's and Howard Stevenson's studies reported in *Frontiers of Entrepreneurship Research: 1983,* ed. J. A. Hornaday, J. A. Timmons, and K. H. Vesper (Babson Park, Mass.: Babson College, 1983).

[18]Arnold Cooper and William Dunkelberg, "A New Look at Business Entry" (San Mateo, Calif.: National Federation of Independent Businesses, March 1984).

People who start companies are more likely to come from families in which their parents or close relatives were in business for themselves. These older people were examples or "models" for the children. Whether they were successful or not probably didn't matter. However, for the children growing up in such a family, the action of starting a new business seems possible—something they can do.

1.5.4   The Experience Factor

The role of experience and know-how is central in successful venture creation.[19] What management skills and competences are necessary for the venture? How do these fit with your own strengths and weaknesses from your cumulative experience and track record? How do your experience and know-how complement those of possible partners? What do they say about the progress and velocity of your "apprenticeship" toward a successful launch? After all, you would not want to depart for your first jump from an airplane without a parachute. What are some effective and timesaving ways to get any needed experience? A large number of studies indicate that 90 percent or more of founders start their companies in the same marketplace and industry that they have been working in.[20]

1.5.5   Acquirable Characteristics and Role Demands

Another important set of factors that founders can profitably consider as part of the start-up process consists of their own talents, attributes, and characteristics.[21] During the past several years new studies about entrepreneurs have tended to confirm what practitioners have known all along: some desirable characteristics are in fact acquirable and learnable, and some attributes are more desirable than others. Do you have the drive, motivation, and intensity of commitment necessary? Do you have the perseverance and tenacity to *make* the venture succeed? Are you willing to "pay the price" in terms of the sacrifices and immersion demanded by the heat of the start-up role? Finding out whether you possess these attributes is part of the apprenticeship. Further, some of the attributes are more desirable than others, especially when you are seeking partners or considering making an investment. Finally, since successful entrepreneurs seem to come in as many sizes, shapes, colors, and descriptions as are imaginable, there doesn't seem to be "one single profile" or "one psychological model." (And, unfortunately, the state of the art in the measurement instruments has not progressed far enough to permit research that can clearly identify and distinguish the essential factors.) Rather, the blend and fit among the founders are what is vital. Is there a talented lead entrepreneur whose capabilities are complemented by those of equally committed partners? Can the partners work together effectively? Are their collective know-how and capacities the critical ones necessary to seize and execute the opportunity? If the answers to these questions are yes, then there is a good fit. Consequently, the chances for success are dramatically improved.

[19] Karl H. Vesper, "New Venture Ideas: Don't Overlook the Experience Factor," *Harvard Business Review;* reprinted in *Growing Concerns, Building and Growing the Smaller Business,* ed. D. E. Gumpert (New York: John Wiley & Sons, 1984), pp. 28–55.

[20] Robert H. Brockhaus, "The Psychology of the Entrepreneur," in *Encyclopedia of Entrepreneurship,* ed. C. Kent, D. Sexton, and K. Vesper (Englewood Cliffs, N.J.: Prentice-Hall, 1982), pp. 50–55, provides a good summary of some of these studies.

[21] J. A. Timmons, "Careful Self-Analysis and Team Assessment Can Aid Entrepreneurs," *Harvard Business Review,* reprinted in *Growing Concerns: Building and Growing the Smaller Business,* ed. D. E. Gumpert (New York: John Wiley & Sons, 1984), pp. 43–52.

1.5.6 Mental Attitudes and Philosophy

Finally, there are some more elusive, tougher-to-define issues: personal attitudes and philosophy, values and ethics. While there is limited research that pinpoints the precise relationship of these matters to entrepreneurial success, practical experience demonstrates that such relationships exist. There appear to be some important attitudes and values that the more successful entrepreneurs share. They see the cup as half-full, rather than as half-empty. They ask "How can I make it work?" rather than dwelling on why it won't work. Their beliefs include such notions as "Bite off more than you can chew, and then chew it" (Roger Babson); "You can do anything you want to do" (Wally Amos—Famous Chocolate Chip Cookies); "You need...to think yourself out of a corner, meet needs, and never, never accept no for an answer" (John Johnson—*Ebony*); and "Never give up" (Carl Sontheimer—Cuisinart).[22] No doubt about it: such attitudes and perseverance are an essential part of the entrepreneurial mind-set.

1.6 THE OPPORTUNITY

1.6.1 An Idea Is Not Necessarily an Opportunity

If there is any single magnet pulling out the entrepreneurial event, it is the opportunity. Some recent work by Howard H. Stevenson of Harvard Business School has lent even further support to the importance that was attributed to this factor in the earlier edition of this book.[23] The core problem does not seem to be the lack of ideas. Entrepreneurs and innovators seem to abound with new ideas. What is the problem then? Simply put, unsuccessful entrepreneurs usually equate an idea with an opportunity; successful entrepreneurs know the difference.

Judging by the failure statistics, presented above, it is apparent that the vast majority of entrepreneurs run out of money before they find enough customers for their "good ideas." A novel idea is not the same as a sound business concept anchored to a marketable idea. Is there really a business opportunity, or just a product or two? Further, the window on the opportunity depends on movement in technology and competitors' thrusts. Not only does the opportunity have an elusive life, but it is a constantly moving target.

The real challenge, then, is recognizing that an opportunity is buried in the often conflicting and contradictory data and signals, in the inevitable noise and chaos of the marketplace. And often, a skillful entrepreneur can shape and create an opportunity where others see little or nothing. After all, if it were simply a matter of using available techniques, checklists, and other screening and evaluation methods, we might have far more than the 470,000 or so ventures in the United States whose sales exceeded $1 million in 1979 and 1980.[24] Why? Because the literature on techniques for screening and evaluating ideas indicates that over 200 such methods have been developed and documented.

---

[22] See the excellent summary of a study of the first 21 inductees into Babson College's Academy of Distinguished Entrepreneurs by John A. Hornaday and Nancy Tieken, "Capturing Twenty-One Heffalumps," in *Frontiers of Entrepreneurship Research: 1983*, ed. J. A. Hornaday, J. A. Timmons, and K. H. Vesper (Babson Park, Mass.: Babson College), pp. 23–50.

[23] See Stevenson's "Paradigm" paper in the *Proceedings from the 75th Anniversary Symposium on Entrepreneurship, July 1983* (Boston: Harvard Business School, 1984).

[24] These included about 33,000 proprietorships and 37,000 partnerships in 1980 and just under 400,000 corporations in 1979, out of a total of nearly 17 million businesses, according to *The State of Small Business, 1982* (Washington, D.C.: SBA, 1983), pp. 199–200.

1.6.2   Window on Opportunity

The more certain you are that you have spotted a viable "window on opportunity," the more effectively you can use your time in preparing to seize it. Pulling together the essential parts of a business plan can take a few calendar months or longer, even when you are allocating most of your time to it; writing it down can take a hundred hours or more as you sharpen your focus. So being quite sure, before beginning to prepare a formal plan, that a serious and compelling opportunity exists can save you valuable time in the end. Knowing which, among a continual flow of opportunities, to focus on and which to say no to, is crucial. Equally important, we should add, is knowing when you do not need, or cannot afford the time necessary, to prepare a full-blown business plan; there are times when action is more appropriate, when the voice of experience tells you that the most important move is to get to that window before it shuts.

1.6.3   An Opportunity for Whom?

The old adage "What is one person's jam is another person's poison" is frequently confirmed in the venture capital business. Different investors will investigate the same venture and come to opposite conclusions. The same holds true for the opportunities facing entrepreneurs. For every manager, engineer, salesperson, or technical person that sheds the "bronze" or even "golden" handcuffs to join a new venture, there are always several who do not view the opportunity as so compelling. Why is this so?

We worked a few years ago with some entrepreneurs from Alaska who were seeking start-up financing there. Imagine finding your opportunity on the Bering Sea, running a small outpost in Bethel, 800 miles west of Anchorage, reachable only by sea and air. Bethel may not be Boston, Dallas, or Silicon Valley, but if you were parking cars for a few dollars an hour, with little future in sight, then it might glimmer with promise. One entrepreneur we worked with went there for a job opportunity. Within two years of his arrival he bought the general store he was running. He subsequently saw even greater opportunities in salmon fishing. In 1980 he expected to gross over $5 million and earn a substantial profit in salmon fishing.

1.6.4   Sizing Up the Opportunity

Defining a good opportunity is no easy matter, as we have suggested. Perhaps a workable definition is that it is an end result that the entrepreneur definitely wants and that is also attainable by the entrepreneur or team; otherwise, why bother? The opportunity depends on a whole host of considerations. For example, some of the more important issues to address include:

What are the principal driving forces and competitive vacuums creating the opportunity? What is behind the opportunity? What are the underlying reasons for the opportunity, and can these be articulated? And how long will they last?

For whom is the opportunity desirable and doable? Time and again, we have found that the personal values and lifestyles of the founders enter heavily into the definition of a good opportunity.

Is there a real need for the product or service? Have the customers been identified, are they reachable, and are they enthusiastic? In short, is there a market?

What are the economics of the opportunity? Are the gross margins and profits sufficient and durable enough to provide a forgiving cushion for error during the steep learning curve that is characteristic of the heat of start-up and necessary to sustain growth? How long will it take to reach a positive cash flow and break even? And how much capital will be required to do this?

Given your alternatives, do the risk-reward trade-offs work in your favor? What needs to be done to shift the balance in the direction you would like? The upside may be exceedingly attractive, but can you absorb the downside, should that occur, in terms both of dollars and of the psychological stress?

1.6.5 Implementation Makes the Difference

In the early 70s entrepreneurs could not turn to a book like this for guidelines to develop a business plan, including examples of actual funded businesses. Today just the opposite is true. Advice about business plan preparation is readily available. Venture capitalists across the country praise the high quality of the business plans they are seeing, and there has never been a greater flow of such plans. With the advent of the microcomputer and spreadsheet software such as Lotus 1–2–3, VisiCalc, Multiplan, and their clones, the agony factor has declined while the time needed to prepare a plan has decreased.

More and more, however, we are reminded that writing the business plan is the easy part (although you won't think so when you do it). It is in the implementation that the real work and challenge begin. What investors, bankers, customers, and prospective key employees want to know is how to make the plan work. Having a superbly prepared document may be a necessary, but far from sufficient, condition for launching and building a million-dollar-plus venture.

Through the cases and other materials in this book we will develop some benchmarks, analytical tools, and rules of thumb that are used to size up an opportunity. At one end of the continuum are the highly selective criteria used by venture capitalists. At the other end might be those appropriate to individual, lifestyle, craftlike businesses. Somewhere in between is a mix that is a good fit, based on your self-assessment of your goals, aspirations, experience, and talents at this time.

1.7 NECESSARY RESOURCES

The third element in our model of new venture creation is the resources required to execute the opportunity, both in starting and growing the company. As can be seen from Exhibit 1.1, these include the very important concepts of a team and a business plan as key tools and talents for identifying, attracting, and managing necessary resources, both inside and outside the business. And time and again, if the founder is credible and has articulated the opportunity, the chances of attracting key people and financing soar once the vision has been pulled together into a cohesive strategy and an implementable business plan.

1.7.1   The Expansion Team

Without a team it is extremely difficult to raise venture capital. As was noted earlier, it is now well established that most experienced investors consider a proven management team to be the most critical success ingredient. But what is not so well known is the importance of a team to the chances of survival *and expansion* in new ventures, whether or not these ventures are candidates for venture capital. We saw earlier that the exceptions to the failure rule were most likely to be firms that managed to grow beyond 20 employees or roughly $1 million in sales. In a large majority of businesses it is quite difficult to do this without a team of at least two key contributors. Take, for example, the CEO of Telesis, one of the emerging high-growth firms in the CAD/CAM business. Before he was recruited by the company's venture capital backers, he was president of one of the early entrants into the office automation business, Vydec Office Systems. At Telesis, the first key addition he made to his management team was a *people* specialist—his former vice president of human resources at Vydec. Unlike some team builders, he did not begin by hiring a marketing, financial, or manufacturing expert. Why was this so?

The CEO knew from his previous experience that usually the greatest single barrier to rapid growth is finding the right people, soon enough. He was anticipating this critical need about a year or two earlier than is done by many expansion team builders.

A final point should be made about the importance of a team for a venture that is experiencing growing pains. There is growing evidence that having the right partner(s) can be invaluable in coping with the high degree of loneliness and stress associated with entrepreneurship.[25]

1.7.2   The Business Plan and Entry Strategy

The preparation of a business plan for a venture that is a real possibility is a cornerstone of this book. Included in the cases are actual business plans, some that were funded by venture capital and others that raised alternative sources of financing and grew multimillion-dollar businesses. Besides these cases, Chapter 13 includes guidelines for developing a business plan and Chapter 14 presents a detailed business plan guide that you will be expected to complete. The guide has been successfully used by hundreds of entrepreneurs to shape and refine their entry strategies and to raise financing for their ventures. It has also been applied by thousands of students in the United States and abroad.

How important is a business plan? Without it raising venture capital or other formal or informal financing is nearly impossible—unless, of course, you don't need it. Nolan Bushnell (founder of Atari, Pizza Time Theaters, and now Catalyst, an early stage venture capital firm) was asked this question by students at Babson College when he was inducted into the Academy of Distinguished Entrepreneurs in 1983. One young woman put it this way: "Do we really have to prepare these business plans? They are a real pain. We sometimes work on one most of the semester and then find out that the business will not work!" Bushnell's response was unequivocal:

---

[25] David Boyd and David E. Gumpert, "Stress, Loneliness, and the Entrepreneur," in *Frontiers of Entrepreneurship Research: 1984* (Babson Park, Mass.: Babson College, 1984).

Absolutely yes. Every time you prepare a business plan, you become a better entrepreneur. It is a lot of work, but it is worth every bit of the effort. Do it.

1.7.3 Minimizing and Controlling Resources

When it comes to resources, entrepreneurs seem to have a quite different mentality, especially as compared to large, established companies. They know that they can get the odds in their favor, even improve the chances of attaining their business plan and personal goals, without having to own the assets and resources. They also manage to get more out of less. Often, their approach is to push ahead with minimum resources. This is a good way to reduce the early risks and exposure, while working through the trial and error process of finding out whether there really is an opportunity and whether it is quite certain to succeed.

Take, for instance, Howard Head's approach to developing the very first metal ski, and subsequently the Prince tennis racket. (He sold the latter in 1982 to Chesebrough-Pond's for about $68 million.) He left his job at a large aircraft manufacturer after World War II. Working with his own savings, on a shoestring, out of his own garage, he began to develop his metal ski. It took over 40 iterations before he finally developed a marketable metal ski. Subsequently, Head Ski dominated the international ski industry through the late 1960s and was sold to AMF. Head is convinced that if he had insisted on having all the right talent, backup, and financing in place before starting to develop the product, he would have failed by wasting it all prematurely.

Early stage entrepreneurs also position themselves so that they can control the resources, which they view as more important than owning the resources. Most large corporations are quite likely to view the situation in just the opposite way.[26] For example, start-up entrepreneurs know that they can stretch limited cash and new capital by renting or leasing new equipment, vehicles, or buildings, instead of buying them. They will take cuts in pay in order to plow funds into growing the business. They work exceptionally hard in the early stages, often 60 hours or more a week, and thereby minimize the need for people resources. And once the business is on a solid footing, it often requires two or three new hires to get nearly the same results in the jobs held initially by the founders.

1.7.4 Outside Professional Resources

One of the very early contributions to the understanding of the role of outside resources indicated that it was one of the key success factors.[27] Finding and properly using the most helpful outsiders—banker, CPA, lawyer, informal advisers, board members, other experts—are among the most easily overlooked challenges that start-up entrepreneurs face. How to find and use such resources and what to look for—and look out for—are addressed in Chapter 11.

1.7.5 Risk Capital Financing

When initially asked what ingredients are most critial to the successful launching of a new company, most people include money among the top three

---

[26]This important notion is well developed in Stevenson's "Paradigm" paper.
[27]Patrick R. Liles, doctoral dissertation, Harvard Business School, 1970.

items, if not first. No doubt about it, you cannot go far without money. After all, it is the fuel in the gas tank that makes the car go. Yet, we deliberately include it *last.* Why?

Because your capacity to raise money is a result of having the other parts of your act together. The financing does not *cause* these other things to happen; in most instances, it *follows* good people who have spotted good opportunities and who demonstrate that they clearly grasp the driving forces that will govern success. Today there is no serious shortage of risk capital. Ironically, more venture capital continues to be available than can be used by new ventures with all the pieces in place.

The same appears to be true of nonventure capital financing. Increasingly, sophisticated bankers, financial institutions, and informal investors back people who have demonstrated that they understand the driving forces needed to succeed in their proposed business.

1.7.6   Implications for Aspiring Entrepreneurs

The implications of all this for aspiring entrepreneurs are simple enough. There are issues and ingredients that need to be included in any consideration of starting a company. There are things you can do about these that can contribute further to stacking the deck in your favor. They are part and parcel of the preparation and apprenticeship.

1.8   MOUNTAIN VENTURES, INC. (A): CASE STUDY

Prepare the MVI case. Consider the following issues:

1. Evaluate the entrepreneurs: What are their strengths and weaknesses, individually and as a team?
2. Would you invest in them if you were convinced that the opportunity was sound? Why or why not?
3. What are the critical skills and resources necessary to succeed in the business? What is needed?
4. What should the founders do now, and why?

MOUNTAIN VENTURES, INC. (A)

In early 1972, at age 31, J. C. Egnew was employed as vice president of manufacturing by Wilderness Products, Inc., a large tent producer. He was responsible for the overall planning and administration of the company's manufacturing operations. The company's sales were about $12 million per year, and it employed over 350 people at three plants. Although the company was growing, Egnew began to encounter basic differences of opinion and philosophy with the owners and top management of the company, particularly over issues of new product development and expansion. Prompted by these differences, Egnew became increasingly intrigued with the possibility of starting his own tent manufacturing company. He discussed his ideas with a co-worker, John F. Moore, the sales service manager.

Wilderness Products had experienced substantial growth in unit volume and dollar sales, but Egnew was troubled about its apparent lack of concern for profits. Drawing from his business school training, he also observed other problems in the company:

There was not one page of formal planning. There was no real organization—everyone was just doing his own thing. And the techniques being used to manage the company weren't keeping up with the rate of growth. These were appropriate for a $1–2 million tent manufacturer, but not one doing $12 million.

There were still other problems with the way the company was being managed. As Egnew put it:

If I asked the production manager, the sales manager, and the president what our capacity was and for a sales forecast, I'd get three very different answers. The company was very sales oriented in a seller's market. So we'd fill up with orders which required too much overtime to produce, so we'd end up with missed delivery schedules and unprofitable sales. It got to the point where I honestly felt something was way out of balance.

During the three years since joining Wilderness Products, Egnew had gained experience in and knowledge of the tent manufacturing industry. He felt that there was a substantial national market for tents and that his current employer was not competing as effectively as it could. In particular, he felt that there was significant potential to manufacture and market a line of camping tents and accessories having broad-based consumer appeal. He felt that such trends as more discretionary income and more leisure time were favorably affecting consumer demand for tents. Further, a U.S. Department of the Interior study estimated that in 1965 Americans went camping 97 million times. It also predicted that camping frequency would increase by more than twice the rate of population growth.[1] Also, federal and state governments were making more public land accessible for public recreation and many private firms were entering the campground business.[2]

Egnew's operating experience in the industry was confirming the impact of these trends. During the previous four years, for example, the six major tent manufacturers had been continually delinquent to customers because they were unable to keep pace with the growing market. Poor deliveries prevailed in this period, while production by the "big six" was expanding at an annual rate of 20 percent. Egnew also knew that strong retail demand had led to a severe erosion of product quality as a result of haphazard industry expansion.

In response to the situation, Egnew decided to try to convince the management that a coordinated plan was needed to pull the business together and make it profitable. During evenings and weekends he and Moore drew up what they considered a sensible long-range plan, and Egnew then discussed the plan with his employer. "I got them to agree to it, but in six months it all went out the window." He concluded: "I didn't have what it takes to convince them to run the business the way I wanted to."

This left him with what he felt were three principal alternatives:

1. Quit and get another job.
2. Get the president fired.
3. Start his own tent manufacturing company.

---

[1] U.S. Department of the Interior, *Outdoor Recreation Trends* (Washington, D.C.: U.S. Government Printing Office, 1967).

[2] Clayne R. Jensen, *Outdoor Recreation in America* (Minneapolis: Burgess, 1970), chap. 4.

Egnew had little net worth and only three years in the business. He was married and had a son. His salary of $21,000 per year provided him with a comfortable standard of living. He wondered whether he wasn't kidding himself, whether it was realistic to go out on his own, and how he might pursue the idea since he had never started a company previously.

Determined to resolve their future by adopting one of the three alternatives that Egnew had identified, Egnew and Moore resolved to meet again for an entire weekend to decide on a strategy.

Personal Backgrounds

J. C. Egnew. J. C. Egnew was born and raised in Indiana. He recalled some of his attitudes, which he attributed to his upbringing:

My dad was a teacher, but a farmer at heart. I remember his thoroughness—"if you're going to do something, do it well." He believed in sticking with things. Both my parents developed in me a high regard for my individual freedom.

This independence apparently also included emancipation from the classroom and attraction to the world of work and basketball. By the time Egnew was 16, he was on his own, working full-time after school. He noted, "I learned a sense of self-responsibility and how to support myself. I made most of my own decisions concerning school and other things. I found work a lot more interesting than school."

In addition to working full-time in high school, J.C. also played basketball. His schoolwork suffered: "I always did what I had to do to get by, and I didn't want to go to college." He graduated from high school 401st out of a class of 439 students.

Following graduation from high school, J.C. entered the University of Evansville, where he received his bachelor of science in mechanical engineering in 1963. He described himself as a loner during college, without a large circle of friends. He became very interested in the cooperative education program, which allowed students to alternate between full-time schooling and work. During co-op he worked for NASA in Huntsville, Alabama, rising from the rank of GS–3 to GS–5 in two years. He graduated in the lower third of his class after an erratic academic performance that included both dean's list and probation. He summed it up: "I hated to take tests, and I was not a crammer."

After graduation he joined NASA in Huntsville as a flight systems test engineer, GS–7, and rose to GS–9 by July 1965. He served as lead test engineer responsible for the conduct of hardware development test programs. This included coordinating and directing about 20 engineers and technicians in formulating, conducting, and evaluating tests and reporting test results.

In July 1965 he was promoted to production test manager for NASA and moved to Bay St. Louis, Mississippi. His responsibilities included the supervision of flight vehicles. By August 1968 he had risen to GS–13. He commented on his work:

I enjoyed getting involved in things where there was no established solution. I liked to find the solutions. I especially liked the new position since it involved work that hadn't been done before. But in about two years most of the problems were solved and it got boring. So I decided to return to school for my master's in industrial management at the University of Tennessee, Knoxville.

John F. Moore. John Moore was born and raised in Columbus, Ohio, one of two sons of a navy career officer who had worked his way up through the ranks. Though his father ran the house "like the commander of a ship," he was quite permissive with his two sons. "He taught us right from wrong. But what he really gave me was the motivation to do things on my own."

In high school John Moore was captain of the swimming, baseball, and football teams. At the same time he worked about 15 hours a week after school in a shoe store, and each summer he worked full-time paving driveways. He graduated in the lower third of his high school class, noting that "I did what I had to do to stay eligible and graduate." His considerable athletic promise earned him a full baseball scholarship to Ohio State University. The lure of fraternity life, particularly its social activities, detracted further from his less than enthusiastic interest in academics. Repeated academic probation caused him to lose his scholarship, so he entered the navy in April 1961. He was honorably discharged in April 1965.

In July 1965 Moore joined North American Rockwell Corporation as a materials requirements analyst, and in early 1968 he became a supervisor in the Support Operations Division. In September 1968 he returned to college and met with more academic success: "Once I went back, I got A's and B's and even won an honors medal in physics."

Upon graduating in June 1970 with a B.S. in industrial management from the University of Tennessee, Knoxville, Moore returned to North American Rockwell for three months as logistics staff assistant in Bay St. Louis, Mississippi. In October 1970, after much urging by J. C. Egnew, he joined Wilderness Products, Inc., as sales service manager.

At Wilderness, he was responsible for customer service, inventory control, transportation, and warehouse activities. This included factory sales to key "house accounts," developing product mix and initiating marketing plans, supervising 30 employees in office areas and transportation and warehousing facilities, and purchasing some accessory products and equipment.

Discussions between Egnew and Moore

In the fall of 1972 Egnew and Moore began a series of thoughtful discussions about what their future might hold. The first topic they raised was a very basic one: the reasons that each of them had for wanting to start his own business. Egnew felt:

As long as my professional talents are being challenged, I have an opportunity to grow, and the rewards for my contributions are commensurate with the marketplace, I'm happy. Everybody likes to have their future tied to a winner. Nobody likes to be in a losing operation. I began to look at alternatives. I saw tremendous opportunities in the tent business that weren't being properly taken care of. I felt there was room for another firm. Then, when I was able to recruit the other key personnel and get a business plan together, I was more sure we had a winner. This was a confidence-building process.

Regarding his financial motivations, Egnew said:

I never really think about the chance to make a big killing. If I'm on target in five, eight, or ten years, at the end of that time I'll be able to do what I want to do. I'll have a new sense of freedom, a sense of independence to do my own thing. Ownership and growth will provide the real rewards. We all dream about making something happen. If you succeed in building your own business, there's no question about who's responsible.

Moore shared similar views:

J. C. was the only one at Wilderness doing anything with any principles in mind or using what we learned in school instead of just shooting from the hip. If we could get organized, we could do it, I felt. I had been exposed to the business. It was dynamic, something new every day, and I liked this. I was excited by the challenge of doing it ourselves. I kept thinking to myself, we could do it!

In addition to challenge, both men appreciated the need to make a total commitment to the business if it was to be a success. Egnew believed:

The commitment to go into business is made when you sever whatever ties you have and say "my livelihood is dependent on this enterprise"—that's when the commitment is made. If the two or three people aren't willing to use most of their key assets for the business, then I wouldn't touch them. So the commitment is also shown when you get everybody to put their bucks in. That's when it all starts.

He also believed that starting salaries were a useful measure of commitment and that investors were right to expect personal and financial commitment from the key team members:

Starting salaries should be lean. A new business needs every possible advantage it can find. If key personnel won't make sacrifices up front, then they won't make them when it gets tough. You should be prepared to make a substantial personal commitment to your business if your haven't already done so. I would be naive to think, "Well, I have this fine educational background, and I have some pretty relevant experience—after all, I'm putting my professional reputation on the line here. What else can you ask for?" "But if the milk turns sour," an investor would point out, "all you have to do is move to some place as far away as southwest Texas and get a 10 or 20 percent salary increase in a new job and you're off and running again, while we're sitting here holding all the empty baskets." That's when it really hit me. If I were investing money in a new business and the two or three key people weren't able to make a significant commitment based on their personal assets, then I sure wouldn't be willing to commit a dime to them. That's the commitment that makes you work a little bit harder and makes you determined that you're going to find a way to succeed. Any investor with sense is going to look for this kind of commitment.

Risks and Rewards

Next, Egnew and Moore discussed their attitudes about risks and rewards in starting a new business. Egnew stated:

If we were to start our own business, I wouldn't waste much time thinking about "what if it doesn't work out?" My thinking is positive. If we can ever afford to blow something, now is the time—we are young and have no heavy debts. The idea or dream of having your own business is one many people have, and here is our opportunity. We are frustated with the way things are going at Wilderness; the opportunity for a better way to do things looks real; and we have a chance to build something.

Moore's comments reflected his confidence in Egnew's optimism:

If we decide to go ahead, I won't have time to worry or think about not making it. I don't feel that it's that much of a risk when we sit here talking about it, I am so hyped up thinking it could work. I guess if we'd both been fired from Wilderness and *had* to start our own company, I would do a bit more worrying. As it is, I am ready to throw in the towel and J. C. keeps the momentum going. It looks like an opportunity to make a lot of money. Wilderness went public in 1968, and one owner with 7 percent of the stock made $600,000. I feel J. C. has it all together, more than any other person I've ever met. I have tremendous respect for him. I am willing to gamble on a good guy, and therefore I feel it is a good gamble.

Start-Up Strategies and Pitfalls

From their previous business training, both Egnew and Moore were aware of the high failure rate of new businesses. Egnew expressed his opinions on this issue:

Most new companies begin with an idea for a new product or service. Few of them survive, and rarely, if ever, does one excel on the strength of the product alone.

You have to put it all together. You can't just have a great idea that's better than anything on the market and have a winner. You also need an organization and a plan. Getting the momentum going is the hardest thing. That's what makes a start-up so risky. All these things have to get moving at the same time—it's like the inertia of a large train. You've got to devote a lot of energy just to get things going.

Moore questioned Egnew on the specifics of "getting things going," and Egnew responded:

You've got to have a detailed business plan. It's an important tool when selling to potential investors. It provides a baseline from which to operate—the marketing plan, the financial aspects, the facilities. It's also a valuable document to help you recruit needed resources. You've got to be able to convince everyone that you're going according to plan, and if you don't have a plan, you won't know. Once you're in business, you'll have things come along that will shake your confidence—and if the business plan is not well founded, these unexpected events will scare the hell out of you and may scare you out of business. The business plan will also help you to be fully convinced that what you're about to do will fly, that you can do what you think you can, and that you can service the debt you're about to take on. When I talk a detailed business plan, I'm talking about a marketing plan, a production plan, and pro forma financial statements which tell you month to month what you expect to happen. These also give you a baseline from which to operate. If you're running over or under, at least you'll know where you are, and you can ask, "How am I going to get where I hope to go?" A detailed business plan with respect to the market plan and financials—if it's in enough depth—can help tell you if your plans are realistic or not. So I can't emphasize a good, solid business plan enough. It's almost impossible to start up effectively without one.

Egnew also felt that the business plan would play an important role in the early confidence-building process after the business was launched:

After start-up you have to realize that everyone is learning their job, including the founders. If you've got a good overall plan established, you'll have more confidence in your decisions and you'll be able to make much better quality decisions because you'll have a ready reference to say, "I've already run the numbers on this, and this is what will happen."

THE OPPORTUNITY

PART I

New Venture Ideas   2

Nothing is more dangerous than an idea, when it's the only one we have.

Alain Emile Chartier

The vitality of thought is in adventure. Ideas won't keep. Something must be done about them. When the idea is new, its custodians have fervor, live for it, and, if need be, die for it.

Alfred North Whitehead

2.1 RESULTS EXPECTED

Upon the completion of this chapter, the accompanying exercises, and the analysis and discussion of the Beantown Seafoods (A) case, you will have:

1. Examined some fallacies about ideas and their role in building a business and identified the important differences between good ideas and good opportunities and between entrepreneurs and inventors.
2. Examined the critical importance of ideas anchored in customer needs.
3. Examined the role of "the experience factor" and how pattern recognition and trial and error iteration can shape sound business ideas.
4. Examined the nature of individual and group creativity and ways to enhance idea development.
5. Identified leading sources of business ideas, networks to access, and methods to help the search.
6. Examined and developed some personal criteria for evaluating and selecting new venture ideas that "fit" you.

2.2 PRESESSION PREPARATION

Complete the creativity exercises in Section 2.5 and the personal criteria inventory in Section 2.8.

2.3 THE GREAT MOUSETRAP FALLACY

Perhaps no one has done a greater disservice to generations of would-be entrepreneurs than Ralph Waldo Emerson. How many times has his famous line been quoted?

If a man can make a better mousetrap than his neighbor, though he builds his house in the woods, the world will make a beaten path to his door.

"The great mousetrap fallacy" was thus spawned, and who knows how many tens of thousands of potential entrepreneurs have been sidetracked, even ruined, by taking the Emerson advice to heart? The myth has lived in the assumption that the core of a successful new enterprise is a novel idea or an invention. Indeed, success is apparently guaranteed if you can just come up with a new idea. And in today's rapidly changing world, if the idea has anything to do with technology, success is even more guaranteed, or so it would seem.

The myth seems to persist despite the lessons of practical experience, noted long ago in the insightful reply to Emerson by O. B. Winters:

The manufacturer who waits for the world to beat a path to his door is a great optimist. But the manufacturer who shows this "mousetrap" to the world keeps the smoke coming out his chimney.

2.3.1   An Idea Does Not Necessarily Equal an Opportunity

The truth of the matter is that ideas, by themselves, are inert, and for all practical purposes, worthless. Take, for instance, the often held belief that if you can obtain a patent for your idea or invention, then you are bound to build a successful business from it. What is a patent really worth? Of course, that is a difficult question to answer, but consider the following illustration.

At a leading New England engineering school where a new ventures course is taught, one assignment asks students to examine the role of inventions and patents in the eventual creation of a business. The students are asked to search through issues of the *Patent Gazette* from 10 years ago and select the 10 patented ideas they believe are most promising. The students are then asked to trace down the inventor and determine how much money was made on these "good ideas." The results are startling, especially if one believes Emerson. Even with the advantages of hindsight and selectivity, on a cumulative basis less than one tenth of 1 percent of these patented "good ideas" have resulted in a financial gain for the inventor.

Why is this so? The lesson has been learned previously by successful entrepreneurs and venture capital investors. There is an enormous difference between an idea and an opportunity that will lead to a successful venture. Most ideas are driven by the creative insight of the individual, often operating in a vacuum, removed from customers and the marketplace. Inventors invent. They seek new ways and new ideas. Entrepreneurs, on the other hand, are driven by opportunity. And opportunity is anchored in customers' needs and a favorable situation, competitive advantages, and timing that add up to one conclusion: we can seize the opportunity, and now is the time.

In short, a sound product or idea is a necessary but not sufficient condition for launching, building, and eventually harvesting a new venture. The entrepreneur is the catalyst who sees how and when an idea can be converted into a successful venture. As Ted Levitt, one of the best known marketing scholars and consultants, has remarked: "Ideas are useless unless used."

Most venture capitalists, if they have survived the past 10 years or more, have learned that no idea or product has ever, by itself, started or run a company, or taken it public. A high-quality management team drives the process. Ideally, having a top-notch idea or innovation, and a first-rate entrepreneurial team, is the best of all worlds. But this doesn't happen very often. The dean of American venture capital, General Georges Doriot, is often quoted for his insistence that he preferred a Grade A entrepreneurial team with a Grade B idea to a Grade B team with a Grade A idea. This view has become one of the standard operating axioms of the venture capital industry today.[1]

One must wonder, given this proven principle, whether General Doriot would have invested in Adam Osborne and his portable computer. Having the best idea first by no means guarantees success. Just ask Mr. Osborne.

2.3.2 Ideas Are a Dime a Dozen

Just listen and look around. What is the flow of ideas for new products and services? How many have you heard of in the past week? How many can you write down in the next five minutes? Try it. The flow of ideas is really quite phenomenal. During the investing boom of the early 1980s, for instance, venture capital investors received as many as 100–200 proposals and business plans *each month.* Yet, only 1–3 percent of these plans actually received financing.

In the first edition of *New Venture Creation* the Idea Generation exercise provided an excellent example of the high volume of ideas that exists. Dozens of teams that have completed the exercise have literally covered the walls with flip-chart paper full of novel ideas. In half an hour hundreds of ideas for products and services can be listed. Narrowing those lists to a few good opportunities is vastly more demanding.

To drive this point home even further, having the best technology or idea often does not make the critical difference in success. Numerous examples can be cited, but consider these:

1. UNIVAC (Sperry-Rand) had the early elegance and technology lead over IBM in computers, but it was never able to seize the significant emerging opportunities in the computer industry.

2. At about the time when one of today's leading minicomputer firms, Data General, was formed in 1968, at least several other new minicomputer ventures were also started. Some of these ventures actually had a "better idea" in the form of more advanced technology. But DG's lead entrepreneur and his team, all under 30 years of age when they started the company, had an entrepreneurial flair and market focus. Later on, the story of this entrepreneurial culture became a best-seller in the book *The Soul of a New Machine.*[2] (It is well worth reading.)

3. In 1969 the then fledgling Cullinet, Inc., raised $500,000 in the then hot new issues stock market. Two years later the firm had spent this initial growth capital and, according to its founder, John Cullinane, still had a payroll of $8,500 to meet. How was the money spent? Through "programmer anarchy," according to Cullinane. He turned the company around by firing the programmers: they did not understand what happiness was. "Happiness," Cullinane said, "is a satisfied customer."[3] By 1977 Cullinane had developed customer-anchored software products and a plan for growth that led to a substantial venture capital investment, at a time when a fraction of the recent venture capital pool was available.

[1]General Doriot, a retired Harvard Business School professor noted for encouraging entrepreneuring among his students, founded American Research and Development Corporation in 1946 in Boston, the first institutional U.S. venture capital firm. AR&D put venture capital on the map when its investment of about $70,000 in 1957 in four young MIT engineers with an idea for a new computer grew to about $350 million—as shares in Digital Equipment Corporation. DEC today is America's second largest computer firm.

[2]Tracy Kidder, *The Soul of a New Machine* (Boston: Little, Brown, 1981).

[3]Comments at his induction into Babson College's Academy of Distinguished Entrepreneurs, April 1984.

4. The pattern of new ventures in microcomputer software is likely to provide numerous other examples of the "better idea without better management" that went nowhere. Hundreds of these small software start-ups are anchored in the invention–better idea mentality. Take, for instance, the clones of VisiCalc, the first spreadsheet software program for microcomputers, and Lotus 1–2–3, the first integrated package for micros to include a spreadsheet, graphics, and database management. Critics and reviewers have reported that some of these new software products are indeed more elegant and sophisticated than the market leaders. But most are unlikely to gain a significant share of market. In mid-1984 a new entrant probably required $5 million and up of initial capital to fund the marketing necessary to launch a new micro-software product and gain attention and distribution in this tumultuous marketplace. Having a top-notch new product is very important, but it is only one of the success ingredients.

2.3.3   Entrepreneurs Are Not Inventors

Somehow the distinction between the inventive genius of a Thomas Edison and the creative entrepreneur is often blurred and confused. No doubt about it: Edison was a remarkable person, but what is less well known is that he earned practically nothing from his many inventions. Many aspiring entrepreneurs, operating unwittingly on the "Edison role model," are bound to become frustrated and disenchanted when their imaginative ideas earn nothing more than admiration from peers.

Exhibit 2.1
The Entrepreneur versus the Inventor

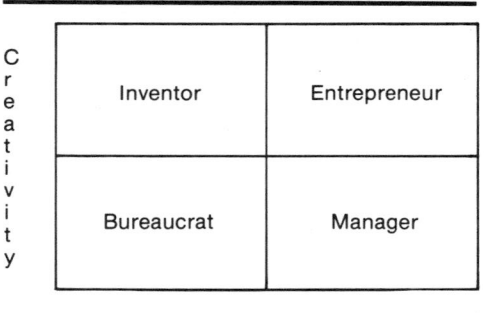

It is quite useful, we believe, to appreciate the differences between the entrepreneur and the inventor. Exhibit 2.1 is a conceptual way of thinking about these differences. Both the entrepreneur and the inventor have a creative flair, but the entrepreneur also has the requisite managerial skills to seize and execute an opportunity, and thereby create a business.

2.3.4   A Caution for Technical Entrepreneurs

Particularly susceptible to the mousetrap fallacy and idea myopia, we have found, is the aspiring, often inexperienced, entrepreneur who possesses an engineering, technical, academic, or research and development background. Why are such non-business-oriented people more vulnerable to placing unwarranted faith in their product or invention?

Part of the reason undoubtedly lies in their backgrounds, educations, and experiences. Perhaps, like Emerson, they have been substantially sheltered in viewpoint and experience from the tough, competitive realities of the business world. One consequence of this is to underestimate, if not seriously downgrade, the importance of entrepreneurial and management talent and what it takes to make a business succeed. There also tends to be a certain disdainful attitude among scientists and some academicians, in particular, toward the "mundane world of business." This attitude contributes to a less realistic estimate of the importance of the entrepreneurial skills and management know-how required to build a business.

Another contributor to the mousetrap fallacy is the mass media, which sometimes portray in a shallow way the ease and genius with which ventures such as Xerox, IBM, and Polaroid made their founders wealthy. Such oversimplified accounts suffer from and promote a similar mousetrap myopia. Unfortunately, these exceptions do not provide a useful rule to guide aspiring entrepreneurs. A guide for dreamers, geniuses, or both—yes, but not for most other entrepreneurs.

The mousetrap fallacy is also reinforced by the technical and scientific orientation to "do it better than ever." A good illustration of this flaw is provided by a Canadian entrepreneur who manufactured truck seats. He related how he and his brother, an engineer, started a business:

My brother developed a new seat for trucks. It was a definite improvement, so we started a business to manufacture and sell them. I knew we could profitably sell the seat he had designed, and we did so. Then we needed more manufacturing capacity—we could sell all we could make. But my brother wasn't as interested in that. He had several ideas on how to *improve* the seat, as well as design some new ones.

If I had listened to him, we would probably be a small custom shop today, or out of business. Instead, we concentrated on making seats that would sell at a profit, rather than just making a better and better seat. Our company has several million dollars of sales today and is profitable.

This is a classic example of how the "do it better than ever" flaw, often found in the technically or scientifically oriented entrepreneur, was overcome.

The stress on perfection—on making the best widget ever and improving it in any minute way possible—places undue emphasis on the product and its technical functioning. And this emphasis, often by necessity, if not by ignorance, excludes sensitive consideration of the ultimate marketplace: the wants and needs of the final user or buyer.

Another factor contributing to the mousetrap fallacy is the tremendous psychological ownership attached to a person's invention or new product (versus the business, as in the previous example). The intense and highly ego-involved personal identity and commitment to an invention or new widget tends to weaken, or preclude entirely, realistic assessment of other crucial aspects of the business—(1) the market potential, (2) the difficulty in developing the product to full completion so that it is ready for the market, (3) the time and effort required to introduce the product and gain customer acceptance, and (4) the real value of the invention—and the failure to make such an assessment can become an obstacle to attracting investors and a management team. An intense level of psychological ownership and involvement is certainly a prerequisite for creating a new business. But a fatal flaw of such ownership and involvement is *narrowness* of focus. Successful entrepreneurs, on the other hand, who build a substantial business possess this same high level of psychological ownership and involvement, but its focal point is the building of the business, rather than just one aspect of it—the idea or product.

2.4 THE EXPERIENCE FACTOR

What is it that enables entrepreneurs to spot an idea for which there is a good venture opportunity? More than anything else, it is, in a word, experience. They have been there before. They have a sense of what will work and what will stumble. And it is important to recognize that relevant experience can be quite independent of one's age—contrast youthful Steve Jobs, Apple Computer founder, with the late Ray Kroc, who founded McDonald's when he was over 50.

Numerous studies point to a common denominator among successful start-ups: in 95 percent of these new firms the founders launch a new venture in the same fundamental marketplace, technology, and industry where they have acquired the bulk of their relevant apprenticeship and management experience. They operate in familiar territory. The more technologically or market sophisticated the venture is, the more important this prior experience seems to be. This does not mean that you cannot launch and grow a successful venture in a business with which you have no experience. Certainly, widespread examples of success exist in numerous nontechnology, service-type businesses and franchises. All we are emphasizing is that one way to get the odds in favor of recognizing a good opportunity buried in a new idea is to get some relevant experience first. What is going on here?

2.4.1 Pattern Recognition

In example after example successful entrepreneurs exhibit an ability to recognize a pattern while it is still taking shape. They recognize that the idea has possibilities for "ringing a customer's bell." It is also noteworthy that these entrepreneurs do not require large, statistically reliable samples and control groups in order to conclude that there is an opportunity. Some actual cases illustrate these points:

1. Since his graduation from Babson College Vincent Keenan had spent 15 years working with leading financial institutions. Before launching his microcomputer software firm, The Financier, he was vice president of the tax shelter group for Dean, Witter. He had extensive experience in managing a large office and dealing with upper-income customers. To meet their sophisticated needs for tax advice and planning, he orchestrated the development of in-house software to keep track of their accounts and assets and provide the analysis of various scenarios. He knew little, in a technical sense, about microcomputers, computer programming, and computers at the time. He used them as tools in his work to meet customer needs. With the advent of the personal computer he saw a pattern that led to his venture: there was a link between the idea (personal financial planning software) and the needs of his customers. He was convinced that a new business could be built around this idea. It was a good opportunity, in his view, since he

was intimately familiar with both the customer's needs and the lack of serious competition. The Financier software has gained recognition as a leader in this rapidly developing industry.

2. Howard Head described how he decided that he could develop the oversized Prince tennis racket into a successful venture. "I saw the pattern again that had worked at Head Ski," he said.[4] "I had proven to myself before that you can take different technology and know-how and apply it to a solution in a new area." Head had been an aeronautical design engineer working with new light metal alloys to build more efficient airfoils during World War II. Although he had limited skiing experience, he concluded that if he could make a metal ski, there would be a significant market due to the limitations of wooden skis. He later tried tennis, with a conventional racket, and realized that there was a need for ball control among newer and learning players. He then set about learning enough about the physics of tennis rackets and surfaces to develop the oversized Prince racket. The company became a major factor in the industry and the second very successful "harvest" for Head.

3. In Texas a less well known young entrepreneur launched a modular home sales business in the late 1970s. He parlayed experience as a loan officer with a large New York City bank into a job with a manufacturer of mobile and modular homes in Texas. This enabled him, over a three-year period, to learn the business and understand the market opportunity. He opened one sales location in a growing suburb about 25 miles from one of the booming larger cities. The business provided him with a decent living, but he looked for ways to expand. By studying his competitors and conducting an analysis of how customers actually went about purchasing a new modular home, he spotted a pattern that meant opportunity. Customers usually shopped at three different locations, each with different models and price ranges, before making a purchase decision. So what did he do? Since his market analysis showed room in his city for three, maybe four, such businesses, he initiated an insightful strategy. He opened two additional lots, each with a different name and with different but complementary lines. Within two years, despite record-high interest rates, his business had tripled to nearly $17 million in annual sales and his only competitor was planning to move. This is an excellent example of how the best ideas invariably deal with ways to provide the customers with what they want, rather than with the product itself.

2.4.2 Iterations: Trial and Error Works

The new business that simply bursts from a flash of brilliance is rare. Sure, such businesses do happen, but they are exceptions. What is usually necessary is a series of trial and error iterations, or repetitions, until the crude idea fits with what the customer is really willing to pay for, and provides high gross margins as well. In technology ventures these iterations often occur during the development and refinement of the prototype. The main issue to be resolved is: Will it work? After all, Howard Head made a total of 40 different metal skis until he finally got one to work consistently.

The hard realities for entrepreneurs are that there are so many variables, and so many constantly changing situations, that refining an idea into an oppor-

[4]Keynote address at the first annual Entrepreneur's Night of the UCLA Graduate School of Business, April 18, 1984, Westwood, California.

tunity necessitates a lot of trial and error experiments. To make matters worse, in creating a venture, there just is not much in the way of theory to guide those experiments. Thus, the role of one's relevant experience becomes paramount once again.

Perhaps that is a major reason why there are numerous examples of the initial product or service being a point of departure for the emerging company. With surprising frequency a major business is built around totally different products or applications than were originally envisioned. Consider these examples:

1. F. Leland Strange, the founder and president of Quadram, maker of graphics, communications, and other "boards" for microcomputers, relayed the story of how he developed his "marketing idea" into a company with $100 million in sales in three years. Not only had Strange been a marketing professor; he had also taught a new ventures course using the first edition of *New Venture Creation*. When asked whether he had developed a business plan to launch his own company, he responded, "Of course." The company had even hit its projected revenues for the first two years. The only thing was, he noted, that it was based on different products than those defined in the original plan![5]

2. Polaroid Corporation, the camera company, was founded on the principle of polarizing light waves, a discovery by Dr. Land that he patented. It was reasoned that such a product would have the compelling safety feature of eliminating head-on nighttime collisions due to "blinding" by the oncoming lights. Conceivably, such polarized lamps could be installed OEM in every vehicle manufactured. The company grew to its present billion-dollar-plus size through a quite different application of the original technology—instant photography—that was not part of its initial growth ideas.

3. IBM, the world's largest mainframe computer manufacturer, and now the market leader in personal computers as well, began in the wire and cable business and later expanded to time clocks. Sales in the 1920s were only a few million dollars a year. The computer business emerged much later.

How important is the original idea to the development of a significant business? By itself, not very. With hindsight it looks very critical. But it is likely to endure and become a business only if it is anchored in the need of the customer, with real benefits and value added. Ideas for new ventures are important, of course, but we think that they tend to be quite overrated, and usually at the expense of ignoring or underemphasizing the other vital driving forces.

Central to the entrepreneurial process are the iterative steps of intelligent trial and error in finding ideas for products and services with significant market opportunity and potential, in revising, retesting, and further reapplying these ideas until a profitable matchup with the customer is achieved. This process is fundamentally a human one: having the capacity to recognize patterns and to seize and execute opportunities.

2.5   ENHANCING CREATIVITY

Can anyone seriously question the potential value of creative thinking in linking the product or service to the customer, devising innovative marketing and sales approaches, solving troublesome problems? No doubt about it, creativity of

[5]Keynote address at the 1984 Babson Entrepreneurship Research Conference, cosponsored by the School of Management, Georgia Institute of Technology, April 23–25, 1984, Atlanta.

all kinds plays a central role in entrepreneuring. The relevant question, then, becomes: Can creativity be enhanced? Fortunately, the answer is yes.

2.5.1 Nature of Creative Thinking

Most people can certainly spot the creativity and creative acts of others. Schoolchildren and college students all seem to know who, among their peers, are the ones with a creative flair. What may not be so well known, however, is that several studies suggest that creativity actually peaks around the first grade. A lot of things account for that. For one thing, one's life tends to become increasingly structured and defined by others and the institutions to which one belongs through adolescence. For another, the development of intellectual discipline, rationality, and rigor in school and in thinking takes on greater proportions during those formative years. A lot of this is probably at the expense of uninhibited, freewheeling creativity. Finally, social pressure may tend to be a taming influence on creativity.

But the good news is that there is considerable evidence that creative thinking can be enhanced. You don't have to be a genius or an artist in order to become a creative thinker. One vital ingredient is to be able to look at the same old problems in new ways, from a different angle. Needless to say, that is not as easy as it sounds, but some knowledgeable experts believe that this skill can be learned by most people with the willingness and patience to apply themselves.

Take, for instance, a group called Synectics in Cambridge, Massachusetts, one of the first organizations—in the early 1950s—to investigate systematically the process of creative thinking and how to harness it.[6] The term *synectics* means the joining together of different or apparently irrelevant parts. Synectics gained experience by applying its principles in order to integrate diverse individuals into problem-defining and problem-solving groups. The theories underlying the synectics approach to developing creativity were threefold:

1. Creative efficiency in people can be markedly increased if they understand the psychological processes by which they operate.
2. In the creative process the emotional component is more important than the intellectual, the irrational more important than the rational.
3. It is the emotional, irrational elements that must be understood in order to increase the probability of success in a problem-solving situation.[7]

The Synectics approach was novel and hands-on. It began with the selection of the groups to attend the training sessions, involved learning the methods and techniques derived from the above principles, and concluded by efforts to integrate the solutions generated by the groups back into the client's business or organization.

One of the authors participated in a training session as a graduate student. Although he was initially skeptical, it became evident that the methods did unlock the thinking process, and they seemed to yield very imaginative solutions. Take, for instance, the first problem assigned to the group: design a vertical anchor for boats. To free thinking from the conventional, rational approach, novel

---

[6]See William J. J. Gordon, *Synectics* (New York: Harper & Row, 1961).
[7]Ibid., p. 6.

techniques were introduced. One involved getting a volunteer from the group to actually lie on the floor, eyes closed, and imagine that *he* was the anchor. With some guidance from the trainer the group urged the "human anchor" to tell them what it felt like to be an anchor on the bottom of the sea!

The group then pushed and tugged at the "anchor" to elicit further imaginative reactions. The uninhibited process of physically and mentally attempting to feel and think what it was like to be some kind of device that would secure a boat vertically elicited both laughter and imagination. Some think that the two are often partners in the creative act.

Amid the hilarity that accompanied such sessions, a genuine respect for the techniques emerged. No doubt about it: Group members conceded that they came up with ideas and creative solutions during these freewheeling, uninhibited voyages into their collective creativity that they had never experienced before.

2.5.2   Left Brain—Right Brain

Since the 1950s a good deal more has been learned about the working of the human brain. Today there is general agreement that the two sides of the brain process information in quite different ways. The left side performs the rational, logical functions, while the right side operates the intuitive and nonrational modes of thought. Of course, we have just one brain and use both sides, actually shifting from one mode to the other. To observe this point in action, we have selected a simple exercise for you to try. It appears in a book by an art teacher who developed a method of teaching drawing based on the newly acquired left-side, right-side insights into the brain's functioning.[8]

It's important that you experience the shift from one mode to the other—the shift from the ordinary verbal, analytic state to the spatial, nonverbal state. By setting up the conditions for this mental shift and experiencing the slightly different feeling it produces, you will be able to recognize and foster this state in yourself—a state in which you will be able to draw.

VASES AND FACES: AN EXERCISE FOR THE DOUBLE BRAIN

The exercises that follow are specifically designed to help you shift from your dominant left-hemisphere mode to your subdominant R-mode. I could go on describing the process over and over in words, but only *you* can experience for yourself this cognitive shift, this slight change in subjective state. As Fats Waller once said, "If you gotta ask what jazz is, you ain't never gonna know." So it is with R-mode state: you must experience the L- to R-mode shift, observe the R-mode state, and in this way come to know it.

VASE-FACES DRAWING 1

You have probably seen the perceptual-illusion drawing of the vase and faces. Looked at one way, the drawing appears to be two faces seen in profile. Then, as you are looking at it, the drawing seems to change and become a vase. One version of the drawing is shown in Exhibit 2.2.

Before you begin. First, read all the directions for the exercise.

1. Draw a profile of a person's head on the *left* side of the paper, facing toward the center. (If you are left-handed, draw the profile on the right side, facing toward the center.) Examples are shown of both the right-handed and left-handed drawings (Exhibits 2.3a

---

[8]Betty Edwards, *Drawing on the Right Side of the Brain* (Boston: Houghton Mifflin, 1979).

Exhibit 2.2

Exhibit 2.3a
For Left-Handers

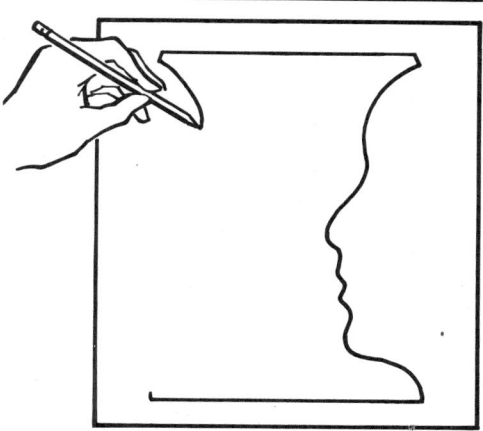

Exhibit 2.3b
For Right-Handers

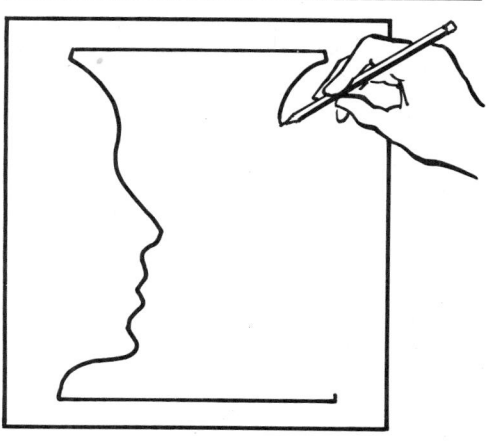

and 2.3b). Make up your own version of the profile if you wish. It seems to help if this profile comes from your own memorized, stored *symbols* for a human profile.

2. Next, draw horizontal lines at the top and bottom of your profile, forming the top and bottom of the vase (Exhibits 2.3a and 2.3b).

3. Now go back over your drawing of the first profile with your pencil. As the pencil moves over the features, *name them to yourself:* forehead, nose, upper lip, chin, neck. Repeat this step at least once. This is an L-mode task: naming symbolic shapes.

4. Next, starting at the top, draw the profile in *reverse.* By doing this, you will *complete the vase.* The second profile should be a reversal of the first in order for the vase to be symmetrical. (Look once more at the example in Exhibit 2.2.) Watch for the faint signals from your brain that you are shifting modes of information processing. You may experience a sense of mental conflict at some point in the drawing of the *second* profile. Observe this. And observe *how you solve the problem.* You will find that you are doing the second profile *differently. This is right-hemisphere-mode drawing.*

Before you read further, do the drawing.

After you finish. Now that you have completed the Vase-Faces drawing, think back on how you did it. The first profile was probably rather rapidly drawn and then, as you were instructed, redrawn while verbalizing the names of the parts as you went back over the features.

This is a left-hemisphere mode of processing: *drawing symbolic shapes from memory and naming them.*

In drawing the second profile (that is, the profile that completes the vase), you may have experienced some confusion or conflict, as I mentioned. To continue the drawing, you had to find a different way, some different process. You probably lost the sense of drawing a profile and found yourself *scanning* back and forth in the space between the profiles, estimating angles, curves, inward-curving and outward-curving shapes, and lengths of line *in relation to* the opposite shapes, which now become *unnamed and unnamable.* Putting it another way, you made constant adjustments in the line you were drawing by checking *where you were* and *where you were going,* by scanning the space between the first profile and your copy in reverse.[9]

In short, you began by drawing a symbol for a *face;* you concluded by drawing a *line*—the same result, but achieved by an entirely different process.

Using medical research as well as her own observations, Edwards has drawn up a list of Left-Mode and Right-Mode Characteristics (see accompanying box).[10] Research indicates, and you yourself have seen, that you can be in either one mode or the other, but not in both modes simultaneously. Therefore, the trick is to tell your left-mode to shut up when you want to approach a problem differently—in a nontemporal, nonverbal way. It works!

For those of you who can take the time, especially if you feel that you "can't draw a straight line," we suggest that you find the book and try a further exercise. It involves copying a line drawing done by Picasso of Igor Stravinsky—only the image is shown upside down. Within a very few minutes you will forget what you are copying and become interested only in how the lines fit together. When you have finished, you will probably be unaware of how much time has elapsed. Best of all, when you turn your drawing right side up, it will look uncannily like Picasso's. How could you have done it? The answer appears to rest in the right side of your brain. Not only is creative thinking very useful, it is also fun.

[9]Ibid., pp. 46–48.
[10]Ibid., p. 40.

A Comparison of Left-Mode and Right-Mode Characteristics

L-Mode	*R-Mode*
Verbal: Using words to name, describe, define.	*Nonverbal:* Awareness of things, but minimal connection with words.
Analytic: Figuring things out step-by-step and part-by-part.	*Synthetic:* Putting things together to form wholes.
Symbolic: Using a symbol to *stand for* something. For example, the sign + stands for the process of addition.	*Concrete:* Relating to things as they are at the present moment.
Abstract: Taking out a small bit of information and using it to represent the whole thing.	*Analogic:* Seeing likenesses between things; understanding metaphoric relationships.
Temporal: Keeping track of time, sequencing one thing after another: Doing first things first, second things second, etc.	*Nontemporal:* Without a sense of time.
Rational: Drawing conclusions based on *reason* and *facts.*	*Nonrational:* Not requiring a basis of reason or facts; willingness to suspend judgment.
Digital: Using numbers as in counting.	*Spatial:* Seeing where things are in relation to other things, and how parts go together to form a whole.
Logical: Drawing conclusions based on logic: one thing following another in logical order—for example, a mathematical theorem or a well-stated argument.	*Intuitive:* Making leaps of insight, often based on incomplete patterns, hunches, feelings, or visual images.
Linear: Thinking in terms of linked ideas, one thought directly following another, often leading to a convergent conclusion.	*Holistic:* Seeing whole things all at once; perceiving the overall patterns and structures, often leading to divergent conclusions.

The author of another recently published book on creativity sums up this attitude:

I like to think of creative thinking as the "sex of our mental lives." Ideas, like organisms, have a life cycle. They are born, they develop, they reach maturity, and the die. So we need a way to generate new ideas. Creative thinking is that means, and like its biological counterpart, it is also pleasurable.[11]

As you might surmise from the book's title, *A Whack on the Side of the Head,* the author takes a lighthearted, but eminently workable, approach to the problem. He has compiled a list of 10 "mental locks" that interfere with creative thinking and suggests ways to unlock them. As you go through the iterations of developing and refining an idea for a product or service that will capture customer enthusiasm, consider his list of creativity blockers:

1. The Right Answer.
2. That's Not Logical.
3. Follow the Rules.
4. Be Practical.
5. Avoid Ambiguity.
6. To Err Is Wrong.
7. Play Is Frivolous.
8. That's Not My Area.
9. Don't Be Foolish.
10. I'm Not Creative.

[11]Roger von Oech, *A Whack on the Side of the Head* (New York: Warner Books, 1983).

As is evident, these "mental locks" are the offspring of left-brain thinking. The obvious implication for an entrepreneur is: What if you tend to be more left-brain than right-brain in your thinking? You may have quite extraordinary logical and rational powers, and develop some quite exquisite technical solutions to a problem, but you never really capture the customer's enthusiasm. Now what?

2.5.3 The Concept of Team Creativity

Individual creativity is stunning when you witness it. But truly creative geniuses are few and far between. What is more, in our rapidly moving, fragile world, customers and the marketplace do not stand still long enough for a creative genius to surface in your venture, if that person is not you. Fortunately, you do not have to rely on a genius-inspired breakthrough to do quite nicely.

What we are continually impressed with is the creativity of a team of people. Time and again, we have observed comparable or better creative solutions to problems evolving from the collective interaction of a small group of people than are arrived at by the same people working individually. Synectics has certainly illustrated this phenomenon. To watch group creativity in action, try the following problem. First, pull together two to four teams of three to five persons each. Have at least five individuals work alone on the problem. Record the various solutions and how much time was required (it should not take more than 15–20 minutes).

Show the following illustration to everyone:

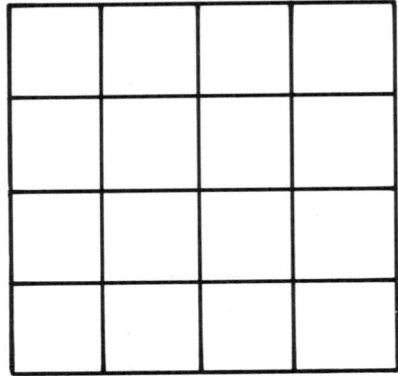

The figure you see is a square box on a single, flat plane. Assume that all of the angles are right angles and that the sides are of equal length. Your task is to count up the *total number of squares* you see in the figure.

Once you have completed the exercise, you can turn to Appendix VIII for an explanation.

These exercises in creativity may hold important implications for entrepreneurs. Two or more heads are very often as good as, if not better than, one. If there is a myth about entrepreneurs and creativity, it is the "fallacy of the one big brain." You do not have to have all of the creativity yourself to build a successful company. But unless there is some strong creativity on your team, you have one strike against you to begin. Again, the team concept surfaces. One good example of this is a company founded by a Babson College graduate with little technical training. He teamed up with a talented inventor-technologist. The entrepreneurial and business know-how of the founder complemented the creative and technical skills of the inventor. The result has been a rapidly growing multimillion-dollar venture in the field of video-based surgical equipment.

2.6 SOURCES OF NEW BUSINESS IDEAS

If you are like most of the people who read this book, the chances are that you already have plenty of ideas that might lead to a new venture. The real challenge, of course, is to identify those ideas that are serious opportunities. The next chapter will focus on that task. But what if you do not have any particular idea for starting a company? Where can you look?

New venture ideas have come from a multitude of sources, contacts, and experiences. In his book *New Venture Strategies*, Karl Vesper suggests a wide variety of potential sources, beyond work experience, including hobbies, social encounters, self-employment, moonlighting, and a deliberate search.[12]

To aid you in a deliberate search, we have compiled a summary of leading sources and information services.

The sources of ideas that will be presented and discussed are not meant to be all-inclusive, but to guide you into some general areas where ideas can be found.

2.6.1 Product-Licensing Information Services

One good way to obtain some exposure to a large number of product ideas that are available from universities, corporations, and independent investors is to subscribe to one of the services that periodically publish data on products available for licensing.

There are a variety of these services, and their publications cover both U.S. and foreign product-license opportunities. The products presented in these publications can range from simple toys and gadgets to sophisticated high-technology products. Some services do a better job than others at screening the products they present, and the amount of product information provided can range from a patent abstract to a one-page description with pictures and proposed licensing terms. To obtain additional information on any product presented, a subscriber must contact the potential licensor. Some services publish the licensor's name and address as part of their product information. Others code their licensor listings, require initial inquiries to go through them, and charge an inquiry fee. The annual subscription price for these information services can range from less than a hundred dollars to much more.

We are familiar with a number of these information services and suggest that you consider subscriptions to one or more of those listed below to locate product or service ideas for your venture.

1. American Bulletin of International Technology Transfer
   554 Wilshire Boulevard
   Los Angeles, California 90036

   Annual subscriptions are $120 for this bimonthly publication, and there is a

---

[12]Karl H. Vesper, *New Venture Strategies* (Englewood Cliffs, N.J.: Prentice-Hall, 1980), chap. 5.

$5-per-item inquiry charge to subscribers. This service provides listings of product and service opportunities sought or offered for licensing by organizations throughout the world.

2. General Electric
   Selected Business Ventures (SBV)
   Business Growth Services
   1 River Road
   Schenectady, New York 12345

Originally a publication for marketing selected GE products, GE's Selected Business Ventures program now identifies new product opportunities available from a number of U.S. and foreign organizations. Products are classified in one or more of eight different categories (e.g., electronic and electromechanical; consumer products; measuring, testing, and controls; and medical). Each month subscribers receive announcements of selected products that are available for licensing in the categories to which they subscribe. An annual subscription to any one product category is $175, with decreasing prices for any additional categories; an annual subscription to all eight categories is $725. Each product is described on a file card that also contains the name and address of the prospective licensor and, sometimes, the proposed licensing terms.

3. Technology Mart
   Thomas Publishing Company
   250 West 34th Street
   New York, New York 10001

Annual subscriptions are $72 for this bimonthly publication, and there is no inquiry fee for subscribers. Technology Mart publishes data on products and processes that are available for international license, divestiture opportunities involving product lines or even corporate divisions, and U.S. government technology that is available for license.

4. Patent Licensing Gazette
   Techni Research Associates, Inc.
   Professional Center Building
   Willow Grove, Pennsylvania 19090

Annual subscriptions are $32 for this bimonthly publication, which provides abstracts of screened patents that are available for licensing from domestic and foreign organizations. Names and addresses of the prospective licensors are given.

5. Government Inventions Available for Licensing
   National Technical Information Service (NTIS)
   U.S. Department of Commerce
   P.O. Box 1533
   Springfield, Virginia 22151

An annual subscription of $165 provides NTIS weekly abstracts of government inventions that are available for licensing. This publication covers government inventions believed to have commercial potential that are available from all major government agencies (e.g., NASA, AEC, and HEW). The descriptions of inventions tend to be very brief and technical. Additional information is available in patent applications. Although government licenses are generally granted on a

nonexclusive basis, some agencies can grant exclusive licenses when this is necessary to attract risk capital to commercialize government technology.

6. International New Product Newsletter
   Box 191
   Back Bay Annex
   Boston, Massachusetts 02116

An annual subscription is $75 for this semimonthly publication, which de-
scribes products and processes that are available for license, primarily from
sources outside the United States. The products and processes included are considered to have reasonably immediate commercial potential.

7. Dr. Dvorkovitz and Associates
   P.O. Box 1748
   Ormond Beach, Florida 32074

Dvorkovitz has the world's largest computerized file of products, processes,
and technology that are available for license. About 8,000 items are listed in
Dvorkovitz's data bank, and these items are replenished and updated by 20 representatives who are in contact with innovating groups in over 50 countries. Data
on available products are supplied weekly as computer printouts or through an
interactive display terminal at the subscriber's location that communicates with
a central computer.

Dvorkovitz's principal customers are major corporations. Dvorkovitz classifies his technology available for license into 99 categories, and the annual price
for a subscriber to monitor any one category is $2,000. The price per additional
category is somewhat discounted, and product information in all categories is
$32,500 per year, including a computer terminal to query the data bank.

2.6.2 Patent Brokers

Patent brokers specialize in marketing patents owned by individual inventors, corporations, universities, or other research organizations to companies or
entrepreneurs seeking new commercially viable products. Some brokers specialize in international product licensing.

Occasionally, a patent broker will purchase an invention and then try to resell it to a manufacturer. More often, a patent broker acts as an agent for an
organization or individual inventor seeking to sell a patent or invention. In this
situation, patent brokers are compensated for their efforts by commissions or flat
fees (from the buyer or the seller, or both) or by a percentage of the royalties
received by the buyer. In some cases of a young cash-short company acquiring
rights to a patent, the broker may take some or all of his fee as stock in the
company.

Over the years, the patent broker's image has occasionally been tarnished by
a few unscrupulous brokers who have taken advantage of individual inventors by
charging them a fee and then doing little to sell their inventions. However, the
acquisition of inventions effected by reputable brokers has resulted in significant
new products. Notable among these was Bausch and Lomb's acquisition, through
National Patent Development Corporation, of the U.S. rights to Hydron, a material (developed in Czechoslovakia) used in contact lenses.

We have been in touch with a number of patent brokers and suggest that one or more of the following might help you find a product for your ventures.

MGA Technology, Inc.
Wrigley Building
400 North Michigan Avenue
Chicago, Illinois 60611

New Product Development Services, Inc.
900 State Line Road
P.O. Box 8424
Kansas City, Missouri 64114

University Patents
875 North Michigan Avenue
Chicago, Illinois 60611

Research Corporation
405 Lexington Avenue
New York, New York 10174

Pegasus International
625 Madison Avenue
New York, New York 10022

National Patent Development Corporation
375 Park Avenue
New York, New York 10022

2.6.3   Industry and Trade Contracts

If you have decided on the industry and market area in which you want to establish a venture, there are a number of contacts you can make and a number of things you can do to seek product ideas for a venture in that industry.

Ideas from Customers. If you are clear enough about the type of product you want to make to be able to identify potential customers, you can meet with them and determine what their needs are and where existing products are deficient or inadequate. For example, if you wanted to enter the biomedical equipment business, discussions with doctors who are heads of medical services at leading hospitals (and potential customers) might lead to product ideas for your venture.

Ideas from Distributors and Wholesalers. Contact those people who distribute the kinds of products you might want to manufacture and sell, and seek their advice on new product requirements. Distributors and wholesalers can have an extensive knowledge of the strengths and weaknesses of existing products and the kinds of product improvements and new products that are needed by their customers.

Ideas from Competitors. Examine closely the products offered by those companies that might be your competitors. If a competitive product is in your area of interest, evaluate whether you can improve on an existing design and come up with a product that can sell against the competition. Your product should not infringe on the patents of your competitor; for many products, however, it is often easy to design around patent claims. Although it's nice to be the one to introduce a product, an imitator who moves quickly with a better product can often achieve a substantial market share. We know of one case in the recreational vehicle field where an improved version of an established trailer accessory achieved sales in excess of $1 million in its introductory year, in spite of the limited experience of the management in that business.

Ideas from Trade Shows. Trade shows covering the industry you want to enter can be an excellent way to examine the products of many of your potential competitors, meet distributors and sales representatives, learn of product and market trends, and identify potential products for your venture.

2.6.4 Former Employers

A number of technology-based businesses in the Boston area were started with products or services based on technology and venture ideas developed by the entrepreneur in a previous employment. In many cases, this technology and idea development was done at research laboratories that were not interested in commercial exploitation of technology and/or under a government contract where the technology was in the public domain. In other cases, entrepreneurs developed ideas to improve products that were purchased and used by their former employers. In yet other cases, the previous employer was not interested in the entrepreneur's ideas for new products, and sold or gave him the rights to use the technology to start his own company. Some companies will even help an entrepreneur to set up a company in return for equity in it.

You should reflect on your current and prior employment and examine whether anything you have done or are doing suggests a product idea that could be the basis of a business. If you do intend to use a product idea that is related or similar to a product manufactured or service provided by a former employer, be careful that you are not infringing on patents or trade secrets of your former employer and that you are not violating any employment contract that may prohibit you from competing with a former employer for a specified period of time after you have left. If you have such a contract or you think that your venture idea may infringe on a prior employer's patents, trade secrets, or other proprietary knowledge, you should consult an attorney before going too far with your venture idea.

2.6.5 Corporations

Almost all corporations engaged in research and development have developed inventions or services that they have not exploited commercially. Usually these inventions do not fit their existing product lines or marketing programs or do not seem to represent a sufficiently large market to be interesting to a large corporation.

A good number of corporations are now seeking to license these kinds of inventions. Some corporations use patent brokers and/or the product-licensing information services to sell their inventions. These same corporations as well as others will also try to sell their technology through their own patent marketing efforts. An entrepreneur who contacts a corporation with a licensing program directly may avoid the costs of a product-licensing information service or a patent broker, but he will not be exposed to a full range of corporate licensing opportunities.

Among the major corporations known to us to have active internal patent marketing efforts are the following:

Gulf and Western
Gulf and Western Invention Development Corporation
1 Gulf and Western Plaza
New York, New York 10023

Kraft Corporation
Research and Development
801 Waukegan Road
Glenview, Illinois

Pillsbury Company
Research and Development Laboratories
311 Second Street SE
Minneapolis, Minnesota 55414

Union Carbide Corporation
Nuclear Division
Oak Ridge, Tennessee 37830

RCA Corporation
Domestic Licensing
1133 Avenue of the Americas
New York, New York 10036

TRW Corporation
Patent and Technology Application Office
Systems Group
1 Space Park
Redondo, California

Lockheed Corporation
Patent Licensing
Missile and Space Division
Sunnyvale, California

2.6.6 Not-for-Profit Research Institutes

These are nonprofit organizations that do research and development under contract to the government and private industry. These organizations also do some internally sponsored research and development to develop new products and processes that can be licensed to private corporations for further development, manufacturing, and marketing. Perhaps the most famous example is Battelle Memorial Institute's participation in the development of xerography and the subsequent license of the technology to the Haloid Corporation, now Xerox. Some of the not-for-profit research institutes with active licensing programs are:

Battelle Memorial Institute
Columbus, Ohio

ITT Research Institute
Chicago, Illinois

Stanford Research Institute
Palo Alto, California

Southwest Research Institute
San Antonio, Texas

2.6.7 Universities

A number of universities that are active in research in the physical sciences seek to license inventions that result from this research. This can be done directly by a university or through an associated foundation that administers its patent program. Massachusetts Institute of Technology (MIT) and California Institute of Technology publish periodic reports that contain abstracts of inventions they own that are available for licensing. Among the universities that have active licensing programs are:

Massachusetts Institute of Technology
California Institute of Technology via the California Research Foundation
University of Wisconsin via the Wisconsin Alumni Research Foundation
Iowa State University via the Iowa State University Research Foundation
Purdue University via the Purdue Research Foundation
University of California
University of Oregon, Innovation Center

However, a number of very good ideas developed in universities never reach the patent offices. Accordingly, another way to find technological opportunities at a university—particularly if you are there as a student or researcher—is to become familiar with the work of researchers in your areas of interest and to evaluate whether anything they are doing could form the basis of a business. They might even join you in such a venture. A number of high-technology businesses in Boston were started this way. One example is a company that was started to manufacture an electro-optical hygrometer that was developed by an MIT student in support of his research. This sort of laboratory contact can also be used to find product opportunities in the laboratories of medical schools.

2.6.8 Professional Contacts

Ideas can also be found by contacting business and professional people in your vicinity who come into contact with inventors seeking to license their patents or to start a business using them. Among the professionals that might be contacted are patent attorneys, accountants, commercial bankers, and venture capitalists.

2.6.9 As a Consultant

A method for obtaining ideas that has often been successful for technically trained entrepreneurs is to provide consulting and one-of-a-kind engineering designs for people in a field of interest to the entrepreneur who needs this service. For example, if you want to establish a medical equipment company, try doing consulting and designing experimental equipment for medical researchers. Or perhaps you can provide engineering consulting to physicists, biologists, or oceanographers needing special kinds of instrumentation. These kinds of activities often lead to prototypes that can be turned into products needed by a number of researchers. One of the authors used this consulting approach to find products for two companies he started. The first company produced psychological testing equipment that evolved from consulting done at the Massachusetts General Hospital; the second designed and manufactured oceanographic instruments that were developed from consulting done for an oceanographic research institute.

2.6.10 Networks

The concept of networking has gained much attention in recent years. No doubt about it: developing an "ole persons' network" of contacts is an important part of entrepreneuring. Such networks can be a stimulant and source of new ideas for businesses, as well as provide valuable contacts with people and resources. Much of this requires personal initiative on an informal basis. But increasingly, in entrepreneurial "hotbeds" around the country, organized networks are cropping up that can facilitate and accelerate the process of making contacts and finding new business ideas. Consider the Boston area, for example, a high-density area of exceptional entrepreneurial activity. Several networking mechanisms have emerged in recent years, including:

1. Babson Entrepreneurial Exchange, an organization of area entrepreneurs, students, and alumni of Babson College who meet several times a year to exchange ideas, make contacts, and help one another with their entrepreneurial activities. The purposes of these gatherings include developing leads for student internships, participating in small workshops for trying out an idea or a business plan, and finding professional assistance. Contact Professor Robert Ronstadt at Babson (617-235-1200).

2. SBANE, the Smaller Business Association of New England, sponsors a monthly session whose sole purpose is to enable those present to meet other entrepreneurs and exchange business cards and ideas (617-890-9070).

3. MIT Enterprise Forum meets monthly to enable entrepreneurs to present their start-up or expansion plan to a large audience (often 100 or more) and a panel consisting of entrepreneurs, venture capitalists, and others. It is an excellent vehicle for learning about new technology ideas, and how technology-based entrepreneurs approach a new venture. Similar forums have recently been created in the Baltimore-Washington area and Los Angeles with MIT alumni and other groups. Contact Paul E. Johnson (616-253-8240).

4. The 128 Venture Group was launched by a former student of ours, Michael Belanger, to create a monthly interchange among entrepreneurs and innovators, management team prospects, and venture capitalists. At each meeting entrepreneurs describe their business idea, managers tell of their relevant experience, and investors hope that they can find their way into a profitable matchup. A group has also been launched in the Baltimore-Washington area (617-259-8776).

5. The Boston Computer Society (BCS) is a leading microcomputer association, with subgroups for entrepreneurs and consultants. Monthly meetings and electronic bulletin boards that can be accessed through a personal computer by modem over the phone provide an excellent way to find and test out ideas. The BCS is an especially valuable source of the latest entrepreneurial thrusts in microcomputer-related hardware and software.

While the Boston and Silicon Valley areas are rich in such entrepreneurial initiatives as these, we are also aware of similar networking opportunities that are emerging in other parts of the nation. We suspect that the following examples have counterparts in many areas of the country.

1. In New York City the American Women's Economic Development Corpora-

tion (AWED) has operated since 1976 as a means for networking and assisting female entrepreneurs (212-347-5195). There are national associations as well, including the Association of Women Entrepreneurs (402-474-2058) and the National Association of Women Business Owners (202-338-8966), with chapters in several major cities.

2. The UCLA Graduate Student Association has created the Entrepreneur's Roundtable to link practicing entrepreneurs with MBA students there. Contact Dean Al Osborne.

3. Wichita State University has initiated an Association of Collegiate Entrepreneurs (ACE), with chapters at colleges around the nation. The first annual gathering of ACE occurred at MIT in April 1984. Attendees we talked to were stimulated and their aspiration levels challenged by the student entrepreneurs they met there. Contact professor Fran Jabara.

2.7 SOURCES OF EXISTING BUSINESSES

The business may not be new, but it is a new venture for the entrepreneur. In addition to the sources noted above, existing business ideas can come from purchasing an ongoing business or acquiring a franchise. In a sense, much of the idea-generating process and the work of converting the idea into an opportunity have been accomplished if the business is operating profitably or has likely future profitability. Such a route to a new venture can be a shortcut, saving time and money, and can reduce the risk as well.

2.7.1 Franchising Ideas

Between 100 and 300 companies have moved into franchising annually in recent years, and the number of franchisors now stands at over 2,000. They account for over 500,000 franchised outlets doing well over $300 billion in sales annually; in fact, the franchise companies account for nearly one third of all retail sales.[13]

Whether you are considering obtaining a franchise or you have an idea or business concept that might be franchised to others, Chapter 9 of this book provides a good current summary of directories, guides, and cautions. Below is a summary of sources that will provide a useful start for a search in this field:

1. *Franchise Opportunity Handbook,* U.S. Department of Commerce, available from Superintendent of Documents, U.S. Government Printing Office, Washington, D.C. 20402. An annual survey of about 900 franchisors, it probably contains more extensive information on franchises than any other publication. $6.50.

2. *The Franchise Annual Handbook and Directory,* edited by Edward L. Dixon (Lewiston, N.Y.: Info Press), lists about 2,000 American and Canadian franchises in each annual edition. $12.95.

3. *Franchising: Proven Techniques for Rapid Company Expansion and Market Dominance,* by David Seltz (New York: McGraw-Hill, 1980), discusses how to go about franchising a business to others.

4. *Franchising World* is the monthly publication of the International Franchise Association (IFA), the largest association of established franchisors, with

[13]David E. Gumpert and Jeffry A. Timmons, *The Encyclopedia of Small Business Resources* (New York: Harper & Row, 1984), p. 277.

over 400 member firms (1015 Connecticut Avenue NW, Washington, D.C. 20036). $60 per year.

5. *Franchising Today* is a semimonthly magazine featuring profiles of successful franchisees and franchisors and developments in franchising (Franchise Technologies, 1201 San Luis Obispo Avenue, Hayward, California 94544). $18 per year.

In addition, *INC.* and *Venture* magazines publish an annual listing of franchise opportunities and run ads monthly on new opportunities in franchising. Similar advertisements can also be found in *The Wall Street Journal.*

2.7.2 Purchasing an Existing Business

The principal sources of listings are newspaper and business publications in your area and business brokers. The latter are listed in the yellow pages. Their transactions generally occur in the $25,000–75,000 range and include many smaller retail businesses, restaurants, and the like. Bank loan officers can be knowledgeable about businesses for sale, as can trust officers. Similarly, bankruptcy judges have a continual flow of ventures in serious trouble. If you have the relevant experience and know-how to operate one of these businesses, there can be some excellent opportunities buried beneath all the financial debris of a bankrupt firm.

Name _____

Date _____

2.8   IDEA GENERATION AND PREFERENCES

2.8.1.   Idea Generation, Sources, and Preferences

Idea Generation

How many times has each of us thought or commented: "I have a great idea for a business!" Or how often have we heard this kind of statement and accompanying examples during a social hour or casual conversation? The answer for most people is probably somewhere between numerous and infinite. Indeed, at one time or another nearly all of us have had what we and others have felt are good ideas for a possible business.

The purpose of the following exercise is to generate as many of these ideas as possible—ones you've heard of or have thought of. Our aim here is to simply generate as many new business ideas as possible—don't try to evaluate them or worry about their implementation. List these ideas below:

Possible New Business Ideas

1.

2.

3.

4.

5.

6.

7.

8.

9.

10.

Idea Sources

Think of as many sources of information—not discussed earlier—as you can for business opportunities, new and existing. List these in the space below:

Idea Sources

Idea Preferences

Step 1.   Think about your personal interests, what you feel you are likely to do very well, and any problems that you would like to make a contribution toward solving. Develop below a list of the possible fields (e.g., retailing, health care, food, pollution control, and real estate) that you feel you definitely would and would not like to be in as of now. List these fields below:

Would Like	*Would Not Like*
1.	1.
2.	2.
3.	3.
4.	4.
5.	5.
6.	6.
7.	7.

Name _____

Date _____

Step 2. Develop a revised list of at least 10 specific businesses—new or existing—or types of businesses that you definitely would and would not want to own and operate. List these below:

Would Want to Own/Operate	*Would Not Want to Own/Operate*
1.	1.
2.	2.
3.	3.
4.	4.
5.	5.
6.	6.
7.	7.
8.	8.
9.	9.
10.	10.

Step 3. Now ask at least three people who know you well to look at your two lists. Do they agree with the lists for you? Would they add or delete any items? Make the changes on your original lists from steps 1 and 2.

Step 4. In Table 2.1 are a number of considerations and characteristics that you might use to determine your personal criteria during the preliminary search for a new business that you would like to start. This exercise will also help you to identify your interests and expertise. Add any other items that you feel are relevant for you. Analyze carefully your New Business Ideas list and your Idea Preferences list for indications of the extent to which the particular consideration is (*a*) personally important to you and (*b*) of genuine interest to you. Also write down any qualifying statements or comments that you would add. Use the space provided in the exercise to complete this step. Indicate for Degree of Importance whether the item is:

> 1 = Very important, a "must have."
> 2 = Desirable, could compromise.
> 3 = Not important.
> 4 = Irrelevant for me.

For example, you may feel that lifestyle and work style and location are more important to you than the size and financial potential of a business, or vice versa. Such personal preferences and values can play a major role in picking a field and business that will suit you.

Name _____

Date _____

2.8.2 Identifying Personal Criteria

Table 2.1

EXERCISE: A SEARCH OF PERSONAL CRITERIA

Degree of Importance
(4 = very important, 1 = unimportant)

1. Location

   a. Geography—a particular area

   _____

   b. Community size and nature

   _____

   c. Community involvement

   _____

   d. Commuting distance, one way

   Less than 15 minutes _____

   16–30 minutes _____

   Over 20 minutes _____

2. Lifestyle and Work Style

   a. Size of Business

   Less than $1 million sales and under 30 employees _____

   More than $1 million sales and 30 employees _____

   More than $10 million sales and 300 employees _____

   b. Rate of Real Growth

   Faster—over 25 percent per year _____

   Moderate—10–15 percent per year _____

   Slower—less than 10 percent per year _____

  c. Work Load

    Over 70 hours, 6 days a week _____

    5–6 days, 55–60 hours per week _____

    5 days, 40–45 hours per week _____

  d. Marriage

    _____

  e. Family

    _____

  f. Travel away from Home

    More than 60 percent _____

    30–50 percent _____

    Less than 30 percent _____

3. Standard of Living

  a. Tight belt, with later capital gains potential

    _____

  b. Average, with limited capital gains

    _____

  c. High income, no capital gains

    _____

  d. Become very rich

    _____

4. Personal Development

  a. Utilize my skills and education

    _____

  b. Opportunity for personal growth and learning

    _____

  c. Enable me to contribute to society

    _____

Name _____

Date _____

5. Status and Prestige

_____

6. Impact on Ecology and Environment

_____

7. Amount of Capital Required

   a. How much? _____

   b. From you _____

   c. From others _____

8. Other Considerations (add any others that you feel are important)

_____

Step 5. Imagine that you have $1,000 to spend in such a way as to reflect your overall sense of priorities among the eight personal criteria items. Indicate below how much of the $1,000 you would allocate to each one; the most important should receive the greatest amount. Some criteria may get no dollars, some may be equal to others, and so on. Once you have done this, then rank the items 1, 2, 3, etc. in order of their importance to you, starting with the *most important item* as number 1. (Note: There are no "right answers" to any of these.)

Characteristic	Share of $1,000	Rank
Location		
Lifestyle and Work Style		
Standard of Living		
Personal Development		
Status and Prestige		
Impact on Ecology and Environment		
Amount of Capital Required		
Other Considerations		

Step 6. Now review the list from step 5 with at least two or three people who know you well. Use them to reality-test and refine your criteria and personal preferences concerning the field of interest and kind of business you would like to start. Below, try to list the fields or types of businesses where you might narrow your search for an idea. Of course, if you already have an idea, this exercise can be a useful way to test its fit with the criteria you have developed in step 5.

Very Attracted	*Somewhat Attracted*	*Unattracted*

Name _____

Date _____

Step 7. Analysis and Discussion. In order to digest and pull together some insights from the exercise, it is useful to exchange your results with some other entrepreneurs. You can do this on your own or as part of a class or training session. The following four steps can aid the exchange.

1. Teams meet for about 30 minutes to discuss their lists of new business ideas and sources. A spokesperson should be prepared to present a summary when the session reconvenes.
2. Session reconvenes and develops total group summary from step 1 (15 minutes).
   a. How many ideas were generated?
   b. How difficult was it to identify ideas?
   c. How many sources were identified, and how difficult was it to determine these?
   d. What implications do the answers to the above questions have concerning the role and importance of the idea?
3. Next, form into trios to exchange and review the Idea Preferences exercise. Use this meeting as an opportunity to compare notes and to reality-test and refine your criteria for selecting a business idea (30 minutes).
4. Class reconvenes to highlight the issues and insights raised in step 3, using various examples from the trios to illustrate these (15 minutes). Then read the summary (5–8 minutes).

Step 8. Closure.   Try to jot down some insights and observations that have emerged from the exercise and discussion. What compelling themes and issues thread through your choices? What insights emerge in terms of your personal values, attitudes, and interests that may bear on what is a "good idea" for you? What issues, conflicts, and trade-offs have been raised that you need to consider further? What implications do you see for selecting a new business opportunity or gaining relevant experience?

2.9 SUMMARY

Our purpose here has been fourfold. First, we aimed to place in a more realistic perspective the role of the idea, invention, or product in the success of a new venture, relative to the lead entrepreneur and the management team. As was disclosed by "the great mousetrap fallacy," a good idea is nothing more than a tool in the hands of an entrepreneur. Ideas are "a dime a dozen," and they are not the same as opportunities; they are a first step in converting one's creativity into an opportunity through trial and error iterations.

Second, new research shows that creativity and intuition rest in the right side of the brain and can be nurtured (some say, even learned). Logic and rationality, the domain of the left-brain, often clash with the freewheeling, intuitive nature of the entrepreneur and lead to many paradoxes. Teams can generate creativity that may not exist in a single individual.

Third, we have attempted to provide some useful sources and guidelines for searching for new business ideas and locating existing ones. There is certainly a lot of help out there. And the advent of the personal computer, news networks, electronic bulletin boards, and information services will make an increasing part of the search possible from your home.

Lastly, and importantly, most entrepreneurs succeed by pursuing ideas that are not only sound business opportunities but also "fit" with their personal criteria, desired lifestyle, and values. Identifying personal criteria speeds up the search process by narrowing the focus and providing guidance on what to say no to. Otherwise, there is such an endless flow of ideas that the search may become the elusive quest for a needle in a haystack.

To illustrate the importance of personal criteria, consider the following:

1. The founder of a major high-technology venture in the Boston area was asked why his headquarters was located practically in downtown Boston, when all the other high-tech firms were on the famous perimeter, Route 128. His reply was: "It's very simple. I wanted to live in Boston because I love the city, and I wanted to be able to walk to work. The rest didn't matter."

2. Two partners founded a small manufacturing firm and retail factory outlet in the camping and backpacking supplies business. They intentionally located the business in a small, almost rural, community 25 miles from a major metropolitan area. The location was decidedly not the ideal location based on consumer traffic and shipping. Further, they deliberately limited their growth to a pace slower than the rapid market growth overall. Why did they do this? They wanted to live in a rural area with their business located equidistant between their two homes and to have a lifestyle that did not place the growth of the business above all else.

3. A young MBA from Chicago had enjoyed spending his summers as a youngster in the lake country of northern Wisconsin. Rather than settle permanently in Chicago and seek a position with his old co-op employer, a major auto producer, he and his wife chose to locate where they had summered in Wisconsin. Entrepreneuring enabled them both to start various small ventures and provided the combination of their preferred lifestyle and their preferred standard of living.

2.10 BEANTOWN SEAFOODS (A): CASE STUDY

This case is an actual start-up idea based on the business plan developed by an undergraduate, disguised as George Halsey, for a New Ventures course at

Northeastern University in 1975. The case will enable you to evaluate his venture idea and to decide whether you might invest in it or consider going to work for the Halseys or joining them as a partner. It will also provide an example of an actual business plan.

BEANTOWN SEAFOODS (A)

In early 1977, as part of a New Ventures course in college, George Halsey developed a business plan for Beantown Seafoods, Inc., (BSI), a fresh fish distribution company started in 1976 by his father.

Following graduation, George joined a large international conglomerate as a product manager. He was successful in his job but frustrated by working in a corporate environment. George saw a lack of focus and direction in the company's marketing attempts. He felt that the company was in the wrong market at the wrong time and believed that new products flopped because they were not carefully researched.

George believed he saw an opportunity to focus his attention on new markets for fresh fish. George was convinced that the business plan defined BSI's market, determined goals, and outlined a plan to meet targets. He told his father he was going to build BSI into a million-dollar sales operation. Daniel Halsey, questioning the worth of formal business plans, replied in disbelief, "A million dollars, are you crazy?" George wondered whether he should take the plunge. After all, wasn't this a good time in his career to "go for it"?

Beantown Seafood's original business plan follows.

Part 1: Beantown Seafood and Its Industry

In February 1976 Daniel Halsey registered Beantown Seafoods as a profit-oriented proprietorship. After 22 years with a national manufacturer of consumer and institutional packaged frozen fish products, Mr. Halsey established Beantown Seafoods in order to meet the increasing national demand for fresh fish.

With two of the nation's largest ocean perch processors morally backing his efforts, the search for potential customers began in the Midwest—an area of the country where perch is heavily consumed.

Today Beantown Seafoods successfully acts as a broker/wholesaler within the fresh fish segment of the commercial fishing industry.

The industry is divided into two major marketing categories: the Industrial category and the Edible Products category. Among the end products of the Industrial category are items such as pet foods and fish oils. As Exhibit 1 demonstrates, this category of the industry has steadily declined over the years, now processing only 33 percent of the industry's total supplies.

The other category of the industry, Edible Products, is divided into three subsegments—frozen, canned, and fresh (the segment Beantown Seafoods competes in). Unfortunately, the U.S. Department of Commerce—the major source of this report's marketing statistics—does not numerically differentiate the fresh and frozen segments. It is estimated, however, that of all Edible Products, fresh fish represents 17 percent of the total category, while frozen and canned fish generate 39 percent and 44 percent, respectively, of the category's business. Exhibit 2 reflects the physical segmentation of the industry.

Exhibit 1
Supply of Fishery Products (in million pounds)

Year	Industrial	Percent Change	Edible	Percent Change	Total	Percent Change
1975	3,289	+2.3	6,559	−6.8	9,848	−3.9
1974	3,215	−54.0	7,037	+4.0	10,252	−25.4
1973	6,989	+20.9	6,764	+12.3	13,753	+16.5
1972	5,781	+9.9	6,023	−3.1	11,804	+2.9
1971	5,261	−14.8	6,213	+9.5	11,474	−3.1
1970	6,173	−47.7	5,674	+1.7	11,847	−31.8
1969	11,802	+29.1	5,579	+15.1	17,381	+24.2
1968	9,142	+29.9	4,849	−10.7	13,991	+12.2
1967	7,037	+30.9	5,432	+5.2	12,469	+18.4
1966	5,372	—	5,163	—	10,535	—

Source: U.S. Department of Commerce.

Exhibit 2
Supply Segmentation of the Commercial Fishing Industry

Total Supply	
Industrial	*Edible Products*
Canned Meal Oils Solubles	Frozen Fresh Canned
Finfish	*Shellfish*
Cod, haddock, perch, flounder, etc.	Lobsters, clams, scallops, etc.

Recently, the United States implemented a more stringent conservation effort to help protect our waters from being overfished—a move primarily designed to curtail the activities of foreign fishing fleets (in particular, the Russian and Japanese fleets), in hopes of revitalizing the American fleet. Within the last 10 years, for instance (1965–75), the total fish supply for the United States has actually increased an average of 3.2 percent per year. Imports have, however, represented a larger share of the U.S. market each year.

As Exhibit 3 reflects, imports accounted for 63 percent of the U.S. Edible

Exhibit 3
Supply of Edible Commercial Fishery Products (in million pounds)

Year	Domestic	Percent	Imported	Percent
1975	2,417	36.8	4,142	63.2
1974	2,328	33.1	4,709	66.9
1973	2,310	34.2	4,454	65.8
1972	2,441	40.5	3,583	59.5
1971	2,537	40.8	3,676	59.2
1970	2,321	40.9	3,353	59.1
1969	2,347	42.1	3,232	57.9
1968	2,368	48.8	2,481	51.2
1967	2,573	47.4	2,859	52.6
1966	2,587	50.1	2,576	49.9

Source: U.S. Department of Commerce.

Products supply in 1975, but in 1965 they had 50 percent of the category. Accordingly, while the foreign fleets have consistently supplied more product, the U.S. fleet has historically harvested the same number of pounds. It is projected, however, that with the 200-mile limit, domestic production should substantially increase over the next five years.[1] (A more complete discussion of the 200-mile limit and its effect on Beantown Seafoods will be provided later in this report.)

Over the years, consumer demand for edible fish has increased too, but at a slower rate than supplies.

Over the last five years, per capita consumption has increased an average of 1.6 percent per year. However, a subsegment within the fresh and frozen category (see Exhibit 4), "Fillets and Steaks," has increased an average of 2.3 percent over the same period. This is important because all fresh fish falls within this subsegment of per capital consumption.

Exhibit 4
Per Capita Consumption (in pounds)

Year	Total	Percent Change	Fresh and Frozen	Percent Change	Steaks and Fillets	Percent Change
1975	46.5	− 4.5	6.8	− 6.9	2.12	− 16.5
1974	48.7	− 26.1	7.3	+ 2.8	2.54	+ 10.9
1973	65.9	+ 16.0	7.1	+ 6.0	2.29	+ 12.2
1972	56.8	+ 1.4	6.7	− 2.9	2.04	− 6.0
1971	56.0	− 4.1	6.9	+ 4.5	2.17	+ 8.0
1970	58.4	− 32.6	6.6	+ 6.4	2.01	+ 8.1
1969	86.6	+ 23.0	6.2	+ 6.9	1.86	+ 13.4
1968	70.4	+ 11.0	5.8	− 4.9	1.64	− 5.7
1967	63.4	+ 17.0	6.1	+ 1.7	1.74	+ 3.6
1966	54.2	− 13.6	6.0	+ 1.7	1.68	+ 3.7

Includes both industrial and edible product categories.
Source: U.S. Department of Commerce.

Part 2: What Is Beantown Seafoods?

In Part 1 we described Beantown Seafoods as a "broker/wholesaler," perhaps a somewhat abstract definition. Let's therefore look at this in more detail.

Beantown Seafoods is classified as a service—presently, simply buying and selling processed fresh fish. Unlike a broker, Beantown Seafoods actually takes possession of the merchandise; we do not, however, have any inventory. Accordingly, Beantown Seafoods doesn't buy fish unless a customer has previously committed to a specific quantity and species of fish. This can work in a number of ways:

1. *Source Initiated.* Here, our suppliers offer *x* amount of a specific species to Beantown Seafoods at *x* price. We in turn call our portfolio of customers, probing their demands and confirming orders. After the final customer has been called, we telephone the supplier with the specific orders. About 65 percent of our business is transacted in this manner.

2. *Customer Initiated.* In a conversation with a customer a request may be made for us to purchase a certain species of fish. Subsequently, we first check

[1] *A Baseline Economic Forecast of the U.S. Fishing Industry* (Washington, D.C.: Superintendent of Documents, 1975).

existing suppliers for product availability and pricing and/or explore new suppliers. At the conclusion of our search we recall the customer with the results (i.e., the price and if supplies enabled us to fill the entire order) and confirm the order. About 30 percent of our business falls within this category.

3. *Beantown Seafoods Initiated.* Occasionally, we will solicit new business from an existing customer by recommending a further diversification of the customer's product line. However, this is a difficult selling task and occurs in only about 5 percent of all transactions.

What are our customers' characteristics? Of the customers we now serve, 95 percent are fish and/or poultry distributors, while the remaining 5 percent are direct retail accounts. The direct retail accounts include a cross section of primarily supermarket chains, but also include a chain of retail fish stores. The bulk of our customers, however, distribute to small retail and fish stores, restaurants, and to supermarkets too.

Last year we tried to survey potential customers, but the results were disappointing and inconclusive. Exhibit 5 is a sample questionnaire.

Exhibit 5
Customer Questionnaire 1, February 1976

1. Does your company presently handle fresh fish? _____ Yes
   _____ No   (Please skip to question 12)

2. Does your company sell freshwater fish?   _____
   ocean fish?   _____
   both freshwater and ocean?   _____

   If "both," what percentage of your sales is from fresh? _____%
   ocean? _____%

3. How many pounds of fresh fish do you sell in a week? _____ lbs.

4. In regard to your answer to 3, what percentage would you estimate is sold to the

   institutional trade? _____%
   retail trade? _____%

5. What species of fresh fish are you presently selling?

Species	Pounds Sold per Week
_____	_____lbs.
_____	_____
_____	_____
_____	_____
_____	_____
_____	_____

6. What percentage of your total 1975 sales did fresh fish represent? _____%

7. How often do you presently obtain fresh fish deliveries?

   _____ times a week
   or
   _____ times a month

8. Are these deliveries flown in? _____
   trucked in? _____

9. Does the majority of the fresh fish you sell come from (please check one)

   the East Coast? _____
   the Gulf? _____
   the West Coast? _____
   the Midwest? _____
   Canada? _____
   any other source? _____

Exhibit 5 *(concluded)*

10. On an average, what's the lapse time between ordering and delivery? _____ days

11. Is this considered a problem for you in any way? _____ Yes _____ No
    If "Yes," why is that so? _____

12. At this point in time, what type of order might you be interested in?

Species	Pounds per Week
_____	_____lbs.
_____	_____
_____	_____
_____	_____
_____	_____

13. What would you prefer in a pack-out for your fresh fish orders? (Please check the one best for you.)

Total Lbs. per Case	Units per Case
_____ 1 to 10 lbs.	_____ 1 unit
_____ 25 to 50	_____ 2 to 3 units
_____ 50 to 75	_____ 4 units
_____ 75 to 100	_____ 5 to 6 units
_____ 100 to 125	_____ 7 units
_____ over 125	_____ Other

14. What type (frequency) of delivery service would be best for you?

    _____ Daily
    _____ 3 to 4 times weekly
    _____ 2 times per week
    _____ 1 time a week
    _____ Once every 6 to 10 days

15. What day of the week would you like delivery?

    _____ Monday
    _____ Tuesday
    _____ Wednesday
    _____ Thursday
    _____ Friday
    _____ Saturday/Sunday
    _____ No preference

16. In this area, how many competitors do you have?

    _____ 1 to 2
    _____ 3
    _____ 4
    _____ 5 to 6
    _____ 7 to 10
    _____ More than 10

17. What would you estimate is your share of market? _____%

Finally, for statistical purposes, we would like to ask you the following questions.

18. Is your company listed in Dun & Bradstreet? _____ Yes _____ No
    If "Yes," what is the company's rating? _____

19. For 1975, were the total dollar sales of your firm: _____ *more* or _____ *less* than $1 million?
    If *"more"*: Is it _____ *more* or _____ *less* than $5 million?
    If *"less"*: Is it _____ *more* or _____ *less* than $500,000?

We greatly appreciate your time. Thank you.

Geographically, our customers are as near as Boston and as far west as Denver. The majority of customers are located in the Midwest, however.

Initially, Beantown Seafoods offered only ocean perch to its customers. As noted earlier, this was primarily because our only suppliers at that time handled perch on an almost exclusive basis.

Within Beantown Seafoods' first 9 to 10 months in business, approximately 95 percent of volume was generated through the sale of perch. Within the last five months, however, we have successfully extended our product line. There were three key factors initiating this change:

1. *Profitability.* To gain recognition within the industry, Beantown Seafoods entered the market on a strategy of low price. Accordingly, our net margin on perch was almost minimal (i.e., 5 percent). Other species, however, offered a higher margin once the customers' orders for the lower-priced perch were obtained.

2. *Customer Demand.* Like Beantown Seafoods, many of our customers too sought new and/or alternate sources of supply. We therefore tried to meet our customers' demands, often resulting in an extension of our product line.

3. *Market Opportunity.* As Beantown Seafoods matured, we saw that many of our competitors maltreated the customers we shared. It was our belief that a possible key to future success was to emphasize service and ambition. One way of accomplishing this would be by showing our customers Beantown Seafoods' full-line capabilities.

Overall, our major objective was to lure new business by demonstrating to our existing customers that Beantown Seafoods was willing to do almost anything to help its customers, in other words, to develop credibility within the industry.

Part 3: The Fresh Fish Market

The Product. One of the most important aspects of success in this segment of the industry is product availability. As mentioned earlier, Beantown Seafoods has two of the nation's largest perch processors on an almost exclusive basis. This has played an essential role in our success to date, especially considering the dwindling availabilities of perch on the open market.

To give a better perspective of the items that Beantown Seafoods sells, Exhibits 6, 7, and 8 outline the products' availability and pricing trends. Exhibit 8 indexes the percent change of price to the percent change of supply.

Over the last five years, fish prices have risen an average of 18.7 percent per year. Per capita consumption of fillets and steaks, however, has increased an average of 2.3 percent per year during that same time period (Exhibit 4). The rise in consumption despite the outpaced rise in prices can be attributed to several key factors:

1. There appears to be more aggressive campaigning on behalf of the national frozen fish manufacturers to introduce consumers to a historically flat section of the freezer case. Companies among these crusaders include Gorton's (now a subsidiary of General Mills), Mrs. Paul's (a subsidiary of RCA), and a host of regional brands (e.g., Van de Kamps in the West, Booth's in the Midwest), plus heavier promotional plans of the chains' private label.

2. Many families looked for main meal alternatives during the meat boycotts in the mid-70s. Many of these families found the lower-cost/high-protein benefits of fish.

Exhibit 6
Fish Supplies (in million pounds)

Species	1976 (pounds)	Percent Change versus Year Ago				
		1976	1975	1974	1973	1972
Butterfish	3.1	−29	+8	+18	+109	−54
Cod	55.8	NC	−5	+17	+8	−12
Cusk	2.8	−9	+5	+3	+32	+22
Flounder	110.6	+4	−3	−5	−1	+4
Haddock	12.8	−21	+97	−1	−29	−46
Hake	14.1	+27	+1	+9	+6	+20
Halibut	20.6	−5	+17	−24	−10	−6
Perch	32.1	NC	−23	−22	−9	−2
Pollock	24.3	+18	+6	+38	+10	+18
Scup	16.0	−5	+9	−7	+31	−8
Total fish	292.2	+2	NC	−1	−1	−4
Clams	81.0	−28	−6	+12	+19	+8
Lobsters	31.7	+9	+3	+1	−1	−12
Scallops	22.0	+88	+36	+6	+8	−3
Total shell	134.7	−12	−2	+9	+14	+2
Total all	426.9	−3	−1	+2	+4	−3

Exhibit 7
Whole Fish Prices

Species	1976 Cents per Pound	Percent Change versus Year Ago				
		1976	1975	1974	1973	1972
Butterfish	28.2	+17	−2	NC	NC	+41
Cod	25.7	+10	+21	+7	+6	+42
Cusk	17.8	+26	+5	+16	+17	+13
Flounder	37.8	+11	+33	+11	+15	+23
Haddock	43.5	+33	−11	−3	+4	+41
Hake	11.6	+24	+11	−8	+26	+25
Halibut	94.2	+40	+32	−2	+6	+109
Perch	13.7	+33	+27	+5	+37	+10
Pollock	13.4	+11	+12	+5	+15	+17
Scup	21.3	NC	+16	−35	+22	−1
Total fish	32.6	+16	+31	+2	+11	+34
Clams	77.4	+114	+13	−1	−9	−3
Lobster	$1.660	−2	+13	+4	+17	+17
Scallops	$1.809	−2	+21	−13	−3	+23
Total shell	$1.152	+58	+18	−5	−2	+4
Total all	58.6	+34	+24	NC	+7	+17

3.   As a result of the products' overall increase in demand, distribution has increased at the retail level. Some retailers which historically carried one brand of frozen fish are now carrying two, while many supermarkets are now adding fresh fish in their deli sections.

In order to maintain momentum at the retail level, supplies of domestic production, the primary source of fresh fish, must increase in the upcoming years. Accordingly, in 1975 the National Marine Fisheries Service (a department within

Exhibit 8
Price Index*

Species	1976	1975	1974	1973	1972
Butterfish	165	91	85	48	306
Cod	110	127	91	98	161
Cusk	138	100	113	89	93
Flouder	107	137	117	116	118
Haddock	168	45	98	146	261
Hake	98	110	84	119	104
Halibut	147	113	129	118	222
Perch	133	165	136	150	112
Pollock	94	106	76	104	99
Scup	105	106	70	93	108
Total fish	114	131	103	112	140
Clams	297	120	88	76	90
Lobster	90	110	103	118	143
Scallops	52	89	82	90	126
Total shell	179	120	87	86	102
Total all	138	125	98	103	121

*An index of 100 would represent the percentage change in price equaling the percentage change in supply. An index below 100 would be interpreted as the percentage change in supply surpassing the percentage change in price (e.g., a supply of +8 percent and a price of −2 percent would equal an index of 91).

the U.S. Department of Commerce) and an independent consultant jointly published a 22-page summary forecasting supplies and prices through 1985. Their projections include:

1. *Total* supplies to increase an average 3.4 percent per year, while prices rise only 3.7 percent.
2. Total *edible product* supplies to increase an average 2.4 percent per year, while their associated prices rise 3.3 percent per year.
3. *Per capita consumption* of total edible products to increase from 35.2 pounds per person in 1975 to 39.7 by 1985—an increase of 13 percent in per capita consumption.

In the final paragraphs of this report, it is stated that these projections were made under the assumption that the U.S. *would not* implement its 200-mile fishing limit. Consequently, its authors state that these figures would be conservative if the pending legislation passed. Therefore, the assumption is made that supplies of domestic production will increase substantially within the next 10 years and that there is a greater probability of increasing per capita consumption, especially within the fillets and steak category.

The Customer. As previously stated, our customers are a combination of fresh fish distributors and direct retail accounts. Most are located in the Midwest, but they extend as far east as Boston and as far west as Denver.

In obtaining a sale from these customers, the most important factor is a combination of price and product availability. But unlike 5 to 10 years ago, another element is growing in importance. Today's retailers are beginning to actively promote their fresh fish sections. Accordingly, service and reliability are playing a more important role each year within the industry.

Service is an important element today because buyers have a multitude of responsibilities, in addition to buying the merchandise. Reliability too is essential—an embarrassing situation for a buyer to set up a fresh fish promotion for the chain, only to find out that his supplier cannot obtain any product!

Beantown Seafoods has recently obtained most of the fresh fish business of a chain of supermarkets in the Rochester, New York, market. According to the head buyer, there were a number of reasons why:

1. Commonly, Beantown Seafoods presented merchandising and promotional ideas to the chain, many of which were accepted and were successful when implemented. Of the chain's current suppliers, Beantown Seafoods was the only supplier offering assistance in the field of marketing.

2. In the recent past, suppliers had shorted the chain on sale items; however, Beantown Seafoods had established itself as being reliable in this area. Often, as an emergency favor, Beantown Seafoods was able to secure the supply our competitors could not obtain.

3. Beantown Seafoods' prices have always been competitive—frequently parity priced, and occasionally lower priced, but consistently an excellent product.

There were other factors mentioned, but these appeared to be our most salable attributes.

The Competition.   We have classified our competition into two categories—primary and secondary. These are further classified as being either just a wholesaler, such as Beantown Seafoods, or as being a wholesaler/processor, having its own production facilities in addition to selling its own output.

Our primary competitors are located on Boston's fish pier and its nearby ports. (This would include Fall River, New Bedford, Gloucester, and Massachusetts' other smaller ports.) Our secondary competitors would subsequently be found in the other areas of New England, primarily in Maine. We consider these firms secondary for the following reasons:

1. On those items in which we compete, there is occasionally a difference in quality and pricing. For instance, Gulf of Maine perch is more desirable than Atlantic perch on the open market and has historically brought a higher price.

2. Most secondary competitors are frozen fish processors and prefer to maintain a low-key profile of their fresh production.

3. Since most of these secondary competitors are outside the Boston market, fishermen are subjected to a local market's pricing policies. Accordingly, there may be a substantial difference in pricing in the locations of our secondary competitors. Frequently, many fishermen in these smaller ports are forced to Boston in order to obtain money for their catch.

There is a third group of competitors, but they are competitive with Beantown Seafoods only under certain circumstances. These competitors are found on the West Coast and in Canada, and normally serve as a very last alternate source for our customers.

Canada is perplexed by the problem of distributing its fresh fish. Its largest port, St. John's, is many road-hours away from the American market. Consequently, American fresh buyers have traditionally had problems with importing fresh Canadian fish.

Although the West Coast has many of the distribution problems solved (attributed to wide-body jets), the quality of its fish falls far below that of the East Coast fish. This is because the Pacific is a warmer body of water, consequently producing a softer fish. Therefore, to help offset this product disadvantage, West Coast fish tend to be much lower priced than Atlantic fish.

As outlined earlier in this report, it is our contention that the key element of future success for Beantown Seafoods is our competitive advantage in service. This includes consistently offering a quality product at a competitive price.

It is, of course, difficult to measure one's success in this segment of the industry. Although sales would be a good indication of success, most firms within the industry are privately held and are therefore scrupulous with regard to whom their financial position is made known. To further complicate the benchmarking problem, the only market trends available are those released by the Commerce Department. As earlier documented, its reports do not numerically differentiate fresh and frozen production. Consequently, a wholesaler such as Beantown Seafoods could only have 0.0001 percent of the total market, yet generate a million dollars in sales. It is because of these problems that Beantown Seafoods must use its own sales in relation to itself to gauge its relative success or failure in today's marketplace.

Part 4: Marketing and Sales Strategy

In developing a strategy, there are two factors which are important: the customer and seasonality.

For marketing purposes, we have classified our marketing areas into two categories: developed markets and expansion markets.

A "developed market" is an area where fresh fish has a high level of distribution, supplying the market with a wide variety of species at competitive prices. Examples of such markets include the New England region, New York State, Cleveland, Chicago, and Detroit. Another characteristic of the developed market is that its buyers are keenly aware of the market's current status—they shop extensively for the lowest price/highest quality. Presently, about 98 percent of Beantown Seafoods' business is in developed markets.

In an "expansion market," fresh fish is distributed on a very limited scale, although a strong frozen fish franchise may have already developed. Examples of such markets are Davenport, Minneapolis, and Phoenix/Tucson.

Obtaining distribution in the expansion markets is difficult. First, a distributor and/or wholesaler must be found that has both the physical capabilities and the ambition to take on this new product. Second, through very different selling, the distributor and/or wholesaler has to be convinced that Beantown Seafoods is *the* company to act as its liaison to the fresh fish market and to completely trust our judgment (i.e., when and what species to buy).

Since these are two separate and distinct marketing groups, Beantown Seafoods has employed two strategies.

Developed Markets

Objectives:

1. To increase the volume of existing customers.
2. To develop customer confidence and loyalty.
3. To find new customers.

Strategy and Tactics. In discovering new customers, Beantown Seafoods has used two resources very successfully: trade references and local truckers.

When shipping product, it is common for a trucker to drop-ship a number of fresh fish orders within a specific geographic region. Through a little probing, we have been able to learn:

1. The customers he's making deliveries for.
2. What species the customer has bought.

Another source for leads has been our existing customers. Again through probing, we have been able to learn of our customers' competitors and their product line. Although as a policy Beantown Seafoods offers its customers product exclusivity within the trading area, the competitor provides us with an alternate source of sales. This has proven to be an effective way of increasing both Beantown Seafoods' sales and customer portfolio.

Another method of increasing Beantown Seafoods' volume, in addition to finding new customers within the developed markets, is by increasing the volume of our existing accounts. To accomplish this objective, we are using two strategies:

1. Obtain increased volume of existing items. For instance, if a customer is currently purchasing 5,000 pounds of perch from Beantown Seafoods each week, we will try to increase the order to 8,000–10,000 pounds.

2. Diversify the product line. Utilizing the above example, Beantown Seafoods would attempt to maintain the perch volume, while recommending a new species (i.e., use Beantown Seafoods as a new source of product).

Within the developed market, price plays an essential role in obtaining the sale. When the market is glutted with product, we sometimes mark up the product no more than 2 cents to 4 cents per pound. In a shortage situation, however, our markups have been as high as 25 cents per pound. In either case, we will not forfeit volume for profit. At this point in time in Beantown Seafoods' history, it is our strategy to obtain increased volume through repeat purchase, hoping to develop credibility and loyalty with each account. Therefore, to greedily overprice our product may severely limit Beantown Seafoods' future growth and profit potential.

Expansion Markets

Soon after Beantown Seafoods was formed, a five-week customer recruitment process was initiated. By traveling from car, each major market between Boston and Denver was investigated. Among the findings of the field trip were the realization and substantiation of fresh fish potential in key underdeveloped markets.

An essential element of success in developing markets where fresh fish has potential is obtaining distribution within supermarkets. Our success in Denver, for instance, is attributed to our helping the chains' distributors develop a program to market the new product. Included in the program were point-of-sale materials (tear-off pads with recipes and display cards), in addition to recommending a promotion theme, schedule, and merchandising tactics (i.e., how much shelf space to allocate to each species and how to package and display the product).

For Beantown Seafoods to develop an expansion market, much time and investment are required. Expansion markets offer, however, a very high profit potential. Unlike the developed markets, expansion markets are less price sensitive because of the markets' lack of experience within the category. This translates into a higher profit margin for both the chain and Beantown Seafoods, offering a quick payback for the initial marketing expenditures. Yet, despite the potential, Beantown Seafoods has decided not to actively pursue expansion markets until 1979–80. There are four key reasons for this delay:

1. At this time, Beantown Seafoods' personnel are occupied full-time in developing existing business and its associated cash base.

2. It's important for Beantown Seafoods to develop a good name with its existing customers to help ensure future growth. Service is our primary selling attribute.

3. To develop these markets, as noted earlier, Beantown Seafoods must be on a sound financial base. It is our strategy, therefore, to utilize the profits from existing accounts to finance our future developmental programs.

4. Through more exposure to the industry we hope to better understand the intricacies and existing problems of fresh fish so as to better programs and presentation to the expansion markets.

Seasonality

Like many products, fresh fish is affected by the seasons, segmented by spring and fall. From April through October suppliers scurry for customers, while the remainder of the year, November through March, fish supplies are limited. It is, however, during these winter months that Beantown Seafoods realizes its higher margins.

As noted earlier, Beantown Seafoods is on an almost exclusive basis with this country's largest perch processors. Consequently, our company is one of the only wholesalers selling perch during the winter months. In many cases, we have developed new customers by their calling us looking for product. Therefore, in light of the product's seasonality, we are using two strategies:

Spring. During the spring months, Beantown Seafoods looks for new sources of supply that will provide product during the fall months. Once we have found a supplier with fall potential, we have established the strategy of giving the processor as much business as possible, in hopes of gaining both credibility and loyalty with the supplier.

Fall. Once we have secured supplies for the fall, we turn our attention to recruiting new customers and business within our existing accounts. Historically, we will not accept a new customer unless it agrees to maintain its account with Beantown Seafoods through the spring/summer months. We have had much success with our strategy of having a continual supply of product in the fall, a selling point many of our primary competitors cannot make.

Part 5: Overall Schedule for 1977–1979

Timing	Activity
1977:	
May–October	1. Seek new sources of supply for fall.
	2. Diversify product line.
November–December	1. Begin legal proceedings for incorporation effective 1/1/78.
	2. Field trip to review suppliers and find new sources.
	3. Begin design of chains' spring program.
	4. Hire part-time shipping clerk and bookkeeper.

Timing		Activity
1978:		
January–March	1.	Incorporate.
	2.	Customer-related field trip to present spring programs and to engage in customer relations activities.
April–June	1.	Hire full-time assistant.
	2.	Move to larger facilities.
	3.	Begin expansion program.
1979:		
January–December	1.	Continuation of expansion program.
	2.	Further diversification of product lines.
	3.	Execute normal seasonal activities.

Part 6: The Management Team

A good management team is composed of individuals who can effectively draw and build from each other's talents and experiences. Accordingly, another factor contributing to Beantown Seafoods' success is its management team.

Currently, the company's only full-time employee is the company's proprietor, Daniel Halsey. After 22 years with a national consumer and institutional frozen fish packaged goods corporation, Daniel Halsey established Beantown Seafoods to meet the increasing national demand for fresh fish—a trend his former employer wished to ignore.

In his former position, Daniel was national sales and promotion manager. His duties included the design and execution of both consumer and trade promotions, in addition to managing the corporation's national brokerage force.

To further strengthen the Beantown Seafoods team, Daniel's two sons, Michael and George, serve as part-time consultants. Michael, a securities salesman in Chicago, serves as Beantown Seafoods' key financial adviser. George, presently employed as a product manager in New York, is involved in consumer marketing and consequently provides Beantown Seafoods with guidance on specific marketing and sales problems.

Beantown Seafoods is essentially a one-man show at this time. Daniel, therefore, is responsible for all aspects of the company—sales, distribution, finance, and accounting. It's normally a 75- to 80-hour workweek. It is planned, however, that by mid-1977 two part-time staff members will join Beantown Seafoods—a shipping clerk and a bookkeeper. As mentioned earlier, a full-time assistant will be hired in 1979 whose primary responsibilities will include the development of an expansion program, in addition to handling the various aspects of the business.

Among Beantown Seafoods' supporting staff are a local CPA and an attorney.

Part 7: Critical Risks and Assumptions

As a service, Beantown Seafoods is highly susceptible to risks which are marketing and/or personnel oriented. The following, however, are the critical risks and assumptions under which Beantown Seafoods operates:

1. Since Beantown Seafoods is a sole proprietorship and a one-man operation, it is essential that Daniel Halsey retain his health.

2. As a one-man operation, it is estimated that Beantown Seafoods is now at its optimal sales level.

3. In order to expand the company's sales base, a full-time employee will be hired within the next 12 to 18 months and will be trained as an assistant to Daniel Halsey.

4. As a broker/wholesaler, Beantown Seafoods is susceptible to more unloyal customers attempting to buy directly from our source. Although this has been attempted in the recent past, Beantown Seafoods has successfully put down the customers' attempts by applying gentle pressure on the supplier.

5. That supplies and prices will remain stable (i.e., there will be no catastrophic natural disasters).

6. That all our customers will pay their bills. (At any one time, a customer may be in debt to us for $10,000 to $30,000. Although we thoroughly check a customer's credit history before accepting an order, a nonpayment of a very large invoice might put a severe financial strain on Beantown Seafoods.)

7. That there will be no legal proceedings implicating Beantown Seafoods in a food poisoning case subsequently finding the company liable.

8. If a fresh fish price war started (yet to happen, however, in the history of this segment of the market), Beantown Seafoods might be one of its first casualties, given the company's present small financial base.

Part 8: The Income Statement

1976:

Beantown Seafoods' first 10 months in business resulted in a profit of over $13,000 on sales of $335,800.

1977:

First-quarter sales and income are acual.

The second-quarter projections were based on the trends of the company's short financial history.

Sales in the third quarter are projected to decline in light of the quarter's increased competitive activities.

1978:

Sales for the year are projected to grow 12 percent, 7.5 percent of which is inflation.

Profits for the year decline to reflect increased expenditures in administrative costs and in developing the expansion program.

1979:

For the year, sales are projected to increase 18 percent. The growth is to be primarily attributed to the attainment of new business through the expansion program.

The company's profits (retained earning) appear weak for the year. Actually, the reduced profits are a result of a combination of increased overhead, investment in expansion programs, and an increase in the owner's withdrawal.

1980:

Now beginning to materialize sales within the expansion markets, sales are projected to increase 27 percent, while profits increase 154 percent.

Exhibit 9

BEANTOWN SEAFOODS
Income Statement

	1976 Total Year	1977					1978				
		1st Qtr.	2d Qtr.	3d Qtr.	4th Qtr.	Total	1st Qtr.	2d Qtr.	3d Qtr.	4th Qtr.	Total
Sales	$335.8	$191.6	$321.9	$285.0	$330.0	$1,128.5	$214.6	$360.5	$319.2	$369.6	$1,263.9
Less: Cost of goods ..	308.3	181.6	286.5	265.0	306.7	1,039.8	198.8	335.6	302.7	332.7	1,169.8
Gross profit	27.5	10.0	35.4	20.0	23.3	88.7	15.5	24.9	16.5	36.9	94.1
(As a percentage of sales)	(8.2%)	(5.2%)	(11.0%)	(7.0%)	(7.1%)	(7.9%)	(7.4%)	(6.9%)	(5.2%)	(10.0%)	(7.4%)
Less:											
Telephone	1.9	0.5	0.7	0.7	0.7	2.6	0.8	0.8	0.8	0.8	3.2
Distribution	5.9	4.3	6.4	5.6	6.6	23.0	4.0	8.3	7.3	8.5	29.0
General and administrative expenses	5.7	1.1	1.4	1.7	1.8	6.0	1.6	2.7	7.4	7.7	19.4
Total expenses	13.5	5.9	8.5	8.0	9.1	31.6	7.3	11.8	15.5	17.0	51.6
Operating profit	14.0	4.1	26.9	11.9	14.2	57.1	8.5	13.1	1.0	20.0	42.6
(As a percentage of sales)	(4.2%)	(2.1%)	(8.4%)	(4.2%)	(4.3%)	(5.1%)	(4.0%)	(3.6%)	(0.3%)	(5.4%)	(3.4%)
Less: Owner's withdrawal	6.3	2.7	7.3	2.3	5.1	17.4	4.0	6.2	0.5	9.3	20.0
Retained earnings	$ 7.7	$ 1.4	$ 19.6	$ 9.6	$ 9.1	$ 39.7	$ 4.5	$ 6.9	$ 0.5	$ 10.5	$ 22.4
(As a percentage of sales)	(2.8%)	(0.7%)	(6.1%)	(3.4%)	(2.7%)	(3.5%)	(2.1%)	(1.9%)	(0.2%)	(2.8%)	(1.8%)

Exhibit 9 *(concluded)*

BEANTOWN SEAFOODS
Income Statement

	1979					1980 Total Year
	1st Qtr.	2d Qtr.	3d Qtr.	4th Qtr.	Total	
Sales	$234.3	$408.8	$375.3	$474.6	$1,493.0	$1,896.3
Less: Cost of goods	213.3	381.5	348.1	428.9	1,371.7	1,728.3
Gross profit	21.1	27.3	27.2	45.7	121.3	168.0
(As a percentage of sales)	(9.0%)	(6.7%)	(7.2%)	(7.5%)	(8.1%)	(8.8%)
Less:						
Telephone	1.0	1.0	1.0	1.0	4.0	5.0
Distribution	6.7	11.7	10.8	13.6	42.8	56.9
General and administrative expenses ..	7.3	9.1	8.7	9.7	34.8	41.7
Total expenses	15.0	21.8	20.5	24.3	81.6	103.6
Operating profit	6.1	5.5	6.7	21.4	39.7	64.4
(As a percentage of sales)	(2.6%)	(1.3%)	(1.8%)	(4.5%)	(2.7%)	(3.4%)
Less: Owner's withdrawal	4.6	4.2	5.1	16.2	30.0	40.0
Retained earnings	$ 1.5	$ 1.3	$ 1.6	$ 5.2	$ 9.6	$ 24.4
(As a percentage of sales)	(0.5%)	(0.3%)	(0.4%)	(1.1%)	(0.6%)	(1.3%)

Part 9: Cash Flow and Proposed Financing

In addition to the items noted in the income statement, the cash flow projections include the cash requirements needed for Beantown Seafoods' expansion program through 1980.

Based on these estimates, Beantown Seafoods' future will be self-financed, and, therefore, Beantown Seafoods will not require outside financial assistance to obtain its objectives.

Exhibit 10

BEANTOWN SEAFOODS
Cashflow

	Cash Flow 1976	1977				1978				1979			
		1st Qtr.	2d Qtr.	3d Qtr.	4th Qtr.	1st Qtr.	2d Qtr.	3d Qtr.	4th Qtr.	1st Qtr.	2d Qtr.	3d Qtr.	4th Qtr.
Cash balance	$ -0-	$ 9.7	$ 10.6	$ 30.2	$ 38.8	$ 46.5	$ 48.9	$ 54.8	$ 51.6	$ 56.3	$ 47.8	$ 35.6	$ 24.9
Add:													
Cash receipts	310.9	168.6	283.3	250.8	290.4	188.8	320.2	280.9	325.2	206.2	359.7	330.3	417.6
Collection of accounts receivable	24.9	23.0	38.6	34.2	39.6	25.7	40.3	38.3	44.3	28.1	49.1	45.0	56.9
Invested capital	2.0	-0-	-0-	-0-	-0-	-0-	-0-	-0-	-0-	-0-	-0-	-0-	-0-
Total receivables	337.8	201.3	332.5	315.2	368.8	261.0	409.4	374.0	421.1	285.9	456.6	410.9	499.4
Less:													
Trade payable	314.2	185.9	292.9	270.7	313.3	203.7	343.9	310.0	341.2	219.9	393.2	358.9	442.5
Administrative	7.6	1.6	2.1	2.4	2.9	3.4	3.5	9.6	12.9	11.3	17.9	18.3	18.1
Leased equipment	-0-	-0-	-0-	1.0	1.0	1.0	1.0	1.4	1.4	2.3	3.7	3.7	3.7
Fixed assets	-0-	0.5	-0-	-0-	-0-	-0-	-0-	0.9	-0-	-0-	-0-	2.0	-0-
Owner's withdrawal	6.3	2.7	7.3	2.3	5.1	4.0	6.2	0.5	9.3	4.6	4.2	5.1	16.2
Total disbursements	328.1	190.7	302.3	276.4	322.3	212.1	354.6	322.4	364.8	238.1	421.0	386.0	480.5
Cash balance	$ 9.7	$ 10.6	$ 30.2	$ 38.8	$ 46.5	$ 48.9	$ 54.8	$ 51.6	$ 56.3	$ 47.8	$ 35.6	$ 24.9	$ 18.9

The Opportunity Focus: Recognizing, Shaping, and Evaluating

To open a business, very easy.
To keep it open, very difficult.

Chinese Fortune Cookie

3.1 RESULTS EXPECTED

This chapter focuses on opportunity recognition and evaluation as a driving force behind entrepreneurial success. Upon completion of the chapter, including working with the Mountain Ventures, Inc. (B), case, you will have:

1. Examined in depth what an attractive opportunity is, for whom it is attractive, and how to recognize it.
2. Identified the patterns and criteria used by successful entrepreneurs and venture capitalists to spot higher-potential venture opportunities.
3. Identified some specific benchmarks that define "forgiving and rewarding economics" in venture opportunities.
4. Determined some leading sources and techniques for obtaining industry and competitor intelligence and market and customer needs assessment.
5. Applied these benchmarks and techniques to an actual new venture situation and prepared a presentation for prospective investors based on the case.

The chapter lays the foundations for conducting an "opportunity screen" of your own venture ideas and for eventually preparing an actual business plan for executing the top opportunity you have identified. A specific guideline for the business plan is found in Chapter 14.

3.2 PRESESSION PREPARATION

Read the chapter; review the Opportunity Screening Guide; and prepare the Mountain Ventures, Inc. (B), case. Begin to apply the benchmarks developed here and in the previous chapter to screen your own ideas and to determine whether one is a "good fit" for you.

3.3 OPPORTUNITY-DRIVEN PROCESS

There are two classes of venture opportunities: (1) those that are profitable and can be harvested and (2) all the rest. The most successful entrepreneurs and venture capital investors work hard to sort out good opportunities among the myriad new business ideas that flow their way. They are *opportunity focused.*[1] As we saw in the last chapter, they know there is a difference between a good idea and a good opportunity, and can spot it. They start with what customers and the marketplace want and do not lose sight of this. The good news is that this is a very situational and judgmental process, which means plenty of room for individual initiative. The bad news is that among the more than 14 million businesses in the United States only about 1 venture in 30 is propelled by entrepreneurs good enough at opportunity spotting and executing to grow their ventures to over $1 million in annual sales.[2]

3.3.1   The Challenge: Recognizing a Good Opportunity

Most entrepreneurs who start a business, particularly if it is their first venture, run out of cash at a faster rate than they bring in customers and profitable sales. There are lots of reasons why this happens, but one thing is for sure: these entrepreneurs have not focused on the right opportunity. Often, the problem is a lack of experience—entrepreneurs who fail initially and learn from the experience usually bounce back and succeed later on.

A sizable part of the problem is that they lack enough experience in specific market areas and in business. As a result, they lack knowledge of the rules of thumb and benchmarks that can guide them in recognizing a good opportunity and saying no to the rest. Take, for instance, one such benchmark from the minicomputer industry. One of the authors worked on a consulting assignment for a firm in this industry with nearly a billion dollars in sales during 1984. Part of the project involved analyzing performance data from 60 computer-related start-ups in the United States since 1975. What was the one leading indicator used to judge the progress of the new firms? Sales per employee was the best clue, in the view of one executive. In this case, an often used industry rule of thumb is $75,000 or more in sales per employee. As a boundary measure, that figure suggests positive performance and a healthy start, while firms with sales of less than $50,000 per employee were considered to be in serious trouble. Interestingly, less than one third of the 60 new firms had achieved sales of $75,000 or more. Of course, there is always the risk of oversimplification, but one can also miss the fundamentals while searching too much for the subtleties. Do you know the sales, profit, and assets per employee benchmarks for the business you want to launch or buy?

The other part of the sorting-out problem is that there is an enormous flow of ideas and opportunities in our country. Think of the process as ideas and opportunities flowing on a three-dimensional conveyor belt through an open window—your "window on opportunity." The speed at which these opportunities flow is variable—the conveyor belt speeds up, slows down, even changes the rate at which this occurs. The window is also constantly opening and closing, on all four sides, representing the volatile and dynamic nature of the marketplace, changes in technology, and competitors' actions.

---

[1] We are especially appreciative to Howard H. Stevenson, Sarofim-Rock professor in entrepreneurship at Harvard Business School, for his helpful suggestions and conceptual framework, which have both reinforced and refocused our original identification of "opportunity analysis" as one of the central driving forces of the new venture process.

[2] *The State of Small Business: A Report of the President, Transmitted to the Congress, March 1983* (Washington, D.C.: SBA, 1984), pp. 199–200.

Given this scenario, the ability to recognize an opportunity when it appears, and the sense of timing to seize it as the window is opening rather than slamming shut, is central to entrepreneurial success. Some of the best examples of this principle—and its rewards and punishments—abound in the emerging microcomputer industry: just ask Adam Osborne (first portable micro) and Mitch Kapor (Lotus 1–2–3). Yet, we often hear, especially from younger, new entrepreneurs, the exhortation: "Go for it! I have nothing to lose now. So what if it doesn't work out. I can do it again. Why wait for a better opportunity?"

The spirit reflected in these comments is commendable. However, while there can be no substitute for actually doing it, such itchiness can be a real mistake unless it is focused on a solid opportunity. Why is this so?

3.3.2 The Lemons and the Pearls Syndrome

The answer to the question lies in a well-known saying among venture capital professionals. Their experience, and the facts, show (see Exhibit 3.1) that it takes considerably longer than most new entrepreneurs might think to determine whether the new venture is a success or a failure. Simply put: The lemons (losers)

Exhibit 3.1
The Lemons and the Pearls

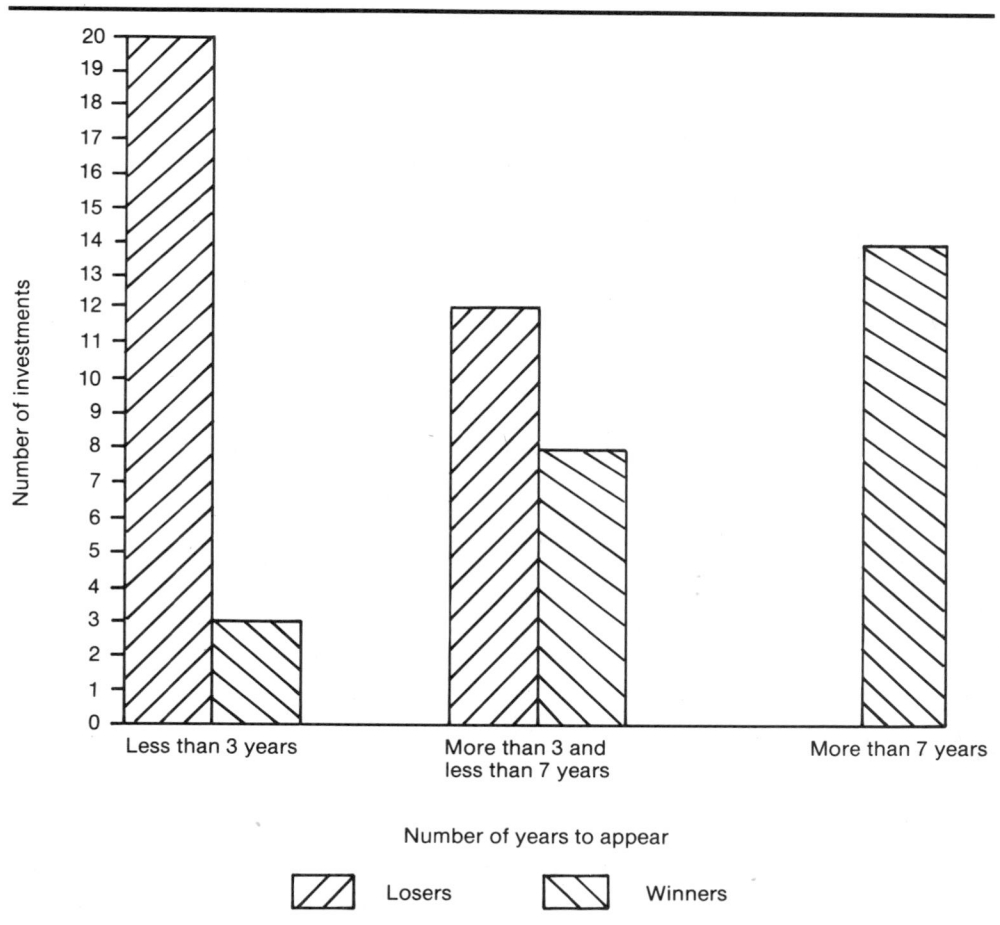

Source: Venture Economics.

ripen in about 2½ years, while the pearls (winners) take 7 or 8 years. (These time frames may be shorter in the more volatile, new technologically innovative areas.) It takes that long for a company backed by new venture capital to succumb or to succeed. Realistically, there is a 7- to 10-year window to which most entrepreneurs are committed before a capital gain is realizable. It is often not so clear-cut along the way either. An extreme example we know of is a Silicon Valley venture capital company that invested in a new firm in 1966. It was not until early 1984 that the venture was successful enough to sell stock to the public and thereby provide a market mechanism to enable the investors to make a capital gain.

The implication for young, aspiring entrepreneurs is even more significant the older you become. Let us say you are 25 years old. If you start a venture now, and it is *not* a good opportunity, or you lack the relevant experience to succeed by yourself—or to attract key people who would make the venture succeed—you will be 27 or 28 by the time you find out that it is not working out. You can try again, as many do. If you fail on the next two, you may be going on 35 years of age with very little to show for it. The wear and tear and burnout of those failures have probably also ended your first marriage, and maybe your second, if you are like most entrepreneurs who have traveled this rocky road. Attracting the money, people, and other support needed to start another company is now very difficult, unless your own pockets are extraordinarily deep. The options now become increasingly limited.

Or let's say you succeed the second time around. The chances are that you will be 35 to 40 years old by the time any personal net worth has grown from the venture. There is plenty of time left to start and grow one or two, maybe even three, "plums," or to keep growing the first one, but for most entrepreneurs, no more.

The message is simple enough: successful venture building takes a lot more time than is commonly believed. While there appear to be "boundless opportunities" for those with the entrepreneurial zest, most new entrepreneurs will be able to seize and attempt to execute only a *very few*. Why is this so?

Judging by Exhibit 3.1, it will take two to three years to determine whether the venture will *not* succeed, and about seven or eight to grow a successful one. Even allowing for one or two false starts—a quite common occurrence—you face the odds of being able to grow and harvest probably one or two ventures. But you probably will not have time for more than three or four ventures during your energetic and productive years. Fortunately, all you need to do is grow and harvest one quite profitable venture whose sales have exceeded several million dollars. The result will be a most satisfying professional life, as well as a quite financially rewarding one.

How important is it that you screen and choose opportunities with great care? Very important. It is no accident that venture capital investors have consistently invested in just 1–3 percent of all the opportunities and ideas that they review. Perhaps there are some lessons in how they sort and evaluate opportunities.

3.4   WHAT IS AN OPPORTUNITY?

Opportunities are situational, and the good ones, we argue, are anchored in high-margin customer needs in an expanding marketplace. For the lead entrepreneur, an attractive opportunity will result in a profitable and harvestable venture that is both *desirable to* and *attainable by* the entrepreneur and, if relevant, the management team. In short, if you do not really want it and you cannot really execute it, then it's not a good opportunity for you.

3.4.1 Opportunity Conditions

What is behind the unusual batting averages of successful entrepreneurs and their venture capital backers? What factors do they pay particular attention to in order to spot and seize an opportunity at the right time? How do they create what may be perceived by others as an "unfair advantage." The broad answer to these questions was addressed earlier (Exhibit 1.1). Far from being a simple matter of completing checklists, good opportunities result from careful screening of key "opportunity conditions" and bold initiative in finding, shaping, and often creating conditions favorable to its execution. Below is a summary of these key conditions, followed by a discussion of each.

The opportunity: Why is it compelling?

Screening and evaluation criteria

The opportunity window: timing and perishability

The economics: How forgiving and rewarding?

Risks, rewards, and trade-offs

Harvest potential

Note that the point of departure here is the opportunity, and implicitly, the customer, the marketplace, and the industry. The fundamental viewpoint is: *What is the opportunity* you are seeking to seize or create, and *why does it exist?* What are the prevailing conditions with the customer, market trends, competitors' vulnerabilities, technology, location, regulatory changes, lead times in market and product innovation, and the economics and capital gains potential of the business that add up to a compelling opportunity? Note further where this screening process *does not begin:* not with "strategy" (strategy derives from the nature of the opportunity conditions); not with financial and spreadsheet analysis (these requirements flow from the former); and not from an estimation of how much the company is worth and who will own what shares. Within the notion of the entire exercise having iterative properties, it is our sense that the opportunity focus is the most fruitful point of departure. Any other starting point usually places the cart squarely before the horse.

Incidentally, this concept is quite proven, hardly original, and by no means limited to product and service ventures. Perhaps the best evidence of how the cart is often placed before the horse comes from the tens of thousands of tax-sheltered investments that had turned sour by the mid-1980s. Many entrepreneurs and investors have apparently learned the lesson the hard way. A good investment is anchored in the fundamental, underlying economic opportunity, not in tax law loopholes that enable one to make the numbers look positive. We learned years back that it is very demanding and difficult to make money in a business that is trying to earn a profit, and business deals that are structured to lose money are not sound long-term opportunities, in our view.

As a practical matter, what do "opportunity conditions" mean?

3.4.2 Benchmarks Used by Successful Entrepreneurs and Venture Capital Investors

One useful way to answer this question is to examine some of the benchmarks used by highly successful entrepreneurs and their venture capital backers to evaluate seed and start-up businesses. The ventures of this group tend to be the cream of the current new venture crop, and they tend to have a technology bias. Yet, this select group by no means has a monopoly on the criteria noted here. Some of the most promising emerging companies have no venture capital at all. If they are in the service sector, or are "cash sales" businesses, their capital requirements are much lower than those of a high-technology manufacturing firm with continual large research and development expenditures. Further, entrepreneurs raise venture capital when they do not have the capital themselves. In today's venture capital market the first round of financing is typically $1–2 million or more for a start-up.[3] Unless you have had a previously successful harvest, then, your options are limited. But there are tens of thousands of self-funded new ventures that are launched and grow into multimillion-dollar enterprises because the founders are driven by these same fundamental opportunity conditions.

In short, we want to emphasize that these benchmarks are *not* the exclusive domain of venture capital. In our view, they mount up to just plain "good business." By knowing them, it is possible to be more selective in screening opportunities, and thereby to improve the odds of success. While the only defensible generality in this business of new ventures may be that you cannot generalize, we believe that these benchmarks can serve as useful and intelligent boundaries. How and to what extent you decide to compromise them in order to fit your needs and objectives is your judgment call. In our experience, "lifestyle entrepreneurs" can also significantly improve the odds of being able to live and work where and how they choose if they too pay attention to these fundamentals and balance the trade-offs carefully.

3.4.3 Venture Capitalists' Start-Up Investing Criteria

Summarized in Exhibit 3.2 are some dominant criteria used by investors to screen seed, start-up, and quite early stage venture opportunities. Usually, the first contact between an entrepreneur and an investor occurs when the entrepreneur calls by phone or forwards a business plan. The investor's initial screening of the opportunity zeroes in on the benchmarks noted here. About 60–70 percent of these proposals are rejected within the first half-hour phone conversation or after a brief review of the business plan. The issues are simple enough: (1) Is there a strong, experienced lead entrepreneur and team? (2) Is there a significant opportunity? and (3) Is there a significant capital gains potential?

The lead entrepreneur and team will be discussed in some detail in subsequent chapters (5–8). The important consideration is the quality of the founders: Do they possess the capacities, relevant experience, commitment, vision, and entrepreneurial zest to execute the opportunity? Most experienced venture capital investors say that about two thirds of their decision is based on their answers to

---

[3] J. A. Timmons, W. Bygrave, and N. Fast, "The Flow of Venture Capital to Highly Innovative Technological Ventures," study for the National Science Foundation; reported in *Frontiers of Entrepreneurship Research: 1984*, ed. J. A. Hornaday, F. Tarpley, J. A. Timmons, and K. H. Vesper (Babson Park, Mass.: Babson College, 1984).

Exhibit 3.2
Venture Capital Investing Criteria

Lead entrepreneur and team
    Relevant experience: general management: complement
    Highly committed plus vision
    Integrity, reliability
    Prior P/L experience in same market and technology
    Entrepreneurial zest

Opportunity driven
    Large ($100M +), rapid growth (30% +) market
    Superior product/service based on proprietary capabilities
    No dominant competitor: niches available
    Lead times—window open
    Rewarding and forgiving economics: 40–50 percent gross
        margins, 10% + PAT, early + CF and BE
    "Unfair" advantages over competition

Harvest potential
    Substantial ROIs (30-50% +)
    Capital gains—IPO, sale

these issues. These judgments evolve by meeting and working with the founders; they are rarely based solely on a 15- or 20-minute phone call.

The opportunity screens have at least some quantitative estimates on which to base one's judgments. The trouble is that the real potential of many start-up opportunities is often inversely related to the data available about market characteristics, shares, competitors, and so on. When these facts and numbers are available, or can be purchased, you can be sure that lots of entrepreneurs and competitors will also obtain them. This is one reason why the entrepreneur's vision and experience are so important in sensing an opportunity. Not only will the data be full of gaps, inaccuracies, and contradictions, but their meaning will be ambiguous. The entrepreneur can see linkages and possibilities where the perfectionist and the timid see chaos and contradiction, and the latter fail to grasp the opportunity and act on it.

Treat these benchmarks as boundaries and thresholds rather than as rigid or precise measures. They are in no particular order, since each business and opportunity situation is unique. The collective experience curves of successful entrepreneurs and investors suggest that these criteria can be one of the most important factors in getting the odds in your favor. Simply put: Fish where the fish are.

1. You have clearly identified your customers and the market segment(s) or niche(s) that you plan to capture. Prototypes of your product or service have gained the enthusiasm of customers to the point that they are your "in-house champions" and readily share their enthusiasm with other prospective customers and investors. Ideally, they have provided "free" space, people, and other resources to enable you to bring the product or service to market sooner. They may agree to advance payments, provide R&D contracts, and possibly even invest in your venture. All of those actions clearly signal that you are meeting an important customer need, with high value-added benefits to the customer and end user, and that your customers are receptive to innovation.

2. A minimum market as large as $100 million or so means that early on you can achieve significant sales with a nonthreatening market share, roughly 5

percent or less. A $1 million sales level would require a 1 percent market share or less. The market can be too large as well, implying a maturity, stability, and level of certainty that translate into lower margins and profitability and competition from Fortune 500–type firms. Consider, as an example, the entry of Apple Computer into the microcomputer industry in 1975, compared to that of a new entrant in 1985. Of course, if you can dominate a considerably smaller market, you can still build a very profitable venture with significant harvest potential even though it is not attractive as a venture capital investment.

3. A market growing at an annual rate of 30–50 percent or more creates a lot of niches for new entrants. It means that the industry, though a bit chaotic, is thriving, upbeat, and looking ahead to opportunities rather than concentrating on the defensive moves against competitors that often characterize mature, slow-growth industries. If a $100 million market is growing at 50 percent yearly, a new venture can attain first-year sales of $1 million by capturing just 2 percent of the increment. This growth rate in such a market also means that it will be a billion-dollar-plus market in a few years (just look at microcomputers) and have plenty of room for innovative entrants that can achieve sales of $50–100 million or more. If you understand the opportunity and you have the commitment and relevant experience to execute it, $1 million is a quite realistic sales level. After all, COMPAQ, the portable microcomputer firm, achieved sales of $110 million in its very first year!

4. There is nothing more forgiving to an entrepreneur than high and durable gross margins (the unit selling price less all direct variable costs). Once the gross margin exceeds 40–50 percent, there is a tremendous cushion built in that permits more errors, mistakes, and rough-hewn learning curves than are possible with margins of 20 percent or less. This in turn means reaching the break-even and a positive cash flow earlier (preferably within the first two years). It is quite common to find gross margins of 60–80 percent or more in high-technology businesses, medical ventures, and the software industry. Think of it this way. If gross margins are just 20 percent, for example, for every $1 increase in fixed costs (insurance, salaries, rent, utilities, etc.) you have to have a sales increase of $5 just to stay at the previous profit level. If gross margins are 75 percent, however, a $1 increase in fixed costs requires a sales increase of just $1.33, instead of $5.

5. The first important corollary to these "forgiving economics" is that they are also very "rewarding." Such high margins often translate into strong and durable profit after taxes of at least 10 percent, and often 15–20 percent or more. (Compare these figures with the latest Fortune 500 results. In 1983 the 500 largest service companies earned net income as a percent of sales typically in the 3–5 percent range and outperformed the 500 industrial group.[4]) This in turn leads to the second corollary. It means higher earnings per share and higher return on stockholders' equity. The higher the after-tax earnings, the greater is the potential "harvest" price of a company, and thus the capital gain, whether the company is sold through an initial public offering (IPO), acquired, or sold privately. (Note: Comparative financial performance ratios for businesses in the field you are considering can be found in the Robert Morris Associates annual statements; see Appendix I for examples of these.)

6. There is no dominant competitor in the marketplace, such as an IBM in mainframe computers. A market share of 40 percent, 50 percent, and especially 60 percent or more usually implies power and influence over suppliers, customers,

[4]*Fortune,* June 11, 1984, pp. 170–94.

pricing, and cost curves that create serious barriers and risks for a new firm. If the dominant competitor is at full capacity in a large and growing market, and is lethargic with regard to innovating or adding capacity, then there may be an entry opportunity. Unfortunately, entrepreneurs usually do not find such sleepy competition in dynamic, emerging industries dense with opportunity. If the market leader has a 20 percent share or less, a new entrant is less vulnerable to the brute force and bullying that a dominant competitor can exert. It is also less likely that the market leader will have the power to erect barriers to your entry and growth.

7. A significant response and lead time, or window, in terms of technological superiority, proprietary protection, plant capacity, market innovation, or distribution is especially important in technology ventures. Such an "unfair advantage" is often achieved by a proprietary product or service, or by a product or service that is very difficult to imitate and cannot be reverse-engineered. These advantages can create barriers to entry or expansion by others. Determining lead time necessitates a good approximation of how fast you and your competitors can respond. In microcomputer software today a six-month edge in getting to the market can be significant, while in automobiles such an edge would be considered insignificant.

In Exhibit 3.3 is a more detailed summary comparison of what might be viewed as "attractive" and "unattractive" opportunities. Again, these can serve as useful boundaries for analysis of opportunities. Do you know the appropriate figures for those ventures that you are considering seriously?

Exhibit 3.3
Criteria for Attractive and Unattractive Opportunities

Criterion	Attractive	Unattractive
Market Issues		
1. Customers	Identified, reachable, and enthusiastic	None yet, unfocused
2. Market size	$100M +	< $10M, unknown, or multibillion $
3. Growth rate	30–50% +	Nil, slow, < 10%
4. Gross margins	40–50% + and durable	< 20% and fragile
5. Attainable market share, year 5 (estimated)	Leader, 20% +	Nil, < 5%
Economics and Harvest Issues		
1. Profit after tax	> 10–15% + and durable	< 5% and fragile
2. Time to break-even	0–2 years	> 2 years
3. Time to positive cash flow	0–2 years	> 2 years
4. ROI potential	25% + / year	< 10% / year
Competitive Advantages Issues		
1. Degree of control over prices, costs, channels of distribution	Moderate-strong	Weak
2. Cost of production, marketing, and distribution	Lowest	High
3. Response and lead time: technology, product and market innovation, and capacity	Have or can gain an edge	No edge
4. Legal, contractual	Proprietary or exclusive	None
Management Team Issues		
1. Entrepreneurial team	Proven	None, unproven
Fatal Flaw Issues		
1. Other issues	Clean	"Fatal flaw"

3.4.4   Fatal Flaws

There is often a "fatal flaw" in opportunities that appear promising at first glance and meet many of the above criteria. Usually such flaws relate to one of the six "opportunity conditions." Consider the following examples of fatal flaws:

1. *Very small market for the product.* One inventor devised an electronic switch that would enable the user to interconnect a personal computer, the home burglar alarm, and the thermostat. At the time there simply were not enough customers who would buy such a device. It is not too hard to be either too early or too late in recognizing the opportunity window.

2. *Overpowering competition and a high cost of entry.* The U.S. automobile industry has examples of ill-fated attempts to enter the industry: Tucker in the late 1940s, Bricklin in the 1970s, and DeLorean in the 1980s. In the 1980s airline deregulation has invited many new entrants, and we can expect similar casualties in the airline industry.

3. *Inability to produce a product at a competitive price.* An example of this was Bowmar's inability to remain competitive in electronic calculators after the producers of large-scale integrated circuits, such as Hewlett-Packard, entered the business. Being unable to achieve and sustain a position as a low-cost producer shortens the life expectancy of the new venture.

4. *Lack of influence and control over product development and component prices.* The entrepreneur has very little control over these if a crucial state-of-the-art component is manufactured and supplied elsewhere. (Economists have long alluded to this issue in terms of vertical integration that is used to gain control of parts and supplies, and thus secure profit margins.) A good example of this was Viatron. Its suppliers were unable to produce several of the semiconductors that Viatron needed at low enough prices to permit Viatron to make the inexpensive computer terminal that it had publicized extensively. This was a significant factor in Viatron's eventual failure.

5. *Inability to expand beyond a one-product company.* Such companies are often driven by an inventor or a technical innovator rather than by an entrepreneur. Perhaps the leading example of this flaw is the failure of Osborne portable computers. After reaching over 1,000 employees, Osborne collapsed in the face of new competition. At this writing, its successor, COMPAQ, may be vulnerable to the same shortcoming.

6. *Overwhelming financial requirements.* Recently, a team of undergraduates proposed to develop a business plan to enter the satellite repair business. The research of these undergraduates indicated that the required start-up capital was in the $50–200-million range. Projects of this magnitude are the domain of government and the megacorporation rather than that of independent entrepreneurs and venture capitalists.

7. *Inability to harvest the opportunity profitably.* Most opportunities become jobs for the self-employed rather than companies with the value and durability to attract buyers. If the venture lacks a sufficient level of the criteria noted in Exhibit 3.2, the chances of realizing a capital gain diminish rapidly. In that event, you may have a "job," but you cannot really get out of the venture in any responsible or financially rewarding way, so you had better love it. In short, it is much easier to get into a business than to get out of it successfully. How many small-scale entrepreneurs have you heard who consider themselves "stuck" in just such

a situation? The owner of a quite successful sporting goods store in a wealthy, historic town near Boston was overheard recently confiding to a friend: "It's really an excellent living, but it is so boring doing the same thing each day; it gets to you."

3.5 AN OPPORTUNITY FOR WHOM?

3.5.1 Risks, Rewards, and Trade-Offs

One of the most challenging parts of the opportunity "juggling act" is figuring out what the balance is likely to be among risks, rewards and trade-offs to decide whether the opportunity is in fact a fit for you. In doing so, the following are worth considering.

First, the upside and the downside are not linear, nor are they on the same continuum. The upside is easy: "success has a thousand sires." The downside is quite another matter: "failure is an orphan." Can you absorb the financial downside in such a way that you can rebound without becoming indentured to debt obligations? If your financial exposure in launching the venture is greater than your net worth, the resources that you can reasonably draw on, and your alternative disposable earnings stream if the venture does not work out, the deal may be too big for you now. Unless you are virtually certain that it will succeed, you are unwittingly buying a ticket to your future bankruptcy. And while today's bankruptcy laws are extremely generous, you have to be able to cope with the psychological burdens of living through such an ordeal. Most of those who have undergone bankruptcy agree that these burdens are infinitely more painful than the financial consequences.

Next, there is the opportunity cost in pursuing any venture opportunity. The truth of the matter is that if you are good enough to grow a successful, multimillion-dollar venture, your talents will be highly valued by medium- to large-sized firms. More than ever before, larger firms are aggressively and creatively seeking entrepreneurs who can manage. Taking a serious look at potential "golden handcuff" alternatives is an important part of sizing up any opportunity.

Take, for instance, a young entrepreneur whom we shall call George Hill. Between the ages of 23 and 29 he played a lead role in starting and growing two firms. Each attained sales of over $5 million in five years. Neither was particularly profitable, and the second, which George launched on his own, closed in its third year. When George began a search for a new job in early 1984, he found a very enthusiastic reception among medium- to large-sized firms. Although his second venture was not even successful and his first cannot be harvested, his entrepreneurial experiences were most unusual. As one observer put it, "He is 29 with the experience of a 50-year-old." The most he had ever earned a year in his own ventures was about $60,000. He had several job offers in the six-figure-plus range.

Third, the opportunities you elect to pursue will *shape* you as an entrepreneur and a person in ways that are hard to imagine. Further, these opportunities—we said that you might have time to execute two to four multimillion-dollar ventures between ages 25 and 50—will successfully *position* you, for better or for worse, for your next opportunity. In the early years it is important to grow the relevant management experience and to gain profit and loss experience.

Last, the trade-offs are very personal. As we saw in Chapter 2, a good opportunity is one that fits with how and where you want to work and live. Eddie Albert reminds us in the hit Broadway play that "you can't take it with you." On the other hand, the wealthy French Baron de Rothschild observed: "You can either eat well, or you can sleep well!" By implication, you cannot do both.

3.6 SOURCES OF INFORMATION FOR OPPORTUNITY SCREENING

Fortunately, there seems to be no shortage of information sources to aid in screening opportunities and honing in on the analysis of the market. With the advent of the personal computer and electronic networks, a huge array of published information, directories, databases, and other sources of market and competitor intelligence is now available, affordable, and accessible from homes and offices. What follows is a summary of leading published sources, data services, computer-based sources, and conventional ways of gathering competitor intelligence.

3.6.1 Published Sources

Trade Associations and Journals. Almost every industry has a trade association and a journal. And these are among the best sources of data about a specific industry. Trade journals print, on a regular basis, market surveys and forecasts. Moreover, the advertisements in trade journals provide an excellent source of information about competitors and their products. Attendance at trade association meetings and conversations with sales representatives can also be good ways of assessing the competition.

The trade associations and journals of various industries can be found in:

Encyclopedia of Associations
(vol. 1, *National Organizations of the United States*)
Gale Research Company
Book Tower
Detroit, Michigan 48226

Ayer Directory of Newspapers, Magazines, and Trade Publications
Ayer Press
West Washington Square
Philadelphia, Pennsylvania 19106

General Marketing Data Sources. In addition to the trade journals, data on the market size and trends in a great many industries can be found in:

Predicasts Basebook
Predicast, Inc.
200 University Circle Research Center
11001 Cedar Avenue
Cleveland, Ohio 11106

U.S. Industrial Outlook
U.S. Department of Commerce
U.S. Government Printing Office
Washington, D.C. 20402

Predicasts Basebook provides abstracts of forecasts for U.S. statistics as well as those for a large number of industries and detailed products.

Sources of Market Studies. In addition to these broad-coverage data sources, market studies of particular industries and products are available from:

Predicasts
200 University Circle Research Center
11001 Cedar Avenue
Cleveland, Ohio 11106

Arthur D. Little
25 Acorn Park
Cambridge, Massachusetts 02140

Business Communications Company
471 Glenbrook Road
Stamford, Connecticut 06906

Frost & Sullivan, Inc.
106 Fulton Street
New York, New York 10038

Morton Research Corporation
1745 Merrick Avenue
Merrick, New York 11566

Theta Technology Corporation
Peer Building
530 Silas Beane Highway
Wethersfield, Connecticut 06109

The prices of the studies and reports provided by these organizations range from $50 to $600. Further, for $150 Predicast will custom-search its library of a half-million abstracts and provide the 300 abstracts that are most relevant to a market research need.

Consumer Expenditures. Data on consumer expenditures at many places in the country can be found in:

Editor & Publisher Market Guide
Editor & Publisher Company
850 Third Avenue
New York, New York 10022

U.S. Census Reports:
  Census of Business
  Census of Housing
  Census of Population
U.S. Bureau of the Census
Superintendent of Documents
Washington, D.C. 20233

Survey of Buying Power
Sales Management, Inc.
630 Third Avenue
New York, New York 10017

Financial Ratios. Information on the financial ratios for various industries that can be useful in evaluating competitive operating practices can be found in:

Annual Statement Studies
Robert Morris Associates
Philadelphia Bank Building
Philadelphia, Pennsylvania 19107

Almanac of Business and Industrial Financial Ratios
Leo Troy
Prentice-Hall
Englewood Cliffs, New Jersey

Guide to Market Data.   For an overall guide to sources of data on consumer and industrial markets:

Data Sources for Business and Market Analysis
Nathalie D. Frank
Scarecrow Press, Inc.
52 Liberty Street
Box 656
Metuchen, New Jersey 08840

If you wish to conduct a limited sampling of your potential market, you might find useful the note "Direct Marketing Information for Entrepreneurs." It was developed at Babson College by Professor Robert Ronstadt and Nancy Tieken, and it is available from Lord Publishing, Dover, Massachusetts 02030.

Guide to Journal Articles.   Journals and periodicals are a large and excellent source of data on products, industries, and markets. The title of an article can be a good clue to what it's about. Some useful directories of articles are:

Readers' Guide to Periodical Literature
Business Periodicals Index
Applied Science and Technology Index
The Wall Street Journal Index

Directories.   The most comprehensive listing of directories is *The Directory of Directories,* which contains a thoroughly described and completely indexed compilation of over 5,000 directories, including all types of rosters, industrial guides, and lists.

Also available from the same source is the *Encyclopedia of Business Information Sources,* which contains specific listings of specialized encyclopedias, handbooks, abstract services, trade associations, manuals, and on-line databases.

Gale Research Company
Book Tower
Detroit, Michigan 48226
(313) 961-2242

3.6.2   Data Services[5]

Association of Computer Users
P.O. Box 9003
Boulder, Colorado 80301
(303) 499-1722

---

[5]Excerpted and used with permission from David E. Gumpert and Jeffry A. Timmons, *The Encyclopedia of Small Business Resources* (New York: Harper & Row, 1984), pp. 376–79.

Like a "Consumer Reports of Computers," the Association of Computer Users makes available reports on the quality of computers in the $15,000–50,000 price range. The reports examine individual machines and are written especially for business users. A dozen reports can vary in price from $150 to $450. Membership is $25.

Bottomline Management Association
10 East 40th Street
New York, New York 10016
(212) 683-5353

Bottomline Management Association sponsors a "dial-an-answer" service on payroll-related problems. Questions concerning payroll taxes, insurance, equal employment opportunity, employee benefits, and recruitment are answered as often as the need arises. The cost of the service is $150 per year. The fee includes regular bulletins that analyze common business problems.

Business Growth Services
General Electric Company
120 Erie Boulevard
Department 392
Schenectady, New York 12305
(518) 385-2577

Business Growth Services provides information on new businesses or products that are immediately available for acquisition or licensing. Its *New Product/ New Business Digest* discloses over 500 unique new products and processes developed by both small and large companies; these new business ventures did not fit General Electric's product lines. The digest costs $45.

Current Industrial Reports
Subscriber Services Section
Bureau of the Census
Washington, D.C. 20233
(301) 763-7472

Current Industrial Reports provides shipment and sales data for over 100 industries. Its tables include data on imports, exports, and shipments, with breakdowns within industries.

Findex
Find/SVP
500 Fifth Avenue
New York, New York 10036
(212) 354-2424

Findex is a directory of market research reports, studies, and surveys that is updated every six months. *Findex* contains descriptions of over 4,000 reports available from 200 publishers, including the publication date, price, and instructions for obtaining copies. These reports cover a wide range of industries and businesses. *Findex* can lessen the outlays of a small business seeking published research on such things as developing technology trends and changes in foreign markets. *Findex* costs $115 annually.

The Information Bank and Advertising and Marketing Intelligence
Mount Pleasant Office Park
1719-A Route 10
Parsipanny, New Jersey 07054
(201) 539-5850

The Information Bank, which is part of the New York Times Company, consists of a database of 60 major worldwide publications, including business and financial journals. Advertising and Marketing Intelligence (AMI) consists of trade journals and public relations statements relating to the advertising and marketing areas. Information for both databases is current within a few days. Any topic or combination of topics can be researched to yield abstracts of relevant newspaper and magazine articles. Applications of this service vary from marketing trend analysis to international finance. For example, such topics as trends in do-it-yourself home improvement and trends in import-export activity could be quite important to certain small businesses. This service might also be used to gather information on prospective merger, acquisition, or takeover candidates.

Both databases are available to small businesses on a fee-for-service basis. The Parsippany office can offer advice on what is available. Research can be performed and an abstract sent on the same day. Full-text copies of articles are also available.

The fee for basic research is $110 per hour. A typical run is usually 12 minutes, or $22.

Information Data Search, Inc.
1463 Beacon Street
Brookline, Massachusetts 02146
(617) 232-1393

Information Data Search (IDS) bills itself as "a modern, one-stop research and information center equipped to answer virtually any question you have on a wide variety of subjects, technical or general." IDS has access to more than 100 computer databases nationwide and thus is in a position to choose those most likely to yield the information that customers request. The costs of the service vary according to the project, with quotes offered before research begins. IDS says that a typical range for services is $14 to $500.

Lockheed DIALOG Information Retrieval Service
3460 Hillview Avenue
Palo Alto, California 94304
(800) 227-1927; California (800) 982-5838

The DIALOG service offers access to more than 30 million journal and newspaper articles, conference papers, and reports from over 100 databases covering all areas of science, technology, business, medicine, social science, current affairs, and the humanities. The service might be applied, for example, to determine how to market a device for the handicapped. For this purpose, an entrepreneur might search a medical database to ascertain product need and search a business database to determine the present state of the market, including competition, dollar sales, and market share.

Department of Commerce Publications
Superintendent of Documents
U.S. Government Printing Office
Washington, D.C. 20402
(202) 783-3238

The U.S. Department of Commerce publishes reports that can help small business owners plan their marketing efforts. The reports are inexpensive and are often found at local libraries. Major Department of Commerce reports include:

The U.S. Industrial Outlook. Contains reports on 200 industries. Important industry developments and patterns are discusssed along with statistics on such things as the total value of shipments, the number of establishments with more than 200 employees and less than 20 employees, exports, and annual rates of change. The 1980 *U.S. Industrial Outlook* contained a section on opportunities for small business in the 1980s.

County Business Patterns. Contains statistics on the number of businesses, by type, in each county. Specific employment and payroll data are included. The number of establishments, broken into nine categories based on the number of employees, is also given for each industry in each county.

NASA Industrial Application Centers. Several universities have information centers to provide technically oriented reports, studies, and literature searches. These centers provide access to over 150 data banks and National Aeronautics and Space Administration (NASA) research. A typical bibliography with 250 to 300 sources costs $100, but fees may range from $30 to thousands of dollars. Fees are discussed before research begins. The information centers are as follows:

Technology Use Studies Center
Southeastern Oklahoma State University
Durant, Oklahoma 74701

Technology Applications Center
University of New Mexico
Albuquerque, New Mexico 87131

Western Research Application Center
University of Southern California
University Park, Los Angeles, California 90007

New England Research Applications Center
Mansfield Professional Park
Stoors, Connecticut 06268

North Carolina Science and Technology Research Center
P.O. Box 12235
Research Triangle Park, North Carolina 27709

Knowledge Availability Systems Center
University of Pittsburgh
Pittsburgh, Pennsylvania 15260

Aerospace Research Application Center
Administration Building
1201 East 38th Street
Indianapolis, Indiana 47401

3.6.3 On-Line Databases

The explosive growth in microcomputers and networks in the past few years has led to enormous growth in the availability of on-line databases and information sources. The fall 1983 issue of *Directory of On-Line Databases* (available from Caudra Associates, Inc., 2001 Wilshire Boulevard, Suite 305, Santa Monica, California 90403) lists about 270 on-line services carrying nearly 1,800 databases produced by 900 organizations. Suppliers of these information services usually charge $50 to $100 per hour of use, and some charge a modest sign-up fee of about $50.[6]

Two of the most significant sources of business information are DIALOG, provided by Lockheed, and Data Resources, Inc. (DRI), databases, containing over 10 million time series as far back as 1929. Exhibit 3.4 below summarizes other on-line databases. Exhibit 3.5 lists the principal links to these various sources of data, such as The Source, CompuServe, Dow-Jones News/Retrieval, and Dialog Information Services.

Exhibit 3.4
A Listing of Some On-Line Databases

Accountants Index
Provider: American Institute of Certified Public Accountants
On-line through: SDC Search Service
Subject: Accounting

Adtrack
Provider: Corporate Intelligence, Inc.
On-line through: Dialog International
Subject: Advertising

Agricola
Provider: U.S. Department of Agriculture
On-line through: BRS, Dialog Information Services, Inc.
Subject: Literature on agriculture

Agriculture Bank
Provider: Data Resources, Inc.
On-line through: Data Resources, Inc.
Subject: Agricultural economic data

American Profiles
Provider: Donnelley Marketing
On-line through: Dun & Bradstreet, Control Data Corporation/Business Information Systems
Subject: Demographics and population, demographics in United States

Balance of Payments
Provider: International Monetary Fund
On-line through: Chase Econometrics/Interactive Data
Subject: International finance

Billboard Information Network
Provider: Billboard Publications, Inc.
On-line through: Billboard Publications, Inc.
Subject: Music and music industry

Book Review Index
Provider: Gale Research Company
On-line through: BRS, Dialog Information Services, Inc.
Subject: Social science and humanities

Books in Print
Provider: R.R. Bowker Company
On-line through: BRS, Dialog Information Services, Inc.
Subject: Books and periodicals—catalogs

[6]*Inc.,* December 1983, p. 214.

Exhibit 3.4 *(continued)*

Commodities Futures
Provider: Call Computer, Inc.
On-line through: Call Computer, Inc.
Subject: Commodities—United States

CompuServe Consumer Information Services
Provider: CompuServe, Inc.
On-line through: CompuServe, Inc.
Subject: Multifaceted information services providing many databases

CompuServe Executive Information Services
Provider: CompuServe, Inc.
On-line through: CompuServe, Inc.
Subject: Multifaceted information services providing many databases

CSS/Quotes +
Provider: Dun & Bradstreet Computer Services, Inc.
On-line through: Dun & Bradstreet Computer Services, Inc.
Subject: Securities—Canada, United States

Dow Jones News and Dow Jones Free-Text
Provider: Dow Jones & Company, Inc.
On-line through: Dow Jones & Company, Inc.
Subject: Business and industry, corporations—finance, news, and economics

EEI Capsule
Provider: Evans Economics, Inc.
On-line through: Control Data Corporation/Business Information Services/Boeing Computer Services Company
Subject: Economics—United States

Foundations
Provider: The Foundation Center
On-line through: Dialog Information Services, Inc.
Subject: Directory, funding sources, and awards

Harvard Business Review
Provider: HBR/ONLINE
On-line through: John Wiley & Sons under agreement with *Harvard Business Review*
Subject: Business management

Horse
Provider: Bloodstock Research Information Services, Inc.
On-line through: Bloodstock Research Information Services, Inc.
Subject: Horses

International Software Database
Provider: Imprint Software Ltd.
On-line through: Dialog Information Services, Inc.
Subject: Computers and computer industry

Legal Resource Index
Provider: Information Access Corporation
On-line through: Dialog Information Services, Inc.
Subject: Law

Legi-Slate
Provider: Legi-Slate, Inc.
On-line through: Legi-Slate, Inc.
Subject: Government, U.S. federal, U.S. state

Medline
Provider: Australian Medicine Network, BLAISE-LINK, DRS
On-line through: Dialog Information Services, Inc., DATA-STAR, DIVDI, MC-KBIC, National Library of Medicine, Japan Information Center of Science and Information Technology
Subject: Biomedicine

Microcomputer Index
Provider: Microcomputer Information Services
On-line through: Dialog Information Services, Inc.
Subject: Computers

Exhibit 3.4 *(concluded)*

National Technical Information Services
Provider: National Technical Information Services
On-line through: BRS, CISTI, DATA-STAR, Dialog Information Services, Inc., ESA-IRS, INKA Karlsruche, SDC Information Services CEDOCAR
Subject: Science and technology

Sociological Abstracts
Provider: Sociological Abstracts, Inc.
On-line through: BRS, DATA-STAR, Dialog Information Services, Inc.
Subject: Sociology

The Source
Provider: Source Telecomputing Corporation
On-line through: The Source
Subject: Contains many information services

Standard & Poor's Industry Financial Data Bank
Provider: Data Resources, Inc., Standard & Poor's Corporation
On-line through: Data Resources Corporation
Subject: Business and Industry—finance, U.S. finance

Source: *Personal Software,* June 1984, p. 1260.

Exhibit 3.5
Connecting to On-Line Databases

Many people who use data communications with a personal computer do so to access on-line databases. There are a number of these databases, covering subjects as diverse as stocks and bonds and thoroughbred bloodlines. The chart below shows subscription charges, storage charges, and connect-time charges for a cross section of on-line services.

Service	Sub-scription	Connect Time	Storage	Monthly Minimum
The Source	$100	$10.75/hr. prime, $7.75/hr. nonprime, 300 baud; 1,200 baud—$5/hr. surcharge prime, $3/hr. nonprime	$0.50/rec first 10 (1 rec = 2k bytes)	$1 storage, $9 connect
CompuServe	$39.95	$6/hr. nonprime, $12.50/hr. prime	First 128k free; $4/wk. per additional 64k	None
Dow Jones News/Retrieval	$75	$1.20/min. prime, $0.90/min. nonprime	None	
Dialog Information Services	None	Typical searches of the databases cost $25 to $125		None
BRS after Dark	$75	$6/hr. to $20/hr. depending on info researched; 6 P.M. local time to 4 A.M. Eastern time.		2 hrs. month

Source: *Personal Software,* p. 127.

Probably the most complete and comprehensive book we have seen is *The Computer Data and Data Source Book,* by Matthew Lesko (New York: Avon Books, 1984).

A word of caution: the "garbage in–garbage out" rule is certainly applicable when it comes to utilizing any of these databases. Unless you have focused questions and know what you are looking for, you may spend more time and money than you can afford. You may dig out loads of information that may be useful and interesting but is not *essential* to the assessment of your opportunity and the shaping of a marketing strategy.

3.6.4 Conventional Competitor Intelligence

How would you like to know your competitors' sales plans, key elements of their corporate strategies, the capacity of their plants and the technology used in them, who their principal suppliers and customers are, and a good bit about new products your rivals have under development? No, you don't have to break any laws to get this information.[7]

The answer is that you would not only like such intelligence but that you have to have it in order to assess effectively the opportunity, risks, and trade-offs. Getting it is probably more difficult in an emerging industry than in a mature field. Nonetheless, a wide range of conventional practices can help to get the odds in your favor by finding out what you need to know about what is happening in the industry, in the market, and among customers. Summarized below are some suggestions:

Trade shows and conferences are a prime place to pick brains and to discover the latest activities of competitors. It never ceases to amaze us how much proprietary information is leaked in "innocent conversations" with engineers, scientists, and salespersons who cannot resist bragging about their latest breakthroughs or initiatives.

Hiring people away from competitors is a frequent occurrence today. To legally challenge such a hiring, according to the *Fortune* article quoted earlier, competitors must prove that your company hired the person with the intention of getting specific trade secrets. A flurry of information gathering by that person immediately prior to resignation is circumstantial evidence of this intention. Students seeking jobs are also sources of important information when they have worked for competitors. They like to brag a bit also!

Consulting firms interviewing competitors claim to be conducting an industry study and promise to share the data they develop. Some of the biggest-name consulting firms get information for their clients in this way.

Debriefing design consultants can pay off in such fields as computers and software, where competitors frequently use the same consultants.

Debriefing competitors' former employees can often provide information damaging to competitors, especially if the employees departed on bad terms.

Encouraging key customers, suppliers, and buyers to talk, a lot, is another tactic that is used to learn as much as possible about the competition.

Obtaining Freedom of Information Act filings can reveal a surprising amount of information from competitors that are doing business with the government. This can be done discreetly through a company that processes such inquiries, FOI Services, Inc., Rockville, Maryland.

Doing reverse engineering can determine costs of production and sometimes even manufacturing methods. According to the *Fortune* article, Advanced Energy Technology, Inc., of Boulder, Colorado, learned firsthand about such tactics. No sooner had it announced a patented new product than it received 50 orders, half of which were from competitors asking for only one or two of the items. (This is also

[7] *Fortune,* "How to Snoop on Your Competitors," May 14, 1984, pp. 28–33.

an excellent example of how filing a patent can negate what might otherwise be a significant market lead time over competitors.)

Less than ethical tactics include conducting phony job interviews and getting customers to put out phony bid requests. And, of course, there are such unscrupulous tactics as lying, cheating, and stealing, which are both illegal and unethical but find their way into practice, partially in response to the enormous stakes and pressures to win, partially as a result of overzealous, blind ambition. You may win the battle, but if it is at the cost of your integrity, you will lose the war for longer-term success.

3.7 MOUNTAIN VENTURES, INC. (B): CASE STUDY

The MVI (B) case is an actual start-up opportunity. The case will enable you to apply the opportunity evaluation concepts and benchmarks presented in the chapter to the analysis of the opportunity in the camping tent industry. Further, it will provide a good basis for honing some opportunity recognition and shaping skills. Suggested preparation questions follow.

3.7.1 Preparation and Team Presentations

In preparation for the next session, analyze the MVI (B) case. Put yourself in the position of Egnew and Moore, the aspiring founders. Be as realistic as possible, and make whatever assumptions you feel are reasonable.

During the next session you will have the opportunity to share your analysis with others in the session. This case will help you to think through how to conduct the kind of venture analysis that will be required to prepare a business plan for your own venture. It will give you a chance to calibrate your own skills in this area and those of some members of your management team.

You should address the questions facing Egnew and Moore at the end of the MVI (B) case. Each team should prepare a 30-minute oral presentation of the case that should cover:

1. What is the opportunity, and why does it exist?
2. Your view of the market, how you would plan to sell and market tents, and the resulting implications.
3. Your product line, prices, and sales projections.
4. Your estimates of financial and manufacturing needs and their implications.
5. The nature of the management team needed, salaries, and equity splits.
6. Any other considerations that you feel are appropriate.

Approach the case and team effort as though MVI were the company that you were trying to start.

This presentation should include an analysis that is as complete as possible, given the information you have. You should not invent unsupported facts or figures, but you may do any outside research that you have time for, if you can support your information.

Once you have completed and presented your MVI (B) case analysis, complete Section 3.7.3.

3.7.2 Mountain Ventures, Inc. (B): Case and Exhibits

MOUNTAIN VENTURES, INC. (B)

By early 1972 J. C. Egnew and John F. Moore had decided to start their own tent manufacturing business. Recognizing the difficulties of starting a new venture and their own inexperience in business, they began to assess their entrepreneurial and management strengths and weaknesses, analyze the feasibility of a new business idea, and develop a business plan in order to secure venture financing. Their investigations indicated that without a complete business plan and a management team with a solid track record, seed capital would be virtually impossible to raise, at least from a reputable source and on reasonable terms.

In late July they were both terminated by their employer, Wilderness Products, Inc., with just a few days' notice, when it was discovered that they were investigating the possibility of launching a competitive tent manufacturing company. Unemployed and, as yet, unfinanced, Egnew and Moore were faced with a serious dilemma: how to start their business in time to take advantage of the 1973 spring tent market.

One of the major hurdles to be overcome in starting their business was a thorough analysis of the venture opportunity. A complete analysis of the general leisure-time, recreational, and industry trends would need to be conducted thoroughly and objectively. Although committed to the venture psychologically, they did not want to launch a venture that had a poor chance of succeeding. A principal aim of their initial venture analysis was to determine whether any major flaws existed in their idea and to decide whether a full business plan was worth preparing. What follows is a summary of some of the market and financial data that the entrepreneurs gathered in order to investigate the potential for their new tent manufacturing business. Also, Exhibits 1 through 4 illustrate several other recreational and outdoor trends related to the general market potential for camping tents.

The Tent Market

The significant tent-producing companies in the continental United States are ranked below, based on 1972 sales:

Kellwood Company	$18,000,000
Sears	10,000,000
Wentzel	8,000,000
Hettrick (Olin Corporation)	15,000,000
Wilderness Products	10,000,000
National Canvas Products	7,000,000
Coleman	4,000,000
Eureka Tent and Awning	3,000,000
Other	3,000,000
Total	$60,000,000

The *Thomas Register* lists a good many other firms in the tent business. Most of these firms are small "mom 'n' pop" operations consisting of those who "custom-produce" (make to order) awnings and tents and other canvas items such as "show tents" and circus-type carnival tents. Others are primarily in the repair business, and some of these have a national market, while others have a regional market only.

Approximately 10 percent of this total tent market consists of tents designed for specific uses (e.g., mountain climbing and backpacking). This factor will limit the general tent market potential for the coming year to $54 million (not accounting for an anticipated 1973 growth factor of 20 percent in the market as a whole). Following is an estimated geographic breakdown of the national tent market that is based on observed industry sales patterns:

	Percent
New England States	22
Metropolitan New York City	13
Mideast (New York, Pennsylvania)	8
Midwest (Corn Belt, Plains)	26
Central Atlantic Coast	4
Southeast	9
Southwest	6
Far West (Coastal)	8
Other	4
Total	100 ($60,000,000)

Sales Fluctuations

It has been an industry practice for retailers to start taking deliveries of tents after January 1, since tents are not usually "Christmas" items. To encourage early order commitments and deliveries, the industry has been allowing "net April 1st" payment terms on tents delivered prior to April. Because delivery service has been poor in the past, it is not unusual for customers to place orders in October and November for tents desired in March or April. Projected sales trends by month for the total tent market follow:

Month	*Percent of Annual Sales*
January	17
February	21
March	15
April	11
May	10
June	6
July	4
August	2
September	3
October	3
November	4
December	5
Total	100

Sales Expenses

The following table shows an estimated sales budget developed by Egnew and Moore for a first year of operation:

One sales representative	$20,000
Travel expenses	3,000
Telephone	3,000
Trade shows	4,000
Catalogs	3,500
Advertising and related	2,500
Miscellaneous	1,000
Total	$37,000

Competitors' Product Lines

Listed below is a comparison of prices among three of the industry leaders for some of the main types of tents available to the consumer. Profit margins do not vary significantly from one type of tent to another.

Prices of the Major Products for Three Major Competitors (1972 published prices)

Style	Size	Wilderness	Hettrick	National
Cabin	7 × 7	$30.80	$ —	
	8 × 10	40.00	47.35	$33.02
	9 × 12	47.95	55.75	50.58
	10 × 16	55.95	65.90	58.48
				—
Cabin—screen	10 × 16	69.75	76.80	—
Umbrella	7 × 7	21.90	21.00	23.82
	9 × 9	32.25	36.80	41.12
Canopy	10 × 10	12.75	—	15.71
	12 × 12	15.45	15.75	18.40
Screenhouse	10 × 10	28.95	33.65	—
Pup tent	5 × 7	4.79	4.75	5.18
	5 × 7	10.80	10.50	10.00
Jvc. umbrella	7 × 7	8.75	9.25	11.16
Trl. awning	8 × 10	13.75	15.80	17.20
	8 × 12	16.35	18.20	18.60

— = Not offered by that competitor.

All prices listed are for the 1972 season and are expected to increase from 10 percent to 12 percent on the average for the coming 1973 season.

The next table presents a comparison of the number of models of each type of tent produced by some of the leading manufacturers.

Comparison of the Number of Models Offered by Five Major Tent Producers

Company	Cabin	Umbrella	Play	Canopy and Screen	Awnings	Nylon	Other*
Wilderness:							
Regular	20	4	5	8	9	6	2
Special	32	3	2	9	2	—	—
Hettrick:							
Regular	12	4	9	7	10	2	6
National	9	6	17	6	14	1	4
Coleman	18	2	2	3	—	1	13
Eureka	9	9	14	11	31	7	13

*Includes ice tents, "flies," wind curtains, etc.

Manufacturing Requirements

A plant site would require about five acres and must include water, power, and sewerage hookup. Productivity is expected to be about $30,000 in sales per unskilled employee per year. It is expected that about $50,000 would have to be spent for various good, used equipment tables; slitting, rewind and sewing machines; pallets; hand trucks; and office equipment. Supplies of raw material have not previously presented a problem.

Financial Considerations

The following is a summary of industry practices relating to the manufacture and sale of tents.

Accounts receivable	75% of all sales prior to April 1 billing. Further, 50% of the accounts will be paid on or before April 1, 35% will be 30 days past due. 10% will be 60 days past due, and 5% will be 90 or more days past due when paid.
Inventories	Monthly inventories will peak in February and be at a minimum level in June.
Work in process	20% of monthly production.
Finished goods	9.3% of monthly sales.
Accounts payable	80% of monthly purchases.
Cost of goods sold	76% of sales.
Gross profit	24% of sales.
General, selling, and administration	Industry average is 15% of sales.

Analyzing the Venture's Feasibility

This preliminary investigation provided the entrepreneurs with a substantial amount of data. Since they began their investigation, several more incomeless weeks had passed. They wondered whether their idea was worth pursuing.

Some new developments of which they had been previously unaware emerged from their investigations. First, they found that the industry was "closed to outsiders," making it very difficult to get useful market information. Second, they found that the sales of the major canvas suppliers for tents had been declining steadily in recent years. Third, they discovered, to their surprise, that no new firms had entered the tent business in the past five to six years, in spite of what they estimated as a growing, seller's market. Further, they learned that a handful of small tent manufacturers had actually failed and gone out of business during this period. What were the market and financial implications and requirements for launching such a venture? How much money would they need, and could it be raised at all? Could the business be profitable, given the preceding factors?

Exhibit 1
National and State Park Systems—Acreage, Visits, and Expenditures, 1950, 1960, and 1970

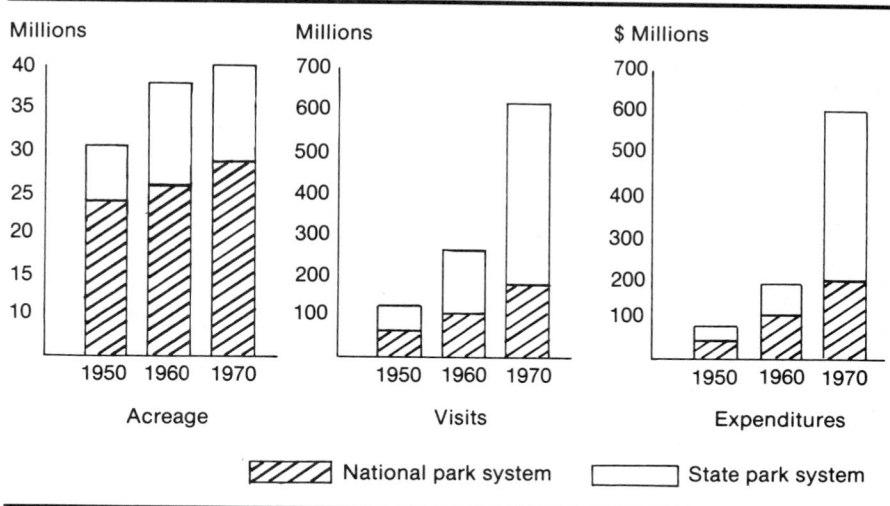

Exhibit 2
Federal Acquisitions and Fund Grants for Outdoor Recreation, 1967–1971 (for years ending June 30)

Item	1967	1968	1969	1970	1971
*Federal real property acquisitions**					
Total acres bought (1,000s)	130.7	144.8	241.4	231.9	105.9
National Park Service	52.6	56.3	124.5	60.4	52.1
Forest Service	78.1	86.0	116.0	156.5	48.9
Bureau of Sport Fisheries and Wildlife	a	2.5	0.9	15.0	4.5
Bureau of Land Management	—	—	—	—	0.4
Cost total ($1,000s)	39.754	29.325	95.377	70.975	87.867
National Park Service	26,139	19,207	81,531	47,098	72,988
Forest Service	13,608	8,894	12,608	22,258	10,210
Bureau of Sport Fisheries and Wildlife	7	1,224	1,238	1,619	4,611
Bureau of Land Management	—	—	—	—	48
Federal matching grants to states					
Total ($1,000s)	82,071	71,585	72,564	49,424	110,500
State recreation resources†	49,639	48,561	26,615	27,677	52,500
County recreation resources	7,953	7,369	12,035	5,931	17,500
Local recreation resources	24,479	15,655	33,924	15,816	40,500
For acquisition	29,935	27,275	37,926	20,610	45,600
For development and/or planning	52,136	44,310	34,638	28,814	64,800

— Represents zero; a = Less than 50 acres.

*Covers land, waters, and improvements.

†Includes grants to District of Columbia, Puerto Rico, Guam, Virgin Islands, and American Samoa.

Source: U.S. National Park Service release.

Exhibit 3
Overnight Stays in Selected Areas Administered by the National Park Service, 1971 (for year ending June 30; 1,000s)

	Total Overnight Stays	Concessioners*	Tents†	Recreation Vehicles	Camping	Hiking	Miscellaneous‡
Total all areas§	13,411	3,434	3,438	4,452	421	1,096	526
Blue Ridge Parkway, Georgia, North Carolina, Virginia	271	48	70	150	2	1	a
Cape Hatteras National Seashore, North Carolina	306	—	113	182	2	—	10
Death Valley National Monument, California, Nevada	280	—	71	204	3	2	—
Glacier National Park, Montana	361	96	90	160	2	11,12	a
Glen Canyon National Recreation Area, Arizona, Utah	444	122	27	133	1	147	13
Grand Canyon National Park, Arizona	804	491	223	91	—	—	—
Grand Teton National Park, Wyoming	593	249	155	153	6	22	9
Great Smoky Mountains National Park, North Carolina, Tennessee	560	7	214	263	19	58	—
Kings Canyon National Park, California	276	14	87	91	6	77	—
Lake Mead National Recreation Area, Arizona, Nevada	749	239	103	223	2	129	53
Olympic National Park, Washington	402	61	109	129	2	101	a
Rocky Mountain National Park, Colorado	276	—	125	116	8	27	—
Shenandoah National Park, Virginia	451	101	105	179	3	57	6
Yellowstone National Park, Idaho, Montana, Wyoming	1,346	545	239	525	8	22	6
Yosemite National Park, California	1,596	659	422	252	42	221	—

— Represents zero; a = less than 500.

* Includes rooms, cabins, campgrounds, and trailer villages.

† Also includes visitors sleeping in cars on the ground.

‡ Includes nights spent aboard boats and overnight stays not elsewhere classified.

§ Includes 97 areas shown separately.

Source: U.S. National Park Service release.

Exhibit 4
Fishing and Hunting Licenses, Number and Cost: 1960–1971 (for years ending June 30)

Item	1960	1965	1968	1969	1970	1971
Fishing licenses (1,000s)						
Total license sales	23,323	24,976	28,787	29,855	31,136	32,384
Resident	20,190	21,576	24,898	25,706	26,814	27,826
Nonresident	3,133	3,400	3,889	4,150	4,322	4,558
Cost to anglers ($1,000s)	52,143	62,857	79,995	87,501	90,864	99,922
Hunting licenses (1,000s)						
Total license sales	18,440	19,372	20,859	21,622	22,184	22,912
Resident	17,808	18,518	19,939	20,600	21,013	21,641
Nonresident	632	854	1,022	1,171	1,271	
Cost to hunters ($1,000s)	60,981	75,173	88,681	95,709	101,608	108,597
Federal duck stamps sold (1,000s)	1,629	1,566	1,934	1,839	2,072	2,394

Sources: U.S. Fish and Wildlife Service, *Federal Aid in Fish and Wildlife Restoration*, Annual, and unpublished data.

Name _____

Date _____

3.7.3　Presentation

MOUNTAIN VENTURES, INC. (B), PRESENTATION

Peer Evaluation and Feedback Form

Each of you should complete the feedback form on the following pages. Be as specific as possible in making comments about other members of your team.

Strengths and Weaknesses. Briefly state on the following page what you feel were the strengths and weaknesses of each member of your team as they appeared to you during the preparation and presentation.

Name	Strengths	Weaknesses
Self		

Name _____

Date _____

Venture Analysis and Management Skills. Indicate below which capabilities of each team member were demonstrated. Distribute 100 points among the members of your team to show which members were strongest in each of the areas listed below. You may give a person from 0 to 100 points. If you give any one person 100 points, the others must receive 0.

Name				*Self*	*Total*
Marketing					100
Financial					100
Technical/ manufacturing operations					100
Teamwork and interpersonal					100
Entrepreneurial characteristics					100
Overall contribution to the team's effort					100

A word of caution: The person with the highest scores in any category may have the best skills in an area, but this is relative: he or she still may not be good enough! And this evaluation may be difficult for you to do—particularly in an area where you do not have skills or expertise.

General Comments. Make any comments or observations that you feel are appropriate to supplement your previous evaluations of each person.

Name
a.

b.

c.

d. Self

Note: Once you have completed this form, tear it out and make a Xerox copy for each
member of your team.

Processing the Feedback (optional for during or outside a formal meeting).   By this time you have probably worked long and hard together on your team's new venture project and in preparing the Mountain Ventures, Inc. (B), case presentation. Since you have come to know one another well, the feedback exercises in this chapter can provide you with a valuable aid to check the reality and accuracy of your various self-assessments and self-perceptions. These integrative feedback exercises should provide a complete reality test for you. Recall that one of the characteristics of effective entrepreneurs is their ability to seek and to use feedback from others and from their environment.

The following steps will enable you and your team to systematically discuss and analyze the feedback that each person received.

Step 1: Team members meet to exchange the MVI Peer Evaluation and Feedback Form. Verbal comments should supplement written evaluations. Allow 30–60 minutes, or more if done outside a regular session.

Step 2: If you have completed Chapter 10, those team members share their other Peer and Professional Feedback Guides (1, 2, 3) to reality-test their own assessments and those of their partners. Allow 30–60 minutes, or more if done outside a regular session.

Venture Opportunity Screening Guide   4 >

Greater than the tread of mighty armies is an idea whose time has come.

Victor Hugo
1852

4.1 RESULTS EXPECTED

This chapter focuses on a specific method of opportunity recognition and evaluation as a driving force behind entrepreneurial success. Upon completion of the chapter, including working with the Venture Opportunity Screening Guide, you will have:

1. Examined in depth the attractiveness of at least one of your high-priority opportunities.
2. Applied some specific benchmarks, criteria, and screening methods used by successful entrepreneurs and venture capitalists to evaluate your own venture idea.
3. Begun to apply the Opportunity Screening Guide to your own new venture ideas in order to focus on the best one for which to develop a business plan.

The chapter lays the foundations for preparing an actual business plan to execute an opportunity you have identified. A specific guideline for the business plan is found in Chapter 14.

4.2 PRESESSION PREPARATION

Read the chapter, and review the Opportunity Screening Guide. Begin to apply the benchmarks developed here and in the previous chapter to screen your own ideas and to determine whether one of them is a good fit for you.

4.3 THE OPPORTUNITY SCREENING GUIDE: WHAT IS IT?

Getting the odds of success in your favor necessitates finding the right opportunity, in the right place, at the right time—no small challenge. In order to describe the business accurately and to develop a sound entry and growth strategy, you need a clear vision and conception of the opportunity. Further, your understanding of the market, production, distribution, service, and financial aspects of the opportunity needs to be concrete enough to determine whether it is sufficiently attractive to pursue. If it is not an attractive business, you are probably better off to continue your search.

Below is a summary outline of suggested contents for the initial screening of any opportunity that you are seriously considering. The outline will enable you either to eliminate an alternative or to follow through and prepare a complete business plan. The tear-out guide can be xeroxed and used to develop notes and a draft. This exercise will help you to concentrate your focus on the key issues pertinent to evaluating an opportunity. Involving potential partners or team members in the task is an excellent way to "try out the marriage" and to find out whether you can work together as well as you had thought. It will also assist you to accelerate the pace and to condense the time span that this task would normally require by a trial and error process. A reasonable expectation is about 20 to 30 hours of effort by you and your team to complete the Opportunity Screening Guide. Depending on the nature of your opportunity, your knowledge, and your access to critical information, this may require more effort, but it will probably not require less.

The following is an outline of the principal issues that need to be resolved early on, which suggest the kinds of information that are needed to do so.

Opportunity Screening Guide Outline

1. The opportunity conditions.
2. Description of the product, service, or activity.
3. Market and customer issues.
4. Competitive advantages issues.
5. Economics and harvest issues.
6. Entrepreneurial team issues.
7. Fatal flaw issues.
8. Idiosyncratic issues.

Name _____

Date _____

4.4 OPPORTUNITY SCREENING GUIDE: COVER PAGE

Prepared by _____

Name of Proposed Venture _____

Proposed Location _____

Date _____

SUMMARY DESCRIPTION OF THE BUSINESS (25 words or less)

4.5 THE OPPORTUNITY CONDITIONS

What conditions are driving the opportunity? Once you have completed the remaining sections of the guide, you can prepare this summary, usually one to two pages in length, with succinct, key points that address the questions below. The summary is developed through iterations as the other issues are analyzed and thought through. Usually these points are not clear initially, as most concepts begin in a fuzzy, ill-defined way, which is normal and acceptable.

What compelling conditions and circumstances are propelling the opportunity? Why does the opportunity exist, now, for you? A sound concept will be technically feasible, enjoy some significant competitive advantages, and have a large and durable potential payoff compared to the time and cost that are required to develop and execute it.

What is the evidence and the reasoning that lead you to conclude that you can seize or create the opportunity?

What is the opportunity window, and how perishable is it?

What is it about the economics, the market conditions, the trends, competitors' vulnerabilities, and your capabilities and advantages that makes the opportunity attractive, and why?

What are the prospects that the venture can be harvested, and are the risks, rewards, and trade-offs acceptable to the founders? If the venture cannot be harvested, is the profitability both durable enough and large enough to meet your goals?

Is the management team convinced that the outcome of executing the opportunity is desirable and that it is able to attain that outcome?

What entry strategy suits the opportunity?

Checkpoint. If you have gotten this far and the answers have eluded you, are still fuzzy, or cannot be articulated, it is time to look for a better opportunity.

4.6   DESCRIPTION OF THE PRODUCT, SERVICE, OR ACTIVITY

4.6.1   Description of the Business

1. What is the business you want to enter? Describe it clearly in 25 words or less.

2. Exactly what products, services, or activities will be sold, and what are the eventual end uses? (If the opportunity is already commercialized, attach photos, specs, or descriptions.)

3. How perishable is the opportunity, and what are the likely windows of obsolescence?

4.6.2   Development Status

1. What is the development status of the product or service? Do you have a prototype, sample of work, or demonstration disk (if software)?

2. How much time and money do you estimate it will take to develop the product or service, test it with customers, and introduce it to the market, license it, or open for business?

3. For intellectual property (software, for example) or proprietary products, indicate the status of any copyrights, trade secrets, or patents and what needs to be done (actions, time, money) to assure the protection of the property or products.

4.6.3 Primary Customers

1. Who are the primary customer groups, and what are the main reasons why they will buy your product or service?

2. What ongoing service, maintenance, and customer support is needed, such as warranty, repair, or training?

4.6.4 Strengths and Weaknesses

1. Describe objectively the strengths and weaknesses of the product, service, or business activity. Whether or not you plan to seek venture capital to execute the opportunity, it is vital to have a realistic view of the vulnerabilities and fragilities of your venture, as well as its strengths.

Checkpoint: It is just possible that you ought to abandon or alter your venture's product or service idea at this point. A realistic estimate of the amount of money and time needed to get the product or service to market, or to be open for business, may be beyond your limits. Even in the abundant venture capital market of the mid-1980s, only 1–3 percent of all proposals receive funding. Typically, the first round of financing is in the $1–2-million range, and to raise over $5 million you need a truly exceptional management team and a concept whose potential rewards are large compared to the risks and the vulnerabilities to obsolescence and competition. The life expectancies of today's technology-based products are often as brief as three to five years.

4.7   MARKET AND CUSTOMER ISSUES

To be an attractive investment, a company should be selling to a market that is large and growing—where a small market share can be a significant sales volume. The company's competition should be profitable, but not so strong as to be overwhelming. And the venture's product must have features and a sales price that will enable it to penetrate the market and/or solve significant problems that customers have with competitive products (e.g., poor quality, late delivery, poor service).

The purpose of a preliminary market evaluation is to obtain some hard facts about the market potential for the venture's product or service, to assess the competition, and to evaluate what is required to bring and sell the product or service to the customer. Such an analysis is not meant to be precise or comprehensive, but it should serve to eliminate from further consideration or study those venture ideas that have obvious market difficulties.

4.7.1 Total Market Size and Trends

1. What is the *approximate* size of the *total potential market* for your kind of product or service? Show past, present, and future market size in units and dollars in Exhibit 4.1. (Use available market data to estimate a range of values.) If you intend to sell only in a local area, region, or state, identify the area and show only its market data.

Exhibit 4.1
Total Market Size

	1983	1984	1985	1986	1987	1988	1989	1990
Sales in units								
Sales in $000								

Indicate the sources of data, comment on the accuracy of the data, and say who did the market research.

4.7.2 Customer and Market Research

1. Who are the specific customers? Can you specifically identify and list them? Can you characterize the primary groups, segments, or niches that you are seeking? Have you, or has a team member, sold directly (face-to-face, telephone, by mail) to the customers?

2. Conduct a customer survey, face-to-face (preferably) or by phone. This survey can be thought of as one of the first interactions to test your idea with potential customers. On the next page, summarize your survey. (This summary will assist you in answering the next few questions, so examine these first.)

Customer Survey
Xerox so that each team member can conduct several interviews

Names of Customers

	1	2	3	4
1. Nature of the customers' business or role				
2. Their reaction to your idea Positive and negative Questions they raised				
3. Specific needs and uses they are seeking				
4. Acceptable selling price, service and support, other key terms				
5. Time frame for their purchase decision				
6. Names of competitive firms and products or services that you learned about				

3. Assume that you have randomly picked 100 persons out of a crowd at a trade show. What are the 5 to 10 most crucial questions that you would like them to answer, and what would you need to know about them in order to identify them as very good customer prospects? What will their answers mean?

    a.

    b.

    c.

    d.

    e.

    f.

    g.

4. Why will these persons buy from you? What are the compelling advantages, benefits, and value-added amounts of your product, service, or activity? How long is the payback to the customer (less than a year, and you have a winner; over three years won't do)?

5. How do these persons buy competitive or substitute products now (e.g., direct sales force, wholesale, retail, through manufacturer's reps or brokers, catalog, direct mail)?

6. Describe the buying decision process (who does the buying, what and who are the influences on the buy, where does the buy occur, and how long does it take from first contact to a close, delivery, and cash receipt?)

4.7.3 Preliminary Market Plan

1. Make a realistic estimate of your sales and market share for the first five years.

	Year				
	19____	19____	19____	19____	19____
Estimate total market (from Exhibit 4.1) Units					
Dollars					
Your estimated share (%)					
Your estimated sales Units					
Dollars					
Percent annual growth Units					
Dollars					

Note. If your business will be done in one city, state, or region, be sure that your market data apply to the area in which you intend to sell and service. Refer to the sources described in Chapter 3, especially *Predicasts Basebook* and *County Business Patterns.*

2. What pricing strategies are workable, and how do you plan to position your pricing, given your level of quality, service, and probable marketing expenditures? Remember, low prices usually mean lower margins and less forgiving and rewarding economics.

3. How do you specifically plan to sell your products (direct, mail order, phone, reps, etc.)? What are the likely sales, marketing, and advertising/trade promotion costs? How will this be done?

4. How do you specifically plan to ship and distribute your products? Are there any special requirements (e.g., refrigeration, speed)? How significant are shipping and distribution costs as a percentage of sales and total costs (i.e., are the products transportation-sensitive)?

Checkpoint. The single largest factor contributing to stillborn ventures, and failure, is a lack of opportunity and market focus. If you were unable to respond to many of the above questions, or do not have much of an idea of how to answer them, then you have a serious obstacle. For one thing, you may have a bad case of "marketing myopia"—especially common among engineers and technologists. For another, you may lack enough experience to tackle the venture at this stage. Or you may simply not be nearly as far along as you had thought, and you may have a lot of work ahead if you want the odds in your favor.

4.8   COMPETITIVE ADVANTAGES ISSUES

4.8.1   Profile of Competitors

1. Are there several kinds of products or services that compete for the same business with the same customers (e.g., a hospital uses both mercury and electronic thermometers)? If this is the case, what are the competing products or services?

2. In Exhibit 4.2, list your major competitors in order of their reputed share of the market. Comment on which is the pricing leader, the quality leader, the most innovative, growing most rapidly, the most aggressive, having problems.

Exhibit 4.2
Competition

Name of Competitor and Address	Estimated Market Share (%)	Estimated Yearly Sales (%)	Major Strengths	Major Weaknesses

3. For each competitor listed under 2, describe in Exhibit 4.3 as much detail as you can its marketing tactics in terms of sales force, normal terms of sale, advertising and promotion tactics, distribution, and service.

Exhibit 4.3
Competitors' Sales Tactics

Description and Selling Force	Selling Terms	Advertising/ Promotion	Distribution	Service

4. Pricing
    What prices do competitors charge for the product/service I sell?

	This Product/Service	*Substitutes*
At retail level		
At wholesale level		
At distributor level		
Other channel		
At manufacturing level		

Do you think that you can be price competitive and make a good profit? Why?

Do you have to charge prices that are similar to those of competitors? Why or why not?

Estimate your:

	$	Percent
Product/service selling price (at _____ level)	_____	_____
Production cost (labor and material) or purchase costs	_____	_____
Gross margin	_____	_____
Fixed costs	_____	_____
Profit before taxes	_____	_____

How profitable are competitors?

Name of Competitor	Profits as Percent of Sales	Past Two Years	Expected This Year	Projected Next Two Years
_____	_____	_____	_____	_____
_____	_____	_____	_____	_____
_____	_____	_____	_____	_____
_____	_____	_____	_____	_____

Industry
average* _____

*Use Robert Morris Associates, D&B, or actual data that you may have.

4.8.2 Competitive Advantages

1. How much can you control and influence prices and costs among customers, suppliers, and the channels of distribution? Indicate how you plan to achieve this leverage.

2. Which competitors enjoy cost advantages and economies of scale in production, advertising and marketing, and distribution? What are your prospects, and under what time-cost constraints, for becoming the low-cost producer and distributor?

3. Do you enjoy, or can you gain, advantages in response and lead times in terms of technology, capacity changes, product, and market innovation?

4. Do you enjoy, or can you gain, any legal or contractual edges, such as proprietary protection or other market exclusivity (e.g., specific franchise or distributor rights)?

5. Specifically, how are competitors fragile and vulnerable, and what is the time window that can be exploited? They may be in disarray from the loss of key people; they may have suffered a recent legal suit involving extensive top-management time; or they may have simply failed to innovate and now need excessive time to catch up.

6. Do you enjoy, or can you gain, with cost-time effectiveness, other "unfair advantages" (strategic, technological, regulatory, people, resource, location, etc.)?

7. What are the financial strengths and weaknesses of competitors' and industry benchmarks? Complete the Robert Morris Associates Exhibit 4.4. for your business, and include any specific data you can about your competitors (see Appendix I for a full description of the RMA data).

Exhibit 4.4
Comparison with RMA Data

RMA data for period ending   Estimates for proposed venture

Asset Size	Under $250M	$250M and Less than $1MM	$1MM and Less than $10MM	$10MM and Less than $50MM	All Sizes
Number of Statements					

Assets
Cash
Marketable securities
Receivables net
Inventory net
All other current
  Total Current
Fixed assets net
All other noncurrent
  Total
	%	%	%	%	%

Liabilities
Due to banks—short-term
Due to trade
Income taxes
Current maturities long-term debt
All other current
  Total Current Debt
Noncurrent debt, unsubordinated
  Total unsubordinated debt
Subordinated debt
Tangible net worth
  Total					

Income Data Net sales Cost of sales Gross profit All other expense net Profit before taxes					
Ratios Quick Current Fixed/Worth Debt/Worth Unsubordinated debt/Capital funds Sales/Receivables Cost sales/Inventory Sales/Working capital Sales/Worth Percent profit before taxes/Worth Percent profit before taxes/Total assets Net sales/Total assets					

4.9 ECONOMICS AND HARVEST ISSUES

1. What gross margins do you anticipate (selling price less direct, variable costs)? Anything over 40–50 percent is considered attractive, and anything under 20 percent is considered unattractive and especially intolerant of the mistakes and steep learning curves of new entrepreneurs.

2. How attractive and durable are the cash flow and profit streams? What is the basis for your conclusions?

3. What is your estimate of the profitability after taxes (use RMA), months to break-even and positive cash flow, and return on equity?

4. What is your best estimate of the capital required to seize the opportunity and to attain break-even sales? To attain your five-year sales estimates?

   a. Prepare a preliminary quarterly cash flow statement for the next two years. (Save up to several days' effort by using one of the microcomputer spreadsheet programs if at all possible—see Chapter 13.) This will enable you to determine a first estimate of how much money is required to launch the business.

   b. Adapt and revise the format suggested on page 131 to your own venture in order to estimate initial start-up capital.

Start-Up Capital Requirements

Start-Up Item	Range of Funds ($000)	Date Will Occur
Plant, equipment, and facilities		
Funds needed to complete product development, build a prototype or demonstration package, complete user documentation or manuals		
Market research		
Set up sales and distribution		
Onetime fees or expenditures (e.g., initial inventory, legal costs to prepare contracts or agreements)		
Lease deposits or other prepayments		
Salaries, rent, phone, insurance premiums for key persons, and other overhead that must be committed before the firm achieves a positive cash flow		
Sales and demo trips to trade shows, customers, media for product introduction		
Up-front marketing outlays to launch the product or service (you may need $5 million or more in the first year to launch a new microcomputer software product)		
Other start-up costs unique to your venture		
Total		

5. How much of this can be raised from asset lenders, such as banks and leasing companies, by financing against inventory, receivables, equipment, real estate, and so forth? Give rough estimates of amounts that can be "bankable loans."

Checkpoint.   Most start-ups run out of cash before they secure enough profitable customers to sustain a positive cash flow. Your preliminary estimates of financial requirements should be within the amount that an investor, a bank, the SBA, or other lenders will be willing to commit to a single venture or that you can personally raise. Are you convinced that the amount is reasonable with respect to the venture's potential and risks? If others are not, what do you know that they do not know (or vice versa)?

6. What are your preliminary estimates of manufacturing and/or staffing, operations, and facilities requirements?

   a. What are the major difficulties (equipment, labor skills, quality standards) in the manufacture of the product or the delivery of the service?

   b. How will you deal with these difficulties, and what is your estimate of the time and money needed to resolve them and begin salable production?

Checkpoint.   It is quite easy to underestimate what it takes to overcome the production and operations problems and deliver your product or service at a competitive price. If you or someone on your team is not experienced and competent in getting the product produced and out the door, you have a major gap to fill.

7. What is your best estimate of the prospects and the time frame for realizing capital gain (industry P/Es, current valuations, future climate)? Do the potential upside and the likelihood of its attainment justify the effort, risks, and requirements?

Checkpoint. Beware of compromising "forgiving and rewarding economics" in a venture you want to start. Life in a new venture can be exhilerating, and very demanding. One way you can get the odds in your favor is to make sure that the opportunity is attractive from an economic and financial standpoint. What is more, such opportunities are just the ones that venture capital investors, informal investors, and savvy entrepreneurs and managers will want to associate with.

4.10 ENTREPRENEURIAL TEAM ISSUES

No doubt about it; the entrepreneurial process is people driven. Investors consider the lead entrepreneur and the key managers to be crucial to creating a successful, profitable business. And even if you do not seek venture capital, the relevant experience and the commitment of the founders are crucial.

1. Are the founders sufficiently committed to the opportunity and the potential outcomes? How much are they personally willing to invest, and guarantee, and what portion of their net worth is this?

2. What management know-how, knowledge of the industry, and other skills are required for the venture's success? Do the founders have the relevant experience to execute the opportunity? If not, can key managers be attracted to the venture?

3. Can the founders instill in new hires the vision and entrepreneurial zest that are needed to sustain high performance and growth?

4. List the roles and contributions that each founder is expected to make, and their anticipated salaries and ownership.

Name	Responsibilities and Contributions	Salary	Ownership Percent

Checkpoint.   Can you do it? Are you fully committed? Equal salaries and stock ownership often indicate that the team has been shaped on naive assumptions. Review Chapter 7 on the team if your structure is a democracy.

4.11   FATAL FLAW ISSUES

4.11.1   Are You Aware of Any?

4.11.2 Major Risks and Problems

Each new business has its risks and problems as well as its opportunities. We have not seen a "perfect deal" as yet, and very few deals are entirely free of difficulties to be overcome. It is important that these difficulties be identified as soon as possible. Usually the entrepreneurs can take steps, early on, to eliminate them or to reduce any negative effects. A recognition of risks and problems also demonstrates to potential investors and prospective management team members that the entrepreneurs are intelligent and realistic and "know their business." Investors will assess the entrepreneurs' handling of such risks and problems as significant indicators of their entrepreneurial ingenuity and resilience. There is nothing more damaging to the new venture proposal than the discovery by investors, a lender, or a prospective partner of negative factors that the entrepreneurs did not know about, did not want to discuss, or cavalierly dismissed.

1. What are the major risks and problems that you see in the proposed business? Indicate their order of importance. Consider especially the reliability of customer orders, their amounts and timing, sales projections, ability to achieve cost and time estimates, and the magnitude, intensity and vindictiveness of your competitors' responses. Time and again, first-time start-up entrepreneurs we have known have overestimated sales and delivery dates and underestimated the costs, effort, and time required to execute the opportunity and reach a positive cash flow.

2. What are the significant trade-offs and assumptions that can affect the execution or outcome? How severe are the downside consequences?

3. What can you do to minimize the above considerations?

4. Overall, how would you rate the risk of the venture: high, medium, or low?

4.12   IDIOSYNCRATIC ISSUES

Each venture—the founders, the timing, the situation—is a unique and specific set of circumstances. Not all of the issues specifically pertinent to every venture can be covered in the Opportunity Screening Guide. You will need to adjust and adapt for particular idiosyncrasies here.

1. Are there any other vital issues or considerations, *unique and situational,* to the nature of the opportunity and proposed business? (We have not included material pertinent to retail establishments, real estate, or location analysis here. Excellent material is available elsewhere, and it is referenced in Chapter 11 on resources.)

Checkpoint. The Opportunity Screening Guide should enable you to determine whether you want to continue and to develop a complete business plan. If you are able to complete the guide with mostly positive results, then a business plan is worth doing. (See Chapter 13 for a detailed guideline and a sample plan, and see Chapter 12 for guidance on using microcomputer spreadsheets for the financial analysis.) If you and your partners are confident that you are on the right track, then keep going.

Note.   *You can now return to Section 4.5, "The Opportunity Conditions," and prepare the summary statement.*

THE FOUNDERS

PART II

The Entrepreneurial Mind   5

> Nothing that sends you to the grave with a smile on your face comes easy.
> Work hard doing what you love. Find out what gives you energy and improve
> on it.
>
> Betty Coster
> Entrepreneur

5.1 RESULTS EXPECTED

The lead entrepreneurs who find opportunities to launch and grow higher-potential ventures—those with profitable sales of $1 million or more—do things differently. Their ambitions, acquired skills, attitudes, and practices and their relevant experience position them to recognize and seize opportunities that others do not see or cannot grasp. Upon completion of this chapter, you will have examined how and why this is so. You will have:

1. Examined frameworks for helping you to discover whether being an entrepreneur *gives you,* rather than takes away, sustaining energy.
2. Examined who can be an entrepreneur, what it takes, and when and why entrepreneurs take the plunge.
3. Explored the entrepreneurial mind: the strategies, approaches, characteristics, and actions that work for entrepreneurs who build higher-potential businesses.
4. Developed some concepts and practical guides for evaluating your entrepreneurial career alternatives and for shaping an entry strategy and "apprenticeship."

5.2 NEW KNOWLEDGE ABOUT THE ENTREPRENEUR

Nearly a decade has passed since the first edition of this book was conceived and written. During that time an unprecedented and explosive rebirth of entrepreneurship has occurred in America, and across the Western world for that matter. Accompanying this trend has been a significant increase in knowledge and research about the entrepreneurial process. One driving force behind this new knowledge has been five research conferences conceived and sponsored by Babson College, beginning in 1981, and cosponsored by Georgia Tech's School of Management (1984) and the Wharton Entrepreneurial Center (1985).[1] We have drawn on

[1] Reported in proceedings from these conferences in *Frontiers of Entrepreneurship Research: 1981, 1982, 1983, 1984, 1985;* ed. J. Hornaday, J. Timmons, K. Vesper, et al.; available from the Center for Entrepreneurial Studies, Babson College, Babson Park, Massachusetts 02157.

over 200 research studies reported at these conferences and on dozens of others reported at other gatherings, such as the Baylor Conference (1980) and the 75th Anniversary Entrepreneurship Symposium held at Harvard Business School in 1983. As the new body of knowledge about entrepreneurship continues to evolve rapidly, much of what we knew previously has been reinforced and refined, some of what we thought we knew has been challenged, and numerous new insights have emerged.

5.2.1 Ten New Discoveries

The major new themes that characterize this flow of research about entrepreneurs and new venture creation can be summarized as follows:

1. *The entrepreneurial and managerial domains* are not mutually exclusive but overlap to a certain extent. The former is more opportunity driven, the latter more resource and "conservation" driven.
2. *Venture financing,* including both the new wave of venture capital financing and other innovative financing techniques, has emerged in the 80s with unprecedented strength, fueling the rebirth of the entrepreneur. Both the know-how about venture financing and the amount of money available are important information for entrepreneurs.
3. *Intrapreneurship,* or entrepreneurship within large organizations, and entrepreneurial cultures and management techniques have gained great attention since *In Search of Excellence* was published.
4. *Entry strategies and career patterns* have been identified that show some important common denominators, issues, and trade-offs.
5. *The great variety among types of entrepreneurs* and in how they have achieved their successes defies notions of any single psychological profile that can predict future success.
6. *The risks and trade-offs* of an entrepreneurial career, particularly its demanding and stressful nature, have been a subject of keen interest, one of relevance to would-be and practicing entrepreneurs alike.
7. *Women and minority entrepreneurs* have emerged in unprecedented numbers and appear to face different obstacles and difficulties than are faced by other entrepreneurs, as well as sharing many things in common with them.
8. *The entrepreneurial spirit may be universal,* judging by the enormous growth of interest in entrepreneurship around the world in the past few years.
9. *The economic and social contributions* of entrepreneurs, venture capitalists, and new companies have been shown to make immensely disproportionate contributions to job creation, innovation, and economic renewal, compared with the contributions made by the 1,000 or so largest companies.
10. *Entrepreneurship education* has become one of the hottest topics at American business and engineering schools; the number of schools teaching a new ventures or similar course has grown from as few as two dozen 10 years ago to nearly 300 at the time of this writing.

In short, we know a good deal more about entrepreneurship than we did 10 years ago, yet we are still looking at the tip of the iceberg.

5.3 A NEW LOOK AT THE ENTREPRENEURIAL MIND

5.3.1 A Matter of Fit

In interpreting and tempering these new research findings and balancing them with our collective real-world and classroom experiences, we have come to refine our own views of higher-potential ventures as shown earlier in Exhibit 1.1.

Exhibit 5.1
The Entrepreneur's Cube

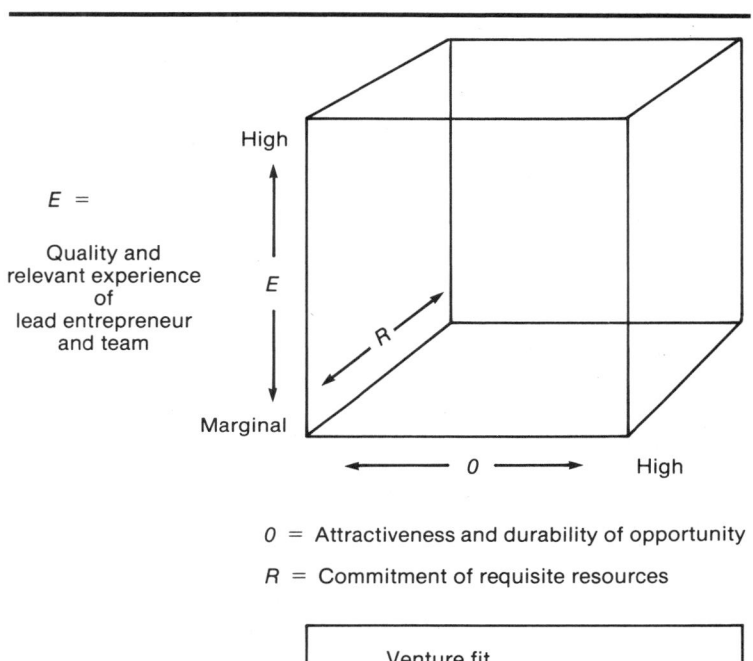

E =

Quality and
relevant experience
of
lead entrepreneur
and team

0 = Attractiveness and durability of opportunity

R = Commitment of requisite resources

Venture fit and potential	$= E \times 0 \times R$

In Exhibit 5.1 these ingredients are represented spatially as "the entrepreneur's cube." In a nutshell, the key ingredients of most successful new ventures fit one another, rarely perfectly, but reasonably so. The extent of this fit and the potential of the venture depend on the quality of the lead entrepreneur and team; the attractiveness, durability, and timeliness of the opportunity; and the extent to which the necessary resources can be marshaled. Thus, for any particular entrepreneurial situation, the greater the volume of the cube, the more the odds are stacked in your favor. For this reason, realistically evaluating the merits and deficiencies of each dimension, and accurately judging the potential and fit represented by this volume, is an important task.

In more practical terms, from Exhibit 1.1, the issues that need attention and resolution are these:

1. The *capabilities, strengths, and weaknesses of the lead entrepreneur* will signal gaps and needs for team members and other resources.
2. The *founding management team* members will add high-value contributions to the venture if they complement and balance the lead entrepreneur, and can work well together.
3. *Relevant experience and know-how* appropriate to a particular venture opportunity can dramatically improve the odds for success. If you—or any of your partners—do not have these, then you will have to acquire them while launching and growing the business. The tuition for such an approach is often greater than most entrepreneurs can afford.
4. Having the *specific management skills and competencies* necessary for the venture to grow and succeed can further enhance the odds. Why stack the deck against yourself if you do not have to?
5. Some *characteristics and attributes* are more desirable than others, and can be learned. Investors and savvy prospective management team members will look for these in you, and you can do the same.
6. The balance of the *risks, rewards, and trade-offs* inherent in the demanding role of lead entrepreneur can be thought through in advance as a way of testing the seriousness of your commitment and that of your partners.
7. The *personal goals and values* of the lead entrepreneur will play a dominant role in the aspiration level, work style and lifestyle, and interpersonal relationships in the venture. Have you thought through what these goals and values are and how they are likely to affect the venture and you?
8. *Certain mental attitudes and philosophies* stimulate, reinforce, and motivate the kind of entrepreneurial zest that can lead to a culture whose self-fulfilling prophecy is success.
9. The *concept of an "apprenticeship"* can assist you in evaluating and resolving these issues, in determining a good fit with any opportunity you consider, and in shaping your own personal and career strategy.

5.3.2 Who Can Be an Entrepreneur?

Anyone who wants to experience the deep, dark canyons of uncertainty and . . . walk the breathtaking highlands of success. But . . . do not plan to walk the latter until you have experienced the former.

The opening quote from the first chapter eloquently answers—in part, at least—the question. While the life of an entrepreneur can be exciting and exhilarating, it is not for everyone. We saw the painful failure statistics in Chapter 1. Yet, the truth of the matter is that nearly anyone in our country can own a business or be self-employed. And judging by some of the latest data, the entrepreneurial wave continues. Take, for instance, the following indicators:[2]

> About 600,000 new corporations were started in 1983. (We estimate that there may have been another 400,000 unincorporated start-ups during the same year.)
>
> Between 1980 and 1982 some 213,000 women became self-employed, while only 47,000 men did so.
>
> By 1982 there were 2.3 million self-employed women, about 10 times the amount a decade earlier, compared to 5 million men in that category.

[2] *New York Times,* March 25, 1984, sec. 3, p. 1.

Despite all these glowing signals, however, there appears to be quite a difference between creating a job for yourself and creating a significant venture.

5.3.3 A Job or a Higher-Potential Venture: What Is the Difference?

Our focus throughout this book has been on the higher-potential venture. As noted in Chapter 1, there are some good reasons for the $1 million in profitable sales guideline. For one thing, the survival odds go up dramatically once this size has been reached. For another, launching, or acquiring and building, a business that will exceed 20 employees is more fun and more challenging than the vast majority of one-person operations. Finally, and perhaps most importantly, a business of this magnitude achieves the critical mass necessary to attract good people and more promising opportunities. As a result, the prospects of realizing a harvest and a capital gain are significantly enhanced. One entrepreneur we worked with summed it up succinctly: "A one-person business makes a living. It takes an organization to make money."

If you cannot grow and harvest a venture, then you may be far better off working your way into a pair of "golden handcuffs" in a medium- to large-sized company. And besides, there is no evidence that suggests it makes any difference to go to college if what you want to do is own and run a modern-day mom 'n' pop store: a boutique, liquor shop, corner convenience store, or tourist agency. Recognize that these latter "ventures" are jobs, and may support two or three people and generate a decent living, but that they are fragile—vulnerable to competition, sudden changes in the community, your own boredom—and are rarely sold for a capital gain that amounts to much. The point is that you do have a choice and that the longer-term consequences of which route you choose are pointedly different.

The "entrepreneurial mind" makes one of the critical differences between traditional very small (one- or two-person) businesses—as well as stagnant or declining large ones—and the higher-potential entrepreneurial ventures that are the focus of this book.

5.3.4 Who Is the Entrepreneur in Higher-Potential Ventures?

Since there has not been a great deal of good, empirical research in this area, we have to draw on the experience and knowledge of practitioners who are intimately familiar with the territory. However, one very recent study provides evidence of what we argued in the first edition (and what our experience confirms): entrepreneurs who *launch and build* fast-growing firms are different from slow-growth entrepreneurs. "What is characteristic is not so much an overall type as a successful, growth-oriented entrepreneurial type.... It is the company builders who are distinctive."[3]

5.3.5 Two Anchors: Creativity and Management Skills

There is mounting evidence that growth-minded entrepreneurs possess not only a creative and innovative flair but also solid management skills and business know-how. These attributes seem to distinguish growth-minded entrepre-

---

[3]N. R. Smith and John B. Miner, "Motivational Considerations in the Success of Technologically Innovative Entrepreneurs," in *Frontiers of Entrepreneurship Research: 1984*, ed. J. Hornaday, F. Tarpley, J. Timmons, and K. Vesper (Babson Park, Mass.: Babson College Center for Entrepreneurial Studies, 1984), pp. 448–95.

Exhibit 5.2
Who Is the Entrepreneur?

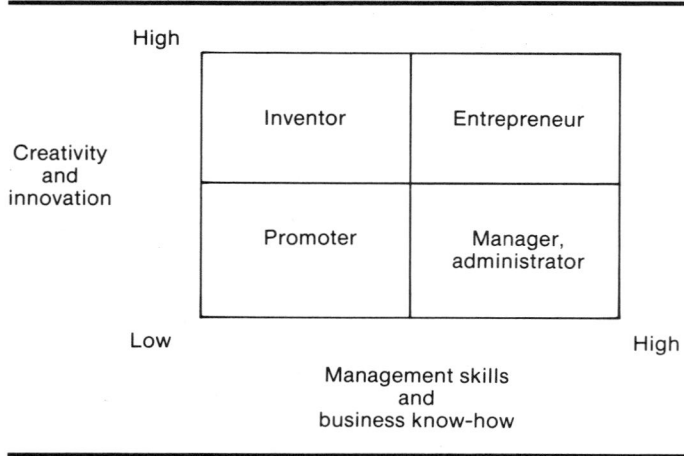

neurs from inventors, promoters, steady state managers, and administrators. Exhibit 5.2 compares growth-minded entrepreneurs with these groups.

Inventors are noted for their creativity. Untold numbers of new ideas and innovations are spawned from just such creativity. Yet, most of these ideas and innovations never become commercial reality, since their inventors often lack the necessary interest or the management and business know-how, or both.

Promoters are often quite creative in the schemes and programs they devise. But these are typically one-shot events or business propositions, with a strong bias toward instant gratification by getting rich quickly. Serious general management skills are often lacking in promoters—they do not need such skills for their role.

Managers have to develop strong managerial skills and business know-how, but they are less known for their creative and innovative solutions, especially in steady state, slow- or no-growth, enterprises. More commonly, they aim for efficiency and effectiveness.

Administrators govern, police, and ensure the smooth operation of the status quo. Their administrative skills are tuned to efficiency as well. Creativity and innovativeness are not only scantly required but may actually be counterproductive in such steady state environments.

The growth-minded entrepreneur has strengths in both creativity and management capabilities. These two driving forces enable him or her not only to conceive and launch a business but also to make it grow and succeed. Or, as the Chinese fortune cookie says: "To open a business, very easy. To keep it open, very difficult."

5.3.6 More Experience and Educated

The profiles and track records of growth-minded entrepreneurs are rich in experience. While there are some outstanding exceptions, such as Steven Jobs, founder of Apple Computer, and Mitch Kapor, founder of Lotus 1–2–3, most founders first acquire substantial relevant business experience. They are more likely to be over 30 than under 30 when they attract the caliber of partners and financial backers necessary to launch and grow a significant venture. They are more likely to have 8–10 years of experience (or more) than less than 5. Among technology-based ventures, the founders are usually college trained and are quite likely to possess an advanced degree. This is not true, as would be expected, among the founders of low-technology or nontechnology businesses, whose prior experience is invariably in basically the same technology, products, and markets in which they plan to launch their new company. Major pluses in the eyes of professional investors—and knowledgeable informal investors, bankers, and others who provide alternatives to venture capital—are general management and marketing experience, including some favorable profit and loss experience. Hundreds of our students have sought out and interviewed at least one such entrepreneur, and about 75 percent of these entrepreneurs have had some direct sales experience.

Growth-minded entrepreneurs usually start the venture with a partner or two. They are likely to have accumulated enough net worth to fund the start-up entirely, or at least to a significant extent. If they have not attained enough net worth to do this, then their track records are impressive enough to give investors and creditors the necessary confidence to provide funding. They have also identified enough reachable customers for their product or service—before they start the business—to break even or become strong enough to attract additional capital before they run out of start-up cash. Finally, they have usually found and nurtured relevant business and other contacts and networks that contribute to the ultimate success of the venture.

5.3.7   Implications for Aspiring Entrepreneurs

The implications of all this are clear: one principal task for an entrepreneur is to determine what kind of an entrepreneur he or she is likely to become, based on background, experience, and drive—and whether these characteristics fit with the opportunity requirements and demands of the potential venture under consideration. If they do, then the entrepreneur can shape a strategy and action plan to make it happen.

5.4   MYTHS AND REALITIES ABOUT ENTREPRENEURS

Folklore and stereotypes about entrepreneurs are remarkably durable, even in these informed and sophisticated times. Despite the fact that we know more about the founders and the process than ever before, certain myths enjoy recurring attention and popularity. Part of the problem is that while generalities may apply to certain types of entrepreneurs and to particular situations, most founders tend to defy generalization. And when some of these observations are applied to growth-minded entrepreneurs who are seeking to build higher-potential businesses, these generalities defy reality as well. Take, for instance, the following examples of myths and realities.

5.4.1   Who Does It?

Myth 1: Entrepreneurs are born, not made.
Reality: We are finding increasing evidence that entrepreneurs are born and

made better—by a combination of work experience, study, and development of "entrepreneurial skills," which we discuss in more detail in this chapter and others. While there is an undeniable core of inborn attributes, which you either have or you don't, it is becoming apparent that possessing these attributes does not necessarily an entrepreneur make and that other attributes of equal importance to successful entrepreneuring can, in fact, be acquired through understanding, hard work, and patience.

Myth 2: Anyone can start a business. It's a matter of luck and guts. All you need is a new idea; then go for it.

Reality: If you want to launch and grow a high-potential venture, you must understand the many things that you must do to get the odds in your favor. You cannot think and act like an inventor, or a promoter, or even a manager; you have got to think and act like an entrepreneur.

Myth 3: Entrepreneurs are gamblers. They roll the dice and take the consequences.

Reality: Successful entrepreneurs take very careful, calculated risks. They get others to share risk with them, thereby lowering their personal exposure. When they find that they can avoid or minimize risks, they do so.

5.4.2   What Does It Take?

Myth 4: You are better off as an independent, lone entrepreneur, owning the whole show yourself.

Reality: It is extremely difficult to grow a venture beyond $1 million in profitable sales by working single-handedly. Higher-potential ventures that succeed usually have multiple founders. Besides, 100 percent of nothing is nothing.

Myth 5: Being an entrepreneur is the only way you can really be your own boss and completely independent.

Reality: Higher-potential entrepreneurs are far from independent, and have many masters and constituencies to serve and juggle. These can include partners, investors, customers, suppliers, creditors, employees, spouse, family, and social and community organizations.

Myth 6:   Entrepreneurs work longer and harder than managers in big companies.

Reality: According to a recent survey of Harvard Business School alumni , a spectrum of "hours per week worked" shows that the self-employed actually work more and less than their corporate counterparts.[4]

Myth 7: Entrepreneurs face greater stress and more pressures, and thus pay a higher price for their role, than do any others.

Reality: Being an entrepreneur is undoubtedly stressful and demanding. But there is no evidence that it is any *more* stressful than numerous other highly demanding professional roles, such as partner in a larger accounting or law firm or head of a large corporation or government agency. And compared to managers in the Harvard study, nearly three times as many entrepreneurs (42 percent) said that they did not plan to retire ever and 73 percent said that they would be entrepreneurs if they had to do it all over. Moreover, most entrepreneurs enjoy what

[4]Howard H. Stevenson, "Who Are the Harvard Self-Employed?" note for *Entrepreneurial Management* (Boston: Harvard Business School, 1985).

they do; they reported more fun than drudgery, and they thrived on the flexibility and innovative aspects of their jobs. Other studies also show that entrepreneurs report very high job satisfaction.

Myth 8: Starting your own company is a risky, hazardous proposition that often ends in failure.

Reality: Success is more common than failure among higher-potential ventures because they are driven by talented and experienced founders in pursuit of attractive opportunities who are able to attract the right people and the financial and other resources that are necessary to make the venture work.

Myth 9: Money is what makes the difference. If you have enough, you will succeed.

Reality: Money is by far the least important ingredient in new venture success. If the other pieces and talents are there, the money will follow.

5.4.3   When Do They Start Ventures?

Myth 10: Start-ups are for the young and energetic.

Reality: While youth and energy may help, it appears that age is no barrier to a start-up. One study showed that nearly 21 percent of the founders were over 40 when they embarked on their entrepreneurial career, that the majority were in their 30s, and that just over one fourth did so by the time they were 25.[5] Further, numerous examples exist of ventures whose founders were over 60.

5.4.4   Why Do They Do It?

Myth 11: Entrepreneurs are motivated solely by the quest for the almighty dollar; they want to make money so that they can spend it.

Reality: Growth-minded entrepreneurs are more driven by building the enterprise and realizing long-term capital gains than by instant gratification through high salaries and perks. Having a sense of personal achievement and accomplishment, feeling in control of their own destinies, and realizing their visions and dreams are also powerful motivators. Money is viewed as a tool and as a way of keeping score.

Myth 12: Entrepreneurs seek power and control over others so that they can feel in charge.

Reality: While many entrepreneurs are driven in this way, most successful growth-minded entrepreneurs are driven in just the opposite way. They are driven by the quest for responsibility, achievement, and results rather than by the quest for power. They thrive on a sense of accomplishment achieved by outperforming the competition rather than on a personal need for power expressed by dominating and controlling others. They gain control by their results.

5.5   ENTREPRENEURS ARE BORN AND MADE BETTER

As recently as 50 years ago a large body of opinion held that leaders were born, not made: you either had it or you did not. Much of this thinking reflected the assumptions and biases of an earlier era when rules were royal and leader-

---

[5]Robert Ronstadt, *Entrepreneurship* (Dover, Mass.: Lord Publishing, 1984).

ship was the prerogative of the aristocracy. Fortunately, such notions have not withstood the test of practice and time, nor the inquisitiveness of researchers of leadership and management. It is widely accepted today that leadership, while an extraordinarily complex subject, depends more on the interconnections among the leader, the task and situation, and those being led than on inborn or inherited attributes alone.

5.5.1   The Entrepreneur: "Special Case" Leader

Today a similar debate on the born/made issue surrounds the entrepreneur. The evidence is mounting, however, that the conclusions will be similar as well. Indeed, the entrepreneur/founder of a higher-potential new venture *is* a special type of leader.

There is also mounting evidence that a good deal about becoming a successful entrepreneur can be learned, but probably not by everyone, nor from everyone. Today about 300 colleges and universities offer courses dealing with start-ups and entrepreneurship, compared to a handful in the early 1970s. And judging by their popularity, these new venture and entrepreneurship curricula have completely captured student interest as well. From our perspective, it is apparent that many of these courses focus on what would-be entrepreneurs and entrepreneurial managers need to know, what works, and how to get going, with this know-how rooted in the know-why provided by useful theories. The students' common sense tells them that these courses are giving them more of what they need to know and do in order to succeed and to grow personally.

It is likely that the now-established field of entrepreneurship will find its place alongside other professional educations. The reason is simple. If you want to be a doctor, dentist, musician, engineer, or lawyer, you seek to attend a professional school to learn what you need to know to succeed. The would-be dentist does not pursue music school, even though he or she may love music. Similarly, entrepreneurially minded students across the country are seeking to test their interests and master the required skills by taking courses on successful new venture creation.

5.5.2   Windows of the Entrepreneurial Apprenticeship

Since entrepreneurs frequently evolve from an entrepreneurial heritage, and are shaped and nurtured by their closeness to entrepreneurs and their experience, the concept of an apprenticeship can be a useful one. Why leave to accident some critical learning opportunities when you do not have to, and can even shape the choices? Certainly, a lot of what you need to know about entrepreneuring—and whether it is really for you—comes from learning-by-doing. Knowing what to prepare for, where the windows for acquiring the relevant exposures lie, when to anticipate these, where to position yourself, and when to move on can be quite useful.

To help you in this regard, Exhibit 5.3 attempts to summarize the key elements of an apprenticeship and experience curve and to relate these elements to age windows.[6]

[6]Professor Timmons wishes to acknowledge the contributions to his thinking here by Mr. Harvey "Chet" Krentzman, entrepreneur, lecturer, author, and nurturer of at least three-dozen growth-minded ventures over the past 20 years.

Exhibit 5.3
Windows of the Entrepreneurial Apprenticeship

Elements of the Apprenticeship and the Experience Curve	Age Window			
	20s	30s	40s	50s
1. Relevant business experience	Low	Moderate to high	Higher	Highest
2. Management skills and know-how	Low to moderate	Moderate to high	High	High
3. Entrepreneurial goals and commitment	Varies widely	Focused high	High	High
4. Drive and energy	Highest	High	Moderate	Lowest
5. Wisdom and judgment	Lowest	Higher	Higher	Highest
6. Focus of apprenticeship	Discussing what you enjoy; learning business, sales, marketing key; profit and loss responsibility	General management Division management Founder	Growing and harvesting	Reinvesting
7. Dominant life-stage issues*	Realizing your "dream" of adolescence and young adulthood		Personal growth and new directions and ventures	Renewal, regeneration, reinvesting in the "system"

*Adapted from Daniel J. Levinson et al., *The Seasons of a Man's Life* (New York: Alfred A. Knopf, 1978).

Lemons and Plums.   These age windows are especially important because of the time that it inevitably takes to create and build any successful activity, whether it is in a new venture or in another organization. There is a saying in the venture capital business that the "lemons," or losers in a portfolio, ripen in about 2½ years and that the "plums," or winners, on the other hand, usually take 7 or 8 years to bear fruit. It simply takes that long to get it all together to the point at which a solid success is evident. Obviously, it can take a shorter or a longer period of time, but seven years is a realistic minimal commitment to have in mind for growing a higher-potential business to a point where a capital gain can be realized. Interestingly, we have heard college presidents, presidents of large corporations, and self-employed professionals say that is about how long it takes to do something significant.

Three-Harvest Limit?   The implications of this time requirement are quite provocative. Assume that you spend the first five years after college or graduate school gaining the relevant experiences that were noted in Section 5.3.6 and are shown in Exhibit 5.3. You are 25 to 30 years of age, maybe 35. How many new ventures can you launch, grow, and successfully harvest, thereby realizing a capital gain? By the age of 50 you might have time for *three*, assuming that everything went according to schedule, which rarely happens. Of course, you do not have to stop then, but realistically, the odds are that you will be slowing down, whether you want to or not.

What is more, it is not uncommon for first-time entrepreneurs to go through some false starts, even a failure or two, in the trial and error process of learning the entrepreneurial ropes (see Chapter 17 for a detailed anatomy of this process). As a result, the first high-potential venture may not be launched until you are in your mid-to-late 30s, so you may grow this one and maybe one more. And, of course, there is always the possibility of staying with the venture and growing it to a larger company, say, $50 million sales or more. But for many ventures, particularly where the technology, competition, marketplace, and regulatory environment—or any combination of these—are rapidly changing, the harvest can be missed completely (see Chapter 18 for more discussion of this important issue).

Paradoxes and Dilemmas of the Windows. Reflecting on Exhibit 5.3 will reveal some paradoxes and dilemmas. For one thing, just when your drive, energy, and ambition are at a peak—usually in your 20s to early 30s—the necessary relevant business experience and management skills are least developed. And that critical element labeled wisdom and judgment is in its infancy. You are straining at the bit to launch and "realize your dream," but usually the deck is stacked against you due to inexperience.

Later on, when you have gained the necessary experience in the "deep, dark canyons of uncertainty and...the breathtaking highlands of success," and have thereby gained wisdom and judgment while focusing your entrepreneurial goals, Mother Nature has begun to recall the vast energy and drive that got you so far.

Other paradoxes are also apparent. You will need patience and perseverance to pursue your long-term vision relentlessly. But you will also need to balance those qualities with the urgency and realism required to make it happen and the flexibility required to stick with the moving opportunity targets, abandon some, and shift to others.

5.5.3 Shaping and Managing the Apprenticeship

It is fair to say that your first 10 years out of school can make you or break you in terms of how well you are prepared for serious entrepreneuring. While it may never be too late, new evidence suggests that the most durable entrepreneurial careers, those found to last 25 years or more, were begun across a broad age spectrum but *after* the person selected prior work or a career to specifically *prepare* for an entrepreneurial career.[7]

Why leave it to chance when you don't have to? Isn't taking charge of your own life and career a part of the thrill and exhilaration of entrepreneuring in the first place? To help you in this matter, Chapter 10 provides an integrated series of self-assessment exercises and a goal-setting exercise that students and practicing entrepreneurs have found extremely valuable. As a woman who founded a rapidly growing medical database and information firm put it: "Self-assessment is the hardest thing for entrepreneurs to do, but if you don't do it, you will really get into trouble." The reason is that if you do not do it, who will?

5.6 THE ENTREPRENEURIAL MIND IN ACTION

Practitioners appear to be well ahead of researchers in coming to a consensus about "the entrepreneurial mind." And, of course, by focusing on start-up and

---

[7]Ronstadt, *Entrepreneurship.*

growth-minded entrepreneurs, rather than all types in all circumstances, some consensus is more likely. Nearly everyone agrees that there is no single profile, or unidimensional psychological or other model, that can accurately define and predict all entrepreneurial behaviors or types, though various efforts have been made to classify different types of entrepreneurs.[8]

Yet, the longer we work with entrepreneurs who launch and build significant businesses—whether or not these entrepreneurs are backed by venture capital—the more we find some common attributes, approaches, and attitudes of vital importance to entrepreneurs. Further, these characteristics suggest a variety of choices about who would be good partners and key managers to complement the lead entrepreneur, and help identify which behaviors seem to work and can be nurtured and developed. This has implications for entrepreneurs, investors, creditors, and prospective partners.

5.6.1   Converging on Acquirable Entrepreneurial Attributes

Increasingly, we have been finding support for our conviction among successful entrepreneurs and venture capital investors and, more recently, academics. Take, for instance, the first 21 inductees into Babson's Academy of Distinguished Entrepreneurs, including such founders as Ken Olson (DEC), An Wang (Wang Computers), Wally Amos (Famous Amos' Chocolate Chip Cookies), Bill Norris (Control Data), Soichiro Honda (Honda Motors), and the late Ray Kroc (McDonald's). The only three attributes and behaviors mentioned by *all* 21 as the principal reasons for their successes were *learnable:*[9]

1. Responding positively to challenges and learning from mistakes.
2. Taking personal initiative.
3. Having great perseverance and determination.

Research undertaken since the first edition of this book has been converging further on some other common attributes. Churchill (1983) proposed a stages model of entrepreneurs and their enterprises and related 11 characteristics of a successful entrepreneur—confirming most of those we noted earlier—to various stages of development of the firms.[10] Smith and Miner, as noted above, found data to distinguish the growth entrepreneurs from the rest of the pack.[11]

These attributes would also appear familiar to the reader of the first edition. Carland and his colleagues summarized the work of 18 researchers and research teams—the summary is shown in Exhibit 5.4—distinguishing the characteristics of entrepreneurs and small business owners.[12] Other researchers, such as Knight,

---

[8]Karl Vesper, *New Venture Strategies* (Englewood Cliffs, N.J.: Prentice-Hall, 1980), chap. 1.

[9]John A. Hornaday and Nancy B. Tieken, "Capturing Twenty-One Heffalumps," in *Frontiers of Entrepreneurship Research: 1983,* ed. J. A. Hornaday, J. A. Timmons, and K. H. Vesper (Babson Park, Mass.: Babson College, 1983), pp. 23–50.

[10]Neil C. Churchill, "Entrepreneurs and Their Enterprises: A Stage Model," in *Frontiers of Entrepreneurship Research: 1983,* ed. J. A. Hornaday, J. A. Timmons, and K. H. Vesper (Babson Park, Mass.: Babson College, 1983), pp. 1–22.

[11]Smith and Miner, "Motivational Considerations," pp. 488–95.

[12]James W. Carland, Frank Hoy, William R. Boulton, and Jo Ann C. Carland, "Differentiating Entrepreneurs from Small Business Owners: A Conceptualization," *Academy of Management Review* 9, no. 2 (1984), pp. 354–59.

Exhibit 5.4
Characteristics of Entrepreneurs

Date	Author(s)	Characteristics	Normative	Empirical
1848	Mill	Risk bearing	X	
1917	Weber	Source of formal authority	X	
1934	Schumpeter	Innovation; initiative	X	
1954	Sutton	Desire for responsibility	X	
1959	Hartman	Source of formal authority	X	
1961	McClelland	Risk taking; need for achievement		X
1963	Davids	Ambition; desire for independence, responsibility; self-confidence		X
1964	Pickle	Drive/mental; human relations; communication ability; technical knowledge		X
1971	Palmer	Risk measurement		X
1971	Hornaday and Aboud	Need for achievement; autonomy; aggression; power; recognition; innovative/independent		X
1973	Winter	Need for power	X	
1974	Borland	Internal locus of control		X
1974	Liles	Need for achievement		X
1977	Gasse	Personal value orientation		X
1978	Timmons	Drive/self-confidence; goal-oriented; moderate risk taker; locus of control; creativity/innovation	X	X
1980	Sexton	Energetic/ambitious; positive setbacks		X
1981	Welsh and White	Need to control; responsibility seeker; self-confidence/drive; challenge taker; moderate risk taker		X
1982	Dunkelberg and Cooper	Growth oriented; independence oriented; craftsman oriented		X

Source: James W. Carland, Frank Hoy, William R. Boulton, and Jo Ann C. Carland, "Differentiating Entrepreneurs from Small Business Owners: A Conceptualization," *Academy of Management Review* 9, no. 2 (1984), p. 356.

report that there are differences between franchised and independent entrepreneurs.[13]

Time and again, the very successful entrepreneurs argue that there are some common denominators that they seek in the people whom they want to surround themselves with so as to build a high-potential business. Take Ken Fisher, for example. He joined Prime Computer in 1975 as president when the company had sales of just $7 million and employed 150. In six years the company grew to $365 million in sales and 4,500 employees. Sales grew at a compounded annual rate of 88 percent, net income at a compounded annual rate of 108 percent, while return on shareholders' equity reached a high of 48.8 percent and topped 35 percent for four consecutive years. During Fisher's stay the Prime share price increased 126 times to its 1981 high, just prior to his resignation. He subsequently formed Encore Computer Corporation with two industry leaders. At a luncheon talk at Babson's 1984 Venture Capital Seminar he made it very clear that "you should look for certain traits—it works: an ego that sustains and drives a person to achieve, stress tolerance, controlled empathy, ability to resolve conflicts, keeping everything in perspective between the business and personal life, and least important of all these, intelligence." He quickly added that "we have done amazing things with people of ordinary intelligence."

[13]R. Knight, "A Comparison of Franchisers and Independent Entrepreneurs," in *Frontiers of Entrepreneurship Research: 1983*, ed. J. A. Hornaday, J. A. Timmons, and K. H. Vesper (Babson Park, Mass.: Babson College, 1983), pp. 167–91.

We do not believe that there is any single set of characteristics that every entrepreneur must have for every venture opportunity. The "fit" concept argues the opportunity is quite situational and depends on the mix and match of the key players and on how promising and forgiving the opportunity is, given the founders' strengths, advantages, and shortcomings. Significantly, among the hundreds of growth-minded entrepreneurs with whom we have worked, *not one* possessed *all* of the highly desirable characteristics noted in Exhibit 5.4 to a high degree. A team might collectively show many of the desired strengths, but even then there is no such thing as a "perfect entrepreneur," as yet.

5.6.2 Using These Insights to Get the Odds in Your Favor

Central to this discussion is the view that you can do something about the desirable characteristics and behaviors. They can be nurtured, developed, and acquired: probably not all of them, nor by anyone, nor at the same pace and proficiency. Most importantly, we believe that would-be, younger entrepreneurs are especially able to improve their odds of success significantly by concentrating on those behaviors and actions that work, nurturing and practicing them and eliminating, or at least ignoring, the rest. It also makes a lot of sense to pay particular attention to picking partners, key business associates, and managers with an eye to complementing your own weaknesses. Having a team whose personal strengths, commitment, and characteristics match or excel the know-how, experience, and management skills of its members can often make the difference between a good and a great venture.

Besides, what is the alternative? To be an ostrich and to ignore looking seriously at what has been successful for others? To ignore the attributes that investors and prospective team members are likely to be seeking in a lead entrepreneur? To stubbornly try to convince yourself that it doesn't matter? To display yourself, and to seek in your partners, key people, and advisers characteristics and behaviors opposite to the "desirable" ones? Fortunately, it is still a free country, and you can certainly proceed as you wish. Before you do so, however, you might want to finish the chapter.

5.6.3 Desirable and Acquirable: A Summary

What follows is a summary of the characteristics and behaviors that can be valuable allies in turning your venture ideas into commercial reality. They represent the synthesis of over 50 research studies compiled for the first edition of this book,[14] updated and revised by subsequent research, including the key contributions noted above, and anchored in and tempered by our own research and experience over the nine years since the first edition was prepared.

1. Total Commitment, Determination, and Perseverance. More than any other single factor, total dedication to success as an entrepreneur can overcome incredible obstacles and setbacks. All of the 21 distinguished entrepreneurs referred to earlier said that this attribute was critical. We have personally seen how sheer determination, and an unwavering commitment to succeed, will even-

---

[14]See these extensive references in Jeffry A. Timmons, Leonard E. Smollen, and Alexander L. M. Dingee, Jr., *New Venture Creation* (Homewood, Ill.: Richard D. Irwin, 1977), pp. 90–91.

tually win out against odds that most people would consider impossible to overcome. It can also compensate enormously for other weaknesses that you may have.

A higher-potential venture whose plans include venture capital financing can expect investors to measure the founders' commitment in several ways. Are you willing to invest a substantial portion of your net worth in the venture, including taking out a second mortgage on your house? Will you take a cut in pay since you will own a major piece of the venture? Have you made other major sacrifices in your lifestyle, family circumstances, and standard of living to make the venture progress far enough to interest outside investors? The harsh reality is that launching and building a higher-potential venture is highly demanding and stressful. You also have to be prepared to lose your job as CEO if your board is controlled by outside investors who do not think your company's performance is as good as they want it to be.

2. Drive to Achieve and Grow. Entrepreneurs are self-starters who appear to others as driven internally by a strong desire to compete, to excel against their self-imposed standards, and to pursue and attain more challenging goals. This "need to achieve" has been well established in the literature on entrepreneurs since McClelland's pioneering work on motivation in the 1950s and 1960s.[15] Seeking out the challenge inherent in a start-up and responding in a positive way, noted by the 21 distinguished entrepreneurs, is achievement motivation in action.

The competitive needs of growth-minded entrepreneurs are to outperform their own previous results rather than to just outperform another person. Having an objective way of keeping score, such as changes in profits, sales, or stock price, is also important. Thus, money is seen as a tool and a way of keeping score rather than as the object of the game.

3. Opportunity and Goal Oriented. One clear pattern among successful growth-minded entrepreneurs is their focus on opportunity rather than resources, structure, or strategy. They start with the opportunity and let their understanding of it guide these other important issues, and thereby do not place the cart before the horse. They are goal oriented and goal directed in their pursuit of opportunities and their execution. Setting high but attainable goals enables them to focus their energies, to be very selective in sorting out opportunities, and to know what to say no to. Having goals and direction also helps them to define priorities and provides them with measures of how well they are performing. It is noteworthy that the Chinese characters for crisis and problem, when combined, mean opportunity.

4. Taking Initiative and Personal Responsibility. The entrepreneur has historically been viewed as an independent and highly self-reliant innovator, the champion (and occasionally the villain) of the free enterprise economy. More modern research and investigation into the entrepreneurial personality have confirmed some of these earlier generalizations, but have refined considerably the ways of focusing on this trait of self-reliance. There is considerable agreement, among researchers and practitioners alike, that effective entrepreneurs actively seek and take initiative. They willingly put themselves in situations where they are personally responsible for the success or failure of the operation. They like to

---

[15]For a more complete description of the need for achievement (n Ach), see Section 5.10, "Postscript: Understanding Entrepreneurial Motivation," at the end of this chapter.

take the initiative in solving a problem or in filling a vacuum where no leadership exists. They also like situations where their personal impact on problems can be measured. Again, this is the doer, action-oriented nature of the entrepreneur expressing itself. In fact, one motto of the entrepreneur might well be: Anything worth doing is worth doing poorly; at least it gets done!

5. Persistent Problem Solving. As we have noted, entrepreneurs who successfully build new enterprises possess an intense level of determination and an intense desire to overcome hurdles, solve a problem, and complete the job. They are not intimidated by difficult situations. In fact, their self-confidence and general optimism seem to translate into a view that the impossible just takes a little longer. Yet, they are neither aimless nor foolhardy in their relentless attack on a problem or obstacle that can impede their business. If the task is extremely easy or perceived to be unsolvable, the entrepreneur will actually give up sooner than others. Other researchers share this view that while entrepreneurs are extremely persistent, they are also realistic in recognizing what they can and cannot do and where they can get help to solve a very difficult but necessary task.

6. Veridical Awareness and a Sense of Humor. The best entrepreneurs we have worked with have a keen awareness of their own and their partner's strengths and weaknesses and of the competitive and other environments that surround and influence them. They are coldly realistic about what they can and cannot do, and they do not delude themselves—which is the definition of "veridical awareness."

This veridical awareness, or "optimistic realism," is often accompanied, we have noticed, by another valuable entrepreneurial trait—a sense of humor. The ability to retain a sense of perspective and to "know thyself"—both thy strengths and thy weaknesses—makes it possible for an entrepreneur to laugh, to ease tensions, and to get an unfavorable situation retracked in a more profitable direction.

7. Seeking and Using Feedback. Unlike lots of people, growth-minded entrepreneurs have an insatiable desire to know how well they are performing. They realize that in order to know how well they are doing, and how to improve their performance, they need to actively seek out, digest, and use feedback. Seeking and using feedback are also central to the habit of learning from mistakes and setbacks and responding in a resilient way to the unexpected. For the same reasons, particularly good entrepreneurs are often described as excellent listeners and quick learners.

As we will see, seeking out people to listen to and learn from has a benefit beyond that of instant feedback for the entrepreneur; it also arouses the interest of the people whose opinions are sought. In this way, the entrepreneur strengthens his supporting network in addition to obtaining the benchmarks he requires.

8. Internal Locus of Control. Successful entrepreneurs believe in themselves. They do not believe that the success or failure of their venture will be governed by fate, luck, or other powerful external forces. They believe that their accomplishments and setbacks lie within their own control and influence, that they can affect the outcome. This attribute is consistent with the achievement motivation drive, the desire to take personal responsibility, and self-confidence.

But there are negatives: overconfidence, arrogance, lack of humility. The entrepreneur should seek to avoid these as assiduously as he seeks to build up a healthy self-confidence.

9. Tolerance for Ambiguity, Stress, and Uncertainty. Ask people working in a large company how sure they are that they will receive their paycheck—assuming that they maintain their present good performance—this month, in two months, in six months, and next year at this time. Invariably, they will say "Virtually for certain," and they will muse at the question. Start-up entrepreneurs face just the opposite levels of certainty: there may be no revenue at the beginning, and if there is, a 90-day sales backlog would be quite an exception. To make matters worse, this uncertainty is compounded by constant changes that introduce ambiguity and stress into every part of the enterprise: jobs are undefined and changing continually, customers are new, co-workers are new, setbacks and surprises are inevitable. And there never seems to be enough time. Lack of organization, structure, and order is a way of life.

Entrepreneurs take all of this in stride and, many would say, actually thrive on the fluidity and excitement of such an ambiguous existence. Job security and retirement generally aren't of any concern to entrepreneurs. In fact, the recent study of self-employed graduates of Harvard Business School showed that 42.5 percent of them planned *never* to retire, while the figure for nonentrepreneurs was about 16 percent.

10. Calculated Risk Taking and Risk Sharing. Successful entrepreneurs are not gamblers. Like the parachutist, they are willing to take a risk. They risk much more than money: they risk their reputations. When they decide to take the plunge, they do so in a very calculated, carefully thought-out manner. They do everything possible to get the odds in their favor, and they appear to avoid unnecessary risks. They reason silently that if you do not have to take the risk, why do it? We have also observed that with more net worth and a successful track record accumulated, they are inclined to take much less risk: they simply do not have to, and they also have much more to lose. Some recent research confirms this pattern. Mitton found three very successful entrepreneurs in California who

initiate and orchestrate actions which, while not risky to themselves, have risk consequences. And while they shun risk, they sustain their courage by the clarity and optimism with which they see the future. They limit the risks they initiate by carefully defining and strategizing their ends and controlling and monitoring their means—and tailoring them both to what they see the future to be. Further, they manage risk by transferring it to others.[16]

Similarly, according to evidence reported by Smith and Miner from an objective test administered to 71 entrepreneurs,

it appears that motives involving self-achievement, avoiding risk, seeking feedback, and personal innovation and a positive orientation to the future are relatively strong in the most successful entrepreneurs.[17]

The strategies of entrepreneurs also include getting others to share the inherent financial and business risks with them: partners put money and reputations on the line; investors do likewise; and creditors join the party, as do customers who advance payments and suppliers who advance credit. And you may

[16]Daryl Mitton, "No Money, Know-How, Know-Who: Formula for Managing Venture Success and Personal Wealth," in *Frontiers of Entrepreneurship Research: 1984,* ed. J. A. Hornaday, F. Tarpley, J. A. Timmons, and K. H. Vesper (Babson Park, Mass.: Babson College, 1984), p. 427.

[17]Smith and Miner, "Motivational Considerations," p. 495.

have to take larger risks when you are just getting started in an entrepreneurial career than are necessary after you are successful. But either way, a carefully calculated, downright cunning approach to risk taking will serve you well.

11. Low Need for Status and Power.[18]   Growth-minded entrepreneurs derive personal motivation from the challenge and excitement of creating and building the enterprise. They are driven by a thirst for achievement rather than by a thirst for status and power. Ironically, their accomplishments, especially if they are very successful, give them power. But it is important to recognize that power and status are a result of their activities and not the need that propels and motivates their actions.

Further, when a strong need to control, influence, and gain power over others characterizes the lead entrepreneur, more often than not the venture gets into trouble. A dictatorial, adversarial, and domineering management style makes it very difficult to attract and keep people who thrive on a thirst for achievement, responsibility, and results. Compliant partners and managers are often chosen. Destructive conflicts often erupt over who has the final say, who is "right," and whose prerogatives are what. Reserved parking spaces, the corner office with the Oriental rug, and the fancy automobiles become symbols of power and status that foster a value system and a culture that are not usually conducive to growth. In such cases, the emphasis is no longer on the opportunity, the customer and market, and the competition.

In fact, we have observed among successful entrepreneurs a well-developed capacity to exert influence *without* formal power. These people are adept at "conflict resolution." They know when to use logic and when to persuade, when to make a concession and when to exact one. In order to run a successful venture, entrepreneurs must learn to get along with many different constituencies, often with conflicting aims—the customer, the supplier, the financial backer, and the creditor, as well as the partners and others on the inside. Arranging an accommodation cannot be done by a formal declaration of "Do as I say"; success comes, rather, when the entrepreneur is a mediator, a negotiator, rather than a dictator.

12. Integrity and Reliability.   Simply put, perhaps the surest way to build and ensure a successful entrepreneurial career—or any other career for that matter—is to insist on personal standards of the highest integrity and reliability. Do what you say you are going to do. To pull for the long haul, such an approach is vital. With it the possibilities are limitless. Your opportunity tree will grow and grow beyond your fondest imagination. Why? Because integrity and reliability are the glue and fiber that bind successful personal and business relationships and make them endure. Investors, partners, customers, and creditors alike value these attributes highly. And sadly, the temptations of a short-term gain often lure too many aspiring entrepreneurs to compromise their integrity, thereby jeopardizing their access to real, enduring opportunities later on. Success achieved without maintaining the highest integrity and reliability is failure. After all, anyone can lie, cheat, or steal, and maybe get away with it once, but this is no way to build an entrepreneurial career.

A recent study of 130 members of the Small Company Management Program at Harvard Business School confirmed how important integrity and reliability

---

[18]For a more complete description of the need for power (n Pow), see Section 5.10.

were in their businesses.[19] Most of them simply said that these attributes were probably the single most important factor in their *long-term* successes.

13. Decisiveness, Urgency, and Patience. One of the paradoxes facing the entrepreneur is the simultaneous need for immediate decisiveness, and getting things done and achieving results right away, and a longer-term view and the patience to manage for the longer haul. The entrepreneur is at once a doer and a visionary. The vision of building a substantial enterprise that will contribute something lasting and relevant to the world, and realizing a capital gain, requires the patience to stick to the task for 5–10 years or more.

14. Dealing with Failure. The ability to use failure experiences as a way of learning, and of better understanding not only your role but also that of others in causing the failure, in order to avoid similar problems in the future is another important entrepreneurial characteristic. There is an old saying to the effect that the cowboy who has never been thrown from a horse undoubtedly has not ridden too many! The iterative, trial and error nature of becoming a successful entrepreneur makes serious setbacks and disappointments an integral part of the learning process. The most effective entrepreneurs are realistic enough to expect such difficulties. Further, they do not become disappointed, discouraged, or depressed by a setback or failure. More typically, they see in adversity and difficult times some opportunities as well, and they doggedly seek to envision victory from situations in which most people can only see defeat. They find promise where others find grounds for pessimism. They see opportunity where others see obstacles.

Entrepreneurs are not afraid of failing. Although intent on succeeding, they are not adverse to the possibility of failing. The persons who fear failure will neutralize whatever achievement motivation they may possess. They will tend to engage in a very easy task, where there is little chance of failure, or in a very difficult (chance) situation where they cannot be held personally responsible if they don't succeed.

15. Team Builder and Hero Maker. Entrepreneurs who create and build substantial enterprises are not the lone wolf, superindependent types.[20] They do not need to collect all of the credit for the effort, nor do they feel the need to prove that they did it "all by myself." Just the opposite characteristics are manifested in their efforts. Not only do they recognize that it is rarely possible to build a substantial business by working alone, but they actively build a team. They have an uncanny ability to make heroes out of the people they attract to the venture by giving responsibility and by sharing credit for accomplishments.

In the corporate setting this hero-making ability is identified as an essential attribute of successful entrepreneurial managers.[21]

The hero makers, of both the independent and corporate varieties, share common attitudes and traits. They are determined to make the pie bigger and better rather than jealously clutching and hoarding a tiny pie that is all theirs. They have a capacity for objective interpersonal relationships as well (Churchill, 1983),

---

[19] J. A. Timmons and H. H. Stevenson, "Entrepreneurship Education in the 80's," presented at the 75th Anniversary Entrepreneurship Symposium, Harvard Business School, Boston, 1983.

[20] For useful insights about the need for affiliation (n Aff), see Section 5.10.

[21] David L. Bradford and Allan R. Cohen, *Managing for Excellence: The Guide to Developing High Performance in Contemporary Organizations* (New York: John Wiley & Sons, 1984).

which enables them to smooth out individual differences of opinion by keeping attention focused on the common goals to be achieved.[22]

Learnable Behaviors. Over the intervening years we have asked students and entrepreneurs one vital question: Which of these and other characteristics can be learned or acquired, and to what extent? A consensus has emerged around characteristics and behaviors discussed above that, yes, you can definitely work on developing, practicing and refining them. Some will require more painstaking effort than others, and much will depend on the individual's motivation to grow. Our sense is that developing these attributes isn't very different from personal growth and learning in many other areas of our lives: people have an astounding capacity to change and learn if they are motivated and committed to do so.

In Chapter 10 an integrated summary of these attributes will enable you to prepare and reflect upon your self-evaluation of these dimensions.

5.6.4 The Not-So-Learnable Attributes

The list of attributes that most experts and observers would argue are more innate than acquired is, fortunately, much shorter. Even today researchers debate extensively whether these attributes can be learned or nurtured to some degree. A friend who is a pediatrician provided a very appropriate analogy of the extent to which certain aspects of our personalities and makeup can be changed. He said that it was like working with fine sandpaper on a large and very hard piece of wood: you can modify its surface, smooth and refine it, but altering its shape is an enormous undertaking.

The following four areas are of this nature. And it is from these "not so learnable" characteristics that the conclusion that entrepreneurs are "born, not made" is undoubtedly derived. While these too are highly desirable givens for any aspiring entrepreneur, it is possible to find quite successful entrepreneurs who lack some of these characteristics or possess each of them to only a modest degree.

1. High Energy, Health, and Emotional Stability. The extraordinary workloads and the stressful demands faced by growth-minded entrepreneurs place a premium on these factors. Although each of them has strong genetic roots, they can be fine tuned and preserved by carefully attending to eating, drinking, and exercise habits and by knowing when to get away for some relaxation.

2. Creativity and Innovativeness. Creativity was once regarded as an exclusively inherited capacity, and most would agree that its roots are strongly genetic. But that may be a surprisingly culture-bound notion, judging by the level of creativity and innovation in the United States compared with that of equally sophisticated cultures that are less creative and innovative. As noted in Chapter 2, a growing school of thought believes that creativity can actually be learned. In new ventures we have seen a collective creativity emerge, much to our delight, from the joint efforts of the founders, where no single individual among them had exceptional creativity.

3. High Intelligence and Conceptual Ability. High intelligence and conceptual ability are certainly great advantages for an entrepreneur. We know of no successful higher-potential venture whose founder would be described as "dumb"

---

[22]Churchill, "Entrepreneurs and Their Enterprises: A Stage Model," pp. 1–22.

or even of "average intelligence." New research on intelligence suggests that it may come in many different shades and forms. This research is quite likely to explain someday what entrepreneurs and businesspeople have known all along: what has been called "street smarts," a nose for business, the entrepreneur's gut feel and instincts, and "ratlike cunning"[23] is a special kind of intelligence that thrives on the entrepreneurial task. Such intelligence might also explain the many school dropouts who go on the become truly extraordinary entrepreneurs.

Take, for instance, the late Colonel Sanders of Kentucky Fried Chicken fame. He has been quoted as saying, "When I got to the point in school where they said *x* equals the unknown quantity *y,* I decided I had learned as much as I could and decided I needed to quit school and go to work!" Needless to say, we are not encouraging you to leave school, if you are there. Our point is that you may have a kind of intelligence that will serve you well as an entrepreneur but does not help you so much in some other situations.

4. Vision and Capacity to Inspire. Those natural, some people say inborn and instinctive, leadership qualities that convey a sense of charisma and boldness and that inspire others, we call vision. All "great leaders" through the ages share these elusive personal characteristics, as do many truly extraordinary entrepreneurs. It is difficult to get anyone to argue that such exceptional personal qualities are other than inborn.

Yet, though your "charisma quotient" may be low, you as the lead entrepreneur are still the leader, and your vision is conveyed by your style of leadership. Your goals and values will establish the atmosphere within which all subsequent activity will unfold. Therefore, we suggest that you not worry about what you weren't born with and that you pay special attention to what you do have: a personal vision and a set of beliefs and ethics that can and should be examined, refined, and disseminated. Your inspiration, regardless of the form it takes, will shape your venture.

Once again, we know of very few entrepreneurs—or others—who have exceptional capacities in all of the areas discussed in this section. If these areas describe your innate talents, then you possess a tremendous potential to be harnessed.

5.6.5 Entrepreneurial Attitudes and Philosophies

We would not spend so much time and space on entreprenuerial attributes if they were merely a summary of current academic research. In fact, they are the very qualities that entrepreneurs themselves believe are in large part responsible for their success. Evidence for this came from our work with the Smaller Company Management Program, noted previously when we asked the men and women who participated an open-ended question: "What do you believe are the most critical concepts, skills, and know-how for running your business—today and five years hence?" Their answers were very revealing: most mentioned mental attitudes and philosophies based on entrepreneurial attributes rather than specific skills or organizational concepts! The entrepreneurs present exuded these attitudes and philosophies throughout our meetings, and we have gathered them together in what might be called an entrepreneur's creed.

---

[23]Our thanks to our colleague Professor Phillip Thurston of Harvard Business School for this insightful term.

1. Figure out how to make it work.
2. Anything is possible if you believe you can do it.
3. If you don't know it can't be done, then you'll go ahead and do it.
4. The cup is half-full, not half-empty.
5. Do things differently.
6. Making money is even more fun than spending it.
7. Take pride in your accomplishments: it's contagious.
8. Make the pie bigger: don't waste time trying to cut smaller slices.

5.6.6 External Role Demands

It is not enough to simply possess a large number and an intense level of entrepreneurial characteristics. Certain external conditions, pressures, and demands are inherent in the role of entrepreneurship. These role requirements have important implications for one's fit with the entrepreneurial task and for the eventual success or failure of a venture. While successful entrepreneurs may share several characteristics in common with successful persons in other careers, their preference for and tolerance of the combination of requirements unique to the entrepreneurial role are major distinguishing features.

We call these role requirements "external" in the sense that they are imposed on every entrepreneur by the nature of the job. You must be able to adapt yourself to them; they are fixed and unforgiving.

Some of these external role requirements are discussed in detail elsewhere in this book: knowledge of the business environment in which you want to launch your venture, apprenticeship and experience, people and team building, creativity. Here, we will focus on four that we have not examined as thoroughly.

1. Accommodation to the Venture: The Need for Total Commitment. The entrepreneur lives under huge, constant pressures—first to survive, then to stay alive, and always to grow and withstand competitors' thrusts. The high-potential venture demands top priority for the entrepreneur's time, emotions, and loyalty. Professor Edgar Schein of MIT has studied several classes that graduated from the Sloan School in the 1950s. He found that there was a similar pattern among entrepreneurs and general managers. The businesses of the entrepreneurs came first by a substantial margin, as did the careers of the general managers. Our own research confirms this. Entrepreneurs must be prepared to "give all" to the building of the business, particularly in the early start-up years. This demand has important implications for decisions relating to marriage, raising a family, and community involvement. To do well in all of these areas while attempting to launch a high-potential venture is not a realistic burden for most people. On the other hand, research on small business owners whose ventures are not in the 15–20 percent of all ventures that are growth-oriented, high-potential firms shows that these business owners can accommodate family and community priorities without damaging the business. In fact, some writers indicate that owners of small businesses are probably dominated as much by personal and family considerations as by the profitability of the business.

2. Stress Generation: The Cost of Accommodation. Stress, the emotional and physiological reaction to external events or circumstances, can be both good and bad for entrepreneurs. In any case, it is inevitable—so the more you understand how you react to stress, the more effectively you can maximize the good, higher-performance results of your reaction and minimize the negative reactions of exhaustion and frustration before they lead to incapacitation.

Two recent surveys by Boyd and Gumpert suggest that very high degrees of both satisfaction and stress characterize founders, to a greater degree than managers, regardless of the success of their ventures.[24] Stress was measured by such physiological symptoms as insomnia, indigestion, and chest pains. Though the founders seemed to accept these discomforts as part of the unavoidable price, the authors remarked that enduring them was not a healthy long-run strategy.

The trade-off needs to be reckoned beyond the immediate situation. An effective strategy measures costs against benefits. . . . The price of corporate health should not be the loss of individual well-being.[25]

Further, the authors attempted to correlate loneliness and stress, arguing that "loneliness is significantly related to negative evaluations of physical self; greater loneliness is associated with tendencies to derogate health and appearance."[26] The study found a high degree of correlation between loneliness and stress and, worse, also found that the two states created a self-destructive cycle. The authors concluded with several practical ways to deal with the problem: first by recognizing its existence and then by controlling its determinants.

Nonetheless, stress in the short haul often produces extraordinary results, through its connection with the type of action essential for entrepreneurs, especially in the start-up stage. Interestingly, once this pattern of producing under pressure has been established, it seems to get locked in; entrepreneurs tend to create new challenges to replace the ones they have met, and to continue to respond to those challenges with a high level of effectiveness. A point to consider in this regard: stopping stressful activity completely may be *more* harmful to your health than sticking with it while attempting to modify it. More than one CEO of our acquaintance who quit cold turkey suffered from months of malaise because he did not allow for a cooling-off period, and one even suffered a heart attack. Like runners, entrepreneurs should probably follow a cooling-down regimen if they decide to decrease their level of activity.

Finally, to put the stress issue into perspective: to date we have seen no evidence that being an entrepreneur is any *more* stressful than engaging in certain other roles or careers that you might also find appealing. As we pointed out in discussing Entrepreneurial Myth 7, the level of stress experienced in numerous other occupations is equally intense. Doctors and nurses, senators, athletes, and even very busy professors all face extraordinary workloads and the same stressful pressures and careers versus family trade-offs that are faced by high-growth entrepreneurs. The personal price you must pay to realize your high ambitions and achieve exceptional goals is high, regardless of career choice.

3. Economic and Professional Values. Business (unlike social or nonprofit) entrepreneurs must share the key values of the free enterprise system: private ownership, profits, capital gains, responsible growth. These dominant eco-

---

[24]D. Boyd and D. E. Gumpert, "The Loneliness of the Start-up Entrepreneur," in *Frontiers of Entrepreneurship Research: 1982* and *1983*, ed. J. A. Hornaday, J. A. Timmons, and K. H. Vesper (Babson Park, Mass.: Babson College), pp. 478-87.

[25]Ibid., 1983, p. 486.

[26]Ibid., 1984, p. 487.

nomic values need not exclude social or other values. But the realities of the competitive market economy seem to require a belief in, or at least a tolerance of, these values.

Personal values, as will be discussed in Chapters 9 and 10, can have a profound effect on the development of the team and on the business itself. An exception to this generalization appears to exist in the area of high-technology entrepreneurship. One study of high-technology entrepreneurs found that aesthetic and theoretical values were strongest. These values of entrepreneurs who spawned their ventures in the research labs of universities, government research centers, or medical laboratories seemed to reflect the environments and backgrounds from which they came.

4. Ethics. In this post-Watergate era, the ethics issue is delicate and controversial. It is generally conceded that the business community has its own ethical standards and that they probably differ markedly from the standards of, say, the religious community. Historically, the entrepreneur has tended to possess what we refer to as situational ethics. The personal ethics of the entrepreneur tend to be defined by the needs and demands of the situation rather than by some external, rigid code of conduct that is applied uniformly, regardless of conditions and circumstances.

Yet, regardless of delicacy and controversy, ethical issues must be addressed—and, in fact, we have expanded and revised the ethics chapter in this book (Chapter 9), which does exactly that. The need to examine your own ethical stance, and that of your partners and associates, is crucial to launching and growing a successful venture. Don't take our word for it; listen to what successful entrepreneurs have to say on the topic:

If the free enterprise system is to survive, the business schools better start paying attention to teaching ethics. They should know that business is built on trust, which depends upon honesty and sincerity.

And:

It doesn't pay *not* to be ethical.

5.6.7 Risks and Rewards

Despite all of the demanding conditions and despite the stressful nature of being a lead entrepreneur and the personal and family sacrifices involved, the bottom line is revealing. Increasing evidence about the careers and job satisfaction of entrepreneurs all points to the same conclusion: if they had to do it over, not only would they become entrepreneurs again,[27] but they would do it earlier in their careers![28] Entrepreneurs report higher personal satisfaction with their lives and their careers than do their managerial counterparts. According to Stevenson, as compared to managers, nearly three times as many entrepreneurs say that they plan never to retire.

---

[27] H. H. Stevenson, "Who Are the Harvard Self-Employed?" in *Frontiers of Entrepreneurship Research 1983*, ed. J. A. Hornaday, J. A. Timmons, and K. H. Vesper (Babson Park, Mass.: Babson College, 1983), pp. 233–54.

[28] Boyd and Gumpert, "Loneliness of the Start-up Entrepreneur," pp. 478–87.

Numerous other studies (for example, Ronstadt) show that independence and living and working where and how they want to are sources of great satisfaction to entrepreneurs.[29]

And financially, there is no doubt that successful growth-minded entrepreneurs enjoy higher incomes and net worths than do career managers in large companies. In addition, the successful harvest of a company usually means a capital gain of several million dollars or more, and with it an entirely new array of very attractive options and opportunities to do whatever the entrepreneur chooses to do with the rest of his or her life.

5.7 THE NON-ENTREPRENEURIAL MIND

Increasingly, we have become convinced that there is also a non-entrepreneurial mind whose characteristics, assumptions, and behaviors spell trouble for a new venture. We have observed attributes of the non-entrepreneurial mind in entrepreneurs who fail, or at least raise enough havoc so that the venture is, at best, one that we would count among the "living dead." We know of no research on this topic, other than broadbrush abstractions about "management as the leading cause of failure." We are intrigued with findings about "hazardous thought patterns" that may contribute to bad judgment among pilots, since there are some parallels between piloting a plane and leading an emerging company.[30] We have observed that some of the hazardous thought patterns that researchers have found among pilots are often prevalent among entrepreneurs who fail. We found the following provocative enough to share for your consideration:

1. Invulnerability. This is a thought pattern of people who feel nothing disastrous could happen to them. They are likely to take unnecessary chances and unwise risks. This behavior obviously has severe implications when flying an airplane or launching a company.

2. Macho. This term describes people who try to prove that they are better than others, that they can beat others. They may try to prove themselves by taking large risks, and they may try to impress others by exposing themselves to danger. While machismo is associated with overconfidence, this thought pattern goes beyond overconfidence. Foolish head-to-head competition and irrational takeover battles may be good examples of macho behavior.

3. Anti-authority. Some people resent control of their actions by any outside authority. Their approach is, "Do not tell me. No one can tell me what to do!" Contrast this thought pattern with the tendency of successful entrepreneurs to seek and use feedback in order to attain their goals and improve their performance and their propensity for seeking team members and the necessary resources to execute their opportunity.

4. Impulsivity. Facing a moment of decision, certain people feel that they must do something, do anything, and do it quickly. They fail to explore the implications of their actions, and they do not review alternatives before acting.

5. Outer-Control. This is the opposite of the internal locus of control characteristic of successful entrepreneurs. People with the trait of outer-control feel

[29] R. C. Ronstadt, "The Decision Not to Become an Entrepreneur," in *Frontiers of Entrepreneurship Research 1983*, pp. 192–212; and R. C. Ronstadt, "Ex-Entrepreneurs and the Decision to Start an Entrepreneurial Career," *Frontiers of Entrepreneurship Research, 1983*, pp. 437–60.

[30] Berl Brechner, "A Question of Judgment," *Flying*, May 1981, pp. 47–52.

that they can do little, if anything, to control what happens to them. If things go well, they attribute it to good luck. If things go poorly, they blame bad luck.

In addition to these thought patterns, we would add three that we have observed.

6. Perfectionist. Time and again, we find that perfectionism is the enemy of the entrepreneur. The time and cost implications of attaining perfection invariably result in the opportunity window being slammed shut by a more decisive and nimble competitor, or disappearing altogether because of a leapfrog in technology. Perfectionism should not be confused with high standards, however.

7. Know-It-All. Entrepreneurs who think they have all the answers usually have very few. To make matters worse, they often fail to recognize what they do not know. Good people and good opportunities find their way elsewhere.

8. Counterdependent. An extreme and severe case of independence can be a limiting mind-set for entrepreneurs. Bound and determined to accomplish things all by themselves, without a particle of help from anyone, these entrepreneurs often end up accomplishing very little. But what they accomplish is *all theirs* to claim.

5.8 IMPLICATIONS

There are undoubtedly other characteristics of the entrepreneurial mind that you can think of. We do not believe that any random set of thought patterns, characteristics, or attitudes is conducive to launching and growing a high-potential venture. The task is simply too complex and demanding. The people who must be drawn to the venture to cause its success, the smart and aware individuals with equally attractive alternatives, seem to partake—in innumerable variations and combinations—in the entrepreneurial core qualities that we have described.

On the other hand, there are certain characteristics that can be fatal for would-be founders of a new venture. We have identified some of them. If you see these—and other—signs of a non-entrepreneurial mind, stop and ask yourself: Would you want to work for people with these non-entrepreneurial attributes? Or have them as partners? Or invest in their business? Or work with them as a customer? Or depend on them to supply your critical components?

5.9 TAKE A GROWTH-MINDED ENTREPRENEUR TO DINNER

Over the years, students have found real value in interviewing a higher-potential entrepreneur. Thus, we suggest that you find one and take that entrepreneur to dinner or convince the entrepreneur to spare an hour of his or her time. Below, we have suggested some questions and guidelines for conducting the interview. Particularly useful criteria for selecting the right person are that he or she has started a company within the past five years, that the company now exceeds $1 million in sales, and that it is profitable. If you do not find an entrepreneur whose venture is profitable, you may learn some of the wrong lessons or some rationalizations.

5.9.1 Purpose of the Interview with an Entrepreneur

The specific purpose for your interview with an entrepreneur is to gain information and insight about the entrepreneur's reasons, strategies, approaches, and motivations for starting and owning a business so as to help you sharpen your own ideas about who an entrepreneur is and what he or she does. The more general purpose is to give you practice in using the interviewing process as a way to gather information and impressions about an unfamiliar topic.

5.9.2 General Suggestions for Interviews

It is our experience that you will learn more if you act more like an interested listener and less like a participant in "20 Questions." You are not administering a test; you are there to learn.

We also find that when you go back over your notes, direct quotes as evidence of the interviewee's motivations or reasons are more useful than such comments as "highly motivated individual"; in other words, learn as many specifics as you can.

If you and the interviewee are *both* comfortable with a small tape recorder, using one to tape the interview can be of great help to you later. However, taping interviews often raises more problems than it solves, so you will have to feel your way and follow your instincts on this matter.

5.9.3 Suggestions for Interviewing an Entrepreneur

Information gathering through the interviewing process is a valuable skill for entrepreneurs to practice, since they can learn a lot in a short time in this way if they thoughtfully prepare for the interview. Your preparation should include the following steps:

1. Define the purpose of the interview.
2. Identify specific questions that you would like to have answered, as well as general areas of information that you would like to know more about. The combination of closed-end questions (How did you get the idea for your venture?) and open-ended ones (Could you tell me about...?) will help keep the interview focused, yet allow for unexpected comments and insights.
3. Contact the person you have selected and make an appointment to see the person, at his or her convenience. Explain why you want to see the person, and set a realistic estimate on how much time you will need.
4. Be prepared to listen, as well as to ask.

After the interview has been completed, you have two more important steps to take:

5. Write the interviewee a note to thank him or her for the time you have been given. This is more than a courtesy; it will also help the interviewee to remember you favorably if you need to contact him or her again.
6. Evaluate the interview. Write down the information in some form that will be helpful to you later on. Make a note both of what you didn't find out and of what you did learn.

5.9.4 Suggested Questions and Format

There is no one "right way" to structure an interview. The one we suggest here has at least two merits, however. It is easy to use because it is chronological. In addition, it has been tested successfully on many occasions.

We suggest asking three open-ended questions, each of which assumes a number of closed-end questions that you can ask directly if the entrepreneur does not supply the information as he is telling his story.

1. Would you tell me about yourself before you started your first venture?
   Entrepreneurial parents, relatives, or close friends?
   Role models?
   Education/military experience? In hindsight, helpful?
   Previous work experience? Helpful?
   In particular, sales or marketing experience? How important was it to starting your company?
2. How did you start your venture?
   How did you spot the opportunity?
   What were your goals?
   How did you evaluate the opportunity in terms of the critical elements for success? the competition? the market?
   What did you do? Find or have partners? Kind of planning? Kind of financing?
   Did you have a start-up business plan of any kind? Tell me about it.
   How much time did it take from the conception to the first day of business? How many hours a day did you spend working on it?
   How much capital did it take? How long did it take to reach a positive cash flow and break-even sales volume? Tell me about the pressures and crises during that early survival period.
   What outside help did you get: experienced advisers? lawyers? accountants? tax experts? patent experts?
   What was your family situation at the time?
   What did you perceive to be your own strengths? weaknesses?
   What did you perceive to be the strengths of your venture? weaknesses?
   What was your most triumphant moment? your worst moment?
3. Once you got going, what happened then?
   What were the most difficult gaps to fill and problems to solve as you began to grow rapidly?
   When you looked for key people as partners, advisers, or managers, were there any personal attributes or attitudes you were especially seeking because you knew they would fit with you and were important to success? Were (or are) there any attributes among partners and advisers that you would definitely try to avoid?
   Have things become more predictable?
   Do you spend more/same/less time with your business now than in the early years?
   Do you feel more managerial and less entrepreneurial?
   In terms of the future, do you plan to harvest? to maintain? to expand?
   When do you plan to retire?
   Have your goals changed? Have you met them?
   Has your family situation changed?
4. In conclusion, we suggest some questions about matters that some entrepreneurs enjoy talking about:
   What do you consider your most valuable asset—the thing that enabled you to "make it"?

If you had it to do over, would you do it again? In the same way? Do something different?

Looking back, what do you feel are the most critical concepts, skills, attitudes, and know-how you needed to get your company started and grown to where it is today? What about five years from now? To what extent can any of these be learned?

Some people say there is a lot of stress to being an entrepreneur. What have you experienced? How would you say it compares with other "hot seat" jobs, such as the head of a big company or a partner in a large law, consulting, or accounting firm?

What are the things that you find personally rewarding and satisfying as an entrepreneur? What have been the rewards, risks, and trade-offs?

Who should try to be an entrepreneur? Can you give me any ideas there?

What advice would you give an aspiring entrepreneur?

5.10 POSTSCRIPT: UNDERSTANDING ENTREPRENEURIAL MOTIVATION

Venture capitalists and entrepreneurs, and behavioral scientists who have examined them share the conclusion that the eventual success of a new venture will depend a great deal on the psychological makeup of the lead entrepreneur. Venture capitalists have learned from experience that there is something different inside a person who builds a successful new company. That something they often refer to as drive, dedication, and determination. Psychologists have also studied this phenomenon among the people who start their own businesses—the entrepreneurs. These comments and the accompanying exercise will provide you with one particularly useful framework for understanding the various motivations of entrepreneurs. They will also help you to recognize these motivations and to apply motivational concepts to the task of assessing yourself.

We hasten to add that there are numerous other ways of thinking about and accounting for human behavior and that the particular framework presented here cannot account for everything. It is included because (1) it is a generally accepted part of the literature on entrepreneurial behavior; (2) it has been used to a considerable extent in actual research, evaluation, and training efforts relating to entrepreneurship; and (3) it combines both depth and breadth in a readily usable frame of reference.

For over 35 years, Dr. David C. McClelland of Harvard University and Dr. John W. Atkinson of the University of Michigan and their colleagues have been seeking to understand individual motivation.[31] They have developed and researched a theory of psychological motivation that has been widely used in the study and practice of management and entrepreneurship. Its applicability to the latter area is the focus of our attention here. Their theory and research suggest that people are motivated by three principal needs: (*a*) the need for achievement (n Ach), (*b*) the need for power (n Pow), and (*c*) the need for affiliation (n Aff).

The relative strengths of each of these needs have important consequences

[31] See J. W. Atkinson, *An Introduction to Motivation* (Princeton, N.J.: D. Van Nostrand, 1964); J. W. Atkinson, ed. *Motives in Fantasy, Action, and Society* (Princeton, N.J.: D. Van Nostrand, 1958); D. C. McClelland, *The Achieving Society* (Princeton, N.J.: D. Van Nostrand, 1961); J. W. Atkinson and N. T. Feather, eds., *A Theory of Achievement Motivation* (New York: John Wiley & Sons, 1966); and D. C. McClelland and D. G. Winter, *Motivating Economic Achievement* (New York: Free Press, 1969).

and implications for a person considering an entrepreneurial career. During the accompanying exercises and subsequent discussions you will have the opportunity to examine several important issues:

1. Which of these needs motivate successful entrepreneurs, and in what way?
2. What is the relationship between each of these needs and entrepreneurship?
3. Are there entrepreneurial strengths and weaknesses that are associated with each of these needs?
4. What is my own motivational profile, and what are its implications for an entrepreneurial career?

In order to address these issues later, we will first learn about the three motivations.

When you think about these three motivations and try to find clues to other people's motivation, keep several precautions in mind. First, what a person says and what a person does, and why, are often not the same thing. You must be careful not to latch on to just one or two words that someone uses and assess his probable motivation by that alone. Second, it is easy to confuse your own motivations with those of another person, whether a superior, partner, friend, or peer. If you are motivated by achievement, you will tend to see that motivation in others and to stress it to the exclusion of the other two motivations. Try to separate your own feelings about what another person says from the words he uses. Third, there is a tendency when you work with n Ach, n Aff and n Pow to attribute motivations to individuals when there are none. Simply because someone says "goals," talks about "people," or uses "strong language" does not mean that he has n Ach, n Aff, or n Pow. There must be some activity or concern before any of the motivations are indicated. You might ask yourself: What seems to turn him or her on? Lastly, remember that people often have some of all three of these motivations and that in different circumstances these three motivations will be more or less prominent. (During a person's life there may be considerable changes in motivations.) Motivations in themselves are neither "good" nor "bad." They are simply ways of describing why people do the things they do.

The Need for Achievement—n Ach

The need for achievement is the need to excel, the need to do a job well. It is the need for measurable personal accomplishment. People with high achievement needs are people who seek out challenging or competitive situations and set goals that are both realistic and achievable. The need for achievement is a primary motivation among most entrepreneurs. It is this need to achieve that psychologists believe provides the inner drive for the unusual accomplishments of starting and building a business. Several behavioral characteristics identify the high achiever:

1. *Competing against a self-imposed standard.* In this situation, the individual engages in an activity where winning or doing better than he or she has done before is a primary concern. A typical example is wanting to win a race or contest or wanting to show that you can do a better job than you did previously, against some objective standard that you set for yourself. Simply beating other people is not n Ach.

2. *Meeting or surpassing a self-imposed standard of excellence.* Such a stan-

dard of excellence does not involve competition with others but is a *self-imposed* standard of high-quality performance. Typical examples include wanting to find a better method and working carefully on a plan. Distinguish between intensity and quality: working hard or fast does not mean that you are concerned about excellence. Only when you demonstrate a concern for accuracy or quality is a self-imposed standard of excellence indicated.

3. *Seeking unique accomplishment.* The individual seeks to accomplish some extraordinary task or use unique methods, for example, an unusual business innovation, that mark him or her as a personal success. This includes seeking to do something that has not been done before.

4. *Using feedback.* The individual likes to get feedback as to how well he or she is doing and is responsive to such concrete feedback. The individual actively seeks information about his or her performance and acts on that information to improve performance.

5. *Setting moderate-risk goals.* The individual sets realistic and challenging goals and works harder to attain such goals when the chances of succeeding are only fair.

6. *Seeking to attain long-term business goals.* Mere mention of a business goal is not the basis for assuming n Ach. There must be evidence of involvement in long-term business goals. This means talking and feeling about goals that lie 5–10 years away and consistently planning how to attain them.

7. *Formulating plans for overcoming personal, environmental, or business obstacles.* The high achiever carefully plans for the future by trying to anticipate any blocks to achieving the desired goals. Evidence of this type of planning can be found in the statements that individuals make about how they have overcome or are planning to overcome any barriers to goal achievement.

The Need for Affiliation—n Aff

To decide whether or not someone shows evidence of affiliation motivation, first look to see whether that person is concerned about attaining an "affiliation goal." Is the goal to build a warm relationship with someone else or to enjoy mutual friendship? There are five categories of indication of the need for affiliation.

1. *Concern with being liked, acceptance, friendship.* In this case, a person talks about wanting to establish, maintain, or restore a close, warm, and friendly relationship with other people.

2. *Attraction to social situations.* Here, the individual expresses a desire to participate in friendly activities such as parties and club reunions and tends to define any gathering in social terms.

3. *Concern about the disruption of a positive interpersonal relationship.* The individual in this situation expresses an emotional concern about separation from someone else, indicating a desire to restore a close relationship that had previously existed.

4. *Concern for people in the work situation.* In this instance, the individual talks about people and working with people as the primary concern in the business life.

5. *Concern for people in non-work settings.* Here, the individual talks about the importance of being with other people as a primary reason for involvement in a spare-time activity.

The need for affiliation exists only when there is some evidence of concern about establishing, maintaining, or restoring a positive emotional relationship with another person. This relationship is best described as a "friendship."

Some personal relationships are not like this. For example, the relationships between father and son, brothers, and lovers, are all relationships between two people, but such relationships do not necessarily have the warm companionship quality embodied in our definition of n Aff. Moreover, these relationships may not be characterized by concern about maintaining or restoring a positive relationship.

The Need for Power—n Pow

In deciding whether a person shows evidence of the need for power, n Pow, you must first look to see whether that person is concerned about attaining an "influence goal." There are four indicators of concern for power:

1. *Powerful actions.* First, these are actions that in themselves express power such as strong, forceful actions that affect others: verbal attacks, threats, or reprimands. Second, these actions might include giving unsolicited help, advice, and support that evidences a concern for power, and goes beyond solving some other person's problem. Third, these actions might include trying to control or influence another person by regulating that person's behavior or conditions of life. Finally, these actions might include trying to influence someone through argument or trying to impress others in the world at large.

2. *Arousing strong emotions in others.* In this instance, the need for power is satisfied by the emotional reaction of others to one's actions—such as delight, awe, despondency, offense, anger, or fear that results from something one has done. Mere interest or listening intently is not sufficient to satisfy this power motivation. The action must arouse strong feelings ("They were absolutely fascinated"), and it must be intentional. Further, the action arousing the strong feelings must be under the control of the power-oriented person.

3. *Concern for reputation, status, or position.* In this case, the individual is concerned about evaluation—about how someone else or the world at large will think of his or her power. Persons whose need for power is widened in this way are concerned about their reputation or status and about other people's views of their powerful position, but they do not necessarily talk about any particular actions that they take relative to this concern. In other words, whether they are basking in the glory of high status or disappointed by their inferior social position, they are concerned only about public evaluation. The standard is externally derived and externally oriented rather than self-imposed.

4. *Outperforming someone else.* The individual engages in an activity where beating the other person or persons is the primary concern. This kind of power-oriented competition is unrelated to any self-imposed standard of excellence but is focused primarily on the desire to beat others.

Remember, powerful words or strong emotions do not necessarily indicate power motivation.

The negative aspects of power motivation are sometimes easier to see than the positive aspects, but bear in mind that successful salespersons and lawyers are effective persuaders. Socialized and civilized power needs have played an important role in influencing people and institutions.[32]

[32]For a good discussion of the positive and negative aspects of power motivation, see David C. McClelland, "Two Faces of Power," in *Organizational Psychology: A Book of Readings,* 2d ed., ed. D. Kolb, I. Rubin, and J. McIntyre (Englewood Cliffs, N.J.: Prentice-Hall, 1974).

Summary of Clues to Individual Motivation

The Need for Achievement (n Ach). The need for achievement is the need to excel, or to do well in a particular task. Indicators are:

1. Competing with a self-imposed, objective standard.
2. Meeting or surpassing a self-imposed standard of excellence.
3. Seeking unique accomplishment.
4. Using feedback.
5. Taking moderate, calculated risks.
6. Seeking to attain long-term business goal.
7. Formulating plans for overcoming personal, environmental, or business obstacles.

The Need for Affiliation (n Aff). The need for affiliation exists when there is evidence of concern about establishing, maintaining, or restoring a positive emotional relationship with another person. Indicators are:

1. Concern with being liked, accepted, befriended.
2. Tendency to see gatherings as social situations.
3. Concern about the disruption of a positive interpersonal relationship.
4. Concern for people in the work situation.
5. Concern for people in spare-time activities.

The Need for Power (n Pow). The need for power exists when an individual's goal is to influence others. Indicators are:

1. Outperforming someone else, irrespective of any objective or self-imposed standard.
2. Showing strong concern for power through powerful actions.
3. Doing things that arouse strong positive or negative emotions in others.
4. Demonstrating concern for reputation or position.

Powerful words or strong emotions do not indicate power motivation. There must be a clear intent to have an impact on others—not just a need to let one's own feelings out.

Once you have studied these concepts thoroughly, complete the following Motivation Prediction exercise. You may refer to the definitions of n Ach, n Aff, and N Pow if necessary, but try to complete as many of the 30 items as you can on your own. The object of the exercise is to strengthen your understanding of the three concepts. At the next class you will compare your solutions with the answers of knowledgeable experts.

Name _____

Date _____

MOTIVATION PREDICTION EXERCISE*

Next to each statement, indicate whether you believe the phrase is indicative of n Ach, n Aff, or n Pow. Check one for each item.

	n Ach	*n Aff*	*n Pow*
1. In everything I do—work, sports, hobbies—I try to set really high standards for myself. Otherwise, where's the fun of it?	_____	_____	_____
2. It's important to establish who's boss when you're in a business situation.	_____	_____	_____
3. My favorite sport is football. I love to see guys really hit.	_____	_____	_____
4. In anything we get involved with, I really think it's important that we set very specific goals. Without goals, our group just goes off in a lot of different directions.	_____	_____	_____
5. In would like my children to become involved in the business rather than spending their time on a lot of artistic nonsense like young people do today.	_____	_____	_____
6. It's people that make up a business, not a lot of stock piled up on the shelves.	_____	_____	_____
7. I really enjoy being with my friends in a pleasant social atmosphere.	_____	_____	_____
8. When you add it up, a person's reputation and standing in the community tell you who he or she is.	_____	_____	_____
9. It's exciting when you have a breakthrough, when you discover a new way of doing something—a way no one has thought of before.	_____	_____	_____
10. When our neighbors installed a swimming pool, my spouse thought it was very important that we put in a somewhat larger one.	_____	_____	_____
11. People think I'm very fortunate to have achieved my financial position, but I've been planning for almost 10 years.	_____	_____	_____
12. Working together in a group to develop a strategy can be satisfying and productive.	_____	_____	_____
13. It is very important for me to be liked by the people I work with.	_____	_____	_____

*This exercise was originally developed by our colleagues George H. Lilwin and Steven K. Trooboff and is used here with their permission.

	n Ach	*n Aff*	*n Pow*
14. I hear a lot about the power of positive thinking. In my opinion, the people who succeed are those who carefully analyze the obstacles, the things that might keep them from achieving their goals.	_____	_____	_____
15. People that can't do as they're told when they are assigned a simple task make me angry.	_____	_____	_____
16. Before we commit ourselves to a new product line, we are pretty careful to examine the various opportunities the market has presented and the particular situation of our competitors.	_____	_____	_____
17. My family and my children mean a great deal to me.	_____	_____	_____
18. I always had respect for my father, and I expect the same from my children.	_____	_____	_____
19. I don't like to get involved in something and then drop it. Success in business is the result of a long-term commitment to what you're doing.	_____	_____	_____
20. I get mad sometimes when people try to infringe upon my prerogatives as owner of this business.	_____	_____	_____
21. I like to understand my employees' personal ambitions so that I can help them.	_____	_____	_____
22. I have to keep control of things in our business, or projects go to pot very quickly.	_____	_____	_____
23. I place a lot of emphasis on relationships because other people can help you achieve your goals.	_____	_____	_____
24. I want to succeed so that I can really do well by the members of my family, who love me very much.	_____	_____	_____
25. I always thought I would enjoy being a teacher or a professor.	_____	_____	_____
26. Kids are really fantastic. I love to spend time with them watching them grow and learn.	_____	_____	_____
27. I used to think that certain personal traits would make it impossible for me to be a successful businessperson, but I have learned how to overcome these problems and how to get where I'm going.	_____	_____	_____
28. I like to get involved in community activities because it gives me a chance to have influence in the community in which I live.	_____	_____	_____
29. My spouse is really a wonderful person, and people often comment on how lucky I am that my spouse is so good-looking.	_____	_____	_____
30. I really like to play competitive sports in which there is an opportunity to excel.	_____	_____	_____

5.11   KEVIN MOONEY (A): CASE STUDY*

KEVIN MOONEY (A)

As the elevator descended silently to the lobby, Kevin Mooney mused confidently about the decision he was facing: whether or not to resign from Price Waterhouse, the prestigious accounting firm, and accept a position with a new, still quite small, software company. He wondered how many of his colleagues at Price Waterhouse would opt to leave the security of a big business for a challenge like the one at Softcorp, Inc. He would be director of international marketing at a small software firm specializing in financial and accounting software packages for mainframe computers. The company's sales were just over $1 million, and it had no international customers. Nobody in the company even had a passport! Kevin thought this opportunity was filled with chances to exercise his entrepreneurial talents. He liked the founders of the company; its products had growth potential; and he would be an important part of the management team, so they said. Yet, the future at Price Waterhouse was very bright. He wondered what he should do.

Kevin Mooney

Kevin gave his father much of the credit for forging his entrepreneurial spirit. Nothing Kevin did was ever quite good enough for his father. His constant criticism made Kevin fiercely independent and willing to take on challenging tasks just to prove to himself that he could do them. Consequently, he often recognized opportunities where others didn't.

During high school in Philadelphia the ham radio club he had organized needed money to buy equipment. Kevin figured the club could raise the money doing what it knew best—working with electrical equipment. He founded his first venture: Rapid Radio Repair at Reasonable Rates, a company which repaired small appliances for neighbors, offering reliable service, pickup, and delivery. The neighbors liked the service, and the venture kept the club running.

After high school Kevin Mooney enrolled at Cornell University as an engineering major. In the early 70s, engineering wasn't a very popular profession, or even a lucrative one, but Kevin thought he needed the discipline engineering offered. His four years at Cornell were successful, although his studies didn't excite him. His real interest was his position as chairman of the Student Finance Commission, which had the responsibility of allocating a $130,000 budget among all the student organizations and activities on campus.

Immediately after graduation Kevin married his high school sweetheart and enrolled in Stanford Business School. He recalled his decision to enroll:

Stanford advised students entering directly from undergraduate school to work for several years before beginning the MBA. I figured that most of the younger students probably followed Stanford's advice. So I decided to enroll right away, learn from *their* work experiences, and save myself some time!

During his two years at Stanford Kevin chose courses which he thought would help him run a small business of his own. Then, before job interviews be-

*This case was prepared by Loretto Crane, Research Assistant, under the direction of Professor Jeffry A. Timmons, as a basis for class discussion rather than to illustrate either effective or ineffective handling of an administrative situation. Copyright © 1984 by Babson College.

Exhibit 1
Kevin Mooney's Résumé

KEVIN MOONEY
Blackwelder 5–G
Stanford, California 94305
(415) 321–6877

JOB OBJECTIVE: To secure a consulting or staff position in corporate or financial planning.

EDUCATION:
1974–1976   STANFORD GRADUATE SCHOOL OF BUSINESS
Candidate for MBA degree in June 1976. Concentration in finance. Selected to represent the Stanford Graduate School of Business on the Journey for Perspective Foundation 1975 international study program abroad. Traveled to Eastern and Western Europe for seminars with business and political leaders. Member of Investment Club and Business Development Association.

1970–1974   CORNELL UNIVERSITY, Ithaca, New York
BS degree in Industrial Engineering and Operations Research in June 1974. Dean's list. Chairman of Cornell Student Finance Commission. Responsibilities included financial planning for more than 100 organizations, allocation of $130,000 of student fees, hiring and directing office staff, and administration of accounts. President of Quill & Dagger Society (senior honorary).

BUSINESS
EXPERIENCE:
Summer 1975   PEAT, MARWICK, MITCHELL & CO., San Francisco, California
Management Consultant. Performed conceptual design and implementation of a centralized purchase order system. Developed complete cost accounting system and contributed in formulating approach and preparing written proposal for a consulting engagement.

Summer 1974   CORNELL UNIVERSITY, Ithaca, New York
Summer Conference Coordinator. Administrative responsibility for summer conference programs. Duties included computer information system development and implementation, personnel administration, and coordination of university departments and facilities.

Summers
1972, 1973   DECISION DATA COMPUTER CORPORATION, Horsham, Pennsylvania
Manufacturing Engineer. Responsibilities included plant layout, tool design, and writing manufacturing instructions.

Additional
Information   Married. Private pilot, currently pursuing additional ratings. Other interests include skiing, photography, swimming, and bicycling.

References   Personal references are on file with the Placement Office and will be forwarded upon request.

---

gan, Kevin and his wife decided that the Pacific Northwest was the place they wanted to live; he planned his company interviews accordingly. (See Exhibit 1.)

Price Waterhouse was interviewing students interested in working in its newly created small business division in Seattle. Although Kevin never planned to be an accountant, the location appealed to him and he thought the job would give him the opportunity to get to know the region's business community. He took the job, and within three months he was generating all his own work, often attending business breakfasts to drum up prospective clients. During the first year he brought five new clients to the firm.

Softcorp, Inc.

One of his many clients was Softcorp, Inc. Founded in 1969 by two men who had worked together at Hewlett-Packard, the company was just beginning to build a reasonable customer base. In the beginning the two founders, Joe Hegarty and Bob Wilson, designed the company's accounting applications packages themselves. Accounts Payable and Fixed Asset Accounting were the company's flagship products and contributed about 90 percent of Softcorp's revenue. Entirely internally funded except for a small line of credit at the bank, Softcorp dedicated its efforts to product development, marketing, and customer support and training. By 1976 it had 29 employees and sales of $1.2 million. (See Exhibit 2.)

Exhibit 2
Softcorp, Inc., Performance, 1974–1976 ($000)

	1974	1975	1976
Annual revenue	$357	$734	$1,217
Installations (cumulative)	383	449	530
Total employees	11	23	29

Hegarty and Wilson first came to Price Waterhouse for help in enhancing their fixed-asset system to incorporate the latest IRS depreciation rules. After three years and no solution, Softcorp's executives were understandably frustated. Kevin Mooney took over their account and resolved the outstanding problems within three months. Mooney's manner and competence impressed the two men, and their relationship thrived. Then, in late 1977, Hegarty and Wilson approached Kevin about the job as director of international marketing.

The Job Negotiations

The offer intrigued Mooney. He saw the opportunities inherent in this small company. He knew little about the general markets for software packages and even less about the international markets. Softcorp was small and undercapitalized, and Kevin wondered what resources would be available to him to launch an international marketing effort.

Kevin worked well with the two founders. He and his wife had been guests at Hegarty's home. In December 1977 Kevin Mooney met with Hegarty and Wilson to discuss the details of the job.

I remember asking them if they knew of any international customers out there who wanted their products. Hegarty just shrugged his shoulders and said, "If there are, we know you'll find them."

I reminded them that I didn't have any operating experience, but that didn't seem to bother them. They seemed very impressed with my competence and my education. Frankly, I don't think I would have hired me!

They offered me a nice salary (a 20 percent increase over what I was making at PW) plus a bonus which would be tied to performance. I raised the question of equity participation. Both men were reluctant to give me any equity up front. They cited examples of two employees who had been given stock, but only after each had demonstrated his commitment and loyalty to the company. They told me that once I had done the same, equity would be a possibility.

The elevator stopped at the lobby. Kevin had just had a last meeting with his boss, Bob Baker. His mentor at Price Waterhouse was disappointed that Kevin would throw away his promising future at Price Waterhouse.

Baker reminded Kevin that promotions would be announced in a few months, and he thought Kevin had a very good shot at being promoted to manager. Baker asked him several questions he couldn't answer: What resources would Softcorp make available to build the international division? How were they planning to measure his performance? What would constitute success or failure?

When the meeting ended, Baker shook Kevin Mooney's hand and said, "Do you realize if you go to Softcorp, you are probably going to fail? Are you prepared for that?" Mooney left the building with Baker's questions running through his mind. Softcorp's offer letter and nondisclosure agreement were in his briefcase, ready for his signature. He had two weeks to make his decision.

Preparation Questions

1. What should Kevin Mooney do, and why?
2. What criteria and considerations should be weighed, and how?
3. Analyze the relevance, risks, and rewards of the two opportunities and their implications for "the entrepreneurial apprenticeship."
4. What additional information would you seek, and how?

The Entrepreneurial Manager 6

> *You have to approach the world as an equal. There is no such thing as being a supplicant. You are trying to work and create a better solution by creating action among a series of people who are relatively equal. . . . We destroy potential entrepreneurs by putting them in a velvet-lined rut, by giving them jobs that pay too much, and by telling them they are too good, before they get adequate intelligence, experience, and responsibility.*
>
> Howard H. Stevenson
> Sarofim-Rock Professor
> Harvard Business School

6.1 RESULTS EXPECTED

There are convergent pressures and skills between the entrepreneur and the manager as a venture accelerates and grows beyond founder-driven and -dominated survival. Key to achieving longer-term, sustained growth, and an eventual harvest, is the development of competencies as an entrepreneurial manager. Upon completion of this chapter you will have:

1. Examined a framework for understanding the entrepreneurial manager.
2. Identified competencies that entrepreneurs need in order to manage start-up, survival, and growth.
3. Completed a Management Competency Inventory in order to assess your own skills and know-how as an entrepreneurial manager.
4. Begun to analyze the implications of your own strengths and weaknesses, such as the need for team members for your venture.

6.2 WHAT IS AN ENTREPRENEURIAL MANAGER?

6.2.1 A Framework for the Entrepreneurial Domain

Increasingly, the evidence suggests that new ventures that flourish beyond survival and grow to become substantial, higher-potential enterprises are more often than not headed by an entrepreneur who is also an effective entrepreneurial manager. For instance, a 1983 *Inc.* survey of the heads of the top 100 ventures showed that the majority of their founders were still the CEOs several years later when the ventures had attained sales of $10 million, $25 million, even $50 million or more. These and other data seem to defy some previous notions that entrepreneurs can start but cannot manage growing companies. The truth is probably somewhere in between. But one thing is apparent: growing a higher-potential venture requires competencies and skills practiced by entrepreneurial managers.

One way to get at these competencies and skills is to study the framework

Exhibit 6.1
Dominant Venture Mode

Venture stage

Seed ⟶ Start-up ⟶ Early ⟶ Expand ⟶ Mature

	Most		High	C
Entrepreneurial domain	New and innovative ventures Early growth Backbone firms	High potential and growth-minded Ventures		h a n g e
	Bureaucratic Custodial "Dinosaurs" Sole proprietorships	Mature Stable Contracting	Low	a n d u n c e r t a i n t y
	Least		Most	

Administrative domain

Exhibit 6.2
The Entrepreneurial Process: Driving Forces

Seed ⟶ Start-up ⟶ Early ⟶ Expand ⟶ Mature

	Most		High	C
Entrepreneurial domain	*Lead entrepreneurs:* Founders' goals, values, commitment Opportunity perception: Customer needs focus Resource minimizing Revolutionary and creative	*Entrepreneurial managers:* Strategic, whole-business focus ventures Opportunity Enterprising management team and innovators Flat/adaptive organization		h a n g e
	Invention: Ideas, technology, product focus Lifestyle, satisfying Survival	Administrators and trustee-custodians Resource ownership Administrative efficiency Formalization of power, procedures control Evolutionary, reactive	Low	a n d u n c e r t a i n t y
	Least		Most	

Administrative domain

developed in Exhibits 6.1 and 6.2. Building on work by Timmons and Stevenson[1] and on Stevenson's "paradigm model," the exhibits graphically illustrate that entrepreneurial and administrative domains exist, with some distinct and some overlapping tasks and behaviors. These domains can provide a useful way to examine and understand the driving forces, the pressures and demands, the stages, and the extent of uncertainty and change facing the entrepreneur. In turn, the competencies and skills required of the entrepreneurial manager can become more evident.

Take Exhibit 6.1, for instance, which portrays what we call the entrepreneurial and administrative domains. Each of the four cells is related to the stage of the venture (upper axis) and to the extent of change and uncertainty accompanying it (right axis) as a result of rapid growth or its absence. Each of the "dominant venture modes" can be characterized by the principal "driving forces" that propel it, as shown in Exhibit 6.2. It is these "driving forces" that serve as the anchors and beacons for the competencies and skills required by entrepreneurial managers, as compared with pure administrators, and by lead start-up entrepreneurs, bureaucrats, or sole proprietors.

Clearly, the entrepreneurial domain—what this edition of *New Venture Creation* is all about—is the two upper cells. In recent years, however, much of business and engineering education has heavily emphasized, and prepared students for life in, the lower two cells. There is nothing wrong with that, but we maintain that a vibrant, growing, entrepreneurial company cannot afford to emphasize the competencies and skills required for administrative efficiency, maintenance tasks, resource ownership, and institutional formalization. Rather, the organizational and managerial skills called for by the entrepreneurial mission requires that greater emphasis be placed on the competencies and broken-field running characteristic of the entrepreneurial manager and the effective general manager in a rapid-growth firm.

6.2.2 Stage, Growth Rate, and Level of Chaos

In a nutshell, the competencies necessary to grow a new venture rapidly beyond start-up and survival are the skills that entrepreneurial managers must possess in order to cope effectively with a high level of change, chaos, and uncertainty. Whether these are affectionately labeled MBWO—management by wandering around, of Hewlett-Packard fame—or management by muddling through, there are some survival and growth skills.

6.2.3 Stages of Growth

One way to visualize some of the differences between management and entrepreneurial skills is through the growth stages of a new venture. Exhibit 6.3 is a representation of this gestation process.[2] The first two or three years—the start-up stage—are by far the most perilous, evidenced by an over 60 percent failure rate among businesses in general. The venture capitalist knows this initial critical

---

[1] J. A. Timmons and H. H. Stevenson, "Entrepreneurship Education in the 80s," presented at the 75th Anniversary Entrepreneurship Symposium, Harvard Business School, Boston, 1983.

[2] For another useful view of the stages of development of a firm and the required management capabilities, see Carroll V. Kroeger, "Management Development and the Small Firm," *California Management Review* 17, no. 1 (Fall 1974), pp. 41–47.

Exhibit 6.3
Stages of New Venture Growth

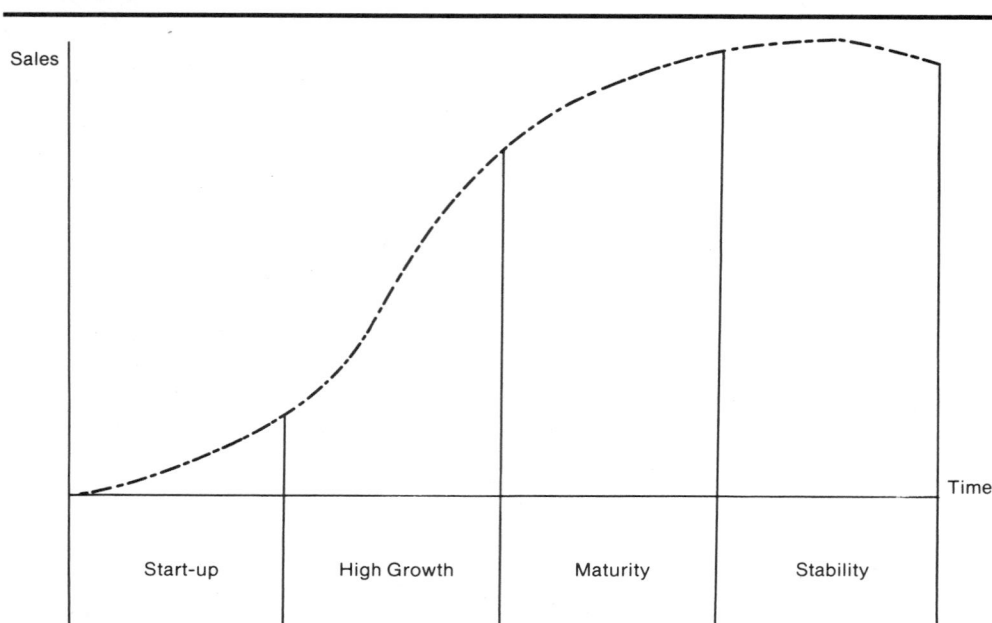

period well: the lemons, it is said, generally ripen in 2½ years. And often, the new business can expect to lose money for the first year or two, depending on the kind of business it is.

These first few years are the critical survival years for the new venture. In perhaps three years, and as long as six or seven, the critical mass of people, market, and financial results and competitive resiliency is usually established. Investor, banker, and customer confidence is earned, and the company is likely to enter a second phase of growth requiring additional financing. The sales may be several million dollars per annum as the new company begins its high-growth stage, typically $2 to $20 million, but there is wide variance. At this point—which can rarely be identified by a date on the calendar until well after the fact—the venture has survived the first critical start-up stage. It has been able to do so by the direct and exhausting drive, energy, and entrepreneurial talent of a lead entrepreneur and a key team member or two.

In most new companies a transition is encountered between the start-up and high-growth entrepreneurial stages and what might be more appropriately called the maturity or managerial stage. In this third stage the key issue for the company is no longer survival; rather, it is one of steady, profitable growth, or stability, depending on the goals and values of the owners. It is generally felt among venture capitalists and researchers that the kind of person with the entrepreneurial spirit required to propel a new venture through start-up and high growth to a multimillion-dollar annual sales level may be different from the person with the managerial capacity to build the new firm as it matures from $5 million to $20–30 million in sales, for example. And further, it is often observed that the entrepreneur who clings to the lead role too long during this maturation process may subsequently limit company growth, if not seriously retard it. In short, a good entrepreneur may not be a good manager, lacking the breadth of management skills and experience required to take the company through the high-growth and maturity stages. Likewise, a manager is not an entrepreneur, lacking in some of the intense personal qualities and orientations that are required to launch a business from ground zero.

6.3 WHAT DO ENTREPRENEURIAL MANAGERS NEED TO KNOW?[3]

In preparation for the 75th Anniversary Entrepreneurship Symposium at the Harvard Business School in 1983, two researchers focused on the nagging question above. Although they had accumulated their own ideas, based on their entrepreneurial experiences, observations, and research, they were not aware of any systematic inquiries into the opinions of practicing entrepreneurs for answers to the question. In particular, they wondered what practicing entrepreneurs would say when asked: What are the critical skills, concepts, practices, and attitudes in running your business today? What about five years from now? One thing was certain: if you want to find out what entrepreneurs need to know, a good way to start is by asking successful entrepreneurs.

6.3.1 What Entrepreneurs Say They Need to Know

During January 1983 over 100 entrepreneurs attended a Smaller Company Management Program at the Harvard Business School, and 60 of them generously agreed to answer some of our questions. The group was composed of middle-aged executives, most of whom were in their mid-30s to early 50s. Nearly half had founded their firms, which ranged in sales from $4 million to $1 billion; over half of the firms had sales of $5–20 million, and over one fourth had sales of $20–50 million. We asked them what they felt were the most important skills and intellectual concepts in running their businesses today and which of these skills and concepts would make the critical difference five years from now. We also asked what they believed were the most important attitudes and philosophies today and how their answers to this question might differ five years hence. With these responses in hand we then asked to what extent they felt that these skills, concepts and attitudes could be learned, at what point in one's education or career this could be done, and what methods or approaches were most effective. Finally, we added two questions that generated thought-provoking responses: first, whether the subject of ethics should be addressed in an entrepreneurship curriculum; and second, how they viewed newly minted MBAs as prospects for employment and what changes were needed in the business school curriculum today.

What follows is a summary of the results of this survey and some of the implications of our findings. While the sampled group is quite select and far from a representative cross section, it can serve as a useful source of feedback and ideas about what really counts in entrepreneurial management in smaller companies. One message is clear: to learn about the education of entrepreneurs, start by asking entrepreneurs.

---

[3]This section is based heavily on the work of Timmons and Stevenson, "Entrepreneurship Education in the 80's."

6.3.2 Ethics and the Entrepreneur

The most startling outcome was the response to the ethics question: 72 percent said that ethics could and should be a part of the curriculum (only 20 percent said no, and two respondents weren't sure). Further discussion of the ethics issue is presented in Chapter 9.

6.3.3 Critical Skills and Concepts: Back to Fundamentals

Another message, though less surprising, was the need to focus on entrepreneurial fundamentals: responsiveness, resiliency, adaptiveness in seizing new opportunities. The responses to our questions about critical skills and concepts echo many of the messages in the recent book *In Search of Excellence.* One of them said that what was vital was "knowing where the competitive threats are and where the opportunities are; an ability to see the customers' needs."

Five years ahead, the executives expected to be faced with an even greater need to be entrepreneurial. As one CEO put it, "You must be able to shoot at a moving target." It is not new to recognize the need for intimate knowledge of the customers and the market, the competition, the products and technology, and the industry. But what may be new is the relatively vital importance that was attached to these, in contrast with the overall content and substance of what business schools attempt to teach. One way we sought to estimate the prevailing emphasis in business school curricula was to list in detail all of the subject titles of leading textbooks and representative course syllabi that we could find. We augmented these titles by examining a list of course coverage sufficient to gain the "business school seal of approval" from the national accrediting organization, the American Association of Collegiate Schools of Business (AACSB). For all required courses—the standard mix of finance, operations, marketing, accounting, human behavior, and so on—we ended up with a list of 501 subjects that were taught and required. Among them we did not find such terms as *customer needs, obtaining orders, serving customers,* or *identifying opportunities.* One could argue that there were some close semantic cousins—product life cycle strategy, for example—but these tended to be buzzwords or to reflect another level of abstracting. (Incidentally, the word *ethics* did not appear on this list of 501 topics.)

Similarly, many respondents recognized and endorsed the importance of people management issues. One of them said that in five years one of the most challenging tasks would be "a leadership role in attracting high-quality people; imparting your vision to them; and holding and motivating them." Many focused on the importance of teamwork and building an organization. Said the head of a manufacturing firm with $10 million in sales: "Understanding people and how to pull them together toward a basic goal will be my main challenge in five years."

The head of a clothing manufacturing business with 225 employees and $6 million in sales shared a view of many that one of the most critical areas where you have leverage and long-term impact is in managing employees: "Treating people honestly and letting them know when they do well goes a long way."

Financial and accounting know-how was also frequently mentioned. Understanding the economics of the business was vital for these entrepreneurs: cash flow and liquidity, incremental revenue, costs and contribution, and simply keeping score.

A number of respondents felt that the ability to conceptualize their business and do strategic planning would be of growing importance, particularly when thinking five years ahead.

But what we found fascinating was the lack of importance assigned to virtually all of the prevailing and highly touted "new management techniques." There was not one mention of a capital asset pricing model, a probabilistic decision tree, beta coefficients, linear programming, or econometric and technological forecasting. Are these techniques examples of the shift away from the practical and toward the theoretical and obscure that was noted at the outset? There is little evidence that these are considered critical skills and concepts by the entrepreneurs.

On the other hand, the microcomputer and related software, and their probable future impact, were seen as important. While only about 6 percent mentioned the computer as important today in running their businesses, nearly a third specifically stressed it when projecting five years hence. As a 61-year-old head of a firm with $6 million sales and 50 employees said, "Five years from now a businessman will not be able to exist without the computer."

Computer literacy was consistently among the top three skills mentioned (the other two were attracting and motivating both subordinates and partners and being even more adaptable and flexible).

Do these founders and heads of reasonably successful firms know something that business schools don't know or have forgotten? Do they have a sense of what really counts in building and running a sizable business? Are they, like the Japanese, reminding our stagnating industries of what they have forgotten about the fundamentals?

A critic might say that little, if anything, of what this survey noted is new, that we've known the importance of these things all along. But much of this has been lost, or at least de-emphasized, in faculty enthusiasm for discovering what is new. Further, is it possible that this inclination is only enhanced by a reward system that encourages research and publishing rather than teaching and course development around the critical areas that contribute to entrepreneurial achievement?

We need to pay a great deal more attention to what the experience and insights of entrepreneurs tell us about educating managers and entrepreneurs alike. One president commented: "You need *not* just know the questions to ask, but how to *cause* the answers, not more questions."

This is a not-so-subtle hint that the trend in business school education has been to overemphasize analysis, resulting in a finely tuned skill among graduates in "analysis-paralysis." One outcome is to become buried in an endless series of "But *why*, mommy?" questions, without ever coming to a decision or taking action.

6.3.4 Instilling Vision in a More Fragile World

A growing sense of the fragility of their enterprises was expressed in the responses. The pace of change and information flow has been accelerating. This may explain in part another revealing theme: a growing concern about perpetuating their institutions. The respondents talked about the long-term challenge of sustaining an entrepreneurial culture and expressed a keen awareness of the burden of instilling a sense of future direction and balance. Many seemed troubled by a growing awareness that the entrepreneurial vigor and commitment of their business partners could not be taken for granted five years from now, though at present this was not an issue. While they frequently noted the critical importance today of being sensitive to employees' needs and alternatives in order to ignite and capture their entrepreneurial drive, their concern for the future was to sustain the motivation and commitment of colleagues and partners.

6.3.5   Attitudes and Philosophies

When we specifically asked the executives what they believed to be the most important skills and concepts in running their business today and in five years, they listed the fundamentals. While this may have been reassuring, it was not surprising. What did surprise us was that about one third failed to mention any skill or concept at all. Rather, they immediately focused on what we have called "attitudes and philosophies" (even though the question covering that subject appeared separately later in the survey).

The attitudes they spoke of included "a willingness to learn about and invest in new techniques"; "to be adaptable"; a "professional attitude"; and "patience." They talked about the importance of "enjoying and being interested in business" and of "the business as a way of life." They mentioned an ability "to activate vision and to instill it in others" and "to have the discipline to sit down and plan" what you aim to do.

When we later asked them directly which "attitudes and philosophies are crucial" today and which would be five years hence, their pens flowed. One impression from their responses was that "this is for real." They could readily articulate what was on their minds. They knew exactly what we were getting at, this gray and elusive area that no one could measure, that many couldn't spot, let alone instill, but whose impact and results were evident to all. What did they say? The acceptance of risk stood out for many. As one executive put it, "Success will go to the honest risk taker who has overcome greed and fear, faces reality, and makes decisions. You must have no fear to admit error and mistakes, but use these to learn and proceed."

The 40-year-old head of a general construction business with 325 employees called it being "risk sensitive within limits; you have to enjoy taking risks rather than avoiding them." Nonetheless, a handful talked about "risk avoidance."

Several talked about "positive mental attitude," a sense of optimism, and "a positive readiness to see the best (not the worst) in employees and customers." Another elaborated this idea with the notion that "we can set goals and reach them; that the future is in our hands and we can influence it." Still others cautioned that there was a need for humility, that "you should keep ego out of the deal"; "egotistical pride will blind and kill." Yet, a handful noted "greed" a "desire to have things," and "more is better" as important attitudes.

The ageless importance of sensitivity to and respect for employees was stressed by a 49-year-old CEO of a firm with $40 million in sales and 400 employees. He put it this way:

It is essential that the separation between management and the average employee be eliminated. Students should be taught to respect employees all the way down to the janitor and accept them as knowledgeable and able persons.

What was particularly revealing was the stress placed on overcoming what we will call "mistake-itis," or the fear of failing and of committing errors. Are entrepreneurs far more tolerant of mistakes and errors than business school professors? Do they have an insight into the process by which entrepreneurs grow and acquire humility at the same time, without losing their zeal? Does the climate in our business schools and most large and slower-growing organizations so stress excellence—nay, perfection—and intense competitiveness that only those who never stumble are rewarded?

6.3.6 Confirmation by Recent McKinsey Study

A recent McKinsey & Co. study of mid-sized growth companies (sales between $25 million and $1 billion, with sales or profit growth of more than 15 percent annually over five years) confirms the importance of many of these same fundamentals of entrepreneurial management.[4] For one thing, these companies practiced opportunity-driven management. According to the study, they achieved their first success with a unique product or a distinctive way of doing business, and often become leaders in market niches. They did this—as our SCMP entrepreneurs insisted—by delivering superior value to customers rather than by low price, and they are highly committed to serving their customers.

For another thing, they put great emphasis on financial control and managing every element of the business: they know how to keep score. As an incentive for their employees, they make extensive use of employee stock ownership programs, with an average of 30 percent of their shares being owned by employees.

And like our SCMP CEOs, they pay great attention to customer closeness. CEOs in the study spent on the average about 10 percent of their time calling on customers, and one in nine spent as much as one third of his or her time in doing so. Other senior executives spent 22 percent of their time calling on customers.

Finally, the CEOs of winning companies were notable for three common traits (resembling the traits of the entrepreneurial mind that we discussed in the previous chapter): perseverance, a builder's mentality, and a strong propensity for taking calculated risks. Their average workweek, incidentally, was 64 hours.

6.3.7 Search for Excellence Ends with the Entrepreneurial Manager

Not surprisingly, the majority of high-performing entrepreneurial managers are often the heads of such emerging companies, rather than of the Fortune 500.

6.4 START-UP AND SURVIVAL COMPETENCIES: A SUMMARY

As we know from listening to and observing successful venture founders, launching a new venture and making it survive depend on a lot of factors, and it is easy to oversimplify how difficult that achievement really is. We believe that one enormous difficulty faced by most would-be entrepreneurs is to know what really works and what really counts. Thus, before discussing the entrepreneurial manager in a growth environment, we will recap the critical competencies and skills that successful entrepreneurs believe are vital to getting a venture off the

---

[4]"How Growth Companies Succeed," reported in *Small Business Report*, July 1984, p. 9.

ground. You will undoubtedly need other competencies and skills to go far, but without these the lifeline of the enterprise is short and the ink is red.

6.4.1 Gaining Customer Commitment

It is very simple: without orders for your product or service you do not really have a business. You may have one waiting to happen, and it may be brilliantly conceived and eloquently articulated in a business plan, but without orders from committed customers there is nothing. Skills in direct selling—of both yourself and your product or service—are critical for a successful start-up. Someone on the founding team—more often than not the lead entrepreneur—must know how to sell, negotiate with, and secure customers.

6.4.2 Positive Cash Flow

Estimating and managing cash flow is the second critical competency for start-up entrepreneurs. Do not run out of cash. If you do so before you secure enough profitable customers, the venture will come to an abrupt halt. Preparing the cash budget and knowing how to use and manage cash flow—made significantly easier with the use of a microcomputer spreadsheet program (see Chapter 12)—are musts for start-up entrepreneurs.

6.4.3 Keeping Score

We have found entrepreneurs who have built multimillion-dollar businesses by understanding and practicing the first two skills, yet do not know how to read, or prepare, an income statement and a balance sheet for their ventures. In our view, business or engineering students can and should have these skills. They are simple enough to learn, and they will make it a great deal easier to deal with the external world, especially with bankers, auditors, and potential investors. We would also add to these scorekeeping skills the concept of break-even analysis.

In short, a highly determined entrepreneur can go a long way with a sound opportunity and these minimal skills. But what about keeping the venture going beyond survival and becoming a higher-potential venture in order to realize a harvest?

6.5 GROWING UP BIG: MANAGING RAPID GROWTH

Consider what the following situations have in common, the pressures and demands they foster, and what it takes to manage each of them effectively.

1. The president of a rapid-growth small computer company sums up what it's like to develop and market new products: "In our business it takes 6–12 months to develop a new computer, ready to bring to the market; and product technology obsolescence is running about 9–12 months."

2. The head of Litton's Microwave Oven Division notes a critical requirement: "In 1981 our sales were $13 million and we had 275 employees. Our long-range plan called for building our sales volume to $100 million in five to seven years (40 percent a year compounded). Having studied the market for the previous

two years, I was convinced that the only limit on our growth was our organization's inability to grow as rapidly as the market opportunities."[5]

3. A middle manager in yet another mushrooming firm finds the pace hectic, with lots of uncertainties and ambiguities. "If you like to know exactly where things are, who's doing what, and when; prefer a structured situation; and need to know exactly where things stand—then you'll go nuts working here."

4. A manufacturing VP comments on his best managers: "They are jugglers that keep all this glued together: they have a knack for blending and balancing the competing, and often conflicting, demands and for creatively solving problems. They aren't distracted by the chaos and confusion—they thrive on it."

No question about it: these managers find that life in a rapid-growth company is unique and very demanding. Managing and growing such a venture are, simply put, a different managerial game. Why is this so? How is the game different? And how do the differences affect management and the organization?

6.5.1   The Entrepreneurial Transition

Higher-potential ventures do not stay small very long. In the process of driving and managing this rapid growth, the venture invariably goes through transitions. These transitions are usually accompanied by various degrees of trauma and confusion. Several writers have described some of these critical stages and the management skills and issues that are most crucial to resolve.[6] Exhibit 6.4 is an effort to characterize some of the crises that are encountered during the entrepreneurial transition. The list is sufficiently awesome to make one wonder: How do entrepreneurial managers deal with all this?

The truth of the matter is that not only do they continue to practice and apply the fundamental launch and survival skills noted above, but they also practice some unique strategic, organizational, and people management skills.

Exhibit 6.4
The Entrepreneurial Transition

New, growing firm ⟶ Small "large" firm

Probable crises:

Erosion of entrepreneurial culture and climate
Confusion, resentment over ambiguous roles, responsibilities, goals
Failure to clone founders
Sharing of power, information, and influence
Delegation versus autonomy and control
Specialization and eroding collaboration
Operating mechanisms and controls
Conflict, divorce among founders

[5]William W. George, "Task Teams for Rapid Growth," *Harvard Business Review,* March–April 1977, p. 71.

[6]L. A. Griener, "Evolution and Revolution as Organizations Grow," *Trials and Rewards of the Entrepreneur* (Boston: Harvard Business Review, 1977), pp. 47–56; and H. N. Woodward, "Management Strategies for Small Companies" (Boston: Harvard Business Review, 1981), pp. 57–66.

6.5.2 Some Unique Requirements

In working closely over the past 15 years with over 1,200 entrepreneurs attempting to raise venture capital to launch rapid-growth companies, we have observed and tried to appreciate the enormousness and uniqueness of their task of launching and piloting a rapid-growth venture. We have worked with a number of Fortune 1000 companies training several hundred managers at all levels. And we have recently worked closely for two years with the top-management team, and nearly all of the managers, of a rapid-growth company.

Several distinguishing characteristics of managing rapid-growth firms are summarized in Exhibit 6.5 and described briefly below:

Exhibit 6.5
The Entrepreneurial Transition

Notable characteristics:

Founder-driven creativity—entrepreneurial culture
Constant change and ambiguity
Time compression, nonlinear
Informal communications, decision making, structure, procedures
Lack of clarity
Lack of formal controls and accountability mechanisms
New jobs and tasks—learning while doing

---

1. *Change* seems to be the only thing that remains constant, and high levels of ambiguity and uncertainty are a way of life; change compounds rapidly, often leading to instability.
2. *Time* is compressed, with shorter leads, lags, and life cycles affecting technology, product development, manufacturing, and marketing. Assimilating rapid changes and being responsive are major organizational challenges.
3. Managers have to deal with *nonlinear* or *unconventional* and often *counterintuitive* decisions and events; these events are stepwise, more often than they are straight-line progressions; and learning curves may be obsolete by the time they are history.
4. *Structures* are more fluid, but clear. There are fewer layers; they are less formal; and they require a high degree of integration and collaboration. The organization has to absorb growth and assimilate change while attaining cohesion, as well as financial and operating control.
5. Most of the firms are *entrepreneurial* in their orientation, management style, values, tasks, and climate. They are better at recognizing and coping with innovation and risk taking. There is a need to accelerate decisions and to respond quickly, as well as to absorb major setbacks.
6. The most effective managers in these organizations possess some special skills that we shall call *entrepreneurial influences*. They use a consensual approach to build a motivated and committed team; they balance conflicting demands and priorities; and they manage conflicts especially adroitly.
7. Lastly, these managers seem to *thrive* on the hectic, at times chaotic, pace and find it challenging and stimulating rather than frustrating or overwhelming.

Let us take a closer look at each of these characteristics of entrepreneurial management.

6.5.3 Time Compressed and Change Compounded

In the rapid-growth environment this phenomenon becomes exaggerated in several ways. There is the constancy of change, which pilfers away that already precious commodity—time. Change creates higher levels of uncertainty, ambiguity, and risk, which, in turn, compound to shrink time. This time compression is also a child of galloping technology, with its relatively minuscule lead times and lag times in bringing new products to market and weathering the storms of rapid obsolescence, compared to stable, slow-growth environments. Consequently, pressures, multiple roles, and the balancing acts required by managers are complex and subject to continuous change.

One net effect of all this is a series of compounding shock waves rolling through the venture by way of new customers, new technologies, new competitors, new markets, and new people. To excel under these conditions requires a resiliency and a responsiveness that are uncommon. Without them these shock waves can lead to a crisis before the real numbers detect it. And it's not difficult to envision the industries where such requirements are commonplace: electronics and aerospace in the 60s, small computers, integrated circuits and silicon chips in the 70s, and telecommunications and microcomputers in the 80s, to note a few.

6.5.4 Nonlinear and Nonparametric

One of the differences in managing rapid growth is what we call the nonlinear and nonparametric events—why? Many events don't follow straight lines or progress arithmetically; rather, they occur in bunches, in stepwise leaps. For instance, the sales force is doubled in 15 months rather than eight years; or manufacturing capacity is tripled in two years with a new Materials Resource Planning (MRP) System and two new plants rather than some increased overtime, followed by a third shift nine months later, and maybe a new plant three years after that. In short, the increments are lurches rather than smooth and digestible steps.

Another characteristic is the relative youth and inexperience accompanying rapid expansion. Most of the pieces in the puzzle are new, even first-time events—technology, applications, customers, the people, the firm itself. As an example, take Prime Computer, a U.S. manufacturer of minicomputers whose sales have grown rapidly in the past five years from $100 million a year to nearly $1.2 billion a year. The average age of all employees in the company was recently reported as less than 29 years; and the firm is barely 10 years old. The founders of Digital Equipment Corporation were approximately 23, 24, and 29 when the company was launched.

One consequence of this youthful pattern is that there are no "normal curves." The explosive birth and growth of a firm such as Apple Computer may be a unique, nonreplicable event. And just when enough experience curves have been accumulated to detect and analyze what might be a "normal curve" of rapid growth, the data are probably obsolete or irrelevant.

There seems to be an entrepreneurial creativity in these firms from the outset. But it is a kind of creativity that is tempered by a keen eye on the market-place and the goal of commercialization. Technological elegance for its own sake may have far less to do with longer-term success than is commonly believed. Unless one's market share is protected by the monopoly of a patent, the technological lead may not be critical. Take the computer industry in the United States as an illustration. In the late 60s and early 70s perhaps as many as 70 new firms were launched to exploit the new technology in small-scale computing. Many industry experts acknowledge that some other firms started at the same time as the dominant industry leaders today, such as Digital Equipment, Data General, Control Data, and Prime Computer, actually had more elegant technology in their products. Yet, most of them lacked the entrepreneurial savvy and ingenuity needed to survive.

This entrepreneurial creativity can be seen in other examples as well. Television did not come about by a succession of improvements in the radio. The jet plane did not emerge from the efforts of the engineers and scientists who were attempting to develop a better and better piston engine plane. If this pattern holds for future technology, the implications are clear: we would not expect the major breakthroughs in energy to come from the oil companies or electrically powered vehicles to come from the automotive industry. Rather, more innovative and entrepreneurial smaller, rapid-growth firms will be the major source of such breakthroughs.

6.5.5   Unconventional and Counterintuitive

Yet another characteristic of managing a rapid-growth venture is a counterintuitive, unconventional pattern of decision making. One example comes from the computer firm noted at the outset. What approach does one take to developing and introducing three new products in such an uncertain, risky marketplace? Each proposed new computer appeared to be going after the same end-user market, and each project head was similarly enthusiastic, confident, and determined about succeeding. Many well-educated MBAs would suggest an analytical process that might consist of the following:

1. Determine the size and growth rates of each market segment.
2. Evaluate the probabilistic estimates of future revenues costs and capital requirements for their accuracy.
3. Compare the discounted, present value cash flow streams that will emerge from each market segment.
4. Select the project with the highest yield versus the required internal rate of return.

One can't really argue with the basic logic or method in this example. Both the logic and the method are fundamentally sound and very useful decision-making tools, when one best alternative exists. But what may be overlooked is that most rapid-growth companies have many excellent alternatives. High-margin opportunities outstrip resources. And, more commonly, the newness of the technology, the immaturity of the marketplace, and the rapid discovery of further applications make it virtually impossible to know which of any three product proposals is "best."

So what did this company do? It supported all three new products at once. And what did it learn? A significant new business was built around each one, with new market niches being discovered simultaneously. Further, the company confirmed its belief that under tumultuous conditions of rapidly changing technology and markets, unconventional approaches can pay off. There is simply not the time, the certainty, or the maturity of information available to provide the "proof" that is possible and desirable in more stable and developed circumstances.

6.5.6 Fluid Structures

Most rapid-growth ventures defy conventional organizational patterns and structures. It is not uncommon to find a firm that has grown $25 million, $50 million, even $150 million a year or more in turnover and still has no formal organization chart. If one does exist, it has some distinguishing features: first, it is inevitably out of date; second, it changes frequently (one firm had eight major reorganizations in its first five years, as it grew to $5 million); third, it is flat, with few management layers and with easy accessibility to the top decision makers; and fourth, it is a fluid structure, not one rigidly defined by policy manuals, detailed procedures, or other early signs of bureaucracy.

There is an informality to the organization as well. But fluidity and informality do not mean casualness or sloppiness when it comes to goals, standards, or clarity of direction and purpose. Rather, they translate into responsiveness and readiness to absorb and assimilate rapid changes while maintaining financial and operational cohesion. These firms don't confuse informality with a lack of discipline.

6.5.7 Different Management Orientation

Managing rapid growth involves some managerial tasks and roles not found in most mature and stable environments. For one thing, the classical obsession that one's responsibility must equal one's authority is often very counterproductive in a rapid-growth venture. If there is an obsession, it's quite different: what is needed to get the job done, attain the goal, or meet the deadline. Getting results usually requires close collaboration with people other than those reporting directly to you. And managers invariably have responsibilities far exceeding their authority. Effective managers need to be especially skillful at managing conflict, resolving differences, balancing multiple viewpoints and demands, and building teamwork and consensus. These tasks are particularly difficult when working with others *outside* one's immediate "chain of formal command," another common role in these firms.

Given these special requirements, what does it take to manage growth successfully? How are rapid-growth firms managed? And what do the effective managers do differently? The answers to these questions come from research and experience.[7]

---

[7]My colleagues at the Forum Corporation (Boston) have conducted some pioneering research in growing firms to detect what distinguishes high-performing managers from the others. Also, over the past dozen years the authors have worked as both consultants and researchers with over 1,000 founders of firms seeking venture capital to propel rapid growth. Following the subsequent growth of many of these ventures has provided us with an additional perspective on the peculiarities of managing rapid growth.

Striking similarities exist between the lead entrepreneurs in the venture capital–spawned companies and the heads of established rapid-growth ventures. For one thing, the latter have often apprenticed under the founders or heads of dynamic firms in new technologies and markets. Their mentors have been entrepreneurs with a flair for innovation and creativity and the capacity to take risks that others don't. It's not surprising, then, that their management style, pace, and intensity often mirror the qualities of their former entrepreneurial bosses.

For another, there are common values that may be more visible to the outsider or to someone unaccustomed to the unusual nature of the rapid-growth environment. These values, always difficult to articulate, and even more elusive to measure, are evident in behavior and attitudes. There is a belief in and a commitment to growth. There is a sense that achievement, improvement, and success are a way of life. There is a sense that "we are in this thing together" and "we will pull together." The priorities seem to focus on goals and the market rather than on whose territory or whose prerogatives are being challenged. Managers appear quite unconcerned about status, power, and personal control. They are more concerned about making sure that tasks, goals, and roles are clear than about whether the organization chart is current or whether their office and rug reflect their current status. Likewise, they are more concerned about the evidence, competence, knowledge, and logic of the arguments affecting a decision than about the title or formal position of the individual doing the arguing.

The common values also express a different view of status: it is earned by accomplishments and cemented in the promise of future achievements. Elegant office space, special privileges, and titles aren't the vogue. Contrast this with a multibillion-dollar, but stagnant, firm in England. Reportedly, no less than 29 different makes and models of automobiles, from Silver Shadow through Mini-Miner, are used in the firm to signify one's position.

Personal power, control, and politics can be a way of life in many larger, stagnant institutions as managers jockey for influence and a piece of a shrinking pie in a zero-sum game. In rapid-growth firms the opposite seems to be true. Since everyone is committed to making the pie larger, a different mentality exists. One's power and influence derive from several sources: achieving not only one's own goals but contributing to the goals of others as well; keeping the overall goal in mind in resolving differences; and developing a reputation as someone who not only gets results but can also manage others and grow managerial talent.

Such a climate attracts and encourages the entrepreneurial achievers. It helps perpetuate the intensity and pace so characteristic of high-growth firms. On the other hand, it is intolerant of the jungle fighter, the self-seeking, and power-thirsting manager. In some ways, this trek toward rapid growth is fragile. It is like the journey of the downhill ski racer whose breathless pace, blinding speed, and relentless attack on the mountain appear reckless and out of control, if not suicidal, to the novitiate. Every meter of the descent appears to flirt with total destruction. And the fragile brink of disaster is often indistinguishable from the brink of victory, except for those who conquer the course.

6.5.8 Entrepreneurial Influence

In rapid-growth companies there appears to be a breed of hybrid managers who fit neither the stereotype of the founding entrepreneur nor that of the middle manager in a large, established company. The particularly effective ones do things differently. They have some unique skills that are especially critical in managing rapid-growth companies and are quite useful elsewhere as well. These "entrepreneurial influence" skills have a great deal to do with the way these managers exert influence over others. But these skills also describe many of the demands and tasks that appear so frequently in rapid-growth firms.

Creating Clarity out of Confusion. These managers have a knack for forging clarity out of the chaos, ambiguity, and constant change that they face. The managers who work with them perceive that these entrepreneurial managers are able to adroitly define and gain agreement on who has what responsibility and authority and who does what with and to whom. Further, they do this in a way that builds motivation and commitment to cross-departmental and corporate goals, not just parochial interests. But this is not perceived by other managers as an effort to jealously carve out and guard personal turf and prerogatives. Rather, it is seen as a genuine effort to clarify roles, tasks, and responsibilities and to ensure accountability and appropriate approvals. This doesn't work unless the manager is seen as willing to relinquish his priorities and power in the interest of an overall goal. It also requires skill in making sure that the appropriate people are included in setting cross-functional or cross-departmental goals and in making decisions. And when this doesn't go as smoothly as was hoped, the most effective managers work it through to an agreement, rather than dash to a shared superior to break the tie.

Managers new to a rapid-growth company who are accustomed to a traditional line-staff, or functional, chain of command, in which "end arounds" and "two-uppers" and "two-downers" are taboo, are often baffled and frustrated in their new role. While some may be quite effective in dealing with their own subordinates, it is an entirely new task to manage and work with peers, others' subordinates, and even superiors outside their chain of command. Getting results from people over whom you have no direct authority whatsoever requires "entrepreneurial influence" skill.

Solving Conflicts and Sharing Power. The most effective managers are creative and skillful in handling conflicts, generating consensus decisions, and sharing their power and information. They are able to get people to open up, instead of clamming up. They get problems out on the table instead of under the rug, and they don't become defensive when others disagree with their views. They seem to know that high-quality decisions require a rapid flow of information in all directions and that knowledge, competence, logic, and evidence should prevail over official status or formal rank in the organization.

The way they manage and resolve conflicts is intriguing. For one thing, they are able to get potential adversaries to be creative and collaborative in making the pie bigger in the interest of an overall organizational goal. They do this by seeking a reconciliation of viewpoints, rather than emphasizing differences, and by blending ideas, rather than playing the role of hard-nosed negotiator or devil's advocate to force their own solution. They are more willing to risk personal vulnerability in this process—often by giving up their own power and resources— than are less effective managers. Perhaps they can do this because they have a clear understanding of the longer-term consequences if they don't: a win-lose, adversarial climate; zero-sum games; less creative problem solving; and a more power- and control-oriented organization that eventually collapses of its own weight and myopia over managerial prerogatives.

The trade-offs aren't easy: at the outset such an approach involves more managers, takes more time, and often appears to yield few immediate results. Up front, it seems like a more painful way to manage. Later on, however, the gains from the motivation, commitment, and teamwork that are anchored in a consensus are striking. For one thing, there is swiftness and decisiveness in actions and follow-through, since the negotiating, compromising, and accepting of priorities are history. For another, new disagreements that emerge generally don't bring progress to a halt, since there is both high clarity and broad acceptance of the overall goal and underlying priorities. Without the up-front consensus each new problem or disagreement might necessitate a time-consuming and painful confrontation and renegotiation simply because that consensus wasn't reached initially. Apparently, the Japanese understand this quite well.

Encouraging Innovation and Calculated Risk Taking. Another form of entrepreneurial influence that these more effective managers use has to do with creativity and innovativeness. Simply stated, they build confidence by encouraging innovation and calculated risk taking, rather than by punishing or criticizing whatever is less than perfect. They also breed independent, entrepreneurial thinking by expecting and encouraging others to find and correct their own errors and to solve their own problems. This does not mean that they follow a "throw them to the wolves" approach. Rather, they are perceived by their peers and other managers as accessible, and willing to help when needed. When it is appropriate, they go to bat for their peers and subordinates, even when they know that they can't always win. And they provide the necessary resources to enable others to do the job.

Building Trust. Finally, and this is probably the most essential ingredient of the entrepreneurial influence process, the most effective managers possess the capacity to generate trust, the oil and glue that bind an organization or a relationship together. They are perceived as trustworthy; they behave in ways that create trust. How do they do this? For one thing, they are straightforward; they do what they say they are going to do. They are neither corporate rumor carriers nor purveyors of gossip. They are open and spontaneous, rather than guarded and cautious in what they say and they are perceived as being honest and direct.

It's not too difficult to envision the kind of track record and reputation that these entrepreneurial managers build for themselves: they get results because they understand that the task of managing in a rapid-growth company usually goes well beyond one's immediate chain of command. They become known as the creative problem solvers who have a knack for blending and balancing multiple views and demands. Their calculated risk taking succeeds more often than it fails. And they have a reputation for developing human capital—they groom and grow other effective growth managers by their example and their mentoring.

Unique Structures and Systems. Achieving coherence while there appears to be chaos requires an awesome level of integration and coordination. New managerial roles and skills are needed. The operating systems—budgets, data processing, order processing, personnel—need to reflect the way in which work really gets done. Equally important, the temptation to formalize procedures, systems, and policies has within it the seeds of demise and destruction.

6.6 CORPORATE ENTREPRENEURIAL MANAGEMENT

One significant consequence of the new wave of entrepreneurship in America is a heightened awareness among large companies. Never before has more attention been paid to the need for entrepreneurship within large structures. What have researchers and writers concluded about how the best-run companies are managed? Surprise, surprise: they are entrepreneurial! They have top and middle managers with a flair for entrepreneurial management! The highest-performing firms encourage and practice many of the entrepreneurial approaches discussed here. Consider some of the recent research that has yielded additional insight into entrepreneurial management within larger companies.

6.6.1 The Change Masters

Rosabeth Moss Kanter, in her 1983 book with this title, argues that American corporations will prosper only to the extent that they understand, initiate, and carry out innovational changes at every level of the organization. She identifies three sets of skills as necessary for entrepreneurial change agents in order to produce integrative, innovation-stimulating environments:

1. Power and persuasion skills.
2. The ability to manage the greater problems accompanying team and employee participation.
3. An understanding of how change is designed and constructed in an organization.

While being a corporate entrepreneur necessitates "buying into" a value system and culture that already exists and has been created by others, many of the practices and competencies are the same. Kanter sums it up this way:

In short, individuals do not have to be doing "big things" in order to have their cumulative accomplishments eventually result in big performance for the company. . . . They are only rarely the inventors of the "breakthrough" system. They are only rarely doing something that is totally unique or that no one, in any organization, ever thought of before. Instead, they are often applying ideas that have proved themselves elsewhere, or they are rearranging parts to create a better result, or they are noting a potential problem before it turns into a catastrophe and mobilizing the actions to anticipate and solve it.[8]

What does this mean for middle managers within large organizations? What do entrepreneurial and innovative middle managers do, and how do their organizations treat them?

6.6.2 Middle Manager as Innovator

In her July–August 1982 *Harvard Business Review* article "Middle Manager as Innovator," Kanter spells out some of the behaviors and practices of entrepreneurial middle managers that she found in her study. To begin with, they are comfortable with change, and see unmet needs as opportunities. Further, they have clarity in their direction, carefully select projects, possess long-time horizons, and see setbacks as temporary. They are known for their thoroughness of preparation, and they operate with a team-oriented, participative management style. Finally, they practice perseverance, persistence, and discretion.

Sound familiar? It should not come as a surprise. After all, what works, works—with size of the organization being no barrier.

Exhibit 6.6 summarizes five companies that Kanter studied, ranging from "most" to "least" entrepreneurial. It provides a useful flavor of how these large

[8]Rosabeth Moss Kanter, *The Change Masters* (New York: Simon & Schuster, 1983), pp. 354–55.

Exhibit 6.6
Characteristics of Five Companies Ranging from Most to Least Entrepreneurial

	Chipco	Radco	Medco	Finco	Utico
Percentage of effective managers with entrepreneurial accomplishments	71%	69%	67%	47%	33%
Current economic trend	Steadily up	Trend up but currently down	Up		
Current "change" issues	Change "normal"; constant change in product generation; proliferating staff and units	Change "normal" in products, technologies; recent changeover to second management generation with new focus	Reorganized about 3–4 years ago to install matrix; "normal" product, technology changes	Change a "shock"; new top-management group from outside reorganizing and trying to add competitive market posture	Change a "shock"; undergoing reorganization to install matrix and add competitive market posture while reducing staff
Organization structure	Matrix	Matrix in some areas; product lines act as quasi divisions	Matrix in some areas	Divisional; unitary hierarchy within divisions; some central services	Functional organization; currently overlaying a matrix of regions and markets
	Decentralized	Mixed	Mixed	Centralized	Centralized
Information flow	Free	Free	Moderately free	Constricted	Constricted
Communication emphasis	Horizontal	Horizontal	Horizontal	Vertical	Vertical
Culture	Clear, consistent, favors individual initiative	Clear, though in transition from emphasis on invention to emphasis on routinization and systems	Clear, pride in company, belief that talent will be rewarded	Idiosyncratic; depends on boss and area	Clear, but top management would like to change it; favors security maintenance, protection
Current "emotional"	Pride in company, team feeling	Uncertainty about changes	Pride in company, team feeling	Low trust, high uncertainty	High certainty, confusion
Rewards	Abundant; include visibility, chance to do more challenging work in the future and to get bigger budget for projects	Abundant; include visibility, chance to do more challenging work in future and to get budgets for projects	Moderately abundant. Conventional	Scarce; primarily monetary	Scarce; promotion, salary freeze; recognition by peers grudging

Source: Rosabeth Moss Kanter, "Middle Managers as Innovators," *Harvard Business Review,* July–August, 1982.

firms differ, and how they are organized to encourage or eradicate entrepreneurial behavior.

6.6.3 Managing for Excellence: The "Postheroic" Managers

In another recent book, *Managing for Excellence,* Bradford and Cohen put some teeth into the implementation and how-to issues that *In Search for Excellence* left unmentioned. How does one get middle managers to pursue and practice the entrepreneurial excellence made famous by Tom Peters and Bob Waterman?

Once again, some of the important fundamentals practiced by team-builder entrepreneurs—who are more intent on getting results than on just getting their own way—are also emulated by effective middle managers. The authors distinguish between the "heroic manager," whose need to be in control may in many instances actually stifle cooperation, and the "postheroic manager," a developer who actually brings about excellence in modern organizations.[9]

In a rapid-growth company the failure of top management to develop entrepreneurial middle management can be fatal. Most rapid-growth businesses enjoy substantial gross margins, often 30 percent, 50 percent, even 60 percent or more. This certainly provides a marvelous cushion for mistakes and errors, and some breathing space as new people learn new jobs in new technologies and markets. Yet, the lagging growth of a cadre of effective middle managers often becomes a bottleneck for the business. And if price competition suddenly appears, margins erode, and the safety cushion with them. If the growing of middle managers has not been attended to, the organization may come unraveled at this point. Paying close attention to the development of managers is vital in the rapid-growth company. An essential first step is linking a plan to grow human capital at the middle-management and supervisory levels with the business strategy.

6.6.4 Creating an Entrepreneurial Culture: The Pepsi Generation

A good example of leading initiatives to foster an entrepreneurial culture is under way at Pepsi Cola Corporation, North America. Its new president, Roger Enrico (Babson College, class of 1965), is doing more than just talking or writing about this.[10] As the new CEO of Pepsi, one of his early initiatives was to develop a strategy and culture to encourage entrepreneurial managers.

He summarized six critical factors:

1. Understand the market: know the business you are in, and stay in that business.
2. Set high performance standards by starting with yourself; develop short-run objectives without sacrificing long-run results.
3. Provide responsive, personal leadership: you don't manage through memos and computer printouts; you do it eyeball to eyeball, and by energizing ideas.
4. Encourage individual initiative.
5. Help others to succeed.
6. Develop your own network for success.

Above all, he advised students to maintain commitment and integrity.

6.6.5 Converging on the Entrepreneurial Manager

Once again, the convergence of these independent viewpoints, coupled with the discussion in the previous chapter on the lead entrepreneur, is far more than coincidental. The messages are too powerful to ignore. Time and again, these fundamentals are echoed: many of the same competencies and practices seem to work. As long as the opportunity is there, and has been spotted, entrepreneurial management actions can convert the opportunity into results. These principles are more important than the size of the organization, its stage of growth, the education of the entrepreneurial manager, or any combination of these.

[9]David Bradford and Allan Cohen, *Managing for Excellence* (New York: John Wiley & Sons, 1984), pp. 3–4.

[10]Based on a talk that Mr. Enrico gave on March 22, 1984, as Executive in Residence at Babson College.

6.7 THE MANAGEMENT COMPETENCY INVENTORY

After you have absorbed the key messages in this chapter about the entrepreneurial manager—especially the sometimes conflicting, sometimes overlapping characteristics of the entrepreneurial domain and the managerial domain illustrated in Exhibits 6.1 and 6.2—we believe that it will be useful for you to assess your management competencies and those of your team. If you consider yourself highly "entrepreneurial," do you or your team members have enough management skills to deal with the entrepreneurial transition in a rapidly growing venture, as summarized in Exhibit 6.4? And, on the other hand, if you consider yourself a competent manager who is joining an entrepreneurial team, will you be able to adapt to the different climate of the entrepreneurial manager as summarized in Exhibit 6.5? This self-knowledge is vital, whether you are to be a lead entrepreneur and must identify what kinds of supporting skills are required or whether you are to educate yourself for a management career.

The Management Competency Inventory is a comprehensive list of management skills. Its seven major dimensions include four key areas of functional skills (marketing, finance, production and operations, and microcomputer skills) and three areas of cross-functional skills (administration, interpersonal work and teamwork, and law and taxation). The determination of whether a particular entrepreneurial team has the required management skills to succeed is a difficult job. The job is also iterative in nature, requiring a continuing review and adjustment as the venture start-up takes shape, particularly while the business plan is developed. Subsequent chapters will link this initial assessment of your own management skills to the forming and building of the team (Chapter 7), the developing of a personal entrepreneurial strategy (Chapter 10) and the developing of the business plan (Chapters 13 and 14).

6.7.1 Directions for Exercise

The purpose of the Management Competency Inventory exercise that follows is fourfold:

1. To introduce management competencies and skills and define them in more detail.
2. To enable you to do an initial diagnosis of where you see yourself on these management competencies and skills.
3. To enable you to begin, on the basis of the diagnosis, to develop your own learning agenda—things you want to learn more about.
4. To provide you with data about your management competencies that, coupled with a knowledge of your venture's management requirements, will enable you to search for team members whose skills complement yours and are necessary for business success.

Complete the Management Competency Inventory prior to the next session. As you go through it, and throughout the book, there are several important points you should keep in mind:

1. This is a self-assessment exercise. There will be an integrated format in Chapter 10 that will enable you to give or receive comments and impressions and to use others as sounding boards to "reality-test" self-perceptions and assess-

ments. How much, if any, of your data you choose to share with others is your decision.

2. Self-assessment, like any other decision process, is most productive when it is made with the benefit of all the available information. With your help a climate can be developed to maximize the necessary information flow.

3. The assumption behind this format is that a systematic recording and analysis of your experiences can (*a*) help you to see where you have been and (*b*) provide some direction regarding how what you have learned about yourself could affect your venture.

4. Finally, a complex set of factors clearly goes into making someone a successful entrepreneur. No individual has all of the managerial skills or personal qualities defined in the exercise. The presence or absence of any single dimension does not guarantee success or failure as an entrepreneur. Knowing that you do not have a certain skill and knowing how to acquire it are clearly as valuable as knowing that you already have it.

In the Management Competency Inventory, you are asked to check the column that most accurately describes your level of expertise and accomplishment in each particular skill area. The three columns to choose from are:

1. Know thoroughly; have proven results doing it.
2. Have limited knowledge; need backup.
3. Unfamiliar; no proven result.

You will also note that at the end of each major skill section (e.g., "Marketing") a space has been left for you to sum the number of checks in each of the three columns. A comparison of the number of checks in the "know well," "limited knowledge," and "unfamiliar" columns of each major skill section should provide a useful way of measuring your overall level of competence in that skill area. If you feel that you have no basis whatsoever for a self-evaluation, you may simply leave the answer spaces blank, although a check in the right-hand column would also be appropriate. And, of course, some technical skills unique to your venture (engineering, designing, etc.) may not be included. Simply add any of these to the list, and evaluate yourself.

Remember, these ratings are the starting point of an effort to reach a realistic assessment of your areas of strength and weakness with regard to management competencies. This assessment will not guarantee or predict either success or failure in a new venture. It will assist you to identify the experiences, resources, and personal management skills important to success, and it will enable you to begin to establish a realistic plan for you to meet those requirements.

In preparing the inventory, it may be helpful to discuss it with people with whom you have worked—on a job, in school, or wherever. We suggest that you reproduce the inventory and distribute copies to as many as five persons who have worked with you as peers, supervisors, or subordinates. More specific suggestions for obtaining and using feedback are contained in Chapter 10.

Name _____

Date _____

6.7.2. Exercise: Management Competency Inventory

For each competency, place a check in the column that best describes your degree of experience and accomplishment in that area. Also, circle the competencies *most* critical to the success of your venture and cross off any irrelevant ones.

	I Know Thoroughly; Have Proven Results Doing It	*I Have Limited Knowledge; Need Backup*	*Unfamiliar; No Proven Results*

1. *Marketing Skills*

   a. *Market Research and Evaluation:*
      Able to design and conduct market research studies and to analyze and interpret study results; familiar with questionnaire design and sampling techniques   _____ _____ _____

   b. *Marketing Planning:*
      Experienced in planning overall sales, advertising, and promotion programs and in deciding on and setting up effective distributor or sales representative systems   _____ _____ _____

   c. *Product Pricing:*
      Able to determine competitive pricing and margin structures and to position products in terms of price; able to develop pricing policies that maximize profits   _____ _____ _____

   d. *Sales Management:*
      Able to organize, supervise, and motivate a direct sales force; able to analyze territory and account sales potential and to manage a sales force to obtain maximum share of market   _____ _____ _____

   e. *Direct Selling:*
      Experience in identifying, meeting, and developing new customers; demonstrated success in closing sales   _____ _____ _____

	I Know Thoroughly; Have Proven Results Doing It	I Have Limited Knowledge; Need Backup	Unfamiliar; No Proven Results
f. *Service:* Able to perceive service needs of particular products; experience in determining service and spare parts requirements, handling customer complaints, and managing a service organization	_____	_____	_____
g. *Distribution Management:* Able to organize and manage the flow of product from manufacturing through distribution channels to ultimate customer; includes familiarity with shipping costs, scheduling techniques, carriers, etc.	_____	_____	_____
h. *Product Management:* Able to integrate market information, perceived needs, R&D, and advertising into a rational product plan; able to understand market penetration and break-even.	_____	_____	_____
i. *New Product Planning:* Experience in new product introductions, including marketing testing, prototype testing, and development of price/ sales/merchandising and distribution plans for new products	_____	_____	_____
Number of checks (out of possible 9)	===============	===============	===============

	I Know Thoroughly; Have Proven Results Doing It	*I Have Limited Knowledge; Need Backup*	*Unfamiliar; No Proven Results*

2. *Operations/Technical Skills*

   a. *Manufacturing Management:*
      Know about the production
      process, machines, personnel, and
      space required to produce the
      product; experience in managing
      production to produce products
      within time, cost, and quality
      constraints

   b. *Inventory Control:*
      Familiar with techniques of
      controlling in-process and
      finished goods inventory of
      materials

   c. *Cost Analysis and Control:*
      Able to calculate labor and
      materials costs, develop standard
      cost system, conduct variance
      analyses, calculate overtime
      labor needs, and manage/control
      costs

   d. *Quality Control:*
      Able to set up inspection systems
      and standards for effective
      control of quality in incoming, in-
      process, and finished materials

   e. *Production Scheduling and Flow:*
      Able to analyze work flow, plan
      and manage production process,
      manage work flow; able to
      calculate schedules and flows for
      rising sales levels

	I Know Thoroughly; Have Proven Results Doing It	*I Have Limited Knowledge; Need Backup*	*Unfamiliar; No Proven Results*

f. *Purchasing:*
Able to identify appropriate sources of supply, negotiate supplier contracts, and manage incoming flow of material into inventory; familiar with economic order quantities and discount advantages

g. *Job Evaluation:*
Able to analyze worker productivity and need for additional help; able to calculate cost-saving aspects of temporary versus permanent help

    Number of checks (out of possible 7)

3. *Financial Skills*

a. *Raising Capital:*
Able to decide how best to acquire funds for start-up and growth; able to forecast funds needs, prepare budgets; familiar with sources and vehicles of short- and long-term financing, formal and informal

b. *Cash Flow Management:*
Able to project cash requirements, set up cash controls, and manage the firm's cash position

c. *Credit and Collection Management:*
Able to develop credit policies and screening criteria; can age receivables and payables; understand use of collection agencies, when to start legal action

	I Know Thoroughly; Have Proven Results Doing It	*I Have Limited Knowledge; Need Backup*	*Unfamiliar; No Proven Results*
d. **Short-Term Financing Alternatives:** Understand payables management, use of interim financing such as bank loans, factoring of receivables, pledging and selling notes and contracts, bills of lading, and bank acceptances; familiar with financial statements and budgeting/profit planning	_____	_____	_____
e. *Familiar with Public and Private Offerings:* Able to develop a business plan and offering memo that can be used to raise capital; familiar with legal requirements of public and private stock offerings	_____	_____	_____
f. *Bookkeeping and Accounting:* Able to determine appropriate bookkeeping and accounting system, including various ledgers and accounts, as company starts and grows	_____	_____	_____
g. *Specific Skills:* Cash flow analysis; break-even analysis; contribution analysis; profit and loss; balance sheet	_____	_____	_____
Number of checks (out of possible 7)	=======	=======	=======

	I Know Thoroughly; Have Proven Results Doing It	*I Have Limited Knowledge; Need Backup*	*Unfamiliar; No Proven Results*
4. *Microcomputer Skills*			
a. Spreadsheet Analysis	_____	_____	_____
b. Word Processing	_____	_____	_____
c. Database Access and Use of Electronic Mail	_____	_____	_____
d. Graphics	_____	_____	_____
Number of checks (out of possible 4)	_____	_____	_____
5. *Administrative Skills*			
a. Problem Solving: Able to anticipate potential problems and to plan to avoid them; able to gather facts about problems, analyze them for *real* causes, and plan effective action to solve the problems; very thorough in dealing with details of particular problems and in follow-through	_____	_____	_____
b. Communication: Able to communicate effectively and clearly—orally and in writing—to media, public, customers, peers, and subordinates	_____	_____	_____
c. Planning: Able to set realistic and attainable goals, identify obstacles to the goals, and develop detailed action plans to achieve the goals; schedule own time very systematically	_____	_____	_____
d. Decision Making: Able to make decisions on best analysis of incomplete data	_____	_____	_____

	I Know Thoroughly; Have Proven Results Doing It	*I Have Limited Knowledge; Need Backup*	*Unfamiliar; No Proven Results*
e. *Project Management:* Skilled in organizing project teams, setting project goals, defining project tasks, and monitoring task completion in the face of problems and cost/ quality constraints	_____	_____	_____
f. *Negotiating:* Able to work effectively in a negotiating situation; able to balance quickly value given and value received	_____	_____	_____
g. *Personnel Administration:* Able to set up payroll, hiring, compensation, and training functions	_____	_____	_____
Number of checks (out of possible 7)	_____	_____	_____

6. *Interpersonal and Team Skills*

   a. *Leadership and Influence:*
      Able to understand the
      relationships among tasks, the
      leader, and the followers; able to
      lead in those situations where
      this is appropriate; willing to
      actively manage, supervise, and
      control activities of others
      through directions, suggestions,
      etc.   _____   _____   _____

   b. *Listening and Trust Building:*
      Able to listen to and understand
      without interrupting or mentally
      preparing my own rebuttal at the
      expense of hearing the message;
      able to build trust   _____   _____   _____

	I Know Thoroughly; Have Proven Results Doing It	I Have Limited Knowledge; Need Backup	Unfamiliar; No Proven Results
c. *Helping:* Able to ask for and provide help and to determine situations where assistance is warranted	_____	_____	_____
d. *Feedback:* Able to provide performance and interpersonal feedback to others that they find useful; able to receive feedback from others without becoming defensive or argumentative	_____	_____	_____
e. *Conflict Management:* Able to confront differences openly and to deal with them until resolution is obtained; able to use evidence and logic; able to share power	_____	_____	_____
f. *Teamwork:* Able to work well with others in pursuing common goals, especially when I have no formal power	_____	_____	_____
g. *Developing Subordinates:* Able to delegate responsibility and to coach subordinates in the development of their managerial capabilities	_____	_____	_____
h. *Climate and Culture Building:* Able to create, by the way I manage, a climate and spirit conducive to high performance; able to press for performance while rewarding work well done; able to encourage innovation, initiative, and calculated risk taking	_____	_____	_____
Number of checks (out of possible 8)	=========	=========	=========

	I Know Thoroughly; Have Proven Results Doing It	I Have Limited Knowledge; Need Backup	Unfamiliar; No Proven Results
7. *Knowledge of Applicable Law*			
a. *Corporate Law:* Familiar with legal issues relating to stock issues, incorporation, distribution agreements, leases, etc.	_____	_____	_____
b. *Contract Law:* Familiar with contract procedures and requirements (government and commercial), including default, warranty, and incentive provisions, fee structures, overhead, G&A allowable, etc.	_____	_____	_____
c. *Patent and Proprietary Rights Laws:* Experienced with preparation and revision of patent applications; able to recognize a strong patent; familiar with claim requirements and proprietary rights	_____	_____	_____
d. *Tax Law:* Familiar with state and federal reporting requirements, Subchapter S, Keogh plans (HR–10), tax shelters, estate planning, fringe benefits, etc.	_____	_____	_____
e. *Real Estate Law:* Familiar with leases, purchase offers, purchase and sale agreements, etc.	_____	_____	_____
f. *Investment Agreement Law:* Familiar with issues relating to term sheets, investment agreements, employment and noncompetition agreements, vesting, restricted stock agreements, etc.	_____	_____	_____
Number of checks (out of possible 6)	========	========	========

6.7.3 **Optional Group Discussion** (1 hour)

Form into groups of three and four persons to discuss the Management Competency Inventory (MCI). These steps should be followed:

Step 1: Each person should share his or her MCI with other members of the group.

Step 2: Use these group discussion guidelines in reviewing each MCI:

    a. How complete and realistic has the person been in his or her self-evaluations? Has each person been honest, objective, and hard-nosed in evaluating the skills and in arriving at the conclusions?

    b. What implications do people see for one another's management skills, strengths, and weaknesses?

    c. What can be done about a particular weakness?

    d. What time implications are there for starting your own business (e.g., how ready are your management skills)?

    e. If you know the other person(s), are you aware of events or past actions that might contribute to this analysis? Are there inferences that might be made or conclusions that might be drawn?

Step 3: The group should summarize this discussion and be prepared to present to the entire group:

    a. The main management skills, strengths, and weaknesses identified. Are there any patterns?

    b. Action recommendations about ways to deal with weaknesses with regard to your personal career and your venture. Be specific.

General Discussion (15–30 minutes)

The entire group can reconvene to summarize the group discussions and the various implications and action alternatives discussed.

6.7.4 Managerial Assessment and Personal Progress (15–20 minutes)

Complete the following self-assessment exercise prior to the next session, whether or not you have participated in a group discussion exercise.

EXERCISE: MANAGERIAL AND ADMINISTRATIVE SKILLS

1. Which of your management skills did your MCI and class discussion highlight as particularly strong?

2. Which of your management skills were highlighted as particularly weak?

3. What comments, if any, did you receive from others or discuss during the class discussion relating to management skills?

4. In what ways has your assessment of your management skills and your entrepreneurial characteristics changed as a result of this entire exercise?

5. In terms of your career and a venture, what are the two or three most important implications and insights of the above in terms of gaining management know-how or experience or of compensating for and overcoming shortcomings identified? What areas do you really need to explore further?

6.8 KEVIN MOONEY (B): CASE STUDY*

KEVIN MOONEY (B)

In March 1978 Kevin Mooney was hard at work in his new job at Softcorp, enjoying the task of setting up the international marketing division. (See Exhibits 1 and 2 for original offer letter and employment agreement.) He reported directly to Joe Hegarty, the president, who Kevin knew had enormous confidence in him. Within three months his responsibilities were expanded to include all of the company's domestic marketing, a function previously managed by Softcorp's vice president, Bob Wilson. Kevin took the new challenge and began developing relationships with advertising agencies and planning the direct mail program.

Problems

Within two months Kevin Mooney's enthusiasm was brought up short with an invitation to lunch with Bob Wilson. During the lunch Wilson expressed shock at the changes Kevin had made in the U.S. marketing policies and anger at not having been consulted. Kevin listened attentively, stunned to see how hurt Wilson was. It had never occurred to him to check with Wilson.

Once he had learned what marketing areas were important to Wilson, he didn't tamper with them. Several months later it was Kevin's turn to invite Wilson to lunch. The lunch was very pleasant; Wilson was surprised and pleased with how much better the U.S. marketing picture looked and complimented Kevin on his job.

Although Kevin Mooney had succeeded in smoothing the relationship between himself and the vice president, he did not spend much time working on building relationships with the other managers at his peer level. He enjoyed his job and liked watching his department succeed, but he didn't like the interdepartmental politics that some of the managers seemed to thrive on.

Personalities

Lack of leadership from both Hegarty and Wilson contributed significantly to the role politics played. Hegarty, the president, was the creative thinker. Personable and charming, he was the idea generator and was comfortable dealing with the big picture, always avoiding the details. Bob Wilson's personality complemented Hegarty's. He was the detail man and very good at making Hegarty's ideas work. Wilson's leadership style was not to issue clear directives to his managers. Instead, he worked to get a consensus, preferring that his managers work out their differences among themselves. Kevin recalled:

Wilson's problem-solving style really was pretty ineffective. Split fights began to occur between the international and domestic divisions. Splits happen when two or more departments have to split a sales commission. I never had any problem splitting commission within my department, and I don't think the VP of domestic had any problem within his. But there was always trouble when we had to split it between us. I just got frus-

---

*This case was prepared by Loretto Crane, Research Assistant, under the direction of Professor Jeffry A. Timmons, as a basis for class discussion rather than to illustrate either effective or ineffective handling of an administrative situation. Copyright © 1984 by Babson College.

trated, sat down and wrote a memo to Wilson suggesting ideas for ways to alleviate the problem. I didn't think my solution was the only one, but I felt it was a start. Instead of getting back to me with his reaction, Wilson sent my memo on to the domestic VP. And nothing was ever resolved!

The International Department

Although Kevin Mooney was not inclined to interact with the other vice presidents, he did have the skills needed to build an international customer base. From the first day, he built the department brick by brick. By early 1979 he had signed the first two agent agreements (companies appointed to represent Softcorp in foreign countries) in England and Australia. Kevin selected companies, which he called "affiliates," already established in the computer service industry. By year-end the international division revenues accounted for almost 100 percent of Softcorp's profits.

By 1980 Scandinavia and Mexico were added to the list of international customers. Kevin Mooney recalled:

We were 120 percent over our plan for the year. I felt that I had demonstrated my commitment to the company and went to Hegarty to see about my getting some equity participation. I was surprised that he didn't remember our conversation about equity during the interview process.

Several weeks later I was flying to Dallas with Bob Wilson. Luckily, I had dug out the letter they had sent me. I showed Bob the letter and told him that I didn't want to pressure him, that the company certainly didn't have to give me any equity, but if that was their decision, Softcorp wasn't the place I wanted to work.

Seeing the letter was apparently quite significant for Wilson. Kevin Mooney was given 1 percent stock participation in Softcorp. (Exhibit 3 is a letter Mooney sent to Hegarty and Wilson.)

In 1981 Mooney was promoted to vice president; Wilson moved to president of Softcorp and Hegarty to chairman. By 1982 the international division had grown to include South Africa, Southeast Asia, and Venezuela; by 1983 new countries included New Zealand, France, Brazil, and Argentina. (See Exhibit 4.)

The Acquisition

Since 1980 Softcorp had considered the idea of going public. Each year, however, these plans were scratched because the company profile was never good enough to attract a market. It lacked timely financial statements; its profits weren't very good; and its performance was erratic. In 1983, however, Softcorp received a bona fide offer from a Fortune 500 firm, Prentiss-McGraw, Inc. (PMI). The firm thought Softcorp fitted well into its portfolio of companies; it saw Softcorp as a growth company with little need to generate healthy profits each year. Furthermore, its deal promised a hands-off approach. It was content to let the founders continue to manage the company. The purchase price was a range between $50 million and $80 million, depending on the company's performance over the next three years. The acquisition, however, had different harvest implications for several members of the management committee, as shown by the equity distribution among the eight management committee members. (See Exhibit 5.)

As a part of the deal, the buyer asked all of us—Hegarty, Wilson, and the six vice presidents—to sign a noncompete agreement and an employment contract guaranteeing that we would work for them for three years. They explained that the employment contract was designed to protect us and that the noncompete agreement was meant to protect them. Everyone but me seemed very ready to sign. One of the VPs wanted the contract to be for five years!

Three of the vice presidents had received their stock options just eight months before the offer, and they weren't entitled to the capital gains tax treatment. PMI promised to provide them with additional compensation because their options would be taxed as ordinary income.

The other two VPs, who each owned 8 percent each in the form of stock, and Hegarty and Wilson were set for life. There I was, standing alone with my 1 percent, now diluted to 0.8 percent, stock, certainly not enough to retire on.

Exhibits 6 and 7 are the employment and noncompete agreement drawn up by PMI's attorneys for execution by Softcorp's executives.

Kevin Mooney's Dilemma

Kevin knew that he was pretty much alone in his reluctance to sign. But he had to consider what was most important to him. He was a young man with a young family. Right now, his job required lots of travel and he wasn't sure he wanted to continue traveling so much. In addition, he loved the job because he could be his own boss and run his own show. He had no idea how PMI's presence would affect that. Whether or not to sign the contract weighed heavily on Kevin's mind.

I thought I had better see a lawyer if for no other reason that to be able to use him as "the bad guy" in all of this. He confirmed my feelings about signing. He told me that I had built a good reputation in the industry and that I could leverage that reputation elsewhere. He told me, "Unless they give you something, don't sign."

Then, at a sales meeting in Hawaii, Wilson cornered me, referring to my reluctance to sign as "the Mooney problem." He told me I was ruining it for the rest of them—that the deal wouldn't go through without my signature.

Kevin wondered how he should proceed.

Preparation Questions

1. Should Kevin Mooney sign the PMI agreement? Why or why not?
2. What are the rights, obligations, liabilities, and responsibilities of the parties to the agreement?
3. What do you see as Kevin's bargaining position? What should be his strategy for dealing with the increasing pressure?
4. What are the consequences of his *actions* for himself, Softcorp, the top-management team at both Softcorp and PMI?
5. What other opportunities should he consider?

Exhibit 1

January 27, 1978

Mr. Kevin Mooney
560 Hillside Avenue
Seattle, Washington 98115

Dear Kevin:

I enjoyed our meeting Tuesday evening, which was obvious due to the seemingly rapid passage of time. As a result of our conversations, I am writing to formalize an invitation to join Softcorp as its Director of International Marketing.

This position would require the development of a reasonably thorough understanding of all of our existing and planned products, as well as the complete marketing approach that is currently being used successfully in the United States.

Following that effort would be a research project to evaluate the various foreign markets in terms of their potential sales volume and concluding in the selection of those markets that could most readily and profitably be undertaken by Softcorp, Inc.

The focus of the position would then shift to one of structuring the type of organization that would be required to implement an effective non-U.S. marketing effort, and would eventually become one of administering the ongoing activities implied by the position's lofty title.

The position would carry an initial starting salary of $26,000 per year. Since the function is new to the company, we would want to review the initial results six months after initial date of employment. Thereafter, such reviews would be annual.

You also would be invited to participate in a medical reimbursement plan that would commence with your initial date of employment. This plan reimburses you for medical expenses not covered by insurance to a limit of $1,000 per year.

We would have no objection to your continued instructional efforts at local educational institutions. The obvious implication here is that such activities would not interfere with the functional requirements of the position.

To the extent that your efforts are successful, in that they generate sales, you would be provided with an overriding level of compensation based on the volume of those sales. That compensation is defined as follows:

Sales	Bonus Percentage
$0–100,000	1
$100,000–300,000	3
$300,000 up	2

This bonus is subject to change on a year-to-year basis as we see what our experience will be. It will be paid quarterly based upon what has been collected.

To preserve and enhance your personal domestic tranquility, the company is willing to absorb the expenses of your spouse should she elect to accompany you on two of your trips each year. It is assumed that the trips mentioned would aggregate approximately two weeks each year.

The position that we are defining is very critical to the future of Softcorp, Inc. We feel that it will take a strong effort over at least a two-year period to accomplish the objectives that we have defined. For this reason, we would ask that you contemplate your acceptance of this offer in the light of a minimum commitment of two years. This would avoid the many problems that we feel would occur if there were to be a break in the continuity of events that we have described.

The last point to be covered is that of equity participation in the company. Both Joe and I are open-minded with regard to stockholder expansion. The issue itself is open for discussion in any performance review that occurs after you have joined the company. Specifically, Kevin, when we recognize that a significant and continuing contribution is being made to the basic strength of the company itself, we would be of a frame of mind to structure an equity position for the individual responsible for that contribution.

We hope you will accept the position that we have offered, because we feel that the company can truly benefit from the talents and skills that you would bring to bear on the outlined function. We also feel that this position offers you an outstanding opportunity for personal and professional growth.

Please be in touch if you have any questions.

Sincerely,

Robert W. Wilson

Robert W. Wilson
President

Exhibit 2

Employment Agreement

This agreement dated 3-13-78 between Softcorp, Inc., a Washington Corporation, having its principal place of business at 381 East Street, Seattle, Washington (hereinafter called the "Company"), and Kevin Mooney, residing at 560 Hillside Avenue, Seattle, Washington 98115 (hereinafter called the "Employee").

In consideration of the mutual covenants herein contained, the parties agree as follows:

Section 1: The Company will employ the Employee and the Employee will serve the Company upon the terms and conditions provided herein, unless terminated as provided herein.

Section 2: During the term of employment hereunder the Employee shall devote his full time during business hours and use his best efforts in furtherance of the business of the Company.

Section 3: At the Company's request, the Employee agrees to assist the Company in every proper way to obtain for its or their own benefit patents for discoveries, inventions, or improvements thereof in any and all countries and all discoveries, inventions, or improvements are to remain the property of the Company whether patented or not.

Section 4: The Employee shall not divulge or communicate to any person or entity other than customers of the Company without the express written consent of the Company any trade secrets, trade knowledge, discoveries, inventions, innovations, computer programs, and other information obtained or conceived by the Company along all lines of work of said Company. During the term of employment hereunder and for a period of two years after the termination of this agreement by any means whatsoever, the Employee shall not within the territorial limits of the United States of America engage in business dealings competitive with the business of the Company with any persons, corporations, or associations and shall not engage as an Employee, Officer, Director, Partner, or Consultant in any business competitive with that of the Company. In the event that this section shall be determined by any court of competent jurisdiction to be unenforceable by reason of its extending for too great a period of time or over too large a geographic area or over too great a range of activities, it shall be interpreted to extend only over the maximum period of time, geographic area, or range of activities as to which it may be enforceable.

Section 5: Any and all notices under this agreement shall be in writing.

Section 6: This agreement supersedes all prior agreements written or oral between the Employee and the Company as of the date of the commencement of employment hereunder and shall constitute the only agreement between the parties for the period of employment hereunder. No provisions of this agreement shall be changed or modified nor shall this agreement be discharged in whole or in part except by an agreement in writing signed by the party against whom such change, modification, or discharge is claimed or sought to be enforced.

Section 7: This agreement shall inure to the benefit of and be binding upon the Company or its successors and assigns. All obligations of the Employee arising under this agreement shall survive the termination of this agreement and shall be binding upon his heirs, executors, and administrators.

Section 8: In the event the Employee leaves the Company voluntarily or is discharged by the Company, this agreement will be terminated except that Section 4 hereof shall survive such termination.

Softcorp, Inc.   Employee

By *Joseph M. Hefferty*   By *Kevin Mooney*

Exhibit 3

Joseph Hegarty   3-17-80
381 East Street   <u>Personal</u>
Seattle, Washington 98115

Dear Joe,

It's 12:45 A.M., and I'm at 30,000 feet en route to San Francisco. I'll attend our seminar there tomorrow and then on to Australia. This flight has been a long one (and I've just started the journey), but it's given me a chance to think about SOFTCORP and the opportunities I've had here.

Let me first thank you sincerely for putting into place the equity plan that Bob described to me last week. Obviously, I appreciate it from a financial standpoint, but equally important, I appreciate the confidence you must have in me to justify such a program.

As you know, equity is something I have felt strongly about since I joined SOFTCORP, and I believe the plan you are implementing is well designed to meet both your objectives and mine. The quantity of stock is sufficient to meet my personal goals as long as we continue our tremendous growth over the next few years. Obviously, this provides strong motivation for me to dedicate my best talents and efforts to this pursuit.

This is also a good opportunity to thank you for the confidence you and Bob have shown in me over the past few years. The experience I've had has been terrific. I hope you've been as satisfied with my performance as I've been with the job. It's been a lot of hard work, but I can't imagine a better place to have done it. I hope the next few years can be as interesting, challenging, and successful as the past few. I'm confident that the international division will continue to grow and prosper and that there's still lots of room for improvement in the U.S. marketing activities.

Thank you for the opportunities you've provided and once again, thank you for the "precious" equity.

Kevin

P.S. I've sent a similar letter to Bob.

Exhibit 4
Softcorp, Inc., Performance, 1977–1983 ($ millions)

	1977	*1978*	*1979*	*1980*	*1981*	*1982*	*1983*
Total sales	$1.7	$3.1	$7.5	$15.6	$26.2	$39.0	$56.0
Profit	$0.048	$0.221	$0.775	$0.910	$1.02	$2.1	$3.6
International			$0.75	$1.5	$3.7	$8.7	$17.0
Employees	57	85	138	251	350	400	640

Exhibit 5
Softcorp, Inc., Distribution of Equity

Frank Hegarty, Chairman	25% stock
Jim Wilson, President	25% stock
Dave Cassidy, VP, Operations	8% stock
Jonathan Latham, VP, Research and Development	8% stock
Richard White, VP, Marketing	0.8% (options)
Roger Fineman, VP, Sales	0.8% (options)
Stephen Marx, VP, Finance and Treasurer	0.8% (options)
Kevin Mooney, VP, International	0.8% stock

Exhibit 6

Shaw & Cartwright
Counselors at Law
60 City Square, N.W.
Seattle, Washington 98100
(206) 227-9740

March 25, 1983

Hand Delivered

R. Kevin Mooney, Vice President
Softcorp, Inc.
381 East Street
Seattle, WA 98115

Dear Kevin:

As promised earlier this week, I am enclosing copies of the following documents, which constitute *all* of the documents to be signed by senior Softcorp officers in connection with the Prentiss-McGraw, Inc., acquisition:

1. *Sellers Agreement.* This has already been signed by the seven senior officers. It contains a covenant not to compete on page 5, with a reference to Appendix A, which lists the termination dates of the covenant for each senior officer.

2. *Sellers' Agent Agreement.* I believe you have not yet seen this agreement, which also has already been signed by all senior officers. Basically, it constitutes a power of attorney granted to Bob and Joe to act on behalf of all sellers throughout the mechanics of the closing, distribution of cash proceeds, etc. and the earn-out period over the next three years. It grants no authority to negotiate or amend individual employment agreements whatsoever.

3. *Employment Agreement.* This has not yet been signed by anyone, but it is proposed that on or immediately before the closing (approximately April 26), all individuals in "tier two" would sign an employment agreement in the form of Exhibit 7, with individual treatment for salaries only. You will especially want to note Section 2 providing for a term of the Agreement through December 31, 1985, and Section 6(c) containing another covenant not to compete continuing for four months after such termination date (i.e., until April 30, 1986).

I would be pleased to attempt to answer any questions you may have regarding any of the above three agreements. If it appears likely that you may be signing any one or more of them, then you will undoubtedly want to secure your personal attorney's views.

I expect to be talking with you next week.

Very truly yours,

John J. Marshall

John J. Marshall

JJM:akl
Enclosures

Exhibit 7

Employment Agreement

This AGREEMENT, dated as of May 4, 1983, between Softcorp, Inc. ("Company"), and R. Kevin Mooney ("Executive").

Witnesseth:

Whereas, the Company, the Prentiss-McGraw, Inc. ("Buyer"), P&M Merger Corporation, a wholly owned subsidiary of Buyer ("Merger Corp."), and Robert W. Wilson and Joseph M. Hegarty, collectively as agent ("Sellers' Agent") for holders, including Executive, of the outstanding shares of capital stock and options to

Exhibit 7 *(continued)*

purchase capital stock of the Company ("Sellers"), have entered into an Agreement and Plan of Merger, dated as of March 21, 1983 (the "Merger Agreement"), pursuant to which Buyer will acquire the Company as a result of the merger of the Merger Corp. with and into the Company (the "Merger");

Whereas, Executive is and has been employed by the Company for more than five years and is currently Vice President—International of the Company;

Whereas, Executive possesses an intimate knowledge of the business and affairs of the Company, its policies, methods, personnel, and problems;

Whereas, the Board of Directors of the Company recognizes that Executive's contribution to the growth and success of the Company has been substantial and desires to assure the Company of Executive's continued employment and to compensate him therefor;

Whereas, Executive desires to be so employed by the Company, on the terms and conditions herein set forth;

Now, therefore, in consideration of the premises and the terms hereinafter set forth, but subject to the consummation of the Merger under the aforesaid Merger Agreement, the parties agree as follows:

1. *Employment.*   After the Effective Date, as that term is defined in the Merger Agreement (the "Effective Date"), the Company shall employ Executive pursuant to the terms of this Agreement. Executive shall hold the office of Vice President—International and, in addition to the duties prescribed for such office, shall have such other duties, responsibilities, and powers as shall be consistent with such office and as may be prescribed from time to time. Executive shall devote substantially all of his business time and attention to the business of the Company. Executive hereby accepts said employment and agrees faithfully to perform said duties in compliance with the policies and procedures applicable to Executive's positions and to render said sevices for the term of his employment. During the term of this Agreement, Company shall not require Executive to change his current domicile to another state.

2. *Term.*   The term of this Agreement shall commence as of the Effective Date and shall continue until December 31, 1985 (the "Termination Date"), unless sooner terminated pursuant to Paragraph 5 hereof. The provisions of Executive's previous employment arrangements with the Company shall continue in effect until the Effective Date, at which time such employment arrangements shall terminate.

3. *Compensation.*

(*a*) During the term of this Agreement, Executive shall be paid, as compensation for his services under this Agreement, as follows:

(*i*) Salary at the rate of $100,000 per annum, payable by check not less often than monthly and not later than the fifteenth day following the expiration of the month in which services are rendered hereunder; and

(ii) Bonus, payable within three (3) months after the end of each year, and based upon the Company's Compensation and Bonus Plan in effect from year to year.

(iii) All salaries and bonuses hereunder shall be reviewed by the Company annually, which reviews shall not result in any reduction of the salaries hereunder.

(*b*) Executive shall be entitled to four weeks' vacation during each calendar year of this Agreement.

(*c*) As an employee of the Company, Executive shall be entitled to the employee welfare benefit, pension, and other benefit plans available to the employees of the Company, which shall not be less than those presently enjoyed by Executive.

4. *Confidential Information.*   In the course of his employment with the Company prior to the date hereof Executive had, and in the course of his employment hereunder Executive will have, access to confidential information and records, data, formulas, specifications, and other trade secrets of the Company, Buyer, and Buyer's affiliates. During and after his employment by the Company, Buyer, or any of Buyer's affiliates, Executive shall not directly or indirectly disclose such information to any person or use any such information, except as required in the course of such employment. All records, files, drawings, documents, models, equipment, and the like relating to the Company's, Buyer's, or any of Buyer's affiliates' business, which Executive shall prepare or use or come into contact with, shall be and remain such company's sole property and shall not be removed from such company's premises without its written consent, except as required in the course of such employment.

5. *Termination.*

(*a*) *Termination for Cause.*   The Company may terminate this Agreement for cause at any time without notice, and thereby cancel all rights and obligations of the parties hereto, except those set forth in Paragraphs 4 and 6(*c*) hereof. For purposes of this Agreement, "cause" shall mean action by Executive involving material breach of the terms of this Agreement which shall not have ceased within ten (10) days after written notice thereof, dishonesty, moral turpitude, or gross obstruction of business operations. If, however, Executive shall dispute whether he was discharged for "cause," then such dispute shall promptly be referred for final determination to binding arbitration in Seattle, Washington, in accordance with the rules and regulations of the American Arbitration Association. Pending such final determination of such dispute, Executive shall continue to participate in the employee welfare benefit, pension, and other benefit plans available to the employees of the company to the extent that such continued participation is permitted under such plans and applicable law, and all compensation which would have been payable to Executive under Paragraph 3 hereof if the Agreement had not been terminated for cause by the Company shall be deposited as it would have become payable in an interest-bearing bank account in any commercial bank doing business in the City of Seattle, Washington, to be held by such bank as escrowee pending such final determination and to be released (together with any interest earned thereon) in accordance with the instructions set forth in such final determination.

Exhibit 7 *(concluded)*

(*b*) *Termination upon Disability.* If, during the term of this Agreement, Executive shall become incapable of fulfilling his obligations hereunder because of injury or physical or mental illness, and such incapacity shall exist or may reasonably be expected upon competent medical opinion to exist for more than six (6) months in the aggregate during any period of twelve (12) consecutive months, the Company may, upon at least thirty (30) days' prior written notice to Executive, terminate all rights and obligations of the parties hereto, except those set forth in Paragraphs 4 and 6(*c*) and except as to payment of compensation in accordance with the terms of the Agreement for a period of at least six (6) months after the commencement of such injury or physical or mental illness.

(*c*) *Termination by Death.* If Executive dies during the term of his employment hereunder, this Agreement shall terminate immediately and any payments due Executive hereunder shall be paid to his legal representative.

6. *General Provisions.*

(*a*) *Assignability.* The rights and duties of the parties hereunder shall not be assignable, except that this Agreement and all rights and obligations hereunder may be assigned by the Company to, and assumed by, any corporation or other business entity which succeeds to all or substantially all of the business of the Company through merger, consolidation, acquisition of assets, or other transaction, upon condition that such assignee or successor assumes all of the obligations of the Company hereunder.

(*b*) *Integration.* This Agreement contains the entire agreement among the parties regarding the employment of Executive and supersedes all prior agreements and undertakings whether oral or written. No amendment to this Agreement may be made except by a writing signed by the party to be bound.

(*c*) *Noncompetition; Specific Enforcement.* Executive agrees that, prior to the applicable date set forth below, he will not directly or indirectly (as a director, officer, partner, employee, manager, consultant, independent contractor, advisor, or otherwise) engage in competition with, or own any interest in, provide any financing for, or perform any service for any business or organization which directly or indirectly engages in competition with any business conducted by the Company or any subsidiary or division of the Company in any area where such business is then conducted:

(*i*) if Executive's employment with the Company terminates on or after the Termination Date, four months after such date of termination;

(*ii*) if Executive's employment with the Company either terminates for "cause" or by voluntary termination prior to the Termination Date, the later of (A) the Termination Date or (B) four months after such date of termination.

The foregoing provisions shall not prohibit Executive's ownership of not more than 1 percent of the outstanding shares of any publicly held corporation or not more than 3 percent of the outstanding shares of any privately held corporation, partnership, or other business entity. In the event of a breach of the provisions of this subparagraph, Executive agrees that the remedy at law may be inadequate and that the Company, in addition to any other remedies, shall be entitled to temporary or permanent injunctive or mandatory relief without the necessity of proving damages. Notwithstanding any of the foregoing to the contrary, if Executive shall be discharged without "cause," there shall immediately upon such termination be no restrictions whatsoever upon the freedom of Executive to engage in competition with the business of the Company.

(*d*) *Waiver.* The waiver by any party of a breach of any provision of this Agreement shall not operate or be construed as a waiver of any subsequent breach of the same provision or of any other provision of this Agreement.

(*e*) *Notices.* Any notice to the Company or Executive hereunder shall be given in writing either by personal delivery or by registered or certified mail, postage prepaid, return receipt requested, addressed to the Company at its principal place of business or to Executive at his home address as then shown on the records of the Company. For purposes of determining compliance with any time limit herein, notice shall be deemed given when personally delivered or on the third business day after the day of such mailing.

(*f*) *Severability.* If, for any reason whatsoever, any one or more of the provisions of this Agreement shall be finally determined to be inoperative, unenforceable, or invalid, by a court of competent jurisdiction, in a particular case or in all cases, such determination shall not render such provision invalid in any other case or render any of the other provisions of this Agreement inoperative, unenforceable, or invalid.

(*g*) *Applicable Law.* The exercise, validity, construction, operation, and effect of the terms and provisions of this Agreement shall be determined in accordance with the laws of the State of Washington.

(*h*) *Captions.* The captions to the paragraphs of this Agreement are for convenience only and shall not be considered or referred to in resolving questions of interpretation.

(*i*) *Counterparts.* This Agreement may be executed in one or more counterparts, each of which shall be deemed an original, but all of which together shall constitute one and the same agreement.

In witness whereof, the parties have executed this Agreement as of the date first above written.

Softcorp, Inc.

By: *Joseph M Hegarty*

_____
Executive

The New Venture Team $\qquad$ 7

> *Conventional wisdom: Every venture needs a balanced team of pros with complementary skills in marketing, production, engineering, and operations.*
>
> *Reality: Every venture needs a founder who understands the need for supporting skills and knows where to find them, when needed.*
>
> Gordon Baty

7.1 RESULTS EXPECTED

This chapter addresses entrepreneurial team building, in the light both of experience and of recent research that has brought some facts and thoughtful analysis to this least understood aspect of new venture creation. Upon completion of the chapter, and the Stock and Salary exercise you will have:

1. Identified and examined the role and significance of the team in building high-potential ventures.
2. Identified some of the important problems associated with new venture teams, myths and realities regarding such teams, and specific methods to resolve the most difficult issues that arise among them.
3. Examined—for your venture—the critical experience, know-how, and skills required to execute the opportunity you have focused on.

7.2 PRESESSION PREPARATION

After reading the chapter, complete the Stock and Salary exercise with your team on a real start-up, or as part of a course business plan project. Prepare and analyze the Beantown Seafoods (B) case in Chapter 8.

7.3 THE NEW VENTURE TEAM

7.3.1 Importance of the Team

No doubt about it there is undoubtedly a strong connection between the quality of a new venture's management team and the growth potential of that venture and its ability to attract venture capital. Accumulating evidence testifies that the management team can make quite a difference in venture success.[1] Consider the following, for example.

[1] Jeffry A. Timmons, "Careful Self-Analysis and Team Assessment Can Aid Entrepreneurs," in *Growing Concerns*, ed. D. E. Gumpert (New York: John Wiley & Sons, 1984), pp. 43–52.

Recall the several studies cited in Chapter 1 that indicated that the survival rate among the firms backed by venture capital was the inverse of the national averages for new firms. Nearly 65 percent to 80 percent or more of the firms backed by venture capital avoid failure, and 10–15 percent do exceedingly well by most standards. More significantly, data reported by Venture Economics, Inc., publisher of *Venture Capital Journal,* show that these venture capital firms must be doing something right: returns on investment of 25–30 percent after tax are the norm, with several of these firms reporting returns of 50 percent or more. Further, the "venture capital 100 index" of venture capital–backed companies that have gone public, reported by *Venture Capital Journal,* has outperformed the Dow-Jones average, the S&P 500, and the OTC market by multiples over the past decade.[2]

A study by Cooper and Bruno of 104 high-technology ventures launched in the 1960s reported that 83.3 percent of the high-growth companies (those achieving sales of $5 million or more annually) were launched by teams, while only 53.8 percent of the 73 discontinued companies had several founders.[3]

This pattern is apparent from an even more recent study by one of the authors, who traced the origins of what he calls the "Route 128 One Hundred," the top firms comprised by the so-called Route 128 new venture phenomenon in the greater Boston area, which has long been known as an entrepreneurial hotbed. Among these firms, annual sales of $16 million were averaged by those up to 5 years old, $49 million by those 6–10 years old, and several hundred million by the more mature ones.[4] It was found that *70 percent of these firms had multiple founders.* Among the 86 firms from which we gained founder information, 38 percent had three or more founders, 17 percent had four or more, and 9 percent had five or more. One firm was launched by a team of eight, which was the largest founding team. (We know of other founding teams this large.)

And, of course, there is a double message in these data. On the one hand, they confirm the notion that teams build substantial companies. On the other, the fact that 30 percent of these firms had single founders suggests that there is ample room for exceptional individual entrepreneurs to make a major difference. Yet, other studies have shown that lone founders are much less likely to build multimillion-dollar-plus ventures. We noted in Chapter 1, for instance, that in this country only about 1 firm in 30 exceeds $1 million in sales.

Finally, the quality of the management team is so important to venture capital investors that they have become more active than ever in helping to shape, and reshape, such teams. One recent study showed, that, in contrast with the 1970s, a significant shift toward such activity had occurred during the recent boom period in venture capital.[5] And a study to examine the nature of venture capital investing in highly innovative technical venture, funded by the National Science Foundation, revealed just how active this role could be.[6]

[2]Most libraries carry *Venture Capital Journal,* the leading industry publication, which is worth examining monthly for details on venture capital investing activity and current trends.

[3]Arnold C. Cooper and Albert V. Bruno, "Success among High Technology Firms," *Business Horizons,* April 1977, p. 20.

[4]Jeffry A. Timmons and Susan Skinner, research assistant, "The Route 128 One Hundred," working paper, Babson College, Wellesley, Massachusetts, 1984.

[5]Jeffry A. Timmons, "Discard Many Old Rules about Raising Venture Capital," in *Growing Concerns,* pp. 273–80.

[6]Jeffry A. Timmons, "Venture Capital: More than Money?" in *Pratt's Guide to Venture Capital Sources,* 8th ed. (Wellesley Hills, Mass.: Venture Economics, 1984), pp. 39–43.

7.3.2 Ventures Backed by Nonventure Capital

One might be quick to conclude that teams are only for firms seeking venture capital. The evidence above suggests otherwise. In addition, the mounting evidence of the loneliness, stress, and pressures that entrepreneurs face[7] argues that the right partner can often play a valuable role in any venture. The key, of course, is the "right" partner.

7.4 ENTREPRENEURIAL TEAM FORMATION

7.4.1 What It Means

The quote at the head of this chapter captures the gist of our view of the team. Our approach to the issue of whether, in fact, you need any team members at all—naturally, not all ventures do—and when they are needed is anchored in the framework originally shown in Exhibit 1.1. Exhibit 7.1 is a closeup of the driving forces that must be considered.

Exhibit 7.1
The Venture Team: What Is Needed?

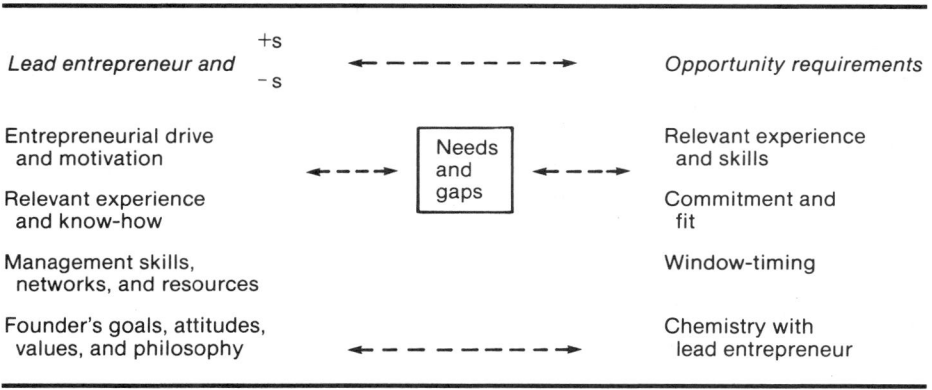

The need for a team depends entirely on the nature of the opportunity and on what the lead entrepreneur brings to the game. What does it take to execute the opportunity and achieve our goals? When is it needed? There are as many approaches to solving these issues as there are ventures with multiple founders. We know of no simple, cookbook solutions to team formation.

What we do know is that the combination of the right team of people can be a most powerful one. Ideally, the team is bound by a shared long-term commitment to growing a substantial business and realizing a capital gain. The whole is, in such instances, greater than the sum of the parts.

7.4.2 What It Does Not Mean

A word about what we do not mean by our emphasis on the new venture team. We do not mean that every venture must start with a full team, who all

---

[7]David Boyd and David Gumpert, "The Loneliness of the Entrepreneur," in *Frontiers in Entrepreneurship Research,* ed. J. A. Hornaday, J. A. Timmons, K. H. Vesper (Babson Park, Mass.: Babson College, 1983), pp. 476–87.

take the plunge into the business simultaneously. Nor do we mean that every venture needs a team or is destined for the new venture graveyard without one. Also, we do not mean that a team must be based on a love-in, friendship, and the like—even though these might help—that is cemented in equality, democracy, and identical participation in ownership of the venture. Finally, we do not envision teams that form like magic and live happily ever after, conflict free. We don't know of any such teams.

7.4.3 Not for Every Entrepreneur

We do recognize that the majority of entrepreneurs seem to prefer the solo venture, or may have acquired a distaste for partners. You may find that you are not a team player and that you do not wish to become one. In that case, a team-founded venture is not for you. We also recognize that some lead entrepreneurs can be happy only if they are in complete control: they want employees, not partners. Others simply do not want to give up control to outside investors, or anyone else for that matter.

Take, for instance, an entrepreneur whom we shall call Ed. Over 10 years ago he founded a high-technology firm that has grown steadily, but slowly, to nearly $2 million in sales. Recently, new patents and technological advances in fiber optics drew much interest from venture capitalists. Yet, he turned down more than one offer of up to $5 million in funding because the investors wanted to own 51 percent or more of his venture. Plainly and simply, he said: "I do not want to give up control of what I have worked so long and hard to create."

Finally, it may take some time for the team to come together as the firm grows. Again, the framework above focuses on the useful issues: What does the opportunity require, and when?

7.5 START-UP ISSUES

The central issues facing a start-up entrepreneur who is attempting to put a team together are simple enough: (1) Who will do and contribute what? (2) Who will own the company? and (3) Who will be paid what? In a subsequent section we will walk through the mechanics of a more "planned approach" that entrepreneurs can use to guide this process. First, there is the question of the climate, goals, and expectations for the new firm.

7.5.1 High Divorce Rate among Founders

At a recent Babson College seminar on "Raising Venture Capital," whose cosponsors were the *Venture Capital Journal* and Coopers, Lybrand, one of the nation's leading attorneys, Richard Testa, addressed an audience of entrepreneurs. Testa's firm deals with start-ups and high-potential ventures (among his clients are over 25 venture capital firms and numerous ventures, including Lotus Development of 1-2-3 fame). His opening comments startled many of the entrepreneurs present:

The only thing that I can tell you with great certainty about this start-up business has to do with you and your partners. I can virtually guarantee you, based on our decade plus of experience, that five years from now at least one of the founders will have left every company represented here today.

Clearly, the breakup of the founding team is a given in the hectic turmoil of start-up ventures today. So what can be done about it?

7.5.2 Establishing the Ground Rules

It is the lead entrepreneur's job to lead. The president sets the stage and ground rules and shapes the climate and culture of the venture. In the final analysis, all of the pressure and responsibility rests on the lead entrepreneur's shoulders. That is why the lead entrepreneur is generally paid substantially more than the number two person and generally owns the largest share of the company. At the Babson College venture capital seminar mentioned earlier, Bill Foster, founder and president of Stratus Computer, was asked whether he and his partners were all equal. His response was revealing: "Yes, we are, except I get paid the most and I own the most stock."

While there is no substitute for actually working together, there are several pre-start-up issues that can be dealt with constructively. For one thing, it is vital to make sure that there is a leader, a CEO, a president—rather than a democracy. Once that is clear—and if it is not, it is time to reconsider—it is essential to determine whether everyone is committed to the same goal. If you want to grow a high-potential venture, the goal is simple: realize a substantial capital gain in the next 5–10 years. All of the stock ownership incentives and rewards should be aimed at reinforcing this goal and its attainment. And if that is not your goal, fine, but do the founders know and agree on what they want out of the venture? In short, performance-based rewards work.

7.5.3 No-Fault Corporate Divorce

In recent years new mechanisms have emerged to foster this longer-term commitment to the success of the venture, while at the same time providing a method for a civilized, "no-fault" corporate divorce. The mechanism used in start-ups is a stock vesting agreement that is attached as a restriction on the "unregistered" stock certificate. Typically, the vesting agreement establishes a period of years, often four or more. During this period the founding stockholders can "earn out" their shares. If a founder decides to leave the company prior to completion of the four-year vesting period, he or she may be required to sell the stock back to the company for the price that was originally paid for it, usually nil. In this instance, the departing shareholder would not own any stock after the departure. Nor would any capital gain windfall be realized by the departing founder. In other cases, founders may vest a certain portion each year, so that they have some shares even if they leave. Such vesting can be weighted toward the last year or two of the vesting period.

Other common restrictions on such "unregistered" stock give management and the board control over the disposition of any of this stock, whether or not the stockholder—founder or key employee—stays with or leaves the company. In effect, the founders and board have to approve the sale of the stock, the terms, and the buyer. This, of course, is generally in the interest of the founders and any outside investors. (See Chapters 15 and 16 for more details on recent changes in the law affecting founders' stock.

In essence, this mechanism confronts the founder-shareholder with the reality that the venture is not a "get rich quick" exercise. Anyone who considers joining the venture will have to take it seriously and be highly committed in order to accept such terms. And for the lead entrepreneur, such requirements can begin to weed out any prospects who lack the appropriate motivation and commitment. Further, requirements of this kind preclude the possibility that the new company will be exploited by a departing shareholder who seeks an outrageous price for his or her stock or, failing to come to terms, resorts to litigation.

Indeed, the unregistered stock mechanism says that you must be prepared to invest several years or more of your intense commitment if you expect to realize a gain. Further, it communicates that no windfall will be realized by temporary partners who have a weak commitment to the venture. In other words, you cannot, as an owner of, say, 10–20 percent or more of the company, leave after a year or so and still keep the stock. The mechanism prevents founders who depart early from sharing in a future capital gain that, in reality, they contributed very little to. Finally, it bases the reward structure exactly where it should be based: on successfully building the business and realizing a capital gain. That necessitates a long-term, serious commitment. And unless all of the founders are convinced that the venture is really going to succeed, these vesting realities may cause them to think twice and to abandon what might otherwise become another marginal venture, loaded with personal loan guarantees, that is not likely to be harvested.

7.5.4 A Word about Trust

Trust raises another of the many paradoxes of entrepreneurship. In the ethics chapter (Chapter 9) and elsewhere we have stressed the importance of integrity in long-term business success. Integrity works, and we believe in it and practice it ourselves. Yet, anyone who knows how things work in the real world is very much aware that it is full of predators, crooks, sharks, frauds, and imposters. Call it "hardball," or what have you. The truth of the matter is that you cannot succeed without trust but that you probably cannot succeed with just blind or naive trust either.

Trust is something that is earned, usually slowly, for it requires a lot of real-world testing. And for the most part, it does not get tested very often, fortunately. This is undoubtedly a major reason why investors prefer to see a team that has worked closely together, that has enjoyed the "breathtaking highlands of success" and walked the "deep, dark canyons of uncertainty" and setbacks together. It is also a major reason why investors are so sensitive to any questionable integrity or ethical practices.

While it may take several years to build solid trust, one thoughtless incident can shatter what is otherwise a good foundation. So what do you do? Work hard at earning and building it, and work even harder to preserve it once you have it. When you have found a partner with whom you share trust, as in a good marriage, you have found something that is invaluable, that no money can buy. Hold on to that partner dearly. Have patience: it takes more than a few weeks or months for most relationships to develop trust. Rely on your instincts and your gut feel: if you, or your spouse or partners, don't feel right about a person, back off or find a way out.

As for outsiders and new relationships, a little cynicism can go a long way. Why proceed blindly and naively? Have you signed agreements, documents, or other contractual obligations without doing your own "due diligence" on the person or firm? If those commitments and obligations turn out to be sour or downright disastrous, have you arranged to protect yourself? Unfortunately, there are more than enough predators out there, just waiting for the innocent with blind trust. If you are unprepared and unprotected, in all likelihood you will become their victim. Unless you do the homework, and digest the details *yourself,* you may be guilty of blind trust that could be costly. Consider the following example.

A young entrepreneur was extremely busy building his part of an international computer-related business. His attorney suggested that he look at a tax-sheltered real estate investment. Not having the time himself, he trusted the attorney, since the attorney had done satisfactory work for him previously and was one of the general partners of the deal. He also reasoned that since he was now earning in excess of $100,000 a year, at age 30, it was time to get other professionals to help him manage his money. After all, his time was better spent on building the business and making money. He never thoroughly read and analyzed the prospectus on the deal. He claimed that it would not have mattered even if he had: he trusted the attorney.

Sadly, the tale does not end happily. The young entrepreneur is likely to lose all, or most, of his $150,000 investment in the deal. His attorney is embroiled in numerous suits for mismanagement of the general partnership. The young entrepreneur and the other limited partners will sue the attorney for malpractice, among other things. With hindsight, of course, it is clear that a little patience and cynicism might have gone a long way.

7.6 PLANNED APPROACH TO TEAM FORMATION

The planned approach to team formation that we advocate grew out of our frustration with the poor success rate of ventures using what, for want of a better term, we shall call the "natural approach."

The formation of new venture teams seems to be a rather idiosyncratic phenomenon. There seem to be a multitude of ways in which venture partners come together. Some teams form by accidents of geography and common interest, others by virtue of past friendships. Some teams form simply because they want to start a business while others have an idea that they feel responds to a market need. Few teams seem to have exactly the same gestation process. Yet, in general, two distinct patterns are identifiable. First, one person has an idea or simply wants to start a business. Then up to three or four associates join this lead entrepreneur as the venture takes form. In the second mode, an entire team, or partnership, forms from the outset based on a shared idea, friendship, experience, or a host of other related factors. These two patterns seem to represent the two principal *natural* processes of team formation.

What becomes of these teams? One study indicates that about 95 percent of the venture teams seeking venture capital never get off the ground.[8] They usually exhaust their own resources, and their commitment, prior to raising the venture capital necessary to launch the venture. Of the ventures that are funded, about 1 in 20 will become very successful in three to five years. Success to the investor

---

[8] *Venture Capital: What It Is and How to Raise It,* based on a report by Frederick E. Finkenauer and Clifton H. W. Maloney, submitted in partial fulfillment of MBA degree requirements, 1965. © 1967 by the President and Fellows of Harvard College.

means a return roughly in excess of five times the original investment in realizable capital gains. Clearly, the odds for a highly successful venture are rather thin. And even if the venture survives, the turnover among team members during the early years probably exceeds the national divorce rate.[9]

It seems that these odds against success, and in favor of venture team "divorces," are largely a result of the *natural* team formation and development process just described. Ironically, a substantial amount of thought usually accompanies the decision of people to go into business together. Yet, an overabundance of the thinking focuses on less critical issues, such as title and corporate name and letterhead, or is misguided, focusing on such matters as what kind of lawyer or accountant is needed, both approaches resulting in poor team formation. Thus, such teams are often ill-conceived from the outset and can easily plunge headlong into unanticipated and unplanned responses to crises, conflicts, and changes.

Fortunately for aspiring entrepreneurs, this formation process need not focus on less critical issues or be misguided. Several fundamental issues can be considered systematically to make team formation and development a more organized, carefully thought-out process. This planned process can assist the new venture team to identify its personnel needs in a methodical way and to do a significantly better job of anticipating and dealing with inevitable crises and conflicts in the early life cycle of the new business. Granted, this distinction between a *natural* process and a *planned* process is a simplistic one, but it is hoped that the focus here may clarify the critical elements and supplement the intuitive approaches that entrepreneurs often rely on.

In evidence, we offer two examples of entrepreneurial teams we have worked with that took advantage of the planned approach in two critical areas: team building and team interaction.

Three technical men formed a company to manufacture unique gold-plating equipment. The existing business had modest annual sales of less than $200,000 and showed little capacity to grow rapidly. Working with us during 1973, the members of the founding team concluded that much of the problem with their company was them! Subsequently, they found a fourth partner with key entrepreneurial skills that they lacked. Nine months later they reported that sales were up to 60 percent and profits were up by 500 percent, with the result that earnings per share had doubled.

And a new kayak manufacturer launched operations in late 1973, aiming for first-year sales of about one-half million dollars. By spring of 1974 shortages spawned by the energy crisis contributed to the difficulties in the way the members of the team were working together. Rather than sweeping these potentially embarrassing but commonly encountered start-up strains under the rug, they recognized the difficulties and sought outside help.

Most of the principles and concepts underlying these approaches are not new. They have found their way into several innovative educational career develop-

---

[9]Note that the Finkenauer and Maloney study did not include smaller businesses, sole proprietorships, small franchises, etc. Its conclusions apply to higher-potential, growth-oriented ventures attempting to raise outside venture capital. Any entrepreneur aspiring to build a substantial, small company will eventually need to consider these team issues.

Exhibit 7.2
A Conceptual Framework for Venture Team Formation: Diagram for Discussion

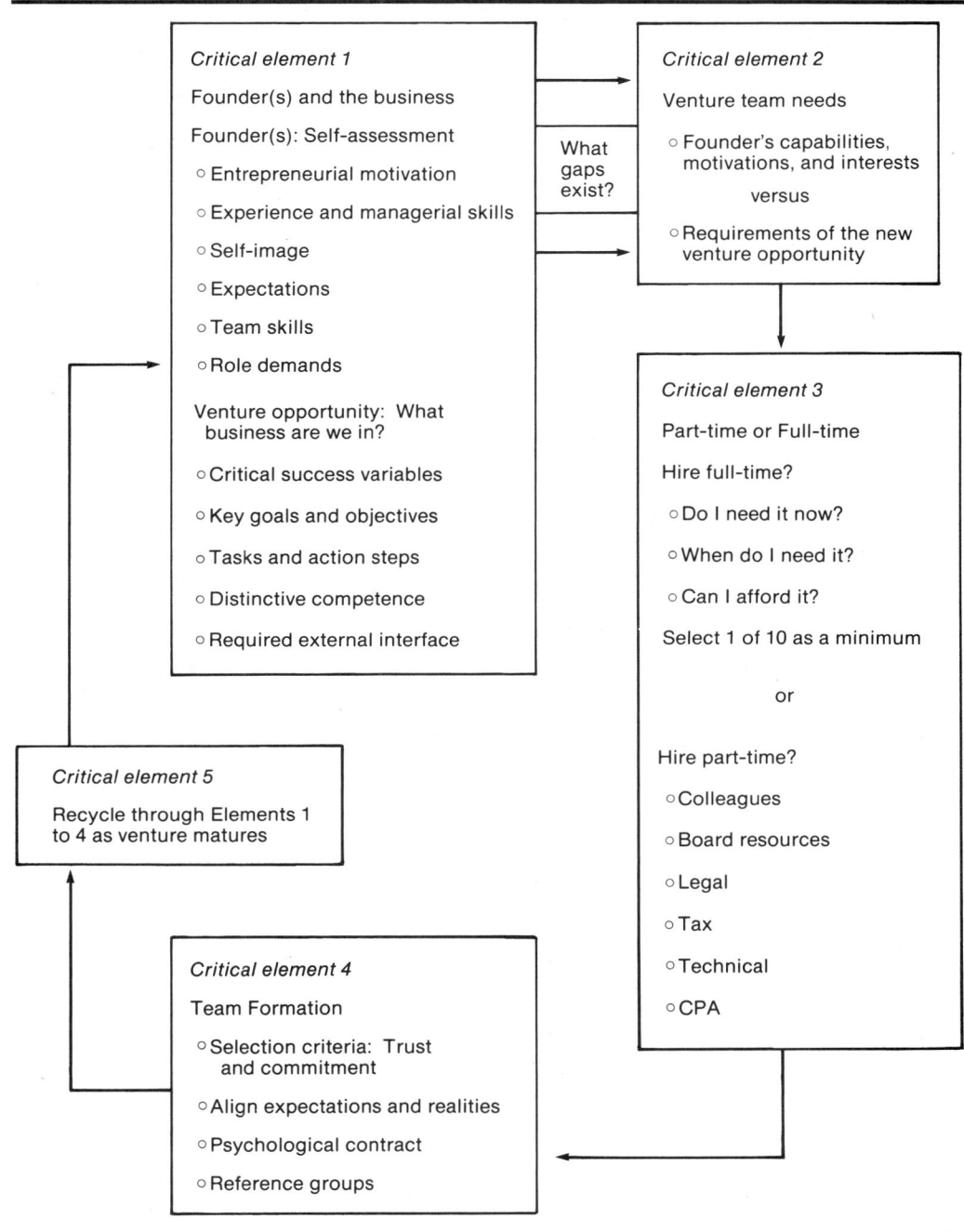

Critical element 1

Founder(s) and the business

Founder(s): Self-assessment

○ Entrepreneurial motivation

○ Experience and managerial skills

○ Self-image

○ Expectations

○ Team skills

○ Role demands

Venture opportunity: What business are we in?

○ Critical success variables

○ Key goals and objectives

○ Tasks and action steps

○ Distinctive competence

○ Required external interface

What gaps exist?

Critical element 2

Venture team needs

○ Founder's capabilities, motivations, and interests

versus

○ Requirements of the new venture opportunity

Critical element 3

Part-time or Full-time

Hire full-time?

○ Do I need it now?

○ When do I need it?

○ Can I afford it?

Select 1 of 10 as a minimum

or

Hire part-time?

○ Colleagues

○ Board resources

○ Legal

○ Tax

○ Technical

○ CPA

Critical element 5

Recycle through Elements 1 to 4 as venture matures

Critical element 4

Team Formation

○ Selection criteria: Trust and commitment

○ Align expectations and realities

○ Psychological contract

○ Reference groups

ment and managerial assessment programs in recent years.[10] However, their specific application to the practice of entrepreneurship is unique.[11]

What follows is a discussion of planned team formation. The conceptual diagram, Exhibit 7.2, should be referred to as each of the five critical elements is discussed.

7.7 CRITICAL ELEMENT ONE: THE FOUNDER AND THE BUSINESS

It is critical to the success of a venture that the founder understand *how* he or she decided to become an entrepreneur and *why* he or she chose the particular business. If we run the risk of redundancy on this topic, it is only because we have seen so many failed ventures that ignored these issues.

7.7.1 Self-Assessment: An Essential Early Task

The material that you have already completed should have given you some insight into your motivations and goals and into what will be demanded of you. By now you should understand more fully the following questions:

1. *Entrepreneurial Motivation:* What are my goals? What is the nature of my commitment? What kind of a risk taker am I? How do I deal with failure? What are my motivations? How do I utilize feedback and seek needed help?
2. *Self-Image and Expectations:* Who am I? What are my expectations and aspirations? What are my family's expectations? What sacrifices are we prepared to make? What lifestyle and values are especially important to me? What about my family?
3. *Role Demands:* What is required of the entrepreneur's job? What does the entrepreneur have to put up with? Are there special demands unique to my venture and industry? Who will do what tasks?

In addition, you should have a realistic idea of what skills you possess, and how they will contribute to the venture. An exercise that appears later in this chapter will help you to answer the following questions:

1. *Expertise and Management Skills:* What is my track record? What are my strengths and weaknesses? What things do I do extremely well—negotiating, marketing, finance, applying technical know-how, or managing people? What do I need to learn? How do others size me up in terms of maturity?
2. *Team Skills:* What interpersonal skills do I have? How do I deal with and resolve differences? How do I feel about teamwork? How do others react to me as a team leader?

7.7.2 Analysis of the Business

Whether the entrepreneur already has an idea or is searching for one, analysis of the potential venture is a critical early need. The fundamental question

---

[10]For example, the work of D. A. Kolb, I. M. Rubin, and J. M. McIntyre, of MIT's Sloan School, *Organizational Psychology: An Experiential Approach*, 2d ed. (Englewood Cliffs, N.J.: Prentice-Hall, 1974); and Ann Howard, "An Assessment of Assessment Centers," *Academy of Management Journal* 17, no. 1 (March 1974), pp. 115–34.

[11]Jeffry A. Timmons, "The Entrepreneurial Team," *Journal of Small Business Management*, October 1975, pp. 36–37.

"What business are we in?" is often neglected. Thorough analysis of at least five key areas helps to sharpen the focus on the fledgling firm's current status and future direction. Furthermore, knowledgeable and articulate treatment of these items is essential for acquiring venture capital. The Opportunity Screening Guide exercise in Chapter 4 should have enabled you to answer the following questions:

1. *Critical Success Variables:* Every industry has ingredients that are critical to success, "absolute musts" if one is to compete at all. Identifying what appear to be the critical success variables in the industry has significant implications for team selection and the ultimate success of the venture.
2. *Goals and Objectives:* What are the most important goals for the first two to three years of the business? These goals may be financial and nonfinancial in nature. Have they been articulated in a specific, measurable, time-phased, and realistic manner?
3. *Tasks and Action Steps:* What key tasks and activities are needed to accomplish the most important goals? Clearly, many areas will be difficult to specify, but more detail is better than less.
4. *Distinctive Competencies:* Ventures usually prosper because they provide a unique product or service or because they secure a market niche. What things will differentiate the venture from its competition?
5. *Required External Interfaces:* Relating the venture effectively to its external environment—technologies, markets, banks, institutions—is required for its survival and growth.[12] What are the venture's critical external relationships, such as lawyers, bankers, customers, suppliers, and regulatory agencies?[13]

Although, by definition, there will be few precise answers to these questions during the early gestation of the venture, best estimates must be developed. Answers to these questions provide important background information for analyzing the needs for an entrepreneurial team.

7.8 CRITICAL ELEMENT TWO: VENTURE TEAM NEEDS

In analyzing the nature of the business, the potential entrepreneur will find that detailed thinking about the business often triggers additional insights into one's own capabilities: What can I do well? What do I want to do? How much time will I have? What are the priorities of tasks? In short, this analysis should attempt to identify the founder's capabilities and limitations and how they match with the requirements of the venture.

7.8.1 Identification of Gaps

What does the venture need in terms of skills and capabilities beyond what the founder brings to it? In a start-up situation the entrepreneur usually wears many hats. To begin with, the more he can personally manage, the better. The nature and demands of the venture will tend to dictate what specific resources are needed. If the founder's strengths, experiences, and preferences do not match most

---

[12]The work of Paul R. Lawrence and Jay W. Lorsch, *Organization and Environment* (Boston: Harvard Business School Division of Research, 1967), documents their research and that of others on this topic.

[13]See Gordon B. Baty, *Entrepreneurship: Playing to Win* (Reston, Va.: Reston Publishing, 1974), chaps. 12, 13, 14, 19, and 23.

of the key tasks and critical variables identified in the analysis of the business, it is probably wise to abort the venture, or at least to thoroughly reappraise it. Certainly, if the founder does not have the needed capabilities, or cannot acquire them in the appropriate time, then someone on the venture team must have them. It is most advantageous for the person-in-charge to know the business thoroughly. In fact, some earlier research in India by McClelland[14] and the work of one of the authors with entrepreneurs in this country[15] suggest that the successful entrepreneurs build on their strengths and former experience, rather than change fields.

In short, it is very difficult to argue that there is any "one best way" to start a business. What seems to be essential is that the founder know the business thoroughly and be committed to the venture's success. Whether the founder's personal strengths are of a technical or managerial nature, or whether the founder's focus is on daily operations or long-term development, other team members must fill the gaps.

7.9 CRITICAL ELEMENT THREE: PART-TIME, FULL-TIME, OR WHAT?

The identification of skills and resource gaps in Critical Element Two is a prerequisite to analysis of whether the venture should hire full-time or part-time or obtain professional services capabilities. The questions that have to be asked are straightforward. The answers are not always self-evident.

First, given the gaps determined in Critical Element Two, specifically what resources does the venture need, in addition to the founder? Second, are these needed now, and are all of them needed? And are they needed five days per week or less? This analysis will require some review of Critical Element One and the priorities now emerging. Third, can the business afford them? Initially, it is uaually best to obtain tax and legal expertise part-time and to obtain some special expertise (e.g., design of an inventory control system) on a one-time basis. Generally, if the resource is required for a onetime or periodic effort, or is peripheral to the key tasks, goals, and activities required by the business in Critical Element One, then the part-time alternative makes sense.

However, if certain expertise is a must for the venture at the outset and the founder cannot provide it, or acquire it soon enough, then one or more people will have to be hired. In essence, new team members should complement, not duplicate, the founder's capabilities. Realistically, there will be overlapping and shared responsibilities. Indeed, most new ventures defy simple categorization such as that implied by a formal organization chart.

The high levels of uncertainty and the very rapid rates of change that characterize the start-up of a new venture require a fluid and highly adaptive form of organization. Such an organization may appear quite amorphous to a manager or engineer accustomed to more highly structured large companies. But an organization that can respond quickly and effectively is a must in the heat of start-up. Moreover, personnel is too scarce and too critical in the new venture to encourage the luxury of duplicated managerial skills.

[14]D. C. McClelland and D. Winter, *Motivating Economic Achievement* (New York: Free Press, 1969).

[15]Jeffry A. Timmons, "Black Is Beautiful—Is It Bountiful?" *Harvard Business Review*, November–December 1971.

7.10 CRITICAL ELEMENT FOUR: TEAM FORMATION—
COURTSHIP, MARRIAGE, A FAMILY

Marriage, with all of its complexities and consequences, is a particularly useful analogy for examining the process of forming an entrepreneurial team. Forming a venture team has many of the characteristics of the courtship and marriage ritual. It involves decisions based in part on emotions and "gut feel." There may well be a certain infatuation among partners, as well as admiration, respect, and even fierce loyalty. Similarly, the complex psychological joys, frustrations, and uncertainties that accompany most normal marriages are also experienced in entrepreneurial teams. For instance, will the new product have a successful introduction (birth)? will it be healthy and grow? will we have more products (children)? will we survive the strains of raising them?

Thus, the choice of partners involves crucial decisions. Granted the prime significance of team selection and formation, it may be helpful to examine some criteria for making these very difficult selection decisions and for approaching team formation on a systematic basis. In addition, hands-on experience in team formation is provided in the last section of this chapter.

7.10.1 Selection Criteria

Like most organizations, new ventures will thrive or wither depending on how well the management team works together. Venture capitalists attach great importance to their assessment of the team's ability to work with the investors. The implications of a poor matchup are clear: the venture begins on a shaky foundation and probably will not make it. Consequently, it is critical to the health of the venture that the team be well formed in terms of psychological and interpersonal factors.

During the early gestation of a venture the founder has a unique opportunity to screen potential partners and to calibrate their commitment, trust, and capabilities. Such an opportunity is provided by the "moonlighting phase" of most start-ups. (Here again, overanxiousness "to do, not talk," and aggressive enthusiasm can be detrimental to the formation of a solid team.) The founder and some selected partners may work together on a business plan, develop a prototype, and actually begin forming a corporation, issuing stock, and working full-time. Indeed, this moonlighting phase can provide a very useful shakedown period for the team and can enable the founder to test the commitment and actual contribution of team members, so that the risks inherent in premature commitment to permanent decisions regarding salary and stock are relatively lower.[16]

To build a substantial business, a partner must be totally committed to the venture and must be totally immersed in it. The success of the venture must be the partner's most important goal. Other priorities, including the partner's family, must come second.[17] Whether such a total immersion commitment exists can be observed during the moonlighting phase and determined through role-playing

[16]The authors are indebted to Mr. Brian Haslett of the Institute for New Enterprise Development for his insightful clarification of this important point.

[17]See, for example, Edgar H. Schein's ongoing research about MIT alumni entrepreneurs, general managers, and technical managers in the proceedings of the Eastern Academy of Management meeting, May 1972, Boston.

with team members. The indicators will include their reactions to such things as heavy workloads, travel, and other possible sacrifices. However, the ultimate test is whether partners are prepared to invest their own money and take the full-time plunge.

Practically speaking, these evaluations are among the most difficult that must be made. There will always be some doubt, a hope for more than the prospective partner can deliver, and there will be a constant recalibration. Eventually, the choice must be made, and the tests of time and working together should prevail over infatuation and premature judgments.

The preparation of the business plan provides an excellent vehicle for zeroing in on exactly who is likely and able to contribute what.

7.10.2   Align Expectations and Realities

If a rigorous analysis has been done in Critical Elements One through Three, this task will be less arduous than it might otherwise be. As noted previously, team members must complement the founder's strengths. This involves identifying potential fits between responsibilities and the tasks to be performed and each person's expertise and capabilities. Diligent efforts should be made to determine who has what responsibility for key tasks and problems during start-up. Such roles cannot be precisely pinned down for all tasks, since some key tasks and problems cannot be anticipated and the actual contributions are not always made by the people who are originally expected to make them. Indeed, maintaining a loose structure with shared responsibility and information is probably desirable for flexibility, rapid learning, and responsive decision making. Therefore, some flexibility must be left for reviewing and revising assigned responsibilities. Often, outside advisers and board members can provide useful insights into this ongoing endeavor. Each team member will usually wear several hats, but the keys seem to be: (*a*) minimize unnecessary duplication of capability or responsibility; (*b*) have team members in the roles or jobs that they are most comfortable with; and (*c*) allow team members to share or even rotate responsibility. The net effect of this approach is to encourage informal sharing of problems and information, while utilizing the strengths of each individual. In addition, this flexibility tends to enable individuals to fill problem vacuums and to respond quickly to changing needs and demands.

One area that can easily be overlooked is the risk-taking orientation of the team as a whole. Successful entrepreneurs appear to be calculated risk takers[18] and risk reducers, and some teams have found it helpful to have a more conservative, lower-risk-taking person on the team. The caution of such a person can help to offset the tendency of overly optimistic and competitive team members to overlook certain dangers, or to overestimate the likelihood of certain gains, as in unduly optimistic sales forecasts. Moreover, setting goals jointly in quantifiable terms helps to clarify the nature of the risks faced.

Before and during the moonlighting phase it is important to encourage each prospective team member to engage in self-assessment similar to that outlined in

---

[18]McClelland and Winter, *Motivating Economic Achievement,* defines moderate risk as in the vicinity of 50–50, rather than a 1 in 100 chance (high risk) or a 99 in 100 chance (low risk). The achievement-motivated entrepreneurial type prefers the challenge and satisfaction of winning with some control over the outcomes, and thus prefers moderate risk.

Critical Element One. Such assessments can provide valuable inputs to the evaluation and trust-building process. Deeper understanding of the individual's personal, life, and family goals and values can greatly facilitate an evaluation of trustworthiness, commitment, and capabilities.

Perhaps most crucial in the team formation process is the creation of realistic expectations for new team members. The founder can be highly influential in helping to establish a viable psychological contract and a climate of trust and straightforwardness. Moreover, by an example of total immersion the founder can encourage greater commitment, higher standards of excellence, and mutual respect among the team members.

7.10.3 Reference Groups and Potential Partners

One easily overlooked aspect of the team creation process is the entrepreneur's source of social and psychological support and reinforcement. Reference groups—groups consisting of individuals with whom there is frequent interaction (family, friends, co-workers), with whom values and interests are shared, and from whom support and approval for activities are derived—have long been known for their influence on behavior.[19] Decisions of all sorts are influenced by the opinions of those persons who are sought for advice, and whose feedback is respected, on such issues as the choice of a college, the choice of a career, and involvement in community affairs. The entrepreneur leads a lonely existence, so that the acceptance or rejection of his career choice by his reference group can have an appreciable effect on his long-term commitment. Although the answers to the following questions will take time to gather, the following basics are worth noting when assessing a prospective team member.

1. Does the spouse think that entrepreneurship is a great idea, and is he or she behind the entrepreneur 100 percent? If no other sources of capital are available and the venture needs additional capital, would a second mortgage on the house be tolerable?

2. Does the spouse accept the "sweat equity" required during the moonlighting phase? Or is he or she reluctant at best or, at worst, downright cynical? The entrepreneur who lacks the support of the spouse and family faces heavy psychological burdens alone and may not have the sustained commitment that is needed when adversity strikes.

3. What about close friends, the people with whom the entrepreneur socializes and enjoys leisure time? How do they feel about someone crazy enough to give up "the good life," risk life savings, and start his or her own business? Again, are such reference group members a source of support and encouragement, or of detraction and negativism?

B. F. Skinner has made us very aware of the power of positive reinforcement in shaping behavior.[20] Reference group approval can be a significant source of positive reinforcement for a person's career choice, and thus for his or her entire self-image, ego, and identity. Indeed, the entrepreneur needs all the help available!

[19] See, for examples, John W. Thibault and Harold H. Kelley, *The Social Psychology of Groups* (New York: John Wiley & Sons, 1966).

[20] See interview with Skinner, *Psychology Today,* December 1972; and B. F. Skinner, *Beyond Freedom and Dignity* (New York: Alfred A. Knopf, 1971).

Knowing something about a prospective team member's reference groups can provide useful insights into the reality and legitimacy of the entrepreneur's own commitment. Ideally, the support for a decision should be there, and if it is not, the founder may have to accept the additional burden of encouraging and supporting the prospective team member in hard times. This burden can be sizable. Granted, the necessary information is very difficult to obtain, and working with a prospective partner for six months or more is clearly more useful than investing precious hours at the outset in attempting to obtain it.

7.11 CRITICAL ELEMENT FIVE: RECYCLE

As noted previously, the task of selecting and building a team is continual. Constant and rapid changes during start-up and the difficult early going require perpetual vigil over the progress and problems of the team. The short fuse of survival has a low tolerance for the sluggishness or ineffectiveness of any member of the team.

7.11.1 In Summary

We have explored the team formation issue. During the part-time moonlighting phase prior to the full-time commitment, several critical elements should be considered.

1. A planned process, rather than a natural evolution, can reduce the chances of failure.
2. The founder or founders should begin with self-assessment in terms of:
    a. Entrepreneurial orientation.
    b. Self-image and expectations.
    c. Expertise and management skills.
    d. Team skills.
3. Analysis of the business is needed to determine what skills and expertise it requires in terms of:
    a. The major goals from start-up through the first three years.
    b. The key tasks and action steps.
    c. The requisites for success.
    d. The firm's distinctive competencies.
    e. The required external interfaces.
4. Comparison of the needs of the venture with the founder's inventory of capabilities will help to identify needs for other team members or outside resources.
5. The formation of a team is like a marriage—it should be approached with great care and thought.
    a. Partners should be picked as one would pick an ideal spouse, and they should complement the founder's personal and business strengths.
    b. A prospective partner's trust and commitment should be carefully calibrated.
    c. Aligning a new team member's expectations with the realities of start-up is crucial, and should begin prior to actual hiring.
    d. Supportive reference groups can facilitate the total immersion of a prospective team member.

Our focus has been on developing a framework for easing the burden of team formation and development. Obviously, it is very time-consuming and demanding to work through each step. Indeed, the impatience of most entrepreneurs would not tolerate a long, drawn-out process. In fact, some entrepreneurs might handle these issues on an intuitive basis and do quite well. But for the impatient, it is cautioned that each of these elements needs to be considered carefully during the preparation of the business plan and the early life of the venture. The order, emphasis, and effort allocation need not match precisely the framework presented here, but to ignore these issues invites eventual disaster. For the patient and careful founder, this framework should help in the analysis of the relevant issues and serve as an aid to individual decision making. And the payoff for creating a highly effective team from the outset can be very substantial.

Finally, our focus here has been on the pre-start-up and early start-up phases of the venture. As a venture matures, the needs, demands, and requirements of the business change. Continual review of each of the critical elements (see Exhibit 7.2) is therefore appropriate.

7.12 TEAM-BUILDING CONCEPTS[21]

The critical ingredients in team building and team formation previously described lay the foundation for a new venture team. Laying this foundation is a continuous process since the requirements of the venture for managerial and entrepreneurial talent change over time. The distinctions between forming and building the team are conceptual since in practice the two overlap. Indeed, it is never too early to begin conscious team-building efforts. The following is an attempt to summarize some ingredients in building team effectiveness. The priorities and skills relevant for the founder or venture manager will be presented in detail.

7.12.1 Three Critical Ingredients

The complex needs and demands of a start-up situation evolve constantly and rapidly. It is nearly impossible to anticipate all of them. Yet, useful concepts for building effective venture teamwork have been provided by research, experience, and practical observations with regard to:

1. Organizational climate.
2. Teamwork and interpersonal skills.
3. Helping skills.

The cumulative effect of managing each of these areas well is to create psychological contracts, realistic expectations, and trust among the venture partners. Clearly, interpersonal skills and psychological strengths and weaknesses tend to govern this dynamic process.

7.12.2 Organizational Climate

For several years now one of the authors and two colleagues have been developing and using the concept of organizational climate to study performance in

[21]Based in part on Jeffry A. Timmons, "The Entrepreneurial Team: Formation and Development," a competitive paper presented at the Annual Meeting of the Academy of Management, Boston, August 1973.

large business organizations.[22] A number of completed studies have led us to three general conclusions:

1. The "climate" of an organization (the perceptions that people have as to the kind of place it is to work in) can have a significant impact on performance.
2. Climate is created both by the expectations people bring to the organization and by the practices and attitudes of the key managers.
3. Managers can manage in ways that create climates conducive to high performance or climates that foster mediocrity or doom.

The climate construct has relevance for new ventures as well. Instructions on climate were included in an early entrepreneurial training program that was well received by prospective entrepreneurs.[23] What, then, should venture founders know about organizational climate, and how can this knowledge contribute to effective team building?

An entrepreneur's style and priorities—particularly, how the entrepreneur manages tasks and people—are well known to the people being managed. They can describe their perceptions of what it is like to work for their manager. They sense, for example, whether there is pressure for high performance standards or whether it is possible to get by with "a pretty good job." They also know whether they are recognized for a job well done or are simply punished for their mistakes; or whether there is an esprit de corps, whether people work well together in their organization. Our research has developed interview guides and questionnaires for measuring perceptions of specific dimensions of organizational climate. This growing body of knowledge can be translated for use in a venture start-up and can contribute significantly to the development of an effective high-performing entrepreneurial team. Before discussing how this managerial tool can be applied to new venture teams, some background should be helpful.

In the course of our investigations we have identified the following six basic dimensions of organizational climate:

Clarity: The degree to which the organization is well organized, concise, and efficient in the way tasks, procedures, and assignments are made and accomplished.

Standards: The degree to which management expects excellent performance and puts pressure on employees to achieve it.

Commitment: The extent to which employees feel committed to the goals and objectives of the organization.

Responsibility: The extent to which members of the organization feel individual responsibility for accomplishing their goals without being constantly monitored and second-guessed.

Recognition: The extent to which employees feel that they are recognized and rewarded in a nonmonetary sense for a job well done, instead of only being punished for mistakes or errors.

---

[22]We are indebted to Jeffry A. Timmons and his colleagues Dr. George H. Litwin and Dr. Stevan K. Trooboff for allowing us to make use of the research findings reported in their as yet unpublished manuscript, "Organizational Climate: The Environments That Shape Our Lives."

[23]Timmons, "Black Is Beautiful."

Teamwork: The extent to which employees feel a sense of cohesion and team spirit, a sense of working well together.

In short, entrepreneurs who are able to create subordinate and colleague perceptions that each of these elements is "high" tend to attain high levels of performance. The founder of a venture can have significant impact on team effectiveness and venture performance by the extent to which he or she succeeds in creating a high-performance climate. Exhibit 7.3 suggests some specific management practices and how they affect an organization's climate. In essence, this exhibit suggests areas of emphasis for building a high-performance climate.

Exhibit 7.3
Relations between Climate Dimensions and Management Practices

Management Practices	*Climate Dimension*
Goal setting, task and project assignment, problem solving, informal interaction	Clarity
Goal setting, individual and group meetings regarding standards, provision of feedback	Standards
Goal setting, task and project assignment, problem solving, informal interaction	Commitment
Individual and group meetings, provision of feedback	Responsibility
Task and project assignment, group meetings, provision of feedback, informal interaction	Recognition
Task and project assignment, group meetings, provision of feedback, informal interaction	Teamwork

Our research suggests that each of the six climate dimensions is important for high performance. Exhibit 7.3 can assist the venture founder or key manager in diagnosing management practice and in planning priorities and emphases to create a positive climate. In addition, it is helpful to examine the general impact of the climate dimensions on the organization's performance and health, since presumably they may not all have equal priority for the venture team. Exhibit 7.4 summarizes these relationships as we know them at this time.

As can readily be seen, changes over time in the competitive demands and requirements of the venture can alter the required emphasis on each climate dimension. This framework provides a general guide for dealing with the critical team-building concept called climate.

Exhibit 7.4
Impact of Organizational Climate Dimensions on Venture Performance and Health

Climate Dimension	*Impact on Performance and Health of the Venture*
Clarity ⟶	Adaptation
Standards ⟶	Profit performance and ROI
Commitment ⟶	Growth performance
Responsibility ⟶	} Individual development
Recognition ⟶	
Teamwork ⟶	Group cohesion

7.12.3 Teamwork and Interpersonal Skills

Most of us have had an unpleasant experience with another person—for example, a salesclerk or a waiter—about which we later remarked, "It wasn't so much what he or she said that blew my stack, but rather how it was said." This section will deal with some of such important "process" issues of teamwork—some of the knowledge about how groups work well together that can be applied to managing a venture team.

Actually, more useful research has been done about team effectiveness than about most other aspects of team formation and development.[24] There are some known characteristics that distinguish effective from ineffective performance in the ways teams operate in accomplishing a task. Some team "survival" exercises in particular have been helpful in adding to this knowledge. These exercises tend to support later research findings on effective team-building behaviors.[25] It is a problem-solving exercise in which individuals rank survival items in order of their importance for survival on the moon, first by themselves and then as a team. Having used the exercise over the past decade with several hundred teams, including prospective new venture teams, we have seen several important lessons emerge. Almost invariably, most of the differences between high- and low-performing teams (as measured against astronauts' rankings) can be accounted for by the process and interpersonal skills evident in the teams. Basically, the evidence suggests that superior teams operate differently in terms of listening and participation, roles performed by team members, resolving leadership issues, using team resources, dealing with disagreements, setting priorities, and establishing a climate. This evidence is relevant to many of the problem-solving, decision-making situations experienced by venture teams. Furthermore, the desirable practices of the superior teams can be learned and utilized by venture founders and team members to facilitate joint problem solving. Exhibit 7.5 summarizes and contrasts these team process characteristics for effective and ineffective performance. Other factors might be added, but those listed appear to be the essential ones. A study of these factors and the effective behavioral practices can serve as a framework for reviewing and improving venture teamwork skills. It should also become evident that these skills or orientations might also be sought when selecting venture team members. Ideally, technical or managerial competence should be accompanied by a capacity to work well with a team.

Two additional factors can also have a significant impact on teamwork. First, as was noted earlier, trust is essential. Second, the entire teamwork process can be facilitated by the compatibility of team members, especially with regard to goals, values, commitment, lifestyles, and work styles. As has been noted, venture aims generally reflect the values and personal needs of the founder and key members. These may relate to such factors as profitability or equity growth, or may place greater emphasis on employment and environmental integrity, traded off against profit maximization. The point is, of course, that the greater the sources of conflict over philosophical issues, which tend to be extremely time-consuming and exhausting to resolve, the more energy is directed away from the primary aims of the venture. Such differences can erode the very foundations of teamwork.

[24]See, for example, R. Likert, *New Patterns of Management* (New York: McGraw-Hill, 1961).
[25]*Psychology Today*, November 1971, p. 51.

Exhibit 7.5
Summary of Team Process Skills

Effective Teams	*Ineffective Teams*
Priorities	
Usually seek a method and criteria for solving problems at outset, rather than "dive in"; are aware of time limitations.	Alligator technique: jump in with arms, legs, and jaws in motion; rarely ask: "What's a good way to solve the problem? How should we go about it, given the time constraints? What resources do we have in the team? What criteria are relevant?"
Climate	
Respect for others' opinions; open to criticism and differences of opinion; sarcasm or put-downs rare; atmosphere encourages thinking, discussion, reasoning, and getting the job done. Willingness to listen and change mind.	Either very friendly or hostile; jovials don't see task seriously—to avoid any conflict; hostiles are full of sarcasm, put-downs that tend to make members clam up; bullies force their solutions. Unwilling to change mind.
Leadership	
No single pattern; elected leaders are accepted as legitimate but don't force their solutions; leadership may be shared, or informal or "natural" leader may guide task; time not wasted in competing for leadership; leadership based on expertise—not authority.	Competition for who will lead team among two or three members; self-appointed, dominant, and aggressive person may take over. Leader tends to force own solution on team, doesn't seek involvement of potential resources.
Roles	
Emphasis on performing task-oriented roles, but someone invariably provides for "maintenance" and group cohesion by good humor and wit.	Typically characterized by absence of task or maintenance roles or by domination of one person.
Participation/listening	
Circular seating arrangements chosen intuitively and facilitate balanced interaction; balanced participation utilizes all team resources; good listening, few interruptions or side conversations; some functional interruptions to avoid waste of time on irrelevant points. Discussion is usually calmer, quieter.	Many interruptions, louder conversations, sometimes shouting; often subgroups engage in conversation; members unwilling to listen to others or to alter own views.
Conflict resolution	
Open confrontation regarding differences of opinion; logic and reason tend to prevail; less emotional; willing to talk out differences, assumptions, reasons, and inferences, and willing to change opinion based on consensus (as a jury does) or near unanimous majority (six or seven must agree). The confrontations can involve considerable emotion.	Usually more emotional and louder; much argumentation rather than reasoning; tend to avoid conflict or differences by compromises, votes, trade-offs, stubborn attachment to individiual solutions. Simple majority vote also used to resolve conflict.

7.12.4 Helping Skills

It is difficult to think of a successful team in organizations or athletics, for example, whose members don't feel that they are helped a great deal by their teammates. This help usually comes in the form of improving technical skills or providing psychological support and reinforcement. Giving and receiving help are skills that are increasingly being acknowledged as important aspects of effective managing.[26] The limited size and resources of most new ventures make helping skills especially critical for members of the entrepreneurial team.

Helping skills involve two distinct elements: (*a*) willingness and ability to seek and receive help from others and (*b*) willingness and ability to give help to

[26]David A. Kolb and Richard E. Boyatzis, "On the Dynamics of the Helping Relationship," *Organizational Psychology: A Book of Readings,* 2d ed., ed. D. Kolb, I. Rubin, and J. McIntyre (Englewood Cliffs, N.J.: Prentice-Hall, 1974), pp. 371–89.

others. Both of these elements are at the core of effective working and consultative relationships. Kolb and Boyatzis suggest that the helping process can be viewed in terms of the task to be accomplished, the motives and self-image of the giver and receiver of help, the psychological climate in which the process takes place, and the feedback that occurs. An understanding of these dynamics of the helping process can further the development of skills in giving and receiving help. Moreover, an analysis of the practices that facilitate or hinder the process will reveal ways to improve the process. Exhibit 7.6 is a summary of some of the important things done by givers and receivers of help that aid or hinder the helping relationship.

Exhibit 7.6
Characteristics of Giving and Receiving Help

Receiver's Behavior That:		*Giver's Behavior That:*	
Facilitates	*Hinders*	*Facilitates*	*Hinders*
1. Can articulate problem.	1. Rigid attachment to my definition of task, problem, solution.	1. Create positive climate.	1. Prejudgments of problem or solution.
2. Ask for help.		2. Nonverbal cues.	2. Predetermined.
3. Belief giver can help me; trust.	2. Poor listening.	3. Effective listening.	3. Poor listening.
4. Openness, honesty.	3. Unwillingness to reexamine problems.	4. Asking probing questions.	4. Taking over the problem.
5. Receptive to help.		5. Help to focus on what receiver can do.	
6. Find helper who cares about my problem.	4. Hostile expectations.		
7. Good listening.			

The focus here has been on the helping skills needed. The summation in Exhibit 7.6 can provide some benchmarks for practicing and improving helping skills. An outside consultant can assist in observing, providing feedback, and developing these skills.

7.12.5 Summary

Successful ventures depend more and more on successful teams, and successful teams, as venture capitalists and behavioral scientists know, have the capacity and skill to meld expertise and to work well together. We saw in Exhibit 7.5 a summary of what effective teams do to work well together. Entrepreneurs, by nature, tend to be loners and self-reliant, yet many leaders of venture teams seem to have at least an intuitive grasp of these important process skills. Successful entrepreneurs are good at building an entrepreneurial climate of teamwork. They may succeed in spite of themselves without some of these skills, but they can increase their effectiveness by using them. A personal aversion to teamwork has obvious implications for a founder or member of a venture team. These limitations can be converted to the new learning goal of acquiring teamwork skills if the founder or member is convinced that such skills are relevant and is willing to acquire them.

Last, the ability to give and receive help is becoming an increasingly important aspect of effective teamwork. Since successful ventures depend on successful teams, team-building skills, which are easily overlooked, deserve major attention from the founding entrepreneur.

7.13 SOME LESSONS ABOUT TEAM-BUILDING PROBLEMS

7.13.1 Overview

Our experience with practicing entrepreneurs struggling with the difficult business of team formation and interaction has convinced us that a conceptual framework is only the first step to successful team efforts. The second step is to form a team and see what happens.

Before you do so, however, consider the following four observations from our involvement with actual entrepreneurial teams.

7.13.2 Some Lessons Learned

First, a competent counselor or adviser who is also knowledgeable about new venture creation can significantly increase the capacity and willingness of the team members to reason out their differences and develop a legitimate consensus. The numerous sensitive issues relating to titles, salary, stock, and responsibilities can become explosive. Often, the crucial intrateam discussions on these thorny issues may lead to a premature disbanding of promising teams with sound business ideas simply because they lack the skill and knowledge to deal with them. Poorly conceived approaches, with a faint consensus and hesitant commitment by some team members, will only lead to post-start-up blues for all concerned.

Second, because each venture is unique, it is preferable for team members to reach a reasoned decision concerning sensitive issues of the types mentioned, rather than try to apply some predetermined model. An essential first step is to help them recognize the key factors that should influence their decisions concerning such matters as ownership and salaries. These factors might include the following: who generated the idea for the venture; who provided the sweat-equity and expertise; the track records of team members relative to the needs of the business; the extent of team members' potential contributions to the firm's goals; the dollars that each team member will invest personally; and the effort that each team member has contributed in preparing the business plan. The very difficult problem of weighing these factors and arriving at an agreement can be facilitated by an outsider who is familiar both with proven approaches and with the behavioral dynamics that will emerge and must be dealt with. Any inclination to treat each team member equally should be considered a serious red flag.

Third, there is a need for an extended "mating dance" among potential partners, preferably during a moonlighting period prior to actually launching the venture. This courtship should be tested thoroughly before ownership and other commitments are solidified, as these are very difficult and costly to alter or revoke once they have been established. Preparing the business plan, discussing and presenting it to potential investors, working on a prototype, and dealing with other prospective team members should all provide unique opportunities to test the potential marriage. Nevertheless, promising ventures are often held back because the lead entrepreneur lacks the funds to pay for moonlighting services. The division of founders' stock sometimes provides an appropriate vehicle for attracting and rewarding early, quality contributions.

Fourth, it should be recognized that regardless of how much time one devotes to team-building tasks and whatever agreements the partners come to, the chances are high that such agreements will become obsolete. Within four to seven years, the initially agreed-upon salaries and stock positions are unlikely to reflect the actual contributions of each team member to the venture's success. This suggests the likelihood that internal adjustments will be required as the venture grows, if stock and salary rewards are to reflect actual performances by team members.

7.13.3 Common Pitfalls

Time and again, we have seen the success of a lead entrepreneur whose own self-assessment had convinced him that he could become an effective team player. Our experience shows that this type of leader has the greatest potential for success and avoids three common pitfalls.

The Leaderless Democracy. This pitfall is what has sometimes been called the "Commune Approach" to forming a new venture team.[27] Two to four entrepreneurs, usually friends or work acquaintances, decide to initiate a venture or buy out a small company together, demonstrating their equality with such democratic trimmings as equal stock ownership, equal salaries, equal office space and cars, and other items symbolizing their peer status. Anyone who has lived through such an investment knows well the problems that this myopic approach fosters. There is no pecking order, so who is in charge? Who makes the final decisions, and how long does it take? How are real differences of opinion resolved without defined leadership roles? While some role overlapping and a sharing and negotiating of decisions are desirable in new venture teams, too much looseness is debilitating. Even sophisticated buy-sell agreements among partners often fail to resolve the conflicts.

The Lead Entrepreneur's Failure to Assess Himself and His Venture. A thorough awareness of one's entrepreneurial and managerial strengths and weaknesses is a key prerequisite to forming a team. Difficulties in putting a sound team together may be due to the lead entrepreneur's unwillingness or inability to identify his own deficiencies and weaknesses and to compensate for them by adding appropriate team members. They may also be due to the lead entrepreneur's lack of understanding of what is really needed to make a new venture grow beyond a million-dollar business.[28] Such a lack of understanding is most likely to exist among technically-oriented people or among people with narrow managerial or entrepreneurial backgrounds (for example, people whose experience has been limited to a business other than the one they wish to launch). A third cause might be the lead entrepreneur's fascination with his own product or idea. Although an emotional attachment to one's brainchild may be essential to generate enthusiasm and commitment, it can also cloud the realities of what it

---

[27] For a more detailed discussion, see Timmons, "The Entrepreneurial Team: Formation and Development."

[28] For a discussion of these entrepreneurial characteristics, see Jeffry A. Timmons, "Entrepreneurial Behavior," *Proceedings, First International Conference on Entrepreneurship*, Center for Entrepreneurial Studies, Toronto, November 1973.

takes to build a substantial business. A first-rate idea or product without a first-rate entrepreneurial team has little appeal to the knowledgeable investor. Over-commitment to any idea usually leads to severe problems.

The Power-Oriented Leader. Whether you are an investor, a prospective team member, or a lead entrepreneur, it is important to be alert to potentially destructive motivation. The early concern for power and control, often resulting in heavy expenditures for status and prestige symbols such as luxury automobiles, plush entertainment, and lush offices, is sometimes called a power orientation. Entrepreneurs who derive their satisfaction in such ways may live well, but they rarely build rapid-growth firms. In contrast, entrepreneurs with an achievement orientation[29] focus on the goal of building a substantial business and approach each new hurdle or disagreement with team members as a problem to be solved rather than as a new round of negotiations to be won or lost.

7.14 THE STOCK AND SALARY EXERCISE

Instructions. Assume that an investor group to which you made a presentation several weeks ago was favorably impressed by your team and your plan for your new venture.

This is an excellent opportunity for your fledgling company. But before the investor group considers you further, it would like you to respond to several questions concerning the company's management and founding organization. It would like you to outline in a brief presentation (10–15 minutes) the following:

1. The various responsibilities and roles to be performed by each member of your team (including titles).
2. A plan to distribute the shares of common stock in your company among the management team. What percentage of the total common shares will be allocated to each team member?
3. The salaries to be paid to each team member during the first one–two years of operation.
4. The fringe benefits that the company plans to provide, including such things as vacations, paid holidays, and health or life insurance.
5. The directors whom you plan to recruit for your board.

Initially, each of you is to work individually; do not consult with any other member of your team. You are to think about the issues and then complete the following form. This will facilitate the preparation of your presentation.

During subsequent session meetings you will work with your team to prepare a presentation outlining your team's approach to these issues.

[29] D. C. McClelland, "Achievement Motivation Can Be Developed," *Harvard Business Review,* November–December 1965.

Name _____

Date _____

STOCK AND SALARY EXERCISE

Complete this form, and bring it to the next session.

1. Roles and Responsibilities.   Indicate below who will do what during the first year or two of your venture. Be as specific as you can, and be sure to include yourself.

Team Member's Name	Title	Key Responsibilities and Tasks
a.		
b.		
c.		
d.		

2. *Reward Structure.* Indicate below the approximate salary and number of shares of stock that you believe each member—including yourself—should have upon the closing of the financing of your new venture.

Name	Approximate Salary	Percent of Shares of Stock Owned
a.		
b.		
c.		
d.		

3. Fringe Benefits. Indicate below what you believe your venture should have in the form of *fringe benefits during the first year or two.*

4. Board of Directors. List the persons who you feel should be on the new firm's board:

	Name	Current Position	Area of Expertise/ Contribution
a.			
b.			
c.			
d.			

Note: At a subsequent session you will join your team to develop your consensus and your summary presentation. If you have a cassette tape recorder, bring it to this session.

Presentation of Results (1–1½ hours).   At the session to present the results of the Stock and Salary exercise, the following should be done:

Step 1:   Each team should develop a brief five-minute presentation to report its consensus on the Stock and Salary exercise completed individually before the session. Allow 30 minutes for each team to prepare its presentation.

Step 2:   Each team should present its conclusions on the blackboard or on flip-chart paper.

Step 3:   The general discussion should focus on the following issues:

    a.   What patterns emerge in the approaches taken by each team? What are the differences and the similarities?

    b.   How difficult or easy was it to reach agreement among team members? Did any issues bog them down?

    c.   If stock or salaries were equal for all team members, why was this so? What risks or problems might such an approach create?

    d.   What criteria, either implicit or explicit, were used to arrive at a decision concerning salaries and stock? Why?

    e.   What lessons and implications concerning the building of an entrepreneurial team emerge from the exercise and discussion?

7.15 EQUITY AND OTHER COMPENSATION: A REWARD SYSTEM[30]

One of the most important issues that new venture teams must face and manage effectively is the issue of how each member of the entrepreneurial team is to be rewarded for effort with stock and other compensation. The apportioning of rewards within the team has a significant impact on the satisfaction of each of the team members, and the division of equity between the internal team and the external investors will affect how much of the venture's equity is available to the team.

7.15.1 The Internal Division: Reward for Performance

When you begin deciding who gets how many shares of stock, who gets how many dollars of salary, and who gets what fringe benefits, a number of difficult issues arise. How should these distributions be made? What criteria are appropriate? What time-tested formulas can we turn to?

There are no simple answers to these questions. What is needed is a thorough commitment by each key team member to confront the issues and work out solutions that reflect the relative contributions of team members as fairly as possible.

The financial rewards of a venture—and these include stock, salary, and fringes—are part of a larger reward system that includes the chance to realize personal goals, exercise autonomy, and develop skills in particular venture roles. Being able to attract and keep high-quality team members depends largely on these financial and psychological rewards. Because these rewards are so important, and because an early stage venture may be extremely limited in what it can offer, the total reward system should be thought through very carefully.

In the absence of easy answers and formulas, we can offer a few guidelines that are based on our experience and that of a number of seasoned venture capitalists. First, the democracy or commune approach can work, but it involves higher risk and more pitfalls than an approach that differentiates among the contributions of the various team members. The different team members usually contribute different amounts to the venture, and the reward system should recognize these differences.

Second, regardless of the contribution of each team member at any given point in time, the probability is high that their contributions will change over time. One team member may perform substantially more or less than anticipated; another team member may have to be replaced; a new member may have to be recruited and added to the existing team. More important than any split of stock and other rewards is the process by which that split is decided and the willingness of each team member to confront the issues openly when decisions have to be made. Such a commitment to dealing with problems will assure that rewards continue to reflect performance.

Third, value and reward should be functions of performance (not just effort) during the entire early life of the venture (three–five years) and should not reflect performance during only one part of this period. Many ventures have been torn apart when the relative contributions of the team members changed dramatically several years after start-up without a significant change in the stock split.

---

[30]We are indebted to John L. Hayes and Brian Haslett for their major contribution and for their permission to use it here.

Finally, what is perceived as a reward will vary among the team members. This depends very much on their personal values, goals, and aspirations. Some may seek long-range capital gains, while others may desire more security and shorter-range income. Before any apportioning of rewards is decided on, it is important to identify what the desired rewards of each team member really are. An entrepreneur can often infer what prospective team members want by careful attention to what they seem to consider important in the deal they are attempting to negotiate.

7.15.2 Timing of Rewards

The rewards that a venture is able to give its entrepreneurial team vary somewhat over the life of the venture. While intangible rewards such as opportunity for self-development and self-realization may be available throughout the life of a venture, some of the financial rewards are more or less appropriate at different stages of the venture's development. A split of stock among the members of the entrepreneurial team will be decided very early in the life of the venture. Once this initial stock split has been decided, changes in the relative stock positions of the team member will not take place unless there are significant changes in the relative contributions of team members. New team members or an external investor might dilute each member's position, but the relative positions will probably remain unchanged. It is therefore extremely important that the split reflect your best estimate of contributed performance over the first several years of the venture.

There are several possible events having implications for the initial stock split that might occur during the early years of your venture. Suppose that any one of the following events takes place:

Case 1. A team member, who has a substantial portion of your company's stock, does not perform and must be replaced 12 months into the venture.

Case 2. A key team member finds a better opportunity and quits 12 months into the venture.

Case 3. A key team member dies in an accident 12 months into the venture.

What will happen to the stock of these team members in each of the above cases? That stock was intended to be a reward for their performance during the first several years of the venture. In Case 1, the venture should have the option of returning the stock to its treasury at the price for which it was purchased—that was the team member's commitment and risk. In Cases 2 and 3, some portion of the stock has been earned and some portion is as yet unearned. The arrangement here needs to be carefully thought out so as to do justice to all parties. In Case 3, the heirs of the former partner are parties to consider.

To protect the venture against such occurrences, several options are available to it when the initial stock splits are made. Stock, once purchased by the team members, may be placed in escrow and then released over a two- or three-year period. This provides a continuing reward for team members. Another option is to structure buy-back agreements that allow the company to repurchase stock under specific circumstances. Whatever mechanism is used, the objective is to avoid the loss or freezing of equity that the business needs to reward the real performers.

Other rewards—salary, stock options, bonus, fringe benefits—can be manipulated more readily to reflect changes in contributed performance. But the use of such rewards is also somewhat dependent on the venture's stage of development. In the early months of a venture salaries will necessarily be low or nonexistent; bonuses and fringe benefits are out of the question at this stage. Salaries, bonuses, and fringe benefits all drain cash from the business. Until profitability has been achieved, cash can always be put to use for operations; and after profitability has been achieved, cash payments will still limit growth. Salaries can become competitive once the venture has passed break-even; and bonuses and fringe benefits should be kept at a minimum until several years of profitability have been demonstrated. Even at that point, however, the owners of the venture will be deciding what trade-off to make between cash rewards and the growth of the venture.

7.15.3 The Value of Contributed Performance

When an entrepreneur or an entrepreneurial team is attempting to decide a fair stock split among the various members of the team, a number of different sides of contribution and performance should be identified and weighed. The contributions of your team members will vary in their nature, extent, and timing. Among the kinds of contributions that are of value to a venture are the following:

1. *The Idea.*
   a. Whose was it?
   b. Are trade secrets or special technology involved?
   c. Has a prototype been developed?
   d. Has research on the product or market been done?
2. *Preparation of the Business Plan That Was Acceptable to the Funding Sources.*
   a. Dollars and hours expended.
3. *Commitment and Risks.*
   a. Percentage of net worth invested in company.
   b. Risk if company fails.
   c. Personal sacrifices.
   d. Willingness to put in long hours and major effort.
   e. Risk of reputation.
   f. Acceptance of a reduced salary.
   g. Time spent already.
4. *Amount of Skills Brought to the Venture.*
   a. Number of skills—marketing, technical, financial, etc.
   b. Importance of skills.
   c. Availability of skills on market.
   d. Experience in the area of the new venture.
   e. Track record.
   f. Number of contacts of value to the venture.
5. *Amount of Responsibility to Be Taken in the Venture.*
   a. Importance of role to venture success.

Items 1 and 2 are frequently overvalued in stock negotiations. In terms of the success of the venture three to five years down the road, it is difficult to justify much more than 15–20 percent for these two items. Commitment, skill, and responsibility play a far greater part in producing venture success. Exactly what each of these is worth must be decided intelligently by every new venture. The above list of considerations should be applied to each team member to attempt to assign fair weights to their relative contributions. Each of these elements has some value; it is up to your team to reach an agreement as to what these values are and to make your agreement flexible enough to allow changes. Remember, it is the contribution over a period of several years that you are attempting to predict and reward. If you predict wrongly, make sure that the venture's capacity to reward is not limited by that error. The reward is buying skills, commitment, and concern; and your venture will need all of these that it can get.

The way you deal with these questions will also determine the investor's view of your credibility. The investor will look for signs of commitment, such as reduced salary and stock in escrow pending demonstrated performance; for a fringe-benefit plan that does not strain a young business; for flexibility in the team, so that, if necessary, a team member can be replaced. Many venture capitalists have faced the task of replacing the lead entrepreneur or a key team member—experience says that this can happen—and you must convince your investor that your venture could survive such a change.

These are very difficult issues to resolve. The stakes for each team member are extremely high, and each team member's feelings of self-worth are inextricably bound up with these issues. Care must be employed to avoid rigid bargaining positions; but these questions must be confronted and resolved in order to develop a strong, committed entrepreneurial team.

The Family Venture

8

Happy families are all alike;
every unhappy family is unhappy in its own way.

Anna Karenina in
Tolstoi, War and Peace, Part I, Chapter 1.

8.1 RESULTS EXPECTED

This chapter addresses a special brand of entrepreneurial team building: the family venture. All the complexities of a regular team are compounded when family members and other relatives become involved in the business. Both experience and recent research have brought some facts and thoughtful analysis to this least understood aspect of new venture creation. Upon completion of the chapter, and analysis and discussion of the Beantown Seafoods (B) case, you will have:

1. Identified and examined the role and significance of the family-based team in building higher-potential ventures.
2. Analyzed some of the important problems associated with new venture teams that involve immediate family members.
3. Examined the "special" team issues inherent in family-owned enterprises and developed resolutions of these issues.

8.2 PRESESSION PREPARATION

After reading the brief textual material, prepare and analyze the Beantown Seafoods (B) case.

8.3 A SPECIAL TYPE OF TEAM: THE FAMILY BUSINESS

8.3.1 Introduction

When you begin your entrepreneurial career, there is a strong possibility that one or more family members already are, or will become, part of the "team." Although we are unaware of any formal studies investigating the percentage of start-ups involving two or more related persons, we ourselves know of a number of such start-ups. At the end of this chapter we have included one example in case form that will provide you with the chance to reflect on the real-life implications of entrepreneurial life in a family business.

Historically, the predominance of family-dominated businesses in the United States has been unquestioned. A recent study suggests that out of every 1 million businesses in the United States, about 980,000 are family-dominated, including some of the largest.[1] Thus, the odds are in favor of your venture falling into the "family business" category.

There are three sets of circumstances in which your entrepreneurial career may become involved with family members:

1. At start-up (or buyout).
2. Joining a recently launched family venture early in its operations.
3. Joining a family business as a second- or third-generation member who hopes to find an entrepreneurial opportunity under the family company umbrella.

Connected with each of these instances is a certain set of problems that may be exacerbated by the fact that your business partner or boss is also your relative. Since surprisingly little research exists on entrepreneurs and family ventures, many of the following remarks are based on firsthand observations of the authors and others who have studied family-owned businesses.

8.3.2 Launching a Venture with a Family Member

Everything that we have said about choosing entrepreneurial teams and practicing entrepreneurial teamwork applies to family teams—but more so. Of special urgency is the need to come to a clear understanding about these questions:

Who is the lead entrepreneur?

What are the specific strengths, and weaknesses, of each member of the team?

What are the backgrounds of each member of the team in other areas of business?

What are the specific responsibilities of each member of the team?

How much money will each member of the team put up, and how will equity be divided?

In our experience it is fatal to the life of a venture to assume that these issues are "understood" because "it's all in the family."

Finally, the family members must decide under what circumstances, and on what terms, nonfamily members will be brought into the venture. While keeping a venture strictly in the family ensures complete control, this approach may also limit growth by discouraging able and potential partners from joining. It may also discourage potential investors who question the growth potential of too tightly held an operation.

It is useful to consider these points in the context of the Beantown Seafoods (B) case.

8.3.3 Joining a Family Venture Early in Its Operation

In a typical scenario for this situation an entrepreneur starts putting a venture together on weekends and evenings, testing its feasibility and starting

---

[1]L. B. Barnes and S. A. Hershon, "Transferring Power in the Family Business," *Harvard Business Review,* July–August 1976, p. 143.

small—with the understanding that a sibling (employed elsewhere or still in school) or a parent will join the venture as it grows. In this instance, the lead entrepreneur has already declared himself or herself and has presumably identified—with the aid of potential family partners, employees, and backers—the areas in which the venture will need help. Here, the questions to ask involve:

> The exact definition of each family member's area of responsibility and of whom he or she will be responsible to.
>
> The type of compensation: salary, bonus, equity shares, or some mixture of these.
>
> An understanding about what will be done if there is a disagreement or if one family member is not pulling his or her weight.
>
> The ante—and whether it can be redeemed if the joining family member changes his mind.

You may think of other important considerations as you reflect upon George Halsey and his brother in the Beantown Seafoods (B) case.

8.3.4 Joining a Family Company as a Second- or Third-Generation Member Looking for an Entrepreneurial Opportunity[2]

This alternative is richer in data, both formal and anecdotal, than the two previous ones—and it is filled with stories of success and failure. We have grouped our facts and opinions around three questions that an entrepreneur considering this option must ask himself or herself:

> What exactly do I intend to accomplish under the family umbrella that I couldn't do as well on my own?

A recent article interviewed entrepreneurial offspring of entrepreneur parents who explicitly chose *not* to join their parents but to start their own ventures.[3] A study of more than 1,000 entrepreneurs and their offspring, referred to in the article, revealed a mixed picture where "half of all children of entrepreneurs chose not to take over their parents' businesses. Size and potential monetary rewards of a business seem to make no difference. Some offspring simply prefer to do things on their own."[4] Is this you?

> What do I wish my role to be? Dutiful apprentice? Head of an autonomous division? Eventual chairman and CEO?

We can cite success stories of entrepreneurs who have clearly defined their goals vis-à-vis the family company in each of these three categories:

---

[2]We do not treat the issue of succession per se in this book. Nonetheless, it becomes an important issue and affects growth strategy as the venture matures. For those interested in additional reading, we suggest: David Ambrose, "Transfer of the Family-Owned Business," *Journal of Small Business Management,* January 1983, pp. 49–56; C. Roland Christensen, *Management Succession in Small and Growing Enterprises* (Boston: Harvard University, 1953); Stanley Davis, "Entrepreneurial Succession," *Administrative Sciences Quarterly,* December 1967; Robert Donnelley, "The Family Business," *Harvard Business Review,* July–August 1964; Renato Tagiuri and John Davis, "Life Stages and Father-Son Working Relationships," working paper HBS 84–26, Division of Research, Graduate School of Business Administration, Harvard University, January 1983; and Barnes and Hershon, "Transferring Power in the Family Business."

[3]Michelle Bekey, "Born and Bred Entrepreneurs," *Venture,* March 1981, pp. 36ff.

[4]D. Alan Jacobowitz, Trenton State College, New Jersey—quoted in Bekey, "Born and Bred Entrepreneurs," p. 37.

a. *The apprentice:* Ira Riklis, son of conglomerateur Meshulam Riklis, of Rapid-American Corporation, worked for his father for one year, developing an ulcer and the conviction that the role was not for him. However, the contacts he made enabled him to start a successful company of his own.[5]
b. *The related business:* Two sons of restauranteur Anthony Athanas, owner of Anthony's Pier 4 in Boston and other restaurants, set up a seafood supply company in Maine, with the intent of having their father be one of their most loyal customers.
c. *The next president:* Of the many examples known to us, we cite that of the Bechtel Corporation, begun by Warren Bechtel for building railroads. His son Steve, Sr., directed the firm into the construction of pipelines and nuclear power plants. Today, Steve, Jr., heads the $3 billion company, which has further diversified.[6]

In each instance, the second-generation entrepreneur made a realistic assessment of the future of his career vis-à-vis the family business and proceeded to position himself accordingly.

> As management in the family firm is presently constituted, how much leeway will I have to try my own ideas—even if they fail?

Your entrepreneurial success within the family business will depend to a great extent on company growth. Is it growing fast enough to accommodate new ideas, new divisions? Is there room for you, or has the company matured and stabilized at its present level of sales? And does management style permit the type of latitude you seek?

A useful chart, showing the characteristics of a company at various stages of growth, may give you a framework within which to answer these questions (Exhibit 8.1).

However, the key to your success within the family firm is probably not to be found on an organization chart. Rather, it will depend on resolving certain personal issues. If you are a son joining your father, there is strong evidence that inherent father-son conflicts become magnified in a business setting.[7] Many founder-fathers regard the company as their child and are unwilling to relinquish any part of their authority over it. In addition, parents do not like to take orders from their children; the generation gap is magnified in the setting of the family business. Often, the second-generation entrepreneur becomes a permanent person-in-waiting.

A survivor of this syndrome describes his good fortune as follows: "Fortunately, my father died one year after I joined the firm."[8] A seasoned observer summarizes the dilemma:

Dad's successor is an entrepreneur in training. He's expected to be the trailblazer when Dad passes on his machete. He's expected to be independent, yet he is forced to work for one of the most domineering bosses in existence, a successful business owner. To make it worse, the "boss" is also the successor's father.[9]

[5]Bekey, "Born and Bred Entrepreneurs."
[6]Barnes and Hershon, "Transferring Power in the Family Business."
[7]Harry Levinson, "Conflicts That Plague Family Business," *Harvard Business Review,* March–April 1977.
[8]Levinson, "Conflicts That Plague Family Business," p. 141.
[9]Leon Danco, *Inside the Family Business* (Cleveland: Center for Family Business, 1980), p. 131.

Exhibit 8.1
Characteristics of Company Growth

Organizational Characteristic	Patterns of the First Stage	Patterns of the Second Stage	Patterns of the Third Stage
Core problem	Survival	Management of growth	Managerial control and allocation of resources
Central function	Fusion of diverse talents and purposes into a unified company	Fission of general authority into specialized functions	Fusion of independent units into an interdependent union of companies
Control systems	Personal (inside); survival in marketplace (outside)	Cost centers and policy formulation (inside); growth potential (outside)	Profit centers and abstract performance criteria (inside); capital expansion potential (outside)
Reward and motivation	Ownership, membership in the family	Salary opportunities and problems of growth	Salary performance bonus, stock options, peer prestige
Management style	Individualistic; direct management	Integrating specialists; collaborative management	Integrating generalists; collection management
Organization:			
Structure	Informal	Functional specialists	Division organizations
CEO's primary task	Direct supervision of employees	Managing specialized managers	Managing generalist managers
Levels of management	Two	At least three	At least four

Source: L. B. Barnes and S. A. Hershon, "Transferring Power in the Family Business," *Harvard Business Review,* July–August 1976, p. 145.

One of the most successful ways of combating parental resistance—endorsed by academics, small business consultants, and entrepreneurs themselves—is this: *acquire practical business experience somewhere else first.*[10] Founding parents have difficulty in believing that their children ever grow up, and a good track record on the outside is one way of helping to overcome this mental block.

In sum, a clear understanding of your family company—objectively (is it growing fast enough to give me the elbow room I need?) and subjectively (is it realistic to think I can overcome the resistance of the older generation?)—is critical to your decision as to whether or not to join the family "team."

8.4 SOME SUGGESTIONS

There are as many combinations of successful and unsuccessful family-based teams as there are family enterprises. There are great extremes of harmony and chaos. Offering any advice is hazardous, but consider the following.

Young entrepreneurs often find their entry into and acceptance by a family company greatly facilitated by having first "earned their spurs" outside the firm, in a relevant job and business. Part of the apprenticeship, then, of someone who contemplates joining a family venture would include an early stint of up to several years in another firm. In that way, you can bring a lot more to the venture, and thereby contribute and gain respect, instead of just being the owner's child.

[10]Barnes and Hershon, "Transferring Power in the Family Business"; Danco, *Inside the Family Business;* Margaret Crane, "How to Keep Families from Feuding," February 1982, pp. 73ff.

There is a national organization called Sons of Bosses (SOBs) and another called Daughters of Bosses (DOBs). These organizations have chapters in many cities. Part of your peer and support network might include one of them. It is reasonably safe to assume that whatever issues you and a parent might be struggling with, there is quite likely a person in that organization who has worked the issue through, or knows someone who has. This shared experience can be very helpful to you and your parents.

8.5 BEANTOWN SEAFOODS (B): CASE STUDY

In preparing the Beantown Seafoods (B) case, consider the following issues:

1. How has BSI done compared to its original projections, and what impact does this have on your earlier view of the opportunity?
2. What have been the actual economics of the venture? How "forgiving and rewarding" a business is it?
3. As a potential buyer, what value would you place on the business? As one of the founders, for what sum would you be willing to sell the business?
4. Be prepared to role-play a meeting between George and his father. What would your objectives be? What proposal would you make concerning your ownership and involvement in the business?
5. What is the nature of the opportunities facing the Halseys at the end of the case?
6. What should George Halsey do, and why?

BEANTOWN SEAFOODS (B)

In early 1981 George Halsey, 27, was contemplating the next step in his entrepreneurial career. He had joined his father's company, Beantown Seafoods, in early 1978—at which point the 18-month-old venture had realized a profit of $13,000 on sales of $70,000. Over the next four years, George had played a key role in building the firm's sales dramatically, to nearly $5 million in 1980.

When George joined the firm, which—at his advice—was a corporation rather than a sole proprietorship, his father, Daniel, agreed to give him 5 percent of the stock for every year that George was employed and the remainder of the shares when Daniel retired in 1984. Back in 1978 Daniel had been skeptical about why George wanted shares. "What is the value of all this? It's just you and I and a desk and a telephone and $70,000 in sales." "Dad," George replied, "I'm going to make it worth something. I'm going to build this business." On this note, both men informally agreed to the arrangement.

By 1981, however, with a projected $6 million in sales, Daniel had indicated that he wasn't sure he was going to keep the "gentleman's agreement"—and George wasn't sure how that would affect his future. After all, it was his original plan—see Beantown Seafoods (A)—and the 90-hour weeks he had spent building the business that had been in great part responsible for the success of the company. Meanwhile, George had married and had a son. While acknowledging the personal growth and excitement of the past four years, George also realized that his father was a difficult man to work with, and was set in his ways about certain aspects of doing business. To make things more difficult, George felt a sense of sadness because his father had never told him how much his efforts had been appreciated.

George was young and had an excellent track record in the industry. He loved the work, begrudging only the long hours that kept him from wife and son. His feelings toward his father were mixed. He felt that he had to do something about the situation soon—but what? And how would it change his future?

Company History: 1976–1978

Beantown Seafoods (BSI) was founded in 1976 by Daniel Halsey in Boston. Daniel intended to establish himself as a broker/wholesaler of fresh fish.[1] At age 55, Daniel had left his position as sales and marketing manager of a major frozen fish company in the wake of an internal corporate shakeup. Daniel, who had worked in the fish industry all his life, saw a niche for himself in the fresh fish area because of two major industry trends. The volume of fish caught was expected to increase after the 200-mile-limit law took effect, and the transportation of fresh fish to the Midwest and West had been greatly simplified by the introduction of wide-bodied jets.

BSI functioned as a service—a buyer and seller of processed (cleaned and filleted) fresh fish. Unlike a broker, however, BSI actually took possession of the fish, though it maintained no inventory. Its orders were received in three ways:

1. *Source Initiated:* The supplier offered BSI a specific amount of fish at a specific price. BSI contacted its customers to determine need and then called the supplier to place an order.
2. *Customer Initiated:* The request for an order came from the customer to BSI, which then checked with a number of suppliers to see whether the order could be filled within the customer's price range. BSI then contacted the customer with the findings and, at the customer's request, placed an order.
3. *BSI Initiated:* Occasionally, BSI would recommend that a customer augment or diversify his product line. If the customer agreed, BSI checked with suppliers and placed the order.

The "hands-on" part of the operation occurred when BSI packaged individual customer orders from the bulk order. The packages would then be shipped by truck to the customer or to the airport.

Because of an agreement with two processors of perch, Beantown Seafoods opened operations with a single species—and targeted the Midwest and Southwest as the prime market area. The small amount of Atlantic fresh fish consumed there had been hauled by truck and was not all that fresh on arrival. In the early 1970s airfreight cost 50 cents/pound; by 1976 the cost had dropped to 10 cents/pound and containers had been developed to hold 3,000 pounds of fish.

However, the airfreight concept had not worked smoothly. Unreliable route scheduling interfered with distribution on a regular basis. For example, wide-bodied jets flew to Florida only in winter months and were routed elsewhere during the summer. In the case of a newly-developed Phoenix market, the Boston-Phoenix route was suddenly dropped, and with it BSI's potential profits.

During 1976–77 George was attending Northeastern Business School in Bos-

[1]See Appendix for a note on the New England fishing industry.

ton. As part of a New Venture Strategy course, he wrote a business plan for Beantown Seafoods, with emphasis on redirecting the marketing strategy and increasing the product line. After graduation he joined a large conglomerate in New York as a product manager, but before long he could no longer resist the challenge of joining his father's company and working to implement his new plans. He joined Beantown Seafoods in early 1978.

Company Operations: 1978–1981

Looking back over the years since he had joined the company, George gave his views of the company's growth and operations.

Market Repositioning

When George joined BSI, the company had a customer base of five; relied heavily on a single species of fish, perch; and shipped almost exclusively by airfreight to its major market, the Midwest. Beginning in 1978, George convinced his father to change the strategy radically. BSI began to compete in the traditional developed markets on the East Coast—supplying supermarkets with fresh fish via trucks. George believed that BSI could penetrate these markets by capitalizing on the chaos that customers felt in the highly fragmented industry and on the dissatisfaction that supermarkets experienced with the existing sources of supply, indicated by a lack of customer loyalty. BSI decided to stake its reputation and its ability to expand operations by providing quality and reliability to its customers; George intended to position BSI as "the buyer's buyer."

One important move on the supply side was to develop a strong chain of suppliers along the East Coast so as to be able to take advantage of the best prices. Since BSI began exclusively as a distributor of perch, George and Daniel had to develop new suppliers of other species. They also had to keep their present perch suppliers happy, and, in the main, this was accomplished by guaranteeing the perch suppliers year-round sales.

On the demand side, two major areas needed attention. BSI had to encourage its old customers (of which there were only five originals) to carry fish other than perch, and it had to find new customers who were receptive to carrying a variety of species. As George described it:

With the perch situation, we saw the kind of control we had. We didn't really understand it. It was kind of like the Arabs. They had all the oil for years and never knew what it really meant. Well, we did the same thing. We knew that we had the perch, and we didn't really twist their arms, but we certainly let it be known we wanted to sell other species. So, if you want the perch, you buy other things. We never came out and said it; we just positioned ourselves that way. That expanded our product line. So our objective now is to continue to try to build up species and downplay the perch.

Now we have maybe 100–150 customers. Our largest customer represents about 5 percent of the whole business. We did that purposely just to try to minimize the risk we'd have from any one customer accounting for a big percent of our sales.

My father had very hard perceptual problems understanding what we were trying to do. At times he tried to hold me back from growing too fast, but I felt the risk was too great if we didn't expand.

As of 1980, Beantown Seafoods sold more than 35 species of fish. Exhibit 1 is a partial listing. The species accounting for most of the 1980 sales were: ocean perch, 22 percent; sole fillets, 18 percent; scallops, 12.2 percent; and cod fillets, 11.4 percent. Exhibit 2 is a complete list of sales by product line.

Almost 100 percent of BSI's sales came from the Midwest in 1976, versus 40 percent in 1980. BSI distributed to markets in Chicago, Detroit, Rochester, Buffalo, Dallas, Houston, Fort Worth, and Los Angeles. Exhibit 3 gives BSI's sales by region for 1980.

Exhibit 1

Fresh haddock fillets		Fresh ocean perch	
Fresh cod fillets		Fresh ocean catfish	
Fresh pollock fillets		Fresh sole fillets	
Fresh hake fillets		Fresh grey sole	
Fresh cusk fillets			
Fresh swordfish		Fresh black sea bass	
Fresh scup (porgies)		Fresh striped bass	
Fresh butterfish		Fresh shark	
Fresh mackerel		Fresh whiting	
Fresh native bluefish		Fresh halibut	
Fresh sea trout		Fresh fluke	
Sea scallops		Littleneck clams	
Bay scallops		Topnecks	
Cape scallops		Cherrystones	
Lobster (chickens)		Quahogs	
Lobster (1¼s)		Steamers	
Lobster (1½s)		Frying clams	
Lobster (2–3s)		Mussels	
Lobster (3+)		Crab	
		Shrimp	

Exhibit 2
Beantown Seafoods Sales by Product Line for Fiscal Year Ending October 31, 1980

Product	$ Sales	Percent of Total
Perch	$1,063,300	22.0%
Sole	867,300	17.9
Scallops	589,800	12.2
Cod	552,500	11.4
Haddock	322,700	6.7
Swordfish	303,300	6.3
Monk	219,300	4.5
Cat/cusk	193,400	4.0
Shellfish	189,800	3.9
Pollock	152,300	3.1
Wholefish	146,800	3.0
Lobster	80,700	1.7
Miscellaneous	68,100	1.4
Shrimp	55,300	1.1
Hake	20,500	0.4
Crab	9,600	0.2
Tuna	4,600	0.1
Frozen	1,300	0.1

Exhibit 3
Beantown Seafoods Sales by Region for Fiscal Year Ending
October 31, 1980

Region	$ Sales	Number of Customers	COGS
Chicago	$ 855,736	12	$ 781,000
Cleveland	1,735,148	13	1,601,035
Rochester/Buffalo	680,383	18	635,318
Detroit	240,944	4	222,403
Boston	147,476	9	134,247
Albany	7,004	2	6,242
Long Island	20,506	1	18,573
Denver	195,273	4	173,040
Los Angeles	234,220	4	211,921
Local Massachusetts	383,000	107	349,600
Miami	169,519	7	142,243
Omaha	19,038	2	18,144
Jackson	33,568	1	30,314
Oakland	4,322	1	3,924
Renn.	30,794	6	28,886
Miscellaneous	28,037	4	25,540
New air business	64,800	N.A.	N.A.
Total	$4,857,800		

George's marketing philosophy can be simply stated: he does not accept the idea that a buyer is ever perfectly content with his existing supplier or his existing business. In the face of resistance, George continues to try to establish new accounts because if he can make a *buyer's* business grow, BSI grows with it.

Understanding the Marketplace: The Suppliers

Fish, like any other commodity, has its own unwritten code of operations, and George and Daniel were determined to learn the business carefully so as to establish trusting relationships and thereby ensure reliability. The three key variables are quality, quantity, and price. The two methods of doing business are at the pier and over the phone. The following anecdotes illustrate the difficult but successful job that BSI has done in establishing good relationships with its suppliers.

Since price varies daily and contracts must be signed days and weeks in advance, some suppliers will sell to the highest bidder regardless of previous arrangements.

You call up one fish plant and order 2,000 pounds of cod fillets. The truck is going to be there at 4 o'clock to pick it up. The supermarket and the supplier (processing plant or wholesaler) agree on a price of $1.40 per pound: a good price for that day. The supplier realized it was a great price and has a chance to sell it for $1.60 per pound. So he sells it. He doesn't notify the supermarket buyer. He just sells it for $1.60 per pound. The supermarket truck is there at 10 minutes until four to pick it up. The supplier says, "I'm sorry. I didn't get the fish off the boat." So here's the supermarket truck with no product on it, and the ad is running in the paper the next day.

To avoid this pitfall, Daniel and George devised several strategies. First, they offered a premium per pound (5–10 cents) to those suppliers who they believed were reliable. Next, they established several groups of informal co-ops along the

East Coast, groups of independent processors with unwritten agreements to trade with others—based on a bond of common trust. These co-ops guaranteed BSI a given supply of fish and set a minimum price; BSI pledged to resell it for at least that price and usually more. This arrangement allowed BSI to get the variety and volume of product it needed.

Another problem has been the relatively high turnover of new suppliers and the difficulty of monitoring the competition. New companies start up overnight; overhead costs are low. New companies disappear; one of BSI's suppliers went out of business overnight when three cutters quit and each went into business for himself.

A third problem hinges on a strategic decision: price versus volume. George's initial plan favored volume and the concomitant buying power that this strategy would bring to the company.

I would rather do a lot of volume for a low profit than a lot of profit with low volume just because of the buying power. Here's an example. There's a guy down on the pier who we've been with since day one of the corporation. But he's always been higher in price. Our sales with him have been pretty consistent. Through the grapevine he learned how significantly we'd grown. He really started to work on price. He originally quoted me $1.80 on cod. The same day he calls back and says, "If I got you $1.50 on cod, how many pounds would you be interested in?" I said, "How many could you get?" He says, "How many would you want? 500? 600? 700?" I said, "Well, how many could you get?" He says, "Maybe 3,000 pounds." I said, "Fine, I'll take them." He says, incredulously, "You want 3,000?" I said, "Yes. If you get more, give me a call." He called back and said, "I can get you another 500–600." I said, "OK. Give them to me." That's buying power.

However, George had to learn about pricing at the wholesale level the hard way, and also about the importance of keeping certain information private. Here is one of his early experiences:

I had to buy some perch from the pier. I was buying 200–300 pounds for two or three different clients. I was buying it at $1.50/pound. One supplier says, "My price is $1.80/pound." I said, "Come on, I'm buying it at $1.50 from everyone else. Why give you $1.80?" He said, "Who are you buying it from at $1.50?" Like a jerk, I said, "I'm buying it from him, him, and him." He said, "My price is $1.80. Take it or leave it." I had to have it, so I took it. Ten minutes later I get three phone calls from the other plants I named. They said, "What are you doing telling this guy what I'm selling to you for?" Like a fool, I got caught with my pants down. So, if you know something, keep it to yourself.

Quality is another problem. It is possible for a supplier to alter the decaying appearance of a less-than-fresh fish by passing it through salt water. "Brining" gives the fish a fresh sheen and is not easy to detect.

A supplier can also pass off one species for another. For instance, there are three sizes of cod fillets: market cod (average $1.50/pound), scrod cod (average $1.40/pound) and anything below scrod cod specifications, called snapper (average $1/pound). On one occasion, a supplier sold scrod to BSI with snapper mixed in. George got a call from the angry customer and confronted the supplier:

Bob, the scrod fillets look beautiful on the top, but when you look down in the box, there's a lot of snapper and broken, raggy fillets. What did you do, machine-cut these? What are you doing, hiring blind people? Bob, there's no way you could miss those raggy fillets. There are snapper in there, and that's really what the objection is. We pay $1.45 for scrod cod, and that's what we expect. Not snapper. I can buy snapper for $1. It's really a short-term gain on your part to do something like that.

Since the industry is small, information travels fast. Like all shrewd commodities traders, Daniel and George have had to learn when to blow the whistle and when to stay mum; whom to trust and whom to stay away from. The result of their experience and sensitivity is reflected on the bottom line—their ability to buy and sell fish.

Understanding the Marketplace: The Customers

The customers, for the most part, are supermarkets. Until recently, few supermarkets carried fresh fish, and those that did carried a limited selection. The supermarkets didn't understand how to market fish to the consumer, and the consumer was not in the habit of buying fresh fish from supermarkets. Thus, the first big job facing Daniel and George had been to help the supermarkets promote fresh fish.

First, the supermarkets had to be convinced of both the reliability and the quality of BSI's service. This meant fresh product, delivered when promised at a prearranged price. Next, the supermarkets had to be educated in how to display the fish, what temperature to hold them at, and how long their "shelf life" was, depending on species. Finally, the supermarkets needed to be educated in point-of-sale and media promotion. Luckily for BSI, the consumer demand for fresh fish had already begun, so the burden of education did not fall solely on Daniel and George. Still, remarked George, "it's been a long educational process for us to try to educate literally thousands of retail stores with only two guys."

The next best sources of customers are retail fish stores. Here, BSI must emphasize the importance of broadening their product line. Getting the customers is only part of the problem; customers can be a tricky lot. George requires the directness from his customers that he demands of himself, and sometimes he has to pressure them to develop this quality. For example, George quoted a customer a price of $1.35/pound for some product. When BSI received payment of $1.25/pound, George reminded the customer of the original quote. The customer's response was that he had recorded it for $1.25. George explained how he handled the situation.

There's nothing you can do about it. You don't know if he did it legitimately or not. But I have an old saying, "I don't get even, I get better." So when things are short and I know I can make more money, I do it. If I normally earn 5 cents a pound and a schmuck calls up, I'll put on 20 cents. If a customer takes advantage of me, I'm going to try to get even with him. On the other hand, if a good customer is in a bind, I'll bend over backwards to get him what he needs at the best price I can.

An unwritten rule in the industry, where the market changes every day, is: whatever you buy that day is at that price. If fish is bought one day but not shipped until the next, if the price dropped in 24 hours, the customer pays the quoted price on the day of sale. George talks about a customer who didn't want to play by the rules:

One customer had 3,000–4,000 pounds of product. When the market price dropped, he called up and said, "Lower your price." We said, "We can't. We're fixed at that price." He said, "Cancel my order." He did that three times, so I won't even talk to him any more. He still calls us because there are only so many kingpins that everything eventually has to come through, and we have slowly developed into one of those kingpins.

BSI makes most of its profit in the winter because it has access to an adequate fish supply. Nonregular customers come back to BSI in the winter. One of its customers wouldn't buy from BSI during the rest of the year because BSI was two cents higher. When supply was short in the winter, the customer came to BSI offering the two-cent difference. George refused his business because he had regular customers who never questioned his pricing.

This unwritten code of George's sometimes makes his customers mad. Some of his customers buy from the Canadians because of their lower prices. George told these customers that he could service them better if they bought from him on a regular basis. In the winter, when BSI carries a full product line, George doesn't sell to them.

George has learned to beat customers at their own games. In another transaction, BSI shipped product to a customer in Chicago. The customer called to say it was bad quality. George said, "OK, I'll take care of it." The customer responded, "How are you going to take care of it?" George said, "Watch." George called him back 10 minutes later and said, "I took care of it. I'm having it picked up by your competitor," another of BSI's accounts. The second account confirmed the shipment's high quality. The first customer never played the game again.

BSI's growth has come through its excellent reputation, not through market research. George believes that market research is not much help in this industry; "market research would probably help tell you a customer's perception of BSI," but George believes that the surest test of a customer's perception is the size and longevity of his account with the firm. "The researcher would have to be careful," he commented. "Otherwise, the customer would probably hang up."

Distribution

BSI ships 80 percent of its product by truck. Shipping costs are subject to fluctuation, since one or two of the trucking firms have a virtual monopoly over their routes.

BSI sells to supermarkets both directly and indirectly, since the company also wholesales to other buyers that resell to the supermarkets. Even though the supermarket pays another markup, it will often choose to do so if it is more convenient to deal with a local wholesaler. Yet, supermarkets often request a quote from BSI to confirm the price quoted by their supplier.

Physical Plant

BSI began operations in the immediate area of the Boston fish pier. In 1980 it relocated several miles inland, in Roxbury, Massachusetts. The area is a deteriorating, forbidding warehouse section of the city. Rent is artificially low. The plant is approximately 3,500 square feet in size. The fish-handling area, though dimly lit and crowded with waist-high tin fish containers, appears to be efficient. In addition to office space, there are a 600-foot freezer and 1,500 square feet of unused space.

Pricing Policies and Strategies

BSI's profit margins compare with those of supermarkets: 1 to 2 percent. Labor accounts for most of the fixed costs.

Daniel and George differ sharply over pricing strategy. Take this example: BSI commits to buy a given amount of fish from a processor at $1.60/pound. If it sells the fish for $1.70/pound, it makes a profit; if the price drops to $1.30/pound, it loses 30 cents/pound. However, the given amount is usually less than the entire volume needed that day, so BSI picks up the rest at the best price it can get.

Daniel expects to sell at a marked-up price in every transaction. Under Daniel's philosophy, BSI would sell the $1.60 cod for $1.70 and the $1.30 cod for $1.45. George, on the contrary, averages the cost of the two together and sells the entire lot for the average amount. He believes that the averaging system works well for his transactions.

George's guiding principle is to go for volume, not price. The lack of seasonality at BSI, which is not typical of the industry, allows it to avoid the shortsighted view of expecting to mark up every individual transaction. The same principle justifies his paying a premium (5 or 10 cents/pound) to reliable suppliers. He sees volume as a buffer if one or two deals go sour.

Suppose the customer starts playing games with you. For example, you sell first-quality codfish to a buyer in Chicago for $1.50/pound. When the product gets to Chicago, the customer calls to say that the quality is questionable and wants 20 cents per pound deducted from the price. There goes your profit. You have to sell a lot of fish to make up for that.

George also buys fish on speculation, that is, without a specific customer order. Historically, BSI bought fish by returning to the processing plants several times a day to purchase small quantities every time a customer called. This was a serious problem for the plants because they had to plan how much fish to buy. George started to give the plants a one-day advance on what his requirements would be. Daniel felt that this was speculation because George didn't know whether the fish would sell or not. He thought the next step was bankruptcy.

In 1979, George successfully gambled on a $15,000 investment in swordfish. In 1980 he speculated on $60,000 of swordfish. He is aware of the risk he is taking. "One of my competitors did the same thing when the FDA first banned swordfish. Well, even if I turned all my swordfish into cat food, I'd probably go bankrupt overnight, so I take two Excedrin every day and hope the FDA will go away."

George sees the greatest opportunity for expanding profit margins on sales in the undeveloped markets, where the concept of selling fresh fish is more unfamiliar and the market will bear the markup. Margins average between 5 and 10 cents/pound in the mature, traditional markets; George estimates that BSI can earn 25–30 cents/pound in the undeveloped markets, a few of which he has already explored. It takes time, however, to develop buyers in distant markets who (1) don't buy fresh fish in volume and (2) don't buy blind from East Coast suppliers whom they don't know and whom they would have to learn to trust. In BSI's experience, winning one influential buyer generally opens the door to other buyers. One supermarket chain feels compelled to carry the same product line as that carried by its competitors. However, George admits that several competitors are going after these markets too.

Employee Relations

George works at being an effective manager. He tries to develop a team spirit among his 10 employees. When recruiting new employees, he tries to evaluate whether they will fit in with the others and he avoids hiring "superstars who I then have to squash." BSI employed a truck driver who believed it was his job just to drive the truck. George says, "In a small company you can't have a guy just to drive the truck. He's got to move boxes, run down to the store to get lunch; he's got to do everything."

George works side by side with his employees in the warehouse. He wears the smell of fish and a green uniform with everyone else. The rapport he's built with his employees conveys to them that he cares about what they're doing. "And every night before they go home, I make sure I say to them, 'Thank you very much for coming in. I appreciate your help.' Because I really do."

BSI has made mistakes and has worked to correct them. Most of them stem from George's implicit trust in the people he works with. At the outset, employee policies were liberal and informal, and began to be abused. Now there is a formal policy for sick leave and a no-personal-loan policy. George and Daniel feel that their casualness was an expensive lesson, but, as George remarked, "you never really know what's going to come up until it's come up."

George has also learned some lessons about whom to hire. Early on, in an effort to expand operations beyond the supermarket customer, George decided to try selling direct to the Boston-area restaurants. BSI hired an experienced restaurant salesman at $20,000 a year to develop this business. George believes in delegating authority, but at the time he did not realize the necessity of monitoring operations as well. Before long, BSI faced serious cash flow problems from the restaurant operation because customers were not paying their bills on time. Sensing imminent disaster, since BSI was a cash-intensive business, George fired the salesman and turned the project over to his brother Timothy, whom Daniel had hired as a supermarket salesman. Timothy hadn't shown much promise in this capacity; George described Timothy as "a social crusader, nonbusiness type with latent entrepreneurial qualities." Taking a chance, George set Timothy up as an independent contractor, while George maintained direct control over the restaurant payment schedule. The new arrangement suited Timothy's temperament well, and restaurant accounts rose to 5 percent of sales. "Timothy is getting kind of cocky now," laughed George. "Now he's thinking of buying from other sources."

George reluctantly admits that he is a victim of the old adage, "Never bring a friend into the business." George hired a friend to coordinate purchasing and distribution from the plants. He perceived his friend to be intelligent, with strong management ability. To his dismay, George discovered that his friend couldn't perform the task that he was hired for. He transferred the friend to the computer control operation and recently gave him a $2,000 raise; George feels that he can't fire him because he is a friend.

George hired another employee who was so good that BSI couldn't hold on to him. George taught Jerry the fish business. He was George's right-hand man for 1½ years before he was hired away by one of BSI's competitors at twice his BSI salary.

Finances

The company was incorporated on November 1, 1977. The financial data on the operating history since 1977 are found in Exhibits 4 through 8.

In 1980 George's objective was to stabilize fixed costs. He kept the number of

Exhibit 4

BEANTOWN SEAFOODS, INC.
Balance Sheet
October 31, 1978
(Inception–November 1, 1977)

Assets

Current assets:

Cash		$ 12,103.26
Accounts receivable		121,138.03
Prepaid items		1,302.90
Total current assets		134,544.19

Property and equipment (at cost):

Office furniture and fixtures	$15,570.88	
Motor vehicle	4,620.00	
	20,190.88	
Less: Accumulated depreciation	3,602.50	16,588.38
Security deposits		945.42
Organization costs, unamortized		364.90
Notes and loans—officer		875.42
		$153,318.31

Liabilities and Stockholders' Equity

Current liabilities:

Accounts payable		$104,336.26
Salaries and wages payable		18,000.00
Chattel mortgage payable—motor vehicle		1,361.16
Notes payable—bank (unsecured)		6,644.76
Taxes withheld, accrued and payable		3,588.50
Total current liabilities		133,930.68

Long-term debt (net):

Chattel mortgage payable—motor vehicle	$ 1,020.87	
Notes payable—bank (unsecured)	3,876.11	4,896.98

Stockholders' equity:
Capital stock—common—no par value:
Authorized—12,500 shares

Issued and outstanding—1,000 shares	2,000.00	
Investment tax credit	2,032.69	
Retained earnings (Exhibit 5)	10,457.96	14,490.65
		$153,318.31

Accompanying accountants' report is an integral part of this unaudited statement.

his labor force stable. He increased volume, hoping that profits would skyrocket. They did. In 1980 net profits quadrupled (see Exhibit 7).

Since trading fish is a cash business, theoretically, the account collection period is short. BSI did not finance receivables until eight months after it started business. Fishermen are paid in cash for their catch. BSI's suppliers have to have cash. BSI pays its processing plants within 14 days. In the early years this was a hard goal. BSI, in turn, must be paid by its customers on time. Accounts over 30 days are bad accounts.

Daniel and George take very little money out of the business. They retain it for working capital, "to try to quicken the pace." Through inattention, BSI's checking account can contain $200,000 at any one time. George does not have the time or the extra personnel to attend to his cash flow right now. He realizes that he's neglecting the management of his working capital, but he sees no alternative at this time.

Exhibit 5

BEANTOWN SEAFOODS, INC.
Statement of Net Income
for the Year Ended October 31, 1978
(Inception—November 1, 1977)

Sales		$2,110,593.17
Cost of sales:		
Purchases	$1,925,244.33	
Freight	14,273.81	
Outside services	18,164.86	
Packaging	2,899.11	
Salaries and wages	19,733.17	1,980,315.28
Gross profit		130,277.89
Operating and administrative expenses:		
Officer's salary	36,000.00	
Bad debts	12,560.16	
Depreciation	5,602.50	
Dues and subscriptions	119.00	
Group insurance	1,891.94	
Insurance	926.00	
Interest expense	426.73	
Miscellaneous expense	987.47	
Motor vehicle operating expense	1,042.37	
Office and postage expense	2,008.14	
Organization costs, amortized	91.22	
Pension expense	24,321.24	
Professional fees	2,820.32	
Rent	3,541.68	
Rental of motor vehicle	3,843.00	
Repairs and maintenance	823.17	
Taxes	4,137.37	
Telephone	11,314.43	
Travel, selling, and promotion	5,630.15	
Utilities	409.74	
Total operating and administrative expenses		118,496.63
Net income from operations		11,781.26
Interest income	496.70	
Other income	361.20	857.90
		12,639.16
Provision for federal income taxes		2,181.20
Net income (transferred to Retained Earnings)		$ 10,457.96

Accompanying accountants' report is an integral part of this unaudited statement.

Because of its inexperience with credit, BSI had some bad accounts in the first few years. In 1976 it was selling product to a fresh fish distributor in LA whose sales to local restaurants ran about $86,000/week. The customer entered the restaurant business himself but neglected to tell BSI. Beantown Seafoods lost $15,000 because of the mail system. It takes five–seven days to receive a check in Boston from the West Coast. By the time the check is processed and mailed back to the customer's bank, marked "insufficient funds," 10–15 days have passed. Meanwhile, BSI was supplying the customer with fish. The original debt was $20,000 until Daniel flew to LA to collect payment. The customer gave Daniel a check for $5,000 as advance payment for more product. BSI never shipped the product.

After this experience, BSI tightened up its credit procedures. It established accounts in local banks in distant markets. The accounts deposit checks directly in the local bank. George calls the bank to confirm that the customer's check will

Exhibit 6

BEANTOWN SEAFOODS, INC.
Balance Sheet
October 31, 1980 and 1979

	1980	1979
Assets		
Current assets:		
Cash	$ 14,719.82	$ 5,766.03
Accounts receivable	610,166.90	271,407.86
Inventory	10,413.70	15,818.45
Prepaid items	1,580.85	2,948.27
Total current assets	636,881.27	295,971.11
Property and equipment (Note 1):		
Motor vehicles	34,506.30	27,799.01
Office furniture and fixtures	17,159.51	17,159.51
Machinery and equipment	480.03	3,109.47
	52,145.84	48,067.99
Less: Accumulated depreciation	16,821.85	10,440.15
Total property and equipment	35,323.99	37,627.84
Other assets:		
Security deposits	5,100.00	5,100.00
Organization costs, unamortized	—	273.70
Notes and loans—others	3,514.51	973.53
Total other assets	8,614.51	6,347.23
	$680,819.77	$339,946.18
Liabilities and Stockholders' Equity		
Current liabilities:		
Accounts payable	$452,752.65	$234,518.30
Chattel mortgages payable	7,724.68	6,148.08
Notes payable—bank	50,000.00	3,876.11
Accrued salaries payable	47,900.00	4,600.00
Accrued pension expense	—	20,000.00
Taxes withheld, accrued and payable	25,855.72	3,941.27
Total current liabilities	584,233.05	273,083.76
Long-term debt (net):		
Chattel mortgages payable	4,236.66	8,065.54
Notes and loans payable—officer	—	33,200.00
Total long-term debt		
Stockholders' equity:		
Capital stock—common—no par value:		
Authorized issue—12,500 shares		
Issued and outstanding—1,000 shares	2,000.00	2,000.00
Investment tax credits	2,996.81	2,286.89
Retained earnings (Exhibit 5)	87,353.25	20,735.99
Total stockholders' equity	92,350.06	25,596.88
	$680,819.77	$339,946.18

See accountants' compilation report.

clear. If it doesn't, BSI doesn't ship the product. It has been able to cut its losses on bad debts from $21,000 in 1979 to $9,800 in 1980 (Exhibit 7).

Another customer filed for Chapter 11 under the Bankruptcy Act with no warning. Both the customer and BSI started in business at the same time. When BSI did its second million, this customer did 12 million. Labor problems in the customer's plant were the beginning of his downfall. He was forced to sell his King Crab inventory that he had bought on speculation at a loss of $1/pound. He declared bankruptcy overnight. It cost BSI $10,000.

Exhibit 7

BEANTOWN SEAFOODS, INC.
Comparative Statement of Net Income and Retained Earnings
For the Years Ended October 31, 1980 and 1979

	1980	1979
Sales	$4,856,970.08	$3,246,522.80
Cost of sales	4,390,982.23	2,985,265.67
Gross profit	465,987.85	261,257.13
Operating and administrative expenses:		
Officers' salaries (including bonuses)	90,187.00	39,270.00
Salaries and wages	87,297.70	38,683.10
Advertising	295.40	14.94
Bad debts	9,838.35	21,103.85
Bank charges	86.00	110.50
Bonuses	8,700.00	8,100.00
Building—maintenance and security	3,095.29	1,030.38
Collection expense	308.96	—
Commissions	12,000.27	163.43
Depreciation	13,043.63	7,637.65
Dues and subscriptions	440.50	143.00
Entertainment	3,765.00	2,429.24
Freight—air	5,265.53	3,051.71
Freight—ground	22,733.33	16,258.32
Group insurance	6,151.53	5,080.57
Insurance	6,453.19	2,684.34
Life insurance expense—officers	3,360.99	3,360.99
Miscellaneous expense	1,991.74	1,267.01
Motor vehicle operating—automobiles	4,795.53	2,235.80
Motor vehicle operating—trucks	2,968.71	3,500.80
Motor vehicle operating—van	1,621.15	—
Office supplies	1,605.42	1,762.98
Outside services	2,220.97	14,666.44
Packaging	20,781.61	6,437.80
Pension fund expense	700.00	20,000.00
Postage	1,000.00	592.90
Professional and consulting fees	6,649.70	3,732.80
Rent	18,000.00	10,697.94
Rental of motor vehicle and equipment	740.65	1,988.94
Repairs and maintenance—automobiles	2,104.20	360.44
Repairs and maintenance—equipment	1,242.42	—
Repairs and maintenance—trucks	2,229.51	1,611.26
Salesmen's expenses	543.78	60.04
Small tools expenses	868.05	527.00
Stationery and printing	1,384.11	2,024.16
Taxes	21,927.56	7,978.05
Telephone	17,948.09	15,015.91
Travel	1,890.66	2,993.73
Utilities	720.25	2,607.35
Total operating and administrative expenses	386,956.78	249,183.37
Net income from operations		
Interest income	1,536.11	780.96
Rental income	2,300.00	2,045.42
Bad debt recovery	600.00	—
WIN reimbursement	9,112.50	—
	13,548.61	2,826.38
Less: Interest expense	6,147.43	3,074.74
Amortization expense	273.70	91.20
Loss on disposal of fixed assets	2,764.26	320.00
	9,185.39	3,485.94
Net income before federal income taxes	83,394.29	11,414.20
Provision for federal income taxes	21,326.76	2,499.06
Less: New Job and WIN credits utilized	4,549.73	1,362.89
	16,777.03	1,136.17
Net income for the year	66,617.26	10,278.03
Retained earnings at beginning of year	20,735.99	10,457.96
Retained earnings at end of year	$ 87,353.25	$ 20,735.99

See accountants' compilation report.

Exhibit 8

BEANTOWN SEAFOODS, INC.
Statement of Changes in Financial Position
For the Year Ended October 31, 1980

Source of funds:
  Operations:
    Net income for the year (net of loss on disposition
      of fixed assets—$2,764.26) .... $ 69,381.52
    Charges to net income not involving capital:
      Depreciation .... $ 13,043.63
      Amortization of organization costs 273.70   13,317.33
        Funds provided from operations 82,698.85
  Investment tax credits acquired and utilized 765.12
  Proceeds from sales of fixed assets 9,450.00
      Total funds provided   92,913.97

Use of funds:
  Acquisition of motor vehicles 22,954.04
  Reduction of chattel mortgages payable 3,828.88
  Reduction of notes and loans payable—officer 33,200.00
  Investment tax credit recaptured 629.20
  Increase in notes and loans receivable 2,540.00
      Total funds used 63,153.10
Net increase in working capital .... $ 29,760.87

Analysis of increase in working capital:

Increase (decrease) in current assets:
  Cash .... $ 8,953.29
  Accounts receivable 338,759.04
  Inventory ....   (5,434.75)
  Prepaid items ....   (1,367.42)
Net increase in current assets   340,910.16

Decrease (increase) in current liabilities:
  Accounts payable .... $(218,234.35)
  Accrued pension expense 20,000.00
  Chattel mortgages payable ....   (1,576.60)
  Notes payable—bank ....   (46,123.89)
  Accrued salaries payable ....   (43,300.00)
  Taxes withheld, accrued and payable ....   (21,914.45)
Net increase in current liabilities ....   (311,149.20)
Net increase in working capital .... $ 29,760.87

See accountants' compilation report.

Summing up the present situation, George comments, "I know a lot about marketing but not much about money."

George's View—A Summary

George likes the freedom and independence of working for himself. The variety of functions he performs as a small business manager is exciting to George.

I am the chief executive officer, and I'm doing the same thing a CEO does at IBM or General Foods except on a smaller scale, and that is very exciting. I feel good that I have direct control over my success and my failures. I can determine my own fate.

In addition to being the CEO, George was the bookkeeper in the first few years of BSI. With the first profits he bought a microcomputer for $18,000. It took nine months to get in operation, but it cut George's bookkeeping time from 30 hours a week to 3. George says the cash was hard to put out, but he knew the computer would allow him the time for selling and managing.

A typical day for George might be as follows: George arrives at the plant by 5 A.M. He takes inventory in the warehouse. By 7 he is in the office talking to the processing plants to begin getting prices. He'll start selling what he knows he has coming in. He'll go back out onto the warehouse floor and begin loading the trucks, then back to selling on the phone again. In between, he may have talked to the insurance company about applying more benefits to the employees or called his bank to find out if he's overdrawn for the day.

Sales volume of BSI has effectively doubled every year since 1976. George believes that planning can be credited for this success. He feels that it is important to have a definite plan of where to concentrate your energy and resources to avoid pursuing routes to the wrong place. George says, "Dad doesn't understand the importance of planning. I guess he thinks we grow because God likes us and that's the way it runs. Well, to a certain degree that's true, but a lot of it is planned growth."

George regards marketing ability as the most important quality required to start your own business. He thinks his father's axiom "You don't *ever* lose money" is a shortsighted philosophy. Daniel would rather not make the transaction than lose money. George concludes that losing money occasionally is inevitable if your first priority is to service customers. He feels that if he doesn't make the transaction, the customer will go somewhere else. George thinks that if he can develop a customer's business, which may include taking a loss some days, revenues will increase in the long run.

LOOKING AHEAD

Strategic Planning for BSI

Sales in 1980 were $4.9 million: an increase of 50 percent over 1979 sales. Sales in 1979 increased 54 percent from 1978. George expects to continue to use his basic selling strategies that have gained them success. At the same time, he realizes the importance of planning for the future. He reports,

Beantown Seafoods will go out of business in 10 years unless we do something different because the market matures and the markets we have developed are going to say "Why do we really need BSI? Why don't we go directly to the processing plant? We can save between 10 and 15 cents per pound." It's important that we do something different.

George plans to remove himself from the day-to-day operations so he can concentrate on ways the company can use its capital to expand. He wants to establish warehouses and sales offices offering full product lines and distribution services in markets on the East Coast, the Gulf, and the West Coast. He anticipates he needs 10 or 15 years, but it is a long-term goal he feels is realistic, "I would love to become the General Motors of the fresh fish industry, so that if a retailer thinks fresh fish, he says 'Beantown Seafoods.'" An immediate goal is to develop the extension markets. BSI is working to develop Minneapolis. Sales to Phoenix and Dallas have grown. BSI's sales report shows that their growth has come from the undeveloped markets. Exhibit 9 reports air business sales in 1980.

Exhibit 9
Beantown Seafoods, Inc., Air Business Analysis
(for fiscal year ending October 31, 1980)

Los Angeles	$224,400
Denver	194,800
Miami	167,900
New air business includes Jackson, Dallas–Fort Worth, Houston, St. Louis, Albuquerque	64,800
Total	$651,900

Another way to expand would be to buy a fish processing plant. By integrating backwards and cutting the fish themselves, BSI could realize another 30 to 40 cents per pound gross profit. This is attractive since gross profits now average 5 cents per pound. However, commitments between processing plants and their suppliers are very private affairs. A processing plant may form an alliance with a fisherman where it buys equipment for the fisherman's boat. He knows that the plant bought it, and he knows that he owes the plant. If he tries to sell his fish elsewhere, the plant reminds him. George feels that these Mafia-like maneuvers are beyond the scope of BSI.

Another idea that captured George's interest was to make fresh fish a branded item. This would change the face of the industry. Fresh fish could be packaged under vacuum in tray packs. Hot dogs are packaged this way, as are fish in Europe. The shelf life of fish would be extended to three or four weeks. The handling of fresh fish at the supermarket level would be eliminated. The risk of perishability would be dramatically reduced.

BSI can set up a tray-packing operation with no capital outlay. George can lease a packing machine from a packaging company that is anxious to use him as a guinea pig. BSI has the physical capacity. Its present plant has 1,500 square feet of unused space. Because BSI would assume the liability for the quality and safety of its packing, insurance rates would increase by $18,000–20,000 per year.

There are risks involved. When vacuum-sealed packages are opened, a gassy smell leaks out. Whether the consumer would continue to purchase fish packaged in this way is a risk. Tray packing could be well received for a few months and then decline because of infrequent repeat purchases. Another risk is that supermarket butchers, some of whom are unionized, would be out of work. An additional risk: Since the packages cannot be packed in ice, the safe delivery of the fish would be determined by whether the trucker keeps his refrigerator unit working.

Daniel Halsey thinks that the risks outweigh the benefits, but George sees the potential of doubling profits in the long run. Daniel's concern is that the fish would be transported incorrectly. George says that BSI already takes this risk every day. George feels that it is a question of being willing to risk the reputation of the corporation.

Eventually, George would like to have a professional board of directors to act as arbitrators between him and his father. George's brother, Michael, a securities analyst in Chicago, has a lot of credibility with Daniel Halsey and often plays the part of arbitrator.

"One thing you have to learn if you start your own business is that your goal should be to get out," says George. "It's not going to last forever, nor are you going to last forever." By hiring and developing the right people now, George is planning for his future exit from the daily operations. "It's an investment," he says. "A union worker puts away wages in a pension fund much the same way I'm investing in people so it will be done the way I want it. When I'm ready to get out or do something else, they'll be there."

George sometimes longs for a life without hard work:

> I'd love to be able to earn a lot of money and do nothing, but I don't know how to do it. It may be selling gold, but I don't know anything about gold. If God sent me a letter and told me how to do it, I'd do it. I'd like to be able to be out playing with my kid all day and go shopping with my wife. But I can't. I have to work for a living.

The Ownership Issue

The future ownership of the company is a frequent argument between George and his father. George has been waiting five years for his father to agree to a shared ownership plan. He trusts his father to be fair. Up until 1980, Daniel believed that the company could go bankrupt at any time. They debate two issues: (1) whether Daniel will share ownership with George and (2) if he does, how they will place a value on BSI.

George says that problems arise when families work together. "There's no question about it. Ordinarily, when faced with a problem, there's a black-and-white answer. Should you do it? Yes or no, and why?" When a family is involved in decisions, there are other considerations that affect the outcome, "things like mothers who don't think the president of a corporation should be doing things the solution might call for." George continues,

> I've gotten to the point with this stock redemption thing with my dad where I've said, "Look, I've had it with you, and I've had it with your waffling on these issues. Either you do it and you do it my way, or else forget it. I'll go out on my own. If I end up competing with you, then I end up competing with you. I'm not going to be subject to any more of this frustration."

As a result, George's brothers and sisters see him as ruthless. They expect him to steal their father's business and start his own company. George feels hurt by their misinterpretation of his intentions. He is desperate to resolve the issue. He wonders whether he's worked five years for nothing. He uses one of his previous jobs to describe his conflict. George was the manager of a radio station at the time Boston was experiencing racial tension over school busing. Most of his employees were black. Witnessing the tension and conflict that his employees felt "ripped my stomach apart." George says, "I have felt as bad in this job at BSI as I did at the radio station."

George has offered his father retirement at a $50,000 salary plus traveling expenses. Daniel was tempted but is not ready to leave the business. He thinks that the business can't run without him. George has offered him 10 percent of the worth of the company and a plan to buy the balance of shares over 10 years.

A BSI customer relates a similar incident:

> "George, I had exactly the same problem. I finally went to my father and said, 'Dad, I don't want to say this, but I'm hoping you're going to die.' My father said, 'I don't want you to think I'm going to die, so here, take the business.'"

In December 1980 Daniel signed over 20 percent ownership to George but retained the stock certificate. George legally owns 20 percent of the company but wonders whether he really does. By January George expects the issue to be concluded.

I'm not going to give him a lot of time to think about this offer. We've been negotiating for five years. There's no room for negotiating any more. If I allow him time, he'll drag it out for years.

George feels that his father doesn't listen to him. He has told Daniel that he's prepared to start his own company. Daniel's response was that George could not get the money. George's bank has offered financial backing. Daniel also does not believe that George is considering this alternative. George hopes his father realizes that he is serious and that he has his father's interests as well as the company's interests at heart. He wants his father to recognize the offer for its fairness.

If George started his own company, it would cause a rift between him and his brothers and sisters. Timothy knows something about the industry and about the value of BSI. He knows that he can get a share of the company by siding with his father. George feels that his family perceives him as an ogre.

If I buy out my father, it's going to be a real threat to Timothy's future goals. It's a problem for me not to be liked anymore by my brothers and sisters, but I can't live my life for them. Dad got really upset when I told him I wasn't living my life for him anymore. I have my own family.

My brothers and sisters see their own financial gains. My brother Michael, the MBA wizard, told my father that if he and I left the business, it would run by itself. Look around. Who would run the business? He had Dad believing that. Dad said we'd get someone in here to run it.

My family doesn't acknowledge that I raised this business from scratch. Our accountant, a mild-mannered fellow, was upset with Dad because he was being so callous about what was transpiring. Frank stood up in a meeting we had together and said, "Jesus Christ, Daniel, what do you think made the business grow—fertilizer?"

So the time has come. As young as I am, fate has a way of being good to me in the long run. For example, on my first co-op job at college, I was working for an ad agency. I got fired because they thought I was looking for a job with another agency. At the time I thought, "How traumatic!" But from there, I went to New York, which was the best thing in the world for me. So I'm looking at this optimistically. I see it, not as a problem, but as a real opportunity. Whatever happens, happens. I'll roll with the punches. If it doesn't work out, I'll just go somewhere else and try something else.

Preparation Questions

1. What do you see as the critical decisions facing George and the company in early 1981?
2. What valuation would you place on Beantown Seafoods in early 1981?
3. What should George Halsey do, and why?
4. Do a break-even for 1977, 1978, and 1979.
5. Evaluate BSI's entry strategy and tactics. How did these differ from the plan?
6. Analyze the financial implications of BSI's pricing and sales strategy.

APPENDIX

The New England Fishing Industry

Descriptions of the New England fishing fleet in the last several years have varied according to the purpose of the speaker or writer. The fleet has been downgraded in order to attract financial support from government, upgraded to get lower interest and insurance rates from industry, romanticized as the "first industry," for Bicentennial purposes, praised for the independence of spirit and action it embodies for America's young men, and mourned for its precipitous decline.[1]

Exhibit 8A–1
U.S. Per Capita Consumption of Fish (in pounds)

	1965	1970	1973	1974	1975	1976	1977	1978
Fish (edible weight)	10.8	11.8	12.9	12.2	12.1	13.0	12.8	12.9
Fresh and frozen	6.0	6.9	7.5	7.0	7.4	8.2	7.8	7.9
Canned	4.3	4.5	5.0	4.8	4.3	4.3	4.6	4.6
Cured	0.5	0.4	0.4	0.4	0.4	0.5	0.4	0.4

Source: U.S. Department of Agriculture, Economics, Statistics, and Cooperative Service.

The U.S. consumption of fish has gradually increased in recent years (see Exhibit 8A–1).

Of the total amount of animal protein consumed by man, fish and shellfish account for approximately 14 percent. Although Americans overwhelmingly prefer meat to fish, the Food and Agriculture Organization of the UN expects the consumption of fish to increase through 1990 at a growth rate higher than that of beef, pork, vegetables, cereal, or milk.

The U.S. coastal waters contain 20 percent of the world's fish resources. Overharvesting and depletion had been allowed until recently. Marine resources are now considered exhaustible.

Groundfish, or bottom fish, caught on the seafloor, are abundant in New England waters. The varieties of New England groundfish consumed by Americans are haddock, cod, ocean perch, yellowtail flounder, whiting, pollock, cust, redfish, and hake.

The two main markets for the New England catch are fresh and frozen fish. There is a smaller market for nonfood fish (fishmeal). Fishing and distribution methods differ for each of these segments.

Because the retail price of fresh fish is higher than that of frozen, most of the groundfish landed by U.S. fishermen is not frozen.

The New England fishing fleet is a collection of diverse-sized fishing vessels that catch a variety of species. Each of the species is subject to different supply and demand conditions and price variations.

The Process

The fishing industry is made up of the producers (the fishermen), the processors (filleters and packagers), and wholesalers and distributors.

[1] Susan Peterson and Leah Smith, *The New England Fishing Industry: A Basis for Management* (Woods Hole, Mass.: Woods Hole Oceanographic Institution, 1977), p. 10.

Boston, New Bedford, and Gloucester, Massachusetts, are the major New England ports where fresh fish is landed. Most of the boats are individually owned and operated by families. Fishermen are represented by organized labor in these ports, although they are not in other New England ports. With the exception of Boston, there is a strong tradition of fathers passing the trade to sons. The union data report that most of the fishermen are between 50 and 60 years of age. Some younger men work as deckhands.

The quantity of fish caught by any one vessel is a function of its type. Since groundfishing in New England is a labor-intensive industry, the ability and experience of the fishermen, which vary from boat to boat, are a major influence on the catch.

New England fishing vessels are small, aged wooden-hulled ships. In 1976 the average age of the boats was 20 years. Their length can range from 20 feet to 140 feet. The smaller boats are used for offshore fishing, and the larger boats for fishing longer distances. Most of the commercial market is supplied by fishermen who fish more than 12 miles off the coast in boats longer than 50 feet weighing 40 tons.

Neither the gear nor the fishing operation has changed significantly in the last 100 years. Much of the operation is still conducted by hand. Electronic gear used to locate schools of fish was introduced after World War II. Otter trawls and purse seines are the more common means used to entrap fish. An otter trawl is a conical net dropped over the side of the boat and dragged along the sea bottom collecting fish. The mouth of the net is held open by otter or trawl boards. A purse seine is a large net that is laid around a school of fish. The ends are closed or pursed to contain the catch.

While at sea, the catch is stored on ice. The boats are not refrigerated.

On arrival in port, the fish is auctioned off before it is unloaded from the ship. Fish is sold for cash at auction on a per pound basis. The price received at auction changes daily, based on supply and demand. Although the quality of the catch will affect its price, the scarcity of the species for sale determines the final selling price. Even though the smaller auctions throughout New England account for most of the fish sold, the price received at the Boston auction sets the regional market price for fish. This is because prices can be artificially controlled at some of the smaller auctions. For example, in New Bedford there are four buyers who conspire to keep prices artificially low. Fishermen are paid on a share system. Until the fish has been auctioned off, the members of the crew don't know what their wages will be. From the gross revenues of the auction sale, the expenses of the trip are deducted. A percentage of the balance is awarded to the crew. Earnings vary from one trip to the next, one day to the next, one season to the next, and one boat to the next.

The fish is unloaded from the hold by a special crew, called "lumpers," who haul the fish with wire baskets. The fish is delivered to the processing plant of the purchaser.

The Economics of the Industry

The commercial fishing industry in the United States is characterized by a lack of technology and capital resources. It has been one of the last U.S. industries to resist technology. The lack of capital has prohibited modernization.

Small individually owned boats cannot compete with foreign fishing vessels that catch and process groundfish in one efficient operation in boats costing $15–20 million to build.

Researchers from Woods Hole Oceanographic Institution offer a reason why fishermen don't favor new technology.

The fact that fishermen are paid by share rather than a fixed salary or hourly wage has several implications for the industry as a whole. For example, the crew may be resistant to changing fishing gear or fishing grounds because the cost of learning is absorbed by all of them rather than by the captain or owner interested in instituting a change. Also, since fewer men on a vessel receive a larger share of the total income, any plan to increse employment would have to consider individual losses of income. Plans to limit effort by requiring archaic gear and therefore requiring more men are also to the disadvantage of the crew. Share systems are usually advantageous to the owner because he assumes men will not be careless with gear or time for which they pay.[2]

Ex-vessel prices of fish are subject to seasonal fluctuations. During the spring and summer months, when the catch increases and demand decreases, prices drop.

The ex-vessel price of fish varies daily based on supply and demand. The retail prices of fish fluctuate far less than the ex-vessel price; therefore, it takes a long time for price increases to be passed on to the consumer.

Distribution and Marketing

After the fish has been landed, it must be filleted and packaged in quantities for sale to wholesalers. This is called processing.

Fresh fish processors can obtain fish in several ways: (1) directly from the fishermen, (2) through auctions, (3) through sales controlled by fish co-ops, or (4) from wholesalers who buy on consignment.

Processing companies have a great deal of influence on the species caught because the fishermen bring to port only what they can sell. Fishermen direct their efforts toward landing species with higher values rather than increasing the volume of fish they land. Many species of fish in New England coastal waters are not commercially fished because there is no market for them.

Most processing companies are also family controlled. Fishermen sellers and processor buyers have informal working alliances that have existed for generations.

Processing plants and fishermen often have formal co-op arrangements that aid in the production and marketing of fresh fish. Co-ops allow commercial fishermen to market their fish collectively. The unit cost of handling fish goes down, and the fishermen experience economies of scale. Other collective benefits are quantity purchases of gear and supplies. Co-ops also arrange financing and operate dock services. To gain higher ex-vessel prices for fishermen, co-op salesmen can spread the sale of a catch over more buyers. In this way, they give the illusion that the fish is scarce and they do not give volume discounts.

Fishermen catch whatever the co-op can sell. If the co-op deals in only a few species of fish, catching new species is discouraged.

[2]Ibid., p. 22.

In ports without co-ops, fishermen are subject to whatever price an auction dealer offers.

Both buyers and processors are affected by the seasonal fluctuations in the volume of fish landed in New England. Idle capacity and transportation arrangements to the markets are the main uncertainties.

Fresh fish is trucked to local markets. Most processors and buyers hire trucking services rather than keeping their own fleet of trucks. Distant markets are supplied via air cargo.

In the last 20 years there has been a shift in the source of supply in New England markets. There is less fish landed today in Boston than in New Bedford and Gloucester, Massachusetts, and in Maine. There has been an accompanying increase in the amount of fish processed outside Massachusetts.

Competition

Brian Veasy, general manager of the New Bedford Seafood Co-op, is quoted as follows:

"Look at it this way. It costs me 90 cents a pound to buy fish from the local boats and fillet and pack them, where I can buy subsidized, duty-free, Canadian fish already filleted and packed for 75 cents. If we weren't a co-op, I wouldn't be buying from the boats here at all."[3]

The fishing industry in Canada is subsidized by the government. The Canadian government subsidizes fuel, makes loan guarantees for boats, and controls most of the fish landed in Canada by centralizing the processing of fresh fish in two plants. In July 1980 Canadian fishermen bought diesel fuel for 39 cents a gallon. Massachusetts fishermen paid 99 cents the same week. The subsidies allow Canadians to flood the U.S. market with fish prices below those for the U.S. catch. Eighty percent of the Canadian catch is exported to the United States. In the late 60s foreign fishing fleets subsidized by the East German, Russian, Japanese, and Polish governments fished in U.S. territorial waters. Factory boats the size of ocean liners cleaned out the ocean within three miles of the U.S. coastline. The Georges Bank fishery, an extension of Cape Cod, was almost totally depleted. Fish was processed, frozen, and stored on the foreign vessels. Typically, the factory boats landed 2,000–3,000 pounds of fish per hour versus the same quantity per day on a traditional U.S. vessel.

They went through each square mile of rich ocean bottom like a combine going through a wheat field, reducing everything from fins and scales to lobster shells into a uniform fish flour which was later made into fish meal, fish cakes, and fertilizer.[4]

U.S. fisherment were clearly outstripped by foreign fishing methods.

In response to the loss of control over its fisheries, the U.S. government passed the Fishery Conservation and Management Act in 1976, which extended control over fish resources to within 200 miles of its coastline. The act is designed to ensure sufficient regeneration of the fish supply in the future. Americans and foreigners alike are subject to quotas. Fishery councils were established to allocate resources first to U.S. fishermen and the surplus to foreign fishermen.

[3]"Plummeting Prices End New England's Fishing Boom," *New York Times,* July 6, 1980, p. 1.
[4]Ibid.

The FCMA has effectively limited the large fleets of foreign factory boats. Prior to FCMA, as many as 2,500 occupied U.S. waters. Since 1977, less than 950 permits have been issued. The foreign catch has dropped by more than one third. The East Coast fishing fleet has increased 30 percent since the passage of the FCMA. In 1978 there was an 8 percent increase in the number of vessels, and in 1979 there was a 20 percent increase. Even though the amount of fish landed has dramatically increased in the last few years, the National Marine Fisheries Service estimates that the average landing per vessel has actually declined in many New England fisheries (Exhibit 8A–2).

Exhibit 8A–2
Aggregate Performance Data—Otter Trawl Fleet (Maine, New Hampshire, Massachusetts), 1974–1979

	1974	1975	1976	1977	1978	1979
Total landings (lbs.)	271,655,129	254,459,727	254,496,205	207,032,489	320,367,919	337,020,568
Total revenue ($)	49,093,988	57,860,618	65,348,495	75,055,295	93,416,891	107,572,789
Total vessels	586	597	599	602	652	780
Lbs./Vessel	463,575	426,230	424,868	493,409	491,361	432,077
$ Nominal/Vessel	83,778	96,918	109,095	124,676	143,277	137,914
$ 1976/Vessel	96,344	100,795	109,095	117,195	126,083	104,814

The Environment

Despite the 200-mile-limit law, observers of the fishing industry feel that it is in a period of decline. Fishermen are expected to incur serious losses because of insufficient government protection via subsidies.

In the late 70s the interest of the U.S. government in the fishing industry grew in response to a concern for the level of contaminants in fish, the possibility of drilling for oil in fishing grounds, and a fishing rights boundary dispute with Canada.

Because of high levels of mercury in swordfish in the 1970s, a ban resulted in all landed swordfish being seized.

Oil companies want to drill for oil in the Georges Bank area of the Gulf of Main (Exhibit 8A–3). Georges Bank, one of the richest fishing grounds in the world, produces 17 percent of the fish consumed in the United States and 14 percent of world fish consumption. It has been estimated that Georges Bank would produce 900 million barrels of oil, enough to supply the needs of the United States for four to five days.

The oil companies claim that oil drilling and fishing are compatible. The U.S. Department of the Interior is reviewing bids from oil companies that want to drill in Georges Bank. Despite a court battle waged by the state of Massachusetts, the Department of the Interior has sold oil leases for rights to drill in Georges Bank. The lieutenant governor of Massachusetts, on behalf of the environmentalists, won the concession from the federal government that the oil companies must conduct biological studies of the area before development can begin. The oil companies have to use the "best available technology" with which to drill.

The danger of an oil spill poisoning the marine environment is great. Pipelines are preferable to tankers in transporting oil, but it is not economical for the oil industry to build a 150–200-mile pipeline to transport the marginal amount of

Exhibit 8A–3
New England Coastline

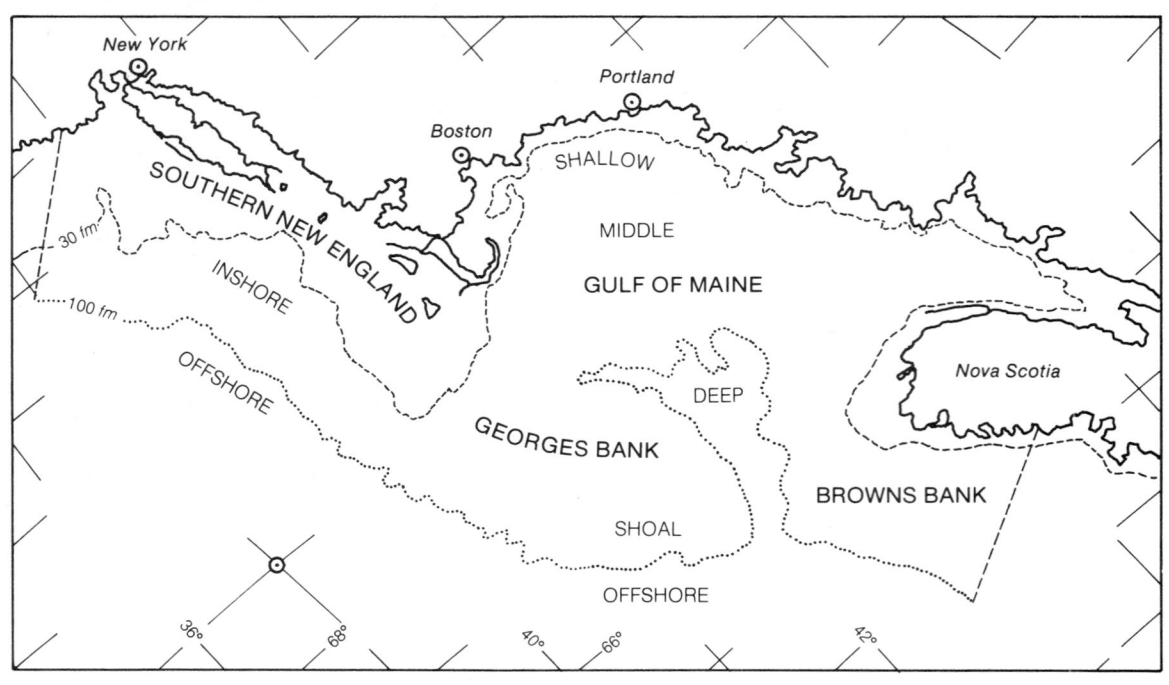

Source: *Sports Fishing Institute*, p. 387, 1979.

oil estimated to be in Georges Bank. Loading oil into tankers in 30-foot seas increases the risk of an oil spill. Since the amount of oil is marginal, it is expected that developers will use cheaper technology to get to the oil. This may lead to a high risk of accidents and of oil discharges into the ocean.

Another environmental consideration is the boundary treaty for fishing rights between the United States and Canada. The dispute is over where and how the Gulf of Maine should be divided (Exhibit 8A–3). The United States claims that Georges Bank in a geographic extension of Cape Cod and therefore belongs to the United States. The Canadians claim that the northeastern corner of Georges Bank is closer to Canada and that the division should be made on the principle of equidistance. The other issue of the treaty is how to allocate the catch between the United States and Canada. The New England fishermen oppose Canada's claim. They feel that the Senate Foreign Relations Committee is trading away their traditional fishing grounds in return for unrelated natural gas and oil agreements with Canada.

Personal Ethics and the Entrepreneur　　9 >

And when at some future date the high court of history sits in judgment on each of us, . . . our success or failure . . . will be measured by the answers to four questions: First, were we truly men of courage. . . . Second, were we truly men of judgment. . . . Third, were we truly men of integrity. . . . Finally, were we truly men of dedication.

John Fitzgerald Kennedy
Inaugural Address
January 9, 1961

9.1　RESULTS EXPECTED

This chapter, and the accompanying session, will focus on personal ethics and entrepreneurship. It will ask you to make some decisions involving ethical choices and then to examine the value system that governed your choices. It will also help you to understand the role of personal ethics in launching an entrepreneurial career.

Upon completion of this chapter and related discussion, you will have:

1. Identified and analyzed some of your personal ethics as they apply to business situations.
2. Made some ethical decisions about business situations described in the chapter and identified and analyzed your ethical values for deciding as you did.
3. Discussed the implications of these ethical decisions with others and identified how they might affect you (the entrepreneur), your partners, your customers, and your competitors.
4. Acquired a background, based on history, philosophy, and research, about the changing and situational nature of business ethics to provide a context for thinking about ethical behavior.
5. Gained some insight into the importance of ethical awareness in the career of a successful entrepreneur.

9.2　PRESESSION PREPARATION

Prepare the Entrepreneurial Decisions exercise in Section 9.3. Be prepared to discuss and defend your choices with other members of the discussion group.

(*Optional:* Complete the Allport-Vernon-Lindsay Personal Values Questionnaire.)

9.3   ENTREPRENEURIAL DECISIONS

9.3.1   Entrepreneurial Decisions Exercise

The following exercise involves considering a number of situations that require a decision. Each situation has four possible decision choices. Select the one that most closely represents the decision that you feel you would make. You will not have all the background information on each question. Instead, you should make whatever assumptions that you feel you would make if you were actually confronted with the decision choices described. In other words, you should feel as much as possible that you are really facing this in life.

This exercise has no "right or wrong answers." Rather, we will use the responses that people select as a basis of subsequent discussion.

1.   Your small manufacturing company is in serious financial difficulty. A large order of your product is ready to be delivered to a key customer when you discover that the product is simply not right. It will not meet all of the performance specifications, will cause problems for your customer, and will require rework in the field; but this, you know, will not become evident until after the customer has received and paid for your order. If you do not ship the order and receive the payment as expected, your business may be forced into bankruptcy. And if you delay the shipment or inform the customer of these problems, you may lose the order and also go bankrupt. What would you do?

_____ *a.*   I would not ship the order, and I would place my firm in voluntary bankruptcy.

_____ *b.*   I would inform the customer and declare voluntary bankruptcy.

_____ *c.*   I would ship the order and inform the customer, after I received payment.

_____ *d.*   I would ship the order and not inform the customer.

2.   You are the cofounder and president of a new venture manufacturing products for the recreational market. Five months after the business has been launched, one of your suppliers informs you that it can no longer supply you with a critical raw material since you are not a large-quantity user. Without the raw material the business cannot continue. Which of the following would you do?

_____ *a.*   I would persuade an alternative supplier to fill my needs even though this will mean that it will no longer be able to supply another, noncompeting small manufacturer, who may thus be forced out of business.

_____ *b.*   I am aware of a sizable stockpile of the raw material at another firm (noncompeting) that I can steal. I steal it.

_____ *c.*   I believe that the supplier could be "persuaded" to meet my needs, but this would necessitate a sizable "under the table" payoff that my company could afford. I make the payoff.

_____ *d.*   In order to secure the raw material from another supplier that would think I am a much larger potential customer, I would grossly overstate my requirements.

3.   You are on a marketing trip for your new venture, calling on the purchasing agent of a major prospective client. Your company is manufacturing an elec-

tronic system that you hope the purchasing agent will buy. During the course of your conversation you notice on the cluttered desk of the purchasing agent several copies of a cost proposal for a system from one of your direct competitors. This purchasing agent has previously reported mislaying several of your own company's proposals and asked for additional copies. The purchasing agent goes out of the room to get you a cup of coffee, leaving you alone with your competitor's proposals less than an arm's length away. What would you do?

_____ *a.* I do nothing but await the man's return.

_____ *b.* I sneak a quick peek at the proposal looking for bottom line numbers.

_____ *c.* I put a copy of the proposal in my briefcase.

_____ *d.* I wait until the man returns and ask his permission to see a copy.

4. You are taking a very difficult chemistry course, which you must pass to maintain your scholarship and to avoid damaging your application for graduate school. Chemistry is not your bag, and because of a just-below-failing average in the course, you will have to receive a 90 or better on the final exam, which is two days away. A janitor, who is aware of your plight, informs you that he found the master stencil for the chemistry final in a trash barrel and saved it. He will make it available to you for a price that you consider to be high but that you could afford. What would you do?

_____ *a.* I tell the janitor thanks but no thanks.

_____ *b.* I report the janitor to the proper officials.

_____ *c.* I buy the exam and keep it to myself.

_____ *d.* I do not buy the exam myself but let some of my friends, who are also flunking the course, know that it is available.

5. You have been working on some financial projections manually for two days now. It seems as if each time you have them completed, your boss shows up with a new assumption or a new "what if" question. If you only had a copy of spreadsheet software for the personal computer like the spreadsheet software that you learned how to use at school, you could plug in the new assumptions and revise the estimates with ease. Instead, it seems that it could take several more days by hand. Then a colleague may have answered your prayers: she offers to let you make a copy of her boyfriend's software—a 1–2–3 type program that she can get. What would you do?

_____ *a.* Readily accept your friend's generous offer and make a copy of the software.

_____ *b.* Decline to copy the software and plug away manually on the numbers.

_____ *c.* Decide to go buy the software yourself, for $300, and hope that you will be reimbursed by the company in the normal month or two.

_____ *d.* Request another extension on an already overdue project date.

9.3.2   Group Discussion of the Entrepreneurial Decisions Exercise

Step 1:   The larger group should be divided into small teams of five or six persons. These teams should preferably be new venture teams that are working on a project together.

Step 2:   Each team should discuss the answers of individual members to the foregoing questions and attempt to arrive at a group consensus regarding an

**Team Summary: Entrepreneurial
Decisions Exercise***

Names: _____

Situation						Team Answer
1.						
2.						
3.						
4.						
5.						

*Record the answer of each team member in each box and the team's solution in the column on the far right.

answer to each of the six decisions. Use the summary sheet below. Allow 20–30 minutes.

Step 3: Each team reports its conclusions to the entire group. These can be recorded on a blackboard or on flip-chart paper.

Step 4: Following a report from each group, the group discussion should focus on:
1. To what extent was a consensus reached by each group?
2. Why was this difficult or easy?
3. What kinds of personal ethics emerged from the group discussion?
4. Did conflicts exist among team members, and how were these resolved or left unresolved?
5. What roles do ethics play, and how important are ethics in the formation of a new venture management team?
6. If you were an investor, would ethics and integrity demonstrated "turn you off"? Why?
7. If the student has judged his or her own conduct as ethically less than perfect, what feelings bother him most (loss of self-respect, a sense of inferiority at not being able to be effective in an "upright" manner, fear of the judgment of others, a combination of these, etc.)?

9.4 SUMMARY DISCUSSION OF THE EXERCISE

The exercise and discussion just completed enabled you to express and examine some of your own ethical standards through the decisions you actually made or did not make. You may have observed that some team members often found it quite difficult to reach agreement on an answer to each of the five situations described. In other teams agreement may have been reached more easily.

The extent of agreement or conflict stemmed from previously held individual beliefs and attitudes toward what is right or wrong, ethical or unethical behavior. Such beliefs and attitudes provide the guidance and directional control system for human behavior. Personal ethics and values thus influence greatly the individual decisions made in the exercise. Because our ethics are very personal and internalized, we may not even be aware of them until we are forced into working out tough decisions under pressure. They govern not only the direction of the team discussion but also the intensity of the feeling and emotion that are displayed during the discussion.

Several important observations should emerge from this exercise:

1. Personal ethics involve internalized beliefs about what is "right" and what is "wrong," and these beliefs differ from individual to individual.
2. Your personal opinion may be altered after you have discussed it with a group.
3. You were only answering the question "What would you do?" You were not being asked to do it. Between the intent and the action lies a large gap that can only be filled by confronting and acting in a number of ambiguous situations.

An awareness of the difference in reactions to "what is ethical" may help you to understand why some aspects of venture creation go wrong for no apparent reason.

Differences among Partners. Innumerable examples can be cited to illustrate that broken partnerships are often traceable to apparent differences in the personal ethics among the members of a management team. To test this generalization for yourself, talk with entrepreneurs who have had a partnership go sour. Ask each partner how important subtleties of personal ethics were and what part they played in the breakup of the partnership. While teams dissolve for myriad reasons, differences in ethics are often prime contributors to such breakups. In fact, difficulties that you may be experiencing in your own venture project team may be explicable in terms of clashes in individual ethics.

Disagreements with Potential Investors. The experienced venture capital investor seeks entrepreneurs with a reputation for integrity, honesty, and ethical behavior. The definition of ethical behavior is necessarily subjective—depending in part on the beliefs of the investor himself and in part on the prevailing ethical climate in the industry sector in which your venture is involved. Evidence that an entrepreneur has engaged in "shady practices" for a short-term gain is a red flag to an experienced investor, who is very likely to decline a proposal from such an entrepreneur. On the other hand, an inexperienced and naive entrepreneur may not understand the operating nuances prevalent in his field of business and may find that his personal views of "right" and "wrong" do not correspond to the rules observed by his competitors. An entrepreneur who is rigidly moralistic in a situation that calls for flexibility is also unlikely to attract investors. Understanding the limits of the "gray area" and how to operate within that area can be critical to the success of your venture—and it takes both experience and sensitivity to tread the line between "savvy" and "shady."

9.4.1 Moralistic, Situational, and Amoral Ethics—A Continuum

One interesting way of examining the question of personal ethics and values is to consider a continuum of the ethical behaviors that can be found in the business world. These behaviors range from the highly rigid and moralistic to the situational and flexible. Of course, some immoral practices are also illegal—deception, fraud, unfair lending,and so forth. And we hasten to emphasize that the entrepreneur should neither encourage nor condone any illegal behavior. Moreover, the moderate risk taker will tend to avoid any overtly illegal or unethical behavior that is perceived as too risky.

Exhibit 9.1 attempts to illustrate how the various suggested responses to the Entrepreneurial Decisions exercise could be viewed along a continuum of behavior from moralistic to illegal or amoral. The choices available in the exercise generally offered responses that ranged from the moralistic (e.g., under no circumstances should one consider doing something that could be considered wrong or even amoral) to the situational (e.g., one should do what the needs and demands of the situation pragmatically require) to the amoral or illegal (one should go beyond the limits of the law and sound situational ethics). Our point here was to enable you to test the limits of your own ethical views, not to encourage or condone amoral or illegal practices. Further, we wanted to illustrate the considerable impact of personal ethics on your relationships with your team members, directors, and investors. And in the real world, of course, creative solutions to those situations that were not included in the exercise might be envisioned.

Exhibit 9.1
A Continuum of Ethical Behavior*

Moralistic	*Situational*	*Amoral, Illegal*
(Rigid and independent code of conduct applied uniformly regardless of the conditions and circumstances)	(Conduct and behavior influenced mainly by the needs and demands of the situation rather than by some rigid external code)	(Conduct and behavior determined without regard for legal or moral constraints)

Entrepreneurial Decisions Exercise Problems	*Positions of answers (to exercise in Section 9.3) tend to reflect their location on the ethical behavior continuum.*			
1. Manufacturing company with faulty product	(a)(b)	(c)		(d)
2. Raw materials shortage	(a)	(c)	(d)	(b)
3. Call on purchasing agent	(a)	(d)	(b)	(c)
4. Final exam	(a)(b)	(d)	(c)	
5. Software	(b)	(c)(d)	(a)	

*It may be of interest to know that the authors debated these classifications of the answers at length and represent the classifications as approximations, recognizing that some of the answers offer no easily agreed-upon classification.

9.5   ETHICS: AN OVERVIEW[1]

9.5.1   Why Include Ethics?

Simply stated, building and maintaining a reputation for high integrity is not only "good business," it is the "right thing" to do. We hear these views echoed from a wide range of sources, and have seen it confirmed in our own experiences. A leading recent example of this was the comment by John Cullinane, founder of Cullinet, Inc., the software firm, during his induction into Babson's Academy of Distinguished Entrepreneurs in 1984.

If you gain financial success at the expense of your integrity, you are not a success at all.

Ironically, when we sought reviews for the revision of this book, we were startled by the comments of one professor who went so far as to chide us:

What do you need a chapter on ethics for? Get rid of it, and replace it with more on making a profit!

We suspect that his experience has been a bit more confined to the classroom than our own.

We felt that the issue was worth exploring further. Were we really off-base on the decision to address the role of ethics in entrepreneurship? One of the authors teamed up with his colleague Howard H. Stevenson, of Harvard Business School, on a research project to seek the views of entrepreneurs and CEOs attending the Small Company Management Program at HBS. We sought to test the relevance of our inclusion of ethics by asking these practitioners a straightforward question: Is there a role for ethics in business education for entrepreneurs?[2]

We reasoned that these entrepreneurs were sufficiently experienced to have some relevant views on the topic. After all, their ages ranged from the early 30s to 60, with an average of around 43; the sales of their quite successful firms were typically $30–40 million and ranged from $4 million to $1 billion; and nearly half of them had actually started their businesses and grown them to their present size. In short, if any group of entrepreneurs had seen ethics in action in the real world, it was this group.

The responses of these entrepreneurs might startle the average person: 72 percent said that ethics could and should be taught as part of the curriculum (only 20 percent said no, and two respondents weren't sure). The most prominently cited reason was that ethical behavior was at the core of long-term business success because it provided the glue that bound enduring successful business and personal relationships together. What's more, the responses reflected a serious and thoughtful awareness of the fragile but vital role of ethics in entrepreneurial attainment. Consider these comments:

If the free enterprise system is to survive, the business schools better start paying attention to teaching ethics. They should know that business is built on trust, which depends upon honesty and sincerity. BS comes out quickly in a small company.

---

[1]The authors wish to acknowledge their debt to Grace M. Dingee for her earlier contributions to this section; to Nancy Tieken of Babson College for her efforts in revising the chapter; and to Profesor David Boyd, Northeastern University, for his thoughtful critique of the chapter and for his contributions to it.

[2]Jeffry A. Timmons and Howard H. Stevenson, "Entrepreneurship Education for the 80s: What Do Entrepreneurs Say?" 75th Anniversary Entrepreneurship Symposium, Harvard Business School, Boston, July 1983.

Another respondent saw ethics as vital to social progress:

If our society is going to move forward, it won't be based on how much money is accumulated in any one person or group. Our society will move forward when all people are treated fairly—that's my simple definition of ethics. I know of several managers, presidents, etc. who you would not want to get between them and their wallets or ambitions.

And another contended that business fared well when judged by ethical conduct standards:

In my experience the business world is by and large the most ethical and law-abiding part of our society.

A 40-year-old head of a real estate and construction firm in the Northeast with 300 employees and $75 million in annual sales saw it differently:

There is so much hypocrisy in today's world that even totally ethical behavior is questioned since many people think it is some new negotiating technique.

A strong consensus emerged in support of a vital role for ethics in the curriculum. One respondent summed it up this way:

Ethics should be addressed, considered, and thoroughly examined; it should be an inherent part of each class and course. . . . Instead of crusading with ethics, it is much more effective to make high ethics an inherent part of business—and it is.

There was keen awareness of the long-term consequences of ethical behavior for the business. As one founder put it: "It doesn't pay not to be ethical." In contrast to this consensus in support of teaching ethics, the subject is virtually untouched in business curricula, apparently because ethics are too delicate or potentially controversial.

9.5.2 Contrary Opinions

Not every businessperson would agree, however, and you should be aware of the type of opposition that the examination of ethics is likely to engender. One entrepreneur who helped to found a large company with international operations cautioned the authors about getting too involved in ethical conjecture. "For God's sake," he warned, "don't forget that 90 percent of the businessman's efforts consist of just plain hard work." He went on to point out the down-to-earth, relentless work atmosphere, with its contradictory demands, within which the individual must find time to identify and analyze his attitude toward what constitutes ethical business behavior.

What, after all, *is* ethical business behavior? Nearly two decades ago, in a provocative article entitled "Is Business Bluffing Ethical?"[3] a businessman asserted that the ethics of business were not those of society but rather those of the poker game. Both business and poker, he argued, required

intimate knowledge of the rules, insight into the psychology of the other players, a bold front, a considerable amount of self-discipline, and an ability to respond swiftly and effectively to opportunities provided by chance.

[3]Albert Z. Carr, "Is Business Bluffing Ethical?" *Harvard Business Review,* January–February 1968, pp. 145–52.

Poker, like business, he continued, did not allow cheating or "unethical" behavior such as trying to get your opponents drunk.

Poker's own brand of ethics is different from the ethical ideals of civilized human relationships. The game calls for distrust of the other fellow. It ignores the claim of friendship. Cunning deception and concealment of one's strength and intentions, not kindness and openheartedness, are vital in poker. No one thinks any the worse of poker on that account. And no one should think any the worse of the game of business because its standards of right and wrong differ from the prevailing traditions of morality in our society.

However, the author's analogy led him to an uncomfortable conclusion:

That most businessmen are not indifferent to ethics in their private lives, everyone will agree. My point is that in their office lives they cease to be private citizens; they become game players who must be guided by a somewhat different set of ethical standards.

As you might suspect, the article—published by the *Harvard Business Review*—provoked a storm of responses by businesspeople who insisted that *their* business ethics were "ethical" and castigated the author for giving "businessmen" a bad name. Nonetheless, the author made a valid point: personal ethics and business ethics are often not in harmony, and by either negotiation or compromise the differences between them must be resolved.

9.5.3 "Strategic Misrepresentation" or Lying?

Another real-life furor about ethics occurred not long ago when *The Wall Street Journal* reported on Professor Howard Raiffa's "Competitive Decision-Making" course at the Harvard Business School.[4] During simulated negotiating sessions students were encouraged to try any tactics at all in order to "win." Lies, which Raiffa termed "strategic misrepresentations," were permissible tactics; Raiffa stated that

in strategic negotiations...it is unfortunately not always true that complete, unadorned open honesty is the best policy.

Again, the protest mail poured into Harvard. *Business and Society Review* elicited comments from several dozen CEOs and professors of business, as well as from the leaders of the Girl Scouts and the Boy Scouts.[5] Many of the replies were in defense of this or that corporation's ethical standards and ethical conduct, and many were moralistic in tone:

Sloan K. Childers, vice president of Phillips Petroleum, wrote:

Even though lying may be categorized as "strategic misrepresentation" it is still lying, and Phillips Petroleum Company does not condone or permit such activity in its operations. The course instructor states that in strategic negotiations it is unfortunately not always true that complete honesty is the best policy. We neither agree with this statement nor permit its implications to be applied by our people. It is our opinion that in business, as in other situations, honesty is always the best policy. I recognize that there are many honest differences of view; however, we do not subscribe to that statement that lying is now an acceptable part of negotiations.[6]

---

[4] *The Wall Street Journal,* January 15, 1979, p. 1.

[5] Leonard H. Orr, ed., "Is Dishonesty Good for Business?" *Business and Society Review,* Summer 1979, pp. 4–19.

[6] Ibid., p. 12.

However, to view the controversy in either-or terms of lying versus telling the truth is to skirt the ethical issues that the negotiating process involves, which after all was the purpose of Raiffa's course. A more thoughtful appreciation of the ethical issues was presented by Richard N. Rosett, then dean of the University of Chicago Business School. He wrote:

In bargaining there often are facts that even the most ethical negotiator will conceal; facts that bear on the strength or weakness of his own position are an example. For this reason, and others, sunshine has proved less attractive in practice than its promise. As to Professor Raiffa's course and the account of it that appeared in *The Wall Street Journal*, I can comment only that newspaper writing does not lend itself readily to expression of subtle or complex ideas. Slightly rearranged, the facts of the article are: in artificially simple, one-time negotiations, students learn that dishonesty may pay; in complicated, repeated negotiations of the sort Harvard graduates often engage in, they learn that honesty often pays better. That lesson would have excited little attention, and consequently would likely not have appeared in *The Wall Street Journal*.

One great advantage of competition is that it provides powerful incentives for ethical behavior even among individuals not so inclined. I have noticed that most businessmen are far less likely to arouse expectations and then not fulfill them than politicians, journalists, clergymen, or university professors.[7]

9.5.4 An Example of Integrity

Imagine the following situation. You are just 27 years of age and have joined a new minicomputer software firm whose sales this year will reach $1.5 million. Your principal goal as vice president of international marketing is to establish profitable distribution for your products in the major industrialized nations. Your stock incentives and your highly leveraged bonus plan place clear emphasis on profitability, rather than volume.

In one European country you have narrowed your choice of distributors to 1, from a field of over 20. It is a top firm, with an excellent track record and management. The chemistry between your team and its team is right. In fact, it is most anxious to do business with you. The normal royalty you pay is about 15 percent, but it is so anxious to have your line that it has expressed its willingness to accept the deal for as little as a 10 percent commission. The other terms of the deal are acceptable to both parties. What do you do?

In this actual case (and in similar situations), the young vice president decided to give the firm the full 15 percent, in spite of the fact that it would have settled for much less. In describing his reasoning, he said that his main goal was

to create a sense of long-term integrity with them. I knew what it would take for them to succeed in gaining the kind of market penetration we were after. I also knew that the economics of their business definitely needed the larger margins from the 15 percent, rather than the smaller royalty. So I figured that if I offered them the full royalty, they would realize I was on their side, and that would create such goodwill that when we did have some serious problems down the road—and you always have them—then we would be able to work together to solve them. And that's exactly what happened. If I had exploited their eagerness to be our distributor, then it only would have come back to haunt me later on.

[7]Ibid., p. 12.

For the record, this approach was apparently quite successful. In five years this international division grew from zero to $18 million in very profitable sales, and the venture was acquired by a large firm for $80 million.

9.5.5 Limitations of Academic Ethics

How have conventional ethical disciplines sought to deal with the business mode? Sometimes they approach the problem by narrowing and defining the scope of inquiry so as to avoid floundering. Thomas Garrett, for instance, tells us reasuringly that

a competitor is ordinarily not an enemy but a rival. As a result, relations with competitors should be governed by basic ethics and the rules of fair play, rather than by the ethics of self-defense and warfare. Unfortunately, an unethical competitor can turn rivalry into ruthless battle. Therefore, there are cases where, all legal remedies having been exhausted, the ethics of self-defense come into play. In the present chapter, we do not treat these cases, but assume that competitors are ethical and engaged in business rather than jungle warfare.[8]

It is convenient for Garrett to assume that "competitors are ethical and engaged in business, rather than jungle warfare." Unfortunately, such writing hasn't enough to say about the real world. In a new business, for example, the severe competitive pressures in our economic system are compounded and magnified. Survival is nearly always a serious issue in the first year or two. The competitive pressures can push entrepreneurs to the limit of their own concept of ethical behavior, if that is what is required to survive or succeed. Compounding this tendency is the importance that both investors and partners place on financial performance and growth.

9.5.6 Usefulness of Academic Ethics

Although academic investigations of ethics seem too removed from the real world to be useful, such studies do have the advantage of bringing perspective to ethical situations at a time when you are not actively engaged in dealing with them, and can provide you with a framework for understanding ethical problems when they arise. One such framework is the Kohlberg Construct (see Exhibit 9.2). It was used in a study of business school students, some of whom had taken a Business Ethics course and some of whom had not.[9] The former showed a progression up the ethical scale; the latter didn't. (This is not to say that a course in business ethics will make you a more ethical businessperson, but it *does* indicate that such a course will make you *more aware* of the pervasiveness of ethical situations in business settings.) Here is an excerpt from that study:

Numerous surveys . . . suggest that managers are experiencing dissonance between personal principles and organizational pressures. The Bok Report has cited "the growing need to define more carefully the ethical standards of corporate executives [and] the social responsibility of business" (1979, p. 1). To prepare tomorrow's leaders for compromis-

---

[8]Thomas Garrett, *Business Ethics* (New York: Appleton-Century-Crofts, 1966), pp. 149–50.

[9]David P. Boyd, "Enhancing Ethical Development by an Intervention Program," unpublished manuscript, Boston, Northeastern University, 1980.

ing encounters, many business schools are adding courses which examine the relationship between social issues and the corporate community.... But will such courses affect student values?

One way to approach this question is to examine value changes which, according to Kohlberg (1969), can be plotted across multiple stages. His construct proceeds from the most elementary value reactions to high levels of personal belief and conscience. The sequence is depicted in Exhibit 9.2.

Exhibit 9.2
Classification of Moral Judgment into Stages of Development

Stage	Orientation	Theme
1	Punishment and obedience	Morality of obedience
2	Instrumental relativism	Simple exchange
3	Interpersonal concordance	Reciprocal role taking
4	Law and order	Formal justice
5	Legitimate social contract	Procedural justice
6	Universal ethical principle	Individual conscience

Source: Adaped from Kohlberg (1967).

In stage 1 "being moral" is synonymous with "being obedient"; the motivation is to avoid condemnation. In stage 2 the individual seeks advantage. Gain is the primary purpose, and interaction does not result in binding personal relationships. Stage 3 orientation is toward pleasing others and winning approval. Proper roles are defined by stereotyped images of majority behavior. Such reciprocity is confined to primary group relations. In stage 4 cooperation is viewed in the context of society as a whole. External laws serve to coordinate moral schemes, and the individual feels committed to the social order. One thus subscribes to formal punishment by police or the courts. In stage 5 there is acknowledgment that reciprocity can be inequitable. New laws and social arrangements may now be invoked as corrective mechanisms. All citizens are assured of fundamental safety and equality.

According to Kohlberg, cognitive structures at the stage 6 level automatically reject credos and actions which the individual considers morally reprehensible.... The referent is a person's own moral framework rather than stereotyped group behavior. Because most of one's fellows endorse a law does not guarantee its moral validity. When confronting social dilemmas, the individual is guided by internal principles that may transcend the legal system. Although these convictions are personal, they are also universal since they have worth and utility apart from the individual espousing them. Kohlberg's final stage thus represents more than mere conformity with state, teacher, or institutional criteria. Rather it indicates one's capacity for decision-making and problem-solving in the context of personal ethical standards.

9.6   THE IMAGE OF THE AMERICAN ENTREPRENEUR: THEN AND NOW

Now, as in the past, America is seen as the land of opportunity. Both abroad and at home, the United States is seen as providing an inviting and nurturing climate for those wishing to start their own enterprises and reap the rewards. In part, this is because the federal government has encouraged, to a greater degree than in any other country, an atmosphere of "laissez-faire"—a hands-off approach toward the regulation of business and commerce. Even such legislation as anti-trust laws, labor-regulation laws, and the graduated income tax has not hampered the growth of entrepreneurship in America. As these laws were enacted in response to society's changing perceptions of what "ethical" business practices constituted, they had the equally desirable effect of forcing many industries to develop their own codes of ethical practices—in large part because they wished to have the freedom to set their own rules, rather than having rules imposed on them by Congress.

As the ethical climate of business has changed, so has the stereotype of the entrepreneur. The "good" and lasting stereotype is personified by Horatio Alger. The "ruthless" stereotypes grew out of the unfettered economic activity in the 19th century, the era of the robber barons, involving acts of industrial sabotage that we would not condone today, though at the time they were regarded as necessary ingredients for success. The battles of Hill and Harriman over the rights of railroads, the alleged sabotage by John D. Rockefeller of his competitors' oil refineries, the exploitation of child labor in New England's textile mills and of black labor on the Southern cotton plantations, and the promoters of "snake oil" and Lydia Pinkham's tonics leave an unsavory aftertaste in the minds of today's more ethically conscious entrepreneurs. For those who judge in hindsight, "entrepreneurs" may still connote a ruthless, scheming group located a good deal lower than the angels.

Yet, the thoughtful historian of American entrepreneurship will recall that our standards were not their standards—and that, regardless of standards, certain American entrepreneurs gave back to society at least as much as they had profited from it, even before the concepts of social consciousness and business ethics were a glimmer in the eye of the American entrepreneur. Regardless of their motivations—social ("noblesse oblige"), practical ("What can you do with $300 million?"), or humanitarian ("Do unto others . . ."')—many entrepreneurs gave as good as they got. We have the Morgan Library, the Rockefeller Foundation (the list is long)—and the extraordinary legacy of Andrew Carnegie.

In retrospect, Carnegie's case is among the most interesting because he described the total change of attitude that came over him after he had amassed his fortune. The son of a Scottish handloom weaver, he was able to amass $300 million in the production of crude steel between 1873 and 1901, and he felt compelled to admit in all candor that the law of competition "insures the survival of the fittest in every department." "The fact that this talent for organization and management is rare among men," Carnegie felt, "is proved by the fact that it invariably secures enormous rewards for its possessor." Carnegie was apparently so satisfied with the correctness of his self-estimate that he did not try to reconcile it with the fact that a protective tariff more than half the amount of the production price of each ton of steel rails[10] effectively excluded the more expensively produced British steel rails from the U.S. market.

That Carnegie's mind was not easy over his fortune, however, is evident from his statement that "I would as soon give my son a curse as the almighty dollar." After 1901, when he sold Carnegie Steel to U.S. Steel under pressure from a combine headed by J. P. Morgan, Carnegie personally supervised the giving of more than $300 million in the United States and Great Britain. Among his gifts to humanity were 2,811 libraries, the Carnegie Endowment for International Peace, and the Carnegie Institute of Technology in Pittsburgh.

[10]W. E. Woodward, *A New American History* (Garden City, N.Y.: Garden City Publishing, 1938), p. 704.

From today's perspective, these ancestral entrepreneurs might be described as having acted in enlightened self-interest. However, when the same sort of entrepreneurial generosity is demonstrated today by such people as Armand Hammer and An Wang, we are more likely to speak of their acts of philanthropy as fulfilling their social contract.

The implications of the American entrepreneurial legacy for today's entrepreneurs are several. They include:

An appreciation of new windows of opportunity that are continually opening in the United States, regardless of government regulation.

An appreciation of how "situational ethical standards" change over time, making judgments about history's "bad guys" suspect.

The realization that the American entrepreneurial tradition has often included valuable gifts to society over and above the jobs that entrepreneurs have provided and the goods and services that they have supplied.

And yet, a touch of suspicion still tinges entrepreneurial activity. As recently as 1975, *Time* magazine suggested, in a thoughtful essay, that a businessman might make the best-qualified candidate for president, but it also noted the "deep-rooted American suspicion of businessmen's motives." Quoting John T. Conner, chairman of Allied Chemical Corporation and former head of Merck & Co., the *Time* essay added, "Anyone with previous business experience becomes immediately suspect. Certain segments think he can't make a decision in the public interest."[11]

As an entrepreneur, the most effective way in which you can counter that type of negative thinking is to be aware of your own ethical attitudes and to build a long-term reputation for the highest integrity and for square dealing.

9.7   ETHICS AND LEGALITY

9.7.1   The Entrepreneur and the Law

When is it ethical to break a law? is a question as old as law itself. From the beginnings of recorded history, in Egypt and the Middle East, a "code of laws" was always accompanied by a human "interpreter of laws," a judge, who decided when breaking the letter of the law did not violate the spirit of the law or the situation that the law was intended to cover. Great moments in history, religion, philosophy, and literature focus on the legal/ethical dilemma, and debating teams would wither away if the dilemma were to disappear. Nonetheless, it is a dilemma of a very serious nature for a practicing entrepreneur, and one that—depending on the entrepreneur's actions—can make or break his or her career.

9.7.2   A Contemporary Legal Dilemma

A more contemporary example of the demands of legality placed on a young entrepreneur is given in the following situation: A small rental service business recently merged with a middle-sized conglomerate. Shortly before the merger, one of the partners in the rental firm had been involved in a severe automobile acci-

---

[11]"Time Essay: New Places to Look for Presidents," *Time*, December 15, 1975, p. 19.

dent, suffering multiple injuries. Although seemingly able to return to work, he knew that the outlook for his health in the immediate future was unpredictable, due to possible aftereffects of the injuries.

Under these circumstances, he was eager, for the sake of his family and his dependent parents, to dispose of some of the stock he had acquired in the merger and make a large portion of his assets liquid. However, federal law does not allow quick profit taking from mergers, and therefore did not allow such a sale. The man thereupon consulted the president and officers of the larger company. They acquiesced in his plans to sell portions of his stock and stated their conviction that no adverse effect on the stock would result.

Still unsure, the man then checked with his lawyer. The federal law in question, he found, had almost never been prosecuted. Having ascertained the risk and probed the rationale of the law as it applied to his case, the man then sold some of the stock he had acquired in the merger, in order to secure his family in the event of his incapacitation or death. He subsequently recovered completely, but this could not have been foreseen.

In this instance, the individual was balancing the ethical imperatives of family against those of the law. He decided that the intrinsic purpose of the law allowed him to act as he did. In addition, he made as thorough a check as possible of the risks involved in his action. He was not satisfied with the decision he made, but he felt that it was the best he could do at the time.

9.7.3 Conflicting Laws

There is another area in which legal questions will particularly concern the entrepreneur: the increasingly frequent situations in which one law directly conflicts with another. A small business investment company in New York City became involved in serious financial trouble. The Small Business Administration stated that the company should begin to liquidate its investments, because otherwise it would be in defiance of its agreement with SBA. However, the Securities and Exchange Commission stated that this liquidation would constitute unfair treatment of stockholders, due to resulting imbalance in the company's portfolios. After a year and a half of agonizing negotiation the company was able to satisfy all the parties, but compromises had to be made on all sides.

A second example of conflicting legal demands involves the Civil Service Code, which states that hiring will include adherence to certain standards. This principle was introduced in the last century to curb the patronage abuses in public service. Recently, however, the problem of encouraging and aiding minorities has led to fair employment acts requiring the public agencies that are guided by Civil Service standards to hire in a nonprejudicial manner—a requirement that may conflict with the requirement that a given test shall serve as the criterion of selection. Without much thinking the reader can understand that both these laws are based on valid ethical intent. But the resolution of such conflicts is no simple matter.

9.7.4 National Laws and International Business

Unlike commercial airline transportation, which is governed by international laws, business has no "international code of ethics." When doing business abroad, entrepreneurs may find that those with whom they wish to do business have little in common with them: no common language, no common historical context for conducting business, and no common set of ethical beliefs about right and wrong and everything in between. In the United States, bribing a high official to obtain a favor is considered both ethically and legally unacceptable; in parts of the Middle East, it is the only way to get things done. What we see as a "bribe," others see as a "tip," as something like what you give the headwaiter at 21 for a good table.

What is the entrepreneur to do? "When in Rome . . ." is one approach. Consulting a lawyer with expertise in international business before doing anything is another. And, assuming that the object of your international business venture is to make money, you must figure out some way that is legally tolerable under the applicable codes of laws and that is ethically tolerable to you, the entrepreneur.

9.7.5   When Do the Ends Justify the Means?

A central question in any ethical discussion concerns the extent to which ignoble means are justified by noble ends, or the extent to which the use of unethical means is justified by assumed ethical ends. As an example of ethical purpose, consider the case of a university agricultural extension service whose goal is to help small farmers to increase their crop productivity. The nature of this service is clearly nonprofit; the end desired is economically constructive; and the ends are profit oriented only in the sense that the farmers may prosper from better crop yields. The service, however, suddenly finds itself in an ethical predicament: to continue being funded, it must provide performance predictions as to the annual increase in crop yield that it can achieve. It is unable to provide performance estimates at the required level of specificity. However, it knows that unless its estimates show substantial increases in crop yields, its funding may be heavily reduced.

The persons who run the service, whose objectives are highly ethical, feel that the presentation of overly optimistic predictions is unethical. However, even such predictions are understandable, and therefore perhaps could be condoned, within the context of the inability of the various groups involved to speak one another's language clearly.

Can there be any completely satisfactory solution to this problem? In this case, the extension service decided, if need be, to fudge the figures. The fact that the funding source finally backed down in its demand ameliorated the immediate problem. But if it had not, there would have been the danger that the individuals in this organization, altruistic though their intentions were, might have begun to think that falsification was the norm and might have forgotten that actions contrary to one's ethical feelings gradually build a debilitating cynicism.

It may therefore be said that, in a personal sense, a noble end never quite justifies a less noble means. In fact, however, the entrepreneur is seldom allowed the luxury of such considerations. The above example shows how one organization responded to pressure. It is a rough rule that the tougher and more uncompromising the pressure and tactics, the greater will be the likelihood of a response in kind. In the political sphere, we have recently seen how the United States was led to overdevelop its means of clandestine surveillance both in its own affairs and in those of other countries. This was due in part to the temptation of improved techniques, but it was also a response to Communist philosophy and ideology, which considered the end as justifying the means. The national confusion over our complicity in this game, when our tradition assumes openness and self-determination, indicates how greatly differing methods may threaten ethical assumptions.

9.7.6 Widening the Entrepreneur's Perspective on Law

In considering the thorny question of legality, it is well to scrutinize not only the authority of the law but also its limitations. In the first place, laws are made with aforethought, and with the deliberate purpose of ensuring justice. They are therefore ethical in intent and deserve respect. In the second place, however, laws are man-made, not God-made. Laws do not anticipate new conditions; they do not always have the effect that they were intended to have; they sometimes conflict with one another; and they are, as they stand, incapable of making judgments where multiple ethical considerations hang in the balance, or actually seem to be at war with one another. Conceivably, the entrepreneur will have to decide ethical questions that involve obligations on many sides: to customers, employees, stockholders, family, partners, and himself, or to a combination of these. The area of the entrepreneur's relations with his partners is of primary importance, as we have seen at the beginning of the chapter.

We hope that the reader will realize that an unquestioning reliance on legality is inadequate in today's world. It is not a matter of rationalizing and legal "waffling," as a term such as *situational ethics* may seem to imply. It is instead a suggestion that energy must be expended, not only on everyday affairs, but also on intelligent, creative criticism over the wider spectrum of our system. Obviously, the average entrepreneur will not have time to embark on crusades to improve every unintelligent law he or she encounters. But the entrepreneur is considered to be an action-oriented person, and action is called for every day.

The good samaritan's intentions are tied to the means of realizing them (and to continual scrutiny to determine whether the good achieved outweighs the bad). It would be unfortunate if the entrepreneur were timid in realizing his potential for combining action with ethical purpose, due to the suspicion that the two motives are unrelated or inimical. There is no reason why they should be considered generically opposed, and, in fact, they can be natural allies. Nevertheless, the individual can expect no substitute in this for his or her own effort and intelligence.

9.8 AN ENTREPRENEURIAL APPROACH TO ETHICS

It is our contention that the entrepreneur's creative, active, and energetic nature equips him or her well to cope with ethical dilemmas. This may raise a few eyebrows, even among practicing entrepreneurs. We can anticipate their responses:

How can we think about ethics when we haven't enough time to even think about running our venture?

Entrepreneurs are doers, not thinkers—and ethics is too abstract a concept to have any bearing on business realities.

When you're struggling to survive, you're not worried about the means you use—you're fighting for one thing: survival.

To this, we answer: "The contemplation of ethical behavior is not unlike poetry—emotion recollected in tranquillity." This chapter is intended to provide one such tranquil opportunity. You have been asked to make decisions in ethically ambiguous situations, and you have had a chance to become more aware of your own ethics and how they can be affected by the ethical climate in which you were forced to make the decisions. During your entrepreneurial career you will have to act in the heat of the moment, but later you must find the energy to recollect: "It didn't feel right," or contrarily, "I couldn't have lived with myself if I hadn't done what I did." In this way, you will continue to gain insight into your own ethical core values and to identify the limits to which your tolerance can be stretched.

In the final analysis, ethics and values are very personal things. As a way to cope with the inevitable conflicts that you will encounter, a first step is developing an awareness of your own explicit and implicit ethical beliefs and of the milieu within which you must compete for survival. An appreciation of this state of affairs is succinctly stated by Fred T. Allen, chairman and president of Pitney-Bowes, Inc.:

As businessmen we must learn to weigh short-term interests against long-term possibilities. We must learn to sacrifice what is immediate, what is expedient, if the moral price is too high. What we stand to gain is precious little compared to what we can ultimately lose.[12]

[12]Letter to the editor, *The Wall Street Journal,* October 17, 1975.

Shaping a Personal Entrepreneurial Strategy

Ninety percent of the world's woe comes from people not knowing them-selves, their abilities, their frailties, and even their real virtues. Most of us go all the way through life as complete strangers to ourselves—so how can we know anyone else?

Sydney J. Harris

For over a dozen years one of the most powerful assignments, according to students, practicing entrepreneurs, and others who have completed it, has been the Personal Strategy Assessment. Consistently, they report that it was one of the most worthwhile assignments that they had ever had. They hasten to add that it was also one of the most demanding.

The Personal Strategy Assessment can be viewed as the personal equivalent of a business plan. The exercises provide an organized framework to help you examine your goals, preferences, and aspirations; your track record—both the ups and downs; the key people and events that have shaped your experience to date; your strengths and weaknesses, and how to overcome the latter through a planned "apprenticeship" and a judicious choice of teammates; and suggestions about how to give feedback to others on their answers and to get feedback on the answers you have given. From these insights and information, you will be in a better position to shape a mid-to-longer-term personal strategy.

10.1 RESULTS EXPECTED

The Personal Strategy Assessment is divided into four parts:

Self-assessing entrepreneurial roots.

Self-assessing entrepreneurial attributes and role requirements.

Goal setting and goal assessing.

Partner, peer, and professional feedback.

Upon completion of these exercises, each of you will have:

1. Given some serious thought to your future.
2. Examined your past accomplishments and setbacks for their entrepreneurial relevance.
3. Matched your personal characteristics and capabilities against what is known about the role requirements of successful entrepreneurs.
4. Elicited the opinions of others about your own assessments, to provide useful "reality testing."

10.2 PRESESSION PREPARATION

To prepare for the self-assessment exercises that follow, you should review:

The information presented about the opportunity and the founders.

The results and self-knowledge gained through completing the Venture Opportunity Screening Guide (Chapters 3 and 4).

The results of the Entrepreneurial Motivation exercise (Chapter 5) and the Management Competencies Inventory (Chapter 6).

Additional preparation might include:

A visit to the campus career counseling service, to complete a battery of aptitude and preference tests.

A look at the book *What Color Is Your Parachute?: A Practical Manual for Job-Hunters and Career-Changers,* by Richard Bolles (Berkeley, Calif.: Ten Speed Press, 1981), an excellent and widely used practical guide for directing you toward the "right" type of job for you.

10.3 SELF-ASSESSING ENTREPRENEURIAL ROOTS: OVERVIEW

One of the principal aims of this book is to expose you in depth and in breadth to the nature, peculiarities, and realities of the entrepreneur and the entrepreneurial role.[1] Further, at a more practical and personal level this book is aimed at helping you to evaluate thoroughly your *attraction* to entrepreneurship and the *fit* between you and the entrepreneurial role and characteristics. Rather than asserting that one simply "is" or "is not" an entrepreneur, we view the issue more as a matter of the relative *fit* among *four principal elements:* (1) the individual, (2) the role, (3) the particular venture opportunity, and (4) the management partners, if they exist. This system's view acknowledges the extreme complexity in predicting or aligning people to careers, especially when both are constantly changing, and the difficulty in accurately measuring enough of the relevant variables to do so. It also recognizes that there is far more to building a substantial new venture than just the presence or absence of a number of behavioral or personality factors. While these are certainly important, how particular shortcomings are compensated for in adapting to continually changing conditions and how effectively entrepreneurial partners complement one another and work together are just as important, if not more important. And unless the opportunity is attractive and attainable, even the very best entrepreneur is unlikely to succeed.

10.3.1 The Self-Assessment Process

Exhibit 10.1 is a flow diagram of the process that you will experience in completing the exercises and the self-assessment and goal-setting units in the book.

The various exercises are designed to place you in situations where you can observe your own characteristics and skills. This requires activity and participa-

[1]The term *entrepreneurial role* is used here to refer to the career of starting, owning, and operating one's own business. The term *role* is commonly used to understand various pressures, demands, rewards, and requirements of a person in a particular job (e.g., entrepreneur, doctor, mayor, plumber). It is also necessary to understand that there are differing pressures from all the various roles that one person could occupy at the same time (e.g., parent, mother, wife, lawyer, friend).

Exhibit 10.1
Flow Diagram of Experiential, Self-Assessment, and Goal-Setting Process

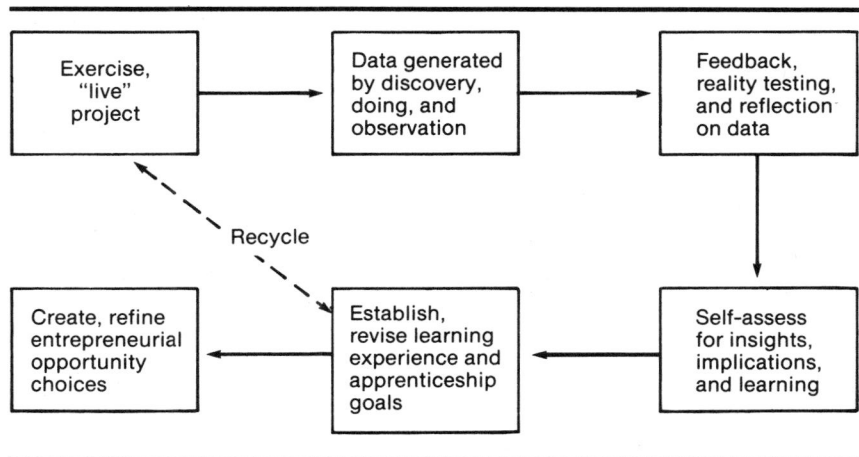

tion on the part of each person. If the assessment of entrepreneurial potential is to be made, one must become very involved in the process of assessment. Only the active participants will be able to make many useful assessments of themselves.

There will be structured opportunities for you to give or receive comments and impressions, to use one another as sounding boards, to "reality-test" self-perceptions and assessments. How much, if any, of the data one chooses to share is one's *own decision*. Self-assessment, like any other decision process, is most productive when it is done with the benefit of all the available information. Care should be taken by each of you to assist in fostering a climate that maximizes the information flow.

Among the important results of the self-assessment approach are that a systematic recording and analysis of one's experience can (*a*) help one see where one has been and (*b*) provide some direction on where one needs to go—things that one can be looking for in future experiences and learning. In addition, there is growing evidence that one's awareness of customers, employees, and the environment is closely linked to effective entrepreneurship.[2]

Finally, a very large number of factors, both personal and environmental, clearly go into making someone a successful entrepreneur. No individual has all of the required managerial skills or personal qualities, and the presence or absence of any single dimension does not guarantee success or failure as an entrepreneur. However, knowing that you do not have a certain attribute or skill and knowing where and how to get it, or how to compensate for it, can be as valuable as already having it.

10.3.2 Great Entrepreneurs Plus Lousy Opportunity Equals Marginal Venture

No doubt about it: silk purses do not come from sows' ears. Even the most talented and committed entrepreneur can hardly be expected to convert a fundamentally unattractive opportunity into a huge success.

[2]Harry Schrage, "The R&D Entrepreneur: Profile of Success," *Harvard Business Review,* November–December 1965.

10.3.3   Maximizing the Self-Assessment Process

All of us possess various personal frames of reference, assumptions, values, and stereotypical notions that will influence our first impressions of one another. In most social situations we all bring out self-images that we want to preserve, protect, and, if and when necessary, defend. A conservative norm usually exists that prohibits people from "telling it like it is." For example, most people won't point out to a stranger with whom they are conversing that a piece of spinach is prominently dangling from that person's front teeth! They would feel that doing this would be too embarrassing for all. It is very difficult to tell a person that he or she is presenting a face or impression that differs from the one that the person thinks is being presented. Such orientations present a potential obstacle to effective processing, and discussion with others, of your self-assessment efforts.

One way to grapple with this problem is to have a framework for looking at what is likely to take place, and some guidelines for giving feedback to others and receiving feedback from others.

The Johari Window (named after Joe Luft and Harry Ingraham) is one conceptual scheme for thinking about this process (see Exhibit 10.2).

Exhibit 10.2
The Johari Window

	Known to Self	Not Known to Self
Known to Others	1. Open area (shared opinions)	2. Blind area (need to know)
Not Known to Others	3. Hidden area (unshared)	4. Unknown area (unconscious)

Source: D. A. Kolb, I. M. Rubin, and J. M. McIntyre, *Organizational Psychology: An Experiential Approach*, 2d ed. (Englewood Cliffs, N.J.: Prentice-Hall, 1974).

Most of us can think about examples for ourselves for boxes 1 and 3 (the open and hidden areas), and we can think of blind areas (box 2) for others, but the unknown area (box 4) is, of course, exactly that.

How can this window apply to entrepreneurs, partners, and investors? Exhibit 10.3 shows how the process of disciplined evaluation by and among the various players can help to "peel the onion" so as to achieve a more thorough picture. The "knowns"—area A—will grow, and the "unknowns"—area B—will shrink to a tolerable size. Since the alternative to this process is ignorance, blindness, and naïveté, isn't it worth the effort to "peel the onion"?

One of the primary benefits of the self-assessment exercises is in helping you to identify "blind spots" (box 2) that could be costly and to examine more carefully some previously hidden assumptions (box 3). Utilizing the conceptual tools and feedback devices presented in the book, you can also benefit from new discovery relating to box 4. It is during the self-assessment exercises and the process of giving and receiving feedback that much of this learning will take place. For this feedback to be helpful, it must be given in such a way that the individual (*a*) understands the

Exhibit 10.3
"Peeling the Onion"

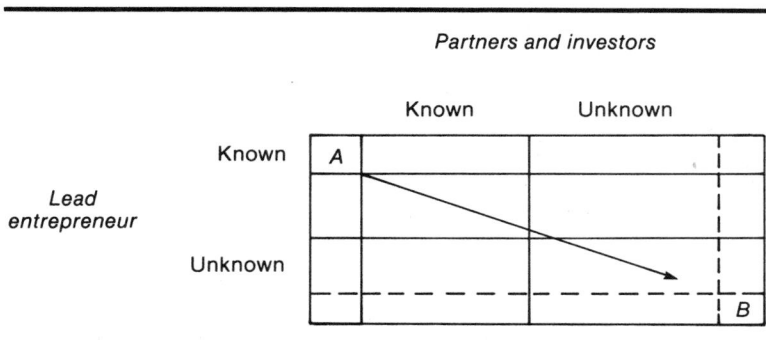

information, (*b*) is able to accept the information, and (*c*) is able to do something about the information. These conditions can be met, but care must be exercised to create a climate that is conducive to the giving and receiving of feedback. The following are some suggestions about how to foster such a climate.

10.3.4 Giving Feedback

Your usefulness as a reality tester for someone else in the session will depend in large part on your interpersonal skills in giving a person your impressions and interpretations of his or her self-assessment data without causing the person to become defensive. The following guidelines should be useful:

1. Perceptions, reactions, and opinions should be presented as such and not as facts. Try to point to *specific* behaviors and situations during the session to illustrate your observation (e.g., "I think you are stronger in marketing skills than you indicated, since you really nailed down the market size when doing the term project").

2. Give the person specific observations, descriptions, and comments that are *not evaluative* in nature. Saying "I think you'd make a great entrepreneur" may be gratifying to one's ego, but it is quite useless in terms of pinpointing strengths and weaknesses and what action needs to be taken. A better example might be: "You seem to take greater than prudent risks, and you might consider finding a more conservative partner to complement you." Feedback is usually more effective if it is given in a manner that communicates acceptance of the receiver as a worthwhile person having a right to be different.

3. Prescriptions or solutions (e.g., "You should do this or that") tend to be counterproductive, especially early in the session. Giving feedback is *not* the same as giving advice or prescriptions. If your prescriptions are wanted, they'll be asked for.

4. Feedback should be concerned with areas in which the person can demonstrate some control over his or her behavior and/or be given ways in which such control can be used for self-improvement or for planning alternative actions.

Feedback should also include a complete discussion of all the things that you react to positively as well as negatively. Beware of only seeing and feeding back to the person either all negative or all positive data. Neither will provide a balanced picture of your perceptions.

5. Ask questions, rhetorically if possible, to help the person look at the data from a different angle and to see things in the way you may see them. For example, saying "I wonder if most entrepreneurs set such difficult goals" is probably better than asserting "You set too difficult goals."

6. Help the person to identify some of the implications of the self-assessment data, in terms of such things as the need for additional or different team members and the need for new learning or experience goals.

10.3.5 Receiving Feedback

Receiving feedback from others, whether you know them well or not at all, can be a most demanding experience. The effectiveness of the discussions of the self-assessment exercises will depend a great deal on how you seek and deal with feedback from others. The following guidelines, while not all-inclusive, can facilitate the process.

1. Avoid becoming defensive, by not taking possible negative comments in a very personal way.

2. Listen carefully to what is being said, and think about it. Avoid "answering" or "debating," or "rationalizing" as to why your opinion may differ. You'll have plenty of time for that latter. Think it over first.

3. Ask for specific comments in areas that you feel are particularly important to you personally and to the success of the venture. Probe for more detail if you are not sure what the feedback says. Paraphrase what you think you heard to check your perception, and ask the other person if that was, in fact, what he or she wanted to say.

4. Ask for help in identifying possible implications of the self-assessment data. Don't worry about reaching final conclusions or decisions. At no point will you arrive at any clean go–no-go appraisal—it just isn't that simple. The process is cumulative, and what you do about weaknesses, for example, is far more important than what the particular weaknesses might be. After all, everyone has weaknesses.

5. Be honest and straightforward in these discussions. Time is too precious and the road to new venture success too treacherous to clutter this activity with game playing or hidden agendas.

6. Seek others within and outside the session to cross-check the feedback you have received and to supplement the session-generated data. This will confirm or deny the accuracy of the feedback.

10.3.6 Instructions for Exercises

Each of the exercises will require some careful thought and concentration. The estimated time to complete the three is 1½–3 hours, depending on how detailed your replies are. Later you are encouraged to exchange these thoughts with others during a structured session.

The structured session will be devoted to an analysis and discussion of the self-assessments. It is designed to enable you to exchange your data from each of the three prework exercises with one or two other persons. This will assist you in analyzing and reality-testing your assessments and identifying their various implications for personal action.

Name _____

Date _____

10.4 SELF-ASSESSING ENTREPRENEURIAL ROOTS: THE EXERCISES

10.4.1 The Personal Preference Exercise

One useful way to begin the very difficult process of assessing yourself and planning your career is to think about your own preferences in terms of lifestyle and work. Couple this with a look into the future: What would you most like to be doing, and how would you like to live? Please give some thought to the following questions. Obviously, there are no "right answers." What is important is that you be honest with yourself in doing the exercise.

1. What *gives you energy*? What would you say are the activities or conditions (circumstances)—both work and nonwork—in which you find the greatest amount of personal energy and satisfaction and sense of enjoyment? These could be such things as reading the Sunday paper, going fishing, working on a problem, and traveling. In other words, these are the things that you *enjoy doing the most* and that energize you. What is it about these things that really motivates you, and why?

2. Now respond to the issue in question 1 in terms of the activities or circumstances that create the greatest amount of personal dissatisfaction, anxiety, or discontent for you. These are the things that you *enjoy the least* and that take away your energy and motivation. Why is this so?

3. Review your two lists, and attempt to rank-order the items that you have listed above.

Most	*Least*
a.	a.
b.	b.
c.	c.
d.	d.
e.	e.
f.	f.
g.	g.

4. Think of yourself 20 to 30 years from now. Describe how you think you would like to spend an ideal month. What would your ideal lifestyle and work style be like? Include such things as income; involvement in work, family, community, and religious or other activities; where and how you would like to live; and who your close friends are likely to be. What is it about this ideal existence that attracts and repels you?

5. Think about all the businesses and types of businesses that you can, and assume that you could go into whichever ones you wished. Make a list of the 10 businesses that you *most* definitely *would* want to enter and the 10 businesses that you *most* definitely *would not* want to enter. Rank-order the lists.

Would Want to Enter	*Would Not Want to Enter*
1.	1.
2.	2.
3.	3.
4.	4.
5.	5.
6.	6.
7.	7.
8.	8.
9.	9.
10.	10.

Do the businesses in each of these lists share any common attributes? What is it about these businesses that you believe would give you energy and motivation, or take them away?

6. Now review your responses to questions 1 through 5. List below those themes, ideas, or characteristics that give you the:

    Most Energy or Enjoyment   *Least Energy or Enjoyment*

7. Have any other themes, patterns, or thought-provokers emerged as a result of completing questions 1 through 6?

10.4.2 The Personal Inventory

Each of us has a personal history that has played and will continue to play a significant role in influencing our values, motivations, attitudes, and behavior. Some of this history may provide some useful insight into your prior entrepreneurial inclinations as well as your future potential fit with an entrepreneurial role. The Personal Inventory will assist you to record and analyze these data.

1. List as many as you can of the self-supporting activities that you have attempted in the past. These might include such things as building something on your own, running a part- or full-time business of your own (paper route, lawn care, auto repairs, etc.), engaging in self-financed education or a hobby, or finding a job or school on your own. Discuss why you became involved and what influenced your decision. Looking back, what did you learn about yourself, self-employment, managing people, and making money? If you resigned or were terminated, what insights emerged for you?

2. Now answer the same questions about any relevant full-time work experience.

3. List the sports, hobbies, and other activities in which you have participated that have an individual rather than a team character (e.g., chess, track, tennis, etc. versus football, etc.). What attracted you to these? What lessons and insights emerged, and how do these apply to your life as an entrepreneur?

4. Have you ever been fired, or have you quit a job? Indicate why, what the circumstances were, and what you might have learned from the experience. What difference has this made?

5. Have you ever changed jobs or relocated? Indicate why, what the circumstances were, and what you might have learned from the experience. How important is it to you to "stay put" and have "roots" or to have a good deal of mobility?

6. List any friends, relatives, or self-employed acquaintances who own and operate their own businesses, or have a profession, such as certified public accountant. How do you view them and their self-employed roles? What have you learned from them about self-employment? The things that attract or repel? The trade-offs? The risks and rewards? Entry strategies that work?

7. If you have ever started a business of your own (part- or full-time), or worked in a small company, list the things that you liked most and least about it and why this was so.

Most   Least

8. If you have ever worked for a larger company (over 500 employees or about $15–20 million in sales), list the things that you liked most and least about your work. Why was this so?

Most   Least

9. Complete this sentence: "I would/would not like to start/acquire (choose one) my own business someday because..."

10. Now review your responses to items 1 through 9. List the activities, reasons, and other factors mentioned that you feel indicate your entrepreneurial strengths, inclinations, and weaknesses.

Try to rank-order the strengths and weaknesses.

Strengths	*Weaknesses*

10.5 ENTREPRENEURIAL ATTRIBUTES AND ROLE REQUIREMENTS: OVERVIEW

Thus far we have presented the notion that successful new ventures are the result of the right combination of (a) a capable and realistic lead entrepreneur with a balanced and compatible entrepreneurial team, (b) a sound business idea and a supporting business plan, and (c) appropriate resources and financing. The first two are prerequisites for raising conventional venture capital. Based on this view of the key ingredients for new venture creation (Chapter 1), we introduced the subsequent notion that the logical and essential next step was the discovery, refinement, and matching of these three crucial elements.

This section discusses what is currently known about the personal characteristics and the various role pressures and requirements that research has linked to entrepreneurship. This knowledge will be particularly useful in assisting you to conduct a thorough and realistic self-appraisal of your entrepreneurial strengths and weaknesses and in helping you to determine your attraction to and suitability for an entrepreneurial career, and especially the venture opportunity you have in mind.

10.5.1 A Matter of Fit with the Venture Opportunity

A considerable amount of research about the personal qualities and behavior of entrepreneurs has been conducted in recent years (see Chapter 5), but the precise identification of entrepreneurial talent remains elusive. More research in this young field of entrepreneurship should yield further insights into our growing body of knowledge about this difficult area. As yet, however, this identification process, using psychological and related methods, remains imprecise—more of an art than a science. While numerous studies have yielded important insights into entrepreneurship, it is important to recognize that the available knowledge may well represent the tip of the iceberg. Drawing on this current knowledge base, however, can yield a substantial improvement over a seat-of-the-pants estimate of one's entrepreneurial potential. The key to such improvement lies in a realistic and thorough self-evaluation by the prospective entrepreneurs. Louis L. Allen, an experienced venture capital investor in small ventures, shares this view of the importance of the role of self-selection:

Unlike the giant firm which has recruiting and selection *experts* to screen the wheat from the chaff, the small business firm, which comprises the most common economic unit in our business systems, cannot afford to employ a personnel manager. . . . More than that, there's something very special about the selection of the owners: they have selected themselves. . . . As I face self-selected top managers across my desk or visit them in their plants or offices I have become more and more impressed with the fact that this self-selection process is far more important to the *success or failure* of the company the man is starting than the monetary aspects of our negotiations.

But how can one wisely self-select when one is unclear about what things to look for and about what is or is not important, in this case, for the entrepreneurial role? This dilemma, common to many job and career choices, will be faced head-on here.

One useful way to confront the dilemma is to view the self-selection and decision-making process as a matter of your relative *fit* with or suitability for various

Exhibit 10.4
A Matter of Fit with Your Venture Opportunity

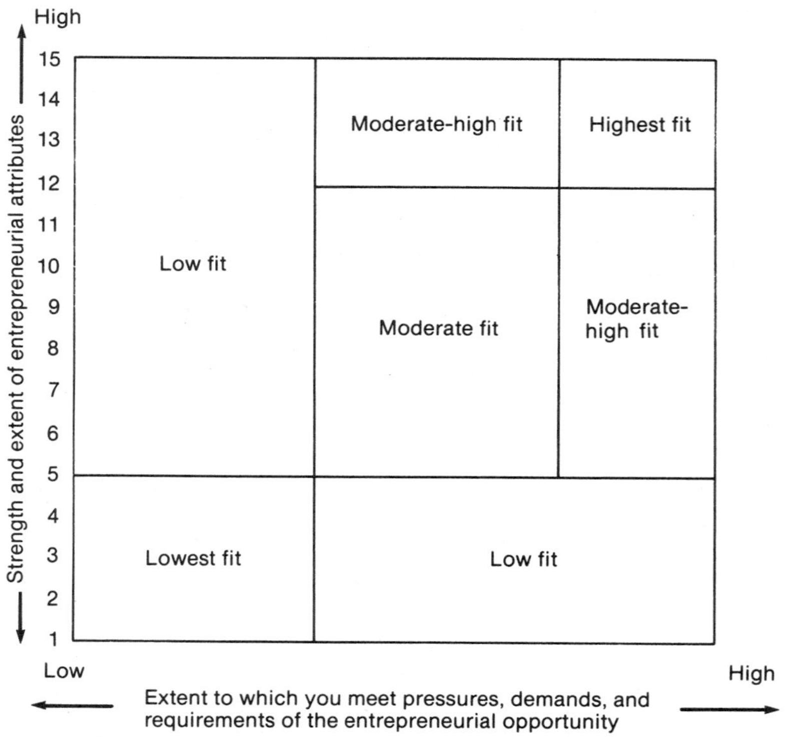

entrepreneurial attributes and the demands and pressures required by the venture opportunity you are pursuing. In addition, complex factors beyond your control—business conditions, political and regulatory changes, luck—can undoubtedly affect the gestation of a new venture. But this reality tends to lend further support to the validity of at least assessing and managing well those things that are within your control. You can certainly do this in the assessment of your likely fit with entrepreneurial characteristics and role requirements.

The idea of "fit," introduced above, enables us to address the three main themes in Parts 1 and 2 of the book: (a) the quality and durability of the opportunity; (b) the attributes, relevant experience, and assertiveness of entrepreneurs; and (c) the pressures, demands, and requirements of an entrepreneurial role. Exhibit 10.4 depicts a conceptual framework that can be useful in assessing your fit with an entrepreneurial opportunity. It will serve as a guide in your efforts to answer for yourself whether (a) you have what it takes to succeed in your venture and (b) you can tolerate the demands that the venture will place on you. While the framework is simple, we want to stress that the process of engaging in an honest, thorough, and realistic self-appraisal is neither simple nor easy. It will require some careful thought, rethought, and time.

In essence, Exhibit 10.4 is a guide for summarizing your self-assessment of the entrepreneurial attributes and role requirements.

10.5.2   Instructions for Exercise

The characteristics and orientations upon which we will focus fall into two categories. The first, which we have labeled "Entrepreneurial Attributes," deals with personal, motivational characteristics of people. The second, which we have labeled "Role Requirements," deals with the demands, pressures, and realities of starting, owning, and operating a substantial business. The purpose of the activity that follows is threefold:

1. To introduce and define these attributes and requirements in more detail.
2. To enable you to do an initial diagnosis of where you see yourself on these attributes and requirements.
3. To begin, on the basis of the diagnosis, to develop your own learning and experience goals for an entrepreneurial or other career—the things you want to learn more about.

As you go through this exercise, to reiterate, you should keep the following important points in mind.

1. This is a self-assessment exercise. Nonetheless, it will be useful to structure opportunities to give or receive comments and impressions from others as sounding boards, to "reality-test" self-perceptions and assessments. How much, if any, of the data you choose to share with others is *your decision*. Of course, the exercise will be of value only to the extent that you are honest and realistic in your approach.

2. At the conclusion of the self-assessment exercises a structured format is provided for you to record and analyze your experiences related to the preceding exercises and the chapter. You may also record your observations and reflections in other than the suggested places and are encouraged to do so if this seems relevant to you.

A benefit of the Entrepreneurial Assessment and Personal Progress guidelines that follow is that a systematic recording and analysis of your experiences can (*a*) help you see where you have been and (*b*) indicate to you how what you have learned about yourself could affect your venture.

3. Finally, a complex set of factors clearly goes into making someone a successful entrepreneur. No individual has all of the managerial skills or personal qualities defined in the various exercises. And even if some individuals did possess most of these skills and traits, their values, role preferences, and lifestyle aims might make them a very poor risk to succeed as entrepreneurs. The presence or absence of any single dimension does not guarantee your success or failure as an entrepreneur. Knowing that you do not have a certain skill and knowing where to get it can be as valuable as knowing that you already have it.

10.6 ENTREPRENEURIAL ATTRIBUTES AND ROLE REQUIREMENTS: THE EXERCISES

10.6.1 Entrepreneurial Attributes

Listed below are a number of characteristics that psychologists, venture capitalists, and practitioners believe to be important for entrepreneurial success. It is unlikely that any one person is exceptionally strong or weak on all of these dimensions. Respond by placing an *X* in the appropriate column as you compare yourself with other businesspersons and entrepreneurs. The most important output of this exercise is an honest, accurate, and realistic self-assessment of how you measure on each of these dimensions.

Please rank yourself on a 5–1 scale, 5 being the strongest and 1 the weakest.

	Strongest		*Average*		*Weakest*
	5	*4*	*3*	*2*	*1*

1. *Total Commitment, Determination, and Perseverance:* The readiness to give your *all* in order to succeed, even if this means sacrifices in family life, a cut in pay, and an incipient ulcer.

2. *Drive to Achieve and Grow:* Self-starting, growth-minded, using objective measures to keep score.

3. *Opportunity and Goal Oriented:* Ability and commitment to set clear goals and objectives that are high and challenging but realistic and attainable.

4. *Taking Initiative and Personal Responsibility:* Desire to seek and take initiative and to put yourself in situations where you are personally responsible for the success or failure of the operation; take the initiative to solve problems or fill leadership vacuums and dislike situations where one's impact on problems cannot be measured; a doer; self-reliant.

5. *Persistent Problem Solving:* Intense and determined desire to complete a task or solve a problem; a strong determination to get the job done.

	Strongest 5	4	Average 3	2	Weakest 1

6. *Veridical Awareness and a Sense of Humor:* Optimistic realism, knowing your weaknesses as well as your strengths and having the ability to retain a sense of perspective.

———   ———   ———   ———   ———

7. *Seeking and Using Feedback:* Demonstrated capacity to seek and use feedback on your performance in order to take corrective action and to improve.

———   ———   ———   ———   ———

8. *Internal Locus of Control:* Hold the belief that one's accomplishments and failures lie within one's personal control and influence, rather than being determined by luck or other external, personally uncontrollable events and circumstances.

———   ———   ———   ———   ———

9. *Tolerance for Ambiguity, Stress, and Uncertainty:* Able, on a continuous basis, to tolerate and live with modest to high levels of ambiguity and uncertainty concerning job and career security, and work-related events; possess sufficient self-confidence that job security and permanency are not important.

———   ———   ———   ———   ———

10. *Calculated Risk Taking and Risk Sharing:* Preference for taking calculated risks, where the chances of winning are neither so small as to be a "gamble" nor so large as to be a "sure thing," but provide a reasonable and challenging opportunity for success; acts to share and reduce risks.

High risk taker; gambler	Calculated risk taker and risk sharer	Low risk taker; conservative

11. *Low Need for Status and Power:* Achievement is the driving force; while power and status may be a result, they are not propellants.

———   ———   ———   ———   ———

	Strongest		Average		Weakest
	5	4	3	2	1

12. *Integrity and Reliability:* High personal standards, unwillingness to compromise them; belief that an excellent reputation is key to long-term success.

13. *Decisiveness, Urgency, and Patience:* Can live with the entrepreneur's paradox: balancing the need to get things done with the need to look down the road and take a longer-range view of what needs to be achieved.

14. *Dealing with Failure:* Ability to use failures as learning experiences and to better understand your role in causing a failure in order to avoid similar problems in the future.

15. *Team Builder and Hero Maker:* Ability to make heroes of the people you attract to the venture, to give responsibility and share credit.

Based on the *opportunity* you have in mind and these preliminary self-ratings of your entrepreneurial characteristics, summarize your best estimate of:

1. Your entrepreneurial strengths:

2. Your entrepreneurial weaknesses:

3. List some specific things that you need to do in order to get the odds of success in your favor or to seek an opportunity that better suits you.

10.6.2 Entrepreneurial Role Requirements

Listed below are a number of entrepreneurial role requirements that psychologists, entrepreneurs, venture capitalists, and practitioners believe to be important for entrepreneurial success. It is unlikely that any one person is exceptionally strong or weak on all of these dimensions, but an entrepreneur should have more strengths than weaknesses and should know which ones are which. Respond by placing an X in the appropriate column as you compare yourself with other businesspersons and entrepreneurs. The most important output of this exercise is an honest, accurate, and realistic assessment of how you stand on each of these requirements.

Please rank yourself on a 5–1 scale, 5 being the strongest and 1 the weakest.

	Strongest 5	4	*Average* 3	2	*Weakest* 1
1. *Accommodation to the Venture:* Extent to which the entrepreneur's career and venture are treated as the number one priority—above family, community, etc.	____	____	____	____	____
2. *Stress Generation:* The cost of accommodation, the need to balance the achievements possible under short-term stress with the ability to relax and ease off when necessary.	____	____	____	____	____
3. *Economic and Professional Values:* Extent to which one believes in and is committed to the conventional economic and financial values of the American system of free enterprise, such as profits, capital gains, private ownership, and earnings per share.	____	____	____	____	____
4. *Ethics:* Esteem in which they are held; extent to which one's business conduct tends to be adapted to the demands and needs of each situation rather than defined by a rigid code of conduct applied uniformly regardless of different conditions and circumstances.	____	____	____	____	____

Based on the *opportunity* you have in mind and these self-ratings of your fit with the entrepreneurial role requirements, summarize your best estimate of:

1. Your strengths:

2. Your weaknesses:

3. Specify the things you need to do, or the issues you need to resolve, in order to pursue the opportunity or seek an alternative.

10.6.3 Entrepreneurial Assessment and Personal Progress

Now review your earlier self-assessments of Entrepreneurial Attributes and Role Requirements. Make whatever additions or modifications you feel are appropriate. Review any of the previous material that you feel would be useful. Then complete the self-assessment questions below.

1. What do you find *most appealing* about entrepreneurship?

2. What do you find *least attractive* about the role demands of entrepreneurship—especially during the first few years?

3. What is it about the specific opportunity you want to pursue that will provide you with sustained energy and motivation? How do you know this?

4. How do the requirements of entrepreneurship—and of your opportunity in particular—especially early sacrifices, total immersion, workload, and long-term commitment fit with your own aims, values, and motivations? What specific conflicts do you anticipate between your aims and values and the demands of entrepreneurship?

5. At this point in time, what appear to be your major entrepreneurial strengths and weaknesses as they pertain to your specific venture opportunity?

Strengths	*Weaknesses*
a.	*a.*
b.	*b.*
c.	*c.*
d.	*d.*
e.	*e.*

6. Overall, how do you seem to stack up against the entrepreneurial attributes and role demands that have been developed so far, compared to other businesspeople you know who have pursued or are pursuing a business like the one you have in mind?

    I rate myself (check one):

Entrepreneurial Attributes		*Role Demands*
_____	Top 1 percent	_____
_____	Top 10 percent	_____
_____	Rest of third	_____
_____	Middle third	_____
_____	Lower third	_____

7. Given the opportunity you have in mind, indicate with an *X* on the Fit Grid below the location that you feel best describes your potential fit and suitability for the venture.

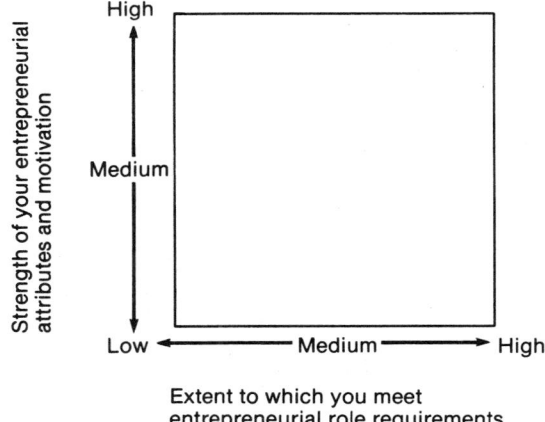

8. What are the implications of these assessments for your current venture opportunity? Is this really for you? What kinds of *partners* would you need? What has to happen now to get the odds of success in your favor?

9. What *other issues* or *questions* have been raised for you thus far to which you would like to have answers?

10.6.4 Suggested Way to Utilize These Assessments (60–90 minutes)

It has proven useful to other entrepreneurs to exchange their exercises with a person or two of their own choosing. Doing this will provide you with a sounding board to assist you in seeking and analyzing a realistic self-appraisal. If you have not already done so, review the earlier sections on giving and receiving feedback.

Step 1: Form into pairs or trios of your own selection.

Step 2: Tear out and exchange your Entrepreneurial Attributes, Role Requirements, and Entrepreneurial Assessment and Personal Progress exercises. It should take 10–15 minutes for each person to read the exercises of the others carefully.

Step 3: Each group member should respond with questions and ideas aimed at helping to sharpen the realism and accuracy of each member's self-assessment. The following kinds of questions may prove useful in facilitating these pair and trio discussions:

   a. Has the person been complete in doing the exercise?

   b. Has the person been honest and realistic in recording his or her thoughts and evaluations and in coming to various inferences and conclusions?

   c. If you know the person, are you aware of omitted events or items that you feel might contribute to the analysis?

   d. Are there alternative inferences or conclusions that might be drawn from these data?

   e. What personal implications seem to exist for the various strengths and weaknesses as they relate to entrepreneurship?

   f. Are there any common threads or patterns of consistency that have not been noted?

   g. Are there other data that the person should gather or consider in connection with these exercises?

Step 4: At the conclusion of the group discussion each person should have identified at least three items for a personal list of things that he or she plans to accomplish. These items should be things that you plan to (*a*) find out, (*b*) think about, and/or (*c*) do. They might include such items as these: talk to three more entrepreneurs about the demands and rewards of entrepreneurship; think about and discuss the lifestyle implications of entrepreneurship for the person I am about to marry.

Step 5: General discussion should summarize the items identified in step 4 and any other issues related to the exercises.

10.7 GOAL SETTING: OVERVIEW

If you don't know where you're going,
any path will take you there.

10.7.1 Introduction: Why Plan? Why Plans Fail

There has been growing evidence in recent years that some important aspects of entrepreneurial behavior can, in fact, be learned.[3] In particular, developing or refining skills in effective goal setting has encouraging implications for aspiring entrepreneurs. In addition, most schools of business and engineering have recognized and included in their curricula such topics as management by objectives (MBO); planning, programming, and budgeting systems (PPBS); and various long-range planning techniques. More recently, career planning and career development courses that include personal planning as a topic have been added. Further, large, well-managed companies commonly have their own version of planning, budgeting, and goal setting throughout the organization. Most of these approaches have in common a balanced emphasis on both the process by which goals are set and the results that they seek.[4] This chapter is intended to enable you to learn about, practice, and apply a method of goal setting that is particularly suitable for entrepreneurship. Goal setting also provides a link between entrepreneurship and management skills.

10.7.2 Why Plan?

More than any other, the old saying at the beginning of this section captures the rationale for establishing personal goals. We've all heard the reasons why *not* to plan: It's out of date as soon as it's written down. No one knows what tomorrow will bring—better opportunities or unknown disasters. It's dangerous to commit to uncertainty; you can't predict the future. The list of such rationalizations can be lengthy. So why plan?

Certainly, we don't know all of the reasons why you should plan, but we have attempted to summarize here some of the important ones:[5]

1. Research shows a close connection between personal and entrepreneurial success and the goal-setting and planning process. As discussed earlier, one of the most striking characteristics of successful entrepreneurs is their attitude toward and use of goal setting.

2. Goal setting helps you to work "smarter," rather than simply "harder." It helps you to come up with a "better way" by considering alternatives. The discipline and process of goal setting, when applied to developing a business plan, for example, enable you to understand and clarify the risks. In turn, goal setting can help you to devise ways both to manage those risks and to reduce them.

---

[3]David C. McClelland, "Achievement Motivation Can Be Developed," *Harvard Business Review,* November–December 1965; David C. McClelland and David G. Winter, *Motivating Economic Achievement* (New York: Free Press, 1969); and Jeffry A. Timmons, "Black Is Beautiful—Is It Bountiful?" *Harvard Business Review,* November–December 1971, p. 81.

[4]See, for examples: George Odiorne, *Management by Objectives—A System of Managerial Leadership* (New York: Pitman Publishing, 1965); and C. L. Hughes, *Goal Setting: Key to Individual and Organizational Effectiveness* (New York: American Management Association, 1965).

[5]The authors acknowledge the contributions of Mr. John L. Hayes, our colleague at the Institute for New Enterprise Development, for his assistance on the material on goal setting.

3. Goal setting keeps you in a "future-oriented" frame of mind. This thinking ahead helps you to anticipate—and thus be more alert for and responsive to—problems, opportunities, and changes that will affect you. It can put you in greater charge of your life.

4. Planning helps you to develop and update a keener strategy by testing the validity of your ideas and approaches with others.

5. A more subtle consequence of proper goal setting is the effect that the goals you are pursuing have on your motivation. Inherent in any goal is some level of effort that is required to attain it. This specific level of effort, once made clear, can be judged in terms of its ease of attainment, which could range from ridiculously easy to impossible. A goal that is ridiculously easy to attain means relatively easy going—there is plenty of time, and it will not take any crash effort to reach the goal. The effect on motivation is that only a mild level of effort is generated. It is also possible to set a goal that is virtually impossible to attain. The individual pursuing the goal knows that it cannot be reached, and his commitment is tempered by the pessimism of knowing that.

The essential element affecting motivation is how individuals *feel* about their goals. Both of the above examples create feelings that detract from the motivation to achieve. Somewhere in between these two examples is the goal that is attainable but will require substantial effort to achieve. The goal is not so difficult to reach that no amount of effort will help in reaching it, nor is it so easy to reach that little effort is needed. The individual who pursues such a challenging but attainable goal is more motivated to work toward than are the individuals who pursue either the easy or the too difficult goal.

6. Goal setting also gives you a "results orientation"—a concern for accomplishment and progress.[6] Once you have stated a specific, time-phases, measurable goal, it will be much easier for you and others to evaluate your performance. Doing this will enable you to see how close you come to achieving your goal. That means taking a lot of responsibility for your actions.

7. Goal setting helps you to manage the risks and uncertainties of the future, but it does not predict the future.

8. The skill and judgment required to establish realistic goals can be effective in managing and coping with what is by nature a stressful role.

We could extend this list of reasons why goal setting can be useful, but the points above are the essential ones. Besides, goal setting must not become too rigid a process; it is intended to provide direction and a point of departure, rather than a lockstep, immutable order.

10.7.3 Disadvantages of Planning[7]

Planning is probably not for everyone. It is not a panacea for lack of personal progress. While the authors share a bias that favors personal planning and goal setting, especially for those with entrepreneurial aspirations, certain risks and limitations must be noted. For some, who may not be entrepreneurs, these drawbacks may offset some of the benefits just discussed.

1. The cautious person who is also anxious about failure may find that set-

---

[6]Peter R. Drucker, *Managing for Results* (New York: Harper & Row, 1964).

[7]For a useful discussion of this issue, see David R. Hampton, "The Planning-Motivation Dilemma," *Business Horizons,* June 1973.

ting personal goals creates a further source of tension and pressure and a heightened fear of failure. The possible mental and physical consequences of such anxiety-inducing activities can be counterproductive for such a person.

2. Establishing goals and plans requires making choices and commitments. It means setting priorities on goals. Inherent in this process is the possibility that future or yet unknown options, which might be more attractive than the one chosen, may become lost or excluded opportunities. This dilemma is central to the decision to commit oneself to a career or a course of action that may take a few years to alter or undo.

3. Commitment to a career-oriented goal, particularly if you are younger and lack much real-world experience, can be premature. For instance, how many of us possess at ages 18 to 20 the accurate information, knowledge, and experience about a particular career or role that are necessary to wisely decide to become an electrical engineer, a pilot, or a businessperson? And for the many who learn from personal, concrete experience what they are and are not good at, and what they do and do not like, the problem of a premature career goal is even greater.

4. For the person who is inclined to be a compulsive and obsessive competitor and achiever, goal setting may have the effect of adding gasoline to the fire. Efficient planning and time management may contribute further to one's total focus on a particular task, project, or career, to the exclusion of family, friends, community, or other responsibilities. This dilemma faces not only aspiring entrepreneurs but anyone pursuing a similarly highly competitive and demanding career.

5. Events and environmental factors entirely beyond one's control may boost or sink the best-laid plans: the Arab oil crisis, a natural disaster, an accidental death, to give some examples. No planning process can foresee all such developments, nor could it necessarily prevent them even if they could be foreseen. Thus, during the demanding early survival stages of a new company, whose life expectancy may at times be estimated in weeks or months, major allocation of time and effort to planning for next year simply does not make sense.[8]

10.7.4 Why Plans Fail[9]

There is perhaps no greater frustration for entrepreneurs and managers than to experience failure with plans seemingly well prepared and well intended. A well-prepared plan consumes precious hours, so it is not only frustrating but downright demoralizing when the plan doesn't seem to work. And this failure, in turn, breeds contempt for the entire planning process, particularly when success has been achieved in the absence of formal planning. Thus, the significant issue is: Why do plans fail?

10.7.5 The Postplanning Syndrome

We are all familiar with the concept of a learning curve. Its ascent is greatest during early mastery of a new task, gradually levels off, and may stabilize or

[8]For a discussion of some approaches to this dilemma, see George A. Steiner, "Approaches to Long Range Planning for Small Business," *California Management Review*, Fall 1967, pp. 3–16.

[9]These sections are based on material prepared by Jeffry A. Timmons from a manuscript by George H. Litwin, Jeffry A. Timmons, and Stevan K. Trooboff, tentatively entitled "Organizational Climate: The Environments That Shape Our Lives."

decline. Similarly, education researchers have discovered that several weeks or a few months following a particular training program, participants often return to their old, routine ways of doing things. Changed behavior in these instances has not been long lasting. And most of us have heard of or observed—or been victims of—the recent graduate of an intensive "management science" or "human development" seminar. The first few days back on the job are characterized by behavior that is incredibly predictable, albeit short-lived: a new enthusiasm, an impressive array of new buzzwords, a prominently displayed "coursebook" and "graduation plaque" on the desk or wall, and exclamations regarding how "we need to (or will) do things differently around here from now on." Now the seasoned greeter of these new behaviors knows that the boss will probably need a week or two to get all of this out of his system, to calm down a bit, and to return to normality. Knowing well how unlikely it is that this enthusiasm and exhortation will endure, the seasoned greeter is at once receptive—at least verbally—and, above all, patient.

By the second Monday after the return the fever has indeed receded to a moderate level: the end is in sight! The routine, occasional tranquillity, and predictable crises of the "old way" will soon return. Ah, yes, and "the best-laid plans of mice and men . . ."

These patterns and outcomes of most training experiences are characteristic of what we might call the postplanning syndrome. The plan doesn't work, so we retreat to the familiar and fall back on the *activity-oriented* routine or, sometimes, crisis management. This routine often becomes counterproductive for the same reason that it was counterproductive prior to the seminar: it lacks or confuses priorities, has no longer-term purpose, and isn't aimed at the attainment of particular objectives. How many times, for example, has someone returned from the day at the office with the following observations? "I was busy all day. But I didn't get a thing done." But plans and planning need not be futile. We contend—and have seen in action—that planning will be effective when critical aspects of the *process* itself are not overlooked. And high-performing entrepreneurs and managers usually approach planning as a *total process*, not as an end result.

10.7.6 Pitfalls of Effective Planning

Central to effective planning is recognizing why plans fail. Simple enough: What are the behaviors or pitfalls that seem to contribute to planning failure, and what must be done to reduce the possibility of failure? While failure is a certainty if you don't work hard, simply working harder is not enough. Working smarter is essential. Working smarter entails an awareness of and a response to six basic reasons why plans fail.

1. No Real Goal. If there is no plan, the plan can't fail. Oddly enough, many people aren't aware of what a goal is. They may allude to some admirable mission such as "improve performance," "growth," or "increased business," but such vagaries are better labeled fantasies than goals. A goal must be concrete. If goals are not specific, measurable, time-phased, and realistic, the plan is very unlikely to work.

2. Failure to Anticipate Obstacles. Obviously, no one can think of every possible contingency, but excessive optimism and overcommitment can seriously impede a sensible effort to constantly anticipate obstacles and pitfalls. Every plan, no matter how carefully prepared, has its limitations and built-in conflicts over priorities and resources. And the fact is that it's often too late to exclaim: "I should have thought of that!" Entrepreneurs who deliberately identify potential obstacles and how to overcome them have superior batting averages for their plans. And effective goal setters know that doing this is not an exercise in identifying the impossible so as to rationalize failure. Rather, they break down into small hurdles that which they may initially perceive as very large obstacles, and then they establish concrete action steps to surmount these hurdles. A plan needs to be flexible and must recognize and provide solutions to the anticipated obstacles if it is to deal with the unknown and unexpected problem.

3. Lack of Progress Milestones and Reviews. Plans that fail often have no concrete milestones and progress review dates, or these are allowed to slip by. The rationale is usually expressed in such ways as these: "It can wait," "I can remember that," or "I know how I'm doing!" Periodic reviews of progress versus the goals set provide "red flags" alerting you to a need for reassessment. And milestones passed provide an important sense of accomplishment, and thus the motivation to succeed further. However, experienced practitioners know that excessive detail and analysis in the review process can detract from the purpose itself—implementation and goal accomplishment. The whole process must be kept simple and must avoid bureaucratic tendencies toward red tape and "checkups." Effective progress reviews simply provide a test of the velocity, direction, and reality of the plan at any point in time.

4. Lack of Commitment. Personal commitment is critical to the success of any plan. Commitment provides the self-motivation to see a plan through to completion. It's quite easy, especially for an entrepreneur, to obtain "lip service" commitment to a plan from a subordinate or a co-worker. But unless and until the people who must implement the plan are *committed* to it, the plan is likely to go unmet. Commitment, though very difficult to create, seems to stem from involvement in the process of developing goals from the outset. Involving subordinates or co-workers in this process generates their interest, their inputs, and more importantly, their ownership in the plan. Discussion that involves negotiating, compromising, and data sharing helps in arriving at goals that are *jointly* established. When a plan doesn't work, it's easy to say, "I told you so; it wasn't *my* plan; it was the boss's!" This is the best indicator that a commitment was never really gained. It implies that collaboration is essential in order to gain commitment to a plan.

For the highly determined entrepreneur, another dilemma is faced on the other side of the commitment coin: the problem of overcommitment. While a zealous supercommitment is necessary to sustain the entrepreneurial spirit, overcommitment can lead to ignoring reality and pressing ahead on a course that is unduly risky and may lead to costly failure. Overcommitment can block out important feedback, distort reality, and confuse perceptions of who is friend or foe. The consequences are apparent to all.

5. Failure to Revise Goals. Not setting goals, anticipating obstacles, reviewing progress, and establishing commitment all contribute to plans gone amiss. An even surer way to torpedo the best-laid plan is failing to reassess and reset goals and plans as dictated by the realities that unfold. New competition, the loss of key personnel, overly ambitious timetables, and a host of other uncertainties rear their ugly heads as a plan is implemented. Inflexibility or stubbornness in the face of such matters forces adherence to what is most likely an unattainable or inappropriate plan. Failure is thus programmed into a plan that has no responsiveness to changes in the environment, internal and external. Progress reviews are wasted if a new situation is not met with a change in emphasis or approach. Such reassessment is simply being practical and realistic. Perhaps new expertise or other help is required. Failing to revise goals when it is appropriate to do so is ignoring reality. Revising goals is a key aspect of the *process* of goal setting. Effective planning provides resiliency in its content.

6. Failure to Learn from Experience. We often observe entrepreneurs doing some of the "right things" noted above, yet they somehow don't seem to learn from what they are doing. They will ignore the feedback that they are receiving ("We're behind schedule, but our budget is holding up"), or they will deny that what has been fed back is even happening ("Go back and check your figures"). Such failures to learn from current and past experience seem to stem in part from an unwillingness to change their way of doing things. Such entrepreneurs comfort in the thought "It's worked before; it must be right." But failing to be proactive learners will prohibit them from ever finding out whether "it" is indeed right, until, of course, it is too late. Flexibility is perhaps the key attribute that is required here.

10.7.7 Summary

In short, plans fail (and subsequently, entrepreneurs fail) because crucial factors are overlooked and critical steps in the planning process are omitted. These omissions are:

1. Specific, measurable, time-phased, realistic goals aren't set.
2. Commitment to success isn't obtained from critical people (you, your team members, and employees).
3. Obstacles aren't anticipated; milestones aren't established to check on progress; provision isn't made for the unforeseen; and alternative strategies aren't developed to handle contingencies.

Moreover, planning should be used to reduce the uncertainty of the future and to *manage* risk and change, *not* to *forecast* the future. Learning from failure, reassessing and resetting goals and plans periodically, is an integral part of this process. Planning can also be used to build team commitment and obtain collaboration. Thus:

1. Plan mutually with team members whose commitment is critical to success.
2. Make performance expectations clear.
3. Create a win-win situation for everyone who is critical to success.
4. Provide and solicit feedback on progress to maintain commitment and keep plans on track.

Last, plans should be *goal oriented* rather than *activity oriented,* and these should not be confused. Working harder is vital to new venture success, but it must also be accompanied by working smarter. Exhibit 10.5 summarizes the ailments of planning and their symptoms and cures.

10.7.8 Instructions for Exercise

During the next hour or so you are going to engage in an activity that most of you have undoubtedly thought about in some ways but have probably never com-

Exhibit 10.5
Planning: Its Ailments, Symptoms, and Cures

Planning	*Symptoms*	*Cure*
1. No Real Goals	Goals are vague, general Goals not specific, measurable, or time-phased No subgoals or action steps Activity oriented, not goal oriented	Set specific, time-phased, measurable goals, subgoals, and action steps. Keep the overall aim in mind. Be opportunistic in pursuing goals.
2. Failure to Anticipate Obstacles	Excessive optimism No alternative strategies No conflicts recognized "Don't worry, I had thought of that" Missed meeting delivery date Missed lead-time forecasts Didn't get support when needed Crises prevail	Be flexible in planning and anticipating as far as possible obstacles and how to overcome them. Face unanticipated obstacles with confidence—there'll always be some. Ask someone else to brainstorm with you, "What could go wrong or get in our way?" Realism is key.
3. Lack of Milestones and Progress Reviews	"It can wait"; "I can remember that" "I'll know how we're doing when we get there—let's play it by ear" Don't really know how you are doing Short-term orientation Can't recall when we last reviewed how we are doing No recent revisions of plan	Set specific task milestones and progress review dates; stick to them and revise when needed. Ask each day, "What did I accomplish today toward reaching my goal?" Ask each day, "What have I learned that will help me to make more rapid progress?"
4. Lack of Commitment	"I told you it wouldn't work—it wasn't *my* plan!" Procrastination Focus on routine, daily activities Failure to meet goals, milestones Failure to develop specific action steps to meet goals Lack of priorities Missed meetings, appointments	Set goals mutually; utilize *joint* review, negotiation, compromise, and data sharing. Meet periodically, and track progress. Encourage informal discussion with team members, both to test and to renew commitment. Keep team members informed about results obtained. Recognize and reward performance that meets your high standards.
5. Failure to Revise Goals	Plan never changes, lacks resiliency Inflexible or stubborn in face of feedback dictating change Goals not met or exceeded greatly Unresponsive to changing situation Help not sought when needed Wasted time or unproductive tasks or activities Activities don't match goal priorities	Meet periodically to review goals and progress and to assess the situation. Change emphasis and approach as appropriate. Create a climate that is tolerant of bad news and invites constructive critiques and feedback.
6. Failure to Learn from Experience	Lost sight of goals Mistake is repeated Feedback is ignored or denied Same routine—same crises as previously Unwillingness to change way of doing things Not asking: "What do we learn from this experience?"	Set improvement and learning objectives. Use milestones, and reassess periodically. Collaborate more frequently in tracking progress and learning. Document at end of one project/plan lessons, benchmarks, guidelines that have emerged. What was learned? Be adaptive, flexible, and responsive to unfolding events. A new venture start-up is full of surprises. Concentrate on producing results, not on reports for their own sake.

mitted to writing. Some people have done neither, and a few are probably not capable of doing it at all, excluding those present, of course. This first goal-setting exercise should be very thought-provoking and stimulating to each of you. It can have significant relevance to and implications for a decision about launching your own venture, and, if you do, when and how. You should therefore take the exercise seriously and work diligently. It is more a writing exercise than a thinking exercise during the first few steps. Each step will have a three-minute time limit, so you will have to work quickly. Later you will have a chance to exchange your work with another person and to discuss the relevance and implications of what you have written.

Name _____

Date _____

10.8 GOAL SETTING: THE EXERCISE

10.8.1 Listing, Prioritizing, and Implementing Goals

Step 1

My Goals by the Time I Am 70

Assume that you will live to be 70 years of age and in reasonably good health. In the next *three minutes,* write below as many as you can of the things that you want to accomplish by age 70. Now go to step 2.

Step 2

My Seven-Year Goals

In the next *three minutes,* write below all the things that you want to accomplish in the next seven years. (If you are an undergraduate, use the next *four* years.) Now go to step 3.

Step 3

My Last-Year-to-Live Goals

Assume that you know that you have exactly one year from today to live. You will enjoy good health in the interim, but will not be able to acquire any more life insurance or borrow an additional large sum of money for a "final fling." Assume further that you could spend that last year of your life doing whatever you want to do. In the next *three* minutes, write below the goals that you would want to accomplish if you had but one year to live. Now go to step 4.

Step 4

My Real Goals

Now tear out the first three lists and lay them side by side. Review each list. You will have six minutes to review and combine the first three lists into one list of your "real goals." Write them below. Now go to step 5.

Step 5

Pair Discussion (20 minutes)

Now is a good juncture to pair up with a person of your choice (or with two persons if there is an odd number). Exchange your "My Real Goals" lists (tear out), and review them. You should help each other to review, refine, and clarify these goal statements, and you should begin to identify their relative importance to you personally. You may find it useful to exchange all four lists, time permitting. The following questions should be helpful in focusing your discussion:

1. How do your goals relate to some of the issues raised previously in the book, particularly work style and lifestyle?
2. How do your goals relate to the creation or acquisition of your own business?
3. Do some of the goals conflict with others?
4. How do your goals relate to your other self-assessments?
5. Can you rank-order the priority of the goals?

Now go to step 6.

Step 6

Identifying Top-Priority Goals

From your list of "My Real Goals" and your Pair Discussion, identify the three goals that you now believe are your *highest-priority* goals. For each one, write down in the space below (*a*) all the *activities,* tasks, or steps that you can take to help you attain the goal and (*b*) all the *obstacles* or hurdles that you feel can prevent you from reaching your goal. You will have 10 minutes to complete this.

	Activities, etc.	*Obstacles*
No. 1 Priority Goal:		
No. 2 Priority Goal:		
No. 3 Priority Goal:		

Now go to steps 7 through 10.

Step 7

Action List

Now review your lists of activities and obstacles in step 6. Cross off the lists *any* activities that cannot be begun or any obstacle that *cannot* be removed in the *next seven days.* You will have four minutes to complete this step.

Step 8

High-Priority Action Items

Now review the remaining items on your lists in step 6. Identify for each of your three highest-priority goals (*a*) the *single most important activity* that you can initiate and (*b*) the *single most important obstacle* that you can remove to help you attain these goals. Circle these items.

Step 9

Establish a Date

Take out your calendar, and set a *date,* a *time,* and, if possible, a place during the *next seven days* to accomplish the high-priority action items you circled in step 8.

Step 10

Small Group Discussion (20 minutes)

If possible, we suggest that teams of four to five persons discuss the exercise with particular attention devoted to the following questions:

1. What was involved? What did we do?
2. What were the differences between what we put on the first two lists and the items on step 6 and later, in terms of concreteness, etc.?
3. Do any of the action items identified in steps 8 and 9 relate to strengths or weaknesses identified previously?
4. What criteria would we now use for judging whether or not we are really setting goals?

10.8.2 Summary

The previous exercise has immersed you in one of the most important ingredients in successful entrepreneurship: effective, realistic goal setting. The process and effort may have been less difficult than you anticipated at first. This rapid simulation of the process has demonstrated the fundamentals of effective goal setting:

1. Setting a *goal.*
2. Establishing a priority.
3. Identifying actions and obstacles.
4. Setting an action step.

The detailed application of these principles to your own career and your entrepreneurial aspirations will take considerably more time and effort. This exercise can be viewed as a step in the appropriate direction, but it does require additional and continual effort.

What Does It Take? Make no mistake; goal setting is a difficult, demanding, and time-consuming process. If you have not done it in a thorough manner previously, you may find it, at first, a somewhat agonizing, as well as rewarding, experience. Few people are effective goal setters; perhaps fewer than 10 percent have ever committed their goals to writing. Perhaps fewer than 50 percent of the adults you know do even mental goal setting, and much of this might be labeled speculative thinking or fantasizing.

Effective goal setting demands four critical *personal* requirements:

1. Your time.
2. Self-discipline.
3. Commitment and dedication to it.
4. Practice and development of the habit.

More important, goal setting can and must be learned for entrepreneurial success. One of the central aims of the chapter and exercise was to assist you in this effort.

Steps to Effective Goal Setting. The goals set by successful entrepreneurs are not dreams, fantasies, or the product of wishful thinking. Nor are they mere predictions or guesses about future outcomes. A goal is far more concrete and specific—it is a decision or choice about future outcomes. Goal setting is a process for managing uncertainties and minimizing risks. Goal setting is the process by which you plan where you want to go, how fast, how to get there, and what to do along the way. It also defines performance so that you can determine progress.

Goals properly set to chart future courses must be carefully defined. Proper goals should meet the following criteria:

1. A goal must be *specific* and *concrete,* rather than abstract and out of focus.
2. A goal must be *measurable.*
3. A goal must be *related to time;* that is, it must be specific about what will be accomplished over a certain time period.
4. A goal must be *realistic* and *attainable.* Simply meeting the first three criteria is not enough; the goal must be challenging but attainable.

Once set, goals should not become static targets. Goal setting is not a task but a process, a way of dealing with the world. A number of distinct steps are involved in this process; these steps are repeated over and over as conditions change.

Step 1. *Establish the goal.* (It must be specific, measurable, time-related, and attainable.)

Step 2. Establish *priorities* (from most to least important goals and action steps); identify potential goal conflicts and trade-offs and how these can be resolved.

Step 3. *Identify potential problems and obstacles* that could prevent you from attaining your goal.

Step 4. Specify the *tasks and action steps* that must be performed to achieve the goal.

Step 5. Indicate how you will *measure the results* that you hope to accomplish.

Step 6. Establish some *milestones* for reviewing the progress that you are making. These should be specific dates on your calendar.

Step 7. Identify the *risks* that are involved in meeting your goal and what must be done to avoid high or low chances of success.

Step 8. Identify and seek out the *help and resources* that may be needed to attain your goal.

Step 9. *Review progress periodically,* and revise goals and plans as feedback and results indicate that such revision is appropriate.

These are the basic ingredients of effective goal setting. Of course, there are numerous ways of actually going about it.[10] Research and practical experience have shown that these ingredients are common to almost all successful planning efforts. We urge you to become familiar with this process, adapt it to your needs, and begin to practice it. Only through effective goal setting will the lessons you learn be translated into personal goals and action steps. And only effective goal setting can produce an action plan that is likely to result in a successful venture.

10.9 PARTNER, PEER, AND PROFESSIONAL FEEDBACK: OVERVIEW

> *And so each venture is a new beginning,*
> *a raid on the inarticulate with shabby equipment*
> *always deteriorating in the general mess*
> *of imprecision of feeling,*
> *undisciplined squads of emotion.*
>
> T. S. Eliot
> (from *Four Quartets*)

10.9.1 Seeking "Outside" Feedback

A source of potentially very useful information, as we related in Section 10.3, is the impressions of people who know us well. Rarely, however, does this information get shared—and for this reason we provided opportunities for giving feedback to and receiving feedback from fellow classmates at the outset of the self-assess-

---

[10]See, for instance, in *Human Behavior,* May 1974, pp. 47–50, an interview with Alan Lakein, a professional who conducts adult goal-setting sessions.

ment exercises. We hope that this experience has (1) made you aware of "blind spots"—things you had not considered before—with regard to both your strengths and weaknesses and (2) reinforced your existing perceptions of both your strengths and weaknesses.

At this point, you are ready to expand your sources of feedback beyond the classroom by going to "outside" peers, potential partners, and professionals to enlist their impressions, in writing, of your entrepreneurial strengths and weaknesses. This set of exercises is aimed toward that objective.

10.9.2   Instructions for Exercises

It is very difficult to find out what your colleagues regard as your strengths and weaknesses. There are many relevant facts: the length of time the person knows you; the degree of rapport that exists between the two of you; the person's areas of knowledge, for example, business skills (Management Skills) and personal characteristics (Entrepreneurial Attributes).

It seems most appropriate, given these facts and the self-assessment focus of this book, that we suggest some issues for you to consider in seeking these impressions and provide you with some guidance on how best to obtain "outside" feedback data.

1. Consider the context in which the person knows you. A business colleague may be better able to comment on your managerial skills. Your partners in a new venture project are potentially excellent sources of feedback. A personal friend may be able to comment on your motivational characteristics or on the possible effects of deciding to become an entrepreneur on your family situation. Your wife or husband, if you are married, is obviously an excellent source of data on the latter. Make copies of the Entrepreneurial Attributes, Role Requirements, and Management Skills forms and of the Feedback Guide. Encourage your colleagues and project partners to fill out as many portions of the forms as they can, based on their knowledge of you.

2. Chat with the person *before* asking him or her to provide any specific written impressions, and indicate the specific areas that you think he or she can best comment on. *One* way to do this is to formulate *your own questions* first. For example, "I've been asking myself the following question. . . . I would really like your impressions in that regard."

3. Encourage the person to describe specific situations or behaviors that have influenced the impressions he or she has developed.

4. The writing of impressions is important for the following reasons: (*a*) The person can take some time to think about the issues after you have spoken with him or her—his answers needn't be "off-the-top" ideas. (*b*) Having the person's answers on paper will help you in the future as you pull together all of your workshop experiences and continue to think more specifically about your potential as an entrepreneur.

10.9.3   Description of Feedback Guides

One copy of a suggested feedback guide has been provided. Feel free to make any additions to the forms that seem appropriate. After speaking with a person and explaining why you are asking him to do this and what you would like him to focus on specifically, leave the impression form with him to complete and return to you.

The person can either mail or deliver his response to you. How you handle this may depend on your decision concerning anonymity. Ideally, you should have all the responses in a few days in order to personally reflect on their content and implications.

How many people you approach for all forms is obviously up to you. The greater their number and the wider the range of their perspectives, the more potential value this exercise will have for you. You should remember that what you say during the preliminary chat with each person will *help him* considerably to provide impressions that will *help you.*

10.10 FEEDBACK GUIDES: THE EXERCISES (Remove pages, and make as many copies as necessary.)

10.10.1 Strengths and Weaknesses

Feedback for: _____
                                        (Name)

Prepared by: _____
                                        (Name)

FEEDBACK GUIDE: PART ONE
STRENGTHS AND WEAKNESSES

1. What are the one or more areas—as an entrepreneur, relevant experience, management know-how—that you see as my greatest potential or existing strengths in terms of succeeding in the venture opportunity we have discussed?

2. What specific situations led you to indicate these as areas of strength?

3. What are the one or more areas—as an entrepreneur, relevant experience, management know-how—that you see as my greatest potential or existing weaknesses in terms of succeeding in the venture opportunity we have discussed?

4. What specific situations led you to indicate these as areas of weakness?

5. Record below any suggestions or "prescriptions" that you think would be helpful for me to consider.

6. Given my venture opportunity, what is your evaluation of my partners? (This assumes you know them, even if casually or in a limited way.) Do they have the relevant experience, know-how, and management competencies to complement my own?

7. Given my venture opportunity, based on your evaluation of my weaknesses, should I consider any additional members for my management team, and what should be their strengths and relevant experience?

10.10.2 Entrepreneurial Attributes Summary

Please complete the following by checking your impressions of my entrepreneurial attributes and management skills.

		Very Strong	*Adequate Enough*	*A Question*	*Real Weakness*	*No Basis to Judge*
a.	Total Commitment, Determination, and Perseverance	_____	_____	_____	_____	_____
b.	Drive to Achieve and Grow	_____	_____	_____	_____	_____
c.	Opportunity and Goal Oriented	_____	_____	_____	_____	_____
d.	Taking Initiative and Personal Responsibility	_____	_____	_____	_____	_____
e.	Persistent Problem Solving	_____	_____	_____	_____	_____
f.	Veridical Awareness and a Sense of Humor	_____	_____	_____	_____	_____
g.	Seeking and Using Feedback	Gambler		Calculated		Conservative
h.	Internal Locus of Control	_____	_____	_____	_____	_____
i.	Tolerance for Ambiguity, Stress, and Uncertainty	_____	_____	_____	_____	_____
j.	Calculated Risk Taking and Risk Sharing	_____	_____	_____	_____	_____
k.	Low Need for Status and Power	_____	_____	_____	_____	_____
l.	Integrity and Reliability	_____	_____	_____	_____	_____
m.	Decisiveness, Urgency, and Patience	_____	_____	_____	_____	_____
n.	Dealing with Failure	_____	_____	_____	_____	_____
o.	Team Builder and Hero Maker	_____	_____	_____	_____	_____

Comments:

ENTREPRENEURIAL ROLE REQUIREMENTS

Please check the appropriate column under the headings below.

		Very Strong	*Adequate Enough*	*A Question*	*Real Weakness*	*No Basis to Judge*
a.	Accommodation to the Venture	_____	_____	_____	_____	_____
b.	Stress Generation	_____	_____	_____	_____	_____
c.	Economic and Professional Values	_____	_____	_____	_____	_____
d.	Ethics	_____	_____	_____	_____	_____

Comments:

10.10.3 Management Skills and Competencies Summary

FEEDBACK GUIDE: PART THREE
MANAGEMENT SKILLS AND COMPETENCIES

Please check the appropriate place on the scale below.

	Major Strength	*Required Threshold*	*Major Weakness*	*No Basis for Judgment*
1. Marketing Skills				
a. Market Research and Evaluation	___	___	___	___
b. Marketing Planning	___	___	___	___
c. Product Pricing	___	___	___	___
d. Sales Management	___	___	___	___
e. Direct Selling	___	___	___	___
f. Service	___	___	___	___
g. Distribution Management	___	___	___	___
h. Product Management	___	___	___	___
i. New Product Planning	___	___	___	___

Comments:

	Major Strength	Required Threshold	Major Weakness	No Basis for Judgment
2. Operations/Technical Skills				
a. Manufacturing Management	_____	_____	_____	_____
b. Inventory Control	_____	_____	_____	_____
c. Cost Analysis and Control	_____	_____	_____	_____
d. Quality Control	_____	_____	_____	_____
e. Production Scheduling and Flow	_____	_____	_____	_____
f. Purchasing	_____	_____	_____	_____
g. Job Evaluation	_____	_____	_____	_____

Comments:

	Major Strength	*Required Threshold*	*Major Weakness*	*No Basis for Judgment*
3. Financial Skills				
a. Raising Capital	___	___	___	___
b. Cash Flow Management	___	___	___	___
c. Credit and Collection Management	___	___	___	___
d. Short-Term Financing Alternatives	___	___	___	___
e. Familiar with Public and Private Stock Offerings	___	___	___	___
f. Bookkeeping and Accounting	___	___	___	___
g. Specific Skills				
Cash Flow Analysis	___	___	___	___
Break-even Analysis	___	___	___	___
Contribution Analysis	___	___	___	___
Profit and Loss	___	___	___	___
Balance Sheet	___	___	___	___

Comments:

		Major Strength	Required Threshold	Major Weakness	No Basis for Judgment
4.	**Micro Computer Skills**				
a.	Spreadsheet Analysis	_____	_____	_____	_____
b.	Word Processing	_____	_____	_____	_____
c.	Database Access and Use of Electronic Mail	_____	_____	_____	_____
d.	Graphics	_____	_____	_____	_____

Comments:

	Major Strength	*Required Threshold*	*Major Weakness*	*No Basis for Judgment*
5. Administrative Skills				
a. Problem Solving	_____	_____	_____	_____
b. Communication	_____	_____	_____	_____
c. Planning	_____	_____	_____	_____
d. Decision Making	_____	_____	_____	_____
e. Project Management	_____	_____	_____	_____
f. Negotiating	_____	_____	_____	_____
g. Personnel Administration	_____	_____	_____	_____

Comments:

	Major Strength	*Required Threshold*	*Major Weakness*	*No Basis for Judgment*
6. Interpersonal and Team Skills				
a. Leadership and Influence	_____	_____	_____	_____
b. Listening and Trust Building	_____	_____	_____	_____
c. Helping	_____	_____	_____	_____
d. Obtaining and Using Feedback	_____	_____	_____	_____
e. Conflict Management	_____	_____	_____	_____
f. Teamwork	_____	_____	_____	_____
g. Developing Subordinates	_____	_____	_____	_____
h. Climate and Culture Building	_____	_____	_____	_____

Comments:

	Major Strength	*Required Threshold*	*Major Weakness*	*No Basis for Judgment*
7. Knowledge of Applicable Law				
a. Corporate Law	_____	_____	_____	_____
b. Contract Law	_____	_____	_____	_____
c. Patent and Proprietary Rights Laws	_____	_____	_____	_____
d. Tax Law	_____	_____	_____	_____
e. Real Estate Law	_____	_____	_____	_____
f. Investment Agreement Law	_____	_____	_____	_____

Comments:

Name _____

Date _____

10.11   ENTREPRENEURIAL ASSESSMENT AND PERSONAL PROGRESS: EXERCISES AND SUMMARY

Complete after you have received and digested peer and partner feedback.

1. What observations and insights have emerged from completing these exercises and discussing them with your peers in terms of your own entrepreneurial career and the specific venture opportunity you have in mind?

2. Below is Exhibit 10.4, discussed earlier in the chapter. Given the venture opportunity you are seeking, how would you rate yourself in terms of a fit with the entrepreneurial attributes and role requirements? Place an *X* in the box to represent where you see yourself now.

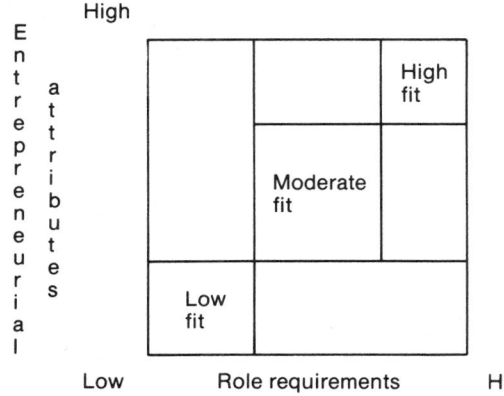

3. Summarize below what you feel are your entrepreneurial strengths and weaknesses with regard to your chosen venture opportunity at this time.

Strengths	*Weaknesses*

4. What personal implications or questions have been raised by these exercises and discussions concerning your potential fit with an entrepreneurial career and your proposed venture?

5. What action is necessary to fill any relevant experience gaps or to resolve any issues raised so far? How do you plan to do this?

By now you should feel that your personal entrepreneurial strategy and planning have begun in earnest. But don't feel that your plan is a prison sentence. It is a point of departure, not a contract of indenture. Believe us, it is not a lockstep life plan; we doubt that there is any such thing, especially for entrepreneurs. The plan certainly can, and will, change over time as you change. Life's events hardly ever unfold predictably or smoothly. Anticipating and adjusting are a vital part of any effective plan.

What is most important is the process and discipline that put you in charge of evaluating and shaping the choices and of initiating action that makes sense for you, rather than letting it just happen. Having a longer-term sense of direction can be both highly motivating and extremely helpful in determining what to say no to (which is much harder than saying yes), and it can temper opportunism and impulsive hunches with a more thoughtful strategic purpose.

Why is that so important? You are what you do. Today's choices, whether or not they are thought out, become tomorrow's track record and résumé. Unthinking opportunism and impulse may end up shaping you in ways that you may not find so attractive 10 years hence. What is worse, they may also result in your failing to obtain just the experiences you need in order to have high-quality opportunities come your way later on.

10.12   KEVIN MOONEY (C): CASE STUDY*

KEVIN MOONEY (C)

In April 1983 the Softcorp-PMI deal went through—without Kevin Mooney's signature on the employment agreement. (See Kevin Mooney (B), Exhibit 7, in Chapter 6.) One week later, just before the management committee was scheduled to meet, Bob Wilson came into Kevin's office.

He told me not to come to the management committee meeting, that all the other VPs were upset that I hadn't signed. They didn't think I had demonstrated any loyalty and commitment to the company, and Bob didn't think we could go on like this.

I missed the meeting and then was given an ultimatum—sign within a week or leave. So I signed. I didn't think I had any choice at that point. I felt a tremendous loyalty to my own staff—the international department was like my own company, and we were really beginning to do some challenging things in the international environment.

Through the rest of the year Kevin Mooney continued to build the international department, exceeding the year's aggressive 75 percent growth plan by 25 percent.

In February 1984 Kevin Mooney was fired.

Wilson came into my office and told me that PMI was unhappy with the working relationship I had with the other VPs. I was surprised at their priorities. I thought the numbers would speak for themselves.

But Bob said there was nothing he could do. He agreed to write a letter saying that I had been fired "without just cause," making my noncompete agreement void and making me eligible to collect my salary under the employment agreement I had signed the year before.

*This case was prepared by Loretto Crane, Research Assistant, under the direction of Professor Jeffry A. Timmons, as a basis for class discussion rather than to illustrate either effective or ineffective handling of an administrative situation. Copyright © 1984 by Babson College.

That evening the Mooneys sat trying to get used to the idea. Kevin's wife was very uncomfortable with the news; she was pregnant with their second child and not working. Kevin called a friend with whom he had discussed his situation on a continuing basis. "Guess what?" he greeted. "I got fired today!" An enthusiastic voice on the other end of the phone blurted out, "Kevin, that's wonderful!"

(Mooney's 1984 résumé is shown in Exhibit 1.)

Exhibit 1

KEVIN MOONEY
560 Hillside Avenue
Seattle, Washington 98115

PROFESSIONAL EXPERIENCE

Softcorp. Inc. (Financial Software Company)   3/78–3/84
Vice President, International. Responsible for start-up and ongoing management of the international division. International gross revenues have grown significantly as follows: 1978—$0, 1979—$750,000, 1980—$1,500,000, 1981—$4,500,000, 1982—$12,500,000, 1983—$17,000,000. At the end of 1983 the total number of direct international employees was approximately 75. The total size of the international organization, including dedicated staff working for overseas representatives, was approximately 150.

Growth in international revenues was achieved through establishment of local sales, marketing, development, and support organizations utilizing a combination of wholly owned subsidiaries, joint ventures, and foreign representatives in the following countries: Canada, United Kingdom, Netherlands, France, Sweden, Norway, Denmark, Finland, Spain, Italy, South Africa, Brazil, Mexico, Venezuela, Peru, Colombia, Australia, New Zealand, Hong Kong, Singapore, Malaysia, Philippines.

Assembled a talented management team to achieve growth and stability in the international organization. This enabled the international division to generate results far in excess of corporate expectations.

Managed all corporate marketing activities (including United States) from 6/78 through 12/80.

Price Waterhouse & Co.   8/76–3/78
Management consultant, specializing in financial planning and control. Participated in broad variety of consulting engagements. Developed purchasing system for large manufacturing company. Designed accounting system for start-up organization. Created business plan used to secure $1.5 million bank financing for new business acquisition. Key participant in development of small business consulting practice.

EDUCATION

Stanford University, MBA, June 1976.
Broad curriculum with particular emphasis on management of smaller, fast-growing organizations. One of two students selected to participate in 1977 "Journey for Perspective" (scholarship program involving three weeks' travel abroad to France, Germany, United Kingdom, Soviet Union, and Czechoslovakia to meet with world leaders in business and government).

Cornell University, B.S., Industrial Engineering and Operations Research, June 1974.
Chairman Student Finance Commission two years. President Quill and Dagger Society (senior honorary society for outstanding contribution to the university).

OTHER

Teaching Activities
Guest lecturer, University of Washington, Graduate Business School. Taught several MBA courses in entrepreneurship, new venture creation, and small business management. Developed all course curricula utilizing variety of teaching methods including case studies, lectures, guest speakers, and general readings. Courses have consistently received highest student ratings.

Interest
Aviation (private pilot with instrument rating), swimming, photography, and fishing.

Preparation Questions

1. Evaluate Kevin Mooney's decision *not* to sign the agreement.
2. What obligations and responsibilities do he and Softcorp *now* have? What are their possible consequences and implications?
3. What should Kevin Mooney do now?

NECESSARY RESOURCES: RECOGNIZING, LOCATING, AND CONTROLLING THEM

PART III

The Entrepreneurial Approach to Resources

11

Another characteristic we observe in good entrepreneurs is a multistage commitment of resources with a minimum commitment at each stage or decision point—in other words, a lack of resources intensity.

Howard H. Stevenson
Harvard Business School

11.1 RESULTS EXPECTED

Successful entrepreneurs view, use, and manage resources differently from the way many large organizations do. This chapter addresses the unique entrepreneurial approach to resources and how it is applied. Upon completion of the chapter you will have:

1. Examined the unique attitudes and assumptions about resources—money, talent, assets—that characterize successful entrepreneurs.
2. Examined ways in which entrepreneurs use and control resources without having to own them.
3. Identified the important issues in the selection and effective utilization of outside professionals such as lawyers, accountants, board members, and consultants.
4. Identified specific sources for finding the resources required to pursue your opportunity.

11.2 PRESESSION PREPARATION

Review the sources noted in Chapters 2 and 3 for finding and evaluating ideas and opportunities. Obtain at the library or bookstore a copy of *The Encyclopedia of Small Business Resources,* ed. D. E. Gumpert and J. A. Timmons (New York: Harper & Row, 1984) and skim its contents. Determine what resources relevant to your opportunity are available in your area and how you will find them.

11.3 THE ENTREPRENEURIAL APPROACH: OPR

11.3.1 OPR = Other People's Resources

Entrepreneurs do things differently. One area in which they appear to defy the conventional wisdom that prevails in many large organizations is their approach to the commitment of resources in pursuit of opportunities. Their attitudes toward the ownership, use, and control of resources as they pursue opportunities are also revealing. They thrive on a *lack of resource intensity.*[1] Their mental set is: How can we pursue this opportunity and accomplish a little more with a little less?

The entrepreneurial approach, at least in the early going, is to minimize the resources necessary to pursue the opportunity—people, money, assets, and so forth—rather than to maximize them. This approach is referred to in colloquial terms as "bootstrapping it." The key to the approach is "Other People's Resources"—OPR. These people include investors, friends, relatives, and business associates who invest in or lend money to the entrepreneur; who, along with a customer or supplier, provide free or inexpensive space, equipment, or other material; who lend people, WATS lines, a word processor, or a Xerox machine—you name it. The barter may be an old friendship and favors, future services or opportunities, or some combination of these.

For example, in one company that grew to $20 million in sales in about 10 years, doing "a little more with a little less" started with the founders. They began with $7,500 in cash, along with liberal use of their credit cards, and they have not had to raise any additional equity capital thus far. They gave more effort for less pay, including pay-holidays in the early years. And when the company grew, the people who took over their old jobs—several with MBAs, by the way—openly acknowledged that it took two new people to do the jobs that each of the founders had performed previously.

Just the opposite approach is often evident in large institutions that are pressured by a trustee, custodial viewpoint: Do we have enough committed resources, plus a cushion, so that we will weather the tough times and not fail? Here, the first question often is "Do we have a big enough head-count and approved budget?" rather than "How can we do it with less?"

Another example of the entrepreneurial approach is the insistence of many entrepreneurs we have known that the worst thing that could have happened to them would have been to have too much money at the outset. Some of the highest-performing new companies in the mid-1980s were launched during 1979–81, a period of miserable economic conditions and high interest rates. Discipline and wisdom are often more readily acquired under the pressure of tight money and lean resources.

Howard Head insists that if he had raised all the money he needed at the outset, he would have failed by spending it all on one of the early, wrong versions of his metal ski. Instead, he developed only a few pairs of skis at a time and went through 40 experimental models before he found one that worked—but before he ran out of money. We have heard similar accounts in connection with hundreds of start-ups. It can be just as hazardous to have too much capital as not enough. An excess of capital seems to tolerate, if not encourage, lack of discipline in management and a more carefree style.

One noticeable difference in the entrepreneurial approach to resources is the way in which founders commit resources. The iterative, trial and error approach—if it works, keep going—that we have described is also part of Stevenson's frame-

[1]Howard H. Stevenson, "A New Paradigm for Entrepreneurial Management," Division of Research, Harvard Business School, 75th Anniversary Entrepreneurship Symposium, Boston, July 1983; we are most appreciative of Stevenson's articulate contribution to this important issue and have drawn on this thinking and on numerous discussions with him (*Proceedings,* 1985).

work. Stevenson sees the commitment of resources as a multistage process—a step at a time rather than an all-at-once, full-blown commitment—that reduces the initial exposure of the entrepreneur and spreads risks among OPRs.

Why do successful entrepreneurs take this approach? They know that their response times have to be short if they are to be competitively vibrant. They know that the decision windows are narrow and move rapidly. Under these normal operating circumstances that entrepreneurs thrive on, it is extremely difficult to predict accurately the resources necessary to execute the opportunity since, as we saw earlier, is also in constant flux. The flexibility gained by a piecemeal commitment of resources can translate into one of those "unfair advantages" that entrepreneurs manage to create for themselves.

11.3.2 Control and Use Rather than Own

Another very important characteristic of the entrepreneurial approach to resources concerns control and use versus ownership. In the start-up and early stages of a venture successful entrepreneurs seek to control and use the resources necessary to execute the opportunity. Unlike many of their corporate or unsuccessful entrepreneurial counterparts, they are not obsessed with *owning* the asset or resource—the building, computer, vehicle, equipment, and so forth. In large firms it is often assumed that virtually all fixed assets will have to be owned in order to control their use. Thus, the decisions center on how they will be acquired and financed, rather than on how to control and use them without having to own them.

What is key is having the use of the resource and the ability to control its development. In the extreme, Stevenson puts it this way:

When it comes to control of resources . . . all I need from a source is the ability to use it. There are people who describe the ideal business as a post office box to which people send cash.[2]

Common examples exist in real estate, where even the largest firms do not employ a top architect; rather, architects are secured on a project-by-project basis. The same is certainly true when it comes to hiring legal assistance, such as that of patent lawyers. Other examples are the hiring of technical consultants, design engineers, and programmers.

One start-up in the minicomputer software industry was anchored by programmers and technical people. Their business plan called for about $300,000 just to get them through the development of the first products. How would they deploy their financial resources? Their first priority was to buy outright an IBM 38 computer for around $150,000. "Why buy it?" they were asked. They replied, "We need to own one." "Why not borrow time, lease one, use slack time at night, etc.?" None of these options appealed to the founders. They were unable to attract venture capital, even though they had an excellent business plan. They did raise about $150,000 from informal, private investors, but since this was not enough money to execute their plan (and asset ownership), they decided to give it back instead of persevering. Would not a more entrepreneurial team have figured out a way to keep going under these conditions? We think so.

Why does this principle of minimal resources work for entrepreneurs? For

[2]H. H. Stevenson, from a talk to the 128 Venture Group, Boston, 1983.

one thing, it effectively reduces the risk of pursuing the opportunity. Less total exposure and capital are required. For another, fixed costs are lowered, thus favorably affecting the break-even. In addition, this smaller up-front resource ownership pattern lowers the cost of exercising the option to abort the venture at any point. Contrast that pattern with the enormous up-front capital commitment of a nuclear power plant and the enormous cost of abandoning the project, such as that experienced by WSPPS and at Seabrook, New Hampshire.

Avoiding the heavy commitment that ownership entails also lowers one's exposure to the risk of obsolescence. It is no wonder that computer leasing caught on early and has prevailed, especially among entrepreneurial ventures. Some might scoff at the practice, driven by the erroneous assumption that "they cannot afford to buy it." The truth of the matter is that not owning provides more entrepreneurial advantages and options.

Consider the inflexibility that you are faced with through permanent commitment to a particular technology, software, or other system. Once the system has been installed and purchased, you are stuck with it. How many people who have suffered with a "lemon" automobile that they bought outright would have been far better off with a leased car? One price of ownership of resources is an inherent inflexibility. Given the rapid flux and uncertainty of market and technology in which most entrepreneurial ventures have to survive, such inflexibility can be a serious curse.

There are, of course, many complications to buy-or-lease decisions, including a host of tax and other issues, and we do not want to make such decisions seem to be simpler than they are. Instead, we want to emphasize that successful entrepreneurs appear to make a strategic choice that favors controlling and using resources rather than owning them.

On the other side of the coin, variable costs do rise as a result of this practice. However, if the entrepreneur has paid particularly keen attention to selecting or shaping an opportunity with the quite "forgiving and rewarding economics" we reviewed in Chapter 3, then there should still be ample gross margins in the venture.

11.3.3 Commit and Decommit Quickly

A final pattern of entrepreneurial resource commitment and use is the capacity to commit and decommit quickly.[3] Larger firms often envy the resiliency and responsiveness that smaller entrepreneurial firms exude. What is behind this? The focus on minimization, control, and use through multistage commitments permits what we have labeled "iterations" in the venture process. It provides the strategic posture from which to conduct the trial and error testing of ideas so common to new ventures, without committing to the end consequences. Think of this rapid commitment and decommitment as enabling "strategic experiments," in Stevenson's words. How many times have you heard entrepreneurs say: "Try it. If it works, keep going." Imagine trying to follow that advice when you are fully committed to the ownership of all the assets and resources in the business, and function in fields of rapid change in markets and technology: microcomputers, computer graphics, CAD/CAM, fiber optics, telecommunications, or software, to name a few.

---

[3]H. H. Stevenson, "A New Paradigm for Entrepreneurial Management."

11.4 OUTSIDE PROFESSIONALS: SELECTION, CARE, AND MANAGEMENT

11.4.1 The Attorney[4]

What do entrepreneurs need to know about the law and lawyers? John Van Slyke, an entrepreneur who also teaches the Entrepreneurial Management course at Harvard Business School, summed it up this way:

In fact, I . . . wonder if we have not reached the point where many serious-minded entrepreneurs with high ambitions should pursue a law degree, either instead of or in addition to an MBA.[5]

He offers some sobering advice and observations about would-be entrepreneurs and the law. For one thing, he has found that students,

in general, have almost no meaningful experience with the law, its people, its processes or its instruments. They emerge from their training with many newly acquired skills in the functional areas of business, but they remain novices about the law and have a lack of skills and a grasp of the fundamentals of business transactions and the legal process. Students also tend to be unaware of their vulnerability. What legal training they do receive is mainly from the subject matter and courses about large corporations. While interesting and partly useful, this is not the kind of knowledge that entrepreneurs need most.[6]

Not surprisingly, lawyers are a particular problem for new entrepreneurs, according to the author, because the latter "have so little direct experience or such limited knowledge that they frequently do not know what or how many questions to ask." His advice is clear:

While lawyers are currently in abundant supply, quality in the profession is so thinly spread that our students are told repeatedly by guest speakers in class at HBS that it is vital to find a good lawyer. Yet experienced businessmen and women know that legal advice is in fact another form of outside expertise which must be managed effectively. But to manage relationships with lawyers effectively, entrepreneurs must know what lawyers do and how they think. Prudent businessmen and women do not wholesalely delegate legal matters to their lawyers, nor do they allow their lawyers to make many decisions for them. After all, the important signatures on contracts, tax forms, and other legal documents are those of the principals, not the lawyers.

No doubt about it: this is a thicket full of potential nightmares for naive and unseasoned entrepreneurs. You can barely stand to live with legal assistance, but you are doomed without it. While we cannot do more than begin to touch the peaks here, we do want to stress the importance of finding competent legal advice and to suggest where your Achilles' heel may be. Judging by the above comments, take your pick.

Important Areas of the Law. The following areas of the law pose potential problems for entrepreneurs and proneness to errors of ignorance. We can only echo the advice of many others that you should be highly selective and that you should expect to get what you pay for.

---

[4]We wish to acknowledge the contributions of John Van Slyke of Harvard Business School and of Gerald Feigen, Office of Advocacy, Small Business Administration, Washington, D.C., who has provided us with input from "Entrepreneurship and the Law," a course that he developed and that he teaches at George Washington University Law School.

[5]John Van Slyke, "What Should We Teach Entrepreneurs about the Law," Division of Research, Harvard Business School, 75th Anniversary Entrepreneurship Symposium, Boston, July 1983, p. 1 (*Proceedings*, forthcoming).

[6]Ibid., p. 2.

1. Form of organization; rights and obligations of officers, shareholders, and directors; what a quorum is; the various options, such as Subchapter S; who can officially call a directors' or stockholders' meeting.

We know of a case where a founder nearly lost his company to the legal maneuvering of the clerk and another shareholder. These two managed to call a directors' meeting, at which they controlled the votes, and not reelect the president before the president could call a stockholders' meeting—at which he controlled the majority. The president found out about the plot, adroitly managed to get his meeting in first, and regained control by not reelecting these other two directors. These things happen, and you need to be aware of what you are getting into when the thick documents are described as "just boilerplate stuff."

2. Contracts, licenses, leases, and agreements, particularly noncompetition employment agreements and agreements governing the vesting rights of shareholders and founders.

An entrepreneur we know obtained one of the best contract lawyers around in matters concerning the sale, leasing, and licensing of software products. Without the subtle but powerful protections devised by both the entrepreneur (such as internal clocks that shut down the software periodically) and the lawyer, the entrepreneur would have faced the loss of $2.5 million in a sale of the business and uncollected fees of over $200,000.

3. Intellectual property protection: patents, trademarks, copyrights, and privileged information.

There is a good deal of uncharted territory here, especially around software, which argues all the more for proceeding carefully. Pushing ahead with the development of software before you have provided yourself with ample protection from the law could be expedient in the short term but disastrous in the long term.

4. SEC, state, and other regulations concerning the securities of your firm, both registered and unregistered, and the advantages and disadvantages of different instruments. There have been many changes in recent years, and we will address these in some detail in Chapter 15.

The long-term consequences of violating any of the securities laws and the potential impact of such violations on your future reputation and options are too great for you to do anything other than tread very cautiously and knowledgeably here.

5. Real estate transactions.

It is hard to imagine an entrepreneur who, at one time or another, will not be involved in various kinds of real estate transactions, from rentals to the purchase and sale of property.

6. Tax implications and changes.

A word of caution: all too frequently, the tail of the accountant's tax avoidance advice wags the dog of good business sense. In our experience, it is very difficult to find and execute an opportunity that can make a good business at a good profit. Worry more about finding good opportunities to make money than about finding situations that will lose it so that you can enjoy a tax shelter, and you will be infinitely better off.

7. Bankruptcy law, options, and the forgivable and nonforgivable liabilities of founders, officers, and directors.

You may have heard of entrepreneurs who did not make deposits to pay the various federal and state taxes, such as unemployment, social security, and workers' compensation, in order to use that cash in their business. They assumed that if the company went bankrupt, the government was out of luck, just like the banks and other creditors. Right? Wrong. In fact, the owners, officers, and often the directors are held personally liable for those obligations even though the company goes under.

While we have undoubtedly missed some subtleties, by and large, these are the core topics. Fortunately for start-up entrepreneurs, in many areas of the country there are a growing number of attorneys who specialize in new ventures and firms with higher growth potential. The best place to start is with your entrepreneurial peers, accountants, bankers, and associates. If you are unable to locate a suitable lawyer in your area through these contacts, then try the following:

1. Check *Pratt's Guide to Venture Capital Sources,* 9th ed. (Wellesley Hills, Mass.: Venture Economics, 1985), and look up the name of a venture capital firm in your area that does start-up investments. Call one of their general partners, and ask for a recommendation for a start-up lawyer.
2. Contact one of the Big 12 accounting offices nearest you, and ask for the partner in charge of the emerging company group. Most of these accounting firms now have such a focus. They can often recommend a lawyer with a good reputation for work with new and smaller firms.
3. Call the local or state bar association.
4. Most larger libraries have a copy of the *Martindale-Hubbell Law Directory,* a national listing of lawyers.

A word of caution. There are many outstanding lawyers who are of enormous benefit to entrepreneurs, but experience has taught us this: assume that lawyers are not businesspeople and that they cannot make the business judgments for you. Their judgments, in many cases, are so contaminated by a desire to provide "perfect" or "fail-safe" protection, that they are totally risk averse. They will discourage you from any bold action. It is the entrepreneur who has to weigh the odds that an unsavory event will happen, the probable consequences, and whether those consequences can be withstood.

Selection, Use, and Compensation. Fortunately, not all of these issues have gone unnoticed. *Inc.* magazine conducted a readership poll not long ago to provide some guidance for entrepreneurs. The results of its questionnaire to about 5,000 subscribers and 5,000 lawyers are revealing. The typical respondent reported sales of $5.1 million, with 62 employees. Of these small companies, 94 percent regularly relied on outside legal counsel, and of the attorneys who responded, 88 percent considered small business clients important to their practices.[7]

What factors enter into the selection of a law firm or attorney? According to the survey, 54 percent said personal contact with a member of the firm. This was followed by reputation, 40 percent, and a prior relationship with the firm, 26 percent. Equally revealing was the fact that the fee was mentioned by only 3 percent. This is not a resource with which to be penny-wise and pound-foolish.[8]

---

[7]Bradford W. Ketchum, Jr., "You and Your Attorney," *Inc.,* June 1982, pp. 51–56.
[8]Ibid., p. 52.

Table 11.1
How Attorneys Are Used

Legal service used (ranked by total mentions)	Annual Company Sales				
	Under $1 Million	$1–2.9 Million	$3–4.9 Million	$5–24.9 Million	$25 Million or More
			Percent of Respondents		
Contracts and agreements	70%	74%	69%	84%	85%
Personal needs of top management	46	58	56	53	38
Formal litigation	34	50	63	61	91
Real estate and insurance matters	32	35	50	51	56
Incorporation	45	34	39	33	24
Estate planning	23	42	48	44	17
Delinquent accounts	20	33	39	34	21
Liability protection	20	17	22	33	41
Copyrights, trademarks, patents	21	19	24	28	38
Mergers and acquisitions	12	14	29	32	47
Employee benefit plans	10	26	19	27	27
Tax planning and review	13	17	22	17	12
Employee stock ownership plans	9	15	10	18	21
Franchising and licensing	13	11	14	14	12
Government-required reports	8	6	6	10	12
Prospectus for public offering	2	1	5	2	18
Labor relations	1	2	2	3	3

The need for legal counsel is obvious when it comes to contracts and lawsuits. But the *Inc.* survey shows that small business managers also rely on company attorneys for personal problems ranging from tax matters to divorce and estate probate. As company size increases, so does the need for advice in such areas as liability, mergers, and benefit plans.

Reprinted with permission, Inc. magazine (June 1982). Copyright © 1982 by Inc. Publishing Corporation, Boston.

Just how attorneys are used depends, of course, on the needs of the venture. Size is a factor here, as can be seen in Table 11.1. Apparently, the newer firms, with sales under $1 million, use attorneys mostly for contracts and agreements (70 percent), the personal needs of top management (46 percent), incorporation (45 percent), and formal litigation (34 percent). It is also noteworthy that contracts and agreements were almost uniformly the predominant use, regardless of the size of the venture. This is certainly consistent with some of our comments above about the important areas of the law.

Obviously, you should pick an attorney with the experience and expertise to deal with the specific issue you have to face. For example, one entrepreneur we know is relocating his business to new office space in a renovated historical building that is being converted into office condominiums. In seeking an attorney, he will not use the two who have handled his other business and personal affairs. Why? Because neither has specific experience with the complicated tax and multiple-ownership issues that arise in office condominium deals involving historical properties. Lastly, as with your partners and investors, the chemistry has to be right, or it won't work.

What about compensation and fees? Take a look at Table 11.2. The messages here are worthwhile: most attorneys are paid on an hourly basis, though retainers and flat fees are paid with increasing frequency among larger ventures; and the amount paid expectedly rises as the firm grows. These data might suggest that if you plan to grow to $5 million in the first five years, you can expect to have legal fees of around $30,000. Have you included these legal fees in your business plan?

Table 11.2
How—and How Much—Attorneys Are Paid

	Under $1 Million	$1–2.9 Million	$3–4.9 Million	$5–24.9 Million	$25 Million or More	All Respondents
			Annual Company Sales			
			Percent of Respondents			
Method						
Hourly rate	67%	67%	72%	73%	63%	69%
Negotiated fee	16	17	15	7	6	14
Retainer	7	12	12	21	28	13
Flat fee	12	9	5	7	3	9
Annual legal fee						
Under $1,000	39	15	5	3	–	20
$1,000–4,999	46	54	44	29	7	43
$5,000–9,999	6	17	31	18	4	14
$10,000–19,999	4	8	13	21	19	11
$20,000 or more	5	6	7	29	70	12
Average annual fee	$4,280	$5,370	$7,270	$15,050	$42,590	$8,400

Regardless of company size, most businesses compensate their attorneys by the hour. However, a few small companies pay negotiated or flat fees, while some larger firms rely on retainers. Among the smallest companies, annual legal expenses are generally less than $5,000.

Reprinted with permission, Inc. magazine (June 1982). Copyright © 1982 by Inc. Publishing Corporation, Boston.

Fortunately, if your venture has higher promise, many law firms will agree to defer charges and to provide a lower-than-normal getting-started rate in order to obtain your business. If they are convinced that your venture might become a $5-million-plus client then you can negotiate reasonable early fees. Note that these figures are based on 1982 prices and have undoubtedly risen since the survey was completed.

11.4.2 The Accountant

The accounting profession has come a long way from the "green-eyeshades" stereotype that is still referred to occasionally. Today virtually all of the larger accounting firms have discovered the enormous client potential of new and entrepreneurial ventures. A significant part of their business strategy in the 1980s has been to cater specifically to new and higher-potential ventures. In the Boston area, for instance, leading Big 8 firms have located a new office for their small business group right off Route 128 in the heart of entrepreneurs' country. This is also happening in other major cities as these firms focus their marketing strategy. This is a big plus for entrepreneurs.

Accountants are often unfairly maligned. As one author puts it:

It is hard for entrepreneurs to fully appreciate accounting and what it can do for them. In fact, many tend to view the accountant as a bean counter, a sort of scorekeeper sitting on the sidelines, rather than as a player on the first team. This is a great mistake.[9]

The real issue, then, is how to find the right accountant for you.

Selecting and Evaluating Your Accountant. The accounting profession is straightforward enough. Whether the firm is small or large, accountants are in

[9]Gordon Baty, *Entrepreneurship for the 80s* (Reston, Va.: Reston Publishing, 1982), p. 107.

the business of selling time, usually on an hourly rate. In larger firms, newer CPAs usually have a goal of billing about 1,600 hours of their time each year, and they often work 2,300 hours or more to do so. At billing rates of $50–100 an hour, the economics work out. Partners may bill at $150, $200, or more per hour. And as with so many other things, you get what you pay for. But how can you be sure you are getting your money's worth?

Consider the following questions:

Does your accountant always seem to take the government's side when computing your taxes? Does he or she have the ready answers to your complex financial accounting questions and never need to look anything up? Does he or she appear either uninterested or uninformed when you ask for advice on issues not related to financial reporting, such as management control, product line profitability, and anti-inflation measures? If so, you may not be getting the accounting services you need and are entitled to.[10]

The authors of the article in which these questions are raised provide some useful suggestions for entrepreneurs who are faced with the problem of selecting a suitable accountant. Of course, you need to start by determining the kind of assistance and services you need. The basic choice is deciding whether to go with a smaller local firm, or one of the four to eight regional firms, or one of the Big 8 large national firms. Several actions are necessary before choosing a large or a small firm, according to the authors:[11]

1. Evaluate the levels of service and attention offered. The chances are that these levels will be higher in a small firm than in a large one.
2. Match your current and developing needs against the CPA firm's competence. The larger firm will be more equipped to handle highly complex or technical problems, while the smaller firm may be preferable for general management advice and assistance because the principals are more likely to be involved in handling the account.
3. Consider the cost: $95 average per hour for a partner in a large firm; $55 for a partner in a small firm. (Add $5 per hour for inflation for each year after 1979, the authors advise.)
4. Think about developing a track record for eventually going public. A series of audits from one of the larger firms is preferable in this case.
5. Perhaps most important, be aware of the chemistry factor.

Probably the best source for an accountant is another entrepreneur who has found a good one. Other sources include bankers, attorneys, and trade groups with chapters in most cities. And once you have reached any significant size, you will have many choices. One firm that one of the authors of this book has worked closely with, for example, had grown to about $5 million in sales and would reach $20 million in the next five years, with ambitions to go public eventually. It put together a brief summary of the firm, its background and track record, and a statement of its needs for both banking and accounting services. The founders were quite startled at the aggressive response they received from several banks and Big 8 firms. As a result, they found new bank and accounting relationships, lowered their costs, and are convinced that they are better served.

---

[10]Neil C. Churchill and Louis A. Werbaneth, Jr., "Choosing and Evaluating Your Accountant," in *Growing Concerns,* ed. David E. Gumpert (New York: John Wiley & Sons and *Harvard Business Review,* 1984), p. 263.

[11]Ibid., p. 265.

Booklets and Information. The Big 8, such as Coopers & Lybrand, Price Waterhouse, and Deloitte Haskins & Sells, are making available to clients free booklets and information that are current and relevant for entrepreneurs. For instance, Coopers & Lybrand has prepared a summary of tax and other filing requirements for emerging businesses as part of its "Emerging Business Services" effort. DHS has prepared such booklets as *Raising Venture Capital* and *Going Public* to aid emerging company entrepreneurs. Price Waterhouse has prepared an excellent summary of the latest changes in the tax laws of particular relevance to entrepreneurs. Ask for these when you contact the emerging business head at one of these firms.

11.4.3 Consultants and Technical Experts[12]

Introduction: Judging among Many Options

You have some savings, an idea for a new business, and some relevant technical expertise and experience. But you know you need a partner who understands the marketplace better than you do. You wonder where to look beyond your circle of friends and associates for such a partner.

Yours is a small business that you run with a checkbook and the cash in a shoebox. The business is beginning to get out of hand, you fear. You want to borrow some money, but your banker is unimpressed with the checkbook stubs and the shoebox. You want to clean up your bookkeeping system and prepare some financial statements, but you aren't sure how to go about it.

Your $1 million specialty business has a limited product line and stable sales. You want to identify potential new products that might fit your existing product line, but you know you need outside research assistance.

The preceding situations are fairly typical of those encountered by would-be and existing entrepreneurs. Whom can these entrepreneurs turn to for help? What kind of quality can they expect in the assistance they find? And how much will it cost?

Unfortunately, there are no easy answers to these questions. Nowhere among small business resources are the options so numerous, the quality so variable, and the costs so unpredictable as in the area of management consulting.

The number of people who call themselves management consultants is large and growing steadily. According to an article in the January 1980 issue of *Venture* magazine, there are between 35,000 and 40,000 private consultants around the country, with the number increasing by perhaps 2,000 annually. Somewhat more than half of the consultants work on their own; the remainder work in firms with up to several hundred people each.

Not all consultants are hired privately, though. Government agencies—primarily the Small Business Administration—can provide consultants to work with small businesses. Some of these consultants are paid by the government, and some volunteer their services. University business professors also act as consultants to small businesses, in some cases on a private basis and in some cases via federally funded programs.

---

[12]Excerpted in part from David E. Gumpert and Jeffry A. Timmons, *The Encyclopedia of Small Business Resources* (New York: Harper & Row, 1984), pp. 48–51.

Also, various private and nonprofit organizations provide management assistance to help entrepreneurs answer specific business questions or weather financial crises. The assistance may be provided by trained consultants or by professionals such as accountants and bankers.

Quality and Cost Factors

Unfortunately, anyone can call himself or herself a consultant. Not surprisingly, there are a good number of self-promoters whose only qualification for being consultants is an interest in making lots of money.

Of course, there are also many skilled consultants who can be of invaluable assistance to small companies. The problem for entrepreneurs is to distinguish between the quacks and the legitimate consultants. As a consultant stated in a May 1980 article about small business consulting in *Inc.* magazine:

There are unscrupulous consultants around, and others who do absolutely stupid things. Sometimes, the small businessman doesn't know what he's getting, and just gets screwed.

Avoiding the frauds isn't enough to ensure that entrepreneurs will be happy with the consultants they choose, though. Entrepreneurs must have a clear idea of what they expect consultants to accomplish. They must also be able to communicate comfortably and effectively with the consultants they hire.

An article in the November–December 1977 *Harvard Business Review* by a management consultant observed:

Management consultants are generally hired for the wrong reasons. Once hired, they are generally poorly employed and loosely supervised. The result is, more often than not, a final report that decorates an executive's bookshelf with as much usefulness as "The Life and Mores of the Pluvianus Aegyptius."

As if choosing consultants weren't tough enough with the problems already described, entrepreneurs also face huge variations in consulting costs. At one end of the spectrum is the Small Business Administration, which provides consultants to small businesses without charge. At the other end are well-known consulting firms that may charge $50,000–100,000 for a minimal marketing or technical feasibility study. In between are consultants who will work for between $100 and $1,000 daily.

While the quality of most products at least roughly correlates with their prices, not so with consultants. The advice rendered by an SBA-sponsored consultant could prove more valuable than that offered by a high-priced consulting firm. Of course, that isn't always the case; the point is, it's difficult to judge consultants solely on the basis of the fees they charge.

Narrowing the Field

Unwieldy and risky as the consulting situation may appear, there are ways of limiting the choices and minimizing the dangers. For one thing, consultants tend to have specialties. While some consultants claim expertise in all aspects of business management or with all size businesses, most will at least indicate the kinds of situations they feel most comfortable and skillful handling. Knowing the kinds of problems they want advice on, then, can help entrepreneurs quickly eliminate inappropriate consultants.

And certainly the high cost of hiring many private consultants will limit the options for most start-up businesses. Because start-up businesses tend to be financially pressed, they are usually best off trying to make use of low-cost educational programs or government-funded management assistance programs of the type described later in this chapter.

What kinds of problems can consultants be most useful in helping to solve? Certainly, the types of problems vary widely between start-up situations and existing businesses.

The *start-up business* requiring help usually needs it to complete critical onetime tasks and decisions that can have a lasting impact on the business and its chances of success. These tasks and decisions relate to assessing business sites, evaluating lease and rental agreements, setting up record and bookkeeping systems, finding business partners, obtaining start-up capital, and formulating initial marketing plans. Obtaining sound outside advice on matters such as these can mean the difference between ultimate success and failure.

The *existing business* tends to face ongoing issues that arise as the business grows and matures; many of these issues, though, are of such a specialized nature that outside advice is helpful in resolving them. Issues that frequently arise include when and how to go about computerizing business tasks, whether to lease or buy major pieces of equipment, how to devise appropriate employee benefit and compensation plans, and whether to change inventory valuation methods. Successfully resolving these and various other issues that come up can clear the way for businesses to move on to new stages of growth.

Sometimes, of course, business owners aren't able to pinpoint the exact nature of the problem their business is having, but they feel they need an unbiased and fresh management expert to look over their businesses. Such entrepreneurs are usually well advised to try to determine the broad nature of their problem—whether it's a personnel problem or a manufacturing problem or a marketing problem—before seeking out consultants. That way they can find consultants who specialize in their area.

Once entrepreneurs make the decision to hire a consultant, they should be hard-nosed and thorough in making their choice. One approach is to identify three or more potential consultants and interview them about their expertise and approach. Those candidates that the entrepreneurs feel most impressed with should be asked to prepare specific proposals for handling the entrepreneurs' situations. These candidates should also be asked for the names of other clients, who should be contacted for their assessments of the consultants.

When a business owner settles on a particular consultant, the two should work out a written agreement specifying the consultant's responsibilities and objectives along with the type and amount of compensation. Some consultants work on an hourly basis; some work on a fixed-fee basis; and some work on a retainer-fee basis.

An article worth reading on the issue summarizes the qualities possessed by the ideal small business consulting firm:[13]

1. A shirt-sleeve approach to the owner-manager's problems.
2. An understanding attitude toward the feelings of the manager and his subordinates.

---

[13]Harvey C. Krentzman and John N. Samaras, "Can Small Business Use Consultants," in *Growing Concerns,* ed. David E. Gumpert (New York: John Wiley & Sons and *Harvard Business Review,* 1984), pp. 243–62.

3. A modest and truthful offer of services, and an ability to produce results.
4. A reasonable and realistic charge for services.
5. A willingness to maintain a continuous relationship.

The hard part is finding the right consultant for your particular needs. Most entrepreneurs underestimate the time it will take to find one who has not only the know-how but also the right chemistry. Not long ago one of the authors sent the CEO of a rapidly growing medical technology products firm to two consultants who worked with emerging, higher-potential firms. Both had excellent reputations; yet, the deciding factor was the chemistry. Contacting some of the consultant's clients is generally very useful. When the president was asked what he learned from the clients of the consultant he finally hired, he said: "They couldn't really pinpoint one thing, but they all said they would not consider starting and growing a company without him!"[14]

11.4.4 Outside Board Members[15]

Deciding to have outside members on the board of directors and deciding whom to choose are, we find, among the more troublesome areas for entrepreneurs. If you are a corporation, you must have a board of directors, elected by the shareholders. If you seek and raise venture capital, it is a virtual given that the investors will be represented on your board. The board, of course, elects the officers, but as long as you own or control the voting shares in your company, the choice of officers is yours. Complications arise especially for start-up entrepreneurs who have to relinquish more than half the shares in their company in order to raise venture capital. So unless you are prepared to accept this, better think twice about raising venture capital this early.

In deciding whether to involve outsiders, a number of considerations are worth careful thought. For one thing, doing so will necessitate greater disclosure of the operations and finances of the business than you are accustomed to. Once you take the plunge with outside directors, it is hard to pull back to your original position. Thus, you need to start with people who are known to you and close enough to be very, very trustworthy, yet able to provide enough distance to be hard-nosed and objective.

Most start-up companies have strategic windows that they go through: raising capital; securing customers; resolving technical issues and producing quality goods; cloning key people; coping with rapid growth, merger, or sale; and so on. By starting with identification of these key strategic tasks one can ask the question: What additional expertise is needed and what relevant experience is missing in my venture that a director could bring? The process is identical to the process of assessing and anticipating additions to the top-management team, described in Chapter 7.

In one venture, for instance, the venture capitalist who first invested in the company was a member of the board and saw it through the first several years of

---

[14]Readers might be interested to know that the "him" is Mr. Joel R. Pitlor, who has his own firm in Damonmill, West Concord, Massachusetts.

[15]We are most appreciative of the insights and knowledge shared with us here by John Van Slyke of Harvard Business School and by Leslie Charm and Karl Youngman, both of whom have served as professional directors and who are entrepreneurs as CEOs and principal shareholders, respectively, of Doktor Pet Centers and Command Performance hair salons.

highly successful growth. The president of the company felt that this director had made vital contributions by helping to recruit key top-management people and gain credibility with potential customers, by being a sounding board and devil's advocate, and by stimulating strategic thinking two years earlier than this would have been done otherwise. However, the director resigned at a point when it was evident that another kind of person was needed: someone who could be invaluable in a public offering.[16]

Selection and Compensation. Finding the appropriate people for your board, once you have decided to include outsiders, is a challenge. Many of the right ones are increasingly cautious about getting involved in new and emerging ventures due to the legal liabilities that directors face in most states. For instance, directors can be held personally liable for the actions of the company and officers. Specific grounds of liability for a director include:

Voting a dividend that renders the corporation insolvent.

In some states, voting for a loan—ultimately in default—out of corporate assets to a director or an officer.

Signing a false corporate document or report.

If the directors act in good faith, they are excused for their involvement in such actions. The problem is, of course, that in start-ups acting in good faith may be no easy matter. It may be complicated by such factors as having a novice management team, financial weaknesses and cash crises that force enormous temptations on management (such as not making proper tax and other withholding deposits), and the lack of corporate information and records capable of serving as a basis for judgment.

To make matters worse, outside stockholders, who may have acquired stock through a private placement or the OTC market, sometimes have unrealistically high expectations and thus cause continual aggravation for the board and the company. Experienced directors also know that it takes more time to work with a venture having $8 million in sales than with one having $35–40 million and that working with the former is riskier. And as if all this were not enough, in many areas there is a climate of litigation that results in vulnerability to legal attack in nearly any reasonable situation.

One immediate solution to these liability concerns is to purchase indemnity insurance for directors. But you have to ask yourself, "If the risks are that bad, do I really need that director in the first place? Or is the director so risk averse that there will not be the kind of commitment to the company I am looking for?"

Most entrepreneurs typically look to their lawyer, banker, insurance adviser, or others nearby for their first outside director. Instead, they should ask, "What does the business need?" and then proceed to find the right person.

A recent *Venture* survey showed that one fourth of the entrepreneurial companies responding had no outside directors and that 16 percent had only one. But those that had outside directors valued them most for their objectivity. Among the respondent companies, incidentally, 58 percent had annual revenues of less than $2 million and 93 percent had sales of under $25 million. In addition, 83 percent of the respondents reported that their companies were profitable, and 64 percent

---

[16]See Jeffry A. Timmons, "Venture Capital: More Than Money?" in *Pratt's Guide to Venture Capital Sources*, 8th ed. (Wellesley Hills, Mass.: Venture Economics), pp. 39–43.

said that they owned a controlling equity interest in their companies. This might account for the somewhat sanguine view expressed in the survey results. And, despite the liability problems noted above, just 11 percent of *Venture*'s respondents reported difficulty in recruiting board members.[17]

The compensation of directors can vary widely. If you are serious about attracting a top-notch outside director, you are asking for at least four days per year for quarterly meetings, each of which is likely to require a day of outside preparation; at least one day for a wild-card meeting to cope with an unanticipated issue; and various phone calls along the way. Fees for such a commitment might run to $10,000–20,000 per year. Often, the directors may get options to purchase 1 or 2 percent or more of the stock in your venture; in some cases, these will be in lieu of any directors' fees. It is reasonable for all of the directors' expenses in attending and preparing for meetings to be reimbursable.

Alternatives to a Formal Board.   The use of advisory boards and quasi boards can be a useful alternative to having formal outside directors. A great deal depends on what the needs of the company are. Such informal boards can bring needed expertise to bear, without the legal entanglements and formalities required of a regular board. You can solicit their objective observations and feedback without the complications and possible embarrassment of having to officially remove someone who is not serving a useful function. Informal advisers are usually much less expensive than directors, with honoraria of $500–1,000 per meeting common.[18]

An informal group of advisers can be a good mechanism for seeing a number of people in action and later selecting one or two of them as regular directors. Such a courtship can enable both parties to assess fairly whether the fit and chemistry are right before formal commitments are made. This can prevent subsequent difficulties and potential litigation if things do not work out.

11.4.5   Networks

Earlier, in Chapters 2 and 3, we addressed the important role that networks, or contacts, play for entrepreneurs. Rather than repeat all of that here, let us urge you to review Sections 2.6.9, 3.6.2, and 3.6.3. Suffice it to say, entrepreneuring is a lonely business, so having some contact with entrepreneurs who are going through or have undergone similar experiences can be invaluable.

But what is much less widely appreciated by most new entrepreneurs is the remarkable extent of interdependence that is necessary to make a venture succeed. The notion of the lone, highly independent entrepreneur, thriving through singular, personal efforts, is not only a myth; it is misleading. Reflect on the multiple resources and constituencies that this book has shown to be part of the successful venture: customers, investors, key people, creditors, the outside professionals discussed in this chapter, and numerous implied others. One consistent theme has been that the most productive sources of many of these essential players come from the entrepreneur's networks and his or her circle of contacts. We cannot urge strongly enough the need for aspiring entrepreneurs to nurture and grow their own relevant networks.

---

[17]"The *Venture* Survey: Who Sits on Your Board?" *Venture*, April 1984, p. 32.

[18]See the article by Harold W. Fox, "Quasi Boards: Useful Small Business Confidants," in *Growing Concerns*, ed. David E. Gumpert (New York: John Wiley & Sons and *Harvard Business Review*, 1984), pp. 307–16.

11.5   OTHER RESOURCES

Since the publication of the first edition of this book, there has been an explosion in information about resources for start-up and other entrepreneurs. You can now pick up such new magazines as *In-Business, Inc.,* and *Venture*—and even the *Harvard Business Review* and *The Wall Street Journal*—and find information that was unavailable when the first edition came out. Incidentally, we strongly recommend that you subscribe to and search these publications regularly, especially the magazines specifically aimed at entrepreneurs.

To complicate the choices even further, there are now over 200 databases and information banks available through personal computer and other networks. These are described in Chapters 2 and 3.

To help entrepreneurs cope with this seemingly endless maze, we recommend one recent book, *The Encyclopedia of Small Business Resources* (New York: Harper & Row, 1984). This book has had particularly good reviews, and it has also elicited numerous favorable comments from entrepreneurs with whom the authors have come in contact. *Forbes,* for example, said:

The authors have methodically brought together, under one cover, the basic sources for information, consulting help and capital for new and small enterprise. Instead of pretending to write a recipe book on starting businesses, they simply took areas where every would-be entrepreneur and most people managing small businesses have questions or encounter problems, and then detailed where to go for help and how much that help might cost, and, sometimes more important, how much time it might take. This is a competent and comprehensive guide in a field in which information is scattered and hard to come by.

More important, entrepreneurs who have used the first edition of *New Venture Creation* and *The Encyclopedia of Small Business Resources* have flatly asserted that these are the only two books you need if you are starting your own company.

Besides, we would consider it indefensible for any self-respecting new ventures professor to fail to promote his own book![19]

With the authors' permission we have excerpted part of the introduction to the book and also included a listing from the table of contents in Table 11.3.

Table 11.3
Table of Contents for *The Encyclopedia of Small Business Resources*

[19]From *The Insider's Guide to Small Business Resources* by David E. Gumpert & Jeffry A. Timmons. Copyright © 1983 by David E. Gumpert & Jeffry A. Timmons. Reprinted by permission of Doubleday & Co., Inc.

Table 11.3 (concluded)

11.5.1 Using *The Encyclopedia of Small Business Resources*

The authors of *The Encyclopedia of Small Business Resources* have attempted to make this book as easy to use as possible, given the varying needs of entrepreneurs and the varying services performed by different sources.

To assist entrepreneurs in quickly identifying sources near to them geographically, the authors have listed sources within every state in the index at the end of the book. Thus, readers can quickly determine the pages on which sources for each of the 50 states are described.

To accommodate the frequently different needs and concerns of entrepreneurs just starting or acquiring businesses for the first time as well as those operating well-established businesses, several chapters have been divided into two sections—one for start-up businesses and one for existing businesses. Not all of the chapters break down that neatly, but even when they don't, the authors indicate within the chapters how start-up and existing businesses can best use the sources described.

Finally, to handle the problem of sources that were appropriate to more than one chapter, heavy use was made of cross-references and a thorough index was assembled. These approaches solve, at least partially, such dilemmas as deciding whether to include an organization for black women entrepreneurs in the chapter on sources for women or in the chapter on sources for minorities. Nonetheless, the authors recommend that entrepreneurs whose situation or circumstances are appropriate to sources in several chapters examine all of those chapters.

11.5.2 Other Practical Books and Information

We also suggest the following:

1. *The Trials and Rewards of the Entrepreneur,* published by *Harvard Business Review* in 1983, is a collection of leading HBR reprints covering a wide range of topics important to start-up and growth-minded entrepreneurs.
2. *Growing Concerns: Building and Managing the Smaller Business,* published by HBR and John Wiley & Sons in 1984, is an even more comprehensive collection of articles, many of which we have referenced here.
3. *The Small Business Report,* published monthly by Small Business Monitoring and Research Company, Inc., 1 Mission Plaza, Monterey, California 93940, contains articles of relevance to entrepreneurs.
4. Both *Inc.* and *Venture* have reprint series that are worth reviewing in order to spot pieces relevant to your situation.
5. Bank of America offers an excellent series entitled *The Small Business Reporter* that covers operations (for example, financial statements and cash flow pitfalls), profiles of specific businesses, and professional management services. Available from BOA, Department 3120, P.O. Box 37000, San Francisco, California 94137.
6. *Entrepreneurship: A Selected Bibliography,* by Professor Robert Ronstadt, Babson College, was prepared in 1982 and is the most complete work of its kind for start-up entrepreneurs.

As is apparent, the problem for start-up entrepreneurs is not a lack of resources. Rather, it is managing the time trade-offs necessary to sort through the mountains of available resources, determining what you really need and picking the ones that fit your situation. Hopefully, the suggestions we have made will narrow that task considerably.

SHOE   Jeff MacNelly

12.1 RESULTS EXPECTED

No doubt about it: the microcomputer is here to stay.[1] In our experience, shared by tens of thousands of start-up entrepreneurs, the sooner you can use the microcomputer and its productivity software for spreadsheets, database management, graphics, word processing, and telecommunications, the better. Upon completion of this chapter, you will have:

1. Examined why there has been an explosion in the use of microcomputers by entrepreneurs and managers.
2. Identified the principal uses and applications of relevant software and what they can do for start-up and growth-minded entrepreneurs.
3. Examined some models that are used to plan cash flow and analyze real estate ventures.
4. Identified some of the potential problems and pitfalls of new microcomputer users and some cautions useful to them.
5. Examined how to "boot" a spreadsheet program on a microcomputer and how to prepare a simple model.

12.2 PRESESSION PREPARATION

Note: Those readers who know how to use the microcomputer and one of the spreadsheet and word-processing programs will find the contents of this chapter quite familiar and can skim it. You should develop cash flow, income statement, and balance sheet models for the venture opportunity you are considering and for

---

[1]The lead author prepared about 80 percent of the manuscript for this book using an IBM-PC with the word-processing program The Final Word and the Lotus 1–2–3 program for spreadsheets. No chapters were handwritten. It was incredibly time and agony saving. Since 1982 all of his writing has been done in this manner, and it will continue to be.

which you are preparing a business plan. Examples are included as exhibits at the end of this chapter and at the end of Chapter 14, "The Business Plan Guide."

Those readers who have not yet used a microcomputer and a spreadsheet program will engage in a "micro-user's start-up" in this chapter. The following activities have been useful to entrepreneurship students and entrepreneurs: (*a*) visit a microcomputer store, and get a demonstration of one of the spreadsheet programs, such as Lotus 1–2–3, VisiCalc, or Multiplan; (*b*) attend an on-campus introductory tutorial on the uses of micros; (*c*) find a friend who can be your "micro guru" during this start-up phase; and if time and resources permit, (*d*) attend a one–three-day commercial course on microcomputer business applications. Once you have done at least (*a*) through (*c*), complete the suggested assignment in the preceding paragraph.

12.3   A NECESSARY SKILL—NOT A HOBBY

Since 1982 every student taking at least one course in the Entrepreneurial Studies program at Babson College—nearly one third of the student body at this point—has been required to learn how to use microcomputers and spreadsheet and word-processing software. (At this writing, this small college with about 1,500 undergraduates has acquired close to 250 DEC Rainbows for use by students and faculty as an important strategic wedge for graduating entrepreneurs and entrepreneurial managers.) Undergraduates, MBAs, and recent alumni have uniformly applauded this requirement and have said that the use of the microcomputer is one of the most valuable skills they have acquired. We are convinced that the microcomputer is a significant timesaving, productivity, and creativity tool for would-be entrepreneurs. Several colleges and universities have gone so far as to require, or provide, a microcomputer for every entering student. This will soon be the case at Babson as well.

At Venture Founders Corporation we have utilized microcomputers and Lotus 1–2–3 to aid entrepreneurs in start-up financial planning, and in Chapter 14 we share a model developed for these purposes that integrates Robert Morris Associates data into the start-up planning process. Microcomputers are also beginning to be used to track the performance of portfolio companies. And two of the authors have used them extensively in their work with new and growing ventures and in their own businesses.

Why all the fuss about microcomputers?

12.4   THE MICROCOMPUTER REVOLUTION: WHY?

12.4.1   Declaration of Independence from Computeritis

Anyone who has had to suffer through a centralized computer department and mainframes, with the usual dosage of computerese, programmer anarchy, MIS arrogance, and access delays can appreciate one of the most significant reasons why micros have caught on. A microcomputer can free you of all these obstacles. You can use a microcomputer when you need it, where you want to do your work, and without waiting in line, logging in, or coming back at 2 A.M. when the mainframe computer is not so overloaded. A microcomputer puts you in charge of your work schedule, rather than the staff assistant at the computer center or the mainframe load at the moment. Perhaps more important, with a microcomputer you safeguard the contents of your files. No one can steal your work unless you leave it lying around on a disk, nor can anyone else access your work by "discovering" your password or tampering with the mainframe files.

12.4.2 Timesaving, Productivity, and Creativity Tool

A colleague was seriously considering the start-up of a new publishing venture. In most ways, the opportunity signals were very encouraging; the relevant experience was there, as was the entrepreneurial commitment. The relevant assumptions about fixed and variable costs, market estimates, and probable start-up resource requirements had been assembled in the usual "back of the envelope" format. What needed to be done next was to generate a detailed monthly cash flow to determine more precisely the economic character of the venture, the quite seasonal nature of the cash inflows and outflows, and what all of this meant in terms of the amount of money needed to launch the business and the potential rewards.

In about 2½ hours all of the assumptions and simple mathematical formulas regarding the revenues and expenditures associated with the start-up were entered into a VisiCalc model (the first spreadsheet program, see below).[2] This took about the same time that it would have taken to record all of these assumptions on paper for subsequent use.

Within another two hours we had played with several different "what ifs" to see what the venture would look like financially over the first 18 months. Three basic scenarios were printed out for subsequent review and analysis. The results were startling: we estimated that the number crunching we had completed in half a day would have taken a week or so to do manually on accounting paper and with the use of a pocket calculator.

More important, we did more than just save significant amounts of time. We obtained a more revealing picture of the venture. We found that we could look more analytically and creatively at the venture than we had previously, or probably would have, with manual methods. While this may not hold true for everyone, it evidently did for us.

Lastly, this analysis significantly altered our perception of the new venture idea, which was abandoned since the risks, uncontrollables, and unknowns appeared to outweigh the potential. This was not at all evident previously. In fact, the lead entrepreneur was all but committed to the launch prior to the analysis. The entrepreneur decided to continue looking at other opportunities and subsequently teamed up with another venture.

12.4.3 Dramatic Cost-Performance Improvement

The technological progress in the computer field in the past 30 years or so can easily be taken for granted. After all, we sent astronauts to the moon 15 years ago. To provide some perspective on this progress, consider the following comparison. If aviation technology had advanced at the same pace, the latest Boeing 767

---

[2]Professor Timmons would like to thank his good friend, colleague, and computer guru, Dudley M. Harde, for showing the way, inspiring his plunge into microcomputers, and revealing the power of their software.

Exhibit 12.1
Evolution of the Microchip

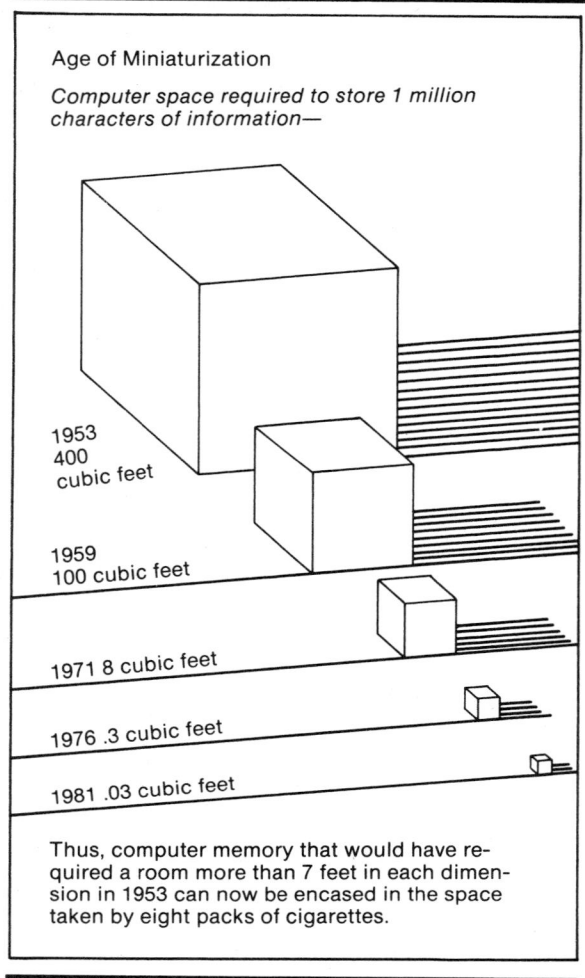

Age of Miniaturization

Computer space required to store 1 million characters of information—

1953
400
cubic feet

1959
100 cubic feet

1971 8 cubic feet

1976 .3 cubic feet

1981 .03 cubic feet

Thus, computer memory that would have required a room more than 7 feet in each dimension in 1953 can now be encased in the space taken by eight packs of cigarettes.

passenger aircraft would be flying at 75,000 miles per hour, using just five gallons of gas to circle the globe in just 20 minutes! In historical terms, the microcomputer industry is sometimes described as being today where the automobile industry was in 1910.

In practical terms, the "chip" has lead a revolution in miniaturization that has made microcomputing possible. This dramatic trend is shown in Exhibit 12.1. In 1953, for instance, 1 million characters (a single-digit letter or number each) could be stored in 400 cubic feet of space, or roughly an area about 7.5 feet on each side. By 1981, less than 20 years later, the 1 million characters could be encased in the space taken by eight packs of cigarettes, or 0.03 cubic feet.

The cost of logic devices that enable the computer to run the programs has declined at about 25 percent per year, and the cost of memory has been decreasing at 40 percent per year. In less than three and two years, respectively, the costs of logic devices and memory are one half of their prior level. These cost curves are, in part, fueling the decline in the prices of microcomputers and memory, which is expected to continue. One result of all this has been a 200-fold increase in computational speed in the past 25 years and a 10,000-fold decrease in cost, size, and energy consumption.

12.4.4 English Spoken Here

Probably the most gratifying discovery for new users of microcomputers is that they actually speak English (and, for foreign entrepreneurs, other languages as well). Virtually all spreadsheet, database, graphics, word-processing, and other programs for micros today have on-screen instructions and information (called the help menu) that are in English, not computerese. One or two simple keystrokes will produce on your screen the information you need to enable you to figure out what to do next.

This eliminates the need to learn computerese, or even the need to learn how to write programs. Some observers have said that requiring a microcomputer user to learn how to write programs is equivalent today to requiring automobile owners to know how to repair their carburetor in order to qualify for a driver's license. It is simply not necessary. And many sophisticated computer users have argued that if the task or problem is important enough to custom-program, then the entrepreneur should be the last one to do it—this job is for highly skilled professionals. Moreover, the trends suggest that in the future entrepreneurs will find it even less necessary to learn how to program than they do today.

12.5 POTENTIAL USES FOR START-UP ENTREPRENEURS: SPREADSHEET IS QUEEN

The origins of the first spreadsheet program for microcomputers reveal its potential relevance for entrepreneurs. It was devised by an MBA student while attending Harvard Business School. At the Harvard Business School the case analyses require an enormous amount of number crunching—cash flows, pro forma income statements and balance sheets, break-even, net present value analyses—and just when final estimates are written on paper, a classmate, or a professor, invariably asks: "What if you assumed such-and-such?" Result: You have to revise the numbers, run the numbers through your pocket calculator one more time, and write them down on paper again.

12.5.1 What Is an Electronic Spreadsheet?

The spreadsheet is nothing more than a piece of accounting paper adapted for use with the microcomputer. Instead of pencil and paper, you use the keyboard to enter the numbers, label the boxes or cells, and define relationships between cells (e.g., Cost of Sales = 60% of Sales). Exhibit 12.2 shows a simple example of cash flow, income, and balance sheet statements prepared using the Lotus 1–2–3 spreadsheet program. After the program disk, such as VisiCalc, 1–2–3, or Multiplan, has been placed in the proper disk drive, the microcomputer is turned on. For 1–2–3 and VisiCalc, for instance, the "/" command (just hit that "/" key) will display a series of cells or boxes into which text, numbers, or formulas can be entered. (See Section 12.9.1 for illustrative step-by-step instructions for "booting,"

Exhibit 12.2
Example of Venture Opportunity Spreadsheet Analysis

OUTPUT GENERATED :

```
****************************
*    Cash Budget    *
****************************
```

	Months											
	1	2	3	4	5	6	7	8	9	10	11	12
CASH BALANCE (Opening)	$50,000	$31,235	$9,073	($18,917)	($50,811)	($85,583)	($122,252)	($173,852)	($228,743)	($293,067)	($359,823)	($431,361)
Plus RECEIPTS: Sales Collections	$2,725	$6,000	$9,675	$13,350	$17,025	$20,700	$24,375	$28,050	$34,350	$38,775	$42,750	$46,425
Other Proceeds	$0	$0	$2,000	$0	$2,000	$5,000	$0	$4,000	$0	$0	$0	$0
Total	$2,725	$6,000	$11,675	$13,350	$19,025	$25,700	$24,375	$32,050	$34,350	$38,775	$42,750	$46,425
Less DISBURSEMENTS: Raw Material Payables	$16,875	$20,625	$26,250	$31,875	$37,500	$43,125	$50,625	$60,000	$67,500	$71,250	$76,875	$82,500
Other Expenses (Accruals)	$4,494	$6,806	$9,169	$11,531	$13,894	$16,256	$19,313	$22,369	$25,706	$28,069	$30,431	$32,794
Fixed Asset Additions	$0	$0	$3,000	$0	$0	$0	$2,400	$0	$0	$0	$0	$0
Lease Expense	$0	$80	$80	$80	$80	$80	$80	$80	$80	$80	$80	$80
Long Term Debt Payments	$0	$5	$5	$5	$5	$5	$5	$5	$5	$5	$5	$5
Other Expenses (Itemized)	$0	$30	$0	$60	$20	$0	$0	$500	$0	$0	$0	$0
"Other Asset" Additions	$0	$0	$10	$0	$0	$0	$0	$0	$0	$0	$0	$0
Federal Taxes (Operations)	$238	$645	$1,048	$1,430	$1,863	$2,285	$2,678	$2,840	$3,915	$4,328	$4,740	$5,153
Total	$21,611	$28,191	$39,561	$44,981	$53,361	$61,751	$75,100	$85,794	$97,206	$103,731	$112,131	$120,531
Net Cash Gain (Loss)	($18,886)	($22,191)	($27,886)	($31,631)	($34,336)	($36,051)	($50,725)	($53,744)	($62,856)	($64,956)	($69,381)	($74,106)
Cumulative Cash Balance	$31,114	$9,044	($18,813)	($50,548)	($85,147)	($121,634)	($172,977)	($227,595)	($291,599)	($358,023)	($429,205)	($505,467)
Financial Income (Expense), net of tax	$121	$29	($104)	($263)	($436)	($618)	($875)	($1,148)	($1,468)	($1,800)	($2,156)	($2,537)
ENDING CASH BALANCE	$31,235	$9,073	($18,917)	($50,811)	($85,583)	($122,252)	($173,852)	($228,743)	($293,067)	($359,823)	($431,361)	($508,004)
Desired Cash Level	$2,000	$2,000	$2,000	$2,000	$2,000	$2,000	$2,000	$2,000	$2,000	$2,000	$2,000	$2,000
Loan Required to Maintain Minimum Cash Level	$0	$0	$20,813	$52,548	$87,147	$123,634	$174,977	$229,595	$293,599	$360,023	$431,205	$507,467
Cash Surplus	$29,114	$7,044	$0	$0	$0	$0	$0	$0	$0	$0	$0	$0

Exhibit 12.2 (continued)

OUTPUT GENERATED :

```
*****************************
*    Income Statement    *
*****************************
```

	Months											
	1	2	3	4	5	6	7	8	9	10	11	12
NET SALES	$5,000	$10,000	$15,000	$20,000	$25,000	$30,000	$35,000	$40,000	$50,000	$55,000	$60,000	$65,000
Allowance for Slippage of Sales Forecast	$1,250	$2,500	$3,750	$5,000	$6,250	$7,500	$8,750	$10,000	$12,500	$13,750	$15,000	$16,250
GROSS SALES	$3,750	$7,500	$11,250	$15,000	$18,750	$22,500	$26,250	$30,000	$37,500	$41,250	$45,000	$48,750
Less: Materials Used	$1,875	$3,750	$5,625	$7,500	$9,375	$11,250	$13,125	$15,000	$18,750	$20,625	$22,500	$24,375
Direct Labor	$375	$750	$1,125	$1,500	$1,875	$2,250	$2,625	$3,000	$3,750	$4,125	$4,500	$4,875
Other Manufacturing Expense	$159	$319	$478	$638	$797	$956	$1,116	$1,275	$1,594	$1,753	$1,913	$2,072
Indirect Labor	$159	$319	$478	$638	$797	$956	$1,116	$1,275	$1,594	$1,753	$1,913	$2,072
COST OF GOODS SOLD	$2,569	$5,138	$7,706	$10,275	$12,844	$15,413	$17,981	$20,550	$25,688	$28,256	$30,825	$33,394
GROSS PROFIT	$1,181	$2,363	$3,544	$4,725	$5,906	$7,088	$8,269	$9,450	$11,813	$12,994	$14,175	$15,356
Less: Sales Expense	$188	$375	$563	$750	$938	$1,125	$1,313	$1,500	$1,875	$2,063	$2,250	$2,438
General and Administrative Expense	$94	$188	$281	$375	$469	$563	$656	$750	$938	$1,031	$1,125	$1,219
Bad Debt Expense	$75	$150	$225	$300	$375	$450	$525	$600	$750	$825	$900	$975
Depreciation Expense, Fixed Assets	$250	$250	$300	$300	$300	$300	$340	$340	$340	$340	$340	$340
Lease Expense	$0	$80	$80	$80	$80	$80	$80	$80	$80	$80	$80	$80
Other Expenses (Itemized Above)	$0	$30	$0	$60	$20	$0	$0	$500	$0	$0	$0	$0
OPERATING PROFIT	$575	$1,290	$2,095	$2,860	$3,725	$4,570	$5,355	$5,680	$7,830	$8,655	$9,480	$10,305
Income Taxes on Operations	$238	$645	$1,048	$1,430	$1,863	$2,285	$2,678	$2,840	$3,915	$4,328	$4,740	$5,153
OTHER FINANCIAL REVENUE (EXPENSE)	$243	$59	($208)	($525)	($871)	($1,236)	($1,750)	($2,296)	($2,936)	($3,600)	($4,312)	($5,075)
Income Tax Provision	$121	$29	($104)	($263)	($436)	($618)	($875)	($1,148)	($1,468)	($1,800)	($2,156)	($2,537)
NET PROFIT	$459	$674	$944	$1,167	$1,427	$1,667	$1,803	$1,692	$2,447	$2,528	$2,584	$2,615

Exhibit 12.2 (continued)

LIST OF ASSUMPTIONS :

Schedule A - Sales and Cost of Sales

Months	1	2	3	4	5	6	7	8	9	10	11
Net Sales $	$5,000	$10,000	$15,000	$20,000	$25,000	$30,000	$35,000	$40,000	$50,000	$55,000	$60,000
Projected Sales, net of slippage	$3,750	$7,500	$11,250	$15,000	$18,750	$22,500	$26,250	$30,000	$37,500	$41,250	$45,000

YEAR	1984	1985	1986	1987	1988
Slippage of Sales Forecast, % of sales.. What if?	25.0%	15.0%	10.0%	10.0%	5.0%
Material Costs, as % of sales	50.0%	48.0%	46.0%	45.0%	45.0%
Direct Labor, as % of sales	10.0%	10.0%	9.0%	9.0%	9.0%
Other m'fg expense (overhead, etc., but exclude depreciation), as % of sales	4.3%	4.3%	4.3%	4.3%	4.3%
Indirect Labor, as % of sales	4.3%	4.3%	4.3%	4.3%	4.3%
Sales expense, as % of sales	5.0%	4.0%	4.0%	4.0%	4.0%
General and Administrative, $	2.5%	2.5%	2.5%	2.5%	2.5%
Federal income tax rate, % of Profit before Tax	50.0%				
What month does this analysis begin? (1-12)	1				
What is the present year?	1984				

Schedule B - Accounts Receivable Aging

	1984	1985	1986	1987	1988
% Collections 0-30 Days	70%	70%	70%	80%	80%
% Collections 30-60 Days	20%	20%	20%	19%	19%
% Collections 60-90 Days	8%	8%	8%	0%	0%
% Uncollectable - Bad Debts	2%	2%	2%	1%	1%

Schedule C - Accounts Payable Aging (Raw Materials)

	1984	1985	1986	1987	1988
% Payments 0-30 Days	100%	100%	80%	80%	80%
% Payments 30-60 Days	0%	0%	20%	20%	20%
% Payments 60-90 Days	0%	0%	0%	0%	0%

Schedule E - Direct Labor, Indirect Labor, M'fg Expense, Selling and G & A Expense, Accruals Aging

	1984	1985	1986	1987	1988
% Payments 0-30 Days	100%	100%	90%	90%	90%
% Payments 30-60 Days	0%	0%	10%	10%	10%

Schedule F - Inventory Assumptions

	1984	1985	1986	1987	1988
What is desired cash level? ($)	$2,000	$5,000	$7,000	$10,000	$10,000
How many months of finished goods inventory on hand?	2	2	3	3	3
How many months of raw materials inventory on hand?	3	3	4	4	4

Schedule G - Financial Revenue and Term Debt Assumptions

	1984	1985	1986	1987	1988
What interest is payed on outstanding loans to maintain desired cash level?	12%	12%	12%	15%	15%
What is your return on a cash surplus?	10%	10%	10%	11%	11%

Exhibit 12.2 (continued)

LIST OF ASSUMPTIONS (PAGE 2):

Schedule H - Beginning Balances, period one

ASSETS:

Cash Balance	$50,000
Accounts Receivable	$100
Raw Materials Inventory	$100
Finished Goods Inventory	$300
Fixed Assets, Depreciable	$3,000
Accumulated Depreciation	$50
Other Assets, net	$200
Total Assets	$53,650

LIABILITIES:

Raw Materials Payable	$100
Accruals Payable	$50
Notes Payable - Banks	$100
Long Term Debt	$100
Contributed Capital	$500
Retained Earnings	$52,800
Total Liabilities + Equity	$53,650

Other - Present Loss Carryforward (-) ($100)

Schedule 1 - Cash Budget, Income Statement Monthly Changes $$

Months	1	2	3	4	5	6	7	8	9	10	11	12
Receipts (Cash Basis):												
Other Proceeds (LTD)	$0	$0	$2,000	$0	$2,000	$0	$0	$4,000	$0	$0	$0	$0
Contributed Capital Additions	$0	$0	$0	$0	$0	$5,000	$0	$0	$0	$0	$0	$0
Dispursements (Cash Basis):												
Long Term Debt Payments	$5	$5	$5	$5	$5	$5	$5	$5	$5	$5	$5	$5
Other Expenses	$0	$30	$0	$60	$20	$0	$0	$500	$0	$0	$0	$0
"Other Asset" Additions, non-depreciable	$0	$0	$10	$0	$0	$0	$0	$0	$0	$0	$0	$0

Schedule J - Fixed Asset Additions

	Asset 1	Asset 2	Asset 3
CURRENT ASSETS:			
Amount	$3,000		
Depreciaiton Period	1		
YEAR 1:			
Amount	$2,400	$3,000	$2,400
Month Bought (1-12)	2	3	7
Depreciation Period or Lease Term	3	5	5
Cash Basis = 1 / Lease = 2	2	1	1
YEAR 2:			
Amount	$3,600	$3,600	$3,600
Month Bought (1-12)	1	6	6
Depreciation Period or Lease Term	5	5	5
Cash Basis = 1 / Lease = 2	1	1	1
YEAR 3:			
Amount	$4,000	$4,000	$5,000
Date Bought	2	3	2
Depreciation Period or Lease Term	3	3	3
Cash Basis = 1 / Lease = 2	2	2	1

NOTE : YEARS FOUR AND FIVE ASSUMPTIONS SAME AS ABOVE

Exhibit 12.2 *(concluded)*

OUTPUT GENERATED :

```
*************************
*    Balance Sheet      *
*************************
      (End of Month)
```

	Months 1	2	3	4	5	6	7	8	9	10	11	12
ASSETS: Cash	$31,135	$8,973	$0	$0	$0	$0	$0	$0	$0	$0	$0	$0
Receivables	$1,125	$2,625	$4,200	$5,850	$7,575	$9,375	$11,250	$13,200	$16,350	$18,825	$21,075	$23,400
Less : Allowance for doubtful accts.	($75)	($225)	($450)	($750)	($1,125)	($1,575)	($2,100)	($2,700)	($3,450)	($4,275)	($5,175)	($6,150)
Net Receivables	$1,200	$2,850	$4,650	$6,600	$8,700	$10,950	$13,350	$15,900	$19,800	$23,100	$26,250	$29,550
Finished Goods Inventory (Net)	$13,144	$31,125	$54,244	$82,500	$115,894	$154,425	$200,663	$254,606	$313,688	$377,906	$447,263	$521,756
Raw Materials Inventory (Net)	$5,625	$9,375	$13,125	$16,875	$20,625	$24,375	$28,125	$33,750	$39,375	$43,125	$46,875	$50,625
CURRENT ASSETS	$50,954	$51,873	$71,119	$104,475	$142,969	$186,600	$237,938	$298,856	$365,963	$435,581	$510,038	$589,631
Fixed Assets	$3,000	$3,000	$6,000	$6,000	$6,000	$6,000	$8,400	$8,400	$8,400	$8,400	$8,400	$8,400
Accumulated Depreciation	$300	$550	$850	$1,150	$1,450	$1,750	$2,090	$2,430	$2,770	$3,110	$3,450	$3,790
Net Fixed Assets	$2,700	$2,450	$5,150	$4,850	$4,550	$4,250	$6,310	$5,970	$5,630	$5,290	$4,950	$4,610
Other Assets	$200	$200	$210	$210	$210	$210	$210	$210	$210	$210	$210	$210
TOTAL ASSETS	$53,854	$54,523	$76,479	$109,535	$147,729	$191,060	$244,458	$305,036	$371,803	$441,081	$515,198	$594,451
LIABILITIES: Notes Payable - Banks	$0	$0	$19,017	$50,911	$85,683	$122,352	$173,952	$228,843	$293,167	$359,923	$431,461	$508,104
Raw Materials Payable	$0	$0	$0	$0	$0	$0	$0	$0	$0	$0	$0	$0
Accruals Payable	$0	$0	$0	$0	$0	$0	$0	$0	$0	$0	$0	$0
Income Tax Payable	$0	$0	$0	$0	$0	$0	$0	$0	$0	$0	$0	$0
Total Current Liabilities	$0	$0	$19,017	$50,911	$85,683	$122,352	$173,952	$228,843	$293,167	$359,923	$431,461	$508,104
Total Long Term Debt	$95	$90	$85	$2,080	$2,075	$4,070	$4,065	$4,060	$8,055	$8,050	$8,045	$8,040
TOTAL LIABILITIES	$95	$90	$19,102	$52,991	$87,758	$126,422	$178,017	$232,903	$301,222	$367,973	$439,506	$516,144
CAPITAL STOCK: Contributed Capital	$500	$500	$500	$500	$500	$5,500	$5,500	$5,500	$5,500	$5,500	$5,500	$5,500
Retained Earnings	$53,259	$53,933	$54,877	$56,044	$57,471	$59,138	$60,941	$62,633	$65,080	$67,608	$70,192	$72,807
TOTAL LIABILITIES AND NET WORTH	$53,854	$54,523	$74,479	$109,535	$145,729	$191,060	$244,458	$301,036	$371,803	$441,081	$515,198	$594,451

that is, starting up, the spreadsheet program on the microcomputer). Once these are entered, they can be changed or saved at the stroke of a key or two.

Built into the program are the necessary commands to enable it to complete whatever calculations you instruct the computer to perform by way of a cell in your spreadsheet. You decide what to enter in the cells and whether to change the entries. For example, you might have the vertical columns represent the months or quarters for your sales estimate. You can write a simple equation that says: Sales will grow at a rate of 10 percent per period, compounded. Thus, the sales in period 2 will be 110 percent of the sales in period 1. That computation will automatically be made once you instruct the computer to make it. You can tell the computer to project the increase for as many periods as you choose, say, 24 months. The program will thus compute what the sales for each cell will be, given those assumptions.

Once you sit down and try the spreadsheet, its power will be self-evident. We suggest a hands-on approach rather than spending time reading books or manuals about how to do it. Have someone sit you down at a micro with one of the spreadsheet programs—and try it.

12.5.2 The Main Use of Spreadsheets: "What If" Modeling

The major advantage of the spreadsheet over manual methods is the time and effort saved once the basic model has been constructed. "What if" questions can be tried out, and the results are shown on the screen nearly instantaneously. Take a cash flow projection, for instance. You can ask: What if sales grow at just 5 percent, instead of 15 percent; and what if we collect only 50 percent of our sales in 30 days, instead of 65 percent? What impact will this have on cash flow? By editing the basic assumptions entered previously, you can, in a matter of seconds, get a complete recalculation of the entire spreadsheet. On the other hand, it could take up to a few hours to revise and recalculate your cash flow manually to determine the effect of those "what if" questions.

One effect of the manual process is that many entrepreneurs simply get worn down, tired out, or bored by the numerical grunt work. They can end up missing important subtleties, settling for untested assumptions, and falling short of a rich analysis, any one of which can have costly consequences later on in the venture.

The same "what if" process can also be applied to the pro forma income statement, the balance sheet, budgeting, and break-even analysis (by altering assumptions about revenues and costs until the cash reaches zero). Using Appendix I, for example, one can envision using Lotus 1–2–3 to link these basic projections to the Robert Morris Associates data. These RMA assumptions, based on actual industry operating results for existing businesses, can be used as comparative boundaries for testing the assumptions about your own venture. Most spreadsheets enable you to apply net present value analysis to the cash flows developed by your model.

Real estate analysis is another microcomputer application of considerable relevance for entrepreneurs. Included in Table 12.1 is a simple model developed with Lotus 1–2–3 to analyze a real estate investment opportunity.[3] In this case, the

---

[3]Developed by Jeffry A. Timmons. For an excellent technical note, obtain "Financial Analysis of Real Property Investments," No. 9-379-193, HBS Case Services, Harvard Business School, Boston, Massachusetts 02163.

Table 12.1
Real Estate Model, Lotus 1–2–3

REAL ESTATE MODEL FOR OFFICE CONDO B:CONDO July 1984 JAT	Per Sq. Ft.	1985	230000 purchase 1986	1987	1988
GROSS RNT 2300	12	27600	27600	27600	27600
Less VACANCIES (5%)		1380	1380	1380	1380
= GROSS REVENUES		26220	26220	26220	26220
Less Rental Fee/Collection (assume ½ mo.)		1150	1150	1150	1150
= NET REVENUE		25070	25070	25070	25070
Less OPERATING EXPENSES Per Sq. Ft. × 2300	4	9200	9200	9200	9200
= OPERATING CASH FLOW		15780	15780	15780	15780
Less FIN. PAYMENTS:					
1st Mortg. Interest (1)		19299	19251	19196	19133
1st Mortg. Principal (1)	nil				
2d Mortg. Interest (2)		0	0	6072	6072
2d Mortg. Principal (2)	nil				
TOTAL FIN. PAYMENTS		19299	19251	25268	25205
= CASH FLOW B. TAXES AND DEPRECIATION		− 3429	− 3381	− 9398	− 9335
Less DEPRECIATION ($80 per sq. ft.) (15 years S.L.)		12267	12267	12267	12267
= TAXABLE INCOME		− 15696	− 15648	− 21665	− 21602
× s TAX RATE (assumes St. + Fed. =)		50%			
= TAX SAVING		− 7848	− 7824	− 10833	− 10801
CASH FLOW AFTER TAXES		4419	4443	1435	715
Less PRINCIPAL REPAYMENT		549	597	652	715
NET A.T. & PRINC. CASH FLOW		3870	3846	783	751

MORTAGE ASSUMPTIONS:
First is 20% down; 14% interest; 30 yrs.
Second is 20% down; 12% interest;
no I or P 1st 2 yrs.; 20 yrs.
Rent increase = 25% after 5 yrs.;
expenses increase = 30%

purchase of 2,300 square feet of office condominium space at $100 per square feet is being analyzed. The first and second mortgage assumptions are noted at the bottom of the exhibit. Once the model has been constructed, one can readily determine the sensitivity points: What is the minimal rent necessary to break even? what if the condo fee exceeds $4 per square foot? what if the depreciation rules are changed to 20 years and straight line? what if the marginal tax rate is 40 percent instead of 50 percent? what if the second mortgage amortization is payable immediately and is based on 15 years instead of 20? The bottom line cash flow, after tax and principal, can be seen in a matter of seconds or minutes by inserting the revised assumptions.

For instance, take the condo fee. If you type in a 5 in place of the 4 and hit the RETURN key, *all* the numbers for all the cells affected will be recalculated and the new bottom line (along with every other new line) will be shown. Whew! Next, you can experiment with the rental rate. What if you can only rent it for $11 per square foot? Enter that new number where the 12 is now, press RETURN, and the results are computed within seconds. In short, you can conduct more refined sensitivity analyses without taking too much time or getting bogged down by all the number crunching. Only 4 years of a 15-year analysis are shown in the exhibit. All of the recalculations for all cells orver the 15 years take a matter of seconds.

The spreadsheet is undoubtedly a very powerful tool. Once you have tried using such a program, it is unlikely that you will revert to the manual method.

A Word of Caution. One potential drawback of spreadsheets that we have seen is the tendency of some entrepreneurs to fixate prematurely on the spreadsheet analysis. They seem to *begin* their business plan with the spreadsheet, rather than focusing initially on the opportunity, defining what it is and how to seize it, and then preparing the financial estimates of what is required. Certainly, this process should manifest the iterations inherent in any new venture. Yet, increasingly, we have seen business plans with elaborate, overkill spreadsheet analyses consisting of multiple scenarios of what might be and including pages and pages of printouts as exhibits. However, these business plans have often failed to answer, or have answered superficially, the much tougher questions about the "opportunity conditions," addressed in Chapter 3 and 4.

12.6 OTHER APPLICATIONS SOFTWARE FOR MICROS

12.6.1 Word Processing

Nearly everyone who has used a word processor has decided to give up the typewriter permanently. Why is this so? From our own experience a word processor is much easier to use than a typewriter, and it completely eliminates the aggravation of typos and the tension induced by the fear of making some—always at the bottom of the page. A word processor also eliminates writer's cramp. It not only saves real time; it saves calendar time. In the preparation of reports, memos, and a manuscript such as the one for this book, it seems to cut in half the time required to get the final document into the right hands.

Even if you cannot type—there are micro programs to teach you to touch-type—word processing can be a productivity saver in many small businesses, especially those that send out repetitive letters, announcements, or other correspondence; that use proposals in which boilerplate sections are slightly modified for each client; and so forth.

12.6.2 Graphics

A picture is worth a thousand words, and now, with integrated software packages such as 1–2–3, you can readily convert the data on your spreadsheet into graphs and line, pie, or bar charts to show estimates, trends, or relationships. Graphics is one of the fastest-growing areas of the computer-related fields, and it is attracting substantial amounts of venture capital as well.

12.6.3 Database Management

Microcomputers can now be used to organize and store records of customers and accounts and other information. As memory costs continue to decline rapidly, more and more capacity will be available at less and less cost. Sorting by code number, by the letters of the alphabet, by size, or by other designated variables can be easily inserted into a database program such as 1–2–3. What is more, you do not need to know how to program to be able to do this. This is not true of all micro database software, however.

12.6.4 Accounting

Numerous software packages of particular importance for the start-up and early stage venture are now available for microcomputers. In Table 12.2 are illustrative examples of the many applications programs that have become commercially available. These provide detailed solutions to problems involving accounts receivable and payable, payroll processing, general ledger, fixed assets, banking, disbursements and check writing, order processing and inventory control, and so on. New packages are becoming available at a rapid rate, and the trend is expected to continue.

Table 12.2
Microcomputer Programs with Accounting Applications

Accounts Receivable
Aged trial balances
Credit checking
Customer Statements
Service charges
Auto billing
Sales territory control
Referral code

Accounts Payable
Vendor profile
Enter vendor invoices
Vendor discounts taken
Current P.O.
Transfer data to disbursements
Order verification
Partial payment to vendor

Payroll
Gross earnings
Up to four pay periods
Preinstalled withholding schedules
Quarterly and year-end reports
Insurance and union dues deductions
Workers' compensation federal/state
Overtime calculations
Expensive distribution
Variable pay rate
Separate federal/state exemptions

General Ledger
Standard accounting
All posting automatic
Audit trails
Debits/credits
Balance sheets, P&L reports
Contra-assets depreciation
Journal adjustments
All modules post to G/L

Fixed Assets
Equipment: Building and leasehold improvements
Newest depreciation methods
Post to contra-assets—G/L
Monthly or yearly depreciation
Detailed reports
Profile report

Banking
Reconcile checking account
Hard copy deposit listing
List by ledger code
P/R check listing
Outstanding check listing
Check register

Disbursements
Payroll check writing
Vendor check writing
Miscellaneous check writing
Calculate tax payments

Order Processing
Sales order entry
Invoicing
Calculate commissions
Discount schedules
Interact with inventory
Interact with A/P
Cash sales
Interact with A/R and P/R
Cash sales

Inventory Control
Perpetual inventory
Cost of inventory
Inventory evaluation
Service file
Issue purchase order
History of items
Markup/profit data
Reorder reports
Inventory activity by up to 10 locations

12.6.5 Income Tax Preparation

Packages are also available to prepare both personal and business tax returns. These promise to be time and aggravation savers. By inputting each month the figures for your year-end tax return, it is possible in early December to run a cumulative return and then to test various year-end tax strategies so as to determine the best option. Similarly, it is possible to pull together the final return in early January—only if you are expecting a refund, of course. While this is no substitute for whatever professional legal and accounting advice you may seek, it could enable you to be far better prepared to focus on the relevant questions.

12.6.6 Other Applications

Several other applications are worth noting. First, for many entrepreneurs electronic mail can be a real time saver by eliminating telephone tag and numerous unsuccessful redials. You simply type, or have typed, your message to another user through an electronic network, accessible through your modem and telephone. The message is stored in the receiver's electronic mailbox until he or she logs in to check the mail and read the message. (Electronic mail has been used through the VAX at Babson College to provide the professors with a constant communications link with Entrepreneurial Studies students and to eliminate phone calls at home.) If you have international or cross-country communications needs that cover several time zones, electronic mail can serve as your own telex, but less expensively. Major networks accessible from home or office by personal computer are available through The Source and CompuServe. Besides electronic mail, these services offer a wide variety of options; weather reports and maps, shopping, Dow-Jones news and stock market information, bulletin boards, and dozens of others. Table 12.3 illustrates many of the other activities that can be performed with a personal computer.

**Table 12.3
Some Things You Can Do on a
Home Computer**

1. *Work with Words*
   Write letters and memos
   Edit reports
   Check and correct your spelling
   Personalize fund-raising form letters

2. *Play Games*
   Win at chess
   Repel invaders
   Solve puzzles
   Coach a football team
   Handicap horse races
   Practice your piloting skills

3. *Learn Things*
   Improve your bridge game
   Brush up on your Spanish
   Help your child learn arithmetic
   Identify the constellations
   Improve your memory
   Teach your child computer programming

Table 12.3 *(concluded)*

---

4. *Talk to Other Computers*

   Tap into airline schedules
   Keep up with stock prices
   Read a newspaper
   Send electronic mail
   Check your daily horoscope
   Get data from your office computer

5. *Manipulate Lists*

   Update Christmas card lists
   Inventory the freezer
   Computerize your telephone file
   Keep an appointment diary
   Keep track of your expense account

6. *Crunch Numbers*

   Forecast corporate cash flow
   Make pricing decisions
   Balance your checkbook
   Manage a stop options portfolio
   Prepare your tax return
   Design a graph
   Analyze a real estate investment

7. *Make Things Run*

   Dial a number until it's answered
   Regulate your shower temperature
   Turn lights on and off when you're away
   Monitor a burglar alarm
   Make toast and coffee

12.7 CAUTIONS AND PITFALLS

On balance, we see the potential payoff as outweighing the costs of the microcomputer applications we have described. As prices continue to decline on hardware and software, the cost-reward potential should become more favorable, and affordable. We are not urging that every reader race out and buy a microcomputer—it is not for everyone. Rather, we are suggesting that if you study your software needs, you may find a cost- and timesaving reason for using a micro.

Several cautions and pitfalls are worth noting, however:

1. *Software choices are more critical than hardware* in determining whether you can benefit from a microcomputer. Invest some time to figure out what the possible uses are and what software will solve your needs. Attending a one–three-day seminar on how to purchase and use a microcomputer can be a real aid to a new user. Tutorials are also available at many colleges and universities.

2. *Garbage in = Garbage out.* The cautions and traps common to traditional mainframe computing also apply to micros. The machine and software are no substitute for clear thinking, logic, and insight. The estimates generated are only as good as the quality of the assumptions, analysis, and logic that have gone into them.

3. *The up-front time investment* can be nontrivial. While one can learn to use one of the spreadsheet programs in as little as 1–3 hours, a word-processing program may take 20 hours and up to master, assuming that you already know how to type.

4. *Internal memory limitations* can be a hidden trap. If you purchase an IBM-

PC, for example, with 128,000 (128k) characters of internal memory, you may find that you can't do much with a program such as 1–2–3. Since the 1–2–3 program itself uses about 93,000 of this memory just to load and operate, you only have room for about another 30,000 characters. How large a spreadsheet can you develop with that? The labels will need 20 characters in width; each month (or period) will need 9 or 10 characters to accommodate sums of 1 million or more (one conservation method is to round to thousands), so 12 months, plus year-end, plus quarters for three more years, plus a year-end sum would require 280 characters at 10 per column. The total width of this spreadsheet would be 280 characters. Thus, if the projection statements exceed more than about 110 lines or rows, the data will not fit on the spreadsheet, and you do not need a very complicated venture to exceed that size. For serious use you need to consider 512k of internal memory, which will not be cost prohibitive.

5. *Disks can be damaged or destroyed* since they are a bit fragile. While they are tougher than we had expected, they do need to be treated gently.

6. *All data files can be lost* unless you are certain to make at least one and even two backup copies. The recommended backup time is at least every 30 minutes. New users will, sooner or later, lose a significant file due to their failure to take this precaution. Once such a loss is experienced, the wisdom needed to avoid this pitfall in the future is often acquired immediately.

7. *The obsolescence of hardware* is inevitable given the embryonic nature of the industry. In our own case, this has not turned out to be a good reason for delaying the purchase of our equipment.

8. *Gremlins can inhabit a microcomputer,* mainly in the way of unanticipated power surges, lightning, phone line static or cut-offs, and other such surprises. You can get surge protection devices, and you can unplug the machine (after *saving* your work) if an electrical storm is brewing.

9. *Microcomputers will enable us to leap tall buildings in a single bound* with approximately the same velocity, trajectory, and rate of descent as we have achieved with any mainframe computer.

12.8 MAKING IT EASIER

Several suggestions, some noted earlier, may make the move to a microcomputer easier.

1. Try it. Rather than spending hours reading manuals, magazines, or even listening to lectures, find a microcomputer and a guru to help you. Sit down with one of the spreadsheet or word-processing programs, and see what it will do. The uniform response among students entirely new to computers of any kind has been: "I can't believe how easy it was. There is really nothing to it. I can do it."

2. The buddy system is an excellent way to compress your learning curve, to help you through the knotty points—we all have some—and to minimize any minor frustrations that you might encounter while getting started. Find someone who is as little as 10 hours ahead of you in mastering a spreadsheet program, and you have found a valuable resource. That person knows how to "boot" the system and what the major commands and help menus are.

3. Subscribe to the microcomputer magazine for the hardware in which you are interested. Nearly all of the major manufacturers—Apple, IBM, Rainbow, etc.—are represented by independent publishers of magazines specifically devoted

to their machine. Libraries carry many of these magazines. Join a local user's group, such as the Boston Computer Society. Such groups are an excellent place for beginners to get help and advice, find shortcuts and new ideas, and locate a "micro guru," if they need one.

4. If you know next to nothing about micros, before wasting time deciding what to buy, attend a one–three-day seminar on how to buy and use a microcomputer. These seminars are available all over the country.

5. Start with software rather than hardware needs in determining whether you should purchase a microcomputer.

6. Take your time. As with many things, rushing into the purchase of a microcomputer can be a costly bit of impatience.

7. Save your work and back it up.

12.9   GETTING STARTED

To illustrate the relative ease of a start-up lesson using a spreadsheet program, we have included an "Introduction to Multiplan" for use with the DEC Rainbow. These step-by-step instructions were prepared for the introductory tutorial on microcomputers for Babson students. They have found it straightforward and workable. We have also included a summary sheet of the commands, showing which keys trigger what responses, and a summary of line commands that explain how to save your work, get help, print out your worksheet, and so on.

There is considerable similarity among the keyboards and commands for the various machines. In our use of several different machines (IBM, COMPAQ, Apple, Rainbow, Tandy, and Commodore) we have found more similarities than differences. The same seems to be true of the main spreadsheet and word-processing programs. We began by learning to use VisiCalc and discovered that learning to use the 1–2–3 spreadsheet was then a breeze. By familiarizing yourself with the introductory steps and the commands, you will have gained a good sense for the command language and keystrokes necessary to make the machine do what you want it to do. You will also have acquired a sense of how uncomplicated it really is.

12.9.1   Introduction to Multiplan

Step 1:   The Rainbow 100

To turn on the Rainbow 100 (technically speaking), first locate the switch to the far left of the disk drive. You'll see a 0 at the bottom of the switch and a 1 at the top. Press in the 1 to turn the power on. If this is done correctly, you should get a message on the screen that asks you to type a particular character in response. **Don't type anything yet!!!**

Step 2:   Inserting the Diskettes

Take the CP/M/Multiplan diskette out of the Multiplan Kit that belongs with the Rainbow you're using. Hold the diskette between thumb and forefinger with the label facing upward. You should see an orange arrow on the top of the diskette to the right of its center. Open the door to drive A (the top drive), and insert the diskette carefully; close the door to the drive. If you want to save files, insert a blank Rainbow diskette (label down arrow to the left) into drive B (the bottom drive); close the door. Remember: Always use drive A to hold your working copy of Multiplan-86 and drive B to hold the diskette that you plan to store data on.

Step 3: Accessing Multiplan

Once your diskettes have been inserted properly, you should press A (no quotes), because your system drive will be drive A. This will load the CP/M operating system, which will enable you to load Multiplan. Type "MP" at the A> prompt to load Multiplan. Within seconds Multiplan-86 will appear on your video screen.

Step 4: Moving the Cursor

The screen is a series of row and column coordinates. Initially, the cursor is positioned at row 1, column 1. You can move the cursor in several ways; the easiest way is to use the arrow keys located at the bottom of the shaded keypad. To move the cursor quickly in any direction, just hold down the proper arrow key. The dimensions of the Multiplan worksheet extend to 255 rows and 63 columns. When you try to move outside these dimensions, Multiplan will beep at you. Now try moving the cursor around. When you're familiar enough with the arrow keys to start building a model, type CTRL/Q (hold down the CONTROL key and press the Q key simultaneously) and the cursor will move back "home" (row 1, column 1).

Step 5: Building Labels

Before you start this step, make sure you've moved the cursor home (see step 4). Type A (for Alpha on the command line—see "Command Line Guide"), then the word SALES. Hit the down arrow key to get you into row 2, column 1. Here, simply type in CST OF GDS. If you make a mistake while typing, use the DELETE/BACKSPACE key (see "Command Sheet Summary"). Once again, hit the down arrow to get to row 3, column 1. Enter the following values in rows 3, 4, 5, and 6 of column 1, respectively:

Row	Label
3	GR PROFIT
4	WAGE EXP
5	OTHER EXP
6	NET INC

Step 6: Building the Model

Move the cursor to row 1, column 2. Enter the value 100. Use the Value command to do this (type V on the command line) if you do not get the "ALPHA/VALUE" prompt, but rather the command line. Press the down arrow to get to row 2, column 2; enter the formula 0.6*R1C2. Hit the down arrow, and enter the following formulas:

Row	Value/Formula
3	+ R1C2 – R2C2
4	20
5	0.15*R1C2
6	+ R3C2 – R4C2 – R5C2

Step 7: Manipulating the Model: The "What If" Process

Move the cursor to row 1, column 2. Hit V for Value, and input 500. Return. What happens? All of the cells whose formulas contain R1C2 change.

Move the cursor to row 4, column 2. In the same way as above, change the value in this cell to 35. Notice that NET INC. changes.

Try changing the formula at R5C2 to 0.21*R1C2.

Move the cursor to R1C2. Type B to Blank this cell, and then return.

Change R1C2 back to 500.

The above examples represented ways in which Multiplan allows you to manipulate your models. Refer to the FORMAT and COPY commands to see how to get a format and to reproduce cells.

Step 8: Expanding the Model

Move the cursor to R1C3. Type V for Value and enter RC[−1]*1.05. This references the cell in the same row and one column left of the current cell and multiplies it by 1.05.

Now type C for COPY and R for Right, then 2 for 2 cells to the right. This copies the same formula as that specified in the current cell to row 1 in columns 4 and 5.

Go to R2C3. Input the formula R[1]C*0.6. This copies the value in the previous row, same column, and multiplies it by 0.6. Copy this formula into the two columns (same row) to the right.

Input the following formulas:

Row	Formula
3	R[2]C − R[− 1]C
4	RC[− 1]
5	0.21*R[− 4]C
6	+ R[− 3]C − R[− 2]C − R[− 1]C

Now use the COPY command to replicate each of these formulas into their corresponding rows in the next two columns. You need only to type C R < ret > for each row. Multiplan anticipates that you want to copy into the same columns you specified before.

Step 9: Manipulating the Expanded Model

Move the cursor to R1C2, and change the value in that cell to 300.

Move the cursor to R4C2, and input 20.

Move the cursor anyway you want, and change anything you want. Watch what happens—if something happens that you don't understand, just ask.

Step 10: Exiting and Saving Your File

Use the Transfer, Save commands to save a copy of your model (you can buy Digital formatted 5¼-inch disks; others won't work). When you type S, the terminal prompt line will ask you to move your file. Just type it in (e.g., JAT B1.0). Once you've saved your work—**but not before**—use the Quit command to exit. You'll get an A> prompt, and you can then turn off the machine and remove the disks. Don't forget to turn the machine off after you've removed the disks and closed the drive doors.

Command Sheet Summary

This sheet is designed for quick reference, not as a replacement for the Multiplan manual. Before using Multiplan, you should review the manual to become familiar with the package. Note: Do not open disk drive doors when the small red light is on.

Command	*Use*
UP ARROW key	Moves the cursor upward on the worksheet.
DOWN ARROW key	Moves the cursor downward on the worksheet.
LEFT ARROW key	Moves the cursor leftward on the worksheet.
RIGHT ARROW key	Moves the cursor rightward on the worksheet.
FIND key	Moves the cursor to the next occupied cell.
CTRL/Q (Control Q)	Moves the cursor HOME (R1, C1).
CTRL/Z (Control Z)	Moves the cursor to the END of the worksheet—(the rightmost, bottommost occupied cell).
NEXT SCREEN/ARROW	Moves the cursor to the next window in the direction of the arrow specified.
SELECT key	Moves the cursor to the next window when the Window Split command is in effect.
HELP key	Causes Multiplan-86 to display HELP information on the screen.
DELETE/BACKSPACE	Deletes, one character at a time, anything you have typed in (to left of cursor).
TAB key	Moves the edit cursor rightward in the menu and among command fields.
SPACEBAR	Moves the edit cursor rightward in the menu.
CTRL/C (Control C)	Halts the command execution; returns you to the menu.
PF1	Acts as WORD LEFT with edit cursor.
PF2	Acts as CHARACTER LEFT with edit cursor.
PF3	Acts as CHARACTER RIGHT with edit cursor.
PF4	Acts as WORD RIGHT with edit cursor.
! key	RECALCULATE: recalculates the entire worksheet. If typed in a formula, the formula will be replaced by its results.
SUM (R1C1:R2C2)	The SUM formula. This is entered into the target cell (i.e., the cell where the sum will be stored). The formula instructs Multiplan to sum the contents of the cells located between the specified coordinates (in this example, row 1, column 1, and row 2, column 2). This is very useful when quarterly data are being summed to arrive at annual figures.
RC[−1]*1.05	An example of referencing a cell in a Multiplan formula. R stands for row, and C for column. Because the C in this example is followed by a −1 in square brackets, Multiplan will look for the value in the cell ONE column to the *left* of the current cell. Use to compound (increases or decreases in a row, e.g., "what if" sales grows at 5% for each time period).
COPY	To replicate a formula across cells instead of having to retype it for each cell (e.g., when compounding sales).
FORMAT	To set the $ format, use F, C, D then TAB to the format code menu to $ (or decimals, %, integers if you wish), then return to execute command.
PRINT	To print out copies of your formulas F, (format), O (options), then TAB to the "Yes" alternative on formulas.
TRANSFER	To SAVE or LOAD a file you want to keep or use now.
EDIT	To revise a value or formula if you made a typo or want to change it. First, use the PF2 and PF3 keys to move the cursor to where you want to make a deletion (the delete key is located above the return key and marked with an X), and then type in the correct value or letter.

Command Line Guide

Alpha. Used to enter or edit ALPHA text terminated by RETURN. An empty string of characters may not be entered using this command.

Blank. Blanks out contents of specified cells.

Copy. Replicates cell contents into other cells. A variety of sources and destinations are provided. Overlapping copying is not permitted. The "from:" and "to:" area must have compatible shapes.

Delete. Deletes (erases) all or parts of rows or columns. Space is closed up; hence, cells to the right of or below the deleted area will move.

Edit. Puts contents of active cell command line into position for editing. Edited value is reassigned to cell when RETURN is pressed.

Format. Presents four options for formatting cells. Use HELP for more details.

Goto. Used to move cell pointer over spreadsheet. With this command you can specify ROW-COL, NAME, and/or WINDOW.

Help. When you can't figure out what to do next, try HELP or ?

Insert. Used to insert new blank cells into the sheet. Existing cells may be moved to make room for the new cells.

Load. See Transfer. (This is a subcommand of the TRANSFER command.)

Lock. Used to protect specified cell contents and formulas from unintentional changes by other commands. The LOCK CELLS command can also be used to unlock cells.

Move. Used to move whole rows or columns from one place to another.

Name. Used to name a cell or a group of cells. The NAME command is also useful for inspecting the existing definitions.

Options. This command lets you turn on or off various options of Multiplan, such as "RECALC" and "MUTE."

Print. Used for the printing of worksheets. Various options are provided (formula printing, printing subsections of worksheet, etc.).

Quit. Ends Multiplan session when confirmed. **This command will not save the active sheet!** Be sure to use the TRANSFER SAVE command to save worksheet before using QUIT—this saves tears in the end.

Save. See Transfer. (This is another subcommand of TRANSFER.)

Sort. You can sort any part of the worksheet using this command. Text values, as well as numeric values, can be sorted.

Transfer. The subcommands of TRANSFER affect the entire active worksheet or saved worksheets. They include: LOAD, SAVE, CLEAR, OPTIONS, DELETE, and RENAME.

Value. Can be used to enter a value or formula in the active cell. The command is completed when RETURN is pressed.

Window. This command is used to control the size, number, and display of "windows" that are subdivisions of the screen. Options include: SPLIT HORIZONTAL, SPLIT VERTICAL, SPLIT TITLES, BORDER, CLOSE, and LINK.

Xternal. This group of commands deals with references to inactive (external) worksheets. Options: COPY, LIST, and USE.

12.10 MODELING THE START-UP

After you have invested a few hours and learned how to use a spreadsheet program on a microcomputer, apply this know-how to the following:

1. In analyzing the cases, develop spreadsheet models for analyzing the cash flow and for projecting income statements and balance sheets. Note that you can tie the after-tax net income to the balance sheet as the retained earnings by simply instructing the cell on the balance sheet labeled to read the after-tax net income figure, less any dividends paid, for the same period from the income statement.

2. Model your own start-up by preparing the same statements for the opportunity you are evaluating or for the business plan that you are developing. Note the illustrative exhibits in Chapter 14, and see Appendix I for the detailed explanation of Robert Morris Associates data.

3. Do the same by preparing a personal budget for the next 12 months and a personal balance sheet. Do you know what your personal net worth is now?

Developing the Business Plan: For Raising Capital and Guiding Growth

13

Voltaire once wrote to a patron: "Madame, enclosed please find the novel you commissioned. It is in two volumes. If I had more time, I could have written it in one."

13.1 RESULTS EXPECTED

This chapter discusses the role and importance of a business plan in defining and articulating how you expect to seize and execute the opportunity you have identified. If you plan to seek venture capital, a business plan is a must. But a business plan is more than a financing device; it is also invaluable in defining and anticipating the potential risks, problems, and trade-offs in a venture.

Upon completion of this chapter, you will have:

1. Examined what a business plan is, who needs to prepare one, and why, and what it is used for.
2. Understood how a business plan can be used as a "dry run" to anticipate and manage better the risks, trade-offs, and problems on paper before the venture is launched.
3. Examine the venture capital investor's need for and use of a business plan in evaluating the management team and the venture opportunity.
4. Recognized the importance of involving your prospective management team in the preparation of the business plan as a means of evaluating potential partners and gaining their commitment.
5. Examined why the business plan is more than a device for raising venture capital, and its role in managing future growth.
6. Examined a sample business plan that entrepreneurs actually used to seek venture capital in order to launch their business.
7. Defined specific action steps that you need to take to develop your business plan and begun to prepare an appropriate plan to meet your needs.

13.2 PRESESSION PREPARATION

Analyze and evaluate the Rapidrill business plan. After reading the chapter and the sample plan, develop a detailed schedule for the completion of each section of the business plan. Anticipate which parts will require the greatest amount of effort. Assign responsibility for various parts to members of your team. Section 13.10 provides a format to assist you in this task.

13.3 OVERVIEW

The business plan is a written document to articulate what the opportunity conditions are, why the opportunity exists, the entry and growth strategy to seize it, and why you and your team have what it takes to execute the plan.[1] If you have never started a business before, the business plan is an excellent way to help you evaluate the opportunity and to guide the start-up. Think of it as a tool to get the odds of implementation on your side. If you have not raised venture capital previously, a business plan is essential for attracting investor attention.

13.4 WHY PREPARE A BUSINESS PLAN?

When a student asked Nolan Bushnell, founder of Atari, Pizza Time Theaters, and now a new venture capital firm, "What I want to know is: Do we really have to prepare the business plans—they are a huge amount of work," Bushnell responded unhesitatingly:

That's exactly what you have to do. There is no way around it; you're doing the best thing. Every time you prepare a business plan, you become a better entrepreneur—I really believe that.[2]

Or take these comments from two MBAs commenting on what they gained from the New Ventures course.

Another lesson is the importance of doing a business plan. It may be a pain in the neck, but it sure does pay off. If I had gone into the venture of importing copperware from France that I was thinking of in the beginning of the semester without going through a detailed analysis of what had to be done to succeed in the business, and without seeing what the market really boiled down to in numbers, I would have fallen flat on my face, probably at a considerable financial loss. My feelings toward the venture were drastically different after the opportunity analysis and business plan than before.

The second MBA had been previously involved in the development of a microcomputer dealership venture.

One of the most important things I have learned is the importance of the business plan. We not only saw it in class, but also heard very successful entrepreneurs talk about how important it is. I wish I had taken the course before my brother-in-law and I started a microcomputer dealership. We really had no idea of what a business plan was. Looking back on it, I realize how awful our presentation to the investors was. We were lucky that most of them were my close friends and the families, and they knew us well. Otherwise, we never would have been able to raise all the capital we needed. Even though we were able to raise enough capital to start operations, the next time I start a business I will make sure I have a complete business plan.

13.4.1 Putting Your Enthusiasm and Vision on Paper

You are enthusiastic about an idea for a new business. You think the business has excellent market prospects and fits well with your skills, experience, personal values, and aspirations.

---

[1] Adapted from an article by Jeffry A. Timmons, "A Business Plan Is More than a Financing Device," *Harvard Business Review*, March–April 1980, pp. 53–59; used with the author's permission.

[2] Comments at a seminar during his induction in 1983 into the Babson College Academy of Distinguished Entrepreneurs.

But what are the most significant risks and problems involved in launching the enterprise? What are its long-term profit prospects? What are its future financing and cash flow requirements? What will be the demands of operating lead times, seasonality, and facility location? What is your marketing and pricing strategy? Can you articulate the answers to these questions, show the evidence for your conclusions—and *put it in writing?*

The development of such a business plan is neither quick nor easy. Properly preparing a business plan can take at least 200 to 300 hours. Squeezing that amount of time into evenings and weekends can make the process stretch out to between 3 and 12 months. One might ask whether such a time-consuming effort is really worth the trouble.

Wouldn't a more effective approach be to have an outside professional quickly prepare the business plan and then have the founders use their time to obtain financing and start the business?

13.4.2 Rewards of Preparation

Keep in mind that the careful preparation of a business plan represents a unique opportunity to think through all facets of a new venture. You can examine the consequences of different strategies and tactics and determine the human and financial requirements for launching and building the venture, all at no risk or cost.

One entrepreneur with whom we worked discovered while preparing a business plan that the major market for his biomedical product was in nursing homes rather than in hospital emergency rooms as he and his physician partner had previously assumed. This realization changed the focus of his entire marketing effort, before it was too late. Had he left the preparation to an outsider, it is unlikely that he would have had the same sense of confidence and commitment to the new strategy.

13.4.3 A Plan's Long-Term Value

Most founders find the business plan to be even more helpful after start-up. As the founder-president of one venture that grew to sales of $14 million in seven years put it:

Once you are in the business, you realize that everyone, including the founders, is learning his or her job. If you have a thoughtful and complete business plan, you have a lot more confidence in your decisions. You have a reference already there to say, "Well I have already run the numbers on inventory, or cost of goods, and this is what will happen."

The business plan can be especially valuable in the important area of product pricing. For instance, the initial strategy of the founders of one new venture was to price its products below the competition, even though the venture had a superior product innovation in a growing market. When the founders consulted outside experts, they were persuaded to price 10 percent over the competition.

By its second year the new company enjoyed pretax profits of $850,000 based on about $9 million in sales. The revised pricing strategy made a significant difference. Without the detailed analysis of the industry and competition that is central to the marketing section of the business plan, it is unlikely that the outside experts would have seen the basis for a different pricing strategy.

Feedback on your business plan by trusted and knowledgeable outsiders can help in refining strategy and making difficult decisions. A Nova Scotia entrepreneur who builds commercial fishing boats recently decided to raise his prices more than 40 percent based on an outside analysis and critique of his business plan. He knew that he would lose two orders, but he also knew that he would make more profit on the remaining three than on all five at the old price. His delivery time would be cut in half as well. He's convinced that the shortened delivery time will lead to additional sales at the higher margins. And with up-front progress payments, he won't have to raise outside equity capital.

The process of developing a business plan can also clarify the venture's financial requirements. An entrepreneur with a three-year-old $1 million business erecting coal-loading sites believed that he needed about $350,000 in expansion capital. After reflecting on a detailed critique of his business plan presentation, he concluded:

> The worst thing I could do right now is put more money into the business. The first thing I should do is get my own backyard more in order. But I will be back in two or three years.

True to his prediction, he returned 2½ years later. His company was now approaching $3 million in sales and had a business plan for expansion that enabled it to obtain a $400,000 debt capital investment without relinquishing any ownership.

13.4.4 From the Investor's Point of View

Once you have convinced yourself and your partners that your venture is viable on paper, can you also convince prospective investors? If you seek out investment capital or loans, you will face much skepticism from venture capital firms, banks, insurance companies, and other financing sources. For example, only 1–5 percent of proposals to venture capital sources for start-up or ongoing financing are actually funded.

An effective business plan will convince the investor that you have identified a high-growth opportunity, that you have the entrepreneurial and management talent to effectively exploit the opportunity, and that you have a rational, coherent, and believable program for doing so.

For the investor the business plan is the single most important screening device. Once the plan has passed initial screening, the investor may request the entrepreneur to make an oral presentation describing key features of the venture. If the investor is still interested, the plan will be given a more detailed evaluation and will become a prime measure of the founder's ability to define and analyze opportunities and problems and to identify and plan actions to deal with them.

Because of the great importance that investors attach to the quality of the entrepreneurs *and* their complete understanding of the business that they are preparing to enter, we cannot overstate the need for writing the plan *yourself.* The investor wants to be sure that what he sees is what he's got—your analysis and understanding of the venture opportunity and your commitment to it. Nothing less will do.

13.4.5 Common Misconceptions

Entrepreneurs tend to downgrade the business plan because of certain false notions that they hold about it. Technical and scientific entrepreneurs share a misconception that we call the "great mousetrap fallacy." They frequently place excessive faith in a product or invention, especially if it is patented. Indeed, technological ideas must be sound, but marketability and marketing know-how generally outweigh technical elegance in the success equation. The new venture discussed earlier reached nearly $40 million in sales; yet, it has no patents on its products.

A second misconception new entrepreneurs often have is that the business plan is essentially a negotiating and selling tool for raising money. It isn't considered relevant or useful beyond that. Indeed, I have heard more than one entrepreneur comment that the plan is "destined for the circular file" once the funds are in the bank.

Such a view is dangerous for several reasons. To prospective partners, investors, or suppliers, it communicates a shallow understanding of the requirements for creating a successful business. It can also signal a promoting quality—a search for fast money and a hope for an early sellout—that creates mistrust of the entrepreneur. If the plan isn't a serious promise of what the team can deliver, should investors believe anything that the founders assert?

A third misconception some entrepreneurs have is the belief that the primary and most important task in the start-up process is to determine whether they can raise money as an indication that their idea is sound. This "cart before the horse" approach usually results in a hastily prepared business plan and exuberant shopping around among prospective investors.

Because most venture capital firms are quite small—often no more than two or three partners—they generally cannot take the time needed to get to know each entrepreneur and to detail the reasons for rejection. They use the business plan for initial screening as well as for making investment decisions. We have met many entrepreneurs who, as long as two years later, still did not understand that they were unable to raise capital because their business plans were deficient.

A fourth misconception is a belief among some entrepreneurs that their particular plan has no fatal flaws. These entrepreneurs ignore the need to test the plan's soundness with knowledgeable outside sources. Entrepreneurs must search for flaws in the market analysis that would make further consideration of the venture unnecessary.

One potential flaw is excessive dependence on outside suppliers for important state-of-the-art components that materially affect product development and prices. Suppliers of Viatron, a computer leasing company that obtained substantial public and private financing in the late 1960s, helped drive the company into bankruptcy in large part because they were unable to produce several semiconductors at prices low enough to enable Viatron to meet its own heavily promoted inexpensive prices.

A final misconception among some start-up and early stage entrepreneurs seeking venture capital is the belief that retaining a minimum 51 percent control of the company is essential. This view seems to assume that control depends on legal percentage ownership rather than on management's behavior. In short, 51 percent of nothing is nothing. Compare this with the 20 percent ownership retained by the four founders of Digital Equipment Corporation.

Sound investment partners do not want to run your company—they invest in you and your team. More than anything else in the early going, the founders' actions are the ultimate controlling influence on the venture.

13.4.6 Business Planning: Not for Everyone, but...

In a recent *Harvard Business Review* article, Phillip Thurston sheds some new light on the role of planning in smaller firms.[3] How can you determine an effective planning process for your venture? After all, business planning is not for everyone.

Consistent with one of the main themes of this book, Thurston suggests that a thorough knowledge of yourself and your business is the place to begin. He also warns against the excesses of the "planning systems" that have emerged in recent years. We agree that there are certainly times when it is more important to "do" than to plan. For instance, when an opportunity that you should seize is perishing at a faster rate than you can complete a business plan articulating it, then you are better off to simply to act.

Nonetheless, Thurston observes that

The smaller companies weathering the current difficult economic times seem to be those following an idea—call it a no-frills, down-to-earth, but clear plan—of how to take advantage of the environment and how to allocate resources.[4]

Aside from the obvious need that entrepreneurs seeking to raise venture capital have for a business plan, what other dimensions, unique to you and your business, might help determine the necessity and the effectiveness of planning for your venture? Thurston suggests the following:

1. Administrative style and ability—the CEO's ability to grasp multiple, interrelated aspects of the business. Some entrepreneurs can keep all that is necessary in their heads and can retrieve it in an orderly fashion.
2. The extent to which the management team wishes to participate in the planning process.
3. The complexity of the business—the simpler it is, the less the need for formal planning.
4. The strength of competition—if your venture needs to be lean, hungry, and tightly disciplined in order to compete and to survive, then a coherent planning process will be more important.
5. The level of uncertainty—if you are in a quite volatile, rapidly changing business, planning of a contingency nature may be more important to survival than if you are in a stable, fairly predictable industry, and preferable to precipitate action.

To these helpful points we would add the notion of "external and other constituencies," including creditors, shareholders, regulators, customers, community groups, and employee groups. The more of these you have to juggle, respond to, and contend with, the greater is the potential payoff in some form of organized and disciplined planning.

Among existing firms not backed by venture capital the "harvest" issue is especially troublesome. Without a venture capital backer the prime motivator and driving force to realize a harvest—along with the skills, know-how, and networks to make it happen—is absent from the deal. We have found that a business

---

[3]Phillip Thurston, "Should Smaller Companies Make Formal Plans?" *Havard Business Review,* September–October 1983, p. 162.

[4]Ibid., p. 182.

plan for an ongoing business can significantly enhance its harvest potential and its selling price. Such a document can articulate why there is a major opportunity for a prospective buyer in much the same way that a start-up business plan does this for venture capital investors.

Finally, the business plan guidelines have been used within existing firms to focus on an internal venture opportunity. Take, for instance, one of the founders of a firm that has grown to $20 million in sales in about a dozen years. He used the business plan in order to present his board and partners with an articulate statement of an opportunity for internal expansion, a new business from within. Certain modifications were necessary, of course, to the start-up guide presented here, but the fundamentals were there.

13.4.7   Some Dos and Don'ts

Before we get into the details of what should be in a business plan, we will set down some important general dos and don'ts for preparing such plans that should be kept in mind as you read the guidelines and begin to write your own plan. These dos and don'ts have come from our own experience with and our reactions to a great many business plans, as well as from some of what has been published on the foibles, pet hates, and preferences of venture capitalists.[5]

1. Do keep the business plan as short as you can without compromising the description of your venture and its potential. Cover the key issues that will interest an investor, and leave the details of secondary importance for a meeting with the investor. Remember, venture capital investors are not patient readers.
2. Don't overdiversify your venture. Focus your attention on one or two product lines and markets. A new or young business does not have the management depth to pursue a number of opportunities.
3. Don't have unnamed, mysterious people on your management team, such the Mr. G., who is currently a financial vice president but will join you later. The investor will want to know early on exactly who Mr. G. is and what his commitment is to your venture.
4. Don't describe technical products or manufacturing processes in a way and with a jargon that only an expert can understand. A venture capitalist does not like to invest in what he doesn't understand or what he thinks you don't understand because you can't explain it to a smart fellow like himself.
5. Don't estimate your sales on the basis of what you can or would like to produce. Do estimate carefully your potential sales, and from these determine the production facility you need.
6. Don't make ambiguous, vague, or unsubstantiated statements. They make you look like a shallow and fuzzy thinker. For example, don't merely say that your markets are growing rapidly. Determine and delineate past, present, and projected future growth rates and market size.
7. Do disclose and discuss any current or potential problems in your venture. If you fail to do this and the venture capitalist discovers them, your credibility will be badly damaged.

---

[5]Charles P. Waite, "The Presentation and Other Key Elements," in *Pratt's Guide to Venture Capital Sources,* 8th ed. (Wellesley Hills, Mass.: Venture Economics, 1984), pp. 36–38.

8. Do involve all of your management team in the preparation of the business plan, as well as any special legal, accounting, or financial help that you may need.

9. Don't claim that you have no competition, or indicate that you expect to "get rich quick." Both are good ways to turn off investors and others who know better.

10. Do recognize that venture capital investors are busy people and there is a need, not only for a short, succinct business plan, but for a concise presentation as well. Many venture capital "fairs" and "forums," such as those sponsored by Georgia Tech, the Commonwealth of Massachusetts, and the American Electronics Association, require entrepreneurs to present their venture in 20 pages and 20 minutes.

11. Don't press for too rapid a decision, or an expression of interest, or conclude too quickly that the investor is ignorant and doesn't understand your business or technology.

12. Do explore more than one alternative source of venture capital financing. As long as the peak investing activity of 1983 and 1984 continues, there will continue to be keen competition for the best ventures.

13. Don't spend money on developing fancy brochures, elaborate slide show presentations, and other "sizzle." Show the "steak."

14. Do be pleasantly persistent and creative in gaining the attention and interest of potential venture capital investors.

15. Don't assume that venture capital is the only, or necessarily the best, source of funding for your venture. It is suitable mainly for a highly selective group of ventures with very high potential.

13.5 GUIDELINES FOR PREPARING BUSINESS PLANS

When an entrepreneur prepares a business plan, he or she must organize and communicate, in writing, the results and conclusions of an analysis of the potential of his or her venture. Most entrepreneurs, even those who have been through a graduate school of business, are not good at doing this.

To help you develop a good business plan, we have prepared the "Business Plan Guide," which can be found on the tear-out pages in Chapter 14. The guidelines it contains are based on our own experience in reviewing a large number of business plans, as well as inputs and critiques from some leading venture capitalists. Intelligent use of the guidelines should result in a complete and professional business plan that makes an orderly presentation of the information necessary to interest a venture capitalist in further evaluating your venture.

Because the guidelines were prepared to be applicable to a wide range of product and service businesses, a slavish compliance with all aspects of the guidelines is neither possible nor desirable. Common sense should be used in applying the guidelines to your specific venture. For example, a plan for a service business need not include a section on manufacturing or, possibly, one on product development. Further, the guidelines are meant to develop business plans for service or product ventures that have the potential to become substantial companies. The guidelines are an "overkill" for the marginal or "mom 'n' pop" businesses (e.g., small motels, machine shops, electronic assemblers) that start and remain small.

But such businesses are of no interest to the venture capital investor and do not require a very comprehensive business plan. However, readers interested in such businesses can and should use selected parts of the business plan guidelines to satisfy themselves as to the viability of their proposed venture and to develop supporting data for bank loan applications.

13.6   WHAT IS IN THE GUIDELINES[6]

In the business plan guidelines there are no questions. The intent is to show you what should be included in a business plan, and why. The issues that you should address in your business plan are spelled out. A sequence and structure are given to you, along with explanations where these are deemed necessary. At first glance, you may feel that you have seen much of this before. In some sections of the guidelines, headings and subheadings from the *Venture Opportunity Screening Guide* in Chapter 4 reappear (market size and trends, competition, etc.). However, there are two important differences in the way you need to treat subjects in your business plan:

1. More detail is called for. This means that you need to spend more time in gathering detailed data, interpreting it, and presenting it clearly.
2. Statements made in a business plan are written with the idea of inducing someone to part with perhaps $500,000 to $2 million, or even more. This means that you must make unambiguous statements that are capable of being supported.

For the purpose of an opportunity screen it may be all right to note (if you cannot do any better): "The size of the target market for our product is in the $30–60-million range, and it is growing at over 15 percent per year." In a business plan, however, that sentence would not get by. The size range would need to be narrowed considerably, or else the reader will have little confidence in this critical number. Second, the phrase "is growing at over 15 percent" is too vague. Does it mean that the market grew at the stated rate between last year and the year before? or on average over the past three years?

Third, "over 15 percent" smacks of imprecision. If you know what the growth rate is, say so, and also explain why it will or will not remain the same. If you don't know what the growth rate is and how it is changing, find out. Statements in a business plan can be taken very seriously by the investor-reader, so you should be able to back them up and defend them. If you are not able to do so, your credibility with an investor will be impaired.

13.7   WHAT IS NOT IN THE BUSINESS PLAN GUIDE

If you are contemplating a new venture in any particular industry or market, there are certain to be a number of special currently critical issues with which you must deal. You should make whatever investigations are needed to develop a list of any special issues that are likely to affect your venture and industry. In the chemical industry, for example, some special issues of significance at present are:

[6]The authors want to acknowledge the useful inputs to this chapter and Chapter 14 made by Brian Haslett.

1. Increasingly strict regulations, at all government levels, covering the use of chemical products and the operation of processes.
2. Diminishing viability of the high capital cost, special-purpose chemical processing plant serving a narrow market.
3. Long delivery times of processing equipment.

In the electronics industry the special issues may be the future availability and price of new kinds of large-scale integrated circuits.

Each industry has a number of special problems and opportunities. If your company is to enter and maintain a position in an industry, you must know what these problems and opportunities are. You will not find them treated in the general-purpose business plan guidelines: you must find them out for yourself. The guidelines should help you to do this because they will require you to examine carefully a number of potentially relevant issues, but it is up to you to determine which issues are especially significant to your venture.

13.8   PREPARING TO WRITE YOUR BUSINESS PLAN

The "Business Plan Guide" in Chapter 14 should be removed, read carefully by you and your management team, and used to guide your preparation of a business plan. You should also review the Venture Opportunity Screening Guide that you prepared as part of the exercises of Chapter 4 and draw on the data developed in that analysis to help you prepare your business plan. Be sure to get your team members to prepare those sections of the business plan that are in their areas of expertise and to collaborate on any sections that require inputs from several business functions (e.g., the manufacturing and operations plan will require marketing and product design data).

13.9   REVIEWING YOUR BUSINESS PLAN

Once you have written your business plan, you should get it reviewed and critiqued before you submit it to any prospective investors. No matter how good you and your team are, you will overlook issues and you will treat aspects of your venture in a manner that is inadequate or less than clear. Good reviewers can point such deficiencies out to you and can give you the benefit of an outside, objective evaluation of your plan. Good reviewers can also act as a sounding board to help you develop alternative solutions to some of your venture's problems as well as answers to some of the questions that investors are likely to ask.

Who should these reviewers be? One should be your attorney to make sure that there are no misleading statements in your plan and that it contains all the information and caveats that should be used in raising money from venture capital investors. (A discussion of the legal aspects of stock offerings for start-up and early stage companies is provided in Chapter 15.) Another reviewer might be a successful entrepreneur, an entrepreneurially oriented corporate executive who has had significant profit and loss responsibility at or above a divisional level, or a venture capitalist who, for whatever reason, would not be a potential investor in your business.

13.10   THE RAPIDRILL BUSINESS PLAN: CASE STUDY

The Rapidrill Corporation case that follows is an actual start-up business plan developed by a team of entrepreneurs to raise venture capital. (The name of the company and other details have been disguised here.) Analyze the business plan from the points of view of a prospective venture capital investor, a customer, and a potential member of the management team. Consider the following questions:

1. What is your evaluation of the opportunity and the business plan, including strengths, weaknesses, omissions, and so forth.
2. Would you invest in Rapidrill? Why or who not? If yes, under what terms? If no, what further evidence would you want in order to make an investment?
3. What valuation would you place on the venture?
4. What is your evaluation of Rapidrill's entry strategy? What changes, if any, would you recommend, or insist upon, before you would invest in the company.

Confidential Plan Number _____

Delivered to _____

BUSINESS PLAN

RAPIDRILL CORPORATION

15 MAIN STREET
NASHVILLE, TENNESSEE
615-365-5749
DECEMBER 10, 1971

SECURITIES OFFERED:
240,000 SHARES OF COMMON STOCK AT $1 PER SHARE

This business plan has been submitted on a confidential basis solely for the benefit of selected, highly qualified investors in connection with the private placement of the above securities and is not for use by any other persons, nor may it be reproduced. By accepting delivery of this plan, the recipient agrees to return this copy to the Corporation at the address listed above if the recipient does not undertake to invest in the Corporation.

TABLE OF CONTENTS

Summary

1. The Industry, the Company, and the Product
2. The Management Team
3. Market Research and Analysis
4. Marketing Plan
5. Design and Development Plans
6. Manufacturing Plan
7. Schedule
8. Risks
9. Financial Plan
10. Proposed Rapidrill Offering

Exhibits

1. Sales and Earnings Forecasts—Fiscal Years Ended September 30, 1972–1976
2. Monthly Sales and Earnings Forecasts—Fiscal Year Ended September 30, 1972
3. Quarterly Sales and Earnings Forecasts—Fiscal Years Ended September 30, 1973–1974
4. Pro Forma Cash Flows—Fiscal Years Ended September 30, 1972–1976
5. Pro Forma Monthly Cash Flows—Fiscal Year Ended September 30, 1972
6. Pro Forma Quarterly Cash Flows—Fiscal Years Ended September 30, 1973–1974
7. Pro Forma Balance Sheets—Fiscal Years Ended September 30, 1971–1976
8. Pro Forma Monthly Balance Sheets—Fiscal Year Ended September 30, 1972
9. Pro Forma Quarterly Balance Sheets—Fiscal Years Ended September 30, 1973–1974
10. 1972–1973 Break-Even Analysis
11. Present and Proposed Capitalization

SUMMARY

Rapidrill was formed in April 1971 and incorporated in the state of Delaware in August 1971 by a highly knowledgeable and experienced team of five executives in response to what they believe to be an attractive business opportunity created by the following conditions:

1. The market for their product, rotary drills, is substantial ($74 million in 1970); has demonstrated a 10 percent annual growth for the past six years; and has strong indicators of accelerated future growth.
2. Prices and margins are attractive (earnings after taxes average 9 percent in the industry) and have been firm.
3. The major existing competitive manufacturers have high costs and high fixed investments, in both manufacturing facilities and distribution organizations. They are also producing drills at near capacity.
4. Rapidrill believes it can achieve cost savings over competitors of from 9 percent to 12 percent in total manufacturing and selling expenses.
5. Rapidrill's ability to accomplish its program is significantly related to the know-how and track record of its management team: their past team efforts increased the market share of the present industry leader from 9 percent to 22 percent of the market in the past five years. The improbability of duplicating this "team" asset by others precludes, for all practical purposes, the effective near-term entry to the market of additional competitors.

As a result of these conditions, Rapidrill believes that it has a unique opportunity to provide superior quality drills at attractive prices, and capture 7.5 percent of the rotary drill market in three years. This market share would produce for Rapidrill forecast sales in 1974 of $7,585,000 and after-tax earnings of $733,000.

Rapidrill is seeking an equity investment of $240,000 to implement the plans described herein. The common stock sold for the $240,000 investment will represent about 35 percent of Rapidrill's outstanding common stock after the offering is completed.

1. THE INDUSTRY, THE COMPANY, AND THE PRODUCT

The Industry

Virtually all mining and medium-to-large-scale construction activities require the penetration and/or removal of significant amounts of rock. Typical applications are as follows:

Surface mining, both coal and metals.
Quarrying.
Water-well drilling.
Highway construction.
Pipeline construction.
Foundation excavations.
Mineral explorations.
Gas- and oil-well drilling.

In the various mining, quarrying, and construction applications that require removal of rock, "blast holes" are drilled into the rock so that it may be blasted into small pieces to facilitate its removal. Similar, though generally much deeper, penetration is required in the drilling of wells or exploration holes.

Over the past 15 years, the "rotary drill," as typically shown in Figure 1, has emerged as the preeminent tool for rock-drilling requirements in the above applications. Its ease of operation and superior productivity have developed in parallel with the larger capacities of complementary equipment, such as loaders, shovels, trucks, and breakers; and have created a market that has expanded from less than $10 million in 1953 to $74 million in 1970.

The principals of Rapidrill have collectively accumulated in excess of 70 years of marketing, engineering, manufacturing, and general management experience with rotary drills and have formed a new company to design and produce rotary drills based on their assessment of conditions in the industry, which they believe create a viable business opportunity favorable to their planned program.

There are 11 manufacturers of rotary drills that presently have a significant share of the market. Only four of these manufacturers produce a line of drills applicable to a broad range of drilling applications and attempt national market coverage. These four manufacturers command about 50 percent of the total market, and all market their drills through equipment distributors. (Ingersol-Rand utilizes "company owned" stores.)

The four manufacturers are:

Indiana Tool, Inc.

Ingersol-Rand

Davey

Joy Manufacturing (Robbins)

They all manufacture a full line of products (gear drives, pumps, etc.) for mining, construction, and industrial markets and share the common characteristic that all gravitated to the manufacture of drills based on their prior experience with the manufacture and packaging of air compressors. This packaging experience coupled with their existing channels of sales to the mining and construction industries created what seemed to be a natural product opportunity.

In the manufacture and packaging of compressors, however, these manufacturers commonly added between 50 and 80 percent of the manufacturing cost content. In a rotary drill, the compressor accounts for less than 10 percent of the total costs and the total value added by the packager is about 25 percent, including the compressor, with the remainder in purchased material. Nevertheless, the manufacture of drills by these companies is accomplished in existing compressor manufacturing facilities with production control systems and overhead structures geared to machine shop operations. These facilities are generally very complex, with high fixed investments, rigidly unionized, and located in high-cost labor areas, all of which leads to rotary drill manufacturing costs that are unnecessarily inflated.

In addition, the product design of rotary drills by these manufacturers has generally been prejudiced by the type and size of compressors in their product line and by their ability to use their own components for mechanical drive systems instead of basing their designs on the optimum utilization of all available components.

Figure 1

While these manufacturing and design decisions use as a rationale higher facility utilization and increased value added, they, in fact force rotary drill designs that do not provide the best solution to market application requirements. And the high-cost labor content adds materially to unnecessarily inflated costs.

Rotary drills can be produced more economically in a simple assembly shop operation, located in a low-rent area, and utilizing the most cost-effective components available (there are 27 manufacturers of compressors in the United States alone).

In combination, the above considerations create a situation whereby a product line of rotary drills may be designed that better satisfies market requirements and that can be produced and distributed at costs significantly below those of the present manufacturers. An opportunity exists for the right new venture to get into the rotary drill business with significant competitive advantages.

The Company

The opportunity for a new manufacturer to enter the rotary drill industry was perceived in April 1971 by a group of five key executives employed by the present industry leader. These executives collectively had more than 70 years of marketing, engineering, manufacturing, and general management experience in the rotary drill business. Their analysis and assessment of conditions in the industry convinced them that there was a viable growth opportunity for a new rotary drill company and that the equity capital requirements for such a new venture were very reasonable (i.e., less than $400,000).

Accordingly, these five executives formed a new company—Rapidrill—to design, manufacture, and sell rotary drills. Rapidrill was formally incorporated in the state of Delaware in August 1971, and the principals invested $128,000 of their funds in it. Rapidrill plans to produce modern, state-of-the-art rotary drills that will be marketed through independent mining and construction equipment distributors.

The Product

The "Rotary Drill" that Rapidrill proposes to make and sell and that is discussed in this plan is a mobile system, either truck- or crawler-mounted, for drilling relatively large holes (generally 6″ to 12″ diameter) in rock formations. The drill is driven at its top by a hydraulic motor. Figure 1 illustrates a typical truck-mounted rig, and Figure 2 shows a crawler-mounted drill rig. Basically, a rotary drill provides a large downthrust and torque force to a drill stem so that a drill bit or hammer can fragment rock at the bottom of the hole being drilled. In addition, compressed air is provided to remove rock cuttings from the hole during the drilling.

Rather than being a simple manufactured product, the rotary drill is in fact a complex technical system design consisting of hydraulic, pneumatic, electrical, and mechanical components integrated into a complete drill rig assembly having a typical value of $100,000. It is significant that for *all* present manufacturers the cost of purchased components for assembled drills is from 60 percent to 70 percent of manufacturing costs. It is also pertinent that no present manufacturer has a sufficient market share to enjoy a "most favored" position with the suppliers of such components.

Figure 2

The strip mining, open-pit mining, construction, quarrying, and water-well-drilling industries utilize rotary drills in their operations. In the various mining, quarrying, and construction operations, blast holes are drilled into the rock overlying the coal or ore, or into the rock structures to be moved. Blasting this waste rock into small pieces enables its removal. An infinite number of different rock structures are encountered in these operations, and a wide range of hole diameters and hole depths are required. In the last 15 years the demand for increased productivity has forced a trend toward faster production of larger, deeper holes, which has best been provided by rotary drills.

While the rotary drills used for drilling blast holes are increasing in size and productivity, the water-well-drilling contractor must cope with problems of mobility. His rotary drill must have the same fast drilling capability, but it must be small enough in size to travel over the public highways and to be set up to drill in small, tight areas—often between buildings.

Product Line

Design studies have been conducted by Rapidrill to determine how to best configure Rapidrill's rotary drills so that they would meet most present drilling requirements and use available components (e.g., trucks, compressors, and diesel engine frames). As a result of these studies, Rapidrill has decided on three basic drill frame sizes:

D–30K for 6″ diameter and smaller holes

D–40K for 6″ to 8″ diameter holes

D–70K for 9″ to 12″ diameter holes

All of these will be hydraulic top-drive drills that are now standard in the drilling industry.

An analysis has also been conducted to determine the suitability of truck- and crawler-mounted versions of each of the above basic drill models for blast hole and well-drilling applications in the principal market segments.

Results of this study are shown in Table 1. Examination of these data shows

Table 1
Percentage of Total Rock-Drilling Applications Met by Rapidrill's Possible Product Lines (by market segment)

Market Segment	Rotary Drill Model					
	D–30K		D–40K		D–70K	
	Truck	Crawler	Truck	Crawler	Truck	Crawler
Wells	70%		90%			
Blast hole drilling						
Coal mining	20	20%	80	50%	30%	30%
Quarrying	30	30	30	30	10	5
Construction	10	5	35	5		
Copper mining			20	30	20	50
Iron mining				20		50

Note: Some overlap exists in the applications for each drill size. For example, 90 percent of all water wells drilled provide water for residential use. These wells are generally 6″ in diameter, and both the D–30K model and the D–40K model can be used to drill them.

that good application coverage can be obtained with only six basic rotary drill models: a truck-mounted D–30K and D–40K for well drilling; a truck-mounted D–30K and D–40K for blast hole drilling; and a crawler-mounted D–40K and D–70K for blast hole drilling. The crawler-mounted version of the D–30K and the truck-mounted version of the D–70K provide insufficient market coverage to warrant their design and manufacture by Rapidrill during its early operations. The data of Table 1 also indicate that the most desirable order of drill development to achieve the earliest coverage of the maximum number of market segments would be: first the D–40K, then the D–30K, and then the D–70K.

Table 2 shows the selected Rapidrill product lines and the relationships among them. Note the high degree of component commonality that can be achieved in the different versions of the basic drill models. The prices shown in Table 2 are list prices to the end user (distributor prices will be about 25 percent lower). Sufficient detail design and component selection have been accomplished to permit accurate cost estimates to be made and to assure that the 25 percent discount to distributors can be achieved.

Table 2
Proposed Rapidrill Models

	Model		
Parameters	D–30K	D–40K	D–70K
Truck-mounted drills			
Well drills			
Hole diameter (inches)	6	6–8	
Rated depth (feet)	1,000–2,000	1,000–2,000	
Bit pressure (pounds)	30,000	40,000	
Bit RPM	0–200	0–200	
Stem length (feet)	20	25	
Compressor	450 CFM–250 psi	750 CFM–250 psi	
Mounting (truck)	T–800 Ford	Crane Carrier	
Estimated weight (pounds)	40,000	56,000	
Selling price	$95,000	$125,000	
Blast hole drills			
Hole diameter (inches)	6	6–8	
Rated depth (feet)	1,000	1,000	
Bit pressure (pounds)	30,000	40,000	
Bit RPM	0–200	0–200	
Stem length (feet)	20	25	
Compressor	450 CFM–250 psi	750 CFM–100 psi 750 CFM–250 psi 900 CFM–50 psi	
Mounting (truck)	T–800 Ford	Crane Carrier	
Estimated weight (pounds)	40,000	56,000	
Selling price	$90,000	$120,000	
Crawler-mounted drills			
Blast hole			
Hole diameter (inches)		6–8	9–12
Rated depth (feet)		1,000	1,000
Bit pressure (pounds)		40,000	70,000
Bit RPM		0–200	0–100
Stem length (feet)		25	30–50
Compressor (psi)		750 CFM–250	1050 CFM–100
Estimated weight (pounds)		60,000	100,000
Selling price		$135,000	$225,000

2. THE MANAGEMENT TEAM

Rapidrill believes that the most important element supporting the feasibility of its proposed program is the strength and proven ability of its management team. Every key functional position in which rotary drill experience would enhance the performance of the company is filled with an individual unquestionably preeminent in the industry.

Perhaps more important than the individual competence of team members is their demonstrated ability to work effectively as a team. Over the last five years, their efforts—and significant effort was required of each of them—increased the market share of their former employer from 9 percent to 22 percent of the total rotary drill market. This 22 percent market share was twice the share of the nearest competitor, and was accomplished with handicaps in capacity, delivery, and costs at least as great as those of any of their competitors.

Consideration of this performance and review of the qualifications of team members are important in judging the validity of Rapidrill's knowledge of the industry and the feasibility of its proposed marketing, product, and manufacturing plans.

The Team

The following tabulation shows ·the organization of Rapidrill management and the responsibility of each member prior to association with Rapidrill.

Rapidrill Organization	*Former Positions with Indiana Tool, Inc., Machinery Division*
S. A. Price, President	Division President
M. F. Einman, VP Marketing	Product Manager, Rotary Drills
F. T. Samuels, VP Engineering	Manager of Engineering
G. A. Miller, VP Finance	Controller
W. D. MacMillan, Manager Manufacturing	Production Superintendent

Qualifications

The following summaries describe the individual qualifications of team members.

Samuel A. Price, President

Mr. Price, age 42, has both B.S. and M.S. degrees in engineering from Michigan State University. His experience includes 15 years of increasing responsibilities in engineering and marketing management and over five years of general management responsibilities in the design, manufacture, and sale of equipment for the mining, construction, and utility markets. This experience was accumulated with General Electric, Dresser Industries, and Indiana Tool, Inc.

In 1963, as general manager of the then new Gas Turbine Division of Dresser Industries, Mr. Price staffed the division (predominantly from outside sources) and supervised the design, fabrication, and installation in customer facilities of over $5-million worth of gas-turbine-powered pipeline booster compressors within 15 months of division start-up. This program was accomplished well within original cost and time objectives.

During the four-year period from 1965 through 1970, under his management as president of the Machinery Division of Indiana Tool, Inc., division sales to the mining and construction markets rose from $17 million per year to $32 million per year and were profitable. This represented the most significant sales and profit growth rate of any of Indiana Tool's divisions and substantial market share improvement in all product lines. The rotary drill product lines accounted for $14 million of those 1970 sales.

Marshal F. Einman, Vice President, Marketing and Sales

Mr. Einman, age 49, attended the Illinois State Teachers College and has prior experience of three years as president of a small privately held company. His 27 years' total experience includes 19 years in marketing and sales of rotary drills with both Hamilton Manufacturing Company and the Machinery Division of Indiana Tool, Inc.

From 1960 to 1971 he was product manager for rotary drills, responsible for domestic and foreign sales, sales forecasting, production requirements, product definition, product pricing, advertising, sales training, and definition of product support programs.

Under his marketing management Indiana Tool's sales of rotary drills rose from $2.5 million in 1960 to $14.4 million in 1970. Much of this sales increase was directly attributable to his personal expertise in drill applications work. He has extensively traveled the United States, and in fact the entire free world, solving difficult drilling problems and promoting drill sales. Recent foreign trips to Australia, Vietnam, the Philippines, Morocco, Spain, Zambia, Rhodesia, and South Africa attest to the worldwide acceptance of his applications and market knowledge.

Mr. Einman is a member of the American Institute of Mining Engineers.

Frank T. Samuels, Vice President, Engineering

Mr. Samuels, age 45, holds degrees in Civil Engineering from Michigan State College, Mechanical Engineering from Worcester Polytechnic Institute, and has done graduate work in Mechanical Engineering at Illinois Institute of Technology. His 24 years of engineering experience include high-pressure hydraulic research with Standard Oil Company of Indiana and 20 years of design responsibility for rotary drills commencing in 1951, when he joined the Hamilton Manufacturing Company as chief engineer. Hamilton Manufacturing, under Mr. Samuels' engineering leadership, pioneered and developed the highly successful hydraulic top-drive rotary drill that has become the standard of the industry.

During this period, and after acquisition of Hamilton Manufacturing by Indiana Tool, Inc., in 1957, in the capacity of chief engineer for Indiana Tool's Machinery Division, he supervised the engineering of over 1,200 rotary drills, ranging in size and application from 5,000-pound high-speed diamond core drills to 200,000-pound crawler-mounted machines used to bore 15″ blast holes in taconite on the Mesabi Range. He has become accepted as the technical leader and innovator in the field. In 1970 he had engineering responsibility for over $32-million worth of mining and construction machinery sales that included $14-million worth of rotary drills.

He is a member of the Society of Automotive Engineers and a registered Professional Engineer in Indiana, Pennsylvania, and New York states.

George A. Miller, Vice President, Finance, Secretary, Treasurer

Mr. Miller, age 32, has a degree in Accounting from Michigan State College and graduate work toward an MBA at Wayne State College.

His initial experience was with Federal-Mogul Corporation, culminating in the position of controller for its Bearings Division plant, where he designed and installed a standard cost system specifically suited for job-shop operations.

In 1966 he joined the Vare Corporation (now Microdot, $170 million annual sales, NYSE) as group controller of its Plastics Division. Promoted to assistant corporate controller, he assisted in the $37-million loan negotiated for the acquisition of Microdot, Inc., by Vare Corporation.

Mr. Miller joined Indiana Tool, Inc., in 1969. As division controller of the $32-million-per-year Machinery Division, he revised and modernized the division's accounting and management reporting systems and worked extensively on financial analysis of new product and manufacturing opportunities.

William D. MacMillan, Manager of Manufacturing

Mr. MacMillan, age 45, has 25 years' experience in directing the operation of machining, welding, and assembly plants. Starting in job shops, he joined Hamilton Manufacturing Company in 1946 as its first employee and assisted in its growth to 100 employees. He was responsible for all manufacturing operations when the company was acquired by Indiana Tool, Inc., in 1957.

With Indiana Tool's Machinery Division, he was superintendent of rotary drill production until 1968, when he was made responsible for the production of all Machinery Division products, and in 1970 accomplished $32 million in shipments. In this capacity he was responsible for directing the scheduling and operations of the rotary drill assembly, portable compressor assembly, and welding and fabricating departments. He initiated many cost reduction programs; most notable was modernizing the welding and fabricating departments and realizing a 30 percent reduction in direct labor cost.

In his total experience Mr. MacMillan directed the assembly and test of over 1,200 rotary drill rigs, an accumulated experience unmatched in the industry.

Compensation and Ownership

Table 3 lists the ownership, the cash investment, and the previous salary of each of Rapidrill's team members. These data demonstrate the dedication, com-

Table 3
Compensation and Ownership of Rapidrill Principals

Principals	Shares Owned	Direct Investment	Annual Salary	Previous Salary	Salary Reduction
S. A. Price	136,000	$ 20,400	$38,000	$62,000*	40%
M. F. Einman	78,000	20,280	25,000	32,000	22
F. T. Samuels	78,000	20,280	25,000	30,000	17
G. A. Miller	42,000	12,600	25,000	27,000	8
W. D. MacMillan	36,000	14,400	18,000	20,000	10
Three district sales managers	(each) 27,000	13,500	24,000	32,000	
Investment total		$128,000			

*Does not include stock options for 4,000 shares of Indiana Tool, Inc.

mitment, and belief of the principals in Rapidrill and their recognition of the relative responsibility and authority of their functional positions.

Future Team Members

In addition to these five principals, three other key personnel are presently committed to Rapidrill's program. These men are district sales managers who collectively account for annual drill sales of $9 million for their present employer and are scheduled to join Rapidrill on March 1, 1972.

Other functional skills will be required in future operations (purchasing, inventory control, etc.) and will be added when operations volume warrants their addition. However, specific rotary drill experience is not felt to be critical in these functional areas.

Board of Directors

Rapidrill's bylaws call for a board of directors of from four to six members. The present directors are Messrs. Price, Einman, Samuels, and Miller, with two directorships reserved for representation of equity investors.

Supporting Professional Services

Rapidrill is presently represented by Walter I. Bobbin of Taylor, Dolan, and Bobbin of Nashville, Tennessee, as general counsel.

The firm of Tanner, Foster, and Company, CPAs, has been retained as independent auditors.

3.   MARKET RESEARCH AND ANALYSIS

Market Description

The rotary drill has enjoyed a steady market growth with an annual growth rate of 10 percent achieved for the last six years and sales of $74 million in 1970. This market is shown graphically in Figure 3, which illustrates the total size of the market, the noncyclic nature of its growth since 1964, and a projection of sales through 1976 showing a 1976 sales forecast of $114 million based on the past seven-year trend.

Market Segmentation. The noncyclic growth performance may be explained principally by the lack of a dominating market segment in the sale of drills. The five principal market segments contributed the following market shares in 1970:

Market Segment	Market Share
Well drills	35%
Quarrying	18
Coal mining	26
Metal mining	10
Construction	11

Figure 3
Market Size and Trends of Rotary Drill Sales

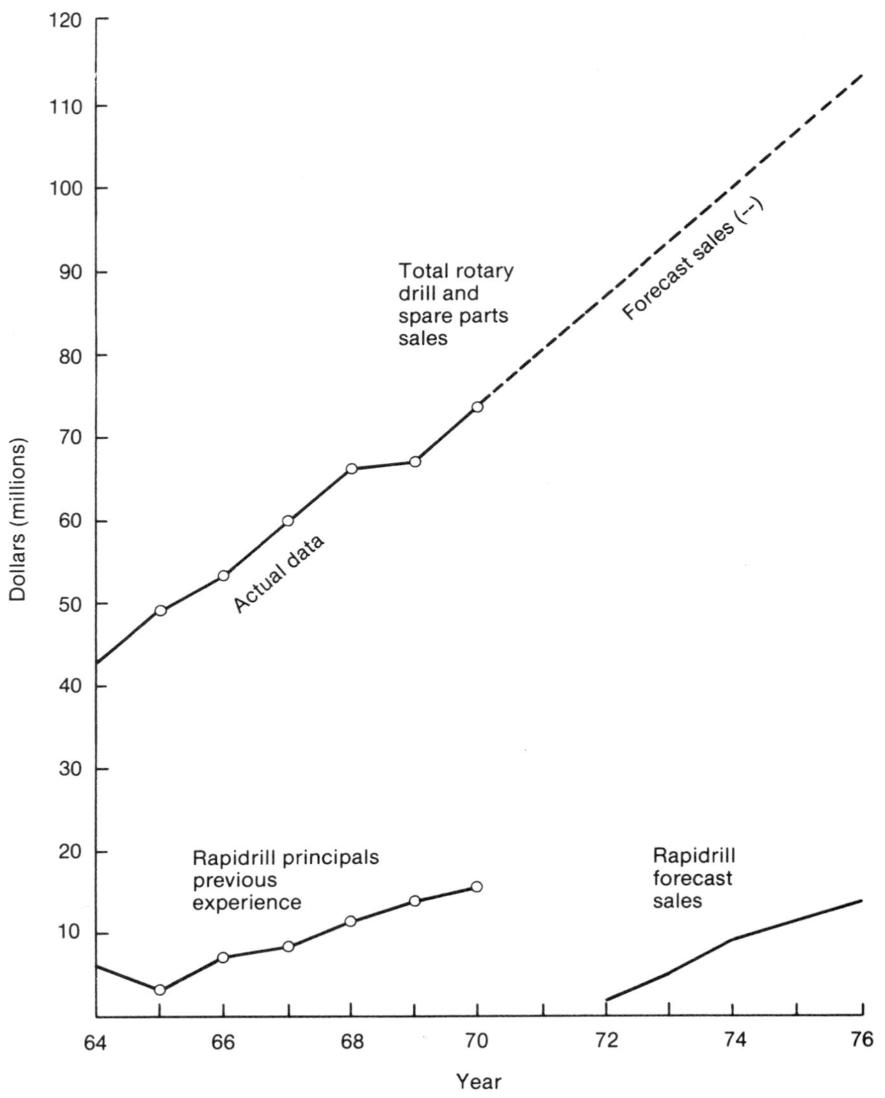

Sources: U.S. Bureau of Mines, Compressed Air and Gas Institute (CAGI), and *Survey of Rotary Drill Manufacturers and Suppliers* by P. J. Lang.

Historically, soft performance in any of these segments has been favorably offset by stronger sales to other segments or by favorable response in those other segments to governmental economic stimulus. For example, highway and dam programs increase construction and quarrying sales, housing starts stimulated by the lowering of interest rates increase water-well drilling, and an interest in alternative energy sources stimulates the surface mining of coal.

Market Trends. The projected future energy shortage and the attendant growth in coal surface-mining production, which requires rock drilling, represent a very significant market opportunity for rotary drill sales over the next 5–10 years.

Figure 4 shows the growth of coal tonnage production over the last 10 years. As shown, virtually the entire growth in production has been accomplished in surface mining. A recent Bureau of Mines forecast, also shown on this curve, projects substantial increases in total coal tonnage production and an increasing trend to surface mining. In 1976 it is estimated that 57 percent of the total production of coal will be mined by surface methods. The bureau further predicts a *tripling* of total coal production by 1985 to meet the nation's energy needs.

Figure 4
U.S. Coal Production

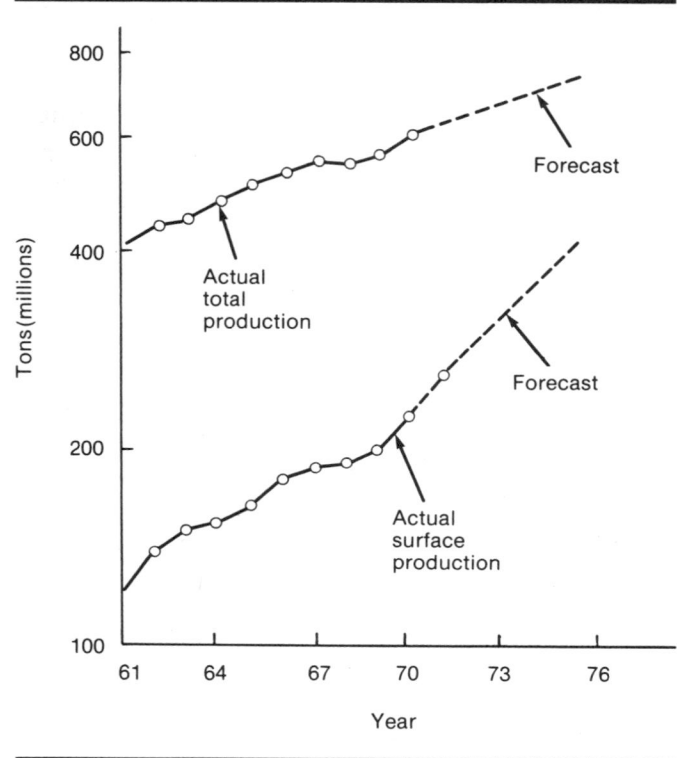

Source: U.S. Bureau of Mines.

The following considerations provide a basis that supports this forecast growth, confirms continuation of the trend to surface-mining operations, and delineates some of the rotary drill market implications:

1. Of the energy reserves in the United States 88 percent are in coal, while at present only 18 percent of the energy consumed is provided by coal. Proven coal reserves are estimated to be sufficient to satisfy all the energy needs of the nation for over 200 years.
2. The Federal Coal Mine Health and Safety Act of 1969 has significantly lowered the productivity of underground coal-mining operations. In the 1960s a typical miner produced 15 tons of coal per day; today this figure has dropped to 10 tons, with two thirds of the decline laid to safety legislation.

3. Recent reverses to environmentalist efforts (e.g., President Nixon's postponement of "clean air" legislation and progress in surface-mine reclamation efforts) have decimated organized opposition to surface mining.
4. Present pending legislation is directed at regulation rather than curtailment of surface-mining activities.
5. Achievement of the above 1986 forecast coal production would require approximately 4,000 drills to be in operation compared to the present 1,000 working drills.

Table 4 shows how market segment sales of rotary drills will change in response to this forecast increase in coal production and illustrates the magnitude of the opportunity that this rapidly growing segment will offer in sales growth.

Table 4
Market Segment Comparison (1970 versus forecast 1974; total unit sales, number of drills)

	1970		1974	
Market Segment	*Sales*	*Percent of Market*	*Sales Forecast*	*Percent of Market*
Water well	250	35	329	31
Quarrying	125	18	159	15
Coal mining	175	26	371	35
Metal mining	70	10	95	9
Construction	80	11	106	10
	700		1,060	

Source: Compressed Air and Gas Institute (CAGI), Bureau of Census, Bureau of Mines, and Driltech Forecast.

Rapidrill believes this coal surface-mining market for rotary drills to be an important opportunity for concentration of its initial effort. Those elements, in addition to this projected segment sales growth, that support this decision will be discussed in the following sections of this plan.

Competition

Table 5 lists all present competitive manufacturers of rotary drills, indicates the range of their product lines, the market segments in which they actively participate, and their approximate present share of the total rotary drill market.

As shown, the 11 manufacturers break down into three general categories that are discussed below.

Large-Drill Manufacturer. Bucyrus-Erie (B-E) manufactures and sells only large drills as a complement to its large-shovel and dragline equipment. It presently has the market for large drills to itself and its 60 units a year produce sales of over $14 million. It sells direct, as it sells its shovels, and has made several abortive excursions into other market segments. These attempts to enter the other drill market segments were unsuccessful primarily because of its unfamiliarity with distributor marketing—the predominant method of selling drills in all but the large-rotary-drill market.

Gardner-Denver has initiated a program to enter the large-drill market. This program was initiated by recruitment of six of B-E's principal engineering person-

Table 5
Rotary Drill Competition

	Product Line*	Market	1970 Share of Total $ Market
Large-drill manufacturers			
Bucyrus-Erie (B-E)	I, L	Coal, metal mining	20%
Broad-line manufacturers			
Indiana Tool, Inc.	S,M,I	All	22
Ingersol-Rand	S,M	All	11
Davey	S+	All	9
Joy (Robbins)	M,I	All except water well	7
			49%
Water-well drill manufacturers			
Gardner-Denver	S,L	Mixed, no iron mining	6%
Failing	S	Water well	5
Koehring Speedstar	S	Water well	5
Schramm	S	Water well	5
Sanderson-Cyclone	S	Water well	5
Winter-Weiss	S	Water well	5
			31%
Rapidrill	S,M,I (L in future)	All	
			100%

* Hole Capability	List Price
S = 6″ or less	$ 60,000– 90,000
M = 6–8″	$110,000–150,000
I = 9–12″	$200,000–250,000
L = 15–17″ or larger	$350,000 up

Note: Both product line and market classifications for the above-listed manufacturers are limited to products that are competitive and markets where efforts are effective. There are some overlaps of both product and market that are not listed; but these are of limited significance.

nel and as yet has produced no significant results. Rapidrill considers this program to be premature and believes that marketing as well as technical know-how will be required in such a program.

Successful quantity gasification or liquid conversion of coal, estimated to be practicable by the late 70s (pilot plants are presently operating), will provide a new and large market for low-sulfur western coal. This new application will require "large" drills and will offer a significant new market opportunity for drill sales and penetration of B-E's dominance of the large-drill market.

Broad-Line Manufacturers. Only four present manufacturers offer a product line applicable to a broad range of market segment applications: Indiana Tool, Inc. (the market leader), Ingersol-Rand, Davey, and Joy Manufacturing.

These manufacturers share several common characteristics:

1. All are compressor manufacturers attracted to drills by their use of compressors.
2. All manufacture an extensive line of mining and construction equipment products in addition to rotary drills.
3. All sell through local equipment distributors. (Ingersol-Rand utilizes "company owned" stores for distribution.)
4. All offer relatively modern machines (5- to 14-year-old designs) with good performance and high productivity. This is more important than price in these

markets. However, all would benefit in both cost and performance by major update of designs.

The drills of these manufacturers are suitable to applications in all market segments, and as a group they account for 49 percent of all drill sales. Most pertinently, this 49 percent includes virtually all of the coal surface-mining drills: the market segment most likely to enjoy significant near-term sales growth. These manufacturers in general have had difficulty in providing sufficient productive capacity to match sales growth, so that their pricing and discounting have been firm over the last seven years. Recent increases in forecast demands will further exacerbate their capacity problem. Accordingly, Rapidrill believes that a new manufacturer can achieve significant drill sales without the disruption of drill pricing structures and that the market segments served by the broad-line drill manufacturers represent the best opportunity for market entry by a new manufacturer.

These manufacturers share one further common characteristic favorable to a new drill manufacturer—they unanimously have a well-deserved reputation for poor service and product support.

Water-Well Drill Manufacturers. Failing, Koehring Speedstar, Schramm, Sanderson-Cyclone, and Winter-Weiss all manufacture only small drills aimed primarily at the low-price portion of the water-well drill market. In general, they distribute and sell most effectively on a regional basis. Of the well drill manufacturers, only Gardner-Denver attempts national distribution and has a broad range of product lines.

The average drill offered by these manufacturers utilizes mechanical drive systems, reciprocating compressors, and other components consistent with a 30- to 40-year-old technology, and most of these manufacturers would have difficulty in developing a modern rotary drill design. While the obsolete design and general poor productivity of these machines is apparent to knowledgeable operators, price remains an important consideration in this market and the low-price drills capture 70 percent to 80 percent of water-well drill sales.

Conversion of the market from cable tool drills to high-quality, hydraulic top-drive rotary drills has been pervasive over the last five years and will continue at a steady rate as operators become familiar with the increase in productivity available through their use of hydraulic drills. Rapidrill plans to achieve its share of water-well drill sales in the high-quality end of the market. However, attempts by Rapidrill to accelerate this conversion and capture an early dominating share of the entire market segment could be met by severe price competition in the price-conscious segment of the market.

Table 6 presents and compares Rapidrill's primary specifications, list prices, and distributor net prices with those of the competition in each of the three hole-capability ranges. In the case of the 6″ or less hole capability, only those competitors that produce high-quality rotary drills and market them nationally are shown and considered. As noted above, Rapidrill does not intend to compete in the low-price, low-quality portion of the well market.

The data of Table 6 show that Rapidrill's proposed drill designs have equal or better specifications than those of its competition and are competitively priced with sufficient margins to provide significantly lower distributor net prices, if required.

Table 6
Comparison of Competing Drills

Manufacturer	Model	Drill Bit Pressure (pounds)	Air Compressor Vol./Pres.	List Price	Distributor Net
6″ or less hole capability					
Rapidrill	D–30K Truck	30,000	450/250	$ 90,000	$ 68,400
Indiana Tool, Inc.	T–650	30,000	450/150	101,120	85,952
Ingersol-Rand	T–3	30,000	600/125	92,080	78,268
Davey	M–8A–HP	30,000	490/250	92,195	78,366
Gardner-Denver	15W	30,000	640/150	102,855	87,427
6″ to 8″ hole capability					
Rapidrill	D–40K Truck	40,000	750/250	120,000	91,200
Indiana Tool, Inc.	T–670	30,000	600/250	120,551	102,468
Ingersol-Rand	T–4	32,000	600/250	120,510	102,433
Rapidrill	D–40K Crawler	40,000	750/250	135,000	102,600
Ingersol-Rand	DM–4	32,000	600/250	139,610	118,668
9″ to 12″ hole capability					
Rapidrill	D–70K Crawler	70,000	900/250	225,000	171,000
Bucyrus-Erie (B-E)	45–R	70,000	900/240	246,977	209,930
Robbins (Joy)	RR–12	70,000	875/250	227,962*	206,518

*Includes new D–9 Caterpillar tractor at $85,000 list.

As noted earlier, the model D–40K rotary drill will be the first product that Rapidrill will produce and market. The design of the D–40K is sufficiently accomplished that reasonably firm detail specifications have been developed for it. Table 7 compares a full range of the features of the D–40K with the best of its present competition with 6″ to 8″ hole capability. As can be seen, the D–40K will have significant superiority in specifications to the machines of either of its competitors and about a 10 percent lower price to the distributor (see Table 6). Rapidrill is able to achieve this lower price without sacrificing profitability through cost savings in purchased components, manufacturing (see Section 6), and selling expenses (see Section 4).

Estimated Market Share and Sales

Rapidrill's sales forecasts for each of its planned rotary drill models for the next five years are shown in Table 8. Sales for truck-mounted D–30K and D–40K drills have been separately estimated for the well-drilling and blast hole–drilling applications of these units. Sales are estimated to rise from $781,000 for the second half of 1972 to $13,680,000 in 1976.

Table 9 shows the total rotary drill market for the next five years, Rapidrill's total sales in each year, and the share of the total rotary drill market that the sales represent. Achievement of Rapidrill's sales forecasts would require its share of the market to rise from 2 percent at the end of the first year to 11.9 percent in the fifth year of operation.

The sales and market share forecasts shown in Tables 8 and 9 are believed to be reasonable—if not conservative—and attainable by the Rapidrill team. There are five principal reasons why Rapidrill believes this to be so:

1. While working for their former employer (Indiana Tool, Inc.), Rapidrill's management team increased that company's share of the total rotary drill market

Table 7
Rotary Drills: Detailed Comparison of Competing Products

	Manufacturer and Model		
	Rapidrill D–40K	Ingersol-Rand T–4	Indiana Tool, Inc. T–670
Hole diameter (inches)	6–8	6–8	6–8
Bit pressure (pounds)	40,000	32,500	30,000
Machine weight (pounds)	56,000	42,000	43,500
Bit speed (RPM range)	0–100 0–150 0–195	0–100	0–86
Bit torque (pounds per inch)	54,000	50,000	36,000
Compressor type	Screw (domestic)	Vane	Screw (imported)
Air volume and pressure	750 @ 100 750 @ 250 900 @ 50	750 @ 150 750 @ 250	600 @ 250
Engine power	Caterpillar 4-cycle diesel	GM 2-cycle diesel	Caterpillar 4-cycle diesel
Horsepower	325	260	300
Drill stem break-out in mast	Yes	Yes	No
Automatic drill stem loader	Yes	Yes	No
Stem loader inside mast	Yes	No	No
Feed rate (FPM)			
Standard	12	12	5.5
Rapid	62	64	40
Retract	110	100	75
Leveling capacity (inches)	48	48	24
Drill stem threads	Low torque 2 thread/inch	High torque 4 thread/inch	High torque 4 thread/inch
Number of best features	17	6	2

Table 8
Rapidrill Corporation Sales Forecast (in $000)

	1972		1973		1974		1975		1976	
	Units	$	Units	$	Units	$	Units	$	Units	$
Models										
D–40K truck-mounted (blast hole)	8	$730	16	$1,459	22	$2,006	29	$ 2,645	36	$ 3,283
D–40K truck-mounted (well)			10	950	14	1,330	20	1,900	24	2,280
D–40K crawler-mounted			7	718	8	821	9	923	12	1,231
D–30K truck-mounted (blast hole)			6	410	8	547	9	616	12	821
D–30K truck-mounted (well)			4	289	12	866	20	1,444	24	1,733
D–70K crawler-mounted					6	1,026	9	1,539	12	2,052
Spares		51		383		989		1,813		2,280
	8		43		70		96		120	
Total		$781		$4,209		$7,585		$10,880		$13,680

Table 9
Rapidrill Market Share Forecast (in 000s)

	1972 1st Year		1973 2d Year	1974 3d Year	1975 4th Year	1976 5th Year
	3d Qtr.	4th Qtr.				
*Total market**	$22,000	$23,000	$94,000	$100,500	$108,000	$114,000
Rapidrill share	1.3%	2.1%	4.4%	7.5%	10.0%	11.9%
*Rapidrill sales**	$290	$490	$4,209	$7,580	$10,880	$13,680

*Both total market figures and Rapidrill sales include spare parts.

from 9 percent to 22 percent in the five-year period from 1965 to 1970. Drill sales during that time went from $4 million to $15 million. Rapidrill's management believes that it should be able to duplicate that kind of performance and capture 11.9 percent of the rotary drill market and $13,680,000 of profitable sales in the first five years of Rapidrill's operation.

2. Rapidrill's marketing team will include three distributor representatives who, as district sales managers, collectively produced annual rotary drill sales of $9 million for their previous employer. They should be able to obtain a large portion of this business for Rapidrill.

3. Rapidrill's distributors (see Section 4) will include three that are among the most effective in the industry. Together these three distributors could absorb all of Rapidrill's projected production in its first two or three operating years.

4. Rapidrill's rotary drills will have performance equal to or better than that of competing units and a lower price to the distributor. The superior drill performance will be achieved by upgrading the design of Rapidrill's machines and using the best and most cost-effective components that are available. Regarding engineering, F. T. Samuels, Rapidrill's vice president of engineering, is recognized as a technical leader in the industry. The selection of components as well as overhead and labor costs (see Section 6) that are less than those of other manufacturers will enable Rapidrill to offer its units to distributors at a price below that of its competition.

5. Rapidrill will offer service, warranty, and application engineering that is superior to that provided by its competition.

4. MARKETING PLAN

Distributor Plan

Rapidrill plans to sell drills through well-established equipment distributors in the mining, construction, and well-drilling industries. Close to 100 percent of all the drills in Rapidrill's proposed model sizes are sold through this channel of sale.

Users, rather than the manufacturers, have created this dominant channel (very favorable to a small independent manufacturer), based on their experience with the present manufacturers' failure to provide service and spare-parts support on a sufficiently localized basis. Distributors, conversely, recognize that their success will ultimately be determined by their ability to support equipment in the field, and are continuously searching for more reliable and maintenance-free product lines, adequately supported by a manufacturer's service and spare-parts programs.

Sufficient dissatisfaction with the product lines and support programs of present competitive manufacturers exists to create a high probability of success for Rapidrill's efforts to establish an effective distributor network.

It will be important during Rapidrill's introduction to the market to have exceptionally strong, well-established distributors. In order to attract such distributors, Rapidrill plans to offer significantly larger than standard industry discounts during an introductory period. Cost estimates have established sufficient manufacturing margins to provide discounts of 24 percent to 26 percent to distributors, compared to a firm industry standard of 15 percent. Such discounts would provide up to 60 percent greater margin to distributors that, on a national average, achieve earnings of 2.5 percent on sales.

In order to minimize Rapidrill's working capital requirements during early periods, these larger discounts will be identified with prompt cash payments for drills, (i.e., 7 percent discount for 15-day payment). Such strategy will further ensure well-financed dealers and will allow a future rationale for decreases in discounts if higher net prices are competitively available.

Over the last three months, Rapidrill has discussed its proposed drill models with three strong, well-established distributors and has tentative agreements with them for the distribution of Rapidrill's drills. These distributors are:

Mining Supplies, Inc.
Gadsden, Alabama

Pierce Mining Equipment Company
Cincinnati, Ohio

Pennsylvania Machinery Company
Scranton, Pennsylvania

These distributors, in the opinion of Rapidrill's principals, are among the most effective drill distributors in the industry. They adequately cover a large part of the coal-mining market for rotary drills, and they could, by themselves, absorb Rapidrill's total forecast production in its first two or three years.

The sales forecast for the next five years (Table 8) projects sales reaching $13,680,000 by 1976. Support of this sales forecast will require only 2 or 3 additional major distributors and a total network of 12 to 14 distributors to achieve adequate national coverage of the total drill market.

Sales Plan

Rapidrill will sell to and support the direct selling efforts of distributors with a team of distributor representatives. It is planned to have at least one distributor representative for every major distributor. Representatives to cover the three above-listed distributors have already committed themselves to join Rapidrill early in 1972. These three men are experienced rotary drill sales managers who presently are collectively responsible for annual drill sales of over $9 million.

Rapidrill believes that its single-product selling requirements and, in particular, the large "ticket" price of rotary drills offer an additional cost advantage to Rapidrill in comparison to its competitors, which sell several products (rotary drills, compressors, diesel engines) to the same distributor. Rapidrill believes that its selling expenses for rotary drills may be maintained at 9 percent of sales (after a sufficient production base is achieved) compared to the 12 percent to 13 percent common to competitive manufacturers. The simplistic explanation for this reduction is that a $100,000 rotary drill is about as easily sold as a $5,000 compressor or a $500 air tool. Rapidrill plans to achieve about $1 million in sales per distributor representative. The industry average for competitors is from $350,000 to $500,000.

Applications Support.   An additional strong influence in rotary drill sales is provided by applications support: the ability to determine for a user the most economic equipment requirements to satisfy his drilling needs.

Rapidrill's principals have market-wide recognition and extensively proven records in providing effective applications services directly to users.

Advertising and Promotion.   Rapidrill's advertising and promotional efforts will be concentrated on those areas shown by experience to be the most effective. These are primarily the exhibition of equipment at trade association shows, particularly regional "buying" shows where immediate sales may be obtained; and demonstration programs where the productivity of drills can be demonstrated on a user's particular job. Rapidrill will maintain at least one rig in inventory for demonstration purposes at all times and plans to offer additional discount incentives to distributors on demonstrator machines. Demonstrator machines are customarily sold by distributors after 100 to 200 hours of operation at about a $1,500 price markdown.

Warranty and Service

Most of the problems that have earned present manufacturers their poor reputations may be attributed to the multiplicity and complexity of the various product lines (compressors, rotary drills, diesel engines, etc.) they manufacture and to plain poor management attention.

Rapidrill believes that proper attention to service, product support, and a competitive warranty posture will enhance market penetration to a degree that pricing in these productivity-conscious market segments would never accomplish alone. Rapidrill's ability to provide such services and support for its drills is definitely aided by the single-product nature of its planned operations.

An initial step in providing good product support is Rapidrill's recently completed study of inventory stocking requirements. This study identified the minimum parts inventory that is required to have a satisfactory response time to predicted customer demands for spare parts.

5.   DESIGN AND DEVELOPMENT PLANS

Rapidrill's planned product line will not require extension of any state-of-the-art technologies. The designs of all competitors are from 5 to 14 years old. The task and the opportunity consist of knowledgeable application of the latest component technology and performance available and an optimum balanced utilization of those components. The result should be significant improvements in product performance at competitive price levels.

Status. The model D–40K series of drills (e.g., truck-mounted well or blast hole and crawler-mounted units) have been selected, for reasons previously discussed, for initial design, development, and market introduction. The development of the D–40K drills will be followed by the design and development of the D–30K truck-mounted well drill and the D–70K crawler-mounted drill, in that order.

It should be emphasized that development and test work on the finished D–40K, D–30K, and D–70K designs should be minimal. The reason for this is that all the components of these drills will be used well within their operating ranges, and testing efforts are principally required to check out control feedback, valve suitability, and other minor design details. After the prototype drills have been tested and their design proven, they will be sold at a slight markdown. This is common practice in the rotary drill industry.

The product design schedule is shown on the master schedule (Figure 6), that is, Section 7.

Parts Grouping. One additional Rapidrill design criterion merits discussion. In the detail design of Rapidrill's product line, "parts grouping" will be utilized. The parts grouping concept defines all optional features, such as compressor size, as a complete and interchangeable group of parts. The parts grouping requirements of the D–40K are shown graphically in Figure 5. The assembly of different versions of a drill model is facilitated by using interchangeable parts groups. Moreover, decisions made by parts group (either on a forecast, lead-time, or max-min basis) permit maximum production feasibility with minimum inventory and simplified production control requirements.

Figure 5
Parts Grouping—Model D-40K

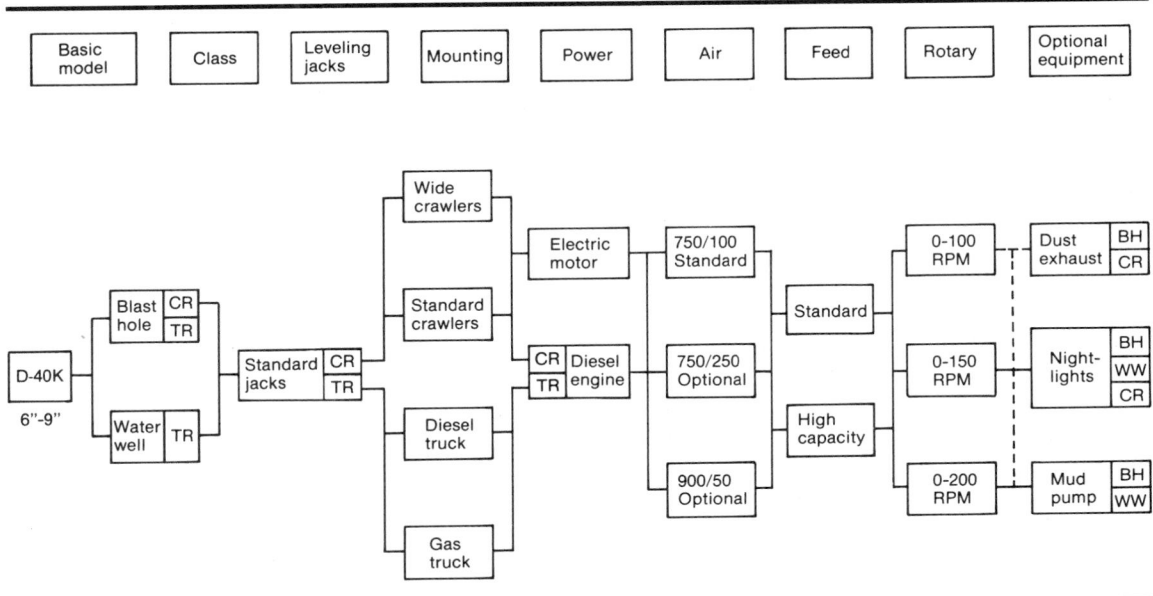

Future Products. The technology of rock drilling and the history of the rotary drill suggest that evolution of drilling equipment will be continuous. Rapidrill believes that in 5–10 years the development of western coal will require "large" drills with higher capacity than that of those presently planned in our product line and that this will present a new, additional (not replacement) market for drills.

Constant desire for improved productivity will eventually create a market for automated operation of drills. Rapidrill plans to be the innovator of such systems and has already discussed a possible joint development program with a hydraulic component manufacturer.

Finally, new methods for mineral exploration and sampling may offer opportunities for innovative drill equipment design. Rapidrill plans to keep abreast of such developments and be an industry leader in the development of any new drilling equipment that might be required.

6. MANUFACTURING PLAN

As previously discussed, Rapidrill's rotary drill will be essentially an engineered package with a high content of purchased components. The nature of the manufacturing efforts consists primarily of fabricating welded mounting and mast structures and assembly of all components into a final drill. Other than minor welding and painting equipment, virtually no high-cost machine tool or other fixed investments are required. Assembly can be accomplished in simple warehouse-type structures with a modest overhead crane capacity. Such structures are available for lease or purchase in virtually every industrial area of the United States.

While most of the value added by the packager consists of this assembly labor, unit production volume is not sufficient to warrant the high fixed cost of a modern assembly line facility (and no present manufacturer has such a facility). Minimizing manufacturing costs then makes low hourly labor rates, worker productivity, efficiency, and flexibility paramount considerations. Such characteristics are not typical of the operations of present competitive drill manufacturers whose plants are rigidly unionized and located in highly industrialized, high-labor-rate locations.

A study by Rapidrill's principals has been conducted to identify the effects of different plant locations on the manufacturing costs of rotary drills. In its evaluation of alternative plant locations, this study considered: labor rates, labor law, labor availability and attitudes, freight and transportation costs, centers of markets, taxes, travel access, facility costs, utility costs, suitability for professional staff, and other pertinent considerations. It concluded that the manufacturing requirements for Rapidrill's operation would best be met in a southeastern city of modest size, in a state with right-to-work laws. After evaluation of several potential locations and detailed analysis of final candidates, Rapidrill has selected the Nashville, Tennessee, area for its plant location. Nashville is well located with respect to rotary drill markets.

Table 10 illustrates some of the results of this evaluation study. It shows the net cost of typical operations in Nashville and compares these to the costs of equivalent operations at the locations of present major drill manufacturers. For the comparisons of Table 10, which shows an average cost advantage of close to 3

Table 10
Comparison of Rapidrill's Operations at Nashville, Tennessee, with Major Competitors' Locations
(base = $10 million annual Rapidrill sales to distributors: 86,000 productive hours)

Location	BLS Index	Direct Labor Cost ($/hr.)	Productive Hour Cost L and OH	Total Cost L and OH (000s)	Freight In and Out (000s)	Total Value-Added Cost (000s)	Nashville Advantage $ (000s)	Nashville Advantage Percent Rapidrill Sales
Nashville	74.2	$2.70	$12.45	$1,071	$196	$1,267	Base	Base
Competitors								
Dallas (G-D)	90.6	3.30	14.70	1,264	191	1,455	$188	2.3%
Franklin, Pa. (ITI)	105.6	3.85	16.70	1,436	150	1,586	319	4.0
Birmingham (Joy)	87.3	3.18	14.25	1,226	157	1,383	116	1.4
West Virginia (I-R)	94.0	3.42	15.26	1,312	139	1,451	184	2.3
Milwaukee (B-E)	104.3	3.79	16.70	1,436	144	1,580	313	3.9
New Jersey (I-R)	98.6	3.59	15.82	1,360	163	1,523	256	3.2
Average:							$229	2.8%

Legend:

G-D = Gardner-Denver
ITI = Indiana Tool, Inc.
Joy = Joy Manufacturing
I-R = Ingersol-Rand

B-E = Bucyrus-Erie
BLS = Bureau of Labor Statistics
L = Labor
OH = Factory overhead (rent, heat, light, etc.)

percent for Rapidrill operations in Nashville, an equal number of productive hours and equal labor productivity and efficiency were assumed for all locations.

Improvements in efficiency and productivity are, in fact, of equal importance and represent a higher potential for cost savings than do the lower labor rates themselves. Estimates of improvements of 20 percent to 25 percent in productivity for a well-managed, open-shop fabrication and assembly operation in Nashville are considered conservative. With typical value added of about 16 percent of manufacturing cost for present rotary drill manufacturers, such productivity improvements would result in an additional 3 percent to 4 percent decrease in total manufacturing costs. For subsequent financial analysis these productivity improvements were assumed to be achieved by Rapidrill over a three-year period, utilizing a 90 percent "learning curve" on assembly operations.

Rapidrill's manufacturing operations will also seek further efficiencies through the use of modern production, inventory control, and purchasing systems that will be focused on reducing the costs of buying, storing, and handling the large content of purchased components used in rotary drills. The implementation of these systems will be significantly aided by employing "parts grouping" techniques (see Section 5) in the product line design. Parts grouping will allow flexibility in assembly scheduling and will minimize inventory requirements.

The total result of such manufacturing operations will be minimum capital equipment and inventory investment and manufacturing costs (after sufficient "learning curve" improvement) from 6 percent to 8 percent below those of present competition. This manufacturing cost reduction, together with the anticipated 3 percent to 4 percent reduction in Rapidrill's selling expenses as compared to those of its competitors, means that Rapidrill's manufacturing and selling costs should be from 9 percent to 12 percent less than those of its competitors. Cost advantages of this order in products with a high purchased content could give Rapidrill a strong competitive advantage.

7. SCHEDULE

Figure 6

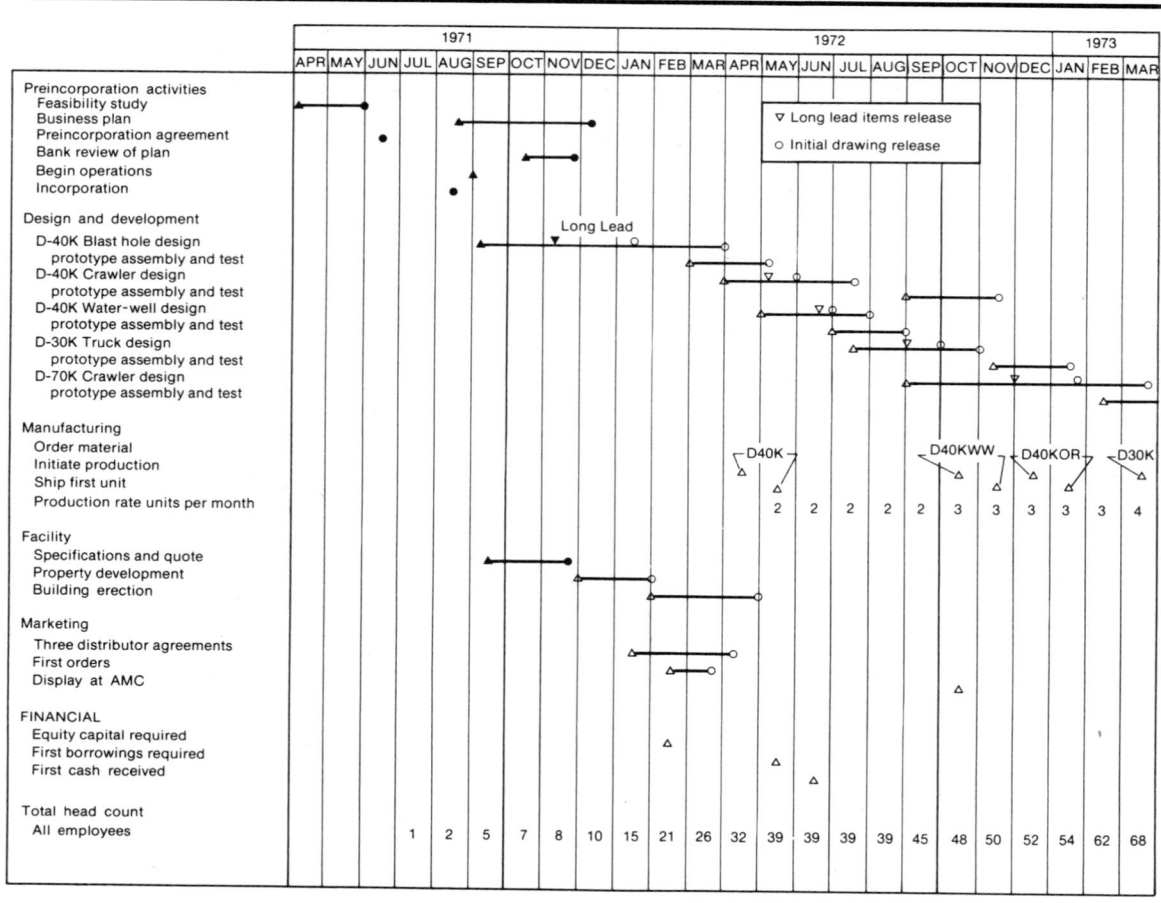

8. RISKS

As with any new venture, there are risks in Rapidrill's plans. Recognition of these risks, evaluation of their severity, and proper contingency planning for their possible occurrences have been considered in Rapidrill's planning.

While the following discussion of specific risks is not intended to be all-inclusive, it is felt to cover those of significant possible impact. Risks are *not* listed in order of probability of occurrence or of degree of possible impact.

1. *Risk:* Legal action by Indiana Tool, Inc. (ITI).

Evaluation: While the departure of its key team members has jeopardized ITI's rotary drill market dominance, it is the opinion of Rapidrill's counsel that no cause for action by ITI has been created. Letters between legal counsel for ITI and Rapidrill have been exchanged, and the prognosis is that the likelihood of further action by ITI is slim.

Contingency: Rapidrill has had policy guidelines prepared by counsel and plans no actions that could be construed as unfair competition or breach of ITI's legal rights.

2. *Risk:* Price cutting by competitors.

Evaluation: Market will absorb everyone's capacity for the next few years. At that time Rapidrill will have sufficient volume to be price competitive with any of its competitors. Historically, existing manufacturers have not responded to new competition with price cuts.

Contingency: Financial planning included generous contingencies in unit costs. If costs are close to present estimates, Rapidrill has immediate ability to reduce its prices and remain profitable.

3. *Risk:* Cost estimates exceeded by engineering and/or manufacturing.

Evaluation: Design has progressed sufficiently so that 60 percent of purchased components are firmly priced. Rapidrill's principals have extensive experience with design and manufacturing start-up phases, so estimates should be accurate.

Contingency: In financials, 10 percent was added to material cost estimates and 100 percent excess assembly time was added to year 1 estimates, and 80 percent to year 2, giving Rapidrill leeway on meeting actual costs.

4. *Risk:* Machine doesn't meet specification performance.

Evaluation: This is considered a low-risk item. Engineering track record of F. T. Samuels is excellent; however, rapid acceptance of Rapidrill units will depend on immediate support of unit in the field.

Contingency: In addition to $25,000 allocated to development testing (2½ times normal), financial planning includes expenditure of $10,000 per unit in field support of first eight units (about five times past experience levels), then progressively less but allowance for significant warranty expenditures. Additional $20,000 allocated for a demonstration program could be directed to development.

5. *Risk:* Sales forecasts not achieved.

Evaluation: Analysis shows a low break-even level (less than 50 percent of year 2 forecasts), and some fixed costs can be delayed to reduce further the break-even if sales are falling well below forecasts.

Contingency: Procurements will be committed for lower-level production than forecast but at forecast rate, allowing time for additional procurements within lead time if sales trend to forecast levels or higher.

6. *Risk:* Delays in design and/or manufacturing.

Evaluation: Delays in design unlikely for first unit since most design work now complete. Delays in either can be minimized to about $20,000 additional cash requirement per month delay. Financial plan shows cash balance of $64,000 for first year-end, allowing, in worst case, a two- to three-month delay.

Contingency: Watch design and manufacturing schedule closely, and expedite procurements closely. An additional $60,000 borrowing is available to Rapidrill in year 2 within debt-equity guidelines; so another three-month contingency could be available.

7. *Risk:* Long-lead-time procurements encountered.

Evaluation: Trucks, diesel engines, compresoors, hydraulic components are on order, with satisfactory shipments promised. Rapidrill's early requirements, two per month, can be met with minor disturbance even if vendors have major problems. Vendors have confirmed this.

Contingency: Closely follow procurements—some purchased components have four- to five-month lead times—and we cannot afford to order backup from other vendors.

8. *Risk:* Economy downturn or fuel shortage affecting sales.

Evaluation: Energy shortages should enhance the sale of drills to mining markets and accelerate rather than deter Rapidrill's growth.

Contingency: Watch signals closely; trend should be apparent before manufacturing is started.

9. *Risk:* Tight money affecting Rapidrill's ability to obtain the required line of credit.

Evaluation: Plan has been reviewed by three largest banks in Nashville, which supported financial assumptions regarding borrowing. Money supply has eased somewhat since those commitments.

Contingency: Secure committed lines of credit in excess of forecast requirements to the limit of reasonable debt-equity ratios.

10. *Risk:* Legislation to curtail strip mining.

Evaluation: In light of the forecast energy shortage and the fact that 10 percent of the nation's energy presently comes from surface-mined coal, this eventuality is considered small.

Contingency: Diversion of initial selling efforts to other market segments. Planned sales of first two years could be achieved in several other market segments.

9. FINANCIAL PLAN

Introduction

Using the sales levels and rotary drill prices developed by the marketing forecast, detailed estimates of material, labor, and burden generated by engineering and manufacturing, and estimates of design, development, and general sales and administrative expenses, detailed financial statements were drawn up depicting the forecast results of Rapidrill's operations for the five years from 1972 to 1976, inclusive. The following assumptions were used in arriving at the results:

1. All operations are performed in a leased facility in Nashville, Tennessee. Labor rates, shipping costs, lease rates, etc., used are consistent with the area.
2. All projections are in 1971 dollars.
3. Interest payments are computed at 15 percent on borrowings. Borrowings will be provided by bank lines of credit.
4. Balance sheet assumptions are:

a. Accounts receivable: 30-day collection through mid-1975; 45 days thereafter.
b. Notes receivable: Average 36-month repayment schedule at 10 percent simple interest. Financing by Rapidrill will commence in the fourth quarter of 1975. Earlier financing to be accomplished utilizing an independent financial institution. Cavanagh Leasing Corporation has expressed interest.
c. Inventories: Four turns per year.
d. Accounts payable: 60-day average through 1975; 36–40 days thereafter.
5. Income taxes include state and federal.
6. Loss for 1972 carried forward and deducted from 1973 income in accordance with IRS Code Section 172.
7. Organizational expenses and initial design cost, estimated to be $14,000 and $240,000, respectively, have been expensed.

Pro forma financial statements are presented as Exhibits 1 through 9, and Exhibit 10 is a break-even chart.

Exhibit 1

RAPIDRILL CORPORATION
Sales and Earnings Forecasts
Fiscal Years Ended September 30, 1972–1976
(000s omitted)

	1972	*1973*	*1974*	*1975*	*1976*
Sales:					
Units	$ 730	$3,827	$6,596	$ 9,067	$11,400
Spares	51	383	989	1,813	2,280
Total	781	4,210	7,585	10,880	13,680
Cost of sales:					
Material	434	2,204	3,722	5,269	6,620
Labor	16	98	201	258	323
Burden	98	387	500	589	631
Total	548	2,689	4,423	6,116	7,574
Gross margin	233	1,521	3,162	4,764	6,106
Percent	29.8	36.1	41.7	43.8	44.6
Selling and marketing	77	430	648	991	1,246
Engineering	74	134	273	425	534
Administration and general	306	483	705	1,103	1,387
Total	457	1,047	1,626	2,519	3,167
Earnings before interest and taxes	(224)	474	1,536	2,245	2,939
Interest expense (income)	5	48	52	(3)	(64)
Earnings before federal and state taxes	(229)	426	1,484	2,248	3,003
Federal and state taxes		214	751	1,137	1,519
Net earnings before extraordinary item	(229)	212	733	1,111	1,484
Extraordinary item—reduction in federal income taxes resulting from carryover of prior years operating losses		114			
Net earnings	$(229)	$ 326	$ 733	$ 1,111	$ 1,484
Percent sales before extraordinary item		5.0	9.7	10.2	10.8
Percent sales after extraordinary item		7.7	9.7	10.2	10.8

Exhibit 2

RAPIDRILL CORPORATION
Monthly Sales and Earnings Forecasts
Fiscal Year Ended September 30, 1972
(000s omitted)

	Oct.	Nov.	Dec.	Jan.	Feb.	Mar.	Apr.	May	June	July	Aug.	Sept.	Total
Sales:													
Units								$92	$182	$92	$182	$182	$730
Spares								6	13	6	13	13	51
								98	195	98	195	195	781
Cost of sales:													
Material								54	109	54	109	108	434
Labor								2	4	2	4	4	16
Burden								12	24	12	25	25	98
								68	137	68	138	137	548
Gross margin								30	58	30	57	58	232
Percent								30.6	29.7	30.6	29.2	29.7	29.8
Selling and marketing						$2	$13	13	13	14	14	15	84
Engineering	$5	$2	$3	$6	$4	7	7	7	8	9	9	10	77
Administration and general	45*	15	14	16	16	17	28	39	29	29	29	29	296
	50	17	17	22	20	26	48	59	50	52	52	54	457
Earnings before interest and taxes	(50)	(17)	(17)	(22)	(20)	(26)	(48)	(20)	8	(22)	5	5	(224)
Interest expense (income)										1	2	2	5
Earnings before federal and state taxes	(50)	(17)	(17)	(22)	(20)	(26)	(48)	(20)	8	(23)	3	3	(229)
Federal and state taxes													
Net earnings	$(50)	$(17)	$(17)	$(22)	$(20)	$(26)	$(48)	$(20)	$8	$(23)	$3	$3	$(229)

*Note: Includes expenses during five months prior to incorporation.

Exhibit 3

RAPIDRILL CORPORATION
Quarterly Sales and Earnings Forecasts
Fiscal Years Ended September 30, 1973–1974
(000s omitted)

	1973					1974				
	1Q	2Q	3Q	4Q	Total	1Q	2Q	3Q	4Q	Total
Sales:										
Units	$764	$874	$1,126	$1,063	$3,827	$1,382	$1,657	$2,086	$1,471	$6,596
Spares	76	88	113	106	383	207	249	313	220	989
	840	962	1,239	1,169	4,210	1,589	1,906	2,399	1,691	7,585
Cost of sales:										
Material	464	516	641	583	2,204	775	937	1,175	834	3,722
Labor	13	20	32	33	98	42	51	61	47	201
Burden	83	88	113	103	387	103	126	152	119	500
	560	624	786	719	2,689	921	1,114	1,388	1,000	4,423
Gross margin	280	338	453	450	1,521	668	792	1,011	691	3,162
Percent	33.3	35.1	36.6	38.5	36.1	42.0	41.6	42.1	40.9	41.7
Selling and marketing	97	98	127	108	430	136	163	205	144	648
Engineering	33	33	33	35	134	68	68	69	68	273
Administration and general	115	117	124	127	483	176	177	176	176	705
	245	248	284	270	1,047	380	408	450	388	1,626

Exhibit 3 (concluded)

	1973					1974				
	1Q	2Q	3Q	4Q	Total	1Q	2Q	3Q	4Q	Total
Earnings before interest and taxes	35	90	169	180	474	288	384	561	303	1,536
Interest expense (income)	11	13	13	11	48	13	18	14	7	52
Earnings before federal and state taxes	24	77	156	169	426	275	366	547	296	1,484
Federal and state taxes	12	39	78	85	214	139	185	277	150	751
Net earnings before extraordinary item	12	38	78	84	212	136	181	270	146	733
Extraordinary item— reduction in federal income taxes resulting from carryover of prior years operating losses	6	21	42	45	114					
Net earnings	$ 18	$ 59	$ 120	$ 129	$ 326	$ 136	$ 181	$ 270	$ 146	$ 733
Percent sales before extraordinary item	1.4	4.0	6.3	7.2	5.0	8.6	9.5	11.2	8.6	9.7
Percent sales after extraordinary item	2.1	6.1	9.7	11.0	7.7	8.6	9.5	11.2	8.6	9.7

Exhibit 4

RAPIDRILL CORPORATION
Pro Forma Cash Flows
Fiscal Years Ended September 30, 1972–1976
(000s omitted)

	1972	1973	1974	1975	1976
Cash receipts:					
Accounts receivable	$ 586	$3,824	$7,320	$10,379	$13,330
Notes receivable					200
Interest				5	64
Total	586	3,824	7,320	10,384	13,594
Cash disbursements:					
Purchases of materials	504	2,178	4,015	5,587	6,698
Manufacturing labor	56	224	418	552	617
Manufacturing overhead	74	183	185	222	225
Warranty expense	20	60	100	100	100
Administration, general, selling, and engineering	453	1,044	1,624	2,518	3,166
Equipment	28	12	12	10	10
Federal and state taxes		100	751	1,137	1,519
Interest	5	48	52	2	
Total	1,140	3,849	7,157	10,128	12,335
Cash provided (drained) by operations	(554)	(25)	163	256	1,259
Investment in long-term notes receivable				163	1,275
Bank borrowing (repayment)	250	(25)	(150)	(75)	
Sale of common stock	280				
Net increase (decrease) in cash balance	$1 (24)	$ (50)	$ 13	$ 18	$ (16)

Exhibit 5

RAPIDRILL CORPORATION
Pro Forma Monthly Cash Flows
Fiscal Year Ended September 30, 1972
(000s omitted)

													1972
	Oct.	Nov.	Dec.	Jan.	Feb.	Mar.	Apr.	May	June	July	Aug.	Sept.	Total
Cash receipts:													
Accounts and notes received...									$ 98	$195	$ 98	$195	$ 586
Interest													
Total									98	195	98	195	586
Cash disbursements:													
Purchases of materials							$ 52		113	115	113	111	504
Manufacturing labor					$ 1	$ 4	8	$ 8	8	9	9	9	56
Manufacturing overhead					11	13	9	9	9	9	7	7	74
Warranty expense							2	3	4	3	4	4	20
Administration, general, selling, and engineering...	$44	$22	$17	$22	19	26	48	49	48	55	50	53	453
Equipment	2			1		10	10			5			28
Federal and state taxes													
Interest										1	2	2	5
Total	46	22	17	23	31	53	129	69	182	197	185	186	1,140
Cash provided (drained) by operations	(46)	(22)	(17)	(23)	(31)	(53)	(129)	(69)	(84)	(2)	(87)	9	(554)
Investment in long-term notes receivable													
Bank borrowing (repayment)								50	100		100		250
Sale of common stock		40			240								280
Net increase (decrease) in cash balance	$(46)	$18	$(17)	$(23)	$209	$(53)	$(129)	$(19)	$ 16	$ (2)	$ 13	$ 9	$ 24
Opening cash balance	88*	42	60	43	20	229	176	47	28	44	42	55	
Closing cash balance 88*	42	60	43	20	229	176	47	28	44	42	55		

*Initial cash balance from investments of principals made prior to October 1, 1971. No corporate expenditures prior to October 1, 1971.

Exhibit 6

RAPIDRILL CORPORATION
Pro Forma Quarterly Cash Flows
Fiscal Years Ended September 30, 1973–1974
(000s omitted)

	1973					1974				
	1Q	2Q	3Q	4Q	Total	1Q	2Q	3Q	4Q	Total
Cash receipts:										
Accounts and notes received	$719	$890	$1,008	$1,207	$3,824	$1,375	$1,848	$2,052	$2,045	$7,320
Interest										
Total	719	890	1,008	1,207	3,824	1,375	1,848	2,052	2,045	7,320
Cash disbursements:										
Purchases of materials	453	531	561	633	2,178	852	1,034	1,028	1,101	4,015
Manufacturing labor	31	45	74	74	224	82	111	112	113	418
Manufacturing overhead	38	52	50	43	183	45	45	48	47	185
Warranty expense	12	14	17	17	60	22	25	26	27	100
Administration, general, selling, and engineering	243	248	283	270	1,044	379	408	449	388	1,624

Exhibit 6 *(concluded)*

	1973					1974				
	1Q	*2Q*	*3Q*	*4Q*	*Total*	*1Q*	*2Q*	*3Q*	*4Q*	*Total*
Equipment................	5	3	2	2	12	5	2	5		12
Federal and state taxes	25	25	25	25	100	191	191	191	178	751
Interest	11	13	13	11	48	13	18	14	7	52
Total	818	931	1,025	1,075	3,849	1,589	1,834	1,873	1,861	7,157
Cash provided (drained) by operations.............	(99)	(41)	(17)	132	(25)	(214)	14	179	184	163
Investment in long-term notes receivable										
Bank borrowing (repayment)..............	100			(125)	(25)	250		(200)	(200)	(150)
Sale of common stock........	—	—	—	—		—	—	—	—	
Net increase (decrease) in cash balance	$ 1	$ (41)	$ (17)	$ 7	$ (50)	$ 36	$ 14	$ (21)	$ (16)	$ 13
Opening cash balance.........	$ 64	$ 65	$ 24	$ 7		$ 14	$ 50	$ 64	$ 43	
Closing cash balance..........	65	24	7	14		50	64	43	27	

Exhibit 7

RAPIDRILL CORPORATION
Pro Forma Balance Sheets
Fiscal Years Ended September 30, 1971–1976
(000s omitted)

	1971	*1972*	*1973*	*1974*	*1975*	*1976*
Current assets:						
Cash	$88	$ 64	$ 14	$ 27	$ 45	$ 29
Accounts receivable		195	581	846	1,360	1,710
Notes receivable.............................					150	1,225
Inventory		393	563	824	1,315	1,502
Total		652	1,158	1,697	2,870	4,466
Property, plant, and equipment cost..............		28	40	52	62	72
Less: Depreciation		5	13	23	33	43
		23	27	29	29	29
Total assets....................................	$88	$675	$1,185	$1,726	$2,899	$4,495
Current liabilities:						
Accounts payable and accrued expenses........		$286	$ 495	$ 453	$ 590	$ 702
Bank loans payable		250	225	75		
Equity:						
Capital stock—common 10¢ par value, 720,000 authorized shares	$37	69	69	69	69	69
Paid-in surplus..............................	51	299	299	299	299	299
Retained earnings...........................		(229)	97	830	1,941	3,425
	88	139	465	1,198	2,309	3,793
Total liabilities and equity......................	$88	$675	$1,185	$1,726	$2,899	$4,495

Exhibit 8

RAPIDRILL CORPORATION
Pro Forma Monthly Balance Sheets
Fiscal Year Ended September 30, 1972
(000s omitted)

	Oct.	Nov.	Dec.	Jan.	Feb.	Mar.	Apr.	May	June	July	Aug.	Sept.
Current assets:												
Cash	$40	$18	$43	$ 20	$229	$176	$ 47	$ 28	$ 44	$ 42	$ 55	$ 64
Accounts receivable								98	195	98	195	195
Notes receivable												
Inventory					13	83	216	283	282	347	337	393
	40	18	43	20	242	259	263	409	521	487	587	652
Property, plant, and equipment—												
at cost	2	2	2	3	3	13	23	23	23	28	28	28
Less: Depreciation						1	2	2	3	4	4	5
	2	2	2	3	3	12	21	21	20	24	24	23
Total assets	$42	$20	$45	$23	$245	$271	$284	$430	$541	$511	$611	$675
Current liabilities:												
Accounts payable and accrued expenses	$ 6	$ 1	$ 1	$ 1	$ 3	$ 55	$116	$232	$235	$228	$225	$286
Bank loans payable								50	150	150	250	250
Equity:												
Capital stock—common 10¢ par value, 720,000 shares authorized	37	45	45	45	69	69	69	69	69	69	69	69
Paid-in surplus	51	83	83	83	299	299	299	299	299	299	299	299
Retained earnings	(50)	(67)	(84)	(106)	(126)	(152)	(200)	(220)	(212)	(235)	(232)	(229)
	36	19	44	22	242	216	168	148	156	133	136	139
Total liabilities and equity	$42	$20	$45	$23	$245	$271	$284	$430	$541	$511	$611	$675

Exhibit 9

RAPIDRILL CORPORATION
Pro Forma Quarterly Balance Sheets
Fiscal Years Ended September 30, 1973–1974
(000s omitted)

	1973				1974			
	1Q	2Q	3Q	4Q	1Q	2Q	3Q	4Q
Current assets:								
Cash	$ 65	$ 24	$ 7	$ 14	$ 50	$ 64	$ 43	$ 27
Accounts receivable	316	388	619	581	795	853	1,200	846
Notes receivable								
Inventory	439	477	424	563	651	630	538	824
	820	889	1,050	1,158	1,496	1,547	1,781	1,697
Property, plant, and equipment—at cost	33	36	38	40	45	47	52	52
Less: Depreciation	7	9	11	13	15	18	20	23
	26	27	27	27	30	29	32	29
Total assets	$846	$916	$1,077	$1,185	$1,526	$1,576	$1,813	$1,726
Current liabilities:								
Accounts payable and accrued expenses	$339	$350	$ 391	$ 495	$ 450	$ 319	$ 486	$ 453
Bank loans payable	350	350	350	225	475	475	275	75
Equity:								
Capital stock—common 10¢ par value, 720,000 shares authorized	69	69	69	69	69	69	69	69
Paid-in surplus	299	299	299	299	299	299	299	299
Retained earnings	(211)	(152)	(32)	97	233	414	684	830
	157	215	336	465	601	782	1,052	1,198
Total liabilities and equity	$846	$916	$1,077	$1,185	$1,526	$1,576	$1,813	$1,726

Exhibit 10
Rapidrill Corporation—1972–1973 Break-Even Analysis

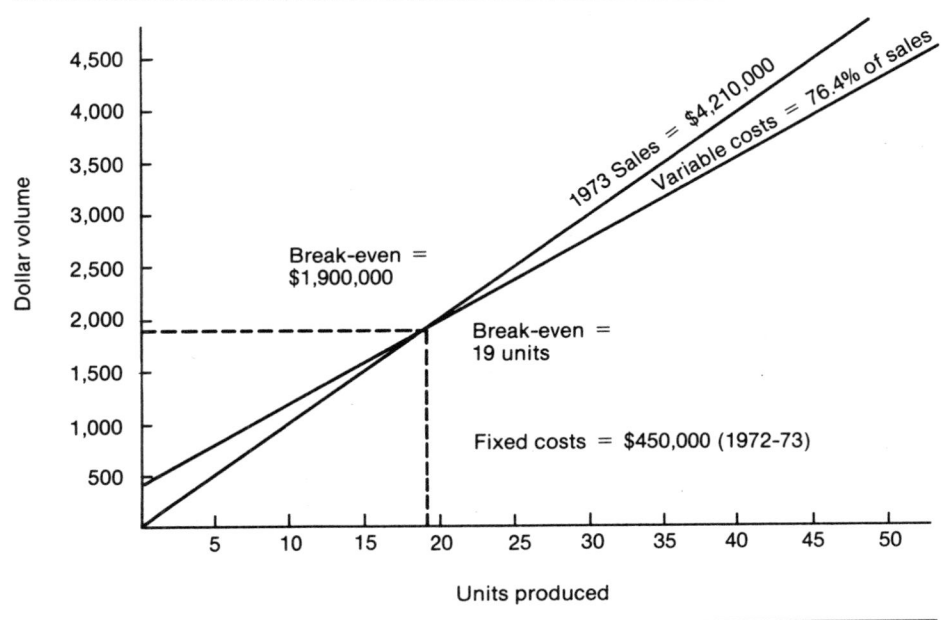

Financial Performance

1. *Sales and Earnings Forecasts* (see Exhibits 1 through 3): Sales of Rapidrill are projected to increase from $730,000 in 1972 to $13,680,000 in 1976. After a projected loss of $229,000 in the first year, after-tax profits are expected to increase from $326,000 in 1973 to $1,484,000 in 1976 (see Exhibit 1). After-tax profit as a percentage of sales is 7.7 percent in the second year of Rapidrill's operation and increases to 10.8 percent in the fifth year. Even if actual sales are one half of those forecast, Rapidrill will be profitable in its second year of operation (see break-even chart, Exhibit 10, and Exhibit 1).

2. *Cash Flow* (see Exhibits 4 through 6): The equity capital raised in this offering, together with the investment of the principals and lines of credit of $250,000 in 1972, $350,000 in 1973, and $475,000 in 1974, should be enough to finance Rapidrill's operations. Ideally, a slightly larger line of credit should be sought to increase Rapidrill's cash in the third and fourth quarters of 1973. Note that the cash flow provided by operations becomes positive in the third year (see Table 14). In the first two years, cash is being used to finance Rapidrill's start-up and working capital. Because bank borrowings are used principally to finance working capital, sales volumes less than forecast will require that less of the line of credit be drawn down.

3. *Balance Sheets* (see Exhibits 7 through 9): Rapidrill's proposed financial plan provides financial strength and liquidity. The lowest ratio of current assets to current liabilities plus bank loans payable is not projected to be less than about 1:2. And much of Rapidrill's inventory consists of standard components and materials that should be readily salable. After the investment of this offering (assumed to be in February 1972), Rapidrill's working capital is estimated not to fall below about $140,000.

Rapidrill's liquidity should hold up reasonably well if sales are somewhat less than forecast. This is because Rapidrill has little invested in fixed assets and bank borrowings are primarily used for working capital. If sales fall from forecasts, current assets, current liabilities, and bank borrowings should tend to drop proportionately and the effect of the sales drop on liquidity or the ratio of current assets to current liabilities plus bank debt should tend to be small.

4. *Break-Even Analysis* (see Exhibit 10): At its currently proposed sales prices and costs, Rapidrill's break-even sales are about 19 units and $1,900,000. Rapidrill recognizes that this may be somewhat high. It is also apparent that a 10 percent increase in Rapidrill's prices would lower the break-even to 12 units and $1,300,000 in sales. Accordingly, Rapidrill will closely watch its competitors' pricing behavior and, if appropriate, consider the possibility of increasing its prices. In any case, if sales volume should drop, it should be possible to lower Rapidrill's fixed cost by cutting back on some of its general and administrative expenses.

Cost Control

Achievement of the financial plan delineated above will depend in significant measure on Rapidrill's ability to control its costs. To do this, Rapidrill's principals will draw on their experience in designing and implementing systems to control the costs of design, development, and manufacturing programs.

Design and development programs will use a job cost reporting system. Each equipment development project will be broken down into subtasks, and labor, overhead, purchased materials, and subcontracting costs will be separately reported for each subtask. Cost reports will be issued every two weeks and the cost and progress to date monitored and compared to budgets. These reports will be monitored by Messrs. Miller, Price, and MacMillan, and weekly meetings will be held to discuss and determine solutions to actual or potential cost problems.

When a drill model (e.g., D–40K) is released for production, a set of standard costs for assembly labor, purchased components, overhead, etc., will be established. Actual costs will be accumulated by subtask and cost category and compared to the standards. Significant differences between actual and standard costs will be evaluated to see if these are due to inefficiencies or are real cost increases. If the former, corrective actions will be identified and taken; if the latter, the standards may need revision. Warranty and field service costs will also be carefully monitored to ensure that Rapidrill's allowance for these is adequate.

Finally, ratio analysis of costs to sale price will be used to identify any cost element that may be deviating significantly from the norms and be cause for concern.

10.   PROPOSED RAPIDRILL OFFERING

Financing

Rapidrill Corporation is incorporated in the state of Delaware and currently has 720,000 shares of 10 cents par value common voting stock authorized, with 451,000 shares issued as of November 30, 1971.

Rapidrill now intends to raise $240,000 through the sale of 240,000 shares of its common voting stock at $1 per share. The common stock sold in this financing will represent about 35 percent of Rapidrill's outstanding common stock after the offering is completed.

Capitalization

Exhibit 11 shows the capitalization of Rapidrill before and after the proposed offering.

Exhibit 11
Rapidrill Corporation—Present and Proposed Capitalization

Stockholders	Shares Owned Pre-Offering	Shares Owned Post-Offering	Percent Ownership Post-Offering	Investment	Cost per Share
S. A. Price	135,000	135,000	19.6%	$ 20,400	$0.15
M. F. Einman	78,000	78,000	11.3	20,280	0.26
F. T. Samuels	78,000	78,000	11.3	20,280	0.26
G. A. Miller	42,000	42,000	6.1	12,600	0.30
W. D. MacMillan	36,000	36,000	5.2	14,400	0.40
J. Jones*	27,000	27,000	3.9	13,500	0.50
D. Mead*	27,000	27,000	3.9	13,500	0.50
S. Ross*	27,000	27,000	3.9	13,500	0.50
Investors of this offering		240,000	34.8	240,000	1.00
	451,000	691,000	100.0%	$368,460	

*These are the three distributor representatives mentioned in Section 2.

Use and Sources of Funds

The money raised in this offering ($240,000), together with the money raised ($128,460) earlier from the sale of stock to Rapidrill's principals and key employees, will be used primarily to design, fabricate, and test the first D–40K truck-mounted rotary drill and to set up a marketing and distribution system. These $368,000 of equity funds will be supplemented by bank borrowings that will be used to finance inventories and receivables. The bank borrowings reach maximums of $250,000 in 1972, $350,000 in 1973, and $475,000 in 1974 (see Pro Forma Cash Flows and Balance Sheets). Rapidrill expects to have a $600,000 to $700,000 revolving line of credit with Nashville banks and has obtained preliminary approval of such a line of credit. Final approval will be contingent on raising the $240,000 of this offering.

Notes to Balance Sheet

Accounts Receivable

Thirty days. Considered to be 100 percent collectible due to financial strength of customers. These customers have demonstrated prompt and consistent payment of invoices in past associations with Rapidrill's principals. The few drills that have been repossessed have repeatedly been sold in the used market for up to 90 percent of their original selling price, thus limiting the loss from an uncollected receivable. Experience of Rapidrill's principals indicates that with proper credit control, industry-wide losses are insignificant.

Notes Receivable

Range from 12 to 60 months in duration. Usually secured by the equipment. Loss expectancy extremely low.

Inventory

Approximately 80 percent value in off-the-shelf, standard, stock items easily returnable; therefore more liquid than custom-specified items.

Accounts Payable

Sixty days, 1972 through second quarter of 1973. Vendors have indicated a willingness to work on these terms during Rapidrill's start-up period.

Loans

Currently negotiating with local banks for a $600,000–700,000 revolving line of credit. Already have had preliminary approvals of loans and now preparing a package to be presented to the credit committees. Final approval contingent on raising $240,000 of this offer.

Retained Earnings

No dividend payments are planned during program.

Rapidrill has 29,000 shares of common stock authorized but unissued. These shares will be used to attract additional management personnel or reserved for future use as stock options to key employees.

Name _____

Date _____

13.11 ACTION STEPS FOR PREPARING A BUSINESS PLAN

This goal-setting exercise is intended to produce a "do list" of very specific tasks that must be accomplished to complete your business plan.[7]

A review of all previous self-assessment and goal-setting exercises in Chapter 9 should be a first step for this exercise. By this time you know how to lay out your goals in specific time-phased and measurable form. We suggest that you use peers and business associates to test the realism, timing, and priorities of your action steps. In doing this, you should review the opportunity screening of your venture and consider which aspects of your venture planning need the most attention and work.

[7]Members of the same venture team should complete this unit working alone at first. They should then work together to integrate their "do lists" and to reach agreement on priorities and responsibilities.

To begin this exercise, list all the tasks that must be accomplished to prepare your business plan starting next week and for four to six weeks thereafter.

List each task in as specific and detailed a form as possible. Break the tasks down to phone calls, meetings, trips, papers written, etc. Try to think of the small tasks that have to be done before the major task can be accomplished (e.g., a trip may be a task, but a series of phone calls may be necessary two weeks earlier to set up the trip). Show who is responsible for each task and when that task will be completed.

Be as specific as possible, and be on the alert for conflicts and lack of reality in your time estimates.

PREPARATION OF DETAILED BUSINESS PLAN

Action Steps	Completion Date	Person Responsible	Priority

Now take a few minutes to place the above-listed action steps on the calendar on the next page. List the action step on the left, with the initials of the person responsible next to the action step. Then place an *x* on the calendar date according to each action step's completion.

When you have placed all of the action steps on the calendar, look carefully for conflicts or lack of realism. Are there any conflicts with your other business or personal activities or those of your associates? Does each of your team members have enough time to accomplish the tasks for which he or she is responsible?

Name _____

Date _____

Week	*1*	*2*	*3*	*4*	*5*	*6*	*7*	*8*	*9*	*10*
Action Step										

The Business Plan Guide

14

He who deliberates fully before taking a step will spend his entire life on one leg.

Chinese Proverb

14.1 RESULTS EXPECTED

This chapter presents detailed guidelines for preparing a business plan. These build on guidelines that have been widely used by venture capitalists and entrepreneurs seeking to launch high-potential ventures. Upon completion of the chapter, you will have:

1. Examined the detailed content of a business plan and what to include in it.
2. Examined an approach to integrating the Lotus 1–2–3 spreadsheet capability with the Robert Morris Associates financial data to improve and facilitate your financial projections.
3. Prepared yourself and your team to write your business plan.

14.2 PRESESSION PREPARATION

Review the previous chapter on developing a business plan and any updates on your Opportunity Screening Guide (with your teammates, if you have any).

14.3 REVIEW OF THE BUSINESS PLAN GUIDE

The original version of the guide was developed at Venture Founders Corporation by our cofounders Leonard E. Smollen and Brian Haslett. It has been used widely for over a dozen years by entrepreneurs and venture capitalists in the United States, Canada, the United Kingdom, and Sweden. The original version leaned heavily toward technology-based, manufacturing businesses. This revised version, developed by Jeffry A. Timmons, builds on the earlier document and its use in our venture capital activities, in his New Venture Creation and Opportunity Analysis and Venture Capital courses, and in his work and research with high-potential ventures and venture capitalists over the past dozen years.

The revised version seeks to retain the many valuable features of the previous guide, while making it more accommodating to nontechnology and non-manufacturing ventures. It also attempts to establish a closer link to the "opportunity focus" and to the concept of a start-up and growth strategy. Finally, it integrates the use of new microcomputer spreadsheet software and the Robert Morris Associates data to facilitate more realistic, yet less agonizing, preparation of the financial projections.

14.4   CONTENTS OF THE GUIDE

Cover Page

I. *Executive Summary*
  A. Summary Description of the Business
  B. The Opportunity and Strategy
  C. The Target Market and Projections
  D. The Competitive Advantages
  E. The Economics, Profitability, and Harvest Potential
  F. The Team
  G. The Offering

II. *The Industry, the Company, and Its Products or Services*
  A. The Industry
  B. The Company
  C. The Products or Services
  D. Entry and Growth Strategy

III. *Market Research and Analysis*
  A. Customers
  B. Market Size and Trends
  C. Competition
  D. Estimated Market Share and Sales
  E. Ongoing Market Evaluation

IV. *The Economics of the Business*
  A. Gross and Operating Margins
  B. Profit Potential and Durability
  C. Fixed, Variable, and Semivariable Costs
  D. Months to Break-Even
  E. Months to Reach Positive Cash Flow

V. *Marketing Plan*
  A. Overall Marketing Strategy
  B. Pricing
  C. Sales Tactics
  D. Service and Warranty Policies
  E. Advertising and Promotion
  F. Distribution

VI. *Design and Development Plans*
  A. Development Status and Tasks
  B. Difficulties and Risks
  C. Product Improvement and New Products

      D. Costs

      E. Proprietary Issues

  VII. *Manufacturing and Operations Plan*

      A. Geographic Location

      B. Facilities and Capacity Improvements

      C. Strategy and Plans

      D. Regulatory and Other Compliances and Approvals and Environmental Issues

 VIII. *Management Team*

      A. Organization

      B. Key Management Personnel

      C. Management Compensation and Ownership

      D. Other Investors

      E. Incentives, Vesting, Employment Agreements

      F. Board of Directors

      G. Other Shareholders, Rights and Restrictions

      H. Supporting Professional Advisers and Services

   IX. *Overall Schedule*

    X. *Critical Risks and Problems*

   XI. *The Financial Plan*

      A. Profit and Loss Forecasts

      B. Pro Forma Cash Flow Analysis

      C. Pro Forma Balance Sheets

      D. Break-Even Chart

      E. Cost Control

  XII. *Proposed Company Offering*

      A. Desired Financing

      B. Securities Offering

      C. Capitalization

      D. Use of Funds

 XIII. *Spreadsheets and Financial Exhibits*

      Exhibit 1. Pro Forma Income Statement

      Exhibit 2. Pro Forma Cash Flows

      Exhibit 3. Pro Forma Balance Sheets

      Exhibit 4. Break-Even Chart

 XIV. *Appendixes*

      Could include such items as:

      A. Lists, specs, pictures of products, systems, software

      B. List of customers, suppliers, references

      C. Appropriate location factors, facilities, or technical analyses

      D. Independent reports by technical experts, consultants

      E. Detailed résumés of founders, key managers

      F. Any critical regulatory, environmental or other compliances, licenses, or approvals

14.5 THE BUSINESS PLAN GUIDE

COVER PAGE

Name of Company
Address
Telephone Number
Date

Securities Offered:

This business plan has been submitted on a confidential basis solely for the benefit of selected, highly qualified investors in connection with the private placement of the above securities and is not for use by any other persons, nor may it be reproduced. By accepting delivery of this plan, the recipient agrees to return this copy to the Corporation at the address listed above if the recipient does not undertake to subscribe to the offering.

I. EXECUTIVE SUMMARY

The principal focus here is to clearly articulate the opportunity conditions and why they exist, who will execute the opportunity and why they are capable of doing so, and how the firm will gain entry and rapid market penetration. Many investors like to read a one–two-page summary that highlights important features, the founders, and opportunities, in order to determine quickly whether or not the venture described is of interest. Does the summary of your venture mirror the "attractive criteria" shown in Exhibit 3.3?

The summary is the last section of your plan to prepare. As you draft each of the other sections, note the one or two sentences and the key facts and numbers that concisely state your main points.

Leave plenty of time to prepare an appealing, succinct, and convincing summary. Really successful public speakers have been known to spend one hour of preparation for each minute of their speech. Remember that the summary is the first thing about you and your venture that a would-be investor, banker, or key manager is going to read, so if it is not appealing and compelling, it will also be the last. You may have spent many weeks on the rest of your plan, and it may be very good. However, if the quality does not come through in your summary, you may not get a chance to make a presentation in person at which you can respond to the difficult questions and clarify misunderstandings or misconceptions.

Your summary should contain brief statements (a paragraph or two) covering the following features of your venture:

A. Summary Description of the Business. You should indicate when the company was formed, what it will do, and what is special or unique about its product, service, or technology. Identify any proprietary technology, trade secrets, or unique capabilities that give you an edge in the marketplace. If the company has existed for a few years, a brief summary of its size and progress is in order.

B. The Opportunity and Strategy. This is the most important summary of what the opportunity is, why it is compelling, and the entry strategy that articulates how you plan to exploit the opportunity and gain rapid market acceptance and penetration. It may be presented in "bullets" of key facts, conditions, competitor vulnerabilities, industry trends and other evidence and logic that add up to the opportunity. Note any plans for growth and expansion beyond the entry products or services.

C. The Target Market and Projections. Identify and briefly explain the market opportunity, who the primary customer groups are, and how you plan to reach them. Include information on the size and growth rate for the market segments or niches that you are seeking, your unit and dollar sales estimates, your anticipated market share, and your pricing position. A brief summary of industry-wide trends is also useful.

D. The Competitive Advantages. Indicate the significant competitive edges that you currently enjoy, or that you can create, as a result of your innovative products, services, and strategies; competitors' weaknesses and vulnerabilities; and any other industry conditions.

E. The Economics, Profitability, and Harvest Potential. Summarize the nature of the "forgiving and rewarding economics" of the venture: gross and operating margins, expected profitability, and how durable the profits appear to be; the relevant time frames to attain break-even and positive cash flow; and the expected return on investment. Include key numbers whenever possible.

F. The Team. Summarize the relevant experience of the lead entrepreneur and any team members, noting previous profit and loss, general management experience, and people management experience. Include numbers that show the size of a division, a project, or prior business you ran.

G. The Offering. Briefly indicate the dollar amount of the equity and/or debt financing that you want, how much of your company you are prepared to offer for that financing, and what principal use will be made of the capital.

II. THE INDUSTRY, THE COMPANY, AND ITS PRODUCTS OR SERVICES

The purpose of this section is to give the investor some context in which to fit all that you are about to tell him concerning your product and its market. This section should clearly present the business that you are or will be in, the product you will offer, the nature of your industry, and the opportunities available to exploit your product.

A. The Industry. Present the current status and prospects for the industry in which the proposed business will operate. Discuss any new products or developments, new markets and customers, new requirements, new companies, and any other national or economic trends and factors that could affect the venture's business positively or negatively. Identify the source of all the information you use to describe industry trends.

B. The Company. Describe briefly what business area your company is in, or intends to enter, what products or service it will offer, and who its principal customers are or will be.

By way of background, give the date your venture was incorporated and describe the identification and development of its products and the involvement of the company's principals in that development.

If your company has been in business for several years and is seeking expansion financing, review its history and cite its prior sales and profit performance. If your company has had setbacks or losses in prior years, discuss these and emphasize what has been done and will be done to prevent a recurrence of these difficulties and improve your company's performance.

C. The Products or Services. The potential investor will be vitally interested in exactly what you are going to sell, what kind of product protection you have, and the opportunities and possible drawbacks of your product or service.

1. Description. Describe in detail the products or services to be sold. Discuss the application of each product or service. Describe the primary end use as well as any significant secondary applications. Emphasize any unique features of the product or service, and highlight any differences between what is currently on the market and what you will offer that will account for your market penetration.

Define the present state of development of the product or service. For products, provide a summary of the functional specifications. Include photographs when available.

2. Proprietary Position. Describe any patents, trade secrets, or other proprietary features. Discuss any head start that you might have that would enable you to achieve a favored or entrenched position in your industry.

3. Potential. Describe any features of your product or service that give it an advantage over the competition. Discuss any opportunities for the expansion of the product line or the development of related products or services. Emphasize your opportunities, and explain how you will take advantage of them.

D. Entry and Growth Strategy. The entry strategy is derived from what the opportunity is asking for: how to gain a foothold in the marketplace and secure rapid market penetration. It is also derived from your competitive advantages and from any weaknesses among competitors that you can exploit, such as their lack of innovation, their slow response time, and their full capacity. Indicate key success variables in your marketing plan (e.g., an innovative product or marketing approach) and your pricing, distribution, advertising, and promotion plans. Summarize how fast you intend to grow, to what size in the first five years, and your growth plans beyond your initial products or services.

III. MARKET RESEARCH AND ANALYSIS

The purpose of this section of the plan is to present enough facts to convince the investor-reader that your venture's product or service has a substantial market in a growing industry and can achieve sales in the face of the competition. The discussion and the guidelines given below should help you do this.

This section of the business plan is one of the most difficult to prepare, but it is one of the most important. Almost all subsequent sections of the business plan depend on the sales estimates that are developed in this section. The sales levels predicted by the market research and analysis directly influence the size of the manufacturing operation, the marketing plan, and the amount of debt and equity capital that you will require. Yet, most entrepreneurs seem to have great difficulty in preparing and presenting market research and analyses that will convince potential investors that the venture's sales estimates are sound and attainable.

Because of the importance of market analysis and the critical dependence of other parts of the plan on the sales projections, we generally advise entrepreneurs to prepare this section of the business plan first. We also advise entrepreneurs to take enough time to do this section very well and to check alternative sources of market data. Consult *The Encyclopedia of Small Business Resources,* D. E. Gumpert and J. A. Timmons (New York:

Harper & Row, 1984) for key numbers such as "market size" and "market growth rates."

A. Customers. Discuss who the customers are for the anticipated application of the product or service. Classify potential customers into relatively homogeneous groups (major market segment) having common, identifiable characteristics. For example, an automotive part might be sold to manufacturers and to parts distributors supplying the replacement market.

Who and where are the major purchasers for the product or service in each market segment? What are the bases of their purchase decisions: price, quality, service, personal contacts, political pressures?

List any potential customers who have expressed an interest in the product or service, and indicate why such interest has been expressed. List any potential customers who have shown no interest in the proposed product or service, and explain why this is so. Explain what you will do to overcome negative customer reaction. If you have an existing business, list your principal current customers and discuss the trends in your sales to them.

B. Market Size and Trends. What is the size of the current total market for the product or service offered? This market size should be determined from available market data sources (see Chapter 3) and from a knowledge of the purchases of competing products by potential customers in each major market segment. Discussions with potential distributors, dealers, sales representatives, and customers can be particularly useful in establishing market size and trends. Describe the size of the total market in both units and dollars. If you intend to sell regionally, show the regional market size. Indicate the sources of the data and describe the methods that have been used to establish current market size. State also the credentials of the people who have done the market research.

Describe the potential annual growth of the total market for your product or service for each major customer group. Total market projections should be made for at least three future years. Discuss the major factors affecting market growth (industry trends, socioeconomic trends, government policy, population shifts), and review previous trends of the market. Any differences between past and projected annual growth rates should be explained. Indicate the sources of all the data and describe the methods that have been used to make projections.

C. Competition. Make a realistic assessment of the strengths and weaknesses of competitive products and services, and name the companies that supply them. State the data sources that have been used to determine the products and the strengths of the competition.

Compare competing products or services on the basis of price, performance, service, warranties, and other pertinent features. A table can be an effective way of presenting these data. Discuss briefly the current advantages and disadvantages of competing products and services, and say why they are not meeting customer needs. Indicate any knowledge of competitors' actions that could lead you to new or improved products and an advantageous position.

Review the strengths and weaknesses of the competing companies. Determine and discuss the share of the market of each competitor-company, its sales, distribution, and production capabilities. Review also the profitability of the competing companies and their profit trend.

Which company is the pricing leader? the quality leader? Discuss why any companies have entered or dropped out of the market in recent years.

Discuss your three or four key competitors and why the customer buys from them. From what you know about their operations, explain why you think that you can capture a share of their business. Discuss what makes you think it will be easy or difficult to compete with them.

D. Estimated Market Share and Sales. Summarize what it is about your product or service that will make it salable in the face of current and potential competition.

Identify any major customers that are willing to make purchase commitments. Indicate the extent of those commitments and why they were made. Discuss which customers could be major purchasers in future years and why.

Based on your assessment of the advantages of your product or service, the market size and trends, customers, the competitors and their products, and the trends of sales in prior years, estimate the share of the market and the sales in units and dollars that you will acquire in each of the next three years. The growth of the company sales in units and its estimated market share should be related to the growth of its industry and customers and the strengths and weaknesses of competitors. The data can best be presented in tabular form, as shown below. The assumptions used to estimate market share and sales should be clearly stated. If yours is an existing business, also indicate the total market, your market share, and sales for two prior years.

Sales and Market Share Data

		1st Year				Year	
		1Q	2Q	3Q	4Q	2	3
Estimated total market	Units						
	Dollars						
Estimated market share, %	Units						
	Dollars						
Estimated sales	Units						
	Dollars						

E. Ongoing Market Evaluation. Explain how you will continue to evaluate your target markets so as to assess customer needs and guide product-improvement programs and new product programs, plan for expansions of your production facility, and guide product/service pricing.

IV. THE ECONOMICS OF THE BUSINESS

This section summarizes the economic and financial characteristics of the business. It should convey the fundamental attractiveness of the opportunity, including the apparent magnitude and durability of margins and profits.

A. Gross and Operating Margins. Describe the magnitude of the gross margins (selling price less variable costs) and operating margins for the products and/or services that you are selling. A table can effectively present such data, especially if there are several different products. Reference the appropriate exhibit for details.

B. Profit Potential and Durability.   Describe the magnitude and expected durability of the profit stream that the business will generate. Reference appropriate industry benchmarks, other competitive intelligence, or your own relevant experience. Address the issue of how perishable or durable the profit stream appears to be, and why, such as barriers to entry that you can create and your technological and market lead time. Indicate where the appropriate exhibits can be found in the plan (e.g., Exhibit 1, "Pro Forma Income Statements").

C. Fixed, Variable, and Semivariable Costs.   Provide a detailed summary of these relevant costs, in dollars and percentages as appropriate, for the various products or services you offer. A table can be a useful way to summarize these and to show the relevant industry benchmarks and the sources of your estimates. Reference the appropriate exhibits in the plan (e.g., Exhibit 1).

D. Months to Break-Even.   Given your entry strategy, marketing plan, and proposed financing, how long will it take to reach a break-even sales level? Reference your break-even chart and calculation in Exhibit 2. Note any significant stepwise changes in your break-even that will occur as you grow, and add substantial capacity. This is often overlooked, along with the delays, learning curves, and erosion of margins that accompany the opening of a new facility.

E. Months to Reach Positive Cash Flow.   Given the above strategy and assumptions, when will the venture attain a positive cash flow? When will you run out of cash? Reference your cash flow analyses in Exhibit 3, and note where the detailed assumptions can be found. Be alert to the points made in IVD about any stepwise changes that may affect the economics and cash flow of the venture.

V.   MARKETING PLAN

The marketing plan describes how the sales projections will be attained. It should detail sales projections and the overall marketing strategy, sales and service policies, pricing, distribution, and advertising strategies that will be used to achieve the estimated market share. The marketing plan should describe *what* is to be done, *how* it will be done, and *who* will do it.

A. Overall Marketing Strategy.   Describe the general marketing philosophy and strategy of the company that develops from the market research and evaluation. This should include a discussion of the following: What kinds of customer groups will be targeted for initial intensive selling effort? for later selling efforts? How will specific potential customers in these groups be identified, and how will they be contacted? What features of the product or service—e.g., quality, price, delivery, warranty—will be emphasized to generate sales? Are there any innovative or unusual marketing concepts that will enhance customer acceptance—e.g., leasing where only sales were previously attempted?

Indicate whether the product or service will initially be introduced nationally or on a regional level. If on a regional basis, explain why and indicate any plans for extending sales to other sections of the country. Discuss any seasonal trends and what can be done to promote sales out of season.

Describe any plans to obtain government contracts as a means of supporting product development costs and overhead.

B. Pricing.   Many entrepreneurs have told us that they plan to sell a superior product for less than their competitors charge. This makes a bad impression for two reasons.

First, if their product is as good as they say it is, they must think that they are very poor salespeople if they think they have to offer it at a lower price than the competition. Second, costs tend to be underestimated. If you start out with low costs and prices, there is little room to maneuver; and price hikes will be tougher to realize than price cuts.

The pricing policy is one of the more important decisions that you will have to make. The "price must be right" to penetrate the market, maintain a market position, and produce profits. Devote ample time to considering a number of pricing strategies, and convincingly present the one you select.

Discuss the prices to be charged for your product and service, and compare your pricing policy with those of your major competitors. Discuss the gross profit margin between manufacturing and ultimate sales costs. Indicate whether this margin is large enough to allow for distribution and sales, warranty, service, amortization of development and equipment costs, and price competition—and still allow you a profit.

Explain how the price you set will enable you to:

1. Get the product or service accepted.
2. Maintain and desirably increase your market share in the face of competition.
3. Produce profits.

Justify any price increases over competitive items on the basis of newness, quality, warranty, and service.

If your product is to be priced lower than the products of your competition, explain how you will do this and maintain profitability—e.g., greater effectiveness in manufacturing and distributing the product, lower labor costs, lower overhead, or lower material costs.

Discuss the relationship of price, market share, and profits. For example, a higher price may reduce volume but result in a higher gross profit. Describe any discount allowance for prompt payment or volume purchases.

C. Sales Tactics. Describe the methods that will be used to make sales and distribute the product or service. Will the company use its own sales force? sales representatives? distributors? Can the company use ready-made manufacturers' sales organizations that are already selling related products? Describe both the initial plans and longer-range plans for a sales force. Discuss the margins to be given to retailers, wholesalers, and salespersons, and compare them to those given by your competition.

If distributors or sales representatives are to be used, describe how they have been selected, when they will start to represent you, and the areas they will cover. Show a table that indicates the buildup of dealers and representatives by month and the expected sales to be made by each dealer. Describe any special policies regarding discounts, exclusive distribution rights, and so forth.

If a direct sales force is to be used, indicate how it will be structured and at what rate it will be built up. If it is to replace a dealer or representative organization, indicate when and how. Show the sales expected per salesperson per year, and what commission incentive and/or salary the salespeople are slated to receive, and compare these figures to the average for your industry.

Present as an exhibit a selling schedule and a sales budget that includes all marketing, promotion, and service costs.

D. Service and Warranty Policies. If your company is offering a product that will require service and warranties, indicate the importance of these to the customers' purchasing decisions and discuss your method of handling service problems. Describe the kind and term of any warranties to be offered, whether service will be handled by company servicers, agencies, dealers and distributors, or factory-return. Indicate the proposed charge for service calls and whether service will be a profitable or break-even operation. Compare your service and warranty policies and practices with those of your principal competitors.

E. Advertising and Promotion. Describe the approaches that the company will use to bring its product to the attention of prospective purchasers. For original equipment manufacturer and industrial products, indicate the plans for trade show participation, trade magazine advertisements, direct mailings, the preparation of product sheets and promotional literature, and the use of advertising agencies. For consumer products, indicate what kind of advertising and promotional campaign is contemplated to introduce the product and what kind of sales aids will be provided to dealers. The schedule and cost of promotion and advertising should be presented. If advertising costs will be a significant part of company expenses, an exhibit showing how and when these costs will be incurred should be included.

F. Distribution. Describe the methods and channels of distribution that you will employ. How sensitive is shipping cost as a percent of the selling price? Note any special issues or problems that need to be resolved or that present potential vulnerabilities. Provide any tables or exhibits that can show the facts that are pertinent here.

VI. DESIGN AND DEVELOPMENT PLANS

If the product, process, or service of the proposed venture requires any design and development before it is ready to be placed on the market, the nature and extent of this work should be fully discussed. The investor will want to know the extent and nature of any design and development and the costs and time required to achieve a marketable product. Such design and development might be the engineering work necessary to convert a laboratory prototype to a finished product; or the design of special tooling; or the work of an industrial designer to make a product more attractive and salable; or the identification and organization of personnel, equipment, and special techniques to implement a service business—e.g., the equipment, new computer software, and skills required for computerized credit checking.

A. Development Status and Tasks. Describe the current status of the product or service, and explain what remains to be done to make it marketable. Describe briefly the competence or expertise that your company has or will acquire to complete this development.

B. Difficulties and Risks. Identify any major anticipated design and development problems, and approaches to their solution. Discuss their possible effect on the schedule, the cost of design and development, and the time of market introduction.

C. Product Improvement and New Products. In addition to describing the development of the initial products, discuss any ongoing design and development work that is planned to keep your product or service competitive and to develop new related products that can be sold to the same group of customers.

D. Costs. Present and discuss a design and development budget. The cost should include labor, materials, consulting fees, and so forth. Design and development costs are often underestimated. This can seriously affect cash flow projections. Accordingly, consider and perhaps show a 15 percent to 30 percent cost contingency. These cost data will become an integral part of the financial plan. (See Section XI, "The Financial Plan.")

E. Proprietary Issues. Describe any patent, trademark, or intellectual property rights that you own or are seeking. Also, note any unresolved issues relating to your proprietary rights that can bear on your timing and your competitive edge. Note any other existing or possible action pending with respect to these, such as disputed rights of ownership.

VII. MANUFACTURING AND OPERATIONS PLAN

The manufacturing and operations plan should describe the kinds of facilities, plant location, space, capital equipment, and labor force (part- and full-time) that are required to provide the company's product or service. For a manufacturing business, discuss your policies on inventory control, purchasing, production control, and "make-or-buy decisions" (i.e., which parts of the product will be purchased and which operations will be performed by your work force). A service business may require particular attention to and focus on an appropriate location, an ability to minimize overhead, and measures for obtaining competitive productivity from a labor force.

The discussion guidelines given below are general enough to cover both product and service businesses. Only those that are relevant to your venture—be its output product or service—should be addressed in the business plan.

A. Geographic Location. Describe the planned geographic location of the business, and discuss any advantages or disadvantages of the site location in terms of wage rates, labor unionization, labor availability, closeness to customers or suppliers, access to transportation, state and local taxes and laws, utilities, and zoning. For a service business, proximity to customers is generally a "must."

B. Facilities and Capacity Improvements. If yours is an existing business, describe the facilities currently used to conduct the business. This should include plant and office space; storage and land areas; and machinery, special tooling, and other capital equipment.

If your venture is a start-up, describe how and when the necessary facilities to start production will be acquired. Discuss whether equipment and space will be leased or acquired (new or used), and indicate the costs and timing of such actions. Indicate how much of the proposed financing will be devoted to plant and equipment. (These cost data will become part of the financial plan.)

Discuss how and when plant space and equipment will be expanded to the capacities required by future sales projections. Discuss any plans to improve or add to existing plant space or to move the facility. Explain future equipment needs, and indicate the timing and cost of meeting them. A three-year planning period should be used for these projections.

C. Strategy and Plans. Describe the manufacturing processes involved in your product's production and any decisions with respect to the subcontracting of component parts as opposed to complete in-house manufacture. The make-or-buy strategy adopted should be determined by consideration of inventory financing, available labor skills, and other nontechnical questions, as well as purely production, cost, and capability issues. Justify your proposed make-or-buy policy. Discuss any surveys of potential subcontractors and suppliers, and indicate who these are likely to be.

Present a production plan that shows cost-volume information at various sales levels of operation with breakdowns of applicable material, labor, purchased components, and factory overhead. Discuss the inventory required at various sales levels. These data will be incorporated into cash flow projections. Explain how any seasonal production loads will be handled without severe dislocation—e.g., by building to inventory or using part-time help in peak periods.

Describe briefly your approach to quality control, production control, and inventory control. Explain what quality control and inspection procedures the company will use to minimize service problems and associated customer dissatisfaction.

D. Regulatory, Other Compliances, Approvals and Environmental Issues. Include here any relevant regulatory requirements unique to your product, process, or service. What approvals are necessary in order to begin operation, such as permits, licenses, and zoning, health, and environmental approvals? What laws or other regulatory compliance are necessary and unique to your business? Note any pending regulatory changes that can affect the nature and timing window on your opportunity, such as occurred in airline deregulation and the AT&T breakup. Are there any legal or contractual obligations that are also pertinent?

VIII. MANAGEMENT TEAM

The management team is the key to turning a good idea into a successful business. Investors look for a committed management team with a proper balance of technical, managerial, and business skills and with experience in doing what is proposed.

Accordingly, this section of the business plan will be of primary interest to potential investors and will significantly influence their investment decisions. It should include a description of the key management personnel and their primary duties, the organizational structure, and the board of directors.

A. Organization. Present in tabular form the key management roles in the company and the individual who will fill each position.

Discuss any current or past situations where the key management people have worked together that indicate how their skills complement each other and result in an effective management team. If any key individuals will not be on board at the start of the venture, indicate when they will join the company.

In a new business it may not be possible to fill each executive role with a full-time person without excessively burdening the overhead of the venture. One solution is to use part-time specialists or consultants to perform some functions. If this is your plan, discuss it and indicate who will be used and when they will be replaced by full-time staff members.

If the company is established and of sufficient size, an organization chart can be appended as an exhibit.

B. Key Management Personnel. Describe the exact duties and responsibilities of each key member of the management team. Include a brief (three- or four-sentence) statement of the career highlights of each individual that focuses on accomplishments that demonstrate his or her ability to perform the assigned role.

Complete résumés for each key management member should be included here or as an exhibit of the business plan. These résumés should stress the training, experience, and accomplishments of each manager in performing functions similar to his or her new role in the venture. Accomplishments should be discussed in concrete terms such as profit and sales improvement, labor management, manufacturing or technical achievements, and ability to meet budgets and schedules.

C. Management Compensation and Ownership. The likelihood of obtaining financing for a start-up is small when the founding management team is not prepared to accept modest initial salaries. If the founders demand substantial salaries in excess of what they received at their prior employment, the potential investor will conclude that their psychological commitment to the venture is a good deal less than it should be.

State the salary that is to be paid to each key person, and compare it with the salary that he received at his last independent job. Set forth the stock ownership planned for the key personnel, the amount of their equity investment (if any), and any performance-dependent stock option or bonus plans that are contemplated.

D. Other Investors. Describe here any other investors in your venture, the number and percentage of the outstanding shares they own, when they were acquired, and at what price.

E. Incentives, Vesting, Employment Agreements. Summarize here any incentive stock option (ISO) or other stock ownership plans that you have in effect, or plan to institute, for key people and employees. Note restrictions on stock and any vesting or other agreements that affect its ownership and disposition, and also note any employment agreements that exist or are contemplated. Eventually, the investor will want to review copies of these documents.

F. Board of Directors. Discuss the company's philosophy as to the size and composition of the board. Identify proposed board members, and include a one- or two-sentence statement on each member's background that shows what he or she can bring to the company.

G. Other Shareholders, Rights and Restrictions. Briefly summarize here any other shareholders in your company and any rights, obligations—such as notes or guarantees—or restrictions associated with them. If all of the shareholders have been accounted for above, simply note that there are no others.

H. Supporting Professional Advisers and Services. State the legal (including patent), accounting, advertising, and banking organizations that you have selected for your venture and—if applicable—the names and affiliations of any close advisers whom you have worked with. Capable, reputable, and well-known individuals and supporting service organizations can not only provide significant direct, professional assistance but can also add to the credibility of your venture. In addition, properly selected professional organizations can help you establish good contacts in the business community, identify potential investors, and help you secure financing.

IX. OVERALL SCHEDULE

A schedule that shows the timing and interrelationship of the major events necessary to launch the venture and realize its objectives is an essential part of a business plan. In addition to being a planning aid and showing deadlines critical to a venture's success, a well-prepared schedule can be an extremely effective sales tool in raising money from potential investors. A well-prepared and realistic schedule demonstrates the ability of the management team to plan for venture growth in a way that recognizes obstacles and minimizes investor risk.

Prepare, as a part of this section, a month-by-month schedule that shows the timing of such activities as product development, market planning, sales programs, production, and operations. Sufficient detail should be included to show the timing of the primary tasks required to accomplish an activity.

Show on the schedule the deadlines or milestones critical to the venture's success. This should include such events as:

1. Incorporation of the venture (for a new business).
2. Completion of design and development.
3. Completion of prototypes (a key date; its achievement is a tangible measure of the company's ability to perform).
4. When sales representatives are obtained.
5. Product display at trade shows.
6. When distributors and dealers are signed up.

7. Order of materials in production quantities.
8. Start of production or operation (another key date because it is related to the production of income).
9. Receipt of first orders.
10. First sales and deliveries (a date of maximum interest because it relates directly to the company's credibility and to its need for capital).
11. Payment of first accounts receivable (cash in).

The schedule should also show the following and their relation to the development of the business:

1. Number of management personnel.
2. Number of production and operations personnel.
3. Additions to plant or equipment.

Discuss in a general way the activities most likely to cause a schedule slippage and what steps you would take to correct such slippages. Discuss the impact of schedule slippages on the venture's operation, especially its potential viability and capital needs. Keep in mind that the time to do things tends to be underestimated—even more than financing requirements. So be realistic about your schedule.

X. CRITICAL RISKS AND PROBLEMS

The development of a business has risks and problems, and the business plan invariably contains some implicit assumptions about them. The discovery of any unstated negative factors by potential investors can undermine the credibility of the venture and endanger its financing.

On the other hand, by identifying and discussing the risks in your venture, you demonstrate your skills as a manager and increase your credibility and that of your venture with a venture capital investor. Taking the initiative on the identification and discussion of risks helps you to demonstrate to the investor that you have thought about them and can handle them. Risks then tend not to loom as large black clouds in the investor's thinking about your venture.

Accordingly, identify and discuss in the business plan the major problems and risks that you think you will have to deal with to develop the venture. This should include a description of the risks relating to your industry, your company and its personnel, your product's market appeal, and the timing and financing of your start-up. Among the risks that might require discussion are:

1. Potential price cutting by competitors.
2. Any potentially unfavorable industry-wide trends.
3. Design or manufacturing costs in excess of estimates.
4. Sales projections not achieved.
5. Product development schedules not met.
6. Difficulties or long lead times encountered in the procurement of parts or raw materials.
7. Difficulties encountered in obtaining a needed bank credit line because of tight money.
8. Larger-than-expected innovation and development costs to stay competitive.

This listing is not meant to be complete but only indicative of the kinds of risks and assumptions that might be discussed.

Indicate which business plan assumptions or potential problems are most critical to the success of your venture. Describe your plans for minimizing the impact of unfavorable developments in each risk area on the success of your venture.

XI. THE FINANCIAL PLAN

The financial plan is basic to the evaluation of an investment opportunity, and it should represent the entrepreneur's best estimates of future operations—your best judgment of the results you believe are realistic and attainable. The purpose of the financial plan is to indicate the venture's potential and its timetable for financial viability. The financial plan can also serve as an operating plan for financial management of the venture.

We have found that the microcomputer and the new spreadsheet programs, such as Lotus 1-2-3, VisiCalc, MultiPlan, and their clones, have been invaluable time savers in modeling the financial requirements necessary to execute the opportunity. We have included here sample pro formas derived from work with 1-2-3, and the formulas that have been developed to run the calculations. Thus, if you have access to a personal computer and 1-2-3, you could enter the model into your computer. (*Note* that you will need at least 256K of memory to run the model on an IBM-PC, and 512K is even better. Anything smaller will not accommodate the program. Simpler models can, of course, be run with 128K, which is still superior, in our opinion, to the manual method.)[1]

These formats integrate the Robert Morris Associates data and financial ratios with the financial statements developed using Lotus 1-2-3. (See Chapter 12 for the relevance and use of microcomputers and their software for entrepreneurs, and Appendix I for detailed information on the RMA financial ratios.) This combination enables you, much more readily than by hand, to apply the relevant financial benchmarks to your venture, in order to evaluate the realism and relevance of your estimates. In addition, we have consistently found that such modeling can greatly enhance the creativity with which you look at your venture and the development of alternative ways of launching it.

A word of caution: We find that the personal computer has led to a fixation by many entrepreneurs on the modeling and number crunching. No doubt about it: the computer is a joy, and fun, compared to the use of pencil, calculator, and erasers. But much of the fixation on developing elaborate models and scenarios is overkill, and, what is worse, as a result of this fixation you invariably lose sight of the most critical factors: the people and the opportunity. Finally, precision does not necessarily mean accuracy. Keep the cart behind the horse.

In developing the financial plan, four basic exhibits must be prepared:

A. *Profit and loss forecasts* for at least the first three years. A yearly summary is also helpful.
B. *Cash flow projections* for the same time span. Remember, happiness is a positive cash flow.
C. *Pro forma balance sheets* at start-up, semiannually in the first year, and at the end of each of the next two years of operation.
D. *Break-even chart and calculation* to show when break-even will be reached and to capture any stepwise changes in break-even that may occur. With higher margin ventures, say, over 40 percent to 60 percent or more, this is less critical than it would be in a lower-margin, more price-sensitive business.

---

[1] We are most appreciative to Mr. Joseph M. Frye, our friend and our partner at Venture Founders Corporation, for making available for use in the revised edition the templates and models that he has developed for evaluating business plans.

In the case of an *existing business seeking expansion capital,* income statements and balance sheets for the current and prior two years should be provided in addition to these estimates.

Sample exhibits have been included in these guidelines.

After you have completed the preparation of the financial exhibits, briefly highlight in writing the important conclusions that can be drawn. These might include the maximum cash requirement and when it will be reached, when you will reach break-even and a positive cash flow, the amount of debt and equity needed, the level of profits as a percentage of sales, how fast any debts are repaid, and so forth.

Finally, on the appropriate exhibits, or in an attachment, specify the assumptions behind the plan, such as how you estimated sales level and growth, collections and payables periods, days' inventory requirements, minimum cash balance, cost of goods, and other line items comparable to the RMA ratios.

A. Profit and Loss Forecasts (see Exhibit 1).   The preparation of pro forma income statements is the planning-for-profit part of financial management. Crucial to the earnings forecasts—as well as other projections—is the sales forecast. The methods for developing sales forecasts have been described in Section II of these guidelines, and the sales data projected in that section should be used here.

Once the sales forecasts are in hand, production costs (or operations costs for a service business) should be budgeted. The level of production or operation that is required to meet the sales forecasts and to fulfill inventory requirements must be determined. The material, labor, service, and manufacturing overhead requirements must be developed and translated into cost data. A separation of the fixed and variable elements of these costs is desirable, and the effect of sales volume on inventory, equipment acquisitions, and manufacturing costs should be taken into account.

Sales expense should include the costs of selling and distribution, storage, discounts, advertising, and promotion. General and administrative expense should include management salaries, secretarial costs, and legal and accounting expenses. Manufacturing or operations overhead includes rent, utilities, fringe benefits, telephone, and so on.

Earnings projections should be prepared monthly in the first year of operation and quarterly in the second and third years.

If these earnings projections are to be useful, they must represent management's realistic and best estimates of probable operating results. Sales or operational cost projections that are either too conservative or too optimistic have little value as aids to policy formulation and decision making.

1. Discussion of Assumptions.   Because of the importance of profit and loss projections as an indication of the potential financial feasibility of a new venture to potential investors, it is extremely important that any assumptions made in their preparation be fully explained and documented. Such assumptions could include the amount allowed for bad debts and discounts and any assumptions made with respect to sales expenses or general and administrative costs being a fixed percentage of costs or sales.

2. Risks and Sensitivity.   Once the income statements have been prepared, draw on Section X of these guidelines and highlight any major risks that could prevent the venture's sales and profit goals from being attained, and the sensitivity of profits to these risks.

This discussion should reflect the entrepreneur's thinking about some of the risks that might be encountered in the firm itself, the industry, and the environment. The discussion could include such things as the effect of a 20 percent reduction in sales projections or the impact of a learning curve on the level of productivity over time.

B. Pro Forma Cash Flow Analysis (see Exhibit 2). For a new venture the cash flow forecast can be more important than the forecasts of profits because it details the amount and timing of expected cash inflows and outflows. Usually the level of profits, particularly during the start-up years of a venture, will not be sufficient to finance operating asset needs. Moreover, cash inflows do not match the outflows on a short-term basis. The cash flow forecast will indicate these conditions and enable management to plan cash needs.

Given a level of projected sales and capital expenditures over a specific period, the cash flow forecast will highlight the need for and timing of additional financing and will indicate the peak requirements for working capital. Management must decide how this additional financing is to be obtained, on what terms, and how it is to be repaid. Part of the needed financing will be supplied by the equity financing (that is sought by this business plan), part by bank loans for one to five years, and the balance by short-term lines of credit from banks. This information becomes part of the final cash flow forecast.

If the venture is in a seasonal or cyclical industry, or is in an industry in which suppliers require a new firm to pay cash, or if an inventory buildup occurs before the product can be sold and produce revenues, the cash flow forecast is crucial to the continuing solvency of the business. A detailed cash flow forecast that is understood and used by management can enable it to direct its attention to operating problems without being distracted by periodic cash crises that should have been anticipated. Cash flow projections should be made for each month of the first year of operation and for each quarter of the second and third years.

1. Discussion of Assumptions. This should include assumptions made on the timing of collection of receivables, trade discounts given, terms of payments to vendors, planned salary and wage increases, anticipated increases in any operating expenses, seasonality characteristics of the business as they affect inventory requirements, inventory turnovers per year, and capital equipment purchases. Thinking about such assumptions when planning your venture is useful for identifying issues that may later require attention if they are not to become significant problems.

2. Cash Flow Sensitivity. Once the cash flow forecast has been completed, discuss the implications for cash needs that possible changes in some of the crucial assumptions would have—e.g., an increase in the receivable collection period or sales below forecasts. This will enable you to test the sensitivity of the cash budget to a variety of assumptions about business factors and to view a wider range of possible outcomes. Investors are vitally interested in this because it helps them to estimate the possibility that you will need more cash sooner than planned.

C. Pro Forma Balance Sheets (see Exhibit 3). The balance sheets are used to detail the assets required to support the projected level of operations and, through liabilities, show how these assets are to be financed. Investors and bankers look to the projected balance sheets to determine whether debt-to-equity ratios, working capital, current ratios, inventory turnover, and so forth are within the acceptable limits required to justify the future financings that are projected for the venture.

Pro forma balance sheets should be prepared at start-up, semiannually for the first year, and at the end of each of the next two years of operation.

D. Break-Even Chart (see Exhibit 4). A break-even chart is a way of determining the level of sales and production that will cover all costs. This includes those costs that vary with the production level (manufacturing labor, material, sales costs) and those that do not vary with the production level (rent, interest charges, executive salaries, etc.). The sales level that just covers all costs is the break-even level for your venture.

It is very useful for the investor and the management to know what the break-even point is, and whether it will be easy or difficult to attain. It is also very desirable that your projected sales be sufficiently larger than the break-even sales so that small perturbations in the venture's performance do not produce losses. You should prepare a break-even chart and discuss how your break-even point might be lowered in case you start to fall short of your sales projections.

E. Cost Control. Your ability to meet your income and cash flow projections will depend critically on your ability to monitor and control costs. For this reason, many investors like to know what sort of accounting and cost control system you have or will use in your business. Accordingly, the financial plan should include a brief description of how you will obtain and report costs, who will be responsible for the control of the various cost elements, how often he or she will obtain cost data, and how you will take action on budget overruns.

XII. PROPOSED COMPANY OFFERING

The purpose of this section of the plan is to indicate how much money is being sought and the nature and amount of the securities that are being offered to the investor and to provide a brief description of the uses that will be made of the capital raised. The discussion and guidelines given below should help you do this.

You should, however, realize that the terms for financing your company that you propose here are the first step in a negotiation process with a venture capital investor that is interested in your "deal." It is very possible that when you close your financing, you will be selling a different kind of security (e.g., convertible debt instead of common stock) for a price different from the one you originally proposed.

A. Desired Financing. Summarize from your cash flow projections how much money is required over the next three years to carry out the development and expansion of your business that has been described. Indicate how much of this capital requirment will be obtained by this offering and how much will be obtained via term loans and lines of credit.

B. Securities Offering. Describe the kind (common stock, convertible debenture, etc.), unit price, and total amount of securities to be sold in this offering. If the securities are not just common stock (e.g., debt with warrants, debt plus stock), indicate interest, maturity, and conversion conditions. Also show the percentage of the company that the investors of this offering will hold after the offering has been completed or after the exercise of any stock conversion or purchase rights in the case of convertible debentures or warrants.

If the securities are being sold as a "private placement" that is exempt from SEC registration (see Chapter 15), you should include the following statement in this part of the plan:

The shares being sold pursuant to this offering are restricted securities and may not be resold readily. The prospective investor should recognize that such securities might be restricted as to resale for an indefinite period of time. Each purchaser will be required to execute a Non-Distribution Agreement that is satisfactory in form to corporate counsel.

C. Capitalization. Present in tabular form the current and proposed (post-offering) number of outstanding shares of common stock. Indicate any shares offered by key management people, and show the number of shares that these people will hold after completion of the proposed financing.

Indicate how many shares of your company's common stock will remain authorized but unissued after the offering and how many of these will be reserved for stock options for future key employees.

  D. Use of Funds. Investors like to know how their money is going to be spent. Provide a brief description of how the capital raised will be used. Summarize as specifically as possible what amount will be used for such things as product design and development, capital equipment, marketing, and general working capital needs.

XIII. SPREADSHEETS AND FINANCIAL EXHIBITS

Exhibit 1
Pro Forma Income Statements

	1st Year (Months)												2d Year Quarters				3d Year Quarters			
	1	2	3	4	5	6	7	8	9	10	11	12	1Q	2Q	3Q	4Q	1Q	2Q	3Q	4Q
Sales Less: Discounts Less: Bad debt provision Less: Materials used																				
Direct labor																				
Manufacturing overhead*																				
Other manufacturing expense (leases)																				
Depreciation																				
Gross profit or (loss)																				
Less: Sales expense Engineering expense General and administrative expense†																				
Operating profit or (loss)																				
Less: Other expense (e.g., interest)																				
Profit (or loss) before taxes																				
Profit after taxes																				

  *Includes rent, utilities, fringe benefits, telephone.
  †Includes office supplies, accounting and legal services, management, etc.

Exhibit 2
Pro Forma Cash Flows

	1st Year (Months)												2d Year Quarters				3d Year Quarters			
	1	2	3	4	5	6	7	8	9	10	11	12	1Q	2Q	3Q	4Q	1Q	2Q	3Q	4Q
Cash balance: Opening																				
Add: Cash receipts:																				
Collection of accounts receivable																				
Miscellaneous receipts																				
Bank loan proceeds																				
Sale of stock																				
Total cash receipts																				
Less: Disbursements:																				
Trade payables																				
Direct labor																				
Manufacturing overhead																				
Leased equipment																				
Sales expense																				
Warranty expense																				
General administrative expense																				
Fixed-asset additions																				
Income tax																				
Loan interest @ _____%																				
Loan repayments																				
Other payments																				
Total disbursements																				
Cash increase (or decrease)																				
Cash balance: Closing																				

Exhibit 3
Pro Forma Balance Sheets

	Start-up Date	1st Year				2d Year	3d Year
		1Q	2Q	3Q	4Q		
Assets							
Cash							
Marketable securities							
Accounts receivable							
Inventories:							
Raw materials and supplies							
Work in process							
Finished goods							
Total inventories							
Prepaid items							
Total current assets							
Plant and equipment							
Less: Accumulated depreciation							
Net plant and equipment							
Deferred charges							
Other assets (identify)							
Total assets							
Liabilities and Stockholders' Equity							
Notes payable to bank							
Accounts payable							
Accruals							
Federal and state taxes accrued							
Other							
Long-term notes							
Other liabilities							
Common stock							
Capital surplus							
Retained earnings							
Stockholders' equity							
Total liabilities and stockholders' equity							

Exhibit 4
Sample Break-Even Chart

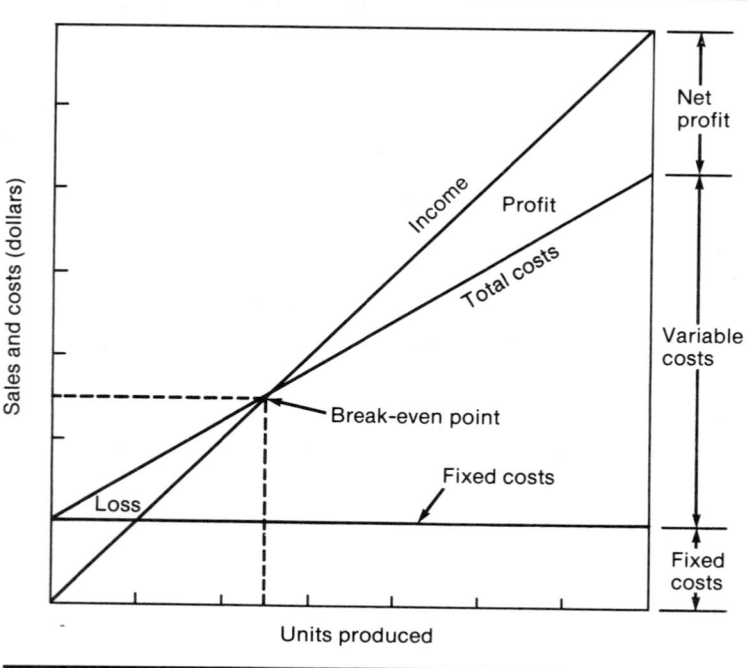

Break-even formula:

SP = Selling price (unit)
VC = Direct or variable costs (e.g., labor, material)
FC = Fixed costs

SP – VC = Gross margin, or "contribution" to profit and fixed costs"

Therefore,

$$\frac{\text{Total fixed costs}}{\text{\$ contribution}} = \text{Number of units required to break even}$$

XIV.   APPENDIXES

Include in this section pertinent information that may be unique to your venture and has not been covered elsewhere. For instance, this information could be product specs or photos, a list of customers as references, or the names of suppliers of critical components; special location factors, facilities, or technical analyses; reports from consultants or technical experts; and any critical regulatory, environmental, or other compliances or approvals that are necessary.

FINANCING ENTREPRENEURIAL VENTURES

PART IV

Sources of Capital 15 >

Money is like a sixth sense without which you cannot make a complete use of the other five.

W. Somerset Maugham
Of Human Bondage

15.1 RESULTS EXPECTED

This chapter will describe the principal sources of capital available to the start-up or the young existing business, the kind of financing that they provide, and their criteria for providing capital.

Upon completion of this chapter, you will:

1. Understand the sources of capital available to your particular venture, based on its type and stage of development.
2. Understand the differences between debt and equity financing and the instances in which each is appropriate.
3. Be able to identify specific sources of capital suitable for your venture, to be included or kept in mind when preparing the "Proposed Company Offering" section of your business plan.

15.2 PRESESSION PREPARATION

Read this chapter. List the sources of financing that would be most appropriate for your venture, in order of preference.

15.3 SOURCES OF CAPITAL: AN OVERVIEW

Every entrepreneur must eventually take on the job of raising money to start, expand, or buy a business or to provide funds for seasonal or temporary business needs. A number of sources of financing and types of capital are available. Some of these can be used to finance a start-up. Others can be used only to provide capital to a going concern. For example, start-ups may be able to obtain money only from friends, relatives, and certain start-up-oriented venture capital groups. On the other hand, existing businesses have a far wider range of financing options available to them, including banks, commercial finance companies, leasing companies and the public sale of stock as well as venture capital firms.

Both the capital sources and the types of financing to be discussed are not all-inclusive, but, based on the authors' experience, they are the sources and types most often used by new and expanding businesses.

15.3.1 Debt versus Equity

Generally speaking, a company's operations can be financed through debt and through some form of equity financing.[1] Short-term debt (one year or less) is required by a business for working capital and is repaid out of the proceeds of its sales. Longer-term borrowings (term loans of one to five years or long-term loans maturing in more than five years) are used for working capital and/or to finance the purchase of property or equipment that serves as collateral for the loans. The most common sources of such debt financing are the commercial banks.

However, the new venture just starting operations has difficulty in obtaining either short- or longer-term bank debt without a substantial cushion of equity financing or long-term debt that is subordinated[2] or junior to all bank debt. With such equity capital or subordinated debt, a bank may lend money to a start-up to some maximum debt-to-equity ratio. As a rough rule of thumb, a start-up *may* be able to obtain debt for working capital purposes that is equal to its equity and subordinated debt. Without much equity capital or subordinated debt the new venture will be unable to obtain much bank debt. As far as the bank is concerned, the start-up has little proven ability to generate the sales, profits, and cash to pay off short-term debt and even less ability to sustain profitable operations over a number of years and retire long-term debt. Even the underlying protection provided by a venture's assets used as loan collateral may be insufficient to obtain bank loans. Asset values can erode with time and, in the absence of adequate equity capital and good management, may provide little real loan security to a bank.[3]

This is not to say that a start-up cannot obtain credit and loans. Sometimes a new venture may obtain long-term financing for a particular piece of equipment from its manufacturer, which will provide a portion of the purchase price as a long-term note. Manufacturers are willing to do this if there is an active market for their used equipment. Long-term debt for a venture might be obtained from a bank if a loan guarantee for 90 percent of the loan can be obtained from the Small Business Administration (SBA). However, the SBA requires that the loans it guarantees be of sound value or so secured as to reasonably ensure repayment. Many new businesses fail to meet this requirement and thus do not qualify for SBA loan guarantees. A new business can also try to reduce its need for long-term debt by leasing some of the equipment it needs. Such leases may be provided by a manufacturer or by a commercial credit company. Until recently, leasing was usually restricted to general-purpose equipment (e.g., oscilloscopes, forklifts) for which there was a large demand. However, several leasing companies have recently introduced programs to lease more specialized equipment to high-technology start-ups that have obtained equity financing from venture capital groups. In

---

[1]In addition to the purchase of common stock, equity financing is meant to include the purchase of both stock and subordinated debt, or subordinated debt with stock conversion features, or warrants to purchase stock.

[2]For lending purposes commercial banks regard such subordinated debt as equity. Venture capital investors normally subordinate their business loans to the loans provided by the bank or other financial institutions.

[3]The bank loan defaults by REITs in 1975 are examples of the failure of assets to provide protection in the absence of sound management and adequate equity capital.

addition to conventional lease payments and typical leasing interest rates, these leasing companies also receive stock purchase warrants to compensate them for their greater risk.

A start-up can sometimes obtain short-term debt financing by negotiating extended credit terms with one or more of its suppliers. A disadvantage of this kind of trade credit is that it restricts the venture's flexibility to select suppliers and reduces its ability to negotiate supplier prices.

The existing business has a much easier job of obtaining debt and equity. Banks, leasing companies, and finance companies will often seek out such businesses and regard them as important customers for secured and unsecured short- and long-term loans. Furthermore, an existing and expanding business will find it easier than the start-up to raise equity capital from private or institutional sources, and on better terms.

Although it may be possible to finance a venture with a great deal of debt and little equity capital, doing this can have a number of disadvantages. A new and growing company is a consumer of capital and therefore ill able to afford the regular payments of interest and principal required with debt financing. Many new ventures that are predominantly debt-financed (i.e., heavily leveraged) are constantly undercapitalized and have continual cash flow problems. These cash flow problems can occupy the time and attention of the venture's management to the detriment of the general development and growth of the venture. The heavy use of debt for starting or expanding a company can also adversely affect the venture's balance sheet and its ability to obtain future debt or equity financing at favorable terms.

On the positive side, debt financing does not dilute the entrepreneurs' equity and the leverage it provides can increase the return on invested capital. But remember that leverage works both ways. In times of tight credit and high interest rates (e.g., 1980–81), a business with a high debt-to-equity ratio is much more likely to have financial difficulty, or even to be driven into bankruptcy, than is a business with more reasonable capitalizations. In this regard, we know of an otherwise successful consumer products company with sales of $30 million that overleveraged its debt (i.e., debt was 8 times equity) and was driven into bankruptcy by the combined effects of rising interest rates and a recession-induced drop in sales.

A new or existing business must obtain both equity and debt financing if it is to have a sound financial foundation for growth without excessive dilution of the entrepreneurs' equity. In the remainder of this chapter we shall discuss the primary sources of such capital and answer such questions as these: What are the sources of short-, medium- and long-term financing? What sources provide capital for start-ups? For existing businesses? What are the financing limits and investment preferences of the various sources? What data must be submitted to obtain financing? What terms and conditions can be expected on particular financings? What are the advantages and disadvantages of the various kinds of financing?

15.4 EQUITY CAPITAL SOURCES

15.4.1 Stages of Venture Development

From whom does a venture obtain venture or equity capital? The answer to this question depends both on the growth potential of the venture—low, moderate or fast—and on the stage of its development. We shall focus our attention on equity capital for the birth and early growth of a venture. Within this time frame we shall consider three stages of development in which a venture may need capital and obtain it from different kinds of investors:

1. *The Seed Stage.* This stage begins with the idea for a business, encompasses the organization and planning of a venture and some R&D, and ends with the creation of a business entity and a business plan.
2. *The Start-up Stage.* This stage begins when a venture is organized and one or two of its principals are actively seeking to complete the development of its products and to obtain sales. The start-up stage ends when the venture can demonstrate some commercial interest in its product. The start-up stage can last anywhere from several months to a year, and a venture need not be profitable at the end of it.
3. *The First Stage.* Companies in their first stage are going organizations. There is some evidence of commercial interest in their products, and there are some sales. However, profits may be one or more years off.

15.4.2 Type and Stage of Venture and Equity Capital

In a 1979 paper William Wetzel presented a useful framework for depicting the sorts of equity capital that are available to three very different "sorts" of companies.[4] These were:

1. *"Lifestyle Firms."* These are firms that have potential annual sales of less than $1 million and are managed by people willing to sacrifice income for the lifestyle afforded by their own small company. These firms have little or no real growth by choice, market size, or circumstance.
2. *"Foundation Firms."* These are firms with potential sales of $1–20 million and from 30 to 600 employees. These firms grow at one to two times the growth rate of the GNP, that is, 10–20 percent per year.
3. *"High-Potential Firms."* These firms have potential sales of $20 million and are growing in excess of 30 percent per year.

Using these three definitions, Wetzel prepared a chart to show the sources of equity capital available to these firms at various stages of their development. The authors have taken the liberty of updating and modifying this chart (see Exhibit 15.1) to reflect the increased availability in 1984 of equity capital from venture capital firms and their appetite for early stage deals.

Note that lifestyle firms are financed almost entirely by personal savings of the entrepreneurs, whereas high-potential firms have a much larger choice of financing alternatives. The entrepreneurs and their associates may also be expected to provide some of the seed capital for foundation and high-potential firms. This may be in the form of forgone salary while the venture is organized and started and/or in actual cash. Venture capital firms investing in an early stage venture like the entrepreneurs to have made some sort of significant financial commitment to the venture. This was an absolute requirement in the 1970s. How-

---

[4]William H. Wetzel, Jr., "The Cost of Availability of Credit and Risk Capital in New England," in *A Region's Struggling Savior: Small Business in New England*, ed. Jeffry A. Timmons and David E. Gumpert (Waltham, Mass.: Small Business Foundation of America), 1979.

Exhibit 15.1
Capital Availability for Different Types of Ventures

Stage of Development	Lifestyle Firms	Foundation Firms	High-Potential Firms
R&D or seed	Personal savings	Personal savings and friendly sources	Personal savings Friendly sources Wealthy individuals Venture capital firms Equity partnerships
Start-up	Personal savings	Wealthy individuals	SBICs Venture capital firms Equity partnerships
Early growth First stage	Personal savings and friendly sources	SBICs	Venture capital firms
Rapid growth	Personal savings and friendly sources	Some venture capital firms Public stock offerings	Venture capital firms Public stock offerings

ever, with the very substantial increase in venture capital since 1980, some ventures are financed with little or no financial investment by the entrepreneurs.

In the sections that follow, we shall briefly describe the characteristics and preferences of each of the equity investors shown in Exhibit 15.1.

15.4.3 "Friendly" Sources of Venture Capital

In addition to the entrepreneurs and their associates, an important source of seed and start-up funds, and of financing at all stages for lifestyle firms, is found among the personal and professional contacts of the entrepreneurs of new ventures. Principal among these are:

1. Family and friends.
2. Professional advisers and business acquaintances.
3. Past employers.
4. Potential customers and suppliers of the new venture.
5. Prospective employees (these may invest or be given stock in return for working at less than their normal compensation).
6. Wealthy businesspeople and private investors who know the entrepreneurs.

These people will generally invest in an opportunistic way, without too much study or "due diligence," and largely on the basis of personal or business relationships with the principals of a new venture. They may also invest at later stages of a venture's development, but the capital then required will usually exceed what they alone can supply.

The entrepreneur and his management team should review their contacts in the categories listed above and determine whether any of them might be interested in making a financial commitment to the venture. As Liles points out, entrepreneurs should take care to know their potential pre-start-up investors well enough to ensure that they are not unethical or just interested in a fast profit with no concern for the entrepreneurs or their ventures.[5]

[5]Patrick R. Liles, *New Business Ventures and the Entrepreneur* (Homewood, Ill.: Richard D. Irwin, 1974), p. 467.

15.4.4 Wealthy Individual Investors

A good deal of the early funding for new ventures has been provided by wealthy individuals.[6] This is especially true outside the centers of organized venture capital (Boston, New York, San Francisco). A number of such people invest more or less regularly in start-up entrepreneurial efforts. They may do this alone or in syndication with other wealthy individuals. Generally, the evaluation of a potential investment by such investors tends to be less thorough than that undertaken by an organized venture capital group, and noneconomic factors (e.g., a desire to be involved with entrepreneurs) may be important to their investment decisions. In the case of a syndicate of such investors, one individual may make the evaluation for the group.

Ex-entrepreneurs who have made money through starting, developing, and selling companies are a good source of start-up capital, as are some wealthy doctors, lawyers, and businesspeople. Although such persons make start-up investments, they often demand more equity for their interest than the entrepreneur may think reasonable. Some of them may try to dominate the venture, and others can get very impatient when sales and profits don't grow as they expected. To avoid legal problems associated with the sale of stock to such investors, review carefully the material in this chapter on the legal aspects of a stock offering.

15.4.5 Professional Venture Capital Groups

The 1980s have seen a metamorphosis in the professional venture capital industry. At present, the organized venture capital community is operating in the most favorable environment in its short history.[7] The reduction in capital gains taxes led to an explosion of new money in 1979, and in 1984 there was 80 times as much new venture capital available as there was 8–10 years earlier. In fact, some say that "too much capital is chasing too few good deals."

This is clearly evident in Exhibit 15.2. In 1983 a staggering $4.5 billion of new money flowed into venture capital funds. The outflow, in the form of investments in portfolio companies, amounted to $2.8 billion. In 1984 the trend continued, according to *Venture Capital Journal.* In 1984, $3.1 billion of new venture capital flowed into the existing pool, raising the total to over $16.5 billion. The total for 1985 may approach $3 billion again. (Note that we are giving gross figures, including all growth stages and all rounds of financing. Proportionately, funds for start-up and seed capital are not large.)

Of equal significance is the amount of money being invested in start-ups, as shown in Exhibit 15.3. According to Timmons and Gumpert:

As recently as 1975, says a National Venture Capital Association study, only 14 percent of investments were in start-ups. In contrast, nearly half of the 51 investors we interviewed in 1980–81 said 30 percent or more of their investments were in start-up ventures. Furthermore, 90 percent of the [venture capital] firms reported that they would consider start-ups. Leading this trend were eight venture capital firms that specialize in start-ups

---

[6]G. Baty, *Initial Financing of the New Research Based Enterprise in New England,* Federal Reserve Bank of Boston Research Report no. 25 (Boston, Mass., 1964); and G. Baty, *Entrepreneurship: Playing to Win* (Reston, Va.: Reston Publishing, 1974), p. 97.

[7]Stanley E. Pratt, *Pratt's Guide to Venture Capital Sources,* 8th ed. (Wellesley, Mass.: Capital Publishing, 1984).

Exhibit 15.2
New Private Capital Committed to Venture Capital Firms ($ millions)

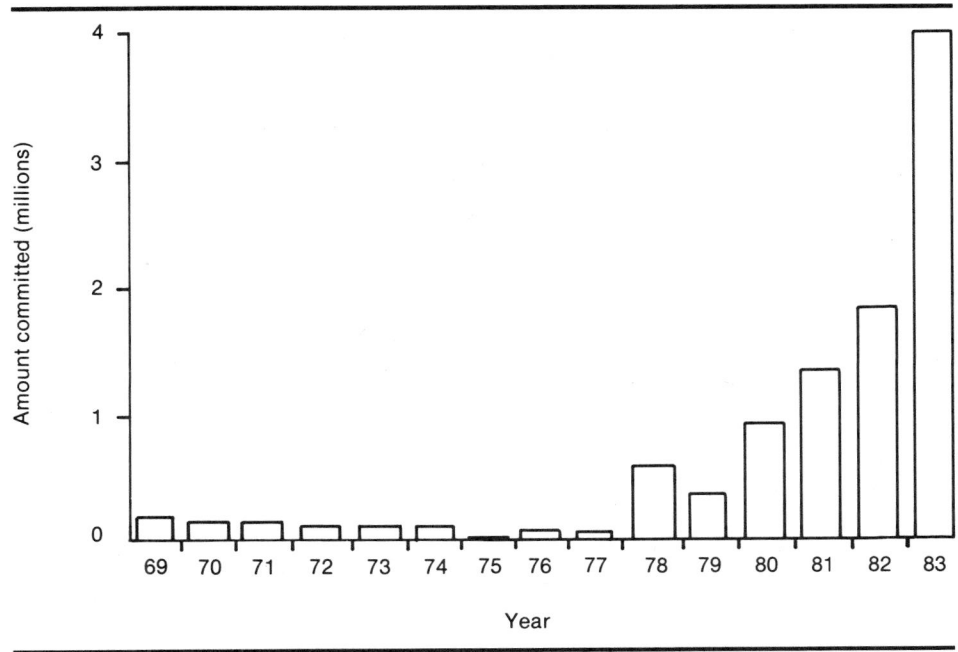

Source: Venture Economics.

Exhibit 15.3
Annual Estimated Disbursements by Venture Capitalists to Portfolio Companies

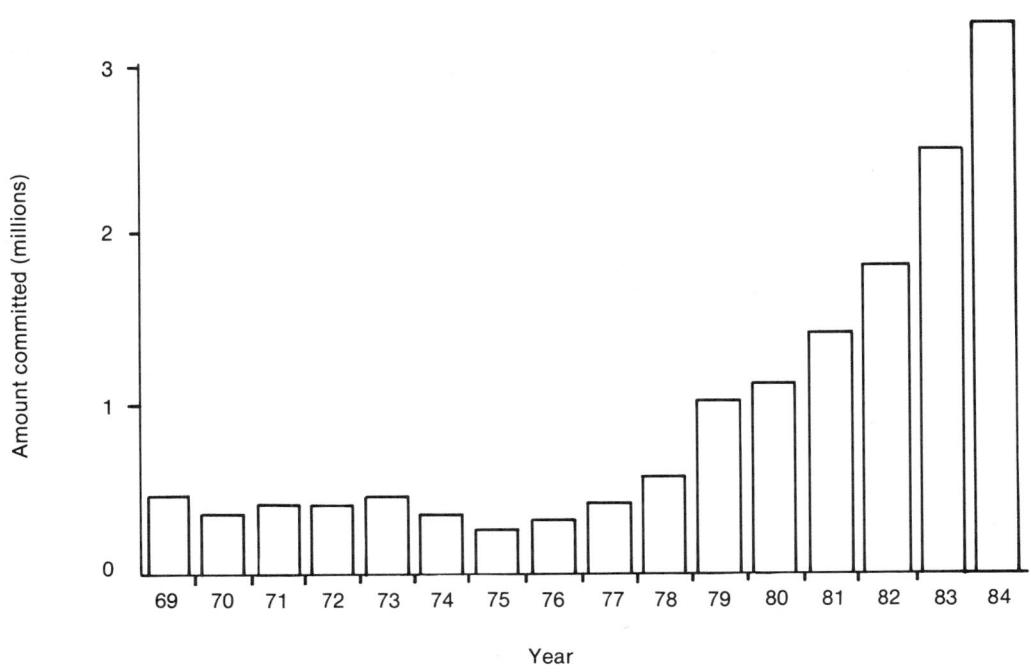

Source: Venture Economics.

and very early stage ventures; they reported that half or more of their investments were in start-up companies.[8]

The interest in start-ups has not been so great since the late 1960s. (Let us hope that we are not facing a boom-bust cycle in the late 1980s similar to the 1969–74 period when start-up financing became very hard to find.)

Some venture capital firms become actively involved financially and managerially in the seed stage of new ventures. Rather than wait for a deal to come to them, they decide on a product or technology that they wish to commercialize and then put their own deal together. This involves assembling a team of entrepreneurs, managers, and technologists; writing business plans; troubleshooting the venture; and providing seed capital alone or in syndication with other venture capital firms. Kleiner Perkins used this approach to get Genentech and Tandem Computer Corporation launched, and the same sort of approach was used by Greylock and J. H. Whitney to start Mass Comp. Sometimes these seed deals are organized as equity partnerships rather than corporations (see the section "Tax Shelter Financing"). The equity partnership allows the early losses of the venture to be flowed directly back to the limited partner investors. This gives the investors a tax deduction that reduces their capital at risk, in return for which the entrepreneurs get to keep more equity than they would in the corporate seed venture.

Capital from a professional venture capital group is very attractive to the entrepreneur. The venture capitalist can bring more than just money to the venture—for example, the experience of having done it before. Moreover, the venture firm has "deep pockets" and contacts with other groups that can facilitate the raising of money as the venture develops.

However, professional venture capital groups have stringent criteria for their investments. They look for ventures with very high growth potential where they can quintuple their investment in five years. Venture capital firms place a very high premium on the quality of the management in a venture. They like to see a management team with complementary business skills headed by someone who has previous entrepreneurial or profit and loss management experience.

Because of the stringent criteria of venture capital firms, no more than 2–4 percent of the ventures contacting such firms receive financing from them. And the equity cost to the entrepreneur can be substantial. Entrepreneurs may give up 35–60 percent of the venture's equity for start-up or seed financing, and by the time several rounds of venture financing have been completed, they may own no more than 10–20 percent of their company's stock.

At the end of 1984 organized venture capital groups consisted of about 700 organizations with a total capital base of over $14 billion. These venture capital sources fell into three main categories, as shown in Exhibit 15.4.

1. Venture Capital Corporations or Partnerships with an Established Capital Base and Professional Management.   There are some 233 venture capital companies and partnerships in the United States. Their investment policies cover a range of preferences as to investment size and the maturity, location, and industry of a venture. Capital for these venture capital companies and partnerships may be provided by: one or more wealthy families, one or more financial institutions (e.g., insurance company, pension fund), and wealthy individuals. Most are organized

---

[8]Jeffry A. Timmons and David E. Gumpert, "Discard Many Old Rules about Getting Venture Capital," *Harvard Business Review,* January–February 1982, pp. 273–80.

Exhibit 15.4
Overview of Venture Capital Sources*

	Private Venture Capital Firms	Small Business Investment Companies (SBICs)†	Corporate/ Industrial/Banks
Estimated number, 1984	233	137	78
Principal objectives and motives	Capital gains 25–40% compounded after tax per year, 5–10 times original investment in 5–10 years	Capital gains same range as private	Windows on technology; tap new talent; acquire new markets; spawn new suppliers; diversification; public relations; use surplus cash; philanthropy; capital gains
Typical size, range, and investments	$500,000–1.5 + million	$250,000–500,000	$10–15 million not unusual
Stage of ventures sought	All stages—20–30% start-ups more common		Later stages; rarely start-ups; seeking markets of $100–200 + million
Outside approval and deals done by firm	Unusual, perhaps 10–12% of firms		Very common, 75% of decisions; review boards and directors.

*We are most appreciative of the assistance of Jane Morris, editor, *Venture Capital Journal,* in providing data for this table.

†Excludes those firms that make debt investments.

Source: David E. Gumpert and Jeffry A. Timmons, *The Encyclopedia of Small Business Resources,* (New York: Harper & Row, 1984), p. 199, with updates.

as limited partnerships in which the fund managers are the general partners and the investors are the limited partners. Today most of these funds prefer to invest upwards of $250,000, though some of the smaller funds will go lower. Most of their investments are in the range of $250,000–750,000. Some of the so-called mega-funds with upwards of $100 million to invest do not like to consider investments of less than $1 million. Their investigation and evaluation of potential investments are thorough and professional. A positive investment decision usually takes from six weeks to three months after the first meeting with the venture's management. Negative decisions are generally reached much faster. Most of their investments are in high-technology businesses, but they will consider investments in most other areas except construction and real estate.

2. SBICs (Small Business Investment Companies). These are licensed by the SBA and can obtain debt capital—$4 in loans for each $1 of private equity—from the federal government (SBA). The SBIC's equity capital is generally supplied by one or more commercial banks, wealthy individuals, and the investing public. There are now about 450 SBICs in the United States, of which about 137 have active venture capital rather than just loan programs; some of these 137 SBICs are affiliates of venture capital firms. SBICs are limited by law to taking minority shareholder positions and to investing no more than 20 percent of their equity capital in any one situation. Because SBICs borrow much of their capital from the SBA and must service this debt, they prefer to make some form of interest-bearing investment. Four common forms of financing are long-term loans with options to buy stock, convertible debentures, straight loans, and in some cases preferred stock. Also, because of their SBA debt, SBICs tend not to finance start-ups and early stage companies but to make investments in more mature companies. SBICs have been an important small business financing source, and in over 21 years they have invested $3 billion in 50,000+ businesses. A typical financing is in the range of $100,000–300,000.

3. *Corporate Venture Capital Groups.*   Some of these are nonfinancial corporations (e.g., Exxon) that have set up their own venture capital groups. Currently, 30–40 of these are active. Most of the corporate venture capital groups are primarily interested in growing their own acquisition candidates, and at the time of their initial investment they may make an arrangement by which they can acquire the entrepreneurs' equity at a future time. Other reasons given for their venture activity are to obtain a "window onto new technologies" (e.g., DEC's investment in Trilogy) and to obtain licenses to manufacture and sell new products. The latter objective was the reason some of the major pharmaceutical companies invested in such biotechnology start-ups as Cetus, which raised $36 million from corporate investors, including Deralb Agresearch and National Distillers in return for rights to use some of the technology from Cetus' genetics research. Notwithstanding this, some corporations (INCO, Analog Devices) have venture capital programs whose objectives are principally capital gains. From an entrepreneur's point of view, obtaining money from corporate venture capital groups may be a plus for these reasons: they have a tendency to overinvest; they are very patient investors, with a time horizon of 10–20 years for returns; and they have been known to supply $10–20 million.[9] A corporate investor is ideal for the genetics start-up, which may take three years to develop a product and five years to get through FDA testing and approvals before there is any prospect of sales.

15.4.6 Public Stock Offerings

During periods of strong bull markets for new issues (e.g., 1980 and 1981), it is possible to raise money for a first-stage and even a start-up from federally registered and underwritten initial public offerings (IPOs). Most of these IPOs (40–50 percent) have been for the "glamorous" high-technology companies. *Inc.* magazine of August 1984 states that "the number of new issues jumped from 281 in 1980 to an astounding 888 in 1983." The 1980 IPOs represented about $1.4 billion, and the 1983 IPOs represented about three times that amount. On the other hand, in the financial environment of 1973–75 it was very difficult to raise money for first-stage or even more mature companies from the public market. And in 1984 the pace of IPOs fell off sharply.

There are two main reasons why a new or young company might want to go public. First, in the right times it will get a higher stock price from an IPO than from a venture capitalist. Second, an IPO establishes a public price for the stock and gives entrepreneurs a sense of wealth—at least on paper, since certain restrictions are placed on the sale of their stock.

Notwithstanding this rationale for a public offering and even if a start-up or early stage company could raise money through such a sale of stock, there are a number of reasons why it should not do so. Principal among these are:

---

[9] A. David Silver, *Up Front Financing: The Entrepreneur's Guide* (New York: John Wiley & Sons, 1982), p. 33.

1. A public offering generally costs more than other ways of raising money (private placements, intrastate offerings) for a small young company. The costs of underwriting fees, legal fees, audits, prospectus, and so forth can be as high as 15–20 percent for public offerings of $400,000 to $1 million.

2. A large amount of management effort, time, and expense is required to comply with SEC regulations and reporting requirements and to maintain the status of a public company. This diversion of management's time and energy from the tasks of running the company can adversely affect the company's performance and growth.

3. The required disclosures to stockholders and, through them, to outsiders can make known information about a company's products, performance, and financial condition that would be better kept secret.

4. The more mature a company is when it makes a public offering, the better are the terms of the offering: a higher valuation can be placed on the company, and the founders can give less equity for the required capital.

5. Managers can become more interested in maintaining the price of the company's stock and computing their capital gains than in running the company. Short-term activities to maintain or increase this year's earnings can take precedence over longer-term programs to build the company and increase its earnings.

6. The liquidity of a company's stock achieved through a public offering may be more apparent than real. Without a sufficient number of shares outstanding and a strong "market maker," there may be no real market for the stock and thus no liquidity.

7. The investment banking firms willing to take a new or unseasoned company public may not be the ones with which you would like to do business and establish a long-term relationship.

How real are these disadvantages? As a result of a survey of 3,000 companies that had had underwritten public offerings over a 10-year period ending in 1971, Howard[10] reported that of 494 companies responding to the survey:

40 percent said that they would not go public if they had the opportunity to make the decision again.

45 percent said that they had severed their relationship with the underwriter that took them public.

Howard also reported that a survey of companies that filed initial registration statements in 1971 showed that of 107 survey respondents that successfully concluded a public offering:

91 percent said that the amount of key management time consumed in the underwriting was a moderate-to-severe problem.

58 percent said that unanticipated costs of the underwriting were a moderate-to-severe problem.

51 percent said that the amount of disclosure required in the offering prospectus was a moderate-to-severe problem.

52 percent said that the pricing of the issue had been a moderate-to-severe problem.

---

[10]Graeme K. Howard, Jr., "Going Public When It Makes Sense," in *Guide to Venture Capital Sources,* 3d ed., Stanley M. Rubel (Chicago: Capital Publishing, 1974), pp. 77–78. Further information about the number of 1971 survey respondents was obtained from a private conversation with Mr. Howard.

Clearly, the disadvantages and potential problems in a public stock offering are quite real.

In spite of the above reasons, at the right time and under the right circumstances a public offering may be the best way for a first-stage or start-up company to raise the money it needs. But this can be true only if a public offering can yield the most net cash for a given amount of equity and if the reasons against a public offering that we have just cited are not serious problems to a company's management. Generally, we believe that a company starting up or in its first stage of development would do better to raise its capital via a private placement to a venture capital investor.

It should be noted that a smaller business making a public offering for less than $5 million can use an SEC Form S–18 Registration statement instead of the more complex Form S–1. The S–18 offering requires less extensive business and management information than does the S–1 and only two years of audited statements rather than the three required for the S–1. The average costs for an S–18 registration are about 65 percent of the costs for an S–1, and the SEC can review the S–18 faster than the S–1.[11]

15.4.7 Private Placements[12]

If you are going to sell securities to raise money from a spectrum of sources that range from friends and relatives to wealthy individuals and professional venture capitalists, you must be aware of certain federal and state laws that regulate such fund-raising activities and how such offerings are made.

A new or very young venture will want to avoid having its sale of securities accidentally classified as a "public offering" and therefore subject to the full gamut of federal securities laws and regulations that govern such issues. Public offerings that have been made unintentionally because of ignorance of the laws and regulations are potentially very damaging. Disgruntled, unsophisticated stockholders can seek rescission of the deal and the return of their invested capital, and this can result in personal liabilities on a company's management and directors.

How then does a new venture offer securities for its pre-start-up, start-up, and first-stage capital so as not to be subject to the federal regulations governing public offerings? The answer is intrastate registration and private placement.

We will briefly discuss below the conditions that must be met to effect the sale of securities to friendly sources, wealthy individuals, or venture capital firms via a private placement. However, because the conditions governing private placements are complex, *you should not undertake such offerings of securities without the advice of an attorney* who is skilled in these matters.

Private placements can be for any amount, and they involve an offering of stock, subordinated debt, convertible debt, or some other option. Most private placements for young companies will be effected under Regulation D, adopted by the Securities and Exchange Commission (SEC) in April 1982. Regulation D facilitates the raising of capital by small businesses by simplifying and expanding

---

[11]SEC, "Form S–18: A Monitoring Report" (Washington, D.C.: SEC, March 1981).

[12]The sources for this section were M. M. Coleman and I. P. Seldie, *A Businessman's Guide to Capital Raising under the Securities Law* (Philadelphia: Packard Press, 1982); and R. H. Kessel, *High Technology Financing in the 80's* (Boston: Pandick Press, 1984).

how securities offerings can be exempted from the regulations governing public offerings. Regulation D defines three separate exemptions that are based on the amount of money being raised. There are different exemption criteria for private placements of up to $500,000, placements of up to $5 million, and placements that have no dollar limit. Very briefly, these exemptions are as follows:

1. For placements of less than $500,000, there are no specific disclosure/information requirements and no limits on the kind or type of purchasers. This makes marketing offerings of this size easier than it was heretofore.

2. For security sales of up to $5 million, the criteria for a public offering exemption get somewhat more difficult. Sales of securities can be made to not more than 35 nonaccredited purchasers and to an unlimited number of accredited purchasers. (Accredited and unaccredited purchasers are defined below.) There are no limits on the number or qualifications of the offerees and no special information requirements for accredited purchasers. If there are nonaccredited as well as accredited purchasers, there are specified information disclosure requirements. Investors must have the opportunity to obtain additional information about the company from its management.

3. For securities sales in excess of $5 million, there may be not more than 35 nonaccredited purchasers and an unlimited number of accredited purchasers. However, the nonaccredited purchasers must be "sophisticated" in investment matters. There are also specific disclosure requirements that are more detailed than those for offerings between $500,000 and $5 million. And investors must have the opportunity to obtain any additional information from the company and its management.

What are accredited, nonaccredited, and sophisticated investors? Accredited investors include:

Institutional investors such as banks, insurance companies, venture capital firms, registered investment companies, and SBICs.

Any person who buys at least $150,000 of the offered security and whose net worth, including that of his or her spouse, is at least five times the purchase price.

Any person who, together with his or her spouse, has a net worth in excess of $1 million at the time of purchase.

Any person whose individual income was in excess of $200,000 in each of the last two years and who expects the same income for the current year.

Directors, executive officers, or general partners of the company or partnership selling the securities.

Certain tax-exempt organizations with more than $500,000 in assets.

These are the accredited investors; everyone else is a nonaccredited investor. Broadly defined, sophisticated investors are wealthy individuals who invest more or less regularly in new and/or early and late stage ventures. They are knowledgeable about the technical and commercial opportunities and risks of the businesses in which they invest. They know what kind of information they want about their prospective investment, and they have the experience and ability needed to obtain and analyze the data provided to them.

In addition to meeting the federal (SEC) regulations described above, private placements must also comply with the state securities laws in each of the states where the securities will be sold. "Blue skying" is what such state registrations are called. Registration is simple in some states and more complex in others. Again, the advice of a skilled securities attorney should be obtained for such state registrations.

15.4.8   1244 Stock

Whenever possible, the stock that is issued should be so-called 1244 stock. This stock has a significant tax advantage for investors. Losses from investing in 1244 stock of up to $25,000 (or $50,000 in the case of a joint tax return) can be deducted from ordinary income in any one year, while gains are taxed at the capital gains rate. To be able to issue 1244 stock, a company must have less than $500,000 of capital and paid-in surplus prior to the issue and no more than $1 million in equity after the 1244 offering. Further, a company must have only one class of stock and it must receive more than one half of its income from sources other than rents and royalties. A 1244 stock-issue plan is adopted by vote of the directors of a company.

15.5   DEBT CAPITAL SOURCES

The principal sources of borrowed capital for new and young businesses are commercial banks, finance companies, leasing companies, factors, and trade credit; the last is an overlooked but important source of funds for the small businessperson. Admittedly, start-ups have more difficulty in borrowing money than do existing businesses. Nevertheless, start-ups managed by an entrepreneur with a track record who can present a sound business plan, can borrow money from one or more sources. The availability of such debt depends, in part, on where the business is located. Debt and leases as well as equity capital are more available to start-up companies in such hotbeds of entrepreneurial activity as Boston and Silicon Valley than, say, in the Midwest. Also, in the former areas there is close contact between the venture capital firms and the banks' high-technology lending officers. This tends to make it easier for start-ups and early stage companies to borrow money.

Exhibit 15.5 (originally prepared by Timmons and Gumpert) summarizes the principal sources of debt capital, the term of their financing, and whether or not they finance start-ups and/or existing businesses.[13]

In what follows, we shall describe the principal forms of debt financing provided by each of these sources. The descriptions include key features, applications of the financing provided, and information about the sort of loan application or other data that must be submitted to a source to obtain financing. Where applicable, restrictions on the use of funds and the investment preferences of the various sources of debt financing are also discussed.

15.5.1   Trade Credit

Trade credit is a very large source of short-term funds for the small business. In fact, trade credit represents 30–40 percent of the current liabilities of nonfinan-

---

[13]David E. Gumpert and Jeffry A. Timmons, *The Encyclopedia of Small Business Resources* (New York: Harper & Row, 1982), p. 160.

Exhibit 15.5
Debt Financing Sources

Source	Type of Business Financed		Term of Financing		
	Start-up	*Existing*	*Short-Term*	*Medium-Term*	*Long-Term*
Trade credit	Yes	Yes	Yes	No	No
Commercial banks	Occasionally with strong equity capital or collateral	Yes	Most frequently	Some	Rare
Finance companies	Rare	Yes	Most frequently	Yes	Rare
Factors	Rare	Yes	Most frequently	Rare	No
Leasing companies	Difficult for some high-tech start-ups with venture capital	Yes	No	Most frequently	Occasionally
Mutual savings banks and savings and loan	Rare	Real estate only	No	No	Real estate
Insurance companies	Rare	Yes	No	No	Yes

cial businesses, with generally higher percentages in small companies. Trade credit is reflected on the balance sheet as accounts payable.

If a small business is able to buy goods and services and to be given—or to take—30, 60, or 90 days to pay for them, that business has essentially obtained a loan of 30 to 90 days. Many small and new businesses will be able to obtain such trade credit when no other form of debt financing is available to them. Suppliers offer such trade credit as a way of getting new customers and will often build the "bad debt" risk into their prices.

The ability of a new business to obtain trade credit will depend on the quality and reputation of its management and on the relationships it establishes with its suppliers. There are no notes, no applications to fill out, and there is no defined repayment date. A word of warning, however: continued nonpayment of trade payables in 60–90 days may cause suppliers to cut off shipments or to ship only on a COD basis. We must also caution that the real financing cost of using trade credit can be very high—for example, undiscounted prices of purchased items for payment in 10 days. Because the real costs of trade credit are seldom expressed as an annual payment, these costs should be analyzed carefully and the new business should shop for the best terms.

Some of the forms that trade credit may take are:

"Extended credit terms."

"Special or seasonal datings." A supplier ships goods in advance of the purchaser's peak selling season and accepts payment 90 or 120 days later during the season.

"Inventory or consignment." Sometimes a supplier will ship inventory on consignment and not require payment until an item has been sold.

"Loan or lease of equipment." Sometimes a supplier will lend or lease specialized equipment to a business that might not be able to obtain it otherwise.

15.5.2 Commercial Banks[14]

Commercial banks like to be no-risk lenders. For their protection they look first to positive cash flow, and then to collateral, and in new and young businesses they are likely to require personal guarantees of the owners' business. Banks prefer to lend to existing businesses that have a track record of sales, profits, and satisfied customers and a current backlog. Bankers' concern about the high failure rates in new businesses can make them less than enthusiastic about making loans to such firms. Notwithstanding this, banks have made loans to start-ups or young businesses that have received strong equity financing from venture capital firms. This is especially true in such centers of entrepreneurial and venture capital activity as Silicon Valley, Boston, and Los Angeles.

Commercial banks are the primary source of debt capital for small and medium-sized businesses (those with less than $5 million in sales). Small business loans may be handled by a bank's small business loan department. Larger loans may require the approval of a loan committee. If a loan exceeds the capability of a local bank, part or all of the loan will be offered to "correspondent" banks in neighboring communities and nearby financial centers. This correspondent network enables the smaller banks in rural areas to handle loans that could not be made otherwise.

Most of the loans made by commercial banks are short-term—for one year or less. Some of these loans are unsecured, and others are secured by receivables, inventories, or other assets. Commercial banks also make a large number of intermediate-term loans (or "term loans") with a maturity of one to five years. On about 90 percent of these term loans the banks require collateral, generally consisting of stocks, machinery, equipment, and real estate. Most term loans are retired by systematic payments over the life of the loan. Apart from real estate mortgages and loans guaranteed by the SBA or a similar organization, commercial banks make few long-term loans with maturities greater than five years.

Banks can also offer a number of services to the small business, such as computerized payroll preparation, letters of credit, international services, lease financing, and money market accounts.

There are almost 14,000 commercial banks in the United States. A complete listing of these banks can be found, arranged by state, in the *American Bank Directory* (Norcross, Ga.: McFadden Business Publications), published semiannually.

Exhibit 15.6 summarizes the kinds of financing that commercial banks can provide to businesses. It shows the primary features of each type of financing, and it notes the considerations and data involved in the bank's financing decision. In addition, the primary distinguishing features of each kind of financing are briefly described below.

Line of Credit. A line of credit is a formal or informal agreement between a bank and a borrower concerning the maximum loan balance that the bank will allow the borrower for a one-year period. Often, the bank will charge a fee of ½–1 percent of the line of credit for a definite commitment to make the loan when requested.

The loan funds are used for seasonal financings such as inventory buildups and receivable financing. It is general practice to repay such loans from the sale

[14]This material is adapted from Leonard E. Smollen, "Commercial Banks and Other Savings Institutions," in *Source Guide for Borrowing Capital* (Wellesley, Mass.: Capital Publishing, 1977).

Exhibit 15.6
Commercial Bank Financing

Financing	Purpose	Term	Collateral	Loan Limit	Payback	Credit Criteria	Data Required	Special Loan Conditions	Typical Interest Rates/Cost Financing
Line of credit	Seasonal financing for inventory buildup, receivable financing, etc.	1 year with 90-day renewable notes, or 1 year installment loan	Can be unsecured or secured by receivables, equipment, inventory, or other assets	40–50% of working capital	Single balloon payment, or Monthly or quarterly installments	1. Character and managerial ability of applicant 2. Uses of money 3. Outlook for business and its industry 4. Ability to pay back as required 5. Satisfactory "cushion" in loan 6. Current ratio 1:1 or greater 7. Debt-to-worth ratio no more than 3:1	1. Completed loan application 2. CPA-prepared financial statements 3. Forecasts of sales, profits, and cash flow 4. Brief description of products, company, industry, and management 5. Justification of loan need and use of funds	Minimum checking account balance of 15–20% of loan Payment of debt once a year and no new debt for 60 days Periodic financial reports Personal guarantee of loan	For prime risks, 1–2% above Federal Reserve rediscount rate For small companies, interest rate is higher
Accounts receivable financing loan	Short-term debt financing for working capital, inventory buildup, and receivables when unsecured debt cannot be obtained	Initially 1 year with renewals Can be extended as revolving line of credit	Accounts receivable Lender has full recourse to borrower for unpaid receivables	70–80% of outstanding receivables	Paid from collection of receivables by borrower or by the bank	Same as 1–4 above plus: 5. Value and collectibility of receivables 6. Quality of firm's debtors	Same as 1–5 above plus: 6. List of receivables showing amount and age of each in 30-day intervals	Only receivables that meet lender's credit standards will be financed Submission of regular financial statements Lender monitoring of books and receivable records	Can be fairly high, e.g., 2–4% above Federal Reserve rediscount rate
Time-sales financing	Short-term debt for working capital and inventory from financing of longer-term installment receivables	Immediate capital from discounted sale of installment contracts	Conditional sales contract for installment purchases Recourse to manufacturer/dealer in the event of loan default Payment obligation of purchaser	Depends on value of installment contract, size of discount taken, and dealer reserve withheld until note is paid	By equipment purchaser in installments to banks or through manufacturer/dealer to bank Payback period less than useful life of equipment	Character, reputation, and stability of manufacturer/dealer Reliability of goods sold on installment contracts Down payment and installments such that amount due is less than resale value Satisfactory current and debt/net worth ratios	Financial statements of dealer/manufacturer Brief description of dealer/manufacturer business and management Credit rating of purchaser Satisfactory installment contract Legal assignment of installment contract to bank	Percentage of installment contract withheld as dealer reserve until note is paid. Amount withheld depends on quality of underlying collateral	Discount of 6–10% from value of installment contract

Exhibit 15.6 (concluded)

Financing	Purpose	Term	Collateral	Loan Limit	Payback	Credit Criteria	Data Required	Special Loan Conditions	Typical Interest Rates/Cost Financing
Unsecured term loan	Intermediate-term financing for working capital, plant, equipment, retiring higher-interest loans	1–5 years	Unsecured or secured by collateral or equipment	Most loans are from $100,000 to $250,000	Retire by equal installments over life of loan. Prepayment of loans usually involves penalty of 1–5% of outstanding balance. A few loans have balloon payment at end	Purpose of loan. Effective use of loan. Long-term profit prospects of company and its industry. Character and effectiveness of management. Fixed-asset values. Adequate future cash flow. Current and forecast financial statements. Satisfactory current and debt/net worth ratios.	Brief business plan that covers: history of company; prospects for company and its industry; current and planned facilities; track record and background of management; financial statements for 2 prior years; forecast income statements, balance sheets, and cash flows for term of loan; justification of loan need and use funds	Current ratios and net working capital held above specified level. Limitation on acquisition of fixed assets. Restriction on major changes in business. Additional term debt prohibited without bank's consent. Bank deposit balance of 15–20% of loan. Management changes requires lender approval. Periodic financial reports. Assets may not be pledged as security to other lenders	Slightly higher than for short-term line of credit. Interest rate can fluctuate with changing rediscount rate. For small companies, rate is higher and depends on company loan size
Chattel mortgage and equipment loan (may also be treated as security agreement under Uniform Commercial Code)	Same as unsecured term loans	Generally 1–5 years. Some for longer term	Equipment, property, and machinery that can be readily disposed of for cash. Can be new equipment purchased with loan	From 100–150% of auction appraisal value or collateral	Same as for unsecured term loans	Same as for unsecured term loans, plus Auction appraisal of collateral	Same as for unsecured term loans, plus Auction appraisal of collateral	Same as for unsecured term loans	1–3% higher than Federal Reserve rediscount rate for larger companies with prime credit ratings. Rates higher for smaller companies

Conditional sales contract	Finance purchase of new equipment	1–5 years and less than equipment life	Legal ownership of equipment resides with seller until buyer has made all payments	60–70% of purchase price	One third of loan down, with balance paid equal installments Down payment and installments such that outstanding loan less than resale value	Market value of equipment financed	Conditional sales contract between buyer and seller	Lending bank has recourse to seller for debt in event of default	Higher than other forms of intermediate-term loans
Plant improvement loan	Finance improvements to plants and facilities	2–10 years	Mortgage on plant and/or property	60–80% of appraised value	Uniform periodic payments over period of loan	Market value of plant	Appraisal of property Current and projected financial statements Track record of management Ability to service loan Justification of loans need	Similar to unsecured term loans	Slightly (1–2%) higher than Federal Reserve rediscount rate

of goods and liquidation of the short-term assets they financed. Lines of credit can be unsecured, but often a bank will require a pledge of inventory, receivables, equipment, or other acceptable assets. Unsecured lines of credit have no lien on any asset of the borrower and no priority over any trade creditor, but they do require that all debt to the principals and stockholders of the company be subordinated to the lines of credit debt.

The line of credit is executed through a series of renewable 90-day notes or through an installment loan that is to be paid up within the year. The renewable 90-day note is the more common practice, and the bank will expect the borrower to completely pay off his open line within a year and to hold a zero loan balance for one to two months. This is known as "resting the line." Commercial banks may also generally require that a borrower maintain a checking account at the bank with a minimum or "compensating" balance of 15–20 percent of the outstanding loan.

For a large, financially sound company, interest rates for "prime risk" line of credit loans will be quoted at about 1–2 percent over the rediscount rate charged by the Federal Reserve. A small firm may be required to pay a higher rate. It should be noted that the true rate of interest will depend on the method of charging interest. If the bank deducts interest in advance (discounts the loan) or the loan is repaid in installments, the effective rate of interest will be higher than the quoted figure. In addition, any "compensating balance" or "resting the line" requirements will increase the effective interest rates.

Accounts Receivable Financing. Accounts receivable financing is short-term financing that involves either the pledge of receivables as collateral for a loan or the sale of receivables (factoring). Accounts receivable loans are made by commercial banks, whereas factoring is done primarily by commercial finance companies and factoring concerns. Only a very limited number of banks do factoring.

Accounts receivable bank loans are made on a discounted value of the receivables pledged. Invoices that do not meet the bank's credit standard will not be accepted as collateral. (Receivables more than 90 days old are not normally accepted.) A bank may make receivable loans on a notification or nonnotification plan. Under the notification plan, the purchaser of goods is informed that his account has been assigned to the bank. Payments are made directly to the bank, which credits them to the borrower's account. Under the nonnotification plan, the borrower collects his accounts as usual and pays off his bank loan.

Accounts receivable loans can often make it possible for a company to secure a loan that it might not obtain otherwise. The loan can be increased as sales and receivables grow. However, receivable loans do have drawbacks. They can be expensive, and receivable financing is sometimes regarded by trade creditors as evidence of a company in financial difficulty.

Time-Sales Finance. Many dealers or manufacturers that offer installment payment terms to purchasers of their equipment cannot, themselves, finance these installment or conditional sales contracts. In such situations, the small-to-medium-sized dealer or manufacturer may sell and assign the installment contract to a bank or sales finance company. (Some very large manufacturers do their own financing through captive finance companies; most very small retailers merely refer their customers to consumer finance companies.) Although commercial banks are becoming more active in the financing of commercial and consumer installment contracts, sales finance companies provide more of this financing, and on more flexible terms.

From the manufacturer's or dealer's point of view, time-sales finance is, in effect, a way of obtaining short-term financing from long-term installment accounts receivable. From the purchaser's point of view, it is a way of term-financing the purchase of new equipment through what is known as conditional sales financing.

Under time-sales financing, the bank purchases installment contracts at a discount from their full value and takes as security an assignment of the manufacturer/dealer's interest in the conditional sales contract. In addition, the bank's financing of the installment notes receivables is with recourse to the seller in the event of loan default by the purchaser. Thus, the bank has the payment obligation of the equipment purchaser, the manufacturer/dealer's security interest in the equipment purchased, and recourse to the manufacturer/dealer in the event of default. The bank also withholds a portion of the payment (5 percent or more) as a dealer reserve until the note is paid. Since the reserve becomes an increasing percentage of the note as the contract is paid off, an arrangement is often made, when multiple contracts are financed, to ensure that the reserve against all contracts will not exceed 20 percent or so.

The purchase price of equipment under a sales financing arrangement includes a "time-sales price differential"—i.e., an increase to cover the discount (typically 6–10 percent) taken by the bank that does the financing. Collection of the installments may be made directly by the bank or indirectly through the manufacturer/dealer.

Unsecured Term Loans. Bank term loans are generally made for periods of from one to five years and may be unsecured or secured. Most of the basic features of bank term loans are the same for secured and unsecured loans. Secured term loans are described below under chattel mortgages and collateral loans.

Term loans provide needed growth capital to companies that could not obtain such capital from the sale of stock. They are also a substitute for a series of short-term loans made with the anticipation of renewal by both the borrower and the lender.

Term loans have three distinguishing features:

1. They are made by banks for periods of up to five years (and occasionally more).
2. Periodic repayment is required.
3. Term loan agreements are designed to fit the special needs and requirements of the borrower; for example, payments can be smaller at the beginning of a loan term and larger at the end.

Because term loans do not mature for a number of years, during which time there could be a significant change in the situation and fortunes of the borrower, the bank must carefully evaluate the prospects and management of the borrowing company. Even the protection afforded by initially strong assets can be wiped out by several years of heavy losses. Term lenders place particular stress on the entrepreneurial and managerial abilities of the borrowing company. The bank will also carefully consider such things as the long-range prospects of the company and its industry, its present and projected profitability, and its ability to generate the cash required to meet the loan payments.

To lessen the risks involved in term loans, the bank will require some restrictive covenants in the loan agreement. These covenants might prohibit additional borrowing, merger of the company, payment of dividends, sales of assets, and so on.

Chattel Mortgages and Equipment Loans. Assigning an appropriate chattel as security is a common way of making secured term loans. The chattel is any machinery, equipment, or business property that is made the collateral of a loan in the same way as a mortgage on real estate. The loan security (chattel) remains with the borrower unless there is default, in which case the chattel goes to the bank. Generally, credit against machinery and equipment is restricted primarily to new or highly serviceable and salable used items.

It should be noted that in many states loans that used to be chattel mortgages are now executed through the security agreement forms of the Uniform Commercial Code (UCC). Chattel mortgages are still used in many places however, and, from custom, many lenders continue to use that term even though the loans are executed through the UCC's security agreements. The term of chattel mortgages is typically from one to five years; some are of longer term.

Conditional Sales Contracts. Conditional sales contracts are used to finance a substantial portion of the new equipment purchased by businesses. Under a sales contract, the buyer agrees to purchase a piece of equipment, make a nominal down payment, and pay the balance in installments over a period of from one to five years. Until payment is complete, the seller holds title to the equipment. Hence, the sale is conditional upon the buyer's completing the payments.

An important and distinguishing feature of this form of financing is that the sales contract is financed by a bank that has recourse to the seller, should the purchaser default the loan. One result of this is that it is easier to finance a new piece of equipment from a machinery dealer than to finance the purchase of a good piece of used equipment at an auction. In the case of new equipment, the bank providing the financing has recourse to a machinery dealer in the event of default. No such recourse is available if the equipment is purchased at an auction and the bank has to dispose of the equipment in the event of loan default. This has occasionally prompted a firm seeking financing on existing and new equipment to sell some of its equipment to a dealer and then to repurchase it, together with new equipment, under a conditional sales contract financed by a bank.

The effective rate of interest on a conditional sales contract is high, running to as much as 15–18 percent if the effect of installment features on the stated interest rate is considered. The purchaser/borrower should make sure that this interest payment will be covered by increased productivity and profitability resulting from the new equipment.

Plant Improvement Loans. Loans made to finance improvements to business properties and plants are called plant improvement loans. They can be intermediate- or long-term, and they are generally secured by a first mortgage on the part of the property or plant that is being improved.

15.5.3 Commercial Finance Companies

The commercial bank is generally the lender of choice for the business. From whom does a business seek loans when the bank says no? The commercial finance company. Silver notes: "Commercial finance company lenders are, for the most part, quite entrepreneurial.... They aggressively seek borrowers.... Their style is exemplified by their most common sentence...:—Okay, let's see how we can make this loan."[15] Commercial finance companies will frequently lend money

[15]Silver, *Up Front Financing,* p. 101.

to companies that do not have positive cash flow. However, this does not imply that finance companies will make loans to companies they consider nonviable. They are, however, more aggressive than banks in their lending practices.

The difference between the lending practice of banks and finance companies arises from the fact that the primary factor in a bank's loan decision is the continuing successful operation of a business and the generation of cash that is more than adequate to repay its loan. On the other hand, the finance company is an asset-based lender. It lends against assets (receivables, inventory, equipment) that it understands, that it knows how and where to liquidate, and whose quick sales and/or collection will be sufficient to repay the loan.

What kinds of asset-backed loans will a finance company make? Generally, liquid assets such as receivables, certain finished goods and raw materials inventory, and, occasionally, equipment. Commercial finance companies lend against the liquidation values of these assets.

In the case of inventories or equipment, liquidation value is the amount that could be realized from an auction or quick sale of these assets. With respect to receivables, finance companies will generally *not* lend against receivables more than 90 days old, federal or state government agency receivables (because they are slow payers), or any receivables whose collection is contingent on the performance of a delivered product. Because of the liquidation criteria, finance companies prefer readily salable inventory items such as electronic components or metal in such commodity forms as billets or standard shapes. Generally, a finance company will not accept inventory as collateral unless it also has receivables. As for equipment loans, these are made only by certain finance companies and against standard equipment such as lathes and milling machines.

How much of the value of the collateral will a finance company lend? Generally, 70–80 percent of acceptable receivables, 40–50 percent of the liquidation value of raw materials and/or finished goods inventory, and 60–70 percent of the liquidation value of equipment—as determined by an appraiser. The equipment loans will be for five years, while the receivable and inventory loans will be for one year. All of these loans will have tough prepayment penalties: the finance company doesn't want to be immediately replaced by a bank when its borrower has improved its credit image.

The data required for a loan from a commercial finance company includes all that would be provided to a bank (see Exhibit 15.6, "Accounts Receivable Financing Loan" and "Chattel Mortgage and Equipment Loan") plus additional details on the assets being used as collateral. For receivable financing, this would include detailed aging of receivables (and payables) and historical data on sales, returns, and collections. For inventory financing, it would include details on the items in inventory, how long they have been there, and their turnover. Requests for equipment loans should be accompanied by details on the date of purchase, the cost of each equipment item, and appraisals if available. If not, the finance company will have such appraisals made.

The advantages of dealing with a commercial finance company are that it will make loans that banks will not and that it can be flexible in their lending arrangements. The price a finance company exacts for this is an interest rate anywhere from 2–6 percent over that charged by a bank, prepayment penalties, and, in the case of receivable loans, recourse to the borrower for unpaid collateralized receivables. Because of their greater risk taking and their asset-based lending, finance companies usually place a larger reporting and monitoring burden on the borrowing firm in order to stay on top of the receivable and inventory serving as loan collateral. Personal guarantees will generally be required from the principals of a business. The finance company will generally reserve the right to reduce the percentage lent against receivables or inventory if it gets "nervous" about the borrower's survivability.

15.5.4   Factors

Factoring is a form of accounts receivable financing. However, instead of being used as collateral against loans, the receivables are sold, at a discounted value, to a factoring company. Some commercial finance companies do factoring. Those whose primary business is factoring are called factors. Like commercial finance companies, the factor provides receivables financing for the company unable to obtain such financing from a bank.

In a standard factoring arrangement the factor buys the client's receivables outright, without recourse, as soon as the client creates them by its shipment of goods to customers. Although the factor has recourse to the borrower for returns, errors in pricing, and so forth, the factor assumes the risk of bad debt losses that develop from receivables that it approves and purchases. Cash can be made available to the client as soon as proof of shipment is provided (old-line factoring) or on the average due date of the invoice (maturity factoring). With maturity factoring the client can often obtain a loan of about 90 percent of the money that the factor would pay him on the maturity date. Most factoring arrangements are for one year.

Factoring fits some businesses better than others. If a business sells on normal credit terms to a customer base that is 75 percent credit rated and has an annual sales volume in excess of $300,000 and a net worth of over $50,000, factoring is a real option. Factoring has become almost traditional in such industries as textiles, furniture manufacturing, clothing manufacturing, toys, shoes, and plastics.

The data required from a business for a receivable loan from a bank will be required by a factor. Because a factor is buying receivables with no recourse, it will analyze carefully the quality and value of a prospective client's receivables. It will want a detailed aging of receivables plus historical data on bad debts, returns, and allowances. It will also investigate the credit history of the customers to whom its client sells, and establish credit limits for each customer. The business client can receive factoring of customer receivables only up to the limits so set.

The cost of financing receivables through factoring is higher than that of borrowing from a bank or finance company. This is because the factor is assuming the credit risk and doing credit investigations and collections as well as advancing funds. A factor generally charges ½–2 percent of the total sales factored as a service charge. There is also an interest charge for monies advanced to a business; the interest rate is usually 2–6 percent above prime. A larger, established business borrowing large sums will command a better interest rate than the small borrower with a onetime, short-term need. Finally, factors will withhold a reserve of 5–10 percent of the receivables purchased.

Factoring is not the cheapest way to obtain capital, but it does quickly turn receivables into cash. Moreover, although more expensive than accounts receivable financing, factoring saves its users credit agency fees, salaries of credit and collection personnel, and bad debt write-offs.

15.5.5 Leasing Companies

The leasing industry has grown substantially in recent years, and lease financing has become an important source of medium-term financing for businesses. There are about 700–800 leasing companies in the United States. In addition to these, many commercial banks and finance companies have leasing departments. Some leasing companies handle a wide variety of equipment, while others specialize in certain types of equipment, for example, machine tools and electronic test equipment.

Common and readily resalable items such as automobiles and trucks, typewriters, and office furniture can be leased by both new and existing businesses. However, the start-up will find it difficult to lease other kinds of industrial, computer, or business equipment without providing a CD to secure the lease or personal guarantees from the founders or a wealthy third party. This does not hold true for high-technology start-ups that have received substantial venture capital. Some of these ventures have received large amounts of lease financing for rather special equipment from equity-oriented lessors that receive some form of stock purchase rights in return for providing the start-up's lease line. In one case known to the authors, one such leasing company provided a $2 million three-year lease line to a start-up with $5 million of equity financing in return for some stock warrants. Two companies doing this sort of venture leasing are Equitec of Oakland, California, with offices in Boston, New York and Dallas, and Intertec of Mill Valley, California. Both of these lease programs are rather recent.

Generally, industrial equipment leases have a term of three–five years, but they run longer in some cases. There can also be lease renewal options for 3–5 percent of the original equipment value per year. Leases are usually structured to return the entire cost of the equipment leased plus finance charges to the lessor.[16] Typically, an up-front payment is required of about 10 percent of the value of the item being leased. The interest rate on equipment leasing may be more or less than that charged for other forms of financing, depending on the equipment leased, the credit of the lessee, the time of the year, and most important, who gets the investment tax credit (ITC). To be eligible for an ITC, a lease must be a "true lease" as defined by the IRS. A "true lease" must have a fair market purchase option for the lessee at the end of the lease: otherwise, the IRS considers the transaction an installment sale. If the lessor receives the ITC, it reduces its interest or finance rate on the lease. Near the end of the lessor's tax year, ITCs have more immediate value and become especially attractive. The result is that leases granting the lessor the ITC and written at year-end can have lower finance/interest charges than leases written earlier in the year. Appropriate consideration of the ITC does not necessarily occur automatically, and the potential lessee should be prepared to raise and negotiate this issue. In most small businesses,

---

[16]Some so-called operating leases do not, over their term, produce revenues equal to or greater than the price of the leased equipment.

cash flow is the paramount concern and it makes good sense to give the lessor the ITC in return for lower lease payments.

Leasing credit criteria are very similar to the criteria used by commercial banks for equipment loans (see Exhibit 15.6). The primary considerations are the value of the equipment leased, the justification of the lease, and the lessee's projected cash flow over the lease term.

Should a business lease equipment? Leasing has certain advantages. It enables a young or growing company to conserve cash and to reduce its requirements for equity capital. Leasing can also be tax advantageous, because payments can be expensed over a shorter period than the depreciation of the same equipment. Finally, leasing provides the flexibility of returning equipment after the lease period if it is no longer needed or if it has become technologically obsolete. The latter can be a particular advantage to companies in high-technology industries. Leasing no longer improves a company's balance sheet, because accounting practice now requires that the value of the equipment leased be capitalized and that a lease liability be shown.

15.6   TAX SHELTER FINANCING

In recent years several forms of tax-advantaged investment have emerged for financing product development and the start-up of new enterprises. The vehicle used for such investments is the limited partnership.

15.6.1   Limited Partnerships: An Overview

In a limited partnership, there are two classes of partners: the limited partners and the general partners. In a general or "ordinary" partnership, all partners have unlimited liability for the actions of the partnership. This is not so in a limited partnership, where the liability of the limited partners—who are the investors—is limited to their capital investment. Only the general partners have unlimited liability. To qualify for limited liability, the limited partners must not participate in the management of the partnership: the general partners manage the activities of the partnership. As in a general partnership, there is no tax at the partnership level for gains or losses realized by the limited partnership. Thus, the limited partnership offers the best of both worlds to its investors: limited liability and a single level of taxation.[17] There is yet another advantage to the limited partnership. Gains and losses may be allocated differently to the limited and general partners. For example, the limited partners may be allocated 90 percent of the losses and 40 percent of the profits and capital gains of the partnership. This permits high-tax-bracket investors to expense for tax purposes most of the losses generally associated with product development and/or starting a new company and thus reduces their capital of risk.

The astute entrepreneur may well ask: Why not make the general partner a corporation and thereby limit the liability of all partners in a limited partnership? Unfortunately, the IRS has also thought of this and has recognized that a

---

[17]We should note that a Subchapter S corporation also provides single level taxation and limited liability. However, the number of investors in a Subchapter S corporation is limited to 25 (including all shareholders or partners of an investing entry) and it does not allow for a different allocation of gains and losses: i.e., shareholders are allocated both gains and in direct proportion to their shareholdings. Notwithstanding this, a Subchapter S can provide some tax advantage to start-up investors.

sole corporate general partner provides limited liability to all participants: almost as if they were shareholders of a corporation. To ensure that a limited partnership with a *sole corporate general partner* is not a "sham" for tax purposes, the IRS has adopted two "safe harbor rules" that such a limited partnership should meet if it is to be taxed as a partnership.[18] These rules are:

1. *Ownership requirements:* The limited partners may not own more than 20 percent of the corporate general partner. This ownership may be in shares or it may be interpreted as a percentage of contributed capital only if the limited partners have made a cash or in-kind investment. In other words, the corporate general partner must have real assets that are at least four times any investment in it by the limited partners.

2. *Capital requirements:* If the capital invested in the partnership is more than $2,500,000, the corporate general partner must have a net worth of at least 10 percent of the partnership's capital at all times. For capital investments less than $2,500,000, the corporate general partner must have a net worth of 15 percent of the partnership's capital, but not more than $250,000.

The above safe harbor rules are only guidelines or opinions promulgated by the IRS, and they do not appear in any formal regulations. Nevertheless, most limited partnerships with a sole corporate general partner will attempt to meet these conditions. The tax considerations are sufficiently complex that an entrepreneur should not set up a limited partnership without expert legal advice. It is essential that the limited partnership be treated for tax purposes as a partnership and not a corporation by the IRS if the limited partners are to receive tax benefits.

The two forms of tax-sheltered investment vehicles that are most popular and most used are the "equity partnership" and the "R&D partnership." Both are discussed below.

15.6.2 Equity Partnerships

The equity partnership is used to start up and operate a business. The basic notion is to flow losses to the limited partners during the start-up and early development phase of a business. Once the venture product has been developed and the business seems to be moving toward profitability, the partnership may assume corporate form, with the limited partners becoming shareholders of the corporation that succeeds the partnership. The legal documents associated with an equity partnership can be complex. Ronald Kessel, an attorney with Herrick & Smith, notes:

Under an elaborate set of agreements, mechanics are established for incorporating the partnership when the business begins to generate taxable income. This raises some very complicated partnership status, incorporation, and reorganization tax issues.[19]

The investors in an equity partnership are primarily interested in long-term capital gains and view the tax shelter features of the vehicle as a way of reducing their capital at risk. Several venture capital firms specialize in investing as a limited partner in an equity partnership. Among these are Venture Founders Cor-

---

[18]Peter C. Reid and Gustave Simons, *Corporate and Executive Tax Sheltered Investments* (New York: Publishing House, 1972), pp. 169–170.

[19]Ronald H. Kessel, *A Securities Lawyer Looks at. . . High Technology Financing in the 80's* (Boston: Pandick Press, 1984), p. 10.

poration of Waltham, Massachusetts, and Crosspoint Ventures of Palo Alto, California. In most equity partnerships a corporation serves as the general partner, with the entrepreneurs as shareholders.

In spite of its elaborate agreements, an equity partnership can be advantageous to the entrepreneur. First, because investors are receiving tax write-offs for part or all of their investment and reducing their capital at risk, the entrepreneur can usually get start-up financing for less equity than would be given to investors in a corporate vehicle. Second, the potential tax savings to investors can serve to stimulate seed and start-up investments by wealthy individual investors. The main disadvantages of the equity partnership are its complexity and the loss of future tax-loss carryforwards by a successor corporation. The tax risk of having the tax-loss flowbacks disallowed lies with the limited partner investors.

15.6.3 R&D Partnerships

R&D partnerships can be and are being used by both start-up and established businesses to fund the development of products. An existing sponsor corporation identifies an R&D or product development program that it wants to fund without showing these expenditures on its income statement. A limited partnership is organized to fund this development work. This partnership funds the sponsoring corporation to actually conduct the R&D. The limited partnership makes payments to the corporation for the R&D it conducts, and the investors receive the benefit of tax deductions for research and development expenses.

If the R&D is successful, ownership of the products developed resides with the limited partnership. Generally, the limited partnership grants the sponsor corporation an option to acquire the technology or product developed in return for a prenegotiated royalty on the subsequent sales of the product. Royalties paid to the limited partners are treated as capital gains by them. To achieve such capital gains treatment, the option must be a real one and not exercisable until at least six months after completion of the R&D:[20] the limited partnership must be seen to bear the risk of the success of the R&D conducted. In a typical R&D partnership the limited partners will have tax write-offs for 70–90 percent of the partners' capital and royalties may run in the 7–10 percent range.[21]

R&D partnerships have acquired a certain notoriety: Storage Technology used one to fund the development of a computer that it later abandoned; and John DeLorean used one for his automobile development. Smaller companies with smaller financing requirements have also used them. Most recently, Telesis (a CAE company) raised a $4.5 million partnership to fund the development of new CAE projects.

In the authors' view, an R&D partnership has several disadvantages. The future payment of royalties can significantly reduce a company's ability to produce cash and profits. Further, an overhanging future royalty payment can be a negative factor in a future equity financing decision by a venture capital firm, because it reduces profitability. As with an equity partnership, an entrepreneur should obtain expert and specialized legal and accounting advice before setting up an R&D partnership.

[20] Ibid., p. 9.

[21] Jane K. Morris, "Tax-Advantaged Financing Sources through Limited Partnerships," in *Pratt's Guide to Venture Capital Sources,* 8th ed., ed. Stanley E. Pratt (Wellesley, Mass.: Capital Publishing, 1984).

15.7 GOVERNMENT FINANCING SOURCES

15.7.1 Federal Sources

In the 1970s there were a number of loan-guarantee, direct loan, and grant programs from at least five federal agencies. Only two have survived into the 1980s: the Small Business Administration's (SBA) direct loan and loan-guarantee programs and the recently (July 1982) authorized Small Business Innovation Research program (SBIR).

Small Business Administration (SBA). The SBA's regular business loan program now includes the special-purpose loan—disaster, export financing, and so forth. Here, we shall focus on the regular business loans, called Section 7A loans by the SBA.

The SBA is often the lender of last resort for entrepreneurs who have been unable to obtain bank loans or other financing. The SBA is a significant source of small business finance, especially for retail establishments. Typically, the SBA provides annually about $2.5 billion in loans and loan guarantees to about 25,000 businesses, and about 6,000–7,000 of these go to new businesses. The SBA's small business loans are used to finance plant construction or expansion, to purchase equipment, and to provide working capital. For SBA purposes, a small business is defined as one that (1) is not dominant in its industry, (2) is independently owned and operated, (3) has a net worth less than $6 million, and (4) has had after-tax profits that averaged less than $2 million for the last two years. In some industries the SBA may use different standards. It is interesting to note that about 95 percent of all businesses in the United States are small by SBA standards.

The SBA has two primary ways of providing financing:

1. *Guaranteed Loans.* Under this approach, a bank makes the actual loan and the SBA guarantees a large portion of the loan: 70–90 percent for loans of over $100,000 and 90 percent for loans of under $100,000. Loans of up to $500,000 can be guaranteed by the SBA. Almost 80 percent of all SBA financial assistance is in the form of loan guarantees. To be eligible for such assistance, the borrower must have been denied loans by two banks.

2. *Direct Loans.* These loans are made directly by the SBA to the borrower. They are not available unless the borrower has been rejected by two banks for a loan with an SBA guarantee. They are limited to $150,000 and are hard to obtain because federal funding for them is limited. Direct loans may be the only financing that some businesses can get, and they carry substantial risk.

SBA business loans can have terms that range from a short period of time to 10 years. In some cases, the term can be extended beyond 10 years. Interest rates on direct loans are set by the government and are prime or less. The banks' interest rate on guaranteed loans is within reasonable limits set by the SBA and is typically 1–2½ percent over prime.

Exhibit 15.7 summarizes the procedures that an established business or a new business should use in applying for SBA loans or loan guarantees. Applications for SBA loans are made by using SBA Form 4 (direct loan application) or Form 4–I (guaranteed bank loan), along with the Statement of Personal History.

The decision of the SBA to make a loan or loan guarantee depends on the applicant's character and track record and on his ability to pay back the loan as demonstrated by past earnings and/or projected cash flows. It also depends on the borrower's having enough of his own and other funds in the business.

Exhibit 15.7
Procedure for Applying for SBA Small Business Loans

For Established Businesses	*For New Businesses*
1. Prepare a current financial statement (balance sheet) listing all assets and all liabilities of the business. Do not include personal items.	1. Describe in detail the type of business to be established.
2. Have an earnings (profit and loss) statement for the previous full year and for the current period to the date of the balance sheet.	2. Describe experience and management capabilites
3. Prepare a current personal financial statement of the owner, or of each partner or stockholder owning 20 percent of more of the corporate stock in the business.	3. Prepare an estimate of how much you or others have to invest in the business and how much you will borrow.
4. List the collateral to be offered as security for the loan, with your estimate of the present market value of each item.	4. Prepare a current financial statement (balance sheet) listing all personal assets and all liabilities. Prepare a detailed projections of earnings for the first year that the business will operate.
5. State amount of the loan required, and explain the exact purpose for which it will be used.	5. List the collateral to be offered as security for the loan, indicating your estimate of the present market value of each item.
6. Take this material with you and see your banker. Ask for a direct bank loan, and if this is declined, ask the bank to make the loan under the SBA's Loan Guaranty Plan or to participate with the SBA in a loan. If the bank is interested in an SBA guaranty or participation loan, ask the banker to contact the SBA for discussion of your application. In most cases of guaranty or participation loans, the SBA will deal directly with the bank.	6. Take this material with you and see your banker. Ask for a direct bank loan, and if this is declined, ask the bank to make the loan under the SBA's Loan Guaranty Plan or to participate with the SBA in a loan. If the bank is interested in an SBA guaranty or participation loan, ask the banker to contact the SBA for discussion of your application. In most cases of guaranty or participation loans, the SBA will deal directly with the bank.
7. If a guaranty or a participation loan is not available, write or visit the nearest SBA office in order to apply for a direct loan. The SBA has 79 field offices and, in addition, sends loan officers to visit many smaller cities on a regularly scheduled basis or as the need is indicated. To speed matters, make your financial information available when you first write or visit the SBA.	7. If a guaranty or a participation loan is not available, write or visit the nearest SBA office in order to apply for a direct loan. The SBA has 79 field offices and, in addition, sends loan officers to visit many smaller cities on a regularly scheduled basis or as the need is indicated. To speed matters, make your financial information available when you first write or visit the SBA.

The advantage of an SBA loan is that "it may be the only game in town." What are some of the disadvantages? Personal guarantees from anyone owning more that 20 percent of the business. A first lien on *"all"* assets of a company. Restrictions on the amounts that can be spent for assets without SBA and/or bank approval. And finally, the amount of time that it can take to get SBA financing. According to Rubin and Goldberg, this can be 2–4 months in metropolitan areas.[22]

Small Business Innovation Research Program (SBIR). Under the Small Business Innovation Development Act, all government agencies with research and development budgets in excess of $100 million must establish SBIR programs. The funding of each SBIR program is a fixed percentage of each agency's R&D budget. There are now 12 agencies participating in the program (see Exhibit 15.8 for the SBIR contacts at each agency).

The SBIR program provides small, technology-based businesses with an op-

---

[22]Richard Rubin and Philip Goldberg, *The Small Business Guide to Borrowing Money* (New York: McGraw-Hill, 1982), p. 115.

Exhibit 15.8
Participating Agency SBIR Representatives

National Aeronautics and Space Administration
Dr. Carl Schwenk
National Aeronautics and Space Administration
SBIR Office—Code RB
600 Independence Avenue, S.W.
Washington, D.C. 20546
(202) 453-2848

National Science Foundation
Mr. Roland Tibbetts
Mr. Ritchie Coryell
SBIR Program Managers
National Science Foundation
1800 G Street, N.W.
Washington, D.C. 20550
(202) 357-7527

Nuclear Regulatory Commission
Mr. Wayne Batson
Office of Nuclear Regulatory Research
Nuclear Regulatory Commission
Washington, D.C. 20460
(301) 427-4250

Department of Education
Dr. Edward Esty
SBIR Program Coordinator
Office of Educational Research and Improvement
Department of Education, Mail Stop 40
Washington, D.C. 20208
(202) 254-8247

Department of Energy
Ms. Gerry Washington
c/o SBIR Program Manager
U.S. Department of Energy
Washington, D.C. 20545
(301) 353-5867

Department of Health and Human Services
Mr. Richard Clinkscales
Director, Office of Small and Disadvantaged Business
  Utilization
Department of Health and Human Services
200 Independence Avenue, S.W., Room 513D
Washington, D.C. 20201
(202) 245-7300

Department of Agriculture
Dr. W. K. Murphey
Office of Grants and Program Systems
Department of Agriculture
West Auditors Building, Room 112
15th and Independence Avenue, S.W.
Washington, D.C. 20251
(202) 475-5022

Department of Commerce
Mr. James P. Maruca
Director, Office of Small and Disadvantaged Business
  Utilization
Department of Commerce, Room 6411
14th and Constitution Avenue, N.W.
Washington, D.C. 20230
(202) 377-1472

Department of Defense
Mr. Horace Crouch
Director, Small Business and Economic Utilization
Office of Secretary of Defense
Room 2A340—The Pentagon
Washington, D.C. 20301
(202) 697-9383

Department of the Interior
Dr. Thomas Henrie
Chief Scientist
U.S. Department of the Interior
2401 E Street, N.W.
Washington, D.C. 20241
(202) 634-1305

Department of Transportation
Mr. George Kovatch
SBIR Program Manager
Transportation Systems Center
Department of Transportation
Kendall Square
Cambridge, Massachusetts 02142
(617) 494-2051

Environmental Protection Agency
Mr. Walter H. Preston
Office of Research and Development
Environmental Protection Agency
401 M Street, S.W.
Washington, D.C. 20460
(202) 382-5744

portunity to obtain grants to finance innovative projects that meet the federal government's R&D needs and, at the same time, have commercial potential.

The SBIR program consists of three phases:

Phase 1 is to evaluate the scientific/technical merit and feasibility of an idea. Financing for this phase is up to $50,000.

Phase 2 continues the development started in Phase 1. Awards are based on the results of the earlier phase, and generally, also require an expression of interest in future financing from a private source. If the Phase 2 work is successful, awards of up to $500,000 may be made in this phase. Only Phase 1 awardees are eligible for Phase 2 awards.

Phase 3 involves the commercialization of the technology and/or products developed in Phase 2 and requires the use of non-SBIR government funding. Ideally, it is hoped that a venture capital firm will provide this sort of financing.

Only small businesses with 500 or fewer employees that are organized for profit are eligible to receive SBIR awards.

The SBIR program was initiated by the National Science Foundation (NSF) in the late 1970s. In fiscal year 1983, the first year of the full program, about $45 million was awarded. It is estimated that $124 million will be awarded in fiscal 1985, and that this will increase to $500 million when the program is fully implemented in 1987. Thus, the SBIR program should become an interesting source of seed funds for technology-oriented businesses.

To apply for an SBIR, entrepreneurs should contact the agency representatives listed in Exhibit 15.8 for a delineation of the research and technology topics of potential interest to each of them. A proposal of no more than 25 pages should be prepared that describes the R&D approach to be used and the qualifications of the people who will do the R&D. A Phase 2 proposal should also indicate the commercial potential and who the Phase 3 financing source might be. Proposals are competitively evaluated to determine the best innovative solutions to an agency's technical topic.

15.7.2 State Sources

Almost every state has some sort of program for providing financial assistance to help companies start up or expand within the state. Some states are more active than others in providing such assistance. Although state programs are principally available to existing businesses, increasing interest is being shown in start-ups. The state's motivation in having such programs is to promote economic development and create jobs within the state.

There are basically three types of *direct* state financial aid programs. The first are state agencies created to provide direct loans, loan guarantees, and sometimes equity capital to businesses. A second form of state aid is provided through Business Development Corporations (BDCs). At any one time about 25–30 states have active BDCs. A BDC is a privately owned corporation that is authorized by the state to promote and assist in the growth and development of businesses in the state. The capital of the BDC comes from the sale of stock and/or loans made to it by financial institutions and private individuals. BDCs can also obtain funds from the SBA, which may only be used to help small businesses. BDCs generally make loans and sometimes provide equity capital to businesses that are too marginal to obtain funds from a bank. Interest rates on loans can range from below prime to 4 percent or so over prime. BDC and/or state agency loans are generally for equipment purchases, facility improvements, and new buildings, and sometimes for working capital. A BDC normally requires the same sort of information from an applicant that a commercial bank requires.

With regard to BDCs, Silver notes that in the smaller states they can be a very active financing source.[23] He notes that Wyoming's BDC is the most active financial institution in the state and has provided all of the financing for some start-ups.

The third state financing program is the industrial revenue bond (IRB). Such bonds are a common form of state financial assistance. IRBs are issued by a state or municipality and use the funds raised to construct or expand plant facilities that are leased to a business. After the bonds are paid back from the lease payments, the user can renew the lease for long periods at favorable rates. It is important to note that the credit supporting these bonds are the lease payments of the renter. Hence, IRBs will generally be issued only to build facilities for a firm with an excellent credit rating.

Obtaining financing from any of the above state sources requires a great deal of patience. Things don't happen quickly in the state bureaucracy.

The financial assistance programs available in each state and whom to contact about them change over time. The most recent compilation of whom to contact can be found in Chapter 4 of *The Encyclopedia for Small Business Resources* by David E. Gumpert and Jeffry A. Timmons.

[23]Silver, *Up Front Financing,* p. 56.

Obtaining Capital $\quad$ 16

A good reputation is more valuable than money.

Publilius Syrus
(First Century B.C. Maxim 108)

16.1 OVERVIEW

Previous chapters have described how to prepare a business plan and the principal sources of equity and debt capital that are available to a start-up or young existing business. This chapter will describe how to use the learning of these earlier chapters to obtain capital for a venture. It is meant to be a practical guide to the mechanics of obtaining equity and/or debt capital. It will describe how to find and contact the principal sources of capital, what sorts of information they will want to see, what sorts of process and decision criteria they use to make a financing decision, how long this decision process typically takes, and what non-financial criteria an entrepreneur or business owner should apply in selecting one source of debt or equity financing over another. The discussion of venture capital financing sources includes a description of how these investors think about pricing a venture and their approach to negotiating and structuring a "deal."

Before getting into any details, it is important to note that the common aspect of a favorable financing decision among all debt and equity financiers is a strong positive appraisal of a venture's management and entrepreneurial capabilities. Without this, the probabilities of obtaining financing from any source to be discussed are nil.

16.2 OBTAINING EQUITY CAPITAL

Entrepreneurs generally find the search for venture (equity) capital to be much more time-consuming, expensive, and frustrating than they ever imagined. For this not to be so, it is important that entrepreneurs take a professional approach to raising capital. They must understand how to find, select, and best present their venture to equity investors—whether "informal sources" of capital (such as the professional acquaintances and/or wealthy individuals described in Chapter 15) or professional venture capital firms.

Before beginning their search for equity capital, the entrepreneurs should have completed a logical, comprehensive, and *readable* business plan. It must be

545

long enough to present the potential of a business but not so long as to bore or discourage the investor-reader. The plan prepared for informal investors can, generally, be less detailed than that prepared for the professional venture capitalist. The entrepreneurs should also have demonstrated their commitment to the venture by investing a significant amount of their time and some of their money in it.

Entrepreneurs should not delay looking for equity capital until they have a serious cash shortage, since it is likely to take six months or more to raise start-up capital if you have not previously succeeded in doing so. In addition to impairing the development of their venture, the lack of planning implicit in this cash shortage can undermine their credibility as good managers and have a negative impact on their ability to negotiate with investors. On the other hand, if entrepreneurs seek and obtain money before they really need it, they may unnecessarily dilute their own equity, as well as erode, inadvertently, the discipline instilled by financial leanness. Entrepreneurs should try to anticipate their cash needs, go as far as they deem prudent on their existing capital, and then properly prepare themselves to raise funds from equity investors. (As noted in Chapter 12, the microcomputer spreadsheet tool can be an invaluable aid.)

When looking for a venture capital investor, an entrepreneur should seek someone (1) who is considering new financing proposals and can provide the required level of capital; (2) who is interested in early stage companies; (3) who understands and has a preference for investments in the industry of the entrepreneur's venture; (4) who can provide good business advice, moral support, and contacts in the business and financial community as well as just venture capital; (5) whom the entrepreneur gets along with; and (6) who is reputable and ethical.

In the sections that follow, we shall describe the process and problems of obtaining capital from both "informal sources" (wealthy individuals and professional acquaintances) and professional venture capital groups.

16.3   INFORMAL SOURCES OF EQUITY CAPITAL

Informal investors are sources of equity capital other than professional venture capital groups, institutional investors, and the public stock markets.[1] They are likely to invest in companies that are smaller, riskier, and with less potential for liquidity than the companies in which a professional venture capitalist is likely to invest. Typically, informal investors are wealthy individuals, successful entrepreneurs, businesspeople, and professionals. As noted in Chapter 15, such investors can be an important source of capital for the "seed" or R&D stages of high-potential firms and for the early stage financing of foundation firms. This is especially true in areas of the country that do not have ready access to professional venture capital groups.

Informal investors are particularly appropriate for financing high-technology inventors before the development of even a prototype; ventures with a capital requirement of between $50,000 and $500,000; ventures with a 5–10-year sales potential of between $2 million and $20 million; and small established, privately held ventures whose sales and profit growth (10–20 percent per year) is not rapid enough to be attractive to a professional venture capital firm.[2] Informal investors

[1]William E. Wetzel, "Informal Investors—When and Where to Look," in *Pratt's Guide to Venture Capital Sources,* 6th ed., ed. Stanley E. Pratt (Wellesley Hills, Mass.: Capital Publishing, 1982), p. 22.
[2]Ibid.

often have noneconomic factors as well as capital gains in mind when they make their investment decisions. A successful entrepreneur may want to help other entrepreneurs get started. A wealthy individual may want to help build new businesses in his or her community. The typical informal investor will invest from $25,000 to $50,000 in any one venture.

16.3.1 Finding Informal Investors

Wetzel notes: "Informal investors, essentially individuals of means and successful entrepreneurs, are a diverse and dispersed group with a preference for anonymity. Creative techniques are required to identify and reach them."[3] Apart from serendipity, such investors learn of investment opportunities from their business associates, fellow entrepreneurs, and friends, many of whom invest together, more or less regularly, in a number of new venture situations. Thus, one informal investor contact can lead the entrepreneur to contacts with others.

In our experience the best way to meet informal investors is to seek advice and referrals from attorneys, accountants, business associates, and entrepreneurs who deal with new ventures and are likely to know such people. Even faculty at an entrepreneur's university can be a source of potential investors. By using the referrer's name, it is generally possible to arrange a meeting with a potential investor. At this meeting the entrepreneur should make a concise presentation of the key features of the proposed venture and his or her qualifications for making it successful. Whether or not the outcome of such a meeting is continued investment interest, the entrepreneur should try to obtain the names of other potential investors from the meeting. If this can be done, the entrepreneur will develop a growing list of potential investors and will find his or her way into one or more networks of informal investors. This process is time-consuming and laborious— but it can succeed. The entrepreneur should avoid meeting with more than one informal investor at the same time. Such meetings often result in negative viewpoints being raised by one investor and reinforced by another. Besides, it is easier to deal with negative reactions and questions from only one investor at a time.

16.3.2 The Informal Investors' Evaluation

More likely than not, more than one meeting will be required to close with potential investors. They will want to review some sort of business plan, meet the full management team, and see any product prototype or design that may exist. The investors will conduct background checks on the venture team and its product potential, usually through someone they know who knows the entrepreneur and the product. The process is not dissimilar to that used by the professional venture capital firm (see below), but it may be less formal and structured. Often, the participation of one investor who is knowledgeable about the product and its market will "trigger" the participation of other investors. If given a choice, the entrepreneur should select informal investors who can be useful advisers and whose objectives are consistent with those of the entrepreneur.

Once the required financial commitments have been obtained, the investors will have some sort of investment agreement drafted by one of their attorneys.

[3]Ibid., p. 22.

This agreement may be somewhat simpler than those used by professional venture capital firms. It may also include some form of a "put" whereby the investors have the right to require the venture to repurchase their stock after a specified number of years at a specified price. If the venture becomes a lifestyle firm, this put will provide the investors with a cash return and satisfy the lifestyle entrepreneurs' desire for complete control of their venture.

16.4 PROFESSIONAL VENTURE CAPITAL INVESTORS

16.4.1 Finding a Venture Capitalist

In trying to decide which venture capital firm to contact, an entrepreneur should seek advice and referrals from accountants, lawyers, investment and commercial bankers, and businesspeople who are knowledgeable about venture capital. These may be people whom the entrepreneur knows or whom he can contact through a mutual acquaintance. Especially good sources of information are other entrepreneurs who have recently tried, successfully or unsuccessfully, to raise money for a venture. There are also several directories of venture capital firms that provide basic data on the investment preferences of venture capital firms throughout the United States; the oldest and most complete of these is the *Guide to Venture Capital Sources,* edited by Stanley Pratt and published by Venture Economics (VE) of Wellesley, Massachusetts. Also available from VE is a computerized database of over 500 venture capital firms, which can be searched to identify the most likely prospects for your venture (617-431-8100). From such sources, the entrepreneur should determine the appetite of target investors for ventures of the age, industry technology, and capital requirements proposed by the entrepreneur. It is also desirable to determine which venture capital firms have money to invest, are actively seeking deals, and have the time and people to investigate new deals. In mid-1984 many venture capital firms were eschewing new deals and concentrating on and reserving capital for companies in their portfolio with problems.

Without this sort of screening of prospective venture capital firms, entrepreneurs increase the time and effort they expend to raise money.

16.4.2 Contacting Venture Capital Firms

Having identified venture capitalists who might be interested in his or her venture, the entrepreneur must avoid contacting such a large number of them that the venture becomes classified as a "shopworn" deal. What this means is that the venture has been seen and turned down by a number, 15 or so, of venture capital investors. Typically, venture capitalists reject in a few hours about 80–90 percent of the venture deals to which they are exposed. Thus, it is inevitable that if enough investors are exposed to a venture deal, there will be enough rejections to classify the deal as shopworn, as these turndowns become known to others in the still close-knit venture capital community. Regardless of the merits of a particular venture, its classification as shopworn will discourage many venture capitalists from making an investment; they don't like to invest in a situation that has been turned down by others in the field.

How can this be avoided? An entrepreneur does want to expose his deal to more than one potential investor—this is no more than good business practice.

However, mass-mailing a business plan to a large number of venture capital investors is not the thing to do. The best way for entrepreneurs to proceed is to identify and contact a small number (5 to 10 of investors that have a reasonable probability of being interested in the entrepreneurs' venture and meet their criteria for a desirable investor.

To receive the proper attention from potential investors, it is desirable that the entrepreneur be properly introduced to them. This can be done by a lawyer, banker, or another entrepreneur who may have suggested a particular investor to the entrepreneur, or, if these people feel uncomfortable about doing this, by someone they know who knows the investor. This referral need not be much more than a telephone call to the investor to tell him that a particular entrepreneur and venture are worthy of his consideration.

Some entrepreneurs who are having difficulty in obtaining such introductions often consider employing a finder, or intermediary. A finder will introduce them to potential investors and receive a fee—up to 5 percent of larger deals and as much as 10 percent of smaller ones—if an introduction results in an investment. We feel that most entrepreneurs will be able to obtain introductions to investors on their own. Notwithstanding this, there are some good, effective finders around—the problem is in knowing who they are. You should also know that some venture capital investors don't like finders or paying finders' fees.

With or without a referral an entrepreneur's initial contact with a potential investor will usually be via a telephone call. During this first contact the entrepreneur will describe his or her venture, its products, the backgrounds of its management team, the amount of capital sought, and the expected performance of the venture two or three years after the investment has been made. The entrepreneur must convey enough of the potential of the venture to persuade the investor to find out more about it.

On the other side, the venture capital investor is making a quick evaluation of the entrepreneur's venture to determine whether it is worth asking the entrepreneur to submit a business plan or, perhaps, make a presentation. Generally, the investor will request to see a business plan before agreeing to meet with an entrepreneur. Somewhere between 60 percent and 80 percent of all ventures presented to a venture capitalist are rejected during this first telephone contact. Venture capitalists will agree to take the next step and review a business plan only if they believe that the entrepreneur and his team appear to have the relevant experience and the required management skills and if the venture's product fulfills a need in a large and growing market.

An entrepreneur should not be discouraged by a rejection at this point. The investor may not like the industry of the venture, may have too many investments in that industry, or may have some other reason for the rejection that is unrelated to the quality of the entrepreneur and the venture. On the other hand, the entrepreneur may have done a poor job presenting the venture, or the investor may perceive some flaw in the venture. In any case, if a venture is rejected, the entrepreneur should review the basic data about the venture and the way the venture is presented to an investor. A recent study by Bruno and Tyebjee, for instance, found that 70 percent of the "rejects" managed to carry on and were in business three years later.[4]

---

[4]A. Bruno and T. Tyebjee, "The One That Got Away," in *Frontiers of Entrepreneurship Research*, ed. J. A. Hornaday, J. A. Timmons, and K. H. Vesper (Babson Park, Mass.: Babson College, 1983), pp. 289–306.

16.4.3 Screening of the Business Plan

Those entrepreneurs and ventures that pass the initial telephone contact are asked to submit their business plans to the investor. On the basis of a quick screening of the business plans (one hour or less) and, perhaps, another telephone call to clarify a point, the venture capital investors will decide whether or not a venture will receive further consideration. Studies of this investor screening process by Bruno and Tyebjee (1984), Timmons, Fast, and Bygrave (1984), Timmons and Gumpert (1982), and Roberts (1983) have shown that it focused on:[5]

1. *The caliber of the management team.* Do they have a successful track record? Do the experience and skills of the principals seem to be up to the job of developing a growth business?
2. *The industry and technology of the venture.* Is the venture in an industry that the investor understands and has previously invested in successfully? Is the venture in a growth and glamour industry?
3. *The uniqueness of the venture.* Does the venture have a unique or really superior product, technology, or skill that can give it a significant competitive advantage?
4. *The financial data.* If the venture is an existing venture, does it have a positive net worth and working capital? Has it borrowed to capacity? Are there any questionable or troublesome assets (overcapitalized patents) or liabilities (unpaid and deferred withholding taxes)? Are the magnitudes of its current and projected sales and profits high enough to be interesting?
5. *The terms of the deal.* How much equity is being offered for how much money? Is this reasonable or very unreasonable?

If, in the screening of the business plan, the investor finds no fatal flaws in the above areas that would be cause for rejecting the venture, the entrepreneur will be asked to make an oral presentation to the investor and his or her associates. At this point, no more than 10–20 percent of all the entrepreneurs who originally contacted the investor are still being considered.

16.4.4 Venture Presentation to the Investor

The oral presentation is an important milestone in the raising of capital from an investor. it is usually the first, and if handled improperly the only, face-to-face opportunity that entrepreneurs have to convince an investor that their venture and management team have substantial potential and are worthy of an investment. The entrepreneur and one to three key members of the management team should prepare for and make the presentation, each individual describing and discussing that part of the business for which he or she will be responsible. The presentation is usually made at the venture capitalist's office in the case of start-ups and early stage ventures. In the case of a venture that is making a product, it is more likely to occur at the venture's facilities. Anywhere from two or three days to two weeks can elapse from the time of telephone contact to the time of the presentation.

[5]A. Bruno and T. Tyebjee, "The Entrepreneur's Search for Capital," *Frontiers of Entrepreneurship Research,* pp. 18–31; J. A. Timmons, N. Fast, and W. D. Bygrave, "Seed and Start-Up Venture Capital Investment in Technological Companies," *Frontiers of Entrepreneurship,* pp. 1–17; and E. Roberts, "Business Planning and Start-Up in High Technology Enterprises," *Frontiers in Entrepreneurship,* pp. 107–17.

The presentation should highlight and discuss the key material in the business plan. Particular stress should be placed on the analysis of the opportunity and market for the venture's products and why those products can establish a market niche against their competition, the unique skills and backgrounds of the key members of the management team that qualify them for their role in the venture; a discussion of the history of the venture, a brief view of projected sales and profits and the key assumptions, and a recognition and discussion of potential risks and problems. It's not a bad idea to use flip-charts for presenting key materials and to bring along prototype product brochures.

Venture capital investors will be interested in the presentation, not only for what they will learn about the venture, but also for the opportunity they will have to meet the entrepreneur and the management team and to judge their individual capabilities and their ability to function as an effective team. Some or all of the venture capital investors present will have read the entrepreneur's business proposal. They will have some hard questions to ask. They will be interested, not only in the answers, but in who answers them and how they are answered. They will be looking for evidence of business knowledge and experience in specific areas of the venture (marketing, finance, etc.) that are of concern to them. If a venture's marketing manager is unable to provide answers that indicate an understanding of the size and growth of the venture's market and the competition, or cannot explain the rationale for a particular sales strategy, the investors may have serious questions about that manager's capability and the venture itself. Similarly, a tendency for the entrepreneur to bypass his management team and answer all questions can raise doubts about the capabilities of the management team and about the entrepreneur's ability to be an effective president. Any attempt by the entrepreneur to dodge tough questions, ignore or appear to be ignorant of risks and problems, or "know all the answers" will be viewed unfavorably by the investors.

After the initial meeting and presentation the venture capitalist will decide either to reject the venture or to go ahead with a serious investigation of the venture and its management. This action should not be viewed as a positive decision but, rather, as the absence of a negative decision. While a venture capitalist is checking out a venture ("doing due diligence"), the entrepreneur can also check out the investor, and should definitely do so. The entrepreneur should discretely and selectively make presentations to a limited number of other venture capitalists, some of whom may be suggested by the interested investor. There are several reasons for doing this. First, if entrepreneurs do not do it, after two to three months of investigation by the venture capitalist they may find themselves with a negative decision, short on cash, and in a poor bargaining position with the investors that they approach subsequently. Second, exposure to more than one venture capitalist is desirable if entrepreneurs are to know the attractiveness and worth of their ventures. Lastly, if the venture requires financing that exceeds the investment limit of one venture firm, other investors will have to be brought into the deal and will want presentations. Further, venture firms often like to involve other venture investors so that there are enough "deep pockets" to provide some or all of the capital for subsequent financings. Notwithstanding this advice, once a venture capitalist has committed to finance a venture and the offer has been accepted, through execution of the "terms sheet," the entrepreneur should not contact other investors without the advice and consent of the lead investor.

16.4.5 Investigation of a Venture

The investigation and analysis of a business by venture capitalists are extensive. The process includes checks on management, the markets for the product, technical feasibility, and detailed financial analysis. As Pratt[6] notes: "One of the best ways to judge a venture capitalist's interest is in the time allocated for substantive investigation." Typically, an investigation takes 6–10 weeks. If a positive decision has not been reached by a venture capitalist by then, it is very likely that such a decision will never be forthcoming. It might require three–four months to obtain a yes, and often up to a year to get a final no from several prospects. Start-ups take longer to assess than later stage ventures.

Venture capitalists agree that the entrepreneur and his management team are the most important factor in the success of a venture capital investment and the growth of a business. Accordingly, much of their evaluation of a business involves getting to know the entrepreneur and the team in depth and observing how they perform in a variety of situations and under stress. These situations can involve requests for more data regarding the venture's market or competitors, or meetings and discussions with the entrepreneurial team in which various aspects of the business (financing, future performance, risks, etc.) as well as the skills, attitudes, motivations, and commitment of the entrepreneur and the team are probed.

The venture capitalist will also have conversations with former employers, business associates, bankers, and technical references to check out the business records and competence of the entrepreneur and his key associates. A credit check is often conducted to make sure that there is nothing dishonest or disreputable about the entrepreneur and the other venture principals.

As part of their investigations, venture capitalists will verify the claims and data about the venture's technology, products, markets, and industry trends. This may be done by talking to such people as the entrepreneur's suppliers, customers, competitors, customers of competitors, and knowledgeable business and technical acquaintances of the venture capitalists in the venture's industry. In many cases, venture capitalists will use a technical consultant to make a market appraisal or to evaluate the technical feasibility of a venture's product. Trade association and industry statistics will be examined to verify market trends, and competitors' track records may be studied to obtain an indication of the venture's growth, profitability, and harvest potential.

When the venture capitalists have assimilated the above kinds of data, they will make an investment decision that will be largely a reasoned judgment using the information they have obtained. If they feel uncomfortable in any way about the venture, they will probably decide not to invest in it. If they make a positive investment decision, negotiations then begin with the entrepreneur regarding the equity to be given up for the required financing and the way in which that financing will be provided. Only about 1–3 percent of all the ventures seen by venture capital investors make it past the final evaluation to a positive decision and the investment of capital.

---

[6]Stanley E. Pratt, "Guidelines for Dealing with Venture Capitalists," in *Pratt's Guide to Venture Capital Sources,* 9th ed. (Wellesley, Mass.: Venture Economics, 1985), pp. 51–53.

16.4.6 Dealing with Rejections

Because such a small percentage of the ventures seeking an investment from the venture capital community obtain it, most entrepreneurs will get more than one rejection in seeking such financing. Good entrepreneurs are persistent, and most will continue to seek financing in the face of a number of rejections over a 9–12-month period. Some entrepreneurs persist for even longer, eventually obtain financing, and go on to build a successful company. Others do not, and the financial and psychic costs of a fruitless search for investors can be substantial—especially if an entrepreneur has quit a job to avoid conflicts with an existing employer and have more time available for fund-raising.

To avoid this sort of experience, entrepreneurs must try to determine the true reason for a rejection. This is not easy. Most venture capitalists will reject a venture by saying:[7] "Interesting venture, but it does not meet our investment criteria," or, "Interesting deal and good management. But we are not lead investors. If you find a strong lead investor, we might be very interested in investing." These are polite ways of saying no. If an entrepreneur is to avoid wasting time and money and, perhaps, be able to turn a rejection into an acceptance, he or she must get some investor to explain the true reason for a rejection. When this is done, the entrepreneur can either correct the flaw in the venture (e.g., obtain an experienced marketing manager) or decide that the venture has basic limitations (e.g., a small market for its products) that make obtaining venture capital improbable, if not impossible.

16.4.7 Negotiating and Structuring the Deal

When the venture capital investor has decided to go ahead with an investment, negotiations will begin with the entrepreneur on the terms of that investment. These negotiations are normally handled by a senior member of the venture capital firm and the president of the venture. In the case of an investment by a syndicate of venture capital firms, one firm will serve as the "lead investor" and conduct negotiations for the investor group.

In the case of early stage deal, financing will be provided to allow the company to achieve one or more specified objectives (e.g., a prototype or sales and profits of a certain amount), with the expectation that additional funds will then be available from current and new investors to take the company to the next stage of its development. If a venture has achieved its objectives, this next round of financing should command a higher price than the earlier one. This staged financing has advantages for both venture capitalists and entrepreneurs; the venture capitalists minimize their financial risk in an early stage investment, and the entrepreneurs who achieve what they promise wind up selling less equity than they would in a single, large early stage financing.

A primary focus of negotiation is on how much the entrepreneur's equity is worth and how much should be purchased by the venture capitalist's investment. But this is not the only issue. The investors may want to purchase a convertible preferred stock, while the entrepreneur may prefer to issue common stock or debt

[7]Burton J. McMurtry and Donald M. Dible, "Objectives of the Venture Capitalist," in *Winning the Money Game,* ed. Donald M. Dible (Santa Clara, Calif.: Entrepreneur Press, 1975), pp. 211–26.

plus stock. Sometimes investors will want a management change if they believe that the venture team is lacking in some skill or if they think the someone else on the team should be president of the company instead of its current leader. The entrepreneur may or may not go along with this. We know of one case where the investors would not invest in a company unless its marketing manager became its president. The company refused to do this and received no financing. Other issues that are the subjects of negotiations are:

- The number of directors' seats allocated to investors. This is usually perceived as a control issue by the entrepreneur, but it usually is not. Management controls a business. Venture investors will not try to intervene unless a business seriously fails to perform as planned. In such a case, the investors may seek management changes via the board of directors.
- The right of investors to have registration rights for their stock in the case of a registered public offering. Underwriters will generally limit the investors' stock coming onto the market with the first public offering.
- The right of investors to have first refusal on subsequent stock offerings. This can be troublesome if earlier stockholders had no such rights.
- Stock vesting agreements whereby the entrepreneurs do not own all of their stock initially but acquire ownership over a period extending from three to five years.
- Employment contracts, and noncompete and proprietary rights agreements between the entrepreneurs and the venture they have proposed. Noncompete agreements are generally nonnegotiable and insisted on by the venture capitalists.

It is very important that entrepreneurs and their management confer and develop positions on these and other potential negotiable issues before entering into negotiations with the investors. With regard to the price per share paid by the investor, entrepreneurs should decide what they would like to get and what they will accept.

During the negotiation the investors will be evaluating the negotiating skills, intelligence, and maturity of the entrepreneur. If investors see anything that shakes their confidence or trust in the entrepreneur's ability, they will probably withdraw from the deal. The entrepreneur should similarly evaluate and react to the investors.

Once the investor and the entrepreneur reach agreement on the amount of equity to be sold for the required investment and on the other terms of the investment, a "terms sheet" will usually be drafted that describes the main features of the investment in plain language. Appendix IV is a sample terms sheet that specifies the essential elements and the potential "deal break-even."

The terms sheet will subsequently be given to an attorney who will prepare an investment agreement (see Appendix III). However, the entrepreneur should realize that the deal is not closed until that formal investment agreement has been signed by both parties.

Throughout the negotiation the entrepreneur should bear in mind that a successful negotiation is one in which both the entrepreneur and the investor believe that they have made a "fair deal." More important than a few percentage points of ownership, one way or the other, is a constructive working relationship between the entrepreneur and the investor. The Genetic Laboratories, Inc., case at the end of this chapter concerns itself with the issues of valuation and investor-entrepreneur negotiations and should be studied.

16.4.8 Valuation and Investor Equity

What considerations influence what percentage of ownership of a venture must be given to a venture capital investor in exchange for his invested capital? Generally, the later the stage of development of a business, the smaller is the percentage of ownership that the venture capitalist expects to receive for a given dollar investment. The equity given to a venture capital investor will be the result of a negotiation. However, this negotiation will take place within certain ranges. These ranges depend a great deal on the entrepreneurial track record of management and on the stage of development and the record of success of the venture being financed. We estimate the ranges of ownership given to a venture capitalist to be as follows:

50–70 percent for the venture capital investor who puts in all of the required funds when a venture is in the start-up stage.

10–40 percent for the venture capitalist who invests in ventures beyond the start-up stage—the percentage depending on the amount invested and on the maturity and track record of the venture.

10–30 percent for the venture capitalist who invests in a seasoned venture that has demonstrated successful performance and needs additional funds to sustain its growth. This venture is likely to have earlier investments of significant size.

If a venture is a start-up with no record of sales or profits, the investor is likely to be taking the vast majority of the financial risk, unless the entrepreneurs are putting up some cash themselves. At this early stage, the venture capital investor views his financial risk to be worth 50–70 percent of the deal, which leaves the entrepreneurial team with 30–50 percent for their skills, efforts, commitment, and so forth. However, if the entrepreneurial team is investing money at the same time that the venture capitalist is doing so, that money should buy stock on the same terms as those of the investor. This purchased stock is added to that received by the entrepreneurs for their skills, efforts, and so on. Note that these estimates will also vary during periods of a highly favorable IPO market accompanied by frenzied venture capital investing, such as occurred in mid-1983.

Most venture capital investors, even those investing at very early stages, recognize the incentive value of the entrepreneurial team's equity position. Thus, most venture capitalists will leave entrepreneurs and their team with an attractive share of the venture or options or warrants to buy such a share. What "attractive" means is negotiable; but few venture capital investors would dilute an entrepreneurial team's share below 20–25 percent at the start-up stage for fear of diluting the team's commitment to the venture.

We should hasten to note that the percentages cited above were typical of the 1981–83 time period, when money was chasing deals. In less heady times, the percentage of equity taken by a venture capitalist will be higher. This was true from 1972 to 1977, and it may again be the case in the last half of the 1980s.

Some of the factors that may persuade a venture capitalist to take less than normal ownership in a start-up or first-stage venture are:

Previous profit responsibility and above-average profit or harvest performance by the lead entrepreneur.

The presence of a complete management team, which means less risk for the investor.

An entrepreneurial team with in-depth and up-to-date knowledge of the target market and substantial previous experience in selling to, and getting orders from, the venture's prospective customers.

A demonstrably strong position for the venture's product or service in terms of patents, know-how, exclusive market, lead time.

The likelihood that substantial additional equity funding will be needed within the next 18 to 24 months, which will dilute the percentage ownership of the entrepreneurial team below the level at which it would feel that it had a real stake in the business.

In ventures beyond the start-up capital stage, the entrepreneurial team is usually able to retain more to the venture's equity when a deal is struck with a venture capital investor. Successful track records of sales and profits demonstrate that a team can work effectively together. This quantifies one of the key risks in the venture and strengthens the entrepreneurial team's bargaining position vis-à-vis the outside investor. Other risks, such as market acceptability of the product and the ability of the venture to sell the product at a profit, are also more quantifiable after some sales and profits have been achieved.

At any stage of a company's development, the question of the percentage of equity purchased by the investor is a result of negotiation. The starting point may be an analytic consideration of the current and projected value of the venture and the return-on-investment objectives of the investor. But this issue of venture valuation is ultimately a subjective one that depends as much as anything else on the value being assigned to ventures of similar age, technology, and potential by the marketplace of venture capital investors at the given time.

Before approaching a venture investor, entrepreneurs would do well to determine what their desired valuation means in terms of prefinancing valuation. For example, if you are trying to raise $2 million for 50 percent of your company, you are saying that its value before any money is invested is $2 million. Can you justify that figure? Confronted in this way, many entrepreneurs cannot.

16.4.9 A Valuation Example

To illustrate how investors might determine a starting point for negotiating the percentage of a venture's equity that they want for their investment, let us examine one way of arriving at such a figure. Suppose that a company is projecting after-tax profits in three years to be $175,000. Also, assume that potential investors believe that these earnings will be achieved. If they don't believe this, investors will make and use their own estimates of a venture's projected earnings. The next assumption is that other companies in the industry of the venture being evaluated are generally valued by investors at six to eight times after-tax earnings. Based on these assumptions, the "value" of the venture being considered in year 3 would be:

$$\$175,000 \times 6 \text{ to } 8 = \$1,050,000 \text{ to } \$1,400,000$$

Two more assumptions are needed for the purposes of this illustration: (*a*) the investor is considering a $200,000 investment and feels that (*b*) a 40 percent per year growth of the original investment for three years would justify the level of risk in the venture. This $200,000 invested today, if it grew at 40 percent per year, would be worth approximately $550,000 at the end of year 3. If a venture is worth $1,050,000 to $1,400,000 at the end of year 3, and the venture capitalist's investment must be worth $550,000 to meet the return objective, the $200,000 put into the venture by the investor today must buy from

$$\frac{\$550,000}{\$1,400,000} \text{ to } \frac{\$550,000}{\$1,050,000}$$

of the company, that is, from 39 percent to 52 percent.

Again, we must emphasize that such valuations are only a starting point because they are based on earnings projections that are reasoned hopes and, usually, unreliable. This is especially true for start-ups that have little or no record of sales or earnings. For this reason, the venture capitalist's valuation of start-ups and early stage deals is highly subjective and largely dependent on the valuation accorded other venture capital deals of the same ilk.

16.4.10   Structuring the Investment

The "present value" formula underlies this example, where PV = present value, FV = future value, i = investment rate of return, and n = the number of years that the investment is held, or:

$$PV = \frac{FV}{(I + i)^n}$$

Thus,

$$\$200,000 = \frac{FV}{(1 + 0.40)^3} = \frac{FV}{2.744}$$

$$FV = \$548,800, \text{ rounded to } \$550,000$$

In order to obtain a greater-than-normal return, the venture capital investors' needs are to invest so that they get—or can get—shares of common stock. Debt, by definition, has a fixed return that is usually not at the level desired by the venture capital investors.

There are three investment instruments that are generally used by venture capitalists for early stage venture investments.

1. Common Stock. This is often used in venture capital financing. Common stockholders have the right to vote on such issues as the composition of the board of directors. They also have the right to the earnings and assets of the firm only after all other expenses, debt, and other obligations have been met. Thus, in most venture situations the common stock investor has little chance to recoup any of the investment if the business moves sideways or fails. On the positive side, the purchase of common stock gives the venture capital investor the most equity for the invested dollar and a large potential for capital gain.

2. Convertible Preferred Stock. In a venture capital financing, this preferred stock is convertible into a number of common stock shares at the option of the investor. Generally, the number of common shares received per share of preferred stock is adjusted upward if stock is subsequently sold at a lower per share price than that of the preferred. This instrument can include gaining voting control over the majority of common shares if performance expectations are not met. Preferred shareholders have a preference over common stockholders (generally management)—but not debtors—in the event of liquidation of the company. Sometimes, 5–10 years after the investment date, the company may be required to redeem at an appreciated value shares of preferred that have not been converted. Currently, convertible preferred stock is the favored form of investment for startups and early stage deals.

3. Subordinated Debt with Conversion Privileges or Warrants. Subordinated debt provides the venture capital investor with the advantages of a debt instrument without restricting a venture's ability to obtain senior debt from banks. It will usually be considered equity by such senior lenders as long as it does not dominate the balance sheet.

Subordinated debt also gives the venture capitalist greater protection if things don't go well than is given to common or preferred stockholders. One way that investors obtain this protection is through an accelerated payment clause in the indenture (debt) agreement that makes the full amount of the loan payable within a specified time of a venture's failure to comply with certain agreed-upon conditions. These conditions might include the venture's agreeing to maintain a minimum working capital or agreeing not to merge or sell certain assets. Because a young venture is not likely to be able to retire the debt, the investor has the power to bankrupt the venture if it doesn't change its operations to meet the terms of the debt agreement. However, we should note that venture capital investors do not want to run the ventures in which they invest. They resort to this only to protect their investment.

A venture capital investor will generally issue subordinated debt with a stock convertible feature or with warrants to purchase stock.[8] Either of these arrangements provides the venture capital investor with an option to purchase common stock and realize the greater-than-normal return that accrues to equity owners in a successful company. At the same time, the venture capitalist can receive interest payments on the debt and has a higher call than common or preferred stock on the assets of the company in the event of liquidation.

16.4.11 Investment Agreements: An Overview

No investment agreement will make a good deal out of a bad one; but an investment agreement could do the opposite if it has not been properly drawn. Investment agreements are complex, and it is likely that the lawyer who drew up a venture's incorporation papers may be ill-suited to counsel an entrepreneur on a venture investment agreement. Entrepreneurs should make sure that the attorneys they consult are experienced in preparing investment agreements. Without such experience the attorney's cost to a venture could be far more than just a legal fee.

---

[8]The difference between convertible subordinated debt and subordinated debt with warrants should be noted. If the warrants are nondetachable, they are equivalent to a conversion feature and the stock must be purchased before the debt has been repaid. However, if the warrants are detachable, then the stock purchase can be made before or after the debt has been repaid, providing the exercise time of the warrants has not run out.

In what follows, we shall present an overview of the objectives and the content of investment agreements. Those readers interested in more detail should consult Appendixes II and III at the end of the book, which present an investment agreement and an in-depth discussion of the legal agreements and documentation.

Objectives of the Investment Agreement. The investment agreement is the document that defines the terms and conditions upon which an investor or investors will make a substantial investment in a venture. If prepared properly, the investment agreement should accomplish the following objectives:

1. Define the amount, type, and terms of the investment (stock, convertible debentures, notes, warrants, etc.).
2. Provide terms that will motivate and retain the entrepreneurial team if it performs as planned.
3. Provide "downside protection" to investors by giving them control of the venture if it is in danger of failing.
4. Provide and protect opportunities for the investor to realize capital gains and liquidity.

In order to meet these objectives, the investment agreement must anticipate and consider a number of future, contingent events. The resultant document can be lengthy and can contain issues that may not have been explicitly discussed during negotiations. The entrepreneur and his attorney should review it carefully and reopen discussions with the investor on any aspects of the agreement that are unacceptable to them.

Contents of an Investment Agreement. There are seven basic categories of terms, conditions, and representations in an investment agreement. A brief discussion of each of these follows:

1. *Description of the investment.* This part of the agreement defines the basic terms of the investment, including the parties to the agreement; the kind, amount, and price of the securities to be issued; and the collateral, guarantees, or subordination associated with debt. If the investment involves warrants for stock or debt conversion privileges, the terms (time limits, price, etc.) of the warrants will be stated.

2. *Preconditions to closing* are things that the venture must do, or supplementary data and agreements that it must submit to the investor, before the investment can be closed. Examples of such preconditions are the execution of employment contracts or the venture's securing a line of credit.

3. *Representations and warranties* are legally binding statements made by the venture's officers that describe the condition of the venture on or before the closing date. For example, the venture will warrant that it is a duly organized corporation in good standing with assets as represented on financial statements.

Although most warranties and representations are made by the venture, there are some that must be made by the investor. For example, if the securities are sold via a private placement, the investor will warrant that the stock is being acquired solely for investment and not with a view to resale or distribution.

4. *Affirmative covenants* define what the venture must do to run its business in a manner that is acceptable to the investor. Requirements to have investors on the venture's board of directors are examples of affirmative covenants.

5. *Negative covenants* define what the venture must not do or must not do without the prior approval of the investor. Restrictions on loans and management salaries are typical negative covenants.

6. *Conditions of default* describes those events that constitute a breach of the investment agreement if they are not corrected within a specified time. One condition of default is a failure to comply with the affirmative or negative covenants.

7. *Remedies.* These are the actions that an investor may take in the event that a condition of default has occurred. Remedies can include acceleration of debt repayment, forfeiture of escrowed stock, or temporary voting rights to control the company's board of directors.

In addition to the investment agreement, the closing of the "deal" generally involves the execution of a number of ancillary agreements. Such agreements might include: noncompete agreements with the entrepreneurial team and employment and stock vesting agreements with key personnel.[9] Supplementary agreements may also be used to give investors preemptive rights (to maintain their percentage ownership of the venture) and rights to include their stock in registered public stock offerings of the venture and to demand one or more registrations for their stock.

16.4.12   The Entrepreneur's Decision

If their venture and management team are particularly attractive, entrepreneurs may find that they have more offers of venture capital than they need. How do they decide which to accept?

In this situation, they should ask themselves what value beyond money a particular venture capitalist can bring to the venture, and then pick those venture capitalists who can provide assistance other than invested capital. As noted by Timmons: "It is far more important whose money you get than how much you get or how much you pay for it."[10] The right venture capitalist can add value in a number of ways. Principal among these are: identifying and helping to recruit key management team members, serving as a sounding board for ideas and plans to solve problems or quicken growth, helping to establish relationships with key customers and/or suppliers, and having "deep pockets" to participate in and syndicate subsequent rounds of financing.

If a choice of venture capitalists is available, entrepreneurs should check out potential investors by talking to the founders of successful and unsuccessful companies that they have backed. Entrepreneurs should also check out a venture capitalist's reputation in the financial community. There will probably not be a unanimity of opinion, but a picture should emerge of which investors are passive and which are helpful, active investors. Entrepreneurs should seek to strike a deal with venture capitalists who can provide contacts and helpful expertise as well as capital, who can provide additional financing when and if required, and who are patient and interested in the long-term development of the company.

Inevitably, entrepreneurs will receive investment offers that place a lower valuation on their venture than they think it merits. How far entrepreneurs should compromise on the valuation of their deal depends partially on the attractiveness of the venture and heavily on the availability of venture capital for early stage ventures. In times of bear markets for new issues, when venture capital for

[9]Stock vesting agreements define how much of an entrepreneur's stock is subject to repurchase at cost if the entrepreneur leaves the employ of the venture for any reason. Generally, an entrepreneur's stock in an early stage venture will not be fully vested (subject to repurchase) until three–five years after the closing of an investment. Appendix V contains a sample vesting agreement.

[10]Jeffry A. Timmons, "Venture Capital: More than Money," in *Pratt's Guide to Venture Capital Sources,* 9th ed., ed. Stanley E. Pratt (Wellesley, Mass.: Venture Economics, 1985), p. 71.

early stage ventures tends to dry up, entrepreneurs may have to accept a good deal less money for the equity offered than they would like—if financing is to be obtained for their ventures. In such a case, they might elect to curtail their operations and wait for a more favorable investment climate. On the other hand, in times of bull markets in new issues and speculative activity, entrepreneurs can obtain investment terms that are much more favorable.

In the final analysis, when the last negotiation is held, the entrepreneur is usually at a considerable disadvantage in bargaining power. As one experienced venture capital attorney put it:

I've been on both sides of the table, and I'd rather be on the side of the venture capitalist any day of the week. It does not matter what the entrepreneur's attorney argues: I know I hold all the trump cards.

16.5 OBTAINING DEBT: DEALING WITH BANKS AND OTHER LENDERS

Choosing a bank—and, more specifically, a banker—is one of the more important decisions that a new or young business will make. A good banking (or other lender) relationship can sometimes mean the difference between the life and death of a business during difficult times. We have seen cases where, other things being equal, one bank has called its loans to a struggling business, causing its demise, and another bank has stayed with its loans and helped a business to survive and prosper. Although we will refer specifically to banks and banking relationships, much of what follows on lending practices and decisions also applies to commercial finance company lenders.

Some banks and bankers will make loans to start-up and early stage ventures, and others will not. Those that will not generally cite the lack of an operating "track record" as the reason for turning down the loan. Lenders that make loans to such ventures usually do so for previously successful entrepreneurs of means or for firms backed by investors with whom they have had prior relationships and whose judgment they trust—for example, established venture capital firms.

In centers of high-technology and venture capital the main officers of major banks will have one or more high-technology lending officers who specialize in making loans to early stage high-technology ventures. Through much experience these bankers have come to understand the market and operating idiosyncrasies, problems, and opportunities of such ventures. They generally have close ties to venture capital firms, and they will refer entrepreneurs to such firms for possible equity financing. The venture capital firms, in turn, will refer their portfolio ventures to the banker for debt financing.

In what follows, we shall discuss some of the things that an entrepreneur should consider in choosing a bank, what is important in a lending decision, and how entrepreneurs should relate to their bankers on an ongoing basis. As we shall see, the banker's lending decision process is similar to that of the venture capitalist in many ways.

16.5.1 Choosing a Banker

Because of the importance of a banking relationship, an entrepreneur should "shop around" before making a choice. The selection of a bank should be based not only on loan interest rates but also on some of the other factors discussed below. Equally important, entrepreneurs should not wait until they have a dire need for funds to try to establish a banking relationship. The choice of a bank and the development of a banking relationship should begin when you don't urgently need the money. When an entrepreneur faces a near-term financial crisis, the venture's financial statements are at their worst and the banker has good cause to wonder about management's financial and planning skills—all to the detriment of the entrepreneur's chances of getting a loan.

Baty[11] and Stancill[12] describe some of the factors that are especially important to an entrepreneur in selecting a bank. These are:

1. *Size of the bank.* The bank selected should be large enough to service a venture's foreseeable loans but not so large as to be relatively indifferent to your business.

2. *Desire and capacity of work with small firms.* Banks differ greatly on this issue. Some banks have special small business loan officers and regard new and early stage ventures as the seeds of very large future accounts. Other banks see new venture loans as merely bad risks.

3. *How will the bank react to problems?* Does the bank tend to call or reduce its loans to small businesses that have problems? When the bank has less capital to lend, will it cut back on small business loans and favor its older, more solid customers?

4. *Is the bank imaginative, creative, and helpful* when a venture has a problem? To quote Baty: "Do they just look at your balance sheet and faint, or do they try to suggest constructive financial alternatives?"[13]

5. *Has the bank had lending experience in your industry,* and especially with young, developing companies? If it has had such experience, your chances of getting a loan are better, it will be more tolerant of problems, and it will be able to help you exploit your opportunities.

6. *Is there good personal chemistry* between you and your prospective lending officer? Remember, "the man you talk to and deal with is the bank."

These are the key criteria that an entrepreneur should take into account in selecting a bank. How does an entrepreneur evaluate a bank against these criteria? First, by consulting accountants, attorneys, and other entrepreneurs who have had dealings with the banks being considered. The experience of entrepreneurs who have dealt with a bank through both good and bad times can be especially useful. Second, by meeting with loan officers at several banks and systematically exploring their attitudes and approaches to their business borrowers. Who meets with you, for how long, and with how many interruptions can be useful measures of a bank's interest in your account. Finally, ask for small business references from each bank's base of borrowers and talk to the entrepreneurs of those firms. Throughout all of these contacts and discussions, check out particular loan officers as well as the bank itself: the bank loan officer is a major determinant of how the bank will deal with you and your venture.

[11]G. B. Baty, *Entrepreneurship: Playing to Win* (Reston, Va.: Reston Publishing, 1974), p. 157.

[12]J. M. Stancill, "Getting the Most from Your Banking Relationship," *Harvard Business Review,* March–April 1980, p. 20.

[13]Baty, *Entrepreneurship,* p. 158.

16.5.2 Approaching and Meeting the Banker

Obtaining a loan is a sales job. Many borrowers tend to forget this. An entrepreneur with an early stage venture must sell himself as well as the viability and potential of his business to the banker. This is much the same situation that the early stage entrepreneur faces with a venture capitalist.

The initial contact with a lender will probably be by telephone. The entrepreneur should be prepared to quickly describe the nature, age and prospects of the venture; the amount of equity financing and who provided it; the prior financial performance of the business; the entrepreneur's experience and background; and the sort of bank financing desired. A referral from a venture capital firm or from a businessperson who knows the banker will be very helpful. If the loan officer agrees to a meeting, he may well request that a business plan and financial statements be sent to him prior to any further contact. A well-prepared business plan and a reasonable amount of equity financing should pique a banker's interest—even for a start-up or very young venture.

The first meeting with a loan officer will probably be at the venture's place of business. The banker will be interested in meeting the members of the management team and seeing how they relate to the entrepreneur and in getting a sense of what sorts of financial controls and reporting are used and how well things seem to be run. A good banker is a well-trained observer of "red flags." He or she may also want to meet one or more of the venture's equity investors. But most of all, the banker is using this meeting to evaluate the integrity and business acumen of those who will ultimately be responsible for the repayment of the loan. Throughout meetings with potential bankers the entrepreneur must convey an air of self-confidence and an optimistic but realistic view of the venture's prospects. If the banker is favorably impressed by what he has seen and read, he will ask for further documents and references and begin to discuss the amount and timing of funds that the bank might lend to the business.

16.5.3 What the Banker Wants to Know

There are four key questions that a banker or other lender will want answered satisfactorily before providing loans:

1. What are you going to do with the money? Does the use of the loan make business sense? Should some or all of the money required be equity capital rather than debt? For new and young businesses, lenders don't like to see total debt-to-equity ratios greater than one. The answer to this question will also determine the type of loan—for example, line of credit or term.

2. How much do you need? You must be prepared to justify the amount requested and to describe how the debt fits into an overall plan for financing and developing the business. Further, the amount of the loan should have enough "cushion" to allow for unexpected developments.

3. When and how will you pay the loan back? This is an important question. Short-term loans for seasonal inventory buildups or for financing receivables are easier to obtain than term loans, especially for early stage businesses. How the loan will be repaid is the "bottom line" question. Presumably, you are borrowing money to finance an activity that will throw off enough cash to repay the loan.

What is your contingency plan if things go wrong? Can you describe the risks and indicate how you will deal with them? Is there a secondary source of repayment, a guarantor of means?

4. When do you need the money? If you need the money tomorrow, forget it. You are a poor planner and manager. If, on the other hand, you will need the money next month or the month after, you have demonstrated an ability to plan ahead. And you have given the banker time to investigate and process a loan application.

One of the best ways for an entrepreneur to answer these questions is by providing the banker with a well-prepared business plan (see Chapters 13 and 14). This plan should contain projections of cash flow, profit and loss, and balance sheets that will demonstrate the need for a loan and how it can be repaid. A well-prepared business plan is vital for the start-up seeking loans. For an existing business, the lender will want much of the information that is in a business plan—if not the plan itself. For an existing business, the lender will also want to review financial statements from prior years prepared or audited by a CPA, a list of aged receivables and payables, the turnover of inventory, and lists of key customers and creditors. He will also want to know that all taxes are paid currently. Finally, he will need to know the details regarding fixed assets and regarding any liens on receivables, inventory, or fixed assets.

The sorts of facts and figures just described should make it fairly easy for an entrepreneur to prepare loan applications and any other paperwork that a bank may require. For examples of actual commercial and SBA loan applications as well as specific guidelines for obtaining bank loans, see David E. Gumpert and Jeffry A. Timmons, *The Encyclopedia of Small Business Resources* (New York: Harper & Row, 1984), chapters 3 and 5. An actual loan agreement is also included so that you will know exactly what covenants and restrictions you must be prepared to live with.

16.5.4   The Lending Decision

The conventional banking wisdom is that lending decisions are based on the "five C's of Credit": Character, Capacity, Capital, Conditions, and Collateral. These decision criteria are the same regardless of the size and nature of the business. It is important for entrepreneurs to understand what these five C's mean to the lender.

1. Character.   Above all else, the banker will only lend money to people he trusts and who impress him as men or women of integrity. More specifically, character means two things to a lender. First, that the borrower has the ability, and will do everything he or she can, to conserve business assets and repay the loan; money will not be squandered. Second, that the borrower is a person of integrity; when the borrower promises to repay a loan, he or she means it. And if this cannot be done, the borrower will have made every possible effort to do so. Good bankers are good judges of people. They will also check the references suggested by the entrepreneur and some that they choose themselves.

2. Capacity.   Does the borrower have the capacity to repay the loan? Does the management have the capacity to use the loan and create the business growth it projects? These are the capacity issues.

3. Capital.   Bankers will want to see an adequate amount of equity capital invested in the business by insiders and or outsiders. First, a cash investment by the entrepreneurs and founders is evidence of their faith in the future of the business. Second, there must be sufficient equity capital so that bankers can safely retain their positions as lenders. Without sufficient equity capital (e.g., a debt-to-equity ratio of no more than 1 to 2), the banker can essentially become a very unwilling shareholder, a position that he does not want to be in.

4. Conditions. According to Belew and old credit hands: "Conditions are what change for the worse after you extend the credit."[14] What are the conditions of this sort that an astute lender will consider? Primarily, whether general business conditions and business conditions within the specific industry of the borrower are such as to give the lender cause for concern or grounds for optimism. Included in such considerations are the nature of the borrower's product and its competitive position in the marketplace. The lender may well know why a loan to fund the expansion of a business is not a wise move at the time of the loan request.

5. Collateral. The lender must decide whether or not the loan should be collateralized, and if so, with what. Also, if the lender forecloses on the fixed-asset collateral, will its sale at auction cover the loan? To whom can the collateral be sold, and for how much? The longer the loan compared to net worth, the more important is the issue of the collateral's value. Established businesses with high credit ratings do most of their short-term borrowings on an unsecured basis. Entrepreneurs with new or early stage businesses will generally be required to back their loans with all the assets of their business, keyperson insurance payable to the bank, and personal guarantees.

16.5.5 Loan Restrictions

To protect themselves against the possibility that things will not go well and/or against poor management practices that might endanger the repayment of a loan, lenders place certain limitations and restrictions in debt agreements. This is true whether or not the loan is collateralized. The kinds of limitations that are placed on borrowers depend to a great extent on the bank's perception of the risk involved. If a company is thought to be a good risk, it should be subject to minimum limitations. On the other hand, a loan to an early stage venture borrower would be viewed as being somewhat risky and would therefore be subject to more restrictions in its loan agreements.

A loan agreement is a document that defines the terms and conditions under which a lender provides capital. With it the lenders do two things: protect their positions as creditor and try to assure repayment of the loan as agreed.

In the loan agreement (as in investment agreements) there are negative and positive covenants. Negative covenants are things that the borrower must not do without the prior approval of the lender. Examples of these are: no further additions to the borrower's total debt, no pledge to others of assets of the borrower, and no payment of dividends. Positive covenants define what the borrower must do. Examples are: maintenance of some minimum net worth or working capital, prompt payment of all federal and state taxes, maintenance of adequate insurance on key people and property, repayment of the loan and interest according to the terms of the agreement, and the submission of periodic financial statements and reports to the lender. Failure to comply with such restrictions and to correct such failure within a specified time can put the loan in default and give the lender the right to accelerate repayment.

---

[14]R. C. Belew, *How to Negotiate Business Loans* (New York: Van Nostrand Reinhold, 1974), p. 167.

Some of these restrictions—for example, a flat restriction on further borrowing—can hinder a company's growth. Such a borrowing limit is often based on the borrower's assets at the time of the loan. Rather than an initially fixed limit, the loan agreement should recognize that as a business grows and as its total assets and net worth increase, the business will need and be able to carry the additional debt required to sustain its growth. Similarly, covenants that require certain minima on working capital or current ratios may be very difficult for highly seasonable business to maintain at all times of the year. Only an analysis of past financial monthly statements can indicate whether such a covenant can be met.

Before borrowing money, an entrepreneur should decide what sorts of restrictions or covenants he or she is prepared to accept. Attorneys and accountants of the company should be consulted before any loan papers are signed. Some restrictions are generally negotiable, and entrepreneurs should negotiate to get terms that their ventures can live with next year as well as today. Once the loan terms have been agreed upon and the loan has been made, the entrepreneur and his venture will be bound by the loan terms.

16.5.6 Summary

The banker will make a lending decision using the criteria we have described. Data for this evaluation will come from meetings with the entrepreneur and his management and from conversations with customers and creditors of the business. Reference checks will be made with former employers and business associates of the entrepreneur and his team. The business plan and loan application will be evaluated, with special attention paid to past and projected financial statements. Particular attention will be given to such financial ratios as current assets to current liabilities, gross margins, net worth to debt, accounts receivable and payable periods, inventory turns, and net profit to sales. The ratios for the borrower's venture will be compared to averages for competitive firms to see how the potential borrower measures up to them and to uncover potential problems.

The entrepreneur-borrower should regard his contacts with the bank as a sales mission and provide required data promptly and in a form that can be readily understood. The better the material that entrepreneurs can supply to demonstrate their business credibility, the easier it will be to obtain a positive lending decision and the faster that decision will be reached. Typically, a lending decision can be made in one to three weeks.

16.5.7 After the Loan: Building a Relationship

After obtaining a loan, entrepreneurs should cultivate a close working relationship with their bankers. Too many businesspeople don't see their lending officers until they need a loan. The astute entrepreneur will take a much more active role with his or her banker. By paying close attention to communicating, entrepreneurs can keep their bankers informed about their businesses and improve their chances of obtaining cooperation from the banks in troubled times as well as larger loans for expansion.

Some of the things that entrepreneurs should do to build a close working relationship with their bankers are fairly simple.[15] In addition to monthly and

---

[15] Baty, *Entrepreneurship*, p. 159.

annual financial statements, bankers should be sent product news releases and any trade articles about the business or its products. The entrepreneur should invite the banker to the venture's facility and should review with him product development plans, the prospects for the business, and any foreseeable new loan needs. Above all, the entrepreneur should get the banker interested in the venture and establish a personal business relationship with him. If this is done, when a new loan is requested, the lending officer will feel better about recommending its approval to the loan committee.

What about bad news? The best action is to never surprise a banker with bad news. Unpleasant surprises are a sign that an entrepreneur is not being candid with his or her banker or that management does not have the business under proper control. Either conclusion by a banker is damaging to the entrepreneur-banker relationship. If a future loan payment cannot be met, entrepreneurs should not panic and avoid their bankers. On the contrary, they should visit their bankers and explain why a loan payment cannot be made and when it will be made. If this is done before the payment due date and the entrepreneur-banker relationship is good, the banker will go along. After all, what else can he or she do? If an entrepreneur has convinced a banker of the viability and future growth of a business, the banker really does not want to call a loan that could bankrupt it. The real key to communicating with a banker is to candidly inform but not scare. In other words, entrepreneurs must indicate that they are aware of adverse events and have a way of dealing with them.

To further build credibility with their bankers, entrepreneurs should borrow before they need to and then repay the loan. This will establish a track record of borrowing and reliable repayment. Entrepreneurs should also make every effort to meet the financial targets that they have set for themselves and discussed with their banker. If this cannot be done, there will be an erosion of the credibility of the entrepreneur, even if the business is growing.

Stancill aptly describes the quid pro quo in a banker-entrepreneur relationship.[16] As a business grows and prospers, bankers have a right to expect an entrepreneur to continue to use them and not go shopping for a better interest rate. In return, entrepreneurs have the right to expect that their bank will continue to provide them with needed loans, particularly during difficult times when a vacillating loan policy could endanger the survival of businesses.

16.6 GENETIC LABORATORIES, INC.: CASE STUDY

GENETIC LABORATORIES, INC.

Summary

Genetic Labs, Inc., was founded in August 1970 by Robert A. Ersek and Arthur A. Beisang as the first commercial sperm bank in the world. The entrepreneurs, with 14 years of combined experience in cryogenic (low-temperature) technology and medical practice, began the company in response to many requests by men wishing to store their semen before having a vasectomy. These men paid a fee for the preservation (freezing) and storage of their semen in liquid nitrogen.

By mid-1972 management realized that partially because of adverse public-

---

[16]Stancill, "Getting the Most from Your Banking Relationship," p. 20.

ity, the sperm bank would not be profitable enough to meet the stockholders' objectives, so new products which had better profit potential were investigated. During this investigation the use of porcine tissue for the treatment of burns was discovered. Using their expertise in low-temperature preservation, Beisang and Ersek developed their current product, an improvement over the competition.

Genetic Laboratories became a public corporation in Minnesota during February 1972.[1] In 1975 the company's major business is manufacturing and marketing porcine tissue dressings (frozen, sterilized tissues taken from the surface of pigskins). These dressings are used in the treatment of burns, skin ulcers (e.g., bedsores), other open skin wounds, and surgical infection. Genetic Labs also buys and then distributes three complementary products.

To compete effectively in the porcine tissue business, Genetic Labs developed and patented a process for quick-thawing the tissue. The company was the first in the industry to emphasize sterile, frozen porcine tissue. This is now a competitive advantage because of the effects of the bacteria which exist in fresh, nonsterile tissue, and the side effects of the antibiotics introduced to inhibit bacterial growth.

Since Genetic's inception in August 1970, sales have increased steadily and losses have declined. The company is now passing its break-even point, and projects its first profitable year in 1975, as is shown in the following table:

Calendar Year	Sales	Operating Profit (Loss)
1971	$ 4,247	($ 5,714)
1972	50,711	(239,796)
1973	130,923	(198,392)
1974	287,371	(42,932)
1975*	574,000	21,364

*Projected

By continuing to offer a high-quality product, having a sound management team, and continuing a recently begun marketing strategy, Genetic Labs expects to achieve the following results from domestic and foreign operations.

Calendar Year	Sales	Profits
1975	$ 574,000	$ 21,364
1976	971,000	92,800
1977	1,562,000	273,292
1978	2,290,000	221,225

$$3x^s = 360K$$
$$5x^s = 600K$$

	P/E		
	5	10	20
	1.1m	2.2m	4.4m
$3x^s$	35%	17%	89%
$5x^s$	55%	29%	13.5%

To achieve these results, Genetic Labs needs $120,000 in equity capital.

[1] A public issue was made on February 7, 1972, under an A Registration; 190,000 shares were offered at $2.50 per share, with net proceeds to the company of $412,000. The stock is traded publicly.

The Company and Its Products

When management realized, in early 1972, that the sperm bank concept was no longer viable, it immediately began to explore the market for other applications of its sophisticated cryogenic techniques.

In July 1972 it was found from market research that porcine tissue (untreated surface tissues from the skin of freshly slaughtered pigs) was being sold to hospitals for burn treatment. Almost all of the porcine tissue being sold was fresh, with a shelf life of 7 to 10 days. It was felt that a significant product improvement could be made using Genetic's knowledge of low-temperature preservation techniques. Starting with fresh hides, a frozen porcine tissue was produced and its viability demonstrated at two large burn units. This took three months and $25,000.

Genetic Labs' frozen porcine tissue has two significant competitive features which set it well ahead of the competition.

The first is guaranteed sterility, achieved by treating the frozen tissue with gamma radiation to kill bacteria and antibiotics.

Since Genetic's product is sterile and free of antibiotic drugs, the Food and Drug Administration could qualify Genetic's product as a device. Most of the competitors' products are heavily contaminated with bacteria and contain significant amounts of antibiotics (to slow bacterial growth), so these products do not have the FDA "approval" that Genetic's product does. The bacteria and antibiotics have created problems at some institutions, such as wound sepsis (infection) and antibiotic toxicity. These flaws in the competitors' products have resulted in several lawsuits against hospitals and doctors because some patients have suffered hearing losses and others have died. This type of situation tends to make potential new users "hedgy."

The second advantage is in ease and use: the quick unthawing time and the longer shelf life.

Genetic's frozen tissue is frozen on a special nylon mesh which allows for rapid thawing. This process is protected by issued patents. The frozen tissue of the major competitor, Burn Treatment Skin Bank (BTSB), takes as long as 45 minutes to thaw, while Genetic's product is ready to use in less than 2 minutes. This is particularly advantageous to nursing personnel because it reduces the preparation time required for treating burns.

Genetic's frozen tissue also has a useful life of at least one year when stored at normal freezer temperatures. This compares to the competitors' products 7 to 10 days' useful life.

Genetic Lab's porcine tissue is available in three sterile forms—fresh frozen, fresh, and lyophilized (freeze-dried). Fresh frozen tissue is porcine tissue that has been frozen and sterilized to kill all bacteria. This type is delivered to the customer while still frozen. Fresh tissue is the fresh frozen product, thawed. This is refrigerated when delivered to the customer. Freeze-dried tissue is sterilized tissue from which most of the water has been removed. This eliminates the need for refrigeration and is more convenient than frozen. However, freeze-dried is less pliable than frozen.

The three complementary products sold by Genetic Labs are: foam burn pads, used to reduce the body pressure from lying in one position for long periods; Dermax, which is a woven elastic bandage used to hold porcine tissue and other dressings in place; and plastic aprons, worn by nurses while caring for burn and skin ulcer patients. These are acquired from manufacturers and distributed by Genetic Labs.

In regard to new products, Genetic Labs has recently developed a kit to be used in treating skin ulcers. This ulcer kit contains four complementary items to treat decubiti and other skin ulcers. Besides porcine tissue, the kit contains a debriding enzyme which removes dead tissue, sterile saline pads for cleansing the would, and foam padding to protect the tissue surrounding the wound. The kit will sell for between $37.50 and $57.50 per unit.

To conveniently treat minor burns and avulsion injuries, an emergency room kit has been developed which is designed specifically for use in hospital emergency rooms. The product contains 33 assorted porcine tissue dressings, and the customer can select either frozen or freeze-dried tissue. The selling price is $255.

Frozen tissue now dominates Genetic's sales picture. Over the next three years frozen tissue will remain the predominant product, with increasing amounts of freeze-dried tissue, ulcer kits, and emergency room kits being sold.

The Industry

Annual porcine tissue sales from 1972 to 1974 were $1,500,000, almost entirely within the burn treatment market. However, there is evidence that porcine tissue has several other uses. A number of medical papers written within the last year indicate that porcine tissue is extremely valuable in the treatment of such skin sores as decubitus ulcers (bed sores), diabetic ulcers, and stasis ulcers (open sores caused when patients cannot be moved for long periods of time). Porcine tissue has also been used successfully to treat avulsions (open soft tissue wounds), surgical infections, and wounds which cannot be closed immediately. These combined markets are potentially larger than the burn treatment market.

There is also a synthetic skin presently on the market for burn treatment, but it will not conform to the natural contours of the body, and when placed on a burn it adheres so strongly that when removed it takes with it the bed of granulation tissue which is necessary for healing. This and the product's inability to perform other basic tasks of natural tissue have limited its applications. Synthetic skin is not viewed as an influence on the market.

The Market—Present and Potential

Currently, about 80 percent of Genetic's porcine tissue sales in the United States are to hospital burn units. Porcine tissue has been available commercially for five years, but no company has yet initiated an aggressive marketing program. From 1972 to 1974, estimated worldwide porcine tissue *sales* were:

1972	$ 700,000
1973	1,200,000
1974	1,500,000

Before 1975, there were few overseas sales.

These sales can be compared to the size of the *potential* markets in the United States:

Major burns	$ 9,700,000
Skin ulcers	41,600,000
Emergency room treatments	2,500,000

Prior to 1975, a mailing was sent to potential foreign distributors who might want to carry porcine tissue. Response to this mailing has led to 1974 foreign sales for Genetic Labs of $82,000, initially in Sweden through a distributor. Genetic Labs is using this same approach worldwide, having tested its usefulness in Sweden.

Other important market developments, mentioned previously, are that porcine tissue is now starting to be used as an effective treatment for skin ulcers, other open skin wounds, and surgical infections. Thus, three major markets now exist for porcine tissue. They are: (*a*) the treatment of burns in hospitals with a special burn unit and in hospitals which do not have a special burn unit; (*b*) the treatment of skin ulcers in hospitals, nursing homes, and other extended care facilities; and (*c*) the treatment of burns and open skin wounds in hospital emergency rooms.

The Competition

There is currently only one major competitor in the market, Burn Treatment Skin Bank (BTSB). In 1974 this company had about 80 percent of the market. Now, in 1975, its share is declining.

Since 1972, three other companies have entered the business. Two have gone out of business, and one is eight months old. This last company has only one customer, and its product is not unique. Also, the incidence of hospitals preparing their own porcine tissue has declined, due to the commercial availability of high-quality tissue from Genetic Labs. Another important occurrence has been the decline of BTSB's sales from a monthly level of $120,000 down to $100,000 and a concurrent increase in Genetic's sales from $10,000 up to $38,000 per month. This growth has been in spite of predatory pricing practices engaged in by BTSB.

A recent communiqué by the FDA recommends the use of sterile porcine dressings as opposed to nonsterile dressings. This, along with Genetic's success in marketing sterile tissue, has caused BTSB to begin supplying frozen sterile tissue. However, BTSB is still identified as a producer of fresh nonsterile tissue by the medical profession. Since Genetic Labs introduced and is now marketing the favored product, Genetic has the potential to become the industry leader.

Marketing Strategy

Genetic plans to sustain the growth in burn unit sales in order to provide a constant cash flow for the company. Existing activities are also being expanded to increase Genetic Labs' share of this market.

Genetic will also develop the domestic skin ulcer market. This is the largest domestic market, and it is important to begin penetration ahead of the competition. At present, individual orders are small and spread over a large number of purchasers. The amount bought per customer per year is only a few hundred dollars. Direct calls will be expensive because the market includes so many customers. Therefore, Genetic Labs will employ mostly direct mail, trade shows, and advertising in medical journals to reach the market.

Another activity will be to increase the foreign market penetration, paralleling the sales method used in Sweden. The method used in Sweden entails contracting with a national distributor of medical products who will carry Genetic's products. This will be done by expanding the number of countries with distributorships. The reason for having several distributors early is to penetrate the market effectively, which will result in a larger long-term sales potential.

The domestic emergency room market will also be developed. This will be part of the overall direct mail program. This is the last priority because the potential market is smaller than the others.

In sum, Genetic labs currently has about 20 percent of the domestic burn treatment market, and BTSB has about 80 percent. However, Genetic proposes to dominate the market within three years by continuing to offer a superior product and as a result of the aggressive marketing program begun earlier this year (1975). To date, the number of customers domestically has more than doubled and porcine tissue distributorships have been negotiated in seven foreign countries.

Company Founders and Management Team

Genetic Labs' founders, Robert A. Ersek, M.D., and Arthur A. Beisang, have a unique mix of skills and experience in the field of low-temperature preservation of living matter, which has been invaluable in enabling them to develop a high-quality porcine teaching product. Their research and teaching have also allowed them to make contacts and develop credibility with the medical profession, a valuable asset in the industry. Arthur Beisang, president, has written more than 20 professional papers in this field.

Also required is technical knowledge of quality control in the field of specialized medical devices. Daniel Holman, vice president of manufacturing, has had extensive experience in monitoring biological assays; both Beisang and Holman have developed their knowledge as a result of managing Genetic Labs. Their talents are demonstrated by the medical profession's acceptance of Genetic's products.

Other skills needed for sales are marketing, managerial, and organizational—all of which presently exist at Genetic Labs. Beisang and Holman have developed considerable managerial and organizational skill by running the business, while the marketing skills were acquired when Ronald Roberts, domestic sales manager, was hired away from Burn Treatment Skin Bank (BTSB). The financial aspects are handled by an outside accountant. As Genetic Labs grows, a full-time vice president of finance will be hired.

The other management team member is Robert Ersek, M.D. Dr. Ersek, cofounder, is medical director. His functions are to evaluate all new products, to research new products which Genetic Labs could market, to contact doctors who have questions about Genetic's products, to handle FDA approval of new products, to review all promotional literature for accuracy, and to continue his research and publishing in cryobiology. Ersek has conducted and led extensive medical research, published more than 20 articles, and has two patents. He also participated in the founding of another medical device company, which currently has sales of $2 million per year.

The overall soundness of Genetic's management team is demonstrated by the fact that this team has brought the company from a $240,000 net loss in 1972 to a $43,000 net loss in 1974. The company is now approaching profitability.

It should also be noted that the lead entrepreneur, Arthur Beisang, is legally blind, but he has not been limited in his research and teaching or in the successful management of Genetic Labs.

Critical Risks and Assumptions

The five major risks are:

1. Price Competition. Burn Treatment Skin Bank's salesmen have been authorized to sell its porcine tissue at discounts of up to 25 percent from the list prices. This maneuver has affected Genetic's ability to sell tissue at full retail price. Genetic has offset this price-cutting by continuing to offer consistently high-quality products and fast service. Genetic also has a very high gross margin (see exhibits at end of case) which has allowed it to withstand this competition.

Genetic's antitrust attorneys have prepared a brief invoking several aspects of the Sherman Anti-Trust Act on BTSB and its parent company, Armour Pharmaceutical. The attorneys' opinion is that antitrust charges could be sustained in a court of law. They are presently negotiating with Armour (Greyhound Corporation) to satisfy damages suffered by Genetic Labs as a result of price-cutting by BTSB. A probable result of these negotiations will be a decrease in price cutting when BTSB is made aware of its allegedly illegal pricing practices.

Genetic Labs is improving its market position at the expense of BTSB. BTSB's porcine tissue represents less than 5 percent of Armour Pharmaceutical's sales, and due to its own price-cutting, its profit margin on this medical product is decreasing. Armour Pharmaceutical may not be willing to put the necessary effort into sustaining their now dominant market position.

2. Ease of Entry. Three new companies have entered the porcine tissue market in the past three years. Only one is still in business. Although the start-up cost is low for this industry, successful entry is difficult because a new company's product quality would be suspected in its early stages. Also, it takes time to gain acceptance with the medical profession, and the market trend is toward a sterile, frozen, quick-thawing product.

Genetic Labs has been issued packaging and processing patents, which gives a measure of protection to the quick-thawing feature of Genetic's porcine products. These patent rights should decrease the chances for success of new competitors. Genetic Labs has both more technical knowledge than a new competitor and credibility with doctors. These two factors will help Genetic Labs withstand new competition.

3. Lack of Working Capital. Genetic Labs has limited capital along with a rapid increase in sales. Although over $400,000 was available to Genetic at its inception, two thirds of that amount was used for the original sperm banking business. With a very limited initial capital investment, Genetic Labs has researched, developed, and marketed a line of porcine tissue and related products.

Management recognizes the need for more capital at this time. It is necessary for Genetic Labs to obtain sufficient capital in order to sustain further sales increases and to fund the development and marketing of product line extensions (such as the skin ulcer kit).

4. Raw Materials Needs. Pigskins must be available in sufficient supply to meet production demands. The present supplier of pigskins has the highest quality and quantity of skins in the United States, as evidenced by the fact that BTSB has changed suppliers and is now purchasing hides from the same supplier as Genetic. Genetic Labs has used hides from other sources and can obtain such hides again, if necessary. A contractual agreement exists with this supplier, which should reduce that risk.

5. Synthetic Substitutes. Porcine tissue dressings are a natural, biological product, and attempts to synthesize such a dressing of less expensive material, with an indefinite shelf life, have gone on since the efficacy of porcine dressings was first reported in 1964. One such commercial synthetic dressing is being marketed by one of the nation's largest pharmaceutical companies. This product has been on the market for two years, and its sales are insignificant. The product has a poor reputation and has cast doubt on the usefulness of synthetic skin because it is not as flexible as natural tissue and rips off some of the patient's skin when removed.

Two other companies are trying to develop synthetic substitutes for natural dressings. Neither has developed any useful facsimiles, and there is no evidence of a breakthrough. Genetic's president believes that a synthetic substitute is many years away.

Break-Even Analysis

Fixed costs for the break-even are:

Salaried employees	$190,300
Rent, leasehold	11,400
Equipment rental	3,589
Van rental	1,484
Wide Area Telephone Service (WATS)	5,832
Insurance	7,950
Accounting	6,460
Depreciation	10,000
Miscellaneous	180
Total	$237,195

The accounting figure also includes computer costs and an annual certified statement for the stockholders. The WATS line costs include only the fixed yearly charge.

The projected 1976 break-even sales level of $685,000, or $57,000 per month, is greater than the 1975 break-even level of $400,000, or $33,000 per month. The increase is due to (1) the president becoming full-time with the venture and (2) the added salesmen to implement the sales plan.

However, as shown in the financial statements, sales will increase to greater than the break-even level, and will be sustained above break-even.

Proposed Financing

Genetic Laboratories, Inc., is a publicly held corporation with 1,200,000 shares issued and 12 million shares authorized.

To carry on an aggressive, profitable marketing program, the company needs $120,000 in equity or subordinated debt. The financing will be used primarily to support a major selling effort to begin in mid-1975.

The minimum cash balance occurs in the first quarter of 1976, with a negative balance of $98,369. A typical cash or liquidity balance for the drug industry is 15 percent of assets. With this balance the cash requirement becomes $123,000, or rounded off, the $120,000 requested.

Exhibit 1
Potential Market for Porcine Tissue ($000s)

Treatment	1975	1976	1977	1978
U.S. market:				
Major burns	$ 9,760	$ 9,820	$ 9,880	$ 9,939
Skin ulcers	41,900	42,100	42,353	42,607
Emergency rooms	2,520	2,530	2,545	2,560
Subtotal	54,180	54,450	54,778	55,105
Foreign market:*				
Major burns	18,673	20,540	22,594	24,853
Skin ulcers	80,080	88,088	96,897	106,586
Emergency rooms	4,813	5,294	5,823	6,405
Subtotal	103,566	113,922	125,314	137,844
Total potential market	$157,746	$168,372	$180,092	$192,949

*Includes Argentina, Austria, Brazil, Denmark, Finland, France, Italy, Mexico, Netherlands, Spain, Sweden, United Kingdom, Venezuela, and West Germany.

Exhibit 2
Projected Sales and Market Share for Porcine Tissue ($000s)*

Category	1975	1976	1977	1978
U.S. potential market	$ 54,180	$ 54,450	$ 54,778	$ 55,105
Genetic *tissue* sales	298	514	852	1,191
Percent of total market	0.55%	0.94%	1.56%	2.16%
Foreign potential market	$103,566	$113,922	$125,314	$137,844
Genetic *tissue* sales	158	276.4	473	700.5
Percent of total market	0.15%	0.24%	0.38%	0.51%

*Not including sperm preservation sales or accessories.

Exhibit 3
Break-Even Chart*

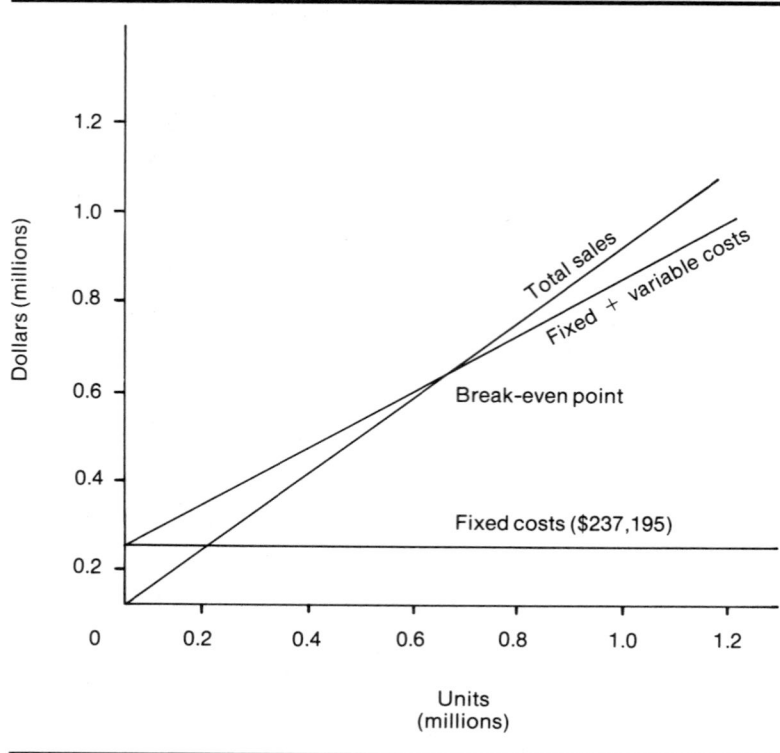

*Based on 1976 figures.

Exhibit 4

GENETIC LABS, INC.
Income Statements
1972–1974

	1972	1973	1974
Net sales and operating revenues	$ 50,711	$130,923	$287,371
Cost of sales and services	138,833	85,780	100,546
Gross margin	(88,122)	45,143	186,825
Selling/administration expense	151,674	243,535	229,757
Operating profit (loss)	(239,796)	(198,392)	(42,932)
Interest income, less interest expense	1,600	325	—
Net income (loss) before taxes	(238,196)	(198,067)	(42,932)
Extraordinary income (loss)	—	45,000	50,000
Net income	$(238,196)	$(153,067)	$ 7,068

Exhibit 5

GENETIC LABS, INC.
Pro Forma Income Statements
1975-1978

	1975	*1976*	*1977*	*1978*
Revenues:				
Accessories	$ 94,000	$156,600	$ 213,000	$ 374,500
Sperm	24,000	24,000	24,000	24,000
Total revenues	574,000	971,000	1,562,000	2,290,000
Expenses:				
Materials	69,081	121,400	195,260	286,300
Direct labor	59,641	104,900	168,700	247,300
Manufacturing overhead	85,492	150,500	242,100	355,000
Other	23,783	41,700	67,168	98,500
Gross margin	336,003	552,500	888,772	1,302,900
General and administrative expense	127,723	193,100	296,780	428,250
Sales expense	176,916	256,600	308,700	422,200
Net operating income	31,364	102,800	283,292	452,450
Depreciation	10,000	10,000	10,000	10,000
Federal taxes	—	—	—	221,225
Net income	$ 21,364	$ 92,800	$ 273,292	$ 221,225

Exhibit 6

GENETIC LABS, INC.
Balance Sheet
For Years Ending December 31, 1972-1974

	1972	*1973*	*1974*
Assets			
Current assets:			
Cash	$ 7,116	$ 24,454	$ 5,333
Certificate of deposit	204,135	—	—
Accounts receivable net of allowance for bad debts	24,449	20,066	51,909
Inventories	1,992	15,833	15,637
Prepaids and other	4,241	4,380	1,847
Total current assets	241,933	64,733	73,907
Plant and equipment	67,666	77,209	76,806
Less: Accumulated depreciation	6,195	15,953	25,275
Net plant and equipment	61,471	61,256	51,531
Deferred charges	—	—	—
Other assets	1,264	2,069	701
Total assets	$305,473	$127,253	$126,139
Liabilities and Stockholders' Equity			
Current liabilities:			
Accounts payable	$ 45,359	$ 27,344	$ 24,762
Notes payable	30,000	2,341	6,371
Accrued expenses	6,333	25,110	2,685
Federal and state taxes	2,986	996	2,243
Other	5,393	4,831	21,878
Total current liabilities	90,071	60,622	57,939
Long-term liabilities:			
Notes payable	—	2,406	—
Other liabilities	6,504	3,519	261
Stockholders' equity:			
Common stock at par (1.2 million shares outstanding as of 7/31/74)	11,820	11,835	12,000
Capital surplus	440,988	445,848	445,848
Retained earnings	(243,910)	(396,977)	(389,909)
Total stockholders' equity	208,898	60,706	67,939
Total liabilities and stockholders' equity	$305,473	$127,253	$126,139

Exhibit 7

GENETIC LABS, INC.
Pro Forma Balance Sheets
For Calendar Years Ended December 31, 1975–1978

Assets		1975		1976		1977		1978
Current assets:								
Cash		$ (30,447)		$ (8,121)		$161,088		$240,883
Marketable securities		—		—		—		—
Accounts receivable		144,375		242,750		390,500		572,500
Inventories:								
Raw materials and supplies	$ 10,286		$ 17,295		$ 28,951		$ 40,787	
Work in process	2,038		3,427		5,719		8,083	
Finished goods	8,625		14,501		24,293		34,200	
Total inventories		20,949		35,233		58,963		83,070
Prepaid items		286		—		—		—
Total current assets		135,163		269,852		610,551		896,453
Plant and equipment	76,995		82,995		88,995		102,995	
Less: Accumulated depreciation	39,934		49,934		59,934		69,934	
Net plant and equipment		37,061		33,061		29,061		33,061
Deferred charges		198		—		—		—
Other assets*		351		—		—		—
Total assets		$172,773		$302,913		$639,612		$929,514
Liabilities and Stockholders' Equity								
Current liabilities:								
Accounts payable		$ 44,648		$ 82,461		$145,740		$206,123
Notes payable		37,020		35,020		33,020		31,020
Accrued expenses		831		1,536		2,516		3,838
Federal and state taxes		971		1,793		2,941		11,913
Other: Prepaid storage		—		—		—		—
Total current liabilities		83,470		120,810		184,217		252,894
Long-term liabilities:								
Long-term notes		—		—		—		—
Other liabilities		—		—		—		—
Stockholders' equity:								
Common stock at par (1.2 million shares)	$ 12,000		$ 12,000		$ 12,000		$ 12,000	
Capital surplus	445,848		445,848		445,848		445,848	
Retained earnings	(368,545)		(275,745)		(2,453)		218,972	
Total stockholders' equity		89,303		182,103		455,395		676,620
Total liabilities and stockholders' equity		$172,773		$302,913		$639,612		$929,314

*No dollar value attached to current proprietary process and patents issues. No value assigned to tax loss of approximately $400,000 carried forward.

LIFE AFTER START-UP

PART V

Entrepreneurs in Action: Some Examples

17

Do not run out of cash.

The Entrepreneur's Maxim

17.1 RESULTS EXPECTED

This chapter gives you the opportunity to consolidate what you have learned so far about putting a venture together and getting it off the ground. It is based on entrepreneurial examples from real life, with comments by the author on "what was learned," what worked and what didn't, and how the iterative process can improve one's odds for venture success. It shows how, in actuality, the three essentials of venture creation—opportunity, people, and resources—come together, and it does not minimize the difficulties that arise. Since a good deal of entrepreneurial learning is by doing, and since the unsuccessful entrepreneur's stumbling block is often the successful entrepreneur's opportunity, we hope that this "dry run" through a number of entrepreneurial incidents will help you to deal more confidently with some of the situations that you and your venture will face.

17.2 PRESESSION PREPARATION

Read the chapter, and list the three lessons that you believe will be the most important in *your* entrepreneurial career.

17.3 ANATOMY OF THE ITERATIVE PROCESS

17.3.1 Introduction

When starting a company, an entrepreneurial team goes through a sequence of steps that could be outlined afterward as milestones or a venture action plan. Some of these steps are defined beforehand and then carried out; some are recognized as they are happening; and some are only noticed after the fact.

It has been the experience and observation of the authors that entrepreneurs can improve their chances of success by laying out, in detail, the steps to be taken in starting and running their businesses. Entrepreneurs who do this step through these milestones or variations of them mentally a number of times. By this method, the sequence, timing, and completeness of the steps can be reality-tested and improved. There is a learning process involved in this mental circulation through the venture milestones. It is far less costly to learn in the mind than through hard experience. In this regard, research has suggested that dart players can actually improve their accuracy by merely thinking about the process of throwing darts. Likewise, thinking about the milestone process of starting a venture should improve the entrepreneur's accuracy.

Meeting venture milestones in actual practice provides even more learning. A study by Lamont of 24 technology-based ventures[1] showed a marked difference in performance between 12 first-generation ventures[2] and 12 second-generation ventures. The second-generation venture was far more product oriented than its first-generation counterpart. The second-generation venture also had a more balanced team, higher initial financing, and higher first-year sales; reached profitability earlier; and had significantly higher profits in its most recent year of operation. This performance indicates, as might be expected, that a learning process occurs for a venture team going through the steps or milestones necessary to start a venture.

If the potential entrepreneur does not have much applicable experience, it may be very hard to start a new venture, let alone make it successful. Even unsuccessful attempts to start a venture will in themselves build up a knowledge of how to start a business successfully. Mental walks through venture action plans will increase the chances for success; this mental exercise, combined with actually trying to meet venture milestones, will cause some learning to happen. Multiple venture creation attempts can help raise the entrepreneur's skill levels over the threshold required to carry out a successful venture "put-together."

The following history will describe one entrepreneur's actual early, unsuccessful attempts to start a business and will serve to indicate the kinds of learning that resulted from these attempts. We hope that this sort of review may reduce some of the trial and error associated with your attempt to launch a venture.

17.3.2 Struggling to Find a Venture: Five Goose Chases

1. The incipient entrepreneur, Charles, received a bachelor of science degree in business administration with a minor in engineering. He knew that he wanted to start a business eventually, but first he wanted to strengthen his engineering abilities. Consequently, he went to work as an engineer in the development laboratory of a chain belt manufacturer, CB Company. He thought he would be working on new product development, which would provide him with experience directly related to starting a new venture. However, before he could do this, he spotted a need in the company for an automatic inspection machine for chain links and successfully proposed to the laboratory director that he develop such a machine for CB's use.

While working on the machine, the laboratory director and Charles, who were graduates of the same school, discussed the possibility of Charles's starting

---

[1]Lawrence M. Lamont, "What Entrepreneurs Learn from Experience," *Journal of Small Business Management,* July 1972, pp. 35–41.

[2]Ibid., p. 36. "The creation of a first generation technology-based enterprise (called a spin-off) occurs when an entrepreneur starts a business to commercialize technology transferred from a previous source of employment. As the new firm develops, it, in turn, becomes a source of technology and entrepreneurs for a second-generation spin-off, and so on."

a company to manufacture a chain link testing instrument that had been developed by the director. With little data they decided that the market for the instrument was not large enough to be the basis for a small company. They did not seriously consider developing an integrated line of chain testing instruments and handling tools to create the business volume necessary for a viable venture.

2. Charles also had venture discussions with Bill, a shop foreman who had worked his way up from the position of machine repair mechanic. Bill was very skillful at grinding machine setup and special machine alterations. Charles and Bill spent many hours in trying to identify a product that could capitalize on the latter's skills. However, the two were unable to define a product that would meet any generalized grinding machine need.

3. Charles also had venture discussions with Tom, a clever mechanical engineer at CB Company. They talked of possible products based on mechanical technology to tie in with Tom's unique design capability. Charles's father, a physicist, was also queried about products, and he said, "Tell me what the market needs, and I might be able to design a product to fit that need." Charles and Tom were unable to identify a potential product or need because they had no detailed knowledge of any marketplace.

4. Charles, Tom, and an electrical engineer, Carl, then tried to come up with ideas. They decided they needed a place to work and began fixing over Carl's chicken coop for this purpose. Between 9 and 10 months later, the engineer had a nicely fixed-over chicken coop, but the team had no ideas for business. The work on the chicken coop had effectively drained 9–10 months of effort away from the more primary goal of finding an idea that met a market need.

5. Two years after Charles's first attempt to identify a venture opportunity, he was drafted into the army. At this time Tom suggested that the team—Charles, Tom, and Carl—design some kind of electromechanical toy. Tom was an exacting craftsman and, as a hobby, had worked on model cars and planes and been very adept at home automobile repair.

After much discussion the field of powered model cars or planes was chosen—based on Tom's experience in building models. A car and a helicopter were picked first, and the car was given priority on the basis of Tom's love and knowledge of cars and the potential difficulty of making a working, powered model helicopter.

Charles and Tom agreed that there must be a market for a properly designed powered model car with the right price. This supposition was based only on the knowledge that model cars and toy trains did sell in enough volume to support a fair-sized industry.

With no market data the team began to design a model-car product based on their own feelings as to what was wanted by the consumer. Charles and Tom provided all of the drive to build a prototype. Carl made a significant contribution to the design of the electrical control. Since Charles was stationed at an army base some distance away, he drove several hundred miles each weekend to work on the car model.

About 10 months after the idea had been conceived, with the part-time effort of Charles and Tom a prototype of a model car was completed. It consisted of a single eight-inch-long model car powered on a restricted track, and its speed and steering were controllable from outside the car. The design appeared to be simple enough to allow low-cost manufacture. With a successful prototype completed, Charles and Tom decided that they would either try to license the model car to an existing manufacturer or start a business to manufacture and sell it.

Developing a Business Strategy. Charles and Tom tried to find somebody with applicable venture experience to discuss how to start a company in the toy field, but failed to find any sources of good advice. Charles attended a large toy manufacturers' sales show in New York to size up the industry. The competitive rat-race image obtained from viewing two hotels full of toy exhibits and from engaging in two days of discussions with toy company representatives left Charles feeling that he wanted nothing to do with starting a company in the toy industry. Further, Charles and Tom both felt completely inadequate to start into large-scale production and consumer distribution of such a toy. It was obvious to the pair of incipient entrepreneurs that only by licensing the car model to a toy manufacturer could they realize some return from their efforts.

Testing the Market. Charles made appointments to display the prototype car model to the Lionel and A. C. Gilbert companies, both manufacturers of toy trains. The chief engineer of Lionel said that the concept was interesting and that an excellent job had been done in reducing it to practice. However, a corporate policy decision had been made at Lionel to get out of the toy field and go into government contracting.

The A. C. Gilbert meeting went better. The board of directors, which happened to be meeting that day, become interested in the model car. Several of the directors "drove" the car around the track and laughed and hugely enjoyed themselves. Although a powered model-car project had already been started at Gilbert, Charles and Tom were told that if only a second car could be added to their track, there was a definite possibility that A. C. Gilbert would be interested in their product.

Reappraising the Potential. At this point, there was a significant question in the minds of the team members about the merits of putting any more effort into the project. It was not obvious that a second car could be put on the track without significant complication and work. Further, it was not at all certain that A. C. Gilbert would really be interested in licensing the model car or that any valid patent could be obtained to protect the idea from being used without compensation.

Charles was now seriously considering a sixth venture try (three years after beginning his venture attempts.) Although Tom agreed to go further in the development of a two-car system, the priority he set on this task was so low that no further developmental progress was made.

17.3.3 Comment: What Was Learned

The five goose chases just described were failures as far as directly starting a new venture was concerned. The goose chases were, however, crude venture action plans that Charles tried to follow. Considerable learning resulted. What was this learning?

Necessity for a Team. In Charles's first venture assessment, it became clear that the laboratory director was not a potential team member and Charles first recognized the need for active partners who would provide complementary skills and who would reinforce one another in the quest for an attractive venture.

In working with the shop foreman, it became very apparent to Charles that there was a combination of abilities in analysis and innovation that was necessary for the development of a standard product. In his later venture attempts Charles did combine with Tom and Carl to obtain such abilities.

Market Awareness. The failure to identify a potentially viable business in the third venture effort led Charles and Tom to go down a dead-end street in the fourth venture effort—that of developing a plant facility (the renovated chicken coop) before product definition. The wasted time involved in this mistake finally brought home the absolute necessity for a clear definition of a product and market in founding a venture. As can be seen, the total lesson was still not learned because Charles and Tom, in the next venture effort, defined a product in a field too competitive for their taste. Further, the toy field required mass production and marketing techniques that were beyond their capabilities. An earlier examination of the toy industry would have shown the entrepreneurs that they were headed for failure.

Positive Lessons Learned from Failure. After five goose chases Charles had learned that he had to have a partner to provide a balance of abilities in a venture effort. He had also identified some of the complementary abilities that he needed in a partner, and he had become aware of the necessity for high quality in these abilities.

Akin to team considerations were those of business contacts. Charles had learned that he had no business contacts from which to get advice. He was convinced that any future venture creation effort he made would include expanding his business horizons and contacts on a planned basis.

A further conclusion was that of the importance of the choice of business field. Charles now realized that an entrepreneur must pick a general field of business (1) that appeals to him or her on a personal basis (the toy field had not appealed), (2) to which he or she can make a significant contribution (this had worked in the choice of the toy field), and (3) that basically requires skills possessed by the entrepreneurial team (the team had not had the production and marketing abilities needed to handle a toy venture).

The major lesson learned from the fifth goose chase was that by taking step-by-step action toward meeting defined goals, two very inexperienced individuals had been able to develop a workable product prototype. This prototype attracted favorable attention from the top management of two leading companies in the chosen field. To Charles, this was coming within shooting distance of success and served to build his venturing self-confidence. Based on all the lessons learned, Charles was convinced that he could use his remaining 10 months' time in the army to get a venture started.

17.4 BIRTH OF THE MASSEY-DICKINSON COMPANY: THE GOOSE IS CAUGHT

Charles had initiated an army transfer to a quiet quartermaster corps laboratory in Boston. He was assigned to a job that required a Ph.D. in mechanical engineering and was completely beyond his trained ability. He could neither learn the job nor design a meaningful research program in his final eight months of army time. Charles decided to use every available minute of his remaining time in the service to initiate a business. In this new venture effort he was determined to use everything he had learned from his previous venturing efforts.

17.4.1 General Business Field for Venture Is Identified

Through library research Charles identified industrial instruments as a growing general field. Through thinking about what was around him, Charles identified the medical equipment and supply field as a second area of interest. Boston, a noted medical research center, seemed an ideal place to base a venture dealing in new medical products. This idea quickly flowered and took precedence in Charles's mind because working in a field that would be of direct help to humanity appealed to him. Library research showed that the medical equipment and supply market was large and that it was growing rapidly compared to other markets. Profit margins in the industry were above average. Charles visited various medical supply houses and concluded that much of the instrumentation, equipment, and specialized medical furniture could be improved. From talking with the supply houses, Charles found that many of the companies manufacturing medical products were small. Therefore, Charles felt that he could start small and be successful. There were existing channels of distribution for medical products that a small company could use, again showing Charles that a new medical venture could establish itself through these channels. Charles and Tom agreed that an effort to develop some medically oriented business on a spare-time basis looked acceptable. They did not regard Carl as a serious team member because of his previous lack of effort after an initial investment of a few hours.

17.4.2 A Potential Business Is Defined

Neither Charles nor Tom were fitted by their experience for starting a company. They had had only development engineering experience with the CB Company. They had had no experience in marketing, production, finance, or in the medical field that they wanted to enter. CB Company had sales of $110 million per year, so working for it had not been a small-company experience.[3] It seemed at first that there was not much to work with.

Charles listed the assets available to him:

1. His ability to live on his wife's pay and his meager army pay for six months while getting a company started.
2. Tom's willingness to work evenings at no cost to the venture.
3. Savings of $12,000
4. The ability of Charles and Tom to design mechanical and electromechanical devices.
5. Proximity to large amounts of active medical records.
6. Proximity to the technological resources of Boston (e.g., libraries, consultants, machine shops, and electronics manufacturing facilities).

Charles decided to offer the one ability that he and Tom had—design of devices—to the medical research community, so that they would be building on their expertise. Their proposed company would design special medical research instruments upon request. After completing the design, the company would subcontract the manufacture of the instruments to eliminate the capital cost of equipping a shop and to retain manufacturing flexibility. The design and subcontract construction of the instruments would be done for a fixed price agreed upon with

---

[3]All dollar figures have been corrected for inflation.

·the customer before work was begun. It was anticipated that many instruments would be built only once but that occasionally there would be repeat orders. This approach of selling services appeared to Charles to be a low-risk, low-profile way of entering the medical field, using what experience the team had as advantageously as possible.

17.4.3 Charles Takes Some Planned Venture Action

Charles visited a well-known senior scientist at MIT who had some contact with the medical research field. The scientist encouraged Charles to proceed with the medical instrument business. He gave Charles the names of several medical researchers. He also mentioned that his son had just been through starting a successful company and might give him some useful tips. Charles visited the son, Jack, who was very helpful. Jack gave Charles the name of a subcontract machine shop that he used and the name of his corporate lawyer. Charles visited the corporate lawyer, who agreed to handle the new firm's legal needs. He recommended that the new firm be a partnership to avoid incorporation costs until it was determined that there was a market, that significant sales were possible, and that a method of limiting personal liability was needed.

Charles visited one of the medical researchers recommended by the MIT scientist. This doctor was located in the Warren Research Building of the Massachusetts General Hospital. The doctor, upon hearing of Charles's design service, asked whether he would be interested in designing and building a new muscle fatigue measuring instrument, based on an old instrument. Charles agreed to return with a proposal. The doctor encouraged Charles about the need for the service he was providing.

Charles also visited a second medical researcher. This medical researcher also encouraged him about the need for special instrument service and recommended a subcontract machine shop that he might use.

17.4.4 Massey-Dickinson Company Is Born

As a result of the several conversations described above, Charles and Tom decided that there was some indication of a need for someone to make special medical instruments. They decided to go ahead with their proposed venture. They now needed a company name. They felt that the name must seem solid and established because the medical field was a conservative one. After many hours of thinking, they chose the name Massey-Dickinson Company. (Massey was Charles's middle name, and Dickinson was Tom's last name.) The name sounded both like Becton Dickinson, a company in the medical field, and like Massey Ferguson, a company in the machinery field, thereby conveying a subliminal feeling of substance and longevity. Individuals' names seemed to the partners to give some personal substance to the company. Incidentally, the company initials were MD, which also seemed appropriate.

17.4.5 More Venture Actions and the First Order

With five months of army time left, Charles began accelerating his level of venture effort. Massey-Dickinson calling cards and letterhead stationery were designed and printed; a telephone answering machine was attached to Charles's apartment telephone; personal contact was made with a local bank; potential subcontracting machine shops were visited; and quotes were obtained for subcontract construction of the muscle fatigue instrument. Then a large number of hours were poured into readying a proposal for that instrument.

Charles submitted the proposal to the doctor, including a three-dimensional drawing of the proposed instrument. The price quoted for the design and the complete instrument was $4,500. (The cost of manufacture, exclusive of engineering, overhead, and profit, was estimated at $3,400. The entrepreneurs had decided to "buy" their first contract to give them some experience.) The doctor gave them a purchase order for the instrument, and Tom began making final drawings, while Charles made a selection of the subcontractor and ordered parts.

17.4.6   The Business Becomes Real, and So Does the Work

As Charles's time in the army came to an end, he was swamped with the detail of supervising the construction of the machine and with visiting more researchers at the Warren Research Building to obtain additional work. His apartment was close to the army laboratory and 10 minutes' drive from the Warren Building. Charles made liberal use of army leave time, three-day weekend passes, evenings, and very extended lunch hours.

Upon separation from the army in July 1957, almost four years after Charles had initiated his first efforts to launch a venture, Massey-Dickinson Company was in business. Its first order was nearing completion; several additional proposals had been submitted to doctors at the Warren Building; and many customer discussions of future orders were under way.

A few months after leaving the army, Charles decided that he couldn't maintain a professional image while operating out of his apartment, so he arranged to rent office space from the subcontractor whom he had found to be the most satisfactory. Charles felt that being next to his major manufacturing facility was efficient and would allow work in progress to be monitored closely. Massey-Dickinson now had an established air about it, with telephone, calling cards, letterhead stationery, office, full-time employee, customers, and a book of pictures showing the several completed and delivered instruments. At this point, Charles was very enthusiastic, putting in a large number of hours per week and handling everything from sweeping the floor to purchasing, subcontract management, engineering, bookkeeping, and selling.

Apart from the rush of productive work on medical equipment, Charles was meeting many other venture milestones at the same time. Examples of these milestones are: equipping office space, moving his offices, hiring a part-time bookkeeper, arranging for typing service, incorporating the partnership, choosing his board of directors, getting product liability insurance, making up a brochure describing the medical equipment development service, broadening his contacts with subcontracting shops and with engineers who could provide backup design services, hiring a mechanical engineer, strengthening his contacts with his bank, and developing a business plan preparatory to raising needed equity money.

17.4.7   Learning from Massey-Dickinson

At the end of one year Charles was loaded with work on special medical instruments. He had hired a disabled mechanical engineer and was also able to draw a small salary from the company. Tom continued to work evenings for no salary. He enjoyed the engineering work as a hobby, but it was becoming evident that he lacked the entrepreneurial drive necessary to create a going business. He enjoyed the security of a larger company. Charles knew he needed to find team members for Massey-Dickinson, but until he had something to offer, his options were limited. In the meantime, Charles was extending his experience and his range of contacts and Massey-Dickinson Company was becoming an experienced company in the medical instrument field.

17.5 A NEW VENTURE ACTION PLAN

As Charles's reputation increased, he saw that the business volume of about $20,000 per month could be increased to support two or three professionals within another 12 months. He felt from his experience in the labs that the market size would not allow much more. To expand further would require a service or product with a larger market potential.

Accordingly, Charles decided to analyze all of the special medical products for areas where a sizable market might be indicated. Eight areas were identified: neurological tools, test-tube handling equipment, cardiographs, medical pumps, medical furniture, programming equipment, data processing equipment, and animal cages. Charles invested significant attention to market testing in each of those areas. The method was simple. Generally, an order could be obtained for one item in the area of interest, for example, a special data integrator. The product would be designed to meet the needs of a more general market. The price obtained would generally defray the cost of manufacture. The engineering design was done on a shoestring. The products were market-tested by a variety of means—from free new product releases in technical journals to papers presented by the involved and interested researchers who were buying the equipment. The proof of the market test would be interested potential customers and sales. A year and a half of this product development effort cost a considerable amount. A bank debt approaching $200,000 based on inventory, work in progress, receivables, and Charles's signature forced Charles to pick the best-looking product and push it into the marketplace.

17.5.1 A Potential Product Business Is Defined and Started

Charles picked behavioral programming equipment to push into the marketplace. This equipment is used to program psychological or physiological tests on humans and animals. The product was an advanced computer-type approach to an old product. The original equipment, built in a laboratory, had been market-tested at a major scientific meeting with good results. Many scientists wanted to buy this equipment or see a catalog. Massey-Dickinson started to move on a standard product. Product design was completed at the same time that orders were being taken from local researchers and a catalog was being written. Charles selected an electronics subcontractor to build the equipment.

Charles, a medical research doctor, an electronics technician from a medical laboratory, and the engineer subcontractor became the entrepreneurial team. Charles was the general manager; Charles and the doctor did systems design; the doctor tested the equipment and made a list of potential buyers; the electronics technician did application engineering and became sales manager; and the subcontractor carried out engineering (on speculation) and manufacture. The work described above may sound simple, but in actuality an immense effort was expended to bring the product to market in time to meet the demand.

The product was sold through display at four scientific meetings a year, selected customer visits, and direct mail. The doctor described to Charles how other companies sold their equipment in this field. Massey-Dickinson followed suit. There were existing companies in the field that had sales of up to $8 million per year. Therefore, the market had a defined size. Charles felt able to cope with it, and he had a sales method that he could control. Also, the market niche was not large enough to attract major competition. The unique solid-state approach of the Massey-Dickinson product gave it a strong edge over existing equipment suppliers.

It was possible to develop the market with a reasonable amount of capital by leaning on the subcontractor to carry inventory and conduct engineering on a speculative basis. Approximately 30 percent of Massey-Dickinson was sold to raise the equity capital necessary for this market development.

17.5.2   Comment: What Was Learned

From the experience of launching Massey-Dickinson, Charles learned a number of specific things, namely, how to:

1. Start a business using subcontractors to maximum advantage.
2. Select subcontractors.
3. Manage subcontract work.
4. Bid complicated jobs accurately.
5. Engineer a variety of instruments and equipment.
6. Make business contacts.
7. Build banking relations.
8. Deal with customers.
9. Make progress according to a venture action plan.

In addition, Charles had acquired considerable general knowledge, including:

1. Knowledge of how to manage an entire business that required the integration of many factors in each management decision.
2. A broad range of specific knowledge on market-study techniques, use of free new product releases, generation of data sheets, exhibiting at trade shows, management of sales representatives and distributors, handling of customers, engineering and management of engineering, management of subcontractors, accurate costing of proposed products, use of patent attorneys, debt and equity financing, use of corporate attorneys, and use of consultants to broaden technical approaches.
3. Through repeated use of subcontractors, how to select good subcontractors and maximize the use of their facilities and assets.
4. How to identify the type of marketplace that fitted his psychological makeup and filled a niche within a large and growing field. The small size of the niche allowed him personal contact with major customers, direct sale to the end user, and reward for high technical performance, which is easily recognized in a small field.

5. Some techniques for analyzing a potential niche:
   a. The size of the niche can be determined from the size of the existing companies in the niche.
   b. Niche customers must be easy to define and reach.
   c. The entrepreneur should know some friendly potential customers in the niche.
6. Reinforcement and refinement of all his previous learning (described earlier in this chapter). For example, he had learned more about the timing problems concerned with taking step-by-step action toward meeting a goal. In short, he learned that during the early stages of a new venture the entrepreneur should not set goals so rigid that they prevent him from responding to actual market feedback. But, on the other hand, the entrepreneur must find and identify his basic goal and put all his energy into its development, at least until a secure base of sales has been obtained.
7. A sense of the dynamic, demanding, and interdependent nature of the goals in a venture action plan. The requirements involved in meeting venture goals came in an unending, demanding stream. He found that the requirements might change even as one worked to fill them. Most of the goals and their requirements were interdependent.

17.6 GEODYNE CORPORATION: ANOTHER GOOSE IS SPOTTED

Charles, the entrepreneur of Massey-Dickinson Company (MD), was busy developing the behavioral programming equipment (M25). A small job he had done at Woods Hole Oceanographic Institute (WHOI) suddenly provided a new opportunity. The scientist at WHOI who had purchased a single instrument from Charles wanted Charles, at no cost to WHOI, to develop a production design of this instrument in return for an order for 12 instruments. The scientist claimed that there would be a market for those instruments with other oceanographers. Conversations with other oceanographers at WHOI and with two fisheries laboratories indicated that there was some potential for the instrument and also a need for other ocean instruments. Further, the staff at WHOI said that significantly increased funding levels were indicated for oceanographic research using measuring instruments. Charles could see the beginnings of a new business field that had the allure of the ocean.

17.6.1 Dilemma

Charles felt a strong desire to create a business concerned with the ocean. With two hours' work in the library he discovered that the federal government purchased large amounts of equipment for ocean research. WHOI represented a significant ocean research customer actually asking him to develop and supply equipment. Starting a second major business effort would dilute effort on M25. But M25 was not sure of major success.

17.6.2 Dilemma Resolved and a Basic Venture-Building Problem Defined

M25 was well along in development, using the subcontractor. The MD sales manager could make all the sales trips that the company could afford. The medical one-of-a-kind business could be tapered off faster than planned, which would free a considerable amount of Charles's time and allow him to develop the oceanographic instrument business.

The major problem that had to be met if an oceanographic equipment business was to be started was the need for increased engineering capacity and instant shop facilities of impressive size. WHOI would not buy major equipment from a cellar-type operation. If Massey-Dickinson could solve this problem, it would have the potential advantage of excluding all other cellar shops from competition. The M25 subcontractor's facility was electronically oriented, with no mechanical shop capability. Further, the facility was unimpressive. The five-man machine shop used for the medical one-of-a-kind work was not up to producing a volume of electromechanical and electronic instruments and had no engineering capability.

17.6.3   Venture Resources Defined

Charles picked a large machine shop on Boston's Route 128 that he had used before. This shop was founded and run by a father (Pete)-and-son (Fred) combination—both were engineers. The shop itself was in an inexpensive but modern, well-organized building. A proposal was made to the founders, and it was agreed that the WHOI instrument order would be taken under the name of Massey-Dickinson. A rough plan of action was laid out for the sharing of the workload, the development and use of capability and resources, and a split of potential ownership, and criteria for market evaluation were established.

The gratis engineering work was to be split between the machine shop and MD. The shop would charge normal rates for its work, and any profit would be split equally between the two groups after the shop's work had been paid for. The shop facility could be shown to WHOI as available for meeting its needs. The shop would also handle the project's telephone calls. If a real market were identified and proven by sales to WHOI and other groups, a separate company would be formed, with ownership split 50–50 between the two companies as partners.

17.6.4   Product Developed

A good, reliable instrument was developed by Charles and his new partner, Fred, and produced by the shop. To make one of the components for the instrument, a special timing device was searched out, tested, and imported in volume from Switzerland. This device was altered and calibrated in the machine shop. It performed a timing function not filled by any commercially available component.

In June 1961, 10 months after receipt of a $35,000 purchase order, the instruments were delivered to WHOI, and they made a good impression. There was particular interest in the unique timing component. After testing, WHOI placed an order for 100 of the timing components at $240 each, to be used on another instrument. These components worked well, and one of the WHOI program managers suggested that Charles and Fred could make the timer and other components for a new type of instrument that WHOI had developed and was testing.

17.6.5   Company Formed

In January 1962 Charles and Fred decided to form a company on paper. Manufacturing would still be done in the machine shop, but the company would have a name, letterhead, calling cards, and a symbol. This move kept the financial commitment low, while presenting a more integrated image to the customer.

The oceanographic equipment business was a second-effort fun thing for both Charles and Fred. It was decided to create a glamour image to go along with the glamour of dealing with the ocean. This fun-thing approach helped to create a flexible attitude in the partners that was a definite asset in laying out the venture action plan.

17.6.6 Company Image

After much effort a company name was created—Geodyne Corporation. This name was specific enough to indicate the type of field but nonlimiting for the expansion that was visualized. Fred designed a company symbol that placed the letters GEODYNE within a world globe form. The design looked so good that an advertising artist did all the graphics necessary for the letterhead, business cards, labels, and data sheet format for a very small fee so that he could carry them in his portfolio.

17.6.7 Company Operations

An incorporation was initiated, with its stock split equally between Charles and Fred. Since Charles had identified a potential instrument business with live customers and had instrument-manufacturing experience, and Fred had a shop facility that provided instant credibility to those customers and also had some instrument experience, the two partners seemed equal in what they were contributing to the venture. Geodyne developed a data sheet on the timing device, using a format drawn up by the advertising artist, and printed it on the copying machine. Later it was printed as a two-color data sheet. At this time WHOI asked Geodyne to start supplying larger numbers of the new instrument that WHOI had developed and had been making itself. Now orders for these instruments and for the first instrument designed by Geodyne began to flow in from other institutions. Oceanographers at these institutions had heard papers presented by WHOI scientists and had seen the instruments demonstrated at WHOI.

17.6.8 Keep That Best Customer

Charles and Fred realized that instruments in use at WHOI were Geodyne's best sales representatives and that WHOI was crucial to early venture success. However, WHOI staff felt that Geodyne had to be located near the institute to properly service WHOI needs. Yet, Charles and Fred did not want to lose the many venture resources available to them in Boston, and it would be inefficient if 90 miles separated them from the plant facility. As a compromise, in the middle of 1962, with sales still under $500,000, Geodyne opened a small technical office next to WHOI in a half-basement of the Woods Hole Inn. The neat office was artistically furnished at low cost and equipped with one each of the instruments and mechanisms that Geodyne was selling. Further, copies of data taken by Geodyne instruments and plotted by WHOI were displayed, along with photos of the instruments in use at sea and photos of the interior and exterior of the machine shop. In short, the office looked functional and businesslike. It created an atmosphere of success and gave an image of the major operation existing in the main facility in Boston.

17.6.9 A Major Hire

To staff the office, a third partner, Paul, a personable ex-WHOI oceanographer and electrical engineer who lived in Woods Hole, was put on Geodyne's payroll at a small salary. The concept of a technical office located near WHOI and staffed by a professional oceanographer kept the institute as an excellent customer. Oceanographers visiting WHOI and perhaps staying at the inn could stop by the office and talk shop and business.

17.6.10 More Customers

The day the office was opened, a government official attending a technical meeting at WHOI walked into the office and said that his agency, the U.S. Public Health Service (UPSHS), wanted to buy what amounted to $3 million worth of equipment! However, it was obvious to Fred and Charles that it would be necessary to prove that Geodyne was more than a paper company in order to close the sale.

17.6.11 More Resources: Directors, Assembly Facility, Capital, and Bank

On the basis of the potential order, a most successful entrepreneur, Jack, who had recently founded and built a major scientific product company, agreed to join the Geodyne board of directors. The seasoned Boston lawyer for this entrepreneur's business also agreed to be on the board. At this time a building belonging to a company that had gone bankrupt came up at auction. It was located directly on Route 128, and as a result, it had significant visibility. The machine shop was only 500 feet away. Charles, Fred, and Pete agreed that a bid should be submitted on the building, and they obtained it for $600,000. In the summer of 1962 the team felt that this move would give substance to Geodyne as a company capable of producing $3 million worth of equipment. They also felt that the risk in buying the building was low because the price was low and because a building directly on Route 128 was a reasonably liquid asset. Further, if the USPHS contract did not materialize, space within the building could be sublet until company sales volume grew to a size capable of supporting the full building.

At the bankruptcy auction of the building the team had picked up at a bargain price some desks, file cabinets, chairs, and workbenches. Several pieces of equipment that had been developed to build WHOI instruments in the machine shop were moved into the newly acquired building. The work to be moved from the machine shop was assembly, testing, packing, shipping, engineering, sales, and administration. All of these factors made it possible to equip the plant for a small capital investment. A sign painter was hired, and the Geodyne symbol was constructed in a 4-foot by 6-foot sign and mounted on the Route 128 front side of the building. The exterior and interior were now assuming the image of a going business. At the start of business a few individuals were shifted from the machine shop payroll to the Geodyne payroll and several new people were hired. Since the work to be conducted in the building was low-skill assembly, it was not difficult to hire the people needed. The idea of going to work for a company manufacturing oceanographic equipment had a lot of allure to many of those hired.

The bank that had serviced both the machine shop and Massey-Dickinson over a number of years had been kept up to date on the progress of Geodyne and its oceanographic equipment. It provided a mortgage for the full purchase price of the building, treating some small improvements that Geodyne had made in the building as the down payment. The bank also agreed to give references to the USPHS if these were called for.

Capital equipment and working capital were necessary to progress further. Charles, Fred, Pete, Paul, and Jack all invested varying amounts in Geodyne. Charles had to find $50,000 to hold his ownership in Geodyne at the level he desired. To do this, he went more heavily in debt to the bank. The bank allowed him to do so because it believed that Geodyne had a tangible value.

The bank was pleased with Charles's and Fred's decision to go full-time in Geodyne. Fred's decision was easy to make—leave a partnership in a job shop for an ocean products company, with the option of returning to the job shop if all did not go well. Charles felt that the dynamic potential of a field just starting, and the romance of manufacturing products related to the ocean, fitted his personality better than did the more stable and established behavioral equipment field. After trying to run Massey-Dickinson in lunch hours for several months, Charles was able to convince the M25 subcontractor to become president of MD on a full-time basis and to merge his company with MD.

17.6.12 Problems

The USPHS official stated that unless Geodyne proved that the data from its instruments could be handled automatically, no contract could be justified. This required a very complex automatic reader that WHOI had been going to develop but had never started. The development of such a device was no minor undertaking. Paul, the oceanographer, worked full-time on finding a subcontractor to do this very specialized job, while Charles worked on developing an in-house machine. To Charles, it rapidly became apparent that building a data-reading machine could never be accomplished in time to win the $3 million contract. Paul found a contractor that produced a general-purpose computer whose optical input could be altered to read the data. He convinced this young company of the excitement and promise of the field and the long-term future of Geodyne. The machine alteration required a very expensive type of movie projector. For the demonstration to USPHS, such a projector was rented, torn apart, and fitted into the system. With several 24-hour work stints the reading technique was demonstrated to the satisfaction of the USPHS.

The USPHS put out a request for a bid on Geodyne-type equipment, and Geodyne submitted the second-to-lowest bid.

17.6.13 More Problems

The lowest bid was rejected because there was no automatic reading. The contract was awarded to Geodyne and then taken away one month later because of direct political intervention caused by the low-bid competitor. Geodyne had demonstrated only a crude prototype data-reading capability. However, the USPHS fought hard to overcome the political pressure. It was willing to fight this battle because the instruments were proven in use and because Geodyne projected a successful, businesslike atmosphere that left the client feeling that delivery, quality, and performance promises would be met. The full $3 million contract was reinstated two months after it had been canceled. Delivery was completed successfully over a period of 18 months, ending in the spring of 1974. This contract gave the company the resources to develop a series of new products and services.

17.6.14 Epilogue

Geodyne built a full team of entrepreneurs, managers, and skilled engineers. At the outset, production was managed by non-equity-owning employees who later received stock options. The company became predominant in the manufacture of buoy-mounted oceanographic instruments. It also successfully provided data processing services based on its instrument capabilities. In 1967 merger with a larger company expanded its services into environmental data collection. Prior to the merger, company sales were just under $7 million per year. Seven years after the merger, total sales of oceanographic instruments and environmental data collection services were approaching $25 million.

17.7 COMMENT: WHAT WAS LEARNED

17.7.1 Interrelationship of Venture Components

You will note that in the case of Geodyne the machine shop became interested because of the product potential from WHOI and WHOI became seriously interested in large volume production from Geodyne because of the involvement of the machine shop. The outside directors were interested in being involved with Geodyne because of its potential for success based on major orders, and the largest of these orders was partly dependent on the company's demonstration of corporate strengths, such as a good board of directors. That order was also dependent on automatic data-reading ability. The data-reading contractor made a major effort to demonstrate an ability to read and process data because of the potential USPHS contract and because of the contractor's belief that Geodyne could successfully supply over $3 million worth of equipment, though the company's sales had been less than $500,000 the year before. The contractor's belief in Geodyne came from the customers' belief in Geodyne, which came partly from the contractor's capability.

This interdependency of venture components is found throughout the young venture. As there is little momentum in an early stage venture, keeping these dependencies in balance is crucial to survival. A later stage company has a momentum that overrides the out-of-balance situations and allows leeway in the correction of difficult situations.

The reader must understand that the full spectrum of interdependencies occurs in the midst of an onrush of daily operating decisions, technical development, response to customers, financing problems, and production difficulties.

The entrepreneur must keep reexamining the venture strategy action plans to make sure that the venture milestones are phasing in correctly and that changing situations are taken into account.

17.7.2 Timing, Cost, and Utility Considerations

There is a fine line to draw on timing and the cost of meeting particular milestones. In the company phone example, you do not want to wait so long to set up a phone-answering method that you create an image of being an unworldly inventor type who will never succeed. On the other hand, if you are running on a very tight budget, you don't want to create operating or capital expenses until these are really necessary. The business phone could be answered by somebody who will always be near it, such as a relative or yourself. It could also be answered by a machine, by an answering service, or by an employee. If you are still developing a prototype in your cellar, you will probably not hire a secretary to answer the phone. Over a period of a year, buying an answering machine ($150) will cost you less than using an answering service ($350), but many people don't like answering machines, so you may decide on the higher-cost answering service for this public relations reason. When you have reached the stage of having a commercial working space, but are still a shoestring operation, you may find an adjacent company willing to have your phone extension and answer it for you at a cost lower than or equal to that of an answering service. This type of solution provides a reasonable business image.

The example of the telephone was picked because it is one of the simpler high-profile venture components that you will use and therefore provides an example that is easy to deal with and understand. Considerations of timing, cost, and utility can get complex, especially when a shoestring venture is watching literally every dollar of expenditure.

Fortunately, many high-image venture components can have a low dollar cost. For the shoestring prestart venture, the entrepreneur's time can often be used in place of capital. This is particularly crucial in the bootstrap operation where the entrepreneur and Aunt Nellie are the only resources for capital. The team, relatives, and friends provide a resource for accomplishing the design of a letterhead or business card or the choice of a company name. The actual cost of printing a letterhead or business card is relatively low. In the case of a venture getting started rapidly with capital already available, these services might be purchased and their execution supervised closely by the venture team. The necessity for close supervision of such services was highlighted when the National Broadcasting Company paid at least $700,000 to develop a company symbol identical to one developed in-house by a local TV station for a few hundred dollars.

With the above comments in mind, examine Table 17.1 and note that many of these steps can be accomplished with the expenditure of time and minimal dollars, if things are done right and timed properly.

Table 17.1
Example of High-Image Venture Components

Component	Comment
Administrative Item	
Company name	Can be developed by the entrepreneurial team.
Letterhead	Could be printed for less than $500.
Mailing label	Could be printed for less than $100.
Calling card	Could be printed for less than $200.
Address	Home address is free. A Post Office box or an office that accepts your mail can be arranged.
Brochure	A simple brochure can cost less than $400.
Business phone	Can cost less than $200 a year.
Answering of phone	Answering service can cost as little as $25–30 per month.
Office	Sometimes can be obtained free from an interested supplier.
Corporation	Legal and filing fees can cost less than $1,200.
Company vehicle	Can have name of corporation painted on your own car.

Table 17.1 *(concluded)*

Component	Comment
Market and product	
Field the company is entering	The choice of an attractive field to enter often costs nothing, while greatly enhancing the image of the venture.
Access to major customers	Oceanographic instrument company specializes in selling services to Woods Hole Oceanographic Laboratory and has friendly contact there. Cost is often entrepreneurial time.
Product idea	Can sometimes be picked up from a purchasing agent or government laboratory at no cost.
Product development paid for by government laboratory or customer	Shows that you know how to use assets at hand. Also gives the feeling of venture getting something free that moves to pocket of investor.
Prototype of product	Can cost anything from a few dollars to six-figure numbers.
Production model	Can cost anything from a few dollars to six-figure numbers.
Production	The company can be producing the product for customers.
Proven market	Can come with the product idea free (e.g., the tent market is well defined).
Market test	Can be made by entrepreneurs or carried out by independent group for a fee.
Business plan	Can be written by entrepreneurial team.
Access to potential customers	Documented by a letter of interest
Articles or papers describing product, authored by company personnel or others	A powerful low-cost selling tool that establishes the credibility of the venture and the product.
New product release in trade publications	The cost is the time to write up and mail the release.
Product literature	Adds significantly to image of activity. Sometimes a Xerox sheet at first.
Testing of product	Can be conducted in company facility and documented at very low cost.
Validated testing of product	Sometimes a potential user will conduct tests at own expense.
Potential patent position	Inventory of ideas recorded, dated, and witnessed, and therefore protected for what they are worth, at cost of time and a notebook.
Patent applications	Cost is a few hundred dollars to get started. Must be examined as to timing and cost effectiveness.
Personal and Institutional Resources	
The lead entrepreneur	Your ability to communicate, entrepreneurial drive, training, business skills, and ability to put the venture together are company assets that are of immense value. These assets do cost the company your incentive equity.
The team	Same comments as above. The team should demonstrate its ability to work together successfully at least on a part-time basis.
Board of directors	A good board can contribute significantly to credibility, general operating decisions, location of resources, potential business. The cost is entrepreneurial time and perhaps a dinner meeting that you pay for. As the company gets stronger, the cost may go up.
Advisers and consultants	Setting up arrangements for future use of consultants establishes credibility for today. The arrangements define fee schedules but don't cost the venture dollars until they are put into action. Both parties benefit.
Good relations with several banks and an accounting firm	Adds to credibility and provides needed services. Again, only activated when needed.
Subcontractor	Can provide production credibility. Further, to win future business, subcontractor may provide aids such as working capital for items subcontracted for, office space, telephone answering, design at very nominal cost or free.
University contacts	In certain businesses, relevant contacts in a university can add credibility and real value to the venture, while giving the university more contact with the outside world.
Progress made to date in putting above pieces together into an integrated venture effort	This costs only the effort that you are making to put the venture together, but it demonstrates your entrepreneurial skill and value.

17.7.3 Cost-Effective Venture Components

The very brief history of Geodyne does display a number of venture components that were utilitarian but created high value. In 1963, one year after Geodyne had moved into its building, a very conservative brokerage house offered to take Geodyne public at a valuation of $10 million. The venture components of marketplace, contact with customers, existing contracts, sales growth, profits, location, Woods Hole office, and quality of team undoubtedly entered into the evaluation. In any case, it is nice to be wanted, but the team members refused the offer because they personally did not need liquidity and the company was financing its development and growth from profits and bank debt.

By careful selection, Geodyne obtained attractive but pivotal venture components at reasonable cost—for example, the name Geodyne, the Route 128 building (which appreciated severalfold), the Woods Hole office, and the entire product line. Presenting a crisp, consistent image of a competent winner helps relations with customers, banks, suppliers, and stockholders. Perhaps most important is the positive effect of the new company on paid employees and on the entrepreneurial team. Very often, if you think you are successful, you are successful.

17.8 COPING WITH PROBLEMS

We turn now from the case study of a single entrepreneur to a variety of real-life incidents, to illustrate how specific venture problems can be handled. These illustrations fall into four general categories:

Anticipating problems.
Identifying problems.
Responding to problems.
Developing strategies for success.

17.8.1 Introduction

Once started, a new venture usually demands far more time from the entrepreneurial team than was predicted or is available. To understand this, imagine yourself in the following situations:

The manufacturing space being rented by your venture proves to be inadequate, and new space must be searched out and altered and a move made; the product brochure being turned out is far harder to write than was envisioned; the major potential customer demands a far more detailed instruction and service manual than was expected; the telephone company doesn't have enough lines for you, so that complaints must be made to it; the sales manager quits, and a new one must be recruited; three important customers in different parts of the country want equipment demonstrated right away, but a major defect has just been discovered in the functioning of the product; the price on the special motor for the product has been increased and the delivery time extended four months; and your wife, while out with your three children, broke her leg.

Time pressures can easily force an entrepreneurial team into a fire-fighting mode, with all its time spent on responding to crises. Therefore, it is worthwhile to try to anticipate what major problems may be encountered in the venture, so that standard operating procedures may cut down the possible crises. Beyond this, the team, when aware of what typical operating problems or incipient crises may confront the venture, will often be subliminally preparing alternative strategic solutions or venture contingency plans. Thus, when the problems occur, they will not cause a major psychological shock.

Anticipation of likely operational problems provides an incentive to establish organized operational methods. Anticipation also increases the team's sensitivity and ability to recognize or identify early stage problems so that proper response can be developed before a problem becomes a major crisis.

17.9   ANTICIPATING VENTURE PROBLEMS

17.9.1   Studies of Venture Problem Experience

This section will expose the reader to problems that might be expected to occur in small ventures, and some specific red flags for recognizing potential problems.

In September 1983 Dun & Bradstreet's business questionnaire was answered by 503 CEOs of businesses with sales under $1 million.[4] They were asked to "rank the following problems according to how seriously they are affecting your business." The seven largest categories for top rank were: cash flow squeeze, 20 percent; inflation, 20 percent; keeping costs under control, 15 percent; finding qualified motivated employees, 12 percent; too much government regulation, 9 percent; inadequate demand, 8 percent; and high interest rates, 8 percent. This compares to a similar 1969 Dun & Bradstreet study quoted in our last edition. The question asked was: "What do you consider your three major business problems?"[5] The answers: competition, 42 percent; personnel, 35 percent; and financing, 18 percent. A Dun & Bradstreet report, "Causes of Business Failure in 1980," lists as underlying causes: incompetence, 44 percent; unbalanced experience, 19 percent; lack of management experience, 16 percent; and lack of experience in the line, 14 percent.[6] The major apparent causes were: inadequate sales, 60 percent; heavy operating expenses, 30 percent; and competitive weakness, 23 percent. A similar 1968 report lists: inadequate sales, 40 percent; and heavy operating expenses, 14 percent.[7]

As Dun & Bradstreet indicates, these apparent causes of failure—for example, competitive weakness and heavy operating expenses—have underlying causes that relate to the skills of the management team and to its ability to develop basic strategy to cope with new situations.

A study by Hoad and Rosko indicates areas of difficulty for new small manufacturers in the following rank order of importance:[8]

[4]James S. Howard, "Annual Survey of Small Business Presidents," *Dun & Bradstreet Reports* (Dun & Bradstreet Credit Services, 99 Church Street, New York, New York 10007), November–December 1983, pp. 18–21.

[5]"Causes of 11,742 Business Failures in 1980," Dun & Bradstreet Credit Services, 99 Church Street, New York, New York 10007.

[6]Ibid.

[7]Report of the President's Task Force on Improving the Prospects of Small Business, *Improving the Prospects of Small Business* (Washington, D.C.: U.S. Government Printing Office, 1970).

[8]I. A. Hoad and J. M. Rosko, *Management Factors Contributing to the Success or Failure of New Small Manufacturers,* Bureau of Business Report no. 44 (Ann Arbor: University of Michigan, Graduate School of Business Administration, 1961).

1. Little drive or ambition on the part of the venture manager.
2. Poor knowledge of marketing.
3. Inadequate experience in the field.
4. Poor knowledge of markets.
5. Poor pricing.
6. Shortage of capital.

The lack of drive or ambition was listed as the cause of difficulty three times as often as the second rank-ordered item, poor knowledge of marketing. Again, it seems apparent that the entrepreneurial team and staff of a small venture are the chief determinants of the venture's success.

The operating problems or causes of failure listed in the above studies give you a generalized view of the problem areas that are encountered. The specific problems of any particular company will vary. As one venture capitalist puts it, "There are 8 or 10 critical variables in any new venture which will be different for each venture but need monitoring to allow management to properly anticipate operating problems. One of the entrepreneurial arts is developing simple ways to get a handle on these critical variables." Examples of such variables would be: orders in hand, number of potential orders being processed by the customer, accounts receivable, cash in the bank, inventory level, work in process, purchases level, production efficiency, and engineering load. The need for this monitoring, the methods used to monitor, and the frequency of monitoring will vary with the venture, its business and cultural environment, and the team and its management style. The following section describes two companies in radically different fields—consumer products and scientific instruments—and lists the critical variables that each venture thought should be monitored in its particular business.

17.9.2 Examples of Key Variables in Two Companies

Here are two quite different key variable lists that we helped two of our entrepreneurial clients to prepare.

A. A manufacturer of textile-related recreational equipment came to understand that the way to beat the competition in his market niche depended on attracting and holding an increasing number of end users. The end users looked for high quality and on-time delivery, which required the company to maintain high operating standards. Having identified these key variables, the manufacturer developed a list of key variables that looked like this:

1. Production schedule tied to worker morale and efficiency.
2. Workload of key people.
3. Orders in hand by a given date.
4. Materials cost.
5. Materials delivery schedule.
6. Quality.
7. Cash flow.
8. Market feedback.

B. In contrast, a manufacturer of oceanographic instruments and systems recognized that his success factors—his key variables—were dependent less on the number of end users (which was relative small) than on the number of major orders being considered or processed.

Because the time it took for a major order to go from the customer's conception of need to receipt of the order by the manufacturer could run from 6 to 18 months, many orders would have to be in process to ensure a steady and growing business. Further, the ratio of orders won to orders lost was crucial. If the success rate dropped, it was almost too late to take corrective action because when a bid was lost to competition, most of the 6–18 months' lead time was gone, and the lost order could not be replaced quickly. Also, the cost to bid large jobs was high and a drop in the success rate meant an increase in overhead.

The founders had the objective of becoming the predominant supplier in the field. Therefore, success in winning certain key contracts was crucial; and it was important in competitive bidding to know manufacturing costs very accurately. Instruments were complex, and it took three years to achieve the accounting accuracy ultimately desired. Competitive pricing, marketing tactics, and political maneuvering all had to be monitored closely. By developing strategies to meet competitive market maneuvering, the company was generally able to neutralize non-objective factors bearing on a prospective purchase and to win its contracts based on technical innovation and performance. Winning on a technical basis required knowledge of the customers' needs, the competitors' equipment strengths and weaknesses, the technical state of the art, and a technical team motivated to come up with the best equipment.

Consequently, the company developed a list of key variables that looked like this:

1. Backlog of orders.
2. Orders being processed or considered by customers.
3. Orders predicted versus orders closed.
4. Entrepreneurial team awareness of the events currently happening to the venture and its environment.
5. Knowledge of manufacturing costs for a wide variety of subassemblies.
6. Competitor pricing.
7. Competitor political action.
8. Customer satisfaction.
9. Reliability of instruments.
10. Ability to process data quickly.
11. State of the art in oceanographic instruments and state of the scientific art that could be applied to the company's instruments.
12. Management and technical team balance.

17.9.3   Specifics of Problem Anticipation

Many entrepreneurs have a list of actions or patterns that might be expected to cause operating problems. Some of these are listed below. However, these factors are so close to the operating mode that they may or may not bear on your particular situation. The following are given as examples of problem-producing conditions to encourage you to develop your own awareness, and your own checklist.

1. Pricing the Product Too Low.   The authors helped a company get started in the capital equipment business. The company's product was better than the best on the market. The entrepreneurial team was pricing the product just under the price of the competition's best product to make sure it would sell. However, the team also felt that the company would have more orders than it could handle. The authors convinced the team to price the product above the competition's price because this would establish the product's superiority by price; and more important, this pricing technique would hold down the number of orders to what could be produced, while increasing company profits. The company's second-year sales were $9 million. Its entire profit was the margin by which the entrepreneurial team had been convinced to raise its prices. This profit added most significantly to the company's total capital and reduced the need for a further investment.

The start-up team is always nervous about getting customers, so there is a tendency to underprice. In a team the marketing people and the salespeople will want to succeed at their function, and a low price will aid them in doing so. Producing profits at that price must be confronted by someone else on the team. Therefore, there is not much incentive for the salespeople to price high. Further, the development engineer is often psychologically inclined to give too much product for a given sales price—so two members of the team may be inclined to push for a product price that is too low.

2. Potential Sales Not Discounted. It is often hard to believe that a customer will not buy what or when he said he would. A mistake that entrepreneurs continue to make is their failure to realize that a customer may buy, but only half as much as he promised. Failure to discount sales predictions accurately can lead to a bad profit performance and cash flow condition.

3. Sales Enthusiasm. The team believes its own sales story and forgets that it has to perform to succeed. No further comment needed.

4. Accepting Business for Which There Is Little Team Experience. The venture should always build on what its team has already done. When the ratio of unknowns to knowns in a project gets high, the risk of failure increases greatly.

5. Overspecification. In a new field the customer often does not know what to specify for performance. If you can leave performance vague, do so. In the capital equipment venture, several years went by with very little specification writing, partly because there was no time. Finally, after several new engineers had been added to the staff, a customer requested a bid with specifications on a new instrument. The engineers wrote the specifications. The founder questioned the specifications, and they were loosened. Founder: "Are you sure you can meet the new specifications now?" Engineer: "Sure, easy!" Well, the specifications were not met without far more work and cost than had been anticipated. The company was hung on its own specifications, which the customer didn't need or want but which the formal procurement and inspection system required the company to meet!

The overspecification concept can be carried to many aspects of the business. For example, when borrowing from the bank, don't promise more performance than you need to. The good feeling that you get from promising more than you need to buys you nothing. However, failure to meet your promise has significant negative implications in a banker's mind.

6. Part-Time People. They can be of great aid, but they do not take your team's ultimate responsibility for success—at least, don't count on it. Further, it is unfair to expect a professional such as a lawyer or a consultant to solve all of your business problems for you. If a lawyer is good, he or she is being paid anywhere from $60 to $300 per hour. If ethical, he or she will try to be as efficient as possible, at that price rate, in getting your job done with minimal hours. The lawyer cannot take your problem home and mull it over for endless hours, as you would.

You can expect sound advice and professional aid but not necessarily detailed creative solutions to your problems. If you have an unusual problem, expect to use the lawyer, accountant, and tax adviser as resources to provide you with the facts you need to solve your particular problem. If they do have the desired final solution, you are that much further ahead.

7. Crying over Spilled Milk.   Your venture will often undertake projects that present considerable risk to the venture if they do not succeed. For example, a nonstandard system may have to be delivered on a tight schedule to a fussy customer. The potential market created by this new system may be large, and the team thinks the advantages outweigh the risks. However, the system constitutes 30 percent of your annual sales, so that failure to perform satisfactorily on the contract could jeopardize the financial stability of the company.

To identify possible problems with the system beyond those that the specialists are worried about and taking care of, try crying over spilled milk. Imagine that the system has failed and that as a result your company is going into bankruptcy. With this urgency at hand, project yourself into this mode and role-play the part of the desperate entrepreneur. What do you feel went wrong? What should you have done to prevent the mistake? Which of the specialists working on the project should have taken what actions? Now, come back to the present, count your blessings, and go take those extra precautionary actions. This example of the nonstandard order is real, and a major problem did occur. The entrepreneur in the case did try the spilled milk method, and he came up with the potential problem, but he did not take action. The venture survived only with an expensive, agonizing effort.

8. Becoming Liquid.   When your venture goes over the counter or merges, don't be so pleased with the upcoming liquidity and advantageous situation that you lose your objectivity concerning the details of the terms. Many of the authors' colleagues have made their fortune through hard years of work and then lost a good part of it when they merged. Venture team members often regard the details of a merger as unattractive paperwork that they prefer to avoid thinking about. But remember, the stakes are big and the downside risk and unknowns are greater in a merger than in most of the dealings that the venture team has gone through to develop the venture to its current maturity.

17.10   IDENTIFYING VENTURE PROBLEMS

The previous section dealt with the anticipation of venture problems, and therefore with the ability to reduce their number, or at least to be aware of their presence early on. However, no matter how organized a group is, some venture problems will suddenly appear in varying states of maturity ranging from a minor difficulty to a full-blown crisis. It may be difficult to recognize or identify these problems in the forest of day-to-day operations. Listed below are patterns that will sometimes indicate a problem.

17.10.1   An Organization of People

The functioning of the full organization of people necessary to make a venture succeed may be the hardest venture factor to monitor and manage. The one or two top team members are often a major key in organizational difficulties.

Are you as a lead team member burdened with a lot of things that should never have reached your desk? A positive answer to this question may indicate worse than a lack of delegation in team and staff function. It may indicate a reverse delegation from partners and subordinates who don't have a clear picture of company goals or policy, or are not capable of handling their positions, or still worse, are willing to take it easy while you do all the work.

How do you, as a lead team member, feel about your work? Do you feel harassed or uncomfortable because you are doing things you don't know how to do? Are you communicating well with your partners? Do you trust your partners' business skills, drive, ethics, need for power, and commitment to the venture? Some serious misgivings about any of the above questions can indicate that you, in relation to the team, are not functioning at full capability, and further, that the team may not be functioning.

It may well be that a group of people calling themselves the entrepreneurial team and staff are not functioning as a working unit. Among the indications that this is so are widely conflicting perceptions of the same event from different team and staff members, repeated inability to come to a consensus, lack of communication of critical information in timely fashion, subordinates making bad decisions, and subordinates making crucial decisions that should have been checked out with the lead entrepreneurs. The statement "We need a system for . . ." may indicate that you need a system, or it may indicate that the person talking thinks, directly or subliminally, that you need a working team.

Another factor to consider is the absence of strategy meetings. This condition often indicates such problems as lack of communication, mistrust of partners, and neglect of day-to-day problems. When the condition exists over a significant number of weeks, however, it clearly indicates a team preference for operations and fire fighting over planning and controlling the venture's direction and fate.

As we have seen, "do lists" are a powerful tool for use in moving the business step by step toward each of its goals. Lack of effective "do lists" on the part of any of the venture's managerial personnel is a warning light that should be heeded.

The formation of cliques that do not communicate with one another signifies the lack of a strong unifying belief in the venture's goals. High employee turnover may be another indicator of low morale and a need for better communication of the unifying company goals. Sometimes the entrepreneurial team will have excessive expectations for the commitment of employees working for pay with no equity incentive. Such expectations can cause frictions and high turnover. It may be possible to note, test, and correct such expectations in conversations with team members.

In success, the entrepreneurial team should remain alert to the problem of arrogance. The business arrogance of believing that you have the key to a successful operating mode for your field may be disastrous if conditions should change. Technical arrogance may lead you into narrow products, dead-end development, or obsolescence; sales arrogance may leave you with some new competitors; and personal arrogance may add a spin-off from your company to your competitors.

17.10.2 The Product or Service

Does the venture's product or service work in testing and in the field under real conditions? The excuses of your personnel for product failure should be verified to your exacting satisfaction. Misunderstanding the extent or cause of failure may lead to large unexpected overruns in development cost. Further, the resultant product may be more expensive than expected, if it can be produced at all. Had these several factors been understood at the time of first failures, the team might have considered the strategy of going in an alternative product direction while the sunk cost was low and there was enough capital left to allow strategic choice.

Another product mistake is simply having too many products. In starting into a new field, the venture may often rapidly develop products to meet customer needs. When it is not apparent which products are going to be crucial to success, this is a valid strategy if development can be worked out on spare time or if the customer pays for it. At some point, however, there will be products that bring little in sales, customer goodwill, or image, while they dilute management, sales, engineering, and service effort as well as working capital.

This dilution of resources must be watched closely because it is one of the more insidious venture dilutions. There will be many defenders of the broad product line, and objective analysis is necessary to keep a line in proper balance.

An endemic problem in small companies is that of service or user manuals and documentation. A system for handling service manuals and documentation should be set up from the start of the venture. In actuality, however, companies often do not set up such systems until they are forced by circumstances to do so. It takes time and experience to write good material concerning a product or service. If the product or service is unique or in a new, growing field, the user will often accept marginal documentation on the first products. Nevertheless, the venture must remain alert to the real costs attached to providing sufficient user information over the long run, and expect to meet this need. As the field matures, there will often be standard requirements for documentation that must be met to compete effectively.

Corollary to the user product information problem is documentation for production of the product. When manufacturing is carried on in-house, a new venture often operates with minimal documentation. The lack of proper documentation may become apparent only when an increase in volume forces the venture to attempt to subcontract the manufacture of subassemblies. The hope is that the proper documentation will be developed before the subcontracts have been let. The first failures of subcontractors to deliver subassemblies that function correctly with the entire product should warn the manufacturer of a continuing problem in this area. As the in-house manufacturing facility grows, documentation also becomes more crucial to facilitate individual and departmental communication and performance. Here, again, the problem will show up as one of quality control.

17.10.3 Sales and Customers

The lifeblood of a company is sales. These are so vital that booked sales will usually be one of the six or eight variables monitored in some fashion. Do not accept excuses for why sales were not closed as predicted. Failure to close sales is a common problem in new ventures. Strategies must be developed to handle the problem immediately. One of the authors was elected as an eleventh hour director of a company that failed to grasp and solve the sales closure problem. The firm received its necessary first major order after it had been closed down irrevocably.

Your company may have good sales but some irate customers. Those irate customers may know something that you should know about your venture. Moreover, with irate customers, you can end up with poor sales.

17.10.4 Financial

An unexpected shortage of cash is, believe it or not, a sign that many new venture entrepreneurs ignore. For example, accounts receivable are overdue, but the team is too busy having fun developing new products to "waste time" doing the dirty work of pursuing accounts. Instead, the bank loan is increased. One of the authors was a participant in that type of problem until a staff member was belatedly assigned full-time work on collecting overdue accounts. A cash shortage may come from many causes. These causes should be understood in depth, and corrective action should be taken.

When expenses run higher than predicted, you should also get nervous. There may be underlying causes other than the obvious ones. It may take time to determine what these causes are; meanwhile, your expenses remain high.

17.10.5 Environment

Your venture exists in the marketplace and the world. If the economy is going down, the effect will eventually get to your venture no matter how insulated you think your business is. Watch out for interest rates going up, loans getting scarce, and accounts receivable stretching out as a result.

17.11 RESPONDING TO VENTURE PROBLEMS

Once the venture problem has been anticipated or identified, it must be dealt with. This section treats this process.

Venture problems or crises may sometimes require only a quick common-sense response on the telephone. In difficult cases, more involved processes may be required. The following steps suggest a possible approach to a complex situation: separate the real problem from the symptoms, and define it in detail; enumerate goals, objectives, and limitations; collect, organize, and analyze data (this may include studies of such matters as cash flow, break-even investment requirement, return on investment, risks-rewards ratio, market direction, patent position, and competitive strength); catalog the available resources; log peripheral factors for consideration; consider previous solutions to similar problems; bring to bear the experience and training of the team and its backup advisers; and use common sense to develop alternative solutions, rank-order the solutions, and choose the best.

Even in the cases where massive data-gathering and analytical effort is expended in preparing for the solution of a venture problem, the actual solution is synthesized in the entrepreneurs' minds through creative cognitive processes. Therefore, mental attitudes are important in achieving high-quality solutions. Further, there are methods other than standard analytical methods that may be used as mental aids to approaching a problem from new directions or with new dimensions. Consideration will be given to a few of these mental attitudes and aids. These attitudes and aids are usually complementary to the methods enumerated above, rather than alternatives.

17.11.1 Keeping a Positive Mental Attitude

It is almost axiomatic that the entrepreneur believes that he or she can control his or her own fate. This and other entrepreneurial characteristics (learning from failure, persistent problem solving, goal orientation) allow a fast bounceback when undesirable events hit the new venture. Some years ago, an entrepreneur was told in July by the director of a federal government office that because of heavy fiscal pressures on the office's budget, the entrepreneur's venture, Inetron, was extremely likely not to be refunded for another 12 months, starting in January. This government office was the venture's only significant customer. The service being supplied was of a specialized nature, and until the venture obtained much more operating experience, it would have almost no market other than this one agency. This was a calculated risk that the venture had taken to achieve its long-term objectives. The office director's comments were disastrous news for the team. It looked as if over two years of intensive work on a unique service would be halted, with grave implications for the survival of the venture. As you can image, a lot of thinking went on in the hotel room that night.

The next morning the lead entrepreneur called the office director and said that there were six possible ways to ease the government's funding with regard to the venture's service; he also said that it seemed impossible that the government would want to stop funding a project that had had initial success and had met significant needs of the government program involved. The office director laughed at the entrepreneur's persistence and invited the team back for further discussions that ended up lasting all morning. The venture team convinced the director that before the end of the year meaningful indications of need for the service could be obtained, sources of supplementary funding lined up, general support from the director's constituency obtained, further positive product performance demonstrated, and a plan outlined for developing self-sufficiency. A specific list of the results that the venture had to obtain by December in order to retain its government funding was hammered out in that morning meeting. The venture achieved these results, was refunded, and has continued to provide a unique successful service since that time.

In the Inetron case, the venture team did not get knocked down psychologically upon hearing a bad prognosis from the director. The team believed that it could influence its own fate by an immediate second approach to the government agency. The approach was: We can and will continue to succeed; here is what we plan to do; your agency can benefit if we succeed together; which parts of our new plan are most significant to your agency; can you help us if we achieve our plans in the next few months? This approach made it hard for the office director to say no to an entrepreneurial force exhibiting determination, resourcefulness, and straightforward drive to continue working on a problem that the agency needed to solve.

In this case, the team was aware of the sales risk involved in dealing with a single large customer. That risk was heightened by the pressures of the agency's constituency concerning the allocation of funding. Therefore, the team was psychologically prepared for a statement of funding cutoff and had considered some possible alternative methods of survival. Awareness of the problem and of alternative solutions is part of a larger mental mode of operation that should be applied by entrepreneurs in everyday operations and problem solving. There are really two parts to this mode that merit review here.

17.11.2 Vision of the Future

The entrepreneur's vision of the future is what pulls him through the present-day details and problems that must be dealt with to get to the future. The ultimate goal of the entrepreneurial team becomes as real or more real to the entrepreneur than present-day life. The management, manufacturing force, product, plant facility, and relationship of the venture to the world of commerce can be seen and felt clearly by the entrepreneur.

The future world can be lived in by the entrepreneur. Living in it makes the entrepreneur more and more aware of future orders of importance, possible future relationships, and differences between future operating conditions and present-day operating conditions. Each walk through the future world gives the entrepreneur more data and dimensions concerning the venture. There may be several models of this future world in the entrepreneur's mind. These models are in transition as factual data eliminates, confirms, or strengthens features of the model or models. When present-day problems occur, the models may be referred to for possible solutions and may give the entrepreneur confidence as unique decisions are made. For instance, an entrepreneurial team was recently trying to establish a price for a new financial management service (FMS). Normally, the fee charged would be based on a percentage of the capital being handled. The costs involved in supplying this proposed new service were too high to allow only 3 or 4 percent to be charged. However, 3 or 4 percent was the standard acceptable management fee for groups that appeared to offer similar services. In group discussions one of the entrepreneurs, projecting into the future model, found it obvious that the new venture being proposed was not a management service but a development operation involving a subsidiary management function. It was, therefore, obvious to the team that management fee precedents did not bear on the setting of the proposed fee.

17.11.3 Total Immersion and Dedication

A corollary and complementary concept to that of the ultimate goal is total immersion. Again, this concept is valid both for problem solving and for day-to-day operations.

Often, members of the entrepreneurial team will immerse themselves totally in their endeavor—operations, the product, the marketplace, the venture environment, competition, current literature, innovations, and so forth. Total immersion works because, with enough intelligent hours applied, one mind or a small group of minds can grasp all the essential details of an entire business and field and make accurate, fast, efficient operating decisions. Larger company competition will generally not engage in total immersion because this requires too much work and time on the part of paid employees. In place of this, the larger company will use more people to attack a particular problem. Adding more people to a decision and action process often means more factors involved, more complication, more time required to move, more reasons not to move, more chances for things to fall through the cracks, and ultimately higher overhead and prices. Thus, the motivated, capable, totally immersed new venture team can carve itself a place in the market based on its ability to make rapid, integrated decisions and to take positive action in a timely, cost-effective way.

Total immersion must last long enough in a new venture to get the company established with some momentum. Once this has been achieved, total immersion becomes less crucial, but elements of it are still required in varying degree. Many ventures continue to operate on this principle long after reaching a solid market position. Digital Equipment Corporation, whose start-up occurred nearly 30 years ago, is now the second largest computer company in the world. Yet, several of its founding entrepreneurs are still operating in a total immersion mode, although they have been able to delegate major authority to new first- and second-level management people, many of whom also operate in a total immersion mode.

17.11.4   Specific Problem-Solving Techniques

Correct definition of the venture problem has already been mentioned as a key factor in problem solving. In defining the problem, one should be careful to avoid defining the symptom rather than the problem itself. In the financial services case mentioned earlier, the symptom of the problem was the inability of the venture to sell its development operation and management service. The improper solution to that improper problem definition might have been to look for a new set of customers. The problem should have been defined as product cost being too high to allow selling in competition with financial management services that the customers viewed as similar to the one proposed. Why is the cost of this service noncompetitive? A development operation plus a management service is being provided. Thus, the answer to the correctly stated venture problem is to sell a new package at a new price to the same customers, rather than to look for new customers.

In the overall problem of putting together the unique development and management package just referred to, the entrepreneurs took three years to assemble the entrepreneurial team, develop the product, gain operational experience and credibility as a going venture, and raise funding to develop the full potential of the package. Many complex problems need a spectrum of resources to allow solution. A clever team can recognize these elements and be on the watch for them.

There is a continual flow of relevant resources and opportunities going by any venture team with respect to time. Time may be treated as a conveyor belt. If the venture team can remain positioned to pick off resources as they pass by the venture, enormous leverage can be obtained by combining these resources over time.

Time acts as capital for the new venture, in the same way that real dollar capital allows a wealthy venture to buy resources all at once when they are needed. For example, in the case of the financial management service mentioned earlier, several specialized and talented individuals who became available over a period of three years were put on the venture's payroll to accomplish very productive and valuable consulting tasks on projects germane to the end goals of the venture. When the time came to place the full development and services product in the marketplace, these individuals were there, tested and trained in new techniques and adding greatly to the credibility of the venture in the eyes of the customer and the potential investor.

In using time as an asset, there is a significant corollary that should be kept in mind. Gauge carefully when you need to commit to the solution of a problem. Often, an entrepreneur, when confronted with a problem, will fall into the good manager syndrome—a problem to be solved should be solved quickly and dispatched. That is not always true. In the development and service venture the first two entrepreneurs could have made early decisions on who the full team would be and the relative position of each team member. This decision was put off until near actual launching of the new product into the marketplace. By that time several members of the team had not proven out and were gone. If entangling legal agreements had been set up with those team members, future venture problems would have been created. In this vein, a common mistake often made by entrepreneurs is to create their corporation long before there is any commonsense need for it. This often forces commitments of bookkeeping, taxes, company name, equity distribution, and job function long before these are necessary.

Another aspect of using time to your advantage in problem solving is that a specific problem may itself change over time, thus opening potential new solutions. An example of this is shown in the previously mentioned case of Inetron and its risky one-government-customer position. The entrepreneurial team had tried to get a market break into a second agency with no success. Finally, a new director in the second agency was appointed who was somewhat more responsive to the potential of the service. Now, because of change, there was opportunity for achieving a solution to the marketing problem.

Even with this change in the agency, it was difficult to reach an agreement with the agency; so the lead entrepreneur, after many go-arounds, handed the ball over to another team member, who thought they could force closure of the sale. Two months later a third member took the ball and carried it farther. Finally, a combination of two team members closed on a contract over two years after the original sales effort had started. A change in circumstances over time, combined with the technique of tossing a discouraging job back and forth among close-knit team members, broke this most difficult marketing problem. It should be pointed out that the team technique works for two reasons. One is that, with each shift, new energy is brought to the problem. The second is the skills and personality of a new team member may provide a new or better fit to the problem. This team approach assumes, of course, that time is available for such shifting to occur.

Solving a problem by using the time techniques described is, in effect, stringing out the problem over time or treating the problem serially. This, in turn, is a form of breaking a problem into pieces, which is a most powerful problem-solving tool.

When confronting a seemingly insoluble, complex problem that must be handled in a fairly short time interval, breaking the problem into pieces sometimes helps. It may be possible to solve each piece separately. Take the easy parts first. Then try breaking down the difficult parts into further pieces. If the pieces can finally be handled, try reassembling the problem and solution and examine the interrelationships of the parts for dysfunctional effects. If these effects can be balanced out with additional solutions, you may have generated an integrated solution to the entire problem.

An example of the break-the-problem-down technique is its use to develop the basic approach that the authors have employed to help understand new venture development. The original problem was: How can one systematically develop new ventures when many informed people feel that the new venture area is one of art rather than science? Three basic venture elements described earlier were defined. In short, idea finding, selection and planning, and venture financing were found to lend themselves to rational searching, cataloging, analytical and synthesizing techniques. This left building the entrepreneurial team. It was the experience of one of the authors that existing psychological techniques could obtain approximate readings on the strengths and weaknesses of individuals. In later contact between behavioral scientists and an author of this book, it became apparent that there was considerable knowledge about the makeup of entrepreneurs and some limited knowledge about team function. This piece-by-piece approach had brought the problem so close to solution that the remaining problems appeared to be, and were, solvable by breaking what remained into further pieces. The break-the-problem-down technique may be used, not only for business problems, but for problems in any area, such as engineering, social, and political problems.

Another highly productive venture problem-solving tool is that of role playing. You imagine yourself in the role of a major or critical component of the problem. If you were trying to design a wind-resistant tower system, you might imagine yourself as the tower and actually feel the forces bearing upon you. In the case of the financial management services company, the entrepreneurs role-played the potential customers to check their acceptance of a higher fee for a unique package. This was carried into developing the written rationale to be given to the customer. In another case, one of the authors role-played his competitors in a highly competitive bidding situation. The author's company won as low bidder by $5,000 on a $500,000 contract.

The above techniques deal with the normal run of venture problems. What do you do with the most difficult problems? A venture problem approach that can occasionally reap large rewards is the silk-purse-out-of-a-sow's-ear method. Take the worst thing that happens to you, and turn it to your advantage.

One of the authors employed this approach when he was unexpectedly drafted into the army. The army duty broke the author's career path, and since he was being used inefficiently, he had a lot of spare time. In the second year of his army duty a transfer to a desired city was arranged; he was then able to spend his weekends, three-day pass time, leave, nights, and lunch hours in starting a medical instrument company. By the time of his separation from the army, a field of business had been chosen, a strategic plan developed, a company founded, customers developed, and an order received and in process.

This silk-purse approach has repeatedly proven successful. Business progress often consists of taking two steps forward and sliding back one. If some of the major slides back can be turned into major forward steps, a venture's business progress should be smoothed and improved.

17.12   STRATEGIES FOR SUCCESS

In summary, we will describe a few entrepreneurial techniques that have proved important to the operating success of certain specific ventures. We make no attempt to deal with standard business operating procedures. A bountiful literature on standard procedures is already in existence. It has been the authors' observation that the learning of effective methods during the operation of a venture is as efficacious when the venture is being run on a shoestring as when it is well capitalized—and perhaps more so. If an entrepreneur has minimal operating experience when starting out in his or her own venture, it may be wise to get some shoestring venture operating experience before trying any major venture effort. There follows a discussion of several special operating philosophies and methods that have worked well for the authors.

17.12.1 The Bandwagon Effect

In developing a successful business, most new ventures need good rapport with outside associates, such as customers, suppliers, bankers, professional support services, and a network of business contacts. The individuals involved in organizations dealing with a new venture are taking some risk in dealing with a fledgling company. As individuals, they like to feel that they are dealing with a winner. This flavor of winning comes through the team's ability to communicate many of the philosophies and considerations that we have already discussed. The team's view of the ultimate goal provides a strong base to talk from. Total immersion results in detailed knowledge of all aspects of the venture, so that organized or, more important, chance questions asked by outsiders get answered correctly and skillfully. Steady step-by-step progress toward defined goals, combined with meeting those goals on or ahead of schedule, builds credibility in the eyes of outside associates.

While all of the above is building momentum, a bandwagon effect is created that in itself adds momentum to the new venture. Outside associates want the tangible benefits of doing business with a growing winner and enjoy associating with success early enough to prove their ability to discern it. This requires that they jump on the bandwagon, which means that they supply the new venture with scarce materials, lend the venture money, and buy the venture's products. The bandwagon will sometimes move faster than the venture, and sometimes it is necessary for the team to push it faster. For instance, when introducing a unique new product to the market, getting the first customer is often a major difficulty. It takes courage to be a first customer. If the venture team is talking with a number of potential customers, it certainly does not hurt the most likely potential customer to hear about the other groups who are, in fact, considering purchase of the new product. With other customers considering jumping on the bandwagon, the bandwagon by definition is going faster. To become the first customer, which is fun, one must now run faster to catch the bandwagon and get that first customer's seat. Therefore, perhaps a purchase decision that would have taken the customer six months in the normal course of events gets made in three months. The Geodyne put-together is an example of the bandwagon effect.

17.12.2 Market Understanding

The lifeblood of a company is its revenue and derived profit. Revenues come from sales in the marketplace. The lead entrepreneur should understand the marketplace well and spend some time in contact with it, regardless of who else on the team is involved with sales and marketing. Any other mode of operation for a new venture needs an overwhelming rationale for proper strategic justification.

17.12.3   The Backdoor Policy

In all operational situations that have any significant risk, it is wise to keep alternative solutions or back doors available. An obvious example is that of keeping a second supplier available in the case of a unique crucial component used in your main product. Another example is that of maintaining good relations with a second banking source even though the main bank you borrow heavily from once per year is very happy with its relationship with your venture.

17.12.4   Communication

Two-way communication that really gets through to the involved parties is difficult to set up, achieve, and maintain. Communication is necessary with all the external associates and the internal members of the venture. Just because you say something and the person responds, doesn't mean that you have really communicated. Particularly in crucial areas, keep testing to make sure that understanding and, you also hope, trust, in fact, exist.

17.12.5   Keep It Simple

George Naylor, a seasoned Boston new venture and corporation lawyer, noted that business should be kept as simple as possible. The more complicated a relationship, the more unknowns, variables, and surprises lie in wait for the entrepreneurial team. Further, the cost of generating legal documents concerning complex relationships is high and the later interpretation of a document may, in itself, cause some surprises. Not all relationships can be kept simple, but aversion to complexity is a good operational reflex to nurture.

17.13   SUMMARY

This chapter has provided examples of how individual entrepreneurs worked through problems and succeeded, and it has pointed out a number of specific lessons that may help you to anticipate, or to avoid, similar problems. However, venturing is by definition a state of flux, so you will have to learn many new lessons yourself.

These entrepreneurial gems may or not apply outside the actual situation from which they were drawn. They do, however, give the reasoning individual a view of how some entrepreneurs attempt to develop and organize an operating philosophy. Do not let the detail in this chapter cause you to lose sight of these important points:

1. A lot can be learned by mentally stepping through a venture action plan—more than once. This learning is increased as the entrepreneur attempts to activate the plan. Failures in activating a plan can cause learning to occur. If the entrepreneur is persistent enough, repeated failures will yield the knowledge necessary to succeed.

2. Making step-by-step progress along a venture action plan is probably the most powerful single method that an entrepreneur can use to obtain success. Only experience will allow the entrepreneur to realize when he has found the proper

venture to pursue, using tightly focused goals. Too early, a tight focus may screen out success. Too late, a tight focus may dissipate energy and time.

3. Your venture's success, particularly in its first year, is dependent on the close-knit, well-balanced, intelligent operation of the entrepreneurial team.

4. The venture plan should be used as a guide to aid in the monitoring of venture progress and performance.

5. A strategic planning team should monitor the company aggressively, guiding it as it grows beyond its original plan or when monitoring indicates the need for a change of direction.

The Harvest and Beyond

18

Shrouds have no pockets.

Sidney Rabb
Chairman of the Board
Stop and Shop, Boston
Founder's Day, 1983—Babson College

18.1 RESULTS EXPECTED

In the final scene of the recent Broadway play *You Can't Take It with You,* starring Eddie Albert as Grandpa Vanderhof, the following revealing exchange occurred between Grandpa and Kirby, a Wall Streeter who was the father of his granddaughter's fiancé, Tony.

Grandpa: Well, what I feel is that Tony's too nice a boy to wake up 20 years from now with nothing in his life but stocks and bonds.

Kirby: How's that?

Grandpa: Yes. Mixed up and unhappy, the way you are.

Kirby [outraged]: I beg your pardon, Mr. Vanderhof. I am a very happy man.

Grandpa: Are you?

Kirby: Certainly I am.

Grandpa: I don't think so. What do you think you get your indigestion from? Happiness? No, sir. You get it because most of your time is spent doing things you don't want to do.

Upon completion of this chapter, you will have:

1. Examined the long-term importance of a harvest mind-set and goal.
2. Identified and examined the principal harvest options.
3. Developed a personal strategy for developing and managing a harvest strategy and beyond.

18.2 IMPORTANCE OF A HARVEST GOAL

More than any other single issue, the harvest separates the real entrepreneurs from the rest of the pack. It is one thing to create a job and a good living for yourself, but it is quite another to do so for many others, including investors. Having a harvest mind-set, anchored in the goal of growing a business that creates enough value to result in a capital gain, is central to entrepreneurial achievement.

18.2.1 Why Is a Harvest Important?

For one thing, a harvest mind-set necessitates a compelling long-term goal to create real value added in whatever business you choose to grow. Otherwise, the business simply will not be worth very much in the marketplace. It is not a "get-rich-quick" mentality common to the promoter and rip-off artist. For another, such a goal creates a high standard and a serious commitment to excellence in results. It can also provide a motivating force and a strategic focus that does not sacrifice customers, employees, and value-added products and services just to maximize quarterly earnings.

There are other good reasons as well. In our experience, the demanding work-load is probably no greater in a harvest-oriented venture than in one that cannot achieve a harvest, and it may actually be less. Nor is it necessarily any more stressful, and may actually be less, especially in those post-40 and -50 years when you can tolerate such pressures less handily. Imagine the plight of the 46-year-old entrepreneur, with three children in college, whose business is overleveraged and on the brink of collapse. Contrast that frightful pressure with the position of the founder and major stockholder of one venture we have been associated with, who, at the same age, recently sold his venture for $15 million.

Consider the options now available to the two entrepreneurs. The choices open to the harvested entrepreneur—compared to the one who has not or cannot reap a substantial profit—seem to rise geometrically. The marketplace has responded; other investors, entrepreneurs, and bankers also respond with new opportunities. Given these factors, is there really a serious choice in the matter?

Finally, there is a very significant societal reason for seeking and building a venture worthy of a harvest. It is such ventures that provide enormous impact and value added in a variety of ways. These are the companies that contribute most disproportionately to technological innovation, to new jobs, to returns for investors, and to economic vibrancy. Within the process of harvest the seeds of renewal and reinvestment are laid. Such a recyling of entrepreneurial talent and capital is at the very heart of our system of private responsibility for economic renewal and individual initiative.

18.3 THE HARVEST OPTIONS

There are six principal avenues by which a company can realize a harvest from the value it has created. These are listed below in the order in which they seem to occur most commonly. You will note that a harvest need not necessarily mean having to sell and leave the company. Each of these paths will be discussed briefly below. No attempt is made here to do more than that since entire books have been written on each of them, including their legal, tax, and accounting intricacies, and it is not possible to do more here than alert the reader to the key issues.

1. The capital cow.
2. The employee stock ownership plan (ESOP).
3. The management buyout.
4. The merger.
5. The outright sale.
6. The public offering.

18.3.1 The Capital Cow

The "capital cow" is to the entrepreneur what the "cash cow" is to the large corporation. In essence, the high margin, profitable venture throws off more cash for personal use than most entrepreneurs have the time, uses, and inclinations to spend it on. The result is a capital- and cash-rich company with enormous capacity for debt and reinvestment. Take, for instance, one firm with which we are familiar. This health-care–related venture was started in the early 1970s, realized early success, and acually went public back then. Several years later the founders decided to buy the company back from the public shareholders and to return it to its closely held status.

Today the company is a Subchapter S (it has fewer than 25 shareholders, enjoys limited liability, and has no corporate income tax obligation) with sales in excess of $50 million. It has generated extra capital in excess of $3 million or so each year. This "capital cow" has enabled the entrepreneurs to invest in several other high-potential ventures, including a leveraged buyout of a $150 million sales division of a larger firm. As a result of this capital surplus, these entrepreneurs have been able to originate venture capital–type investments with even further upside potential.

18.3.2 The ESOP

Among closely held companies, the employee stock ownership plan has become a very popular method for creating a valuation mechanism for the stock, which has no formal market. It is also a vehicle through which founders can realize some liquidity from their stock by sales to the plan and other employees. And since the ESOP usually creates widespread ownership of stock among employees, it is viewed as a positive motivational device as well.

18.3.3 The Management Buyout

Another avenue by which founders can realize a gain from the business is to sell it to existing partners or other key managers in the business. Unless the buyers have the cash up front—which is rarely the case—such sales can be very fragile and vulnerable to realization of less than the full gain. The main reason for this is that these buyouts typically require the seller to take a limited amount of cash up front and a note for the balance of the purchase price over several years. The buying entrepreneurs want to stretch this payment as long as possible, while the seller wants it earlier rather than later. And if the purchase price is linked to the future profitability of the business, the seller is totally dependent on the ability and integrity of the buyers.

Under such an arrangement, one way to lower the purchase price is to grow the business as fast as possible, spending on new products and people and showing very little profit along the way. In five years the marginally profitable business is acquired at a bargain price, yet is positioned for excellent earnings in the next two or three years. This is one of several reasons why most advisers tell selling entrepreneurs to get the cash price up front.

18.3.4   The Merger

Merging with another firm is still another way for founders to realize a gain. Recently, one of the authors worked with two founders to consummate a merger with another company. These entrepreneurs had developed some high-quality training programs for the rapidly emerging personal computer industry. Their backgrounds were in computers, rather than in marketing or general management, and they had major gaps as an entrepreneurial team. Their results in the first five years of their existence reflected this as well. Their sales were under $500,000; they tended to develop custom programs only; and they did no marketing. They were unable to attract any venture capital investors, even during the hot market of 1982.

Another $15 million firm had an excellent reputation for its management training programs, a Fortune 1000 customer base with a rebuy rate of over 70 percent, and requests from the field sales force for programs to train managers to use personal computers. The marriage was consummated within about six months from the initial meeting between the founders of the two firms.

The deal was as follows: The buyer obtained 80 percent of the shares of the smaller firm in order to consolidate the revenues and earnings from the merged company into its own financial statements. The two founders of the smaller firm retained a 20 percent ownership in their firm; they also had employment contracts, and they are now treated like other officers in the parent company. The buyer provided nearly $1.5 million of capital advances during the first year of the new business. A "put" will enable the founders to realize a gain on their 20 percent, depending on the venture's performance over the next few years.

The two founders are now reporting to the president of the parent firm, and one founder of the parent firm has taken a key executive position with them. This type of approach is common for mergers between closely held firms.

18.3.5   The Outright Sale

Most advisers of entrepreneurs who are attempting to harvest their venture insist that the outright sale is the ideal route to go. Cash up front is preferred over most stock, even though the latter can result in a tax-free exchange. The problem is, of course, the volatility and unpredictability of the stock price of the purchasing company. Many an entrepreneur has been left with a fraction of the original purchase when the stock price of the buyer's company declined steadily. Often, the acquiring company wants to lock key management into employment contracts for up to several years. Whether this makes sense depends on the goals and circumstances of the individual entrepreneur.[1]

18.3.6   The Public Offering

Probably the most sacred "business school cow" of all—other than the cash cow—is to take your company public. The vision or fantasy of having one's venture listed on the stock exchanges, even over-the-counter, arouses all the passions

---

[1]See several relevant articles on selling your company in *Growing Concerns,* ed. David Gumpert (New York: John Wiley & Sons, 1984), part 5, pp. 332–98.

of greed, glory, and greatness. For many would-be entrepreneurs, this aspiration is unquestioned—and enormously appealing. Yet, for all but a chosen few, taking your company public, and then living with it, may be far more trouble—and expensive—than it is worth.[2]

Consider the following table when contemplating the odds of going public, regardless of the real costs and consequences:

Year	Number of Small Firm New Issues
1969	698
1975	5
1983	888
1984	450 (estimated)

Even in the two hottest new issues markets in the past 25 years, a relatively small number of companies have gone public. A fraction of these were new or very young ventures. Of course, the Lotus, Compaq, and Apple Computers of the world do get unprecedented attention and fanfare. But these firms are truly exceptions to the rule.

What are the realities of going public for many smaller firms? It can be a very expensive and time-consuming proposition. And just because your stock is listed does not mean that the founders can realize a liquid gain. SEC restrictions on the timing and amount of stock that officers, directors, and insiders can dispose of in the public market have become increasingly severe. As a result, it can take several years after an initial public offering before a liquid gain is possible.

18.4 CRAFTING A HARVEST STRATEGY

A consistent pattern has characterized entrepreneurs and the harvest issue. First, when the company is launched, struggles for survival, and begins its ascent, usually the farthest thing from the founder's mind is selling out. Psychologically, this is equivalent to complete abandonment of his or her very own "baby." The intense feeling of parentage, personal involvement, and identity can be as strongly felt with an entrepreneur's new venture as with a new family. And, some youngsters will argue, even more so!

Time and again, the founder does not even consider selling out—especially when things are finally going well—until terror is experienced in the form of possibly losing the whole company. This usually comes in an unexpected way: a new technology threatens to leapfrog over the current product line; a large competitor suddenly appears in a small market that management thought it had to itself; or a major account is lost, and the reasons elude the current management team. Invariably, the company is suddenly for sale: at the wrong time, for the wrong reasons, and thus, for the wrong price. A sense of panic grips the founders and shareholders of the closely held firm. So what can one do about all this?

This is an enormously complicated and difficult area, and we know of no simple solutions. There are some guidelines and cautions that can help to shape strat-

[2]See the article by Richard Salomon, "Second Thoughts on Going Public," in *Trials and Rewards of the Entrepreneur,* ed. David E. Gumpert (Boston: *Harvard Business Review,* 1983).

egy. These have evolved from the particularly successful efforts of one colleague and, to a lesser extent, from our own experiences.[3]

First, the crafting of harvest strategy is more sensible if done within a medium-to-long time frame, at least a 3-to-5-year window, and as long as 7 to 10 years. While each industry and each venture within it is unique, this patient horizon also fits with the "lemons and plums" time frame that experienced venture capital investors understand. Most successful companies required several years to launch and build. There are clearly better and worse times in which to sell a company, and patience can be invaluable.

Second, the other side of the patience coin is not to panic as a result of precipitate events. Selling under duress is usually the worst of all worlds.

Third, if impatience is the enemy of an attractive harvest, then greed is its executioner. We knew of an excellent small firm in New England, nearly 80 years old, with the third generation of succesful family leadership at the helm. Profitable growth had attracted a number of prospective acquirers, and a bona fide offer for over $25 million was made after discussion with one suitor. The owners became convinced that this "great little company" was worth considerably more; they held out. Before long, there were no buyers; market circumstances changed unfavorably, coupled with skyrocketing interest rates. Then things got worse. Soon thereafter, the company collapsed financially, ending up in bankruptcy. Greed was the executioner.

Fourth, advisers with a "harvest mind-set" are in very short supply—so start looking well before you think you will need harvest advice. It is extremely difficult to find someone to help you craft a harvest strategy while you are growing the business, and to maintain both objectivity about its value and the patience and skill to maximize it. The major problem seems to be that people who sell businesses—investment bankers or business brokers—are performing the same economic role and function as real estate brokers. In essence, their incentive is the commission on the deal during a quite short time frame, usually a matter of months. Contrast this with our colleague Mr. Pitlor, who works with the lead entrepreneur for five years or more, helping to shape and implement strategy for the whole business, so that it is positioned in the most favorable way to spot and respond to harvest opportunities when they appear.

One good example of this is a company called HTC, Inc., a leading edge innovator in developing vapor-phase technology for soldering printed circuit boards. When Pitlor began working with this company in 1977, it was basically a one-person, garage shop venture, with no marketable product as yet. The best the founder could do in raising venture capital was just $10,000 for 10 percent of the venture, from a firm that was very reluctant to invest a dime. Pitlor worked closely with the lead entrepreneur, so that he knew the intricacies of the market, the industry, the competitors, the customers, and the internal management capabilities as the firm grew to nearly $7 million in sales in 1984. As a pair, who could have a better grasp of the value and potential timing for a harvest than HTC's founder and Pitlor? Judging by the recent sale of the company for $15 million cash to a larger firm, their patience, long-term positioning, and close involvement paid off.

---

[3]We are indebted to our colleague Mr. Joel R. Pitlor, Concord, Massachusetts, for sharing some of the notions that have worked so well for him and his entrepreneurial clients. He has successfully worked over several years with a handful of companies to achieve a harvest, usually realizing a price as much as twice the valuation estimated by knowledgeable investment bankers and merger and acquisition specialists.

18.5 SOME SOBERING HARVEST LESSONS

So as not to tip the scales too optimistically, we include at this point a few of the lessons and insights that entrepreneurs say are the most difficult to acquire in their journey to a harvest, and that students and would-be entrepreneurs often lack or underestimate.

18.5.1 As Ye Sow . . .

Clearly, harvesting is a nonissue until something begins to sprout—and most start-from-scratch entrepreneurs agree that securing customers and generating continuing sales revenue are much harder and take much longer than even they could have imagined. There is a vast difference between the existing revenue stream of an ongoing business and creating revenue where none exists. Further, the ease with which those revenue estimates can be cast and manipulated on a microcomputer spreadsheet belies the time and effort necessary to turn those projections into cash.

So, while we counsel the inclusion of a harvest strategy in the long-range planning process, we emphatically emphasize that you should direct all of your entrepreneurial efforts in the start-up years toward getting those seeds planted, and showing some healthy sprouts, before you take the time to deal with how those sprouts can best be harvested.

18.5.2 Extent of Required Commitment and Personal Trade-Offs

There is an enormous gap between reading about it, talking about it, listening about it, and doing it. The immersion, the workload, the sacrifices for your family, the wear and tear, and often the burnout experienced by entrepreneurs are real. For instance, we know one computer software entrepreneur who has been very successful. Working alone for several years, he has developed highly sophisticated software for the banking industry. At this writing, he is closing in on a harvest through the sale of his venture to a major financial institution. Yet, he is the first to insist that he cannot stand the computer business for another day. He says he is sick of it, nearly burned out from the cumulative exhaustion of nearly 15 years in the business. He will do almost anything to get out of the business. Imagine trying to position your company for sale effectively and to negotiate a deal for a premium price when your emotional and physical fatigue have created such mental sea-anchors. If you were the buyer, how would you detect this man's frailty, and thus negotiate a bargain price?

And some entrepreneurs, even with what most of us would agree has been raging success, wonder whether the price of victory has been too high.

One very successful entrepreneur put it this way:

What difference does it make if you win, have $20 million in the bank—I know several who do—and you are a basket case, your family has been washed out, and your kids are a wreck?

18.5.3 Years Required to Accumulate After-Tax Cash and Net Worth

If you believe the popular press and government statistics, there are more millionaires than ever in America. About 1 million persons in the United States today are millionaires—their net worth exceeds $1 million—or about 1 percent of the working population. There are two serious flaws with these impressive num- bers. To begin with, a million dollars, sadly, is not really all that much money today as a result of high inflation. To illustrate, the popular TV show of the 50s and 60s, "The Millionaire," in which John Beresford Tipton routinely gave as- tounded recipients a check for $1 million, today would have to be renamed "The *Four* Millionaire." The increase merely keeps up with inflation over the period.

The second flaw is that lottery and Irish sweepstakes winners become instant millionaires, but entrepreneurs do not. The number of years it usually takes to accumulate such a net worth is a far cry from the instant millionaire, get-rich- quick-and-easy impression associated with lottery winners or the fantasy TV writers. For the vast majority of entrepreneurs, it takes 10, 15, even 20 years or more to build a significant net worth. Doing so is neither quick nor painless.

18.6   BEYOND THE HARVEST: PERPETUATING THE PROCESS

The opening lines in the chapter say it all: you can't take it with you. But the majority of highly successful entrepreneurs we know of seem to accept a responsi- bility to renew and perpetuate the very system that has treated them so well. Some of the following data often surprise people.

1. Consider the sources of college endowments and income from gifts. A few years ago we discovered that over half of the endowment at MIT has come from gifts of stock and other assets made by the founders of companies. A recent study of Babson College alumni showed that up to eight times as many entrepreneurs made the larger gifts to the college, compared with other graduates.[4]

2. Among the most generous and enthusiastic contributors to the Harvard Business School are the graduates of the Smaller Company Management Pro- gram, a short, nondegree course for the heads of smaller firms. The same pattern is also true among HBS alumni: entrepreneurs lead the way.

3. Entrepreneurs who have harvested very often heavily reinvest their lead- ership skills and money in a wide variety of civic and community activities. These include the symphony orchestra, museums, and local colleges and universities. Postharvest entrepreneurs lead fund-raising campaigns, serve on boards, and devote many hours to other voluntary work. A young Swedish couple, after spend- ing a six-month "apprenticeship" with venture capital firms in Silicon Valley and New York, was "astounded at the extent to which these entrepreneurs and ven- ture capitalists engage in such voluntary, civic activities," in sharp contrast to the Swedish pattern of paid government bureaucrats performing many of the same services.

4. Successful postharvest entrepreneurs also reinvest their efforts and re- sources in the next generation of entrepreneurs and opportunities. Somehow they are keenly aware that our unique American system of opportunity and mobility will not perpetuate itself through osmosis. Its continuing existence depends in large part on this self-renewal process. Further, we do not find a "take the money and run—hide it in a Swiss bank account" mentality among the entrepreneurs with whom we have been associated.

[4]John A. Hornaday, "Patterns of Alumni Giving," in *Frontiers of Entrepreneurship Research, 1984* (Bab- son Park, Mass.: Babson College, 1984).

What motivates successful entrepreneurs to behave this way? We sense that they implicitly know that perpetuating the system we have is far too important, and too delicate, to be left to anyone else. They have learned the hard lessons. The innovation, the job creation, the economic renewal and vibrancy are all results of the entrepreneurial process. The complicated and little understood process is not caused by government—though it can certainly be impeded by it. Nor is it caused by the stroke of a legislative pen, though it can be ended by such a stroke. Rather, it is created by entrepreneurs, investors and hardworking people in pursuit of opportunities. Fortunately, entrepreneurs seem to accept a disproportionate share of the responsibility for making sure that the process is renewed. And judging by the new wave of U.S. entrepreneurship in the 1980s, both the marketplace and society are once again prepared to allocate the rewards to entrepreneurs that are commensurate with their acceptance of responsibility and their delivery of results.

18.7 TIMMONS' SEVEN SECRETS OF SUCCESS

The following are included for your contemplation and amusement.

1. The first secret is: there are no secrets. Understanding and practicing the fundamentals discussed here, along with hard work, will get results.
2. The second secret is: as soon as there is a secret, everyone else knows about it too. Searching for secrets is a mindless exercise.
3. Happiness is a positive cash flow.
4. Teach a person to work for others, and you feed him or her for a year; teach a person to be an entrepreneur, and you feed him or her, and others, for a lifetime.
5. Do not run out of cash.
6. Entrepreneurial success is fundamentally a human process rather than a financial or technological process. *You* can make an enormous difference.
7. Happiness is a positive cash flow.

APPENDIXES

PROJECTION OF FINANCIAL STATEMENTS—AND THE PREPARATORY
USE OF WORKSHEET SCHEDULES FOR BUDGETS†

I don't know about other credit men, but without exception, all the budgets that I have seen were submitted without supporting schedules showing the source of the figures being used. Without this source, the budgets left me with an uneasy feeling of nebulous value and questionable accuracy, because it was impossible to check back any figures used.

I will be the first one to admit that I am not an expert in the preparation of "Projection of Financial Statements" (RMA Form C–117), but I'd say that it is impossible to complete these forms with any consistent degree of accuracy without the prior preparation of supporting schedules. In fact, the easiest, quickest—and possibly the only—way to complete the budget form is to sit down beforehand and gather up all the necessary information in a logical, concise, and intelligent manner in the form of "worksheet schedules." This article is directed primarily to the preparation and use of such schedules.

For purposes of illustration, I am going to deal with a hypothetical company, Sample Company, Inc. Starting out with (1) a 12/31/59 balance sheet and income statement (which the reader can find in the first column of the accompanying completed C–117) and (2) with certain additional pertinent financial facts (given below for the reader), my goal was to project Sample Company's financial statements monthly for 1960—i.e., to complete C–117. Each of the five schedules I had to prepare before tackling C–117 are reproduced in the article, and, following the schedules, there is presented a line-by-line explanation of the entries made on C-117.

Here are the necessary pertinent facts about Sample Company, established by competent management opinions:

*Reprinted with permission. The Robert Morris Associates, 1616 Philadelphia National Bank Building, Philadelphia, Pennsylvania 19107.

†By Chester G. Zimmerman, Director of Loan Review, American National Bank and Trust Company of Chicago, Chicago, Illinois. Reprinted from the April 1961 issue of the *Bulletin* (now *The Journal of Commercial Bank Lending*) published by Robert Morris Associates, The National Association of Bank Loan and Credit Officers, 1432 Philadelphia National Bank Bldg., Philadelphia, Pa. 19107. (Copyright 1961, Robert Morris Associates.)

Sales Proposed (see Schedule A for detail by month)	$12,000,000
Cost Figures—1959 percentages to be used	
Inventory supply on hand—45 days' supply, based upon next month's material costs with December inventory the same as at the beginning.	
Accounts Receivable Collections:	
January through April	15 days
May and June	30 days
July and August 50% in 30 days, 25% in 60 days, 25% in 90 days	
September 75% in 30 days, 25% in 60 days	
October through November	30 days
December	20 days
Trade payments every 15 days	
Additions to fixed assets (equally over the year)	$120,000 per annum
Depreciation (equally over the year)	$ 72,000 per annum
Direct Labor, Indirect Labor, and Manufacturing Expenses Paid Every 15 Days	
Sales Expense—5% of Sales—Paid by End of Month	
General and Administrative Expense—2½% of Sales—Paid by End of Month	
Minimum Cash Balances to be Carried	$250,000
Monthly Payments on Long-Term Obligations	$ 5,000
Borrowing Will Be in Multiples of	$ 50,000

The first logical schedule to be prepared ("A") would be the proposed sales, cost of sales, and other expenses making up the profit and loss figures for the coming year. These data complete the upper third of the form, and, because of the segregation of expenses, some details are brought forward to additional schedules to support cash projections and balance sheet data.

Schedule "A" projects by month:

Cost of Sales (85% based upon 1959 percentages)
Material Costs (80% of cost of sales based upon 1959 percentages)
Direct Labor Costs (10% of cost of sales—1959 percentages)
Indirect Labor Costs (5% of cost of sales—1959 percentages)
Manufacturing Overhead (5% of cost of sales—exclusive of depreciation—1959 percentages)
Sales Expense (5% of sales)
General and Administrative Expense (2½% of sales)

WORK SHEET SCHEDULES TO SUPPORT PROJECTION OF FINANCIAL STATEMENTS —

SAMPLE COMPANY, INC.

SCHEDULE "A" — SALES AND COST OF SALES PROJECTED FOR 1960 (000) Omitted

Details	January	February	March	April	May	June	July	August	September	October	November	December	Totals
Net Sales	$800	$800	$1,500	$1,200	$800	$600	$400	$700	$1,000	$1,500	$1,500	$1,200	$12,000
Material Costs—80% of Cost of Sales	544	544	1,020	816	544	408	272	476	680	1,020	1,020	816	8,160
Direct Labor—10% of Cost of Sales	68	68	128	102	68	50	34	60	84	128	126	102	1,018
Mfg. Overhead (Excl. Deprec.)													
5% of Cost of Sales	34	34	64	51	34	25	17	30	42	64	63	51	509
Indirect Labor—5% of Cost of Sales	34	34	64	51	34	25	17	30	42	64	63	51	509
Cost of Sales—85% of Sales	680	680	1,276	1,020	680	508	340	596	848	1,276	1,272	1,020	10,196
Gross Profit	120	120	224	180	120	92	60	104	152	224	228	180	1,804
Sales Expense—5% of Sales	40	40	75	60	40	30	20	35	50	75	75	60	600
General & Admin. Expense—2½% of Sales	20	20	37	30	20	15	10	17	25	38	37	30	299
Operating Profit before Deprec. & Taxes	$60	$60	$112	$90	$60	$47	$30	$52	$77	$111	$116	$90	$905

Material Costs are brought into Schedule "C".

Direct Labor and Manufacturing Overhead are brought into Schedule "E".

Sales Expenses and General & Administrative Expenses are combined for Line 25.

Depreciation is set forth on Line 12. Income Tax is provided at 50% (for ease in computation) and added to total of Line 48 less payments made on Line 27

Line 15 is net profit which is added to previous month balance of Line 56 for current month total for Line 56

SCHEDULE "B" — ACCOUNTS RECEIVABLE OUTSTANDINGS AND COLLECTIONS (000) Omitted

	January	February	March	April	May	June	July	August	September	October	November	December	Totals
Balance—Beginning of Month	$366	$400	400	750	600	800	600	400	900	1,450	1,925	1,500	
Add: Sales	800	800	1,500	1,200	800	600	400	700	1,000	1,500	1,500	1,200	$12,000
Total	$1,166	$1,200	$1,900	$1,950	$1,400	$1,400	$1,000	$1,100	$1,900	$2,950	$3,425	$2,700	
Balance—End of Month—Based on Collection Terms	400	400	750	600	800	600	400	900	1,450	1,925	1,500	800	
Cash Collections	$766	$800	$1,150	$1,350	600	800	600	200	450	$1,025	$1,925	$1,900	$11,566
Collection Terms—in Days	15	15	15	15	30	30	30	60 & 90	257 — 60 & 90	30	30	20	

Balance — End of Month listed on Line 36

Monthly Cash Collections listed on Line 17

SCHEDULE "C" — MATERIAL FLOW AND PURCHASES (000) Omitted

	January	February	March	April	May	June	July	August	September	October	November	December	Totals
Beginning Inventory	$788	$816	$1,530	$1,224	$816	$612	$408	$711	$1,020	$1,530	$1,530	$1,224	$8,160
Less: Materials Used from Schedule "A"	544	544	1,020	816	544	408	272	476	680	1,020	1,020	816	8,160
Net Remaining before Required Purchases	244	272	510	408	272	204	136	238	340	510	510	408	
Add: Purchases Required	572	1,258	714	408	340	204	578	782	1,190	1,020	714	380	
Ending Inventory—45 Days' Supply	$816	$1,530	$1,224	$816	$612	$408	$714	$1,020	$1,530	$1,530	$1,224	$788	$8,160

"Purchases Required" are brought forward to Schedule "D" to obtain cash disbursements and accounts payable at end of month

"Purchase Required" is always an amount which when added to the "net inventory" results in the pre-computed ending inventory

Ending inventories are set forth on Line 37

SCHEDULE "D" — ACCOUNTS PAYABLE — CASH FLOW — 15 DAY TERMS (000) Omitted

	January	February	March	April	May	June	July	August	September	October	November	December	Totals
Accounts Payable—Beginning of Month	$311	$286	$629	$357	$204	$170	$102	$289	$391	$595	$510	$357	
Add: Monthly Purchases Required—Schedule "B"	572	1,258	714	408	340	204	578	782	1,190	1,020	714	380	$8,160
Total	$913	$1,514	$1,343	$765	$541	$374	$680	$1,071	$1,581	$1,615	$1,224	$737	
Less Accounts Payable—End of Month	286	629	357	204	170	102	289	391	595	510	357	190	
Cash Disbursed on Trade Payables	$627	$915	$986	$561	$353	272	391	680	986	$1,105	$867	$517	$8,311

Cash Disbursed is listed on Line 22

Accounts Payable—End of month are listed on Line 47

SCHEDULE "E" — DIRECT LABOR, MANUFACTURING EXPENSES AND INDIRECT LABOR — ACCRUALS AND CASH DISBURSED (000) Omitted

	January	February	March	April	May	June	July	August	September	October	November	December	Totals
Accruals—Beginning of Month	$95	$68	$68	$128	$102	$68	$50	$31	$60	$84	$128	$126	
Add: Monthly Expense from Schedule "A" of 3 totals	136	136	256	204	136	100	68	120	168	256	252	204	$2,036
Total	$231	$204	$324	$332	$238	$168	$118	$154	$228	$340	$380	$330	
Less: Accruals—End of Month—Paid 15 days	68	68	128	102	68	50	34	60	84	128	126	102	
Cash Disbursed	$163	$136	$196	$230	$170	$118	$84	$94	$144	$212	$254	$228	$2,029

Accruals — End of Month listed on Line 51

Cash Disbursed listed on Lines 23 and 24

Sample Company, Inc.: Source of Figures for Budget Form

Line No.	Source
1	Sales from Schedule A
2	Material costs from Schedule A
3	Direct Labor from Schedule A
4	Manufacturing Overhead from Schedule A
5	Indirect Labor from Schedule A
6	Cost of Goods Sold from Schedule A
7	Gross Profit—Line 1 less Line 6
8	Sales Expense—Schedule A
9	General and Administrative Expenses—Schedule A
11	Line 7 less totals of Lines 8, 9, and 10
12	Depreciation—from Preliminary Facts
13	50% for purposes of illustration (or current tax rate) or Difference between Line 11 less Line 12
14	
15	Line 11 less total of Lines 12, 13, and 14
16	Balance of Line 33 (from previous month)
17	Monthly Cash Collections from Schedule B
20	Bank Loan Proceeds—an amount to be added (Line 20) to the difference of Line 21 less Line 32 to equal cash balances (Line 33) of not less than $250,000. Borrowings to be made in multiples of $50,000.
21	Totals of Lines 16 through 20
22	Cash Disbursed on Trade Payables from Schedule D
23 24 }	Cash Disbursed from Schedule E
25	Total of Lines 8 and 9 above
26	Monthly amounts of fixed-asset additions from preliminary facts
27	Balance on Line 48 (from actual balance sheet) distributed in March and June, with 25% of the amount in excess of $100,000 of estimated income taxes payable in September and December
30	Balance on Line 49 (actual) distributed in accordance with terms of payment
31	When bank loans are outstanding if Line 21 exceeds Line 32 (without Line 31 added in), any amount which reduces cash balances (Line 33) to not less than $250,000 should be placed in Line 31
32	Totals of Lines 22 to 31
33	The difference between Line 21 less Line 32—at no time to be less than $250,000
34	From Line 33
36	Balance—End of Month—from Schedule B
37	Ending Inventory—from Schedule C
39	Totals of Lines 34 through 38
40	Line 26 less Line 12 added to outstanding of previous month
41	No change—brought across from actual
44	No change—brought across from actual
45	Total of Lines 39 through 44
46	Total of Line 20 less total of Line 31 added to previous month balance
47	Accounts Payable end of month from Schedule D
48	Previous month balance plus Line 13 less Line 27
49	(Current Maturities—Term Debt) year-end actual total less payments on Line 30, plus maturities of Line 53 becoming current obligations
51	Accruals end of month from Schedule E
52	Total of Lines 46 through 51
53	(Term Debt) Outstanding balance (from actual) less maturities becoming current obligations
54	(Total Liabilites) Total of Lines 52 and 53
56 57 }	Previous month outstanding balance plus Line 15
58	Total of Lines 54 and 56
59	Line 39 less Line 52

rma

'77 annual statement studies

fiscal year-ends 6/30/76 through 3/31/77

with other sources of composite
financial data

Published by Robert Morris Associates, Philadelphia, Pa.

CHEMICALS & ALLIED PRODUCTS — SIC# 5161   WHOLESALERS   DRUGS, DRUG PROPRIETARIES & DRUGGISTS' SUNDRIES — SIC# 5122

0-250M (23)	250M-1MM (65)	1-10MM (72)	10-50MM (5)	ALL (165)	ASSET SIZE / NUMBER OF STATEMENTS	0-250M (16)	250M-1MM (26)	1-10MM (58)	10-50MM (15)	ALL (115)
%	%	%	%	%	**ASSETS**	%	%	%	%	%
7.9	7.7	6.9		10.9	Cash & Equivalents	9.6	5.5	3.6	8.9	6.6
34.3	35.0	33.6		30.4	Accts & Notes Rec - Trade(net)	30.3	28.4	32.3	26.8	29.1
32.2	28.8	24.6		28.5	Inventory	39.9	44.6	44.6	41.2	42.7
1.0	2.3	2.5		1.8	All Other Current	.7	1.2	2.0	1.9	1.9
75.4	73.9	67.7		71.6	Total Current	80.6	79.6	82.4	78.7	80.3
14.8	19.4	25.5		21.9	Fixed Assets (net)	8.3	12.2	11.8	16.4	14.3
.3	.7	.8		.6	Intangibles (net)	.0	1.0	.6	1.1	.9
9.5	5.9	6.0		6.0	All Other Non-Current	11.1	7.2	5.1	3.8	4.5
100.0	100.0	100.0		100.0	Total	100.0	100.0	100.0	100.0	100.0
					LIABILITIES					
12.6	10.2	9.5		7.6	Notes Payable-Short Term	10.9	10.6	13.3	3.6	7.9
4.0	2.8	3.5		2.5	Cur. Mat.-L/T/D	2.2	2.7	1.2	.9	1.1
22.2	26.0	28.4		29.5	Accts & Notes Payable - Trade	30.4	31.2	29.2	26.9	28.0
10.2	5.4	5.4		4.6	Accrued Expenses	3.8	6.1	4.3	5.1	4.8
2.8	3.9	5.1		7.4	All Other Current	1.0	2.8	1.8	1.5	1.7
51.7	48.3	51.9		51.6	Total Current	48.3	53.4	49.8	38.0	43.4
15.8	12.1	10.2		9.3	Long Term Debt	16.1	7.4	9.5	8.2	8.7
2.2	2.0	2.4		2.5	All Other Non-Current	0	7.2	1.3	3.2	2.5
30.4	37.7	35.5		36.6	Net Worth	35.6	32.0	39.4	50.6	45.3
100.0	100.0	100.0		100.0	Total Liabilities & Net Worth	100.0	100.0	100.0	100.0	100.0
					INCOME DATA					
100.0	100.0	100.0		100.0	Net Sales	100.0	100.0	100.0	100.0	100.0
64.9	75.6	80.5		79.5	Cost Of Sales	73.5	71.7	82.1	79.7	80.5
35.1	24.4	19.5		20.5	Gross Profit	26.5	28.3	17.9	20.3	19.5
29.1	21.3	16.2		16.3	Operating Expenses	23.3	25.3	15.0	16.2	16.0
6.0	3.0	3.2		4.2	Operating Profit	3.2	3.0	2.9	4.1	3.5
1.1	.6	.2		.3	All Other Expenses (net)	-.3	.4	.7	.3	.5
4.9	2.4	3.1		3.9	Profit Before Taxes	3.5	2.6	2.2	3.8	3.1
					RATIOS					
2.1	2.0	1.7		1.9	Current	1.9	2.3	2.0	2.9	2.1
1.6	1.5	1.4		1.4		1.7	1.6	1.7	2.1	1.7
1.1	1.2	1.1		1.1		1.5	1.2	1.3	1.8	1.4
1.2	1.1	1.1		1.1	Quick	1.5	1.1	.9	1.4	1.1
.9	.9	.8		.8		1.0	.7	.7	.9	.8
.6	.6	.6		.6		.4	.3	.6	.8	.5
26 14.3	28 13.1	33 10.9	31 11.7		Sales/Receivables	23 16.1	22 16.9	28 13.1	29 12.6	27 13.5
41 8.8	36 10.1	46 7.9	42 8.6			30 12.2	42 8.7	39 9.4	38 9.7	38 9.6
72 5.1	54 6.8	60 6.1	57 6.4			47 7.8	52 7.0	54 6.7	44 8.3	49 7.4
42 8.6	26 13.8	24 15.0	28 13.2		Cost of Sales/Inventory	50 7.3	56 6.5	49 7.4	60 6.1	54 6.8
60 6.1	44 8.3	42 8.6	46 7.9			74 4.9	79 4.6	62 5.9	63 5.8	66 5.4
87 4.2	73 5.0	64 5.7	70 5.2			104 3.5	118 3.1	87 4.2	69 5.3	87 4.2
7.9	7.6	10.4		8.3	Sales/Working Capital	7.7	6.1	6.9	5.0	6.6
8.9	13.9	14.9		13.9		9.2	8.6	10.7	7.5	9.3
44.4	34.3	38.9		36.9		20.0	21.0	16.4	9.4	15.1
13.0	11.8	12.1		12.1	EBIT/Interest	7.4	13.8	10.1	29.4	11.3
(19) 6.0	(50) 3.2	(51) 4.7	(123) 4.7			(12) 4.6	(23) 4.6	(43) 5.2	(12) 12.3	(90) 5.1
3.3	1.7	2.0		1.9		2.1	1.8	1.8	4.3	2.0
	4.1	5.6		4.9	Cash Flow/Cur. Mat. L/T/D		4.7	11.2	27.4	8.9
(32) 2.1	(41) 3.7	(83) 2.9			(12) 2.9	(28) 2.8	(10) 8.4	(55) 2.9	
1.0	1.6	1.1				1.2	1.3	2.5	1.3
.1	.2	.3		.2	Fixed/Worth	.1	.1	.1	.1	.1
.3	.5	.6		.3		.2	.3	.2	.2	.2
1.6	1.2	1.0		1.1		.5	.9	.4	.5	.5
.8	.9	1.1		1.0	Debt/Worth	1.3	1.0	1.1	.6	1.0
1.9	2.2	1.9		2.0		1.7	1.7	1.7	1.0	1.6
7.3	3.5	3.6		3.6		2.4	5.0	2.9	1.4	2.9
88.5	35.1	36.0		37.5	% Profit Before Taxes/Tangible Net Worth	52.2	37.8	28.9	29.0	34.2
(20) 45.0	17.1	(71) 23.3	(161) 22.4			(15) 31.1	(22) 16.2	17.5	(110) 19.7	18.1
15.3	10.8	10.3		10.8		8.2	9.2	10.1	7.5	9.8
21.1	10.8	13.9		14.1	% Profit Before Taxes/Total Assets	19.0	13.7	11.0	14.0	13.8
10.7	5.4	8.3		7.4		10.9	6.7	7.3	10.0	7.8
4.4	3.0	3.2		3.2		3.7	3.0	2.7	2.0	3.3
65.2	60.8	41.9		53.3	Sales/Net Fixed Assets	113.6	85.9	81.8	51.6	81.2
29.2	20.5	14.9		17.8		48.0	26.8	42.6	33.4	36.3
11.7	9.6	9.3		9.7		14.5	16.0	22.3	23.1	17.7
3.9	4.0	3.8		3.8	Sales/Total Assets	3.8	3.8	4.0	3.5	3.9
2.7	3.2	2.8		2.9		3.1	2.7	3.2	3.0	3.1
1.9	2.3	2.3		2.2		2.6	1.9	2.4	2.8	2.4
.7	.4	.6		.5	% Depr., Dep., Amort./Sales	.3	.4	.2	.3	.3
(19) 1.1	(61) .9	(70) 1.0	(155) 1.0			(13) .5	(23) .7	(51) .4	(14) .5	(101) .5
1.9	1.7	2.1		1.8		1.0	1.3	.7	.9	.9
.9	.2	.2		.3	% Lease & Rental Exp/Sales	.7	.6	.4		.5
(18) 1.6	(36) 1.0	(43) .7	(100) .9			(13) 1.4	(18) 1.0	(36) .6	(74)	.9
2.9	1.2	1.4		1.5		4.7	2.2	1.3		1.5
3.7	2.2	1.2		1.6	% Officers' Comp/Sales	3.9	2.4	.9		1.3
(15) 6.5	(35) 3.4	(33) 1.7	(84) 3.1			(13) 5.9	(14) 3.6	(25) 1.5	(54)	2.4
8.8	6.4	3.1		5.2		8.7	5.0	2.2		4.9
9612M	117496M	803504M	196173M	926785M	Net Sales ($)	8699M	43413M	662937M	800390M	1515439M
3346M	37519M	216024M	106577M	363466M	Total Assets ($)	2604M	14802M	206362M	267752M	491420M

Robert M... Assoc... 1977   M = $thousand   MM = $million

DEFINITION OF RATIOS
INTRODUCTION

Below the common size balance sheet and income statement presented on each data page are series of ratios which have been computed from the financial statement data. Each ratio has three values: the upper quartile, median, and lower quartile. For any given ratio, these figures are calculated by first computing the value of the ratio for *each* financial statement in the sample. These values are then arrayed—"listed"—in an order from the strongest to the weakest. (We acknowledge that, for certain ratios, there may be differences of opinion concerning what is a strong or a weak value. RMA has resolved this problem by following general banking guidelines consistent with sound credit practice in its presentation of data.)

In such an array of ratio values, the figure which falls in the middle between the strongest and the weakest ratios is the *median*. The figure that falls halfway between the median and the strongest ratio is the *upper quartile*. The figure that falls halfway between the median and the weakest ratio is the *lower quartile*. The median and quartile values will always be shown on the data pages in the order indicated below:

Upper Quartile
Median
Lower Quartile

There are several reasons for using medians and quartiles instead of an average. One is to eliminate the influence which values in an "unusual" statement would have on an average. The method used more accurately reflects the ranges of ratio values than would a straight averaging method.

It is important to understand that the spread (range) between the upper and lower quartiles represents the middle 50% of all the companies in a sample. Ratio values greater than the upper or less than the lower quartiles, therefore, begin to approach "unusual" values.

For some ratio values, you will occasionally see an entry that is other than a conventional number. These unusual entries are defined as follows:

(1) *INF*—This stands for infinity, a value so large as to be beyond any practical value. It is the result of the denominator having the value of zero in a ratio calculation. With respect to the ratios sales/working capital, debt/worth, and fixed/worth, the value $\pm$ *INF* may occasionally appear as a quartile or median. This is the result of interpolation between positive and negative values in the nonlinear arrays typical of these ratios.

(2) *999.8*—When a ratio value equals 1,000 or more, it also becomes an "unusual" value and is given the "999.8" designation. This is considered to be a close enough approximation to the actual atypically large value.

(3) *.0*—In a few places in this book, we encounter a negative value so minute that, when rounded, it becomes zero. We have used the symbol " .0" to reflect this, but it is important to recognize that it is the result of rounding a *negative* number.

Throughout the *Statement Studies*, the ratio values have been omitted whenever there were less than ten statements in a sample. Occasionally, the number of statements used in a ratio array will differ from the number of statements in a sample because certain elements of data may not be present in all financial statements. In these cases, the number of statements used is shown in parentheses to the left of the array.

In interpreting ratios, the "strongest" or "best" value is not always the largest numerical value, nor is the "weakest" always the lowest numerical value. The following description of each of the ratios. appearing in the *Statement Studies* will provide details regarding the arraying of the values.

The ratios in the *Statement Studies* are grouped into five principal categories: liquidity, coverage, leverage, operating, and specific expense items.

LIQUIDITY RATIOS

Liquidity is a measure of the quality and adequacy of current assets to meet current obligations as they come due.

CURRENT RATIO

Computation: Total current assets divided by total current liabilities.

$$\frac{\text{total current assets}}{\text{total current liabilities}}$$

Interpretation: This ratio is a rough indication of a firm's ability to service its current obligations. Generally, the higher the current ratio, the greater the "cushion" between current obligations and a firm's ability to pay them. The stronger ratio reflects a numerical superiority of current assets over current liabilities. However, the composition and quality of current assets is a critical factor in the analysis of an individual firm's liquidity.

The ratio values are arrayed from the highest positive to the lowest positive.

QUICK RATIO

Computation: Cash and equivalents plus accounts and notes receivable (trade) divided by total current liabilities.

$$\frac{\text{cash \& equivalents + accounts \& notes receivable (trade)}}{\text{total current liabilities}}$$

Interpretation: Also known as the "ACID TEST" ratio, it is a refinement of the current ratio and is a more conservative measure of liquidity. The ratio expresses the degree to which a company's current liabilities are covered by the most liquid current assets. Generally, any value of less than 1 to 1 implies a reciprocal "dependency" on inventory or other current assets to liquidate short-term debt.

The ratio values are arrayed from the highest positive to the lowest positive.

If the number of statements used in the calculation of this ratio differs from the sample size used in the asset category column, the sample size for each ratio will be printed in parentheses to the left of the array.

SALES/RECEIVABLES

Computation: Net sales divided by accounts and notes receivable (trade) .

$$\frac{\text{net sales}}{\text{accounts \& notes receivable (trade)}}$$

Interpretation: This ratio measures the number of times accounts and notes receivable (trade) turn over during the year. The higher the turnover of receivables, the shorter the time between sale and cash collection. For example, a company with sales of $720,000 and receivables of $120,000 would have a sales/receivables ratio of 6.0, which means receivables turn over six times a year. If a company's receivables appear to be turning slower than the rest of the industry, further research is needed and the quality of the receivables should be examined closely.

A problem with this ratio is that it compares one day's receivables, shown at statement date, to total annual sales and does not take into consideration seasonal fluctuations. An additional problem in interpretation may arise when there is a large proportion of cash sales to total sales.

When the receivables figure is zero, the quotient will be infinity (INF) and represents the best possible ratio. The ratio values are therefore arrayed starting with infinity (INF) and then from the numerically highest to the numerically lowest value. The only time a zero will appear in the array is when the sales figure is low and the quotient rounds off to zero. By definition, this ratio cannot be negative.

Days' Receivables: The sales/receivables ratio will have a figure printed in bold type directly to the left of the array. This figure is the days' receivables.

Computation: The sales/receivables ratio divided into 365 (the number of days in one year).

$$\frac{365}{\text{sales/receivable ratio}}$$

Interpretation: This figure expresses the average time in days that receivables are outstanding. Generally, the greater number of days outstanding, the greater the probability of delinquencies in accounts receivable. A comparison of a company's daily receivables may indicate the extent of a company's control over credit and collections. The terms offered by a company to its customers, however, may differ from terms within the industry and should be taken into consideration.

In the example above, 365 : 6 = 61—i.e., the average receivable is collected in 61 days.

COST OF SALES/INVENTORY

Computation: Cost of sales divided by inventory.

$$\frac{\text{Cost of Sales}}{\text{Inventory}}$$

Interpretation: This ratio measures the number of times inventory is turned over during the year. High inventory turnover can indicate better liquidity or superior merchandising. Conversely it can indicate a shortage of needed inventory for sales. Low inventory turnover can indicate poor liquidity, possible overstocking, obsolescence, or in contrast to these negative interpretations a planned inventory buildup in the case of material shortages. A problem with this ratio is that it compares one day's inventory to cost of goods sold and does not take seasonal fluctuations into account. When the inventory figure is zero, the quotient will be infinity (INF) and represents the best possible ratio. The ratio values are arrayed starting with infinity (INF) and then from the numerically highest to the numerically lowest value. The only time a zero will appear in the array is when the cost of sales figure is very low and the quotient rounds off to zero.

Days' Inventory
The cost of sales inventory ratio will have a figure printed in bold type directly to the left of the array. This figure is the days' inventory.

Computation: The cost of sales/inventory ratio divided into 365 (the number of days in one year).

$$\frac{365}{\text{cost of sales/inventory ratio}}$$

Interpretation: Division of the inventory turnover ratio into 365 days yields the average length of time units are in inventory.

SALES/WORKING CAPITAL

Computation: Net sales divided by net working capital (current assets less current liabilities equals net working capital).

$$\frac{\text{Net Sales}}{\text{Net Working Capital}}$$

Interpretation: Working capital is a measure of the margin of protection for current creditors. It reflects the ability to finance current operations. Relating the level of sales arising from operations to the underlying working capital measures how efficiently working capital is employed. A low ratio may indicate an inefficient use of working capital while a very high ratio often signifies overtrading —a vulnerable position for creditors.

If working capital is zero, the quotient is infinity (INF). If working capital is negative, the quotient is negative. The ratio values are arrayed from the lowest positive to the highest positive, to infinity, and then from the highest negative to the lowest negative.

The value ± INF may occasionally appear as a quartile or median. This is the result of interpolation between positive and negative values in the nonlinear array typical of this ratio.

COVERAGE RATIOS

Coverage ratios measure a firm's ability to service debt.

EARNINGS BEFORE INTEREST AND TAXES (EBIT)/INTEREST

Computation: Earnings (profit) before annual interest expense and taxes divided by annual interest expense.

$$\frac{\text{Earnings Before Interest \& Taxes}}{\text{Annual Interest Expense}}$$

Interpretation: This ratio is a measure of a firm's ability to meet interest payments. A high ratio may indicate that a borrower would have little difficulty in meeting the interest obligations of a loan. This ratio also serves as an indicator of a firm's capacity to take on additional debt.

Only those statements which reported annual interest expense were used in the calculation of this ratio. If the number of statements used in the calculation of these ratios differed from the sample size used in the asset category column, the sample size for each ratio will be printed in parentheses to the left of the array. If there were less than 10 ratios in an array, no entry will be shown. The ratio values are arrayed from the highest positive to the lowest positive and then from the lowest negative to the highest negative.

CASH FLOW/CURRENT MATURITIES LONG-TERM DEBT

Computation: Net profit plus depreciation, depletion, and amortization expenses, divided by the current portion of long-term debt.

$$\frac{\text{Net Profit} + \text{Depreciation, Depletion, Amortization Expenses}}{\text{Current Portion of Long-Term Debt}}$$

Interpretation: This ratio expresses the coverage of current maturities by cash flow from operations. Since cash flow is the primary source of debt retirement, this ratio measures the ability of a firm to service principal repayment and is an indicator of additional debt capacity. Although it is misleading to think that all cash flow is available for debt service, the ratio is a valid measure of the ability to service long-term debt.

Only data for *corporations* which have the following items were used;
    (1) Profit or loss after taxes (positive, negative, or zero)
    (2) A positive figure for Depreciation/Depletion/Amortization expenses
    (3) A positive figure for current maturities of long-term debt

If the number of ratios used differed with the total number of firms reported in a column, the sample size is printed to the left of the array. If less than 10 ratios were available, the array was not printed. Ratio values are arrayed from the highest to lowest positive and then from the lowest to the highest negative.

LEVERAGE RATIOS

Highly leveraged firms (those with heavy debt in relation to net worth) are more vulnerable to business downturns than those with lower debt to worth positions. While leverage ratios help to measure this vulnerability, it must be remembered that they vary greatly depending on the requirements of particular industry groups.

FIXED/WORTH

Computation: Fixed assets (net of accumulated depreciation) divided by tangible net worth.

$$\frac{\text{Net Fixed Assets}}{\text{Tangible Net Worth}}$$

Interpretation: This ratio measures the extent to which owner's equity (capital) has been invested in plant and equipment (fixed assets). A lower ratio indicates a proportionately smaller investment in fixed assets in relation to net worth, and a better "cushion" for creditors in case of liquidation. Similarly, a higher ratio would indicate the opposite situation. The presence of substantial leased fixed assets (not shown on the balance sheet) may deceptively lower this ratio.

Fixed assets may be zero, in which case the quotient is zero. If tangible net worth is zero, the quotient is infinity (INF). If tangible net worth is negative, the quotient is negative. The ratio values are arrayed from the lowest positive to the highest positive, infinity, and then from the highest negative to the lowest negative.

The value ± INF may occasionally appear as a quartile or median. This is the result of interpolation between positive and negative values in the nonlinear array typical of this ratio.

DEBT/WORTH

Computation: Total liabilities divided by tangible net worth.

$$\frac{\text{Total Liabilities}}{\text{Tangible Net Worth}}$$

Interpretation: This ratio expresses the relationship between capital contributed by creditors and that contributed by owners. It expresses the degree of protection provided by the owners for the creditors. The higher the ratio, the greater the risk being assumed by creditors. A lower ratio generally indicates greater long-term financial safety. A firm with a low debt/worth ratio usually has greater flexibility to borrow in the future. A more highly leveraged company has a more limited debt capacity.

Tangible net worth may be zero, in which case the ratio is infinity (INF). Tangible net worth may also be negative which results in the quotient being negative. The ratio values are arrayed from the lowest to highest positive, infinity, and then from the highest to lowest negative.

The value ± INF may occasionally appear as a quartile or median. This is the result of interpolation between positive and negative values in the nonlinear array typical of this ratio.

OPERATING RATIOS

Operating ratios are designed to assist in the evaluation of management performance.

% PROFITS BEFORE TAXES/TANGIBLE NET WORTH

Computation: Profit before taxes divided by tangible net worth and multiplied by 100.

$$\frac{\text{Profit Before Taxes}}{\text{Tangible Net Worth}} \times 100$$

Interpretation: This ratio expresses the rate of return on tangible capital employed. While it can serve as an indicator of management performance, the analyst is cautioned to use it in conjunction with other ratios. A high return, normally associated with effective management, could indicate an under-capitalized firm. Whereas, a low return, usually an indicator of inefficient management performance, could reflect a highly capitalized, conservatively operated business.

This ratio has been multiplied by 100 since it is shown as a percentage.

Profit before taxes may be zero, in which case the ratio is zero. Profits before taxes may be negative resulting in negative quotients. Firms with negative tangible net worth have been omitted from the ratio arrays. Negative ratios will therefore only result in the case of negative profit before taxes. If the tangible net worth is zero, the quotient is infinity (INF). If there are less than 10 ratios for a particular size class, the result is not shown. The ratio values are arrayed starting with infinity (INF), and then from the highest to the lowest positive values, and from the lowest to the highest negative values.

% PROFIT BEFORE TAXES/TOTAL ASSETS

Computation: Profit before taxes divided by total assets and multiplied by 100.

$$\frac{\text{Profit Before Taxes}}{\text{Total Assets}} \times 100$$

Interpretation: This ratio expresses the pre-tax return on total assets and measures the effectiveness of management in employing the resources available to it. If a specific ratio varies considerably from the ranges found in this book, the analyst will need to examine the makeup of the assets and take a closer look at the earnings figure. A heavily depreciated plant and a large amount of intangible assets or unusual income or expense items will cause distortions of this ratio.

This ratio has been multiplied by 100 since it is shown as a percentage. If profit before taxes is zero, the quotient is zero. If profit before taxes is negative, the quotient is negative. These ratio values are arrayed from the highest to the lowest positive and then from the lowest to the highest negative.

SALES/NET FIXED ASSETS

Computation: Net sales divided by net fixed assets (net of accumulated depreciation).

$$\frac{\text{Net Sales}}{\text{Net Fixed Assets}}$$

Interpretation: This ratio is a measure of the productive use of a firm's fixed assets. Largely depreciated fixed assets or a labor intensive operation may cause a distortion of this ratio.

If the net fixed asset figure is zero, the quotient is infinity (INF). The only time a zero will appear in the array will be when the net sales figure is low and the quotient rounds off to zero. These ratio values cannot be negative.

They are arrayed from infinity (INF) and then from the highest to the lowest positive values.

SALES/TOTAL ASSETS

Computation: Net sales divided by total assets.

$$\frac{\text{Net Sales}}{\text{Total Assets}}$$

Interpretation: This ratio is a general measure of a firm's ability to generate sales in relation to total assets. It should be used only to compare firms within specific industry groups and in conjunction with other operating ratios to determine the effective employment of assets.

The only time a zero will appear in the array will be when the net sales figure is low and the quotient rounds off to zero. The ratio values cannot be negative. They are arrayed from the highest to the lowest positive values.

EXPENSE TO SALES RATIOS

The following three ratios relate specific expense items to net sales and express this relationship as a percentage. Comparisons are convenient because the item, net sales, is used as a constant. Variations in these ratios are most pronounced between capital and labor intensive industries.

% DEPRECIATION, DEPLETION, AMORTIZATION/SALES

Computation: Annual depreciation, amortization, and depletion expenses divided by net sales and multiplied by 100.

$$\frac{\text{Depreciation, Amortization, Depletion Expenses}}{\text{Net Sales}} \times 100$$

% LEASE AND RENTAL EXPENSES/SALES

Computation: Annual lease and rental expenses divided by net sales and multiplied by 100.

$$\frac{\text{Lease \& Rental Expenses}}{\text{Net Sales}} \times 100$$

% OFFICERS' COMPENSATION/SALES

Computation: Annual officers' compensation divided by net sales and multiplied by 100.

$$\frac{\text{Officers' Compensation}}{\text{Net Sales}} \times 100$$

Only statements showing a positive figure for each of the expense categories shown above were used. If the number of statements used in an array differs from the sample population for an asset size category, the number of statements used is shown in parentheses to the left of the array. When there are less than 10 ratios, the array is not printed. The ratios are arrayed from the lowest to highest positive values.

SIC NUMBERS APPEARING IN THE STATEMENT STUDIES

SIC No.	Page	SIC No.	Page	SIC No.	Page
0161	186	2065	51	2512	59
0181	185	2074	56	2514	57
0211	182	2075	56	2515	56
0212	181	2076	56	2522	57
0251	183	2082	45	2541	58
0781	185	2084	46	2542	58
0782	185	2085	46	2621	85
0783	185	2086	183	2631	85
1211	182	2087	45	2642	84
1311	184	2091	51	2643	84
1381	193 & 200	2211	94	2648	84
1442	184	2221	94	2651	85
1521	191 & 199	2231	94	2652	85
1522	191 & 199	2241	97	2653	85
1541	191 & 199	2252	95 & 96	2654	85
1542	191 & 199	2253	96	2655	85
1611	192 & 199	2254	96	2711	89
1622	192 & 199	2257	96	2721	89
1623	197 & 202	2258	96	2731	87
1711	195 & 201	2261	95	2732	86
1721	194 & 200	2262	95	2751	87
1731	189 & 198	2272	97	2752	88
1741	193 & 200	2282	98	2761	88
1742	195 & 201	2311	42	2789	86
1743	197 & 202	2321	42	2791	90
1752	190 & 198	2327	41	2821	49
1761	196 & 201	2328	41	2831	47
1771	189 & 198	2335	43	2833	47
1791	196 & 201	2337	44	2834	47
1794	190 & 198	2341	44	2841	50
2011	54	2342	43	2844	49
2013	55	2351	39	2851	48
2016	54	2352	39	2861	48
2021	52	2371	39	2865	48
2022	52	2391	38	2873	47
2023	52	2392	40	2874	47
2024	52	2394	37	3021	91
2026	52	2421	63	3111	61
2033	52	2431	62	3143	60
2034	52	2435	61	3144	60
2037	53	2441	63	3161	60
2041	53	2451	100	3171	60
2048	55	2452	62	3172	60
2051	50	2511	58	3251	91

Appendix II: The Legal Process of Venture Capital Investment*

Richard J. Testa

Richard J. Testa is a partner in the Boston law firm of Testa, Hurwitz & Thibeault. He and his firm have served as counsel for several professional venture capital companies as well as for a large number of businesses that have been financed by venture capital sources, including Lotus 1–2–3.

Section I. General Considerations Relating to Legal Documentation

A key element in the attainment of a successful relationship between a young business enterprise and its venture capital investors is the careful crafting of the legal structure of the investment transaction. Venture capital investing is a long-term commitment of support to a company. As such, the parties involved in structuring and implementing the investment transaction must bring to the process a sensitivity to the changing and different objectives and requirements (financial, legal, personal, etc.) of the business and its principal participants. The legal documents must foresee the evolution of the enterprise from a development stage start-up to a publicly held company or viable acquisition candidate. Not only do the investment documents represent a charter of the legal rights of the parties spanning the growth cycle of the business, but they also set the tone of the relationships between the management/entrepreneurs and the financial backers of the enterprise, serving as a model for resolution of their often differing interests.

Despite increasing standardization of the venture capital process, it remains, fundamentally, highly idiosyncratic, with each transaction reflecting the particular chemistry between entrepreneur and investor. Accordingly, there exists no such thing as the "perfect model" of legal documentation for the investment transaction. Each deal should be tailored to reflect the unique combination of styles and interests involved. Generally, however, each transaction will encompass the following common set of documents:

1. *The term sheet,* summarizing in broad stroke the principal financial and other terms of the investment.
2. *The investment agreement,* detailing the terms of purchase and provisions of the securities (equity or debt) being acquired.
3. *The stockholders agreement,* containing restrictions upon the transfer and voting of securities by management and (occasionally) investors.

*Reprinted from the 8th edition of *Pratt's Guide to Venture Capital Sources,* 1984, with the permission of the author and publisher. Venture Economics, Wellesley Hills, Massachusetts.

4. *Employee stock purchase or stock option agreements,* governing the current and future allocation of equity in the business to key employees.
5. *Employee confidentiality and proprietary rights agreements,* assuring the retention by the business of its valuable trade secrets and business rights.
6. *Legal opinion* of company counsel.

Section II. The Term Sheet

The handshake "agreement" between investor and entrepreneur is often set forth in a writen term sheet or letter of intent. Although the term sheet may take a variety of forms, from a cursory and informal letter to a more detailed and formal memorandum, it is intended to accomplish the following purposes:

1. To reflect the agreed-upon valuation of the business and to quantify the proposed allocation of that value between the entrepreneurs and investors.
2. To summarize key financial and legal terms of the transaction which will serve as the basis for preparing definitive legal documents.
3. On occasion, to impose enforceable legal obligaions upon the parties, such as requiring payment of expenses in the event the investment does not close or prohibiting negotiations with other parties pending the completion of the transaction.

Above all, the term sheet should be used by the venture captialist to elicit those concerns of the entrepreneurs which, if unaddressed and unresolved, might later develop into "deal killers." For example, if the venture capitalist intends to require that the entrepreneurs submit their stock ownership in the enterprise to buy-back or forfeiture restrictions in the event they sever employment, such a condition should be covered in the term sheet since it encroaches in an area in which the entrepreneur will be especially sensitive. Similarly sensitive topics are the composition of the board of directors and matters relating to the terms of employment of the entrepreneurs.

Section III. The Investment Agreement

A. Principal Purposes and Legal Consequences

The long-form investment agreement has four principal business objectives:

1. Most importantly, it sets forth the detailed substantive terms of the investment.
2. It serves as the basic disclosure document in which the relevant historical, business, financial, and legal data relating to the enterprise are set forth or referenced.
3. It presents, through the use of conditions precedent to closing, a "stop-action" photograph or image of the issuer that must exist at the time of closing. The level of detail of this photograph will vary depending upon the round of financing involved in the transaction and the simplicity or complexity of the company's operations.
4. It defines the several business parameters within which the enterprise must operate in the future. The several commandments to management range from relatively simple "thou shall not's" to complex "thou shalt's."

The legal effect of the investment agreement is similar to that of many commercial contracts. The most common consequence of a breach of agreement in the capital investment context is the ability of the investor to refuse to close the transaction because of the company's failure to satisfy a condition precedent or the existence of a significant misrepresentation by the company. Once the closing has occurred, remedies in the nature of recission are rare. Moreover, while claims for damages do arise, they are uncommon in the high-risk venture area. Common remedies available for breach of covenant are specific performance and injunctive relief. As a practical matter, however, remedies that are self-executing, such as ratchet-down provisions in an antidilution formula or extraordinary voting rights granted to a class of preferred stock, are more formidable than those remedies which frequently amount to waving a stick in the air, such as accelerated repayment of debt securities.

B. Description of the Transaction

The investment agreement memorializes the terms of the transaction. Consequently, the agreement should include a description of the securities being purchased, the purchase price, and a requirement that the securities be properly authorized.

If the investor acquires a note (whether or not convertible) or a stock purchase warrant, the form of the security should be attached as an exhibit to the investment agreement. If the investor acquires a class of stock other than conventional common stock, the terms of the class of stock as set forth in the corporate charter should be attached to the investment agreement as an exhibit.

If more than one investor participates in the financing, they may be listed or referenced in an exhibit to the agreement. In some cases, the company will execute separate but identical investment agreements with the other investors. A condition of each investor's obligation to purchase may be that identical investment agreements have been executed simultaneously with each investor, such agreements have not been amended and are in full force on the closing date, and a specified minimum number of dollars has been raised by the company.

In some transactions, the entire investment will not be made available to the company at a single closing. The purchase may be made in two or more installments over fixed periods of time, in which event the major condition precedent to closing each successive installment is the absence of any material adverse changes affecting the company since the initial closing. In a "staged" investment, the purchase of additional securities at subsequent closings is conditioned upon the accomplishment of certain financial or operational goals, such as the attainment of specified revenue levels or completion of development work on a new product, as well as the absence of adverse changes. A stage investment serves as an incentive to management to proceed diligently with the development of its product as outlined in its business plan and enables the venture capitalist to target his investment with a maximum impact on the development of the business.

C. Representations and Warranties of the Company

It is a rare issuer company that is totally "clean," that is, a company which has no stated exceptions to the several business, financial, and legal topics addressed by the representation and warranty section of the investment agreement. Only a new start-up company with neither employees nor sales is likely to fall into this category. Since the venture capitalist has already conducted a thorough factual review of the company's business prior to issuing his term sheet or letter of intent, the representations and warranties are not intended to "screen" the company for suitability as an investment (although the disclosure of significant adverse information not previously known to the investor may scuttle the investment) but rather to provide full disclosure of the fine details of the company's operations which may be relevant in advising management with regard to the future conduct of the business.

The following list of specific representations and warranties are common in most venture capital investment agreements. Each category is prefaced by an affirmative declaration or affirmation of compliance, subject to stated exceptions which are normally appended as an exhibit.

1. *Organization and authority:* The company is properly organized, in good standing, and has legal authority to conduct its business.
2. *Corporate action:* All necessary actions under state corporate law, and the company's corporate charter and bylaws, have been taken to authorize and perform the transaction.
3. *Governmental approvals:* All consents and approvals of governmental agencies necessary to complete the transaction have been obtained. In particular, this covers compliance with federal and state securities laws.
4. *Absence of litigation:* No litigation or other proceedings exist, or are threatened, which would adversely affect the company's business or the financing transaction.
5. *Employment of key personnel:* No restrictions exist relating to employment of key personnel or use of business information, particularly as a result of prior employment of such personnel by another enterprise.
6. *Compliance with other agreements:* No violations of the company's corporate charter, bylaws, or other valid agreements exist, or will exist as a result of the financing.
7. *Ownership of properties and assets:* The company possesses sufficient ownership rights in its business assets, particularly its proprietary rights and other intangible assets, to conduct its business.
8. *Financial information:* Audited and internal unaudited financial statements have been prepared in accordance with generally accepted accounting principles and fairly present the financial position and operating results of the company. Statements as to specific categories of items, such as inventory valuation and status of accounts receivables, may be included. No adverse changes have occurred since the date of the most recent financial statements furnished.
9. *Transactions with insiders:* Disclosure is made of any direct or indirect transactions between the company and its directors, officers, and stockholders.
10. *Third-party guaranties or investments:* Absence of continuing financial involvements with third parties.
11. *Compliance with federal securities laws:* Certification that the transaction complies with federal and state securities laws, including the possibility that the transaction may be integrated with other securities sales.
12. *Disclosure:* The business plan used to seek financing is accurate and complete, and all material disclosures have been made to investors either in the business plan or in legal documents relating to the transaction.

13. *Brokerage:* Disclosure of any finder's or broker's fees or commissions payable in connection with the transaction.

14. *Capitalization:* Description of the company's authorized capitalization and status of outstanding securities, including warrants, options, and convertible securities. Any transfer restrictions, repurchase rights, or preemptive rights are also described, as well as registration rights.

D. Covenants and Undertakings of the Company

The covenants section of the investment agreement contains several affirmative and negative undertakings of the company relating to the future conduct of its affairs. Affirmative covenants are actions, positions, or results that the company promises to achieve or undertake. Negative covenants are actions, positions, or results that the company promises to avoid.

If, under the terms of the investment agreement, the board of directors is to be controlled by inside management, the covenants are frequently extensive. In an equity-oriented venture capital investment, however, where the investors will frequently control the board of directors, the covenants are often kept to a minimum. In such a situation, the affirmative covenants might merely provide that the investor will receive periodic financial information and will be represented on the board. The negative covenants might limit only the company's ability to amend its corporate charter or merge or sell its assets without the investor's consent. A venture capital firm with board control will generally rely upon this control to influence the development of a company and will not, as a rule, find it necessary to impose extensive contractual restrictions on the conduct of the business by insisting on strict affirmative and negative covenants.

Both affirmative and negative covenants may remain in effect as long as the investors hold any of the investment securities or, alternatively, may terminate upon the occurrence of certain events, such as the completion of an initial public offering, conversion of debt-oriented convertible securities into equity, or mere passage of time.

Among the customary *affirmative* covenants which are found in venture capital investment agreements are the following:

1. *Payment of taxes and claims:* The company will pay all lawful taxes, assessments, and levies upon it or its income or property before they become in default. This covenant sometimes provides that all trade debt and principal and interest on debt securities acquired by the investor will be paid when due.

2. *Property and liability insurance:* The company will maintain insurance against hazards and risks and liability to persons and property to the extent customary for companies engaged in the same or similar businesses.

3. *Maintenance of corporate existence:* The company will maintain its corporate existence and all rights, licenses, patents, copyrights, trademarks, etc. useful in its business, and will engage only in the type of business described in the business plan.

4. *Legal compliance:* The company will comply with all applicable laws and regulations in the conduct of its business.

5. *Access to premises:* The investor or his representative will generally be permitted to inspect the company's facilities, books, and records. To the extent that confidentiality of corporate business information may be compromised

by such rights of access, investors generally agree to confidentiality restrictions or to limiting access to lead or other major investors.

6. *Accounts and reports:* The company may be asked by the investor to agree to maintain a standard system of accounting in accordance with generally accepted accounting principles consistently applied, and to keep full and complete financial records.

7. *Repair and maintenance:* The company will keep all necessary equipment and property in good repair and condition, as required to permit the business to be properly conducted.

8. *Approval of budgets:* The investor will frequently require management to produce comprehensive annual budgets for approval by the investor or by the board of directors. Revisions of the budget during the year may also require advance approval.

9. *Protection of proprietary rights:* The company will agree to take all necessary steps to protect proprietary developments made in the future, including causing all key employees to sign confidentiality and proprietary rights and agreements.

10. *Compliance with key agreements:* The company will enforce its rights under key agreements, such as the stockholders agreement, and will cause future stockholders to join the agreement.

11. *Life insurance:* The investor will often require the company to maintain insurance on the lives of key officers and employees. The face amount in some cases may be as much as the purchase price of the securities, and the insurance proceeds are often payable directly to the investor, particularly if the investor holds debt securities.

12. *Board of directors:* Venture capital firms will generally seek assurances that they will be represented on the company's board of directors. The right to be represented on the board may be backed up by voting agreements with the principal stockholders. If the investor is not to be represented on the board, the company may be required to notify the investor of the time and place of board meetings and to permit the investor or his representative to attend such meetings. Frequency of board meetings and financial arrangements may also be covered.

13. *Financial and operating statements:* The company will invariably agree to provide the investor with detailed financial and operating information. The information to be provided may include annual, quarterly, and sometimes monthly reports of sales, production, shipments, profits, cash balances, receivables, payables, and backlog; all statements filed with the Securities and Exchange Commission or other agencies; notification of significant lawsuits or other legal proceedings; and any other information that the investor may need for his own voluntary or involuntary filing requirements. Particularly where an investor is acquiring debt securities or preferred stock containing extensive financial and other covenants, financial statements are required to be accompanied by a certificate from the company's chief executive or financial officer and, in the case of audited financial statements, its auditors, to the effect that the company is in compliance with all provisions of the investment agreement. The right to receive financial information is often terminated when the company goes public in order to avoid dissemination of "inside" information. Although companies generally concede the legitimate in-

terests of investors to receive business information, negotiation over the scope and form of this information may be considerable in view of the operational burden and potential liabilities it can impose upon management.

14. *Current ratio, working capital, or net worth:* These covenants normally are included only in debt financings and are agreements to maintain the current ratio, working capital, or net worth, either at a minimum amount or as specified for various time periods. They may be keyed to projections made by the company; accordingly, care should be taken by the company in preparing the business plan to project financial results and conditions which management is comfortable in undertaking to attain on a contractual basis.

15. *Use of proceeds:* The use of funds may be broadly stated in terms of the business of the company, or it may be narrowly defined with reference to a specific financing plan.

In contrast to affirmative covenants, which generally exhort the company to undertake actions which it would ordinarily choose to take in the normal course, the negative covenants contained in the investment agreement serve to limit the company from actions it otherwise might be inclined to take, unless the investors have consented in advance. Typically these negative covenants relate to matters which would affect the fundamental nature of the business in which the investment has been made (e.g., mergers and acquisitions) or would alter the balance of control between the investors and entrepreneurs reached in the investment agreement. Since the negative covenants limit the scope of managerial flexibility, they are often the subject of sharp negotiation. As suggested above, there is a trade-off between the degree of investor control of the voting power and board of directors and the strictness of the negative covenants imposed on the company. Many typical negative covenants are described below:

1. *Mergers, consolidations, and sale or purchase of assets:* Mergers, consolidations, acquisitions, and the like are generally prohibited without the investor's advance approval. Liquidation and dissolution of the company and the sale, lease, or other disposition of substantial assets without consent may also be barred. Restrictions may also be placed on the company's purchase of capital assets.

2. *Dealings with related parties:* The company will covenant that no transactions between the company and any officers, directors, or stockholders of the company shall be effected unless on an arm's-length basis and on terms no less favorable to the company than could be obtained from nonrelated persons. Approval of all transactions with affiliates by either the board or the investors may be required.

3. *Change in business:* The company will not change the nature of its business as described in its business plan.

4. *Charter amendments:* The investor may prohibit the company from amending its corporate charter or bylaws without the consent of the investor. More narrowly drawn covenants might prohibit only certain specified actions (such as a change in the capital structure) without the investor's consent.

5. *Distributions and redemptions:* The company typically agrees not to make any dividend distributions to stockholders. Dividends may be prohibited until a given date or may be limited to a fixed percentage of profits above a set amount. In addition, the company may covenant not to repurchase or redeem

any of its securities except in accordance with the terms of the securities purchased by the investor (e.g., redeemable preferred stock), employee plans (e.g., forfeiture of stock upon termination of employment), or agreements with stockholders (e.g., right of first refusal).

6. *Issuance of stock or convertible securities:* The investor may prohibit the company from issuing any securities that would result in dilution of the investor's position. This includes restrictions on the issuance of securities of the type purchased by the investor and any securities convertible into such securities at a price less than that paid by the investor. Alternatively, such an issuance could result in an improved conversion rate for the securities purchased by the investor. Frequently these covenants are included in the terms of the securities themselves.

7. *Liens and encumbrances:* The investment agreement (generally for debt-oriented securities, including redeemable preferred stock) may provide for restrictions on liens, pledges, and other encumbrances, with exceptions for such liabilities as real estate mortgages. Separate restrictions can be placed on leases of real property or equipment.

8. *Indebtedness:* The company may agree to restrictions on future indebtedness, with exceptions for institutional senior borrowings, indebtedness on personal property purchase money obligations, and trade indebtedness, up to certain limits in the ordinary course of business. Again, this provision is most typical of investments in debt-oriented securities.

9. *Investments:* Restrictions against investing in other companies may be imposed by the investor. Exceptions are made for investments in subsidiaries.

10. *Employee compensation:* The company may agree to limit employment and other personal service contracts of management or key personnel to a maximum term and a maximum amount of annual compensation.

11. *Financial covenants:* Negative financial covenants are frequently imposed upon a company in a debt-oriented investment, such as prohibiting key ratios or financial conditions from exceeding certain limits or limiting the company from incurring losses in excess of a certain amount. Semantics often determine whether a financial covenant is affirmative or negative in nature. Clear definition of financial and accounting terms is critical. In lieu of defaulting on securities, failure to comply with financial covenants may trigger adjustments in conversion ratios of securities or give rise to preferential voting or other rights for the investor.

In addition to the numerous affirmative and negative covenants described above, the venture capital investment agreement will customarily contain a number of more complex undertakings by the company, which are generally set apart in the agreement. Two of the more typical of these covenants pertain to registration rights and rights to participate in future financings. Another such provision, indemnification of the investors for breach of the investment agreement, is also discussed briefly below:

1. *Registration rights:* The right to register securities for public sale under the Securities Act of 1933 and state securities laws represents the most advantageous vehicle for a venture capital investor to achieve liquidity and realize a return on his investment. The potential of an enterprise to achieve a size conducive to a public offering is an imperative of most venture capital invest-

ments; accordingly, the right of the investor to participate in the public market for the company's securities is an area in which the venture capitalist will concede few limitations on his flexibility of action. Registration rights are intricately bound up in the complexities of federal and state securities regulation and must be thoroughly understood by the investor and his counsel. The key elements of a registration rights provision in a venture capital investment agreement generally include the following:

a. *Securities available for registration:* Registrable securities will invariably be limited to common stock, including shares issuable on conversion of other securities. After-acquired common stock may also be included. If the investor is participating in a second- or third-round financing, he must consider to what extent his registration rights will be coordinated or "pooled" with registration rights granted to investors in previous financings.

b. *"Piggyback" registration rights:* Investors will have the right to include shares in any registration which the company undertakes either for its own benefit or for the account of other holders of securities. Exceptions are generally made for registrations involving employee stock plans or acquisitions. "Piggyback" registrations will frequently be unlimited in number on the theory that no significant burden is imposed on the company by requiring it to include additional shares in a registration which it is otherwise undertaking. Except for the company's initial public offering, investors may be guaranteed a minimum participation in "piggyback" registrations.

c. *Demand registration rights:* Investors frequently obtain the right to require an issuer to register their shares upon demand and without regard to the registration of shares for the account of any other person. Demand rights assure the investor access to the public market. Theoretically, unrestricted demand registration rights enable an investor to force a company to go public; as a practical matter, demand rights are rarely, if ever, used to this end, although their presence may influence the decision of a company to go public. Because of the expense involved, demand rights may be limited in number, unless registration is available on a short-form registration statement such as Form S–3. In addition, investors may agree to limit the exercise of demand rights to the holders of a minimum specified percentage of registrable securities to avoid unduly small registrations.

d. *Marketing rights:* "Piggyback" registration rights generally contain provisions enabling the managing underwriters to cut back on a pro rata basis the number of shares to be registered by selling securityholders if, in the underwriters' opinion, such a cutback is necessary or desirable to market the public issue effectively. If securityholders other than the venture capital investors also hold registration rights, the relative marketing priorities of the various groups, including management, in the event of a cutback must be addressed.

e. *Indemnification:* Each party will agree to indemnify the other against liabilities for which it is responsible arising out of a registration. Although the extensive indemnification provisions of an underwriting agreement will frequently supersede the terms of the investment agreement, they are nevertheless important because underwriters will typically look to the company and any major selling shareholders for indemnification on a joint and several basis and will leave those parties to their own devices to allocate any liabilities among themselves.

f. *Procedural covenants:* Many registration rights provisions contain undertakings to comply with certain procedural matters involved in a registration, such as participation in the preparation of a registration statement, qualification under state securities laws, and entitlement to legal opinions and accountants' comfort letters.

g. *Availability of Rule 144:* The company will agree that once it has gone public, it will file all reports and take all other action necessary to enable the investors to sell shares in the public market under the exemption from registration contained in Rule 144 under the Securities Act of 1933.

h. *Expenses of registration:* Because of the cost involved in a registration of securities, investors will typically require the company to agree at the time of the initial investment to bear the expenses of registration, exclusive of underwriters' discounts or commissions.

2. *Rights to future financings:* Venture capitalists often insist upon a right to participate in future financings by the company. On the upside, this offers the investor an opportunity to maintain or increase his interest in the success of the enterprise; on the downside, the investor receives some protection against dilution or loss of his initial investment in the event financing must be sought under distress situations. The right to participate may include:

a. *Rights of first refusal* to assume the entire financing (each investor on a pro rata basis with other members of the investor group).

b. *Preemptive rights* to participate in the financing on a pro rata basis with all other securityholders of the company.

c. *Rights of prior negotiation* to discuss and negotiate financing opportunities with the company prior to the company making offers to others.

3. *Indemnification for breach of agreement:* Particularly in the case of start-ups, venture capital investors may require founders and/or top management to share personal responsibility for the representations and warranties made by the company in the investment agreement and to indemnify the investors for any breaches thereof. From the investors' point of view, imposing the specter of personal liability on the insiders can be an effective means of assuring complete and accurate disclosure of all material business information. Indemnification by insiders also circumvents the anomaly of investors seeking indemnification from the company out of the capital which they have invested in the business. On the other hand, personal liability for disclosure matters which may be outside his reasonable knowledge may be an unfair burden to place on the entrepreneur. For this reason, in cases where personal responsibility for representations and warranties is desired, care should be taken to focus that responsibility in areas of special knowledge of the entrepreneur (e.g., ownership of proprietary rights, compliance with prior employment arrangements, etc.) and to distinguish between the risks assumed by the company and those assumed by the individual (e.g., unqualified representations versus "best knowledge" representations). Termination of indemnification obligations often occurs after a stated period of time, usually not exceeding two years, or after the issuance of audited financial statements covering a one- or two-year period.

E. Conditions to Closing

The use of "conditions precedent to closing" in the investment agreement, or more appropriately the satisfaction of conditions at or prior to the closing, is a device used for two principal purposes. The most obvious is to guarantee certain fundamentals relating to the securities and the particular transaction, with favorable legal opinions being a classic example. In addition, conditions are used as negotiating tools to change or affect the affairs of the company. For example, a common closing condition may involve the contemporaneous execution of a bank loan agreement satisfactory to the investor or the consummation of a significant commercial transaction with a customer.

Many venture financings contemplate a simultaneous signing of the investment agreement and closing. Consequently, there is no technical need for a set of conditions designed to cover the time period between execution of the agreement and a subsequent closing. Notwithstanding a simultaneous signing and closing, the use of express conditions serves to expedite the negotiations and to assist the closing process by serving as a checklist of actions to be taken in connection with the implementation of the transaction.

Conditions that are commonly seen in the capital formation process include: opinion of counsel for the company; opinion of counsel for the investor; execution of the several ancillary agreements, including employment, noncompetition, and stock restriction agreements; elections and resignations of directors; and compliance certificates by senior management. Descriptions of certain of these ancillary agreements and documents are included in Section IV below.

Section IV. Terms of Investment Securities

A. General Considerations and Descriptions

Selection of the appropriate investment security for a specific transaction will depend upon the relative importance to the venture capitalist and the issuer of a number of factors, including the level of risk of the venture, investment objectives of the investors, capital requirements of the company, the relative interests and contributions of other securityholders, the degree to which management control by the investors is desirable, liquidity of the securities, and so on. Among the securities which are commonly used in a venture capital financing are:

Common stock.
Convertible preferred stock.
Convertible debt.
Nonconvertible preferred stock or debt coupled with common stock or common stock purchase warrants.

Generally the venture capitalists will prefer to invest in a senior security which is convertible into, or carries rights to purchase, common equity. A convertible senior security affords the investor downside protection, in terms of the opportunity to recover the investment on a priority basis through redemption, repayment, or liquidation preferences, with the upside potential of a liquid equity security traded at significantly appreciated values in the public market. Discussion of the relative merits and disadvantages of the various types of investment securities is beyond the scope of this article. Described in the following sections, however, are certain of the principal provisions of typical preferred stock and debt securities.

B.   Principal Terms of Preferred Stock

Preferred stock is the investment security most frequently involved in venture capital financings because of the flexibility it offers the company and the investor in tailoring the critical issues of the investment—principally management control and recovery/return on investment. Typically the preferred stock utilized in a venture transaction is convertible into common stock and contains redemption provisions designed to enable the investor to recoup his investment if the enterprise fails to achieve its anticipated success. Convertible preferred stock provisions should address the following major issues:

1. *Dividends:* "Plain vanilla" convertible preferred stock does not generally carry mandatory dividend rights. Preferred will, however, participate with common to the extent dividends are declared. If dividends are desired, they may be on a cumulative or noncumulative basis. Cash flow considerations will affect the ability of a start-up to pay dividends.

2. *Liquidation:* Holders of preferred stock will have a priority claim to assets of the corporation over the common stockholders in a liquidation. The liquidation preference will typically equal the original purchase price of the security plus accrued dividends. Participating preferred may also share pari passu with common stock after the liquidation preference has been distributed. Convertible preferred stock provisions usually permit the investors to elect liquidation treatment in the event of a merger or acquisition.

3. *Voting rights:* Convertible preferred stock votes with the common stock on all matters and is entitled to one vote for each share of common into which the preferred may be converted. In addition, the holders of convertible preferred stock, voting separately as a class, may have the right to veto certain corporate transactions affecting the convertible preferred stock (such as the issuance of senior securities, mergers, acquisitions, and amendment of stock terms). Other preferential voting rights may include:

    a. Class vote for election of directors.

    b. Extraordinary voting rights to elect a majority of the board of directors upon a breach of the terms of the convertible preferred stock, such as a failure to pay dividends or make mandatory redemptions or default in the performance of financial or other covenants which may be contained in the convertible preferred stock provisions or underlying investment agreement.

4. *Conversion:* Holders of convertible preferred stock may convert their shares into common stock at their discretion (except as limited by automatic conversion obligations). Conversion provisions should address the following matters:

    a. Automatic conversion upon the occurrence of certain events, principally the completion of a public offering or the attainment of specified financial goals.

    b. Mechanics of conversion.

    c. Conversion ratio, usually expressed by a formula based upon original purchase price, which initially yields a 1-for-1 conversion factor.

    d. Adjustment of conversion ratio to take into account (1) stock splits, stock dividends, consolidations, etc. and (2) "dilutive" common stock issuances, that is, sales of common stock at prices lower than those paid by the investors.

   e. Certification of adjusted conversion ratios by independent accountants.

     The nature of the antidilution adjustments can have a dramatic effect on the number of common shares issuable upon conversion. "Rachet-down" antidilution provisions apply the lowest sale price for any shares of common stock (or equivalents) as the adjusted conversion value.

     "Formula" or "weighted average" antidilution provisions adjust the conversion value by application of a weighted average formula based upon both sale price and number of common shares sold. Antidilution provisions generally carve out a predetermined pool of shares which may be issued to employees without triggering an adjustment of the conversion ratio.

5. *Redemption:* Redemption offers the investor a means of recovering his initial investment and the issuer an opportunity to eliminate the preferential rights held by the holders of the senior security. Topics to be addressed include:

   a. Optional or mandatory redemption.

   b. Stepped-up redemption price or redemption premium designed to provide investors a certain appreciated return on the investment (NB: "unreasonable redemption premium" issue under IRC Section 305).

   c. Desirability of a sinking fund.

   d. Redemption call by the company.

     It should be noted that the prospect of mandatory redemption or redemption upon call by the issuer may force the holder of convertible preferred stock to exercise his conversion privilege lest he lose the upside potential of his investment.

C. Principal Terms of Debt Securities

     The purchase of debt securities will enable the venture capitalist to receive a current return on his investment through receipt of interest payments. In the case of a convertible debt instrument, the interest rate will be below market rates because of the equity feature coupled with it. Although the terms of convertible debt may be structured to resemble preferred stock in many aspects, significant differences between the two securities do exist. First, debt securities do not carry the right to vote for the election of directors or on other stockholder matters. Accordingly, the investor's ability to influence management of the company directly is diminished and he must resort to voting agreements and proxies in order to participate in the election of directors or, alternatively, rely on indirect means of influence such as the affirmative and negative covenants contained in the investment agreement. It should further be noted that the investor's status as a creditor of the company in any bankruptcy proceedings may be affected by principles of "equitable subordination" to the extent that such equity-like control is exercised. Second, the investor's right to receive interest under a debt instrument is more secure than the right to receive dividends on a preferred stock, inasmuch as payment of dividends may be restricted by state corporate laws relating to legally available funds and by the requirement that dividends must be declared by the board of directors. Finally, although a debt security may rank prior to preferred stock in terms of a claim on corporate assets in liquidation, this advantage is at the cost of creating a weaker balance sheet, which may have adverse effects in terms of trade and commercial bank credit, even where subordination provisions are present.

The following principal issues are generally addressed in the structuring of a venture capital investment in debt securities:

1. *Interest rate:* Interest will be at a fixed rate, below market if debt is convertible or coupled with common stock or stock purchase warrants. Because of cash flow considerations of the issuer, interest payments may be deferred for a period of time.
2. *Repayment:* Repayment of principal is often scheduled in quarterly, semi-annual, or annual installments commencing four to six years into the term, or in a single payment at maturity.
3. *Optional prepayment:* The company may elect to prepay the debt, often at a premium. Since prepayment will have the effect of extinguishing any conversion rights, the right to prepay will be deferred generally to such time as initial principal installments fall due. Issuance of stock purchase warrants in lieu of conversion will avoid this problem.
4. *Conversion:* The debt instrument may be converted into common stock at a fixed price at any time. Conversion terms, including antidilution provisions, will be similar to those of convertible preferred stock.
5. *Subordination:* Debt is generally subordinated to bank and other institutional borrowings and may thus be viewed as equity by lenders. Complex subordination provisions are often required to regulate the relationships between senior lenders and subordinated noteholders in the event of defaults, insolvency, etc.
6. *Affirmative and negative covenants:* Debt instruments are tied into extensive affirmative and negative undertakings by the company, which are usually contained in the purchase agreement. In addition to standard covenants used in a venture capital financing, these may include lengthy financial covenants of the variety typical in a commercial lending transaction.
7. *Defaults:* Defaults include material breaches of representations and warranties, breach of covenants which are not remedied within a cure period, nonpayment of principal and interest on debt instrument, acceleration (cross-default) of senior debt, insolvency, and events of bankruptcy.
8. *Security:* Generally a debt instrument will be issued to a venture capitalist on an unsecured basis, although collateral is sometimes given in asset-based transactions such as leveraged buy-outs. Another common exception to the general rule is an SBIC financing, in which adequate collateral and personal guarantees are often required.

Section V. Ancillary Agreements and Documents

A. Stockholders Agreement

The stockholders agreement is designed to control the transfer and voting of the equity securities of the company so that stable ownership and management of the enterprise may be maintained for the term of the investment. This is accomplished through restrictions on the sale of stock by insiders, which have the effect of limiting the stockholder group to persons who are known quantities to the investors, and through voting agreements, which assure that the balanced composition of the board of directors will be perpetuated. The principal provisions contained in a typical stockholders agreement to achieve these results are:

1. *Right of first refusal:* Key management stockholders will grant the company and/or the investors the right to purchase their shares on the same terms as those contained in a bona fide offer from a third party. Investors participate in the right of first refusal on a pro rata basis and have oversubscription rights to acquire any offered shares which are not picked up by another investor. Rights of first refusal are generally *not* extended to the company or insiders by the investors since the existence of such terms would tend to chill any sale of an entire block of shares by the investors to a third party. Transfers of shares by way of gift to members of an insider's family or as collateral in a bona fide loan transaction are permitted, provided the transferee or pledgee also agrees to be bound by the agreement.

2. *Buy-out provisions:* Some stockholder agreements provide that the company and/or the investors will have an option to purchase the shares of any insider at fair market value upon the occurrence of certain contingencies, such as death, personal bankruptcy, or attachment of shares by legal process. Detailed procedures, usually involving one or more appraisals by disinterested persons, are provided to assure a fair valuation of the stock.

3. *Right to participate in insider sales:* Although philosophically at odds with a right of first refusal, a stockholder agreement may provide that the investors have a right to participate alongside management insiders in any sale to third parties. Although rarely exercised, this right limits the ability of management to bail out of the company leaving the investors at risk to recover their investment. Often this right of cosale is triggered only by a sale which would have the effect of transferring actual or effective voting control to a third party.

4. *Voting requirements:* All parties will generally agree to vote all shares for the election of directors in favor of specified nominees of the respective groups.

Restrictions under applicable state law need to be examined to determine the legality of stockholder agreements in any given jurisdiction, as well as to verify compliance with state procedural and substantive requirements. Unless otherwise limited by state law (10 years in Massachusetts), stockholder agreements will generally terminate upon the earlier of a public offering by the company or the expiration of a stated period of time.

B. Employee Stock Purchase Agreements

Venture capital investors typically insist that appropriate equity incentives be implemented to attract, retain, and motivate key employees. Both the entrepreneurs and investors are willing to suffer dilution of their respective equity interests (anywhere in a range from 5 percent to 15 percent of fully diluted equity) to achieve this end. The investment agreement will specify a pool of shares to be set aside for employee purchases and exempt the issuance of those shares from the various negative covenants, antidilution provisions, and preemptive rights contained in the investment agreement and the terms of the investment securities. Establishment of appropriate employee stock plans is frequently a condition of closing of the investment. Incentive objectives and tax considerations play a significant role in determining the shape of an employee equity program. Among the typical employee equity incentives are the following:

1. *Stock purchase plans,* providing for an outright sale to key employees, often at a bargain price, with the company retaining on option to repurchase the shares on a lapsing basis (generally over four or five years) if the employee terminates employment for any reason.

2. *Incentive stock options,* enabling the employee to purchase shares with advantageous tax consequences at the fair market value on the date the option was granted.

3. *Nonqualified stock options,* which may be granted in amounts which exceed the aggregate dollar limitations for incentive stock options under the Internal Revenue Code and which may have exercise prices less than fair market value and other terms not available under incentive stock options.

4. *"Junior" common stock,* which is an equity security bearing only a percentage of the voting, dividend, liquidation, and other rights of a straight common stock and which is automatically converted into common stock upon the attainment of certain specified objectives, such as revenue and profit goals. Although "junior" common stock was a popular incentive vehicle through the end of 1983, its continued use and attractiveness as a method of compensating management have been called into question by recent actions taken by the Securities and Exchange Commission and proposed to be taken by the Financial Accounting Standards Board (FASB).

In all circumstances (other than incentive stock options) consideration must be given to the application of Section 83 of the Internal Revenue Code to issuances of stock to employees. Section 83 provides that an employee is required to recognize income in respect of property (including corporate securities) transferred to him in connection with the performance of services in an amount equal to the difference between the fair value of the property and the amount paid therefor. In the case of property subject to restrictions which lapse over time (such as forfeiture restrictions or repurchase options), the income is recognized at the time the restrictions lapse. Thus, an employee who acquires stock at a low purchase price in the early years of an enterprise and whose rights to those shares "vest" as forfeiture restrictions lapse over a period of years will recognize income based on the appreciated value of those shares as each installment lapses. Section 83(b) of the Code ameliorates the harsh effect of this provision by permitting a taxpayer to elect to include the value of the transferred property in income in the year of receipt by filing a special election.

In a recent decision (*Alves et al.* v. *Commissioner,* 79 TC 864, CCH Tax Court Reports Dec. 39, 501 (1982)), the Tax Court applied Section 83 to a founding stockholder of a new company who acquired shares subject to a repurchase option granted to the company and exercisable upon his termination of employment prior to the end of a specified period. As a result of this decision, founding stockholders should consider taking the precaution of filing Section 83(b) elections when shares are initially acquired in order to prevent assessment of significant tax liabilities when those shares vest at appreciated values in later years.

C. Employee Confidentiality and Proprietary Rights Agreements

Protection and preservation of the "intellectual capital" of an enterprise are of paramount importance to the venture capital investor, especially where the portfolio company is engaged in product development activities on the leading edge of technologies. To secure the company's claim to its valuable proprietary and business rights, investors are increasingly requiring that founders and other key employees enter into confidential nondisclosure and invention agreements with the company. These agreements typically provide that the employee (1) will not disclose company trade secrets or rights to third parties or use such rights for any purpose, in each case other than in connection with the company's business; and (2) will disclose and convey to the company all inventions developed by the employee during the course of employment. Such agreements often contain acknowledgment that the individual is not bound by any obligations to a former employer which would prevent or restrict his employment with the company and that his performance of services for the company does not involve the violation of the proprietary rights of any former employer. Founding stockholders may also agree to noncompetition covenants.

D. Legal Opinion

The favorable legal opinion of company counsel generally covers the legality of the securities, compliance with state and federal securities laws, and related matters. If the company is involved in litigation, company counsel may be requested to express a position. Likewise, if patents are critical to the company's business, a favorable opinion of patent counsel may also be required. A common error is to confuse the opinion of legal counsel with due diligence. Counsel is not a surety for business or legal uncertainties; the opinion is not a substitute for factual investigation.

Appendix III: Outline of an Investment Agreement

What follows is a detailed outline of the contents of a venture investment agreement. The main sections of a typical agreement are briefly described, and many of the terms that might appear in each section are noted. However, not all of the terms listed will appear in an investment agreement. Venture capital investors select terms from among those listed (and some not listed) to best serve their needs in a particular venture investment situation. For more detail on investment agreements we recommend the papers by Gardner[1] and Stewart.[2]

1. Description of the Investment

This section of the agreement defines the basic terms of the investment. It includes descriptions of the:

a. Amount and type of investment.
b. Securities to be issued.
c. Guarantees, collateral subordination, and payment schedules associated with any notes.
d. Conditions of closing: time, place, method of payment.

When investment instruments are involved that carry warrants or debt conversion privileges, the agreement will completely describe them. This description will include the:

a. Time limits on the exercise of the warrant or conversion of the debt.
b. Price and any price changes that vary with the time of exercise.
c. Transferability of the instruments.
d. Registration rights on stock acquired by the investor.
e. Dilution resulting from exercise of warrants or debt conversion.
f. Rights and protections surviving after conversion, exercise, or redemption.

---

[1] W. F. Gardner, Jr., "Venture Capital Financing: A Lawyer's Checklist," *Business Lawyer,* January 1971, p. 997.

[2] M. D. Stewart, "Venture Capital: Semi-Industry," *Venture Capital,* Publication 44–1092 (New York: Practicing Law Institute, 1973), p. 29.

2. Preconditions to Closing

This section covers what the venture must do or what ancillary agreements and documents must be submitted to the investor before the investment can be closed. These agreements and documents may include:

a. Corporate documents; e.g., bylaws, articles of incorporation, resolutions authorizing sale of securities, tax status certificates, list of stockholders, and directors.
b. Audited financial statements.
c. Any agreements for simultaneous additional financing from another source or for lines of credit.
d. Ancillary agreements; e.g., employment contracts, stock option agreements, keyman insurance policies, stock repurchase agreements.
e. Copies of any leases or supply contracts.

3. Representations and Warranties by the Venture

This section contains legally binding statements made by the venture's officers that describe its condition on or before the closing date of the investment agreement. The venture's management will warrant:

a. That it is a duly organized corporation in good standing.
b. That its action in entering into an agreement is authorized by its directors, allowed by its bylaws and charter, legally binding upon the corporation, and not in breach of any other agreements.
c. If a private placement, that the securities being issued are exempt from registration under the Securities Act of 1933 as amended and under state securities law and that registration is not required under the Securities Exchange Act of 1934.
d. That the capitalization, shares, options, directors, and shareholders of the company are as described (either in the agreement or an exhibit).
e. That no trade secrets or patents will be used in the business that are not owned free and clear or if rights to use them have not been acquired.
f. That no conflicts of interest exist in their entering the agreement.
g. That all material facts and representations in the agreement and exhibits are true as of the date of closing (includes accuracy of business plan and financials).
h. That the venture will fulfill its part of the agreement so long as all conditions are met.
i. That any patents, trademarks, or copy rights owned and/or used by the company are as described.
j. That the principal assets and liabilities of the company are as described in attached exhibits.
k. That there are no undisclosed obligations, litigations, or agreements of the venture of a material nature not already known to all parties.
l. That any prior-year income statements and balance sheets are accurate as presented and have been audited and that there have been no adverse changes since the last audited statements.
m. That the venture is current on all tax payments and returns.

4. Representations and Warranties by the Investor

This section contains any legally binding representations made by the investor. They are much smaller in number than those made by the company. The investor may warrant:

a. If a corporation, that it is duly organized and in good standing.

b. If a corporation, that its action in entering into an agreement with the venture is authorized by its directors, allowed by its bylaws and charter, legally binding upon the corporation, and not in breach of any existing agreements.

c. If a private placement, that the stock being acquired is for investment and not with a view to or for sale in connection with any distribution.

d. The performance of his or her part of the contract if all conditions are met.

5. Affirmative Covenants

In addition to the above representations and warranties, the company in which the investor invests usually has a list of affirmative covenants with which it must comply. These could include agreeing to:

a. Pay taxes, fees, duties, and other assessments promptly.

b. File all appropriate government or agency reports.

c. Pay debt principal and interest.

d. Maintain corporate existence.

e. Maintain appropriate books of accounts and keep a specified auditing firm on retainer.

f. Allow access to these records to all directors and representatives of the investor.

g. Provide the investor with periodic income statements and balance sheets.

h. Preserve and provide for the investor's stock registration rights as described in the agreement.

i. Maintain appropriate insurance, including keyman insurance with the company named as beneficiary.

j. Maintain minimum net worth, working capital, or net assets levels.

k. Maintain the number of investor board seats prescribed in the agreement.

l. Hold the prescribed number of directors' meetings.

m. Comply with all applicable laws.

n. Maintain corporate properties in good condition.

o. Notify the investor of any events of default of the investment agreement within a prescribed period of time.

p. Use the investment proceeds substantially in accordance with a business plan that is an exhibit to the agreement.

6. Negative Covenants

These covenants define what a venture must not do, or must not do without prior investor approval; such approval not to be unreasonably withheld. A venture usually agrees not to do such things as:

a. Merge, consolidate with, acquire, or invest in any form of organization.

b. Amend or violate the venture's charter or bylaws.

c. Distribute, sell, redeem, or divide stock except as provided for in the agreement.

d. Sell, lease, or dispose of assets whose value exceeds a specified amount.
e. Purchase assets whose value exceeds a specified amount.
f. Pay dividends.
g. Violate any working capital or net worth restrictions described in the investment agreement.
h. Advance to, loan to, or invest in individuals, organizations, or firms except as described in the investment agreement.
i. Create subsidiaries.
j. Liquidate the corporation.
k. Institute bankruptcy proceedings.
l. Pay compensation to its management other than as provided for in the agreement.
m. Change the basic nature of the business for which the firm was organized.
n. Borrow money except as provided for in the agreement.
o. Dilute the investors without giving them the right of first refusal on new issues of stock.

7. Conditions of Default

This section describes those events that constitute a breach of the investment agreement if not corrected within a specified time and under which an investor can exercise specific remedies. Events that constitute default may include:

a. Failure to comply with the affirmative or negative covenants of the investment agreement.
b. Falsification of representations and warranties made in the investment agreement.
c. Insolvency or reorganization of the venture.
d. Failure to pay interest or principal due on debentures.

8. Remedies

This section describes the actions available to an investor in the event that a condition of default occurs. Remedies depend on the form an investment takes. For a common stock investment, the remedies could be:

a. Forfeiture to the investor of any stock of the venture's principals that was held in escrow.
b. The investor receiving voting control through a right to vote some or all of the stock of the venture's principals.
c. The right of the investor to "put" his stock to the company at a predetermined price.

For a debenture, the remedies might be:

a. The full amount of the note becoming due and payable on demand.
b. Forfeiture of any collateral used to secure the debt.

In the case of a preferred stock investment, the remedy can be special voting rights (e.g., the right to vote the entrepreneurs' stock) to obtain control of the board of directors.

9. Other Conditions

A number of other clauses that cover a diverse group of issues often appear in investment agreements. Some of the more common issues covered are:

a. Who will bear the costs of closing the agreement; this is often born by the company.

b. Who will bear the costs of registration of the investors' stocks; again, the investors like this to be borne by the company for the first such registration.

c. Right of first refusal for the investor on subsequent company financings.

Appendix IV: Sample Terms Sheet

BLACK BOX TECHNOLOGY, INC.
Summary of Principal Terms

Amount: $_____

Security: ____ shares of Convertible Preferred Stock ("Preferred") at a price of $____ per share ("Original Purchase Price")

Rights, Preferences, Privileges, and Restrictions of Preferred Stock:

1. *Dividend Provisions:* The Preferred Stock shall be entitled to dividends at the same rate as the Common Stock ("Common") (based on the number of shares of Common into which the Preferred is convertible on the date the dividend is declared).

2. *Liquidation Preference:* In the event of any liquidation of the Company, the Preferred will be entitled to receive in preference to the Common an amount equal to the Original Purchase Price.

3. *Redemption:* The Company will redeem the Preferred in three equal annual installments commencing six (6) years from the date of purchase by paying in cash a total amount equal to the Original Purchase Price.

4. *Conversion:* The Preferred will be convertible at any time, at the option of the holder, into shares of Common Stock of the Company at an initial conversion price equal to the Original Purchase Price. Initially, each share of Preferred is convertible into one share of Common Stock. The conversion price will be subject to adjustment as provided in paragraph 6 below.

5. *Automatic Conversion:* The Preferred will be automatically converted into Common, at the then applicable conversion price, in the event of an underwritten public offering of shares of Common at a price per share that is not less than five times the Original Purchase Price in an offering resulting in gross proceeds to the Company of not less than $10 million.

6. *Antidilution Provisions:* The conversion price of the Preferred Stock will be subject to adjustment to prevent dilution in the event that the Company is-

sues additional shares (other than the Reserved Employee Shares described under "Reserved Employee Shares" below) at a purchase price less than the applicable conversion price. The conversion price will be subject to adjustment on a weighted basis which takes into account issuances of additional shares at prices below the applicable conversion price.

7. *Voting Rights:* Except with respect to election of directors, the holder of a share of Preferred will have the right to that number of votes equal to the number of shares of Common issuable upon conversion of the Preferred at the time the record for the vote is taken. Election of directors will be as described under "Board Representation" below.

8. *Protective Provisions:* Consent of the holders of at least two thirds of the Preferred will be required for any sale by the Company of a substantial portion of its assets, any merger of the Company with another entity, each amendment of the Company's articles of incorporation, and for any action which (i) alters or changes the rights, preferences, or privileges of the Preferred materially and adversely; (ii) increases the authorized number of shares of Preferred Stock; or (iii) creates any new class of shares having preference over or being on a parity with the Preferred.

Information Rights:

The Company will timely furnish the investors with annual, quarterly and monthly financial statements. Representatives of the investors will have the right to inspect the books and records of the Company.

Registration Rights:

1. *Demand Rights:* If investors holding at least 50 percent of the Preferred (or Common issued upon conversion of the Preferred) request that the Company file a Registration Statement covering at least 20 percent of the Common issuable upon conversion of the Preferred, the Company will use its best efforts to cause such shares to be registered.

   The Company will not be obligated to effect more than two registrations (other than on Form S–3) under these demand right provisions.

2. *Registrations on Form S–3:* Holders of 10 percent or more of the Preferred (or Common issued upon conversion of the Preferred) will have the right to require the Company to file an unlimited number of Registration Statements on Form S–3 (but no more than two per year).

3. *Piggyback Registration:* The investors will be entitled to "piggyback" registration rights on all registrations of the Company.

4. *Registration Expenses:* All registration expenses (exclusive of underwriting discounts and commissions or special counsel fees of a selling shareholder) shall be borne by the Company.

Board Representation:

The Board will consist of ____ members. The holders of the Preferred will have the right to designate ____ directors; the holders of the Common (exclusive of the Investors) will have the right to designate ____ directors; and the remaining ____ directors will be unaffiliated persons elected by the Common and the Preferred voting as a single class.

Key Man Insurance:

As determined by the Board of Directors.

Preemptive Right to Purchase New Securities:

If the Company proposes to offer additional shares (other than Reserved Employee Shares or shares issued in the acquisition of another company), the Company will first offer all such shares to the investors on a pro rata basis. This preemptive right will terminate upon an underwritten public offering of shares of the Company.

Stock Restriction and Stockholders Agreements:

All present holders of Common Stock of the Company who are employees of, or consultants to, the Company will execute a Stock Restriction Agreement with the Company pursuant to which the Company will have an option to buy back at cost a portion of the shares of Common Stock held by such person in the event that such shareholder's employment with the Company is terminated prior to the expiration of 48 months from the date of employment; 25 percent of the shares will be released each year from the repurchase option based upon continued employment by the Company. In addition, the Company and the Investors will have a right of first refusal with respect to any employee's shares proposed to be resold or, alternatively, the right to participate in the sale of any such shares to a third party, which rights will terminate upon a public offering.

Reserved Employee Shares:

The Company may reserve up to _____ shares of Common Stock for issuance to employees of the Company (the "Reserved Employee Shares"). The Reserved Employee Shares will be issued from time to time under such arrangements, contracts, or plans as are recommended by management and approved by the Board.

Noncompetition, Proprietary Information, and Inventions Agreement:

Each officer and key employee of the Company designated by the investors will enter into a noncompetition, proprietary information, and inventions agreement in a form reasonably acceptable to the investors.

The Purchase Agreement:

The purchase of the Preferred will be made pursuant to a Stock Purchase Agreement drafted by counsel to the Investors and reasonably acceptable to the Company and the Investors, which agreement shall contain, among other things, appropriate representations and warranties of the Company, covenants of the Company reflecting the provisions set forth herein, and appropriate conditions of closing.

Expenses:

The Company will bear the legal fees and other out-of-pocket expenses of the investors with respect to the transaction.

Appendix V: Sample Vesting and Stock Restriction Agreement

Agreement, dated as of September 30, 1983, between Venture x, a Massachusetts corporation (the "Company"), and Investor y (the "Stockholder").

Whereas, the Company has previously sold shares of its common stock ("Common Stock") to the Stockholder; and

Whereas, the Company is amending its Articles of Organization to remove certain provisions set forth therein which restrict the transfer of its Common Stock; and

Whereas, the parties desire to retain and impose certain restrictions on the shares of Common Stock presently owned by the Stockholders and on any new, additional, or different shares of the capital stock of the Company which may at any time be issued to the Stockholder as a result of a recapitalization, stock dividend, split-up, combination, or exchange of or on the Common Stock of the Company (collectively, all such Common Stock and any other such shares being referred to as "Shares");

Now, therefore, in consideration of the covenants and agreements set forth herein, and the mutual benefits which the parties anticipate from the performance thereof, the parties agree as follows.

1. Repurchase of Shares on Termination of Employment Relationship. Subject to the lapse provisions hereinafter set forth, if at any time the Stockholder's employment or consulting relationship with the Company is terminated for any reason whatsoever, including death or disability, the Company shall have the right (but not the obligation) to require the Stockholder to sell to the Company all or any part of the Shares at the cash price paid by the Stockholder therefor.

The Company's right of repurchase set forth in this Section 3 to purchase part or all of the Shares shall lapse as follows:

a. As to 100 percent of the Shares on November 30, 1983, if at least $180,000 in funding has not been received by the Company on or before such date.

b. If such funding has been received on or before such date, at the rate of 25 percent of such Shares each year for four years effective annually on the anniversary of this agreement.

The Company may exercise its right of repurchase of such Shares by giving written notice to the Stockholder or to his estate, personal representative, or beneficiary ("Estate") at any time within 90 days of the termination of the Stockholder's employment with the Company, specifying the number of Shares to be sold to the Company. Such notice shall be effective only as to Shares as to which the Company's repurchase rights have not lapsed as of the date of such notice. Once such notice has been given, no further lapsing of such right of repurchase shall occur.

2. Procedure for Sale of Shares. In any notice given by the Company pursuant to Section 1 hereof, the Company shall specify a closing date for the repurchase transaction described therein. At the closing, the repurchase price shall be payable by the Company's check against receipt of certificates representing all Shares so repurchased. Upon the date of any such notice from the Company to the Stockholder or his Estate, the interest of the Stockholder in the Shares specified in the notice for repurchase shall automatically terminate, except for the Stockholder's right to receive payment from the Company for such Shares.

3. Right of First Refusal. If the Stockholder desires to sell all or any part of any Shares as to which the repurchase rights of the Company under Section 1 hereof have lapsed and an offeror ("the Offeror") has made an offer therefor, which offer the Stockholder desires to accept, the Stockholder desires to accept, the Stockholder shall: (i) obtain in writing an irrevocable and unconditional bona fide offer (the "Bona Fide Offer") for the purchase thereof from the Offeror; and (ii) give written notice (the "Option Notice") to the Company setting forth his desire to sell such Shares, which Option Notice shall be accompanied by a photocopy of the original executed Bona Fide Offer and shall set forth at least the name and address of the Offeror and the price and terms of the Bona Fide Offer. Upon receipt of the Option Notice, the Company shall have an option to purchase any or all of such Shares specified in the Option Notice, such option to be exercisable by giving, within 30 days after receipt of the Option Notice, a written counternotice to the Stockholder. If the Company elects to purchase any or all of such Shares, it shall be obligated to purchase, and the Stockholder shall be obligated to sell to the Company, such Shares at the price and terms indicated in the Bona Fide Offer within 60 days from the date of receipt by the Company of the Option Notice.

The Stockholder may sell, pursuant to the terms of the Bona Fide Offer, any or all of such Shares not purchased by the Company for 30 days after expiration of the Option Notice, or for 30 days following a failure by the Company to purchase such Shares within 60 days of giving its counternotice of an intent to purchase such Shares; provided, however, that the Stockholder shall not sell such Shares to the Offeror if the Offeror is a competitor of the Company and the Company gives written notice to the Stockholder within 30 days of its receipt of the Option Notice stating that the Stockholder shall not sell his Shares to the Offeror; and provided, further, that prior to the sale of such Shares to the Offeror, the Offeror shall execute an agreement with the Company pursuant to which the Offeror agrees not to become a competitor of the Company and further agrees to be subject to the restrictions set forth in this Agreement. If any or all of such Shares are not sold pursuant to a Bona Fide Offer within the times permitted above, the unsold Shares shall remain subject to the terms of this Agreement.

The refusal rights of the Company set forth in Section 3 of this Agreement shall remain in effect until a distribution, if ever, to the public of shares of Common Stock for an aggregate public offering price of at least $3 million or more pursuant to a registration statement filed under the Securities Act of 1933, or a successor statute, at which time this Agreement will automatically expire.

Because the Shares cannot be readily purchased or sold in the open market, and for other reasons, the Stockholder and the Company acknowledge that the parties will be irreparably damaged in the event that this Agreement is not specifically enforced. Upon a breach or threatened breach of the terms, covenants, and/or conditions of this Agreement by any of the parties hereto, the other party shall, in addition to all other remedies, be entitled to a temporary or permanent injunction, without showing any actual damage, and/or a decree for specific performance, in accordance with the provisions hereof.

4. Adjustments. If there shall be any change in the Common Stock of the Company through merger, consolidation, reorganization, recapitalization, stock dividend, split-up, combination, or exchange of shares, or the like, all of the terms and provisions of this Agreement shall apply to any new, additional, or different shares or securities issued with respect to the Shares as a result of such event, and the repurchase price and the number of shares or other securities that may be repurchased under this Agreement shall be appropriately adjusted by the Board of Directors of the Company, whose determination shall be conclusive.

5. Restrictions on Transfer. The Stockholder agrees during the term of this Agreement that he will not sell, assign, transfer, pledge, hypothecate, mortgage, or otherwise encumber or dispose of, by gift or otherwise (except to the Company), all or any of the Shares now or hereafter owned by him except as permitted by this Agreement.

The Company may place a legend on any stock certificate representing any of the Shares reflecting the restrictions on transfer and the Company's right of repurchase set forth herein and may make an appropriate notation on its stock records with respect to the same.

6. Waiver of Restrictions. The Company may at any time waive any restriction imposed by any Section of this Agreement with respect to all or any portion of any of the Shares.

7. No Obligation as to Employment. The Company is not by reason of this Agreement obligated to start or continue the Stockholder in any employment or consulting capacity.

8. Successors and Assigns. This Agreement shall be binding on and inure to the benefit of the Company's successors and assigns and the Stockholder's transferees of the Shares, heirs, executors, administrators, legal representatives, and assigns. Without limiting the foregoing, the Company is specifically permitted to assign its repurchase rights under Sections 1, 2, and 3 hereof.

9. Notices. All notices and other communications provided for or contemplated by this Agreement shall be delivered by hand or sent by certified mail, return receipt requested, addressed as follows:

If to the Company:

If to the Stockholder: At his address set forth below

or to such other address as the addressee may specify by written notice pursuant to this Section 10. Notices or communications sent by mail shall be deemed to have been given on the date of mailing. In the event of the Stockholder's death or incapacity, any notice or communication from the Company may, at the Company's option, be addressed either to the Stockholder at his last address specified pursuant to this Section 10 or to the Stockholder's Estate.

10. Governing Law.   This Agreement shall be governed by and construed in accordance with the laws of the Commonwealth of Massachusetts.

11. Amendments; Waivers.   Changes, amendments, or modifications in or additions to or waivers of any provision under or of this Agreement may be made only by a written instrument executed by the parties hereto. Any waiver of any provision of this Agreement shall not excuse compliance with any other provision of this Agreement. Notwithstanding the foregoing, no course of dealing or delay on the part of either party in exercising any right shall operate as a waiver thereof or otherwise prejudice the rights of such holder.

The Stockholder acknowledges that the issuance of the Shares to the Stockholder hereunder satisfies and discharges in full any previous understanding between the Company and the Stockholder regarding the issuance of the Company's stock or option rights with respect thereto, and the Stockholder waives any preemptive rights he has to purchase any capital stock of the Company.

12. Captions.   Captions are for convenience only and shall not be deemed to be a part of this Agreement.

In witness whereof, the undersigned have caused this Agreement to be executed as an instrument under seal as of the day and year first above written.

Appendix VI: Dun & Bradstreet: Industry Norms and Key Business Ratios

Contents

Source: Dun & Bradstreet, 1983 Edition. Reprinted with permission.

Background

The Library Edition, *Industry Norms and Key Business Ratios,* hereafter referred to as *Industry Norms,* is specifically produced for libraries only as a reference tool. This book is made possible through the over 1 million financial statements in the Dun's Financial Profiles computerized database. This file consists of U.S. corporations, partnerships, and proprietorships, both public and privately owned, in all size ranges, and includes over 800 different lines of business as defined by the U.S. Standard Industrial Classification (SIC) code numbers. Our data are collected weekly, maintained daily, and constantly edited and updated by the Dun's Financial Profiles Department. All of these factors combine to make this financial information unequaled anywhere for scope and timeliness.[1]

It should be noted that only general data are supplied in the Library Edition; however, for more detailed asset/geographical breakdowns of these data, a set of industry norm books are also published by Dun & Bradstreet for the corporate marketplace in the following five industry volumes:

1. *Agriculture/Mining/Construction/Transportation/Communication/Utilities*
2. *Manufacturing*
3. *Wholesaling*
4. *Retailing*
5. *Banking/Finance/Insurance/Real Estate/Services*

All five segments are available in three different formats (for a total of 15 books). The three formats are as follows:

1. *Industry Norms* for last three years ("Full File").
2. *Industry Norms* for the most recent year ("Partial file").
3. *Key Business Ratios* (only) for the most recent year.

Note that the *Industry Norms* books contain "typical" balance sheets and income statements, and "common-size" financial figures, as well as key business ratios. The *Key Business Ratios* books contain 14 indicators of performance.

Industry Norm Format

At the top of each industry norm will be identifying information: SIC code number and short title. Beside the year date, in parentheses, is the number of companies in the sample. The "typical" balance sheet figures are in the first column and the "common-size" balance sheet figures are in the second. The respective income statements begin with the item "Net Sales," and the respective key business ratios begin with the item "Ratios." The latter are further broken down, or refined, into the median and the upper quartile and lower quartile.

The Common-Size Financial Statement

The common-size balance sheet and income statement present each item of the financial statement as a percentage of its respective aggregate total. Common-size percentages are computed for all statement items of all the individual companies used in the industry sample. An average for each statement item is then determined and presented as the industry norm.

---

[1]To provide the most current information available, fiscal years July 1–June 30 were utilized to calculate the Norms.

This enables the analyst to examine the current composition of assets, liabilities, and sales of a particular industry.

The Typical Financial Statement

The typical balance sheet figures are the result of translating the common-size percentages into dollar figures. They permit, for example, a quick check of the relative size of assets and liabilities between one's own company and that company's own line of business.

After the common-size percentages have been computed for the particular sample, the actual financial statements are then sequenced by both total *assets* and total *sales,* with the median, or midpoint, figure in both these groups serving as the "typical" amount. We then compute the typical balance sheet and income statement dollar figures by multiplying the common-size percentages for each statement item by their respective total amounts.

(For example, if the median total assets for an SIC category are $669,599, and the common-size figure for cash is 9.2 percent, then by multiplying the two we derive a cash figure of $61,603 for the typical balance sheet.)

Key Business Ratios

The 14 key business ratios are broken down into median figures, with upper and lower quartiles, giving the analyst an even more refined set of figures to work with. These ratios cover all those critical areas of business performance, with indicators of solvency, efficiency, and profitability. They provide a profound and well-documented insight into all aspects for everyone interested in the financial workings of business—business executives and managers, credit executives, bankers, lenders, investors, academicians, students.

In the ratio tables appearing in this book, the figures are broken down into the median—which is the midpoint of all companies in the sample—and the upper quartile and lower quartile—which are midpoints of the upper and lower halves.

Upper-quartile figures are not always the highest numerical value, nor are lower-quartile figures always the lowest numerical value. The quartile listings reflect judgmental ranking; thus, the upper quartile represents the best condition in any given ratio and is not necessarily the highest numerical value. (For example, see the items Total Liabilities-to-Net Worth or Collection Period, where a lower numerical value represents a better condition.)

Each of the 14 ratios is calculated individually for every concern in the sample. These individual figures are then sequenced for each ratio according to condition (best to worst), and the figure that falls in the middle of this series becomes the median (or midpoint) for that ratio in that line of business. The figure halfway between the median and the best condition of the series becomes the upper quartile; and the number halfway between the median and the least favorable condition of the series is the lower quartile.

In a statistical sense, each median is considered the *typical* ratio figure for a concern in a given category.

Appendix VII: Summary of Federal and State Start-Up Requirements

If you are starting a venture, the chances are that you know you have to file something somewhere, but we are willing to bet that you have *no idea* of how much potential paperwork may lie ahead. Depending on the complexity of the situation, you may need to hire a lawyer or an accountant; however, there are also state and federal agencies that, for free, can assist you in routine filings.

To give you a sense of what lies ahead, we reproduce two summary sheets:

Do I Have to Register My Business?

Taxes and Insurance

Do I Have to Register My Business?

What kinds of registration you have to file, what kinds of records you have to keep, and what kinds of taxes you have to pay depend to a large extent on whether your business is going to operate as a single proprietorship, a general partnership, a limited partnership, an ordinary corporation, or a Subchapter S corporation. That is why you probably want to consult a lawyer and an accountant before you decide on your form of business organization.

If your business is going to be a single proprietor–owned business under your own name, you need not be bothered with registration.

If your business is going to be a single proprietorship under some other name (e.g., Quality Plumbing), you have to register with the town or city in which you operate. This is what is commonly known as a "DBA" (Doing Business As).

If your business is going to be a general partnership, you will have to register with the town or city in which you will operate.

If your business is going to have any limited partners, you will have to register with the secretary of state's office in the state capital.

If your business is going to be a corporation, you have to file corporation papers with the secretary of state's office in the state capital.

You need to register with the U.S. Internal Revenue Service and get an employer's ID number if your business is going to be a partnership or a corporation, regardless of whether you are planning to have employees, *and* if your business is going to be a single proprietorship with employees.

You will need a number from the state department of revenue to collect sales taxes or be exempted from paying sales taxes, if your state has a sales tax.

You should also check with the local city/town hall and the state division of registration to see whether you need a license for the line of business you plan to be in.

Taxes and Insurance

Taxes

Below is a list of business taxes that you should be concerned about, although some of them might not apply to your particular business. The list does not include federal and state income taxes that you withhold from employees and forward to the government.

Social security taxes
Federal unemployment tax
Federal corporation income tax
Federal highway use tax
State sales tax
State unemployment tax
State minimum corporate tax
State meals tax
State excise tax
Local property tax

Insurance

Below is a list of insurance coverages that you might consider. They are listed in their order of importance:

Workers' compensation—mandatory
Automobile insurance—mandatory
Liability insurance—essential
Fire insurance—essential
Business interruption insurance—desirable
Crime insurance—desirable
Group life insurance for you and your employees
Group health insurance for you and your employees
Disability insurance for you and your employees
Key man insurance
Fidelity bond

Consult a highly recommended underwriter for your insurance coverage.

A booklet called *Insurance Checklist for Small Businesses* (no. 148) is available free from the U.S. Small Business Administration by calling a toll-free number 1-800-433-7212.

Appendix VIII: Solution to "Creative Squares"

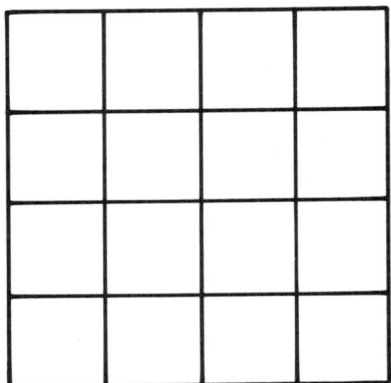

16	single squares
1	large square
4	corners, 2×2
4	corners, 3×3
4	middle, 2×2
1	center, 2×2
30	Total

Annotated Bibliography*

GENERAL BACKGROUND AND REFERENCE

The Encyclopedia of Small Business Resources, by David E. Gumpert and Jeffry A. Timmons (New York: Harper & Row, 1984). Published in hard cover by Doubleday in 1982 as *The Insider's Guide to Small Business Resources.*

    A topic-by-topic listing of sources for information, consulting help, and capital for new and small enterprise. "This is a competent and comprehensive guide in a field in which information is scattered and hard to come by" (Forbes).

Encyclopedia of Entrepreneurship, ed. C. Kent, D. Sexton, and K. H. Vesper (Englewood Cliffs, N.J.: Prentice-Hall, 1982).

    A fine collection of research articles by the leading academicians on many aspects of the entrepreneurial process: the entrepreneur, the venture, the environment, the history, the nonacademic literature, and suggestions for further research.

Entrepreneurship for the Eighties, by Gordon Baty (Englewood Cliffs, N.J.: Prentice-Hall, 1981).

    A breezy, practical walk-through of starting a new venture by someone who has done it.

Entrepreneurship: Text, Cases, and Notes, by Robert Ronstadt (Dover, Mass.: Lord Publishing, 1984).

    This text was designed for classroom use, but potential and practicing entrepreneurs can find much of interest here. The text takes a career perspective on entrepreneurship and includes two useful chapters on how to make quantitative assessments and how to deal with qualitative issues.

Frontiers of Entrepreneurship Research: 1981, 1982, 1983, 1984, 1985, ed. J. A. Hornaday, J. A. Timmons, F. Tarpley, and K. H. Vesper (Babson Park, Mass.: Babson College).

*Portions of the Bibliography are adapted from *The Encyclopedia of Small Business Resources,* by David E. Gumpert and Jeffry A. Timmons (New York: Harper & Row, 1984).

These five volumes include the complete proceedings of five annual conferences on entrepreneurship research. The data-based papers cover every aspect of the venture creation process. The authors are from academia, government, and the private sector, both in this country and abroad. These documents are the most comprehensive existing compendium of research into entrepreneurship.

Growing Concerns, edited by David E. Gumpert (New York: John Wiley & Sons, 1984).

This is a compendium of articles about emerging growth ventures that have appeared in the *Harvard Business Review.*

New Business Ventures and the Entrepreneur, by Howard H. Stevenson, Michael J. Roberts, and H. Irving Grousbeck (Homewood, Ill.: Richard D. Irwin, 1985).

This book, an update and revision of Patrick Liles's 1974 publication bearing the same title, contains cases and technical notes on specific aspects of venture creation.

Trials and Rewards of the Entrepreneur, articles reprinted from the *Harvard Business Review* (Harvard College, 1984).

These articles, written between 1964 and 1982, deal with various aspects of the merging, growing, and maturing venture. It is nice to have them all under the same cover.

EDUCATION AND TRAINING SOURCES

A. For Start-Ups

Entrepreneurship and Venture Management, by Clifford M. Baumback and J. R. Mancuso (Englewood Cliffs, N.J.: Prentice-Hall, 1975).

A good book of readings on starting and operating a small business.

New Venture Strategies, by Karl Vesper (Englewood Cliffs, N.J.: Prentice-Hall, 1980).

Informative discussion of start-up approaches that have worked for others. Liberal use of actual examples and anecdotes makes it readable and worthwhile. Vesper is one of the leading gurus of entrepreneurship.

B. For Existing Small Businesses

U.S. Small Business Administration
U.S. Small Business Administration
1441 L Street, N.W.
Washington, D.C. 20416

SBA has about 300 publications covering all aspects of small business management for a wide range of businesses. These publications present facts, figures, and techniques in readable, nontechnical form. Some of the best-sellers include:

Management Training. Excellent summary of SBA's publications and materials.
Management Aids for Small Manufacturers.
Small Marketers Aids. Suggestions, checklists, guidelines for small retail, wholesale, and service firms.

Small Business Management Series (35 vols.). Covers various businesses and problems.

Starting and Managing Series. Covers various businesses.

Managing for Profits. A pragmatic, how-to guide.

Buying and Selling a Small Business.

Protecting the Small Business Cash Flow Lifeline (Office of Advocacy, January 1980). Excellent discussion of 55 practices frequently used to cope with tight money conditions and a weak economy.

Non-SBA books for existing small buinesses include the following:

How to Organize and Operate a Small Business, 6th ed., by Clifford M. Baumback and Kenneth Lawyer (Englewood Cliffs, N.J.: Prentice-Hall, 1979).

Probably the leading college text on the subject.

Small Business Management Fundamentals, 2d ed., by Dan Steinhoff (New York: McGraw-Hill, 1978).

A good nuts-and-bolts textbook.

Small Business Reporter (San Francisco, CA: Bank of America).

An excellent collection of reports on starting and managing specific types of businesses and on the problems of such businesses.

CONSULTANTS AND MANAGEMENT ASSISTANCE

Four major associations and publications provide information and directories on management consultants:

Institute of Management Consultants
19 West 44th Street
New York, New York 10036
(212) 921-2885

Consultants News
Templeton Road
Fitzwilliam, New Hampshire 03447
(603) 585-2200

Association of Management Consultants
331 Madison Avenue
New York, New York 10017
(212) 687-2825

Association of Consulting Management Engineers, Inc.
230 Park Avenue
New York, New York 10017
(212) 697-9693

Consulting: A Complete Guide to a Profitable Career, by Robert E. Kelley (New York: Charles Scribner's Sons, 1981).

Kelley is widely recognized in academic circles as an expert on consulting. He is also a fine writer.

"How to Get a Good Consultant," *Harvard Business Review,* November–December 1977.

FEDERAL GOVERNMENT FINANCING SOURCES

Catalog of Federal Domestic Assistance. Issued by the Office of Management and Budget; available from the Superintendent of Documents, U.S. Government Printing Office, Washington, D.C. 20402; $20; published annually.

This approximately 1,000-page catalog is an exceptional document for the entrepreneur who wants to explore every possible source of federal assistance. It lists and briefly describes each and every federal loan, grant, training, and assistance program. Included within each program description are vital statistics, such as the total amount of funds available, expected future funds, the number of grants or loans made, and where to get further information. The one drawback to the volume is that it requires some patience to use, because business-related program information is mixed in with education, defense, and social welfare program information.

Business Services and Information, The Guide to the Federal Government, by Management Information Exchange (New York: John Wiley & Sons, 1979).

This 300-page book is a directory of federal services and information of specific interest to businesses of all sizes.

Small Business Guide to Government. Issued by and available from U.S. Small Business Administration, Office of Advocacy, 1441 L Street, N.W., Washington, D.C. 20416; free.

This 72-page booklet lists the names, addresses, and telephone numbers of government agencies that are of particular interest to small business owners. It provides a similar listing for small business trade groups.

Business Loans: A Guide to Money Sources and How to Approach Them Successfully, by Rick Stephan Hayes (New York: CBI Publishing, 1980).

This book about small business financing devotes some 60 pages to describing and advising about government loan programs, federal, state, and local. It also devotes more than 200 pages to the mechanics of preparing loan proposals. Much of the material on government loans reads as though it came straight from government manuals and has become outdated with the Reagan administration cutbacks, but the book contains some useful information on agency attitudes and approaches.

How to Finance Your Small Business with Government Money: SBA Loans, by Rick Stephan Hayes and John Cotton Howell (New York: John Wiley & Sons; 1980).

The first 24 pages of this 165-page book are devoted to explaining the various SBA lending programs. The remainder of the book is purportedly a guide to preparing SBA loan applications, but in reality it is a guide to preparing a loan proposal for any number of potential lenders. It instructs readers on putting together market surveys, pro forma balance sheets, cash flow statements, and other basic financial information required by any lender.

STATE AND LOCAL GOVERNMENT ASSISTANCE

Sourceguide for Borrowing Capital, by Leonard E. Smollen, Mark Rollinson, and Stanley M. Rubel (Wellesley Hills, Mass.: Capital Publishing, 1977).

This book contains two quite useful chapters on state financing sources. One chapter, by the late Stanley M. Rubel, is a description and listing of business development corporations and other organizations. A second chapter, by Mark Rollinson, examines in detail revenue bond programs in each state. Both chapters also contain useful advice about exploiting state financing sources. The book's only real weakness is that it is beginning to become somewhat outdated as new state programs are added and others are changed.

COMMERCIAL FINANCE

The Small Business Guide to Borrowing Money, by Richard L. Rubin and Philip Goldberg (New York: McGraw-Hill, 1980).

Conceptually similar to the Hayes book, though a little shorter and with fewer sample forms. Includes selected listings of venture capital firms and SBICs. Good discussion of how to work with different sources.

Financing the Growing Small Business, by Thomas J. Martin (New York: Holt, Rinehart & Winston, 1980).

An excellent book on financing the small firm. It contains many practical examples, guidelines, and suggestions. Also includes a glossary, valuation guides, and present value tables.

VENTURE CAPITAL

Venture Economics
16 Laurel Avenue, P.O. Box 348
Wellesley Hills, Massachusetts 02181
(617) 431-8100

Capital Publishing Corporation has long been recognized as the most authoritative source of information on the venture capital industry, with its monthly *Venture Capital Journal,* reference books on business development, and seminars for entrepreneurs and investors. Capital Publishing has also recently developed an information services, research, and consulting division called Venture Economics, which uses a proprietary database built up over the past 20 years. Venture Economics clients are generally investors who are looking at industry trends, but entrepreneurs should find the *Journal* and the book *Guide to Venture Capital Sources* extremely valuable.

Pratt's Guide to Venture Capital Sources, 9th ed., ed. Stanley E. Pratt (1985).

Contains articles written by experts on such subjects as business plan preparation techniques, guidelines for working with venture capitalists, raising and using venture capital, and going public. It also contains information on more than 700 venture capital companies and more than 60 small business underwriters.

ASSISTANCE FOR MINORITY BUSINESSES

Black Enterprise
Earl G. Graves Publishing Company
295 Madison Avenue
New York, New York 10017
(212) 889-8820

Black Enterprise, published monthly, offers the most comprehensive and entertaining coverage of minority business of any publication. It provides updates of developments in government assistance to minority business, along with profiles of successful black entrepreneurs. It also includes articles, similar to those in *Ebony* magazine, on black lifestyles and neighborhoods. The annual subscription rate is $10.

National Minority Business Campaign
1201 12th Avenue N.
Minneapolis, Minnesota 55411

This nonprofit organization publishes three directories and booklets on an annual or semiannual basis. These are:

Try Us: National Minority Business Directory (known simply as *Try Us*)

Guide to Obtaining Minority Business Directories (known simply as *Guide*)

Purchasing People in Major Corporations (known simply as *Purchasing People*)

Try Us lists 4,300 minority businesses that have at least regional sales, with a brief description of each company's products or services. Minority firms are listed without charge. The directory costs $14.

Guide lists by state 200 organizations that have compiled minority firm listings in their areas. It costs $3.

Purchasing People lists purchasing officials and minority vendor program coordinators of the 750 largest companies in the country. It costs $4.

ASSISTANCE FOR WOMEN

Superintendent of Documents
U.S. Government Printing Office
Washington, D.C. 20402

A Directory of Federal Government Business Assistance Programs for Women; free.

This guide was put together by several federal agencies.

The Guide to the U.S. Department of Commerce for Women Business Owners; $2.75.

Describes Department of Commerce efforts to aid women entrepreneurs just starting out and already operating businesses.

Women and the Small Business Administration and *Women's Handbook: How the SBA Can Help You Go into Business.*

Both publications, which describe SBA programs of potential use for women entrepreneurs, are available free from local SBA offices or the central SBA office:

U.S. Small Business Administration
Office of Women's Business Enterprise
U.S. Small Business Administration
1441 L Street, N.W.
Washington, D.C. 20416

The Women's Guide to Starting a Business, by Claudia Jessup and Genie Hipps, rev. ed. (New York: Holt, Rinehart & Winston, 1979).

This book offers advice on starting and operating small businesses, with chapters on evaluating business ideas, financing, advertising, accounting, and marketing. It also includes interviews with 30 entrepreneurs, along with a bibliography and an information source list.

Women and the Business Game: Strategies for Successful Ownership, by Charlotte Taylor (New York: Cornerstone Library, 1980).

A thoughtful and clearly written guide to starting and operating a small business. The title is misleading, though, since the book's advice is mainly the sort addressed to entrepreneurs in general by various other guides to starting small businesses. At the end the book lists information sources of particular interest to women entrepreneurs.

The New Entrepreneurs: Women Working from Home, by Terri P. Tepper and Nona Dawe Tepper (New York: Universe Books, 1980).

This book essentially consists of 40 profiles of women who started businesses at home, with their own accounts of how they learned to operate their businesses and the obstacles they encountered. Among the women profiled are a shoemaker, an antique dealer, a pastry chef, and craft specialists.

The Entrepreneurial Woman: How She Thinks and Copes: How She Starts and Succeeds in Her Own Business, by Sandra Winston (New York: Newsweek Books, 1979).

This book also consists mostly of case histories of women who have started small enterprises. *Inc.* magazine in its September 1979 issue was critical of the book for including "an endless series of self-help checklists" and for being "condescending" to readers.

Women's Networks: The Complete Guide to Getting a Better Job: Advancing Your Career and Feeling Great as a Woman through Networking, by Carol Kleiman (New York: Lippincott & Crowell, 1980).

This book offers an overview of the network concept together with advice on setting up and using networks of different types. It also lists women's organizations around the country that promote the network concept.

FRANCHISING

For Prospective and Operating Franchisees

Franchise Opportunities Handbook, U.S. Department of Commerce. Available from Superintendent of Documents, U.S. Government Printing Office, Washington, D.C. 20402; $6.50.

This annual survey of about 900 franchisors probably provides more extensive information on the franchises it covers than any other publication. Information on each franchise includes number of outlets, length of time in business, capital needed for starting a franchise, financing assistance available from the franchisor, and training and managerial assistance available from the franchisor.

Your Fortune in Franchises, by Richard P. Finn (Chicago: Contemporary Books, 1979).

Finn's book is a worthwhile introductory text for prospective franchisees. It explains such things as how to investigate opportunities, financial elements to consider, franchisor rights, site selection, training, promotion, financial management, and special opportunities for minority and female franchisees. Among the several hundred franchisors listed in the book are detailed appraisals of the six best franchising opportunities; there are also examples of franchises in each business category.

The Franchise Annual Handbook and Directory, edited by Edward L. Dixon (Lewiston, N.Y.: Info Press).

This sourcebook lists about 2,000 American and Canadian franchises in each annual edition, as well as general information and advice for potential franchisees. Though it has more listings, it provides less information than does *Franchise Opportunities Handbook.*

IFA Membership Directory and *Investigate before Investing: Guidance for Prospective Franchisees* (Washington, D.C.: International Franchise Association); $5 for both.

The *Directory* lists all IFA members, along with the number of franchises belonging to each, length of time in business, and investment required for enfranchisement. *Investigate before Investing* is a booklet that explains how to evaluate franchising opportunities.

Franchise Index/Profile, the U.S. Small Business Administration. Available from Superintendent of Documents, U.S. Government Printing Office, Washington, D.C. 20402; $2.

This book provides guidance on the pros and cons of franchising and on evaluating individual franchisors.

Franchising and Business Opportunities: Rules and Guides, Franchise and Business Opportunities Program, Federal Trade Commission, Washington, D.C. 20580; free.

This booklet explains the FTC's disclosure rules in the layperson's terms.

1980 Directory of Franchising Organizations (New York: Pilot Books, 1980).

This book contains a listing of only about 100 franchisors, with a one- or two-line description and oversimplified investment figures for each. It also has a superficial three-page discussion of franchising and a nine-point evaluation checklist. Overall, it contains the least amount of useful information of all the sources listed here.

For Prospective and Operating Franchisors

Franchising in the Economy, U.S. Department of Commerce. Available from Superintendent of Documents, U.S. Government Printing Office, Washington, D.C. 20402; $4.75.

Published annually, this book is mainly a statistical compilation of the influence of franchises in the American economy. It also provides information on foreign franchise markets and general advice for the franchisor on approaching different countries as potential franchise markets.

FTC Franchising Rule: The IFA Compliance Kit, by Carl E. Zwisler III and Andrew A. Caffey (Washington, D.C.: International Franchise Association, 1979); $40 to members, $80 to nonmembers.

This book, which comes in a three-ring binder, contains a history and analysis of the Federal Trade Commission franchising disclosure rule so as to enable franchisors to comply with it. The book also provides an outline of state disclosure requirements.

How to Organize a Franchise Advisory Council (Washington, D.C.: International Franchise Association, 1979); $5 to members, $10 to nonmembers.

This book provides detailed advice and directions to franchisors on how to help set up trade associations of franchisees to aid in communication and cooperation among franchisees and between franchisors and franchisees.

The Franchise Option, by DeBanks M. Henward III and William Ginalski (Phoenix, Ariz.: Franchise Group Publishers, 1980).

This book provides advice on franchising businesses, with a view toward planning and implementing franchising systems.

Franchising: Proven Techniques for Rapid Company Expansion and Market Dominance, by David Seltz (New York: McGraw-Hill, 1980).

This book discusses how to go about franchising a business. It also describes other types of business expansion techniques.

Franchising World, the International Franchise Association; $60 per year.

This monthly publication provides information on developing franchising trends, along with detailed information on IFA member public relations and advertising programs. It also includes updates on legal issues and industry profiles.

Continental Franchise Review, National Research Publications, Inc., 720 South Colorado Boulevard, Denver, Colorado 80222; $105 per year.

This newsletter is published twice monthly and provides an analysis of the existing franchising situation and climate.

For Prospective and Operating Franchisees and Franchisors

Franchising Today, Franchise Technologies, 1201 San Luis Obispo Avenue, Hayward, California 94544; ϕ18 per year.

This magazine comes out semimonthly and features profiles of successful franchisors and franchisees. The magazine reports on legal developments, international franchising, and new technologies. It also offers advice to both prospective franchisees and franchisors on getting started in their respective endeavors.

GOVERNMENT PROCUREMENT

The $100 Billion Market: How to Do Business with the U.S. Government, by Herman Holtz (New York: AMACOM, 1980).

Offers a good overview of the federal procurement process. The writer's informal, breezy style makes for easy reading. His approach is hardheaded—he acknowledges the various obstacles to obtaining government contracts but argues that the businesses that are best prepared can make out profitably in the procurement game.

Besides advising the reader on how best to understand and exploit the system, he provides an extensive appendix of relevant publications and government procurement offices.

Government Contracts: Proposalmanship and Winning Strategies, by Herman Holtz (New York: Plenum Press, 1979).

This book is more specialized than the previous one, concentrating on negotiated contracts as opposed to fixed-price contracts. Gives a good feeling for the breadth of opportunity available and the amount of effort required to obtain negotiated contracts. Written in the same breezy style as the previous book.

How to Get Started in Government Business, by Eli Chappe (Suffern, N.Y.: Danbury Press, 1979).

This is a manual that provides detailed instructions on selling products to the federal government. Though services are not covered, much of the material applies to services as well. The book is intended for novices in the area of federal procurement, but it actually assumes that the reader has something of an overview of the procurement process. It sets out 27 steps for small business owners to follow in selling to the government, along with describing markets and listing agencies and other contacts. Without some background on the process, however, the reader quickly becomes lost in going through the details of 27 steps. The 120-page manual is also packed with abbreviations that are confusing even though they're explained in a two-page listing. Readers who have some familiarity with the procurement process, however, can benefit from the details and advice offered.

Various subsets of regulations exist that aren't covered in the above two publications, however. Searching out all of the procurement regulations involves going through the multivolume *Code of Federal Regulations* and ordering the appropriate volume on procurement regulations. An index to the code can be ordered for $8.50; major libraries have the volumes of the code available for perusal. Specific volumes cost between $8 and $10 each.

U.S. Government Purchasing and Sales Directory (Washington, D.C.: U.S. Government Printing Office); $5.50.

Lists the products and services purchased by military and civilian agencies along with the appropriate purchasing offices to be contacted. Also lists types of surplus property sold, with contacts.

GSA Supply Catalog; $5.50.

Lists items commonly purchased by the GSA.

Doing Business with the Federal Government; free. Available from GSA, Washington, D.C. 20405, or from local GSA Business Service Centers.

Provides an overview of the federal procurement process in fairly understandable language. Not surprisingly, it stresses all the assistance potentially available from the GSA.

Selling to the Military; $4.

Gives instructions on the procedures for selling to the armed forces and lists major buying offices within the military, along with descriptions of their purchasing activities.

Commerce Business Daily; $105 annually via first-class mail, $80 via second-class mail.

Ostensibly lists all purchases being planned by all federal agencies, so that any company that feels qualified can seek to bid on the work. In reality, it lists only about 10 percent of intended purchases. Still, it's a good source for the newcomer to discover potential government markets, since it's the most complete single listing of what government agencies are planning to buy. Available for perusal at all SBA, Commerce Department, and GSA offices.

Contractor Paths to Grief with Some Solutions; free.

This booklet, published by the SBA, describes some of the commonest problems that small businesses encounter in doing business with the government. It's surprisingly frank for a government publication and is valuable for this reason alone. This and several other SBA publications on selling to the federal government are available from the SBA, 1441 L Street, N.W., Washington, D.C. 20416.

FOREIGN TRADE—EXPORTING

World Trade Information Center
One World Trade Center
New York, New York 10048
(212) 466-3068

The World Trade Information Center does research for individual businesses to locate overseas contacts, statistics, and market reports. Its basic fee is $30 hourly for most services.

The federal government issues a variety of publications that track foreign economic and trading trends. The publications listed can all be obtained from:

Superintendent of Documents
U.S. Government Printing Office
Washington, D.C. 20402
(202) 783-3238

Among the publications are the following:

Foreign Economic Trends, a series of publications issued by the U.S. Foreign Service on business developments and economic indicators in more than 100 countries; $50 annually.

Overseas Business Reports, a publication issued irregularly that provides current and detailed marketing information, trade outlooks, and market profiles; $40 annually.

Global Market Surveys, a series of publications providing detailed information on 15–20 of the best foreign markets for the products of various American industries. Prices vary according to the survey.

Country Market Sectoral Surveys, a series of publications that pinpoint the best exporting opportunities in particular foreign countries. Prices vary.

International Economic Indicators, a quarterly publication that presents a wide variety of comparative economic statistics for the United States and seven major competitor countries for recent periods. Annual subscriptions, $10.

Business International Corporation
One Dag Hammarskjold Plaza
New York, New York 10017
(212) 750-6300

Business International Corporation issues a variety of publications on foreign trade trends around the world. Its publications also offer guidance on financing foreign operations and on investing abroad. Prices vary.

Foreign Trade Marketplace (Detroit: Gale Research, 1977).

This directory lists organizations, government agencies, and companies and provides export and import procedures, trading zones, and other information regarding foreign trade.

Committee for Small Business Exports
Box 6
Aspen, Colorado 81611
(303) 925-7567

The Committee for Small Business Exports is a lobbying organization that was formed in 1979 for the purpose of pressing federal legislators and bureaucrats to aid small business exporting. Its members in 30 states include small manufacturing, trading, export management, and consulting companies. Any company with up to $100 million in annual sales is eligible for membership. An internal newsletter keeps members informed of activities. Dues are $100 annually for companies with less than $3 million in annual sales and $200 for larger companies.

Complete Export Guide Manual, by Steve Murphy (Manhattan Beach, Calif.: SJM & Associates, 1980).

This book is concerned mostly with the documentation that must accompany exported products. It also offers exporting rules for over 150 different countries.

SMALL BUSINESS LOBBYING AND SERVICE ORGANIZATIONS

Encyclopedia of Associations (Detroit: Gale Research).

This three-volume annual publication lists and describes 14,000 associations in alphabetical order within broad categories. Besides providing addresses, phone numbers, and officials to contact, the publication includes number of members, staff sizes, and member services.

National Trade and Professional Associations of the United States and Canada and Labor Unions (Washington, D.C.: Columbia Books).

This volume lists 6,300 national trade associations, labor unions, and professional and scientific societies. The listings are in alphabetical order, but not by category. The volume provides names, addresses, phone numbers, membership sizes, annual budget, staff sizes, and similar information along with one- or two-line descriptions.

NEWSPAPERS AND PERIODICALS

For timely, often provocative, information for and about entrepreneurs we suggest the following publications:

Harvard Business Review, "Growing Concerns," Soldiers Field Road, Boston, Massachusetts 02163.

In Business, Box 323, Emmaus, Pennsylvania 18049.

Inc. Magazine, 38 Commercial Wharf, Boston, Massachusetts 02110.

Small Business Reporter, Bank of America, San Francisco, California.

Venture, 35 West 45th Street, New York, New York 10036.

The Wall Street Journal publishes a regular feature on small business, and the *New York Times* frequently has items of interest to entrepreneurs.

Index

This book has been set using a Quadex/Compugraphic 8400 CRT phototypesetting system in 11 and 10 point Century Schoolbook, leaded 2 points. Part numbers are 24 point Helvetica Medium and chapter numbers are 18 point Helvetica Bold. Part titles and chapter titles are 18 point Helvetica Bold. The overall type area is 40 by 55 picas.

Sixth Edition

CHEMISTRY
The Central Science

Theodore L. Brown
University of Illinois

H. Eugene LeMay, Jr.
University of Nevada

Bruce E. Bursten
The Ohio State University

x

Prentice Hall, Englewood Cliffs, NJ 07632

ISBN 0-13-336405-4

Acquisitions editor: *Paul Banks*
Editor-in-chief: *Tim Bozik*
Development editor: *Robert J. Weiss*
Editorial/production supervision: *Barbara Grasso Mack*
Supplements editor: *Mary Hornby*
Design director: *Florence Dara Silverman*
Interior design and page layout: *Lorraine Mullaney*
Cover design: *Bruce Kenselaar*
Project manager: *Trudy Pisciotti*
Photo editor: *Lorinda Morris-Nantz*
Photo researcher: *Yvonne Gerin*
Cover photo: *Grant Heilman Photography, Inc.*

Chapter opening photos: 1. Dr. John R. Dickle/Science Photo Library/Photo Researchers
2. IBM Research 3. Richard Megna/Fundamental Photographs 4. Richard Megna/
Fundamental Photographs 5. Chris Collins/Stock Market 6. Alan Hicks/Allstock
7. Richard Megna/Fundamental Photographs 8. Georg Gerster/Comstock 9. Omikron/
Photo Researchers 10. Sheila Beougher/Gamma-Liaison 11. Charles Krebs/Stock Market
12. David Parker/IMI/University of Birmingham High TC Consortium/SPL/Photo Researchers
13. Craig Tuttle/Stock Market 14. Richard Megna/Fundamental Photographs 15. Chad
Ehlers/Allstock 16. Tom Tracy/Stock Market 17. Charles Seaborn/Odyssey/Chicago
18. NASA 19. Diane Schiumo/Fundamental Photographs 20. Dr. Jeremy Burgess/Science
Photo Library/Photo Researchers 21. NASA 22. Ralph Starkweather/Westlight
23. Michael Dalton/Fundamental Photographs 24. Arthur Meyerson/The Image Bank
25. Paul Hurd/Allstock 26. Orion Press/Westlight

© 1994, 1991, 1988, 1985, 1981, 1977 by Prentice-Hall, Inc.
A Paramount Communications Company
Englewood Cliffs, New Jersey 07632

Printed in the United States of America
10 9 8 7 6 5 4 3 2 1

ISBN 0-13-336405-4

Prentice-Hall International (UK) Limited, *London*
Prentice-Hall of Australia Pty. Limited, *Sydney*
Prentice-Hall Canada Inc., *Toronto*
Prentice-Hall Hispanoamericana, S.A., *Mexico*
Prentice-Hall of India Private Limited, *New Delhi*
Prentice-Hall of Japan, Inc., *Tokyo*
Simon & Schuster Asia Pte. Ltd., *Singapore*
Editora Prentice-Hall do Brasil, Ltda., *Rio de Janeiro*

*To our students,
whose enthusiasm and curiosity
have often inspired us,
and whose questions and
suggestions have sometimes
taught us.*

Brief Contents

Contents

Dr. John R. Dickle/Science Photo Library/Photo Researchers

Richard Megna/Fundamental Photographs

3 Stoichiometry: Calculations with Chemical Formulas and Equations 67

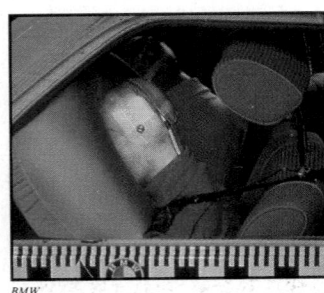

BMW

4 Aqueous Reactions and Solution Stoichiometry 104

LIST OF THE ELEMENTS WITH THEIR SYMBOLS AND ATOMIC WEIGHTS

Element	Symbol	Atomic number	Atomic weight	Element	Symbol	Atomic number	Atomic weight	Element	Symbol	Atomic number	Atomic weight
Actinium	Ac	89	227.0278	Hahnium [b]	Ha	105	(262)	Protactinium	Pa	91	231.0359
Aluminum	Al	13	26.98154	Helium	He	2	4.00260	Radium	Ra	88	226.0254
Americium	Am	95	(243)[a]	Holmium	Ho	67	164.9304	Radon	Rn	86	(222)
Antimony	Sb	51	121.757	Hydrogen	H	1	1.00794	Rhenium	Re	75	186.207
Argon	Ar	18	39.948	Indium	In	49	114.82	Rhodium	Rh	45	102.9055
Arsenic	As	33	74.9216	Iodine	I	53	126.9045	Rubidium	Rb	37	85.4678
Astatine	At	85	(210)	Iridium	Ir	77	192.22	Ruthenium	Ru	44	101.07
Barium	Ba	56	137.33	Iron	Fe	26	55.847	Rutherfordium [b]	Rf	104	(261)
Berkelium	Bk	97	(247)	Krypton	Kr	36	83.80	Samarium	Sm	62	150.36
Beryllium	Be	4	9.01218	Lanthanum	La	57	138.9055	Scandium	Sc	21	44.9559
Bismuth	Bi	83	208.9804	Lawrencium	Lr	103	(260)	Selenium	Se	34	78.96
Boron	B	5	10.81	Lead	Pb	82	207.2	Silicon	Si	14	28.0855
Bromine	Br	35	79.904	Lithium	Li	3	6.941	Silver	Ag	47	107.8682
Cadmium	Cd	48	112.41	Lutetium	Lu	71	174.967	Sodium	Na	11	22.98977
Calcium	Ca	20	40.078	Magnesium	Mg	12	24.305	Strontium	Sr	38	87.62
Californium	Cf	98	(251)	Manganese	Mn	25	54.9380	Sulfur	S	16	32.066
Carbon	C	6	12.011	Mendelevium	Md	101	(258)	Tantalum	Ta	73	180.9479
Cerium	Ce	58	140.12	Mercury	Hg	80	200.59	Technetium	Tc	43	(98)
Cesium	Cs	55	132.9054	Molybdenum	Mo	42	95.94	Tellurium	Te	52	127.60
Chlorine	Cl	17	35.453	Neodymium	Nd	60	144.24	Terbium	Tb	65	158.9254
Chromium	Cr	24	51.996	Neon	Ne	10	20.1797	Thallium	Tl	81	204.383
Cobalt	Co	27	58.9332	Neptunium	Np	93	237.048	Thorium	Th	90	232.0381
Copper	Cu	29	63.546	Nickel	Ni	28	58.69	Thulium	Tm	69	168.9342
Curium	Cm	96	(247)	Niobium	Nb	41	92.9064	Tin	Sn	50	118.710
Dysprosium	Dy	66	162.50	Nitrogen	N	7	14.0067	Titanium	Ti	22	47.88
Einsteinium	Es	99	(252)	Nobelium	No	102	(259)	Tungsten	W	74	183.85
Erbium	Er	68	167.26	Osmium	Os	76	190.2	Uranium	U	92	238.0289
Europium	Eu	63	151.96	Oxygen	O	8	15.9994	Vanadium	V	23	50.9415
Fermium	Fm	100	(257)	Palladium	Pd	46	106.42	Xenon	Xe	54	131.29
Fluorine	F	9	18.998403	Phosphorus	P	15	30.97376	Ytterbium	Yb	70	173.04
Francium	Fr	87	(223)	Platinum	Pt	78	195.08	Yttrium	Y	39	88.9059
Gadolinium	Gd	64	157.25	Plutonium	Pu	94	(244)	Zinc	Zn	30	65.39
Gallium	Ga	31	69.72	Polonium	Po	84	(209)	Zirconium	Zr	40	91.224
Germanium	Ge	32	72.61	Potassium	K	19	39.0983	[106] [b]		106	(263)
Gold	Au	79	196.9665	Praseodymium	Pr	59	140.9077	[107]		107	(262)
Hafnium	Hf	72	178.49	Promethium	Pm	61	(145)	[108]		108	(265)
								[109]		109	(266)

[a] Approximate values for radioactive elements are listed in parentheses.
[b] The official name and symbol have not been agreed to.

5 Energy Relationships in Chemistry: Thermochemistry   139

6 Electronic Structure of Atoms   174

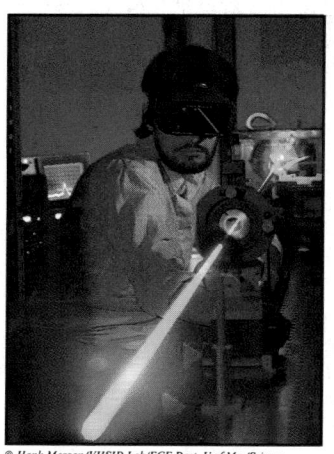

© Hank Morgan/VHSID Lab/ECE Dept. U of Ma./Science
Source/Photo Researchers

Richard Megna/Fundamental Photographs

V. Faint/The Image Bank

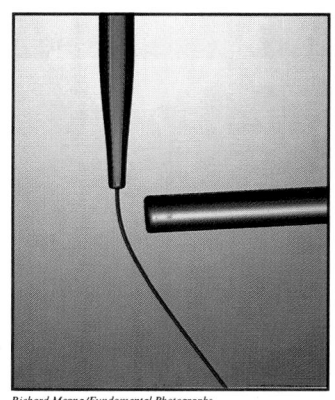

Richard Megna/Fundamental Photographs

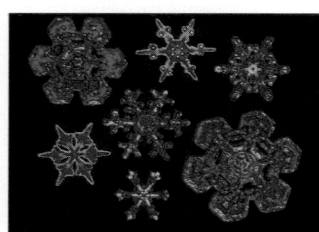
© Scott Camazine/Photo Researchers

12 Modern Materials   413

David Parker/IMI/University of Birmingham High TC
Consortium/SPL/Photo Researchers

13 Properties of Solutions   447

Craig Tuttle/Stock Market

Richard Megna/Fundamental Photographs

14 Chemical Kinetics   487

15 Chemical Equilibrium   533

Richard Megna/Fundamental Photographs

Charles Seaborn/Odyssey/Chicago

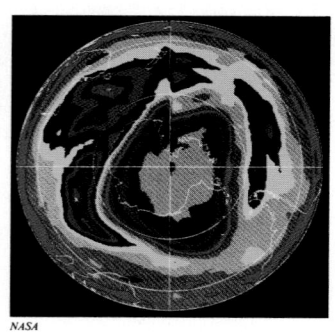
NASA

18 Chemistry of the Environment   661

19 Chemical Thermodynamics   691

Dr. Jeremy Burgess/Science Photo Library/Photo Researchers

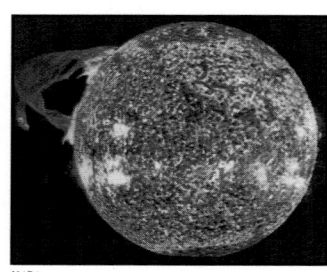

NASA

Ralph Starkweather/Westlight

Roberto DeGugliemo/Science Photo Library/Photo Researchers

Contents   **xvii**

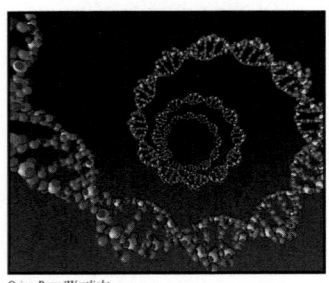

Orion Press/Westlight

© Jim Zuckerman/Westlight

Chemical Applications and Essays

 ## CHEMISTRY AT WORK

 ## A CLOSER LOOK

CHEMISTRY AND LIFE

STRATEGIES IN CHEMISTRY

Using the Annotated Instructor's Edition

The Annotated Instructor's Edition (AIE) of *Chemistry: The Central Science* is the most convenient and comprehensive tool available for your classroom. Conversations with chemistry instructors from universities and colleges throughout the country have made it clear that the commodity in shortest supply is time. This AIE is designed to reduce the amount of time needed to prepare for the demands of the lecture hall. At the same time it enables you to maximize the effectiveness of the many other resources available to you. In particular, Prentice Hall provides an extremely comprehensive package of supplements, including several newly developed multimedia tools, which are described in the Preface.

The AIE consists of the complete student version of the textbook, plus an overlay of commentary designed to support your lectures with appropriate supplemental information. Of course, some experienced professors of general chemistry might find the information provided to be thoroughly familiar. But for instructors rotating into general chemistry once every 3 or 4 years, for those teaching the course for the first time, for graduate assistants, and even for those with a great deal of experience, we hope to provide the utmost in convenience in teaching. The major categories of annotations are listed below. Note that they are displayed in blue type in the margins of the text.

 Lecture demonstrations: One or two chemical demonstrations are suggested in each chapter and are highlighted by the Erlenmeyer flask at a relevant point in the text. While the source for each demonstration is listed in the annotation, the full description is found in the accompanying *Instructors' Resource Manual.*

 Transparencies: An icon of a transparency projector provides quick identification of the 200 tables and figures that are duplicated in the accompanying boxed set of full-color acetates.

 Additional references: Designated by an icon of a book, these complete bibliographic citations suggest additional information or sources that will enrich your presentation, and provide ideas for extra assigned reading.

Learning goals: These marginal notes reprint the learning goals for each text section, as found in the Student Study Guide.

Teaching notes: This commentary suggests useful strategies in presenting key information.

Common misconceptions: Based on extended classroom experience, this set of remarks alerts the instructor to the errors inexperienced students are prone to make.

Points of emphasis: By repeating key points discussed in the adjacent text, this category signals the desirability of providing a slightly different perspective or emphasis so that the student is exposed to multiple entry points of understanding for major topics.

Special thanks are due to Gilbert Yang of the University of Southern California, who was responsible for revising and coordinating the annotations program in the AIE.

Preface

To the Student

Chemistry: The Central Science, Sixth Edition, has been written to introduce you to modern chemistry. During the many years we have been practicing chemists, we have found chemistry to be an exciting intellectual challenge and an extraordinarily rich and varied part of our cultural heritage. We hope that as you advance in your study of chemistry, you will share with us some of that enthusiasm and appreciation. We also hope that you will come to realize the importance of chemistry in your everyday life. As authors, we have, in effect, been engaged by your instructor to help you learn chemistry. Based on the comments of students and instructors who have used this book in its previous editions, we believe that we have done that job well. Of course, we expect the text to continue to evolve through future editions. We invite you to write to us to tell us what you like about the book, so that we will know where we have helped you most. Also, we would like to learn of any shortcomings, so that we might further improve the book in subsequent editions. Our addresses are given at the end of the Preface.

Using this Text

Learning chemistry requires both the assimilation of many new concepts and the development of analytical skills. To assist you in these goals, we have interspersed throughout the text hundreds of *Sample Exercises.* Each exercise illustrates the use of a key concept or skill. The accompanying solution illustrates the reasoning required to answer the exercise. Paired with every Sample Exercise is a *Practice Exercise,* which addresses the same concept. You can test your understanding by working the Practice Exercise and comparing your answer with the one that is given.

To help you visualize abstract ideas, we have included *full-color illustrations,* including photographs, diagrams, conceptual artwork, and graphs. Several important concepts and calculations are presented schematically through the use of *flow diagrams.* We believe you will find the illustrations and their captions to be very helpful as you read the text.

Four kinds of *supplemental essays* appear throughout the text to aid and enrich your studies. The *Chemistry at Work* sections discuss interesting applications of the concepts in the text to everyday life. The *Chemistry and Life* essays emphasize the integration of basic chemical concepts in biology and medicine. The essays titled *A Closer Look* augment the chapter material by delving more deeply into a topic. Finally, in the essays titled *Strategies in Chemistry,* we offer some general advice on how to succeed in learning chemistry.

At the end of each chapter you will find a *Summary* that points out the chapter highlights. The list of *Key Terms* gives the vocabulary that has been introduced in the chapter. The terms listed here are printed in boldface type in the chapter and also appear in the end-of-book *Glossary.*

The *Exercises* at the end of each chapter test your understanding of the material. Many exercises are grouped according to topic, and they are also arranged in matched pairs. Both exercises in a pair deal with the same principle or procedure, so if you have difficulty with a particular exercise, its companion will provide you with further practice. The answer to one member of each pair is given in a section at the back of the book. *Additional exercises* appear at the end of each chapter's exercise set. The additional exercises test your ability to solve problems that are not identified by topic. These exercises often combine ideas from more than one part of the chapter. The additional exercises and the matched-pair exercises whose answers appear near the end of the book are numbered in color. The more challenging exercises are marked with brackets.

Finally, you should note that there are several *Appendices* near the back of the book, as well as useful tables in the front and back inside covers.

Supplemental Materials

Because we realize that you will encounter challenging material in this course, Prentice Hall has made available to you several valuable supplements. One key supplement is *Chemistry Explorer Software,* an interactive software program that is based on worked examples and problems from the book. *Chemistry Explorer Software* enables you to simulate experiments on your computer and manipulate different elements of these experiments to see how they affect the results. This software also provides graphs and spreadsheets to help you analyze data. Thus, *Chemistry Explorer Software* is a valuable tool for helping you learn the basic concepts and skills you will need in your chemistry course.

Of particular use to chemistry students is the *Student's Guide* by James C. Hill of California State University. The student guide follows the same chapter sequence as the text. Each chapter in the guide contains an overview, topical summaries and additional exercises, and tests for each chapter section.

Advice for Studying Chemistry

Keep up with your studying day to day. New material builds on the old. It is important not to fall behind; if you do, you will find it much harder to follow the lectures and discussions on current topics. Trying to "cram" just before an exam is generally a very ineffective way to study chemistry.

Focus your study. The amount of information you will receive in your chemistry course can sometimes seem overwhelming. The number of facts and details in a first course in chemistry is enough to challenge any student, and it is essential to recognize those concepts and skills that are particularly important. Listen intently for what your lecturer and teaching assistant emphasize. Pay attention to the skills stressed in the sample exercises and homework assignments. Notice the italicized statements in the text, and study the concepts presented in the chapter summaries.

Keep good lecture notes, so that you have a clear and concise record of the required material. You will find it easier to take useful notes if you *skim topics in the text before they are covered in lecture.* To skim a chapter, first read the introduction and summary. Then quickly read through the chapter, skipping Sample Exercises and supplemental sections. Pay attention to section heads and subheads, which give you a feeling for the scope of topics. Avoid the feeling that you must learn and understand everything right away.

After lecture, *carefully read the topics covered in class.* You will probably need to read assigned material more than once to master it. As you read, pay particular attention to the Sample Exercises. Once you think you understand a Sample Exercise, test your understanding by working the accompanying Practice Exercise.

Finally, *attempt all of the assigned end-of-chapter exercises.* Working out these exercises provides necessary practice in recalling and using the essential ideas of the chapter. You cannot learn merely by observing; you must be a participant. In particular, there is little value in merely copying answers from the Solutions Manual or from another student. If, however, you really get stuck on a problem, get help. Spending more than 20 minutes on a single exercise is rarely effective unless you know that it is particularly challenging.

To the Instructor

Philosophy

Throughout the evolution of this text, certain goals have guided our writing efforts. The first is that a text should endeavor to show students the usefulness of chemistry in their major areas of study as well as in the world around them. It has been our experience that as students become aware of the importance of chemistry to their own goals and interests, they become more enthusiastic about learning the subject. With this in mind, we have attempted, as much as space and our imaginations permit, to bring in interesting and significant applications of the subject matter. We attempt to show that chemistry is indeed the *central science.* At the same time, of course, we seek to provide students with the necessary background in modern chemistry for their specialized studies, including more advanced chemistry courses.

Second, we want to show not only that chemistry provides the basis for much of what goes on in our world, but that it is a vital, continually developing science. We have tried to keep the book up-to-date in terms of new concepts and applications and to convey some of the excitement of the field.

Third, we feel that any text should be written to the students and not just to their instructors. We have sought to keep our writing clear and interesting and the book attractive and well illustrated. Furthermore, we have provided numerous in-text study aids for students. A more subtle aspect of this student orientation is the care we have taken to describe problem-solving strategies.

Organization

In the present edition, the first five chapters give a largely macroscopic, phenomenological view of chemistry. They introduce basic concepts, such as nomenclature, stoichiometry, and thermochemistry, that provide the necessary background for many of the laboratory experiments usually performed in general chemistry. Chapter 4 gives a brief, early treatment of chemical reactions in aqueous solutions.

The next four chapters (Chapters 6–9) deal with electronic structure and bonding. The focus then changes to the next level of the organization of matter: the states of matter (Chapters 10 and 11) and solutions (Chapter 13). Also included in this section is a chapter on the chemistry of modern materials (Chapter 12), which builds on the student's understanding of chemical bonding and intermolecular interactions and their relationships to the properties of matter.

The next several chapters examine the factors that determine the speed and extent of chemical reactions: kinetics (Chapter 14), equilibria (Chapters 15–17), thermodynamics (Chapter 19), and electrochemistry (Chapter 20). Also in this section is an optional chapter on environmental chemistry (Chapter 18), in which the concepts developed in preceding chapters are applied to a discussion of the atmosphere and hydrosphere.

After a discussion of nuclear chemistry (Chapter 21), the final chapters survey the chemistry of nonmetals, metals, organic chemistry, and biochemistry (Chapters 22–26). These chapters are developed in a parallel fashion and can be treated in any order.

Although our chapter sequence provides a fairly standard organization, we recognize that not everyone teaches all of the topics in exactly our order. We have therefore structured our writing so that instructors can make common changes in teaching sequence with no loss in student comprehension. In particular, many instructors prefer to introduce gases (Chapter 10) after stoichiometry or after thermochemistry rather than with states of matter. The chapter on gases has been written to permit this change with *no* disruption in the flow of material. It is also possible to treat the balancing of redox equations (Sections 20.1 and 20.2) earlier, after the introduction of oxidation numbers in Section 8.10, or even with the introduction to redox reactions in Section 4.6.

We have always attempted to introduce students to *descriptive chemistry* by integrating examples throughout the text. You will find pertinent and relevant examples of "real" chemistry woven into all of the chapters as a means to illustrate principles and applications. Some chapters, of course, more directly address the properties of elements and their compounds, especially Chapters 4, 7, 12, 18, and 22–26. We also incorporate descriptive chemistry in the end-of-chapter exercises.

Changes in this Edition

Our major goal in the sixth edition has been to strengthen an already strong textbook while retaining its effective and popular style. The traditional strengths of *Chemistry: The Central Science* include its clarity of writing, its scientific accuracy and currency, its strong end-of-chapter exercises, and its consistency in level of coverage.

In making changes to this edition, we have tried to be responsive to the feedback we have received from the faculty and students who used the fifth edition. Students have appreciated the *student-friendly* style of writing, and we have preserved this style in the sixth edition. Sections that struck students as hard to follow have been rewritten and, when possible, augmented with improved artwork. In order to make the text easier for students to use, we have maintained a *clean design* in the layout of the book.

The text also contains *improvements in artwork* that help convey the beauty and excitement of chemistry. The program of *molecular art and line diagrams* has been improved to help students better visualize three-dimensional concepts on a two-dimensional page. *New photographs* have been added throughout the book. Our goal has been to use color in a nondistracting way to help emphasize important points, to focus the student's attention, and to make the text attractive and inviting.

We have increased the emphasis on concept-oriented learning throughout the text. *Sample exercises* have been rewritten with more explicit explanations of the thought processes and intermediate calculations. *Flow diagrams* are used whenever possible to provide a visual summary of critical concepts and important relationships. A new icon used in the text, *concept links,* provides easy-to-see cross-references to pertinent earlier material in the text. New essays titled *Strategies in Chemistry* emphasize paradigms used to learn chemistry more effectively and to provide advice on problem solving. The essay at the end of Chapter 26 reminds students that the introductory course is only the beginning of the excitement of learning chemistry.

In response to shifts in student interests, the text contains *greater emphasis on chemistry in the life sciences.* Much of the material that was contained previously in a separate chapter on biochemistry (Chapter 27 of the fifth edition) has been incorporated in earlier chapters. New essays titled *Chemistry and Life* underscore the importance of basic chemical concepts in biology and medicine. In Chapter 26 of the sixth edition, *organic chemistry and biochemistry are combined,* which allows a smoother transition between these two advanced topics. The chapter has been written to allow an instructor to teach only the organic chemistry portion if desired.

We have kept the text fresh by keeping it *current.* References to current events help students relate their studies of chemistry with their everyday life experiences. Students are exposed to new developments in chemistry, such as the excitement surrounding the discovery of buckminsterfullerene. Finally, the sixth edition has an *increased focus on the positive aspects of chemistry,* but without neglecting the problems that can arise in an increasingly technological world. Our goal is to help students appreciate the real-world perspective of chemistry and the ways in which chemistry affects their lives.

Supplements

To accompany the text, Prentice Hall has assembled a very thorough supplements package that will benefit both you and your students. In addition to our standard supplements such as the study guide and laboratory manual, we now offer a number of multimedia items. The key supplements are described below.

- *Chemistry Explorer Software* This is an interactive simulation program based on worked problems and examples from the text. It allows students to manipulate variables and physical parameters in performing experiments to observe how these manipulations affect the results. It also provides data analysis tools such as spreadsheets and graphs.

- *Prentice Hall Chemistry Laserdisc* This "visual encyclopedia" combines demonstration experiments, still images from both the text and outside sources, molecular animations, and brief application segments emphasizing new frontiers in chemistry.

- *Prentice Hall Multimedia Chemistry Presenter* The laserdisc and the Explorer software can be used separately, or they can be combined through *Prentice Hall Multimedia Chemistry Presenter.* This modular classroom presentation tool organizes and drives the media components and allows the instructor to customize available resources.

- *Prentice Hall/The New York Times Themes of the Times* To emphasize the importance and relevance of chemistry in everyday life, we once again offer this unique supplement produced through the joint efforts of Prentice Hall and *The New York Times. Themes of the Times* consists of a series of *Times* articles relating to chemistry that are reproduced to resemble an actual edition of the *Times.*

- *Solutions to Exercises* by Roxy Wilson of the University of Illinois. This manual contains the answers to the end-of-chapter exercises in the book. Three different versions are available: one with answers to all the black-numbered questions; one with answers to all the red-numbered questions; and one with answers to all the questions. With the instructor's permission these manuals may be made available to students.

- *Instructor's Resource Manual* Available in both electronic and paper formats, this manual provides detailed lecture outlines on a chapter-by-chapter basis. Also, lecture schedules to accommodate a two-semester or three-quarter sequence, or a schedule emphasizing descriptive chemistry, provide a quick guide to assignments. Other useful features of the *Instructor's Resource Manual* are the complete lecture demonstrations referenced in the Annotated Instructor's Edition, cross-referencing of all other supplements available for Brown/LeMay/Bursten, weekly quizzes, and chapter summaries. By providing the *Instructor's Resource Manual* electronically we hope to give you quick access to a wealth of material that can be immediately personalized to your needs. Call up a given chapter outline on your computer screen, annotate it to fit your needs, and print it out.

- *Student's Guide* Authored by James C. Hill of California State University, Sacramento, the student guide has proved over the years to be an excellent companion volume to *Chemistry: The Central Science.* Each chapter is keyed to the text material and follows a basic format that includes an overview of the chapter, format that includes an overview of the chapter, topical summaries and additional exercises, study exercises, and sectional tests.

- *Chemical Problem Solving Using Dimensional Analysis,* 3rd Ed., by Robert Nakon. This supplement provides hundreds of problems for the student to work, and their solutions.

- *Laboratory Experiments,* by John Nelson and Kenneth Kemp. This long-established and time-tested volume contains 40 experiments, all of them retained or refined from previous editions.

- ***Instructor's Edition to the Laboratory Experiments*** This manual contains the student's version of the lab manual plus answers to all questions, tips on safety and disposal of chemicals, suggestions for handling of chemicals and equipment, and related information.
- ***Introduction to Semimicro Qualitative Analysis,*** 7th Ed., by J. J. Lagowski and C. H. Sorum. This is a valuable tool for instructors who emphasize qualitative analysis in their general chemistry courses. This supplement consists of two parts. Part One focuses on the theories and techniques behind qualitative analysis; Part Two contains a number of time-tested experiments.
- ***Transparency Pack*** Prentice Hall can make available approximately 240 full-color acetates, all of them taken from the text.
- ***The Prentice Hall Test Manager 2.0*** and ***Test Item File*** These supplements now consist of over 2500 items, available in paperback or on floppy disk, for IBM® and MacIntosh® computers. As a major innovation, Test Manager allows you to add your own questions and to automatically alternate ordering of questions. New features of Test Manager 2.0 include complete control over print options as well as export of tests to Word or WordPerfect. In addition, telephone testing services are available.
- ***Chemical Concepts and Techniques Video*** A 100-minute videotape has been specifically developed for use in conjunction with Brown/LeMay/Bursten. Divided into ten segments of 10 minutes each, the video highlights important concepts of chemistry through a variety of visual media including electron microscopy, computer animation, and other tape technology.
- ***Chemistry Toolkit*** Available at no additional charge. Part One of the Toolkit consists of a chapter-by-chapter guide to the mathematics used throughout the Sixth Edition. Part Two is a guide to career planning and chemistry. It highlights the value of chemistry training in business and other careers not specifically related to chemistry. Part Three looks at the special requirements of writing in chemistry, focusing particularly on the lab notebook.
- ***Spreadsheet Chemistry*** by Gary Breneman and Jerry Parker. Finally, in the software category, a very special book is available for use in conjunction with EXCEL®. *Spreadsheet Chemistry* provides a means for quickly calculating numerical results from theory, experimental data, and questions posed about changes in conditions that govern chemical systems. Topics addressed include electron distribution in atoms and molecules, thermodynamic quantities, ideal- and real-gas behaviors, and oxidation-reduction reactions.

To receive a copy of any of these supplements, please contact your local sales representative.

Acknowledgments

This book owes its final shape and form to the assistance and hard work of many people. Several colleagues reviewed the manuscript and helped us immensely by sharing their insights and criticizing our initial writing efforts. We would like especially to thank the following:

Joe F. Allen	Clemson University
Patricia A. Basili	Prince George's Community College
Linda S. Brunauer	Santa Clara University
Joe Cantrell	Miami University
Dana Chatellier	University of Delaware
Larry Epstein	University of Pittsburgh
Natalie Foster	Lehigh University
Thomas A. Furtsch	Tennessee Technological University
Henry Gehrke	South Dakota State University
L. Peter Gold	Pennsylvania State University
Gregory J. Grant	The University of Utah
Nicholas Kildahl	Worcester Polytechnic Institute
Paul Kreiss	Anne Arundel Community College
Robert M. Kren	University of Michigan - Flint
William M. Litchman	University of New Mexico
Peter Lykos	Illinois Institute of Technology
Joel T. Mague	Tulane University
Richard S. Mitchell	Arkansas State University
Paul N. Noble	California State University - Sacramento
Gordon A. Parker	The University of Michigan - Dearborn
Helen Place	Washington State University
Robert A. Pribush	Butler University
Theodore Sakano	Rockland Community College
Jack H. Stocker	University of New Orleans
Klaus H. Theopold	University of Delaware
Charles Trapp	University of Louisville
Gilbert K. Yang	University of Southern California

We would also like to express our sincere appreciation to our colleagues at Prentice Hall who have worked so hard to make this edition possible: Diana Farrell and Tim Bozik, our chemistry editors, who contributed imagination and energy to this project; Bob Weiss, our fine developmental editor, whose tenacious attention to detail, ideas for improving our exposition, and gentle prodding about deadlines were invaluable to this revision; and Barbara Grasso, our production editor, who efficiently and with good cheer managed the incredibly complex task of bringing the design, photos, artwork, and writing together.

Many others were intimately involved in the complex task of putting together this textbook and deserve special recognition: Richard Megna and Kip Peticolas of Fundamental Photographs, whose photographs brought our crude drawings to life with considerable artistic flair; Roxy Wilson (University of Illinois) for performing the difficult job of working end-of-chapter exercises and checking our calculations; Nicholas Kildahl (Worcester Polytechnic Institute) and Linda Brunauer (Santa Clara University) for their helpful proofreading and criticism; and Gilbert Yang (University of Southern California) for his efforts in preparing the Annotated Instructor's Edition of the text.

Finally, our thanks to all the students and faculty who gave us comments and suggestions about *Chemistry: The Central Science,* Fifth Edition. You will see many of your suggestions incorporated into the sixth edition.

Theodore L. Brown
School of Chemical Sciences
University of Illinois
Urbana, IL 61801

H. Eugene LeMay, Jr.
Department of Chemistry
University of Nevada
Reno, NV 89557

Bruce E. Bursten
Department of Chemistry
The Ohio State University
Columbus, OH 43210

The New York Times and Prentice Hall are sponsoring *Themes of the Times,* a program designed to enhance student access to current information of relevance in the classroom.

Through this program, the core subject matter provided in the text is supplemented by a collection of time-sensitive articles from one of the world's most distinguished newspapers, *The New York Times.* These articles demonstrate the vital, ongoing connection between what is learned in the classroom and what is happening in the world around us.

To enjoy the wealth of information of *The New York Times* daily, a reduced subscription rate is available. For information, call toll-free: 1-800-631-1222.

Prentice Hall and *The New York Times* are proud to cosponsor *Themes of the Times.* We hope it will make the reading of both textbooks and newspapers a more dynamic, involving process.

About the Authors

Theodore L. Brown received his Ph.D. from Michigan State University in 1956. Since that time he has been a member of the faculty of the University of Illinois, Urbana-Champaign, where he is Professor of Chemistry. He served as Vice Chancellor for Research and as Dean, The Graduate College during 1980–1986, and as Founding Director of the Beckman Institute, 1987–1993.

Professor Brown has been an Alfred P. Sloan Research Fellow, and has also been awarded a Guggenheim Fellowship. He has held several offices with the American Chemical Society. In 1972 he was awarded the American Chemical Society Award for Research in Inorganic Chemistry, and in 1993 he received the American Chemical Society Award for Distinguished Service in the Advancement of Inorganic Chemistry. He is a member of the Governing Board of Chemical Abstracts Services, of the Advisory Council of the Directorate of Education and Human Resources of the National Science Foundation, and of the Council of the Government-University-Industry Research Roundtable.

H. Eugene LeMay, Jr., received his B.S. degree in Chemistry from Pacific Lutheran University (Washington) and his Ph.D. in Chemistry in 1966 from the University of Illinois (Urbana). He then joined the faculty of the University of Nevada, Reno, where he is currently Professor of Chemistry and Freshman-Chemistry Coordinator. He has also served as Associate Chairman and Acting Chairman of the Chemistry Department. He has enjoyed Visiting Professorships at the University of North Carolina at Chapel Hill, at the University College of Wales in Great Britain, and at U.C.L.A.

Professor LeMay is a popular and effective teacher, who has taught thousands of students during nearly 30 years of university teaching. Known for the clarity of his lectures and his sense of humor, he has received several university awards for his teaching at both the undergraduate and graduate levels, including the University Distinguished Teacher of the Year Award. When not teaching and writing, Professor LeMay enjoys time with his family, photography, and hiking.

Bruce E. Bursten received his S.B. degree in chemistry from the University of Chicago and his Ph.D. from the University of Wisconsin in 1978. Following two years as a National Science Foundation Postdoctoral Fellow at Texas A&M University, he joined the faculty of The Ohio State University, where he is currently Professor of Chemistry.

Professor Bursten has been a Camille and Henry Dreyfus Foundation Teacher-Scholar and an Alfred P. Sloan Foundation Research Fellow. At Ohio State, he has received the University Distinguished Teaching Award, the Arts and Sciences Student Council Outstanding Teaching Award, and the University Distinguished Scholar Award. In addition to his teaching and research activities, he presently serves as Secretary of the Division of Inorganic Chemistry of the American Chemical Society.

Introduction: Some Basic Concepts 1

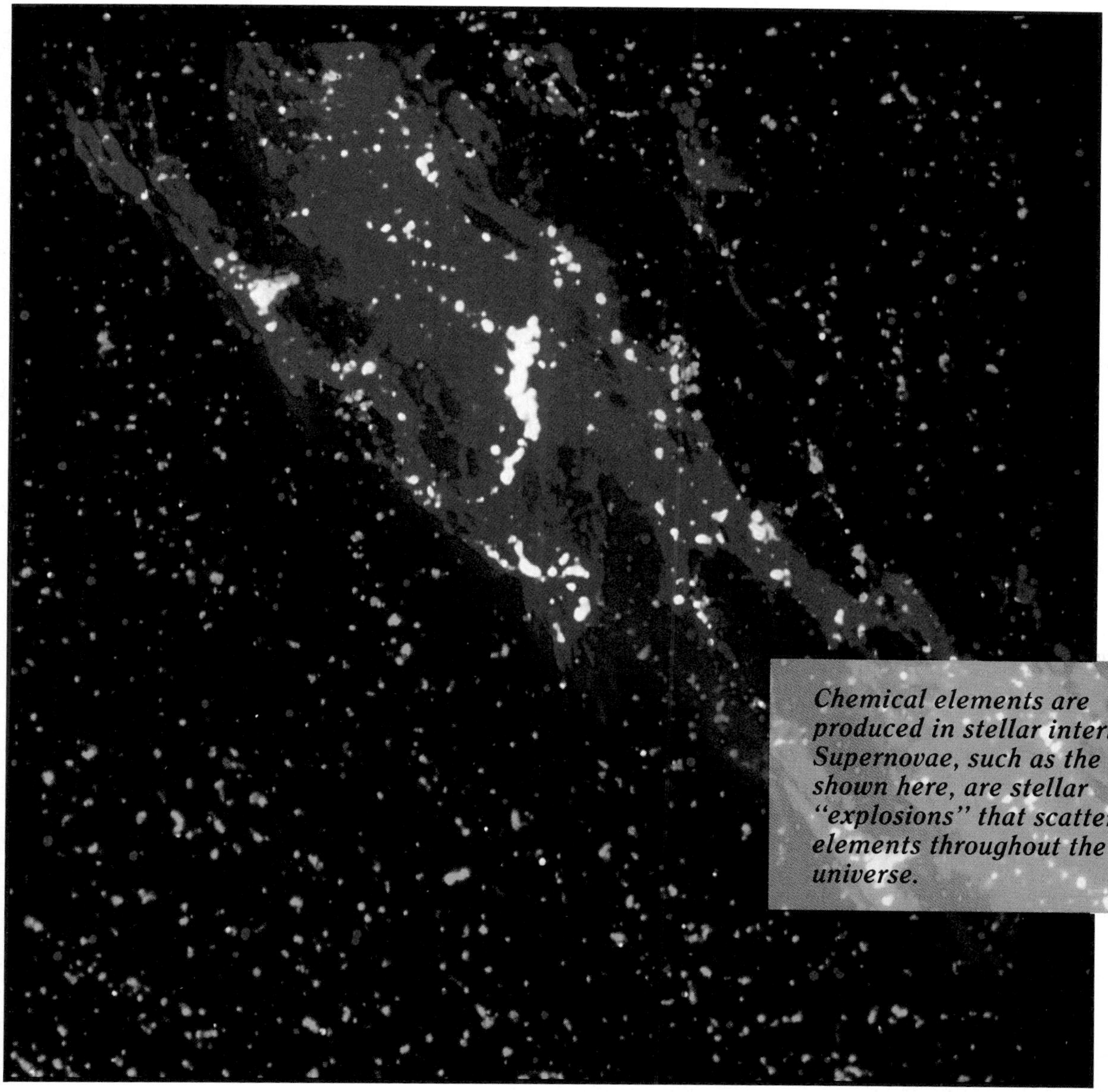

Chemical elements are produced in stellar interiors. Supernovae, such as the one shown here, are stellar "explosions" that scatter the elements throughout the universe.

CONTENTS

The greatest inventions are those inquiries which tend to increase the power of man over matter.

— BENJAMIN FRANKLIN (1706–1790)

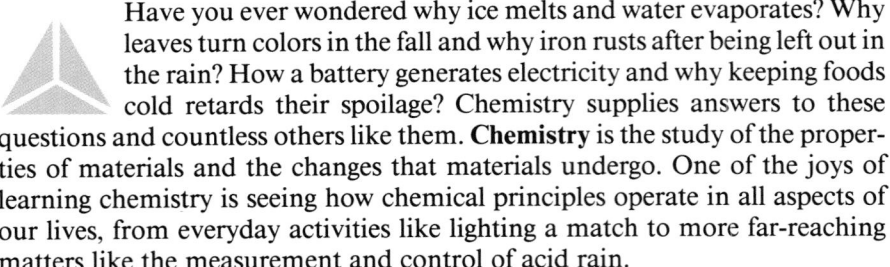

Have you ever wondered why ice melts and water evaporates? Why leaves turn colors in the fall and why iron rusts after being left out in the rain? How a battery generates electricity and why keeping foods cold retards their spoilage? Chemistry supplies answers to these questions and countless others like them. **Chemistry** is the study of the properties of materials and the changes that materials undergo. One of the joys of learning chemistry is seeing how chemical principles operate in all aspects of our lives, from everyday activities like lighting a match to more far-reaching matters like the measurement and control of acid rain.

Our knowledge of chemistry has benefited us in many ways. We have developed plastics and polymers that are used in almost every facet of our lives. We have discovered pharmaceutical chemicals that enhance our health and prolong our lives. We have increased food production through the development of fertilizers and pesticides. Indeed, we produce vast amounts of chemicals that touch our lives in a variety of ways. Unfortunately, some of these chemicals also have the potential for harming our health or environment. It is in our best interest as educated citizens and consumers to understand the profound effects, both positive and negative, that chemicals have on our lives and to strike an informed balance about their uses.

Most of you are studying chemistry, however, not merely to satisfy your curiosity or to become more informed consumers or citizens, but because it is an essential part of your curriculum. Your major might be biology, engineering, agriculture, geology, or some other field. Why do so many diverse subjects share an essential tie to chemistry? The answer is that chemistry, by its very nature, is the *central science*. Our interactions with the material world raise basic questions about the materials around us. What are their compositions and properties? How do they interact with us and their environment? How, why, and when do they undergo change? These questions are important whether the material is a modern polymer involved in the production of high-tech computer chips, an aged pigment used by a Renaissance painter, or an extraterrestrial material collected during a space mission (Figure 1.1). Chemistry provides answers to these and countless other questions. For this reason, chemistry will probably play a significant role in your future. You will be better prepared for the future if you increase your understanding of chemical principles.

This text introduces you to chemical facts and concepts not as ends in themselves but as a means to help you understand the world around you. We hope that you find this to be an enjoyable and fascinating experience as well as an educational one. As with any discipline, we must begin by learning some basic ideas and vocabulary. In this chapter, we focus on some fundamental concepts about matter and scientific measurements.

1.1 Introduction to Matter

Our present understanding of the changes we see around us—such as the melting of ice and the burning of wood—is intimately tied to our understand-

(a)

(b)

(c)

FIGURE 1.1 (a) A microscopic view of a computer chip. (b) A Renaissance painting, "L'alchemista." (c) A "moon rock" collected from the lunar surface. (John Walsh/Photo Researchers; Scala/Art Resource; NASA)

ing of the nature and composition of matter. **Matter** is the physical material of the universe; it is anything that occupies space and has mass.

Matter can exist in three physical *states:* gas (also known as vapor), liquid, and solid (Figure 1.2). These states differ in some of their simple observable properties. A *gas* has no fixed volume or shape; rather, it conforms to the volume and shape of its container. A gas can be compressed to occupy a smaller volume, or it can expand to occupy a larger one. A **liquid** has a distinct volume independent of its container but has no specific shape. It assumes the shape of

Learning Goal 1: Differentiate among the three states of matter.

FIGURE 1.2 The three physical states of water are common and familiar to us: water vapor, liquid water, and ice. We cannot see water vapor. What we see when we look at steam or clouds is tiny droplets of liquid water dispersed through the water vapor. In this photo we see both the liquid and solid states of water. (Robert W. Hernandez)

1.1 Introduction to Matter **3**

Chemistry and the Chemical Industry

Many people are familiar with common household chemicals such as those shown in Figure 1.3, but few realize how huge and important the chemical industry is. Domestic and foreign sales of chemicals and related products manufactured in the United States total about $300 billion annually. The chemical industry employs about 10 percent of all scientists and engineers and is our only nonsubsidized industry with a positive balance of payments to foreign countries, more than $15 billion annually. In fact, the chemical industry contributes more to the U.S. economy than does the automotive industry. Vast amounts of chemicals are produced each year and serve as raw materials for a variety of uses, including the manufacture of metals, plastics, fertilizers, pharmaceuticals, fuels, paints, adhesives, pesticides, synthetic fibers, microprocessor chips, and numerous other products. Table 1.1 lists the top 10 chemicals produced in the United States in 1992. We will discuss many of these substances and their uses as the course progresses.

People who have degrees in chemistry hold a variety of positions in industry, government, and academia. Those who work in the chemical industry find positions as laboratory chemists, carrying out experiments to develop new products (research and development), analyzing materials (quality control), or assisting customers in using products (sales and service). Those with more experience or training may work as managers or company directors. There are also alternate careers that a chemistry degree prepares you for such as teaching, medicine, biomedical research, information science, environmental work, technical sales, work with government regulatory agencies, and patent law.

FIGURE 1.3 Many common supermarket products have very simple chemical compositions. (Richard Megna/ Fundamental Photographs)

TABLE 1.1 △ The Top 10 Chemicals Produced by the Chemical Industry in 1992[a]

Table 1.1

Rank	Chemical	Formula	1992 Production (billions of pounds)	Principal end uses
1	Sulfuric acid	H_2SO_4	88.80	Fertilizers, chemical manufacturing
2	Nitrogen	N_2	58.70	Fertilizers
3	Oxygen	O_2	42.38	Steel, welding
4	Ethylene	C_2H_4	40.41	Plastics, antifreeze
5	Ammonia	NH_3	35.95	Fertilizers
6	Lime	CaO	34.72	Paper, cement, steel
7	Phosphoric acid	H_3PO_4	25.36	Fertilizers
8	Sodium hydroxide	$NaOH$	24.02	Aluminum production, soap
9	Propylene	C_3H_6	22.60	Plastics, gasoline
10	Chlorine	Cl_2	22.28	Bleaches, plastics, water purification

[a] *Source: Chemical and Engineering News,* April 12, 1993, p. 11.

the portion of the container that it occupies. A **solid** has both a definite shape and a definite volume; it is rigid. Neither liquids nor solids can be compressed to any appreciable extent.

Substances

Most forms of matter that we encounter — for example, the air we breathe (a gas), gasoline for cars (a liquid), and a sidewalk on which we walk (a solid) — are not chemically pure. We can, however, resolve, or separate, these kinds of matter into different pure substances. A **pure substance** (from here on referred to simply as a *substance*) is matter that has a fixed composition and distinct properties. For example, seawater can be separated into several different substances, the most abundant of which are water and ordinary table salt (sodium chloride).

Point of Emphasis: Pure substances contain only one kind of matter.

Physical and Chemical Properties

Every substance has a unique set of *properties* — characteristics that allow us to recognize it and to distinguish it from other substances. These properties can be grouped into two categories: physical and chemical. **Physical properties** are those that we can measure without changing the basic identity of the substance. They include color, odor, density, melting point, boiling point, and hardness. **Chemical properties** describe the way a substance may change or "react" to form other substances. For example, a common chemical property is *flammability,* the tendency of a substance to burn in the presence of oxygen.

Learning Goal 2: Distinguish between physical and chemical properties and also between physical and chemical changes.

Physical and Chemical Changes

As with the properties of substances, the changes that substances undergo can be classified as either physical or chemical. During **physical changes,** a substance changes its physical appearance but not its basic identity. The evaporation of water is a physical change. When water evaporates, it changes from the liquid state to the gas state, but it is still water; it has not changed into any other substance. All **changes of state** (for example, from liquid to gas or from liquid to solid) are physical changes.

    In **chemical changes** (also called **chemical reactions**), a substance is transformed into a chemically different substance. For example, when hydrogen burns in air it undergoes a chemical change in which it is converted to water.

    Chemical changes can be dramatic. The following account describes a young man's first experiences with chemical reactions. The writer is Ira Remsen, who later became the author of a popular chemistry text published in 1901. The chemical reaction that he observed is shown in Figure 1.4.

Point of Emphasis: Physical changes *do not* alter the identity of a substance.

Teaching Note: Physical changes involve changes in appearance but do not alter the identity of a substance. Chemical changes alter the identity of a substance; they *may* involve changes in appearance as well.

Lee R. Summerlin, Christie L. Borgford, and Julie B. Ealy, "Ira Remsen's Investigation of Nitric Acid," *Chemical Demonstrations, A Sourcebook for Teachers,* Volume 2 (Washington: American Chemical Society, 1987), pp. 4–5.

> While reading a textbook of chemistry, I came upon the statement "nitric acid acts upon copper," and I determined to see what this meant. Having located some nitric acid, I had only to learn what the words "act upon" meant. In the interest of knowledge I was even willing to sacrifice one of the few copper cents then in my possession. I put one of them on the table, opened a bottle labeled "nitric acid," poured some of the liquid on the copper, and prepared to make an observation. But what was this wonderful thing which I beheld? The cent was already changed, and it was no

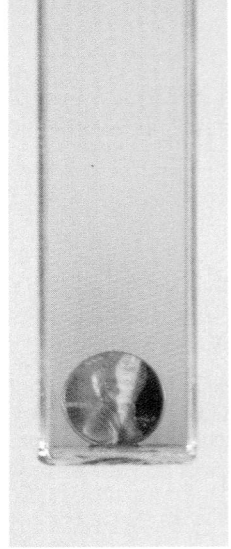

small change either. A greenish-blue liquid foamed and fumed over the cent and over the table. The air became colored dark red. How could I stop this? I tried by picking the cent up and throwing it out the window. I learned another fact: nitric acid acts upon fingers. The pain led to another unpremeditated experiment. I drew my fingers across my trousers and discovered nitric acid acts upon trousers. That was the most impressive experiment I have ever performed. I tell of it even now with interest. It was a revelation to me. Plainly the only way to learn about such remarkable kinds of action is to see the results, to experiment, to work in the laboratory.

Mixtures

Most of the matter we encounter consists of combinations of different substances. Chemists use the term **mixtures** to refer to combinations of two or more substances in which each substance retains its own chemical identity and hence its own properties. Some mixtures, such as sand, rocks, and wood, do not have the same composition, properties, and appearance throughout. Such mixtures are *heterogeneous* [Figure 1.5(a)]. Mixtures that are uniform throughout are *homogeneous.* Air is a homogeneous mixture of the gaseous substances nitrogen, oxygen, and smaller amounts of other substances. The nitrogen in air has all the properties that pure nitrogen does. Salt, sugar, and many other sub-

Learning Goal 3: Distinguish among elements, compounds, and mixtures.

Point of Emphasis: *Heterogeneous mixtures* have variable compositions in different parts of a sample.

Point of Emphasis: *Homogeneous mixtures* are uniform throughout the sample and are also called *solutions.* Solutions can be gaseous, liquid, or solid, although we usually think of them as liquids.

(a)

(b)

FIGURE 1.5 (*a*) Many common materials, including rocks, are heterogeneous. This photo shows a rock containing a copper mineral called malachite. (*b*) Homogeneous mixtures are called solutions. Many substances, including the blue solid shown in this photo (copper sulfate), dissolve in water to form solutions. (© Paul Silverman, 1990/Fundamental Photographs; Richard Megna/Fundamental Photographs)

A CLOSER LOOK

The Scientific Method

Chemistry is an experimental science. The idea of using experiments to understand nature seems like such a natural pattern of thought to us now, but there was a time, before the seventeenth century, when experiments were rarely used. The ancient Greeks, for example, did not rely on experiments to test their ideas.

Although two different scientists rarely approach the same problem in exactly the same way, there are guidelines for the practice of science that have come to be known as the **scientific method.** These guidelines are outlined in Figure 1.6. We begin by collecting information, or *data,* by observation and experiment. However, the collection of information is not the ultimate goal. The goal is to find a pattern or sense of order in our observations and to understand the origin of this order.

As we perform our experiments, we may begin to see patterns that lead us to a *tentative explanation* or **hypothesis** that guides us in planning further experiments. Eventually, we may be able to tie together a great number of observations in terms of a single statement or equation called a scientific law. A **scientific law** *is a concise verbal statement or a mathematical equation that summarizes a broad variety of observations and experiences.* We tend to think of the laws of nature as the basic rules under which nature operates. However, it is not so much that matter obeys the laws of nature, but rather that the laws of nature describe the behavior of matter.

At many stages of our studies, we may propose explanations of why nature behaves in a particular way. If a hypothesis is sufficiently general and is continually effective in predicting facts yet to be observed, it is called a theory or model. A **theory** *is an explanation of the general principles of certain phenomena with considerable evidence or facts to support it.*

As we proceed through this text, we will rarely have the opportunity to discuss the doubts, conflicts, clashes of personalities, and revolutions of perception that have led to our present ideas. We need to be aware that just because we can spell out the results of science so concisely and neatly in textbooks does not mean that scientific progress is smooth, certain, and predictable. Some of the ideas we have presented in this text took centuries to develop and involved large numbers of scientists. We gain our view of the natural world by standing on the shoulders of the scientists who came before us. Take advantage of this view. As you study, exercise your imagination. Don't be afraid to ask daring questions when they occur to you. You may be fascinated by what you discover!

Figure 1.6

FIGURE 1.6 The scientific method is a general approach to problems that involves making observations, seeking patterns in the observations, formulating hypotheses to explain the observations, and testing these hypotheses by further experiments. Those hypotheses that withstand such tests and prove themselves useful in explaining and predicting behavior become known as theories.

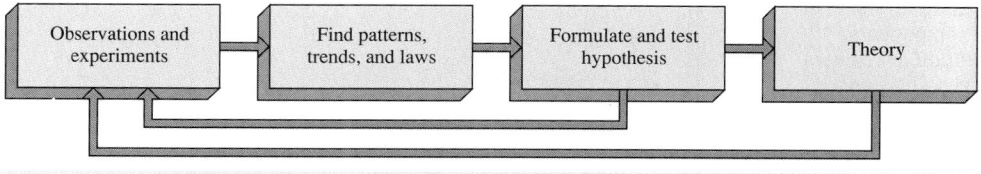

stances dissolve in water to form homogeneous mixtures [Figure 1.5(b)]. Homogeneous mixtures are also called **solutions.** Air is a gaseous solution; gasoline is a liquid solution; brass is a solid solution.

The compositions of mixtures can vary widely. Because each component of a mixture retains it own properties, however, we can separate a mixture into its component substances by taking advantage of the differences in their physical properties. For example, a heterogeneous mixture of iron filings and gold filings could be sorted individually by color into iron and gold. A more clever

Point of Emphasis: The compositions of mixtures can vary greatly.

FIGURE 1.7 Separation by filtration. A mixture of a solid and a liquid is poured through a porous medium, in this case filter paper. The liquid passes through the paper while the solid remains on the paper. (Donald Clegg and Roxy Wilson)

approach would be to use a magnet to attract the iron filings and leave the gold ones behind. We can also use differences in chemical properties to separate mixtures into their components. Of course, chemical reactions will change some of the substances into others. In the case of our mixture of iron and gold, we could take advantage of an important chemical difference between these metals: Many acids dissolve iron but not gold. Thus, if we put our mixture into an appropriate acid, the iron will dissolve and the gold will be left behind. The two could then be separated by *filtration,* a procedure illustrated in Figure 1.7. We would have to use other chemical reactions, which we will learn about later, to transform the dissolved iron back into metal.

We can separate homogeneous mixtures into their components in similar ways. For example, water has a much lower boiling point than table salt. If we boil a solution of salt and water, the water will evaporate and the salt will be left behind. We could use a tube with cold walls (a condenser) to change the water vapor back into liquid (Figure 1.8). This process is called *distillation.*

The differing abilities of substances to adhere to the surfaces of various solids such as paper and starch can also be used to separate mixtures. This is the

FIGURE 1.8 A simple apparatus for the separation of a sodium chloride solution (salt water) into its components. Boiling the solution evaporates the water, which is condensed and collected in the receiving flask. After all the water has boiled away, pure sodium chloride remains in the boiling flask.

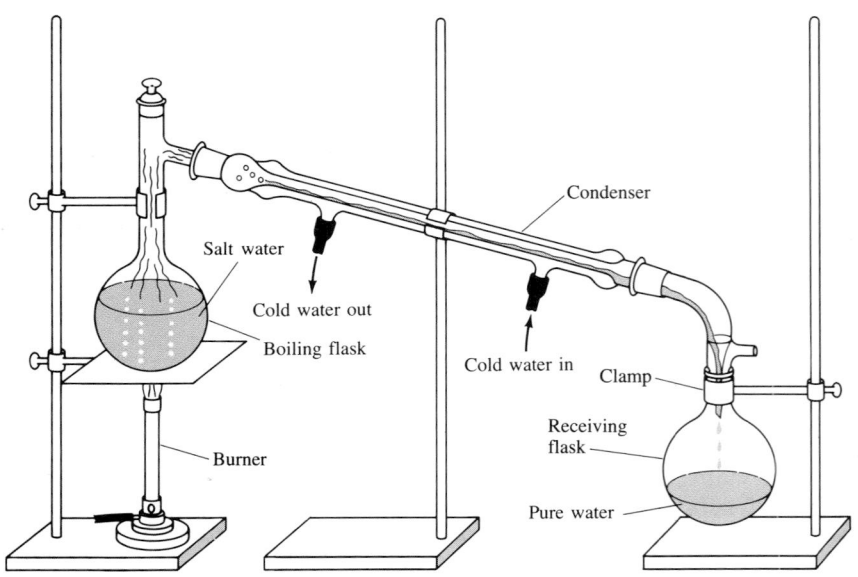

FIGURE 1.9 Separation of ink into components by paper chromatography. (*a*) Water begins to move up the paper. (*b*) Water moves past the ink spot, dissolving different components of the ink at different rates. (*c*) Water has separated the ink into its several different components. (© Richard Megna, 1990/Fundamental Photographs)

(*a*)   (*b*)   (*c*)

basis of *chromatography* (literally "the writing of colors"), a technique that can give beautiful and dramatic results. An example of the chromatographic separation of ink is shown in Figure 1.9.

1.2 Elements and Compounds

Pure subtances have a constant, invariable composition. We can classify subtances as either elements or compounds. **Elements** are substances that cannot be decomposed into simpler subtances by chemical means. **Compounds,** in contrast, can be decomposed by chemical means into two or more elements. Figure 1.10 summarizes the classification of matter into mixtures, compounds, and elements.

Point of Emphasis: *Elements* cannot be decomposed by chemical means. *Compounds* can be decomposed into simpler substances by chemical means. Compounds are composed of elements.

FIGURE 1.10 Classification of matter resulting in the categories of compounds and elements.

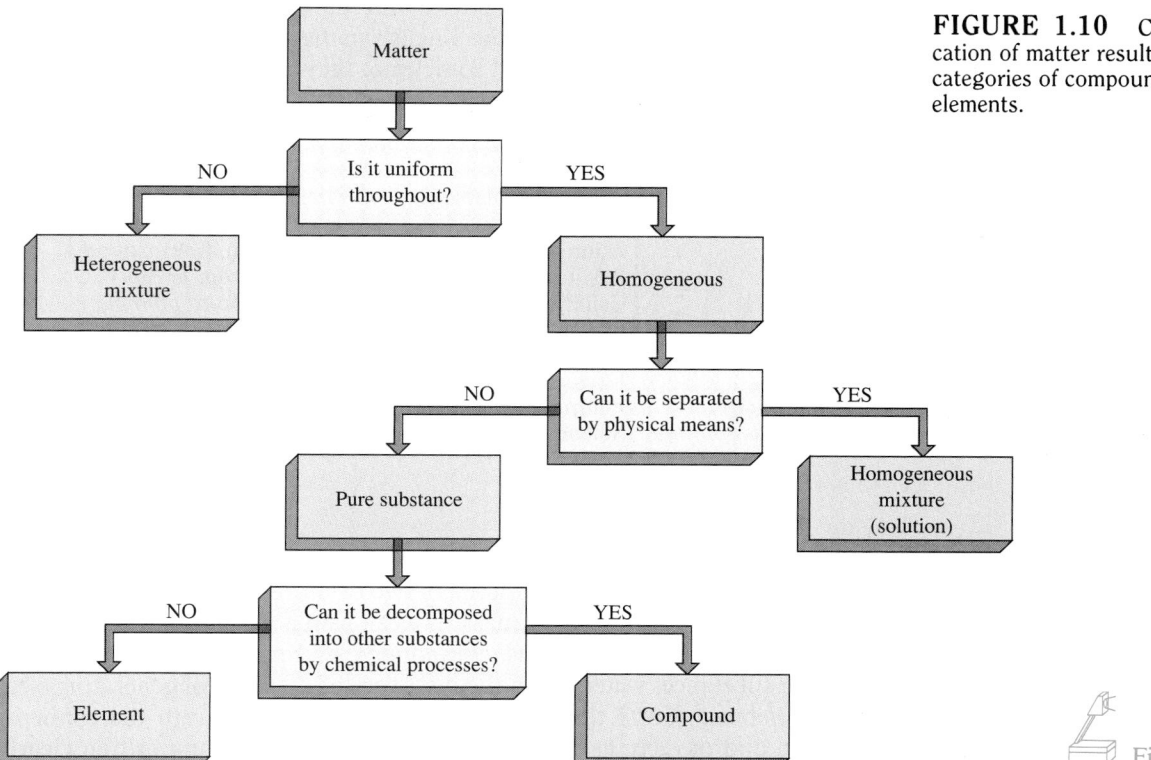

Figure 1.10

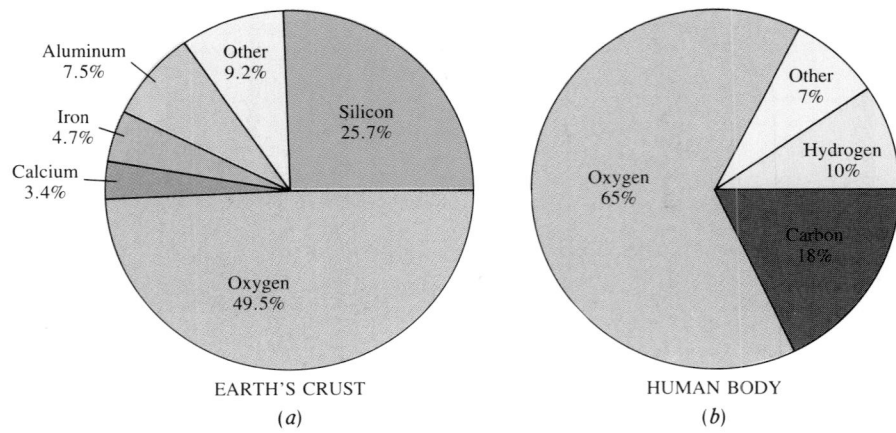

EARTH'S CRUST
(*a*)

HUMAN BODY
(*b*)

FIGURE 1.12 Decomposition of the compound water into the elements hydrogen and oxygen by passing a direct electrical current through it.

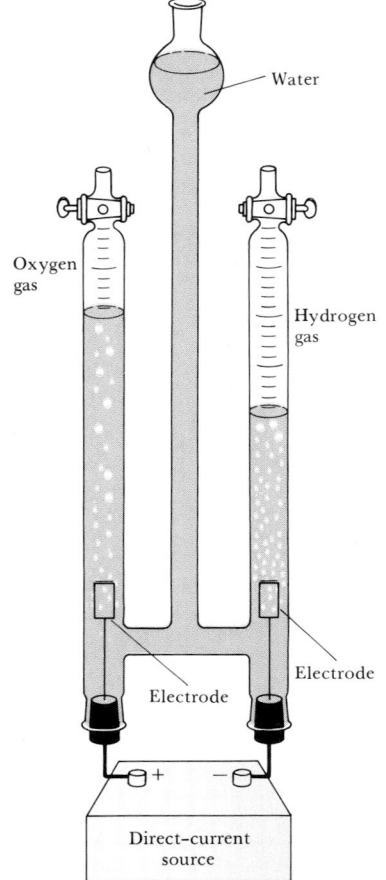

Elements

Elements are the basic substances out of which all matter is composed. In light of the seemingly endless variety of materials in our world, it is perhaps surprising that there are only 109 known elements (as of 1992). They vary greatly in abundance, as shown in Figure 1.11. For example, over 90 percent of the mass of the earth's crust consists of only five elements: oxygen, silicon, aluminum, iron, and calcium. In contrast, over 90 percent of the mass of the human body is accounted for by just three elements: oxygen, carbon, and hydrogen.

Some of the more familiar elements are listed in Table 1.2 along with the chemical abbreviations — or *symbols* — that we use to denote them. All of the known elements are listed on the front inside cover of this text. The symbol for an element consists of one or two letters, with the first letter capitalized. These symbols are often derived from the English name for the element (first and second columns in Table 1.2), but sometimes they are derived from a foreign name instead (third column). You will need to know these symbols and to learn others as we encounter them in the text.

TABLE 1.2 △ **Some Common Elements and Their Symbols**

Carbon (C)	Aluminum (Al)	Copper (Cu, from *cuprum*)
Fluorine (F)	Barium (Ba)	Iron (Fe, from *ferrum*)
Hydrogen (H)	Calcium (Ca)	Lead (Pb, from *plumbum*)
Iodine (I)	Chlorine (Cl)	Mercury (Hg, from *hydrargyrum*)
Nitrogen (N)	Helium (He)	Potassium (K, from *kalium*)
Oxygen (O)	Magnesium (Mg)	Silver (Ag, from *argentum*)
Phosphorus (P)	Platinum (Pt)	Sodium (Na, from *natrium*)
Sulfur (S)	Silicon (Si)	Tin (Sn, from *stannum*)

Compounds

Compounds are substances composed of two or more elements united chemically in definite proportions by mass. We can gain a clearer understanding of the distinctions among elements, compounds, and mixtures by examining a common substance, water. With the discovery of methods of generating electricity, chemists found that water could be decomposed into the elements hydrogen and oxygen, as shown in Figure 1.12. This decomposition clearly

TABLE 1.3 △ Comparison of Water, Hydrogen, and Oxygen

	Water	Hydrogen	Oxygen
Physical state[a]	Liquid	Gas	Gas
Normal boiling point	100°C	−253°C	−183°C
Density[a]	1.00 g/mL	0.084 g/L	1.33 g/L
Combustible?	No	Yes	No

[a] At room temperature and atmospheric pressure.

indicates that water is not an element. However, it is not merely a mixture of hydrogen and oxygen either. The properties of water are much different from those of its constituent elements, as seen in Table 1.3. Furthermore, the composition of water is not variable. Pure water, regardless of its source, consists of 11 percent hydrogen and 89 percent oxygen by mass.

The observation that the elemental composition of a pure compound is always the same is known as the **law of constant composition** (or the **law of definite proportions**). It was first put forth by the French chemist Joseph Louis Proust (1754–1826) in about 1800. Although this law has been known for almost 200 yr, the general belief persists among some people that a fundamental difference exists between compounds prepared in the laboratory and the corresponding compounds found in nature. However, a pure compound has the same composition and properties regardless of its source. Both chemists and nature must use the same elements and operate under the same natural laws. Differences in composition and properties between substances indicate that the compounds are not the same or that they differ in purity.

Point of Emphasis: The properties of a compound are different from those of a mixture of its constituent elements.

1.3 Units of Measurement

Many properties of matter are *quantitative;* that is, they are associated with numbers. When a number represents a measured quantity, the units of that quantity must always be specified. To say that the length of a pencil is 17.5 is meaningless. To say that it is 17.5 centimeters (cm) properly specifies the length. The units used for scientific measurements are those of the **metric system.** Metric units are based on the decimal system; that is, they are related by powers of 10.

The metric system, which was first developed in France during the late eighteenth century, is used as the system of measurement in most countries throughout the world. The United States has traditionally used the English system, although use of the metric system has become more common in recent years. For example, the contents of most canned goods and soft drinks in grocery stores are now given in metric as well as in English units. Figure 1.13 illustrates the application of the metric system to another aspect of our culture.

SI Units

In order to simplify and modernize the metric system, an international agreement was reached in 1960 specifying a particular choice of metric units for use in scientific measurements. These preferred units are called **SI units,** after the French *Système International d'Unités.* The SI system has seven *base units*

Learning Goal 5: List the basic SI units and the common metric prefixes and their meanings.

from which all other units are derived. Table 1.4 lists these base units and their symbols. In this chapter, we will consider three of these units, those for length, mass, and temperature.

The SI system employs a series of prefixes to indicate decimal fractions or multiples of various units. For example, the prefix *milli-* represents a 10^{-3} fraction of a unit: A milligram (mg) is 10^{-3} gram (g), a millimeter (mm) is 10^{-3} meter (m), and so forth. Table 1.5 presents the prefixes most commonly en-

TABLE 1.4 △ SI Base Units

Physical quantity	Name of unit	Abbreviation
Mass	Kilogram	kg
Length	Meter	m
Time	Second	s[a]
Electric current	Ampere	A
Temperature	Kelvin	K
Luminous intensity	Candela	cd
Amount of substance	Mole	mol

[a] The abbreviation sec is frequently used.

Table 1.5

TABLE 1.5 △ Selected Prefixes Used in the SI System

Prefix	Abbreviation	Meaning	Example
Mega-	M	10^6	1 megameter (Mm) = 1×10^6 m
Kilo-	k	10^3	1 kilometer (km) = 1×10^3 m
Deci-	d	10^{-1}	1 decimeter (dm) = 0.1 m
Centi-	c	10^{-2}	1 centimeter (cm) = 0.01 m
Milli-	m	10^{-3}	1 millimeter (mm) = 0.001 m
Micro-	μ[a]	10^{-6}	1 micrometer (μm) = 1×10^{-6} m
Nano-	n	10^{-9}	1 nanometer (nm) = 1×10^{-9} m
Pico-	p	10^{-12}	1 picometer (pm) = 1×10^{-12} m
Femto-	f	10^{-15}	1 femtometer (fm) = 1×10^{-15} m

[a] This is the Greek letter mu (pronounced "mew").

countered in chemistry. In using the SI system and in working problems throughout this text, it is important to have a comfortable familiarity with exponential notation. If you are unfamiliar with exponential notation or want to review it, refer to Appendix A.1.

Although non-SI units are being phased out, there are still some that are commonly used by scientists. Whenever we first encounter a non-SI unit in the text, the proper SI unit will also be given.

Length and Mass

The SI base unit of *length* is the meter (m), a distance only slightly longer than a yard. The relations between the English and metric system units that we will use most frequently in this text appear on the back inside cover. We will discuss how to convert English units into metric units, and vice versa, in Section 1.5. For the moment, it is more important to understand clearly the use of the prefixes given in Table 1.5.

Mass* is a measure of the amount of material in an object. The SI base unit of mass is the kilogram (kg), which is equal to about 2.2 lb. This base unit is unusual because it uses a prefix, *kilo-,* instead of the word *gram* alone. We obtain other units for mass by adding prefixes to the word *gram.*

> ### SAMPLE EXERCISE 1.1
>
> What is the name given to the unit that equals (a) 10^{-9} gram; (b) 10^{-6} second; (c) 10^{-3} meter?
>
> **SOLUTION** In each case we can refer to Table 1.5, finding the prefix related to each of the decimal fractions: (a) nanogram, ng; (b) microsecond; μs; (c) millimeter, mm.
>
> ### PRACTICE EXERCISE
>
> What fraction of a second is a picosecond, ps?   ***Answer:*** 10^{-12} second

Temperature

We sense temperature as a measure of the hotness or coldness of an object. Indeed, temperature determines the direction of heat flow. Heat always flows spontaneously from a substance at higher temperature to one at lower temperature. Thus, we feel the influx of energy when we touch a hot object, and we know that the object is at a higher temperature than our hand.

The temperature scales commonly employed in scientific studies are the Celsius and Kelvin scales. The **Celsius scale** is widely used in chemistry. It was originally based on the assignment of 0°C to the freezing point of water and 100°C to its boiling point at sea level (Figure 1.14). The **Kelvin scale,** however, is the SI temperature scale. This scale is based on the properties of gases, and its origins will be considered in Chapter 10. Zero on this scale is the lowest attainable temperature, −273.15°C, a temperature referred to as *absolute zero.* Both the Celsius and Kelvin scales have equal-sized units—that is, a kelvin is the same size as a degree Celsius. Thus, the Kelvin and Celsius scales are related as follows:

$$K = {}^\circ C + 273.15 \qquad\qquad [1.1]$$

---

* Mass and weight are often incorrectly thought to be the same. The *weight* of an object, however, is the force that the mass exerts because of gravity. In space, where gravitational forces are very weak, an astronaut can be weightless, but he or she cannot be *massless.* In fact, the astronaut's mass in space is the *same* as it is on the earth.

The freezing point of water, 0°C, is 273.15 K (Figure 1.14). Notice that we do not use a degree sign (°) with temperatures on the Kelvin scale.

The common temperature scale in the United States is the *Fahrenheit scale,* which is not generally used in scientific studies. On the Fahrenheit scale, water freezes at 32°F and boils at 212°F. There are 100° between the freezing point and the boiling point on the Celsius scale, and there are 180° between these points on the Fahrenheit scale (Figure 1.14). Consequently, the two scales are related as follows:

$$°C = \frac{100}{180}(°F - 32°) = \frac{5}{9}(°F - 32°) \qquad [1.2]$$

or, equivalently

$$°F = \frac{9}{5}(°C) + 32° \qquad [1.3]$$

SAMPLE EXERCISE 1.2

If a weather forecaster predicts that the temperature for the day will reach 31°C, what is the predicted temperature **(a)** in K; **(b)** in °F?

SOLUTION
(a) K = 31 + 273 = 304 K
(b) °F = $\frac{9}{5}$(31°C) + 32°
   = 56° + 32°
   = 88°F

PRACTICE EXERCISE

Ethylene glycol, the major ingredient in antifreeze, boils at 199°C. What is the boiling point in **(a)** K; **(b)** °F?   ***Answers:*** **(a)** 472 K; **(b)** 390°F

FIGURE 1.14 Comparison of the Kelvin, Celsius, and Fahrenheit temperature scales.

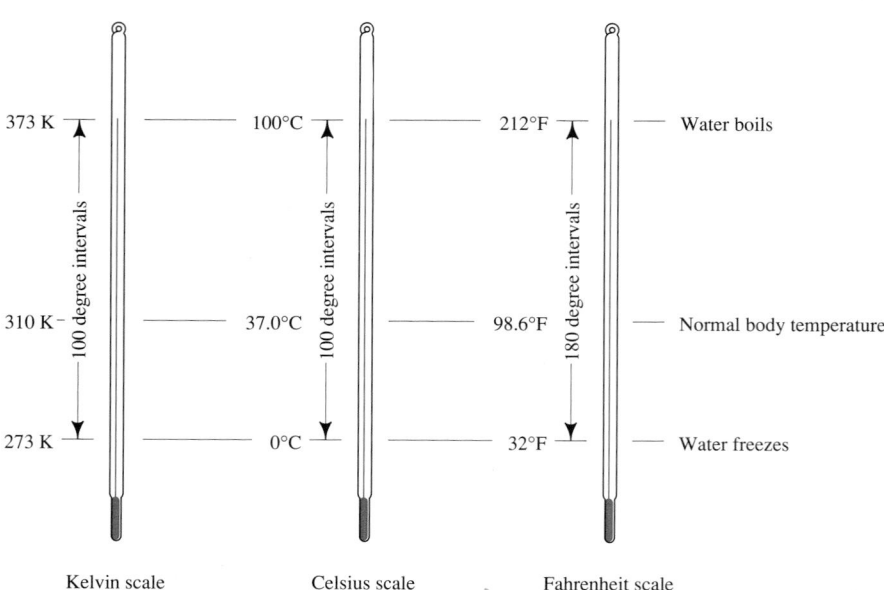

373 K	100°C	212°F	Water boils
310 K	37.0°C	98.6°F	Normal body temperature
273 K	0°C	32°F	Water freezes

Kelvin scale   Celsius scale   Fahrenheit scale

Derived SI Units

The seven SI base units are used to derive the units of other quantities. To do so, we use the base units in equations that define the physical quantity. For example, speed is defined as the ratio of distance to elapsed time. Thus, the SI unit for speed is the SI unit for distance (length) divided by the SI unit for time, m/s, which we read as "meters per second." We will encounter many derived units, such as those for force, pressure, and energy, later in this text. In this chapter, we examine two simple but important derived units, those for volume and density.

Volume

The *volume* of a cube is given by its length cubed, (length)^3. Thus, the basic SI unit of volume is the cubic meter, or m^3, the volume of a cube that is 1 m on each edge. Because this is a very large volume, smaller units are commonly used for most applications of chemistry. The cubic centimeter, cm^3, (sometimes written as cc), is one such unit. The cubic decimeter, dm^3, is also used. This volume is more commonly known as the *liter* (L) and is slightly larger than a quart. The liter is the first metric unit that we have encountered that is *not* an SI unit. There are 1000 milliliters (mL) in a liter (Figure 1.15), and each milliliter is the same volume as a cubic centimeter: 1 mL = 1 cm^3. The terms *milliliter* and *cubic centimeter* are used interchangeably in expressing volume.

The devices used most frequently in chemistry to measure volume are illustrated in Figure 1.16. Syringes, burets, and pipets allow the delivery of liquids with more accuracy than do graduated cylinders. Volumetric flasks are used to contain specific volumes of liquid.

Point of Emphasis: 1 mL ≡ 1 cc ≡ 1 cm^3.

Common Misconception: Students sometimes interchange the words "millimeter" and milliliter."

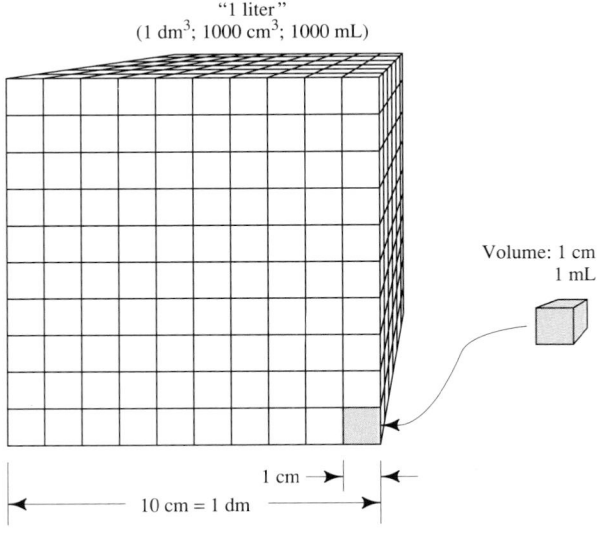

Volume: 1 cubic decimeter
"1 liter"
(1 dm^3; 1000 cm^3; 1000 mL)

Volume: 1 cm
1 mL

1 cm

10 cm = 1 dm

FIGURE 1.15 Comparison of 1 L and 1 mL.

FIGURE 1.16 Common devices used in chemistry laboratories for the measurement and delivery of volumes of liquid. The graduated cylinder, syringe, and buret are used to deliver variable volumes of liquid; the pipet is used to deliver a specific volume of a liquid; the volumetric flask contains a specific volume of liquid.

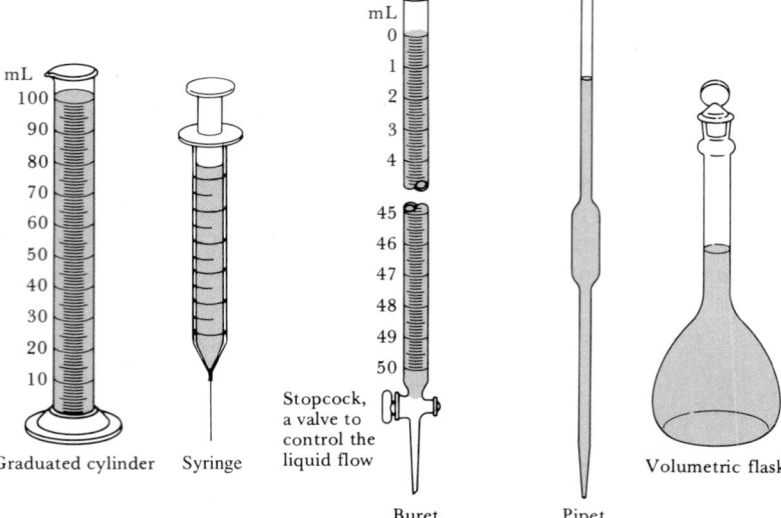

Graduated cylinder   Syringe   Stopcock, a valve to control the liquid flow   Buret   Pipet   Volumetric flask

Learning Goal 7: Perform calculations involving density.

TABLE 1.6 △ Densities of Some Selected Substances at 25°C

Substance	Density (g/cm³)
Air	0.001
Balsa wood	0.16
Water	1.00
Table salt	2.16
Iron	7.9
Gold	19.32

Common Misconception: Students often equate density with mass. However, density and mass are not the same. *Density* refers to the *ratio* of mass to volume for the sample.

Density

Density is widely used to characterize substances. It is defined as the amount of mass in a unit volume of the substance:

$$\text{Density} = \frac{\text{mass}}{\text{volume}} \qquad [1.4]$$

Although the basic SI unit of density is kg/m^3, density is more commonly expressed in units of grams per cubic centimeter (g/cm^3). The densities of some common substances are listed in Table 1.6. It is no coincidence that the density of water is 1.00 g/cm^3; the gram was originally defined as the mass of 1 cm^3 of water at a specific temperature.

The terms *density* and *weight* are sometimes confused. A person who says that iron weighs more than air generally means that iron has a higher density than air; 1 kg of air has the same mass as 1 kg of iron, but the iron is confined to a smaller volume, thereby giving it a higher density.

SAMPLE EXERCISE 1.3

(a) Calculate the density of mercury if 1.00×10^2 g occupies a volume of 7.36 cm^3.
(b) Calculate the mass of 65.0 cm^3 of mercury.

SOLUTION

(a) $\text{Density} = \dfrac{\text{mass}}{\text{volume}} = \dfrac{1.00 \times 10^2 \text{ g}}{7.36 \text{ cm}^3} = 13.6 \text{ g/cm}^3$

(b) Solving Equation 1.4 for mass gives

$$\text{Mass} = \text{volume} \times \text{density}$$

Using the density of mercury that we calculated in part (a) gives

$$\text{Mass} = (65.0 \text{ cm}^3)(13.6 \text{ g/cm}^3) = 884 \text{ g}$$

PRACTICE EXERCISE

A student needs 15.0 g of ethanol (ethyl alcohol) for an experiment. If the density of the alcohol is 0.789 g/mL, how many milliliters of alcohol are needed? *Answer:* 19.0 mL

Chemistry in the News

Because chemistry is so central to our lives, it is not surprising that we can read about it in the news nearly every day. Some of the news is good, such as recent breakthroughs in the development of new pharmaceuticals, materials, and products. Some of the news is more somber, dealing with the negative effects of chemicals on the environment or on society in general. The "chemical headlines" listed below indicate both the advances promised by chemistry and current problems that involve chemistry. An important aspect of being a student of chemistry is to become more aware of the chemistry that is continually going on around you. We hope that as you proceed through this text, your awareness and understanding of the impact of chemistry on your everyday life will be increased.

"Researchers Seek New Source for Promising Anticancer Drug"

A natural product called taxol has shown very promising results in the treatment of a variety of cancers, including ovarian and breast cancers. Taxol is obtained from the bark of the Pacific yew tree (Figure 1.17), which grows in the forests of the western United States and Canada. Although the Pacific yew is not a rare plant, it is less abundant now than in the past because of extensive lumbering operations in the areas in which it grows.

Taxol is present in tree bark in only low concentrations. The procedures for isolating it from the bark are difficult and low-yielding. The trees, which are slow-growing, must be killed to harvest the bark. It takes about three trees to provide sufficient drug for a course of treatment for one patient. As a result, there is widespread concern for the long-term survival of the Pacific yew because demand for the drug is very great. Furthermore, because of the laborious procedures involved in obtaining the drug, it is very expensive.

Several chemical research groups are attempting to synthesize taxol from simple starting materials. Other chemists are attempting to synthesize the drug from related compounds that can be extracted from the leaves and twigs of various yew trees and bushes. Others are searching for similar compounds that are just as potent. Still another approach is to develop plant tissue cultures in which the drug is formed. Such cell cultures could then be produced on a large scale, and the drug extracted from them.

"Researchers Act to Cut Auto Pollution Further"

Tailpipe catalytic converters are very successful in reducing air pollution, eliminating over 75 percent of the air pollutants emitted by car engines—including between 96 and 98 percent of the carbon monoxide. Air

FIGURE 1.17 The bark of the Pacific yew tree is grown and extracted to obtain a small amount of taxol, a promising anticancer drug. (Entheos)

quality in some areas is still so poor, however, that even this reduction is not enough. Scientists have observed that in a 30-km (20-mi) commute, half the emissions of certain pollutants occur in the first 5 to 6 km (3 to 4 mi) while the converter is cold. The efficiency of the converter increases with temperature. One method of further reducing emissions that is under development is a preheated converter (Figure 1.18). Automakers are also working on moving the converter closer to the engine to heat it faster. We will discuss how temperature and catalysts affect the speed of chemical reactions in Chapter 14.

"Key Signal of Cells Found to Be a Common Gas"

A simple and familiar chemical, nitric oxide, has been found to be important in controlling many vital functions in the body. It had escaped attention until now because it survives in the body for a mere 5 s or so and because it bears no resemblance to any known biological regulator. The new findings show that it is a messenger molecule involved in a wide range of activities. It mediates the control of blood pressure. It helps the immune system kill invading parasites that enter cells. It stops cancer cells from dividing and spreading. It transmits signals between brain cells, and it contributes to the large-scale death of brain cells that can debilitate people who have suffered strokes. Drug companies have started investigating how this discovery can be used to develop new drugs to control blood pressure, treat migraine

FIGURE 1.18 Electrically heated catalytic converters are currently being tested as a way of further reducing the quantity of air pollutants emitted by automobiles. (W. R. Grace)

headaches, and help protect brain cells threatened by degenerative diseases and strokes. If you want to read more on this topic, see: S. H. Snyder and D. S. Brett, "Biological Roles of Nitric Oxide," *Scientific American,* 266(5), 68–77 (May 1992).

"Arctic Ozone Loss: Outlook Is Bleak"

The National Aeronautics and Space Administration (NASA) has reported stratospheric ozone depletion of about 10 percent in certain Arctic regions. The studies on ozone loss and its causes have been subjects of major articles in newspapers and news magazines (Figure 1.19).

Ozone is a form of the element oxygen whose molecules contain three atoms of oxygen each, as we discuss in Chapters 2 and 7. It is less common than the "usual" form of oxygen, which contains two atoms per molecule. The action of sunlight on oxygen produces a layer of ozone in the stratosphere more than 10 km above the earth's surface. This ozone layer serves as a natural sun screen, filtering out harmful ultraviolet radiation that can cause skin cancer and cataracts.

In the mid-1980s, scientists detected a thinning of the ozone layer over Antarctica, a problem referred to as the "ozone hole." The discovery of a depletion in the Northern Hemisphere has been more recent. The causes for the ozone depletion have been the subject of much study and debate in the scientific community. Many hypotheses have been put forth, including the idea that volcanic activity plays a role. One of the most compelling ideas is that a class of substances called chlorofluorocarbons (CFCs) are involved in triggering the ozone loss. These substances are widely used as refrigerants, aerosol propellants, cleaning solvents, and foaming agents for plastics. Normally, CFC molecules are unreactive. When exposed to sunlight, however, they

produce chlorine atoms which react with ozone, decomposing it into normal oxygen. This discovery has led to intense research activity seeking substances that can be used as replacements for CFCs. We will discuss the topic of ozone depletion further in Chapter 18.

"New Class of Superconductors Pushing Temperatures Higher"

Since the early 1900s, scientists have been aware that when certain metals and alloys are cooled, they become *superconductors*—materials that conduct electricity with no resistance (and hence no power loss). The ability to utilize such materials could lead to huge advances in, for example, the transmission of energy, biomedical imaging, and solid-state electronic devices. Until the mid-1980s, however, superconductivity had been observed only at extremely low temperatures (23 K and below). In 1986, two researchers in Switzerland discovered that certain chemical compounds called *metal oxides* were superconductors at about 30 K, a significant jump in the superconducting temperature. Since that discovery, chemical modification of the metal oxides has led to the production of new materials that exhibit superconductivity at temperatures greater than 100 K. We discuss the story of high-temperature superconductors in more detail in Chapter 12.

FIGURE 1.19 News of decreasing ozone levels in the upper atmosphere and their potential effects has generated a great deal of interest and concern among scientists and among the public at large. (Copyright 1992 Time Inc. Reprinted by permission.)

Intensive and Extensive Properties

Temperature and density are examples of **intensive properties,** properties whose values do not depend on the amount of material chosen. Two samples of a liquid can have the same temperature, though one has a volume of one cup and the other fills a bathtub. Likewise, the density of mercury, calculated in Sample Exercise 1.3, is 13.6 g/cm³ regardless of the size of the sample. In contrast, both volume and mass are **extensive properties,** properties whose values depend on the amount of material. Similarly, the *heat content* of a sample (the total amount of heat "held" by a sample) is an extensive property. Note the important distinction between temperature, an intensive property, and heat content, an extensive property. We will examine heat content and its relation to temperature in Chapter 5.

Point of Emphasis: *Intensive properties* do not depend on the sample size; *extensive properties* do depend on the size of the sample.

1.4 Uncertainty in Measurement

In scientific work, we recognize two kinds of numbers: *exact numbers* (those whose values are known exactly) and *inexact numbers* (those whose values have some uncertainty). Exact numbers are those that have defined values or are integers that result from counting numbers of objects. For example, by definition, there are exactly 12 eggs in a dozen, exactly 1000 g in a kilogram, and exactly 2.54 cm in an inch. The number 1 in any conversion factor between units, as in 1 m = 1.0936 yd, is also an exact number.

Numbers obtained by measurement are always *inexact.* There are always inherent limitations in the equipment used to measure quantities (equipment errors), and there are differences in how different people make the same measurement (human errors). Suppose that 10 students with 10 different balances are given the same dime to weigh. The 10 measurements will vary slightly. The balances might be calibrated slightly differently, and there might be differences in how each student reads the mass from the balance. Remember: *Uncertainties always exist in measured quantities.*

Precision and Accuracy

Two terms are usually used in discussing the uncertainties in measured values: precision and accuracy. **Precision** is a measure of how closely individual measurements agree with one another. **Accuracy** refers to how closely individual measurements agree with the correct, or "true" value. The analogy of darts stuck in a dart board pictured in Figure 1.20 illustrates the difference between the two terms.

In general, the more precise a measurement, the more accurate it will be. We gain confidence in the accuracy of a measurement if we obtain nearly the same value in many different experiments. Thus, in the laboratory, you will often perform several different "trials" of the same experiment. It is possible, however, for a precise value to be inaccurate. If a very sensitive balance is poorly calibrated, for example, the masses measured will be inaccurate even if they are precise.

Common Misconception: The terms "accurate" and "precise" are often incorrectly used interchangeably.

FIGURE 1.20 The distribution of darts on a target illustrates the distinction between accuracy and precision.

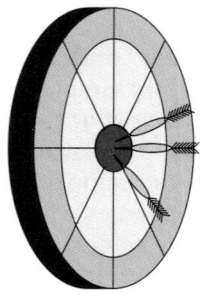
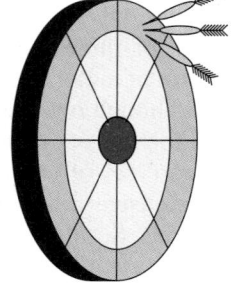
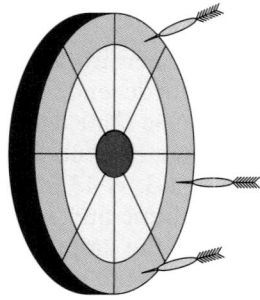

Good accuracy
Good precision

Poor accuracy
Good precision

Poor accuracy
Poor precision

Figure 1.20

Significant Figures

Suppose you weigh a dime on a balance capable of measuring to the nearest 0.0001 g. You could report the mass as 2.2405 ± 0.0001 g. The $\pm$ notation (read "plus or minus 0.0001") is a useful way to express the uncertainty of a measurement. In much scientific work, we drop the $\pm$ notation with the understanding that an uncertainty of at least one unit exists in the last digit of the measured quantity. That is, *measured quantities are generally reported in such a way that only the last digit is uncertain.* All digits, including the uncertain one, are called **significant figures.** The number 2.2405 has five significant figures. The number of significant figures indicates the preciseness of a measurement.

Learning Goal 8: Determine the number of significant figures in a measured quantity.

SAMPLE EXERCISE 1.4

What is the difference between 4.0 g and 4.00 g?

SOLUTION Many people would say there is no difference, but a scientist would note the difference in the number of significant figures in the two measurements. The value 4.0 has two significant figures, while 4.00 has three. This implies that the second measurement is more precise. A mass of 4.0 g indicates that the mass is between 3.9 and 4.1 g; the mass is 4.0 ± 0.1 g. A measurement of 4.00 g implies that the mass is between 3.99 and 4.01 g; the mass is 4.00 ± 0.01 g.

PRACTICE EXERCISE

A balance has a precision of ± 0.001 g. A sample that weighs about 25 g is weighed on this balance. How many significant figures should be reported for this measurement? *Answer:* 5

The following guidelines apply to determining the number of significant figures in a measured quantity:

1. All nonzero digits are significant—457 cm (three significant figures); 2.5 g (two significant figures).
2. Zeros between nonzero digits are significant—1005 kg (four significant figures); 1.03 cm (three significant figures).
3. Zeros to the left of the first nonzero digit are not significant; they merely indicate the position of the decimal point—0.02 g (one significant figure); 0.0026 cm (two significant figures).

4. Zeros that fall both at the end of a number and to the right of the decimal point are significant—0.0200 g (three significant figures); 3.0 cm (two significant figures).

5. When a number ends in zeros but contains no decimal point, the zeros may or may not be significant—130 cm (two or three significant figures); 10,300 g (three, four, or five significant figures). We describe how to remove this ambiguity below.

The use of exponential notation (Appendix A) avoids the potential ambiguity of whether the zeros at the end of a number are significant (rule 5). For example, a mass of 10,300 g can be written in exponential notation showing three, four, or five significant figures:

1.03×10^4 g   (three significant figures)
1.030×10^4 g   (four significant figures)
1.0300×10^4 g   (five significant figures)

In these numbers all the zeros to the right of the decimal point are significant (rules 2 and 4). (All significant figures come before the exponent; the exponential term does not add to the number of significant figures.)

Exact numbers can be treated as if they have an infinite number of significant figures. This rule applies to many definitions between units. Thus, when we say, "There are 12 inches in 1 foot," the number 12 is exact, and we need not worry about the number of significant figures in it.

SAMPLE EXERCISE 1.5

How many significant figures are in each of the following numbers (assume that each number is a measured quantity): (a) 4.003; (b) 6.023×10^{23}; (c) 5000?

SOLUTION
(a) Four; the zeros are significant figures. (b) Four; the exponential term does not add to the number of significant figures. (c) One, two, three, or four. In this case, the ambiguity could have been avoided by using standard exponential notation. Thus 5×10^3 has only one significant figure; 5.00×10^3 has three.

PRACTICE EXERCISE

How many significant figures are in each of the following measurements:
(a) 3.549 g   (b) 2.3×10^4 cm   (c) 0.00134 m³?
Answers: (a) four   (b) two   (c) three

Significant Figures in Calculations

In carrying measured quantities through calculations, observe this point: The precision of the result is limited by the precision of the measurements. *In multiplication and division the result must be reported as having no more significant figures than the measurement with the fewest significant figures.* When the result contains more than the correct number of significant figures, it must be rounded off.

For example, the area of a rectangle whose edge lengths are 6.221 cm and 5.2 cm should be reported as 32 cm²:

Area = (6.221 cm)(5.2 cm) = 32.3492 cm² ⟶ round off to 32 cm²

We round off to two significant figures because 5.2 cm has only two significant figures.

In rounding off numbers, look at the leftmost digit to be dropped:

1. If the leftmost digit to be removed is less than 5, the preceding number is left unchanged. Thus, rounding 7.248 to two significant figures gives 7.2.
2. If the leftmost digit is 5 or greater, the preceding number is increased by 1. Rounding 4.735 to three significant figures gives 4.74, and rounding 2.376 to two significant figures gives 2.4.

The guidelines used to determine the number of significant figures in multiplication and division cannot be used for *addition and subtraction.* For these operations, *the result should be reported to the same number of decimal places as that of the term with the least number of decimal places.* In the following example the uncertain digits appear in color:

This number limits   20.4   ⟵ one decimal place
the number of significant   1.322 ⟵ three decimal places
figures in the result ⟶   83   ⟵ zero decimal places
                 104.722 ⟶ round off to 105
                     (one uncertain digit)

SAMPLE EXERCISE 1.6

A person's height is measured to be 67.50 in. What is this height in centimeters?

SOLUTION There are 2.54 cm in an inch; this is an exact number and can be treated as if it had an infinite number of significant figures. The precision of the answer is thus limited by the measurement in inches and should be reported to four significant figures (67.50 has four significant figures). The answer is

$$(67.50 \text{ in.})\left(2.54 \frac{\text{cm}}{\text{in.}}\right) = 171.45 \text{ cm, which is rounded to } 171.5 \text{ cm}$$

PRACTICE EXERCISE

There are 1609.4 m in a mile. How many meters are in a distance of 1.35 mi?
Answer: 2.17×10^3 m

SAMPLE EXERCISE 1.7

A gas at 25°C exactly fills a container previously determined to have a volume of 1.05×10^3 cm³. The container plus gas are weighed and found to have a mass of 837.6 g. The container, when emptied of all gas, has a mass of 836.2 g. What is the density of the gas at 25°C?

SOLUTION The mass of the gas is just the difference in the two masses: (837.6 − 836.2) g = 1.4 g. Notice that 1.4 g has only two significant figures, even though the masses from which it is obtained have four.

From the definition of density we have

$$\text{Density} = \frac{\text{mass}}{\text{volume}} = \frac{1.4 \text{ g}}{1.05 \times 10^3 \text{ cm}^3}$$

$$= 1.3 \times 10^{-3} \text{ g/cm}^3 = 0.0013 \text{ g/cm}^3$$

There are two significant figures in this quantity, corresponding to the smaller number of significant figures in the two numbers that form the ratio.

It is important to have a feeling for significant figures when you use a calculator, because calculators ordinarily display more digits than are significant. For example, a typical calculator would give 1.3333333×10^{-3} as the answer to the calculation in Sample Exercise 1.7. This result must be rounded off because of the uncertainties in the measured quantities used in the calculation.

When a calculation involves two or more steps, retain at least one additional digit—past the number of significant figures—for intermediate answers. This procedure ensures that small errors from rounding at each step do not combine to affect the final result. In using a calculator, you may enter the numbers one after another, rounding only the final answer. Accumulated round-off errors often account for small differences between results you obtain and answers given in the text for numerical problems.

Point of Emphasis: In a long calculation, round-off errors can be minimized by rounding off only the final answer.

1.5 Dimensional Analysis

Throughout the text, we use an approach called **dimensional analysis** as an aid in problem solving. In dimensional analysis, we carry units through all calculations. Units are multiplied together, divided into each other, or "canceled." Dimensional analysis will help ensure that the solutions to problems yield the proper units. Moreover, dimensional analysis provides a systematic way of solving many numerical problems and of checking our solutions for possible errors.

The key to using dimensional analysis is the correct use of conversion factors to change one unit into another. A **conversion factor** is a fraction whose numerator and denominator are the same quantity expressed in different units. For example, 2.54 cm and 1 in. are the same length, 2.54 cm = 1 in. This relationship allows us to write two conversion factors:

Learning Goal 10: Interconvert metric and English-system measurements using dimensional analysis.

$$\frac{2.54 \text{ cm}}{1 \text{ in.}} \qquad \frac{1 \text{ in.}}{2.54 \text{ cm}}$$

The first of these factors is used when we want to convert inches to centimeters. For example, the length in centimeters of an object that is 8.50 in. long is given by

Teaching Note: Because the numerator and denominator express the same quantities (only in different units), the value of the conversion factor is exactly 1.

$$\text{Number of centimeters} = (8.50 \text{ in.}) \frac{2.54 \text{ cm}}{1 \text{ in.}} = 21.6 \text{ cm}$$

Desired unit

Given unit

Note that the units of inches in the denominator of the conversion factor cancel the units of inches in the data we were given (8.50 *inches*). The centimeters in the numerator of the conversion factor become the units of the final answer. In general, the units multiply and divide as follows:

$$\text{Given unit} \times \frac{\text{desired unit}}{\text{given unit}} = \text{desired unit}$$

If the desired units are not obtained in a calculation, then an error must have been made somewhere. Careful inspection of units often reveals the source of the error.

SAMPLE EXERCISE 1.8

A man weighs 185 lb. What is his mass in grams?

SOLUTION   From the back inside cover we have 1 lb = 453.6 g. In order to cancel pounds and leave grams, we will use the conversion factor with grams in the numerator and pounds in the denominator:

$$\text{Mass in grams} = (185 \text{ lb})\left(\frac{453.6 \text{ g}}{1 \text{ lb}}\right) = 8.39 \times 10^4 \text{ g}$$

Note that the answer can be given only to three significant figures.

PRACTICE EXERCISE

By using a conversion factor from the back inside cover, determine the length in kilometers of a 500.0-mi automobile race.   *Answer:* 804.7 km

We can use more than one conversion factor in the solution of a problem. For example, suppose we want to know the length in inches of an 8.00-m rod. The table at the end of the text doesn't give the relationship between meters and inches. It *does* give the relationship between centimeters and inches, though, and we know that 1 m = 100 cm. Thus, we can convert first from meters to centimeters, and then from centimeters to inches:

Length in inches
    = (length in m)(factor converting m → cm)(factor converting cm → in.)

The relationship between meters and centimeters gives us the first conversion factor. Because we need to cancel meters, we write meters in the denominator:

$$\frac{100 \text{ cm}}{1 \text{ m}}$$

We then use the relationship 2.54 cm = 1 in. to write the second conversion factor with the desired units, inches, in the numerator:

$$\frac{1 \text{ in.}}{2.54 \text{ cm}}$$

Thus, we have

$$\text{Number of inches} = (8.00 \text{ m})\left(\frac{100 \text{ cm}}{1 \text{ m}}\right)\left(\frac{1 \text{ in.}}{2.54 \text{ cm}}\right) = 315 \text{ in.}$$

The conversion factors above convert from length to length or, more generally, from one unit of a given measure to another unit of the same measure. We also have conversion factors that convert from one measure to a different one. The density of a substance, for example, is a conversion factor between mass and volume. Suppose that we want to know the mass in grams of a cubic inch (1.00 in.³) of gold, which has a density of 19.3 g/cm³. The density gives us the following conversion factors:

$$\frac{19.3 \text{ g}}{1 \text{ cm}^3} \qquad \frac{1 \text{ cm}^3}{19.3 \text{ g}}$$

Because the answer we want is a mass in grams, we can see that we will use the first of these factors, which has mass in grams in the numerator. To use this factor, however, we must first relate cubic centimeters to cubic inches. We know the factor for converting from inches to centimeters, and the cube of this gives us the desired conversion factor:

$$\left(\frac{2.54 \text{ cm}}{1 \text{ in.}}\right)^3 = \frac{(2.54)^3 \text{ cm}^3}{(1)^3 \text{ in.}^3} = \frac{16.39 \text{ cm}^3}{1 \text{ in.}^3}$$

Teaching Note: Students often fail to perform an algebraic function on *both* the units and the numerical value in a conversion. Caution students that when squaring a unit conversion, the numerical part of the factor *and* the unit must be squared. When cubing a unit conversion, the numerical part of the factor *and* the unit must be cubed.

Notice that both the numbers and the units are cubed. Also, because 2.54 is an exact number, we can retain as many digits of $(2.54)^3$ as we need. We have used four, one more than the number of digits in the density (19.3 g/cm³). Applying our conversion factors, we can now solve the problem:

$$\text{Mass in grams} = (1.00 \text{ in.}^3)\left(\frac{16.39 \text{ cm}^3}{1 \text{ in.}^3}\right)\left(\frac{19.3 \text{ g}}{1 \text{ cm}^3}\right) = 316 \text{ g}$$

The final answer is reported to three significant figures, the same number as in 19.3.

Summary of Dimensional Analysis

In using dimensional analysis to solve problems, we will always ask three questions:

1. *What data are we given in the problem?*
2. *What quantity do we wish to obtain in the problem?*
3. *What conversion factors do we have available to take us from the given quantity to the desired one?*

If you carry the units through during your calculations, you will always know whether you are using the correct conversion factors. Finally, whenever you finish a calculation, look at the numerical value of your answer (as well as the units) and ask yourself whether your answer makes any sense.

When solving numerical problems, always ask yourself whether your answer makes sense. (*Calvin and Hobbes.* Copyright 1986 Universal Press Syndicate. Reprinted with permission. All rights reserved.)

SAMPLE EXERCISE 1.9

What is the mass in grams of 1.00 gal of water? The density of water is 1.00 g/mL.

SOLUTION   Following the procedure summarized above, we note the following:

1. We are given 1.00 gal of water.
2. We wish to obtain the mass in grams.
3. We have the following conversion factors either given, commonly known, or available on the back inside cover of the text:

$$\frac{1.00 \text{ g water}}{1 \text{ mL water}} \qquad \frac{1 \text{ L}}{1000 \text{ mL}} \qquad \frac{1 \text{ L}}{1.057 \text{ qt}} \qquad \frac{1 \text{ gal}}{4 \text{ qt}}$$

We realize that the first of these conversion factors must be used as written (with grams in the numerator) to give the desired result. We also realize that the last conversion factor must be inverted in order to cancel gallons. The solution is given by

$$\text{Mass in grams} = (1.00 \text{ gal of water})\left(\frac{4 \text{ qt}}{1 \text{ gal}}\right)\left(\frac{1 \text{ L}}{1.057 \text{ qt}}\right)\left(\frac{1000 \text{ mL}}{1 \text{ L}}\right)\left(\frac{1.00 \text{ g}}{1 \text{ mL}}\right)$$

$$= 3.78 \times 10^3 \text{ g water}$$

PRACTICE EXERCISE

A car travels 28 mi per gallon of gasoline. How many kilometers per liter will it go?   *Answer:* 12 km/L

SAMPLE EXERCISE 1.10

A certain printed page has an average of 25 words per square inch of paper. The average length of the words is 5.3 letters. What is the average number of letters per square centimeter of paper?

SOLUTION   We are given the "print density" in units of words per square inch. We want to convert this to a print density in units of letters per square centimeter. We are given the relation 1 word = 5.3 letters and, from the back inside cover, 1 in. = 2.54 cm. The solution is given by

$$\text{Number of letters/cm}^2 = \left(\frac{25 \text{ words}}{1 \text{ in.}^2}\right)\left(\frac{5.3 \text{ letters}}{1 \text{ word}}\right)\left(\frac{1 \text{ in.}}{2.54 \text{ cm}}\right)^2$$

$$= 21 \text{ letters/cm}^2$$

PRACTICE EXERCISE

In a certain part of the country, there is an average of 710 people per square mile and 0.72 telephones per person. What is the average number of telephones in an area of 5.0 km²?   *Answer:* 9.9×10^2 telephones

For Review

Summary

Chemistry is the study of the properties, composition, and changes of matter. Matter exists in three states: gas, liquid, and solid. Most matter consists of a mixture of substances. Mixtures can be either homogeneous or heterogeneous; homogeneous mixtures are called solutions. There are two types of pure substances: elements and compounds. Each substance has a unique set of physical and chemical properties that can be used to identify it. Matter can undergo physical changes and chemical changes (chemical reactions).

Measurements in chemistry are made using the metric system. Special emphasis is placed on a particular set of metric units called SI units, which are based on the meter, kilogram, and second as the basic units of length, mass, and time, respectively. The metric system employs a set of prefixes to indicate decimal fractions or multiples of the base units.

All measured quantities are inexact to some extent. The number of significant figures indicates the exactness of the measurement. Certain rules must be followed so that a calculation involving measured quantities is reported to the proper number of significant figures.

In the dimensional analysis approach to problem solving we keep track of units as we carry measurements through calculations. The units are multiplied together, divided into each other, or canceled like algebraic quantities. Obtaining the proper units for the final result is an important means of checking the method of calculation. In converting units, and in several other types of problems, conversion factors can be used. These factors are ratios constructed from valid relations between equivalent quantities.

Key Terms

chemistry
matter (Sec. 1.1)
gas (Sec. 1.1)
liquid (Sec. 1.1)
solid (Sec. 1.1)
pure substance (Sec. 1.1)
physical properties (Sec. 1.1)
chemical properties (Sec. 1.1)
physical changes (Sec. 1.1)
changes of state (Sec. 1.1)
chemical changes (Sec. 1.1)
chemical reactions (Sec. 1.1)
scientific method (Sec. 1.1)
hypothesis (Sec. 1.1)
scientific law (Sec. 1.1)
theory (Sec. 1.1)
mixtures (Sec. 1.1)
solutions (Sec. 1.1)

elements (Sec. 1.2)
compounds (Sec. 1.2)
law of constant composition (Sec. 1.2)
law of definite proportions (Sec. 1.2)
metric system (Sec. 1.3)
SI units (Sec. 1.3)
mass (Sec. 1.3)
Celsius scale (Sec. 1.3)
Kelvin scale (Sec. 1.3)
density (Sec. 1.3)
intensive property (Sec. 1.3)
extensive property (Sec. 1.3)
precision (Sec. 1.4)
accuracy (Sec. 1.4)
significant figures (Sec. 1.4)
dimensional analysis (Sec. 1.5)
conversion factor (Sec. 1.5)

Exercises

Introduction to Matter

1.1. Identify each of the following substances as a gas, a liquid, or a solid under ordinary conditions of temperature and pressure: **(a)** mercury; **(b)** sodium bicarbonate (baking soda); **(c)** hydrogen; **(d)** carbon monoxide.

1.2. Give the state of matter (gas, liquid, or solid) for each of the following under normal conditions: **(a)** oxygen; **(b)** iron; **(c)** isopropyl alcohol (used as rubbing alcohol); **(d)** sodium chloride (table salt).

1.3. Indicate which of the following processes are physical processes and which are chemical processes: **(a)** corrosion of aluminum metal; **(b)** cutting a diamond; **(c)** burning gasoline; **(d)** boiling water.

1.4. A match is lit and held under a cold piece of metal. The following observations are made: **(a)** The match burns. **(b)** The metal gets warmer. **(c)** Water condenses on the metal. **(d)** Soot (carbon) is deposited on the metal. Which of these occurrences are due to physical changes and which are due to chemical changes?

1.5. In the process of attempting to characterize a substance, a chemist makes the following observations: The substance is a silvery-white, lustrous metal. It melts at 649°C and boils at 1105°C. Its density at 20°C is 1.738 g/cm^3. The substance burns in air, producing an intense white light. It reacts with chlorine to give a brittle, white solid. The substance can be pounded into thin sheets or drawn into wires. It is a good conductor of electricity. Which of these characteristics are physical properties and which are chemical properties?

1.6. Classify the following observations about a substance as either physical or chemical properties: **(a)** color; **(b)** melting point; **(c)** reactivity with water; **(d)** boiling point; **(e)** state of matter under ordinary conditions; **(f)** flammability; **(g)** density; **(h)** electrical conductivity; **(i)** decomposition products upon heating.

1.7. Classify each of the following as a pure substance or a mixture; if a mixture, indicate whether it is homogeneous or heterogeneous: **(a)** a chocolate-chip cookie; **(b)** water; **(c)** vodka; **(d)** a pure gold coin.

1.8. Classify each of the following as a pure substance or a mixture; if a mixture, indicate whether it is homogeneous or heterogeneous: **(a)** air; **(b)** gasoline; **(c)** iodine crystals; **(d)** salad dressing.

Elements and Compounds

1.9. Give the chemical symbol for each of the following elements: **(a)** carbon; **(b)** sodium; **(c)** iron; **(d)** phosphorus; **(e)** potassium; **(f)** chlorine; **(g)** nitrogen; **(h)** silver.

1.10. Identify the chemical elements represented by the following symbols: **(a)** He; **(b)** Mg; **(c)** Pb; **(d)** S; **(e)** F; **(f)** Zn; **(g)** Cu; **(h)** Ar.

1.11. In 1807, the English chemist Humphry Davy passed an electric current through molten potassium hydroxide and isolated a bright, shiny, reactive substance. He claimed the discovery of a new element, which he named potassium. In those days, before the advent of modern instruments, what was the basis on which one could claim that a substance was an element?

1.12. A solid white substance A is heated strongly in the absence of air. It decomposes to form a new white substance B and a gas C. The gas has exactly the same properties as the product obtained when carbon is burned in an excess of oxygen. What can we say about whether solids A and B and the gas C are elements or compounds?

Units and Measurement

1.13. What basic SI units are appropriate for expressing the following quantities: **(a)** the diameter of the earth; **(b)** the surface area of a tennis ball; **(c)** the volume of a gasoline tank; **(d)** the mass of a brick; **(e)** the speed of light; **(f)** the temperature of the air?

1.14. What basic SI units are appropriate for expressing quantities having the following units? **(a)** square miles; **(b)** quarts; **(c)** tons; **(d)** days; **(e)** yards; **(f)** degrees Fahrenheit.

1.15. What decimal power do the following abbreviations represent: **(a)** d; **(b)** c; **(c)** f; **(d)** μ; **(e)** M; **(f)** k; **(g)** n; **(h)** m; **(i)** p?

1.16. Use appropriate metric prefixes to write the following measurements without use of exponents: **(a)** 3.4×10^{-12} m; **(b)** 4.8×10^{-6} mL; **(c)** 7.23×10^3 g; **(d)** 2.35×10^{-6} m³; **(e)** 5.8×10^{-9} s; **(f)** 3.45×10^{-3} mol.

1.17. What type of quantity (for example, length, volume, density) do the following units indicate? **(a)** μL; **(b)** cm²; **(c)** mm³; **(d)** mg/L; **(e)** ps; **(f)** nm; **(g)** K.

1.18. Indicate whether the following are measurements of length, area, volume, mass, density, time, or temperature: **(a)** 5 ns; **(b)** 3.2 kg/L; **(c)** 0.88 pm; **(d)** 540 km²; **(e)** 173 K; **(f)** 2 mm³; **(g)** 23°C.

1.19. Perform the following conversions: **(a)** 454 mg to g; **(b)** 5.0×10^{-8} m to nm; **(c)** 0.076 mL to μL; **(d)** 1.55 kg/m³ to g/L.

1.20. Convert **(a)** 3.05×10^5 g to kg; **(b)** 0.0025 μm to pm; **(c)** 3.45×10^{-8} s to ns; **(d)** 4.5×10^8 pm³ to m³.

1.21. **(a)** A sample of chloroform, a liquid once used as an anesthetic, has a mass of 37.25 g and a volume of 25.0 mL. What is its density? **(b)** The density of platinum is 23.4 g/cm³. Calculate the mass of 50.0 cm³ of platinum. **(c)** The density of magnesium is 1.74 g/cm³. What is the volume of 175 g of this metal?

1.22. **(a)** A cube of plastic 1.2×10^{-5} km on a side has a mass of 1.1 g. What is its density in g/cm³? Will this material float on water? (Materials that are less dense than water will float.) **(b)** The density of liquid bromine is 3.12 g/mL. What is the mass of 0.500 L of bromine? **(c)** The density of a piece of ebony wood is 1.20 g/cm³. What is the volume of 8.74 kg of this wood?

1.23. Make the following temperature conversions: **(a)** 68°F to °C; **(b)** −36.7°C to °F; **(c)** −15°C to K; **(d)** 415 K to °F; **(e)** 1500°F to K.

1.24. **(a)** The temperature on a hot summer day is 92°F. What is the temperature in °C? **(b)** The melting point of sodium chloride (table salt) is 804°C. What is this temperature in kelvins? **(c)** Mercury freezes at 234.28 K. What is its freezing point in °F?

Uncertainty in Measurement

1.25. Indicate which of the following are exact numbers: **(a)** the number of inches in a mile; **(b)** the diameter of a dime; **(c)** the mass of a 12-oz bag of potato chips; **(d)** the number of ounces in a pound; **(e)** the number of micrometers in a kilometer; **(f)** the number of inches in a kilometer.

1.26. Indicate which of the following are exact numbers: **(a)** the mass of a Nerf ball; **(b)** the number of seconds in a year; **(c)** the surface area of a penny; **(d)** the temperature of the surface of the sun; **(e)** the number of mL in a cubic foot of water; **(f)** the number of pages in this book.

1.27. What is the number of significant figures in each of the following measured quantities? **(a)** 122 g; **(b)** 0.002796 s; **(c)** 8.07 mm; **(d)** 0.01050 L; **(e)** 5.7750×10^{-4} cm³.

1.28. Indicate the number of significant figures in each of the following measured quantities: **(a)** 3.141 cm; **(b)** 0.000050 m²; **(c)** 3,480,200 s; **(d)** −1.200°C; **(e)** 1.0800×10^{-2} L.

1.29. Round each of the following numbers to four significant figures: **(a)** 12,345,670; **(b)** 2.35500; **(c)** 456,500; **(d)** 3.218×10^3; **(e)** 0.000657030; **(f)** 100,500.1.

1.30. Round each of the following numbers to three significant figures: **(a)** 10.000; **(b)** 0.05000; **(c)** 23,000; **(d)** 1.565×10^1; **(e)** 9,834.05; **(f)** −1235.

1.31. Carry out the following operations and express the answers with the appropriate number of significant figures: **(a)** 1.23056 + 67.809; **(b)** 23.67 − 500; **(c)** 890.05 × 12.3; **(d)** 88,132/22.500.

1.32. Carry out the following operations and express the answer with the appropriate number of significant figures: **(a)** 324.55 − (6104.5/22.3); **(b)** $[(285.3 \times 10^6) - (12.000 \times 10^3)] \times 22.8954$; **(c)** $(0.0045 \times 30,000.0) + (283 \times 12)$; **(d)** $869 \times [1255 - (3.45 \times 10^3)]$.

Dimensional Analysis

1.33. Perform the following conversions: **(a)** 3.60 mi to m; **(b)** 2.00 days to s; **(c)** $1.95/gal to dollars per liter; **(d)** 5.0 pm/μs to m/s; **(e)** 85.00 mi/hr to m/s; **(f)** 33.35 ft³ to cm³.

1.34. Make the following conversions: **(a)** 7.5 ft to cm; **(b)** 4.45 qt to mL; **(c)** 35.7 in/hr to mm/s; **(d)** 2.00 yd³ to m³; **(e)** $3.99 per pound to pennies per gram; **(f)** 1.57 g/mL to kg/m³.

1.35. **(a)** If the gasoline tank on a compact car has a capacity of 12 U.S. gal, what is its capacity in liters? **(b)** If a bee flies at an average speed of 3.4 m/s, what is its average speed in mi/hr? **(c)** What is the engine piston displacement in liters of an engine whose displacement is listed as 320 in³?

1.36. **(a)** How many liters of wine can be held in a wine barrel whose capacity is 31 gal? **(b)** The recommended adult dose of Elixophyllin, a drug used to treat asthma, is 6 mg/kg of body mass. Calculate the dose in milligrams for a 170-lb person. **(c)** If an automobile is able to travel 244 mi on 11.2 gal of gasoline, what is the gas mileage in km/L?

1.37. The density of air at ordinary atmospheric pressure and 25°C is 1.19 g/L. What is the mass, in kilograms, of the air in a room that measures 8.2 × 13.5 × 2.75 m?

1.38. The maximum allowable concentration of carbon monoxide in urban air is 10 mg/m³ over an 8-hr period. At this level, what mass of carbon monoxide is present in a room measuring 8 × 12 × 20 ft?

1.39. Mercury is traded by the "flask," a unit that has a mass of 34.5 kg. What is the volume of a flask of mercury if the density of mercury is 13.6 g/mL?

1.40. The Morgan silver dollar has a mass of 26.73 g. By law, it was required to contain 90 percent silver, with the remainder being copper. **(a)** When the coin was minted in the late 1800s, silver was worth $1.18 per troy ounce (31.1 g). At this price, what is the value of the silver in the silver dollar? **(b)** Today, silver sells for $3.70 per troy ounce. How many silver dollars are required to obtain $25.00 of pure silver?

1.41. In March 1989, the *Exxon Valdez* ran aground and spilled 240,000 barrels of crude petroleum off the coast of Alaska. One barrel of petroleum is equal to 42 gal. How many milliliters of petroleum were spilled?

1.42. A pound of coffee beans yields 50 cups of coffee (4 cups = 1 qt). How many milliliters of coffee can be obtained from 1 g of coffee beans?

Additional Exercises

1.43. You are told that a substance is either a gas or a liquid. What additional information do you need to determine which it is?

1.44. Which of the following are intensive properties: **(a)** mass; **(b)** density; **(c)** temperature; **(d)** area; **(e)** color; **(f)** volume.

1.45. Consider the following description of the element bromine: "Bromine is a reddish-brown liquid at room temperature. It vaporizes readily to form a red vapor. It boils at 58.8°C and freezes at −7.2°C. The density of the vapor is 7.59 g/L, and the density of the liquid is 3.12 g/mL (at 20°C). The element reacts readily with many metals including iron and aluminum." Indicate which of the properties in this description are physical and which are chemical.

1.46. **(a)** What is the difference between a hypothesis and a theory? **(b)** What is difference between a theory and a scientific law? Which addresses how matter behaves, and which addresses why it behaves that way?

1.47. A sample of ascorbic acid (vitamin C) is synthesized in the laboratory. It contains 1.50 g of carbon and 2.00 g of oxygen. Another sample of ascorbic acid isolated from citrus fruits contains 6.35 g of carbon. How many grams of oxygen does it contain? Which law does this illustrate?

1.48. Give the derived SI units for each of the following quantities in terms of base SI units: **(a)** acceleration = distance/time²; **(b)** force = mass × acceleration; **(c)** work = force × distance; **(d)** pressure = force/area; **(e)** power = work/time.

1.49. Magnesium is used in automobile wheels because it is "lighter" than steel. What is a more scientifically correct statement of this?

1.50. Helium has the lowest boiling point of any liquid, −268.9°C. What is this temperature in kelvins? In °F?

1.51. Is the use of significant figures in each of the following statements appropriate? Why or why not? **(a)** The 1976 circulation of *Reader's Digest* was 17,887,299. **(b)** There are more than 1.4 million people in the United States who have the surname Brown. **(c)** The average annual rainfall in San Diego, California, is 20.54 in. **(d)** The population of East Lansing, Michigan, was 51,237 in 1979.

1.52. The annual production of sodium hydroxide in the United States in 1991 was 24.39 billion pounds. **(a)** How many grams of sodium hydroxide were produced in that year? **(b)** The density of sodium hydroxide is 2.130 g/cm³. How many cubic kilometers were produced?

1.53. You are given a bottle that contains 2.36 mL of a yellow liquid. The total mass of the bottle and the liquid is 5.26 g. The empty bottle weighs 3.01 g. What is the density of the liquid?

[1.54]. An 8.47-g sample of a solid is placed in a 25.00-mL flask. The remaining volume in the flask is filled with benzene in which the solid is insoluble. The solid and the benzene together weigh 24.54 g. The density of the benzene is 0.879 g/mL. What is the density of the solid?

1.55. The distance from Earth to the moon is approximately 240,000 mi. **(a)** What is this distance in millimeters?

(b) The Concorde SST has an airspeed of about 2400 km/hr. If the Concorde could fly to the moon, how many megaseconds would it take?

1.56. The U.S. quarter has a mass of 5.67 g and is approximately 1.55 mm thick. **(a)** How many quarters would have to be stacked to reach 575 ft, the height of the Washington Monument? **(b)** How much would this stack weigh? **(c)** How much money would this stack contain? **(d)** At this writing, the national debt is $4.2 trillion. How many stacks like the one described would be necessary to pay off this debt?

1.57. In the United States, water used for irrigation is measured in acre-feet. An acre-foot of water covers an acre to a depth of 1 ft. An acre is 4840 yd². An acre-foot is enough water to supply two typical households for 1.00 yr. Desalinated water costs about $2000 per acre-foot. **(a)** How much does desalinated water cost per liter? **(b)** How much would it cost one household per year if it were the only source of water?

1.58. A piece of aluminum foil measuring 12.0 in. by 15.5 in. has a mass of 5.175 g. Aluminum has a density of 2.70 g/cm³. What is the thickness of the foil in millimeters?

1.59. A cylindrical container of radius r and height h has a volume of $\pi r^2 h$. **(a)** Calculate the volume in cubic centimeters of a cylinder with a radius of 16.5 cm and a height of 22.3 cm. **(b)** Calculate the volume in cubic meters of a cylinder that is 6.3 ft high and 2.0 ft in diameter. **(c)** Calculate the mass in kilograms of a volume of mercury equal to the volume of the cylinder in part (b). The density of mercury is 13.6 g/cm³ (see Sample Exercise 1.3).

1.60. A cylindrical glass tube 15.0 cm in length is filled with ethanol. The mass of ethanol needed to fill the tube is found to be 9.64 g. Calculate the inner diameter of the tube in centimeters. The density of ethanol is 0.789 g/mL.

[1.61]. Gold is alloyed (mixed) with other metals to increase its hardness in making jewelry. **(a)** Consider a piece of gold jewelry that weighs 9.85 g and has a volume of 0.675 cm³. The jewelry contains only gold and silver, which have densities of 19.3 g/cm³ and 10.5 g/cm³, respectively. Assuming that the total volume of the jewelry is the sum of the volumes of the gold and silver that it contains, calculate the percentage of gold (by mass) in the jewelry. **(b)** The relative amount of gold in an alloy is commonly expressed in units of karats. Pure gold is 24 karats, and the percentage of gold in an alloy is given as a percentage of this value. For example, an alloy that is 50 percent gold is 12 karats. State the purity of the gold jewelry in karats.

[1.62]. Chromatography (Figure 1.9) is a simple but reliable method for separating a mixture into its constituent substances. Suppose you are using chromatography to separate a mixture of two substances. How would you know whether the separation is successful? Can you propose a means of quantifying how good or how poor the separation is?

[1.63]. Suppose you are given a sample of a homogeneous liquid. What would you do to determine whether it is a solution or a pure substance?

[1.64]. Using the *Handbook of Chemistry and Physics* or a similar source of data, determine: **(a)** the solid element with the greatest density; **(b)** the solid element with the highest known melting point; **(c)** the element with the lowest known melting point; **(d)** the only two elements that are liquids at room temperature (about 20°C).

2 Atoms, Molecules, and Ions

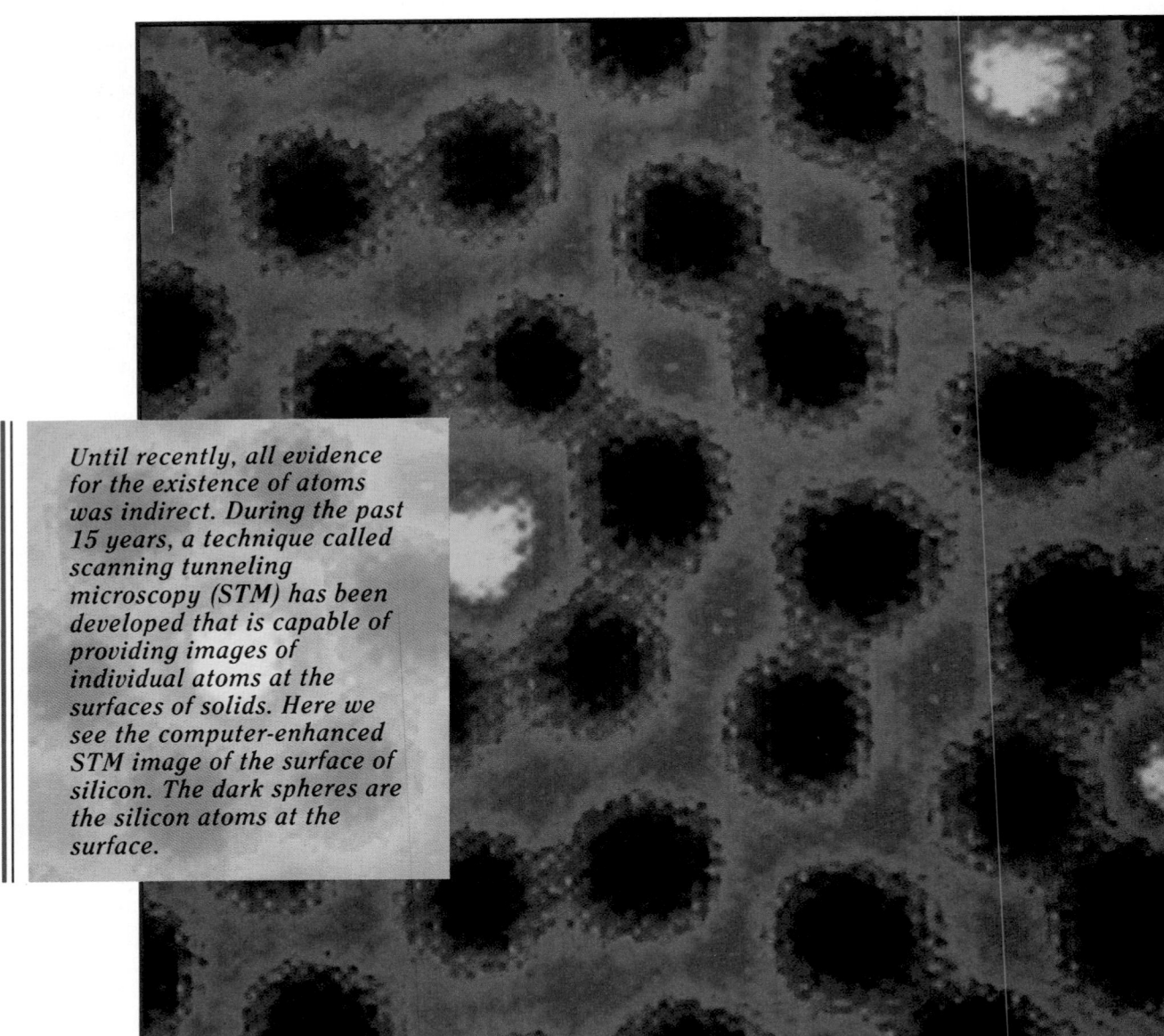

Until recently, all evidence for the existence of atoms was indirect. During the past 15 years, a technique called scanning tunneling microscopy (STM) has been developed that is capable of providing images of individual atoms at the surfaces of solids. Here we see the computer-enhanced STM image of the surface of silicon. The dark spheres are the silicon atoms at the surface.

In the previous chapter, we noted that chemistry is concerned with the properties of materials. When we observe that iron rusts, diamonds are hard, or nitroglycerin is explosive, we are dealing with the *macroscopic* world, the world of our everyday senses. However, the perspective of chemistry in seeking to understand the properties of matter involves the *microscopic* world, the world of atoms and molecules. Chemists make their observations in the macroscopic world, but they think in terms of the microscopic world.

The classification of substances as elements, compounds, and mixtures, which provides us with a system for organizing basic chemical information, deals with the macroscopic world. It is the microscopic view of matter, however, that forms the basis for understanding why elements and compounds react in the ways they do and why they exhibit specific physical properties. In this chapter, we will introduce the fascinating microscopic world of atoms. We will examine some basic concepts of atomic structure and briefly discuss the formation of molecules and ions. Finally, we will consider the systematic procedure used to name compounds.

2.1 The Atomic Theory of Matter

Greek philosophers pondered the question, Can matter be divided endlessly into smaller and smaller pieces, or is there a point at which it cannot be divided any further? Most of these philosophers, including Plato and Aristotle, believed that matter was infinitely divisible. One person who disagreed with this view was Democritus (460–370 B.C.). He argued that matter is composed of small, indivisible particles which he called *atomos,* meaning "indivisible."

Despite Democritus's proposition, however, the erroneous idea that matter could be divided infinitely was widely believed until the early nineteenth century. During this long period, scientists were continually accumulating information on how substances react with one another. As these scientists discovered patterns of reactivity that seemed inconsistent with the idea of infinitely divisible matter, Democritus's notion of atoms reemerged.

A meaningful *atomic theory* was finally published during the period 1803–1807 by John Dalton, an English schoolteacher (Figure 2.1). Dalton designed his theory to explain several experimental observations. His efforts were so insightful that his theory has remained basically intact up to the present.

The essence of Dalton's atomic theory of matter is summarized in the following postulates:

1. Each element is composed of extremely small particles called atoms.
2. All atoms of a given element are identical; the atoms of different elements are different and have different properties (including different masses).
3. Atoms of an element are not changed into different types of atoms by chemical reactions; atoms are neither created nor destroyed in chemical reactions.
4. Compounds are formed when atoms of more than one element combine; a given compound always has the same relative number and kind of atoms.

FIGURE 2.1 John Dalton (1766–1844) was the son of a poor English weaver. Dalton began teaching at the age of 12; he spent most of his years in Manchester, where he taught both grammar school and college. His lifelong interest in meteorology led him to study gases and hence to chemistry and eventually to the atomic theory. (Library of Congress)

Dalton's theory provides us with a conceptual picture of matter. As shown in Figure 2.2, we can visualize matter as being composed of tiny particles called atoms (see also Figure 2.3). **Atoms** are the basic building blocks of matter. They are the smallest units of an element. ∞ (Sec. 1.2) An *element* is composed of only one kind of atom. In *compounds,* the atoms of two or more elements combine in definite arrangements [Figure 2.2(b)]. *Mixtures* do not involve the intimate interactions between atoms that are found in compounds [Figure 2.2(c)].

Dalton's theory explains several simple laws of chemical combination that were known at the time. One of these was the *law of constant composition* (Section 1.2): In a given compound, the relative number and kind of atoms are constant. This law is the basis of postulate 4. Another fundamental chemical

FIGURE 2.2 Differences between elements, compounds, and mixtures as visualized through Dalton's atomic theory. (*a*) Elements are composed of small particles called atoms. All atoms of a given element are identical; atoms of different elements are different. (*b*) Compounds involve atoms of two or more elements combined in definite arrangements. (*c*) Mixtures have variable compositions. There is no restriction on the relative number of atoms of elements 1 and 2.

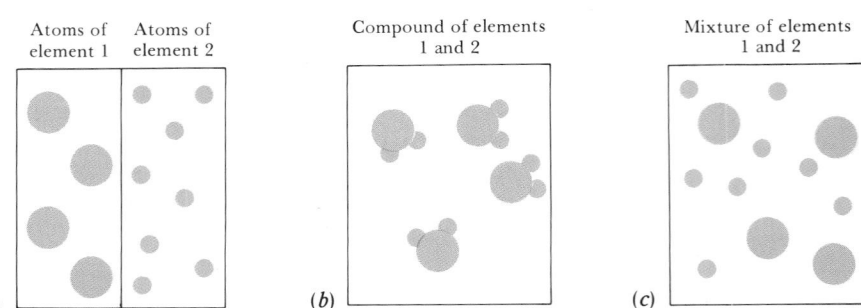

law was the *law of conservation of mass* (also known as the *law of conservation of matter*): The total mass of materials present after a chemical reaction is the same as the total mass before the reaction. This law is the basis for postulate 3. Dalton argued that atoms retain their identities during chemical reactions and that chemical reactions consist of the rearrangement of the atoms to give new chemical combinations.

A good theory should not only explain the known facts but should also predict new ones. Dalton used his theory to deduce the *law of multiple proportions:* If two elements A and B combine to form more than one compound, then the masses of B that can combine with a given mass of A are in the ratio of small whole numbers. We can illustrate this law by considering the substances water and hydrogen peroxide, both of which consist of the elements hydrogen and oxygen. We find that, in forming water, 8.0 g of oxygen reacts with 1.0 g of hydrogen. In hydrogen peroxide, there are 16.0 g of oxygen per 1.0 g of hydrogen. In other words, the ratio of the mass of oxygen per gram of hydrogen in the two compounds is 2 : 1. Using the atomic theory, we can conclude that hydrogen peroxide contains twice as many atoms of oxygen per hydrogen atom as does water.

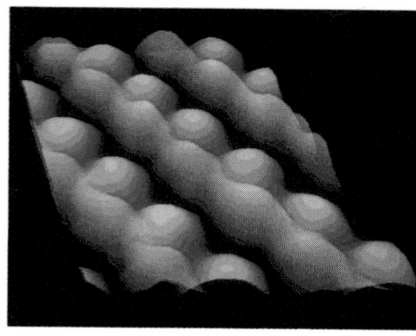

FIGURE 2.3 An image of the surface of the semiconductor GaAs (gallium arsenide) as obtained by a technique called tunneling electron microscopy. The color was added to the image by computer to distinguish the gallium atoms (blue spheres) from the arsenic atoms (red spheres). (IBM Research)

2.2 The Discovery of Atomic Structure

Scientists presently have a large arsenal of sophisticated equipment with which to measure the properties of individual atoms in great detail. Consequently, we now know a great deal about the structure of atoms. However, only 150 years ago very little was known about atoms beyond what was contained in Dalton's atomic theory. Dalton and his contemporaries viewed the atom as an indivisible object, like a tiny, indestructible, unchangeable ball. By 1850, scientists had begun to accumulate data indicating that the atom is composed of even smaller particles. Before we summarize the current model of atomic structure, we will consider a few of the most important experiments that led to that model. In order to understand these experiments we need to keep in mind a basic rule regarding the behavior of electrically charged particles: *Like charges repel each other; unlike charges attract.*

Cathode Rays and Electrons

In the mid-1800s, scientists began to study electrical discharge through partially evacuated tubes (tubes that had been pumped almost empty of air), such as those shown in Figure 2.4. A high voltage produces radiation within the tube. This radiation became known as **cathode rays** because it originated from the negative electrode, or cathode. Although the rays themselves could not be seen, their movement could be detected because the rays cause certain materials, including glass, to *fluoresce,* or give off light. (Television picture tubes are cathode-ray tubes; a television picture is the result of fluorescence from the television screen.) In the absence of magnetic or electric fields, cathode rays travel in straight lines. However, magnetic and electric fields "bend" the rays in the manner expected for negatively charged particles. Moreover, a metal plate exposed to cathode rays acquired a negative charge. These observations of the properties of cathode rays suggested that the radiation consists of a stream of

Point of Emphasis: Conservation means something cannot be created nor destroyed. Here, it applies to matter (mass). Later, it will be applied to energy.

Teaching Note: Until recently, computer terminals were popularly referred to as CRTs (cathode-ray tubes). They are now commonly called VDTs (video display terminals).

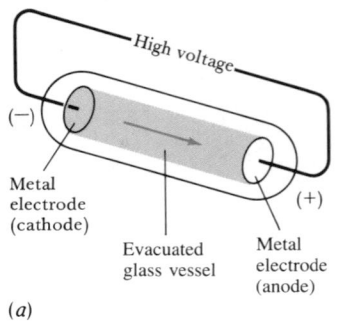

(a)

(b)

(c)

FIGURE 2.4 (*a*) In a cathode-ray tube, electrons move from the negative electrode (cathode) to the positive electrode (anode). (*b*) A photo of a cathode-ray tube containing a fluorescent screen to show the path of the cathode rays. (*c*) The path of the cathode rays is deflected by the presence of a magnet. (© Richard Megna/Fundamental Photographs)

negatively charged particles, which we now call *electrons.* In addition, it was found that the cathode rays emitted by different cathode materials were the same. All of these observations led to the conclusion that electrons are a basic component of matter.

In 1897, the British physicist J. J. Thomson (Figure 2.5) measured the ratio of the electrical charge to the mass of the electron using a cathode-ray tube such as that shown in Figure 2.6. When only the magnetic field is turned on, the

FIGURE 2.5 J. J. Thomson (1856–1940) was appointed professor of physics at Cambridge University when he was not quite 28 years old. He received the Nobel Prize in physics in 1906 for his characterization of the electron. (The Granger Collection)

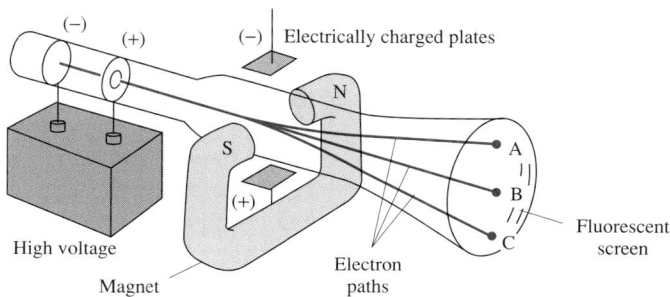

High voltage

Magnet

Electron paths

N

S

(+)

(−)

(+)

(−) Electrically charged plates

A

B

C

Fluorescent screen

Figure 2.6

electron strikes point A of the tube. When the magnetic field is off and the electric field is on, the electron strikes point C. When both the magnetic and electric fields are off or when they are balanced so as to cancel each other's effects, the electron strikes point B. By carefully and quantitatively determining the effects of magnetic and electric fields on the motion of the cathode rays, Thomson was able to determine the charge-to-mass ratio of 1.76×10^8 coulombs per gram.*

Once the charge-to-mass ratio of the electron was known, a scientist who could measure either the charge or the mass of an electron could easily calculate the other quantity. In 1909, Robert Millikan (1868–1953) of the University of Chicago succeeded in measuring the charge of an electron by performing an experiment known as the "Millikan oil-drop experiment" (Figure 2.7). He then calculated the mass of the electron by using his value for the charge, 1.60×10^{-19} C, and Thomson's charge-to-mass ratio, 1.76×10^8 C/g:

$$\text{Mass} = \frac{1.60 \times 10^{-19} \text{ C}}{1.76 \times 10^8 \text{ C/g}} = 9.10 \times 10^{-28} \text{ g}$$

Using slightly more accurate values, we obtain the presently accepted value for the mass of the electron, 9.10939×10^{-28} g. This mass is about 2000 times smaller than that of hydrogen, the lightest atom.

Figure 2.7

* The coulomb (C) is the SI unit for electrical charge.

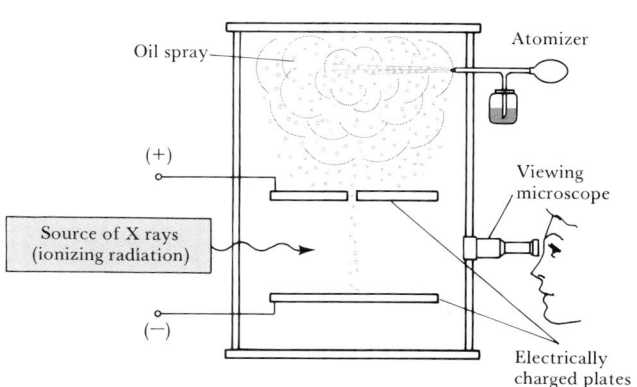

Oil spray

Atomizer

(+)

Source of X rays (ionizing radiation)

Viewing microscope

(−)

Electrically charged plates

2.2 The Discovery of Atomic Structure   **37**

Radioactivity

Other discoveries also grew out of studies of cathode rays. In 1895, Wilhelm Roentgen (1845–1923) found that when cathode rays struck certain materials, a new type of invisible ray was emitted. Unlike cathode rays, these new rays passed unimpeded through many objects, and they were unaffected by magnetic fields. He also found that they produced an image on photographic plates. Roentgen called this startling new phenomenon *X-rays*. Today we know that X-rays are a high-energy form of radiation.

When Roentgen announced the discovery of X-rays in December 1895, he caused a frenzy within the scientific community. A few months later, the French scientist Henri Becquerel (1852–1908) made an equally startling discovery. Becquerel had been studying substances that become luminous after exposure to sunlight, a phenomenon referred to as *phosphorescence.* After Roentgen's announcement, Becquerel sought to determine whether phosphorescent substances emitted X-rays. While working with a phosphorescent uranium mineral, Becquerel accidentally discovered that, even in the dark, the mineral spontaneously produced high-energy radiation. This spontaneous emission of radiation is called **radioactivity.** At Becquerel's suggestion, Marie Sklodowska Curie (Figure 2.8) and her husband, Pierre, began their famous experiments to isolate the radioactive components of the mineral, called pitchblende.

Further study of the nature of radioactivity, principally by the British scientist Ernest Rutherford (1871–1937), revealed three types of radiation: alpha (α), beta (β), and gamma (γ) radiation. Each type differs in its response to an electric field, as shown in Figure 2.9. Both α and β radiation are bent by the

Learning Goal 3: Cite the evidence from studies of radioactivity for the existence of subatomic particles.

Point of Emphasis: X-rays and γ radiation are true electromagnetic radiation, whereas α and β radiation are actually streams of particles—helium nuclei and electrons, respectively.

FIGURE 2.8 Marie Sklodowska Curie (1867–1934). When M. Curie presented her doctoral thesis, it was described as the greatest single contribution of any doctoral thesis in the history of science. Among other things, two new elements, polonium and radium, had been discovered. In 1903, Becquerel, M. Curie, and her husband, Pierre, were jointly awarded the Nobel Prize in physics. In 1911, M. Curie won a second Nobel Prize, this time in chemistry. Irene Curie, daughter of Marie and Pierre Curie, was also a scientist. She and her husband, Frederic Joliot, shared the 1935 Nobel Prize in chemistry for their work in artificial production of radioactive substances. (The Bettman Archive)

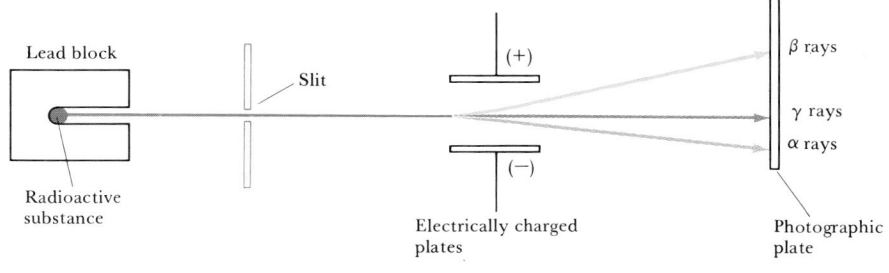

Figure 2.9

electric field, although in opposite directions. In contrast, γ radiation is not affected by the electric field.

Rutherford showed that both α and β rays consist of fast-moving particles, which were called α and β particles. In fact, β particles are high-speed electrons and can be considered the radioactive equivalent of cathode rays. The α particles are much more massive than the β particles and have a positive rather than negative charge. In units of the charge of the electron, β particles have a charge of $1-$, and α particles a charge of $2+$. Rutherford showed further that α particles combine with electrons to form atoms of helium. He thus concluded that an α particle consists of the positively charged core of the helium atom. He further concluded that γ radiation is high-energy radiation similar to X-rays; it does not consist of particles.

The Nuclear Atom

With the growing evidence that the atom is composed of even smaller particles, attention was given to how the particles fit together. In the early 1900s, J. J. Thomson proposed a model for the structure of atoms. He reasoned that because electrons comprise only a very small fraction of the mass of an atom, they probably were responsible for an equally small fraction of the atom's size. He proposed that the atom consisted of a uniform positive sphere of matter in which the electrons were embedded, as shown in Figure 2.10. This model became known as the "plum-pudding" model, after the name of a traditional English dessert. Thomson's atomic model was very short-lived.

In 1910, Rutherford and his coworkers performed an experiment that led to the downfall of Thomson's model. Rutherford was studying the angles at which α particles were scattered as they passed through a thin gold foil. He had found only slight scattering, on the order of 1 degree, which was consistent with Thomson's model. One day Hans Geiger, an associate of Rutherford's, proposed that Ernest Marsden, a 20-year-old undergraduate working in their laboratory, get some experience in conducting such experiments. Rutherford suggested that Marsden see if α particles were scattered through large angles. In Rutherford's own words:

I may tell you in confidence that I did not believe they would be since we knew that the α particle was a very massive particle with a great deal of energy. . . . Then I remember two or three days later Geiger coming to me in great excitement and saying, "We have been able to get some α particles coming backwards." . . . It was quite the most incredible event that has ever happened to me in my life. It was almost as if you fired a 15-inch shell into a piece of tissue paper and it came back and hit you.

Learning Goal 4: Describe the experimental evidence for the nuclear nature of the atom.

FIGURE 2.10 J. J. Thomson's "plum-pudding" model of the atom. He pictured the small electrons to be embedded in the atom much like raisins in a pudding or like seeds in a watermelon. Ernest Rutherford proved this model wrong.

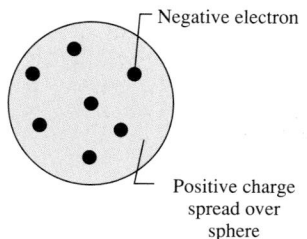

Rutherford and his coworkers observed that almost all of the α particles passed directly through the foil without deflection. However, a few were deflected, some even bouncing back in the direction from which they had come, as shown in Figure 2.11.

By 1911, Rutherford was able to explain these observations; he postulated that most of the mass of the atom, and all of its positive charge, reside in a very small, extremely dense region which he called the **nucleus.** Most of the total volume of the atom is empty space in which electrons move around the nucleus. In the α-scattering experiment, most α particles pass directly through the foil because they do not encounter the minute nucleus; they merely pass through the empty space of the atom. Occasionally an α particle comes into the close vicinity of a gold nucleus, however. The repulsion between the highly charged gold nucleus and the α particle is strong enough to deflect the less massive α particle, as depicted in Figure 2.12.

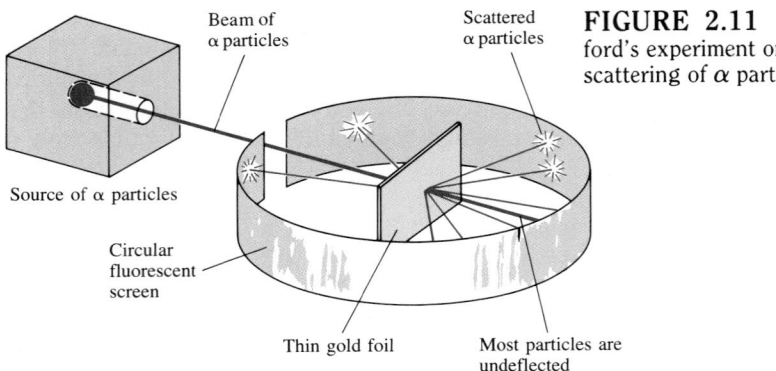

FIGURE 2.11 Rutherford's experiment on the scattering of α particles.

Figure 2.11

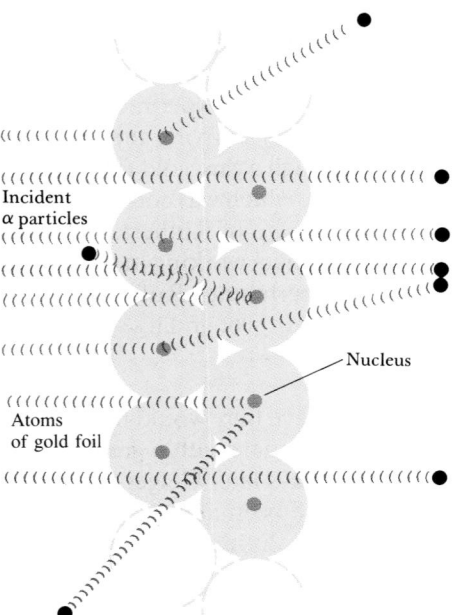

FIGURE 2.12 Rutherford's model explaining his experiment on the scattering of α particles (Figure 2.11). The gold foil is actually several thousand atoms thick. Both the α particles and the gold nuclei are positively charged; according to Coulomb's law, like charges repel one another. Thus, when an α particle collides with (or passes very close to) a gold nucleus, it is strongly repelled. The less massive α particle is deflected from its path by this repulsive interaction. Because the gold nuclei are extremely small, only a small fraction of the particles is deflected.

Figure 2.12

 A CLOSER LOOK

Basic Forces

There are four basic forces, or interactions, known in nature: gravity, electromagnetism, and the strong and the weak nuclear forces. *Gravitational forces* act between all objects in proportion to their masses. Gravitational forces between atoms or subatomic particles are so small that they are of no chemical significance.

Electromagnetic forces act between electrically charged or magnetic objects. Electric and magnetic forces are intimately related. Electric forces are of fundamental importance in understanding the chemical behavior of atoms. The magnitude of the electrical force between two charged particles is given by *Coulomb's law:* $F = kQ_1Q_2/d^2$, where Q_1 and Q_2 are the magnitudes of the charges on the two particles, d is the distance between their centers, and k is a constant determined by the units for Q and d. A negative value for the force indicates attraction, and a positive value indicates repulsion.

All nuclei except those of hydrogen atoms contain two or more protons. Because like charges repel, the electrical repulsion would cause the protons to fly apart if a stronger force did not keep them together in the nucleus. This stronger force is called the *strong nuclear force.* It acts between subatomic particles that are extremely close together, as they are in the nucleus. At this small distance this force is stronger than the electrical force, so the nucleus holds together. The *weak nuclear force* is weaker than the electric force but stronger than gravity. We are aware of its existence only because it shows itself in certain types of radioactivity.

Subsequent experimental studies led to the discovery of both positive particles (*protons*) and neutral particles (*neutrons*) in the nucleus. Protons were discovered in 1919 by Rutherford. Neutrons were discovered in 1932 by the British scientist James Chadwick (1891–1972). We examine these particles more closely in the next section.

2.3 The Modern View of Atomic Structure

Since the time of Rutherford, physicists have learned much about the detailed composition of atomic nuclei. In the course of these discoveries the list of particles that make up nuclei has grown long and continues to increase. As chemists, we can take a very simple view of the atom, because only three subatomic particles — the **proton, neutron,** and **electron** — have a bearing on chemical behavior.

The charge of an electron is -1.602×10^{-19} C, and that of a proton is $+1.602 \times 10^{-19}$ C. The quantity 1.602×10^{-19} C is called the **electronic charge.** For convenience, the charges of atomic and subatomic particles are usually expressed as multiples of this charge rather than in coulombs. Thus, the charge of the electron is $1-$, and that of the proton is $1+$. Neutrons are uncharged; that is, they are electrically neutral (which is how they received their name). Because atoms have an equal number of electrons and protons, they have no net electrical charge.

Protons and neutrons reside together in the nucleus of the atom, which, as Rutherford proposed, is extremely small. The vast majority of an atom's volume is the space in which the electrons move. The electrons are attracted to the protons in the nucleus by the force that exists between particles of opposite electrical charge. In later chapters we will see that the strength of the attractive forces between electrons and nuclei can be used to explain many of the differences between different elements.

Learning Goal 5: Give the approximate size, relative mass, and charge of an atom, proton, neutron, and electron.

Learning Goal 6: Describe the composition of the atom in terms of protons, neutrons, and electrons.

Barrie M. Peake, "The Discovery of the Electron, Proton, and Neutron," *J. Chem. Educ.* **1989,** *66,* 738.

TABLE 2.1 △ Comparison of the Proton, Neutron, and Electron

Particle	Charge	Mass (amu)
Proton	Positive (1+)	1.0073
Neutron	None (neutral)	1.0087
Electron	Negative (1−)	5.486×10^{-4}

Teaching Note: 1 amu = 1.66054×10^{-24} g. 1 g = 6.02214×10^{23} amu.

diameter of atoms

100 - 500 pm

diameter of nuclei

~ 10^{-2} pm

(~ 10^{-4} Å)

Point of Emphasis: 1 Å = 10^{-10} m = 100 pm = 0.1 nm.

Atoms have extremely small masses. For example, the mass of the heaviest known atom is on the order of 4×10^{-22} g. Because it would be cumbersome to continually have to express such small masses in grams, we instead use a unit called the *atomic mass unit,* or amu.* An amu equals 1.66054×10^{-24} g. A proton has a mass of 1.0073 amu, a neutron 1.0087 amu, and an electron 5.486×10^{-4} amu. The masses of the proton and neutron are very nearly equal, and both are much greater than that of an electron. In fact, it would take 1836 electrons to equal the mass of 1 proton. Thus, the nucleus contains most of the mass of an atom. Table 2.1 summarizes the charges and masses of the subatomic particles. We will have more to say about atomic masses in Section 3.3.

Atoms are extremely small; most of them have diameters between 1×10^{-10} m and 5×10^{-10} m, or 100–500 pm. Another convenient, although non-SI, unit of length used to express atomic dimensions is the **angstrom** (Å). One angstrom equals 10^{-10} m. Thus, atoms have diameters on the order of 1–5 Å. For example, the diameter of a chlorine atom is 200 pm, or 2.0 Å. Both picometers and angstroms are commonly used to express the dimensions of atoms and molecules, and you should be familiar with both units.

Sample Exercise 2.1 illustrates further how very small atoms are compared to more familiar objects.

SAMPLE EXERCISE 2.1

The diameter of a U.S. penny is 19 mm. The diameter of a copper atom, by comparison, is only 2.6 Å. How many copper atoms could be arranged side by side in a straight line across the diameter of a penny?

SOLUTION
The unknown is the number of Cu atoms. We can take the relationship 1 Cu atom = 2.6 Å as a conversion factor relating number of atoms and distance. Thus, we can start with the diameter of the penny, first converting this distance into angstroms and then using the diameter of the Cu atom:

$$\text{Cu atoms} = (19 \text{ mm})\left(\frac{10^{-3} \text{ m}}{1 \text{ mm}}\right)\left(\frac{1 \text{ Å}}{10^{-10} \text{ m}}\right)\left(\frac{1 \text{ Cu atom}}{2.6 \text{ Å}}\right)$$

$$= 7.3 \times 10^7 \text{ Cu atoms}$$

That is, 73 million copper atoms could sit side by side across a penny!

PRACTICE EXERCISE

The diameter of a carbon atom is 1.5 Å. **(a)** Express this diameter in picometers. **(b)** How many carbon atoms could be aligned side by side in a straight line across the width of a pencil line that is 0.10 mm wide?   *Answers:* **(a)** 150 pm; **(b)** 6.7×10^5 C atoms

---

* The SI abbreviation for the atomic mass unit is merely u. We will use the more common abbreviation amu.

The diameters of atomic nuclei are on the order of 10^{-4} Å, only a small fraction of the diameter of the atom as a whole. If the atom were scaled upward in size so that the nucleus was 2 cm in diameter (about the diameter of a penny), the atom would have a diameter of 200 m (about twice the length of a football field). Because the tiny nucleus carries most of the mass of the atom in such a small volume, it has an incredible density—on the order of 10^{13}–10^{14} g/cm^3. A matchbox full of material of such density would weigh over 2.5 billion tons! Astrophysicists have suggested that the interior of a collapsed star may reach nearly this density.

An illustration of the atom that incorporates the features we have just discussed is shown in Figure 2.13. The electrons, which take up most of the volume of the atom, play the major role in chemical reactions. The significance of representing the region containing the electrons as an indistinct cloud will become clear in later chapters when we consider the energies and spatial arrangements of the electrons.

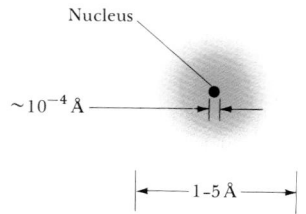

FIGURE 2.13 Schematic cross-sectional view through the center of an atom. The nucleus, which contains protons and neutrons, is the location of virtually all the mass of the atom. The rest of the atom is the space in which the light, negatively charged electrons move.

Point of Emphasis: Electrons occupy most of the volume of the atom but account for only a small fraction of its mass.

Learning Goal 7: Write the chemical symbol for an element having been given its mass number and atomic number, and perform the reverse operation.

Point of Emphasis: All atoms of the same element have the same number of protons and electrons, but they may have different numbers of neutrons.

Teaching Note: Inside the front cover of the text is a list of the elements with names, symbols, atomic numbers, and atomic weights.

Point of Emphasis: In referring to a specific isotope, use the symbolism $^A_Z Sy$, where Sy is the symbol for the element, A is the mass number (number of protons and neutrons) of the isotope, and Z is the atomic number (number of protons) of the element.

Isotopes, Atomic Numbers, and Mass Numbers

What makes an atom of one element different from an atom of another element? The answer to this question centers on the number of protons in the nucleus of the atom: *All atoms of an element have the same number of protons in the nucleus.* The specific number of protons is different for different elements. Furthermore, because an atom has no net electrical charge, the number of electrons in it must equal its number of protons. For example, all atoms of the element carbon have six protons and six electrons. Most carbon atoms also have six neutrons, although some have more and some have less.

Atoms of a given element that differ in the number of neutrons, and consequently in mass, are called **isotopes.** The symbol $^{12}_6C$ or simply ^{12}C (read "carbon twelve," carbon-12) represents the carbon atom with six protons and six neutrons. The number of protons, which is called the **atomic number,** is shown by the subscript. The atomic number of each element is listed with the name and symbol of the element on the front inside cover of the text. Because all atoms of a given element have the same atomic number, the subscript is redundant and hence is often omitted. The superscript is called the **mass number;** it is the total number of protons plus neutrons in the atom. For example, some carbon atoms contain six protons and eight neutrons and are consequently represented as ^{14}C (read "carbon fourteen"). Several isotopes of carbon are listed in Table 2.2.

We will generally use the notation with subscripts and superscripts only when making reference to a particular isotope of an element. An atom of a specific isotope is called a **nuclide.** Thus, an atom of $^{14}_6C$ is referred to as a $^{14}_6C$

TABLE 2.2 △ **Some of the Isotopes of Carbon**[a]

Symbol	Number of protons	Number of electrons	Number of neutrons
^{11}C	6	6	5
^{12}C	6	6	6
^{13}C	6	6	7
^{14}C	6	6	8

[a] Almost 99 percent of the carbon found in nature consists of ^{12}C.

nuclide. We will have more to say about the isotopic compositions of the elements in Section 3.3 when we examine atomic masses.

All atoms are made up of protons, neutrons, and electrons. Because these particles are the same in all atoms, the difference between atoms of distinct elements (gold and oxygen, for example) is due entirely to the difference in the number of subatomic particles in each atom. We can therefore consider an atom to be the smallest sample of an element, because breaking an atom into subatomic particles destroys its identity.

SAMPLE EXERCISE 2.2

How many protons, neutrons, and electrons are in an atom of ^{197}Au?

SOLUTION According to the list of elements given on the front inside cover of this text, gold has an atomic number of 79. Consequently, an ^{197}Au atom has 79 protons, 79 electrons, and $197 - 79 = 118$ neutrons.

PRACTICE EXERCISE

How many protons, neutrons, and electrons are in a ^{39}K atom?   *Answer:* 19 protons, 19 electrons, and 20 neutrons.

SAMPLE EXERCISE 2.3

Hydrogen has three isotopes, with mass numbers 1, 2, and 3. Write the complete chemical symbol for each of them.

SOLUTION Hydrogen has atomic number 1, so all atoms of hydrogen contain one proton. The three isotopes are therefore represented by $^1_1$H, $^2_1$H, and $^3_1$H.

PRACTICE EXERCISE

Give the complete chemical symbol for the nuclide that contains 18 protons, 18 electrons, and 22 neutrons.   *Answer:* $^{40}_{18}$Ar

Point of Emphasis: ^{1}H = hydrogen (protium); ^{2}H = deuterium; ^{3}H = tritium.

2.4 The Periodic Table

Dalton's atomic theory set the stage for a vigorous growth in chemical experimentation during the early 1800s. As the body of chemical observations grew and the list of known elements expanded, attempts were made to find regularities in chemical behavior. These efforts culminated in the development of the periodic table in 1869. We will have much to say about the periodic table in later chapters, but it is so important and useful that you should become acquainted with it now.

Many elements show very strong similarities to each other. For example, lithium (Li), sodium (Na), and potassium (K) are all soft, very reactive metals. The elements helium (He), neon (Ne), and argon (Ar) are very nonreactive gases. If the elements are arranged in order of increasing atomic number, their chemical and physical properties are found to show a repeating, or periodic, pattern. For example, each of the soft, reactive metals—lithium, sodium, and potassium—comes immediately after one of the nonreactive gases—helium, neon, and argon— as shown in Figure 2.14. The arrangement of elements in order of increasing atomic number, with elements having similar properties placed in vertical columns, is known as the **periodic table**. The periodic table is shown in Figure 2.15 and is also given on the front inside cover of the text. You will see large periodic tables hung on the walls of most chemistry classrooms—

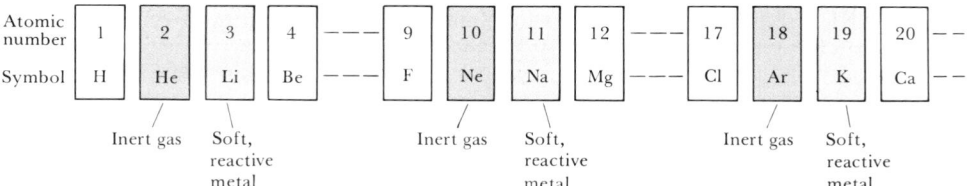

FIGURE 2.14 Arranging the elements by atomic number illustrates the periodic, or repeating, pattern in properties that is the basis of the periodic table.

a testimony to their usefulness. You may notice slight variations in periodic tables from one book to another, or between those in the lecture hall and in the text. These are matters of style or concern the particular information included; there are no fundamental differences.

The elements in a column of the periodic table are known as a **family** or **group.** The labeling of the families is basically arbitrary, and three different labeling schemes are in common use, two of which are shown in Figure 2.15. The top set of labels, which have A and B designations, is widely used in North America. Roman numerals, rather than Arabic ones, are often employed in this scheme. For example, group 7A is often labeled VIIA. Europeans use a similar convention that numbers the columns from 1A through 8A and then from 1B

FIGURE 2.15 Periodic table of the elements, showing the division of elements into metals, metalloids, and nonmetals.

Figure 2.15

1A 1																	8A 18
1 H	2A 2												3A 13	4A 14	5A 15	6A 16	7A 17	2 He
3 Li	4 Be												5 B	6 C	7 N	8 O	9 F	10 Ne
11 Na	12 Mg	3B 3	4B 4	5B 5	6B 6	7B 7	8	8B 9	10	1B 11	2B 12		13 Al	14 Si	15 P	16 S	17 Cl	18 Ar
19 K	20 Ca	21 Sc	22 Ti	23 V	24 Cr	25 Mn	26 Fe	27 Co	28 Ni	29 Cu	30 Zn		31 Ga	32 Ge	33 As	34 Se	35 Br	36 Kr
37 Rb	38 Sr	39 Y	40 Zr	41 Nb	42 Mo	43 Tc	44 Ru	45 Rh	46 Pd	47 Ag	48 Cd		49 In	50 Sn	51 Sb	52 Te	53 I	54 Xe
55 Cs	56 Ba	57 La	72 Hf	73 Ta	74 W	75 Re	76 Os	77 Ir	78 Pt	79 Au	80 Hg		81 Tl	82 Pb	83 Bi	84 Po	85 At	86 Rn
87 Fr	88 Ra	89 Ac	104 Rf	105 Ha	[106]	[107]	[108]	[109]										

58 Ce	59 Pr	60 Nd	61 Pm	62 Sm	63 Eu	64 Gd	65 Tb	66 Dy	67 Ho	68 Er	69 Tm	70 Yb	71 Lu
90 Th	91 Pa	92 U	93 Np	94 Pu	95 Am	96 Cm	97 Bk	98 Cf	99 Es	100 Fm	101 Md	102 No	103 Lw

Metals

Metalloids

Nonmetals

TABLE 2.3 △ Family Names for Some of the Groups in the Periodic Table

Group	Name	Elements
1A	Alkali metals	Li, Na, K, Rb, Cs, Fr
2A	Alkaline earth metals	Be, Mg, Ca, Sr, Ba, Ra
6A	Chalcogens ("chalk formers")	O, S, Se, Te, Po
7A	Halogens ("salt formers")	F, Cl, Br, I, At
8A	Noble gases (or inert gases or rare gases)	He, Ne, Ar, Kr, Xe, Rn

Table 2.3

FIGURE 2.16 Some familiar examples of metals and nonmetals. The nonmetals (from bottom left) are sulfur (yellow powder), iodine (dark, shiny crystals), bromine (reddish-brown liquid and vapor in glass vial), and three samples of carbon (black charcoal powder, diamonds, and graphite in the pencil lead). The metals are in the form of an aluminum wrench, copper pipe, lead shot, silver coins, and gold nuggets. (Richard Megna/Fundamental Photographs)

through 8B, thereby giving the label 7B (or VIIB) instead of 7A to the family headed by fluorine (F). In an effort to eliminate this confusion, the International Union of Pure and Applied Chemistry (IUPAC) has proposed a new convention that numbers the groups from 1 through 18 with no A or B designations, as shown in the second set of labels in Figure 2.15. We will use the traditional North American convention.

Elements that belong to the same group often exhibit some similarities in their physical and chemical properties. You can see, for example, that the "coinage metals"—copper (Cu), silver (Ag), and gold (Au)–all belong to group 1B. As their name suggests, the coinage metals are used throughout the world to make coins. Many other groups in the periodic table have family names. For example, the members of group 1A—lithium, sodium, potassium, rubidium (Rb), cesium (Cs), and francium (Fr)—are known as the *alkali metals.* The names of several of the groups in the periodic table are given in Table 2.3. You should note the origins of these family names; they arise from some of the chemical characteristics of each group, as we will discuss in later chapters.

We will learn in Chapters 6 and 7 that the elements in a family of the periodic table have similar properties because they have the same type of arrangement of electrons at the periphery of their atoms. However, we need not wait until then to make good use of the periodic table; after all, the table in pretty much its current form was invented by chemists who knew nothing of the electronic structures of atoms! We can use the table, as they intended, to correlate the behaviors of elements and to aid in remembering many facts. You will find it helpful to refer to the periodic table frequently in studying the remainder of this chapter.

Even in our first viewing of the periodic table, we can see patterns in the physical properties of the elements. All the elements on the left side and in the middle of the periodic table (except for hydrogen) are **metallic elements,** or **metals.** The majority of elements are metallic. Metals share many characteristic properties, such as luster and high electrical and heat conductivity. All metals, with the exception of mercury (Hg), are solids at room temperature. The metals are separated from the **nonmetallic elements** by a diagonal steplike line that runs from boron (B) to astatine (At), as shown in Figure 2.15. Hydrogen, although on the left side of the periodic table, is also a nonmetal. At room temperature some of the nonmetals are gaseous, some are liquid, and some are solid. They generally differ from the metals in appearance (Figure 2.16) and in other physical properties. Many of the elements that lie along the line that separates metals from nonmetals, such as antimony (Sb), have properties that fall between those of metals and nonmetals. These elements are often referred to as **metalloids.**

Radioactive Isotopes and the Chernobyl Accident

On April 26, 1986, the worst nuclear reactor accident in history occurred at Chernobyl, Russia (Figure 2.17). While testing a modification to the reactor, the operators of the power plant inexcusably bypassed the reactor's emergency protection systems. Because the safety system was bypassed, the reactor overheated. As a result, cooling water used to remove heat from the reactor core was converted quickly to steam. The increasing pressure eventually caused the reactor to explode, blowing off its 1000-ton concrete lid. The contents of the core of the reactor were blown into the atmosphere. Dust from the explosion was dispersed through the atmosphere, settling to the earth over a wide area. By July 1986, significant levels of radioactive isotopes from Chernobyl were found in the Canadian arctic and the western United States, as well as in the soil and vegetation of most parts of Europe.

The primary fuel used in the reactor was an isotope of uranium, ^{235}U. The ^{235}U produces many radioactive nuclides as byproducts. Of these nuclides, ^{131}I, ^{134}Cs, ^{137}Cs, and ^{90}Sr are particularly noteworthy because of their long-term effects on human health. Iodine, cesium, and strontium move readily into the human food chain. Radioactive ^{131}I, like the nonradioactive isotopes of iodine, concentrates in the thyroid gland. Cesium is chemically similar to the essential nutrient potassium, which is above it in the alkali metal family. Radioactive cesium can therefore be mistaken for potassium by living organisms and thus gain entry to cells. Strontium, which is below calcium in the alkaline earth family, can replace calcium in bone tissue. Once inside the body, all these radioactive isotopes can induce cancer. The Chernobyl accident is therefore expected to increase the number of cancer deaths in the coming decades, although exact predictions are impossible to make.

Want to read more? We recommend: C. H. Atwood, "Chernobyl—What Happened?," *Journal of Chemical Education*, 65, 1037–1041 (1988).

FIGURE 2.17 The Chernobyl nuclear power plant, site of a major accident in April 1986. (Photo by V. Zufarov, Tass/Sovfoto)

SAMPLE EXERCISE 2.4

Which of the following elements would you expect to show the greatest similarity in chemical and physical properties: Li, Be, F, S, Cl?

SOLUTION The elements F and Cl should be most alike because they are in the same family (group 7A, the halogen family).

PRACTICE EXERCISE

Locate P (phosphorus) and K (potassium) on the periodic table. Give the atomic number of each and label each a metal, metalloid or nonmetal. ***Answer:*** P, atomic number 15, is a nonmetal; K, atomic number 19, is a metal.

2.5 Molecules and Ions

We have seen that the atom is the smallest representative sample of an element. However, only the noble gas elements are normally found in nature as isolated atoms. Most matter is composed of molecules or ions, both of which are formed from atoms.

Molecules and Chemical Formulas

A **molecule** is an assembly of two or more atoms tightly bound together. The resultant "package" of atoms behaves in many ways as a single, distinct object, just as a television set composed of many parts can be recognized as a single object. We will discuss the forces that hold the atoms together (the chemical bonds) in Chapters 8 and 9.

Many elements are found in nature in molecular form; that is, two or more of the same type of atom are bound together. For example, oxygen as it is normally found in air consists of molecules that contain two oxygen atoms. We represent this molecular form of oxygen by the **chemical formula** O_2 (read "oh two"). The subscript in the formula tells us that two oxygen atoms are present in each molecule. Any molecule that is made up of two atoms is said to be a **diatomic molecule.** Oxygen also exists in another molecular form known as *ozone.* Molecules of ozone consist of three oxygen atoms, so its chemical formula is O_3. Even though "normal" oxygen (O_2) and ozone are both composed only of oxygen atoms, they exhibit very different chemical and physical properties. For example, O_2 is essential for life, but O_3 is toxic; O_2 is odorless, whereas O_3 has a sharp, pungent smell.

The elements that normally occur as diatomic molecules are hydrogen, oxygen, nitrogen, and the halogens. Their locations in the periodic table are shown in Figure 2.18. When we speak of the substance hydrogen, we mean H_2 unless we explicitly indicate otherwise. Likewise, when we speak of oxygen, nitrogen, or any of the halogens, we are referring to O_2, N_2, F_2, Cl_2, Br_2, or I_2. Thus, the properties of oxygen and hydrogen listed in Table 1.3 are those of O_2 and H_2. Other forms of these elements behave much differently.

Molecules of compounds contain more than one type of atom. For example, a molecule of water consists of two hydrogen atoms and one oxygen atom. It is therefore represented by the chemical formula H_2O (read "aitch two oh"). Lack of a subscript on the O implies one atom of O per molecule. Another compound composed of these same elements is hydrogen peroxide, H_2O_2. The properties of these two compounds are very different.

Common Misconception: Students often interpret *molecules* as the particles described by *any* chemical formula. Molecules consist of discrete (well-defined) units and consequently only exist for covalent species, not for ionic or interstitial species.

Teaching Note: Such different chemical formulas of an element are known as *allotropes.* Allotropes differ in their chemical and physical properties. See Chapter 7.

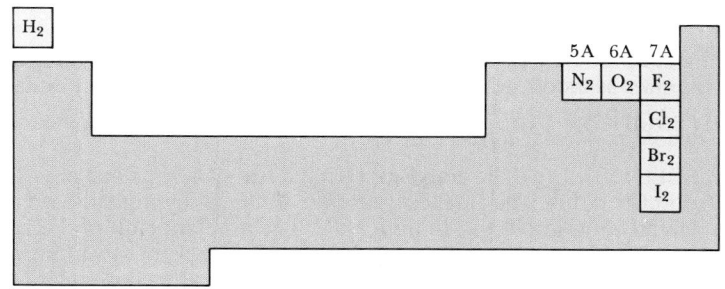

Several common molecules are shown in Figure 2.19. You can see that the composition of each molecule is given by its chemical formula. Note also that these substances are composed only of nonmetallic elements. *Most molecular substances that we will encounter contain only nonmetals.*

Molecular, Empirical, and Structural Formulas

Chemical formulas that indicate the *actual* numbers and types of atoms in a molecule are called **molecular formulas.** (The formulas in Figure 2.19 are molecular formulas.) Chemical formulas that give only the *relative* number of atoms of each type in a ~~molecule~~ are called **empirical** or **simplest formulas.** The subscripts in an empirical formula are always the smallest whole-number ratios; conversely, the subscripts in a molecular formula are always integral multiples of the subscripts in the empirical formula of the substance. For example, the empirical formula for hydrogen peroxide is HO; its molecular formula is H_2O_2. The empirical formula for ethylene is CH_2; its molecular formula is C_2H_4. For many substances, the empirical formula and molecular formula are identical, as in the case of water, H_2O.

Learning Goal 9: Distinguish among empirical formulas, molecular formulas, and structural formulas.

Point of Emphasis: An *empirical formula* gives the simplest whole-number ratio of elements in a compound. A *molecular formula* gives the actual number of atoms of each element in a molecular compound. A *structural formula* is a pictorial representation of a molecular formula.

Point of Emphasis: The subscripts in the molecular formula of a substance are always an integral multiple of the subscripts in the empirical formula of that substance.

FIGURE 2.19 Representation of some common simple molecules.

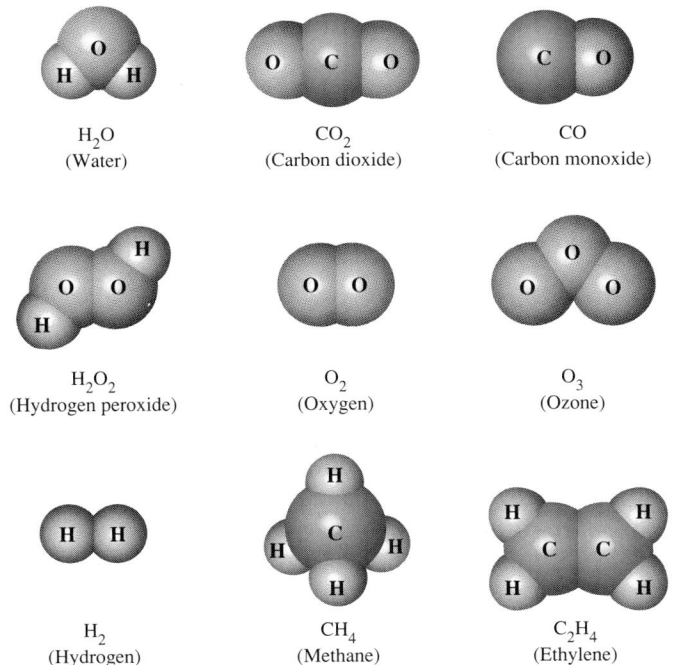

H_2O
(Water)

CO_2
(Carbon dioxide)

CO
(Carbon monoxide)

H_2O_2
(Hydrogen peroxide)

O_2
(Oxygen)

O_3
(Ozone)

H_2
(Hydrogen)

CH_4
(Methane)

C_2H_4
(Ethylene)

 Figure 2.19

2.5 Molecules and Ions **49**

SAMPLE EXERCISE 2.5

Write the empirical formulas for the followng molecules: **(a)** glucose, a substance also known as blood sugar and as dextrose, whose molecular formula is $C_6H_{12}O_6$; **(b)** nitrous oxide, a substance used as an anesthetic and commonly called laughing gas, whose molecular formula is N_2O.

SOLUTION **(a)** The empirical formula has subscripts that are the smallest whole-number ratios. The smallest ratios are obtained by dividing each subscript by the largest common factor, in this case 6. The resultant empirical formula is CH_2O.
  (b) Because the subscripts in N_2O are already the lowest integral numbers, the empirical formula for nitrous oxide is the same as its molecular formula N_2O.

PRACTICE EXERCISE

Give the empirical formula for the substance whose molecular formula is Si_2H_6.
Answer: SiH_3

Molecular formulas are preferred over empirical formulas because they provide more information. Many substances do not exist as discrete molecules, however, and for these we can write only empirical formulas. For example, the element carbon normally exists in extended three-dimensional structures rather than as isolated atoms or molecules. Because there are no distinct molecules of carbon in this structure, we cannot write a molecular formula. The empirical formula for any element is simply the symbol for that element, so carbon is represented by its symbol, C.
  Often the formula of a molecule is written to show how its atoms are joined together. For example, the formulas for water and hydrogen peroxide can be written as follows:

Water   Hydrogen peroxide

Such formulas are known as **structural formulas.** The lines between the symbols for the elements represent the bonds that hold the respective atoms together. These formulas indicate which atoms are attached to which; however, they do not necessarily tell anything about the shapes of molecules (that is, about the actual angles at which the atoms are joined together).

Ions

The nucleus of an atom is unchanged by ordinary chemical processes, but atoms can readily gain or lose electrons. If electrons are removed or added to a neutral atom, a charged particle called an **ion** is formed. An ion with a positive charge is called a **cation** (pronounced CAT-ion); a negatively charged ion is called an **anion** (AN-ion). For example, the sodium atom, which has 11 protons and 11 electrons, easily loses one electron. The resulting cation has 11 protons and 10 electrons, and hence has a net charge of 1 +. The net charge on an ion is represented by a superscript; +, 2+, and 3+ mean a net charge resulting from the loss of one, two, or three electrons, respectively. The superscripts −, 2−, and 3 − represent net charges resulting from the gain of one, two, or three electrons, respectively. The formation of the Na^+ ion from an Na atom is shown schematically below:

$$11p^+ \quad 11e^- \Big) \xrightarrow[\text{electron}]{\text{Lose one}} 11p^+ \quad 10e^- \Big)$$

Na atom $\qquad\qquad$ Na^+ ion

Chlorine, with 17 protons and 17 electrons, often gains an electron in chemical reactions, producing the Cl^- ion:

$$17p^+ \quad 17e^- \Big) \xrightarrow[\text{electron}]{\text{Gain one}} 17p^+ \quad 18e^- \Big)$$

Cl atom $\qquad\qquad$ Cl^- ion

In general, metal atoms tend to lose electrons, and nonmetal atoms tend to gain electrons.

SAMPLE EXERCISE 2.6

Give the complete chemical symbols for the following ions: **(a)** The ion with 26 protons, 30 neutrons, and 24 electrons; **(b)** the phosphorus ion with 16 neutrons and 18 electrons.

SOLUTION   **(a)** The element whose atoms have 26 protons (atomic number 26) is Fe (iron). The mass number of this particular isotope is $26 + 30 = 56$ (the sum of the protons and neutrons). Because the ion has two more protons than electrons, it has a net charge of $2+$. Thus, the complete symbol for the ion is $^{56}_{26}Fe^{2+}$.

(b) By referring to a periodic table or table of elements, we see that phosphorus (symbol P) has an atomic number of 15. Thus, each atom has 15 protons. Its mass number is $15 + 16 = 31$. Because the ion has 15 protons and 18 electrons (three more electrons than protons), its net charge is $3-$. Thus, the complete symbol for the ion is $^{31}_{15}P^{3-}$.

Through most of the rest of our discussions, we will focus on the net charges of ions and not concern ourselves with their mass numbers.

PRACTICE EXERCISE

How many protons and electrons does the Se^{2-} ion possess?   *Answer:* 34 protons and 36 electrons

In addition to simple ions such as Na^+ and Cl^-, there are **polyatomic ions** such as NO_3^- (nitrate ion) and SO_4^{2-} (sulfate ion). These ions consist of atoms joined together as in a molecule, but they have a net positive or negative charge. We will consider further examples of polyatomic ions in Section 2.6.

The chemical properties of ions are greatly different from those of the atoms from which they are derived. The change of an atom or molecule to an ion is like that from Dr. Jekyll to Mr. Hyde: Although the body may be essentially the same (plus or minus a few electrons), the behavior is much different.

Predicting Ionic Charges

Learning Goal 11: Use the periodic table to predict the charges of monatomic ions.

Many atoms gain or lose electrons so as to end up with the same number of electrons as the noble gas closest to them in the periodic table. The members of the noble gas family are chemically very nonreactive and form very few compounds. We might deduce that this is because their electron arrangements are very stable. Nearby elements can obtain these same stable arrangements by losing or gaining electrons. For example, loss of one electron from an atom of sodium leaves it with the same number of electrons as the neutral neon atom (atomic number 10). Similarly, when chlorine gains an electron, it ends up with 18, the same as argon (atomic number 18). We will content ourselves with this simple observation in explaining the formation of ions until later chapters in which we consider chemical bonding.

SAMPLE EXERCISE 2.7

Predict the charges expected for the most stable ions of barium and oxygen.

SOLUTION   Refer to the periodic table. Barium has atom number 56. The nearest noble gas is xenon, atomic number 54. Barium can obtain the stable arrangement of 54 electrons by losing two of its electrons, thereby forming the Ba^{2+} cation.

Oxygen has atomic number 8. The nearest noble gas is neon, atomic number 10. Oxygen can obtain this stable electron arrangement by gaining two electrons, thereby forming an anion of $2-$ charge, O^{2-}.

PRACTICE EXERCISE

Predict the charge of the most stable ion of aluminum.   *Answer:* $3+$

The periodic table is very useful for remembering the charges of ions, especially those of the elements on the left and right sides of the table. As Figure 2.20 shows, the charges of these ions relate in a simple way to their positions in the table. On the left side of the table, we see, for example, that the group 1A elements (the alkali metals) form $1+$ ions, and the group 2A elements (the alkaline earths) form $2+$ ions. On the other side of the table, the group 7A elements (the halogens) form $1-$ ions, and the group 6A elements form $2-$ ions. As we shall see later in the text, many of the other groups do not lend themselves to such simple rules.

Figure 2.20

FIGURE 2.20 Charges of some common ions found in ionic compounds. Notice that the steplike line that divides metals from nonmetals also separates cations from anions.

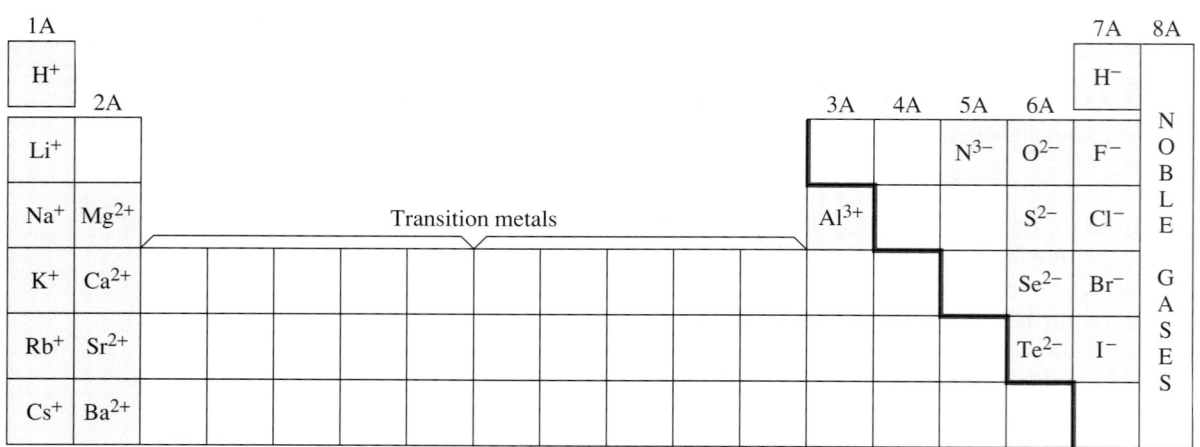

Ionic Compounds

A great deal of chemical activity involves the transfer of electrons between substances. Ions form when one or more electrons transfer from one neutral atom to another. Such a scenario is depicted in Figure 2.21: When elemental sodium is allowed to react with elemental chlorine, an electron transfers from a neutral sodium atom to a neutral chlorine atom. We are left with an Na^+ ion and a Cl^- ion. But that is not the end of the matter. Because objects of opposite charge attract, the Na^+ and the Cl^- ions bind together to form NaCl, an ionic compound. An **ionic compound** is a compound that contains positively charged ions and negatively charged ions.

We can often tell whether a compound is ionic (consisting of ions) or molecular (consisting of molecules) from its composition. In general, cations are metal ions; anions are nonmetal ions. Consequently, *ionic compounds are generally combinations of metals and nonmetals,* as in NaCl. In contrast, *molecular compounds are generally composed of nonmetals only,* as in H_2O.

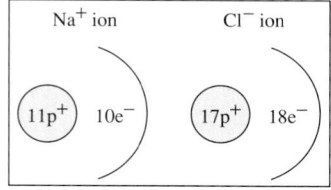

FIGURE 2.21 The transfer of an electron from a neutral Na atom to a neutral Cl atom leads to the formation of a Na^+ ion and a Cl^- ion.

SAMPLE EXERCISE 2.8

Which of the following compounds would you expect to be ionic: N_2O, Na_2O, $CaCl_2$, SF_4?

SOLUTION We would predict that the ionic compounds are Na_2O and $CaCl_2$ because they are composed of a metal combined with a nonmetal. The other two compounds, which are composed entirely of nonmetals, are molecular.

PRACTICE EXERCISE

Which of the following compounds are molecular: CI_4, FeS, P_4O_6, PbF_2?
Answer: CI_4 and P_4O_6

Point of Emphasis: Ionic compounds are generally combinations of metal ions (positively charged) and nonmetal ions (negatively charged).

The ions in ionic compounds are arranged in three-dimensional structures. The arrangement of Na^+ and Cl^- ions in NaCl is shown in Figure 2.22. Because there is no discrete molecule of NaCl, we are able to write only an empirical formula for this substance. In fact, only empirical formulas can be written for most ionic compounds.

FIGURE 2.22 Arrangement of ions in solid sodium chloride, NaCl.

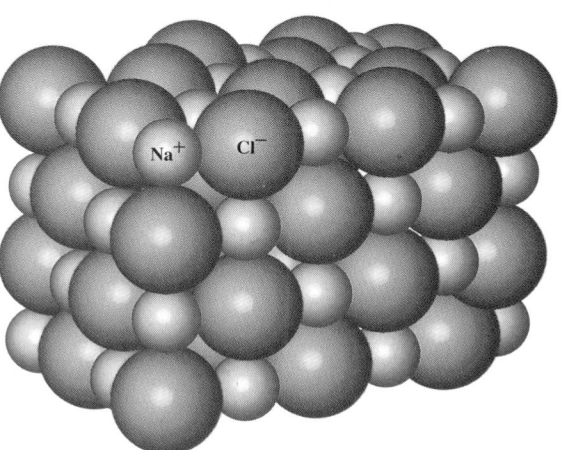

Figure 2.22

STRATEGIES IN CHEMISTRY

Pattern Recognition

Someone has said that drinking at the fountain of knowledge in a chemistry course is like drinking from a fire hydrant. It's true that the pace can sometimes seem brisk. More to the point, however, we can drown in the facts if we don't see the general patterns. The value of recognizing patterns and learning rules and generalizations is that they free us from learning many individual facts. They tie ideas together, so we don't get lost in the details.

Many students struggle with chemistry because they don't see how the topics relate to one another, how ideas tie together to form the fabric of the discipline. They therefore treat every idea and problem as being unique, instead of as an example or application of a general rule, procedure, or relationship. Begin to notice the structure of the topic. Pay attention to the trends and rules that are given to summarize a large body of information. Notice, for example, how atomic structure helps us understand the existence of isotopes (as seen in Table 2.2) and how the periodic table aids us in remembering the charges of ions (as seen in Figure 2.20). You may surprise yourself by observing patterns that are not even explicitly spelled out yet. Perhaps you've even noticed certain trends in chemical formulas. Moving across the periodic table from element 11, Na, we find that the elements form compounds with F with the following compositions: NaF, MgF_2, and AlF_3. Does this trend continue? Do SiF_4, PF_5, and SF_6 exist? Indeed they do. If you have picked up on trends like this from the scraps of information you've seen, you're ahead of the game, and you've already prepared yourself for some topics we will address in later chapters.

It is a simple matter to write the empirical formula for an ionic compound if we know the charges of the ions of which it is composed. Chemical compounds are always electrically neutral. Consequently, the ions in an ionic compound always occur in such a ratio that the total positive charge is equal to the total negative charge. Thus, there is one Na^+ to one Cl^- giving NaCl, one Ba^{2+} to two Cl^- giving $BaCl_2$, and so forth.

As you consider these and other examples, you will see that if the charges on the cation and anion are equal, the subscript on each ion will be 1. If the charges are not equal, the charge on one ion (without its sign) will become the subscript on the other ion:

$$Mg^{2+} \quad N^{3-} \longrightarrow Mg_3N_2$$

SAMPLE EXERCISE 2.9

What are the empirical formulas of the compounds formed by (a) Al^{3+} and Cl^- ions; (b) Al^{3+} and O^{2-} ions; (c) Mg^{2+} and NO_3^- ions?

SOLUTION (a) Three Cl^- ions are required to balance the charge of one Al^{3+} ion. Thus, the formula is $AlCl_3$.

(b) Two Al^{3+} ions are required to balance the charge of three O^{2-} ions (that is, the total positive charge is $6+$, and the total negative charge is $6-$). Thus, the formula is Al_2O_3. (c) Two NO_3^- ions are needed to balance the charge of one Mg^{2+}. Thus, the formula is $Mg(NO_3)_2$. In this case the formula for the entire negative ion must be enclosed in parentheses so that it is clear that the subscript 2 applies to all the atoms of that ion.

PRACTICE EXERCISE

Write the empirical formulas for the compounds formed by the following ions: (a) Na^+ and PO_4^{3-}; (b) Zn^{2+} and SO_4^{2-}; (c) Fe^{3+} and CO_3^{2-}. *Answers:* (a) Na_3PO_4; (b) $ZnSO_4$; (c) $Fe_2(CO_3)_3$

2.6 Naming Inorganic Compounds

As you proceed in your study of this text and in chemistry laboratory work, you will need to refer to specific chemical substances by name. We present here some of the basic rules for naming simple compounds. You may not have immediate use for some of the rules, but they are gathered here in one place for your convenience to use whenever a question of *nomenclature,* or naming of substances, arises.

There are now over 10 million known chemical substances. Naming them all would be a hopelessly complicated task if each had a special name independent of all the others. Many important substances that have been known for a long time, such as water, H_2O, and ammonia, NH_3, do have individual, traditional names. For most substances, however, we rely upon a set of rules that lead to an informative, systematic name for each substance.

One of the earliest classification schemes in chemistry was the distinction between inorganic and organic compounds. *Organic compounds* contain carbon, usually in combination with hydrogen, oxygen, nitrogen, or sulfur. All other compounds are called *inorganic compounds.* Early chemists associated organic compounds with plants and animals, and they associated inorganic compounds with the nonliving portion of our world. This distinction is no longer pertinent. A great number of organic compounds have now been prepared that do not occur in nature. We will discuss naming of organic compounds in Chapter 26. In this section, we will consider the basic rules for naming inorganic compounds, beginning with those that are ionic.

Ionic Compounds: Cations

The names of ionic compounds are based on the names of the ions of which they are composed. For example, NaCl is called sodium chloride after the Na^+ or sodium ion and the Cl^- or chloride ion. The positive ion (cation) is always named first and listed first in writing the formula for the compound. The negative ion (anion) is named and written last. To see how the names of these ions arise, consider first the naming of positive ions.

Ions may be monatomic (composed of a single atom) or polyatomic (formed from two or more atoms). The vast majority of monoatomic cations are formed from metallic elements. These ions take the name of the element itself:

Na^+ sodium ion Zn^{2+} zinc ion Al^{3+} aluminum ion

If an element can form more than one positive ion, the positive charge of the ion is indicated by a Roman numeral in parentheses following the name of the metal:

Fe^{2+} iron(II) ion Cu^+ copper(I) ion

Fe^{3+} iron(III) ion Cu^{2+} copper(II) ion

At this stage, you have no way of knowing which elements commonly form more than one type of cation. This need not be a source of difficulty. If there is any doubt in your mind, use the Roman numeral designation of charge as part

Learning Goal 13: Write the name of a simple inorganic compound, having been given its chemical formula, and perform the reverse operation.

FIGURE 2.23 Compounds of ions of the same element but with different charge can be very different in appearance. Both substances shown are complex salts of iron with K^+ and CN^- ions. The one on the left is potassium ferrocyanide, which contains the Fe(II) bound to CN^- ions. The one on the right is potassium ferricyanide, which contains the Fe(III) bound to CN^- ions. Both substances are used extensively in blueprinting and other dyeing processes. (Richard Megna/Fundamental Photographs)

of the name. It is never wrong to do so, even though it may sometimes be unnecessary. Iron and copper are examples of elements known as *transition metals*, metals that occur in the block of elements from 3B to 2B of the periodic table. The transition metals often form two or more different monatomic cations.

An older method still widely used for distinguishing between two differently charged ions of a metal is to apply the ending *-ous* or *-ic*. These endings represent the lower and higher charged ions, respectively. They are added to the root of the Latin name of the element:

$$Fe^{2+} \quad \text{ferrous ion} \qquad Cu^+ \quad \text{cuprous ion}$$
$$Fe^{3+} \quad \text{ferric ion} \qquad Cu^{2+} \quad \text{cupric ion}$$

Compounds of differently charged ions of the same element generally exhibit very different properties, including physical appearance (Figure 2.23).

The only common polyatomic cations are those given below:

$$NH_4^+ \quad \text{ammonium ion} \qquad Hg_2^{2+} \quad \text{mercury(I) or mercurous ion}$$

The name mercury(I) ion is given to Hg_2^{2+} because it can be considered to consist of two Hg^+ ions. Mercury also occurs as the monatomic Hg^{2+} ion, which is known as the mercury(II) or mercuric ion.

Ionic Compounds: Anions

Monatomic anions (those derived from a single atom) are most commonly formed from atoms of the nonmetallic elements. They are named by dropping the ending of the name of the element and adding the ending *-ide:*

$$H^- \quad \text{hydride ion} \qquad O^{2-} \quad \text{oxide ion} \qquad N^{3-} \quad \text{nitride ion}$$
$$F^- \quad \text{fluoride ion} \qquad S^{2-} \quad \text{sulfide ion} \qquad P^{3-} \quad \text{phosphide ion}$$

Only a few common polyatomic ions end in *-ide:*

$$OH^- \quad \text{hydroxide ion} \qquad CN^- \quad \text{cyanide ion}$$
$$O_2^{2-} \quad \text{peroxide ion} \qquad N_3^- \quad \text{azide ion}$$

Table 2.4 lists the most common cations and anions. Notice that many of the anions are polyatomic and contain oxygen. Anions of this kind are referred to as **oxyanions.** A particular element such as sulfur may form more than one oxyanion. When this occurs, there are rules for indicating the relative numbers of oxygen atoms in the anion. When an element forms only two oxyanions, the name of the one that contains more oxygen ends in *-ate;* the name of the one with less oxygen ends in *-ite:*

$$NO_2^- \quad \text{nitrite ion} \qquad SO_3^{2-} \quad \text{sulfite ion}$$
$$NO_3^- \quad \text{nitrate ion} \qquad SO_4^{2-} \quad \text{sulfate ion}$$

TABLE 2.4 △ Common Ions

Positive ions (cations)	Negative ions (anions)

1+
 Ammonium (NH_4^+)
 Cesium (Cs^+)
 Copper(I) or cuprous (Cu^+)
 Hydrogen (H^+)
 Lithium (Li^+)
 Potassium (K^+)
 Silver (Ag^+)
 Sodium (Na^+)
	1−
	 Acetate ($C_2H_3O_2^-$)
	 Azide (N_3^-)
	 Bromide (Br^-)
	 Chlorate (ClO_3^-)
	 Chloride (Cl^-)
	 Cyanide (CN^-)
	 Dihydrogen phosphate ($H_2PO_4^-$)
	 Fluoride (F^-)
	 Hydride (H^-)
	 Hydrogen carbonate or bicarbonate
	   (HCO_3^-)
	 Hydrogen sulfate or bisulfate
	   (HSO_4^-)
	 Hydroxide (OH^-)
	 Iodide (I^-)
	 Nitrate (NO_3^-)
	 Nitrite (NO_2^-)
	 Perchlorate (ClO_4^-)
	 Permanganate (MnO_4^-)
	 Thiocyanate (SCN^-)

2+ Barium (Ba^{2+}) Cadmium (Cd^{2+}) Calcium (Ca^{2+}) Cobalt(II) or cobaltous (Co^{2+}) Copper(II) or cupric (Cu^{2+}) Iron(II) or ferrous (Fe^{2+}) Lead(II) or plumbous (Pb^{2+}) Magnesium (Mg^{2+}) Manganese(II) or manganous (Mn^{2+}) Mercury(I) or mercurous (Hg_2^{2+}) Mercury(II) or mercuric (Hg^{2+}) Nickel (Ni^{2+}) Strontium (Sr^{2+}) Tin(II) or stannous (Sn^{2+}) Zinc (Zn^{2+})	**2−** Carbonate (CO_3^{2-}) Chromate (CrO_4^{2-}) Dichromate ($Cr_2O_7^{2-}$) Hydrogen phosphate (HPO_4^{2-}) Oxide (O^{2-}) Peroxide (O_2^{2-}) Sulfate (SO_4^{2-}) Sulfide (S^{2-}) Sulfite (SO_3^{2-})
3+ Aluminum (Al^{3+}) Chromium(III) or chromic (Cr^{3+}) Iron(III) or ferric (Fe^{3+})	**3−** Nitride (N^{3-}) Phosphate (PO_4^{3-}) Phosphide (P^{3-})

When the series of anions of a given element extends to three or four members, as with the oxyanions of the halogens, prefixes are also employed. The prefix *hypo-* indicates less oxygen, and the prefix *per-* indicates more oxygen:

ClO^- hypochlorite ion (one less oxygen than chlorite)

ClO_2^- chlorite ion (one less oxygen than chlorate)

ClO_3^- chlorate ion

ClO_4^- perchlorate ion (one more oxygen than chlorate)

Notice that if you memorize the rules just indicated, you need know only the name for one oxyanion in a series to deduce the names for the other members. The rules for naming anions are summarized in Figure 2.24.

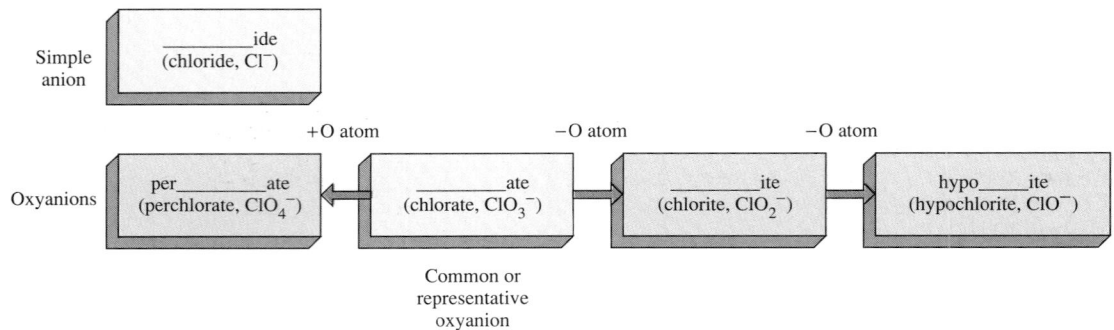

Figure 2.24

FIGURE 2.24 A summary of the procedure for naming anions. The root of the name (such as "chlor" for chlorine) goes in the blank.

SAMPLE EXERCISE 2.10

The formula for the selenate ion is SeO_4^{2-}. Write the formula for the selenite ion.

SOLUTION The selenite ion should have one less oxygen than the selenate ion; hence, SeO_3^{2-}.

PRACTICE EXERCISE

The formula for the bromate ion is BrO_3^-. Write the formula for the hypobromite ion. **Answer:** BrO^-

Because many names of ions predate the establishment of systematic rules, there are many exceptions to these rules. For example, the permanganate ion is MnO_4^-; we thus expect that the manganate ion should be MnO_3^-, but this ion is unknown. The name manganate ion is given to the species MnO_4^{2-}.

Many polyatomic anions that have high charges readily add one or more hydrogen ions (H^+) to form anions of lower charge. These ions are named by prefixing the word *hydrogen* or *dihydrogen,* as appropriate, to the name of the hydrogen-free anion. An older method, which is still used, is to use the prefix *bi-:*

HCO_3^- hydrogen carbonate (or bicarbonate) ion

HSO_4^- hydrogen sulfate (or bisulfate) ion

$H_2PO_4^-$ dihydrogen phosphate ion

We are now in a position to combine the names of cations and anions to name and write the formulas for ionic compounds. The following examples illustrate the relationship between formula and name:

Point of Emphasis: Names of ionic compounds follow the form: cation name + anion name, without reference to how many of each ion are present.

barium bromide	$BaBr_2$	copper(II) nitrate or cupric nitrate	$Cu(NO_3)_2$
aluminum oxide	Al_2O_3	mercury(I) chloride or mercurous chloride	Hg_2Cl_2

SAMPLE EXERCISE 2.11

Name the following compounds: (a) K_2SO_4; (b) $Ba(OH)_2$; (c) $FeCl_3$.

SOLUTION   (a) This compound is composed of K^+ and SO_4^{2-} ions. Because K^+ is called the potassium ion and SO_4^{2-} is called the sulfate ion, the name of the compound is potassium sulfate. (b) This compound is composed of Ba^{2+} and OH^- ions. Ba^{2+} is the barium ion: OH^- is the hydroxide ion. Thus, the compound is called barium hydroxide. (c) This compound is composed of Fe^{3+}, which is called iron(III) or ferric ion, and chloride ions, Cl^-. The compound is iron(III) chloride or ferric chloride.

PRACTICE EXERCISE

Name the following compounds: (a) NH_4Cl; (b) Cr_2O_3; (c) $Co(NO_3)_2$.
Answers: (a) ammonium chloride; (b) chromium(III) oxide; (c) cobalt(II) nitrate

SAMPLE EXERCISE 2.12

Write the chemical formulas for the following compounds: (a) calcium carbonate; (b) stannous fluoride; (c) iron(II) perchlorate.

SOLUTION   (a) The calcium ion is Ca^{2+}; the carbonate ion is CO_3^{2-}. Because of the charges of each ion, there will be one Ca^{2+} ion for each CO_3^{2-} in the compound, giving the empirical formula $CaCO_3$. (b) The stannous ion, also known as the tin(II) ion, is Sn^{2+}. The fluoride ion is F^-. Two F^- ions are needed to balance the positive charge of Sn^{2+}, giving the formula SnF_2. This compound is a tooth-decay preventative that was common in many toothpastes a few years ago. (c) The iron(II) ion is Fe^{2+}; the perchlorate ion is ClO_4^-. Two ClO_4^- ions are required to balance the charge on one Fe^{2+}, giving $Fe(ClO_4)_2$.

These examples should indicate the importance of remembering the charges of the common ions. Indeed, you should begin to learn as many of the entries in Table 2.4 as possible.

PRACTICE EXERCISE

Give the chemical formula for (a) magnesium sulfate; (b) silver sulfide; (c) lead(II) nitrate.   *Answers:* (a) $MgSO_4$; (b) Ag_2S; (c) $Pb(NO_3)_2$

Acids

The important class of compounds known as acids is named in a special way. For our present purposes, an *acid* is defined as a substance whose molecules yield hydrogen ions (H^+) when dissolved in water. Whenever we encounter the chemical formula for an acid at this stage of the course, it will be written with H as the first element, as in HCl and H_2SO_4. The formula of any acid consists of an anionic group whose charge is balanced by one or more H^+ ions, as seen in the examples in the table below. The name of the acid is related to the name of the anion. Anions whose names end in *-ide* have associated acids that have the *hydro-* prefix and an *-ic* ending, as in these examples:

Anion	Corresponding acid
Cl^- (chloride)	HCl (hydrochloric acid)
S^{2-} (sulfide)	H_2S (hydrosulfuric acid)

Many of the most important acids are derived from oxyanions. If the anion has an *-ate* ending, the corresponding acid is given an *-ic* ending. Anions whose names end in *-ite* have associated acids whose names end in *-ous*. Prefixes in the name of the anion are retained in the name of the acid. These rules are illustrated by the oxyacids of chlorine:

Anion	Corresponding acid
ClO^- (hypochlor*ite*)	$HClO$ (hypochlor*ous* acid)
ClO_2^- (chlor*ite*)	$HClO_2$ (chlor*ous* acid)
ClO_3^- (chlor*ate*)	$HClO_3$ (chlor*ic* acid)
ClO_4^- (perchlor*ate*)	$HClO_4$ (perchlor*ic* acid)

Figure 2.25 summarizes the relationships between the names of acids and anions.

SAMPLE EXERCISE 2.13

Name the following acids: (a) HCN; (b) HNO_3; (c) H_2SO_4; (d) H_2SO_3.

SOLUTION (a) The anion from which this acid is derived is CN^-, the cyanide ion. Because this ion has an *-ide* ending, the acid is given a *hydro-* prefix and an *-ic* ending: hydrocyanic acid. Only water solutions of HCN are referred to as hydrocyanic acid: the pure compound is called hydrogen cyanide. (b) Because NO_3^- is the nitrate ion, HNO_3 is called nitric acid (the *-ate* ending of the anion is replaced with an *-ic* ending in naming the acid). (c) Because SO_4^{2-} is the sulfate ion, H_2SO_4 is called sulfuric acid. (d) Because SO_3^{2-} is the sulfite ion, H_2SO_3 is sulfurous acid (the *-ite* ending of the anion is replaced with an *-ous* ending).

PRACTICE EXERCISE

Give the chemical formulas for (a) hydrobromic acid; (b) phosphoric acid.
Answers: (a) HBr; (b) H_3PO_4

FIGURE 2.25 Summary of the way in which anion names and acid names are related. Notice that the prefixes *per* and *hypo* are retained in going from the anion to the acid.

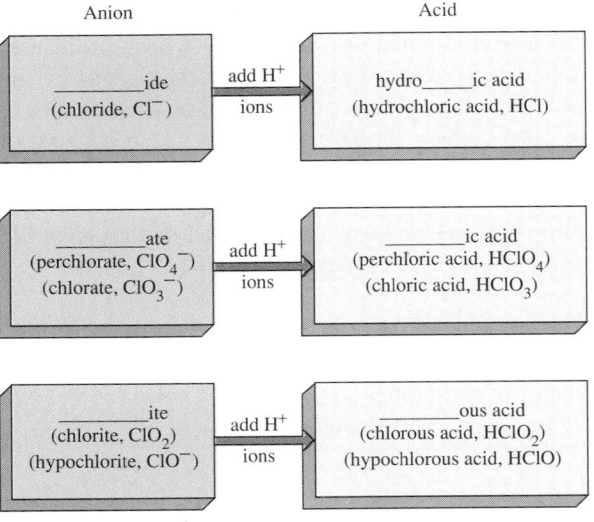

Figure 2.25

Molecular Compounds

The procedures for naming binary (two-element) molecular compounds are similar to those for naming ionic compounds. In these molecular compounds it is possible to associate a more positive nature with one element in the molecule and a more negative one with the other element. The elements become more positive as you move to the left and down on the periodic table. They become more negative as you move to the right and toward the top. The element with the more positive nature is named first and also appears first in the chemical formula. The second element is named with an *-ide* ending. For example, the name for HCl is hydrogen chloride. (This is the name used when referring to the pure compound; water solutions of HCl are referred to as hydrochloric acid; see Figure 2.26.)

Often a pair of elements can form several different molecular compounds. For example, carbon and oxygen form CO and CO_2. To distinguish these compounds from one another, the prefixes given in Table 2.5 are used to denote the numbers of atoms of each element present. Thus, CO is called carbon *mon*oxide, and CO_2 is called carbon *di*oxide. When the prefix ends in *a* or *o* and the name of the anion begins with a vowel (such as *oxide*), the *a* or *o* is often dropped. The prefix *mono-* is usually omitted for the first-named element. A few examples follow:

Cl_2O dichlorine monoxide NF_3 nitrogen trifluoride

N_2O_4 dinitrogen tetroxide P_4S_{10} tetraphosphorus decasulfide

It is important to realize that you cannot predict the formulas of most molecular substances in the same way you predict the formulas of ionic compounds. That is why we name them using prefixes that explicitly indicate their composition. We will discuss the basis for their compositions in Chapter 8.

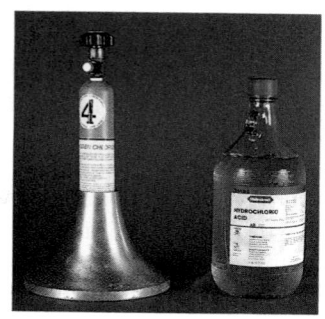

FIGURE 2.26 Hydrogen chloride, which is a gas at room temperature, is shown in a compressed-gas cylinder (left). Hydrochloric acid, which is a water solution of hydrogen chloride, is shown in a glass bottle (right). (Donald Clegg and Roxy Wilson)

TABLE 2.5 △ **Prefixes Used in Naming Binary Compounds Formed Between Nonmetals**

Prefix	Meaning
Mono-	1
Di-	2
Tri-	3
Tetra-	4
Penta-	5
Hexa-	6
Hepta-	7
Octa-	8
Nona-	9
Deca-	10

SAMPLE EXERCISE 2.14

Name the following compounds: **(a)** SO_2; **(b)** PCl_5; **(c)** N_2O_3.

SOLUTION Because the compounds consist entirely of nonmetals, you should expect that they are molecular rather than ionic. Using the prefixes in Table 2.5, we have **(a)** sulfur dioxide, **(b)** phosphorus pentachloride, and **(c)** dinitrogen trioxide.

PRACTICE EXERCISE

Give the chemical formula for **(a)** silicon tetrabromide; **(b)** disulfur dichloride. *Answers:* **(a)** $SiBr_4$; **(b)** S_2Cl_2

For Review

Summary

Atoms are the basic building blocks of matter; they are the smallest units of an element that can combine with other elements. Atoms are composed of a nu-cleus (containing protons and neutrons) and electrons that move around the nucleus. We considered some of the historically significant experiments that led to this model of the atom: Thomson's experiments on the behavior of cathode rays (a stream of electrons) in magnetic and electric fields, Millikan's oil-drop experiment, Becquerel's and Rutherford's studies on radioactivity, and Rutherford's studies on the scattering of α particles by thin metal foils.

Elements can be classified by atomic number, the number of protons in the nucleus of an atom. All atoms of a given element have the same atomic number. The mass number of an atom is the sum of the numbers of protons and neutrons. Atoms of the same element that differ in mass number are known as isotopes.

The periodic table is an arrangement of the elements in order of increasing atomic number. Elements with similar properties are placed in vertical columns. The elements in a column are known as a periodic family or group. The metallic elements, which comprise the majority of the elements, dominate the left side and middle of the table; the nonmetallic elements are located on the upper right side.

Atoms can combine to form molecules. Atoms can also either gain or lose electrons, thereby forming charged particles called ions. Metals tend to lose electrons, becoming positively charged ions (cations). Nonmetals tend to gain electrons, forming negatively charged ions (anions). Because ionic compounds are electrically neutral, containing both cations and anions, they usually contain both metallic and nonmetallic elements. Compounds composed of molecules (molecular compounds) usually contain only nonmetallic elements.

The chemical formulas used for ionic compounds are empirical formulas. The empirical formula of an ionic compound can be written readily if the charges of the ions are known. Although empirical formulas can also be written for molecular substances, the molecular formula is preferred because it gives the actual number of each type of atom in a molecule of the substance. Structural formulas show the order in which the atoms in a molecule are connected.

A set of systematic rules has been developed for naming inorganic compounds. We considered ionic compounds, acids, and binary molecular compounds.

Key Terms

atoms
law of multiple proportions (Sec. 2.1)
cathode rays (Sec. 2.2)
radioactivity (Sec. 2.2)
nucleus (Sec. 2.2)
proton (Sec. 2.3)
neutron (Sec. 2.3)
electron (Sec. 2.3)
electronic charge (Sec. 2.3)
angstrom (Sec. 2.3)
isotopes (Sec. 2.3)
atomic number (Sec. 2.3)
mass number (Sec. 2.3)
nuclide (Sec. 2.3)
periodic table (Sec. 2.4)
family (group) (Sec. 2.4)

metallic elements (metals) (Sec. 2.4)
nonmetallic elements (nonmetals) (Sec. 2.4)
metalloids (Sec. 2.4)
molecule (Sec. 2.5)
chemical formula (Sec. 2.5)
diatomic molecule (Sec. 2.5)
molecular formula (Sec. 2.5)
empirical formula (simplest formula) (Sec. 2.5)
structural formula (Sec. 2.5)
ion (Sec. 2.5)
cation (Sec. 2.5)
anion (Sec. 2.5)
polyatomic ions (Sec. 2.5)
ionic compound (Sec. 2.5)
oxyanion (Sec. 2.6)

Exercises

Atomic Theory

2.1. Using the atomic theory, explain the difference in the following two statements: **(a)** Nitrogen dioxide is a *compound* of nitrogen and oxygen. **(b)** Air is a *mixture* composed mostly of nitrogen and oxygen.

2.2. How does the atomic theory account for the fact that when 1.000 g of water is decomposed into its elements, 0.111 g of hydrogen and 0.889 g of oxygen are obtained regardless of the source of the water?

2.3. A chemist prepared a series of compounds containing only sulfur and fluorine and determined the amount of each element in each compound:

Compound	Mass of sulfur (g)	Mass of fluorine (g)
A	23.2	55.0
B	16.6	9.8
C	19.3	68.6

(a) Calculate the mass of fluorine per gram of sulfur in each compound. (b) How do the numbers in part (a) support the atomic theory?

2.4. A chemistry student finds that 15.20 g of nitrogen will react with 17.37 g, 34.74 g, or 43.43 g of oxygen to form three different compounds. (a) Calculate the mass of oxygen per gram of nitrogen in each compound. (b) How do the numbers in part (a) support the atomic theory?

2.5. Natural gas (methane) burns in the presence of oxygen to produce water, carbon dioxide, and heat. We know that 4.0 g of natural gas requires 16.0 g of oxygen for complete combustion and that 9.0 g of water is produced in this reaction. Can the mass of carbon dioxide produced be determined from this information? Explain.

2.6. When the magnesium foil within a flashbulb burns, the flashbulb undergoes no change in mass. When a sample of magnesium ribbon burns in open air, the sample gains mass. What is the difference between these two experiments? Does the second observation violate the law of conservation of mass? Explain.

Atomic Structure

2.7. What was the evidence used to conclude that cathode rays consist of negatively charged particles?

2.8. A negatively charged particle is directed between two electrically charged plates such as those shown in Figure 2.9. (a) Why does the path of the charged particle bend? (b) As the charge on the plates is increased, would you expect the bending to increase, decrease, or stay the same? (c) As the mass of the particle is increased, would you expect the bending to increase, decrease, or stay the same?

2.9. Static electricity, such as that given to a piece of amber by rubbing it with wool, is due to a buildup of electrons. A sample of amber is measured to have a static charge of 3.24×10^{-6} C. How many excess electrons are on the piece of amber?

2.10. Millikan determined the charge on the electron by studying the static charges on oil drops falling in an electric field. A student carried out this experiment using several oil drops for her measurements and calculated the charges on the drops. She obtained the following data:

Droplet	Calculated charge (C)
A	1.60×10^{-19}
B	3.15×10^{-19}
C	4.81×10^{-19}
D	6.31×10^{-19}

What is the significance of the fact that the droplets carried different charges? What conclusion can the student draw from these data regarding the charge of the electron? What value (and to how many significant figures) should she report for the electronic charge?

2.11. Why is Rutherford's nuclear model of the atom more consistent with the results of the α-particle-scattering experiment than Thomson's "plum pudding" model?

2.12. What differences would you expect if beryllium foil were used instead of gold foil in the α-particle-scattering experiment depicted in Figures 2.11 and 2.12?

2.13. The diameter of the cesium (Cs) atom is about 4.7 Å. (a) Express this distance in nanometers (nm); in picometers (pm). (b) How many cesium atoms would have to be lined up to span 1.0 cm?

2.14. If 1.0×10^8 sodium (Na) atoms could be arranged side by side, they would form a straight line measuring 3.1 cm. What is the diameter of an Na atom?

2.15. How many protons, neutrons, and electrons are in the following atoms: (a) ^{20}Ne; (b) ^{39}K; (c) ^{48}Ti; (d) ^{80}Br; (e) ^{109}Ag; (f) ^{137}Ba?

2.16. Each of the following nuclides is used in medicine. Indicate the number of protons and neutrons in each nuclide: (a) cobalt-60; (b) iodine-131; (c) technetium-99; (d) phosphorus-32; (e) chromium-51; (f) iron-59.

2.17. Fill in the gaps in the following table:

Symbol	^{19}F	^{74}As			
Protons			56		
Neutrons			81	71	
Electrons				51	78
Mass no.					196

2.18. Fill in the gaps in the following table:

Symbol	^{31}P				
Protons		26			80
Neutrons		30			
Electrons				53	
Atomic no.			50		
Mass no.			119	127	201

2.19. Write the correct symbol, with both superscript and subscript, for each of the following (use the list of elements on the front inside cover): (a) the isotope of sodium with mass 23; (b) the nuclide of vanadium that contains 28 neutrons; (c) an α particle; (d) the isotope of chlorine with mass 37; (d) the nuclide of magnesium that has an equal number of protons and neutrons.

2.20. The uranium isotope used to generate nuclear power has 143 neutrons in its nucleus. The most common isotope of uranium has 146 neutrons in its nucleus. What are the full chemical symbols, with both superscript and subscript, for these isotopes of uranium?

The Periodic Table; Molecules and Ions

2.21. For each of the following elements, write its chemical symbol, locate it in the periodic table, and indicate whether it is a metal, metalloid, or nonmetal: (a) manganese; (b) phosphorus; (c) aluminum; (d) argon; (e) iodine; (f) chromium; (g) germanium.

2.22. Locate each of the following elements in the periodic table, indicate whether it is a metal, metalloid, or nonmetal, and give the name of the element: (a) S; (b) Se; (c) Hg; (d) Ca; (e) Ne; (f) Be; (g) Zn.

2.23. For each of the following elements, write its chemical symbol, determine the name of the group to which it belongs (Table 2.3), and indicate whether it is a metal, metalloid, or nonmetal: (a) chlorine; (b) xenon; (c) lithium; (d) barium; (e) sulfur.

2.24. Classify each of the group 6A elements (the chalcogens) as a metal, metalloid, or nonmetal.

2.25. Which conveys more information, the empirical formula of a compound or its molecular formula? Explain.

2.26. Two compounds have the same empirical formula. Do they necessarily have the same molecular formula?

2.27. Write the empirical formula corresponding to each of the following molecular formulas: (a) N_2O_4; (b) C_6H_{12}; (c) $C_4H_2O_4$; (d) P_2O_5; (e) $C_6H_{12}O_6$; (f) SO_3.

2.28. From the following list, find the groups of compounds that have the same empirical formula: C_2H_2, N_2O_4, C_2H_4, C_6H_6, NO_2, C_3H_6, C_4H_8.

2.29. Fill in the gaps in the following table:

Symbol	$^{37}Cl^-$	$^{88}Sr^{2+}$			
Protons			21	28	
Neutrons			23	31	16
Electrons				26	18
Net charge			3+		3-

2.30. Fill in the gaps in the following table:

Symbol	$^{17}O^{2-}$	$^{52}Cr^{3+}$		
Protons			38	34
Neutrons			50	45	74
Electrons				36	54
Net charge			2+		1-

2.31. Each of the following elements is capable of forming an ion in chemical reactions. By referring to the periodic table, predict the charge found on the most stable ion formed by each: (a) Mg; (b) S; (c) Al; (d) K; (e) Br; (f) Y.

2.32. Which of the following ions would you *not* expect to form: (a) F^+; (b) S^{2-}; (c) Be^-; (d) P^{3-}; (e) Br^-; (f) K^{2+}?

2.33. Predict the empirical formula for the ionic compound formed by (a) Ca^{2+} and Br^-; (b) NH_4^+ and Cl^-; (c) Al^{3+} and $C_2H_3O_2^-$; (d) K^+ and SO_4^{2-}; (e) Mg^{2+} and PO_4^{3-}; (f) Ba^{2+} and OH^-.

2.34. Predict the empirical formula for the ionic compound formed from each of the following pairs of elements: (a) Na, S; (b) Ca, F; (c) Mg, O; (d) Al, O; (e) Be, S; (f) Li, N.

2.35. Predict whether each of the following compounds is molecular or ionic; (a) NO_2; (b) BF_3; (c) Li_2O; (d) Sc_2O_3; (e) CsBr; (f) PF_5; (g) NF_3; (h) LaP.

2.36. Which of the following are ionic substances and which are molecular: (a) CaO; (b) $SiCl_4$; (c) $Mg(NO_3)_2$; (d) NOCl; (e) B_2H_6; (f) CH_3OH; (g) Ag_2SO_4?

Naming Inorganic Compounds

2.37. Distinguish between the following ions: sulfate, sulfite, sulfide, and hydrogen sulfate.

2.38. Give the chemical formula for (a) chlorite ion; (b) chloride ion; (c) chlorate ion; (d) perchlorate ion; (e) hypochlorite ion.

2.39. Provide names for the following ionic compounds: (a) $ZnCl_2$; (b) $Ca(CN)_2$; (c) $Cu(OH)_2$; (d) $Ba(NO_3)_2$; (e) K_3PO_4; (f) Hg_2S; (g) $(NH_4)_2SO_4$; (h) FeF_3; (i) Na_2CrO_4; (j) $Cr_2(CO_3)_3$.

2.40. Name the following ionic compounds: (a) Al_2O_3; (b) $Cu(ClO_4)_2$; (c) $NiCO_3$; (d) $SnBr_2$; (e) $Fe(OH)_2$; (f) $KMnO_4$; (g) $Pb(C_2H_3O_2)_2$; (h) $Zn(H_2PO_4)_2$; (i) Li_2SO_3; (j) $(NH_4)_2Cr_2O_7$.

2.41. Give the chemical formula for each of the following ionic compounds: (a) calcium nitride; (b) iron(II) sulfide; (c) chromium(III) sulfate; (d) copper(II) acetate; (e) calcium bicarbonate; (f) potassium hypochlorite.

2.42. Give the chemical formula for each of the following ionic compounds: (a) iron(III) oxide; (b) magnesium phosphate; (c) sodium peroxide; (d) ferrous nitrate; (e) calcium hydride; (f) zinc hydrogen sulfate.

2.43. Provide the name or chemical formula, as appropriate, for each of the following acids: (a) nitric acid; (b) hydroiodic acid; (c) sulfurous acid; (d) $HClO_2$; (e) H_3PO_4; (f) H_2CO_3.

2.44. Give the name or chemical formula, as appropriate, for each of the following acids: (a) HBr; (b) $HBrO_4$; (c) HNO_2; (d) hypochlorous acid; (e) iodic acid; (f) sulfuric acid.

2.45. Give the name or chemical formula, as appropriate, for each of the following molecular substances: (a) N_2O_5; (b) IF_7; (c) XeO_3; (d) silicon tetrachloride; (e) hydrogen selenide; (f) tetraphosphorus hexoxide.

2.46. Provide the name or chemical formula, as appropriate, for the following molecular substances: (a) SF_6; (b) Cl_2O_7; (c) ICl_3; (d) carbon disulfide; (e) hydrogen cyanide; (f) dinitrogen tetroxide.

2.47. Write the chemical formula for each substance mentioned in the following word descriptions (use the front inside cover to find the symbols for the elements you don't know). (a) Zinc carbonate can be heated to form zinc oxide and carbon dioxide. (b) On treatment with hydrofluoric acid, silicon dioxide forms silicon tetrafluoride and water. (c) Sulfur dioxide reacts with water to form sulfurous acid. (d) The substance hydrogen phosphide is commonly called phosphine. (e) Perchloric acid reacts with cadmium to form cadmium(II) perchlorate. (f) Vanadium(III) bromide is a colored solid.

2.48. Assume that you encounter the following phrases in your reading. What is the chemical formula for each substance mentioned? (a) Potassium chlorate is used as a laboratory source of oxygen. (b) Sodium hypochlorite is used as a household bleach. (c) Ammonia is important in the synthesis of fertilizers such as ammonium nitrate. (d) Hydrofluoric acid is used to etch glass. (e) The smell of rotten eggs is due to hydrogen sulfide. (f) When hydrochloric acid is added to sodium bicarbonate (baking soda), carbon dioxide gas forms.

Additional Exercises

2.49. Describe the contributions to atomic theory made by the following scientists: (a) Dalton; (b) Thomson; (c) Millikan; (d) Rutherford.

2.50. It is common in chemistry to assume that the mass of a cation is the same as that of its parent atom. (a) Using data in Table 2.1, determine the number of significant figures that must be reported before the difference in mass of ^1H and $^1H^+$ is significant. (b) What percentage of the mass of a ^1H atom does the electron represent?

2.51. Fill in the gaps in the following table:

Symbol	^{35}Cl	$^{55}Mn^{2+}$			
Protons			16		38
Neutrons			17	43	49
Electrons				36	36
Net charge			0	3−	

2.52. Deuterium and tritium are the names given to the isotopes of hydrogen that have one and two neutrons in the nucleus, respectively. (a) Write the full chemical symbols for deuterium and tritium. (b) Describe the similarities and differences between an atom of deuterium and one of tritium.

2.53. An unknown element, X, reacts with chlorine to form an ionic compound whose empirical formula is XCl_2. If the ion of X has 18 electrons, identify the element.

2.54. From the following list of elements—Ar, H, Ga, Al, Ca, Br, Ge, K, O—pick the one that best fits each description; use each element only once: (a) an alkali metal; (b) an alkaline earth metal; (c) a noble gas; (d) a halogen; (e) a metalloid; (f) a nonmetal listed in group 1A; (g) a metal that forms a 3+ ion; (h) a nonmetal that forms a 2− ion; (i) an element that resembles aluminum.

[2.55]. Hydrocarbons are molecules that contain only carbon and hydrogen. A hydrocarbon with empirical formula CH contains 0.923 g of carbon per gram of hydrocarbon; the remaining mass is hydrogen. Listed below is the carbon content per gram of substance for several common hydrocarbons:

Hydrocarbon	Grams of carbon per gram of hydrocarbon
Methane	0.750
Ethylene	0.857
Ethane	0.800
Propane	0.818
Butane	0.828

(a) For the hydrocarbon with empirical formula CH, calculate the mass of H that combines with 1 g of C. (b) For the hydrocarbons listed in the table, calculate the mass of H that combines with 1 g of C. (c) By comparing the results for part (b) to those for part (a), determine small-number ratios of hydrogen atoms per carbon atom for the hydrocarbons in the table. (d) Write empirical formulas for the hydrocarbons in the table.

2.56. The following are pairs of anions and cations without their charges given. For each pair, indicate the charge on the cation and the anion, provide an empirical formula for the ionic compound that results from these, and provide the proper name for the compounds: (a) NH_4, SO_4; (b) Ca, HCO_3; (c) Al, HSO_4; (d) K, CrO_4; (e) Na, $C_2H_3O_2$; (f) Ag, S; (g) Be, Br; (h) K, Te.

2.57. Give the chemical names of each of the following familiar compounds: (a) NaCl (table salt); (b) $NaHCO_3$ (baking soda); (c) NaOCl (in many bleaches); (d) NaOH (caustic soda); (e) $(NH_4)_2CO_3$ (smelling salts); (f) $CaSO_4$ (plaster of paris).

2.58. Many familiar substances have common, unsystematic names. For each of the following, give the correct systematic name: (a) saltpeter, KNO_3; (b) soda ash, Na_2CO_3; (c) lime, CaO; (d) muriatic acid, HCl; (e) epsom salt, $MgSO_4$; (f) milk of magnesia, $Mg(OH)_2$.

2.59. Many ions and compounds have very similar names, and there is great potential for confusing them. Write the correct chemical formulas to distinguish between (a) calcium sulfide and calcium hydrogen sulfide; (b) hydrobromic acid and bromic acid; (c) aluminum nitride and aluminum nitrite; (d) iron(II) oxide and iron(III) oxide; (e) ammonia and ammonium ion; (f) potassium sulfite and potassium bisulfite; (g) mercurous chloride and mercuric chloride; (h) chloric acid and perchloric acid.

2.60. Iodic acid has the molecular formula HIO_3. Write the formulas for the following: (a) the iodate anion; (b) the periodate anion; (c) the hypoiodite anion; (d) hypoiodous acid; (e) periodic acid.

[2.61]. Using a suitable reference such as the *Handbook of Chemistry and Physics,* look up the following information for sulfur; (a) the number of known isotopes; (b) the natural abundance of the four most abundant isotopes.

[2.62]. Using the *Handbook of Chemistry and Physics,* find the density, melting point, and boiling point for PF_3.

Stoichiometry: Calculations with Chemical Formulas and Equations

3

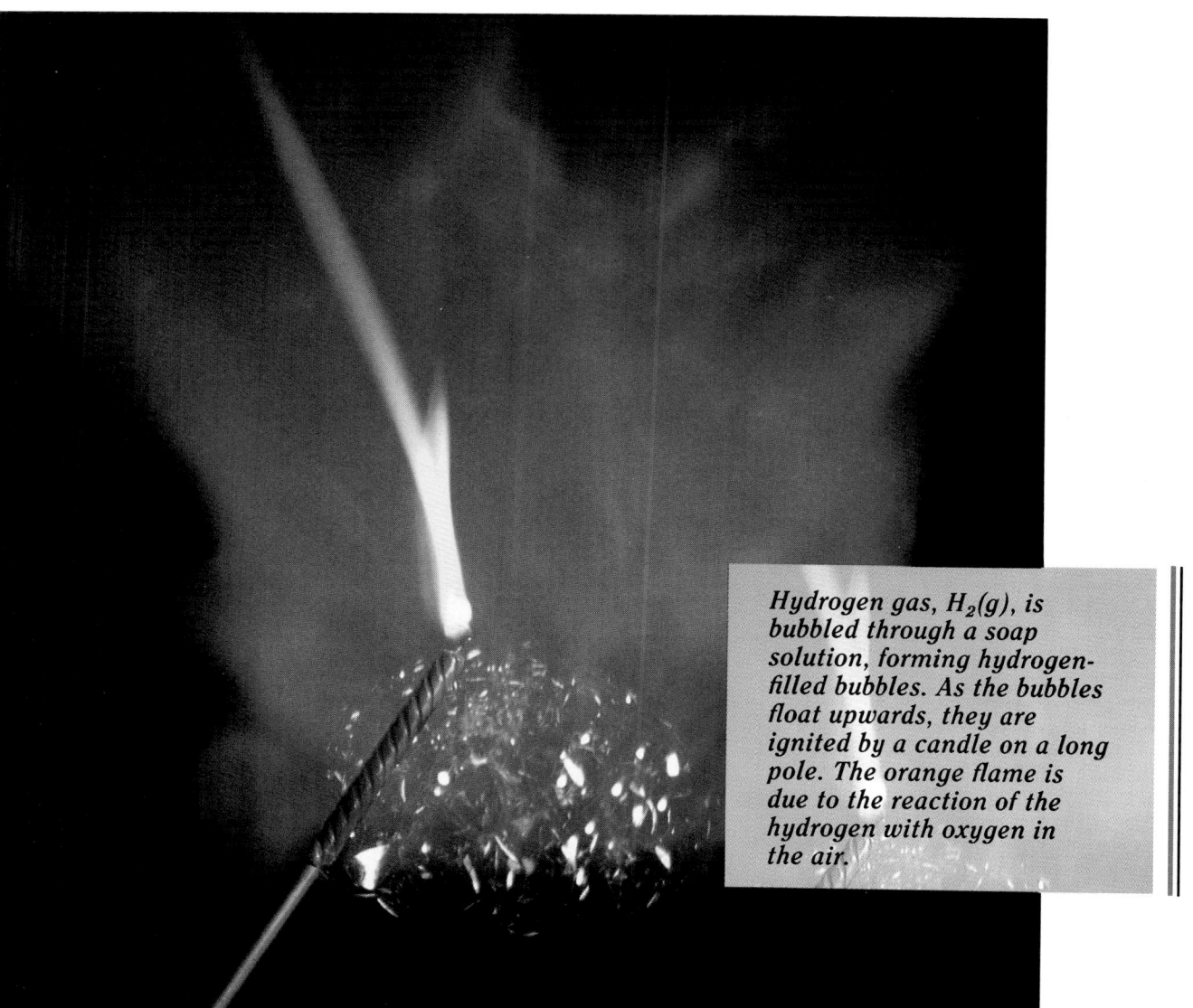

Hydrogen gas, $H_2(g)$, is bubbled through a soap solution, forming hydrogen-filled bubbles. As the bubbles float upwards, they are ignited by a candle on a long pole. The orange flame is due to the reaction of the hydrogen with oxygen in the air.

CONTENTS

Point of Emphasis: The *law of conservation of mass* (or matter) states that mass is neither created nor destroyed in a chemical reaction.

Point of Emphasis: *Stoichiometry* literally means *measurement of elements.* The relationship among the numbers of reactant and product species produces a balanced chemical equation.

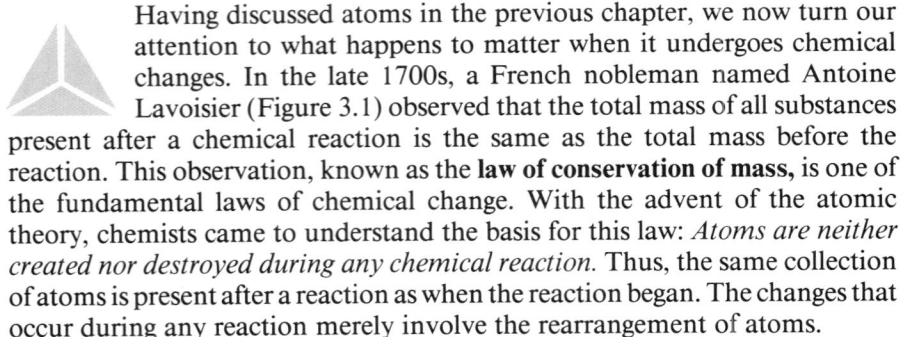

Having discussed atoms in the previous chapter, we now turn our attention to what happens to matter when it undergoes chemical changes. In the late 1700s, a French nobleman named Antoine Lavoisier (Figure 3.1) observed that the total mass of all substances present after a chemical reaction is the same as the total mass before the reaction. This observation, known as the **law of conservation of mass,** is one of the fundamental laws of chemical change. With the advent of the atomic theory, chemists came to understand the basis for this law: *Atoms are neither created nor destroyed during any chemical reaction.* Thus, the same collection of atoms is present after a reaction as when the reaction began. The changes that occur during any reaction merely involve the rearrangement of atoms.

In this chapter, we begin to examine the quantitative nature of chemical formulas and chemical reactions. This area of study is known as **stoichiometry** (pronounced stoy-key-OM-uh-tree), a name derived from the Greek words *stoicheion* ("element") and *metron* ("measure"). The law of conservation of mass will serve as one of the guiding principles in our discussions.

Stoichiometry is an essential tool in chemistry. Such diverse problems, for example, as measuring the concentration of ozone in the atmosphere, determining the potential yield of gold from an ore, and assessing the suitability of different processes for converting coal into gaseous fuels all involve aspects of stoichiometry.

3.1 Chemical Equations

Chemical reactions are represented in a concise way by **chemical equations.** For example, when hydrogen, H_2, burns, it reacts with oxygen, O_2, in the air to

FIGURE 3.1 Antoine Lavoisier (1734–1794), as pictured in a nineteenth-century French engraving. Lavoisier conducted many important studies on combustion reactions. Here he is shown experimenting to determine the composition of water by igniting a mixture of hydrogen and oxygen with an electric spark. Unfortunately, Lavoisier's career was cut short by the French Revolution. He was not only a member of the French nobility but also a tax collector. He was guillotined in 1794 during the final months of the Reign of Terror. He is now generally considered to be the father of modern chemistry because of his reliance on carefully controlled experiments and his use of quantitative measurements. (The Granger Collection)

form water, H_2O. We write the chemical equation for this reaction as follows:

$$2H_2 + O_2 \longrightarrow 2H_2O \qquad\qquad [3.1]$$

We read the + sign to mean "reacts with" and the arrow as "produces." The chemical formulas on the left of the arrow represent the starting substances, called **reactants.** The substances produced in the reaction, called **products,** are shown to the right of the arrow. The numbers in front of the formulas are called *coefficients*. (As in algebraic equations, the numeral 1 is usually not written.)

Because atoms are neither created nor destroyed in any reaction, a chemical equation must have an equal number of atoms of each element on each side of the arrow. When this condition is met, the equation is said to be *balanced.* For example, on the right side of Equation 3.1 there are two molecules of H_2O, each containing two atoms of hydrogen and one atom of oxygen. Thus, $2H_2O$ (read "two molecules of H_2O") contains $2 \times 2 = 4$ H atoms and $2 \times 1 = 2$ O atoms. Because there are also 4 H atoms and 2 O atoms on the left side of the equation, the equation is balanced.

Before we can write the chemical equation for a reaction, we must determine by experiment those substances that are reactants and those that are products. Once we know the chemical formulas of the reactants and products in a reaction, we can write the unbalanced chemical equation. We then balance the equation by determining the coefficients that provide equal numbers of each type of atom on each side of the equation. Generally, whole-number coefficients are used.

In balancing equations, it is important to understand the difference between a coefficient in front of a formula and a subscript in a formula. Refer to Figure 3.2. Notice that changing a subscript in a formula—from H_2O to H_2O_2, for example—changes the identity of the chemical. The substance H_2O_2, hydrogen peroxide, is quite different from water. *Subscripts should never be changed in balancing an equation.* In contrast, placing a coefficient in front of a formula changes only the *amount* and not the *identity* of the substance; $2H_2O$ means two molecules of water, $3H_2O$ means three molecules of water, and so forth.

To illustrate the process of balancing equations, consider the reaction that occurs when methane, CH_4, the principal component of natural gas, burns in air to produce carbon dioxide gas, CO_2, and liquid water, H_2O. Both of these products contain oxygen atoms that come from O_2 in the air. We say that

Chemical symbol	Meaning		Composition
H_2O	One molecule of water:		Two H atoms and one O atom
$2H_2O$	Two molecules of water:		Four H atoms and two O atoms
H_2O_2	One molecule of hydrogen peroxide:		Two H atoms and two O atoms

FIGURE 3.2 Illustration of the difference between a subscript in a chemical formula and a coefficient in front of the formula. Notice that the number of atoms of each type (listed under composition) is obtained by multiplying the coefficient and the subscript associated with each element in the formula.

Figure 3.2

combustion in air is "supported by oxygen," meaning that oxygen is a reactant. The unbalanced equation is

$$CH_4 + O_2 \longrightarrow CO_2 + H_2O \qquad \text{(unbalanced)} \qquad [3.2]$$

Notice that one molecule of CH_4 contains the same number of C atoms (one) as does one molecule of CO_2. Therefore, the coefficients for these substances *must* be the same, and we choose them both to be 1 as we start the balancing process. However, the reactant CH_4 contains more H atoms (four) than does the product H_2O (two). If we place a coefficient 2 in front of H_2O, there will be four H atoms on each side of the equation:

$$CH_4 + O_2 \longrightarrow CO_2 + 2H_2O \qquad \text{(unbalanced)} \qquad [3.3]$$

It is usually best to balance first those elements that occur in only one substance on each side of the equation. In our example, both C and H appear in only one reactant and, separately, in one product each, so we begin by focusing attention on CH_4. We consider first carbon and then hydrogen.

At this stage, the products have more total O atoms (four, two from CO_2 and two from $2H_2O$) than the reactants have (two). If we place a coefficient 2 in front of O_2, we complete the balancing by making the number of O atoms equal on both sides of the equation:

$$CH_4 + 2O_2 \longrightarrow CO_2 + 2H_2O \qquad \text{(balanced)} \qquad [3.4]$$

The balanced equation is shown schematically in Figure 3.3. For most purposes, a balanced equation should contain the smallest whole-number coefficients, as in this example.

The approach we have taken to balancing Equation 3.4 is largely trial and error. We balance each kind of atom in succession, adjusting coefficients as necessary. This approach works for most chemical equations. Verifying that an equation is balanced is easier than actually balancing one, so you should practice balancing equations until you are comfortable with this process.

The physical state of each chemical in a chemical equation is often indicated parenthetically. We use the symbols (g), (l), (s), and (aq) for gas, liquid,

FIGURE 3.3 Balanced chemical equation for the combustion of CH_4. The drawings of the molecules involved call attention to the conservation of atoms through the reaction.

Figure 3.3

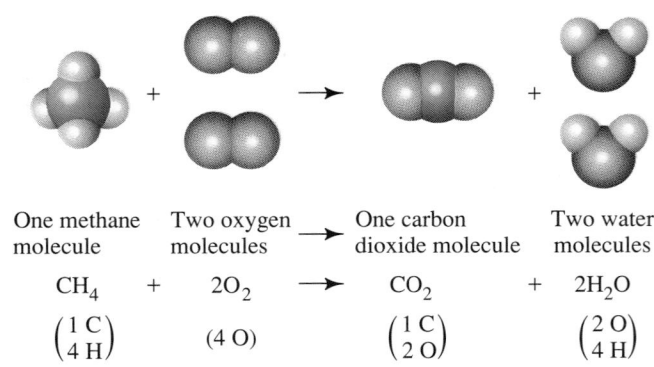

One methane molecule	Two oxygen molecules		One carbon dioxide molecule	Two water molecules
CH_4	+	$2O_2$	$\longrightarrow$ CO_2	+ $2H_2O$
$\begin{pmatrix} 1\,C \\ 4\,H \end{pmatrix}$		$(4\,O)$	$\begin{pmatrix} 1\,C \\ 2\,O \end{pmatrix}$	$\begin{pmatrix} 2\,O \\ 4\,H \end{pmatrix}$

solid, and aqueous (water) solution, respectively. Thus, the balanced equation above can be written

Point of Emphasis: The physical states of the reactants and products are often indicated by the symbols (g), (l), (s), (aq), for gas, liquid, solid, and aqueous (water) solutions, respectively.

$$CH_4(g) + 2O_2(g) \longrightarrow CO_2(g) + 2H_2O(l) \qquad [3.5]$$

Often the conditions under which the reaction proceeds appear above or below the arrow between the two sides of the equation. For example, the temperature or pressure at which the reaction occurs could be so indicated. The symbol Δ is often placed above the arrow to indicate the addition of heat.

SAMPLE EXERCISE 3.1

Balance the following equation:

$$Na(s) + H_2O(l) \longrightarrow NaOH(aq) + H_2(g)$$

SOLUTION We begin by counting the atoms of each kind on both sides of the arrow. The Na and O atoms are balanced (one Na and one O on each side), but there are two H atoms on the left and three H atoms on the right. To increase the number of H atoms on the left, we place a coefficient 2 in front of H_2O:

$$Na(s) + 2H_2O(l) \longrightarrow NaOH(aq) + H_2(g)$$

This choice is merely a trial beginning, but as we shall see, it starts us on the correct path. Now that we have $2H_2O$, we need to regain the balance in O atoms. We can do so by moving to the other side of the equation and putting a coefficient 2 in front of NaOH:

$$Na(s) + 2H_2O(l) \longrightarrow 2NaOH(aq) + H_2(g)$$

This brings the H atoms into balance, but it requires that we move back to the left and put a coefficient 2 in front of Na to rebalance the Na atoms:

$$2Na(s) + 2H_2O(l) \longrightarrow 2NaOH(aq) + H_2(g)$$

Finally, we check the number of atoms of each element and find that we have two Na atoms, four H atoms, and two O atoms on each side of the equation. The equation is therefore balanced.

PRACTICE EXERCISE

Balance the following equations by providing the missing coefficients:
(a) __C_2H_4 + __O_2 $\longrightarrow$ __CO_2 + __H_2O
(b) __Al + __HCl $\longrightarrow$ __$AlCl_3$ + __H_2
Answers: (a) 1, 3, 2, 2; (b) 2, 6, 2, 3

3.2 Patterns of Chemical Reactivity

Our discussion in Section 3.1 focused on how to balance chemical equations given the reactants and products for the reaction. We did not try to say anything about the type of reaction or to predict the products. Discussing this matter is a bit of a diversion from the basic theme of this chapter. However, an introductory discussion now will help you feel more at ease with the reactions used to illustrate concepts in the chapter.

Learning Goal 2: Predict the products of a chemical reaction, having seen a suitable analogy.

Using the Periodic Table

We may identify reactants and products experimentally by their properties. However, we can often predict what will happen in a reaction if we have seen a similar reaction before. Naturally, recognizing a general pattern of reactivity for a class of substances gives you a broader understanding than merely memorizing a large number of unrelated reactions. The periodic table can be a powerful ally in this regard. For example, knowing that sodium, Na, reacts with water, H_2O, to form NaOH and H_2 (see Sample Exercise 3.1), we can predict what happens when potassium, K, is placed in water. Both sodium and potassium are in the same family of the periodic table (the alkali metal family, family 1A). We would expect them to behave similarly, producing the same kinds of products. Indeed, this prediction is correct:

$$2K(s) + 2H_2O(l) \longrightarrow 2KOH(aq) + H_2(g) \qquad [3.6]$$

In fact, all alkali metals react with water to form their hydroxide compounds and hydrogen. If we let M represent any alkali metal, we can write the general reaction as follows:

$$2M(s) + 2H_2O(l) \longrightarrow 2MOH(aq) + H_2(g) \qquad [3.7]$$

Alkali metal + water $\longrightarrow$ Metal hydroxide + hydrogen

Figure 3.4 shows photographs of the reactions of sodium and of potassium with water. In the chapters ahead, we will sometimes encounter reactions that are characteristic of a particular family of elements. We will also see some reactions that are characteristic of particular classes of compounds. For example, different combustible carbon compounds almost always form the same products when they burn in air.

Combustion in Air

Combustion reactions are rapid reactions that produce a flame. Most of the combustion reactions we observe involve O_2 from air as a reactant. Equation 3.5 and Practice Exercise 3.1(a) illustrate a general class of reactions involving the burning or combustion of hydrocarbon compounds (compounds that contain only carbon and hydrogen, such as CH_4 and C_2H_6).

Point of Emphasis: Although they may differ in the vigor of reaction, members of a family on the periodic table tend to react in similar ways.

Learning Goal 3: Predict the products of the combustion reactions of hydrocarbons and simple compounds containing C, H, and O atoms.

FIGURE 3.4 The reaction of sodium with water (*a*) and of potassium with water (*b*). An acid-base indicator (phenolphthalein) has been added to both solutions; the pink color indicates the presence of hydroxide ions in the solution. Although the overall reactions of the two metals with water are very similar, potassium reacts more vigorously, as evidenced by the formation of steam and smoke. (Donald Clegg and Roxy Wilson)

(*a*)

(*b*)

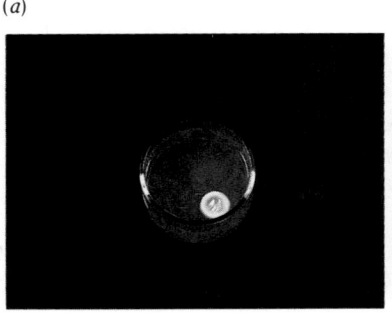
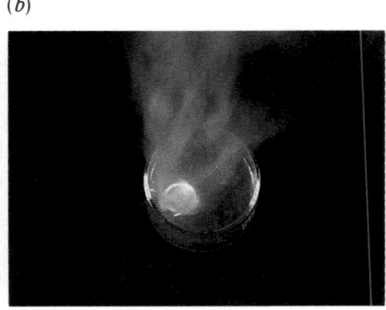

When hydrocarbons are combusted, they react with O_2 to form CO_2 and H_2O.* The number of molecules of O_2 required in the reaction and the number of molecules of CO_2 and H_2O formed depend on the composition of the hydrocarbon. For example, the combustion of propane, C_3H_8, a gas used for cooking and home heating, is described by the following equation:

$$C_3H_8(g) + 5O_2(g) \longrightarrow 3CO_2(g) + 4H_2O(l) \qquad [3.8]$$

The blue flame produced when propane burns is shown in Figure 3.5.

Combustion of compounds containing oxygen atoms as well as carbon and hydrogen (for example, CH_3OH and $C_6H_{12}O_6$) also produce CO_2 and H_2O. The simple rule that hydrocarbons and related compounds form CO_2 and H_2O when they burn in air summarizes the behavior of about 3 million compounds. Many compounds that our bodies use as energy sources, such as the sugar glucose, $C_6H_{12}O_6$, likewise react in our bodies with O_2 to form CO_2 and H_2O.

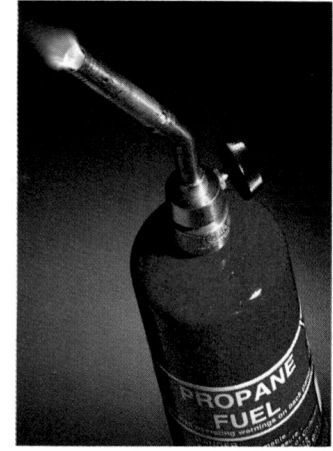

FIGURE 3.5 Propane, C_3H_8, burns in air, producing a blue flame. The liquid propane vaporizes and mixes with air as it escapes from the bottle through the nozzle. The combustion reaction between C_3H_8 and O_2 produces CO_2 and H_2O along with a high temperature. (Richard Megna/Fundamental Photographs)

SAMPLE EXERCISE 3.2

Write the balanced chemical equation for the reaction that occurs when methanol, $CH_3OH(l)$, is burned in air.

SOLUTION We first recall that when any compound containing C, H, and O is combusted, it reacts with the $O_2(g)$ in air to produce $CO_2(g)$ and $H_2O(l)$. Thus, the unbalanced equation is

$$CH_3OH(l) + O_2(g) \longrightarrow CO_2(g) + H_2O(l)$$

Because CH_3OH has only one C atom, we can start balancing the equation using the coefficient 1 for CO_2. Because CH_3OH has four H atoms, we place a coefficient 2 in front of H_2O to balance the H atoms:

$$CH_3OH(l) + O_2(g) \longrightarrow CO_2(g) + 2H_2O(l)$$

This gives four O atoms among the products and three among the reactants (one in CH_3OH and two in O_2). We can use the fractional coefficient $\frac{3}{2}$ in front of O_2 to provide four O atoms among the reactants (there are $\frac{3}{2} \times 2 = 3$ O atoms in $\frac{3}{2}O_2$):

$$CH_3OH(l) + \tfrac{3}{2}O_2(g) \longrightarrow CO_2(g) + 2H_2O(l)$$

Although the equation is now balanced, it is not in its most conventional form because it contains a fractional coefficient. If we multiply each side of the equation by 2, we will remove the fraction and achieve the following balanced equation:

$$2CH_3OH(l) + 3O_2(g) \longrightarrow 2CO_2(g) + 4H_2O(l)$$

PRACTICE EXERCISE

Write the balanced chemical equation for the reaction that occurs when ethanol, $C_2H_5OH(l)$, is burned in air.
Answer: $C_2H_5OH(l) + 3O_2(g) \longrightarrow 2CO_2(g) + 3H_2O(l)$

Point of Emphasis: Here, combustion is a reference to *complete combustion,* which yields CO_2 and H_2O. *Incomplete combustion* occurs when the amount of oxygen is insufficient; it yields CO rather than CO_2 as a product.

Combination and Decomposition Reactions

Table 3.1 summarizes two other simple types of reactions, combination and decomposition reactions. In **combination reactions,** two or more substances

Point of Emphasis: *Combination reactions* are characterized by two or more substances reacting together to form a single product. These are *often* reactions of free elements to form a compound.

---

* When there is an insufficient quantity of O_2 present, carbon monoxide, CO, will be produced. Even more severe restriction of O_2 will cause the production of fine particles of carbon that we call soot. *Complete* combustion produces CO_2. Unless specifically stated to the contrary, we will take *combustion* to mean *complete combustion.*

TABLE 3.1 △ Combination and Decomposition Reactions

Combination reactions

$$A + B \longrightarrow C$$
$$C(s) + O_2(g) \longrightarrow CO_2(g)$$
$$N_2(g) + 3H_2(g) \longrightarrow 2NH_3(g)$$
$$CaO(s) + H_2O(l) \longrightarrow Ca(OH)_2(s)$$

Two reactants combine to form a single product. Many elements react with one another in this fashion to form compounds.

Decomposition reactions

$$C \longrightarrow A + B$$
$$2KClO_3(s) \longrightarrow 2KCl(s) + 3O_2(g)$$
$$PbCO_3(s) \longrightarrow PbO(s) + CO_2(g)$$

A single reactant breaks apart to form two or more substances. Many compounds behave in this fashion when heated.

Table 3.1

react to form one product. There are many examples of such reactions, especially those in which different elements combine to form compounds. For example, magnesium metal burns in air with a dazzling brilliance to produce magnesium oxide, as shown in Figure 3.6:

$$2Mg(s) + O_2(g) \longrightarrow 2MgO(s) \qquad [3.9]$$

This reaction is employed in flashbulbs used in photography. The bulbs are filled with magnesium ribbon and oxygen gas. Passage of an electric current through the magnesium causes it to ignite, producing heat and light as MgO forms.

Point of Emphasis: *Decomposition reactions* are characterized by the breaking down of a single substance to form two or more products.

In a **decomposition reaction,** one substance undergoes a reaction to produce two or more other substances. Many compounds undergo decomposition reactions when they are heated. For example, many metal carbonates decompose to form metal oxides and carbon dioxide when heated:

$$CaCO_3(s) \longrightarrow CaO(s) + CO_2(g) \qquad [3.10]$$

The decomposition of $CaCO_3$ is an important commercial process. Limestone or seashells, which are both primarily $CaCO_3$, are heated to prepare CaO, which is known as lime or quicklime. Over 1.5×10^{10} kg (16 million tons) of CaO are used in the United States each year, principally in making glass, in obtaining iron from its ores, and in making mortar to bind bricks.

As a further example, the decomposition of sodium azide, NaN_3, is used to inflate safety airbags in automobiles (Figure 3.7). The decomposition reaction rapidly releases $N_2(g)$, which inflates the airbag:

$$2\,NaN_3(s) \longrightarrow 2\,Na(s) + 3\,N_2(g) \qquad [3.11]$$

FIGURE 3.6 Magnesium metal burns with a brilliant flame. (Dr. E. R. Degginger)

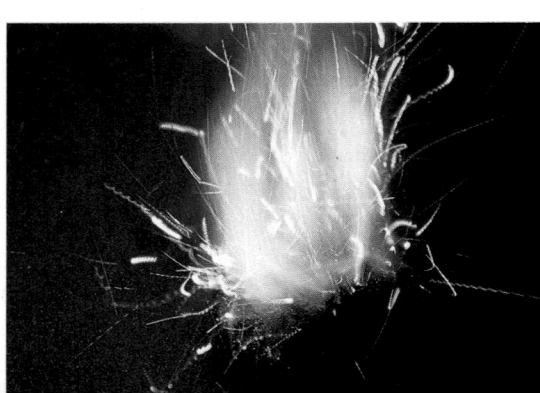

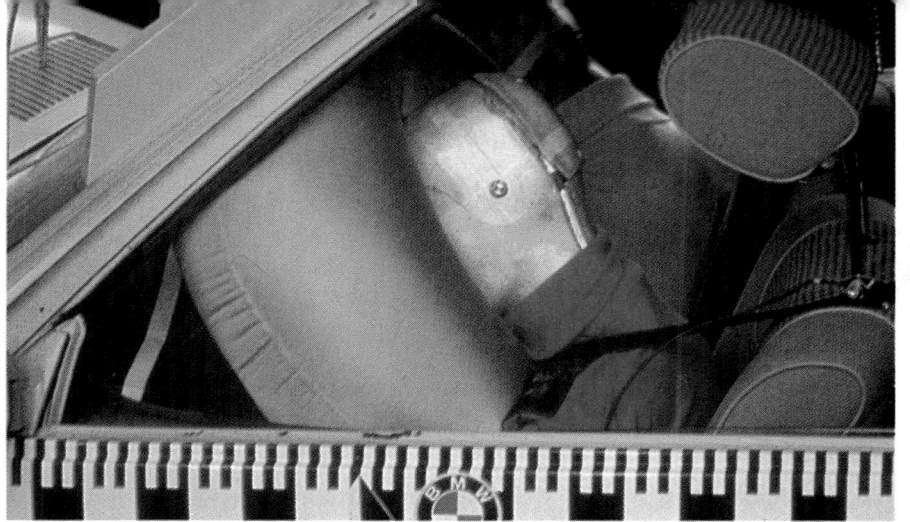

FIGURE 3.7 The decomposition of sodium azide, $NaN_3(s)$, is used to inflate automobile airbags. When properly ignited, the NaN_3 decomposes rapidly, forming nitrogen gas, $N_2(g)$, which expands the airbag. (BMW)

The system is designed so that an impact causes the ignition of a detonator cap, which in turn causes NaN_3 to decompose explosively. A small quantity of NaN_3 (about 100 g) forms a large quantity of gas (about 50 L).

We will consider additional types of reactions in the next chapter when we examine reactions in aqueous solutions.

3.3 Atomic and Molecular Weights

Chemical formulas and chemical equations have a *quantitative* significance; that is, the subscripts in formulas and the coefficients in equations represent precise quantities. The formula H_2O is not merely an abbreviation for the word *water:* it indicates that a molecule of this substance contains exactly two atoms of hydrogen and one atom of oxygen. Similarly, the chemical equation for the combustion of propane — $C_3H_8(g) + 5O_2(g) \longrightarrow 3CO_2(g) + 4H_2O(l)$, shown in Equation 3.8 — indicates more than the qualitative idea that propane reacts with O_2 to form CO_2 and H_2O. The equation is a quantitative statement that the combustion of one molecule of C_3H_8 requires five molecules of O_2 and produces exactly three molecules of CO_2 and four of H_2O. Although we cannot directly count atoms or molecules, we can indirectly determine their numbers if we know the masses of atoms. Therefore, before we can pursue the quantitative aspects of chemical formulas or equations further, we must explore the concept of atomic and molecular masses.

The Atomic Mass Scale

Although scientists of the nineteenth century knew nothing about subatomic particles, they were aware that atoms of different elements have different masses. They found, for example, that each 100 g of water contains 11.1 g of hydrogen and 88.9 g of oxygen. Thus, water contains $88.9/11.1 = 8$ times as much oxygen, by mass, as hydrogen. Once scientists understood that water contains two hydrogen atoms for each oxygen, they concluded that an oxygen atom must weigh $2 \times 8 = 16$ times as much as a hydrogen atom. Hydrogen, the lightest atom, was arbitrarily assigned a relative mass of 1 (no units), and atomic masses of other elements were determined relative to this value. Thus, oxygen was assigned an atomic mass of 16.

Today we can measure the masses of individual atoms with a high degree of accuracy. For example, we know that the hydrogen-1 atom has a mass of 1.6735×10^{-24} g and the oxygen-16 atom has a mass of 2.6561×10^{-23} g. As we saw in Section 2.3, it is convenient to use a unit called the **atomic mass unit** (amu) in dealing with these extremely small masses:

$$1 \text{ amu} = 1.66054 \times 10^{-24} \text{ g} \quad \text{and} \quad 1 \text{ g} = 6.02214 \times 10^{23} \text{ amu}$$

Point of Emphasis: The amu is defined by assigning a mass of exactly 12 amu to the ^{12}C isotope of carbon. This assignment is universally accepted convention.

The amu is defined by assigning a mass of exactly 12 amu to the ^{12}C isotope of carbon. In these units, the mass of the hydrogen-1 atom is 1.0080 amu and that of the oxygen-16 atom is 15.995 amu.

Average Atomic Masses

Learning Goal 4: Calculate the atomic weight of an element given the abundances and masses of its isotopes.

Most elements occur in nature as mixtures of isotopes. ∞ (Sec. 2.3) We can determine the average atomic mass of an element by using the masses of its various isotopes and their relative abundances. For example, naturally occurring carbon is composed of 98.892 percent ^{12}C and 1.108 percent ^{13}C. The masses of these nuclides are 12 amu (exactly) and 13.00335 amu, respectively. We calculate the average atomic mass of carbon as follows:

$$(0.98892)(12 \text{ amu}) + (0.01108)(13.00335 \text{ amu}) = 12.011 \text{ amu}$$

Point of Emphasis: Atomic weight = Σ [(isotope mass) $\times$ (fractional isotope abundance)] over all isotopes of the element.

The average atomic mass of each element (expressed in amu) is also known as its **atomic weight.** Although the term *average atomic mass* is more proper, the term *atomic weight* has become common. The atomic weights of the elements are listed both in the periodic table and in the table of elements, which are found inside the front cover of this text.

$\parallel$ **SAMPLE EXERCISE 3.3**

Naturally occurring chlorine is 75.53 percent ^{35}Cl, which has an atomic mass of 34.969 amu, and 24.47 percent ^{37}Cl, which has an atomic mass of 36.966 amu. Calculate the average atomic mass (that is, the atomic weight) of chlorine.

SOLUTION As shown in the example above, the average atomic mass is found by multiplying the abundance of each isotope by its atomic mass and summing these products. Thus, we have

Average atomic mass $= (75.53\%)(34.969 \text{ amu}) + (24.47\%)(36.966 \text{ amu})$

$= (0.7553)(34.969 \text{ amu}) + (0.2447)(36.966 \text{ amu})$

$= 26.41 \text{ amu} + 9.05 \text{ amu}$

$= 35.46 \text{ amu}$

The average is between the masses of the two isotopes, as expected.

PRACTICE EXERCISE

Three isotopes of silicon occur in nature: ^{28}Si (92.21 percent), which has a mass of 27.97693 amu; ^{29}Si (4.70 percent), which has a mass of 28.97649 amu; and ^{30}Si (3.09 percent), which has a mass of 29.97376 amu. Calculate the atomic weight of silicon. *Answer:* 28.09 amu

Formula and Molecular Weights

The **formula weight** of a substance is merely the sum of the atomic weights of each atom in its chemical formula. For example, H_2SO_4, sulfuric acid, has a formula weight of 98.0 amu:*

$$FW = 2(AW \text{ of } H) + (AW \text{ of } S) + 4(AW \text{ of } O)$$
$$= 2(1.0 \text{ amu}) + 32.0 \text{ amu} + 4(16.0 \text{ amu})$$
$$= 98.0 \text{ amu}$$

Here we have rounded off the atomic weights to one place beyond the decimal point. We will round off the atomic weights in this way for most problems.

If the chemical formula of a substance is its molecular formula, then the formula weight is also called the **molecular weight.** For example, the molecular formula for glucose (the sugar transported by the blood to body tissues in order to provide energy) is $C_6H_{12}O_6$. The molecular weight of glucose is therefore

$$MW = 6(12.0 \text{ amu}) + 12(1.0 \text{ amu}) + 6(16.0 \text{ amu})$$
$$= 180.0 \text{ amu}$$

With ionic substances such as NaCl that exist as three-dimensional arrays of ions (Figure 2.22), it is inappropriate to speak of molecules. Thus, we cannot write molecular formulas and molecular weights for such substances. The formula weight of NaCl is

$$FW = 23.0 \text{ amu} + 35.5 \text{ amu}$$
$$= 58.5 \text{ amu}$$

SAMPLE EXERCISE 3.4

Calculate the formula weight of **(a)** sucrose, $C_{12}H_{22}O_{11}$ (table sugar); **(b)** calcium nitrate, $Ca(NO_3)_2$.

SOLUTION **(a)** By adding the weights of the atoms in sucrose we find it to have a formula weight of 342.0 amu:

$$12 \text{ C atoms} = 12(12.0 \text{ amu}) = 144.0 \text{ amu}$$
$$22 \text{ H atoms} = 22 (1.0 \text{ amu}) = 22.0 \text{ amu}$$
$$11 \text{ O atoms} = 11(16.0 \text{ amu}) = \underline{176.0 \text{ amu}}$$
$$342.0 \text{ amu}$$

(b) If a chemical formula has parentheses, the subscript outside the parentheses is a multiplier for all atoms inside. Thus for $Ca(NO_3)_2$ we have

$$1 \text{ Ca atom} = 1(40.1 \text{ amu}) = 40.1 \text{ amu}$$
$$2 \text{ N atoms} = 2(14.0 \text{ amu}) = 28.0 \text{ amu}$$
$$6 \text{ O atoms} = 6(16.0 \text{ amu}) = \underline{96.0 \text{ amu}}$$
$$164.1 \text{ amu}$$

PRACTICE EXERCISE

Calculate the formula weight of **(a)** $Al(OH)_3$; **(b)** CH_3OH.   *Answers:* **(a)** 78.0 amu; **(b)** 32.0 amu

---

* The abbreviation AW is used for atomic weight, FW for formula weight, and MW for molecular weight.

A CLOSER LOOK

The Mass Spectrometer

The most direct and accurate means for determining atomic and molecular weights is provided by the **mass spectrometer.** The operation of this instrument is shown in Figure 3.8. A gaseous sample is introduced into the instrument at A and then bombarded by a stream of high-energy electrons at B. Collisions between the electrons and the atoms or molecules of the gas produce positive ions, mostly with a $1+$ charge. These ions are accelerated toward a negatively charged wire grid (C). After they pass through the grid, they encounter two slits that allow only a narrow beam of ions to pass through. This beam then passes between the poles of a magnet, which deflects the ions into a curved path. For ions with the same charge, the extent of deflection depends on mass—the more massive the ion, the less the deflection.

The ions are thereby separated according to their masses. By continuously changing either the strength of the magnetic field or the accelerating voltage on the negatively charged grid, ions of varying masses can be selected to enter the detector at the end of the instrument.

A graph of the intensity of the signal from the detector versus the mass of the ion is called a *mass spectrum.* The mass spectrum of mercury, shown in Figure 3.9, reveals the presence of several isotopes. Analysis of a mass spectrum gives both the masses of the ions reaching the detector and their relative abundances. The abundances are obtained from the intensities of their signals. Knowledge of the atomic mass and the abundance of each isotope allows us to calculate the average atomic mass of an element, as discussed in Section 3.3.

FIGURE 3.8 Diagram of a mass spectrometer.

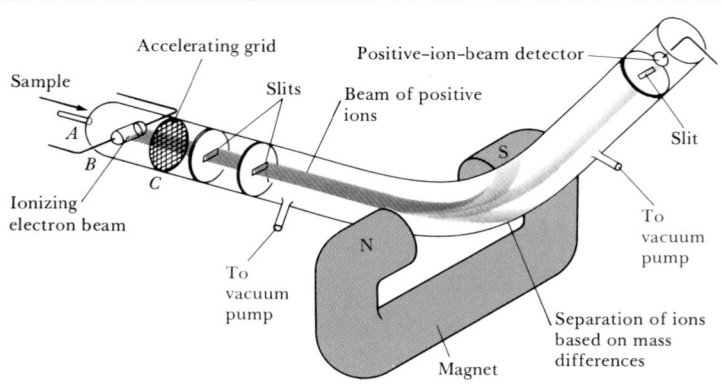

Figure 3.8

FIGURE 3.9 Mass spectrum of Hg^+ ions in mercury vapor.

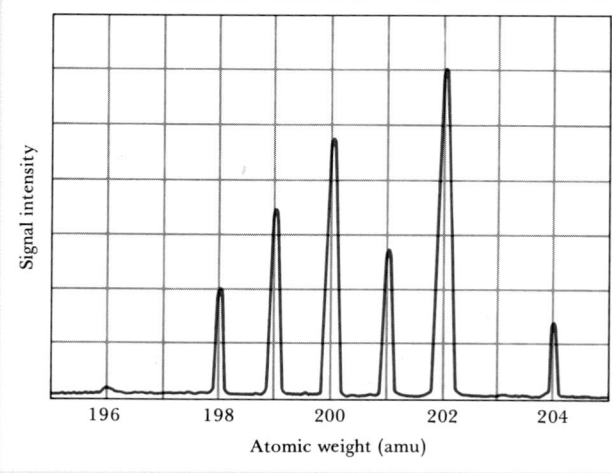

Percentage Composition from Formulas

Occasionally we must calculate the *percentage composition* of a compound (that is, the percentage by mass contributed by each element in the substance). For example, we may wish to compare the calculated composition of a substance with that found experimentally in order to verify the purity of the compound. Calculating percentage composition is a straightforward matter if the chemical formula is known. The calculation of such percentages is illustrated in Sample Exercise 3.5.

SAMPLE EXERCISE 3.5

Calculate the percentage composition of $C_{12}H_{22}O_{11}$.

SOLUTION In general, the percentage of a given element in a compound is given by

$$\frac{(\text{Atoms of element})(\text{AW})}{\text{FW of compound}} \times 100$$

The formula weight of $C_{12}H_{22}O_{11}$ is 342 amu (Sample Exercise 3.4). Therefore, the percentage composition is

$$\%C = \frac{12(12.0 \text{ amu})}{342 \text{ amu}} \times 100 = 42.1\%$$

$$\%H = \frac{22(1.0 \text{ amu})}{342 \text{ amu}} \times 100 = 6.4\%$$

$$\%O = \frac{11(16.0 \text{ amu})}{342 \text{ amu}} \times 100 = 51.5\%$$

The same elemental composition is obtained from the empirical formula of a substance as from its molecular formula. In Section 3.5 we shall see how the experimentally determined percentage composition of a compound can be used to calculate the empirical formula of the compound.

PRACTICE EXERCISE

Calculate the percentage of nitrogen, by mass, in $Ca(NO_3)_2$.   ***Answer:*** 17.1 percent

---

3.4 The Mole

Even the smallest samples that we deal with in the laboratory contain enormous numbers of atoms, ions, or molecules. For example, a teaspoon of water (about 5 mL) contains 2×10^{23} water molecules! It is convenient to have a special unit for describing such large numbers of objects.

In everyday life, we use counting units like dozen (12 objects) and gross (144 objects) to deal with large quantities. In chemistry, the unit we use for dealing with atoms, ions, and molecules is the **mole,** abbreviated mol.* A mole is defined as the amount of matter that contains as many objects (atoms, molecules, or whatever objects we are considering) as the number of atoms in exactly 12 g of ^{12}C. From numerous experiments, scientists have determined

---

* The term *mole* comes from the Latin word *moles,* meaning "a mass." The term *molecule* is the diminutive form of this word and means "a small mass."

the number of atoms in this quantity of ^{12}C to be 6.0221367×10^{23}. This number is given a special name: **Avogadro's number,** in honor of Amedeo Avogadro (1776–1856), an Italian scientist. For most purposes, we will use 6.02×10^{23} for Avogadro's number throughout the text. You should remember this number.

A mole of ions, molecules, or anything else contains Avogadro's number of these objects:

$$1 \text{ mol } ^{12}C \text{ atoms} = 6.02 \times 10^{23} \text{ } ^{12}C \text{ atoms}$$
$$1 \text{ mol } H_2O \text{ molecules} = 6.02 \times 10^{23} \text{ } H_2O \text{ molecules}$$
$$1 \text{ mol } NO_3^- \text{ ions} = 6.02 \times 10^{23} \text{ } NO_3^- \text{ ions}$$

Avogadro's number is so large that it is difficult to imagine. Spreading 6.02×10^{23} marbles over the surface of the entire earth would produce a layer about 3 mi thick!

SAMPLE EXERCISE 3.6

How many C atoms are in 0.350 mol of $C_6H_{12}O_6$?

SOLUTION Our strategy is to use Avogadro's number, which provides the conversion factor between the number of moles of $C_6H_{12}O_6$ and the number of molecules of $C_6H_{12}O_6$: 1 mol $C_6H_{12}O_6$ = 6.02×10^{23} molecules $C_6H_{12}O_6$. Once we know the number of molecules of $C_6H_{12}O_6$, we can use the chemical formula of the substance, which tells us that each molecule contains 6 C atoms:

$$\text{C atoms} = (0.350 \text{ mol } C_6H_{12}O_6)\left(\frac{6.02 \times 10^{23} \text{ molecules}}{1 \text{ mol } C_6H_{12}O_6}\right)\left(\frac{6 \text{ C atoms}}{1 \text{ molecule}}\right)$$
$$= 1.26 \times 10^{24} \text{ C atoms}$$

The magnitude of our answer is reasonable, being on the order of magnitude of Avogadro's number.

PRACTICE EXERCISE

How many nitrogen atoms are in 0.25 mol of $Ca(NO_3)_2$? ***Answer:*** 3.0×10^{23}

Molar Mass

A single ^{12}C atom has a mass of 12 amu, whereas a single ^{24}Mg atom is twice as massive, 24 amu (to two significant figures). Because a mole always has the same number of particles, a mole of ^{24}Mg must be twice as massive as a mole of ^{12}C atoms. Because a mole of ^{12}C weighs 12 g (by definition), then a mole of ^{24}Mg must weigh 24 g. Notice that the mass of a single atom of an element (in amu) is numerically equal to the mass (in grams) of 1 mol of atoms of that element. This fact is true regardless of the element:

One ^{12}C atom weighs 12 amu; 1 mol ^{12}C weighs 12 g.
One ^{24}Mg atom weighs 24 amu; 1 mol ^{24}Mg weighs 24 g.
One ^{197}Au atom weighs 197 amu; 1 mol ^{197}Au weighs 197 g.

The mass in grams of 1 mol of a substance is called its **molar mass.** *The molar mass (in grams) of any substance is always numerically equal to its formula weight (in amu):*

Teaching Note: Avogadro's number is also the number of amu per gram, i.e., the conversion factor between amu and gram is 6.02×10^{23} amu/g.

Irving R. Tannenbaum, "How Large Is A Mole?," *J. Chem. Educ.* **1990,** *67,* 481.

Point of Emphasis: The molar mass (in grams) is numerically equivalent to the formula weight (in amu).

TABLE 3.2 △ Mole Relationships

Name	Formula	Formula weight (amu)	Mass of 1 mol of formula units (g)	Number and kind of particles in 1 mol
Atomic nitrogen	N	14.0	14.0	6.02×10^{23} N atoms
Molecular nitrogen	N_2	28.0	28.0	{ 6.02×10^{23} N_2 molecules $2(6.02 \times 10^{23})$ N atoms
Silver	Ag	107.9	107.9	6.02×10^{23} Ag atoms
Silver ions	Ag^+	107.9[a]	107.9	6.02×10^{23} Ag^+ ions
Barium chloride	$BaCl_2$	208.2	208.2	{ 6.02×10^{23} $BaCl_2$ units 6.02×10^{23} Ba^{2+} ions $2(6.02 \times 10^{23})$ Cl^- ions

[a] Recall that the electron has negligible mass; thus ions and atoms have essentially the same mass.

One H_2O molecule weighs 18.0 amu; 1 mol H_2O weighs 18.0 g.
One NO_3^- ion weighs 62.0 amu; 1 mol NO_3^- weighs 62.0 g.
One NaCl unit weighs 58.5 amu; 1 mol NaCl weighs 58.5 g.

Further examples of mole relationships are shown in Table 3.2. Figure 3.10 shows 1-mol quantities of several substances.

The first entries in Table 3.2, those for N and N_2, point out the importance of stating the chemical form of a substance exactly when we use the mole concept. Suppose you read that 1 mol of nitrogen is produced in a particular reaction. You might interpret this statement to mean 1 mol of nitrogen atoms (14.0 g). Unless otherwise stated, what was probably meant is 1 mol of nitrogen molecules, N_2 (28.0 g), because N_2 is the usual chemical form of the element. To avoid ambiguity it is important to state explicitly the chemical form being discussed. Using the chemical formula N_2 or referring to the substance as "dinitrogen" avoids ambiguity.

Point of Emphasis: When a substance is referred to by name, the context must be used to identify it correctly. For example, N vs. N_2, or O vs. O_2 vs. O_3. The correct formula weight (or molar mass) and the correct number of atoms represented depend on the identification.

FIGURE 3.10 One mole each of several substances. Clockwise from top: $C_{12}H_{22}O_{11}$ (sucrose), H_2O, Hg, S, NaCl, Cu, Pb. The colored compound in the center is $K_2Cr_2O_7$. (Richard Megna/Fundamental Photographs)

SAMPLE EXERCISE 3.7

What is the mass of 1 mol of glucose, $C_6H_{12}O_6$?

SOLUTION By adding the atomic weights of the atoms in glucose, we find it to have a formula weight of 180.0 amu:

$$
\begin{array}{lll}
6 \text{ C atoms} = 6(12.0 \text{ amu}) = & 72.0 \text{ amu} \\
12 \text{ H atoms} = 12(1.0 \text{ amu}) = & 12.0 \text{ amu} \\
6 \text{ O atoms} = 6(16.0 \text{ amu}) = & \underline{96.0 \text{ amu}} \\
& 180.0 \text{ amu}
\end{array}
$$

Hence 1 mol of $C_6H_{12}O_6$ has a mass of 180.0 g; that is, $C_6H_{12}O_6$ has a molar mass of 180.0 g.

Glucose is sometimes called dextrose. Also known as blood sugar, glucose is found widely in nature, occurring, for example, in honey and fruits. Other types of sugars used as food must be converted into glucose in the stomach or liver before they are used by the body as energy sources. Because glucose requires no conversion, it is often given intravenously to patients who need immediate nourishment.

PRACTICE EXERCISE

Calculate the molar mass of $Ca(NO_3)_2$.   *Answer:* 164.1 g

Interconverting Masses, Moles, and Numbers of Particles

The conversions of mass to moles and of moles to mass are frequently encountered in calculations using the mole concept. These calculations are made easy through dimensional analysis, as illustrated in the next two sample exercises.

SAMPLE EXERCISE 3.8

How many moles of glucose, $C_6H_{12}O_6$, are in **(a)** 538 g and **(b)** 1.00 g of this substance?

SOLUTION **(a)** One mole of $C_6H_{12}O_6$ has a mass of 180.0 g (Sample Exercise 3.7). Therefore, there must be more than 1 mol in 538 g of this substance. Using

$$1 \text{ mol } C_6H_{12}O_6 = 180.0 \text{ g } C_6H_{12}O_6$$

to write the appropriate conversion factor, we have

$$\text{Moles } C_6H_{12}O_6 = (538 \text{ g } C_6H_{12}O_6)\left(\frac{1 \text{ mol } C_6H_{12}O_6}{180.0 \text{ g } C_6H_{12}O_6}\right)$$

$$= 2.99 \text{ mol}$$

(b) In this case there must be less than 1 mol.

$$\text{Moles } C_6H_{12}O_6 = (1.00 \text{ g } C_6H_{12}O_6)\left(\frac{1 \text{ mol } C_6H_{12}O_6}{180.0 \text{ g } C_6H_{12}O_6}\right)$$

$$= 5.56 \times 10^{-3} \text{ mol}$$

Notice that the number of moles is always the mass divided by the molar mass.

PRACTICE EXERCISE

How many moles of $NaHCO_3$ are present in 5.08 g of this substance?
Answer: 0.0605 mol

SAMPLE EXERCISE 3.9

What is the mass, in grams, of 0.433 mol of $Ca(NO_3)_2$? The molar mass of $Ca(NO_3)_2$ is 164.1 g.

SOLUTION Using 1 mol $Ca(NO_3)_2 = 164.1$ g $Ca(NO_3)_2$ to write the appropriate conversion factor, we have

$$\text{Grams } Ca(NO_3)_2 = (0.433 \text{ mol } Ca(NO_3)_2)\left(\frac{164.1 \text{ g } Ca(NO_3)_2}{1 \text{ mol } Ca(NO_3)_2}\right)$$

$$= 71.1 \text{ g } Ca(NO_3)_2$$

The mass of a certain number of moles of a substance is always the number of moles times the molar mass.

PRACTICE EXERCISE

What is the mass, in grams, of 6.33 mol of $NaHCO_3$?   *Answer:* 532 g

In the introduction to Section 3.3, we noted that the concept of atomic weights is important because it permits us to count atoms indirectly by weighing samples. The mole concept provides the bridge between masses and numbers of particles. To illustrate how we can interconvert masses and numbers of particles, let's calculate the number of copper atoms in a traditional copper penny. Such a penny weighs 3 g, and we'll assume that it is 100 percent copper:

Teaching Note: When working examples, place the flow diagram grams $\longrightarrow$ moles $\longrightarrow$ atoms on the board first and work the problem numerically below it.

$$\text{Cu atoms} = (3 \text{ g Cu})\left(\frac{1 \text{ mol Cu}}{63.5 \text{ g Cu}}\right)\left(\frac{6.02 \times 10^{23} \text{ Cu atoms}}{1 \text{ mol Cu}}\right)$$

$$= 3 \times 10^{22} \text{ Cu atoms}$$

Notice how we were able to use dimensional analysis (Section 1.5) in a straightforward manner to go from grams to numbers of atoms. The molar mass and Avogadro's number are used as conversion factors to convert grams $\longrightarrow$ moles $\longrightarrow$ atoms as summarized in Figure 3.11. Notice also that our answer is a very large number. Any time you calculate the number of atoms, molecules, or ions in an ordinary sample of matter, you can expect the answer to be very large. On the other hand, the number of moles in a sample will usually be much smaller, often less than 1.

SAMPLE EXERCISE 3.10

How many glucose molecules are in 5.23 g of $C_6H_{12}O_6$?

SOLUTION Our strategy is summarized in Figure 3.11. We need to convert the given quantity, 5.23 g $C_6H_{12}O_6$, to moles $C_6H_{12}O_6$, which can then be converted to give the desired quantity, molecules $C_6H_{12}O_6$. The first conversion uses the molar mass of $C_6H_{12}O_6$: 1 mol $C_6H_{12}O_6 = 180$ g $C_6H_{12}O_6$. The second conversion uses Avogadro's number:

Molecules $C_6H_{12}O_6$

$$= (5.23 \text{ g } C_6H_{12}O_6)\left(\frac{1 \text{ mol } C_6H_{12}O_6}{180 \text{ g } C_6H_{12}O_6}\right)\left(\frac{6.02 \times 10^{23} \text{ molecules } C_6H_{12}O_6}{1 \text{ mol } C_6H_{12}O_6}\right)$$

$$= 1.75 \times 10^{22} \text{ molecules}$$

The answer is reasonable. Because the mass we began with is less than a mole, there should be less than 6.02×10^{23} molecules.

PRACTICE EXERCISE

How many oxygen atoms are present in 4.20 g of $NaHCO_3$?   *Answer:* 9.03×10^{22}

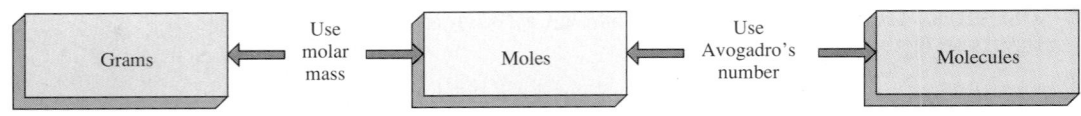

FIGURE 3.11 Outline of the procedure used to interconvert the mass of a substance in grams and the number of molecules of that substance. The number of moles of the substance is central to the calculation.

Figure 3.11

Learning Goal 6: Calculate the empirical formula of a compound, having been given appropriate analytical data such as elemental percentages or the quantity of CO_2 and H_2O produced by combustion.

3.5 Empirical Formulas from Analyses

Point of Emphasis: *Empirical* means experimentally determined.

Point of Emphasis: The empirical formula gives the ratio of atoms of each type of compound. Therefore, always convert to moles when calculating empirical formulas.

The empirical formula for a substance tells us the relative number of atoms of each element it contains. Thus, the formula H_2O indicates that water contains two H atoms for each O atom. This ratio also applies on the molar level; thus, 1 mol of H_2O contains 2 mol of H atoms and 1 mol of O atoms. Conversely, the ratio of the number of moles of each element in a compound gives the subscripts in a compound's empirical formula. Thus, the mole concept provides a way of calculating the empirical formulas of chemical substances, as shown in the following examples.

Mercury forms a compound with chlorine that is 73.9 percent mercury and 26.1 percent chlorine by mass. This means that if we had a 100-g sample of the solid it would contain 73.9 g of mercury, Hg, and 26.1 g of chlorine, Cl. (Any size sample can be used in problems of this type, but we use 100 g to make the calculation of mass from percentage easy.) We divide each of these masses by the appropriate atomic weight to obtain the number of moles of each element in 100 g:

$$73.9 \text{ g Hg} \left(\frac{1 \text{ mol Hg}}{200.6 \text{ g Hg}} \right) = 0.368 \text{ mol Hg}$$

$$26.1 \text{ g Cl} \left(\frac{1 \text{ mol Cl}}{35.5 \text{ g Cl}} \right) = 0.735 \text{ mol Cl}$$

Teaching Note: Be careful! Due to experimental or round-off errors, the coefficients may come out close to whole numbers (see text). You should then round them off to that whole number. However, if the coefficients come out close to common fractions (e.g., 1/4, 1/3, 1/2), the formula should be multiplied by the least common denominator (4, 3, 2, respectively) and *not* rounded.

We then divide the larger number of moles by the smaller to obtain the ratio 1.99 mol Cl/1 mol Hg. Because of experimental errors, the results of an analysis may not lead to exact integers for the ratios of moles. The ratio obtained in this case is very close to 2, and we can confidently conclude that the formula for the compound is $HgCl_2$. This is the simplest, or empirical, formula because it uses as subscripts the smallest set of integers that express the correct ratios of atoms present. ∞ (Sec. 2.5) The general procedure for determining empirical formulas is outlined in Figure 3.12.

SAMPLE EXERCISE 3.11

Ascorbic acid (vitamin C) contains 40.92 percent C, 4.58 percent H, and 54.50 percent O by mass. What is the empirical formula of ascorbic acid?

SOLUTION As outlined in Figure 3.12, we *first* assume that we have 100 g of material (although any number can be used). In 100 g of ascorbic acid, we will have 40.92 g C, 4.58 g H, and 54.50 g O.

Second, we calculate the number of moles of each element in 100 g of the compound:

$$\text{Moles C} = (40.92 \text{ g C}) \left(\frac{1 \text{ mol C}}{12.01 \text{ g C}} \right) = 3.407 \text{ mol C}$$

$$\text{Moles H} = (4.58 \text{ g H}) \left(\frac{1 \text{ mol H}}{1.008 \text{ g H}} \right) = 4.54 \text{ mol H}$$

$$\text{Moles O} = (54.50 \text{ g O}) \left(\frac{1 \text{ mol O}}{16.00 \text{ g O}} \right) = 3.406 \text{ mol O}$$

Third, we determine the simplest whole-number ratio of moles by dividing each number of moles by the smallest number of moles, 3.406:

$$\text{C:} \frac{3.407}{3.406} = 1 \qquad \text{H:} \frac{4.54}{3.406} = 1.33 \qquad \text{O:} \frac{3.406}{3.406} = 1$$

The ratio for H is too far from 1 to attribute the difference to experimental error; in fact, it is quite close to $1\frac{1}{3}$. This suggests that if we multiply the ratio by 3, we will obtain whole numbers:

$$\text{C:H:O} = 3(1:1.33:1) = 3:4:3$$

The whole-number ratio gives us the subscripts for the empirical formula. Thus, the empirical formula is $C_3H_4O_3$.

PRACTICE EXERCISE

A 5.325-g sample of methyl benzoate, a compound used in the manufacture of perfumes, is found to contain 3.758 g of carbon, 0.316 g of hydrogen, and 1.251 g of oxygen. What is the empirical formula of this substance?   *Answer:* C_4H_4O

Molecular Formula from Empirical Formula

Remember that the formula obtained from percentage compositions is always the empirical formula. We can obtain the molecular formula from the empirical formula if we know the molecular weight of the compound. *The subscripts in the molecular formula of a substance are always a whole-number multiple of the corresponding subscripts in its empirical formula.* ∞ (Sec. 2.5) The multiple is found by comparing the formula weight of the empirical formula with the molecular weight. For example, in Sample Exercise 3.11, we saw that the empirical formula of ascorbic acid is $C_3H_4O_3$, giving a formula weight of $3(12.0 \text{ amu}) + 4(1.0 \text{ amu}) + 3(16.0 \text{ amu}) = 88.0 \text{ amu}$. The experimentally determined molecular weight is 176 amu. Thus, the molecule has twice the

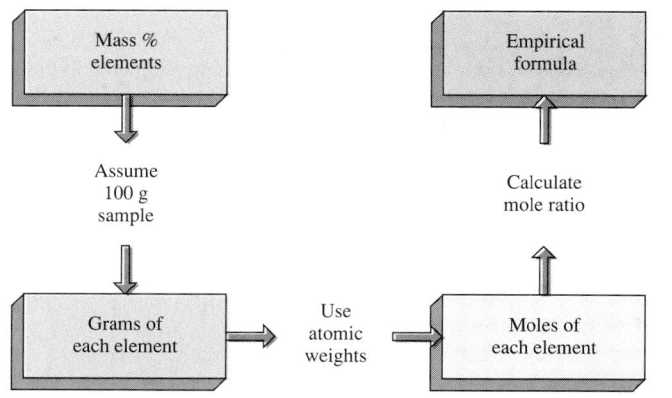

FIGURE 3.12 Outline of the procedure used to calculate the empirical formula of a substance from its percentage composition. The procedure is also summarized as "percent to mass, mass to moles, divide by small, multiply 'til whole."

Figure 3.12

mass ($176/88.0 = 2.00$) and must therefore have twice as many atoms as the empirical formula. The subscripts in the empirical formula must be multiplied by 2 to obtain the molecular formula: $C_6H_8O_6$.

SAMPLE EXERCISE 3.12

Mesitylene, a hydrocarbon that occurs in small amounts in crude oil, has an empirical formula of C_3H_4. The experimentally determined molecular weight of this substance is 121 amu. What is the molecular formula of mesitylene?

SOLUTION   To find the molecular formula, we first calculate the formula weight of the empirical formula: $3(12.0 \text{ amu}) + 4(1.0 \text{ amu}) = 40.0 \text{ amu}$.

Next, we divide the formula weight into the molecular weight to give the factor by which the subscripts in C_3H_4 must be multiplied:

$$\frac{MW}{FW} = \frac{121}{40.0} = 3.02$$

Only whole-number ratios make physical sense because we must be dealing with whole atoms. The 3.02 in this case results from a small experimental error in the molecular weight. We therefore multiply each subscript in the empirical formula by 3 to give the molecular formula: C_9H_{12}.

PRACTICE EXERCISE

Ethanol, the alcohol contained in alcoholic beverages, is composed of 52.2 percent C, 13.0 percent H, and 34.8 percent O by mass. Its molar mass is 46.0 g/mol. **(a)** What is the empirical formula of ethanol? **(b)** What is its molecular formula?
Answers: **(a)** C_2H_6O; **(b)** C_2H_6O

Combustion Analysis

When a compound containing carbon and hydrogen is combusted in an apparatus such as that shown in Figure 3.13, all the carbon of the compound is converted to CO_2, and all the hydrogen to H_2O. The amount of CO_2 produced can be measured by determining the mass increase in the CO_2 absorber. Similarly, the amount of H_2O formed is determined from the increase in mass of the water absorption tube. We can then use the masses of CO_2 and H_2O to determine the amounts of C and H in the original compound.

Point of Emphasis: Combustion analysis works only if complete combustion occurs: fuel $+ O_2 \longrightarrow CO_2 + H_2O$

As an example of this procedure, let's consider a sample of isopropyl alcohol, a substance sold as rubbing alcohol. The compound is known to contain only C, H, and O. Combustion of 0.255 g of isopropyl alcohol produces

FIGURE 3.13   Apparatus for determining the percentages of carbon and hydrogen in a compound. Copper oxide serves to oxidize traces of carbon and carbon monoxide to carbon dioxide, and to oxidize hydrogen to water. Magnesium perchlorate, $Mg(ClO_4)_2$, is used to absorb water, whereas sodium hydroxide, NaOH, absorbs carbon dioxide.

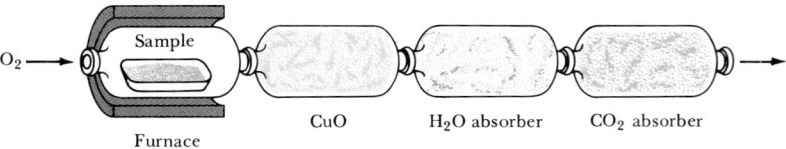

One important aspect of chemistry is problem solving, including being able to deal with "word problems," problems that are stated verbally but have a numerical answer. The key to success with problem solving is practice. As you practice, you will find that you can improve your skills by following these steps:

Step 1. Understand the problem. One of the most important aids in problem solving is having a thorough understanding of the problem. Unfortunately, many students begin to think about how they are going to solve the problem before they even understand what it is asking. Watch out for this trap because it can block your reasoning process. Read the problem for understanding. What does it say? Pick out the important information and write it down. Draw any diagrams or pictures that will help you visualize the problem. Do not be concerned with how to solve the problem at this time.

Step 2. Identify the unknown and the given data. If you did not do so in step 1, identify the quantity that you need to obtain (the unknown) and the given data. [Some data may not be given explicitly; you may be expected to know certain quantities (like Avogadro's number) or to look them up in tables (like atomic weights).]

Step 3. Set up the problem. Consider the possible paths between the given information and the unknown. What principles or equations relate the known data to the unknown? Write down the appropriate equations or relationships. The point of this step is to develop a *strategy* for solving the problem. This may involve a single step or a series of steps with intermediate answers.

Step 4. Solve the problem. Use the known information and the suitable equations or relationships to solve for the unknown. Be careful with significant figures, signs, and units.

Step 5. Check the solution. Read the problem again to make sure you have found all the solutions the problem asks for. Does your answer make sense? That is, is the answer outrageously large or small, or is it in the ballpark? Finally, are the units and significant figures correct?

0.561 g CO_2 and 0.306 g H_2O. From these two bits of experimental information, we can calculate the quantities of C and H in the sample. To calculate the number of grams of C in 0.561 g of CO_2, we can use the mole concept:

$$(0.561 \text{ g } CO_2)\left(\frac{1 \text{ mol } CO_2}{44.0 \text{ g } CO_2}\right)\left(\frac{1 \text{ mol } C}{1 \text{ mol } CO_2}\right)\left(\frac{12.0 \text{ g C}}{1 \text{ mol } C}\right) = 0.153 \text{ g C}$$

Similarly, we can calculate the number of grams of H in 0.306 g of H_2O:

$$(0.306 \text{ g } H_2O)\left(\frac{1 \text{ mol } H_2O}{18.0 \text{ g } H_2O}\right)\left(\frac{2 \text{ mol } H}{1 \text{ mol } H_2O}\right)\left(\frac{1.01 \text{ g H}}{1 \text{ mol } H}\right) = 0.0343 \text{ g H}$$

Because the compound contains only C, H, and O, the amount of O in the compound must be

$$0.255 \text{ g} - (0.153 \text{ g} + 0.0343 \text{ g}) = 0.068 \text{ g}$$

Point of Emphasis: If the compound contains only C, H, and O, the mass of the oxygen is the difference between the total mass and the masses of C and H.

From these data, we can now calculate the number of moles of each element present in the sample:

$$\text{Moles C} = (0.153 \text{ g C})\left(\frac{1 \text{ mol C}}{12.0 \text{ g C}}\right) = 0.0128 \text{ mol C}$$

$$\text{Moles H} = (0.0343 \text{ g H})\left(\frac{1 \text{ mol H}}{1.01 \text{ g H}}\right) = 0.0340 \text{ mol H}$$

$$\text{Moles O} = (0.068 \text{ g O})\left(\frac{1 \text{ mol O}}{16.0 \text{ g O}}\right) = 0.0043 \text{ mol O}$$

The relative number of moles of each element is found by dividing each number by the smallest number, 0.0043. The ratio of C : H : O so obtained is 2.98 : 7.91 : 1. The first two numbers are close to the whole numbers 3 and 8, giving the empirical formula C_3H_8O.

3.6 Quantitative Information from Balanced Equations

Learning Goal 8: Calculate the mass of a particular substance produced or used in a chemical reaction (mass-mass problem).

The mole concept allows us to use the quantitative information available in a balanced chemical equation on a practical, macroscopic level. Consider the following balanced equation:

$$2H_2(g) + O_2(g) \longrightarrow 2H_2O(l) \qquad\qquad [3.12]$$

The coefficients tell us that two molecules of H_2 react with each molecule of O_2 to form two molecules of H_2O. It follows that the relative numbers of moles are identical to the relative numbers of molecules:

$2H_2(g)$	+	$O_2(g)$	$\longrightarrow$	$2H_2O(l)$
2 molecules		1 molecule		2 molecules
$2(6.02 \times 10^{23}$ molecules)		6.02×10^{23} molecules		$2(6.02 \times 10^{23}$ molecules)
2 mol		1 mol		2 mol

Point of Emphasis: Chemical equations are technically written to represent numbers of atoms, ions, molecules, and so forth. Equations can be *interpreted* as representing the numbers of moles of atoms, ions, molecules, and so forth.

The coefficients in a balanced chemical equation can be interpreted both as the relative numbers of molecules (or formula units) involved in the reaction and as the relative numbers of moles.

The quantities 2 mol H_2, 1 mol O_2, and 2 mol H_2O, which are given by the coefficients in Equation 3.12, are called *stoichiometrically equivalent quantities*. The relationship between these quantities can be represented as follows:

$$2 \text{ mol } H_2 \approxeq 1 \text{ mol } O_2 \approxeq 2 \text{ mol } H_2O$$

where the symbol $\approxeq$ is taken to mean "stoichiometrically equivalent to." In other words, Equation 3.12 shows 2 mol of H_2 and 1 mol of O_2 forming 2 mol of H_2O. These stoichiometric relations can be used to give conversion factors for relating quantities of reactants and products in a chemical reaction. For example, the number of moles of H_2O produced from 1.57 mol of O_2 can be calculated as follows:

$$\text{Moles } H_2O = (1.57 \ \cancel{\text{mol } O_2}) \left(\frac{2 \text{ mol } H_2O}{1 \ \cancel{\text{mol } O_2}} \right)$$

$$= 3.14 \text{ mol } H_2O$$

As an additional example, consider the combustion of butane, C_4H_{10}, the fuel in disposable cigarette lighters:

$$2C_4H_{10}(l) + 13O_2(g) \longrightarrow 8CO_2(g) + 10H_2O(l) \qquad [3.13]$$

Suppose we want to calculate the mass of CO_2 that is produced in burning 1.00 g of C_4H_{10}. The coefficients in Equation 3.13 tell us how the amount of C_4H_{10} consumed is related to the amount of CO_2 produced: 2 mol $C_4H_{10} \simeq$ 8 mol CO_2. In order to use this relationship, however, we must use the molar mass of C_4H_{10} to convert grams of C_4H_{10} to moles of C_4H_{10}. Because 1 mol C_4H_{10} = 58.0 g C_4H_{10}, we have

$$\text{Moles } C_4H_{10} = (1.00 \ \cancel{\text{g } C_4H_{10}}) \left(\frac{1 \text{ mol } C_4H_{10}}{58.0 \ \cancel{\text{g } C_4H_{10}}} \right)$$

$$= 1.72 \times 10^{-2} \text{ mol } C_4H_{10}$$

Richard L. Poole, "Teaching Stoichiometry: A Two-Cycle Approach," *J. Chem. Educ.* **1989,** *66,* 57.

We can then use the stoichiometric factor from the balanced equation, 2 mol $C_4H_{10} \simeq$ 8 mol CO_2, to calculate moles of CO_2:

$$\text{Moles } CO_2 = (1.72 \times 10^{-2} \ \cancel{\text{mol } C_4H_{10}}) \left(\frac{8 \text{ mol } CO_2}{2 \ \cancel{\text{mol } C_4H_{10}}} \right)$$

$$= 6.88 \times 10^{-2} \text{ mol } CO_2$$

Finally, we can calculate the mass of the CO_2, in grams, using the molar mass of CO_2: 1 mol CO_2 = 44.0 g CO_2:

$$\text{Grams } CO_2 = (6.88 \times 10^{-2} \ \cancel{\text{mol } CO_2}) \left(\frac{44.0 \text{ g } CO_2}{1 \ \cancel{\text{mol } CO_2}} \right)$$

$$= 3.03 \text{ g } CO_2$$

Thus, the conversion sequence is

Teaching Note: When working examples, place a flow diagram similar to: grams$_1$ $\longrightarrow$ moles$_1$ $\longrightarrow$ moles$_2$ $\longrightarrow$ grams$_2$ on the board first, and work the problem numerically below it. The 1's and 2's can represent any combination of reactants and products.

These steps can be combined in a single sequence of factors:

$$\text{Grams } CO_2 = (1.00 \ \cancel{\text{g } C_4H_{10}}) \left(\frac{1 \text{ mol } C_4H_{10}}{58.0 \ \cancel{\text{g } C_4H_{10}}} \right) \left(\frac{8 \ \cancel{\text{mol } CO_2}}{2 \ \cancel{\text{mol } C_4H_{10}}} \right) \left(\frac{44.0 \text{ g } CO_2}{1 \ \cancel{\text{mol } CO_2}} \right)$$

$$= 3.03 \text{ g } CO_2$$

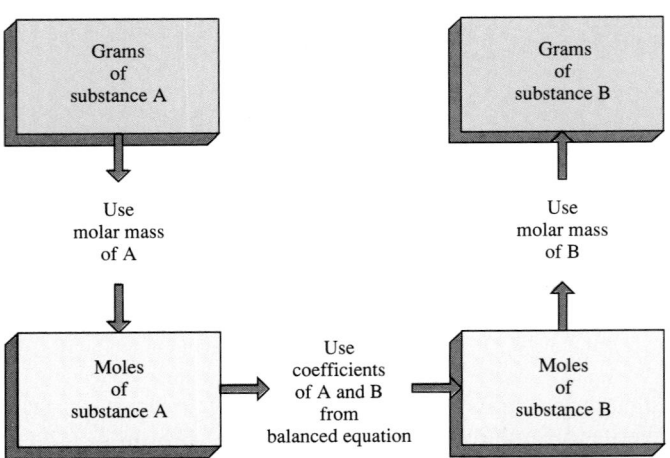

FIGURE 3.14 Outline of the procedure used to calculate the number of grams of a reactant consumed or of a product formed in a reaction, starting with the number of grams of one of the other reactants or products.

We can similarly calculate the amount of O_2 consumed or H_2O produced in this reaction. To calculate the amount of O_2 consumed, we again rely on the coefficients in the balanced equation to give us the appropriate stoichiometric factor: $2 \text{ mol } C_4H_{10} \hateq 13 \text{ mol } O_2$:

$$\text{Grams } O_2 = (1.00 \text{ g } C_4H_{10}) \left(\frac{1 \text{ mol } C_4H_{10}}{58.0 \text{ g } C_4H_{10}} \right) \left(\frac{13 \text{ mol } O_2}{2 \text{ mol } C_4H_{10}} \right) \left(\frac{32.0 \text{ g } O_2}{1 \text{ mol } O_2} \right)$$

$$= 3.59 \text{ g } O_2$$

Figure 3.14 summarizes the general approach used to calculate the quantities of substances consumed or produced in chemical reactions. As we have seen, the balanced chemical equation tells us the relative numbers of moles of reactants and products involved in the reaction.

SAMPLE EXERCISE 3.13

How many grams of water are produced in the combustion of 1.00 g of glucose, $C_6H_{12}O_6$:

$$C_6H_{12}O_6(s) + 6O_2(g) \longrightarrow 6CO_2(g) + 6H_2O(l)$$

SOLUTION The chemical equation gives the relation between the amount of $C_6H_{12}O_6$ and the amount of H_2O in the reaction: $1 \text{ mol } C_6H_{12}O_6 \hateq 6 \text{ mol } H_2O$. To use this information, however, we must *first* convert the amount of $C_6H_{12}O_6$ from grams to moles:

$$\text{Moles } C_6H_{12}O_6 = (1.00 \text{ g } C_6H_{12}O_6) \left(\frac{1 \text{ mol } C_6H_{12}O_6}{180 \text{ g } C_6H_{12}O_6} \right)$$

Second, we use the chemical equation to calculate moles of H_2O:

$$\text{Moles } H_2O = (1.00 \text{ g } C_6H_{12}O_6) \left(\frac{1 \text{ mol } C_6H_{12}O_6}{180 \text{ g } C_6H_{12}O_6} \right) \left(\frac{6 \text{ mol } H_2O}{1 \text{ mol } C_6H_{12}O_6} \right)$$

Third, we convert moles of H_2O to grams:

$$\text{Grams H}_2\text{O} = (1.00 \text{ g C}_6\text{H}_{12}\text{O}_6)\left(\frac{1 \text{ mol C}_6\text{H}_{12}\text{O}_6}{180 \text{ g C}_6\text{H}_{12}\text{O}_6}\right)\left(\frac{6 \text{ mol H}_2\text{O}}{1 \text{ mol C}_6\text{H}_{12}\text{O}_6}\right)\left(\frac{18.0 \text{ g H}_2\text{O}}{1 \text{ mol H}_2\text{O}}\right)$$

$$= 0.600 \text{ g H}_2\text{O}$$

The steps can be summarized in a diagram like that in Figure 3.14:

An average person ingests 2 L of water daily and eliminates 2.4 L. The difference is produced in the metabolism of foodstuffs. (*Metabolism* is a general term used to describe all the chemical processes of a living animal or plant.) The desert rat (kangaroo rat) is able to take great advantage of its metabolic water to help it survive in the dry desert. In fact, it apparently never drinks water.

PRACTICE EXERCISE

A common laboratory method for preparing small amounts of O_2 involves the decomposition of $KClO_3$: $2KClO_3(s) \longrightarrow 2KCl(s) + 3O_2(g)$. How many grams of O_2 can be prepared from 4.50 g of $KClO_3$? **Answer:** 1.77 g

SAMPLE EXERCISE 3.14

Solid lithium hydroxide is used in space vehicles to remove exhaled carbon dioxide. The lithium hydroxide reacts with gaseous carbon dioxide to form solid lithium carbonate and liquid water. How many grams of carbon dioxide can be absorbed by each 1.00 g of lithium hydroxide?

SOLUTION Using the verbal description of the reaction, we can write the unbalanced chemical equation:

$$\text{LiOH}(s) + \text{CO}_2(g) \longrightarrow \text{Li}_2\text{CO}_3(s) + \text{H}_2\text{O}(l)$$

The balanced equation is

$$2\text{LiOH}(s) + \text{CO}_2(g) \longrightarrow \text{Li}_2\text{CO}_3(s) + \text{H}_2\text{O}(l)$$

The problem can be solved by a stepwise conversion of grams of LiOH to moles of LiOH to moles of CO_2 to grams of CO_2. The conversion from grams of LiOH to moles of LiOH requires this substance's formula weight (6.94 + 16.00 + 1.01 = 23.95). The conversion of moles of LiOH to moles of CO_2 is based on the balanced chemical equation: 2 mol LiOH $\cong$ 1 mol CO_2. To convert the number of moles of CO_2 to grams, we must use the formula weight of CO_2: 12.01 + 2(16.00) = 44.01:

$$(1.00 \text{ g LiOH})\left(\frac{1 \text{ mol LiOH}}{23.95 \text{ g LiOH}}\right)\left(\frac{1 \text{ mol CO}_2}{2 \text{ mol LiOH}}\right)\left(\frac{44.01 \text{ g CO}_2}{1 \text{ mol CO}_2}\right) = 0.919 \text{ g CO}_2$$

PRACTICE EXERCISE

Propane, C_3H_8, is a common fuel used for cooking and home heating. What mass of O_2 is consumed in the combustion of 1.00 g of propane? **Answer:** 3.64 g

CO$_2$ and the Greenhouse Effect

Coal and petroleum provide the fuels that we use to generate electricity, move our vehicles, heat our homes, and power our industrial machinery. These fuels are composed primarily of hydrocarbons and other carbon-containing substances. As we have seen, the combustion of 1.00 g of C$_4$H$_{10}$ produces 3.03 g of CO$_2$. In similar fashion, a gallon (3.78 L) of gasoline (density = 0.70 g/mL and approximate composition C$_8$H$_{18}$) produces about 8 kg (18 lb) of CO$_2$. It should not be surprising, therefore, that combustion of fuels releases a tremendous amount of CO$_2$ into the atmosphere, about 20 billion tons annually.

Much CO$_2$ is absorbed into oceans, incorporated into carbonate minerals, or used by plants in photosynthesis. Nevertheless, we are now generating CO$_2$ much faster than it is being absorbed. Chemists have systematically monitored atmospheric CO$_2$ concentrations since 1958. Analysis of air trapped in ice cores taken from Antarctica and Greenland permits us to determine the atmospheric levels of CO$_2$ during the past 160,000 years. These measurements reveal that the level of CO$_2$ remained fairly constant from the last ice age some 10,000 years ago until roughly the beginning of the Industrial Revolution, about 300 years ago. Since that time, the concentration of CO$_2$ has increased by about 25 percent (Figure 3.15).

Although CO$_2$ is a minor component of the atmosphere, it plays a significant role in trapping heat near the surface of the planet. By absorbing radiant heat, it acts much like the glass over a greenhouse. For this reason, we often refer to CO$_2$ and other heat-trapping gases as greenhouse gases, and we call the warming caused by these gases the *greenhouse effect*. Some scientists believe that the accumulation of CO$_2$ and other heat-trapping gases such as CH$_4$ has begun to change the climate of our planet. Other scientists point out, however, that the factors affecting climate are complex and incompletely understood.

One possible long-term outcome of global warming is the melting of the polar icecaps, causing a rise in the sea level, which could lead to the flooding of low-lying coastal areas. Other effects are shifts in rainfall distribution over the continental land masses. If we are to reverse the present trends, we must develop new energy sources, intensify energy conservation efforts, and halt deforestation throughout the globe. We will examine the greenhouse effect more closely in Chapter 18.

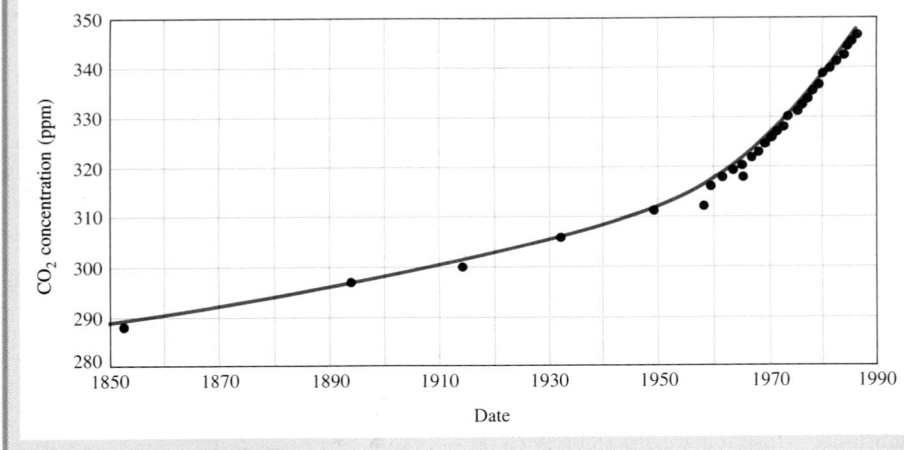

FIGURE 3.15 The concentration of atmospheric CO$_2$ over the past 140 years. Data before 1958 come from analyses of air trapped in bubbles of glacial ice. The concentration in ppm (vertical scale) is the number of molecules of CO$_2$ per million (10^6) molecules of air. CO$_2$ is a relatively minor component of air, but its presence has significant consequences.

3.7 Limiting Reactants

Suppose you have 10 slices of bread and 7 pieces of bologna and you wish to make sandwiches using one slice of bologna and two slices of bread per sandwich. You will be able to make only five sandwiches before you run out of

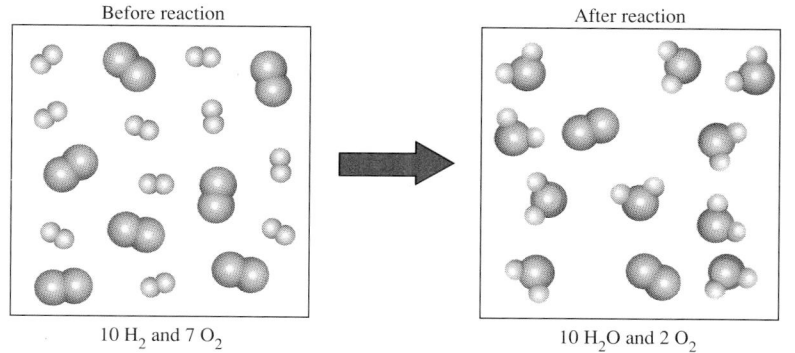

Before reaction   After reaction

10 H$_2$ and 7 O$_2$ 10 H$_2$O and 2 O$_2$

FIGURE 3.16 Diagram showing the complete consumption of a limiting reagent in a reaction. Because the H$_2$ is completely consumed, it is the limiting reagent in this case. Because there is a stoichiometric excess of O$_2$, some is left over at the end of the reaction.

Figure 3.16

bread. You will have two slices of bologna left over. The amount of available bread limits the number of sandwiches.

An analogous situation occurs in chemical reactions when one of the reactants is used up before the others. The reaction stops as soon as any one of the reactants is totally consumed, leaving the excess reactants as leftovers. Suppose, for example, that we have a mixture of 10 mol H$_2$ and 7 mol O$_2$, which we cause to react to form water:

$$2H_2(g) + O_2(g) \longrightarrow 2H_2O(l)$$

Because 2 mol H$_2$ $\approx$ 1 mol O$_2$, the number of moles of O$_2$ needed to react with all the H$_2$ is

$$\text{Moles } O_2 = (10 \text{ mol } H_2)\left(\frac{1 \text{ mol } O_2}{2 \text{ mol } H_2}\right)$$

$$= 5 \text{ mol } O_2$$

Point of Emphasis: Always convert the amounts of reactants into molar quantities and use the reaction stoichiometry to determine the limiting reagent.

Because 7 mol O$_2$ was available at the start of the reaction, 7 mol O$_2$ − 5 mol O$_2$ = 2 mol O$_2$ will be present when the H$_2$ is all consumed. This situation is shown on a molecular scale in Figure 3.16.

The reactant that is completely consumed in a reaction is called the **limiting reactant** or **limiting reagent** because it determines, or limits, the amount of product formed. The other reactants are sometimes called *excess reactants* or *excess reagents*. In our example, H$_2$ is the limiting reactant, which means that once all the H$_2$ has been consumed, the reaction stops; O$_2$ is the excess reactant, and some is left over when the reaction stops.

Learning Goal 9: Determine the limiting reagent in a reaction.

SAMPLE EXERCISE 3.15

Part of the SO$_2$ that is introduced into the atmosphere ends up being converted to sulfuric acid, H$_2$SO$_4$. The net reaction is

$$2SO_2(g) + O_2(g) + 2H_2O(l) \longrightarrow 2H_2SO_4(aq)$$

How much H$_2$SO$_4$ can be formed from 5.0 mol of SO$_2$, 1.0 mol of O$_2$, and an unlimited quantity of H$_2$O?

SOLUTION The number of moles of O_2 needed for complete consumption of 5.0 mol of SO_2 is

$$\text{Moles } O_2 = (5.0 \text{ mol } SO_2) \left(\frac{1 \text{ mol } O_2}{2 \text{ mol } SO_2} \right) = 2.5 \text{ mol } O_2$$

The complete conversion of SO_2 to H_2SO_4 requires more O_2 than is available. We therefore conclude that some of the SO_2 will not be consumed. O_2 is the limiting reactant. We use the quantity of the limiting reactant, O_2, to calculate the quantity of H_2SO_4 produced.

$$\text{Moles } H_2SO_4 = (1.0 \text{ mol } O_2) \left(\frac{2 \text{ mol } H_2SO_4}{1 \text{ mol } O_2} \right) = 2.0 \text{ mol } H_2SO_4$$

We might note that in forming 2.0 mol of H_2SO_4, 2.0 mol of SO_2 is consumed. Therefore, 3.0 mol of SO_2 is left over. SO_2 is the excess reactant.

PRACTICE EXERCISE

Consider the reaction $2Al(s) + 3Cl_2(g) \longrightarrow 2AlCl_3(s)$. A mixture of 1.5 mol of Al and 3.0 mol of Cl_2 are allowed to react. **(a)** What is the limiting reactant? **(b)** How many moles of $AlCl_3$ are formed?   *Answers:* **(a)** Al; **(b)** 1.5 mol

Another approach to the problem of the limiting reactant is to calculate the amount of product that could be formed from each of the given amounts of reactants, assuming they were all completely consumed. The reagent that leads to the smallest amount of product is the limiting reactant.

Common Misconception: Students often combine the amounts of product calculated from each reactant when working with limiting reagents. The reagent that leads to the smallest amount of product is the limiting reagent. The amount of product formed in the reaction is the *smallest calculated amount, not the sum.*

SAMPLE EXERCISE 3.16

Consider the following reaction:

$$2Na_3PO_4(aq) + 3Ba(NO_3)_2(aq) \longrightarrow Ba_3(PO_4)_2(s) + 6NaNO_3(aq)$$

Suppose that a solution containing 3.50 g of Na_3PO_4 is mixed with a solution containing 6.40 g of $Ba(NO_3)_2$. How many grams of $Ba_3(PO_4)_2$ can be formed?

SOLUTION From the balanced equation we have the following stoichiometric relations:

$$2 \text{ mol } Na_3PO_4 \rightleftharpoons 3 \text{ mol } Ba(NO_3)_2 \rightleftharpoons 1 \text{ mol } Ba_3(PO_4)_2$$

The mass of 1 mol of each substance can be found by determining the formula weight for each substance. The results are as follows:

$$1 \text{ mol } Na_3PO_4 = 164 \text{ g } Na_3PO_4$$
$$1 \text{ mol } Ba(NO_3)_2 = 261 \text{ g } Ba(NO_3)_2$$
$$1 \text{ mol } Ba_3(PO_4)_2 = 602 \text{ g } Ba_3(PO_4)_2$$

Let us now calculate the amount of product that could be formed from each of our given amounts of reactants, assuming that each in turn is the limiting reactant. Assuming first that Na_3PO_4 is completely consumed gives:

$$\text{Grams } Ba_3(PO_4)_2 = (3.50 \text{ g } Na_3PO_4) \left(\frac{1 \text{ mol } Na_3PO_4}{164 \text{ g } Na_3PO_4} \right)$$
$$\times \left(\frac{1 \text{ mol } Ba_3(PO_4)_2}{2 \text{ mol } Na_3PO_4} \right) \left(\frac{602 \text{ g } Ba_3(PO_4)_2}{1 \text{ mol } Ba_3(PO_4)_2} \right)$$
$$= 6.42 \text{ g } Ba_3(PO_4)_2$$

Assuming that $Ba(NO_3)_2$ is completely consumed gives:

$$\text{Grams } Ba_3(PO_4)_2 = (6.40 \text{ g } Ba(NO_3)_2)\left(\frac{1 \text{ mol } Ba(NO_3)_2}{261 \text{ g } Ba(NO_3)_2}\right)$$

$$\times \left(\frac{1 \text{ mol } Ba_3(PO_4)_2}{3 \text{ mol } Ba(NO_3)_2}\right)\left(\frac{602 \text{ g } Ba_3(PO_4)_2}{1 \text{ mol } Ba_3(PO_4)_2}\right)$$

$$= 4.92 \text{ g } Ba_3(PO_4)_2$$

The lesser quantity, 4.92 g, is the amount of $Ba_3(PO_4)_2$ that can form, indicating that $Ba(NO_3)_2$ is the limiting reactant.

PRACTICE EXERCISE

A strip of zinc metal weighing 2.00 g is placed in an aqueous solution containing 2.50 g of silver nitrate, causing the following reaction to occur:

$$Zn(s) + 2AgNO_3(aq) \longrightarrow 2Ag(s) + Zn(NO_3)_2(aq)$$

How many grams of Ag will form?   *Answer:* 1.59 g

Theoretical Yields

The quantity of product that is calculated to form when all of the limiting reactant reacts is called the **theoretical yield.** The amount of product actually obtained in a reaction is called the *actual yield.* The actual yield is almost always less than (and can never be greater than) the theoretical yield. There are many reasons for this difference. For example, part of the reactants may not react, or they may react in a way different from that desired (side reactions). In addition, it is not always possible to recover all of the reaction product from the reaction mixture. The **percent yield** of a reaction relates the actual yield to the theoretical (calculated) yield:

Point of Emphasis: The actual yield can *never* be greater than the theoretical yield. Therefore, percent yields must be less than or equal to 100 percent.

$$\text{Percent yield} = \frac{\text{actual yield}}{\text{theoretical yield}} \times 100 \qquad [3.14]$$

For example, in the experiment described in Sample Exercise 3.16, we calculate that 4.92 g of $Ba_3(PO_4)_2$ should form when 3.50 g of Na_3PO_4 is mixed with 6.40 g of $Ba(NO_3)_2$. This is the theoretical yield of $Ba_3(PO_4)_2$ in the reaction. If the actual yield turned out to be 4.70 g, the percent yield would be

$$\frac{4.70 \text{ g}}{4.92 \text{ g}} \times 100 = 95.5\%$$

SAMPLE EXERCISE 3.17

Adipic acid, $H_2C_6H_8O_4$, is a raw material used for the production of nylon. It is made commercially by a controlled reaction between cyclohexane, C_6H_{12}, and O_2:

$$2C_6H_{12} + 5O_2 \longrightarrow 2H_2C_6H_8O_4 + 2H_2O$$

(a) Assume that you carry out this reaction starting with 25.0 g of cyclohexane, and that cyclohexane is the limiting reactant. What is the theoretical yield of adipic acid?

(b) If you obtain 33.5 g of adipic acid from your reaction, what is the percent yield of adipic acid?

SOLUTION **(a)** The theoretical yield is merely the calculated quantity of adipic acid formed in the reaction:

$$\text{Grams } H_2C_6H_8O_4 = (25.0 \text{ g } C_6H_{12}) \left(\frac{1 \text{ mol } C_6H_{12}}{84.0 \text{ g } C_6H_{12}} \right)$$

$$\times \left(\frac{2 \text{ mol } H_2C_6H_8O_4}{2 \text{ mol } C_6H_{12}} \right) \left(\frac{146 \text{ g } H_2C_6H_8O_4}{1 \text{ mol } H_2C_6H_8O_4} \right)$$

$$= 43.5 \text{ g } H_2C_6H_8O_4$$

(b) Using the definition of percent yield, Equation 3.14, we have

$$\text{Percent yield} = \frac{\text{actual yield}}{\text{theoretical yield}} \times 100 = \frac{33.5 \text{ g}}{43.5 \text{ g}} \times 100 = 77.0\%$$

PRACTICE EXERCISE

Imagine that you are working on ways to improve the process by which iron ore containing Fe_2O_3 is converted into iron. In your tests you carry out the following reaction on a small scale:

$$Fe_2O_3(s) + 3CO(g) \longrightarrow 2Fe(s) + 3CO_2(g)$$

(a) If you start with 150 g of Fe_2O_3 as the limiting reagent, what is the theoretical yield of Fe? **(b)** If the actual yield of Fe in your test was 87.9 g, what was the percent yield? *Answers:* **(a)** 105 g Fe; **(b)** 83.7%

For Review

Summary

The law of conservation of mass states that the total mass of the products of a chemical reaction is the same as the total mass of the reactants. The same numbers of atoms of each type are present before and after a chemical reaction. A balanced equation shows equal numbers of atoms of each element on each side of the equation, consistent with the law of conservation of mass. Equations are balanced by placing coefficients in front of the chemical formulas for the reactants and products of a reaction.

You can sometimes predict the products of a reaction from a knowledge of similar reactions and by using the periodic table. Among the reaction types seen in this chapter are (1) combustion reactions in oxygen, in which a hydrocarbon reacts with O_2 to form CO_2 and H_2O; (2) combination reactions, in which two reactants combine to form one product; and (3) decomposition reactions, in which a single reactant forms two or more products.

Much quantitative information can be determined from chemical formulas and equations by using atomic weights. The atomic weight (average atomic mass) of an element can be calculated from the relative abundances and masses of that element's isotopes. Atomic weights are conveniently expressed in atomic mass units (amu). The amu is defined by assigning a mass of exactly 12 amu to the ^{12}C atom. The formula weight of a compound equals the sum of the atomic weights of the atoms in its formula. If the formula is a molecular formula, the formula weight is also called the molecular weight. The mass spectrometer provides the most direct and accurate means of experimentally determining atomic and molecular weights.

A mole of any substance is Avogadro's number (6.022×10^{23}) of formula units of that substance. The mass of a mole of atoms, molecules, or ions is the formula weight of that material expressed in grams (the molar mass). For example, a single molecule of H_2O weighs 18 amu; a mole of H_2O weighs 18 g. The mole concept is very useful in chemistry, and knowing how to interconvert grams and moles for any substance is important.

The empirical formula of any substance can be determined from its percent composition by calculating the relative number of moles of each atom in 100 g of the substance. If the substance is molecular in nature, its molecular formula can be determined from the empirical formula if the molecular weight is known.

The mole concept can be used to calculate the relative quantities of reactants and products involved in chemical reactions. The coefficients in a balanced equation give the relative numbers of moles of these substances. A limiting reactant is the reactant that is completely consumed in a reaction. When it is gone, the reaction stops, thus limiting the quantities of products formed.

Key Terms

law of conservation of mass
stoichiometry
chemical equation (Sec. 3.1)
reactants (Sec. 3.1)
products (Sec. 3.1)
combustion reaction (Sec. 3.2)
combination reaction (Sec. 3.2)
decomposition reaction (Sec. 3.2)
atomic mass unit (Sec. 3.3)
atomic weight (Sec. 3.3)

formula weight (Sec. 3.3)
molecular weight (Sec. 3.3)
mass spectrometer (Sec. 3.3)
mole (Sec. 3.4)
Avogadro's number (Sec. 3.4)
molar mass (Sec. 3.4)
limiting reactant (reagent) (Sec. 3.7)
theoretical yield (Sec. 3.7)
percent yield (Sec. 3.7)

Exercises

Balancing Chemical Equations

3.1. (a) What scientific principle or law is used in the process of balancing chemical equations? (b) What are the symbols used to represent gases, liquids, solids, and aqueous solutions in chemical equations? (c) What is the difference between P_4 and 4P in a chemical equation?

3.2. (a) What is the difference between a reactant and a product in a chemical equation? (b) In balancing equations, why shouldn't subscripts in chemical formulas be changed? (c) Is the following chemical equation, as written, consistent with the law of conservation of mass?

$$H_2SO_4(aq) + Ca(OH)_2(aq) \longrightarrow H_2O(l) + CaSO_4(s)$$

Why or why not?

3.3. Balance the following equations by providing the missing coefficients:
(a) $\_N_2O_5(g) + \_H_2O(l) \longrightarrow \_HNO_3(aq)$
(b) $\_(NH_4)_2Cr_2O_7(s) \longrightarrow \_N_2(g) + \_Cr_2O_3(s) + \_H_2O(l)$
(c) $\_PCl_3(l) + \_H_2O(l) \longrightarrow \_H_3PO_3(aq) + \_HCl(aq)$
(d) $\_Mg_3N_2(s) + \_HCl(aq) \longrightarrow \_MgCl_2(aq) + \_NH_4Cl(aq)$
(e) $\_C_6H_6(l) + \_O_2(g) \longrightarrow \_CO_2(g) + \_H_2O(l)$
(f) $\_C_3H_5NO(g) + \_O_2(g) \longrightarrow \_CO_2(g) + \_NO_2(g) + \_H_2O(l)$

3.4. Balance the following equations:
(a) $La_2O_3(s) + H_2O(l) \longrightarrow La(OH)_3(aq)$
(b) $FeO(s) + O_2(g) \longrightarrow Fe_2O_3(s)$
(c) $NCl_3(aq) + H_2O(l) \longrightarrow NH_3(aq) + HOCl(aq)$
(d) $C_5H_{10}O(l) + O_2(g) \longrightarrow CO_2(g) + H_2O(g)$
(e) $NO_2(g) + H_2O(l) \longrightarrow HNO_3(aq) + NO(g)$
(f) $Fe(OH)_3(s) + H_2SO_4(aq) \longrightarrow Fe_2(SO_4)_3(aq) + H_2O(l)$

3.5. Write a balanced chemical equation to correspond to each of the following descriptions: (a) When sulfur trioxide gas reacts with water, a solution of sulfuric acid forms. (b) Boron sulfide, $B_2S_3(s)$, reacts violently with water to form dissolved boric acid, H_3BO_3, and hydrogen sulfide gas. (c) Phosphine, $PH_3(g)$, combusts in oxygen gas to form gaseous water and solid tetraphosphorus decaoxide. (d) When solid mercury(II) nitrate is heated, it decomposes to form solid mercury(II) oxide, gaseous nitrogen dioxide, and oxygen. (e) When hydrogen sulfide gas is passed over solid hot iron(III) hydroxide, the resultant reaction produces solid iron(III) sulfide and gaseous water.

3.6. Write balanced chemical equations to correspond to each of the following descriptions: (a) When ammonia gas, $NH_3(g)$, is passed over hot liquid sodium metal, hydrogen gas is released and sodium amide, $NaNH_2$, is formed as a solid product. (b) Solid zinc metal reacts with sulfuric acid to form hydrogen gas and an aqueous solution of zinc sulfate. **(c)** When solid potassium nitrate is heated, it decomposes to form solid potassium nitrite and oxygen gas. **(d)** When liquid phosphorus trichloride is added to water, it reacts violently to form aqueous phosphorous acid, $H_3PO_3(aq)$, and aqueous hydrochloric acid. **(e)** Copper metal reacts with hot concentrated sulfuric acid to form aqueous copper(II) sulfate, sulfur dioxide gas, and water.

Patterns of Chemical Reactivity

3.7. Write a balanced chemical equation for the reaction that occurs when **(a)** $C_7H_{16}(l)$ is combusted in air; **(b)** $CH_3OC_2H_5(l)$ burns in air; **(c)** Rb(s) reacts with water; **(d)** Mg(s) reacts with $Cl_2(g)$.

3.8. Write a balanced chemical equation for the reaction that occurs when **(a)** styrene, $C_8H_8(l)$, burns in air; **(b)** the gasoline additive MTBE (methyl tertiary-butyl ether), $C_5H_{12}O(l)$, is combusted in air; **(c)** lithium metal is added to water; **(d)** $BaCO_3(s)$ is heated.

3.9. Balance the following equations and indicate whether they are combustion, combination, or decomposition reactions:
(a) $KClO_3(s) \longrightarrow KCl(s) + O_2(g)$
(b) $C_7H_8O_2(l) + O_2(g) \longrightarrow CO_2(g) + H_2O(l)$
(c) $Cr(s) + Cl_2(g) \longrightarrow CrCl_3(s)$
(d) $SO_3(g) \longrightarrow SO_2(g) + O_2(g)$

3.10. Balance the following equations and indicate whether they are combustion, combination, or decomposition reactions:

(a) $C_5H_6O(l) + O_2(g) \longrightarrow CO_2(g) + H_2O(g)$
(b) $H_2O_2(l) \longrightarrow H_2O(l) + O_2(g)$
(c) $CaO(s) + H_2O(l) \longrightarrow Ca(OH)_2(aq)$
(d) $Li(s) + N_2(g) \longrightarrow Li_3N(s)$

3.11. From the hints provided, write complete balanced equations for the following reactions: **(a)** Reaction of potassium with liquid ammonia is very much like reaction of this metal with water. **(b)** Combustion of nitromethane, $CH_3NO_2(g)$, leads to $NO_2(g)$ as one of the products. **(c)** Fluorine, like oxygen, can support combustion. For example, methane, $CH_4(g)$, can "burn" in an atmosphere of $F_2(g)$.

3.12. Using a periodic table or the hints provided, write complete balanced equations for the following reactions: **(a)** Combustion of $Si_2H_6(g)$. **(b)** Combustion of $CH_3SH(g)$ leads to $SO_2(g)$ as one of the products. **(c)** Magnesium metal undergoes a vigorous combination reaction when exposed to chlorine gas.

Atomic and Molecular Weights

3.13. **(a)** What isotope is used as the standard in establishing the atomic mass scale? **(b)** What is an atomic mass unit?

3.14. **(a)** What is the mass in amu of a carbon-12 atom? **(b)** If the mass of a carbon-12 atom were redefined to be exactly 20 new mass units (nmu), what would be the mass of an average hydrogen atom in new mass units?

3.15. Only two isotopes of boron occur naturally: ^{10}B (mass = 10.013 amu; abundance = 19.78 percent) and ^{11}B (mass = 11.009 amu; abundance = 80.22 percent). Calculate the average atomic mass (atomic weight) of boron.

3.16. The element neon consists of three isotopes with masses 19.99, 20.99, and 21.99 amu. The relative abundances of these three isotopes are 90.92, 0.25, and 8.83 percent, respectively. From these data, calculate the average atomic mass of neon.

3.17. In GaAs, 48.20 percent of the mass is gallium, and the rest is arsenic. If a relative atomic mass scale were established with the mass of arsenic assigned a value of exactly 100, what would be the relative atomic mass of gallium?

3.18. In his determination of the atomic weight of the element zinc, Berzelius determined in 1818 that the mass ratio of Zn to O in the oxide of zinc was 4.032. He thought that the formula of the compound was ZnO_2. Assuming an atomic weight of 16.00 for oxygen, what value does this give for the atomic weight of zinc? By comparing this with the presently accepted value, what can you say about Berzelius's assumption? If it was in error, what should it have been?

3.19. Determine the formula weights of each of the following compounds: **(a)** SO_3; **(b)** C_2F_6; **(c)** $(NH_4)_2Cr_2O_7$; **(d)** $Mg(C_2H_3O_2)_2$; **(e)** $CH_3OC_2H_5$.

3.20. Determine the formula weights of each of the following compounds: **(a)** acetylene, C_2H_2, a gas used in welding; **(b)** ammonium sulfate, $(NH_4)_2SO_4$, a substance used as a nitrogen fertilizer; **(c)** ascorbic acid, $C_6H_8O_6$, also known as vitamin C; **(d)** $PtCl_2(NH_3)_2$, a chemotherapy agent called cisplatin; **(e)** the male sex hormone testosterone, $C_{19}H_{28}O_2$.

3.21. Calculate the percentage by mass of each element in the following compounds: **(a)** SO_3; **(b)** CCl_4; **(c)** CH_3OH; **(d)** $Ca(NO_3)_2$; **(e)** $(NH_4)_2SO_4$.

3.22. Calculate the percentage by mass of the indicated element in each of the following compounds:
(a) nitrogen in nitrous oxide, N_2O, known as laughing gas and used as an anesthetic in dentistry; **(b)** carbon in benzoic acid, $C_7H_6O_2$, a substance used as a food preservative; **(c)** magnesium in $Mg(OH)_2$, the active ingredient in milk of magnesia; **(d)** nitrogen in urea, $(NH_2)_2CO$, a compound used as a nitrogen fertilizer; **(e)** hydrogen in pentyl acetate, $CH_3CO_2C_5H_{11}$, responsible for the odor of bananas.

3.23. The mass spectrum of H_2 is taken under conditions that prevent decomposition into H atoms. The two naturally occurring isotopes of hydrogen are ^1H (mass = 1.00783 amu; abundance = 99.985 percent) and ^2H (mass = 2.01411 amu; abundance = 0.015 percent). **(a)** How many peaks will the mass spectrum have? **(b)** Give the relative atomic masses of each of these peaks. (c) Which peak will be the largest, and which will be the smallest?

✓ [3.24]. The element bromine consists of two isotopes. The mass spectrum of molecular bromine, Br_2, consists of three peaks:

Mass (amu)	Relative size
157.84	0.2534
159.84	0.5000
161.84	0.2466

(a) What is the origin of each peak (that is, of what isotopes does each consist)? (b) What is the mass of each isotope? (c) Determine the average molecular mass of a Br_2 molecule. (d) Determine the average atomic mass of a bromine atom. (e) Calculate the abundances of the two isotopes.

The Mole

✓ 3.25. The mole is a key concept in chemistry. (a) Define the term *mole*. (b) What is Avogadro's number? (c) What is the relationship between the formula weight of a substance and its molar mass?

3.26. (a) What is the mass, in grams, of a mole of ^{12}C? (b) How many carbon atoms are present in a mole of ^{12}C? (c) What is the mass, in grams, of a single ^{12}C atom?

✓ 3.27. A sample of glucose, $C_6H_{12}O_6$, contains 2.0×10^{22} atoms of carbon. (a) How many atoms of hydrogen does it contain? (b) How many molecules of glucose does it contain? (c) How many moles of glucose does it contain? (d) What is the mass of this sample in grams?

3.28. A sample of the female sex hormone estradiol, $C_{18}H_{24}O_2$, contains 1.0×10^{20} atoms of hydrogen. (a) How many atoms of carbon does it contain? (b) How many molecules of estradiol does it contain? (c) How many moles of estradiol does it contain? (d) What is the mass of this sample in grams?

3.29. (a) What is the molar mass of copper(II) nitrate, $Cu(NO_3)_2$? (b) What is the mass, in grams, of 0.320 mol of $Cu(NO_3)_2$? (c) How many moles of $Cu(NO_3)_2$ are present in 5.20 g of this substance? (d) How many N atoms are present in 5.25 mg of $Cu(NO_3)_2$?

3.30. Aspartame, the artificial sweetener marketed as Nu-traSweet, has a molecular formula $C_{14}H_{18}N_2O_5$. (a) What is the mass of 1.00 mol of aspartame? (b) How many moles are present in 65.7 g of aspartame? (c) What is the mass, in grams, of 0.842 mol of aspartame? (d) How many hydrogen atoms are present in 4.33 mg of aspartame?

✓ 3.31. Calculate the mass, in grams, of each of the following: (a) 0.00650 mol SO_2; (b) 4.58×10^{22} atoms of Ar; (c) 1.25×10^{20} molecules of caffeine, $C_8H_{10}N_4O_2$.

3.32. Calculate the mass, in grams, of each of the following: (a) 0.0795 mol of aspirin, $C_9H_8O_4$; (b) 3.25×10^{20} molecules of ozone, O_3; (c) 5.64×10^{24} molecules of cholesterol, $C_{27}H_{46}O$.

3.33. Calculate the number of molecules present in each of the following samples: (a) 0.350 mol acetylene, C_2H_2, a fuel used in welding; (b) a 500-mg tablet of vitamin C, $C_6H_8O_6$; (c) an average snowflake containing 5.0×10^{-5} g of H_2O.

3.34. Calculate the number of molecules in (a) 0.0850 mol propane, C_3H_8, a hydrocarbon fuel; (b) a 100-mg tablet of paracetamol, $C_8H_9O_2N$, an analgesic sold under the name Tylenol; (c) a tablespoon of table sugar, $C_{12}H_{22}O_{11}$, weighing 12.6 g.

✓ 3.35. The allowable concentration level of vinyl chloride, C_2H_3Cl, in the atmosphere in a chemical plant is 2.05×10^{-6} g/L. How many moles of vinyl chloride in each liter does this represent? How many molecules per liter?

3.36. About 25 μg minimum of tetrahydrocannabinol (THC), the active ingredient in marijuana, is required to produce intoxication. The molecular formula of THC is $C_{21}H_3O_2$. How many moles of THC does this 25 μg represent? How many molecules?

Empirical Formulas

3.37. What is the difference between an empirical formula and a molecular formula?

✓ 3.38. Explain why percentage compositions can be used to give empirical formulas but not necessarily molecular formulas.

✓ 3.39. Determine the empirical formula of each of the following compounds if a sample contains (a) 0.0230 mol C and 0.0615 mol H; (b) 5.28 g Sn and 3.37 g F; (c) 87.5 percent N and 12.5 percent H by mass.

3.40. Give the empirical formula of each of the following compounds if a sample contains (a) 0.104 mol Na, 0.052 mol S, and 0.156 mol O; (b) 11.66 g iron and 5.01 g oxygen; (c) 40.0 percent C, 6.7 percent H, and 53.3 percent O.

✓ 3.41. Determine the empirical formulas of the compounds with the following compositions by mass: (a) 10.4 percent C, 27.8 percent S, and 61.7 percent Cl; (b) 21.7 percent C, 9.6 percent O, and 68.7 percent F.

3.42. Determine the empirical formulas of the compounds with the following compositions by mass: **(a)** 32.79 percent Na, 13.02 percent Al, and 54.19 percent F; **(b)** 62.1 percent C, 5.21 percent H, 12.1 percent N, and 20.7 percent O.

3.43. Determine the empirical and molecular formulas of each of the following substances: **(a)** epinephrine (adrenaline), a hormone secreted into the bloodstream in times of danger or stress: 59.0 percent C, 7.1 percent H, 26.2 percent O, and 7.7 percent N by mass; MW about 180 amu; **(b)** nicotine, a component of tobacco: 74.1 percent C, 8.6 percent H, and 17.3 percent N by mass; molar mass = 160 ± 5 g.

3.44. Determine the empirical and molecular formulas of each of the following substances: **(a)** ethylene glycol, the substance used as the primary component of most antifreeze solutions: 38.7 percent C, 9.7 percent H, and 51.6 percent O by mass; MW = 62.1 amu; **(b)** caffeine, a stimulant found in coffee: 49.5 percent C, 5.15 percent H, 28.9 percent N, and 16.5 percent O by mass; molar mass about 195 g.

3.45. Cyclopropane, a substance used with oxygen as a general anesthetic, contains only two elements, carbon and hydrogen. When 1.00 g of this substance is completely combusted, 3.14 g of CO_2 and 1.29 g of H_2O are produced. What is the empirical formula of cyclopropane?

3.46. The characteristic odor of pineapple is due to ethyl butyrate, a compound containing carbon, hydrogen, and oxygen. Combustion of 2.78 mg of ethyl butyrate produces 6.32 mg of CO_2 and 2.58 mg of H_2O. What is the empirical formula of the compound?

3.47. Epsom salts, a strong laxative used in veterinary medicine, is a hydrate, which means that a certain number of water molecules are included in the solid structure. The formula for epsom salts can be written as $MgSO_4 \cdot xH_2O$, where x indicates the number of moles of water per mole of $MgSO_4$. When 5.061 g of this hydrate is heated to 250°C, all the water of hydration is lost, leaving 2.472 g of $MgSO_4$. What is the value of x?

3.48. Washing soda, a compound used to prepare hard water for washing laundry, is a hydrate. Its formula can be written as $Na_2CO_3 \cdot xH_2O$, where x is the number of moles of H_2O per mole of Na_2CO_3. When a 2.558-g sample of washing soda is heated at 125°C, all the water of hydration is lost, leaving 0.948 g of Na_2CO_3. What is the value of x?

[3.49]. Fungal laccase, a blue protein found in wood-rotting fungi, is approximately 0.39 percent copper by mass. If a laccase molecule contains four copper atoms, what is its approximate molecular weight?

[3.50]. Hemoglobin, the oxygen-carrying protein in red blood cells, has four iron atoms per molecule and contains 0.340 percent iron by mass. Calculate the molar mass of hemoglobin.

Calculations Based on Chemical Equations

3.51. Why is it essential to use balanced chemical equations in solving stoichiometry problems?

3.52. What parts of chemical equations give information about the relative numbers of moles of reactants and products involved in a reaction?

3.53. The alcohol in "gasohol" burns according to the following equation:

$$C_2H_5OH(l) + 3O_2(g) \longrightarrow 2CO_2(g) + 3H_2O(l)$$

(a) How many moles of CO_2 are produced when 5.00 mol of C_2H_5OH is burned in this way? **(b)** How many grams of CO_2 are produced when 5.00 g of C_2H_5OH is burned in this way?

3.54. The complete combustion of octane, C_8H_{18}, a component of gasoline, proceeds as follows:

$$2C_8H_{18}(l) + 25O_2(g) \longrightarrow 16CO_2(g) + 18H_2O(l)$$

(a) How many moles of O_2 are needed to burn 5.00 mol of C_8H_{18}? **(b)** How many grams of O_2 are needed to burn 5.00 g of C_8H_{18}? **(c)** Octane has a density of 0.692 g/mL at 20°C. How many grams of O_2 are required to burn 5.00 mL of C_8H_{18}?

3.55. Hydrofluoric acid, HF (aq), cannot be stored in glass bottles because compounds called silicates in the glass are attacked by the HF(aq). For example, sodium silicate, Na_2SiO_3, reacts in the following way:

$$Na_2SiO_3(s) + 8HF(aq) \longrightarrow$$
$$H_2SiF_6(aq) + 2NaF(aq) + 3H_2O(l)$$

(a) How many moles of HF are required to dissolve 1.50 mol of Na_2SiO_3 in this reaction? **(b)** How many grams of NaF form when 3.00 mol of HF reacts in this way? **(c)** How many grams of Na_2SiO_3 can be dissolved by 3.00 g of HF?

3.56. The fermentation of glucose, $C_6H_{12}O_6$, produces ethyl alcohol, C_2H_5OH, and CO_2:

$$C_6H_{12}O_6(aq) \longrightarrow 2C_2H_5OH(aq) + 2CO_2(g)$$

(a) How many moles of CO_2 are produced when 0.450 mol of $C_6H_{12}O_6$ reacts in this fashion? **(b)** How many grams of $C_6H_{12}O_6$ are needed to form 5.00 mol of C_2H_5OH? **(c)** How many grams of CO_2 form when 5.00 g of C_2H_5OH are produced?

3.57. The reusable booster rockets of the U.S. space shuttle use a mixture of aluminum, Al, and ammonium perchlorate, NH_4ClO_4, for fuel. The reaction between these substances is as follows:

$$3Al(s) + 3NH_4ClO_4(s) \longrightarrow$$
$$Al_2O_3(s) + AlCl_3(s) + 3NO(g) + 6H_2O(g)$$

What mass of ammonium perchlorate should be used in the fuel mixture for each kilogram of aluminum?

3.58. A chemical plant uses electrical energy to decompose aqueous solutions of NaCl to give Cl_2, H_2, and NaOH:

$$2NaCl(aq) + 2H_2O(l) \longrightarrow 2NaOH(aq) + H_2(g) + Cl_2(g)$$

If the plant produces 1.4×10^6 kg (1400 metric tons) of Cl_2 daily, estimate the quantities of H_2 and NaOH produced.

3.59. Many antacids contain aluminum hydroxide, $Al(OH)_3$, as their active ingredient. **(a)** Write the balanced chemical equation for the reaction of HCl in stomach acid with solid $Al(OH)_3$ to form water and aqueous $AlCl_3$. **(b)** How many grams of HCl react with 2.50 g of $Al(OH)_3$?

Limiting Reactants; Theoretical Yields

3.61. (a) Define the terms *limiting reagent* and *excess reagent*. **(b)** Why are the amounts of products formed in a reaction determined only by the amount of the limiting reagent?

3.62. (a) Define the terms *theoretical yield, actual yield,* and *percent yield*. **(b)** Why is the actual yield in a reaction almost always less than the theoretical yield?

3.63. A manufacturer of bicycles has 5350 wheels, 3133 frames, and 2785 handlebars. **(a)** How many bicycles can be manufactured using these parts? **(b)** How many parts of each kind are left over? **(c)** Which part is like a limiting reactant in that it limits the production of bicycles?

3.64. A bottling plant has 121,550 bottles with a capacity of 355 mL, 125,000 caps, and 53,575 L of beverage. **(a)** How many bottles can be filled and capped? **(b)** How much of each item is left over? **(c)** Which component limits the production?

3.65. Silicon carbide, SiC, is commonly known as carborundum. This hard substance, which is used commercially as an abrasive, is made by heating SiO_2 and C to high temperatures:

$$SiO_2(s) + 3C(s) \longrightarrow SiC(s) + 2CO(g)$$

(a) How many grams of SiC are formed by complete reaction of 5.00 g of SiO_2? **(b)** How many grams of C are required to react with 5.00 g of SiO_2? **(c)** How many grams of SiC can form when 2.50 g of SiO_2 and 2.50 g of C are allowed to react? **(d)** In part (c), which reactant is the limiting reactant and which is the excess reactant? **(e)** In part (c), how much of the excess reactant remains after the limiting reactant is completely consumed?

3.66. One of the steps in the commercial process for converting ammonia to nitric acid involves the conversion of NH_3 to NO:

$$4NH_3(g) + 5O_2(g) \longrightarrow 4NO(g) + 6H_2O(g)$$

(a) How many grams of NO are formed by complete reaction of 2.50 g of NH_3? **(b)** How many grams of O_2 are required to react with 2.50 g of NH_3? **(c)** How many grams

3.60. Automotive airbags inflate when sodium azide, NaN_3, rapidly decomposes to the elements. **(a)** Write a balanced chemical equation for this reaction. **(b)** How many grams of NaN_3 are required to form 1.00 g of N_2? **(c)** How many grams of NaN_3 are required to produce 12.0 ft^3 of $N_2(g)$ if the gas has a density of 1.25 g/L?

of NO form when 1.50 g of NH_3 reacts with 1.00 g of O_2? **(d)** In part (c), which reactant is the limiting reactant and which is the excess reactant? **(e)** In part (c), how much of the excess reactant remains after the limiting reactant is completely consumed?

3.67. Consider the following reaction:

$$H_2S(g) + 2NaOH(aq) \longrightarrow Na_2S(aq) + 2H_2O(l)$$

How many grams of Na_2S are formed if 2.05 g of H_2S is bubbled into a solution containing 1.84 g of NaOH, assuming that the limiting reagent is completely consumed?

3.68. Ethylene, C_2H_4, burns in air:

$$C_2H_4(g) + 3O_2(g) \longrightarrow 2CO_2(g) + 2H_2O(l)$$

How many grams of CO_2 can form when a mixture of 2.93 g of C_2H_4 and 5.29 g of O_2 is ignited, assuming only the reaction above occurs?

3.69. A student reacts benzene, C_6H_6, with bromine, Br_2, in an attempt to prepare bromobenzene, C_6H_5Br:

$$C_6H_6 + Br_2 \longrightarrow C_6H_5Br + HBr$$

(a) What is the theoretical yield of bromobenzene in this reaction when 30.0 g of benzene reacts with 65.0 g Br_2? **(b)** If the actual yield of bromobenzene was 56.7 g, what was the percentage yield?

3.70. Azobenzene, $C_{12}H_{10}N_2$, is an important intermediate in the manufacture of dyes. It can be prepared by the reaction between nitrobenzene, $C_6H_5NO_2$, and triethylene glycol, $C_6H_{14}O_4$, in the presence of zinc and potassium hydroxide:

$$2C_6H_5NO_2 + 4C_6H_{14}O_4 \xrightarrow[\text{KOH}]{\text{Zn}}$$
$$C_{12}H_{10}N_2 + 4C_6H_{12}O_4 + 4H_2O$$

(a) What is the theoretical yield of azobenzene when 115 g of nitrobenzene and 327 g of triethylene glycol are allowed to react? **(b)** If the reaction yields 55 g of azobenzene, what is the percent yield of azobenzene?

Additional Exercises

3.71. Balance the following equations:
(a) $PBr_5(s) + H_2O(l) \longrightarrow H_3PO_4(aq) + HBr(aq)$
(b) $Li_3N(s) + H_2O(l) \longrightarrow NH_3(g) + LiOH(aq)$
(c) $C_4H_9OH(l) + O_2(g) \longrightarrow CO_2(g) + H_2O(l)$

3.72. Write the balanced chemical equation for the complete combustion of butyric acid, $C_4H_8O_2$, a compound produced when butter becomes rancid.

[3.73]. Which would be larger: an atomic mass unit based on the current standard, or one based on the mass of a beryllium-9 atom set at exactly 9 amu? Explain briefly. (Beryllium-9 is the only naturally occurring isotope of beryllium.)

[3.74]. Gallium (Ga) consists of two naturally occurring isotopes with masses of 68.926 and 70.926 amu. (a) How many protons and neutrons are in the nucleus of each isotope? Write the complete atomic symbol for each, showing the atomic number and mass number. (b) The average atomic mass of Ga is 69.72 amu. Calculate the abundance of each isotope.

3.75. Calculate the percent by mass of the indicated element in each of the following compounds: (a) the percent samarium (Sm) in Co_5Sm, an alloy used to form permanent magnets in very lightweight headsets such as the Sony Walkman; (b) the percentage of C in dopamine, $C_8H_{11}O_2N$, a neurotransmitter.

3.76. Aluminum oxide, Al_2O_3, occurs in nature as the mineral corundum. This mineral, which is noted for its hardness, has a density of 3.97 g/cm^3. Calculate the number of Al atoms in 10.0 cm^3 of Al_2O_3.

3.77. The molecule pyridine, C_5H_5N, adsorbs on the surfaces of certain metal oxides. A 5.0-g sample of finely divided zinc oxide, ZnO, was found to adsorb 0.068 g of pyridine. (a) How many pyridine molecules are adsorbed? (b) What is the ratio of pyridine molecules to formula units of zinc oxide? (c) If the surface area of the oxide is 48 m^2/g, what is the average area of surface per adsorbed pyridine molecule?

[3.78]. An element X forms an iodide XI_3 and a chloride XCl_3. The iodide is quantitatively converted to the chloride when it is heated in a stream of chlorine:

$$2XI_3 + 3Cl_2 \longrightarrow 2XCl_3 + 3I_2$$

If 0.5000 g of XI_3 is treated, 0.2360 g of XCl_3 is obtained. (a) Calculate the atomic weight of the element X. (b) Identify the element X.

[3.79]. One of the earliest accurate formula weight measurements involved measurement of the weight ratio of $KClO_3$ to KCl, based on decomposition of $KClO_3$:

$$2KClO_3(s) \longrightarrow 2KCl(s) + 3O_2(g)$$

In 1911 Stähler and Meyer measured this ratio and found it to be 1.64382. Using only this ratio and the presently accepted atomic weight of oxygen, calculate the formula weight for KCl. Compare this calculated formula weight with the presently accepted value.

[3.80]. Stas reported in 1865 that he had reacted a weighed amount of pure silver with nitric acid and had recovered all the silver as pure silver nitrate, $AgNO_3$. The mass ratio of Ag to $AgNO_3$ was found to be 0.634985. Using only this ratio and the presently accepted values for the atomic weights of silver and oxygen, calculate the atomic weight of nitrogen. Compare this calculated atomic weight with the currently accepted value.

3.81. The koala bear dines exclusively on eucalyptus leaves. Its digestive system detoxifies the eucalyptus oil, a poison to other animals. The chief constituent in eucalyptus oil is a substance called eucalyptol, which contains 77.87 percent C, 11.76 percent H, and the remainder O. (a) What is the empirical formula for this substance? (b) A mass spectrum of eucalyptol shows a peak at about 154 amu. What is the molecular formula of the substance?

3.82. Vanillin, the dominant flavoring in vanilla, contains three elements: C, H, and O. When 1.05 g of this substance is completely combusted, 2.43 g of CO_2 and 0.50 g of H_2O are produced. What is the empirical formula of vanillin?

[3.83]. An oxybromate compound, $KBrO_x$, where x is unknown, is analyzed and found to contain 52.92 percent Br. What is the value of x?

[3.84]. A mixture of pure AgCl and pure AgBr is found to contain 60.94% Ag by mass. What are the mass percentages of Cl and Br in the mixture?

3.85. The fizz produced when an Alka-Seltzer tablet is dissolved in water is due to the reaction between sodium bicarbonate, $NaHCO_3$, and citric acid, $H_3C_6H_5O_7$:

$$3NaHCO_3(aq) + H_3C_6H_5O_7(aq) \longrightarrow$$
$$3CO_2(g) + 3H_2O(l) + Na_3C_6H_5O_7(aq)$$

How many grams of citric acid should be used for each 1.00 g of sodium bicarbonate?

3.86. The fat stored in the hump of a camel is a source of both energy and water. Calculate the mass of H_2O produced by metabolism of 2.0 kg of fat, assuming the fat consists entirely of tristearin ($C_{57}H_{110}O_6$), a typical animal fat, and that during metabolism, tristearin reacts with O_2 to form only CO_2 and H_2O.

[3.87]. HCN is a poisonous gas. The lethal dose is approximately 300 mg HCN per kilogram of air when inhaled. (a) Calculate the amount of HCN that gives the lethal dose in a small laboratory room measuring 12 ft × 15 ft × 8.0 ft. The density of air at 26°C is 0.00118 g/cm^3. (b) If the HCN is formed by reaction of NaCN with an acid such as H_2SO_4, what mass of NaCN gives the lethal dose in the room?

$$2NaCN(s) + H_2SO_4(aq) \longrightarrow Na_2SO_4(aq) + 2HCN(g)$$

(c) HCN forms when synthetic fibers containing Orlon or Acrilan burn. Acrilan has an empirical formula of CH_2CHCN, and so HCN is 50.9 percent of the formula by mass. If a rug that measures 12 ft × 15 ft and contains 30 oz of Acrilan fibers per square yard of carpet burns, will a lethal dose of HCN be generated in the room? Assume that the yield of HCN from the fibers is 20 percent and that the carpet is 50 percent consumed.

3.88. A mixture of $N_2(g)$ and $H_2(g)$ is caused to react in a closed container to form ammonia, $NH_3(g)$. The reaction ceases before either reactant has been totally consumed. At this stage, 2.0 mol N_2, 2.0 mol H_2, and 2.0 mol NH_3 are present. How many moles of N_2 and H_2 were present originally?

3.89. Chloromycetin is an antibiotic with the formula $C_{11}H_{12}O_5N_2Cl_2$. A 1.03-g sample of an ophthalmic ointment containing chloromycetin was chemically treated to convert its chlorine into Cl^- ions. The Cl^- was precipitated as AgCl. If the AgCl weighed 0.0129 g, calculate the mass percentage of chloromycetin in the sample.

[3.90]. A mixture containing $KClO_3$, $KHCO_3$, K_2CO_3, and KCl was heated, producing CO_2, O_2, and H_2O gases according to the following equations:

$$2KClO_3(s) \longrightarrow 2KCl(s) + 3O_2(g)$$

$$2KHCO_3(s) \longrightarrow K_2O(s) + H_2O(g) + 2CO_2(g)$$

$$K_2CO_3(s) \longrightarrow K_2O(s) + CO_2(g)$$

The KCl does not react under the conditions of the reaction. If 100.0 g of the mixture produces 1.80 g of H_2O, 13.20 g of CO_2, and 4.00 g of O_2, what was the composition of the original mixture? (Assume complete decomposition of the mixture.)

3.91. A particular coal contains 2.8 percent sulfur by mass. When this coal is burned, the sulfur is converted into $SO_2(g)$. This SO_2 is reacted with CaO to form $CaSO_3(s)$. If the coal is burned in a power plant that uses 2000 tons of coal per day, what is the daily production of $CaSO_3$?

3.92. When a mixture of 10.0 g of acetylene, C_2H_2, and 10.0 g of oxygen, O_2, is ignited, the resultant combustion reaction produces CO_2 and H_2O. (a) Write the balanced chemical equation for this reaction. (b) Which reactant is the limiting reactant in this reaction? (c) How many grams of C_2H_2, O_2, CO_2, and H_2O are present after the reaction?

3.93. Aspirin, $C_9H_8O_4$, is produced from salicylic acid, $C_7H_6O_3$, and acetic anhydride, $C_4H_6O_3$:

$$C_7H_6O_3 + C_4H_6O_3 \longrightarrow C_9H_8O_4 + HC_2H_3O_2$$

(a) How much salicylic acid is required to produce 1.5×10^2 kg of aspirin, assuming that all of the salicylic acid is converted to aspirin? (b) How much salicylic acid would be required if only 80 percent of the salicylic acid is converted to aspirin? (c) What is the theoretical yield of aspirin if 185 kg of salicylic acid is allowed to react with 125 kg of acetic anhydride? (d) If the situation described in part (c) produces 182 kg of aspirin, what is the percentage yield?

[3.94]. Hydrogen and chlorine both have two naturally occurring isotopes: ^1H (1.0078 amu; 99.985 percent abundance) and ^2H (2.0140 amu; 0.015 percent abundance), ^{35}Cl (34.969 amu; 75.53 percent abundance) and ^{37}Cl (36.966 amu; 24.47 percent abundance). (a) How many peaks would be expected in a mass spectrum of $HCl(g)$? (b) At what molecular weights will peaks be observed? (c) What should be the relative intensities of the peaks? (d) The mass spectrum of a compound HX shows eight peaks. What can you conclude about the element X?

4 Aqueous Reactions and Solution Stoichiometry

When a copper wire is placed in an aqueous solution of silver nitrate, crystals of silver metal form on the copper surface.

Water is a truly remarkable substance. Because water is one of the most abundant compounds on the earth, we sometimes tend to take its unique chemical and physical properties for granted. However, we shall see time and time again throughout this text that water possesses many unusual properties. For example, it melts and boils at much higher temperatures than other substances of comparable molar mass, and it is one of the few substances that expands upon freezing. All these properties of water are essential to support life on earth.

One of the most important properties of water is its ability to dissolve a wide variety of substances. Solutions in which water is the dissolving medium are called **aqueous solutions.** Many of the chemical reactions that take place around us and affect our lives involve substances dissolved in water. Nutrients dissolved in blood are carried to our cells, where they enter into reactions that help keep us alive. Automobile parts rust when they come into frequent contact with aqueous solutions that contain various dissolved substances. Spectacular limestone caves, such as Mammoth Cave in Kentucky (Figure 4.1), were formed by the dissolving action of underground water containing carbon dioxide:

$$CaCO_3(s) + H_2O(l) + CO_2(aq) \longrightarrow Ca(HCO_3)_2(aq) \qquad [4.1]$$

Recall from Section 3.1 that the symbol $CO_2(aq)$ means that the carbon dioxide is dissolved in water.

In this chapter we will consider some common types of reactions that occur in aqueous solutions. Chances are that you have already studied some aspects of aqueous chemistry in the laboratory portion of your course. Much of the chemistry we will discuss involves the reactions of three categories of substances: acids, bases, and salts. Before we consider these substances and their reactions, however, we need to address two background questions: How do we express solution composition? What are the chemical forms in which substances occur in aqueous solutions?

Point of Emphasis: *Aqueous means dissolved in water.*

FIGURE 4.1 Mammoth Cave in Kentucky. The great vaults in these and similar caves were formed by the action of water containing dissolved CO_2 on limestone formations. (National Park Service, Mammoth Cave National Park)

4.1 Solution Composition

A *solution* is a homogeneous mixture of two or more substances. ∞ (Sec. 1.1) One of these substances is called the **solvent;** it is usually the component that is present in the greater quantity. The other substances in the solution are known as **solutes;** they are said to be dissolved in the solvent. For example, when a small amount of sodium chloride, NaCl, is mixed with a large quantity of water, we refer to water as the solvent and sodium chloride as the solute.

Molarity

Scientists use the term **concentration** to designate the amount of solute dissolved in a given quantity of solvent or solution. The concept of concentration is an intuitive one: The greater the amount of solute that is dissolved in a certain amount of solvent, the more concentrated the resulting solution. In chemistry we often need to express the concentrations of solutions quantitatively. We shall see in this and later chapters that many of the properties of solutions depend directly on their concentrations.

The most widely used way of quantifying concentration in chemistry is **molarity.** The molarity (symbol M) of a solution is defined as the number of moles of *solute* in a liter of *solution* (soln):

$$Molarity = \frac{moles\ solute}{volume\ of\ soln\ in\ liters} \qquad [4.2]$$

A 1.00 molar solution (written 1.00 M) contains 1.00 mol of solute in every liter of solution. Figure 4.2 shows the preparation of 250 mL of a 1.00 M solution of $CuSO_4$ in a 250-mL volumetric flask. First 0.250 mol of $CuSO_4$ (39.9 g) is weighed out and placed in the volumetric flask. Water is added to

FIGURE 4.2 Procedure for preparation of 0.250 L of 1.00 M solution of $CuSO_4$. (*a*) Weigh out 0.250 mol (39.9 g) of $CuSO_4$ (formula weight = 159.6 amu). (*b*) Put the $CuSO_4$ (solute) into a 250-mL volumetric flask and add a small quantity of water. (*c*) Dissolve the solute by swirling the flask. (*d*) Add more water until the solution just reaches the calibration mark etched on the neck of the flask. Shake the stoppered flask to ensure complete mixing. (Donald Clegg and Roxy Wilson)

(*a*)

(*b*)

(*c*)

(*d*)

dissolve the salt, and the resultant solution is diluted to a total volume of 250 mL. The molarity of the solution is (0.250 mol $CuSO_4$)/(0.250 L soln) = 1.00 M.

SAMPLE EXERCISE 4.1

Calculate the molarity of a solution made by dissolving 23.4 g of sodium sulfate, Na_2SO_4, in enough water to form 125 mL of solution.

SOLUTION   From Equation 4.2 we have

$$\text{Molarity} = \frac{\text{moles } Na_2SO_4}{\text{liters soln}}$$

We first use the formula weight of Na_2SO_4 to calculate the number of moles of Na_2SO_4:

$$\text{Moles } Na_2SO_4 = (23.4 \text{ g } Na_2SO_4)\left(\frac{1 \text{ mol } Na_2SO_4}{142 \text{ g } Na_2SO_4}\right) = 0.165 \text{ mol } Na_2SO_4$$

We then make certain that the volume of solution is expressed in liters:

$$\text{Liters soln} = (125 \text{ mL})\left(\frac{1 \text{ L}}{1000 \text{ mL}}\right) = 0.125 \text{ L}$$

Thus, the molarity is

$$\text{Molarity} = \frac{0.165 \text{ mol } Na_2SO_4}{0.125 \text{ L soln}} = 1.32 \frac{\text{mol } Na_2SO_4}{\text{L soln}} = 1.32 \text{ } M$$

PRACTICE EXERCISE

Calculate the molarity of a solution made by dissolving 5.00 g of $C_6H_{12}O_6$ in sufficient water to form 100 mL of solution.   *Answer:* 0.278 M

If we know the molarity of a solution, we can easily calculate the number of moles of solute in a given volume. Thus, molarity is a conversion factor between volume of solution and moles of solute. Calculation of the number of moles of HNO_3 in 2.0 L of 0.200 M HNO_3 solution illustrates the conversion of volume to moles:

$$\text{Moles } HNO_3 = (2.0 \text{ L soln})\left(\frac{0.200 \text{ mol } HNO_3}{1 \text{ L soln}}\right)$$

$$= 0.40 \text{ mol } HNO_3$$

Notice how dimensional analysis can be used in this conversion if we express molarity as moles/liter soln. Notice also that to obtain moles we multiplied liters and molarity: moles = liters × molarity. To illustrate the conversion of moles to volume, consider the calculation of the volume of 0.30 M HNO_3 solution required to supply 2.0 mol of HNO_3:

Point of Emphasis: Moles solute = (volume of solution in liters) × molarity

$$\text{Liters soln} = (2.0 \text{ mol } HNO_3)\left(\frac{1 \text{ L soln}}{0.30 \text{ mol } HNO_3}\right)$$

$$= 6.7 \text{ L soln}$$

Point of Emphasis: Volume of solution = moles solute/molarity

In this case, dimensional analysis makes it clear that we need to use the reciprocal of molarity to convert moles to volume: liters = moles × 1/M.

SAMPLE EXERCISE 4.2

How many grams of Na_2SO_4 are required to make 0.350 L of 0.500 M Na_2SO_4?

SOLUTION

$$M\ Na_2SO_4 = \frac{moles\ Na_2SO_4}{liters\ soln}$$

Thus,

$$Moles\ Na_2SO_4 = liters\ soln \times M\ Na_2SO_4$$

$$= (0.350\ \cancel{L\ soln}) \left(\frac{0.500\ mol\ Na_2SO_4}{1\ \cancel{L\ soln}} \right)$$

$$= 0.175\ mol\ Na_2SO_4$$

Because each mole of Na_2SO_4 weighs 142 g, the required number of grams of Na_2SO_4 is

$$(0.175\ \cancel{mol\ Na_2SO_4}) \left(\frac{142\ g\ Na_2SO_4}{1\ \cancel{mol\ Na_2SO_4}} \right) = 24.9\ g\ Na_2SO_4$$

PRACTICE EXERCISE

(a) How many grams of Na_2SO_4 are there in 15 mL of 0.50 M Na_2SO_4? **(b)** How many milliliters of 0.50 M Na_2SO_4 solution are required to supply 0.038 mol of this salt?   *Answers:* **(a)** 1.1 g; **(b)** 76 mL

Dilution

Solutions that are used routinely in the laboratory are often purchased or prepared in concentrated form (called *stock solutions*). For example, hydrochloric acid, HCl, is purchased as a 12 M solution (concentrated hydrochloric acid). Solutions of lower concentrations can then be obtained by adding water,* a process called **dilution.**

When solvent is added to dilute a solution, the number of moles of solute remains unchanged.

$$Moles\ solute\ before\ dilution = moles\ solute\ after\ dilution \qquad [4.3]$$

Because number of moles $= M \times$ liters, we can write

$$(Initial\ molarity)(initial\ volume) = (final\ molarity)(final\ volume)$$

$$M_{initial} V_{initial} = M_{final} V_{final} \qquad [4.4]$$

Suppose you wanted to prepare 250 mL of 0.10 M $CuSO_4$ solution by diluting 1.0 M $CuSO_4$. You can calculate the volume of the more concentrated solution that must be diluted:

$$(1.0\ M)\ (V_{initial}) = (0.10\ M)(250\ mL)$$

$$V_{initial} = \frac{(0.10\ M)(250\ mL)}{1.0\ M} = 25\ mL$$

Thus, this dilution is achieved by withdrawing 25 mL of the 1.0 M solution using a pipet, adding it to a 250-mL volumetric flask, and then diluting it to a

---

* In diluting a concentrated acid or base, the acid or base should be added to water and then further diluted by addition of more water. Adding water directly to concentrated acid or base can cause spattering because of the intense heat generated.

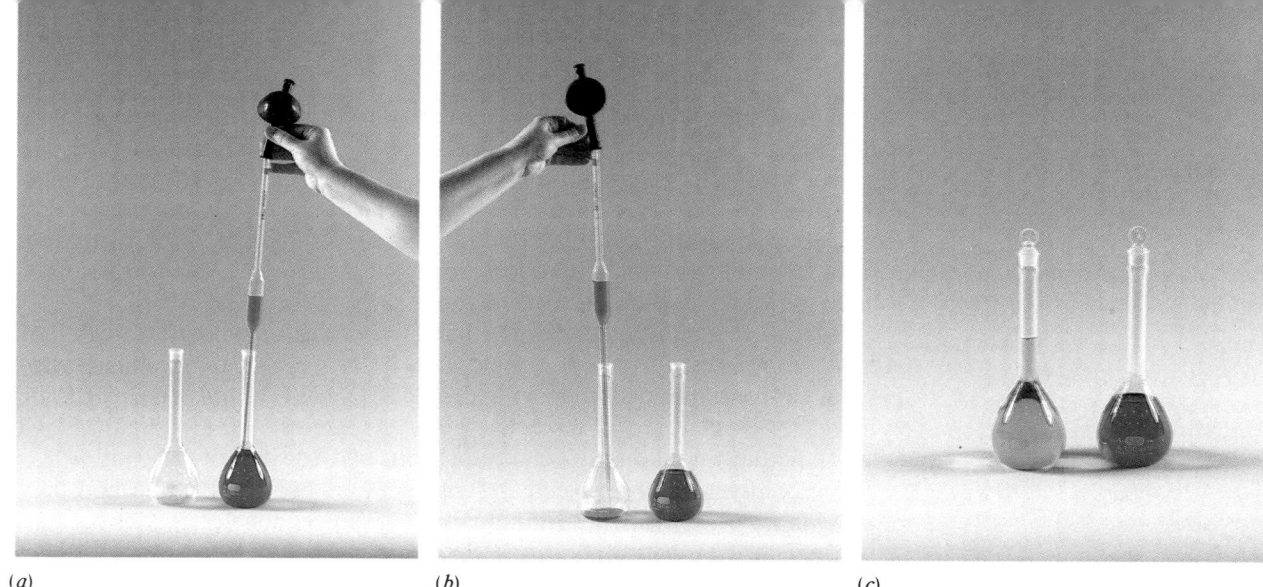

(a)   (b)   (c)

FIGURE 4.3 Procedure for preparation of 250 mL of 0.10 M CuSO$_4$ by dilution of 1.0 M CuSO$_4$. (a) Draw 25 mL of the 1.0 M solution into a pipet. (b) Add this amount to a 250-mL volumetric flask. (c) Add water to dilute the solution to a total volume of 250 mL. (Donald Clegg and Roxy Wilson)

final volume of 250 mL, as shown in Figure 4.3. Notice that the diluted solution is less intensely colored than the concentrated one.

SAMPLE EXERCISE 4.3

How much 3.0 M H$_2$SO$_4$ would be required to make 500 mL of 0.10 M H$_2$SO$_4$?

SOLUTION Using Equation 4.4, $M_{initial}V_{initial} = M_{final}V_{final}$, we can write

$$V_{initial} = \frac{M_{final}V_{final}}{M_{initial}}$$

$$= \frac{(0.10\ M)(500\ mL)}{3.0\ M} = 17\ mL$$

We see that if we start with 17 mL of 3.0 M H$_2$SO$_4$ and dilute it to a total volume of 500 mL, the desired 0.10 M solution will be obtained.

PRACTICE EXERCISE

How many milliliters of 5.0 M K$_2$Cr$_2$O$_7$ solution must be diluted in order to prepare 250 mL of 0.10 M solution?   *Answer:* 5.0 mL

4.2 Electrolytes

What happens to a solute when it is dissolved in water? Imagine preparing two aqueous solutions, one by dissolving a teaspoon of table salt (sodium chloride) in a cup of water, and the other by dissolving a teaspoon of table sugar (sucrose) in a cup of water. Both solutions are clear and colorless. How do they differ? One way, which might not be immediately obvious, is in their electrical conductivity: the salt solution is a good conductor of electricity, whereas the sugar solution does not conduct well.

 Bassam Z. Shakha-shiri, "Conductivity and Extent of Dissociation of Acids in Aqueous Solution," *Chemical Demonstrations: A Handbook for Teachers of Chemistry, Volume 3* (Madison: The University of Wisconsin Press, 1989), pp. 140–45.

Figure 4.4

Recall that solid NaCl consists of Na^+ and Cl^- ions in an orderly arrangement (Figure 2.22). When NaCl is dissolved in water, Na^+ and Cl^- ions are dispersed throughout the solution; the ionic solid *dissociates* into ions in solution. Although water itself is a poor conductor of electricity, the presence of ions causes aqueous solutions to become good conductors. For this reason, solutes that exist as ions in solution are called **electrolytes.** Not surprisingly, soluble ionic compounds are electrolytes.

Many other substances dissolve in water to form ions, even though they are not ionic compounds. For example when HCl *(g)* dissolves in water, it forms H^+ and Cl^- ions; it *ionizes* to form hydrochloric acid, HCl*(aq)*. Like NaCl*(aq)*, HCl*(aq)* consists entirely of dissociated ions. As a result, 1.0 L of a 1.0 *M* HCl solution actually contains 1.0 mol of H^+ ions and 1.0 mol of Cl^- ions.

By contrast, many molecular substances do not form ions when they dissolve in water. We call these nonionizing substances **nonelectrolytes** because they form nonconducting solutions. Sucrose, $C_{12}H_{22}O_{11}$, is a nonelectrolyte. The aqueous solution of sucrose discussed above contains neutral sucrose molecules dispersed throughout the water.

A device such as that shown in Figure 4.4 can be used to test whether ions are present in a solution, provided the solution is not too dilute. If ions are present, they permit electrical charges to move between the electrodes immersed in the solution. The ions complete the electrical circuit, causing the light bulb to glow. The larger the concentration of ions in solution, the greater the electrical current, and the brighter the bulb glows.

Strong and Weak Electrolytes

Substances such as NaCl and HCl that exist in solution almost completely as ions are called **strong electrolytes.** Nearly all ionic compounds are strong elec-

FIGURE 4.4 A device for distinguishing solutions containing strong electrolytes, weak electrolytes, and nonelectrolytes. In (*a*) the bulb glows brightly because the ions present in the strong electrolytic solution provide a large number of electrical current carriers. In (*b*) the bulb glows weakly because the solution of a weak electrolyte has comparatively few ions to serve as current carriers. In (*c*) the bulb does not glow at all because the nonelectrolytic solution has no charged species to serve as current carriers.

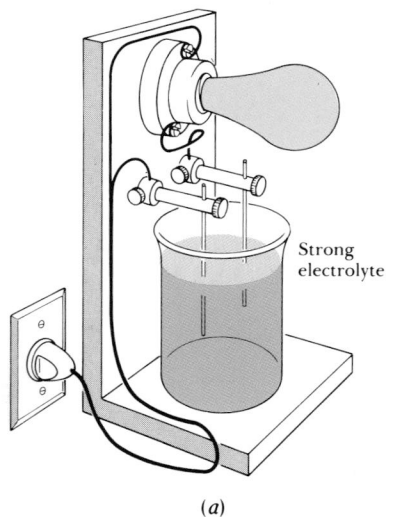

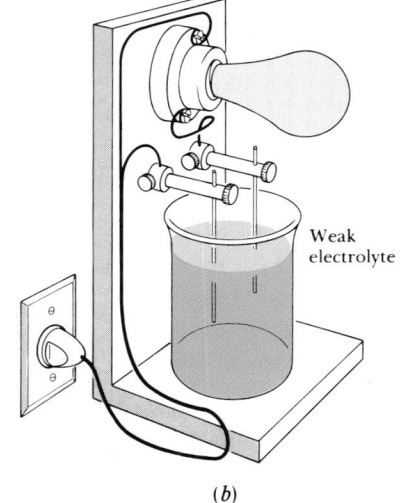

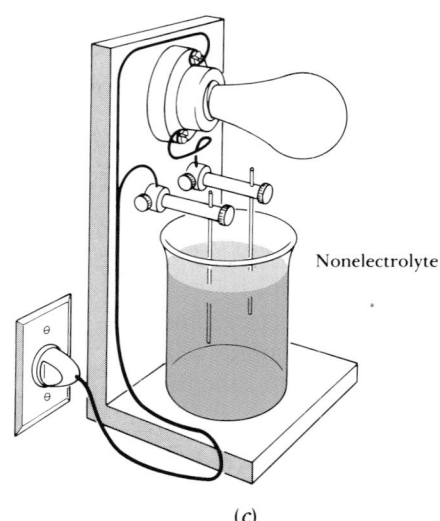

(*a*) Strong electrolyte

(*b*) Weak electrolyte

(*c*) Nonelectrolyte

trolytes. We can usually infer the nature of the ions present in a solution of an ionic compound from the chemical name of the substance. For example, sodium sulfate, Na_2SO_4, dissociates into sodium ions, Na^+, and sulfate ions, SO_4^{2-}. It is important for you to remember the formulas and charges of common ions (Table 2.4) to understand the forms in which ionic compounds exist in solution.

Teaching Note: The difference between strong electrolytes and weak electrolytes is qualitative and somewhat arbitrary.

SAMPLE EXERCISE 4.4

What are the molar concentrations of all ions present in a 0.025 M aqueous solution of calcium nitrate?

SOLUTION Calcium nitrate is an ionic compound composed of calcium ions, Ca^{2+}, and nitrate ions, NO_3^-. Because most soluble ionic compounds are strong electrolytes, we may correctly predict that each mole of $Ca(NO_3)_2$ that dissolves dissociates into 1 mol of Ca^{2+} and 2 mol of NO_3^-. Thus a solution that is 0.025 M in $Ca(NO_3)_2$ is 0.025 M in Ca^{2+} and 2×0.025 $M = 0.050$ M in NO_3^-.

PRACTICE EXERCISE

How many moles of Cl^- ions are present in 0.25 L of 0.015 M $NiCl_2$ solution?
Answer: 0.0075 mol

Some compounds ionize only slightly upon dissolving in water. For example, in a 1.0 M solution of acetic acid, $HC_2H_3O_2$, most of the solute is present as $HC_2H_3O_2$ molecules. Only a small fraction (about 1 percent) of the $HC_2H_3O_2$ is present as H^+ and $C_2H_3O_2^-$ ions. Compounds that only partly ionize in a solution are called **weak electrolytes.**

We must be careful not to confuse the extent to which an electrolyte dissolves with whether it is strong or weak. For example, $HC_2H_3O_2$ is extremely soluble in water but is a weak electrolyte. In contrast, $Ba(OH)_2$ is not very soluble, but the amount of the substance that does dissolve dissociates almost completely. Therefore, $Ba(OH)_2$ is a strong electrolyte.

When a weak electrolyte such as acetic acid ionizes in solution, we write the reaction in the following manner:

$$HC_2H_3O_2(aq) \rightleftharpoons H^+(aq) + C_2H_3O_2^-(aq) \qquad [4.5]$$

The double arrow means that the reaction is significant in both directions. At any given moment, some $HC_2H_3O_2$ molecules are ionizing to form H^+ and $C_2H_3O_2^-$. At the same time, H^+ and $C_2H_3O_2^-$ ions are recombining to form $HC_2H_3O_2$. The balance between these opposing processes determines the relative concentrations of neutral molecules and ions. This balance, which produces a state of **chemical equilibrium,** varies from one weak electrolyte to another. Chemical equilibria are extremely important, and we will devote several later chapters to examining them.

Chemists use a double arrow to represent the ionization of weak electrolytes and a single arrow to represent the ionization of strong electrolytes. For example, because HCl is a strong electrolyte, we write the equation for the ionization of HCl as follows:

Common Misconception: The symbol for equilibrium ($\rightleftharpoons$) is not to be confused with the double-headed arrow ($\longleftrightarrow$). Students often incorrectly interchange these symbols.

$$HCl(aq) \longrightarrow H^+(aq) + Cl^-(aq) \qquad [4.6]$$

The single arrow indicates that the H^+ and Cl^- ions have no tendency to recombine in water to form HCl molecules.

4.3 Acids, Bases, and Salts

Acids, bases, and salts are among the most familiar compounds that we encounter (Figure 4.5). They are also the most common electrolytes.

Acids are substances that are able to ionize to form a hydrogen ion and thereby increase the concentration of H^+ (aq) ions in aqueous solutions. Because a hydrogen atom consists of a proton and an electron, H^+ is simply a proton. Thus, acids are often called proton donors. Examples of acids are HCl, HNO_3, and $HC_2H_3O_2$.

Molecules of different acids can ionize to form different numbers of H^+ ions. Both HCl and HNO_3 are examples of *monoprotic* acids, which yield one H^+ per molecule of acid. Sulfuric acid, H_2SO_4, is an example of a *diprotic* acid, one that yields two H^+ per molecule of acid. The ionization of H_2SO_4 and other diprotic acids occurs in two steps:

$$H_2SO_4(aq) \longrightarrow H^+(aq) + HSO_4^-(aq) \qquad [4.7]$$

$$HSO_4^-(aq) \rightleftharpoons H^+(aq) + SO_4^{2-}(aq) \qquad [4.8]$$

Although H_2SO_4 is a strong electrolyte, only the first ionization is complete. Thus, aqueous solutions of sulfuric acid contain a mixture of H^+ (aq), $HSO_4^-(aq)$, and $SO_4^{2-}(aq)$.

Bases

Bases are substances that can react with or accept H^+ ions. Hydroxide ions, OH^-, are basic because they readily react with H^+ ions to form water:

$$H^+(aq) + OH^-(aq) \longrightarrow H_2O(l) \qquad [4.9]$$

Thus, we can also define a base as any substance that increases the concentration of $OH^-(aq)$ when added to water. Ionic hydroxide compounds such as NaOH, KOH, and $Ca(OH)_2$ are among the most common bases. When dissolved in water, they dissociate into their separate ions, introducing OH^- ions into the solution. Compounds that do not contain OH^- ions can also be bases. For example, ammonia, NH_3, is a common base. When added to water, it

FIGURE 4.5 Some common acids (*left*), bases (*center*), and salts (*right*) that are household products. (Robert Mathena/Fundamental Photographs)

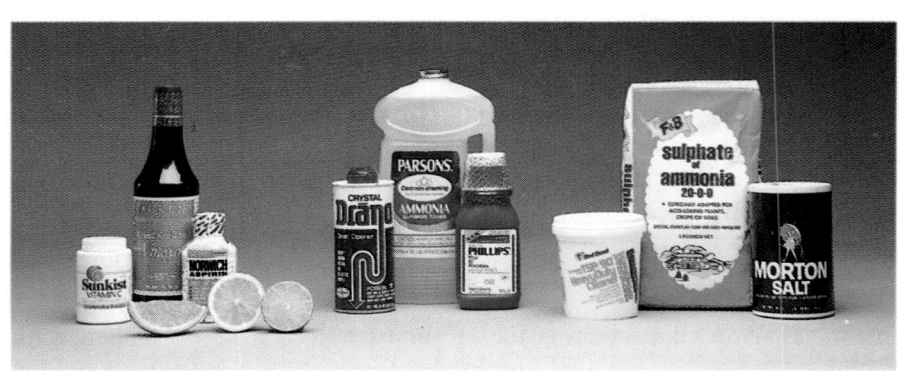

accepts an H^+ ion from the water molecule and thereby increases the concentration of OH^- ions in the water (Figure 4.6):

$$NH_3(aq) + H_2O(l) \rightleftharpoons NH_4^+(aq) + OH^-(aq) \qquad [4.10]$$

Because only a small fraction of the NH_3 (about 1 percent) forms NH_4^+ and OH^- ions, ammonia is a weak electrolyte.

Acids and bases that are strong electrolytes (completely ionized in solution) are referred to as **strong acids** and **strong bases.** Those that are weak electrolytes (partly ionized) are referred to as **weak acids** and **weak bases.** Strong acids are more reactive than weak acids when the reactivity depends only on the concentration of $H^+(aq)$. The reactivity of an acid, however, can depend on the anion as well as on $H^+(aq)$. For example, hydrofluoric acid, HF, is a weak acid; a 0.1 M solution of HF is only 8 percent ionized. However, HF is very reactive and vigorously attacks many substances, including glass. This reactivity is due to the combined action of $H^+(aq)$ and $F^-(aq)$.

Table 4.1 lists the common strong acids and bases. You should commit these to memory. We can make several observations about the acids and bases listed in this table. First, some of the most common and familiar acids, such as HCl, HNO_3, and H_2SO_4, are strong. Second, three of the strong acids result from combining a hydrogen atom and a halogen atom. (HF is a weak acid.) Third, the list of strong acids is very short. Most acids are weak. Fourth, the only common strong bases are the hydroxides of Li^+, Na^+, K^+, Rb^+, and Cs^+ (the alkali metals, group 1A) and the hydroxides of Ca^{2+}, Sr^{2+}, and Ba^{2+} (the heavy alkaline earths, group 2A). The most common weak base is NH_3.

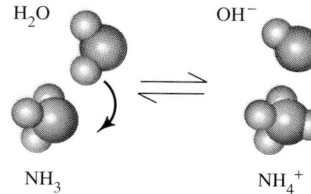

FIGURE 4.6 An H_2O molecule acts as a proton donor (acid) and NH_3 as a proton acceptor (base). Only a fraction of the NH_3 reacts with H_2O; NH_3 is a weak electrolyte.

Salts

Salts are ionic compounds that can be formed by replacing one or more of the hydrogen ions of an acid by a different positive ion. For example, replacing the H^+ ion of HCl with Na^+ gives the salt NaCl. Similarly, replacing two H^+ ions of H_2SO_4 with Ni^{2+} gives the salt $NiSO_4$. Almost all salts are strong electrolytes. The only exceptions are some salts of the heavy metals such as mercury and lead. For example, $HgCl_2$ and $Pb(C_2H_3O_2)_2$ are weak electrolytes.

Acids, bases, and salts are among the most important compounds in industry and in the chemical laboratory. Table 4.2 lists several acids, bases, and salts and the amount of each compound produced annually in the United States. You can see that these substances are produced in enormous quantities.

Teaching Note: Salts can be thought of as ionic compounds that are neither acids nor bases.

TABLE 4.1 △ Common Strong Acids and Bases

Strong acids	Strong bases
Chloric, $HClO_3$ Hydrobromic, HBr Hydrochloric, HCl Hydroiodic, HI Nitric, HNO_3 Perchloric, $HClO_4$ Sulfuric, H_2SO_4	Group 1A metal hydroxides (LiOH, NaOH, KOH, RbOH, CsOH) Heavy group 2A metal hydroxides [$Ca(OH)_2$, $Sr(OH)_2$, $Ba(OH)_2$]

TABLE 4.2 △ U.S. Production of Some Acids, Bases, and Salts in 1992

Compound	Formula	Annual production (kg)	Principal uses and end products
Acids			
Sulfuric	H_2SO_4	4.0×10^{10}	Fertilizers (70%), metallurgy (10%), petroleum (5%)
Phosphoric	H_3PO_4	1.1×10^{10}	Fertilizers (90%), detergents (5%)
Nitric	HNO_3	6.8×10^9	Fertilizers (80%), plastics (10%), explosives (5%)
Bases			
Ammonia	NH_3	1.6×10^{10}	Fertilizers (80%), plastics and fibers (10%)
Calcium hydroxide (lime)	$Ca(OH)_2$	1.5×10^{10}	Metallurgy (40%), water treatment (25%), chemicals (10%)
Sodium hydroxide (caustic soda)	$NaOH$	1.1×10^{10}	Chemicals (50%), pulp and paper (20%)
Salts			
Sodium carbonate (soda ash)	Na_2CO_3	9.3×10^9	Glass (50%), chemicals (25%)
Ammonium nitrate	NH_4NO_3	6.6×10^9	Fertilizers (90%)

Identifying Strong and Weak Electrolytes

Learning Goal 4: Predict whether a substance is a non-electrolyte, strong electrolyte, or weak electrolyte from its chemical formula.

Learning Goal 5: Predict the ions formed by electrolytes when they dissociate or ionize.

The following generalizations are useful in recognizing which substances are strong electrolytes and which are weak:

1. Most *salts* are strong electrolytes.
2. Most *acids* are weak electrolytes. However, HCl, HBr, HI, HNO_3, H_2SO_4, $HClO_3$, and $HClO_4$ are strong acids.
3. The common strong *bases* are the hydroxides of the alkali metals and the heavy alkaline earths. Ammonia, NH_3, is a weak electrolyte.
4. Most other substances are nonelectrolytes.

SAMPLE EXERCISE 4.5

Classify each of the folowing substances as a nonelectrolyte, weak electrolyte, or strong electrolyte: $CaCl_2$, HNO_3, CH_3OH (methanol), $HCHO_2$ (formic acid), KOH.

SOLUTION One approach is to identify those substances that are acids, bases, or salts. Salts are ionic compounds and as such tend to be compounds of metals with nonmetals. Only one of the substances, $CaCl_2$, is a salt. Like most salts, $CaCl_2$ is a strong electrolyte.

Two of the substances, HNO_3 and $HCHO_2$, are acids. We should recognize HNO_3 as nitric acid, a common strong acid (a strong electrolyte). The name of $HCHO_2$ given in the question identifies it as an acid. (Recall that the chemical formulas of acids are generally written with H listed first.) Because most acids are weak acids, our best guess would be that $HCHO_2$ is a weak acid (weak electrolyte). This is correct.

The bases that we have discussed so far are NH_3 and metal hydroxides. There is one base, KOH, in the list. It is one of the common strong bases (a strong electrolyte) because it is a hydroxide of an alkali metal.

The remaining compound, CH_3OH, is not an acid, base, or salt. Although CH_3OH has an OH group, it is not a *metal* hydroxide and thus not a base; CH_3OH is a nonelectrolyte.

PRACTICE EXERCISE

Predict which one of the following 0.1 *M* solutions in water will cause the light bulb in the apparatus in Figure 4.4 to glow most brightly: C_2H_5OH (ethanol), $HC_2H_3O_2$ (acetic acid), $NaC_2H_3O_2$ (sodium acetate). *Answer:* $NaC_2H_3O_2$

Neutralization Reactions

Solutions of acids and bases have very different properties. Acids have a sour taste, whereas bases have a bitter taste.* Acids can change the colors of certain dyes in a specific way that differs from the effect of a base (Figure 4.7). For example, the dye known as litmus is changed from blue to red by an acid, and from red to blue by a base. In addition, acidic and basic solutions differ in chemical properties in several important ways that we will explore in this chapter and in later chapters.

When a solution of an acid is mixed with a solution of a base, a **neutralization reaction** occurs. The products of the reaction have none of the characteristic properties of either acidic or basic solutions. For example, when 1 mol of hydrochloric acid is mixed with a solution containing 1 mol of sodium hydroxide, the products of the reaction are water and the salt sodium chloride:

$$\text{HCl}(aq) + \text{NaOH}(aq) \longrightarrow \text{H}_2\text{O}(l) + \text{NaCl}(aq) \qquad [4.11]$$
$$\text{(acid)} \qquad \text{(base)} \qquad \text{(water)} \qquad \text{(salt)}$$

In general, *a neutralization reaction between an acid and a metal hydroxide produces water and a salt.*

FIGURE 4.7 The acid-base indicator bromthymol blue is blue in basic solution and yellow in acidic solution. The left flask shows the indicator in the presence of a base, aqueous ammonia (here labeled as ammonium hydroxide). The right flask shows the indicator in the presence of hydrochloric acid, HCl. (Richard Megna/Fundamental Photographs)

Point of Emphasis: Neutralization reactions involve an acid reacting with a base to produce an aqueous solution of a salt and water, where water is the product of the reaction of the H^+ and OH^- ions.

SAMPLE EXERCISE 4.6

Write a balanced equation for the reaction of hydrobromic acid, HBr, with barium hydroxide, Ba(OH)_2, in aqueous solution.

SOLUTION The products of the acid-base reaction are a salt and water. The salt is that formed from the cation of the base, Ba(OH)_2, and the anion of the acid, HBr. The charge on the barium ion is $2+$ (see Table 2.4), and that on the bromide ion is $1-$. Therefore, to maintain electrical neutrality, the formula for the salt must be BaBr_2. The unbalanced equation for the neutralization reaction is therefore

$$\text{HBr}(aq) + \text{Ba(OH)}_2(aq) \longrightarrow \text{H}_2\text{O}(l) + \text{BaBr}_2(aq)$$

To balance the equation we must provide two molecules of HBr to furnish the two Br^- ions and to supply the two H^+ ions needed to combine with the two OH^- ions of the base. The balanced equation is thus

$$2\text{HBr}(aq) + \text{Ba(OH)}_2(aq) \longrightarrow 2\text{H}_2\text{O}(l) + \text{BaBr}_2(aq)$$

PRACTICE EXERCISE

Write a balanced equation for the reaction between phosphoric acid, H_3PO_4, and potassium hydroxide, KOH. *Answer:* $\text{H}_3\text{PO}_4 + 3\text{KOH} \longrightarrow 3\text{H}_2\text{O} + \text{K}_3\text{PO}_4$

4.4 Ionic Equations

In writing chemical equations for reactions in solution, it is often useful to indicate explicitly whether the dissolved substances are present *predominantly*

---

* Tasting chemical solutions is, of course, not a good practice. However, we have all had acids such as ascorbic acid (vitamin C), acetylsalicylic acid (aspirin), and citric acid (in citrus fruits) in our mouths, and we are familiar with their characteristic sour taste. It differs from the taste of soaps, which are mostly basic.

as ions or as molecules. Consider again the neutralization reaction between HCl and NaOH:

$$HCl(aq) + NaOH(aq) \longrightarrow H_2O(l) + NaCl(aq)$$

An equation written in this fashion, showing the complete chemical formulas of the reactants and products, is called a **molecular equation.** This term is a bit of a misnomer in this case, because HCl, NaOH, and NaCl are strong electrolytes. We can therefore write the chemical equation to indicate that they are completely ionized in solution:

$$H^+(aq) + Cl^-(aq) + Na^+(aq) + OH^-(aq) \longrightarrow$$
$$H_2O(l) + Na^+(aq) + Cl^-(aq) \quad [4.12]$$

An equation written in this form — with all soluble strong electrolytes shown as ions — is known as a *complete ionic equation.*

Notice that $Na^+(aq)$ and $Cl^-(aq)$ appear in identical forms on both sides of Equation 4.12. Ions that appear in identical forms among both the reactants and products of a complete ionic equation are called **spectator ions.** When spectator ions are omitted from the equation (they cancel out like algebraic quantities), we are left with the **net ionic equation.** In the present example, omitting the spectator ions $Na^+(aq)$ and $Cl^-(aq)$ gives

$$H^+(aq) + OH^-(aq) \longrightarrow H_2O(l) \quad [4.13]$$

The net ionic equation includes only those ions and molecules that are directly involved in the reaction. Because charge is conserved in reactions, the sum of the charges of the ions must be the same on both sides of a balanced net ionic equation.

Net ionic equations are widely used because they can illustrate the similarities between large numbers of reactions involving electrolytes. For example, Equation 4.13 expresses the essential feature of the neutralization reaction between *any* strong acid and *any* strong base: $H^+(aq)$ and $OH^-(aq)$ ions combine to form H_2O. Thus, a net ionic equation helps us appreciate that more than one set of reactants can lead to the same net reaction. The molecular equation, on the other hand, identifies the actual reactants that participate in a reaction.

In order to write an ionic equation, you need to ask yourself two questions. First, is the substance soluble? Second, if it is soluble, is it a strong electrolyte? Only if the answers to both these questions are yes should the substance be written in ionic form. Only soluble strong electrolytes are written in ionic form. Soluble weak electrolytes, soluble nonelectrolytes, and insoluble substances (whether solid, liquid, or gas) are written in "molecular" form. Finally, spectator ions are omitted from net ionic equations.

SAMPLE EXERCISE 4.7

Write the net ionic equation for neutralization of *two* of the acidic hydrogens of phosphoric acid by sodium hydroxide in aqueous solution.

SOLUTION   The chemical formula for phosphoric acid is H_3PO_4. The formula for sodium hydroxide is NaOH. Sodium hydrogen phosphate, Na_2HPO_4, is the salt formed when two H^+ ions from H_3PO_4 are replaced by two Na^+. The other product is

Learning Goal 6:   Identify the spectator ions and write the net ionic equations for solution reactions starting with their molecular equations.

Teaching Note: Writing the net ionic equation makes it easier for students to focus on the ions participating in a chemical reaction. It is important to remember that, although they do not appear in the net ionic equation, the spectator ions are still present in solution.

Common Misconception: Students commonly fail to see that the net ionic equation of an acid-base neutralization reaction between strong acids and strong bases is always the same; that is, $H^+(aq) + OH^-(aq) \longrightarrow H_2O(l)$.

H_2O. The unbalanced molecular equation for the reaction is

$$H_3PO_4(aq) + NaOH(aq) \longrightarrow H_2O(l) + Na_2HPO_4(aq)$$

Balancing this equation gives

$$H_3PO_4(aq) + 2NaOH(aq) \longrightarrow 2H_2O(l) + Na_2HPO_4(aq)$$

Because H_3PO_4 is not on the list of common strong acids, we would predict that it is a weak acid. This prediction is indeed correct. Both NaOH and Na_2HPO_4 are strong electrolytes; Na_2HPO_4 ionizes to form $2Na^+(aq)$ and $HPO_4^{2-}(aq)$ ions. Thus, the complete ionic equation for the reaction is

$$H_3PO_4(aq) + 2Na^+(aq) + 2OH^-(aq) \longrightarrow 2H_2O(l) + 2Na^+(aq) + HPO_4^{2-}(aq)$$

Elimination of the spectator ions, $2Na^+(aq)$, gives the net ionic equation:

$$H_3PO_4(aq) + 2OH^-(aq) \longrightarrow 2H_2O(l) + HPO_4^{2-}(aq)$$

In sum, the weak acid H_3PO_4 reacts with the basic hydroxide ion to form water and the aqueous hydrogen phosphate ion. Notice that each side of this balanced net ionic equation has a total charge of $2-$.

PRACTICE EXERCISE

Write the net ionic equation for the reaction between aqueous solutions of HF and $Ba(OH)_2$. **Answer:** $HF(aq) + OH^-(aq) \longrightarrow H_2O(l) + F^-(aq)$

4.5 Metathesis Reactions

In the molecular equations for many aqueous reactions, positive ions (cations) and negative ions (anions) appear to exchange partners. These reactions conform to the following general equation:

$$AX + BY \longrightarrow AY + BX \qquad [4.14]$$

Example: $AgNO_3(aq) + KCl(aq) \longrightarrow AgCl(s) + KNO_3(aq)$

Such reactions are known as **metathesis reactions** (meh-TATH-eh-sis, which is the Greek word for "to transpose"). Acid-base neutralization reactions involving ionic hydroxides are a type of metathesis reaction. The H^+ from the acid combines with the OH^- from the base to form H_2O; the anion of the acid and the cation of the base form the salt.

For a metathesis reaction to lead to a net change in a solution, ions must be removed from the solution. In general, three chemical processes can lead to the removal of ions from solution, thus serving as a *driving force* for metathesis to occur:

1. The formation of an insoluble solid (called a precipitate)
2. The formation of either a soluble weak electrolyte or a soluble nonelectrolyte
3. The formation of a gas that escapes from solution.

In the following sections, we further examine these types of metathesis reactions.

Learning Goal 7: Predict the products of metathesis reactions (including both neutralization and precipitation reactions), and write balanced chemical equations for them.

Learning Goal 8: Identify the driving force for any metathesis reaction.

Point of Emphasis: One of the following is needed to drive a metathesis reaction: the formation of a precipitate, the generation of a gas, the production of a weak electrolyte, or the production of a nonelectrolyte.

L. R. Summerlin, Christie L. Borgford, and Julie B. Ealy, "Name That Precipitate," *Chemical Demonstrations, A Sourcebook for Teachers, Volume 2* (Washington: American Chemical Society, 1987), pp. 121–23.

Learning Goal 9: Use solubility rules to predict whether a precipitate will form when electrolytic solutions are mixed.

Precipitation Reactions

Metathesis reactions that result in the formation of an insoluble solid are known as **precipitation reactions.** A **precipitate** is an insoluble solid formed by a reaction in solution. As an example, consider the reaction between a solution of potassium iodide, KI, and a solution of lead nitrate, $Pb(NO_3)_2$. When the two solutions are mixed, a yellow precipitate forms, as shown in Figure 4.8. This precipitate is lead iodide, PbI_2, a salt that has a very low solubility in water.

The **solubility** of a substance is the amount of that substance that can be dissolved in a given quantity of solvent. Only 1.2×10^{-3} mol of PbI_2 dissolves in a liter of water at $25\,°C$. In our discussions, any substance whose solubility is less than 0.01 mol/L will be referred to as *insoluble.*

Solubility Rules

Can we predict whether a precipitate will form when solutions are mixed? In order to do so, we must have some knowledge of the solubilities of different compounds. Unfortunately, there are no rules based on simple physical properties such as ionic charge to guide us. Experimental observations, however, have led to a set of empirical solubility rules for ionic compounds. For example, experiments demonstrate that all ionic compounds that contain the nitrate anion, NO_3^-, are soluble in water. Table 4.3 presents a summary of solubility rules for ionic compounds based on the anion in the compound. If you look closely, you will also see an important generalization based on the cation of the compound: *All common ionic compounds of the alkali metal ion (group 1A) and of the ammonium ion, NH_4^+, are soluble in water.*

We can use Table 4.3 to predict whether a precipitate forms when two solutions are mixed. For example, $Mg(NO_3)_2$ and NaOH are both water-soluble according to the rules presented in Table 4.3. If a solution of $Mg(NO_3)_2$ is mixed with a solution of NaOH, the possible metathesis products are $Mg(OH)_2$ and $NaNO_3$:

$$Mg(NO_3)_2(aq) + 2NaOH(aq) \longrightarrow Mg(OH)_2 + 2NaNO_3 \qquad [4.15]$$

FIGURE 4.8   The addition of a colorless solution of potassium iodide, KI, to a colorless solution of lead nitrate, $Pb(NO_3)_2$, produces a yellow precipitate of lead iodide, PbI_2. (Lawrence Migdale/Photo Researchers)

TABLE 4.3 △ Solubility Rules for Common Ionic Compounds in Water

	Mainly water soluble
NO_3^-	All nitrates are soluble.
$C_2H_3O_2^-$	All acetates are soluble.
Cl^-	All chlorides are soluble except $AgCl$, Hg_2Cl_2, and $PbCl_2$.
Br^-	All bromides are soluble except $AgBr$, Hg_2Br_2, $PbBr_2$, and $HgBr_2$.
I^-	All iodides are soluble except AgI, Hg_2I_2, PbI_2, and HgI_2.
SO_4^{2-}	All sulfates are soluble except $CaSO_4$, $SrSO_4$, $BaSO_4$, $PbSO_4$, Hg_2SO_4, and Ag_2SO_4.

	Mainly water insoluble
S^{2-}	All sulfides are insoluble except those of the 1A and 2A elements and $(NH_4)_2S$.
CO_3^{2-}	All carbonates are insoluble except those of the 1A elements and $(NH_4)_2CO_3$.
PO_4^{3-}	All phosphates are insoluble except those of the 1A elements and $(NH_4)_3PO_4$.
OH^-	All hydroxides are insoluble except those of the 1A elements, $Ba(OH)_2$, $Sr(OH)_2$, and $Ca(OH)_2$.

From Table 4.3 we see that $Mg(OH)_2$ is insoluble and thus will form a precipitate. The other product, $NaNO_3$, is soluble; the Na^+ and NO_3^- ions will remain in solution as spectator ions:

$$Mg(NO_3)_2(aq) + 2NaOH(aq) \longrightarrow Mg(OH)_2(s) + 2NaNO_3(aq) \quad [4.16]$$

The precipitation of $Mg(OH)_2$ is the first step in the reactions used to extract magnesium metal from seawater.

SAMPLE EXERCISE 4.8

Write balanced molecular, ionic, and net ionic equations for the precipitation reactions (if any) that occur when solutions of the following compounds are mixed: (a) $BaCl_2$ and Na_2SO_4; (b) KCl and Na_2SO_4.

SOLUTION (a) Both $BaCl_2$ and Na_2SO_4 are soluble and ionize to give Ba^{2+}, Cl^-, Na^+, and SO_4^{2-} ions. The possible precipitation products are $BaSO_4$ and $NaCl$. The $BaSO_4$ is insoluble according to the rule given in Table 4.3 for SO_4^{2-} compounds. Therefore, the molecular equation is

$$BaCl_2(aq) + Na_2SO_4(aq) \longrightarrow BaSO_4(s) + 2NaCl(aq)$$

Recall that in writing ionic equations, the formulas of soluble electrolytes are written in ionic form. Thus, the ionic equation is

$$Ba^{2+}(aq) + 2Cl^-(aq) + 2Na^+(aq) + SO_4^{2-}(aq) \longrightarrow$$
$$BaSO_4(s) + 2Na^+(aq) + 2Cl^-(aq)$$

Both $Na^+(aq)$ and $Cl^-(aq)$ are spectator ions. The net ionic equation is

$$Ba^{2+}(aq) + SO_4^{2-}(aq) \longrightarrow BaSO_4(s)$$

(b) Both reactants are soluble and ionize in solution. There are no possible insoluble salts resulting from reaction. Both $NaCl$ and K_2SO_4 are soluble. Therefore, there is no reaction; the solutes merely mix in the solution.

Reactions in Which a Weak Electrolyte or Nonelectrolyte Forms

Point of Emphasis: Water is a nonelectrolyte.

We have seen that metathesis reactions occur when ions are removed from solution as solid precipitates. Ions can also interact to form a weak electrolyte or nonelectrolyte that remains dissolved in the solution. Acid-base neutralization reactions, in which H^+ and OH^- ions react to form water, are the most common reactions of this type. Even water-insoluble hydroxides react with acids. For example, $Mg(OH)_2(s)$, which is sold as a milky-white suspension called milk of magnesia, dissolves when it reacts with $HCl(aq)$:

$$Mg(OH)_2(s) + 2HCl(aq) \longrightarrow MgCl_2(aq) + 2H_2O(l) \qquad [4.17]$$

This reaction is illustrated in Figure 4.9.

Insoluble metal oxides also react with acids because the oxide ion can combine with two H^+ ions to give water. For instance, $NiO(s)$ reacts with HNO_3 (Figure 4.10):

Molecular equation:

$$NiO(s) + 2HNO_3(aq) \longrightarrow Ni(NO_3)_2(aq) + H_2O(l) \qquad [4.18]$$

Net ionic equation:

$$NiO(s) + 2H^+(aq) \longrightarrow Ni^{2+}(aq) + 2H_2O(l) \qquad [4.19]$$

Metals are often washed with acid before electroplating in order to remove any oxide coating that might be on the surface of the metal.

FIGURE 4.9 (a) Milk of magnesia is a suspension of magnesium hydroxide, $Mg(OH)_2(s)$, in water. (b) The magnesium hydroxide dissolves upon the addition of hydrochloric acid, $HCl(aq)$. (c) The final clear solution contains soluble $MgCl_2(aq)$, shown in Equation 4.17. (Richard Megna/Fundamental Photographs)

(a)

(b)

(c)

(*a*)   (*b*)

FIGURE 4.10   (*a*) Nickel oxide (NiO), nitric acid (HNO₃), and water. (*b*) The NiO is insoluble in water but reacts with HNO₃ to give a green solution of Ni(NO₃)₂. (Richard Megna/Fundamental Photographs)

A net reaction will also occur when ions are removed from solution by the formation of a weak electrolyte such as a weak acid. For example, reaction of HCl with $NaC_2H_3O_2$ results in the formation of acetic acid, $HC_2H_3O_2$, a weak acid:

Molecular equation:

$$HCl(aq) + NaC_2H_3O_2(aq) \longrightarrow HC_2H_3O_2(aq) + NaCl(aq) \quad [4.20]$$

Net ionic equation:

$$H^+(aq) + C_2H_3O_2^-(aq) \longrightarrow HC_2H_3O_2(aq) \quad [4.21]$$

Reactions in Which a Gas Forms

Sometimes the product of a metathesis reaction is a gas that has a low solubility in water. For example, hydrogen sulfide, H_2S, the substance that gives rotten eggs their foul odor, forms when a strong acid such as HCl(*aq*) reacts with a metal sulfide such as Na_2S:

Molecular equation:

$$2HCl(aq) + Na_2S(aq) \longrightarrow H_2S(g) + 2NaCl(aq) \quad [4.22]$$

Net ionic equation:

$$2H^+(aq) + S^{2-}(aq) \longrightarrow H_2S(g) \quad [4.23]$$

Carbonates and sulfites also react with acids to form gases. In these cases, metathesis reactions form carbonic acid, H_2CO_3, and sulfurous acid, H_2SO_3, respectively. These acids, however, are too unstable to be isolated as pure

CHEMISTRY AT WORK

Antacids

The stomach secretes acids to help digest foods. These acids, which include hydrochloric acid, are about $0.1\ M$ in H^+. The stomach and digestive tract are normally protected from the corrosive effects of stomach acid by a mucosal lining. Holes can develop in this lining, however, that allow the acid to attack the underlying tissue and cause painful damage. These holes, which are known as *ulcers*, can be caused by the secretion of excess acid or by a weakness in the digestive lining. Between 10 and 20 percent of Americans suffer from ulcers at some point in their lives, and many others experience occasional indigestion or heartburn due to high levels of digestive acids.

As chemists, we can address the problem of excess stomach acid in two simple ways: (1) removing the excess acid, or (2) decreasing the production of acid. *Antacids* are simple bases that neutralize the digestive acids. Most antacids are sold as common, over-the-counter drugs (Figure 4.11). Their ability to neutralize acids is due to the hydroxide, carbonate, or bicarbonate ions they contain. Table 4.4 lists the active ingredients in some popular antacids.

There is no ideal formulation for antacids. Preparations containing $Al(OH)_3$ tend to cause constipation, whereas those containing $Mg(OH)_2$ act as laxatives. (This is one reason for formulations that contain both

TABLE 4.4 △ Some Common Antacids

Commercial name	Acid-neutralizing agents
Alka-Seltzer	$NaHCO_3$
Amphojel	$Al(OH)_3$
Di-Gel	$Mg(OH)_2$ and $CaCO_3$
Milk of magnesia	$Mg(OH)_2$
Maalox	$Mg(OH)_2$ and $Al(OH)_3$
Mylanta	$Mg(OH)_2$ and $Al(OH)_3$
Rolaids	$NaAl(OH)_2CO_3$
Tums	$CaCO_3$

ingredients.) Antacids containing calcium ions have been advertised as calcium supplements useful in combating osteoporosis (see the Chemistry at Work box in Section 7.6). Calcium, however, stimulates acid production after it is absorbed, a phenomenon known as acid rebound. Thus, calcium-containing antacids are somewhat out of favor with physicians.

The newer generation of antiulcer drugs, such as Tagamet, Zantac, and Prilosec, use the second approach described above. These pharmaceuticals inhibit the production of gastric acids by acting on acid-producing cells in the lining of the stomach.

FIGURE 4.11 Some common antacids. (Coco McCoy/Rainbow)

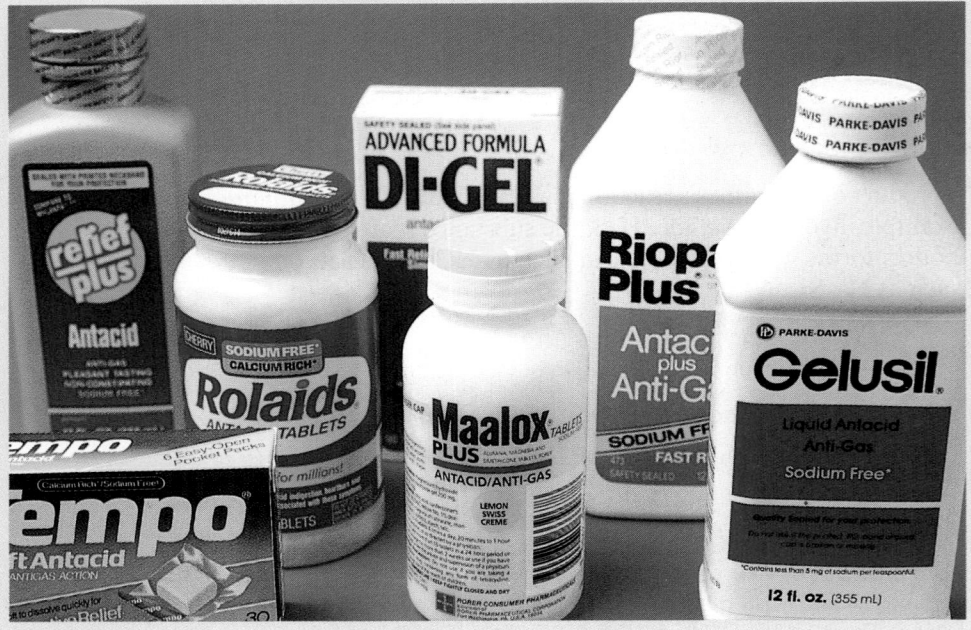

compounds; if present in solution in sufficient concentrations, they decompose:

$$H_2CO_3(aq) \longrightarrow H_2O(l) + CO_2(g) \qquad [4.24]$$

$$H_2SO_3(aq) \longrightarrow H_2O(l) + SO_2(g) \qquad [4.25]$$

For example, when hydrochloric acid is added to sodium bicarbonate, the following metathesis occurs:

$$HCl(aq) + NaHCO_3(aq) \longrightarrow NaCl(aq) + H_2CO_3(aq) \qquad [4.26]$$

The resultant H_2CO_3 decomposes readily into H_2O and CO_2, causing bubbles to form, as shown in Figure 4.12. The overall reaction is

Molecular equation:

$$HCl(aq) + NaHCO_3(aq) \longrightarrow NaCl(aq) + H_2O(l) + CO_2(g) \qquad [4.27]$$

Net ionic equation:

$$H^+(aq) + HCO_3^-(aq) \longrightarrow H_2O(l) + CO_2(g) \qquad [4.28]$$

Both $NaHCO_3$ and Na_2CO_3 are used as acid neutralizers in acid spills. The bicarbonate or carbonate salt is added until the fizzing due to the formation of $CO_2(g)$ stops. Sometimes sodium bicarbonate is used as an antacid to soothe an upset stomach. In that case, the HCO_3^- reacts with stomach acid to form $CO_2(g)$. The fizz of Alka-Seltzer tablets is due to the reaction of sodium bicarbonate and citric acid in the tablets.

FIGURE 4.12 Carbonates react with acids to form carbon dioxide gas. Here $NaHCO_3$ (white solid) reacts with hydrochloric acid; the bubbles contain CO_2. (Richard Megna/ Fundamental Photographs)

L. R. Summerlin, Christie L. Borgford, and Julie B. Ealy, "A Hand-Held Reaction: Production of Ammonia Gas," *Chemical Demonstrations, A Sourcebook for Teachers, Volume 2* (Washington: American Chemical Society, 1987), p. 38.

SAMPLE EXERCISE 4.9

Write balanced complete ionic and net ionic equations for any reactions that occur when the following compounds are mixed: **(a)** $Cr(C_2H_3O_2)_2(aq)$ and $HNO_3(aq)$; **(b)** $FeCO_3(s)$ and $HCl(aq)$; **(c)** $PbS(s)$ and $H_2SO_4(aq)$.

SOLUTION In each case, we examine the possible products of metathesis to determine whether a net reaction should occur.

(a) The molecular equation for this reaction is similar to Equation 4.20. Both reactants are soluble strong electrolytes that are therefore written in ionic form: $Cr^{2+}(aq)$, $C_2H_3O_2^-(aq)$, $H^+(aq)$, and $NO_3^-(aq)$. We can see that acetic acid, $HC_2H_3O_2$, a soluble weak electrolyte, can be formed by metathesis. The other metathesis product, $Cr(NO_3)_2$, should be soluble, according to the rules in Table 4.3. Because it is a soluble strong electrolyte, it is written in ionic form as $Cr^{2+}(aq)$ and $NO_3^-(aq)$.

Complete ionic:

$$Cr^{2+}(aq) + 2C_2H_3O_2^-(aq) + 2H^+(aq) + 2NO_3^-(aq) \longrightarrow$$
$$Cr^{2+}(aq) + 2HC_2H_3O_2(aq) + 2NO_3^-(aq)$$

Net ionic:

$$2C_2H_3O_2^-(aq) + 2H^+(aq) \longrightarrow 2HC_2H_3O_2(aq)$$

We can simplify the net ionic equation by dividing all the coefficients by 2:

$$C_2H_3O_2^-(aq) + H^+(aq) \longrightarrow HC_2H_3O_2(aq)$$

(b) This reaction is similar to Equation 4.27, but the reactant carbonate is an insoluble solid. Insoluble carbonates react with acids in much the same way as soluble ones do, liberating $CO_2(g)$.

Complete ionic:

$$FeCO_3(s) + 2H^+(aq) + 2Cl^-(aq) \longrightarrow Fe^{2+}(aq) + 2Cl^-(aq) + H_2O(l) + CO_2(g)$$

Net ionic:

$$FeCO_3(s) + 2H^+(aq) \longrightarrow Fe^{2+}(aq) + H_2O(l) + CO_2(g)$$

(c) This reaction resembles Equation 4.22. Most ionic sulfides will react with acids even though they are insoluble. From Table 4.3, we see that $PbSO_4$ is insoluble. Remember also that H_2SO_4 in aqueous solution ionizes primarily into H^+ and HSO_4^- ions.

Complete ionic:

$$PbS(s) + H^+(aq) + HSO_4^-(aq) \longrightarrow PbSO_4(s) + H_2S(g)$$

The net ionic equation is identical to the complete ionic equation; there are no spectator ions.

PRACTICE EXERCISE

Write the net ionic equations for the following reactions: **(a)** Solid sodium hypochlorite reacts with aqueous hydrochloric acid; **(b)** solid silver sulfite reacts with aqueous hydrobromic acid.   *Answers:* **(a)** $NaOCl(s) + H^+(aq) \longrightarrow Na^+(aq) + HOCl(aq)$; **(b)** $Ag_2SO_3(s) + 2H^+(aq) + 2Br^-(aq) \longrightarrow 2AgBr(s) + SO_2(g) + H_2O(l)$

4.6 Reactions of Metals

FIGURE 4.13 Corrosion at the terminals of a battery caused by attack of the metal by sulfuric acid from the battery. (Dr. E. R. Degginger)

Have you ever noticed corrosion at the terminals of an automobile battery? What we term *corrosion* is the conversion of a metal into a metal compound by a reaction between the metal and some substance in its environment. The most common corrosion reactions involve oxygen, water, acids, or salts as reactants. The corrosion shown in Figure 4.13 results from the reaction of battery acid, H_2SO_4, with the metal clamp.

Oxidation and Reduction

When a metal undergoes corrosion, it loses electrons and forms cations. For example, calcium is vigorously attacked by acids to form calcium, Ca^{2+}, ions:

$$Ca(s) + 2H^+(aq) \longrightarrow Ca^{2+}(aq) + H_2(g) \qquad [4.29]$$

When an atom, ion, or molecule has become more positively charged (that is, when it has lost electrons), we say that it has been *oxidized*. Loss of electrons by a substance is called **oxidation**. Thus, Ca, which has no net charge, is oxidized (undergoes oxidation) in Equation 4.29, forming Ca^{2+}.

The term *oxidation* is used because the first reactions of this sort to be studied thoroughly were reactions with oxygen. Many metals react directly with O_2 in air to form metal oxides. In these reactions, the metal loses electrons to

FIGURE 4.14 Calcium metal oxidizes readily in air. The surface of the metal on the left is already dull due to the formation of oxide. The sample on the right is appreciably oxidized. (Richard Megna / Fundamental Photographs)

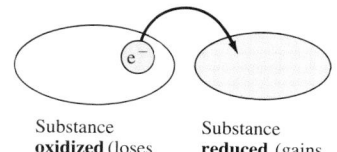

Substance **oxidized** (loses electron)   Substance **reduced** (gains electron)

FIGURE 4.15 Oxidation is the loss of electrons by a substance; reduction is the gain of electrons by a substance. Oxidation of one substance is always accompanied by reduction of another.

oxygen, forming an ionic compound of the metal ion and oxide ion. For example, when calcium metal is exposed to air, the bright metallic surface of the metal tarnishes as CaO forms (Figure 4.14):

$$2Ca(s) + O_2(g) \longrightarrow 2CaO(s) \qquad [4.30]$$

The analogous reaction of iron with oxygen in the presence of water is responsible for the formation of rust, an oxide of iron.

As Ca is oxidized in Equation 4.30, oxygen is transformed from neutral O_2 to the O^{2-} ion. When an atom, ion, or molecule has become more negatively charged (gained electrons), we say that it is *reduced;* the gain of electrons by a substance is called **reduction.** When one reactant loses electrons, another reactant must gain them; the oxidation of one substance is always accompanied by the reduction of another as electrons are transferred between them, as shown in Figure 4.15. We will examine oxidation and reduction more closely in Chapter 20.

Point of Emphasis: Oxidation is the loss of electrons by a substance.

Point of Emphasis: Reduction is the gain of electrons by a substance.

FIGURE 4.16 Many metals, such as the iron in the nail shown here, react with acids such as sulfuric acid to form hydrogen gas. The bubbles are due to the hydrogen gas. (Dr. E. R. Degginger)

Oxidation of Metals by Acids and Salts

Many metals react with acids to form salts and hydrogen gas. For example, magnesium metal reacts with hydrochloric acid to form magnesium chloride and hydrogen gas:

$$\text{Metal} + \text{acid} \longrightarrow \text{salt} + \text{hydrogen}$$
$$Mg(s) + 2HCl(aq) \longrightarrow MgCl_2(aq) + H_2(g) \qquad [4.31]$$

Similarly, iron reacts with sulfuric acid (see Figure 4.16):

$$Fe(s) + H_2SO_4(aq) \longrightarrow FeSO_4(aq) + H_2(g) \qquad [4.32]$$

In each instance, the metal is oxidized by the acid to form the metal cation; the H^+ ion of the acid is reduced to form H_2.

The oxidation of iron by acids occurs when acidic foods are cooked in cast-iron cookware, providing a useful dietary source of iron. Half a cup of spaghetti sauce contains only 3 mg of iron. However, spaghetti sauce simmered several hours in an iron pot increases in iron content to at least 50 mg.

SAMPLE EXERCISE 4.10

Write the balanced molecular and net ionic equations for the reaction of aluminum with hydrobromic acid.

SOLUTION We recall from Section 2.6 that aluminum tends to form Al^{3+} ions. We therefore expect that the reaction of $Al(s)$ with $HBr(aq)$ will form $H_2(g)$ and the salt of Al^{3+} and Br^-:

$$2Al(s) + 6HBr(aq) \longrightarrow 2AlBr_3(aq) + 3H_2(g)$$

Both HBr and $AlBr_3$ are strong electrolytes. When the complete ionic equation is written, we see that Br^- is a spectator ion:

$$2Al(s) + 6H^+(aq) + 6Br^-(aq) \longrightarrow 2Al^{3+}(aq) + 6Br^-(aq) + 3H_2(g)$$

Thus, the net ionic equation is

$$2Al(s) + 6H^+(aq) \longrightarrow 2Al^{3+}(aq) + 3H_2(g)$$

PRACTICE EXERCISE

Write the balanced molecular and net ionic equation for the reaction between sulfuric acid and lead.
Answer: $Pb(s) + H_2SO_4(aq) \longrightarrow PbSO_4(s) + H_2(g)$
$Pb(s) + H^+(aq) + HSO_4^-(aq) \longrightarrow PbSO_4(s) + H_2(g)$

When a metal is oxidized by acid, the H^+ ions are reduced to H_2. Metals can also be oxidized by aqueous solutions of various salts. For example, iron metal is oxidized to Fe^{2+} by aqueous solutions of Ni^{2+}, such as $Ni(NO_3)_2(aq)$:

Molecular equation:

$$Fe(s) + Ni(NO_3)_2(aq) \longrightarrow Fe(NO_3)_2(aq) + Ni(s) \qquad [4.33]$$

Net ionic equation:

$$Fe(s) + Ni^{2+}(aq) \longrightarrow Fe^{2+}(aq) + Ni(s) \qquad [4.34]$$

Point of Emphasis: When one substance is oxidized, another substance must be reduced.

Notice that the oxidation of iron in the above equations is accompanied by the reduction of Ni^{2+} to Ni. Remember: *Whenever one substance is oxidized, some other substance must be reduced.*

The Activity Series

Learning Goal 10: Use the activity series to predict whether a reaction will occur when a metal is added to an aqueous solution of either a metal salt or an acid; write the balanced molecular and net ionic equations for the reaction.

Why does a reaction such as Equation 4.33 occur? Can we predict whether a certain metal will be oxidized by acids or by salts of other metals? These questions are of practical import as well as chemical interest. For example, Equation 4.33 tells us that it would be unwise to store a solution of nickel nitrate in an iron container, for the solution would dissolve the container. When a metal is oxidized, it appears to be eaten away as it reacts to form various compounds. Extensive oxidation can lead to the failure of metal machinery parts or the deterioration of metal structures.

Different metals vary in the ease with which they are oxidized. For example, zinc metal is oxidized by aqueous solutions of copper(II), but silver metal is not. We conclude that zinc loses electrons more readily than does silver; that is, zinc is easier to oxidize than silver.

A list of metals arranged in order of decreasing ease of oxidation is called an **activity series.** Table 4.5 gives the activity series for many of the most common metals. Hydrogen is also included in the table. The metals at the top of the table are most easily oxidized; that is, they react most readily to form compounds. Notice that the alkali metals and alkaline earth metals are at the top. They are called the *active metals.* The metals at the bottom of the activity series are very stable and form compounds less readily. Notice also that the transition elements from groups 8B and 1B are at the bottom of the list. These metals, which are used in making coins and jewelry, are called noble metals because of their low reactivity.

The activity series can be used to predict the outcome of reactions between metals and either metal salts or acids. *Any metal on the list can be oxidized by the ions of elements below it.* For example, copper is above silver in the series. Thus, copper metal will be oxidized by silver ions, as pictured in Figure 4.17.

$$Cu(s) + 2Ag^+(aq) \longrightarrow Cu^{2+}(aq) + 2Ag(s) \qquad [4.35]$$

Once again we note that the oxidation of copper is accompanied by a reduction reaction, namely, the reduction of silver ions to silver metal.

Copper is below iron in the activity series. Therefore, we expect that iron(II) ions cannot oxidize copper metal. Indeed, no reaction occurs when copper metal is added to a solution of iron(II) sulfate.

FIGURE 4.17 The reaction between copper metal and a solution of silver nitrate. The product, silver metal, is evident on the surface of the copper wires. The other product, copper(II) nitrate, produces the blue color in the solution. (Fundamental Photographs)

Point of Emphasis: Elements that lie near the top of the list in Table 4.5 are referred to as *active metals.*

TABLE 4.5 △ **Activity Series of Metals**

Metal	Oxidation reaction			
Lithium	Li	$\longrightarrow$	Li^+	$+ \; e^-$
Potassium	K	$\longrightarrow$	K^+	$+ \; e^-$
Barium	Ba	$\longrightarrow$	Ba^{2+}	$+ \; 2e^-$
Calcium	Ca	$\longrightarrow$	Ca^{2+}	$+ \; 2e^-$
Sodium	Na	$\longrightarrow$	Na^+	$+ \; e^-$
Magnesium	Mg	$\longrightarrow$	Mg^{2+}	$+ \; 2e^-$
Aluminum	Al	$\longrightarrow$	Al^{3+}	$+ \; 3e^-$
Manganese	Mn	$\longrightarrow$	Mn^{2+}	$+ \; 2e^-$
Zinc	Zn	$\longrightarrow$	Zn^{2+}	$+ \; 2e^-$
Chromium	Cr	$\longrightarrow$	Cr^{3+}	$+ \; 3e^-$
Iron	Fe	$\longrightarrow$	Fe^{2+}	$+ \; 2e^-$
Cobalt	Co	$\longrightarrow$	Co^{2+}	$+ \; 2e^-$
Nickel	Ni	$\longrightarrow$	Ni^{2+}	$+ \; 2e^-$
Tin	Sn	$\longrightarrow$	Sn^{2+}	$+ \; 2e^-$
Lead	Pb	$\longrightarrow$	Pb^{2+}	$+ \; 2e^-$
Hydrogen	H_2	$\longrightarrow$	$2H^+$	$+ \; 2e^-$
Copper	Cu	$\longrightarrow$	Cu^{2+}	$+ \; 2e^-$
Silver	Ag	$\longrightarrow$	Ag^+	$+ \; e^-$
Mercury	Hg	$\longrightarrow$	Hg^{2+}	$+ \; 2e^-$
Platinum	Pt	$\longrightarrow$	Pt^{2+}	$+ \; 2e^-$
Gold	Au	$\longrightarrow$	Au^{3+}	$+ \; 3e^-$

Ease of oxidation decreases

Table 4.5

SAMPLE EXERCISE 4.11

Will an aqueous solution of iron(II) chloride oxidize magnesium metal? If so, write the balanced molecular and net ionic equations for the reaction.

SOLUTION We see in Table 4.5 that Mg is above Fe in the activity series, which indicates that a reaction will occur. To write the equations, we must remember the charges of common ions. Magnesium is always present in compounds as the Mg^{2+} ion; the chloride ion is Cl^-. Thus, the compound formed is $MgCl_2$. The balanced molecular equation is

$$Mg(s) + FeCl_2(aq) \longrightarrow MgCl_2(aq) + Fe(s)$$

Both $FeCl_2$ and $MgCl_2$ are soluble salts (see Table 4.3). Thus, they are strong electrolytes and can be written in ionic form. When we do this, we find that Cl^- is a spectator ion. The net ionic equation is

$$Mg(s) + Fe^{2+}(aq) \longrightarrow Mg^{2+} + Fe(s)$$

As the net ionic equation clearly shows, Mg is oxidized and Fe^{2+} is reduced in this reaction.

PRACTICE EXERCISE

Which of the following metals will be oxidized by $Pb(NO_3)_2$: Zn, Cu, Fe?
Answer: Zn and Fe

Only those metals above hydrogen in the activity series are able to react with acids to form H_2. For example, Ni reacts with $HCl(aq)$ to form H_2:

$$Ni(s) + 2HCl(aq) \longrightarrow NiCl_2(aq) + H_2(g) \qquad [4.36]$$

Because elements below hydrogen in the activity series are not oxidized by H^+, Cu does not react with $HCl(aq)$. Interestingly, copper *does* react with nitric acid, as shown earlier in Figure 1.4. However, this reaction is not a simple oxidation of copper by the H^+ ions of the acid. Instead, the metal is oxidized to Cu(II) by the nitrate ion of the acid, accompanied by the formation of brown nitrogen dioxide, $NO_2(g)$:

$$Cu(s) + 4HNO_3(aq) \longrightarrow Cu(NO_3)_2(aq) + 2H_2O(l) + 2NO_2(g) \qquad [4.37]$$

You might wonder what substance is being reduced as copper is oxidized in Equation 4.37. In this case, the NO_2 results from the reduction of NO_3^-. We shall examine reactions of this type in more detail in Chapter 20.

4.7 Solution Stoichiometry

In Chapter 3, we examined the procedures for calculating the quantities of reactants and products involved in a chemical reaction. Recall that the coefficients in a balanced equation give the relative number of moles of reactants and products. ∞ (Sec. 3.6) To use this information, we have to convert the amounts of substances involved in a reaction into moles. When we are dealing with grams of a substance, as we were in Chapter 3, we use the molar mass to

A CLOSER LOOK

The Aura of Gold

Among the metals, gold occupies a unique place in the record of humankind. Gold has been known since the earliest records of human existence (Figure 4.18). Throughout history, people have cherished gold, have fought for it, and have died for it.

The physical and chemical properties of gold have served to make it a special metal. First, its intrinsic beauty and rarity have made it precious. Second, gold is soft and can be easily formed into artistic objects, jewelry, and coins; we shall discuss these properties at greater length in Chapter 7. Third, gold is one of the least active metals (Table 4.5). It is not oxidized in air and does not react with water. It is unreactive toward basic solutions and nearly all acidic solutions. As a result, gold can be found in nature as a pure element rather than combined with oxygen or other elements, which accounts for its early discovery.

Many of the early studies of the reactions of gold arose from the practice of alchemy, in which people attempted to turn cheap metals, such as lead, into gold. Alchemists discovered that gold can be dissolved in a 3:1 mixture of concentrated hydrochloric and nitric acids, known as *aqua regia* (royal water). The action of nitric acid on gold is similar to that on copper (Equation 4.37) in that the nitrate ion, rather than H^+, oxidizes the metal to Au^{3+}. The Cl^- ions interact with the gold cation to form highly stable $AuCl_4^-$ ions. The net ionic equation for the reaction of gold with aqua regia is

$$Au(s) + NO_3^-(aq) + 4H^+(aq) + 4Cl^-(aq) \longrightarrow$$
$$AuCl_4^-(aq) + 2H_2O(l) + NO(g)$$

Notice that, as was the case for dissolving copper in nitric acid, a nitrogen-containing gas is produced, in this case colorless nitric oxide, $NO(g)$. In Chapter 24, we shall see that gold can also be dissolved in aqueous solutions of CN^- in the presence of O_2.

Besides its value for jewelry and currency, gold is also important in the health professions. Because of its resistance to corrosion by acids and other substances found in saliva, gold is an ideal metal for use in dental fillings. The pure metal is too soft to use for fillings, so it is combined with other metals to form *alloys,* which we shall discuss in Chapter 24. Gold compounds also have useful therapeutic applications. For example, salts of Au^+ may be used in the treatment of certain types of rheumatoid arthritis (Figure 4.19).

FIGURE 4.18   An ornate gold artifact from the tomb of the Egyptian King Tutankhamen. This object was fashioned in about 1350 B.C. (Archaeological Museum, Cairo, Egypt. © Photograph by Erich Lessing/Art Resource, New York)

FIGURE 4.19   Myochrysine® is an example of a gold salt used to treat certain types of arthritis. (Merck & Co., Inc.)

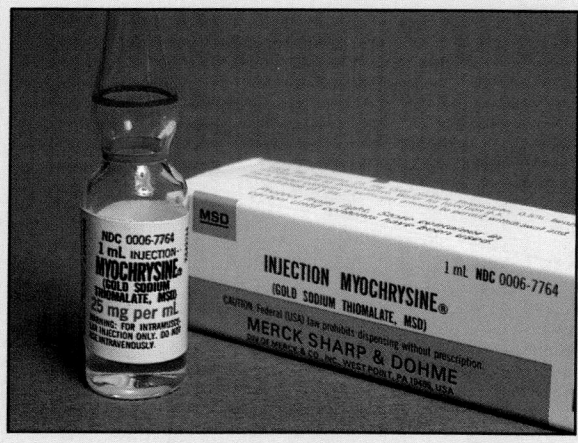

achieve this conversion. When we are working with solutions of known molarity, however, we use the molarity and volume to determine the number of moles. As we saw in Section 4.1, moles solute $= M \times L$. This approach is illustrated in the following sample exercise and is summarized in Figure 4.20.

SAMPLE EXERCISE 4.12

How many moles of H_2O form when 25.0 mL of 0.100 M HNO_3 solution is completely neutralized by NaOH?

SOLUTION   The product of the molar concentration of a solution and its volume in liters gives the number of moles of solute (Section 4.1):

$$\text{Moles } HNO_3 = M \times L = \left(0.100 \ \frac{\text{mol } HNO_3}{L}\right)(0.0250 \ L)$$
$$= 2.50 \times 10^{-3} \text{ mol } HNO_3$$

The relationship between the number of moles of HNO_3 and the number of moles of H_2O is given by the balanced chemical equation for the reaction. Because this is an acid-base neutralization reaction, we know that HNO_3 and NaOH react to form H_2O and the salt containing Na^+ (the cation of the base) and NO_3^- (the anion of the acid), $NaNO_3$, as shown in the following molecular equation:

$$HNO_3(aq) + NaOH(aq) \longrightarrow H_2O(l) + NaNO_3(aq)$$

Thus, 1 mol $HNO_3 \simeq 1$ mol H_2O. Therefore,

$$\text{Moles } H_2O = 2.50 \times 10^{-3} \text{ mol } HNO_3 \left(\frac{1 \text{ mol } H_2O}{1 \text{ mol } HNO_3}\right)$$
$$= 2.50 \times 10^{-3} \text{ mol } H_2O$$

Had the question asked for the number of grams of H_2O instead of the number of moles, we would proceed in the same way and then convert moles of H_2O into grams using its molar mass (18.0 g/mol); 0.0450 g of H_2O is produced.

PRACTICE EXERCISE

What volume of 0.500 M HCl(aq) is required to react completely with 0.100 mol of $Pb(NO_3)_2(aq)$, forming a precipitate of $PbCl_2(s)$?   ***Answer:*** 0.400 L

 Figure 4.20

FIGURE 4.20   Outline of the procedure used to solve stoichiometry problems that involve measured (laboratory) units of mass, solution concentration (molarity), or volume.

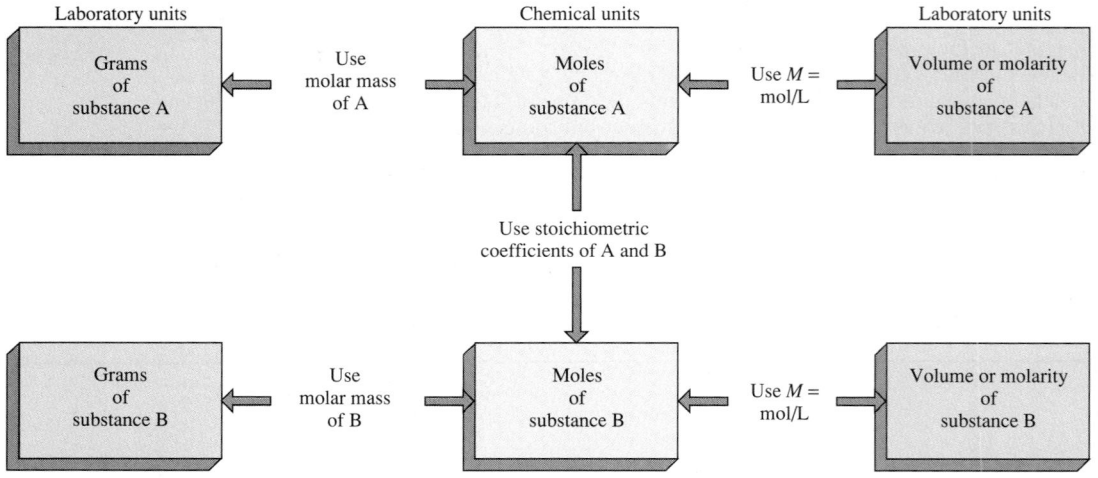

Titrations

We will end this chapter by addressing an important question: How can we determine the concentration of a solution? One common way is to use a second solution of known concentration, called a **standard solution,** that undergoes a specific chemical reaction of known stoichiometry with the solution of unknown concentration. This procedure is known as a **titration.** As an example, suppose we have an HCl solution of unknown concentration and an NaOH solution we know to be 0.100 *M*. To determine the concentration of the HCl solution, we take a specific volume of that solution, say 20.00 mL. We then slowly add the standard NaOH solution to it until the neutralization reaction between the HCl and NaOH is complete. The point at which stoichiometrically equivalent quantities are brought together is known as the **equivalence point** of the titration.

In order to titrate an unknown with a standard solution, there must be some way to determine when the equivalence point of the titration has been reached. In acid-base titrations, dyes known as acid-base **indicators** are used for this purpose. For example, the dye known as phenolphthalein is colorless in acidic solution but is red in basic solution. If we add phenolphthalein to an unknown solution of acid, the solution will be colorless. We can then add standard base from a buret until the solution barely turns from colorless to red. This color change indicates that the acid has been neutralized and the drop of base that caused the solution to become colored has no acid to react with. The solution therefore becomes basic, and the dye turns red. The color change signals the *end point* of the titration, which usually coincides very nearly with the equivalence point. Care must be taken to choose indicators whose end points correspond to the equivalence point of the titration. We will consider this matter in Chapter 17. The titration procedure is summarized in Figure 4.21.

Learning Goal 11: Calculate the concentration or mass of solute in a sample from titration data.

Teaching Note: The equivalence point of a titration is the point where the stoichiometrically correct number of moles of each reactant is present. The end point of a titration is the point where the indicator changes. They are not the same, although we choose an indicator that will change as close to the equivalence point as possible.

FIGURE 4.21 Procedure for titrating an acid against a standardized solution of NaOH. (*a*) A known quantity of acid is added to a flask. (*b*) An acid-base indicator is added, and standardized NaOH is added from a buret. (*c*) Equivalence point is signaled by a color change in the indicator.

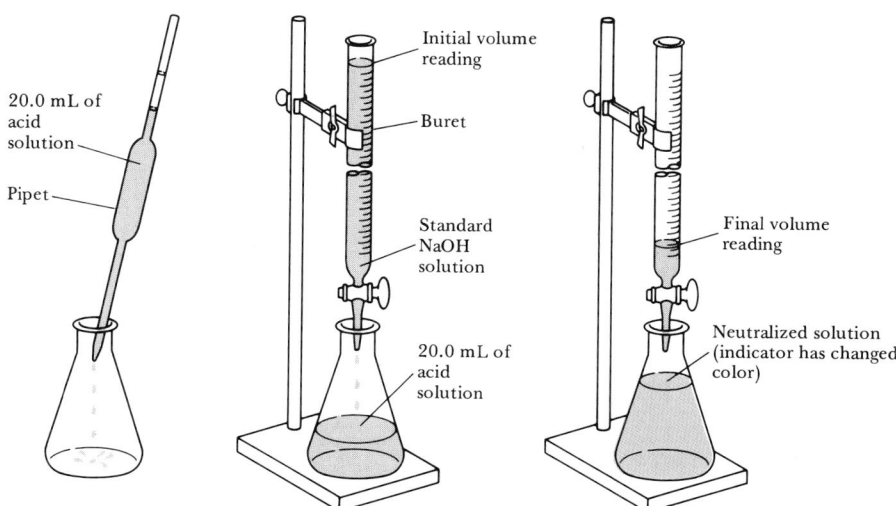

STRATEGIES IN CHEMISTRY

Analyzing Chemical Reactions

In this chapter you have been introduced to a great number of chemical reactions. A major difficulty that students face in trying to master material of this sort is gaining a "feel" for what happens when chemicals are allowed to react. In fact, you might marvel at the ease with which your professor or teaching assistant can figure out the results of a chemical reaction. One of our goals in this textbook is to help you become more adept at predicting the outcome of reactions. The key to gaining this "chemical intuition" is understanding how to categorize reactions and how to use your knowledge to reach a logical conclusion.

There are so many individual reactions in chemistry that memorizing them all is a futile task. It is far more fruitful to try to use pattern recognition to determine the general category of reaction, such as metathesis or oxidation of metals. Thus, when you are faced with the challenge of predicting the outcome of a chemical reaction, you should ask yourself a number of pertinent questions: What are the reactants in the reaction? Are they electrolytes or nonelectrolytes? Are there any reactants that might not be immediately obvious, such as water from the solution, or oxygen or carbon dioxide from the atmosphere? Will metathesis of the reactants produce any chemical change? Can any gases be formed? Can the reactants undergo oxidation or reduction? By asking questions such as these, you should be able to reach a reasonable answer as to what might happen during the reaction. You might not always be correct, but if you keep your wits about you, you will not be far off.

Of course, one of the greatest tools available to us in chemistry is experimentation. If you perform an experiment in which two solutions are mixed, you can make observations that help you understand what is happening. For example, using the information in Table 4.3 to predict whether a precipitate will form is not nearly as exciting as actually seeing the precipitate form, as in Figure 4.8. The laboratory portion of your course reinforces the material you learn in lecture; your observations in the laboratory will make your lecture material easier to master.

SAMPLE EXERCISE 4.13

One method used commercially to peel potatoes is to soak them in a solution of NaOH for a short time, remove them from the NaOH, and spray off the peel. The concentration of NaOH is normally in the range 3 to 6 M. The NaOH is analyzed periodically. In one such analysis, 45.7 mL of 0.500 M H_2SO_4 is required to react completely with a 20.0-mL sample of NaOH:

$$H_2SO_4(aq) + 2NaOH(aq) \longrightarrow 2H_2O(l) + Na_2SO_4(aq)$$

What is the concentration of the NaOH solution?

SOLUTION

$$\text{Moles } H_2SO_4 = (45.7 \text{ mL soln}) \left(\frac{1 \text{ L soln}}{1000 \text{ mL soln}} \right) \left(0.500 \frac{\text{mol } H_2SO_4}{\text{L soln}} \right)$$

$$= 2.28 \times 10^{-2} \text{ mol } H_2SO_4$$

According to the balanced equation, 1 mol $H_2SO_4 \cong 2$ mol NaOH. Therefore,

$$\text{Moles NaOH} = (2.28 \times 10^{-2} \text{ mol } H_2SO_4) \left(\frac{2 \text{ mol NaOH}}{1 \text{ mol } H_2SO_4} \right)$$

$$= 4.56 \times 10^{-2} \text{ mol NaOH}$$

Knowing the number of moles of NaOH present in 20.0 mL of solution allows us to calculate the concentration of this solution:

$$\text{Molarity NaOH} = \frac{\text{mol NaOH}}{\text{L soln}}$$

$$= \left(\frac{4.56 \times 10^{-2} \text{ mol NaOH}}{20.0 \text{ mL soln}}\right)\left(\frac{1000 \text{ mL soln}}{1 \text{ L soln}}\right)$$

$$= 2.28 \frac{\text{mol NaOH}}{\text{L soln}} = 2.28 \ M$$

Thus, the solution is too dilute and needs to be replaced.

PRACTICE EXERCISE

What is the molarity of an NaOH solution if 48.0 mL is needed to neutralize 35.0 mL of 0.144 M H_2SO_4? The equation for the chemical reaction is given in the above Sample Exercise.   *Answer:* 0.210 M

SAMPLE EXERCISE 4.14

The quantity of Cl^- in a water supply is determined by titrating the sample with Ag^+:

$$Ag^+(aq) + Cl^-(aq) \longrightarrow AgCl(s)$$

What mass of chloride ion is present in a 10.0-g sample of the water if 20.2 mL of 0.100 M Ag^+ is required to react with all the chloride in the sample?

SOLUTION   We must first determine the number of moles of Ag^+ used in the titration:

$$(20.2 \text{ mL soln}) \left(\frac{1 \text{ L soln}}{1000 \text{ mL soln}}\right)\left(0.100 \frac{\text{mol Ag}^+}{\text{L soln}}\right) = 2.02 \times 10^{-3} \text{ mol Ag}^+$$

From the balanced equation, we see that 1 mol $Ag^+ \simeq$ 1 mol Cl^-. Therefore, the sample must contain 2.02×10^{-3} mol of Cl^-:

$$\text{Moles Cl}^- = (2.02 \times 10^{-3} \text{ mol Ag}^+)\left(\frac{1 \text{ mol Cl}^-}{1 \text{ mol Ag}^+}\right)$$

$$= 2.02 \times 10^{-3} \text{ mol Cl}^-$$

The number of moles of Cl^- can then be converted to grams:

$$\text{Grams Cl}^- = (2.02 \times 10^{-3} \text{ mol Cl}^-)\left(\frac{35.5 \text{ g Cl}^-}{1 \text{ mol Cl}^-}\right)$$

$$= 7.17 \times 10^{-2} \text{ g Cl}^-$$

We might note that the mass percentage of Cl^- in the water is

$$\% \text{ Cl}^- = \frac{7.17 \times 10^{-2} \text{ g Cl}^-}{10.0 \text{ g soln}} \times 100 = 0.717\%$$

Chloride ion is one of the major ions in water and sewage. Ocean water contains 1.92 percent Cl^-. Whether water containing Cl^- exhibits a salty taste depends on the other ions present. If the only accompanying ions are Na^+ ions, a salty taste may be detected with as little as 0.03 percent Cl^-.

PRACTICE EXERCISE

What mass of chloride ion is present in a sample of water if 15.7 mL of 0.108 M $AgNO_3$ is required to titrate the sample? Refer to Sample Exercise 4.14 for the reaction.   *Answer:* 0.0602 g

For Review

Summary

The composition of a solution expresses the relative quantities of solvent and solutes that it contains. The molarity is the number of moles of solute per liter of solution. This concentration unit allows us to interconvert solution volume and number of moles of solute. Solutions of known molarity can be formed either by weighing out the solute and diluting it to a known volume or by diluting a more concentrated solution of known concentration.

Substances that exist in solution as ions are called electrolytes. Substances that are completely ionized in solution are called strong electrolytes, whereas those that are partially ionized are called weak electrolytes. The most important electrolytes are acids, bases, and salts.

Acids are proton donors; they increase the concentration of $H^+(aq)$ in aqueous solutions to which they are added. Bases are proton acceptors; they increase the concentration of $OH^-(aq)$ in aqueous solutions. When solutions of acids and bases are mixed, a neutralization reaction results. The neutralization reaction between an acid and a metal hydroxide produces water and a salt.

Chemical equations can be written to show whether dissolved substances are present in solution predominantly as ions or molecules. In a net ionic equation, those ions that go through the reaction unchanged (spectator ions) are omitted.

One significant class of reactions involving ions is metathesis, which includes both neutralization and precipitation reactions. Metathesis requires a driving force such as the formation of a precipitate, a gas, a weak electrolyte, or a nonelectrolyte. Solubility rules help in determining whether a precipitate will form. The gases commonly formed in metathesis are H_2S, CO_2, and SO_2. The most common nonelectrolyte produced in metathesis is H_2O.

Many metals are oxidized by O_2 and by acids and salts. Many metals react with acids to form a salt and H_2. Metals can also be oxidized by the salts of other metals. Comparing such reactions allows us to rank metals according to their ease of oxidation. A list of metals arranged in order of decreasing ease of oxidation is called an activity series. Any metal on the list can be oxidized by ions of metals below it in the series.

In the process called titration, we bring a solution of known concentration (a standard solution) into reaction with a solution of unknown concentration in order to determine the unknown concentration or the quantity of solute in the unknown.

Key Terms

aqueous solution
solvent (Sec. 4.1)
solutes (Sec. 4.1)
concentration (Sec. 4.1)
molarity (Sec. 4.1)
dilution (Sec. 4.1)
electrolyte (Sec. 4.2)
nonelectrolyte (Sec. 4.2)
strong electrolyte (Sec. 4.2)
weak electrolyte (Sec. 4.2)
chemical equilibrium (Sec. 4.2)
acids (Sec. 4.3)
bases (Sec. 4.3)
strong acids (Sec. 4.3)
strong bases (Sec. 4.3)
weak acids (Sec. 4.3)
weak bases (Sec. 4.3)

salts (Sec. 4.3)
neutralization reaction (Sec. 4.3)
molecular equation (Sec. 4.4)
spectator ions (Sec. 4.4)
net ionic equation (Sec. 4.4)
metathesis reaction (Sec. 4.5)
precipitation reaction (Sec. 4.5)
precipitate (Sec. 4.5)
solubility (Sec. 4.5)
oxidation (Sec. 4.6)
reduction (Sec. 4.6)
activity series (Sec. 4.6)
standard solution (Sec. 4.7)
titration (Sec. 4.7)
equivalence point (Sec. 4.7)
indicators (Sec. 4.7)

Exercises

Solution Composition: Molarity

✓ **4.1.** Is the concentration of a solution an intensive or an extensive property?

✓ **4.2.** Suppose you prepare 500 mL of a 0.10 M solution of some salt and then accidently spill some of it. What happens to the concentration of the solution left in the container?

4.3. A certain volume of a 0.50 M solution contains 3.5 g of a certain salt. What mass of the salt is present in the same volume of a 2.50 M solution?

✓ **4.4.** What is the difference between 0.50 mol HCl and 0.50 M HCl?

4.5. (a) Calculate the molarity of a solution that contains 0.0575 mol NH_4Cl in 400 mL of solution. (b) How many moles of HNO_3 are present in 35.0 mL of a 3.50 M solution of nitric acid? (c) How many milliliters of 1.50 M KOH solution are needed to supply 0.250 mol of KOH?

4.6. (a) Calculate the molarity of a solution made by dissolving 0.0834 mol Na_2SO_4 in enough water to form 650 mL of solution. (b) How many moles of $KMnO_4$ are present in 75.0 mL of a 0.168 M solution? (c) How many milliliters of 11.6 M HCl solution are needed to obtain 0.175 mol of HCl?

4.7. Calculate the number of grams of solute present in each of the following solutions:
(a) 0.200 L of 0.125 M KBr
(b) 100 mL of 0.150 M Na_2SO_4
(c) 250 mL of 0.0500 M $KBrO_3$
(d) 50.0 mL of 1.70 M $C_6H_{12}O_6$

4.8. Calculate the molar concentration of solute in each of the following solutions:
(a) 0.250 L containing 5.75 g of $NaNO_3$
(b) 100.0 mL containing 22.57 g of H_2SO_4
(c) 50.0 mL containing 1.48 g of $AgNO_3$
(d) 2.00 L containing 138 g of $NiCl_2 \cdot 6H_2O$

4.9. Starting with solid sucrose, $C_{12}H_{22}O_{11}$, describe how you would prepare 250 mL of 0.150 M sucrose solution.

4.10. How would you prepare 100.0 mL of 0.02000 M $AgNO_3$ solution starting with pure solute?

4.11. Describe how you would prepare 500 mL of 0.100 M $C_{12}H_{22}O_{11}$ starting with 2.00 L of 1.50 M $C_{12}H_{22}O_{11}$.

4.12. An experiment calls for you to use 200 mL of 1.0 M HNO_3 solution. All you have available is a liter bottle of 6.0 M HNO_3. How would you prepare the desired solution?

[**4.13**]. Pure acetic acid, known as *glacial* acetic acid, is a liquid with a density of 1.049 g/mL at 25°C. Calculate the molarity of a solution of acetic acid made by dissolving 10.00 mL of glacial acetic acid at 25°C in enough water to make 100.0 mL of solution.

[**4.14**]. Glycerol, $C_3H_8O_3$, is a substance used extensively in the manufacture of cosmetics, foodstuffs, antifreeze, and plastics. Glycerol is a water-soluble liquid of density 1.2656 g/mL at 15°C. Calculate the molarity of a solution of glycerol made by dissolving 40.000 mL glycerol at 15°C in enough water to make 250.00 mL of solution.

Electrolytes

4.15. Although pure water is a poor conductor of electricity, we are cautioned not to operate electrical appliances around water. Why?

4.16. Suppose you are given a 0.50 M solution of an unknown solute and a 0.50 M solution of glucose, a nonelectrolyte. Could you use an apparatus such as that in Figure 4.4 to determine whether the unknown solute is an electrolyte?

4.17. Classify each of the following aqueous solutions as a nonelectrolyte, weak electrolyte, or strong electrolyte: (a) HBrO; (b) HNO_3; (c) KOH; (d) $CoSO_4$; (e) sucrose, $C_{12}H_{22}O_{11}$; (f) O_2.

4.18. Classify each of the following substances as a nonelectrolyte, weak electrolyte, or strong electrolyte in water: (a) HF; (b) ethanol, C_2H_5OH; (c) NH_3; (d) $KClO_3$; (e) $Cu(NO_3)_2$.

4.19. Indicate the total concentration of all solute species present in each of the following solutions: (a) 0.14 M NaOH; (b) 0.25 M $CaBr_2$; (c) 0.25 M CH_3OH: (d) a mixture of 50.0 mL of 0.20 M $KClO_3$ and 25.0 mL of 0.20 M Na_2SO_4.

4.20. Indicate the total concentration of each ion present in the solution formed by mixing: (a) 20.0 mL of 0.100 M HCl and 10.0 mL of 0.220 M HCl; (b) 15.0 mL of 0.300 M Na_2SO_4 and 10.0 mL of 0.100 M NaCl; (c) 3.50 g of KCl in 60.0 mL of 0.500 M $CaCl_2$ solution (assume no volume change).

4.21. Which will have the highest concentration of potassium ion, 0.20 M KCl, 0.15 M K_2CrO_4, or 0.080 M K_3PO_4?

4.22. Which will contain the greater number of moles of chloride ion, 40.0 mL of 0.35 M NaCl or 25.0 mL of 0.25 M $CaCl_2$?

Acids, Bases, and Salts

4.23. An aqueous solution of an unknown solute is tested with litmus paper and found to be acidic. The solution is weakly conducting compared with a solution of NaCl of the same concentration. Which of the following substances could the unknown be: KOH, NH_3, HNO_3, $KClO_2$, H_3PO_3, CH_3COCH_3?

4.24. Label each of the following substances as an acid, base, salt, or none of the above. Indicate whether the substance exists in aqueous solution entirely in molecular form, entirely as ions, or as a mixture of molecules and ions. **(a)** HF; **(b)** acetonitrile, CH_3CN; **(c)** $NaClO_4$; **(d)** $Ba(OH)_2$.

4.25. What is the difference between: **(a)** a monoprotic acid and a diprotic acid; **(b)** a weak acid and a strong acid; **(c)** an acid and a base?

4.26. Explain the following observations: **(a)** NH_3 contains no OH^- ions, and yet its aqueous solutions are basic; **(b)** HF is called a weak acid, and yet it is very reactive.

4.27. Why do we use a single arrow in the chemical equation for the ionization of HNO_3 but a double arrow for the ionization of HCN?

4.28. Although sulfuric acid is a strong electrolyte, a 0.1 M aqueous solution of H_2SO_4 is not 0.2 M in $H^+(aq)$. Explain.

4.29. Complete and balance the following equations:
(a) $Ba(OH)_2(s) + HNO_3(aq) \longrightarrow$
(b) $H_3PO_4(aq) + KOH(aq) \longrightarrow$
(c) $Y(OH)_3(s) + H_2SO_4(aq) \longrightarrow$

4.30. Identify the salt produced in each of the following neutralization reactions: **(a)** Aqueous acetic acid is neutralized by aqueous sodium hydroxide; **(b)** solid calcium hydroxide is dissolved in hydroiodic acid; **(c)** aqueous ammonia is neutralized by hydrochloric acid.

Ionic Equations: Metathesis Reactions

4.31. Write balanced net ionic equations for the following reactions and identify the spectator ion or ions present in each:
(a) $Pb(NO_3)_2(aq) + Na_2SO_4(aq) \longrightarrow$
$$PbSO_4(s) + 2NaNO_3(aq)$$
(b) $Zn(s) + 2HCl(aq) \longrightarrow ZnCl_2(aq) + H_2(g)$
(c) $FeO(s) + 2HClO_4(aq) \longrightarrow H_2O(l) + Fe(ClO_4)_2(aq)$

4.32. Balance the following equations and then write their balanced net ionic equations:
(a) $Cr(OH)_3(s) + HNO_3(aq) \longrightarrow H_2O(l) + Cr(NO_3)_3(aq)$
(b) $Na_2CO_3(aq) + HCl(aq) \longrightarrow$
$$H_2O(l) + CO_2(g) + NaCl(aq)$$
(c) $CuBr_2(aq) + NaOH(aq) \longrightarrow Cu(OH)_2(s) + NaBr(aq)$

4.33. Explain what is meant by the term *driving force* when referring to metathesis reactions. What are the driving forces in each of the reactions in Exercise 4.32?

4.34. Give a specific example of a metathesis that occurs because of each of the following driving forces: **(a)** formation of an insoluble solid; **(b)** formation of a gas; **(c)** formation of a weak electrolyte or nonelectrolyte.

4.35. Using solubility rules or reasonable extensions of them, predict whether each of the following compounds is soluble in water: **(a)** Ag_2S; **(b)** $CaCl_2$; **(c)** $CsBr$; **(d)** $SrCO_3$; **(e)** $(NH_4)_2SO_4$.

4.36. Predict whether each of the following compounds is soluble in water: **(a)** K_3PO_4; **(b)** $Pb(C_2H_3O_2)_2$; **(c)** $Ga(OH)_3$; **(d)** NaCN; **(e)** $BaSO_4$.

4.37. Separate samples of a solution of an unknown salt are treated with dilute solutions of HBr, H_2SO_4, and NaOH. A precipitate forms only with H_2SO_4. Which of the following cations could the solution contain: K^+; Pb^{2+}; Ba^{2+}?

4.38. Separate samples of a solution of an unknown salt are treated with dilute $AgNO_3$, $Pb(NO_3)_2$, and $BaCl_2$. Precipitates form in all three cases. Which of the following anions could be the anion of the unknown salt: Br^-; SO_4^{2-}; NO_3^-?

4.39. Write balanced net ionic equations for the reactions, if any, that occur between
(a) ZnS(s) and HCl(aq);
(b) $Na_2CO_3(aq)$ and $BaCl_2(aq)$;
(c) $Na_3PO_4(aq)$ and HBr(aq);
(d) $Ba(OH)_2(aq)$ and HCl(aq);
(e) $Sr(C_2H_3O_2)_2(aq)$ and $NiSO_4(aq)$;
(f) $ZnSO_3(aq)$ and HCl(aq);
(g) $Pb(NO_3)_2(aq)$ and $H_2S(aq)$;
(h) $Fe(OH)_3(s)$ and $HClO_4(aq)$.

4.40. Write balanced net ionic equations for the reactions, if any, that occur when each of the following pairs is mixed:
(a) $H_2SO_4(aq)$ and $BaCl_2(aq)$;
(b) NaCl(aq) and $(NH_4)_2SO_4(aq)$;
(c) $AgNO_3(aq)$ and $Na_2CO_3(aq)$;
(d) KOH(aq) and $HNO_3(aq)$;
(e) $Ca(OH)_2(aq)$ and $HC_2H_3O_2(aq)$;
(f) $K_2SO_3(s)$ and $H_2SO_4(aq)$;
(g) $Pb(NO_3)_2(aq)$ and $MgSO_4(aq)$.

Reactions of Metals

4.41. Where, in general, do the most easily oxidized metals occur in the periodic table? Where do the least easily oxidized metals occur in the periodic table?

4.42. Why are platinum and gold called noble metals? Why are the alkali metals and alkaline earth metals called active metals?

4.43. Write balanced molecular and net ionic equations for the reactions of **(a)** hydrochloric acid with nickel; **(b)** sulfuric acid with iron; **(c)** hydrobromic acid with zinc; **(d)** acetic acid, $HC_2H_3O_2$, with magnesium.

4.44. Write balanced molecular and net ionic equations for the reactions of **(a)** manganese with sulfuric acid; **(b)**

chromium with hydrobromic acid; **(c)** tin with hydrochloric acid; **(d)** aluminum with formic acid, $HCHO_2$.

4.45. Based on the activity series (Table 4.5), what is the outcome of each of the following reactions?
(a) $Al(s) + NiCl_2(aq) \longrightarrow$
(b) $Ag(s) + Pb(NO_3)_2(aq) \longrightarrow$
(c) $Cr(s) + NiSO_4(aq) \longrightarrow$
(d) $Mn(s) + HBr(aq) \longrightarrow$
(e) $H_2(g) + CuCl_2(aq) \longrightarrow$
(f) $Ba(s) + H_2O(l) \longrightarrow$

4.46. Using the activity series (Table 4.5), write balanced chemical equations for the following reactions. If no reaction occurs, simply write NR. **(a)** Zinc metal is added to a solution of silver nitrate; **(b)** iron metal is added to a solution of aluminum sulfate; **(c)** hydrochloric acid is added to cobalt metal; **(d)** hydrogen gas is bubbled through an aqueous solution of $FeCl_2$; **(e)** lithium metal is added to water.

4.47. The metal cadmium tends to form Cd^{2+} ions. The following observations are made: (i) When a strip of zinc metal is placed in $CdCl_2(aq)$, cadmium metal is deposited on the strip. (ii) When a strip of cadmium metal is placed in $Ni(NO_3)_2(aq)$, nickel metal is deposited on the strip.

(a) Write net ionic equations to explain each of the observations made above. **(b)** What can you conclude about the position of cadmium in the activity series? **(c)** What experiments would you perform to allow you to locate more precisely the position of cadmium in the activity series?

4.48. **(a)** Use the following reactions to prepare an activity series for the halogens: $Br_2(aq) + 2NaI(aq) \longrightarrow 2NaBr(aq) + I_2(aq)$; $Cl_2(aq) + 2NaBr(aq) \longrightarrow 2NaCl(aq) + Br_2(aq)$. **(b)** Relate the positions of the halogens in the periodic table with their locations in this activity series. **(c)** Predict whether reaction occurs when the following reagents are mixed: $Cl_2(aq)$ and $KI(aq)$; $Br_2(aq)$ and $LiCl(aq)$.

4.49. Although neither hydrochloric acid nor nitric acid by itself can dissolve gold, aqua regia, which is a mixture of the two, does dissolve gold. Explain why a mixture of the two acids is necessary.

4.50. Hydrochloric acid does not dissolve glass. By contrast, hydrofluoric acid, $HF(aq)$, is a weak acid that dissolves glass and must therefore be stored in plastic containers. Do you think that the ability of hydrofluoric acid to dissolve glass is due primarily to the action of $H^+(aq)$ on glass?

Solution Stoichiometry; Titrations

4.51. **(a)** What volume of 0.105 M $HClO_4$ solution is required to neutralize 50.00 mL of 0.0875 M NaOH? **(b)** What volume of 0.158 M HCl is required to neutralize 2.87 g of $Mg(OH)_2$? **(c)** If 25.8 mL of $AgNO_3$ is required to precipitate all the Cl^- ion in a 895-mg sample of KCl (forming AgCl), what is the molarity of the $AgNO_3$ solution? **(d)** If 35.8 mL of 0.117 M HCl solution is required to neutralize a solution of KOH, how many grams of KOH must be present in the solution?

4.52. **(a)** How many milliliters of 0.210 M HCl are needed to neutralize completely 35.0 mL of 0.101 M $Ba(OH)_2$ solution? **(b)** How many milliliters of 3.50 M H_2SO_4 are needed to neutralize 75.0 g of NaOH? **(c)** If 45.2 mL of $BaCl_2$ solution is needed to precipitate all of the sulfate in a 544-mg sample of Na_2SO_4 (forming $BaSO_4$), what is the molarity of the solution? **(d)** If 42.7 mL of 0.250 M HCl solution is needed to neutralize a solution of $Ca(OH)_2$, how many grams of $Ca(OH)_2$ must be present in the solution?

4.53. Some sulfuric acid is spilled on a lab bench. It can be neutralized by sprinkling sodium bicarbonate on it and then mopping up the resultant solution. The sodium bicarbonate reacts with sulfuric acid in the following way:

$$2NaHCO_3(s) + H_2SO_4(aq) \longrightarrow$$
$$Na_2SO_4(aq) + 2CO_2(g) + 2H_2O(l)$$

Sodium bicarbonate is added until the fizzing due to the

formation of $CO_2(g)$ stops. If 25 mL of 6.0 M H_2SO_4 was spilled, what is the minimum mass of $NaHCO_3$ that must be added to the spill to neutralize the acid?

4.54. The distinctive odor of vinegar is due to acetic acid, $HC_2H_3O_2$. Acetic acid reacts with sodium hydroxide in the following fashion:

$$HC_2H_3O_2(aq) + NaOH(aq) \longrightarrow$$
$$H_2O(l) + NaC_2H_3O_2(aq)$$

If 2.50 mL of vinegar requires 34.9 mL of 0.0960 M NaOH to reach the equivalence point in a titration, how many grams of acetic acid are in a 1.00-qt sample of this vinegar?

4.55. A sample of solid $Ca(OH)_2$ is allowed to stand in contact with water at 30°C for a long time, until the solution contains as much dissolved $Ca(OH)_2$ as it can hold. A 100-mL sample of this solution is withdrawn and titrated with 5.00×10^{-2} M HBr. It requires 48.8 mL of the acid solution for neutralization. What is the molarity of the $Ca(OH)_2$ solution? What is the solubility of $Ca(OH)_2$ in water, at 30°C, in grams of $Ca(OH)_2$ per 100 mL of solution?

4.56. In the laboratory, 6.67 g of $Sr(NO_3)_2$ is dissolved in enough water to form 0.750 L. A 0.100-L sample is withdrawn from this stock solution and titrated with a 0.0460 M solution of Na_2CrO_4. What volume of Na_2CrO_4 solution is required to precipitate all the $Sr^{2+}(aq)$ as $SrCrO_4$?

Additional Exercises

4.57. Calculate the molarity of the solution produced by mixing **(a)** 50.0 mL of 0.200 M NaCl and 100.0 mL of 0.100 M NaCl; **(b)** 24.5 mL of 1.50 M NaOH and 20.5 mL of 0.850 M NaOH. (Assume that the volumes are additive.)

4.58. A solution is made by mixing 50.0 mL of 6.00 M HCl, 100.0 mL of 1.00 M HCl, and enough water to make 250.0 mL of solution. What is the molarity of HCl in the final solution?

4.59. Using modern analytical techniques it is possible to detect sodium ions in concentrations as low as 50 pg/mL. What is this detection limit expressed in **(a)** molarity of Na^+; **(b)** Na^+ ions per cubic centimeter?

4.60. You choose to investigate some of the solubility rules for two ions not listed in Table 4.3, the chromate ion, CrO_4^{2-}, and the oxalate ion, $C_2O_4^{2-}$. You are given solutions (A, B, C, D) of four water-soluble salts:

Solution	Solute	Color of solution
A	Na_2CrO_4	Yellow
B	$(NH_4)_2C_2O_4$	Colorless
C	$AgNO_3$	Colorless
D	$CaCl_2$	Colorless

When these solutions are mixed, the following observations are made:

Expt. number	Solns mixed	Result
1	A + B	No precipitate, yellow solution
2	A + C	Red precipitate forms
3	A + D	No precipitate, yellow solution
4	B + C	White precipitate forms
5	B + D	White precipitate forms
6	C + D	White precipitate forms

(a) Write net ionic equations for the reaction that occurs in each of the experiments. **(b)** Identify the precipitate formed, if any, in each of the experiments. **(c)** Based on these limited observations, which ion tends to form the more soluble salts, chromate or oxalate?

4.61. Antacids are often used to relieve pain and promote healing in the treatment of mild ulcers. Write balanced net ionic equations for the reactions that occur between the HCl(aq) in the stomach and each of the following substances used in various antacids: **(a)** $Al(OH)_3(s)$; **(b)** $Mg(OH)_2(s)$; **(c)** $MgCO_3(s)$; **(d)** $NaAl(CO_3)(OH)_2(s)$; **(e)** $CaCO_3(s)$.

4.62. Suppose you have a solution that might contain any or all of the following cations: Ni^{2+}, Ag^+, Sr^{2+}, and Mn^{2+}. Addition of HCl solution causes a precipitate to form. After filtering off the precipitate, H_2SO_4 solution is added to the resultant solution and another precipitate forms. This is filtered off, and a solution of NaOH is added to the resulting solution. No precipitate is observed. Which ions are present in each of the precipitates? Which of the four ions listed above must be absent from the original solution?

4.63. Titanium(IV) ion, Ti^{4+}, can be reduced to Ti^{3+} by the careful addition of zinc metal. **(a)** Write the net ionic equation for this process. **(b)** Would it be appropriate to use this reaction as a means of including titanium in the activity series of Table 4.5? Why or why not?

4.64. Use Table 4.5 to predict which of the following ions can be reduced to their metal forms by reacting with zinc: **(a)** Na^+ (aq); **(b)** Pb^{2+} (aq); **(c)** Mg^{2+} (aq); **(d)** Fe^{2+} (aq); **(e)** Cu^{2+} (aq); **(f)** Al^{3+} (aq). Write the balanced net ionic equation for each reaction that occurs.

[4.65]. Lanthanum metal forms cations with a charge of $3+$. Consider the following observations about the chemistry of lanthanum: When lanthanum metal is exposed to air, a white solid (compound A) is formed that contains lanthanum and one other element. When lanthanum metal is added to water, gas bubbles are observed, and a different white solid (compound B) is formed. Both A and B dissolve in hydrochloric acid to give a clear solution. When the solution from either A or B is evaporated, a soluble white solid (compound C) remains. If compound C is dissolved in water and sulfuric acid is added, a white precipitate (compound D) forms. **(a)** Propose identities for the substances A, B, C, and D. **(b)** Write net ionic equations for all the reactions described above. **(c)** Based on the observations above, what can be said about the position of lanthanum in the activity series (Table 4.5)?

4.66. The Pt^{4+} ion can be stabilized in aqueous solution by interacting with six Cl^- ions to form the $PtCl_6^{2-}$ ion. How does this observation help explain why platinum metal dissolves in aqua regia but not in hydrochloric or nitric acid alone?

4.67. Tartaric acid, $H_2C_4H_4O_6$, has two acidic hydrogens. The acid is often present in wines and precipitates from solution as the wine ages. A solution containing an unknown concentration of the acid is titrated with NaOH. It requires 22.62 mL of 0.2000 M NaOH solution to titrate both acidic protons in 40.00 mL of the tartaric acid solution. Write a balanced net ionic equation for the neutralization reaction and calculate the molarity of the tartaric acid solution.

[4.68]. The arsenic in a 1.22-g sample of a pesticide was converted to AsO_4^{3-} by suitable chemical treatment. It was then titrated using Ag^+ to form Ag_3AsO_4 as a precipitate. If it took 25.0 mL of 0.102 M Ag^+ to reach the equivalence point in this titration, what is the percentage of arsenic in the pesticide?

[4.69]. Federal regulations set an upper limit of 50 parts per million (ppm) of NH_3 in the air in a work environment (that is, 50 mL NH_3 per 10^6 mL of air). The density of $NH_3(g)$ at room temperature is 0.771 g/L. Air from a manufacturing operation was drawn through a solution containing 100 mL of 0.0105 M HCl. The NH_3 reacts with HCl as follows:

$$NH_3(aq) + HCl(aq) \longrightarrow NH_4Cl(aq)$$

After drawing air through the acid solution for 10.0 min at a rate of 10.0 L/min, the acid was titrated. The remaining acid required 13.1 mL of 0.0588 M NaOH to reach the equivalence point. **(a)** How many grams of NH_3 were drawn into the acid solution? **(b)** How many ppm of NH_3 were in the air? **(c)** Is this manufacturer in compliance with regulations?

Energy Relationships in Chemistry: Thermochemistry

5

The head of a "strike-anywhere match" contains $KClO_3$, P_4S_3, ground glass, and the oxides of zinc and iron, all bound by glue. The head is ignited by the heat of friction, which causes a vigorous, energy-liberating reaction between the $KClO_3$ and P_4S_3. This reaction then ignites the wood of the matchstick.

Teaching Note: Entropy and Gibbs free energy are covered in Chapter 19, as are the relationships among enthalpy, entropy, and free energy.

When you eat an orange, the sugar it contains reacts in your body with oxygen to form CO_2 and H_2O. During this chemical process, one other important change occurs—energy is released. The food you eat is the fuel that your body uses to operate your muscles and to maintain proper body temperature. This example illustrates a general point: Chemical reactions involve changes in energy. Some reactions, like the oxidation of sugar, liberate energy. Others, like the splitting of water into hydrogen and oxygen, require energy. At the present time, over 90 percent of the energy produced in our society comes from chemical reactions, principally from the combustion of coal, petroleum products, and natural gas.

The study of energy and its transformations is known as **thermodynamics** (Greek: *therme,* "heat"; *dynamis,* "power"). This area of study began during the Industrial Revolution as the relationships among heat, work, and the energy content of fuels were studied in an effort to maximize the performance of steam engines. Thermodynamics is important not only to chemistry but to other areas of science and to engineering as well. It touches our daily lives as we use energy for manufacturing, travel, and communications. Thermodynamics relates to such diverse topics as the metabolism of foods, the operation of batteries, and the design of engines.

In this chapter, we examine the relationships between chemical reactions and energy changes. This aspect of thermodynamics is called **thermochemistry.**

5.1 The Nature of Energy

The concept of matter has always been an easy notion to grasp because matter can be seen and felt. Energy, on the other hand, is a more abstract concept. To gain insight into this important idea, let's consider a simple process that requires us to expend energy, such as lifting a barbell (Figure 5.1).

Gravity causes an attraction between the barbell and the ground. This gravitational attraction is an example of a force. A **force** is any kind of push or pull exerted on an object. In our example, the force of gravity "pulls" the barbell to the ground. In chemistry, we are more concerned with other forces. For example, positively charged nuclei exert a "pull" on negatively charged electrons.

When we lift a barbell against the force of gravity, we perform work. Similarly, when we increase the distance between a proton and an electron, we perform work to overcome the attractive force between them. The **work,** w, that we do in moving objects against a force equals the product of the force, F, and the distance, d, that the object is moved:

$$w = F \times d \qquad [5.1]$$

Energy, in the form of work, must be used to move an object against a force. It requires more work to lift a heavy barbell than a light one because the gravitational force exerted on the heavy barbell is greater.

As we lift barbells, we also notice that we feel warmer. Our bodies generate heat as we perform this task. **Heat** is the energy that is transferred from one object to another because of a difference in temperature. As we get hotter, we transfer heat from our bodies to our surroundings. As we lift barbells, then, we expend energy in the forms of work and heat.

FIGURE 5.1 Lifting a barbell requires energy in the form of mechanical work to overcome the force of gravity. If the force of gravity acting on the barbell is denoted as F, then the work, w, required to lift the barbell a distance, d, off the ground is $w = F \times d$. (Paul J. Sutton/Duomo)

Our example teaches us that work and heat are the two ways that we experience energy changes in our macroscopic environment. **Energy** *is the capacity to do work or to transfer heat.* We can gain further insight into the concept of energy by noting that objects possess energy because of their motions and their positions. That is, objects, whether they are barbells or molecules, can possess energy in two ways: as kinetic energy and as potential energy.

Common Misconception: Students often confuse the terms *power* and *energy.*

Kinetic and Potential Energy

Kinetic energy is the energy of motion. The magnitude of the kinetic energy, E_k, of an object depends on its mass, m, and velocity, v:

$$E_k = \tfrac{1}{2} mv^2 \qquad\qquad [5.2]$$

This equation expresses quantitatively what our experience teaches — that both the mass and speed of an object determine how much work it can accomplish. For example, the more massive a hammer is and the faster it moves, the more work it can accomplish with each blow in pounding a nail. Molecules and their component parts are in motion and thereby possess kinetic energy.

An object can also possess energy by virtue of its position relative to other objects. This stored energy is called **potential energy.** It is a result of the attractions and repulsions an object experiences in relation to other objects. A brick held high in the air has potential energy because of the force of gravity acting on it. As it falls, its potential energy is converted into kinetic energy, and the brick does work on whatever object it strikes. Likewise, an electron has potential energy when located near a proton because of the attractive electrostatic force between them.

Learning Goal 1: Give examples of different forms of energy.

In some contexts, you may see other forms of energy discussed, such as *chemical energy* or *thermal energy.* These forms of energy can be understood as kinetic or potential energy at the atomic or molecular level. For example, the chemical energy of gasoline can be regarded as potential energy stored in the arrangements of the electrons and nuclei within the molecules that compose the gasoline. Thermal energy is the energy associated with the random motion of molecules and can therefore be understood in terms of kinetic energy. Heat is just the transfer of thermal energy between two objects whose molecules have different average kinetic energies. The energy flows from the hotter object (whose molecules have the larger average kinetic energy) to the colder object (whose molecules have the smaller average kinetic energy).

Point of Emphasis: Heat flows from regions of higher temperature to regions of lower temperature.

Energy Units

The SI unit for energy is the **joule,** J (pronounced "jool"), in honor of James Prescott Joule (1818–1889), a British scientist who investigated work and heat; $1 \text{ J} = 1 \text{ kg-m}^2/\text{s}^2$. A mass of 2 kg moving at a velocity of 1 m/s possesses a kinetic energy of 1 J:

Learning Goal 2: List the important units in which energy is expressed, and convert from one unit to another.

$$E_k = \tfrac{1}{2} mv^2 = \tfrac{1}{2} (2 \text{ kg})(1 \text{ m/s})^2 = 1 \text{ kg-m}^2/\text{s}^2 = 1 \text{ J}$$

A joule is not a large amount of energy, and we will often use kilojoules (kJ) in discussing the energy liberated or required by chemical reactions.

Traditionally, energy changes accompanying chemical reactions have been expressed in calories, a non-SI unit still widely used in chemistry, biology,

Point of Emphasis: With mass expressed in kilograms and velocity expressed in meters per second, kinetic energy has the units of joules ($1 \text{ J} = 1 \text{ kg-m}^2/\text{s}^2$).

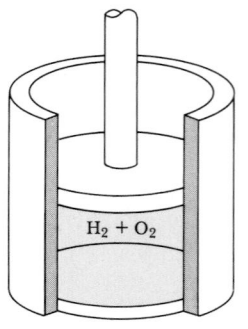

FIGURE 5.2 Hydrogen and oxygen gases in a cylinder. If we are interested in studying only the properties of the gases, the gases are the system and the cylinder and piston are considered part of the surroundings.

Point of Emphasis: The contents of the vessel are the *system;* everything else comprises the *surroundings.*

and biochemistry. A **calorie** (cal) was originally defined as the amount of energy required to raise the temperature of 1 g of water by 1°C. It is now defined in terms of the joule:

$$1 \text{ cal} = 4.184 \text{ J (exactly)}$$

A related energy unit used in nutrition is the nutritional *Calorie* (note that this unit is capitalized): 1 Cal = 1000 cal or 1 kcal.

Systems and Surroundings

When we study energy changes, we focus our attention on a limited and well-defined part of the universe. The portion we single out for study is called the **system;** everything else is called the **surroundings.** When we observe a chemical reaction in the laboratory, the chemicals usually constitute the system. The container and everything beyond it are considered the surroundings. The systems we can most readily study are those that exchange energy but not matter with their surroundings. As an example, consider a mixture of hydrogen gas, H_2, and oxygen gas, O_2, in a cylinder, as illustrated in Figure 5.2. The system in this case is just the hydrogen and oxygen; the cylinder, piston, and everything beyond them (including us) are the surroundings. If the hydrogen and oxygen react to form water, energy is liberated:

$$2H_2(g) + O_2(g) \longrightarrow 2H_2O(l) + \text{energy}$$

Although the chemical form of the hydrogen and oxygen atoms in the system is changed by this reaction, the system has not lost or gained mass; it undergoes no exchange of matter with its surroundings. However, it does exchange energy with its surroundings in the form of heat and work. These are quantities that we can measure.

Lowering the Energy of the System

A basic fact of nature, and one that governs many processes in chemistry, is that *systems tend to attain as low an energy as possible.* For example, consider a bicyclist at the top of a steep hill, as shown in Figure 5.3. Because of the force of gravity, the potential energy of the bicyclist and her bicycle (which compose the

Teaching Note: Systems tend to move "downhill" in an energetic sense.

FIGURE 5.3 A bicycle at the top of a hill (left) has a high potential energy. As the bicycle proceeds down the hill (right), the potential energy is converted into kinetic energy; the potential energy is lower at the bottom than at the top. Energy is transferred from the system (the bicycle) to the surroundings by friction and air resistance.

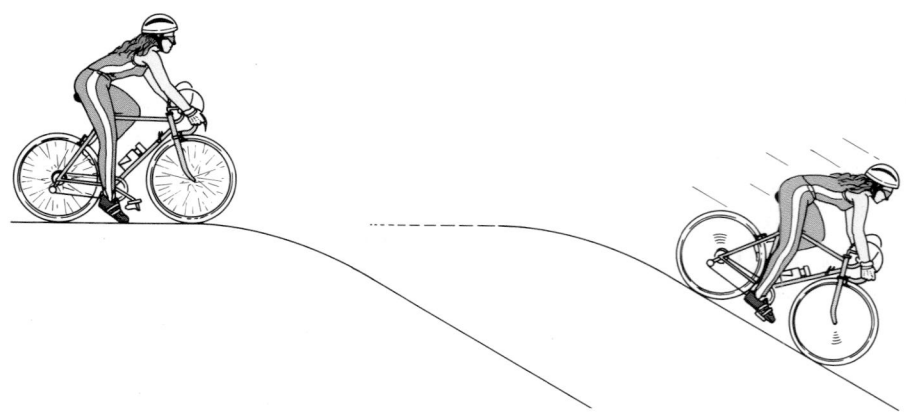

system) is much greater at the top of the hill than it would be at the bottom. As a result, the bicycle easily proceeds down the hill with no effort on the part of the rider. As it does so, the stored potential energy of the system is converted into kinetic energy, which can do work on, and transfer heat to, the surroundings.

We will see throughout this text that a great many chemical reactions follow this fundamental idea as well. Systems with a high potential energy are less stable and more likely to undergo change than systems with a low potential energy. Like the bicycle in Figure 5.3, chemical reactants move spontaneously toward a lower potential energy when possible.

5.2 The First Law of Thermodynamics

When you drop a stone, its potential energy is converted to kinetic energy as it falls. Conversely, when you lift a barbell, its kinetic energy is converted to potential energy. In general, energy can be converted from one form to another. Scientists have found, however, that energy can be neither created nor destroyed: *Energy is conserved.* The total energy lost by a system equals the total energy gained by its surroundings. Likewise, the total energy gained by a system equals that lost by its surroundings. This important observation is known as the *law of conservation of energy.* Because it is the most elementary of thermodynamic concepts, it is also known as the **first law of thermodynamics.**

Learning Goal 3: Define the first law of thermodynamics both verbally and by means of an equation.

Point of Emphasis: The first law of thermodynamics *is* the law of conservation of energy.

Internal Energy

The total energy of a system is the sum of all the kinetic and potential energies of its component parts. For the system shown in Figure 5.2, total energy includes not only the motions and interactions of the H_2 and O_2 molecules themselves but also of their component nuclei and electrons. This total energy is called the **internal energy** of the system. Because there are so many types of motions and interactions, we cannot determine the exact energy of any system of practical interest. We can, however, measure the *changes* in internal energy that accompany chemical and physical processes.

We define the change in internal energy, which we represent as ΔE (read "delta E"),* as the difference between the internal energy of the system at the completion of a process and that at the beginning:

Point of Emphasis: *Total energy* (E) is conserved; it can be transferred between the system and the surroundings.

Point of Emphasis: The term Δ or *change in* always refers to the value of the final state minus that of the initial state.

$$\Delta E = E_{\text{final}} - E_{\text{initial}} \qquad [5.3]$$

Thermodynamic quantities such as ΔE have three parts: a number and a unit giving the magnitude of the change, and a sign giving the direction. A *positive* ΔE results when $E_{\text{final}} > E_{\text{initial}}$, indicating that the system has gained energy from its surroundings. A negative ΔE is obtained when $E_{\text{final}} < E_{\text{initial}}$, indicating that the system has lost energy to its surroundings.

In a chemical reaction, the initial state of the system refers to the reactants, and the final state refers to the products. When hydrogen and oxygen react to form water, the system loses energy; the energy content of the products is less than that of the reactants, and ΔE for the process is negative. This means that

Learning Goal 4: Describe how the change in the internal energy of a system is related to the exchange of heat and work between the system and its surroundings.

---

* The symbol Δ is commonly used to denote *change.* For example, a change in volume can be represented by ΔV.

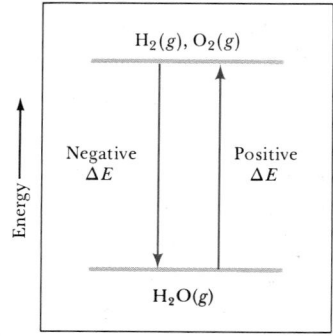

FIGURE 5.4 A system composed of $H_2(g)$ and $O_2(g)$ has a greater energy content than one composed of $H_2O(l)$. The system loses energy (negative ΔE) when H_2 and O_2 are converted to H_2O. It gains energy (positive ΔE) when H_2O is decomposed into H_2 and O_2.

FIGURE 5.5 Heat, q, absorbed by the system and work, w, done on the system are both positive quantities. Both serve to increase the internal energy, E, of the system: $\Delta E = q + w$.

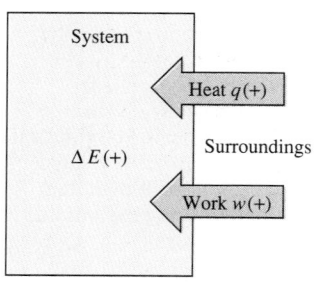

the internal energy of the hydrogen and oxygen is greater than that of water, as shown in the *energy diagram* in Figure 5.4.

Relating ΔE to Heat and Work

As we noted in Section 5.1, any system can exchange energy with its surroundings in two general ways: as heat or as work. The internal energy of a system changes in magnitude as heat is added to or removed from the system, or as work is done on it or by it. We can use these ideas to write a very useful algebraic expression of the first law of thermodynamics. When a system undergoes any chemical or physical change, the accompanying change in its internal energy, ΔE, is given by the heat added to or liberated from the system, q, plus the work done on or by the system, w:

$$\Delta E = q + w \qquad [5.4]$$

Heat added to the system is assigned a positive sign. Likewise, *work done on the system is positive* (Figure 5.5). Both the heat added to the system and the work done on it increase the internal energy. On the other hand, both the heat lost by the system and the work done by the system on its surroundings are negative; they reduce the internal energy. For example, if the system absorbs 50 J of heat and does 10 J of work on its surroundings, $q = 50$ J and $w = -10$ J. Thus, $\Delta E = 50$ J $+ (-10$ J$) = 40$ J.*

SAMPLE EXERCISE 5.1

The hydrogen and oxygen gases in the cylinder illustrated in Figure 5.2 are ignited. As the reaction occurs, the system loses 550 J of heat to its surroundings. The reaction also causes the piston to move upward as the gas expands. It is determined that the expanding gas does 240 J of work on the surroundings as it pushes against the atmosphere. What is the change in the internal energy of the system?

SOLUTION From the sign conventions for q and w, we have $q = -550$ J and $w = -240$ J (that is, energy flows from the system both as heat and as work). Using Equation 5.4, we have

$$\Delta E = q + w = (-550 \text{ J}) + (-240 \text{ J}) = -790 \text{ J}$$

Thus, 790 J of energy has been transferred from the system to the surroundings.

PRACTICE EXERCISE

Calculate ΔE for a process in which the system absorbs 65 J of heat and also receives 12 J of work from its surroundings. *Answer:* 77 J

State Functions

Although scientists usually have no way of knowing the precise value of the internal energy of a system, they do know that it has a fixed value for a given set of conditions. The conditions that influence this energy include the temperature and pressure. Furthermore, the total internal energy of a system is proportional to the total quantity of matter in the system; energy is an extensive property. ∞ (Sec. 1.3)

---

* Equation 5.4 is sometimes written $\Delta E = q - w$. When written this way, work done *by* the system is defined as positive. This convention has merit in the many engineering applications that focus interest on a machine that does work on its surroundings.

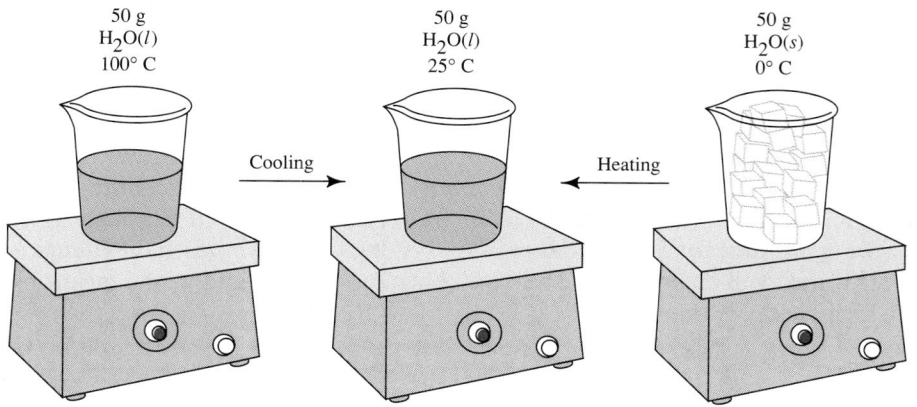

FIGURE 5.6 Internal
energy, a state function,
depends only on the present
state of the system and not on
the path by which it arrived at
that state. The internal energy
of 50 g of water at 25°C is the
same whether the water is
cooled from a higher
temperature to 25°C or is
obtained by melting 50 g of ice
and then warming to 25°C.

Suppose we define our system as 50 g of water at 25°C, as in Figure 5.6. Our system could have arrived at that state by our cooling 50 g of water from 100°C or by our melting 50 g of ice and subsequently warming the water to 25°C. The internal energy of the water is the same in either case. The internal energy of a system is a **state function,** a property of a system that is determined by specifying its condition, or its state (in terms of temperature, pressure, location, and so forth). *The value of a state function does not depend on the particular history of the sample, only on its present condition.* Because E is a state function, ΔE depends only on the initial and final states of the system and not on how the change occurs.

Learning Goal 5: Define the term *state function,* and de-scribe its importance in ther-mochemistry.

Point of Emphasis: State functions do not depend on pathway, only on the *initial* and *final* states.

An analogy may help you to understand the difference between quantities that are state functions and those that are not. Imagine that you are traveling between Chicago and Denver. Chicago is 660 ft above sea level, whereas Denver is 5280 ft above sea level. No matter what route you take, the altitude change will be the same, 4620 ft. The distance you travel, however, will depend on your route. Altitude is analogous to a state function, whereas distance traveled is not.

Although some thermodynamic quantities are state functions, others are not. For example, the work done by a system in a given process is not a state function. Rather, it depends on the manner in which the process is carried out. As an example, let's consider a flashlight battery as our system and let the change in the system be the complete discharge of the battery at constant temperature. If the battery is discharged in a flashlight [Figure 5.7(a)], no

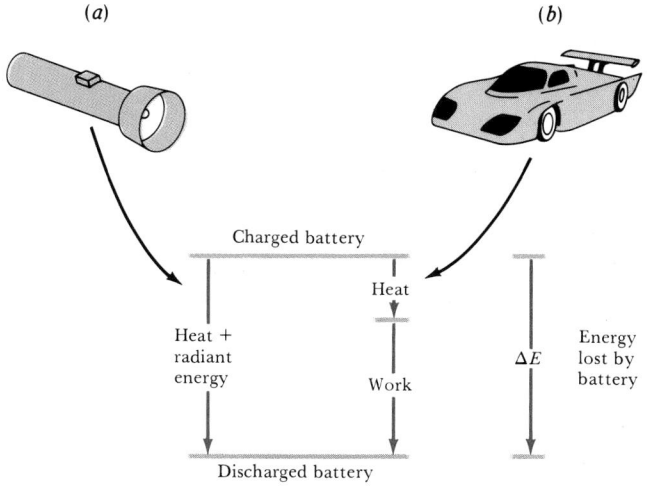

(a)

(b)

Charged battery

Heat

Heat +
radiant
energy

Work

ΔE

Energy
lost by
battery

Discharged battery

FIGURE 5.7 When a
battery is discharged in lighting
a flashlight, all the energy of
the battery appears as radiant
energy and heat; no work is
done. When the battery is used
in the toy car, work is done in
moving the car from place to
place. Thus, the work done by
the system (the battery) is not
a state function because its
magnitude depends on the
particular path by which the
system gets from its initial to
its final state.

Figure 5.7

mechanical work is accomplished. All the energy lost from the battery appears as radiant energy and heat. If the battery is used in a mechanical toy [Figure 5.7(b)], the same change in state of the battery produces mechanical work and heat. The change in state of the system, and thus the change in ΔE, are the same in both cases. However, the amount of work done in the two cases is different, as is the amount of heat released. We see from this example that although ΔE is always the same for a given change in the system, the way in which the change is performed will determine the relative contributions of q and w, the means by which energy is transferred.

5.3 Heat and Enthalpy Changes

When a process occurs in an open container, such as a beaker, most of the energy gained or lost by the system is in the form of heat. Only tiny amounts of work are usually involved as the system expands or contracts, causing it to change volume (move) against the force of the atmosphere. Thus, the heat gained or lost accounts for most of the change in the energy of the system. Heat flows between system and surroundings until the two are at the same temperature.

When a reaction or physical change occurs in which the system absorbs heat, we say that the process is **endothermic** (*endo-* is a prefix meaning "into"). In that case, heat flows *into* the system from its surroundings. Consider an endothermic process occurring in a container that is initially at room temperature. If we, as part of the surroundings, touch the container, it feels cold to us because heat has passed from our hands to the container.

A process that results in the evolution of heat is **exothermic** (*exo-* is a prefix meaning "out of"); that is, heat flows *out* of the system and into its surroundings. If we touch a container in which an exothermic reaction is occurring, it feels warm because heat has passed from the container to our hands. The combustion of gasoline is an exothermic process; the melting of ice is an endothermic process. Figure 5.8 shows further examples of endothermic and exothermic processes.

FIGURE 5.8 (*a*) When ammonium thiocyanate, NH_4SCN, and barium hydroxide octahydrate, $Ba(OH)_2 \cdot 8H_2O$, are mixed at room temperature, an endothermic reaction occurs: $2NH_4SCN(s) + Ba(OH)_2 \cdot 8H_2O(s) \longrightarrow Ba(SCN)_2(aq) + NH_3(aq) + 8H_2O(l)$. As a result of this reaction, the temperature of the system drops from about $20°C$ to the temperature shown on the digital thermometer, $-9°C$. (*b*) The reaction of powdered aluminum with Fe_2O_3 (known as the thermite reaction) is highly exothermic. Once started, the reaction proceeds vigorously to form Al_2O_3 and molten iron: $2Al(s) + Fe_2O_3(s) \longrightarrow Al_2O_3(s) + 2Fe(l)$. (Richard Megna/Fundamental Photographs)

(*a*)

(*b*)

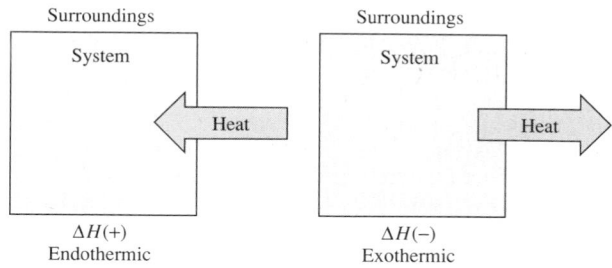

FIGURE 5.9 (*a*) If the system absorbs heat, ΔH will be positive ($\Delta H > 0$). (*b*) If the system loses heat, ΔH will be negative ($\Delta H < 0$).

Enthalpy

Most physical and chemical changes, including those in living systems, take place under the essentially constant pressure of the earth's atmosphere. In the laboratory, for example, reactions are generally carried out in containers that are open to the atmosphere. Chemists use a special symbol, H, and a special name, **enthalpy** (from the Greek word *enthalpein,* meaning "to warm") in dealing with the heat absorbed or released under constant pressure. Although heat is merely the energy that transfers between a system and its surroundings when they are at different temperatures, it is convenient to think of the process as if heat were flowing, causing the "heat content" of the system to change. In this view of the process, the enthalpy of the system would be its heat content.

We cannot measure the enthalpy of a system, but we can measure the *change in enthalpy,* which we represent by the symbol ΔH. *The change in enthalpy, ΔH, equals the heat, q_P, added to or lost by the system when the process occurs under constant pressure:*

Point of Emphasis: The heat exchanged in a reaction at constant pressure is ΔH.

$$\Delta H = q_P \qquad [5.5]$$

(We put a subscript P on q to remind ourselves that we are considering a special case where pressure is constant.)

ΔH represents the difference between the enthalpy of the system at the completion of a process and that at the beginning:

Learning Goal 6: Define enthalpy, and relate the enthalpy change in a process occurring at constant pressure to the heat added to or lost by the system during the process.

$$\Delta H = H_{\text{final}} - H_{\text{initial}}$$

A *positive* ΔH results when $H_{\text{final}} > H_{\text{initial}}$, indicating that the system has gained heat from the surroundings (an *endothermic process*), as shown in Figure 5.9(a). A *negative* ΔH is obtained when $H_{\text{final}} < H_{\text{initial}}$, indicating that the system has lost heat to its surroundings (an *exothermic process*), as shown in Figure 5.9(b). Like energy, the enthalpy of a system is a state function; that is, *the enthalpy of a system does not depend on the history of the system, only on its present condition.* Because H is a state function, ΔH depends only on the initial and final states of the system and not on how the change occurs.

5.4 Enthalpies of Reaction

Because $\Delta H = H_{\text{final}} - H_{\text{initial}}$, the enthalpy change for a chemical reaction is given by the enthalpy of the products minus that of the reactants:

Relating Energy and Enthalpy

We have seen that the change in the energy of a system is given by Equation 5.4: $\Delta E = q + w$. This equation allows us to understand better how ΔE and ΔH differ. To explore this difference, we must examine a common kind of work, that associated with the expansion or compression of a gas. For example, expanding gases from the combustion of gasoline in the cylinders of an automobile engine do work on the pistons, and this work eventually turns the wheels. Expanding gases from an open reaction vessel also do work in pushing back the atmosphere, but this work is lost to us; it accomplishes nothing in a practical sense. However, all kinds of work, whether useful or not, must be considered if we desire to keep track of all the energy changes of a system.

To better understand the work accomplished by expanding gases, consider a gas confined to a cylinder with a movable piston, as shown in Figure 5.10. A downward force, F, acts on the piston. The pressure on the gas is defined as the ratio of this force to the area, A, of the piston. That is, $P = F/A$. We will assume that the piston itself is weightless and that the only force acting on it is the weight of the earth's atmosphere. This pressure is called the *atmospheric pressure*. We will have more to say about atmospheric pressure and about the properties of gases in Chapter 10; at this point, we need only be aware that the atmosphere exerts a pressure, which we will assume is constant.

Suppose the expanding gas causes the piston to move a distance, Δh. The magnitude of the work accomplished by the moving piston is given by the product of the force and the distance:

$$\text{Work} = \text{force} \times \text{distance} = F \times \Delta h$$

Rearranging the equation that defines pressure, $P = F/A$, gives $F = P \times A$. Thus,

$$\text{Work} = F \times \Delta h = P \times A \times \Delta h$$

The volume change, ΔV, resulting from the piston moving is given by the product of the area of the piston and the distance it moves: $\Delta V = A \times \Delta h$. Thus,

$$\text{Work} = P \times A \times \Delta h = P \times \Delta V$$

This derivation gives the magnitude of the work, but what about its sign? Because an expanding gas does work on its surroundings, the work must be negative. For an expanding gas, ΔV is a positive quantity, and P is positive under all circumstances. In order for work, w, to be negative when P and ΔV are positive, we must introduce a negative sign:

$$w = -P \, \Delta V \qquad [5.6]$$

Substituting $w = -P \, \Delta V$ into Equation 5.4 and using q_P as our symbol for the heat gained or lost by the system under a constant applied pressure, we have

$$\Delta E = q_P - P \, \Delta V$$

Because $q_P = \Delta H$, we can make a further substitution to give

$$\Delta E = \Delta H - P \, \Delta V \qquad [5.7]$$

That is, the energy change, ΔE, of the system is given by the energy that enters or leaves as heat, ΔH, and the energy that the system expends or gains as work as it changes its volume, $-P \, \Delta V$.

The volume change accompanying many reactions is close to zero, making $P \, \Delta V$, and therefore the difference between ΔE and ΔH, small. For example, the combustion of a mole of $H_2(g)$ to form $H_2O(g)$ gives $\Delta E = -240.6$ kJ, and $\Delta H = -241.8$ kJ. We will not concern ourselves with the conversion between ΔE and ΔH elsewhere in the text. The important point is that because the difference is generally small, chemists tend to think of energy changes in most chemical reactions in terms of ΔH.

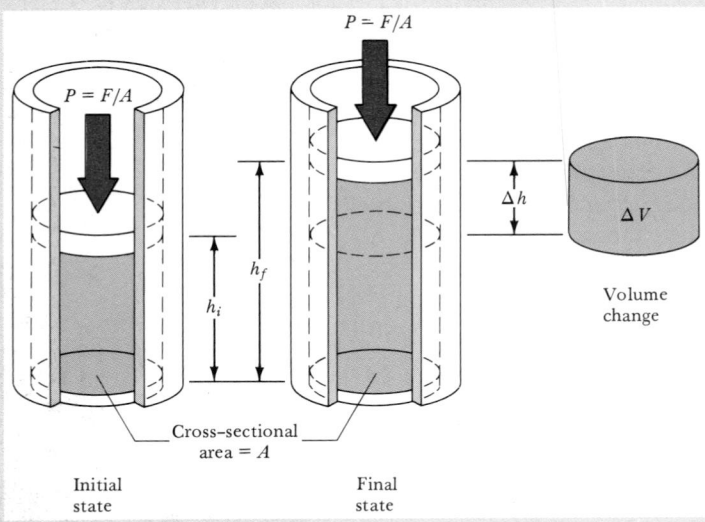

P = F/A

Δh

ΔV

Volume change

hf

hi

Cross-sectional area = A

Initial state

Final state

FIGURE 5.10 A piston moving a distance, Δh, against a pressure, P, does work on the surroundings. The amount of work done is given by the product of the pressure and the change in volume of the gas: $w = -P\Delta V$.

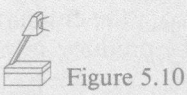

Figure 5.10

(a)

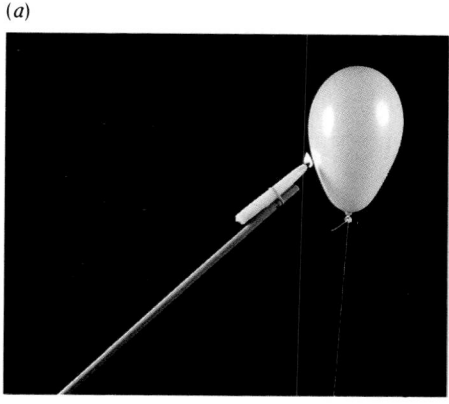

(b)

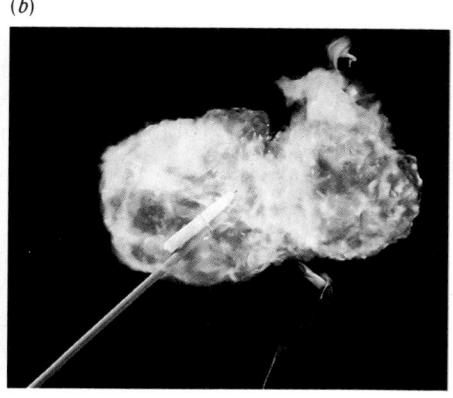

(c)

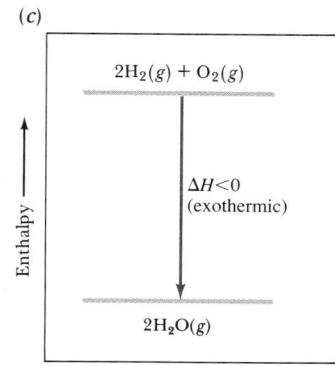

FIGURE 5.11 (*a*) A candle is held near a balloon filled with hydrogen gas and oxygen gas. (*b*) The $H_2(g)$ ignites, reacting with $O_2(g)$ to form $H_2O(g)$. The resultant explosion produces the yellow ball of flame. The system gives off heat to its surroundings, decreasing in enthalpy. (*c*) The energy diagram for this reaction, showing the exothermic character of the reaction. (Donald Clegg and Roxy Wilson)

$$\Delta H = H(\text{products}) - H(\text{reactants}) \qquad [5.8]$$

The enthalpy change that accompanies a reaction is called the *enthalpy of reaction* or merely the *heat of reaction* and is sometimes written ΔH_{rxn} ("rxn" is a commonly used abbreviation for "reaction").

We will often find it convenient to give the ΔH for a reaction together with the associated chemical equation. For example, consider the combustion of hydrogen (Figure 5.11). When the reaction is controlled so that 2 mol $H_2(g)$ burn to form 2 mol $H_2O(g)$ at a constant pressure, 483.6 kJ of heat is released by the system. We can summarize this information as follows:

$$2H_2(g) + O_2(g) \longrightarrow 2H_2O(g) \qquad \Delta H = -483.6 \text{ kJ} \qquad [5.9]$$

The negative sign for ΔH tells us that this reaction is exothermic. Notice that ΔH is reported at the end of the balanced equation, with no explicit mention of the amount of chemicals involved. In such cases, it is understood that the coefficients in the balanced equation represent the number of moles of reactants and products producing the associated enthalpy change. Balanced chemical equations that show the associated enthalpy change in this way are called *thermochemical equations*.

The enthalpy change accompanying a chemical reaction can also be represented in an *enthalpy diagram* such as that shown in Figure 5.11*(c)*. The fact that the combustion of $H_2(g)$ is exothermic indicates that the products in the reaction possess a lower enthalpy than the reactants. Using the analogy of the bicyclist in Figure 5.3, we can think of exothermic reactions as going "downhill" in enthalpy. Because the reaction of hydrogen with oxygen is highly exothermic and rapid at high temperatures, it can occur with explosive violence, as demonstrated by the disastrous explosions of the German airship *Hindenburg* in 1937 and the space shuttle *Challenger* in 1986 (Figure 5.12).

The following guidelines are helpful in using thermochemical equations and enthalpy diagrams:

FIGURE 5.12 The tragic explosion of the space shuttle *Challenger* was a result of the uncontrolled exothermic reaction between hydrogen and oxygen. Hydrogen, stored as a liquid, is the fuel used to propel space shuttles out of the earth's gravitational pull. (NASA)

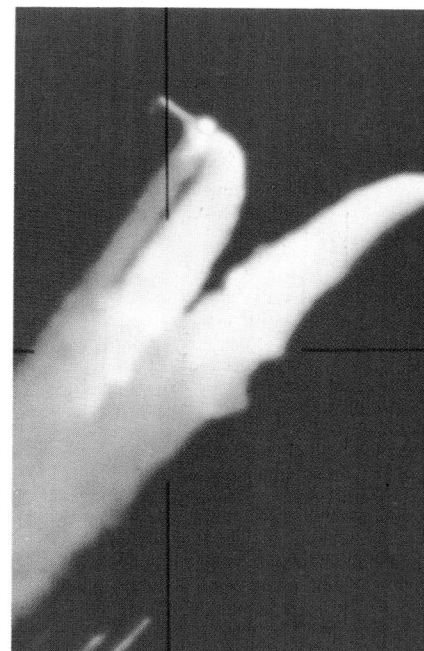

Teaching Note: Enthalpy is an extensive property; see Section 1.3.

Learning Goal 7: Sketch an energy diagram like that shown in Figure 5.13, given the enthalpy changes in the processes involved, and associate the sign of ΔH with whether the process is exothermic or endothermic.

Learning Goal 8: Calculate the quantity of heat involved in a reaction at constant pressure given the quantity of reactants and the enthalpy change for the reaction on a mole basis.

Lee R. Summerlin, Christie L. Borgford, and Julie B. Ealy, "Flaming Cotton," *Chemical Demonstrations, A Sourcebook for Teachers, Volume 2* (Washington: American Chemical Society, 1987), p. 102.

Lee R. Summerlin and James L. Ealy, Jr., "Endothermic Reaction: Ammonium Nitrate," *Chemical Demonstrations, A Sourcebook for Teachers* (Washington: American Chemical Society, 1985), p. 43.

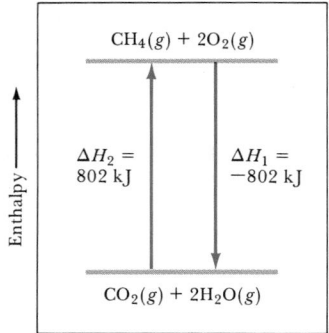

FIGURE 5.13 Reversing a reaction changes the sign but not the magnitude of the enthalpy change: $\Delta H_2 = -\Delta H_1$.

1. *Enthalpy is an extensive property.* This fact means that the magnitude of ΔH is directly proportional to the amount of reactant consumed in the process. Consider the combustion of methane to form carbon dioxide and water. It is found experimentally that 802 kJ of heat is produced when 1 mol of CH_4 is burned in a constant-pressure system:

$$CH_4(g) + 2O_2(g) \longrightarrow CO_2(g) + 2H_2O(g) \qquad \Delta H = -802 \text{ kJ} \quad [5.10]$$

Because the combustion of 1 mol of CH_4 with 2 mol of O_2 produces 802 kJ of heat, the combustion of twice this quantity (2 mol of CH_4 with 4 mol of O_2) produces twice as much heat, 1604 kJ.

SAMPLE EXERCISE 5.2

How much heat is released when 4.50 g of methane gas is burned in a constant-pressure system? (Use the information given in Equation 5.10.)

SOLUTION According to Equation 5.10, 802 kJ is produced when 1 mol CH_4 is burned at constant pressure ($\Delta H = -802$ kJ). We can treat this information as a stoichiometric relationship: 1 mol $CH_4 \,\widehat{=}\, -802$ kJ. To use this relationship, however, we must convert grams of CH_4 to moles of CH_4. By adding the atomic weights of C and 4H, we have 1 mol $CH_4 = 16.0$ g CH_4. Thus, we can use the appropriate conversion factors to convert grams of CH_4 to moles of CH_4 to kilojoules:

$$\text{Heat} = (4.50 \text{ g } CH_4)\left(\frac{1 \text{ mol } CH_4}{16.0 \text{ g } CH_4}\right)\left(\frac{-802 \text{ kJ}}{1 \text{ mol } CH_4}\right) = -226 \text{ kJ}$$

The negative sign indicates that 226 kJ is released by the system into the surroundings.

PRACTICE EXERCISE

Ammonium nitrate can decompose by the following reaction:

$$NH_4NO_3(s) \longrightarrow N_2O(g) + 2H_2O(g) \qquad \Delta H = -37.0 \text{ kJ}$$

Calculate the quantity of heat produced when 2.50 g of NH_4NO_3 decomposes at constant pressure. ***Answer:*** -1.16 kJ

2. *The enthalpy change for a reaction is equal in magnitude but opposite in sign to ΔH for the reverse reaction.* For example, when Equation 5.10 is reversed, ΔH for the process is $+802$ kJ:

$$CO_2(g) + 2H_2O(g) \longrightarrow CH_4(g) + 2O_2(g) \qquad \Delta H = 802 \text{ kJ} \quad [5.11]$$

When we reverse a reaction, we reverse the roles of the products and the reactants; the reactants in a reaction become the products of the reverse reaction, and so forth. From Equation 5.8, we can see that reversing the products and reactants leads to the same magnitude but a change in sign for ΔH. This relationship is diagramed for Equations 5.10 and 5.11 in Figure 5.13.

3. *The enthalpy change for a reaction depends on the state of the reactants and products.* If the product in the combustion of methane (Equation 5.10) were liquid H_2O instead of gaseous H_2O, ΔH would be -890 kJ instead of -802 kJ. More heat is available for transfer to the surround-

CHEMISTRY AT WORK

Using Exothermic Reactions to Warm Food

In a modern army, food rations are called "meals, ready to eat," or MREs. The key aspect of these rations is that they can be warmed without benefit of a stove or campfire. The pouch that contains the food is attached to a perforated fiberboard container (called a flameless ration heater). This heater contains chemicals that react with water to produce heat. When the pouch is placed in a bag and water added, the food reaches about 60°C in about 15 min (Figure 5.14).

The heater contains magnesium metal, which reacts with water:

$$Mg(s) + 2H_2O(l) \longrightarrow Mg(OH)_2(s) + H_2(g)$$
$$\Delta H = -353 \text{ kJ}$$

This reaction is normally very slow because magnesium metal has a film of oxide, MgO, on its surface, which protects the metal from further oxidation by either O_2 or H_2O. In order for magnesium to react rapidly with water, this barrier must be penetrated. The reaction of magnesium with water is greatly accelerated in the presence of iron and ordinary salt, NaCl. As we saw in Section 4.6, a less active metal (such as Fe) will promote the corrosion (oxidation) of an active metal (such as Mg). Therefore, the flameless ration heater contains a mixture of Mg, Fe, and NaCl.

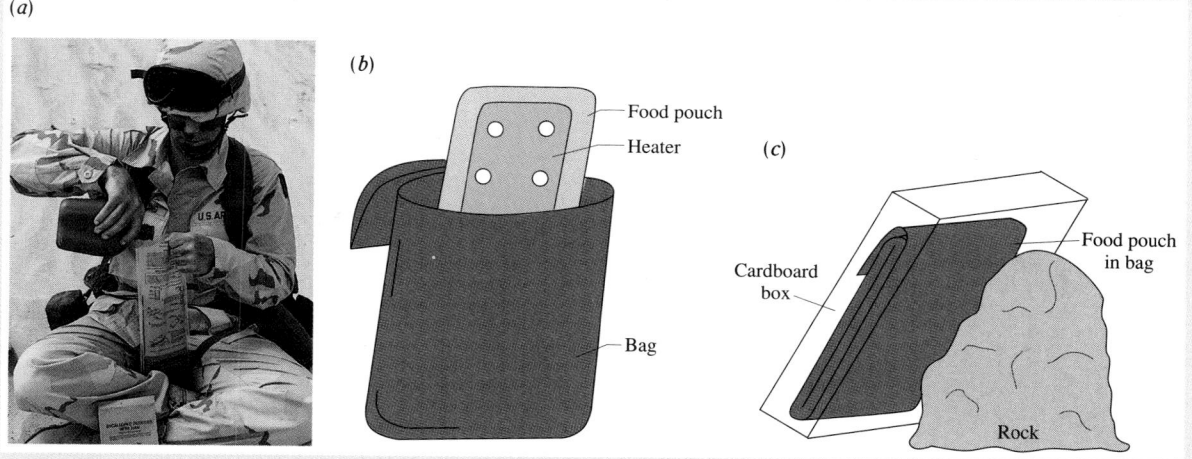

FIGURE 5.14 (a) A soldier adding water to a MRE. (b) The food pouch of a MRE with an attached chemical heater containing Mg, Fe, and NaCl. The pouch and heater are placed in a plastic bag, and water is added. (c) The bag and its contents are placed in a box and situated so water does not run out. (Photo courtesy of Natick Development and Engineering Center)

---

ings because 88 kJ is released when 2 mol of gaseous water is condensed to the liquid state:

$$2H_2O(g) \longrightarrow 2H_2O(l) \qquad \Delta H = -88 \text{ kJ} \qquad [5.12]$$

Therefore, the states of the reactants and products must be specified. In addition, we will generally assume that the reactants and products are both at the same temperature, 25°C, unless otherwise indicated.

Point of Emphasis: The physical states of the reactants and products need to be considered when calculating ΔH.

The enthalpy change associated with a given chemical process is often of great significance. In the sections that follow, we will consider some ways in which we can evaluate this important quantity. As we shall see, ΔH_{rxn} can be either directly determined by experiment or calculated from a knowledge of the enthalpy changes associated with other reactions by invoking the first law of thermodynamics.

5.5 Calorimetry

The value of ΔH can be determined experimentally by measuring the heat flow accompanying a reaction at constant pressure. When heat flows into or out of a substance, the temperature of the substance changes. Experimentally, we can determine the heat flow associated with a chemical reaction by measuring the temperature change it produces. The measurement of heat flow is called **calorimetry;** an apparatus that measures heat flow is called a **calorimeter.**

Heat Capacity and Specific Heat

Learning Goal 9: Define the terms *heat capacity* and *specific heat.*

When an object sits in the sun and absorbs heat, its temperature changes. The temperature change experienced by a body when it absorbs a certain amount of energy is determined by its **heat capacity.** We define the heat capacity of an object as the amount of heat required to raise its temperature by 1 K (or 1 °C). The greater the heat capacity of a body, the more heat it requires to produce a given rise in temperature. For example, a swimming pool has a much greater heat capacity than a fish tank. Much more heat is required to raise the temperature of water in a swimming pool from 15 °C to 25 °C than to produce the same temperature change in a fish tank.

Point of Emphasis: Molar heat capacity is heat capacity expressed on a per-mole basis.

For pure substances, the heat capacity is usually given for a specified amount of the substance. The heat capacity of 1 mol of a substance is called its **molar heat capacity.** The heat capacity of 1 g of a substance is called its *specific heat capacity,* or merely its **specific heat.** The specific heat of a substance can be determined experimentally by measuring the temperature change, ΔT, that a known mass, m, of the substance undergoes when it gains or loses a specific quantity of heat, q:

Point of Emphasis: Specific heat is heat capacity expressed on a per-gram basis.

Learning Goal 10: Calculate any one of the following quantities given the other three: heat, quantity of material, temperature change, and specific heat.

$$\text{Specific heat} = \frac{\text{quantity of heat transferred}}{(\text{grams of substance}) \times (\text{temperature change})}$$

$$= \frac{q}{m \times \Delta T} \qquad [5.13]$$

For example, 209 J is required to increase the temperature of 50.0 g of water by 1.00 K. Thus, the specific heat of water is

$$\text{Specific heat} = \frac{209\ \text{J}}{(50.0\ \text{g})(1.00\ \text{K})} = 4.18\ \frac{\text{J}}{\text{g-K}}$$

It is important to note that a temperature change in kelvins is equal in magnitude to the temperature change in degrees Celsius: $\Delta T = 1\ \text{K} = 1\ °\text{C}$. Remember that when the sample gains heat (positive q), the temperature of the sample increases (positive ΔT).

The specific heats of several substances are listed in Table 5.1. The specific heat of liquid water is one of the highest known. It is, for example, about five

TABLE 5.1 △ Specific Heats at 298 K

Substance	Specific heat (J/g-K)	Substance	Specific heat (J/g-K)
Elements		Compounds	
Al(s)	0.90	CaCO₃(s)	0.85
C(s)	0.71	CCl₄(l)	0.86
Fe(s)	0.45	H₂O(l)	4.18
Hg(l)	0.14		

times as great as that of aluminum metal. The high specific heat of water makes our body's important task of maintaining a constant body temperature, 37°C, much easier. The adult body is about 60 percent water by mass and consequently has the ability to absorb or release considerable energy with little effect on its temperature.

We can calculate the quantity of heat that a substance has gained or lost by using its specific heat together with its measured mass and temperature change. Rearranging Equation 5.13, we have

$$q = \text{(specific heat)} \times \text{(grams of substance)} \times \Delta T \qquad [5.14]$$

SAMPLE EXERCISE 5.3

(a) How much heat is required to raise the temperature of 250 g of water (about 1 cup) from 22°C (about room temperature) to near its boiling point, 98°C? The specific heat of water is 4.18 J/g-K. **(b)** What is the molar heat capacity of water?

SOLUTION **(a)** The water undergoes a temperature change of $\Delta T = 98°C - 22°C = 76°C = 76$ K. Using Equation 5.14, we have

$$q = \text{(specific heat of H}_2\text{O)} \times \text{(grams of H}_2\text{O)} \times \Delta T$$
$$= (4.18 \text{ J/g-K})(250 \text{ g})(76 \text{ K}) = 7.9 \times 10^4 \text{ J}$$

(b) The molar heat capacity is the heat capacity of 1 mol of substance. Using the atomic weights of hydrogen and oxygen, we have 1 mol H_2O = 18.0 g H_2O. From the specific heat given in part (a), we have

$$\text{Molar heat capacity} = (4.18 \text{ J/g-K})\left(\frac{18.0 \text{ g}}{1 \text{ mol}}\right) = 75.2 \text{ J/mol-K}$$

PRACTICE EXERCISE

(a) Large beds of rocks are used in some solar-heated homes to store heat. Calculate the quantity of heat absorbed by 50.0 kg of rocks if their temperature increases by 12.0°C. (Assume that the specific heat of the rocks is 0.82 J/g-K.) **(b)** What temperature change would these rocks undergo if they absorbed 450 kJ of heat? *Answer:* **(a)** 4.9×10^5 J; **(b)** 11 K = 11°C increase

Constant-Pressure Calorimetry

The techniques and equipment employed in calorimetry depend on the nature of the process being studied. For many reactions, such as those occurring in solution, it is a simple matter to control pressure so that ΔH is measured directly. (Recall that $\Delta H = q_P$.) Although the calorimeters used for highly accurate work are precision instruments, a very simple "coffee cup" calorimeter, such as that shown in Figure 5.15, is often used in general chemistry labs to

FIGURE 5.15 "Coffee cup" calorimeter, in which reactions occur at constant pressure.

Thermometer

Glass stirrer

Cork stopper

Two Styrofoam cups nested together containing reactants in solution illustrate the principles of calorimetry. Because the calorimeter is not sealed, the reaction occurs under the essentially constant pressure of the atmosphere. The heat of a reaction is determined from the temperature change of a known quantity of solution in the calorimeter. Because the calorimeter prevents the gain or loss of heat from its surroundings, the heat released by the reaction, $-q_{rxn}$, equals that gained by the solution, q_{soln}. Thus,

$$q_{rxn} = -q_{soln} = -(\text{specific heat of solution}) \times (\text{grams of solution}) \times \Delta T$$

For dilute solutions, the specific heat of the solution will be approximately the same as that of water, 4.18 J/g-K. As expected, a temperature increase (positive ΔT) means that the reaction is exothermic (negative q_{rxn}).

SAMPLE EXERCISE 5.4

When a student mixes 50 mL of 1.0 M HCl and 50 mL of 1.0 M NaOH in a coffee cup calorimeter, the temperature of the resultant solution increases from 21.0°C to 27.5°C. Calculate the enthalpy change for the reaction, assuming that the calorimeter loses only a negligible quantity of heat, that the total volume of the solution is 100 mL, that its density is 1.0 g/mL, and that its specific heat is 4.18 J/g-K.

SOLUTION Because the total volume of the solution is 100 mL, the mass of the solution is

$$(100 \text{ mL})(1.0 \text{ g/mL}) = 100 \text{ g}$$

The temperature change is 27°C − 21.0°C = 6.5°C = 6.5 K. Because the temperature increases, the reaction must be exothermic:

$$q_{rxn} = -(\text{specific heat of solution}) \times (\text{grams of solution}) \times \Delta T$$
$$= -(4.18 \text{ J/g-K})(100 \text{ g})(6.5 \text{ K}) = -2700 \text{ J} = -2.7 \text{ kJ}$$

Because the process occurs at constant pressure, $\Delta H = q_P = -2.7$ kJ. To put the enthalpy change on a molar basis, we use the fact that the number of moles of HCl and NaOH is given by the product of the respective solution volumes (50 mL = 0.050 L) and concentrations:

$$(0.050 \text{ L})(0.10 \text{ mol/L}) = 0.050 \text{ mol}$$

Thus, the enthalpy change per mole of HCl or NaOH is

$$\Delta H = -2.7 \text{ kJ}/0.050 \text{ mol} = -54 \text{ kJ/mol}$$

PRACTICE EXERCISE

When 50.0 mL of 0.100 M AgNO$_3$ and 50.0 mL of 0.100 M HCl are mixed in a constant-pressure calorimeter, the temperature of the mixture increases from 22.30°C to 23.11°C. The temperature increase is caused by the following reaction:

$$AgNO_3(aq) + HCl(aq) \longrightarrow AgCl(s) + HNO_3(aq)$$

Calculate ΔH for this reaction, assuming that the combined solution has a mass of 100.0 g and a specific heat of 4.18 J/g-°C. *Answer:* −68,000 J/mol = −68 kJ/mol

Bomb Calorimetry (Constant-Volume Calorimetry)

One of the most important types of reactions studied by means of calorimetry is combustion. ∞ (Sec. 3.2)   A compound, usually an organic compound, is allowed to react completely with excess oxygen. Equation 5.10 is an example of such a reaction. Combustion reactions are most conveniently studied by means of a **bomb calorimeter,** a device shown schematically in Figure 5.16. The substance to be studied is placed in a small cup within a sealed vessel called a *bomb.*

FIGURE 5.16 Cutaway view of a bomb calorimeter, in which reactions occur at constant volume.

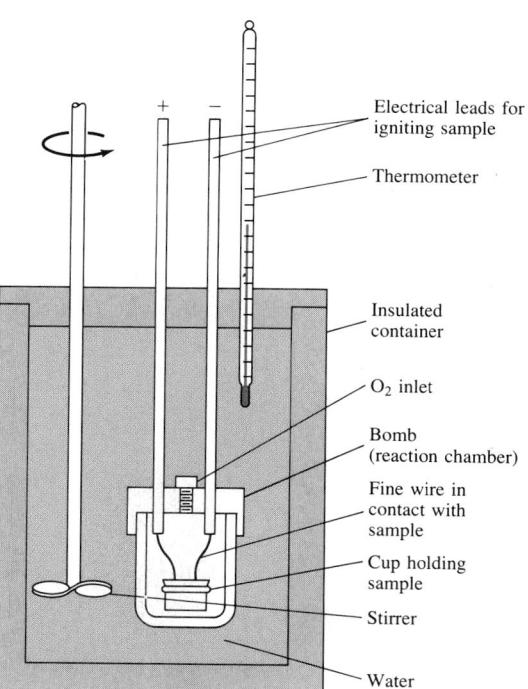

Electrical leads for igniting sample

Thermometer

Insulated container

O_2 inlet

Bomb (reaction chamber)

Fine wire in contact with sample

Cup holding sample

Stirrer

Water

Figure 5.16

The bomb, which is designed to withstand high pressures, has an inlet valve for adding oxygen and also has electrical contacts to initiate the combustion reaction. After the sample has been placed in the bomb, the bomb is sealed and pressurized with oxygen. It is then placed in the calorimeter, which is essentially an insulated container, and covered with an accurately measured quantity of water. When all the components within the calorimeter have come to the same temperature, the combustion reaction is initiated by passing an electrical current through a fine wire that is in contact with the sample. When the wire gets sufficiently hot, the sample ignites.

Heat is evolved (released) when combustion occurs. This heat is absorbed by the calorimeter contents, causing a rise in the temperature of the water. The temperature of the water is very carefully measured before reaction and then after reaction when the contents of the calorimeter have again arrived at a common temperature. The heat evolved in the combustion of the sample is absorbed by its surroundings, namely, the calorimeter contents.

To calculate the heat of combustion from the measured temperature increase in the calorimeter, it is necessary to know the heat capacity of the calorimeter, $C_{calorimeter}$. This is normally ascertained by combusting a sample that gives off a known quantity of heat. For example, it is known that combustion of exactly 1 g of benzoic acid, $C_7H_6O_2$, in a bomb calorimeter produces 26.38 kJ of heat. Suppose that 1 g of benzoic acid is combusted in our calorimeter and it causes a temperature increase of 5.022°C. The heat capacity of the calorimeter is then given by 26.38 kJ/5.022°C = 5.253 kJ/°C. Once we know the value of the heat capacity of the calorimeter, we can measure temperature changes produced by other reactions, and from these we can calculate the heat, q, evolved in the reaction:

$$q_{evolved} = -C_{calorimeter} \times \Delta T \qquad [5.15]$$

Learning Goal 11: Calculate the heat capacity of the calorimeter, given the temperature change and quantity of material involved; also calculate the heat evolved or absorbed in a process from a knowledge of the heat capacity of the system and its temperature change.

SAMPLE EXERCISE 5.5

Hydrazine, N_2H_4, and its derivatives are widely used as rocket fuels. The combustion of hydrazine with oxygen produces $N_2(g)$ and $H_2O(g)$:

$$N_2H_4(l) + O_2(g) \longrightarrow N_2(g) + 2H_2O(g)$$

When 1.00 g of hydrazine is burned in a bomb calorimeter, the temperature of the calorimeter increases by 3.51°C. If the calorimeter has a heat capacity of 5.510 kJ/°C, what is the quantity of heat evolved? What amount of heat is evolved upon combustion of a mole of N_2H_4?

SOLUTION   The quantity of heat evolved is simply the heat capacity times the temperature change (Equation 5.15).

$$-\left(\frac{5.510 \text{ kJ}}{1°C}\right) 3.51°C = -19.3 \text{ kJ}$$

Because this is the amount of heat that results from combustion of 1.00 g of hydrazine, the amount released by combustion of 1 mol of N_2H_4 is

$$\left(\frac{-19.3 \text{ kJ}}{1 \text{ g } N_2H_4}\right)\left(\frac{32.0 \text{ g } N_2H_4}{1 \text{ mol } N_2H_4}\right) = -618 \text{ kJ/mol } N_2H_4$$

PRACTICE EXERCISE

A 0.5865-g sample of lactic acid, $HC_3H_5O_3$, is burned in a calorimeter whose heat capacity is 4.812 kJ/°C. The temperature increases from 23.10°C to 24.95°C. Calculate the heat of combustion of lactic acid per gram and per mole.
Answer: −15.2 kJ/g; −1370 kJ/mol

Because the reactions in a bomb calorimeter occur under constant-volume rather than constant-pressure conditions, the heat transferred corresponds to the energy change, ΔE, rather than the enthalpy change, ΔH. It is possible to correct the measured heat changes to obtain ΔH values, but the corrections are usually small, and we will not concern ourselves with them.

5.6 Hess's Law

Many enthalpies of reaction have been measured and tabulated. In this section and the next, we will see that it is often possible to calculate the ΔH for a reaction from the tabulated ΔH values of other reactions. Thus, it is not necessary to make calorimetric measurements for all reactions.

Because enthalpy is a state function, the enthalpy change, ΔH, associated with any chemical process depends only on the amount of matter that undergoes change and on the nature of the initial state of the reactants and the final state of the products. This means that if a particular reaction can be carried out in one step or in a series of steps, the sum of the enthalpy changes associated with the individual steps must be the same as the enthalpy change associated with the one-step process. As an example, the combustion of methane gas, $CH_4(g)$, to form $CO_2(g)$ and liquid water can be thought of as occurring in two steps: (1) the combustion of $CH_4(g)$ to form $CO_2(g)$ and gaseous water, $H_2O(g)$, and (2) the condensation of gaseous water to form liquid water, $H_2O(l)$. The enthalpy change for the overall process is simply the sum of the enthalpy changes for these two steps:

$$CH_4(g) + 2O_2(g) \longrightarrow CO_2(g) + 2H_2O(g) \qquad \Delta H = -802 \text{ kJ}$$
(Add)
$$\underline{2H_2O(g) \longrightarrow 2H_2O(l) \qquad\qquad\qquad \Delta H = -88 \text{ kJ}}$$
$$CH_4(g) + 2O_2(g) + 2H_2O(g) \longrightarrow CO_2(g) + 2H_2O(l) + 2H_2O(g) \quad \Delta H = -890 \text{ kJ}$$

Net equation:

$$CH_4(g) + 2O_2(g) \longrightarrow CO_2(g) + 2H_2O(l) \qquad \Delta H = -890 \text{ kJ}$$

To obtain the net equation, the sum of the reactants of the two equations is placed on one side of the arrow, and the sum of the products on the other side. Because $2H_2O(g)$ occurs on both sides of the arrow, it can be canceled like an algebraic quantity that appears on both sides of an equal sign.

Hess's law states that *if a reaction is carried out in a series of steps, ΔH for the reaction will be equal to the sum of the enthalpy changes for the individual steps.* The overall enthalpy change for the process is independent of the number of steps or the particular nature of the path by which the reaction is carried out. We can therefore calculate ΔH for any process, as long as we find a route for which ΔH is known for each step. This important fact permits us to use a relatively small number of experimental measurements to calculate ΔH for a vast number of different reactions.

Hess's law provides a useful means of calculating energy changes that are difficult to measure directly. For instance, it is not possible to measure directly the enthalpy of combustion of carbon to form carbon monoxide. Combustion of 1 mol of carbon with $\frac{1}{2}$ mol of O_2 produces not only CO but also CO_2, leaving some carbon unreacted. However, both solid carbon and carbon monoxide can be completely burned in O_2 to produce CO_2. We can use the enthalpy changes of these reactions to calculate the heat of combustion of C to CO, as shown in Sample Exercise 5.6.

Point of Emphasis: If a reaction is multiplied or divided by a number (whole or fractional), the ΔH must also be multiplied or divided by that same number.

Learning Goal 12: State Hess's law, and apply it to calculate the enthalpy change in a process, given the enthalpy changes in other processes that could be combined to yield the reaction of interest.

Teaching Note: This is a direct consequence of the fact that enthalpy is a state function.

SAMPLE EXERCISE 5.6

The enthalpy of combustion of C to CO_2 is -393.5 kJ/mol C, and the enthalpy of combustion of CO to CO_2 is -283.0 kJ/mol CO:

$$(1) \quad C(s) + O_2(g) \longrightarrow CO_2(g) \qquad \Delta H = -393.5 \text{ kJ}$$
$$(2) \quad CO(g) + \tfrac{1}{2}O_2(g) \longrightarrow CO_2(g) \qquad \Delta H = -283.0 \text{ kJ}$$

Using these data, calculate the enthalpy of combustion of C to CO:

$$(3) \quad C(s) + \tfrac{1}{2}O_2(g) \longrightarrow CO(g)$$

SOLUTION In order to use equations (1) and (2), we need to arrange them so that C(s) is on the reactant side and CO(g) is on the product side of the arrow, as we see in the target reaction, equation (3). Because equation (1) has C(s) as a reactant, we can use that equation just as it is. Notice that the target reaction has CO(g) as a product. Thus, we need to turn equation (2) around so that CO(g) is a product. Remember that when reactions are turned around, the sign of ΔH is reversed. We arrange the two equations so that they can be added to give the target equation:

$$C(s) + O_2(g) \longrightarrow CO_2(g) \qquad\qquad \Delta H = -393.5 \text{ kJ}$$
$$\underline{CO_2(g) \longrightarrow CO(g) + \tfrac{1}{2}O_2(g) \qquad \Delta H = 283.0 \text{ kJ}}$$
$$C(s) + \tfrac{1}{2}O_2(g) \longrightarrow CO(g) \qquad\qquad \Delta H = -110.5 \text{ kJ}$$

When we add the two equations, $CO_2(g)$ appears on both sides of the arrow and therefore cancels out. Likewise, $\frac{1}{2}O_2(g)$ is eliminated from each side when the two equations are summed.

Point of Emphasis: If a reaction is reversed, then the sign of ΔH must be switched.

PRACTICE EXERCISE

Carbon occurs in two forms, graphite and diamond. The enthalpy of combustion of graphite is -393.5 kJ/mol, and that of diamond is -395.4 kJ/mol:

$$C(\text{graphite}) + O_2(g) \longrightarrow CO_2(g) \qquad \Delta H = -393.5 \text{ kJ}$$

$$C(\text{diamond}) + O_2(g) \longrightarrow CO_2(g) \qquad \Delta H = -395.4 \text{ kJ}$$

Calculate ΔH for the conversion of graphite to diamond:

$$C(\text{graphite}) \longrightarrow C(\text{diamond})$$

Answer: $+1.9$ kJ

SAMPLE EXERCISE 5.7

Calculate ΔH for the reaction

$$2C(s) + H_2(g) \longrightarrow C_2H_2(g)$$

given the following reactions and their respective enthalpy changes:

$$C_2H_2(g) + \tfrac{5}{2}O_2(g) \longrightarrow 2CO_2(g) + H_2O(l) \qquad \Delta H = -1299.6 \text{ kJ}$$

$$C(s) + O_2(g) \longrightarrow CO_2(g) \qquad \Delta H = -393.5 \text{ kJ}$$

$$H_2(g) + \tfrac{1}{2}O_2(g) \longrightarrow H_2O(l) \qquad \Delta H = -285.9 \text{ kJ}$$

SOLUTION Because the target equation has C_2H_2 as a product, we turn the first equation around; the sign of ΔH is therefore changed. Because the target equation has $2C(s)$ as a reactant, we multiply the second equation and its ΔH by 2. Because the target equation has H_2 as a reactant, we keep the third equation as it is. We then add the three equations and their enthalpy changes in accordance with Hess's law:

$$
\begin{array}{ll}
2CO_2(g) + H_2O(l) \longrightarrow C_2H_2(g) + \tfrac{5}{2}O_2(g) & \Delta H = \quad 1299.6 \text{ kJ} \\
2C(s) + 2O_2(g) \longrightarrow 2CO_2(g) & \Delta H = -787.0 \text{ kJ} \\
H_2(g) + \tfrac{1}{2}O_2(g) \longrightarrow H_2O(l) & \Delta H = -285.9 \text{ kJ} \\
\hline
2C(s) + H_2(g) \longrightarrow C_2H_2(g) & \Delta H = \quad 226.7 \text{ kJ}
\end{array}
$$

When the equations are added, there are $2CO_2$, $\tfrac{3}{2}O_2$, and H_2O on both sides of the arrow. These are canceled in writing the net equation.

PRACTICE EXERCISE

Calculate ΔH for the reaction

$$NO(g) + O(g) \longrightarrow NO_2(g)$$

given the following information:

$$NO(g) + O_3(g) \longrightarrow NO_2(g) + O_2(g) \qquad \Delta H = -198.9 \text{ kJ}$$

$$O_3(g) \longrightarrow \tfrac{3}{2}O_2(g) \qquad \Delta H = -142.3 \text{ kJ}$$

$$O_2(g) \longrightarrow 2O(g) \qquad \Delta H = \quad 495.0 \text{ kJ}$$

Answer: -304.1 kJ

The first law of thermodynamics, in the form of Hess's law, teaches us that we can never expect to obtain more (or less) energy from a chemical reaction by changing the method of carrying out the reaction. For example, for the reaction of methane, CH_4, and oxygen, O_2, to form CO_2 and H_2O, we may envision the reaction to occur either directly or with the initial formation of CO, which is then subsequently combusted. This set of choices is illustrated in Figure 5.17. Because ΔH is a state function, either path produces the same change in the enthalpy content of the system. That is, $\Delta H_1 = \Delta H_2 + \Delta H_3$.

FIGURE 5.17 The
quantity of heat generated by
combustion of CH_4 is
independent of whether the
reaction takes place in one or
more steps ($\Delta H_1 = \Delta H_2 + \Delta H_3$).

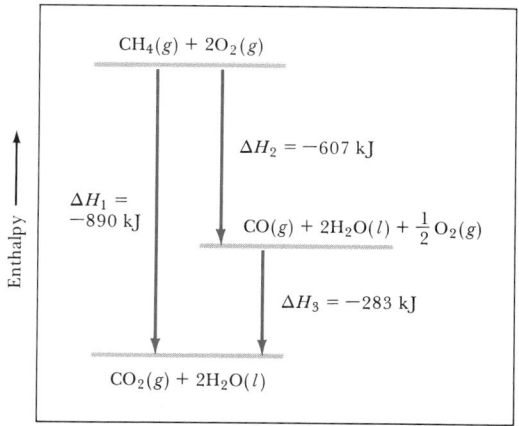

5.7 Enthalpies of Formation

By using the methods we have just discussed, we can calculate the enthalpy changes for a great many reactions from a few tabulated ΔH values. Many experimental data are tabulated according to the type of process. For example, extensive tables exist of *enthalpies of vaporization* (ΔH for converting liquids to gas), *enthalpies of fusion* (ΔH for melting solids), *enthalpies of combustion* (ΔH for combusting a substance in oxygen), and so forth. A particularly important process used for tabulating thermochemical data is the formation of a compound from its constituent elements. The enthalpy change associated with this process is called the **enthalpy of formation** (or *heat of formation*) and is labeled ΔH_f, where the subscript *f* indicates that the substance has been *formed* from its elements.

The magnitude of any enthalpy change depends on the conditions of temperature, pressure, and state (gas, liquid, or solid, crystalline form) of the reactants and products. The **standard state** for a substance is the form most stable at the particular temperature of interest and at standard atmospheric pressure (1 atm; see Section 10.2). When a reaction occurs with all reactants and products in their standard states, we refer to its enthalpy change as the *standard enthalpy of reaction, $\Delta H°$*, where the superscript ° indicates standard conditions. The temperature usually chosen for tabulating data is 298 K (25°C). Thus, the **standard enthalpy of formation** of a compound, $\Delta H_f°$, is the change in enthalpy that accompanies the formation of 1 mol of that substance from its elements, with all substances in their standard states. For example, the standard enthalpy of formation for ethanol, C_2H_5OH, is the enthalpy change for the following reaction:

$$2C(\text{graphite}) + 3H_2(g) + \tfrac{1}{2}O_2(g) \longrightarrow C_2H_5OH(l)$$

$$\Delta H_f° = -277.7 \text{ kJ} \quad [5.16]$$

The elemental source of oxygen is O_2, not O or O_3, because O_2 is the stable form of oxygen at 25°C and standard atmospheric pressure. Similarly, the elemental source of carbon is graphite and not diamond, because the former is the stable (lower-energy) form at 25°C and standard atmospheric pressure. The conversion of graphite to diamond requires the addition of energy:

$$C(graphite) \longrightarrow C(diamond) \qquad \Delta H° = 1.88 \text{ kJ} \qquad [5.17]$$

The most stable form of hydrogen under standard conditions is $H_2(g)$, so this is used as the source of hydrogen in Equation 5.16.

The stoichiometry of formation reactions always indicates that 1 mol of the desired substance is produced, as in Equation 5.16. As a result, enthalpies of formation are reported in kJ/mol of the substance. Several standard enthalpies of formation are given in Table 5.2. A more complete table is provided in Appendix C. By definition, *the standard enthalpy of formation of the most stable form of any element is zero* because there is no formation reaction needed when the element is already in its standard state. Thus, the values of $\Delta H_f°$ for $C(graphite)$, $H_2(g)$, $O_2(g)$, and the standard states of other elements are zero by definition.

Teaching Note: Appendix C has an extensive list of standard enthalpy values.

Point of Emphasis: For the most stable form of an element at standard conditions, $\Delta H_f°$ has a value of zero.

Learning Goal 15: Calculate the enthalpy change in a reaction occurring at constant pressure, given the standard enthalpies of formation of each reactant and product.

Point of Emphasis: The sums must be completed before subtracting.

Using Enthalpies of Formation to Calculate Enthalpies of Reaction

We can determine the standard enthalpy change for any reaction, $\Delta H_{rxn}°$, by using standard enthalpies of formation and Hess's law. We sum the enthalpies of formation of all reaction products, taking care to multiply each molar enthalpy of formation by the coefficient of that substance in the balanced equation. From this, we subtract a similar sum of the enthalpies of formation for the reactants:

$$\Delta H_{rxn}° = \sum n\Delta H_f°(\text{products}) - \sum m\Delta H_f°(\text{reactants}) \qquad [5.18]$$

The symbol Σ (sigma) means "the sum of," and n and m are the stoichiometric coefficients of the chemical reaction. For example, we can calculate $\Delta H°$ for the combustion of propane from the $\Delta H_f°$ values of the products and reactants:

$$C_3H_8(g) + 5O_2(g) \longrightarrow 3CO_2(g) + 4H_2O(l) \qquad [5.19]$$

$$\Delta H_{rxn}° = [3\Delta H_f°(CO_2) + 4\Delta H_f°(H_2O)] - [\Delta H_f°(C_3H_8) + 5\Delta H_f°(O_2)] \qquad [5.20]$$

TABLE 5.2 △ Standard Enthalpies of Formation, $\Delta H_f°$, at 25°C

Substance	Formula	$\Delta H_f°$(kJ/mol)	Substance	Formula	$\Delta H_f°$(kJ/mol)
Acetylene	$C_2H_2(g)$	226.7	Hydrogen chloride	$HCl(g)$	−92.30
Ammonia	$NH_3(g)$	−46.19	Hydrogen fluoride	$HF(g)$	−268.6
Benzene	$C_6H_6(l)$	49.04	Hydrogen iodide	$HI(g)$	25.9
Calcium carbonate	$CaCO_3(s)$	−1207.1	Methane	$CH_4(g)$	−74.85
Calcium oxide	$CaO(s)$	−635.5	Methanol	$CH_3OH(l)$	−238.6
Carbon dioxide	$CO_2(g)$	−393.5	Propane	$C_3H_8(g)$	−103.85
Carbon monoxide	$CO(g)$	−110.5	Silver chloride	$AgCl(s)$	−127.0
Diamond	$C(s)$	1.88	Sodium bicarbonate	$NaHCO_3(s)$	−947.7
Ethane	$C_2H_6(g)$	−84.68	Sodium carbonate	$Na_2CO_3(s)$	−1130.9
Ethanol	$C_2H_5OH(l)$	−277.7	Sodium chloride	$NaCl(s)$	−411.0
Ethylene	$C_2H_4(g)$	52.30	Sucrose	$C_{12}H_{22}O_{11}(s)$	−2221
Glucose	$C_6H_{12}O_6(s)$	−1260	Water	$H_2O(l)$	−285.8
Hydrogen bromide	$HBr(g)$	−36.23	Water vapor	$H_2O(g)$	−241.8

FIGURE 5.18 Because ΔH is a state function, $\Delta H_1 = \Delta H_2 + \Delta H_3$. Note that ΔH_2 is $-\Delta H_f^\circ(C_3H_8)$, whereas ΔH_3 is $4\,\Delta H_f^\circ(H_2O) + 3\,\Delta H_f^\circ(CO_2)$. That is, the enthalpy change for combustion of C_3H_8 equals the sum of the enthalpy changes for converting the reactants into the standard states of the elements and then forming the products from the elements. This same result is given by Equation 5.19, because $\Delta H_f^\circ(O_2)$ is zero.

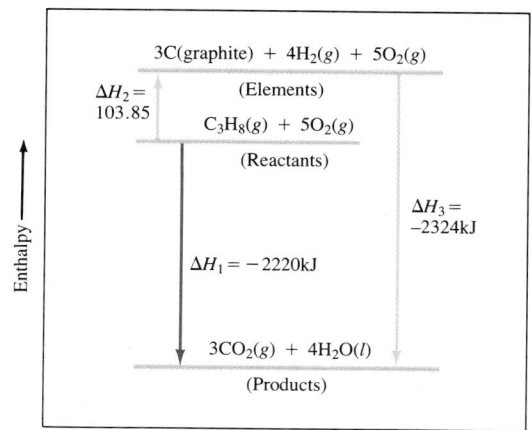

Figure 5.18

Because $O_2(g)$ is the most stable form of the element, $\Delta H_f^\circ(O_2) = 0$. The other enthalpies of formation can be obtained from Table 5.2, giving

$$\Delta H_{rxn}^\circ = \left[(3\text{ mol }CO_2)\left(-393.5\,\frac{kJ}{\text{mol }CO_2}\right) + (4\text{ mol }H_2O)\left(-285.8\,\frac{kJ}{\text{mol }H_2O}\right)\right]$$
$$- \left[(1\text{ mol }C_3H_8)\left(-103.85\,\frac{kJ}{\text{mol }C_3H_8}\right) + (5\text{ mol }O_2)\left(0\,\frac{kJ}{\text{mol }O_2}\right)\right]$$
$$= (-2324\text{ kJ}) - (-103.85\text{ kJ})$$
$$= -2220\text{ kJ}$$

The general relationship expressed in Equation 5.18 is just an application of Hess's law. It follows directly from the fact that H is a state function. This fact allows calculation of the enthalpy change for any reaction from the energies required to convert the initial reactants into elements and then combine the elements into the desired products. This reaction pathway is shown in Figure 5.18 for the combustion of propane.

SAMPLE EXERCISE 5.8

Compare the quantity of heat produced by combustion of 1.00 g of propane, C_3H_8, with that produced by 1.00 g of benzene, C_6H_6.

SOLUTION The example worked in the text gave $\Delta H^\circ = -2220$ kJ for the combustion of a mole of propane. The molecular weight of propane is 44.0 amu. Therefore, the heat produced per gram is

$$(-2220\text{ kJ/mol})\left(\frac{1\text{ mol}}{44.0\text{ g}}\right) = -50.5\text{ kJ/g}$$

For 1 mol of benzene:

$$C_6H_6(l) + \tfrac{15}{2}O_2(g) \longrightarrow 6CO_2(g) + 3H_2O(l)$$

Using Equation 5.18 and data in Table 5.2, we have

$$\Delta H_{rxn}^\circ = [6\Delta H_f^\circ(CO_2) + 3\Delta H_f^\circ(H_2O)] - [\Delta H_f^\circ(C_6H_6) + \tfrac{15}{2}\,\Delta H_f^\circ(O_2)]$$
$$= 6(-393.5\text{ kJ}) + 3(-285.8\text{ kJ}) - (49.04\text{ kJ})$$
$$= (-2361 - 857.4 - 49.04)\text{ kJ}$$
$$= -3267\text{ kJ}$$

The molecular weight of benzene is 78.0 amu. Therefore, the heat produced per gram of benzene is

$$(-3267 \text{ kJ/mol})\left(\frac{1 \text{ mol}}{78.0 \text{ g}}\right) = -41.9 \text{ kJ/g}$$

Both propane and benzene are hydrocarbons. As a rule of thumb, the energy obtained from the combustion of a gram of hydrocarbon is between 40 and 50 kJ.

PRACTICE EXERCISE

Using the standard enthalpies of formation listed in Table 5.2, calculate the enthalpy change for the combustion of 1 mol of ethanol:

$$C_2H_5OH(l) + 3O_2(g) \longrightarrow 2CO_2(g) + 3H_2O(l)$$

Answer: -1366.7 kJ

SAMPLE EXERCISE 5.9

The standard enthalpy change for the reaction

$$CaCO_3(s) \longrightarrow CaO(s) + CO_2(g)$$

is 178.1 kJ. From the values for the standard enthalpies of formation of $CaO(s)$ and $CO_2(g)$ given in Table 5.2, calculate the standard enthalpy of formation of $CaCO_3(s)$.

SOLUTION   The standard enthalpy change in the reaction is

$$\Delta H^\circ_{rxn} = [\Delta H^\circ_f(CaO) + \Delta H^\circ_f(CO_2)] - \Delta H^\circ_f(CaCO_3)$$

Inserting the known values, we have

$$178.1 \text{ kJ} = -635.5 \text{ kJ} - 393.5 \text{ kJ} - \Delta H^\circ_f(CaCO_3)$$

Solving for $\Delta H^\circ_f(CaCO_3)$ gives

$$\Delta H^\circ_f(CaCO_3) = -1207.1 \text{ kJ/mol}$$

PRACTICE EXERCISE

Given the following standard enthalpy of reaction, use the standard enthalpies of formation in Table 5.2 to calculate the standard enthalpy of formation of $CuO(s)$:

$$CuO(s) + H_2(g) \longrightarrow Cu(s) + H_2O(l) \qquad \Delta H^\circ = -130.6 \text{ kJ}$$

Answer: -155.2 kJ/mol

5.8 Foods and Fuels

Most chemical reactions used to produce heat are combustion reactions. The energy released when 1 g of a material is combusted is often called its **fuel value.** Because all heats of combustion are exothermic, it is common to report fuel values without their associated negative sign. The fuel value of any food or fuel can be measured by calorimetry.

Foods

Most of the energy our bodies need comes from carbohydrates and fats. Carbohydrates are decomposed in the intestines into glucose, $C_6H_{12}O_6$. Glucose is soluble in blood and is known as blood sugar. It is transported by the blood to cells, where it reacts with O_2 in a series of steps, eventually producing $CO_2(g)$, $H_2O(l)$, and energy:

$$C_6H_{12}O_6(s) + 6O_2(g) \longrightarrow 6CO_2(g) + 6H_2O(l) \qquad \Delta H^\circ = -2816 \text{ kJ}$$

The breakdown of carbohydrates is rapid, so their energy is quickly supplied to the body. However, the body stores only a very small amount of carbohydrates. The average fuel value of carbohydrates is 17 kJ/g (4 kcal/g).

Like carbohydrates, fats produce CO_2 and H_2O in both their metabolism and their combustion in a bomb calorimeter. The reaction of tristearin, $C_{57}H_{110}O_6$, a typical fat, is as follows:

$$2C_{57}H_{110}O_6(s) + 163O_2(g) \longrightarrow 114CO_2(g) + 110H_2O(l)$$
$$\Delta H^\circ = -75,520 \text{ kJ}$$

The body puts the chemical energy from foods to different uses: to maintain body temperature, to drive muscles, and to construct and repair tissues. Any excess energy is stored as fats. Fats are well suited to serve as the body's energy reserve for at least two reasons: (1) They are insoluble in water, which permits their storage in the body; and (2) they produce more energy per gram than either proteins or carbohydrates, which makes them efficient energy sources on a mass basis. The average fuel value of fats is 38 kJ/g (9 kcal/g).

In the case of proteins, metabolism in the body produces less energy than combustion in a calorimeter does because the products are different. Proteins contain nitrogen, which is released in the bomb calorimeter as N_2. In the body, this nitrogen ends up mainly as urea, $(NH_2)_2CO$. Proteins are used by the body mainly as building materials for organ walls, skin, hair, muscle, and so forth. On the average, the metabolism of proteins produces 17 kJ/g (4 kcal/g), the same as for carbohydrates.

The fuel values for a variety of common foods are shown in Table 5.3. Labels on packaged foods show the amounts of carbohydrate, fat, and protein contained in an average serving, as well as the energy value of the serving (Figure 5.19). The amount of energy our bodies require varies considerably depending on such factors as weight, age, and muscular activity. About 100 kJ per kilogram of body weight per day is required to keep the body functioning at a minimal level. An average 70-kg person expends about 800 kJ/hr when doing light work, such as slow walking or light gardening. Strenuous activity, such as

FIGURE 5.19 Labels of processed foods have information about the quantities of different nutrients in an average serving. (Richard Megna/Fundamental Photographs)

TABLE 5.3 △ Fuel Values and Compositions of Some Common Foods

	Approximate composition (% by mass)			Fuel value	
	Protein	Fat	Carbohydrate	kJ/g	kcal/g
Apples (raw)	0.4	0.5	13	2.5	0.59
Beer[a]	0.3	0	1.2	1.8	0.42
Bread (white, enriched)	9	3	52	12	2.8
Cheese (cheddar)	28	37	4	20	4.7
Eggs	13	10	0.7	6	1.4
Fudge	2	11	81	18	4.4
Green beans (frozen)	1.9	—	7.0	1.5	0.38
Hamburger	22	30	—	15	3.6
Milk	3.3	4.0	5.0	3.0	0.74
Peanuts	26	39	22	23	5.5

[a] Beers typically contain 3.5 percent ethanol, which has fuel value.

Table 5.3

running, often requires 2000 kJ/hr or more. When the energy content of our food exceeds the energy we expend, our body stores the surplus as fat.

SAMPLE EXERCISE 5.10

(a) A 28-g (1-oz) serving of a popular breakfast cereal served with 120 mL ($\frac{1}{2}$ cup) of skim milk provides 8 g protein, 26 g carbohydrates, and 2 g fat. Using the average fuel values of these kinds of substances, estimate the amount of food energy in this serving. (b) A person of average weight uses about 100 Cal/mi when running or jogging. How many servings of this cereal provide the fuel value requirements for running 3 mi?

SOLUTION (a)

$$(8 \text{ g protein})\left(\frac{17 \text{ kJ}}{1 \text{ g protein}}\right) + (26 \text{ g carbohydrate})\left(\frac{17 \text{ kJ}}{1 \text{ g carbohydrate}}\right)$$
$$+ (2 \text{ g fat})\left(\frac{38 \text{ kJ}}{1 \text{ g fat}}\right) = 650 \text{ kJ (to two significant figures)}$$

This corresponds to 160 kcal:

$$(650 \text{ kJ})\left(\frac{1 \text{ kcal}}{4.18 \text{ kJ}}\right) = 160 \text{ kcal}$$

Recall that the dietary Calorie is equivalent to 1 kcal. Thus, the serving provides 160 Cal.

$$\textbf{(b) } \text{Servings} = (3 \text{ mi})\left(\frac{100 \text{ Cal}}{1 \text{ mi}}\right)\left(\frac{1 \text{ serving}}{160 \text{ Cal}}\right) = 2 \text{ servings}$$

PRACTICE EXERCISE

(a) Dry red beans contain 62 percent carbohydrate, 22 percent protein, and 1.5 percent fat. Estimate the fuel value of these beans. (b) Very light activity like reading or watching television uses about 7 kJ/min. How many minutes of such activity can be sustained by the energy provided by a can of chicken noodle soup containing 13 g protein, 15 g carbohydrate, and 5 g fat? *Answer:* (a) 15 kJ/g; (b) 95 min.

Fuels

Learning Goal 17: List the major sources of energy on which humankind must depend, and discuss the likely availability of these for the foreseeable future.

The elemental compositions and fuel values of several common fuels are compared in Table 5.4. During the combustion of fuels, carbon is converted to CO_2 and hydrogen is converted to H_2O, both of which have large negative enthalpies of formation. Consequently, the greater the percentage of carbon and hydrogen in a fuel, the higher its fuel value. Compare, for example, the compositions and

TABLE 5.4 △ Fuel Values and Compositions of Some Common Fuels

	Approximate elemental composition (%)			
	C	H	O	Fuel value (kJ/g)
Wood (pine)	50	6	44	18
Anthracite coal (Pennsylvania)	82	1	2	31
Bituminous coal (Pennsylvania)	77	5	7	32
Charcoal	100	0	0	34
Crude oil (Texas)	85	12	0	45
Gasoline	85	15	0	48
Natural gas	70	23	0	49
Hydrogen	0	100	0	142

fuel values of bituminous coal and wood. The coal has a higher fuel value because of its greater carbon content.

The average daily energy consumption per person in the United States amounts to about 8.8×10^5 kJ. This amount is about 100 times greater than the individual food-energy requirement. We are a very energy-intensive society. Figure 5.20 gives the sources of the energy consumed annually in the United States.

Coal, petroleum, and natural gas, which are our major sources of energy, are known as **fossil fuels.** All are thought to have formed over millions of years from the decomposition of plants and animals. All are presently being depleted far more rapidly than they are being formed. **Natural gas** consists of gaseous hydrocarbons, compounds of hydrogen and carbon. It varies in composition, but it contains primarily methane, CH_4, with small amounts of ethane, C_2H_6, propane, C_3H_8, and butane, C_4H_{10}. We determined the fuel value of propane and benzene (another hydrocarbon) in Sample Exercise 5.8. **Petroleum** is a liquid composed of hundreds of compounds. Most of these compounds are hydrocarbons, with the remainder being mainly organic compounds containing sulfur, nitrogen, or oxygen. **Coal,** which is solid, contains hydrocarbons of high molecular weight as well as compounds containing sulfur, oxygen, and nitrogen. The sulfur in petroleum and coal is important from the standpoint of air pollution, as we shall discuss in Chapter 18.

Coal is the most abundant fossil fuel; it constitutes 80 percent of the fossil fuel reserves of the United States and 90 percent of those of the world. However, the use of coal presents a number of problems. Coal is a complex mixture of substances, and it contains components that produce air pollution. Because it is a solid, recovery from its underground deposits is expensive and often dangerous. Furthermore, coal deposits are not always close to the locations where energy use is high, so there are often substantial shipping costs as well.

Some experts feel that coal could be used most effectively if it were converted to a gaseous form, often called **syngas** (for "*syn*thesis *gas*"). In such a conversion the sulfur is removed, thereby decreasing air pollution when the syngas is burned. Syngas could be easily transported in pipelines and could supplement our diminishing supplies of natural gas. Gasification of coal requires the addition of hydrogen to coal. Typically, the coal is pulverized and treated with superheated steam. The product contains a mixture of CO, H_2, and CH_4, all of which can be used as fuels. However, conditions are maintained to maximize production of CH_4. A simplified schematic showing some of the reactions that occur is given in Figure 5.21.

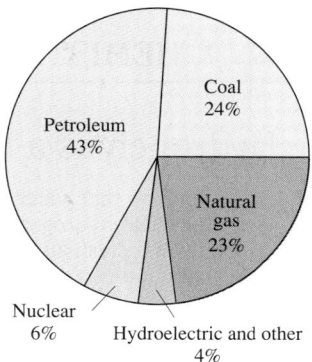

FIGURE 5.20 Sources of energy consumed in the United States.

FIGURE 5.21 Basic processes involved in the gasification of coal to form synthesis gas (syngas). A catalyst is a substance that increases the speed of a reaction without itself being consumed in the reaction.

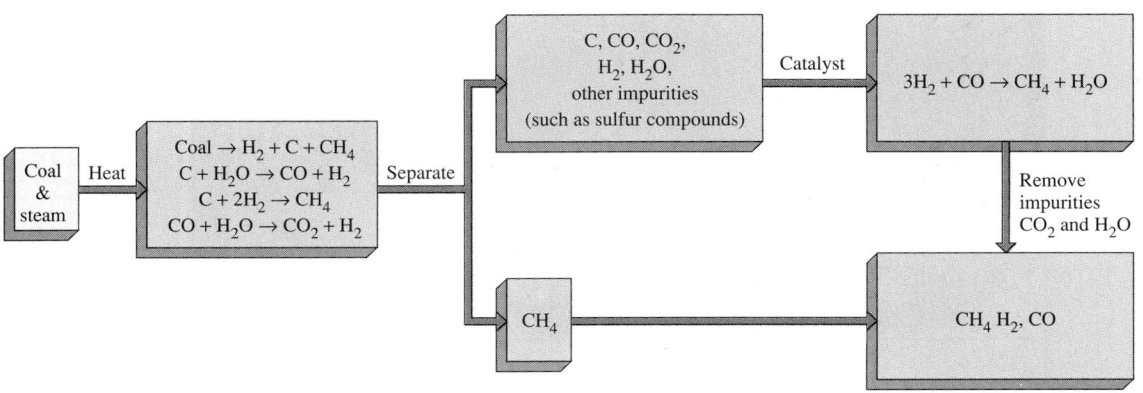

Hydrogen as a Fuel

I believe that water will one day be employed as a fuel, that hydrogen and oxygen which constitutes it will furnish an inexhaustible source of heat and light. /Jules Verne, *The Mysterious Island* (1870).

As this quotation indicates, hydrogen, H_2, has long been recognized as a very attractive fuel. Hydrogen has a very high fuel value (Table 5.4), and its combustion produces water, a "clean" by-product with no negative environmental effects. However, hydrogen cannot be used as a primary energy source because there is so little H_2 in nature. Most hydrogen is produced by decomposing water or hydrocarbons. This decomposition requires energy; in fact, because of heat losses, more energy must be used to generate hydrogen than can be reclaimed when the hydrogen is subsequently used as a fuel. However, should large, cheap sources of energy become available (as might be the case in solar-power generation), a portion of this energy could be used to generate hydrogen, which is both portable and storable.

Hydrogen can also be made from the treatment of coal with superheated steam:

$$\text{Coal} + H_2O(g) \longrightarrow CO(g) + H_2(g)$$

The conversion of high-sulfur coal to hydrogen is especially important because the sulfur is removed in this process: The direct burning of high-sulfur coal generates emissions that are particularly harmful to the environment (Chapter 18). Hydrogen can also be generated from methane, the principal component of natural gas:

$$CH_4(g) + H_2O(g) \longrightarrow CO(g) + 3H_2(g)$$

Once generated, hydrogen could serve as a convenient energy carrier. It would be cheaper to transport hydrogen using existing natural-gas pipelines than to transport electrical energy. Because present industrial technology is based on combustible fuels, hydrogen from the decomposition of water could replace petroleum and natural gas as these fuels become scarcer and more expensive. Hydrogen-fueled internal combustion engines suitable for automobiles have already been developed; they are 20 percent to 50 percent more efficient than gasoline engines (Figure 5.22).

Of course, there are drawbacks to the use of hydrogen as a fuel. Most notable among these is the explosive flammability of hydrogen gas (Figures 5.11 and 5.12). A promising solution to this problem is the use of metal alloys to store hydrogen. For example, an alloy of iron and titanium acts as a "sponge" in which the hydrogen gas combines with the alloy to form a fine, silvery powder. Heating the powder safely releases the hydrogen gas for use as a fuel. Such storage systems are much safer than the storage of hydrogen as a gas or liquid.

FIGURE 5.22 A prototype car powered by hydrogen gas. The hydrogen is safely stored in a metal alloy that holds enough hydrogen for the car to travel 120 mi. The car emits only water vapor in the exhaust gas, which allows it to meet extremely tough emission standards. (Chrystyna Czajkowsky/AP/Wide World Photos)

Other Energy Sources

Of the various sources of energy that could serve as alternatives to fossil fuels, only nuclear and solar energies are potentially capable of furnishing sufficient quantities of energy to satisfy the world's needs. Nuclear power currently supplies about 6 percent of the gross energy consumed in the United States. Issues related to the use of nuclear reactors for energy production are discussed in Chapter 21.

Solar energy is the world's largest energy source. On a clear day, about 1 kJ of solar energy reaches each square meter of the earth's surface every second. The solar energy that falls on only 0.1 percent of the land area of the United States is equivalent to all the energy that this nation currently uses. Harnessing this energy is difficult, however, because it is dilute (it is distributed over a wide area) and it fluctuates with time and weather conditions. The effective use of solar energy will depend on the development of some means of storing the energy collected for use at a later time. Any practical means for doing this will almost certainly involve use of an endothermic chemical process that can be reversed at a later time to release heat. One such reaction is the following:

$$CH_4(g) + H_2O(g) + heat \rightleftharpoons CO(g) + 3H_2(g) \qquad [5.21]$$

This reaction can be made to proceed in the forward direction at high temperatures, which can be obtained directly in a solar furnace. The CO and H_2 formed in the reaction could then be reacted later, with the resulting evolution of heat put to useful work.

Solar energy can be converted directly into electricity by use of photovoltaic devices, sometimes called *solar cells.* The efficiencies of solar energy conversion by use of such devices have increased dramatically during the past few years as a result of intensive research efforts. Photovoltaics are vital to the generation of power for satellites. However, for large-scale generation of useful energy at the earth's surface, they are not yet practical because of high unit cost. Even if the costs are reduced, some means must be found to store the energy produced by the solar cells because the sun shines only intermittently and during only part of the day at any place. Once again, the solution to this problem will almost certainly be to use the energy to run a chemical reaction in the direction in which it is endothermic.

 # For Review

Summary

Thermodynamics is the study of heat, work, and energy and the rules that govern their interconversions. Energy is the capacity to do work or to transfer heat. Work is the energy expended to move an object against a force. Heat is the energy that is transferred as a result of a temperature difference between two bodies.

The joule (J) is the SI unit of energy: 1 J = 1 kg-m²/s². Another common energy unit is the calorie (cal). A calorie is the quantity of energy necessary to increase the temperature of 1 g of water by 1 °C: 1 cal = 4.184 J.

To study thermodynamic properties, we define some specific amount of matter as our system and study the interactions between this system and its surroundings. The first law of thermodynamics (the law of conservation of energy) tells us that energy is conserved; the energy lost by a system equals that gained by its surroundings. Systems tend to gain stability by attaining as low an energy as possible.

On a molecular level, the internal energy, E, of a system is due to the kinetic and potential energies of its component parts. An object possesses kinetic energy because of its motion, and potential energy because of its position. We do not in general know the magnitude of this internal energy, but we can measure the changes in internal energy, ΔE, that accompany changes in the system.

The internal energy of a system changes as the system exchanges heat with its surroundings, has work done on it by the surroundings, or does work on the surroundings: $\Delta E = q + w$. The internal energy is a state function; E depends only on the state or condition of the system and not on the details of how it came to be in that state.

The heat gained or lost by a system at constant pressure is called the enthalpy change, represented by the symbol ΔH. The quantity is positive for endothermic processes (those that absorb heat) and negative for exothermic ones (those that give off heat).

The quantity of heat absorbed or evolved in chemical and physical processes is measured experimentally by calorimetry. A calorimeter measures the temperature change accompanying the process being investigated. The magnitude of the temperature change that an object undergoes when it absorbs a certain quantity of heat depends on its heat capacity. The molar heat capacity of a substance is the heat required to raise the temperature of 1 mol of the substance by 1 K. The specific heat of a substance is the heat required to raise the temperature of 1 g of the substance by 1 K. The quantity of heat transferred to a substance is given by the product of its mass, specific heat, and temperature change. If the system is at constant pressure, the heat flow equals ΔH for the process. A bomb calorimeter is a constant-volume device used to measure the heat evolved when a substance is combusted in oxygen.

Because enthalpy is a state function, ΔH depends only on the initial and final states of the system, and not on how the change occurs. Thus, the enthalpy change for a given chemical process is the same whether the process is carried out in one step or in a series of steps. Hess's law states this fact in a very useful form: If a reaction is carried out in a series of steps, ΔH for the reaction will be equal to the sum of the enthalpy changes for the steps. This means that we can calculate the enthalpy change for any reaction as long as we can find a route for which ΔH is known for each step. Tabulated values for the standard enthalpy of formation, ΔH_f°, are particularly helpful for such calculations.

The standard enthalpy of formation of a substance is defined as the enthalpy change for the formation of a mole of that substance from the elements, with all reactants and products in their standard states. The standard state refers to the conditions of 1 atm pressure, with each reactant and product in its stable form (gas, liquid, or solid) at the temperature in question, usually 298 K (25°C). By convention, the enthalpies of formation of elements in their standard states are zero. The enthalpy change in any reaction can be calculated from the enthalpies of formation of the reactants and products in the reaction:

$$\Delta H_{rxn}^\circ = \sum n \, \Delta H_f^\circ (\text{products})$$
$$- \sum m \, \Delta H_f^\circ (\text{reactants})$$

The fuel value of any substance or mixture is defined as the heat energy released when a gram of that material is combusted. We considered briefly the fuel values of some common foods and fuels, including various forms of fossil fuels.

Key Terms

thermodynamics
thermochemistry
force (Sec. 5.1)
work (Sec. 5.1)
heat (Sec. 5.1)
energy (Sec. 5.1)
kinetic energy (Sec. 5.1)
potential energy (Sec. 5.1)

joule (Sec. 5.1)
calorie (Sec. 5.1)
system (Sec. 5.1)
surroundings (Sec. 5.1)
first law of thermodynamics (Sec. 5.2)
internal energy (Sec. 5.2)
state function (Sec. 5.2)
endothermic (Sec. 5.3)

exothermic (Sec. 5.3)
enthalpy (Sec. 5.3)
calorimetry (Sec. 5.5)
calorimeter (Sec. 5.5)
heat capacity (Sec. 5.5)
molar heat capacity (Sec. 5.5)
specific heat (Sec. 5.5)
bomb calorimeter (Sec. 5.5)
Hess's law (Sec. 5.6)

enthalpy of formation (Sec. 5.7)
standard state (Sec. 5.7)
standard enthalpy of formation (Sec. 5.7)
fuel value (Sec. 5.8)
fossil fuels (Sec. 5.8)
natural gas (Sec. 5.8)
petroleum (Sec. 5.8)
coal (Sec. 5.8)
syngas (Sec. 5.8)

Exercises

Nature of Energy

5.1. (a) What is work? (b) How do we determine the amount of work done given the magnitude of the associated force?

5.2. (a) What is heat? (b) Under what conditions is heat transferred from one system to another?

5.3. Identify the force present and explain whether work is being performed in the following cases: (a) Two positively charged particles are held a fixed distance from one another. (b) You lift a paper clip off the top of a desk.

5.4. Identify the force present and explain whether work is being performed when (a) two magnets are pulled apart; (b) a spring is stretched to twice its normal length.

5.5. (a) Calculate the kinetic energy in joules of a 45-g golf ball moving at 61 m/s. (b) Convert this energy to calories. (c) What happens to this energy when the ball strikes a tree?

5.6. At 20°C (approximately room temperature), the average velocity of N_2 molecules in air is 1050 mi/hr. (a) What is the average speed in m/s? (b) What is the kinetic energy (in joules) of a N_2 molecule moving at this speed? (c) What is the total kinetic energy of 1 mol of N_2 molecules moving at this speed?

5.7. In much engineering work, it is common to use the British thermal unit (Btu). A Btu is the amount of heat required to raise the temperature of 1 lb of water by 1°F. Calculate the number of joules in a Btu.

5.8. A watt is a measure of power (the rate of energy change) equal to 1 J/s. Calculate the number of joules in a kilowatt-hour.

First Law of Thermodynamics

5.9. (a) Verbally state the first law of thermodynamics. (b) Define the term *system*. (c) How is the energy change of a system related to that of its surroundings?

5.10. (a) Write an equation that expresses the first law of thermodynamics. (b) Define the term *surroundings*. (c) How does the energy change of the surroundings relate to that of the system?

5.11. Calculate ΔE and indicate whether the internal energy of the system has increased or decreased in the following cases: (a) A system absorbs 145 J of heat and does 167 kJ of work; (b) $q = -3.0$ kJ and $w = -750$ J; (c) a system releases 128 J of heat while the surroundings does 143 J of work on it.

5.12. Calculate the change in internal energy of the system and indicate whether the internal energy of the system has increased or decreased in the following cases: (a) A gas ex-

pands very rapidly, so that there is no heat exchange with the surroundings; in the expansion it does 450 J of work on the surroundings. (b) A chemist heats 200 g of water from 30°C to 40°C, a process that requires approximately 8360 J of heat. (c) A gas contracts as it is cooled; it has 300 J of work done on it and loses 146 J of heat to its surroundings.

5.13. (a) What is meant by the term *state function?* (b) Give an example of a quantity that is a state function and one that is not. (c) Is temperature a state function? Why or why not?

5.14. Indicate which of the following is independent of the path by which a change occurs: (a) the change in potential energy when a book is transferred from table to shelf; (b) the heat evolved when a cube of sugar is oxidized to $CO_2(g)$ and $H_2O(g)$; (c) the work accomplished in burning a gallon of gasoline.

Enthalpy

5.15. (a) If the enthalpy of a system is lower after a process has occurred, is the process exothermic or endothermic? (b) What is the sign of ΔH for the process? (c) For a system under a constant pressure, what is the relationship between

the change in enthalpy and the amount of heat exchanged with the surroundings?

5.16. (a) If a system increases its enthalpy, is ΔH positive or negative for the process? (b) Is the process exothermic or endothermic? **(c)** Under what conditions is ΔH for a system equal to the heat that it exchanges with its surroundings?

✓ **5.17.** Classify the following processes as endothermic or exothermic: **(a)** A match burns. **(b)** Ice melts. **(c)** Molten metal solidifies. **(d)** Sodium metal reacts with water. **(e)** Rubbing alcohol evaporates.

✓ **5.18.** Predict the sign of ΔH for each of the following processes: **(a)** $H_2O(l) \longrightarrow H_2O(g)$; **(b)** $C_2H_4(g) + 3O_2(g) \longrightarrow 2CO_2(g) + 2H_2O(g)$; **(c)** $NaOH(aq) + HCl(aq) \longrightarrow H_2O(l) + NaCl(aq)$ (the temperature of the solution increases); **(d)** $2H_2O(g) \longrightarrow 2H_2(g) + O_2(g)$.

[5.19]. A gas is confined to a cylinder under constant atmospheric pressure, as illustrated in Figure 5.2. When the gas undergoes a particular chemical reaction, it releases 135 kJ of heat to its surroundings and does 63 kJ of P-V work on its surroundings. What are the values of ΔH and ΔE for this process?

[5.20]. A gas is confined to a cylinder under constant atmospheric pressure, as illustrated in Figure 5.2. When 600 J of heat is added to the gas, it expands and does 140 J of work on the surroundings. What are the values of ΔH and ΔE for this process?

✓ **5.21.** The complete combustion of $CH_3OH(l)$ to form $H_2O(l)$ and $CO_2(g)$ at constant pressure produces 726.7 kJ of heat per mole of CH_3OH. **(a)** Write a balanced thermochemical equation for this reaction. **(b)** Draw an enthalpy diagram for the reaction.

5.22. The decomposition reaction of $NH_3(g)$ to form $N_2(g)$ and $H_2(g)$ at constant pressure requires 46.19 kJ of heat per mole of NH_3. **(a)** Write a balanced thermochemical equation for the reaction. **(b)** Draw an enthalpy diagram for the reaction.

✓ **5.23.** Consider the following reaction:

$$2N_2(g) + O_2(g) \longrightarrow 2N_2O(g) \qquad \Delta H = +163.2 \text{ kJ}$$

(a) Is the reaction exothermic or endothermic? **(b)** Calculate the amount of heat transferred when 10.0 g of $N_2O(g)$

forms by this reaction at constant pressure. **(c)** How many grams of nitrogen gas must react to produce an enthalpy change of 1.00 kJ? **(d)** How many kilojoules of heat are produced when 15.0 g of $N_2O(g)$ is decomposed into $N_2(g)$ and $O_2(g)$ at constant pressure?

5.24. Consider the following reaction:

$$2Na(s) + Cl_2(g) \longrightarrow 2NaCl(s) \qquad \Delta H = -821.8 \text{ kJ}$$

(a) Is the reaction exothermic or endothermic? **(b)** Calculate the amount of heat transferred when 8.0 g of $Na(s)$ reacts according to this reaction at constant pressure. **(c)** How many grams of NaCl are produced during an enthalpy change of 10.0 kJ? **(d)** How many kilojoules of heat are absorbed when 25.0 g of $NaCl(s)$ is decomposed into $Na(s)$ and $Cl_2(g)$ at constant pressure?

✓ **5.25.** When solutions containing silver ions and chloride ions are mixed, silver chloride precipitates:

$$Ag^+(aq) + Cl^-(aq) \longrightarrow AgCl(s) \qquad \Delta H = -65.5 \text{ kJ}$$

(a) Calculate ΔH for formation of 0.200 mol of AgCl by this reaction. **(b)** Calculate ΔH for formation of 2.50 g of AgCl. **(c)** Calculate ΔH when 0.350 mol of AgCl dissolves in water.

5.26. A common means of forming small quantities of oxygen gas in the laboratory used to be to heat $KClO_3$:

$$2KClO_3(s) \longrightarrow 2KCl(s) + 3O_2(g) \qquad \Delta H = -89.4 \text{ kJ}$$

For this reaction, calculate ΔH for the formation of **(a)** 0.345 mol of O_2; **(b)** 7.85 g of KCl; **(c)** 9.22 g of $KClO_3$ from KCl and O_2.

5.27. Which of the following has the highest enthalpy at a given temperature and pressure: $H_2O(s)$, $H_2O(l)$, or $H_2O(g)$? Which has the lowest enthalpy?

5.28. Consider the following reaction:

$$3O_2(g) \longrightarrow 2O_3(g) \qquad \Delta H = +284.6 \text{ kJ}$$

Under the conditions of this reaction, does $O_2(g)$ or $O_3(g)$ have the higher enthalpy? Explain.

Calorimetry

✓ **5.29.** **(a)** What is the specific heat of water? **(b)** What is the heat capacity of 348 g of water? **(c)** How many kilojoules of heat are needed to raise the temperature of 2.06 kg of water from 35.14°C to 76.37°C?

5.30. **(a)** What is the molar heat capacity of water? **(b)** What is the heat capacity of 6.35 mol of water? **(c)** How many kilojoules of heat are needed to raise the temperature of 165 mol of water from 10.55°C to 47.32°C?

✓ **5.31.** The specific heat of ethanol is 2.46 J/g-K. How many joules of heat are required to heat 193 g of ethanol from 19.00°C to 35.00°C?

5.32. The specific heat of lead is 0.129 J/g-K. How many joules of heat are required to raise the temperature of 382 g of lead from 22.50°C to 37.20°C?

✓ **5.33.** When a 6.50-g sample of solid sodium hydroxide dissolves in 100.0 g of water in a coffee cup calorimeter

(Figure 5.15), the temperature rises from 21.6°C to 37.8°C. Calculate ΔH (in kJ/mol NaOH) for the solution process

$$NaOH(s) \longrightarrow Na^+(aq) + OH^-(aq)$$

Assume that the specific heat of the solution is the same as that of pure water.

5.34. When a 4.25-g sample of solid ammonium nitrate dissolves in 60.0 g of water in a coffee cup calorimeter (Figure 5.15), the temperature drops from 22.0°C to 16.9°C. Calculate ΔH (in kJ/mol NH_4NO_3) for the solution process

$$NH_4NO_3(s) \longrightarrow NH_4^+(aq) + NO_3^-(aq)$$

Assume that the specific heat of the solution is the same as that of pure water.

✓ **5.35.** A 1.80-g sample of octane, C_8H_{18}, was burned in a bomb calorimeter whose total heat capacity is 11.66 kJ/°C. The temperature of the calorimeter and its contents increased from 21.36°C to 28.78°C. What is the heat of combustion per gram of octane? Per mole of octane?

5.36. A 2.20-g sample of quinone, $C_6H_4O_2$, is burned in a bomb calorimeter whose total heat capacity is 7.854 kJ/°C. The temperature of the calorimeter increases from 23.44°C to 30.57°C. What is the heat of combustion per gram of quinone? Per mole of quinone?

5.37. Under constant-volume conditions, the heat of combustion of benzoic acid, $HC_7H_5O_2$, is 26.38 kJ/g. A 1.200-g sample of benzoic acid is burned in a bomb calorimeter. The temperature of the calorimeter increases from 22.45°C to 26.10°C. **(a)** What is the total heat capacity of the calorimeter? **(b)** If the calorimeter contained 1.500 kg of water, what is the heat capacity of the calorimeter when it contains no water? **(c)** What temperature increase would be expected in this calorimeter if the 1.200-g sample of benzoic acid were combusted when the calorimeter contained 1.000 kg of water?

5.38. Under constant-volume conditions, the heat of combustion of glucose is 15.57 kJ/g. A 2.500-g sample of glucose is burned in a bomb calorimeter. The temperature of the calorimeter increased from 20.55°C to 23.25°C. **(a)** What is the total heat capacity of the calorimeter? **(b)** If the calorimeter contained 2.700 kg of water, what is the heat capacity of the dry calorimeter? **(c)** What temperature increase would be expected in this calorimeter if the glucose sample had been combusted when the calorimeter contained 2.000 kg of water?

Hess's Law

5.39. State Hess's law. Why is it important to thermochemistry?

5.40. What is the connection between the fact that H is a state function and Hess's law?

5.41. From the following enthalpies of reaction:

$$2SO_2(g) + O_2(g) \longrightarrow 2SO_3(g) \qquad \Delta H = -196 \text{ kJ}$$
$$2S(s) + 3O_2(g) \longrightarrow 2SO_3(g) \qquad \Delta H = -790 \text{ kJ}$$

calculate the enthalpy change for the reaction

$$S(s) + O_2(g) \longrightarrow SO_2(g)$$

5.42. Calculate ΔH for

$$2F_2(g) + 2H_2O(l) \longrightarrow 4HF(g) + O_2(g)$$

given that

$$H_2(g) + F_2(g) \longrightarrow 2HF(g) \qquad \Delta H = -537 \text{ kJ}$$
$$2H_2(g) + O_2(g) \longrightarrow 2H_2O(l) \qquad \Delta H = -572 \text{ kJ}$$

5.43. From the following enthalpies of reaction:

$$H_2(g) + F_2(g) \longrightarrow 2HF(g) \qquad \Delta H = -537 \text{ kJ}$$
$$C(s) + 2F_2(g) \longrightarrow CF_4(g) \qquad \Delta H = -680 \text{ kJ}$$
$$2C(s) + 2H_2(g) \longrightarrow C_2H_4(g) \qquad \Delta H = +52.3 \text{ kJ}$$

calculate ΔH for the reaction of ethylene with F_2:

$$C_2H_4(g) + 6F_2(g) \longrightarrow 2CF_4(g) + 4HF(g)$$

5.44. Given the following data:

$$2C_2H_6(g) + 7O_2(g) \longrightarrow 4CO_2(g) + 6H_2O(l)$$
$$\Delta H = -3120 \text{ kJ}$$
$$C(s) + O_2(g) \longrightarrow CO_2(g) \qquad \Delta H = -394 \text{ kJ}$$
$$2H_2(g) + O_2(g) \longrightarrow 2H_2O(l) \qquad \Delta H = -572 \text{ kJ}$$

use Hess's law to calculate ΔH for the reaction

$$2C(s) + 3H_2(g) \longrightarrow C_2H_6(g)$$

Enthalpies of Formation

5.45. Write a balanced thermochemical equation depicting the formation of 1 mol of each compound from its elements in their standard states, using Appendix C to obtain the standard enthalpy of formation of each. **(a)** $NH_3(g)$; **(b)** $NOCl(g)$; **(c)** $CH_3OH(l)$; **(d)** $KClO_3(s)$.

5.46. Write balanced equations that describe the formation of the following compounds from their elements in their standard states, and use Appendix C to obtain their enthalpies of formation: **(a)** $HC_2H_3O_2(l)$; **(b)** $NaHCO_3(s)$; **(c)** $NH_4NO_3(s)$; **(d)** $FeCl_3(s)$

5.47. The following reaction is known as the thermite reaction:

$$2Al(s) + Fe_2O_3(s) \longrightarrow Al_2O_3(s) + 2Fe(s)$$

This highly exothermic reaction is used for welding massive units, such as propellers for large ships. Using enthalpies of formation from Appendix C, calculate $\Delta H°$ for this reaction.

5.48. Many cigarette lighters contain liquid butane, $C_4H_{10}(l)$. Using enthalpies of formation, calculate the quantity of heat produced when 1.0 g of butane is completely combusted in air.

5.49. Using values from Appendix C, calculate the standard enthalpy change for each of the following reactions:
(a) $CO(g) + 2NH_3(g) \longrightarrow NH_4CN(s) + H_2O(g)$;
(b) $NH_4NO_3(s) \longrightarrow N_2O(g) + 2H_2O(g)$;
(c) $P_4O_6(s) + 2O_2(g) \longrightarrow P_4O_{10}(s)$;
(d) $KClO_3(s) + 3PCl_3(l) \longrightarrow 3POCl_3(l) + KCl(s)$.

5.50. Using values from Appendix C, calculate the standard enthalpy change for each of the following reactions:
(a) $2NOCl(g) \longrightarrow 2NO(g) + Cl_2(g)$;
(b) $N_2(g) + 3H_2(g) \longrightarrow 2NH_3(g)$;
(c) $HC_2H_3O_2(l) \longrightarrow CH_4(g) + CO_2(g)$;
(d) $4NH_3(g) + 5O_2(g) \longrightarrow 4NO(g) + 6H_2O(g)$.

5.51. Calcium carbide, CaC_2, reacts with water to form acetylene, C_2H_2, and $Ca(OH)_2$. From the following enthalpy of reaction data and the data in Appendix C, calculate ΔH_f° for $CaC_2(s)$:

$$CaC_2(s) + 2H_2O(l) \longrightarrow Ca(OH)_2(s) + C_2H_2(g)$$
$$\Delta H^\circ = -127.2 \text{ kJ}$$

5.52. Complete combustion of acetone, C_3H_6O, results in the liberation of 1790 kJ:

$$C_3H_6O(l) + 4O_2(g) \longrightarrow 3CO_2(g) + 3H_2O(l)$$
$$\Delta H^\circ = -1790 \text{ kJ}$$

Using this information together with the data in Appendix C, calculate the enthalpy of formation of acetone.

5.53. Calculate the standard enthalpy of formation of solid $Mg(OH)_2$, given the following data:

$$2Mg(s) + O_2(g) \longrightarrow 2MgO(s) \qquad \Delta H^\circ = -1203.6 \text{ kJ}$$
$$Mg(OH)_2(s) \longrightarrow MgO(s) + H_2O(l)$$
$$\Delta H^\circ = +37.1 \text{ kJ}$$
$$2H_2(g) + O_2(g) \longrightarrow 2H_2O(l) \qquad \Delta H^\circ = -571.7 \text{ kJ}$$

5.54. Calculate the standard enthalpy of formation of gaseous diborane, B_2H_6, using the following thermochemical information:

$$4B(s) + 3O_2(g) \longrightarrow 2B_2O_3(s) \qquad \Delta H^\circ = -2509.1 \text{ kJ}$$
$$2H_2(g) + O_2(g) \longrightarrow 2H_2O(l) \qquad \Delta H^\circ = -571.7 \text{ kJ}$$
$$B_2H_6(g) + 3O_2(g) \longrightarrow B_2O_3(s) + 3H_2O(l)$$
$$\Delta H^\circ = -2147.5 \text{ kJ}$$

Foods and Fuels

5.55. A particular brand of potato chips contains 15 g carbohydrate, 1 g protein, and 10 g fat per serving. Estimate the number of Calories provided by a serving.

5.56. A pound of peanut brittle contains 214 g of carbohydrate, 146 g of fat, and 79 g of protein. What is the fuel value in kilojoules in a 50-g bar of peanut brittle? How many Calories does it provide?

5.57. The heat of combustion of fructose, $C_6H_{12}O_6$, is -2812 kJ/mol. If a freshly harvested Golden Delicious apple weighing 4.23 oz (120 g) contains 16.0 g of fructose, what caloric content does the fructose contribute to the apple?

5.58. The heat of combustion of ethanol, $C_2H_5OH(l)$, is -1371 kJ/mol. A 12-oz (355-mL) bottle of beer contains 3.7 percent ethanol by mass. Assuming the density of the beer to be 1.0 g/mL, what caloric content does the alcohol in a bottle of beer have?

5.59. The standard enthalpies of formation of gaseous propyne, C_3H_4, propylene, C_3H_6, and propane, C_3H_8, are $+185.4$, $+20.4$, and -103.8 kJ/mol, respectively. **(a)** Calculate the heat evolved per mole on combustion of each substance to yield $CO_2(g)$ and $H_2O(g)$. **(b)** Calculate the heat evolved on combustion of 1 kg of each substance. **(c)** Which is the most efficient fuel in terms of heat evolved per unit mass?

5.60. From the following data for three prospective fuels, calculate which could provide the most energy per unit volume.

Fuel	Density at 20°C (g/cm³)	Molar enthalpy of combustion (kJ/mol)
Nitroethane, $C_2H_5NO_2(l)$	1.052	-1348
Ethanol, $C_2H_5OH(l)$	0.789	-1371
Diethyl ether, $(C_2H_5)_2O(l)$	0.714	-2727

Additional Exercises

5.61. Based on your experience, is heat added or removed from the system when water freezes? Is it an exothermic or an endothermic process? How about the melting of ice?

5.62. When a mole of dry ice, $CO_2(s)$, is converted to $CO_2(g)$ at atmospheric pressure and $-78°C$, the heat absorbed by the system exceeds the increase in internal energy of the CO_2. Why is this so? What happens to the remaining energy?

5.63. An expanding gas absorbs 1.55 kJ of heat. If its internal energy increases by 1.32 kJ, does the system do work on its surroundings or have work done on it? What quantity of work is involved?

[5.64]. Limestone stalactites are formed in caves by the following reaction:

$$Ca^{2+}(aq) + 2HCO_3^-(aq) \longrightarrow$$
$$CaCO_3(s) + CO_2(g) + H_2O(l)$$

If 1 mol of $CaCO_3$ forms at 298 K under 1 atm pressure, the reaction performs 2.47 kJ of expansion work, pushing back the atmosphere as the gaseous CO_2 forms. At the same time, 38.95 kJ of heat is absorbed from the environment. What are the values of ΔH and of ΔE for this reaction?

5.65. When fruits and grains are fermented, glucose is converted to ethyl alcohol:

$$C_6H_{12}O_6(s) \longrightarrow 2C_2H_5OH(l) + 2CO_2(g)$$
$$\Delta H = -69.4 \text{ kJ}$$

(a) Is this reaction exothermic or endothermic? **(b)** Which has higher enthalpy, the reactants or the products of this reaction? **(c)** Calculate ΔH for the formation of 5.00 g of C_2H_5OH. **(d)** What quantity of heat is liberated when 95.0 g of C_2H_5OH is formed at constant pressure?

✓ **5.66.** A house is being designed to have passive solar energy features. Brickwork is to be incorporated into the interior of the house to act as a heat absorber. Each brick weighs approximately 1.8 kg. The specific heat of the brick is 0.85 J/g-K. How many bricks will need to be incorporated into the interior of the house to provide the same total heat capacity as 1000 gal of water?

[5.67]. A coffee cup calorimeter of the type shown in Figure 5.15 contains 150 g of water at 24.6°C. A 110-g block of molybdenum metal is heated to 100°C and then placed in the water in the calorimeter. The temperature of the water rises to 28.0°C, at which point it stops rising. What is the specific heat of molybdenum metal? Ignore the heat capacity of the plastic cups.

✓ **5.68.** When 50.0 mL of 1.00 M $CuSO_4$ and 50.0 mL of 2.00 M KOH are mixed in a constant-pressure calorimeter, the temperature of the mixture rises from 21.5°C to 27.7°C. From these data, calculate ΔH for the process

$$CuSO_4(aq;\ 1\ M) + 2KOH(aq;\ 2\ M) \longrightarrow$$
$$Cu(OH)_2(s) + K_2SO_4(aq;\ 0.5\ M)$$

Assume that the calorimeter absorbs only a negligible quantity of heat, that the total volume of the solution is 100.0 mL, and that the specific heat and density of the solution following mixing are the same as that of pure water.

[5.69]. **(a)** When a 0.235-g sample of benzoic acid is combusted in a bomb calorimeter, a 1.642°C rise in temperature is observed. When a 0.265-g sample of caffeine, $C_8H_{10}O_2N_4$, is burned, a 1.525°C rise in temperature is measured. Using the value 26.38 kJ/g for the heat of combustion of benzoic acid, calculate the heat of combustion per mole of caffeine at constant volume. **(b)** Assuming that there is an uncertainty of 0.002°C in each temperature reading and that the masses of samples are measured to 0.001 g, what is the estimated uncertainty in the value calculated for the heat of combustion per mole of caffeine?

[5.70]. Aspirin is produced commercially from salicylic acid, $C_7O_3H_6$. A large shipment of salicylic acid is contaminated with boric oxide, which, like salicylic acid, is a white powder. The heat of combustion of salicylic acid at constant volume is known to be -3.00×10^3 kJ/mol. Boric oxide, because it is fully oxidized, does not burn. When a 3.556-g sample of the contaminated salicylic acid is burned in a bomb calorimeter, the temperature increases 2.556°C. From previous measurements, the heat capacity of the calorimeter is known to be 13.62 kJ/K. What is the amount of boric oxide in the sample, in terms of percent by mass?

5.71. Calculate the standard enthalpy changes for the following reactions. Indicate which are endothermic and which are exothermic.

(a) $2H_2O_2(l) \longrightarrow 2H_2O(l) + O_2(g)$
(b) $CaO(s) + CO_2(g) \longrightarrow CaCO_3(s)$
(c) $N_2H_4(g) + O_2(g) \longrightarrow N_2(g) + 2H_2O(g)$

5.72. Titanium tetrachloride reacts with water to form titanium dioxide and hydrogen chloride:

$$TiCl_4(l) + 2H_2O(l) \longrightarrow TiO_2(s) + 4HCl(g)$$
$$\Delta H° = 67.0\ kJ$$

$\Delta H_f°$ for $TiCl_4(l)$ is -804.2 kJ/mol. Using additional information from Appendix C, determine $\Delta H_f°$ for $TiO_2(s)$.

5.73. The two common sugars, glucose, $C_6H_{12}O_6$, and sucrose, $C_{12}H_{22}O_{11}$, are both carbohydrates. Their standard enthalpies of formation are given in Table 5.2. Using these data: **(a)** Calculate the molar enthalpy of combustion to $CO_2(g)$ and $H_2O(l)$ for the two sugars. **(b)** Calculate the enthalpy of combustion per gram of each sugar. **(c)** How do your answers to part (b) compare to the average fuel value of carbohydrates discussed in Section 5.8?

5.74. Burning methane in oxygen can produce three different carbon-containing products: soot (very fine particles of graphite), $CO(g)$, and $CO_2(g)$. **(a)** Write three balanced equations for the reaction of methane gas with oxygen to produce these three products. In each case, assume that $H_2O(l)$ is the only other product. **(b)** Determine the standard enthalpies for the reactions in part (a). **(c)** Why, if the oxygen supply is adequate, is $CO_2(g)$ the predominant carbon-containing product of the combustion of methane?

5.75. Acetylene, C_2H_2, and benzene, C_6H_6, are hydrocarbons that have the same empirical formula. Benzene is an example of an "aromatic" hydrocarbon, one that is unusually stable because of its structure. **(a)** By using the data in Appendix C, determine the standard enthalpy change for the reaction $3C_2H_2(g) \longrightarrow C_6H_6(l)$. **(b)** Which has greater enthalpy, 3 mol of acetylene gas or 1 mol of liquid benzene? **(c)** Determine the fuel value in kJ/g for acetylene and benzene.

[5.76]. Ammonia, NH_3, boils at -33°C; at this temperature, it has a density of 0.81 g/cm³. The enthalpy of formation of $NH_3(g)$ is -46.2 kJ/mol, and the enthalpy of vaporization of $NH_3(l)$ is 4.6 kJ/mol. Calculate the enthalpy change when 1 L of liquid NH_3 is burned in air to give $N_2(g)$ and $H_2O(g)$. How does this compare with ΔH for the complete combustion of a liter of liquid methanol, CH_3OH [density at 25°C = 0.792 g/cm³, and enthalpy of formation $\Delta H_f°(CH_3OH(l)) = -239$ kJ/mol]?

[5.77]. Three common hydrocarbons that contain four carbons are listed below, along with their standard enthalpies of formation:

Hydrocarbon	Formula	$\Delta H_f°$(kJ/mol)
1,3-Butadiene	$C_4H_6(g)$	111.9
1-Butene	$C_4H_8(g)$	1.2
n-Butane	$C_4H_{10}(g)$	-124.7

(a) For each of these, calculate the molar enthalpy of combustion to $CO_2(g)$ and $H_2O(l)$. **(b)** Calculate the fuel value in kJ/g for each of these compounds. **(c)** For each hydrocarbon, determine the percentage of hydrogen by mass. **(d)** By comparing your answers for parts (b) and (c), propose a relationship between hydrogen content and fuel value in hydrocarbons.

6

Electronic Structure of Atoms

In "neon" signs, light is produced when the electrons in an electrically excited gas atom relax to a lower energy state. Different gases produce light of different colors.

In the preceding chapters, we considered some basic ideas about chemistry that have helped us understand how substances behave. Our goal, however, is not merely to understand *how* substances behave but to understand *why* they behave as they do. Why, for example, are sodium and potassium both reactive metals? Why do hydrogen and chlorine combine to form HCl and not some other composition? Why is CO_2 molecular and not ionic?

When atoms react, it is their outer parts, their electrons, that interact. Electrons hold the key to understanding why substances behave as they do. We refer to the arrangements of electrons in atoms as their **electronic structure.** The electronic structure of an atom relates not only to the number of electrons that an atom possesses but also to where they can be found and to what energies they possess. As we shall see, electrons do not behave like anything we are familiar with in the macroscopic world. Understanding their behavior was a major scientific development, one that produced a new way of perceiving nature on the atomic level. In this chapter, we seek to describe the electronic structures of atoms and relate them to the positions of the elements in the periodic table. In later chapters, we will see how electronic structure is used to explain trends in the periodic table and to understand the bonding between atoms.

6.1 The Wave Nature of Light

Much of our present understanding of the electronic structure of atoms has come from analysis of the light emitted or absorbed by substances. To understand the basis for our current model of electronic structure, therefore, we must first learn more about light. The light that we can see with our eyes, *visible light,* is a type of **electromagnetic radiation.** Electromagnetic radiation carries energy through space and is therefore also known as *radiant energy.* There are actually many types of electromagnetic radiation in addition to ordinary or visible light. These different forms — such as the radio waves that carry music to our radios, the infrared radiation from a glowing fireplace, and the X-rays used by a dentist — may *seem* very different from one another, yet they share certain fundamental characteristics.

All types of electromagnetic radiation move through a vacuum at a speed of 3.00×10^8 m/s, the "speed of light." Furthermore, all have wavelike characteristics similar to those of waves that move through water. Water waves are the result of energy imparted to the water, perhaps by the dropping of a stone, the movement of a boat, or the force of wind on the water surface. This energy is expressed as the up-and-down movements of the water.

If we look at a cross section of a water wave (Figure 6.1), we see that it is periodic: The pattern of peaks and troughs repeats itself at regular intervals. The distance between successive peaks (or troughs) is called the **wavelength.** The number of complete wavelengths, or *cycles,* that pass a given point in 1 s is the **frequency** of the wave. We could measure the frequency of a water wave by counting the number of times per second that a cork bobbing on the water moves through a complete cycle of upward and downward motion.

Electromagnetic radiation has both electric and magnetic components. Its wave characteristics are due to the periodic oscillations of these components. We can assign a frequency and wavelength to electromagnetic radiation, as illustrated in Figure 6.2. Because all electromagnetic radiation moves at the

Learning Goal 1: Describe the wave properties and characteristic speed of propagation of radiant energy (electromagnetic radiation).

Point of Emphasis: Electronic structure is more important than any other single feature in describing how elements behave chemically.

Joseph D. Caparick, "Introduction to Atomic Structure: Demonstrations and Labs," *J. Chem. Educ.* 1988, *65,* 892.

Teaching Note: The term *light* is often used to describe electromagnetic radiation that is visible to us. In general, all electromagnetic radiation can be called light.

Point of Emphasis: All forms of electromagnetic radiation, including visible light, radio waves, and X-rays, share certain fundamental characteristics.

FIGURE 6.1 Characteristics of water waves. (*a*) The distance between corresponding points on each wave is called the *wavelength*. (*b*) The number of times per second that the cork bobs up and down is called the *frequency*.

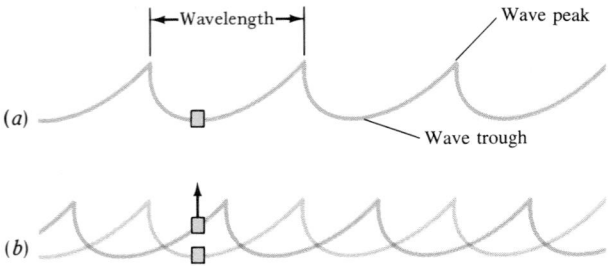

(*a*)
Wavelength
Wave peak
Wave trough

(*b*)

speed of light, wavelength and frequency are related. If the wavelength is long, there will be fewer cycles of the wave passing a point per second; thus, the frequency will be low. Conversely, for a wave to have a high frequency, the distance between the peaks of the wave must be small (short wavelength). This inverse relationship between the frequency and the wavelength of electromagnetic radiation can be expressed as a simple equation: The product of the frequency of the radiation, v (nu), and its wavelength, λ (lambda), equals the speed of light, c:

$$v\lambda = c \qquad [6.1]$$

Wavelength is expressed in units of length. Figure 6.3 shows the various types of electromagnetic radiation arranged in order of increasing wavelength, a display called the *electromagnetic spectrum*. Notice that the wavelengths span a tremendous range. The wavelengths of gamma rays are similar to the diameters of atomic nuclei, whereas those of radio waves can be longer than a football field. Notice also that visible light, which corresponds to wavelengths of about 400 to 700 nm, is an extremely small portion of the electromagnetic spectrum.

FIGURE 6.2 Wave characteristics of radiant energy. Radiant energy is associated with periodic changes in the electric and magnetic fields. Notice that the shorter the wavelength, the higher the frequency. The wavelength in (*b*) is one-third as great as that in (*a*), and its frequency is therefore three times as great. The *amplitude* of the wave is the vertical distance from the midline of the wave to its peak. It relates to the intensity of the radiation. Here both waves have the same amplitude.

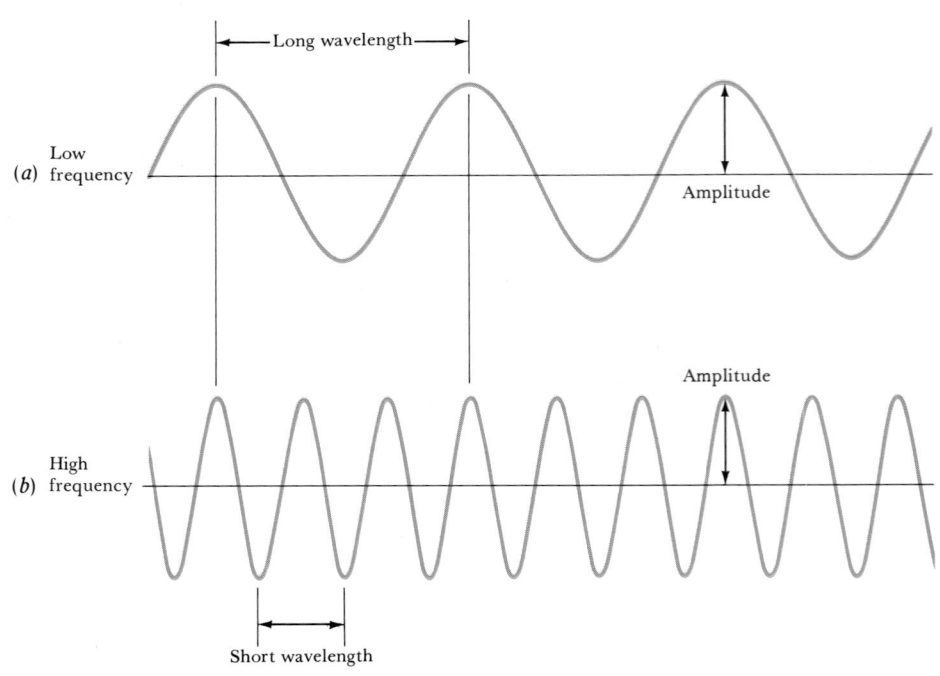

(*a*) Low frequency
Long wavelength
Amplitude

(*b*) High frequency
Amplitude
Short wavelength

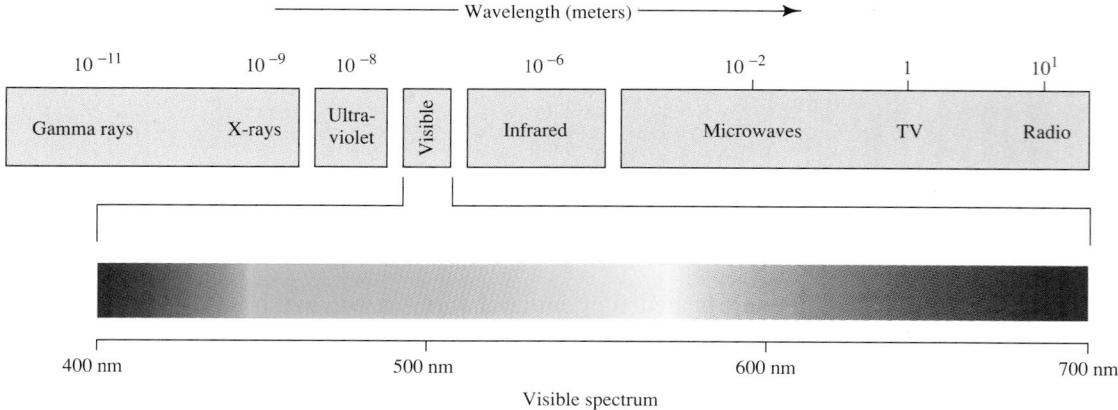

FIGURE 6.3 Wavelengths of electromagnetic radiation characteristic of various regions of the electromagnetic spectrum. Notice that color can be expressed quantitatively by wavelength.

Visible light can be seen because of chemical reactions that it triggers in our eyes. The unit of length normally chosen to express wavelength depends on the type of radiation, as shown in Table 6.1.

Frequency is expressed in cycles per second, a unit also called a *hertz* (Hz). Because it is understood that cycles are involved, the units of frequency are normally given simply as "per second," which is denoted by s^{-1} or /s. For example, a frequency of 820 kilohertz (kHz), a typical frequency for an AM radio station, could be written as $820,000 \ s^{-1}$.

TABLE 6.1 △ Common Wavelength Units for Electromagnetic Radiation

Unit	Symbol	Length (m)	Type of radiation
Angstrom	Å	10^{-10}	X-ray
Nanometer	nm	10^{-9}	Ultraviolet, visible
Micrometer	μm	10^{-6}	Infrared
Millimeter	mm	10^{-3}	Infrared
Centimeter	cm	10^{-2}	Microwave
Meter	m	1	TV, radio

SAMPLE EXERCISE 6.1

The yellow light given off by a sodium vapor lamp used for public lighting has a wavelength of 589 nm. What is the frequency of this radiation?

SOLUTION The relationship between the wavelength (which is given) and the frequency (which is our unknown) is given by Equation 6.1. Solving this equation for frequency gives $v = c/\lambda$. When we insert the values for c and λ, we note that the units of length in these two quantities are different. We can convert the wavelength from nanometers to meters, so the units cancel:

$$v = \frac{c}{\lambda} = \left(\frac{3.00 \times 10^8 \ m/s}{589 \ nm}\right)\left(\frac{1 \ nm}{10^{-9} \ m}\right) = 5.09 \times 10^{14} \ s^{-1}$$

This high frequency is reasonable because of the short wavelength. The units are proper because frequency has units of "per second" or s^{-1}.

6.2 Quantum Effects and Photons

Learning Goal 3: Explain the essential feature of Planck's quantum theory, namely, that the smallest increment, or quantum, of radiant energy of frequency, v, that can be emitted or absorbed is hv, where h is Planck's constant.

Teaching Note: Max Planck received the 1918 Nobel prize in physics for his work on the quantum theory.

When solids are heated, they emit radiation, as seen in the red glow of an electric stove burner and the bright white light of a tungsten light bulb. The wavelength distribution of the radiation depends on temperature, a "red-hot" object being cooler than a "white-hot" one. In the late 1800s, a number of physicists were studying this phenomenon, trying to understand the relationship between the temperature and the intensity and wavelengths of the emitted radiation. The prevailing laws of physics could not account for the observations.

In 1900, Max Planck (Figure 6.4) solved the problem by making a daring assumption: He assumed that energy can be released (or absorbed) by atoms only in "chunks" of some minimum size. Planck gave the name **quantum** (meaning "fixed amount") to the smallest quantity of energy that can be emitted or absorbed as electromagnetic radiation. He proposed that the energy, E, of a single quantum equals a constant times the frequency:

$$E = hv \qquad [6.2]$$

The constant h, known as *Planck's constant,* has a value of 6.63×10^{-34} joule-seconds (J-s). According to Planck's theory, energy is always emitted or absorbed in whole-number multiples of hv, for example, hv, $2hv$, $3hv$, and so forth. We say that the allowed energies are *quantized* (that is, their values are restricted to certain quantities).

FIGURE 6.4 Max Planck (1858–1947), physicist. Born in Kiel, Germany, Planck was the son of a law professor at the University of Kiel. When he announced his intention to study physics, Planck was warned that all the major discoveries had already been made in this field. Nevertheless, Planck became a physicist and in 1892 was named professor of physics at the University of Berlin. In 1900, he presented a paper before the Berlin Physical Society that launched one of the greatest intellectual revolutions in the history of science. Planck was awarded the Nobel prize in physics in 1918. (Library of Congress)

SAMPLE EXERCISE 6.2

Calculate the smallest increment of energy (that is, the quantum of energy) that an object can absorb from yellow light whose wavelength is 589 nm.

SOLUTION We obtain the magnitude of a quantum of energy from Equation 6.2, $E = h\nu$. The value of Planck's constant is given both in the text above and in the table of physical constants on the back inside cover of the text: $h = 6.63 \times 10^{-34}$ J-s. The frequency, ν, is calculated from the given wavelength, as shown in Sample Exercise 6.1: $\nu = c/\lambda = 5.09 \times 10^{14}$ s^{-1}. Thus, we have

$$E = (6.63 \times 10^{-34} \text{ J-s})(5.09 \times 10^{14} \text{ s}^{-1})$$
$$= 3.37 \times 10^{-19} \text{ J}$$

Planck's theory tells us that an atom or molecule emitting or absorbing radiation whose wavelength is 589 nm cannot lose or gain energy by radiation except in multiples of 3.37×10^{-19} J. It cannot, for example, gain 5.00×10^{-19} J from this radiation because this amount is not a multiple of 3.37×10^{-19} J.

If one quantum of radiant energy supplies 3.37×10^{-19} J, then one mole of these quanta will supply $(6.02 \times 10^{23} \text{ quanta})(3.37 \times 10^{-19} \text{ J/quantum})$, which equals 2.03×10^5 J. (Quanta is the plural of quantum.) This is the magnitude of enthalpies of reactions. ⚯ (Sec. 5.4) Indeed, radiation can cause chemical bonds to break, producing what are called *photochemical reactions*.

PRACTICE EXERCISE

A laser that emits light energy in pulses of short duration has a frequency of 4.69×10^{14} s^{-1} and deposits 1.3×10^{-2} J of energy during each pulse. How many quanta of energy does each pulse deposit? (Hint: First calculate the energy of one quantum of this frequency.)   ***Answer:*** 4.2×10^{16} quanta

If the notion of quantized rather than continuous energies seems strange, it might be helpful to draw an analogy with some musical instruments, specifically a violin and a piano (Figure 6.5). A violinist can play every pitch between two notes (say B and C) by changing the position of the fingers on the strings; the pitch of a violin can be varied continuously. In contrast, a pianist can change notes only by a set amount. It is not possible to play any notes between B and C. We could say, therefore, that the notes on a piano are quantized. Quantized energies can also be likened to climbing a ladder. You can stop only *on* rungs, not *between* them.

FIGURE 6.5   The pitch of a violin can be varied continuously, but that of a piano can be varied only in steps; the notes on the piano are quantized. (Four By Five/Superstock; © Christian Steiner)

If Planck's quantum theory is correct, why aren't its effects more obvious in our everyday experience? You will note that Planck's constant is an extremely small number. Thus, a quantum of energy, $h\nu$, will be an extremely small amount. Planck's rules regarding the gain or loss of energy are always the same, whether we are concerned with objects on the size scale of our ordinary experience or with microscopic objects. For macroscopic objects, such as humans, the gain or loss of a quantum of energy is completely unnoticed. When dealing with matter at the atomic level, however, the impact of quantized energies is far more significant.

The Photoelectric Effect

Figure 6.6

A few years after Planck presented his theory, scientists began to see its applicability to a great many experimental observations. It soon became apparent that Planck's theory had within it the seeds of a revolution in the way the physical world is viewed. In 1905, Albert Einstein (1879–1955) used Planck's quantum theory to explain the *photoelectric effect,* which is illustrated in Figure 6.6. Experiments had shown that light shining on a clean metallic surface causes the surface to emit electrons. For each metal, there is a minimum frequency of light below which no electrons are emitted. For example, light with a frequency of $4.60 \times 10^{14}\,\mathrm{s^{-1}}$ or greater will cause cesium metal to eject electrons, but light of lower frequency has no effect.

To explain the photoelectric effect, Einstein assumed that the radiant energy striking the metal surface is a stream of tiny energy packets. Each energy packet behaves like a tiny particle of light and is called a **photon**. Extending Planck's quantum theory, Einstein deduced that each photon must have an energy proportional to the frequency of the light: $E = h\nu$. Thus, radiant energy itself is quantized.

When a photon strikes the metal, its energy is transferred to an electron in the metal. A certain amount of energy is required for the electron to overcome the attractive forces that hold it within the metal. If the photons of the radiation have less energy than this energy threshold, the electron cannot escape from the

FIGURE 6.6 The photoelectric effect. When photons of sufficiently high energy strike a metal surface, electrons are emitted from the metal, as in (*a*). The photoelectric effect is the basis of the photocell shown in (*b*). The emitted electrons are drawn toward the other electrode, which is a positive terminal. As a result, current flows in the circuit. Photocells are used in photographic light meters as well as in numerous other electronic devices.

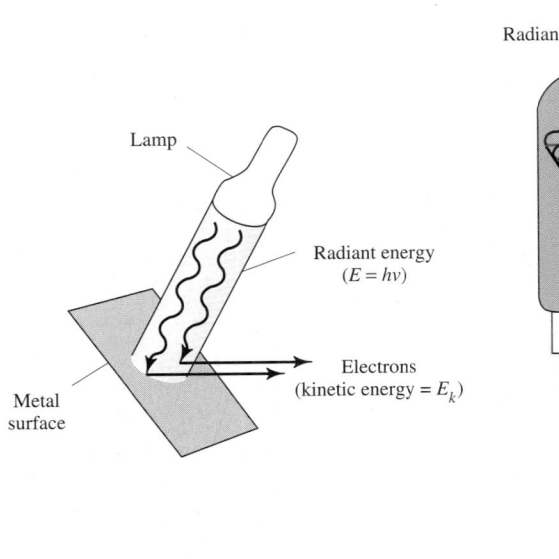

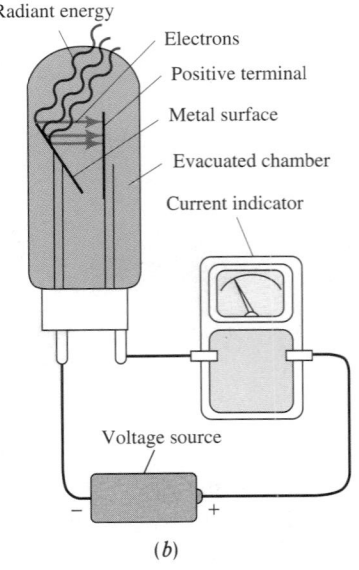

(*a*)

(*b*)

FIGURE 6.7 Niels Bohr (1885–1962), a Danish physicist, born and educated in Copenhagen. From 1911 to 1913, he studied in England, working first with J. J. Thomson at Cambridge University and then with Ernest Rutherford at the University of Manchester. He published his quantum theory of the atom in 1914 and was awarded the Nobel Prize in physics in 1922. (Alan W. Richards/AP/Wide World)

metal surface, even if the light beam is intense. If a photon does have sufficient energy, the electron is emitted. If a photon has more than the minimum energy required to free an electron, the excess appears as the kinetic energy of the emitted electron.

Point of Emphasis: The kinetic energy of the emitted electron is lower than the energy of the incident photon.

The idea that the energy of light depends on its frequency helps us understand the diverse effects that different kinds of electromagnetic radiation have on matter. For example, the high frequency (short wavelength) of X-rays (Figure 6.3) causes photons of this kind to have high energy, sufficient to cause tissue damage and even cancer. Thus, signs are normally posted around X-ray equipment warning us of high-energy radiation. On the other hand, we are constantly surrounded by radio waves, which pose no health danger partly because their low frequencies (long wavelengths) cause their photons to have low energies.

Einstein's theory of light has posed a dilemma. Is light a wave, or does it consist of particles? To date, the only way to resolve this dilemma is to adopt what might seem to be an unusual position: We must consider light to possess both wavelike and particlelike properties. As we shall see in Section 6.4, this dual nature (wavelike and particlelike) is also characteristic of matter.

FIGURE 6.8 Monochromatic light being emitted by a laser. (Hank Morgan/VHSID Lab/ECE Dept., U of MA/Science Source/Photo Researchers)

6.3 Bohr's Model of the Hydrogen Atom

The work of Planck and Einstein paved the way for understanding how electrons are arranged in atoms. An important step occurred in 1913 when the Danish physicist Niels Bohr (Figure 6.7) offered a theoretical explanation of line spectra, another phenomenon that had puzzled scientists in the nineteenth century.

Line Spectra

A particular source of radiant energy may emit a single wavelength, as in the light from a laser (Figure 6.8). Radiation composed of a single wavelength is said to be *monochromatic.* However, most common radiation sources, including light bulbs and stars, produce radiation containing many different wavelengths. When radiation from such sources is separated into its different wave-

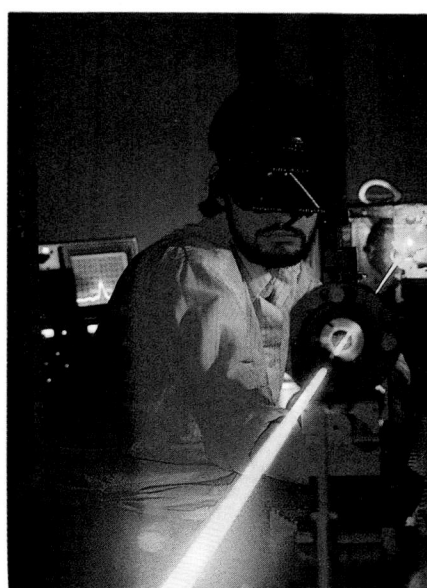

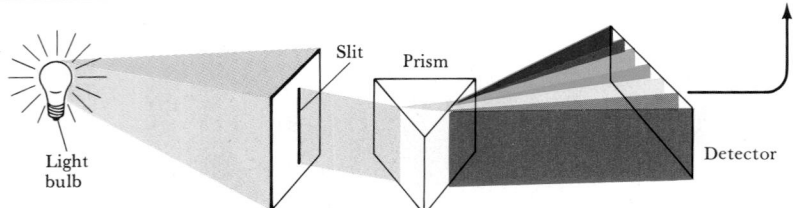

FIGURE 6.9 A continuous visible spectrum is produced when a narrow beam of white light is passed through a prism. The white light could be sunlight or light from an incandescent lamp.

Learning Goal 5: Explain the origin of the expression *line spectra.*

length components, a **spectrum** is produced. Figure 6.9 shows how "white" light from a light bulb can be dispersed by a prism. The spectrum so produced consists of a continuous range of colors: Violet merges into blue, blue into green, and so forth, with no blank spots. This rainbow of colors, containing light of all wavelengths, is called a **continuous spectrum.** The most familiar example of a continuous spectrum is the rainbow, produced by the dispersal of sunlight by raindrops or mist.

Not all radiation sources produce a continuous spectrum. When different gases are placed under reduced pressure in a tube and a high voltage is applied, the gases emit different colors of light (Figure 6.10). The light emitted by neon gas is the familiar red-orange glow of many "neon" lights (many neon lights actually contain other gases); sodium vapor emits the yellow light characteristic of some modern street lights. When light coming from such tubes is passed through a prism, only lines of a few wavelengths are present in the resultant spectra, as shown in Figure 6.12. The colored lines are separated by black

FIGURE 6.10 Different gases emit light of different characteristic colors upon excitation in an electrical discharge: (*a*) H; (*b*) Hg; (*c*) N. (Richard Megna/Fundamental Photographs)

(*a*)   (*b*)   (*c*)

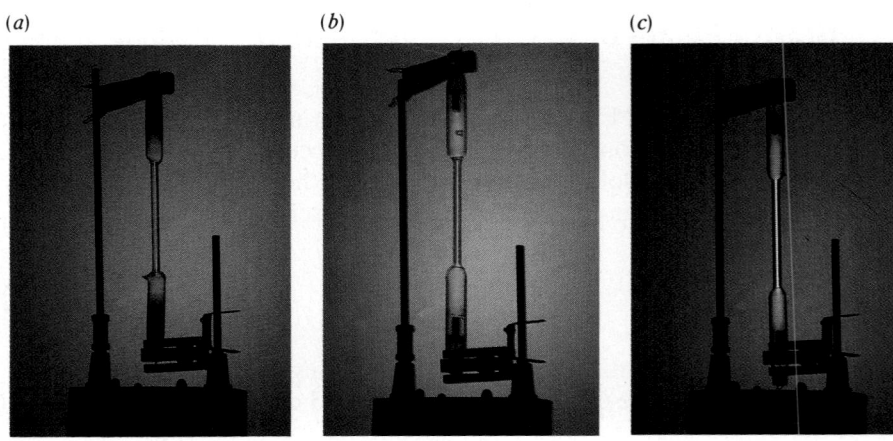

A CLOSER LOOK

Discovery of Helium

The spectrum of the radiation emitted by a substance is called an *emission spectrum*. The line spectrum of hydrogen shown in Figure 6.12 is an emission spectrum. Substances also exhibit *absorption spectra*. When continuous electromagnetic radiation, such as that from a light bulb, passes through a substance, certain wavelengths may be absorbed. The spectrum of the radiation that passes through is called an absorption spectrum. The absorption spectrum of hydrogen consists of what looks like a continuous spectrum interrupted by black lines at 656.3 nm, 486.3 nm, and the other wavelengths found in the emission spectrum. The absorption spectrum of hydrogen is a line spectrum that is complementary to its emission spectrum.

Each element has a characteristic line spectrum that can be used to identify it. Figure 6.11 shows the spectrum of the light emitted by the sun. Notice that there are several dark bands in the spectrum. Because of its high temperature, the core of the sun emits a continuous spectrum of radiation; however, elements that are present in the outer regions of the sun, where the temperatures are not so high, absorb radiation at characteristic wavelengths. Absorptions due to hydrogen, helium, iron, and other atoms give rise to the dark bands evident in Figure 6.11.

Helium was first discovered in 1868 from a similar spectrum of our sun. Some of the absorption lines of the sun's spectrum could not be matched with those of any element then known. It was concluded that the sun contained an element previously unknown on earth. This element was named helium after *helios*, the Greek word for "sun." Helium was subsequently isolated and characterized in the laboratory in 1895.

FIGURE 6.11 Spectrum of the sun's radiation. Notice the presence of dark lines, called *Fraunhofer lines*, due to absorption of radiation by hydrogen and other atoms at the outer limits of the sun. The lower spectrum is that of an incandescent source of the same temperature as the sun's surface. (Courtesy Bausch & Lomb)

FIGURE 6.12 The line spectra of (*a*) H; (*b*) Hg. (Courtesy Sargent-Welch Scientific Co.)

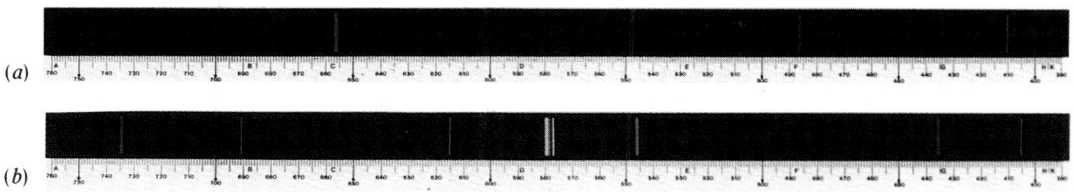

(*a*)

(*b*)

Figure 6.13

FIGURE 6.13   Energy levels in the hydrogen atom from the Bohr model. The arrows refer to the transitions of the electron from one allowed energy state to another. Only the lowest six energy levels are shown.

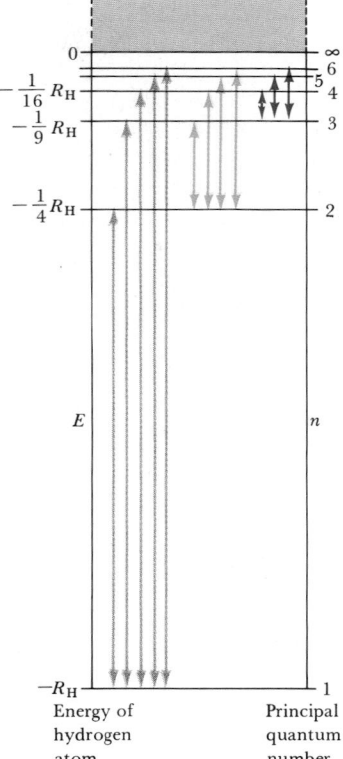

regions, which correspond to wavelengths that are absent in the light. A spectrum containing radiation of only specific wavelengths is called a **line spectrum.**

When scientists first detected the line spectrum of hydrogen in the mid-1800s, they were fascinated by its simplicity. In 1885, a Swiss schoolteacher named Johann Balmer observed that the frequencies of the four lines of hydrogen shown in Figure 6.11 fit an intriguingly simple formula:

$$\nu = C\left(\frac{1}{2^2} - \frac{1}{n^2}\right) \qquad n = 3, 4, 5, 6 \qquad [6.3]$$

In this formula, C is a constant equal to 3.29×10^{15} s^{-1}. How could the remarkable simplicity of this equation be explained? It took nearly 30 more years to answer this question, as we will see in the next section.

Bohr's Model

After Rutherford's discovery of the nuclear nature of the atom (Section 2.2), scientists thought of the atom as a "microscopic solar system" in which electrons orbited the nucleus. In explaining the line spectrum of hydrogen, Bohr started with this idea, assuming that electrons move in circular orbits around the nucleus. According to classical physics, however, an electrically charged particle (such as an electron) that moves in a circular path should continuously lose energy by emitting electromagnetic radiation. As the electron loses energy, it should spiral into the nucleus. Bohr approached this problem in much the same way that Planck had approached the problem of the nature of the radiation emitted by hot objects: He assumed that the prevailing laws of physics were inadequate to describe atoms. Furthermore, he adopted Planck's idea that energies are quantized. He proposed that only orbits of certain radii, corresponding to certain definite energies, are permitted. An electron in a permitted orbit has a specific energy and is said to be in an "allowed" energy state. An electron in an allowed energy state will not radiate energy and therefore will not spiral into the nucleus.

Using concepts from physics, Bohr showed that if the orbits of the electron in a hydrogen atom are restricted, the energies that the electron can possess are given by

$$E_n = (-R_H)\left(\frac{1}{n^2}\right) \qquad [6.4]$$

The constant R_H is called the *Rydberg constant* and has the value of 2.18×10^{-18} J. The integer n, called the *principal quantum number,* corresponds to the different allowed orbits for the electron. Thus, an electron in the first orbit (the one closest to the nucleus) has $n = 1$, an electron in the next allowed orbit further from the nucleus has $n = 2$, and so forth. Figure 6.13 shows the energy levels of the electron in a hydrogen atom.

All the energies given by Equation 6.4 are negative. The lower (more negative) the energy is, the more stable the atom will be. (One way to remember this convention is to think of a ball rolling down a stairway. The ball will naturally proceed to the bottom stair; it is most stable when its potential energy is lowest.) The lowest energy state (analogous to the bottom stair) is that for which $n = 1$. This is called the **ground state** of the atom. When the electron is in a higher (less negative) energy orbit—namely, $n = 2$ or higher—the atom is said to be in an **excited state.**

What happens to the orbit radius and the energy as n becomes infinitely large? The radius increases as n^2; we reach a point at which the electron is completely separated from the nucleus. The energy for $n = \infty$ becomes

$$E_\infty = (-2.18 \times 10^{-18} \text{ J}) \left(\frac{1}{\infty^2}\right) = 0$$

Thus, the state in which the electron is removed from the nucleus is the reference, or zero-energy, state of the hydrogen atom. It is important to remember that this zero-energy state is *higher* in energy than the states with negative energies.

In addition to assuming that the orbits and hence the energy states of the electron are quantized, Bohr also assumed that the electron can change from one energy state to another by absorbing or emitting radiant energy. Radiant energy must be absorbed for an electron to move to a higher energy state (one with a larger principal quantum number), which corresponds to moving the electron further from the nucleus. Conversely, radiant energy is emitted when the electron moves to a lower energy state. The change in the energy, ΔE, is given by the difference between the energy of the final state of the electron, E_f, and the initial state, E_i:

$$\Delta E = E_f - E_i$$

Substituting the expression for the energy of the electron, Equation 6.4, gives

$$\Delta E = \left(\frac{-R_H}{n_f^2}\right) - \left(\frac{-R_H}{n_i^2}\right) = -R_H \left(\frac{1}{n_f^2} - \frac{1}{n_i^2}\right) = R_H \left(\frac{1}{n_i^2} - \frac{1}{n_f^2}\right)$$

The frequency of the radiant energy corresponds exactly to the energy difference between the energy states: $\Delta E = h\nu$. Thus, Bohr was able to write

$$\Delta E = h\nu = (R_H) \left(\frac{1}{n_i^2} - \frac{1}{n_f^2}\right) \qquad [6.5]$$

A positive value of ΔE results when $n_f > n_i$, indicating that radiant energy is absorbed. When ΔE is negative, radiant energy is emitted as the electron moves from a higher to lower energy ($n_i > n_f$).

By solving Equation 6.5 for ν, we can see the relationship between Balmer's formula—Equation 6.3—and Bohr's result. Only those lines for which $n_f = 2$ appear in the visible portion of the spectrum. Thus, Balmer had a factor of $\frac{1}{2}^2$ in his formula. Balmer's constant, C, equals R_H (that is, 2.18×10^{-18} J) divided by Planck's constant, h.

SAMPLE EXERCISE 6.3

Calculate the wavelength of light that corresponds to the transition of the electron from the $n = 4$ to the $n = 2$ state of the hydrogen atom. Is the light absorbed or emitted by the atom?

SOLUTION   We use Equation 6.5, substituting $n_i = 4$ and $n_f = 2$ because these are the quantum numbers for the initial and final energy states, respectively:

Point of Emphasis: The *ground state* for hydrogen is the one in which the electron is in the lowest energy orbit, $n = 1$. If the electron is in any other orbit, it is in an *excited state.*

Point of Emphasis: Arithmetically, $1/\infty = 0$. Because the energies of the orbits are all negative, the zero-energy state is high in energy.

Learning Goal 8:   Calculate the energy difference between any two allowed energy states of the electron in hydrogen.

Point of Emphasis: By convention, differences of energies in chemistry (ΔH, ΔE, etc.) are always the value at the final state minus the value at the initial state. This is necessary for the arithmetic sign of the result to be correct.

Teaching Note: Although ΔE can be positive or negative depending on whether energy was absorbed or emitted, the energy of the photon involved is always positive.

Teaching Note: Other series of spectral lines for hydrogen carry names of scientists: Lyman ($n_f = 1$), Paschen ($n_f = 3$), and Brackett ($n_f = 4$).

Teaching Note: Bohr's model did an equally good job of explaining the other series of lines in the hydrogen spectrum.

$$\Delta E = h\nu = R_H \left(\frac{1}{n_i^2} - \frac{1}{n_f^2} \right)$$

$$\nu = \frac{R_H}{h} \left(\frac{1}{n_i^2} - \frac{1}{n_f^2} \right)$$

$$= \frac{2.18 \times 10^{-18} \text{ J}}{6.63 \times 10^{-34} \text{ J-s}} \left(\frac{1}{4^2} - \frac{1}{2^2} \right)$$

$$= \frac{2.18 \times 10^{-18} \text{ J}}{6.63 \times 10^{-34} \text{ J-s}} \left(\frac{1}{16} - \frac{1}{4} \right)$$

$$= \frac{2.18 \times 10^{-18} \text{ J}}{6.63 \times 10^{-34} \text{ J-s}} \left(-\frac{3}{16} \right)$$

$$= -6.17 \times 10^{14} \text{ s}^{-1}$$

The negative sign indicates that light with a frequency of $6.17 \times 10^{14} \text{ s}^{-1}$ is emitted by the atom. We expect this; the electron is moving from a higher to a lower energy state, so energy is released. The wavelength of the emitted light is given by Equation 6.1:

$$\lambda = \frac{c}{\nu} = \frac{3.00 \times 10^8 \text{ m/s}}{6.17 \times 10^{14} \text{ s}^{-1}}$$

$$= 4.86 \times 10^{-7} \text{ m} = 486 \text{ nm}$$

This is the wavelength of the green emission line in the spectrum of hydrogen (Figure 6.12). All of the emission lines shown in Figure 6.12 correspond to transitions of the electron from higher orbits to the $n = 2$ orbit.

PRACTICE EXERCISE

Calculate the wavelength of the hydrogen line that corresponds to the transition of the electron from the $n = 4$ to the $n = 1$ state. *Answer:* 97.3 nm, in the ultraviolet portion of the electromagnetic spectrum.

Teaching Note: The Bohr model, with slight variation, describes any 1 e⁻ system satisfactorily.

Bohr's model was very important because it introduced the idea of quantized energy states for electrons in atoms. This feature is incorporated into our current model of the atom. However, Bohr's model was adequate for explaining only atoms and ions with a single electron, such as H, He^+, and Li^{2+}. It could not explain the atomic spectra of other atoms or ions, except in a rather crude way. Consequently, Bohr's model was eventually replaced by a new way of viewing atoms that maintains the concept of quantized energy states but adds further applications of Planck's quantum theory.

6.4 The Dual Nature of the Electron

Teaching Note: Louis Victor de Broglie received the 1929 Nobel prize in physics for his work on the wave nature of the electron.

In the years following Bohr's development of a model for the hydrogen atom, the dual nature of radiant energy became a familiar concept. Depending on the experimental circumstances, radiation appears to have either a wavelike or a particlelike (photon) character. Louis de Broglie (1892–1987), who was working on his Ph.D. thesis in physics at the Sorbonne in Paris, made a daring extension of this idea. If radiant energy could, under appropriate conditions, behave as though it were a stream of particles, could not matter under appropriate conditions possibly show the properties of a wave? Suppose that the electron in orbit around the nucleus of a hydrogen atom could be thought of as a wave, with a characteristic wavelength. De Broglie suggested that the electron in its circular path about the nucleus has associated with it a particular wavelength. He went on to propose that the characteristic wavelength of the electron or of any other particle depends on its mass, m, and velocity, v:

$$\lambda = \frac{h}{mv} \qquad [6.6]$$

Learning Goal 9: Calculate the characteristic wavelength of a particle from a knowledge of its mass and velocity.

Point of Emphasis: For a given velocity, the higher the mass of the particle, the shorter the wavelength.

(h is Planck's constant). The quantity mv for any object is called its **momentum.** De Broglie used the term **matter waves** to describe the wave characteristics of material particles.

Because de Broglie's hypothesis is applicable to all matter, any object of mass m and velocity v would give rise to a characteristic matter wave. However, Equation 6.6 indicates that the wavelength associated with an object of ordinary size, such as a golf ball, is so tiny as to be completely out of the range of any possible observation. This is not so for electrons because their mass is so small.

SAMPLE EXERCISE 6.4

What is the characteristic wavelength of an electron with a velocity of 5.97×10^6 m/s? (The mass of the electron is 9.11×10^{-28} g.)

SOLUTION The value of Planck's constant, h, is 6.63×10^{-34} J-s (recall that $1\ J = 1\ kg\text{-}m^2/s^2$).

$$\lambda = \frac{h}{mv}$$

$$= \frac{6.63 \times 10^{-34}\ \text{J-s}}{(9.11 \times 10^{-28}\ \text{g})(5.97 \times 10^6\ \text{m/s})} \left(\frac{1\ \text{kg-m}^2/s^2}{1\ \text{J}} \right) \left(\frac{10^3\ \text{g}}{1\ \text{kg}} \right)$$

$$= 1.22 \times 10^{-10}\ \text{m} = 0.122\ \text{nm}$$

By comparing this value with the wavelengths of electromagnetic radiations shown in Figure 6.3, we see that the characteristic wavelength is about the same as that of X-rays.

PRACTICE EXERCISE

At what velocity must a neutron be moving in order for it to exhibit a wavelength of 500 pm? The mass of a neutron is given in the table on the back inside cover of the text. *Answer:* 7.92×10^2 m/s

Within a few years after de Broglie published his theory, the wave properties of the electron were demonstrated experimentally. Electrons were diffracted by crystals, just as X-rays are diffracted.

The technique of electron diffraction has been highly developed. In the electron microscope, the wave characteristics of electrons are used to obtain pictures of tiny objects. The electron microscope is an important tool for studying surface phenomena at very high magnifications. Figure 6.14 is an example of an electron microscope picture. Such pictures are powerful demonstrations that tiny particles of matter can indeed behave as waves.

FIGURE 6.14 Electron micrograph of a single influenza virus. In an electron microscope, the wave behavior of a stream of electrons is utilized in the same way that a conventional microscope uses the wave behavior of a beam of light. The virion (particle) has been magnified about 400,000 times. (CNRI/Science Photo Library/Photo Researchers)

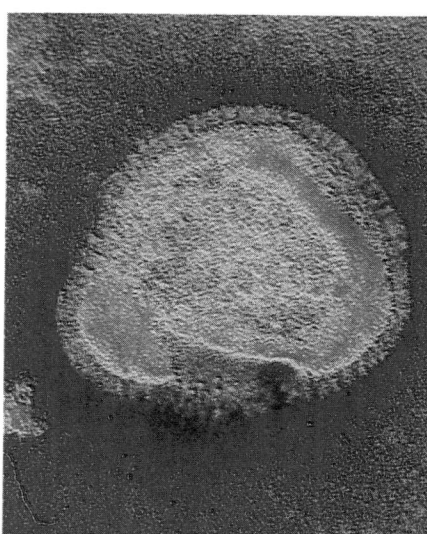

The Uncertainty Principle

The discovery of the wave properties of matter raised some new and interesting questions about classical physics. Consider, for example, a ball rolling down a ramp. By using classical physics, we can calculate *exactly* its position, its direc-

A CLOSER LOOK

Measurement and the Uncertainty Principle

Whenever any measurement is made, some uncertainty exists. Our experience with objects of ordinary dimensions, like balls or trains or laboratory equipment, indicates that the uncertainty of a measurement can be decreased by using more precise instruments. In fact, we might expect that the uncertainty in a measurement can be made indefinitely small. However, the uncertainty principle states that there is an actual limit to the accuracy of measurements. This limit is not a restriction on how well instruments can be made; rather, it is inherent in nature. This limit has no practical consequences when we are dealing with ordinary-sized objects, but its implications are enormous when we are dealing with subatomic particles, such as electrons.

To measure an object, we must disturb it, at least a little, with our measuring device. Imagine that you use a flashlight to locate a large rubber ball in a dark room. You see the ball when the light from the flashlight bounces off the ball and strikes your eyes. When a beam of photons strikes an object of this size, it does not alter its position or momentum to any practical extent. Imagine, however, that you wish to locate an electron by similarly bouncing light off it into some detector. Objects can be located to an accuracy no greater than the wavelength of the radiation used. Thus, if we want an accurate position measurement for an electron, we must use a short

wavelength. This means that photons of high energy must be employed. The more energy the photons have, the more momentum they impart to the electron when they strike it, which changes the electron's motion in an unpredictable way. The attempt to measure accurately the electron's position introduces considerable uncertainty in its momentum; the act of measuring the electron's position at one moment makes our knowledge of its future position inaccurate.

Suppose, then, that we use photons of longer wavelength. Because these photons have lower energy, the momentum of the electron is not so appreciably changed during measurement, but its position will be correspondingly less accurately known. This is the essence of the uncertainty principle: *There is an uncertainty in either the position or the momentum of the electron that cannot be reduced beyond a certain minimum level.* The more accurately one is known, the less accurately the other is known. Although we can never know with certainty the exact position and motion of the electron, we can talk about the probability of the electron being at certain locations in space. In the next section, we introduce a model of the atom that provides the probability of finding electrons of specific energies at certain positions in atoms.

Learning Goal 10: Describe the uncertainty principle, and explain the limitations it places on our ability to define simultaneously the location and momentum of a subatomic particle, particularly an electron.

tion of motion, and its speed of motion at any time. Can we do the same for an electron that exhibits wave properties? A wave extends in space, and its location is not precisely defined. We might therefore anticipate that it is not possible to determine exactly where an electron is located at a specific time.

The German physicist Werner Heisenberg (Figure 6.15) concluded that the dual nature of matter places a fundamental limitation on how precisely we

FIGURE 6.15 Werner Heisenberg (1901–1976). This photograph was taken in 1924 at the University of Göttingen, where he delivered the lecture that qualified him for a university chair. Heisenberg turned down a professorship at Göttingen for a postdoctoral assistantship with Niels Bohr at Copenhagen. While working with Bohr, he formulated his famous uncertainty principle. Shortly thereafter, at the age of 25, he became Germany's youngest full professor, as chair for theoretical physics at the University of Leipzig. He demonstrated intense ambition and a nearly insatiable drive for distinction as the best at everything he did. At 32, he was one of the youngest scientists to receive the Nobel Prize. (Photo by Professor Friedrich Hund, Werner Heisenberg Archive, Werner Heisenberg Institut, Max Planck Institut for Physik.)

can know both the location and the momentum of any object. The limitation becomes important only when we deal with matter at the subatomic level, that is, with masses as small as that of an electron. Heisenberg's principle is called the **uncertainty principle.** When applied to the electrons in an atom, this principle states that it is inherently impossible for us to know simultaneously both the exact momentum of the electron and its exact location in space. Thus, it is not appropriate to imagine the electrons as moving in well-defined circular orbits about the nucleus.

De Broglie's hypothesis and Heisenberg's uncertainty principle set the stage for a new and more broadly applicable theory of atomic structure. In this new approach, any attempt to define precisely the instantaneous location and momentum of the electrons is abandoned. The wave nature of the electron is recognized, and the electron's behavior is described in terms appropriate to waves.

6.5 Quantum Mechanics and Atomic Orbitals

In 1926, the Austrian physicist Erwin Schrödinger (1887–1961) proposed an equation, now known as Schrödinger's wave equation, that incorporates both the wavelike and particlelike behavior of the electron. His work opened a new way of dealing with subatomic particles known as *quantum mechanics* or *wave mechanics.* The application of Schrödinger's equation requires advanced calculus, and we will not be concerned with the details of his approach. We will, however, consider qualitatively the results he obtained because they give us a powerful new way to view electronic structure. Let's begin by examining the electronic structure of the simplest atom, hydrogen.

Solving Schrödinger's equation leads to a series of mathematical functions called **wave functions** that are usually represented by the symbol ψ (the Greek lowercase letter *psi*). Although the wave function itself has no direct physical meaning, the square of the wave function, ψ^2, provides information about an electron's location when it is in an allowed energy state. For the hydrogen atom, the allowed energies are the same as those predicted by the Bohr model. However, the Bohr model assumes that the electron is in a circular orbit of some particular radius about the nucleus. In the quantum-mechanical model, the electron's location cannot be described so simply. The uncertainty principle suggests that if we know the momentum of the electron with high accuracy, our knowledge of its location is very uncertain. Thus, we cannot hope to specify the location of an individual electron around the nucleus. Rather, we must be content with a kind of statistical knowledge. In the quantum-mechanical model, we therefore speak of the *probability* that the electron will be in a certain region of space at a given instant. As it turns out, the square of the wave function, ψ^2, at a given point in space represents the probability that the electron will be found at that location. For this reason, ψ^2 is called the **probability density.**

One way of representing the probability of finding the electron in various regions of an atom is shown in Figure 6.16. In this figure, the density of the dots represents the probability of finding the electron. The regions with a high density of dots correspond to relatively large values for ψ^2. **Electron density** is another way of expressing probability: Regions where there is a high probability of finding the electron are said to be regions of high electron density. In Section 6.6, we will say more about the ways in which we can represent electron density.

Teaching Note: Werner Heisenberg received the 1932 Nobel prize in physics for his uncertainty principle.

Teaching Note: Picture a busy intersection photographed at night. With a short exposure, you get a clear image of the position of every car, but you cannot tell how fast they are going or whether they are going forward or backward or are about to swerve or turn. With a time-lapsed exposure, you can tell from the streaks of light the speed and direction of each car, but you cannot tell where each one currently is. You can know position or path, not both.

Learning Goal 11: Explain the concepts of orbital, electron density, and probability as used in the quantum-mechanical model of the atom. Explain the physical significance of ψ^2.

Teaching Note: Unlike Bohr and his predecessors, who started with a preconceived notion of atomic shape in their models, Schrödinger started with the measurable energies of the atom and worked toward the description of the atom. In a very real way, Schrödinger worked the problem backward.

FIGURE 6.16 Electron-density distribution in the ground state of the hydrogen atom.

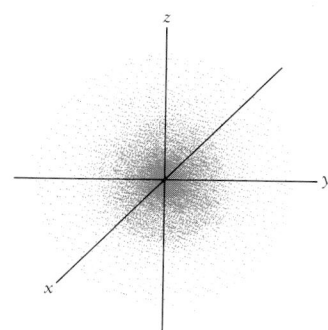

Orbitals and Quantum Numbers

Learning Goal 12: Describe
the quantum numbers n, l,
and m_l used to define an orbital in an atom, and list the
limitations placed on the
values each may have.

Point of Emphasis: The
wave equation does not give a
trajectory for the electron,
only the regions around the
nucleus where it is most likely
to be found.

Teaching Note: The quan-
tum numbers are parameters
in the solution of the wave
equation.

Teaching Note: Erwin
Schrödinger received the 1933
Nobel prize in physics (with
Paul Dirac) for the wave
equation.

The complete solution to Schrödinger's equation for the hydrogen atom yields a set of wave functions and a corresponding set of energies. These wave functions are called **orbitals.** Each orbital describes a specific distribution of electron density in space, as given by its probability density. An orbital therefore has both a characteristic energy and a characteristic shape. For example, the lowest energy orbital in the hydrogen atom has an energy of -2.18×10^{-18} J and the shape illustrated in Figure 6.16. Note that an *orbital* (quantum-mechanical model) is not the same as an *orbit* (Bohr model).

The Bohr model introduced a single quantum number, n, to describe an orbit. The quantum-mechanical model uses three quantum numbers, n, l, and m_l, to describe an orbital. We will consider what information we obtain from each of these and how they are interrelated.

1. The *principal quantum number, n,* can have integral values of 1, 2, 3, and so forth. As n increases, the orbital becomes larger, and the electron spends more time farther from the nucleus. An increase in n also means that the electron has a higher energy and is therefore less tightly bound to the nucleus. For hydrogen, $E_n = -(2.18 \times 10^{-18} \text{ J})(1/n^2)$, as in the Bohr model.

2. The second quantum number — the *azimuthal quantum number, l* — can have integral values from 0 to $n - 1$ for each value of n. This quantum number defines the shape of the orbital. (We will consider these shapes in Section 6.6.) The value of l for a particular orbital is generally designated by the letters s, p, d, and f,* corresponding to l values of 0, 1, 2, and 3, respectively, as summarized below.

Value of l	0	1	2	3
Letter used	s	p	d	f

3. The *magnetic quantum number, m_l,* can have integral values between l and $-l$, including zero. This quantum number describes the orientation of the orbital in space. (The orientations will be considered in Section 6.6.)

A collection of orbitals with the same value of n is called an **electron shell.** For example, all the orbitals with $n = 3$ are said to be in the third shell. One or more orbitals with the same set of n and l values is called a **subshell.** Each subshell is designated by a number (the value of n) and a letter (s, p, d, or f, corresponding to the value of l). For example, all of the orbitals of an atom with $n = 3$ and $l = 1$ are collectively referred to as $3p$ orbitals and are said to be in the $3p$ subshell. The possible values of the three quantum numbers through $n = 4$ (the fourth shell) are summarized in Table 6.2.

The restrictions on the possible values of the quantum numbers give rise to a pattern that is very important:

1. Each shell is divided into the number of subshells equal to the principal quantum number, n, for that shell. The first shell consists of only the $1s$

---

* The letters s, p, d, and f come from the words *sharp, principal, diffuse,* and *fundamental,* which were used to describe certain features of spectra before quantum mechanics was developed.

TABLE 6.2 △ Relationship Among Values of n, l, and m_l through $n = 4$

n	l	Subshell designation	m_l	Number of orbitals in subshell
1	0	$1s$	0	1
2	0	$2s$	0	1
	1	$2p$	1, 0, −1	3
3	0	$3s$	0	1
	1	$3p$	1, 0, −1	3
	2	$3d$	2, 1, 0, −1, −2	5
4	0	$4s$	0	1
	1	$4p$	1, 0, −1	3
	2	$4d$	2, 1, 0, −1, −2	5
	3	$4f$	3, 2, 1, 0, −1, −2, −3	7

Table 6.2

subshell; the second shell consists of two subshells, $2s$ and $2p$; the third shell consists of three subshells, $3s$, $3p$, and $3d$. Thus, every shell has an s subshell; every shell beginning with the second has a p subshell; every shell beginning with the third has a d subshell, and so forth.

2. Each subshell is divided into orbitals. Each s subshell consists of one orbital; each p subshell consists of three orbitals; each d subshell consists of five orbitals; each f subshell consists of seven orbitals. (Notice that these are the odd numbers, 1, 3, 5, 7.)

Figure 6.17 shows the number and relative energies of all hydrogen atom orbitals through $n = 3$. Each box represents an orbital; orbitals of the same

Figure 6.17

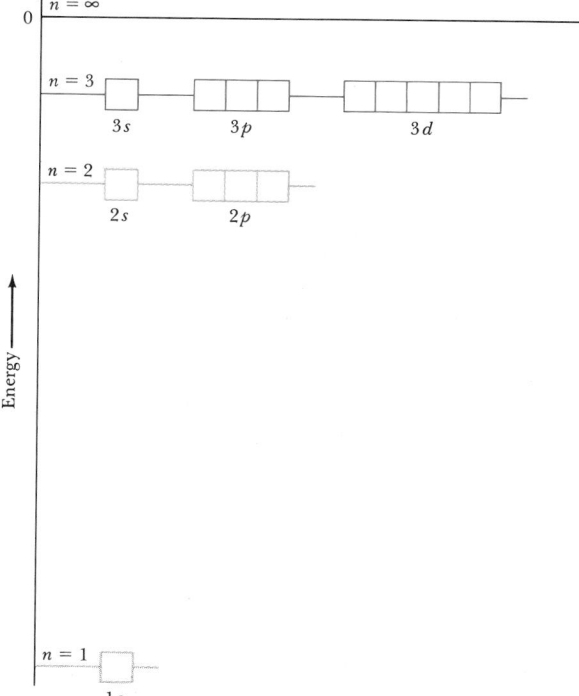

FIGURE 6.17 Orbital energy levels in the hydrogen atom and in hydrogenlike ions (those containing just one electron). Note that all orbitals with the same value for the principal quantum number, n, have the same energy. This is true only in one-electron systems.

subshell, such as the 2*p*, are grouped together. When the electron is in the lowest energy orbital (the 1*s* orbital), the hydrogen atom is said to be in its *ground state*. When the electron is in any other orbital, the atom is in an *excited state*. At ordinary temperatures, essentially all hydrogen atoms are in their ground states. The electron may be promoted to an excited-state orbital by absorption of a photon of appropriate energy.

SAMPLE EXERCISE 6.5

(a) Without referring to Table 6.2, predict the number of subshells in the fourth shell (that is, for $n = 4$). (b) Give the label for each of these subshells. (c) How many orbitals are in each of these subshells?

SOLUTION (a) There are four subshells in the fourth shell, corresponding to the four possible values of l (0, 1, 2, and 3).

(b) These subshells are labeled 4*s*, 4*p*, 4*d*, and 4*f*. The number given in the designation of a subshell is the principal quantum number, n; the following letter designates the value of the azimuthal quantum number, l.

(c) There is one 4*s* orbital (when $l = 0$, there is only one possible value of m_l: 0). There are three 4*p* orbitals (when $l = 1$, there are three possible values of m_l: 1, 0, and -1). There are five 4*d* orbitals (when $l = 2$, there are five allowed values of m_l: 2, 1, 0, -1, -2). There are seven 4*f* orbitals (when $l = 3$, there are seven permitted values of m_l: 3, 2, 1, 0, -1, -2, -3).

PRACTICE EXERCISE

(a) What is the designation for the subshell with $n = 5$ and $l = 1$? (b) How many orbitals are in this subshell? (c) Indicate the values of m_l for each of these orbitals.
Answers: (a) 5*p*; (b) 3; (c) 1, 0, -1

6.6 Representations of Orbitals

In our discussion of orbitals, we have so far emphasized their energies. But the wave function also provides information about the electron's location in space when it is in a particular allowed energy state. We need to examine the ways that we can picture the orbitals.

The *s* Orbitals

The lowest-energy (most stable) orbital, the 1*s* orbital, is spherically symmetric, as shown in Figure 6.16. Figures of this type, showing electron density, are one of the several ways we have to help us visualize orbitals. This figure indicates that the probability of finding the electron around the nucleus decreases as we move away from the nucleus in any direction. When the probability function, ψ^2, for the 1*s* orbital is graphed as a function of the distance from the nucleus, r, it rapidly approaches zero, as shown in Figure 6.18(*a*). This effect indicates that the electron, which is drawn toward the nucleus by electrostatic attraction, is unlikely ever to get very far from the nucleus.

If we similarly consider the 2*s* and 3*s* orbitals of hydrogen, we find that they are also spherically symmetric. Indeed, *all s* orbitals are spherically symmetric. The manner in which the probability function, ψ^2, varies with r for the 2*s* and 3*s* orbitals is shown in Figure 6.18(*b*) and (*c*). Notice that for the 2*s* orbital, ψ^2 goes to zero and then increases again in value before finally approaching zero at a larger value of r. The intermediate regions where ψ^2 goes to zero are called **nodal surfaces,** or simply **nodes.** The number of nodes increases with increasing value for the principal quantum number, n. The 3*s* orbital

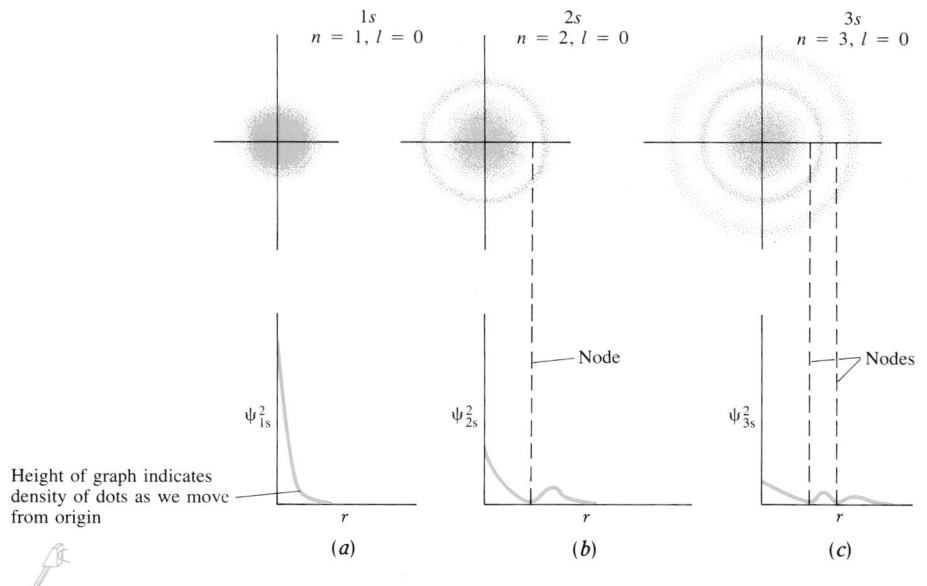

Height of graph indicates density of dots as we move from origin

(a)   (b)   (c)

Figure 6.18

FIGURE 6.18 Electron-density distribution in $1s$, $2s$, and $3s$ orbitals. The lower part of the figure shows how the electron density, represented by ψ^2, varies as a function of distance from the nucleus. In the $2s$ and $3s$ orbitals, the electron-density function drops to zero at certain distances from the nucleus. The spherical surfaces around the nucleus at which ψ^2 is zero are called *nodes.*

FIGURE 6.19 Contour representations of the $1s$, $2s$, and $3s$ orbitals. The relative radii of the spheres correspond to a 90 percent probability of finding the electron within each sphere.

possesses two nodes, as illustrated in Figure 6.18(c). Notice also that as n increases, the electron is more and more likely to be located farther from the nucleus. That is, the size of the orbital increases as n increases.

The most widely used method of representing orbitals is to display a boundary surface that encloses some substantial fraction, say 90 percent, of the total electron density for the orbital. For the s orbitals, these contour representations are merely spheres. The contour or boundary surface representations of the $1s$, $2s$, and $3s$ orbitals are shown in Figure 6.19. They have the same shape, but they differ in size. Although the details of how the electron density varies within the surface are lost in these representations, this is not a serious disadvantage. It turns out that for more qualitative discussions, the most important features of orbitals are their relative sizes and their shapes. These features are adequately represented by contour diagrams.

The p Orbitals

The distribution of electron density for a $2p$ orbital is shown in Figure 6.20(a). As we can see from this figure, the electron density is not distributed in a

FIGURE 6.20 (a) Electron-density distribution of a $2p$ orbital. (b) Contour representations of the three $2p$ orbitals. Note that the subscript on the orbital label indicates the axis along which the orbital lies.

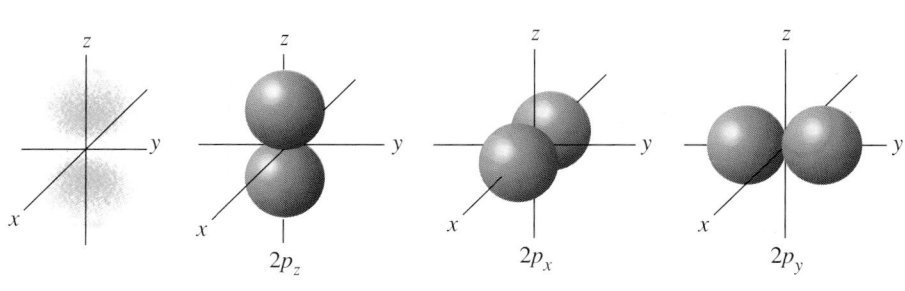

Figure 6.20

(a)   (b)

spherically symmetric fashion as in an *s* orbital. Instead, the electron density is concentrated on two sides of the nucleus, separated by a node at the nucleus; we often say that this orbital has two lobes. It is useful to recall that we are making no statement of how the electron is moving within the orbital; Figure 6.20(*a*) portrays the *averaged* distribution of the 2*p* electron in space.

Each shell beginning with $n = 2$ has three *p* orbitals. For example, there are three 2*p* orbitals, three 3*p* orbitals, and so forth. The orbitals of a given subshell have the same size and shape but differ from each other in orientation. The contour surfaces of the three 2*p* orbitals are shown in Figure 6.20(*b*). It is convenient to label these as the $2p_x$, $2p_y$, and $2p_z$ orbitals. The letter subscript indicates the axis along which the orbital is oriented. As it turns out, there is no necessary connection between one of these subscripts and a particular value of m_l. To explain why this is so would require discussion of material beyond the scope of an introductory text. Like *s* orbitals, *p* orbitals increase in size as we move from 2*p* to 3*p* to 4*p*, and so forth.

The *d* and *f* Orbitals

In the third shell and beyond, we encounter the *d* orbitals. There are five 3*d* orbitals, five 4*d* orbitals, and so forth. As in the case of the *p* orbitals, the different *d* orbitals in a given shell have different orientations in space. The most useful representations of the 3*d* orbitals are shown in Figure 6.21. Notice that four of these orbitals have lobes centered in the plane indicated by the subscript on the orbital label. The lobes of both the d_{xy} and $d_{x^2-y^2}$ orbitals lie in the *xy* plane. However, the lobes of the $d_{x^2-y^2}$ orbital lie along the *x* and *y* axes, whereas the lobes of the d_{xy} orbital lie between the axes. The lobes of the d_{xz} and d_{yz} orbitals also lie between the respective axes. The one orbital of unique shape is the d_{z^2}, which has two lobes along the *z* axis and a "doughnut" in the *xy* plane.

Figure 6.21

FIGURE 6.21 Contour representations of the five 3*d* orbitals.

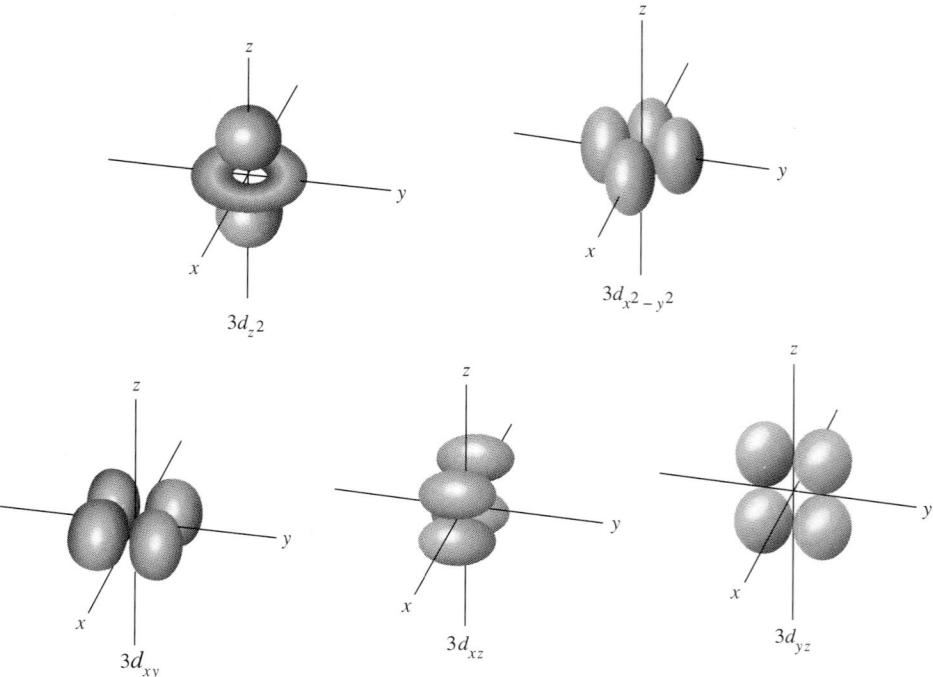

Although the d_{z^2} orbital looks different, it has the same energy as the other four d orbitals.

The representations of higher d orbitals are very much like those for the $3d$. The contour representations shown in Figure 6.21 are commonly employed for all d orbitals, regardless of principal quantum number.

There are seven equivalent f orbitals (for which $l = 3$) for each value of n of 4 or greater. The f orbitals are difficult to represent in three-dimensional contour diagrams. We shall have no need to concern ourselves with orbitals having values for l greater than 3.

As we shall see in Chapter 9, an understanding of the number and shapes of atomic orbitals is important to a proper understanding of the molecules formed by combining atoms. Your instructor may ask you to memorize the orbital representations shown in Figures 6.19 through 6.21.

6.7 Orbitals in Many-Electron Atoms

We have seen that quantum mechanics leads to a very elegant description of the hydrogen atom. The hydrogen atom is the simplest atom, of course, because it has only one electron. How does our description of atomic electronic structure have to be changed when we discuss atoms with two or more electrons? Fortunately, we can describe an atom with more than one electron (a *many-electron* atom) in terms of orbitals like those for hydrogen. Thus, we can continue to designate orbitals as $1s$, $2p_x$, and so forth. Furthermore, these orbitals have the same shapes as the corresponding hydrogen orbitals.

Although the shapes of the orbitals for many-electron atoms are the same as those for hydrogen, the presence of more than one electron greatly changes the energies of the orbitals. In hydrogen, the energy of an orbital depends only on its principal quantum number, n (Figure 6.17); the $3s$, $3p$, and $3d$ subshells all have the same energy, for instance. In a many-electron atom, however, the electron-electron repulsions cause different subshells to be at different energies, as shown in Figure 6.22. For example, the $2s$ subshell is lower in energy than the $2p$ subshell. To understand why this is so, we need to consider the forces between the electrons and how these forces are affected by the shapes of the orbitals.

Point of Emphasis: The varying energies of the subshells in the many-electron atom is the biggest difference between the descriptions of the many-electron atom and the single-electron atom.

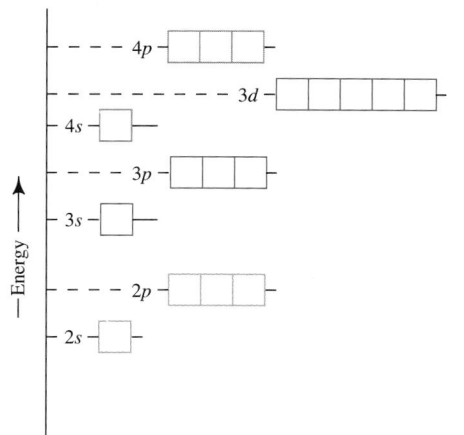

FIGURE 6.22 Ordering of orbital energy levels in many-electron atoms, through the $4p$ orbitals. As in Figure 6.17, which shows the orbital energy levels for the hydrogen atom, each box represents an orbital. Note that orbitals in different subshells differ in energy.

Figure 6.22

Effective Nuclear Charge

In a many-electron atom, each electron is simultaneously attracted to the nucleus and repelled by the other electrons. In general, there are so many electron-electron repulsions that we cannot analyze the situation exactly. We can, however, estimate the energy of each electron by considering how it interacts with the *average* environment created by the nucleus and all the other electrons in the atom. This approach allows us to treat each electron individually.

Any electron density between the nucleus and the electron of interest will reduce the nuclear charge acting on that electron. The net positive charge attracting the electron is called the **effective nuclear charge.** The effective nuclear charge, Z_{eff}, equals the number of protons in the nucleus, Z, minus the average number of electrons, S, that are between the nucleus and the electron in question:

$$Z_{eff} = Z - S \qquad [6.7]$$

Thus, the positive charge experienced by outer-shell electrons is always less than the full nuclear charge because the inner-shell electrons partly offset the positive charge of the nucleus. The inner electrons are said to shield or screen the outer electron from the full charge of the nucleus. This effect, which is called the **screening effect,** is illustrated in Figure 6.23.

Energies of Orbitals

The extent to which an electron will be screened by the other electrons depends on its electron distribution as we move outward from the nucleus. For a given value of n, this distribution differs for each subshell. Consider the orbitals for which $n = 3$. An electron in the $3s$ orbital is more likely to be close to the nucleus than an electron in the $3p$ orbital; an electron in the $3p$ orbital, in turn,

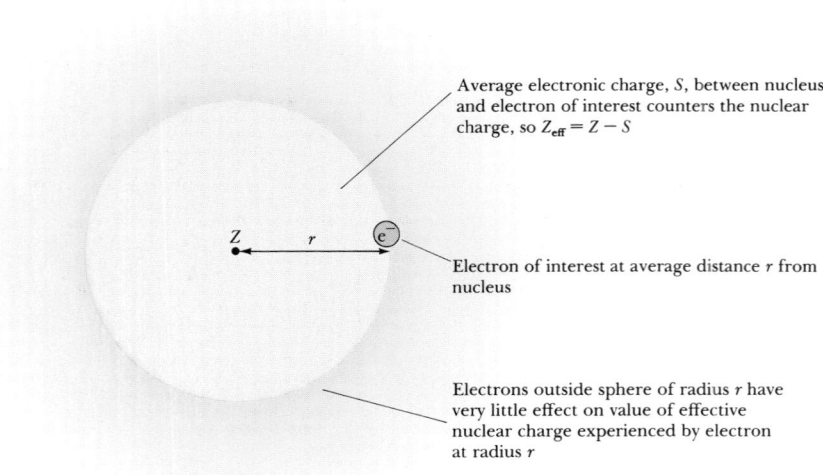

FIGURE 6.23 Shielding of the nuclear charge, Z, from an electron by other electrons in an atom. As an example, if the nuclear charge were 5 and the sphere of radius r contained three electrons, the effective nuclear charge at the radius of the sphere would be $5 - 3 = 2$. This approach allows us to treat multi-electron atoms like a hypothetical atom with one electron and a positive nuclear charge of Z_{eff}.

Average electronic charge, S, between nucleus and electron of interest counters the nuclear charge, so $Z_{eff} = Z - S$

Electron of interest at average distance r from nucleus

Electrons outside sphere of radius r have very little effect on value of effective nuclear charge experienced by electron at radius r

has a greater probability of being close to the nucleus than one in the $3d$ orbital. As a result, the $3s$ electrons experience the least shielding, and the $3d$ electrons the most. Thus, the $3s$ electrons experience a larger Z_{eff} than do the $3p$ electrons, which in turn experience a larger Z_{eff} than do the $3d$ electrons. We can generalize these observations: *In a many-electron atom, for a given value of n, Z_{eff} decreases with increasing value of l.*

The energy of an electron depends on the effective nuclear charge, Z_{eff}. Because Z_{eff} is larger for the $3s$ electrons, they have a lower energy (that is, they are more stable) than the $3p$, which in turn are lower in energy than the $3d$. Again, we can generalize: *In a many-electron atom, for a given value of n, the energy of an orbital increases with increasing value of l.* The relative energies of orbitals in a many-electron atom are shown in Figure 6.22. Figure 6.22 is a *qualitative* energy-level diagram; the exact energies and their spacings differ from one atom to another. Notice that all orbitals of a given subshell (such as the $3d$ orbitals) still have the same energy, just as they do in the hydrogen atom. Orbitals that have the same energy are said to be **degenerate**.

Point of Emphasis: The concept of *orbital degeneracy* often arises later in chemistry.

SAMPLE EXERCISE 6.6

Based on the energy-level diagram in Figure 6.22, would you expect the average distance from the nucleus of a $3d$ electron to be greater or less than that of a $2p$ electron? Explain.

SOLUTION   The energy of the $2p$ orbitals is considerably lower than for the $3d$. This indicates that Z_{eff} for the $2p$ electron is much greater than that for an electron in the $3d$ orbital. The increased attractive interaction is due to a smaller average distance of the $2p$ electron from the nucleus.

PRACTICE EXERCISE

The sodium atom has 11 electrons. Two of these occupy a $1s$ orbital, two occupy a $2s$ orbital, and one occupies a $3s$ orbital. Which of these s electrons experiences the smallest effective nuclear charge?   *Answer:* The electron in the $3s$ orbital

Electron Spin and the Pauli Exclusion Principle

At the beginning of this chapter, we stated that one of our goals was to determine the electronic structures of atoms. We have now seen that we can use orbitals to describe many-electron atoms. What, however, determines the orbitals in which electrons reside? That is, how do the electrons of a many-electron atom populate the available orbitals? To answer this question, we must consider an additional property of the electron.

When scientists studied the line spectra of many-electron atoms in great detail, they noticed a very puzzling feature: Lines that were originally thought to be single were actually closely spaced pairs. This meant, in essence, that there were twice as many energy levels as there were "supposed" to be. In 1925, the Dutch physicists George Uhlenbeck and Samuel Goudsmit proposed a solution to this dilemma. They postulated that electrons have an intrinsic property, called **electron spin.** If we view the electron as a tiny sphere, we can envision it as spinning on its own axis.*

By now it probably does not surprise you to learn that electron spin is quantized. This observation led to the assignment of a new quantum number

Learning Goal 15: Explain the concepts of electron spin and the electron spin quantum number.

Point of Emphasis: For most discussions of the electron, the two spins ($\pm 1/2$) are indistinguishable.

---

* As we discussed earlier, the electron has both particlelike and wavelike properties. Thus, the picture of an electron as a spinning charged sphere is, strictly speaking, not correct. It is a useful conceptual picture of electron spin, however.

A CLOSER LOOK

Experimental Evidence for Electron Spin

Even before electron spin had been proposed, there was experimental evidence that electrons had an additional property that needed explanation. In 1921, Otto Stern and Walter Gerlach succeeded in separating a beam of neutral atoms into two groups by passing them through an inhomogeneous magnetic field. Their experiment is diagramed in Figure 6.24. Let us assume that they used a beam of hydrogen atoms (in actuality, they used silver atoms). We would normally expect that neutral atoms would not be affected by a magnetic field. However, the magnetic field arising from the electron's spin interacts with the magnet's field, deflecting the atom from its straight-line path. As shown in Figure 6.24, the magnetic field splits the beam in two, suggesting that there are two (and only two) equivalent values for the electron's own magnetic field. The Stern-Gerlach experiment could be readily interpreted once it was realized that there are exactly two values for the spin of the electron. These values will produce equal magnetic fields that are opposite in direction.

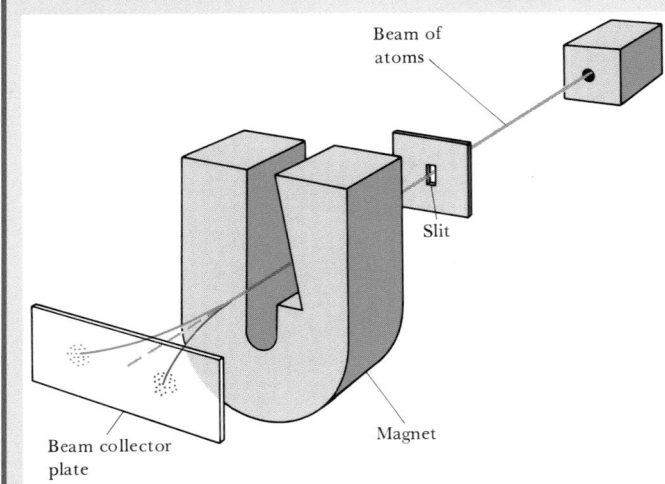

FIGURE 6.24 Diagrammatic illustration of the Stern-Gerlach experiment. A beam of atoms is allowed to pass through an inhomogeneous magnetic field. Atoms in which the electron-spin quantum number (m_s) of the unpaired electron is $+\frac{1}{2}$ are deflected in one direction, whereas those in which m_s is $-\frac{1}{2}$ are deflected in the other.

Beam of atoms

Slit

Beam collector plate

Magnet

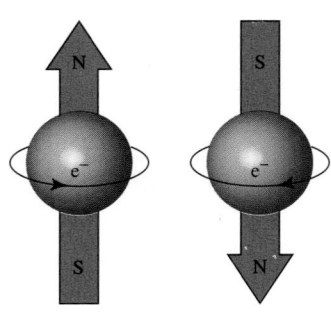

FIGURE 6.25 The electron behaves as if it were spinning about an axis through its center. The two directions of spin correspond to the two possible values for the spin quantum number, m_s.

for the electron, in addition to n, l, and m_l that we have already discussed. This new quantum number, the **electron spin quantum number,** is denoted m_s (the subscript s stands for *spin*). Only two possible values are allowed for m_s, $+\frac{1}{2}$ or $-\frac{1}{2}$, which we interpret as indicating the two opposite directions in which the electron can spin. A spinning charge produces a magnetic field. The two opposite directions of spin produce oppositely directed magnetic fields, as shown in Figure 6.25. These two opposite magnetic fields lead to the splitting of spectral lines into closely spaced pairs.

Electron spin is crucial for understanding the electronic structures of atoms. In 1925, the Austrian-born physicist Wolfgang Pauli (1900–1958) discovered the principle that governs the arrangements of electrons in many-electron atoms. The **Pauli exclusion principle** states that *no two electrons in an atom can have the same set of four quantum numbers n, l, m_l, and m_s.* For a given orbital (1s, $2p_z$, and so forth), the values of n, l, and m_l are fixed. Thus, if we want to put more than one electron in an orbital *and* satisfy the Pauli exclusion principle, our only choice is to assign different m_s values to the electrons. Because there are only two such values, we conclude that *an orbital can hold a maximum of two electrons, and they must have opposite spins.* This restriction allows us to index the electrons in an atom, giving their quantum numbers and thereby defining the region in space where each electron is most likely to be found. It also provides the key to one of the great problems in chemistry — understanding the structure of the periodic table of the elements. We shall discuss these issues in the next two sections.

Teaching Note: Wolfgang Pauli received the 1945 Nobel prize in physics for the exclusion principle.

6.8 Electron Configurations

Point of Emphasis: No two electrons in an atom can have the same set of four quantum numbers, n, l, m_l, m_s.

We are now in a position to consider the arrangements of electrons in atoms. The way in which the electrons are distributed among the various orbitals is called the **electron configuration.** The most stable, or ground, electron configuration of an atom is that in which the electrons are in the lowest possible energy states. If there were no restrictions on the possible values for the quantum numbers of the electrons, all the electrons would crowd into the $1s$ orbital because it is the lowest in energy (Figure 6.22). The Pauli exclusion principle, however, tells us that there can be at most two electrons in any single orbital. Thus, the orbitals are filled in order of increasing energy, with no more than two electrons per orbital. For example, consider the lithium atom, which has three electrons. (Recall that the number of electrons in a neutral atom is equal to its atomic number, Z.) The $1s$ orbital can accommodate two of the electrons. The third one goes into the next lowest energy orbital, the $2s$.

We can summarize any electron configuration by writing the symbol for the occupied subshell and adding a superscript to indicate the number of electrons in that subshell. For example, for lithium we write $1s^2 2s^1$ (read "$1s$ two, $2s$ one"). We can also show the arrangement of the electrons in the following way:

Li   [↑↓] [↑]

$1s$ $2s$

In this kind of representation, which we shall call an **orbital diagram,** each orbital is represented by a box and each electron by a half-arrow. A half-arrow pointing upward (↑) represents an electron with a positive spin quantum number ($m_s = +\frac{1}{2}$), and a downward half-arrow (↓) represents an electron with a negative spin quantum number ($m_s = -\frac{1}{2}$). This pictorial representation of electron spin is quite convenient. In fact, chemists and physicists often refer to electrons as "spin-up" and "spin-down" rather than specifying the value for m_s.

Electrons having opposite spins are said to be *paired* when they are in the same orbital. An *unpaired electron* is not accompanied by a partner of opposite spin. In the lithium atom, the two electrons in the $1s$ orbital are paired, and the electron in the $2s$ orbital is unpaired.

Writing Electron Configurations

Learning Goal 16: Write the electron configuration for any element.

It is informative to consider how the electron configurations of the elements change as we move from element to element across the periodic table. Hydrogen has one electron, which occupies the $1s$ orbital in its ground state:

H   [↑] : $1s^1$

$1s$

CHEMISTRY AT WORK

Nuclear Spin and Magnetic Resonance Imaging

A major challenge facing medical diagnosis is to see inside the human body from the outside. Until recently, this was accomplished primarily by using X-rays to yield images of human bones, muscles, and organs. However, there are several drawbacks to using X-rays for medical imaging. First, X-rays do not give well-resolved images of overlapping physiological structures. Moreover, because damaged or diseased tissue often yields the same image as healthy tissue, X-rays frequently fail to detect illness or injuries. Finally, X-rays are high-energy radiation that can cause physiological harm, even in low doses.

In the 1980s, a new technique called *magnetic resonance imaging* (MRI) moved to the forefront of medical imaging technology. The foundation of MRI is a phenomenon called nuclear magnetic resonance (NMR), which was discovered in the mid-1940s. Today, NMR has become one of the most important spectroscopic methods used in chemistry. It is based on the observation that, like electrons, the nuclei of many elements possess an intrinsic spin. Like electron spin, nuclear spin is quantized. For example, the nucleus of ^{1}H (a proton) has two possible nuclear-spin quantum numbers, $+\frac{1}{2}$ and $-\frac{1}{2}$. The hydrogen nucleus is the most common one studied by NMR.

A spinning hydrogen nucleus acts like a tiny magnet. In the absence of external effects, the two spin states have the same energy. However, when the nuclei are placed in an external magnetic field, they can align either parallel or opposed (antiparallel) to the field, depending

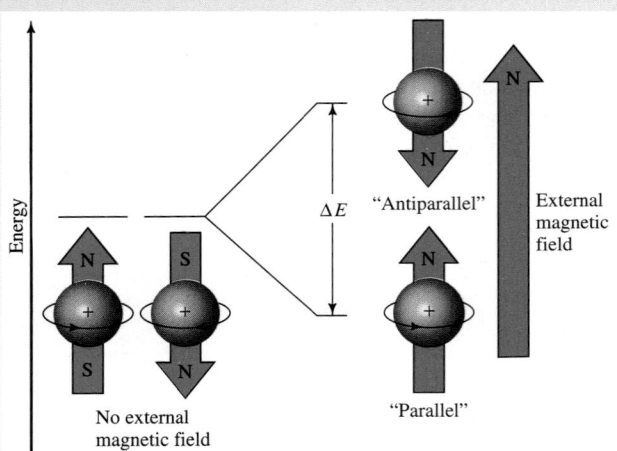

FIGURE 6.26 Like electron spin, nuclear spin generates a small magnetic field and has two allowed values. In the absence of an external magnetic field (left), the two spin states have the same energy. If an external magnetic field is applied (right), the parallel alignment of the nuclear magnetic field is lower in energy than the antiparallel alignment. The energy difference, ΔE, is in the radio-frequency portion of the electromagnetic spectrum.

The choice of a spin-up electron here is arbitrary; we could equally well show the ground state with one spin-down electron in the $1s$ orbital.

The next element, helium, has two electrons. Because two electrons with opposite spins can occupy an orbital, both of helium's electrons are in the $1s$ orbital:

$$\text{He} \quad \boxed{\uparrow\downarrow} : \quad 1s^2$$
$$\qquad\quad {}_{1s}$$

The two electrons present in helium complete the filling of the first shell. This arrangement represents a very stable configuration, as is evidenced by the chemical inertness of helium.

on their spin. The parallel alignment is lower in energy than the antiparallel one (Figure 6.26) by a certain amount, ΔE. If the nuclei are irradiated with photons with energy equal to ΔE, the spin of the nuclei can be "flipped," that is, excited from the parallel to the antiparallel alignment. Detection of the flipping of nuclei between the two spin states leads to an NMR spectrum. The radiation used in an NMR experiment is in the radio-frequency range, typically 100 to 500 MHz.

Because hydrogen is a major constituent of aqueous body fluids and fatty tissue, the hydrogen nucleus is the most convenient one for study by MRI. In MRI, a person's body is placed in a strong magnetic field. By irradiating the body with pulses of radio-frequency radiation and using sophisticated detection techniques,

tissue can be imaged at specific depths within the body, giving pictures with spectacular detail (Fig. 6.27). The ability to sample at different depths allows medical technicians to construct a three-dimensional picture of the body.

MRI has none of the disadvantages of X-rays. Diseased tissue appears very different from healthy tissue, resolving overlapping structures at different depths in the body is much easier, and the radio-frequency radiation is not harmful to humans in the doses used. The major drawback of MRI is expense: The current cost of a new MRI instrument for clinical applications is over $1 million.

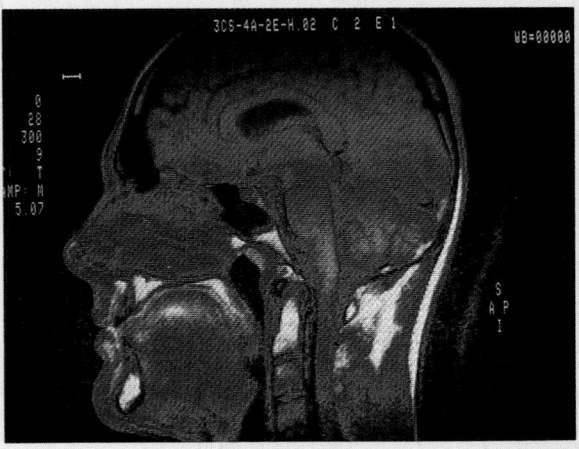

FIGURE 6.27 An MRI image of a human head, showing the structures of a normal brain, airways, and facial tissues. (Philippe Plailly/Science Photo Library/Photo Researchers)

The electron configurations of lithium and several elements that follow it in the periodic table are shown in Table 6.3. For the third electron of lithium, the change in principal quantum number represents a large jump in energy and a corresponding jump in the average distance of the electron from the nucleus. It represents the start of a new shell of electrons. As you can see by examining the periodic table, lithium represents the start of a new row of the periodic table. It is the first member of the alkali metals family (group 1A).

The element that follows lithium is beryllium; its electron configuration is $1s^2 2s^2$ (Table 6.3). Boron, atomic number 5, has the electron configuration $1s^2 2s^2 2p^1$. The fifth electron must be placed in a $2p$ orbital because the $2s$ orbital is filled. Because all the three $2p$ orbitals are of equal energy, it doesn't matter which $2p$ orbital is occupied.

TABLE 6.3 △ Electron Configurations of Several Lighter Elements

Element	Total electrons	Orbital diagram					Electron configuration
		$1s$	$2s$	$2p$		$3s$	
Li	3	↑↓	↑				$1s^2 2s^1$
Be	4	↑↓	↑↓				$1s^2 2s^2$
B	5	↑↓	↑↓	↑			$1s^2 2s^2 2p^1$
C	6	↑↓	↑↓	↑ ↑			$1s^2 2s^2 2p^2$
N	7	↑↓	↑↓	↑ ↑ ↑			$1s^2 2s^2 2p^3$
Ne	10	↑↓	↑↓	↑↓ ↑↓ ↑↓			$1s^2 2s^2 2p^6$
Na	11	↑↓	↑↓	↑↓ ↑↓ ↑↓		↑	$1s^2 2s^2 2p^6 3s^1$

Learning Goal 17: State the Pauli exclusion principle and Hund's rule, and illustrate how they are used in writing the electronic structures of the elements.

Teaching Note: If the highest-energy occupied orbitals are degenerate, then the number of unpaired electrons with the same spin should be maximized.

With the next element, carbon, we come to a new situation. We know that the sixth electron must go into a $2p$ orbital. However, does this new electron go into the $2p$ orbital that already has one electron, or into one of the others? This question is answered by **Hund's rule,** which states that *for degenerate orbitals, the lowest energy is attained when the number of electrons with the same spin is maximized.* This means that electrons will occupy orbitals singly to the maximum extent possible, with their spins parallel. Thus, for a carbon atom to achieve its lowest energy, the two $2p$ electrons will have the same spin. In order for this to happen, the electrons must be in different $2p$ orbitals, as shown in Table 6.3. We see that a carbon atom in its ground state has two unpaired electrons. Similarly, for nitrogen in its ground state, Hund's rule requires that the three $2p$ electrons singly occupy each of the three $2p$ orbitals. This is the only way that all three electrons can have the same spin. For oxygen and fluorine, we need to place four and five electrons, respectively, in the $2p$ orbitals. In order to achieve this, we must pair up electrons in the $2p$ orbitals, as we will see in Sample Exercise 6.7.

Hund's rule is based in part on the fact that electrons repel one another. By occupying different orbitals, the electrons remain as far as possible from one another, thus minimizing electron-electron repulsions.

The filling of the $2p$ subshell is complete at neon (Table 6.3), which has a stable configuration with eight electrons (an *octet*) in the outermost shell. We next encounter sodium, atomic number 11, marking the beginning of a new row of the periodic table. Sodium has a single $3s$ electron beyond the stable configuration of neon. We can abbreviate the electron configuration of sodium as follows:

$$\text{Na} \quad [\text{Ne}]3s^1$$

Point of Emphasis: Most important chemical phenomena and reactions make use of only the outermost (valence) electrons.

The symbol [Ne] represents the electron configuration of the 10 electrons of neon, $1s^2 2s^2 2p^6$. Writing the electron configuration in this manner helps us focus attention on the outermost electrons of the atom. The outer electrons are the ones largely responsible for the chemical behavior of an element. For example, we can write the electron configuration of lithium as follows:

$$\text{Li} \qquad [\text{He}]2s^1$$

By comparing this with the electron configuration for sodium, it is easy to appreciate why lithium and sodium are so similar chemically: They have the same type of outer-shell electron configuration. All the members of the alkali metal family (group 1A) have a single s electron beyond a noble-gas configuration. The outer-shell electrons are often referred to as **valence electrons.** The electrons in the inner shells are called the **core electrons.**

Point of Emphasis: The observed stability of a full octet of electrons in the s and p orbitals is the basis of important bonding descriptions (Chapter 8).

SAMPLE EXERCISE 6.7

Draw the orbital diagram representation for the electron configuration of oxygen, atomic number 8.

SOLUTION The ordering of orbitals is shown in Figure 6.22. Two electrons each go into the $1s$ and $2s$ orbitals. This leaves four electrons for the three $2p$ orbitals. Following Hund's rule, we put one electron into each $2p$ orbital until all three have one each. The fourth electron must then be paired up with one of the three electrons already in a $2p$ orbital, so that the correct representation is

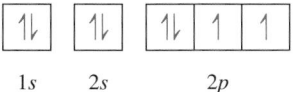

$$1s \qquad 2s \qquad 2p$$

The corresponding electron configuration is written $1s^2 2s^2 2p^4$ or $[\text{He}]2s^2 2p^4$. The $1s^2$ or $[\text{He}]$ electrons are the inner-shell or core electrons of the oxygen atom. The $2s^2 2p^4$ electrons are the outer-shell or valence electrons.

PRACTICE EXERCISE

Write the electron configuration of phosphorus, element 15.
Answer: $1s^2 2s^2 2p^6 3s^2 3p^3 = [\text{Ne}]3s^2 3p^3$

The noble-gas element argon marks the end of the row started by sodium. The configuration for argon is $1s^2 2s^2 2p^6 3s^2 3p^6$. The element following argon in the periodic table is potassium (K), atomic number 19. In all its chemical properties, potassium is clearly a member of the alkali metal family. The experimental facts about the properties of potassium leave no doubt that the outermost electron of this element occupies an s orbital. But this means that the highest-energy electron has *not* gone into a $3d$ orbital, which we might naively have expected it to do. In this case the ordering of energy levels is such that the $4s$ orbital is lower in energy than the $3d$.

Following complete filling of the $4s$ orbital (this occurs in the calcium atom), the next set of equivalent orbitals to be filled is the $3d$. (You will find it helpful as we go along to refer often to the periodic table on the front inside cover.) Beginning with scandium and extending through zinc, electrons are added to the five $3d$ orbitals until they are completely filled. Thus, the fourth row of the periodic table is 10 elements wider than the two previous rows. These 10 elements are known as **transition elements** or **transition metals.** Note the position of these elements in the periodic table.

In accordance with Hund's rule, electrons are added to the $3d$ orbitals singly until all five orbitals have one electron each. Additional electrons are then placed in the 3*d* orbitals with spin pairing until the shell is completely filled. The orbital diagram representations and electron configurations of two transition elements are as follows:

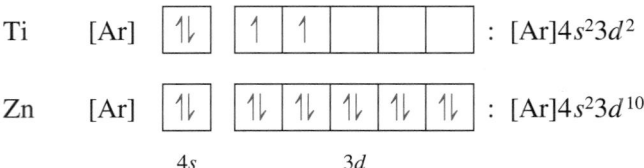

Upon completion of the 3*d* transition series, the 4*p* orbitals begin to be occupied, until the completed octet of outer electrons $(4s^2 4p^6)$ is reached with krypton (Kr), atomic number 36. Krypton is another of the noble gases. Rubidium (Rb) marks the beginning of the fifth row of the periodic table. This row is in every respect like the preceding one, except that the value for *n* is 1 greater. The sixth row of the table begins similarly to the preceding one: one electron in the 6*s* orbital of cesium (Cs) and two electrons in the 6*s* orbital of barium (Ba). The next element, lanthanum (La), represents the start of the third series of transition elements. But with cerium (Ce), element 58, a new set of orbitals, the 4*f*, enter the picture. The energies of the 5*d* and 4*f* orbitals are very close. For lanthanum itself, the 5*d* orbital energy is just a little lower than the 4*f*. However, for the elements immediately following lanthanum, the 4*f* orbital energies are a little lower, so that the 4*f* orbitals fill before the 5*d* orbitals.

There are seven equivalent 4*f* orbitals, corresponding to the seven allowed values of m_l, ranging from 3 to -3. Thus it requires 14 electrons to fill the 4*f* orbitals completely. The 14 elements corresponding to the filling of the 4*f* orbitals are elements 58 to 71, known as the **rare-earth,** or **lanthanide, elements.** In order not to make the periodic table unduly wide, the rare-earth elements are set together below the other elements. The properties of the rare-earth elements are all quite similar, and they occur together in nature. For many years it was virtually impossible to separate them from one another.

After the rare-earth series, the third transition element series is completed, followed by the filling of the 6*p* orbitals. This brings us to radon (Rn), heaviest of the noble-gas elements. The final row of the periodic table begins as the one before it. The **actinide elements,** of which uranium (U, element 92) and plutonium (Pu, element 94) are the best known, are built up by completion of the 5*f* orbitals. Most of the actinides are not found in nature.

6.9 Electron Configurations and the Periodic Table

Our rather brief survey of electron configurations of the elements has taken us through the periodic table. We have seen that the electron configurations of elements are related to their location in the periodic table. The periodic table is structured so that elements with the same type of outer-shell electron configuration are arranged in columns. For example, for groups 2A and 3A we have

Group 2A		Group 3A	
Be	[He]$2s^2$	B	[He]$2s^22p^1$
Mg	[Ne]$3s^2$	Al	[Ne]$3s^23p^1$
Ca	[Ar]$4s^2$	Ga	[Ar]$3d^{10}4s^24p^1$
Sr	[Kr]$5s^2$	In	[Kr]$4d^{10}5s^25p^1$
Ba	[Xe]$6s^2$	Tl	[Xe]$4f^{14}5d^{10}6s^26p^1$
Ra	[Rn]$7s^2$		

If you understand how the periodic table is organized, it is not necessary to memorize the order in which orbitals fill. You can write the electron configuration of an element based on its location in the periodic table. The pattern is summarized in Figure 6.28. Notice that the elements can be grouped in terms of the *type* of orbital into which the electrons are placed. On the left are *two* columns of elements. These elements, known as the alkali metals and alkaline earth metals, are those in which the outer-shell *s* orbitals are being filled. On the right is a block of *six* columns. These are the elements in which the outermost *p* orbitals are being filled. The *s* block and the *p* block of the periodic table contain the **representative** or **main-group elements.** In the middle of the table is a block of *ten* columns that contains the transition metals. These are the elements in which the *d* orbitals are being filled. Below the main portion of the table are two rows that contain *fourteen* columns. These elements are often referred to as the **f-block metals** because they are the ones in which the *f* orbitals are being filled.

Learning Goal 18: Describe what we mean by the *s*, *p*, *d*, and *f* blocks of elements.

FIGURE 6.28 Block diagram of the periodic table showing the groupings of the elements according to the type of orbital being filled with electrons.

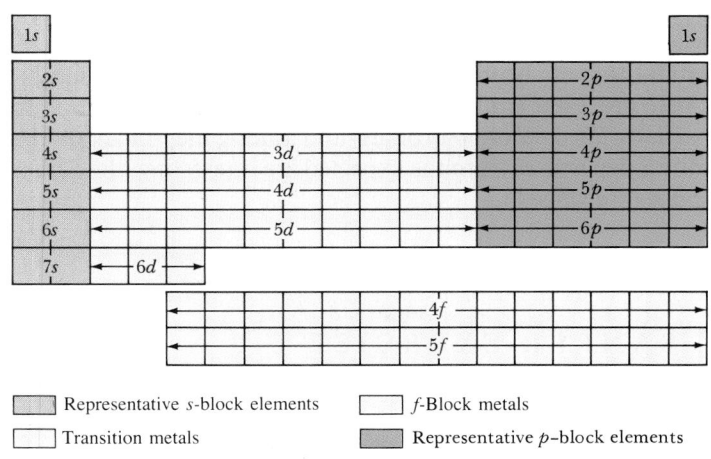

Figure 6.28

Recall that the numbers 2, 6, 10, and 14 are precisely the number of electrons that can fill the s, p, d, and f subshells, respectively. Recall also that the 1s subshell is the first s subshell, the 2p is the first p subshell, the 3d is the first d subshell, and the 4f is the first f subshell.

Learning Goal 19: Write the electron configuration and valence electron configuration for any element once you know its place in the periodic table.

SAMPLE EXERCISE 6.8

What is the characteristic outer-shell electron configuration of the group 7A elements, the halogens?

SOLUTION   The first member of the halogen family is fluorine, atomic number 9. The abbreviated form of the electron configuration for fluorine is

$$\text{F} \qquad [\text{He}]2s^2 2p^5$$

Similarly, the abbreviated form of the electron configuration for chlorine, the second halogen, is

$$\text{Cl} \qquad [\text{Ne}]3s^2 3p^5$$

From these two examples we see that the characteristic outer-shell electron configuration of a halogen is $ns^2 np^5$, where n ranges from 2 in the case of fluorine to 6 in the case of astatine.

PRACTICE EXERCISE

What family of elements is characterized by having an ns^2 outer-electron configuration?   **Answer:** the alkaline earth metals, group 2A

In some cases, electrons shift from one orbital to another in ways that appear to violate the rules we have just discussed. For example, the ground electron configuration of chromium is $[\text{Ar}]4s^1 3d^5$ rather than $[\text{Ar}]4s^2 3d^4$, as we might have expected. Similarly, the configuration of copper is $[\text{Ar}]4s^1 3d^{10}$ instead of the expected $[\text{Ar}]4s^2 3d^9$. This anomalous behavior is largely a consequence of the closeness of the 3d and 4s orbital energies. It frequently occurs when there are enough electrons to lead to precisely half-filled sets of degenerate orbitals (as in chromium) or to a completely filled d subshell (as in copper). There are a few similar cases among the heavier transition metals (those with partially filled 4d or 5d orbitals) and among the f-block metals. Although these minor departures from the expected are interesting, they are not of great chemical significance.

Judith A. Strong, "The Periodic Table and Electron Configurations," *J. Chem. Educ.* **1986**, *63*, 834.

SAMPLE EXERCISE 6.9

Write the electron configuration for the element bismuth, atomic number 83.

SOLUTION   We can do this by simply moving across the periodic table one row at a time and writing the occupancies of the orbital corresponding to each row (refer to Figure 6.28).

First row	$1s^2$
Second row	$2s^22p^6$
Third row	$3s^23p^6$
Fourth row	$4s^23d^{10}4p^6$
Fifth row	$5s^24d^{10}5p^6$
Sixth row	$6s^24f^{14}5d^{10}6p^3$
Total:	$1s^22s^22p^63s^23p^63d^{10}4s^24p^64d^{10}4f^{14}5s^25p^65d^{10}6s^26p^3$

Note that 3 is the lowest possible value that n may have for a d orbital, and that 4 is the lowest possible value of n for an f orbital.

The total of the superscripted numbers should equal the atomic number of bismuth, 83. The electrons may be listed, as shown above, in the order of increasing major quantum number. However, it is also possible to list them in the sequence read from the periodic table: $1s^22s^22p^63s^23p^64s^23d^{10}4p^65s^24d^{10}5p^66s^24f^{14}5d^{10}6p^3$.

It is a simple matter to write the abbreviated electron configuration of an element using the periodic table. First locate the element of interest (in this case element 83) and then move backward until the first noble gas is encountered (in this case Xe, element 54). Thus the inner core is [Xe]. The outer electrons are then read from the periodic table as before. Moving from Xe to Cs, element 55, we find ourselves in the sixth row. Moving across this row to Bi gives us the outer electrons. The complete electron configuration is thus $[Xe]6s^24f^{14}5d^{10}6p^3$ or $[Xe]4f^{14}5d^{10}6s^26p^3$.

PRACTICE EXERCISE

Use the periodic table to write the electron configurations for the following atoms by giving the appropriate noble-gas inner core plus the electrons beyond it: **(a)** Co (atomic number 27); **(b)** Te (atomic number 52).   *Answers:* **(a)** $[Ar]4s^23d^7$ or $[Ar]3d^74s^2$; **(b)** $[Kr]5s^24d^{10}5p^4$ or $[Kr]4d^{10}5s^25p^4$

SAMPLE EXERCISE 6.10

Draw the orbital diagram representation for zirconium, atomic number 40; show only those electrons beyond the krypton inner core.

SOLUTION   Zirconium has four electrons beyond the nearest noble gas, krypton, atomic number 36. Examining the periodic table, we see that zirconium is a transition element from the fifth row of the table. This means that its outermost electrons are in $5s$ and $4d$ orbitals. Two electrons occupy the $5s$ orbital; two must be placed in the five $4d$ orbitals. As indicated by Hund's rule, the $4d$ electrons occupy separate orbitals. Thus, we have

Learning Goal 20:   Write the orbital diagram representations for electron configurations of atoms.

PRACTICE EXERCISE

Using orbital diagrams for the outer electrons, determine the number of unpaired electrons in **(a)** Ni (atomic number 28); **(b)** Br (atomic number 35)   *Answers:* **(a)** 2; **(b)** 1

Table 6.4 gives a complete list of the ground electron configurations of the elements. You should use this table to check your answers as you practice writing electron configurations. We have written these configurations as they would be read off the periodic table. As we have seen in Sample Exercise 6.9, they are sometimes written with orbitals of a given principal quantum number grouped together.

TABLE 6.4 △ The Electron Configurations of the Elements

Atomic number	Symbol	Electron configuration	Atomic number	Symbol	Electron configuration	Atomic number	Symbol	Electron configuration
1	H	$1s^1$	37	Rb	$[Kr]5s^1$	73	Ta	$[Xe]6s^24f^{14}5d^3$
2	He	$1s^2$	38	Sr	$[Kr]5s^2$	74	W	$[Xe]6s^24f^{14}5d^4$
3	Li	$[He]2s^1$	39	Y	$[Kr]5s^24d^1$	75	Re	$[Xe]6s^24f^{14}5d^5$
4	Be	$[He]2s^2$	40	Zr	$[Kr]5s^24d^2$	76	Os	$[Xe]6s^24f^{14}5d^6$
5	B	$[He]2s^22p^1$	41	Nb	$[Kr]5s^14d^4$	77	Ir	$[Xe]6s^24f^{14}5d^7$
6	C	$[He]2s^22p^2$	42	Mo	$[Kr]5s^14d^5$	78	Pt	$[Xe]6s^14f^{14}5d^9$
7	N	$[He]2s^22p^3$	43	Tc	$[Kr]5s^24d^5$	79	Au	$[Xe]6s^14f^{14}5d^{10}$
8	O	$[He]2s^22p^4$	44	Ru	$[Kr]5s^14d^7$	80	Hg	$[Xe]6s^24f^{14}5d^{10}$
9	F	$[He]2s^22p^5$	45	Rh	$[Kr]5s^14d^8$	81	Tl	$[Xe]6s^24f^{14}5d^{10}6p^1$
10	Ne	$[He]2s^22p^6$	46	Pd	$[Kr]4d^{10}$	82	Pb	$[Xe]6s^24f^{14}5d^{10}6p^2$
11	Na	$[Ne]3s^1$	47	Ag	$[Kr]5s^14d^{10}$	83	Bi	$[Xe]6s^24f^{14}5d^{10}6p^3$
12	Mg	$[Ne]3s^2$	48	Cd	$[Kr]5s^24d^{10}$	84	Po	$[Xe]6s^24f^{14}5d^{10}6p^4$
13	Al	$[Ne]3s^23p^1$	49	In	$[Kr]5s^24d^{10}5p^1$	85	At	$[Xe]6s^24f^{14}5d^{10}6p^5$
14	Si	$[Ne]3s^23p^2$	50	Sn	$[Kr]5s^24d^{10}5p^2$	86	Rn	$[Xe]6s^24f^{14}5d^{10}6p^6$
15	P	$[Ne]3s^23p^3$	51	Sb	$[Kr]5s^24d^{10}5p^3$	87	Fr	$[Rn]7s^1$
16	S	$[Ne]3s^23p^4$	52	Te	$[Kr]5s^24d^{10}5p^4$	88	Ra	$[Rn]7s^2$
17	Cl	$[Ne]3s^23p^5$	53	I	$[Kr]5s^24d^{10}5p^5$	89	Ac	$[Rn]7s^26d^1$
18	Ar	$[Ne]3s^23p^6$	54	Xe	$[Kr]5s^24d^{10}5p^6$	90	Th	$[Rn]7s^26d^2$
19	K	$[Ar]4s^1$	55	Cs	$[Xe]6s^1$	91	Pa	$[Rn]7s^25f^26d^1$
20	Ca	$[Ar]4s^2$	56	Ba	$[Xe]6s^2$	92	U	$[Rn]7s^25f^36d^1$
21	Sc	$[Ar]4s^23d^1$	57	La	$[Xe]6s^25d^1$	93	Np	$[Rn]7s^25f^46d^1$
22	Ti	$[Ar]4s^23d^2$	58	Ce	$[Xe]6s^24f^15d^1$	94	Pu	$[Rn]7s^25f^6$
23	V	$[Ar]4s^23d^3$	59	Pr	$[Xe]6s^24f^3$	95	Am	$[Rn]7s^25f^7$
24	Cr	$[Ar]4s^13d^5$	60	Nd	$[Xe]6s^24f^4$	96	Cm	$[Rn]7s^25f^76d^1$
25	Mn	$[Ar]4s^23d^5$	61	Pm	$[Xe]6s^24f^5$	97	Bk	$[Rn]7s^25f^9$
26	Fe	$[Ar]4s^23d^6$	62	Sm	$[Xe]6s^24f^6$	98	Cf	$[Rn]7s^25f^{10}$
27	Co	$[Ar]4s^23d^7$	63	Eu	$[Xe]6s^24f^7$	99	Es	$[Rn]7s^25f^{11}$
28	Ni	$[Ar]4s^23d^8$	64	Gd	$[Xe]6s^24f^75d^1$	100	Fm	$[Rn]7s^25f^{12}$
29	Cu	$[Ar]4s^13d^{10}$	65	Tb	$[Xe]6s^24f^9$	101	Md	$[Rn]7s^25f^{13}$
30	Zn	$[Ar]4s^23d^{10}$	66	Dy	$[Xe]6s^24f^{10}$	102	No	$[Rn]7s^25f^{14}$
31	Ga	$[Ar]4s^23d^{10}4p^1$	67	Ho	$[Xe]6s^24f^{11}$	103	Lr	$[Rn]7s^25f^{14}6d^1$
32	Ge	$[Ar]4s^23d^{10}4p^2$	68	Er	$[Xe]6s^24f^{12}$	104	Rf	$[Rn]7s^25f^{14}6d^2$
33	As	$[Ar]4s^23d^{10}4p^3$	69	Tm	$[Xe]6s^24f^{13}$	105	Ha	$[Rn]7s^25f^{14}6d^3$
34	Se	$[Ar]4s^23d^{10}4p^4$	70	Yb	$[Xe]6s^24f^{14}$	106	[106]	$[Rn]7s^25f^{14}6d^4$
35	Br	$[Ar]4s^23d^{10}4p^5$	71	Lu	$[Xe]6s^24f^{14}5d^1$	107	[107]	$[Rn]7s^25f^{14}6d^5$
36	Kr	$[Ar]4s^23d^{10}4p^6$	72	Hf	$[Xe]6s^24f^{14}5d^2$	108	[108]	$[Rn]7s^25f^{14}6d^6$
						109	[109]	$[Rn]7s^25f^{14}6d^7$

For Review

Summary

Radiant energy moves through a vacuum at the "speed of light," $c = 3.00 \times 10^8$ m/s. It has wavelike characteristics that allow it to be described in terms of wavelength, λ, and frequency, v, which are interrelated: $c = \lambda v$. The dispersion of radiation into its component wavelengths produces a spectrum. If all wavelengths are present, the spectrum is said to be continuous; if only certain wavelengths are present, it is called a line spectrum.

The quantum theory describes the minimum amount of radiant energy that an object can gain or lose, $E = hv$; this smallest quantity is called a quantum. A quantum of radiant energy is called a photon. The quantum theory was used to explain the photoelectric effect and the line spectrum of the hydrogen atom. The absorptions or emissions of light by an atom, which produce its line spectrum, correspond to energy changes of electrons within the atom; the energy of the electron in an atom is quantized.

Electrons exhibit wave properties and can be described by a wavelength, $\lambda = h/mv$. Discovery of the wave properties of the electron led to the uncertainty principle, which indicates that the position and momentum of an electron can be determined simultaneously with only limited accuracy.

In the quantum-mechanical model of the hydrogen atom we speak of the probability of the electron being found at a particular point in space. Although the positions of the electrons are defined in this averaged sense, their energies are precisely known. Each allowed state of an electron in the atom corresponds to a particular set of values for three quantum numbers. Each such allowed energy state is termed an orbital. An orbital is described by a combination of an integer and letters, corresponding to the three values for the quantum numbers. The principal quantum number, n, is indicated by the integers 1, 2, 3, ... This quantum number relates most directly to the size and energy of an orbital. The azimuthal quantum number, l, is indicated by the letters, s, p, d, f, and so on, corresponding to values of l of 0, 1, 2, 3, ... The l quantum number defines the shape of the orbital. The magnetic quantum number, m_l, describes the orientation of the orbital in space. For example, the three $3p$ orbitals are designated $3p_x$, $3p_y$, and $3p_z$, the subscript letters indicating the axis along which the orbital is oriented.

Restrictions on the values of the three quantum numbers give rise to the following allowed subshells:

$1s$

$2s$, $2p$

$3s$, $3p$, $3d$

$4s$, $4p$, $4d$, $4f$

.
.
.

There is one orbital in an s subshell, three in a p subshell, five in a d subshell, and seven in an f subshell. The contour representations are the most generally useful way to visualize the spatial characteristics of the orbitals.

In many-electron atoms, we saw that the electron configurations can be written by placing electrons into orbitals in the following order:

$1s$, $2s$, $2p$, $3s$, $3p$, $4s$, $3d$, $4p$, . . .

Subshells with a given principal quantum number, such as the $3s$, $3p$, and $3d$ subshells, do not have the same energies. This fact can be understood in terms of the effective nuclear charge and the average distance of an electron from the nucleus in each of these subshells.

The Pauli exclusion principle places a limit of two on the number of electrons that can occupy any one atomic orbital. These two electrons differ in their electron-spin quantum number, m_s. As the electrons populate orbitals of equal energy, they do not pair up until each orbital contains one electron; this observation is called Hund's rule. Using the relative energies of the orbitals, the Pauli exclusion principle, and Hund's rule, it is possible to write the electron configuration of any atom. When we do so, we see that the elements in any given family in the periodic table have the same type of electron arrangements in their outermost shells. For example, the electron configurations of the halogens fluorine and chlorine are [He]$2s^22p^5$ and [Ne]$3s^23p^5$, respectively. This periodicity in electron configurations, summarized in Figure 6.28, allows us to write the electron configuration of an element from its position in the periodic table.

Key Terms

electronic structure
electromagnetic radiation (Sec. 6.1)
wavelength (Sec. 6.1)
frequency (Sec. 6.1)
quantum (Sec. 6.2)
photon (Sec. 6.2)
spectrum (Sec. 6.3)

continuous spectrum (Sec. 6.3)
line spectrum (Sec. 6.3)
ground state (Sec. 6.3)
excited state (Sec. 6.3)
momentum (Sec. 6.4)
matter waves (Sec. 6.4)
uncertainty principle (Sec. 6.4)

wave functions (Sec. 6.5)
probability density (Sec. 6.5)
electron density (Sec. 6.5)
orbitals (Sec. 6.5)
electron shell (Sec. 6.5)
subshell (Sec. 6.5)
nodal surfaces (nodes) (Sec. 6.6)
effective nuclear charge (Sec. 6.7)
screening effect (Sec. 6.7)
degenerate (Sec. 6.7)
electron spin (Sec. 6.7)
electron spin quantum number (Sec. 6.7)

Pauli exclusion principle (Sec. 6.7)
electron configuration (Sec. 6.8)
orbital diagram (Sec. 6.8)
Hund's rule (Sec. 6.8)
valence electrons (Sec. 6.8)
core electrons (Sec. 6.8)
transition elements (Sec. 6.8)
transition metals (Sec. 6.8)
rare-earth (lanthanide) elements (Sec. 6.8)
actinide elements (Sec. 6.8)
representative (main-group) elements (Sec. 6.9)
f-block metals (Sec. 6.9)

Exercises

Radiant Energy

6.1. What are the basic SI units for (a) the wavelength of light, (b) the frequency of light, and (c) the speed of light?

6.2. What is the relationship between the wavelength and the frequency of a light wave? What range of wavelength (in nanometers) encompasses the visible portion of the electromagnetic spectrum?

6.3. List the following types of electromagnetic radiation in order of increasing wavelength: (a) the gamma rays produced by a radioactive nuclide used in medical imaging; (b) radiation from an FM radio station at 93.1 MHz on the dial; (c) a radio signal from an AM radio station at 680 kHz on the dial; (d) the yellow light from sodium-vapor street lights; (e) the red light of a light-emitting diode, such as in a calculator display.

6.4. List the following types of electromagnetic radiation in order of increasing wavelength: (a) the infrared radiation emitted by a hot electric stove burner; (b) the X-rays used in medical diagnosis; (c) the ultraviolet (UV) light from a sunlamp; (d) radiation from a microwave oven; (e) the green light from a traffic signal.

6.5. (a) What is the wavelength of radiation whose frequency is 6.24×10^{14} s^{-1}? (b) What is the frequency of radiation whose wavelength is 3.55 μm? (c) Would you be able to see either of the radiations specified in parts (a) and (b)? (d) What distance does light travel in 2.50 min?

6.6. (a) What is the wavelength of radiation whose frequency is 8.73×10^8 s^{-1}? (b) What is the frequency of radiation whose wavelength is 650 nm? (c) Would you be able to detect either of the radiations specified in parts (a) and (b) with an infrared detector? (d) What distance does light travel in 4.2 ns?

6.7. A neon light emits radiation of 616-nm wavelength. What is the frequency of this radiation? Using Figure 6.3, predict the color associated with this wavelength.

6.8. Excited barium atoms emit visible light whose frequency is 6.59×10^{14} s^{-1}. What is the wavelength of this light? Use Figure 6.3 to predict its color.

Quantum Effects and Photons

6.9. What do we mean when we say energy is quantized?

6.10. Why don't we notice the quantization of energy in everyday activities?

6.11. (a) Calculate the smallest increment of energy (a quantum) that can be emitted or absorbed at a wavelength of 405 nm. (b) Calculate the energy of a photon of frequency 6.3×10^{13} s^{-1}. (c) What wavelength of radiation has photons of energy 2.83×10^{-19} J?

6.12. (a) Calculate the smallest increment of energy (a quantum) that can be emitted or absorbed at a wavelength of 803 nm. (b) Calculate the energy of a photon of frequency 7.9×10^{14} s^{-1}. (c) What frequency of radiation has photons of energy 1.88×10^{-18} J?

6.13. Under appropriate conditions, copper emits X-rays that have a characteristic wavelength of 1.54 Å. Calculate and compare the energy of photons of these X-rays to those emitted by a microwave source that radiates at a frequency of 5.87×10^{10} s^{-1}.

6.14. (a) Calculate and compare the energy of a photon of wavelength 8.7 μm with that of wavelength 160 nm. (b) Using Figure 6.3, identify the region of the electromagnetic spectrum to which each belongs.

6.15. A high-powered laser is pulsed for a period of 100 ns. During that time, it emits a signal with a total energy of 8300 J. If the wavelength of the signal is 351 nm, how many photons have been emitted?

6.16. If the human eye receives a 1.45×10^{-17} J signal from photons whose wavelength is 550 nm, how many photons have hit the eye?

6.17. The energy from radiation can be used to cause the rupture of chemical bonds. A minimum energy of 495 kJ/mol is required to break the oxygen-oxygen bond in O_2. What is the longest wavelength of radiation that possesses the necessary energy to break the bond? What type of electromagnetic radiation is this?

6.18. A certain photographic film requires a minimum radiation energy of 80 kJ/mol to cause exposure. What is the longest wavelength of radiation that possesses the necessary energy to expose the film? Could this film be used for infrared photography?

6.19. Potassium metal must absorb radiation with a minimum frequency of 5.57×10^{14} s^{-1} before it can emit an electron from its surface via the photoelectric effect. **(a)** What is the minimum energy required to produce this effect? **(b)** What wavelength radiation will provide a photon of this energy? **(c)** Using Figure 6.3, identify the region of the electromagnetic spectrum to which this radiation belongs. **(d)** If potassium is irradiated with light whose wavelength is 510 nm, what is the maximum possible kinetic energy of the emitted electrons?

6.20. It requires a minimum energy of 277 kJ/mol to eject electrons from calcium metal via the photoelectric effect. **(a)** What is the energy per photon? **(b)** What is the minimum frequency of light required? **(c)** What is the wavelength of this light? **(d)** If calcium is irradiated with light whose wavelength is 350 nm, what is the maximum possible kinetic energy of the emitted electrons?

Bohr's Model; Matter Waves

6.21. What is the difference between continuous spectra and line spectra?

6.22. How does the Bohr theory explain the line spectrum of hydrogen?

6.23. Is energy emitted or absorbed when the following electronic transitions occur in hydrogen? **(a)** from $n = 5$ to $n = 1$; **(b)** from an orbit of radius 0.53 Å to one of radius 4.77 Å. **(c)** completely removing the electron from the atom when it is in the $n = 2$ state.

6.24. Indicate whether energy is emitted or absorbed when the following electronic transitions occur in hydrogen: **(a)** from $n = 2$ to $n = 4$; **(b)** from an orbit of radius 8.48 Å to one with radius 2.12 Å; **(c)** removing the electron from the atom when it is in the $n = 3$ state.

6.25. For each of the following electronic transitions in the hydrogen atom, calculate the energy, frequency, and wavelength of the associated radiation: **(a)** from $n = 1$ to $n = 3$; **(b)** from $n = 2$ to $n = 5$; **(c)** from $n = 6$ to $n = 7$. Will the radiation be absorbed or emitted during these transitions?

6.26. For each of the following electronic transitions in the hydrogen atom, calculate the energy, frequency, and wavelength of the associated radiation: **(a)** from $n = 4$ to $n = 1$; **(b)** from $n = 5$ to $n = 3$; **(c)** from $n = 6$ to $n = 2$. Will the radiation be absorbed or emitted during these transitions?

6.27. What wavelength of light is emitted when an electron moves from the $n = 5$ to the $n = 2$ state in hydrogen?

Using Figure 6.12, identify the line in the emission spectrum that corresponds to this transition.

6.28. What wavelength of light is necessary to excite a hydrogen atom from its ground state to its lowest-energy excited state ($n = 2$)? What type of radiation is necessary to make this transition occur?

6.29. Use the de Broglie relationship to determine the wavelengths of the following objects: **(a)** an 85-kg person skiing at 60 km/hr; **(b)** a 50-g golf ball traveling at 400 m/s; **(c)** a lithium atom moving at 6.5×10^5 m/s.

6.30. Calculate the wavelengths of the following objects: **(a)** a 3000-lb automobile moving at 55 mi/hr; **(b)** a baseball weighing 5.0 oz (1 oz = 28.3 g) thrown at a speed of 89 mi/hr; **(c)** a helium atom moving at a speed of 8.5×10^5 m/s.

6.31. Neutron diffraction is an important technique for determining the structures of molecules. Calculate the velocity of a neutron that has a characteristic wavelength of 0.88 Å. (Refer to the back inside cover for the mass of the neutron.)

6.32. The electron microscope has been widely used to obtain highly magnified images of biological and other types of materials. When an electron is accelerated through 100 V, it attains a speed of 5.93×10^6 m/s. What is the characteristic wavelength of this electron? Is the wavelength comparable to the size of atoms?

Quantum Mechanics and Atomic Orbitals

6.33. In the quantum-mechanical description of the hydrogen atom, what is the physical significance of the square of the wave function, ψ^2?

6.34. In the Bohr model of the ground state of hydrogen, the electron orbits the nucleus with a radius of 0.53 Å. Is this also true in the quantum-mechanical description of the hydrogen atom? Explain.

6.35. **(a)** For $n = 5$, what are the possible values of l? **(b)** For $l = 2$, what are the possible values of m_l?

6.36. (a) For $n = 4$, what are the possible values of l? (b) For $l = 3$, what are the possible values of m_l?

6.37. Give the values for n, l, and m_l (a) for each orbital in the $4d$ subshell; (b) for each orbital in the $n = 3$ shell.

6.38. Give the values for n, l, and m_l (a) for each orbital in the $4f$ subshell; (b) for each orbital in the $n = 2$ shell.

6.39. Which of the following are permissible sets of quantum numbers for an electron in a hydrogen atom: (a) $n = 2$, $l = 1$, $m_l = 1$; (b) $n = 1$, $l = 0$, $m_l = -1$; (c) $n = 4$, $l = 2$, $m_l = -2$; (d) $n = 3$, $l = 3$, $m_l = 0$? For those combinations that are permissible, write the appropriate designation for the subshell to which the orbital belongs (that is, $1s$, and so on).

6.40. Which of the following sets of quantum numbers are allowed for an electron in a hydrogen atom: (a) $n = 1$, $l = 1$, $m_l = 0$; (b) $n = 3$, $l = 0$, $m_l = 0$; (c) $n = 4$, $l = 1$, $m_l = -1$; (d) $n = 2$, $l = 1$, $m_l = 2$? For those combinations that are allowed, write the designation for the subshell to which the orbital belongs.

6.41. Which of the following are permissible subshells for an electron in an excited state of hydrogen: $3f$, $3d$, $6p$, $3s$, $2d$?

6.42. Which of the following are permissible subshells for an electron in an excited state of hydrogen: $5f$, $1p$, $4d$, $5s$, $2f$?

6.43. Sketch the contour representation for the following types of orbitals: (a) s; (b) p_x; (c) $d_{x^2-y^2}$.

6.44. Sketch the contour representation for the following types of orbitals: (a) p_y; (b) d_{xz}; (c) d_{z^2}.

6.45. (a) What are the similarities and differences between a $2s$ and a $3s$ orbital? (b) What are the similarities and differences between a $2s$ and a $2p_x$ orbital? (c) Which of these ($2s$, $2p_x$, $3s$) is highest in energy?

6.46. Both Li^{2+} and H have only one electron but differ in nuclear charge. How does the $2s$ orbital of Li^{2+} resemble and how does it differ from the $2s$ orbital of hydrogen?

Many-Electron Atoms

6.47. Which quantum numbers must be the same in order that orbitals be degenerate (have the same energy) (a) in a hydrogen atom, and (b) in a many-electron atom?

6.48. Within a given shell, how do the energies of the s, p, d, and f subshells compare for a many-electron atom? How do the energies of the orbitals of a given subshell compare?

6.49. Explain why the effective nuclear charge experienced by a $3s$ electron in iron is greater than that for a $3d$ electron.

6.50. Compare the average distance from the nucleus of a $2s$ electron in neon with that for a $2p$ electron.

6.51. Explain why the effective nuclear charge experienced by a $3s$ electron in magnesium is larger than that experienced by a $3s$ electron in sodium.

6.52. Which should experience a greater effective nuclear charge, a $4s$ electron in titanium or a $4s$ electron in copper?

6.53. What is the maximum number of electrons that can occupy each of the following subshells: (a) $3d$; (b) $4s$; (c) $2p$; (d) $5f$?

6.54. What is the maximum number of electrons in an atom that can have the following quantum numbers: (a) $n = 3$; (b) $n = 4$, $l = 2$; (c) $n = 4$, $l = 3$, $m_l = 2$; (d) $n = 2$, $l = 1$, $m_l = 0$, $m_s = -\frac{1}{2}$?

6.55. List the possible values of the four quantum numbers for each electron in the ground-state lithium atom.

6.56. List the possible values of the four quantum numbers for a $2p$ electron in beryllium.

Electron Configurations

6.57. Write the electron configurations for the following atoms using the appropriate noble-gas inner core for abbreviation: (a) Ca; (b) Ge; (c) Br; (d) Co; (e) Eu; (f) Hf.

6.58. Write the electron configurations for the following atoms using the appropriate noble-gas inner core for abbreviation: (a) Cs; (b) Mn; (c) Ni; (d) Sb; (e) Lu; (f) Pb.

6.59. Draw the orbital diagrams for the valence electrons of each of the following elements: (a) Si; (b) Te; (c) Fe; (d) Eu; (e) Bi. How many unpaired electrons would you expect in each of these?

6.60. Using orbital diagrams, determine the number of unpaired electrons in each of the following atoms: (a) B; (b) Ga; (c) Sn; (d) Ru; (e) Ir.

6.61. Identify the specific element that has the following electron configuration: (a) $1s^2 2s^2 2p^4$; (b) $[Ne]3s^2 3p^5$; (c) $[Ar]4s^1$; (d) $[Ar]4s^1 3d^5$

6.62. Identify the group of elements that corresponds to the following electron configurations: (a) [noble gas]ns^1; (b) [noble gas]$ns^2 np^3$; (c) [noble gas]$ns^2(n-1)d^{10}np^2$; (d) [noble gas]$ns^2(n-1)d^6$

6.63. Consider the two electromagnetic waves shown below:

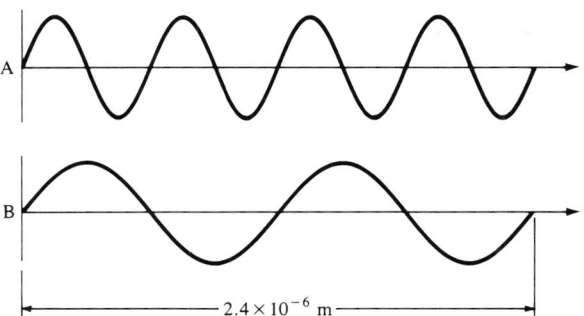

(a) What is the wavelength of wave A? Of wave B? (b) What is the frequency of wave A? Of wave B? (c) Identify the regions of the electromagnetic spectrum to which waves A and B belong.

6.64. Certain elements emit light of a specific color when they are burned. Historically, chemists used such "flame tests" to determine whether specific elements were present in a sample. Some characteristic wavelengths for some of the elements are:

Ag	328.1 nm	Fe	372.0 nm
Au	267.6 nm	K	404.7 nm
Ba	455.4 nm	Mg	285.2 nm
Ca	422.7 nm	Na	589.6 nm
Cu	324.8 nm	Ni	341.5 nm

(a) For each of these elements, determine the color associated with its flame. (b) Which element emits the most energetic light? The least energetic light? (c) When burned, a sample of an unknown substance is found to emit light of frequency 6.59×10^{14} s^{-1}. Which of the above elements is probably in the sample?

6.65. The planetary space probe *Voyager 2* has sent pictures from Neptune to Earth, a distance of 2.82×10^9 mi. How long did it take for the pictures transmitted from *Voyager 2* to reach Earth?

6.66. The laser in an audio compact disc player uses light whose wavelength is 780 nm. (a) What is the frequency of this radiation? (b) What is the energy (in joules) of a single photon of this wavelength?

6.67. Chlorophyll absorbs blue light, $\lambda = 460$ nm, and emits red light, $\lambda = 660$ nm. Calculate the net energy change in the chlorophyll system (in kilojoules) when a mole of 460-nm photons is absorbed and a mole of 660-nm photons is emitted.

6.68. An argon-ion laser emits light whose wavelength is 488 nm. (a) Calculate the energy of a photon of this light. (b) The power of lasers is measured in watts, a unit of power equal to the energy in joules it radiates per second (1 W = 1 J/s). How many photons are delivered by a laser rated at 10 W if the light pulse lasts 1.5 μs?

[6.69]. A phototube, such as that illustrated in Figure 6.6(b), is a device used to measure the intensity of light. In a certain experiment, when light of wavelength 550 nm is shined on the phototube, electrons are emitted at the rate of 8.6×10^{-13} C/s. Assume that each photon that impinges on the phototube emits one electron. How many photons per second are striking the phototube? How much energy per second is the phototube absorbing?

[6.70]. The stratospheric ozone (O_3) layer helps to protect us from harmful ultraviolet radiation. It does so by absorbing ultraviolet light and falling apart into an O_2 molecule and an oxygen atom, a process known as *photodissociation:*

$$O_3(g) \longrightarrow O_2(g) + O(g)$$

Use the data in Appendix C to calculate the enthalpy change for this reaction. What is the maximum wavelength a photon can have if it is to possess sufficient energy to cause this dissociation? In what portion of the spectrum does this wavelength occur?

[6.71]. Microwave ovens emit microwave radiation that is absorbed by water. The absorbed radiation is converted to heat that is transferred to other components of the food. Suppose that the microwave radiation has a wavelength of 12.5 cm. How many photons are required to increase the temperature of 100 mL of water from 20°C to 100°C if all the energy of the photons is converted to heat?

6.72. When the light from a neon light is dispersed in a prism to form a spectrum, the spectrum is not continuous; rather, it consists of several sharp lines, each of a specific frequency. Explain in general terms why a line spectrum is produced.

[6.73]. The energy required to completely remove an electron from an individual atom is called its ionization energy. The ionization of a hydrogen atom can be calculated by assuming the electron is moved from the $n = 1$ (ground state) to the $n = \infty$ state. Calculate the ionization energy of the hydrogen atom. Express this energy on a mole basis (as kJ/mol).

6.74. Hydrogen displays an emission line in the infrared region of the spectrum, at 1875.6 nm. Determine the values of n for the two energy levels that are responsible for this emission.

[6.75]. Heisenberg's uncertainty principle can be expressed mathematically as $\Delta x \cdot \Delta p \geq h/2\pi$, where Δx and Δp denote the uncertainty in position and momentum, respectively, and h is Planck's constant. (a) An electron has a speed of 3.0×10^6 m/s. If the accuracy with which this can be measured is 1.0 percent, what is the minimum uncertainty in the position of the electron? (b) Repeat the calculation in part (a), but for a 12-g bullet whose speed is 200 m/s. (c) Compare the results for parts (a) and (b): How does each compare with the size of the object itself? (Remember that momentum is mass times velocity: $p = mv$.)

6.76. What is the subshell designation for each of the following cases: **(a)** $n = 2$, $l = 0$; **(b)** $n = 4$, $l = 2$; **(c)** $n = 5$, $l = 1$; **(d)** $n = 3$, $l = 2$; **(e)** $n = 4$, $l = 3$?

6.77. Indicate the number of orbitals that can have each of the following designations: **(a)** $n = 5$; **(b)** $3p$; **(c)** $4f$; **(d)** $5d_{xy}$; **(e)** $6s$; **(f)** $4d$.

6.78. In a chlorine atom, which electrons experience the largest effective nuclear charge? Which experience the smallest?

6.79. The quantum numbers listed below are for four different electrons in the same atom. Arrange them in order of increasing energy. Indicate whether any two have the same energy.
(a) $n = 4$, $l = 0$, $m_l = 0$, $m_s = \frac{1}{2}$;
(b) $n = 3$, $l = 2$, $m_l = 1$, $m_s = \frac{1}{2}$;
(c) $n = 3$, $l = 2$, $m_l = -2$, $m_s = -\frac{1}{2}$;
(d) $n = 3$, $l = 1$, $m_l = 1$, $m_s = -\frac{1}{2}$.

6.80. Why can the $2p$ subshell of an atom hold more electrons than the $2s$ subshell?

6.81. Using only a periodic table as a guide, write the complete electron configurations for the following atoms: **(a)** Cd; **(b)** As; **(c)** La; **(d)** Pd; **(e)** S.

6.82. The Stern-Gerlach experiment illustrated in Figure 6.24 was carried out using a beam of silver atoms. Draw the orbital-diagram representation for the valence electron configuration of silver. How many unpaired electrons does this atom have?

6.83. Consider the ground electron configurations for the elements of the fourth row of the periodic table. **(a)** Which of these will have no unpaired electrons? **(b)** Which will have one unpaired electron? **(c)** Which will have the most unpaired electrons?

6.84. For each of the following electron configurations, determine the element to which it corresponds and determine whether it is a ground- or an excited-state electron configuration: **(a)** [He]$2s^1 2p^5$; **(b)** [Ar]$4s^2 3d^{10} 4p^5$; **(c)** [Ne]$3s^2 3p^2 4s^1$; **(d)** [Kr]$5s^2 4d^{10} 5p^1$.

[6.85]. Cite evidence to support or refute the following claims: **(a)** The energy levels of a hydrogen atom are quantized. **(b)** The electron in a hydrogen atom can be located exactly. **(c)** Electrons possess spin. **(d)** The effective nuclear charge experienced by a $3p$ electron in a Cl⁻ ion is less than that experienced by a $3p$ electron in a neutral Cl atom. **(e)** The actinide elements are the only ones that have electrons residing in f orbitals.

Periodic Properties of the Elements

The red, blue, and yellow colors in fireworks are produced by salts of strontium, copper, and sodium, respectively.

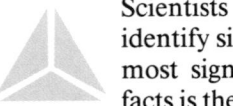

CONTENTS

Point of Emphasis: The *valence orbitals* are those that are occupied beyond the orbitals of the preceding noble gas. These orbitals do not necessarily have the highest values of n.

N. K. Goh and L. S. Chia, "Using the Learning Cycle to Introduce Periodicity," *J. Chem. Educ.* 1989, 66, 747.

Scientists constantly seek ways to organize facts so that they can identify similarities, differences, and trends among these facts. The most significant tool for organizing and remembering chemical facts is the periodic table. As we saw in Chapter 6, the periodic table arises from the periodic nature of electron configurations. Elements in the same column contain the same number of electrons in their outer-shell orbitals, or **valence orbitals.** For example, N($[He]2s^2 2p^3$) and As($[Ar]4s^2 3d^{10} 4p^3$) are both members of group 5A; the similarity in their electronic structures leads to many similarities in their properties.

When we compare N and As, however, it is apparent that they exhibit differences as well as similarities (Figure 7.1). Some clues as to the distinctions of these elements are evident in the *differences* in their configurations. The outermost electrons of N are in the second shell, whereas those of As are in the fourth shell. Also, As has a completely filled $3d$ subshell, whereas N has no electrons in d orbitals. We shall see that electron configurations can be used to explain differences as well as similarities in the properties of elements.

In this chapter, we shall use the electronic structure of atoms to gain a deeper understanding of how the properties of elements change as we move across a row or down a column of the periodic table. We shall see that for many properties, the trends within a row or column form patterns. Our discussion will begin with a brief history of the periodic table.

7.1 Development of the Periodic Table

The discovery of new chemical elements has been an ongoing process since ancient times (Figure 7.2). Certain elements, such as gold and silver, appear in nature in elemental form and were thus discovered thousands of years ago. In contrast, some elements are radioactive and intrinsically unstable. We know about them only because of twentieth-century technological developments.

The majority of the elements, although stable, are dispersed widely in nature and are incorporated into numerous compounds. Thus, for centuries, scientists were unaware of their existence. Finally, in the early nineteenth century, advances in chemistry made it easier to isolate elements from their

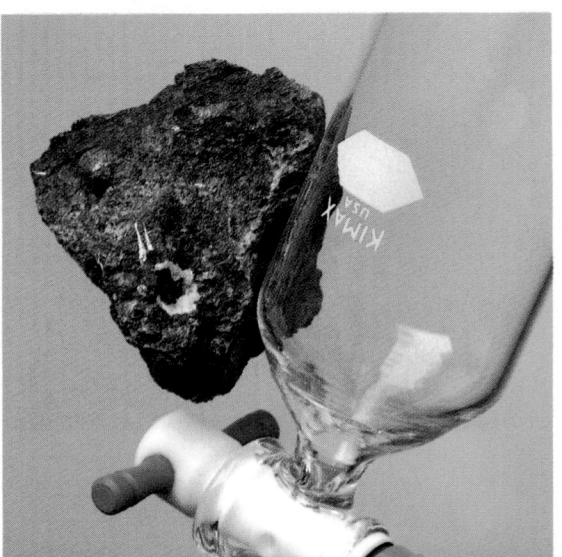

FIGURE 7.1 Nitrogen (right) and arsenic (left) are both group 5A elements. As such, they have many chemical similarities. However, they also have many differences, including, as shown here, the forms they take as elements. Nitrogen is a colorless diatomic gas (here shown enclosed in a glass container), whereas arsenic is a gray, solid metalloid. (Richard Megna/ Fundamental Photographs)

H																	He
Li	Be											B	C	N	O	F	Ne
Na	Mg											Al	Si	P	S	Cl	Ar
K	Ca	Sc	Ti	V	Cr	Mn	Fe	Co	Ni	Cu	Zn	Ga	Ge	As	Se	Br	Kr
Rb	Sr	Y	Zr	Nb	Mo	Tc	Ru	Rh	Pd	Ag	Cd	In	Sn	Sb	Te	I	Xe
Cs	Ba	La	Hf	Ta	W	Re	Os	Ir	Pt	Au	Hg	Tl	Pb	Bi	Po	At	Rn
Fr	Ra	Ac	Rf	Ha	[106]	[107]	[108]	[109]									

Ce	Pr	Nd	Pm	Sm	Eu	Gd	Tb	Dy	Ho	Er	Tm	Yb	Lu
Th	Pa	U	Np	Pu	Am	Cm	Bk	Cf	Es	Fm	Md	No	Lr

▢ Ancient Times	▢ 1735-1843	▢ 1894-1918			
▢ Middle Ages-1700	▢ 1843-1886	▢ 1923-1961	▢ 1965-		

FIGURE 7.2 Periodic table showing the dates of discovery of the elements. [V. Ringnes, *Journal of Chemical Education,* 66, 731 (1989)]

compounds. As a result, the number of known elements more than doubled from 31 in 1800 to 63 by 1865.

As the number of known elements increased, scientists began to investigate the possibilities of classifying them in useful ways. In 1869, Dmitri Mendeleev in Russia (Figure 7.3) and Lothar Meyer in Germany published nearly identical schemes for classifying the elements. Both scientists noted that similar chemical and physical properties recur periodically when the elements are arranged in order of increasing atomic weight. Scientists at that time had no knowledge of atomic numbers. Atomic weights, however, generally increase with increasing atomic number, so both Mendeleev and Meyer unwittingly

FIGURE 7.3 Dmitri Mendeleev. Mendeleev rose from very poor beginnings to a position of great eminence in nineteenth-century science. He was born in Siberia, the youngest child in a family of at least 14. His mother endured great personal sacrifice to make it possible for him to enroll in a university in Saint Petersburg. Mendeleev proved to be a brilliant student in science and mathematics and eventually was able to study in France and Germany. He spent most of his career as a professor of chemistry at the University of Saint Petersburg. Despite his eminence as a scientist, he was often in trouble because of his liberal, unorthodox opinions. (Library of Congress)

TABLE 7.1 △ Comparison of the Properties of Eka-Silicon Predicted by Mendeleev with the Observed Properties of Germanium

Property	Mendeleev's predictions for eka-silicon (made in 1871)	Observed properties of germanium (discovered in 1886)
Atomic weight	72	72.59
Density (g/cm³)	5.5	5.35
Specific heat (J/g-K)	0.305	0.309
Melting point (°C)	High	947
Color	Dark gray	Grayish white
Formula of oxide	XO_2	GeO_2
Density of oxide (g/cm³)	4.7	4.70
Formula of chloride	XCl_4	$GeCl_4$
Boiling point of chloride (°C)	A little under 100	84

arranged the elements in proper sequence. The tables of elements advanced by Mendeleev and Meyer were the forerunners of the modern periodic table.

Although Mendeleev and Meyer came to essentially the same conclusion about the periodicity of the properties of the elements, Mendeleev is given credit for advancing his ideas more vigorously and stimulating much new work in chemistry. His insistence that elements with similar characteristics be listed in the same families forced him to leave several blank spaces in his table. For example, both gallium (Ga) and germanium (Ge) were at that time unknown. Mendeleev boldly predicted their existence and properties, referring to them as eka-aluminum and eka-silicon, after the elements they appear under in the periodic table. When these elements were discovered, their properties were found to match closely those predicted by Mendeleev, as illustrated in Table 7.1. The accuracy of Mendeleev's predictions did much to promote the acceptance of the periodic table.

In 1913, just 2 years after Rutherford had proposed the nuclear model of the atom, Henry Moseley (1887–1915) discovered the concept of atomic numbers. Moseley bombarded different elements with energetic electrons and studied the resultant X-rays. He observed that the frequencies of the X-rays were different for each element. He was able to arrange these frequencies in order by assigning each element a unique whole number, which he called the *atomic number*. He correctly proposed that the atomic number is the charge on the nucleus of the atom. We know today that the atomic number equals not only the number of protons in the nucleus of an atom but also the number of electrons in that atom. In the sections that follow, we shall examine how the arrangement of electrons helps determine an element's chemical properties.

7.2 Electron Shells in Atoms

When we move down a column of the periodic table, we change the principal quantum number, n, of the valence orbitals of the atoms. In Section 6.5, we referred to all the orbitals with the same value of n as a *shell*. The origin of this term actually predates the quantum-mechanical model of the atom. Even before Bohr had proposed his theory of the hydrogen atom, the American chemist Gilbert N. Lewis (1875–1946) had used his understanding of chemical behavior to suggest that electrons in atoms are arranged in spherical shells around the nucleus. How does the quantum-mechanical description of electron configurations correspond to Lewis's idea of electron shells? Consider the noble gases helium, neon, and argon, whose electron configurations follow:

$$He \quad 1s^2$$

$$Ne \quad 1s^2 2s^2 2p^6$$

$$Ar \quad 1s^2 2s^2 2p^6 3s^2 3p^6$$

The total electronic charge distribution in these atoms can be accurately calculated using large computers. These distributions are shown in Figure 7.4. The quantity plotted on the vertical axis is called the *radial electron density*. It corresponds to the probability of finding the electron at a particular distance from the nucleus. As Figure 7.4 shows, the radial electron density does not fall off continuously as we move away from the nucleus. Rather, it shows maxima corresponding to distances at which there are higher probabilities of finding electrons. These maxima correspond to Lewis's idea of shells of electrons; however, these shells are diffuse and overlap considerably.

Helium shows a single shell, neon two, and argon three. Each of these maxima is due mainly to electrons that have the same principal quantum number, n. Thus, for helium the $1s$ electrons show a maximum in radial electron density at about 0.3 Å. In argon, the maximum in the $1s$ radial electron density occurs at only 0.05 Å. The second maximum, which occurs at a larger radial distance, is due to both the $2s$ and $2p$ electrons. The third maximum is due to $3s$ and $3p$ electrons.

Why is the $1s$ shell in argon so much closer to the nucleus than the $1s$ shell in helium? The reason is clear when we recall that the nuclear charge of helium is only $2+$, whereas that for argon is $18+$. Because the $1s$ electrons are the innermost electrons of the atom, they are not shielded from the nucleus very effectively by other electrons. Thus, as the nuclear charge increases, the $1s$ electrons are "pulled" closer and closer to the nucleus. Similarly, the $n = 2$ shell of argon is closer to the nucleus than that of neon: Even though the $n = 3$ shell

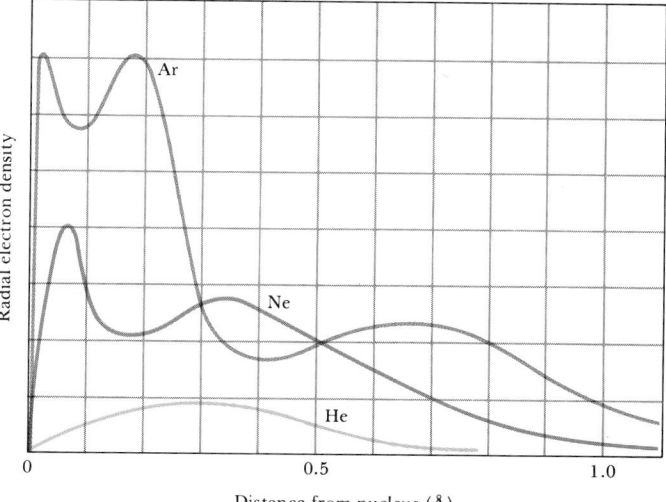

FIGURE 7.4 Radial electron-density graphs for the first three noble-gas elements, He, Ne, and Ar. The maxima that occur in the radial electron density correspond to electrons with the same value of the principal quantum number, n.

Figure 7.5

FIGURE 7.5 Atomic radius versus atomic number. The noble gases are not included in this graph because there is no simple way of relating their radii to those of the other elements on the basis of solid-state structure determinations. Gaps in the graph are due to lack of experimental data. The violet symbols mark the beginning of a period (alkali metals), and the yellow ones mark the halogens.

weakly shields the $n = 2$ shell in argon, this is more than offset by the attraction due to the greater nuclear charge of argon.

Now that we have some understanding of the electronic structure of atoms, we can examine some properties of atoms that depend largely on their electron configurations. We shall consider three properties that provide important insights into chemical behavior: atomic size, ionization energy, and electron affinity.

7.3 Sizes of Atoms

We often think of atoms as hard, spherical objects. One conclusion we can draw from the quantum-mechanical model, however, is that an atom does not have a sharply defined boundary. This is evident in Figure 7.4. The electron-density distributions illustrated do not end abruptly at some distance from the nucleus; rather, they decrease slowly with increasing distance. Thus, atoms do not have boundaries that fix their sizes. Nevertheless, it is possible to estimate the **atomic radius** — the radius of an atom — by assuming that atoms are spherical objects that touch each other when they are bonded together in molecules. For example, the Br—Br distance in Br_2 is 2.28 Å;* we might then say that the radius of the Br atom is half this distance, 1.14 Å. Similarly, in compounds containing carbon-carbon bonds, the C—C distance is found to be very close to 1.54 Å. We can thus assign an atomic radius of 0.77 Å to carbon. If our concept of an atomic radius is going to be very useful, these atomic radii should remain nearly constant when the atom is bound to another element. Thus, the distance between carbon and bromine in a C—Br bond should be 1.14 + 0.77 Å, or

---

* Remember: The angstrom (1 Å = 10^{-10} m), although a convenient metric unit for atomic measurements of length, is not an SI unit. The most commonly used SI unit for such measurements is the picometer (1 pm = 10^{-12} m). 1 Å = 100 pm.

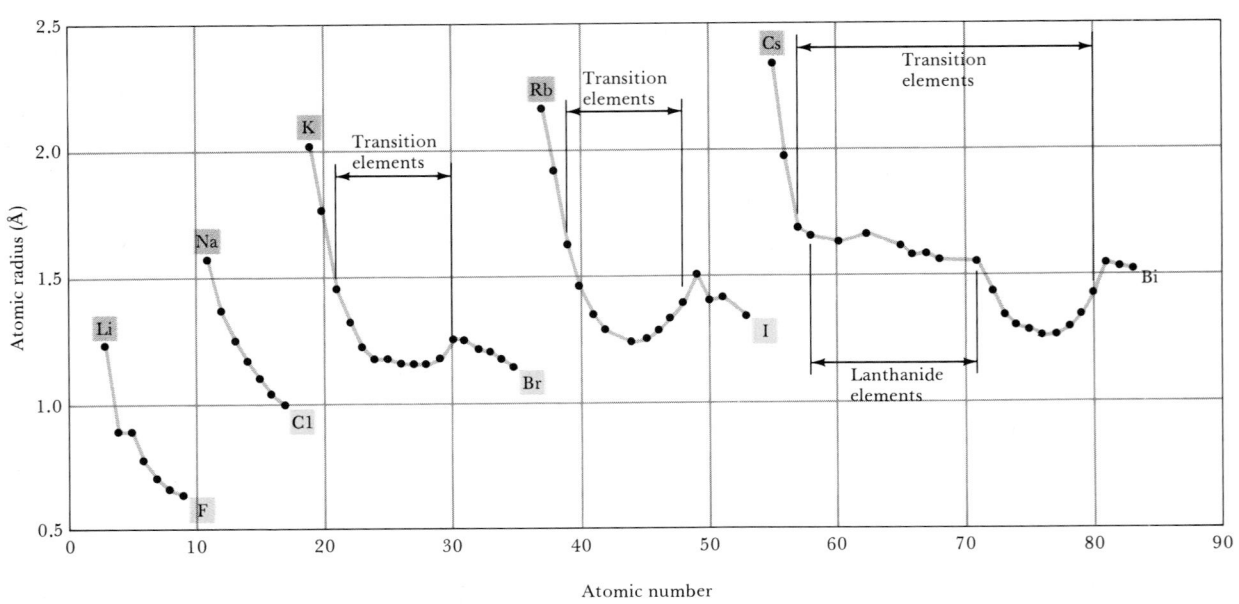

1.91 Å. It turns out that carbon-bromine bonds in various compounds are about this length.

Atomic radii have been obtained for many elements, based on a large body of experimental data. These radii are graphed in Figure 7.5 as a function of atomic number. Provided we keep in mind that there are uncertainties in these values because of the means by which they are obtained, we can discern some interesting trends in the data:

1. Within each group (column), the atomic radius tends to increase going from top to bottom.
2. Within each period (row), the atomic radius tends to decrease moving left to right.

These general trends, which are summarized in Figure 7.6, are the result of two factors that determine the size of the outermost orbital: its principal quantum number and the effective nuclear charge acting on its electrons. Increasing the principal quantum number increases the size of the orbital; increasing the effective nuclear charge reduces the size.

Proceeding across any row of the table, the number of core electrons remains the same, while the nuclear charge increases. The electrons that are added to counterbalance the increasing nuclear charge are very ineffective in shielding each other. The effective nuclear charge therefore increases steadily, while the principal quantum number remains constant. For example, the inner $1s^2$ electrons of lithium ($1s^2 2s^1$) shield the outer $2s$ electron from the $3+$ charged nucleus. Consequently, the outer electron experiences an effective nuclear charge of about $1+$. For beryllium ($1s^2 2s^2$), the effective nuclear charge experienced by each outer $2s$ electron is larger; in this case the inner $1s^2$ electrons are shielding a $4+$ nucleus, and each $2s$ electron only partially shields the other from the nucleus. As the effective nuclear charge increases, the electrons are drawn closer to the nucleus. Thus, the radius of the atom decreases as we proceed from left to right.

In going down a column of elements, the effective nuclear charge remains relatively constant, while the principal quantum number increases. Thus, the size of the valence orbital, and consequently of the atomic radius, increases.

SAMPLE EXERCISE 7.1

Referring to a periodic table, arrange the following atoms in order of increasing size: O, S, F.

SOLUTION Notice that F is to the right of O in the same period; thus we expect that F is smaller than O. Now notice that S is below O in group 6A: hence S is larger than O. The resultant order of increasing radii is F < O < S.

PRACTICE EXERCISE

Arrange the following atoms in order of increasing atomic radius: Na, Be, Mg.
Answer: Be < Mg < Na

7.4 Ionization Energy

The strength with which an atom holds its electrons is an important indicator of its chemical behavior. The **ionization energy** of an atom measures how strongly

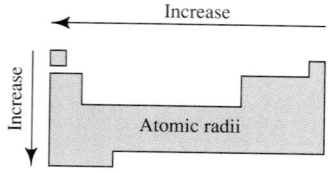

FIGURE 7.6 General trends in atomic radii of *s*- and *p*-block elements with position in the periodic table.

an atom holds its electrons; ionization energy is the minimum energy required to remove an electron from the ground state of the isolated gaseous atom. The *first ionization energy*, I_1, is the energy needed to remove the first electron. For example, the first ionization energy for the sodium atom is the energy required for the following process:

$$Na(g) \longrightarrow Na^+(g) + e^- \qquad [7.1]$$

The *second ionization energy*, I_2, is the energy needed for the removal of the second electron, and so forth for successive removals of additional electrons. Thus, I_2 for the sodium atom is the energy associated with the following process:

$$Na^+(g) \longrightarrow Na^{2+}(g) + e^- \qquad [7.2]$$

The higher the ionization energy, the more difficult it is to remove an electron.

Ionization energies for the elements sodium through argon are listed in Table 7.2. Notice that the ionization energies for an element increase in magnitude as successive electrons are removed: $I_1 < I_2 < I_3$, and so forth. This trend arises because the positive nuclear charge that provides the attractive force remains the same, whereas the number of electrons, which produce repulsive interactions, steadily decreases. As a result, the effective nuclear charge experienced by the remaining electrons increases. The greater the effective nuclear charge, the greater the energy required to remove an electron.

A second important feature of the data in Table 7.2 is the sharp increase in ionization energy that occurs when an inner-shell electron is removed. For example, consider silicon, whose electron configuration is $1s^2 2s^2 2p^6 3s^2 3p^2$ or $[Ne]3s^2 3p^2$. The ionization energies increase steadily from 786 kJ/mol to 4354 kJ/mol for the loss of the four electrons in the 3s and 3p subshells. Removal of the fifth electron, which comes from the 2p subshell, requires much more energy: 16,100 kJ/mol. The large jump in energy occurs because the inner-shell 2p electron is much closer to the nucleus and experiences a much greater effective nuclear charge than do the valence-shell 3s and 3p electrons. Every element exhibits a large increase in ionization energy when electrons are removed from its noble-gas core. This observation supports the idea that only the outermost electrons, those beyond the noble-gas core, are involved in the sharing and transfer of electrons that give rise to chemical change. The inner electrons are too tightly bound to the nucleus to be lost from the atom or even shared with another atom.

Point of Emphasis: Ionization energies of the atomic elements are always positive; that is, energy is absorbed from the surroundings. The ionizations are endothermic.

Learning Goal 3: Explain the observed changes in values of the successive ionization energies for a given atom.

Point of Emphasis: Due to the large increase in the ionization energy when the electron comes from the next lower value of n, it is seldom necessary to consider ionizations that take more electrons than needed to achieve a noble-gas electron configuration.

Point of Emphasis: These easily removed electrons are the valence electrons.

TABLE 7.2 △ Successive Values of Ionization Energies, I, for the Elements Sodium Through Argon (kJ/mol)

Element	I_1	I_2	I_3	I_4	I_5	I_6	I_7
Na	496	4560		(Inner-shell electrons)			
Mg	738	1450	7730				
Al	577	1816	2744	11,600			
Si	786	1577	3228	4354	16,100		
P	1060	1890	2905	4950	6270	21,200	
S	999	2260	3375	4565	6950	8490	27,000
Cl	1256	2295	3850	5160	6560	9360	11,000
Ar	1520	2665	3945	5770	7230	8780	12,000

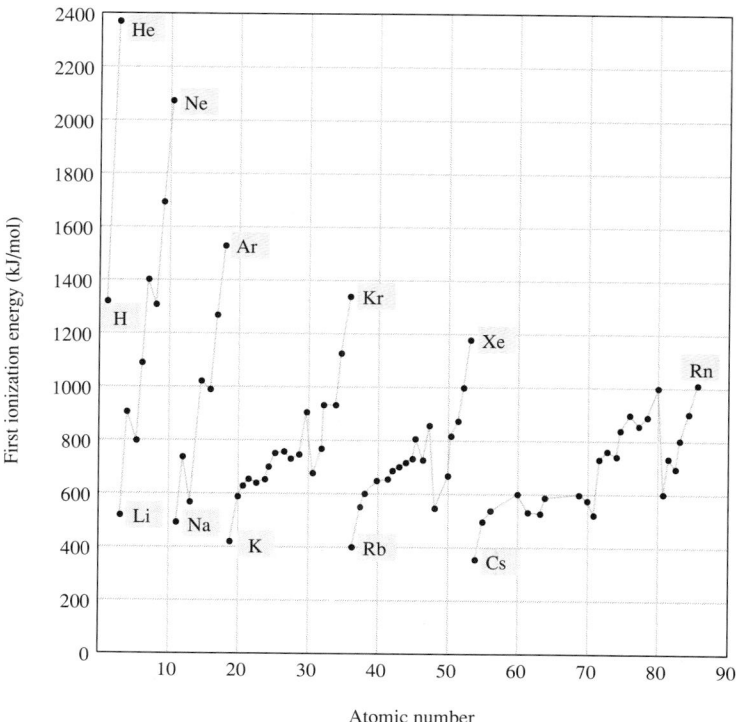

Figure 7.7

Periodic Trends in Ionization Energies

We have seen that, for a given element, the ionization energy increases as we remove successive electrons. What trends do we observe in the ionization energies as we move from one element to another in the periodic table? Figure 7.7 shows a graph of the first ionization energies, I_1, versus atomic number. An overall periodicity in I_1 is evident, as noted in the following trends:

1. Within each period, I_1 generally increases with increasing atomic number. The alkali metals show the lowest ionization energy in each row, and the noble gases the highest. There are slight irregularities in this trend that we will overlook for the moment.
2. Within each group, ionization energy generally decreases with increasing atomic number. For example, less energy is required to remove an electron from a potassium atom than from a lithium atom.

These general trends are summarized in Figure 7.8.

A few simple considerations help to explain these trends. The energy needed to remove an electron from the outer shell depends on both the effective nuclear charge and the average distance of the electron from the nucleus. Either increasing the effective nuclear charge or decreasing the distance from the nucleus increases the attraction between the electron and the nucleus. As this attraction increases, it becomes harder to remove the electron, and thus the ionization energy increases. As we move across a period, there is both an increase in effective nuclear charge and a decrease in atomic radius, causing the ionization energy to increase. However, as we move down a column, the atomic

Learning Goal 4: Explain the general variations in first ionization energies among the elements, as shown in Figure 7.7, and relate these variations to variations in atomic radii.

Point of Emphasis: Within a period, I_1 generally increases as you move to the right. Within a group, I_1 generally decreases as you move down.

FIGURE 7.8 General trends in first ionization energies.

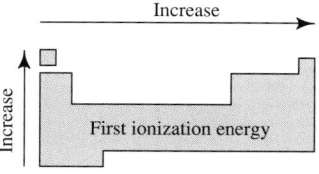

radius increases, while the effective nuclear charge remains essentially constant. Thus, the attraction between the nucleus and the electron decreases in this direction, causing the ionization energy to decrease.

The irregularities within a given period are somewhat more subtle but are readily explained. For example, the decrease in ionization in going from beryllium ($[He]2s^2$) to boron ($[He]2s^22p^1$) arises because the electrons in the filled $2s$ orbital are more effective at shielding the electrons in the $2p$ subshell than they are at shielding each other. This is essentially the same reason that in many-electron atoms, the $2p$ orbital is at a higher energy than the $2s$ (Figure 6.22). The decrease in ionization energy on going from nitrogen ($[He]2s^22p^3$) to oxygen ($[He]2s^22p^4$) is due to repulsion of paired electrons in the p^4 configuration. (Remember that, according to Hund's rule, each electron in the p^3 configuration resides in a different p orbital.)

For the fourth, fifth, and sixth periods, we see several sequences of elements that have similar values of I_1, with only a slight trend toward increasing I_1 with increasing atomic number. From the periodic table, we see that these sequences correspond to the transition metal and f-block elements. In general, periodic trends are not as dramatic in the properties of these elements as they are for the representative elements.

SAMPLE EXERCISE 7.2

Referring to the periodic table, select the atom from the following list that has the greatest first ionization energy: S, Cl, Se, Br.

SOLUTION Because ionization energy tends to increase as we move from the bottom of any family to the top, S and Cl should have greater ionization energies than Se and Br. Because the ionization energy increases as we move left to right in any period, Cl should have a greater ionization energy than S. Thus, Cl has the largest ionization energy of these four elements.

PRACTICE EXERCISE

Which of the following atoms—B, Al, C, and Si—has the lowest ionization energy?   *Answer:* Al

7.5 Electron Affinities

Atoms not only lose electrons to form positively charged ions, they also gain them to form negatively charged ones. The ionization energy measures the energy changes associated with removing electrons from gaseous atoms. The energy change that occurs when an electron is added to a gaseous atom or ion measures the attraction or affinity for the added electron and is called the **electron affinity.**

For most neutral atoms and for all positively charged ions, energy is released when an electron is added. For example, the addition of an electron to a neutral chlorine atom is accompanied by an energy change of -349 kJ/mol, the negative sign indicating that the process is exothermic. ∞ (Sec. 5.3)

$$Cl(g) + e^- \longrightarrow Cl^-(g) \qquad \Delta E = -349 \text{ kJ/mol} \qquad [7.3]$$

Thus, we say that chlorine has an electron affinity of -349 kJ/mol.* The greater the attraction between the species and the added electron, the more exothermic the process. On the other hand, the energy changes for adding an electron to anions and to some atoms are positive, meaning that work must be done to force the electron onto the species, forming an unstable anion.

Figure 7.9 shows the variation of electron affinities of the first 20 elements in the periodic table. Notice that the electron affinities have a definite periodic pattern. The general trend is for the electron affinity to become increasingly negative (stronger binding of an electron) as we move across each period toward the halogens. The halogens, which are one electron shy of a filled p subshell, have the most negative electron affinities. By picking up an electron, they form very stable negative ions with noble-gas electron configurations. On the other hand, elements of group 2A (Be, Mg, and Ca) and group 8A (He, Ne, and Ar) have positive electron affinities, so adding an electron requires energy. The 2A elements have filled s subshells in their valence shell, while the 8A elements have both s and p subshells filled. In both families, an added electron must therefore reside in a higher energy orbital. The 5A elements (N and P) also represent an interesting situation. These elements have half-filled p subshells, so that an added electron must be placed in an orbital that is already occupied, resulting in larger electron-electron repulsions. As a result, these elements have electron affinities that are either near zero or only slightly negative.

---

* Two sign conventions are used for electron affinity. In most introductory texts, including this one, the thermodynamic sign convention is used: A negative sign indicates that the addition of an electron is an exothermic process, as in the electron affinity given for chlorine, -349 kJ/mol. Historically, however, electron affinity has been defined as the energy *released* when an electron is added to a gaseous atom or ion. Because 349 kJ/mol are released when an electron is added to Cl(g), the electron affinity is then given as $+349$ kJ/mol.

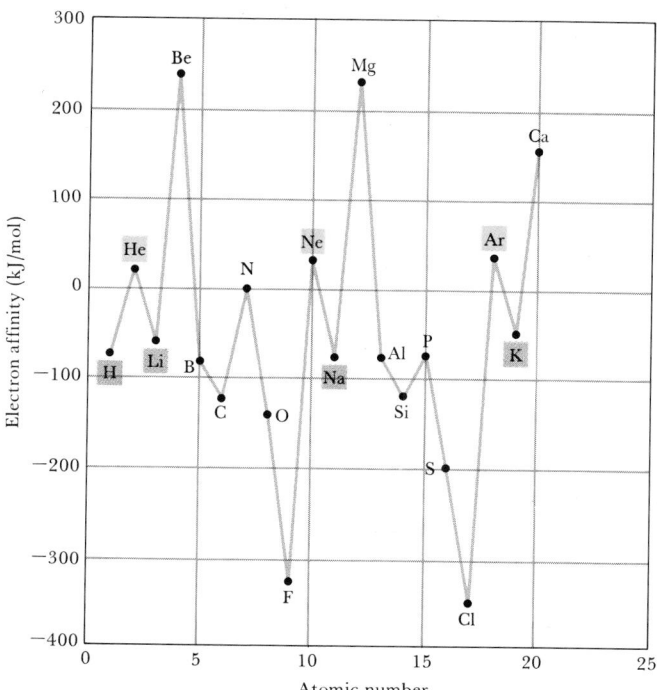

FIGURE 7.9 Electron affinity versus atomic number. The violet symbols mark the beginning of a period (alkali metals), and the yellow ones mark the end (noble gases).

Lee R. Summerlin,
Christie L. Borgford,
and Julie B. Ealy, "Halogens
Compete for Electrons,"
*Chemical Demonstrations, A
Sourcebook for Teachers, Volume 2* (Washington: American Chemical Society, 1987),
pp. 60–61.

Electron affinities do not change greatly as we go down a group. For example, consider the electron affinities of the halogens, listed in Table 7.3. For F, the added electron goes into a $2p$ orbital, for Cl a $3p$ orbital, for Br a $4p$ orbital, and so forth. Thus, as we proceed from F to I, the average distance of the added electron from the nucleus steadily increases, causing the electron-nucleus attraction to decrease. The orbital that holds the outermost electron is increasingly spread out, however, as we proceed from F to I, reducing the electron-electron repulsions. A lower electron-nucleus attraction is thus counterbalanced by lower electron-electron repulsions.

TABLE 7.3 △ Electron Affinities of Hydrogen and the Halogens

Element	Ion formed	E (kJ/mol)
H	H^-	-73
F	F^-	-332
Cl	Cl^-	-349
Br	Br^-	-325
I	I^-	-295

7.6 Metals, Nonmetals, and Metalloids

Point of Emphasis: With the exception of the noble gases, few elements exist in nature as uncombined atoms.

We will have frequent opportunity to use the concepts of atomic radii, ionization energies, and electron affinities in the chapters ahead. It is important to note, however, that these are properties of individual atoms. With the exception of the noble gases, none of the elements exist in nature as isolated individual atoms. To get a broader understanding of the properties of elements, we must also examine periodic trends in properties that involve large collections of atoms, which are the properties that we usually observe.

Learning Goal 6: Describe the periodic trends in metallic and nonmetallic behavior.

One of the fundamental periodic trends of this sort is the division of elements into the categories of metals, nonmetals, and metalloids, first introduced in Section 2.4. This classification is shown in Figure 7.10. Roughly three-quarters of the elements are metals, and these are situated in the left and middle portions of the table. The nonmetals are located at the top right corner, and the metalloids lie between the metals and nonmetals. Notice that hydrogen, which is located at the top left corner, is a nonmetal. It is for this reason that we set off hydrogen from the remaining group 1A elements. Some of the distinguishing properties of metals and nonmetals are summarized in Table 7.4. As

Point of Emphasis: Despite its placement in column 1A, hydrogen is a nonmetal.

TABLE 7.4 △ Characteristic Properties of Metallic and Nonmetallic Elements

Metallic elements	Nonmetallic elements
Distinguishing luster	Nonlustrous; various colors
Malleable and ductile as solids	Solids are usually brittle, may be hard or soft
Good thermal and electrical conductivity	Poor conductors of heat and electricity
Most metallic oxides are basic, ionic solids	Most nonmetallic oxides are molecular, acidic compounds
Exist in aqueous solution mainly as cations	Exist in aqueous solution mainly as anions or oxyanions

1A																	8A
1 **H**	2A											3A	4A	5A	6A	7A	**2** **He**
3 **Li**	**4** **Be**											**5** **B**	**6** **C**	**7** **N**	**8** **O**	**9** **F**	**10** **Ne**
11 **Na**	**12** **Mg**	3B	4B	5B	6B	7B		8B		1B	2B	**13** **Al**	**14** **Si**	**15** **P**	**16** **S**	**17** **Cl**	**18** **Ar**
19 **K**	**20** **Ca**	**21** **Sc**	**22** **Ti**	**23** **V**	**24** **Cr**	**25** **Mn**	**26** **Fe**	**27** **Co**	**28** **Ni**	**29** **Cu**	**30** **Zn**	**31** **Ga**	**32** **Ge**	**33** **As**	**34** **Se**	**35** **Br**	**36** **Kr**
37 **Rb**	**38** **Sr**	**39** **Y**	**40** **Zr**	**41** **Nb**	**42** **Mo**	**43** **Tc**	**44** **Ru**	**45** **Rh**	**46** **Pd**	**47** **Ag**	**48** **Cd**	**49** **In**	**50** **Sn**	**51** **Sb**	**52** **Te**	**53** **I**	**54** **Xe**
55 **Cs**	**56** **Ba**	**57** **La**	**72** **Hf**	**73** **Ta**	**74** **W**	**75** **Re**	**76** **Os**	**77** **Ir**	**78** **Pt**	**79** **Au**	**80** **Hg**	**81** **Tl**	**82** **Pb**	**83** **Bi**	**84** **Po**	**85** **At**	**86** **Rn**
87 **Fr**	**88** **Ra**	**89** **Ac**	**104** **Rf**	**105** **Ha**	[106]	[107]	[108]	[109]									

58 **Ce**	**59** **Pr**	**60** **Nd**	**61** **Pm**	**62** **Sm**	**63** **Eu**	**64** **Gd**	**65** **Tb**	**66** **Dy**	**67** **Ho**	**68** **Er**	**69** **Tm**	**70** **Yb**	**71** **Lu**
90 **Th**	**91** **Pa**	**92** **U**	**93** **Np**	**94** **Pu**	**95** **Am**	**96** **Cm**	**97** **Bk**	**98** **Cf**	**99** **Es**	**100** **Fm**	**101** **Md**	**102** **No**	**103** **Lw**

Metals

Metalloids

Nonmetals

FIGURE 7.10 The periodic table, showing metals, metalloids, and nonmetals.

Figure 7.10

you might expect, a close relationship exists between electron configurations and the properties of metals, nonmetals, and metalloids.

Metals

Most metals look much alike, exhibiting a characteristic metallic luster (Figure 7.11). Metals exhibit good electrical and thermal conductivity. They are malle-

Aluminum Copper Vanadium

Nickel Tin Zirconium

FIGURE 7.11 Metals are readily recognized by their characteristic luster. (Dr. E. R. Degginger)

able (can be pounded into thin sheets), ductile (can be drawn into wire), and can be formed into various shapes. All are solids at room temperature except mercury (melting point $= -39°C$), which is a liquid. Two metals melt at slightly above room temperature: cesium at 28.4°C and gallium at 29.8°C. At the other extreme, many metals melt at very high temperatures. For example, chromium melts at 1900°C.

Metals tend to have low ionization energies and are consequently oxidized (lose electrons) when they undergo chemical reaction. The relative ease of oxidation of common metals was discussed earlier, in Section 4.6. As we noted then, many metals are oxidized by a variety of common substances including O_2 and acids.

Figure 7.12 shows the charges of some common ions. As we noted in Section 2.5, the charges of the alkali metals are always $1+$ and those of the alkaline earth metals are always $2+$ in their compounds. For each of these families, the outer s electrons are easily lost, yielding a noble-gas electron configuration. The charges of the transition metal ions do not follow an obvious pattern. Many transition metal ions have $2+$ charges, but $1+$ and $3+$ are also encountered. One of the characteristic features of the transition metals is their ability to form more than one positive ion. For example, iron may be $2+$ in some compounds and $3+$ in others. We will consider the electron configurations of these ions in Section 8.2.

Compounds of metals with nonmetals tend to be ionic substances. For example, most metal oxides and halides are ionic solids. To illustrate, the reaction between nickel metal and oxygen produces nickel oxide, an ionic solid containing Ni^{2+} and O^{2-} ions:

$$2Ni(s) + O_2(g) \longrightarrow 2NiO(s) \qquad [7.4]$$

The oxides are particularly important because of the great abundance of oxygen in our environment.

Most metal oxides are *basic oxides;* those that dissolve in water react to form metal hydroxides, as in the following examples:

Figure 7.12

FIGURE 7.12 Charges of some common ions found in ionic compounds. Notice that the steplike line that divides metals from nonmetals also separates cations from anions. Ions shown in tan have the same number of electrons as the nearest noble-gas atom.

1A	2A	\ Transition metals \											3A	4A	5A	6A	7A	8A
H^+																	H^-	N O B L E G A S E S
Li^+															N^{3-}	O^{2-}	F^-	
Na^+	Mg^{2+}												Al^{3+}		P^{3-}	S^{2-}	Cl^-	
K^+	Ca^{2+}				Cr^{3+}	Mn^{2+}	Fe^{2+} Fe^{3+}	Co^{2+}	Ni^{2+}	Cu^+ Cu^{2+}	Zn^{2+}					Se^{2-}	Br^-	
Rb^+	Sr^{2+}									Ag^+	Cd^{2+}			Sn^{2+}		Te^{2-}	I^-	
Cs^+	Ba^{2+}								Pt^{2+}	Au^+ Au^{3+}	Hg_2^{2+} Hg^{2+}			Pb^{2+}	Bi^{3+}			

Metal oxide + water ⟶ metal hydroxide

$$Na_2O(s) + H_2O(l) \longrightarrow 2NaOH(aq) \qquad [7.5]$$

$$CaO(s) + H_2O(l) \longrightarrow Ca(OH)_2(aq) \qquad [7.6]$$

As noted in Section 4.5, metal oxides also demonstrate their basicity by reacting with acids to form salts and water:

Metal oxide + acid ⟶ salt + water

$$MgO(s) + 2HCl(aq) \longrightarrow MgCl_2(aq) + H_2O(l) \qquad [7.7]$$

$$NiO(s) + H_2SO_4(aq) \longrightarrow NiSO_4(aq) + H_2O(l) \qquad [7.8]$$

Ronald L. Rich, "Periodicity in the Acid-Base Behavior of Oxides and Hydroxides," *J. Chem. Educ.* **1985**, *62*, 44.

SAMPLE EXERCISE 7.3

(a) Write the chemical formula for aluminum oxide. (b) Would you expect this substance to be a solid, liquid, or gas at room temperature? (c) Write the balanced chemical equation for the reaction of aluminum oxide with nitric acid.

SOLUTION (a) In all its compounds, aluminum has a 3+ charge, Al^{3+}; the oxide ion is O^{2-}. Consequently, the chemical formula of aluminum oxide is Al_2O_3.

(b) Because aluminum oxide is the oxide of a metal, we would expect it to be a solid. Indeed it is, and it happens to have a very high melting point, 2072°C.

(c) Metal oxides generally react with acids to form salts and water. In this case the salt is aluminum nitrate, $Al(NO_3)_3$. The balanced equation is

$$Al_2O_3(s) + 6HNO_3(aq) \longrightarrow 2Al(NO_3)_3(aq) + 3H_2O(l)$$

PRACTICE EXERCISE

Write the balanced chemical equation for the reaction between copper(II) oxide and sulfuric acid.   ***Answer:*** $CuO(s) + H_2SO_4(aq) \longrightarrow CuSO_4(aq) + H_2O(l)$

Nonmetals

Nonmetals vary greatly in appearance (Figure 7.13). They are not lustrous and are generally poor conductors of heat and electricity. The melting points of

FIGURE 7.13 Nonmetals are very diverse in their appearances. Shown here are (left to right) sulfur, white phosphorus (stored under water), bromine, and carbon. (Dr. E. R. Degginger)

nonmetals are generally lower than those of metals (although diamond, a form of carbon, melts at 3570°C). Seven nonmetals exist under ordinary conditions as diatomic molecules. Included in this list are gases (H_2, N_2, O_2, F_2, and Cl_2), one liquid (Br_2), and one volatile solid (I_2). The remaining nonmetals are solids that can be hard like diamond or soft like sulfur.

Nonmetals, in reacting with metals, tend to gain electrons and become anions. For example, the reaction of aluminum with bromine produces aluminum bromide, an ionic compound containing the bromide ion, Br^-, and the aluminum ion, Al^{3+}:

$$\text{Metal} + \text{nonmetal} \longrightarrow \text{salt}$$

$$2Al(s) + 3Br_2(l) \longrightarrow 2AlBr_3(s) \qquad\qquad [7.9]$$

Notice in Figure 7.12 that the nonmetals commonly gain enough electrons to fill their outer p subshell completely, giving a noble-gas electron configuration.

SAMPLE EXERCISE 7.4

Predict the formulas of compounds formed between (a) Ba and Te; (b) Ga and Br.

SOLUTION (a) Notice the location of these elements in the periodic table. The charge on a barium ion is 2+; the charge on a tellurium ion (telluride) is 2−, like that of oxides and sulfides. Thus, the formula of the compound is BaTe. (b) Gallium is in group 3A. Like the more familiar aluminum ion, gallium forms a 3+ ion. Bromine forms a 1− ion (bromide). Thus, the formula is $GaBr_3$.

PRACTICE EXERCISE

Predict the formula of the compound formed by Rb and Se.   *Answer:* Rb_2Se

Compounds composed entirely of nonmetals are molecular substances. For example, the oxides, halides, and hydrides of the nonmetals are molecular substances that tend to be gases, liquids, or low-melting solids.

Most nonmetal oxides are *acidic oxides;* those that dissolve in water react to form acids, as in the following examples:

$$\text{Nonmetal oxide} + \text{water} \longrightarrow \text{acid}$$

$$CO_2(g) + H_2O(l) \longrightarrow H_2CO_3(aq) \qquad\qquad [7.10]$$

$$P_4O_{10}(s) + 6H_2O(l) \longrightarrow 4H_3PO_4(aq) \qquad\qquad [7.11]$$

The reaction of carbon dioxide with water (Figure 7.14) accounts for the acidity of carbonated water, and, to some extent, rainwater. Because sulfur is present in varying amounts in oil and coal, combustion of these common fuels produces sulfur dioxide and sulfur trioxide. These substances dissolve in water to produce *acid rain,* a major pollution problem in many parts of the world. The acidity of nonmetal oxides is also illustrated by the fact that they dissolve in basic solutions to form salts, as in the following examples:

$$\text{Nonmetal oxide} + \text{base} \longrightarrow \text{salt} + \text{water}$$

$$CO_2(g) + 2NaOH(aq) \longrightarrow Na_2CO_3(aq) + H_2O(l) \qquad\qquad [7.12]$$

$$SO_3(g) + 2KOH(aq) \longrightarrow K_2SO_4(aq) + H_2O(l) \qquad\qquad [7.13]$$

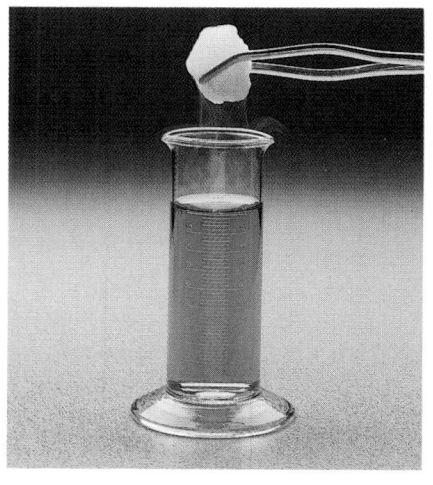
(a)

(b)

SAMPLE EXERCISE 7.5

Write the balanced chemical equations for the reactions of solid selenium dioxide with **(a)** water; **(b)** sodium hydroxide.

SOLUTION **(a)** Selenium dioxide is SeO_2. Its reaction with water is like that of carbon dioxide (Equation 7.10):

$$SeO_2(s) + H_2O(l) \longrightarrow H_2SeO_3(aq)$$

(It doesn't matter that SeO_2 is a solid and CO_2 is a gas; the point is that both are soluble nonmetal oxides.)

(b) The reaction with sodium hydroxide is like the reaction summarized by Equation 7.12:

$$SeO_2(s) + 2NaOH(aq) \longrightarrow Na_2SeO_3(aq) + H_2O(l)$$

PRACTICE EXERCISE

Write the balanced chemical equation for the reaction of tetraphosphorus hexoxide with water. **Answer:** $P_4O_6(s) + 6H_2O(l) \longrightarrow 4H_3PO_3(aq)$

Point of Emphasis: Metalloids have properties that are intermediate between metallic and nonmetallic.

Metalloids

Metalloids have properties intermediate between those of metals and nonmetals. They may have *some* characteristic metallic properties but lack others. For example, silicon *looks* like a metal (Figure 7.15), but it is brittle rather than malleable and is a much poorer conductor of heat and electricity than metals. Several of the metalloids, most notably silicon, are electrical semiconductors and are the principal elements used in the manufacture of integrated circuits and computer chips.

Trends in Metallic and Nonmetallic Character

The more fully an element exhibits the physical and chemical properties characteristic of metals, the greater its **metallic character.** Similarly, we can speak of the *nonmetallic character* of an element. Metallic and nonmetallic character exhibit some important periodic trends, summarized in Figure 7.16 and in the following list:

FIGURE 7.15 A large crystal of elemental silicon, which is a metalloid. Although it looks metallic, silicon is brittle and is a poor thermal and electrical conductor as compared to metals. Large crystals of ultrapure silicon are sliced into very thin wafers for use in integrated circuits. (Richard Megna/Fundamental Photographs)

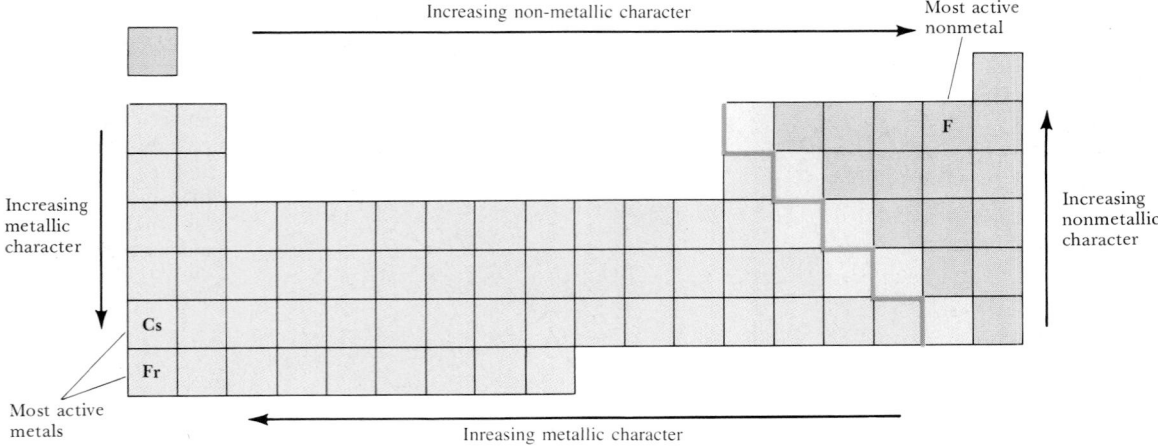

FIGURE 7.16 Periodic trends in metallic and nonmetallic character. Notice the positions of the most active metals and the most active nonmetal.

1. *Metallic character is strongest for the elements in the leftmost part of the periodic table and tends to decrease as we move to the right in any period.* For example, as we move across the fourth period from K to Kr, the ease with which each element loses electrons decreases. This is, of course, the same trend that we observed in the I_1 values for the elements. ∞ (Sec. 7.4) For the fourth period, K displays the greatest reactivity toward substances that readily accept electrons, such as oxygen.

2. *Within any group of representative elements, the metallic character increases progressively from top to bottom.* For example, Ba loses electrons more readily than Mg. This rule is generally not followed among the transition metals. The first-row transition metals are generally more active than those in the second or third rows. For example, Fe is a more active metal than Ru or Os.

   A decrease in metallic character corresponds to an increase in nonmetallic character. Thus, nonmetallic character increases moving from left to right across a period and decreases moving down a family.

Learning Goal 8: Write balanced equations for simple reactions between the active metals (groups 1A and 2A) and the nonmetals (groups 6A and 7A).

Learning Goal 9: Describe the general physical and chemical behavior of the alkali metals and alkaline earth metals, and explain how their chemistry relates to their position in the periodic table.

7.7 Group Trends: The Active Metals

Our discussion of atomic size, ionization energy, electron affinity, and metallic character gives some indication of the way the periodic table can be used to organize and remember facts. Not only do elements in a family possess general similarities, but there are also trends as we move through a family or from one family to another. In this section, we shall use the periodic table and our knowledge of electron configurations to examine the chemistry of the **alkali metals** (group 1A) and the **alkaline earth metals** (group 2A). In the following section, we shall look at the group trends in selected families of nonmetals.

Group 1A: The Alkali Metals

The alkali metals are soft, metallic solids (Figure 7.17). All have characteristic metallic properties such as a silvery, metallic luster and high thermal and electrical conductivities. The name *alkali* comes from an Arabic word meaning "ashes." Many compounds of sodium and potassium, the two most abundant alkali metals, were isolated from wood ashes by early chemists. The names soda ash and potash are still sometimes used for the carbonate salts Na_2CO_3 and K_2CO_3, respectively.

Some of the physical and chemical properties of the alkali metals are given in Table 7.5. Notice that the elements have low densities and melting points and that these properties vary in a fairly regular way with increasing atomic number. We can also see some of the expected trends as we move down the family, such as increasing atomic radius and decreasing first ionization energy. The alkali metals have the lowest I_1 values of the elements (Figure 7.7), which reflects the relative ease with which their outer s electron can be removed. As a result, the alkali metals are all very reactive, readily losing one electron to form ions with a $1+$ charge:

$$M \longrightarrow M^+ + e^- \qquad [7.14]$$

(The symbol M in this equation and others represents any one of the alkali metals.) The alkali metals are the most active metals (Section 4.6) and thus exist

1A
3 Li
11 Na
19 K
37 Rb
55 Cs
87 Fr

Joseph D. Ciparick and Richard F. Jones, "A Variation on the Demonstration of the Properties of the Alkali Metals," *J. Chem. Educ.* **1989,** *66, 438.*

TABLE 7.5 △ Some Properties of the Alkali Metals

Element	Electron configuration	Melting point (°C)	Density (g/cm³)	Atomic radius (Å)	I_1 (kJ/mol)
Lithium	[He]$2s^1$	181	0.53	1.52	520
Sodium	[Ne]$3s^1$	98	0.97	1.86	496
Potassium	[Ar]$4s^1$	63	0.86	2.27	419
Rubidium	[Kr]$5s^1$	39	1.53	2.48	403
Cesium	[Xe]$6s^1$	29	1.90	2.65	376

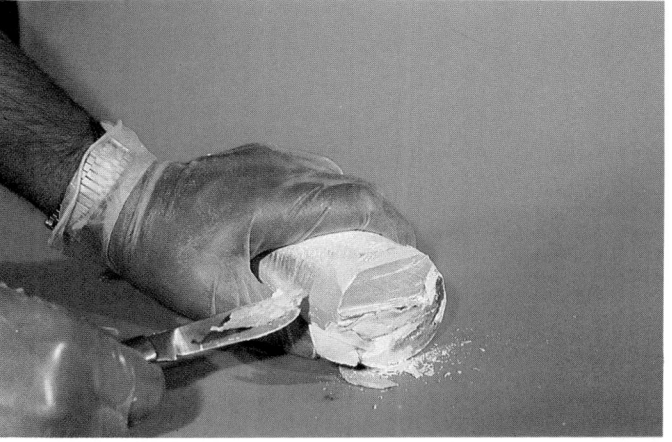

FIGURE 7.17 Sodium and the other alkali metals are soft. Here we see sodium being cut with a knife. The shiny metallic surface quickly tarnishes as the metal reacts with oxygen in the air. (H. E. LeMay, Jr.)

Point of Emphasis: *Electrolysis* is the process by which passing an electrical current through a substance causes a reaction.

in nature only as compounds. The metals can be obtained by passing an electric current through a molten salt, a process known as *electrolysis.* For example, sodium is prepared commercially by the electrolysis of molten NaCl. The electrical energy is used to remove electrons from Cl^- ions and to force them onto Na^+ ions:

$$2Cl^- \longrightarrow Cl_2 + 2e^- \qquad [7.15]$$

$$2Na^+ + 2e^- \longrightarrow 2Na \qquad [7.16]$$

We will discuss electrolysis in detail in Chapter 20.

Learning Goal 10: Write balanced equations for the reaction of hydrogen with metals to form metal hydrides.

Not surprisingly, the chemistry of the alkali metals is dominated by their tendency to lose an electron, thus forming a $1+$ cation (Equation 7.14). The metals combine directly with most nonmetals. For example, they react with hydrogen to form solid hydrides, with sulfur to form solid sulfides, and with chlorine to form solid chlorides:

$$2M(s) + H_2(g) \longrightarrow 2MH(s) \qquad [7.17]$$

$$2M(s) + S(s) \longrightarrow M_2S(s) \qquad [7.18]$$

$$2M(s) + Cl_2(g) \longrightarrow 2MCl(s) \qquad [7.19]$$

Point of Emphasis: Hydride is the anion of hydrogen, H^-. It has the electron configuration $1s^2$. The formation of an anion is one of the properties of hydrogen that makes it different from the alkali metals, with which it is often grouped.

In the hydrides of the alkali metals (LiH, NaH, and so forth), hydrogen is present as H^-, called the **hydride ion**. The hydride ion is to be distinguished from the hydrogen ion, H^+, formed when a hydrogen atom loses its electron.

The alkali metals react vigorously with water, producing hydrogen gas and solutions of alkali metal hydroxides:

$$2M(s) + 2H_2O(l) \longrightarrow 2MOH(aq) + H_2(g) \qquad [7.20]$$

These reactions are very exothermic. In many cases, enough heat is generated to ignite the H_2, producing a fire or explosion (Figure 7.18). This reaction is most violent in the case of the heavier members of the family, in keeping with their weaker hold on the single outer-shell electron.

The reactions between the alkali metals and oxygen are more complex. When oxygen reacts with metals, metal oxides, which contain the O^{2-} ion, are usually formed. Indeed, lithium shows this reactivity:

$$4Li(s) + O_2(g) \longrightarrow 2Li_2O(s) \qquad [7.21]$$
$$\text{lithium oxide}$$

In contrast, the other alkali metals all form metal peroxides, which contain the O_2^{2-} ion. For example,

$$2Na(s) + O_2(g) \longrightarrow Na_2O_2(s) \qquad [7.22]$$
$$\text{sodium peroxide}$$

Potassium, rubidium, and cesium also form compounds that contain the O_2^- ion, called superoxides:

$$K(s) + O_2(g) \longrightarrow KO_2(s) \qquad [7.23]$$
$$\text{potassium superoxide}$$

FIGURE 7.18 Potassium reacts so vigorously with water that the hydrogen evolved bursts into flame. The pink color of the acid-base indicator phenolphthalein indicates the presence of OH⁻ ions generated during the reaction. (Richard Megna/Fundamental Photographs)

You should realize that the reactions shown in Equations 7.22 and 7.23 are somewhat surprising; in most cases, the reaction of oxygen with a metal forms the metal oxide.

As is evident from Equations 7.20 through 7.23, the alkali metals are extremely reactive toward water and oxygen. Because of this, the metals are usually stored under a hydrocarbon, such as kerosene or mineral oil.

Alkali metal salts and their aqueous solutions are colorless unless they contain a colored anion like the yellow CrO_4^{2-}. Color is produced when an electron in an atom is excited from one energy level to another by visible radiation. Alkali metal ions, having lost their outermost electrons, have no electrons that can be excited by visible radiation.

When alkali metal compounds are placed in a flame, they emit characteristic colors, as shown in Figure 7.19. The alkali metal ions are reduced to

FIGURE 7.19 Flame test for (a) Li (crimson red), (b) Na (yellow), and (c) K (lilac). (H. E. LeMay, Jr.)

(a)

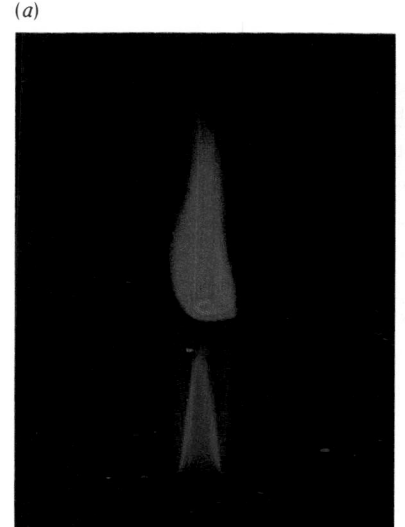

(b)

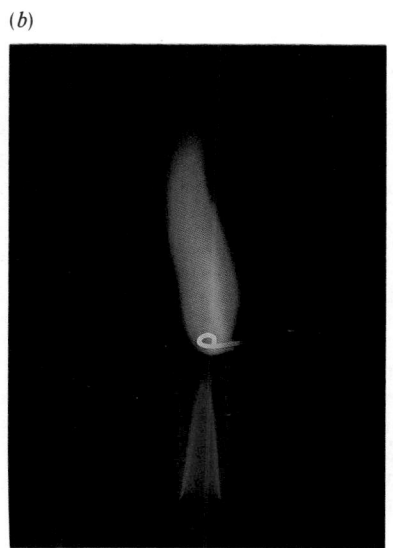

(c)

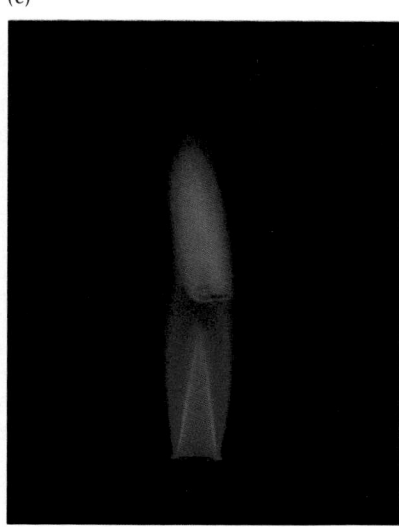

gaseous metal atoms in the lower, central region of the flame. The atoms are electronically excited by the high temperature of the flame; they then emit energy in the form of visible light as they return to the ground state. For example, sodium gives a yellow flame due to emission at 589 nm. This wavelength is produced by transition of the excited valence electron from the $3p$ to the $3s$ subshell.

SAMPLE EXERCISE 7.6

Write balanced chemical equations for the reactions of cesium with **(a)** $H_2(g)$; **(b)** $Cl_2(g)$; **(c)** $H_2O(l)$.

SOLUTION By analogy to the equations above, we have

$$2Cs(s) + H_2(g) \longrightarrow 2CsH(s)$$
$$2Cs(s) + Cl_2(g) \longrightarrow 2CsCl(s)$$
$$2Cs(s) + 2H_2O(l) \longrightarrow 2CsOH(aq) + H_2(g)$$

In each case, cesium forms a $1+$ ion in its compounds, Cs^+. The hydride ion, chloride ion, and hydroxide ion all have $1-$ charges: H^-, Cl^-, and OH^-

PRACTICE EXERCISE

Solid sodium hydride reacts with water to form an aqueous solution of sodium hydroxide and hydrogen gas. Write a balanced chemical equation for this reaction. ***Answer:*** $NaH(s) + H_2O(l) \longrightarrow NaOH(aq) + H_2(g)$

Group 2A: The Alkaline Earth Metals

2A
4   Be
12   Mg
20   Ca
38   Sr
56   Ba
88   Ra

Like the alkali metals, the group 2A elements are all solids with typical metallic properties, some of which are listed in Table 7.6. Compared with the alkali metals, the alkaline earth metals are harder, are more dense, and melt at higher temperatures.

The first ionization energies of the alkaline earth elements are low, but not as low as those of the alkali metals. Consequently, the alkaline earths are less reactive than their alkali metal neighbors. As we have noted in Section 7.4, the ease with which the elements lose electrons decreases as we move across the periodic table from left to right and increases as we move down a family. Thus, beryllium and magnesium, the lightest members of the family, are the least reactive.

The trend of increasing reactivity within the family is illustrated by the behavior of the elements toward water. Beryllium does not react with water or steam, even when heated red hot. Although magnesium does not react with liquid water, it does react with steam to form magnesium oxide and hydrogen:

TABLE 7.6 △ **Some Properties of the Alkaline Earth Metals**

Element	Electron configuration	Melting point (°C)	Density (g/cm³)	Atomic radius (Å)	I_1 (kJ/mol)
Beryllium	[He]$2s^2$	1287	1.85	1.12	899
Magnesium	[Ne]$3s^2$	649	1.74	1.60	738
Calcium	[Ar]$4s^2$	839	1.55	1.97	590
Strontium	[Kr]$5s^2$	768	2.63	2.15	549
Barium	[Xe]$6s^2$	727	3.62	2.22	503

CHEMISTRY AND LIFE

$$Mg(s) + H_2O(g) \longrightarrow MgO(s) + H_2(g) \qquad [7.24]$$

Calcium and the elements below it react readily with water at room temperature (although more slowly than the alkali metals adjacent to them in the periodic table), as shown in Figure 7.20:

$$Ca(s) + 2H_2O(l) \longrightarrow Ca(OH)_2(aq) + H_2(g) \qquad [7.25]$$

The above two reactions are illustrative of the dominant pattern in the reactivity of the alkaline earth elements—the tendency to lose their two outer s electrons and form $2+$ ions. For example, magnesium reacts with chlorine at room temperature to form $MgCl_2$, and it burns with dazzling brilliance in air to give MgO (Figure 3.6):

$$Mg(s) + Cl_2(g) \longrightarrow MgCl_2(s) \qquad [7.26]$$
$$2Mg(s) + O_2(g) \longrightarrow 2MgO(s) \qquad [7.27]$$

In the presence of O_2, magnesium metal is protected from many chemicals by a thin surface coating of water-insoluble MgO. Thus, even though it is high in the activity series (Section 4.6), Mg can be incorporated into lightweight structural alloys used in, for example, automobile wheels (so-called mag wheels). The heavier alkaline earth metals (Ca, Sr, and Ba) are even more reactive toward nonmetals than magnesium and must be stored in such a way as to protect them from oxidation by O_2 and H_2O.

Like the $1+$ ions of the alkali metals, the $2+$ ions of the alkaline earth elements have a noble-gas electron configuration. As such, they form colorless or white compounds unless they are combined with a colored anion. The heavier alkaline earths have characteristic flames. The calcium flame is brick red, strontium is crimson red, and barium is green. The strontium flame produces the familiar red color of flares and fireworks.

FIGURE 7.20 Calcium metal reacts with water to form hydrogen gas and calcium hydroxide, $Ca(OH)_2$. (Dr. E. R. Degginger)

7.8 Group Trends: Selected Nonmetals

Hydrogen

Teaching Note: Due to the fact that hydrogen shares little in common with the other members of group 1A other than outer-shell electron configuration and common cationic charge, some sources have placed hydrogen by itself above the center of the periodic table.

Learning Goal 11: Write balanced equations for the reaction of hydrogen with nonmetals such as oxygen and chlorine.

The first element in the periodic table, hydrogen, has a $1s^1$ electron configuration and is usually placed above the alkali metals. However, it is a unique element and does not truly belong to any family. Hydrogen is a nonmetal that occurs as a colorless diatomic gas, $H_2(g)$, under most conditions. Whereas the chlorides and oxides of metals tend to be solids at room temperature, HCl is a gas, and H_2O is a liquid.

Owing to the complete absence of nuclear shielding of its sole electron, the ionization energy of hydrogen, 1312 kJ/mol, is markedly higher than that of the active metals. In fact, it is comparable to I_1 of other nonmetals, such as oxygen and chlorine. Hydrogen generally reacts with other nonmetals to form molecular compounds. These reactions can be quite exothermic, as evidenced by the combustion reaction between hydrogen and oxygen to form water:

$$2H_2(g) + O_2(g) \longrightarrow 2H_2O(l) \qquad \Delta H° = -571.7 \text{ kJ} \qquad [7.28]$$

We have also seen that hydrogen reacts with active metals to form solid metal hydrides, which contain the H^- ion. For example,

$$2Na(s) + H_2(g) \longrightarrow 2NaH(s) \qquad [7.29]$$

$$Ca(s) + H_2(g) \longrightarrow CaH_2(s) \qquad [7.30]$$

Teaching Note: The historical name for group 6A is the *chalcogens* (KAL-ke-jens), meaning "chalk formers."

The aqueous chemistry of hydrogen, which was introduced in Chapter 4, is dominated by the $H^+(aq)$ ion. We shall take up its study in detail in Chapter 16.

Group 6A: The Oxygen Family

As we proceed down group 6A, the increase in metallic character is clearly evident. Oxygen is a colorless gas at room temperature; all of the others are solids. Oxygen, sulfur, and selenium are typical nonmetals. Tellurium has some metallic properties and is classified as a metalloid. Polonium, which is radioactive and quite rare, is a metal. Some of the physical properties of the group 6A elements are given in Table 7.7.

As we saw in Section 2.5, oxygen is encountered in two molecular forms, O_2 and O_3. The O_2 form is the common one. People generally mean O_2 when they say "oxygen," although the name *dioxygen* is more descriptive. O_3 is called **ozone**. The two forms of oxygen are examples of **allotropes**. Allotropes are

TABLE 7.7 △ Some Properties of the Group 6A Elements

Element	Electron configuration	Melting point (°C)	Density	Atomic radius (Å)	I_1 (kJ/mol)
Oxygen	$[He]2s^22p^4$	−219	1.43 g/L	0.73	1314
Sulfur	$[Ne]3s^23p^4$	112	2.07 g/cm³	1.03	999
Selenium	$[Ar]4s^23d^{10}4p^4$	217	4.79 g/cm³	1.40	941
Tellurium	$[Kr]5s^24d^{10}5p^4$	452	6.24 g/cm³	1.60	869
Polonium	$[Xe]6s^24f^{14}5d^{10}6p^4$	254	9.32 g/cm³	1.64	813

different forms of the same element in the same state (in this case, both forms are gases). About 21 percent of dry air consists of O_2 molecules. Ozone, which is toxic and has a pungent odor, is present in very small amounts in the upper atmosphere and in polluted air. It is also formed from O_2 in electrical discharges, such as in lightning storms and around electrical machinery:

Learning Goal 12: Describe the allotropy of oxygen.

Bassam Z. Shakhashiri, "Preparation and Properties of Oxygen," *Chemical Demonstrations: A Handbook for Teachers of Chemistry, Volume 2* (Madison: The University of Wisconsin Press, 1985), pp. 137–41.

$$3O_2(g) \longrightarrow 2O_3(g) \qquad \Delta H° = 284.6 \text{ kJ} \qquad [7.31]$$

As indicated by the endothermic nature of this reaction, ozone is less stable than O_2.

Oxygen has a great tendency to attract electrons from other elements (in other words, to *oxidize* them). As we have discussed, oxygen in combination with metals is almost always present as the oxide, O^{2-}, ion. This ion has a noble-gas configuration and is particularly stable. As shown in Equation 7.28, the formation of nonmetal oxides is also often very exothermic and thus energetically favorable.

Learning Goal 13: Explain the dominant chemical reactions of oxygen, and relate this behavior to its position in the periodic table.

In our discussion of the alkali metals, we noted two less common oxygen anions, namely, the peroxide, O_2^{2-}, and superoxide, O_2^-, ions. Compounds of these ions often react with themselves to produce an oxide and O_2. For example, aqueous hydrogen peroxide, H_2O_2, slowly decomposes into water and O_2 at room temperature:

Point of Emphasis: Other than when combined with fluorine or in the peroxide anion (O_2^{2-}) or the superoxide anion (O_2^-), oxygen forms a divalent anion (O^{2-}), called *oxide.*

$$2H_2O_2(aq) \longrightarrow 2H_2O(l) + O_2(g) \qquad \Delta H° = -196.1 \text{ kJ} \qquad [7.32]$$

For this reason, bottles of aqueous hydrogen peroxide are topped with caps that are able to release the $O_2(g)$ produced before the pressure inside becomes too great (Figure 7.21).

After oxygen, the most important member of group 6A is sulfur. Sulfur also exists in several allotropic forms, the most common and stable of which is

FIGURE 7.21 Hydrogen peroxide bottles are topped with caps that "don't fit right." The cap allows any excess pressure of $O_2(g)$ to be released from the bottle. Hydrogen peroxide is often stored in dark-colored or opaque bottles to minimize exposure to light, which accelerates its decomposition. (Richard Megna/ Fundamental Photographs)

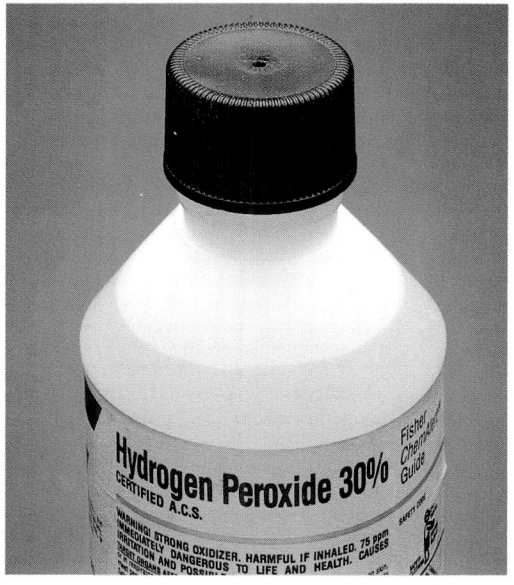

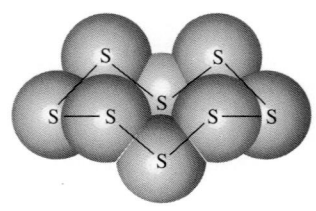

FIGURE 7.22 Structure of S_8 molecules as found in the most common allotropic form of sulfur at room temperature.

the yellow solid with molecular formula S_8. This molecule consists of an eight-membered ring of sulfur atoms, as shown in Figure 7.22.

Like oxygen, sulfur has a tendency to gain electrons from other elements to form sulfides, which contain the S^{2-} ion. This is particularly true for the active metals, as in the example of sodium metal reacting with $S_8(s)$:

$$16Na(s) + S_8(s) \longrightarrow 8Na_2S(s) \qquad [7.33]$$

Most sulfur in nature is present as metal sulfide compounds. Because sulfur is below oxygen in the periodic table, its tendency to form sulfide anions is not as great as that of oxygen to form oxide ions. As a result, the chemistry of sulfur is more complex and varied than that of oxygen. In fact, sulfur or sulfur-containing compounds (including those in coal and petroleum) can be burned in oxygen, yielding mainly sulfur dioxide:

$$S_8(s) + 8O_2(g) \longrightarrow 8SO_2(g) \qquad [7.34]$$

As we shall discuss further in Chapter 18, SO_2 is one of the principal air pollutants and is the major cause of acid rain.

Group 7A: The Halogens

7A

| 9 F |
| 17 Cl |
| 35 Br |
| 53 I |
| 85 At |

The group 7A elements are known as the **halogens,** after the Greek words *halos* and *gennao,* meaning "salt formers." Some of the properties of these elements are given in Table 7.8. Astatine, which is both extremely rare and radioactive, is omitted because many of its properties are not yet known.

As we move from group 6A to group 7A, the nonmetallic behavior of the elements increases, as we would expect. Unlike the group 6A elements, all the halogens are typical nonmetals. Their melting and boiling points increase with increasing atomic number. Fluorine and chlorine are gases at room temperature, bromine is a liquid, and iodine is a solid. Each element consists of diatomic molecules: F_2, Cl_2, Br_2, and I_2. Fluorine gas is pale yellow; chlorine gas has a yellow-green color; bromine liquid is reddish brown and readily forms a reddish-brown vapor; and solid iodine is grayish black and readily forms a violet vapor (Figure 7.23).

The halogens have among the most negative electron affinities (Figure 7.9). Thus, it is not surprising that the chemistry of the halogens is dominated by their tendency to gain electrons from other elements to form halide ions:

$$X_2 + 2e^- \longrightarrow 2X^- \qquad [7.35]$$

TABLE 7.8 △ Some Properties of the Halogens

Element	Electron configuration	Melting point (°C)	Density	Atomic radius (Å)	I_1 (kJ/mol)
Fluorine	[He]$2s^22p^5$	−219	1.81 g/L	0.72	1681
Chlorine	[Ne]$3s^23p^5$	−101	3.21 g/L	0.99	1256
Bromine	[Ar]$4s^23d^{10}4p^5$	−7.3	3.19 g/cm³	1.14	1143
Iodine	[Kr]$5s^24d^{10}5p^5$	114	4.94 g/cm³	1.33	1009

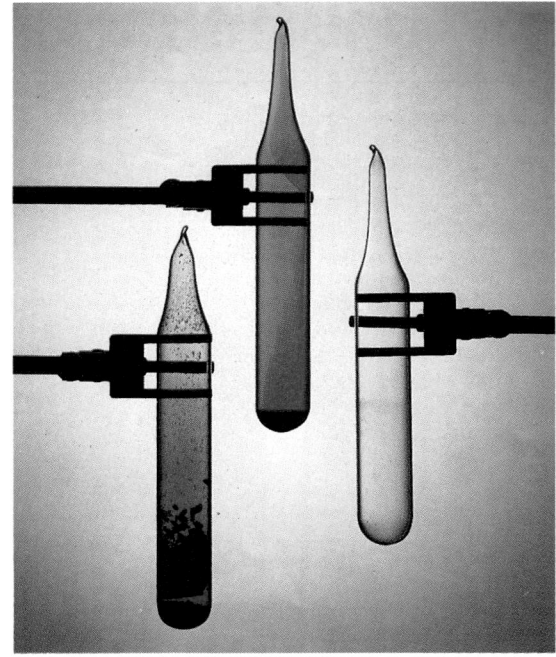

FIGURE 7.23 Chlorine, Cl_2 (right), is a greenish-yellow gas at room temperature and at ordinary pressure. Bromine, Br_2 (middle), is a reddish-brown liquid that vaporizes readily to form a vapor of the same color. (Notice the dark liquid below the vapor.) Iodine, I_2 (left), is a grayish-black solid that readily vaporizes (sublimes) to form a violet vapor. (Notice the dark solid below the vapor.) (Dr. E. R. Degginger)

(In this and subsequent equations, X indicates any one of the halogen elements.) Fluorine and chlorine are more reactive than bromine and iodine. In fact, fluorine removes electrons from almost any substance with which it comes into contact, including water, and usually does so very exothermically, as in the following examples:

$$2Na(s) + F_2(g) \longrightarrow 2NaF(s) \qquad\qquad \Delta H° = -1147 \text{ kJ} \qquad [7.36]$$

$$2H_2O(l) + 2F_2(g) \longrightarrow 4HF(aq) + O_2(g) \qquad \Delta H° = -758.7 \text{ kJ} \qquad [7.37]$$

As a result, fluorine gas is difficult and dangerous to use, requiring special apparatus.

Chlorine is the most industrially useful of the halogens. In 1992, total production was 22.3 billion pounds, making it the tenth most produced chemical in the United States. Chlorine is usually produced by the electrolysis of molten NaCl (Equations 7.15 and 7.16) or by the electrolysis of *brine,* a concentrated aqueous solution of NaCl:

$$2NaCl(aq) + 2H_2O(l) \xrightarrow{\text{electricity}} 2NaOH(aq) + H_2(g) + Cl_2(aq) \qquad [7.38]$$

Unlike fluorine, chlorine reacts slowly with water to form relatively stable aqueous solutions of HCl and HOCl (hypochlorous acid):

$$Cl_2(g) + H_2O(l) \longrightarrow HCl(aq) + HOCl(aq) \qquad [7.39]$$

Chlorine is often added to drinking water and swimming pools, where the HOCl(aq) that is generated serves as a disinfectant.

Discovery of the Noble Gases

None of the noble gases was known when Mendeleev proposed his periodic table. Their discovery created considerable scientific controversy but proved invaluable in understanding chemical behavior. The first significant hint of their existence was obtained during the early 1890s in the laboratories of the British physicist Lord Rayleigh. Rayleigh was involved in a program of making exact measurements of the densities of simple gases. During his studies he discovered a discrepancy between the densities of nitrogen obtained from air and nitrogen obtained from chemical reactions, as in the decomposition of ammonia:

$$2NH_3(g) \longrightarrow N_2(g) + 3H_2(g)$$

FIGURE 7.24 Sir William Ramsay (1852–1916), from the *Vanity Fair* series of caricatures. He was one of the principals in the discovery and study of the noble gases. He was awarded the Nobel Prize in chemistry in 1904 for this work. (The Granger Collection)

When all the other gases then known were removed from air, the remaining nitrogen was found to have a density of 1.2572 g/L at 0°C and standard atmospheric pressure. However, the density of nitrogen from chemical sources was found to be 1.2506 g/L under the same conditions. The difference was slight but reproducible. In April 1894, Rayleigh published a paper devoted entirely to the matter of the densities of nitrogen from the two sources. This report excited the interest of the British chemist Sir William Ramsay (Figure 7.24), who began to study the atmospheric nitrogen.

Rayleigh and Ramsay deduced that air must contain a previously unidentified component. They were able to isolate small quantities of this substance and measure some of its properties. The gas was composed of a new element with an atomic weight of 39.95 amu, which presented some problems in placing the element in the periodic table. Based on its atomic weight, the element would fall between potassium (K) and calcium (Ca), but this placement made no chemical sense. The scientists met with a second surprise: The element had no chemical reactivity. Try as they may, they were unable to form any compounds of the element. They consequently named the element *argon,* which means "the lazy one" in Greek.

Rayleigh and Ramsay publicly announced the discovery of argon in August 1894. Chemists found the existence of this curious element hard to believe, and many ingenious but erroneous alternative proposals were put forth for its identity. In January 1895, Ramsay presented a paper on the discovery of argon before the Royal Society. Over 800 people assembled to hear him.

Later that same year, Ramsay isolated helium (He), the lightest of the noble gases, from uranium ores. The helium in these ores forms when alpha particles produced in radioactive decay (Section 2.2) pick up electrons. During the spring and summer of 1898, Ramsay and his coworkers isolated three additional noble gases from air: neon (Ne), krypton (Kr), and xenon (Xe). The discovery of these elements contributed to a partial resolution of the problem of argon's location in the periodic table. Clearly, there is an entire family of elements whose most obvious characteristic is their lack of chemical reactivity. The atomic weights of family members other than argon placed them after the halogens, a position that made chemical sense. The apparent problem of argon's position in the periodic table was finally resolved by Moseley's work (Section 7.1), which led to arranging elements by their atomic numbers.

The halogens react directly with most metals to form ionic halides. The halogens also react with hydrogen to form gaseous hydrogen halide compounds:

$$H_2(g) + X_2 \longrightarrow 2HX(g) \qquad [7.40]$$

These compounds are all very soluble in water and dissolve to form the hydrohalic acids. As we discussed in Section 4.3, HCl(*aq*), HBr(*aq*), and HI(*aq*) are strong acids, whereas HF(*aq*) is a weak acid.

Group 8A: The Noble Gases

8A

The group 8A elements, known as the **noble gases,** are all nonmetals that are gases at room temperature. They are all *monoatomic* (that is, they consist of single atoms rather than molecules). Some physical properties of the noble-gas elements are given in Table 7.9. The high radioactivity of Rn has inhibited the study of its chemistry.

The noble gases are characterized by completely filled s and p subshells. All elements of group 8A have large first ionization energies, and we see the expected decrease as we move down the column. Because the noble gases possess such stable electron configurations, they are exceptionally unreactive. In fact, until the early 1960s the elements were called the *inert gases* because they were thought to be incapable of forming chemical compounds. In 1962, Neil Bartlett at the University of British Columbia reasoned that the ionization energy of Xe might be low enough to allow it to form compounds. In order for this to happen, Xe would have to react with a substance with an extremely high ability to remove electrons from other substances, such as fluorine. Bartlett synthesized the first noble-gas compound by reacting Xe with the fluorine-containing compound PtF_6. Xenon also reacts directly with $F_2(g)$ to form the molecular compounds XeF_2, XeF_4, and XeF_6 (Figure 7.25). Krypton has a higher I_1 value than xenon and is therefore less reactive. In fact, only a single stable compound of krypton is known, KrF_2. No compounds of He, Ne, or Ar are yet known; they still warrant the label "inert."

8A
2 He
10 Ne
18 Ar
36 Kr
54 Xe
86 Rn

Point of Emphasis: The noble gases are the only elements that are stable in the form of monatomic gases.

Learning Goal 15: Explain the very low chemical reactivity of the noble gas elements.

TABLE 7.9 △ Some Properties of the Noble Gases

Element	Electron configuration	Boiling point (K)	Density (g/L)	Atomic radius (Å)	I_1 (kJ/mol)
Helium	$1s^2$	4.2	0.18	0.53	2372
Neon	$[He]2s^22p^6$	27.1	0.90	0.71	2080
Argon	$[Ne]3s^23p^6$	87.3	1.78	0.98	1520
Krypton	$[Ar]4s^23d^{10}4p^6$	120	3.75	1.12	1351
Xenon	$[Kr]5s^24d^{10}5p^6$	165	5.90	1.31	1170
Radon	$[Xe]6s^24f^{14}5d^{10}6p^6$	211	9.73	—	1037

FIGURE 7.25 Crystals of XeF_4. (Argonne National Laboratory)

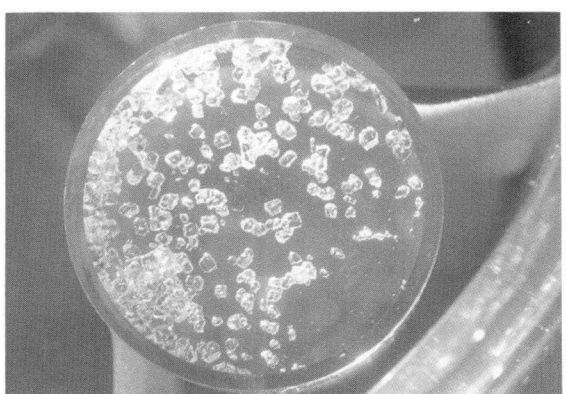

For Review

Summary

Many properties of atoms exhibit periodic character. Among the most important of these are atomic radii, ionization energy, and electron affinity. Electron configurations and the periodic table help us understand the trends in these properties. In general, atomic radii increase as we go down a column and decrease as we proceed left to right in a row. Ionization energies show exactly the opposite behavior: They tend to decrease as we move down a column and increase as we proceed from left to right in a row.

There is also periodicity in the classification of the elements as metals, nonmetals, or metalloids. Most elements are metals; they occupy the left side and the middle of the periodic table. Nonmetals appear in the upper-right section of the table. Metalloids occupy a narrow band between the metals and nonmetals.

Metals have a characteristic luster. They are good electrical and thermal conductors. Metals tend to transfer electrons to other substances to form cations when they react. The compounds of metals with nonmetals, such as the oxides, hydrides, and chlorides, are mostly ionic solids. Metal oxides are basic; they react with acids to form salts and water.

Nonmetals lack metallic luster. Several are gases at room temperature. When nonmetals react with metals, the nonmetal generally gains electrons from the metal to become an anion. Compounds composed entirely of nonmetals are molecular; thus, the oxides, hydrides, and chlorides of the nonmetals are usually gases, liquids, or solids that melt at low temperatures. Nonmetal oxides are acidic; they tend to react with bases to form salts and water.

Metallic character increases as we move down a family of representative elements; it also increases moving to the left in any period. Metallic character is strongest for elements at the bottom left of the periodic table; nonmetallic character is greatest for elements in the upper right.

We use electron configurations to help understand many of the chemical and physical properties of families of the representative elements. The alkali metals (group 1A) are soft metals of low density that melt at low temperatures. They have the lowest ionization energies of the elements. As a result, they are very reactive, easily losing their outer s electron to give $1+$ ions. The metals in group 2A, the alkaline earth metals, are harder, are more dense, and melt at higher temperatures than the alkali metals. They are also very reactive, readily losing their two outer s electrons to yield $2+$ ions.

Hydrogen is a nonmetal and exists as a diatomic molecule, H_2. Hydrogen tends to form molecular compounds with other nonmetals, such as oxygen or the halogens. Hydrogen also reacts with active metals to give metal hydrides, ionic compounds that contain the H^- ion. Oxygen and sulfur are the most important of the group 6A elements. Oxygen is usually found as a diatomic molecule, O_2. Ozone, O_3, is an important allotrope of oxygen. Oxygen has a strong tendency to take electrons from other substances, hence oxidizing them. In combination with metals, oxygen is usually found as the oxide ion, O^{2-}. Alkali metal peroxides and superoxides are formed on reaction of the heavier alkali metals with O_2. Sulfur is most commonly found as S_8 molecules.

The group 7A elements are the halogens. They are all nonmetals that exist as diatomic molecules. The halogens have the highest electron affinities of the elements. As a result, their chemistry is dominated by their tendency to gain an electron to form $1-$ ions.

The members of group 8A are called the noble gases. They are characterized by completely filled s and p subshells, which are very stable electron configurations. As a result, the noble gases exhibit very low chemical reactivity, and only the heavier members of the family—Kr, Xe, and Rn—form compounds.

Key Terms

valence orbitals
atomic radius (Sec. 7.3)

ionization energy (Sec. 7.4)
electron affinity (Sec. 7.5)

metallic character (Sec. 7.6)
alkali metals (Sec. 7.7)
alkaline earth metals (Sec. 7.7)
hydride ion (Sec. 7.7)

ozone (Sec. 7.8)
allotropes (Sec. 7.8)
halogens (Sec. 7.8)
noble gases (Sec. 7.8)

Exercises

Periodic Table; Electron Shells

7.1. **(a)** What was the basis on which Mendeleev constructed his periodic table? **(b)** What was Moseley's contribution to the development of the periodic table?

7.2. Why did Mendeleev leave blanks in his table? How did he predict the properties of the elements that belonged in these blanks?

7.3. How can a plot of the radial electron density of an atom be used to determine the number of electron shells in the atom?

7.4. Sketch the radial electron-density graph (like that in Figure 7.4) for Kr.

7.5. Arrange the following atoms in order of increasing distance of the $n = 3$ shell from the nucleus: Ti, Rh, P, K, and Mg.

7.6. Why is the $n = 2$ electron shell in neon closer to the nucleus than the same shell in carbon?

Sizes of Atoms

7.7. Why does the quantum-mechanical description of many-electron atoms make it difficult to define the term *atomic radius?*

7.8. What assumptions are made in assigning radii to atoms?

7.9. The distance between chlorine atoms in Cl_2 is 1.99 Å; the P—Cl distance in PCl_3 is 2.04 Å. Based on these distances, determine the atomic radii of Cl and P.

7.10. The distance between fluorine atoms in F_2 is 1.42 Å; the N—F distance in NF_3 is 1.37 Å. Based on these distances, determine the atomic radii of F and N.

7.11. How do atomic radii change as we move **(a)** from left to right in the periodic table? **(b)** From top to bottom in

a group in the periodic table? **(c)** Arrange the following atoms in order of increasing atomic radius: B, Al, Si, and Ge.

7.12. By referring to the periodic table, arrange the following atoms in order of increasing atomic size: **(a)** Mg, F, P, O and Ca; **(b)** In, Ar, Rb, Ge, and He.

7.13. Why does the He atom have a smaller atomic radius than the hydrogen atom? Why is the He atom smaller than the Ne atom?

7.14. Why do the sizes of atoms change as we move **(a)** from left to right in the periodic table? **(b)** From top to bottom in a group in the periodic table?

Ionization Energies; Electron Affinities

7.15. Write equations that show the processes corresponding to the second and third ionization energies of a scandium atom.

7.16. The fourth ionization energy of sulfur is 4565 kJ/mol. Write the chemical equation that corresponds to this energy.

7.17. Why is the second ionization energy of lithium much greater than that of beryllium?

7.18. Why is the second ionization energy of K much greater than its first ionization energy?

7.19. Based on their positions in the periodic table, select the atom with the larger first ionization energy from each of the following pairs: **(a)** B, F; **(b)** N, P; **(c)** Hf, Cs; **(d)** O, P; **(e)** Ga, Ge.

7.20. For each of the following pairs, indicate which element has the larger first ionization energy: **(a)** P, Cl; **(b)** Al, Ga; **(c)** Cs, La; **(d)** Si, N. In each case provide an explanation in terms of electron configuration and effective nuclear charge.

7.21. What is the trend in first ionization energies as you proceed across the fourth period from K to Kr? How does this compare with the trend in atomic sizes?

7.22. What is the trend in first ionization energies as you proceed down the group 8A elements? How does this compare with the trend in atomic sizes?

7.23. Is the effective nuclear charge operating on the $3s$ electron greater in Al^{2+} or in Si^{3+}? How do the data in Table 7.2 provide support for your answer?

7.24. Although SiO_2—which can be thought of as containing Si^{4+} ions—is common, AlO_2 is not a known compound. Explain this fact in terms of the data in Table 7.2.

7.25. The addition of an electron to Cl is an exothermic process. In contrast, addition of an electron to Ar is an endothermic process. Account for this difference in terms of the electron configurations of the two elements.

7.26. Addition of an electron to Na(g) is a slightly exothermic process, whereas addition of an electron to Mg(g) is strongly endothermic. Explain this difference in terms of the electron configurations of the two elements.

Properties of Metals and Nonmetals

7.27. Use the periodic table to arrange the following pure, solid elements in order of increasing electrical conductivity at room temperature: Ge, Ca, S, and Si. Explain the reason for the order you chose.

7.28. Use the periodic table to arrange the following elements in order of increasing melting point: Al, F, Na, and Mg. Explain the reason for the order you chose.

7.29. For each of the following pairs, which element will have the greater metallic character: **(a)** Li or Be; **(b)** Li or Na; **(c)** Sn or P; **(d)** B or Al?

7.30. **(a)** Arrange the following elements in order of increasing metallic character: As, P, Bi, Sb, N. **(b)** Arrange the following elements in order of increasing nonmetallic character: S, Hg, Ge, F, In.

7.31. Which of the following oxides are ionic, and which are molecular: N_2O, Na_2O, CaO, CO, P_2O_5, Cl_2O_7, Fe_2O_3? Explain the reason for your choices.

7.32. Which of the following compounds are solids at room temperature, and which are gases: NO, Na_2S, BaO, CO_2, $PbCl_2$, OF_2, MgF_2? Explain the reason for your choices.

7.33. What is meant by the terms *acidic oxide* and *basic oxide?* Give an example of each.

7.34. Arrange the following oxides in order of increasing acidity: CO_2, MgO, Al_2O_3, SO_3, BaO, SiO_2, and P_2O_5.

7.35. Write balanced chemical equations for the following reactions: **(a)** sodium oxide with water; **(b)** copper(II) oxide with nitric acid; **(c)** sulfur trioxide with water; **(d)** selenium dioxide with aqueous sodium hydroxide.

7.36. Write balanced chemical equations for the following reactions: **(a)** dichlorine heptoxide with water; **(b)** iron(II) oxide with hydrochloric acid; **(c)** barium oxide with water; **(d)** carbon dioxide with aqueous potassium hydroxide.

Group Trends in Metals and Nonmetals

7.37. Compare the elements sodium and magnesium with respect to the following properties: **(a)** electron configuration; **(b)** most common ionic charge; **(c)** first ionization energy; **(d)** reactivity toward water; **(e)** atomic radius. Account for the differences between the two elements.

7.38. Compare the elements rubidium and silver with respect to the following properties: **(a)** electron configuration; **(b)** most common ionic charge; **(c)** reactivity; **(d)** atomic radius (see Figure 7.5). Account for the differences between the two elements.

7.39. **(a)** Why is strontium more reactive than beryllium toward water? **(b)** Why is the product of reacting sodium with oxygen somewhat surprising?

7.40. Why is calcium generally less reactive than potassium?

7.41. Write a balanced chemical equation for the reaction that occurs in each of the following cases: **(a)** Potassium is added to water. **(b)** Barium is added to water. **(c)** Lithium is heated in nitrogen, forming lithium nitride. **(d)** Magnesium burns in oxygen.

7.42. Write a balanced chemical equation for the reaction that occurs in each of the following cases: **(a)** Sodium vapor reacts with bromine vapor. **(b)** Hydrogen gas is bubbled through molten sodium. **(c)** Lithium is burned in oxygen. **(d)** Strontium oxide is added to water.

7.43. Explain, in terms of electron configurations, why hydrogen exhibits properties similar to those of both Li and F.

7.44. **(a)** Write balanced equations for the reaction of sodium with chlorine and for the reaction of hydrogen with chlorine. What are the similarities and differences among the products of these two reactions? **(b)** Write balanced equations for the reaction of fluorine with calcium and for the reaction of hydrogen with calcium. What are the similarities among the products of these two reactions?

7.45. Compare the elements oxygen and fluorine with respect to the following properties: **(a)** electron configuration; **(b)** most common ionic charge; **(c)** first ionization energy; **(d)** reactivity toward water; **(e)** reactivity toward hydrogen; **(f)** atomic radius. Account for the differences between the two elements.

7.46. Compare the elements fluorine and chlorine with respect to the following properties: **(a)** electron configuration; **(b)** most common ionic charge; **(c)** first ionization energy; **(d)** reactivity toward water; **(e)** electron affinity; **(f)** atomic radius. Account for the differences between the two elements.

7.47. Until the early 1960s, the group 8A elements were called inert gases. Why is this name no longer used?

7.48. Why does xenon react with fluorine whereas neon does not?

7.49. Write a balanced chemical equation for the reaction that occurs in each of the following cases: **(a)** Sulfur reacts with lithium. **(b)** Ozone decomposes to dioxygen. **(c)** Aqueous potassium bromide is electrolyzed. **(d)** Chlorine reacts with calcium.

7.50. Write a balanced chemical equation for the reaction that occurs in each of the following cases: **(a)** Iodine reacts with lithium. **(b)** Sulfur is burned in air. **(c)** Krypton reacts with fluorine. **(d)** Oxygen reacts with potassium.

7.51. **(a)** Which would you expect to be a better conductor of electricity, tellurium or iodine? **(b)** How does a molecule of sulfur (in its most common room-temperature form) differ from a molecule of oxygen? **(c)** Why is chlorine generally more reactive than bromine?

7.52. **(a)** Why does xenon react with fluorine but not with iodine? **(b)** When we talk of "molecular oxygen," why do we mean O_2 rather than O_3? **(c)** Why must a special apparatus be used to carry out reactions with fluorine gas?

Additional Exercises

7.53. By examining the modern periodic table, find as many examples as you can of the violations of Mendeleev's periodic law that the chemical and physical properties of the elements are periodic functions of their atomic weight.

7.54. Explain why the radii of atoms do not increase uniformly as the atomic number of the atom increases.

7.55. Why is the second ionization energy, I_2, of an atom always larger than the first, I_1?

7.56. Arrange the following elements in terms of **(a)** increasing first ionization energy and **(b)** increasing atomic radius: O, Se, C, Si, F.

7.57. The successive ionization energies for boron are 801, 2430, 3670, 25,000, and 32,800 kJ/mol. **(a)** Why do the values increase with successive ionization? **(b)** Why is there such a large change in ionization energy in moving from the third to the fourth ionization energy? **(c)** Why are the values for the first four ionization energies greater than the corresponding values for aluminum (Table 7.2)?

7.58. The ions Na^+ and Mg^{2+} occur in compounds, but Na^{2+} and Mg^{3+} do not. Explain.

7.59. Atomic radii normally increase going down a group in the periodic table. Suggest a reason why hafnium breaks this rule, as shown by the following data.

Atomic radii (Å)			
Sc	1.62	Ti	1.47
Y	1.80	Zr	1.60
La	1.87	Hf	1.59

[7.60]. By examining the distances between ions in a salt it is possible to define *ionic radii* in a manner similar to the way that atomic radii were defined. Listed below are the atomic and ionic (2+) radii for calcium and zinc:

Radii (Å)			
Ca	1.97	Ca^{2+}	1.00
Zn	1.34	Zn^{2+}	0.74

(a) Explain why the atomic radius of calcium is larger than that of zinc. **(b)** Suggest a reason why the difference in the ionic radii is much less than the difference in the atomic radii.

7.61. The radii of Li and its ions are Li (135 pm), Li^+ (60 pm), and Li^{2+} (18 pm). Explain why the radius decreases from Li to Li^{2+}. Predict how the radius of Be^{2+} would compare with that of Li^{2+}.

7.62. As you go down a group in the periodic table, the change in electron affinity is not nearly as great as the change in first ionization energy. Explain.

7.63. The energy changes for adding an electron to F and the O^- ion are given below:

$$F(g) + e^- \longrightarrow F^-(g) \qquad \Delta E = -332 \text{ kJ/mol}$$
$$O^-(g) + e^- \longrightarrow O^{2-}(g) \qquad \Delta E = +710 \text{ kJ/mol}$$

(a) What can be said about the electron configurations of F and O^-? **(b)** What is the essential difference in these two processes? **(c)** What prediction can you make concerning the electron affinity of gaseous N^{2-}?

[7.64]. On the basis of electron configurations, explain the following observations: **(a)** The first ionization energy of phosphorus is greater than that of sulfur. **(b)** The electron affinity of nitrogen is lower (less negative) than those of both carbon and oxygen. **(c)** The second ionization energy of oxygen is greater than that of fluorine. **(d)** The third ionization energy of manganese is greater than those of both chromium and iron.

[7.65]. What is the electron affinity of the $Na^+(g)$ ion? Explain your reasoning.

[7.66]. Make a graph of all of the second ionization energies, I_2, listed in Table 7.2, as a function of atomic number. Account for the general trend in the series from Mg through Ar. Account for the exceptionally large value for Na. Suggest why the value for Al is larger than one might expect from the general trend.

[7.67]. There are certain similarities in properties that exist between the first member of any periodic family and the element located below it and to the right in the periodic table. For example, in some ways Li resembles Mg, Be resembles Al, and so forth. This observation is called the *diagonal relationship*. In terms of what we have learned in this chapter, offer a possible explanation for this relationship.

[7.68]. The ionization energy of the oxygen *molecule* is the energy required for the following process:

$$O_2(g) \longrightarrow O_2^+(g) + e^-$$

The energy needed for this process is 1175 kJ/mol, very similar to the first ionization energy of Xe. Would you expect O_2 to react with F_2? If so, suggest a product or products of this reaction.

[7.69]. The elements at the bottom of groups 1A, 2A, 6A, 7A, and 8A — Fr, Ra, Po, At, and Rn — are all radioactive. As a result, much less is known about their physical and chemical properties than for the elements above them. Based upon what we have learned in this chapter, which of these five elements would you expect (a) to have the most metallic character; (b) to have the most nonmetallic character; (c) to have the largest ionization energy; (d) to have the smallest ionization energy; (e) to have the greatest (most negative) electron affinity; (f) to have the largest atomic radius; (g) to resemble least in appearance the element immediately above it; (h) to have the highest melting point; (i) to react most readily with water?

[7.70]. Using the *Handbook of Chemistry and Physics*, determine whether the physical properties of tellurium (density, melting point, boiling point, and so on) most closely resemble those of its neighbor to the left, to the right, or above it in the periodic table. Which would you expect the chemical properties of tellurium to most closely resemble?

Basic Concepts of Chemical Bonding

8

One million tons of salt awaiting shipment near a saltworks.

CONTENTS

Deep within the earth, below the city of Detroit and beneath the rolling plains of Kansas, lie enormous deposits of the white mineral halite. This substance, also known as sodium chloride, NaCl, was deposited in these and other places millions of years ago, when extensive primordial seas dried upon the changing surface of the earth. Sodium chloride is the most abundant dissolved substance present in seawater and is found in human body tissues in large quantities. However, it is most familiar to us as ordinary table salt. This substance consists of sodium ions and chloride ions, Na^+ and Cl^-.

Water, H_2O, is even more plentiful. We drink it, swim in it, and use it as a cooling agent. It is essential to life as we know it. This substance is composed of molecules.

Why are some substances composed of ions and others composed of molecules? The key to this question is found in the electronic structures of the atoms involved, which we studied in Chapters 6 and 7, and in the nature of the chemical forces within the compounds. In this chapter and the next, we shall examine the relationships between electronic structure, chemical bonding forces, and the properties of substances. As we do this, we shall find it useful to classify chemical forces into three broad groups: (1) ionic bonds, (2) covalent bonds, and (3) metallic bonds. Figure 8.1 shows examples of substances in which we find these types of bonds.

The term **ionic bond** refers to the electrostatic forces that exist between ions of opposite charge. As we shall see, ions may be formed from atoms by the transfer of one or more electrons from one atom to another. Ionic substances generally result from the interaction of metals from the far left side of the periodic table with nonmetallic elements from the far right side (excluding the noble gases, group 8A).

A **covalent bond** results from the sharing of electrons between two atoms. The most familiar examples of covalent bonding are seen in the interactions of nonmetallic elements with one another.

FIGURE 8.1 Examples of substances in which (a) ionic, (b) covalent, and (c) metallic bonds are found. (Richard Megna/Fundamental Photographs)

(a)   Calcium fluoride   (b)   Bromine   (c)   Gold

Magnesium oxide   Sodium chloride   Sulfur   Sugar   Magnesium   Copper

Metallic bonds are found in solid metals such as copper, iron, and aluminum. In the metals, each metal atom is bonded to several neighboring atoms. The bonding electrons are relatively free to move throughout the three-dimensional structure. Metallic bonds give rise to such typical metallic properties as high electrical conductivity and luster. We will postpone further discussion of metallic bonding until Chapter 24. We shall start our discussion by examining the preferred arrangements of electrons in atoms when they form chemical compounds.

8.1 Lewis Symbols and the Octet Rule

The electrons that take part in chemical bonding are called **valence electrons.** (The term *valence,* which comes from the Latin *valere,* "to be strong," relates to the formation of chemical bonds.) Valence electrons are the ones that reside in the incompletely filled outer electron shell of an atom. ⟲ (Sec. 6.8) **Electron-dot symbols** (also known as **Lewis symbols,** after G. N. Lewis) are a simple and convenient way of showing the valence electrons of atoms and keeping track of them in the course of bond formation. The electron-dot symbol for an element consists of the chemical symbol for the element plus a dot for each valence electron. For example, sulfur has the electron configuration $[Ne]3s^23p^4$; its electron-dot symbol therefore shows six valence electrons:

$$\cdot \overset{\cdot\cdot}{\underset{\cdot\cdot}{S}} \cdot$$

Notice that the dots are placed on the four sides of the atomic symbol: the top, the bottom, and the left and right sides. Each side can accommodate up to two electrons, as seen in the other examples shown in Table 8.1.

The number of valence electrons of any representative element is the same as the column number of the element in the periodic table. For example, the electron-dot symbols for both oxygen and sulfur, members of family 6A, show six dots.

Atoms often gain, lose, or share electrons to achieve the same number of electrons as the noble gas closest to them in the periodic table. The noble gases, you will recall, have very stable electron arrangements, as evidenced by their high ionization energies, low affinity for additional electrons, and general lack of chemical reactivity. Because all noble gases (except He) have eight valence electrons, many atoms undergoing reactions also end up with eight valence electrons. This observation has led to what is known as the **octet rule:** Atoms tend to gain, lose, or share electrons until they are surrounded by eight valence electrons. An octet of electrons can be thought of as four pairs of valence electrons arranged around the atom. An example is the configuration for Ne in Table 8.1. Of course, because He has only two electrons, atoms near it in the periodic table, such as H, tend to obtain an arrangement of two electrons. As we shall see, there are many exceptions to the octet rule. Nevertheless, it provides a useful framework for introducing many important concepts of bonding.

TABLE 8.1 △ Electron-Dot Symbols

Element	Electron configuration	Electron-dot symbol
Li	$[He]2s^1$	Li·
Be	$[He]2s^2$	·Be·
B	$[He]2s^22p^1$	·B·
C	$[He]2s^22p^2$	·C·
N	$[He]2s^22p^3$	·N:
O	$[He]2s^22p^4$	:O:
F	$[He]2s^22p^5$	·F:
Ne	$[He]2s^22p^6$	:Ne:

FIGURE 8.2 The reaction between sodium metal and chlorine gas to form sodium chloride. (*a*) A container of chlorine gas (left) and sodium metal (right). (*b*) Formation of NaCl begins as sodium is added to the chlorine. (*c*) The reaction a few minutes later. The reaction is strongly exothermic, giving off both heat and light. (Donald Clegg and Roxy Wilson)

(*a*)   (*b*)   (*c*)

8.2 Ionic Bonding

When sodium metal is brought into contact with chlorine gas, Cl_2, a violent reaction ensues (see Figure 8.2). The product of this reaction is sodium chloride, NaCl, a substance composed of Na^+ and Cl^- ions:

$$2Na(s) + Cl_2(g) \longrightarrow 2NaCl(s)$$

These ions are arranged throughout the solid NaCl in a regular three-dimensional array, as shown in Figure 8.3.

Figure 8.3

FIGURE 8.3 (*a*) The crystal structure of sodium chloride. Each of the Na^+ ions is surrounded by six Cl^- ions, and each Cl^- ion is surrounded by six Na^+ ions. This is made clearer in (*b*), in which the cubic arrangement of the lattice is emphasized.

(*a*)

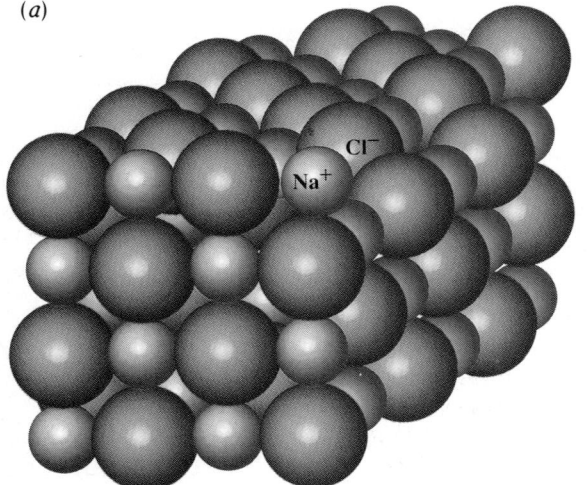

(*b*)

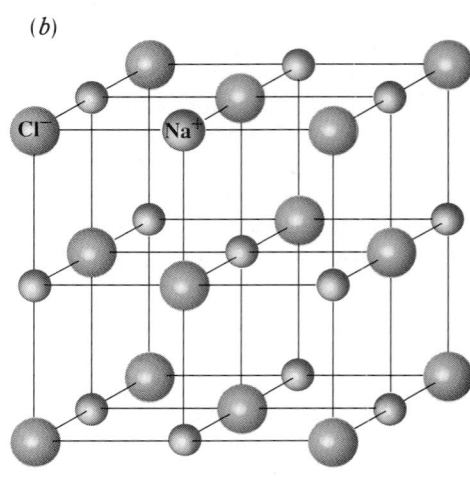

The formation of Na^+ from Na and of Cl^- from Cl_2 indicates that an electron has been lost by a sodium atom and gained by a chlorine atom. Such electron transfer to form oppositely charged ions occurs when the atoms involved differ greatly in their attraction for electrons. Our example of NaCl is rather typical for ionic compounds; it involves a metal of low ionization energy and a nonmetal with a high affinity for electrons. Using electron-dot symbols (and showing a chlorine atom rather than the Cl_2 molecule), we can represent this reaction as follows:

$$Na \cdot \; + \; \cdot \ddot{\underset{..}{Cl}} : \longrightarrow Na^+ + \left[: \ddot{\underset{..}{Cl}} : \right]^- \qquad [8.1]$$

The arrow indicates the transfer of an electron from the Na atom to the Cl atom. Each ion has an octet of electrons, the octet on Na^+ being the $2s^2 2p^6$ electrons that lie below the single $3s$ valence electron of the Na atom. We've put a bracket around the chloride ion to emphasize that all eight electrons are located exclusively on the Cl^- ion.

Energetics of Ionic Bond Formation

As seen in Figure 8.2, the reaction of sodium with chlorine to form sodium chloride is *very* exothermic. Indeed, if we examine the heats of formation of the ionic compounds listed in Appendix C, we find that all are quite negative. What are the factors that make the formation of ionic compounds so exothermic?

In Equation 8.1, we represented the formation of NaCl in terms of the transfer of electrons from Na to Cl. However, as we saw when we discussed ionization energies, the loss of electrons from an atom is always an endothermic process. ∞ (Sec. 7.4) Removing an electron from Na(g) to form $Na^+(g)$ requires 496 kJ/mol. On the other hand, when a nonmetal gains an electron, the process is generally exothermic, as seen in the electron affinities of the elements. ∞ (Sec. 7.5) Adding an electron to Cl(g) releases 349 kJ/mol. If the transfer of an electron from one atom to another were the only factor in forming an ionic bond, the overall process would rarely be exothermic. For example, removing an electron from Na(g) and adding it to Cl(g) requires $496 - 349 = 147$ kJ/mol of energy.

The principal reason that ionic compounds are stable is the attraction between ions of unlike charge. This attraction draws the ions together, releasing energy and causing the ions to form a solid array or lattice such as that shown for NaCl in Figure 8.3. A measure of just how much stabilization results from the arranging of oppositely charged ions in an ionic solid is given by the **lattice energy**. *The lattice energy is the energy required to separate completely a mole of a solid ionic compound into its gaseous ions.* To get a picture of this process for NaCl, imagine that the structure shown in Figure 8.3 expands from within, so that the distances between the ions increase until the ions are very far apart. This process requires 788 kJ/mol, which is the value of the lattice energy:

$$NaCl(s) \longrightarrow Na^+(g) + Cl^-(g) \qquad \Delta H_{lattice} = +788 \text{ kJ/mol} \qquad [8.2]$$

Table 8.2 lists the lattice energy of NaCl and of several other ionic compounds. Notice that all are large, positive values, indicating that the ions are strongly attracted to one another in these solids. The energy released by the attraction between ions of unlike charge more than makes up for the endother-

	$\Delta H_f , kJ/mol$
Li Cl(s)	−408.3
Na Cl(s)	−410.9
K Cl(s)	−435.9
Rb Cl(s)	−430.5
MgCl₂(s)	−641.6
CaCl₂(s)	−795.8

Learning Goal 3: Describe the origin of the energy terms that lead to stabilization of ionic lattices.

Point of Emphasis: Lattice energy is always endothermic (ΔH is positive).

TABLE 8.2 △ Lattice Energies for Some Ionic Compounds

Compound	Lattice energy (kJ/mol)
LiF	1024
LiI	744
NaF	911
NaCl	788
NaI	693
KF	815
KBr	682
KI	641
MgF_2	2910
$SrCl_2$	2130
MgO	3938

mic nature of ionization energies, making the formation of ionic compounds an exothermic process. The strong interactions also cause most ionic materials to be hard, brittle materials with high melting points. (NaCl melts at 801°C.)

The magnitude of the lattice energy of a solid depends on the charges of the ions, their sizes, and the way they are arranged in the solid. The potential energy (Section 5.1) of two interacting charged particles is given by

$$E = k \frac{Q_1 Q_2}{d} \qquad [8.3]$$

In this equation, Q_1 and Q_2 are the charges on the particles, d is the distance between their centers, and k is a constant, 8.99×10^9 J-m/C². Equation 8.3 indicates that the attractive interaction between two oppositely charged ions increases as the magnitudes of their charges increase and as the distance between their centers decreases. Thus, for a given arrangement of ions, the lattice energy increases as the charges on the ions increase and as their radii decrease. The magnitude of lattice energies depends primarily on the ionic charges because ionic radii do not vary over a very wide range.

Point of Emphasis: The magnitude of the lattice energy depends primarily on the amount of charge on the ionic species.

SAMPLE EXERCISE 8.1

Arrange the following ionic compounds in order of increasing lattice energy: LiF, KBr, and MgO.

SOLUTION   LiF consists of Li^+ and F^- ions, KBr of K^+ and Br^- ions, and MgO of Mg^{2+} and O^{2-} ions. According to Equation 8.3, the electrostatic attraction between oppositely charged ions increases with the charge on the ions. For this reason, we expect the lattice energy of MgO, which has 2+ and 2− ions, to be the greatest of the three. To compare LiF and KBr, we need to determine in which substance the ions are closer together. Because the radius of a Li atom is less than that of a K atom, we might expect that a Li^+ ion is smaller than a K^+ ion. Similarly, we expect that F^- is a smaller ion than Br^-. (We will discuss the sizes of ions in Section 8.3.) Therefore, the distance between the ions in LiF should be less than the distance between the ions in KBr, and the lattice energy of LiF should be greater than that of KBr. Table 8.2 confirms the order KBr < LiF < MgO.

PRACTICE EXERCISE

Which substance would you expect to have the greater lattice energy, FeO or Fe_2O_3?   *Answer:* Fe_2O_3

Electron Configurations of Ions

Learning Goal 4: Predict on the basis of the periodic table the probable formulas of ionic substances formed between common metals and nonmetals.

Our analysis of the energetics of ionic bond formation helps us understand why many ions tend to have noble-gas electron configurations. The amounts of energy required to empty the valence shell of many metal atoms are not substantial, and so the energy released in forming the ionic lattice ($-\Delta H_{lattice}$) is sufficient to compensate for this process. However, the magnitude of the lattice energy is not large enough to compensate for removal of electrons from the noble-gas core of the atom. Thus, for example, we find Na^+ but not Na^{2+} in compounds:

Point of Emphasis: Recall that the ionization energy jumps markedly after all the valence electrons have been removed.

Na: $1s^2\ 2s^2\ 2p^6\ 3s^1 = [Ne]\ 3s^1$

Na^+: $1s^2\ 2s^2\ 2p^6 = [Ne]$

Na^{2+}: $1s^2\ 2s^2\ 2p^5$

▲ A CLOSER LOOK

The Born-Haber Cycle

The lattice energy cannot be determined directly by experiment. It can, however, be calculated by envisioning the formation or an ionic compound as occurring in a series of well-defined steps. We can then use Hess's law (Section 5.6) to put these steps together in a way that gives us the lattice energy for the compound. By so doing, we construct a **Born-Haber cycle,** a thermochemical cycle named after the German scientists Max Born (1882–1970) and Fritz Haber (1868–1934), who introduced it to analyze the factors leading to the stability of ionic compounds.

In the Born-Haber cycle for NaCl, we consider the formation of NaCl(s) from the elements Na(s) and $Cl_2(g)$ by two different routes, as shown in Figure 8.4. The enthalpy change for the direct route is the heat of formation of NaCl(s):

$$Na(s) + \tfrac{1}{2}Cl_2(g) \longrightarrow NaCl(s)$$
$$\Delta H_f^\circ[NaCl(s)] = -410.9 \text{ kJ} \quad [8.4]$$

The indirect route consists of five steps. First we generate gaseous atoms of sodium by vaporizing sodium metal. Then we form gaseous atoms of chlorine by breaking the bond in the Cl_2 molecule. The enthalpy changes for these processes are available to us as enthalpies of formation (Appendix C):

$$Na(s) \longrightarrow Na(g) \quad \Delta H_f^\circ[Na(g)] = 107.7 \text{ kJ} \quad [8.5]$$
$$\tfrac{1}{2}Cl_2(g) \longrightarrow Cl(g) \quad \Delta H_f^\circ[Cl(g)] = 121.7 \text{ kJ} \quad [8.6]$$

Notice that both of these processes are endothermic; energy is required to generate gaseous sodium and chlorine atoms.

In the next two steps, we remove the electron from Na(g) to form $Na^+(g)$ and then add the electron to Cl(g) to form $Cl^-(g)$. The enthalpy changes for these processes equal the ionization energy of Na and the electron affinity of Cl, respectively: ⚬⚬ (Secs. 7.4, 7.5)

$$Na(g) \longrightarrow Na^+(g) + e^- \quad \Delta H = I_1(Na) = 496 \text{ kJ} \quad [8.7]$$
$$Cl(g) + e^- \longrightarrow Cl^-(g) \quad \Delta H = E(Cl) = -349 \text{ kJ} \quad [8.8]$$

Finally, we combine the gaseous sodium and chloride ions to form solid sodium chloride. Because this process is just the reverse of the lattice energy (breaking a solid into ions), the enthalpy change is the negative of the lattice energy, the quantity that we wish to determine:

$$Na^+(g) + Cl^-(g) \longrightarrow NaCl(s)$$
$$\Delta H = -\Delta H_{lattice} = ? \quad [8.9]$$

The sum of the five steps in the indirect path gives us the NaCl(s) from Na(s) and $\tfrac{1}{2}Cl_2(g)$. Thus, from Hess's law we know that the sum of the enthalpy changes for these five steps equals that for the direct path, Equation 8.4:

$$\Delta H_f^\circ[NaCl(s)] = \Delta H_f^\circ[Na(g)] + \Delta H_f^\circ[Cl(g)] + I_1(Na) - E(Cl) - \Delta H_{lattice} \quad [8.10]$$

$$-411 \text{ kJ} = 108 \text{ kJ} + 122 \text{ kJ} + 496 \text{ kJ} - 349 \text{ kJ} - \Delta H_{lattice}$$

Solving for $\Delta H_{lattice}$:

$$\Delta H_{lattice} = 108 \text{ kJ} + 122 \text{ kJ} + 496 \text{ kJ} - 349 \text{ kJ} + 411 \text{ kJ} = 788 \text{ kJ}$$

Thus the lattice energy of NaCl is 788 kJ/mol.

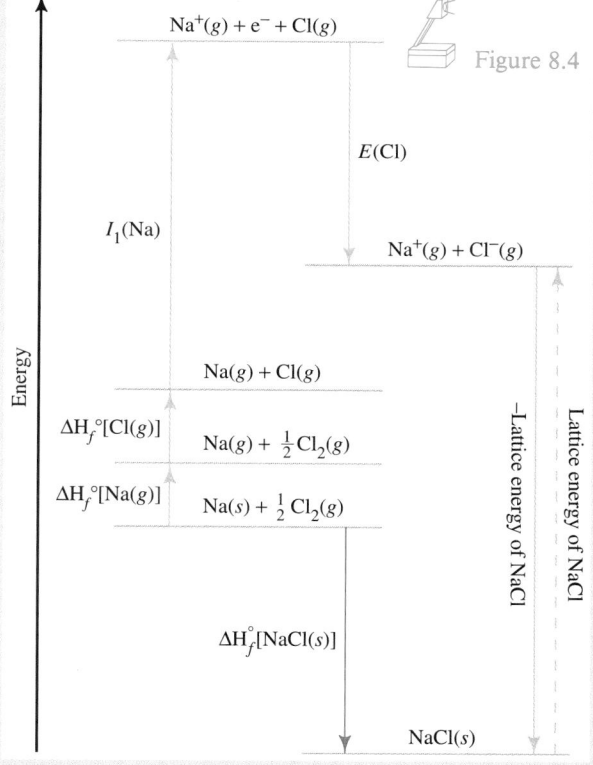

Figure 8.4

FIGURE 8.4 A Born-Haber cycle shows the energetic relationships in the formation of ionic solids from the elements. In this example, the enthalpy of formation of NaCl(s) from elemental sodium and chlorine (Equation 8.4) is equal to the sum of the energies of several individual steps (Equations 8.5 through 8.9) by Hess's law.

Similarly, addition of electrons to nonmetals is either exothermic or only slightly endothermic as long as electrons are being added to the valence shell. To add further electrons, however, requires a tremendous amount of energy, more than is available from the lattice energy. Thus, for example, we find Cl^- but not Cl^{2-} in compounds:

$$Cl: \quad 1s^2\, 2s^2\, 2p^6\, 3s^2\, 3p^5 = [Ne]\, 3s^2\, 3p^5$$

$$Cl^-: \quad 1s^2\, 2s^2\, 2p^6\, 3s^2\, 3p^6 = [Ar]$$

$$Cl^{2-}: \quad 1s^2\, 2s^2\, 2p^6\, 3s^2\, 3p^6\, 4s^1 = [Ar]\, 4s^1$$

The electron configurations of the transition metals present an interesting case. The lattice energies of ionic compounds are generally large enough to compensate for the loss of up to only three electrons from atoms. Thus, we find cations having charges of $1+$, $2+$, or $3+$ in ionic compounds. Because most transition metals have more than three electrons beyond a noble-gas core, attainment of a noble-gas configuration for these ions is not feasible. For example, metals of group 1B (Cu, Ag, Au) often occur as $1+$ ions (as in CuBr and AgCl). Silver possesses a $[Kr]4d^{10}5s^1$ electron configuration. In forming Ag^+, the $5s$ electron is lost, leaving a completely filled $4d$ subshell. As in this example, transition metals generally do not form ions with noble-gas configurations. The octet rule, although useful, is clearly limited in scope.

The fact that the $5s$ electron is removed before the $4d$ electron in forming Ag^+ is noteworthy. *When a positive ion is formed from an atom, electrons are always lost first from the subshell with the largest value of n.* Thus, a transition metal always loses the outer s electrons before it loses electrons from the underlying d subshell. As a further example, consider Fe, which has the electron configuration $[Ar]3d^64s^2$. Removal of two electrons gives the Fe^{2+} ion, whose electron configuration is $[Ar]3d^6$. Removal of an additional electron gives the Fe^{3+} ion whose electron configuration is $[Ar]3d^5$.

SAMPLE EXERCISE 8.2

Write the electron configuration for the Co^{2+} ion and for the Co^{3+} ion.

SOLUTION Cobalt (atomic number 27) has an electron configuration of $[Ar]3d^74s^2$. To form a $2+$ ion, two electrons must be removed. As discussed in the text above, the $4s$ electrons are removed before the $3d$ electron. Consequently, the Co^{2+} ion has an electron configuration of $[Ar]3d^7$. To form Co^{3+} requires the removal of an additional electron; the electron configuration for this ion is $[Ar]3d^6$.

PRACTICE EXERCISE

Write the electron configuration for the Cr^{3+} ion.   *Answer:* $[Ar]3d^3$

Polyatomic Ions

This is a good point at which to review Table 2.4, which lists the common ions. ∞ (Sec. 2.6)   Many common ions are polyatomic. Examples include the ammonium ion, NH_4^+, and the carbonate ion, CO_3^{2-}. In polyatomic ions, two or more atoms are bound together by predominantly covalent bonds. They form a stable grouping that carries a charge, either positive or negative. We will examine the covalent bonding forces in these ions in Chapter 9. For now, you must realize only that the group of atoms as a whole acts as a charged species in forming an ionic compound with an ion of opposite charge.

8.3 Sizes of Ions

Ionic size plays a crucial role in determining the structure and stability of ionic solids. For example, the sizes of ions are important in determining both the way in which the ions pack in a solid and the lattice energy of the solid. Ionic size is also a major factor governing the properties of ions in solution. For example, a small difference in ionic size is often sufficient for one metal ion to be biologically important and another not to be.

The size of an ion depends on its nuclear charge, the number of electrons it possesses, and the orbitals in which the outer-shell electrons reside. Consider first the relative sizes of an ion and its parent atom. Positive ions are formed by removing one or more electrons from the outermost region of the atom. Thus, the formation of a cation not only vacates the most spatially extended orbitals, it also decreases the total electron-electron repulsions. As a consequence, *cations are smaller than their parent atoms,* as illustrated in Figure 8.5. The opposite is true of negative ions. When electrons are added to form an anion, the increased electron-electron repulsions cause the electrons to spread out more in space. Thus, *anions are larger than their parent atoms.*

It is also important to note that *for ions of the same charge, size increases as we go down a family in the periodic table.* This trend is seen in Figure 8.5 and also in Table 8.3, which gives the radii for several ions with noble-gas electron configurations. As the principal quantum number of the outer occupied orbital of an ion increases, the size of both the ion and its parent atom increases.

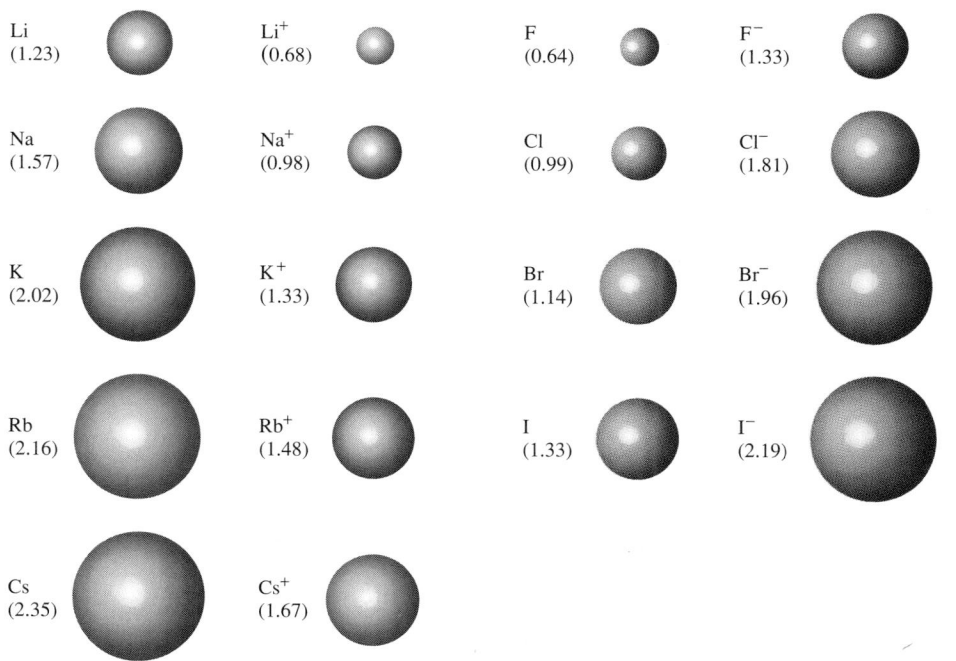

Li (1.23)   Li$^+$ (0.68)   F (0.64)   F$^-$ (1.33)

Na (1.57)   Na$^+$ (0.98)   Cl (0.99)   Cl$^-$ (1.81)

K (2.02)   K$^+$ (1.33)   Br (1.14)   Br$^-$ (1.96)

Rb (2.16)   Rb$^+$ (1.48)   I (1.33)   I$^-$ (2.19)

Cs (2.35)   Cs$^+$ (1.67)

FIGURE 8.5 Relative sizes of atoms and ions. The values in parentheses are radii (Å).

Figure 8.5

TABLE 8.3 △ Radii (Å) of Ions with Noble-Gas Electron Configurations

Group 1A		Group 2A		Group 3A, 3B		Group 6A		Group 7A	
Li^+	0.68	Be^{2+}	0.30			O^{2-}	1.45	F^-	1.33
Na^+	0.98	Mg^{2+}	0.65	Al^{3+}	0.45	S^{2-}	1.90	Cl^-	1.81
K^+	1.33	Ca^{2+}	0.94	Sc^{3+}	0.68	Se^{2-}	2.02	Br^-	1.96
Rb^+	1.48	Sr^{2+}	1.10	Y^{3+}	0.90	Te^{2-}	2.22	I^-	2.19
Cs^+	1.67	Ba^{2+}	1.31						

SAMPLE EXERCISE 8.3

Arrange the following atoms and ions in order of decreasing size: Mg^{2+}, Ca^{2+}, and Ca.

SOLUTION Cations are smaller than their parent atoms; thus Ca^{2+} is smaller than the Ca atom. Because Ca is below Mg in group 2A of the periodic table, Ca^{2+} is larger than Mg^{2+}. These observations lead to the following order: $Ca > Ca^{2+} > Mg^{2+}$.

PRACTICE EXERCISE

Which of the following atoms and ions is largest: S^{2-}, S, O^{2-}.   *Answer:* S^{2-}

Learning Goal 6: Explain the concept of an isoelectronic series and the origin of changes in ionic radius within such a series.

The effect of varying nuclear charge on ionic radii is seen in the variation in radius in an **isoelectronic series** of ions. The term *isoelectronic* means that the ions possess the same number of electrons. For example, each ion in the series O^{2-}, F^-, Na^+, Mg^{2+}, and Al^{3+} has 10 electrons arranged in a $1s^2 2s^2 2p^6$ electron configuration like that of neon. The nuclear charge in this series increases steadily in the order listed. (Recall that the charge on the nucleus of an atom or monoatomic ion is given by the atomic number of the element.) Because the number of electrons remains constant, the radius of the ion decreases with increasing nuclear charge, as the electrons are more strongly attracted to the nucleus:

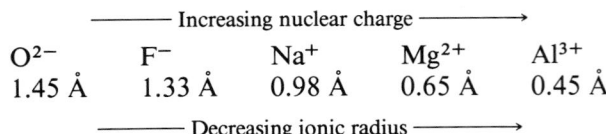

Increasing nuclear charge ⟶

O^{2-}	F^-	Na^+	Mg^{2+}	Al^{3+}
1.45 Å	1.33 Å	0.98 Å	0.65 Å	0.45 Å

⟵ Decreasing ionic radius ⟶

Notice the positions of these elements in the periodic table and also their atomic numbers. The nonmetal anions precede the noble gas Ne in the table. The metal cations follow Ne. Oxygen, the largest ion in this isoelectronic series, has the lowest atomic number, 8. Aluminum, the smallest of these ions, has the highest atomic number, 13.

SAMPLE EXERCISE 8.4

Arrange the ions S^{2-}, Cl^-, K^+, and Ca^{2+} in order of decreasing size.

SOLUTION This is an isoelectronic series of ions, with all ions having 18 electrons. In an isoelectronic series, size decreases as the nuclear charge (atomic number) of the ion increases. The atomic numbers of the ions are S (16), Cl (17), K (19), and Ca (20). Thus the ions decrease in size in the following order: $S^{2-} > Cl^- > K^+ > Ca^{2+}$.

PRACTICE EXERCISE

Which of the following ions is largest: Rb^+, Sr^{2+}, Y^{3+}?   *Answer:* Rb^+

8.4 Covalent Bonding

We have seen that ionic substances possess several characteristic properties. They are usually brittle substances with high melting points. They are usually crystalline, meaning that the solids have flat surfaces that make characteristic angles with one another. Ionic crystals can often be cleaved; that is, they break apart along smooth, flat surfaces. The characteristics of ionic substances result from the electrostatic forces that maintain the ions in a rigid, well-defined, three-dimensional arrangement such as that illustrated in Figure 8.3.

Learning Goal 7: Describe general differences in physical properties between substances with ionic bonds and those with covalent bonds.

The vast majority of chemical substances do not have the characteristics of ionic materials; water, gasoline, banana peelings, hair, antifreeze, and plastic bags are examples. Most of the substances with which we come in daily contact tend to be gases, liquids, or solids with low melting points. Many vaporize readily—for example, mothball crystals. Many in their solid forms are pliable rather than rigidly crystalline—for example, paraffin and plastic bags.

For the very large class of substances that do not behave like ionic substances, we need a different model for the bonding between atoms. G. N. Lewis reasoned that an atom might acquire a noble-gas electron configuration by sharing electrons with other atoms. A chemical bond formed by sharing a pair of electrons is called a **covalent bond.**

The hydrogen molecule, H_2, furnishes the simplest possible example of a covalent bond. Using Lewis symbols, formation of the H_2 molecule by combination of two hydrogen atoms can be represented as

$$H \cdot \ + \ \cdot H \longrightarrow \left(H \!:\! H \right)$$

The shared pair of electrons provides each hydrogen atom with two electrons in its valence shell (the $1s$) orbital, so that in a sense it has the electron configuration of the noble gas helium (the shared electrons are counted with both atoms). Similarly, when two chlorine atoms combine to form the Cl_2 molecule, we have

$$:\!\overset{..}{\underset{..}{Cl}}\!\cdot \ + \ \cdot\overset{..}{\underset{..}{Cl}}\!: \ \longrightarrow \ \left(:\!\overset{..}{\underset{..}{Cl}}\!:\!\overset{..}{\underset{..}{Cl}}\!: \right)$$

Each chlorine atom, by sharing the bonding electron pair, acquires eight electrons (an octet) in its valence shell. It thus achieves the noble-gas electron configuration of argon. The structures shown above for H_2 and Cl_2 are called **Lewis structures.** In writing Lewis structures, we usually show each electron pair shared between atoms as a line, and the unshared electron pairs as dots. The Lewis structures for H_2 and Cl_2 are shown as follows:

Teaching Note: Shared pairs of electrons are sometimes represented by a pair of dots.

$$H\!-\!H \qquad :\!\overset{..}{\underset{..}{Cl}}\!-\!\overset{..}{\underset{..}{Cl}}\!:$$

Of course, the shared pairs of electrons are not located in fixed positions between nuclei. Figure 8.6 shows the distribution of electron density in the H_2 molecule. Notice that electron density is concentrated between the nuclei. The two atoms are bound into the H_2 molecule principally because of the electrostatic attractions of the two positive nuclei for the concentration of negative charge between them. In Chapter 9, in which we start with the Lewis symbols of the atoms, we shall look more closely at the use of orbitals to describe the

FIGURE 8.6 Electron distribution in the H_2 molecule.

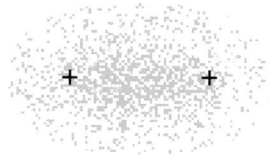

electron density within molecules. Meanwhile, our discussions will rely primarily on Lewis structures.

For the nonmetals, the number of valence electrons is the same as the group number. Therefore, one might predict that 7A elements, such as F, would form one covalent bond to achieve an octet; 6A elements, such as O, would form two covalent bonds; 5A elements, such as N, would form three covalent bonds; and 4A elements, such as C, would form four covalent bonds. These predictions are borne out in many compounds. For example, consider the simple hydrides of the nonmetals of the second row (period) of the periodic table:

$$H-\ddot{\underset{\cdot\cdot}{F}}: \qquad H-\underset{\underset{H}{|}}{\ddot{O}}: \qquad H-\underset{\underset{H}{|}}{\overset{\cdot\cdot}{N}}-H \qquad H-\underset{\underset{H}{|}}{\overset{\overset{H}{|}}{C}}-H$$

Thus, the Lewis model succeeds in accounting for the compositions of compounds of nonmetals, in which covalent bonding predominates.

Multiple Bonds

The sharing of a pair of electrons constitutes a single covalent bond, generally referred to simply as a **single bond.** In many molecules, atoms attain complete octets by sharing more than one pair of electrons between them. When two electron pairs are shared, two lines are drawn, representing a **double bond.** A **triple bond** corresponds to the sharing of three pairs of electrons. Such **multiple bonding** is found, for example, in the N_2 molecule:

$$:\overset{\cdot}{\underset{\cdot}{N}}\cdot + \cdot\overset{\cdot}{\underset{\cdot}{N}}: \longrightarrow :N:::N: \qquad (\text{or } :N\equiv N:)$$

Because each nitrogen atom possesses five electrons in its valence shell, the sharing of three electron pairs is required to achieve the octet configuration. The properties of N_2 are in complete accord with this Lewis structure. Nitrogen gas is a diatomic gas with exceptionally low reactivity that results from the very stable nitrogen-nitrogen bond. Study of the structure of N_2 reveals that the nitrogen atoms are separated by only 1.10 Å. The short $N\equiv N$ bond distance is a result of the triple bond between the atoms. From structure studies of many different substances in which nitrogen atoms share one or two electron pairs, we have learned that the average distance between bonded nitrogen atoms varies with the number of shared electron pairs:

N—N	N=N	N≡N
1.47 Å	1.24 Å	1.10 Å

As a general rule, the distance between bonded atoms decreases as the number of shared electron pairs increases.

Carbon dioxide, CO_2, provides a further example of a molecule containing multiple bonds:

$$:\overset{\cdot}{\underset{\cdot\cdot}{O}}: + \cdot\overset{\cdot}{\underset{\cdot}{C}}\cdot + :\overset{\cdot}{\underset{\cdot\cdot}{O}}: \longrightarrow \ddot{\underset{\cdot\cdot}{O}}::C::\ddot{\underset{\cdot\cdot}{O}} \qquad (\text{or } \ddot{\underset{\cdot\cdot}{O}}=C=\ddot{\underset{\cdot\cdot}{O}})$$

8.5 Bond Polarity and Electronegativity

The electron pairs shared between two different atoms are not necessarily shared equally. We can visualize two extreme cases in the degree to which electron pairs are shared. On the one hand, we have bonding between two identical atoms, as in Cl_2 or N_2, where the electron pairs must be equally shared. At the other extreme, illustrated by NaCl, there will be essentially no sharing of electrons. We know that in this case the compound is best described as composed of Na^+ and Cl^- ions. The $3s$ electron of the Na atom is, in effect, transferred completely to chlorine. The bonds occurring in most covalent substances fall somewhere between these extremes.

The concept of **bond polarity** is useful in describing the sharing of electrons between atoms. A **nonpolar bond** is one in which the electrons are shared equally between two atoms. In a **polar covalent bond,** one of the atoms exerts a greater attraction for the electrons than the other. If the difference in relative ability to attract electrons is large enough, an ionic bond is formed.

Electronegativity

We use a quantity called electronegativity to estimate whether a given bond will be nonpolar, polar covalent, or ionic. **Electronegativity** is defined as the ability of an atom *in a molecule* to attract electrons to itself. The greater an atom's electronegativity, the greater its ability to attract electrons to itself. The electronegativity of an atom in a molecule is related to its ionization energy and electron affinity, which are properties of isolated atoms. The ionization energy measures how strongly the atom holds on to its electrons. Likewise, the electron affinity is a measure of how strongly the atom attracts additional electrons. An atom with a very negative electron affinity and high ionization energy will both attract electrons from other atoms and resist having its electrons attracted away; it will be highly electronegative.

Figure 8.7 shows electronegativity values for many of the elements. Fluorine is the most electronegative element, with an electronegativity of 4.0. The least electronegative element, cesium, has an electronegativity of 0.7. The values for all other elements lie between these extremes.

FIGURE 8.7 Electronegativities of the elements.

Figure 8.7

1A																	
H 2.1	2A											3A	4A	5A	6A	7A	
Li 1.0	**Be** 1.5											**B** 2.0	**C** 2.5	**N** 3.0	**O** 3.5	**F** 4.0	
Na 0.9	**Mg** 1.2	3B	4B	5B	6B	7B		8B		1B	2B	**Al** 1.5	**Si** 1.8	**P** 2.1	**S** 2.5	**Cl** 3.0	3.0–4.0
K 0.8	**Ca** 1.0	**Sc** 1.3	**Ti** 1.5	**V** 1.6	**Cr** 1.6	**Mn** 1.5	**Fe** 1.8	**Co** 1.9	**Ni** 1.9	**Cu** 1.9	**Zn** 1.6	**Ga** 1.6	**Ge** 1.8	**As** 2.0	**Se** 2.4	**Br** 2.8	2.0–2.9
Rb 0.8	**Sr** 1.0	**Y** 1.2	**Zr** 1.4	**Nb** 1.6	**Mo** 1.8	**Tc** 1.9	**Ru** 2.2	**Rh** 2.2	**Pd** 2.2	**Ag** 1.9	**Cd** 1.7	**In** 1.7	**Sn** 1.8	**Sb** 1.9	**Te** 2.1	**I** 2.5	1.5–1.9
Cs 0.7	**Ba** 0.9	**La** 1.0	**Hf** 1.3	**Ta** 1.5	**W** 1.7	**Re** 1.9	**Os** 2.2	**Ir** 2.2	**Pt** 2.2	**Au** 2.4	**Hg** 1.9	**Tl** 1.8	**Pb** 1.9	**Bi** 1.9	**Po** 2.0	**At** 2.2	Below 1.5

Note that each horizontal row of the table generally exhibits a steady increase in electronegativity from left to right, that is, from the most metallic to the most nonmetallic elements. Notice also that, with some exceptions (especially within the transition metals), electronegativity decreases with increasing atomic number in any one group. This is what we might expect, because we know that ionization energies tend to decrease with increasing atomic number in a group and electron affinities don't change very much. You do not need to memorize numerical values for electronegativity. However, you should know the periodic trends so that you can predict which of two elements is more electronegative.

Electronegativity and Bond Polarity

We can use the difference in electronegativity between two atoms to gauge the polarity of the bonding between them. Consider the three fluorine-containing compounds listed below:

Compound	F_2	HF	LiF
Electronegativity difference	$4.0 - 4.0 = 0$	$4.0 - 2.1 = 1.9$	$4.0 - 1.0 = 3.0$
Type of bond	Nonpolar	Polar covalent	Ionic

In F_2, the electrons are shared equally between the fluorine atoms, and the bond is nonpolar. In HF, the fluorine atom has a greater electronegativity than the hydrogen atom. Consequently, the sharing of electrons is unequal (the bond is polar), with the more electronegative fluorine attracting electron density from hydrogen. We represent this situation in the following two ways:

$$\overset{\delta+ \;\; \delta-}{H-F} \quad \text{or} \quad \overset{\longrightarrow}{H-F}$$

The $\delta+$ and $\delta-$ are meant to represent partial positive and negative charges, respectively. (The symbol δ is the Greek lowercase letter "delta.") The arrow represents the pull of electron density off the hydrogen by the fluorine, leaving the hydrogen with a partial positive charge; the head of the arrow points in the direction in which the electrons are attracted, toward the more electronegative atom. In LiF, the far greater electronegativity of fluorine as compared to lithium leads to the complete transfer of the valence electron of Li to F. This transfer results in the formation of Li^+ and F^- ions; the resultant bond is therefore ionic.

We shall consider the molecular consequences of bond polarities further in Chapter 9. For now, remember: *The greater the difference in electronegativity, the more polar the bond.*

SAMPLE EXERCISE 8.5

Which bond is more polar: **(a)** B—Cl or C—Cl; **(b)** P—F or P—Cl? Indicate in each case which atom has the partial negative charge.

SOLUTION **(a)** The difference in the electronegativities of chlorine and boron is $3.0 - 2.0 = 1.0$; the difference between chlorine and carbon is $3.0 - 2.5 = 0.5$. Consequently, the B—Cl bond is the more polar; the chlorine atom carries the partial negative charge because it has a higher electronegativity. We should be able to reach this same conclusion without using a table of electronegativities; instead, we can rely on periodic trends. Because boron is to the left of carbon in the periodic table, we would predict that it has a lower attraction for electrons. Chlorine, being on the right side of the table, has a strong attraction for electrons. The most polar bond will be the one between the atoms having the lowest attraction for electrons (boron) and the highest attraction (chlorine).

(b) Because fluorine is above chlorine in the periodic table, we would predict it to be more electronegative. Consequently, the P—F bond will be more polar than the P—Cl bond. You should compare the electronegativity differences for the two bonds to verify this prediction. The fluorine atom carries the partial negative charge.

PRACTICE EXERCISE

Which of the following bonds is most polar: S—Cl, S—Br, Se—Cl, or Se—Br?
Answer: Se—Cl

8.6 Drawing Lewis Structures

Lewis structures are useful in understanding the bonding in many compounds and are used frequently when discussing the properties of molecules. Drawing Lewis structures is an important skill, especially in mastering the material in this chapter and the next. Thus, you should practice writing Lewis structures. To do so, you should follow a regular procedure. First we'll outline the procedure, and then we'll go through several examples to show its application.

1. *Sum the valence electrons from all atoms.* (Use the periodic table as necessary to help you determine the number of valence electrons in each atom.) For an anion, add an electron to the total for each negative charge. For a cation, subtract an electron for each positive charge. Don't worry about keeping track of which electrons come from which atoms. Only the total number is important.

2. *Write the symbols for the atoms to show which atoms are attached to which, and connect them with a single bond* (a dash or two dots, representing two electrons). Atoms are often written in the order in which they are connected in the molecule or ion, as in HCN. When a central atom has a group of other atoms bonded to it, we usually write the central atom first, as in CO_3^{2-} and SF_4. In other cases, you may need more information before you can draw the Lewis structure.

3. *Complete the octets of the atoms bonded to the central atom.* (Remember, however, that hydrogen can have only two electrons.)

4. *Place any leftover electrons on the central atom,* even if doing so results in more than an octet.

5. *If there are not enough electrons to give the central atom an octet, try multiple bonds.* Use one or more of the unshared pairs of electrons on the atoms bonded to the central atom to form double or triple bonds.

SAMPLE EXERCISE 8.6

Draw the Lewis structure for phosphorus trichloride, PCl_3.

SOLUTION *First,* we sum the valence electrons. Phosphorus (group 5A) has five valence electrons, and each chlorine (group 7A) has seven. The total number of valence-shell electrons is therefore $5 + (3 \times 7) = 26$.

Second, we arrange the atoms to show which atom is connected to which, and we draw a single bond between them. There are various ways the atoms might be

Point of Emphasis: Lewis structures are much easier to write and the results are more consistently correct when students follow the method outlined here. Reproducible logic is the key.

Learning Goal 11: Using the periodic table, write the Lewis structures for molecules and ions containing covalent bonds.

James Allen Carroll, "Drawing Lewis Structures without Anticipating Octets," *J. Chem. Educ.* **1986,** *63,* 28.

Melvin E. Zandler and Erach R. Talaty, "The '6N + 2 Rule' for Writing Lewis Octet Structures," *J. Chem. Educ.* **1984,** *61,* 124.

arranged. However, in binary (two-element) compounds, the first element listed in the chemical formula is generally surrounded by the remaining atoms. Thus, we begin with a skeleton structure that shows single bonds between phosphorus and each chlorine:

$$Cl-P-Cl$$
$$|$$
$$Cl$$

(It is not crucial to place the atoms in exactly this arrangement; Lewis structures are not usually drawn to show geometry. However, it is important to show correctly which atoms are bonded to which.)

Third, complete the octets on the atoms bonded to the central atom. Placing octets around each Cl atom accounts for 24 electrons:

$$:\ddot{C}l-P-\ddot{C}l:$$
$$|$$
$$:\ddot{C}l:$$

Fourth, place the remaining two electrons on the central atom, completing the octet around that atom as well:

$$:\ddot{C}l-\ddot{P}-\ddot{C}l:$$
$$|$$
$$:\ddot{C}l:$$

This structure gives each atom an octet, so we stop at this point. (Remember that in achieving an octet, the bonding electrons are counted for both atoms.)

PRACTICE EXERCISE

(a) How many valence electrons should appear in the Lewis structure for CH_2Cl_2? **(b)** Draw the Lewis structure. (The central atom is C.)   *Answers:* **(a)** 20;   **(b)**

$$H$$
$$|$$
$$:\ddot{C}l-C-\ddot{C}l:$$
$$|$$
$$H$$

SAMPLE EXERCISE 8.7

Draw the Lewis structure for HCN.

SOLUTION   Hydrogen has one valence-shell electron, carbon (group 4A) has four, and nitrogen (group 5A) has five. The total number of valence-shell electrons is therefore $1 + 4 + 5 = 10$. Again there are various ways we might choose to arrange the atoms. Because hydrogen can accommodate only one electron pair, it always has only one single bond associated with it in any compound. This fact causes us to reject C—H—N as a possible arrangement. The remaining two possibilities are H—C—N and H—N—C. The first is the arrangement found experimentally. You might have guessed this to be the atomic arrangement because the formula is written with the atoms in this order. Thus we begin with a skeleton structure that shows single bonds between hydrogen, carbon, and nitrogen:

$$H-C-N$$

These two bonds account for four electrons. If we then place the remaining six electrons around N to give it an octet, we do not achieve an octet on C:

$$H-C-\ddot{N}:$$

We therefore try a double bond between C and N, using an unshared pair of electrons that we had placed on N. Again, there are fewer than eight electrons on C, so we try a triple bond. This structure gives an octet around both C and N:

$$H-C\equiv N:$$

PRACTICE EXERCISE

Draw the Lewis electron dot structure for the NO^+ ion.   ***Answer:*** $[:N \equiv O:]^+$

SAMPLE EXERCISE 8.8

Draw the Lewis structure for the BrO_3^- ion.

SOLUTION   Bromine (group 7A) has seven valence electrons, and oxygen (group 6A) has six. An extra electron is added to account for the ion having a 1− charge. The total number of valence-shell electrons is therefore $7 + (3 \times 6) + 1 = 26$. After putting in the single bonds and distributing the unshared electron pairs, we have

$$\left[:\ddot{O} - \ddot{Br} - \ddot{O}: \atop \quad :\ddot{O}: \right]^-$$

For oxyanions—BrO_3^-, SO_4^{2-}, NO_3^-, CO_3^{2-}, and so forth—the oxygen atoms surround the central nonmetal atom. Notice here and elsewhere that the Lewis structures of ions are written in brackets with the charge shown at the upper right.

PRACTICE EXERCISE

Draw the Lewis structure for the PO_4^{3-} ion.

Answer:
$$\left[\begin{array}{c} :\ddot{O}: \\ | \\ :\ddot{O} - P - \ddot{O}: \\ | \\ :\ddot{O}: \end{array} \right]^{3-}$$

8.7 Resonance Structures

We sometimes encounter substances in which the known arrangement of atoms is not adequately described by a single Lewis structure. The structural chemistry of nonmetallic elements affords several examples. Consider ozone, O_3, about which we shall have much to say in Chapter 18. This fascinating substance consists of bent molecules with both O—O distances the same, as shown in Figure 8.8. Because each oxygen atom contributes 6 valence-shell electrons, the ozone molecule has 18 valence-shell electrons. In writing the Lewis structure, we find that we must have one double bond to attain an octet of electrons about each atom:

$$:\ddot{O}{\diagdown}^{\ddot{O}}{\diagup}_{O:}$$

But this structure cannot by itself be correct, because it requires that one O—O bond be different from the other, contrary to the observed structure; we would expect the O=O double bond to be shorter than the O—O single bond. However, in drawing the Lewis structure we could just as easily have put the O=O bond on the left:

$$_{O}{\diagup}^{\ddot{O}}{\diagdown}_{O:}$$

The two alternative Lewis structures for ozone are equivalent except for the placement of electrons. Equivalent Lewis structures of this sort are called **reso-**

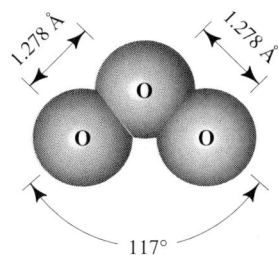

FIGURE 8.8   Molecular structure of ozone, O_3.

1.278 Å   1.278 Å

117°

Teaching Note: Not all resonance structures are necessarily equivalent. Some possible structures may be better than others. Formal charges are a way of determining which structures are favored. See "A Closer Look: Formal Charge and Lewis Structures."

Formal Charge and Lewis Structures

The concept of **formal charge** is sometimes used as an aid in deciding between alternative Lewis structures. The formal charge is largely a means of "bookkeeping" for the valence electrons. It is the charge an atom would have if all atoms had the same electronegativity. To calculate the formal charge on any atom in a Lewis structure, we assign electrons to the atom as follows:

1. *All* the unshared (nonbonding) electrons are assigned to the atom on which they are found.
2. *Half* the bonding electrons are assigned to each atom in the bond.

The formal charge of an atom equals *the number of valence electrons in the isolated atom, minus the number of electrons assigned to the atom in the Lewis structure.*

   Let's illustrate these rules by calculating the formal charges on the C and N atoms in the cyanide ion, CN^-:

$$[:C \equiv N:]^-$$

We first count the number of electrons assigned to the C atom. There are 2 from the nonbonding pair of electrons, and 3 from the 6 electrons in the triple bond, for a total of 5. The number of valence electrons on a neutral C atom (group 4A) is 4. Thus, the formal charge on C is $4 - 5 = -1$. For N, there are 2 nonbonding electrons and 3 electrons from the triple bond. The number of valence electrons on a neutral N atom (group 5A) is 5. Thus, the formal charge on N is $5 - 5 = 0$. We indicate the formal charges in the Lewis formula by inserting circled charges near the atoms:

$$[:C \equiv N:]^- \overset{\ominus}{}$$

Because the ion as a whole has a charge of $1-$, the formal charges of all atoms must sum to $1-$.

   To see how the idea of formal charge can help in making a distinction between alternative Lewis structures, consider the thiocyanate ion, NCS^-. There are three possible orders for the atoms in this ion. For each, we can write a Lewis structure that yields an octet about each atom. For each structure, we can then calculate the formal charge on each atom:

Formal	$[\ddot{N}=C=\ddot{S}]^-$	$[C=S=\ddot{N}]^-$	$[\ddot{S}=N=\ddot{C}]^-$
charge	−1 0 0	−2 +2 −1	0 +1 −2

   As a general rule, *when several Lewis structures are possible, the most stable one will be that in which the atoms bear the smallest formal charges, and any negative formal charges reside on the more electronegative atoms.*

   The Lewis structure on the left is clearly superior to the other two in producing the smallest variations in formal charge among the atoms. Furthermore, it is more reasonable to place a negative charge on N than on the less electronegative C atom. This suggests that the arrangement shown on the left is the preferred structure for the ion; indeed, it is the observed structure:

$$[\overset{\ominus}{\ddot{N}}=C=\ddot{S}]^-$$

   Although the concept of formal charge is useful in helping to decide between alternative Lewis structures, keep in mind that *formal charges do not represent real charges on atoms.* Electronegativity differences between atoms are important in determining the actual charge distributions in molecules and ions.

Learning Goal 12: Write resonance forms for molecules or polyatomic ions that are not adequately described by a single Lewis structure.

nance structures or **resonance forms.** To describe the structure of ozone properly, we write both Lewis structures and indicate that the real molecule is described by an average of the structures suggested by the two resonance forms:

The double-headed arrow indicates that the structures shown are resonance forms.

   Insight into the meaning of resonance structures can be gained from a simple analogy: A medieval European who had traveled to Africa described a rhinoceros as having the characteristics of two mythical creatures, a unicorn and a dragon. It was not a unicorn one second and a dragon the next but sort of a

Teaching Note: The double headed arrow (⟷) is specifically reserved for indicating that two or more structures are resonance forms. This symbol must not be used in other contexts, for example, equilibria.

blend of the two. Likewise, if a molecule (or ion) has two or more resonance structures, the molecule is a blend of these structures. The molecule *does not* oscillate rapidly between two or more different forms. There is only one form of the molecule. For example, there is a single kind of ozone molecule, which has two equivalent O—O bonds whose lengths are intermediate between the lengths of O—O single bonds and O=O double bonds. The molecule can be visualized as a blend of its two resonance structures. We write resonance structures only because a single Lewis structure inadequately describes the electron distribution in the molecule.

As an additional example of resonance structures, consider the nitrate ion, NO_3^-, one of the most commonly encountered anions. Three equivalent Lewis structures can be drawn, each with a different location for the double bond:

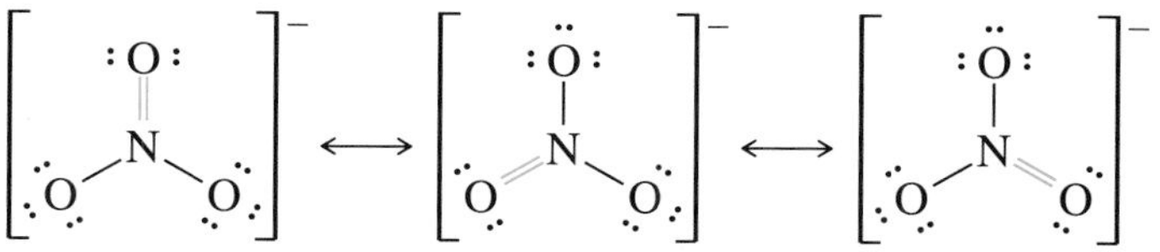

Notice that the arrangement of nuclei is the same in each structure; only the placement of electrons differs. In writing resonance structures, the same atoms must be bonded to one another in all structures, so that the only differences are in the arrangements of electrons. All three Lewis structures taken together adequately describe the nitrate ion, which has three equal N—O distances.

Teaching Note: The resulting bonds are sometimes referred to as 1 1/3 bonds, although that description is more valid in molecular orbital theory. See Section 9.6.

SAMPLE EXERCISE 8.9

Which has the shorter sulfur-oxygen bonds, SO_3 or SO_3^{2-}?

SOLUTION The sulfur atom has 6 valence-shell electrons, as does oxygen. Thus, SO_3 contains 24 valence-shell electrons. In writing the Lewis structure, we see that there are three equivalent resonance structures that can be drawn:

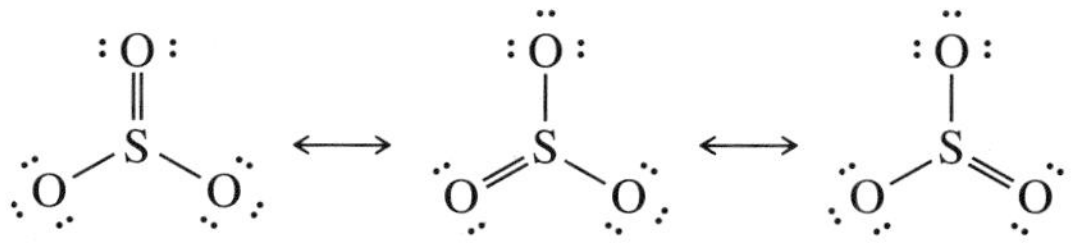

Because the actual molecule is a blend of these structures, each S—O bond distance should be about one-third of the way between that of a single and that of a double bond. That is, they should be shorter than single bonds but not as short as double bonds.

The SO_3^{2-} ion has 26 electrons, leading to the following Lewis structure:

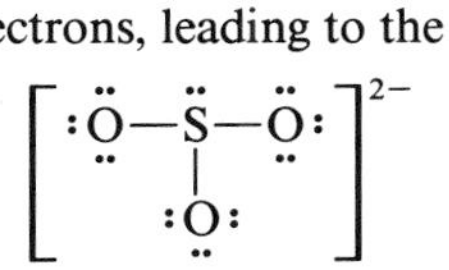

In this case, the S—O bonds are single bonds.

Our analysis of each case suggests that SO_3 should have the shorter S—O bonds and SO_3^{2-} the longer ones. This agrees with experiment; the S—O bond length in SO_3 is 1.42 Å, whereas that in SO_3^{2-} is 1.51 Å.

PRACTICE EXERCISE

Draw two equivalent resonance structures for the NO_2^- ion.

Answer:

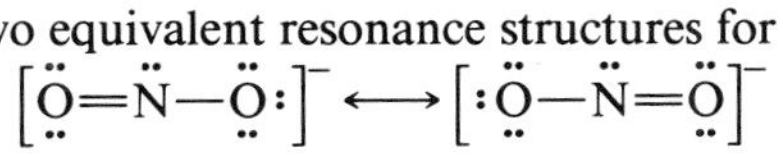

8.8 Exceptions to the Octet Rule

Common Misconception: Students often believe that the octet rule cannot be violated. They need to understand that the term *exception* does not mean such molecules are rare. Indeed, there are many exceptions to the octet rule.

Learning Goal 13: Write the Lewis structures for molecules and ions containing covalent molecules that have an odd number of electrons, a deficiency of electrons or an expanded octet.

The octet rule is so simple and useful in introducing the basic concepts of bonding that you might assume that it is always obeyed. In Section 8.2, however, we noted its limitation in dealing with ionic compounds of the transition metals. The octet rule also fails in many situations involving covalent bonding. These exceptions to the octet rule are of three main types:

1. Molecules with an odd number of electrons
2. Molecules in which an atom has less than an octet
3. Molecules in which an atom has more than an octet.

Odd Number of Electrons

In the vast majority of molecules, the number of electrons is even, and complete pairing of electron spins occurs. However, in a few molecules such as ClO_2, NO, and NO_2, the number of electrons is odd. For example, NO contains $5 + 6 = 11$ valence electrons. Obviously, complete pairing of these electrons is impossible, and an octet around each atom cannot be achieved.

Less Than an Octet

A second type of exception occurs when there are fewer than eight electrons around an atom in a molecule or ion. This is also a relatively rare situation and is most often encountered in compounds of boron and beryllium. For example, let's consider boron trifluoride, BF_3. If we follow the procedure on page 263 for drawing Lewis structures, then through the first four steps we have the following structure:

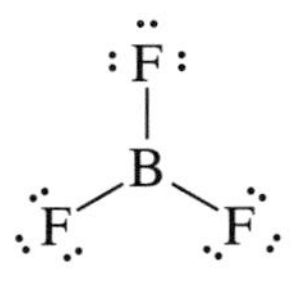

We see that there are only six electrons around the boron atom. We could complete the octet around boron by forming a double bond. In so doing, we see that there are three such equivalent resonance structures:

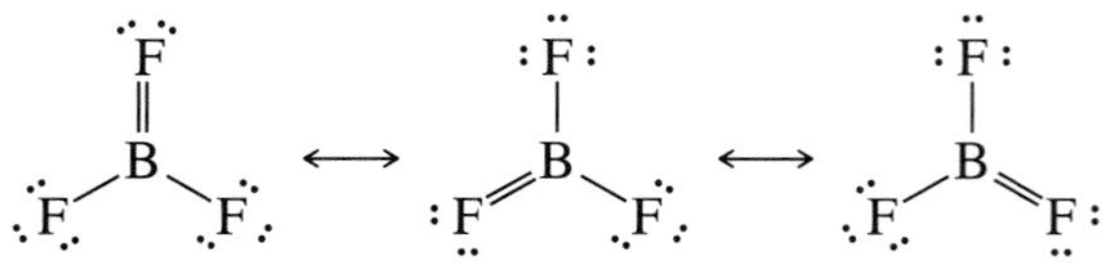

Teaching Note: If you have included the Closer Look section on formal charge, it follows that the six-electron structure of BF_3 should be most stable, with all atoms having formal charges of zero.

However, in forming these Lewis structures, we have forced a fluorine atom to share additional electrons with the boron atom. This is inconsistent with the high electronegativity of fluorine: We don't expect the fluorine atoms to share additional electrons with the boron atom.* We conclude that the Lewis struc-

* When there is a double bond between B and F, the F atom has a formal charge of 1+, and the less electronegative B atom has a formal charge of 1−, an unfavorable situation.

tures in which there is a B=F double bond are less important than the one in which there is less than an octet around boron:

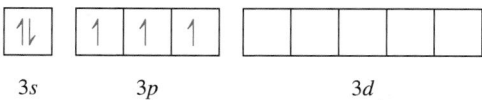

Most important   Less important

We usually represent BF_3 solely by the leftmost resonance structure in which there are only six electrons around boron. The chemical behavior of BF_3 is consistent with this representation. Thus, BF_3 reacts very energetically with molecules that have an unshared pair of electrons that can be used to form a bond with boron. For example, it reacts with ammonia, NH_3, to form the compound NH_3BF_3:

$$\underset{\underset{H}{|}}{\overset{\overset{H}{|}}{H{-}N}}: \;+\; B\!\!\overset{\overset{F}{\diagup}}{\underset{\underset{F}{\diagdown}}{{-}F}} \;\longrightarrow\; \underset{\underset{H}{|}}{\overset{\overset{H}{|}}{H{-}N}}{-}B\!\!\overset{\overset{F}{\diagup}}{\underset{\underset{F}{\diagdown}}{{-}F}}$$

In this stable compound boron has an octet of electrons.

More Than an Octet

The third and largest class of exceptions consists of molecules or ions in which there are more than eight electrons in the valence shell of an atom. As an example, consider PCl_5. When we draw the Lewis structure for this molecule, we are forced to "expand" the valence shell and place 10 electrons around the central phosphorus atom:

$$:\!\overset{..}{Cl}\!-\!\overset{\overset{\textstyle :\overset{..}{Cl}:}{|}}{\underset{\underset{\textstyle :\overset{..}{Cl}:}{|}}{P}}\!\!\overset{\overset{\textstyle \overset{..}{Cl}:}{\diagup}}{\underset{\underset{\textstyle \overset{..}{Cl}:}{\diagdown}}{}}$$

Other examples of molecules and ions with "expanded" valence shells are SF_4, AsF_6^-, and ICl_4^-. The corresponding molecules with a second-period atom, such as NCl_5 and OF_4, do *not* exist. Let's take a look at why expanded valence shells are observed only for elements in period 3 and beyond in the periodic table.

    The octet rule works as well as it does because the representative elements usually employ only an ns and three np valence-shell orbitals in bonding, and these orbitals hold eight electrons. Because elements of the second period have only $2s$ and $2p$ orbitals available for bonding, they can never have more than an octet of electrons in their valence shells. However, from the third period on, the elements have unfilled nd orbitals that can be used in bonding. For example, the orbital diagram for the valence shell of a phosphorus atom is as follows:

Point of Emphasis: Attaining more electrons than an octet is common for third-period elements and ones lower in the periodic table. Second-period elements cannot exceed the octet.

$\uparrow\downarrow$	$\uparrow$	$\uparrow$	$\uparrow$					

    $3s$ $3p$ $3d$

Although third-period elements such as phosphorus often satisfy the octet rule, as in PF_3, they also often exceed it by using their empty d orbitals to accommodate additional electrons.

Size also plays an important role in determining whether an atom can accommodate more than eight electrons. The larger the central atom, the larger the number of atoms that can surround it. The occurrences of expanded valence shells therefore increase with increasing size of the central atom. The size of the surrounding atoms is also important. Expanded valence shells occur most often when the central atom is bonded to the smallest and most electronegative atoms, such as F, Cl, and O.

SAMPLE EXERCISE 8.10

Draw the Lewis structure for ICl_4^-.

SOLUTION Iodine (group 7A) has 7 valence electrons; each chlorine (group 7A) also has 7; an extra electron is added to account for the $1-$ charge of the ion. Therefore, the total number of valence electrons is $7 + 4(7) + 1 = 36$. The I atom is the central atom in the ion. Putting 8 electrons around each Cl atom (including a pair of electrons between I and each Cl to represent the single bonds between these atoms) requires $8 \times 4 = 32$ electrons. We are thus left with $36 - 32 = 4$ electrons to be placed on the larger iodine:

Therefore, iodine has 12 electrons around it, exceeding the common octet of electrons.

PRACTICE EXERCISE

Which of the following atoms is never found with more than an octet of electrons around it: S, C, P, Br? *Answer:* C

8.9 Strengths of Covalent Bonds

Point of Emphasis: Bond-dissociation energy is the energy *required* to break a bond.

Learning Goal 14: Relate bond energies to bond strengths, and use bond energies to estimate ΔH for reactions.

Point of Emphasis: Individual bond energies (for example, the first, second, third, and fourth C-H bond energies in CH_4) usually differ from the average bond energy.

The stability of a molecule can be related to the strengths of the covalent bonds it contains. The strength of a covalent bond between two atoms is determined by the energy required to break that bond. The **bond-dissociation energy,** also called the **bond energy,** is the enthalpy change, ΔH, required to break a particular bond in a mole of gaseous substance. For example, the dissociation energy for the bond between chlorine atoms in the Cl_2 molecule is the energy required to dissociate a mole of Cl_2 into chlorine atoms:

$$:\ddot{C}l-\ddot{C}l:(g) \longrightarrow 2 :\ddot{C}l\cdot(g) \qquad \Delta H = D(Cl-Cl) = 242 \text{ kJ}$$

We use the designation D(bond type) in this equation and elsewhere to represent bond-dissociation energies.

It is a relatively easy matter to assign bond energies to bonds in diatomic molecules. As we have seen, the bond energy is just the energy required to break the diatomic molecule into its component atoms. However, for bonds that occur only in polyatomic molecules (such as the C—H bond), we must often utilize average bond energies. For example, the enthalpy change for the process shown below (called *atomization*) can be used to define an average bond strength for the C—H bond:

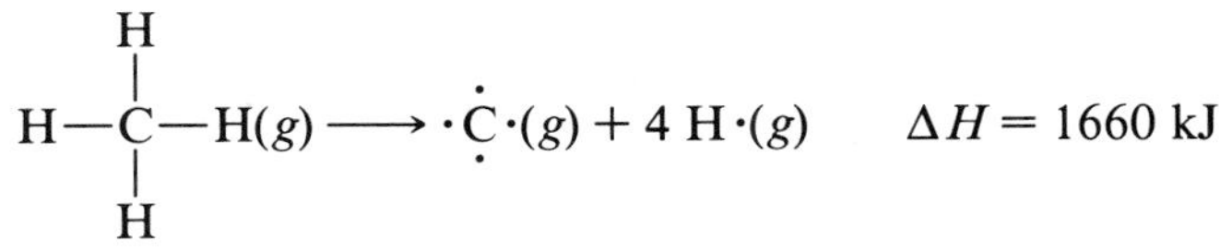

$$H-\overset{\displaystyle H}{\underset{\displaystyle H}{\overset{|}{\underset{|}{C}}}}-H(g) \longrightarrow \cdot\ddot{C}\cdot(g) + 4\,H\cdot(g) \qquad \Delta H = 1660\ \text{kJ}$$

Because there are four equivalent C—H bonds in methane, the heat of atomization is equal to the total bond energies of the four C—H bonds. Therefore, the average C—H bond energy is $D(C-H) = (1660/4)\ \text{kJ/mol} = 415\ \text{kJ/mol}$.

The bond energy for a given set of atoms, say C—H, depends on the rest of the molecule of which it is a part. However, the variation from one molecule to another is generally small. This supports the idea that the bonding electron pairs are localized between atoms. If we consider C—H bond strengths in many different compounds, we find that the average strength is 413 kJ/mol, which compares closely with the 415 kJ/mol value calculated from CH_4.

Table 8.4 lists several average bond energies. Notice that *the bond energy is always a positive quantity;* energy is always required to break chemical bonds. Conversely, energy is released when a bond forms between two gaseous atoms or molecular fragments. Of course, the greater the bond energy, the stronger the bond.

A molecule with strong chemical bonds generally has less tendency to undergo chemical change than does one with weak bonds. This relationship between strong bonding and chemical stability helps explain the chemical form in which many elements are found in nature. For example, Si—O bonds are

TABLE 8.4 △ Average Bond Energies (kJ/mol)

Single bonds

C—H	413	N—H	391	O—H	463	F—F	155
C—C	348	N—N	163	O—O	146		
C—N	293	N—O	201	O—F	190	Cl—F	253
C—O	358	N—F	272	O—Cl	203	Cl—Cl	242
C—F	485	N—Cl	200	O—I	234		
C—Cl	328	N—Br	243			Br—F	237
C—Br	276			S—H	339	Br—Cl	218
C—I	240			S—F	327	Br—Br	193
C—S	259	H—H	436	S—Cl	253		
		H—F	567	S—Br	218	I—Cl	208
Si—H	323	H—Cl	431	S—S	266	I—Br	175
Si—Si	226	H—Br	366			I—I	151
Si—C	301	H—I	299				
Si—O	368						

Multiple bonds

C=C	614	N=N	418	O_2	495
C≡C	839	N≡N	941		
C=N	615			S=O	523
C≡N	891			S=S	418
C=O	799				
C≡O	1072				

among the strongest ones that silicon forms. It is not surprising therefore that SiO_2 and other substances containing Si—O bonds (silicates) are so common; it is estimated that over 90 percent of the earth's crust is composed of SiO_2 and silicates. We shall discuss these compounds in greater detail in Chapter 23.

Bond Energies and the Enthalpy of Reactions

We can use the average bond energies given in Table 8.4 to estimate the enthalpies of chemical reactions in which bonds are broken and new ones are made. This procedure enables us to estimate quickly whether a given reaction will be endothermic ($\Delta H > 0$) or exothermic ($\Delta H < 0$), even if we do not know ΔH_f^0 for all the chemical species involved. Our strategy for estimating reaction enthalpies is straightforward: (1) We determine which bonds are being broken in the reaction and sum the bond energies of these bonds. This sum is the total amount of energy that must be supplied to break bonds during the reaction. (2) We determine which bonds are being formed in the reaction and sum these bond energies. This total is the amount of energy released by bond formation during the reaction. (3) The enthalpy of the reaction is estimated as the total energy required to break bonds, minus the total bond energy of the new bonds formed:

$$\Delta H = \Sigma \text{ (bond energies of bonds broken)} -$$
$$\Sigma \text{ (bond energies of bonds formed)} \quad [8.11]$$

As an example, consider the reaction between 1 mol of chlorine and 1 mol of methane:

$$\text{Cl—Cl}(g) + \text{H—CH}_3(g) \longrightarrow \text{H—Cl}(g) + \text{Cl—CH}_3(g) \quad [8.12]$$

In the course of this reaction, the following bonds are broken and made:

$$
\begin{aligned}
&\text{Bonds broken:} && \text{1 mol Cl—Cl, 1 mol C—H} \\
&\text{Bonds formed:} && \text{1 mol H—Cl, 1 mol C—Cl}
\end{aligned}
$$

Using Equation 8.11 and the data in Table 8.4, we estimate the enthalpy of the reaction as

$$
\begin{aligned}
\Delta H &= [D(\text{Cl—Cl}) + D(\text{C—H})] - [D(\text{H—Cl}) + D(\text{C—Cl})] \\
&= (242 \text{ kJ} + 413 \text{ kJ}) - (431 \text{ kJ} + 328 \text{ kJ}) \\
&= -104 \text{ kJ}
\end{aligned}
$$

We see that the reaction is exothermic because the bonds in the products (especially the H—Cl bond) are stronger than those in the reactants (especially the Cl—Cl bond).

We usually use bond energies to estimate ΔH for a reaction only if we do not have all the needed ΔH_f^0 values readily at hand. Thus, in the example above we cannot calculate the enthalpy from ΔH_f^0 values and Hess's law because ΔH_f^0 for $CH_3Cl(g)$ is not given in Appendix C (although we could certainly find that ΔH_f^0 in other sources). It is also important to remember that bond energies are derived for gaseous molecules and that they are often averaged values. Nonetheless, the use of bond energies often gives a result very close to the correct value, as illustrated in Sample Exercise 8.11.

SAMPLE EXERCISE 8.11

Using Table 8.4, estimate ΔH for the following reaction (where we show explicitly the bonds involved in the reactants and products):

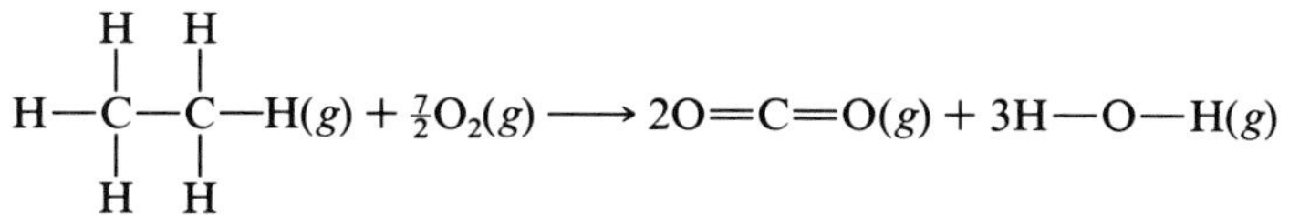

$$H{-}\underset{\underset{H}{|}}{\overset{\overset{H}{|}}{C}}{-}\underset{\underset{H}{|}}{\overset{\overset{H}{|}}{C}}{-}H(g) + \tfrac{7}{2}O_2(g) \longrightarrow 2O{=}C{=}O(g) + 3H{-}O{-}H(g)$$

SOLUTION Among the reactants, we must break six C—H bonds and a C—C bond in C_2H_6; we also break $\tfrac{7}{2}O_2$ bonds. Among the products, we form four C=O bonds (two in each CO_2) and six O—H bonds (two in each H_2O). Using Equation 8.11 and data from Table 8.4, we have

$$\begin{aligned}
\Delta H &= 6D(C{-}H) + D(C{-}C) + \tfrac{7}{2}D(O_2) - 4D(C{=}O) - 6D(O{-}H) \\
&= 6(413 \text{ kJ}) + 348 \text{ kJ} + \tfrac{7}{2}(495 \text{ kJ}) - 4(799 \text{ kJ}) - 6(463 \text{ kJ}) \\
&= 4558 \text{ kJ} - 5974 \text{ kJ} \\
&= -1416 \text{ kJ}
\end{aligned}$$

This estimate can be compared with the value of -1428 kJ calculated from more accurate thermochemical data; the agreement is excellent.

PRACTICE EXERCISE

Using Table 8.4, estimate ΔH for the following reaction:

$$H{-}\underset{\underset{H}{|}}{N}{-}\underset{\underset{H}{|}}{N}{-}H(g) \longrightarrow N{\equiv}N(g) + 2H{-}H(g)$$

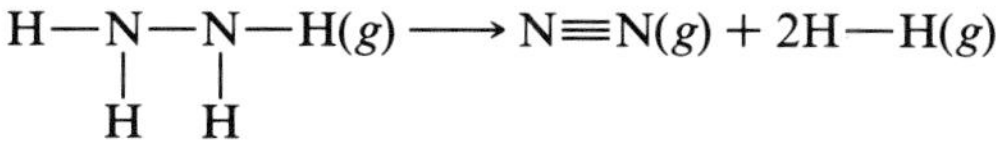

Answer: -86 kJ

Bond Strength and Bond Length

Just as we can define an average bond strength, we can also define an average bond length for a number of common bond types. Some of these are listed in Table 8.5. Of particular interest to us here is the relationship among bond strength, bond length, and the number of bonds between the atoms. For exam-

TABLE 8.5 △ Average Bond Lengths for Some Single, Double, and Triple Bonds

Bond	Bond length (Å)	Bond	Bond length (Å)
C—C	1.54	N—N	1.47
C=C	1.34	N=N	1.24
C≡C	1.20	N≡N	1.10
C—N	1.43	N—O	1.36
C=N	1.38	N=O	1.22
C≡N	1.16		
		O—O	1.48
C—O	1.43	O=O	1.21
C=O	1.23		
C≡O	1.13		

Explosives

Enormous amounts of energy can be stored in chemical bonds. Perhaps the most graphic example of the chemical energy stored in bonds is in the chemistry of explosives. An explosive is a liquid or solid substance that satisfies three principal criteria: (1) It must decompose very exothermically; (2) the products of its decomposition must be gaseous, so that a tremendous gas pressure accompanies the decomposition; and (3) its decomposition must occur extremely rapidly. The combination of these three effects leads to the violent generation of heat and gases that we associate with explosions (Figure 8.9).

What are the most desirable products into which an explosive should decompose? Ideally, to give the most exothermic reaction, an explosive should have weak chemical bonds, and it should decompose into many small molecules with very strong bonds. Looking at

FIGURE 8.9 Explosives being used in the demolition of buildings. (V. Faint/The Image Bank)

bond energies (Table 8.4), we see that the $N\equiv N$, $C\equiv O$, and $C=O$ bonds are among the strongest. Not surprisingly, explosives are usually designed to produce $N_2(g)$, $CO(g)$, and $CO_2(g)$. Water vapor is nearly always produced as well.

Many common explosives are organic molecules that contain nitro (NO_2) or nitrate (NO_3) groups attached to a carbon backbone. The structures of two of the most familiar explosives, glyceryl trinitrate (more commonly called nitroglycerin) and trinitrotoluene (TNT), are shown at top right.

Nitroglycerin

TNT

Nitroglycerin is a pale-yellow, oily liquid. It is highly *shock-sensitive:* Merely shaking the liquid can cause its explosive decomposition into nitrogen, carbon dioxide, water, and oxygen gases:

$$4C_3H_5N_3O_9(l) \longrightarrow$$
$$6N_2(g) + 12CO_2(g) + 10H_2O(g) + O_2(g)$$

The high energies of the bonds in the N_2 molecules (941 kJ/mol), CO_2 molecules (2×799 kJ/mol), and water molecules (2×463 kJ/mol) make this reaction enormously exothermic. Nitroglycerin is an exceptionally unstable explosive because it is in nearly perfect *explosive balance:* Ideally, with the exception of a small amount of $O_2(g)$ produced, the only products are N_2, CO_2, and H_2O. Note also that, unlike combustion reactions (Section 3.2), explosions are entirely self-contained. No other reagent, such as $O_2(g)$, is needed for the explosive decomposition.

Because nitroglycerin is so unstable, it is difficult to use as a controllable explosive. The Swedish inventor Alfred Nobel (1833–1896) found that mixing nitroglycerin with an absorbent solid material such as diatomaceous earth gives a solid explosive *(dynamite)* that is much safer than liquid nitroglycerin. Nobel's discovery was hugely profitable and led to his endowment of the Nobel Prizes and other philanthropic causes.

ple, we can use data in Tables 8.4 and 8.5 to compare the bond lengths and bond energies of carbon-carbon single, double, and triple bonds:

C—C	C=C	C≡C
1.54 Å	1.34 Å	1.20 Å
348 kJ/mol	614 kJ/mol	839 kJ/mol

As the number of bonds between the carbon atoms increases, the bond energy increases and the bond length decreases; that is, the carbon atoms are held more closely and more tightly together. In general, *as the number of bonds between two atoms increases, the bond grows shorter and stronger.*

8.10 Oxidation Numbers

In this chapter we have considered two kinds of bonds, ionic and covalent. We have seen (Section 8.5) that when a covalent bond forms between two atoms with different electronegativities, the bonding electrons lie somewhat closer to the more electronegative atom. For example, in HCl, the bonding is polar covalent with the electrons in the H—Cl bond displaced toward the more electronegative Cl atom:

$$H \overset{+\ \longrightarrow}{\underset{\cdot\cdot}{:}\overset{\cdot\cdot}{Cl}:}$$

The H atom therefore carries a partial positive charge, and the Cl atom a partial negative one.

In keeping track of electrons, it is sometimes helpful to assign charges to atoms by assigning shared electrons to the more electronegative atom. In HCl, this procedure gives Cl eight valence-shell electrons, one more than the neutral atom. We have in effect given a −1 charge to the chlorine. Hydrogen, stripped of its electron, is assigned a charge of +1.

Charges assigned in this fashion are called **oxidation numbers** or **oxidation states.** The oxidation number of an atom is the charge that results when the electrons in a covalent bond are assigned to the more electronegative atom; it is the charge an atom would possess *if* the bonding were ionic. In HCl, the oxidation number of H is +1 and that of Cl is −1. (In writing oxidation numbers, we will write the sign before the number to distinguish them from actual electronic charges, which we write with the number first.)

Oxidation numbers do not correspond to real charges on the atoms, except in the special case of simple ionic substances. Nevertheless, they are useful in a variety of situations. Their most frequent uses are in naming compounds, in balancing chemical equations for reactions in which changes in oxidation numbers occur, and in examining trends in chemical properties.

Although we can determine oxidation numbers for atoms using Lewis structures and electronegativities as we have done for HCl, we seldom use this procedure. It is generally easier to determine oxidation numbers using the following set of rules.

1. *The oxidation number of an element in its elemental form is zero.* For an isolated atom — like an N atom, where there is no bonding and no net

A. A. Woolf, "Oxidation Numbers and their Limitations," *J. Chem. Educ.* **1988,** *65,* 45.

Learning Goal 15: Assign oxidation numbers to atoms in molecules and ions.

Point of Emphasis: Assigning oxidation numbers in a covalent compound is like asking the question "If this were an ionic compound, what would the ion charges be?"

Joel M. Kauffman, "Simple Method for Determination of Oxidation Numbers of Atoms In Compounds," *J. Chem. Educ.* **1986,** *63,* 474.

charge — the oxidation state must be 0. It is also zero for any elemental substance in which there is bonding. For example, in Na metal, N_2, Cl_2, and P_4 the bonding electrons are shared equally between identical atoms, giving each atom an oxidation state of 0.

2. *The oxidation number of a monoatomic ion is the same as its charge.* For example, the oxidation number of sodium in Na^+ is $+1$, and that of sulfur in S^{2-} is -2.

3. *In binary compounds (those with two different elements), the element with greater electronegativity is assigned a negative oxidation number equal to its charge in simple ionic compounds of the element.* For example, consider the oxidation state of Cl in PCl_3. Cl is more electronegative than P. In its simple ionic compounds, chlorine appears as the chloride ion, Cl^-. Thus, in PCl_3, Cl is assigned an oxidation number of -1.

4. *The sum of the oxidation numbers equals zero for an electrically neutral compound and equals the overall charge for an ionic species.* For example, PCl_3 is a neutral molecule. Thus, the sum of the oxidation numbers of the P and Cl atoms must equal zero. Because the oxidation number of each Cl in this compound is -1 (rule 3), the oxidation number of P must be $+3$. In like manner, the sum of the oxidation numbers of C and O in CO_3^{2-} must equal -2. The oxidation number of O in this ion is -2, because O is more electronegative than C and -2 is the charge on the oxide ion (rule 3). Therefore, the oxidation number on C must be $+4$, because $+4 + 3(-2) = -2$.

The periodic table provides us with many additional guidelines for assigning oxidation numbers. As shown in Figure 8.10, oxidation numbers exhibit periodic trends. Some observations are particularly helpful. The alkali metals (group 1A) exhibit only the oxidation state of $+1$ in their compounds. The alkaline earth metals (group 2A) are always found in compounds in the $+2$ oxidation state. The most commonly encountered element in group 3A, Al, is always found in the $+3$ oxidation state.

The most electronegative element, F, is always found in compounds in the -1 oxidation state. Oxygen in compounds is nearly always in the -2 oxidation state. The only common exception to this general rule occurs in peroxides. In the peroxide ion, O_2^{2-}, and in molecular peroxides, such as H_2O_2, oxygen has an oxidation number of -1. Hydrogen has an oxidation number of $+1$ when it is bonded to a more electronegative element (most nonmetals) and of -1 when bonded to a less electronegative element (most metals).

FIGURE 8.10 Common nonzero oxidation numbers for elements with atomic numbers 3 through 39. Notice that the maximum and minimum oxidation states (through which lines have been drawn for emphasis) are a periodic function of atomic number.

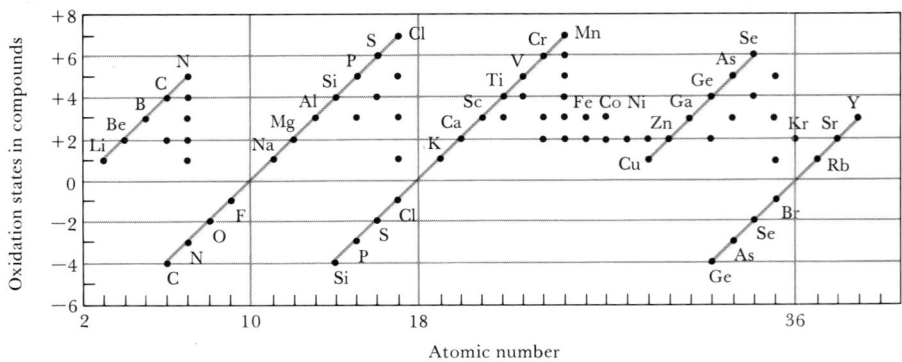

SAMPLE EXERCISE 8.12

Determine the oxidation state of sulfur in each of the following: **(a)** H_2S; **(b)** S_8; **(c)** SCl_2; **(d)** Na_2SO_3; **(e)** SO_4^{2-}.

SOLUTION **(a)** This is a binary (two-element) compound. Because S is more electronegative than H, S must have a negative oxidation number equal to its ionic charge (rule 3). Thus, S has an oxidation number of -2. This is consistent with the oxidation number of $+1$ expected for H.

(b) Because this is an elemental form of sulfur, the oxidation state of S is 0 (rule 1).

(c) Chlorine is more electronegative than sulfur. Therefore, the Cl in this binary compound must have a negative oxidation number equal to its ionic charge (rule 3), which is -1. The sum of the oxidation numbers must equal zero (rule 4). Letting x equal the oxidation number of S, we have $x + 2(-1) = 0$. Consequently, the oxidation state of S, x, must be $+2$.

(d) Sodium, an alkali metal, is always found in compounds in the $+1$ oxidation state. Oxygen has a common oxidation state of -2. If we let x equal the oxidation number of S, we have $2(+1) + x + 3(-2) = 0$. Therefore, the oxidation number of S in this compound is $+4$.

(e) The oxidation state of O is -2. The sum of the oxidation numbers equals -2, the net charge of the SO_4^{2-} ion. Letting x equal the oxidation number of S, we have $x + 4(-2) = -2$. From this relation we conclude that the oxidation state of S is $+6$.

These examples illustrate the range of oxidation states exhibited by sulfur, from -2 to $+6$. In general, the most negative oxidation state of a nonmetal corresponds to the number of electrons that must be added to the atom to give it an octet. In this case, S, which belongs to periodic family 6A, has six valence-shell electrons. Thus, two more are needed to give it an octet, as in the S^{2-} ion. The most positive oxidation state, in this case $+6$, corresponds to loss of all valence-shell electrons.

PRACTICE EXERCISE

What is the oxidation state of the underlined element in each of the following: **(a)** $\underline{P}_2O_5$; **(b)** $Na\underline{H}$; **(c)** $\underline{Cr}_2O_7^{2-}$; **(d)** $\underline{Sn}Br_4$; **(e)** $Ba\underline{O}_2$?   *Answers:* **(a)** $+5$; **(b)** -1; **(c)** $+6$; **(d)** $+4$; **(e)** -1

Oxidation Numbers and Nomenclature

We saw in Section 2.6 that there are two general approaches to naming binary compounds (compounds composed of two elements), one used for ionic compounds and the other for molecular ones. In both approaches, the name of the less electronegative element is given first, followed by the name of the more electronegative element, modified to have an *-ide* ending. Compounds that are ionic are given names based on their component ions, including the charge of the cation if it is variable. Those that are molecular are named using the prefixes listed in Table 2.5 to indicate the number of atoms of each kind in the substance:

Learning Goal 16: Assign acceptable names to simple inorganic compounds and ions.

Ionic		*Molecular*	
MgH_2	magnesium hydride	H_2S	dihydrogen sulfide
FeF_2	iron(II) fluoride	OF_2	oxygen difluoride
Mn_2O_3	manganese(III) oxide	Cl_2O_3	dichlorine trioxide

Point of Emphasis: The use of oxidation states in names (the Stock notation) is becoming the preferred method of naming compounds, especially for metal-containing compounds.

The dividing line between the two approaches, however, is not always clear, and both approaches are often applied to the same substances. For example, TiO_2, which is a commercially important white paint pigment, is sometimes referred to as titanium(IV) oxide but is more commonly called titanium dioxide.

Binary Oxides

The concepts discussed in this chapter help us organize and understand many important chemical observations. To illustrate this point, let's consider the binary compounds of oxygen, which we treated briefly in Sections 7.6 and 7.8.

With an electronegativity of 3.5, oxygen is more electronegative than all other elements except fluorine. Because metals tend to have low electronegativities, oxides of metals in low oxidation states (especially +1 and +2) are usually ionic solids with large lattice energies (Table 8.2). As a result, these metal oxides typically have high melting points (Table 8.6). Many metal oxides are therefore used as heat-resistant materials, such as firebrick and ceramics. Many other applications of metal oxides, such as the use of Y_2O_3 in fluorescent lights (Figure 8.11), also depend on the high thermal stability of these materials.

Because they contain the O^{2-} ion, ionic metal oxides are basic. ∞ (Sec. 7.6) For example, CaO, also known as lime, is an important commercial base: It reacts with water to form $Ca(OH)_2$. Similarly, Na_2O dissolves in water to form NaOH. In keeping with their high lattice energies, most metal oxides are rather insoluble in water.

The electronegativity of most nonmetals is sufficiently high that nonmetal oxides are not ionic. Rather, these elements form molecular oxides that contain polar covalent bonds with oxygen. These substances are typically gases, liquids, or solids with low melting points. Nonmetal oxides, especially those in which the nonmetal is in a high oxidation state, are generally acidic. ∞ (Sec. 7.6) For example, chlorine(VII) oxide, Cl_2O_7, dissolves in water to form perchloric acid, $HClO_4$:

$$Cl_2O_7(l) + H_2O(l) \longrightarrow 2HClO_4(aq)$$

Notice that Cl has an oxidation state of +7 in both Cl_2O_7 and $HClO_4$. When two nonmetals are in the same oxidation state, the acidity of the oxide increases with increasing electronegativity of the element. For example, in both SO_2 and SeO_2 the oxidation number of the central atom is +4. Because S is more electronegative than Se, SO_2 is more acidic than SeO_2.

FIGURE 8.11 Yttrium oxide, Y_2O_3, is a white solid. Here we see the red fluorescence of a sample of yttrium oxide caused by the UV lamp seen in the background. This oxide material is used to coat the walls of fluorescent lamps and TV picture tubes to enhance the red light they produce. This use of Y_2O_3 relies on its thermal stability at high operating temperature. (Courtesy of GTE Products Corporation)

In general, the acidity of oxides increases with increasing oxidation state of the element. A fascinating example of this trend is seen in the oxides of the transition metals. For example, manganese(II) oxide, MnO, is an ionic solid with a high melting point that has the same structure as NaCl. Although insoluble in water, MnO is strongly basic. It dissolves in acid, neutralizing the acid and giving Mn^{2+} ions:

$$MnO(s) + 2H^+(aq) \longrightarrow Mn^{2+}(aq) + H_2O(l)$$

In contrast, manganese(VII) oxide, Mn_2O_7, is a liquid that dissolves readily in water to form a strongly acidic solution.

Finally, there are certain oxides that exhibit *both* acidic and basic properties. These oxides, which are usually insoluble in water, are soluble in both acids and bases. They are called *amphoteric* (from the Greek *amphoteros*, meaning "each of two"). Most of the representative elements that form amphoteric oxides lie near the diagonal line in the periodic table that divides metals from nonmetals. For example, aluminum oxide, Al_2O_3, is amphoteric and reacts with both acids and bases:

$$Al_2O_3(s) + 6HCl(aq) \longrightarrow 2AlCl_3(aq) + 3H_2O(l)$$

$$Al_2O_3(s) + 6NaOH(aq) \longrightarrow 2Na_3AlO_3(aq) + 3H_2O(l)$$

We shall consider amphoterism again in Chapter 17, when we discuss acids and bases and solubility in more detail.

TABLE 8.6 △ Melting Points of Some Metal Oxides

Oxide	Melting point (°C)
Na_2O	1132
TiO_2	1857
Al_2O_3	2045
BeO	2530
CaO	2610
MgO	2826

One reason for the overlap in the two approaches to nomenclature is that compounds of metals in higher oxidation states tend to be molecular rather than ionic. For example, $SnCl_4$ [tin tetrachloride or tin(IV) chloride] is a colorless liquid that freezes at $-33°C$ and boils at $114°C$; Mn_2O_7 [dimanganese heptoxide or manganese(VII) oxide] is a green liquid that freezes at $5.9°C$. Recall that ionic compounds are solids at room temperature. When we see the formula of a compound containing a metal in a high oxidation state (above $+3$), we should not be surprised that it does not exhibit the general properties of ionic compounds. We will make wide use of oxidation numbers in later chapters to explain trends in chemical behavior.

SAMPLE EXERCISE 8.13

In your reading, you encounter the following names: (a) chromium(VI) oxide, and (b) phosphorus(V) sulfide. Give the chemical formula for these substances and suggest alternative names.

SOLUTION   (a) The name indicates that chromium has an oxidation state of $+6$. The oxidation state of oxygen in oxides is -2. To have a charge balance, the chemical formula must be CrO_3. This compound is also named chromium trioxide.
     (b) The name indicates that the phosphorus has an oxidation state of $+5$. The oxidation state of sulfur in sulfides is -2. Thus, the chemical formula is P_2S_5. This compound would more properly be named diphosphorus pentasulfide.

PRACTICE EXERCISE

Write the chemical formula for manganese dioxide, and give its name in terms of the oxidation state of manganese.   *Answers:* MnO_2; manganese(IV) oxide

For Review

Summary

In this chapter, we have dealt with the interactions that lead to the formation of chemical bonds. The tendencies of atoms to gain, lose, or share their valence electrons to form bonds can often be viewed in terms of attempts to achieve a noble-gas electron configuration (the octet rule).

Ionic bonding results from the complete transfer of electrons from one atom to another, with formation of a three-dimensional lattice of charged particles. The stabilities of ionic substances result from the powerful electrostatic attractive forces between an ion and all the surrounding ions of opposite charge. These interactions are measured by the lattice energy. The magnitude of the lattice energy depends primarily on the charges and sizes of the ions. In general, lattice energies increase as the charges of the ions increase and as their sizes decrease.

Cations are smaller than their parent atoms; anions are larger than their parent atoms. For ions of the same charge, size increases going down a family. For an isoelectronic series, size decreases with increasing nuclear charge (atomic number). Not all ions have noble-gas configurations. Many transition metal ions do not. In forming transition metal ions, the atom first loses its outer s electrons.

Covalent bonding results from the sharing of electrons. The octet rule is useful in describing this sharing. We can represent shared electron-pair structures of molecules by means of Lewis structures, which show the sharing of electron pairs between atoms. The sharing of one pair of electrons produces a single bond; the sharing of two or three pairs of electrons between atoms produces double and triple bonds, respectively.

It is important to recognize that even in covalent bonding, electrons may not be shared equally between two atoms. Electronegativity is a measure of the ability of an atom to compete with other atoms for the electrons shared between them. Highly electronegative elements strongly attract electrons. The electronegativities of the elements, which show a regular periodic relationship, are an important guide to chemical behavior. We shall be using the concept of electronegativity often throughout the text. The difference in electronegativities of bonded atoms is used to determine the polarity of a bond.

Sometimes a single Lewis structure is inadequate to represent a particular molecule, but an average of two or more Lewis structures does form a satisfactory representation. In these cases, the Lewis structures are called resonance forms. Sometimes the octet rule is not obeyed; this situation occurs mainly when a large atom is surrounded by small, electronegative atoms like F, O, or Cl. In such instances, the large atom has unfilled d orbitals in its valence shell to accommodate more than an octet of electrons. Thus, expanded octets are observed for atoms in the third period and beyond in the periodic table.

The strength of a covalent bond is measured by its bond energy. The strengths of covalent bonds increase with the number of electron pairs shared between two atoms. We can use bond energies to estimate the enthalpy changes during chemical reactions.

It is sometimes convenient to attribute charges to atoms by assigning shared electrons to the more electronegative atom. The resultant whole number charges, called oxidation numbers, are of great value in helping us to organize chemical facts, to balance equations, and to name compounds.

Key Terms

ionic bond
covalent bond
metallic bond
valence electrons (Sec. 8.1)
electron-dot symbols (Lewis symbols) (Sec. 8.1)
octet rule (Sec. 8.1)
lattice energy (Sec. 8.2)
Born-Haber cycle (Sec. 8.2)
isoelectronic series (Sec. 8.3)
covalent bond (Sec. 8.4)
Lewis structures (Sec. 8.4)
single bond (Sec. 8.4)

double bond (Sec. 8.4)
triple bond (Sec. 8.4)
multiple bonding (Sec. 8.4)
bond polarity (Sec. 8.5)
nonpolar bond (Sec. 8.5)
polar covalent bond (Sec. 8.5)
electronegativity (Sec. 8.5)
formal charge (Sec. 8.7)
resonance structures (forms) (Sec. 8.7)
bond-dissociation energy (Sec. 8.9)
bond energy (Sec. 8.9)
oxidation numbers (states) (Sec. 8.10)

Exercises

Lewis Symbols and Ionic Bonding

8.1. (a) What are the valence electrons of an atom? (b) How many valence electrons does a nitrogen atom possess?

8.2. (a) What is the octet rule? (b) How many electrons must a sulfur atom gain to achieve an octet?

8.3. Write the Lewis symbols for (a) silicon, Si; (b) sodium, Na; (c) selenium, Se; (d) aluminum, Al.

8.4. What is the Lewis symbol for each of the following atoms or ions: (a) Br; (b) Mg; (c) Ca^{2+}; (d) F^-.

8.5. Use Lewis symbols to diagram the reaction that occurs between Li and F atoms to give LiF.

8.6. Using Lewis symbols, diagram the reaction that occurs between Mg and Cl.

8.7. Predict the chemical formula of the ionic compound formed between the following pairs of elements: (a) Al and F; (b) K and S; (c) Mg and N; (d) Ba and O.

8.8. Indicate whether each of the following formulas is likely to represent a stable compound and give an explanation for your answer: (a) Rb_2O; (b) BaF; (c) Mg_2O; (d) $ScBr_3$; (e) Na_3N.

8.9. Write the electron configuration for each ion and state which possess a noble-gas configuration: (a) I^-; (b) Se^{2-}; (c) Sr^{2+}; (d) Ni^{2+}; (e) Pb^{2+}.

8.10. Write the electron configuration for each ion and state which possess a noble-gas configuration: (a) As^{3-}; (b) Ag^+; (c) Cs^+; (d) Co^{2+}; (e) Sc^{3+}.

8.11. (a) Define the term *lattice energy*. (b) Which factors govern the magnitude of the lattice energy of a compound?

8.12. Does the lattice energy of an ionic solid increase or decrease as (a) the charges of the ions increase; (b) as the sizes of the ions increase?

8.13. Energy is required to remove two electrons from Ca to form Ca^{2+} and is also required to add two electrons to O to form O^{2-}. Why, then, is CaO stable relative to the free elements?

8.14. List the individual steps used in constructing a Born-Haber cycle for the formation of $CaBr_2$ from the elements. Which of these steps would you expect to be exothermic?

8.15. The lattice energy of LiH is 858 kJ/mol, whereas that for MgH_2 is 2790 kJ/mol. Account for the large difference in these two quantities.

8.16. Explain the following trends in lattice energy: (a) MgO > MgS; (b) LiF > CsBr; (c) CaO > KF.

[8.17]. Use data from Appendix C, Table 7.3, and Table 7.5 to calculate the lattice energy of RbCl. Is this value greater than or less than the lattice energy of NaCl? Explain.

[8.18]. By using data from Appendix C, Table 7.3, Table 7.6, and the value of the second ionization energy for Ca, 1145 kJ/mol, calculate the lattice energy of CaF_2. Is this value greater than or less than the lattice energy of NaF? Explain.

Sizes of Ions

8.19. Explain the following variations in atomic or ionic radii: (a) $I^- > I > I^+$; (b) $Ca^{2+} > Mg^{2+} > Be^{2+}$; (c) $Fe^{2+} > Fe^{3+}$.

8.20. (a) Why are monoatomic anions larger than the corresponding neutral atoms? (b) Why are monoatomic cations smaller than the corresponding neutral atom?

8.21. (a) What is an isoelectronic series? (b) Which neutral atom is isoelectronic with each of the following ions: Cl^-; Se^{2-}; Mg^{2+}?

8.22. Select the ions or atoms from each of the following sets that are isoelectronic with each other: (a) K^+, Rb^+, Ca^{2+}; (b) Cu^+, Ca^{2+}, Sc^{3+}; (c) S^{2-}, Se^{2-}, Ar; (d) Fe^{2+}, Co^{3+}, Mn^{2+}.

8.23. Why do the radii of isoelectronic ions decrease with increasing nuclear charge?

8.24. Explain the following variations in atomic or ionic radii: (a) $P^{3-} > S^{2-} > Cl^-$; (b) $Br^- > Kr > Rb^+$.

8.25. Arrange the atoms and ions in each of the following sets in order of increasing size: (a) Li^+, Rb^+, K^+; (b) Br^-, Na^+, Mg^{2+}; (c) Ar, Cl^-, S^{2-}, K^+; (d) Cl, Cl^-, Ar.

8.26. For each of the following sets of atoms and ions, arrange the members in order of increasing size: (a) Se^{2-}, Te^{2-}, Se; (b) Co^{3+}, Fe^{2+}, Fe^{3+}; (c) Ca, Ti^{4+}, Sc^{3+}; (d) Be^{2+}, Na^+, Ne.

Covalent Bonding, Electronegativity, and Bond Polarity

8.27. Use Lewis symbols and Lewis structures to diagram the formation of H_2S from H and S atoms.

8.28. Using Lewis symbols and Lewis structures, diagram the formation of NF_3 from N and F atoms.

8.29. Give the Lewis structure of a molecule with (a) a double bond; (b) a triple bond.

8.30. How does the number of shared electron pairs between atoms affect the distance between the atoms?

8.31. (a) What is meant by the term *electronegativity?* (b) Which element has the greatest electronegativity?

8.32. (a) How does the electronegativity of the elements generally vary as you proceed from left to right in a row of the periodic table? (b) What is the general trend in electronegativity as you proceed down a family of the periodic

table? (c) How do the periodic trends in electronegativity relate to those for ionization energy and electron affinity?

8.33. By referring only to the periodic table, arrange the members of each of the following sets in order of increasing electronegativity: (a) O, P, S; (b) Mg, Al, Si; (c) S, Cl, Br; (d) C, Si, N.

8.34. Using only the periodic table, select the most electronegative atom in each of the following sets: (a) Be, B, C, Si; (b) Cl, S, Br, Se; (c) Si, Ge, Al, Ga; (d) K, Ca, As, Se.

8.35. Which of the following bonds are polar: (a) P—O; (b) S—S; (c) H—Br; (d) C—N; (e) As—F? Which is the more electronegative atom in each polar bond?

8.36. Arrange the bonds in each of the following sets in order of increasing polarity: (a) N—F, N—Cl, N—Br; (b) H—F, O—F, B—F; (c) N—N, N—P, N—O.

Lewis Structures; Resonance Structures

8.37. Draw the Lewis structures for (a) PH_3; (b) BrO_3^-; (c) CO; (d) $HClO_2$ (H is bonded to O); (e) $SeCl_2$.

8.38. Write the Lewis structures for (a) BH_4^-; (b) H_2O_2 (the O atoms are bonded to each other); (c) HOCl; (d) C_2H_2 (the C atoms are bonded to each other); (e) ONCl.

8.39. Draw resonance structures for each of the following: (a) SO_3; (b) $C_2O_4^{2-}$ (each C atom is bonded to two O atoms and to the other C); (c) HNO_3 (H is bonded to O); (d) ClO_3.

8.40. Draw the resonance forms for the following: (a) NO_2^-; (b) CO_3^{2-}; (c) SCN^-; (d) HCO_2^- (H and both O atoms are bonded to C).

8.41. Predict the ordering of the C—O bond lengths in CO, CO_2, and CO_3^{2-}.

8.42. Based on their Lewis structures, predict the ordering of N—O bond lengths in NO^+, NO, NO_2^-, and NO_3^-.

8.43. Calculate the formal charge on the indicated atom in each of the following molecules or ions: (a) the central oxygen atom in O_3; (b) phosphorus in PF_6^-; (c) nitrogen in NO_2; (d) iodine in ICl_3; (e) chlorine in $HClO_4$ (H is bonded to O).

8.44. Use the concept of formal charge to choose the more likely skeleton structure in each of the following cases: (a) NNO or NON; (b) HCN or HNC; (c) NOBr or ONBr; (d) NSC⁻ or SNC⁻ or SCN⁻.

Exceptions to the Octet Rule

8.45. What is the most common kind of exception to the octet rule?

8.46. Why does the octet rule not hold for many compounds containing elements in the third period of the periodic table and beyond?

8.47. Draw the Lewis structures for each of the following compounds. Identify those that do not obey the octet rule and explain why they do not. (a) NO_2; (b) GeF_4; (c) TeF_4; (d) BCl_3; (e) XeF_4.

8.48. Draw the Lewis structures for each of the following ions. Identify those that do not obey the octet rule and explain why they do not. (a) SO_3^{2-}; (b) BH_3; (c) I_3^-; (d) AsF_6^-; (e) O_2^-.

8.49. In the vapor phase, $BeCl_2$ exists as a discrete molecule. (a) Draw the Lewis structure of this molecule using only single bonds. Does this Lewis structure satisfy the octet rule? (b) What other resonance forms are possible that satisfy the octet rule? (c) Using formal charges, select the resonance form that is most important.

8.50. (a) Describe the molecule chlorine dioxide, ClO_2, in terms of three possible resonance structures. (b) Do any of these resonance structures satisfy the octet rule? Why or why not? (c) Using formal charges, select the resonance structure(s) that is (are) most important.

Bond Energies

8.51. Using the bond energies tabulated in Table 8.4, estimate ΔH for each of the following gas-phase reactions:

(a)
$$H—\underset{\underset{H}{|}}{\overset{\overset{H}{|}}{C}}—O—H + H—Br \longrightarrow$$
$$H—\underset{\underset{H}{|}}{\overset{\overset{H}{|}}{C}}—Br + H—O—H$$

(b)
$$H—\underset{\underset{Cl}{|}}{\overset{\overset{Cl}{|}}{C}}—Cl + O \longrightarrow Cl—\overset{\overset{O}{\|}}{C}—Cl + H—Cl$$

(c) $C≡O + H—O—H \longrightarrow H—H + O=C=O$

8.52. Using bond energies (Table 8.4), estimate ΔH for the following gas-phase reactions:

(a)
$$\underset{H}{\overset{H}{>}}C=C\underset{H}{\overset{H}{<}} + H—O—O—H \longrightarrow$$
$$H—O—\underset{\underset{H}{|}}{\overset{\overset{H}{|}}{C}}—\underset{\underset{H}{|}}{\overset{\overset{H}{|}}{C}}—O—H$$

(b)
$$\underset{H}{\overset{H}{>}}C=C\underset{H}{\overset{H}{<}} + H—C≡N \longrightarrow$$
$$H—\underset{\underset{H}{|}}{\overset{\overset{H}{|}}{C}}—\underset{\underset{H}{|}}{\overset{\overset{H}{|}}{C}}—C≡N$$

(c)
$$2 Cl—\underset{\underset{Cl}{|}}{N}—Cl \longrightarrow N≡N + 3 Cl—Cl$$

8.53. Using the bond energies in Table 8.4, estimate the enthalpy change for each of the following gas-phase reactions:
(a) $HCN + 3H_2 \longrightarrow CH_4 + NH_3$
(b) $HBr + 2F_2 \longrightarrow BrF_3 + HF$

8.54. Using bond energies (Table 8.4), estimate ΔH for the following gas-phase reactions:
(a) $CO + 2H_2 \longrightarrow CH_3OH$
(b) $CH_2=CH_2 + F_2 \longrightarrow CH_2F—CH_2F$

8.55. Given the following bond dissociation energies, calculate the average bond energy for the Ti—Cl bond.

	ΔH (kJ/mol)
$TiCl_4(g) \longrightarrow TiCl_3(g) + Cl(g)$	335
$TiCl_3(g) \longrightarrow TiCl_2(g) + Cl(g)$	423
$TiCl_2(g) \longrightarrow TiCl(g) + Cl(g)$	444
$TiCl(g) \longrightarrow Ti(g) + Cl(g)$	519

[8.56]. Using the ΔH_f^0 values in Appendix C for $C_2H_6(g)$, $C(g)$, and $H(g)$, and the average C—H bond energy from Table 8.4, calculate the C—C bond energy in ethane, C_2H_6. How does this value compare to the average C—C bond energy given in Table 8.4?

Oxidation Numbers

8.57. Determine the oxidation number of the underlined element in each of the following: **(a)** $\underline{P}_4$; **(b)** $\underline{As}_2O_3$; **(c)** $NaH\underline{C}O_3$; **(d)** $Na_3\underline{P}O_4$; **(e)** $\underline{N}O^+$; **(f)** $\underline{Br}F_3$; **(g)** $K_2\underline{O}_2$; **(h)** $Pb\underline{S}O_4$.

8.58. Determine the oxidation number of the underlined element in each of the following: **(a)** $\underline{S}F_4$; **(b)** $\underline{Hg}_2Cl_2$; **(c)** $\underline{Co}Cl_4^{2-}$; **(d)** $\underline{Xe}OF_4$; **(e)** $K\underline{Mn}O_4$; **(f)** $\underline{N}O_2^-$; **(g)** $\underline{Cl}O_4^-$; **(h)** $\underline{U}O_2^{2+}$.

8.59. What are the maximum and minimum oxidation numbers exhibited by **(a)** N; **(b)** Se; **(c)** Ca; **(d)** Mn?

8.60. What are the maximum and minimum oxidation numbers exhibited by **(a)** As; **(b)** Br; **(c)** Sc; **(d)** Cr?

8.61. Give the name or chemical formula, as appropriate, for each of the following substances: **(a)** iron(III) fluoride; **(b)** molybdenum(VI) oxide; **(c)** arsenic(V) bromide; **(d)** V_2O_3; **(e)** CoF_3; **(f)** MnS.

8.62. Give the name or chemical formula, as appropriate, for each of the following substances: **(a)** manganese(IV) oxide; **(b)** gallium(III) sulfide; **(c)** selenium(VI) fluoride; **(d)** Cu_2O; **(e)** ClF_3; **(f)** TeO_3.

8.63. Indicate the oxidation states of the elements that undergo a change in oxidation state in each of the following reactions:
(a) $Xe(g) + 2F_2(g) \longrightarrow XeF_4(g)$
(b) $2CuSO_4(aq) + 4KI(aq) \longrightarrow$
$$2CuI(s) + 2K_2SO_4(aq) + I_2(s)$$
(c) $NH_3(g) + 3Cl_2(g) \longrightarrow NCl_3(g) + 3HCl(g)$
(d) $I_2(aq) + SO_2(aq) + 2H_2O(l) \longrightarrow$
$$2HI(aq) + H_2SO_4(aq)$$
(e) $2PbS(s) + 3O_2(g) \longrightarrow 2PbO(s) + 2SO_2(g)$

8.64. Indicate the oxidation states of the elements that undergo a change in oxidation state in each of the following reactions:
(a) $2KI(aq) + F_2(g) \longrightarrow 2KF(aq) + I_2(s)$
(b) $MnO_2(s) + 4HCl(aq) \longrightarrow$
$$MnCl_2(aq) + Cl_2(aq) + 2H_2O(l)$$
(c) $2H_2O_2(aq) \longrightarrow 2H_2O(l) + O_2(g)$
(d) $2CH_4(g) + O_2(g) \longrightarrow 2CH_3OH(g)$
(e) $5Fe^{2+}(aq) + MnO_4^-(aq) + 8H^+(aq) \longrightarrow$
$$5Fe^{3+}(aq) + Mn^{2+}(aq) + 4H_2O(l)$$

Additional Exercises

8.65. In each of the following examples of a Lewis symbol, indicate the group in the periodic table in which the element X belongs: **(a)** $\cdot \overset{\cdot}{X} \cdot$; **(b)** $\cdot X \cdot$; **(c)** $: \overset{\cdot}{X} \cdot$.

8.66. Which of the following contain metal ions that do not have noble-gas electron configurations: **(a)** CuCl; **(b)** CdO; **(c)** TiO_2; **(d)** ScF_3.

8.67. Write the electron configurations for **(a)** Ni^{2+}; **(b)** Cr^{3+}; **(c)** Bi^{3+}; **(d)** Sc^{3+}.

8.68. The $+2$ oxidation state is common for transition metal ions. Explain why this might be expected.

8.69. Explain the following trend in lattice energies: LiH, 858 kJ/mol; NaH, 782 kJ/mol; KH, 699 kJ/mol; RbH, 674 kJ/mol.

8.70. From the ionic radii given in Table 8.3, calculate the potential energy of each of the following ion pairs, assuming that they are separated by the sum of their ionic radii (the magnitude of the electronic charge is given on the back inside cover): **(a)** Mg^{2+}, O^{2-}; **(b)** Na^+, Br^-.

[8.71]. From the ionic radii given in Table 8.3, calculate the potential energy of a Na^+ and Cl^- ion pair that are just touching (the magnitude of the electronic charge is given on the back inside cover). Calculate the energy of a mole of such pairs. How does this value compare with the lattice energy of NaCl (Table 8.2)? Explain the difference.

[8.72]. The electron affinity of oxygen is -141 kJ/mol, corresponding to the reaction

$$O(g) + e^- \longrightarrow O^-(g)$$

The lattice energy of SrO is 3369 kJ/mol. Using these data, along with data from Table 7.6 and Appendix C, calculate the "second electron affinity" of oxygen, corresponding to the reaction

$$O^-(g) + e^- \longrightarrow O^{2-}(g)$$

8.73. Although I_3^- is known, F_3^- is not. Using Lewis structures, explain why F_3^- does not form.

8.74. Based on the positions of the elements in the periodic table, select the most polar and least polar bond from the following list: P—N, P—O, P—P, P—S.

8.75. Three Lewis structures that can be drawn for N_2O are $: N \equiv N - \overset{\cdot\cdot}{\underset{\cdot\cdot}{O}} :$, $: \overset{\cdot\cdot}{N} - N \equiv O :$, and $: \overset{\cdot\cdot}{N} = N = \overset{\cdot\cdot}{\underset{\cdot\cdot}{O}} :$. Using formal charges, which of these three resonance forms is likely to be the most important?

8.76. Use the concepts of formal charge and electronegativity to explain why the best Lewis structure of BF_3 is the one with less than an octet around boron.

8.77. The two sulfur-oxygen bonds in sulfur dioxide, SO_2, are equal in length and short (1.43 Å). **(a)** Write a Lewis structure for SO_2 that satisfies the octet rule. Would you expect more than one resonance form for this Lewis structure? **(b)** Write a Lewis structure in which there is an expanded valence shell for sulfur. Would you expect more than one resonance form for this Lewis structure? **(c)** For the Lewis structures in (a) and (b), determine the formal charge for the atoms in SO_2. **(d)** If the criterion of minimizing the formal charges is used, would the Lewis structure from (a) or from (b) be a better one for SO_2? [After you cover Chapter 9, you might want to read more about the Lewis structures of SO_2. See G. H. Purser, *Journal of Chemical Education,* 66, 710 (1989).]

8.78. Ammonia is produced directly from nitrogen and hydrogen by using the *Haber process.* The chemical reaction is

$$N_2(g) + 3H_2(g) \longrightarrow 2NH_3(g)$$

(a) Use bond energies (Table 8.4) to estimate whether this reaction is exothermic or endothermic. **(b)** Compare the enthalpy change you calculate in (a) to the true enthalpy change as obtained using ΔH_f° values.

8.79. An important reaction for the conversion of natural gas to other useful hydrocarbons is the conversion of methane to ethane:

$$2CH_4(g) \longrightarrow C_2H_6(g) + H_2(g)$$

In practice, this reaction is carried out in the presence of oxygen, which converts the hydrogen produced to water:

$$2CH_4(g) + \tfrac{1}{2}O_2(g) \longrightarrow C_2H_6(g) + H_2O(g)$$

Use bond energies (Table 8.4) to estimate ΔH for these two reactions. Why is the conversion of methane to ethane more favorable when oxygen is used?

[8.80]. The hydrogen molecule can, in principle, break apart into either neutral atoms or ions, as shown in the following reactions:

$$H_2(g) \longrightarrow H(g) + H(g)$$
$$H_2(g) \longrightarrow H^+(g) + H^-(g)$$

The bond energy of an H—H bond is defined by the first reaction. By using bond energies (Table 8.4), electron affinities (Table 7.3), and the ionization energy of hydrogen (1312 kJ/mol), determine ΔH for the second reaction. Based on a comparison of the enthalpy changes for these reactions, which should be the preferred means by which hydrogen molecules break apart?

[8.81]. The enthalpy of formation of $NH(g)$ at 25 °C is 360 kJ/mol. From this value, and using the data in Table 8.4, calculate the N—H bond dissociation energy in NH.

8.82. Two compounds are *isomers* if they have the same chemical formula but a different arrangement of atoms. Use bond energies (Table 8.4) to estimate ΔH for ~~these two reactions. Why is the conversion of methane to ethane more favorable when oxygen is used?~~ *each of the following isomerization reactions and indicate which isomer has the lower enthalpy.*

(a)

Ethanol   Dimethyl ether

(b)

Ethylene oxide   Acetaldehyde

(c)

Cyclopentene   Pentadiene

(d)

Methyl isocyanide   Acetonitrile

[8.83]. With reference to the Chemistry at Work box on explosives: **(a)** Use bond energies to estimate the enthalpy change for the explosion of 1.00 g of nitroglycerin. **(b)** Write a balanced equation for the decomposition of TNT. Assume that, upon explosion, TNT decomposes into $N_2(g)$, $CO_2(g)$, $H_2O(g)$, and $C(s)$.

8.84. Assign oxidation states to the indicated atom: **(a)** N in hydrazine, N_2H_4, a substance that has been employed as a rocket fuel; **(b)** S in sodium thiosulfate, $Na_2S_2O_3$, sometimes called "hypo" and used as a "fixer" in black-and-white photography; **(c)** N in ammonium sulfate, $(NH_4)_2SO_4$, used as a fertilizer; **(d)** Cl in chlorine trifluoride, ClF_3, used in nuclear reactor fuel processing; **(e)** As in diarsenic trisulfide, As_2S_3, used as a yellow pigment.

8.85. A white solid, melting at 1115 °C and insoluble in water but slightly soluble in aqueous NaOH, is likely to be which of the following: SrO; GeO_2; SeO_2; N_2O_3? Explain.

[8.86]. The bond lengths of carbon-carbon, carbon-nitrogen, carbon-oxygen, and nitrogen-nitrogen single, double, and triple bonds are listed in Table 8.5. Plot bond energy (Table 8.4) versus bond length for these bonds. What do you conclude about the relationship between bond length and bond energy? What do you conclude about the relative strengths of C—C, C—N, C—O, and N—N bonds?

Molecular Geometry and Bonding Theories

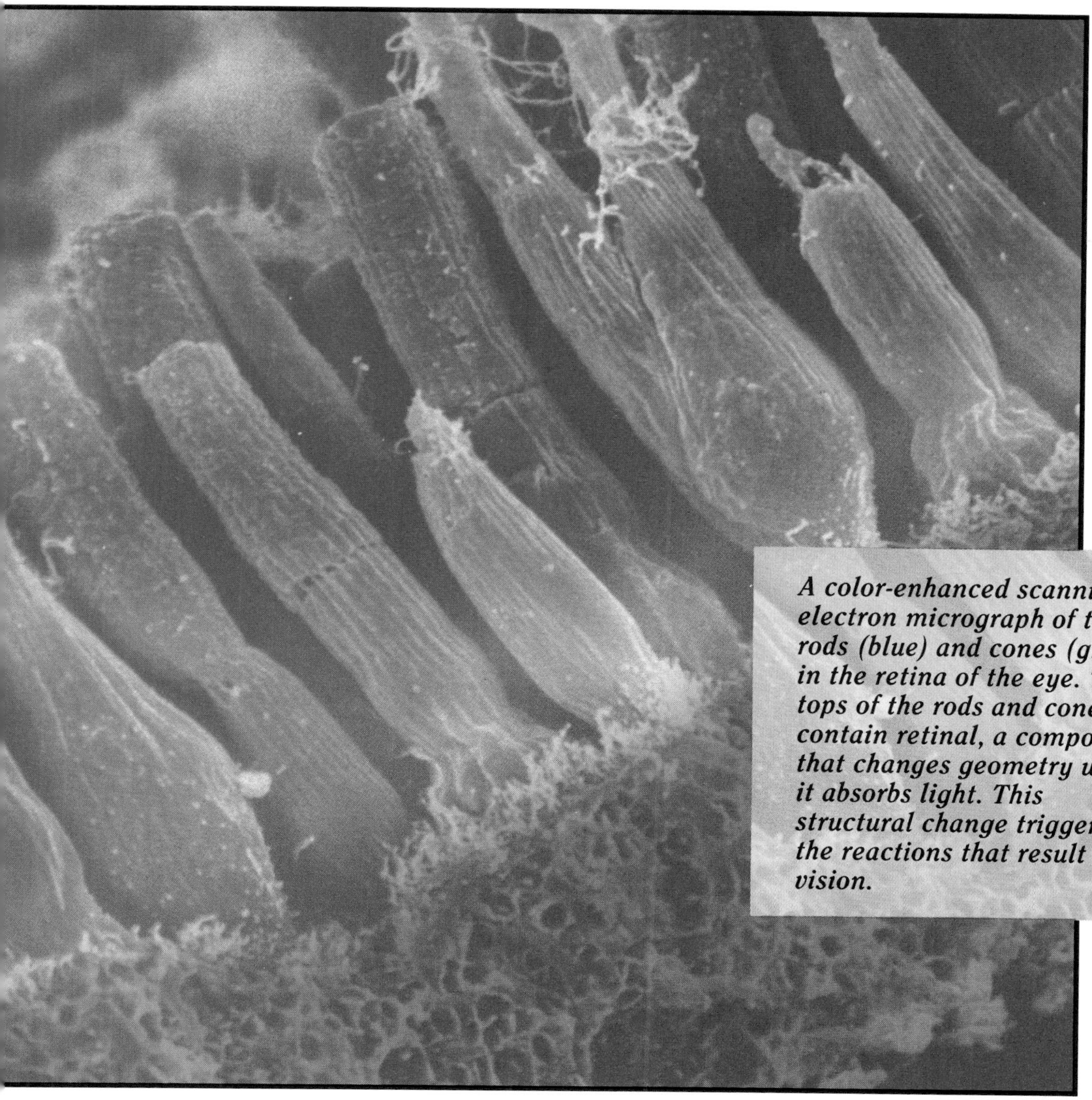

A color-enhanced scanning electron micrograph of the rods (blue) and cones (green) in the retina of the eye. The tops of the rods and cones contain retinal, a compound that changes geometry when it absorbs light. This structural change triggers the reactions that result in vision.

CONTENTS

The size and shape of a molecule of a particular substance, together with the strength and polarity of its bonds, largely determine the physical and chemical properties of that substance. Some of the most dramatic examples of the importance of size and shape are seen in biochemical reactions. For example, a small change in the size or shape of a drug molecule may enhance its effectiveness or reduce its side effects.

Even the sensations of smell and vision depend in part on molecular shape. When you smell the aroma of freshly baked bread, molecules from the bread stimulate receptor sites in your nose. The shapes and sizes of the molecules determine their ability to fit properly on these receptor sites. The interactions between the molecules and the receptors sensitize nerve endings that transmit impulses to the brain. The brain then identifies these impulses as a particular aroma. The nose is so good at molecular recognition that two substances may produce different sensations of odor even when their molecular structures differ as subtly as your right hand differs from your left.

In this chapter, we shall use three models to direct our discussion of molecular geometry and bonding. First, we consider how the shapes of molecules can be described and predicted using a simple model based largely on Lewis structures and the idea of electron-electron repulsions (the VSEPR model). We then examine a model of molecular bonding (the valence bond theory) that helps us understand why molecules form bonds and why they have the shapes they do. Finally, we discuss a model of chemical bonding (the molecular orbital theory) that provides additional insight into the energetics of bond formation and into the electronic structures of molecules.

9.1 Molecular Geometries

In Chapter 8, we used Lewis structures to account for the formulas of covalent compounds. Lewis structures, however, do not indicate the shapes of molecules. Rather, they simply show the number and types of bonds between atoms. For example, the Lewis structure of carbon tetrachloride tells us only that four Cl atoms are bonded to a central C atom by four single bonds:

$$:\ddot{C}l:$$
$$|$$
$$:\ddot{C}l-C-\ddot{C}l:$$
$$|$$
$$:\ddot{C}l:$$

Point of Emphasis: *Tetrahedron* means "four faces."

Point of Emphasis: A tetrahedron can be constructed by placing the central atom at the center of a cube and placing the peripheral atoms at four opposing corners:

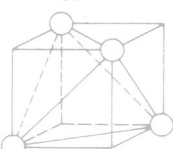

The Lewis structure is drawn with the atoms in the same plane. However, as shown in Figure 9.1, the actual three-dimensional arrangement of the atoms has the Cl atoms at the corners of a *tetrahedron,* a geometrical object with four corners and four faces, each of which is an equilateral triangle.

The overall shape of a molecule is determined by its **bond angles,** the angles made by the lines joining the nuclei of the atoms in the molecule. The bond angles of a molecule, together with the bond lengths (Section 8.9), accurately define the size and shape of the molecule. In CCl_4, all four C—Cl bonds are the same length (1.78 Å), and all six Cl—C—Cl angles have the same value (109.5°, which is characteristic of a tetrahedron). Thus, the size and shape of CCl_4 are completely described by stating that it is tetrahedral with C—Cl bonds of length 1.78 Å.

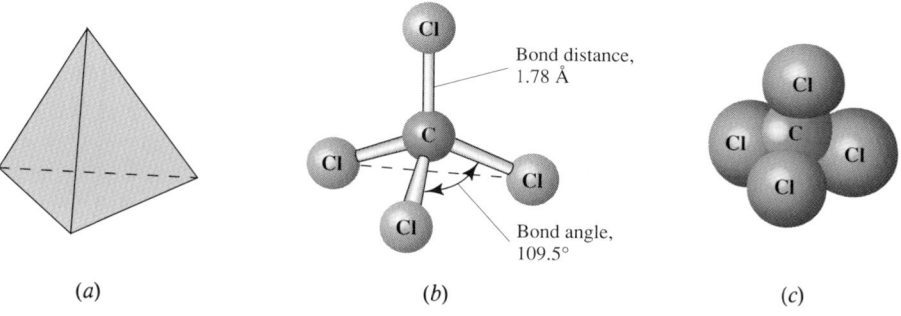

(a)   (b)   (c)

FIGURE 9.1 (a) A tetrahedron is an object with four faces and four vertices. Each face is an equilateral triangle. (b) The geometry of the CCl_4 molecule. Each C—Cl bond in the molecule points toward a vertex of a tetrahedron. All the C—Cl bonds are the same length, and all the Cl—C—Cl bond angles are the same. This type of drawing of CCl_4 is called a "ball-and-stick" model. (c) A representation of CCl_4 called a "space-filling" model. It shows the relative sizes of the atoms, but the geometry is somewhat harder to see.

 Figure 9.1

In describing molecular geometries, we shall first consider molecules of the type AB_n, in which a central A atom is bonded to two or more B atoms. Although an enormous number of different molecules of this kind exist, the shapes they exhibit are rather limited. For example, the shape of an AB_2 molecule must be either linear (bond angle = 180°) or bent (bond angle ≠ 180°). Figure 9.2 shows these and several other common molecular geometries. We see that several different geometries can be exhibited by, for example, AB_3 molecules, and it is natural for us to ask whether the geometries of molecules can be predicted. The answer is that they can be, at least when A is a nonmetal. To do so, we use the **valence-shell electron-pair repulsion (VSEPR) model.** Although the name is rather imposing, the model is quite simple.

The Valence-Shell Electron Pair Repulsion Model

Imagine taking two identical balloons and tying them together at their ends. As shown in Figure 9.3(a), the balloons naturally orient themselves so that each is pointing away from the other. They do so in order to minimize the interactions between themselves; that is, they try to "get out of each other's way" as much as possible. If we add a third balloon, the balloons orient themselves toward the

Learning Goal 1: Relate the number of electron pairs in the valence shell of an atom in a molecule to their geometrical arrangement around the atom.

Figure 9.2

FIGURE 9.2 The geometries of some simple molecules.

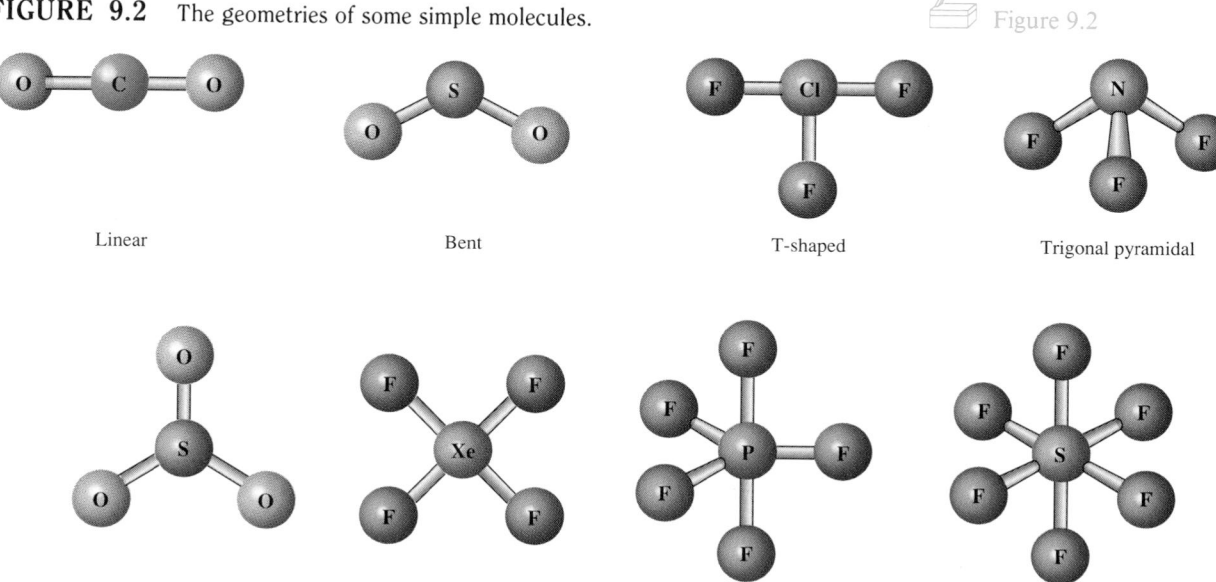

Linear   Bent   T-shaped   Trigonal pyramidal

Trigonal planar   Square planar   Trigonal bipyramidal   Octahedral

9.1 Molecular Geometries   **287**

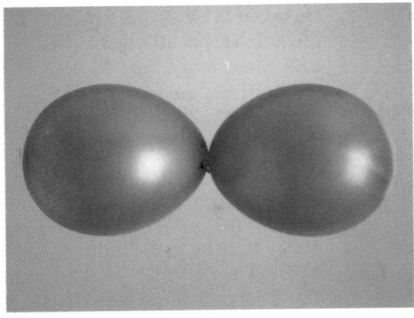
(a)

(b)

(c)

FIGURE 9.3 Balloons tied together at their ends naturally adopt their lowest-energy arrangement. (*a*) Two balloons adopt a linear arrangement. (*b*) Three balloons adopt a trigonal planar arrangement. (*c*) Four balloons adopt a tetrahedral arrangement. (Kristen Brochman/Fundamental Photographs)

vertices of an equilateral triangle [Figure 9.3(*b*)]. If we add a fourth balloon, the balloons naturally adopt a tetrahedral shape, as shown in Figure 9.3(*c*). We see that there is an optimum geometry for each number of balloons.

We have seen that atoms are bonded to each other in molecules by the sharing of pairs of valence-shell electrons. Electron pairs repel one another. Therefore, like the balloons in Figure 9.3, electron pairs try to stay out of each other's way. *The best arrangement of a given number of electron pairs is the one that minimizes the repulsions among them.* This simple idea is the basis of the VSEPR model. In fact, the analogy between electron pairs and balloons is so close that the same preferred geometries are found in both cases. Thus, as shown in Figure 9.3, two electron pairs are arranged *linearly*, three pairs are arranged in a *trigonal planar* fashion, and four are arranged *tetrahedrally*. These arrangements, together with those for five electron pairs (*trigonal bipyramidal*) and six electron pairs (*octahedral*), are summarized in Table 9.1. As we shall see, the shape of a molecule or ion can be related to these five basic arrangements of electron pairs.

Predicting Molecular Geometries

In drawing Lewis structures (Section 8.6), we see that there are two types of valence-shell electron pairs: **bonding pairs,** which are shared by atoms in bonds, and **nonbonding pairs** (also called *lone pairs*). For example, the Lewis structure of ammonia reveals three bonding pairs and one nonbonding pair around the central nitrogen atom:

$$H - \overset{\cdot\cdot}{N} - H \quad \text{nonbonding pair}$$
$$\underset{H}{|} \quad \text{bonding pairs}$$

The electron-pair repulsions about the nitrogen are minimized when these four electron pairs are arranged tetrahedrally (Table 9.1). Hence, the arrangement of electron pairs, known as the **electron-pair geometry,** around the nitrogen atom in NH_3 is tetrahedral, as shown in Figure 9.4.

TABLE 9.1 △ Electron-Pair Geometries as a Function of the Number of Electron Pairs

Number of electron pairs	Arrangement of electron pairs	Electron-pair geometry	Predicted bond angles
2	180°	Linear	180°
3	120°	Trigonal planar	120°
4	109.5°	Tetrahedral	109.5°
5	90° 120°	Trigonal bipyra- midal	120° 90°
6	90° 90°	Octahedral	90°

Table 9.1

When we experimentally determine the structure of a molecule, we locate the atoms, not the electron pairs. The **molecular geometry** of a molecule (or ion) is the arrangement of the *atoms* in space. We can predict the molecular geometry of a molecule from its electron-pair geometry. In NH_3, for example, the three bonding pairs point toward three of the vertices (corners) of a tetrahedron. The hydrogen atoms are therefore located at three of the vertices of a tetrahedron that has the nitrogen atom at its center. The nonbonding electron pair on nitrogen points toward the fourth vertex (Figure 9.4). Thus, the VSEPR model

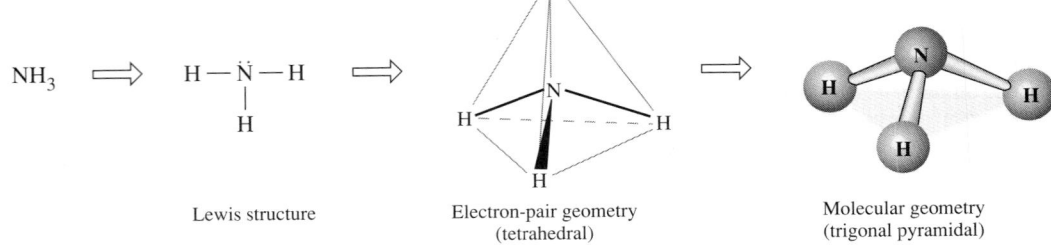

NH_3 ⟹ H—N̈—H ⟹ ⟹

|
H

Lewis structure   Electron-pair geometry   Molecular geometry
                              (tetrahedral)   (trigonal pyramidal)

FIGURE 9.4   The molecular geometry of NH_3 is predicted by first writing the Lewis structure, then using the VSEPR model to determine the electron-pair geometry, and finally focusing on the atoms themselves to describe the molecular structure.

correctly predicts that the atoms in NH_3 do not all lie in a plane; rather, NH_3 resembles a tetrahedral molecule but with an atom missing.

When describing the shapes of molecules, we always give the *molecular* geometry rather than the *electron-pair* geometry. For example, we describe the shape of NH_3 as *trigonal pyramidal.* Even though the electron-pair geometry of NH_3 is tetrahedral, the arrangement of the atoms is a trigonal pyramid (a pyramid with a triangular base).

As the example of NH_3 in Figure 9.4 shows, the following steps are used to predict molecular geometries with the VSEPR model:

1. Sketch the Lewis dot structure of the molecule or ion.
2. Count the total number of electron pairs around the central atom and arrange them in the way that minimizes electron-pair repulsions (see Table 9.1).
3. Describe the molecular geometry in terms of the angular arrangement of the *bonding* pairs. (The angular arrangement of the bonding pairs corresponds to the angular arrangement of the bonded atoms.)

In the following discussions, we apply the VSEPR model first to molecules and ions that obey the octet rule and then to those that have expanded octets.

Four or Fewer Valence-Shell Electron Pairs

The molecular geometries that can arise when a central atom has four or fewer valence-shell electron pairs are summarized in Table 9.2. These geometries are important because they include all of the commonly occurring structural types found for molecules or ions that obey the octet rule. Application of the VSEPR model to molecules containing double or triple bonds reveals one further rule: *A double or triple bond has essentially the same effect on bond angles as a single bond and is therefore counted as one bonding pair (that is, one electron region) when predicting geometry.* For example, in Table 9.2 we count the two C=O double bonds in the Lewis structure for CO_2 as two electron pairs.

Common Misconception: Students often confuse the *electron-pair* geometry with the *molecular* geometry. You must stress that the molecular geometry *is a consequence* of the electron-pair geometry.

Learning Goal 2: Predict the geometrical structure of a molecule or ion from its Lewis structure.

Teaching Note: Referring to nonbonded electron pairs, single bonds, and multiple bonds as *regions of electron density* may help relieve any confusion that might arise from treating the various kinds of electron pairs differently.

TABLE 9.2 △ Electron-Pair Geometries and Molecular Shapes for Molecules with Two, Three, and Four Electron Pairs About the Central Atom

Total electron pairs	Electron-pair geometry	Bonding pairs	Nonbonding pairs	Molecular geometry	Example
2	 Linear	2	0	 Linear	$\ddot{O}=C=\ddot{O}$
3	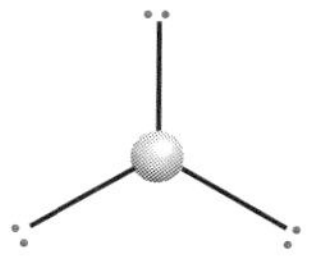 Trigonal planar	3	0	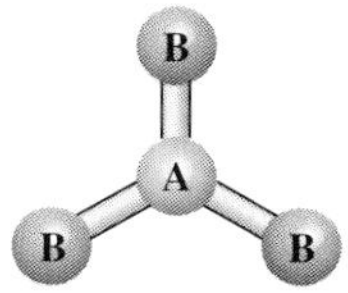 Trigonal planar	$\begin{array}{c} :\ddot{F}: \\ | \\ B \\ :\ddot{F} \quad \ddot{F}: \end{array}$
		2	1	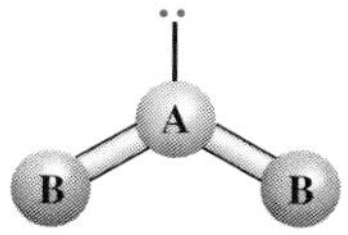 Bent	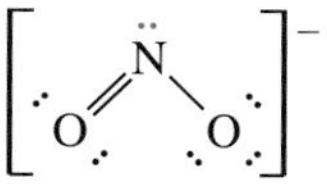 $\left[:\ddot{O} \quad \overset{\cdot\cdot}{N} \quad \ddot{O}: \right]^{-}$
4	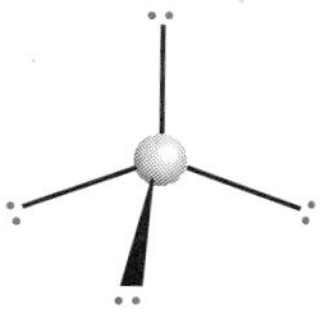 Tetrahedral	4	0	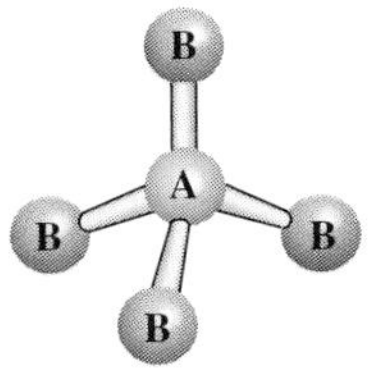 Tetrahedral	$\begin{array}{c} H \\ | \\ C \\ H \overset{}{\underset{H}{\diagup \quad \diagdown}} H \end{array}$
		3	1	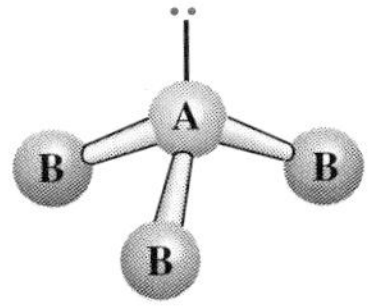 Trigonal pyramidal	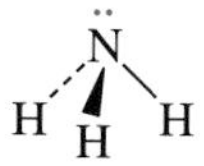 $H \overset{\overset{\cdot\cdot}{N}}{\underset{H}{\diagup \quad \diagdown}} H$
		2	2	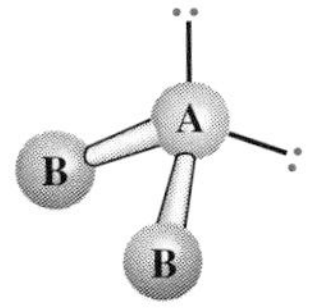 Bent	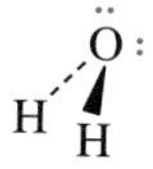 $H \overset{\ddot{O}:}{\underset{H}{\diagup \quad}}$

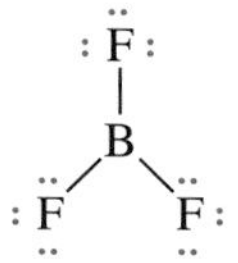

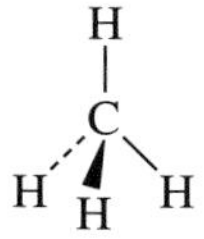

Table 9.2

SAMPLE EXERCISE 9.1

Using the VSEPR model, predict the molecular geometries of the following: **(a)** $SnCl_3^-$; **(b)** O_3.

SOLUTION **(a)** The Lewis structure for the $SnCl_3^-$ ion is as follows:

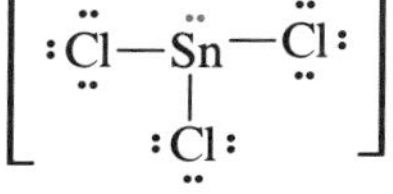

$$\left[:\ddot{Cl}-\overset{}{Sn}-\ddot{Cl}: \atop \underset{:\ddot{Cl}:}{|} \right]$$

The central Sn atom is surrounded by one nonbonding electron pair and three single bonds. Thus, the electron-pair geometry is tetrahedral. That is, the four electron pairs are disposed at the corners of a tetrahedron. Three of the corners are occupied by the bonding pairs of electrons. The molecular geometry is thus trigonal pyramidal:

(b) Two resonance structures for the O_3 molecule can be drawn:

$$:\ddot{O}-\ddot{O}=\ddot{O} \longleftrightarrow \ddot{O}=\ddot{O}-\ddot{O}:$$

Both resonance structures show one nonbonding electron pair, one single bond, and one double bond about the central O atom. When we predict geometry, a double bond is counted as one electron pair. Thus, the arrangement of valence-shell electrons is trigonal planar. Two of these positions are occupied by O atoms, so the molecule has a bent shape:

As this example illustrates, when a molecule exhibits resonance, any one of the resonance structures can be used to predict the geometry.

PRACTICE EXERCISE

Predict the electron-pair geometry and the molecular geometry for **(a)** H_2S; **(b)** $CO_3{}^{2-}$. ***Answers:*** **(a)** tetrahedral, bent; **(b)** trigonal planar, trigonal planar

The Effect of Nonbonding Electrons and Multiple Bonds on Bond Angles

Learning Goal 3: Explain why unshared electron pairs exert a greater repulsive interaction on other pairs than do shared pairs.

We can refine the VSEPR model to predict and explain slight distortions of molecules from the ideal geometries summarized in Table 9.2. For example, consider methane, CH_4, ammonia, NH_3, and water, H_2O. All three have tetrahedral electron-pair geometries, but their bond angles differ slightly:

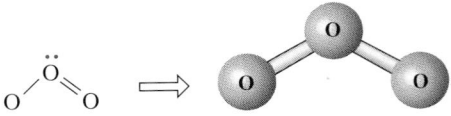

Teaching Note: The positive charge on the second nucleus attracts the bonding electron pair, keeping the shape more compact than is the case with a nonbonding pair.

Notice that the bond angles decrease as the number of nonbonding electron pairs increases. Bonding pairs are attracted by the two nuclei of the bonded atoms. By contrast, nonbonding electrons move under the attractive influence of only one nucleus and thus spread out more in space. As a result, *nonbonding electron pairs exert greater repulsive forces on adjacent electron pairs and thus tend to compress the angles between the bonding pairs.* Using the analogy in

292   Chapter 9   Molecular Geometry and Bonding Theories

Figure 9.3, we can envision nonbonding electron pairs as represented by slightly larger and fatter balloons than bonding pairs.

Because multiple bonds contain a higher electronic-charge density than do single bonds, multiple bonds also affect bond angles. Notice how the bond angles in the formaldehyde molecule, H_2CO, differ from the ideal $120°$ angles:

$$\begin{array}{c} H \\ \diagdown ^{122°} \\ 116°C{=}O \\ \diagup ^{122°} \\ H \end{array}$$

The double bond seems to act much like a nonbonding pair of electrons, reducing the $H{-}C{-}H$ bond angle from $120°$ to $116°$. *Electrons in multiple bonds, like nonbonding pairs, exert a greater repulsive force on adjacent electron pairs than do single bonds.*

Geometries of Molecules with Expanded Valence Shells

When the central atom of a molecule is from the third period of the periodic table and beyond, that atom may have more than four electron pairs around it. ∞ (Sec. 8.8) Molecules with five or six electron pairs around the central atom display a variety of molecular geometries, as shown in Table 9.3.

The most stable electron-pair geometry for five electron pairs is the trigonal bipyramid (two trigonal pyramids sharing a common base). Unlike the electron-pair geometries we have seen to this point, the trigonal bipyramid contains two geometrically distinct types of electron pairs. Two pairs are called *axial pairs,* and the remaining three are called *equatorial pairs,* as shown in Figure 9.5. In an axial position, an electron pair is situated $90°$ from the three equatorial pairs. In an equatorial position, an electron pair is situated $120°$ from the other two equatorial pairs and $90°$ from the two axial pairs.

Suppose a molecule has five electron pairs, one of which is a nonbonding pair. Will the nonbonding pair occupy an axial or an equatorial position? Because we could place the lone pair at two distinct sites, we must determine which site will minimize the electron-pair repulsion. Electron-pair repulsions are much greater when pairs are situated $90°$ from each other than when they are at $120°$. Because they are $90°$ from only two other pairs, the equatorial pairs

FIGURE 9.5 Trigonal bipyramidal arrangement of five electron pairs about a central atom. There are two geometrically distinct types of electron pairs, two axial and three equatorial pairs. Unshared electron pairs occupy the equatorial positions.

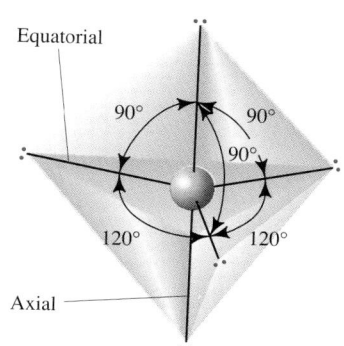

Equatorial

$90°$ $90°$

$90°$

$120°$ $120°$

Axial

TABLE 9.3 △ Electron-Pair Geometries and Molecular Shapes for Molecules with Five and Six Electron Pairs About the Central Atom

Number of electron pairs	Electron-pair geometry	Bonding pairs	Nonbonding pairs	Molecular geometry	Example
5	Trigonal bipyramidal	5	0	Trigonal bipyramidal	PCl_5
		4	1	Seesaw	SF_4
		3	2	T-shaped	ClF_3
		2	3	Linear	XeF_2
6	Octahedral	6	0	Octahedral	SF_6
		5	1	Square pyramidal	BrF_5
		4	2	Square planar	XeF_4

Table 9.3

experience less repulsion than do the axial pairs, which are 90° from *three* other pairs. Because nonbonding pairs exert larger repulsions than bonding pairs, they always occupy the equatorial positions, as shown in Table 9.3.

The most stable electron-pair geometry for six electron pairs is the *octahedron*. As shown in Figure 9.6, an octahedron is a solid object with six vertices and eight faces, each of which is an equilateral triangle. In an octahedral molecule such as SF_6 (Figure 9.2), the central atom is located in the center and the electron pairs point toward the six vertices. All the angles in an octahedron are 90° or 180°, and all six positions are equivalent. Therefore, if a molecule has five bonding pairs of electrons and one nonbonding pair, it makes no difference where we place them on the octahedron. However, when there are two non-bonding electron pairs, their repulsions are minimized by placing them on opposite sides of the octahedron, as shown in Table 9.3.

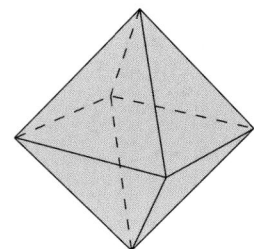

FIGURE 9.6 An octahedron is an object with eight faces and six vertices. Each face is an equilateral triangle.

SAMPLE EXERCISE 9.2

Using the VSEPR model, predict the molecular geometry of **(a)** SF_4; **(b)** IF_5.

SOLUTION **(a)** The Lewis dot structure for SF_4 is

$$\text{:}\overset{..}{F} \quad \overset{..}{F}\text{:}$$
$$\underset{\text{:}\overset{..}{F}}{\overset{S}{}} \quad \overset{..}{F}\text{:}$$

The sulfur has five valence-shell electron pairs around it. Each pair points toward a corner of a trigonal bipyramid. The one nonbonding pair occupies an equatorial position. The four bonding electron pairs occupy the remaining four positions:

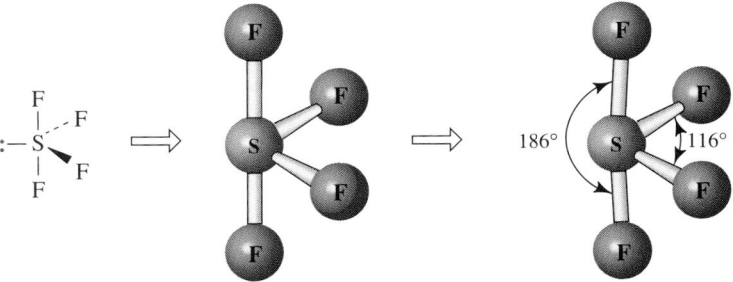

The experimentally observed structure is shown on the right. From this structure, we can infer that the unshared electron pair resides in an equatorial position, as pre-dicted. Note that the axial and equatorial S—F bonds are slightly bent back away from the nonbonding electron pair, suggesting that they are pushed by the nonbond-ing electron pair, which has a greater repulsive effect.

(b) The Lewis structure of IF_5 (nonbonding pairs excluded from F) is

$$\begin{array}{c} F \\ | \\ F-\overset{..}{I}-F \\ \diagup \;\; | \\ F \;\; F \end{array}$$

The iodine has six pairs of valence-shell electrons around it, five of them bonding pairs. The electron pairs should point toward the corners of an octahedron. The geometrical arrangement of atoms is therefore square pyramidal (Table 9.3).

Point of Emphasis: The name *octahedron* means "eight faces."

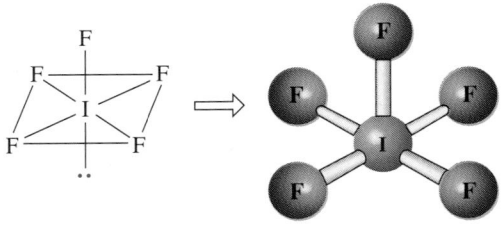

PRACTICE EXERCISE

Predict the molecular geometries of **(a)** ClF_3; **(b)** ICl_4^-.   *Answers:* **(a)** T-shaped; **(b)** square planar

Point of Emphasis: The geometry around atoms is crucial to understanding reactions in future courses in organic chemistry, inorganic chemistry, and biochemistry.

Molecules with No Single Central Atom

The molecules and ions whose structures we have thus far considered contain only a single central atom. The VSEPR model, however, can be readily extended to more complex molecules. Consider the acetic acid molecule, whose Lewis structure is shown below:

$$\begin{array}{ccc} H & \ddot{\text{O}}\text{:} & \\ | & \| & \\ H-C-C- & \ddot{\text{O}}-H \\ | & & \\ H & & \end{array}$$

Using the VSEPR model, we can predict the geometry around the leftmost C atom, the central C atom, and the rightmost O atom.

Notice that the leftmost C has four electron pairs around it, all of them bonding pairs. Thus, the geometry around that atom is tetrahedral. The central C has effectively three bonding pairs around it (counting the double bond as if it were one pair). Thus, the geometry around that atom is trigonal planar. The O atom has four electron pairs, giving it a tetrahedral electron-pair geometry. However, only two of these pairs are bonding pairs, so the molecular geometry around O is bent. The molecular geometry is shown in Figure 9.7.

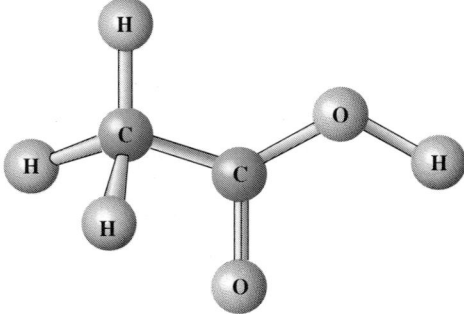

FIGURE 9.7   The molecular structure of acetic acid, $HC_2H_3O_2$.

SAMPLE EXERCISE 9.3

Predict the approximate values for the H—O—C and O—C—O bond angles in oxalic acid:

$$\text{H}-\overset{..}{\underset{..}{\text{O}}}-\overset{\overset{:\text{O}:}{\|}}{\text{C}}-\overset{\overset{:\text{O}:}{\|}}{\text{C}}-\overset{..}{\underset{..}{\text{O}}}-\text{H}$$

SOLUTION To predict the H—O—C bond angle, consider the number of electron pairs around the central O of this angle. Because there are four electron pairs (two single bonds and two nonbonding electron pairs), the electron-pair geometry is tetrahedral, and thus the bond angle is approximately 109°.

In the case of the O—C—O bond angle, the central C atom is surrounded by a double bond and two single bonds. To predict their arrangement, we count the double bond as a single bond, so we have three electron pairs. Thus the electron-pair geometry is trigonal planar, and the bond angle is approximately 120°.

PRACTICE EXERCISE

Predict the C—C—C bond angle in the following molecule:

$$\text{H}-\overset{\overset{\text{H}}{|}}{\underset{\underset{\text{H}}{|}}{\text{C}}}-\text{C}\equiv\text{C}-\text{H}$$

Answer: 180°

9.2 Polarity of Molecules

The shape of a molecule and the polarity of its bonds together determine the charge distribution in the molecule. A molecule is said to be **polar** if its centers of negative and positive charge do not coincide. Because one end of a polar molecule has a slight negative charge and the other a slight positive charge, polar molecules are also called **dipoles.** If there are no charges on the opposite ends of a molecule, or if the charges have the same sign, the molecule is not a dipole and is therefore *nonpolar.*

Any diatomic molecule with a polar bond (Section 8.5) is a polar molecule. For example, the HF molecule is polar, having a concentration of negative charge on the more electronegative F atom, leaving the less electronegative H atom as the positive end:

$$\overset{+\longrightarrow}{\text{H}-\text{F}}$$

The arrow denotes the shift in electron density toward the fluorine atom.

Polar molecules align themselves in an electric field, as shown in Figure 9.8. They also align themselves with respect to each other and with respect to ions. The negative end of one polar molecule and the positive end of another attract each other. Polar molecules are likewise attracted to ions. The negative end of a polar molecule is attracted to a positive ion; the positive end is attracted to a negative ion. These interactions are important in explaining the properties of liquids, solids, and solutions, as you will see in Chapters 11, 12, and 13.

Teaching Note: The "crossed" end of the arrow can be thought of as a plus (+) sign and is used to designate the positive end of a dipole.

FIGURE 9.8 Polar molecules align themselves in an electric field, with their negative ends pointing toward the positive plate.

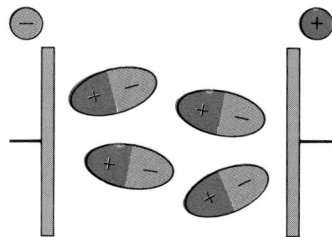

The degree of polarity of a molecule is measured by its **dipole moment.**
The dipole moment, μ, is defined as the product of the charge at either end of the
dipole, Q, times the distance, r, between the charges: $\mu = Qr$. Therefore, the
dipole moment increases as the quantity of charge that is separated increases
and as the distance between the positive and negative centers increases.

Dipole moments are generally reported in debyes (D), a unit equaling
3.33×10^{-30} coulomb-meters (C-m). For example, the dipole moment of HCl
is 1.08 D. What does this value tell us about the separation of charge in the
molecule? The bond length in HCl is 1.27 Å. The dipole moment produced by a
full positive and a full negative charge (1.60×10^{-19} C) separated by 1.27 Å
(1.27×10^{-10} m) is 2.03×10^{-29} C-m $= 6.10$ D. The actual dipole moment is
much smaller than this because the H—Cl bond is polar covalent rather than
ionic. If we examine other hydrogen halides (Table 9.4), we find that the dipole
moment decreases from HF to HI, which corresponds to the decrease in the
electronegativity of the halide.

TABLE 9.4 △ **Bond Lengths, Electronegativity Differences, and Dipole
Moments of the Hydrogen Halides**

Compound	Bond length (Å)	Electronegativity difference	Dipole moment (D)
HF	0.92	1.9	1.82
HCl	1.27	0.9	1.08
HBr	1.41	0.7	0.82
HI	1.61	0.4	0.44

The Polarity of Polyatomic Molecules

The polarity of a molecule containing more than two atoms depends on both
the polarities of the bonds and the geometry of the molecule. For each polar
bond in a molecule, we can consider the *bond dipole,* that is, the dipole moment
due only to the two atoms bonded together. We must then ask what *overall*
dipole moment results from adding up the individual bond dipoles. For example, consider the CO_2 molecule, which is linear. As shown in Figure 9.9(*a*), each
C—O bond is polar and, because the C—O bonds are identical, the bond
dipoles are equal in magnitude.

Does the fact that both C—O bonds are polar mean that the CO_2 molecule is polar? Not necessarily. Bond dipoles and dipole moments are *vector*
quantities; that is, they have both a magnitude and a direction. The overall
dipole moment of a polyatomic molecule is the sum of its bond dipoles. Both
the magnitudes *and* the directions of the bond dipoles must be considered in

this sum of vectors. The two bond dipoles in CO_2, although equal in magnitude,
are exactly opposite in direction. Adding them together is the same as adding
two numbers that are equal in magnitude but opposite in sign, such as $100 +
(-100)$: The bond dipoles, like the numbers, "cancel" each other. Therefore,
the overall dipole moment of CO_2 is zero. Note that the oxygen atoms in CO_2 do
carry a partial negative charge and that the carbon atom carries a partial positive
charge, as we expect for polar bonds. Even though the individual bonds are

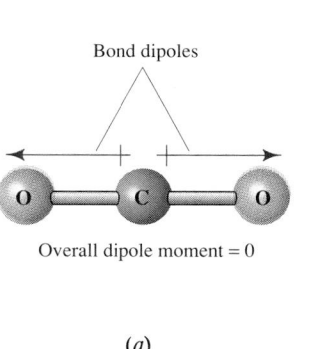

Bond dipoles

Overall dipole moment = 0

(a)

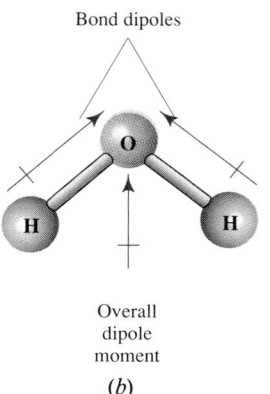

Bond dipoles

Overall dipole moment

(b)

FIGURE 9.9 The overall dipole moment of a molecule is the sum of its bond dipoles. (a) In CO_2, the bond dipoles are equal in magnitude but exactly oppose each other. The overall dipole moment is zero. (b) In H_2O, the bond dipoles are also equal in magnitude but do not exactly oppose each other. The molecule has a nonzero overall dipole moment.

polar, the geometry of the molecule dictates that the overall dipole moment be zero.

Now let's consider H_2O, which is a bent molecule with two polar bonds [Figure 9.9(b)]. Again, both the bonds are identical, so the bond dipoles are equal in magnitude. Because the molecule is bent, however, the bond dipoles do not directly oppose each other and therefore do not cancel each other. Hence, the water molecule has an overall dipole moment ($\mu = 1.84$ D). The oxygen atom carries a partial negative charge, and the hydrogen atoms each have a partial positive charge. The polarity of H_2O molecules is demonstrated in Figure 9.10, which shows that a stream of water is deflected by an electrically charged glass rod.

Figure 9.11 shows several other examples of polar and nonpolar molecules, all of which have polar bonds. Notice that the molecules in which the central atom is symmetrically surrounded by identical atoms (BF_3 and CCl_4) are nonpolar. For AB_n molecules in which all the B atoms are the same, certain symmetrical geometries—linear (AB_2), trigonal planar (AB_3), tetrahedral and square planar (AB_4), trigonal bipyramidal (AB_5), and octahedral (AB_6)—must lead to nonpolar molecules regardless of how polar the individual bonds are.

(a)

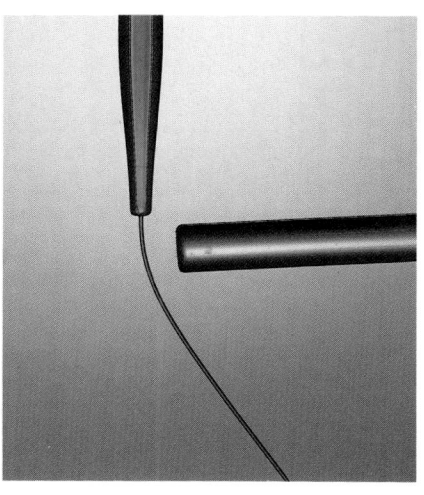

(b)

FIGURE 9.10 Whether or not a liquid is composed of polar molecules can be shown by placing a charged rod near a stream of the liquid. (a) A nonpolar liquid such as hexane (dyed red) is undeflected. (b) A polar liquid such as water (dyed blue) is deflected because the molecules are attracted toward the charge.

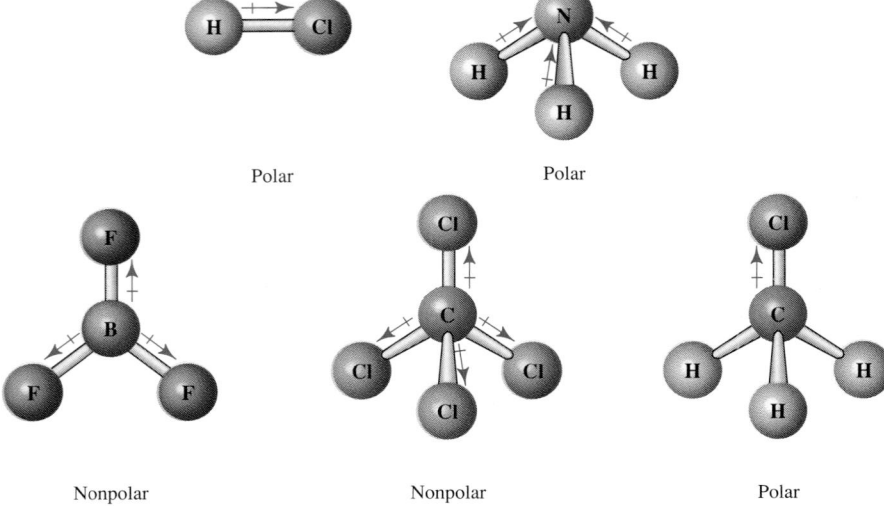

FIGURE 9.11 Examples of molecules with polar bonds. Some of these molecules are nonpolar because their bond dipoles cancel one another.

Polar   Polar

Nonpolar   Nonpolar   Polar

 Figure 9.11

SAMPLE EXERCISE 9.4

Predict whether the following molecules are polar or nonpolar: **(a)** BrCl; **(b)** SO_2; **(c)** SF_6.

SOLUTION **(a)** Chlorine is more electronegative than bromine. Consequently, BrCl will be polar with chlorine carrying the negative charge:

$$Br-Cl$$

Experimentally, the dipole moment of the molecule is 0.57 D. All diatomic molecules with polar bonds are polar molecules.

(b) Because oxygen is more electronegative than sulfur, the molecule has polar bonds. Several resonance forms for SO_2 can be written (see Exercise 8.77):

$$:\ddot{O}-\ddot{S}=\ddot{O}: \longleftrightarrow :\ddot{O}=\ddot{S}-\ddot{O}: \longleftrightarrow :\ddot{O}=\ddot{S}=\ddot{O}:$$

For each of these, the VSEPR model predicts a bent geometry. Because the molecule is bent, the bond dipoles do not cancel and the molecule is polar ($\mu = 1.62$ D):

(c) Fluorine is more electronegative than sulfur. The bond dipoles therefore point toward fluorine. The six S—F bonds are arranged in an octahedral fashion around the central sulfur:

The symmetrical octahedral geometry of the molecule leads to cancellation of the bond dipoles, and the molecule is nonpolar ($\mu = 0$).

PRACTICE EXERCISE

Are the following molecules polar or nonpolar: **(a)** NF_3; **(b)** BCl_3? *Answers:* **(a)** polar; **(b)** nonpolar

9.3 Covalent Bonding and Orbital Overlap

The VSEPR model provides a simple means for predicting the shapes of molecules. However, it does not explain why bonds exist between atoms. In developing theories of covalent bonding, chemists have approached the problem from another direction, namely, using quantum mechanics. How can we explain bonding and account for the geometries of molecules in terms of atomic orbitals? The marriage of Lewis's notion of electron-pair bonds to the idea of atomic orbitals leads to a model of chemical bonding called **valence bond theory.** By extending this approach to include the ways in which atomic orbitals can mix with one another, we obtain a picture that corresponds nicely to the VSEPR model.

In the Lewis theory, covalent bonding occurs when atoms share electrons. Such sharing concentrates electron density between the nuclei. In the valence bond theory, the buildup of electron density between two nuclei is visualized as occurring when a valence atomic orbital of one atom merges with that of another atom. The orbitals are then said to share a region of space, or to **overlap.** The overlap of orbitals allows two electrons of opposite spin to share the common space between the nuclei, forming a covalent bond.

The approach of two H atoms to form H_2 is depicted in Figure 9.12(*a*). Each atom has a single electron in a $1s$ orbital. As the orbitals overlap, electron density is concentrated between the nuclei. Because the electrons are simultaneously attracted to both nuclei, they hold the atoms together, forming a covalent bond.

The idea of orbital overlap producing a covalent bond applies equally well to other molecules. For example, consider the HCl molecule. Chlorine has the electron configuration $[Ne]3s^2 3p^5$. All of the valence orbitals of chlorine are full except one $3p$ orbital, which contains a single electron. This electron pairs up with the single electron of H to form a covalent bond. Figure 9.12(*b*) shows the overlap of the $3p$ orbital of Cl with the $1s$ orbital of H. Likewise, we can explain the covalent bond in the Cl_2 molecule in terms of the overlap of the $3p$ orbital of one atom with the $3p$ orbital of another, as shown in Figure 9.12(*c*).

Raymond F. Peterson and David F. Treagust, "Grade-12 Students' Misconceptions of Covalent Bonding and Structure," *J. Chem. Ed.* **1989,** *66,* 459.

FIGURE 9.12 The overlap of orbitals to form covalent bonds. Each orbital has one unpaired electron, giving a shared pair of electrons in the bond. (*a*) The bond in H_2 results from the overlap of two $1s$ orbitals from two H atoms. (*b*) The bond in HCl results from the overlap of a $1s$ orbital of H and one of the lobes of a $3p$ orbital of Cl. (*c*) The bond in Cl_2 results from the overlap of two $3p$ orbitals from two Cl atoms.

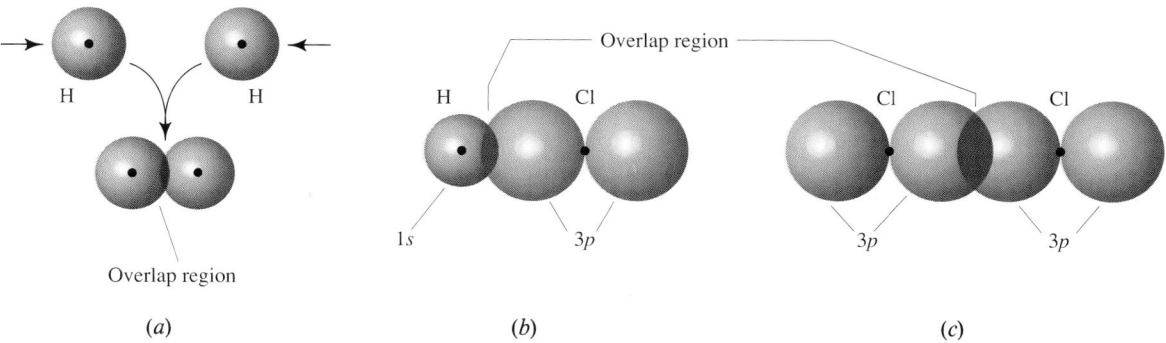

FIGURE 9.13 The change in potential energy during the formation of the H_2 molecule. The minimum in the energy, at 0.74 Å, represents the equilibrium bond distance. The energy at that point, -436 kJ/mol, corresponds to the energy change for formation of the H—H bond.

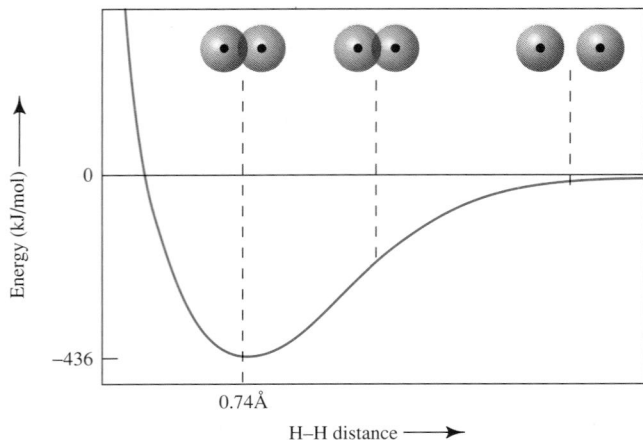

Figure 9.13

There is always an optimum distance between the two bonded nuclei in any covalent bond. This fact is illustrated in Figure 9.13, which shows how the potential energy of the system changes as two H atoms come together to form an H_2 molecule. As the distance between the atoms decreases, the overlap between their $1s$ orbitals increases. Because of the resultant increase in electron density between the nuclei, the potential energy of the system decreases. That is, the strength of the bond increases, as shown by the decrease in the energy on the curve. However, the curve also shows that as the atoms come very close together, the energy increases rapidly. This rapid increase is due mainly to the electrostatic repulsion between the nuclei, which becomes significant at short internuclear distances. The internuclear distance at a minimum of the potential-energy curve corresponds to the observed bond length. Thus, the observed bond length is the distance at which the attractive forces between unlike charges (electrons and nuclei) are balanced by the repulsive forces between like charges (electron-electron and nucleus-nucleus).

9.4 Hybrid Orbitals

Although the idea of orbital overlap allows us to understand the formation of covalent bonds, it is not always so simple to apply this idea to polyatomic molecules. For polyatomic molecules, we must explain not only the number of bonds formed but also their observed geometries. The approach taken by valence bond theory to rationalize geometries is illustrated by considering the BeF_2 molecule.

sp Hybrid Orbitals

Heating the salt BeF_2 to high temperatures generates gaseous molecules of BeF_2, whose Lewis structure is

$$:\!\overset{..}{F}\!-\!Be\!-\!\overset{..}{F}\!:$$

The VSEPR model predicts that this molecule is linear; indeed, experiments show that the molecule is linear with two identical Be—F bonds. How can we use valence bond theory to describe the bonding in linear BeF_2? We have no problem with the fluorine atoms, because the electron configuration of F ($1s^2 2s^2 2p^5$) tells us that there is an unpaired electron in a $2p$ orbital. This $2p$ electron can be paired with an unpaired electron from the Be atom to form a polar covalent bond. However, we are now faced with a more difficult question: Which orbitals on the Be atom overlap with those on the F atoms to form the Be—F bonds?

The orbital diagram for a ground-state Be atom is as follows:

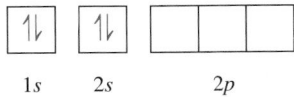

$1s$ $2s$ $2p$

Because it has no unpaired electrons, the Be atom in its ground state is incapable of forming bonds with the fluorine atoms. We can envision the atom obtaining the ability to form two bonds by "promoting" one of the $2s$ electrons to a $2p$ orbital:

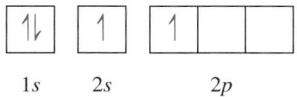

$1s$ $2s$ $2p$

Because the $2p$ orbital is of higher energy than the $2s$, this promotion requires energy. The Be atom now has two unpaired electrons and can therefore form two polar covalent bonds with the F atoms. The Be $2s$ orbital would be used to form one of the bonds, and a $2p$ orbital would be used for the other. We certainly would not expect these two bonds to be identical. Therefore, although the promotion of an electron allows the formation of two Be—F bonds, we still haven't explained the structure of BeF_2.

We can solve our dilemma by envisioning a "mixing" of the $2s$ orbital and one of the $2p$ orbitals to generate two new orbitals, as shown in Figure 9.14. Like p orbitals, each of the new orbitals has two lobes. However, unlike p orbitals, one lobe is much larger than the other. The two new orbitals are identical in shape, but their large lobes point in opposite directions. We have created two **hybrid orbitals,** orbitals that we form by mixing two or more atomic orbitals on an atom, a procedure called **hybridization.** In this case, we have hybridized one s and one p orbital, so we call each hybrid an *sp hybrid orbital.*

For the Be atom of BeF_2, we write the orbital diagram for the formation of two *sp* hybrid orbitals as follows:

$1s$ $2sp$ $2p$

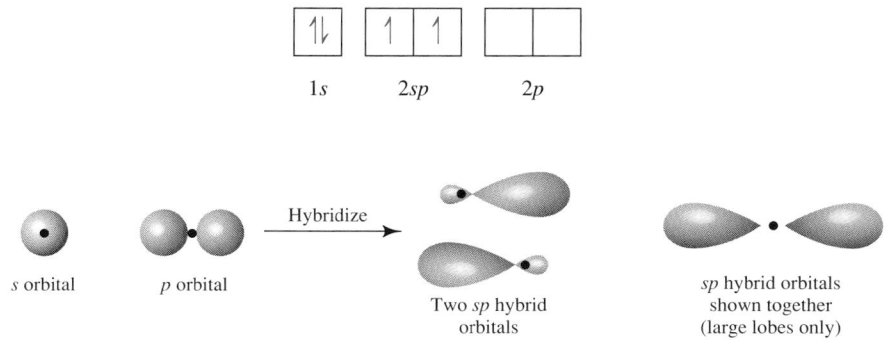

s orbital   *p* orbital

Hybridize →

Two *sp* hybrid orbitals

sp hybrid orbitals shown together (large lobes only)

FIGURE 9.14 One *s* orbital and one *p* orbital can hybridize to form two equivalent *sp* hybrid orbitals. The two hybrid orbitals have their large lobes pointing in opposite directions, 180° apart.

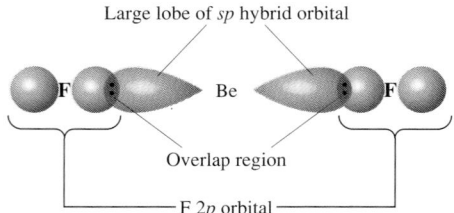

FIGURE 9.15 The formation of two equivalent Be—F bonds in BeF$_2$. Each of the *sp* hybrid orbitals on Be overlaps with a 2*p* orbital on F to form an electron-pair bond.

Figure 9.15

The electrons in the *sp* hybrid orbitals can form shared electron bonds with the two fluorine atoms (Figure 9.15). Because the *sp* hybrid orbitals are equivalent to one another but point in opposite directions, BeF$_2$ has two identical bonds and a linear geometry.

As noted above, the promotion of a 2*s* electron to a 2*p* orbital in Be requires energy. Why, then, do we envision the formation of hybrid orbitals? Hybrid orbitals have one large lobe and can therefore be directed at other atoms more effectively than can unhybridized atomic orbitals. Hence, they can overlap more strongly with the orbitals of other atoms than can atomic orbitals, and stronger bonds result. The energy released by the formation of chemical bonds more than offsets the energy that must be expended to promote electrons.

sp² and *sp³* Hybrid Orbitals

Whenever we mix a certain number of atomic orbitals, we get the same number of hybrid orbitals. Each of these hybrid orbitals is equivalent to the others but points in a different direction. Thus, mixing one 2*s* and one 2*p* orbital yields two equivalent *sp* hybrid orbitals that point in opposite directions (Figure 9.14). Other combinations of atomic orbitals can be hybridized to obtain different geometries. For example, in BF$_3$, a 2*s* electron on the B atom can be promoted to a vacant 2*p* orbital. Mixing the 2*s* and two of the 2*p* orbitals yields three equivalent *sp²* (pronounced "s-p-two") hybrid orbitals:

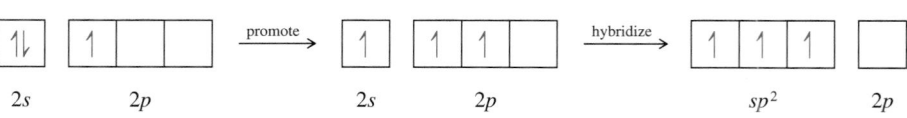

The three *sp²* hybrid orbitals lie in the same plane, 120° apart from one another (Figure 9.16). They are used to make three equivalent bonds with the three fluorine atoms, leading to the trigonal planar geometry of BF$_3$.

An *s* orbital can also mix with all three *p* orbitals in the same subshell. For example, the carbon atom in CH$_4$ forms four equivalent bonds with the four hydrogen atoms. We envision this process as resulting from the mixing of the 2*s* and all three 2*p* atomic orbitals of carbon to create four equivalent *sp³* (pronounced "s-p-three") hybrid orbitals:

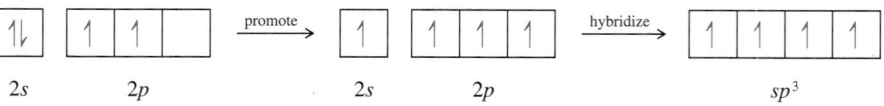

Each of the *sp³* hybrid orbitals has a large lobe that points toward a vertex of a tetrahedron, as shown in Figure 9.17. These hybrid orbitals can be used to form

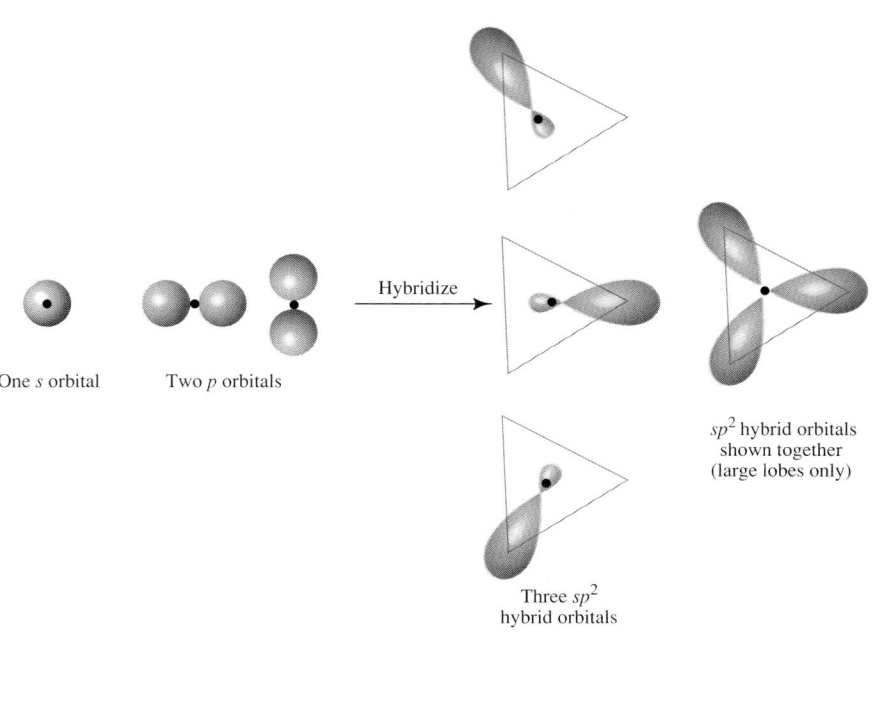

FIGURE 9.16 One *s* orbital and two *p* orbitals can hybridize to form three equivalent *sp*² hybrid orbitals. The large lobes of the hybrid orbitals point toward the corners of an equilateral triangle.

One *s* orbital   Two *p* orbitals

Hybridize

*sp*² hybrid orbitals shown together (large lobes only)

Three *sp*²
hybrid orbitals

Figure 9.16

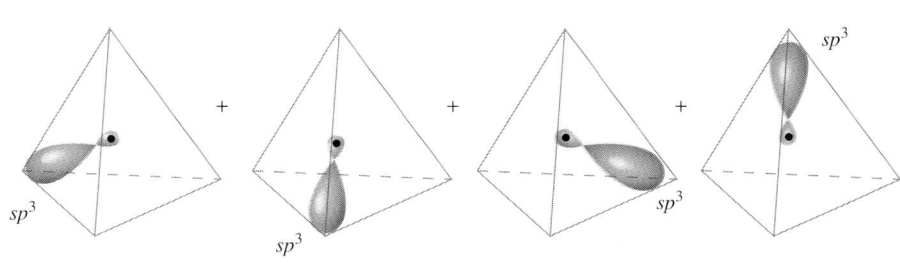

FIGURE 9.17 Formation of four *sp*³ hybrid orbitals from a set of one *s* orbital and three *p* orbitals.

x s + x p_x + p_y + x p_z

Hybridize to form four *sp*³ hybrid orbitals

sp^3 + sp^3 + sp^3 + sp^3

Shown together (large lobes only)

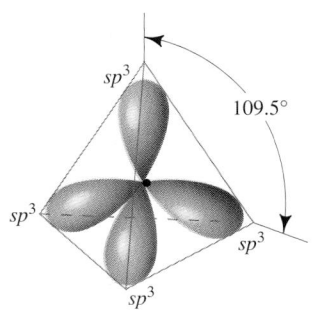

sp^3
sp^3
sp^3
sp^3
sp^3
109.5°

Figure 9.17

9.4 Hybrid Orbitals   **305**

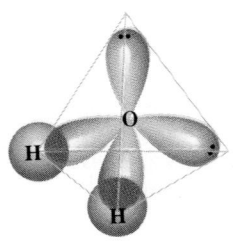

FIGURE 9.18 The bonding in H_2O can be envisioned in terms of sp^3 hybridization of the orbitals on O. Two of the four hybrid orbitals overlap with $1s$ orbitals of H to form covalent bonds. The other two hybrid orbitals are occupied by nonbonding pairs of electrons.

two-electron bonds by overlap with the atomic orbitals of another atom, for example, H. Thus, within valence bond theory, we can describe the bonding in CH_4 as the overlap of four equivalent sp^3 hybrid orbitals on C with the $1s$ orbitals of the four H atoms to form four equivalent bonds.

The idea of hybridization is used in a similar way to describe the bonding in molecules containing nonbonding pairs of electrons. For example, in H_2O, the electron-pair geometry around the central O atom is approximately tetrahedral. Thus, the four electron pairs can be envisioned as occupying sp^3 hybrid orbitals. Two of these orbitals contain nonbonding pairs of electrons, while the other two are used in forming bonds with hydrogen atoms, as shown in Figure 9.18.

Hybridization Involving d Orbitals

Atoms in the third period and beyond can also use d orbitals to form hybrid orbitals. Mixing one s orbital, three p orbitals, and one d orbital leads to five sp^3d hybrid orbitals. These hybrid orbitals are directed at the vertices of a trigonal bipyramid. The formation of sp^3d hybrids is exemplified by the phosphorus atom in PF_5:

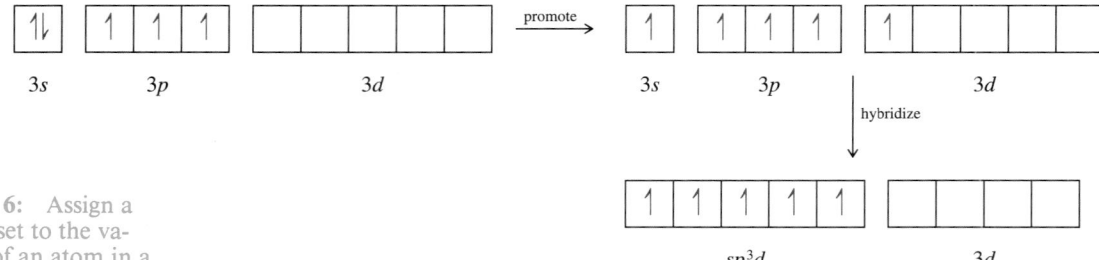

Similarly, mixing one s orbital, three p orbitals, and two d orbitals gives six sp^3d^2 hybrid orbitals, which are directed at the vertices of an octahedron. The use of d orbitals in constructing hybrid orbitals nicely corresponds to the notion of an expanded valence shell. ∞ (Sec. 8.8) The geometrical arrangements characteristic of hybrid orbitals are summarized in Table 9.5.

Summary

You should realize that the purpose of hybrid orbitals is to provide a convenient model for using valence bond theory to describe covalent bonds in molecules. The picture of hybrid orbitals has limited predictive value; that is, we cannot say in advance that the nitrogen atom in NH_3 uses sp^3 hybrid orbitals. When we know the molecular geometry, however, we can employ the concept of hybridization to describe the atomic orbitals used by the central atom in bonding. We therefore use the following steps to predict the hybrid orbitals used by an atom in bonding:

1. Draw the Lewis structure for the molecule or ion.
2. Determine the electron-pair geometry using the VSEPR model.
3. Specify the hybrid orbitals needed to accommodate the electron pairs based on their geometrical arrangement (Table 9.5).

TABLE 9.5 △ Geometrical Arrangements Characteristic of Hybrid Orbital Sets

Atomic orbital set	Hybrid orbital set	Geometry	Examples
s,p	Two sp	Linear (180°)	BeF_2, $HgCl_2$
s,p,p	Three sp^2	Trigonal planar (120°)	BF_3, SO_3
s,p,p,p	Four sp^3	Tetrahedral (109.5°)	CH_4, NH_3, H_2O, NH_4^+
s,p,p,p,d	Five sp^3d	Trigonal bipyramidal (90°, 120°)	PF_5, SF_4, BrF_3, $SbCl_5^{2-}$
s,p,p,p,d,d	Six sp^3d^2	Octahedral (90°, 90°)	SF_6, ClF_5, XeF_4, SiF_6^{2-}

Table 9.5

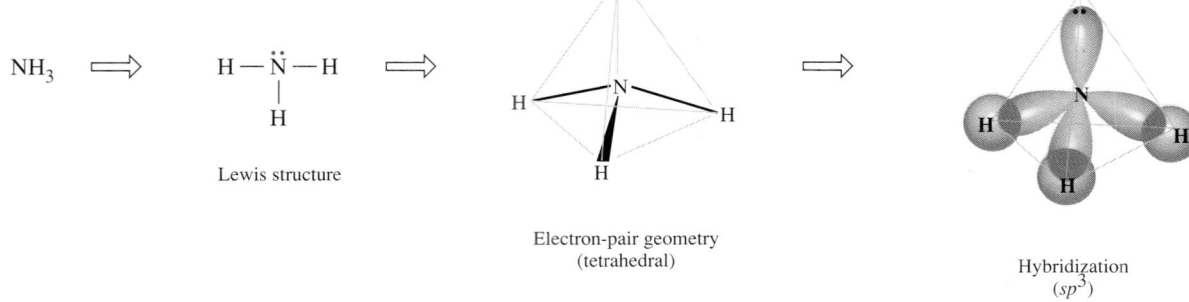

NH$_3$ $\Longrightarrow$

H $-$ $\ddot{\text{N}}$ $-$ H
$\quad$ |
$\quad$ H

Lewis structure

$\Longrightarrow$

Electron-pair geometry
(tetrahedral)

$\Longrightarrow$

Hybridization
(sp^3)

FIGURE 9.19 The hybrid orbitals used by N in the NH$_3$ molecule is predicted by first writing the Lewis structure, then using the VSEPR model to determine the electron-pair geometry, and then specifying the hybrid orbitals needed to accommodate the electron pairs based on their number and geometrical arrangement. Notice that this is essentially the same procedure as that used to determine molecular structure (Figure 9.4), except the final focus is on the location of the electron pairs rather than the location of the atoms.

Figure 9.19

These steps are illustrated in Figure 9.19, which shows how the hybridization employed by N in NH$_3$ is determined.

SAMPLE EXERCISE 9.5

Indicate the hybridization of orbitals employed by the central atom in each of the following: **(a)** NH$_2^-$; **(b)** SF$_4$ (see Sample Exercise 9.2).

SOLUTION **(a)** As shown in Figure 9.19, we *first* determine the Lewis structure of NH$_2^-$;

$$\left[\text{H} \!:\! \ddot{\underset{..}{\text{N}}} \!:\! \text{H} \right]^{-}$$

Second, we determine the electron-pair geometry around N using the VSEPR model. Because there are four electron pairs around N, we conclude that the electron-pair geometry is tetrahedral.

Third, we specify the hybridization that gives a tetrahedral electron-pair geometry, namely, sp^3 (Table 9.5). Two of the sp^3 hybrid orbitals contain nonbonding pairs of electrons, and the other two contain bonding pairs that are shared with hydrogen.

(b) The Lewis structure and electron-pair geometry of SF$_4$ are shown in Sample Exercise 9.2. We see that there are five pairs of valence-shell electrons around S, giving rise to the trigonal bipyramidal electron-pair geometry. With an expanded octet of 10 electrons, the use of a d orbital on the sulfur is required. The trigonal bipyramidal electron-pair geometry corresponds to the sp^3d hybridization (Table 9.5). One of the hybrid orbitals contains a nonbonding pair of electrons; the other four are used in bonding.

PRACTICE EXERCISE

Predict the electron-pair geometry and the hybridization of the central atom in **(a)** SO$_3^{2-}$; **(b)** SF$_6$. *Answers:* **(a)** tetrahedral, sp^3; **(b)** octahedral, sp^3d^2

9.5 Multiple Bonds

In each of the covalent bonds that we have considered thus far, the electron density is concentrated symmetrically about the line that connects the nuclei (the *internuclear axis*). That is, the line joining the two nuclei passes through the middle of the overlap region. These bonds are all called **sigma (σ) bonds.** Thus, the overlap of two *s* orbitals as in H_2 [Figure 9.12(*a*)], the overlap of an *s* and a *p* orbital as in HCl [Figure 9.12(*b*)], the overlap between two *p* orbitals as in Cl_2 [Figure 9.12(*c*)], and the overlap of a *p* orbital with an *sp* hybrid orbital as in BeF_2 (Figure 9.15) are all examples of σ bonds.

   To describe multiple bonding, we must consider a second kind of bond that results from the overlap between two *p* orbitals oriented perpendicularly to the internuclear axis (Figure 9.20). This sideways overlap of *p* orbitals produces a **pi (π) bond.** A π bond is a covalent bond in which the overlap regions lie above and below the internuclear axis. Unlike a σ bond, there is no probability of finding the electron in a π bond on the internuclear axis. Because the total overlap in the π bonds tends to be less than that in a σ bond, π bonds are generally weaker than σ bonds.

   In almost all cases, single bonds are σ bonds. A double bond consists of one σ bond and one π bond, and a triple bond consists of one σ bond and two π bonds:

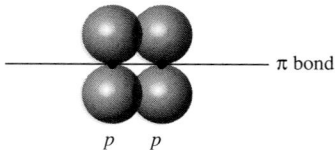

H—H
One σ bond

C=C (with H's)
One σ bond plus one π bond

:N≡N:
One σ bond plus two π bonds

   To see how these ideas are used, consider ethylene, C_2H_4, which possesses a C=C double bond. The bond angles in ethylene are all approximately 120° (Figure 9.21), suggesting that each carbon atom uses sp^2 hybrid orbitals (Figure 9.16) to form σ bonds with the other carbon and with two hydrogens. Because carbon has four valence electrons, after sp^2 hybridization one electron remains in the *unhybridized* 2*p* orbital:

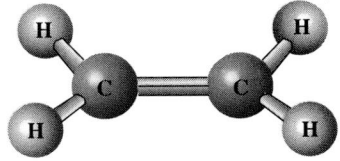

2*s*   2*p*   2*s*   2*p* sp^2 2*p*

The unhybridized 2*p* orbital is directed perpendicular to the plane that contains the three sp^2 hybrid orbitals.

   Each sp^2 hybrid orbital on a carbon atom contains one electron. Figure 9.22 shows how the four C—H σ bonds are formed by the overlap of sp^2 hybrid orbitals on C with the 1*s* orbitals on each hydrogen atom. We therefore use eight electrons to form four electron-pair bonds. The C—C σ bond is formed by the overlap of two sp^2 hybrid orbitals, one on each carbon atom, and requires two more electrons. The C_2H_4 molecule has a total of 12 valence electrons, 10 of which are used to form one C—C and four C—H σ bonds.

FIGURE 9.20   Formation of a π bond by overlap of two *p* orbitals. The two regions of overlap constitute one π bond.

FIGURE 9.21   The molecular geometry of ethylene, C_2H_4.

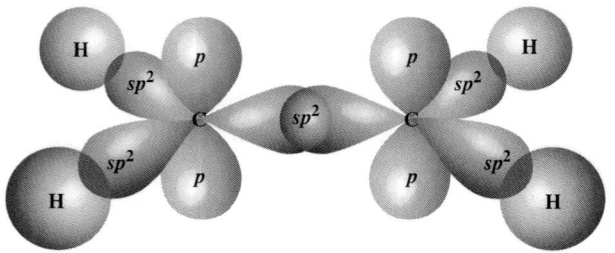

FIGURE 9.22 Hybridization of carbon orbitals in ethylene. The σ bonding framework, formed from sp^2 hybrid orbitals on the carbon atoms, determines the observed structure of the molecule.

Figure 9.22

Figure 9.23

FIGURE 9.23 Formation of the π bond in ethylene by overlap of the $2p$ orbitals on each carbon atom. Note that the centers of charge density in the π bond are above and below the bond axis, whereas in the σ bonds, the centers of charge density lie on the bond axes. The two lobes constitute one π bond.

The remaining two valence electrons reside in the unhybridized $2p$ orbitals, one electron on each of the carbon atoms. These $2p$ orbitals can overlap with one another in a sideways fashion, as shown in Figure 9.23. The resultant electron density is concentrated above and below the C—C bond axis; this is therefore a π bond (Figure 9.20). Thus, the C=C double bond in ethylene consists of one σ bond and one π bond.

Although we cannot experimentally observe a π bond directly (all we can observe are the positions of the atoms), the structure of ethylene provides strong support for its presence. First, the C—C bond length in ethylene (1.34 Å) is much shorter than that in compounds with C—C single bonds (1.54 Å), consistent with the presence of a C=C double bond. Second, all six atoms in C_2H_4 lie in the same plane. Only when the two CH_2 fragments lie in the same plane can the $2p$ orbitals that comprise the π bond achieve a good overlap. If the π bond were not present, there would be no reason to expect the two CH_2 fragments of ethylene to lie in the same plane. Because π bonds require that portions of a molecule be planar, they can introduce rigidity into molecules. This molecular rigidity can strongly affect the properties of substances, as we shall see in Chapter 12.

Triple bonds can also be explained by using hybrid orbitals. Consider acetylene, C_2H_2, a linear molecule containing a triple bond: H—C≡C—H. The linear geometry suggests that each carbon atom uses sp hybrid orbitals to form σ bonds with the other carbon and one hydrogen. Each carbon atom then has two remaining unhybridized $2p$ orbitals at right angles to each other and to the axis of the sp hybrid set (Figure 9.24). These p orbitals overlap to form a pair of π bonds. Thus, the triple bond in acetylene consists of one σ bond and two π bonds.

Although it is possible to make π bonds from d orbitals, the only kind of π bond that we shall consider is that formed by the overlap of p orbitals. This π bond can form only if unhybridized p orbitals are present on the bonded atoms. Therefore, only atoms having sp or sp^2 hybridization can be involved in such π bonding. Furthermore, double and triple bonds (and hence π bonds) are more common in molecules with small atoms, especially C, N, and O. Larger atoms, such as S, P, and Si, form π bonds less readily.

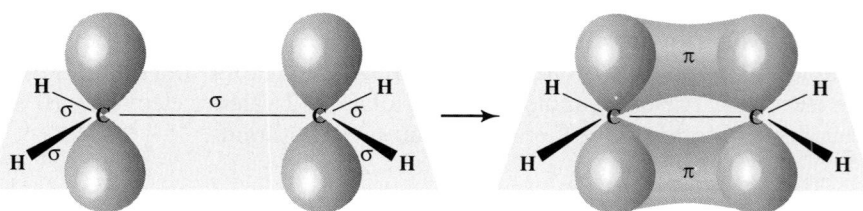

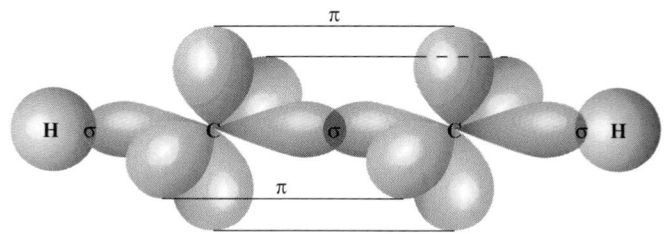

FIGURE 9.24 Formation of two π bonds in acetylene, C_2H_2, from the overlap of two sets of carbon $2p$ orbitals.

Figure 9.24

SAMPLE EXERCISE 9.6

Formaldehyde, which is a planar molecule, has the following Lewis structure:

$$\begin{array}{c} H \\ \diagdown \\ C{=}O{:} \\ \diagup \\ H \end{array}$$

Describe the bonding in formaldehyde in terms of an appropriate set of hybrid orbitals at the carbon atom.

SOLUTION Using the VSEPR model, we would predict the bond angles around C to be about 120° (trigonal-planar geometry). The 120° bond angles about the central atom suggest sp^2 hybrid orbitals for the σ bonds (Table 9.5). There remains a $2p$ orbital on carbon, perpendicular to the plane of the three σ bonds.

    Using the VSEPR model, we predict that the two unshared electron pairs on oxygen and the O—C σ bond will be in a trigonal plane, with approximately 120° angles between them. There also remains a $2p$ orbital on oxygen, perpendicular to the plane of the three σ bonds. This orbital overlaps with the similarly oriented $2p$ orbital on carbon to form a π bond between carbon and oxygen, as illustrated in Figure 9.25.

FIGURE 9.25
Formation of σ and π bonds in formaldehyde, H_2CO.

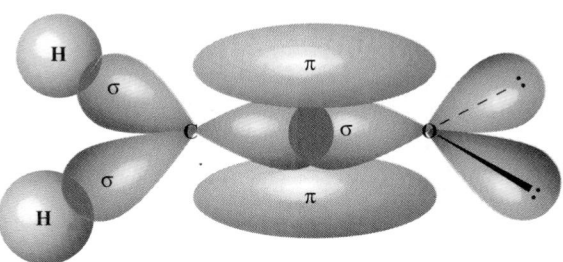

PRACTICE EXERCISE

Consider the acetonitrile molecule:

$$\begin{array}{c} H \\ | \\ H{-}C{-}C{\equiv}N{:} \\ | \\ H \end{array}$$

(a) Predict the bond angles around each carbon; **(b)** give the hybridizations on both carbon atoms; **(c)** determine the total number of σ and π bonds in the molecule.
Answers: **(a)** 109° around the leftmost C and 180° on the rightmost C; **(b)** sp^3, sp; **(c)** five σ bonds and two π bonds.

The Chemistry of Vision

In recent years, scientists have begun to understand the complex chemistry that produces the sensation of vision. Vision begins when light is focused by the lens onto the retina, the layer of cells lining the interior of the eyeball. The retina contains "photoreceptor" cells known as rods and cones (seen in the chapter-opening photograph). The rods are sensitive to dim light and are used in night vision. The cones are sensitive to colors. The tops of the rods and cones contain a complex molecule called *rhodopsin*. Rhodopsin consists of a protein, called *opsin*, bonded to a reddish-purple pigment called *retinal*. Structural changes around a double bond in the retinal portion of the molecule trigger a series of chemical reactions that result in vision.

Double bonds between atoms are stronger than single bonds between the same atoms (Table 8.4). For example, a C=C double bond is stronger [$D(C=C) = 614$ kJ/mol] than a C—C single bond [$D(C—C) = 348$ kJ/mol], though not twice as strong. Our recent discussions now allow us to appreciate another aspect of double bonds, the stiffness or rigidity that they introduce into molecules.

Imagine taking the —CH$_2$ group of the ethylene molecule and rotating it relative to the other —CH$_2$ group as shown in Figure 9.26. This rotation destroys the overlap of p orbitals, breaking the π bond, a process that requires considerable energy. Thus, the presence of a double bond restricts the rotation of the bonds in a molecule. In contrast, molecules can rotate almost freely around the bond axis in single (σ) bonds because this motion has no effect on orbital overlap. This rotation allows molecules with single bonds to twist and fold almost as if their atoms were attached by hinges.

Our vision depends on the rigidity of double bonds in retinal. In its normal form, retinal is held rigid by its double bonds in the geometry shown on the left in Figure 9.27. (The structure of the *opsin* portion of the molecule is not pertinent to our discussion.) When light enters the eye, it is absorbed by the rhodopsin, and the energy is used to break the π-bond portion of the indicated double bond. The molecule then rotates around this bond, changing its molecular geometry. The retinal then separates from the opsin, triggering the reactions that produce a nerve impulse that the brain interprets as the sensation of vision. It takes as few as five closely spaced molecules reacting in this fashion to produce the sensation of vision. Thus, only five photons of light are necessary to stimulate the eye.

The retinal slowly reverts to its original form and reattaches to the opsin. The slowness of this process helps explain why intense bright light causes temporary blindness. The light causes all the retinal to separate from opsin, leaving no further molecules to absorb light.

FIGURE 9.26 Schematic illustration of rotation about a carbon-carbon double bond in ethylene. The overlap of the p orbitals that form the π bond is lost in the rotation. For this reason, rotation about double bonds does not occur readily.

π bond

H

H

H

90° rotation around double bond

H

H

H

H

H

FIGURE 9.27 When rhodopsin absorbs visible light, the π component of the double bond shown in red breaks, allowing rotation that produces a change in molecular geometry.

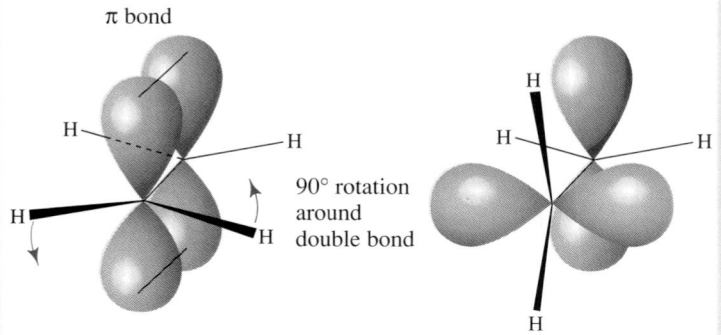

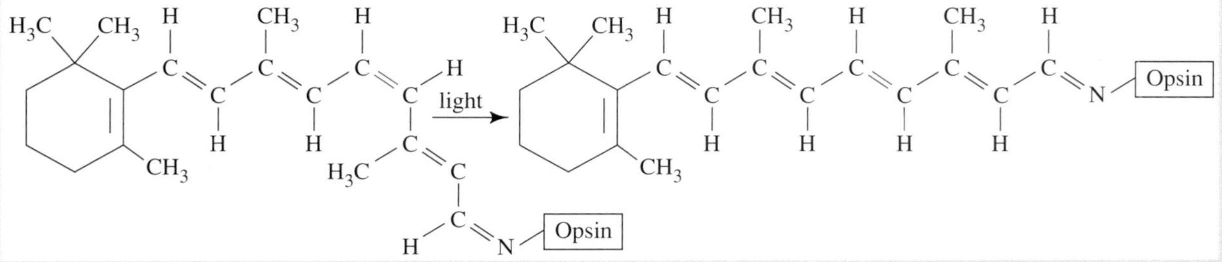

Delocalized Bonding

In each of the molecules we have discussed in this chapter, the bonding electrons are *localized*. By this we mean that the σ and π electrons are associated totally with the two atoms forming the bond. In some molecules, particularly those with more than one resonance form, we cannot accurately describe the bonding as localized. Benzene, C_6H_6, is an example of such a molecule. Benzene has two resonance forms:

All six C—C bonds in benzene are of equal length—1.40 Å—intermediate between the values for a C—C single bond (1.54 Å) and a C=C double bond (1.34 Å). The molecule is planar, and the bond angles around each carbon are 120°.

To describe the bonding in benzene in terms of hybrid orbitals, we first choose a hybridization scheme consistent with the geometry of the molecule. Because each carbon is surrounded by three atoms at 120° angles, the appropriate hybrid set is sp^2. Six C—C σ bonds and six C—H σ bonds are formed from the sp^2 hybrid orbitals, as shown in Figure 9.28(a). This leaves a $2p$ orbital on each carbon that is oriented perpendicularly to the plane of the molecule. The situation is very much like that in ethylene, except that we now have six carbon $2p$ orbitals arranged in a ring [Figure 9.28(b)].

FIGURE 9.28 The σ and π bond networks in benzene, C_6H_6. (a) The C—C and C—H σ bonds all lie in the plane of the molecule and are formed by using carbon sp^2 hybrid orbitals. (b) Each carbon atom has an unhybridized $2p$ orbital that lies perpendicular to the molecular plane. (c) A representation of the smearing out, or delocalization, of three C—C π bonds among the six carbon atoms.

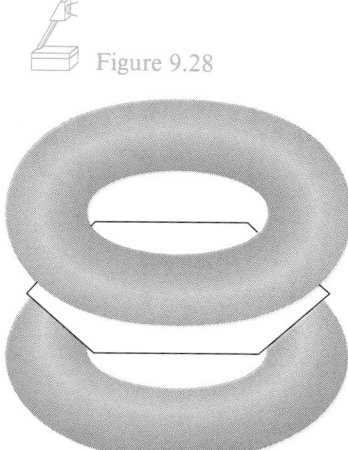
Figure 9.28

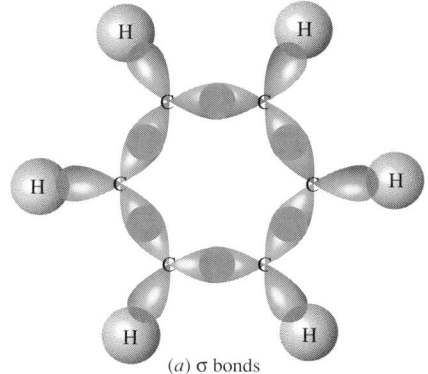

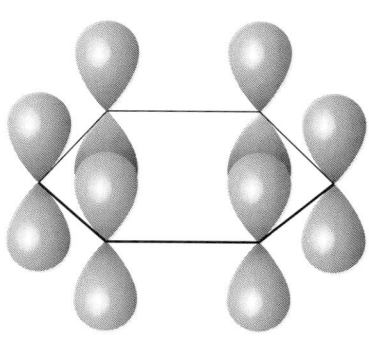

(a) σ bonds

(b) $2p$ atomic orbitals

(c) Delocalized π bonds

Learning Goal 8: Explain
the concept of delocalization
in π bonds.

Sture Nordholm,
"Delocalization—The Key
Concept of Covalent Bond-
ing," *J. Chem. Ed.* **1988,** *65,*
581.

Point of Emphasis: This
method of depiction is commonly used for organic compounds.

Common Misconception:
Students often label the vertices without putting in the
hydrogen atoms. If a vertex is
labeled with the symbol for
carbon, then all the attached
hydrogens must be drawn in.

Each of the 2*p* orbitals in benzene has one electron in it, so three π bonds can be formed. Now, if localized π bonds were formed between pairs of carbon atoms, the molecule would have three short double bonds and three longer single bonds. This corresponds exactly to the situation described by either of the individual Lewis structures above. However, a description that better reflects *both* resonance structures is to envision the three π bonds "smeared out" among all six carbon atoms, as shown in Figure 9.28(*c*). This model leads to the description of each bond between neighboring carbon atoms as an average of a single bond and a double bond, consistent with the observed C—C bond lengths in benzene.

Because we cannot describe the π bonds in benzene in terms of electron-pair bonds between neighboring atoms, we say that the π bonds are **delocalized** among the six carbon atoms. Delocalization of the electrons in its π bonds gives benzene a special stability. For example, bromine readily attacks the π bond of ethylene, but the π-bonding system in benzene is far less reactive.

It is common to represent benzene by omitting the hydrogen atoms attached to carbon and showing only the carbon-carbon framework with the vertices unlabeled. The π bonds are shown either by using one of the Lewis structures or by placing a circle in the center of the carbon ring:

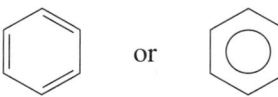

The representation on the left gives a better sense of the number of electrons used in forming C—C σ and π bonds, but it implies localized bonding. The representation on the right correctly shows the delocalization of the π bonds, but it does not explicitly indicate the number of electrons used in forming these bonds. Chemists use both representations of benzene interchangeably.

General Conclusions

On the basis of all the examples we've seen, we can formulate a few general conclusions that are helpful in using the concept of hybrid orbitals to discuss molecular structures.

1. Every pair of bonded atoms shares one or more pairs of electrons. In every bond, at least one pair of electrons is localized in the space between the atoms, in a σ bond. The appropriate set of hybrid orbitals used to form the σ bonds between an atom and its neighbors is determined by the observed geometry of the molecule. The relationship between hybrid orbital set and geometry about an atom is given in Table 9.5.

2. The electrons in σ bonds are localized in the region between two bonded atoms and do not make a significant contribution to the bonding between any other two atoms.

3. When atoms share more than one pair of electrons, the additional pairs are in π bonds. The centers of charge density in a π bond lie above and below the bond axis.

4. Molecules with two or more resonance forms can have π bonds that extend over more than two bonded atoms. Electrons in π bonds that extend over more than two atoms are said to be delocalized.

9.6 Molecular Orbitals

Valence bond theory and hybrid orbitals allow us to move in a straightforward way from Lewis dot structures to rationalizing the observed geometries of molecules in terms of atomic orbitals. For example, we can use this theory to understand why methane has the formula CH_4, how the carbon and hydrogen atomic orbitals are used to form electron-pair bonds, and why the arrangement of the C—H bonds about the central carbon is tetrahedral. This model, however, does not explain all aspects of bonding. It is not successful, for example, in describing the excited states of molecules, which we must understand in order to explain how molecules absorb light, giving them color.

Some aspects of bonding are better explained by another model called **molecular orbital theory.** In Chapters 6 and 7, we saw that electrons in atoms exist in allowed energy states, which we call atomic orbitals. In a similar way, molecular orbital theory predicts that electrons in molecules exist in allowed energy states called **molecular orbitals.**

Molecular orbitals have many of the same characteristics as atomic orbitals. For example, molecular orbitals hold a maximum of two electrons (with opposite spins), they have definite energies, and their electron-density distributions can be visualized by using contour representations, as we did when we discussed atomic orbitals. Molecular orbitals, however, are associated with the entire molecule.

The Hydrogen Molecule

To get some sense of the approach taken in molecular orbital theory, consider the hydrogen molecule, H_2. Whenever two atomic orbitals overlap, two molecular orbitals form. Thus, the overlap of the $1s$ orbitals of two hydrogen atoms to form H_2 produces the two molecular orbitals pictured in Figure 9.29.

The lower-energy molecular orbital of H_2 concentrates electron density between the two hydrogen nuclei and is called the **bonding molecular orbital.** This sausage-shaped molecular orbital results from summing the two atomic orbitals so that the atomic orbital wave functions enhance each other in the bond region. Because an electron in this molecular orbital is strongly attracted to both nuclei, the electron is more stable (at lower energy) than it is in the $1s$ orbital of the hydrogen atom. Because it concentrates electron density between

A. B. Sanningrahi and Tapas Kar, "Molecular Orbital Theory of Bond Order and Valency," *J. Chem. Ed.* 1988, *65*, 674.

Learning Goal 9: Explain the concept of orbital overlap and the reason why overlap may in some cases be zero because of symmetry.

Learning Goal 10: Describe how molecular orbitals are formed by overlap of atomic orbitals.

Teaching Note: The linear combination of atomic orbitals (LCAO) method is the most straightforward approach to molecular orbital theory.

Teaching Note: This orbital overlap resulting in two molecular orbitals is very much like the mixing of two atomic orbitals to form hybrid orbitals. The difference is that the two atomic orbitals used to form molecular orbitals are on two different nuclei.

Figure 9.29

FIGURE 9.29 Contour representations of the combination of two hydrogen $1s$ atomic orbitals into two molecular orbitals of H_2. In the bonding molecular orbital, σ_{1s} (the molecular orbital at lower energy), the atomic orbitals combine constructively, leading to a buildup of electron density between the nuclei. In the antibonding molecular orbital σ_{1s}^* (the molecular orbital at higher energy), the orbitals combine destructively in the bonding region: The two atomic orbitals partially cancel each other, leading to an exclusion of electron density from the region between the nuclei. Note that the σ_{1s}^* orbital has a node between the two nuclei.

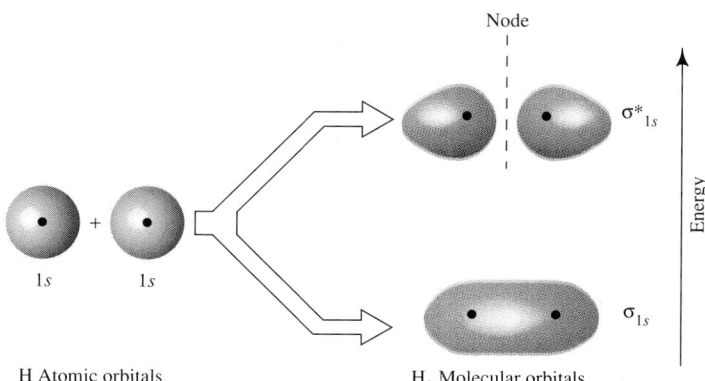

Node

σ^*_{1s}

Energy

σ_{1s}

$1s$ $1s$

H Atomic orbitals

H_2 Molecular orbitals

the nuclei, the bonding molecular orbital holds the atoms together in a covalent bond.

The higher-energy molecular orbital in Figure 9.29 has very little electron density between the nuclei and is called the **antibonding molecular orbital.** Instead of enhancing each other in the region between the nuclei, the atomic orbitals cancel each other in this region, and the greatest electron density is on opposite sides of the nuclei. Thus, this molecular orbital excludes electrons from the very region in which a bond must be formed. An electron in this molecular orbital is actually repelled from the bonding region and is therefore less stable (at higher energy) than it is in the $1s$ orbital of a hydrogen atom.

The electron density in both the bonding and the antibonding molecular orbitals of H_2 is centered about an imaginary line passing through the two nuclei (see Figure 9.29). Molecular orbitals of this type are called **sigma (σ) molecular orbitals.** The bonding sigma molecular orbital of H_2 is labeled σ_{1s}, the subscript indicating that the molecular orbital is formed from two $1s$ orbitals. The antibonding sigma orbital of H_2 is labeled σ_{1s}^*, the asterisk denoting that the orbital is antibonding.

The interaction between two $1s$ orbitals to form σ_{1s} and σ_{1s}^* molecular orbitals can be represented by an **energy-level diagram** (also called a **molecular orbital diagram**), like those in Figure 9.30. Such diagrams show the interacting atomic orbitals in the left and right columns and the molecular orbitals in the middle column. Note that the bonding molecular orbital, σ_{1s}, is lower in energy than the atomic $1s$ orbitals, whereas the antibonding orbital, σ_{1s}^*, is higher in energy than the $1s$ orbitals. Like atomic orbitals, each molecular orbital can accommodate two electrons with their spins paired (Pauli exclusion principle).

The molecular orbital diagram of the H_2 molecule is shown in Figure 9.30(a). Each H atom has one electron, so there are two electrons in H_2. These two electrons occupy the lower-energy bonding (σ_{1s}) molecular orbital with their spins paired. Electrons occupying a bonding molecular orbital are called *bonding electrons*. Because the σ_{1s} orbital is lower in energy than the isolated $1s$ orbitals, the H_2 molecule is more stable than the two separate H atoms.

In contrast, the hypothetical He_2 molecule would have four electrons to fill its molecular orbitals, as shown in Figure 9.30(b). Because only two electrons can be placed in the σ_{1s} orbital, the other two must be placed in the σ_{1s}^*. The energy decrease resulting from the two electrons in the bonding molecular orbital is offset by the energy increase from the two electrons in the antibonding

FIGURE 9.30 Energy-level diagram for (a) the H_2 molecule, and (b) the hypothetical He_2 molecule.

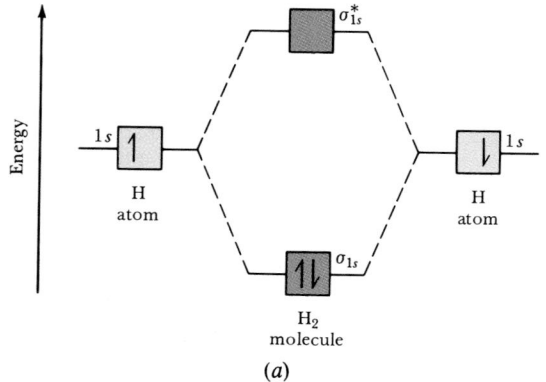

(a)

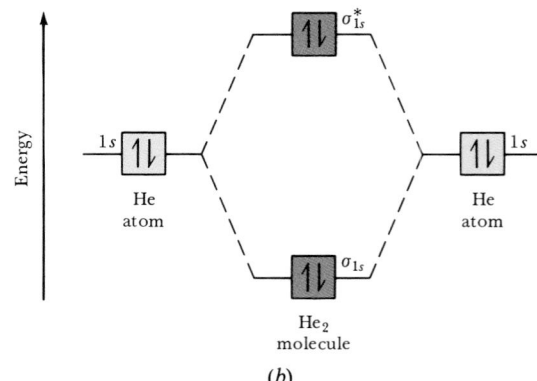

(b)

orbital.† Hence, He_2 is not a stable molecule. Molecular orbital theory correctly predicts that hydrogen forms diatomic molecules but helium does not.

Bond Order

In molecular orbital theory, the stability of a covalent bond is related to its **bond order,** defined as follows:

Bond order = $\frac{1}{2}$(number of bonding electrons

$-$ number of antibonding electrons)

That is, the bond order is half the difference between the number of bonding electrons and the number of antibonding electrons. We take half the difference because we are used to thinking of bonds in terms of pairs of electrons. *A bond order of 1 represents a single bond, a bond order of 2 represents a double bond, and a bond order of 3 represents a triple bond.* Because molecular orbital theory also treats molecules with an odd number of electrons, bond orders of $\frac{1}{2}$, $\frac{3}{2}$, or $\frac{5}{2}$ are possible.

Because H_2 has two bonding electrons and no antibonding ones (Figure 9.30), it has a bond order of $\frac{1}{2}(2 - 0) = 1$. Because He_2 has two bonding electrons and two antibonding ones [Figure 9.30(b)], it has a bond order of $\frac{1}{2}(2 - 2) = 0$. A bond order of 0 means that no bond exists.

SAMPLE EXERCISE 9.7

What is the bond order of the He_2^+ ion? Would you expect this ion to be stable relative to the separated He atom and He^+ ion?

SOLUTION   The energy-level diagram for this system is shown in Figure 9.31. The He_2^+ ion has a total of three electrons. Two are placed in the bonding orbital, the third in the antibonding orbital. Thus, the bond order is

$$\text{Bond order} = \frac{1}{2}(2 - 1) = \frac{1}{2}$$

Because the bond order is greater than 0, the He_2^+ molecular ion is predicted to be stable relative to the separated He and He^+. Formation of He_2^+ in the gas phase has been demonstrated in laboratory experiments.

FIGURE 9.31   Energy-level diagram for the He_2^+ ion.

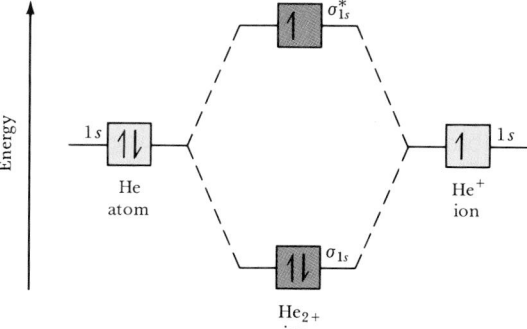

PRACTICE EXERCISE

Determine the bond order of the H_2^- ion.   *Answer:* $\frac{1}{2}$

---

† In fact, antibonding molecular orbitals are slightly more unfavorable than bonding orbitals are favorable. Whenever there is an equal number of electrons in bonding and antibonding orbitals, the energy is higher than it is for the isolated atoms; no bond is formed.

9.7 Second-Period Diatomic Molecules

Just as we treated the bonding in H_2 by using molecular orbital theory, we can also consider the molecular orbital description of other diatomic molecules. In this section, we shall restrict our discussion to *homonuclear* diatomic molecules (those composed of two identical atoms) of elements in the second period. As we shall see, the procedure for determining the distribution of electrons in these molecules closely follows the one we used for H_2.

Second-period atoms have more than one atomic orbital. We shall therefore consider some rules that will simplify the construction of molecular orbitals from the atomic orbitals. Further, we shall look at some rules that govern the way in which we place electrons in molecular orbitals:

1. The number of molecular orbitals formed equals the number of atomic orbitals combined.
2. Atomic orbitals combine most effectively with other atomic orbitals of similar energy.
3. The effectiveness with which two atomic orbitals combine is proportional to their overlap with one another; that is, as the overlap increases, the bonding orbital is lowered in energy, and the antibonding orbital is raised in energy.
4. Each molecular orbital can accommodate at most two electrons, with their spins paired (Pauli exclusion principle).
5. When molecular orbitals have the same energy, one electron enters each orbital (with parallel spins) before spin pairing occurs (Hund's rule).

Molecular Orbitals for Li_2 and Be_2

Teaching Note: *Star Trek* fans will be disappointed to know that dilithium, Li_2, isn't a solid and exists only at very high temperatures!

Lithium, the first element of the second period, has a $1s^2 2s^1$ electron configuration. When lithium metal is heated above its boiling point ($1347\,°C$), Li_2 molecules are found in the vapor phase. The Lewis structure for Li_2 indicates a Li—Li single bond. We shall now address the description of the bonding in Li_2 in terms of molecular orbitals.

Because the $1s$ and $2s$ orbitals of Li are so different in energy, we may assume that the $1s$ orbital on one Li atom interacts only with the $1s$ orbital on the other atom (rule 2.). Likewise, the $2s$ orbitals interact only with each other. The resulting energy-level diagram is shown in Figure 9.32. The $1s$ orbitals combine to form σ_{1s} and σ_{1s}^* bonding and antibonding orbitals, as they did for H_2. The $2s$ orbitals interact with one another in exactly the same way, producing bonding (σ_{2s}) and antibonding (σ_{2s}^*) molecular orbitals. Because the $2s$ orbitals of Li extend farther from the nucleus than do the $1s$, the $2s$ orbitals overlap more effectively. As a result, the energy separation between the σ_{2s} and σ_{2s}^* orbitals is greater than that for the $1s$-based molecular orbitals. Note that, despite being an antibonding orbital, the σ_{1s}^* molecular orbital is lower in energy than the σ_{2s} bonding orbital. The $1s$ orbitals of Li are so much lower in energy that their antibonding orbital is still well below the $2s$-based bonding orbital.

Each Li atom has three electrons, so six electrons must be placed in the molecular orbitals of Li_2. As shown in Figure 9.32, these occupy the σ_{1s}, σ_{1s}^*, and σ_{2s} molecular orbitals, each with two electrons. There are four electrons in bonding orbitals and two in antibonding orbitals, so the bond order equals

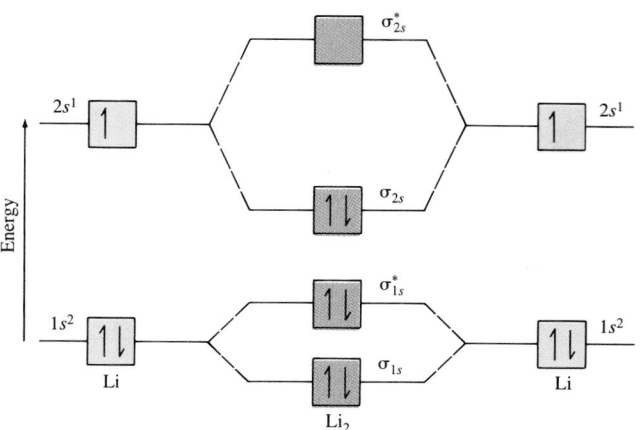

FIGURE 9.32 Energy-level diagram for the Li_2 molecule.

$\frac{1}{2}(4-2)=1$. The molecule has a single bond, in accord with its Lewis structure.

Because both the σ_{1s} and σ_{1s}^* molecular orbitals of Li_2 are completely filled, the $1s$ orbitals contribute almost nothing to the bonding. The single bond in Li_2 is due essentially to the interaction of the valence $2s$ orbitals on the Li atoms. This example illustrates the general rule that *filled atomic subshells usually do not contribute significantly to bonding in molecule formation.* The rule is equivalent to our use of only the valence electrons when drawing Lewis structures. Thus, we need not consider further the $1s$ orbitals while discussing the other second-period diatomic molecules.

The molecular orbital description of Be_2 follows readily from the energy-level diagram for Li_2. Each Be atom has four electrons ($1s^2 2s^2$), so we must place eight electrons in molecular orbitals. Thus, we completely fill the σ_{1s}, σ_{1s}^*, σ_{2s}, and σ_{2s}^* molecular orbitals. We have an equal number of bonding and antibonding electrons, so the bond order equals 0. Thus, Be_2 does not exist.

Point of Emphasis: It is common to include only valence-shell orbitals in energy-level diagrams.

Molecular Orbitals from $2p$ Atomic Orbitals

Before we can consider the next molecule, B_2, we must look at the molecular orbitals that result from combining $2p$ atomic orbitals. The interaction between p orbitals is shown in Figure 9.33, where we have arbitrarily chosen the internuclear axis to be the z axis. The $2p_z$ orbitals face each other in a "head-to-head" fashion. Just as we did for the s orbitals, we can combine the $2p_z$ orbitals in two ways. One combination concentrates electron density between the nuclei and is therefore a bonding molecular orbital. The other combination excludes electron density from the bonding region; it is an antibonding molecular orbital. In each of these molecular orbitals, the electron density lies along the line through the nuclei. Hence, they are σ molecular orbitals: σ_{2p} and σ_{2p}^*.

The other $2p$ orbitals overlap in a sideways fashion and thus concentrate electron density on opposite sides of the line through the nuclei. Molecular orbitals of this type are called **pi (π) molecular orbitals.** We get one π bonding molecular orbital by combining the $2p_x$ atomic orbitals and another one from the $2p_y$ atomic orbitals. These two π_{2p} molecular orbitals have the same energy; they are degenerate. Likewise, we get two degenerate π_{2p}^* antibonding molecular orbitals.

FIGURE 9.33 Contour representations of the molecular orbitals formed by the $2p$ orbitals on two atoms. Each time we combine two atomic orbitals, we obtain two molecular orbitals, one bonding and one antibonding. In (*a*) the *p* orbitals overlap "head-to-head" to form a σ bond. In (*b*) and (*c*) they overlap "sideways" to form π bonds.

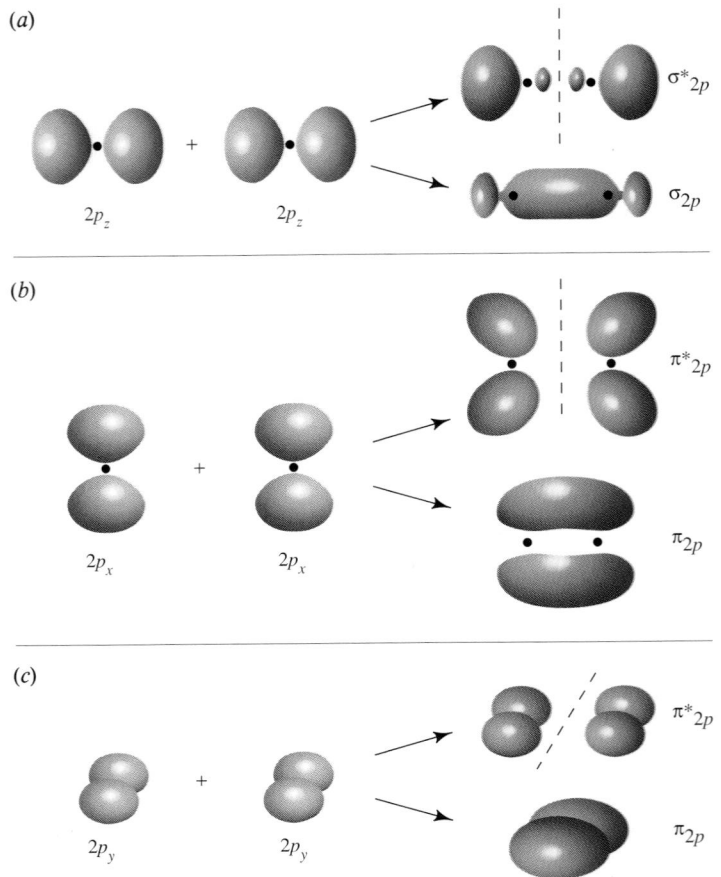

Figure 9.33

The $2p_z$ orbitals on two atoms point directly at one another. Hence, the overlap of two $2p_z$ orbitals is greater than that for two $2p_x$ or $2p_y$ orbitals. From rule 3, we therefore expect the σ_{2p} molecular orbital to be lower in energy (more stable) than the π_{2p} molecular orbitals. Similarly, the σ_{2p}^* molecular orbital should be higher in energy (less stable) than the π_{2p}^* molecular orbitals. This would indeed be the case were it not for the influence of the $2s$ atomic orbitals, as we shall see shortly.

Electron Configurations for B₂ Through F₂

The elements boron through fluorine all have valence $2s$ and $2p$ electrons. We can use the energy-level diagram in Figure 9.34 to discuss all the homonuclear diatomic molecules of these elements. This diagram is as we would expect, with one exception: We see that the σ_{2p} molecular orbital is at a higher energy than the π_{2p} molecular orbitals, contrary to what we would expect from rule 3. This reversal in ordering is the result of an unfavorable interaction between the σ_{2p} molecular orbital and the σ_{2s} molecular orbital. Both of these orbitals try to concentrate electron density between the nuclei on the internuclear axis and, because they are not very different in energy, they can interact. The σ_{2p} molecu-

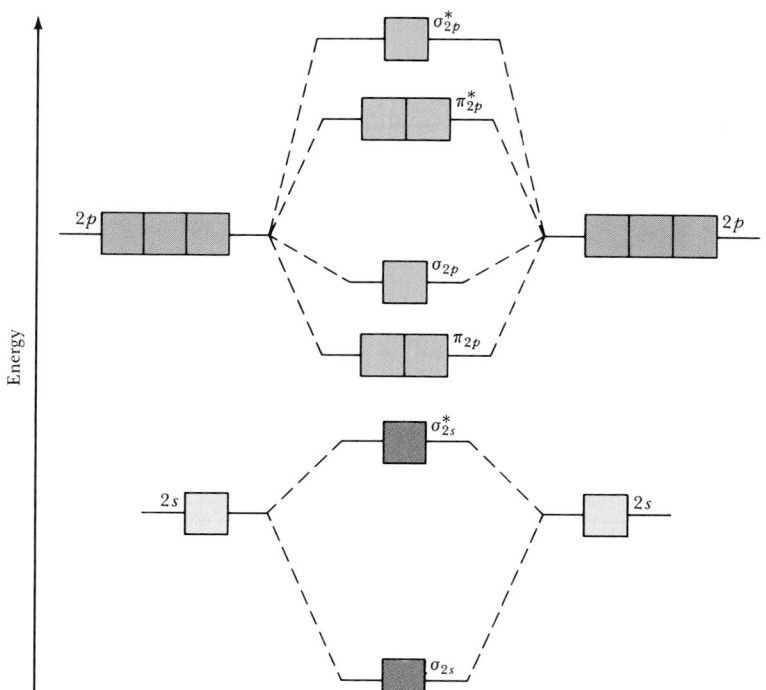

Figure 9.34

lar orbital is literally pushed upward in energy to the point where it is above the π_{2p} orbitals, and the σ_{2s} molecular orbital is pushed down in energy.†

Given the energy ordering of the molecular orbitals shown in Figure 9.34, it is a simple matter to determine the electron configurations for the second-period diatomic molecules. For example, a boron atom has three valence electrons (remember, we are ignoring the inner-shell $1s$ electrons). Thus, for B_2 we must place six electrons in molecular orbitals. Four of these fully occupy the σ_{2s} and σ_{2s}^* molecular orbitals, leading to no net bonding. The last two electrons are put in the π_{2p} bonding molecular orbitals; one electron is put in each π_{2p} orbital with the same spin (rule 5). Therefore, B_2 has a bond order of 1. Each time we move to the right in the second period, two more electrons must be placed in the diagram. For example, on moving to C_2, we have two more electrons than in B_2, and these electrons also are placed in the π_{2p} molecular orbitals, completely filling them. The electron configurations and bond orders for the diatomic molecules B_2 through F_2 are given in Table 9.6.

Electron Configurations and Molecular Properties

It is interesting to compare the electronic structures of these diatomic molecules with their observable properties. The behavior of a substance in a magnetic field provides an important insight into the arrangements of its electrons. Molecules

---

† The interaction between the σ_{2p} and σ_{2s} molecular orbitals decreases as we move from left to right in the second period. As a result, the σ_{2p} orbital is higher in energy than the π_{2p} orbitals for B_2, C_2, and N_2. For O_2, F_2, and Ne_2, the σ_{2p} orbital is lower in energy than the π_{2p} orbitals.

TABLE 9.6 △ Molecular Orbital Electron Configurations and Some Experimental Data for Several Second-Row Diatomic Molecules

Molecular orbital	B₂	C₂	N₂	O₂	F₂
σ*2p					
π*2p				↑ ↑	↑↓ ↑↓
σ2p			↑↓	↑↓	↑↓
π2p	↑ ↑	↑↓ ↑↓	↑↓ ↑↓	↑↓ ↑↓	↑↓ ↑↓
σ*2s	↑↓	↑↓	↑↓	↑↓	↑↓
σ2s	↑↓	↑↓	↑↓	↑↓	↑↓
Bond order	1	2	3	2	1
Bond energy (kJ/mol)	290	620	941	495	155
Bond length (Å)	1.59	1.31	1.10	1.21	1.43
Magnetic behavior	Paramagnetic	Diamagnetic	Diamagnetic	Paramagnetic	Diamagnetic

Table 9.6

with one or more unpaired electrons are attracted into a magnetic field. The more unpaired electrons in a species, the stronger the force of attraction. This type of magnetic behavior is called **paramagnetism.**

Substances with no unpaired electrons are weakly repelled from a magnetic field. This property is called **diamagnetism.** Diamagnetism is a much weaker effect than paramagnetism. A straightforward method for measuring the magnetic properties of a substance, illustrated in Figure 9.35, involves weighing the substance in the presence and absence of a magnetic field. If the substance is paramagnetic, it will appear to weigh more in the magnetic field; if it is diamagnetic, it will appear to weigh less. The magnetic behaviors observed for the diatomic molecules of the second-period elements agree with the electron configurations shown in Table 9.6.

The electron configurations can also be related to the bond distances and bond-dissociation energies of the molecules. As bond orders increase, bond

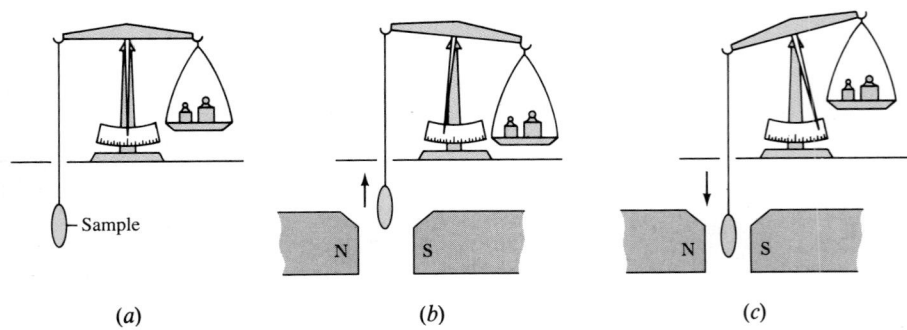

FIGURE 9.35   Experiment for determining the magnetic properties of a sample. (*a*) The sample is first weighed in the absence of a magnetic field. (*b*) When a field is applied, a diamagnetic sample tends to move out of the field and thus appears to have a lower mass. (*c*) A paramagnetic sample is drawn into the field and thus appears to gain mass. Paramagnetism is a much stronger effect than is diamagnetism.

Sample

(*a*)   (*b*)   (*c*)

CHEMISTRY AT WORK

Organic Dyes

The chemistry of color has fascinated people since ancient times. The brilliant colors around you—those of your clothes, the photographs in this book, the foods you eat—are due to the selective absorption of light by chemicals. Light excites electrons in molecules. In a molecular orbital picture, we can envision light exciting an electron from a filled molecular orbital to an empty one at higher energy. Because the molecular orbitals have definite energies, only light of the proper wavelengths can excite electrons. The situation is analogous to the atomic line spectra. ∞ (Sec. 6.3) If the appropriate wavelength for exciting electrons is in the visible portion of the electromagnetic spectrum, the substance will appear colored: Certain wavelengths of white light are absorbed, others are not. For example, a red traffic light appears red because only red light is transmitted through the lens. The other wavelengths of visible light are absorbed by it.

In using molecular orbital theory to discuss the absorptions of light by molecules, it is useful to focus on two molecular orbitals in particular. The *highest occupied molecular orbital* (HOMO) is the molecular orbital of highest energy that has electrons in it. The *lowest unoccupied molecular orbital* (LUMO) is the molecular orbital of lowest energy that does not have electrons in it. In N_2, for example, the HOMO is the π_{2p} molecular orbital and the LUMO is the π_{2p}^* molecular orbital (Table 9.6). The energy difference between the HOMO and the LUMO—known as the HOMO-LUMO gap—is related to the minimum energy needed to excite an electron in the molecule. Colorless or white substances usually have such a large HOMO-LUMO gap that visible light is not energetic enough to excite an electron to the higher level. For example, the minimum energy needed to excite an electron in N_2 corresponds to light with a wavelength of less than 200 nm, which is far into the ultraviolet part of the spectrum (Figure 6.3). As a result, N_2 cannot absorb any visible light and is therefore colorless.

Many of the rich colors with which we are familiar are due to *organic dyes,* organic molecules that strongly absorb selected wavelengths of visible light. The first synthetic dye, called mauveine or aniline purple, was discovered by accident in 1856 as a derivative of coal tar (Figure 9.36). Its discoverer, William Perkin, was 18 years old at the time; he immediately quit school to commercialize his discovery, thus spawning the coal-tar dye industry. The design of new dyes that are "tuned" to absorb very specific wavelengths of light is an important part of today's chemical industry.

Organic dyes contain extensively delocalized π electrons. The molecules contain atoms that are predominantly sp^2 hybridized, like the carbon atoms in

FIGURE 9.36 Perkin's original sample of mauveine, the first synthetic organic dye ever made. The yarn in the background has been colored by mauveine. Also shown is an old sample of alizarin, another organic dye. (Science Museum, London. Photo © Michael Halford)

benzene (Figure 9.28). This leaves one unhybridized p orbital to form π bonds with neighboring atoms. The p orbitals are arranged so that electrons can be delocalized throughout the entire molecule; we say that the π bonds are *conjugated.* The HOMO-LUMO gap in such molecules gets smaller as the number of conjugated double bonds increases. For example, consider butadiene, C_4H_6, a molecule that has alternating carbon-carbon double and single bonds:

The representation on the right is the shorthand notation that chemists use for organic molecules. There are implicitly carbon atoms at the ends of the straight segments, and there are implicitly enough hydrogen atoms to make a total of four bonds at each carbon. Butadiene is planar, so the unhybridized p orbitals on the carbons are pointing in the same direction. The π electrons are delocalized among the four carbon atoms; the double bonds are conjugated.

Because butadiene has only two conjugated double bonds, it still has a fairly large HOMO-LUMO gap. Butadiene absorbs light at 217 nm, still well into the ultraviolet part of the spectrum. It is therefore colorless. If we keep adding new conjugated double bonds, however, the HOMO-LUMO gap keeps shrinking until visible light is absorbed. For example, the molecule shown below is β-carotene, the substance chiefly responsible for the bright orange color of carrots.

Because β-carotene contains 11 conjugated double bonds, its π electrons are very extensively delocalized. It absorbs light of wavelength 500 nm, in the middle of the visible part of the spectrum. The human body converts β-carotene into vitamin A, which in turn is converted into retinal, a component of *rhodopsin,* found in the retinas of your eyes. (See the Chemistry and Life box in Section 9.5.) The absorption of visible light by rhodopsin is a major reason why "visible" light is indeed visible. There thus seems to be a good basis for the maxim that eating carrots is good for your eyesight.

distances decrease and bond-dissociation energies increase. Notice the short bond distance and high bond-dissociation energy of N_2, whose bond order is 3. The N_2 molecule does not react readily with other substances to form nitrogen compounds. The high bond order of the molecule helps explain its exceptional stability. We should also note that molecules with the same bond orders do not have the same bond distances and bond-dissociation energies. Bond order is only one factor influencing these properties. Other factors, including the nuclear charges and the extent of orbital overlap, also contribute.

The bonding in the dioxygen molecule, O_2, is especially interesting. The Lewis structure of this molecule shows a double bond and complete pairing of electrons:

$$\ddot{O}=\ddot{O}$$

The short O—O bond distance (1.21 Å) and the relatively high bond-dissociation energy (495 kJ/mol) of the molecule are in agreement with the presence of a double bond. However, the molecule is found to contain two unpaired electrons. The paramagnetism of O_2 is demonstrated in Figure 9.37. Although the Lewis structure fails to account for the paramagnetism of O_2, molecular orbital theory correctly predicts that there are two unpaired electrons in the π_{2p}^{*} orbital of the molecule (Table 9.6). The molecular orbital description also correctly indicates a bond order of 2.

Teaching Note: The explanation of the origin of the two unpaired electrons in O_2 is one of the factors that has made molecular orbital theory so popular.

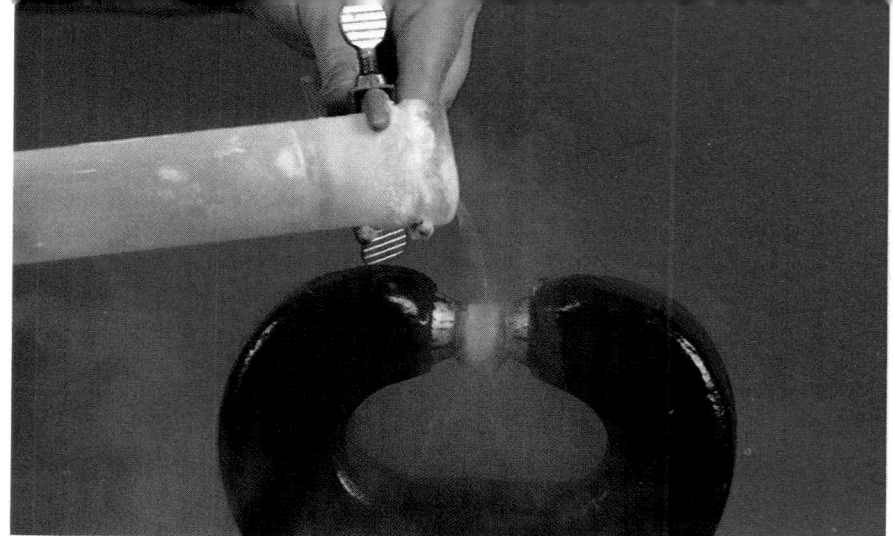

FIGURE 9.37 Liquid O_2 being poured between the poles of a magnet. Because the O_2 is paramagnetic, it is attracted into the magnetic field and forms a bridge between the magnetic poles. (Donald Clegg and Roxy Wilson)

SAMPLE EXERCISE 9.8

Predict the following properties of O_2^+: **(a)** number of unpaired electrons; **(b)** bond order; **(c)** bond-dissociation energy and bond length.

SOLUTION **(a)** The O_2^+ ion has one electron less than O_2. The electron removed from O_2 to form O_2^+ is one of the two unpaired π^* electrons (see Table 9.6). Therefore, O_2^+ should have just one unpaired electron left.

(b) The molecule has eight bonding electrons (the same number as O_2) and three antibonding ones (one less than O_2). Thus, its bond order is

$$\text{Bond order} = \tfrac{1}{2}(8 - 3) = 2\tfrac{1}{2}$$

(c) The bond order of O_2^+ is between that for O_2 (bond order 2) and N_2 (bond order 3). Thus, the bond-dissociation energy and bond length should be about midway between those for O_2 and N_2, approximately 720 kJ/mol and 1.15 Å, respectively. The observed bond-dissociation energy and bond length of the ion are 625 kJ/mol and 1.123 Å, respectively.

PRACTICE EXERCISE

Predict the magnetic properties and bond order of **(a)** the peroxide ion, O_2^{2-}; **(b)** the acetylide ion, C_2^{2-} *Answers:* **(a)** diamagnetic, 1; **(b)** diamagnetic, 3

For Review

Summary

In this chapter, we've applied the basic principles of chemical bonding to several important areas of chemical structure and behavior. The three-dimensional structures of molecules are determined by the distances between bonded atoms and by the directions of chemical bonds with respect to one another around a particular atom. The valence-shell electron-pair repulsion (VSEPR) model explains these relative directions in terms of the repulsions that exist between electron pairs. According to this model, electron pairs around an atom orient themselves so as to minimize electrostatic repulsions; that is, they remain as far apart as possible. By recognizing that unshared electron pairs take up more space (exert greater repulsive forces) than shared electron pairs, we can account for the departures of bond angles from idealized values and explain many other aspects of molecular structure.

The shape of a molecule and the bond polarities determine whether the molecule will be polar. The degree of polarity of a molecule is measured by its dipole moment.

The Lewis model for covalent bonding introduced in Chapter 8 can be extended to account for the geometric properties of molecules. In valence bond theory, we imagine that the atoms in a molecule are bonded to one another by electron pairs that occupy pairs of overlapping atomic orbitals. The extent to which the atomic orbitals share the same region of space, called overlap, is important in determining the amount of stability that results from bond formation. The bonds directed along the internuclear axes are called σ bonds.

It is possible to formulate hybrid orbitals on an atom that are directed toward each of the surrounding atoms. These orbitals are made up of mixtures of the familiar s, p, and d atomic orbitals. Depending on the number of valence-shell electron pairs around an atom, a particular set of hybrid orbitals can be formulated that corresponds to the electron-pair geometry around the atom. For example, sp^3 hybrid orbitals are directed toward the corners of a tetrahedron.

In addition to the σ bonds, which determine the geometry of the bonding around a particular atom, there may be also π bonds constructed from remaining, unhybridized atomic orbitals. Thus, a double bond, consisting of a σ and a π bond, or a triple bond, consisting of a σ and two π bonds, may be formed. In some molecules the π bonds may extend, or be delocalized, over several atoms. Delocalization of the π electrons in a cyclic structure, such as in benzene, leads to a special stability.

The coming together of atoms to form molecules may be viewed also as the coming together of atomic orbitals to form molecular orbitals. Atomic orbitals may combine with one another in various ways. The rules for combining atomic orbitals on atoms to form molecular orbitals allow us to account very well for the observed properties of the diatomic molecules formed by the first several elements of the periodic table. The molecular orbital model is particularly impressive in explaining why the O_2 molecule contains two unpaired electrons.

Key Terms

bond angle (Sec. 9.1)
valence-shell electron-pair repulsion (VSEPR) model (Sec. 9.1)
bonding pair (Sec. 9.1)
nonbonding pair (Sec. 9.1)
electron-pair geometry (Sec. 9.1)
molecular geometry (Sec. 9.1)
polar (Sec. 9.2)
dipoles (Sec. 9.2)
dipole moment (Sec. 9.2)
valence bond theory (Sec. 9.3)
overlap (Sec. 9.3)
hybrid orbital (Sec. 9.4)
hybridization (Sec. 9.4)

sigma (σ) bond (Sec. 9.5)
pi (π) bond (Sec. 9.5)
delocalized electrons (Sec. 9.5)
molecular orbital theory (Sec. 9.6)
molecular orbital (Sec. 9.6)
bonding molecular orbital (Sec. 9.6)
antibonding molecular orbital (Sec. 9.6)
sigma (σ) molecular orbital (Sec. 9.6)
energy-level diagram (Sec. 9.6)
molecular orbital diagram (Sec. 9.6)
bond order (Sec. 9.6)
pi (π) molecular orbital (Sec. 9.7)
paramagnetism (Sec. 9.7)
diamagnetism (Sec. 9.7)

Exercises

Molecular Geometry; the VSEPR Model

9.1. Describe the characteristic electron-pair geometry of each of the following numbers of electron pairs about a central atom: **(a)** 3; **(b)** 4; **(c)** 5; **(d)** 6.

9.2. Indicate the number of electron pairs about a central atom, given the following angles between them: **(a)** 120°; **(b)** 180°; **(c)** 109°; **(d)** 90°.

9.3. What is the difference between the electron-pair geometry and the molecular geometry of a molecule? Use the water molecule as an example in your discussion.

9.4. What is the molecular geometry of a molecule that has **(a)** two bonding pairs and one nonbonding pair of electrons; **(b)** three bonding pairs and one nonbonding pair of electrons; **(c)** two bonding pairs and two nonbonding pairs of electrons; **(d)** three bonding pairs and two nonbonding pairs of electrons.

9.5. Give the electron-pair geometry and the molecular geometry for: **(a)** Cl_2O; **(b)** N_2O; **(c)** SO_3; **(d)** SO_3^{2-}; **(e)** PF_4^+; **(f)** PF_4^-.

9.6. Give the electron-pair geometry and the molecular geometry for: **(a)** SCl_2; **(b)** Cl_2SO; **(c)** ICl_2^-; **(d)** PCl_3; **(e)** ICl_3; **(f)** CO_3^{2-}.

9.7. The molecules NF_3, BF_3, and ClF_3 all have molecular formulas of the type XF_3, but the molecules have different molecular geometries. Predict the shape of each molecule and explain the origin of the differing shapes.

9.8. The molecules SiF_4, SF_4, and XeF_4 all have molecular formulas of the type XF_4, but the molecules have different molecular geometries. Predict the shape of each molecule and explain the origin of the differing shapes.

9.9. The three species NO_2^+, NO_2, and NO_2^- all have a central N atom. The ONO bond angles in the three species

are 180°, 134°, and 115°, respectively. Explain this variation in bond angles.

9.10. The three species NH_2^-, NH_3, and NH_4^+ have H—N—H bond angles of 105°, 107°, and 109°, respectively. Explain this variation in bond angles.

9.11. Give approximate values for the indicated bond angles in the following molecules:

9.12. Give the approximate values for the indicated bond angles in the following molecules:

Molecular Polarity

9.13. Indicate whether the following molecules are polar or nonpolar: **(a)** BrCl; **(b)** SO_2; **(c)** SO_3; **(d)** PH_3; **(e)** $SiCl_4$; **(f)** SF_4.

9.14. Predict whether the following molecules possess dipole moments: **(a)** HCN; **(b)** CS_2; **(c)** BF_3; **(d)** HCF_3; **(e)** XeF_4; **(f)** C_2H_4.

9.15. Despite the larger electronegativity difference between the bonded atoms, $BeCl_2(g)$ has no dipole moment, whereas $SCl_2(g)$ does possess one. Account for this difference in polarity.

9.16. The PF_3 molecule has a dipole moment of 1.03 D, but BF_3 has a dipole moment of zero. How can you explain the difference?

9.17. Dichloroethylene, $C_2H_2Cl_2$, has the following geometries (isomers), each of which is an individual substance:

A pure sample of one of these substances is found experimentally to have a dipole moment of zero. Can we determine which of the three substances was measured?

9.18. Dichlorobenzene, $C_6H_4Cl_2$, exists in three different forms (isomers), called *ortho, meta,* and *para:*

ortho   meta   para

Which of these would have a nonzero dipole moment? Explain.

Orbital Overlap; Hybrid Orbitals

9.21. **(a)** What is meant by the term *orbital overlap?* **(b)** What is the significance of overlapping orbitals in valence bond theory? **(c)** What two fundamental concepts are incorporated in valence bond theory?

9.22. Draw sketches illustrating the overlap between the following orbitals on two atoms: **(a)** the $2s$ orbital on each; **(b)** the $2p_z$ orbital on each (assume that the atoms are on the z axis); **(c)** the $2s$ orbital on one and the $2p_z$ orbital on the other.

9.23. Without referring to tables or figures in the chapter, indicate the designation for the hybrid orbitals formed from each of the following combinations of atomic orbitals: **(a)** one s and two p; **(b)** one s, three p, and one d; **(c)** one s, three p, and two d. What bond angles are associated with each?

9.24. Without referring to tables or figures in the chapter, indicate the hybridization and bond angles associated with each of the following electron-pair geometries: **(a)** linear; **(b)** tetrahedral; **(c)** trigonal planar; **(d)** octahedral; **(e)** trigonal bipyramidal.

9.25. Draw the Lewis structure of ClO_3^-. What is its electron-pair geometry and molecular shape? Describe the bonding of the molecule, using hybrid orbitals.

9.26. Draw the Lewis structure of NF_3. What is its electron-pair geometry and molecular shape? Describe the bonding of the molecule using hybrid orbitals.

9.27. Indicate the hybrid orbital set used by the central atom in each of the following molecules and ions: **(a)** BI_3; **(b)** NCl_3; **(c)** $AlCl_4^-$; **(e)** PF_5; **(f)** SF_6.

9.28. For each of the following molecules and ions, predict the molecular geometry (including approximate bond angles) and indicate the hybrid orbitals on the central atom: **(a)** OF_2; **(b)** SO_3^{2-}; **(c)** PO_4^{3-}; **(d)** ICl_2^-; **(e)** XeF_4; **(f)** PF_6^-.

Multiple Bonds

9.29. What is the difference between a σ bond and a π bond? Which is generally the stronger?

9.30. How many σ and how many π bonds are generally part of **(a)** a double bond; **(b)** a triple bond?

9.31. If an atom uses an sp^2 hybrid orbital set, how many unhybridized p orbitals in the same valence shell remain on the atom? How many π bonds can the atom form?

9.32. Indicate the number of unhybridized p orbitals on a particular atom available for π bonding when the following hybrid orbital sets are used: **(a)** sp; **(b)** sp^3; **(c)** sp^3d^2.

9.33. Consider the Lewis structure for glycine, the simplest amino acid:

(a) What are the approximate bond angles about each of the two carbon atoms, and what are the hybridizations of the orbitals on each of them? **(b)** What are the hybridizations of the orbitals on the two oxygens and the nitrogen atom, and what are the approximate bond angles at the nitrogen? **(c)**

What is the total number of σ bonds in the entire molecule, and what is the total number of π bonds?

9.34. The compound whose Lewis structure is shown below is acetylsalicylic acid, better known as aspirin:

(a) What are the approximate values of the bond angles marked 1, 2, and 3? **(b)** What hybrid orbitals are used about the central atom of each of these angles? **(c)** How many σ bonds are in the molecule?

9.35. What is the difference between a localized π bond and a delocalized one?

9.36. Is the π bond in NO_2^- localized or delocalized? How do you know?

9.19, 9.20

9.19. The bond length in HBr is 1.41 Å, and its dipole moment is 0.82 D. **(a)** Calculate the electronic charge of H and Br, assuming that the charges are centered on the atoms. **(b)** What percentage of the charge of an electron does this charge represent?

9.20. The bond length in HF is 91.7 pm, and its dipole moment is 1.82 D. **(a)** Calculate the electronic charge on H and F, assuming that the charges are centered on the atoms. **(b)** What percentage of the charge of an electron does this represent?

9.37. The bonds between O atoms in O_3 are shorter than O—O single bonds but longer than O=O double bonds. Explain in terms of (a) resonance forms, and (b) delocalized bonding in the molecule.

9.38. (a) Draw the three resonance structures for the carbonate ion. (b) Predict the geometry of this ion. (c) What is the hybridization of the atomic orbitals of C in this ion? (d) Describe the delocalized π bonding in this ion.

Molecular Orbitals

9.39. How do bonding and antibonding molecular orbitals differ with respect to (a) energies; (b) the spatial distribution of electron density?

9.40. How do σ and π molecular orbitals differ with respect to the spatial distribution of electron density? Sketch the shapes of the σ_{2p} and π_{2p} molecular orbitals.

9.41. What is meant by the following terms: (a) bond order; (b) paramagnetism; (c) energy-level diagram?

9.42. How do bond order, bond length, and bond energy correlate for a series of bonds between the same two elements?

9.43. If we assume that the energy-level diagram for homonuclear diatomic molecules (Figure 9.34) can be applied to heteronuclear diatomic molecules and ions, predict the bond order and magnetic behavior of the following: (a) CO; (b) NO^-; (c) CN^-; (d) OF.

9.44. Using Figures 9.32 and 9.34 as a guide, give the molecular orbital electron configuration for each of the following cations: (a) Li_2^+; (b) B_2^+; (c) C_2^+; (d) Ne_2^{2+}. In each

case, indicate whether the addition of an electron would increase or decrease the stability of the species.

9.45. The ions O_2^-, O_2^{2-}, and O_2^+ occur in several compounds. Compare these three ions with O_2 by listing the four in order of increasing bond length.

9.46. List the members of the following series in order of increasing bond length: N_2^+, N_2, N_2^-.

9.47. Provide explanations for the following observations about molecular orbital energy-level diagrams: (a) The σ_{1s} molecular orbital in H_2 is lower in energy than the σ_{1s}^* molecular orbital. (b) The σ_{1s}^* molecular orbital in H_2 is higher in energy than the atomic H $1s$ orbitals. (c) In Li_2, the energy separation between the σ_{1s} and σ_{1s}^* molecular orbitals is less than that between the σ_{2s} and σ_{2s}^* molecular orbitals.

9.48. Explain the following observations: (a) In Li_2, the σ_{1s}^* antibonding molecular orbital is lower in energy than the σ_{2s} bonding molecular orbital. (b) In B_2, there are two degenerate π_{2p} molecular orbitals. (c) In B_2, the π_{2p}^* molecular orbitals are lower in energy than the σ_{2p}^* molecular orbital.

Additional Exercises

9.49. Predict the molecular geometry of (a) AsF_3; (b) OCN^-; (c) H_2CO; (d) I_3^-.

9.50. The H—P—H bond angle in PH_3 is $93°$; in PH_4^+ it is $109.5°$. Account for this difference.

9.51. When applying the VSEPR model, we count double and triple bonds as a single pair of electrons. Present an argument as to why this is justified.

9.52. From their Lewis structures, determine the number of σ and π bonds in each of the following molecules or ions: (a) CO_2; (b) NCS^-; (c) SO_4^{2-}; (d) $HCO(OH)$ which has an H and two O atoms attached to C.

9.53. There are two compounds of the formula $Pt(NH_3)_2Cl_2$:

$$\begin{array}{cc} NH_3 & Cl \\ | & | \\ Cl-Pt-Cl & Cl-Pt-NH_3 \\ | & | \\ NH_3 & NH_3 \end{array}$$

The compound on the right, known as *cisplatin,* is used in cancer therapy. Both compounds have a square planar geometry. Which compound has a nonzero dipole moment?

[9.54]. The water molecule, H_2O, has O—H bonds of length 0.96 Å, and the H—O—H angle is $104.5°$. The di-

pole moment of the water molecule is 1.85 D. (a) In what directions do the bond dipoles of the O—H bonds point? In what direction does the dipole moment vector of the water molecule point? (b) Calculate the magnitude of the bond dipole for the O—H bonds. (Note: You will need to use vector addition to do this.)

[9.55]. By using vector addition, prove that the dipole moment of BF_3 must be zero even though the bond dipoles are not zero.

[9.56]. The Lewis structure for allene is

$$\begin{array}{cc} H & H \\ \diagdown & \diagup \\ C=C=C \\ \diagup & \diagdown \\ H & H \end{array}$$

Make a sketch of the structure of this molecule that is analogous to Figure 9.24. In addition, answer the following two questions: (a) Is the molecule planar? (b) Does it have a nonzero dipole moment?

9.57. Consider the unstable molecule called diimine, HN=NH. (a) Draw the Lewis structure. (b) Use the VSEPR model to predict the molecular geometry. (c) Indicate the hybrid orbitals used by the nitrogen atoms. (d) Sketch the formation of σ and π bonds in the molecule from the hybrid and unhybridized orbitals. (e) It is found experimentally that the dipole moment of diimine is zero. Is this consistent with your molecular geometry? Is there a geometry for the molecule, with the same Lewis structure, that could have a nonzero dipole moment?

9.58. A compound composed of 2.1 percent H, 29.8 percent N, and 68.1 percent O has a molar mass of approximately 50 g/mol. **(a)** What is the molecular formula of the compound? **(b)** What is its Lewis structure if H is bonded to O? **(c)** What is the geometry of the molecule? **(d)** What is the hybridization of orbitals around the N atom? **(e)** How many σ and how many π bonds are there in the molecule?

9.59. Cumene hydroperoxide, for which the structure is

$$
\begin{array}{c}
O-O-H \\
| \\
CH_3-C-CH_3 \\
| \\
\bigcirc
\end{array}
$$

is an intermediate in the formation of phenol, C_6H_5OH, an important industrial chemical. Indicate the hybrid orbital set employed by all the carbon and oxygen atoms of cumene hydroperoxide.

9.60. The nitrogen-nitrogen bond lengths in N_2H_4, N_2F_2, and N_2 are 1.45, 1.25, and 1.10 Å, respectively. How can this trend be explained?

[9.61]. The azide ion, N_3^-, is a linear ion with two N—N bonds of equal length, 1.16 Å. **(a)** Draw a Lewis structure for the azide ion. **(b)** With reference to Table 8.5, is the observed N—N bond length consistent with your Lewis structure? **(c)** What hybridization scheme would you expect at each of the nitrogen atoms in N_3^-? **(d)** Show which hybridized and unhybridized orbitals are involved in the formation of σ and π bonds in N_3^-. **(e)** It is often observed that σ bonds that involve an sp hybrid orbital are shorter than those that involve only sp^2 or sp^3 hybrid orbitals. Can you propose a reason for this? Is this observation applicable to the observed bond lengths in N_3^-?

9.62. Use average bond energies (Table 8.4) to estimate ΔH for the atomization of benzene, C_6H_6:

$$C_6H_6(g) \longrightarrow 6C(g) + 6H(g)$$

Compare the value to that obtained by using ΔH_f° data given in Appendix C and Hess's law. To what do you attribute the large discrepancy in the two values?

[9.63]. The reaction of three molecules of fluorine gas with an Xe atom produces the substance xenon hexafluoride, XeF_6:

$$Xe(g) + 3F_2(g) \longrightarrow XeF_6(g)$$

(a) Draw a Lewis structure for XeF_6. **(b)** If you try to use the VSEPR model to predict the molecular geometry of XeF_6, you run into a problem. What is it? **(c)** What could you do to attempt to resolve the difficulty in part (b)? **(d)** Suggest a hybridization scheme for the Xe atom in XeF_6. **(e)** The molecule IF_7 has a *pentagonal bipyramidal* structure (five equatorial fluorine atoms at the vertices of a regular penta-

gon and two axial fluorine atoms). Based on the structure of IF_7, suggest a structure for XeF_6.

[9.64]. In ozone, O_3, the two oxygen atoms on the ends of the molecule are equivalent to one another. **(a)** What is the best choice of hybridization scheme for the atoms of ozone? **(b)** For one of the resonance forms of ozone, which of the orbitals are used to make bonds and which are used to hold nonbonding pairs of electrons? **(c)** Which of the orbitals can be used to make a delocalized π system? **(d)** How many electrons are delocalized in the π system of ozone?

9.65. Butadiene, C_4H_6, is a planar molecule that exhibits the following carbon-carbon bond lengths:

$$
\begin{array}{c}
H_2C \overset{1.34\,\text{Å}}{=\!=\!=} CH \overset{1.48\,\text{Å}}{-\!-\!-} CH \overset{1.34\,\text{Å}}{=\!=\!=} CH_2
\end{array}
$$

Compare these bond lengths to the average bond lengths listed in Table 8.5. Can you explain any differences?

9.66. Consider the following species: H_2, H_2^+, H_2^-, He_2^+, He_2. **(a)** Predict how the bond strength of these species varies. (List them in order of increasing bond strength.) **(b)** List them in order of increasing bond length.

9.67. Would either Ne_2 or Ne_2^+ be expected to exist? Explain.

9.68. The fact that B_2 is paramagnetic is consistent with the π_{2p} molecular orbitals being lower in energy than the σ_{2p} molecular orbital in Figure 9.34. Why must this be the energy ordering of these molecular orbitals for B_2?

[9.69]. The nitric oxide molecule, NO, is a *heteronuclear* diatomic molecule (one that consists of two different atoms). We shall assume that the energy-level diagram for homonuclear diatomic molecules (Figure 9.34) can be applied to NO. **(a)** In terms of molecular orbitals, write the electron configuration for the NO molecule. **(b)** Would NO be diamagnetic or paramagnetic? **(c)** In chemical reactions, NO readily loses one electron to form the NO^+ ion. Why is this consistent with the electronic structure of NO? **(d)** Predict the order of the N—O bond strengths in NO, NO^+, and NO^-. **(e)** With what neutral homonuclear diatomic molecules are the NO^+ and NO^- ions isoelectronic (same number of electrons)?

[9.70]. Consider the methyl cation, CH_3^+. **(a)** Predict the molecular geometry of CH_3^+. **(b)** Would you expect the molecular geometry of the methyl anion, CH_3^-, to be the same as or different from that of CH_3^+? **(c)** The lowest-energy bonding molecular orbital of CH_3^+ results from adding the $1s$ orbitals of the three hydrogen atoms to the $2s$ orbital of the carbon atom. Produce a sketch analogous to Figure 9.29 that shows the formation of this molecular orbital.

[9.71]. Many compounds of the transition-metal elements contain direct bonds between metal atoms. We shall assume that the z axis is defined as the metal-metal bond axis. **(a)** Which of the $3d$ orbitals (Figure 6.21) can be used to make a σ bond between metal atoms? **(b)** Sketch the σ_{3d} bonding and σ_{3d}^* antibonding molecular orbitals. **(c)** Sketch the energy-level diagram for the Sc_2 molecule, assuming that only the $3d$ orbital from part (a) is important. **(d)** What is the bond order in Sc_2?

Gases 10

Tornados are among the most awesome and terrifying natural phenomena. The birth of a tornado begins with a low pressure area, an area in which the pressure of the atmosphere is unusually low.

CONTENTS

Point of Emphasis: Gases may be monatomic, diatomic, or polyatomic.

Point of Emphasis: A vapor is the gaseous form of any substance that is usually a liquid or solid at room temperature.

In the past several chapters, we have learned about electronic structures of atoms and about how atoms combine to form molecules and ionic substances. In everyday life, however, we encounter matter not on the atomic or molecular scale but as the large collections of atoms or molecules that we recognize as solids, liquids, and gases. ⚬ (Sec. 1.1) In the next few chapters we will consider some important characteristics of these states of matter. This chapter will focus on gases; in Chapter 11 we will discuss liquids and solids.

We are surrounded by an atmosphere composed of a mixture of gases that we refer to as air. We breathe air to absorb oxygen, O_2, which supports human life. We also encounter gases in countless other situations. For example, chlorine gas, Cl_2, is used to purify drinking water. Acetylene gas, C_2H_2, is used in welding. Carbon dioxide, CO_2, and methane, CH_4, are among the gases known as *greenhouse gases*, which are implicated in global warming (Chapter 18). Although different gases may vary widely in their chemical properties, they share many physical properties. Our goal in this chapter is to gain a deeper understanding of the physical properties of gases.

10.1 Characteristics of Gases

Air consists primarily of oxygen and nitrogen. About 78 percent of the molecules in the air are N_2 molecules, and about 21 percent are O_2 molecules. Several other nonmetallic elements also exist as gases under ordinary conditions of temperature and pressure: H_2, F_2, Cl_2, and the noble gases He, Ne, Ar, Kr, and Xe. Many molecular compounds are also gases. Table 10.1 lists a few of the more common gaseous compounds. Notice that all of these gases are composed entirely of nonmetallic elements. Furthermore, all have simple molecular formulas and, therefore, low molar masses.

Substances that are liquids or solids under ordinary conditions can usually also exist in the gaseous state, where they are often referred to as **vapors.** The substance H_2O, for example, can exist as liquid water, solid ice, or water vapor. Under the right conditions, a substance can coexist in all three states of matter, or *phases,* at the same time. A thermos bottle containing a mixture of ice and water at 0°C has some water vapor in the gas phase over the liquid and solid phases.

TABLE 10.1 △ Some Common Compounds That Are Gases

Formula	Name	Characteristics
HCN	Hydrogen cyanide	Very toxic, slight odor of bitter almonds
HCl	Hydrogen chloride	Toxic, corrosive, choking odor
H_2S	Hydrogen sulfide	Very toxic, odor of rotten eggs
CO	Carbon monoxide	Toxic, colorless, odorless
CO_2	Carbon dioxide	Colorless, odorless
CH_4	Methane	Colorless, odorless, flammable
N_2O	Nitrous oxide	Colorless, sweet odor, laughing gas
NO_2	Nitrogen dioxide	Toxic, red-brown, irritating odor
NH_3	Ammonia	Colorless, pungent odor
SO_2	Sulfur dioxide	Colorless, irritating odor

Gases differ significantly from solids and liquids in several respects. For example, a gas expands spontaneously to fill its container. Consequently, the volume of a gas equals the volume of the container in which it is held. As a result, gases are highly compressible: When pressure is applied to a gas, its volume readily decreases. In contrast, solids and liquids do not expand to fill their containers, and solids and liquids are not readily compressible.

Gases form homogeneous mixtures with each other regardless of the identities or relative proportions of the component gases. For example, when water and gasoline are poured into a bottle, the water vapor and gasoline vapors above the liquids form a homogeneous gas mixture. The two liquids, in contrast, do not mix and remain as separate layers.

The characteristic properties of gases arise because the individual molecules are relatively far apart. For example, in the air we breathe, the molecules take up only about 0.1 percent of the total volume, with the rest being empty space. Thus, each molecule behaves largely as though the others weren't present. As a result, different gases behave similarly, even though they are made up of different molecules. In contrast, the individual molecules in a liquid are close together and occupy perhaps 70 percent of the total space. The attractive forces among the molecules keep the liquid together.

10.2 Pressure

Among the most readily measured properties of a gas are its temperature, volume, and pressure. It is not surprising, therefore, that many early studies of gases focused on relationships among these properties. We have already discussed volume and temperature. ∞ (Sec. 1.3) Let us now consider the concept of pressure.

In general terms, **pressure** conveys the idea of a force, a push that tends to move something else in a given direction. Pressure, P, is, in fact, the force, F, that acts on a given area, A:

$$P = \frac{F}{A} \qquad [10.1]$$

Gases exert a pressure on any surface with which they are in contact. For example, the gas in an inflated balloon exerts a pressure on the inside surface of the balloon.

Atmospheric Pressure and the Barometer

Because of gravity, our atmosphere exerts a downward force and consequently a pressure upon the earth's surface. The force F exerted by any object is the product of its mass, m, times its acceleration, a: $F = ma$. The earth's gravity exerts an acceleration of 9.8 m/s². A column of air 1 m² in cross section extending through the atmosphere has a mass of roughly 10,000 kg (Figure 10.1). The force exerted by this column is

$$F = (10{,}000 \text{ kg})(9.8 \text{ m/s}^2) = 1 \times 10^5 \text{ kg-m/s}^2 = 1 \times 10^5 \text{ N}$$

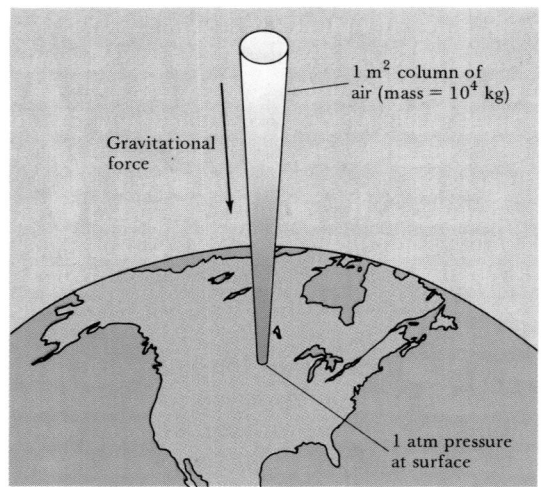

FIGURE 10.1 Illustration of the manner in which the earth's atmosphere exerts pressure at the surface of the planet. The mass of a column of atmosphere 1 m² in cross-sectional area and extending to the top of the atmosphere exerts a force of 1.01×10^5 N.

1 m² column of air (mass = 10^4 kg)

Gravitational force

1 atm pressure at surface

Figure 10.1

The SI unit for force is kg-m/s² and is called the *newton* (N): 1 N = 1 kg-m/s². The pressure exerted by the column is the force divided by its cross-sectional area, A:

$$P = \frac{F}{A} = \frac{1 \times 10^5 \text{ N}}{1 \text{ m}^2} = 1 \times 10^5 \text{ N/m}^2 = 1 \times 10^5 \text{ Pa} = 1 \times 10^2 \text{ kPa}$$

Point of Emphasis: 1 Pa≡1 N/m² 1 Joule≡1 m³·Pa

Analogy: When you are washing dishes notice that an inverted glass filled with water remains filled until the rim is lifted above the surface of the wash water.

Figure 10.2

FIGURE 10.2 Mercury barometer invented by Torricelli.

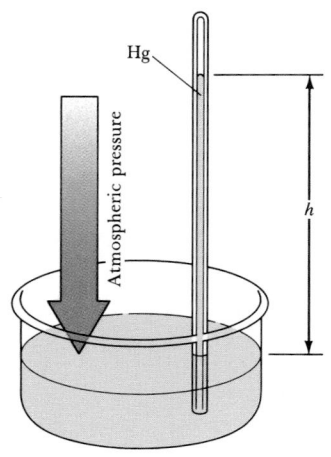

Hg

Atmospheric pressure

h

The SI unit of pressure is N/m². It is given the name **pascal** (Pa) after Blaise Pascal (1623–1662), a French mathematician and scientist: 1 Pa = 1 N/m². We see that the atmospheric pressure at sea level is about 100 kPa. Of course, the actual atmospheric pressure at any location depends on weather conditions as well as on altitude.

Atmospheric pressure can be measured by use of a mercury *barometer* (Figure 10.2). Such a barometer can be made from a glass tube more than 760 mm long which is closed at one end. The tube is completely filled with mercury and inverted into a dish that contains additional mercury. Care must be taken that no air gets into the tube. Some of the mercury flows out when the tube is inverted, but a column of mercury remains in the tube. The space in the tube above the mercury is nearly a vacuum; only a negligible amount of mercury vapor occupies it.

The mercury surface in the dish experiences the full force, or weight, of the Earth's atmosphere. Because there is no air (and therefore no atmospheric pressure) above the mercury in the tube, the mercury is pushed up the tube until the pressure due to the mass of the mercury column balances the atmospheric pressure. Thus, the height of the mercury column changes as the atmospheric pressure changes.

Standard atmospheric pressure, which corresponds to the typical pressure at sea level, is the pressure sufficient to support a column of mercury 760 mm in height. In SI units, this pressure equals 1.01325×10^5 Pa. It is used to define some common non-SI units used to express gas pressures: the **atmosphere** (atm) and the *millimeter of mercury* (mm Hg). The latter unit is also called the **torr,**

after the Italian scientist Evangelista Torricelli (1608 – 1647), who invented the barometer:

$$1 \text{ atm} = 760 \text{ mm Hg} = 760 \text{ torr} = 1.01325 \times 10^5 \text{ Pa} = 101.325 \text{ kPa}$$

Note that the units mm Hg and torr are the same: 1 torr = 1 mm Hg.

In this text, we will usually express gas pressure in units of atm or torr. You should make certain that you are comfortable converting gas pressures from one set of units to another.

SAMPLE EXERCISE 10.1

(a) Convert 0.357 atm to torr. (b) Convert 6.6×10^{-2} torr to atm. (c) Convert 147.2 kPa to torr.

SOLUTION   In solving problems of this type, we will use dimensional analysis. The relationships given above for the various units of pressure are used to generate the conversion factors we need. (a) We convert atmospheres to torr by using the conversion factor derived from 760 torr = 1 atm:

$$(0.357 \text{ atm}) \left(\frac{760 \text{ torr}}{1 \text{ atm}} \right) = 271 \text{ torr}$$

Note that the units cancel in the required manner.
(b) We use the same relationship that we did in part (a). Dimensional analysis tells us that we must use the conversion factor in the following way:

$$(6.6 \times 10^{-2} \text{ torr}) \left(\frac{1 \text{ atm}}{760 \text{ torr}} \right) = 8.7 \times 10^{-5} \text{ atm}$$

(c) The relationship 760 torr = 101.325 kPa allows us to derive an appropriate conversion factor for this problem:

$$(147.2 \text{ kPa}) \left(\frac{760 \text{ torr}}{101.325 \text{ kPa}} \right) = 1104 \text{ torr}$$

PRACTICE EXERCISE

In countries that use the metric system — for example, Canada — atmospheric pressure in weather reports is given in units of kPa. Convert a pressure of 745 torr to kPa.   *Answer:* 99.3 kPa

Pressures of Enclosed Gases and Manometers

We use various devices to measure the pressures of enclosed gases. The simple tire gauges used to measure the pressure of air in automobile tires give the pressure over and above atmospheric pressure. In laboratories, we sometimes use a simple device called a *manometer,* whose principle of operation is similar to that of a barometer. Figure 10.3(a) shows a closed-tube manometer, a device normally used to measure pressures below atmospheric pressure. The pressure is just the difference in the heights of the mercury levels in the two arms.

An open-tube manometer, like that pictured in Figure 10.3(b) and (c), is often employed to measure gas pressures that are near atmospheric pressure. The difference in the heights of the mercury levels in the two arms of the manometer relates the gas pressure to atmospheric pressure. If the pressure of the enclosed gas is the same as atmospheric pressure, the levels in the two arms

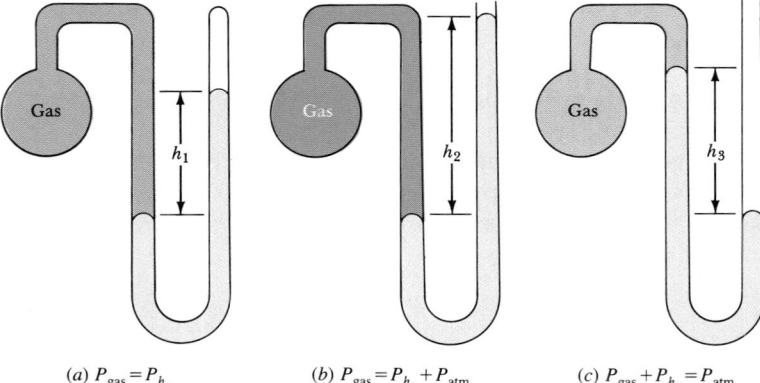

FIGURE 10.3 Closed-end manometer (*a*) and open-end manometers (*b* and *c*). In (*b*) gas pressure exceeds atmospheric pressure; in (*c*) gas pressure is less than atmospheric pressure.

Figure 10.3

(a) $P_{gas} = P_{h_1}$ (b) $P_{gas} = P_{h_2} + P_{atm}$ (c) $P_{gas} + P_{h_3} = P_{atm}$

are equal. If the pressure of the enclosed gas is greater than atmospheric pressure, mercury is forced higher in the arm exposed to the atmosphere, as in Figure 10.3(*b*). Conversely, if atmospheric pressure exceeds the gas pressure, the mercury is higher in the arm exposed to the gas, as in Figure 10.3(*c*).

Although mercury is the liquid most often used in a manometer, other liquids can be employed. For a given pressure difference, the difference in heights of the liquid levels in the two arms of the manometer is inversely proportional to the density of the liquid. That is, the greater the density of the liquid, the smaller the difference in column heights. The high density of mercury (13.6 g/mL) allows us to build smaller manometers than we could with less dense liquids.

SAMPLE EXERCISE 10.2

On a certain day, the barometer in a laboratory indicates that the atmospheric pressure is 764.7 torr. A sample of gas is placed in a vessel attached to an open-end mercury manometer. A meter stick is used to measure the height of the mercury above the bottom of the manometer. The level of mercury in the open-end arm of the manometer has a measured height of 136.4 mm, and that in the arm that is in contact with the gas has a height of 103.8 mm. What is the pressure of the gas in atmospheres?

SOLUTION Because the level of mercury in the open arm is higher than that in the enclosed arm, the pressure of the gas is greater than atmospheric pressure, as in Figure 10.3(*b*). The difference in height between the two arms gives the amount by which the pressure of the gas exceeds atmospheric pressure. Because a mercury manometer is used, the height difference directly measures the pressure difference in mm Hg or torr. Thus, the pressure of the gas is equal to the atmospheric pressure plus the difference in height between the two arms of the manometer:

$$P_{gas} = P_{atm} + \text{(difference in height of arms)}$$
$$= 764.7 \text{ torr} + (136.4 \text{ torr} - 103.8 \text{ torr})$$
$$= 797.3 \text{ torr}$$

Finally, we convert the pressure of the gas to atmospheres:

$$P_{gas} = (797.3 \text{ torr}) \left(\frac{1 \text{ atm}}{760 \text{ torr}} \right) = 1.049 \text{ atm}$$

Note that in order to use an open-end manometer, we must know the value of the atmospheric pressure.

PRACTICE EXERCISE

A vessel connected to an open-end mercury manometer is filled with gas to a pressure of 0.835 atm. The atmospheric pressure is 755 torr. **(a)** In which arm of the manometer will the level of mercury be higher? **(b)** What is the height difference between the two arms of the manometer?   *Answers:* **(a)** The level in the arm attached to the gas is higher. **(b)** 120 mm

10.3 The Gas Laws

Experiments with a large number of gases reveal that four variables are usually sufficient to define the state, or condition, of a gas: temperature, T, pressure, P, volume, V, and the quantity of matter, which is usually expressed as the number of moles, n. The equations that express the relationships among P, T, V, and n are known as the *gas laws.*

Learning Goal 3: Describe how a gas responds to changes in pressure, volume, temperature, and quantity of gas.

The Pressure–Volume Relationship: Boyle's Law

If the pressure on a balloon is decreased, the balloon expands. That is why weather balloons expand as they rise through the atmosphere (Figure 10.4). Conversely, when a volume of gas is compressed, the pressure of the gas increases. The first person to investigate the relationship between the pressure of a gas and its volume was the British chemist Robert Boyle (1627–1691).

Bassam Z. Shakhashiri, "Boyle's Law," *Chemical Demonstrations: A Handbook for Teachers of Chemistry, Volume 2* (Madison: The University of Wisconsin Press, 1985), pp. 14–19.

FIGURE 10.4   The volume of gas in this weather balloon will increase as it ascends into the high atmosphere, where the atmospheric pressure is lower than on the earth's surface. (NASA/Science Course/Photo Researchers)

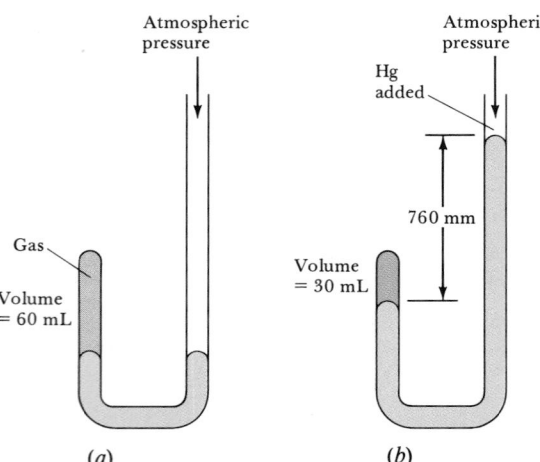

FIGURE 10.5 An illustration of Boyle's experiment. In (a) the volume of the gas trapped in the J-tube is 60 mL when the gas pressure is 760 torr. When additional mercury is added, as shown in (b), the trapped gas is compressed. The volume is 30 mL when its total pressure is 1520 torr, corresponding to atmospheric pressure plus the pressure exerted by the 760-mm column of mercury.

Teaching Note: The equation PV = constant describes a hyperbola.

FIGURE 10.6 Graphs based on Boyle's law: (a) pressure versus volume; (b) volume versus $1/P$.

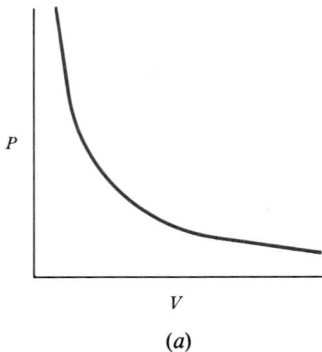

(a)

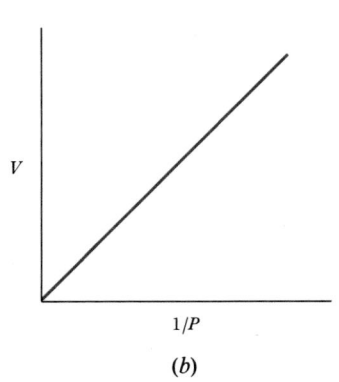

(b)

To perform his gas experiments, Boyle used a J-shaped tube like that shown in Figure 10.5. A quantity of gas is trapped in the tube behind a column of mercury. Boyle changed the pressure on the gas by adding mercury to the tube. He found that the volume of the gas decreased as the pressure increased. For example, doubling the pressure caused the gas volume to decrease to one-half its original value.

Boyle's law, which summarizes these observations, states that *the volume of a fixed quantity of gas maintained at constant temperature is inversely proportional to the pressure.* When two measurements are inversely proportional, one gets smaller as the other gets larger. Boyle's law can be expressed in mathematical terms:

$$V = \text{constant} \times \frac{1}{P} \quad \text{or} \quad PV = \text{constant} \qquad [10.2]$$

The value of the constant depends on the temperature and the amount of gas in the sample. The graph of P versus V in Figure 10.6(a) shows the type of curve always obtained for a given quantity of gas at a fixed temperature. A linear relationship is obtained when V is plotted versus $1/P$, as shown in Figure 10.6(b).

We see an application of Boyle's law every time we breathe. Between breaths, the gas pressure inside the lungs equals atmospheric pressure. The volume of the lungs is governed by the rib cage, which can expand and contract, and the diaphragm, a muscle beneath the lungs that can act as a plunger. Inhalation occurs when the rib cage expands and the diaphragm moves downward. Both of these actions serve to increase the volume of the lungs, thus decreasing the gas pressure inside the lungs. The atmospheric pressure forces air into the lungs until the pressure in the lungs once again equals atmospheric pressure. Exhalation involves the reverse process: The rib cage contracts and the diaphragm moves up, both of which decrease the volume of the lungs. Air is forced out of the lungs by the increase in pressure caused by this reduction in volume.

(a)

(b)

(c)

FIGURE 10.7 As liquid nitrogen ($-196\,°C$) is poured over a balloon, the gas in the balloon is cooled and the volume decreases. (Richard Megna/Fundamental Photographs)

The Temperature–Volume Relationship: Charles's Law

Hot-air balloons rise because air expands as it is heated. The warm air in the balloon is less dense than the surrounding cool air at the same pressure. The difference in density causes the balloon to ascend. Similarly, a balloon will shrink when it is cooled, as seen in Figure 10.7.

The relationship between gas volume and temperature was discovered in 1787 by the French scientist Jacques Charles (1746–1823). Charles found that the volume of a fixed quantity of gas at constant pressure increases linearly with temperature. Some typical data are shown in Figure 10.8. Notice that the extrapolated (extended) line (which is dashed) through the data points passes through $-273.15\,°C$. Note also that the gas is predicted to have zero volume at this temperature. Of course, this condition is never fulfilled because all gases liquefy or solidify before reaching this temperature.

Lee R. Summerlin, Christie L. Borgford, and Julie B. Ealy, "Charles's Law: The Relationship Between Volume and Temperature of a Gas" *Chemical Demonstrations, A Sourcebook for Teachers, Volume 2* (Washington: American Chemical Society, 1987), p. 23.

FIGURE 10.8 Volume of an enclosed gas as a function of temperature at constant pressure. The dashed line is an extrapolation to temperatures at which the substance is no longer a gas.

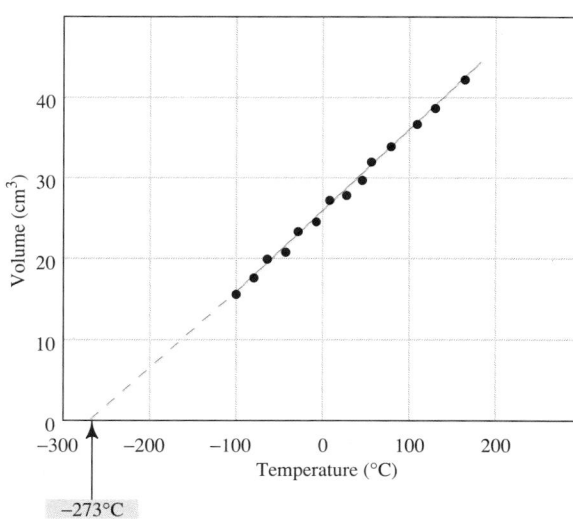

In 1848, William Thomson (1824–1907), a British physicist whose title was Lord Kelvin, proposed an absolute-temperature scale, now known as the Kelvin scale. On this scale 0 K, which is called *absolute zero,* equals −273.15°C. In terms of the Kelvin scale, **Charles's law** can be stated as follows: *The volume of a fixed amount of gas maintained at constant pressure is directly proportional to its absolute temperature.* Thus, doubling absolute temperature, say from 200 K to 400 K, causes the gas volume to double. Mathematically, Charles's law takes the following form:

$$V = \text{constant} \times T \qquad \text{or} \qquad \frac{V}{T} = \text{constant} \qquad [10.3]$$

The value of the constant depends on the pressure and amount of gas.

The Quantity–Volume Relationship: Avogadro's Law

As we add gas to a balloon, the balloon expands. The volume of a gas is affected not only by pressure and temperature but by the amount of gas as well. The relationship between the quantity of a gas and its volume follows from the work of Joseph Louis Gay-Lussac (1778–1823) and Amadeo Avogadro.

Gay-Lussac is one of those extraordinary figures in the history of science who could truly be called an adventurer. He was interested in lighter-than-air balloons, and in 1804 he made an ascent to 23,000 ft, an exploit that set the altitude record for several decades. In order to control lighter-than-air balloons better, Gay-Lussac carried out several experiments on the properties of gases. In 1808, he discovered the *law of combining volumes:* At a given pressure and temperature, the volumes of gases that react with one another are in the ratios of small whole numbers. For example, two volumes of hydrogen gas react with one volume of oxygen to form two volumes of water vapor, as shown in Figure 10.9.

Three years later, Amadeo Avogadro (Section 3.4) interpreted Gay-Lussac's observation by proposing what is now known as **Avogadro's hypothesis:** *Equal volumes of gases at the same temperature and pressure contain equal numbers of molecules.* To illustrate, suppose we have three 1-L bulbs containing Ar, N_2, and H_2, respectively (Figure 10.10), and that each gas is at the same pressure and temperature. According to Avogadro's hypothesis, these bulbs contain equal numbers of gaseous particles, although the masses of the substances in the bulbs differ greatly. Experiments show that 1 mol of any gas (that is, 6.02×10^{23} gas molecules) at 1 atm and 0°C occupies approximately 22.4 L.

FIGURE 10.9 Gay-Lussac's experimental observation of combining volumes shown together with Avogadro's explanation of this phenomenon.

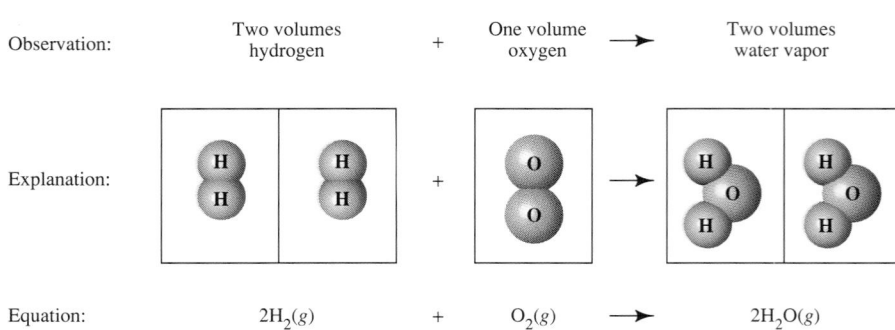

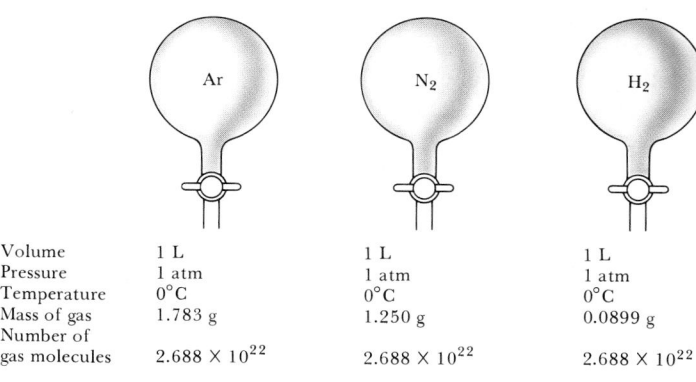

Avogadro's law follows from Avogadro's hypothesis: *The volume of a gas maintained at constant temperature and pressure is directly proportional to the number of moles of the gas.* That is,

$$V = \text{constant} \times n \qquad [10.4]$$

Thus, doubling the number of moles of gas will cause the volume to double if T and P remain constant.

10.4 The Ideal-Gas Equation

In the preceding section, we examined three historically important gas laws. Each was obtained by holding two variables constant in order to see how the other variables affect each other. Using the symbol $\propto$ which is read "is proportional to," we have

Boyle's law: $\quad V \propto \dfrac{1}{P} \qquad$ (constant n, T)

Charles's law: $\quad V \propto T \qquad$ (constant n, P)

Avogadro's law: $\quad V \propto n \qquad$ (constant P, T)

We can combine these relationships to make a more general gas law:

$$V \propto \frac{nT}{P}$$

If we call the proportionality constant R, we have

$$V = R\left(\frac{nT}{P}\right)$$

Rearranging, we have this relationship in its more familiar form:

$$PV = nRT \qquad [10.5]$$

Learning Goal 4: Use the ideal-gas equation to solve for one variable (P, V, n, or T) given the other three variables or information from which they can be determined.

TABLE 10.2 △
Numerical Values of the Gas Constant, R, in Various Units

Units	Numerical value
L-atm/mol-K	0.08206
cal/mol-K	1.987
J/mol-K[a]	8.314
m³-Pa/mol-K[a]	8.314
L-torr/mol-K	62.36

[a] SI unit.

Point of Emphasis: In working with gases, the most commonly used values of R are 0.08206 L-atm/mol-K and 62.36 L-torr/mol-K.

Point of Emphasis: The standard conditions for gas behavior (0°C, 1 atm) are *not* the same as the standard conditions in thermodynamics and thermochemistry (25°C, 1 atm).

This equation is known as the **ideal-gas equation.** An **ideal gas** is a hypothetical gas whose pressure, volume, and temperature behavior is completely described by the ideal-gas equation.

The term R in the ideal-gas equation is called the **gas constant.** The value and units of R depend on the units of P, V, n, and T. Temperature must *always* be expressed on an absolute-temperature scale, normally the Kelvin scale. The quantity of gas, n, is normally expressed in moles. The units chosen for pressure and volume are most often atm and liters, respectively. However, other units can be used. Table 10.2 shows the numerical value for R in various units. As we saw in the Closer Look box in Section 5.3, the product PV has the units of energy. Therefore, the units of R can include calories or joules. In working problems with the ideal-gas equation, the units of P, V, n, and T must agree with the units in the gas constant. Throughout this chapter, we will use the value $R = 0.08206$ L-atm/mol-K (four significant figures) or 0.0821 L-atm/mol-K (three significant figures) whenever we use the ideal-gas equation.

Now suppose we have 1.000 mol of an ideal gas at 1.000 atm and 0.00°C (273.15 K). Then, from the ideal-gas equation, the volume of the gas is given by

$$V = \frac{nRT}{P} = \frac{(1.000 \text{ mol})(0.08206 \text{ L-atm/mol-K})(273.15 \text{ K})}{1.000 \text{ atm}} = 22.41 \text{ L}$$

The conditions 0°C and 1 atm are referred to as the **standard temperature and pressure (STP).** Many properties of gases are tabulated for these conditions. The volume occupied by 1 mol of ideal gas at STP, 22.41 L, is known as the *molar volume* of an ideal gas at STP.

The ideal-gas equation does not always accurately describe real gases. For example, the measured volume, V, for given conditions of P, n, and T, might differ from the volume calculated from $PV = nRT$. Ordinarily, the difference between ideal and real behavior is so small that we may ignore it. We will examine deviations from ideal behavior in Section 10.10.

SAMPLE EXERCISE 10.3

Calcium carbonate, $CaCO_3(s)$, decomposes upon heating to give $CaO(s)$ and $CO_2(g)$. A sample of $CaCO_3$ is decomposed, and the carbon dioxide is collected in a 250-mL flask. After the decomposition is complete, the gas has a pressure of 1.3 atm at a temperature of 31°C. How many moles of CO_2 gas were generated?

SOLUTION We first ask ourselves which quantity in the ideal-gas equation we seek. In this exercise, we want to find the number of moles, n. It is usually helpful to tabulate the information given in the problem and to convert the values to units consistent with those for R (0.0821 L-atm/mol-K). In this case, the values of the other three variables in the ideal-gas equation—P, V, and T—are given in the problem:

$$P = 1.3 \text{ atm}$$

$$V = 250 \text{ mL} = 0.25 \text{ L}$$

$$T = 31°C = (31 + 273) \text{ K} = 304 \text{ K}$$

Remember: *Absolute temperature must always be used when the ideal-gas equation is solved.*

We now rearrange the ideal-gas equation (Equation 10.5) to solve for n:

$$n = \frac{PV}{RT}$$

$$n = \frac{(1.3\ \text{atm})(0.25\ \text{L})}{(0.0821\ \text{L-atm/mol-K})(304\ \text{K})} = 0.013\ \text{mol}\ CO_2$$

Notice that proper cancellation of units ensures that we have properly rearranged the ideal-gas equation and have converted to the correct units.

PRACTICE EXERCISE

A flashbulb contains 2.4×10^{-4} mol of O_2 gas at a pressure of 1.9 atm and a temperature of 19°C. What is the volume of the flashbulb in cubic centimeters?
Answer: 3.0 cm³

SAMPLE EXERCISE 10.4

A sample of argon gas is confined to a 1.00-L tank at 27.0°C. The pressure in the tank is 4.15 atm. The gas is allowed to expand into a larger vessel. Upon expansion, the temperature of the gas drops to 15.0°C, and the pressure drops to 655 torr. What is the final volume of the gas?

SOLUTION Let us begin by making a table of the information we are given. We note that we must convert temperature to kelvins, and, in order to use the usual value of R, we convert the final pressure, 655 torr, to atmospheres.

	Pressure	Volume	Moles, n	Temperature
Initial	4.15 atm	1.00 L	?	300 K
Final	0.862 atm	?	?	288 K

Notice that we are missing two of the four quantities we need to determine the final state of the gas. However, upon rereading the problem, we note that the quantity of gas, n, does not change. Therefore, if we can determine the amount of gas that was initially present, we can use that value to determine the final volume of the gas.

We can use the ideal-gas equation to determine the number of moles of gas, n, by using the quantities for the initial condition of the gas:

$$n = \frac{PV}{RT} = \frac{(4.15\ \text{atm})(1.00\ \text{L})}{(0.0821\ \text{L-atm/mol-K})(300\ \text{K})} = 0.168\ \text{mol}$$

We can now use this value of n, along with the other data for the final state of the gas, to calculate the final volume of the gas:

$$V = \frac{nRT}{P} = \frac{(0.168\ \text{mol})(0.0821\ \text{L-atm/mol-K})(288\ \text{K})}{0.862\ \text{atm}} = 4.62\ \text{L}$$

Dimensional analysis shows that our final value has the proper units of volume. Notice also that the final volume is larger than the initial volume. This result is what we expect because the problem stated that the gas expanded into a larger vessel.

PRACTICE EXERCISE

A 0.50-mol sample of oxygen gas is confined at 0°C in a cylinder with a movable piston, such as that shown in Figure 5.2. The gas has an initial pressure of 1.0 atm. The gas is then compressed by the piston so that its final volume is half the initial volume. The final pressure of the gas is 2.2 atm. What is the final temperature of the gas in degrees Celsius?   *Answer:* 27°C

The ideal-gas equation, like many other equations you will encounter in chemistry and elsewhere, is a relationship among several different experimentally measured variables. The ideal-gas equation contains four experimental quantities—P, V, n, and T—and one constant—R. Depending on the type of problem, we might need to solve the ideal-gas equation for any of the four quantities.

Student sometimes have difficulty extracting the necessary information from problems involving many variables. By using a systematic procedure, such as the one we used in Sample Exercises 10.3 and 10.4, you should be able to minimize the difficulties in solving such problems. Any time that you encounter a problem involving several variables, we suggest that you do the following:

1. Tabulate the information. You should read problems carefully to determine (a) which quantity is the unknown, and (b) the values of the variables needed to solve the equation. Every time you encounter a numerical value, jot down the information you are being given. Consider, for example, the following statements: "A barometer in the laboratory indicated that atmospheric pressure was 755 torr. A manometer was used to determine that the pressure of the gas was 43 torr greater than atmospheric pressure." We can use these statements to determine the pressure of the gas as a sequence of equations:

$$P_{atm} = 755 \text{ torr}; \qquad P_{gas} = P_{atm} + 43 \text{ torr} = (755 + 43) \text{ torr} = 798 \text{ torr}$$

In many cases, constructing a table of the given information will be useful.

2. Convert to appropriate units. As you have already seen, we often use several different units to express the same quantity. You must make certain that quantities are converted to the proper units by using the correct conversion factors. In using the ideal-gas equation, for example, we usually use the value of R that has units of L-atm/mol-K. If you are given a pressure in torr, you will need to convert it to atmospheres.

3. If a single equation relates the variables, rearrange the equation to solve for the unknown. You should make certain that you are comfortable using algebra

Learning Goal 5: Use the gas laws, including the combined gas law, to calculate how one variable of a gas (P, V, n, or T) responds to changes in one or more of the other variables.

Point of Emphasis: *Any* of the gas laws can be derived from the ideal-gas equation.

Relationship Between the Ideal-Gas Equation and the Gas Laws

The simple gas laws that we discussed in Section 10.3, such as Boyle's law, are special cases of the ideal-gas equation. For example, when the quantity of gas and the temperature are held constant, n and T have fixed values. Therefore, the product nRT is the product of three constants and must itself be a constant:

$$PV = nRT = \text{constant} \qquad \text{or} \qquad PV = \text{constant} \qquad [10.6]$$

Thus, we have Boyle's law. We see that if n and T are constant, the individual values of P and V can change, but the product PV must remain constant.

Similarly, Charles's law is a special case of the ideal-gas equation in which n and P are constant:

$$V = \left(\frac{nR}{P}\right) T = \text{constant} \times T \qquad \text{or} \qquad \frac{V}{T} = \text{constant} \qquad [10.7]$$

to solve the equation for the desired variable. In the case of the ideal-gas equation, the following algebraic rearrangements will all be used at one time or another:

$$P = \frac{nRT}{V}; \qquad V = \frac{nRT}{P}; \qquad n = \frac{PV}{RT}; \qquad T = \frac{PV}{nR}$$

4. *Use dimensional analysis.* Dimensional analysis enables you to check that you have solved the equation correctly. If the units of the quantities in the equation cancel properly to give the units of the desired variable, you have probably used the equation correctly.

One note of caution is in order: Sometimes you will not be given values for the necessary variables directly. Rather, you will be given the values of other quantities that can be used to determine the needed variables. For example, suppose you are trying to use the ideal-gas equation to calculate the pressure of a gas. You are given the temperature of the gas, but you are not given explicit values for n and V. However, the problem states that "the sample of gas contains 0.15 mol of gas per liter." We turn this statement into the expression

$$\frac{n}{V} = 0.15 \text{ mol/L}$$

Solving the ideal-gas equation for pressure yields

$$P = \frac{nRT}{V} = \left(\frac{n}{V}\right) RT$$

Thus, we can solve the equation even though we are not given specific values for n and V. We shall examine how to use the density and molar mass of a gas in this fashion in Section 10.5.

As we have continuously stressed, the most important thing you can do to become proficient in solving problems is to practice by solving the assigned exercises at the end of the chapter.

Thus, the ideal-gas equation predicts a linear relationship between volume and absolute temperature, extrapolating to zero volume at 0 K (Figure 10.8). Again, we must remind ourselves that real gases lose their gaseous properties before absolute zero is reached.

If both n and V in the ideal-gas equation are fixed, the pressure and temperature of the gas obey the following simple relation:

$$P = \left(\frac{nR}{V}\right) T = \text{constant} \times T \qquad \text{or} \qquad \frac{P}{T} = \text{constant} \qquad [10.8]$$

Thus, if a confined gas is heated at constant volume, the pressure increases linearly with temperature.

We can use relationships such as Equations 10.6 through 10.8 to solve problems involving gases even though we might not know explicit values for all four variables P, V, n, and T. The following sample exercise illustrates this point.

SAMPLE EXERCISE 10.5

The gas pressure in an aerosol can is 1.5 atm at 25°C. Assuming that the gas inside obeys the ideal-gas equation, what would the pressure be if the can were heated to 450°C?

SOLUTION   Let us again proceed by tabulating the information that we are given. We will use subscripts 1 and 2 to represent the initial and final states, respectively. Because the volume and quantity of gas do not change, we see that $V_2 = V_1$ and $n_2 = n_1$.

	P	V	n	T
Initial	1.5 atm	V_1	n_1	298 K
Final	P_2	V_1	n_1	723 K

Because n and V are constant, the ratio P/T is a constant (Equation 10.8). Thus, even though we do not know the values of n and V, P/T must be constant. In other words,

$$\frac{P_1}{T_1} = \frac{P_2}{T_2}$$

$$P_2 = P_1 \left(\frac{T_2}{T_1}\right)$$

$$P_2 = (1.5 \text{ atm}) \left(\frac{723 \text{ K}}{298 \text{ K}}\right) = 3.6 \text{ atm}$$

This answer is intuitively reasonable—increasing the temperature of a gas increases its pressure. It is evident from this example why aerosol cans carry a warning not to incinerate.

PRACTICE EXERCISE

A large natural-gas storage tank is arranged so that the pressure is maintained at 2.20 atm. On a cold day in December when the temperature is -15°C (4°F), the volume of gas in the tank is 28,500 ft³. What is the volume of the same quantity of gas on a warm July day when the temperature is 31°C (88°F)?   *Answer:* 33,600 ft³

We are often faced with the situation in which P, V, and T all change for a fixed number of moles of gas. Because n is constant under these circumstances, the ideal-gas equation gives

$$\frac{PV}{T} = nR = \text{constant}$$

If we represent the initial and final conditions of pressure, temperature, and volume by subscripts 1 and 2, respectively, we can write the following expression:

$$\frac{P_1 V_1}{T_1} = \frac{P_2 V_2}{T_2} \tag{10.9}$$

If you now take another look at Sample Exercise 10.4, you will see that we could have answered the question directly by using Equation 10.9. Doing so would simplify the problem by avoiding the intermediate calculation of n.

Point of Emphasis: The subscripts "1" and "2" are arbitrary and only serve to keep each V associated with the correct P.

346   Chapter 10   Gases

10.5 Molar Mass and Gas Densities

Learning Goal 6: Calculate the molar mass of a gas, given gas density under specified conditions of temperature and pressure. Also, calculate gas density under stated conditions, knowing molar mass.

We can make many applications of the ideal-gas equation in measuring and calculating gas density. Density has the units of mass per unit volume. We can arrange the gas equation to obtain

$$\frac{n}{V} = \frac{P}{RT}$$

Now n/V has the units of moles per liter. Suppose that we multiply both sides of this equation by the molar mass, $\mathcal{M}$, which is the number of grams in 1 mol of a substance:

$$\frac{n\mathcal{M}}{V} = \frac{P\mathcal{M}}{RT} \qquad [10.10]$$

The product of the quantites n/V and $\mathcal{M}$ equals the density, as we see when we examine their units:

$$\frac{\text{Moles}}{\text{Liter}} \times \frac{\text{grams}}{\text{mole}} = \frac{\text{grams}}{\text{liter}}$$

Point of Emphasis: The densities of liquids and solids are usually expressed in g/mL, whereas the densities of gases are usually expressed in g/L.

Thus, the density of the gas is given by the expression on the right in Equation 10.10:

$$d = \frac{P\mathcal{M}}{RT} \qquad [10.11]$$

This relationship can be arranged to calculate the molar mass of a gas:

$$\mathcal{M} = \frac{dRT}{P} \qquad [10.12]$$

Lee R. Summerlin and James L. Ealy, Jr., "Determining the Molecular Weight of a Gas: Flick Your Bic," *Chemical Demonstrations, A Sourcebook for Teachers,* (Washington: American Chemical Society, 1985), p. 17.

S A M P L E   E X E R C I S E   1 0 . 6

What is the density of carbon tetrachloride vapor at 714 torr and 125°C?

SOLUTION The molar mass of CCl_4 is $12.0 + (4)(35.5) = 154$ g/mol. We must remember to convert temperature to the Kelvin scale and to convert pressure to atmospheres. Using Equation 10.11 we see

$$d = \frac{(714 \text{ torr})(1 \text{ atm}/760 \text{ torr})(154 \text{ g/mol})}{(0.0821 \text{ L-atm/mol-K})(398 \text{ K})} = 4.43 \text{ g/L}$$

P R A C T I C E   E X E R C I S E

The mean molar mass of the atmosphere at the surface of Titan, Saturn's largest moon, is 28.6 g/mol. The surface temperature is 95 K, and the pressure is 1.6 earth atm. Assuming ideal behavior, calculate the density of Titan's atmosphere. *Answer:* 5.9 g/L

SAMPLE EXERCISE 10.7

A large flask is evacuated and found to weigh 134.567 g. It is then filled to a pressure of 735 torr at 31°C with a gas of unknown molar mass and then reweighed; its mass is 137.456 g. The flask is then filled with water and again weighed; its mass is now 1067.9 g. Assuming that the ideal-gas equation applies, what is the molar mass of the unknown gas? (The density of water at 31°C is 0.997 g/cm³.)

SOLUTION First we must determine the volume of the flask. This is given by the difference in weights of the empty flask and the flask filled with water, divided by the density of water at 31°C, which is 0.997 g/cm³:

$$V = \frac{1067.9 \text{ g} - 134.6 \text{ g}}{0.997 \text{ g/cm}^3} = 936 \text{ cm}^3$$

Because the mass of the gas is 137.456 g − 134.567 g = 2.889 g, its density is 2.889 g/0.936 L = 3.09 g/L. Using Equation 10.12, we have

$$\mathcal{M} = \frac{dRT}{P}$$

$$= \frac{(3.09 \text{ g/L})(0.0821 \text{ L-atm/mol-K})(304 \text{ K})}{(735/760) \text{ atm}}$$

$$= 79.7 \text{ g/mol}$$

PRACTICE EXERCISE

One method for accurately determining the molar mass of a gas is to measure its density as a function of pressure. The graph of the quantity d/P against pressure is extrapolated to zero pressure to obtain a limiting value. In one set of experiments a certain gas was shown to have a limiting value d/P of 2.86 g/L-atm at 0°C. Calculate the molar mass. *Answer:* 64.1 g/mol

10.6 Gas Mixtures and Partial Pressures

Thus far we have considered only the behavior of pure gases—those that consist of only one substance in the gaseous state. How do we deal with gases composed of a mixture of two or more different substances? While studying the properties of air, John Dalton (Section 2.1) observed that the *total pressure of a mixture of gases equals the sum of the pressures that each would exert if it were present alone.* The pressure exerted by a particular component of a mixture of gases is called the **partial pressure** of that gas, and Dalton's observation is known as **Dalton's law of partial pressures.**

If we let P_t be the total pressure, and P_1, P_2, and so forth, be the partial pressures of the gases in the mixture, we can write Dalton's law as follows:

$$P_t = P_1 + P_2 + P_3 + \cdots \qquad [10.13]$$

This equation implies that each gas in the mixture behaves independently of the others, as we can see by the following analysis. Let n_1, and n_2, and so forth, be the number of moles of each of the gases in the mixture, and n_t be the total number of moles of gas ($n_t = n_1 + n_2 + n_3 + \cdots$).

If each of the gases obeys the ideal-gas equation, we can write

$$P_1 = n_1 \left(\frac{RT}{V}\right), \qquad P_2 = n_2 \left(\frac{RT}{V}\right), \qquad P_3 = n_3 \left(\frac{RT}{V}\right), \qquad \text{and so forth.}$$

All the gases experience the same temperature and volume. Therefore, by substituting into Equation 10.13, we obtain

$$P_t = (n_1 + n_2 + n_3 + \cdots)\frac{RT}{V} = n_t\left(\frac{RT}{V}\right) \qquad [10.14]$$

That is, the total pressure at constant temperature and volume is determined by the total number of moles of gas present, whether that total represents just one substance or a mixture.

SAMPLE EXERCISE 10.8

A gaseous mixture made from 6.00 g O_2 and 9.00 g CH_4 is placed in a 15.0-L vessel at 0°C. What is the partial pressure of each gas, and what is the total pressure in the vessel?

SOLUTION Because each gas behaves independently, we can calculate the pressure that each would exert if the other were not present. We must first convert the mass of each gas to moles:

$$n_{O_2} = (6.00 \text{ g } O_2)\left(\frac{1 \text{ mol } O_2}{32.0 \text{ g } O_2}\right) = 0.188 \text{ mol } O_2$$

$$n_{CH_4} = (9.00 \text{ g } CH_4)\left(\frac{1 \text{ mol } CH_4}{16.0 \text{ g } CH_4}\right) = 0.563 \text{ mol } CH_4$$

We can now use the ideal-gas equation to calculate the partial pressure of each gas:

$$P_{O_2} = \frac{n_{O_2}RT}{V} = \frac{(0.188 \text{ mol})(0.0821 \text{ L-atm/mol-K})(273 \text{ K})}{15.0 \text{ L}} = 0.281 \text{ atm}$$

$$P_{CH_4} = \frac{n_{CH_4}RT}{V} = \frac{(0.563 \text{ mol})(0.0821 \text{ L-atm/mol-K})(273 \text{ K})}{15.0 \text{ L}} = 0.841 \text{ atm}$$

According to Dalton's law (Equation 10.13), the total pressure in the vessel is the sum of the partial pressures:

$$P_t = P_{O_2} + P_{CH_4} = 0.281 \text{ atm} + 0.841 \text{ atm} = 1.122 \text{ atm}$$

PRACTICE EXERCISE

What is the total pressure exerted by a mixture of 2.00 g of H_2 and 8.00 g of N_2 at 273 K in a 10.0-L vessel?   *Answer:* 2.86 atm

Partial Pressures and Mole Fractions

Because each gas in a mixture behaves independently, we can easily relate the amount of a given gas in a mixture and its partial pressure. For an ideal gas $P = nRT/V$, and so we can write

$$\frac{P_1}{P_t} = \frac{n_1RT/V}{n_tRT/V} = \frac{n_1}{n_t} \qquad [10.15]$$

The ratio n_1/n_t is called the mole fraction of gas 1, which we denote X_1. The **mole fraction,** X, is a dimensionless number that expresses the ratio of the number of moles of one component to the total number of moles in the mixture. We can rearrange Equation 10.15 to give

$$P_1 = \left(\frac{n_1}{n_t}\right)P_t = X_1 P_t \qquad [10.16]$$

Thus, the partial pressure of a gas in a mixture is its mole fraction times the total pressure.

As an example, the mole fraction of N_2 in air is 0.78 (that is, 78 percent of the molecules in air are N_2 molecules). If the total barometric pressure is 760 torr, then the partial pressure of N_2 is

$$P_{N_2} = (0.78)(760 \text{ torr}) = 590 \text{ torr}$$

This result makes intuitive sense: Because N_2 comprises 78 percent of the mixture, it contributes 78 percent of the total pressure.

SAMPLE EXERCISE 10.9

A study of the effects of certain gases on plant growth requires a synthetic atmosphere composed of 1.5 mol percent CO_2, 18.0 mol percent O_2, and 80.5 mol percent Ar. **(a)** Calculate the partial pressure of O_2 in the mixture if the total pressure of the atmosphere is to be 745 torr. **(b)** If this atmosphere is to be held in a 120-L space at 295 K, how many moles of O_2 are needed?

SOLUTION **(a)** The mole percent is just the mole fraction times 100. Therefore, the mole fraction of O_2 is 0.180. Using Equation 10.16, we have

$$P_{O_2} = (0.180)(745 \text{ torr}) = 134 \text{ torr}$$

(b) Tabulating the given variables and changing them to appropriate units, we have

$$P_{O_2} = (134 \text{ torr})\left(\frac{1 \text{ atm}}{760 \text{ torr}}\right) = 0.176 \text{ atm}$$

$$V = 120 \text{ L}$$

$$n_{O_2} = ?$$

$$R = 0.0821 \frac{\text{L-atm}}{\text{mol-K}}$$

$$T = 295 \text{ K}$$

Solving the ideal-gas equation for n_{O_2}, we have

$$n_{O_2} = P_{O_2}\left(\frac{V}{RT}\right) = (0.176 \text{ atm})\frac{120 \text{ L}}{(0.0821 \text{ L-atm/mol-K})(295 \text{ K})} = 0.872 \text{ mol}$$

PRACTICE EXERCISE

From data gathered by *Voyager 1*, scientists have estimated the composition of the atmosphere of Titan, Saturn's largest moon. The total pressure on the surface of Titan is 1220 torr. The atmosphere consists of 82 mol percent N_2, 12 mol percent Ar, and 6.0 mol percent CH_4. Calculate the partial pressure of each of these gases in Titan's atmosphere. *Answer:* 1.0×10^3 torr N_2, 1.5×10^2 torr Ar, and 73 torr CH_4

10.7 Volumes of Gases in Chemical Reactions

A knowledge of the properties of gases is important for chemists because gases are often reactants or products in chemical reactions. For this reason, we are often faced with calculating the volumes of gases required as reactants or produced as products in reactions. We saw in Chapter 3 that the coefficients in balanced chemical equations tell us the relative amounts (in moles) of reactants and products in a reaction. The number of moles of a gas, of course, is related to P, V, and T.

SAMPLE EXERCISE 10.10

The industrial synthesis of nitric acid involves the reaction of nitrogen dioxide gas with water:

$$3NO_2(g) + H_2O(l) \longrightarrow 2HNO_3(aq) + NO(g)$$

How many moles of nitric acid can be prepared using 450 L of NO_2 at a pressure of 5.00 atm and a temperature of 295 K?

SOLUTION The balanced chemical equation tells us that 3 mol of NO_2 will produce 2 mol of HNO_3 in the reaction. To use this information, we must first determine the number of moles of NO_2:

$$n = \frac{PV}{RT} = \frac{(5.00 \text{ atm})(450 \text{ L})}{(0.0821 \text{ L-atm/mol-K})(295 \text{ K})} = 92.9 \text{ mol}$$

From here we can use the number of moles of NO_2 and the coefficients in the balanced equation to calculate the number of moles of HNO_3:

$$92.9 \text{ mol } NO_2 \left(\frac{2 \text{ mol } HNO_3}{3 \text{ mol } NO_2} \right) = 61.9 \text{ mol } HNO_3$$

PRACTICE EXERCISE

In the first step in the industrial process for making nitric acid, ammonia reacts with oxygen at 850°C and 5.00 atm in the presence of a suitable catalyst. The following reaction occurs:

$$4NH_3(g) + 5O_2(g) \longrightarrow 4NO(g) + 6H_2O(g)$$

How many liters of $NH_3(g)$ at 850°C and 5.00 atm are required to react with 1.00 mol of $O_2(g)$ in this reaction? **Answer:** 14.8 L

Collecting Gases over Water

An experiment that often comes up in the course of laboratory work involves determining the number of moles of gas collected from a chemical reaction. Sometimes this gas is collected over water. For example, solid potassium chlorate, $KClO_3$, can be decomposed by heating it in a test tube in an arrangement shown in Figure 10.11. The balanced equation for the reaction is

$$2KClO_3(s) \longrightarrow 2KCl(s) + 3O_2(g) \qquad [10.17]$$

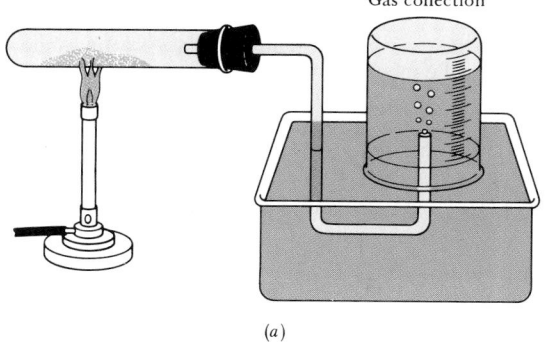

(a)

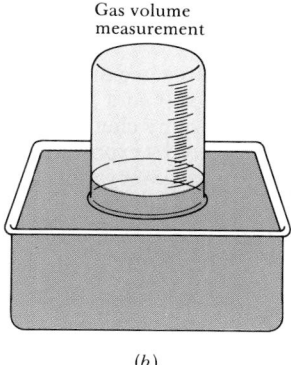

(b)

FIGURE 10.11 (a) Collection of gas over water. (b) When the gas has been collected, the bottle is raised or lowered so that the heights of the water inside and outside the collection vessel are equalized. The total pressure of the gases inside the vessel is then equal to the atmospheric pressure.

The oxygen gas is collected in a bottle that is initially filled with water and inverted in a water pan.

The volume of gas collected is measured by raising or lowering the bottle as necessary until the water levels inside and outside the bottle are the same. When this condition is met, the pressure inside the bottle is equal to the atmospheric pressure outside. The total pressure inside is the sum of the pressure of gas collected and the pressure of water vapor in equilibrium with liquid water:

$$P_{total} = P_{gas} + P_{H_2O} \qquad [10.18]$$

The pressure exerted by water vapor, P_{H_2O}, at various temperatures is shown in Appendix B.

SAMPLE EXERCISE 10.11

A sample of $KClO_3$ is partially decomposed (Equation 10.17), producing O_2 gas that is collected over water as in Figure 10.11. The volume of gas collected is 0.250 L at 26°C and 765 torr total pressure. (a) How many moles of O_2 are collected? (b) How many grams of $KClO_3$ were decomposed? (c) When dry, what volume would the O_2 gas collected occupy at the same temperature and pressure?

SOLUTION   (a) If we tabulate the information presented in the problem, we will see that values are given for V and T. In order to calculate the unknown, n_{O_2}, we also must know the pressure of O_2 in the system. We therefore first need to determine the partial pressure of O_2 gas in the mixture of O_2 and H_2O vapor collected over water. The partial pressure of the O_2 gas is the difference between the total pressure, 765 torr, and the pressure of the water vapor at 26°C, 25 torr (Appendix B):

$$P_{O_2} = 765 \text{ torr} - 25 \text{ torr} = 740 \text{ torr}$$

We can use the ideal-gas equation to solve for the number of moles of O_2, which gives us

$$n_{O_2} = \frac{P_{O_2}V}{RT} = \frac{(740 \text{ torr})(1 \text{ atm}/760 \text{ torr})(0.250 \text{ L})}{(0.0821 \text{ L-atm/mol-K})(299 \text{ K})} = 9.92 \times 10^{-3} \text{ mol } O_2$$

(b) From Equation 10.17, we have 2 mol $KClO_3 \simeq 3$ mol O_2. The molar mass of $KClO_3$ is 122.6 g/mol. Thus, we can convert the moles of O_2 that we found in part (a) to moles of $KClO_3$ and grams of $KClO_3$:

$$(9.92 \times 10^{-3} \text{ mol } O_2)\left(\frac{2 \text{ mol } KClO_3}{3 \text{ mol } O_2}\right)\left(\frac{122.6 \text{ g } KClO_3}{1 \text{ mol } KClO_3}\right) = 0.811 \text{ g } KClO_3$$

(c) The original gas mixture contained both O_2, at a partial pressure of 740 torr, and water vapor, with a partial pressure of 25 torr. We are now going to remove the water vapor, leaving dry O_2. The dry O_2 will have a pressure of 765 torr at the same temperature as before. The volume it will occupy thus follows from Boyle's law:

$$V_2 = \frac{P_1V_1}{P_2} = \frac{(740 \text{ torr})(0.250 \text{ L})}{(765 \text{ torr})} = 0.242 \text{ L}$$

Notice that we did not need to convert the pressures to atmospheres. As long as the units for P_1 and P_2 are the same, they will cancel.

Many chemical compounds that react with water and water vapor would be degraded by exposure to wet gas. Thus, in research laboratories, gases are often dried by passing wet gas over a substance that absorbs water (a *desiccant*), such as calcium sulfate, $CaSO_4$. Calcium sulfate crystals are sold as a desiccant under the tradename Drierite.

PRACTICE EXERCISE

Ammonium nitrite, NH_4NO_2, decomposes upon heating to form N_2 gas:

$$NH_4NO_2(s) \longrightarrow N_2(g) + 2H_2O(g)$$

When a sample of NH_4NO_2 is decomposed in a test tube, as in Figure 10.11, 511 mL of N_2 gas is collected over water at 26°C and 745 torr total pressure. How many grams of NH_4NO_2 were decomposed?   *Answer:* 1.26 g

10.8 Kinetic-Molecular Theory

The ideal-gas equation describes *how* gases behave, but it doesn't explain *why* they behave as they do. For example, why does a gas expand when heated at constant pressure? Or why does its pressure increase when the gas is compressed at constant temperature? To understand the physical properties of gases, we need a model that helps us picture what happens to gas particles as experimental conditions such as pressure or temperature change. Such a model, known as the **kinetic-molecular theory,** was developed over a period of about 100 years, culminating in 1857 when Rudolf Clausius (1822 – 1888) published a complete and satisfactory form of the theory.

The kinetic-molecular theory (the theory of moving molecules) is summarized by the following statements:

1. Gases consist of large numbers of molecules that are in continuous, random motion. (The word *molecule* is used here to designate the smallest particle of any gas; some gases, such as the noble gases, consist of uncombined atoms.)
2. The volume of all the molecules of the gas is negligible compared to the total volume in which the gas is contained.
3. Attractive and repulsive forces between gas molecules are negligible.
4. Energy can be transferred between molecules during collisions, but the *average* kinetic energy of the molecules does not change with time, as long as the temperature of the gas remains constant. In other words, the collisions are perfectly elastic.
5. The average kinetic energy of the molecules is proportional to absolute temperature. At any given temperature the molecules of all gases have the same average kinetic energy.

The kinetic-molecular theory gives us an understanding of both pressure and temperature at a molecular level. The pressure of a gas is caused by collisions of the molecules with the walls of the container, as shown in Figure 10.12. The magnitude of the pressure is determined both by how often and how "hard" the molecules strike the walls.

The absolute temperature of a gas is a measure of the *average* kinetic energy of its molecules. If two different gases are at the same temperature, their molecules have the same average kinetic energy. If the temperature of a gas is doubled (say from 200 K to 400 K), the average kinetic energy of its molecules doubles. Thus, molecular motion increases with increasing temperature.

Although the molecules in a sample of gas have an *average* kinetic energy and hence an average speed, the individual molecules move at varying speeds. At any instant, some of them are moving rapidly, others more slowly. Figure 10.13 illustrates the distribution of molecular speeds within nitrogen gas at 0°C (blue line) and at 100°C (red line). The curve tells us the fraction of molecules moving at each speed. Notice that at higher temperatures a greater fraction of

Teaching Note: The average kinetic energy of a gas depends only on the temperature of the gas.

FIGURE 10.12 The pressure of a gas is caused by collisions of the gas molecules with the walls of their container.

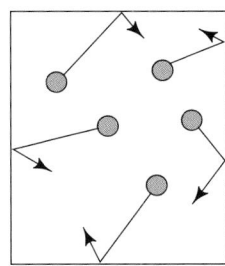

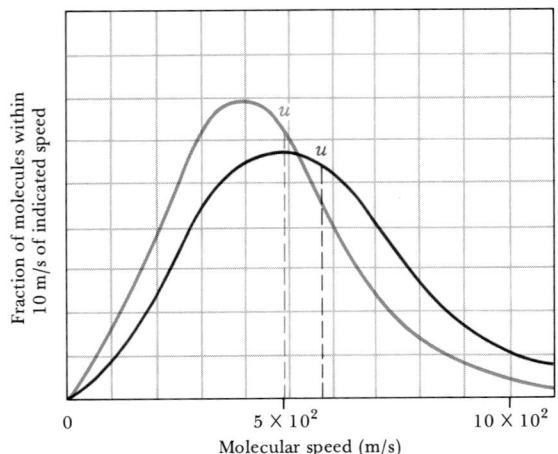

FIGURE 10.13 Distribution of molecular speeds for nitrogen at 0°C (blue line) and 100°C (red line).

 Figure 10.13

molecules is moving at greater speeds; the distribution curve has shifted toward higher speeds and hence toward higher average kinetic energy.

Figure 10.13 also shows the value of the **root-mean-square (rms) speed,** u, of the molecules at each temperature. This quantity is the speed of a molecule possessing average kinetic energy. The rms speed is not quite the same as the average (mean) speed. The difference between the two, however, is small.*

The rms speed is important because the average kinetic energy of the gas molecules, ϵ, is related directly to u^2:

$$\epsilon = \tfrac{1}{2}mu^2 \qquad\qquad [10.19]$$

where m is the mass of the molecule. Because mass doesn't change with temperature, the rms speed (and also the average speed) of molecules must increase as temperature increases.

Application to the Gas Laws

The empirical observations of gas properties as expressed in the various gas laws are readily understood in terms of the kinetic-molecular theory. The following examples illustrate this point.

1. *Effect of a volume increase at constant temperature:* The fact that temperature remains constant means that the average kinetic energy of the gas molecules remains unchanged. This in turn means that the rms speed of the molecules, u, is unchanged. However, if the volume is increased, the molecules must move a longer distance between collisions. Consequently, there are fewer collisions per unit time with the container walls, and

---

* To illustrate the difference between rms speed and average speed, suppose that we have four objects with speeds of 4.0, 6.0, 10.0, and 12.0 m/s. Their average speed is $\tfrac{1}{4}(4.0 + 6.0 + 10.0 + 12.0) = 8.0$ m/s. The rms speed, u, however, is the square root of the average squared speeds of the molecules:

$$\sqrt{\tfrac{1}{4}(4.0^2 + 6.0^2 + 10.0^2 + 12.0^2)} = \sqrt{74.0} = 8.6 \text{ m/s}$$

For an ideal gas, the average speed equals $0.921 \times u$. Thus the average speed is directly proportional to the rms speed, and the two are in fact nearly equal.

The Ideal-Gas Equation

Beginning with the postulates of the kinetic-molecular theory, it is possible to derive the ideal-gas equation. Rather than proceed through a derivation, let's consider in somewhat qualitative terms how the ideal-gas equation might follow. As we have seen, pressure is force per unit area. ⟶ (Sec. 10.2) The total force of the molecular collisions on the walls, and hence the pressure produced by these collisions, depends both on how strongly the molecules strike the walls (impulse imparted per collision) and on the rate at which these collisions occur:

$P \propto$ impulse imparted per collision $\times$ rate of collisions

For a molecule traveling at the rms speed, u, the impulse imparted by a collision with a wall depends on the momentum of the molecule; that is, it depends on the product of its mass and speed, mu. The rate of collisions is proportional to both the number of molecules per unit volume, n/V, and their speed, u. If there are more molecules in a container, there will be more frequent collisions with the container walls. As the molecular speed increases or the volume of the container decreases, the time required for molecules to traverse the distance from one wall to another is reduced, and the molecules collide more frequently with the walls. Thus, we have

$$P \propto mu \times \frac{n}{V} \times u \propto \frac{nmu^2}{V} \qquad [10.20]$$

Because the average kinetic energy, $\frac{1}{2}mu^2$, is proportional to temperature, we have $mu^2 \propto T$. Making this substitution into Equation 10.20 gives

$$P \propto \frac{n(mu^2)}{V} \propto \frac{nT}{V} \qquad [10.21]$$

Let us now convert the proportionality sign to an equal sign by expressing n as the number of moles of gas; we then insert a proportionality constant—R, the molar gas constant:

$$P = \frac{nRT}{V} \qquad [10.22]$$

This expression, of course, is the familiar ideal-gas equation.

pressure decreases. Thus, the model accounts in a simple way for Boyle's law.

2. *Effect of a temperature increase at constant volume:* An increase in temperature means an increase in the average kinetic energy of the molecules, and thus an increase in u. If there is no change in volume, there will be more collisions with the walls per unit time. Furthermore, the change in momentum in each collision increases (the molecules strike the walls harder). Hence the model explains the observed pressure increase.

SAMPLE EXERCISE 10.12

A sample of O_2 gas initially at STP is transferred from a 2-L container to a 1-L container at constant temperature. What effect does this change have on (a) the average kinetic energy of O_2 molecules; (b) the average speed of O_2 molecules; (c) the total number of collisions of O_2 molecules with the container walls in a unit time; (d) the number of collisions of O_2 molecules with a unit area of container wall in a unit time?

SOLUTION (a) The average kinetic energy of the O_2 molecules is determined only by temperature. The average kinetic energy is not changed by the compression of O_2 from 2 L to 1 L at constant temperature. (b) If the average kinetic energy of O_2 molecules doesn't change, the average speed remains constant. (c) The total number of collisions with the container walls in a unit time must increase, because the molecules are moving within a smaller volume but with the same average speed as before. Under these conditions they must encounter a wall more frequently. **(d)** The number of collisions with a unit area of wall increases because the total number of collisions with the walls is higher and the area of wall is smaller than before.

PRACTICE EXERCISE
How is the rms speed of N_2 molecules in a gas sample changed by **(a)** an increase in temperature; **(b)** an increase in volume of sample; **(c)** mixing with a sample of Ar at the same temperature? *Answers:* **(a)** increases; **(b)** no effect; **(c)** no effect

10.9 Molecular Effusion and Diffusion

According to the kinetic-molecular theory, the average kinetic energy of *any* collection of gas molecules, $\frac{1}{2}mu^2$, has a specific value for a given temperature of the gas. Thus, a gas composed of light particles, such as He, will have the same average kinetic energy as one composed of much heavier particles, such as Xe, provided the two gases are at the same temperature. The mass, m, of the particles in the lighter gas is smaller than that in the heavier gas. Consequently, the particles of the lighter gas must have a higher rms speed, u, than the heavier one. An equation that expresses this fact quantitatively can be derived from the theory:

$$u = \sqrt{\frac{3RT}{M}} \qquad [10.23]$$

Teaching Note: For *all* gases at the same temperature, the average kinetic energies are identical.

Teaching Note: At a fixed temperature, the average speed of a lighter gas is greater than that of a heavier gas.

Notice that the molar mass, M, appears in the denominator. Thus, the less massive the gas molecules, the higher the rms speed, u. Figure 10.14 shows the distribution of molecular speeds for several different gases at 25°C. Notice how the distributions are shifted toward higher speeds for gases of lower molar masses.

SAMPLE EXERCISE 10.13
Calculate the rms speed, u, of a N_2 molecule at 25°C.

SOLUTION In using Equation 10.23, we should convert each quantity to SI units so that all the units are compatible:

$T = 25 + 273 = 298$ K

$M = 28.0$ g/mol $= 28.0 \times 10^{-3}$ kg/mol

$R = 8.314$ J/mol-K $= 8.314$ kg-m^2/s^2-mol-K   (These units follow from the fact that 1 J $= 1$ kg-m^2/s^2)

$$u = \sqrt{\frac{3(8.314 \text{ kg-m}^2/\text{s}^2\text{-mol-K})(298 \text{ K})}{28.0 \times 10^{-3} \text{ kg/mol}}} = 5.15 \times 10^2 \text{ m/s}$$

This corresponds to a speed of 1150 mi/hr.

PRACTICE EXERCISE
What is the rms speed of a He atom at 25°C?   *Answer:* 1.36×10^3 m/s

The dependence of molecular speeds on mass has several interesting consequences, two of which we will consider here. The first phenomenon is called **effusion,** which is the escape of gas molecules through a tiny hole such as a pinhole in a balloon. The rate of effusion depends on the molecular mass of the

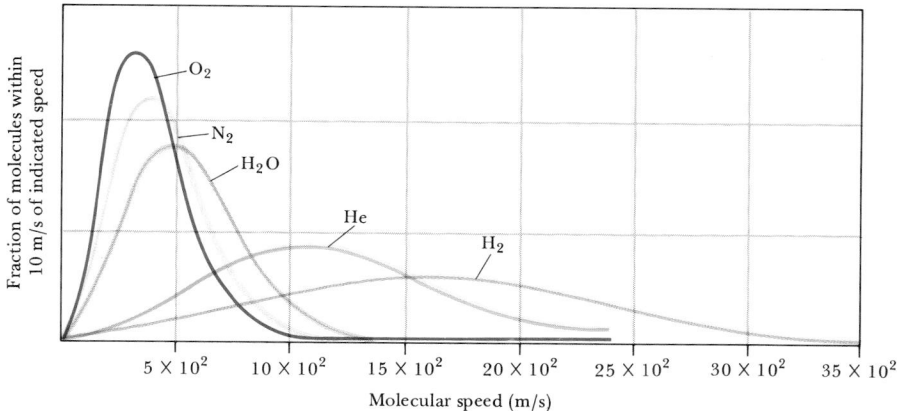

Figure 10.14

gas (Figure 10.15). The second is **diffusion,** which is the spread of one substance throughout a space or throughout a second substance. For example, the molecules of a perfume diffuse through a room.

Graham's Law of Effusion

In about 1830, Thomas Graham discovered that the effusion rate of a gas is inversely proportional to the square root of its molar mass. Assume that we have two gases at the same initial pressure contained in identical containers, each with an identical pinhole in one wall. Let the rate of effusion be called r. **Graham's law** states that

$$\frac{r_1}{r_2} = \sqrt{\frac{\mathcal{M}_2}{\mathcal{M}_1}}$$ [10.24]

Equation 10.24 compares the *rates* of effusion of two different gases; the lighter gas effuses more rapidly.

Common Misconception: *Effusion* and *diffusion* are very commonly confused. *Effusion* is the leakage of a gas through a small aperture. *Diffusion* is the spread of a gas throughout open space.

Learning Goal 10: Describe how the relative rates of effusion and diffusion of two gases depend on their molar masses (Graham's law).

(a)

(b)

FIGURE 10.15 Light atoms or molecules effuse through the pores of a balloon faster than heavy atoms or molecules. (*a*) Two balloons are filled to the same volume, one with helium and the other with nitrogen. (*b*) After 48 hr, the helium-filled balloon is smaller than the nitrogen-filled one; helium effuses out of the balloon faster than nitrogen. (Richard Megna/Fundamental Photographs)

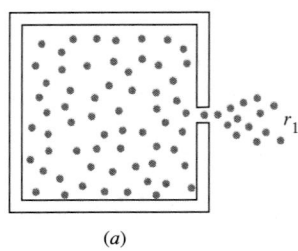

(a)

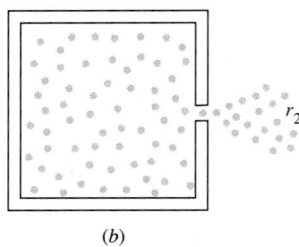

(b)

FIGURE 10.16 Effusion of gases through a pinhole. In this illustration the molar mass of gas molecules in (*a*) is higher than in (*b*). The rate of effusion, r_1, from box (*a*), is slower than r_2, from box (*b*), in accordance with Equation 10.24.

Figure 10.16

FIGURE 10.17 Schematic illustration of the diffusion of a gas molecule. For clarity, no other gas molecules in the container are shown. The path of the molecule of interest begins at the dot. Each short segment of line represents travel between collisions. The red arrow indicates the net distance traveled by the molecule.

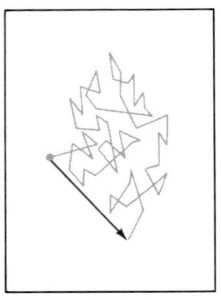

Figure 10.16 helps us understand the basis of Graham's law. The only way for a molecule to escape one of the boxes is for it to "collide" with the pinhole. The number of such collisions will increase as the speed of the gas molecules increases; the faster the molecules are moving, the greater the likelihood that a molecule will hit the pinhole and effuse. In fact, the rate of effusion is directly proportional to the rms speed of the molecules. Because R and T are constant, we have from Equation 10.23:

$$\frac{r_1}{r_2} = \frac{u_1}{u_2} = \sqrt{\frac{3RT/\mathcal{M}_1}{3RT/\mathcal{M}_2}} = \sqrt{\frac{\mathcal{M}_2}{\mathcal{M}_1}} \qquad [10.25]$$

SAMPLE EXERCISE 10.14

An unknown gas composed of homonuclear diatomic molecules effuses at a rate that is only 0.355 times that of O_2 at the same temperature. What is the identity of the unknown gas?

SOLUTION We can use Graham's law of effusion, Equation 10.24, to determine the molar mass of the unknown gas. If we let r_x and M_x represent the rate of effusion and molar mass of the unknown gas, Equation 10.24 gives

$$\frac{r_x}{r_{O_2}} = \sqrt{\frac{\mathcal{M}_{O_2}}{\mathcal{M}_x}}$$

Thus

$$\frac{r_x}{r_{O_2}} = 0.355 = \sqrt{\frac{32.0\ \text{g/mol}}{M_x}}$$

We now solve for the unknown molar mass, M_x:

$$\frac{32.0\ \text{g/mol}}{M_x} = (0.355)^2 = 0.126$$

$$M_x = \frac{32.0\ \text{g/mol}}{0.126} = 254\ \text{g/mol}$$

Because we are told that the unknown gas is composed of homonuclear diatomic molecules, this molar mass must represent twice the atomic weight of the atoms in the unknown gas. We conclude that the unknown gas is I_2.

PRACTICE EXERCISE

Calculate the ratio of the effusion rates of N_2 and O_2, r_{N_2}/r_{O_2}. *Answer:* $r_{N_2}/r_{O_2} = 1.07$

Diffusion and Mean Free Path

Diffusion, like effusion, is faster for light molecules than for heavy ones. In fact, the relative rates of diffusion of two gases under identical experimental conditions is also given by Equation 10.24. The ratio of the rates is inversely proportional to the square root of the ratio of the molar masses. Nevertheless, molecular collisions make diffusion more complicated than effusion.

We can see from the horizontal scale in Figure 10.13 that the speeds of molecules are quite high. The average speed of N_2 at room temperature is 515 m/s (1150 mi/hr). Yet we know that if someone opens a vial of perfume at one end of a room, some time elapses, perhaps a few minutes, before the odor is detected at the other end. The diffusion of gases is much slower than molecular speeds because of molecular collisions. These collisions occur quite frequently for a gas at atmospheric pressure—about 10^{10} times per second for each molecule. Because of these collisions, the direction of motion of a gas molecule is

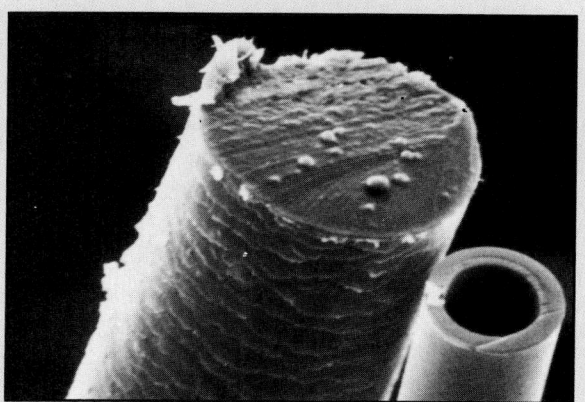
Gas Separations

The fact that lighter molecules move at higher average speeds than heavier ones has many interesting consequences and applications. To use one dramatic example, the effort to develop the atomic bomb during World War II required scientists to separate the relatively low-abundance uranium isotope ^{235}U (0.7 percent) from the much more abundant ^{238}U (99.3 percent). This task was accomplished by converting the uranium into a volatile compound, UF_6, which boils at 56°C. The gaseous UF_6 was allowed to pass through porous barriers. The slight difference in molar mass between the compounds of the two isotopes caused the molecules to move at slightly different rates:

$$\frac{r_{235}}{r_{238}} = \sqrt{\frac{352.04}{349.03}} = 1.0043$$

Thus, the gas initially appearing on the opposite side of the barrier was very slightly enriched in the lighter molecule. The diffusion process was repeated thousands of times, leading to a nearly complete separation of the two nuclides of uranium.

The rate of diffusion of a gas through a porous medium is not always determined solely by the molecular mass of the gas molecules. Even weak interactions between the molecules of gas and the molecules of the porous medium will affect the rate. Attractive intermolecular interactions, which we will discuss in more detail in the next chapter, slow the rate at which a gas molecule passes through the narrow passages of the porous medium.

The medium's molecules may attract one substance in a mixture more than another. Thus, the rates of diffusion of a mixture's components through a medium are not uniform. Dow Chemical Company has recently developed a method of separating gaseous mixtures into their components by using the difference in the rate at which molecules pass through a porous membrane. Figure 10.18 shows Dow's tiny hollow fiber made of polyolefin, an organic polymer (see Chapter 12). The fiber is smaller than a human hair. Its walls are permeable to the passage of N_2 and O_2. However, O_2 and water vapor diffuse through the fiber walls considerably more readily than does N_2. To take advantage of this property, thousands of the fibers are formed into bundles. Compressed air is introduced around the outside of the bundles. The gas stream taken from inside the fibers is selectively enriched in O_2. The gas stream on the outside of the fibers is correspondingly enriched in N_2.

FIGURE 10.18 Polyolefin fibers used to carry out gas separations. The solid cylinder is a human hair. Gases such as nitrogen and oxygen differ significantly in the rate at which they pass through the wall of the hollow fiber. This difference in permeability provides the basis for gas separations. (Dow Chemical Company)

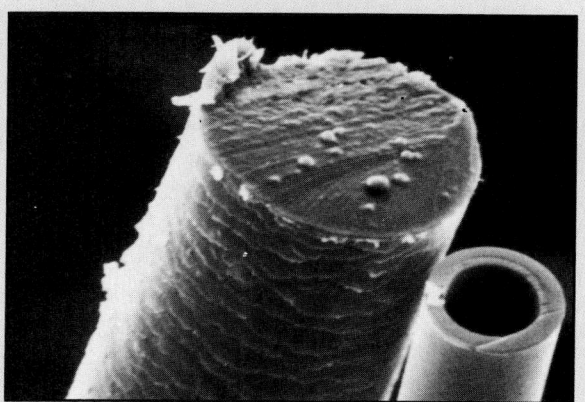

constantly changing. Therefore, the diffusion of a molecule from one point to another consists of many short, straight-line segments as collisions buffet it around in random directions, as depicted in Figure 10.17. First the molecule moves in one direction, then in another, at one instant at high speed, next at low speed.

The average distance traveled by a molecule between collisions is called the **mean free path.** The higher the density of a gas, the smaller the mean free path. That is, the more molecules there are in a given volume, the shorter the average distance traveled between collisions. The mean free path for air molecules at sea level is about 60 nm (6×10^{-6} cm). At about 100 km in altitude, where the air density is much lower, the mean free path is about 10 cm, about 1 million times longer than at the earth's surface.

Analogy: Imagine walking through a shopping mall. When the mall is very crowded (high pressure), the average distance you can walk before bumping into someone else is short (short mean free path). When the mall is empty (low pressure), you can walk a long way (long mean free path) before bumping into someone else.

10.10 Deviations from Ideal Behavior

Although the ideal-gas equation is a very useful description of gases, all real gases fail to obey the relationship to some degree. The extent to which a real gas departs from ideal behavior may be seen by slightly rearranging the ideal-gas equation:

$$\frac{PV}{RT} = n \qquad\qquad [10.26]$$

Learning Goal 11: Explain the origin of deviations shown by real gases from the relationship $PV/RT = 1$ for a mole of an ideal gas.

Learning Goal 12: Cite the general conditions of P and T under which real gases most closely approximate ideal-gas behavior.

For a mole of ideal gas ($n = 1$), the quantity PV/RT equals 1 at all pressures. In Figure 10.19, PV/RT is plotted as a function of P for 1 mol of several different gases. At high pressures, the deviation from ideal behavior ($PV/RT = 1$) is large and is different for each gas. Clearly, real gases do not behave ideally at high pressure. At lower pressures (usually below 10 atm), however, the deviations from ideal behavior are small, and we can use the ideal-gas equation without generating serious error.

The deviation from ideal behavior also depends on temperature. Figure 10.20 shows graphs of PV/RT vs. P for 1 mol of N_2 at three different temperatures. As temperature increases, the properties of the gas more nearly approach that of the ideal gas. In general, the deviations from ideal behavior increase as temperature decreases, becoming significant near the temperature at which the gas is converted into a liquid.

The basic assumptions of the kinetic-molecular theory give us insight into why real gases deviate from ideal behavior. The molecules of an ideal gas are assumed to occupy no space and have no attractions for one another. *Real molecules, however, do have finite volumes, and they do attract one another.* As shown in Figure 10.21, the free, unoccupied space in which molecules can

FIGURE 10.19 *PV/RT* versus pressure for 1 mol of several gases at 300 K. The data for CO_2 pertain to a temperature of 313 K because CO_2 liquefies under high pressure at 300 K.

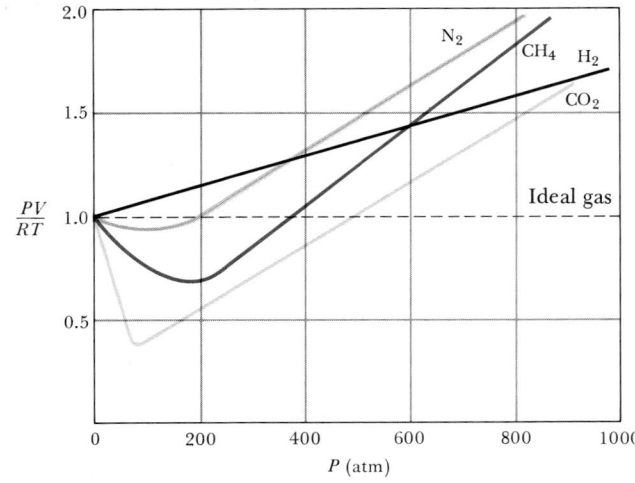

FIGURE 10.20 *PV/RT* versus pressure for 1 mol of nitrogen gas at three different temperatures. As temperature increases, the gas more closely approaches ideal behavior.

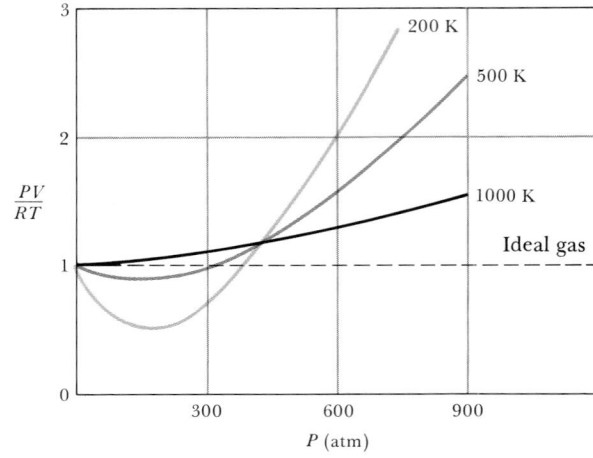

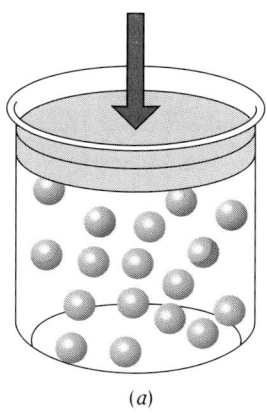
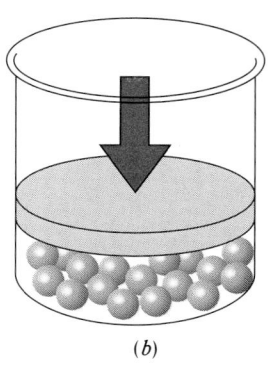

(a)   (b)

FIGURE 10.21 Illustration of the effect of the finite volume of gas molecules on the properties of a real gas at high pressure. In (a), at low pressure, the volume of the gas molecules is small compared with the container volume. In (b), at high pressure, the volume of the gas molecules themselves is a large fraction of the total space available.

move is somewhat less than the container volume. At relatively low pressures, the volume of the gas molecules is negligible compared to the container volume. Thus, the free volume available to the molecules is essentially the entire volume of the container. As the pressure increases, however, the free space in which the molecules can move becomes a smaller fraction of the container volume.

In addition, the attractive forces between molecules come into play at short distances, as when molecules are crowded together at high pressures. Because of these attractive forces, the impact of a given molecule with the wall of the container is lessened. If we could stop the action in a gas, the position of the molecules might resemble the illustration in Figure 10.22. The molecule about to make contact with the wall experiences the attractive forces of nearby molecules. These attractions lessen the force with which the molecule hits the wall. As a result, the pressure is less than that of an ideal gas. This effect serves to decrease PV/RT, as seen in Figure 10.19. When the pressure is sufficiently high, the volume effects discussed above dominate, and PV/RT increases.

Temperature determines how effective attractive forces between gas molecules are. As the gas is cooled, the average kinetic energy decreases, while intermolecular attractions remain constant. In a sense, cooling a gas deprives molecules of the energy they need to overcome their mutual attractive influence. The effects of temperature shown earlier in Figure 10.20 illustrate this point very well. Notice that as temperature increases, the negative departure of PV/RT from ideal-gas behavior disappears. The difference that remains at high temperature stems mainly from the effect of the finite volumes of the molecules.

Point of Emphasis: Gases deviate from ideality at *high* pressures.

Point of Emphasis: Gases deviate from ideality at *low* temperatures.

The van der Waals Equation

Engineers and scientists who work with gases at high pressures often cannot use the ideal-gas equation to predict the pressure-volume properties of gases because departures from ideal behavior are too large. One of the earliest and most useful equations developed to predict the behavior of real gases was proposed by the Dutch scientist Johannes van der Waals (1837–1923).

The ideal-gas equation predicts that the pressure of a gas is

$$P = \frac{nRT}{V} \qquad \text{(ideal gas)}$$

FIGURE 10.22 Effect of attractive intermolecular forces on the pressure exerted by a gas on its container walls. The molecule that is about to strike the wall in the figure experiences attractive forces from nearby molecules, and its impact on the wall is thereby lessened. The attractive forces become significant only under high-pressure conditions, when the average distance between molecules is small.

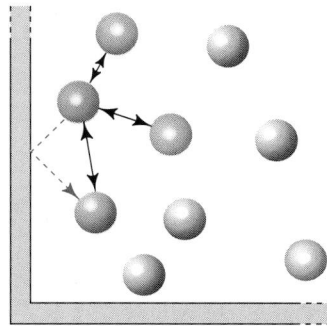

Van der Waals recognized that, for a real gas, this expression would have to be corrected for the two effects we discussed above: the finite volume occupied by the gas molecules, and the attractive forces between the gas molecules. He introduced two constants, a and b, to make these corrections:

$$P = \underbrace{\frac{nRT}{V - nb}}_{\substack{\text{Correction for} \\ \text{volume of molecules}}} - \underbrace{\frac{n^2a}{V^2}}_{\substack{\text{Correction for} \\ \text{molecular attractions}}} \qquad [10.27]$$

Learning Goal 13: Explain the origins of the correction terms to P and V that appear in the van der Waals equation.

The volume is decreased by the factor nb, which accounts for the finite volume occupied by the gas molecules (Figure 10.21). The van der Waals constant b is a measure of the actual volume occupied by a mole of gas molecules; b has units of L/mol. The pressure is in turn decreased by the factor n^2a/V^2, which accounts for the attractive forces between the gas molecules (Figure 10.22). The unusual form of this correction results because the attractive forces between pairs of molecules increase as the square of the number of molecules per unit volume, $(n/V)^2$. Hence the van der Waals constant a has units of L^2-atm/mol^2. The magnitude of a reflects how strongly the gas molecules attract each other.

Equation 10.27 is generally rearranged to give the usual form of the **van der Waals equation:**

$$\left(P + \frac{n^2a}{V^2} \right)(V - nb) = nRT \qquad [10.28]$$

The van der Waals constants a and b are different for each gas. Values of these constants for several gases are listed in Table 10.3. Note that the values of both a and b generally increase with an increase in mass of the molecule and with an increase in the complexity of its structure.

TABLE 10.3 △ Van der Waals Constants for Gas Molecules

Substance	a (L^2-atm/mol^2)	b (L/mol)
He	0.0341	0.02370
Ne	0.211	0.0171
Ar	1.34	0.0322
Kr	2.32	0.0398
Xe	4.19	0.0510
H_2	0.244	0.0266
N_2	1.39	0.0391
O_2	1.36	0.0318
Cl_2	6.49	0.0562
H_2O	5.46	0.0305
CH_4	2.25	0.0428
CO_2	3.59	0.0427
CCl_4	20.4	0.1383

SAMPLE EXERCISE 10.15

If 1.000 mol of an ideal gas were confined to 22.41 L at 0.0°C, it would exert a pressure of 1.000 atm. Use the van der Waals equation and the constants in Table 10.3 to estimate the pressure exerted by 1.000 mol of $Cl_2(g)$ in 22.41 L at 0.0°C.

SOLUTION Using Equation 10.27, we have

$$P = \frac{nRT}{V - nb} - \frac{n^2a}{V^2}$$

Substituting $n = 1.000$ mol, $R = 0.08206$ L-atm/mol-K, $T = 273.2$ K, $V = 22.41$ L, $a = 6.49$ L^2 atm/mol², and $b = 0.0562$ L/mol:

$$P = \frac{(1.000 \text{ mol})(0.08206 \text{ L-atm/mol-K})(273.2 \text{ K})}{22.41 \text{ L} - (1.000 \text{ Mol})(0.0562 \text{ L/mol})}$$
$$- \frac{(1.000 \text{ mol})^2(6.49 \text{ L}^2\text{-atm/mol}^2)}{(22.41 \text{ L})^2}$$
$$= 1.003 \text{ atm} - 0.013 \text{ atm} = 0.990 \text{ atm}$$

Notice that 1.003 atm is the pressure corrected for molecular volume. This value is higher than the ideal value, 1.000 atm, because the volume in which the molecules are free to move is smaller than the container volume, 22.41 L. Thus, the molecules must collide more frequently with the container walls. The second factor, 0.013 atm, corrects for intermolecular forces. The intermolecular attractions between molecules reduce the pressure to 0.990 atm. We can conclude, therefore, that the intermolecular attractions are the main cause of the slight deviation of $Cl_2(g)$ from ideal behavior under the stated experimental conditions.

PRACTICE EXERCISE

Consider a sample of 1.000 mol of $CO_2(g)$ confined to a volume of 3.000 L at 0.0°C. Calculate the pressure of the gas using **(a)** the ideal-gas equation, and **(b)** the van der Waals equation. *Answer:* **(a)** 7.473 atm; **(b)** 7.182 atm

For Review

Summary

To describe the state or condition of a gas, we must specify four variables: pressure, temperature, volume, and quantity of gas. Volume is usually measured in liters (L), and temperature in kelvins. Pressure is defined as the force per unit area. It is expressed in SI units as pascals, Pa (1 Pa = 1 N/m² = 1 kg/m-s²), or more commonly in torr or in atmospheres (atm). One atmosphere pressure equals 101.325 kPa, or 760 torr. A barometer is often used to measure the atmospheric pressure. A manometer can be used to measure the pressure of enclosed gases.

The ideal-gas equation, $PV = nRT$, is the equation of state for an ideal gas. Most gases at pressures of about 1 atm and temperatures of 300 K and above obey the ideal-gas equation reasonably well. We can use the ideal-gas equation to calculate variations in one variable when one or more of the others are changed. For example, for a constant quantity of gas at constant temperature, the volume of the gas is inversely proportional to the pressure (Boyle's law). Similarly, for a constant quantity of gas at constant pressure, the volume of a gas is directly proportional to temperature (Charles's law). Avogadro's law states that at constant temperature and pressure the volume of a gas is directly proportional to the quantity of gas, that is, to the number of gas molecules. In gas mixtures, the total pressure is the sum of the partial pressures that each gas would exert if it were present alone under the same conditions (Dalton's law of partial pressures). In all applications of the ideal-gas equation we must remember to convert temperatures to the absolute-temperature scale, the Kelvin scale.

Using the ideal-gas equation, we can relate the density of a gas to its molar mass: $\mathcal{M} = dRT/P$. We can also use the ideal-gas equation to solve problems involving gases as reactants or products in chemical reactions. We saw that in calculating the quantity of gas collected over water, correction must be made for the partial pressure of water vapor in the container.

The kinetic-molecular theory accounts for the properties of an ideal gas in terms of a set of assumptions about the nature of gases. Briefly, these assumptions are that molecules are in continuous chaotic motion; that the volume of gas molecules is negligible in relation to the volume of their container; that the gas molecules have no attractive forces for one another; and that the average kinetic energy of the gas molecules is proportional to absolute temperature.

The molecules of a gas do not all have the same kinetic energy at a given instant. Their speeds are distributed over a wide range; the distribution varies with the molar mass of the gas and with temperature.

The root-mean-square (rms) speed, u, varies in proportion to the square root of absolute temperature and inversely with the square root of molar mass: $u = (3RT/\mathcal{M})^{1/2}$. It follows that the rate at which a gas escapes (effuses) through a tiny hole is inversely proportional to the square root of its molar mass (Graham's law). Because molecules undergo frequent collisions with one another, the mean free path—the mean distance traveled between collisions—is short. Collisions between molecules limit the rate at which a gas molecule can diffuse through the space occupied by other gas molecules.

Departures from ideal behavior increase in magnitude as pressure increases and as temperature decreases. The extent of nonideality of a real gas can be seen by examining the quantity PV/RT for 1 mol of the gas as a function of pressure; for an ideal gas this quantity is exactly 1 at all pressures. Real gases depart from ideal behavior because the molecules possess finite volume and because the molecules experience attractive forces for one another upon collision. The van der Waals equation is an equation of state for gases that modifies the ideal-gas equation to represent more faithfully the pressure and volume behavior of real gases.

Key Terms

vapors (Sec. 10.1)
pressure (Sec. 10.2)
pascal (Sec. 10.2)
standard atmospheric pressure (Sec. 10.2)
atmosphere (Sec. 10.2)
torr (Sec. 10.2)
Boyle's law (Sec. 10.3)
Charles's law (Sec. 10.3)
Avogadro's hypothesis (Sec. 10.3)
Avogadro's law (Sec. 10.3)
ideal-gas equation (Sec. 10.4)
ideal gas (Sec. 10.4)

gas constant (Sec. 10.4)
standard temperature and pressure (STP) (Sec. 10.4)
partial pressure (Sec. 10.6)
Dalton's law of partial pressures (Sec. 10.6)
mole fraction (Sec. 10.6)
kinetic-molecular theory (Sec. 10.8)
root-mean-square (rms) speed (Sec. 10.8)
effusion (Sec. 10.9)
diffusion (Sec. 10.9)
Graham's law (Sec. 10.9)
mean free path (Sec. 10.9)
van der Waals equation (Sec. 10.10)

Exercises

Gas Characteristics; Pressure

10.1. Elemental chlorine, Cl_2, is a gas at room temperature and 1 atm pressure, whereas bromine, Br_2, is a liquid. The density of Cl_2 under these conditions is 2.90 g/L, whereas that of Br_2 is 3.19 g/cm³. Explain on a molecular basis why these two elements differ so greatly in density.

10.2. Although water and carbon tetrachloride, $CCl_4(l)$, do not mix, their vapors form homogeneous mixtures. Explain.

10.3. Consider two people of the same mass standing in a room. One person is standing normally, and the other is standing on one foot. **(a)** Does one person exert a greater force on the floor than the other? **(b)** Does one person exert a greater pressure on the floor than the other?

10.4. Explain why the height of mercury in a mercury barometer is independent of the diameter of the mercury column.

10.5. **(a)** How high must a column of water be to exert a pressure equal to that of a column of mercury that is 760 mm high? **(b)** What is the pressure on the body of a diver if he is 25 ft below the surface of the water?

10.6. Dibutylphthalate is a nonvolatile liquid with a density of 1.05 g/mL. The density of mercury is 13.6 g/mL. Assuming that the maximum atmospheric pressure is 760 torr, what would be the minimum height of a barometer based on dibutylphthalate?

10.7. Perform the following conversions: **(a)** 0.660 atm to kilopascals; **(b)** 347 torr to atmospheres; **(c)** 825 mm Hg to atmospheres; **(d)** 0.917 atm to torr.

10.8. Perform the following conversions: **(a)** 98,200 Pa to atmospheres; **(b)** 1.43 atm to mm Hg; **(c)** 659 mm Hg to torr; **(d)** 1.00×10^3 torr to atmospheres.

10.9. In the United States, barometric pressures are reported in inches of mercury (in. Hg). On a beautiful summer day in Chicago, the barometric pressure is 30.45 in. Hg. **(a)** Convert this pressure to torr. **(b)** A meteorologist explains the nice weather by referring to a "high-pressure area." In light of your answer to part (a), explain why this term makes sense.

10.10. **(a)** On Titan, the largest moon of Saturn, the atmospheric pressure is 1.6 earth atmospheres. What is the atmospheric pressure of Titan in kilopascals? **(b)** On Venus the surface atmospheric pressure is about 90 earth atmospheres. What is the Venusian atmospheric pressure in kilopascals?

10.11. Suppose that a woman weighing 130 lb and wearing high-heeled shoes momentarily places all her weight on the heel of one foot. If the area of the heel is 0.50 in.^{2}, calculate the pressure exerted on the underlying surface in kilopascals.

10.12. An aluminum cube with edges 20.0 cm in length rests on a flat surface. The density of aluminum is 2.70 g/cm^3. Calculate the pressure in pascals exerted by the cube on the surface.

10.13. **(a)** Is it necessary to know the atmospheric pressure to use a closed-end manometer such as that in Figure 10.3(a)? Explain. **(b)** Is it necessary to know the barometric pressure to use an open-end manometer such as that in Figure 10.3(b)? Explain.

10.14. An open-end manometer containing mercury is connected to a container of gas. What is the pressure of the enclosed gas in torr in each of the following situations? **(a)** The mercury in the arm attached to the gas is 27 mm lower than in the one open to the atmosphere; atmospheric pressure is 0.981 atm. **(b)** The mercury in the arm attached to the gas is 5.6 cm higher than in the one open to the atmosphere; atmospheric pressure is 1.03 atm.

The Gas Laws; The Ideal-Gas Equation

10.15. **(a)** What do we mean when we say two quantities are directly proportional? Inversely proportional? **(b)** Is volume of a gas directly or inversely proportional to pressure? To absolute temperature? To the quantity of gas?

10.16. Write an equation or proportionality expression that expresses each of the following statements: **(a)** For a given quantity of gas at constant temperature, the product of pressure and volume is constant. **(b)** For a given temperature and pressure, the volume of a gas is proportional to the number of moles of gas present. **(c)** For a given volume and quantity of gas, the pressure is proportional to the absolute temperature. **(d)** For a given quantity of gas, the product of pressure and volume is proportional to absolute temperature.

10.17. A fixed quantity of gas at a constant temperature exhibits a pressure of 715 torr and occupies a volume of 10.7 L. Use Boyle's law to calculate the following: **(a)** the volume the gas will occupy if the pressure is increased to 1.40 atm; **(b)** the pressure of the gas if the volume is increased to 15.5 L.

10.18. A fixed quantity of gas at a constant pressure occupies a volume of 6.75 L at a temperature of 31.0°C. Use Charles's law to calculate the following: **(a)** the volume the gas will occupy if the temperature is increased to 125°C; **(b)** the temperature in degrees Celsius at which the volume of the gas will be 5.00 L.

10.19. **(a)** How is the law of combining volumes explained by Avogadro's hypothesis? **(b)** Consider a 1.0-L flask containing neon gas and a 1.5-L flask containing xenon gas. Both gases are at the same pressure and temperature. According to Avogadro's law, what can be said about the ratio of the number of atoms in the two flasks?

10.20. Nitrogen and hydrogen gases react to form ammonia gas:

$$N_2(g) + 3H_2(g) \longrightarrow 2NH_3(g)$$

At a certain temperature and pressure, 0.70 L of N_2 reacts with 2.1 L of H_2. If all the N_2 and H_2 are consumed, what volume of NH_3, at the same temperature and pressure, will be produced?

10.21. **(a)** What is an ideal gas? **(b)** Write the ideal-gas equation and give the units used for each term in the equation when $R = 0.0821$ L-atm/mol-K.

10.22. **(a)** What conditions are represented by the abbreviation STP? **(b)** What is the molar volume of an ideal gas at STP? **(c)** Room temperature is often assumed to be 25°C. Calculate the molar volume of an ideal gas at room temperature.

10.23. Calculate each of the following quantities for an ideal gas: **(a)** the pressure, in atmospheres, if 2.59×10^{-2} mol occupies 121 mL at −15°C; **(b)** the quantity of gas, in moles, if 4.65 L at 35°C has a pressure of 1150 torr; **(c)** the volume of the gas, in liters, if 1.76 mol has a pressure of 0.76 atm at a temperature of 47°C; **(d)** the absolute temperature of the gas at which 9.87×10^{-2} mol occupies 164 mL at 722 torr.

10.24. For an ideal gas, calculate the following quantities: **(a)** the pressure of the gas if 1.04 mol occupies 21.8 L at 25°C; **(b)** the volume occupied by 6.72×10^{-3} mol at 265°C and a pressure of 23.0 torr; **(c)** the number of moles in 1.50 L at 37°C and 725 torr; **(d)** the temperature at which 0.270 mol occupies 15.0 L at 2.54 atm.

10.25. A deep breath of air has a volume of 1.05 L at a pressure of 740 torr and body temperature, 37°C. Calculate the number of molecules in the breath.

10.26. A neon sign is made of glass tubing whose inside diameter is 2.0 cm and whose length is 4.0 m. If the sign contains neon at a pressure of 1.5 torr at 35°C, how many grams of neon are in the sign? (The volume of a cylinder is $\pi r^2 h$.)

10.27. At 36°C and 1.00 atm pressure, a gas occupies a volume of 0.600 L. How many liters will it occupy **(a)** at 0°C and 0.205 atm; **(b)** at STP?

10.28. Chlorine is widely used to purify municipal water supplies and to treat swimming pool waters. Suppose that the volume of a particular sample of Cl_2 is 6.18 L at 740 torr and 33°C **(a)** What volume will the Cl_2 occupy at 107°C and 680 torr? **(b)** What volume will the Cl_2 occupy at STP? **(c)** At what temperature will the volume be 3.00 L if the pressure is 8.00×10^2 torr? **(d)** At what pressure will the volume be 5.00 L if the temperature is 67°C?

10.29. Many gases are shipped in high-pressure containers. Consider a steel tank whose volume is 42.0 L and which contains O_2 gas at a pressure of 18,000 kPa at 23°C. **(a)** What mass of O_2 does it contain? **(b)** What volume would the gas occupy at STP?

10.30. Fluorine gas, which is dangerously reactive, is shipped in stainless steel cylinders of 30.0-L capacity at a pressure of 160 lb/in.^{2} at 26°C. **(a)** What mass of F_2 is contained in a cylinder? **(b)** What volume would the gas occupy at STP?

10.31. In an experiment recently reported in the scientific literature, male cockroaches were made to run at different speeds on a miniature treadmill while their oxygen consumption was measured. The average cockroach running at 0.08 km/hr consumed 0.8 mL of O_2 at 1 atm pressure and 24°C per gram of insect weight per hour. **(a)** How many moles of O_2 would be consumed in 1 hr by a 5.2-g cockroach moving at this speed? **(b)** This same cockroach is caught by a child and placed in a 1-qt fruit jar with a tight lid. Assuming the same level of continuous activity as in the research, will the cockroach consume more than 20 percent of the available O_2 in a 48-hr period? (Air is 21 mol percent O_2.)

10.32. After the large eruption of Mount St. Helens in 1980, gas samples from the volcano were taken by sampling the downwind gas plume. The unfiltered gas samples were passed over a gold-coated wire coil to absorb mercury (Hg) present in the gas. The mercury was recovered from the coil by heating it, and then analyzed. In one particular set of experiments, scientists found a mercury vapor level of 1800 ng of Hg per cubic meter in the plume, at a gas temperature of 10°C. Calculate **(a)** the partial pressure of Hg vapor in the plume; **(b)** the number of Hg atoms per cubic meter in the gas; **(c)** the total mass of Hg emitted per day by the volcano if the daily plume volume was 1600 km^3.

Density and Molar Mass

10.33. **(a)** Calculate the density of NO_2 gas at 1.00 atm and 35°C. **(b)** Calculate the molar mass of a gas if 4.40 g occupies 3.50 L at 560 torr and 41°C.

10.34. **(a)** Calculate the density of sulfur tetrafluoride vapor at 600 torr and 100°C. **(b)** Calculate the molar mass of a gas if it has a density of 3.67 g/L at 15°C and 825 torr.

10.35. Cyanogen, a highly toxic gas, is composed of 46.2 percent C and 53.8 percent N by mass. At 25°C and 750 torr, 1.05 g of cyanogen occupies 0.500 L. What is the molecular formula of cyanogen?

10.36. Cyclopropane, a gas used with oxygen as a general anesthetic, is composed of 85.7 percent C and 14.3 percent H by mass. If 1.56 g of cyclopropane has a volume of 1.00 L at 0.984 atm and 50.0°C, what is the molecular formula of cyclopropane?

10.37. In the Dumas-bulb technique for determining the molar mass of an unknown liquid, you vaporize the sample of a liquid that boils below 100°C in a boiling-water bath and determine the mass of vapor required to fill the bulb (see Figure 10.23). From the following data, calculate the molar mass of the unknown liquid: mass of unknown

vapor, 1.012 g; volume of bulb, 354 cm^3; pressure, 742 torr; temperature, 99°C.

FIGURE 10.23

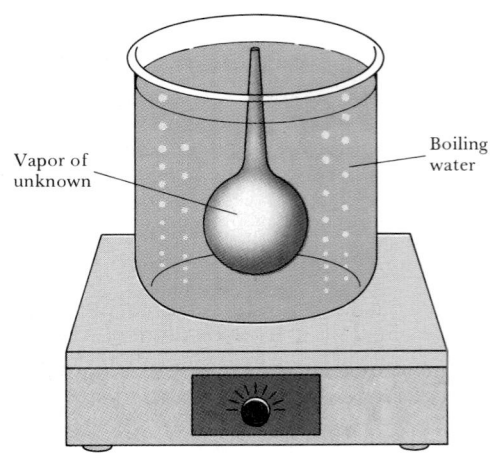

Vapor of unknown

Boiling water

10.38. The molar mass of a volatile substance was determined by the Dumas bulb method described in Exercise 10.37. The unknown vapor had a mass of 0.846 g; the volume of the bulb was 354 cm³, pressure 752 torr, temperature 100°C. Calculate the molar mass of the unknown vapor.

Partial Pressures

10.39. (a) Define the term *partial pressure*. (b) State Dalton's law of partial pressures.

10.40. Can the partial pressures of the components of an enclosed mixture of gases be measured with a manometer? If not, how are the partial pressures determined?

10.41. A mixture containing 0.432 mol He(g), 0.357 mol Ne(g), and 0.103 mol Ar(g) is confined in a 7.00-L vessel at 25°C. (a) Calculate the partial pressure of each of the gases in the mixture. (b) Calculate the total pressure of the mixture.

10.42. A mixture containing 5.00 g each of $CH_4(g)$, $C_2H_4(g)$, and $C_4H_{10}(g)$ is contained in a 1.50-L flask at a temperature of 0°C. (a) Calculate the partial pressure of each of the gases in the mixture. (b) Calculate the total pressure of the mixture.

10.43. A mixture of gases contains 0.45 mol N_2, 0.25 mol O_2, and 0.10 mol CO_2. If the total pressure of the mixture is 1.32 atm, what is the partial pressure of each component?

10.44. A mixture of gases contains 3.50 g of N_2, 1.30 g of H_2, and 5.27 g of NH_3. If the total pressure of the mixture is 2.50 atm, what is the partial pressure of each component?

10.45. Consider a mixture of two gases, A and B, confined to a closed vessel. A quantity of a third gas, C, is added to the same vessel at the same temperature. How does the addition of gas C affect the following: (a) the partial pressure of gas A; (b) the total pressure in the vessel; (c) the mole fraction of gas B?

10.46. A 5.00-L vessel contains a mixture of 6.00 g $SO_2(g)$ and 7.50 g $SO_3(g)$ at 18°C. If the vessel is heated to 60°C, calculate the change (if any) in the following quantities: (a) the partial pressure of SO_2; (b) the total pressure of the mixture; (c) the mole fraction of SO_3.

10.47. A quantity of N_2 gas originally held at 4.60 atm pressure in a 1.00-L container at 26°C is transferred to a 10.0-L container at 20°C. A quantity of O_2 gas originally at 3.50 atm and 26°C in a 5.00-L container is transferred to this same container. What is the total pressure in the new container?

10.48. Consider the arrangement of bulbs shown in Figure 10.24. Each of the bulbs contains a gas at the pressure shown. What is the pressure of the system when all the stopcocks are opened, assuming that the temperature remains constant? (We can neglect the volume of the capillary tubing connecting the bulbs.)

FIGURE 10.24

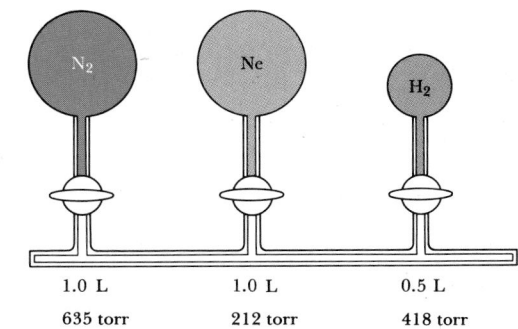

Volume	1.0 L	1.0 L	0.5 L
Pressure	635 torr	212 torr	418 torr

Quantities of Gases in Chemical Reactions

10.49. Calcium hydride, CaH_2, reacts with water to form hydrogen gas:

$$CaH_2(s) + 2H_2O(l) \longrightarrow Ca(OH)_2(aq) + 2H_2(g)$$

This reaction is sometimes used to inflate life rafts, weather balloons, and the like, where a simple, compact means of generating H_2 is desired. How many grams of CaH_2 are needed to generate 10.0 L of H_2 gas if the partial pressure of H_2 is 740 torr at 23°C?

10.50. Magnesium can be used as a "getter" in evacuated enclosures, to react with the last traces of oxygen. (The magnesium is usually heated by passing an electric current through a wire or ribbon of the metal.) If an enclosure of 0.382 L has a partial pressure of O_2 of 3.5×10^{-6} torr at 27°C, what mass of magnesium will react according to the following equation?

$$2Mg(s) + O_2(g) \longrightarrow 2MgO(s)$$

10.51. The metabolic breakdown of glucose, $C_6H_{12}O_6$, in our bodies produces CO_2, which is expelled from our lungs as gas:

$$C_6H_{12}O_6(s) + 6O_2(g) \longrightarrow 6CO_2(g) + 6H_2O(l)$$

Calculate the volume of dry CO_2 produced at body temperature (37°C) and 1.00 atm when 5.00 g of glucose is consumed in this reaction.

10.52. Ammonium sulfate, an important fertilizer, can be prepared by the reaction of ammonia with sulfuric acid:

$$2NH_3(g) + H_2SO_4(aq) \longrightarrow (NH_4)_2SO_4(aq)$$

Calculate the volume of $NH_3(g)$ needed at 20°C and 25.0 atm to react with 150 kg of H_2SO_4.

10.53. Hydrogen gas is produced when zinc reacts with sulfuric acid:

$$Zn(s) + H_2SO_4(aq) \longrightarrow ZnSO_4(aq) + H_2(g)$$

Exercises **367**

If 124 mL of wet H_2 is collected over water at 24°C and a barometric pressure of 725 torr, how many grams of Zn have been consumed? (The vapor pressure of water is tabulated in Appendix B.)

10.54. Small quantities of oxygen gas are sometimes generated in the laboratory by heating $KClO_3$ in the presence of MnO_2 as a catalyst:

$$2KClO_3(s) \longrightarrow 2KCl(s) + 3O_2(g)$$

What volume of O_2 is collected over water at 23°C by reaction of 0.2890 g of $KClO_3$ if the barometric pressure is 742 torr? (The vapor pressure of water is tabulated in Appendix B.)

Kinetic-Molecular Theory; Graham's Law

10.55. Suppose you have two 1-L flasks, one containing N_2 at STP, the other containing SF_6 at STP. How do these systems compare with respect to (a) number of molecules? (b) density? (c) average kinetic energy of the molecules? (d) rate of effusion through a pinhole leak?

10.56. Vessel A contains H_2 gas at 0°C and 1 atm. Vessel B contains O_2 gas at 20°C and 0.5 atm. The two vessels have the same volume. (a) Which vessel contains more molecules? (b) Which contains more mass? (c) In which vessel is the average kinetic energy of molecules higher? (d) In which vessel is the rms speed of molecules higher?

10.57. Indicate which of the following statements regarding the kinetic-molecular theory of gases are correct. For those that are false, formulate a correct version of the statement. (a) The average kinetic energy of a collection of gas molecules at a given temperature is proportional to $\mathcal{M}^{1/2}$. (b) The gas molecules are assumed to exert no forces on each other. (c) All the molecules of a gas at a given temperature have the same kinetic energy. (d) The volume of the gas molecules is negligible in comparison to the total volume in which the gas is contained.

10.58. What change or changes in the state of a gas bring about each of the following effects? (a) The number of impacts per unit time on a given container wall increases. (b) The average energy of impact of molecules with the wall of the container decreases. (c) The average distance between gas molecules increases. (d) The average speed of molecules in the gas mixture is increased.

10.59. (a) Place the following gases in order of increasing average molecular speed at 25°C: CO, SF_6, H_2S, Cl_2, HI. (b) Calculate the rms speed of CO at 25°C.

10.60. (a) Place the following gases in order of increasing average molecular speed at 300 K: CO_2, N_2O, HF, F_2, H_2. (b) Calculate and compare the rms speeds of H_2 and CO_2 at 300 K.

10.61. Hydrogen has two naturally occurring isotopes, ^1H and ^2H. Chlorine also has two naturally occurring isotopes, ^{35}Cl and ^{37}Cl. Thus, hydrogen chloride gas consists of four distinct types of molecules: $^1H^{35}Cl$, $^1H^{37}Cl$, $^2H^{35}Cl$, and $^2H^{37}Cl$. Place these four molecules in order of increasing rate of effusion.

10.62. As discussed in the Chemistry at Work box in Section 10.9, enriched uranium is produced via gaseous diffusion of UF_6. Suppose a process were developed to allow diffusion of gaseous uranium atoms, U(g). Calculate the ratio of diffusion rates for ^{235}U and ^{238}U and compare it to the ratio for UF_6 given in the essay.

10.63. A gas of unknown molecular mass was allowed to effuse through a small opening under constant pressure conditions. It required 72 s for 1 L of the gas to effuse. Under identical experimental conditions it required 28 s for 1 L of O_2 gas to effuse. Calculate the molar mass of the unknown gas. (Remember that the faster the rate of effusion, the shorter the time required for effusion of 1 L; that is, rate and time are inversely proportional.)

10.64. Arsenic(III) sulfide sublimes readily, even below its melting point of 320°C. The molecules of the vapor phase are found to effuse through a tiny hole at 0.28 times the rate of effusion of Ar atoms under the same conditions of temperature and pressure. What is the molecular formula of arsenic(III) sulfide in the gas phase?

Nonideal-Gas Behavior

10.65. (a) Under what experimental conditions of temperature and pressure do gases usually behave nonideally? (b) What two properties or characteristics of gas molecules cause them to behave nonideally?

10.66. The planet Jupiter has a mass 318 times that of Earth, and its surface temperature is 140 K. Mercury has a mass 0.05 times that of Earth, and its surface temperature is between 600 and 700 K. On which planet is the atmosphere more likely to obey the ideal-gas law? Explain.

10.67. Explain how the function PV/RT can be used to show how gases behave nonideally at high pressures.

10.68. (a) What causes real gases to have values of PV/RT that are less than those of an ideal gas? (b) What causes PV/RT to be greater for real gases than for an ideal gas? (c) Why does the difference in PV/RT values for real gases and ideal gases become smaller as the temperature increases?

10.69. Based on their respective van der Waals constants (Table 10.3), is Ar or CO_2 expected to behave more nearly like an ideal gas at high pressures? Explain.

10.70. Briefly explain the significance of the constants a and b in the van der Waals equation.

10.71. Calculate the pressure that CCl_4 will exert at 40°C if 1.00 mol occupies 28.0 L, assuming that (a) CCl_4 obeys the ideal-gas equation; (b) CCl_4 obeys the van der Waals equation. (Values for the van der Waals constants are given in Table 10.3.)

10.72. It turns out that the van der Waals constant b is equal to four times the total volume actually occupied by the molecules of a mole of gas. Using this figure, calculate the fraction of the volume in a container actually occupied by Ar atoms (a) at STP; (b) at 100 atm pressure and 0°C. (Assume for simplicity that the ideal-gas equation still holds.)

Additional Exercises

10.73. Suppose the mercury used to make a barometer has a few small droplets of water trapped in it that rise to the top of the mercury in the tube. Will the barometer show the correct atmospheric pressure? Explain.

10.74. The *Hindenburg* was a famous hydrogen-filled dirigible that exploded in 1937. If the *Hindenburg* held 2.0×10^5 m^3 of hydrogen gas at 27°C and 1.0 atm, what mass of hydrogen was present?

10.75. Propane, C_3H_8, liquefies under modest pressure, allowing a large amount to be stored in a container. (a) Calculate the number of moles of propane gas in a 1.00-L container at 3.00 atm and 27°C. (b) Calculate the number of moles of liquid propane that can be stored in the same volume if the density of the liquid is 0.590 g/mL. (c) Explain why more moles are present in the liquid.

10.76. To minimize the rate of evaporation of the tungsten filament, 10^{-5} mol of argon is placed in a 200-cm^3 light bulb. What is the pressure of argon in the light bulb at 23°C?

10.77. Some aerosol spray cans will explode if their internal pressure exceeds 3.0 atm. If an aerosol can has a pressure of 2.2 atm at 24°C, at what temperature will its pressure equal 3.0 atm?

10.78. Assume that a single cylinder of an automobile engine has a volume of 600.0 cm^3. (a) If the cylinder is full of air at 80°C and 0.980 atm, how many moles of O_2 are present? (The mole fraction of O_2 in dry air is 0.2095.) (b) How many grams of C_8H_{18} could be combusted by this quantity of O_2 assuming complete combustion with formation of CO_2 and H_2O?

10.79. If the partial pressure of ozone, O_3, in the stratosphere is 3.0×10^{-3} atm and the temperature is 250 K, how many ozone molecules are in a liter?

10.80. Nickel carbonyl, $Ni(CO)_4$, is one of the most toxic substances known. The present maximum allowable concentration in laboratory air during an 8-hr workday is 1 part in 10^9. Assume 24°C and 1 atm pressure. What mass of $Ni(CO)_4$ is allowable in a laboratory that is 110 m^2 in area, with a ceiling height of 2.7 m?

10.81. Ammonia, $NH_3(g)$, and hydrogen chloride, $HCl(g)$, react to form solid ammonium chloride, $NH_4Cl(s)$:

$$NH_3(g) + HCl(g) \longrightarrow NH_4Cl(s)$$

Two 2.00-L flasks at 25°C are connected by a stopcock, as shown in Figure 10.25. One flask contains 5.00 g $NH_3(g)$, and the other contains 5.00 g $HCl(g)$. When the stopcock is opened, the gases react until one is completely consumed. (a) Which gas will remain in the system after the reaction is complete? (b) What will be the final pressure of the system after the reaction is complete? (Neglect the volume of the ammonium chloride formed.)

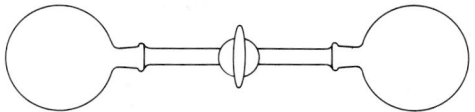

FIGURE 10.25

[10.82]. A mixture of methane, CH_4, and acetylene, C_2H_2, occupies a certain volume at a total pressure of 70.5 torr. The sample is burned, forming CO_2 and H_2O. The H_2O is removed, and the remaining CO_2 is found to have a pressure of 96.4 torr at the same volume and temperature as the original mixture. What fraction of the gas was acetylene?

[10.83]. A gaseous mixture of O_2 and Kr has a density of 1.104 g/L at 435 torr and 300 K. What is the mole percent O_2 in the mixture?

[10.84]. Gaseous iodine pentafluoride, IF_5, can be prepared by the reaction of solid iodine and gaseous fluorine:

$$I_2(s) + 5F_2(g) \longrightarrow 2IF_5(g)$$

A 5.00-L flask is charged with 10.0 g I_2 and 10.0 g F_2, and the reaction proceeds until one of the reagents is completely consumed. After the reaction, the temperature in the flask is 125°C. After the reaction is complete (a) what is the partial pressure of IF_5 in the flask? (b) What is the mole fraction of IF_5 in the flask?

[10.85]. A glass vessel fitted with a stopcock has a mass of 337.428 g when evacuated. When filled with Ar, it has a mass of 339.712 g. When evacuated and refilled with a mixture of Ne and Ar, under the same conditions of temperature and pressure, it weighs 339.218 g. What is the mole percent of Ne in the gas mixture?

10.86. A balloon made of rubber permeable to small molecules is filled with helium to a pressure of 1 atm. This balloon is then placed in a box that contains pure hydrogen, also at a pressure of 1 atm. Will the balloon expand or contract? Explain.

[10.87]. The density of a gas of unknown molar mass was measured as a function of pressure at 0°C:

Pressure (atm)	1.00	0.666	0.500	0.333	0.250
Density (g/L)	2.3074	1.5263	1.1401	0.7571	0.5660

(a) Determine a precise molar mass for the gas. (Hint: Graph d/P versus P.) (b) Why is d/P not a constant as a function of pressure?

[10.88]. Consider the apparatus shown in Figure 10.25. A gas at 1 atm pressure is contained in the left flask, and the right flask is evacuated. When the stopcock is opened, the gas expands to fill both flasks. Only a very small temperature change is noted when this expansion occurs. Explain how this observation relates to assumption 3 of the kinetic-molecular theory.

10.89. On the same plot, qualitatively sketch the distribution of molecular speeds for (a) Kr(g) at −50°C; (b) Kr(g) at 0°C; (c) Ar(g) at 0°C.

[10.90]. Large amounts of nitrogen gas are used in the manufacture of ammonia, principally for use in fertilizers. Suppose 80.00 kg of $N_2(g)$ is stored in a 1000.0-L metal cylinder at 300°C. (a) Calculate the pressure of the gas assuming ideal-gas behavior. (b) By using data in Table 10.3, calculate the pressure of the gas according to the van der Waals equation. (c) Under the conditions of this problem, which correction dominates, the one for finite volume of gas molecules or the one for attractive interactions?

Intermolecular Forces, Liquids, and Solids

11

Water droplets on a green plant. Many of the important properties of water, such as it being a liquid at room temperature, are a consequence of the attractions between water molecules.

CONTENTS

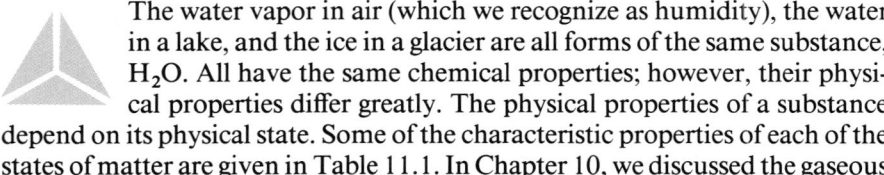

The water vapor in air (which we recognize as humidity), the water in a lake, and the ice in a glacier are all forms of the same substance, H_2O. All have the same chemical properties; however, their physical properties differ greatly. The physical properties of a substance depend on its physical state. Some of the characteristic properties of each of the states of matter are given in Table 11.1. In Chapter 10, we discussed the gaseous state in some detail. In this chapter, we turn our attention to the physical properties of liquids and solids.

Many of the substances that we will consider are molecular. In fact, virtually all substances that are liquids at room temperature are molecular substances. Covalent bonds, which are forces *within* molecules, influence molecular shape, bond energies, and many aspects of chemical behavior. The physical properties of molecular liquids and solids, however, are due largely to **intermolecular forces,** the forces that exist *between* molecules. We first encountered intermolecular forces in Section 10.10, where we saw that attractions between gas molecules led to deviations from ideal-gas behavior. By understanding the nature and strength of intermolecular forces, we can begin to relate the composition and structure of molecules to their physical properties.

Teaching Note: Although termed *intermolecular forces,* these forces hold many large molecules, such as DNA, in their characteristic shapes.

11.1 The Kinetic-Molecular Description of Liquids and Solids

In Chapter 10, we learned that the physical properties of gases can be understood in terms of the kinetic-molecular theory. Gases consist of a collection of widely separated molecules in constant, chaotic motion. The average kinetic energy of the molecules is much larger than the average energy of the attractions between them. The lack of strong attractive forces between molecules allows a gas to expand to fill its container.

In liquids, the intermolecular attractive forces are strong enough to hold molecules close together. Thus, liquids are much denser and far less compressible than gases. Unlike gases, liquids have a definite volume, independent of the size and shape of their container. The attractive forces in liquids are not strong enough, however, to keep the molecules from moving past one another. Thus, liquids can be poured, and they assume the shapes of their containers.

TABLE 11.1 △ **Some Characteristic Properties of the States of Matter**

Gas	Assumes both the volume and shape of container
	Is compressible
	Diffusion within a gas occurs rapidly
	Flows readily
Liquid	Assumes the shape of the portion of the container it occupies
	Does not expand to fill container
	Is virtually incompressible
	Diffusion within a liquid occurs slowly
	Flows readily
Solid	Retains its own shape and volume
	Is virtually incompressible
	Diffusion within a solid occurs extremely slowly
	Does not flow

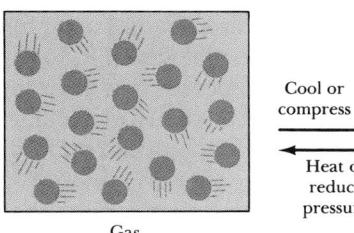
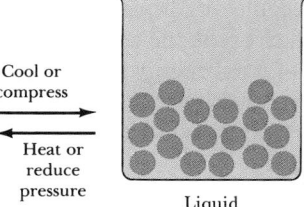
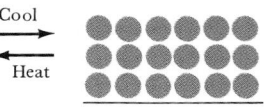

Gas

Total disorder; much empty space; particles have complete freedom of motion; particles far apart.

Liquid

Disorder; particles or clusters of particles are free to move relative to each other; particles close together.

Crystalline solid

Ordered arrangement; particles are essentially in fixed positions; particles close together.

FIGURE 11.1 Molecular-level comparison of gases, liquids, and solids. The particles can be atoms, ions, or molecules. The density of particles in the gas phase is exaggerated as compared with most real situations.

Figure 11.1

In solids, the intermolecular attractive forces are strong enough not only to hold molecules close together but virtually to lock them in place. Solids, like liquids, are not very compressible because the molecules have little free space between them. Often the molecules take up positions in a highly regular pattern. Solids that possess highly ordered structures are said to be *crystalline.* (The transition from a liquid to a crystalline solid is rather like the change that occurs on a military parade ground when the troops are called to formation.) Because the particles of a solid are not free to undergo long-range movement, solids are rigid.

Figure 11.1 compares the three states of matter. The particles that compose the substance can be individual atoms, as in Ar; molecules, as in H_2O; or ions, as in NaCl. The state of a substance depends largely on the balance between the kinetic energies of the particles and the interparticle energies of attraction. The kinetic energies, which depend on temperature, tend to keep the particles apart and moving. The interparticle attractions tend to draw the particles together. Those substances that are gases at room temperature have weaker interparticle attractions than those that are liquids; those that are liquids have weaker attractions than those that are solids. Because the particles in a solid or liquid are fairly close together compared to those of a gas, we often refer to solids and liquids as *condensed phases.*

We can change a substance from one state to another by heating or cooling, which changes the average kinetic energy of the particles. For example, NaCl, which is a solid at room temperature, melts at 804°C and boils at 1465°C under 1 atm pressure. Conversely, N_2O, which is a gas at room temperature, liquefies at −88.5°C and solidifies at −102.4°C under 1 atm pressure.

Increasing the pressure on a substance forces the molecules closer together, which in turn increases the strength of intermolecular forces. For example, propane, C_3H_8, is a gas at room temperature and 1 atm pressure. Liquefied propane (LP) gas is a liquid at room temperature because it is stored under much higher pressure.

Learning Goal 1: Employ the kinetic-molecular model to explain the differences in motion of particles in gases, liquids, and solids and how these relate to their states.

11.2 Intermolecular Forces

The strengths of intermolecular forces of different substances vary over a wide range. However, they are generally much weaker than ionic or covalent bonds. For example, only 16 kJ/mol is required to overcome the intermolecular at-

FIGURE 11.2 Illustration of the preferred orientation of dipolar molecules toward ions. The negative end of the dipolar molecule is oriented toward a cation (*a*), the positive end toward an anion (*b*).

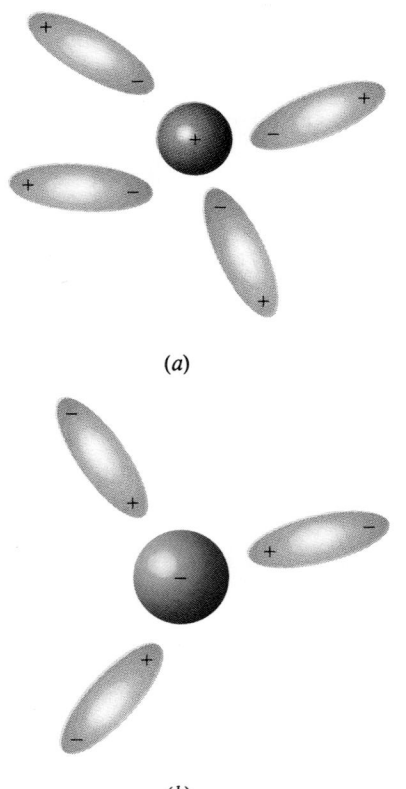

(*a*)

(*b*)

tractions between HCl molecules in liquid HCl in order to vaporize it. In contrast, the energy required to break the covalent bond to dissociate HCl into H and Cl atoms is 431 kJ/mol. Less energy is required to vaporize a liquid or to melt a solid than to break covalent bonds in molecules. Thus, when a molecular substance like HCl changes from solid to liquid to gas, the molecules remain intact.

Many properties of liquids, including their *boiling points*, reflect the strengths of the intermolecular forces. A liquid boils when bubbles of its vapor form within the liquid. The molecules of a liquid must overcome their attractive forces in order to separate and form a vapor. The stronger the attractive forces, the higher the temperature at which the liquid boils. Similarly, the *melting points* of solids increase with an increase in the strengths of the intermolecular forces.

Three types of intermolecular attractive forces are known to exist between neutral molecules: dipole-dipole forces, London dispersion forces, and hydrogen-bonding forces. These forces are also called *van der Waals forces* after Johannes van der Waals, who developed the equation for predicting the deviation of gases from ideal behavior. ∞ (Sec. 10.10) Another kind of attractive force, the ion-dipole force, is important in solutions. As a group, intermolecular forces tend to be less than 15 percent as strong as covalent or ionic bonds. As we consider these forces, notice that each is electrostatic in nature, involving attractions between positive and negative species.

Ion-Dipole Forces

An **ion-dipole force** exists between an ion and the partial charge on the end of a polar molecule. Polar molecules are dipoles; they have a positive end and a negative end. ∞ (Sec. 9.2) For example, HCl is a polar molecule because of the difference in the electronegativities of the H and Cl atoms. The extent of the charge separation in a polar molecule is measured by its dipole moment. The dipole moment of HCl is 1.08 Debyes (D).

Positive ions are attracted to the negative end of a dipole, whereas negative ions are attracted to the positive end, as shown in Figure 11.2. The magnitude of the interaction energy depends on the charge on the ion (Q), the dipole moment of the molecule (μ), and the distance from the center of the ion to the midpoint of the dipole (d): $E \propto Q\mu/d^2$.

Ion-dipole forces are especially important in solutions of ionic substances in polar liquids, for example, a solution of NaCl in water. We will have more to say about such solutions in Section 13.1.

Dipole-Dipole Forces

A **dipole-dipole force** exists between neutral polar molecules. Polar molecules attract each other when the positive end of one molecule is near the negative end of another, as in Figure 11.3(*a*) and (*b*). Dipole-dipole forces are effective only when polar molecules are very close together, and they are generally weaker than ion-dipole forces.

In liquids, dipolar molecules are free to move with respect to one another. They will sometimes be in an orientation that is attractive, and sometimes in an orientation that is repulsive. Two molecules that are attracting each other spend more time near each other than do two that are repelling each other. Thus, the

FIGURE 11.3 Variation in the dipole-dipole interaction with orientation. In (*a*) and (*b*), the dipoles are aligned so as to produce an attractive interaction. In (*c*) and (*d*), the interactions are repulsive.

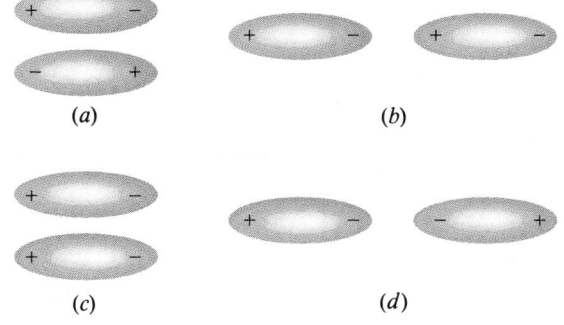

(*a*)　　　　　　　　(*b*)

(*c*)　　　　　　　　(*d*)

overall effect is a net attraction. When we examine various liquids, we find clear evidence that *for molecules of approximately equal mass and size, the strengths of intermolecular attractions increase with increasing polarity.* We can see this trend for the liquids listed in Table 11.2: The boiling points increase with increasing magnitude of the dipole moment.

Point of Emphasis: For molecules of approximately equal mass and size, the strengths of intermolecular forces increase with increasing polarity.

London Dispersion Forces

What kind of interparticle forces can exist between nonpolar atoms or molecules? Clearly, there can be no dipole-dipole forces when the particles are nonpolar. Yet the fact that nonpolar gases can be liquefied tells us that there must be some kind of attractive interactions between the particles. The origin of this attraction was first proposed in 1930 by Fritz London, a German-American physicist. London recognized that the motion of electrons in an atom or molecule can create an *instantaneous* dipole moment. Let's consider helium atoms as an example.

In a collection of helium atoms, the *average* distribution of the electrons about each nucleus is spherically symmetrical. The atoms are nonpolar and possess no permanent dipole moment. The instantaneous distribution of the electrons, however, can be different from the average distribution. For example, if we could freeze the motion of the electrons in a helium atom at any given instant, both electrons could be on one side of the nucleus. At just that instant, then, the atom would have an instantaneous dipole moment. Because electrons repel one another, the motions of electrons on one atom influence the motions of electrons on its near neighbors. Thus, the temporary dipole on one atom can induce a similar dipole on an adjacent atom, causing the atoms to be attracted

TABLE 11.2 △ Molecular Masses, Dipole Moments, and Boiling Points of Several Simple Organic Substances

Substance	Molecular mass (amu)	Dipole moment, μ (D)	Boiling point (K)
Propane, $CH_3CH_2CH_3$	44	0.1	231
Dimethyl ether, CH_3OCH_3	46	1.3	248
Methyl chloride, CH_3Cl	50	2.0	249
Acetaldehyde, CH_3CHO	44	2.7	294
Acetonitrile, CH_3CN	41	3.9	355

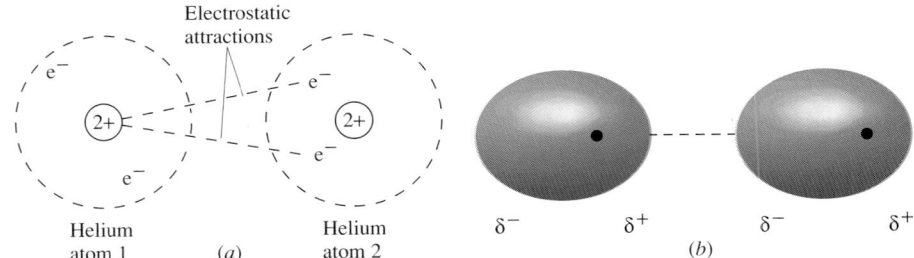

FIGURE 11.4 Two schematic representations of the instantaneous dipoles on two adjacent helium atoms, showing the electrostatic attraction between them.

Teaching Note: London dispersion forces are also commonly called London forces or dispersion forces.

Point of Emphasis: London dispersion forces tend to increase in strength with increasing molecular weight.

Point of Emphasis: In general, the more electrons an atom has, the more polarizable it is.

to each other as shown in Figure 11.4. This attractive interaction is called the **London dispersion force** (or merely the dispersion force). This force is significant only when molecules are very close together.

The ease with which the charge distribution in a molecule can be distorted by an external electric field is called its **polarizability.** We can think of the polarizability of a molecule as a measure of the "squashiness" of its electron cloud; the greater the polarizability of a molecule, the more easily its electron cloud can be distorted to give a momentary dipole, which leads to stronger London dispersion forces. In general, larger molecules tend to have greater polarizabilities because they have a greater number of electrons and their electrons are farther from the nuclei. Therefore, the strength of the London dispersion forces tends to increase with increasing molecular size. Because molecular size and mass generally parallel each other, *dispersion forces tend to increase in strength with increasing molecular weight.* Thus, the boiling points of the substances listed in Table 11.3 increase with increasing molecular weight.

The shapes of molecules can also play a role in the magnitudes of dispersion forces. For example, *n*-pentane* and neopentane, illustrated in Figure 11.5, have the same molecular formula, C_5H_{12}, yet the boiling point of *n*-pentane is 27 K higher than that of neopentane. The difference can be traced to the different shapes of the two molecules. The overall attraction between molecules is greater in the case of *n*-pentane because the molecules can come in contact over the entire length of the long, somewhat cylindrically shaped molecule. Less contact is possible between the more nearly spherical molecules of neopentane.

Dispersion forces operate between all molecules, whether they are polar or nonpolar. In fact, dispersion forces between polar molecules can contribute more to *overall* attractive forces than do dipole-dipole forces. For example, the fact that the boiling point of HBr (206.2 K) is higher than that of HCl (189.5 K) indicates that the overall attractive forces are stronger for HBr. The stronger attractive forces for HBr cannot be attributed to greater dipole-dipole forces,

---

* The *n* in *n*-pentane is an abbreviation for the word *normal.* A normal hydrocarbon is one whose carbon atoms are arranged in a straight chain.

TABLE 11.3 △ Boiling Points of the Halogens and Noble Gases

Halogen	Boiling point (K)	Noble gas	Boiling point (K)
F_2	85.1	He	4.6
Cl_2	238.6	Ne	27.3
Br_2	332.0	Ar	87.5
I_2	457.6	Kr	120.9
		Xe	166.1

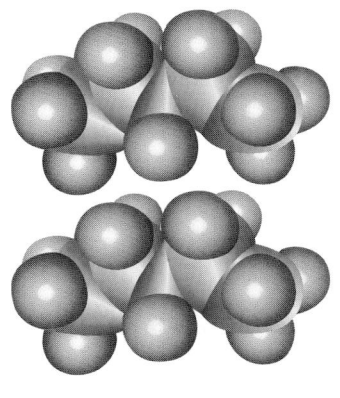
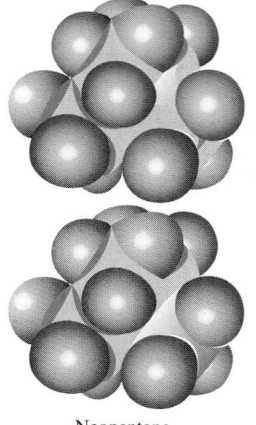

n-Pentane   Neopentane

FIGURE 11.5 Illustration of the effect of molecular shape on intermolecular attraction. The boiling point of *n*-pentane is 309.4 K, and that of neopentane is 282.7 K.

because HBr is less polar than HCl (0.82 D compared to 1.08 D). Because HBr is more massive and polarizable than HCl, however, the dispersion forces are stronger in HBr, and these lead to stronger overall attractive forces for it.

It is difficult to make generalizations about the relative strengths of intermolecular attractions unless we restrict ourselves to comparing molecules of either similar size and shape or similar polarity and shape. If molecules are of similar size and shape, dispersion forces are approximately equal, and therefore attractive forces increase with increasing polarity. If molecules are of similar polarity and shape, attractive forces tend to increase with increasing molecular mass because dispersion forces are greater.

SAMPLE EXERCISE 11.1

Which of the following substances is most likely to exist as a gas at room temperature and normal atmospheric pressure: P_4O_{10}, Cl_2, AgCl, or I_2?

SOLUTION In essence, the question asks which substance has the weakest intermolecular attractive forces. The weaker these forces, the more likely the substance is to exist as a gas at any given temperature and pressure. We should therefore select Cl_2, because it is a nonpolar molecule and also has the lowest molecular weight. In fact, Cl_2 does exist as a gas at room temperature and normal atmospheric pressure, whereas the others are solids. Of the other substances, AgCl is least likely to be a gas because it exists as Ag^+ and Cl^- ions with very strong ionic bonds holding the ions within the solid.

PRACTICE EXERCISE

Of Br_2, Ne, HCl, and N_2, which is likely to have **(a)** the largest intermolecular dispersion forces; **(b)** the largest dipole-dipole attractive forces?   *Answers:* **(a)** Br_2; **(b)** HCl

Hydrogen Bonding

Figure 11.6 shows the boiling points of the simple hydrides of group 4A and 6A elements. In general, the boiling point increases with increasing molecular weight, owing to increased dispersion forces. The notable exception to this trend is H_2O, whose boiling point is much higher than we would expect on the basis of its molecular weight. In addition, NH_3 and HF also have abnormally

Teaching Note: The boiling point of neon (AW ≈ 20 amu) is 27.3 K, whereas that of water (MW ≈ 18 amu) is 373.15 K.

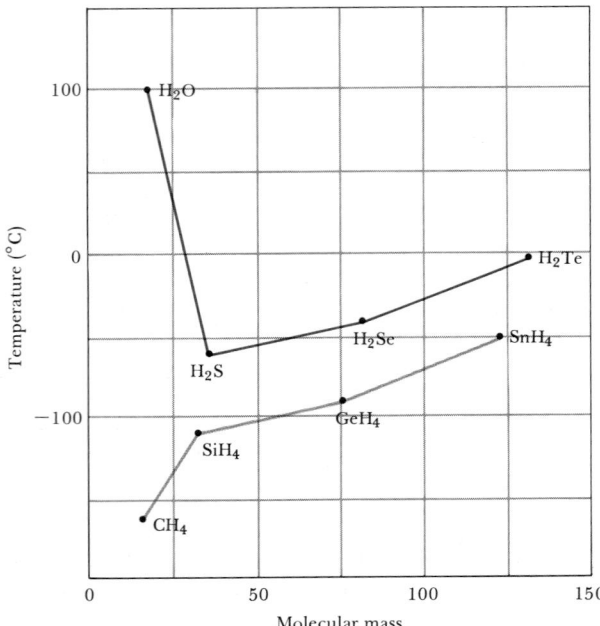

Figure 11.6

Point of Emphasis: Hydrogen bonding is a special type of dipole-dipole attraction.

FIGURE 11.7 Examples of hydrogen bonding. The solid lines represent covalent bonds; the red dotted lines represent hydrogen bonds.

high boiling points. These compounds also have many other characteristics that distinguish them from other substances of similar molecular weight and polarity. For example, water has a high melting point, a high specific heat, and a high heat of vaporization. Each of these properties indicates that the intermolecular forces between H_2O molecules are abnormally strong.

These strong intermolecular attractions result from hydrogen bonding. **Hydrogen bonding** *is a special type of intermolecular attraction that exists between the hydrogen atom in a polar bond (particularly an H—F, H—O, or H—N bond) and an unshared electron pair on a nearby electronegative ion or atom (usually an F, O, or N atom on another molecule).* For example, a hydrogen bond exists between the H atom in an HF molecule and the F atom of an adjacent HF molecule, F—H···F—H (where the dots represent the hydrogen bond between the molecules). Several additional examples are shown in Figure 11.7.

Hydrogen bonds can be considered unique dipole-dipole attractions. Because F, N, and O are so electronegative, a bond between hydrogen and any of these three elements is quite polar, with hydrogen at the positive end:

$$N—H \qquad O—H \qquad F—H$$

The hydrogen atom has no inner core of electrons. Thus, the positive side of the bond dipole has the concentrated charge of the partially exposed, nearly bare proton of the hydrogen nucleus. This positive charge is attracted to the negative charge of an electronegative atom in a nearby molecule. Because the electron-poor hydrogen is so small, it can approach an electronegative atom very closely and thus interact strongly with it.

▲ A CLOSER LOOK

Trends in Hydrogen Bonding

If the hydrogen bond is the result of an electrostatic interaction between the X—H bond dipole and an unshared electron pair on another atom, Y, then the strength of hydrogen bonding should increase as the X—H bond dipole increases. Thus, for the same Y, we would expect hydrogen-bonding strength to increase in the series

$$N-H\cdots Y < O-H\cdots Y < F-H\cdots Y$$

This is indeed true. But what property of Y dictates the strength of the hydrogen bonding? The atom Y must possess an unshared electron pair that attracts the positive end of the X—H dipole. This electron pair must not be too diffuse in space; if the electrons occupy too large a volume, the X—H dipole does not experience a strong, directed attraction. For this reason, we find that hydrogen bonding is not very strong unless Y is a small, highly electronegative atom, specifically N, O, or F. Among these three elements, we find that hydrogen bonding is stronger when the electron pair is not attracted *too*

strongly to its own nucleus. The electronegativity of Y is a good measure of this aspect. For example, the electronegativity of nitrogen is less than that of oxygen. Nitrogen is thus a better donor of the electron pair to the X—H bond. For a given X—H, hydrogen-bond strength increases in the order

$$X-H\cdots F < X-H\cdots O < X-H\cdots N$$

When X and Y are the same, the energy of hydrogen bonding increases in the order

$$N-H\cdots N < O-H\cdots O < F-H\cdots F$$

When the Y atom carries a negative charge, the electron pair is able to form especially strong hydrogen bonds. The hydrogen bond in the $F-H\cdots F^-$ ion is among the strongest known; the reaction

$$F^-(g) + HF(g) \longrightarrow FHF^-(g)$$

has a ΔH value of about -155 kJ/mol.

The energies of hydrogen bonds vary from about 4 kJ/mol to 25 kJ/mol or so. Thus, they are much weaker than ordinary chemical bonds (see Table 8.4). Nevertheless, hydrogen bonding is generally much stronger than dipole-dipole or dispersion forces and therefore has important consequences for the properties of many substances, including those in biological systems.

One of the most remarkable consequences of hydrogen bonding is found in comparing the density of ice to that of liquid water. In most substances, the molecules in the solid are more densely packed than in the liquid. Thus, the solid phase is denser than the liquid phase (Figure 11.8). By contrast, the density of ice at 0°C (0.917 g/mL) is less than that of liquid water at 0°C (1.00 g/mL).

Teaching Note: Ice will melt under sufficient external pressure. For example, the pressure exerted by the blade of an ice skate melts the ice, forming a thin layer of water upon which the skate easily slides.

FIGURE 11.8 As with most substances, the solid phase of paraffin is denser than the liquid phase, and the solid therefore sinks below the liquid (left). In contrast, the solid phase of water, ice, is less dense than its liquid phase (right). (Richard Megna/Fundamental Photographs)

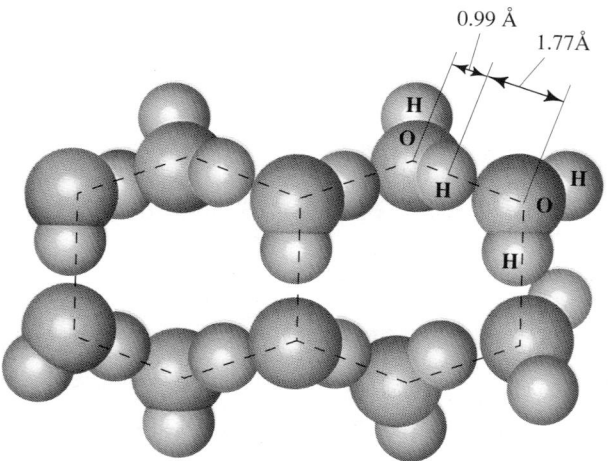

0.99 Å

1.77Å

FIGURE 11.9 Arrangement of water molecules in ice. Each hydrogen atom on one water molecule is oriented toward a nonbonding pair of electrons on an adjacent water molecule. In the full structure each oxygen atom has a hydrogen bond with two O—H groups.

The low density of ice compared to that of water can be understood in terms of hydrogen-bonding interactions between water molecules. The interactions in the liquid are random. However, when water freezes, the molecules assume the ordered, open arrangement shown in Figure 11.9, which leads to a less dense structure for ice compared to that of water: A given mass of ice occupies a greater volume than does the same mass of liquid water. The structure of ice permits the maximum number of hydrogen-bonding interactions between the H_2O molecules. The hexagonal arrangement of water molecules in ice leads to the characteristic hexagonal shape of small crystals of ice, such as snowflakes (Figure 11.10).

The density of ice compared to water profoundly affects life on Earth. Because ice is less dense than water, ice floats (Figure 11.8). When ice forms in cold weather, it covers the top of the water, thereby insulating the water below. If ice were more dense than water, ice forming at the top of a lake would sink to the bottom, and the lake could freeze solid. Most aquatic life could not survive under these conditions. The expansion of water upon freezing is also what causes water pipes to break in freezing weather (Figure 11.11).

Let us now put *all* the intermolecular forces we have discussed in perspective. To summarize, we have seen that we can usually identify the dominant

FIGURE 11.10 These computer-enhanced photographs of snowflakes show their characteristic hexagonal shape, which originates with the hexagonal arrangement of water molecules in ice (Figure 11.9). (Scott Camazine/Photo Researchers)

intermolecular forces in a condensed phase by considering the atoms, molecules, or ions of which the substance is composed. Figure 11.12 presents a systematic way of choosing the most important intermolecular forces for a given type of system.

SAMPLE EXERCISE 11.2

List the substances $BaCl_2$, H_2, CO, HF, and Ne in order of increasing boiling points.

SOLUTION   The boiling point depends in part on the attractive forces in the liquid. These are stronger for ionic substances than for molecular ones, so $BaCl_2$ has the highest boiling point. The intermolecular forces of the remaining substances depend on molecular weight, polarity, and hydrogen bonding. The other molecular weights are H_2 (2), CO (28), HF (20), and Ne (20). The boiling point of H_2 should be the lowest because it is nonpolar and has the lowest molecular weight. The molecular weights of CO, HF, and Ne are roughly the same. Because HF can hydrogen bond, it has the highest boiling point of the three. Next is CO, which is slightly polar and has the highest molecular weight. Finally, Ne, which is nonpolar, comes last of these three. The predicted boiling points are therefore

$$H_2 < Ne < CO < HF < BaCl_2$$

The actual normal boiling points are H_2 (20 K), Ne (27 K), CO (83 K), HF (293 K), and $BaCl_2$ (1813 K).

PRACTICE EXERCISE

Which of the following can form hydrogen bonds with H_2O: **(a)** CH_3OCH_3; **(b)** CH_4; **(c)** NH_4^+?   *Answer:* CH_3OCH_3 and NH_4^+

FIGURE 11.11   Water is one of the few substances that expands upon freezing. The expansion is due to the open structure of ice relative to that of liquid water. (Richard Megna/Fundamental Photographs)

FIGURE 11.12   Flowchart of the major types of intermolecular forces. The strength of the forces generally increases proceeding from left to right.

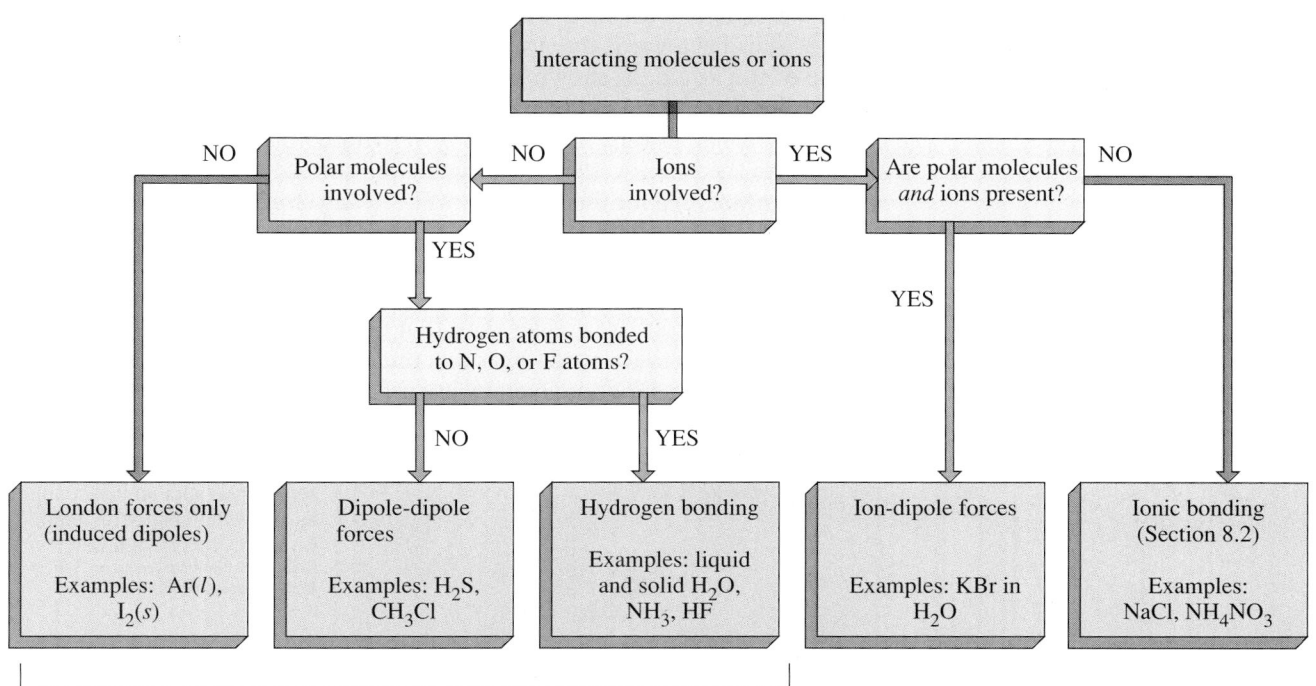

FIGURE 11.13 The Society of Automotive Engineers (SAE) has established numbers to indicate the viscosity of motor oils. The higher the number, the greater the viscosity at any given temperature. The SAE 40 motor oil on the left is more viscous and flows more slowly than the less viscous SAE 10 oil on the right. (Kristen Brochmann/Fundamental Photographs)

FIGURE 11.14 Molecular-level view of the intermolecular forces acting on a molecule at the surface of a liquid compared to those in the interior.

11.3 Properties of Liquids: Viscosity and Surface Tension

Now that we have introduced intermolecular forces, we can consider some of the properties of liquids and solids. In this section, we examine two important properties of liquids: viscosity and surface tension.

Viscosity

Some liquids, such as molasses and motor oil, flow very slowly, whereas others, such as water and gasoline, flow easily. The resistance of a liquid to flow is called its **viscosity**. The greater a liquid's viscosity, the more slowly it flows. Viscosity can be measured by timing how long it takes a certain amount of the liquid to flow through a thin tube under gravitational force. More viscous liquids take longer (Figure 11.13). Viscosity can also be determined by measuring the rate at which steel spheres fall through the liquid. The spheres fall more slowly as the viscosity increases.

Viscosity is related to the ease with which individual molecules of the liquid can move with respect to one another. It thus depends on the attractive forces between molecules and on whether structural features exist that cause the molecules to become entangled. Viscosity decreases with increasing temperature because at higher temperature the greater average kinetic energy of the molecules more easily overcomes the attractive forces between molecules.

Surface Tension

When water is placed on a waxy surface, it "beads up," forming distorted spheres. This behavior is due to an imbalance of intermolecular forces at the surface of the liquid, as shown in Figure 11.14. Notice that molecules in the interior are attracted equally in all directions, whereas those at the surface experience a net inward force. This inward force pulls molecules from the surface into the interior, thereby reducing the surface area. (Spheres have the smallest surface area for their volume.) The inward force also makes the molecules at the surface pack closely together, causing the liquid to behave almost as if it had a skin. This effect permits a carefully placed needle to float on the surface of water and some insects to "walk" on water (Figure 11.15), even though their densities are greater than that of water.

A measure of the inward forces that must be overcome in order to expand the surface area of a liquid is given by its surface tension. **Surface tension** is the

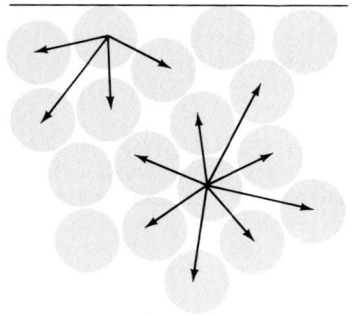

FIGURE 11.15 Surface tension permits an insect such as the water strider to "walk" on water. (© 1977 Michael P. Godomski, National Audubon Society, Photo Researchers, Inc.)

energy required to increase the surface area of a liquid by a unit amount. For example, the surface tension of water at 20°C is 7.29×10^{-2} J/m², which means that an energy of 7.29×10^{-2} J must be supplied to increase the surface area of a given amount of water by 1 m². Water has a high surface tension because of its strong hydrogen bonds. The surface tension of mercury is even higher (4.6×10^{-1} J/m²) because of even stronger metallic bonds between the atoms of mercury.

Forces that bind like molecules to one another, such as the hydrogen bonding in water, are called *cohesive forces*. Forces that bind a substance to a surface are called *adhesive forces*. Water placed in a glass tube adheres to the glass because of the adhesive forces between water and glass. The curved upper surface, or *meniscus,* of the water is therefore U-shaped (Figure 11.16). For mercury, however, the meniscus is curved downward where the mercury contacts the glass. In this case, the cohesive forces between the mercury atoms are much greater than the adhesive forces between the mercury atoms and the glass.

When a small-diameter glass tube, or capillary, is placed in water, water rises in the tube. The rise of liquids up very narrow tubes is called **capillary action.** The adhesive forces between the liquid and the walls of the tube tend to increase the surface area of the liquid. The surface tension of the liquid tends to reduce the area, thereby pulling the liquid up the tube. The liquid climbs until the adhesive and cohesive forces are balanced by the force of gravity on the liquid. Capillary action helps water and dissolved nutrients to move upward through plants.

11.4 Changes of State

Many important properties of liquids and solids relate to the ease with which they change from one state to another. Everyone has seen examples of such changes. Water left uncovered in a glass for several days evaporates. An ice cube left in a warm room quickly melts. Solid CO_2 (sold as Dry Ice) *sublimes* at room temperature; that is, it changes directly from the solid to the vapor state. In general, each state of matter can change into either of the other two states. Figure 11.17 shows the name associated with each of these transformations. These transformations are called **phase changes** or changes of state.

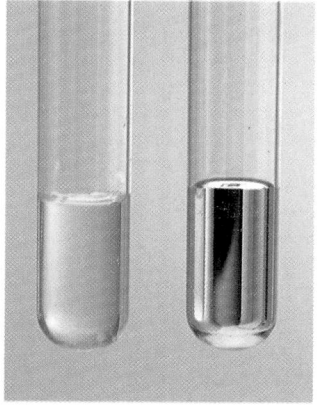

FIGURE 11.16 Comparison of the shape of the water meniscus in a glass tube and the shape of the mercury meniscus. (Richard Megna/ Fundamental Photographs)

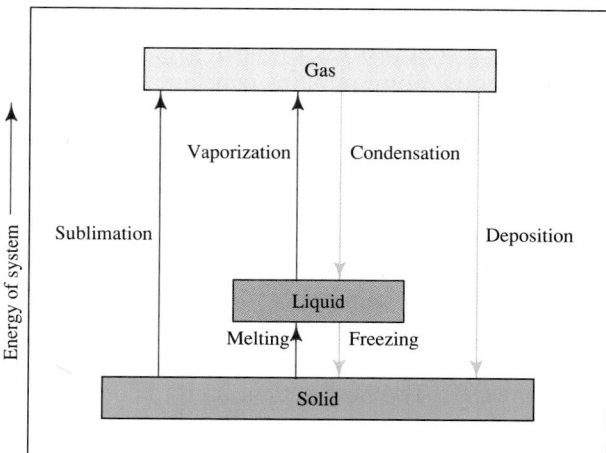

FIGURE 11.17 Energy changes accompanying phase changes between the three states of matter, and the names associated with them.

Bassam Z. Shakha-shiri, "Evaporation As an Endothermic Process," *Chemical Demonstrations: A Handbook for Teachers of Chemistry, Volume 3* (Madison: The University of Wisconsin Press, 1989), pp. 249–251.

Teaching Note: Recall from Chapter 5 that reactions that require heat energy are termed *endothermic*.

Point of Emphasis: In this context, fusion is the same as melting.

Norman C. Craig, Brian J. Brown, William S. Chamness, and Elaine B. Mulvey, "A Computer-Simulated Experiment on Vapor-Liquid Phase Equilibrium," *J. Chem. Educ.* **1988**, *65*, 792.

Point of Emphasis: The sequence: heat solid → melt → heat liquid → boil → heat gas is endothermic. The sequence: cool gas → condense → cool liquid → freeze → cool solid is exothermic.

Point of Emphasis: The system must be well mixed so that the temperature throughout the sample is uniform.

Energy Changes Accompanying Changes of State

Each change of state is accompanied by a change in the energy of the system. Whenever a change of state involves going to a less ordered state, energy must be supplied to overcome intermolecular forces. Thus, energy is required to melt a solid. The attractive forces that hold particles in fixed positions in the solid must be overcome to form the liquid. Likewise, vaporization requires energy. The attractive forces that hold particles close to each other in the liquid must be overcome to form the gas. Sublimation also requires energy. As the strengths of the intermolecular forces increase, the amounts of energy required to cause a change of state also increase.

The melting process for a solid is also referred to as *fusion.* Thus, the enthalpy change associated with melting a solid is often called the enthalpy of fusion, or **heat of fusion,** which we denote ΔH_{fus}. The heat of fusion of ice is 6.01 kJ/mol. The heat needed for the vaporization of a liquid is called the **heat of vaporization** (or enthalpy of vaporization), denoted ΔH_{vap}. The heat of vaporization of water is 40.67 kJ/mol. Notice that the heat of fusion is smaller than the heat of vaporization. Less energy is needed to allow particles to move past one another than to separate them totally.

The cooling effect accompanying vaporization is evident when we get out of a swimming pool. As the water evaporates from our skin, it removes heat from our bodies. The evaporation of water through perspiring is important in keeping our bodies cool on hot days and during strenuous exercise. A refrigerator also relies on the cooling effect accompanying vaporization. Its mechanism contains an enclosed gas, usually Freon-12, CCl_2F_2, that can be liquefied under pressure. The Freon absorbs heat as it evaporates, thus cooling the interior of the refrigerator. The Freon vapor is then recycled to a compressor where it is again liquefied.

Because melting, vaporization, and sublimation are endothermic processes, the reverse processes (freezing, condensation, and deposition) are all exothermic. That is why, for example, steam can cause severe burns. When steam comes in contact with skin, it condenses, releasing considerable heat.

Heating Curves

Suppose we heat a sample of ice that is initially at $-25°C$ and 1 atm pressure. What happens? The addition of heat causes the temperature of the ice to increase. As long as the temperature is below $0°C$, the sample remains frozen as ice. When the temperature reaches $0°C$, the ice begins to melt. Because melting is an endothermic process, the heat we add at $0°C$ is used to convert ice to water, and the temperature remains constant until all the ice has melted. Once we reach this point, the further addition of heat causes the temperature of the liquid water to increase.

We can plot the processes described above as a *heating curve,* which is a graph of the temperature of the system versus the amount of heat added. Figure 11.18 shows a heating curve for heating ice at $-25°C$ to steam at $125°C$ under a constant pressure of 1 atm. Heating the ice from $-25°C$ to $0°C$ is represented by the line segment *AB* in Figure 11.18, while the conversion of ice at $0°C$ to water at $0°C$ leads to the horizontal segment *BC*. Adding additional heat increases the temperature of the water until the temperature reaches $100°C$ (segment *CD*). The heat is then used to convert water to steam at a constant

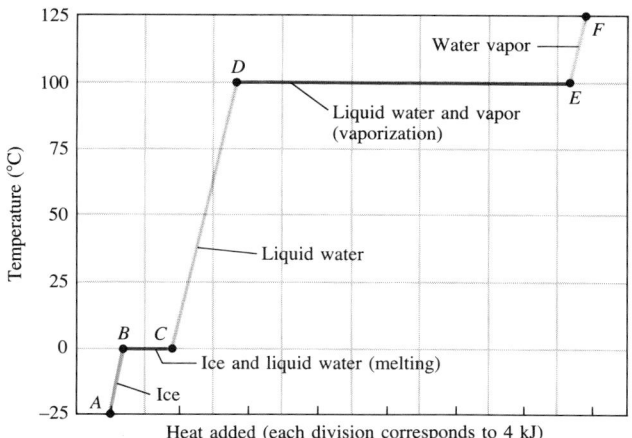

FIGURE 11.18 Heating curve for the transformation of water at $-25°C$ to $125°C$ at a constant pressure of 1 atm.

Figure 11.18

temperature of 100°C (segment *DE*). Once all the water has been converted to steam, the steam is heated to its final temperature of 125°C (segment *EF*).

We can calculate the enthalpy change of the system for each of the segments of the heating curve. In segments *AB, CD*, and *EF*, we are heating a single phase from one temperature to another. As we saw in Section 5.5, the amount of heat needed to raise the temperature of a substance is given by its specific heat or molar heat capacity. The greater the specific heat of a substance, the more heat we must add to accomplish a certain temperature increase. Because the specific heat of water is greater than that of ice, the slope of segment *CD* is less than that of segment *AB*; we must add more heat to water to achieve a 1°C temperature change than is needed to warm the same quantity of ice by 1°C.

In segments *BC* and *DE*, we are converting one phase to another at a constant temperature. The temperature remains constant during these phase changes because the added energy is used to overcome the attractive forces between molecules rather than to increase their average kinetic energy. For segment *BC*, in which ice is converted to water, the enthalpy change can be calculated by using ΔH_{fus}, while for segment *DE* we use ΔH_{vap}. In the following Sample Exercise, we calculate the total enthalpy change for the heating curve in Figure 11.18.

SAMPLE EXERCISE 11.3

Calculate the enthalpy change upon converting 1.00 mol of ice at $-25°C$ to water vapor (steam) at 125°C under a constant pressure of 1 atm. The specific heats of ice, water, and steam are 2.09 J/g-K, 4.18 J/g-K, and 1.84 J/g-K, respectively. For H_2O, $\Delta H_{fus} = 6.01$ kJ/mol, and $\Delta H_{vap} = 40.67$ kJ/mol.

SOLUTION We can calculate the enthalpy change for each segment and then sum them to get the total enthalpy change (Hess's law). For segment *AB* in Figure 11.18, we are adding enough heat to ice to increase its temperature by 25°C. Remember that a temperature change of 25°C is the same as a temperature change of 25 K. We can use the specific heat of ice to calculate the enthalpy change during this process:

AB: $\Delta H = (1.00 \text{ mol})(18.0 \text{ g/mol})(2.09 \text{ J/g-K})(25 \text{ K}) = 940 \text{ J} = 0.94 \text{ kJ}$

For segment *BC* in Figure 11.18, in which we convert ice to water at 0°C, we can use the molar enthalpy of fusion directly:

BC: $\Delta H = (1.00 \text{ mol})(6.01 \text{ kJ/mol}) = 6.01 \text{ kJ}$

The enthalpy changes for segments *CD, DE,* and *EF* can be calculated in similar fashion:

CD: $\Delta H = (1.00 \text{ mol})(18.0 \text{ g/mol})(4.18 \text{ J/g-K})(100 \text{ K}) = 7520 \text{ J} = 7.52 \text{ kJ}$

DE: $\Delta H = (1.00 \text{ mol})(40.67 \text{ kJ/mol}) = 40.67 \text{ kJ}$

EF: $\Delta H = (1.00 \text{ mol})(18.0 \text{ g/mol})(1.84 \text{ J/g-K})(25 \text{ K}) = 830 \text{ J} = 0.83 \text{ kJ}$

The total enthalpy change is the sum of the changes of the individual steps:

$$\Delta H = 0.94 \text{ kJ} + 6.01 \text{ kJ} + 7.52 \text{ kJ} + 40.67 \text{ kJ} + 0.83 \text{ kJ} = 55.97 \text{ kJ}$$

PRACTICE EXERCISE

What is the enthalpy change during the process in which 100.0 g of water at 50.0°C is cooled to ice at −30.0°C? (Use the specific heats and enthalpies for phase changes given in the Sample Exercise above.) ***Answer:*** $-20.9 \text{ kJ} - 33.4 \text{ kJ} - 6.3 \text{ kJ} = -60.6 \text{ kJ}$

We cool a substance by removing heat from it. As noted in the above practice exercise, cooling is an exothermic process; the system must release heat to become cooler. We sometimes observe some unusual behavior of vapors and liquids upon careful, controlled cooling. For example, under the right conditions we can cool liquid water to a temperature well below 0°C without forming ice. We say that the water is *supercooled.*

We can understand supercooling by considering the molecular structure of solids and liquids. When we cause a solid to undergo a phase change to a liquid, we are increasing the kinetic energy of the molecules sufficiently to break the intermolecular forces that hold the solid in a rigid order. When we cool a liquid, the kinetic energy of the molecules decreases to the point at which the formation of a well-ordered phase is favorable. However, the molecules need to organize themselves properly in order for the solid to form. We rarely observe supercooled water in nature because particles of dust and other solid surfaces provide good sites for the growth of ice crystals to begin.

Critical Temperature and Pressure

Gases can be liquefied by compressing them at a suitable temperature. As temperature rises, however, gases become more difficult to liquefy because of the increasing kinetic energies of their molecules. For every substance there exists a temperature above which the gas cannot be liquefied, regardless of the pressure. The highest temperature at which a substance can exist as a liquid is

TABLE 11.4 △ Critical Temperatures and Pressures of Selected Substances

Substance	Critical temperature (K)	Critical pressure (atm)
Ammonia, NH_3	405.6	111.5
Argon, Ar	150.9	48
Carbon dioxide, CO_2	304.3	73.0
Dinitrogen, N_2	126.1	33.5
Dioxygen, O_2	154.4	49.7
Freon-12, CCl_2F_2	384.7	39.6
Water, H_2O	647.6	217.7

Supercritical Fluid Extraction

At ordinary pressures, a substance above its critical temperature behaves as an ordinary gas. However, as pressure increases up to several hundred atmospheres, its character changes. Like a gas, it still expands to fill the confines of its container, but its density approaches that of a liquid. (For example, the critical temperature of water is 374.4 °C, and its critical pressure is 217.7 atm. At this temperature and pressure, the density of water is 0.4 g/mL.) It is perhaps more appropriate to speak of a substance at critical temperature and pressure as a *supercritical fluid* rather than as a gas.

Like liquids, supercritical fluids can behave as solvents, dissolving a wide range of substances. This ability forms the basis of a system for separating the components of mixtures, a process known as supercritical fluid extraction. The solvent power of a supercritical fluid increases as its density increases. Conversely, lowering its density (either by decreasing pressure or increasing

temperature) causes the supercritical fluid and the dissolved material to separate. With skillful manipulation of temperature and pressure, it is possible to separate the components of very complicated mixtures.

The process of supercritical fluid extraction is now under extensive study in the chemical, food, drug, and energy industries. A process for removing caffeine from green coffee beans by extraction with supercritical carbon dioxide has been in commercial operation for several years. At the proper temperature and pressure, the CO_2 removes caffeine from the beans but leaves the flavor and aroma components, producing decaffeinated coffee. Other applications of supercritical CO_2 extraction include removal of nicotine from tobaccos and removal of oil from potato chips, producing a lower-calorie product that is less greasy but has the same flavor and texture.

---

called its **critical temperature.** The **critical pressure** is the pressure required to bring about liquefaction at this critical temperature. The greater the intermolecular attractive forces, the more readily a gas is liquefied, and thus the higher the critical temperature of the substance.

The critical temperatures and pressures of substances are often of considerable importance to engineers and other people working with gases because they provide information about the conditions under which gases liquefy. Sometimes we want to liquefy a gas; other times we want to avoid liquefying it. It is useless to try to liquefy a gas by applying pressure if the gas is above its critical temperature. For example, O_2 has a critical temperature of 154.4 K. It must be cooled below this temperature before it can be liquefied by pressure. In contrast, ammonia has a critical temperature of 405.6 K. Thus, it can be liquefied at room temperature (approximately 295 K) by compressing the gas to a sufficient pressure. The critical temperatures and pressures of some selected substances are given in Table 11.4.

11.5 Vapor Pressure

We have seen that molecules can escape from the surface of a liquid into the gas phase by vaporization or evaporation. Suppose we conduct an experiment in which we place a quantity of ethyl alcohol (ethanol) in an evacuated, closed container such as that in Figure 11.19. The ethanol will quickly begin to evaporate. As a result, the pressure exerted by the vapor in the space above the liquid

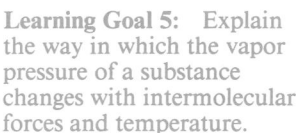

FIGURE 11.19 Illustration of the equilibrium vapor pressure over liquid ethanol. In (*a*) we imagine that no ethanol molecules exist in the gas phase; there is zero pressure in the cell. In (*b*) the rate at which molecules of ethanol leave the surface equals the rate at which gas molecules pass into the liquid phase. Thus, the rates of condensation and of vaporization are equal. This produces a stable vapor pressure that does not change with time, as long as temperature remains constant.

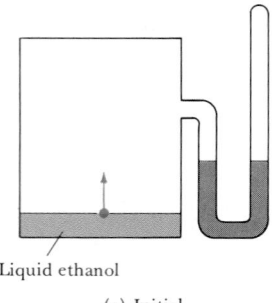
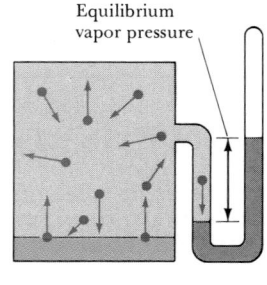

Equilibrium vapor pressure

Liquid ethanol

(*a*) Initial   (*b*) At equilibrium

will begin to increase. After a short time, the pressure of the vapor will attain a constant value, which we call the **vapor pressure** of the substance.

Explaining Vapor Pressure on the Molecular Level

The molecules of a liquid move at various speeds. Figure 11.20 shows the distribution of kinetic energies of the particles at the surface of a liquid at two temperatures. The distribution curves are like those shown earlier for gases (Figures 10.13 and 10.14). At any instant, some of the molecules on the surface of the liquid possess sufficient energy to escape from the attractive forces of their neighbors. The weaker the attractive forces, the larger the number of molecules that are able to escape into the gas phase, and hence the higher the vapor pressure.

At any particular temperature, the movement of molecules from the liquid to the gas phase goes on continuously. However, as the number of gas-phase molecules increases, the probability increases that a molecule in the gas phase will strike the liquid surface and stick there, as shown in Figure 11.19(*b*). Eventually, the rate at which molecules return to the liquid is exactly equal to the rate at which they escape. The number of molecules in the gas phase then reaches a steady value, and the pressure of the vapor at this stage becomes constant.

The condition in which two opposing processes are occurring simultaneously at equal rates is called a **dynamic equilibrium.** A liquid and its vapor are in equilibrium when evaporation and condensation occur at equal rates. The

FIGURE 11.20 Distribution of kinetic energies of surface molecules of a hypothetical liquid at two different temperatures. The minimum energy needed to escape from the surface depends on the magnitude of the attractive forces between molecules. The fraction of molecules having sufficient kinetic energy to escape the liquid is given by the shaded area. Notice that the fraction of molecules that can escape the liquid increases with increasing temperature.

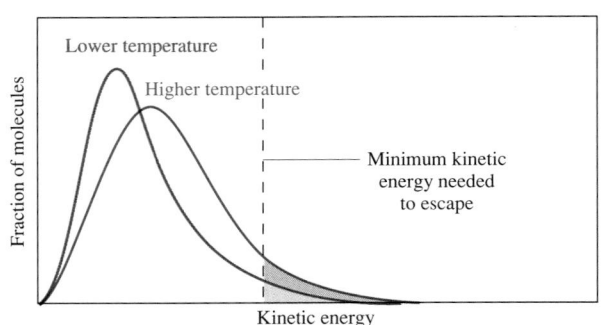

Lower temperature

Higher temperature

Fraction of molecules

Minimum kinetic energy needed to escape

Kinetic energy

Figure 11.20

observer may conclude that nothing is occurring during an equilibrium because there is no net change in the system. In fact, a great deal is happening; molecules continuously pass from the liquid state to the gas state and from the gas state to the liquid state. All equilibria between different states of matter possess this dynamic character. *The vapor pressure of a liquid is the pressure exerted by its vapor when the liquid and vapor states are in dynamic equilibrium.*

Volatility, Vapor Pressure, and Temperature

When vaporization occurs in an open container, as when water evaporates from a bowl, the vapor spreads away from the liquid. Little, if any, is recaptured at the surface of the liquid. Equilibrium never occurs, and the vapor continues to form until the liquid evaporates to dryness. Substances with high vapor pressure (such as gasoline) evaporate more quickly than substances with low vapor pressure (such as motor oil). Liquids that evaporate readily are said to be **volatile.**

Common Misconception: The adjective *volatile* is often used imprecisely (especially by the news media) with vague connotations ranging from corrosive to hazardous to flammable. The definition given here is the only one used in chemistry.

Hot water evaporates more quickly than cold water because vapor pressure increases with temperature. We see this effect in Figure 11.20: As the temperature of a liquid is increased, the molecules move more energetically, and a greater fraction can therefore escape more readily from their neighbors. Figure 11.21 depicts the variation in vapor pressure with temperature for four common substances that differ greatly in volatility. Note that in all cases the vapor pressure increases nonlinearly with increasing temperature.

Learning Goal 6: Describe the relationship between the pressure on the surface of a liquid and the boiling point of the liquid.

Vapor Pressure and Boiling Point

A liquid boils when its vapor pressure equals the external pressure acting on the surface of the liquid. At this point, bubbles of vapor are able to form within the interior of the liquid. The temperature of boiling increases with increasing external pressure. The boiling point of a liquid at 1 atm pressure is called its **normal boiling point.** From Figure 11.21, we see that the normal boiling point of water is 100°C.

Point of Emphasis: The term *boiling point* is often used to refer to the *normal boiling point,* that is, the boiling point at 1.0 atm external pressure. If the external pressure is varied, the boiling point will also vary.

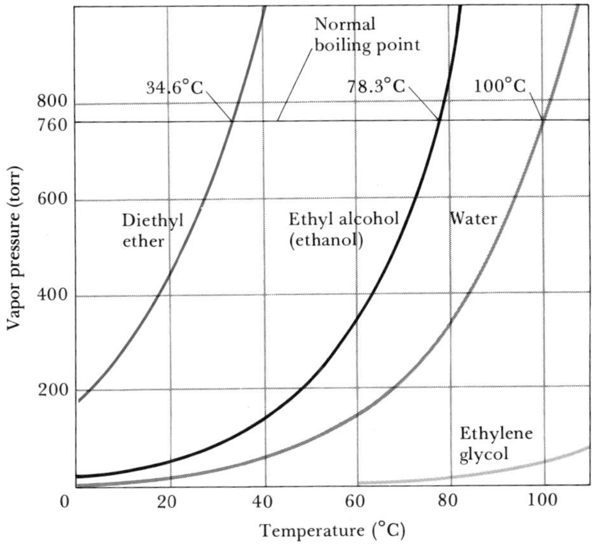

FIGURE 11.21 Vapor pressure of four common liquids shown as a function of temperature. The temperature at which the vapor pressure is 760 torr is the normal boiling point of each liquid.

Figure 11.21

A CLOSER LOOK

The Clausius-Clapeyron Equation

You might have noticed that the plots of the variation of vapor pressure with temperature shown in Figure 11.21 have a distinct shape: Each curves sharply upward to a higher vapor pressure with increasing temperature. The relationship between vapor pressure and temperature is given by an equation called the *Clausius-Clapeyron equation*:

$$\ln P = \frac{-\Delta H_{vap}}{RT} + C \qquad [11.1]$$

In this equation, T is the absolute temperature, R is the gas constant (8.3145 J/mol-K), ΔH_{vap} is the enthalpy of vaporization per mole of substance, and C is a constant. We see that the Clausius-Clapeyron equation predicts

that a graph of $\ln P$ versus $1/T$ should give a straight line with a slope equal to $-\Delta H_{vap}/R$. Thus, we can use a plot of vapor pressure versus temperature to determine the enthalpy of vaporization of a substance.

As an example of the application of the Clausius-Clapeyron equation, the vapor-pressure data for ethanol shown in Figure 11.21 are graphed in Figure 11.22 as $\ln P$ versus $1/T$. Note that the data lie on a straight line with a negative slope. We can use the slope of the line to determine ΔH_{vap} for ethanol. We can also extrapolate the line to obtain values for the vapor pressure of ethanol at temperatures above and below the temperature range for which we have data.

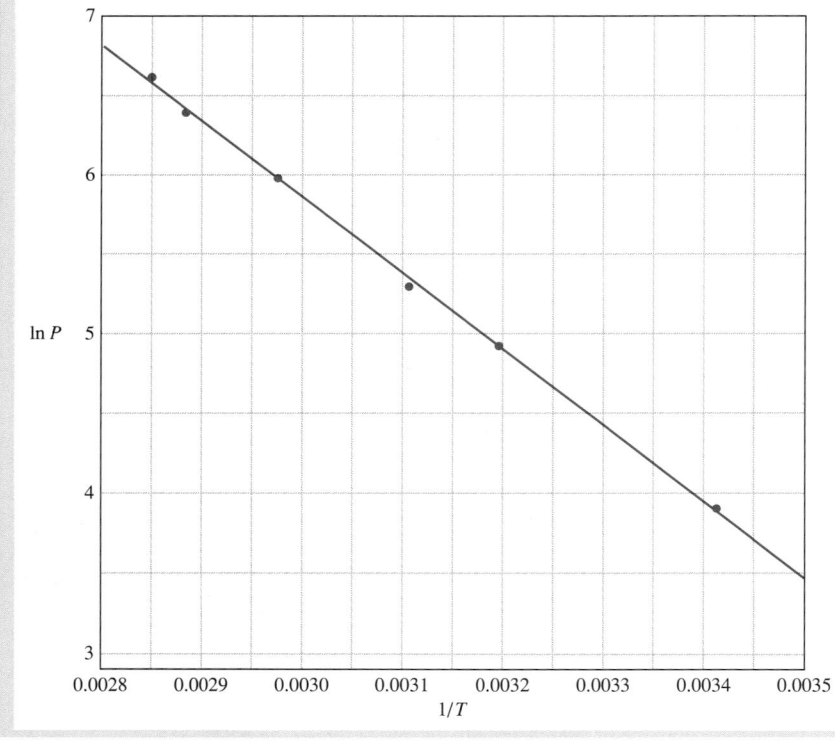

FIGURE 11.22 Application of the Clausius-Clapeyron equation, Equation 11.1, to the vapor-pressure-versus-temperature data for ethanol. The slope of the line equals $-\Delta H_{vap}/R$.

The boiling point is important to many processes that involve heating liquids, including cooking. The time required to cook food depends on the temperature. As long as water is present, the maximum temperature of the cooking food is the boiling point of water. Pressure cookers work by allowing steam to escape only when it exceeds a predetermined pressure; the pressure above the water can therefore increase above atmospheric pressure. The higher pressure causes water to boil at a higher temperature, thereby allowing the food to get hotter and so cook more rapidly. The effect of pressure on boiling point also explains why it takes longer to cook food at higher elevations than at sea level. At higher altitudes the atmospheric pressure is lower, and so water boils at a lower temperature.

SAMPLE EXERCISE 11.4

Use Figure 11.21 to estimate the boiling point of diethyl ether under an external pressure of 600 torr.

SOLUTION   The boiling point is the temperature at which the vapor pressure is equal to the external pressure. From Figure 11.21, we see that the boiling point at 600 torr is about 27°C, which is close to room temperature. We can make a flask of diethyl ether boil at room temperature by using a vacuum pump to lower the pressure above the liquid to about 600 torr.

PRACTICE EXERCISE

At what external pressure will ethanol have a boiling point of 60°C?
Answer: About 350 torr

11.6 Phase Diagrams

The equilibrium between a liquid and its vapor is not the only dynamic equilibrium that can exist between states of matter. Under appropriate conditions of temperature and pressure, a solid can be in equilibrium with its liquid state or even with its vapor state. A **phase diagram** is a graphical way to summarize the conditions under which equilibria exist between the different states of matter. It also allows us to predict the phase of a substance that is stable at any given temperature and pressure.

The general form of a phase diagram for a substance that exhibits three phases is shown in Figure 11.23. The diagram contains three important curves, each of which represents the conditions of temperature and pressure at which the various phases can coexist at equilibrium.

Learning Goal 7:   Draw a phase diagram of a substance given appropriate data, and use a phase diagram to predict which phases are present at any given temperature and pressure.

Teaching Note: A phase diagram allows one to predict whether a substance will be a gas, liquid, or solid at a given temperature and pressure.

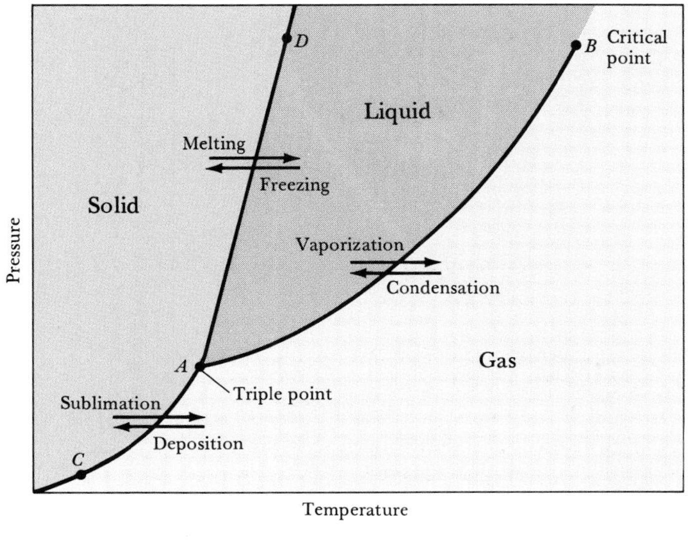

FIGURE 11.23   General shape for a phase diagram of a system exhibiting three phases: gas, liquid, and solid.

Figure 11.23

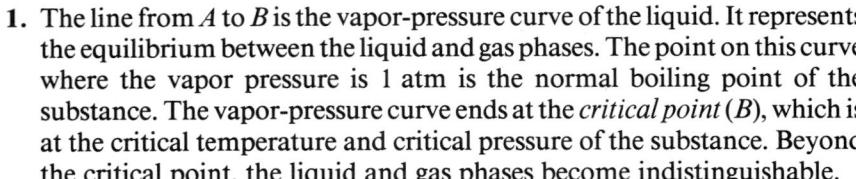

1. The line from A to B is the vapor-pressure curve of the liquid. It represents the equilibrium between the liquid and gas phases. The point on this curve where the vapor pressure is 1 atm is the normal boiling point of the substance. The vapor-pressure curve ends at the *critical point* (B), which is at the critical temperature and critical pressure of the substance. Beyond the critical point, the liquid and gas phases become indistinguishable.

2. The line AC represents the variation in the vapor pressure of the solid as it sublimes at different temperatures.

3. The line from A through D represents the change in melting point of the solid with increasing pressure. This line normally slopes slightly to the right as pressure increases. For most substances, the solid is denser than the liquid; therefore, an increase in pressure usually favors the more compact solid phase. Thus, higher temperatures are required to melt the solid at higher pressures. The *melting point* of a substance is identical to its *freezing point*. The two differ only in the temperature direction from which the phase change is approached. The melting point at 1 atm is the **normal melting point.**

Point A, where the three curves intersect, is known as the **triple point.** All three phases are at equilibrium at this temperature and pressure. Any other point on the three curves represents an equilibrium between two phases. Any point on the diagram that does not fall on a line corresponds to conditions under which only one phase is present. Notice that the gas phase is the stable phase at low pressures and high temperatures. The conditions under which the solid phase is stable extend to low temperatures and high pressures. The stability range for liquids lies between the other two regions.

The Phase Diagrams of H_2O and CO_2

Figure 11.24 shows the phase diagrams of H_2O and CO_2. Notice that the solid-liquid equilibrium (melting point) line of CO_2 is normal; its melting point increases with increasing pressure. On the other hand, the melting point of H_2O

Figure 11.24

FIGURE 11.24 Phase diagram of (*a*) H_2O and (*b*) CO_2. The axes are not drawn to scale in either case. In (*a*), for water, note the triple point A (0.0098°C, 4.58 torr), the normal melting (or freezing) point B (0°C, 1 atm), the normal boiling point C (100°C, 1 atm), and the critical point D (374.4°C, 217.7 atm). In (*b*), for carbon dioxide, note the triple point X (−56.4°C, 5.11 atm), the normal sublimation point Y (−78.5°C, 1 atm), and the critical point Z (31.1°C, 73.0 atm).

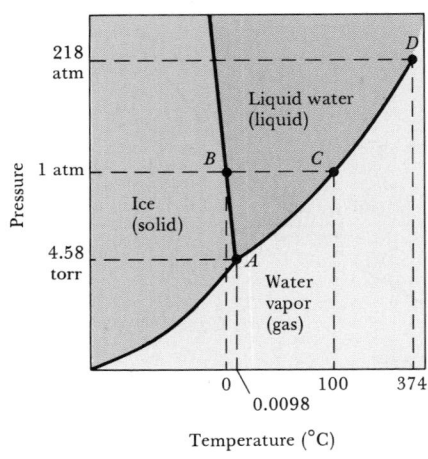

(*a*)

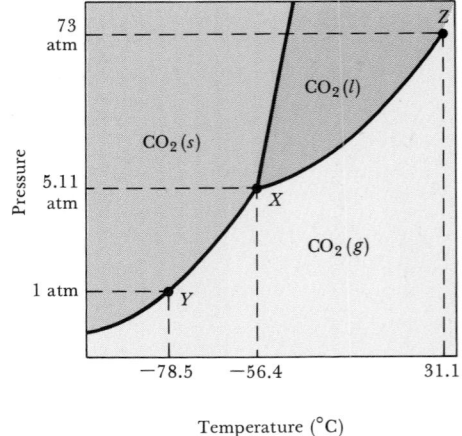

(*b*)

decreases with increasing pressure. Water is among the very few substances whose liquid form is more compact than its solid form. ∞ (Sec. 11.2)

The triple point of H_2O (0.0098°C and 4.58 torr) is at much lower pressure than that of CO_2 (−56.4°C and 5.11 atm). For CO_2 to exist as a liquid, the pressure must exceed 5.11 atm. Consequently, solid CO_2 does not melt but rather sublimes when heated at 1 atm. Thus, CO_2 does not have a normal melting point; instead, it has a normal sublimation point, −78.5°C. Because CO_2 sublimes rather than melts as it absorbs energy at ordinary pressures, solid CO_2 (Dry Ice) is a convenient coolant. For water (ice) to sublime, however, its vapor pressure must be below 4.58 torr. Freeze-drying of food is accomplished by placing frozen food in a low-pressure chamber (below 4.58 torr) so that the ice in it sublimes.

SAMPLE EXERCISE 11.5

Referring to Figure 11.25, describe any changes in the phases present when H_2O is **(a)** kept at 0°C while the pressure is increased from that at point 1 to that at point 5 (vertical line); **(b)** kept at 1.00 atm while the temperature is increased from that at point 6 to that at point 9 (horizontal line).

SOLUTION **(a)** At point 1, H_2O exists totally as a vapor. At point 2, a solid-vapor equilibrium exists. Above that pressure, at point 3, all the H_2O is converted to a solid. At point 4, some of the solid melts, and an equilibrium between solid and liquid is achieved. At still higher pressures, all the H_2O melts, so that only the liquid phase is present at point 5.

 (b) At point 6, the H_2O exists entirely as a solid. When the temperature reaches point 4, the solid begins to melt, and an equilibrium condition occurs between the solid and the liquid phases. At a yet higher temperature, point 7, the solid has been converted entirely to a liquid. When point 8 is encountered, vapor forms and a liquid-vapor equilibrium is achieved. Upon further heating, to point 9, the H_2O is converted entirely to the vapor phase.

PRACTICE EXERCISE

Using Figure 11.24(*b*), describe what happens when the following changes are made in a CO_2 sample initially at 1 atm and −60°C. **(a)** Pressure increases at constant temperature to 60 atm. **(b)** Temperature increases from −60°C to −20°C at constant 60 atm pressure. ***Answers:*** **(a)** $CO_2(g) \longrightarrow CO_2(s)$; **(b)** $CO_2(s) \longrightarrow CO_2(l)$

FIGURE 11.25 Phase diagram of H_2O.

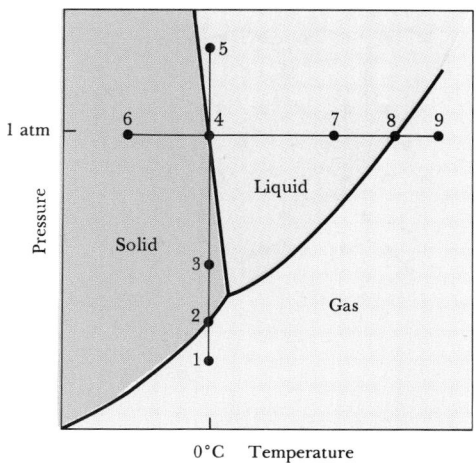

(a)

(b)

(c)

FIGURE 11.26 Crystalline solids come in a variety of forms and colors. (*a*) Calcite, (*b*) fluorite twin crystals, (*c*) quartz. (Runk, Schoenberger/Grant Heilman Photography)

11.7 Structures of Solids

Throughout the remainder of this chapter we will focus on how the properties of solids relate to their structures and bonding. Solids can be either crystalline or amorphous (noncrystalline). A **crystalline solid** is a solid whose atoms, ions, or molecules are ordered in well-defined arrangements. These solids usually have flat surfaces or faces that make definite angles with one another. The orderly stacks of particles that produce these faces also cause the solids to have highly regular shapes (Figure 11.26). Quartz and diamond are examples of crystalline solids.

An **amorphous solid** (from the Greek words for "without form") is a solid whose particles have no orderly structure. These solids lack well-defined faces and shapes. Many amorphous solids are mixtures of molecules that do not stack together well. Most others are composed of large, complicated molecules. Familiar amorphous solids include rubber and glass.

Quartz, SiO_2, is a crystalline solid with a three-dimensional structure like that shown in Figure 11.27(*a*). When quartz melts (at about 1600°C), it becomes a viscous, tacky liquid. Although the silicon-oxygen network remains largely intact, many Si—O bonds are broken, and the rigid order of the quartz is lost. If the melt is rapidly cooled, the atoms are unable to return to an orderly arrangement. An amorphous solid known as quartz glass or silica glass results [Figure 11.27(*b*)].

FIGURE 11.27 Schematic comparisons of (*a*) crystalline SiO_2 (quartz) and (*b*) amorphous SiO_2 (quartz glass). The blue dots represent silicon atoms; the red dots represent oxygen atoms. The structure is actually three-dimensional and not planar as drawn. The unit shown as the basic building block (silicon and three oxygens) actually has four oxygens, the fourth coming out of the plane of the paper and capable of bonding to other silicon atoms.

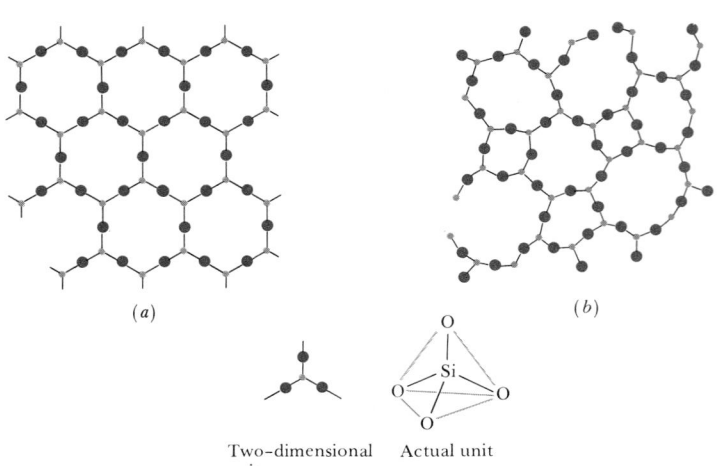
(a)

(b)

Two-dimensional unit   Actual unit

Because the particles of an amorphous solid lack any long-range order, intermolecular forces vary in strength throughout a sample. Thus, amorphous solids do not melt at specific temperatures. Instead, they soften over a temperature range as intermolecular forces of various strengths are overcome. A crystalline solid, on the other hand, melts at a specific temperature.

Unit Cells

The order characteristic of crystalline solids allows us to convey a picture of an entire crystal by looking at only a small part of it. We can think of the solid as being built up by stacking together identical building blocks, much as a brick wall is formed by stacking individual, identical bricks. The repeating unit of a solid—the crystalline "brick"—is known as the **unit cell.** A simple two-dimensional example appears in the sheet of wallpaper shown in Figure 11.28. There are several ways of choosing the repeat pattern, or unit cell, of the design, but the choice is usually the smallest one that shows clearly the symmetry characteristic of the entire pattern.

A crystalline solid can be represented by a three-dimensional array of points, each of which represents an identical environment within the crystal. Such an array of points is called a **crystal lattice.** We can imagine forming the entire crystal structure by arranging the contents of the unit cell repeatedly on a network of points.

Figure 11.29 shows a crystal lattice and its associated unit cell. In general, unit cells are parallelepipeds (six-sided figures whose faces are parallelograms). Each unit cell can be described in terms of the lengths of the edges of the cell (a, b, and c) and by the angles between these edges (α, β, and γ), as shown in Figure 11.29. The lattices of all crystalline compounds can be described in terms of seven basic types of unit cells. The simplest of these is the cubic unit cell, in which all the sides are equal in length and all the angles are 90°.

FIGURE 11.28 Wallpaper design showing a characteristic repeat pattern. Each dashed blue square denotes the unit cell of the repeat pattern.

Point of Emphasis: The unit cell is the smallest repeating unit of a solid.

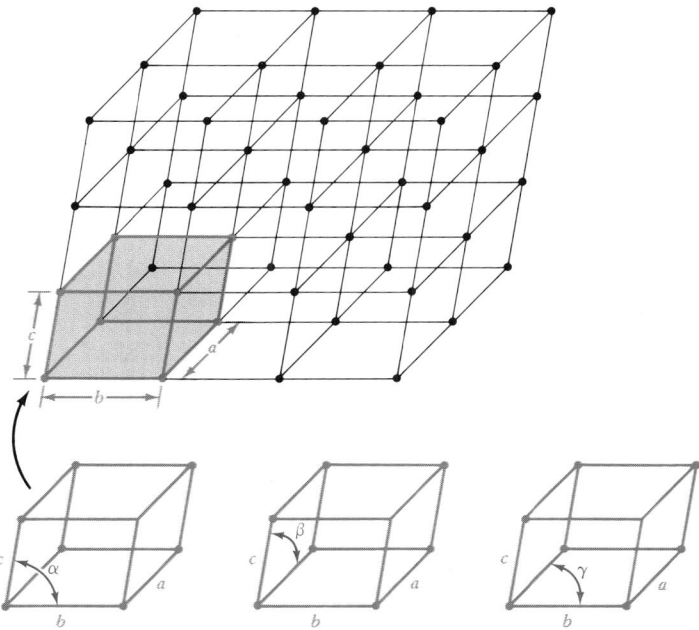

FIGURE 11.29 Simple crystal lattice and its associated unit cell. Each view of the unit cell shows one of the characteristic angles between unit-cell axes. Angle α is the angle between the b and c axes; β is the angle between the a and c axes; γ is the angle between the a and b axes.

FIGURE 11.30 The three types of unit cells found in cubic lattices.

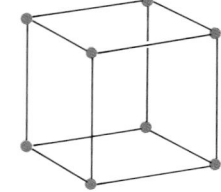 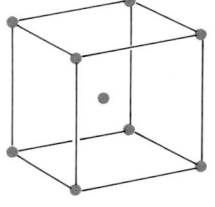 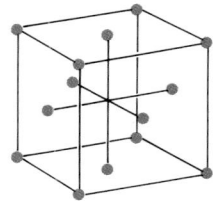

Primitive cubic   Body-centered cubic   Face-centered cubic

There are three kinds of cubic unit cells, as illustrated in Figure 11.30. When lattice points are at the corners only, the unit cell is described as **primitive cubic.** When a lattice point also occurs at the center of the unit cell, the cell is known as **body-centered cubic.** A third type of cubic cell has lattice points at the center of each face, as well as at each corner, an arrangement known as **face-centered cubic.**

FIGURE 11.31 Portion of the crystal lattice of NaCl, illustrating two ways of defining its unit cell. Gray spheres represent Na$^+$ ions, and green spheres represent Cl$^-$ ions. Colored lines define the unit cell. In (a) Cl$^-$ ions are at the corners of the unit cell. In (b) Na$^+$ ions are at the corners of the unit cell. Both of these choices for the unit cell are acceptable; both have the same volume, and in both cases identical points are arranged in a face-centered-cubic fashion.

The Crystal Structure of Sodium Chloride

It is instructive to examine the crystal structure of NaCl (Figure 11.31). This figure shows two ways of locating the lattice points so they are in identical environments. In Figure 11.31(a), the points are centered on the Cl$^-$ ions; in Figure 11.31(b), they are centered on Na$^+$. In both cases, the structure possesses a lattice with a face-centered-cubic unit cell. The cubic character of the unit cell is reflected in the shapes of well-formed crystals of NaCl, Figure 11.32.

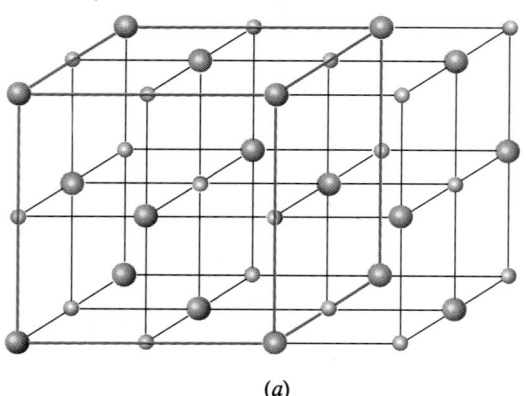

(a)

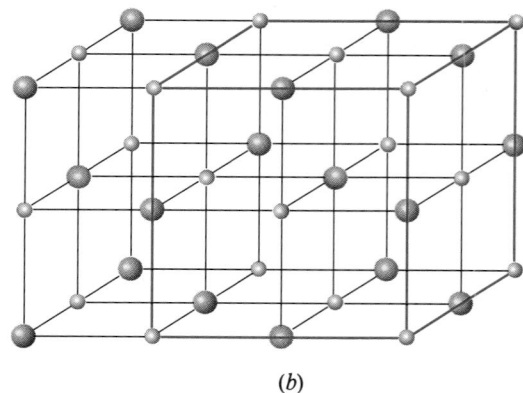

(b)

FIGURE 11.32 Crystals of NaCl, showing well-defined crystal planes based on the underlying cubic structure. (Dr. E. R. Degginger)

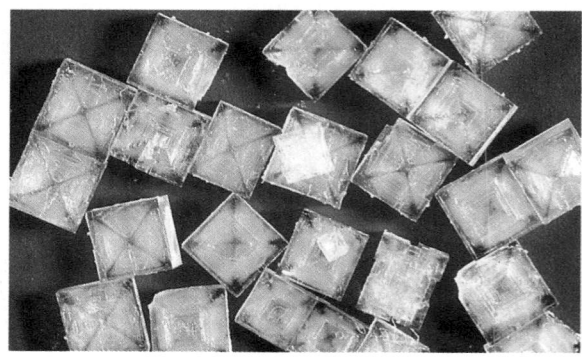

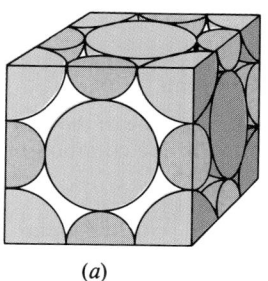
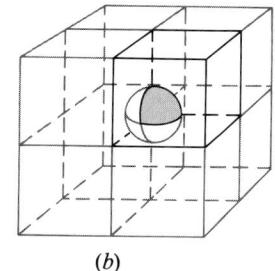
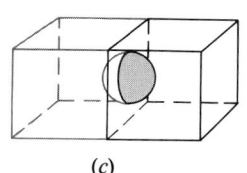

(a)   (b)   (c)

FIGURE 11.33 (a) The unit cell of NaCl showing the relative sizes of the Na⁺ ions (gray) and Cl⁻ ions (green). Notice that only portions of most of the ions lie within the boundaries of the single unit cell. (b) The sharing of a corner atom or ion by eight unit cells. (c) The sharing of a face-centered atom or ion by two unit cells.

In Figure 11.31, the Na^+ and Cl^- ions have been moved apart so the symmetry of the structure can be seen more clearly. In this representation, no attention is paid to the relative sizes of the ions. In contrast, Figure 11.33(a) provides a representation that shows the relative sizes of the ions and how they fill the unit cell. Notice that the particles at the corners, edges, and faces do not lie wholly within the unit cell. Instead, these particles are shared by other unit cells. A particle at a corner is shared by eight unit cells [Figure 11.33(b)], one at the center of a face is shared by two [Figure 11.33(c)], and one at the edge is shared by four. Table 11.5 summarizes the fraction of an atom that occupies a unit cell for various positions.

The total cation-to-anion ratio of a unit cell must be the same as that for the entire crystal. Therefore, within the unit cell of NaCl there must be an equal number of Na^+ and Cl^- ions. Similarly, the unit cell for $CaCl_2$ would have one Ca^{2+} for each two Cl^-, and so forth.

TABLE 11.5 △
Fraction of an Atom That Occupies a Unit Cell for Various Positions in the Unit Cell

Position in unit cell	Fraction in unit cell
Center	1
Face	1/2
Edge	1/4
Corner	1/8

SAMPLE EXERCISE 11.6

Determine the net number of Na^+ and Cl^- ions in the NaCl unit cell (Figure 11.33).

SOLUTION There is one-fourth of a Na^+ on each edge, a whole Na^+ in the center of the cube (refer also to Figure 11.31), one-eighth of a Cl^- on each corner, and one-half of a Cl^- on each face. Thus, we have the following:

$$Na^+: \quad (\tfrac{1}{4} \, Na^+ \text{ per edge})(12 \text{ edges}) = 3 \, Na^+$$

$$(1 \, Na^+ \text{ per center})(1 \text{ center}) = 1 \, Na^+$$

$$Cl^-: \quad (\tfrac{1}{8} \, Cl^- \text{ per corner})(8 \text{ corner}) = 1 \, Cl^-$$

$$(\tfrac{1}{2} \, Cl^- \text{ per face})(6 \text{ faces}) = 3 \, Cl^-$$

Thus, the unit cell contains four Na^+ and four Cl^-. This result agrees with the compound's stoichiometry: one Na^+ for each Cl^-.

PRACTICE EXERCISE

The element iron crystallizes in a form called α-iron, which has a body-centered-cubic unit cell. How many iron atoms are in the unit cell? **Answer:** two

SAMPLE EXERCISE 11.7

The geometric arrangement of ions in crystals of LiF is the same as that in NaCl. The unit cell of LiF is 4.02 Å on an edge. What is the density of LiF?

SOLUTION Because the arrangement of ions in LiF is the same as that in NaCl, a unit cell of LiF will contain four Li^+ and four F^- ions (Sample Exercise 11.6). Density is a measurement of mass per unit volume. Thus, we can calculate the density of LiF by the mass contained in a unit cell and by the volume of the unit cell. The mass contained in one unit cell is

$$4(6.94 \text{ amu}) + 4(19.0 \text{ amu}) = 103.8 \text{ amu}$$

The volume of a cube of length a on an edge is a^3, so the volume of the unit cell is $(4.02 \text{ Å})^3$. We can now calculate the density, converting to the common units of g/cm³:

$$\text{Density} = \frac{103.8 \text{ amu}}{(4.02 \text{ Å})^3} \left(\frac{1 \text{ g}}{6.02 \times 10^{23} \text{ amu}}\right)\left(\frac{1 \text{ Å}}{10^{-8} \text{ cm}}\right)^3 = 2.65 \text{ g/cm}^3$$

This value agrees with that found by simple density measurements. The size and contents of the unit cell are therefore consistent with the macroscopic density of the substance.

PRACTICE EXERCISE

The body-centered cubic unit cell of a particular crystalline form of iron is 2.8664 Å on each side. Calculate the density of this form of iron. *Answer:* 7.878 g/cm³

Close Packing of Spheres

The structures adopted by crystalline solids are those that bring particles in closest contact to maximize the attractive forces between them. In many cases, the particles that make up the solids are spherical or approximately so. Such is the case for atoms in metallic solids. Many molecules can also be approximated as spheres, as seen for CH_4 in Figure 11.34. It is therefore instructive to consider how equal-sized spheres can pack most efficiently (that is, with the minimum amount of empty space).

The most efficient arrangement of a layer of equal-sized spheres is shown in Figure 11.35(a). Each sphere is surrounded by six others in the layer. A second layer of spheres will pack efficiently in the depressions of the first layer

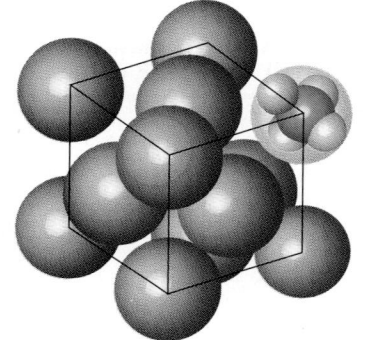

FIGURE 11.34 Unit cell of solid methane. Each large sphere represents a CH_4 molecule, as shown in the upper right.

FIGURE 11.35 Close packing of equal-sized spheres. (*a*) One layer; each sphere is in contact with six others. (*b*) Spheres in the second layer sit in the depressions of the first layer. (*c*) In the hexagonal close-packed structure, each sphere in the third layer sits directly over a sphere in the first layer. (*d*) In the cubic close-packed structure, the spheres in the third layer are not directly over the first-layer spheres.

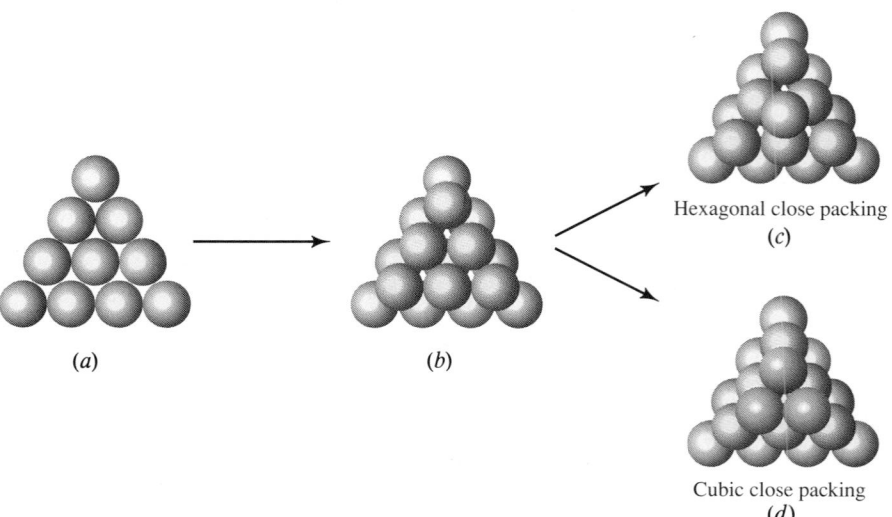

Hexagonal close packing
(*c*)

Cubic close packing
(*d*)

(*a*)

(*b*)

[Figure 11.35(b)]. The spheres of the third layer likewise sit in the depressions of the second layer. However, there are two types of depressions, and they result in different structures.

If the spheres of the third layer are placed immediately above those of the first layer, as shown in Figure 11.35(c), the result is a structure known as **hexagonal close packing.** The third layer repeats the first layer, the fourth layer repeats the second layer, and so forth, giving a layer sequence *ABABAB* . . . . The stacking sequence in the hexagonal close-packed structure is viewed from a different perspective in Figure 11.36(a).

If the spheres of the third layer are placed in slightly different positions, as shown in Figure 11.35(d), the resulting structure is known as **cubic close packing.** In this case the fourth layer repeats the first layer, giving a layer sequence *ABCABC* . . . . The stacking sequence is pictured in Figure 11.36(b). Although it cannot be seen in either Figure 11.35(d) or Figure 11.36(b), the unit cell of the cubic close-packed structure is face-centered cubic.

In both of the close-packed structures, each sphere has 12 equidistant nearest neighbors: 6 in one plane, 3 above that plane, and 3 below, as seen in Figure 11.36. We say that each sphere has a **coordination number** of 12. The coordination number is the number of particles immediately surrounding a particle in the crystal structure. In both types of close packing, 74 percent of the total volume of the structure is occupied by spheres; 26 percent is empty space between the spheres. By comparison, each sphere in the body-centered-cubic structure has a coordination number of 8, and only 68 percent of the space is occupied. In the simple cubic structure, the coordination number is 6, and only 52 percent of the space is occupied.

When unequal-sized spheres are packed in a lattice, the large particles sometimes assume one of the close-packed arrangements, with small particles occupying the holes between the large spheres. For example, in Li_2O the oxide ions assume a cubic close-packed structure, and the Li^+ ions occupy small cavities that exist between oxide ions.

FIGURE 11.36 (a) Hexagonal close packing. In this arrangement, the atoms of the third layer lie directly over those in the first layer. Thus, the order of layers is *ABABAB*. (b) Cubic close packing. In this arrangement, the atoms of the third layer are not directly over those in the first but are offset by a bit. As a result, the layers are arranged vertically as *ABCABC*.

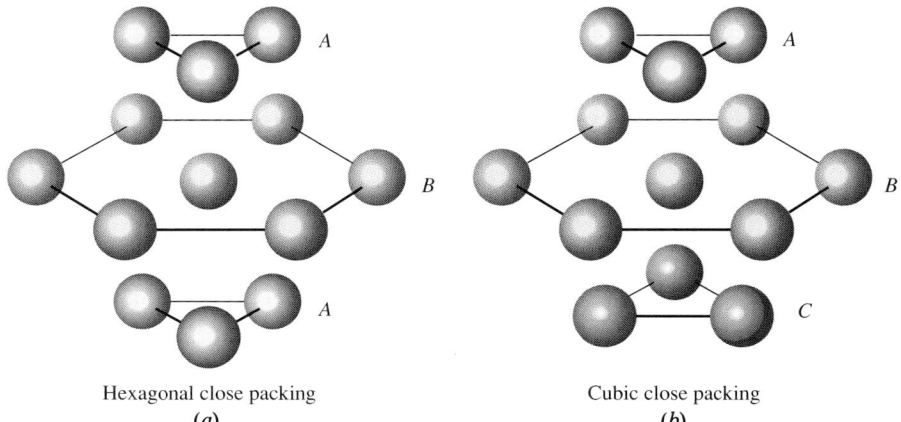

Hexagonal close packing
(a)

Cubic close packing
(b)

Figure 11.36

▲ A CLOSER LOOK

X-Ray Diffraction by Crystals

When light waves pass through a narrow slit, they are scattered in such a way that the wave seems to spread out. This physical phenomenon is called *diffraction*. When light passes through many evenly spaced narrow slits (a *diffraction grating*), the scattered waves interact to form a series of light and dark bands, known as a diffraction pattern. The most effective diffraction of light occurs when the wavelength of the light and the width of the slits are similar in magnitude.

The spacing of the layers of atoms in solid crystals is usually about 2 to 20 Å. The wavelengths of X-rays are also in this range. Thus, a crystal can serve as an effective diffraction grating for X-rays. **X-ray diffraction** results from the scattering of X-rays by a regular arrangement of atoms, molecules, or ions. Much of what we know about crystal structures has been obtained by studies of X-ray diffraction by crystals, a technique known as *X-ray crystallography*. Figure 11.37 depicts the diffraction of a

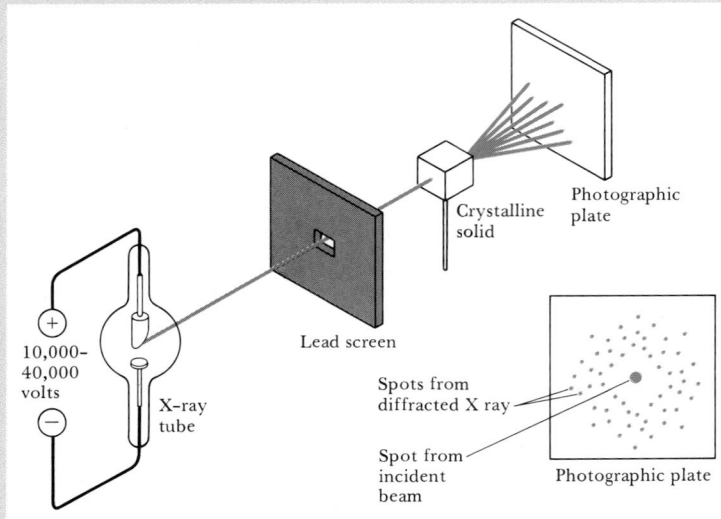

FIGURE 11.37 In X-ray crystallography, an X-ray beam is diffracted by a crystal. The diffraction pattern can be recorded as dark spots where the diffracted X-rays strike a photographic plate.

11.8 Bonding in Solids

Learning Goal 11: Predict the type of solid (molecular, covalent network, ionic, or metallic) formed by a substance, and predict its general properties.

The physical properties of crystalline solids, such as their melting points and hardnesses, depend both on the arrangements of particles and on the attractive forces between them. Table 11.6 on page 402 classifies solids according to the types of forces between particles in solids.

Molecular Solids

Molecular solids consist of atoms or molecules held together by intermolecular forces (dipole-dipole forces, London dispersion forces, and hydrogen bonds). Because these forces are weak, molecular solids are soft. Furthermore, they normally have relatively low melting points (usually below 200°C). Most substances that are gases or liquids at room temperature form molecular solids at low temperature. Examples include Ar, H_2O, and CO_2.

beam of X-rays as it passes through a crystal. The diffraction pattern of spots on the photographic film in Figure 11.37 depends on the particular arrangement of atoms in the crystal. Thus, different types of crystals will give different diffraction patterns. In 1913, the English father and son scientists William and Lawrence Bragg determined how the spacing of layers in crystals leads to different X-ray diffraction patterns. Partly because of their work, it is possible to work backward from the diffraction pattern to deduce the arrangement of atoms that produced the diffraction.

One of the most famous X-ray diffraction patterns is the one for crystals of the genetic material DNA (Figure 11.38), which was obtained in the early 1950s. Working from photographs such as this one, Francis

Crick, Rosalind Franklin, James Watson, and Maurice Wilkins determined the double-helix structure of DNA, one of the most important discoveries in molecular biology.

Today, X-ray crystallography is used extensively to determine the structures of molecules in crystals. The instruments used to measure X-ray diffraction, known as *X-ray diffractometers,* are now computer-controlled, making the collection of diffraction data highly automated. The diffraction pattern of a crystal can be determined very accurately and quickly (sometimes in a matter of hours). Computer programs are then used to analyze the diffraction data and determine the arrangement and structure of the molecules in the crystal.

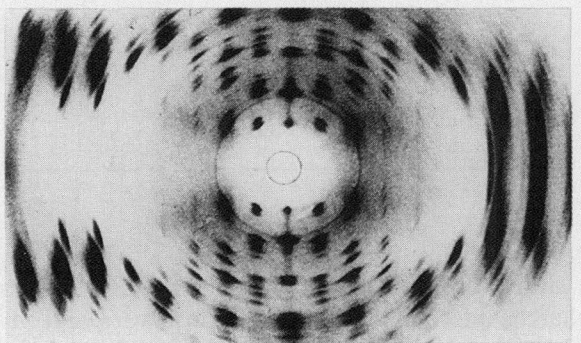

FIGURE 11.38   The X-ray diffraction photograph of one form of crystalline DNA, taken in the early 1950s. From the pattern of dark spots, the double-helical shape of the DNA molecule was deduced. (Science Source/Photo Researchers)

The properties of molecular solids depend not only on the strengths of the forces that operate between molecules but also on the abilities of the molecules to pack efficiently in three dimensions. For example, benzene, C_6H_6, is a highly symmetrical planar molecule. It has a higher melting point than toluene, a compound in which one of the hydrogen atoms of benzene has been replaced by a CH_3 group (Figure 11.39). The lower symmetry of toluene molecules prevents them from packing as efficiently as benzene molecules. As a result, the

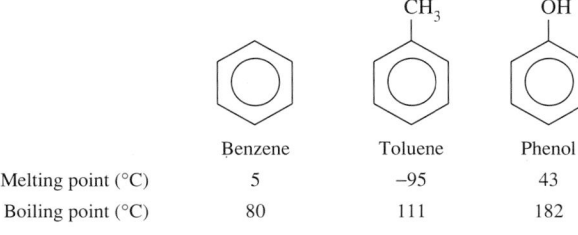

FIGURE 11.39   Comparative melting and boiling points for benzene, toluene, and phenol.

	Benzene	Toluene	Phenol
Melting point (°C)	5	−95	43
Boiling point (°C)	80	111	182

TABLE 11.6 △ Types of Crystalline Solids

Type of solid	Form of unit particles	Forces between particles	Properties	Examples
Molecular	Atoms or molecules	London dispersion, dipole-dipole forces, hydrogen bonds	Fairly soft, low to moderately high melting point, poor thermal and electrical conduction	Argon, Ar; methane, CH_4; sugar, $C_{12}H_{22}O_{11}$; Dry Ice, CO_2
Covalent-network	Atoms that are connected in a covalent-bond network	Covalent bonds	Very hard, very high melting point, often poor thermal and electrical conduction	Diamond, C; quartz, SiO_2
Ionic	Positive and negative ions	Electrostatic attractions	Hard and brittle, high melting point, poor thermal and electrical conduction	Typical salts—for example, NaCl, $Ca(NO_3)_2$
Metallic	Atoms	Metallic bonds	Soft to very hard, low to very high melting point, excellent thermal and electrical conduction, malleable and ductile	All metallic elements—for example, Cu, Fe, Al, W

intermolecular forces that depend on close contact are not as effective, and the melting point is lower. In contrast, the boiling point of toluene is higher than that of benzene, indicating that the intermolecular attractive forces are larger in liquid toluene than in liquid benzene. Figure 11.39 also presents the melting and boiling points of another substituted-benzene compound, phenol. The melting and boiling points of phenol are both higher than those of benzene because of the hydrogen-bonding ability of the OH group of phenol.

Covalent-Network Solids

Covalent-network solids consist of atoms held together in large networks or chains by covalent bonds. Because covalent bonds are much stronger than intermolecular forces, these solids are much harder and have higher melting points than molecular solids. Two of the most familiar examples of covalent-network solids are diamond and graphite, two allotropes of carbon. Other examples include quartz, SiO_2, silicon carbide, SiC, and boron nitride, BN.

In diamond, each carbon atom is bonded to four other carbon atoms as shown in Figure 11.40(a). This interconnected three-dimensional array of strong carbon-carbon single bonds contributes to diamond's unusual hardness. Industrial-grade diamonds are employed in the blades of saws for the most demanding cutting jobs. In keeping with its structure and bonding, diamond also has a high melting point, 3550°C.

In graphite, the carbon atoms are arranged in layers of interconnected hexagonal rings as shown in Figure 11.40(b). Each carbon atom is bonded to

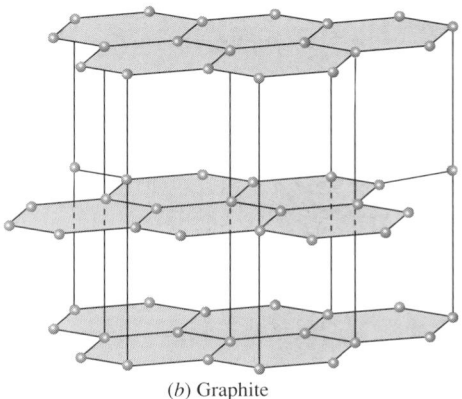

FIGURE 11.40 Structures of (*a*) diamond and (*b*) graphite.

(*a*) Diamond   (*b*) Graphite

three others in the layer. The distance between adjacent carbon atoms in the plane, 1.42 Å, is very close to the C—C distance in benzene, 1.395 Å. In fact, the bonding resembles that of benzene, with delocalized π bonds extending over the layers. ∞ (Sec. 9.5) Electrons move freely through the delocalized orbitals, making graphite a good conductor of electricity along the layers. (If you have ever taken apart a flashlight battery, you know that the central electrode in the battery is made of graphite.) The layers, which are separated by 3.41 Å, are held together by weak dispersion forces. The layers readily slide past one another when rubbed, giving the substance a greasy feel. Graphite is used as a lubricant and in making the "lead" in pencils. Figure 11.41 is a photomicrograph of graphite that reveals its layered structure.

FIGURE 11.41 Piece of graphite photographed with an electron microscope (magnified about 15 million times). The bright bands are layers of carbon atoms that are only 3.41 Å apart. (P. A. Marsch and A. Voet. J. M. Hunder Corp.)

"Buckyball"

Until the mid-1980s, pure solid carbon was thought to exist in only two forms: diamond and graphite, both of which are covalent-network solids. In 1985, a group of researchers led by Richard Smalley and Robert Curl of Rice University in Houston and Harry Kroto of the University of Sussex in England made a startling discovery. They vaporized a sample of graphite with an intense pulse of laser light and used a stream of helium gas to carry the vaporized carbon into a mass spectrometer (see the Closer Look box in Section 3.3). The mass spectrum showed peaks corresponding to clusters of carbon atoms, with a particularly strong peak corresponding to molecules composed of 60 carbon atoms, C_{60}.

The fact that C_{60} clusters were so preferentially formed led the group to propose a radically different form of carbon, namely, C_{60} molecules that were nearly spherical in shape. They proposed that the carbon atoms of C_{60} form a "ball" with 32 faces, of which 12 are pentagons and 20 are hexagons, exactly like a soccer ball (Figure 11.42). The shape of this molecule is reminiscent of the geodesic dome invented by the U.S. engineer and philosopher R. Buckminster Fuller, and so C_{60} was whimsically named "buckminsterfullerene," or "buckyball" for short.

In 1990, a group of U.S. and German scientists found that appreciable amounts of buckyball can be prepared by electrically evaporating graphite in an atmosphere of helium gas. About 14 percent of the resulting soot consists of C_{60} and a related molecule, C_{70}, for which an egg-shaped geometry is proposed. Because these forms of elemental carbon are molecules, they can be dissolved much more easily than diamond or graphite (Figure 11.43).

The discovery of a molecular form of solid carbon is truly remarkable. The chemistry of these molecules, now generally called fullerenes, will lead to the development of some very new chemistry of carbon in the years to come. For example, it is possible to place a metal atom inside a buckyball, generating a molecule in which a metal atom is completely enclosed by the carbon sphere. The properties of such molecules might be very different from those of any molecules known to date.

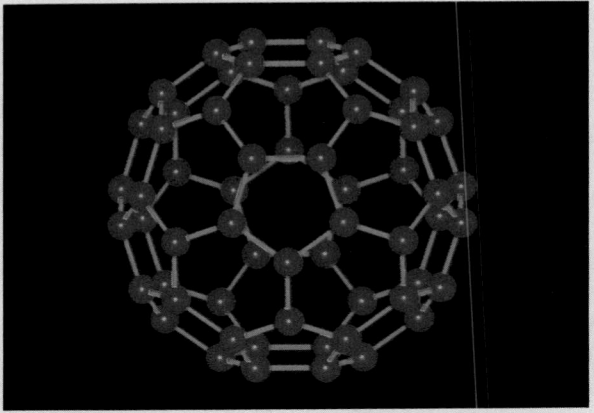

FIGURE 11.42 The buckminsterfullerene molecule, C_{60}, has a highly symmetric structure in which the 60 carbon atoms sit at the vertices of a truncated icosahedron —the same geometry as a soccer ball. (Clive Freeman/Biosym Technologies/Science Photo Library/Photo Researchers)

FIGURE 11.43 Unlike diamond and graphite, the new molecular forms of carbon can be dissolved in organic solvents. The orange solution at left is a solution of C_{70} in *n*-hexane, which is a colorless liquid. The magenta solution at right is a solution of buckyball, C_{60}, in *n*-hexane. (Robert L. Whetten, UCLA)

Teaching Note: For ionic attraction, $E \propto \dfrac{Q^+Q^-}{d}$. There is also a contribution to the energy due to short-range interactions.

Ionic Solids

Ionic solids consist of ions held together by ionic bonds. ∞ (Sec. 8.2) The strength of an ionic bond depends strongly on the charges of the ions. Thus,

NaCl, in which the ions have charges of $1+$ and $1-$, has a melting point of $801\,^\circ$C, whereas MgO, in which the charges are $2+$ and $2-$, melts at $2852\,^\circ$C.

The structures of simple ionic solids can be classified as a few basic types. The NaCl structure is a representative example of one type. Other compounds that possess this same structure include LiF, KCl, AgCl, and CaO. Three other common types of crystal structures are shown in Figure 11.44.

The structure adopted by an ionic solid depends largely on the charges and relative sizes of the ions. In the NaCl structure, for example, the Na^+ ions have a coordination number of 6: Each Na^+ ion is surrounded by 6 Cl^- ion nearest neighbors. In the CsCl structure [Figure 11.44(a)], by comparison, each Cs^+ ion is surrounded by 8 Cl^- ions. The increase in the coordination number as the alkali metal ion is changed from Na^+ to Cs^+ is a consequence of the larger size of Cs^+ compared to Na^+.

In the zinc blende, ZnS, structure [Figure 11.44(b)], the S^{2-} ions adopt a face-centered-cubic arrangement, with the smaller Zn^{2+} ions arranged so they are each surrounded tetrahedrally by four S^{2-} ions. CuCl also adopts this structure.

In the fluorite, CaF_2, structure [Figure 11.44(c)] the Ca^{2+} ions are shown in a face-centered-cubic arrangement. As required by the chemical formula of the substance, there are twice as many F^- ions in the unit cell as there are Ca^{2+} ions. Other compounds that have the fluorite structure include $BaCl_2$ and PbF_2.

Metallic Solids

Metallic solids consist entirely of metal atoms. Metallic solids usually have hexagonal close-packed, cubic close-packed (face-centered-cubic), or body-centered-cubic structures. Thus, each atom typically has 8 or 12 adjacent atoms.

FIGURE 11.44   Unit cells of some common types of crystal structures found for ionic solids: (a) CsCl; (b) ZnS (zinc blende); (c) CaF_2 (fluorite).

Figure 11.44

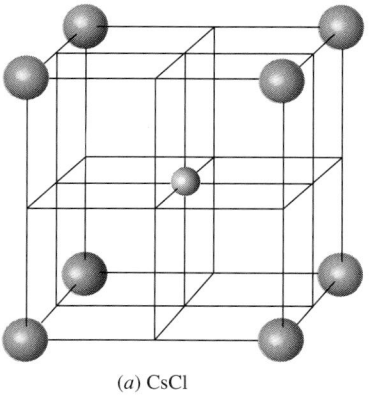

(a) CsCl

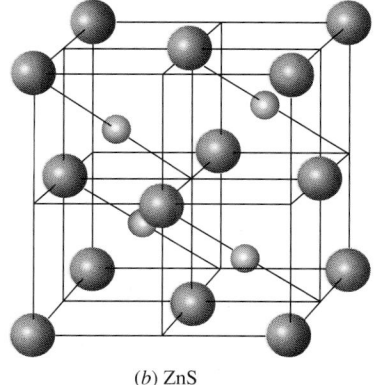

(b) ZnS

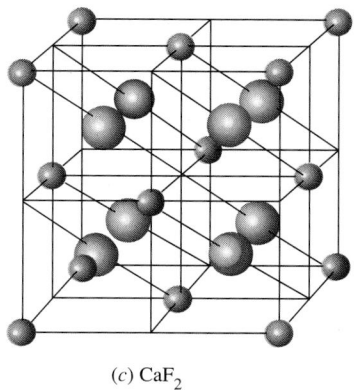

(c) CaF_2

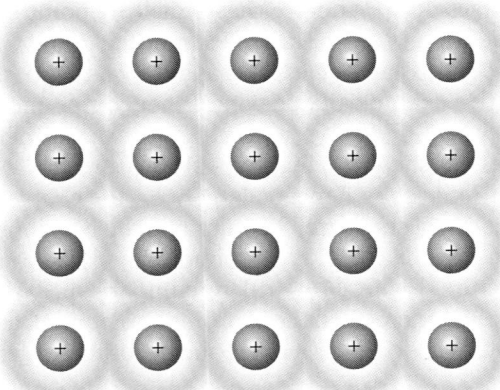

FIGURE 11.45 A cross section of a metal. Each sphere represents the nucleus and inner-core electrons of a metal atom. The surrounding colored "fog" represents the mobile sea of electrons that binds the atoms together.

The bonding in metals is too strong to be due to London dispersion forces, and yet there are not enough valence electrons for ordinary covalent bonds between atoms. The bonding is due to valence electrons that are delocalized throughout the entire solid. In fact, we can visualize the metal as an array of positive ions immersed in a sea of delocalized valence electrons, as shown in Figure 11.45.

Metals vary greatly in the strength of their bonding, as is evidenced by their wide range of physical properties such as hardness and melting point. In general, however, the strength of the bonding increases as the number of electrons available for bonding increases. Thus, sodium, which has only one valence electron per atom, melts at 97.5°C, whereas chromium, with six electrons beyond the noble-gas core, melts at 1890°C. The mobility of the electrons explains why metals are good conductors of heat and electricity. The bonding and properties of metals will be examined more closely in Chapter 24.

 # For Review

Summary

Substances that are gases or liquids at room temperature are usually composed of molecules. In gases, the intermolecular attractive forces are negligible compared to the kinetic energies of the molecules; thus, the molecules are widely separated and undergo constant, chaotic motion. In liquids, the intermolecular forces are strong enough to keep the molecules in close proximity; nevertheless, the molecules are free to move with respect to one another. Solids are composed of atoms, molecules, or ions. The interparticle attractive forces are strong enough to restrain motion and to force the particles to occupy specific locations in a three-dimensional arrangement.

Three types of intermolecular forces exist between neutral molecules: dipole-dipole, London dispersion, and hydrogen bonding. Ion-dipole forces are important in solutions. London dispersion forces operate between all molecules. The relative strengths of the dipole-dipole and dispersion forces depend on the polarity, polarizability, size, and shape of the molecule. Dipole-dipole forces increase in strength with increasing polarity. Dispersion forces tend to increase in strength with increasing molecular mass. Hydrogen bonding occurs in compounds containing O—H, N—H, and F—H bonds. Hydrogen bonds are generally stronger than dipole-dipole or dispersion forces.

The stronger the intermolecular forces, the greater the viscosity, or resistance to flow, of a liquid. The surface tension of a liquid also increases as intermolecular forces increase in strength. Surface tension is a measure of the tendency of a liquid to maintain a minimum surface area. The adhesion of a liquid to the walls of a narrow tube and the cohesion of the liquid account for capillary action and for the formation of a meniscus.

A substance may exist in more than one state of matter, or phase. Changes of a solid to liquid (melting), solid to gas (sublimation), and liquid to gas (vaporization) are all endothermic processes. That is, the heats of melting (also called fusion), sublimation, and vaporization are all positive quantities. The reverse processes are thus exothermic. A gas cannot be liquefied by application of pressure if the temperature is above its critical temperature.

The vapor pressure of a liquid measures the tendency of the liquid to evaporate. The vapor pressure is the partial pressure of the vapor when it is in equilibrium with the liquid. The equilibrium is a dynamic process in which the rate of transfer of molecules from the liquid to the vapor equals the rate of transfer from the vapor to the liquid. The higher the vapor pressure of a liquid, the more readily it evaporates and the more volatile it is said to be. Vapor pressure increases nonlinearly with temperature. Boiling occurs when the vapor pressure equals the external pressure. The normal boiling point is the temperature at which the vapor pressure equals 1 atm.

The equilibria between the solid, liquid, and gas phases of a substance as a function of temperature and pressure are displayed on a phase diagram. Equilibria between any two phases are indicated by a line. The point on the diagram at which all three phases coexist in equilibrium is called the triple point.

Solids whose particles are arranged in a regularly repeating pattern are said to be crystalline. Those whose particles show no such order are said to be amorphous.

The essential structural features of a crystalline solid can be represented by its unit cell, the smallest part of the crystal that can, by simple displacement, reproduce the three-dimensional structure. The three-dimensional structures of crystals can also be represented by their crystal lattices. The points in a crystal lattice represent positions in the structure where there are identical environments. The structures of crystalline solids can be determined from their X-ray diffraction patterns.

Many solids have a close-packed structure in which spherical particles are arranged so as to leave the minimal amount of empty space. Two closely related forms of close packing, cubic close packing and hexagonal close packing, are possible. In both, each sphere has a coordination number of 12.

The properties of solids depend both on the arrangements of particles and on the attractive forces between them. Molecular solids, which consist of atoms or molecules held together by intermolecular forces, are soft and low-melting. Covalent-network solids, which consist of atoms held together by covalent bonds that extend throughout the solid, are hard and high-melting. Ionic solids are hard and brittle and have high melting points. Metallic solids, which consist of metal cations held together by a sea of electrons, exhibit a wide range of properties.

Key Terms

intermolecular forces
ion-dipole force (Sec. 11.2)
dipole-dipole force (Sec. 11.2)
London dispersion force (Sec. 11.2)
polarizability (Sec. 11.2)
hydrogen bonding (Sec. 11.2)
viscosity (Sec. 11.3)
surface tension (Sec. 11.3)
capillary action (Sec. 11.3)
phase changes (Sec. 11.4)
heat of fusion (Sec. 11.4)
heat of vaporization (Sec. 11.4)

critical temperature (Sec. 11.4)
critical pressure (Sec. 11.4)
vapor pressure (Sec. 11.5)
dynamic equilibrium (Sec. 11.5)
volatile (Sec. 11.5)
normal boiling point (Sec. 11.5)
phase diagram (Sec. 11.6)
normal melting point (Sec. 11.6)
triple point (Sec. 11.6)
crystalline solid (Sec. 11.7)
amorphous solid (Sec. 11.7)
unit cell (Sec. 11.7)

crystal lattice (Sec. 11.7)
primitive cubic (Sec. 11.7)
body-centered cubic (Sec. 11.7)
face-centered cubic (Sec. 11.7)
hexagonal close packing (Sec. 11.7)
cubic close packing (Sec. 11.7)

coordination number (Sec. 11.7)
X-ray diffraction (Sec. 11.7)
molecular solids (Sec. 11.8)
covalent-network solids (Sec. 11.8)
ionic solids (Sec. 11.8)
metallic solids (Sec. 11.8)

Exercises

Kinetic-Molecular Theory

11.1. Compare the degree of order within a solid to that within a liquid. What properties of solids and liquids reflect the difference in the degree of order?

11.2. For which of the following pairs is the degree of order of the two phases most similar: a gas and a liquid; a gas and a solid; a liquid and a solid?

11.3. Account for the difference in the compressibility of gases, liquids, and solids.

11.4. For a given substance, the densities of the liquid and solid phases are usually very similar and very different from the density of the gas. Explain.

11.5. Why does increasing the temperature cause a substance to change in succession from a solid to a liquid to a gas?

11.6. Explain why compressing a gas at constant temperature can cause it to liquefy.

Intermolecular Forces

11.7. Define and give an example of each of the following types of intermolecular forces: **(a)** dipole-dipole force; **(b)** ion-dipole force; **(c)** London dispersion force; **(d)** van der Waals force; **(e)** hydrogen bond.

11.8. Which type of intermolecular attractive force operates between: **(a)** all molecules; **(b)** polar molecules; **(c)** the hydrogen atom of a polar bond and a nearby electronegative atom?

11.9. What kind of attractive forces dominate in the following systems: **(a)** solid NaCl; **(b)** liquid xenon; **(c)** an aqueous solution of potassium bromide; **(d)** frozen water?

11.10. What kind of attractive forces must be overcome to **(a)** boil water; **(b)** melt KCl; **(c)** sublime I_2; **(d)** boil H_2S?

11.11. The dipole moments of HCl and HI are 1.08 D and 0.44 D, respectively. **(a)** Which of these substances will have the greater dipole-dipole interactions? **(b)** Which of these substances will have the greater London dispersion forces?

11.12. Molecular nitrogen, N_2, and carbon monoxide, CO, are isoelectronic and nearly equal in molecular mass. Explain why the boiling point of $CO(l)$ is slightly higher than that of $N_2(l)$.

11.13. **(a)** What is meant by the term *polarizability?* **(b)** Which of the following atoms would you expect to be most polarizable: O, S, Se, or Te? Explain. **(c)** Put the following molecules in order of increasing polarizability: $GeCl_4$, CH_4, $SiCl_4$, SiH_4, $GeBr_4$.

11.14. **(a)** Why does the strength of dispersion forces increase with increasing polarizability? **(b)** Explain how the observation that helium can be liquefied provides evidence for the existence of dispersion forces. **(c)** How do the strengths of dispersion forces vary with molecular size?

11.15. Which member of each of the following pairs of substances would you expect to have the higher boiling point: **(a)** N_2 or O_2; **(b)** CH_4 or SiH_4; **(c)** NaCl or CH_3Cl; **(d)** C_2H_5Cl or C_2H_5OH? Explain.

11.16. Rationalize the difference in boiling point between the members of the following pairs of substances: **(a)** HF (20°C) and HCl (−85°C); **(b)** $CHCl_3$ (61°C) and $CHBr_3$ (150°C); **(c)** Br_2 (59°C) and ICl (97°C); **(d)** $CH_3CH_2CH_2CH_3$ (0°C) and $(CH_3)_3CH$ (−10°C).

11.17. Cite three properties of water that can be attributed to the existence of hydrogen bonding.

11.18. **(a)** Why does water expand when it freezes? **(b)** Why do snowflakes have a hexagonal shape? **(c)** Give an example of the biological significance of the fact that ice is less dense than water.

Viscosity and Surface Tension

11.19. How do the viscosity and surface tension of liquids change as the intermolecular forces become stronger?

11.20. How do the viscosity and surface tension of liquids change as temperature increases?

11.21. Explain the following observations: **(a)** The viscosity of ethanol, CH_3CH_2OH, is greater than that of ether, $CH_3CH_2OCH_2CH_3$. **(b)** In contact with a narrow capillary tube made of polyethylene, water forms a concave-downward meniscus like that of mercury in a glass tube.

11.22. Explain the following observations: **(a)** The surface tension of $CHBr_3$ is greater than that of $CHCl_3$. **(b)** As temperature increases, oil flows faster through a narrow tube. **(c)** Raindrops that collect on a waxed automobile hood take on a nearly spherical shape.

Changes of State

11.23. Name all the possible phase changes that can occur between different states of matter. Which of these are exothermic and which are endothermic?

11.24. Explain the following observations: **(a)** During the cold winter months, snow often gradually disappears without melting. **(b)** The heat of fusion for any substance is generally lower than its heat of vaporization. **(c)** Ethyl chloride, C_2H_5Cl, boils at 12°C. When liquid C_2H_5Cl under pressure is sprayed on a surface at atmospheric pressure, the surface is cooled considerably. **(d)** When heated above 279°C, carbon disulfide, CS_2, cannot be liquefied regardless of how great the pressure exerted on the gas.

11.25. For many years, drinking water has been cooled in hot climates by evaporating it from the surfaces of canvas bags or porous clay pots. How many grams of water can be cooled from 35°C to 22°C by the evaporation of 10 g of water? The heat of vaporization of water in this temperature range is 2.4 kJ/g. The heat capacity of water per gram is 4.18 J/g-K.

11.26. Freon-12, CCl_2F_2, is used as a refrigerant. Its heat of vaporization is 289 J/g. What mass of Freon-12 must evaporate in order to freeze 100 g of water initially at 18°C?

(The heat of fusion of water is 334 J/g; the heat capacity of water per gram is 4.18 J/g-K.)

11.27. Freon-11, which has the chemical formula CCl_3F, has a normal boiling point of 23.8°C. The specific heats of $CCl_3F(l)$ and $CCl_3F(g)$ are 0.87 J/g-K and 0.59 J/g-K, respectively. The heat of vaporization for the compound is 24.75 kJ/mol. Calculate the heat required to convert 10.0 g of Freon-11 from a liquid at −50.0°C to a gas at 50.0°C.

11.28. Ethanol, C_2H_5OH, melts at −114°C and boils at 78°C. The enthalpy of fusion of ethanol is 5.02 kJ/mol, and its enthalpy of vaporization is 38.56 kJ/mol. The specific heats of solid and liquid ethanol are 0.97 J/g-K and 2.3 J/g-K, respectively. How much heat is required to convert 50.0 g of ethanol at −150°C to the vapor phase at 78°C?

11.29. **(a)** What does the critical temperature tell us about the conditions required for liquefaction of gases? **(b)** What is the significance of the critical pressure of a substance?

11.30. **(a)** Which of the substances listed in Table 11.4 can be liquefied at room temperature (25°C)? **(b)** Which of the substances listed in Table 11.4 can be liquefied at the temperature of liquid nitrogen (−196°C)?

Vapor Pressure and Boiling Point

11.31. Explain why the boiling point of a liquid varies substantially with pressure, whereas the melting point of a solid depends little on pressure.

11.32. Explain how each of the following affects the vapor pressure of a liquid: **(a)** surface area; **(b)** temperature; **(c)** intermolecular attractive forces; **(d)** volume of the liquid; **(e)** pressure of the air above the liquid.

11.33. Place the following substances in order of increasing volatility: CH_4, CBr_4, CH_2Cl_2, CH_3Cl, $CHBr_3$, CH_2Br_2. Explain your answer.

11.34. Phosphorus trichloride, PCl_3, is more volatile than arsenic trichloride, $AsCl_3$, at 25°C. **(a)** Which substance has the greater intermolecular forces? Explain. **(b)** Which substance has the higher vapor pressure at 25°C? **(c)** Which substance will have the higher boiling point?

11.35. Two pans of water are on different burners of a stove. One pan of water is boiling vigorously, while the other is boiling gently. What can be said about the temperature of the water in the two pans?

11.36. Explain the following observations: **(a)** Water evaporates more quickly on a hot, dry day than on a hot,

humid day. **(b)** It takes longer to boil eggs at high altitudes than at lower ones.

11.37. **(a)** Use the vapor pressure curve in Figure 11.21 to estimate the boiling point of ethanol at 200 torr. **(b)** Use the vapor-pressure table in Appendix B to determine the boiling point of water when the external pressure is 12 torr.

11.38. **(a)** Suppose the pressure inside a pressure cooker reaches 1.3 atm. By using the vapor-pressure table in Appendix B, estimate the temperature at which water will boil in this cooker. **(b)** Use the vapor-pressure curve in Figure 11.21 to estimate the external pressure under which diethyl ether will boil at 20°C.

11.39. Reno, Nevada, is about 4500 ft above sea level. If the barometric pressure is 680 torr in Reno, at what temperature will water boil? Refer to Appendix B.

11.40. Mt. Kilimanjaro in Tanzania is the tallest peak in Africa (19,340 ft). If the barometric pressure at the top of the mountain is 350 torr, at what temperature will water boil there? Refer to Appendix B.

Phase Diagrams

11.41. Why does the line on a phase diagram that separates the gas and liquid phases end rather than going to infinite pressure and temperature?

11.42. What is the significance of the triple point of a phase diagram?

11.43. Refer to Figure 11.24(a) and describe all the phase changes that would occur in each of the following cases. (a) Water vapor originally at 1.0×10^{-3} atm and $-0.10°C$ is slowly compressed at constant temperature until the final pressure is 10 atm. (b) Water originally at $-10°C$ and 0.30 atm is heated at constant pressure until the temperature is 80.0°C.

11.44. Refer to Figure 11.24(b) and describe the phase changes (and the temperatures at which they occur) when CO_2 is heated from $-80°C$ to $-20°C$ at (a) a constant pressure of 3 atm; (b) a constant pressure of 6 atm.

11.45. The normal melting and boiling points of O_2 are $-218°C$ and $-183°C$, respectively. Its triple point is at $-219°C$ and 1.14 torr, and its critical point is at $-119°C$ and 49.8 atm. (a) Sketch the phase diagram for O_2, showing the four points given above and indicating the area in which each phase is stable. (b) Which is denser, $O_2(s)$ or $O_2(l)$? Explain. (c) As it is heated, will solid O_2 sublime or melt under a pressure of 1 atm?

11.46. The normal melting and boiling points of xenon are $-112°C$ and $-107°C$, respectively. Its triple point is at $-121°C$ and 282 torr, and its critical point is at 16.6°C and 57.6 atm. (a) Sketch the phase diagram for Xe, showing the four points given above and indicating the area in which each phase is stable. (b) Will Xe(s) float on Xe(l)? Explain. (c) If Xe gas is cooled under an external pressure of 100 torr, will it undergo condensation or deposition? Explain.

Structures of Solids

11.47. How does an amorphous solid differ from a crystalline one?

11.48. Amorphous silica has a density of about 2.2 g/cm³, whereas the density of crystalline quartz is 2.65 g/cm³. Account for this difference in density.

11.49. What is a unit cell? What properties does it have?

11.50. Calculate the net number of spheres in (a) a primitive cubic unit cell; (b) a body-centered-cubic unit cell; (c) a face-centered-cubic unit cell.

11.51. Silver metal crystallizes in a cubic close-packed structure (face-centered-cubic unit cell). (a) How many silver atoms are in a unit cell? (b) What is the coordination number of each silver atom? (c) Assume that the silver atoms can be represented as spheres, as shown in Figure 11.46. If each Ag atom has a radius of 1.44 Å , what is the length of a side of the unit cell? (d) Calculate the density of silver metal.

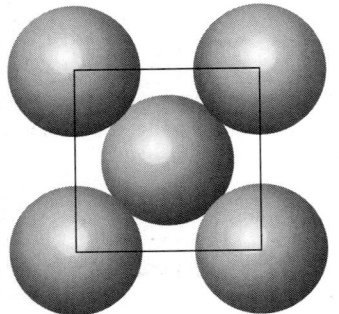

FIGURE 11.46

11.52. Lead crystallizes in a face-centered-cubic unit cell that has an edge length of 4.95 Å. The atom in the center of the face is in contact with the corner atoms, as shown in Figure 11.46. (a) Calculate the atomic radius of lead. (b) Calculate the density of lead metal.

11.53. What is the coordination number of each sphere in (a) a three-dimensional, close-packed array of equal-sized spheres; (b) a primitive cubic structure; (c) a body-centered-cubic lattice?

11.54. What is the coordination number of (a) Na^+ in the NaCl structure, Figure 11.31; (b) Zn^{2+} in the ZnS unit cell, Figure 11.44(b); (c) Ca^{2+} in the CaF_2 unit cell, Figure 11.44(c)?

11.55. Nickel oxide, NiO, crystallizes in the NaCl type of crystal structure (Figure 11.31). The length of an edge of the unit cell of NiO is 4.18 Å. Calculate the density of NiO.

11.56. Clausthalite is a mineral composed of lead selenide, PbSe. The mineral adopts a NaCl-type structure. The density of PbSe at 25°C is 8.27 g/cm³. Calculate the length of an edge of the PbSe unit cell.

11.57. An element crystallizes in a body-centered-cubic lattice. The edge of the unit cell is 2.86 Å, and the density of the crystal is 7.92 g/cm³. Calculate the atomic weight of the element.

11.58. KCl has the same structure as NaCl. The length of the unit cell is 628 pm. The density of KCl is 1.984 g/cm³, and its formula mass is 74.55. Using this information, calculate Avogadro's number.

Bonding in Solids

11.59. What kinds of attractive forces exist between particles in (a) molecular crystals; (b) covalent-network crystals; (c) ionic crystals; (d) metallic crystals?

11.60. Indicate the type of crystal (molecular, metallic, covalent-network, or ionic) each of the following would form upon solidification: (a) HBr; (b) Ar; (c) Mn; (d) $Co(NO_3)_2$; (e) C; (f) paradichlorobenzene (moth balls).

11.61. Name two substances that form covalent-network solids.

11.62. Covalent bonding occurs in both molecular and covalent-network solids. Why do these two kinds of solids differ so greatly in their hardness and melting point?

11.63. For each of the following pairs of substances, predict which will have the higher melting point and indicate why: (a) KBr, Br_2; (b) SiO_2, CO_2; (c) Se, CO; (d) NaF, MgF_2.

11.64. For each of the following compounds, predict which will have the higher melting point and indicate why: (a) C_6Cl_6, C_6H_6; (b) HF, HCl; (c) KO_2, SiO_2; (d) Ar, Xe.

11.65. You are given a white substance that sublimes at 3000°C; the solid is a nonconductor of electricity and is insoluble in water. Which type of solid (Table 11.6) might this substance be?

11.66. A white substance melts with some decomposition at 730°C. As a solid it is a nonconductor of electricity, but it dissolves in water to form a conducting solution. Which type of solid (Table 11.6) might the substance be?

[11.67]. A certain form of AgI adopts the zinc blende structure [Figure 11.44(b)]. The density of the salt is 5.69 g/cm^3. (a) Calculate the length of a side of the unit cell. (b) Calculate the distance between the Ag^+ and I^- ions in the structure.

[11.68]. The mineral uraninite, UO_2, adopts a fluorite structure [Figure 11.44(c)] in which the length of an edge of the unit cell is 5.468 Å. (a) Will the uranium ions be represented by the larger or the smaller spheres in Figure 11.44(c)? Explain. (b) Calculate the density of uraninite.

Additional Exercises

11.69. Using the thermodynamic data listed in Appendix C, calculate ΔH for the following processes at 25°C:

$$Br_2(l) \longrightarrow Br_2(g) \qquad Br_2(g) \longrightarrow 2Br(g)$$

$$I_2(s) \longrightarrow I_2(g) \qquad I_2(g) \longrightarrow 2I(g)$$

(a) For Br_2, discuss the relative magnitudes of the enthalpy changes for phase changes compared to those for bond breaking. (b) Discuss the trends in the enthalpy changes as one compares those for Br_2 to those for I_2.

11.70. (a) Which of the following substances can exhibit dipole-dipole attractions between its molecules: CO_2, SO_2, H_2, IF, HBr, CCl_4? (b) Which of the following substances exhibit hydrogen bonding in their liquid and solid states: CH_3NH_2, CH_3F, PH_3, HCOOH?

11.71. Two isomers of the planar compound 1,2-dichloro-ethylene are shown below along with their melting and boiling points:

	cis isomer	trans isomer
Melting point (°C)	−80.5	−50
Boiling point (°C)	60.3	47.5

(a) Which of the two isomers will have the stronger dipole-dipole forces? Is this prediction borne out by the data presented above? (b) Based on the data presented above, which isomer packs more efficiently in the solid phase?

11.72. In dichloromethane, CH_2Cl_2 ($\mu = 1.60$ D), the dispersion force contribution to the intermolecular attractive forces is about five times larger than the dipole-dipole contribution. Would you expect the relative importance of the two kinds of intermolecular attractive forces to differ (a) in dibromomethane ($\mu = 1.43$ D); (b) in difluoromethane ($\mu = 1.93$ D)? Explain.

11.73. What measurable physical property of a liquid relates to each of the following: (a) its ability to flow; (b) the temperature at which its vapor pressure equals the pressure on the surface of the liquid; (c) its tendency to bead up on a surface for which it exhibits no appreciable adhesive forces; (d) the amount of heat that must be added to vaporize it.

11.74. The units that are usually used to express viscosity are kg/m-s. With reference to Figure 11.13, explain why these units are sensible ones for viscosity.

11.75. Trimethylamine, $(CH_3)_3N$, and propylamine, $CH_3CH_2CH_2NH_2$, have fishy, ammonia-like odors. Explain why propylamine has a lower vapor pressure than trimethylamine.

11.76. Ethylene glycol, the major component of antifreeze, is a slightly viscous liquid that is not very volatile at room temperature and boils at 198°C. Its chemical formula is $CH_2(OH)CH_2(OH)$. Pentane, C_5H_{12}, which has about the same molecular weight, is a nonviscous liquid that is highly volatile at room temperature and whose boiling point is 36°C. Explain the differences in the physical properties of the two substances.

11.77. Liquid butane, C_4H_{10}, is stored in cylinders to be used as a fuel. Suppose 3.00 L of butane at 17°C and 735 torr is removed from a cylinder. How much heat must be added to vaporize this much butane if its heat of vaporization is 21.3 kJ/mol?

11.78. The heat of sublimation of a substance, ΔH_{sub}, can be estimated as $\Delta H_{fus} + \Delta H_{vap}$. Use Hess's law to rationalize this approximation.

11.79. By using data in Appendix B, determine the mass of water vapor you would expect to find in a bathroom measuring 4.0 m × 4.0 m × 3.0 m if water at 40°C has been left in the bathtub.

[11.80]. The following table gives the vapor pressure of hexafluorobenzene, C_6F_6, as a function of temperature:

Temperature (K)	Vapor pressure (torr)
280.0	32.42
300.0	92.47
320.0	225.1
330.0	334.4
340.0	482.9

(a) By plotting these data in a suitable fashion, determine whether the Clausius-Clapeyron equation is obeyed. If so, use your plot to determine ΔH_{vap} for C_6F_6. (b) Use these data to determine the boiling point of the compound.

[11.81]. Suppose that the vapor pressure of a substance is measured at two different temperatures. (a) By using the Clausius-Clapeyron equation, Equation 11.1, derive the following relationship between the vapor pressures P_1 and P_2 and the absolute temperatures at which they were measured, T_1 and T_2:

$$\ln \frac{P_1}{P_2} = -\frac{\Delta H_{vap}}{R}\left(\frac{1}{T_1} - \frac{1}{T_2}\right)$$

(b) The melting point of potassium is 62.3°C. Molten potassium has a vapor pressure of 10.00 torr at 443°C and a vapor pressure of 400.0 torr at 708°C. Use these data and the equation in part (a) to calculate the heat of vaporization of liquid potassium. (c) By using the equation in part (a) and the data given in part (b), calculate the boiling point of potassium. (d) Calculate the vapor pressure of liquid potassium at 100°C.

[11.82]. The following data present the temperatures at which certain vapor pressures are achieved for dichloromethane, CH_2Cl_2, and methyl iodide, CH_3I:

Vapor pressure (torr):	10.0	40.0	100.0	400.0
T for CH_2Cl_2 (°C):	−43.3	−22.3	−6.3	24.1
T for CH_3I (°C):	−45.8	−24.2	−7.0	25.3

(a) Which of the two substances is expected to have the greater dipole-dipole forces? Which is expected to have the greater London dispersion forces? Based on your answers, explain why it is difficult to predict which compound would be more volatile. (b) Which compound would you expect to have the higher boiling point? Check your answer in a reference book such as the *Handbook of Chemistry and Physics*. (c) The order of volatility of these two substances changes as the temperature is increased. What quantity must be different for the two substances in order for this phenomenon to occur? (d) Substantiate your answer for part (c) by drawing an appropriate graph.

[11.83]. We might guess that the Clausius-Clapeyron equation (Equation 11.1) would be applicable also to the vapor-pressure data for a solid. Use this equation to estimate the heat of sublimation of ice from the following data:

Temperature (°C)	Vapor pressure (torr)
−20.0	0.640
−16.0	1.132
−12.0	1.632
−8.0	2.326
−4.0	3.280
0.0	4.579

[11.84]. Chromium crystallizes in a body-centered-cubic unit cell whose edge length is 2.884 Å. If the atoms touch along the body diagonal of the unit cell, calculate the atomic radius of a Cr atom.

11.85. In a typical X-ray crystallography experiment, X-rays of wavelength $\lambda = 0.71$ Å are generated by bombarding molybdenum metal with an energetic beam of electrons. Why are these X-rays more effectively diffracted by crystals than is visible light?

[11.86]. (a) Assume that all the bonds in buckminsterfullerene are carbon-carbon single bonds. How many bonds are there in the molecule? (b) The valence of carbon atoms is usually 4. If we wish to have each carbon atom of C_{60} achieve a valence of 4, how many of the bonds from part (a) will be double bonds?

[11.87]. (a) The density of diamond [Figure 11.40(a)] is 3.5 g/cm³, and that of graphite [Figure 11.40(b)] is 2.3 g/cm³. Based on the structure of buckminsterfullerene (Figure 11.42), what would you expect for its density relative to these other forms of carbon? (b) X-ray diffraction studies of buckminsterfullerene show that it has a face-centered-cubic lattice of C_{60} molecules. The length of a side of the unit cell is 14.2 Å. Calculate the density of buckminsterfullerene.

Modern Materials *12*

The levitation of a small magnet by a ceramic superconductor, which is being cooled in liquid nitrogen. The magnet floats in space because the superconductor excludes magnetic fields. Ceramic semiconductors, discovered in 1986, are subjects of intensive worldwide research because of their many potential applications.

CONTENTS

Since the beginning of the modern era of chemistry in the nineteenth century, one of the important goals of chemical research has been the discovery and development of materials with useful properties. Chemists have invented both entirely new substances and the means for processing naturally occurring materials to form fibers, films, coatings, adhesives, and substances with special electrical, magnetic, or optical properties. Today, we have entered a new era in which advances in technology will depend more than ever upon the discovery and development of useful new materials. Here are some examples of how these materials will affect all aspects of our lives in the near future:

1. They will make possible electronic-display devices that are thin and light, for example, a television set that can be mounted on the wall like a picture.
2. They will serve as repositories of vast quantities of information. Already the storage of information in a tiny space is possible (Figure 12.1), although not yet ready for widespread use. In the future, this technology will develop as a practical means of accessing information.
3. The expected lifetimes of biological replacement parts such as hip and knee joints will increase from the present 10 yr or less to the lifetime of the recipient.
4. Solar-cell technology for energy conversion with practical efficiencies will lead to more widespread utilization of solar energy.
5. Catalytic converters that reduce automobile pollution more effectively will contribute to improvements in the environment at lower costs.

In this chapter, we will discuss the properties and applications of several kinds of materials. The aim is to show how we can understand many special physical or chemical properties in terms of the principles we have discussed in earlier chapters. We will see that the observable properties of materials are the result of atomic- and molecular-level structures and processes. At this stage of the text, we cannot cover all kinds of materials. Instead, we will examine four types: liquid crystals, polymers, ceramics, and thin films.

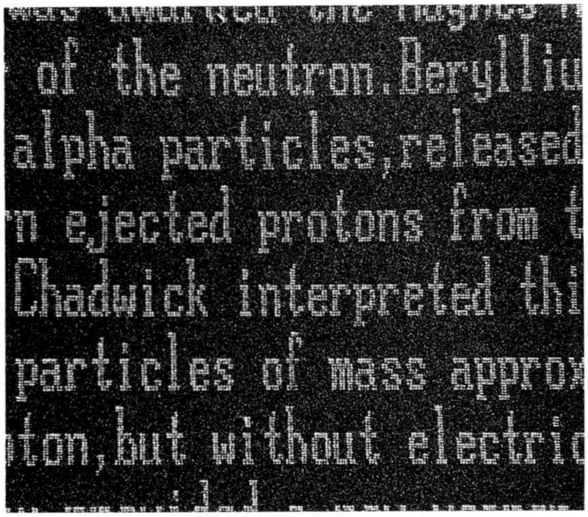

FIGURE 12.1 A portion of the *Encyclopedia Brittanica* written into an AlF_3 surface using an electron beam. The diameter of the beam is only 0.5 nm. At this scale, the entire contents of the *Encyclopedia Brittanica* would be contained within the area of the period at the end of this sentence. (Courtesy of Professor Colin Humphreys, University of Cambridge)

12.1 Liquid Crystals

We have seen that when a solid is heated to its melting point, the added thermal energy overcomes the intermolecular attractions that provide molecular order to the solid. ∞ (Sec. 11.1)   The liquid that forms is characterized by random molecular orientation and considerable molecular motion. Some substances, however, exhibit more complex behavior as their solids are heated.

In 1888, Frederick Reinitzer, an Austrian botanist, discovered that an organic compound he was studying, called cholesteryl benzoate, has interesting and unusual properties. When heated, the substance melts at 145°C to form a milky liquid, and at 179°C the milky liquid suddenly becomes clear. When the substance is cooled, the reverse processes occur: The clear liquid turns milky at 179°C (Figure 12.2), and the milky liquid solidifies at 145°C. Reinitzer's work represents the first systematic report of what we now call a **liquid crystal.**

Instead of passing directly from the solid to the liquid phase when they are heated, some substances, such as cholesteryl benzoate, pass through an intermediate, liquid-crystalline phase that has some of the structure of solids and some of the freedom of motion possessed by liquids. Because of the partial ordering, liquid crystals may be very viscous and possess properties intermediate between those of the solid and liquid phases. The region in which they exhibit these properties is marked by sharp transition temperatures, as in Reinitzer's example.

Learning Goal 1:   Recount the ways in which a liquid-crystalline phase differs from an ordinary (isotropic) liquid phase.

FIGURE 12.2   (*a*) Molten cholesteryl benzoate at a temperature above 179°C. In this temperature region, the substance is a clear, isotropic liquid. Note that the printing on the surface of the beaker in back of the sample test tube is readable. (*b*) Cholesteryl benzoate at a temperature between 179°C and 145°C, the melting point of cholesteryl benzoate. In this temperature interval, cholesteryl benzoate exhibits a milky liquid-crystalline phase. (© Richard Megna/Fundamental Photographs)

(*a*)

(*b*)

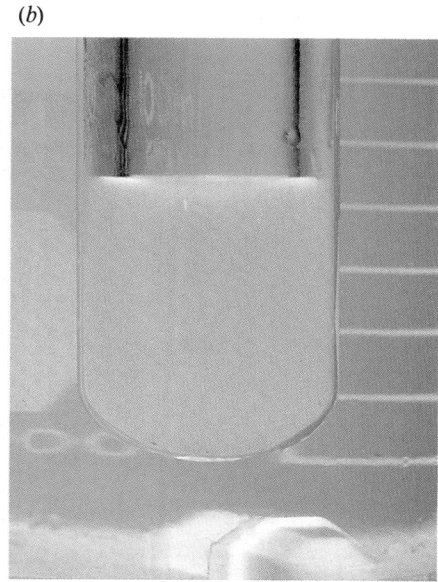

Point of Emphasis: The forces causing alignment of liquid-crystalline molecules are intermolecular forces. See Chapter 11.

From the time of their discovery in 1888 until about 30 years ago, liquid crystals were largely a laboratory curiosity. They are now widely used as pressure and temperature sensors and in the displays of electrical devices such as digital watches, calculators, and laptop computers (Figure 12.3). These uses of liquid crystals result from the fact that the weak intermolecular forces that hold the molecules together in a liquid crystal are easily affected by changes in temperature, pressure, and electromagnetic fields.

Types of Liquid-Crystalline Phases

Point of Emphasis: The molecules of liquid-crystalline substances tend to have a stiff, rodlike shape.

Substances that form liquid crystals are often composed of long, rodlike molecules. In the normal liquid phase, these molecules are oriented in random directions [Figure 12.4(a)]. Liquid-crystalline phases, by contrast, exhibit some ordering of the molecules. Depending on the degree of ordering, liquid crystals can be divided into three categories: nematic, smectic, and cholesteric.

Learning Goal 2: Distinguish among the major classes of liquid-crystalline phases.

In the **nematic liquid-crystalline phase,** the molecules are aligned along their long axes, but there is no ordering with respect to the ends of the molecules [Figure 12.4(b)]. The arrangement of the molecules is like that of a handful of pencils whose ends are not aligned.

Graeme Patch and Gregory A. Hope, "Preparation and Properties of Liquid Crystals," *J. Chem. Educ.* 1985, *62,* 454.

In the **smectic liquid-crystalline phases,** the molecules exhibit additional ordering beyond that of the nematic phase. The smectic phases resemble a handful of pencils whose ends are more nearly aligned. There are different kinds of smectic phases, designated by the letters A, B, C, and so forth. In the smectic A phase, the molecules are arranged in layers, with their long axes perpendicular to the layers [Figure 12.4(c)]. Other smectic phases display different types of alignments. For example, in the smectic C phase, the molecules are aligned with their long axes tilted relative to the layers in which the molecules are stacked [Figure 12.4(d)].

Some examples of molecules that exhibit nematic and smectic phases are shown in Figure 12.5. The molecular structure of the first of these is shown in

FIGURE 12.3 A laptop computer with a liquid-crystal display (LCD) panel. (Apple Computer, Inc.)

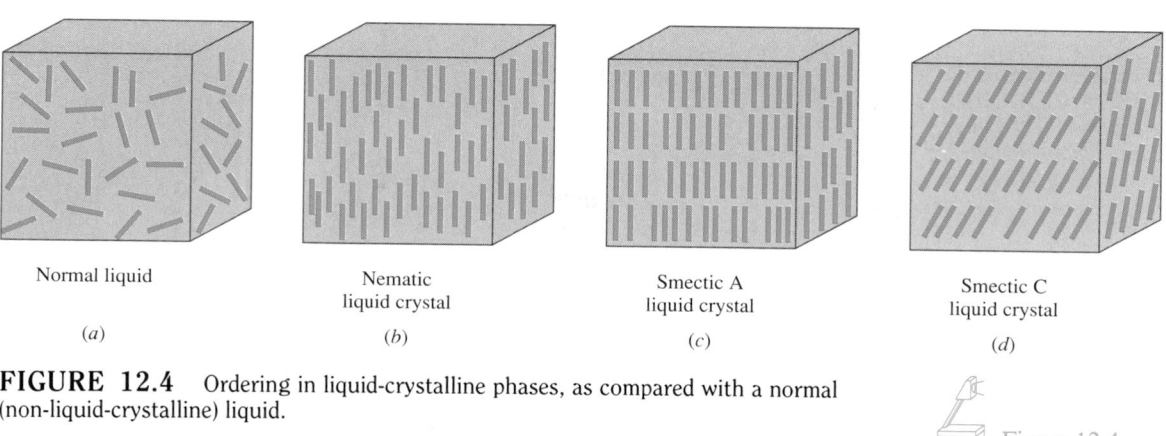

Normal liquid
(a)

Nematic
liquid crystal
(b)

Smectic A
liquid crystal
(c)

Smectic C
liquid crystal
(d)

FIGURE 12.4 Ordering in liquid-crystalline phases, as compared with a normal (non-liquid-crystalline) liquid.

Figure 12.4

Figure 12.6. Notice that all of these molecules are long and oriented in one direction like the pencils in our analogy. The $C=N$ and $N=N$ double bonds and the benzene rings add stiffness to these molecules. (Recall from Section 9.5 that molecules cannot twist around double bonds.) Because these molecules are long, stiff, and thin, there is no room for them to tumble. Rather, the molecules order themselves quite naturally along their long axes. They can, however, rotate around their axes and slide parallel to one another. In the smectic phase, the intermolecular forces between the molecules (such as London dispersion forces, dipole-dipole attractions, and hydrogen bonds) limit the ability of the molecules to slide past one another.

FIGURE 12.5 Structures of some typical liquid crystals.

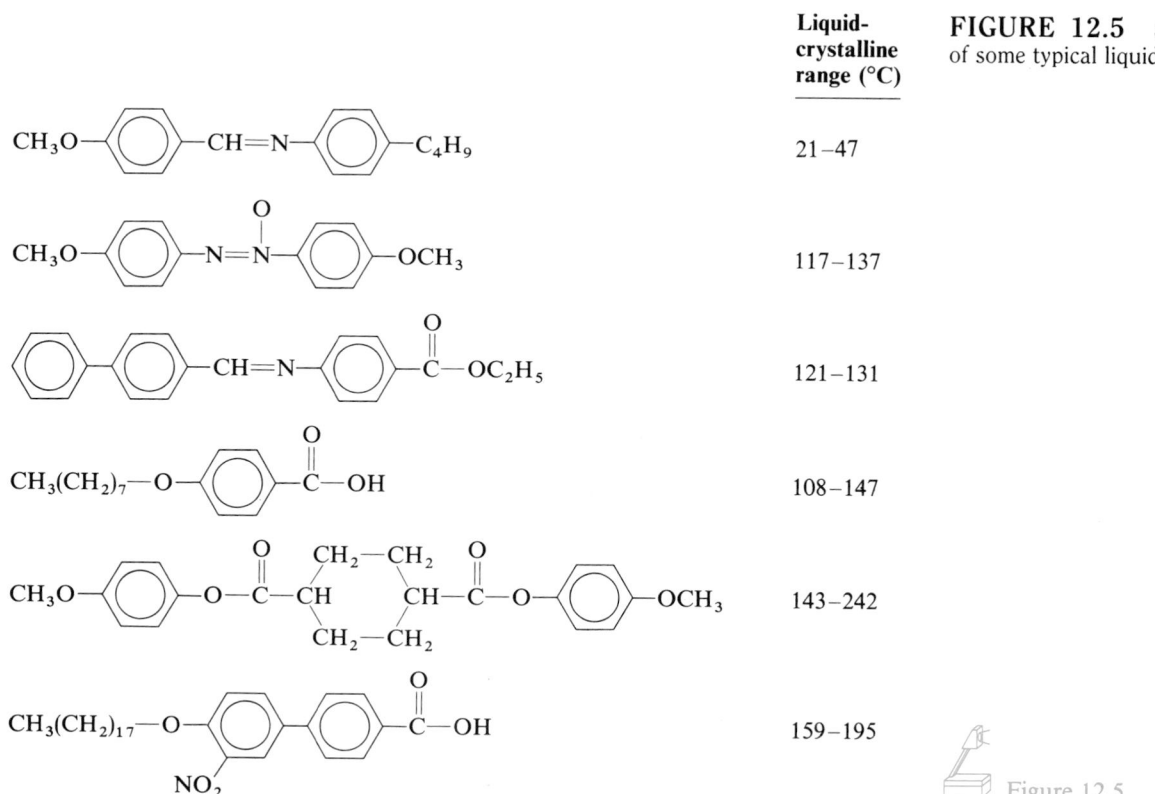

	Liquid-crystalline range (°C)
CH_3O—〇—$CH=N$—〇—C_4H_9	21–47
CH_3O—〇—$N=N$—〇—OCH_3 (with O on N)	117–137
〇—〇—$CH=N$—〇—$C-OC_2H_5$ (C=O)	121–131
$CH_3(CH_2)_7$—O—〇—$C-OH$ (C=O)	108–147
CH_3O—〇—$O-C-CH$ ... $CH-C-O$—〇—OCH_3	143–242
$CH_3(CH_2)_{17}$—O—〇—〇—$C-OH$, NO_2	159–195

Figure 12.5

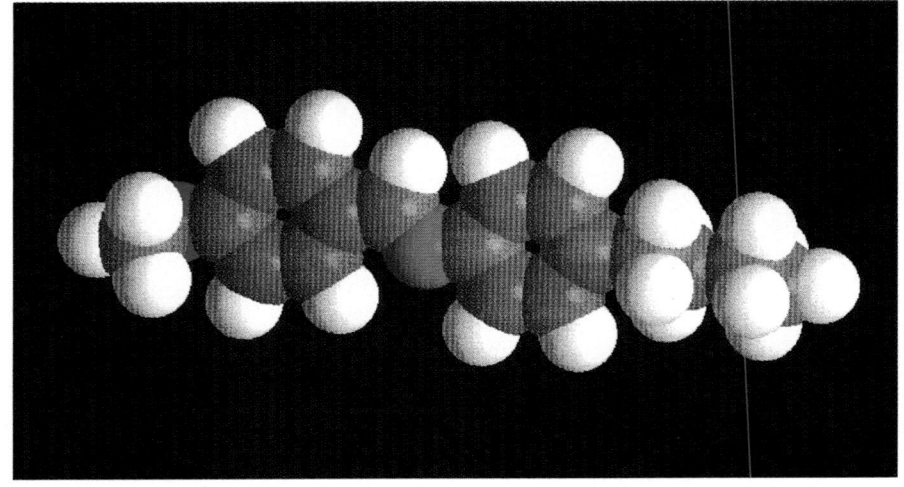

FIGURE 12.6 Three-dimensional structure of $CH_3OC_6H_4CH=NC_6H_4C_4H_9$ (the first compound listed in Figure 12.5), which is liquid-crystalline in the range 21°C to 47°C.

Figure 12.7 shows the ordering of the **cholesteric liquid-crystalline phase.** The molecules are aligned along their long axes as in nematic liquid crystals, but they are arranged in layers with the molecules in each plane twisted slightly in relation to the molecules in the planes above and below. These liquid crystals derive their name from the fact that many derivatives of cholesterol, such as the one that Reinitzer studied, adopt this structure. One such molecule is cholesteryl octanoate, whose molecular and three-dimensional structures are shown in Figure 12.8. Even though this is a rather complex molecule, it can be described approximately as a flat rod with a flexible tail. In the liquid crystal, the molecules sit side by side in layers. The tail, however, causes one layer to be twisted relative to the next. The slight twist in their orientation from layer to layer tends to make these liquid crystals colored. Changes in temperature and pressure change the order and hence the color (Figure 12.9). These liquid crystals have been used to monitor temperature changes in situations where conventional methods are not feasible. For example, they can detect hot spots in microelectronic circuits, which may signal flaws.

Teaching Note: In the past few years, fever thermometers that change color when touched to the forehead have become common.

FIGURE 12.7
(*a*) Ordering in a cholesteric liquid crystal. The molecules in successive layers are oriented at a characteristic angle with respect to those in adjacent layers, to avoid unfavorable interactions. The result is a screwlike axis, as shown in (*b*).

Figure 12.7

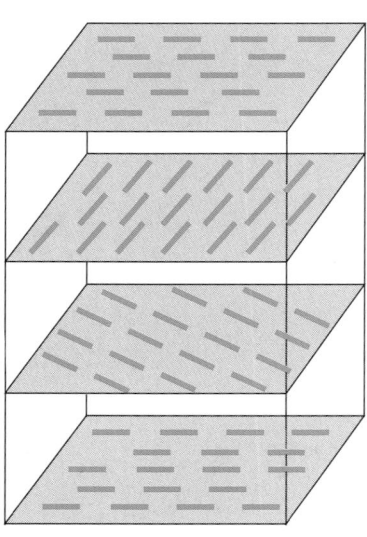

Cholesteric structure

(*a*)

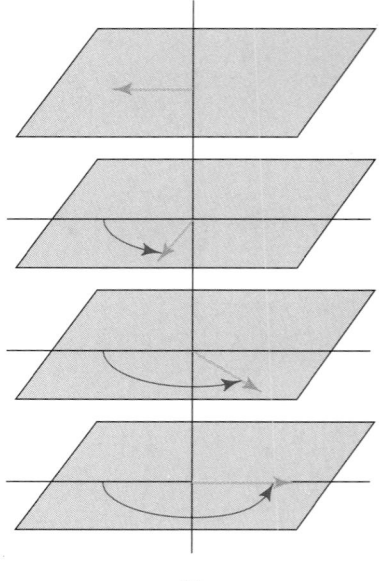

(*b*)

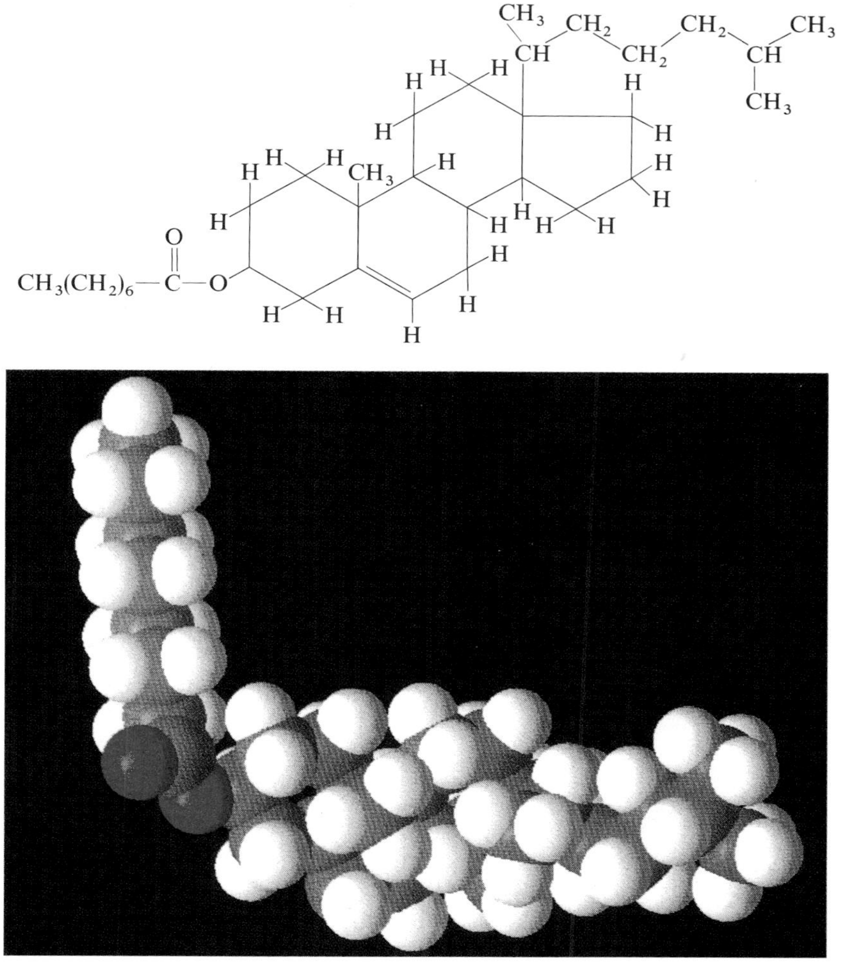

(a)

$CH_3(CH_2)_6$—C—O

(b)

FIGURE 12.8
(a) Molecular structure of cholesteryl octanoate. Note that the rings in this molecule are not benzene rings. Each corner of the rings has a carbon atom and as many attached hydrogen atoms or other bonds as needed to satisfy the carbon atom valency of four. (b) A three-dimensional model of cholesteryl octanoate.

FIGURE 12.9 Color change in a cholesteric liquid-crystalline material as a function of temperature. (Richard Megna/Fundamental Photographs)

CHEMISTRY AT WORK

Liquid-Crystal Displays

Liquid crystals are widely used in electrically controlled liquid-crystal display (LCD) devices in watches, calculators, and computer screens, as illustrated in Figure 12.3. These applications arise from the ability of an applied electrical field to cause a change in the orientation of liquid-crystal molecules and thus affect the optical properties of a layer of liquid-crystalline material.

LCDs come in a variety of designs, but the structure shown in Figure 12.10 is typical. The liquid-crystalline material is placed between two glass plates coated with transparent, electrically conducting material, as shown in Figure 12.10(a). In a typical watch or calculator display, the light that strikes the display surface first passes through a thin sheet called a *polarizer*, which passes only light rays that lie along a certain direction. When no voltage is applied, the polarized light passes through the liquid crystal, is reflected at the bottom, and emerges again through the cover plate. Thus, the surface appears bright. An applied voltage changes the orientation of the liquid-crystal molecules. As a result, the polarized light does not pass through the liquid-crystalline phase. The areas of the display to which the voltage has been applied thus appear dark.

The top electrode surface is divided into tiny areas. Applying a voltage to combinations of these areas forms letters, numerals, or other figures. Figure 12.10(b) shows how a numeric display capable of forming any numeral is made up of seven segments.

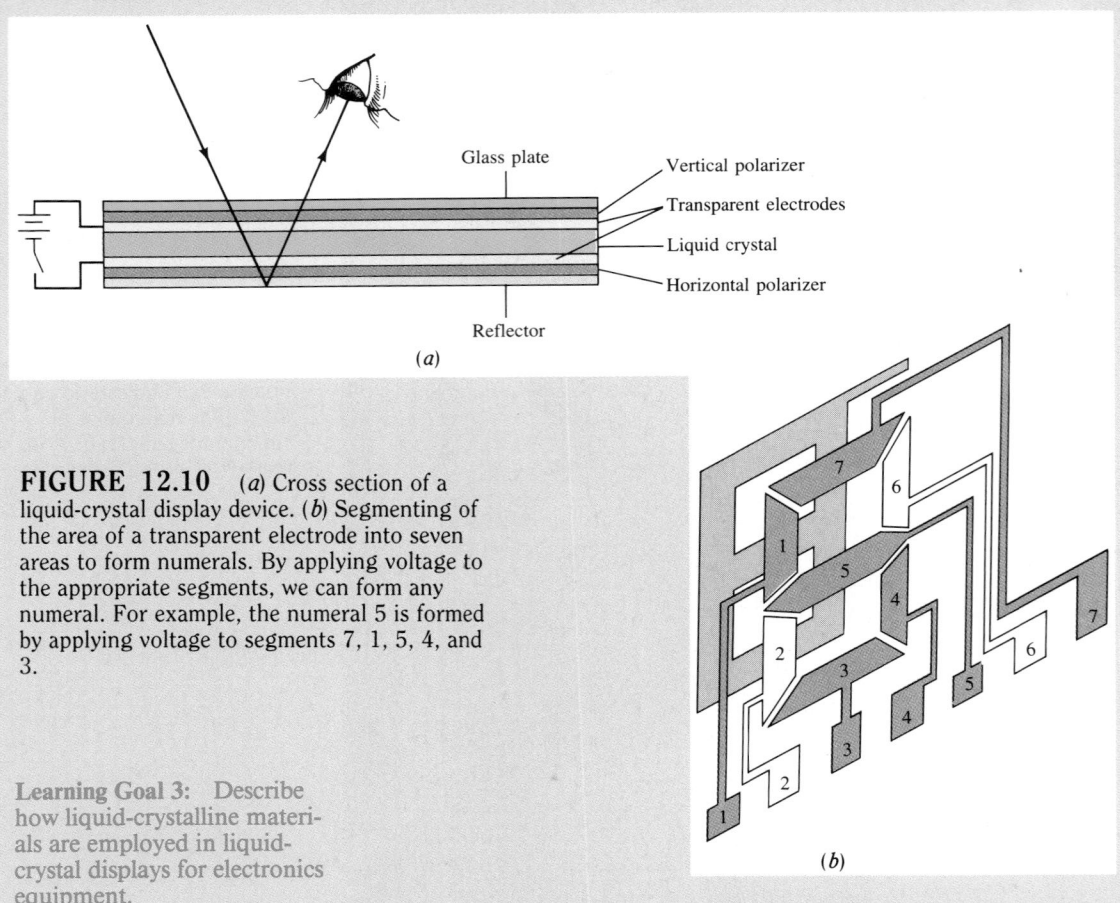

FIGURE 12.10   (*a*) Cross section of a liquid-crystal display device. (*b*) Segmenting of the area of a transparent electrode into seven areas to form numerals. By applying voltage to the appropriate segments, we can form any numeral. For example, the numeral 5 is formed by applying voltage to segments 7, 1, 5, 4, and 3.

Learning Goal 3: Describe how liquid-crystalline materials are employed in liquid-crystal displays for electronics equipment.

SAMPLE EXERCISE 12.1

Which of the following substances is most likely to exhibit liquid-crystalline behavior?

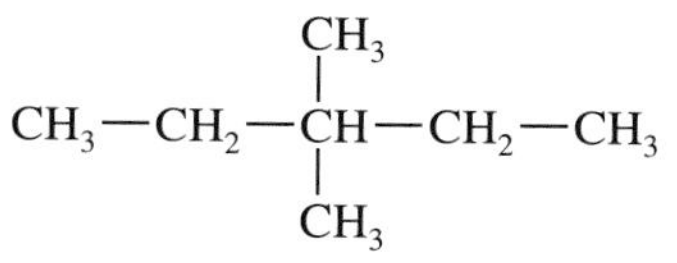

$$CH_3-CH_2-\underset{\underset{CH_3}{|}}{\overset{\overset{CH_3}{|}}{CH}}-CH_2-CH_3$$

(i)

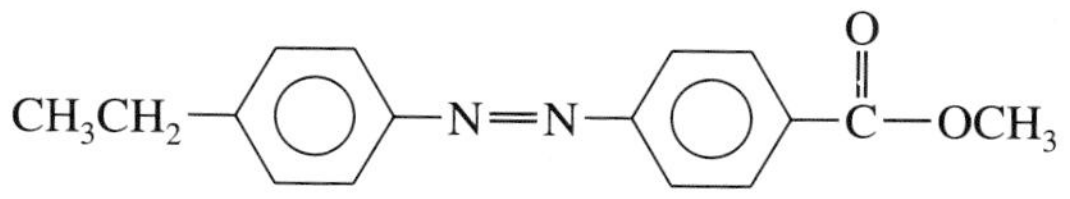

$$CH_3CH_2-\bigcirc-N=N-\bigcirc-\overset{\overset{O}{\|}}{C}-OCH_3$$

(ii)

$$\bigcirc-CH_2-\overset{\overset{O}{\|}}{C}-O^-Na^+$$

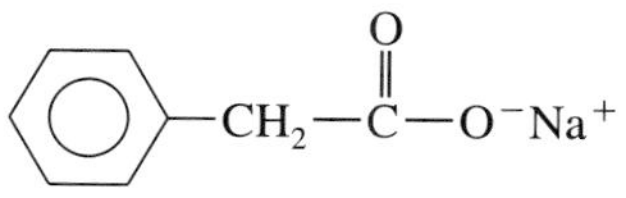

(iii)

SOLUTION Molecule (i) is not likely to be liquid-crystalline because it does not have a long axial structure. Molecule (iii) is ionic; the generally high melting points of ionic materials (Section 8.2) and the absence of a characteristic long axis make it unlikely that this substance will exhibit liquid-crystalline behavior. Molecule (ii) possesses the characteristic long axis and the kinds of structural features that are often seen in liquid crystals (Figure 12.5).

PRACTICE EXERCISE

Suggest a reason why the following molecule, *n*-decane, does not exhibit liquid-crystalline behavior:

$$CH_3CH_2CH_2CH_2CH_2CH_2CH_2CH_2CH_2CH_3$$

Answer: Because rotation can occur around carbon-carbon single bonds, molecules whose backbone consists of C—C single bonds are too flexible; the molecules tend to coil in random ways and thus are not rodlike.

12.2 Polymers

Our discussions of chemistry to this point have focused primarily on molecules of fairly low molecular mass. However, in nature we find many substances of very high molecular mass, running into millions of amu. Starch and cellulose abound in plants; proteins and nucleic acids are found in both plants and animals. In 1827, Jons Jakob Berzelius coined the word **polymer** (from the Greek *polys,* "many," and *meros,* "parts") to denote molecular substances of high molecular mass formed by the *polymerization* (joining together) of **monomers,** molecules with low molecular masses. Starch and cellulose are formed by polymerization of the monomer glucose, the structure of which is shown in Figure 12.11. Starch and cellulose differ only in the different spatial arrangements of the linkages joining the glucose molecules.

For a long time, humans have used naturally occurring polymers to form useful materials. The spinning of wool, the tanning of leather, and the manu-

FIGURE 12.11 The structure of glucose, the monomer from which starch and cellulose are formed.

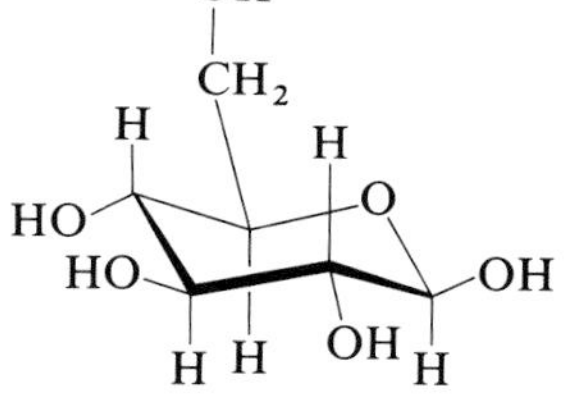

Point of Emphasis: *Polymerization reactions* link small monomeric units together to form very large molecules called *polymers.*

Learning Goal 5: Explain how a polymer is formed from monomers via (a) addition polymerization and (b) condensation polymerization.

facture of natural rubber are all examples of processing natural polymers. During the past 50 years or so, chemists have learned to form synthetic polymers by polymerizing monomers through controlled chemical reactions. A great many of these synthetic polymers have a backbone of carbon-carbon bonds. Carbon atoms have an exceptional ability to form strong, stable bonds with one another.

The simplest example of a polymerization reaction is the formation of *polyethylene* from ethylene molecules. In this reaction, the double bond in each ethylene molecule "opens up," and two of the electrons originally in this bond are used to form new C—C single bonds with two other ethylene molecules:

Ethylene   Polyethylene

Teaching Note: Polymerization reactions are usually exothermic.

Polymerization that occurs through such coupling of monomers using their multiple bonds, with no other products formed in the reaction, is termed **addition polymerization.**

We can write the polymerization reaction this way:

$$n\,CH_2{=}CH_2 \longrightarrow \left[\!\!\begin{array}{c} H\ \ H \\[-2pt] |\ \ \ | \\[-2pt] C{-}C \\[-2pt] |\ \ \ | \\[-2pt] H\ \ H \end{array}\!\!\right]_n \qquad [12.1]$$

Bassam Z. Shakhashiri, "Polyurethane Foam," *Chemical Demonstration: A Handbook for Teachers of Chemistry, Volume 1* (Madison: The University of Wisconsin Press, 1983), pp. 216–218.

Here the letter n is the large number—ranging from hundreds to many thousands—of monomer molecules (ethylene in this case) that react to form one large polymer molecule. Within the polymer, a repeat unit (the unit in brackets) appears along the entire chain. The ends of the chain are capped by carbon-hydrogen bonds or by some other bond so that the end carbons have four bonds.

Point of Emphasis: *Addition polymers* are formed by double bonds opening and shifting the electrons into the region where the new bond is formed. No other products are formed in these reactions.

Polyethylene is a very important material; about 10 million tons is produced in the United States each year. Although its formula is the most simple of all the organic polymers, it is not readily formed from ethylene. Only after many years of research were the right conditions and appropriate catalysts identified for manufacturing a commercially useful polymer. Today, many different forms of polyethylene, varying widely in physical properties, are known. Polymers of other chemical compositions provide still greater variety in physical and chemical properties. Table 12.1 lists several other common polymers that are obtained by addition polymerization.

Raymond B. Seymour, "Polymers Are Everywhere," *J. Chem. Educ.* **1988,** *65,* 327.

Point of Emphasis: *Condensation polymers* are created by bonding two monomer molecules end-to-end and producing a small molecule such as water, in addition to the polymer.

A second general kind of reaction used to synthesize commercially important polymers is **condensation polymerization.** In a **condensation reaction,** two molecules are joined to form a larger molecule by elimination of a small molecule such as H_2O. For example, an amine (a compound containing the —NH_2) group will react with a carboxylic acid (a compound containing the —COOH group) to form a bond between N and C together with the formation of H_2O:

$$-\overset{\overset{\displaystyle H}{|}}{N}\underbrace{-H + H-O}-\overset{\overset{\displaystyle O}{\|}}{C}- \longrightarrow -\overset{\overset{\displaystyle H}{|}}{N}-\overset{\overset{\displaystyle O}{\|}}{C}- + H_2O \qquad [12.2]$$

In the formation of nylon, a *diamine*—a compound with a —NH_2 group at each end—is caused to react with a *diacid*—a compound with a —COOH group at each end. For example, nylon 6,6, which is a specific kind of nylon, is formed when a diamine that has six carbon atoms and an amino group on each end is caused to react with adipic acid, which has six carbon atoms:

$$n\,H_2N\!\!-\!\!(CH_2)_6\!\!-\!\!NH_2 + n\,HOC\!\!-\!\!(CH_2)_4\!\!-\!\!C\!\!-\!\!OH \longrightarrow \left[-NH(CH_2)_6NH-C(CH_2)_4C-\right]_n \qquad [12.3]$$

$$\underset{\text{Diamine}}{} \qquad \underset{\text{Adipic acid}}{} \qquad \underset{\text{Nylon 6,6}}{}$$

TABLE 12.1 △ Polymers of Commercial Importance

Polymer	Structure	Uses	Quantity (tons/yr)*
Addition polymers:			
Polyethylene	$+CH_2-CH_2+_n$	Films, packaging, bottles	10,000,000
Polypropylene	$\left[CH_2-CH\atopCH_3\right]_n$	Kitchenware, fibers, appliances	4,200,000
Polystyrene	$\left[CH_2-CH(C_6H_5)\right]_n$	Packaging, disposable food containers, insulation	2,500,000
Polyvinyl chloride	$\left[CH_2-CH\atopCl\right]_n$	Pipe fittings, clear film for meat packaging	5,000,000
Condensation polymers:			
Polyurethane	$\left[C-NH-R-NH-C-O-R'-O\right]_n$ ‖O ‖O R, R' = for example, —CH_2—CH_2—	"Foam" furniture stuffing, spray-on insulation, automotive parts, footwear, water-protective coatings	780,000
Polyethylene terephthalate (a polyester)	$\left[OCH_2-CH_2-O-C(C_6H_4)C\right]_n$ ‖O ‖O	Tire cord, magnetic tape, apparel, soft-drink bottles	2,000,000
Nylon 6,6	$\left[NH-(CH_2)_6NH-C-(CH_2)_4-C\right]_n$ ‖O ‖O	Home furnishings, apparel, carpet fibers, fishing line	1,300,000 (all nylons)

Source: Chemical and Engineering News, April 12, 1993, p. 16.

CHEMISTRY AT WORK

Recycling Plastics

If you look at the bottom of a plastic container, you are likely to see a recycle symbol containing a number, as seen in Figure 12.12. The number in the middle of the recycle symbol and the abbreviation below it indicate the kind of polymer from which the container is made, as summarized in Table 12.2. (The chemical structures of these polymers are shown in Table 12.1.) These symbols make it possible to sort the containers by their composition. In general, the lower the number, the greater the ease with which the material can subsequently be recycled.

TABLE 12.2 △ Categories Used for Recycling Polymeric Materials in the United States

Number	Abbreviation	Polymer
1	PETE	Polyethylene terephthalate
2	HDPE	High density polyethylene
3	V	Polyvinyl chloride (PVC)
4	LDPE	Low density polyethylene
5	PP	Polypropylene
6	PS	Polystyrene
7		Others

FIGURE 12.12 Plastic containers have symbols stamped on the bottom, indicating their composition. (Richard Megna/Fundamental Photographs)

A condensation reaction occurs on each end of the diamine and the acid. The components of H_2O are split out, and N—C bonds are formed between molecules. Table 12.1 lists nylon 6,6 and some other common polymers obtained by condensation polymerization. Notice that these polymers have backbones containing N or O atoms as well as C atoms. In Chapter 26, we will see that proteins are also condensation polymers.

Types of Polymers

Before we continue this discussion of polymers, we should clarify the meanings of some commonly used terms. The word **plastic** is generally applied to materials that can be formed into various shapes, usually by the application of heat and pressure. **Thermoplastic** materials can be reshaped. For example, plastic milk containers are made from polyethylene of high molecular mass. These containers can be melted down and the polymer recycled for some other use. In contrast, a **thermosetting plastic** is shaped through certain irreversible chemical processes and therefore cannot be reshaped readily.

The term **elastomer** is applied to a material that exhibits rubbery or elastic behavior. When subjected to stretching or bending, it regains its original shape upon removal of the distorting force, provided that it has not been distorted beyond some elastic limit. Some polymers can also be formed into *fibers* that, like hair, are very long in relation to cross-sectional area and are not elastic.

Structures and Physical Properties of Polymers

The simple structural formulas given above for polyethylene and other polymers are deceptive. Because each carbon atom in polyethylene is surrounded by four bonds, the atoms are arranged in a tetrahedral fashion, so that the chain is not straight as we have depicted it. Furthermore, the atoms are relatively free to rotate around the single (sigma) C—C bonds. Thus, rather than being straight and rigid, the chains are very flexible, folding readily. The flexibility in the molecular chains causes the polymer material to be very flexible.

Polymers are amorphous (noncrystalline) materials. Rather than exhibiting well-defined crystalline phases with sharp melting points, they soften over a range of temperatures. They may, however, possess short-range order in some regions of the solid, with chains lined up in regular arrays as shown in Figure 12.13. The extent of such ordering is indicated by the *degree of crystallinity* of the polymer. The crystallinity of a polymer can frequently be enhanced by mechanical stretching or pulling to align the chains as the molten polymer is drawn through small holes, as shown in Figure 12.14. Intermolecular forces between the polymer chains hold the chains together in the ordered, crystalline regions, making the polymer denser, harder, less soluble, and more resistant to heat. Table 12.3 shows how the properties of polyethylene change as the degree of crystallinity increases.

The simple linear structure of polyethylene is conducive to intermolecular interactions that lead to crystallinity. However, the degree of crystallinity in polyethylene is strongly dependent on the average molecular mass. Polymerization results in a mixture of *macromolecules* (large molecules) with varying n and hence varying molecular masses. So-called low-density polyethylene used in forming films and sheets has an average molecular mass in the range of 10^4 amu and has substantial chain branching. That is, there are side chains off the main chain of the polymer, much like spur lines that branch from a main railway line. These branches inhibit the formation of crystalline regions, reducing the density of the material. High-density polyethylene, used to form bottles, drums, and pipes, has an average molecular mass in the range of 10^6 amu. This form has less branching and consequently a higher degree of crystallinity. Low-density and high-density polyethylene are illustrated in Figure 12.15.

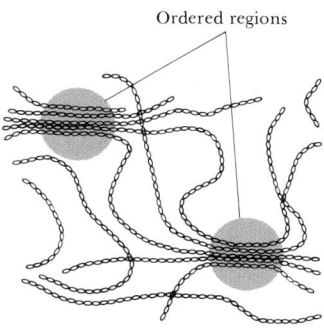

FIGURE 12.13 Interactions between polymer chains. In the circled regions, the forces that operate between adjacent polymer-chain segments lead to ordering analogous to the ordering in crystals.

Figure 12.13

Learning Goal 6: Explain how processing affects the properties of synthetic polymer fibers and how it relates to molecular orientations in the fiber.

Learning Goal 7: Explain what is meant by the term *crystallinity* in polymers, and indicate how the polymer properties generally vary with degree of crystallinity.

Teaching Note: In a sample of a polymer, not all of the molecules will have the same molecular mass; i.e., the values of n will be different. Thus, the *average* molecular mass is often used.

TABLE 12.3 △ Properties of Polyethylene as a Function of Crystallinity

	Degree of crystallinity				
	55%	62%	70%	77%	85%
Melting point (°C)	109	116	125	130	133
Density (gm/cm³)	0.92	0.93	0.94	0.95	0.96
Stiffness[a]	25	47	75	120	165
Yield stress[a]	1700	2500	3300	4200	5100

* These test results show that the mechanical strength of the polymer increases with increased crystallinity. The physical units for the stiffness test are psi $\times 10^{-3}$ (psi = pounds per square inch); those for the yield stress test are psi. Discussion of the exact meaning and significance of these tests is beyond the scope of this text.

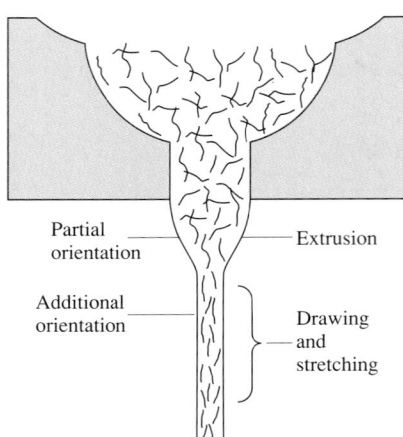

FIGURE 12.14 Extrusion and drawing of polymeric material to form a fiber. As the extruded material is drawn, the individual polymer molecules align along the direction in which the stretch occurs.

Partial orientation — Extrusion

Additional orientation — Drawing and stretching

The properties of polymeric materials can be extensively modified by adding substances with lower molecular mass. For example, substances may be added to provide protection against degradation of the material in sunlight. In other cases, **plasticizers** are added to reduce the extent of interactions between

FIGURE 12.15
(*a*) Schematic illustration of the structure of low-density polyethylene (LDPE) and a typical use of LDPE film to form food-storage bags. (*b*) Schematic illustration of the structure of high-density polyethylene (HDPE) and 1-gal containers formed from HDPE. (© Richard Megna/Fundamental Photographs)

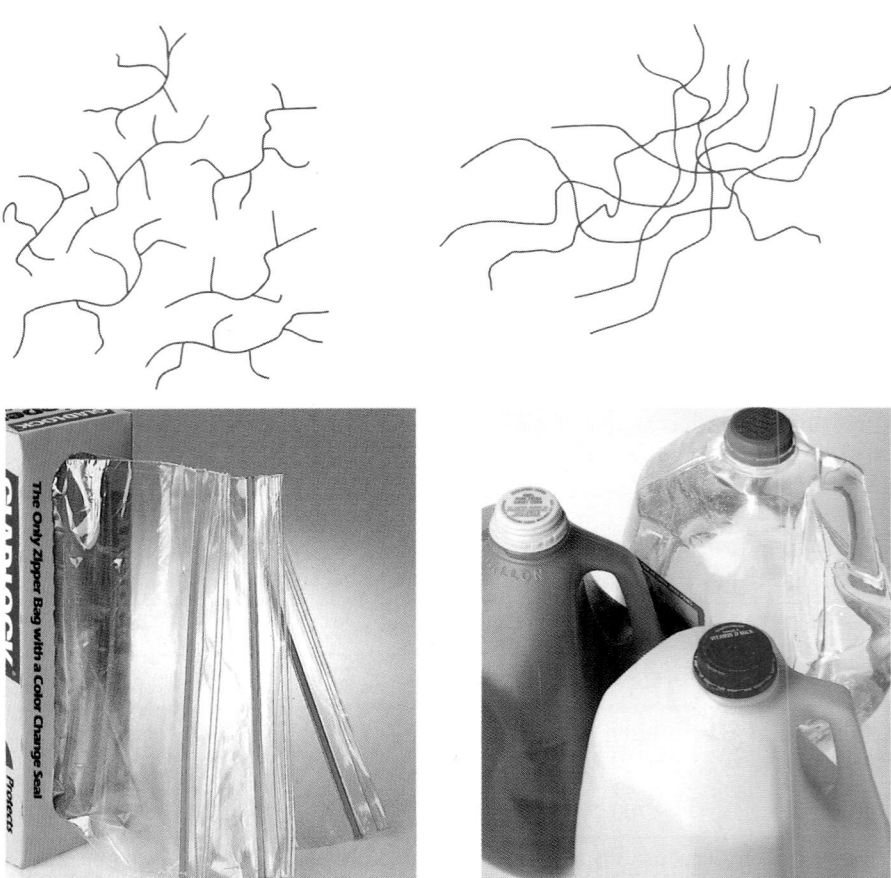

(*a*)   (*b*)

Kevlar, An Advanced Material

Polymers are used today in many ways that were entirely unanticipated at the time of their discovery. For example, nylon is not used merely as a fiber, which was its initial application. It is also used in the manufacture of bearings, insulators, fishing line, and tire cord. These extended applications for nylon and other polymers have stimulated a strong demand for new "super" fibers with the heat resistance of asbestos, the stiffness of glass, and strengths much greater than steel.

One new substance that has many of these properties is called Kevlar and has the following chemical structure:

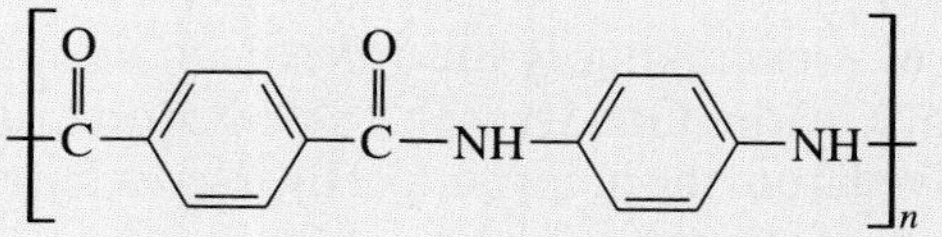

The average molecular mass of each polymer chain is 10^5 amu. Kevlar owes its special properties to the way in which the polymer molecules interact with one another, as illustrated in Figure 12.16. Notice that the individual chains are hydrogen-bonded to adjacent chains. This hydrogen-bonding network causes the chains to align, forming a sheet structure.

Kevlar has many exceptional properties due to the strong bonding in the individual polymer chains, the strong hydrogen-bonding network in the sheets, and the regular arrangement of the sheets in the fibers. Kevlar ropes have replaced steel ropes and cables in many applications, especially on offshore oil drilling platforms. For a given diameter, Kevlar ropes in seawater have 20 times the strength of steel. Because it has very good high-temperature stability, Kevlar is used in protective gloves and clothing worn by firefighters. It is also a major component in very strong and damage-resistant structures such as the hull of the racing craft shown in Figure 12.17.

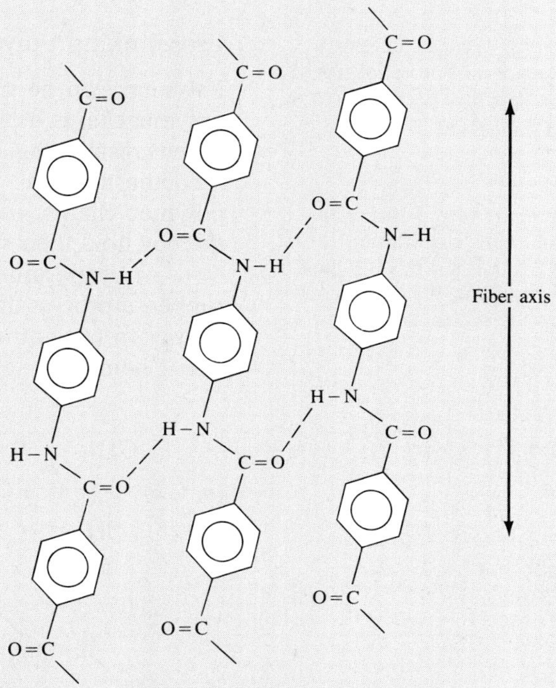

FIGURE 12.16 Hydrogen bonding structure in sheets of Kevlar molecules.

FIGURE 12.17 The *KAAMA* offshore racer. The hull of this craft is reinforced with Kevlar. (E.I. Du Pont de Nemours & Co, Textile Fibers Department KEVLAR Special Products)

Learning Goal 8: Describe the chemical and intermolecular structure of Kevlar, and account for the unusually high strength and thermal stability of fibers formed from this substance.

chains and thus to make the polymer more pliable. As an example, polyvinyl chloride (PVC) (Table 12.1) is a hard, rigid material of high molecular mass that is used to manufacture sewer pipes. When blended with a suitable substance of lower molecular mass, however, it forms a flexible polymer that can be used to make rain boots and doll parts. In some applications, the plasticizer in a plastic object may be lost over time because of evaporation. As this happens, the plastic loses its flexibility and becomes subject to cracking.

Crosslinking Polymers

Polymers can be made stiffer by introducing chemical bonds between the polymer chains, as illustrated in Figure 12.18. Forming bonds between chains is called **crosslinking**. The greater the number of crosslinks in a polymer, the more rigid the material. Whereas thermoplastic materials consist of independent polymer chains, thermosetting ones become crosslinked when heated and thereby hold their shapes.

An important example of crosslinking is the *vulcanization* of natural rubber, a process discovered by Charles Goodyear in 1839. Natural rubber is formed from a liquid resin derived from the inner bark of the *Hevea brasiliensis* tree. Chemically, it is a polymer of isoprene, C_5H_8:

$$(n+2) \quad \underset{\underset{CH_2}{}}{\overset{CH_3}{}}C\!\!-\!\!C\overset{H}{\underset{CH_2}{}} \quad \longrightarrow$$

Isoprene

$$\cdots CH_2{}^{CH_3}\!\!C\!\!=\!\!C^H{}_{CH_2}\!\!\left[CH_2{}^{CH_3}\!\!C\!\!=\!\!C^H{}_{CH_2}\right]_n\!\!CH_2{}^{CH_3}\!\!C\!\!=\!\!C^H{}_{CH_2}\cdots \qquad [12.4]$$

Rubber

Because rotation about the carbon-carbon double bond does not readily occur, the orientation of the groups bound to the carbons is rigid. In naturally occurring rubber, the chain extensions are on the same side of the double bond, as shown in Equation 12.4. This form is called *cis*-polyisoprene; the prefix *cis*- is derived from a Latin phrase meaning "on this side."

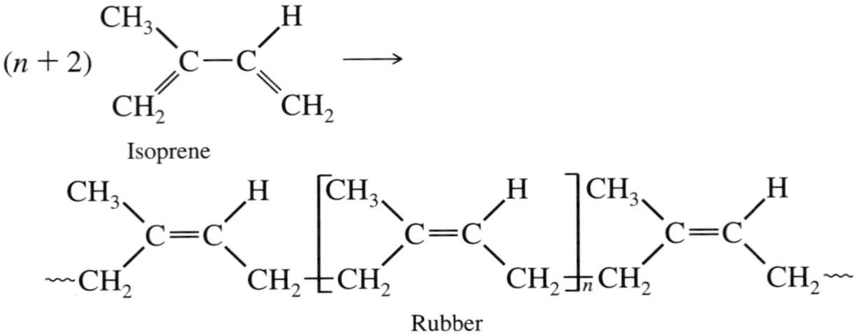

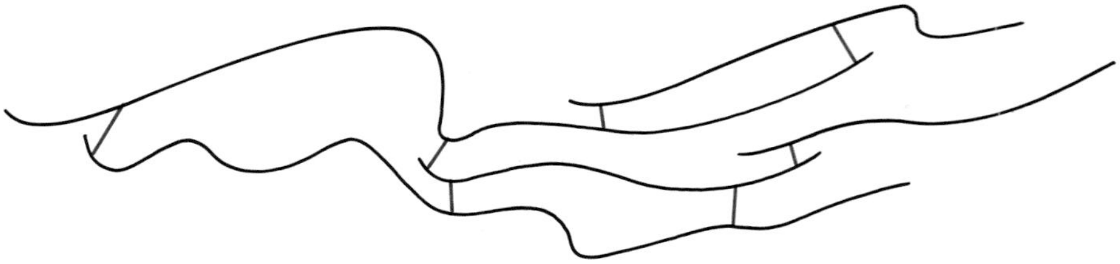

FIGURE 12.18 Crosslinking of polymer chains. The crosslinking groups constrain the relative motions of the polymer chains, making the material harder and less flexible.

Natural rubber is not a useful plastic because it is too soft and too chemically reactive. Goodyear accidentally discovered that adding sulfur to rubber and then heating the mixture makes the rubber harder and reduces its susceptibility to oxidation or other chemical attack. The sulfur changes rubber into a thermosetting polymer by crosslinking the polymer chains through reactions at some of the double bonds, as shown schematically in Figure 12.19. Crosslinking about 5 percent of the double bonds creates a flexible, resilient rubber. When the rubber is stretched, the crosslinks help prevent the chains from slipping, so that the rubber retains its elasticity.

Bassam Z. Shakhashiri, "Polybutadiene (Jumping Rubber)," *Chemical Demonstration: A Handbook for Teachers of Chemistry, Volume 1* (Madison: The University of Wisconsin Press, 1983), pp. 231–234.

FIGURE 12.19 The structure of natural rubber is disclosed in (*a*). The carbon-carbon double bonds marked in red are opened as two sulfur atoms are added to form an interchain link. This crosslinking, shown in (*b*), is referred to as *vulcanization*.

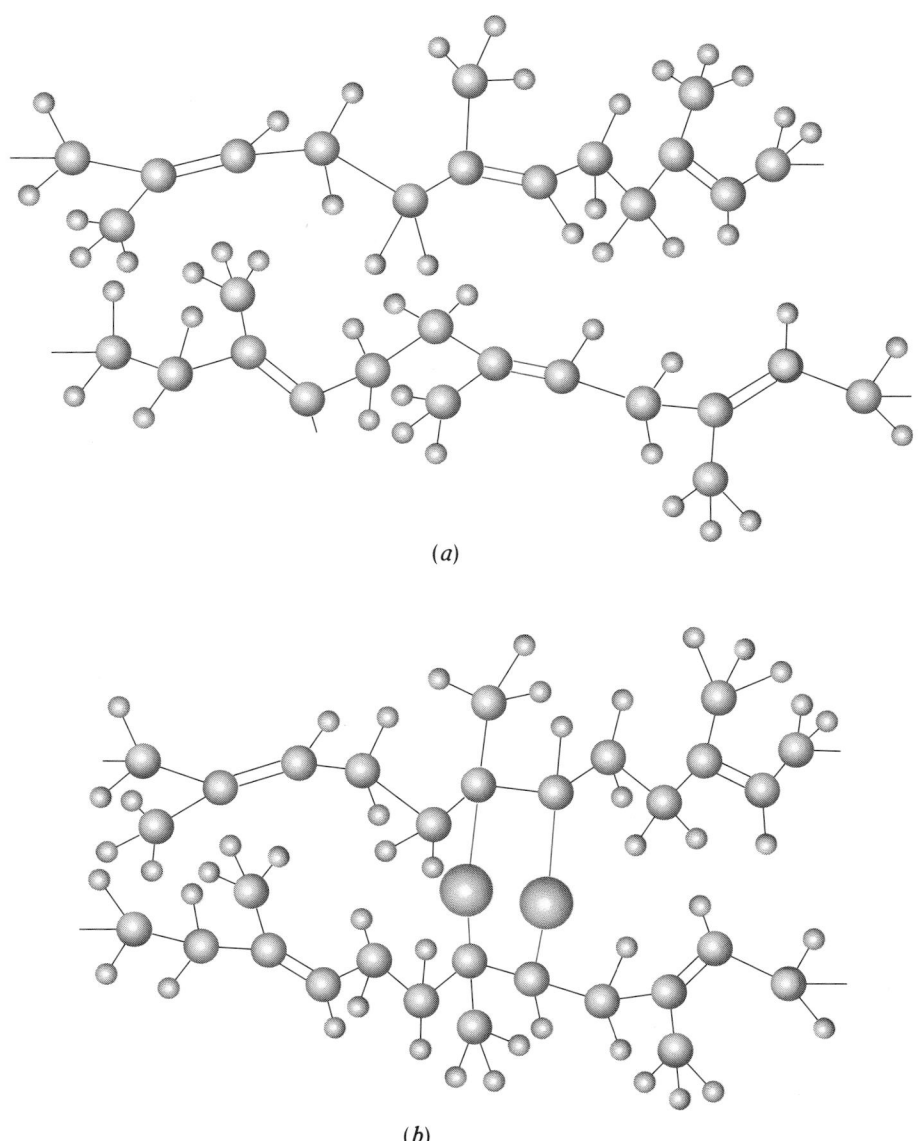

(*a*)

(*b*)

SAMPLE EXERCISE 12.2

What mass of sulfur per gram of isoprene, C_5H_8, is required to establish a crosslink with every isoprene unit, as shown in Figure 12.19?

SOLUTION   We see from the figure that each crosslink involves two sulfur atoms and two isoprene, C_5H_8, units. That is, the ratio of S to C_5H_8 is 1:1. Thus, we have

$$(1.0 \text{ g } C_5H_8)\left(\frac{1 \text{ mol } C_5H_8}{68.6 \text{ g } C_5H_8}\right)\left(\frac{1 \text{ mol S}}{1 \text{ mol } C_5H_8}\right)\left(\frac{32.1 \text{ g S}}{1 \text{ mol S}}\right) = 0.47 \text{ g S}$$

PRACTICE EXERCISE

In a particular vulcanization process, 0.67 g S was used per 10 g polyisoprene. Assuming that all the sulfur reacted to form crosslinks, what is the percentage of cross-linking in the product?   *Answer:* 14 percent

A further example of crosslinking is found in the polymer formed by melamine and formaldehyde, illustrated in Figure 12.20. Although it is not obvious from this two-dimensional drawing, the crosslinking extends in three dimensions, creating a hard, rigid, chemically stable material. This class of thermosetting polymers is found in products such as dinnerware, coatings, and table tops (Formica).

12.3 Ceramics

Ceramics are inorganic, nonmetallic, solid materials. They can be crystalline or noncrystalline. Noncrystalline ceramics include glass and a few other materials with amorphous structures. Ceramics can possess a covalent network structure, ionic bonding, or some combination of the two.   ∞ (Sec. 11.8, Table 11.6)   They are normally hard and brittle and are stable to very high temperatures. Familiar examples of ceramic materials are pottery, china, cement, roof tiles, refractory bricks used in furnaces, and the insulators in spark plugs.

Ceramic materials come in a variety of chemical forms, including *silicates* (silica, SiO_2, with metal oxides), *oxides* (oxygen and metals), *carbides* (carbon

FIGURE 12.20   (*a*) A condensation reaction between formaldehyde and two melamine molecules begins the formation of a polymer. (*b*) The structure of the melamine-formaldehyde polymer, a highly crosslinked material.

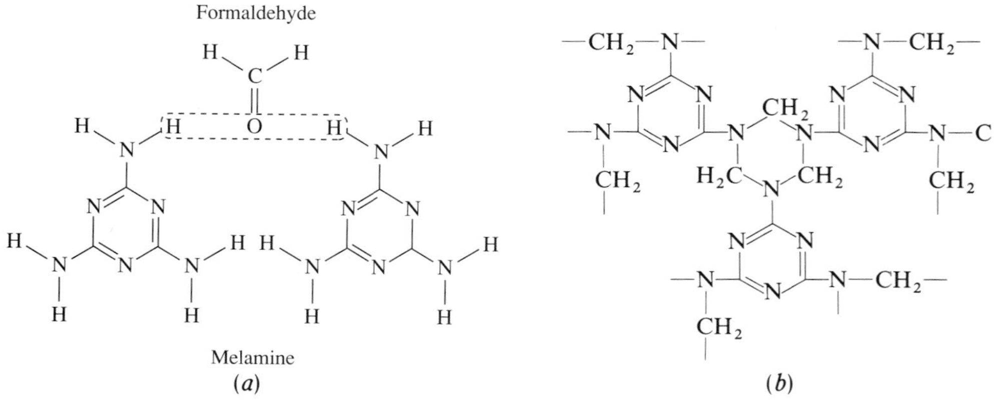

Melamine
(a)

(b)

TABLE 12.4 △ Properties of Some Ceramic and Selected Nonceramic Materials

Material	Melting point (°C)	Density (g/cm³)	Hardness (mohs)[a]	Modulus of elasticity[b]	Coefficient of thermal expansion[c]
Alumina, Al_2O_3	2050	3.8	9	34	8.1
Silicon carbide, SiC	2800	3.2	9	65	4.3
Zirconia, ZrO_2	2660	5.6	8	24	6.6
Beryllia, BeO	2550	3.0	9	40	10.4
Mild steel	1370	7.9	5	17	15
Aluminum	660	2.7	3	7	24

[a] The Mohs scale is based on the relative ability of a material to scratch another, softer material. The larger the number, the harder the material.
[b] A measure of the stiffness of a material when subjected to a load ($MPa \times 10^4$). The larger the number, the stiffer the material.
[c] In units of K ($\times 10^{-6}$). The larger the number, the greater the size change upon heating or cooling.

and metals), *nitrides* (nitrogen and metals), and *aluminates* (alumina, Al_2O_3, with metal oxides). Although most ceramic materials contain metal ions, some do not. Table 12.4 lists a few ceramic materials and contrasts their properties with those of metals.

Ceramics are highly resistant to heat, corrosion, and wear, do not readily deform under stress, and are less dense than the metals used for high-temperature applications. Some ceramics used in aircraft, missiles, and spacecraft weigh only 40 percent as much as the metal component they replace (Figure 12.21). In spite of these many advantages, the use of ceramics as engineering materials has been limited because of their extremely brittle nature. Whereas a metal component might suffer a dent when struck, a ceramic part typically shatters because the bonding prevents the atoms from sliding over one another. Ceramic components are also difficult to manufacture free of defects. Indeed, high fabrica-

Learning Goal 12: Indicate the advantages and disadvantages of engineering ceramics as compared with other materials in various applications.

FIGURE 12.21 A variety of ceramic parts made of silicon nitride, Si_3N_4. These ceramic components can replace metal parts in engines and/or be used in other applications where high temperatures and wear are involved. (Photo courtesy GTE Laboratories, Incorporated)

tion costs and uncertain component reliability are barriers that must be overcome before ceramics are more widely used to replace metals and other structural materials. Attention has therefore focused in recent years on the processing of ceramic materials, as well as on the formation of composite ceramic materials and the development of thin ceramic coatings on conventional materials.

Processing of Ceramics

Ceramic parts often develop random, undetectable microcracks and voids (hollow spaces) during processing. These defects are more susceptible to stress than the rest of the ceramic. Thus, they are generally the origin of part failures due to cracking and fracture. To "toughen" a ceramic — that is, to increase its resistance to fracture — scientists frequently produce very pure uniform particles of the ceramic material that are less than a micrometer ($\frac{1}{1000}$ of a millimeter) in diameter. These are then *sintered* (heated at high temperature under pressure so that the individual particles bond together) to form the desired object.

Learning Goal 13: Describe the sol-gel process for forming ceramic materials.

The **sol-gel process** is an important method of forming extremely fine particles of uniform size. A typical sol-gel procedure begins with a metal alkoxide. An alkoxide contains organic groups bonded to a metal atom through oxygen atoms. Alkoxides are produced when the metal is reacted with an alcohol, which is an organic compound containing an OH group bonded to carbon. To illustrate this process, we will use titanium as the metal and ethyl alcohol, CH_3CH_2OH, as the alcohol:

$$Ti(s) + 4CH_3CH_2OH(l) \longrightarrow Ti(OCH_2CH_3)_4(s) + 2H_2(g) \quad [12.5]$$

The alkoxide product, $Ti(OCH_2CH_3)_4$, is dissolved in an appropriate alcohol solvent. Water is then added, which reacts with the alkoxide to form $Ti-OH$ groups and to regenerate the ethyl alcohol:

$$Ti(OCH_2CH_3)_4(soln) + 4H_2O(l) \longrightarrow Ti(OH)_4(s) + 4CH_3CH_2OH(l) \quad [12.6]$$

The $Ti(OH)_4$ is present at this stage as a *sol,* a suspension of extremely small particles. The acidity or basicity of the sol is adjusted to cause water to be split out from between two of the $Ti-OH$ bonds:

$$(HO)_3Ti-O-H(s) + H-O-Ti(OH)_3(s) \longrightarrow$$
$$(HO)_3Ti-O-Ti(OH)_3(s) + H_2O(l) \quad [12.7]$$

This is another example of a condensation reaction, a reaction that involves the splitting out of a small molecule such as H_2O from between two reactants. ∞ (Sec. 12.2) In the above reaction, condensation also occurs at some of the other OH groups bonded to the central titanium atom, producing a three-dimensional network. The resultant material, called a *gel,* is a suspension of extremely small particles with the consistency of gelatin. When this material is heated carefully at 200°C to 500°C, all the liquid is removed, and the gel is converted to a finely divided metal oxide powder with particles in the range of 0.003 to 0.1 μm in diameter. Figure 12.22 shows SiO_2 particles formed with remarkably uniform, spherical shapes by a precipitation process similar to the sol-gel process.

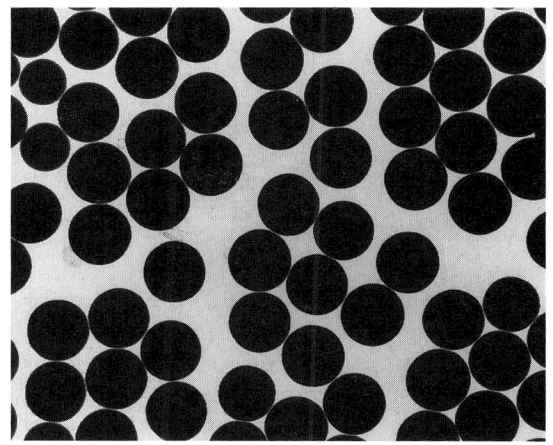

FIGURE 12.22 Uniformly sized spheres of amorphous silica, SiO_2, formed by precipitation from an alcohol solution of $Si(OCH_3)_4$ upon addition of water and ammonia. The average diameter of these spheres is 550 nm. (Professor C. Zukowki, University of Illinois, Urbana-Champaign)

The sol-gel process is particularly useful in producing ceramic coatings and films. The gel is simply applied and then heated to form the ceramic product. It is more difficult to form a ceramic object with a complex three-dimensional shape. One possible approach is to add the gel to a casting and heat it to drive out the liquid component. However, when this is done there is considerable shrinkage, and it is difficult to prevent formation of void spaces and other imperfections. Another approach is to form a useful object from the ceramic powder. The finely divided material, possibly mixed with other powders, is compacted under pressure and then sintered at high temperature. The temperatures required are about 1650°C for alumina, 1700°C for zirconium oxide, and 2050°C for silicon carbide. During sintering, the ceramic particles partially coalesce without actually melting (compare the sintering temperatures with the melting temperatures listed in Table 12.4).

Ceramic Composites

Ceramic objects are much tougher when they are formed from a complex mixture of two or more materials. Such a mixture is called a **composite.** The most effective composites are formed by addition of *ceramic fibers* to a ceramic material. Thus, the composite consists of a ceramic matrix containing embedded fibers of a ceramic material, which may or may not be of the same chemical composition as the matrix.

Learning Goal 14: Give examples of ceramic composites, and indicate their potential advantages over noncomposite ceramic materials.

By definition, a fiber has a length at least 100 times its diameter. Fibers typically have great strength with respect to loads applied along the long axis. When they are embedded in a matrix, they strengthen it by resisting deformations that exert a stress on the fiber along its long axis.

The formation of ceramic fibers is illustrated by the case of silicon carbide, SiC, or carborundum. The first step in the production of SiC fibers is the synthesis of a polymer, polydimethylsilane:

$$-\underset{\underset{CH_3}{|}}{\overset{\overset{CH_3}{|}}{Si}} - \left[\underset{\underset{CH_3}{|}}{\overset{\overset{CH_3}{|}}{Si}} \right]_n - \underset{\underset{CH_3}{|}}{\overset{\overset{CH_3}{|}}{Si}} -$$

When this polymer is heated to about 400°C, it converts to a material that has alternating carbon and silicon atoms along the chain:

$$-\underset{\underset{CH_3}{|}}{\overset{\overset{H}{|}}{Si}}-\left[CH_2-\underset{\underset{CH_3}{|}}{\overset{\overset{H}{|}}{Si}}\right]_n-CH_2-\underset{\underset{CH_3}{|}}{\overset{\overset{H}{|}}{Si}}-$$

Fibers formed from this polymer are then heated slowly to about 1200°C in a nitrogen atmosphere to drive off all the hydrogen and all carbon atoms other than those that directly link the silicon atoms. The final product is a ceramic material of composition SiC, in the form of fibers ranging in diameter from 10 to 15 μm. By similar procedures, beginning with an appropriate organic polymer, ceramic fibers of other compositions—such as boron nitride, BN—can be fabricated. When the ceramic fibers are added to a ceramic material processed as described above, the resulting product has a much higher resistance to catastrophic crack failure.

Applications of Ceramics

Teaching Note: Ceramic composites are being actively studied as replacement materials in aircraft parts.

Teaching Note: Piezoelectric crystals are used in portable gas stove igniters and in some butane cigarette lighters.

FIGURE 12.23 A thermistor temperature sensor. The electrical resistance of the ceramic element at the ends of the wires decreases reproducibly with increasing temperature. Therefore, the device can be used to measure temperature after it is calibrated. (© Richard Megna/ Fundamental Photographs)

Ceramics, particularly new ceramic composites, are widely used in the cutting-tool industry. For example, alumina reinforced with silicon carbide whiskers (extremely fine fibers) is used to cut and machine cast iron and harder nickel-based alloys. Ceramic materials are also used in grinding wheels and as abrasives because of their exceptional hardness (Table 12.4). Silicon carbide is the most widely used abrasive.

Ceramic materials play an important role in the electronics industry. Semiconductor integrated circuits are typically mounted on a ceramic substrate, usually alumina. Some ceramics, notably quartz (crystalline SiO_2), are **piezoelectric,** which means that they generate an electrical potential when subjected to mechanical stress. This property enables us to use piezoelectric materials to control frequencies in electronic circuits, as in quartz watches and ultrasonic generators.

Thermistors are ceramic materials with limited electrical conductivity that increases with temperature. Thermistors are widely used in devices that measure or control temperature. They are also used as heating elements and electrical switches. Figure 12.23 shows a thermistor used as a temperature sensor.

One of the most highly publicized uses of ceramic materials is in the manufacture of ceramic tiles for the surfaces of space shuttle vehicles to protect against overheating on reentry into the earth's atmosphere (Figure 12.24). The tiles are made of short, high-purity silica fibers reinforced with aluminum borosilicate fibers. The material is formed into blocks, sintered at over 1300°C, and then cut into tiles. The tiles have a density of only 0.2 g/cm³, yet they are able to keep the shuttle's aluminum skin below 180°C while sustaining a surface temperature of up to 1250°C.

Superconducting Ceramics

In 1911, Dutch physicist H. Kamerlingh Onnes discovered that when mercury is cooled below 4.2 K it loses all resistance to the flow of an electrical current.

FIGURE 12.24 Workers apply thermally insulating ceramic tiles to the body of the space shuttle orbiter. (Lyndon B. Johnson Space Center, NASA)

Since that discovery, scientists have found that many substances exhibit this "frictionless" flow of electrons. This property has become known as **superconductivity.** Substances that exhibit superconductivity do so only when cooled below a particular temperature, called the **superconducting transition temperature, T_c.** The observed values of T_c are generally very low. In fact, before the 1980s, the highest value that had been observed for T_c was about 23 K for a niobium-germanium compound.

In 1986, J. G. Bednorz and K. A. Müller, working at the IBM research laboratories in Zürich, Switzerland, discovered superconductivity above 30 K in a ceramic oxide containing lanthanum, barium, and copper. This material represents the first **superconducting ceramic.** That discovery, for which Bednorz and Müller received the Nobel Prize in 1987, set off a flurry of research activity all over the world. Before the end of 1986, scientists had verified the onset of superconductivity at 95 K in a compound of yttrium-barium-copper oxide, $YBa_2Cu_3O_7$. At the time of this writing, the highest temperature for onset of zero resistance has been 133 K, which was achieved in another complex copper oxide, $HgBa_2Ca_2Cu_3O_{8+x}$, where x represents a slight excess of oxygen.

The discovery of so-called high-temperature (high-T_c) superconductivity is of great significance. Using materials that carry electrical current with zero resistance could save great amounts of energy in many applications, including electrical generators and large electric motors, and could lead to the production of smaller and faster computer chips. In addition, superconducting materials exhibit a property, called the *Meissner effect,* in which they exclude from their volume all magnetic fields. For this reason, engineers might be able to use these materials to design magnetically levitated trains (Figure 12.25). All these applications became feasible only with the discovery of high-temperature superconductivity, because the cost of maintaining extremely low temperatures is very high. The only readily available safe coolant at temperatures below 77 K is liquid helium, which costs about $10 per liter. However, for materials that undergo the superconducting transition at temperatures well above 77 K, liquid nitrogen, which costs only about $0.50 per liter, can be used.

One of the most widely studied ceramic superconductors is $YBa_2Cu_3O_7$, whose structure is shown in Figure 12.26. The unit cell is defined by the lines; a

Learning Goal 15: Define the term *superconductivity,* and give an example of a superconducting ceramic oxide.

FIGURE 12.25 The Meissner effect, demonstrated in the chapter-opening photo, has numerous potential applications. Here we see an experimental magnetically levitated train near Miyazaki, Japan. (© Chuck O'Rear/West Light)

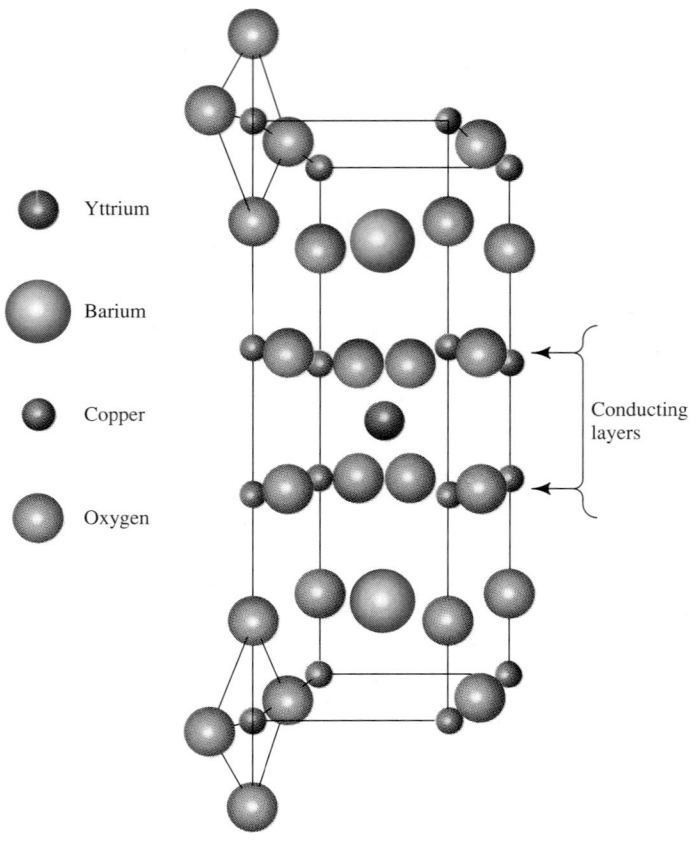

FIGURE 12.26 Unit cell of $YBa_2Cu_3O_7$. A few oxygen atoms that fall outside the unit cell are also shown to illustrate the arrangement of oxygen atoms about each copper atom. The unit cell is defined by the lines that describe a rectangle.

Yttrium

Barium

Copper

Oxygen

Conducting layers

FIGURE 12.27 A wire coil of the high-temperature superconductor $YBa_2Cu_3O_7$. The wire was formed by extruding it from a paste of reactant materials and shaping it into a coil before heating to form the ceramic oxide. (Argonne National Laboratory)

few oxygen atoms that lie outside the unit cell are also shown to illustrate the arrangement of oxygens about each copper atom. Extensive work on modifying this and related copper oxide superconductors by introducing other atoms, called dopants, in various atomic positions indicates that the conductivity and superconductivity take place in the copper oxide planes. The Cu^{2+} ions have a $[Ar]3d^9$ electron configuration with a single electron in the $3d_{x^2-y^2}$ orbital. Although the mechanism of conduction and superconduction is not yet well understood, the fact that the lobes of the $3d_{x^2-y^2}$ orbital point toward the neighboring O^{2-} ions is believed to be important.

The new superconducting ceramic materials have immense promise, but a great deal of research is needed before they can be applied on a practical basis. At present it is difficult to mold ceramics, which are brittle materials, into useful shapes like wires on a large scale. Although science has made some progress in this area (Figure 12.27), the attainable current densities (that is, the current that can be carried by a wire of a certain cross-sectional area) are not yet high enough for many applications. A related problem is the tendency of ceramics to interact with their environment, particularly with water and carbon dioxide. For example, the reaction of $YBa_2Cu_3O_7$ with atmospheric water liberates O_2 and forms $Ba(OH)_2$, $Y_2BaCu_3O_5$, and CuO. Because these materials are so reactive, they must be protected against long-term exposure to the atmosphere.

The discovery of new high-temperature superconducting materials with superior properties and the fabrication of useful devices from the known superconducting materials are subjects of very active research. Even so, scientists estimate that the new discoveries will not be translated into important practical applications for several years. In time, however, this new class of ceramic materials will likely become part of our everyday lives.

12.4 Thin Films

Thin films were first used for decorative purposes. In the seventh century, artists learned how to paint a pattern on a ceramic object with a silver salt solution and then heat the painted object to cause decomposition of the salt, leaving a thin film of metallic silver. Thin films are used today for decorative or protective purposes, to form conductors, resistors, and other types of films in microelectronic circuits, to form photovoltaic devices for conversion of solar energy to electricity, and for many other applications (Figure 12.28). A thin film might be made of any kind of material, including metals, metal oxides, or organic substances.

FIGURE 12.28 The glass panels forming the outer wall of this building have a thin film of metal, which acts to reflect a significant fraction of the outdoor light. The reflective glass provides privacy, reduces interior glare, and reduces the cooling load on the building in hot weather. The building is the Allied Bank, Dallas, Texas, designed by I. M. Pei. (© Wes Thompson/The Stock Market)

The term **thin film** does not have a precise definition. In general, it refers to films with thickness ranging from 0.1 μm to about 300 μm. It does not normally refer to coatings such as paint and varnish, which are typically much thicker. For a thin film to be useful, it should possess all or most of the following properties: (a) It should be chemically stable in the environment in which it is to be used; (b) it should adhere well to the substrate it covers; (c) it should have a uniform thickness; (d) it should be chemically pure or of controlled chemical composition; and (e) it should have a low density of imperfections. In addition to these general characteristics, special properties might be required for certain applications. For example, the film might need to be an insulator or a semiconductor, or to possess special optical or magnetic properties.

A thin film must adhere to its underlying substrate if it is to perform usefully. Because the film is inherently fragile, it must depend on the substrate for structural support. To attain that support, the film must be bound to the substrate by strong forces. The bonding forces may be chemical in nature; that is, a chemical reaction at the interface can connect the film to the underlying material. For example, when a metal oxide is deposited on glass, the oxide lattices of the metal oxide and the glass blend at the interface, forming a thin zone of intermediate composition. In these cases, the bonding energies between the film and the substrate are of the same magnitudes as chemical bonds, in the range of 250 to 400 kJ/mol. In some cases, however, the bonding between the film and the substrate is based solely on intermolecular van der Waals and electrostatic forces, as might be the case when an organic polymer film is deposited on a metal surface. The energies that bind the film to the substrate in such cases might be in the range of 50 to 100 kJ/mol. Thus, films in which only bonding of this sort is present are not as robust.

Uses of Thin Films

Thin films are very important in microelectronics. They are employed as conductors, resistors, and capacitors. Thin films are widely used as optical coatings on lenses (Figure 12.29) to reduce the amount of light reflected from the lens surface and to protect the lens. Thin metallic films have been used for a long time as protective coatings on metals. They are usually deposited from solu-

FIGURE 12.29 The lenses of these binoculars are coated with a ceramic thin film to reduce reflectance and protect the softer glass against scratching. (© Kristen Brochman/Fundamental Photographs)

tions by the use of electrical currents, as in silver plating and "chrome" plating. (We will defer discussion of electrochemical methods for forming films until Chapter 20.) Metal tool surfaces are coated with ceramic thin films to increase their hardness. For example, a hard steel drill bit may be coated with a thin film of titanium nitride or tungsten carbide (Figure 12.30). Although it is not evident to the consumer, nearly every glass bottle purchased is coated with one or more thin films. The films are applied to the glass to reduce scratching and abrasion and to increase lubricity, that is, the ease with which bottles can slide by one another. The most common thin film is one of tin oxide, SnO_2.

Formation of Thin Films

Thin films are formed by a variety of techniques. We will discuss three of the most commonly used methods: vacuum deposition, sputtering, and chemical-vapor deposition.

Vacuum deposition is used to form thin films of substances that can be vaporized or evaporated without destroying their chemical identities. These substances include metals, metal alloys, and simple inorganic compounds such as oxides, sulfides, fluorides, and chlorides. For example, optical lenses are coated with inorganic materials such as MgF_2, Al_2O_3, and SiO_2. The material to be deposited as a thin film is heated—either electrically or by electron bombardment—in a high-vacuum chamber with a pressure of 10^{-5} torr or less. The process is shown diagrammatically in Figure 12.31. To obtain a film of uniform thickness, all parts of the surface to be coated must be equally accessible to the vapor phase from which the thin-film material is deposited. Sometimes this uniformity is obtained by rotating the piece to be coated.

Sputtering involves the use of a high voltage to remove material from a source, or target. Atoms removed from the target are carried through the ionized gas within the chamber and deposited on the substrate. The target surface is the negative electrode, or cathode, in the circuit, and the substrate may be attached to the positive electrode, or anode. Figure 12.32 depicts this process. The chamber contains an inert gas such as argon that is ionized in the high-voltage field. The positively charged ions are accelerated toward the target surface, which they strike with sufficient energy to dislodge atoms of the target material. Many of these atoms are accelerated toward the substrate surface. On striking it, they form a thin film.

FIGURE 12.30 The tip of this masonry drill bit has been coated with a thin film of tungsten carbide to impart hardness and resistance against wear. (© Richard Megna/Fundamental Photographs)

Learning Goal 17: Explain how thin films are formed by vacuum deposition, sputtering, and chemical vapor deposition.

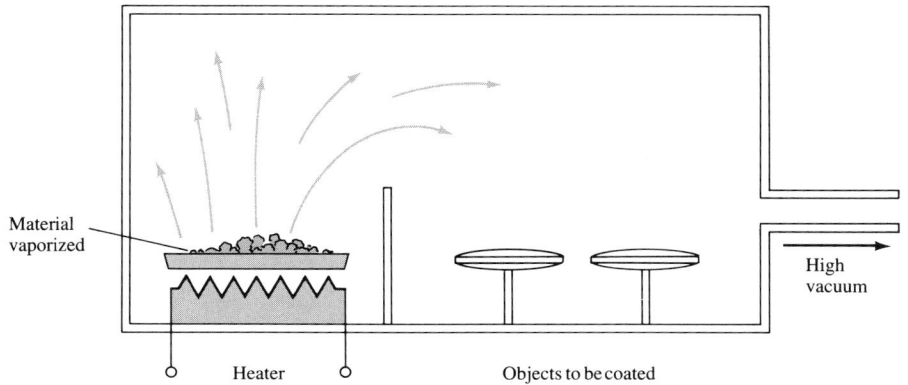

Material vaporized

Heater — Objects to be coated

High vacuum

FIGURE 12.31 A schematic illustration of a vacuum-deposition apparatus.

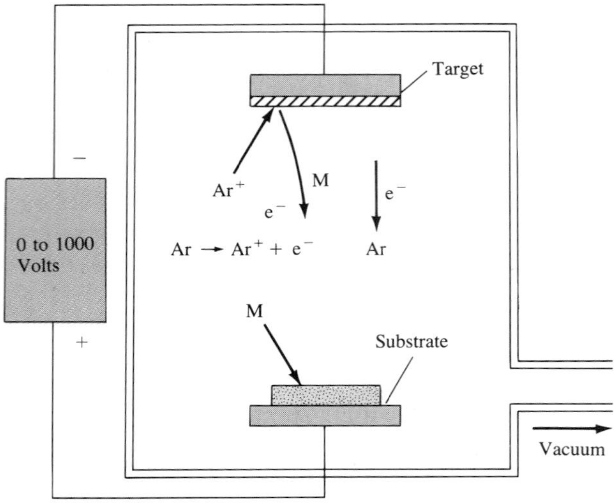

FIGURE 12.32 A schematic illustration of a sputtering apparatus.

The sputtered atoms have a lot of energy. The initial atoms striking the surface may penetrate several atomic layers into the substrate, which helps to ensure good adhesion of the thin-film layer to the substrate. An additional advantage of sputtering is that it is possible to change the target material from which the sputtered atoms arise without disturbing the system, so that multilayer thin films can be formed.

Sputtering is widely used to form thin films of such elements as silicon, titanium, niobium, tungsten, aluminum, gold, and silver. It is also employed to form thin films of refractory materials such as carbides, borides, and nitrides on metal tool surfaces, to form soft lubricating films such as molybdenum disulfide, and to apply antiglare coatings of metal oxides to optical equipment. It is even possible with appropriate equipment to sputter nonconducting organic polymers.

In **chemical-vapor deposition,** the surface is coated with a volatile, stable chemical compound at a temperature below the melting point of the surface. The compound then undergoes some form of chemical reaction to form a stable, adherent coat. For example, titanium tetrabromide is evaporated, and the gaseous $TiBr_4$ is mixed with hydrogen. The mixture is then passed over a surface heated to about 1300°C. The heated substrate is ordinarily a ceramic such as silica or alumina. The metal halide undergoes reaction with hydrogen to form a coating of titanium metal:

$$TiBr_4(g) + 2H_2(g) \longrightarrow Ti(s) + 4HBr(g) \qquad [12.8]$$

Similarly, it is possible to make silicon films by decomposition of $SiCl_4$ in the presence of H_2 at 1100°C to 1200°C:

$$SiCl_4(g) + 2H_2(g) \longrightarrow Si(s) + 4HCl(g) \qquad [12.9]$$

Films of silica, SiO_2, are formed by decomposition of $SiCl_4$ in the presence of both H_2 and CO_2 at 600°C to 900°C:

CHEMISTRY AT WORK

Diamond Coatings

Besides being one of the hardest known substances, diamond is also highly resistant to corrosion. At the present time, commercial diamonds are widely used to strengthen cutting and grinding tools. These diamonds are embedded in the tools and are not intimately and uniformly part of the material.

Scientists have recently developed procedures for applying ultrathin layers of synthetic diamond coatings on materials. Diamond films promise to give diamond's hardness and durability to a variety of materials—glass, paper, plastics, metals, and semiconductor devices, for example. Imagine scratchproof glass; cutting tools that virtually never need sharpening (Figure 12.33); surfaces that are chemical-resistant. Because diamond is compatible with biological tissue, it also can be used to coat prosthetic materials and biosensors.

One procedure for generating diamond films involves exposing a mixture of methane gas, CH_4, and hydrogen gas, H_2, to intense microwave radiation in the presence of the object to be coated. Under appropriate conditions, the CH_4 decomposes, depositing a thin film of diamond. The H_2 dissociates into atomic hydrogen, which impedes formation of graphite. Atomic hydrogen reacts faster with graphite than with diamond, effectively removing graphite from the growing film. Although the process is not fundamentally expensive or sophisticated, its widespread commercial application is still some years away. Researchers are presently trying to reduce the deposition temperatures, increase the deposition rate, and develop techniques for coating the surfaces of a wider variety of sizes and shapes than is now practical.

FIGURE 12.33 Two cutting-tool inserts of the same composition and used under similar conditions. The one on the left has been coated with a diamond film and shows less wear at the cutting edge. (Photomicrographs courtesy of William Drawl, Pennsylvania State University; *Chemical Engineering News* **1989**, May 15, p. 37)

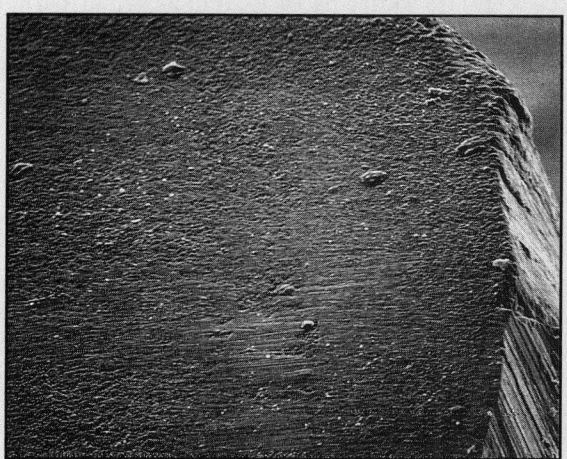 

$$SiCl_4(g) + 2H_2(g) + 2CO_2(g) \longrightarrow SiO_2(s) + 4HCl(g) + 2CO(g) \quad [12.10]$$

Films of silicon nitride, Si_3N_4, can be formed by the reaction of silane, SiH_4, with ammonia at 900°C to 1100°C:

$$3SiH_4(g) + 4NH_3(g) \longrightarrow Si_3N_4(s) + 12H_2(g) \quad\quad [12.11]$$

For Review

Summary

In this chapter, we have considered four important classes of modern materials: liquid crystals, polymers, ceramics, and thin films. Liquid crystals are substances that exhibit one or more ordered phases in a temperature range above the melting point of the solid. In a nematic liquid crystal, the molecules are aligned along a common direction, but the ends of the molecules are not lined up. In smectic phases, the ends of the molecules are lined up as well, so that the molecules form sheets. Nematic and smectic phases are generally composed of molecules with fairly rigid, rodlike shapes. The cholesteric liquid-crystalline phase is composed of molecules that form ordered layers of molecules. The most important applications of liquid-crystalline materials are in screens for portable computers and in other digital-display devices such as watches and calculators.

A polymer contains many identical molecules (monomers) joined together to form a molecular chain. Two of the most important kinds of reactions that join monomers into polymers are addition polymerization, exemplified by the formation of polyethylene, and condensation polymerization, exemplified by the formation of nylon 6,6. The properties of a given polymer vary with the average length of the chain and with the degree of branching along the chain.

Plastics are materials that can be formed into particular shapes using heat and pressure. Thermoplastic materials can be reshaped, whereas thermosetting plastics, once formed, are not readily reshaped. An elastomer is a material that, when stretched or bent, regains its original shape upon removal of the distorting force.

Polymers are considered amorphous materials, but they may possess regions in which the molecules are aligned. These regions are referred to as being *crystalline;* they impart hardness and raise the temperature at which the materials soften. A plasticizer is a substance with a low molecular mass that is added to a polymer to disrupt partially the alignment of the polymer molecules, thus imparting greater flexibility to the material.

Greater hardness and lower flexibility can be achieved in polymers by crosslinking, that is, by forming chemical bonds between polymer chains. An example is the vulcanization of rubber, which occurs when natural rubber is heated with sulfur. Sulfur atoms bridge between adjacent polymer chains, making the rubber harder and less subject to decomposition.

Ceramics are inorganic materials that typically exhibit hardness, rigidity, and high-temperature stability. Ceramics find use in a variety of applications where metals, wood, or plastics were traditionally used. The use of ceramics in many applications is limited by their brittle nature, which makes them susceptible to catastrophic failure through crack formation. Ceramics can be toughened (made resistant to cracking) by sintering of extremely small particles. One important method for forming small ceramic particles of uniform size is called the sol-gel process. Ceramics can also be made tougher by forming a composite, which is a solid mixture of two or more component materials.

Certain ceramic materials, including quartz, are piezoelectric; that is, they develop an electrical potential upon deformation. A thermistor is a ceramic whose electrical resistance decreases with increasing temperature. Superconducting ceramics are relatively new materials that exhibit no electrical resistance below a certain transition temperature. The superconducting transition temperatures for ceramic superconductors, such as $YBa_2Cu_3O_7$, are higher than for any nonceramic superconductors.

A thin film is a layer of one substance, ranging in thickness from $0.1\ \mu m$ to perhaps several hundred micrometers, covering an underlying substrate. Thin films are formed primarily by vacuum deposition, in which a substance is sublimed onto the substrate. A second method, called sputtering, involves use of a high-voltage gaseous discharge. In chemical-vapor deposition, a substance is deposited on a surface, after which a chemical reaction forms the desired film.

Key Terms

liquid crystal (Sec. 12.1)
nematic liquid-crystalline phase (Sec. 12.1)
smectic liquid-crystalline phase (Sec. 12.1)
cholesteric liquid-crystalline phase (Sec. 12.1)
polymer (Sec. 12.2)
monomer (Sec. 12.2)
addition polymerization (Sec. 12.2)
condensation polymerization (Sec. 12.2)
condensation reaction (Sec. 12.2)
plastic (Sec. 12.2)
thermoplastic (Sec. 12.2)
thermosetting plastic (Sec. 12.2)
elastomer (Sec. 12.2)
plasticizers (Sec. 12.2)

crosslinking (Sec. 12.2)
ceramics (Sec. 12.3)
sol-gel process (Sec. 12.3)
composite (Sec. 12.3)
piezoelectric (Sec. 12.3)
thermistors (Sec. 12.3)
superconductivity (Sec. 12.3)
superconducting transition temperature (T_c) (Sec. 12.3)
superconducting ceramic (Sec. 12.3)
thin film (Sec. 12.4)
vacuum deposition (Sec. 12.4)
sputtering (Sec. 12.4)
chemical-vapor deposition (Sec. 12.4)

Exercises

12.1. What is the difference between a liquid crystal and a liquid? Between a liquid crystal and a crystal?

12.2. A solid has molecular-level order in all three dimensions, whereas a liquid has no long-range order. Does a liquid crystal possess any molecular order? Explain.

12.3. What observations made by Reinitzer on cholesteryl benzoate suggested that this substance possesses a liquid-crystalline phase?

12.4. How does a liquid-crystalline material behave differently from one that is not liquid-crystalline?

12.5. What are the most common characteristics of the shapes of liquid-crystalline substances?

12.6. All the liquid-crystalline materials listed in Figure 12.5 possess backbones containing benzene rings; several also have N=N or C=N double bonds. What roles do these groups play in causing the substances to exhibit liquid-crystalline behavior?

12.7. Name the three major classes of liquid-crystalline phases and indicate the distinctions among them.

12.8. What is the difference between the smectic A phase and the smectic C phase of liquid crystals?

12.9. When a second substance is dissolved in a substance that has a liquid-crystalline phase, only a small concentration of solute is often sufficient to eliminate formation of the liquid-crystalline phase. Why?

12.10. The molecules shown in Figure 12.5 all possess polar groups, that is, groupings of atoms that give rise to fairly large dipole moments within the molecules. In terms of the factors that give rise to intermolecular interactions (Section 11.2), how might the presence of such polar groups enhance the tendency toward liquid-crystal formation?

Polymers

12.11. What is a polymer? What is a monomer?

12.12. What structural feature is common to all monomers that undergo addition polymerization?

12.13. Write a chemical equation that represents the formation of polychloroprene from chloroprene,

$$CH_2=CH-\underset{\underset{Cl}{|}}{C}=CH_2$$

(Polychloroprene is employed in highway-pavement seals, expansion joints, conveyor belts, and wire and cable jacketing.)

12.14. Write a chemical equation that describes the formation of polyacrylonitrile from acrylonitrile,

$$CH_2=\underset{\underset{CN}{|}}{CH}$$

(Polyacrylonitrile is employed in home furnishings, craft yarns, wearing apparel, and many other uses.)

12.15. What is a condensation reaction? How can condensation reactions be used to form polymers?

12.16. An ester is a compound formed by a condensation reaction between a carboxylic acid and an alcohol. Use the index to find the discussion of esters in Chapter 26 and give an example of a reaction forming an ester. How might this kind of reaction be used to form a polymer (a polyester)?

12.17. Write a chemical equation representing the formation of poly(phenylene oxide) by condensation polymerization of 2,6-dimethyl-*p*-hydroxyphenol,

HO—⟨benzene ring with CH₃ groups at 2,6 positions⟩—OH

[Poly(phenylene oxide) is employed in fabricating automotive parts, appliances, and computer chassis.]

12.18. The nylon Nomex has the following structure:

⟨structure of Nomex polymer⟩

Draw the structures of the two monomeric compounds that yield Nomex as a polymerization product when subjected to a condensation reaction.

12.19. How does the hardness of a polymeric material change with **(a)** increasing crystallinity; **(b)** crosslinking; **(c)** addition of a plasticizer; **(d)** increasing strength of intermolecular bonding between chains; **(e)** branching of chains?

12.20. **(a)** What molecular features make a polymer flexible or rubbery? **(b)** Why are most polymers amorphous materials?

12.21. Provide a brief description of each of the following: **(a)** elastomer; **(b)** thermoplastic; **(c)** thermosetting plastic.

12.22. Provide a brief description or definition of each of the following: **(a)** plasticizer; **(b)** crosslinking; **(c)** condensation reaction.

Ceramics

12.23. List the potential advantages of ceramics as engineering materials over other materials such as plastics and metals.

12.24. List some of the ways in which ceramics differ from polymers in terms of molecular structure and physical properties.

12.25. Silicon carbide, SiC, has the three-dimensional structure shown in Figure 12.34. Describe how the bonding and structure of SiC lead to its great thermal stability (to 2700°C) and exceptional hardness.

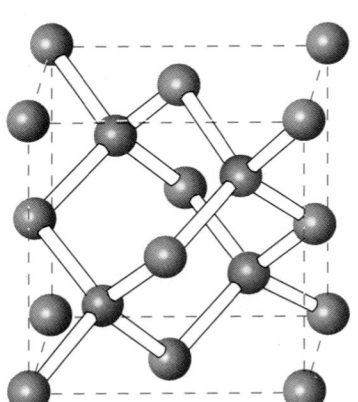

FIGURE 12.34

12.26. Account for each of the following applications of ceramic materials in terms of the electronic structure of the substance: **(a)** Zirconia, ZrO_2, is employed in high-temperature engine blocks and in gas turbine rotors. **(b)** The compound $Mg_3Al_2(SiO_4)_3$, a garnet mineral, is employed as the abrasive material in sandpaper.

12.27. Why are ceramic materials generally brittle?

12.28. Describe the steps that can be taken to increase the resistance of ceramic materials to mechanical failure.

12.29. In a sol-gel process, a metal alkoxide is reacted with water to produce a metal hydroxide, which then undergoes condensation reactions to yield a polymeric network of metal-oxygen-metal linkages. Suggest a reason why the process is not simply begun with the metal hydroxide.

12.30. In a typical insulator composed primarily of Al_2O_3, the solid is formed by sintering grains of Al_2O_3 that are 5 to 10 μm in diameter. What is the reason behind sintering small particles to form a larger solid piece?

12.31. What is a composite? In what respects is a ceramic composite likely to be an improvement over the primary ceramic material from which it is formed?

12.32. Ceramic materials typically fail by catastrophic crack propagation. Offer an explanation of how the addition of ceramic fibers to a ceramic matrix toughens the material against this.

12.33. What property or properties of the ceramic material are most important in each of the following applications of ceramics: **(a)** thermistor temperature sensor; **(b)** silicon carbide-reinforced machine cutting tool; **(c)** silicon dioxide substrate for a semiconductor integrated circuit; **(d)** silicon carbide gas turbine rotor in an aircraft engine?

12.34. What general properties of ceramic materials are important in the use of ceramic tiles to protect space shuttle vehicles against overheating during reentry into the earth's atmosphere?

12.35. How does a superconducting material differ in its electrical properties from ordinary electrical conductors?

12.36. In what ways does the superconducting ceramic $YBa_2Cu_3O_7$ differ from superconducting materials known before 1980?

Thin Films

12.37. What is meant by the term "thin film"?

12.38. For a thin film to be useful, what properties should it have?

12.39. List the characteristics that would be desirable in a thin film of tantalum carbide applied to the surface of a cutting tool to impart hardness.

12.40. What properties does a thin coat of SnO_2 impart to glass?

12.41. List three general methods by which thin films are formed.

12.42. Indicate the method or methods applicable to formation of a thin film of each of the following materials: **(a)** MgO; **(b)** Teflon, an organic polymer of empirical formula CF_2; **(c)** titanium.

Additional Exercises

12.43. Why don't substances with molecular backbones consisting entirely of C—C single bonds exhibit liquid-crystalline behavior?

[12.44]. A particular liquid-crystalline substance has the phase diagram shown in Figure 12.35. By analogy with the phase diagram for a non-liquid-crystalline substance (Section 11.6), label the areas as to the phase present.

FIGURE 12.35

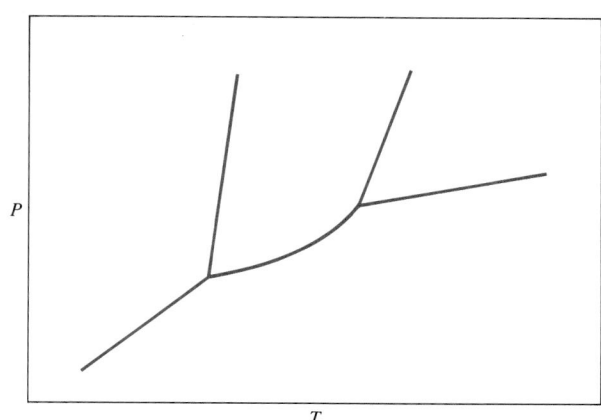

[12.45]. The operation of a liquid-crystal display, as illustrated in Figure 12.10, depends upon a change in the orientation of the molecules in an electric field. Suppose the molecules in a nematic substance were aligned as follows in the absence of an applied electrical potential:

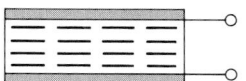

How would these molecules be aligned when an electrical potential is applied by connecting a battery across the contacts? What molecular properties would be likely to cause such a realignment to occur? (Hint: See Section 11.2.)

12.46. Polyethylene has London dispersion forces operating between chains. Nylon has hydrogen bonding. Compare the strengths of these two kinds of intermolecular attractive forces. How would you expect this difference to affect the hardness of these two polymers?

12.47. Teflon is a polymer formed by the polymerization of $F_2C=CF_2$. What is the structure of this polymer? What kind of polymerization reaction is used to form it?

[12.48]. Polypropylene is an addition polymer formed from propylene, $CH_3—CH=CH_2$. Depending on the conditions under which it is made, polypropylene can vary greatly in crystallinity, elasticity, and density. It has a much wider range of properties in these respects than does polyethylene. Account for these observations in light of the comparative structures of the two polymers.

12.49. Classify each of the following as a ceramic, polymer, or liquid crystal.

(a)
$$\left[\begin{array}{c} CH_3 \\ | \\ CH_2-C- \\ | \\ COOCH_3 \end{array}\right]_n$$

(b) $LiNbO_3$

(c) SiC

(d)
$$\left[\begin{array}{c} CH_3 \\ | \\ Si \\ | \\ CH_3 \end{array}\right]_n$$

(e) $CH_3O-\!\!\!\bigcirc\!\!\!-N=N-\!\!\!\bigcirc\!\!\!-OCH_3$ (with O above N=N)

12.50. Ceramics are generally brittle, subject to crack failure, and stable to high temperatures. In contrast, plastics are generally deformable under stress and have limited thermal stability. Discuss these differences in terms of the structures and bonding in the two classes of materials.

12.51. In most applications of ceramic composites, the matrix and the added fiber should have closely similar coefficients of thermal expansion. Why is this so?

[12.52]. In ceramic composites, a strong interaction between the embedded fibers and the matrix host is essential. What kinds of interactions might exist in these systems? How would the high-temperature processing of the ceramic be likely to affect the nature of the interactions?

12.53. Write balanced chemical equations to describe: **(a)** formation of a silicon carbide whisker by the two-step thermal decomposition of poly(dimethylsilane) (two equations); **(b)** formation of a thin film of niobium by thermal decomposition of $NbBr_5$ on a hot surface under an H_2 atmosphere; **(c)** formation of $Si(OCH_2CH_3)_4$ by reaction of $SiCl_4$ with ethyl alcohol; **(d)** polymerization of styrene,

$$\langle\bigcirc\rangle\!-\!CH\!=\!CH_2,$$

to form polystyrene.

[12.54]. In the superconducting ceramic $YBa_2Cu_3O_7$, what is the average oxidation state of copper, assuming that Y and Ba are in their expected oxidation states? Yttrium can be replaced with a rare-earth element such as La, and Ba can be replaced with other similar elements without fundamentally changing the superconducting properties of the material. However, general replacement of copper by any other element leads to a loss of superconductivity. In what respects is the electronic structure of copper different from that of the other two metallic elements in this compound?

12.55. List an application of thin films that involves each of the following characteristics or types of material: **(a)** an electrical conductor; **(b)** a metal oxide; **(c)** a hard ceramic material.

[12.56]. Whereas thin films of metal oxides can be formed by vacuum deposition, a general rule is that inorganic compounds having anionic components with names ending in -ite or -ate cannot be successfully vacuum-deposited. Why is this so?

[12.57]. Indicate the nature of the film formed by thermal decomposition on a heated surface of each of the following: **(a)** SiH_4 with H_2 as carrier gas, in the presence of CO_2 (CO is a product); **(b)** $TiCl_4$ in the presence of water vapor; **(c)** $GeCl_4$ in the presence of H_2 as carrier gas.

Properties of Solutions

13

A wave breaking in the Pacific Ocean off of Cape Kiwanda, Oregon. Ocean water is a complex aqueous solution of many dissolved substances, of which sodium chloride is highest in concentration.

CONTENTS

Most of the materials that we encounter in everyday life are mixtures of pure substances. Many of these mixtures are homogeneous; that is, their components are uniformly intermingled on a molecular level. Homogeneous mixtures are called *solutions*. ∞ (Secs. 1.1, 4.1) Examples of solutions abound in the world around us. The air we breathe is a solution of several gases. Brass is a solid solution of zinc in copper. The fluids that run through our bodies are solutions, carrying a great variety of essential nutrients, salts, and other materials.

Solutions may be gases, liquids, or solids (Table 13.1). Each of the substances in a solution is called a *component* of the solution. As we saw in Chapter 4, the *solvent* is normally the component present in greatest amount. Other components are called *solutes*. Because liquid solutions are the most common, we will focus our attention on them in this chapter. We will be particularly concerned with aqueous solutions of ionic substances because of their central importance in chemistry and in our daily lives.

In Chapter 11, we considered the various types of intermolecular forces that exist between molecules and ions. In this chapter, we will see that these forces are also involved in the interactions between solutes and solvents. We will start this chapter by examining the molecular processes and energetics involved in forming a solution from a solvent and a solute.

13.1 The Solution Process

A solution is formed when one substance disperses uniformly throughout another. With the exception of gas mixtures, all solutions involve substances in a condensed phase. We learned in Chapter 11 that substances in the liquid and solid states experience intermolecular attractive forces that hold the individual particles together. Intermolecular forces also operate between a solute particle and the solvent that surrounds it.

Any of the various kinds of intermolecular forces that we discussed in Chapter 11 can operate between solute and solvent particles in a solution. As a general rule, we expect solutions to form when the attractive forces between solute and solvent are comparable in magnitude with those that exist between the solute particles themselves or between the solvent particles themselves. For example, the ionic substance NaCl dissolves readily in water because the attractive interaction between the ions and the polar H_2O molecules overcomes the lattice energy of NaCl(s).

Point of Emphasis: The only difference between the intermolecular forces at work in pure substances (Chapter 11) and the intermolecular forces at work in solutions is that the forces in solution are among unlike particles (solute and solvent).

TABLE 13.1 △ **Examples of Solutions**

State of solution	State of solvent	State of solute	Example
Gas	Gas	Gas	Air
Liquid	Liquid	Gas	Oxygen in water
Liquid	Liquid	Liquid	Alcohol in water
Liquid	Liquid	Solid	Salt in water
Solid	Solid	Gas	Hydrogen in palladium
Solid	Solid	Liquid	Mercury in silver
Solid	Solid	Solid	Silver in gold

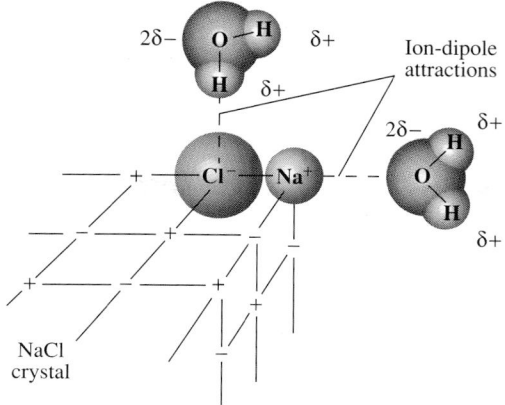

FIGURE 13.1 Interactions between H_2O molecules and the Na^+ and Cl^- ions of a NaCl crystal.

Figure 13.1

When NaCl is added to water, the water molecules orient themselves on the surface of the NaCl crystals, as shown in Figure 13.1. The positive end of the water dipole is oriented toward the Cl^- ions, and the negative end of the water dipole is oriented toward the Na^+ ions. The ion-dipole attractions between Na^+ and Cl^- ions and water molecules are sufficiently strong to pull these ions from their positions in the crystal.

Once separated from the crystal, the Na^+ and Cl^- ions are surrounded by water molecules, as shown in Figure 13.2. Such interactions between solute and solvent molecules are known as **solvation.** When the solvent is water, the interactions are known as **hydration.**

Point of Emphasis: *Solvation* is a general term and can be used regardless of the solvent. *Hydration* is a specific term and is used only when water is the solvent.

Energy Changes and Solution Formation

Sodium chloride dissolves in water because the water molecules have a sufficient attraction for the Na^+ and Cl^- ions to overcome the attraction of these two ions for one another in the crystal. To form an aqueous solution of NaCl, water molecules must also separate from one another to make room for the solute particles. This example suggests that there are three attractive interactions involved in solution formation:

1. Solute-solute interactions
2. Solvent-solvent interactions
3. Solute-solvent interactions

Learning Goal 1: Describe the energy changes that occur in the solution process in terms of solute-solute, solvent-solvent, and solute-solvent attractive forces; describe the role of disorder in the solution process.

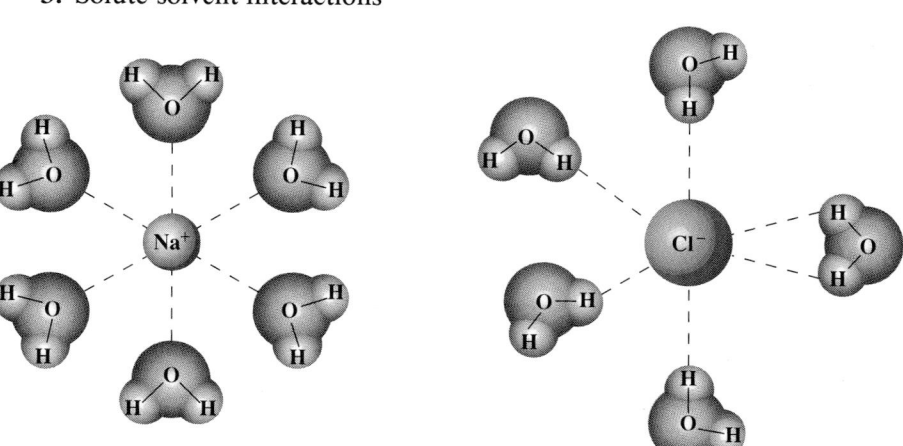

FIGURE 13.2 Hydrated Na^+ and Cl^- ions. The negative ends of the water dipole point toward the positive ion. The positive ends of the water dipole point toward the negative ion. We do not know whether one or both positive hydrogens are oriented toward the negative ion.

Figure 13.2

13.1 The Solution Process **449**

The overall enthalpy change in forming a solution, ΔH_{soln}, is the sum of the enthalpy changes that correspond to each of these three interactions:

$$\Delta H_{soln} = \Delta H_1 + \Delta H_2 + \Delta H_3$$

Figure 13.3 depicts the enthalpy change for each process. Separation of the solute particles from one another requires an input of energy to overcome their attractive interactions. This process is therefore endothermic (positive ΔH_1). The separation of solvent molecules from one another is similarly endothermic (positive ΔH_2). These first two steps require that energy be added to the system. However, when the solute and solvent particles are allowed to interact, we have an exothermic process (negative ΔH_3) that releases energy from the system.

As shown in Figure 13.3, the formation of a solution can be either exothermic or endothermic. For example, when sodium hydroxide, NaOH, is added to water, the resultant solution gets quite warm; $\Delta H_{soln} = -44.48$ kJ/mol. In contrast, the dissolution of ammonium nitrate, NH_4NO_3, is endothermic: $\Delta H_{soln} = 26.4$ kJ/mol. Ammonium nitrate has been used to make instant ice packs, which are used to treat athletic injuries (Figure 13.4).

A solution will not form if ΔH_{soln} is too endothermic. The solvent-solute interaction must be strong enough to make ΔH_3 comparable in quantity to $\Delta H_1 + \Delta H_2$. This is why ionic solutes like NaCl do not dissolve in nonpolar liquids like gasoline. The nonpolar hydrocarbon molecules of the gasoline would experience only weak attractive interactions with the ions, and these interactions would not go very far toward compensating for the energies required to separate the ions from one another.

By similar reasoning, we can understand why a polar liquid such as water does not form solutions with a nonpolar liquid such as octane, C_8H_{18}. The water molecules experience strong hydrogen-bonding interactions with one another (Section 11.2); these attractive forces would need to be overcome to disperse the water molecules throughout the nonpolar liquid. The energy re-

FIGURE 13.3 Analysis of the enthalpy changes accompanying the solution process: ΔH_1 is the enthalpy required to separate solute particles; ΔH_2 is the enthalpy required to separate solvent particles; ΔH_3 is the enthalpy released when solute and solvent particles interact with each other. The figure on the left shows a net exothermic heat of solution, whereas the one on the right shows a net endothermic heat of solution.

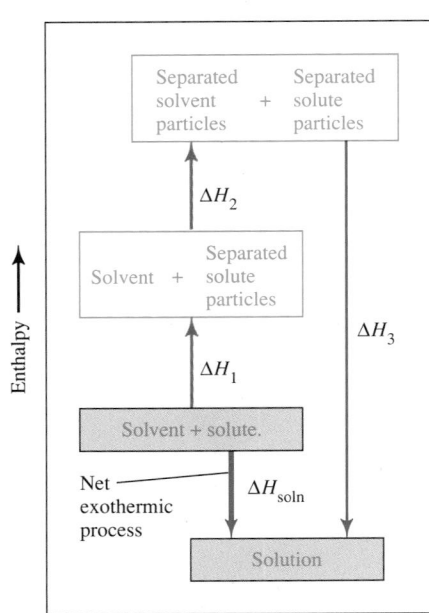
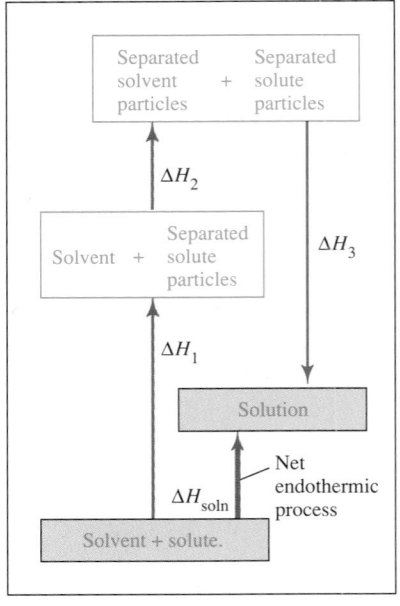

Figure 13.3

FIGURE 13.4 Photo of an instant ice pack containing ammonium nitrate, used to treat athletic injuries. To activate the ice pack, the container is kneaded, breaking the seal separating solid NH_4NO_3 from water. (© Richard Megna/Fundamental Photographs)

FIGURE 13.5 Formation of a homogeneous solution between CCl_4 and C_6H_{14} upon removal of a barrier separating the two liquids. The solution in (b) is more disordered, or random in character, than the separate liquids before solution formation (a).

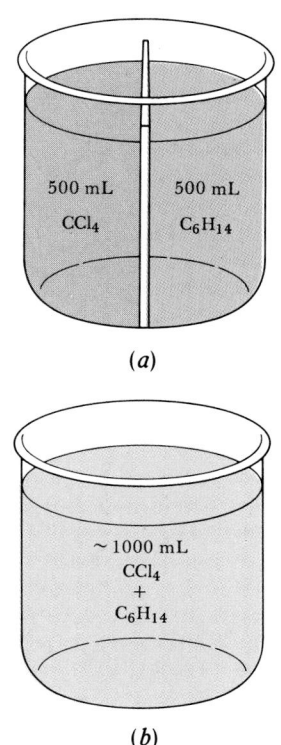

quired to separate the H_2O molecules is not recovered in the form of attractive interactions between H_2O and C_8H_{18} molecules.

Solution Formation, Spontaneity, and Disorder

When two nonpolar substances such as CCl_4 and hexane, C_6H_{14}, are mixed, they readily dissolve in one another in all proportions. The attractive forces between molecules in both of these substances are London dispersion forces. The two substances have similar boiling points: CCl_4 boils at $77\,°C$, and C_6H_{14} boils at $69\,°C$. It is therefore reasonable to suppose that the magnitudes of the attractive forces between molecules are comparable in the two substances. When the two are mixed, there is little or no energy change. Yet the dissolving process occurs spontaneously; that is, it occurs to an appreciable extent without any extra input of energy from outside the system. Two distinct factors are involved in processes that occur spontaneously. The most obvious is energy; the other is disorder.

If you let go of a book, it falls to the floor because of gravity. At its initial height, it has a potential energy higher than when it is on the floor. Unless it is restrained, the book falls and so loses energy. This fact leads us to the first basic principle identifying spontaneous processes and the direction they take: *Processes in which the energy content of the system decreases tend to occur spontaneously.* Spontaneous processes tend to be exothermic. ∞ (Sec. 5.3) Change occurs in the direction that leads to a lower energy content.

However, we can think of processes that do not result in a lower energy— or that may even be endothermic—and still occur spontaneously. For example, NH_4NO_3 readily dissolves in water, even though the solution process is endothermic. The mixing of CCl_4 and C_6H_{14} provides another simple example. All such processes are characterized by an increase in the disorder, or randomness, of the system. Suppose that we could suddenly remove a barrier that separates 500 mL of CCl_4 from 500 mL of C_6H_{14}, as in Figure 13.5(a). Before

A CLOSER LOOK

Hydrates

Frequently, hydrated ions remain in crystalline salts that are obtained by evaporation of water from aqueous solutions. Common examples include $FeCl_3 \cdot 6H_2O$ [iron(III) chloride hexahydrate] and $CuSO_4 \cdot 5H_2O$ [copper(II) sulfate pentahydrate]. The $FeCl_3 \cdot 6H_2O$ consists of $Fe(H_2O)_6^{3+}$ and Cl^- ions; the $CuSO_4 \cdot 5H_2O$ consists of $Cu(H_2O)_4^{2+}$ and $SO_4(H_2O)^{2-}$ ions. Water molecules can also occur in positions in the crystal lattice that are not specifically associated with either a cation or an anion. $BaCl_2 \cdot 2H_2O$ (barium chloride dihydrate) is an example. Compounds such as $FeCl_3 \cdot 6H_2O$, $CuSO_4 \cdot 5H_2O$, and $BaCl_2 \cdot 2H_2O$, which contain a salt and water combined in definite proportions, are known as *hydrates;* the water associated with them is called *water of hydration.* Figure 13.6 shows an example of a hydrate and the corresponding anhydrous (water-free) substance.

FIGURE 13.6 Samples of hydrated copper sulfate, $CuSO_4 \cdot 5H_2O$ (left), and anhydrous $CuSO_4$ (right). (Dr. E. R. Degginger)

the barrier is removed, each liquid occupies a volume of 500 mL. We know that we can find all the CCl_4 molecules in the 500 mL to the left of the barrier and all the C_6H_{14} molecules in the 500 mL to the right. When equilibrium has been established after removal of the barrier, the two liquids together occupy a volume of about 1000 mL.* Formation of a homogeneous solution has resulted in increased disorder, or randomness, in that the molecules of each substance are now distributed in a volume twice as large as that which they occupied before mixing. This example illustrates our second basic principle: *Processes in which the disorder of the system increases tend to occur spontaneously.*

When molecules of different types are brought together, an increase in disorder occurs spontaneously unless the molecules are restrained by sufficiently strong intermolecular forces or by physical barriers. Thus, because of the strong bonds holding the sodium and chloride ions together, sodium chloride does not spontaneously dissolve in gasoline. Conversely, gases spontaneously expand unless restrained by their containers; in this case intermolecular forces are too weak to restrain the molecules. We shall discuss spontaneous processes again in Chapter 19. At that time, we shall consider the balance between the tendencies toward lower energy and toward increased disorder in greater detail. For the moment, we need to be aware that, in most cases, the formation of a solution is favored by the increase in disorder that accompanies mixing. Consequently, a solution will form unless solute-solute or solvent-solvent interactions are too strong relative to the solute-solvent interactions.

---

* The slight change in total volume that may occur upon mixing is unimportant for our example.

(a)

(c)   (b)

FIGURE 13.7 (*a*) Nickel metal and hydrochloric acid. (*b*) Nickel reacts slowly with hydrochloric acid, forming $NiCl_2(aq)$ and $H_2(g)$. (*c*) $NiCl_2(s)$ is obtained when the solution from (*b*) is evaporated to dryness. (© Richard Megna/Fundamental Photographs)

Solution Formation and Chemical Reactions

In all our discussions of solutions, we must be careful to distinguish the *physical* process of solution formation from *chemical* processes that lead to a solution. For example, nickel metal is dissolved on contact with hydrochloric acid solution. The following chemical reaction occurs (see Equation 4.36):

$$Ni(s) + 2HCl(aq) \longrightarrow NiCl_2(aq) + H_2(g) \qquad [13.1]$$

In this instance, the chemical form of the substance being dissolved is changed. If the solution is evaporated to dryness, $Ni(s)$ is not recovered as such; instead, $NiCl_2(s)$ is recovered (Figure 13.7). In contrast, when $NaCl(s)$ is dissolved in water, it can be recovered by evaporation of its solution to dryness. Our focus throughout this chapter is on solutions from which the solute can be recovered unchanged from the solution.

Point of Emphasis: Dissolution is often a chemical process. However, in most situations encountered in this chapter, it can be considered a physical process.

13.2 Ways of Expressing Concentration

The concentration of a solution can be expressed either qualitatively or quantitatively. The terms *dilute* and *concentrated* are used to describe a solution

Point of Emphasis: The terms *dilute* and *concentrated* are only intended as qualitative references to concentration.

qualitatively. A solution with a relatively small concentration of solute is said to be dilute; one with a large concentration is said to be concentrated.

Several quantitative expressions of concentration are used in chemistry. One of the simplest is the **mass percentage** of a component in a solution, given by

$$\text{Mass \% of component} = \frac{\text{mass of component in soln}}{\text{total mass of soln}} \times 100 \quad \text{[13.2]}$$

where we have abbreviated *solution* as "soln." Thus, a solution of hydrochloric acid that is 36 percent HCl by mass contains 36 g of HCl for each 100 g of solution.

We often express the concentrations of very dilute solutions in **parts per million (ppm),** defined as

$$\text{ppm of component} = \frac{\text{mass of component in soln}}{\text{total mass of soln}} \times 10^6 \quad \text{[13.3]}$$

We see that a solution whose solute concentration is 1 ppm contains 1 g of solute for each million (10^6) grams of solution or, equivalently, 1 mg of solute per kilogram of solution. Because the density of water is 1 g/mL, 1 kg of a dilute aqueous solution will have a volume very close to 1 L. Thus, 1 ppm also corresponds to 1 mg of solute per liter of solution. The acceptable maximum concentrations of toxic or carcinogenic substances are often expressed in ppm. For example, the maximum allowable concentration of arsenic in drinking water in the United States is 0.05 ppm, that is, 0.05 mg of arsenic per liter of water. For solutions that are even more dilute, *parts per billion (ppb)* is used. A concentration of 1 ppb represents 1 g of solute per billion (10^9) grams of solution, or 1 microgram (μg) of solute per liter of solution.

Learning Goal 2: Define *mass percentage, parts per million, mole fraction, molarity,* and *molality,* and calculate concentrations in any of these units.

Point of Emphasis: The statement that the density of a dilute aqueous solution is identical to that of pure water (1g/mL) is a valid assumption at normal temperatures (to two significant figures).

SAMPLE EXERCISE 13.1

(a) A solution is made by dissolving 13.5 g of glucose, $C_6H_{12}O_6$, in 0.100 kg of water. What is the mass percentage of solute in this solution? (b) A 2.5-g sample of groundwater was found to contain 5.4 μg of Zn^{2+}. What is the concentration of Zn^{2+} in parts per million?

SOLUTION   (a) We calculate the mass percentage by using Equation 13.2. The mass of the solution is the sum of the mass of solute (glucose) and the mass of solvent (water). Because 0.100 kg equals 100 g,

$$\text{Mass \% of glucose} = \frac{\text{mass glucose}}{\text{mass soln}} \times 100 = \frac{13.5 \text{ g}}{13.5 \text{ g} + 100 \text{ g}} \times 100 = 11.9\%$$

The mass percentage of water in this solution is $(100 - 11.9)\% = 88.1\%$.
(b) Because 1 μg is 1×10^{-6} g, 5.4 $\mu g = 5.4 \times 10^{-6}$ g. Thus,

$$\text{ppm} = \frac{\text{mass of solute}}{\text{mass of soln}} \times 10^6 = \frac{5.4 \times 10^{-6} \text{ g}}{2.5 \text{ g}} \times 10^6 = 2.2 \text{ ppm}$$

PRACTICE EXERCISE

A commercial bleaching solution contains 3.62 mass percent sodium hypochlorite, NaOCl. What is the mass of NaOCl in a bottle containing 2500 g of bleaching solution?   *Answer:* 90.5 g of NaOCl

Mole Fraction, Molarity, and Molality

We often use concentration expressions based on the number of moles of one or more components of the solution. The three we use most commonly are mole fraction, molarity, and molality. Recall from Section 10.6 that the *mole fraction* of a component of a solution is given by

$$\text{Mole fraction of component} = \frac{\text{moles of component}}{\text{total moles all components}} \quad [13.4]$$

The symbol X is commonly used for mole fraction, with a subscript to indicate the component of interest. For example, the mole fraction of HCl in a hydrochloric acid solution is represented as X_{HCl}. The sum of the mole fractions of all components of a solution must equal 1.

We introduced *molarity (M)* in Section 4.1. Recall that the molarity of a solute in a solution is defined as

$$\text{Molarity} = \frac{\text{moles solute}}{\text{liters soln}} \quad [13.5]$$

The **molality** of a solution, denoted m, is defined as the number of moles of solute per kilogram of solvent:

$$\text{Molality} = \frac{\text{moles solute}}{\text{kilograms of solvent}} \quad [13.6]$$

Notice the difference between molarity and molality. Because these two ways of expressing concentration are so similar, they can be easily confused. Molarity is defined in terms of the volume of *solution,* whereas molality is defined in terms

Point of Emphasis: The difference between the definitions of molarity (M) and molality (m) and between their respective notations and pronunciations must be emphasized to avoid confusion.

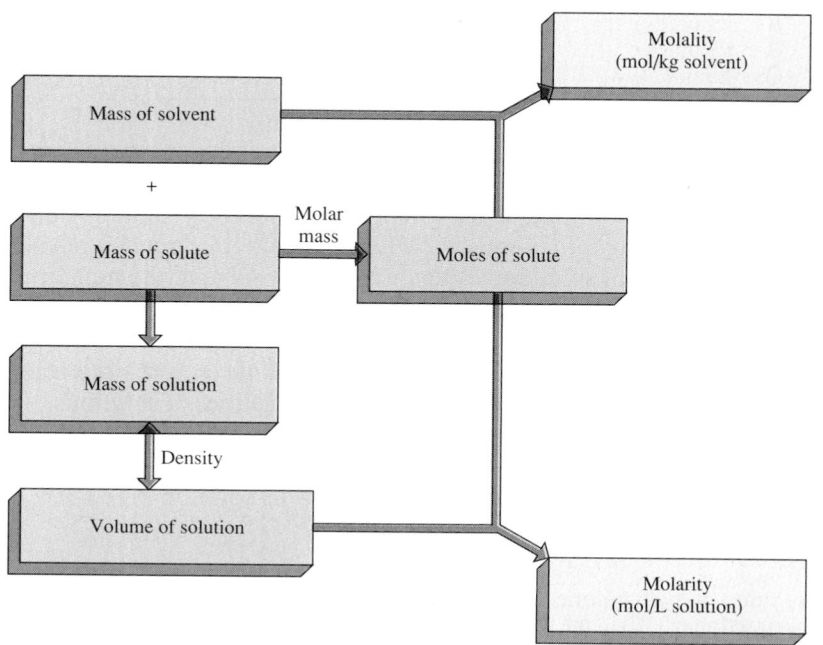

FIGURE 13.8 Diagram of the interconversions used in calculation of the molarity and molality of solutions.

A CLOSER LOOK

Normality

The concentration units that we have just discussed appear throughout the rest of this chapter and elsewhere in this text. However, one further concentration expression, called *normality,* may be encountered in other places. Normality (abbreviated N) is defined as the number of *equivalents* of solute per liter of solution:

$$\text{Normality} = \frac{\text{equivalents solute}}{\text{liters soln}} \quad [13.7]$$

An equivalent is defined according to the type of reaction being examined. For acid-base reactions, an equivalent of an acid is the quantity that supplies 1 mol of H^+; an equivalent of a base is the quantity reacting with 1 mol of H^+. In an oxidation-reduction reaction, an equivalent is the quantity of substance that gains or loses 1 mol of electrons.

An equivalent is always defined in such a way that 1 equivalent of reagent A will react with 1 equivalent of reagent B. For example, in acid-base reactions, 1 mol H^+ (1 equivalent of acid) reacts with 1 mol OH^- (1 equivalent of base). Similarly, in oxidation-reduction reac-

tions, for each mole of electrons lost by one substance (1 equivalent), 1 mol must be gained by another substance (1 equivalent).

Table 13.2 gives the masses of 1 equivalent of several substances in either acid-base or oxidation-reduction reactions. For example, when H_2SO_4 reacts as an acid to form SO_4^{2-}, it loses *two* H^+ ions. Thus, 1 mol of H_2SO_4 (98.0 g) will be 2 equivalents. If 1 mol of H_2SO_4 is dissolved in sufficient water to form 1 L of solution, its concentration can be expressed as either 1 M or 2 N:

$$\frac{1\ \text{mol}}{1\ \text{L}} = 1\ M \qquad \frac{2\ \text{equivalents}}{1\ \text{L}} = 2\ N$$

Likewise, a 0.255 M solution of H_2SO_4 will be 2 × 0.255 = 0.510 N. The normality of the H_2SO_4 solution is twice its molarity. Normality is always a whole-number multiple of molarity. In acid-base reactions, the whole number is the number of H^+ or OH^- available in a formula unit of the substance. In oxidation-reduction reactions, the whole number is the number of electrons gained or lost by one formula unit of the substance.

TABLE 13.2 △ Equivalent-Mass Relationships

Reactant	Product	Reaction type	Mass of 1 mol of reactant (g)	Mass of 1 equivalent of reactant (g)
H_2SO_4	SO_4^{2-}	Acid (2 H^+)	98.0	98.0/2 = 49.0
$Al(OH)_3$	Al^{3+}	Base (3 OH^-)	78.0	78.0/3 = 26.0
$KMnO_4$	Mn^{2+}	Reduction (5 e^-)	158.0	158.0/5 = 31.6
$KMnO_4$	MnO_2	Reduction (3 e^-)	158.0	158.0/3 = 52.7
$Na_2C_2O_4$	CO_2	Oxidation (2 e^-)	134.0	134.0/2 = 67.0

of the mass of *solvent.* A 1.50 molal (written 1.50 m) solution contains 1.50 mol of solute for every kilogram of solvent. A 1.50 M solution contains 1.50 mol of solute for every liter of solution. (When water is the solvent, the molality and molarity of a dilute solution are numerically about the same, because 1 kg of solvent is nearly the same as 1 kg of solution, and 1 kg of the solution has a volume of about 1 L.) Figure 13.8 outlines some of the conversions that are often involved in calculating the molarities and molalities of solutions.

The molality of a given solution does not vary with temperature because masses do not vary with temperature. Molarity, however, changes with temperature because of the expansion or contraction of the solution.

Point of Emphasis: For more concentrated solutions, the density of the solution is needed to relate molarity and molality.

Learning Goal 3: Convert concentration in one concentration unit into any other (given the density of the solution where necessary).

SAMPLE EXERCISE 13.2

A solution of hydrochloric acid contains 36 percent HCl by mass. **(a)** Calculate the mole fraction of HCl in the solution. **(b)** Calculate the molality of HCl in the solution.

(c) What additional information would you need to calculate the molarity of the solution?

SOLUTION (a) It is often helpful in problems involving mass percentages to assume a certain total mass. Let us assume that there is exactly 100 g of solution. The solution contains 36 g of HCl and $(100 - 36)\,g = 64\,g$ of H_2O. To calculate the mole fraction of HCl, we first convert mass to moles and then use Equation 13.4:

$$\text{Moles HCl} = (36 \text{ g HCl}) \left(\frac{1 \text{ mol HCl}}{36.5 \text{ g HCl}} \right) = 0.99 \text{ mol HCl}$$

$$\text{Moles H}_2\text{O} = (64 \text{ g H}_2\text{O}) \left(\frac{1 \text{ mol H}_2\text{O}}{18 \text{ g H}_2\text{O}} \right) = 3.6 \text{ mol H}_2\text{O}$$

$$X_{\text{HCl}} = \frac{\text{moles HCl}}{\text{moles H}_2\text{O} + \text{moles HCl}} = \frac{0.99}{3.6 + 0.99} = \frac{0.99}{4.6} = 0.22$$

(b) To calculate the molality of HCl in the solution, we use Equation 13.6, where water is the solvent. We calculated the number of moles of HCl in part (a), and the mass of solvent is $64\,g = 0.064$ kg.

$$\text{Molality of HCl} = \frac{0.99 \text{ mol HCl}}{0.064 \text{ kg H}_2\text{O}} = 15 \, m$$

(c) In order to calculate the molarity of the solution, we need to know the volume of solution. If we were given the density of the solution, we could convert the mass of solution to volume of solution and then calculate the molarity.

PRACTICE EXERCISE

(a) Calculate the mole fraction of NaOCl in a commercial bleach solution containing 3.62 mass percent NaOCl in water. (b) What is the molality of a solution made by dissolving 36.5 g of naphthalene, $C_{10}H_8$, in 420 g of toluene, C_7H_8? **Answers: (a)** 9.00×10^{-3}; **(b)** $0.678 \, m$

SAMPLE EXERCISE 13.3

Given that the density of a solution of 5.0 g of toluene and 225 g of benzene is 0.876 g/mL, calculate **(a)** the molarity of the solution; **(b)** the mass percentage of solute.

SOLUTION (a) The total mass of the solution is equal to the mass of the solvent plus the mass of the solute:

$$\text{Mass soln} = 5.0 \text{ g} + 225 \text{ g} = 230 \text{ g}$$

The density of the solution is used to convert the mass of the solution to its volume:

$$\text{Milliliters soln} = (230 \text{ g}) \left(\frac{1 \text{ mL}}{0.876 \text{ g}} \right) = 263 \text{ mL}$$

The number of moles of solute is:

$$\text{Moles C}_7\text{H}_8 = (5.0 \text{ g C}_7\text{H}_8) \left(\frac{1 \text{ mol C}_7\text{H}_8}{92 \text{ g C}_7\text{H}_8} \right) = 0.054 \text{ mol}$$

Molarity is moles of solute per liter of solution:

$$\text{Molarity} = \frac{\text{moles C}_7\text{H}_8}{\text{liter soln}} = \left(\frac{0.054 \text{ mol C}_7\text{H}_8}{263 \text{ mL soln}} \right) \left(\frac{1000 \text{ mL soln}}{1 \text{ L soln}} \right) = 0.21 \, M$$

By comparison, the molality of this solution is $0.24 \, m$.
(b) The mass percentage of solute is calculated as follows:

$$\text{Mass \% C}_7\text{H}_8 = \frac{5.0 \text{ g C}_7\text{H}_8}{5.0 \text{ g C}_7\text{H}_8 + 225 \text{ g C}_6\text{H}_6} \times 100 = \frac{5.0 \text{ g}}{230 \text{ g}} \times 100 = 2.2\%$$

13.3 Saturated Solutions and Solubility

As a solid solute begins to dissolve in a solvent, the concentration of solute particles in solution increases, and so the chances of their colliding with the surface of the solid increase (Figure 13.9). Such a collision may result in the solute particle becoming attached to the solid. This process, which is the opposite of the solution process, is called **crystallization.** Thus, two opposing processes occur in a solution in contact with undissolved solute. This situation is represented in Equation 13.8 by use of a double arrow:

$$\text{Solute} + \text{solvent} \underset{\text{crystallize}}{\overset{\text{dissolve}}{\rightleftarrows}} \text{solution} \qquad [13.8]$$

When the rates of these opposing processes become equal, no further net increase in the amount of solute in solution occurs. This balance is another example of *dynamic equilibrium,* similar to that discussed in Section 11.5 where the processes of evaporation and condensation were considered.

A solution that is in equilibrium with undissolved solute is said to be **saturated.** Additional solute will not dissolve if added to a saturated solution. The amount of solute needed to form a saturated solution in a given quantity of

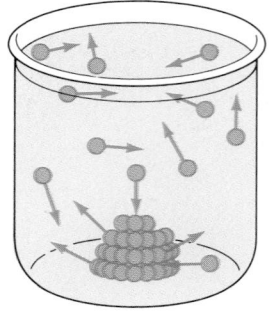

FIGURE 13.9 Movement of solute particles in solvent containing excess solute. Both dissolution and crystallization occur.

Point of Emphasis: *Crystallization* is the reverse of *dissolution.*

Point of Emphasis: Only *saturated* solutions are in a dynamic equilibrium.

FIGURE 13.10 Sodium acetate readily forms supersaturated solutions in water. When a seed crystal of $NaC_2H_3O_2$ is added (*a*), excess $NaC_2H_3O_2$ crystallizes from solution (*b* and *c*). (© Richard Megna/Fundamental Photographs)

(*a*)

(*b*)

(*c*)

 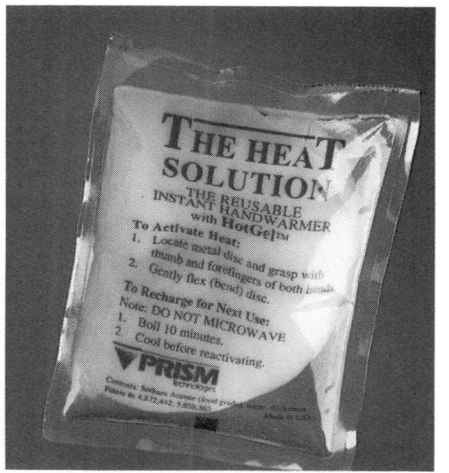

(a)   (b)

FIGURE 13.11 Portable heat packs often use crystallization of a supersaturated solution to generate heat. When the solution is induced to crystallize (either by introduction of a seed crystal or by mechanical motion of a metal plate), heat is released. The heat pack can be reused by heating it to a temperature high enough to redissolve all the solute. (Richard Megna/Fundamental Photographs)

solvent is known as the **solubility** of that solute. For example, the solubility of NaCl in water at 0°C is 35.7 g per 100 mL of water. This is the maximum amount of NaCl that can be dissolved in water to give a stable, equilibrium solution at that temperature.

It is, of course, possible to dissolve less solute than that needed to form a saturated solution. Thus, we might choose to form a solution containing only 10.0 g of NaCl per 100 mL of water at 0°C. The solution is then said to be **unsaturated.**

Under suitable conditions, it is possible to form solutions that contain a greater amount of solute than that needed to form a saturated solution. Such solutions are said to be **supersaturated.** These solutions can sometimes be prepared by saturating a solution at high temperature and then carefully cooling it to a temperature at which the solute is less soluble. Supersaturated solutions result for much the same reason as supercooled liquids (Section 11.4): In order for crystallization to occur, the molecules of solute must arrange themselves properly to form crystals. Because the solute molecules in a supersaturated solution are in an unfavorable state, supersaturated solutions are unstable. The addition of a small crystal of the solute (a *seed crystal*) provides a template for crystallization of the excess solute, leading to a saturated solution in contact with excess solid (Figure 13.10).

When the solute molecules in a supersaturated solution crystallize, energy is released as a result of the favorable solute-solute interactions. This energy is usually released as heat. For this reason, supersaturated solutions of $NaC_2H_3O_2$ are used to make instant heat packs (Figure 13.11). The exothermic crystallization of $NaC_2H_3O_2$ from the supersaturated solution is initiated by mechanical mixing or by squeezing out a seed crystal from a small compartment in the pack.

Point of Emphasis: *Solubility* is the measure, usually in g/100 mL, of how much solute can dissolve before saturation is reached.

Lee R. Summerlin, Christie L. Borgford, and Julie B. Ealy, "Supersaturation," *Chemical Demonstrations, A Sourcebook for Teachers, Volume 2* (Washington: American Chemical Society, 1987), p. 119.

13.4 Factors Affecting Solubility

The extent to which one substance dissolves in another depends on the nature of both the solute and the solvent. It also depends on temperature and, at least for gases, on pressure.

TABLE 13.3 △
**Solubilities of Several
Gases in Water at
20°C, with 1 atm Gas
Pressure**

Gas	Solubility (M)
N_2	6.9×10^{-4}
CO	1.04×10^{-3}
O_2	1.38×10^{-3}
Ar	1.50×10^{-3}
Kr	2.79×10^{-3}

$$CH_3\overset{\overset{\displaystyle O}{\|}}{C}CH_3$$

Acetone

$$CH_3CH_2\overset{\overset{\displaystyle O}{\|}}{C}CH_2CH_3$$

Diethyl ketone

Point of Emphasis: Pairs of solute and solvent that are able to mix with each other *in all proportions* are said to be *miscible.* Pairs of solute and solvent that *do not* dissolve in each other to any appreciable degree are said to be *immiscible.* Combinations that dissolve in each other in *some, but not all,* proportions are not covered by these terms. We refer to these as being partially soluble.

Solute-Solvent Interactions

Our discussion of the solution process enables us to understand many observations regarding solubilities. As a simple example, consider the data in Table 13.3 for the solubilities of various simple gases in water. Note that solubility increases with increasing molecular mass. The attractive forces between the gas and solvent molecules are mainly of the London dispersion type, which increase with increasing size and mass of the gas molecules. When a chemical reaction occurs between the gas and solvent, much higher gas solubilities result. We will encounter instances of this in later chapters, but as a simple example, the solubility of Cl_2 in water under the same conditions given in Table 13.3 is 0.102 M. This is much higher than would be predicted from the trends in the table, based on just molecular mass. We can infer from this that dissolving Cl_2 in water is accompanied by some kind of chemical process. The use of chlorine as a bactericide in municipal water supplies and swimming pools is based on its chemical reaction with water.

Polar liquids tend to dissolve readily in polar solvents. For example, acetone, a polar molecule whose structure is shown at the left, mixes in all proportions with water. Pairs of liquids that mix in all proportions are said to be **miscible,** and liquids that do not mix are termed **immiscible.** Water and hexane, C_6H_{14}, for example, are immiscible. Diethyl ketone (see structure at left), which is similar to acetone but has a higher molecular mass, dissolves in water to the extent of about 47 g per liter of water at 20°C, but it is not completely miscible.

Hydrogen-bonding interactions between solute and solvent may lead to high solubility. For example, water is completely miscible with ethanol, CH_3CH_2OH. The CH_3CH_2OH molecules are able to form hydrogen bonds with water molecules as well as with each other (Figure 13.12). Because of this hydrogen-bonding ability, the solute-solute, solvent-solvent, and solute-solvent forces are not appreciably different within a mixture of CH_3CH_2OH and H_2O. There is no significant change in the environment of the molecules as they are mixed. The increase in disorder accompanying mixing therefore plays a significant role in formation of the solution.

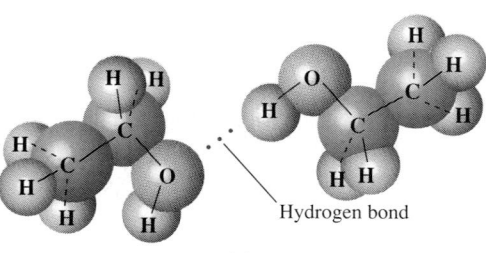

(a)

FIGURE 13.12 Hydrogen-bonding interactions between ethanol molecules (a) and between water and ethanol molecules (b).

Figure 13.12

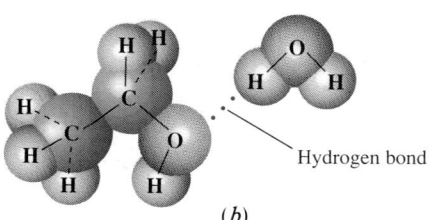

(b)

TABLE 13.4 △ Solubilities of Some Alcohols in Water

Alcohol	Solubility in H_2O (mol/100 g H_2O at 20°C)[a]
CH_3OH (methanol)	∞
CH_3CH_2OH (ethanol)	∞
$CH_3CH_2CH_2OH$ (propanol)	∞
$CH_3CH_2CH_2CH_2OH$ (butanol)	0.11
$CH_3CH_2CH_2CH_2CH_2OH$ (pentanol)	0.030
$CH_3CH_2CH_2CH_2CH_2CH_2OH$ (hexanol)	0.0058
$CH_3CH_2CH_2CH_2CH_2CH_2CH_2OH$ (heptanol)	0.0008

[a] The infinity symbol indicates that the alcohol is completely miscible in water.

Learning Goal 4: Rationalize the solubilities of substances in various solvents in terms of their molecular structures and intermolecular forces.

The number of carbon atoms in an alcohol affects its solubility in water, as shown in Table 13.4. As the length of the carbon chain increases, the polar OH group becomes an ever smaller part of the molecule, and the molecule becomes more like a hydrocarbon. The solubility of the alcohol decreases correspondingly. If the number of OH groups along the carbon chain increases, more solute-water hydrogen bonding is possible, and solubility generally increases. Glucose, $C_6H_{12}O_6$, has five OH groups on a six-carbon framework, which makes the molecule very soluble in water (83 g dissolve in 100 mL of water at 17.5°C). The glucose molecule is shown in Figure 13.13.

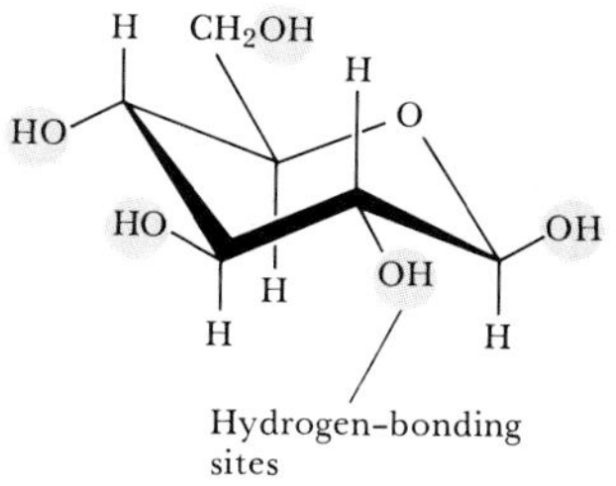

FIGURE 13.13 Structure of glucose. Colored spheres indicate sites capable of hydrogen-bonding with water.

Examination of pairs of substances such as those listed in the preceding paragraphs has led to an important generalization: *Substances with similar intermolecular attractive forces tend to be soluble in one another.* This generalization is often simply stated as *"like dissolves like."* Nonpolar substances are soluble in nonpolar solvents; ionic and polar solutes are soluble in polar solvents. Network solids like diamond and quartz are not soluble in either polar or nonpolar solvents because of the strong bonding forces within the solid.

Teaching Note: "Like dissolves like" is a useful rule of thumb when predicting solubilities.

SAMPLE EXERCISE 13.4

Predict whether each of the following substances is more likely to dissolve in carbon tetrachloride, CCl_4, which is nonpolar, or in water, which is polar: C_7H_{16}, $NaHCO_3$, HCl, I_2.

SOLUTION Both C_7H_{16} and I_2 are nonpolar. We would therefore predict that they would be more soluble in CCl_4 than in H_2O. $NaHCO_3$ is ionic, and HCl is polar covalent. Water would be a better solvent than CCl_4 for these two substances.

PRACTICE EXERCISE

Which of the following is most likely to be miscible with water?

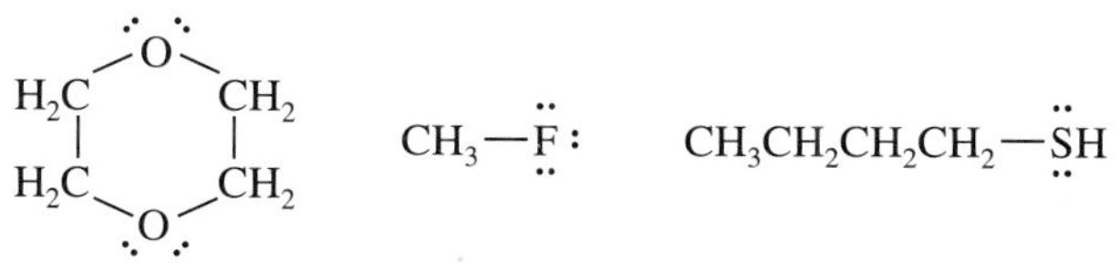

Dioxane   Methyl fluoride   Butyl mercaptan

Answer: dioxane

CHEMISTRY AND LIFE

Fat- and Water-Soluble Vitamins

Vitamins B and C are water-soluble. Vitamins A, D, E, and K are soluble in nonpolar solvents and in the fatty tissue of the body (which is nonpolar). Because of their water solubility, vitamins B and C are not stored to any appreciable extent in the body, and so foods containing these vitamins should be included in the daily diet. In contrast, the fat-soluble vitamins are stored in sufficient quantities to keep vitamin-deficiency diseases from appearing even after a person has subsisted for a long period on a vitamin-deficient diet. With the ready availability of vitamin supplements, cases of hypervitaminosis, an illness caused by an excessive amount of vitamins, are now being seen by physicians in this country. Because the body can store only the fat-soluble vita-

mins, true hypervitaminosis has been observed solely for these vitamins.

The different solubility patterns of the water-soluble vitamins and the fat-soluble ones can be rationalized in terms of the structures of the molecules. The chemical structures of vitamin A (retinol) and of vitamin C (ascorbic acid) are shown below. Note that the vitamin A molecule is an alcohol with a very long carbon chain. It is nearly nonpolar, and because the OH group is such a small part of the molecule, the molecule resembles the long-chain alcohols listed in Table 13.4. In contrast, the vitamin C molecule is smaller and has more OH groups that can form hydrogen bonds with water. It is somewhat like glucose, discussed above.

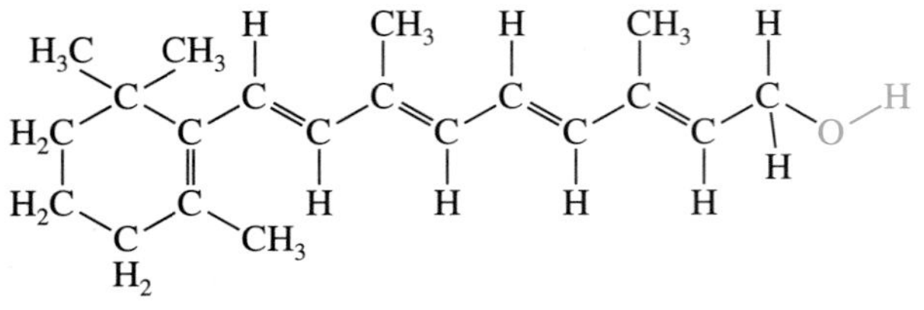

Vitamin A 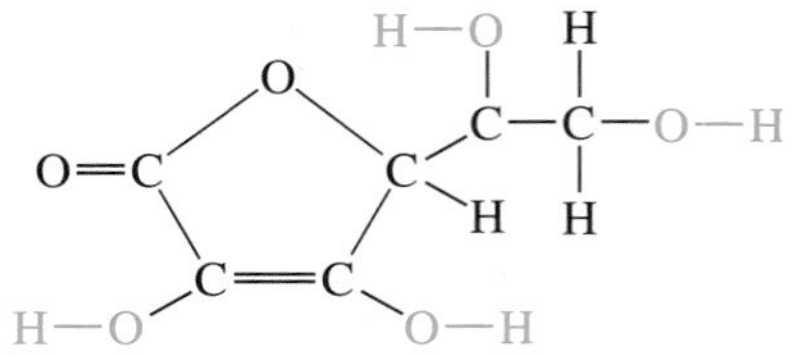   Vitamin C

Pressure Effects

Learning Goal 5: Describe the effects of pressure and temperature on solubilities.

Point of Emphasis: The solubility of a gas increases as the pressure of the gas over the liquid increases. The solubility of solids and liquids is not very dependent on the pressure.

The solubility of a gas in any solvent is increased as the pressure of the gas over the solvent increases. By contrast, the solubilities of solids and liquids are not appreciably affected by pressure. We can understand the effect of pressure on the solubility of a gas by considering the dynamic equilibrium illustrated in Figure 13.14. Suppose that we have a gaseous substance distributed between the gas and solution phases. When equilibrium is established, the rate at which gas molecules enter the solution equals the rate at which solute molecules escape from the solution to enter the gas phase. The small arrows in Figure 13.14(a) represent the rates of these opposing processes. Now suppose that we exert added pressure on the piston and compress the gas above the solution, as shown in Figure 13.14(b). If we reduced the volume to half its original value, the pressure of the gas would increase to about twice its original value. The rate at which gas molecules strike the surface to enter the solution phase would therefore increase. Thus, the solubility of the gas in the solution would increase until an equilibrium is again established; that is, solubility increases until the rate at

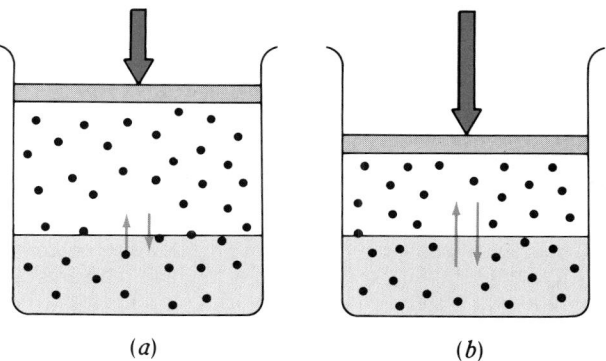

FIGURE 13.14 Effect of pressure on the solubility of a gas. When the pressure is increased, as in (b), the rate at which gas molecules enter the solution increases. The concentration of solute molecules at equilibrium increases in proportion to the pressure.

(a)   (b)

which gas molecules enter the solution equals the rate at which solute molecules escape from the solvent, as indicated by the arrows in Figure 13.14(b). Thus, the solubility of the gas should increase in direct proportion to the pressure.

The relationship between pressure and solubility is expressed in terms of a simple equation known as **Henry's law:**

$$C_g = kP_g \qquad\qquad [13.9]$$

where C_g is the solubility of the gas in the solution phase (usually expressed as molarity), P_g is the partial pressure of the gas over the solution, and k is a proportionality constant known as the *Henry's law constant.* The Henry's law constant is different for each solute-solvent pair. It also varies with temperature. As an example, the solubility of N_2 gas in water at 25°C and 0.78 atm pressure is 5.3×10^{-4} M. The Henry's law constant for N_2 in water is thus given by $(5.3 \times 10^{-4}$ mol/L$)/0.78$ atm $= 6.8 \times 10^{-4}$ mol/L-atm. If the partial pressure of N_2 is doubled, Henry's law predicts that the solubility in water will also be doubled to 1.06×10^{-3} M.

Bottlers use the effect of pressure on solubility in producing carbonated beverages such as champagne, beer, and many soft drinks. These are bottled under a carbon dioxide pressure slightly greater than 1 atm. When the bottles are opened to the air, the partial pressure of CO_2 above the solution is decreased, the solubility of CO_2 decreases, and CO_2 bubbles out of the solution.

Point of Emphasis: The Henry's law constant is different for each solute-solvent pair at each different temperature.

SAMPLE EXERCISE 13.5

Calculate the concentration of CO_2 in a soft drink that is bottled with a partial pressure of CO_2 of 4.0 atm over the liquid at 25°C. The Henry's law constant for CO_2 in water at this temperature is 3.1×10^{-2} mol/L-atm.

SOLUTION Henry's law, Equation 13.9, can be applied in a straightforward fashion:

$$C_g = kP_g = (3.1 \times 10^{-2} \text{ mol/L-atm})(4.0 \text{ atm})$$
$$= 0.12 \text{ mol/L} = 0.12 \ M$$

PRACTICE EXERCISE

Calculate the concentration of CO_2 in a soft drink after the bottle is opened and sits at 25°C under a CO_2 partial pressure of 3.0×10^{-4} atm.   *Answer:* 9.3×10^{-6} M

CHEMISTRY AND LIFE

Blood Gases and Deep-Sea Diving

Deep-sea divers rely on compressed air for their oxygen supply. According to Henry's law, the solubilities of gases increase with pressure. If a diver is suddenly exposed to atmospheric pressure, where the solubility of gases is less, bubbles form in the bloodstream and in other fluids of the body. These bubbles affect nerve impulses and give rise to the disease known as "the bends," or decompression sickness. Nitrogen is the main problem because it has the highest partial pressure in air and because it can be removed only through the respiratory system. Oxygen is consumed in metabolism. Substitution of helium for nitrogen minimizes this effect because

helium has a much lower solubility in biological fluids than does N_2. Jacques Cousteau's divers on *Conshelf III* used a mixture of 98 percent helium and 2 percent oxygen. At the high pressures (10 atm) experienced by the divers, this percentage of oxygen gives an oxygen partial pressure of about 0.2 atm, which is the partial pressure in normal air at 1 atm. If the oxygen partial pressures become too great, the urge to breathe is reduced, CO_2 is not removed from the body, and CO_2 poisoning occurs. At excessive concentrations in the body, carbon dioxide acts as a neurotoxin, interfering with nerve conduction and transmission.

Temperature Effects

The solubility of most solid solutes in water increases as the temperature of the solution increases. Thus, more sucrose, $C_{12}H_{22}O_{11}$, can be dissolved in hot water than in cold water, the basis for making "rock candy" and some other confections. Figure 13.15 shows the effect of temperature on the solubilities of several ionic substances in water. Note that, in general, the solubility increases with increasing temperature. There are a few exceptions to this rule, however, as is evident in the curve for $Ce_2(SO_4)_3$.

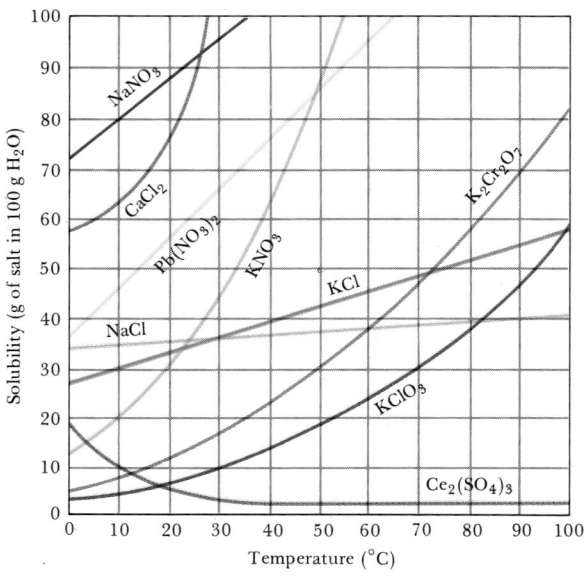

FIGURE 13.15 Solubilities of several common ionic solids as a function of temperature.

Figure 13.15

FIGURE 13.16
Solubilities of several gases in water as a function of temperature. Note that solubilities are in units of millimoles per liter, for a constant pressure of 1 atm in the gas phase.

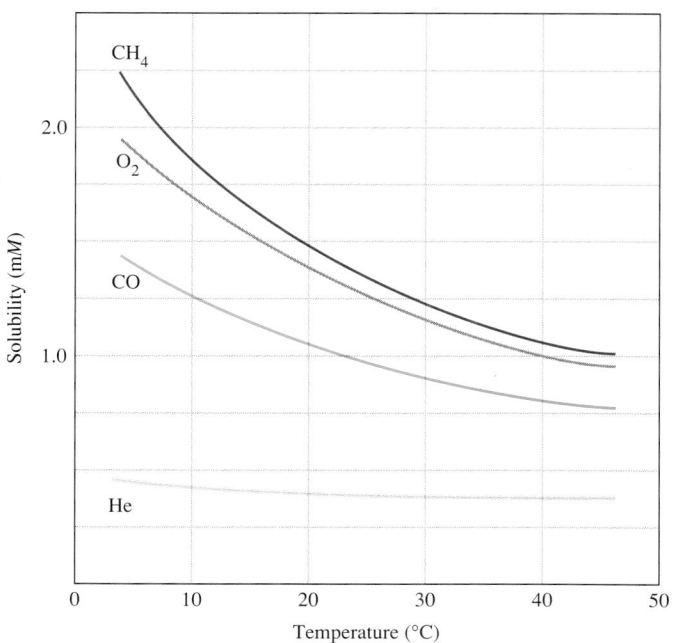

Figure 13.16

In contrast to solid solutes, the solubility of gases in water *decreases* with increasing temperature (Figure 13.16). If a glass of cold tap water is warmed, bubbles of air are seen on the inside of the glass. Similarly, carbonated beverages go "flat" as they are allowed to warm; as the temperature of the solution increases, the solubility of CO_2 decreases, and $CO_2(g)$ escapes from the solution. The decreased solubility of O_2 in water as temperature increases is one of the effects of *thermal pollution* of lakes and streams. The effect is particularly serious in deep lakes because warm water is less dense than cold water. It therefore tends to remain on top of cold water, at the surface. This situation impedes the dissolving of oxygen into the deeper layers, thus stifling the respiration of all aquatic life needing oxygen. Fish may suffocate and die in these circumstances.

Teaching Note: The decrease in gas solubility as temperature increases is primarily a function of kinetic energy. As temperature increases, so does the kinetic energy of the dissolved gas molecules. The increased kinetic energy makes it easier for the gas molecules to escape the solution.

13.5 Colligative Properties

Some physical properties of solutions differ in important ways from those of the pure solvent. For example, pure water freezes at 0°C, but aqueous solutions freeze at lower temperatures. Ethylene glycol is added to the water in radiators of cars as an antifreeze to lower the freezing point of the solution. It also raises the boiling point of the solution above that of pure water, permitting operation of the engine at a higher temperature.

The lowering of the freezing point and the raising of the boiling point are examples of physical properties of solutions that depend on the *quantity* (concentration) but not the *kind* of solute particles. Such properties are called **colligative properties.** (*Colligative* means "depending on the collection"; colligative properties depend on the collective effect of the number of solute particles.) In addition to freezing-point lowering and boiling-point elevation, there

Learning Goal 6: Describe the effects of solute concentration on the vapor pressure, boiling point, freezing point, and osmotic pressure of a solution, and calculate any of these properties given appropriate concentration data.

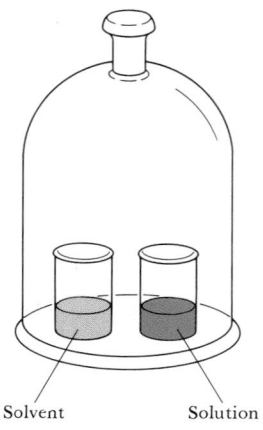

Solvent   Solution

(a)

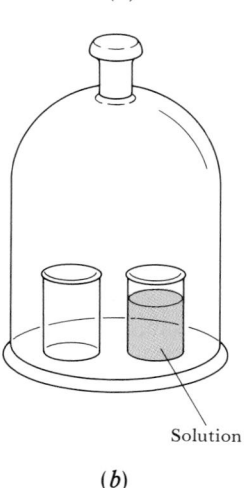

Solution

(b)

FIGURE 13.17 Experiment showing that a solution possesses a lower vapor pressure than does the pure solvent.

are two other colligative properties: vapor-pressure reduction and osmotic pressure.

Lowering the Vapor Pressure

The effect of a nonvolatile solute on the vapor pressure of a volatile solvent is illustrated by the simple experiment shown in Figure 13.17. Two beakers are place side by side in a sealed enclosure. One beaker contains pure water, the other, an equal volume of an aqueous solution of sugar. Gradually, the volume of the sugar solution increases, while the volume of the pure water decreases. Eventually, all the water transfers to the sugar solution, as shown in Figure 13.17(b). How do we explain this result?

Let's refer to back to Section 11.5, particularly Figure 11.19. Recall that the vapor pressure over a liquid is the result of a dynamic equilibrium: The rate at which molecules leave the liquid surface for the gas phase equals the rate at which gas-phase molecules return to the surface of the liquid. A nonvolatile solute added to the liquid reduces the capacity of the solvent molecules to move from the liquid phase to the vapor phase, as shown in Figure 13.18. At the same time, however, there is no change in the rate at which solvent molecules in the gas phase return to the liquid. The shift in equilibrium due to the solute reduces the vapor pressure over the solution. The vapor pressure over the pure solvent is thus higher than that over the solution.

Return to the experiment shown in Figure 13.17. You should now see why the solvent transfers from the beaker holding pure water to the one holding the sugar solution. The vapor pressure necessary to achieve equilibrium with the pure solvent is higher than that required with the solution. Consequently, as the pure solvent seeks to reach equilibrium by forming vapor, the solution seeks to reach equilibrium by removing molecules from the vapor phase. A net movement of solvent molecules from the pure solvent to the solution results. The process continues until no free solvent remains.

The *extent* to which a nonvolatile solute lowers the vapor pressure is proportional to its concentration. Doubling the concentration of solute doubles its effect. In fact, the reduction in vapor pressure is roughly proportional to the total concentration of solute particles, whether they are neutral or charged. For example, 1.0 mol of a nonelectrolyte, such as glucose, produces essentially the same reduction in vapor pressure in a given quantity of water as does 0.5 mol of NaCl, a strong electrolyte. Both solutions have 1.0 mol of particles because 0.5 mol of NaCl dissociates to give 0.5 mol of $Na^+(aq)$ and 0.5 mol of $Cl^-(aq)$. ∞ (Sec. 4.2)

Point of Emphasis: The rate of condensation is *not* changed by the addition of a nonvolatile solute. The rate of vaporization is *slowed* by the addition of a nonvolatile solute.

Point of Emphasis: The more nonvolatile solute present in a solution, the greater the decrease in the solution's vapor pressure.

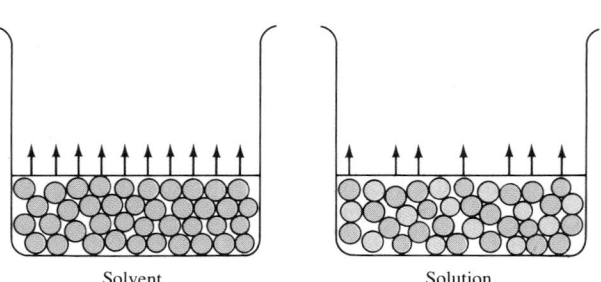

Solvent   Solution

FIGURE 13.18
A nonvolatile solute reduces the rate of vaporization of the solvent.

Raoult's Law

Quantitatively, the vapor pressure of solutions containing nonvolatile solutes is given by **Raoult's law,** Equation 13.10, where P_A is the vapor pressure of the solution, X_A is the mole fraction of the solvent, and P_A° is the vapor pressure of the pure solvent:

$$P_A = X_A P_A^\circ \qquad [13.10]$$

Teaching Note: Note the similarity between Raoult's law ($P_A = X_A P_A^\circ$) and the expression for partial pressures derived from Dalton's law ($P_A = X_A P_{tot}$).

For example, the vapor pressure of water is 17.5 torr at 20°C. Imagine holding the temperature constant while adding glucose, $C_6H_{12}O_6$, to the water so that the resulting solution has $X_{H_2O} = 0.80$ and $X_{C_6H_{12}O_6} = 0.20$. According to Equation 13.10, the vapor pressure of water over the solution will be 14 torr:

$$P_{H_2O} = (0.80)(17.5 \text{ torr}) = 14 \text{ torr}$$

SAMPLE EXERCISE 13.6

Glycerin, $C_3H_8O_3$, is a nonvolatile nonelectrolyte with a density of 1.26 g/mL. Calculate the vapor pressure at 25°C of a solution made by adding 50.0 mL glycerin to 500.0 mL of water. The vapor pressure of pure water at 25°C is 23.8 torr (Appendix B).

SOLUTION To apply Raoult's law, Equation 13.10, we must calculate the mole fraction of water in the solution:

$$\text{Moles } C_3H_8O_3 = (50.0 \text{ mL } C_3H_8O_3)\left(\frac{1.26 \text{ g } C_3H_8O_3}{1 \text{ mL } C_3H_8O_3}\right)$$
$$\times \left(\frac{1 \text{ mol } C_3H_8O_3}{92.1 \text{ g } C_3H_8O_3}\right) = 0.684 \text{ mol}$$

$$\text{Moles } H_2O = (500.0 \text{ mL } H_2O)\left(\frac{1.00 \text{ g } H_2O}{1 \text{ mL } H_2O}\right)\left(\frac{1 \text{ mol } H_2O}{18.0 \text{ g } H_2O}\right) = 27.8 \text{ mol}$$

$$X_{H_2O} = \frac{\text{mol } H_2O}{\text{mol } H_2O + \text{mol } C_3H_8O_3} = \frac{27.8}{27.8 + 0.684} = 0.976$$

We now use Raoult's law to calculate the vapor pressure of water for the solution:

$$P_{H_2O} = X_{H_2O} P_{H_2O}^\circ = (0.976)(23.8 \text{ torr}) = 23.2 \text{ torr}$$

The vapor pressure of the solution has been lowered by 0.6 torr relative to that of pure water.

PRACTICE EXERCISE

The vapor pressure of pure water at 110°C is 1070 torr. A solution of ethylene glycol and water has a vapor pressure of 1.00 atm at 110°C. Assuming that Raoult's law is obeyed, what is the mole fraction of ethylene glycol in the solution?
Answer: 0.290

Recall that the definition of an ideal gas is a gas described by the ideal-gas equation. Similarly, an **ideal solution** is a solution that obeys Raoult's law. Real solutions best approximate ideal behavior when the solute concentration is low and when the solute and solvent have similar molecular sizes and similar types of intermolecular attractions.

Many solutions do not obey Raoult's law exactly: They are not ideal solutions. If the intermolecular forces between solvent and solute are weaker

Point of Emphasis: Solutions are more likely to behave ideally when the solute concentration is low and when both solute and solvent are similar in size and intermolecular forces are nonpolar.

A CLOSER LOOK

Ideal Solutions with Two or More Volatile Components

Solutions sometimes have two or more volatile components. For example, gasoline is a complex solution containing several volatile substances. To gain some understanding of such mixtures, consider an ideal solution containing two components, A and B. The partial pressures of A and B vapors above the solution are given by Raoult's law:

$$P_A = X_A P_A^\circ \quad \text{and} \quad P_B = X_B P_B^\circ$$

The total vapor pressure over the solution is the sum of the partial pressures of each volatile component:

$$P_{total} = P_A + P_B = X_A P_A^\circ + X_B P_B^\circ$$

As an example of such a solution, consider a mixture of benzene, C_6H_6, and toluene, C_7H_8, containing 1 mol of benzene and 2 mol of toluene ($X_{ben} = 0.33$ and $X_{tol} = 0.67$). At 20°C, the vapor pressures of the pure substances are

$$\text{Benzene:} \quad P_{ben}^\circ = 75 \text{ torr}$$
$$\text{Toluene:} \quad P_{tol}^\circ = 22 \text{ torr}$$

Thus, the partial pressures of benzene and toluene above the solution are

$$P_{ben} = (0.33)(75 \text{ torr}) = 25 \text{ torr}$$
$$P_{tol} = (0.67)(22 \text{ torr}) = 15 \text{ torr}$$

The total pressure is

$$P_{total} = 25 \text{ torr} + 15 \text{ torr} = 40 \text{ torr}$$

These results indicate that the vapor is richer in the more volatile component, benzene. The mole fraction of benzene in the vapor is given by the ratio of its vapor pressure to the total pressure (See Equation 10.16):

$$X_{ben} \text{ in vapor} = \frac{P_{ben}}{P_{total}} = \frac{25 \text{ torr}}{40 \text{ torr}} = 0.63$$

Although benzene comprises only 33 percent of the molecules in the solution, it comprises 63 percent of the molecules in the vapor.

When ideal solutions are in equilibrium with their vapor, the more volatile component of the mixture will be relatively richer in the vapor. This fact forms the basis of the important technique of *distillation.* This technique is used to separate (or partially separate) mixtures containing one or more volatile components. Distillation is the procedure by which a "moonshiner" obtains whiskey using a "still" and by which petrochemical plants achieve the separation of crude petroleum into

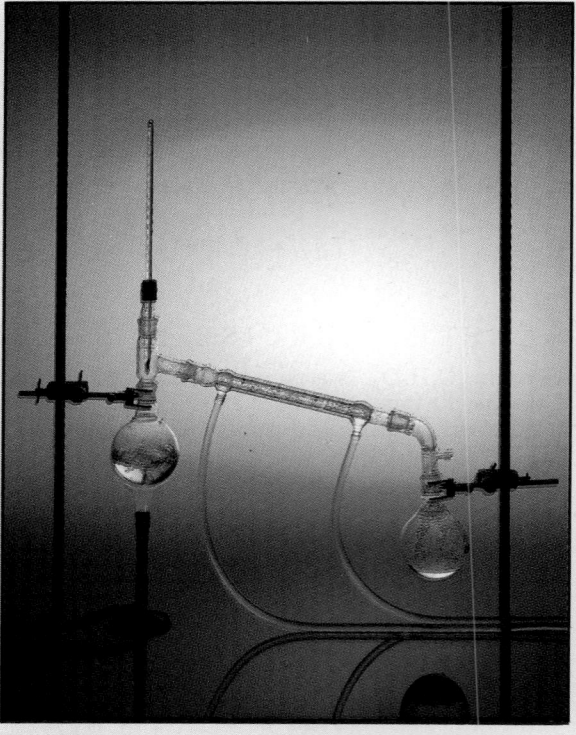

FIGURE 13.19 Simple laboratory distillation setup, showing the distillation of an aqueous solution. Open flames should be avoided when heating flammable liquids such as benzene and toluene. (© Richard Megna/ Fundamental Photographs)

gasoline, diesel fuel, lubricating oil, and so forth. It is also used routinely on a small scale in the laboratory. Figure 13.19 shows a simple laboratory distillation apparatus. Imagine that the solution in the distillation flask is a mixture of benzene and toluene. As the mixture is heated to its boiling point, the more volatile benzene will concentrate in the vapor. The vapor is condensed in the cooler part of the apparatus (the condenser) and collected. The liquid may be distilled again to enrich it further in the more volatile component. A specially designed *fractional distillation* apparatus can achieve in a single operation a degree of separation that would be equivalent to several successive simple distillations.

than those between solvent and solvent and between solute and solute, then the solvent vapor pressure tends to be greater than predicted by Raoult's law. Conversely, when the interactions between solute and solvent are exceptionally strong, as might be the case when hydrogen bonding exists, the solvent vapor pressure is lower than Raoult's law predicts. Although you should be aware that these departures from ideal solution occur, we will ignore them for the remainder of this chapter.

Boiling-Point Elevation

In Sections 11.5 and 11.6, we examined the vapor pressures of pure substances and how they can be used to construct phase diagrams. How will the phase diagram of a solution, and hence its boiling and freezing points, differ from those of the pure solvent? The addition of a nonvolatile solute lowers the vapor pressure of the solution. Thus, as shown in Figure 13.20, the vapor-pressure curve of the solution (blue line) will be shifted downward relative to the vapor-pressure curve of the pure liquid (black line); at any given temperature, the vapor pressure of the solution is lower than that of the pure liquid. Recall that the normal boiling point of a liquid is the temperature at which its vapor pressure equals 1 atm. ∞ (Sec. 11.5) At the normal boiling point of the pure liquid, the vapor pressure of the solution will be less than 1 atm (Figure 13.20). Therefore, a higher temperature is required to attain a vapor pressure of 1 atm. Thus, the boiling point of the solution is higher than that of the pure liquid.

The increase in boiling point, ΔT_b (relative to the boiling point of the pure solvent), is directly proportional to the number of solute particles per mole of solvent molecules. We know that molality expresses the number of moles of solute per 1000 g of solvent, which represents a fixed number of moles of solvent. Thus, ΔT_b is proportional to molality:

$$\Delta T_b = K_b m \qquad [13.11]$$

Point of Emphasis: In both the boiling-point elevation and the freezing-point depression, the concentration of solute must be expressed in *molality*.

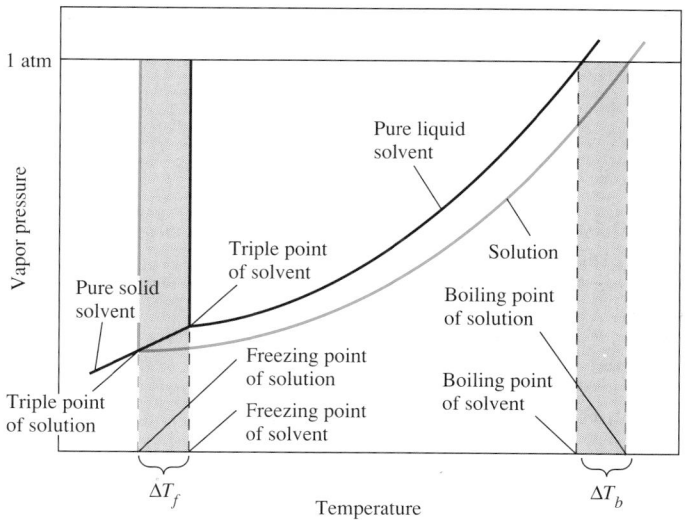

FIGURE 13.20 Phase diagrams for a pure solvent and for a solution of a nonvolatile solute. The vapor pressure of the solid solvent is unaffected by the presence of solute if the solid freezes out without containing a significant concentration of solute, as is usually the case.

Figure 13.20

The magnitude of K_b, which is called the **molal boiling-point-elevation constant,** depends only on the solvent. Some typical values for several common solvents are given in Table 13.5.

For water, K_b is $0.52\,^\circ C/m$; therefore, a $1\ m$ aqueous solution of sucrose or any other aqueous solution that is $1\ m$ in nonvolatile solute particles will boil at a temperature $0.52\,^\circ C$ higher than pure water. It is important to realize that the boiling-point elevation is proportional to the number of solute particles present in a given quantity of solution. When NaCl dissolves in water, 2 mol of solute particles—1 mol of Na^+ and 1 mol of Cl^-—are formed for each mole of NaCl that dissolves. Therefore, a $1\ m$ solution of NaCl in water causes a boiling-point elevation twice as large as a $1\ m$ solution of a nonelectrolyte such as sucrose.

Point of Emphasis: For a solution of an ionic compound, the concentration of solute particles is the sum of the concentrations of all of the ions formed upon dissociation.

Freezing-Point Depression

The lower vapor pressure of a solution relative to the pure liquid also affects the freezing point of the solution. The explanation is a bit more subtle than that used above for boiling-point elevation, but we can proceed as follows.

When a solution freezes, crystals of pure solvent usually separate out; the solute molecules are not normally soluble in the solid phase of the solvent. For example, when aqueous solutions are partially frozen, the solid that separates out is almost always pure ice. As a result, the part of the phase diagram in Figure 13.20 that represents the vapor pressure of the solid is the same as that for the pure liquid. The vapor pressure curves for the liquid and solid phases meet at the triple point. ∞ (Sec. 11.6)   In Figure 13.20, we see that the triple point of the solution must be at a lower temperature than in the pure liquid because of the lower vapor pressure of the solution compared to that of the pure liquid.

The freezing point of a solution is the temperature at which the first crystals of pure solvent begin to form in equilibrium with the solution. Recall from Section 11.6 that the line representing the solid-liquid equilibrium rises nearly vertically from the triple point. Because the triple-point temperature of the solution is lower than that of the pure liquid, the freezing point of the solution will also be lower than that of the pure liquid.

Like the boiling-point elevation, the decrease in freezing point, ΔT_f, is directly proportional to the molality of the solute:

$$\Delta T_f = K_f m \qquad [13.12]$$

TABLE 13.5 △ Molal Boiling-Point-Elevation and Freezing-Point-Depression Constants

Solvent	Normal boiling point (°C)	K_b (°C/m)	Normal freezing point (°C)	K_f (°C/m)
Water, H_2O	100.0	0.52	0.0	1.86
Benzene, C_6H_6	80.1	2.53	5.5	5.12
Ethanol, C_2H_5OH	78.4	1.22	−114.6	1.99
Carbon tetrachloride, CCl_4	76.8	5.02	−22.3	29.8
Chloroform, $CHCl_3$	61.2	3.63	−63.5	4.68

The values of K_f, the **molal freezing-point-depression constant,** for several common solvents are given in Table 13.5. For water, K_f is $1.86°C/m$; therefore, a $0.5\ m$ aqueous solution of NaCl or any aqueous solution that is $1\ m$ in nonvolatile solute particles will freeze $1.86°C$ lower than pure water. The freezing-point lowering caused by solutes explains the use of antifreeze in cars (Sample Exercise 13.7) and the use of calcium chloride, $CaCl_2$, to melt ice on roads during winter.

SAMPLE EXERCISE 13.7

Automotive antifreeze consists of ethylene glycol, $C_2H_6O_2$, a nonvolatile nonelectrolyte. Calculate the boiling point and freezing point of a 25.0 mass percent solution of ethylene glycol in water.

SOLUTION   In order to use the molal boiling-point-elevation and freezing-point-depression constants, we must express the concentration of the solution as molality. Let us assume for convenience that we have 1000 g of solution. Because the solution is 25.0 mass percent ethylene glycol, the masses of ethylene glycol and water in the solution are 250 and 750 g, respectively. The molality of the solution is obtained as follows:

$$\text{Molality} = \frac{\text{moles } C_2H_6O_2}{\text{kilograms } H_2O}$$

$$= \left(\frac{250\text{ g } C_2H_6O_2}{750\text{ g } H_2O}\right)\left(\frac{1\text{ mol } C_2H_6O_2}{62.0\text{ g } C_2H_6O_2}\right)\left(\frac{1000\text{ g } H_2O}{1\text{ kg } H_2O}\right) = 5.38\ m$$

We now use Equations 13.11 and 13.12 to calculate the changes in the boiling and freezing points:

$$\Delta T_b = K_b m = (0.52°C/m)(5.38\ m) = 2.8°C$$

$$\Delta T_f = K_f m = (1.86°C/m)(5.38\ m) = 10.0°C$$

Hence, the boiling and freezing points of the solution are

$$\text{Boiling point} = (\text{normal b.p. of solvent}) + \Delta T_b$$

$$= 100.0°C + 2.8°C = 102.8°C$$

$$\text{Freezing point} = (\text{normal f.p. of solvent}) - \Delta T_f$$

$$= 0.0°C - 10.0°C = -10.0°C$$

Notice that the boiling point has been elevated and the freezing point depressed compared to those of the pure solvent, water.

PRACTICE EXERCISE

Calculate the freezing point of a solution containing 0.600 kg of $CHCl_3$ and 42 g of eucalyptol, $C_{10}H_{18}O$, a fragrant substance found in the leaves of eucalyptus trees. *Answer:* $-65.6°C$

SAMPLE EXERCISE 13.8

List the following aqueous solutions in order of their expected freezing points: $0.050\ m$ $CaCl_2$; $0.15\ m$ NaCl; $0.10\ m$ HCl; $0.050\ m$ $HC_2H_3O_2$; $0.10\ m$ $C_{12}H_{22}O_{11}$.

SOLUTION   First notice that $CaCl_2$, NaCl, and HCl are strong electrolytes, $HC_2H_3O_2$ is a weak electrolyte, and $C_{12}H_{22}O_{11}$ is a nonelectrolyte. The molality of each solution in total particles is as follows:

$0.050\ m$ $CaCl_2$	($0.15\ m$ in particles)
$0.15\ m$ NaCl	($0.30\ m$ in particles)
$0.10\ m$ HCl	($0.20\ m$ in particles)
$0.050\ m$ $HC_2H_3O_2$	(between 0.050 and 0.10 m in particles)
$0.10\ m$ $C_{12}H_{22}O_{11}$	($0.10\ m$ in particles)

Because the freezing points depend on the total molality of particles in solution, the expected ordering is: 0.15 m NaCl (lowest freezing point), 0.10 m HCl, 0.050 m $CaCl_2$, 0.10 m $C_{12}H_{22}O_{11}$, 0.050 m $HC_2H_3O_2$ (highest freezing point).

PRACTICE EXERCISE

Which of the following solutes will produce the largest increase in boiling point upon addition to 1 kg of water: 1 mol of $Co(NO_3)_2$, 2 mol of KCl, or 3 mol of C_2H_5OH? **Answer:** 2 mol of KCl

Osmosis

Bassam Z. Shakhashiri, "Osmotic Pressure of a Sugar Solution," *Chemical Demonstrations: A Handbook for Teachers of Chemistry, Volume 3* (Madison: The University of Wisconsin Press, 1989), pp. 286–89.

Point of Emphasis: In osmosis, there is net movement of solvent from the side with the higher solvent concentration (lower solute concentration) to the side with lower solvent concentration (higher solute concentration). Concentrations in the calculation of osmotic pressure are expressed in *molarity*.

Teaching Note: When sufficient pressure is exerted to halt osmosis, solvent molecules are still moving back and forth across through the membrane. Because equal numbers of molecules are moving in both directions, no *net* transfer of solvent occurs.

Certain materials—including many membranes in biological systems and synthetic substances such as cellophane—are *semipermeable*. That is, when in contact with a solution, they permit the passage of some molecules but not others. They often permit the passage of small solvent molecules such as water but block the passage of larger solute molecules or ions. This semipermeable character is due to a network of tiny pores within the membrane.

Consider a situation in which only solvent molecules are able to pass through a membrane. If such a membrane is placed between two solutions of different concentration, solvent molecules move in both directions through the membrane. However, the concentration of *solvent* is higher in the solution containing less solute than in the more concentrated one. Therefore, the rate of passage of solvent from the less concentrated to the more concentrated solution is greater than the rate in the opposite direction. Thus, there is a net movement of solvent molecules from the less concentrated solution into the more concentrated one. This process is called **osmosis.** The important point to remember is that *the net movement of solvent is always toward the solution with the higher solute concentration.*

Figure 13.21(*a*) shows two solutions separated by a semipermeable membrane. Solvent moves through the membrane from right to left, as if the solutions were driven to attain equal concentrations. As a result, the liquid levels in the two arms become uneven. Eventually, the pressure difference resulting from the uneven heights of the liquid in the two arms becomes so large that the net flow of solvent ceases, as shown in Figure 13.21(*b*). Alternatively, we may

FIGURE 13.21 Osmosis: (*a*) net movement of solvent from the solution with low solute concentration into the solution with high solute concentration; (*b*) osmosis stops when the column of solution on the left becomes high enough to exert sufficient pressure to stop the osmosis.

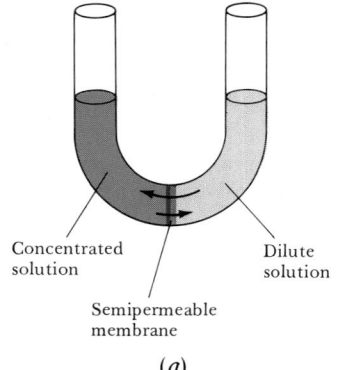
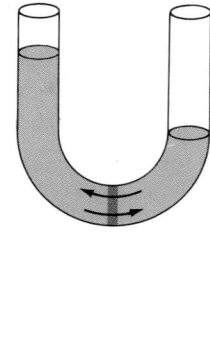

Concentrated solution

Dilute solution

Semipermeable membrane

(*a*)

(*b*)

Figure 13.21

apply pressure to the left arm of the apparatus, as shown in Figure 13.22, to halt the net flow of solvent. The pressure required to prevent osmosis is known as the **osmotic pressure**, π, of the solution. The osmotic pressure is found to obey a law similar in form to the ideal-gas law: $\pi V = nRT$, where V is the volume of the solution, n is the number of moles of solute, R is the ideal-gas constant, and T is the temperature on the Kelvin scale. From this equation, we can write

$$\pi = \left(\frac{n}{V}\right) RT = MRT \qquad [13.13]$$

where M is the molarity of the solution.

If two solutions of identical osmotic pressure are separated by a semipermeable membrane, no osmosis will occur. The two solutions are said to be *isotonic*. If one solution is of lower osmotic pressure, it is described as being *hypotonic* with respect to the more concentrated solution. The more concentrated solution is said to be *hypertonic* with respect to the dilute solution.

Osmosis plays a very important role in living systems. For example, the membranes of red blood cells are semipermeable. Placement of a red blood cell in a solution that is hypertonic relative to the intracellular solution (the solution within the cells) causes water to move out of the cell, as shown in Figure 13.23. This causes the cell to shrivel, a process known as *crenation*. Placement of the cell in a solution that is hypotonic relative to the intracellular fluid causes water to move into the cell. This causes rupturing of the cell, a process known as *hemolysis*. People needing replacement of body fluids or nutrients who cannot be fed orally are given solutions by intravenous (IV) infusion, which feeds nutrients directly into the veins. To prevent crenation or hemolysis of red blood cells, the IV solutions must be isotonic with the intracellular fluids of the cells.

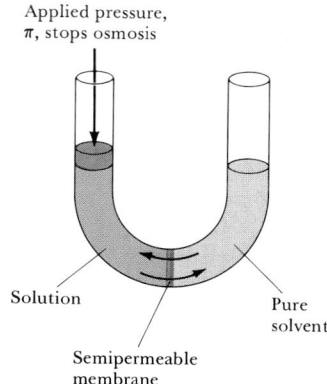

FIGURE 13.22 Applied pressure on the left arm of the apparatus stops net movement of solvent from the right side of the semipermeable membrane. This applied pressure is known as the osmotic pressure of the solution.

FIGURE 13.23 Osmosis through the semipermeable membrane of a red blood cell: (*a*) crenation caused by movement of water from the cell; (*b*) hemolysis caused by movement of water into the cell.

SAMPLE EXERCISE 13.9

The average osmotic pressure of blood is 7.7 atm at 25°C. What concentration of glucose, $C_6H_{12}O_6$, will be isotonic with blood?

SOLUTION

$$\pi = MRT$$

$$M = \frac{\pi}{RT} = \frac{7.7 \text{ atm}}{\left(0.0821 \dfrac{\text{L-atm}}{\text{mol-K}}\right)(298 \text{ K})} = 0.31 \ M$$

In clinical situations, the concentrations of solutions are generally expressed in terms of mass percentages. The mass percentage of a 0.31 M solution of glucose is 5.3 percent. The concentration of NaCl that is isotonic with blood is 0.16 M because NaCl ionizes to form two particles, Na^+ and Cl^- (a 0.155 M solution of NaCl is 0.310 M in particles). A 0.16 M solution of NaCl is 0.9 mass percent in NaCl. Such a solution is known as a physiological saline solution.

PRACTICE EXERCISE

What is the osmotic pressure at 20°C of a 0.0020 M sucrose, $C_{12}H_{22}O_{11}$, solution? ***Answer:*** 0.048 atm, or 37 torr

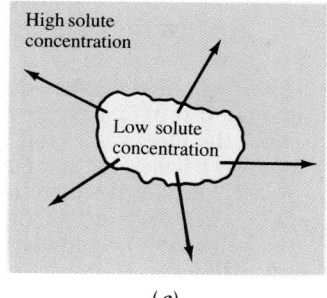

(*a*)

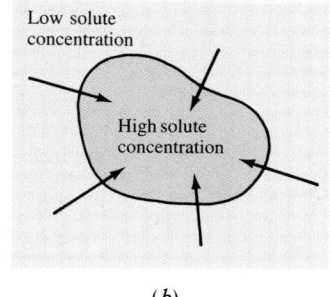

(*b*)

There are many interesting examples of osmosis. A cucumber placed in concentrated brine loses water via osmosis and shrivels into a pickle. A carrot

A CLOSER LOOK

Learning Goal 7: Explain the difference between the magnitude of changes in colligative properties caused by electrolytes compared to those caused by nonelectrolytes.

Colligative Properties of Electrolyte Solutions

We have observed that the colligative properties of solutions depend on the total concentration of solute particles, regardless of whether the particles are ions or molecules. Thus, we would expect a 0.100 m solution of NaCl to have a freezing-point depression of $(0.200\ m) \times (1.86°C/m) = 0.372°C$ because it is 0.100 m in $Na^+(aq)$ and 0.100 m in $Cl^-(aq)$. However, the measured freezing-point depression, 0.348°C, is not quite this large. The situation is similar for other strong electrolytes. For example, a 0.100 m solution of KCl freezes at $-0.344°C$.

The difference between the expected and observed colligative properties for strong electrolytes is due to electrostatic attractions between ions. As the ions move about in solution, ions of opposite charge collide and "stick together" for brief moments. While they are together, they behave as a single particle, called an **ion pair** (Figure 13.24). The number of independent particles is thereby reduced, causing a reduction in the freezing-point depression (as well as in the boiling-point elevation, the vapor-pressure reduction, and the osmotic pressure).

One measure of the extent to which electrolytes dissociate is the *van't Hoff factor, i.* This factor is the ratio of the actual value of a colligative property to the value calculated assuming the substance to be a nonelectrolyte. For example, using the freezing-point depression, we have

$$i = \frac{\Delta T_f(\text{measured})}{\Delta T_f(\text{calculated for nonelectrolyte})} \quad [13.14]$$

The ideal value of i can be determined for a salt by noting the number of ions per formula unit. For example, for NaCl the ideal van't Hoff factor is 2 because the salt consists of one Na^+ and one Cl^- per formula unit; for K_2SO_4, it is 3, the three ions being two K^+ and one SO_4^{2-}. In the absence of any information about the actual value of i for a solution, we will use the ideal value in calculations.

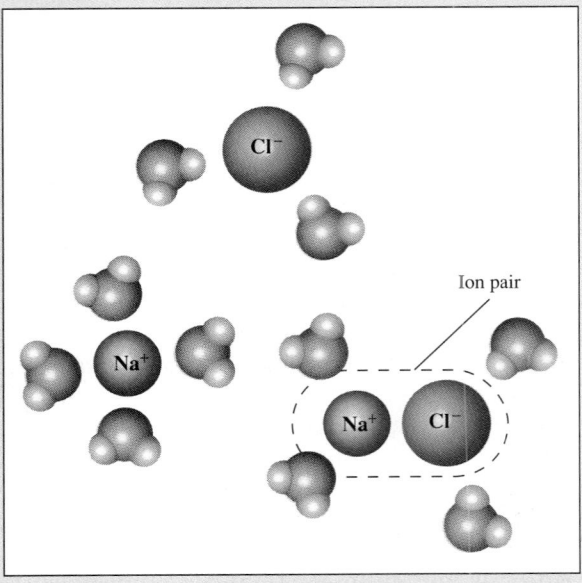

FIGURE 13.24 A solution of NaCl contains not only separated $Na^+(aq)$ and $Cl^-(aq)$ ions but ion pairs as well.

Table 13.6 gives the observed van't Hoff factors for several substances at different dilutions. Two trends are evident in these data. First, dilution affects the value of i for electrolytes; the more dilute the solution, the more closely i approaches the ideal or limiting value. Thus, the extent of ion pairing in electrolyte solutions decreases upon dilution. Second, the lower the charges on the ions, the smaller the departure of i from the limiting value, because the extent of ion pairing decreases as the charges of ions decrease. Both trends are consistent with simple electrostatics: The force of interaction between charged particles decreases as their separation increases and as their charges decrease.

TABLE 13.6 △ van't Hoff Factors for Several Substances at 25°C

Compound	Concentration			
	0.100 m	0.0100 m	0.00100 m	Limiting value
Sucrose	1.00	1.00	1.00	1.00
NaCl	1.87	1.94	1.97	2.00
K_2SO_4	2.32	2.70	2.84	3.00
$MgSO_4$	1.21	1.53	1.82	2.00

that has become limp because of water loss to the atmosphere can be placed in water. Water moves into the carrot through osmosis, making it firm once again. People who eat a lot of salty food experience water retention in tissue cells and intercellular spaces because of osmosis. The resultant swelling or puffiness is called *edema*. Movement of water from soil into plant roots and subsequently into the upper portions of the plant is due at least in part to osmosis. The preservation of meat by salting and of fruit by adding sugar protects against bacterial action. Through the process of osmosis, a bacterium on salted meat or candied fruit loses water, shrivels, and dies.

In osmosis, water moves from an area of high water concentration (low solute concentration) into an area of low water concentration (high solute concentration). Such movement of a substance from an area where its concentration is high to an area where it is low is spontaneous. Biological cells transport not only water but also other select materials through their membrane walls. This permits entry of nutrients and allows for disposal of waste materials. In some cases, substances must be moved from an area of low concentration to one of high concentration. This movement is called *active transport*. It is not spontaneous and so requires expenditures of energy by the cell.

Point of Emphasis: Osmosis is spontaneous, requiring no external energy expenditure. Active transport is not spontaneous and requires an external energy source.

Determination of Molar Mass

The colligative properties of solutions provide a useful means of experimentally determining molar mass. Any of the four colligative properties could be used to determine molar mass. The procedures are illustrated in Sample Exercises 13.10 and 13.11.

Learning Goal 8: Determine the concentration and molar mass of a nonvolatile nonelectrolyte from its effect on the colligative properties of a solution.

SAMPLE EXERCISE 13.10

A solution of an unknown nonvolatile nonelectrolyte was prepared by dissolving 0.250 g in 40.0 g of CCl_4. The normal boiling point of the resultant solution increased by $0.357°C$. Calculate the molar mass of the solute.

SOLUTION Using Equation 13.11, we have

$$\text{Molality} = \frac{\Delta T_b}{K_b} = \frac{0.357°C}{5.02°C/m} = 0.0711\ m$$

Thus the solution contains 0.0711 mol of solute per kilogram of solvent. The solution was prepared from 0.250 g of solute and 40.0 g of solvent. The number of grams of solute in a kilogram of solvent is therefore

$$\frac{\text{Grams solute}}{\text{Kilograms } CCl_4} = \left(\frac{0.250 \text{ g solute}}{40.0 \text{ g } CCl_4}\right)\left(\frac{1000 \text{ g } CCl_4}{1 \text{ kg } CCl_4}\right) = \frac{6.25 \text{ g solute}}{1 \text{ kg } CCl_4}$$

Notice that a kilogram of solvent contains 6.25 g, which from the ΔT_b measurement must be 0.0711 mol. Therefore,

$$0.0711 \text{ mol} = 6.25 \text{ g}$$

$$1 \text{ mol} = \frac{6.25 \text{ g}}{0.0711} = 87.9 \text{ g}$$

Therefore, $\mathcal{M} = 87.9$ g/mol

PRACTICE EXERCISE

Camphor, $C_{10}H_{16}O$, melts at $179.8°C$; it has a particularly large freezing-point depression constant, $K_f = 40°C/m$. When 0.186 g of an organic substance of unknown molar mass is dissolved in 22.01 g of liquid camphor, the freezing point of the mixture is found to be $176.7°C$. What is the approximate molar mass of the solute? *Answer:* 109 g/mol

SAMPLE EXERCISE 13.11

The osmotic pressure of an aqueous solution of a certain protein was measured in order to determine its molar mass. The solution contained 3.50 mg of protein dissolved in sufficient water to form 5.00 mL of solution. The osmotic pressure of the solution at 25°C was found to be 1.54 torr. Calculate the molar mass of the protein.

SOLUTION Using Equation 13.13, we can calculate the molarity of the solution:

$$\text{Molarity} = \frac{\pi}{RT} = \frac{(1.54 \text{ torr})\left(\dfrac{1 \text{ atm}}{760 \text{ torr}}\right)}{\left(0.0821 \dfrac{\text{L-atm}}{\text{mol-K}}\right)(298 \text{ K})} = 8.28 \times 10^{-5} \frac{\text{mol}}{\text{L}}$$

Because the volume of the solution is 5.00 mL = 5.00×10^{-3} L, the number of moles of protein must be

$$\text{Moles} = (8.28 \times 10^{-5} \text{ mol/L})(5.00 \times 10^{-3} \text{ L}) = 4.14 \times 10^{-7} \text{ mol}$$

The molar mass is the number of grams per mole of the substance. The sample has a mass of 3.50 mg = 3.50×10^{-3} g. The molar mass is the number of grams divided by the number of moles:

$$\frac{\text{Grams}}{\text{Moles}} = \frac{3.50 \times 10^{-3} \text{ g}}{4.14 \times 10^{-7} \text{ mol}} = 8.45 \times 10^{3} \text{ g/mol}$$

Because small pressures can be measured easily and accurately, osmotic pressure measurements provide an excellent way to determine the molecular weights of very large molecules.

PRACTICE EXERCISE

A sample of 2.05 g of the plastic polystyrene was dissolved in enough toluene to form 100 mL of solution. The osmotic pressure of this solution was found to be 1.21 kPa at 25°C. Calculate the molar mass of the polystyrene. **Answer:** 4.20×10^{4} g/mol

13.6 Colloids

Learning Goal 9: Describe how a colloid differs from a true solution.

Teaching Note: The particle sizes in true solutions are generally in the range of 1 to 10 Å in diameter.

When finely divided clay particles are dispersed through water, they do not remain suspended but eventually settle out of the water because of the gravitational pull. The dispersed clay particles are much larger than molecules and consist of many thousands or even millions of atoms. In contrast, the dispersed particles of a solution are of a molecular size. Between these extremes is the situation in which dispersed particles are larger than molecules but not so large that the components of the mixture separate under the influence of gravity. These intermediate types of dispersions or suspensions are called **colloidal dispersions,** or simply **colloids.** Colloids are on the dividing line between solutions and heterogeneous mixtures. Like solutions, colloids can be gases, liquids, or solids. Examples of each are listed in Table 13.7.

The size of the dispersed particle is the property used to classify a mixture as a colloid. Colloid particles range in diameter from approximately 10 to 2000 Å. Solute particles are smaller. The colloid particle may consist of many atoms, ions, or molecules, or it may even be a single giant molecule. For example, the hemoglobin molecule, which carries oxygen in blood, has molecular dimensions of 65 Å × 55 Å × 50 Å and a molecular weight of 64,500 amu.

TABLE 13.7 △ Types of Colloids

Phase of colloid	Dispersing (solvent-like) substance	Dispersed (solute-like) substance	Colloid type	Example
Gas	Gas	Gas	—	None (all are solutions)
Gas	Gas	Liquid	Aerosol	Fog
Gas	Gas	Solid	Aerosol	Smoke
Liquid	Liquid	Gas	Foam	Whipped cream
Liquid	Liquid	Liquid	Emulsion	Milk
Liquid	Liquid	Solid	Sol	Paint
Solid	Solid	Gas	Solid foam	Marshmallow
Solid	Solid	Liquid	Solid emulsion	Butter
Solid	Solid	Solid	Solid sol	Ruby glass

Although colloid particles may be so small that the dispersion appears uniform even under a microscope, they are large enough to scatter light very effectively. Consequently, most colloids appear cloudy or opaque unless they are very dilute. (Homogenized milk is a colloid.) Furthermore, because they scatter light, a light beam can be seen as it passes through a colloidal suspension, as shown in Figure 13.25. This scattering of light by colloidal particles, known as the **Tyndall effect,** makes it possible to see the light beam coming from the projection housing in a smoke-filled theater or the light beam from an automobile on a dusty dirt road.

Bassam Z. Shakhashiri, "Color of the Sunset: The Tyndall Effect," *A Handbook for Teachers of Chemistry, Volume 3* (Madison: The University of Wisconsin Press, 1989), pp. 353–357.

Hydrophilic and Hydrophobic Colloids

The most important colloids are those in which the dispersing medium is water. Such colloids are frequently referred to as **hydrophilic** (water-loving) or **hydrophobic** (water-hating). Hydrophilic colloids are most like the solutions that we have previously examined. In the human body, the extremely large molecules that make up such important substances as enzymes and antibodies are kept in

FIGURE 13.25 Illustration of the Tyndall effect. The vessel on the left contains a colloidal suspension, that on the right a solution. Note that the path of the beam through the colloidal suspension is clearly seen because the light is scattered by the colloidal particles. Light is not scattered by the individual solute molecules in the solution. (© Richard Megna/Fundamental Photographs)

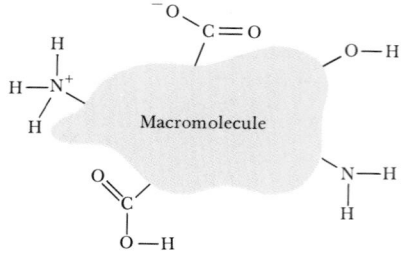

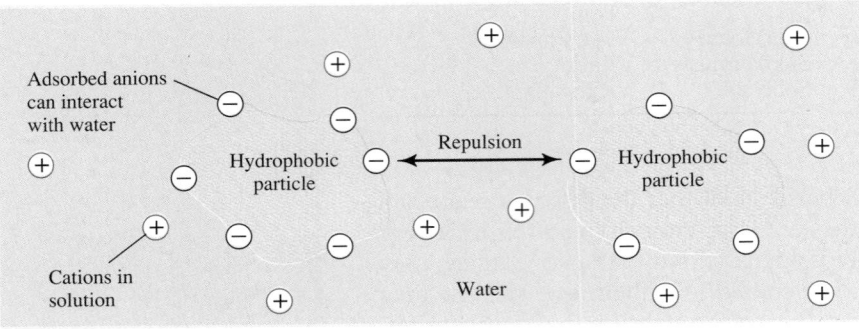

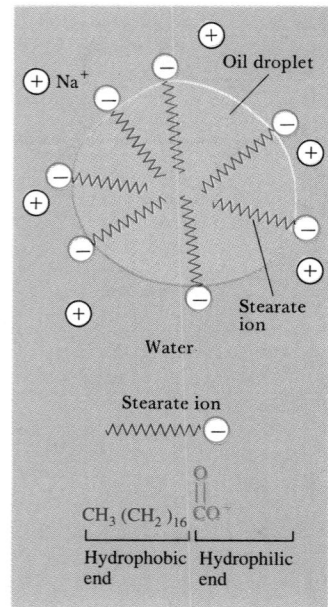

FIGURE 13.26 Examples of hydrophilic groups at the surface of a giant molecule (macromolecule) that help keep the molecule suspended in water.

FIGURE 13.27 Schematic representation of the stabilization of a hydrophobic colloid by adsorbed ions.

FIGURE 13.28 Stabilization of an emulsion of oil in water by stearate ions.

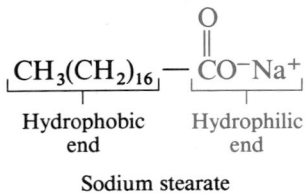

Hydrophobic end   Hydrophilic end

Sodium stearate

suspension by interaction with surrounding water molecules. The molecules fold so that polar, or charged, groups can interact with water molecules at the periphery of the molecules. These hydrophilic groups generally contain oxygen or nitrogen. Some examples are shown in Figure 13.26.

Hydrophobic colloids can be prepared in water only if they are stabilized in some way. Otherwise, their natural lack of affinity for water causes them to separate from the water. Hydrophobic colloids can be stabilized by adsorption of ions on their surface, as shown in Figure 13.27. (*Adsorption* refers to adherence to a surface. It differs from *absorption,* which means passage into the interior, as when water is absorbed by a sponge.) These adsorbed ions can interact with water, thereby stabilizing the colloid. At the same time, the mutual repulsion between colloid particles with adsorbed ions of the same charge keeps the particles from colliding and so getting larger.

Hydrophobic colloids can also be stabilized by the presence of other hydrophilic groups on their surfaces. For example, small droplets of oil are hydrophobic. They do not remain suspended in water; instead, they separate, forming an oil slick on the surface of the water. Addition of sodium stearate, whose structure is shown at the left, or any similar substance having one end that is hydrophilic (polar, or charged) and one that is hydrophobic (nonpolar), will stabilize a suspension of oil in water, as shown in Figure 13.28. The hydrophobic ends of the stearate ions interact with the oil droplet, and the hydrophilic ends point out toward the water with which they interact.

These concepts have an interesting application in our own digestive system. When fats in our diet reach the small intestine, a hormone causes the gallbladder to excrete a fluid called bile. Among the components of bile are compounds that have chemical structures similar to sodium stearate; that is,

Sickle-Cell Anemia

Our blood contains a complex protein called *hemoglobin* that is responsible for carrying oxygen from our lungs to other parts of our body. In the genetic disease known as *sickle-cell anemia,* hemoglobin molecules are abnormal: They have lower solubility, especially in the unoxygenated form. Consequently, as much as 85 percent of the hemoglobin in the red blood cells crystallizes from solution. This distorts the cells into a sickle shape, as shown in Figure 13.29. These clog the capillaries, thus causing gradual deterioration of the vital organs. The disease is hereditary, and if both parents carry the defective genes, it is likely that their children will possess only abnormal hemoglobin. Such children seldom survive more than a few years after birth. The reason for the insolubility of hemoglobin in sickle-cell anemia can be traced to a change in one part of the molecule.

Normal hemoglobin molecules have an amino acid in their makeup that has a side chain protruding from the main body of the molecule:

$$-CH_2-CH_2-\overset{\displaystyle O}{\overset{\displaystyle \|}{C}}-OH$$

Normal

Notice that this side chain terminates in a polar group, which contributes to the solubility of the hemoglobin molecule in water. In the hemoglobin molecules of persons suffering from sickle-cell anemia, the side chain is of a different type:

$$-\underset{\displaystyle CH_3}{\overset{\displaystyle |}{CH}}-CH_3$$

Abnormal

This abnormal group of atoms is nonpolar (hydrophobic), and its presence leads to the aggregation of this defective form of hemoglobin into particles too large to remain suspended in biological fluids.

FIGURE 13.29 Electron micrograph showing normal red blood cells (left) and sickled red blood cells (right). (Bill Longcore/Photo Researchers)

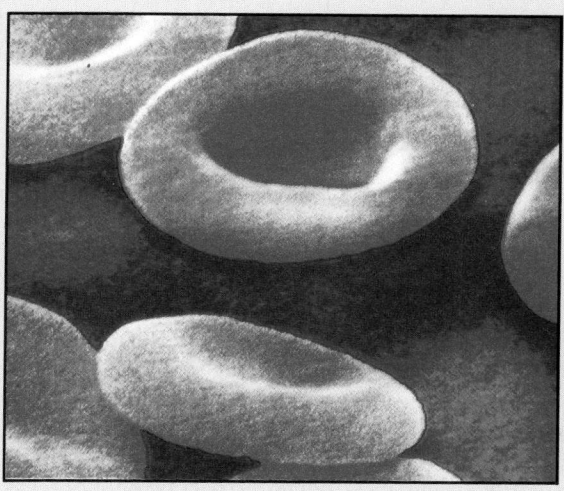

they have a hydrophilic (polar) end and a hydrophobic (nonpolar) end. These compounds emulsify the fats present in the intestine and thus permit digestion and absorption of fat-soluble vitamins through the intestinal wall. The term *emulsify* means "to form an emulsion," that is, a suspension of one liquid in another (Table 13.7). A substance that aids in the formation of an emulsion is called an emulsifying agent. If you read the labels for foods and other materials, you will observe that a variety of chemicals are used as emulsifying agents. These chemicals typically have a hydrophilic end and a hydrophobic end, as in the examples in the text above.

Removal of Colloidal Particles

Colloidal particles frequently must be removed from a dispersing medium, as in the removal of smoke from stacks or butterfat from milk. Because colloidal particles are so small, they cannot be extracted by simple filtration. The colloidal particles must be enlarged, a process called *coagulation.* The resultant larger particles can then be separated by filtration or merely by allowing them to settle out of the dispersing medium.

Heating or adding an electrolyte to the mixture may bring about coagulation. Heating the colloidal dispersion increases the particle motion and so the number of collisions. The particles increase in size as they stick together after colliding. The addition of electrolytes causes neutralization of the surface charges of the particles, thereby removing the electrostatic repulsions that inhibit their coming together. The effect of electrolytes is seen in the depositing of suspended clay in a river as it mixes with salt water. This results in the formation of river deltas wherever rivers empty into oceans or other salty bodies of water.

Semipermeable membranes can also be used to separate ions from colloidal particles, because the ions can pass through the membrane but the colloid particles cannot. This type of separation is known as *dialysis.* This process is used in the purification of blood in artificial kidney machines. Our kidneys are responsible for removing the waste products of metabolism from blood. In a kidney machine, blood is circulated through a dialyzing tube immersed in a washing solution. That solution is isotonic in ions that must be retained by the blood but is lacking the waste products. Wastes therefore dialyze out of the blood, but the ions do not.

For Review

Summary

Solutions are homogeneous mixtures of atoms, ions, or molecules. The relative amounts of solute and solvent in a solution can be described qualitatively (dilute or concentrated solutions) or quantitatively (in terms of weight percentage, parts per million, mole fraction, molarity, molality, and normality).

A saturated solution is one in which dissolved and undissolved solute are in dynamic equilibrium. The solubility of a solute is its concentration in a saturated solution. Solubility depends on the relative magnitudes of solute-solute, solute-solvent, and solvent-solvent attractive forces as well as on the change in disorder accompanying mixing. Although the solution process can be either endothermic or exothermic, solutions form only if the solute-solvent interaction is comparable in magnitude to the solute-solute and solvent-solvent interactions. Solubility therefore depends on the identity of the solute and the solvent (like dissolves like).

For most ionic solutes in water, solubility increases with increasing temperature. For gases, solubility generally decreases with increasing temperature and increases with increasing pressure. As described by Henry's law, the solubility of a gas is proportional to its partial pressure above the solution.

Some physical properties of solutions are colligative; that is, they depend on the concentration of the particles present and not on their chemical identity. Four colligative properties were discussed: the lowering of vapor pressure, the increase in boiling point, the decrease in freezing point, and osmotic pressure. Osmosis is the passage of solvent through a semipermeable membrane from a solution with a lower solute concentration into one with a higher solute concentration. Osmotic pressure is the pressure that must be applied to a solution to prevent osmosis into a solution from a pure solvent. Colligative properties can be used to determine the molar masses of nonvolatile nonelectrolytes.

True solutions can be differentiated from colloids on the basis of particle size. Colloids play important roles in many chemical and biological systems.

Key Terms

solvation (Sec. 13.1)
hydration (Sec. 13.1)
mass percentage (Sec. 13.2)
parts per million (ppm) (Sec. 13.2)
molality (Sec. 13.2)
crystallization (Sec. 13.3)
saturated solution (Sec. 13.3)
solubility (Sec. 13.3)
unsaturated solution (Sec. 13.3)
supersaturated solution (Sec. 13.3)
miscible (Sec. 13.4)
immiscible (Sec. 13.4)
Henry's law (Sec. 13.4)

colligative properties (Sec. 13.5)
Raoult's law (Sec. 13.5)
ideal solution (Sec. 13.5)
molal boiling-point-elevation constant (Sec. 13.5)
molal freezing-point-depression constant (Sec. 13.5)
osmosis (Sec. 13.5)
osmotic pressure (Sec. 13.5)
ion pair (Sec. 13.5)
colloidal dispersions (colloids) (Sec. 13.6)
Tyndall effect (Sec. 13.6)
hydrophilic (Sec. 13.6)
hydrophobic (Sec. 13.6)

Exercises

The Solution Process

13.1. Why are solvent-solvent, solute-solute, and solvent-solute intermolecular forces important in determining how soluble a solute is in a solvent?

13.2. Dissolving $NH_4NO_3(s)$ in water is an endothermic process. Explain this observation in terms of the enthalpy changes for each step of the solution process.

13.3. Indicate the type of solute-solvent interaction (Section 11.2) that should be most important in each of the following solutions: (a) KBr in water; (b) hexane, C_6H_{14}, in gasoline; (c) ammonia in water; (d) HCl in acetonitrile, CH_3CN.

13.4. What is the most important solute-solvent intermolecular force (Section 11.2) in each of the following solutions: (a) HF in water; (b) toluene, C_7H_8, in cyclohexane, C_6H_{12}; (c) NaOH in water; (d) iodine, I_2, in CCl_4?

13.5. The phrase "like dissolves like" is often used as a rule of thumb for solubility. Explain the basis of this rule in terms of intermolecular forces.

13.6. Which member of each of the following pairs is the more soluble in water: (a) CH_3CH_3 or CH_3OH; (b) C_2H_5OH or CH_3OCH_3; (c) CH_2Cl_2 or $CaCl_2$? Explain in each case.

13.7. In terms of intermolecular forces, explain each of the following observations: (a) KCl is insoluble in C_6H_6; (b) $Br_2(l)$ is more soluble than $I_2(s)$ in CCl_4.

13.8. Give an explanation in terms of intermolecular forces for each of the following observations: (a) Methanol, CH_3OH, is not soluble in cyclohexane, C_6H_{12}; (b) chloroform, $CHCl_3$, is soluble in water to the extent of only 1 g per 100 g of water but is miscible in ethanol, C_2H_5OH.

13.9. The intermolecular forces in hexane, C_6H_{14}, and heptane, C_7H_{16}, are very similar. (a) Explain why ΔH_{soln} for the mixing of hexane and heptane is nearly zero. (b) Given that $\Delta H_{soln} \approx 0$, explain why hexane and heptane mix spontaneously.

13.10. The enthalpy of solution of KBr in water is about +19.8 kJ/mol. The process, then, is endothermic. Never-theless, the solubility of KBr in water is relatively high. Why does the solution process, although endothermic, proceed?

Concentration of Solutions

13.11. (a) Calculate the mass percentage of Na_2SO_4 in a solution containing 10.5 g Na_2SO_4 in 175 g of water. (b) An ore contains 5.0 g of gold per ton of ore. What is the concentration of gold in ppm?

13.12. (a) What is the mass percentage of iodine, I_2, in a solution containing 0.050 mol I_2 in 50.0 g of CCl_4? (b) Seawater contains 0.412 g of Ca^{2+} per kilogram of water. What is the concentration of Ca^{2+} in ppm?

13.13. Calculate the mole fraction of methyl alcohol, CH_3OH, in the following solutions: (a) 6.00 g of CH_3OH in 480 g of H_2O; (b) 4.13 g of CH_3OH in 48.6 g of CCl_4.

13.14. Calculate the mole fraction of ethylene glycol, $C_2H_6O_2$, in the following solutions: (a) 120 g of $C_2H_6O_2$ dissolved in 120 g of water; (b) 120 g of $C_2H_6O_2$ dissolved in 1.20 kg of acetone, C_3H_6O.

13.15. Calculate the molarity of the following solutions: (a) 10.5 g NaCl in 350.0 mL of solution; (b) 40.7 g $LiClO_4 \cdot 3H_2O$ in 125 mL of solution; (c) 40.0 mL of 1.50 M HNO_3 diluted to 0.500 L.

13.16. What is the molarity of each of the following solutions: (a) 25.0 g MgI_2 in 0.200 L of solution; (b) 3.40 g $Cr(NO_3)_3 \cdot 9H_2O$ in 75.0 mL of solution; (c) 75.0 mL of 6.00 M H_2SO_4 diluted to 1.00 L?

13.17. Calculate the molality of each of the following solutions: (a) 13.0 g of benzene, C_6H_6, dissolved in 17.0 g of carbon tetrachloride, CCl_4; (b) 5.85 g NaCl dissolved in 0.250 L of water.

13.18. Calculate the molality of each of the following solutions: (a) 2.1 g of sulfur, S_8, dissolved in 95.0 g of naphthalene, $C_{10}H_8$; (b) 1.50 mol of NaCl dissolved in 15.0 mol water.

13.19. The density of acetonitrile, CH_3CN, is 0.786 g/mL, and the density of methanol, CH_3OH, is 0.791 g/mL. A solution is made by dissolving 20.0 mL CH_3OH in 100.0 mL CH_3CN. (a) What is the mole fraction of methanol in the solution? (b) What is the molality of the solution? (c) Assuming that the volumes are additive, what is the molarity of CH_3OH in the solution?

13.20. The density of toluene, C_7H_8, is 0.867 g/mL, and the density of thiophene, C_4H_4S, is 1.065 g/mL. A solution is made by dissolving 15.0 g of thiophene in 250.0 mL of toluene. (a) Calculate the mole fraction of thiophene in the solution. (b) Calculate the molality of thiophene in the solution. (c) Assuming that the volumes of the solute and solvent are additive, what is the molarity of thiophene in the solution?

13.21. A solution containing 66.0 g of acetone, C_3H_6O, and 46.0 g of H_2O has a density of 0.926 g/mL. Calculate (a) the mass percentage; (b) the mole fraction; (c) the molality; (d) the molarity of H_2O in this solution.

13.22. A sulfuric acid solution containing 571.6 g of H_2SO_4 per liter of solution has a density of 1.329 g/cm³. Calculate (a) the mass percentage; (b) the mole fraction; (c) the molality; (d) the molarity of H_2SO_4 in this solution.

13.23. Commercial concentrated nitric acid is 69 percent HNO_3 by mass and has a density of 1.42 g/mL. What is the molarity of this solution?

13.24. Commercial concentrated aqueous ammonia is 28 percent NH_3 by mass and has a density of 0.90 g/mL. What is the molarity of this solution?

13.25. Calculate the number of moles of solute present in each of the following solutions: (a) 214 mL of 0.122 M $MgCl_2$; (b) 3.50 μL of 2.00 M HCl; (c) 156 mL of 0.0455 M $(NH_4)_2CrO_4$.

13.26. Calculate the number of moles of solute present in each of the following solutions: (a) 60.0 g of an aqueous solution that is 1.25 percent KI by mass; (b) 250 g of an aqueous solution that is 0.460 percent NaCl by mass; (c) 0.600 L of 1.25 M H_2SO_4.

13.27. Describe how you would prepare each of the following aqueous solutions, starting with solid KBr: (a) 1.40 L of 1.5×10^{-2} M KBr; (b) 250 g of 0.400 m KBr; (c) 1.50 L of a solution that is 12.0 percent KBr by mass (the density of the solution is 1.10 g/mL); (d) a 0.200 M solution of KBr that contains just enough KBr to precipitate 21.0 g of AgBr from a solution containing 0.480 mol of $AgNO_3$.

13.28. Describe how you would prepare each of the following aqueous solutions: (a) 0.500 L of 0.200 M Na_2CO_3 solution, starting with solid Na_2CO_3; (b) 150 g of a solution that is 1.00 m in $(NH_4)_2SO_4$, starting with the solid solute; (c) 1.50 L of a solution that is 20.0 percent of $Pb(NO_3)_2$ by mass (the density of the solution is 1.20 g/mL), starting with solid solute; (d) a 0.50 M solution of HCl that would just neutralize 5.0 g of $Ba(OH)_2$, starting with 6.0 M HCl.

[13.29]. (a) In a certain reaction, Zn^{2+} is reduced to zinc metal. What is the normality of a solution that contains 4.50 g of ZnI_2 per 100.0 mL of solution? (b) What is the molarity of a 0.135 N solution of H_3PO_4 for an acid-base neutralization reaction in which two of the three hydrogen atoms of H_3PO_4 react?

[13.30]. (a) In a certain reaction, Sn^{2+} is oxidized to Sn^{4+}. How many equivalents are present in 10.0 mL of 0.0500 M $SnBr_2$ solution? (b) For the following net ionic reaction, calculate the normality of a solution containing 0.500 g $KMnO_4$ per 100.0 mL of solution:

$$8H^+(aq) + MnO_4^-(aq) + 5Fe^{2+}(aq) \longrightarrow Mn^{2+}(aq) + 5Fe^{3+}(aq) + 4H_2O(l)$$

Saturated Solutions: Factors Affecting Solubility

13.31. (a) What is meant by the term *saturated solution?* (b) What is meant by the term *supersaturated solution?* (c) How can supersaturated solutions be formed?

13.32. The solubility of sodium acetate, $NaC_2H_3O_2$, in water at $0°C$ is 119 g per 100 mL of H_2O. At $100°C$, the solubility of sodium acetate is 170 g per 100 mL of H_2O. A solution is made by adding 150 g sodium acetate to 100 mL of H_2O. (a) Would the solution be saturated at $0°C$? (b) Would the solution be saturated at $100°C$? (c) When the solution is carefully cooled from $100°C$ to $0°C$, crystallization does not occur. Explain what has happened.

13.33. By referring to Figure 13.15, determine whether the addition of 50 g of each of the following ionic solids to 100 g of water at $50°C$ will lead to a saturated solution: (a) $NaNO_3$; (b) KCl; (c) $K_2Cr_2O_7$; (d) $Pb(NO_3)_2$.

13.34. By referring to Figure 13.15, determine whether the addition of 20 g of each of the following ionic solids to 100 g of water at $20°C$ will lead to a saturated solution: (a) KNO_3; (b) $KClO_3$; (c) NaCl; (d) $Ce_2(SO_4)_3$.

13.35. How do the solubilities of most ionic compounds in water change with temperature? How about gases in water?

13.36. How do the solubilities of gases, liquids, and solids in water change with pressure? State Henry's law.

13.37. The Henry's law constant for helium gas in water at $30°C$ is 3.7×10^{-4} M/atm; that for N_2 at $30°C$ is 6.0×10^{-4} M/atm. If the two gases are each present at 2.5 atm pressure, calculate the solubility of each gas.

13.38. The partial pressure of O_2 in air at sea level is 0.21 atm. Using the data in Table 13.3, together with Henry's law, calculate the molar concentration of O_2 in the surface water of a lake saturated with air at $20°C$.

Colligative Properties

13.39. What characteristic of a solution determines its colligative properties?

13.40. Which of the following are colligative properties of solutions? (a) density; (b) vapor-pressure lowering; (c) osmotic pressure; (d) mass percentage of solute; (e) boiling-point elevation.

13.41. State Raoult's law and explain it on a molecular basis.

13.42. (a) What is an ideal solution? (b) Explain how you would determine whether a solution of known composition is ideal.

13.43. (a) Calculate the mass of ethylene glycol, $C_2H_6O_2$, that must be added to 1.00 kg of ethanol, C_2H_5OH, to reduce its vapor pressure by 8.1 torr at $35°C$. The vapor pressure of pure ethanol at $35°C$ is 1.00×10^2 torr. (b) Calculate the mass of KBr that must be added to 0.500 kg of water to reduce the vapor pressure by 6.50 torr at $50°C$. (Vapor-pressure data for water are given in Appendix B.)

13.44. Calculate the vapor pressure of water above a solution prepared by adding (a) 10.0 g of lactose, $C_{12}H_{22}O_{11}$, to 82.0 g of water at 338 K; (b) 5.00 g of sodium sulfate, Na_2SO_4, to 115 g of water at 338 K; (c) 32.5 g of glycerin, $C_3H_8O_3$, to 120 g of water at 338 K. (The vapor pressure of water is given in Appendix B.)

[13.45]. At $63.5°C$, the vapor pressure of H_2O is 175 torr, and that of ethanol, C_2H_5OH, is 400 torr. A solution is made by mixing equal masses of H_2O and C_2H_5OH. (a) What is the mole fraction of ethanol in the solution? (b) Assuming ideal-solution behavior, what is the vapor pressure of the solution at $63.5°C$? (c) What is the mole fraction of ethanol in the vapor above the solution?

[13.46]. At $20°C$ the vapor pressure of benzene, C_6H_6, is 75 torr, and that of toluene, C_7H_8, is 22 torr. Assume that benzene and toluene form an ideal solution. (a) What is the composition in mole fraction of a solution that has a vapor pressure of 40 torr at $20°C$? (b) What is the mole fraction of benzene in the vapor above the solution described in part (a)?

13.47. By using data from Table 13.5, calculate the freezing and boiling points of each of the following solutions: (a) 0.45 m ethylene glycol in ethanol; (b) 6.7 g of $C_{10}H_8$ in 150 g of chloroform; (c) 5.0 g CsI in 50.0 mL of water.

13.48. By using data from Table 13.5, calculate the freezing and boiling points of each of the following solutions: (a) 0.15 m glucose in ethanol; (b) 20.0 g $C_{12}H_{26}$ in 0.350 kg of CCl_4; (c) 2.75 g of $MgCl_2$ in 80.0 mL of water.

13.49. List the following aqueous solutions in order of increasing boiling point: 0.030 m glycerin; 0.020 m KBr; 0.030 m benzoic acid, $HC_7H_5O_2$.

13.50. List the following aqueous solutions in order of decreasing freezing point: 0.080 m glucose; 0.060 m LiBr; 0.030 m $Zn(NO_3)_2$.

13.51. An aqueous solution freezes at $-8.95°C$. What is the boiling point of the solution?

13.52. A solution made by adding a nonvolatile nonelectrolyte to carbon tetrachloride boils at $80.9°C$. What is the freezing point of the solution?

13.53. Urea, $(NH_2)_2CO$, is the product of protein metabolism in mammals. What is the osmotic pressure of an aqueous solution containing 1.10 g of urea in 100 mL of solution at $20°C$?

13.54. Seawater contains 3.4 g of salts for every liter of solution. Assuming that the solute consists entirely of NaCl (over 90 percent is), calculate the osmotic pressure of seawater at $20°C$.

13.55. Adrenaline is the hormone that triggers release of extra glucose molecules in times of stress or emergency. A solution of 0.64 g of adrenaline in 36.0 g at CCl_4 causes an elevation of $0.49°C$ in the boiling point. What is the molar mass of adrenaline?

13.56. Lauryl alcohol is obtained from coconut oil and is used to make detergents. A solution of 5.00 g of lauryl alcohol in 0.100 kg of benzene freezes at $4.1°C$. What is the molar mass of this substance?

13.57. Lysozyme is an enzyme that breaks bacterial cell walls. A solution containing 0.150 g of this enzyme in 210 mL of solution has an osmotic pressure of 0.953 torr at $25°C$. What is the molar mass of this substance?

13.58. A dilute sugar solution prepared by mixing 16.0 g of an unknown sugar with sufficient water to form 0.200 L of solution is found to have an osmotic pressure of 2.86 atm at $25°C$. What is the molar mass of this substance?

13.59. The osmotic pressure of a 0.010 M aqueous solution of $CaCl_2$ is found to be 0.674 atm at $25°C$. **(a)** Calculate the van't Hoff factor, i, for the solution. **(b)** How would you expect the value of i to change as the solution becomes more concentrated?

13.60. **(a)** Using data from Table 13.6, calculate the freezing points of 0.100 m NaCl and 0.100 m $MgSO_4$. **(b)** To what features of these compounds can you ascribe the difference in the values calculated in part (a)?

Colloids

13.61. Distinguish between solutions and colloids. Give an example of each.

13.62. Explain how observation of the passage of a beam of light through a liquid can be used to distinguish between a solution and a colloidal dispersion. Account for the different behavior in the two cases.

13.63. Indicate whether each of the following is a hydrophilic or a hydrophobic colloid: **(a)** butterfat in homogenized milk; **(b)** hemoglobin in blood; **(c)** vegetable oil in a salad dressing.

13.64. Explain how each of the following factors operates in determining the stability or instability of a colloidal dispersion: **(a)** particulate mass; **(b)** hydrophobic character; **(c)** charges on colloidal particles.

13.65. What are the usual reasons that colloid particles do not coalesce into larger particles upon collision? How can colloids be coagulated?

13.66. Explain the following observations: **(a)** Soaps (for example, sodium stearate) will stabilize a colloidal dispersion of oil in water; **(b)** milk curdles upon addition of acid.

Additional Exercises

13.67. The enthalpies of solution of hydrated salts are generally more positive than those of anhydrous materials. For example, ΔH of solution for KOH is -57.3 kJ/mol, and that for $KOH \cdot H_2O$ is -14.6 kJ/mol. Similarly, ΔH_{soln} for $NaClO_4$ is $+13.8$ kJ/mol, and that for $NaClO_4 \cdot H_2O$ is $+22.5$ kJ/mol. Explain this effect in terms of the enthalpy contributions to the solution process depicted in Figure 13.3.

13.68. Butylated hydroxytoluene (BHT) has the following molecular structure:

BHT

It is widely used as a preservative in a variety of foods, including dried cereals, cooking oils, and canned goods. The average person in the United States consumes about 2 mg of BHT daily. In terms of its structure, would you expect it to be readily excreted from the body or found stored in body fat? (Incidentally, BHT is not known to have any harmful properties; it is, in fact, a known antiviral agent.)

13.69. An aqueous solution is 10.0 percent NaCl by mass. The density of the solution is 1.071 g/mL. **(a)** What is the molality of the solution? **(b)** What is the molarity of the solution?

13.70. Acetonitrile, CH_3CN, is a polar organic solvent that dissolves a wide range of solutes, including many salts. The density of a 1.80 M acetonitrile solution of LiBr is 0.826 g/cm³. Calculate the concentration of the solution in **(a)** molality; **(b)** mole fraction of LiBr; **(c)** mass percentage of CH_3CN.

13.71. Copper(II) sulfate, $CuSO_4$, is commonly used to reduce the growth of algae in lakes, ponds, and water reservoirs. An aqueous solution of $CuSO_4$ that is 18.0 percent by mass has a density of 1.208 g/mL. Copper(II) sulfate is commonly available as the pentahydrate, $CuSO_4 \cdot 5H_2O$. What mass of this substance must be used to make up 8.00 L of a solution that is 18.0 percent by mass? What is the molarity of this solution?

13.72. A solution is made by dissolving 2.16 g of benzoic acid, $HC_7H_5O_2$, in 180 mL of CCl_4, density 1.59 g/mL.

Another solution is prepared by dissolving the same quantity of benzoic acid in 180 mL of C_2H_5OH, density 0.782 g/mL. (a) Calculate the mole fractions and molalities in each case. (b) Assuming that the density of the solution is the same as that of pure solvent, calculate the molarity in each case. (c) Compare the molarities and molalities of these solutions and comment on their relative magnitudes.

13.73. Sodium metal dissolves in liquid mercury to form a solution called a sodium amalgam. The densities of $Na(s)$ and $Hg(l)$ are 0.97 g/cm^3 and 13.6 g/cm^3, respectively. A sodium amalgam is made by dissolving 1.0 cm^3 $Na(s)$ in 20.0 cm^3 $Hg(l)$. Assume that the final volume of the solution is 21.0 cm^3. (a) Calculate the molality of Na in the solution. (b) Calculate the molarity of Na in the solution. (c) For dilute aqueous solutions, the molality and molarity are generally near equal in value. Is that the case for the sodium amalgam described here? Explain.

13.74. A saturated solution of sucrose, $C_{12}H_{22}O_{11}$, is made by dissolving excess table sugar in a flask of water. There are 50 g of undissolved sucrose crystals at the bottom of the flask, in contact with the saturated solution. The flask is stoppered and set aside. A year later, a single large crystal of mass 50 g is at the bottom of the flask. Explain how this experiment provides evidence for a dynamic equilibrium between the saturated solution and the undissolved solute.

13.75. The solubility of samarium(III) chloride, $SmCl_3$, in water is 92.4 g per 100 mL H_2O at 10°C. A solution is made by adding 500 g $SmCl_3$ to 500 mL H_2O at 10°C. (a) Will the solution be saturated? (b) What is the molality of the solution?

[13.76]. Fluorocarbons (compounds that contain both carbon and fluorine) are commonly used as refrigerants. The compounds listed below are all gases at 25°C, and their solubilities in water at 25°C and 1 atm fluorocarbon pressure are given as mass percentages:

Fluorocarbon	Solubility (mass %)
CF_4	0.0015
$CClF_3$	0.009
CCl_2F_2	0.028
$CHClF_2$	0.30

(a) For each fluorocarbon, calculate the molality of a saturated solution. (b) Explain why the molarity of each of the solutions should be very close numerically to the molality. (c) Based on their molecular structures, account for the differences in the solubility of the four fluorocarbons. (d) Calculate the Henry's law constant at 25°C for $CHClF_2$ and compare its magnitude to that for N_2 (6.8 × 10⁻⁴ mol/L-atm). Can you account for the difference in magnitude?

13.77. Concern has grown in many parts of the United States regarding a possible health hazard arising from the presence of the radioactive gas radon (Rn) in well water obtained from aquifers that lie in rock deposits. A sample consisting of various gases contains 3.5 × 10⁻⁶ mole fraction of radon. This gas at a total pressure of 36 atm is shaken with water at 30°C. Assume that the solubility of radon in water with 1 atm pressure of the gas over the solution at 30°C is 7.27 × 10⁻³ M. Calculate the molar concentration of radon in the water.

13.78. Explain why deep-sea divers breathe a mixture of helium and oxygen rather than a mixture of nitrogen and oxygen during dives.

13.79. A "canned heat" product used to warm chafing dishes consists of a homogeneous mixture of ethyl alcohol, C_2H_5OH, and paraffin that has an average formula $C_{24}H_{50}$. What mass of C_2H_5OH should be added to 620 kg of the paraffin in formulating the mixture if the vapor pressure of ethyl alcohol at 35°C over the mixture is to be 8 torr? The vapor pressure of pure ethyl alcohol at 35°C is 100 torr.

[13.80]. The cooling system of an automobile is filled with a solution formed by mixing equal volumes of water (density = 1.00 g/mL) and ethylene glycol, $C_2H_6O_2$ (density = 1.12 g/mL). Estimate the freezing point and boiling point of the mixture.

13.81. Calculate the freezing point of a 0.100 m solution of K_2SO_4 (a) ignoring interionic attractions; (b) taking interionic attractions into consideration.

13.82. When 10.0 g of mercuric nitrate, $Hg(NO_3)_2$, is dissolved in 1.00 kg of water, the freezing point of the solution is −0.172°C. When 10.0 g of mercuric chloride, $HgCl_2$, is dissolved in 1.00 kg of water, the solution freezes at −0.0685°C. Use these data to determine which is the stronger electrolyte, $Hg(NO_3)_2$ or $HgCl_2$.

[13.83]. A 0.0200 m solution of hydrofluoric acid freezes at −0.043°C. Calculate the percentage ionization of this weak acid.

[13.84]. Carbon disulfide, CS_2, boils at 46.30°C and has a density of 1.261 g/mL. (a) When 0.250 mol of a nondissociating solute is dissolved in 400.0 mL of CS_2, the solution boils at 47.46°C. What is the molal boiling-point-elevation constant for CS_2? (b) When 5.39 g of a nondissociating unknown is dissolved in 50.0 mL of CS_2, the solution boils at 47.08°C. What is the molecular weight of the unknown?

[13.85]. At 35°C the vapor pressure of acetone, $(CH_3)_2CO$, is 360 torr, and that of chloroform, $CHCl_3$, is 300 torr. Acetone and chloroform can form weak hydrogen bonds between one another as shown below.

A solution composed of an equal number of moles of acetone and chloroform has a vapor pressure of 250 torr at 35°C. (a) What would be the vapor pressure of the solution if it exhibited ideal behavior? (b) Use the existence of hydrogen bonds between acetone and chloroform molecules to explain the deviation from ideal behavior. (c) Based on the behavior of the solution, predict whether the mixing of acetone and chloroform is an exothermic ($\Delta H_{soln} < 0$) or endothermic ($\Delta H_{soln} > 0$) process.

[13.86]. A mixture of solid NaCl and solid sucrose, $C_{12}H_{22}O_{11}$, has an unknown composition. When 15.0 g of the mixture is dissolved in enough water to make 500 mL of solution, the solution exhibits an osmotic pressure of 6.41 atm at 25°C. Determine the mass percentage of NaCl in the mixture.

[13.87]. A lithium salt used in lubricating grease has the formula $LiC_nH_{2n-1}O_2$. The salt is soluble in water to the extent of 0.036 g per 100 g of water at 25°C. The osmotic pressure of this solution is found to be 57.1 torr. Assuming that molality and molarity in such a dilute solution are the same and that the lithium salt is completely dissociated in the solution, determine an appropriate value of n in the formula for the salt.

[13.88]. In the bell jar experiment shown in Figure 13.17, 20.0 mL of a 0.050 M aqueous solution of a nonvolatile nonelectrolyte is placed in the left beaker, and 20 mL of a 0.030 M aqueous solution of NaCl is placed in the right beaker. What are the volumes in the two beakers when equilibrium is attained?

Chemical Kinetics 14

When heated in air, steel wool does not burn. It burns vigorously, however, forming Fe_2O_3 when heated and then placed in pure oxygen, as shown here. The different behaviors in air and pure oxygen are due to the different concentrations of O_2 in the two environments. The concentrations of reactants influence reaction rates.

Chemistry is by its very nature concerned with change. Substances with well-defined properties are converted by chemical reactions into other materials with different properties. Chemists want to know which new substances are formed from a given set of starting reactants. However, it is equally important to know how rapidly chemical reactions occur and to understand the factors that control their speeds. For example, what factors are important in determining how rapidly foods spoil? What determines the rate at which steel rusts? How do you design a rapidly setting material for dental fillings? Which biochemical reaction rates determine the contraction and relaxation of smooth muscle in the arteries of the heart? Which factors control the rate at which fuel burns in an auto engine?

The area of chemistry concerned with the speeds, or rates, at which reactions occur is called **chemical kinetics.** In this chapter, we shall learn how to express and determine the rates at which reactions occur. We shall see that the rates of chemical reactions are affected by several factors, most notably:

1. *The concentrations of the reactants:* Most chemical reactions proceed faster if the concentration of one or more of the reactants is increased. For example, steel wool burns with difficulty in air, which contains 20 percent O_2, but bursts into a brilliant white flame in pure oxygen, as shown in the chapter-opening photograph.

2. *The temperature at which the reaction occurs:* The rates of chemical reactions increase as temperature is increased. It is for this reason that we refrigerate perishable foods such as milk. The bacterial reactions that lead to the spoiling of milk proceed much more rapidly at room temperature than they do at the lower temperatures of a refrigerator.

3. *The presence of a catalyst:* The rates of many reactions can be increased by adding a substance known as a *catalyst.* We will see that a catalyst increases the rate of a reaction without being consumed in the reaction. The physiology of most living species depends crucially on *enzymes,* protein molecules that act as catalysts, increasing the rates of selected biochemical reactions.

4. *The surface area of solid or liquid reactants or catalysts:* Reactions that involve solids often proceed faster as the surface area of the solid is increased. For example, a medicine in the form of a tablet will dissolve in the stomach and enter the bloodstream more slowly than the same medicine in the form of a fine powder.

We shall consider all the above factors as we proceed through this chapter. We shall also consider what chemical kinetics can teach us about how chemical reactions occur at the molecular level.

14.1 Reaction Rates

The speed of any event is measured by the change that occurs in a given interval of time. For example, the speed of an automobile is expressed in terms of a change in position in a certain amount of time; the units we use to measure this speed are usually miles per hour (mi/hr). Similarly, the speed of a reaction, or the **reaction rate,** is expressed as the change in concentration of a reactant or product in a certain amount of time. The units of reaction rates are usually

Teaching Note: As will be discussed, chemical reactions occur at all temperatures but are faster at higher temperature.

Learning Goal 1: Express the rate of a given reaction in terms of the variation in concentration of a reactant or product substance with time.

488   Chapter 14   Chemical Kinetics

molarity per second (M/s). As an example, consider the reaction that occurs when butyl chloride, C_4H_9Cl, is placed in water. The resulting reaction produces butyl alcohol, C_4H_9OH, and hydrochloric acid:

$$C_4H_9Cl(l) + H_2O(l) \longrightarrow C_4H_9OH(aq) + HCl(aq) \qquad [14.1]$$

Point of Emphasis: For slow reactions, time is often expressed in minutes or hours.

Suppose that we prepare a 0.1000 M solution of C_4H_9Cl in water and then measure the concentration of C_4H_9Cl at various times after the solution is prepared. Because C_4H_9Cl is consumed during the reaction, its concentration decreases with time, as shown in the first two columns of Table 14.1. The average rate of the reaction over any time interval is equal to the decrease in the concentration of C_4H_9Cl divided by the time in which that change occurs:

Learning Goal 2: Calculate the average rate over an interval of time, given the concentrations of a reactant or product at the beginning and end of that interval.

$$\text{Average rate} = \frac{\text{decrease in concentration of } C_4H_9Cl}{\text{length of time interval}}$$

$$= -\frac{\Delta[C_4H_9Cl]}{\Delta t} \qquad [14.2]$$

As noted in Section 5.2, the Greek letter delta, Δ, is read "change in"; thus, Δt is the change in time between the beginning and end of the interval:

Point of Emphasis: The negative sign in Equation 14.2 denotes *loss* of the reactant.

$$\Delta t = (\text{time at end of interval}) - (\text{time at beginning of interval})$$
$$= (\text{final time}) - (\text{initial time})$$

Teaching Note: The term *change in* a quantity always refers to the final value minus the initial value.

The brackets around C_4H_9Cl in Equation 14.2 indicate the concentration of the substance. Thus, $\Delta[C_4H_9Cl]$ is the change in the concentration of C_4H_9Cl during the time interval:

Teaching Note: Square brackets denote the concentration of the species within the brackets, e.g. [A] is read: "the concentration of A."

$$\Delta[C_4H_9Cl] = [C_4H_9Cl]_{\text{final time}} - [C_4H_9Cl]_{\text{initial time}}$$

The subscripts on $[C_4H_9Cl]$ indicate when the concentrations were measured.

Because $[C_4H_9Cl]$ decreases as the reaction proceeds, $\Delta[C_4H_9Cl]$ is negative. The negative sign in Equation 14.2 makes the average rate a positive quantity; reaction rates are always positive quantities. We call $-\Delta[C_4H_9Cl]/\Delta t$ the *rate of disappearance* of C_4H_9Cl.

Lee R. Summerlin and James L. Ealy, Jr., "The Old Nassau Clock Reaction," *Chemical Demonstrations, A Sourcebook for Teachers* (Washington: American Chemical Society, 1985), p. 77.

TABLE 14.1 △ **Rate Data for Reaction of C_4H_9Cl with Water**

Time (s)	$[C_4H_9Cl]$ (M)	Average rate (M/s)
0.0	0.1000	
50.0	0.0905	1.90×10^{-4}
100.0	0.0820	1.70×10^{-4}
150.0	0.0741	1.58×10^{-4}
200.0	0.0671	1.40×10^{-4}
300.0	0.0549	1.22×10^{-4}
400.0	0.0448	1.01×10^{-4}
500.0	0.0368	0.80×10^{-4}
800.0	0.0200	0.56×10^{-4}
10,000	0	

FIGURE 14.1 Concentration of butyl chloride, C_4H_9Cl, as a function of time. The dots represent the experimental data from the first two columns of Table 14.1; the colored line is the smooth curve drawn to connect the data points. The reaction rate at any time is given by the slope of the tangent to the curve at that time. The slope of the tangent is defined as the vertical change divided by the horizontal change in the tangent, that is, $\Delta[C_4H_9Cl]/\Delta t$. Tangents have been drawn that touch the curve at $t = 0$ and $t = 600$ s. The calculation of the slope at $t = 600$ s is performed in the body of the text. The slope at $t = 0$ is calculated in Sample Exercise 14.1.

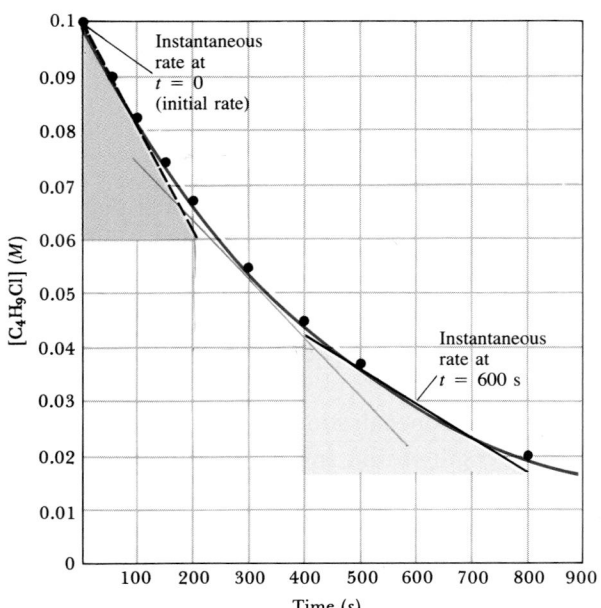

Figure 14.1

We can use the data in the first two columns of Table 14.1 to calculate the average rate of disappearance of C_4H_9Cl for the various time intervals. For example, from $t = 0.0$ s to $t = 50.0$ s, $[C_4H_9Cl]$ decreases from 0.1000 M to 0.0905 M. Therefore, the average rate over this 50.0-s interval is

$$\text{Average rate} = -\frac{[C_4H_9Cl]_{t=50.0\,s} - [C_4H_9Cl]_{t=0.0\,s}}{50.0\,s - 0.0\,s}$$

$$= -\frac{(0.0905 - 0.1000)\,M}{(50.0 - 0.0)\,s} = 1.90 \times 10^{-4}\,M/s$$

The calculated average rate for each time interval is shown in the third column of Table 14.1. Notice that the average rate steadily decreases as the reaction proceeds. At some point, the reaction essentially stops; there is no longer any change in concentration with time.

We can also see this decrease in rate if we display the data graphically, as in Figure 14.1. The dots represent the experimental data from the first two columns of Table 14.1. Using this curve we can determine the **instantaneous rate;** this is the rate at a particular time as opposed to the average rate over an interval of time. The instantaneous rate is obtained from the straight-line tangent that touches the curve at the point of interest. We have drawn two such tangents in Figure 14.1, one at $t = 0$ and the other at $t = 600$ s. The slopes of these tangents give the instantaneous rates at these times.* For example, at 600 s we have

$$\text{Instantaneous rate} = -\frac{(0.017 - 0.042)\,M}{(800 - 400)\,s} = 6.2 \times 10^{-5}\,M/s$$

We will usually refer to the instantaneous rate merely as the rate.

---

* You may wish to review briefly the idea of graphical determination of slopes by referring to Appendix A. If you are familiar with calculus, you may recognize that the average rate approaches the instantaneous rate as the time interval approaches zero. This limit, in the notation of calculus, is represented as $-d[C_4H_9Cl]/dt$.

SAMPLE EXERCISE 14.1

(a) Using the data in Table 14.1, calculate the average rate of disappearance of C_4H_9Cl over the time interval from 50.0 to 150.0 s. (b) Using Figure 14.1, estimate the instantaneous rate of disappearance of C_4H_9Cl at $t = 0$ (the initial rate).

SOLUTION (a) Using data from Table 14.1, we have

$$\text{Average rate} = -\frac{\Delta[C_4H_9Cl]}{\Delta t}$$

$$= -\frac{(0.0741 - 0.0905)\ M}{(150.0 - 50.0)\ s} = 1.64 \times 10^{-4}\ M/s$$

(b) The initial rate is given by the slope of the dashed line in Figure 14.1. The slope of a straight line is given by the change in the vertical axis divided by the corresponding change in the horizontal axis. The straight line falls from $[C_4H_9Cl] = 0.100$ to $0.060\ M$ in the time change from 0 to 200 s. Thus, the instantaneous rate is

$$\text{Rate} = -\frac{(0.060 - 0.100)\ M}{(200 - 0)\ s} = 2.0 \times 10^{-4}\ M/s$$

PRACTICE EXERCISE

Using Figure 14.1, estimate the instantaneous rate of disappearance of C_4H_9Cl at $t = 300$ s.   *Answer:* $1.1 \times 10^{-4}\ M/s$

Reaction Rates and Stoichiometry

In the reaction of butyl chloride with water, Equation 14.1, we expressed the rate in terms of the change in the concentration of C_4H_9Cl. We could equally well have expressed the rate in terms of the change in the concentration of C_4H_9OH. Because C_4H_9OH is a product of the reaction, its concentration increases with time. The quantity $\Delta[C_4H_9OH]/\Delta t$, which we call the *rate of appearance* of C_4H_9OH, is therefore positive. According to the chemical equation for the reaction, one mole of C_4H_9OH is produced for each mole of C_4H_9Cl consumed. Thus, the rate of appearance of C_4H_9OH equals the rate of disappearance of C_4H_9Cl:

$$\text{Rate} = -\frac{\Delta[C_4H_9Cl]}{\Delta t} = \frac{\Delta[C_4H_9OH]}{\Delta t}$$

We can always express the rate of a reaction in terms of the disappearance of any reactant or the appearance of any product. In general, the stoichiometry of the reaction tells us the relationship between these. For example, in the reaction

$$2HI(g) \longrightarrow H_2(g) + I_2(g)$$

we can measure the rate of disappearance of HI or the rate of appearance of either H_2 or I_2. Because 2 mol of HI disappear for each mole of H_2 or I_2 that forms, the rate of disappearance of HI is twice the rate of appearance of H_2 or I_2. To equate the rates we must therefore divide the rate of disappearance of HI by 2 (its coefficient in the balanced chemical equation):

$$\text{Rate} = -\frac{1}{2}\frac{\Delta[HI]}{\Delta t} = \frac{\Delta[H_2]}{\Delta t} = \frac{\Delta[I_2]}{\Delta t}$$

In general, for the reaction

$$aA + bB \longrightarrow cC + dD$$

the rate is given by

$$\text{Rate} = -\frac{1}{a}\frac{\Delta[A]}{\Delta t} = -\frac{1}{b}\frac{\Delta[B]}{\Delta t} = \frac{1}{c}\frac{\Delta[C]}{\Delta t} = \frac{1}{d}\frac{\Delta[D]}{\Delta t} \qquad [14.3]$$

When we speak of the rate of a reaction without specifying a particular reactant or product, we will mean it in this sense.*

SAMPLE EXERCISE 14.2

(a) How is the rate of disappearance of ozone related to the rate of appearance of oxygen in the following equation: $2O_3(g) \rightarrow 3O_2(g)$? (b) If the rate of appearance of O_2, $\Delta[O_2]/\Delta t$, is 6.0×10^{-5} M/s at a particular instant, what is the value of the rate of disappearance of O_3, $-\Delta[O_3]/\Delta t$, at this same time?

SOLUTION (a) Using the coefficients in the balanced equation, we have

$$\text{Rate} = -\frac{1}{2}\frac{\Delta[O_3]}{\Delta t} = \frac{1}{3}\frac{\Delta[O_2]}{\Delta t}$$

(b) Using the relationship from part (a), we have

$$-\frac{\Delta[O_3]}{\Delta t} = \frac{2}{3}\frac{\Delta[O_2]}{\Delta t} = \frac{2}{3}(6.0 \times 10^{-5} \ M/s) = 4.0 \times 10^{-5} \ M/s$$

PRACTICE EXERCISE

The decomposition of N_2O_5 proceeds according to the equation

$$2N_2O_5(g) \longrightarrow 4NO_2(g) + O_2(g)$$

If the rate of decomposition of N_2O_5 at a particular instant in a reaction vessel is 4.2×10^{-7} M/s, what is the rate of appearance of (a) NO_2; (b) O_2? *Answers:* (a) 8.4×10^{-7} M/s; (b) 2.1×10^{-7} M/s

14.2 The Dependence of Rate on Concentration

The decreasing rate of reaction with passing time that is evident in Figure 14.1 is quite typical of reactions. Reaction rates diminish as the concentrations of reactants diminish. Conversely, rates generally increase when reactant concentrations are increased.

One way of studying the effect of concentration on reaction rate is to determine the way in which the rate at the beginning of a reaction depends on the starting concentrations. To illustrate this approach, consider the following reaction:

$$NH_4^+(aq) + NO_2^-(aq) \longrightarrow N_2(g) + 2H_2O(l)$$

---

* Equation 14.3 does not hold true if substances other than C and D are formed in significant amounts during the course of the reaction. For example, sometimes intermediate substances build in concentration before forming the final products. In that case, the relationship between the rate of disappearance of reactants and the rate of appearance of products will not be given by Equation 14.3. All reactions whose rates we consider in this chapter obey Equation 14.3.

We might study the rate of this reaction by measuring the concentration of NH_4^+ or NO_2^- as a function of time or by measuring the volume of N_2 collected. Because of the 1 : 1 stoichiometry of the reaction, all of these rates will be equal.

Once we determine the initial reaction rate (the instantaneous rate at $t = 0$) for various starting concentrations of NH_4^+ and NO_2^-, we can tabulate the data as shown in Table 14.2. These data indicate that changing either $[NH_4^+]$ or $[NO_2^-]$ changes the reaction rate. Notice that if we double $[NH_4^+]$ while holding $[NO_2^-]$ constant, the rate doubles (compare experiments 1 and 2). If $[NH_4^+]$ is increased by a factor of 4 (compare experiments 1 and 3), the rate changes by a factor of 4, and so forth. These results indicate that the rate is proportional to $[NH_4^+]$ raised to the first power. When $[NO_2^-]$ is similarly varied while $[NH_4^+]$ is held constant, the rate is affected in the same manner. We conclude that the rate is also directly proportional to the concentration of NO_2^-. We can express the overall concentration dependence as follows:

$$\text{Rate} = k[NH_4^+][NO_2^-] \qquad [14.4]$$

Teaching Note: Equation 14.4 follows from the original observation that the rate $\propto$ $[NH_4^+][NO_2^-]$.

Learning Goal 4: Explain the meaning of the term *rate constant,* and state the units associated with rate constants.

Such an expression, which shows how the rate depends on the concentrations of reactants, is called a **rate law.** The constant, k, in the rate law is called the **rate constant.**

If we know the rate law for a reaction and its rate for a set of reactant concentrations, we can calculate the value of the rate constant, k. For example, using the data in Table 14.2 and the results from experiment 1, we can substitute into Equation 14.4:

$$5.4 \times 10^{-7}\ M/s = k(0.0100\ M)(0.200\ M)$$

Solving for k gives

$$k = \frac{5.4 \times 10^{-7}\ M/s}{(0.0100\ M)(0.200\ M)} = 2.7 \times 10^{-4}\ M^{-1}\ s^{-1}$$

You may wish to satisfy yourself that this same value of k is obtained using any of the other experimental results given in Table 14.2.

Once we have both the rate law and the value of the rate constant for a reaction, we can calculate the rate of reaction for any set of concentrations. For

TABLE 14.2 △ Rate Data for the Reaction of Ammonium and Nitrite Ions in Water at 25°C

Experiment number	Initial NH_4^+ concentration (M)	Initial NO_2^- concentration (M)	Observed initial rate (M/s)
1	0.0100	0.200	5.4×10^{-7}
2	0.0200	0.200	10.8×10^{-7}
3	0.0400	0.200	21.5×10^{-7}
4	0.0600	0.200	32.3×10^{-7}
5	0.200	0.0202	10.8×10^{-7}
6	0.200	0.0404	21.6×10^{-7}
7	0.200	0.0606	32.4×10^{-7}
8	0.200	0.0808	43.3×10^{-7}

example, using the rate law in Equation 14.4, and $k = 2.7 \times 10^{-4} \, M^{-1} \, s^{-1}$, we can calculate the rate for $[NH_4^+] = 0.100 \, M$ and $[NO_2^-] = 0.100 \, M$:

$$\text{Rate} = (2.7 \times 10^{-4} \, M^{-1} \, s^{-1})(0.100 \, M)(0.100 \, M) = 2.7 \times 10^{-6} \, M/s$$

Note that if the concentration of either NH_4^+ or NO_2^- were doubled, the rate of production of N_2 and H_2O likewise would double.

Reaction Order

The rate laws for most reactions have the general form

$$\text{Rate} = k[\text{reactant 1}]^m[\text{reactant 2}]^n \; . \; . \; . \qquad\qquad [14.5]$$

The exponents m and n in Equation 14.5 are called **reaction orders,** and their sum is the **overall reaction order.** For example, the rate law for the reaction of NH_4^+ with NO_2^- (Equation 14.4) contains the concentration of NH_4^+ raised to the first power. Thus, the reaction order in NH_4^+ is 1; the reaction is *first order* in NH_4^+. It is also first order in NO_2^-. The overall reaction order is $1 + 1 = 2$; we say the reaction is *second order overall.*

The following are some further examples of rate laws:

Point of Emphasis: The coefficients of the balanced chemical equation do not necessarily correspond to the reaction orders in the rate law.

Teaching Note: Some reactions show a negative or fractional dependence on reactant concentrations. Some even show a dependence on the concentration of accumulating products.

$$2N_2O_5(g) \longrightarrow 4NO_2(g) + O_2(g) \qquad \text{Rate} = k[N_2O_5] \qquad [14.6]$$
$$CHCl_3(g) + Cl_2(g) \longrightarrow CCl_4(g) + HCl(g) \qquad \text{Rate} = k[CHCl_3][Cl_2]^{1/2} \quad [14.7]$$
$$H_2(g) + I_2(g) \longrightarrow 2HI(g) \qquad\qquad\qquad \text{Rate} = k[H_2][I_2] \qquad [14.8]$$

Notice that the reaction orders do not necessarily correspond to the coefficients in the balanced chemical equation. *The values of these exponents are determined experimentally.* In most rate laws, reaction orders are 0, 1, or 2. However, we also occasionally encounter rate laws in which the reaction order is fractional (such as Equation 14.7) or even negative.

Units of Rate Constants

The units of the rate constant depend on the overall reaction order of the rate law. For example, in a reaction that is second order overall, the units of the rate constant must satisfy

$$\text{Units of rate} = (\text{units of rate constant})(\text{units of concentration})^2$$

Hence, in our usual units of concentration and time,

Teaching Note: Sometimes molarity (M) is written as mol/L. Thus $M^{-1}s^{-1} \equiv L/$mol-s.

$$\text{Units of rate constant} = \frac{\text{units of rate}}{(\text{units of concentration})^2} = \frac{M/s}{M^2} = M^{-1} \, s^{-1}.$$

SAMPLE EXERCISE 14.3

(a) What are the overall reaction orders for the reactions described in Equations 14.6 and 14.7? **(b)** What are the usual units of the rate constant for the rate law for Equation 14.6?

SOLUTION **(a)** The overall reaction order is the sum of the powers to which all the concentrations of reactants are raised in the rate law. The reaction in Equation 14.6 is first order in N_2O_5 and first order overall. The reaction in Equation 14.7 is first order in $CHCl_3$ and one-half order in Cl_2. The overall reaction order is three-halves.

(b) For the rate law for Equation 14.6, we have

Units of rate = (units of rate constant)(units of concentration)

So

$$\text{Units of rate constant} = \frac{\text{units of rate}}{\text{units of concentration}} = \frac{M/s}{M} = s^{-1}.$$

Notice that the units of the rate constant for the first-order reaction are different from those for the second-order reaction discussed in the text above.

PRACTICE EXERCISE

(a) What is the reaction order of the reactant H_2 in Equation 14.8? **(b)** What are the units of the rate constant for Equation 14.7?   *Answers:* **(a)** 1; **(b)** $M^{-1/2} s^{-1}$

Using Initial Rates to Determine Rate Laws

The rate law for any chemical reaction must be determined experimentally; it cannot be predicted by merely looking at the chemical equation. We often determine the rate law for a reaction by the same method we applied to the data in Table 14.2: We observe the effect of changing the initial concentrations of the reactants on the initial rate of the reaction. If a reaction is zero order in a particular reactant, changing its concentration will have no influence on rate (as long as some of the reactant is present). If the reaction is first order in a reactant, changes in the concentration of that substance will produce proportional changes in the rate. Thus, doubling the concentration will double the rate, and so forth. When the rate law is second order in a particular reactant, doubling its concentration increases the rate by a factor of $2^2 = 4$, tripling its concentration causes the rate to increase by a factor of $3^2 = 9$, and so forth.

   In working with rate laws, be careful not to confuse the rate constant for a reaction with the reaction rate. The rate of a reaction depends on the concentrations of reactants; the rate constant does not. As we shall see later in this chapter, the rate constant and consequently the reaction rate are affected by temperature and the presence of a catalyst.

Learning Goal 5:   Determine the rate law from experimental results that show how concentration affects rate.

Learning Goal 6:   Calculate rate, rate constants, or reactant concentration, given two of these together with the rate law.

SAMPLE EXERCISE 14.4

The initial rate of a reaction $A + B \longrightarrow C$ was measured for several different starting concentrations of A and B, with the results given below:

Experiment number	[A] (M)	[B] (M)	Initial rate (M/s)
1	0.100	0.100	4.0×10^{-5}
2	0.100	0.200	4.0×10^{-5}
3	0.200	0.100	16.0×10^{-5}

Using these data, determine **(a)** the rate law for the reaction; **(b)** the magnitude of the rate constant; **(c)** the rate of the reaction when [A] = 0.050 M and [B] = 0.100 M.

SOLUTION   (a) We may assume that the rate law has the following form: Rate = $k[A]^m[B]^n$. Our task is to deduce the values of m and n. Notice that when [A] is held constant and [B] is doubled, the rate remains the same (compare experiments 1 and 2). We conclude that the concentration of B has no influence on the reaction rate. The rate law is therefore zero order in B. Experiments 1 and 3 indicate that doubling

[A] increases the rate fourfold. This result indicates that rate is proportional to $[A]^2$; the reaction is second order in A. The rate law is

$$\text{Rate} = k[A]^2[B]^0 = k[A]^2$$

This same conclusion could be reached in a more formal way by taking the ratio of the rates from two experiments:

$$\frac{\text{Rate 2}}{\text{Rate 1}} = \frac{4.0 \times 10^{-5}\ M/s}{4.0 \times 10^{-5}\ M/s} = 1$$

Using the rate law, then, we have

$$1 = \frac{\text{rate 2}}{\text{rate 1}} = \frac{k[0.100\ M]^m[0.200\ M]^n}{k[0.100\ M]^m[0.100\ M]^n} = \frac{[0.200]^n}{[0.100]^n} = 2^n$$

But 2^n equals 1 only if $n = 0$. We can deduce the value of m in a similar fashion:

$$\frac{\text{Rate 3}}{\text{Rate 1}} = \frac{16.0 \times 10^{-5}\ M/s}{4.0 \times 10^{-5}\ M/s} = 4$$

Using the rate law gives

$$4 = \frac{\text{rate 3}}{\text{rate 1}} = \frac{k[0.200\ M]^m[0.100\ M]^n}{k[0.100\ M]^m[0.100\ M]^n} = \frac{[0.200]^m}{[0.100]^m} = 2^m$$

The fact that $2^m = 4$ indicates that $m = 2$.

(b) Using the rate law and the data from experiment 1, we have

$$k = \frac{\text{rate}}{[A]^2} = \frac{4.0 \times 10^{-5}\ M/s}{(0.100\ M)^2} = 4.0 \times 10^{-3}\ M^{-1}\ s^{-1}$$

(c) Using the rate law from part (a) and the rate constant from part (b), we have

$$\text{Rate} = k[A]^2 = (4.0 \times 10^{-3}\ M^{-1}\ s^{-1})(0.050\ M)^2 = 1.0 \times 10^{-5}\ M/s$$

Because [B] is not part of the rate law, it is immaterial to the rate, provided that there is at least some B present to react with A.

PRACTICE EXERCISE

A particular reaction was found to depend on the concentration of the hydrogen ion, $[H^+]$. The initial rates varied as a function of $[H^+]$ as follows:

$[H^+]$ (M)	0.0500	0.100	0.200
Initial rate (M/s)	6.4×10^{-7}	3.2×10^{-7}	1.6×10^{-7}

(a) What is the order of the reaction in $[H^+]$? **(b)** Predict the initial reaction rate when $[H^+] = 0.400\ M$.   *Answers:* **(a)** -1 (the rate is *inversely* proportional to $[H^+]$); **(b)** $0.8 \times 10^{-7}\ M/s$

14.3 Change of Concentration with Time

A rate law tells us how the rate of a reaction changes at a particular temperature as we change reactant concentrations. Rate laws can be converted into equations that tell us what the concentrations of the reactants or products are at any time during the course of a reaction. The mathematics required involves calculus. We don't expect you to be able to perform the calculus operations; however, you should be able to use the resulting equations. We shall apply this conversion to two of the simplest rate laws — those that are first order overall and those that are second order overall.

First-Order Reactions

A **first-order reaction** is one whose rate depends on the concentration of a single reactant raised to the first power. For a reaction of the sort A $\longrightarrow$ products, the rate law is

$$\text{Rate} = -\frac{\Delta[A]}{\Delta t} = k[A]$$

Using calculus, this equation can be transformed into an equation that relates the concentration of A at the start of the reaction, $[A]_0$, to its concentration at any other time t, $[A]_t$:

$$\ln[A]_t - \ln[A]_0 = -kt \quad \text{or} \quad \ln\frac{[A]_t}{[A]_0} = -kt \qquad [14.9]$$

The function "ln" is the natural logarithm (Appendix A.2).*
    Equation 14.9 can be rearranged:

$$\ln[A]_t = -kt + \ln[A]_0 \qquad [14.10]$$

This equation has the form of the general equation for a straight line, $y = mx + b$, in which m is the slope and b is the y-intercept of the line (see Appendix A.4):

$$\ln [A]_t = -k \cdot t + \ln[A]_0$$
$$\quad\quad\downarrow \quad\quad\quad \downarrow \quad\downarrow \quad\quad\quad \downarrow$$
$$\quad y \quad = \quad m \,\cdot x + \quad b$$

Thus, for a first-order reaction, a graph of $\ln [A]_t$ versus time gives a straight line with a slope of $-k$ and a y-intercept of $\ln [A]_0$.
    The conversion of methyl isonitrile to acetonitrile is an example of a first-order reaction:

$$H_3C-N\equiv C: \quad \longrightarrow \quad H_3C-C\equiv N: \qquad [14.11]$$
$$\text{Methyl isonitrile} \qquad\qquad\quad \text{Acetonitrile}$$

Figure 14.2(a) shows how the pressure of methyl isonitrile varies with time as it rearranges in the gas phase at 198.9°C. We can use pressure as a unit of concentration for a gas because, from the ideal-gas law, the number of moles per unit volume is directly proportional to pressure. Figure 14.2(b) shows a plot of the natural logarithm of the pressure versus time, a plot that yields a straight line. The slope of this line is $-5.11 \times 10^{-5}\,s^{-1}$. (You should verify this for yourself, remembering that your result may vary slightly from ours because of inaccuracies associated with reading the graph.) Because the slope of the line equals $-k$, we see that the rate constant for this reaction equals $5.11 \times 10^{-5}\,s^{-1}$.

---

* In terms of base-10 or common logarithms, Equation 14.9 can be written as

$$\log[A]_t - \log[A]_0 = -\frac{kt}{2.30} \quad \text{or} \quad \log\frac{[A]_t}{[A]_0} = -\frac{kt}{2.30}$$

The factor 2.30 arises from the conversion of natural logarithms to base-10 logarithms.

Learning Goal 7: Use the equations

$$\ln[A]_t = -kt + \ln[A]_0$$
$$\ln\left(\frac{[A]_0}{[A]_t}\right) = kt$$

to determine (a) the concentration of a reactant or product at any time after a reaction has started, (b) the time required for a given fraction of sample to react, or (c) the time required for the concentration of a reactant to reach a certain level.

Teaching Note: Equation 14.9 is the result of the integration

$$\int_{[A]_0}^{[A]_t} \frac{d[A]}{[A]} = -k \int_0^t dt.$$

Point of Emphasis: Note that this rate law is defined in terms of the natural logarithm. Using the natural logarithm relieves students of keeping track of where the factor 2.30 goes.

H. Alan Rowe and Morris Brown, "Practical Enzyme Kinetics," *J. Chem. Educ.* **1988,** *65,* 548.

Learning Goal 8: Use the equations

$$\ln[A]_t = -kt + \ln[A]_0$$
$$\frac{1}{[A]_t} = \frac{1}{[A]_0} + kt$$

to determine graphically whether the rate law for a reaction is first or second order.

Teaching Note: The natural logarithm of any value is dimensionless.

FIGURE 14.2 (a) Variation in the pressure of methyl isonitrile, CH_3NC, with time at 198.9°C during the reaction $CH_3NC \longrightarrow CH_3CN$. (b) A plot of the natural logarithm of the CH_3NC pressure as a function of time.

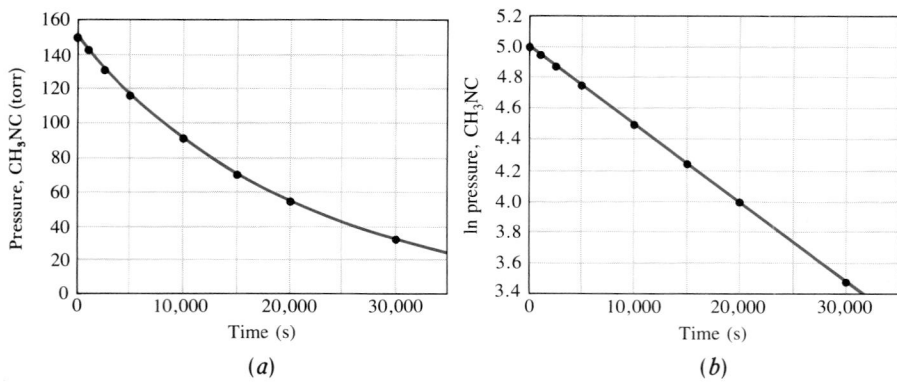

Figure 14.2

For a first-order reaction, Equation 14.9 or 14.10 can be used to determine (1) the concentration of a reactant remaining at any time after the reaction has started, (2) the time required for a given fraction of a sample to react, or (3) the time required for a reactant concentration to reach a certain level.

SAMPLE EXERCISE 14.5

The first-order rate constant for the decomposition of a certain insecticide in water at 12°C is 1.45 yr^{-1}. A quantity of this insecticide is washed into a lake in June, leading to a concentration of 5.0×10^{-7} g/cm^3 of water. Assume that the effective temperature of the lake is 12°C. **(a)** What is the concentration of the insecticide in June of the following year? **(b)** How long will it take for the concentration of the insecticide to drop to 3.0×10^{-7} g/cm^3?

SOLUTION **(a)** Substituting $k = 1.45$ yr^{-1}, $t = 1.00$ yr, and $[\text{insecticide}]_0 = 5.0 \times 10^{-7}$ g/cm^3 into Equation 14.10 gives

$$\ln[\text{insecticide}]_{t=1 \text{ yr}} = -(1.45 \text{ yr}^{-1})(1.00 \text{ yr}) + \ln(5.0 \times 10^{-7})$$

We use the ln function on a calculator to evaluate the second term on the right, giving

$$\ln[\text{insecticide}]_{t=1 \text{ yr}} = -1.45 + (-14.51) = -15.96$$

To obtain $[\text{insecticide}]_{t=1 \text{ yr}}$ we use the inverse natural logarithm, or e^x, function on the calculator. Enter -15.96 followed by the e^x key (on some calculators, you may have to enter -15.96, followed by the INV key, followed by the ln key):

$$[\text{insecticide}]_{t=1 \text{ yr}} = e^{-15.96} = 1.2 \times 10^{-7} \text{ g/cm}^3$$

Note that the concentration units for $[A]_t$ and $[A]_0$ must be the same.
   (b) Again substituting into Equation 14.10, with $[\text{insecticide}]_t = 3.0 \times 10^{-7}$ g/cm^3, gives

$$\ln(3.0 \times 10^{-7}) = -(1.45 \text{ yr}^{-1})(t) + \ln(5.0 \times 10^{-7})$$

Solving for t gives

$$t = -[\ln(3.0 \times 10^{-7}) - \ln(5.0 \times 10^{-7})]/1.45 \text{ yr}^{-1}$$
$$= -(-15.02 + 14.51)/1.45 \text{ yr}^{-1} = 0.35 \text{ yr}$$

PRACTICE EXERCISE

The decomposition of N_2O_5 according to the equation

$$2N_2O_5(g) \longrightarrow 4NO_2(g) + O_2(g)$$

has a first-order rate law. The rate constant k has the value $8.5 \times 10^{-3}\,s^{-1}$. If the initial pressure of N_2O_5 is 240 torr, what will its pressure be after 300 s? ***Answer:*** 18.7 torr

Half-life

The **half-life** of a reaction, $t_{1/2}$, is the time required for the concentration of a reactant to drop to one-half of its initial value. That is $[A]_{t_{1/2}} = \frac{1}{2}[A]_0$. We can determine the half-life of a first-order reaction by substituting $[A]_{t_{1/2}}$ into Equation 14.9:

Learning Goal 9: Explain the concept of reaction half-life, and describe the relationship between half-life and rate constant for a first-order reaction.

$$\ln \frac{\frac{1}{2}[A]_0}{[A]_0} = -kt_{1/2}$$

$$\ln \frac{1}{2} = -kt_{1/2}$$

$$t_{1/2} = -\frac{\ln \frac{1}{2}}{k} = \frac{0.693}{k} \qquad [14.12]$$

Point of Emphasis: For a first-order reaction, $t_{1/2} = 0.693/k$ and is constant throughout the reaction.

Notice that $t_{1/2}$ for a first-order rate law is independent of the initial concentration of reactant. Thus, the half-life is the same at any time during the reaction. If, for example, the concentration of the reactant is $0.120\,M$ at some moment in the reaction, it will be $\frac{1}{2}(0.120\,M) = 0.060\,M$ one half-life later. The concept of half-life is widely used in describing radioactive decay. This application is discussed in detail in Section 21.4.

The data for the first-order rearrangement of methyl isonitrile at $198.9\,^\circ C$ are graphed in Figure 14.3. The first half-life is shown at 13,300 s. At a time 13,300 s later, the isonitrile concentration has decreased to one-half of one half, or one-fourth the original concentration. *In a first-order reaction the concentration of the reactant decreases by $\frac{1}{2}$ in each of a series of regularly spaced time intervals, namely, $t_{1/2}$.*

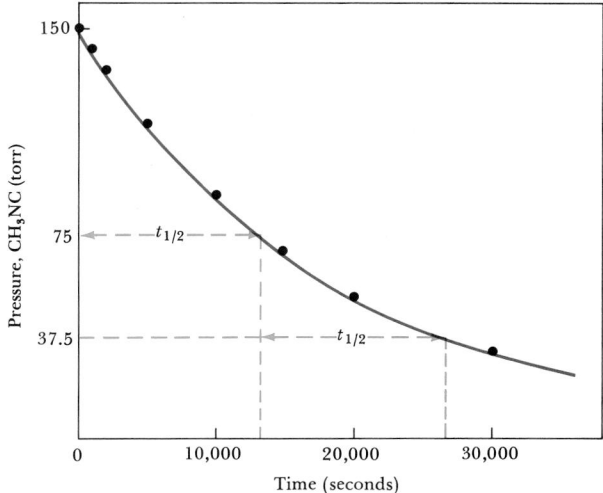

FIGURE 14.3 Pressure of methyl isonitrile as a function of time. Two successive half-lives of the rearrangement reaction, Equation 14.11, are shown.

Figure 14.3

SAMPLE EXERCISE 14.6

From Figure 14.1 estimate the half-life of the reaction of C_4H_9Cl with water.

SOLUTION   From the figure, we see that the initial value of $[C_4H_9Cl]$ is 0.100 M. The half-life for this first-order reaction is the time required for $[C_4H_9Cl]$ to decrease to 0.050 M. This point occurs at approximately 340 s. At the end of the second half-life, which should occur at 680 s, the concentration should have decreased by yet another factor of 2, to 0.025 M. Inspection of the graph shows that this is indeed the case.

PRACTICE EXERCISE

Using Equation 14.12, calculate $t_{1/2}$ for the reaction described in Practice Exercise 14.5.   **Answer:** 81.5 s

Second-Order Reactions

Learning Goal 10: Determine the rate law for a given higher-order reaction from the appropriate data.

A **second-order reaction** is one whose rate depends on the reactant concentration raised to the second power or on the concentrations of two different reactants, each raised to the first power. For a reaction that is second order in just one reactant, A, the rate law is given by

$$Rate = k[A]^2$$

Teaching Note: Equation 14.13 is the result of the integration

$$\int_{[A]_0}^{[A]_t} \frac{d[A]}{[A]^2} = -k \int_0^t dt.$$

Relying on calculus, this rate law can be used to derive the following equation:

$$\frac{1}{[A]_t} = kt + \frac{1}{[A]_0} \qquad [14.13]$$

Michael G. Silvestri and Charles E. Dills, "A Kinetic Study of the Diels-Alder Reaction: An Experiment Illustrating Simple Second-Order Reaction Kinetics," *J. Chem. Educ.* **1989,** *66,* 690.

This equation, like Equation 14.10, has the form of a straight line ($y = mx + b$). If the reaction is second order, a plot of $1/[A]_t$ versus t will yield a straight line with a slope equal to k and a y-intercept equal to $1/[A]_0$. One way to distinguish between first- and second-order rate laws is to graph both ln $[A]_t$ and $1/[A]_t$ against t. If the ln $[A]_t$ plot is linear, the reaction is first order; if the $1/[A]_t$ plot is linear, the reaction is second order.

Point of Emphasis: To determine if a reaction obeys a first- or second-order rate law, plot both $\ln[A]_t$ and $1/[A]_t$ *vs* t. Only one plot will be linear, indicating the molecularity of the reaction.

Using Equation 14.13, we can show that the half-life of a second-order reaction is

$$t_{1/2} = \frac{1}{k[A]_0} \qquad [14.14]$$

We see that, unlike that of first-order reactions, the half-life of a second-order reaction is dependent on the initial concentration of reactant.

Teaching Note: For a second-order reaction, the half-life will change throughout the course of the reaction.

SAMPLE EXERCISE 14.7

The following data were obtained for the gas-phase decomposition of nitrogen dioxide at 300°C, $2NO_2(g) \longrightarrow 2NO(g) + O_2(g)$:

Time (s)	$[NO_2]$ (M)
0.0	0.0100
50.0	0.0079
100.0	0.0065
200.0	0.0048
300.0	0.0038

Is the reaction first or second order in NO_2?

SOLUTION   To test whether the reaction is first or second order, we can construct plots of ln $[NO_2]$ and $1/[NO_2]$ against time. In doing so, we will find it useful to prepare the following table from the data given:

Time (s)	$[NO_2]$ (M)	ln $[NO_2]$	$1/[NO_2]$
0.0	0.0100	−4.61	100
50.0	0.0079	−4.84	127
100.0	0.0065	−5.04	154
200.0	0.0048	−5.34	208
300.0	0.0038	−5.57	263

As Figure 14.4 shows, only the plot of $1/[NO_2]$ versus time is linear. Thus the reaction obeys a second-order rate law: Rate = $k[NO_2]^2$. From the slope of this straight-line graph we have that $k = 0.543$ M^{-1} s^{-1} for the disappearance of NO_2.

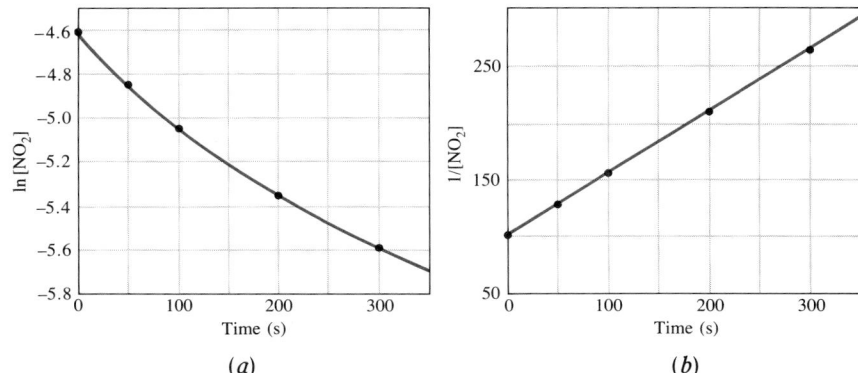

(a)   (b)

FIGURE 14.4   Plots of the kinetic data for the reaction $2NO_2(g) \longrightarrow 2NO(g) + O_2(g)$ at 300°C. The plot of $\ln[NO_2]$ versus time (a) is not linear; consequently, the reaction is not first order in NO_2. The plot of $1/[NO_2]$ versus time (b) is linear; the reaction is second order in NO_2.

Figure 14.4

PRACTICE EXERCISE

What is the half-life measured from time $t = 0$ for the decomposition of NO_2, as represented by the tabular data above?   ***Answer:*** 184 s

A reaction may also be second order by having a first-order dependence of the rate on each of two reagents; that is, rate = $k[A][B]$. It is possible to derive an expression for the variation in concentrations of A and B with time. However, we will not consider this and other more complicated rate laws in this text.

14.4 Temperature and Rate

The rates of most chemical reactions increase as the temperature rises. Examples of this generalization surround us. Plants grow more rapidly in warm weather than in cold. Food cooks faster in boiling water than in merely hot water, and it spoils faster at room temperature than when it is refrigerated. We can literally see the effect of temperature on the rate of a chemical reaction by observing a *chemiluminescent* reaction, a chemical reaction that produces light. Fireflies produce their characteristic glow through a chemiluminescent reaction. Another common example of chemiluminescence is the light produced by Cyalume light sticks. Light sticks contain chemicals in two compartments separated by a divider. When the divider is broken and the chemicals mix, chemiluminescence results. The greater the rate of the reaction, the greater the amount of light produced. Figure 14.5 demonstrates the effect of temperature on the light emitted by Cyalume light sticks. The light stick in hot water produces more light than the one immersed in cold water.

The effect of temperature on rate is expressed in the rate constant, whose magnitude changes with temperature. For example, consider the first-order arrangement of methyl isonitrile (Equation 14.11). Figure 14.6 shows the experimentally determined rate constant for this reaction as a function of temperature. The rate constant, and hence the rate of reaction, increases rapidly with temperature, approximately doubling for each 10°C rise in temperature. Why does temperature, or for that matter even concentration, affect reaction rates? One appealing explanation is provided by the collision model of chemical kinetics.

The Collision Model

Learning Goal 11: Use the collision model of chemical reactions to explain how reactions occur at the molecular level.

The central idea of the **collision model** is that *molecules must collide to react.* The greater the number of collisions occurring per second, the greater the reaction rate. This idea allows us to understand the effect of concentration on rate: As the concentration of reactant molecules increases, the number of collisions increases, leading to an increase in reaction rate. The collision model also allows us to understand the effect of temperature: We know from the kinetic-molecular theory of gases that increasing the temperature increases molecular velocities. ∞ (Sec. 10.8) As molecules move faster, they collide harder (with more energy) and more frequently, increasing reaction rates. However, the matter is not entirely this simple. For most reactions, *only a small fraction of collisions actually lead to reaction.*

FIGURE 14.5 Temperature affects the rate of the chemiluminescence reaction in Cyalume light sticks. The light stick in hot water (left) glows more brightly than the one in cold water (right); the reaction is faster and produces more light at the higher temperature. (© Richard Megna/Fundamental Photographs)

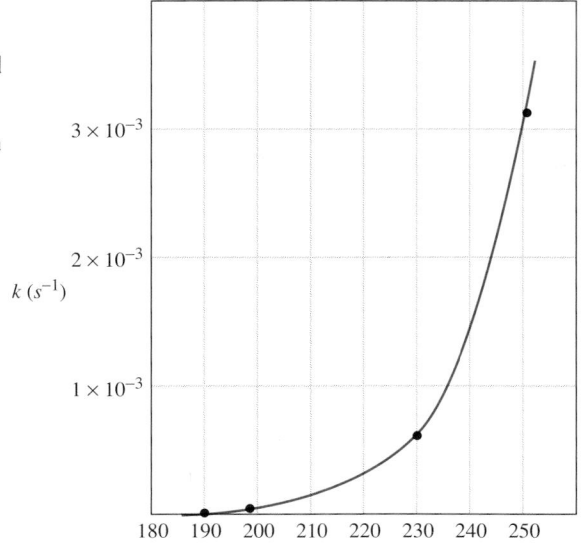

FIGURE 14.6 Variation in the first-order rate constant for the rearrangement of methyl isonitrile as a function of temperature. (The four points indicated are used in connection with Sample Exercise 14.8.)

$k\ (s^{-1})$

3×10^{-3}

2×10^{-3}

1×10^{-3}

180 190 200 210 220 230 240 250

For example, in a mixture of H_2 and I_2 at ordinary temperatures and pressures, each molecule undergoes about 10^{10} collisions per second. If every collision between H_2 and I_2 resulted in the formation of HI, the reaction would be over in much less than a second. Instead, at room temperature the reaction proceeds very slowly. Only about 1 in every 10^{13} collisions produces a reaction. What keeps the reaction from occurring more rapidly?

Activation Energy

In 1888, the Swedish chemist Svante Arrhenius suggested that molecules must possess a certain minimum amount of energy in order to react. According to the collision model, this energy comes from the kinetic energies of the colliding molecules. Upon collision, the kinetic energy of the molecules can be used to stretch or bend bonds in ways that lead to chemical reaction. The situation is like that of two colliding automobiles. If the cars are moving fast enough when they collide, they will undergo structural changes. The kinetic energy of the cars is used to rearrange their structures. On the other hand, if the automobiles touch ever so softly, say bumper against bumper, there will be no damage. Likewise, if molecules are moving too slowly, with too little kinetic energy, they merely bounce off one another without changing.

We see that if molecules have sufficient kinetic energy, their collisions can cause chemical bonds to break or form, producing a chemical reaction. In order to react, colliding molecules must have a total kinetic energy equal to or greater than some minimum value. The minimum energy required to initiate a chemical reaction is called the **activation energy**, E_a. The value of E_a varies from reaction to reaction.

The situation during reactions is rather like that shown in Figure 14.7. The boulder is initially at position A. It will be at a lower energy (more stable) at position B. To get from position A to position B, however, it must acquire enough energy to get over the hill blocking its passage. In the same way, molecules may require a certain minimum energy to break existing bonds during a

Learning Goal 12: Explain the concept of activation energy and how it relates to the variation of reaction rate with temperature.

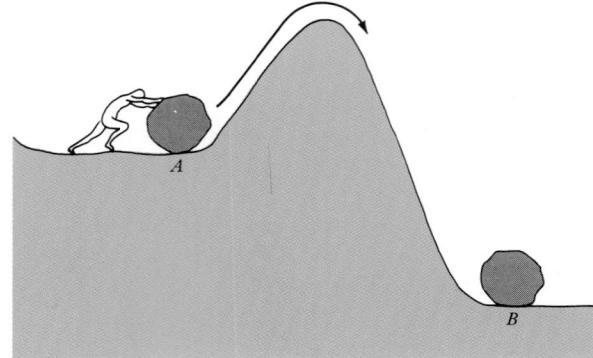

chemical reaction. As an example, in the rearrangement of methyl isonitrile to acetonitrile, we might imagine passing through an intermediate state in which the N≡C portion of the molecule is sitting sideways:

$$H_3C-N\equiv C: \longrightarrow \left[H_3C\cdots \overset{\displaystyle C}{\underset{\displaystyle N}{\parallel}} \right] \longrightarrow H_3C-C\equiv N:$$

The change in the energy of the molecule during the reaction is shown in Figure 14.8. The diagram shows that energy must be supplied to stretch the bond between the H_3C group and the N≡C group so as to allow the N≡C group to rotate. After the N≡C group has twisted sufficiently, the C—C bond begins to form, and the energy of the molecule drops. Thus, the barrier represents the energy necessary to force the molecule through the relatively unstable intermediate state to the final product. The energy barrier between the starting molecule and the highest energy along the reaction pathway is the activation energy, E_a. The particular arrangement of atoms at the top of the barrier is called the **activated complex** or **transition state.**

The conversion of $H_3C-N\equiv C$ to $H_3C-C\equiv N$ is exothermic. Figure 14.8 therefore shows the product as having a lower energy than the reactant. The energy change for the reaction, ΔE, has no effect on the rate of the reaction; rather, the rate depends solely on the magnitude of E_a. Notice that the reverse

Point of Emphasis: For the reverse reaction, the roles of reactant and product have been switched. Therefore, $\Delta E = E_{final} - E_{initial}$ has the same magnitude but opposite sign as ΔE for the forward reaction.

FIGURE 14.8 Energy profile for the rearrangement of methyl isonitrile. The molecule must surmount the activation-energy barrier before it can form the product, acetonitrile.

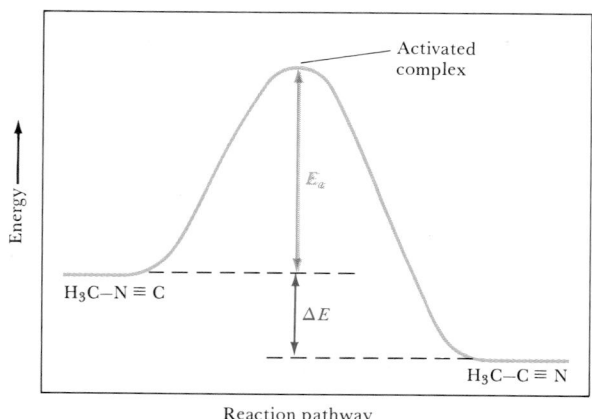

Figure 14.8

reaction is endothermic. The activation barrier for the reverse reaction is equal to the sum of ΔE and E_a for the forward reaction.

Energy is transferred between molecules through collisions. Thus, within a certain period of time, any particular isonitrile molecule might acquire enough energy to overcome the energy barrier and be converted into acetonitrile. Recall that in a gas sample the molecules have a distribution of velocities and hence a distribution of kinetic energies. ∞ (Sec. 10.8) Figure 14.9 shows the distribution of kinetic energies for two different temperatures, comparing them with the minimum energy needed for reaction, E_a. Notice that at the higher temperature, a much greater fraction of the molecules has kinetic energy greater than E_a, which leads to a much greater rate of reaction.

In addition to the requirement that the reactant species collide with sufficient energy to begin to rearrange bonds, an orientational requirement exists. The relative orientations of the molecules during their collisions determine whether the atoms are suitably positioned to form new bonds. For example, consider the reaction of Cl atoms with NOCl:

$$Cl + NOCl \longrightarrow NO + Cl_2$$

The reaction will take place if the collision brings Cl atoms together to form Cl_2, as shown in Figure 14.10(a). On the other hand, the collision shown in Figure 14.10(b) will be ineffective and will not yield products. Thus, collisions must occur not only with sufficient energy but also with suitable orientation in order to cause reaction.

The Arrhenius Equation

Arrhenius noted that, for most reactions, the increase in rate with increasing temperature is nonlinear, as in the example shown in Figure 14.6. He found that most reaction-rate data obeyed the equation

$$k = Ae^{-E_a/RT} \qquad [14.16]$$

where k is the rate constant. This equation is called the **Arrhenius equation.** The term E_a is the activation energy, R is the gas constant (8.314 J/mol-K), and T is absolute temperature. The term A is constant, or nearly so, as temperature is varied. Called the **frequency factor,** A is related to the frequency of collisions and the probability that the collisions are favorably oriented for reaction. No-

Keith J. Laidler, "Just What Is a Transition State?," *J. Chem. Educ.,* **1988,** *64,* 540.

Point of Emphasis: According to collision theory, the reactants must (1) collide with sufficient energy, and (2) collide in the proper orientation in order for the reaction to occur.

Learning Goal 13: Determine the activation energy for a reaction from a knowledge of how the rate constant varies with temperature (the Arrhenius equation).

Point of Emphasis: The values of A and E_a are specific to each chemical reaction.

Figure 14.9

FIGURE 14.9 Distribution of kinetic energies in a sample of gas molecules at two different temperatures. At the higher temperature a larger number of molecules has higher energy. Thus, a larger fraction at any one instant will have more than the minimum energy required for reaction.

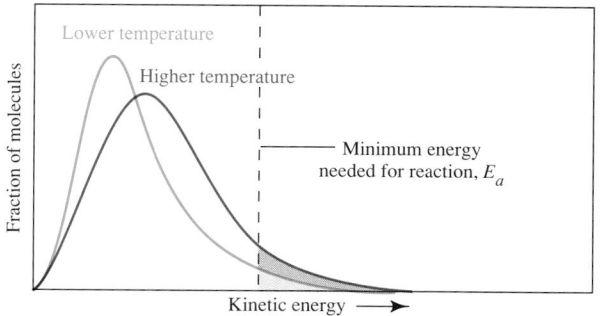

(a) Effective collision

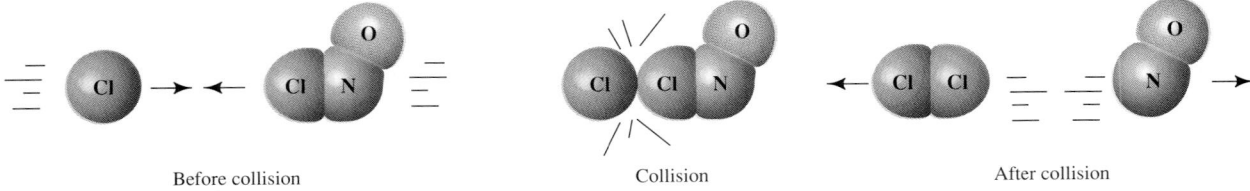

Before collision   Collision   After collision

(b) Ineffective collision

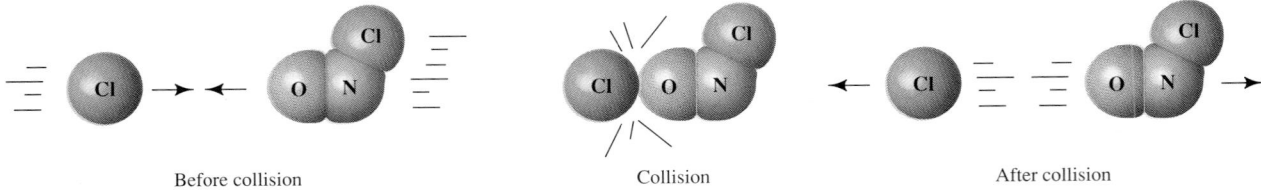

Before collision   Collision   After collision

FIGURE 14.10   Two possible ways that Cl atoms and NOCl molecules can collide. (a) If molecules are oriented properly, a sufficiently energetic collision will lead to reaction. (b) If the orientation of the colliding molecules is wrong, no reaction occurs.

Figure 14.10

tice that as the magnitude of E_a increases, k becomes smaller. Thus, reaction rates decrease as the energy barrier increases.

Taking the natural log of both sides of Equation 14.16, we have

$$\ln k = -\frac{E_a}{RT} + \ln A \qquad [14.17]$$

Point of Emphasis: The absolute temperature (in Kelvin) must be used.

Equation 14.17 has the form of a straight line; it predicts that a graph of $\ln k$ versus $1/T$ will be a line with a slope equal to $-E_a/R$ and a y-intercept equal to $\ln A$.

We can also use Equation 14.17 to evaluate E_a in a nongraphical way if we know the rate constant of a reaction at two or more temperatures. For example, suppose that at two different temperatures T_1 and T_2, a reaction has rate constants k_1 and k_2. For each condition, we have

$$\ln k_1 = -\frac{E_a}{RT_1} + \ln A \qquad \text{and} \qquad \ln k_2 = -\frac{E_a}{RT_2} + \ln A$$

Subtracting $\ln k_2$ from $\ln k_1$ gives

$$\ln k_1 - \ln k_2 = \left(-\frac{E_a}{RT_1} + \ln A\right) - \left(-\frac{E_a}{RT_2} + \ln A\right)$$

Simplifying this equation and rearranging it gives

$$\ln \frac{k_1}{k_2} = \frac{E_a}{R}\left(\frac{1}{T_2} - \frac{1}{T_1}\right) \qquad [14.18]$$

Seeing the Transition State

The details of how chemical reactions occur—the events that happen as reactants turn into products—have long fascinated chemists. In the laboratory, you will probably perform experiments that allow you to monitor how long a reaction takes to occur. In so doing, you will observe the result of the passage of reactants through the transition state into products (as in, for example, Figure 14.8), usually on the time scale of several minutes. What happens when the reactants reach the transition state, the energetic "top of the mountain" between reactants and products? The nature of the transition state—how molecules collide, transfer energy, break and make bonds—is the focus of the field of chemistry called *molecular reaction dynamics*. This is an extremely important field of modern chemical research. The 1986 Nobel Prize for Chemistry was awarded jointly to Dudley Herschbach, Yuan Lee, and John Polanyi for their pioneering research in reaction dynamics.

Transition states are very unstable and extremely short-lived; they exist for incomprehensibly short periods of time before falling apart into products or back into reactants. Research in reaction dynamics requires the design of elaborate experiments to take "snapshots" of the transition state, often using pulses of laser light that are extremely short in duration. Recent advances in laser design have allowed chemists to take faster and faster pictures of transition states falling apart into products, on the time scale of femtoseconds (1 fs = 10^{-15} s)!

One of the first examples of chemistry studied on the femtosecond time scale was the dissociation of ICN by light, a so-called photofragmentation reaction:

$$ICN(g) \xrightarrow{\text{Light}} [I \cdots CN] \longrightarrow I(g) + CN(g)$$

Activated
complex

The absorption of light by an ICN molecule excites the molecule and ultimately leads to breaking of the I—C bond. In the activated complex that results from the absorption of light, the iodine and carbon atoms are still within bonding distance of one another. In 1987, by using laser pulses less than 100 fs in duration, chemists at the California Institute of Technology determined that it takes only a few hundred femtoseconds for the activated complex to fall apart. Studies such as these hold great promise for providing detailed pictures of how molecules react.

The laser apparatus needed for femtosecond-time-scale studies is extremely complex (Figure 14.11). Excruciating care is required to isolate the equipment from vibrations that could change the distance that the laser light travels. In 1 fs, light travels only 3×10^{-7} m (0.3 μm), and so even a minute vibration would throw off the timing of the snapshots.

FIGURE 14.11 Part of the apparatus at the California Institute of Technology for performing laser experiments on the femtosecond time scale. (Dr. Ahmed H. Zewail, California Institute of Technology)

Point of Emphasis: In this context, R is usually expressed in common energy units, such as 8.314 J/mol-K.

Equation 14.18 provides a convenient way to calculate the rate constant, k_1, at some temperature, T_1, when we know the activation energy and the rate constant, k_2, at some other temperature, T_2.

SAMPLE EXERCISE 14.8

The following table shows the rate constants for the rearrangement of methyl isonitrile at various temperatures (these are the data that are graphed in Figure 14.6).

Temperature (°C)	k (s^{-1})
189.7	2.52×10^{-5}
198.9	5.25×10^{-5}
230.3	6.30×10^{-4}
251.2	3.16×10^{-3}

(a) From these data calculate the activation energy for the reaction. (b) What is the value of the rate constant at 430.0 K?

SOLUTION (a) We must first convert the temperatures from degrees Celsius to kelvins. We then take the inverse of each temperature, $1/T$, and the natural log of each rate constant, $\ln k$. This gives us the following table:

T (K)	$1/T$ (K^{-1})	$\ln k$
462.9	2.160×10^{-3}	-10.59
472.1	2.118×10^{-3}	-9.85
503.5	1.986×10^{-3}	-7.37
524.4	1.907×10^{-3}	-5.76

A graph of $\ln k$ versus $1/T$ results in a straight line, as shown in Figure 14.12. The slope of the line is obtained by choosing two well-separated points, as shown, and using the coordinates of each:

$$\text{Slope} = \frac{\Delta y}{\Delta x} = \frac{-6.6 - (-10.4)}{0.00195 - 0.00215} = -1.9 \times 10^4$$

Because logarithms have no units, the numerator in this equation is dimensionless. The denominator has the units of $1/T$, namely, K^{-1}. Thus, the overall units for the

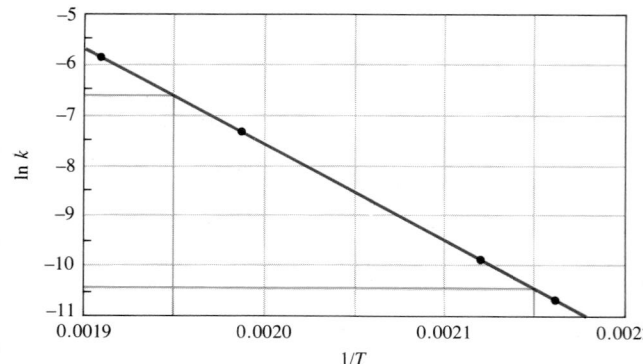

FIGURE 14.12 The natural logarithm of the rate constant for the rearrangement of methyl isonitrile as a function of $1/T$. The linear relationship is predicted by the Arrhenius equation.

slope are K. The slope is equal to $-E_a/R$. We use the value for the molar gas constant R in units of J/mol-K (Table 10.2). We thus obtain

$$\text{Slope} = -\frac{E_a}{R}$$

$$E_a = -(\text{slope})(R) = -(-1.9 \times 10^4 \text{ K})\left(8.31\ \frac{\text{J}}{\text{mol-K}}\right)\left(\frac{1\ \text{kJ}}{1000\ \text{J}}\right)$$

$$= 160\ \text{kJ/mol}$$

Note that we report the activation energy to two significant figures; we are limited by the precision with which we can read the graph in Figure 14.12.

(b) To determine the rate constant, k_1, at 430.0 K, we can use Equation 14.18 with $E_a = 160$ kJ/mol, $k_2 = 2.52 \times 10^{-5}$ s^{-1}, $T_2 = 462.9$ K, and $T_1 = 430.0$ K:

$$\ln\left(\frac{k_1}{2.52 \times 10^{-5}\ \text{s}^{-1}}\right) = \left(\frac{160\ \text{kJ/mol}}{8.31\ \text{J/mol-K}}\right)\left(\frac{1}{462.9\ \text{K}} - \frac{1}{430.0\ \text{K}}\right)\left(\frac{1000\ \text{J}}{1\ \text{kJ}}\right) = -3.18$$

Thus,

$$\frac{k_1}{2.52 \times 10^{-5}\ \text{s}^{-1}} = e^{-3.18} = 4.15 \times 10^{-2}$$

$$k_1 = (4.15 \times 10^{-2})(2.52 \times 10^{-5}\ \text{s}^{-1}) = 1.04 \times 10^{-6}\ \text{s}^{-1}$$

Note that the units k_1 are the same as those of k_2.

PRACTICE EXERCISE

Estimate the rate constant for the rearrangement of methyl isonitrile at 280°C.
Answer: 2.14×10^{-2} s^{-1}

14.5 Reaction Mechanisms

A balanced equation for a chemical reaction indicates the substances that are present at the start of the reaction and those produced at the end. However, it provides no information about how the reaction occurs. The process by which a reaction occurs is called the **reaction mechanism.** At the most sophisticated level, a reaction mechanism will describe in great detail the order in which bonds are broken and formed and the changes in relative positions of the atoms in the course of the reaction. We will begin with more rudimentary descriptions of how reactions occur.

Learning Goal 14: Explain what is meant by the mechanism of a reaction using the terms *elementary steps, rate-determining step,* and *intermediate.*

Elementary Steps

We have seen that reactions take place as a result of collisions between reacting molecules. For example, the collision between methyl isonitrile, CH_3NC, and some other molecule can provide the energy to allow the CH_3NC to rearrange:

Similarly, the reaction of NO and O_3 to form NO_2 and O_2 appears to occur as a result of a single collision involving suitably oriented and sufficiently energetic NO and O_3 molecules:

$$NO(g) + O_3(g) \longrightarrow NO_2(g) + O_2(g) \qquad [14.19]$$

Both of these processes occur in a single event or step and are called **elementary steps** (or elementary processes).

The number of molecules that participate as reactants in an elementary step defines the **molecularity** of the step. If a single molecule is involved, the reaction is said to be **unimolecular**. The rearrangement of methyl isonitrile is a unimolecular process. Elementary steps involving the collision of two reactant molecules are said to be **bimolecular**. The reaction between NO and O_3 (Equation 14.19) is bimolecular. Elementary steps involving the simultaneous collision of three molecules are said to be **termolecular**. Termolecular steps are far less probable than unimolecular or bimolecular processes and are rarely encountered. The chance that four or more molecules will collide simultaneously with any regularity is even more remote; consequently, such collisions are never proposed as part of a reaction mechanism.

The net change represented by a balanced chemical equation often occurs by a *multistep mechanism,* which consists of a sequence of elementary steps. For example, consider the reaction of NO_2 and CO:

$$NO_2(g) + CO(g) \longrightarrow NO(g) + CO_2(g) \qquad [14.20]$$

Below 225°C, this reaction appears to proceed in two elementary steps, each of which is bimolecular. First, two NO_2 molecules collide, and an oxygen atom is transferred from one to the other. The resultant NO_3 then transfers an oxygen atom to CO during a collision between these molecules:

$$NO_2(g) + NO_2(g) \longrightarrow NO_3(g) + NO(g)$$
$$NO_3(g) + CO(g) \longrightarrow NO_2(g) + CO_2(g)$$

Point of Emphasis: As in Hess's law, elementary steps *must* sum to give the net reaction.

The elementary steps in a multistep mechanism must always add to give the chemical equation of the overall process. In the present example, the sum of the elementary steps is

$$2NO_2(g) + NO_3(g) + CO(g) \longrightarrow NO_2(g) + NO_3(g) + NO(g) + CO_2(g)$$

Common Misconception: Students often confuse intermediates with activated complexes or transition states; they are not the same thing. Intermediates have some stability, however limited (i.e., are local energy minima), whereas activated complexes are inherently unstable (i.e., are local energy maxima).

Simplifying this equation by eliminating substances that appear on both sides of the arrow gives the net equation for the process, Equation 14.20. Because NO_3 is neither a reactant nor a product in the overall reaction — it is formed in one elementary step and consumed in the next — it is called an **intermediate.** Multistep mechanisms involve one or more intermediates.

SAMPLE EXERCISE 14.9

It has been proposed that the conversion of ozone into O_2 proceeds in two steps:

$$O_3(g) \longrightarrow O_2(g) + O(g)$$
$$O_3(g) + O(g) \longrightarrow 2O_2(g)$$

(a) Describe the molecularity of each step in this mechanism. (b) Write the equation for the overall reaction. (c) Identify the intermediate, if any.

SOLUTION   (a) The first elementary step involves a single reactant and is consequently unimolecular. The second step, which involves two reactant molecules is bimolecular.
   (b) Adding the two elementary steps gives

$$2O_3(g) + O(g) \longrightarrow 3O_2(g) + O(g)$$

Because $O(g)$ appears in equal amounts on both sides of the equation, it can be eliminated to give the net equation for the chemical process:

$$2O_3(g) \longrightarrow 3O_2(g)$$

   (c) The intermediate is $O(g)$. It is neither an original reactant nor a final product but is formed in one step and consumed in another.

PRACTICE EXERCISE

For the following reaction of $Mo(CO)_6$,

$$Mo(CO)_6 + P(CH_3)_3 \longrightarrow Mo(CO)_5P(CH_3)_3 + CO$$

the proposed mechanism is

$$Mo(CO)_6 \longrightarrow Mo(CO)_5 + CO$$
$$Mo(CO)_5 + P(CH_3)_3 \longrightarrow Mo(CO)_5P(CH_3)_3$$

(a) Is the proposed mechanism consistent with the equation for the overall reaction? (b) Identify the intermediate or intermediates.   *Answers:* (a) yes, the two equations add to yield the equation for the reaction; (b) $Mo(CO)_5$

Rate Laws of Elementary Processes

In Section 14.2, we stressed that rate laws must be determined experimentally; they cannot, in general, be predicted from the coefficients of balanced chemical equations. Now we are in a position to understand why. What we will see is that the reaction mechanism — the elementary steps of the reaction and their relative speeds — rather than the chemical equation for the overall process determines the rate law. Indeed, the rate law for a reaction can be determined from its mechanism if the slow step is known. The rate law derived from the mechanism, however, must agree with the experimental rate law, or the mechanism is incorrect. Let's examine the rate laws for elementary steps and then consider how they relate to the overall rate law for a reaction that occurs by a multistep mechanism.

   The rate law of any elementary step is based directly on its molecularity. For example, consider the general unimolecular process

Point of Emphasis: The rate law of an elementary step *does* follow from the coefficients of the balanced equation of the step.

$$A \longrightarrow products$$

As the number of A molecules increases, the number that decompose in a given interval of time will increase proportionally. Thus, the rate of a unimolecular process will be first order:

$$Rate = k[A]$$

   Similarly, the rate laws for bimolecular steps are second order overall, and those for termolecular ones are third order, as shown in Table 14.3. Notice how the rate law for each kind of elementary step follows directly from the molecularity of that step. Keep in mind, however, that we cannot tell by merely looking

TABLE 14.3 △ Elementary Steps and Their Rate Laws

Molecularity	Elementary step	Rate law
*Uni*molecular	A $\longrightarrow$ products	Rate $= k[A]$
*Bi*molecular	A + A $\longrightarrow$ products	Rate $= k[A]^2$
*Bi*molecular	A + B $\longrightarrow$ products	Rate $= k[A][B]$
*Ter*molecular	A + A + A $\longrightarrow$ products	Rate $= k[A]^3$
*Ter*molecular	A + A + B $\longrightarrow$ products	Rate $= k[A]^2[B]$
*Ter*molecular	A + B + C $\longrightarrow$ products	Rate $= k[A][B][C]$

at a balanced chemical equation whether the reaction involves one or several elementary steps. One of the great challenges in chemical kinetics is to determine the elementary steps that lead to the experimentally observed rate law for the overall reaction. We don't expect you to propose mechanisms at this stage of your training. You will be expected, however, to propose rate laws given the mechanisms or to distinguish between mechanisms based on experimental data.

SAMPLE EXERCISE 14.10

If the following reaction occurs in a single elementary step, predict the rate law:

$$O_3(g) + NO(g) \longrightarrow NO_2(g) + O_2(g)$$

SOLUTION The elementary step is bimolecular, involving the collision of one molecule of O_3 with one molecule of NO. The rate law will therefore be first order in each reactant and second order overall:

$$\text{Rate} = k[O_3][NO]$$

Only by performing experiments can we verify that the rate law is indeed first order in both O_3 and NO and determine what the value of k is.

PRACTICE EXERCISE

(a) Write the rate law for the following reaction, assuming it involves a single elementary step:

$$2NO(g) + Br_2(g) \longrightarrow 2NOBr(g)$$

(b) Is a single-step mechanism likely for this reaction?   *Answers:* (a) rate $= k[NO]^2[Br_2]$; (b) no, because termolecular reactions are very rare

Rate Laws of Multistep Mechanisms

Most chemical reactions occur by mechanisms that involve more than one elementary step. Often, one of the steps is much slower than the others. The overall rate of a reaction cannot exceed the rate of the slowest elementary step of its mechanism. Because the slow step limits the overall reaction rate, it is called the **rate-determining step.**

To understand better the concept of a rate-determining step, it is helpful to think of a toll road with two toll plazas (Figure 14.13). We will measure the rate at which cars exit the toll road. Cars enter the toll road at point 1 and pass through toll plaza A. They then pass an intermediate point 2 before passing

Learning Goal 15: Derive the rate law for a reaction that has a rate-determining step, given the elementary steps and their relative speeds; or, conversely, choose a plausible mechanism for a reaction given the rate law.

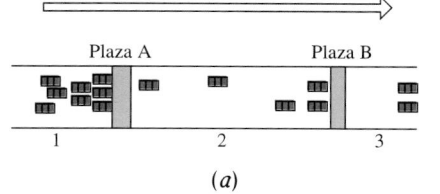

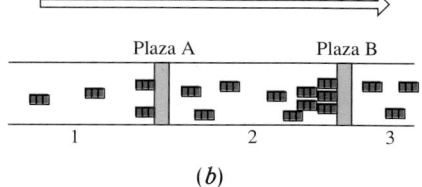

Plaza A   Plaza B   Plaza A   Plaza B

1   2   3   1   2   3

(a)   (b)

FIGURE 14.13   The flow of traffic on a toll road is limited by the flow of traffic through the slowest toll plaza. As cars pass from point 1 to point 2, they pass through plaza A; from point 2 to point 3, they pass through plaza B. In (a), the rate at which cars can reach point 3 is limited by how quickly they can get through plaza A; getting from point 1 to point 2 is the rate-determining step. In (b), getting from point 2 to point 3 is the rate-determining step. Traffic builds up in the intermediate stretch of road between the two toll plazas.

through toll plaza B. Upon exiting, they pass point 3. We can therefore envision this trip along the toll road as occurring in two elementary steps:

Step 1:   Point 1 $\longrightarrow$ point 2   (through plaza A)
Step 2:   Point 2 $\longrightarrow$ point 3   (through plaza B)

Overall: Point 1 $\longrightarrow$ point 3   (through plazas A and B)

Now suppose that several of the gates at toll plaza A are malfunctioning so that traffic backs up behind it [Figure 14.13(a)]. The rate at which cars can get to point 3 is limited by the rate at which they can get through the traffic jam at plaza A. Thus, step 1 is the rate-determining step of the journey along the toll road. If, on the other hand, traffic flows quickly through plaza A but gets backed up at plaza B [Figure 14.13(b)], there will be a buildup of cars in the intermediate region between the plazas. In this case, step 2 is the rate-determining step: The rate at which cars can travel the toll road is limited by the rate at which they can pass through plaza B.

In the same way, the slowest step in a multistep reaction determines the overall rate. By analogy to Figure 14.13(a), the rate of a faster step following the rate-determining step does not affect the overall rate. If the slow step is not the first one, as in Figure 14.13(b), the faster preceding steps produce intermediate products that accumulate before being consumed in the slow step. Furthermore, *the rate-determining step governs the rate law for the overall reaction.*

As an example of a slow first step determining the rate law of a reaction, consider the reaction of NO_2 and CO to produce NO and CO_2 (Equation 14.20). It is found experimentally that the rate law is second order in NO_2 and zero order in CO: Rate = $k[NO_2]^2$. Can we propose a reaction mechanism that is consistent with this rate law? Consider the following two-step mechanism.*

Step 1: $NO_2(g) + NO_2(g) \xrightarrow{k_1} NO_3(g) + NO(g)$ (slow) Rate = $k[NO_2]^2$
Step 2: $NO_3(g) + CO(g) \xrightarrow{k_2} NO_2(g) + CO_2(g)$ (fast) Rate = $k[NO_3][CO]$

Overall: $NO_2(g) + CO(g) \longrightarrow NO(g) + CO_2(g)$

*The subscript on the rate constant identifies the elementary step involved. Thus, k_1 is the rate constant for step 1, k_2 is the rate constant for step 2, and so forth. A negative subscript refers to the rate constant for the reverse of an elementary step. For example, k_{-1} is the rate constant for the reverse of the first step.

Teaching Note: The problem of solving traffic congestion as if it were a chemical system has been worked on by Ilya Prigogine, the 1977 Nobel Prize winner in Chemistry.

Lee R. Summerlin and James L. Ealy, Jr., "A Traffic Light Reaction," *Chemical Demonstrations, A Sourcebook for Teachers* (Washington: American Chemical Society, 1985), p. 79.

David W. Ball, "Another Auto Analogy: Rate Determining Steps," *J. Chem. Educ.* **1987**, *64*, 486.

Step 2 is much faster than step 1; that is, $k_2 \gg k_1$. Step 1 is rate-determining. Thus, the rate of the overall reaction equals the rate of step 1, and the rate law of the overall reaction equals the rate law of step 1. Step 1 is a bimolecular process that has the rate law

$$\text{Rate} = k_1[NO_2]^2$$

Thus, the rate law predicted by this mechanism agrees with the one observed experimentally.

Could we propose a one-step mechanism for the above reaction? We might suppose that the overall reaction is a single bimolecular elementary process that involves the collision of a molecule of NO_2 with one of CO. However, the rate law predicted by this mechanism would be

$$\text{Rate} = k[NO_2][CO]$$

Because this mechanism predicts a rate law different from that observed experimentally, we can rule it out.

Mechanisms with an Initial Fast Step

It is not easy to derive the rate law for a mechanism in which an intermediate is a reactant in the rate-determining step. This situation arises in multistep mechanisms when the first step is *not* rate-determining. Let us consider one example, the gas-phase reaction of nitric oxide, NO, with bromine, Br_2:

$$2NO(g) + Br_2(g) \longrightarrow 2NOBr(g) \qquad [14.21]$$

The experimentally determined rate law for this reaction is second order in NO and first order in Br_2:

$$\text{Rate} = k[NO]^2[Br_2] \qquad [14.22]$$

We seek a reaction mechanism that is consistent with this rate law. One possibility is that the reaction occurs in a single termolecular step:

$$NO(g) + NO(g) + Br_2(g) \longrightarrow 2NOBr(g) \qquad \text{Rate} = k[NO]^2[Br_2] \quad [14.23]$$

This does not seem likely, however, because termolecular processes are so rare. Let us consider an alternative mechanism that does not invoke termolecular steps:

$$\text{Step 1:} \qquad NO(g) + Br_2(g) \underset{k_{-1}}{\overset{k_1}{\rightleftharpoons}} NOBr_2(g) \qquad \text{(fast)}$$

$$\text{Step 2:} \quad NOBr_2(g) + NO(g) \xrightarrow{k_2} 2NOBr(g) \qquad \text{(slow)}$$

Because the second step is the slow, rate-determining step, the rate of the overall reaction is governed by the rate law for that step:

$$\text{Rate} = k_2[NOBr_2][NO] \qquad [14.24]$$

A CLOSER LOOK

Evidence of Mechanism

The basic procedure in establishing the mechanism of a chemical reaction is first to determine the rate law experimentally. One or more elementary steps are then postulated that account for that rate law and for other experimental observations. That a mechanism gives a rate law that agrees with the observed one does not prove that the mechanism is correct. Often several mechanisms can be envisioned that give rise to the same rate law. To distinguish among such mechanisms, chemists might search for proposed intermediates or carry out other types of studies. As an example, consider the following reaction:

$$O^+(g) + NO(g) \longrightarrow NO^+(g) + O(g)$$

This reaction occurs in the upper atmosphere. The rate law for this reaction is as follows: Rate $= k[O^+][NO]$, and the reaction is believed to occur in a single elementary step. However, we may ask whether the reaction involves the breaking of the NO bond and the formation of a new bond between N and O^+, or whether it involves merely the transfer of an electron from NO to O^+. These two possibilities are shown in Figure 14.14. The question of which of these mechanisms is operative is answered by performing the reaction using O^+ that has been highly enriched in the rare isotope ^{18}O. Because this isotope is present to the extent of only 0.2 percent in nature, the NO contains only 0.2 percent $N^{18}O$. By measuring the location of ^{18}O in the reaction products, the two mechanisms can be distinguished (see Figure 14.14). The experiment indicates that no ^{18}O is incorporated into NO^+; the experimental results are therefore consistent with the electron-transfer pathway but not the atom-transfer pathway.

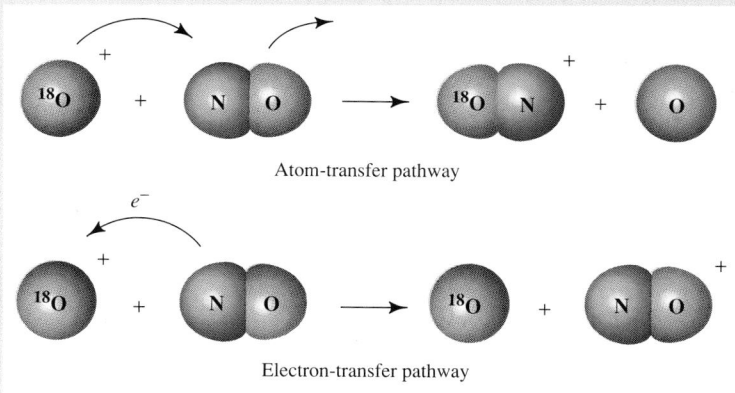

Atom-transfer pathway

Electron-transfer pathway

FIGURE 14.14 Alternative pathways for the reaction $O^+ + NO \longrightarrow O + NO^+$. The results of experiments using ^{18}O labeling show that the reaction proceeds according to the electron-transfer pathway.

However, NOBr$_2$ is an intermediate generated in step 1. Intermediates are usually unstable molecules that have a low, unknown concentration. Thus, we have a problem in that our rate law depends on the unknown concentration of an intermediate. Fortunately, with the aid of some assumptions, we can express the concentration of NOBr$_2$ in terms of the concentrations of NO and Br$_2$. We first assume that NOBr$_2$ is intrinsically unstable. There are two ways for NOBr$_2$ to be consumed after it is formed: Either it can react with NO to form NOBr, or it can fall back apart into NO and Br$_2$. The first of these possibilities is step 2, a slow process. The second is the reverse of step 1, a unimolecular process:

$$NOBr_2(g) \xrightarrow{k_{-1}} NO(g) + Br_2(g) \qquad [14.25]$$

Because step 2 is slow, we assume that most of the NOBr$_2$ falls apart according to Equation 14.25. Thus, we have both the forward and reverse reactions of step

Teaching Note: This is closely related to the *steady-state approximation.*

1 occurring much faster than step 2. We can therefore assume further that the first step achieves an equilibrium in which the rates of the forward and reverse reactions are equal:

$$k_1[NO][Br_2] \quad = \quad k_{-1}[NOBr_2]$$

Rate of forward reaction   Rate of reverse reaction

Solving for [NOBr$_2$], we have

$$[NOBr_2] = \frac{k_1}{k_{-1}}[NO][Br_2]$$

Substituting this relationship into the rate law for the rate-determining step (Equation 14.24), we have

$$\text{Rate} = k_2 \frac{k_1}{k_{-1}}[NO][Br_2][NO] = k[NO]^2[Br_2]$$

This is consistent with the experimental rate law (Equation 14.22). The experimental rate constant k is equal to $k_2 k_1/k_{-1}$. This mechanism, which involves only unimolecular and bimolecular processes, is far more probable than the single termolecular step (Equation 14.23).

    In general, *whenever a fast step precedes a slow one, we can solve for the concentration of an intermediate by assuming that an equilibrium is established in the fast step.*

SAMPLE EXERCISE 14.11

Show that the following mechanism for Equation 14.21 also produces a rate law consistent with the experimentally observed one:

Step 1: $NO(g) + NO(g) \underset{k_{-1}}{\overset{k_1}{\rightleftharpoons}} N_2O_2(g)$ (fast, equilibrium)

Step 2: $N_2O_2(g) + Br_2(g) \xrightarrow{k_2} 2NOBr(g)$ (slow)

SOLUTION   The second step is rate-determining, and so the overall rate is

$$\text{Rate} = k_2[N_2O_2][Br_2]$$

We solve for the concentration of the intermediate N_2O_2 by assuming that an equilibrium is established in step 1; thus, the rates of the forward and reverse reactions in step 1 are equal:

$$k_1[NO]^2 = k_{-1}[N_2O_2]$$

$$[N_2O_2] = \frac{k_1}{k_{-1}}[NO]^2$$

Substituting this expression into the rate expression gives

$$\text{Rate} = k_2 \frac{k_1}{k_{-1}}[NO]^2[Br_2] = k[NO]^2[Br_2]$$

Thus, this mechanism also yields a rate law consistent with the experimental one.

PRACTICE EXERCISE

The first step of a mechanism involving the reaction of bromine is

$$Br_2(g) \underset{k_{-1}}{\overset{k_1}{\rightleftharpoons}} 2Br(g) \qquad \text{(fast, equilibrium)}$$

What is the expression relating the concentration of $Br(g)$ to that of $Br_2(g)$?

Answer: $[Br] = \left(\dfrac{k_1}{k_{-1}}[Br_2]\right)^{1/2}$

14.6 Catalysis

A **catalyst** is a substance that changes the speed of a chemical reaction without itself undergoing a permanent chemical change in the process. Catalysts are very common; most reactions occurring in the human body, in the atmosphere, in the oceans, or in industrial chemical processes are affected by catalysts.

In your laboratory work, you may have carried out the reaction in which oxygen is produced by heating potassium chlorate, $KClO_3$:

$$2KClO_3(s) \overset{\Delta}{\longrightarrow} 2KCl(s) + 3O_2(g)$$

In the absence of a catalyst, $KClO_3$ does not readily decompose in this manner, even on strong heating. However, mixing black manganese dioxide, MnO_2, with the $KClO_3$ before heating causes the reaction to occur much more readily. The MnO_2 can be recovered largely unchanged from this reaction, and so the overall chemical process is clearly still the same. Thus, MnO_2 acts as a catalyst for decomposition of $KClO_3$.

Much industrial chemical research is devoted to the search for new and more effective catalysts for reactions of commercial importance. Extensive research efforts also are devoted to finding means of inhibiting or removing certain catalysts that promote undesirable reactions, such as those involved in corrosion of metals, aging, and tooth decay.

Homogeneous Catalysis

A catalyst that is present in the same phase as the reacting molecules is a **homogeneous catalyst.** Examples abound both in solution and in the gas phase. Consider, as an example, the decomposition of aqueous hydrogen peroxide, $H_2O_2(aq)$, into water and oxygen:

$$2H_2O_2(aq) \longrightarrow 2H_2O(l) + O_2(g) \qquad [14.26]$$

In the absence of a catalyst, this reaction occurs at an extremely slow rate. Many different substances are capable of catalyzing the reaction; among these is bromine, Br_2. The bromine reacts with hydrogen peroxide in acidic solution, forming bromide ion and liberating oxygen:

$$Br_2(aq) + H_2O_2(aq) \longrightarrow 2Br^-(aq) + 2H^+(aq) + O_2(g) \qquad [14.27]$$

Learning Goal 16: Describe the effect of a catalyst on the energy requirements for a reaction.

Lee R. Summerlin and James L. Ealy, Jr., "Catalytic Decomposition of Hydrogen Peroxide: Foam Production," *Chemical Demonstrations, A Sourcebook for Teachers* (Washington: American Chemical Society, 1985), p. 71.

Teaching Note: Chlorine atoms are catalysts for ozone destruction in the stratosphere. See Chapter 18.

If this were the complete reaction, bromine would not be a catalyst, because it undergoes chemical change in the reaction. It happens, however, that hydrogen peroxide reacts with bromide ion in acidic solution to form bromine:

$$2Br^-(aq) + H_2O_2(aq) + 2H^+(aq) \longrightarrow Br_2(l) + 2H_2O(l) \quad [14.28]$$

The overall sum of Equations 14.27 and 14.28 is just Equation 14.26. We see that bromine is indeed a catalyst in the reaction because it speeds the overall reaction without itself undergoing any net change. You should convince yourself that the bromide ion, Br^-, can also catalyze Equation 14.26. Figure 14.15 shows the effect of adding bromide ion on the decomposition of an aqueous hydrogen peroxide solution.

On the basis of the Arrhenius expression for a chemical reaction, Equation 14.16, the rate constant k is determined by the activation energy, E_a, and the frequency factor, A. A catalyst may affect the rate of reaction by altering the value for either E_a or A. The most dramatic catalytic effects come from lowering E_a. As a general rule, *a catalyst lowers the overall activation energy for a chemical reaction.* The lowering of E_a by a catalyst is shown in Figure 14.16.

A catalyst usually lowers the overall activation energy for a reaction by providing a completely different mechanism for the reaction. The examples given above involve a reversible, cyclic reaction of the catalyst with the reactants. For example, in the decomposition of hydrogen peroxide, two successive reactions of H_2O_2, with bromine and then with bromide, take place. Because these two reactions together serve as a catalytic pathway for hydrogen peroxide decomposition, *both* of them must have significantly lower activation energies than the uncatalyzed decomposition, as shown schematically in Figure 14.17.

Heterogeneous Catalysis

A **heterogeneous catalyst** exists in a different phase from the reactant molecules, usually as a solid in contact with either gaseous reactants or with reactants in a liquid solution. Many industrially important reactions are catalyzed by the

FIGURE 14.15 Effect of added NaBr on the decomposition of $H_2O_2(aq)$ solution (*a*). Very soon after adding colorless NaBr solution to an H_2O_2 solution, the solution turns brown because Br_2 is formed (Equation 14.28). (*b*) After a time, when the Br_2 concentration has built up, decomposition of H_2O_2 (Equation 14.27) occurs at a rapid pace with evolution of O_2. (Donald Clegg and Roxy Wilson)

(*a*)

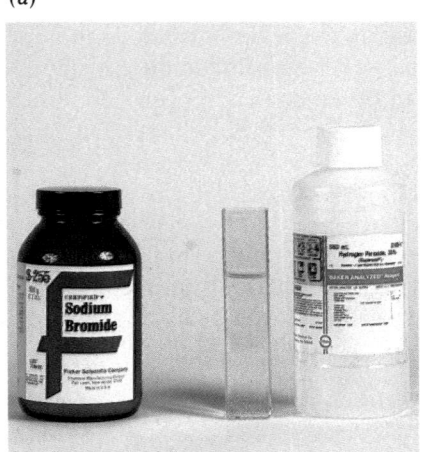

(*b*)

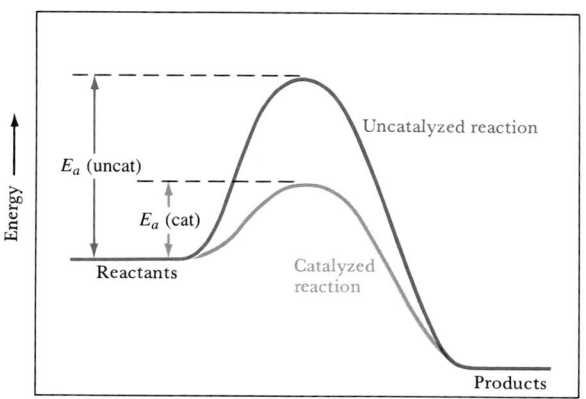

FIGURE 14.16 Energy profiles for catalyzed and uncatalyzed reactions. The catalyst functions in this example to lower the activation energy for reaction. Notice that the energies of reactants and products are unchanged by the catalyst.

surfaces of solids. For example, hydrocarbon molecules are rearranged to form gasoline with the aid of what are called "cracking" catalysts (see the Chemistry at Work box in Section 26.1). Heterogeneous catalysts are often composed of metals or metal oxides. Because the catalyzed reaction occurs on the surface, special methods are often used to prepare catalysts so that they have very large surface areas.

The initial step in heterogeneous catalysis is usually **adsorption** of reactants. *Adsorption* refers to the binding of molecules to a surface, whereas *absorption* refers to the uptake of molecules into the interior of another substance. ∞ (Sec. 13.6) Adsorption occurs because the atoms or ions at the surface of a solid are extremely reactive. Unlike their counterparts in the interior of the substance, they have unfulfilled valence requirements. The unused bonding capability of surface atoms or ions may be used to bond molecules from the gas or solution phase to the surface of the solid. In practice, not all the atoms or ions of the surface are reactive; various impurities may be adsorbed at the surface, and these may occupy many potential reaction sites and block further reaction. The places where reacting molecules may become adsorbed are called **active sites.** The number of active sites per unit amount of catalyst depends on the nature of the catalyst, on its method of preparation, and on its treatment before use.

 Figure 14.17

FIGURE 14.17 Energy profiles for the uncatalyzed decomposition of hydrogen peroxide and for the reaction as catalyzed by Br_2. The catalyzed reaction involves two successive steps, each of which has a lower activation energy than the uncatalyzed reaction.

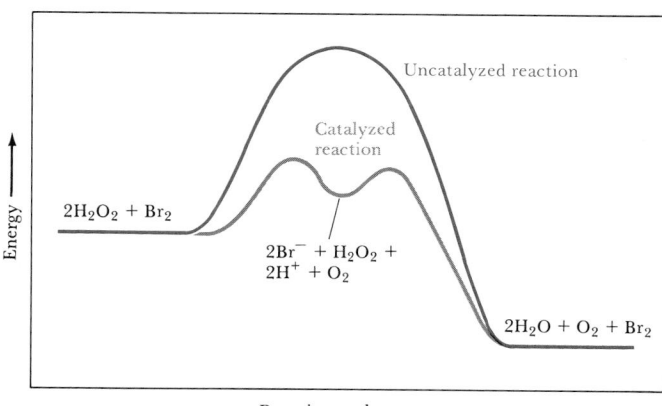

As an example of heterogeneous catalysis, consider the reaction of hydrogen with ethylene to form ethane:

$$\begin{array}{c}
\text{H}\!\!\diagdown \qquad \diagup\text{H} \\
\qquad\text{C}=\text{C} \qquad + \text{H}_2 \longrightarrow \\
\text{H}\!\!\diagup \qquad \diagdown\text{H}
\end{array}
\qquad
\begin{array}{c}
\text{H}\!\!\diagdown \qquad \diagup\text{H} \\
\text{H}-\text{C}-\text{C}-\text{H} \\
\text{H}\!\!\diagup \qquad \diagdown\text{H}
\end{array}
\qquad [14.29]$$

Ethylene   Ethane

In the absence of a catalyst, this reaction occurs slowly. However, in the presence of a very finely powdered metal such as nickel, palladium, or platinum, the reaction occurs rather easily at room temperature, under a few hundred atmospheres of hydrogen pressure. The mechanism by which reaction occurs is shown diagrammatically in Figure 14.18. Both ethylene and hydrogen are adsorbed at the metal surface [Figure 14.18(a)]. The adsorption of hydrogen results in breaking of the H—H bond and formation of two M—H bonds, where M represents the metal surface [Figure 14.18(b)]. The hydrogen atoms are relatively free to move about the surface. When they encounter an adsorbed ethylene, the hydrogen may become bound to the carbon [Figure 14.18(c)]. The carbon thus acquires four σ bonds about it, which reduces its tendency to remain adsorbed at the metal. When the other carbon also acquires a hydrogen, the ethane molecule is released from the surface [Figure 14.18(d)]. The active site is ready to adsorb another ethylene molecule and thus begin the cycle again.

FIGURE 14.18 Mechanism for reaction of ethylene with hydrogen on a catalytic surface. (a) The hydrogen and ethylene are adsorbed at the metal surface. (b) The H—H bond is broken to give adsorbed hydrogen atoms. (c) These migrate to the adsorbed ethylene and bond to the carbon atoms. (d) As C—H bonds are formed, the adsorption of the molecule to the metal surface is decreased, and ethane is released.

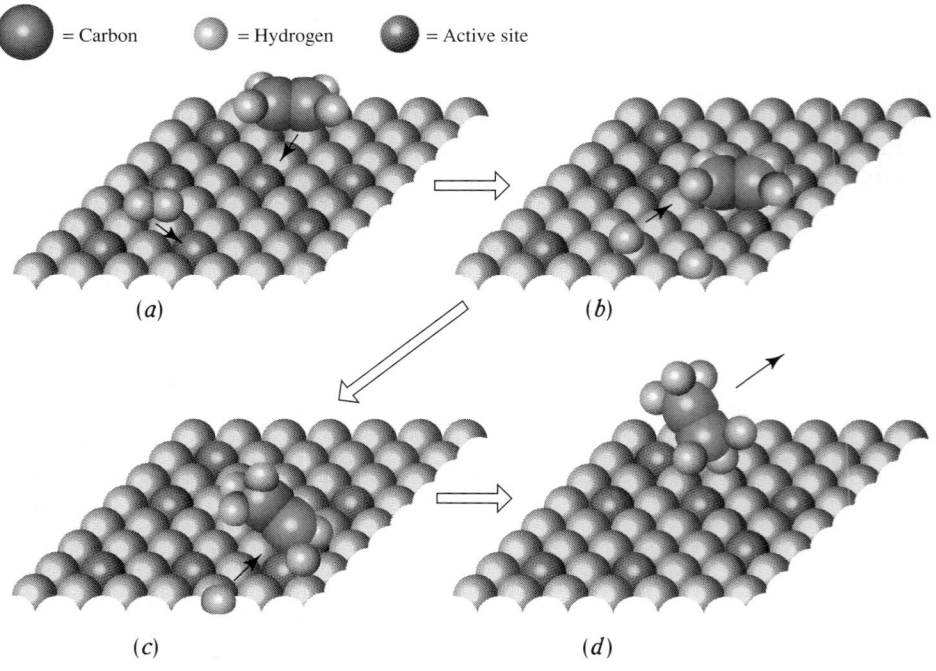

= Carbon   = Hydrogen   = Active site

(a)　(b)　(c)　(d)

Figure 14.18

CHEMISTRY AT WORK

Catalytic Converters

Heterogeneous catalysis plays a major role in the fight against urban air pollution. Two components of automobile exhausts that are involved in the formation of photochemical smog are nitrogen oxides and unburned hydrocarbons of various types (Section 18.4). In addition, automobile exhausts may contain considerable quantities of carbon monoxide. Even with the most careful attention to engine design and fuel characteristics, it is not possible under normal driving conditions to reduce the contents of these pollutants to an acceptable level in the exhaust gases coming from the engine. It is therefore necessary somehow to remove them from the exhaust gases before they are vented to the air. This removal is accomplished in the *catalytic converter*.

The catalytic converter, illustrated in Figure 14.19, must perform two distinct functions: (1) oxidation of CO and unburned hydrocarbons to carbon diox-

ide and water, and (2) reduction of nitrogen oxides to nitrogen gas:

$$CO, \text{hydrocarbons } (C_xH_y) \xrightarrow{O_2} CO_2 + H_2O$$
$$NO, NO_2 \longrightarrow N_2$$

These two functions require two distinctly different catalysts, and so the development of a successful catalyst system is a very difficult challenge. The catalysts must be effective over a wide range of operating temperatures; they must continue to be active in spite of the poisoning action of various gasoline additives emitted along with the exhaust; they must be sufficiently rugged to withstand exhaust gas turbulence and the mechanical shocks of driving under various conditions for thousands of miles.

FIGURE 14.19 Illustration of the arrangement and functions of a catalytic converter.

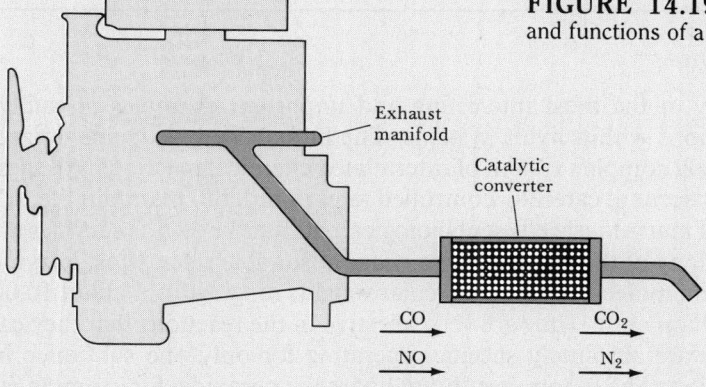

FIGURE 14.20 A stainless-steel catalytic converter used in automobiles. The zig-zag pattern of the metal foil provides favorable passage of exhaust gases and increases the surface area. Microscopic whiskers of aluminum oxide are grown on the stainless steel to anchor a coating that contains the noble-metal catalysts. The catalysts promote the conversion of exhaust gases into CO_2, H_2O, and N_2. (AC Rochester Division, GMC)

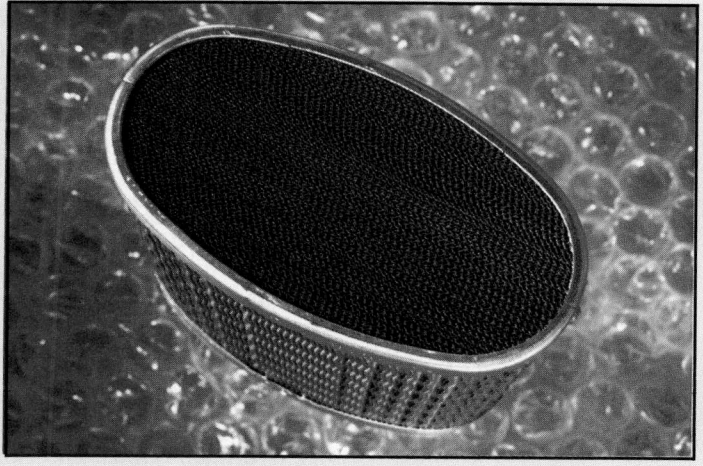

14.6 Catalysis   **521**

Catalysts that promote the combustion of CO and hydrocarbons are, in general, the transition-metal oxides and noble metals such as platinum. As an example, a mixture of two different metal oxides—CuO and Cr_2O_3, for example—might be used. These materials are supported on a structure (Figure 14.20) that allows the best possible contact between the flowing exhaust gas and the catalyst surface. Either bead or honeycomb structures made from alumina, Al_2O_3, and impregnated with the catalyst may be employed. Such catalysts operate by first adsorbing oxygen gas, also present in the exhaust gas. This adsorption weakens the O—O bond in O_2, so that oxygen atoms are in effect available for reaction with adsorbed CO to form CO_2. Hydrocarbon oxidation probably proceeds somewhat similarly, with the hydrocarbons first being adsorbed by rupture of a C—H bond.

The most effective catalysts for reduction of NO to yield N_2 and O_2 are transition-metal oxides and noble metals, the same kinds of materials that catalyze the oxidation of CO and hydrocarbons. The catalysts that are most effective in one reaction, however, are usually much less effective in the other. It is therefore necessary to have two different catalytic components.

Catalytic converters are remarkably efficient heterogeneous catalysts. The automotive exhaust gases are in contact with the catalyst for only 100 to 400 ms. In this very short time, 96 percent of the hydrocarbons and CO are converted to CO_2 and H_2O. The emission of nitrogen oxides is reduced by 76 percent.

Of course, there are costs as well as benefits associated with the use of catalytic converters. Some of the metals used in the converters are very expensive. Catalytic converters currently account for 35 percent of the platinum and 73 percent of the rhodium used in the United States. Both of these metals are far more expensive than gold. In addition, the catalysts are incompatible with lead-containing antiknock agents that used to be commonly added to gasoline to improve engine performance. Additives such as tetramethyl lead, $Pb(CH_3)_4$, and tetraethyl lead, $Pb(C_2H_5)_4$, "poison" the catalyst; that is, they bind to and block active catalytic sites, decreasing the catalytic activity. Partly because of the severe catalyst poisoning that results from the use of leaded fuels, cars built since 1975 have been engineered for use with unleaded gas.

Enzymes

Many of the most interesting and important examples of catalysis involve reactions within living systems. The human body is characterized by an extremely complex system of interrelated chemical reactions. All these reactions must occur at carefully controlled rates in order to maintain life. A large number of marvelously efficient biological catalysts known as **enzymes** are necessary for many of these reactions to occur at suitable rates. Most enzymes are large protein molecules with molecular weights ranging from about 10,000 to about 1 million amu. They are very selective in the reactions that they catalyze, and some are absolutely specific, operating for only one substance in only one reaction. The decomposition of hydrogen peroxide, for example, is an important biological process. Because hydrogen peroxide is strongly oxidizing, it can be physiologically harmful. For this reason, the blood and livers of mammals contain an enzyme, *catalase,* that catalyzes the decomposition of hydrogen peroxide into water and oxygen (Figure 14.21).

The reaction that a given enzyme catalyzes occurs at a specific site on the enzyme called the *active site.* The substances that undergo reaction at this site are called **substrates.** A simple explanation for the specificity of enzymes is provided by the **lock-and-key model,** illustrated in Figure 14.22. The substrate is pictured as fitting neatly into a special place on the enzyme (the active site), much like a specific key fitting into a lock. The combination of the enzyme and the substrate is called the *enzyme-substrate complex.* Although the figure shows both the active site and its complementary substrate as having rigid shapes, there is often a fair amount of flexibility in the active site. Thus, the active site may change shape as it binds the substrate. The binding between the substrate and the active site involves intermolecular forces such as dipole-dipole attractions, hydrogen bonds, and London dispersion forces.

FIGURE 14.21 The addition of ground-up beef liver to hydrogen peroxide causes rapid decomposition into water and oxygen. The decomposition is catalyzed by the enzyme *catalase.* Grinding the liver breaks open the cells so that reaction takes place extracellularly. (© Richard Megna/ Fundamental Photographs)

As the substrate molecules enter the active site, they are somehow activated so that they are capable of extremely rapid reaction. This activation may result from the withdrawal or donation of electron density at a particular bond by the enzyme. In addition, in the process of fitting into the active site, the substrate molecule may be distorted and thus made more reactive. Once the reaction occurs, the products then depart, allowing another substrate molecule to enter.

The activity of an enzyme is destroyed if some molecule in the solution is able to bind strongly to the active site and block the entry of the substrate. Such substances are called *enzyme inhibitors.* Nerve poisons and certain toxic metal ions such as lead and mercury are believed to act in this way to inhibit enzyme activity. Some other poisons act by attaching elsewhere on the enzyme, thereby distorting the active site so the substrate no longer fits.

Enzymes are enormously more efficient than ordinary nonbiochemical catalysts. The number of individual catalyzed reaction events occurring at a particular active site, called the *turnover number,* is generally in the range of 10^3 to 10^7 per second. Such large turnover numbers correspond to very low activation energies.

Teaching Note: Some scientists, especially those working with biological systems, have started using the term *catalyst* to mean specifically a substance that accelerates a reaction and the term *inhibitor* to refer to a substance that slows a reaction.

FIGURE 14.22 The lock-and-key model for enzyme action. The correct substrate is recognized by its ability to fit the active site of the enzyme, forming the enzyme-substrate complex. After the reaction of the substrate is complete, the products separate from the enzyme.

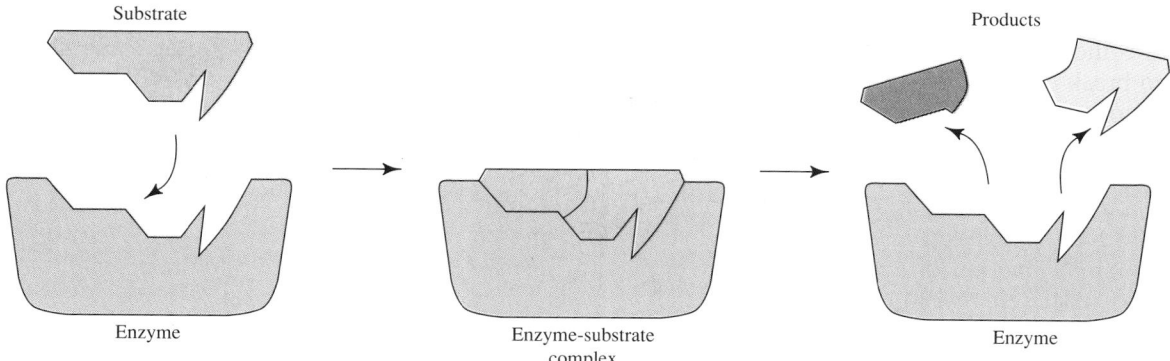

For Review

Summary

In this chapter, we have discussed ways of expressing reaction rates and the factors that influence these rates, namely, concentration, temperature, and catalysts. Rates are expressed as changes in concentration per unit of time; typically, for reactions in solution, the units are M/s. The quantitative relationship between rate and concentration is expressed by the rate law, which often has the following form: Rate = $k[\text{reactant 1}]^m[\text{reactant 2}]^n$. . . . The constant k in the rate law is called the rate constant; the exponents m, n, and so forth, are called reaction orders. The rate law depends not on the overall reaction but on the mechanism by which it occurs. Thus, rate laws cannot ordinarily be determined from the coefficients in the balanced chemical equation but must be determined by experiment.

In a first-order reaction, the reaction rate is proportional to the concentration of a single reactant raised to the first power: Rate = $k[\text{A}]$. In such cases, $\ln [\text{A}]_t = -kt + \ln [\text{A}]_0$, where $[\text{A}]_t$ is the concentration of reactant A at time t, k is the rate constant, and $[\text{A}]_0$ is the initial concentration of reactant A. Thus, a graph of $\ln [\text{A}]_t$ versus time yields a straight line of slope $-k$. First-order reactions are also characterized by having a constant half-life, which is related to the rate constant: $t_{1/2} = 0.693/k$. Reactions more complex than first order yield different expressions for the rate constant and half-life. For example, for second-order reactions, rate = $k[\text{A}]^2$, the following relationship holds: $1/[\text{A}]_t = 1/[\text{A}]_0 + kt$; thus, in this case a graph of $1/[\text{A}]_t$ versus time yields a straight line.

Reactions occur as a result of collisions between molecules. Collisions bring atoms together so that new chemical bonds can form. In addition, when molecules collide, part of their kinetic energies may be used to break old bonds. Of course, not all collisions lead to a reaction. In order for a reaction to occur, molecules must collide with sufficient energy and proper orientation. The minimum energy required for a reaction to occur is called the activation energy. When the activation energy is appreciable, only a very small fraction of all collisions between reactants provide the energy required to surmount the activation-energy barrier and form the products of the

reaction. By increasing the temperature of a system, we can increase the fraction of molecules whose kinetic energies exceed the activation energy and thereby increase the reaction rate. From the manner in which the rate constant for a reaction varies with temperature, it is possible to determine the activation energy, E_a, for a reaction using the Arrhenius equation: $\ln k = \ln A - E_a/RT$. A graph of $\ln k$ versus $1/T$ yields a straight line whose slope is $-E_a/R$.

From a knowledge of the rate law for a reaction and with other experimental information, a picture of how the reaction proceeds may be formulated. The overall reaction may occur in a series of elementary steps or in a single elementary step. Elementary steps (or elementary processes) may be unimolecular, bimolecular, or termolecular, depending on whether one, two, or three molecules, respectively, are involved as reactants. The rate law of an elementary step is related directly to its molecularity. Therefore, unimolecular reactions have first-order rate laws, and bimolecular reactions have second-order rate laws. Termolecular reactions, which are very rare, have third-order rate laws.

The sequence of elementary steps by which a reaction proceeds is known as its reaction mechanism. If a reaction proceeds by a multistep mechanism, one of the elementary steps may be much slower than the others and so be the rate-determining step. The rate-determining step governs the rate law for the overall process.

A catalyst speeds a reaction without itself undergoing a net chemical change. It does so by providing a different mechanism for the reaction, one having a lower activation-energy barrier. Catalysts may be either homogeneous—that is, in the same phase with the reactants—or heterogeneous—in a separate phase. Heterogeneous catalysts are particularly important in large-scale industrial chemical processes and in applications such as the catalytic converter of an automobile. Enzymes are biological catalysts. The lock-and-key mechanism pictures the catalysis as occurring as the substrate is bound to the active site of the enzyme.

Key Terms

chemical kinetics
reaction rate (Sec. 14.1)
instantaneous rate (Sec. 14.1)
rate law (Sec. 14.2)
rate constant (Sec. 14.2)
reaction order (Sec. 14.2)
overall reaction order (Sec. 14.2)
first-order reaction (Sec. 14.3)
half-life (Sec. 14.3)
second-order reaction (Sec. 14.3)
collision model (Sec. 14.4)
activation energy (Sec. 14.4)
activated complex (Sec. 14.4)
transition state (Sec. 14.4)
Arrhenius equation (Sec. 14.4)
frequency factor (Sec. 14.4)

reaction mechanism (Sec. 14.5)
elementary steps (Sec. 14.5)
molecularity (Sec. 14.5)
unimolecular (Sec. 14.5)
bimolecular (Sec. 14.5)
termolecular (Sec. 14.5)
intermediate (Sec. 14.5)
rate-determining step (Sec. 14.5)
catalyst (Sec. 14.6)
homogeneous catalyst (Sec. 14.6)
heterogeneous catalyst (Sec. 14.6)
adsorption (Sec. 14.6)
active sites (Sec. 14.6)
enzymes (Sec. 14.6)
substrate (Sec. 14.6)
lock-and-key model (Sec. 14.6)

Exercises

Reaction Rates

14.1. For each of the following reactions, indicate how the rate of disappearance of each reactant is related to the rate of appearance of each product:
(a) $2H_2O(g) \longrightarrow 2H_2(g) + O_2(g)$
(b) $CO(g) + 2H_2(g) \longrightarrow CH_3OH(g)$
(c) $S_2O_8^{2-}(aq) + 2I^-(aq) \longrightarrow 2SO_4^{2-}(aq) + I_2(aq)$

14.2. For each of the following reactions, indicate how the rate of disappearance of each reactant is related to the rate of appearance of each product:
(a) $N_2(g) + 3H_2(g) \longrightarrow 2NH_3(g)$
(b) $2NO(g) + Cl_2(g) \longrightarrow 2NOCl(g)$
(c) $B_2H_6(g) + 3O_2(g) \longrightarrow B_2O_3(s) + 3H_2O(g)$

14.3. (a) Consider the combustion of $H_2(g)$, $2H_2(g) + O_2(g) \longrightarrow 2H_2O(g)$. If hydrogen is burning at the rate of 4.6 mol/s, what is the rate of consumption of oxygen? What is the rate of formation of water vapor? (b) The reaction $2NO(g) + Cl_2(g) \longrightarrow 2NOCl(g)$ is carried out in a closed vessel. If the partial pressure of NO is decreasing at the rate of 30 torr/min, what is the rate of change of the total pressure of the vessel?

14.4. (a) Consider the combustion of methane, $CH_4(g) + 2O_2(g) \longrightarrow CO_2(g) + 2H_2O(g)$. If the concentration of CH_4 is decreasing at the rate of 0.40 M/s, what are the rates of change in the concentrations of CO_2 and H_2O? (b) If the rate of increase in NH_3 pressure in a closed reaction vessel from the reaction $N_2(g) + 3H_2(g) \longrightarrow 2NH_3(g)$ is 100 torr/hr, what is the rate of change of the total pressure in the vessel?

14.5. The rate of disappearance of H^+ was measured for the following reaction:

$$CH_3OH(aq) + HCl(aq) \longrightarrow CH_3Cl(aq) + H_2O(l)$$

The following data were collected:

Time (min)	$[H^+]$ (M)
0.0	1.85
79.0	1.67
158.0	1.52
316.0	1.30
632.0	1.00

Calculate the average rate of reaction for the time interval between each measurement.

14.6. The rearrangement of methyl isonitrile, CH_3NC, was studied in the gas phase at 215°C, and the following data were obtained:

Time (s)	$[CH_3NC]$ (M)
0	0.0165
2,000	0.0110
5,000	0.00591
8,000	0.00314
12,000	0.00137
15,000	0.00074

Calculate the average rate of reaction for the time interval between each measurement.

14.7. Using the data provided in Exercise 14.5, make a graph of $[H^+]$ versus time. Draw tangents to the curve at $t = 100$ and $t = 500$ min. Determine the rates at these times.

14.8. Using the data provided in Exercise 14.6, make a graph of $[CH_3NC]$ versus time. Draw tangents to the curve at $t = 3500$ and $t = 13,500$ s. Determine the rates at these times.

Rate Laws

14.9. The decomposition of N_2O_5 in carbon tetrachloride proceeds as follows: $2N_2O_5 \longrightarrow 4NO_2 + O_2$. The rate law is first order in N_2O_5. At $45°C$, the rate constant is $6.08 \times 10^{-4} s^{-1}$. **(a)** Write the rate law for the reaction. **(b)** What is the rate of reaction when $[N_2O_5] = 0.100\ M$? **(c)** What happens to the rate when the concentration of N_2O_5 is doubled to $0.200\ M$?

14.10. Consider the following reaction:

$$2NO(g) + 2H_2(g) \longrightarrow N_2(g) + 2H_2O(g)$$

(a) The rate law for this reaction is first order in H_2 and second order in NO. Write the rate law. **(b)** If the rate constant for this reaction at 1000 K is $6.0 \times 10^4\ M^{-2} s^{-1}$, what is the reaction rate when $[NO] = 0.050\ M$ and $[H_2] = 0.010\ M$? **(c)** What is the reaction rate at 1000 K when the concentration of NO is doubled, to $0.10\ M$, while the concentration of H_2 is $0.010\ M$?

14.11. Consider the following reaction:

$$CH_3Br(aq) + OH^-(aq) \longrightarrow CH_3OH(aq) + Br^-(aq)$$

The rate law for this reaction is first order in CH_3Br and first order in OH^-. When $[CH_3Br]$ is $0.010\ M$ and $[OH^-]$ is $0.10\ M$, the reaction rate at 298 K is 0.28 M/s. **(a)** What is the value of the rate constant? **(b)** What are the units of the rate constant? **(c)** What would happen to the rate if the concentration of OH^- were tripled?

14.12. The reaction $2NO(g) + O_2(g) \longrightarrow 2NO_2(g)$ is second order in NO and first order in O_2. When $[NO] = 0.030\ M$ and $[O_2] = 0.040\ M$, the observed rate is $7.2 \times 10^{-5}\ M/s$. **(a)** What is the value of the rate constant? **(b)** What are the units of the rate constant? **(c)** What would happen to the rate if the concentration of NO were decreased by a factor of 2?

14.13. What are the rate laws for two reactions of the type $A + B \longrightarrow C$ if the following observations are made: **(a)** For the first reaction, doubling the concentration of A doubles the rate, whereas doubling the concentration of B has no effect on the rate. **(b)** For the second reaction, tripling the concentration of A triples the rate, whereas tripling the concentration of B increases the rate by a factor of 9.

14.14. If the rate for a reaction behaves in the following way, what is the rate law? **(a)** Doubling the concentration of reactant A causes the rate to increase by a factor of 4,

whereas tripling the concentration of reactant B triples the rate. **(b)** When the concentration of reactant X is cut in half, the rate is unaffected, whereas when the concentration of reactant Y is cut in half, the rate is reduced to one-half its initial value.

14.15. The following data were collected for the rate of disappearance of NO in the reaction $2NO(g) + O_2(g) \longrightarrow 2NO_2(g)$:

Experiment	[NO] (M)	[O$_2$] (M)	Initial rate (M/s)
1	0.0126	0.0125	1.41×10^{-2}
2	0.0252	0.0250	1.13×10^{-1}
3	0.0252	0.0125	5.64×10^{-2}

Determine the rate law and the value of the rate constant.

14.16. The following data were measured for the reaction $BF_3(g) + NH_3(g) \longrightarrow F_3BNH_3(g)$:

Experiment	[BF$_3$] (M)	[NH$_3$] (M)	Initial rate (M/s)
1	0.250	0.250	0.2130
2	0.250	0.125	0.1065
3	0.200	0.100	0.0682
4	0.350	0.100	0.1193
5	0.175	0.100	0.0596

(a) What is the rate law for the reaction? **(b)** What is the overall order of the reaction? **(c)** What is the value of the rate constant for the reaction?

14.17. The following data were collected for the gas-phase reaction between nitric oxide and bromine at $273°C$:

$$2NO(g) + Br_2(g) \longrightarrow 2NOBr(g)$$

14.3

#14.5

$$\frac{-30\text{ tan}}{\text{min}} - \frac{15\text{ tan}}{\text{min}} + \frac{30\text{ tan}}{\text{min}} = -\frac{15\text{ tan}}{\text{min}}$$

average rate

#14.3

$$2NO + Cl_2 \longrightarrow 2NOCl$$

$$Rate = -\frac{\Delta[NO]}{\Delta t} = \frac{30 \text{ torr decrease}}{\text{min}}$$

$$\frac{\Delta[Cl_2]}{\Delta t} = \frac{1}{2} \cdot \frac{-\Delta[NO]}{\Delta t} = \frac{15 \text{ torr decrease}}{\text{min}}$$

$$\frac{\Delta[NOCl]}{\Delta t} = -\frac{\Delta[NO]}{\Delta t} = \frac{30 \text{ torr increase}}{\text{min}}$$

Rate of change in total pressure must tell decrease/increase ...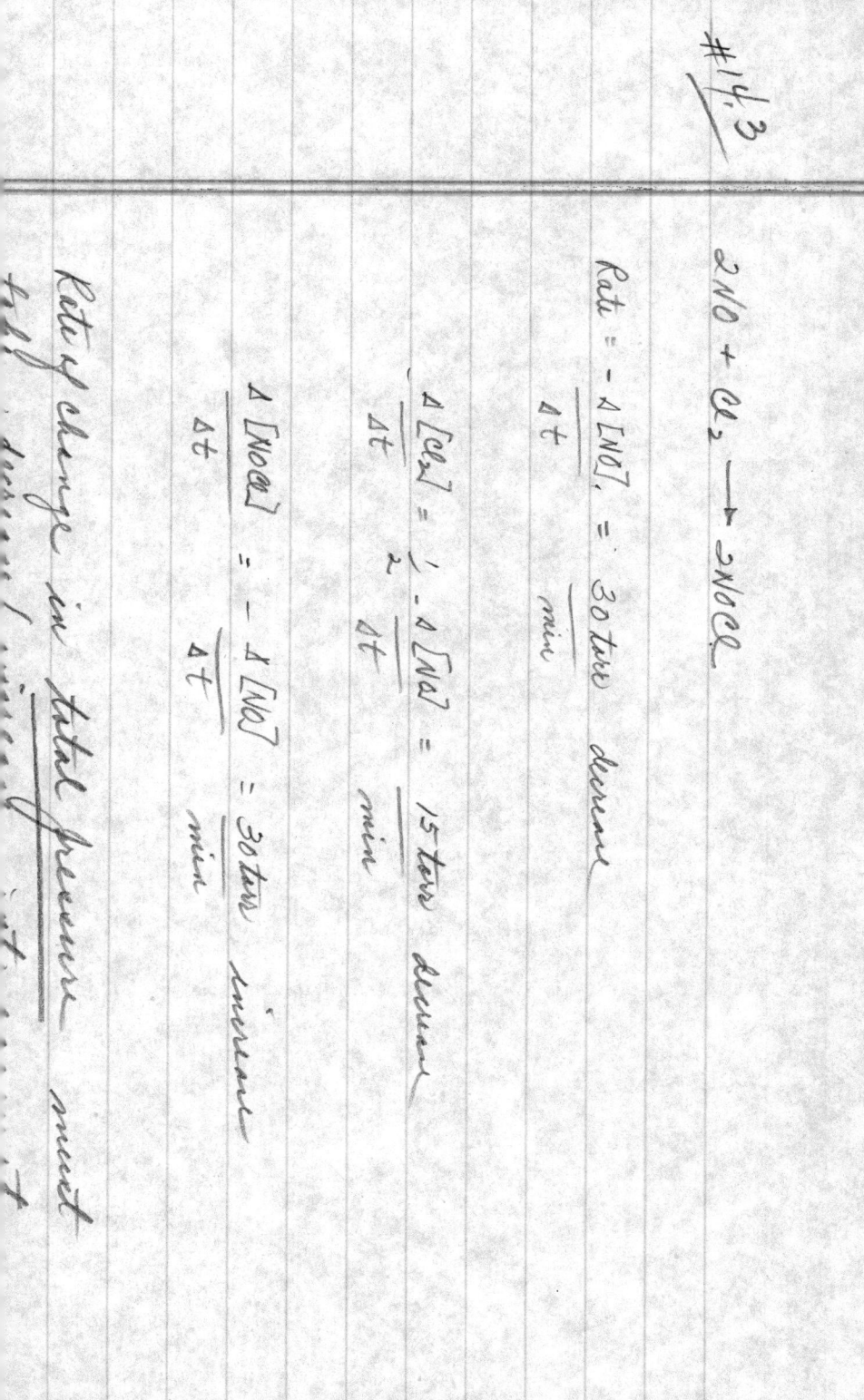

Experiment	[NO] (M)	[Br$_2$] (M)	Initial rate of appearance of NOBr (M/s)
1	0.10	0.10	12
2	0.10	0.20	24
3	0.20	0.10	48
4	0.30	0.10	108

(a) Determine the rate law. (b) Calculate the value of the rate constant for the appearance of NOBr. (c) How is the rate of appearance of NOBr related to the rate of disappearance of Br$_2$? (d) What is the rate of appearance of NOBr when [NO] = 0.15 M and [Br$_2$] = 0.25 M? (e) What is the rate of disappearance of Br$_2$ when [NO] = 0.075 M and [Br$_2$] = 0.185 M?

14.18. Consider the reaction of peroxydisulfate ion, $S_2O_8^{2-}$, with iodide ion, I^-, in aqueous solution:

$$S_2O_8^{2-}(aq) + 3I^-(aq) \longrightarrow 2SO_4^{2-}(aq) + I_3^-(aq)$$

At a particular temperature, the rate of this reaction varies with reactant concentrations in the following manner:

Experiment	[S$_2$O$_8^{2-}$] (M)	[I$^-$] (M)	$\dfrac{-\Delta[S_2O_8^{2-}]}{\Delta t}$ (M/s)
1	0.038	0.060	1.4×10^{-5}
2	0.076	0.060	2.8×10^{-5}
3	0.076	0.030	1.4×10^{-5}

(a) Write the rate law for the rate of disappearance of $S_2O_8^{2-}$. (b) What is the value of the rate constant for the disappearance of $S_2O_8^{2-}$? (c) What is the rate of disappearance of $S_2O_8^{2-}$ when [$S_2O_8^{2-}$] = 0.025 M and [I^-] = 0.100 M? (d) What is the rate of appearance of SO_4^{2-} when [$S_2O_8^{2-}$] = 0.025 M and [I^-] = 0.050 M?

$$Rate = -\frac{\Delta\,[S_2O_8^{2-}]}{\Delta t} = k\,[S_2O_8^{2-}]\,[I^-]$$

$$k = 6.1 \times 10^{-3}\ L\,mol^{-1}\,s^{-1}$$

Change of Concentration with Time

14.19. Define the term *half-life*. What is unique about the half-life of first-order reactions?

14.20. It takes 36 min for the concentration of a substance to decrease to 25 percent of its initial value. If the decomposition is first order, what is the half-life for the process?

14.21. The thermal decomposition of $N_2O_5(g)$ to form $NO_2(g)$ and $O_2(g)$ is a first-order reaction. The rate constant for the reaction is 5.1×10^{-4} s^{-1} at 318 K. What is the half-life of this process?

14.22. The gas-phase decomposition of N_2O to form N_2 and O_2 is first order in N_2O. At 1000 K, the half-life for this process is 0.91 s. What is the rate constant at this temperature?

14.23. The first-order rate constant for the decomposition of N_2O_5 to NO_2 and O_2 at 70°C is 6.82×10^{-3} s^{-1}. Suppose we start with 0.300 mol of $N_2O_5(g)$ in a 0.500-L container. (a) How many moles of N_2O_5 will remain after 1.5 min? (b) How many minutes will it take for the quantity of N_2O_5 to drop to 0.030 mol? (c) What is the half-life of N_2O_5 at 70°C?

14.24. The first-order rate constant for the decomposition of a certain antibiotic in water at 20°C is 1.65 yr^{-1}. (a) If a 6.0×10^{-3} M solution of the antibiotic is stored at 20°C, what will its concentration be after 3 months? After 1 year? (b) How long will it take for the concentration of the solution to drop to 1.0×10^{-3} M? (c) What is the half-life of the antibiotic solution?

14.25. The reaction

$$SO_2Cl_2(g) \longrightarrow SO_2(g) + Cl_2(g)$$

is first order in SO_2Cl_2. Using the following kinetic data, determine the magnitude of the first-order rate constant:

Time (s)	Pressure SO$_2$Cl$_2$ (atm)
0	1.000
2,500	0.947
5,000	0.895
7,500	0.848
10,000	0.803

14.26. From the following data for the first-order gas-phase rearrangement of CH_3NC at 215°C, calculate the first-order rate constant and half-life for the reaction:

Time (s)	Pressure CH$_3$NC (torr)
0	502
2,000	335
5,000	180
8,000	95.5
12,000	41.7
15,000	22.4

14.27. The decomposition of N_2O_5 has been studied in carbon tetrachloride solution at 45°C. The following data were obtained:

Time (min)	$[N_2O_5]$ (M)
0.0	0.90
5.0	0.75
10.0	0.63
20.0	0.44
50.0	0.15

Time (s)	$[NO_2]$ (M)
0.0	0.100
5.0	0.017
10.0	0.0090
15.0	0.0062
20.0	0.0047

(a) Is the reaction first order or second order with respect to N_2O_5? (b) What is the value of the rate constant?

14.28. The gas-phase decomposition of NO_2 to form NO and O_2 is studied at 383°C, giving the following data:

(a) Is the reaction first order or second order with respect to the concentration of NO_2? (b) What is the value of the rate constant?

Temperature and Rate

14.29. What factors determine whether a collision between two molecules will lead to a chemical reaction?

14.30. Show how O_3 and NO molecules might collide to produce O_2 and ONO molecules. How might they collide in a way that cannot produce a reaction?

14.31. For the reaction $2N_2O_5(g) \longrightarrow 4NO_2(g) + O_2(g)$, the activation energy, E_a, and overall ΔE are 100 kJ/mol and -23 kJ/mol, respectively. (a) Sketch the energy profile for this reaction. (b) What is the activation energy for the reverse reaction?

14.32. For the uncatalyzed decomposition of $H_2O_2(aq)$ to form $H_2O(l)$ and $O_2(g)$, the activation energy and overall ΔE are 75.3 kJ/mol and -98.1 kJ/mol, respectively. (a) Sketch the energy profile for this reaction. (b) What is the activation energy for the reverse reaction?

14.33. Based on their activation energies and energy changes, which of the following reactions would be fastest and which would be slowest? (a) $E_a = 30$ kJ/mol; $\Delta E = -10$ kJ/mol; (b) $E_a = 45$ kJ/mol, $\Delta E = 15$ kJ/mol; (c) $E_a = 60$ kJ/mol, $\Delta E = 10$ kJ/mol.

14.34. Which of the reactions in Exercise 14.33 will be fastest in the reverse direction? Which will be slowest?

14.35. Two reactions have identical values for E_a. Does this ensure that they will have the same rate constant if run at the same temperature? Explain.

14.36. Two similar reactions have the same rate constant at 25°C, but at 35°C one of the reactions has a higher rate constant than the other. Account for these observations.

14.37. The gas-phase decomposition of HI into H_2 and I_2 is found to have $E_a = 182$ kJ/mol. The rate constant at 700°C is 1.57×10^{-5} M^{-1} s^{-1}. What is the value of k at (a) 600°C; (b) 800°C?

14.38. The rate constant, k, for a reaction is 3.0×10^{-2} s^{-1} at 0°C. Calculate k at 75°C if (a) $E_a = 47.8$ kJ/mol; (b) $E_a = 125$ kJ/mol.

14.39. The rate of the reaction

$$CH_3COOC_2H_5(aq) + OH^-(aq) \longrightarrow$$
$$CH_3COO^-(aq) + C_2H_5OH(aq)$$

was measured at several temperatures, and the following data were collected:

Temperature (°C)	k (M^{-1} s^{-1})
15	0.0521
25	0.101
35	0.184
45	0.332

Using these data, construct a graph of ln k versus $1/T$. Using your graph, determine the value of E_a.

14.40. The temperature dependence of the rate constant for the reaction

$$CO(g) + NO_2(g) \longrightarrow CO_2(g) + NO(g)$$

is tabulated below. Calculate E_a and A.

Temperature (K)	k (M^{-1} s^{-1})
600	0.028
650	0.22
700	1.3
750	6.0
800	23

[14.41]. For a particular reaction, raising the temperature from $27°C$ to $37°C$ increases the rate by a factor of 2. What is the activation energy for the reaction?

[14.42]. The activation energy of a reaction is 38.2 kJ/mol. How many times faster will the reaction occur at $40°C$ than at $0°C$?

Reaction Mechanisms

14.43. Explain the difference among unimolecular, bimolecular, and termolecular elementary processes. Why are termolecular processes very rare?

14.44. Can the rate law for a general reaction $A + B \longrightarrow C$ be predicted without knowing the reaction mechanism? If it is specified that the reaction is an elementary step, what do you know about the rate law of the reaction?

14.45. What is the molecularity of each of the following elementary processes? Write the rate law for each.
(a) $N_2O(g) + Cl(g) \longrightarrow N_2(g) + ClO(g)$
(b) $Cl_2(g) \longrightarrow 2Cl(g)$
(c) $NO(g) + Cl_2(g) \longrightarrow NOCl_2(g)$

14.46. What is the molecularity of each of the following elementary processes? Write the rate law for each.
(a) $NO(g) + O_3(g) \longrightarrow NO_2(g) + O_2(g)$
(b) $CO(g) + Cl_2(g) \longrightarrow COCl_2(g)$
(c) $O_3(g) \longrightarrow O_2(g) + O(g)$

14.47. The following mechanism has been proposed for the reaction of NO with H_2 to form N_2O and H_2O:

$$NO(g) + NO(g) \longrightarrow N_2O_2(g)$$
$$N_2O_2(g) + H_2(g) \longrightarrow N_2O(g) + H_2O(g)$$

(a) Show that the elementary steps of the proposed mechanism add to provide a balanced equation for the reaction. (b) Write a rate law for each elementary step in the mechanism. (c) Identify any intermediates in the mechanism. (d) The observed rate law is: Rate $= k[NO]^2[H_2]$. If the proposed mechanism is correct, what can we conclude about the relative speeds of the first and second steps?

14.48. The balanced equation for the oxidation of HBr is $4HBr(g) + O_2(g) \longrightarrow 2H_2O(g) + 2Br_2(g)$. The following mechanism has been proposed:

$$HBr + O_2 \longrightarrow HOOBr$$
$$HOOBr + HBr \longrightarrow 2HOBr$$
$$HOBr + HBr \longrightarrow H_2O + Br_2$$

(a) Indicate whether the elementary steps of the proposed mechanism add to give the balanced equation for the reaction. (Hint: You may need to multiply all the coefficients of a given elementary step by some integer before adding.) (b) Write the rate law for each elementary step. (c) Identify any intermediates in the mechanism. (d) The reaction is found to be first order with respect to both HBr and O_2. Neither HOBr nor HOOBr is detected among the products. What can you conclude about the rate-determining step?

14.49. Consider the following reaction:

$$H_2(g) + 2ICl(g) \longrightarrow 2HCl(g) + I_2(g)$$

The rate law for this reaction is first order in both H_2 and ICl: Rate $= k[H_2][ICl]$. Which of the following mechanisms are consistent with the observed rate law?
(a) $2ICl(g) + H_2(g) \longrightarrow 2HCl(g) + I_2(g)$
  (termolecular reaction)
(b) $H_2(g) + ICl(g) \longrightarrow HI(g) + HCl(g)$ (slow)
  $HI(g) + ICl(g) \longrightarrow HCl(g) + I_2(g)$ (fast)
(c) $H_2(g) + ICl(g) \longrightarrow HI(g) + HCl(g)$ (fast)
  $HI(g) + ICl(g) \longrightarrow HCl(g) + I_2(g)$ (slow)
(d) $H_2(g) + ICl(g) \longrightarrow HCII(g) + H(g)$ (slow)
  $H(g) + ICl(g) \longrightarrow HCl(g) + I(g)$ (fast)
  $HCII(g) \longrightarrow HCl(g) + I(g)$ (fast)
  $I(g) + I(g) \longrightarrow I_2(g)$ (fast)

14.50. The reaction $2NO(g) + Cl_2(g) \longrightarrow 2NOCl(g)$ obeys the rate law, rate $= k[NO]^2[Cl_2]$. The following mechanism has been proposed for this reaction:

$$NO(g) + Cl_2(g) \longrightarrow NOCl_2(g)$$
$$NOCl_2(g) + NO(g) \longrightarrow 2NOCl(g)$$

(a) What would the rate law be if the first step were rate-determining? (b) Based on the observed rate law, what can we conclude about the relative rates of the two steps?

Catalysis

14.51. How does a catalyst increase the rate of a reaction?

14.52. In older texts, catalysts were sometimes defined as substances that speed up a chemical reaction without taking part in the reaction. In what way is this definition misleading? How might the definition be modified to correct it?

14.53. What is the difference between a homogeneous and a heterogeneous catalyst?

14.54. Why is the activity of a heterogeneous catalyst highly dependent on its method of preparation and prior treatment?

14.55. NO catalyzes the decomposition of N_2O, possibly by the following mechanism:

$$NO(g) + N_2O(g) \longrightarrow N_2(g) + NO_2(g)$$

$$2NO_2(g) \longrightarrow 2NO(g) + O_2(g)$$

(a) What is the chemical equation for the overall reaction? (b) Why is NO considered a catalyst and not an intermediate? (c) Is this an example of homogeneous catalysis or heterogeneous catalysis? (d) If the first step in the mechanism is the slow step, what is the rate law for the reaction?

14.56. The oxidation of SO_2 to SO_3 is catalyzed by NO_2. The reaction proceeds as follows:

$$NO_2(g) + SO_2(g) \longrightarrow NO(g) + SO_3(g)$$

$$2NO(g) + O_2(g) \longrightarrow 2NO_2(g)$$

(a) Show that the two reactions can be summed to give the overall oxidation of SO_2 by O_2 to give SO_3. (b) Why do we consider NO_2 a catalyst and not an intermediate in this reaction? (c) Is this an example of homogeneous catalysis or heterogeneous catalysis?

14.57. A reaction in solution is catalyzed by metallic iron. Would you expect a solid chunk of iron metal or an equal mass of finely ground iron filings to be a more effective catalyst? Explain.

14.58. Many metallic catalysts, particularly the precious-metal ones, are often deposited as very thin films on a substance of high surface area per unit mass, such as alumina, Al_2O_3, or silica, SiO_2. Why is this an effective way of utilizing the catalyst material?

14.59. When D_2 is reacted with ethylene, C_2H_4, in the presence of a finely divided catalyst, ethane with two deuteriums, $CH_2D—CH_2D$, is formed. (Deuterium, D, is an isotope of hydrogen of mass 2.) Very little ethane forms in which two deuteriums are bound to one carbon, for example, $CH_3—CHD_2$. Explain why this is so in terms of the sequence of steps involved in the reaction.

14.60. Suppose that the hydrogens on ethylene (Equation 14.29) were replaced by bulky organic groups such as $—CH_3$. What effect do you think this would have on the ease with which the compound could undergo reaction with H_2 using a nickel metal catalyst? Explain.

14.61. Describe in qualitative terms how an enzyme works. What is meant by the *active site* of an enzyme?

14.62. In terms of the lock-and-key model, what characteristics must an enzyme inhibitor possess?

14.63. Solutions of dilute (about 3 percent) hydrogen peroxide are stable for long periods of time, especially if a small amount of a stabilizer is added. However, when such a solution is poured onto an open cut or wound, the hydrogen peroxide decomposes very rapidly with evolution of oxygen gas and formation of water. How can you account for this result?

14.64. Enzymes have a special sensitivity to temperature different from that of other catalysts. Figure 14.23 shows the typical response of enzyme activity to temperature. The activity of enzymes generally increases up to some value near the normal temperature of the organism in which it is found and then decreases thereafter. Account for this behavior. (Hint: The shape of the enzyme is maintained by intermolecular forces.)

FIGURE 14.23

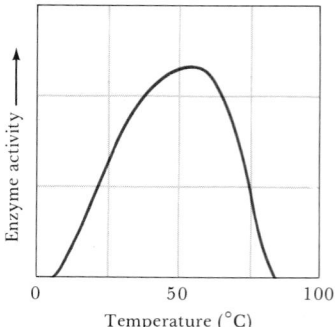

Additional Exercises

14.65. List three factors that can be varied to change the rate of a chemical reaction. Explain, on a molecular level, how each exerts its influence.

14.66. Hydrogen sulfide, H_2S, is a common and troublesome pollutant in industrial wastewaters. One way to remove this substance is to treat the water with chlorine, in which case the following reaction occurs:

$$H_2S(aq) + Cl_2(aq) \longrightarrow S(s) + 2H^+(aq) + 2Cl^-(aq)$$

The rate of this reaction is first order in each reactant. The rate constant for disappearance of H_2S at $28°C$ is $3.5 \times 10^{-2}\ M^{-1}s^{-1}$. If at a given time the concentration of H_2S is $1.6 \times 10^{-4}\ M$ and that of Cl_2 is $0.070\ M$, what is the rate of formation of Cl^-?

14.67. The following data have been measured for the reaction $CH_3Cl(g) + H_2O(g) \longrightarrow CH_3OH(g) + HCl(g)$:

Experiment	[CH₃Cl] (M)	[H₂O] (M)	Initial rate (M/s)
1	0.500	0.500	22.700
2	0.750	0.500	34.050
3	0.500	0.750	51.075
4	0.500	0.250	5.675
5	0.750	0.125	2.128

(a) What is the rate law for the reaction? (b) What is the overall order of the reaction? (c) What is the value of the rate constant for the reaction?

14.68. Consider the following reaction between mercury(II) chloride and oxalate ion:

$$2HgCl_2(aq) + C_2O_4^{2-}(aq) \longrightarrow$$
$$2Cl^-(aq) + 2CO_2(g) + Hg_2Cl_2(s)$$

The initial rate of this reaction was determined for several concentrations of $HgCl_2$ and $C_2O_4^{2-}$, and the following rate data were obtained:

Experiment	$[HgCl_2]$ (M)	$[C_2O_4^{2-}]$ (M)	Rate (M/s)
1	0.105	0.15	1.8×10^{-5}
2	0.105	0.30	7.1×10^{-5}
3	0.052	0.30	3.5×10^{-5}
4	0.052	0.15	8.9×10^{-6}

(a) What is the rate law for this reaction? (b) What is the value of the rate constant? (c) What is the reaction rate when the concentration of $HgCl_2$ is 0.080 M and that of $C_2O_4^{2-}$ is 0.10 M if the temperature is the same as that used to obtain the data shown above?

14.69. Urea, NH_2CONH_2, is the end product in protein metabolism in animals. The decomposition of urea in 0.1 M HCl occurs according to the reaction

$$NH_2CONH_2(aq) + H^+(aq) + 2H_2O(l) \longrightarrow$$
$$2NH_4^+(aq) + HCO_3^-(aq)$$

The reaction is first order in urea. When [urea] = 0.200 M, the rate at 61.05°C is 8.56×10^{-5} M/s. (a) What is the value for the rate constant, k? (b) What is the concentration of urea in this solution after 5.00×10^3 s if the starting concentration is 0.500 M? (c) What is the half-life for this reaction at 61.05°C?

14.70. Sulfuryl chloride, SO_2Cl_2, decomposes in the gas phase into sulfur dioxide, SO_2, and chlorine, Cl_2. The concentration of SO_2Cl_2 is monitored over time. It is found that a plot of ln $[SO_2Cl_2]$ versus time is linear, and that in 240 s the concentration decreases from 0.400 M to 0.280 M. (a) What is the rate constant for the reaction $SO_2Cl_2(g) \longrightarrow SO_2(g) + Cl_2(g)$? (b) What is the half-life of the reaction?

14.71. Cyclopentadiene, C_5H_6, reacts with itself to form dicyclopentadiene, $C_{10}H_{12}$. A 0.0400 M solution of C_5H_6 was monitored as a function of time as the reaction $2C_5H_6 \longrightarrow C_{10}H_{12}$ proceeded. The following data were collected:

Time (s)	$[C_5H_6]$ (M)
0.0	0.0400
50.0	0.0300
100.0	0.0240
150.0	0.0200
200.0	0.0174

Plot $[C_5H_6]$ versus time, ln $[C_5H_6]$ versus time, and $1/[C_5H_6]$ versus time. What is the order of the reaction? What is the value of the rate constant?

14.72. A sample of polluted water was oxidized with O_2 at 25°C. The percentage of organic matter in the sample that was oxidized varied with time in the following manner:

Time (days)	1	2	3	4	5	6	7	10	20
Organic matter oxidized (%)	21	37	50	60	68	75	80	90	99

Is the oxidation process first or second order? What is the rate constant for this reaction?

14.73. The first-order rate constant for hydrolysis of a particular organic compound in water varies with temperature as follows:

Temperature (K)	Rate constant (s^{-1})
300	1.0×10^{-5}
320	5.0×10^{-5}
340	2.0×10^{-4}
355	5.0×10^{-4}

From these data calculate the activation energy in units of kJ/mol.

14.74. The activation energy for the reaction

$$2NO_2(g) \longrightarrow 2NO(g) + O_2(g)$$

is 114 kJ/mol. If $k = 0.75$ M^{-1} s^{-1} at 600°C, what is the value of k at 500°C?

14.75. The decomposition of hydrogen peroxide is catalyzed by iodide ion. The catalyzed reaction is thought to proceed by a two-step mechanism:

$$H_2O_2(aq) + I^-(aq) \longrightarrow H_2O(l) + IO^-(aq) \quad \text{(slow)}$$
$$IO^-(aq) + H_2O_2(aq) \longrightarrow H_2O(l) + O_2(g) + I^-(aq) \quad \text{(fast)}$$

(a) Assuming that the first step of the mechanism is rate-determining, predict the rate law for the overall process. (b) Write the chemical equation for the overall process. (c) Identify the intermediate, if any, in the mechanism.

[14.76]. The following mechanism has been proposed for the gas-phase reaction of chloroform, $CHCl_3$, and chlorine:

Step 1: $\quad Cl_2(g) \underset{k_{-1}}{\overset{k_1}{\rightleftharpoons}} 2Cl(g) \quad$ (fast)

Step 2: $\quad Cl(g) + CHCl_3(g) \overset{k_2}{\longrightarrow} HCl(g) + CCl_3(g)$ (slow)

Step 3: $\quad Cl(g) + CCl_3(g) \overset{k_3}{\longrightarrow} CCl_4(g) \quad$ (fast)

(a) What is the overall reaction? (b) What are the intermediates in the mechanism? (c) What is the molecularity of each of the elementary steps? (d) What is the rate-determining step? (e) What is the rate law predicted by this mechanism? (Hint: The overall reaction order is not an integer.)

[14.77]. In hydrocarbon solution, the gold compound $(CH_3)_3AuPH_3$ decomposes into ethane, C_2H_6, and a different gold compound, $(CH_3)AuPH_3$. The following mechanism is proposed for the decomposition of $(CH_3)_3AuPH_3$:

Step 1: $(CH_3)_3AuPH_3 \underset{k_{-1}}{\overset{k_1}{\rightleftharpoons}} (CH_3)_3Au + PH_3$ (fast)

Step 2: $(CH_3)_3Au \xrightarrow{k_2} C_2H_6 + (CH_3)Au$ (slow)

Step 3: $(CH_3)Au + PH_3 \xrightarrow{k_3} (CH_3)AuPH_3$ (fast)

(a) What is the overall reaction? (b) What are the intermediates in the mechanism? (c) What is the molecularity of each of the elementary steps? (d) What is the rate-determining step? (e) What is the rate law predicted by this mechanism? (f) What would be the effect on the reaction rate of adding PH_3 to the solution of $(CH_3)_3AuPH_3$?

14.78. A certain physiologically important first-order reaction has an activation energy equal to 45.0 kJ/mol at normal body temperature (37°C). Without a catalyst, the rate constant for the reaction is $5.0 \times 10^{-4}\,s^{-1}$. To be effective in the human body, where the reaction is catalyzed by an enzyme, the rate constant must be at least $2.0 \times 10^{-2}\,s^{-1}$. If the activation energy is the only factor affected by the presence of the enzyme, by how much must the enzyme lower the activation energy of the reaction to achieve the desired rate?

[14.79]. We have seen in this chapter that the hydrogenation of ethylene to form ethane is heterogeneously catalyzed by nickel metal. One particular study found that at low C_2H_4 pressure, the rate of hydrogenation of C_2H_4 was first order with respect to C_2H_4 pressure. However, with all other factors remaining constant, the rate of hydrogenation was found to be zero order with respect to ethylene pressure at high pressures of C_2H_4. (a) What is the significance of a zero-order dependence, insofar as the rate of reaction is concerned? (b) Suggest an explanation for why the reaction rate has a zero-order dependence on ethylene pressure at high ethylene pressures.

14.80. One of the many remarkable enzymes in the human body is carbonic anhydrase, which catalyzes the interconversion of carbonic acid with carbon dioxide and water. If it were not for this enzyme, the body could not rid itself rapidly enough of the CO_2 accumulated by cell metabolism. The enzyme catalyzes the dehydration (release to air) of up to 10^7 CO_2 molecules per second. Which components of this description correspond to the terms *enzyme, substrate,* and *turnover number?*

14.81. The enzyme invertase catalyzes the conversion of sucrose, a disaccharide, to invert sugar, a mixture of glucose and fructose. When the concentration of invertase is 3×10^{-7} M and the concentration of sucrose is 0.01 M, invert sugar is formed at the rate of 2×10^{-4} M/s. When the sucrose concentration is doubled, the rate of formation of invert sugar is doubled also. Assuming that the enzyme-substrate model is operative, is the fraction of enzyme tied up as complex large or small? Explain. Addition of inositol, another sugar, causes a decrease in the rate of formation of invert sugar. Suggest a mechanism by which this occurs.

Chemical Equilibrium 15

Carlsbad Caverns, New Mexico. Chemical equilibria are involved in numerous natural phenomena, including the reactions that result in the formation of limestone caves such as this. The cave itself results from the dissolving of limestone, $CaCO_3$, by water containing CO_2. The formation of the stalactites and stalagmites is due to reverse reaction, the precipitation of $CaCO_3$. The equilibrium reaction is $CaCO_3(s) + H_2O(l) + CO_2(g) \rightleftharpoons Ca^{2+}(aq) + 2HCO_3^-(aq)$.

CONTENTS

Carl W. David, "An Elementary Discussion of Chemical Equilibrium," *J. Chem. Educ.* 1988, 65, 407.

Point of Emphasis: The term *dynamic equilibrium* is also commonly used.

Point of Emphasis: At equilibrium, Rate$_{forward}$ = Rate$_{reverse}$. See Chapter 14.

In the laboratory portion of this course, you have had the opportunity to observe a number of chemical reactions. When a reaction "stopped"—when colors stopped changing, gases stopped evolving, and so forth—you probably assumed that the reactants had been completely converted to products. In many cases, however, chemical reactions come to an apparent halt before the reaction is complete. As an example, consider the dissociation of colorless N_2O_4 gas into brown NO_2 gas:

$$N_2O_4(g) \longrightarrow 2NO_2(g)$$

Colorless   Brown

When pure, frozen N_2O_4 is warmed above its boiling point (21.2 °C), the gas in the sealed tube progressively turns darker as a result of the formation of NO_2 (Figure 15.1). Eventually, the color change stops even though there is still N_2O_4 in the tube. We are left with a mixture of N_2O_4 and NO_2 in which the concentrations of the gases no longer change.

The condition in which the concentrations of all reactants and products cease to change with time is called **chemical equilibrium.** *Chemical equilibrium occurs when opposing reactions are proceeding at equal rates:* The rate at which the products are formed from the reactants equals the rate at which the reactants are formed from the products. For equilibrium to occur, neither reactants nor products can escape from the system.

We have already seen several instances of equilibria. For example, the vapor above a liquid is in equilibrium with the liquid phase. ∞ (Sec. 11.5) The rate at which molecules escape from the liquid into the gas phase equals the rate at which molecules in the gas phase strike the surface and become part of the liquid. As another example, in a saturated solution of sodium chloride, the solid sodium chloride is in equilibrium with the ions dispersed in water. ∞ (Sec. 13.3) The rate at which ions leave the solid

FIGURE 15.1 (*a*) Frozen N_2O_4 is nearly colorless. (*b*) As N_2O_4 is warmed above its boiling point, it is partly converted to brown $NO_2(g)$. (*c*) Eventually the color stops changing, even though there is still $N_2O_4(g)$ in the tube. The two gases are in equilibrium. (© Richard Megna/Fundamental Photographs)

(*a*)

(*b*)

(*c*)

surface equals the rate at which other ions are removed from the liquid to become part of the solid.

Chemical equilibria are of importance in explaining a great many natural phenomena and play important roles in many industrial processes. In this and the next two chapters, we will explore chemical equilibria in some detail. In this chapter, we will learn how to express the equilibrium position of a reaction in quantitative terms, and we will study the factors that determine the relative concentrations of reactants and products at equilibrium. We begin by exploring the relationship between the rates of opposing reactions and how this relationship leads to chemical equilibrium.

15.1 The Concept of Equilibrium

At equilibrium, the rate at which products are produced from reactants equals the rate at which reactants are produced from products. We can use some of the concepts developed in Chapter 14 to illustrate how equilibrium is reached. Let's imagine that we have a simple reaction A $\longrightarrow$ B, and that both this reaction and its reverse (B $\longrightarrow$ A) are elementary processes. As we learned in Section 14.5, the rates of these unimolecular reactions are

$$\text{Forward reaction:} \quad \text{A} \longrightarrow \text{B} \quad \text{Rate} = k_f[\text{A}] \qquad [15.1]$$

$$\text{Reverse reaction:} \quad \text{B} \longrightarrow \text{A} \quad \text{Rate} = k_r[\text{B}] \qquad [15.2]$$

where k_f and k_r are the rate constants for the forward and reverse reactions, respectively.

Now, let us suppose that we start with pure compound A. As A reacts to form compound B, the concentration of A decreases while the concentration of B increases [Figure 15.2(a)]. As [A] decreases, the rate of the forward reaction decreases, as shown in Figure 15.2(b). Likewise, as [B] increases, the rate of the reverse reaction increases. Eventually, the reaction reaches a point at which the forward and reverse rates are the same [Figure 15.2(b)]; compounds A and B are in equilibrium. At equilibrium, therefore,

$$k_f[\text{A}] = k_r[\text{B}]$$

$$\underset{\substack{\text{Forward} \\ \text{rate}}}{\phantom{k_f[\text{A}]}} \quad \underset{\substack{\text{Reverse} \\ \text{rate}}}{\phantom{k_r[\text{B}]}}$$

Figure 15.2

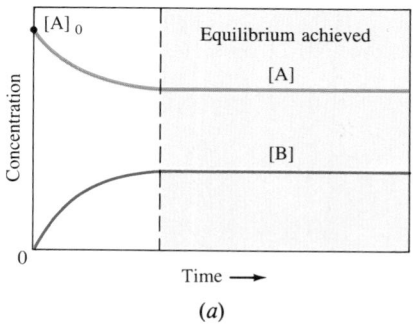

(a)

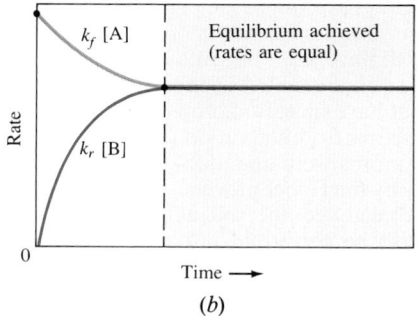

(b)

FIGURE 15.2 Achieving chemical equilibrium for the reaction A $\rightleftharpoons$ B. (a) The reaction of pure compound A, with initial concentration $[\text{A}]_0$. After a time, the concentrations of A and B do not change. The reason is that (b) the rates of the forward reaction ($k_f[\text{A}]$) and the reverse reaction ($k_r[\text{B}]$) become equal.

Nitrogen Fixation and the Haber Process

Of all the chemical reactions that humans have learned to carry out and control for their own purposes, the synthesis of ammonia from hydrogen and atmospheric nitrogen is one of the most important. Plant growth requires a substantial store of nitrogen in the soil, in a form usable by plants. The quantity of food required to feed the ever-increasing human population far exceeds the amount that could be produced if we relied solely on naturally available nitrogen in the soil.

The only widely available source of nitrogen is the N_2 present in the atmosphere. The problem thus becomes one of "fixing" atmospheric N_2, that is, converting it to compounds that plants can use. This process is called *nitrogen fixation.*

The N_2 molecule is exceptionally unreactive, in large part because of the strong triple bond between the nitrogen atoms. ∞ (Sec. 8.4) For this reason, fixation is not easy to achieve. In nature, the fixation of N_2 is carried out by special nitrogen-fixing bacteria that grow on the roots of certain plants such as clover and alfalfa.

In 1912, the German chemist Fritz Haber (Figure 15.3) developed a process, which still bears his name, for synthesizing ammonia directly from nitrogen and hydrogen (Equation 15.4). The process is sometimes called the *Haber-Bosch process* to also honor Karl Bosch, the engineer who developed the equipment for the industrial production of ammonia. The engineering needed to implement the Haber process requires the use of temperatures and pressures (approximately 500°C and 200 atm) that were difficult to achieve at that time.

The Haber process provides a historically interesting example of the complex impact of chemistry on our lives. At the start of World War I in 1914, Germany was dependent on nitrate deposits in Chile for the nitrogen-containing compounds needed to manufacture explosives. During the war, the Allied naval blockade of South America cut off this supply. However, by fixing nitrogen from air, Germany was able to continue production of explosives. Experts have estimated that World War I would have ended several years before 1918 had it not been for the Haber process.

From these unhappy beginnings as a major factor in international warfare, the Haber process has become the world's principal source of fixed nitrogen. The same process that prolonged World War I has enabled scientists to manufacture fertilizers that have increased crop yields, thereby saving millions of people from starvation. In 1992, 36 billion pounds of ammonia were manufactured in the United States, mostly by the Haber process. The ammonia can be applied directly to the soil as fertilizer (Figure 15.4). It can also be converted into ammonium salts—for example, ammonium sulfate, $(NH_4)_2SO_4$, or ammonium hydrogen phosphate, $(NH_4)_2HPO_4$—that in turn are used as fertilizers.

FIGURE 15.3 Fritz Haber (1868–1934), the German chemist who developed the process for synthesizing ammonia from nitrogen and hydrogen. (German Information Center).

Haber was a patriotic German who gave enthusiastic support to his nation's war effort. He served as chief of Germany's Chemical Warfare Service during World War I and developed the use of chlorine as a poison-gas weapon. Consequently, the decision to award him the Nobel Prize for Chemistry in 1918 was the subject of considerable controversy and criticism. The ultimate irony, however, came in 1933 when Haber was expelled from Germany because he was Jewish.

FIGURE 15.4 Liquid ammonia, produced by the Haber process, can be added directly to the soil as a fertilizer. Agricultural use is the largest single application of manufactured NH_3. (Farmland Industries)

Rearranging this equation gives

$$\frac{[B]}{[A]} = \frac{k_f}{k_r} = \text{a constant} \qquad [15.3]$$

We see that at equilibrium the ratio of the concentrations of A and B equals a constant. (We will consider this constant in Section 15.2.) It makes no difference whether we start with A or B, or even with some mixture of the two. At equilibrium, the ratio of their concentrations equals a definite value.

Once equilibrium is established, the concentrations of A and B do not change. This does *not* mean that A and B stop reacting, however. On the contrary, the equilibrium is *dynamic.* ∞ (Sec. 11.5) Compound A is still converted to compound B, and B to A, but *both processes occur at the same rate.* To indicate that the reaction proceeds in both the forward and reverse directions, we use a double arrow:

$$A \rightleftharpoons B$$

This example illustrates that opposing reactions naturally lead to an equilibrium situation. In order to examine equilibrium for a real chemical system, we will focus on an extremely important chemical reaction, namely, the synthesis of ammonia from nitrogen and hydrogen:

$$N_2(g) + 3H_2(g) \rightleftharpoons 2NH_3(g) \qquad [15.4]$$

This reaction is the basis for the **Haber process** for synthesizing ammonia.

15.2 The Equilibrium Constant

The Haber process consists of putting together N_2 and H_2 in a high-pressure tank at a total pressure of several hundred atmospheres, in the presence of a catalyst, and at a temperature of a few hundred degrees Celsius. Under these conditions, the two gases react to form ammonia. But the reaction does not lead to complete consumption of the N_2 and H_2. Rather, at some point the reaction appears to stop, with all three components of the reaction mixture present at the same time. The manner in which the concentrations of H_2, N_2, and NH_3 vary with time is shown in Figure 15.5(*a*). The situation is analogous to the one shown in Figure 15.2(*a*). The relative amounts of N_2, H_2, and NH_3 present at

Figure 15.5

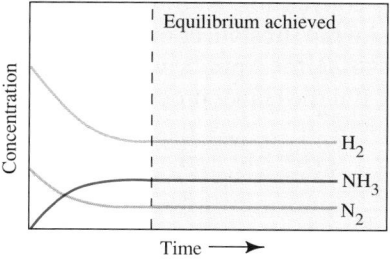

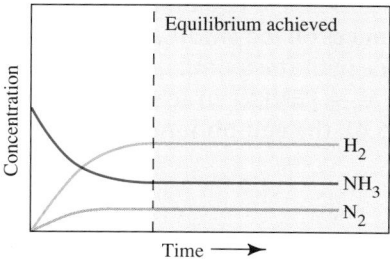

FIGURE 15.5 Variation in concentrations in the approach to equilibrium for $N_2 + 3H_2 \rightleftharpoons 2NH_3$. (*a*) The equilibrium is approached beginning with H_2 and N_2 in the ratio 3:1. (*b*) The equilibrium is approached beginning with NH_3.

equilibrium do not depend on the amount of catalyst present. However, they do depend on the relative amounts of H_2 and N_2 with which the reaction was begun. Furthermore, if only ammonia is placed in the tank under the same reaction conditions, at equilibrium there is again a mixture of N_2, H_2, and NH_3. The variations in concentrations as a function of time for this situation are shown in Figure 15.5(*b*). At equilibrium, the relative concentrations of H_2, N_2, and NH_3 are the same, regardless of whether the starting mixture was a 3 : 1 molar ratio of H_2 and N_2 or pure NH_3. *The equilibrium condition can be reached from either direction.*

Earlier, we saw that when the reaction A $\rightleftharpoons$ B reaches equilibrium, the ratio of the concentrations A and B has a constant value (Equation 15.3). A similar relationship governs the concentrations of N_2, H_2, and NH_3 at equilibrium. If we were systematically to change the relative amounts of the three gases in the starting mixture and then analyze the gas mixtures at equilibrium, we could determine the relationship among the equilibrium concentrations. Chemists carried out studies of this kind on other chemical systems in the nineteenth century, before Haber's work. In 1864, Cato Maximilian Guldberg (1836–1902) and Peter Waage (1833–1900) postulated their **law of mass action,** which expresses the relationship between the concentrations of the reactants and products at equilibrium in any reaction. Suppose we have the general reaction

$$aA + bB \rightleftharpoons pP + qQ \qquad [15.5]$$

where A, B, P, and Q are the chemical species involved, and *a*, *b*, *p*, and *q* are their coefficients in the balanced chemical equation. According to the law of mass action, the equilibrium condition is expressed by the equation

$$K_c = \frac{[P]^p[Q]^q}{[A]^a[B]^b} \qquad [15.6]$$

(As before, the square brackets in this equation signify molar concentrations.) We call this relationship the **equilibrium expression** (or the equilibrium-constant expression) for the reaction. The constant K_c, which we call the **equilibrium constant,** is the numerical value obtained when we substitute actual equilibrium concentrations into the equilibrium expression. The subscript *c* indicates that concentration (expressed in molarity) is used.

In general, the numerator of the equilibrium expression is the product of the concentrations of all substances on the product side of the chemical equation, each raised to the power of its coefficient in the balanced equation. The denominator is similarly given in terms of the substances on the reactant side of the chemical equation. (Remember that the convention is to write the substances on the *product* side in the *numerator* and the substances on the *reactant* side in the *denominator*.) For the reaction A $\rightleftharpoons$ B, the equilibrium expression is $K_c = [B]/[A]$, in accord with Equation 15.3. For the Haber process (Equation 15.4), the equilibrium expression is

$$K_c = \frac{[NH_3]^2}{[N_2][H_2]^3}$$

Note that once we know the balanced chemical equation for an equilibrium, we can write the equilibrium expression even if we don't known the reaction mechanism. *The equilibrium expression depends only on the stoichiometry of the reaction, not on its mechanism.*

The value of the equilibrium constant at any given temperature does not depend on the initial concentrations of reactants and products. It also does not matter whether other substances are present, as long as they do not react with a reactant or product. The value of the equilibrium constant does vary with temperature, however.

We can illustrate how the law of mass action was discovered empirically by considering the gas-phase equilibrium between dinitrogen tetroxide and nitrogen dioxide:

$$N_2O_4(g) \rightleftharpoons 2NO_2(g) \qquad [15.7]$$

Point of Emphasis: The notation K_c is a reminder that the amounts of materials are expressed as molar concentrations.

Figure 15.1 shows this equilibrium being reached after starting with pure N_2O_4. Because NO_2 is a dark-brown gas and N_2O_4 is colorless, the amount of NO_2 in the mixture can be determined by measuring the intensity of the brown color of the gas mixture.

The equilibrium expression for Equation 15.7 is

$$K_c = \frac{[NO_2]^2}{[N_2O_4]} \qquad [15.8]$$

How can we determine the numerical value for K_c and verify that it is constant regardless of the starting concentrations of NO_2 and N_2O_4? We could perform experiments in which we start with several sealed tubes containing different concentrations of NO_2 and N_2O_4, as summarized in Table 15.1. The tubes are kept at 100°C until no further change in the color of the gas is noted. We then analyze the mixtures and determine the equilibrium concentrations of NO_2 and N_2O_4, as shown in Table 15.1.

To evaluate the equilibrium constant, K_c, the equilibrium concentrations are inserted into the equilibrium expression, Equation 15.8. For example, using the first set of data, $[NO_2] = 0.0172\ M$ and $[N_2O_4] = 0.00140\ M$:

Point of Emphasis: For a particular reaction, the value of the equilibrium constant varies with temperature.

$$K_c = \frac{[NO_2]^2}{[N_2O_4]} = \frac{(0.0172)^2}{0.00140} = 0.211$$

TABLE 15.1 △ Initial and Equilibrium Concentrations (Molarities) of NO_2 and N_2O_4 in the Gas Phase at 100°C

Experiment	Initial N_2O_4 concentration (M)	Initial NO_2 concentration (M)	Equilibrium N_2O_4 concentration (M)	Equilibrium NO_2 concentration (M)	K_c
1	0.0	0.0200	0.00140	0.0172	0.211
2	0.0	0.0300	0.00280	0.0243	0.211
3	0.0	0.0400	0.00452	0.0310	0.213
4	0.0200	0.0	0.00452	0.0310	0.213

Proceeding in the same way, the values of K_c for the other samples were calculated, as listed in Table 15.1. Note that the value for K_c is constant ($K_c = 0.212$ within the limits of experimental error) even though the initial concentrations vary. Furthermore, the results of experiment 4 show that equilibrium can be attained beginning with N_2O_4 as well as with NO_2. That is, equilibrium can be approached from either direction. Figure 15.6 shows how both experiments 3 and 4 result in the same equilibrium mixture even though one begins with 0.0400 M NO_2 and the other with 0.0200 M N_2O_4.

Point of Emphasis: Equilibrium constants have no units.

Notice that no units are given for the values of K_c in Table 15.1 or in the calculation above. The common practice is to write equilibrium constants as dimensionless quantities.

SAMPLE EXERCISE 15.1

Write the equilibrium expression for K_c for the following reactions:
(a) $2O_3(g) \rightleftharpoons 3O_2(g)$
(b) $2NO(g) + Cl_2(g) \rightleftharpoons 2NOCl(g)$

SOLUTION (a) As indicated by Equation 15.6, the equilibrium expression has the form of a quotient. The numerator contains the concentrations of the substances on the product side of the chemical equation, each raised to a power equal to its coefficient in the balanced equation. The denominator is similarly obtained using the substances on the reactant side of the equation:

$$K_c = \frac{[O_2]^3}{[O_3]^2}$$

(b) In this case, we have

$$K_c = \frac{[NOCl]^2}{[NO]^2[Cl_2]}$$

PRACTICE EXERCISE

Write the equilibrium constant expression for $H_2(g) + I_2(g) \rightleftharpoons 2HI(g)$.
Answer: $K_c = [HI]^2/[H_2][I_2]$

Expressing Equilibrium Constants in Terms of Pressure, K_p

When the reactants and products in a chemical equation are gases, we can formulate the equilibrium expression in terms of partial pressures (in atmo-

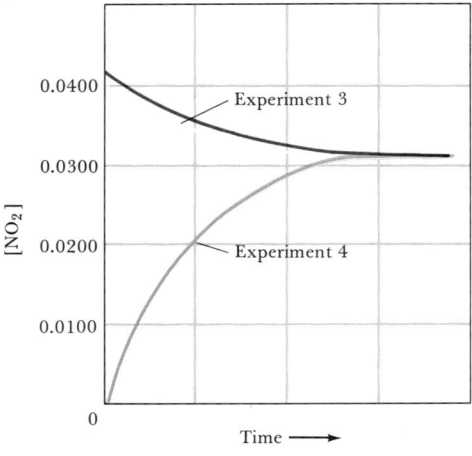

FIGURE 15.6 As seen in Table 15.1, the same equilibrium mixture is produced starting with either 0.0400 M NO_2 (experiment 3) or 0.0200 M N_2O_4 (experiment 4).

Figure 15.6

spheres) instead of molar concentrations. When partial pressures are used in the equilibrium expression, we represent the equilibrium constant as K_p (where the subscript p stands for pressure). For example, consider again the equilibrium between dinitrogen tetroxide and nitrogen dioxide:

$$N_2O_4(g) \rightleftharpoons 2NO_2(g)$$

We can write the equilibrium expression for this reaction in two ways:

$$K_c = \frac{[NO_2]^2}{[N_2O_4]} \quad \text{and} \quad K_p = \frac{P_{NO_2}^2}{P_{N_2O_4}}$$

Point of Emphasis: The notation K_p is a reminder that the amounts of materials are expressed as gas pressures.

Because the numerical values of K_c and K_p will generally be different, we must take care to indicate which we are using by means of these subscripts. We will examine the relationship between K_c and K_p in Section 15.4.

Point of Emphasis: When $K \gg 1$, there are more products than reactants, and the reaction is said to lie to the right. When $K \ll 1$, there are more reactants than products, and the reaction is said to lie to the left.

The Magnitude of Equilibrium Constants

Equilibrium constants can be very large or very small. The magnitude of the constant provides us with important information about the equilibrium mixture. For example, consider the reaction of carbon monoxide and chlorine gases at 100°C to form phosgene, $COCl_2$, a highly toxic gas that was used as a poison-gas weapon in World War I. (Phosgene is currently used in the manufacture of certain polymers and insecticides.)

$$CO(g) + Cl_2(g) \rightleftharpoons COCl_2(g) \qquad K_c = \frac{[COCl_2]}{[CO][Cl_2]} = 4.57 \times 10^9$$

In order for the equilibrium constant to be so large, the numerator of the equilibrium expression must be much larger than the denominator. Thus, the equilibrium concentration of $COCl_2$ must be much greater than that of CO or Cl_2; an equilibrium mixture of the three gases is essentially pure $COCl_2$. We say that the equilibrium *lies to the right,* that is, toward the product side. Likewise, an equilibrium constant much less than 1 indicates that the equilibrium mixture contains mostly reactants. We then say that the equilibrium *lies to the left.* In general,

$K \gg 1$: Equilibrium lies to the right; products favored.

$K \ll 1$: Equilibrium lies to the left; reactants favored.

These situations are summarized in Figure 15.7.

FIGURE 15.7 The equilibrium expression has products in the numerator and reactants in the denominator. (*a*) When $K \gg 1$, there are more products than reactants at equilibrium, and the equilibrium is said to lie to the right. (*b*) When $K \ll 1$, there are more reactants than products at equilibrium, and the equilibrium is said to lie to the left.

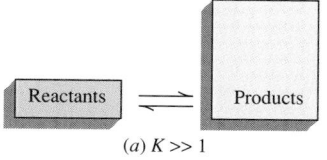

(*a*) $K \gg 1$

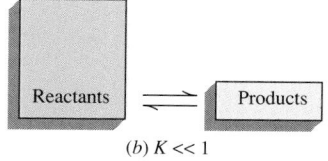

(*b*) $K \ll 1$

SAMPLE EXERCISE 15.2

The reaction of N_2 with O_2 to form NO might be considered a means of "fixing" nitrogen:

$$N_2(g) + O_2(g) \rightleftharpoons 2NO(g)$$

The value for the equilibrium constant for this reaction at 25°C is $K_c = 1 \times 10^{-30}$. Describe the feasibility of this reaction for nitrogen fixation.

SOLUTION Because K_c is so small, very little NO will form at 25°C. The equilibrium lies to the left, favoring the reactants. Consequently, this reaction is an extremely poor choice for nitrogen fixation, at least at 25°C.

PRACTICE EXERCISE

The equilibrium constant for the reaction $H_2(g) + I_2(g) \rightleftharpoons 2HI(g)$ varies with temperature in the following way: $K_c = 794$ at 298 K; $K_c = 54$ at 700 K. Is the formation of HI favored more at the higher or lower temperature?   *Answer:* at the lower temperature because of the larger K_c value

The Direction of the Chemical Equation and K

Because an equilibrium can be approached from either direction, the direction in which we write the chemical equation for an equilibrium is arbitrary. For example, we have seen that we can represent the NO_2/N_2O_4 equilibrium as

$$N_2O_4(g) \rightleftharpoons 2NO_2(g)$$

For this equation, we can write

$$K_c = \frac{[NO_2]^2}{[N_2O_4]} = 0.212 \qquad \text{(at 100°C)} \qquad [15.9]$$

We could equally well consider this same equilibrium in terms of the reverse reaction:

$$2NO_2(g) \rightleftharpoons N_2O_4(g)$$

The equilibrium expression is then given by

$$K_c = \frac{[N_2O_4]}{[NO_2]^2} = \frac{1}{0.212} = 4.72 \qquad \text{(at 100°C)} \qquad [15.10]$$

Point of Emphasis: For the value of an equilibrium constant to be meaningful, we must specify how the equilibrium reaction is written; i.e., which species are written on the product side and which are written on the reactant side.

Notice that Equation 15.10 is just the reciprocal of Equation 15.9. *The equilibrium expression for a reaction written in one direction is the reciprocal of the one for the reaction written in the reverse direction.* Consequently, the numerical value of the equilibrium constant for the reaction written in one direction is the reciprocal of that for the reverse reaction. Both expressions are equally valid, but it is meaningless to say that the equilibrium constant for the NO_2/N_2O_4 equilibrium is 0.212 or 4.72 unless we indicate how the equilibrium reaction is written and also specify the temperature.

SAMPLE EXERCISE 15.3

(a) Write the equilibrium expression for K_c for the following reaction:

$$2NO(g) \rightleftharpoons N_2(g) + O_2(g)$$

(b) Using information in Sample Exercise 15.2, determine the value of this equilibrium constant at 25°C:

SOLUTION   (a) Writing products over reactants, we have

$$K_c = \frac{[N_2][O_2]}{[NO]^2}$$

(b) The reaction is just the reverse of the one given in Sample Exercise 15.2. Thus, both the equilibrium expression and the value of the equilibrium constant are the reciprocals of those for the reverse reaction:

$$K_c = \frac{1}{1 \times 10^{-30}} = 1 \times 10^{30}$$

Either way we express the equilibrium among NO, N_2, and O_2, we see that the equilibrium at 25°C lies on the side that favors N_2 and O_2.

PRACTICE EXERCISE

For the formation of NH_3 from N_2 and H_2, $N_2(g) + 3H_2(g) \rightleftharpoons 2NH_3(g)$, $K_p = 4.34 \times 10^{-3}$ at 300°C. What is the value of K_p for the reverse reaction?
Answer: 2.30×10^2

15.3 Heterogeneous Equilibria

Many equilibria of importance, such as the hydrogen-nitrogen-ammonia system, involve substances all in the same phase. Such equilibria are called **homogeneous equilibria.** On the other hand, the substances in equilibrium may be in different phases, giving rise to **heterogeneous equilibria.** As an example, consider the decomposition of calcium carbonate:

$$CaCO_3(s) \rightleftharpoons CaO(s) + CO_2(g) \qquad [15.11]$$

This system involves a gas in equilibrium with two solids. If we write the equilibrium expression for this process in the usual way, we obtain

$$K_c = \frac{[CaO][CO_2]}{[CaCO_3]} \qquad [15.12]$$

This example presents a problem we have not encountered previously: How do we express the concentration of a solid substance? The concentration of a pure substance, liquid or solid, equals its density divided by its molar mass, $\mathcal{M}$:

$$\frac{\text{Density}}{\mathcal{M}} = \frac{g/cm^3}{g/mol} = \frac{mol}{cm^3}$$

The density of a pure liquid or solid is a constant at any given temperature and changes very little with temperature. Thus, the effective concentration of a pure solid or liquid is a constant, regardless of how much pure solid or liquid is present. We can use this fact to simplify the equilibrium expression. For example, Equation 15.12 simplifies to

$$K_c = \frac{(\text{constant 1})[CO_2]}{\text{constant 2}}$$

where constant 1 is the concentration of CaO and constant 2 is the concentration of $CaCO_3$. Moving the constants to the left side of the equation, we have

$$K_c' = K_c \frac{\text{constant 2}}{\text{constant 1}} = [CO_2] \qquad [15.13]$$

Point of Emphasis: Homogeneous reactions have all substances in one phase. Heterogeneous reactions have substances in two or more phases.

Point of Emphasis: Pure solids and pure liquids have essentially constant concentrations.

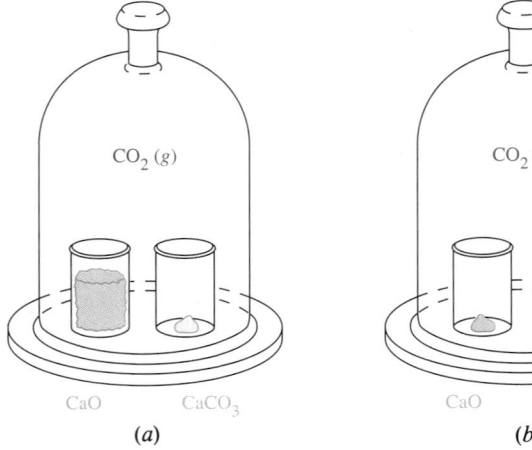

CO_2 (g) CO_2 (g)

CaO $CaCO_3$ CaO $CaCO_3$

(a)   (b)

We have in effect excluded the concentrations of the solids from the equilibrium expression.

We can generalize this result to other situations involving not only pure solids but pure liquids as well: *If a pure solid or a pure liquid is involved in a heterogeneous equilibrium, its concentration is not included in the equilibrium expression for the reaction.* The concentrations of gases and substances in solution, however, are included in equilibrium expressions because these concentrations can vary.

Equation 15.13 tells us that, at a given temperature, an equilibrium among CaO, $CaCO_3$, and CO_2 will always lead to the same concentration of CO_2 as long as all three components are present. As shown in Figure 15.8, we would have the same pressure of CO_2 regardless of the relative amounts of CaO and $CaCO_3$. Of course, if one of the three components is missing, we cannot have an equilibrium. *Even though they do not appear in the equilibrium expression, the pure solids and liquids participating in the reaction must be present for an equilibrium to be established.*

SAMPLE EXERCISE 15.4

Each of the mixtures listed below was placed in a closed container and allowed to stand. Which of these mixtures is capable of attaining the equilibrium expressed by Equation 15.11): **(a)** pure $CaCO_3$; **(b)** CaO and a pressure of CO_2 greater than the value of K_p; **(c)** some $CaCO_3$ and a pressure of CO_2 greater than the value of K_p; **(d)** $CaCO_3$ and CaO?

SOLUTION   Equilibrium can be reached in all cases except (c) as long as sufficient quantities of solids are present. In **(a)**, $CaCO_3$ simply decomposes, forming CaO(s) and $CO_2(g)$, until the equilibrium pressure of CO_2 is attained. There must be enough $CaCO_3$, however, to allow the CO_2 pressure to reach equilibrium. In **(b)**, CO_2 combines with the CaO present until its pressure decreases to the equilibrium value. In **(c)**, equilibrium can't be attained because there is no way in which the CO_2 pressure can decrease so as to attain its equilibrium value. In **(d)**, the situation is essentially the same as in (a); $CaCO_3$ decomposes until equilibrium is attained. The presence of CaO initially makes no difference.

PRACTICE EXERCISE

Which one of the following substances—$H_2(g)$, $H_2O(g)$, $O_2(g)$—when added to $Fe_3O_4(s)$ in a closed container at high temperature, permits attainment of equilibrium in the reaction $3Fe(s) + 4H_2O(g) \rightleftharpoons Fe_3O_4(s) + 4H_2(g)$?   ***Answer:*** Only $H_2(g)$

SAMPLE EXERCISE 15.5

Write the equilibrium expressions for K_c and K_p for each of the following reactions:
(a) $CO_2(g) + H_2(g) \rightleftharpoons CO(g) + H_2O(l)$
(b) $SnO_2(s) + 2CO(g) \rightleftharpoons Sn(s) + 2CO_2(g)$

SOLUTION **(a)** The equilibrium expressions are

$$K_c = \frac{[CO]}{[CO_2][H_2]} \quad \text{and} \quad K_p = \frac{P_{CO}}{P_{CO_2}P_{H_2}}$$

(Because H_2O appears in the reaction as a pure liquid, its concentration does not appear in the equilibrium expression.)
   (b) The equilibrium expressions are

$$K_c = \frac{[CO_2]^2}{[CO]^2} \quad \text{and} \quad K_p = \frac{P_{CO_2}^2}{P_{CO}^2}$$

(Because SnO_2 and Sn are both pure solids, their concentrations do not appear in the equilibrium expression.)

PRACTICE EXERCISE

Write the equilibrium expressions for K_c and K_p for the reaction $3Fe(s) + 4H_2O(g) \rightleftharpoons Fe_3O_4(s) + 4H_2(g)$. **Answer:** $K_c = [H_2]^4/[H_2O]^4$; $K_p = P_{H_2}^4/P_{H_2O}^4$

15.4 Calculating Equilibrium Constants

One of the first tasks confronting Haber when he approached the problem of ammonia synthesis was finding the magnitude of the equilibrium constant for the synthesis of NH_3 at various temperatures. If the value of K for Equation 15.4 were very small, then the amount of NH_3 in an equilibrium mixture would be small relative to N_2 and H_2. Clearly, if the equilibrium lies too far to the left, it would not be possible to develop a satisfactory synthesis of ammonia.

   Haber and his co-workers therefore evaluated the equilibrium constants for this reaction at various temperatures. The method they employed is analogous to that described in constructing Table 15.1: They started with various mixtures of N_2, H_2, and NH_3, allowed them to achieve equilibrium at a specific temperature, and measured the concentrations of all three gases at equilibrium. Because the equilibrium concentrations of all products and reactants were known, the equilibrium constant could be calculated directly from the equilibrium expression.

SAMPLE EXERCISE 15.6

In one of their experiments, Haber and co-workers introduced a mixture of hydrogen and nitrogen into a reaction vessel and allowed the system to attain chemical equilibrium at 472°C. The equilibrium mixture of gases was analyzed and found to contain 0.1207 M H_2, 0.0402 M N_2, and 0.00272 M NH_3. From these data, calculate the equilibrium constant, K_c, for

$$N_2(g) + 3H_2(g) \rightleftharpoons 2NH_3(g)$$

SOLUTION

$$K_c = \frac{[NH_3]^2}{[N_2][H_2]^3} = \frac{(0.00272)^2}{(0.0402)(0.1207)^3} = 0.105$$

PRACTICE EXERCISE

Nitryl chloride, NO_2Cl, is in equilibrium in a closed container with NO_2 and Cl_2:

$$2NO_2Cl(g) \rightleftharpoons 2NO_2(g) + Cl_2(g)$$

At equilibrium the concentrations of the substances in the equilibrium are $[NO_2Cl] = 0.00106 \ M$, $[NO_2] = 0.0108 \ M$, and $[Cl_2] = 0.00538 \ M$. From these data, calculate the equilibrium constant, K_c. **Answer:** 0.558

Learning Goal 2: Numerically evaluate K_c (or K_p) from a knowledge of the equilibrium concentrations (or pressures) of reactants or products, or from the initial concentrations and the equilibrium concentration of at least one substance.

We often don't know the equilibrium concentrations of all chemical species in an equilibrium. However, if we know the equilibrium concentration of at least one species, we can generally use the stoichiometry of the reaction to deduce the equilibrium concentrations of the other species in the chemical equation. We will use the following procedure to do this:

1. Tabulate the known initial and equilibrium concentrations of all species involved in the equilibrium.
2. For those species for which both the initial and equilibrium concentrations are known, calculate the change in concentration that occurs as the system reaches equilibrium.
3. Use the stoichiometry of the reaction to calculate the changes in concentration for all the other species in the equilibrium.
4. From the initial concentrations and the changes in concentration, calculate the equilibrium concentrations. These are used to evaluate the equilibrium constant.

We illustrate the procedure in Sample Exercise 15.7.

SAMPLE EXERCISE 15.7

A mixture of 5.00×10^{-3} mol of H_2 and 1.00×10^{-2} mol of I_2 is placed in a 5.00-L container at 448°C and allowed to come to equilibrium. Analysis of the equilibrium mixture shows that the concentration of HI is $1.87 \times 10^{-3} \ M$. Calculate K_c at 448°C for the reaction

$$H_2(g) + I_2(g) \rightleftharpoons 2HI(g)$$

SOLUTION *First,* we tabulate the initial and equilibrium concentrations of all the species in the equilibrium. In our table we also provide space for listing the changes in concentrations. As shown below, it is convenient to use the chemical equation as the heading for the table.

In this exercise, the initial concentrations of H_2 and I_2 must be calculated:

$$[H_2]_{initial} = \frac{5.00 \times 10^{-3} \text{ mol}}{5.00 \text{ L}} = 1.00 \times 10^{-3} \ M$$

$$[I_2]_{initial} = \frac{1.00 \times 10^{-2} \text{ mol}}{5.00 \text{ L}} = 2.00 \times 10^{-3} \ M$$

Thus, the first entries in the table are:

	$H_2(g)$	$+$	$I_2(g)$	$\rightleftharpoons$	$2HI(g)$
Initial	$1.00 \times 10^{-3} \ M$		$2.00 \times 10^{-3} \ M$		$0 \ M$
Change					
Equilibrium					$1.87 \times 10^{-3} \ M$

Second, we calculate the change in concentration of HI, using the initial and equilibrium values. The change is the difference between the initial and equilibrium values, $1.87 \times 10^{-3} \ M$.

Third, we use the stoichiometry of the reaction to calculate the changes in the other species. The balanced chemical equation indicates that for each 2 mol of HI formed, 1 mol of H_2 must be consumed. Thus, the amount of H_2 consumed is

$$\left(1.87 \times 10^{-3} \frac{\text{mol HI}}{\text{L}}\right)\left(\frac{1 \text{ mol } H_2}{2 \text{ mol HI}}\right) = 0.935 \times 10^{-3} \text{ mol } H_2/\text{L}$$

The same line of reasoning gives us the amount of I_2 consumed, which is also 0.935×10^{-3} *M*.

Fourth, we calculate the equilibrium concentrations, using the initial concentrations and the changes. The equilibrium concentration of H_2 is the initial concentration minus that consumed:

$$[H_2] = 1.00 \times 10^{-3} M - 0.935 \times 10^{-3} M = 0.065 \times 10^{-3} M$$

Likewise, the equilibrium concentration of I_2 is

$$[I_2] = 2.00 \times 10^{-3} M - 0.935 \times 10^{-3} M = 1.065 \times 10^{-3} M$$

The filled-in table now looks like this:

	$H_2(g)$ $+$	$I_2(g)$ $\rightleftharpoons$	$2HI(g)$
Initial	$1.00 \times 10^{-3} M$	$2.00 \times 10^{-3} M$	$0 M$
Change	$-0.935 \times 10^{-3} M$	$-0.935 \times 10^{-3} M$	$+1.87 \times 10^{-3} M$
Equilibrium	$0.065 \times 10^{-3} M$	$1.065 \times 10^{-3} M$	$1.87 \times 10^{-3} M$

Finally, now that we know the equilibrium concentration of each reactant and product, we can use the equilibrium expression to calculate the equilibrium constant:

$$K_c = \frac{[HI]^2}{[H_2][I_2]} = \frac{(1.87 \times 10^{-3})^2}{(0.065 \times 10^{-3})(1.065 \times 10^{-3})} = 51$$

PRACTICE EXERCISE

Sulfur trioxide decomposes at high temperature in a sealed container: $2SO_3(g) \rightleftharpoons 2SO_2(g) + O_2(g)$. Initially the vessel is charged at 1000 K with $SO_3(g)$ at a concentration of 6.09×10^{-3} *M*. At equilibrium, the SO_3 concentration is 2.44×10^{-3} *M*. Calculate the value for K_c at 1000 K.   ***Answer:*** 4.07×10^{-3}

Relating K_c and K_p

The ideal-gas equation (Section 10.4) permits us to convert between atmospheres and molarity and therefore to convert between K_p and K_c:

Learning Goal 3: Interconvert K_c and K_p.

$$PV = nRT$$

$$P = \left(\frac{n}{V}\right) RT = MRT$$

where n/V (the number of moles per liter) is concentration in molarity, *M*. As a result of the relationship between pressure and molarity, a general expression relating K_p and K_c can be written

$$K_p = K_c(RT)^{\Delta n} \qquad\qquad [15.14]$$

The quantity Δn in this equation is the change in the number of moles of gas upon going from reactants to products. It is equal to the number of moles of

Common Misconception: Students frequently arrive at the wrong sign for Δn. In the expression $K_p = K_c(RT)^{\Delta n}$, note that K_p is on the left and $\Delta n =$ product moles of gas − reactant moles of gas.

gaseous products minus the number of moles of gaseous reactants. For example, in the reaction

$$H_2(g) + I_2(g) \rightleftharpoons 2HI(g)$$

there are 2 mol of HI (the coefficient in the balanced equation); there are also 2 mol of gaseous reactants ($1H_2 + 1I_2$). Therefore, $\Delta n = 2 - 2 = 0$, and $K_p = K_c$ for this reaction.

SAMPLE EXERCISE 15.8

Using the value of K_c obtained in Sample Exercise 15.6, calculate K_p for

$$N_2(g) + 3H_2(g) \rightleftharpoons 2NH_3(g)$$

at 472°C.

SOLUTION   The relationship between K_c and K_p is given by Equation 15.14. There are 2 mol of gaseous products ($2NH_3$) and 4 mol of gaseous reactants ($1N_2 + 3H_2$). Therefore, $\Delta n = 2 - 4 = -2$. (Remember that Δ functions are always based on products minus reactants.) The temperature, T, is $273 + 472 = 745$ K. The value for the ideal-gas constant, R, is 0.0821 L-atm/mol-K. The value of K_c from Sample Exercise 15.6 is 0.105. We therefore have

$$K_p = \frac{P_{NH_3}^2}{P_{N_2}P_{H_2}^3} = K_c(RT)^{\Delta n} = (0.105)(0.0821 \times 745)^{-2} = 2.81 \times 10^{-5}$$

PRACTICE EXERCISE

For the equilibrium $2SO_3(g) \rightleftharpoons 2SO_2(g) + O_2(g)$ at temperature 1000 K, K_c has the value 4.07×10^{-3}. Calculate the value for K_p.   *Answer:* 0.334

15.5 Applications of Equilibrium Constants

We have seen that the magnitude of K indicates the extent to which a reaction will proceed. If K is very large, the reaction will tend to proceed far to the right; if K is much less than 1, the equilibrium mixture will contain mainly reactants. The equilibrium constant also allows us (1) to predict the direction in which a reaction mixture will proceed to achieve equilibrium, and (2) to calculate the concentrations of reactants and products once equilibrium has been reached.

Predicting the Direction of Reaction

Suppose we place a mixture of 2.00 mol of H_2, 1.00 mol of N_2, and 2.00 mol of NH_3 in a 1.00-L container at 472°C. Will N_2 and H_2 react to form more NH_3? If we insert the starting molar concentrations of N_2, H_2, and NH_3 into the equilibrium expression, we have

$$\frac{[NH_3]^2}{[N_2][H_2]^3} = \frac{(2.00)^2}{(1.00)(2.00)^3} = 0.500$$

According to Sample Exercise 15.6, at this temperature $K_c = 0.105$. Therefore, the quotient $[NH_3]^2/[N_2][H_2]^3$ will need to change from 0.500 to 0.105 for the system to achieve equilibrium. This change can happen only if $[NH_3]$ decreases and $[N_2]$ and $[H_2]$ increase. Thus, the reaction proceeds toward equilibrium with the formation of N_2 and H_2 from the NH_3; the reaction proceeds from right to left.

When we substitute reactant and product concentrations into the equilibrium expression as we did above, the result is known as the **reaction quotient** and is represented by the letter Q. The reaction quotient will equal the equilibrium constant, K, only if the concentrations are such that the system is at equilibrium: $Q = K$ only at equilibrium. We have seen that when the reaction quotient is larger than K, substances on the right side of the chemical equation will react to form substances on the left; the reaction moves from right to left in approaching equilibrium: If $Q > K$, the reaction moves from right to left. Conversely, if $Q < K$, the reaction will achieve equilibrium by forming more products (it moves from left to right). These relationships are summarized in Table 15.2.

SAMPLE EXERCISE 15.9

At 448°C the equilibrium constant, K_c, for the reaction

$$H_2(g) + I_2(g) \rightleftharpoons 2HI(g)$$

is 50.5. Predict how the reaction will proceed to reach equilibrium at 448°C if we start with 2.0×10^{-2} mol of HI, 1.0×10^{-2} mol of H_2, and 3.0×10^{-2} mol of I_2 in a 2.0-L container.

SOLUTION The initial concentrations are

$$[HI] = 2.0 \times 10^{-2} \text{ mol}/2.0 \text{ L} = 1.0 \times 10^{-2} \text{ } M$$

$$[H_2] = 1.0 \times 10^{-2} \text{ mol}/2.0 \text{ L} = 5.0 \times 10^{-3} \text{ } M$$

$$[I_2] = 3.0 \times 10^{-2} \text{ mol}/2.0 \text{ L} = 1.5 \times 10^{-2} \text{ } M$$

The reaction quotient is

$$Q = \frac{[HI]^2}{[H_2][I_2]} = \frac{(1.0 \times 10^{-2})^2}{(5.0 \times 10^{-3})(1.5 \times 10^{-2})} = 1.3$$

Because $Q < K_c$, [HI] will need to increase and $[H_2]$ and $[I_2]$ decrease to reach equilibrium; the reaction will proceed from left to right.

PRACTICE EXERCISE

At 1000 K the value of K_c for the reaction $2SO_3(g) \rightleftharpoons 2SO_2(g) + O_2(g)$ is 4.07×10^{-3}. Calculate the value for Q and predict the direction in which the reaction will proceed toward equilibrium if the initial concentrations of reactants are $[SO_3] = 2 \times 10^{-3}$ M; $[SO_2] = 5 \times 10^{-3}$ M; $[O_2] = 3 \times 10^{-2}$ M. *Answer:* $Q = 0.2$; the reaction will proceed from right to left, forming SO_3.

Calculation of Equilibrium Concentrations

Chemists frequently need to calculate equilibrium concentrations. Our approach in solving problems of this type is similar to the one we used for evaluating equilibrium constants: We tabulate the initial concentrations, the changes in these concentrations, and the final equilibrium concentrations. Usually we end up using the equilibrium expression to derive an equation that must be solved for an unknown quantity, as demonstrated in Sample Exercise 15.10.

SAMPLE EXERCISE 15.10

For the Haber process, $N_2(g) + 3H_2(g) \rightleftharpoons 2NH_3(g)$, $K_p = 1.45 \times 10^{-5}$ at 500°C. In an equilibrium mixture of the three gases at 500°C, the partial pressure of H_2 is

0.928 atm and that of N_2 is 0.432 atm. What is the partial pressure of NH_3 in this equilibrium mixture?

SOLUTION We are told that the mixture is in equilibrium, and so we need not worry about initial concentrations. We tabulate the equilibrium pressures of the gases as follows:

$$N_2(g) + 3H_2(g) \rightleftharpoons 2NH_3(g)$$

Equilibrium pressure (atm): 0.432 0.928 x

Because we do not know the equilibrium pressure of NH_3, we represent it with a variable, x. At equilibrium, the pressures must satisfy the equilibrium expression:

$$K_p = \frac{P_{NH_3}^2}{P_{N_2}P_{H_2}^3} = \frac{x^2}{(0.432)(0.928)^3} = 1.45 \times 10^{-5}$$

We now rearrange the equation to solve for x:

$$x^2 = (1.45 \times 10^{-5})(0.432)(0.928)^3 = 5.01 \times 10^{-6}$$

$$x = \sqrt{5.01 \times 10^{-6}} = 2.24 \times 10^{-3} \text{ atm} = P_{NH_3}$$

We can always double-check our answer by using it to recalculate the value of the equilibrium constant:

$$K_p = \frac{(2.24 \times 10^{-3})^2}{(0.432)(0.928)^3} = 1.45 \times 10^{-5}$$

PRACTICE EXERCISE

At 500 K, the equilibrium constant K_p for the reaction

$$PCl_5(g) \rightleftharpoons PCl_3(g) + Cl_2(g)$$

has the value 0.497. In an equilibrium mixture at 500 K, the partial pressure of PCl_5 is 0.860 atm and that of PCl_3 is 0.350 atm. What is the partial pressure of Cl_2 in the equilibrium mixture?   *Answer:* 1.22 atm

Learning Goal 5: Use the equilibrium constant to calculate equilibrium concentrations.

In many situations, we will know the value of the equilibrium constant and the initial concentrations of all species. We will then need to solve for the equilibrium concentrations. This usually entails treating as a variable the change in concentration as equilibrium is achieved. The stoichiometry of the reaction gives us the relationship between the changes in the concentrations of all the reactants and products, as illustrated in Sample Exercises 15.11 and 15.12.

SAMPLE EXERCISE 15.11

A 1.000-L flask is filled with 1.000 mol of H_2 and 2.000 mol of I_2 at 448°C. The value of the equilibrium constant, K_c, for the reaction

$$H_2(g) + I_2(g) \rightleftharpoons 2HI(g)$$

at 448°C is 50.5. What are the concentrations of H_2, I_2, and HI in the flask at equilibrium?

SOLUTION Unlike Sample Exercise 15.10, here we are not given any of the equilibrium concentrations. We must develop some relationships that relate the initial concentrations to those at equilibrium. The procedure is similar in many regards to that outlined in Sample Exercise 15.7.

First, we construct a table in which we tabulate the initial concentrations: $[H_2] = 1.000\ M$, $[I_2] = 2.000\ M$, and $[HI] = 0$.

Second, we use the stoichiometry of the chemical equation to determine the changes in concentrations that occur as the reaction proceeds to equilibrium. Clearly, the concentration of HI cannot be zero at equilibrium. (That would give $Q = 0$; in contrast, $K_c = 50.5$.) The concentrations of H_2 and I_2 will decrease as equilibrium is established, and that of HI will increase. Let's represent the change in concentration of H_2 by the variable x. The balanced chemical equation tells us the relationship between the changes in the concentrations of the three gases: For each x moles of H_2 per liter that react, x moles of I_2 per liter are also consumed, and $2x$ moles of HI per liter are produced.

Third, we use the initial concentrations and the concentration changes to express the equilibrium concentrations. With all of our entries, we now have the following table:

	$H_2(g)$ $+$	$I_2(g)$ $\rightleftharpoons$	$2HI(g)$
Initial	1.000 M	2.000 M	0 M
Change	$-x$ M	$-x$ M	$+2x$ M
Equilibrium	$(1.000 - x)$ M	$(2.000 - x)$ M	$2x$ M

Fourth, we substitute the equilibrium concentrations into the equilibrium expression and solve for the single unknown, x:

$$K_c = \frac{[HI]^2}{[H_2][I_2]} = \frac{(2x)^2}{(1.000 - x)(2.000 - x)} = 50.5$$

Expanding this expression leads to a quadratic equation in x:

$$4x^2 = 50.5(x^2 - 3.000x + 2.000)$$

$$46.5x^2 - 151.5x + 101.0 = 0$$

Solving the quadratic equation (Appendix A.3) leads to two solutions for x:

$$x = \frac{-(-151.5) \pm \sqrt{(-151.5)^2 - 4(46.5)(101.0)}}{2(46.5)} = 2.323 \text{ or } 0.935$$

The first of these solutions, $x = 2.323$, when substituted into the expressions for the equilibrium concentrations, gives "negative" concentrations of H_2 and I_2. A negative concentration is not chemically meaningful, so we reject this solution. We use the other solution, $x = 0.935$, to find the equilibrium concentrations:

$$[H_2] = 1.000 - x = 0.065 \ M$$

$$[I_2] = 2.000 - x = 1.065 \ M$$

$$[HI] = 2x = 1.870 \ M$$

Finally, we can double-check our solution by putting these numbers into the equilibrium expression:

$$K_c = \frac{[HI]^2}{[H_2][I_2]} = \frac{(1.870)^2}{(0.065)(1.065)} = 50.5$$

Whenever we need to use the quadratic equation to solve an equilibrium problem, one of the solutions will not be physically meaningful and can be rejected.

PRACTICE EXERCISE

For the equilibrium $PCl_5(g) \rightleftharpoons PCl_3(g) + Cl_2(g)$, the equilibrium constant K_p has the value 0.497 at 500 K. A gas cylinder at 500 K is charged with $PCl_5(g)$ at an initial pressure of 1.66 atm. What are the equilibrium pressures of PCl_5, PCl_3, and Cl_2 at this temperature? *Answer:* $P_{PCl_5} = 0.97$ atm; $P_{PCl_3} = P_{Cl_2} = 0.693$ atm

SAMPLE EXERCISE 15.12

As we saw in Sample Exercise 15.6, the equilibrium constant for the Haber process at 472°C is $K_c = 0.105$. A 2.00-L flask is filled with 0.500 mol of NH_3 and is allowed to reach equilibrium at 472°C. What are the equilibrium concentrations of NH_3, N_2, and H_2?

Point of Emphasis: For the equation $0 = ax^2 + bx + c$, the solution x is given by the quadratic formula:

$$x = -b \pm \sqrt{\frac{b^2 - 4ac}{2a}}$$

Point of Emphasis: When solving for x, especially when using the quadratic formula, it is imperative to check if the answer obtained is reasonable. For example, solutions that yield negative concentrations can be eliminated.

William R. Smith and Ronald W. Missen, "Chemical Equilibrium and Polynomial Equations: Beware of Roots," *J. Chem. Educ.* **1989,** *66,* 489.

SOLUTION To achieve equilibrium, NH_3 will be converted into N_2 and H_2. The initial concentration of $NH_3(g)$ is $(0.500 \text{ mol})/(2.00 \text{ L}) = 0.250\ M$. The balanced equation tells us that for every $2x$ moles of NH_3 per liter that decompose, x moles of N_2 per liter and $3x$ moles of H_2 per liter will be produced. We can therefore construct the following table:

$$N_2(g) \;+\; 3H_2(g) \rightleftharpoons \; 2NH_3(g)$$

Initial	$0\ M$	$0\ M$	$0.250\ M$
Change	$+x\ M$	$+3x\ M$	$-2x\ M$
Equilibrium	$x\ M$	$3x\ M$	$(0.250 - 2x)\ M$

The equilibrium concentrations must satisfy the equilibrium expression:

$$K_c = \frac{[NH_3]^2}{[N_2][H_2]^3} = \frac{(0.250 - 2x)^2}{(x)(3x)^3} = 0.105$$

Expanding $x(3x)^3$ gives $27x^4$; multiplying both sides of the equation by 27, we have

$$\frac{(0.250 - 2x)^2}{x^4} = (27)(0.105) = 2.835$$

We can solve this equation by taking the square root of both sides, converting it to a quadratic equation:

$$\frac{0.250 - 2x}{x^2} = \sqrt{2.835} = 1.684$$

$$1.684x^2 + 2x - 0.250 = 0$$

Solving the quadratic equation yields $x = 0.114$ or $x = -1.30$. The second of these leads to negative concentrations and is therefore rejected. We are left with the following equilibrium concentrations:

$$[N_2] = x = 0.114\ M$$
$$[H_2] = 3x = 0.342\ M$$
$$[NH_3] = 0.250 - 2x = 0.022\ M$$

PRACTICE EXERCISE

A 1.00-L flask is filled with 0.500 mol of HI at 448°C. Using the equilibrium constant given in Sample Exercise 15.11, determine the concentrations of H_2, I_2, and HI at equilibrium. (Note: You need not use the quadratic equation to solve this problem.) *Answer:* $[H_2] = [I_2] = 0.0549\ M$; $[HI] = 0.390\ M$

15.6 Factors Affecting Equilibrium: Le Châtelier's Principle

In developing his process for making ammonia from N_2 and H_2, Haber sought the factors that might be varied to increase the yield of NH_3. Using the values of the equilibrium constant at various temperatures, he calculated the equilibrium amounts of NH_3 formed under a variety of conditions. The results of some of his calculations are shown in Table 15.3. Notice that the percent of NH_3 present at equilibrium decreases with increasing temperature and increases with increasing pressure. We can understand these effects in terms of a principle first put forward by Henri-Louis Le Châtelier* (1850–1936), a

---

* Pronounced "le-SHOT-lee-ay."

TABLE 15.3 △ Effect of Temperature and Total Pressure on the Percentage of Ammonia Present at Equilibrium, Beginning with a 3:1 Molar H_2/N_2 Mixture

Temperature (°C)	Total pressure (atm)			
	200	300	400	500
400	38.7	47.8	54.9	60.6
450	27.4	35.9	42.9	48.8
500	18.9	26.0	32.2	37.8
600	8.8	12.9	16.9	20.8

French industrial chemist. **Le Châtelier's principle** can be stated as follows: *If a system at equilibrium is disturbed by a change in temperature, pressure, or the concentration of one of the components, the system will shift its equilibrium position so as to counteract the effect of the disturbance.*

In this section, we will use Le Châtelier's principle to make qualitative predictions about the response of a system at equilibrium to various changes in external conditions. We will consider three ways that a chemical equilibrium can be disturbed: (1) adding or removing a reactant or product, (2) changing the pressure, and (3) changing the temperature.

Change in Reactant or Product Concentrations

A system at equilibrium is in a dynamic state; the forward and reverse processes are occurring at equal rates, and the system is in a state of balance. An alteration in the conditions of the system may disturb the state of balance. If this occurs, the equilibrium shifts until a new state of balance is attained. Le Châtelier's principle states that the shift will be in the direction that minimizes or reduces the effect of the change. Therefore, *if a chemical system is at equilibrium and we add a substance (either a reactant or a product), the reaction will shift so as to reestablish equilibrium by consuming part of the added substance. Conversely, removal of a substance will result in the reaction moving in the direction that forms more of the substance.*

As an example, consider an equilibrium mixture of N_2, H_2, and NH_3:

$$N_2(g) + 3H_2(g) \rightleftharpoons 2NH_3(g)$$

Addition of H_2 would cause the system to shift so as to reduce the concentration of H_2 toward its original value. This can occur only if the equilibrium shifts to form more NH_3. At the same time, the quantity of N_2 would also be reduced slightly. This situation is illustrated in Figure 15.9. Addition of more N_2 to the equilibrium would likewise cause a shift in the direction of forming more NH_3. On the other hand, if we add NH_3 to the system at equilibrium, the concentrations will adjust to reduce the NH_3 concentration toward its original value; that is, some of the added ammonia will decompose to form N_2 and H_2.

We can reach the same conclusions by considering the effect of adding or removing a substance on the reaction quotient. ∞ (Sec. 15.5) For example, removal of NH_3 from an equilibrium mixture gives

$$\frac{[NH_3]^2}{[N_2][H_2]^3} = Q < K_c$$

Lee R. Summerlin and James L. Ealy, Jr., "Equilibrium and Le Châtelier's Principle," *Chemical Demonstrations, A Sourcebook for Teachers* (Washington: American Chemical Society, 1985), pp. 51–52.

Learning Goal 6: Explain how the relative equilibrium quantities of reactants and products are shifted by changes in temperature, pressure, or the concentrations of substances in the equilibrium reaction.

Teaching Note: Consider changing the concentration or pressure of a substance in a reaction at equilibrium as creating a stress. The removal of something creates a "deficit stress," and adding something creates an "excess stress." Reactions will always respond to stress by reducing the deficit (making more of what was removed) or by reducing the excess (consuming some of what was added). This description works regardless of which side of the reaction is changed.

Point of Emphasis: If you add a substance to a reaction at equilibrium, the reaction will shift to consume some of the added substance. If you remove a substance from a reaction at equilibrium, the reaction will shift to produce more of the removed substance.

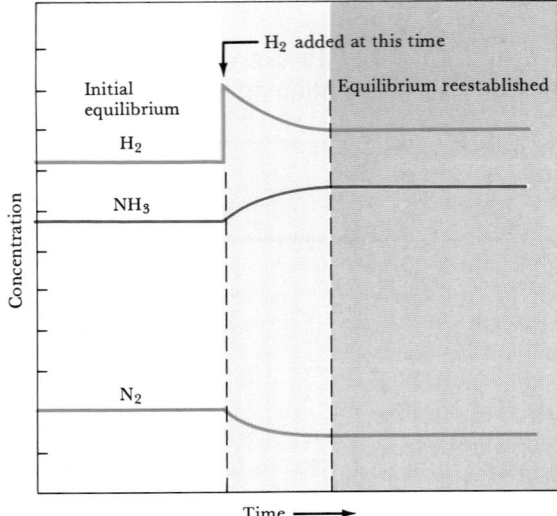

FIGURE 15.9 When H_2 is added to an equilibrium mixture of N_2, H_2, and NH_3, a portion of the H_2 reacts with N_2 to form NH_3, thereby establishing a new equilibrium position.

Figure 15.9

Because $Q < K_c$, the reaction shifts from left to right, forming more NH_3 and decreasing $[N_2]$ and $[H_2]$ to restore a new equilibrium that is still governed by K_c.

If the products of a reaction can be removed continuously, the reacting system can be continuously shifted to form more products. The yield of NH_3 in the Haber process can be increased dramatically by liquefying the NH_3; the liquid NH_3 is removed, and the N_2 and H_2 are recycled to form more NH_3. The general way this is accomplished is shown in Figure 15.10. If a reaction is

FIGURE 15.10 Schematic diagram summarizing the industrial production of ammonia. Incoming N_2 and H_2 gases are heated to approximately 500°C and passed over a catalyst. The resultant gas mixture is allowed to expand and cool, causing NH_3 to liquefy. Unreacted N_2 and H_2 gases are recycled.

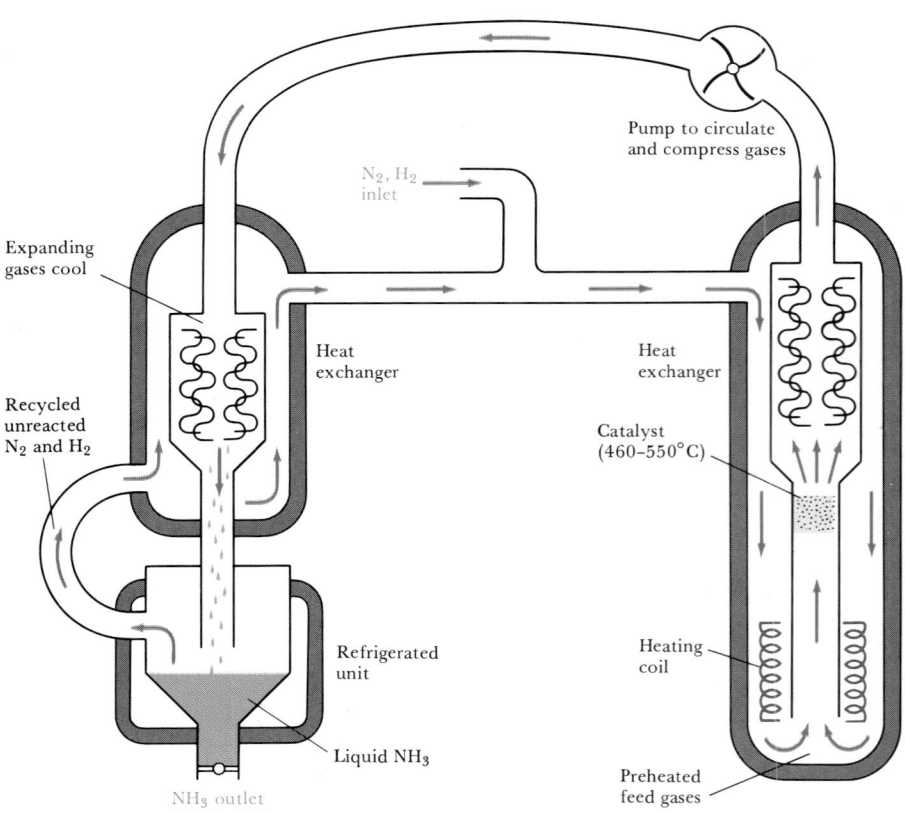

554

operated so that equilibrium cannot be achieved because of the escape of products, or if the equilibrium constant is very large, the reaction will proceed essentially to completion. In such instances, the chemical equation for the reaction is usually given with a single arrow: reactants $\longrightarrow$ products.

Effects of Volume and Pressure Changes

If a system is at equilibrium and its volume is decreased, thereby increasing its total pressure, Le Châtelier's principle indicates that the system will respond by shifting its equilibrium position to reduce the pressure. A system can reduce its pressure by reducing the total number of gas molecules; fewer molecules of gas exert a lower pressure. Thus, *reducing the volume of a gaseous equilibrium mixture causes the system to shift in the direction that reduces the number of moles of gas.* Conversely, increasing the volume causes a shift in the direction that produces more gas molecules.

For example, let's consider the equilibrium $N_2O_4(g) \rightleftharpoons 2NO_2(g)$, which we saw in Figure 15.1. What happens if the total pressure of an equilibrium mixture is increased by decreasing the volume? According to Le Châtelier's principle, the equilibrium shifts to the side that reduces the total number of moles of gas, which in this case is the reactant side. We therefore expect NO_2 to be converted into N_2O_4 as equilibrium is reestablished. Indeed, we see that the gas mixture gets lighter in color as brown NO_2 is converted into colorless N_2O_4 (Figure 15.11).

For the reaction

$$N_2(g) + 3H_2(g) \rightleftharpoons 2NH_3(g)$$

there are 2 mol of gas on the right side of the chemical equation ($2NH_3$) and 4 mol of gas on the left ($1N_2 + 3H_2$). Consequently, an increase in pressure (decrease in volume) leads to the formation of more NH_3; the reaction shifts toward the side with fewer gas molecules. In the case of the reaction

$$H_2(g) + I_2(g) \rightleftharpoons 2HI(g)$$

Point of Emphasis: If you change the pressure of a participating substance in a reaction at equilibrium, the reaction will shift to counter that change.

Lee R. Summerlin and James L. Ealy, Jr., "Equilibrium in the Gas Phase," *Chemical Demonstrations, A Sourcebook for Teachers* (Washington: American Chemical Society, 1985), pp. 60–61.

FIGURE 15.11 (a) An equilibrium mixture of brown $NO_2(g)$ and colorless $N_2O_4(g)$ held in a gas-tight syringe. (b) The volume and hence the pressure is changed by moving the plunger. When the pressure is increased, the mixture turns darker as the concentration of both gases is increased. The mixture is no longer in a state of equilibrium. (c) Equilibrium is reestablished when some $NO_2(g)$ is converted to $N_2O_4(g)$, thereby decreasing the number of gas molecules to accommodate the decreased volume. The color is lighter than in (b) because of the decrease in the concentration of $NO_2(g)$.
(© Richard Megna/Fundamental Photographs)

(a)

(b)

(c)

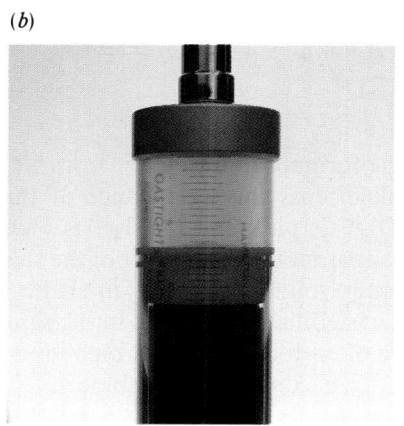
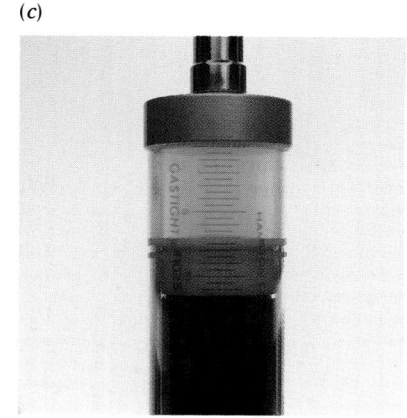

the number of moles of gaseous products equals the number of moles of gaseous reactants; therefore, changing the pressure will not influence the position of the equilibrium.

Keep in mind that pressure-volume changes do not change the value of K as long as the temperature remains constant. Rather, they change the concentrations of the gaseous substances. In Sample Exercise 15.6, we calculated K_c for an equilibrium mixture at 472°C that contained $[H_2] = 0.1207\ M$, $[N_2] = 0.0402\ M$, and $[NH_3] = 0.00272\ M$. The value of K_c is 0.105. Consider what happens if we suddenly reduce the volume of the system by half. If there were no shift in equilibrium, this volume change would cause the concentrations of all substances to double, giving $[H_2] = 0.2414\ M$, $[N_2] = 0.0804\ M$, and $[NH_3] = 0.00544\ M$. The reaction quotient would then no longer equal the equilibrium constant:

$$Q = \frac{[NH_3]^2}{[N_2][H_2]^3} = \frac{(0.00544)^2}{(0.0804)(0.2414)^3} = 2.62 \times 10^{-2}$$

Because $Q < K_c$, the system is no longer at equilibrium. Equilibrium will be reestablished by increasing $[NH_3]$ and decreasing $[N_2]$ and $[H_2]$ until $Q = K_c = 0.105$. Therefore, the equilibrium shifts to the right as Le Châtelier's principle predicts.

It is possible to change the total pressure of the system without changing its volume. For example, pressure increases if additional amounts of any of the reacting components are added to the system. We have already seen how to deal with a change in concentration of a reactant or product. The total pressure within the reaction vessel might also be increased by addition of a gas that is not involved in the equilibrium. For example, argon might be added to the ammonia equilibrium system. This addition would not alter the partial pressures of any of the reacting components and therefore would not cause a shift in equilibrium.

Point of Emphasis: For a change in pressure to have any effect on the amounts of the participants in an equilibrium mixture, the partial pressure of at least one participant species must change.

Effect of Temperature Changes

Learning Goal 7: Explain how the change in equilibrium constant with change in temperature is related to the enthalpy change in the reaction.

Changes in concentrations or total pressure cause shifts in equilibrium without changing the value of the equilibrium constant. In contrast, almost every equilibrium constant changes in value as the temperature changes. For example, consider the following equilibrium, which is established when cobalt(II) chloride, $CoCl_2$, is dissolved in hydrochloric acid, $HCl(aq)$:

$$Co(H_2O)_6^{2+}(aq) + 4Cl^-(aq) \rightleftharpoons CoCl_4^{2-}(aq) + 6H_2O(l) \qquad \Delta H > 0 \quad [15.15]$$

Pale pink   Deep blue

Lee R. Summerlin and James L. Ealy, Jr., "Effect of Temperature Change on Equilibrium: Cobalt Complex," Chemical Demonstrations, A Sourcebook for Teachers (Washington: American Chemical Society, 1985), p. 53.

The formation of $CoCl_4^{2-}$ from $Co(H_2O)_6^{2+}$ is an endothermic process. We shall discuss the significance of this enthalpy change shortly. Because $Co(H_2O)_6^{2+}$ is pink and $CoCl_4^{2-}$ is blue, the position of this equilibrium is readily apparent from the color of the solution. Figure 15.12(a) shows a room-temperature solution of $CoCl_2$ in $HCl(aq)$. Both $Co(H_2O)_6^{2+}$ and $CoCl_4^{2-}$ are present in significant amounts in the solution; the violet color results from the presence of both the pink and blue ions. When the solution is heated [Figure 15.12(b)], it becomes intensely blue in color, indicating that the equilibrium has

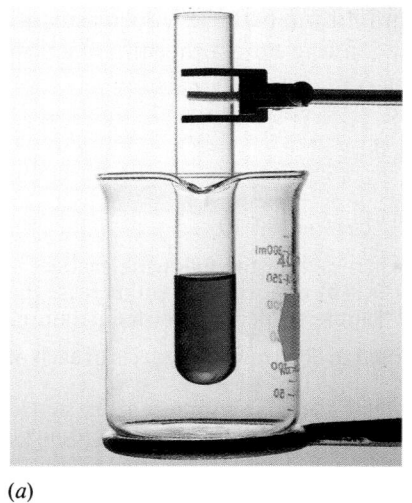

(a)   (b)   (c)

FIGURE 15.12 The effect of temperature on the equilibrium $Co(H_2O)_6^{2+}(aq) + 4Cl^-(aq) \rightleftharpoons CoCl_4^{2-}(aq) + 6H_2O(l)$. (a) At room temperature, both the pink $Co(H_2O)_6^{2+}$ and blue $CoCl_4^{2-}$ ions are present in significant amounts, giving a violet color to the solution. (b) Heating the solution shifts the equilibrium to the right, forming more blue $CoCl_4^{2-}$. (c) Cooling the solution shifts the equilibrium to the left, toward pink $Co(H_2O)_6^{2+}$. (© Richard Megna/Fundamental Photographs)

shifted so as to form more $CoCl_4^{2-}$. Cooling the solution, as in Figure 15.12(c), leads to a more pink solution, indicating that the equilibrium has shifted to produce more $Co(H_2O)_6^{2+}$. How can we explain the dependence of this equilibrium on temperature?

We can deduce the rules for the temperature dependence of the equilibrium constant by applying Le Châtelier's principle. A simple way to do this is to treat heat as if it were a chemical reagent. In an endothermic reaction, we can consider heat as a reactant, whereas in an exothermic reaction, we can consider heat as a product:

Endothermic: Reactants + *heat* $\rightleftharpoons$ products

Exothermic: Reactants $\rightleftharpoons$ products + *heat*

When heat is added to the system, the equilibrium shifts in the direction that absorbs heat. In an endothermic reaction, such as Equation 15.15, heat is absorbed as reactants are converted to products; thus, the equilibrium shifts to the right, in the direction of products, and K increases. Thus, in the case of Equation 15.15, heating the solution leads to the formation of more $CoCl_4^{2-}$, as observed in Figure 15.12(b). In an exothermic reaction, the opposite occurs. Heat is absorbed as products are converted to reactants, and so the equilibrium shifts to the left and K decreases. We can summarize these results as follows:

Endothermic: Increasing T results in an increase in K.

Exothermic: Increasing T results in a decrease in K.

Cooling a reaction has the opposite effect of heating it. As we remove heat from the system, the equilibrium shifts to the side that produces heat. Thus, cooling an endothermic reaction shifts the equilibrium to the left, decreasing K. We observed this effect in Figure 15.12(*c*). Cooling an exothermic reaction shifts the equilibrium to the right, increasing K.

SAMPLE EXERCISE 15.13

Consider the following equilibrium:

$$N_2O_4(g) \rightleftharpoons 2NO_2(g) \qquad \Delta H° = 58.0 \text{ kJ}$$

In what direction will the equilibrium shift when each of the following changes is made to a system at equilibrium? **(a)** Add N_2O_4; **(b)** remove NO_2; **(c)** increase the total pressure by adding $N_2(g)$; **(d)** increase the volume; **(e)** decrease the temperature?

SOLUTION Le Châtelier's principle can be used to determine the effects of each of these changes.

    (a) The system will adjust so as to decrease the concentration of the added N_2O_4; the equilibrium consequently shifts to the right, in the direction of products.

    (b) The system will adjust to this change by shifting to the side that produces more NO_2; thus, the equilibrium shifts to the right.

    (c) Adding N_2 will increase the total pressure of the system, but N_2 is not involved in the reaction. The partial pressures of NO_2 and N_2O_4 are unchanged, and there is no shift in the position of the equilibrium.

    (d) The system will shift in the direction that occupies a larger volume (more gas molecules); thus, the equilibrium shifts to the right. (This is the opposite of the effect observed in Figure 15.11.)

    (e) The reaction is endothermic; therefore, we can imagine heat as a reagent on the reactant side of the equation. Decreasing the temperature will shift the equilibrium in the direction that produces heat, and so the equilibrium shifts to the left, toward the formation of more N_2O_4. Note that only this last change also affects the value of the equilibrium constant, K.

PRACTICE EXERCISE

For the reaction

$$PCl_5(g) \rightleftharpoons PCl_3(g) + Cl_2(g) \qquad \Delta H° = 87.9 \text{ kJ}$$

in what direction will the equilibrium shift when **(a)** $Cl_2(g)$ is added; **(b)** the temperature is increased; **(c)** the volume of the reaction system is decreased; **(d)** $PCl_5(g)$ is added?   ***Answers:*** **(a)** left: additional $PCl_5(g)$ is formed; **(b)** right: increased dissociation of $PCl_5(g)$ occurs; **(c)** left: more $PCl_5(g)$ is formed; **(d)** right: additional $PCl_3(g)$ and $Cl_2(g)$ are formed.

SAMPLE EXERCISE 15.14

Using the standard heat of formation data in Appendix C, determine the standard enthalpy change for the reaction

$$N_2(g) + 3H_2(g) \rightleftharpoons 2NH_3(g)$$

Determine how the equilibrium constant for this reaction should change with temperature.

SOLUTION Recall that the standard enthalpy change for a reaction is given by the sum of the standard molar enthalpies of formation of the products, each multiplied by its coefficient in the balanced chemical equation, less the same quantities for the reactants. At 25°C, $\Delta H_f°$ for $NH_3(g)$ is -46.19 kJ/mol. The $\Delta H_f°$ values for $H_2(g)$ and $N_2(g)$ are zero by definition, because the enthalpies of formation of the elements in their normal states at 25°C are defined as zero (Section 5.7). Because 2 mol of NH_3 is formed, the total enthalpy change is

$$2 \text{ mol}(-46.19 \text{ kJ/mol}) - 0 = -92.38 \text{ kJ}$$

The reaction in the forward direction is exothermic. An increase in temperature causes the reaction to shift in the *reverse* direction—in our example, in the direction of less NH_3 and more N_2 and H_2. This is what occurs, as reflected in the values for K_p presented in Table 15.4. Notice that K_p changes very markedly with change in temperature and that it is larger at lower temperatures. This is a matter of great practical importance. To form ammonia at a reasonable rate requires higher temperatures. Yet at higher temperatures, the equilibrium constant is smaller, and so the percentage conversion to ammonia is smaller. To compensate for this, higher pressures are needed because high pressure favors ammonia formation.

PRACTICE EXERCISE

Using the thermodynamic data in Appendix C, determine the enthalpy change for the reaction

$$2POCl_3(g) \rightleftharpoons 2PCl_3(g) + O_2(g)$$

Use this result to determine how the equilibrium constant for the reaction should change with temperature. ***Answer:*** $\Delta H° = 508$ kJ; the equilibrium constant for the reaction will increase with increasing temperature.

TABLE 15.4 △ Variation in K_p for the Equilibrium $N_2 + 3H_2 \rightleftharpoons 2NH_3$ as a Function of Temperature

Temperature (°C)	K_p
300	4.34×10^{-3}
400	1.64×10^{-4}
450	4.51×10^{-5}
500	1.45×10^{-5}
550	5.38×10^{-6}
600	2.25×10^{-6}

The Effect of Catalysts

What happens if we add a catalyst to a chemical system that is at equilibrium? As shown in Figure 15.13, a catalyst lowers the barrier between the reactants and products. Notice that the activation energy of the forward reaction is lowered to the same extent as that for the reverse reaction. The catalyst thereby increases the rates of both the forward and reverse reactions by exactly the same factor. As a result, *a catalyst increases the rate at which equilibrium is achieved, but it does not change the composition of the equilibrium mixture.* The value of the equilibrium constant for a reaction is not affected by the presence of a catalyst.

The rate at which a reaction approaches equilibrium is an important practical consideration. As an example, let us again consider the synthesis of ammonia from N_2 and H_2. In designing a process for ammonia synthesis, Haber had to deal with a rather serious problem. He had to cope with a rapid decrease in equilibrium constant with increasing temperature, as shown in Table 15.4. At temperatures sufficiently high to give a satisfactory reaction rate, the amount of ammonia formed was too small. The solution to this dilemma

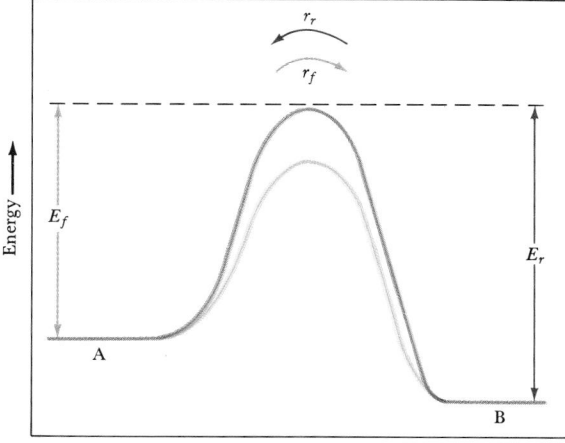

Figure 15.13

Reaction pathway

FIGURE 15.13 Schematic illustration of chemical equilibrium in the reaction $A \rightleftharpoons B$. When equilibrium is attained, the rate of the forward reaction, r_f, equals the rate of the reverse reaction r_r. A catalyst lowers the energy of the transition state, as shown by the green curve. Thus, the activation energy is lowered for both the forward and the reverse reactions. As a result, the rates of forward and reverse reactions in the catalyzed reaction are increased by the same factor.

CHEMISTRY AT WORK

Controlling Nitrogen Oxide Emissions

The formation of NO from N_2 and O_2 provides another interesting example of the practical importance of changes in equilibrium constant and reaction rate with temperature. The balanced equation and the standard enthalpy change for the reaction are

$$\tfrac{1}{2}N_2(g) + \tfrac{1}{2}O_2(g) \rightleftharpoons NO(g)$$
$$\Delta H° = 90.4 \text{ kJ} \quad [15.16]$$

The reaction is endothermic; that is, heat is absorbed when NO is formed from the elements. By applying Le Châtelier's principle, we deduce that an increase in temperature will shift the equilibrium in the direction of more NO. The equilibrium constant, K_c, for formation of 1 mol of NO from the elements at 300 K is only about 10^{-15}. On the other hand, at a much higher temperature, about 2400 K, the equilibrium constant is 10^{13} times as large, about 0.05. The manner in which K_c for reaction Equation 15.16 varies with temperature is shown in Figure 15.14.

This graph helps to explain why NO is a pollution problem. In the cylinder of a modern high-compression auto engine, the temperatures during the fuel-burning part of the cycle may be on the order of 2400 K. Also, there is a fairly large excess of air in the cylinder. These conditions provide an opportunity for the formation of some NO. After the combustion, however, the gases are quickly cooled. As the temperature drops, the equilibrium of Equation 15.16 shifts strongly to the left, that is, in the direction of N_2 and O_2. But the lower temperatures also mean that the rate of the reaction is decreased. The NO formed at high temperatures is essentially "frozen" in that form as the gas cools.

The gases exhausting from the cylinder are still quite hot, perhaps 1200 K. At this temperature, as shown in Figure 15.14, the equilibrium constant for formation of NO is much smaller. However, the rate of conversion of NO to N_2 and O_2 is too slow to permit much loss of NO before the gases are cooled still further. Removing the NO from the exhaust gases depends on finding a catalyst that will work at the temperatures of the exhaust gases and that will cause conversion of NO into something harmless to the environment. If a catalyst could be found that would convert the NO back into N_2 and O_2, the equilibrium would be sufficiently favorable. It has not proved possible to find a catalyst capable of withstanding the grueling conditions found in automobile exhaust systems that can catalyze the conversion of NO into N_2 and O_2. Instead, the catalysts used are designed to catalyze the reaction of NO with H_2 or CO.

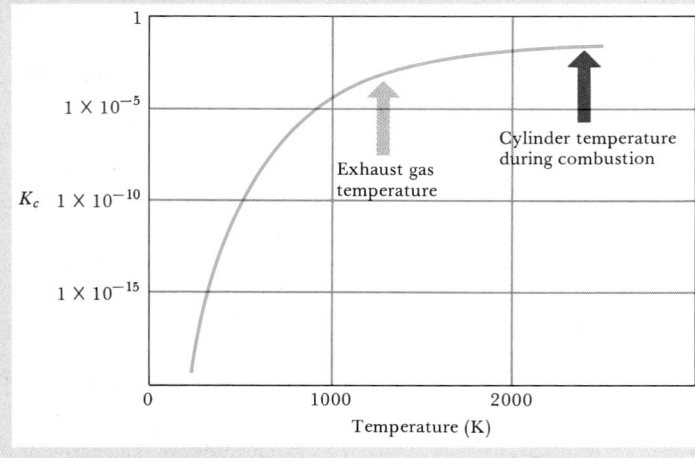

FIGURE 15.14 Variation in the equilibrium constant for the reaction $\tfrac{1}{2}N_2(g) + \tfrac{1}{2}O_2(g) \rightleftharpoons NO(g)$ as a function of temperature. It is necessary to use a log scale for K_c because the values of K_c vary over such a large range.

was to develop a catalyst that would produce a reasonably rapid approach to equilibrium at a sufficiently low temperature so that the equilibrium constant was still reasonably large. The development of a catalyst thus became the focus of Haber's research efforts.

After trying different substances to see which would be most effective, Haber finally settled on iron mixed with metal oxides. Variants of the original catalyst formulations are still used. These catalysts make it possible to obtain a reasonably rapid approach to equilibrium at temperatures around 400°C to 500°C and with gas pressures of 200 to 600 atm. The high pressures are needed to obtain a satisfactory degree of conversion at equilibrium. You can see from Table 15.3 that if an improved catalyst could be found — one that would lead to sufficiently rapid reaction at temperatures lower than 400°C to 500°C — it would be possible to obtain the same degree of equilibrium conversion at much lower pressures. This would result in great savings in the cost of equipment for ammonia synthesis. In view of the growing need for nitrogen as fertilizer, the fixation of nitrogen is a process of ever-increasing importance.

For Review

Summary

If the reactants and products of a reaction are kept in contact, a chemical reaction can achieve a state in which the forward and reverse reactions are occurring at equal rates. This condition is known as chemical equilibrium. A system at equilibrium does not change with time. For such a system, we can define an equilibrium constant, K. At equilibrium, the equilibrium constant equals the equilibrium expression, which is given by the product of the concentrations of the products, each raised to the power of its coefficient in the balanced chemical equation, divided by a like product of reactant concentrations. The equilibrium constant changes with temperature but is not affected by changes in relative concentrations of any reacting substance or by pressure or the presence of catalysts. In heterogeneous equilibria, the concentrations of pure solids or liquids are absent from the equilibrium expression.

If concentrations are expressed in molarity, we label the equilibrium constant K_c; if the concentration units are atmospheres, we use K_p. The constants K_c and K_p are related by the following equation: $K_p = K_c(RT)^{\Delta n}$. A large value for K_c or K_p indicates that the equilibrium mixture contains more products than reactants. A small value for the equilibrium constant means the equilibrium lies toward the reactant side.

The reaction quotient, Q, is found by substituting reactant and product concentrations into the equilibrium expression. If the system is at equilibrium, $Q = K$. However, if $Q \neq K$, nonequilibrium conditions apply; when $Q < K$, the reaction will move toward equilibrium by forming more products (the reaction moves from left to right); when $Q > K$, the reaction will proceed from right to left. Knowledge of the value of K_c or K_p permits calculation of the equilibrium concentrations of reactants and products.

Le Châtelier's principle states that if we disturb a system that is at equilibrium, the equilibrium will shift to minimize the disturbing influence. The effects of adding (or removing) reactants or products and of changing pressure, volume, or temperature can be predicted using this principle. Catalysts affect the speed at which equilibrium is reached but do not affect K.

Key Terms

chemical equilibrium
Haber process (Sec. 15.1)

law of mass action (Sec. 15.2)
equilibrium expression (Sec. 15.2)

equilibrium constant (Sec. 15.3)
homogeneous equilibria (Sec. 15.3)
heterogeneous equilibria (Sec. 15.3)

reaction quotient (Sec. 15.5)
Le Châtelier's principle (Sec. 15.6)

Exercises

The Concept of Equilibrium; Equilibrium Expressions

15.1. Explain what is incorrect about the following statements: **(a)** At equilibrium, the reaction stops; no more reactants are transformed into products. **(b)** At equilibrium, there are equal amounts of reactants and products.

15.2. A flask contains a saturated aqueous NaCl solution that is in contact with 10.0 g of undissolved NaCl powder. The flask is stoppered and left undisturbed. A year later it is observed that the system contains a single, large 10.0-g crystal of NaCl in contact with the solution. Explain how this observation can be used to support the notion that equilibrium is a dynamic process.

15.3. For a certain elementary process A $\rightleftharpoons$ B, the forward rate constant is 6.2×10^6 s^{-1} and the reverse rate constant is 4.8×10^3 s^{-1}. What is the value of the equilibrium constant for the reaction?

15.4. Consider the reaction A + B $\rightleftharpoons$ C + D. We will assume that both the forward and reverse reactions are elementary processes. Show that the equilibrium constant can be expressed as a ratio of the rate constants for the forward and reverse reactions.

15.5. Write the equilibrium expressions for K_c for the following reactions. In each case, indicate whether the reaction is homogeneous or heterogeneous.
(a) $H_2(g) + Cl_2(g) \rightleftharpoons 2HCl(g)$
(b) $2N_2O_5(g) \rightleftharpoons 4NO_2(g) + O_2(g)$
(c) $CH_4(g) + 2H_2S(g) \rightleftharpoons CS_2(g) + 4H_2(g)$

(d) $C(s) + CO_2(g) \rightleftharpoons 2CO(g)$
(e) $H_2(g) + FeO(s) \rightleftharpoons H_2O(g) + Fe(s)$

15.6. Write the equilibrium expressions for K_c and K_p for the following reactions. In each case, indicate whether the reaction is homogeneous or heterogeneous.
(a) $2CO_2(g) \rightleftharpoons 2CO(g) + O_2(g)$
(b) $2H_2S(g) + 3O_2(g) \rightleftharpoons 2H_2O(g) + 2SO_2(g)$
(c) $Zn(s) + 2HCl(g) \rightleftharpoons ZnCl_2(s) + H_2(g)$
(d) $4NH_3(g) + 3O_2(g) \rightleftharpoons 2N_2(g) + 6H_2O(l)$
(e) $NH_4NO_2(s) \rightleftharpoons N_2(g) + 2H_2O(l)$

15.7. The equilibrium constant for the reaction

$$2SO_3(g) \rightleftharpoons 2SO_2(g) + O_2(g)$$

is $K_c = 2.4 \times 10^{-3}$ at 700°C.
(a) Calculate K_c for $2SO_2(g) + O_2(g) \rightleftharpoons 2SO_3(g)$.
(b) Does the equilibrium favor SO$_2$ and O$_2$, or does it favor SO$_3$ at this temperature?

15.8. The equilibrium constant for the reaction

$$2NO(g) \rightleftharpoons N_2(g) + O_2(g)$$

is $K_c = 2.4 \times 10^3$ at 2000°C.
(a) Calculate K_c for $N_2(g) + O_2(g) \rightleftharpoons 2NO(g)$.
(b) Does the equilibrium favor NO, or does it favor N$_2$ and O$_2$?

Calculating Equilibrium Constants

15.9. Gaseous hydrogen iodide is placed in a closed container at 425°C, where it partially decomposes to hydrogen and iodine: $2HI(g) \rightleftharpoons H_2(g) + I_2(g)$. At equilibrium, it is found that $[HI] = 3.53 \times 10^{-3}$ M; $[H_2] = 4.79 \times 10^{-4}$ M; and $[I_2] = 4.79 \times 10^{-4}$ M. What is the value of K_c at this temperature?

15.10. At temperatures near 800°C, steam passed over hot coke (a form of carbon obtained from coal) reacts to form CO and H$_2$:

$$C(s) + H_2O(g) \rightleftharpoons CO(g) + H_2(g)$$

The mixture of gases that results is an important industrial fuel called *water gas*. When equilibrium is achieved at 800°C, $[H_2] = 4.0 \times 10^{-2}$ M, $[CO] = 4.0 \times 10^{-2}$ M, and $[H_2O] = 1.0 \times 10^{-2}$ M. Calculate K_c at this temperature.

15.11. A mixture of 0.100 mol of NO, 0.050 mol of H$_2$, and 0.100 mol of H$_2$O is placed in a 1.00-L vessel. The

following equilibrium is established:

$$2NO(g) + 2H_2(g) \rightleftharpoons N_2(g) + 2H_2O(g)$$

At equilibrium $[NO] = 0.062$ M. **(a)** Calculate the equilibrium concentrations of H$_2$, N$_2$, and H$_2$O. **(b)** Calculate K_c.

15.12. A mixture of 1.374 g of H$_2$ and 70.31 g of Br$_2$ is heated in a 2.00-L vessel at 700 K. These substances react as follows:

$$H_2(g) + Br_2(g) \rightleftharpoons 2HBr(g)$$

At equilibrium, the vessel is found to contain 0.566 g of H$_2$. **(a)** Calculate the equilibrium concentrations of H$_2$, Br$_2$, and HBr. **(b)** Calculate K_c.

15.13. **(a)** At 1285°C, $K_c = 1.04 \times 10^{-3}$ for the reaction

$$Br_2(g) \rightleftharpoons 2Br(g)$$

What is the value of K_p for this reaction at this temperature? **(b)** The equilibrium constant for the reaction

$$CO_2(g) + H_2(g) \rightleftharpoons CO(g) + H_2O(g)$$

is $K_p = 0.11$ at 700 K. What is the value of K_c at this temperature?

15.14. **(a)** At 700°C, $K_c = 416$ for the reaction

$$2SO_2(g) + O_2(g) \rightleftharpoons 2SO_3(g)$$

What is the value of K_p at this temperature? **(b)** The equilibrium constant for the reaction

$$2Cl_2(g) + 2H_2O(g) \rightleftharpoons 4HCl(g) + O_2(g)$$

is $K_p = 0.0752$ at 480°C. What is the value of K_c at this temperature?

15.15. Phosphorus trichloride gas and chlorine gas react to form phosphorus pentachloride gas: $PCl_3(g) + Cl_2(g) \rightleftharpoons PCl_5(g)$. A gas vessel is charged with a mixture of $PCl_3(g)$ and $Cl_2(g)$, which is allowed to equilibrate at 450 K. At equilibrium, the partial pressures of the three gases are $P_{PCl_3} = 0.124$ atm, $P_{Cl_2} = 0.157$ atm, and $P_{PCl_5} =$

Applications of Equilibrium Constants

15.19. At 100°C, the equilibrium constant for the reaction $COCl_2(g) \rightleftharpoons CO(g) + Cl_2(g)$ has the value of $K_c = 2.19 \times 10^{-10}$. Are the following mixtures of $COCl_2$, CO, and Cl_2 at equilibrium? If not, indicate the direction that the reaction must proceed to achieve equilibrium. **(a)** $[COCl_2] = 5.00 \times 10^{-2}$ M, $[CO] = 3.31 \times 10^{-6}$ M, $[Cl_2] = 3.31 \times 10^{-6}$ M; **(b)** $[COCl_2] = 3.50 \times 10^{-3}$ M, $[CO] = 1.11 \times 10^{-5}$ M, $[Cl_2] = 3.25 \times 10^{-6}$ M; **(c)** $[COCl_2] = 1.45$ M, $[CO] = [Cl_2] = 1.56 \times 10^{-6}$ M.

15.20. As shown in Table 15.4, K_p for the equilibrium

$$N_2(g) + 3H_2(g) \rightleftharpoons 2NH_3(g)$$

is 4.51×10^{-5} at 450°C. Each of the mixtures listed below may or may not be at equilibrium at 450°C. Indicate in each case whether the mixture is at equilibrium; if it is not at equilibrium, indicate the direction (toward product or toward reactants) in which the mixture must shift to achieve equilibrium: **(a)** 105 atm NH_3, 35 atm N_2, 495 atm H_2; **(b)** 35 atm NH_3, 595 atm H_2, no N_2; **(c)** 26 atm NH_3, 42 atm H_2, 202 atm N_2; **(d)** 105 atm NH_3, 55 atm H_2, 5.0 atm N_2.

15.21. At 2000°C, the equilibrium constant for the reaction

$$N_2(g) + O_2(g) \rightleftharpoons 2NO(g)$$

is $K_c = 4.1 \times 10^{-4}$. If the initial concentrations of N_2 and O_2 are 0.20 M and 0.10 M, respectively, what is the equilibrium concentration of NO?

15.22. For the equilibrium

$$Br_2(g) + Cl_2(g) \rightleftharpoons 2BrCl(g)$$

at 400 K, $K_c = 7.0$. If 0.50 mol of Br_2 and 0.50 mol Cl_2 are introduced into a 1.0-L container at 400 K, what will be the equilibrium concentration of BrCl?

1.30 atm. **(a)** What is the value of K_p at this temperature? **(b)** Does the equilibrium favor reactants or products?

15.16. At 500 K, the equilibrium constant for the reaction $2NO(g) + Cl_2(g) \rightleftharpoons 2NOCl(g)$ is $K_p = 52.0$. An equilibrium mixture of the three gases has partial pressures of 0.095 atm and 0.171 atm for NO and Cl_2, respectively. What is the partial pressure of NOCl in the mixture?

15.17. A flask is charged with 0.50 atm of $N_2O_4(g)$ and 0.50 atm $NO_2(g)$ at 25°C. The equilibrium reaction is given in Equation 15.7. After reaching equilibrium, the partial pressure of N_2O_4 is 0.60 atm. **(a)** Calculate the equilibrium pressure of NO_2. **(b)** Calculate the value of K_p at 25°C.

15.18. A sample of nitrosyl bromide, NOBr, decomposes according to the following equation:

$$2NOBr(g) \rightleftharpoons 2NO(g) + Br_2(g)$$

An equilibrium mixture in a 5.00-L vessel at 100°C contains 3.22 g of NOBr, 3.08 g of NO, and 4.19 g of Br_2. **(a)** Calculate K_c. **(b)** Calculate K_p. **(c)** What is the total pressure exerted by the mixture of gases?

15.23. At 1285°C, the equilibrium constant for the reaction $Br_2(g) \rightleftharpoons 2Br(g)$ is $K_c = 1.04 \times 10^{-3}$. A 0.200-L vessel containing an equilibrium mixture of the gases has 0.245 g $Br_2(g)$ in it. What is the mass of $Br(g)$ in the vessel?

15.24. For the reaction $H_2(g) + I_2(g) \rightleftharpoons 2HI(g)$, $K_p = 55.3$ at 700 K. In a 2.000-L flask containing an equilibrium mixture of the three gases, there are 0.056 g H_2 and 4.36 g I_2. What is the mass of HI in the flask?

15.25. For the equilibrium

$$C(s) + CO_2(g) \rightleftharpoons 2CO(g)$$

$K_p = 167.5$ at 1000°C. What is the partial pressure of CO_2 that is in equilibrium with CO whose partial pressure is 0.500 atm?

15.26. For the equilibrium

$$2NOBr(g) \rightleftharpoons 2NO(g) + Br_2(g)$$

$K_p = 0.416$ at 373 K. If the pressures of NOBr(g) and NO(g) are equal, what is the equilibrium pressure of $Br_2(g)$?

15.27. At 21.8°C, $K_c = 1.2 \times 10^{-4}$ for the following reaction:

$$NH_4HS(s) \rightleftharpoons NH_3(g) + H_2S(g)$$

Calculate the equilibrium concentrations of NH_3 and H_2S if a sample of solid NH_4HS is placed in a closed vessel and allowed to decompose until equilibrium is reached.

15.28. At 80°C, the equilibrium constant K_p is 1.57 for the following reaction:

$$PH_3BCl_3(s) \rightleftharpoons PH_3(g) + BCl_3(g)$$

(a) Calculate the equilibrium pressures of $PH_3(g)$ and $BCl_3(g)$ if a sample of PH_3BCl_3 is placed in a closed vessel at 80°C and allowed to decompose until equilibrium is attained. (b) What is the minimum amount of PH_3BCl_3 that must be placed in a 0.500-L vessel at 80°C if equilibrium is to be attained?

15.29. For the reaction $I_2(g) + Br_2(g) \rightleftharpoons 2IBr(g)$, $K_c = 280$ at 150°C. Suppose that 0.500 mol IBr is placed in a 1.000-L flask and allowed to reach equilibrium at this tem-

perature. What are the equilibrium concentrations of IBr, I_2, and Br_2?

15.30. At 250°C, the reaction

$$PCl_5(g) \rightleftharpoons PCl_3(g) + Cl_2(g)$$

has an equilibrium constant $K_c = 1.80$. If 0.100 mol PCl_5 is added to a 5.00-L vessel, what are the concentrations of PCl_5, PCl_3, and Cl_2 at equilibrium at this temperature?

Le Châtelier's Principle

15.31. In the reaction

$$6CO_2(g) + 6H_2O(l) \rightleftharpoons C_6H_{12}O_6(s) + 6O_2(g)$$
$$\Delta H° = 2816 \text{ kJ}$$

how is the equilibrium yield of $C_6H_{12}O_6$ affected by (a) increasing P_{CO_2}; (b) increasing temperature; (c) removing CO_2; (d) increasing the total pressure; (e) removing part of the $C_6H_{12}O_6$; (f) adding a catalyst?

15.32. Consider the following equilibrium system:

$$C(s) + CO_2(g) \rightleftharpoons 2CO(g) \qquad \Delta H° = 119.8 \text{ kJ}$$

If the reaction is at equilibrium, what would be the effect of (a) adding $CO_2(g)$; (b) adding $C(s)$; (c) adding heat; (d) increasing the pressure on the system by decreasing the volume; (e) adding a catalyst; (f) removing $CO(g)$?

15.33. How do the following changes affect the value of the equilibrium constant for an exothermic reaction: (a)

removal of a reactant or product; (b) decrease in the volume; (c) decrease in the temperature; (d) addition of a catalyst?

15.34. Using the thermochemical data in Appendix C, calculate $\Delta H°$ for the reaction

$$CO(g) + 2H_2(g) \rightleftharpoons CH_3OH(l)$$

(a) If you want to maximize the equilibrium yield of methanol in this reaction, would you use a high or a low temperature? (b) Does the equilibrium constant for this reaction increase or decrease with increasing temperature? (c) Assuming equal pressures of CO and H_2, how would the extent of conversion of the gas mixture to methanol, CH_3OH, vary with total pressure?

Additional Exercises

15.35. Both the forward and reverse reactions of the following equilibrium are believed to be elementary steps:

$$CO(g) + Cl_2(g) \rightleftharpoons COCl(g) + Cl(g)$$

At 25°C, the rate constants for the forward and reverse reactions are 1.4×10^{-28} M^{-1} s^{-1} and 9.3×10^{10} M^{-1} s^{-1}, respectively. (a) What is the value for the equilibrium constant at 25°C? (b) Are reactants or products more plentiful at equilibrium?

15.36. A mixture of CH_4 and H_2O is passed over a nickel catalyst at 1000 K. The emerging gas is collected in a 5.00-L flask and is found to contain 8.62 g of CO, 2.60 g of H_2, 43.0 g of CH_4, and 48.4 g of H_2O. Assuming that equilibrium has been reached, calculate K_c for the reaction

$$CH_4(g) + H_2O(g) \rightleftharpoons CO(g) + 3H_2(g)$$

15.37. A mixture of H_2, S, and H_2S is held in a 1.00-L vessel at 90°C until the following equilibrium is achieved:

$$H_2(g) + S(s) \rightleftharpoons H_2S(g)$$

At equilibrium, the mixture contains 0.46 g of H_2S and 0.40 g H_2. (a) Write the equilibrium expression for this reaction. (b) What is the value of K_c for the reaction at this temperature? (c) Why can we ignore the amount of S when doing the calculation in part (b)?

15.38. At 500 K, 1.00 mol of NOCl(g) is introduced into a 1.00-L container. At equilibrium, 9.0 percent of the NOCl(g) is dissociated:

$$2NOCl(g) \rightleftharpoons 2NO(g) + Cl_2(g)$$

Calculate the value of K_c for this equilibrium at 500 K.

15.39. A mixture of 3.0 mol of SO_2, 4.0 mol of NO_2, 1.0 mol of SO_3, and 4.0 mol of NO is placed in a 2.0-L vessel. The following reaction takes place:

$$SO_2(g) + NO_2(g) \rightleftharpoons SO_3(g) + NO(g)$$

When equilibrium is reached at 700°C, the vessel is found to contain 1.0 mol of SO_2. (a) Calculate the equilibrium concentrations of SO_2, NO_2, and SO_3, and NO. (b) Calculate the value of K_c for this reaction at 700°C.

15.40. Consider the hypothetical reaction $A(g) \rightleftharpoons 2B(g)$. A flask is charged with 0.75 atm of pure A, after which it is allowed to reach equilibrium at 0°C. At equilibrium, the partial pressure of A is 0.50 atm. (a) What is the total pressure in the flask at equilibrium? (b) What is the value of K_p? (c) What is the value of K_c?

[15.41]. As shown in Table 15.4, at 300°C the equilibrium constant for the reaction $N_2(g) + 3H_2(g) \rightleftharpoons 2NH_3(g)$ is $K_p = 4.34 \times 10^{-3}$. Pure NH_3 is placed in a 1.000-L flask and allowed to reach equilibrium at this temperature. There is 0.753 g NH_3 in the equilibrium mixture. (a) What are the masses of N_2 and H_2 in the equilibrium mixture? (b) What was the initial mass of ammonia placed in the vessel? (c) What is the total pressure in the vessel?

15.42. At 1558 K, the equilibrium constant, K_c, for the reaction

$$Br_2(g) \rightleftharpoons 2Br(g)$$

is 1.04×10^{-3}. If a 0.200-L vessel contains 4.53×10^{-2} mol of Br_2 at equilibrium, how many moles of Br are present?

15.43. For the equilibrium

$$2IBr(g) \rightleftharpoons I_2(g) + Br_2(g)$$

$K_c = 8.5 \times 10^{-3}$ at 150°C. If 0.040 mol of IBr is placed in a 1.00-L container, what is the concentration of this substance after equilibrium is reached?

15.44. For the equilibrium

$$PH_3BCl_3(s) \rightleftharpoons PH_3(g) + BCl_3(g)$$

$K_p = 0.052$ at 60°C. (a) Calculate K_c. (b) Some solid PH_3BCl_3 is added to a closed 0.500-L vessel at 60°C; the vessel is then charged with 0.0216 mol of $BCl_3(g)$. What is the equilibrium concentration of PH_3?

[15.45]. Write the equilibrium expression for the equilibrium

$$C(s) + CO_2(g) \rightleftharpoons 2CO(g)$$

The table below shows the relative mole percentages of $CO_2(g)$ and $CO(g)$ at a total pressure of 1 atm for several temperatures. Calculate the value of K_c at each temperature. Is the reaction exothermic or endothermic? Explain.

Temperature (°C)	CO_2 (mol %)	CO (mol %)
850	6.23	93.77
950	1.32	98.68
1050	0.37	99.63
1200	0.06	99.94

15.46. Solid NH_4HS is introduced into an evacuated flask at 24°C. The following reaction takes place:

$$NH_4HS(s) \rightleftharpoons NH_3(g) + H_2S(g)$$

At equilibrium, the total pressure (for NH_3 and H_2S taken together) was 0.614 atm. What is K_p for this equilibrium at 24°C?

[15.47]. A 0.831-g sample of SO_3 is placed in a 1.00-L container and heated to 1100 K. The SO_3 undergoes decomposition to SO_2 and O_2.

$$2SO_3(g) \rightleftharpoons 2SO_2(g) + O_2(g)$$

At equilibrium, the total pressure in the container is 1.300 atm. Find the values of K_p and K_c for this reaction at 1100 K.

15.48. Nitric oxide, NO, reacts readily with chlorine gas as follows:

$$2NO(g) + Cl_2(g) \rightleftharpoons 2NOCl(g)$$

At 700 K, the equilibrium constant, K_p, for this reaction is 0.26. Predict the behavior of each of the following mixtures at this temperature: (a) $P_{NO} = 0.15$ atm, $P_{Cl_2} = 0.31$ atm, and $P_{NOCl} = 0.11$ atm; (b) $P_{NO} = 0.12$ atm, $P_{Cl_2} = 0.10$ atm, and $P_{NOCl} = 0.050$ atm; (c) $P_{NO} = 0.15$ atm, $P_{Cl_2} = 0.20$ atm, and $P_{NOCl} = 5.10 \times 10^{-3}$ atm.

15.49. At 900°C, $K_c = 0.0108$ for the reaction

$$CaCO_3(s) \rightleftharpoons CaO(s) + CO_2(g)$$

A mixture of $CaCO_3$, CaO, and CO_2 is placed in a 10.0-L vessel at 900°C. For the following mixtures, will the amount of $CaCO_3$ increase, decrease, or remain the same as the system approaches equilibrium?
(a) 25.0 g $CaCO_3$, 25.0 g CaO, and 15.0 g CO_2.
(b) 1.50 g $CaCO_3$, 15.0 g CaO, and 4.75 g CO_2.
(c) 35.0 g $CaCO_3$, 20.5 g CaO, and 2.50 g CO_2.

15.50. Consider the reaction

$$2CO(g) + O_2(g) \rightleftharpoons 2CO_2(g) \qquad \Delta H° = -514.2 \text{ kJ}$$

In which direction will the equilibrium move if (a) CO_2 is added; (b) CO_2 is removed; (c) the volume is increased; (d) the pressure is increased; (e) the temperature is increased?

15.51. NiO is to be reduced to nickel metal in an industrial process by use of the reaction

$$NiO(s) + CO(g) \rightleftharpoons Ni(s) + CO_2(g)$$

At 1600 K, the equilibrium constant for the reaction is 600. If a CO pressure of 150 torr is to be employed in the furnace and total pressure never exceeds 760 torr, will reduction occur?

15.52. Nickel carbonyl, $Ni(CO)_4$, is an extremely toxic liquid with a low boiling point. Nickel carbonyl results from the reaction of nickel metal with carbon monoxide. For temperatures above the boiling point (42.2°C) of $Ni(CO)_4$, the reaction is

$$Ni(s) + 4CO(g) \rightleftharpoons Ni(CO)_4(g)$$

Nickel that is more than 99.9 percent pure can be produced by the *carbonyl process:* Impure nickel is reacted with CO at 50°C, which produces $Ni(CO)_4(g)$. The $Ni(CO)_4$ is then heated to 200°C to decompose it back into $Ni(s)$ and $CO(g)$. (a) Write the equilibrium expression for the above reaction. (b) Given the temperatures used for the steps in the carbonyl process, do you think the above reaction is endothermic or exothermic? (c) In the early days of automobiles, nickel-plated exhaust pipes were used. Even though the equilibrium constant for the above reaction is very small at the temperature of automotive exhaust gases, the exhaust pipes quickly corroded. Explain why this occurred.

[15.53]. At 700 K, the equilibrium constant for the reaction

$$CCl_4(g) \rightleftharpoons C(s) + 2Cl_2(g)$$

is $K_p = 0.76$. A flask is charged with 2.00 atm of CCl_4, which is then allowed to reach equilibrium at 700 K. (a) What is the value of K_c for this reaction at 700 K? (b) What fraction of the CCl_4 is converted into C and Cl_2? (c) What are the partial pressures of CCl_4 and Cl_2 at equilibrium?

[15.54]. At 25°C, the equilibrium constant for the reaction

$$NH_4SH(s) \rightleftharpoons NH_3(g) + H_2S(g)$$

is $K_p = 0.120$. A 10.0-L flask is charged with 0.100 atm of pure $NH_3(g)$ at 25°C. Solid NH_4SH is then added until there is excess unreacted solid remaining. (a) Why does no reaction occur until the NH_4SH is added? (b) What is the total pressure in the flask at equilibrium? (c) What is the minimum mass, in grams, of NH_4SH that must be added in order to achieve equilibrium?

[15.55]. The reaction $PCl_3(g) + Cl_2(g) \rightleftharpoons PCl_5(g)$ has $K_p = 0.0870$ at 300°C. A flask is charged with 0.30 atm PCl_3, 0.60 atm Cl_2, and 0.10 atm PCl_5 at this temperature. (a) Use the reaction quotient to determine the direction the reaction must proceed in order to reach equilibrium. (b) Calculate the equilibrium partial pressures of the gases. (c) What effect will increasing the volume of the system have on the mole fraction of PCl_5 in the mixture? (d) The reaction is exothermic. What effect will increasing the temperature of the system have on the mole fraction of PCl_5 in the mixture?

[15.56]. An equilibrium mixture of H_2, I_2, and HI at 458°C contains 2.24×10^{-2} M H_2, 2.24×10^{-2} M I_2, and 0.155 M HI in a 5.00-L vessel. What are the equilibrium concentrations when equilibrium is reestablished following the addition of 0.100 mol of HI?

[15.57]. Consider the hypothetical reaction $A(g) + 2B(g) \rightleftharpoons 2C(g)$, for which $K_c = 0.25$ at some temperature. A 1.00-L reaction vessel is loaded with 1.00 mol of compound C, which is allowed to reach equilibrium. Let the variable x represent the number of mol/L of compound A present at equilibrium. (a) In terms of x, what are the equilibrium concentrations of compounds B and C? (b) What limits must be placed on the value of x so that all concentrations are positive? (c) By putting the equilibrium concentrations (in terms of x) into the equilibrium expression, derive an equation that can be solved for x. (d) The equation from part (c) is a *cubic* equation (one that has the form $ax^3 + bx^2 + cx + d = 0$). In general, cubic equations cannot be solved in closed form. However, you can estimate the solution by plotting the cubic equation in the allowed range of x that you specified in part (b). The point at which the cubic equation crosses the y axis is the solution. (e) From the plot in part (d), estimate the equilibrium concentrations of A, B, and C. (You can check the accuracy of your answer by substituting these concentrations into the equilibrium expression.)

15.58. At 1200 K, the approximate temperature of automobile exhaust gases (Figure 15.14), the equilibrium constant K_p, for the reaction

$$2CO_2(g) \rightleftharpoons 2CO(g) + O_2(g)$$

is about 1×10^{-13}. Assuming that the exhaust gas (total pressure 1 atm) contains 0.2 percent CO by volume, 12 percent CO_2, and 3 percent O_2, is the system at equilibrium with respect to the above reaction? Based on your conclusion, would the CO concentration in the exhaust be lowered or increased by a catalyst that speeds up the reaction above?

15.59. Suppose that you worked at the U.S. Patent Office and a patent application came across your desk claiming that a newly developed catalyst was much superior to the Haber catalyst for ammonia synthesis because the catalyst led to much greater equilibrium conversion of N_2 and H_2 into NH_3 than the Haber catalyst under the same conditions. What would be your response?

15.60. The hypothetical reaction $A + B \rightleftharpoons C$ occurs in the forward direction in a single step. The energy profile of the reaction is shown in Figure 15.15. (a) Is the forward or reverse reaction faster at equilibrium? (b) Would you expect the equilibrium to favor reactants or products? (c) In general, how would a catalyst affect the energy profile shown? (d) How would a catalyst affect the ratio of the rate constants for the forward and reverse reactions? (e) How would you expect the equilibrium constant of the reaction to change with increasing temperature?

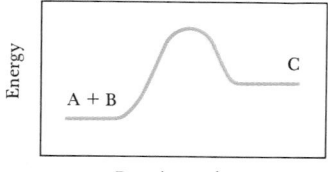

Reaction pathway

FIGURE 15.15

[15.61]. Consider the equilibrium $A \rightleftharpoons B$ discussed in Equations 15.1 through 15.3. Assume that the only effect of a catalyst on the reaction is to lower the activation energies of the forward and reverse reactions, as shown in Figure 15.13. Using the Arrhenius equation (Section 14.4), prove that the equilibrium constant is the same for the catalyzed reaction as for the uncatalyzed one.

Acid-Base Equilibria 16

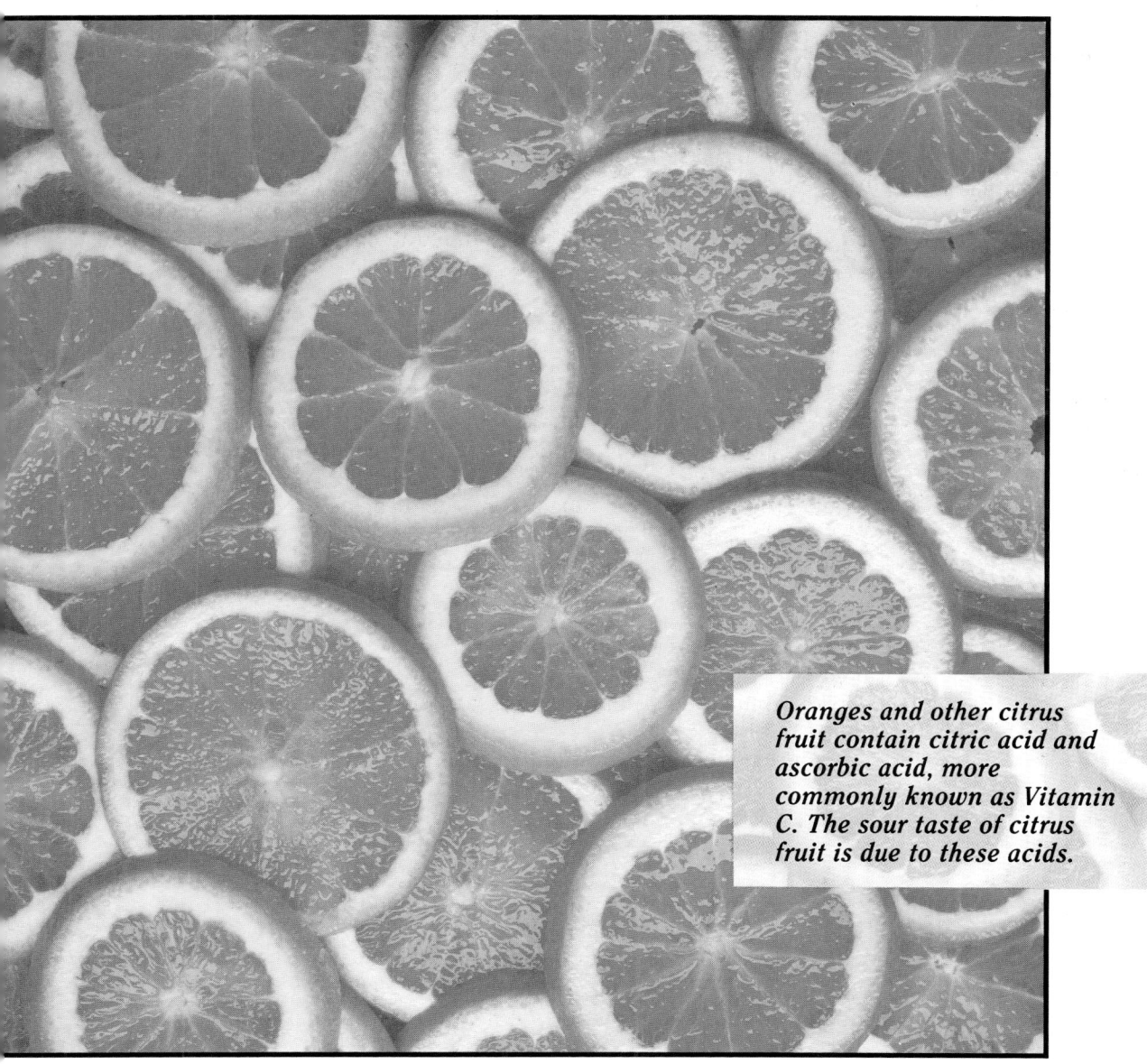

Oranges and other citrus fruit contain citric acid and ascorbic acid, more commonly known as Vitamin C. The sour taste of citrus fruit is due to these acids.

CONTENTS

Acids and bases are important in numerous chemical processes that occur around us, from industrial processes to biological ones, from reactions in the laboratory to those in our environment. The time required for a metal object immersed in water to corrode, the ability of an aquatic environment to support fish and plant life, and the fate of pollutant chemicals washed out of the air by rain are all critically dependent upon the acidity or basicity of the solution.

We have encountered acids and bases many times in earlier discussions. For example, much of Chapter 4 focused on the reactions of these important substances. In this chapter, we will reexamine acids and bases, applying the principles of chemical equilibrium. We will see how to describe the aqueous equilibria quantitatively. We will also examine the relationship between acid or base strength and chemical structure.

Earlier, we introduced acids and bases as substances that increase the concentrations of $H^+(aq)$ and $OH^-(aq)$, respectively. ∞ (Sec. 4.3) If an aqueous solution contains more H^+ than OH^-, the solution is *acidic*. Likewise, if the solution contains more OH^- than H^+, the solution is *basic*. We also saw that H^+ and OH^- ions react with one another to form water during neutralization reactions (Equation 4.13). Why are these two ions of such major importance in our discussions of aqueous chemistry? Is there a relationship between the concentrations of these ions in an aqueous solution? To answer these questions, we will first examine the dissociation of water molecules into $H^+(aq)$ and $OH^-(aq)$, a process that is central to our discussion of acids and bases.

Teaching Note: Acid-base neutralization reactions are discussed in Section 4.3.

16.1 The Dissociation of Water

Pure water is a rather poor conductor of electricity because there are very few ions to permit the conduction of electrical current. ∞ (Sec. 4.2) Indeed, pure water consists almost entirely of H_2O molecules. Water does ionize into H^+ and OH^- ions to a very small extent, however, a process we can represent most simply by the following equilibrium:

$$H_2O(l) \rightleftharpoons H^+(aq) + OH^-(aq) \qquad [16.1]$$

Learning Goal 1: Explain what is meant by the autoionization of water, and write the ion-product constant expression for this process.

We call this process the **autoionization** of water. At room temperature, only about one out of every 10^8 molecules is ionized at any given instant. No individual molecule remains ionized for long; the equilibria are extremely rapid.

The equilibrium expression for the autoionization reaction is

$$K = \frac{[H^+][OH^-]}{[H_2O]}$$

Teaching Note: Other liquid solvents, such as NH_3, also undergo autoionization.

The concentration of water in aqueous solutions is typically very large, about 55 M, and remains essentially constant for dilute solutions. We therefore exclude the concentration of water from equilibrium expressions for aqueous solutions, just as we exclude the concentrations of pure solids and liquids from equilibrium expressions for heterogeneous reactions. ∞ (Sec. 15.3) Thus, we can write the equilibrium expression for the autoionization of water as

$$K[H_2O] = K_w = [H^+][OH^-]$$

The product of two constants, K and $[H_2O]$, defines a new constant, K_w. This important equilibrium constant is called the **ion-product constant** for water. At 25°C, K_w has the value of 1.0×10^{-14}. This is an important equilibrium constant. You should memorize this expression:

$$K_w = [H^+][OH^-] = 1.0 \times 10^{-14} \qquad \text{[16.2]}$$

Equation 16.2 is valid for aqueous solutions as well as for pure water. A solution for which $[H^+] = [OH^-]$ is said to be *neutral*. In most solutions, H^+ and OH^- concentrations are not equal. As the concentration of one of these ions increases, the concentration of the other must decrease so that the ion product equals 1.0×10^{-14}. In acidic solutions, $[H^+]$ exceeds $[OH^-]$. In basic solutions, the reverse is true: $[OH^-]$ exceeds $[H^+]$.

SAMPLE EXERCISE 16.1

Calculate the values of $[H^+]$ and $[OH^-]$ in a neutral solution at 25°C.

SOLUTION By definition, in a neutral solution, $[H^+]$ equals $[OH^-]$. Let us call the concentration of each of these species in neutral solution x. Using Equation 16.2, we have

$$[H^+][OH^-] = (x)(x) = 1.0 \times 10^{-14}$$
$$x^2 = 1.0 \times 10^{-14}$$
$$x = 1.0 \times 10^{-7} = [H^+] = [OH^-]$$

In an acid solution, $[H^+]$ is greater than 1.0×10^{-7} M; in a basic solution $[H^+]$ is less than 1.0×10^{-7} M.

PRACTICE EXERCISE

Indicate whether each of the following solutions is neutral, acidic, or basic: **(a)** $[H^+] = 2 \times 10^{-5}$ M; **(b)** $[OH^-] = 3 \times 10^{-9}$ M; **(c)** $[OH^-] = 1 \times 10^{-7}$ M.
Answers: **(a)** acidic; **(b)** acidic; **(c)** neutral

SAMPLE EXERCISE 16.2

Calculate the concentration of $H^+(aq)$ in **(a)** a solution in which $[OH^-]$ is 0.010 M; **(b)** a solution in which $[OH^-]$ is 2.0×10^{-9} M.

SOLUTION In this problem and all that follow, we assume, unless stated otherwise, that the temperature is 25°C.
  (a) Using Equation 16.2, we have

$$[H^+][OH^-] = 1.0 \times 10^{-14}$$
$$[H^+] = \frac{1.0 \times 10^{-14}}{[OH^-]} = \frac{1.0 \times 10^{-14}}{0.010}$$
$$= 1.0 \times 10^{-12} \ M$$

This solution is basic because $[OH^-] > [H^+]$
  (b) In this instance

$$[H^+] = \frac{1.0 \times 10^{-14}}{[OH^-]} = \frac{1.0 \times 10^{-14}}{2.0 \times 10^{-9}} = 5.0 \times 10^{-6} \ M$$

This solution is acidic because $[H^+] > [OH^-]$.

The Proton in Water

Point of Emphasis: The terms hydrogen ion, proton, and H^+ are equivalent and are used interchangeably.

In Equation 16.1, water molecules form $H^+(aq)$. An H^+ ion is simply a proton with no surrounding valence electron. This small, positively charged particle interacts strongly with the lone pair electrons of water molecules to form hydrated hydrogen ions. For example, the interaction of a proton with one water molecule forms the **hydronium ion, $H_3O^+(aq)$**:

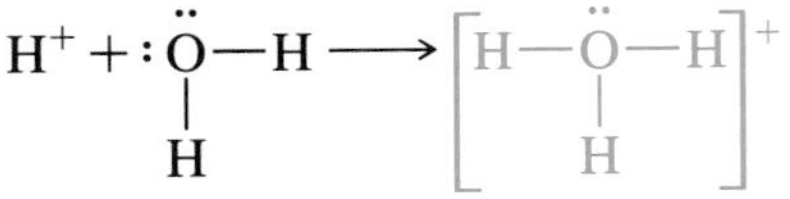

$$H^+ + :\overset{..}{O}{-}H \longrightarrow \left[H{-}\overset{..}{O}{-}H \right]^+ \qquad [16.3]$$

Teaching Note: The H^+ ion actually forms clusters with water, of which H_3O^+ is the simplest.

The formation of hydronium ions is one of the complex features of the interaction of the H^+ ion with the hydrogen-bond network of liquid water. In fact, the H_3O^+ ion can form hydrogen bonds to additional H_2O molecules to generate larger clusters of hydrated hydrogen ions, such as $H_5O_2^+$ and $H_9O_4^+$ (Figure 16.1).

Chemists use $H^+(aq)$ and $H_3O^+(aq)$ interchangeably to represent the hydrated proton. In terms of the hydronium ion, the autoionization of water is written as a reaction between two water molecules, with the proton being transferred from one to the other:

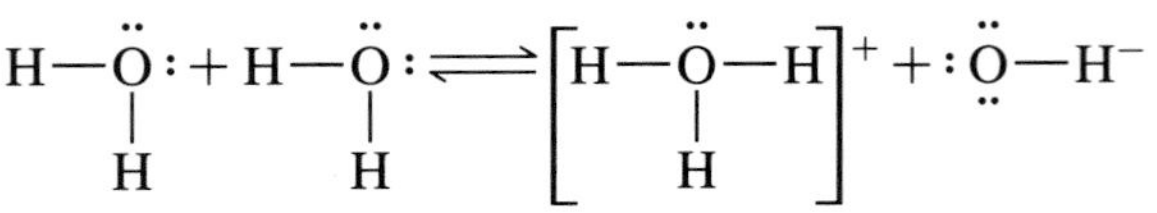

$$H{-}\overset{..}{O}: + H{-}\overset{..}{O}: \rightleftharpoons \left[H{-}\overset{..}{O}{-}H \right]^+ + :\overset{..}{O}{-}H^- \qquad [16.4]$$

Figure 16.1

FIGURE 16.1 Two possible structural forms for the proton in water, in addition to H_3O^+. There is good experimental evidence for the existence of both these species.

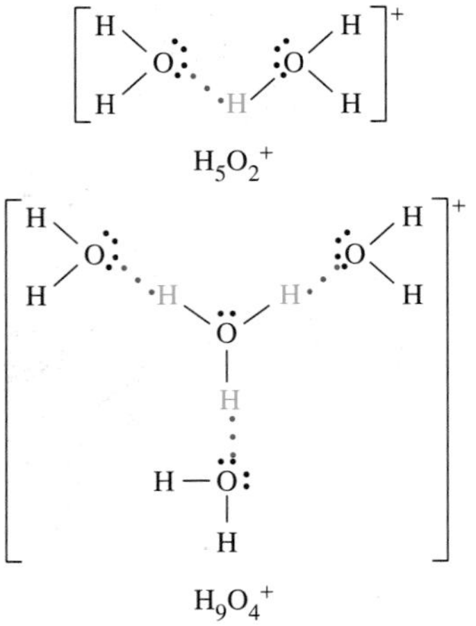

Because the concentration of $H_2O(l)$ does not enter into the expression for K_w, the value of K_w is the same regardless of whether H^+ or H_3O^+ is used:

$$K_w = [H^+][OH^-] = [H_3O^+][OH^-] = 1.0 \times 10^{-14} \qquad \text{(at } 25°\text{C)} \quad [16.5]$$

16.2 Brønsted-Lowry Acids and Bases

Now that we have some understanding of the relationship between $[H^+]$ and $[OH^-]$, let's examine again how we define acids and bases. From the earliest days of experimental chemistry, scientists recognized acids and bases by their characteristic properties. Acids have a sour taste (for example, citric acid in lemon juice) and cause certain dyes to change color (for example, litmus turns red on contact with acids). Bases have a bitter taste, feel slippery (soap is a good example), and neutralize acids.

Chemists sought to relate the properties of acid and base solutions to their composition and molecular structure. One of the first definitions of acids and bases was suggested by the Swedish chemist Svante Arrhenius (1859–1927) in the 1880s. According to the Arrhenius definition, *acids are substances that, when dissolved in water, increase the concentration of H^+ ions.* Likewise, *bases are substances that, when dissolved in water, increase the concentration of OH^-*

ions. As noted in the preceding section, increasing the concentration of one of these ions leads to a decrease in the concentration of the other.

Hydrogen chloride is an example of an Arrhenius acid. Hydrogen chloride gas is highly soluble in water because of its chemical reaction with water, which produces hydrated H^+ and Cl^- ions:

$$HCl(g) \xrightarrow{\text{H}_2\text{O}} H^+(aq) + Cl^-(aq) \qquad [16.6]$$

The aqueous solution of HCl is known as hydrochloric acid. Concentrated hydrochloric acid is 37 to 38 percent HCl by mass and is 12 M in HCl.

Proton-Transfer Reactions

We can also represent the formation of hydrochloric acid (Equation 16.6) as a reaction between an HCl molecule and a water molecule to form hydronium and chloride ions:

$$HCl(g) + H_2O(l) \longrightarrow H_3O^+(aq) + Cl^-(aq) \qquad [16.7]$$

In this reaction, the acid molecule, HCl, transfers a proton to the H_2O molecule (Figure 16.2).

The Danish chemist Johannes Brønsted (1879–1947) and the English chemist Thomas Lowry (1874–1936) recognized that the Arrhenius definition of acids and bases could be made more general. In 1923, Brønsted and Lowry independently proposed that acid-base behavior could be regarded as the ability of substances to transfer protons. According to their definition, *an acid is a substance capable of donating a proton, and a base is a substance capable of accepting a proton.* In these terms, when HCl dissolves in water (Equation 16.7), HCl acts as a **Brønsted-Lowry acid** (it donates a proton to H_2O), and H_2O acts as a **Brønsted-Lowry base** (it accepts a proton from HCl), as shown in Figure 16.2.

Because the emphasis in the Brønsted-Lowry concept is on proton transfer, the concept is also applicable to reactions that do not occur in aqueous solution. For example, in the reaction between HCl and NH_3, a proton is transferred from the acid HCl to the base NH_3:

$$\ddot{\underset{\cdot\cdot}{Cl}}{-}H + :\underset{|}{\overset{|}{N}}{-}H \longrightarrow :\ddot{\underset{\cdot\cdot}{Cl}}:^- + \left[H-\underset{\underset{H}{|}}{\overset{\overset{H}{|}}{N}}-H \right]^+ \qquad [16.8]$$

This reaction can occur in the gas phase. The hazy film that forms on the windows of general chemistry laboratories and on glassware in the lab is largely solid NH_4Cl formed by the gas-phase reaction of HCl and NH_3 (Figure 16.3).

As another example comparing the relationship between the Arrhenius definitions and the Brønsted-Lowry definitions of acids and bases, consider an aqueous solution of ammonia, in which the following equilibrium occurs:

$$NH_3(aq) + H_2O(l) \rightleftharpoons NH_4^+(aq) + OH^-(aq) \qquad [16.9]$$

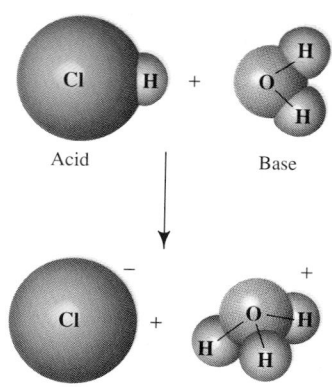

Acid   Base

FIGURE 16.2 When a proton is transferred from HCl to H_2O, HCl acts as the acid and H_2O acts as the base.

Figure 16.2

Learning Goal 2: List the general properties that characterize acidic and basic solutions, and identify the ions responsible for these properties.

Learning Goal 3: Define Brønsted-Lowry acid, Brønsted-Lowry base, and conjugate acid-base pair; identify the conjugate base associated with a given Brønsted-Lowry acid and the conjugate acid associated with a given Brønsted-Lowry base.

FIGURE 16.3 The HCl(*g*) escaping from concentrated hydrochloric acid and the NH_3(*g*) escaping from aqueous ammonia (here labeled ammonium hydroxide) combine to form a white fog of $NH_4Cl(s)$. (© Richard Megna/Fundamental Photographs)

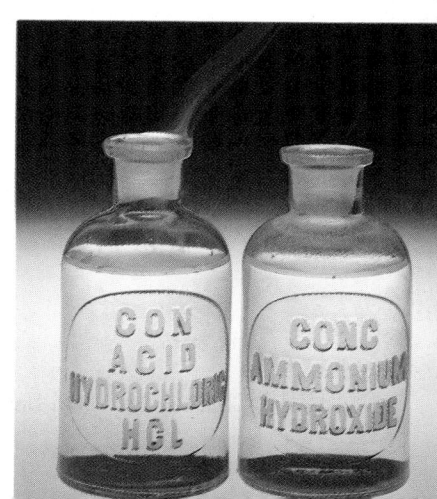

Ammonia is an Arrhenius base because the addition of ammonia to water leads to an increase in the concentration of $OH^-(aq)$. It is also a Brønsted-Lowry base because it accepts a proton from H_2O. The H_2O molecule in Equation 16.9 acts as a Brønsted-Lowry acid because it donates a proton to the NH_3 molecule.

Conjugate Acid-Base Pairs

In any acid-base equilibrium, both the forward reaction (to the right) and the reverse reaction (to the left) involve proton transfers. For example, consider the reaction of an acid, which we will denote HA, with water:

$$HA(aq) + H_2O(l) \rightleftharpoons A^-(aq) + H_3O^+(aq) \qquad [16.10]$$

In the forward reaction, HA donates a proton to H_2O. Therefore, HA is the Brønsted-Lowry acid, and H_2O is the Brønsted-Lowry base. In the reverse reaction, the H_3O^+ ion donates a proton to the A^- ion; H_3O^+ is the acid, and A^- is the base. Note that when the acid HA donates a proton, it leaves behind a substance, A^-, that acts as a base. Likewise, when H_2O acts as a base, it generates H_3O^+, which can act as an acid.

An acid and a base such as HA and A^- that differ only in the presence or absence of a proton are called a **conjugate acid-base pair.*** Every acid has a **conjugate base,** formed by the removal of a proton from the acid. For example, OH^- is the conjugate base of H_2O, and A^- is the conjugate base of HA. Every base has associated with it a **conjugate acid,** formed by the addition of a proton to the base. Thus, H_3O^+ is the conjugate acid of H_2O, and HA is the conjugate acid of A^-.

In any acid-base (proton-transfer) reaction, we can "tie together" the conjugate acid-base pairs. For example, consider the reaction between nitrous acid, HNO_2, and water:

$$HNO_2(aq) + H_2O(l) \rightleftharpoons NO_2^-(aq) + H_3O^+(aq) \qquad [16.11]$$

Acid — Base — Conjugate base — Conjugate acid (remove H^+ / add H^+)

Likewise, for the reaction between NH_3 and H_2O (Equation 16.9), we have

$$NH_3(aq) + H_2O(l) \rightleftharpoons NH_4^+(aq) + OH^-(aq) \qquad [16.12]$$

Base — Acid — Conjugate acid — Conjugate base (add H^+ / remove H^+)

Notice that an acid can be a charged species, such as NH_4^+, or a neutral species, such as HNO_2. Similarly, bases can be neutral or charged. Note also

* The word *conjugate* means "joined together as a pair."

that some substances can act as an acid in one reaction and as a base in another. For example, H_2O is a Brønsted-Lowry base in its reaction with HNO_2 (Equation 16.11) and a Brønsted-Lowry acid in its reaction with NH_3 (Equation 16.12). A substance that is capable of acting as either an acid or a base is called **amphoteric.**

Teaching Note: A substance that can act as an acid or as a base, depending on circumstance, is said to be *amphoteric*.

SAMPLE EXERCISE 16.3

(a) What is the conjugate base of each of the following: $HClO_4$; H_2S; PH_4^+; HCO_3^-?
(b) What is the conjugate acid of each of the following: CN^-; SO_4^{2-}; H_2O; HCO_3^-?

SOLUTION **(a)** To find the conjugate base of each substance, remove *one* proton (H^+) from the formula of the substance. Thus, the conjugate base of $HClO_4$ is ClO_4^-. The other conjugate bases are HS^-, PH_3, and CO_3^{2-}. **(b)** To find the conjugate acid of each substance, add *one* proton to the formula of the substance: HCN, HSO_4^-, H_3O^+, H_2CO_3.

Notice that the hydrogen carbonate ion, HCO_3^-, is amphoteric: It can act as either an acid or a base.

PRACTICE EXERCISE

Write the formula for the conjugate acid of each of the following: HSO_3^-; F^-; PO_4^{3-}; CO. *Answers:* H_2SO_3; HF; HPO_4^{2-}; HCO^+.

SAMPLE EXERCISE 16.4

The hydrogen sulfite ion, HSO_3^-, is amphoteric. **(a)** Write an equation for the reaction of HSO_3^- with water in which the ion acts as an acid. **(b)** Write an equation for the reaction of HSO_3^- with water in which the ion acts as a base. In both cases, identify the conjugate acid-base pairs.

SOLUTION **(a)** In order to behave as a Brønsted-Lowry acid, HSO_3^- must serve as a proton donor to water, which acts as a base:

$$HSO_3^-(aq) + H_2O(l) \rightleftharpoons SO_3^{2-}(aq) + H_3O^+(aq)$$

SO_3^{2-} is the conjugate base of HSO_3^-, and H_3O^+ is the conjugate acid of H_2O.

(b) For HSO_3^- to serve as a base, it must accept a proton from water, which acts as an acid in this case:

$$HSO_3^-(aq) + H_2O(l) \rightleftharpoons H_2SO_3(aq) + OH^-(aq)$$

Notice that the reverse of this reaction is the neutralization of sulfurous acid, H_2SO_3, by hydroxide ion, OH^-.

PRACTICE EXERCISE

When lithium oxide, Li_2O, is dissolved in water, the solution turns basic from the reaction of the oxide ion, O^{2-}, with water. Write the reaction that occurs and identify the conjugate acid-base pairs.
Answer: $O^{2-}(aq) + H_2O(l) \rightleftharpoons OH^-(aq) + OH^-(aq)$. OH^- is the conjugate acid of the base O^{2-}. OH^- is also the conjugate base of the acid H_2O.

Conjugate Acid-Base Strengths

If we arrange acids in order of their ability to donate a proton, we see an interesting and important fact: The more readily a substance gives up a proton, the less readily its conjugate base accepts a proton. Similarly, the more readily a base accepts a proton, the less readily its conjugate acid gives up a proton. In other words, *the stronger an acid, the weaker its conjugate base; the weaker an acid, the stronger its conjugate base.* Thus, if we know something about the strength of an acid (its ability to donate protons), we also know something about the strength of its conjugate base (its ability to accept protons). For example,

Point of Emphasis: The stronger an acid is, the weaker its conjugate base is.

HCl is a strong acid. ∞ (Sec. 4.3) Therefore, its conjugate base, Cl⁻, must be a very poor proton acceptor.

Figure 16.4 displays some common acids and their conjugate bases. $H^+(aq)$ is the strongest proton donor that can exist at equilibrium in aqueous solution. Thus acids listed above $H^+(aq)$ in Figure 16.4 completely transfer protons to water to form $H^+(aq)$. Likewise, $OH^-(aq)$ is the strongest base that can exist at equilibrium in aqueous solution. Any stronger proton acceptor will react completely with water, removing a proton to form OH^- ions.

Teaching Note: $H^+(aq)$ and $OH^-(aq)$ are, respectively, the strongest possible acid and base that can exist at equilibrium in aqueous solution. Stronger acids and bases simply react with the water to liberate $H^+(aq)$ and $OH^-(aq)$ ions. This effect is known as the *leveling effect*.

SAMPLE EXERCISE 16.5

Hydrocyanic acid, HCN, is ionized in water to a lesser extent than an HF solution of the same concentration. What is the conjugate base of HCN? Is it a stronger or weaker base than F⁻?

SOLUTION The conjugate base of HCN is CN⁻, the ion that remains after a proton has been lost to the solvent. HCN dissociates to a lesser extent than HF, which means that the tendency of the reverse reaction to occur is greater. In the reverse reaction the conjugate base, CN⁻, accepts a proton from the solvent. In other words, CN⁻ is a stronger base than F⁻.

PRACTICE EXERCISE

The dimethylammonium ion, $(CH_3)_2NH_2^+$, is a weak acid, ionized to a slight degree in water. **(a)** What is the conjugate base of the dimethylammonium ion? **(b)** How does the strength of this base compare with that of Cl⁻? *Answers:* **(a)** dimethylamine, $(CH_3)_2NH$; **(b)** dimethylamine is a stronger base than Cl⁻.

FIGURE 16.4 Relative strengths of some common conjugate acid-base pairs, which are listed opposite one another in the two columns.

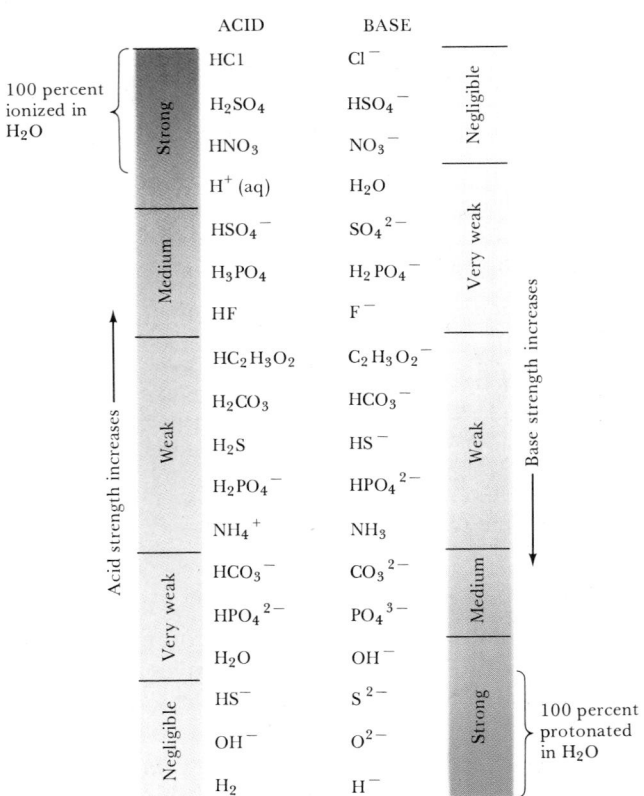

Figure 16.4

16.3 The pH Scale

The concentration of $H^+(aq)$ in an aqueous solution is usually quite small. For convenience, we therefore usually express $[H^+]$ in terms of **pH**, which is defined as the negative logarithm in base 10 of $[H^+]$:*

$$pH = -\log [H^+] \qquad [16.13]$$

If you need to review the use of logs, see Appendix A.

We can use Equation 16.13 to calculate the pH of a neutral solution at 25°C, that is, one in which $[H^+] = 1.0 \times 10^{-7}\ M$:

$$pH = -\log (1.0 \times 10^{-7}) = -(-7.00) = 7.00$$

The pH of a neutral solution is 7.00.

What happens to the pH of a solution as we make the solution acidic? An acidic solution is one in which $[H^+] > 1.0 \times 10^{-7}\ M$. Because of the negative sign in Equation 16.13, *the pH decreases as [H+] increases.* For example, consider an acidic solution in which $[H^+] = 1.0 \times 10^{-3}\ M$. The pH of this solution is

$$pH = -\log (1.0 \times 10^{-3}) = -(-3.00) = 3.00$$

At 25°C, the pH of an acidic solution is less than 7.

Similarly, let's consider a basic solution, one in which $[OH^-] > 1.0 \times 10^{-7}\ M$. Suppose $[OH^-] = 2.0 \times 10^{-3}$. We can use Equation 16.2 to calculate $[H^+]$ for this solution, and Equation 16.13 to calculate the pH:

$$[H^+] = \frac{K_w}{[OH^-]} = \frac{1.0 \times 10^{-14}}{2.0 \times 10^{-3}} = 5.0 \times 10^{-12}\ M$$

$$pH = -\log (5.0 \times 10^{-12}) = 11.30$$

We see that the pH of a basic solution is greater than 7. The relationships among $[H^+]$, $[OH^-]$, and pH are summarized in Table 16.1.

The pH values characteristic of several familiar solutions are shown in Figure 16.5. Notice that a change in $[H^+]$ by a factor of 10 causes the pH to

Learning Goal 4: Define *pH;* calculate pH from a knowledge of $[H^+]$ or $[OH^-]$, and perform the reverse operation.

Point of Emphasis: In chemistry, pH is one of the few logarithmic functions that is actually defined in terms of the common (base 10) logarithm.

Point of Emphasis: Lower values of pH correspond to higher concentrations of H^+.

TABLE 16.1 △ Relationships Among $[H^+]$, $[OH^-]$, and pH, at 25°C

Solution type	$[H^+]$ (M)	$[OH^-]$ (M)	pH Value
Acidic	$> 1.0 \times 10^{-7}$	$< 1.0 \times 10^{-7}$	< 7.00
Neutral	$= 1.0 \times 10^{-7}$	$= 1.0 \times 10^{-7}$	$= 7.00$
Basic	$< 1.0 \times 10^{-7}$	$> 1.0 \times 10^{-7}$	> 7.00

* As noted earlier, $[H^+]$ and $[H_3O^+]$ are used interchangeably. Thus, you might sometimes see pH defined as $-\log [H_3O^+]$.

FIGURE 16.5 Values of pH for some more common solutions. The pH scale in this figure is shown to extend from 0 to 14 because nearly all solutions commonly encountered have pH values in that range. In principle, however, the pH values for strongly acidic solutions can be less than 0, and for strongly basic solutions can be greater than 14.

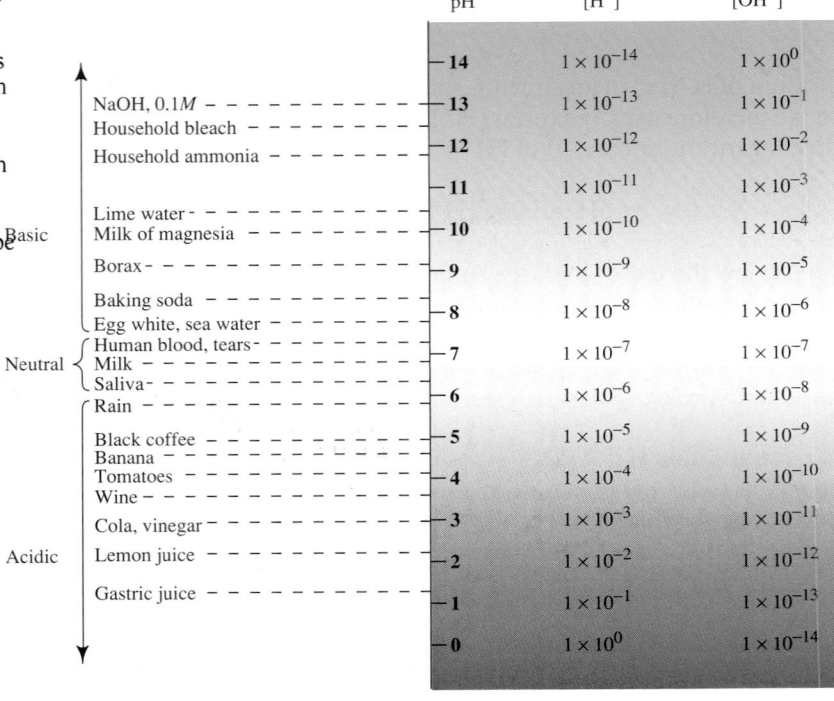

change by 1. For example, a solution of pH 6 has 10 times the concentration of $H^+(aq)$ that a solution of pH 7 has.

SAMPLE EXERCISE 16.6

Calculate the pH values for the two solutions described in Sample Exercise 16.2.

SOLUTION **(a)** In the first instance we found $[H^+]$ to be 1.0×10^{-12} M. Because $\log 10^x = x$, we can calculate the pH quite readily:

$$pH = -\log(1.0 \times 10^{-12}) = -(-12.00) = 12.00$$

The rule for using significant figures with logs is that *the number of decimal places in the log equals the number of significant figures in the original number* (see Appendix A). Because 1.0×10^{-12} has two significant figures, the pH has two decimal places, 12.**00**. **(b)** For the second solution, $[H^+] = 5.0 \times 10^{-6}$ M. Thus the pH equals $-\log(5.0 \times 10^{-6})$. Before performing the calculation, it is helpful to make an estimate of the pH. To do so, we bracket the concentration by its closest powers of 10: $10^{-6} < 5.0 \times 10^{-6} < 10^{-5}$. We therefore expect the pH of the solution to be between 5 (the pH for $[H^+] = 10^{-5}$ M) and 6 (the pH for $[H^+] = 10^{-6}$ M). You should use an estimation of pH to check whether your final answer is reasonable.

On most calculators, calculation of the pH can be performed with the following keystrokes:

$$\boxed{5}\;\boxed{.}\;\boxed{0}\;\boxed{EE}\;(\text{or}\;\boxed{EXP})\;\boxed{+/-}\;\boxed{6}\;\boxed{\log}\;\boxed{+/-}$$

We see that the pH $= -\log(5.0 \times 10^{-6}) = -(-5.30) = 5.30$.

PRACTICE EXERCISE

(a) In a sample of lemon juice, $[H^+]$ is 3.8×10^{-4} M. What is the pH? **(b)** A commonly available window-cleaning solution has a $[H^+]$ of 5.3×10^{-9} M. What is the pH? *Answers:* **(a)** 3.42; **(b)** 8.28

SAMPLE EXERCISE 16.7

A sample of freshly pressed apple juice has a pH of 3.76. Calculate $[H^+]$.

SOLUTION Because the pH is between 3 and 4, we know immediately that $[H^+]$ will be between 10^{-3} and 10^{-4} M. From the equation defining pH, we have

$$pH = -\log[H^+] = 3.76$$

Thus
$$\log[H^+] = -3.76$$

To find $[H^+]$ we need to determine the *antilog* of -3.76. Many calculators have an antilog function (sometimes labeled INV log), which allows us to perform the calculation with the following key sequence:

$$\boxed{3}\ \boxed{.}\ \boxed{7}\ \boxed{6}\ \boxed{+/-}\ \boxed{\text{INV}}\ \boxed{\log}$$

The result, expressed in standard exponential notation, is 1.7×10^{-4} M. Some calculators rely on 10^x or y^x functions to find antilogs: antilog $(-3.76) = 10^{-3.76} = 1.7 \times 10^{-4}$. Consult the user's manual for your calculator to find out how to perform the antilog operation. Notice that the number of significant figures in $[H^+]$ equals the number of decimal places in the pH (2).

PRACTICE EXERCISE

A solution formed by dissolving an antacid tablet has a pH of 9.18. Calculate $[H^+]$.   ***Answer:*** $[H^+] = 6.6 \times 10^{-10}$ M

The negative log is also a convenient way of expressing the magnitudes of other small quantities. We use the convention that the negative log of a quantity is labeled p(quantity). For example, one can express the concentration of OH^- as pOH:

$$pOH = -\log[OH^-] \qquad [16.14]$$

By taking the log of both sides of Equation 16.2 and multiplying through by -1, we can obtain

$$pH + pOH = -\log K_w = 14.00 \qquad [16.15]$$

This expression is often convenient to use. We will see later (Section 16.7) that the pX notation is also useful in dealing with equilibrium constants.

Teaching Note: Acid and base equilibrium constants are also commonly expressed as the pX functions pK_a and pK_b. See Section 16.7.

Measuring pH

The pH of a solution can be measured quickly and accurately with a *pH meter* (Figure 16.6). A complete understanding of how these important devices work requires a knowledge of electrochemistry, a subject we take up in Chapter 20. In brief, a pH meter consists of a pair of electrodes connected to a meter capable of measuring small voltages, on the order of millivolts. A voltage, which varies with the pH, is generated when the electrodes are placed in a solution. This voltage is read by the meter, which is calibrated to give pH.

The electrodes used with pH meters come in many shapes and sizes, depending on their intended use. Electrodes have even been developed that are so small that they can be inserted into single living cells in order to monitor the pH of the cell medium. Pocket-sized pH meters are also available for use in environmental studies, in monitoring industrial effluents, and in agricultural work.

FIGURE 16.6 A digital pH meter. (© Richard Megna/ Fundamental Photographs)

Teaching Note: Early indicators were made from plant extracts. Today, many indicators are still derived from plants.

Bassam Z. Shakhashiri, "Acid-Base Indicators Extracted from Plants," *Chemical Demonstrations: A Handbook for Teachers of Chemistry, Volume 3* (Madison: The University of Wisconsin Press, 1989), pp. 50–57.

Teaching Note: The color of an acid-base indicator in its transition pH range is determined by the proportion of indicator molecules that exist in each of the two possible forms.

Learning Goal 5: Identify the common strong acids and bases, and calculate the pH of their aqueous solutions given their concentrations.

Although less precise, *acid-base indicators* are often used to measure pH. An acid-base indicator is a colored substance that can exist in either an acid or a base form. The two forms are different colors. If you know the pH at which the indicator turns from one form to the other, you can determine whether a solution has a higher or lower pH than this value. For example, litmus, one of the most common indicators, changes color in the vicinity of pH 7. However, the color change is not very sharp. Red litmus indicates a pH of about 5 or lower, and blue litmus indicates a pH of about 8 or higher.

Some of the more common indicators are listed in Figure 16.7. We see from this figure that methyl orange, for example, changes color over the pH interval from 3.1 to 4.4. Below pH 3.1 it is in the acid form, which is red. In the interval between 3.1 and 4.4 it is gradually converted to its basic form, which has a yellow color. By pH 4.4 the conversion is complete, and the solution is yellow. Paper tape that is impregnated with various indicators and comes complete with a comparator color scale is widely used for approximate determinations of pH.

16.4 Strong Acids and Bases

The chemistry of an aqueous solution often depends critically on the pH of the solution. It is therefore important that we examine how to determine the pH for solutions of acids or bases. The simplest cases are those involving strong acids and strong bases. Recall that strong acids and bases are *strong electrolytes:* They exist in aqueous solution entirely as ions, leaving no undissociated molecules in solution. ∞ (Sec. 4.3) There are relatively few common strong acids and bases, and we listed these substances in Table 4.1.

Strong Acids

The six most common strong acids are HCl, HBr, HI, HNO_3, $HClO_4$, and H_2SO_4. Thus, an aqueous solution of nitric acid, HNO_3, consists entirely of

FIGURE 16.7 The pH ranges for the color changes of some common acid-base indicators. Most indicators have a useful range of about 2 pH units.

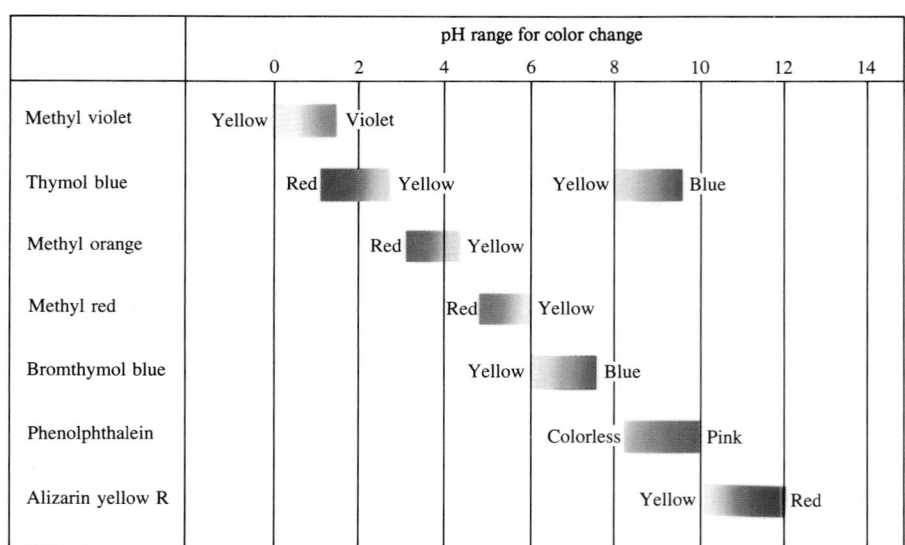

$H^+(aq)$ and $NO_3^-(aq)$:

$$HNO_3(aq) \longrightarrow H^+(aq) + NO_3^-(aq) \qquad \text{(complete ionization)} \quad [16.16]$$

Notice that we have not used an equilibrium arrow for Equation 16.16 because the reaction lies entirely to the right side, namely, as ions. ∞ (Sec. 4.2)

In an aqueous solution of a strong acid, the acid is normally the only significant source of H^+ ions.* As a result, calculation of the pH of a solution of a strong acid is quite simple because $[H^+]$ equals the original concentration of the acid. For example, in a 0.20 M solution of $HNO_3(aq)$, $[H^+] = [NO_3^-] = 0.20$ M; the concentration of undissociated HNO_3 molecules is virtually zero (Equation 16.16).

SAMPLE EXERCISE 16.8

What is the pH of a 0.040 M solution of $HClO_4$?

SOLUTION   We recognize that $HClO_4$ is a strong acid. Because it is a strong acid, it is completely ionized, giving $[H^+] = [ClO_4^-] = 0.040$ M. The pH of the solution is given by pH $= -\log (0.040) = 1.40$.

PRACTICE EXERCISE

An aqueous solution of HNO_3 has a pH of 2.66. What is the concentration of the acid?   *Answer:* 0.0022 M

Strong Bases

There are also relatively few common strong bases. The most common soluble strong bases are the ionic hydroxides of the alkali metals (group 1A) and the heavier alkaline earth metals (group 2A), such as NaOH, KOH, and $Ca(OH)_2$. These compounds completely dissociate into ions in aqueous solution. Thus, a solution labeled 0.30 M NaOH consists of 0.30 M $Na^+(aq)$ and 0.30 M $OH^-(aq)$; there are no undissociated NaOH molecules.

Because strong bases dissociate entirely into ions in aqueous solution, calculating the pH of a solution of a strong base is also straightforward, as shown in Sample Exercise 16.9.

SAMPLE EXERCISE 16.9

What is the pH of a 0.011 M solution of $Ca(OH)_2$?

SOLUTION $Ca(OH)_2$ is a strong base that dissociates in water to give two OH^- ions per formula unit. Thus, the concentration of $OH^-(aq)$ in the solution is 2 × (0.011 M) = 0.022 M. We can calculate the pH of the solution in two equivalent ways. First, we could use Equation 16.2 to calculate $[H^+]$ and then use Equation 16.13 to calculate the pH:

$$[H^+] = \frac{1.0 \times 10^{-14}}{0.022} = 4.6 \times 10^{-13} \ M \qquad pH = -\log (4.6 \times 10^{-13}) = 12.34$$

Alternatively, we could use $[OH^-]$ directly to calculate pOH and then use Equation 16.14 to calculate the pH:

$$pOH = -\log (0.022) = 1.66 \qquad pH = 14.00 - pOH = 12.34$$

---

* If the concentration of the acid is 10^{-6} M or less, we also need to consider H^+ ions that result from the autoionization of H_2O. Normally, the concentration of H^+ from H_2O is so small that it can be ignored.

PRACTICE EXERCISE

What is the concentration of a solution of KOH for which the pH is 11.89?
Answer: 7.8×10^{-3} *M*

Although all the hydroxides of the alkali metals (group 1A) are strong electrolytes, LiOH, RbOH, and CsOH are not encountered commonly in the laboratory. The hydroxides of all of the alkaline earths (group 2A) except Be are also strong electrolytes. However, they have limited solubilities and consequently are used only when high solubility is not critical. The compound $Mg(OH)_2$ has an especially low solubility (9×10^{-3} g/L of water at 25°C). The least expensive and most common of the alkaline earth hydroxides is $Ca(OH)_2$, with a solubility of 0.97 g/L at 25°C.

Basic solutions are also created when substances react with water to form $OH^-(aq)$. The most common of these is the oxide ion. Ionic metal oxides, especially Na_2O and CaO, are often used in industry when a strong base is needed. Each mole of O^{2-} reacts with water to form 2 mol of OH^-, leaving virtually no O^{2-} remaining in the solution:

$$O^{2-}(aq) + H_2O(l) \longrightarrow 2OH^-(aq) \qquad [16.17]$$

Thus, a solution formed by dissolving 0.010 mol of $Na_2O(s)$ in a liter of water will have $[OH^-] = 0.020$ *M* and hence a pH of 12.30.

Ionic hydrides and nitrides also react with H_2O to form OH^-:

$$H^-(aq) + H_2O(l) \longrightarrow H_2(g) + OH^-(aq) \qquad [16.18]$$
$$N^{3-}(aq) + 3H_2O(l) \longrightarrow NH_3(aq) + 3OH^-(aq) \qquad [16.19]$$

Because the anions (O^{2-}, H^-, and N^{3-}) are stronger bases than OH^- (the conjugate base of H_2O), they are able to remove a proton from H_2O.

Point of Emphasis: Oxide (O^{2-}) is too strong a base to exist in water. It rapidly reacts with water, as shown in Equation 16.17. Hydride (H^-) and nitride (N^{3-}) similarly react with water.

16.5 Weak Acids

Most acidic substances are weak acids that only partially ionize in solution. We can express the extent to which a weak acid ionizes by using the equilibrium constant for the ionization reaction. We can represent a general acid by the formula HA, where A^- is the conjugate base of the acid. The ionization equilibrium for HA is given by

$$HA(aq) \rightleftharpoons H^+(aq) + A^-(aq) \qquad [16.20]$$

The corresponding equilibrium expression is

$$K_a = \frac{[H^+][A^-]}{[HA]} \qquad [16.21]$$

The subscript *a* on K_a denotes that it is an equilibrium constant for an acid, and K_a is called the **acid-dissociation constant.**

Table 16.2 shows the names, structures, and K_a values for several weak acids. A more complete listing is given in Appendix D. Many weak acids are

Point of Emphasis: Warn students not to confuse a *weak acid* (small K_a) with a *dilute acid* (low concentration).

Bassam Z. Shakhashiri, "Differences Between Acid Strength and Concentration," *Chemical Demonstrations: A Handbook for Teachers of Chemistry, Volume 3* (Madison: The University of Wisconsin Press, 1989), pp. 136–39.

TABLE 16.2 △ Some Weak Acids in Water at 25°C[a]

Acid	Molecular formula	Structural formula[a]	Conjugate base	K_a
Hydrofluoric	HF	H—F	F⁻	6.8×10^{-4}
Nitrous	HNO_2	H—O—N=O	NO_2^-	4.5×10^{-4}
Benzoic	$HC_7H_5O_2$	$H-O-\overset{\displaystyle O}{\overset{\|}{C}}-C_6H_5$	$C_7H_5O_2^-$	6.5×10^{-5}
Acetic	$HC_2H_3O_2$	$H-O-\overset{\displaystyle O}{\overset{\|}{C}}-\overset{\displaystyle H}{\underset{\displaystyle H}{\overset{\|}{\underset{\|}{C}}}}-H$	$C_2H_3O_2^-$	1.8×10^{-5}
Hypochlorous	HClO	H—O—Cl	ClO⁻	3.0×10^{-8}
Hydrocyanic	HCN	H—C≡N	CN⁻	4.9×10^{-10}
Phenol	HOC_6H_5	H—O—C_6H_5	$C_6H_5O^-$	1.3×10^{-10}

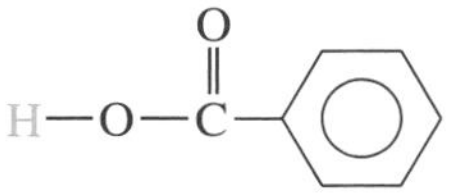

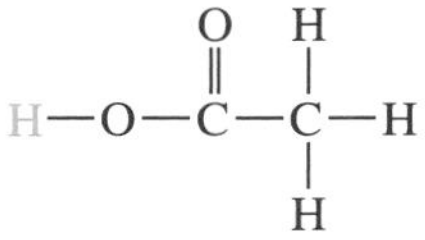

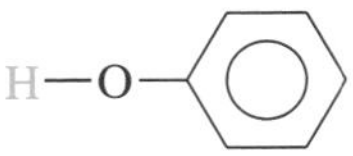

[a] The proton that ionizes is shown in blue.

organic compounds composed entirely of carbon, hydrogen, and oxygen. These compounds usually contain some hydrogen atoms bonded to carbon atoms and some bonded to oxygen atoms. In almost all cases, the hydrogen atoms bonded to carbon do not ionize in water; the acidic behavior of these compounds is due to the hydrogen atoms attached to oxygen atoms.

The magnitude of K_a indicates the tendency of the hydrogen atom to ionize: *The larger the value of K_a, the stronger the acid.* For example, hydrofluoric acid, HF, is the strongest acid listed in Table 16.2, and phenol, HOC_6H_5, is the weakest. Notice that K_a is typically less than 10^{-3}.

In order to calculate the pH of solutions of weak acids, we will use many of the skills for solving equilibrium problems that we developed in Section 15.5. In many cases, the small magnitude of K_a allows us to use approximations to simplify the problem.

SAMPLE EXERCISE 16.10

A student prepared a 0.10 M solution of formic acid, $HCHO_2$, and measured its pH using a pH meter of the type illustrated in Figure 16.6. The pH at 25°C was found to be 2.38. **(a)** Calculate K_a for formic acid at this temperature. **(b)** What percentage of the acid is ionized in this 0.10 M solution?

SOLUTION **(a)** The first step in solving any equilibrium problem is to write the equation for the equilibrium reaction. The ionization equilibrium for formic acid can be written as follows:

$$HCHO_2(aq) \rightleftharpoons H^+(aq) + CHO_2^-(aq)$$

The equilibrium expression is

$$K_a = \frac{[H^+][CHO_2^-]}{[HCHO_2]}$$

From the measured pH we can calculate $[H^+]$:

$$pH = -\log [H^+] = 2.38$$
$$\log [H^+] = -2.38$$
$$[H^+] = 4.2 \times 10^{-3}\ M$$

We can do a little accounting to determine the concentrations of the species involved in the equilibrium. We first imagine that the solution consists of $0.10\ M$ of $HCHO_2$ molecules. We then consider the ionization of the acid into H^+ and CHO_2^-. For each H^+ ion produced in solution, one CHO_2^- anion also forms, and there is a loss of one $HCHO_2$ molecule:

	$HCHO_2(aq)$	$\rightleftharpoons$ $H^+(aq)$	$+$ $CHO_2^-(aq)$
Initial	$0.10\ M$	0	0
Change	$-4.2 \times 10^{-3}\ M$	$+4.2 \times 10^{-3}\ M$	$+4.2 \times 10^{-3}\ M$
Equilibrium	$(0.10 - 4.2 \times 10^{-3})\ M$	$4.2 \times 10^{-3}\ M$	$4.2 \times 10^{-3}\ M$

Notice that the amount of $HCHO_2$ that ionizes is very small in comparison with the initial concentration of the acid. To the number of significant figures we are using, the subtraction yields just $0.10\ M$:

$$(0.10 - 4.2 \times 10^{-3})\ M \approx 0.10\ M$$

We can now insert the equilibrium concentrations into the expression for K_a:

$$K_a = \frac{(4.2 \times 10^{-3})(4.2 \times 10^{-3})}{0.10} = 1.8 \times 10^{-4}$$

(b) The percentage of acid that ionizes is given by the concentration of H^+ or CHO_2^- at equilibrium, divided by the initial acid concentration, times 100:

$$\text{Percent ionization} = \frac{[H^+] \times 100}{[HCHO_2]} = \frac{(4.2 \times 10^{-3}) \times 100}{0.10} = 4.2\ \text{percent}$$

PRACTICE EXERCISE

Niacin, one of the B vitamins, has the following molecular structure:

A $0.020\ M$ solution of niacin has a pH of 3.26. What is the acid-dissociation constant, K_a, for the ionizable proton? **Answer:** 1.5×10^{-5}

Calculating pH for Solutions of Weak Acids

Using the value for K_a we can calculate the concentration of $H^+(aq)$ in a solution of a weak acid. For example, consider acetic acid, $HC_2H_3O_2$, the substance responsible for the characteristic odor and acidity of vinegar. Let's calculate the pH of a $0.30\ M$ solution of acetic acid at $25\,°C$.

Our *first* step is to write the ionization equilibrium for acetic acid:

$$HC_2H_3O_2(aq) \rightleftharpoons H^+(aq) + C_2H_3O_2^-(aq) \qquad [16.22]$$

Note from the Lewis structure for acetic acid, shown in Table 16.2, that the hydrogen that ionizes is the one attached to an oxygen atom. We write this hydrogen separate from the others in the formula to emphasize that only this one hydrogen is readily ionized.

The *second* step is to write the equilibrium expression and the value for the equilibrium constant. From Table 16.2 we have $K_a = 1.8 \times 10^{-5}$. Thus, we can write the following:

$$K_a = \frac{[H^+][C_2H_3O_2^-]}{[HC_2H_3O_2]} = 1.8 \times 10^{-5} \qquad [16.23]$$

As the *third* step, we need to express the concentrations that make up the equilibrium expression. This can be done with a little accounting, as described in Sample Exercise 16.10. Because we want to find the equilibrium value for $[H^+]$, let us call this quantity x. The concentration of acetic acid before any of it ionizes is 0.30 M. The equation for the equilibrium tells us that for each molecule of $HC_2H_3O_2$ that ionizes, one $H^+(aq)$ and one $C_2H_3O_2^-(aq)$ are formed. Consequently, if x moles per liter of $H^+(aq)$ form at equilibrium, x moles per liter of $C_2H_3O_2^-(aq)$ must also form, and x moles per liter of $HC_2H_3O_2$ must be ionized. This gives rise to the following equilibrium concentrations:

$$HC_2H_3O_2(aq) \rightleftharpoons H^+(aq) + C_2H_3O_2^-(aq)$$

Initial	0.30 M	0	0
Change	$-x\ M$	$+x\ M$	$+x\ M$
Equilibrium	$(0.30 - x)\ M$	$x\ M$	$x\ M$

As the *fourth* step of the problem, we need to substitute the equilibrium concentrations into the equilibrium expression. The substitutions give the following equation:

$$K_a = \frac{[H^+][C_2H_3O_2^-]}{[HC_2H_3O_2]} = \frac{(x)(x)}{0.30 - x} = 1.8 \times 10^{-5} \qquad [16.24]$$

This expression leads to a quadratic equation in x, which we could solve by using the quadratic formula. However, we can simplify the problem by noting that the value of K_a is quite small. As a result, we anticipate that the equilibrium will lie far to the left, and x will probably be very small compared to the initial concentration of acetic acid. Thus, we will *assume* that x is negligible compared to 0.30, so that $0.30 - x$ is essentially equal to 0.30:

Point of Emphasis: The criteria for making this approximation are discussed below.

$$0.30 - x \approx 0.30$$

As we shall see, we can (and should!) check the validity of this assumption when we finish the problem.

By using this assumption, Equation 16.24 now becomes

$$K_a = \frac{x^2}{0.30} = 1.8 \times 10^{-5}$$

Solving for x, we have

$$x^2 = (0.30)(1.8 \times 10^{-5}) = 5.4 \times 10^{-6}$$

$$x = \sqrt{5.4 \times 10^{-6}} = 2.3 \times 10^{-3}$$

$$[H^+] = x = 2.3 \times 10^{-3} \ M$$

$$pH = -\log(2.3 \times 10^{-3}) = 2.64$$

Point of Emphasis: When in doubt, work the problem assuming $([HA]_0 - x) \approx [HA]_0$. After solving for x, compare x to $[HA]_0$. If $x \geq 5$ percent of $[HA]_0$, rework the problem using the quadratic formula.

We should now go back and check the validity of our simplifying assumption that $0.30 - x \approx 0.30$. Indeed, the value of x that we determined is so small that, for this number of significant figures, the assumption is entirely valid. We are thus satisfied that the assumption was a reasonable one to make. Because x represents the moles per liter of acetic acid that ionize, we see that, in this particular case, less than 1 percent of the acetic acid molecules ionize:

Learning Goal 7: Calculate the percent ionization for a weak acid, knowing its concentration in solution and the value of K_a.

$$\text{Percent ionization of } HC_2H_3O_2 = \frac{0.0023 \ M}{0.30 \ M} \times 100 = 0.77 \text{ percent}$$

As a general rule, if the quantity x is more than about 5 percent of the initial value, it is better to use the quadratic formula. You should always make certain to check the validity of any simplifying assumptions after you have finished solving a problem.

Point of Emphasis: The validity of any assumptions made during the solution of a problem should be verified after the fact.

Finally, we can compare the pH value of this weak acid to a solution of a strong acid of the same concentration. The pH of the 0.30 M solution of acetic acid is 2.64. By comparison, the pH of a 0.30 M solution of a strong acid such as HCl is $-\log(0.30) = 0.52$. As expected, the pH of a solution of a weak acid is higher (less acidic) than that of a solution of a strong acid of the same molarity.

SAMPLE EXERCISE 16.11

Calculate the pH of a 0.20 M solution of HCN. (Refer to Table 16.2 or Appendix D for the value of K_a.)

SOLUTION Proceeding as in the example worked out above, we write both the chemical equation for the ionization reaction that forms $H^+(aq)$ and the equilibrium (K_a) expression for the reaction:

$$HCN(aq) \rightleftharpoons H^+(aq) + CN^-(aq)$$

$$K_a = \frac{[H^+][CN^-]}{[HCN]} = 4.9 \times 10^{-10}$$

Next we tabulate the concentrations of the species involved in the equilibrium reaction, letting $x = [H^+]$:

	$HCN(aq)$ $\rightleftharpoons$	$H^+(aq)$ +	$CN^-(aq)$
Initial	0.20 M	0	0
Change	$-x \ M$	$+x \ M$	$+x \ M$
Equilibrium	$(0.20 - x) \ M$	$x \ M$	$x \ M$

Substituting the equilibrium concentrations from the table into the equilibrium expression yields

$$K_a = \frac{(x)(x)}{0.20 - x} = 4.9 \times 10^{-10}$$

We next make the simplifying approximation that x, the amount of acid that dissociates, is small in comparison with the initial concentration of acid; that is, $0.20 - x \simeq 0.20$. Thus,

$$\frac{x^2}{0.20} = 4.9 \times 10^{-10}$$

Solving for x, we have

$$x^2 = (0.20)(4.9 \times 10^{-10}) = 0.98 \times 10^{-10}$$
$$x = \sqrt{0.98 \times 10^{-10}} = 9.9 \times 10^{-6} \, M = [H^+]$$

Notice that 9.9×10^{-6} is much smaller than 5 percent of 0.20, the initial HCN concentration. Our simplifying approximation is therefore appropriate. We now calculate the pH of the solution:

$$pH = -\log[H^+] = -\log(9.9 \times 10^{-6}) = 5.00$$

PRACTICE EXERCISE

The K_a for niacin (Practice Exercise 16.10) is 1.5×10^{-5}. What is the pH of a 0.010 M solution of niacin?   *Answer:* 3.41

The result obtained in Sample Exercise 16.11 is typical of the behavior of weak acids; the concentration of $H^+(aq)$ is only a small fraction of the concentration of the acid in solution. Of course, those properties of the acid solution that relate directly to the concentration of $H^+(aq)$, such as electrical conductivity and rate of reaction with an active metal, are much less in evidence for a solution of a weak acid than for a solution of a strong acid. Figure 16.8 illustrates an experiment often carried out in the chemistry laboratory to demonstrate the difference in concentration of $H^+(aq)$ in weak and strong acid solutions of the same concentration. The rate of reaction with the metal is much faster for the solution of a strong acid. Reactions in which the rate depends on $[H^+]$ are common and are especially important in biological systems.

Figure 16.9 compares how the electrical conductivities of HCl and HF solutions vary with concentration. The conductivity of the strong acid increases approximately in proportion to its concentration. In contrast, the conductivity of the weak acid is much less than that of the strong acid and does not vary linearly with the acid concentration. The nonlinearity of the graph arises from the fact that the percentage of acid ionized varies with the acid concentration.

(a)   (b)

FIGURE 16.8 Demonstration of the relative rates of reaction of two acid solutions of the same concentration with an active metal. (*a*) The flask on the left contains 1 M $HC_2H_3O_2$; the one on the right contains 1 M HCl. Each balloon contains the same amount of magnesium metal. (*b*) When the Mg metal is dropped into the acid, H_2 is formed. The rate of H_2 formation is clearly higher for the 1 M HCl solution on the right. (Donald Clegg and Roxy Wilson)

FIGURE 16.9 Electrical conductivity versus concentration for solutions of HCl, a strong acid, and HF, a weak acid.

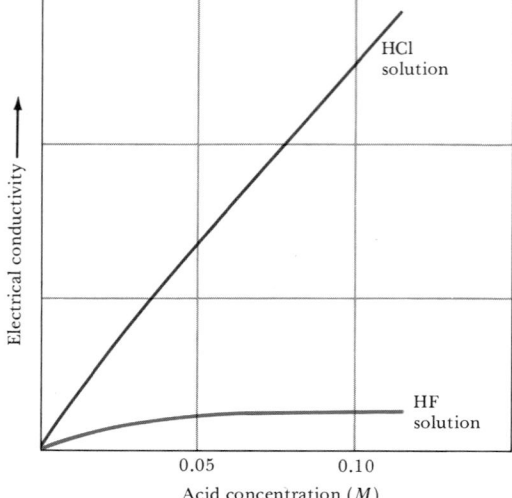

 Figure 16.9

Point of Emphasis: The percentage ionization of a weak acid varies with the acid's concentration.

The degree of ionization increases as the concentration of the acid decreases, as illustrated in Sample Exercise 16.12.

SAMPLE EXERCISE 16.12

Calculate the percentage of HF molecules ionized in **(a)** a 0.10 M HF solution; **(b)** a 0.010 M HF solution.

SOLUTION **(a)** The equilibrium reaction and equilibrium concentrations are as follows:

	$HF(aq)$ $\rightleftharpoons$	$H^+(aq)$ +	$F^-(aq)$
Initial	0.10 M	0	0
Change	$-x$ M	$+x$ M	$+x$ M
Equilibrium	$(0.10 - x)$ M	x M	x M

The equilibrium expression is

$$K_a = \frac{[H^+][F^-]}{[HF]} = \frac{(x)(x)}{0.10 - x} = 6.8 \times 10^{-4}$$

When we try solving this equation using the approximation $0.10 - x = 0.10$ (that is, by neglecting the concentration of acid that ionizes in comparison with the initial concentration), we obtain $x = 8.2 \times 10^{-3}$ M. Because this value is greater than 5 percent of 0.10 M, we should work the problem without the approximation, using the quadratic formula. Rearranging our equation and writing it in standard quadratic form, we have

$$x^2 = (0.10 - x)(6.8 \times 10^{-4})$$
$$= 6.8 \times 10^{-5} - (6.8 \times 10^{-4})x$$
$$x^2 + (6.8 \times 10^{-4})x - 6.8 \times 10^{-5} = 0$$

Solution of this equation by use of the standard quadratic formula,

$$x = \frac{-b \pm \sqrt{b^2 - 4ac}}{2a}$$

586   Chapter 16   Acid-Base Equilibria

gives

$$x = \frac{-6.8 \times 10^{-4} \pm \sqrt{(6.8 \times 10^{-4})^2 + 4(6.8 \times 10^{-5})}}{2}$$

$$= \frac{-6.8 \times 10^{-4} \pm 1.65 \times 10^{-2}}{2}$$

Of the two solutions, only the one that gives a positive value for x is physically reasonable. Thus,

$$x = [H^+] = [F^-] = 7.9 \times 10^{-3} \, M$$

From our result we can calculate the percent of molecules ionized:

$$\text{Percent ionization of HF} = \frac{\text{concentration ionized}}{\text{original concentration}} \times 100$$

$$= \frac{7.9 \times 10^{-3} \, M}{0.10 \, M} \times 100 = 7.9\%$$

(b) Proceeding similarly for the 0.010 M solution, we have

$$\frac{x^2}{0.010 - x} = 6.8 \times 10^{-4}$$

Solving the resultant quadratic expression, we obtain

$$x = [H^+] = [F^-] = 2.3 \times 10^{-3} \, M$$

The percentage of molecules ionized is

$$\frac{0.0023}{0.010} \times 100 = 23\%$$

Notice that in diluting the solution by a factor of 10, the percentage of molecules ionized increases by a factor of 3. This conclusion is what we would expect from Le Châtelier's principle. ∞ (Sec. 15.6) There are more "particles" or reaction components on the right side of the equation than on the left. Dilution causes the reaction to shift in the direction of the larger number of particles because this counters the effect of the decreasing concentration of particles.

PRACTICE EXERCISE

Calculate the percentage of niacin molecules ionized in **(a)** the solution in Practice Exercise 16.11; **(b)** a $1.0 \times 10^{-3} \, M$ solution of niacin.   *Answers:* **(a)** 3.9%; **(b)** 11.5%

Polyprotic Acids

Many acids have more than one proton that can ionize. These acids are known as **polyprotic acids.** For example, each of the protons in sulfurous acid, H_2SO_3, can ionize in successive steps:

$$H_2SO_3(aq) \rightleftharpoons H^+(aq) + HSO_3^-(aq) \qquad K_{a1} = 1.7 \times 10^{-2} \quad [16.25]$$

$$HSO_3^-(aq) \rightleftharpoons H^+(aq) + SO_3^{2-}(aq) \qquad K_{a2} = 6.4 \times 10^{-8} \quad [16.26]$$

The acid-dissociation constants for the above equilibria are labeled K_{a1} and K_{a2}. The numbers on the constants refer to the particular proton of the acid that is ionizing. Thus, K_{a2} always refers to the equilibrium involving removal of the second proton of a polyprotic acid.

In the above example, K_{a2} is much smaller than K_{a1}. This trend is intuitively reasonable; on the basis of electrostatic attractions, we would expect a

Point of Emphasis: The term *polyprotic* means "many protons." The term is used to describe acids with more than one ionizable proton.

TABLE 16.3 △ Acid-Dissociation Constants of Some Common Polyprotic Acids

Name	Formula	K_{a1}	K_{a2}	K_{a3}
Ascorbic	$H_2C_6H_6O_6$	8.0×10^{-5}	1.6×10^{-12}	
Carbonic	H_2CO_3	4.3×10^{-7}	5.6×10^{-11}	
Citric	$H_3C_6H_5O_7$	3.5×10^{-4}	1.7×10^{-5}	4.0×10^{-7}
Oxalic	$H_2C_2O_4$	5.9×10^{-2}	6.4×10^{-5}	
Phosphoric	H_3PO_4	7.5×10^{-3}	6.2×10^{-8}	4.2×10^{-13}
Sulfurous	H_2SO_3	1.7×10^{-2}	6.4×10^{-8}	
Sulfuric	H_2SO_4	Large	1.2×10^{-2}	
Tartaric	$H_2C_4H_4O_6$	1.0×10^{-3}	4.6×10^{-5}	

Ascorbic acid
(vitamin C)

Citric acid

Point of Emphasis: The K_a values for successive losses of protons from polyprotic acids generally decrease at least by a factor of 10^3.

Teaching Note: The K_a value for strong acids is often simply described as "large."

positively charged proton to be lost more readily from the neutral H_2SO_3 molecule than from the negatively charged HSO_3^- ion. This observation is general: *It is always easier to remove the first proton from a polyprotic acid than the second.* Similarly, for an acid with three ionizable protons, it is easier to remove the second proton than the third. Thus, the K_a values become successively smaller as successive protons are ionized.

The acid-dissociation constants for a few common polyprotic acids are given in Table 16.3. A more complete list is given in Appendix D. The structures for ascorbic and citric acids are shown in the margin. Notice that the K_a values for successive losses of protons from these acids usually differ by a factor of at least 10^3. Notice also that the value of K_{a1} for sulfuric acid is listed simply as "large." Sulfuric acid is a strong acid with respect to the ionization of the first proton. Thus, the reaction for the ionization of the first proton lies completely to the right:

$$H_2SO_4(aq) \longrightarrow H^+(aq) + HSO_4^-(aq) \qquad \text{(complete ionization)}$$

As seen in Table 16.3, HSO_4^- is a weak acid for which $K_{a2} = 1.2 \times 10^{-2}$.

Because K_{a1} is so much larger than subsequent dissociation constants for these polyprotic acids, almost all the $H^+(aq)$ in the solution comes from the first ionization reaction. As long as successive K_a values differ by a factor of 10^3 or more, it is possible to obtain a satisfactory estimate of the pH of polyprotic acid solutions by considering only K_{a1}.

SAMPLE EXERCISE 16.13

The solubility of CO_2 in pure water at 25°C and 0.1 atm pressure is 0.0037 M. The common practice is to assume that all of the dissolved CO_2 is in the form of carbonic acid, H_2CO_3, which is produced by reaction between the CO_2 and H_2O:

$$CO_2(aq) + H_2O(l) \rightleftharpoons H_2CO_3(aq)$$

What is the pH of a 0.0037 M solution of H_2CO_3?

SOLUTION H_2CO_3 is a polyprotic acid; the two acid dissociation constants, K_{a1} and K_{a2} (Table 16.3), differ by more than a factor of 10^3. Consequently, the pH can be determined by considering only K_{a1}, thereby treating the acid as if it were a monoprotic acid. Proceeding as in Sample Exercises 16.11 and 16.12, we can write the equilibrium reaction and equilibrium concentrations as follows:

$$H_2CO_3(aq) \rightleftharpoons H^+(aq) + HCO_3^-(aq)$$

Initial	0.0037 M	0	0
Change	$-x\ M$	$+x\ M$	$+x\ M$
Equilibrium	$(0.0037 - x)\ M$	$x\ M$	$x\ M$

The equilibrium expression is as follows:

$$K_{a1} = \frac{[H^+][HCO_3^-]}{[H_2CO_3]} = \frac{(x)(x)}{0.0037 - x} = 4.3 \times 10^{-7}$$

Because K_{a1} is small, we make the simplifying approximation that x is small so that $0.0037 - x \simeq 0.0037$. Thus,

$$\frac{(x)(x)}{0.0037} = 4.3 \times 10^{-7}$$

Solving for x, we have

$$x^2 = (0.0037)(4.3 \times 10^{-7}) = 1.6 \times 10^{-9}$$
$$x = [H^+] = [HCO_3^-] = \sqrt{1.6 \times 10^{-9}} = 4.0 \times 10^{-5}\ M$$

The small value of x indicates that our simplifying assumption was justified. The pH is therefore

$$pH = -\log [H^+] = -\log (4.0 \times 10^{-5}) = 4.40$$

If we are asked to solve for $[CO_3^{2-}]$, we will need to use K_{a2}. Let's illustrate that calculation. Using the values of $[HCO_3^-]$ and $[H^+]$ calculated above, and setting $[CO_3^{2-}] = y$, we have the following initial and equilibrium concentration values:

	$HCO_3^-(aq)$ $\rightleftharpoons$	$H^+(aq)$	$+\ CO_3^{2-}(aq)$
Initial	$4.0 \times 10^{-5}\ M$	$4.0 \times 10^{-5}\ M$	0
Change	$-y\ M$	$+y\ M$	$+y\ M$
Equilibrium	$(4.0 \times 10^{-5} - y)\ M$	$(4.0 \times 10^{-5} + y)\ M$	$y\ M$

Assuming that y is small compared to 4.0×10^{-5}, we have

$$K_{a2} = \frac{[H^+][CO_3^{2-}]}{[HCO_3^-]} = \frac{(4.0 \times 10^{-5})(y)}{4.0 \times 10^{-5}} = 5.6 \times 10^{-11}$$
$$y = 5.6 \times 10^{-11}\ M = [CO_3^{2-}]$$

The value calculated for y is indeed very small in comparison to 4.0×10^{-5}, showing that our assumption was justified. It also shows that the ionization of HCO_3^- is negligible in comparison to that of H_2CO_3 as far as production of H^+ is concerned. However, it is the *only* source of CO_3^{2-}, which has a very low concentration in the solution.

Our calculations thus tell us that in a solution of carbon dioxide in water most of the CO_2 is in the form of CO_2 or H_2CO_3, a small fraction ionizes to form H^+ and HCO_3^-, and an even smaller fraction ionizes to give CO_3^{2-}.

PRACTICE EXERCISE

Calculate the pH and concentration of oxalate ion, $[C_2O_4^{2-}]$, in a 0.020 M solution of oxalic acid, $H_2C_2O_4$ (see Table 16.3).   *Answers:* pH = 1.80; $[C_2O_4^{2-}] = 6.4 \times 10^{-5}\ M$

16.6 Weak Bases

Many substances behave as weak bases in water. Such substances react with water, removing protons from H_2O, thereby forming the conjugate acid of the base and OH^- ions:

$$\text{Weak base} + H_2O \rightleftharpoons \text{conjugate acid} + OH^- \qquad [16.27]$$

The most commonly encountered weak base is ammonia:

$$NH_3(aq) + H_2O(l) \rightleftharpoons NH_4^+(aq) + OH^-(aq) \qquad [16.28]$$

The equilibrium expression for this reaction can be written as

$$K = \frac{[NH_4^+][OH^-]}{[NH_3][H_2O]} \qquad [16.29]$$

Because the concentration of water is essentially constant, the $[H_2O]$ term is incorporated into the equilibrium constant, giving

$$K[H_2O] = K_b = \frac{[NH_4^+][OH^-]}{[NH_3]} \qquad [16.30]$$

The constant K_b is called the **base-dissociation constant,** by analogy with the acid-dissociation constant, K_a, for weak acids. *The constant K_b always refers to the equilibrium in which a base reacts with H_2O to form the conjugate acid and OH^-.* Table 16.4 lists the names, formulas, Lewis structures, equilibrium reactions, and values of K_b for several weak bases in water. Appendix D includes a more extensive list. Notice that these bases contain one or more lone pairs of electrons. A lone pair is necessary to form the bond with H^+. Notice also that in the neutral molecules the lone pairs are on nitrogen atoms and that the other bases are anions of weak acids.

Learning Goal 8: Calculate the pH for a weak base solution in water, given the base concentration and K_b; calculate K_b given the base concentration and pH.

SAMPLE EXERCISE 16.14

Calculate the concentration of OH^- in a 0.15 M solution of NH_3.

SOLUTION We use essentially the same procedure here as used in solving problems involving the ionization of acids. The first step is to write the ionization reaction and the corresponding equilibrium (K_b) expression:

$$NH_3(aq) + H_2O(l) \rightleftharpoons NH_4^+(aq) + OH^-(aq)$$

$$K_b = \frac{[NH_4^+][OH^-]}{[NH_3]} = 1.8 \times 10^{-5}$$

We then tabulate the equilibrium concentrations involved in the equilibrium:

	$NH_3(aq)$	+	$H_2O(l) \rightleftharpoons$	$NH_4^+(aq)$	+	$OH^-(aq)$
Initial	0.15 M		—	0		0
Change	$-x\,M$		—	$+x\,M$		$+x\,M$
Equilibrium	$(0.15 - x)\,M$		—	$x\,M$		$x\,M$

(Notice that we ignore the concentration of H_2O, because it is not involved in the equilibrium expression.) Inserting these quantities into the equilibrium expression gives the following:

$$K_b = \frac{[NH_4^+][OH^-]}{[NH_3]} = \frac{(x)(x)}{0.15 - x} = 1.8 \times 10^{-5}$$

Because K_b is small, we can neglect the small amount of NH_3 that reacts with water, as compared to the total NH_3 concentration; that is, we can neglect x in comparison to 0.15 *M*. Then we have

$$\frac{x^2}{0.15} = 1.8 \times 10^{-5}$$

$$x^2 = (0.15)(1.8 \times 10^{-5}) = 0.27 \times 10^{-5}$$

$$x = [NH_4^+] = [OH^-] = \sqrt{2.7 \times 10^{-6}} = 1.6 \times 10^{-3}\ M$$

Notice that the value obtained for x is only about 1 percent of the NH_3 concentration, 0.15 *M*. Therefore, our neglect of x in comparison with 0.15 is justified.

PRACTICE EXERCISE

Which of the following compounds should produce the highest pH as a 0.05 *M* solution: pyridine, methylamine, or nitrous acid? ***Answer:*** methylamine

TABLE 16.4 △ Weak Bases and Their Aqueous Solution Equilibria

Base	Lewis structure	Conjugate acid	Equilibrium reaction	K_b
Ammonia (NH_3)	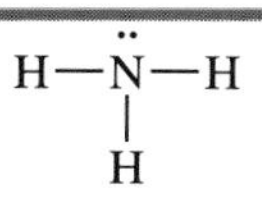	NH_4^+	$NH_3 + H_2O \rightleftharpoons NH_4^+ + OH^-$	1.8×10^{-5}
Pyridine (C_5H_5N)		$C_5H_5NH^+$	$C_5H_5N + H_2O \rightleftharpoons C_5H_5NH^+ + OH^-$	1.7×10^{-9}
Hydroxylamine (H_2NOH)	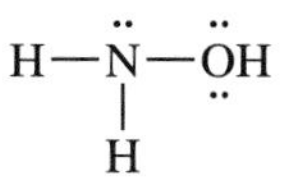	H_3NOH^+	$H_2NOH + H_2O \rightleftharpoons H_3NOH^+ + OH^-$	1.1×10^{-8}
Methylamine (NH_2CH_3)	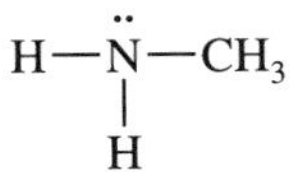	$NH_3CH_3^+$	$NH_2CH_3 + H_2O \rightleftharpoons NH_3CH_3^+ + OH^-$	4.4×10^{-4}
Hydrosulfide ion (HS^-)	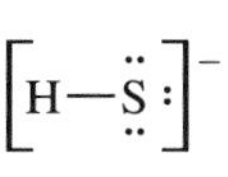	H_2S	$HS^- + H_2O \rightleftharpoons H_2S + OH^-$	1.8×10^{-7}
Carbonate ion (CO_3^{2-})	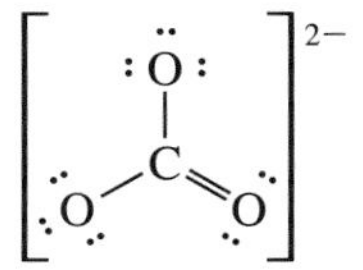	HCO_3^-	$CO_3^{2-} + H_2O \rightleftharpoons HCO_3^- + OH^-$	1.8×10^{-4}
Hypochlorite ion (ClO^-)	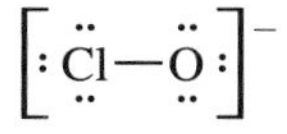	HClO	$ClO^- + H_2O \rightleftharpoons HClO + OH^-$	3.3×10^{-7}

CHEMISTRY AT WORK

Amines and Amine Hydrochlorides

Many amines with low molecular weights have unpleasant "fishy" odors. Amines and NH_3 are produced by the anaerobic (absence of O_2) decomposition of dead animal or plant matter. Two such amines with very disagreeable odors are $H_2N(CH_2)_4NH_2$, known as *putrescine*, and $H_2N(CH_2)_5NH_2$, known as *cadaverine*.

Many drugs, including quinine, codeine, caffeine, and amphetamine (Benzedrine), are amines. Like other amines, these substances are weak bases; the amine nitrogen is readily protonated by treatment with an acid. The resulting products are called *acid salts*. If we use A as the abbreviation for an amine, the acid salt formed by reaction with hydrochloric acid can be written as AH^+Cl^-. (It is sometimes written as $A \cdot HCl$ and referred to as a hydrochloride.) For example, amphetamine hydrochloride is the acid salt formed by treating amphetamine with HCl:

$$\langle\bigcirc\rangle-CH_2-\underset{\underset{CH_3}{|}}{CH}-\overset{..}{N}H_2(aq) + HCl(aq) \longrightarrow$$

Amphetamine

$$\langle\bigcirc\rangle-CH_2-\underset{\underset{CH_3}{|}}{CH}-NH_3^+Cl^-(aq)$$

Amphetamine hydrochloride

Such acid salts are less volatile, more stable, and generally more water-soluble than the corresponding neutral amines. Many drugs that are amines are sold and administered as acid salts. Some examples of over-the-counter medications that contain amine hydrochlorides as active ingredients are shown in Figure 16.10.

FIGURE 16.10 Over-the-counter medications in which an amine hydrochloride is a major active ingredient. (Donald Clegg and Roxy Wilson)

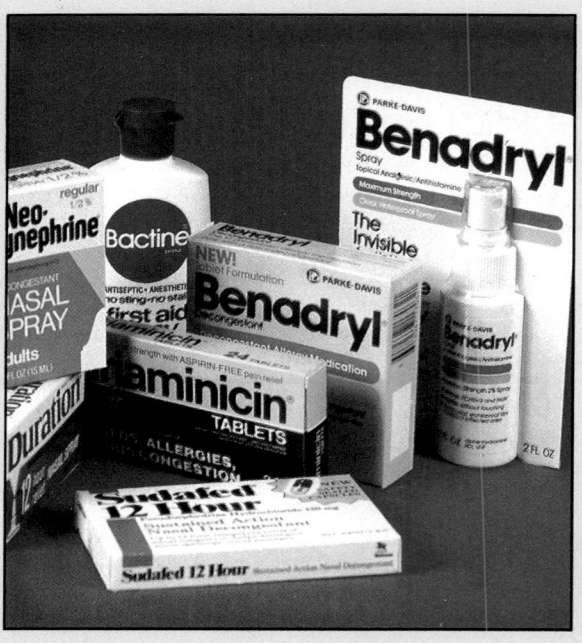

Types of Weak Bases

We know that weak acids are substances that contain partially ionizable protons. What chemical properties cause a substance to behave as a weak base? Weak bases fall into two general categories. The first are neutral substances that contain an atom with a lone pair of electrons that can serve as a proton acceptor. The largest group of such bases, including all of the neutral bases listed in Table 16.4, contain a nitrogen atom. These substances include ammonia and other compounds of nitrogen and hydrogen, such as hydrazine, N_2H_4. Closely related to ammonia is the class of compounds called **amines**. In amines, one or more of the N—H bonds in NH_3 is replaced with a bond between N and C. Thus, the replacement of one N—H bond in NH_3 with a N—CH_3 bond leads to methylamine, NH_2CH_3. Like ammonia, amines can extract a proton from a

Point of Emphasis: *Amines are covalent compounds that contain a nitrogen bonded to three other atoms by single bonds.*

water molecule by forming an additional N—H bond, as shown below for methylamine.

$$H-\underset{\underset{H}{|}}{\overset{..}{N}}-CH_3(aq) + H_2O(l) \rightleftharpoons \left[H-\underset{\underset{H}{|}}{\overset{\overset{H}{|}}{N}}-CH_3 \right]^+ (aq) + OH^-(aq) \quad [16.31]$$

The second general class of weak bases is composed of the anions of weak acids. Consider, for example, an aqueous solution of sodium hypochlorite, NaClO. This salt dissolves in water to give Na^+ and ClO^- ions. The Na^+ ion is always a spectator ion in acid-base reactions. ∞ (Sec. 4.4) However, the ClO^- ion is the conjugate base of a weak acid, hypochlorous acid. Consequently, the ClO^- ion acts as a weak base in water:

$$ClO^-(aq) + H_2O(l) \rightleftharpoons HClO(aq) + OH^-(aq) \quad K_b = 3.3 \times 10^{-7} \quad [16.32]$$

SAMPLE EXERCISE 16.15

A solution is made by adding solid sodium hypochlorite, NaClO, to enough water to make 2.00 L of solution. If the solution has a pH of 10.50, how many moles of NaClO were added to the water?

SOLUTION NaClO is an ionic compound consisting of Na^+ and ClO^- ions. As such, it is a strong electrolyte that completely dissociates in solution into Na^+, which is a spectator ion, and ClO^- ion, which is a weak base with $K_b = 3.3 \times 10^{-7}$ (Equation 16.32). We wish to determine the concentration of ClO^- in solution that would generate enough OH^- ion to raise the pH to 10.50.

We first calculate the concentration of $OH^-(aq)$ at equilibrium. We can calculate $[OH^-]$ by using either Equation 16.2 or Equation 16.15; we shall use the latter method here:

$$pOH = 14.00 - pH = 14.00 - 10.50 = 3.50$$
$$[OH^-] = 10^{-3.50} = 3.2 \times 10^{-4} \, M$$

This concentration is high enough that we can assume that Equation 16.32 is the only source of OH^-; that is, we can neglect any OH^- produced by the autoionization of H_2O. We now assume a value x for the initial concentration of ClO^- and solve the equilibrium problem in the usual way:

	$ClO^-(aq)$ +	$H_2O(l)$ ⇌	$HClO(aq)$ +	$OH^-(aq)$
Initial	$x \, M$	—	0	0
Change	$-3.2 \times 10^{-4} \, M$	—	$+3.2 \times 10^{-4}$	$+3.2 \times 10^{-4}$
Final	$(x - 3.2 \times 10^{-4}) \, M$	—	$+3.2 \times 10^{-4}$	$+3.2 \times 10^{-4}$

We now use the expression for the base-dissociation constant to solve for x:

$$K_b = \frac{[HClO][OH^-]}{[ClO^-]} = \frac{(3.2 \times 10^{-4})^2}{x - 3.2 \times 10^{-4}} = 3.3 \times 10^{-7}$$

Thus,

$$x = \frac{(3.2 \times 10^{-4})^2}{3.3 \times 10^{-7}} + (3.2 \times 10^{-4}) = 0.31 \, M$$

We say that the solution is 0.31 M in NaClO, even though some of the ClO⁻ ions have reacted with water. Because the solution is 0.31 M in NaClO and the total volume of solution is 2.00 L, 0.62 mol of NaClO is the amount of the salt that was added to the water.

PRACTICE EXERCISE

A solution of NH_3 in water has a pH of 10.50. What is the molarity of the solution?   *Answer:* 0.0060 M

16.7 Relation Between K_a and K_b

Learning Goal 9: Determine the relationship between the strength of an acid and that of its conjugate base; calculate K_b from a knowledge of K_a and vice-versa.

We've seen in a qualitative way that the stronger acids have the weaker conjugate bases. The fact that this qualitative relationship exists suggests that we might be able to find a quantitative relationship. Let's explore this matter by considering the NH_4^+ and NH_3 conjugate acid-base pair. Each of these species reacts with water:

$$NH_4^+(aq) \rightleftharpoons NH_3(aq) + H^+(aq) \qquad [16.33]$$

$$NH_3(aq) + H_2O(l) \rightleftharpoons NH_4^+(aq) + OH^-(aq) \qquad [16.34]$$

Each of these equilibria is expressed by a characteristic dissociation constant:

$$K_a = \frac{[NH_3][H^+]}{[NH_4^+]} \qquad K_b = \frac{[NH_4^+][OH^-]}{[NH_3]}$$

Now notice something very interesting and important. When Equations 16.33 and 16.34 are added together, the NH_4^+ and NH_3 species cancel, and we are left with just the autoionization of water:

$$NH_4^+(aq) \rightleftharpoons NH_3(aq) + H^+(aq)$$
$$\underline{NH_3(aq) + H_2O(l) \rightleftharpoons NH_4^+(aq) + OH^-(aq)}$$
$$H_2O(l) \rightleftharpoons H^+(aq) + OH^-(aq)$$

Point of Emphasis: When the addition of two equilibria yields a third, the product of the equilibrium constants for the equilibria being added is equal to the equilibrium constant for the third.

To determine what we should do about the equilibrium constants for the added reactions, we make use of a rule that can be derived from the general principles governing chemical equilibria: *When two reactions are added to give a third reaction, the equilibrium constant for the third reaction is given by the product of the equilibrium constants for the two added reactions.* In general, if

$$\text{Reaction 1} + \text{reaction 2} = \text{reaction 3}$$

then

$$K_1 \times K_2 = K_3$$

Applying this to our present example, if we multiply K_a and K_b, we obtain the following result:

$$K_a \times K_b = \left(\frac{[NH_3][H^+]}{[NH_4^+]}\right)\left(\frac{[NH_4^+][OH^-]}{[NH_3]}\right)$$
$$= [H^+][OH^-] = K_w$$

Thus the result of multiplying K_a times K_b is just the ion-product constant, K_w (Equation 16.2). This is, of course, just what we would expect because addition of Equations 16.33 and 16.34 gave us just the autoionization equilibrium for water, for which the equilibrium constant is K_w.

This relationship is so important that it should receive special attention: *The product of the acid-dissociation constant for an acid and the base-dissociation constant for its conjugate base is the ion-product constant for water:*

$$K_a \times K_b = K_w \qquad [16.35]$$

Point of Emphasis: For a conjugate acid-base pair, $K_a \times K_b = K_w$

As the strength of an acid increases (larger K_a), the strength of its conjugate base must decrease (smaller K_b), so that the product $K_a \times K_b$ remains equal to 1.0×10^{-14}. This product is illustrated by the data shown in Table 16.5.

Using Equation 16.35 we can calculate K_b for any weak base if we know K_a for its conjugate acid. Similarly, we can calculate K_a for a weak acid if we know K_b for its conjugate base. As a practical consequence, ionization constants are often listed for only one member of a conjugate acid-base pair. For example, Appendix D does not contain K_b values for the anions of weak acids because these can be readily calculated from the tabulated K_a values for their conjugate acids.

If you have the occasion to look up the values for acid- or base-dissociation constants in a chemistry handbook, you may find them expressed as pK_a or pK_b, that is, as $-\log K_a$ or $-\log K_b$. ∞ (Sec. 16.3) Equation 16.35 can be put in terms of pK_a and pK_b by taking the negative log of both sides:

Point of Emphasis: Chemists define pK_a and pK_b as they do pH; that is, $pK_a = -\log(K_a)$ and $pK_b = -\log(K_b)$.

$$pK_a + pK_b = pK_w = 14.00 \qquad [16.36]$$

Point of Emphasis: For a conjugate acid-base pair, $pK_a + pK_b = 14$

This form is particularly useful when the tabulated pK value is that for the conjugate acid or base of the substance of interest. Often the dissociation constants for bases are tabulated as pK_a values for the corresponding conjugate acids. An example, morphine, a nitrogen-containing base, is listed as the protonated cation, with $pK_a = 7.87$. This means that for the reaction

$$C_{17}H_{19}O_3NH^+(aq) \rightleftharpoons C_{17}H_{19}O_3N(aq) + H^+(aq)$$

Morphine

the equilibrium constant, K_a, has the value $K_a = 10^{-7.87} = 1.3 \times 10^{-8}$. The reaction

$$C_{17}H_{19}O_3N(aq) + H_2O(l) \rightleftharpoons C_{17}H_{19}O_3NH^+(aq) + OH^-(aq)$$

TABLE 16.5 △ Some Conjugate Acid-Base Pairs

Acid	K_a	Base	K_b
HNO_3	(Strong acid)	NO_3^-	(Negligible basicity)
HF	6.8×10^{-4}	F^-	1.5×10^{-11}
$HC_2H_3O_2$	1.8×10^{-5}	$C_2H_3O_2^-$	5.6×10^{-10}
H_2CO_3	4.3×10^{-7}	HCO_3^-	2.3×10^{-8}
NH_4^+	5.6×10^{-10}	NH_3	1.8×10^{-5}
HCO_3^-	5.6×10^{-11}	CO_3^{2-}	1.8×10^{-4}
OH^-	(Negligible acidity)	O^{2-}	(Strong base)

is described by equilibrium constant K_b. Using Equation 16.36 and $pK_a = 7.87$, we have

$$pK_b = 14.00 - pK_a = 14.00 - 7.87 = 6.13$$

Thus, $K_b = 10^{-6.13} = 7.4 \times 10^{-7}$.

SAMPLE EXERCISE 16.16

Calculate **(a)** the base-dissociation constant, K_b, for the fluoride ion, F^-; **(b)** the acid-dissociation constant, K_a, for the ammonium ion, NH_4^+.

SOLUTION   **(a)** K_b for F^- is not included in Table 16.4 or in Appendix D. However, K_a for its conjugate acid, HF, is given in Table 16.2 and Appendix D as $K_a = 6.8 \times 10^{-4}$. We can therefore use Equation 16.35 to calculate K_b:

$$K_b = \frac{K_w}{K_a} = \frac{1.0 \times 10^{-14}}{6.8 \times 10^{-4}} = 1.5 \times 10^{-11}$$

(b) K_b for NH_3 is listed in Table 16.4 and in Appendix D as $K_b = 1.8 \times 10^{-5}$. Using Equation 16.35, we can calculate K_a for the conjugate acid, NH_4^+:

$$K_a = \frac{K_w}{K_b} = \frac{1.0 \times 10^{-14}}{1.8 \times 10^{-5}} = 5.6 \times 10^{-10}$$

PRACTICE EXERCISE

(a) Which of the following anions has the largest base-dissociation constant: NO_2^-, PO_4^{3-}; N_3^-? **(b)** The base quinoline has the structure

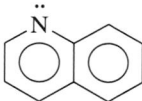

Its conjugate acid is listed in handbooks as having a pK_a of 4.90. What is the base-dissociation constant for quinoline?   *Answers:* **(a)** PO_4^{3-}; **(b)** 7.9×10^{-10}

16.8 Acid-Base Properties of Salt Solutions

Even before you began this chapter, you were undoubtedly aware of many substances that are acidic, such as HNO_3, HCl, and H_2SO_4, and others that are basic, such as NaOH and NH_3. However, our recent discussions have indicated that ions can also exhibit acidic or basic properties. For example, we calculated K_a for NH_4^+ and K_b for F^- in Sample Exercise 16.16. Such behavior implies that salt solutions can be acidic or basic. Before proceeding with further discussions of acids and bases, let's summarize some features of salts that should bring their acid and base properties into sharper focus.

We can assume that when salts dissolve in water they are completely ionized; nearly all salts are strong electrolytes. Consequently, the acid-base properties of salt solutions are due to the behavior of their cations and anions. Many ions are able to react with water to generate $H^+(aq)$ or $OH^-(aq)$. This type of reaction is often called **hydrolysis.**

The anions, A^-, derived from weak acids, HA, react with water to produce OH^- ions and are thus basic:

$$A^-(aq) + H_2O(l) \rightleftharpoons HA(aq) + OH^-(aq) \qquad [16.37]$$

In contrast, the anions of strong acids, such as the NO_3^- ion, are not basic and consequently do not influence pH.

Anions that still have ionizable protons, such as HSO_3^-, are amphoteric: They are capable of acting as either acids or bases (Sample Exercise 16.4). Their behavior toward water will be determined by the relative magnitudes of K_a and K_b for the ion, as shown in Sample Exercise 16.17.

SAMPLE EXERCISE 16.17

Predict whether the salt Na_2HPO_4 will form an acidic or basic solution on dissolving in water.

SOLUTION   The two possible reactions that HPO_4^{2-} may undergo on addition to water are

$$HPO_4^{2-}(aq) \rightleftharpoons H^+(aq) + PO_4^{3-}(aq) \qquad [16.38]$$

$$HPO_4^{2-}(aq) + H_2O \rightleftharpoons H_2PO_4^-(aq) + OH^-(aq) \qquad [16.39]$$

Depending on which of these has the larger equilibrium constant, the ion will cause the solution to be acidic or basic. The value of K_a for Equation 16.38, as shown in Table 16.3, is 4.2×10^{-13}. We must calculate the value of K_b for Equation 16.39 from the value of K_a for its conjugate acid, $H_2PO_4^-$. We make use of the relationship shown in Equation 16.35.

$$K_a \times K_b = K_w$$

We want to know K_b for the base HPO_4^{2-}, knowing the value of K_a for the conjugate acid $H_2PO_4^-$:

$$K_b(HPO_4^{2-}) \times K_a(H_2PO_4^-) = K_w = 1.0 \times 10^{-14}$$

Because K_a for $H_2PO_4^-$ is 6.2×10^{-8} (Table 16.3), we calculate K_b for HPO_4^{2-} to be 1.6×10^{-7}. This is more than 10^5 times larger than K_a for HPO_4^{2-}; thus the reaction shown in Equation 16.39 predominates over that in Equation 16.38, and the solution is basic.

PRACTICE EXERCISE

Predict whether the dipotassium salt of citric acid, $K_2HC_6H_5O_7$, will form an acidic or basic solution in water (see Table 16.3 for data).   *Answer:* acidic

All cations except those of the alkali metals and the heavier alkaline earths (Ca^{2+}, Sr^{2+}, and Ba^{2+}) act as weak acids in water solution. Because the alkali metal and alkaline earth cations do not hydrolyze in water, the presence of any of these ions in solution does not influence pH. It may surprise you that metal ions, such as Al^{3+}, and the transition metal ions form weakly acidic solutions. We can take this observation for now as a point of fact. The reasons for this behavior are discussed in Section 16.10.

Among the cations that produce an acidic solution is, of course, NH_4^+, which is the conjugate acid of the base NH_3. The NH_4^+ ion dissociates in water as follows:

$$NH_4^+(aq) \rightleftharpoons H^+(aq) + NH_3(aq) \qquad [16.40]$$

The pH of a solution of a salt can be qualitatively predicted by considering the cation and anion of which the salt is composed. A convenient way to do this is to consider the relative strengths of the acids and bases from which the salt is derived.*

Learning Goal 10:   Predict whether a particular salt solution will be acidic, basic, or neutral.

---

* These rules apply to what can be called *normal salts.* These salts are ones that contain no ionizable protons on the anion. The pH of an acid salt (such as $NaHCO_3$ or NaH_2PO_4) is affected not only by the hydrolysis of the anion but also by its acid dissociation, as shown in Sample Exercise 16.17.

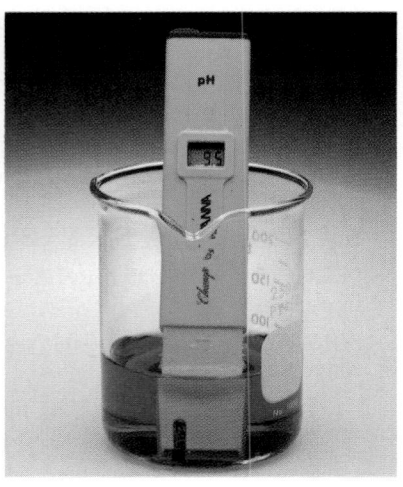

(a)   (b)   (c)

FIGURE 16.11   Depending on the ions involved, salt solutions can be neutral, acidic, or basic. These three solutions contain the acid-base indicator bromthymol blue. (a) A NaCl solution is neutral; (b) a NH_4Cl solution is acidic; (c) a NaClO solution is basic. (© Richard Megna/Fundamental Photographs)

1. *Salt derived from a strong base and a strong acid:* Examples are NaCl and $Ca(NO_3)_2$, which are derived from NaOH and HCl and from $Ca(OH)_2$ and HNO_3, respectively. Neither cation nor anion hydrolyzes. The solution has a pH of 7.

2. *Salt derived from a strong base and a weak acid:* In this case the anion is a relatively strong conjugate base. Examples are NaClO and $Ba(C_2H_3O_2)_2$. The anion hydrolyzes to produce $OH^-(aq)$ ions. The solution has a pH above 7.

3. *Salt derived from a weak base and a strong acid:* In this case the cation is a relatively strong conjugate acid. Examples are NH_4Cl and $Al(NO_3)_3$. The cation hydrolyzes to produce $H^+(aq)$ ions. The solution has a pH below 7.

4. *Salt derived from a weak base and a weak acid:* Examples are $NH_4C_2H_3O_2$, NH_4CN, and $FeCO_3$. Both cation and anion hydrolyze. The pH of the solution depends upon the extent to which each ion hydrolyzes. The pH of a solution of NH_4CN is greater than 7 because CN^- ($K_b = 2.0 \times 10^{-5}$) is more basic than NH_4^+ ($K_a = 5.6 \times 10^{-10}$) is acidic. Consequently, CN^- hydrolyzes to a greater extent than NH_4^+ does.

Figure 16.11 demonstrates the influence of several salts on pH.

SAMPLE EXERCISE 16.18

List the following solutions in order of increasing pH: (i) 0.1 M $Co(ClO_4)_2$; (ii) 0.1 M RbCN; (iii) 0.1 M $Sr(NO_3)_2$; (iv) 0.1 M $KC_2H_3O_2$.

SOLUTION   The most acidic solution will be (i), which has a metal ion that undergoes hydrolysis and an anion derived from a strong acid. Solution (iii) should have pH of about 7 because it is derived from an alkaline earth cation and the anion of a strong acid. Neither of these ions undergoes hydrolysis to any appreciable extent. Solutions (ii) and (iv) are both derived from an alkali metal ion, which does not undergo hydrolysis, and an anion of a weak acid. Anion hydrolysis should lead to a basic solution in both cases, but solution (ii) will be more strongly basic because CN^- is a stronger base than $C_2H_3O_2^-$. We see that the order of pH is 0.1 M $Co(ClO_4)_2$ < 0.1 M $Sr(NO_3)_2$ < 0.1 M $KC_2H_3O_2$ < 0.1 M RbCN.

PRACTICE EXERCISE

In each case below, indicate which salt will form the more acidic (or less basic) 0.010 M solution: **(a)** $NaNO_3$, $Fe(NO_3)_3$; **(b)** KBr, KBrO; **(c)** CH_3NH_3Cl, $BaCl_2$; **(d)** NH_4NO_2, NH_4NO_3.   *Answers:* **(a)** $Fe(NO_3)_3$; **(b)** KBr; **(c)** CH_3NH_3Cl; **(d)** NH_4NO_3

16.9 Acid-Base Behavior and Chemical Structure

We have seen that when a substance is dissolved in water, it may behave as an acid, behave as a base, or exhibit no acid-base properties. How does the chemical structure of a substance determine which of these behaviors will be exhibited by the substance? For example, why do some substances that contain OH groups behave as bases, releasing OH^- ions into solution, whereas others behave as acids, ionizing to release H^+? Why are some acids stronger than others? In this section, we will briefly address the effects of chemical structure on acid-base behavior.

Effect of Bond Polarity and Bond Strength

Any molecule containing H can potentially act as an acid. However, a substance HX will transfer a proton only if the H—X bond is already polarized in the following way:

$$\overset{+\quad\longrightarrow}{\text{H—X}}$$

In ionic hydrides such as NaH, the reverse is true; the H atom possesses a negative charge and behaves as a proton acceptor (Equation 16.18). Nonpolar H—X bonds, such as the H—C bond in CH_4, produce neither acidic nor basic solutions.

    Another factor that helps determine whether a molecule containing an H—X bond will donate a proton is the strength of the bond. Very strong bonds are less easily ionized than are weaker ones. This factor is of importance, for example, in the case of the hydrogen halides. The H—F bond is the most polar H—X bond. You therefore might expect that HF would be a very strong acid if the first rule were all that mattered. However, the energy required to dissociate HF into H and F atoms is much higher than it is for the other hydrogen halides, as shown in Table 8.4. As a result, HF is a weak acid, whereas all the other hydrogen halides are strong acids in water.

    A third factor that affects the ease with which a hydrogen atom ionizes from HX is the stability of the conjugate base, X^-. In general, the greater the stability of the conjugate base, the stronger the acid. The strength of an acid is often a combination of all three factors: the polarity of the H—X bond, the strength of the H—X bond, and the stability of the conjugate base, X^-.

    These factors can be used to relate the acid-base properties of the hydride of an element to its position in the periodic table. In any horizontal row of the table, the most basic hydrides are on the left, the most acidic hydrides on the

Learning Goal 11: Explain how relative acid strength relates to the polarity and strength of the H—X bond.

Point of Emphasis: In general, the more polar the H—X bond, the stronger the acid, and the weaker the H—X bond, the stronger the acid.

right. For example, in the second row of the table, NaH is a basic hydride. On addition to water it reacts to form $OH^-(aq)$, as described by Equation 16.18. On the right-hand side of the row, the acidity increases in the order $PH_3 < H_2S < HCl$. This general trend is related to the increasing electronegativity of the element as we move from left to right in any horizontal row. In general, *metal hydrides are either basic or show no pronounced acid-base properties in water,* whereas *nonmetal hydrides range from showing no pronounced acid-base properties to being acidic.* Note that the base ammonia, NH_3, is an exception to this rule.

In any vertical row of nonmetallic elements there is a tendency toward increasing acidity with increasing atomic number. For example, among the group 6A elements the acid dissociation constants vary in the order $H_2O < H_2S < H_2Se < H_2Te$. This order arises primarily because the bond strengths steadily decrease in this series as the central atom grows larger and the overlaps of atomic orbitals grow smaller. Figure 16.12 illustrates the application of these general correlations to the nonmetal hydrides of periods 2 and 3.

Oxyacids

Learning Goal 12: Predict the relative acid strengths of oxyacids.

Many common acids contain one or more O—H bonds. For example, sulfuric acid contains two such bonds:

$$H-\overset{\displaystyle :\overset{..}{O}:}{\underset{\displaystyle :\underset{..}{O}:}{\overset{|}{\underset{|}{S}}}}-\overset{..}{O}-H$$

Acids in which OH groups and possibly additional oxygen atoms are bound to a central atom are called **oxyacids.** The OH group is also present in bases. What factors determine whether an OH group will behave as a base or as an acid? Let's consider an OH group bound to some atom Y, which might in turn have other groups attached to it:

$$\overset{\diagdown}{\underset{\diagup}{Y}}-O-H$$

FIGURE 16.12 Acid-base properties of the nonmetal hydrides (relative to water) of periods 2 and 3.

	GROUP			
	4A	5A	6A	7A
Period 2	CH₄ No acid or base properties	NH₃ Weak base	H₂O ———	HF Weak acid
Period 3	SiH₄ No acid or base properties	PH₃ Weak base	H₂S Weak acid	HCl Strong acid

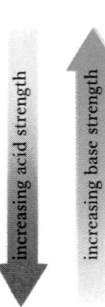

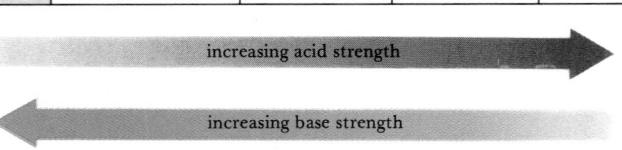

increasing acid strength

increasing base strength

At one extreme, Y might be a metal, such as Na, K, or Mg. The pair of electrons shared between Y and O is then completely transferred to oxygen, and an ionic compound involving OH^- is formed. Because of the charge that surrounds it, the oxygen of the OH^- ion does not strongly attract to itself the electron pair it shares with hydrogen. That is, the O—H bond in OH^- is not strongly polarized. Therefore, the hydrogen of OH^- has no tendency to transfer to the solvent as $H^+(aq)$. Such compounds therefore behave as bases.

When Y is an element of intermediate electronegativity, around 2.0, the bond to O is more covalent in character, and the substance does not readily lose OH^-. Elements with electronegativities in this range include B, C, P, As, and I (Figure 8.7).

Whether such substances will behave as acids in water depends on the ease with which the proton is lost from oxygen. As a general rule, as the ability of group Y to attract electrons increases, so will the acidity of the substance, for two reasons: First, the O—H bond becomes more polar, thereby favoring loss of H^+ (Figure 16.13). Second, because the conjugate base is usually an anion, its stability generally increases as the electronegativity of Y increases.

Many oxyacids contain additional electronegative atoms (usually O) bonded to the central atom Y. By the same reasoning used above, the strength of an acid will increase as additional electronegative atoms bond to the central atom Y: The additional electronegative atoms help polarize the O—H bond and help stabilize the conjugate base.

We can summarize these ideas as two simple rules that relate the acid strength of oxyacids to the electronegativity of Y and to the number of groups attached to Y:

1. *For oxyacids that have the same structure, acid strength generally increases with increasing electronegativity of the central atom Y. For example, the strength of the hypohalous acids, which have the structure H—O—Y, increases as the electronegativity of Y increases (Table 16.6).*

TABLE 16.6 △ Electronegativity Values (EN) of Y and Acid-Dissociation Constants (K_a) of the Hypohalous Acids, H—O—Y

Acid	EN of Y	K_a
HClO	3.0	3×10^{-8}
HBrO	2.8	2×10^{-9}
HIO	2.5	2×10^{-11}

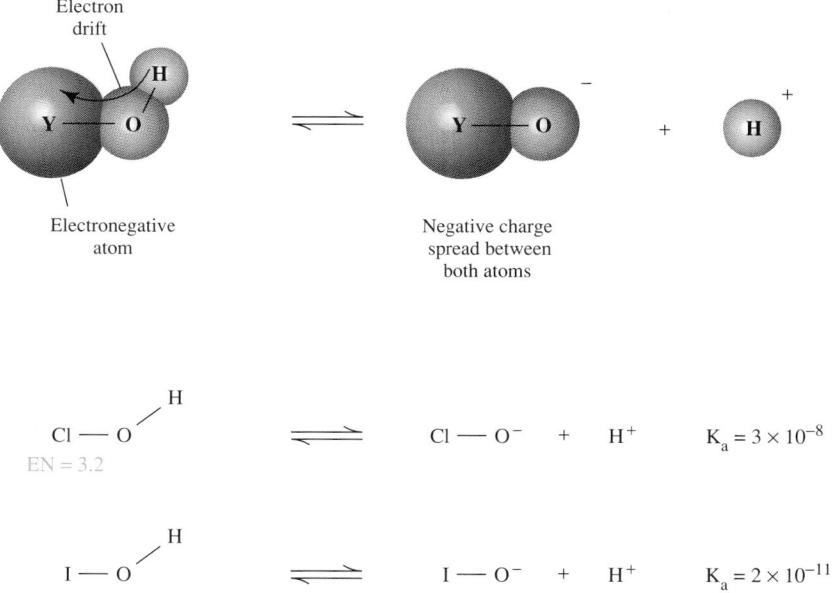

FIGURE 16.13 As the electronegativity of the atom Y attached to an O—H group increases, the ease with which the hydrogen atom is ionized increases. The drift of electrons toward atom Y further polarizes the O—H bond, which favors ionization. In addition, the electronegativity of atom Y will help stabilize the conjugate base, which also leads to a stronger acid. As shown, for example, HClO is a stronger acid than HIO because Cl is more electronegative than I.

Teaching Note: The increased ability to "spread out" the negative charge as the number of oxygen atoms increases can be seen in the corresponding increase in the number of equivalent resonance structures in the Lewis diagram.

2. *For oxyacids that have the same central atom Y, acid strength increases as the number of oxygen atoms attached to Y increases.* Because oxygen atoms are highly electronegative, increasing the number of oxygen atoms will increase the ability of the conjugate base to "spread out" its negative charge and increase the polarity of the O—H bond. For example, the strength of the oxyacids of chlorine steadily increases from hypochlorous acid, HClO, to perchloric acid, $HClO_4$:

Increasing acid strength →

$$
\text{H—O—Cl} \qquad \text{H—O—Cl—O} \qquad \text{H—O—Cl—O} \qquad \text{H—O—Cl—O}
$$

Hypochlorous	Chlorous	Chloric	Perchloric
+1	+3	+5	+7

Chlorine oxidation numbers

Notice that this correlation can be stated in another but equivalent way: In a series of oxyacids, the acidity increases as the oxidation number of the central atom increases.

SAMPLE EXERCISE 16.19

Arrange the compounds in each of the following series in order of increasing acid strength: **(a)** AsH_3, HI, NaH, H_2O; **(b)** H_2SeO_3, H_2SeO_4, H_2O.

SOLUTION **(a)** The elements from the left side of the periodic table form the most basic hydrides because the hydrogen in these compounds carries a negative charge. Thus NaH should be the most basic hydride on the list. Because arsenic is a less electronegative element than oxygen, we might expect that AsH_3 would be a weak base toward water. That is also what we would predict by an extension of the trends shown in Figure 16.12. Further, we expect that the hydrides of the halogens, as the most electronegative element in each period, will be acidic relative to water. Finally, HI is one of the strong acids in water. Thus the order of increasing acidity is NaH < AsH_3 < H_2O < HI.

   (b) The acidity of oxyacids increases as the number of oxygen atoms bonded to the central atom increases. Thus, H_2SeO_4 will be a stronger acid than H_2SeO_3; in fact, we note that the Se atom in H_2SeO_4 is in its maximum positive oxidation state, and so we expect it to be a comparatively strong acid, much like H_2SO_4. H_2SeO_3 is an oxyacid of a nonmetal that is similar to H_2SO_3. As such, we expect that H_2SeO_3 is able to donate a proton to H_2O, indicating that H_2SeO_3 is a stronger acid than H_2O. We see that the order of increasing acidity is H_2O < H_2SeO_3 < H_2SeO_4.

PRACTICE EXERCISE

In each of the following pairs, choose the compound that leads to the more acidic (or less basic) solution: **(a)** HBr, HF; **(b)** PH_3, H_2S; **(c)** HNO_2, HNO_3; **(d)** H_2SO_3, H_4SiO_4.   *Answers:* **(a)** HBr; **(b)** H_2S; **(c)** HNO_3; **(d)** H_2SO_3

Carboxylic Acids

Another large group of acids is illustrated by acetic acid, $HC_2H_3O_2$, the structure of which is as follows:

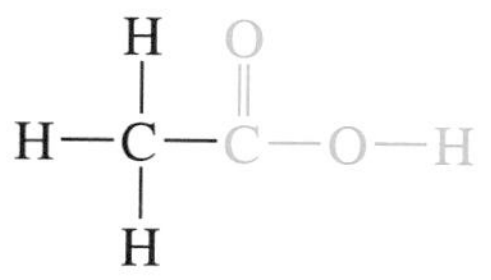

$$H-\overset{\overset{\displaystyle H}{|}}{\underset{\underset{\displaystyle H}{|}}{C}}-\overset{\overset{\displaystyle O}{\|}}{C}-O-H$$

The portion of the structure shown in blue is called the *carboxyl group,* which is often written as COOH. Thus, the chemical formula of acetic acid is often written as CH_3COOH, where only the hydrogen atom in the carboxyl group can be ionized. Acids that contain a carboxyl group are called **carboxylic acids,** which is the largest group of organic acids. Formic acid and benzoic acid, whose structures are drawn below, are further examples of this large and important class of acids.

Point of Emphasis: Carboxylic acids are organic compounds that have the general formula R—COOH, where R is either hydrogen or a chain of carbon-based groups.

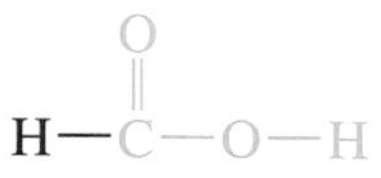

$$H-\overset{\overset{\displaystyle O}{\|}}{C}-O-H$$

Formic acid

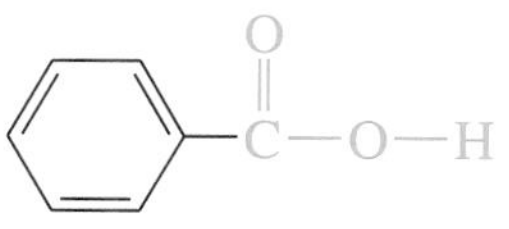

Benzoic acid

As we have seen, acetic acid is fairly acidic ($K_a = 1.8 \times 10^{-5}$); in contrast, methanol, CH_3OH, is not an acid in water. Two factors contribute to the acidic behavior of carboxylic acids. First, the additional oxygen atom attached to the carboxyl group carbon increases the polarity of the O—H bond and helps to stabilize the conjugate base. Second, the conjugate base of a carboxylic acid (a *carboxylate anion*) can exhibit resonance (Section 8.7), which contributes further to the stability of the anion by spreading the negative charge over several atoms:

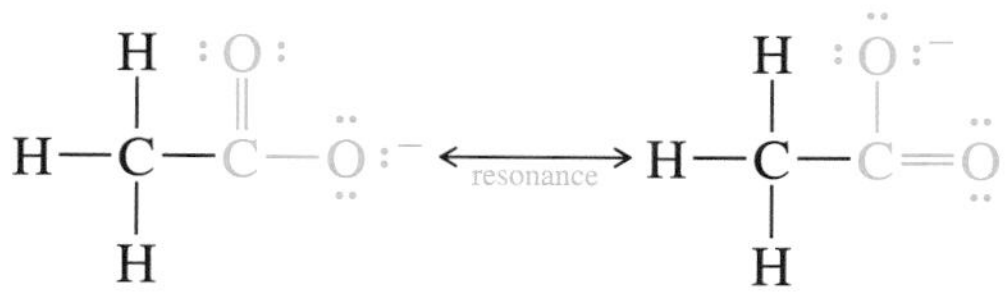

The acid strength of carboxylic acids also increases as the number of electronegative atoms in the acid increases. For example, trifluoroacetic acid, CF_3COOH, has $K_a = 5.0 \times 10^{-1}$; the replacement of three hydrogen atoms of acetic acid with more electronegative fluorine atoms leads to a great increase in acid strength.

16.10 Lewis Acids and Bases

For a substance to be a proton acceptor (that is, a base in the Brønsted-Lowry sense), that substance must possess an unshared pair of electrons for binding the proton. For example, we have seen that NH_3 acts as a proton acceptor. Using Lewis structures, we can write the reaction between H^+ and NH_3 as follows:

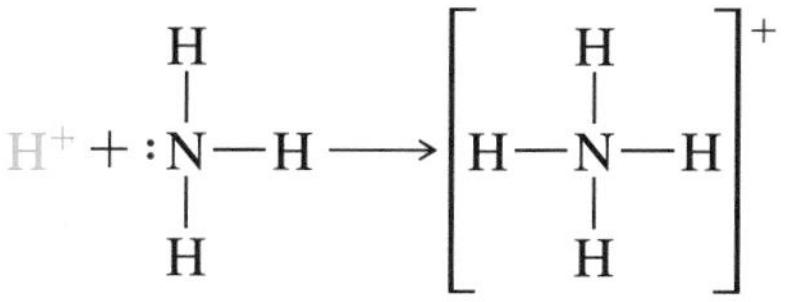

$$H^+ + :\overset{\overset{\displaystyle H}{|}}{\underset{\underset{\displaystyle H}{|}}{N}}-H \longrightarrow \left[H-\overset{\overset{\displaystyle H}{|}}{\underset{\underset{\displaystyle H}{|}}{N}}-H\right]^+ \qquad [16.41]$$

The Amphoteric Behavior of Amino Acids

You are probably aware that *amino acids* are the building blocks of proteins. The general structure of amino acids is shown below, where different amino acids have different R groups attached to the central carbon atom.

$$: N - C - C - O - H$$

Amine group (basic)   Carboxyl group (acidic)

For example, in *glycine,* which is the simplest amino acid, R is a hydrogen atom, whereas in *alanine* R is a CH_3 group:

$$H_2N - C - COOH \qquad H_2N - C - COOH$$

Glycine   Alanine

Amino acids contain a carboxyl group and can therefore serve as acids. They also contain an NH_2 group, characteristic of amines (Section 16.6), and thus they can also act as bases. Therefore, amino acids are amphoteric. For glycine, we might expect that the acid and base reactions with water would be as follows:

Acid: $H_2N-CH_2-COOH(aq) + H_2O(l) \rightleftharpoons$
$\qquad H_2N-CH_2-COO^-(aq) + H_3O^+(aq)$ [16.42]

Base: $H_2N-CH_2-COOH(aq) + H_2O(l) \rightleftharpoons$
$\qquad H_3N-CH_2-COOH^+(aq) + OH^-(aq)$ [16.43]

The pH of a solution of glycine in water is about 6.0, indicating that it is a slightly stronger acid than a base.

The acid-base chemistry of amino acids is somewhat more complicated than shown in Equations 16.42 and 16.43, however. Because the COOH can act as an acid and the NH_2 group can act as a base, amino acids undergo a "self-contained" Brønsted-Lowry acid-base reaction in which the proton of the carboxyl group is transferred to the basic nitrogen atom:

$$H - N - C - C - OH \rightleftharpoons$$

proton transfer

Neutral molecule

$$H - N^+ - C - C - O^- \qquad [16.44]$$

Zwitterion

Although the form of the amino acid on the right side of Equation 16.44 is electrically neutral overall, we see that it has a positively charged end and a negatively charged end. A molecule of this type is called a *zwitterion* (German for "hybrid ion").

Do amino acids exhibit any properties indicating that they behave as zwitterions? If so, they should show behavior that is similar to that of ionic substances. ⊂⊃ (Sec. 8.2) Crystalline amino acids (Figure 16.14) have relatively high melting points, usually above 200°C; this property is characteristic of ionic solids. Amino acids are far more soluble in water than in nonpolar solvents. In addition, the dipole moments of amino acids are large, consistent with a large separation of charge in the molecule. We see that the ability of amino acids to act simultaneously as acids and bases has important effects on their properties.

FIGURE 16.14 Crystals of *lysine,* one of the amino acids found in proteins. The crystals are colorless; they are viewed here under polarized light, which causes them to appear multicolored. Many of the properties of amino acids, such as the high melting point of these crystals, are consistent with their formulation as *zwitterions.* (Paul Silverman/Fundamental Photographs)

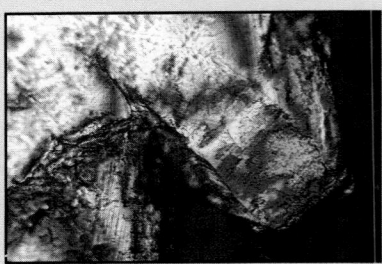

G. N. Lewis was the first to notice this aspect of acid-base reactions. He proposed a definition of acid and base that emphasizes the shared electron pair: A **Lewis acid** is defined as an electron-pair acceptor, and a **Lewis base** as an electron-pair donor.

Glen T. Seaborg, "The Research Style of Gilbert N. Lewis: Acids and Bases," *J. Chem. Educ.* **1984**, *61*, 93.

Learning Goal 13: Define acid or base in terms of the Lewis concept.

Every base that we have discussed thus far—whether it be OH^-, H_2O, an amine, or an anion—is an electron-pair donor. Everything that is a base in the Brønsted-Lowry sense (a proton acceptor) is also a base in the Lewis sense (an electron-pair donor). However, in the Lewis theory, a base can donate its electron pair to something other than H^+. The Lewis definition therefore greatly increases the number of species that can be considered acids; H^+ is a Lewis acid, but not the only one. For example, consider the reaction between NH_3 and BF_3. This reaction occurs because BF_3 has a vacant orbital in its valence shell. ∞ (Sec. 8.8) It therefore acts as an electron-pair acceptor (a Lewis acid) toward NH_3, which donates the electron pair:

$$
\begin{array}{ccc}
\underset{\text{Base}}{
\begin{array}{c}
\ \ \ \text{H}\ \ \ \ \text{F}\\
\ \ \ \ |\ \ \ \ \ | \\
\text{H}-\text{N:}+\text{B}-\text{F}\\
\ \ \ \ |\ \ \ \ \ | \\
\ \ \ \text{H}\ \ \ \ \text{F}
\end{array}} & \longrightarrow &
\begin{array}{c}
\ \ \ \text{H}\ \ \ \ \text{F}\\
\ \ \ \ |\ \ \ \ \ | \\
\text{H}-\text{N}-\text{B}-\text{F}\\
\ \ \ \ |\ \ \ \ \ | \\
\ \ \ \text{H}\ \ \ \ \text{F}
\end{array}
\end{array}
$$

Our emphasis throughout this chapter has been on water as the solvent and on the proton as the source of acidic properties. In such cases, we find the Brønsted-Lowry definition of acids and bases to be the most useful. In fact, when we speak of a substance as being acidic or basic, we are usually thinking of aqueous solutions and using these terms in the Arrhenius or Brønsted-Lowry sense. The advantage of the Lewis theory is that it allows us to treat a wider variety of reactions, including those that do not involve proton transfer, as acid-base reactions. To avoid confusion, a substance like BF_3 is rarely called an acid unless it is clear from the context that we are using the term in the sense of the Lewis definition. Instead, substances that function as electron-pair acceptors are referred to explicitly as "Lewis acids."

Lewis acids include molecules that, like BF_3, have an incomplete octet of electrons. In addition, many simple cations can function as Lewis acids. For example, Fe^{3+} interacts strongly with cyanide ions to form the ferricyanide ion, $Fe(CN)_6^{3-}$:

$$Fe^{3+} + 6:C{\equiv}N:^- \longrightarrow [Fe(C{\equiv}N:)_6]^{3-}$$

The Fe^{3+} ion has vacant orbitals that accept the electron pairs donated by the CN^- ions; we will learn more in Chapter 25 about just which orbitals are used by the Fe^{3+} ion. That the metal ion is highly charged also contributes to the interaction with CN^- ions.

Some compounds with multiple bonds can behave as Lewis acids. For example, the reaction of carbon dioxide with water to form carbonic acid, H_2CO_3, can be pictured as an attack by a water molecule on CO_2, in which the water acts as an electron-pair donor and the CO_2 as an electron-pair acceptor, as shown in the margin. The electron pair of one of the carbon-oxygen double bonds is moved onto the oxygen, leaving a vacant orbital on the carbon that can act as an electron-pair acceptor. We have shown the shift of these electrons with arrows. After forming the initial acid-base product, a proton moves from one oxygen to another, thereby forming carbonic acid:

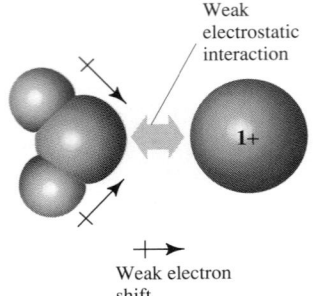

Weak electrostatic interaction

Weak electron shift

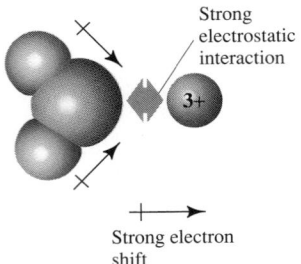

Strong electrostatic interaction

Strong electron shift

FIGURE 16.15 Interaction of a water molecule with a cation of 1+ charge or 3+ charge. The interaction is much stronger with the smaller ion of higher charge.

Learning Goal 14: Predict the relative acidities of solutions of metal salts from a knowledge of metal-ion charges and ionic radii.

$$H \overset{\curvearrowleft}{\underset{}{}} : \ddot{O} : \qquad\qquad H - \ddot{O} :$$

(structural formula reaction)

$$H - O - C \longrightarrow H - O - C$$

A similar kind of Lewis acid-base reaction takes place when any oxide of a nonmetal dissolves in water to form an acidic solution.

Hydrolysis of Metal Ions

The Lewis concept is also helpful in explaining why solutions of many metal ions show acidic properties. ∞ (Sec. 16.8) For example, a solution of $Cr(NO_3)_3$ is quite acidic. A solution of $ZnCl_2$ is also acidic, though to a lesser extent. To understand why this is so, we must examine the interaction between a metal ion and water molecules.

Because metal ions are positively charged, they attract the unshared electron pairs of water molecules. It is primarily this interaction, referred to as *hydration*, that causes salts to dissolve in water. ∞ (Sec. 13.1) The process of hydration is a Lewis acid-base interaction in which the metal ion acts as a Lewis acid and the water molecules as Lewis bases. When the water molecule interacts with the positively charged metal ion, electron density is drawn from the oxygen, as illustrated in Figure 16.15. This flow of electron density causes the O—H bond to become more polarized; as a result, water molecules bound to the metal ion, M, are more acidic than those in the bulk solvent.

As an example of how a hydrated metal ion can serve as an acid, consider the hydrated Fe^{3+} ion, $Fe(H_2O)_6^{3+}$, which we usually represent simply as $Fe^{3+}(aq)$. This ion acts as a source of protons:

$$Fe(H_2O)_6^{3+}(aq) \rightleftharpoons Fe(H_2O)_5(OH)^{2+}(aq) + H^+(aq) \qquad [16.45]$$

FIGURE 16.16 The pH values of 1.0 M solutions of a series of nitrate salts, as estimated using acid-base indicators. From left to right, $NaNO_3$, $Ca(NO_3)_2$, $Zn(NO_3)_2$, and $Al(NO_3)_3$. (Donald Clegg and Roxy Wilson)

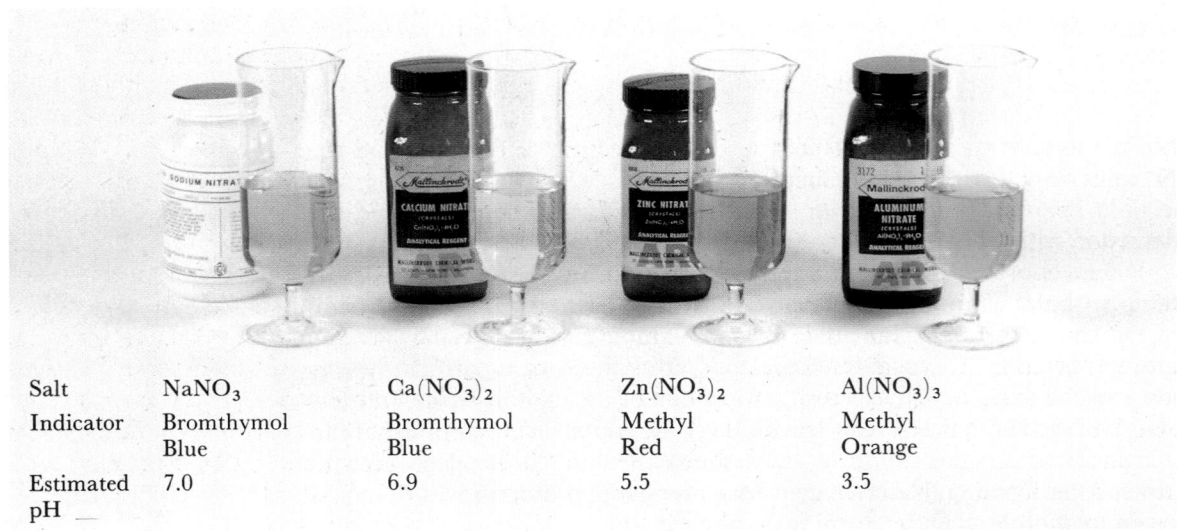

Salt	NaNO₃	Ca(NO₃)₂	Zn(NO₃)₂	Al(NO₃)₃
Indicator	Bromthymol Blue	Bromthymol Blue	Methyl Red	Methyl Orange
Estimated pH	7.0	6.9	5.5	3.5

The acid-dissociation constant for this hydrolysis reaction has the value $K_a = 2 \times 10^{-3}$, indicating that $Fe^{3+}(aq)$ is a fairly strong acid. Acid-dissociation constants for hydrolysis reactions generally increase with increasing charge and decreasing radius of the ion (Figure 16.15). Thus, the Cu^{2+} ion, which has a smaller charge and a larger radius than Fe^{3+}, forms less acidic solutions than Fe^{3+}: The K_a for $Cu^{2+}(aq)$ is 1×10^{-8}. The acid hydrolysis of a number of salts of metal ions is demonstrated in Figure 16.16. Note that the Na^+ ion, which is large and has only a 1+ charge, exhibits no acid hydrolysis and yields a neutral solution.

For Review

Summary

In this chapter we have considered the general properties of acidic and basic solutions, with emphasis on water as a solvent. We have seen that acidic solutions are those that contain more $H^+(aq)$ than $OH^-(aq)$. The hydrogen ion is strongly bound to water; for this reason the hydronium ion, $H_3O^+(aq)$, is often used to represent the predominant form of H^+ in water. Basic solutions contain more $OH^-(aq)$ than $H^+(aq)$.

Water spontaneously ionizes to a slight degree (autoionization), forming $H^+(aq)$ and $OH^-(aq)$. The extent of ionization is expressed by the ion-product constant for water:

$$K_w = [H^+][OH^-] = 1.0 \times 10^{-14} \quad (25\,^\circ C)$$

This relationship describes not only pure water, but aqueous solutions as well. Thus, as $[H^+]$ increases, $[OH^-]$ decreases. Because the concentration of water is effectively constant in dilute solutions, $[H_2O]$ is omitted from the ion-product expression for water as well as from other equilibrium expressions associated with reactions in aqueous solution.

The Brønsted-Lowry concept of acids and bases emphasizes the transfer of protons (H^+) from acids to bases. A Brønsted-Lowry acid is a substance that donates a proton (H^+) to another substance; a Brønsted-Lowry base is a substance that accepts a proton from another substance. The conjugate base of a Brønsted-Lowry acid is the species that remains when a proton is removed from the acid. Together, the acid and its conjugate base are called a conjugate acid-base pair. The acid-base strengths of conjugate acid-base pairs are related: The stronger an acid, the weaker its con-

jugate base; the weaker an acid, the stronger its conjugate base. Water is an example of a substance that can function as either a Brønsted-Lowry acid or base. Such substances are called amphoteric.

Strong acids are strong electrolytes, ionizing completely in aqueous solution. The common strong acids are HCl, HBr, HI, HNO_3, $HClO_4$, and H_2SO_4. Strong acids have conjugate bases that are weaker proton acceptors than H_2O.

Basic solutions are produced by ionic hydroxides such as NaOH and by substances that react with water to increase $[OH^-]$. Strong bases have conjugate acids that are weaker proton donors than H_2O. Common strong bases are the hydroxides and oxides of the alkali metals and the heavier alkaline earths.

Weak acids are weak electrolytes; only part of the molecules exist in solution in ionized form. The extent of ionization is expressed by the acid-dissociation constant, K_a, which is the equilibrium constant for the reaction $HA(aq) \rightleftharpoons H^+(aq) + A^-(aq)$.

Polyprotic acids, such as H_2SO_3, have more than one ionizable proton. These acids have more than one acid-dissociation constant: K_{a1}, K_{a2}, and so forth. These constants decrease in magnitude in the order $K_{a1} > K_{a2} > K_{a3}$.

Weak bases include NH_3, amines, and the anions of weak acids. The extent to which a weak base reacts with water to generate OH^- and the conjugate acid of the base is measured by the base-dissociation constant, K_b. This is the equilibrium constant for the reaction $B(aq) + H_2O(l) \rightleftharpoons HB^+(aq) + OH^-(aq)$, where B is the base.

The stronger an acid, the weaker its conjugate base; the weaker an acid, the stronger its conjugate base. This qualitative observation is expressed quantitatively by $K_a \times K_b = K_w$ (where K_a and K_b are dissociation constants for conjugate acid-base pairs).

The acid-base properties of salts can be ascribed to the behavior of their respective cations and anions. The reaction of ions with water with a resultant change in pH is called hydrolysis. The cations of strong bases (the alkali metal ions and alkaline earth metal ions) and the anions of strong acids do not undergo hydrolysis.

The tendency of a substance to show acidic or basic characteristics in water can be correlated reasonably well with chemical structure. Acid character

requires the presence of a highly polar H—X bond, promoting loss of hydrogen as H^+ on reaction with water. Basic character, on the other hand, requires the presence of an available pair of electrons. By considering the effects of changes in structure, it is possible to predict how a given structural change is likely to alter the acidity or basicity.

The Lewis concept of acids and bases emphasizes the shared electron pair rather than the proton. An acid is defined as an electron-pair acceptor, a base as an electron-pair donor. The Lewis concept is more general than the Brønsted-Lowry concept because it can apply to cases in which the acid is some substance other than H^+.

Key Terms

autoionization (Sec. 16.1)
ion-product constant (Sec. 16.1)
hydronium ion (Sec. 16.1)
Brønsted-Lowry acid (Sec. 16.2)
Brønsted-Lowry base (Sec. 16.2)
conjugate acid-base pair (Sec. 16.2)
conjugate base (Sec. 16.2)
conjugate acid (Sec. 16.2)
amphoteric (Sec. 16.2)
pH (Sec. 16.3)

acid-dissociation constant (Sec. 16.5)
polyprotic acids (Sec. 16.5)
base-dissociation constant (Sec. 16.6)
amines (Sec. 16.6)
hydrolysis (Sec. 16.8)
oxyacids (Sec. 16.9)
carboxylic acids (Sec. 16.9)
Lewis acid (Sec. 16.10)
Lewis base (Sec. 16.10)

Exercises

Introduction; Dissociation of Water

16.1. Although HCl and H_2SO_4 have very different properties as pure substances, their aqueous solutions possess many common properties. List some general properties of these solutions and explain their common behavior in terms of the species present.

16.2. Although pure NaOH and CaO have very different properties, their aqueous solutions possess many common properties. List some general properties of these solutions and explain their common behavior in terms of the species present.

16.3. (a) What is meant by the term *autoionization*? (b) Explain why pure water is a poor conductor of electricity. (c) You are told that an aqueous solution is acidic. What does this statement mean?

16.4. (a) Write a chemical equation that illustrates the autoionization of water. (b) Write the expression for the ion-product constant for water, K_w. Why is $[H_2O]$ omitted

from this expression? (c) A solution is described as basic. What is meant by this statement?

16.5. Indicate whether each of the following solutions is acidic, basic, or neutral: (a) 0.008 M H^+; (b) 0.0004 M OH^-; (c) 1.5×10^{-10} M H^+; (d) $[H^+] = 1.00 \times 10^{-7}$ M; (e) 5.0×10^{-7} M OH^-.

16.6. Determine whether each of the following solutions is acidic, basic, or neutral: (a) $[H^+] = [OH^-]$; (b) 4.0×10^{-5} M OH^-; (c) 6.5×10^{-7} M H^+; (d) $[H^+] = 0.00000000050$ M; (e) $[OH^-] = 0.00000010$ M.

16.7. Calculate $[OH^-]$ for each of the following solutions: (a) $[H^+] = 0.0050$ M; (b) $[H^+] = 1.3 \times 10^{-9}$ M; (c) A solution in which $[OH^-]$ is 100 times greater than $[H^+]$.

16.8. Calculate the concentration of $H^+(aq)$ in each of the following solutions: (a) $[OH^-] = 4.5 \times 10^{-11}$ M; (b) $[OH^-] = 1.50$ M; (c) A solution in which $[H^+]$ is five times greater than $[OH^-]$.

Brønsted-Lowry Acids and Bases

16.9. **(a)** What is the difference between the Arrhenius and the Brønsted-Lowry definitions of an acid? **(b)** $NH_3(g)$ and $HCl(g)$ react to form the ionic solid $NH_4Cl(s)$ (Figure 16.3). Which substance is the Brønsted-Lowry acid in this reaction? Which is the Brønsted-Lowry base?

16.10. What is the difference between the Arrhenius and the Brønsted-Lowry definitions of a base? **(b)** When ammonia is dissolved in water, it behaves both as an Arrhenius base and as a Brønsted-Lowry base. Explain.

16.11. Give the conjugate base of the following Brønsted-Lowry acids: **(a)** H_2S; **(b)** HNO_3; **(c)** $HClO$; **(d)** HCO_3^-; **(e)** NH_4^+.

16.12. Give the conjugate acid of the following Brønsted-Lowry bases: **(a)** NH_3; **(b)** ClO_3^-; **(c)** PO_4^{3-}; **(d)** HCO_3^-; **(e)** H_2S.

16.13. Identify the acid, the base, the conjugate acid, and the conjugate base in each of the following reactions:
(a) $NH_2^-(aq) + H_2O(l) \longrightarrow NH_3(aq) + OH^-(aq)$
(b) $H_2C_2O_4(aq) + H_2O(l) \rightleftharpoons HC_2O_4^-(aq) + H_3O^+(aq)$
(c) $H^+(aq) + HPO_4^{2-}(aq) \rightleftharpoons H_2PO_4^-(aq)$

16.14. Identify the acid, the base, the conjugate acid, and the conjugate base in each of the following equilibria:
(a) $HC_2O_4^-(aq) + CO_3^{2-}(aq) \rightleftharpoons$
$$C_2O_4^{2-}(aq) + HCO_3^-(aq)$$
(b) $PH_4^+(aq) + H_2O(l) \rightleftharpoons PH_3(aq) + H_3O^+(aq)$
(c) $NH_4^+(aq) + CN^-(aq) \rightleftharpoons NH_3(aq) + HCN(aq)$

16.15. Which of the following would you expect to be the stronger Brønsted-Lowry acid: **(a)** NH_3 or H_2O; **(b)** $HClO_4$ or HF? Briefly explain your choice.

16.16. Which of the following would you expect to be the stronger Brønsted-Lowry base: **(a)** CN^- or Cl^-; **(b)** NO_3^- or CO_3^{2-}? Briefly explain your choice.

16.17. What is meant by stating that a substance is *amphoteric*? **(b)** Write an equation for the autoionization of water that demonstrates that water is amphoteric.

16.18. Write an equation for the reaction in which $H_2PO_4^-(aq)$ acts as a base in $H_2O(l)$. **(b)** Write an equation for the reaction in which $H_2PO_4^-(aq)$ acts as an acid in $H_2O(l)$. **(c)** What is the conjugate acid of $H_2PO_4^-$? What is its conjugate base?

The pH Scale

16.19. Indicate whether the following are acidic, basic, or neutral: **(a)** pH = 3.50; **(b)** pH = 11.43; **(c)** pOH = 7.00; **(d)** pOH = 2.94.

16.20. Indicate whether the following are acidic, basic, or neutral: **(a)** pH = 7.00; **(b)** pH = −0.57; **(c)** pOH = 12.31; **(d)** pOH = 6.50.

16.21. Calculate the pH of each of the following: **(a)** $3.6 \times 10^{-3} M H^+$; **(b)** $[H^+] = 0.047 M$; **(c)** pOH = 5.33; **(d)** $6.7 \times 10^{-2} M OH^-$.

16.22. Calculate the pH of each of the following: **(a)** $4.2 \times 10^{-5} M H^+$; **(b)** $[H^+] = 1.20 M$; **(c)** pOH = 11.21; **(d)** $0.92 M OH^-$.

16.23. Calculate $[H^+]$ for solutions with the following pH values: **(a)** 4.78; **(b)** 12.32; **(c)** −0.67; **(d)** 7.1.

16.24. Calculate $[H^+]$ and $[OH^-]$ for each of the following: **(a)** pH = 6.21; **(b)** pOH = 1.00; **(c)** pH = 9.88; **(d)** pOH = 7.5.

16.25. At normal body temperature, 37°C, $K_w = 2.4 \times 10^{-14}$. Calculate $[H^+]$, $[OH^-]$, pH, and pOH for a neutral aqueous solution at this temperature.

16.26. Deuterium oxide (D_2O, where D = deuterium, the hydrogen-2 nuclide) has an ion-product constant, K_w, of 8.9×10^{-16} at 20°C. Calculate $[D^+]$, $[OD^-]$, pD, and pOD for pure (neutral) D_2O at this temperature.

16.27. By what factor does $[H^+]$ change for a pH change of **(a)** 2.00 units; **(b)** 0.50 units?

16.28. Consider two solutions, solution A and solution B. $[H^+]$ in solution A is 500 times greater than that in solution B. What is the difference in the pH values of the two solutions?

Strong Acids and Bases

16.29. **(a)** What is a strong acid? **(b)** A solution is labeled 0.500 M HCl. What is $[H^+]$ for the solution? **(c)** Which of the following are strong acids: HF, HCl, HBr, HI?

16.30. **(a)** What is a strong base? **(b)** A solution is labeled 0.125 M $Sr(OH)_2$. What is $[OH^-]$ for the solution? **(c)** Is the following statement true or false? Because $Mg(OH)_2$ is not very soluble, it cannot be a strong base. Explain.

16.31. Calculate the pH of each of the following strong acid solutions: **(a)** 0.025 M HNO_3; **(b)** 0.824 g of $HClO_4$ in 0.500 L of solution; **(c)** 5.00 mL of 1.5 M HCl diluted to 100 mL; **(d)** a mixture formed by adding 10.0 mL of 0.020 M HCl to 30.0 mL of 0.010 M HI.

16.32. Calculate the pH of each of the following strong acid solutions: **(a)** $1.8 \times 10^{-4} M$ HBr; **(b)** 1.02 g of HNO_3 in 250 mL of solution; **(c)** 2.00 mL of 0.500 M $HClO_4$ diluted to 50.0 mL; **(d)** a solution formed by mixing 10.0 mL of 0.0100 M HBr with 20.0 mL of $2.50 \times 10^{-3} M$ HCl.

16.33. Calculate $[OH^-]$ and pH for each of the following strong base solutions: **(a)** 0.050 M KOH; **(b)** 2.33 g of NaOH in 500 mL of solution; **(c)** 10.0 mL of 0.150 M

Ca(OH)$_2$ diluted to 500 mL; (d) a solution formed by mixing 10.0 mL of 0.015 M Ba(OH)$_2$ with 30.0 mL of 6.8 × 10^{-3} M NaOH.

16.34. Calculate [OH$^-$] and pH for (a) 3.5 × 10^{-4} M Sr(OH)$_2$; (b) 1.50 g of LiOH in 250 mL of solution; (c) 1.00 mL of 0.095 M NaOH diluted to 2.00 L; (d) a solution formed by adding 5.00 mL of 0.0105 M KOH to 15.0 mL of 3.5 × 10^{-3} M Ca(OH)$_2$.

[16.35]. Calculate the pH of a solution made by adding 2.00 g of lithium oxide, Li$_2$O, to enough water to make 0.600 L of solution.

[16.36]. Calculate the pH of a solution made by adding 5.00 g of sodium hydride, NaH, to enough water to make 0.900 L of solution.

Weak Acids and Bases

16.37. Relying on your knowledge of strong acids and using Table 16.2, indicate which of the following is the strongest and which is the weakest acid: HNO$_2$; HClO$_4$; HClO; HC$_2$H$_3$O$_2$.

16.38. Using Table 16.2 and your knowledge of strong acids, select the strongest and the weakest acid in the following list: HF; HCN; HC$_7$H$_5$O$_2$; HBr.

16.39. Lactic acid, HC$_3$H$_5$O$_3$, has one acidic hydrogen. A 0.10 M solution of lactic acid has a pH of 2.44. Calculate K_a.

16.40. A 0.050 M solution of KHCrO$_4$ has a pH of 3.80. Calculate K_a for HCrO$_4^-$.

16.41. Calculate the pH of each of the following solutions (K_a and K_b values are given in Appendix D): (a) 0.175 M hydrazoic acid, HN$_3$; (b) 0.040 M propionic acid, HC$_3$H$_5$O$_2$; (c) 0.050 M ethylamine, C$_2$H$_5$NH$_2$.

16.42. Determine the pH of each of the following solutions (K_a and K_b values are given in Appendix D): (a) 0.045 M hypochlorous acid; (b) 0.0068 M phenol; (c) 0.080 M hydroxylamine.

16.43. Calculate the pH of a 0.020 M solution of iodic acid, HIO$_3$. (The value of K_a is given in Appendix D.)

16.44. Calculate [OH$^-$] and pH for a 0.00200 M solution of dimethylamine, (CH$_3$)$_2$NH. The value of K_b is given in Appendix D.

16.45. Calculate the percent ionization of hydrazoic acid, HN$_3$, in solutions of each of the following concentrations (K_a given in Appendix D): (a) 0.400 M; (b) 0.100 M; (c) 0.0400 M.

16.46. Calculate the percent ionization of HCrO$_4^-$ in solutions of each of the following concentrations (K_a given in Appendix D): (a) 0.250 M; (b) 0.0800 M; (c) 0.0200 M.

16.47. A 0.200 M solution of a weak acid HX is 9.4 percent ionized. Using this information, calculate [H$^+$], [X$^-$], [HX], and K_a for HX.

16.48. A 0.100 M solution of bromoacetic acid, CH$_2$BrCOOH, is 13.2 percent ionized. Using this information, calculate [CH$_2$BrCOO$^-$], [H$^+$], [CH$_2$BrCOOH], and K_a for bromoacetic acid.

[16.49]. Show that for a weak acid the percent ionization should vary as the inverse square root of the acid concentration.

[16.50]. For solutions of a weak acid, a graph of pH versus the log of the initial acid concentration should be a straight line. What is the magnitude of the slope of that line?

[16.51]. Citric acid, which is present in citrus fruits, is a triprotic acid (Table 16.3). Calculate the pH of a 0.050 M solution of citric acid. Explain any approximations or assumptions that you make in your calculations.

[16.52]. Tartaric acid is found in many plants (grapes, for example). It is partly responsible for the dry texture of certain wines. Calculate the pH of a 0.025 M solution of tartaric acid, for which the acid dissociation constants are listed in Table 16.3. Explain any approximations or assumptions that you make in your calculation.

16.53. Write the balanced net ionic equation for the reaction of each of the following bases with water. Also write the base-dissociation-constant expression for each substance: (a) propylamine, C$_3$H$_7$NH$_2$; (b) cyanide ion, CN$^-$; (c) formate ion, CHO$_2^-$.

16.54. Write the balanced net ionic equation for the reaction of each of the following bases with water. Also write the base-dissociation-constant expression for each substance: (a) hydrazine, H$_2$NNH$_2$; (b) methylamine, CH$_3$NH$_2$; (c) benzoate ion, C$_6$H$_5$CO$_2^-$.

K_a–K_b Relationship; Acid-Base Properties of Salts

16.55. (a) Show that the ionization reaction of HCN and the reaction of CN$^-$ with water can be added to give the autoionization reaction of water. (b) Write the equilibrium constants for the reactions in part (a) and show that their product gives K_w.

16.56. (a) Write a chemical equation that shows the reaction of the phenolate ion, C$_6$H$_5$O$^-$, as a base with water. (b) Although the acid-dissociation for phenol, C$_6$H$_5$OH, is

listed in Appendix D, the base-dissociation constant K_b for the phenolate ion is not. Explain why it is not necessary to list both K_a for phenol and K_b for phenolate ion.

16.57. Using the values of K_a from Appendix D, calculate the base-dissociation constant for each of the following species: (a) nitrite ion, NO$_2^-$; (b) azide ion, N$_3^-$; (c) hydrogen phosphate ion, HPO$_4^{2-}$; (d) formate ion, CHO$_2^-$.

16.58. Using the values of K_b from Appendix D, calculate K_a for each of the following species: **(a)** dimethylammonium ion, $(CH_3)_2NH_2^+$; **(b)** hydrazinium ion, $H_3NNH_2^+$; **(c)** pyridinium ion, $C_5H_5NH^+$; **(d)** hydroxylammonium ion, $HONH_3^+$.

16.59. Calculate $[OH^-]$ and pH for each of the following solutions: **(a)** 0.10 M NaCN; **(b)** 0.080 M Na_2CO_3; **(c)** a mixture that is 0.10 M in $NaNO_2$ and 0.20 M in $Ca(NO_2)_2$.

16.60. Calculate $[OH^-]$ and pH for each of the following solutions: **(a)** 0.10 M NaF; **(b)** 0.10 M Na_2S; **(c)** a mixture that is 0.085 M in $NaC_2H_3O_2$ and 0.055 M in $Ba(C_2H_3O_2)_2$.

16.61. Indicate whether each of the following substances would form an acidic, basic, or neutral solution in water: **(a)** $KC_2H_3O_2$; **(b)** $NaHCO_3$; **(c)** CH_3NH_3Br; **(d)** KNO_2.

16.62. Indicate whether each of the following substances would form an acidic, basic, or neutral solution in water: **(a)** $NaHC_2O_4$; **(b)** CsI; **(c)** $Al(NO_3)_3$; **(d)** NH_4CN.

16.63. Sorbic acid, $HC_6H_7O_2$, is a weak monoprotic acid with $K_a = 1.7 \times 10^{-5}$. Its salt (potassium sorbate) is added to cheese to inhibit the formation of mold. What is the pH of a solution containing 4.93 g of potassium sorbate in 0.500 L of solution?

16.64. Trisodium phosphate, Na_3PO_4, is available in hardware stores as TSP and is used as a cleaning agent. The label on a box of TSP warns that the substance is very basic (caustic or alkaline). What is the pH of a solution containing 50.0 g of TSP in a liter of solution?

Acid-Base Character and Chemical Structure

16.65. How does the acid strength of an oxyacid depend on **(a)** the electronegativity of the central atom; **(b)** the number of nonprotonated oxygen atoms in the molecule?

16.66. **(a)** How does the strength of an acid vary with the polarity and strength of the H—X bond? **(b)** How does the acidity of the hydride of an element vary as a function of the electronegativity of the element? How does this relate to the position of the element in the periodic table?

16.67. Based on their compositions and structures, select the member of each of the following pairs that is the stronger acid: **(a)** H_2SO_3 or H_2SeO_3; **(b)** H_3PO_4 or H_3PO_3; **(c)** H_2SO_3 or H_2CO_3.

16.68. Based on their compositions and structures and on conjugate acid-base relationships, select the member of each of the following pairs that is the stronger base: **(a)** BrO^- or BrO_2^-; **(b)** BrO^- or ClO^-; **(c)** HPO_4^{2-} or $H_2PO_4^-$.

16.69. Indicate whether each of the following statements is true or false. For those that are false, correct the statement so that it is true. **(a)** In general, the acidity of hydrides increases from left to right in a given row of the periodic table. **(b)** In a series of acids that have the same central atom, acid strength increases with the number of hydrogen atoms bonded to the central atom. **(c)** Hydrotelluric acid, H_2Te, is a stronger acid than H_2S because Te has a higher electronegativity than S.

16.70. Indicate whether each of the following statements is true or false. For those that are false, correct the statement so that it is true. **(a)** Acid strength in a series H_nX increases with increasing size of X. **(b)** For acids of the same structure but differing electronegativity of the central atom, acid strength decreases with increasing electronegativity of the central atom. **(c)** The strongest acid of all is HF because fluorine is the most electronegative element.

Lewis Acids and Bases

16.71. Prepare a table in which you compare the definitions of acids and bases according to the Lewis, Brønsted-Lowry, and Arrhenius theories. Which is the most general; that is, which includes the others within its scope? Explain.

16.72. For each of the following descriptive statements, provide an interpretation in terms of the Brønsted-Lowry theory, the Lewis theory, or both, as appropriate. **(a)** Hydrogen bromide, HBr, dissolves in water to form an acidic solution. **(b)** Sodium hydride, NaH, reacts with water to form a basic solution. **(c)** Pyridine reacts with sulfur dioxide in a dry organic solvent to form pyridine-SO_2:

(d) Sulfur dioxide, SO_2, dissolves in water to form an acidic solution.

16.73. Identify the Lewis acid and Lewis base in each of the following reactions:

(a) $Fe(ClO_4)_3(s) + 6H_2O(l) \longrightarrow$
$$Fe(H_2O)_6^{3+}(aq) + 3ClO_4^-(aq)$$
(b) $CN^-(aq) + H_2O(l) \rightleftharpoons HCN(aq) + OH^-(aq)$
(c) $(CH_3)_3N(g) + BF_3(g) \rightleftharpoons (CH_3)_3NBF_3(s)$
(d) $HIO(lq) + NH_2^-(lq) \rightleftharpoons NH_3(l) + IO^-(lq)$
    (lq denotes liquid ammonia as solvent)

16.74. Identify the Lewis acid and Lewis base in each of the following reactions:
(a) $HNO_2(aq) + OH^-(aq) \rightleftharpoons NO_2^-(aq) + H_2O(l)$
(b) $FeBr_3(s) + Br^-(aq) \rightleftharpoons FeBr_4^-(aq)$
(c) $Zn^{2+}(aq) + 4NH_3(aq) \rightleftharpoons Zn(NH_3)_4^{2+}(aq)$
(d) $SO_2(g) + H_2O(l) \rightleftharpoons H_2SO_3(aq)$

16.75. Which member of each of the following pairs would you expect to produce the more acidic aqueous solution: **(a)** LiI or CdI_2; **(b)** $Fe(NO_3)_3$ or $Ca(NO_3)_2$; **(c)** $CrCl_2$ or $CrCl_3$?

16.76. Which member of each of the following pairs would you expect to be the stronger Lewis acid: **(a)** BH_4^- or BH_3; **(b)** S_8 or SO_3; **(c)** NaH or HBr; **(d)** Mo^{4+} or Zn^{2+}?

Additional Exercises

16.77. Calculate $[H^+]$ for each of the following solutions: **(a)** urine, pH 6.1; **(b)** lemon juice, pH 2.1; **(c)** gastric juice, pH 1.4; **(d)** household ammonia, pH 11.9. Indicate in each case whether the solution is acidic, basic, or neutral.

16.78. Arrange the following bases in order of their tendency to combine with protons, putting the strongest base first: NH_3, H_2O, OH^-, $C_2H_3O_2^-$, Br^-.

[16.79]. Liquid ammonia can undergo the following autoionization reaction:

$$NH_3(l) + NH_3(l) \rightleftharpoons NH_4^+(lq) + NH_2^-(lq)$$

The phase lq indicates that the ion is dissolved in liquid ammonia. **(a)** Identify the conjugate acid-base pairs in the above equilibrium. **(b)** Write the equilibrium expression for the above equilibrium. **(c)** It is customary to exclude $[NH_3(l)]$ from the equilibrium expression for part (b). Explain. **(d)** At $-50°C$, the value of the equilibrium constant is 1×10^{-30}. At this temperature, what is the concentration of $NH_4^+(lq)$ in pure liquid ammonia? **(e)** A solution is made by dissolving $NH_4Cl(s)$ in liquid ammonia. Is the solution "acidic," "basic," or "neutral"? Explain your answer.

16.80. The dye bromthymol blue, abbreviated HBb, is a weak acid whose ionization can be represented as

$$HBb(aq) \rightleftharpoons H^+(aq) + Bb^-(aq)$$

Which way will this equilibrium shift when NaOH is added? The acid form of the dye is yellow, whereas its conjugate base is blue. What color is the NaOH solution containing this dye?

16.81. Calculate the number of moles of each of the following substances that must be present in 0.200 L of solution to form a solution with pH 3.25: **(a)** HCl; **(b)** $HC_7H_5O_2$; **(c)** HF.

16.82. Hemoglobin plays a part in a series of equilibria involving protonation-deprotonation and oxygenation-deoxygenation. The overall reaction is approximately as follows:

$$HbH^+(aq) + O_2(aq) \rightleftharpoons HbO_2(aq) + H^+(aq)$$

(where Hb stands for hemoglobin, and HbO_2 for oxyhemoglobin). **(a)** The concentration of O_2 is higher in the lungs and lower in the tissues. What effect does high $[O_2]$ have on the position of this equilibrium? **(b)** The normal pH of blood is 7.4. What is $[H^+]$ in normal blood? Is the blood acidic, basic, or neutral? **(c)** If the blood pH is lowered by the presence of large amounts of acidic metabolism products, a condition known as *acidosis* results. What effect does lowering blood pH have on the ability of hemoglobin to transport O_2?

16.83. Saccharin, a sugar substitute, is a weak acid with $pK_a = 11.68$ at $25°C$. It ionizes in aqueous solution as follows:

$$HNC_7H_4SO_3(aq) \rightleftharpoons H^+(aq) + NC_7H_4SO_3^-(aq)$$

What is the pH of a 0.10 M solution of this substance?

16.84. The active ingredient in aspirin is acetylsalicylic acid, $HC_9H_7O_4$, a monoprotic acid with $K_a = 3.3 \times 10^{-4}$ at $25°C$. What is the pH of a solution obtained by dissolving two aspirin tablets, each containing 325 mg of acetylsalicylic acid, in 250 mL of water?

[16.85]. What is the pH of a 1.0×10^{-8} M solution of HNO_3?

[16.86]. A hypothetical acid H_2X is both a strong acid and a polyprotic acid. **(a)** Calculate the pH of a 0.050 M solution of H_2X, assuming that only one proton ionizes per acid molecule. **(b)** Calculate the pH of the solution from part (a), now assuming that both protons of each acid molecule completely ionize. **(c)** In an experiment, it is observed that the pH of a 0.050 M solution of H_2X is 1.27. Comment on the relative acid strengths of H_2X and HX^-. **(d)** Would a solution of the salt NaHX be acidic, basic, or neutral? Explain.

[16.87]. What are the concentrations of H^+, $H_2PO_4^-$, HPO_4^{2-}, and PO_4^{3-} in a 0.100 M solution of H_3PO_4?

16.88. Ephedrine, a central nervous system stimulant, is used in nasal sprays as a decongestant. This compound is a weak organic base:

$$C_{10}H_{15}ON(aq) + H_2O(l) \rightleftharpoons$$
$$C_{10}H_{15}ONH^+(aq) + OH^-(aq)$$

K_b has the value 1.4×10^{-4}. What pH would you expect for a 0.035 M solution of ephedrine, assuming that no other substances are present? What is the value of pK_a for the conjugate acid, ephedrine hydrochloride?

16.89. Codeine, $C_{18}H_{21}NO_3$, is a weak organic base. A 5.0×10^{-3} M solution of codeine has a pH of 9.95. Calculate the value of K_b for this substance.

[16.90]. **(a)** Using dissociation constants from Appendix D, determine the value for the equilibrium constant for each of the following reactions. (Remember that when reactions are added, the corresponding equilibrium constants are multiplied.)

(i) $HCO_3^-(aq) + OH^-(aq) \rightleftharpoons CO_3^{2-}(aq) + H_2O(l)$
(ii) $NH_4^+(aq) + CO_3^{2-}(aq) \rightleftharpoons NH_3(aq) + HCO_3^-(aq)$

(b) We usually use single arrows for reactions when the forward reaction is appreciable (K much greater than 1) or when products escape from the system so that equilibrium is not achieved. If we follow this convention, which of these equilibria might be written with a single arrow?

[16.91]. Many moderately large organic molecules containing basic nitrogen atoms are not very soluble in water as neutral molecules, but they are frequently much more soluble as their acid salts. Assuming that pH in the stomach is 2.5, indicate whether each of the following compounds would be present in the stomach as the neutral base or in the protonated form: nicotine, $K_b = 7 \times 10^{-7}$; caffeine, $K_b = 4 \times 10^{-14}$; strychnine, $K_b = 1 \times 10^{-6}$; quinine, $K_b = 1.1 \times 10^{-6}$.

[16.92]. A 1.00 m solution of HF freezes at $-1.90°C$. (a) Based on the freezing-point lowering, calculate the fraction of HF that is ionized at this temperature. (b) What is the value of K_a for HF at $-1.90°C$?

[16.93]. The amino acid glycine, $H_2N—CH_2—COOH$, can undergo the following equilibria in water:

$H_2N—CH_2—COOH + H_2O \rightleftharpoons$
$\qquad H_2N—CH_2—COO^- + H_3O^+ \qquad K_a = 4.3 \times 10^{-3}$

$H_2N—CH_2—COOH + H_2O \rightleftharpoons$
$\qquad H_3N—CH_2—COOH^+ + OH^- \qquad K_b = 6.0 \times 10^{-5}$

(a) Use the values of K_a and K_b to estimate the equilibrium constant for the intramolecular proton transfer to form a zwitterion:

$\qquad H_2N—CH_2—COOH \rightleftharpoons {}^+H_3N—CH_2—COO^-$

What assumptions did you need to make?
(b) What is the pH of a 0.050 M aqueous solution of glycine?
(c) What would be the predominant form of glycine in a solution with pH 13? With pH 1?

16.94. The K_a values for phenol, C_6H_5OH, and benzoic acid, C_6H_5COOH, are both listed in Table 16.2. Based on the chemical structure of these two compounds, explain why one is a stronger acid than the other.

[16.95]. The Lewis structure for acetic acid is shown in Table 16.2. Replacement of hydrogen atoms on the carbon by chlorine atoms causes an increase in acidity, as follows:

Acid	Formula	$K_a(25°C)$
Acetic	CH_3COOH	1.8×10^{-5}
Chloroacetic	$CH_2ClCOOH$	1.4×10^{-3}
Dichloroacetic	$CHCl_2COOH$	3.3×10^{-2}
Trichloroacetic	CCl_3COOH	2×10^{-1}

Using Lewis structures as the basis of your discussion, explain the observed trend in acidities in the series. Calculate the pH of a 0.10 M solution of each acid.

17 Additional Aspects of Aqueous Equilibria

A coral reef in the western Pacific Ocean. Coral reefs are formed by the deposition of solid carbonates from dissolved minerals and carbon dioxide in the ocean water.

Water is the most common and most important solvent on this planet. In a sense, it is the solvent of life. It is difficult to imagine how living matter in all its complexity could exist with any liquid other than water as solvent. Water occupies its position of importance not only because of its abundance but also because of its exceptional ability to dissolve a wide variety of substances. Aqueous solutions encountered in nature, such as biological fluids and seawater, contain many solutes. Consequently, many equilibria take place simultaneously in these solutions.

In this chapter, we take a step toward understanding such complex solutions by looking first at further applications of acid-base equilibria. We then broaden our discussion to include two additional types of aqueous equilibria, those involving slightly soluble salts and those forming metal complexes in solution.

17.1 The Common-Ion Effect

In Chapter 16, we examined the equilibrium concentrations of ions in solutions containing a weak acid or a weak base. We now consider solutions that contain not only a weak acid, such as acetic acid, $HC_2H_3O_2$, but also a soluble salt of that acid, such as $NaC_2H_3O_2$. What happens when $NaC_2H_3O_2$ is added to a solution of $HC_2H_3O_2$? Because $C_2H_3O_2^-$ is a weak base, it isn't surprising that the pH of the solution increases; that is, $[H^+]$ decreases. However, we will find it instructive to view this effect from the perspective of Le Châtelier's principle. ∞ (Sec. 15.6)

Like most salts, $NaC_2H_3O_2$ is a strong electrolyte. Consequently, it dissociates completely in aqueous solution to form Na^+ and $C_2H_3O_2^-$ ions. On the other hand, $HC_2H_3O_2$ is a weak electrolyte that ionizes as follows:

$$HC_2H_3O_2(aq) \rightleftharpoons H^+(aq) + C_2H_3O_2^-(aq) \qquad [17.1]$$

The addition of $C_2H_3O_2^-$, from $NaC_2H_3O_2$, causes this equilibrium to shift to the left, thereby decreasing the equilibrium concentration of $H^+(aq)$:

$$HC_2H_3O_2(aq) \rightleftharpoons H^+(aq) + C_2H_3O_2^-(aq)$$

Addition of $C_2H_3O_2^-$ shifts equilibrium, reducing $[H^+]$

We see that the dissociation of the weak acid $HC_2H_3O_2$ decreases when we add the strong electrolyte $NaC_2H_3O_2$, which has an ion in common with it. We can generalize this observation, which we call the **common-ion effect:** The dissociation of a weak electrolyte is decreased by adding to the solution a strong electrolyte that has an ion in common with the weak electrolyte. Sample Exercises 17.1 and 17.2 illustrate how equilibrium concentrations may be calculated when a solution contains a mixture of a weak electrolyte and a strong electrolyte that have a common ion. You will see that the procedures are similar to those encountered for weak acids and weak bases in Chapter 16.

Point of Emphasis: In this situation, the soluble salt of the weak acid's conjugate base is simply a source of the conjugate base.

Point of Emphasis: The common-ion effect is predicted from Le Châtelier's principle.

Learning Goal 1: Predict qualitatively and calculate quantitatively the effect of an added common ion on the pH of an aqueous solution of a weak acid or base.

SAMPLE EXERCISE 17.1

What is the pH of a solution made by adding 0.30 mol of acetic acid, $HC_2H_3O_2$, and 0.30 mol of sodium acetate, $NaC_2H_3O_2$, to enough water to make 1.0 L of solution?

SOLUTION In any problem in which we need to determine the pH of a solution containing a mixture of solutes, it is helpful to proceed by a series of logical steps:

First, identify the major species in solution and consider their acidity or basicity. Because $HC_2H_3O_2$ is a weak electrolyte and $NaC_2H_3O_2$ is a strong electrolyte, the major species in the solution are $HC_2H_3O_2$ (a weak acid), Na^+ (which is neither acidic nor basic), $C_2H_3O_2^-$ (which is the conjugate base of $HC_2H_3O_2$), and H_2O (which is a very weak acid or base).

Second, identify the important equilibrium reaction. Because H_2O is a much weaker acid than $HC_2H_3O_2$, the pH of the solution will be controlled by the dissociation equilibrium of $HC_2H_3O_2$, which involves both $HC_2H_3O_2$ and $C_2H_3O_2^-$:

$$HC_2H_3O_2(aq) + H_2O(l) \rightleftharpoons H_3O^+(aq) + C_2H_3O_2^-(aq)$$

(We could, of course, have written this equilibrium using $H^+(aq)$, as we did in Equation 17.1.) Remember that because $NaC_2H_3O_2$ was added to the solution, the values of $[H_3O^+]$ and $[C_2H_3O_2^-]$ are not the same. The Na^+ ion is merely a spectator ion and will have no influence on the pH. ∞ (Sec. 16.8)

Third, calculate the initial and equilibrium concentrations of each of the species that participates in the equilibrium. We can tabulate the concentrations much as we have in solving other equilibrium problems. ∞ (Sec. 15.5)

$$HC_2H_3O_2(aq) + H_2O(l) \rightleftharpoons H_3O^+(aq) + C_2H_3O_2^-(aq)$$

Initial	0.30 M	—	0	0.30 M
Change	$-x$ M	—	$+x$ M	$+x$ M
Equilibrium	$(0.30 - x)$ M	—	x M	$(0.30 + x)$ M

Notice that the equilibrium concentration of $C_2H_3O_2^-$ (the common ion) is the initial concentration due to the $NaC_2H_3O_2$ (0.30 M) plus the change in concentration (x) due to the ionization of $HC_2H_3O_2$.

The equilibrium expression is

$$K_a = 1.8 \times 10^{-5} = \frac{[H_3O^+][C_2H_3O_2^-]}{[HC_2H_3O_2]}$$

(The dissociation constant for $HC_2H_3O_2$ at 25°C is from Appendix D; addition of $NaC_2H_3O_2$ does not change the value of this constant.) Substituting the equilibrium concentrations into the equilibrium expression gives

$$K_a = 1.8 \times 10^{-5} = \frac{x(0.30 + x)}{0.30 - x}$$

Because K_a is small, we assume that x is small compared to the original concentrations of $HC_2H_3O_2$ and $C_2H_3O_2^-$ (0.30 M each). We can therefore simplify our equation before solving for x:

$$K_a = 1.8 \times 10^{-5} \approx \frac{x(0.30)}{0.30}$$

$$x = 1.8 \times 10^{-5} M = [H_3O^+]$$

The resulting value of x is indeed small relative to 0.30, justifying the approximation made in simplifying the problem.

Fourth, calculate the pH from the equilibrium concentration of $H_3O^+(aq)$:

$$pH = -\log(1.8 \times 10^{-5}) = 4.74$$

In Section 16.5 we calculated that a 0.30 M solution of $HC_2H_3O_2$ has a pH of 2.64, corresponding to $[H_3O^+] = 2.3 \times 10^{-3}$ M. Thus, the addition of $NaC_2H_3O_2$ has substantially decreased $[H_3O^+]$, as expected from Le Châtelier's principle.

PRACTICE EXERCISE

Calculate the pH of a solution containing 0.16 M nitrous acid, HNO_2 ($K_a = 4.5 \times 10^{-4}$), and 0.10 M potassium nitrite, KNO_2. **Answer:** 3.14

SAMPLE EXERCISE 17.2

Calculate the fluoride-ion concentration and pH of a solution containing 0.10 mol of HCl and 0.20 mol of HF in 1.0 L of solution.

SOLUTION   Because HCl is a strong acid and HF is a weak acid, the major species in solution are H^+, Cl^-, HF, and the solvent, H_2O. The problem asks for $[F^-]$, which is formed by ionization of HF. Thus, the important equilibrium is

$$HF(aq) \rightleftharpoons H^+(aq) + F^-(aq)$$

Note that we have written the equilibrium in terms of $H^+(aq)$ rather than $H_3O^+(aq)$. Both representations of the hydrated hydrogen ion are equally valid.

Now we can tabulate the initial and equilibrium concentrations of each species involved in this equilibrium (the Cl^- is merely a spectator ion):

	$HF(aq)$	$\rightleftharpoons$	$H^+(aq)$	$+$	$F^-(aq)$
Initial	0.20 M		0.10 M		0
Change	$-x$ M		$+x$ M		$+x$ M
Equilibrium	$(0.20 - x)$ M		$(0.10 + x)$ M		x M

The equilibrium constant, from Appendix D, is 6.8×10^{-4}. Thus,

$$K_a = 6.8 \times 10^{-4} = \frac{[H^+][F^-]}{[HF]} = \frac{(0.10 + x)(x)}{0.20 - x}$$

If we assume that x is small relative to 0.10 or 0.20 M, this expression simplifies to give

$$\frac{(0.10)(x)}{0.20} = 6.8 \times 10^{-4}$$

$$x = \frac{0.20}{0.10}(6.8 \times 10^{-4}) = 1.4 \times 10^{-3} \, M = [F^-]$$

This F^- concentration is substantially smaller than it would be in a 0.20 M solution of HF with no added HCl. The common ion, H^+, has repressed the dissociation of HF. The concentration of $H^+(aq)$ is

$$[H^+] = (0.10 + x) \, M \approx 0.10 \, M$$

Thus, pH = 1.00. Notice that $[H^+]$ is for all practical purposes due entirely to the HCl; the HF makes a negligible contribution by comparison.

PRACTICE EXERCISE

Calculate the formate-ion concentration and pH of a solution that is 0.050 M in formic acid, $HCHO_2$ ($K_a = 1.8 \times 10^{-4}$), and 0.100 M in HNO_3. **Answer:** $[CHO_2^-] = 9.0 \times 10^{-5}$; pH = 1.00

Sample Exercises 17.1 and 17.2 both involve weak acids. The ionization of a weak base is also decreased by the addition of a common ion. For example, the addition of NH_4^+ (as from the strong electrolyte NH_4Cl) causes the base-dissociation equilibrium of NH_3 to shift to the left, decreasing the equilibrium concentration of OH^- and lowering the pH:

$$NH_3(aq) + H_2O(l) \rightleftharpoons NH_4^+(aq) + OH^-(aq) \qquad [17.2]$$

Addition of NH_4^+ shifts equilibrium, reducing $[OH^-]$

17.2 Acid-Base Titrations

Learning Goal 2: Calculate the concentration of each species present in a solution formed by mixing an acid and a base.

We have seen that we need to consider the common-ion effect whenever we have a solution that contains both a weak acid and its conjugate base in appreciable concentrations. We encounter such solutions when we examine acid-base reactions. For example, in Section 4.7 we briefly described acid-base *titration*, a common procedure in which we quantitatively add a base to an acid or an acid to a base. We noted that acid-base indicators can be used to signal the equivalence point of a titration (the point at which stoichiometrically equivalent quantities of acid and base have been brought together). In this section, we shall examine more closely how the pH of a solution changes during a titration.

Learning Goal 3: Describe the form of the titration curves for titration of a strong acid by a strong base, a weak acid by a strong base, or a strong acid by a weak base.

A graph of pH as a function of added titrant is called a **titration curve**. A typical apparatus for measuring a titration curve is illustrated in Figure 17.1. The titrant is added to the solution by buret, and the pH is continually monitored by using a pH meter (Figure 16.6). We shall first examine the titration curves of strong acids and strong bases, in which the only important reaction is the neutralization reaction between $H^+(aq)$ and $OH^-(aq)$. We shall then ad-

FIGURE 17.1 A typical setup for using a pH meter to measure a titration curve. In this case, a standard solution of NaOH (the titrant) is added by buret to a solution of HCl that is to be titrated. The solution is stirred during the titration to ensure uniform composition.

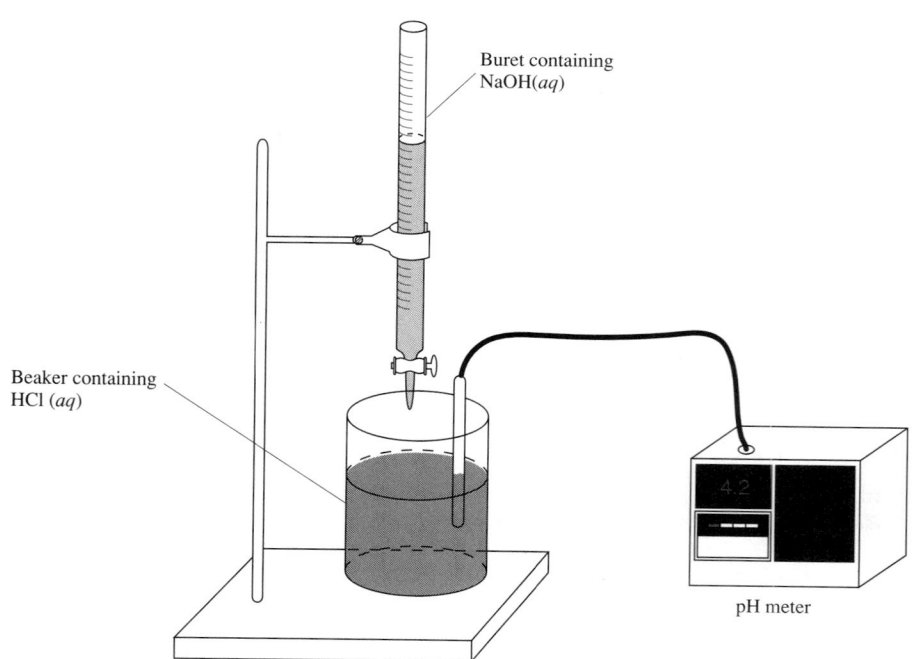

Buret containing NaOH(*aq*)

Beaker containing HCl (*aq*)

pH meter

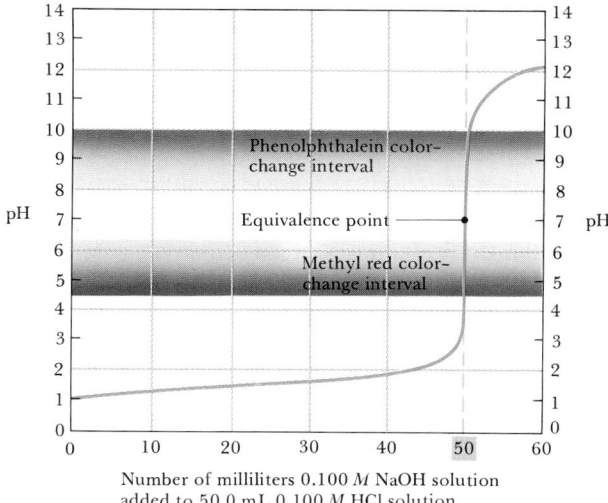

Figure 17.2

FIGURE 17.2 The pH curve for titration of a solution of a strong acid with a solution of a strong base, in this case HCl and NaOH.

Number of milliliters 0.100 M NaOH solution added to 50.0 mL 0.100 M HCl solution

dress titrations involving weak acids and bases, which will require more careful consideration of the common-ion effect.

Strong Acid–Strong Base Titrations

The titration curve produced when a strong base is added to a strong acid has the general shape shown in Figure 17.2. This curve depicts the pH change that occurs as 0.100 M NaOH is added to 50.0 mL of 0.100 M HCl. The pH can be calculated at various stages of the titration. The pH of the solution before the addition of any base is determined by the initial concentration of the strong acid: pH $= -\log(0.100) = 1.000$ for 0.100 M HCl. Thus, the pH starts out low.

As NaOH is added, the pH increases slowly at first and then rapidly in the vicinity of the equivalence point. The pH of the solution before the equivalence point is determined by the concentration of acid that has not yet been neutralized by base. The pH at the equivalence point is the pH of the resultant salt solution. Because the salt produced by the reaction of a strong acid and a strong base (in this case NaCl) does not hydrolyze (Section 16.8), the equivalence point occurs at pH 7.00. The pH of the solution after the equivalence point is determined by the concentration of the excess base in the solution.

Common Misconception: Students often believe that the pH at the equivalence point is 7.00 (neutral). The pH at the equivalence point is 7.00 *only* for a strong acid-strong base titration.

SAMPLE EXERCISE 17.3

Calculate the pH when the following quantities of 0.100 M NaOH solution have been added to 50.00 mL of 0.100 M HCl solution: **(a)** 49.00 mL; **(b)** 49.90 mL; **(c)** 50.10 mL; **(d)** 51.00 mL.

Learning Goal 4: Calculate the pH at any point, including the equivalence point, in acid-base titrations.

SOLUTION   (a) As the NaOH solution is added to the HCl solution, H$^+$(aq) reacts with OH$^-$(aq) to form H$_2$O. In order to determine the pH of the resultant solution, we must first determine how many moles of H$^+$ were originally present and how many moles of OH$^-$ were added. We can then calculate how many moles of each ion remain after the neutralization reaction. In order to calculate [H$^+$], and hence pH, we must also remember that the volume of the solution increases as we add titrant to the solution, thus diluting the concentration of all solutes present.

The number of moles of H$^+$ in the original solution is

$$(0.05000 \text{ L soln}) \left(\frac{0.100 \text{ mol H}^+}{1 \text{ L soln}} \right) = 5.00 \times 10^{-3} \text{ mol H}^+$$

and the number of moles of OH^- in 49.00 mL of 0.100 M NaOH is

$$(0.04900 \text{ L soln}) \left(\frac{0.100 \text{ mol } OH^-}{1 \text{ L soln}} \right) = 4.90 \times 10^{-3} \text{ mol } H^+$$

Thus, there are more moles of H^+ present than OH^-. Each mole of OH^- will react with a mole of H^+, leaving

$$(5.00 \times 10^{-3} \text{ mol}) - (4.90 \times 10^{-3} \text{ mol}) = 1.0 \times 10^{-4} \text{ mol } H^+(aq)$$

After the titrant has been added, the solution has a volume of 50.00 mL + 49.00 mL = 99.00 mL (we assume that the volumes can be added). Thus, the concentration of $H^+(aq)$ is

$$\frac{1.0 \times 10^{-4} \text{ mol}}{0.0990 \text{ L soln}} = 1.0 \times 10^{-3} \ M$$

The corresponding pH is 3.00.

To answer (b), (c), and (d) of the exercise we proceed in the same way. In each case, we calculate the amount of added OH^-, compare that with the amount of H^+ originally present, and determine what amount of H^+ or OH^- exists in excess over the other. The concentration is then calculated from a knowledge of the total volume of the solution. By proceeding in this way we can construct a table of pH versus volume of added NaOH solution, as shown in Table 17.1. By graphing the pH as a function of the volume of added NaOH, we obtain the titration curve shown in Figure 17.2.

PRACTICE EXERCISE

Calculate the pH when the following quantities of 0.100 M HCl have been added to 25.00 mL of 0.100 M NaOH solution: (a) 24.90 mL; (b) 25.00 mL; (c) 25.10 mL. *Answers:* (a) 10.30; (b) 7.00; (c) 3.70

Because the pH change for a strong acid–strong base titration is very large near the equivalence point, the indicator for the titration need not change color precisely at 7.00. Most strong acid–strong base titrations are carried out using phenolphthalein as an indicator, because its color change is dramatic (Figure 17.3). From Figure 16.7, we see that this indicator changes color in the pH range 8.3 to 10. Thus, a slight excess of NaOH must be present to cause the observed color change. However, such a tiny excess of base is required to bring about the color change that no serious error is introduced. Similarly, methyl red, which changes color in the slightly acidic range (Figure 17.4), could also be used.

Titration of a solution of a strong base with a solution of a strong acid would yield an entirely analogous curve of pH versus added acid. In this case, however, the pH would be high at the outset of the titration and low at its completion, as shown in Figure 17.5.

TABLE 17.1 △ Titration of 50.00 mL of 0.100 M HCl Solution with 0.100 M NaOH Solution

Volume of HCl	Volume of NaOH	Total volume	Moles H^+	Moles OH^-	Molarity of excess ion	pH
50.00	0.00	50.00	5.00×10^{-3}	0.00	0.100	1.00
50.00	49.00	99.00	5.00×10^{-3}	4.90×10^{-3}	1.0×10^{-3} (H^+)	3.00
50.00	49.90	99.90	5.00×10^{-3}	4.99×10^{-3}	1×10^{-4} (H^+)	4.0
50.00	50.10	100.10	5.00×10^{-3}	5.01×10^{-3}	1×10^{-4} (OH^-)	10.0
50.00	51.00	101.00	5.00×10^{-3}	5.10×10^{-3}	1.0×10^{-3} (OH^-)	11.00
50.00	60.00	110.00	5.00×10^{-3}	6.00×10^{-3}	9.09×10^{-3} (OH^-)	11.96

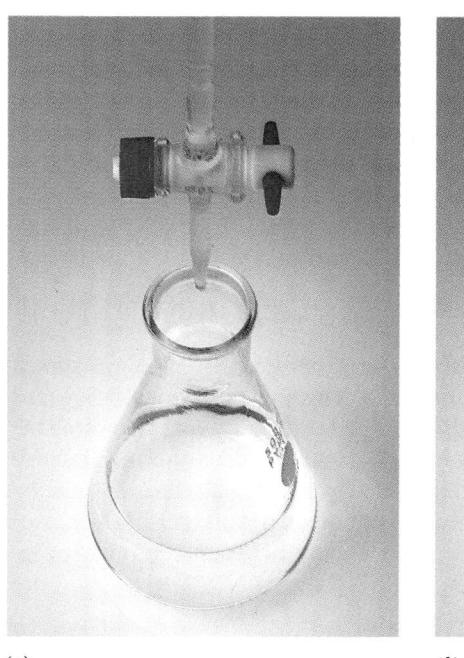

(a)

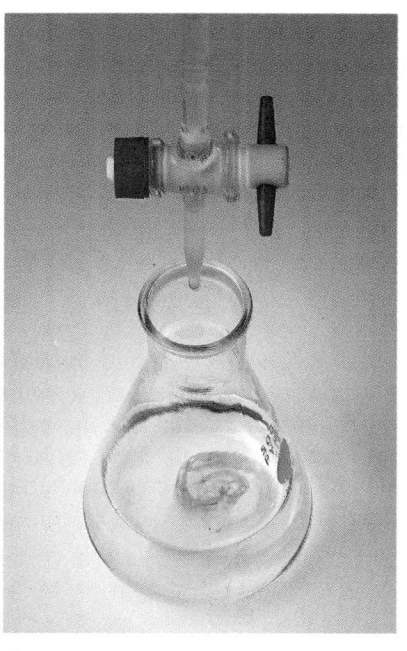

(b)

(c)

FIGURE 17.3 Change in appearance of a solution containing phenolphthalein indicator as base is added. Before the endpoint, the solution is colorless (*a*). As the endpoint is approached, a pale pink color forms where the base is added (*b*). At the endpoint, this pale pink color extends throughout the solution after the mixing. As more base is added, the intensity of the pink color increases (*c*). (© Richard Megna/Fundamental Photographs)

(a)

(b)

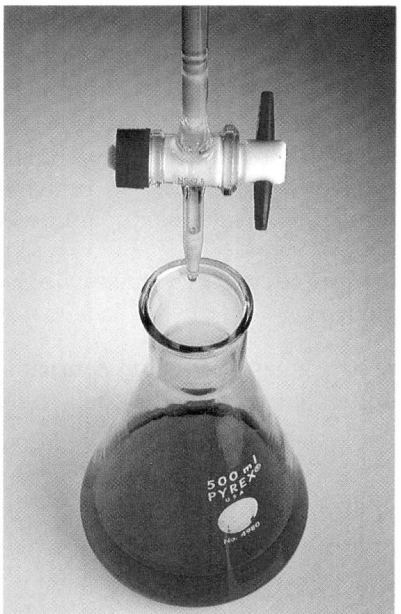

FIGURE 17.4 Change in appearance of a solution containing methyl red indicator in the pH range 4.2 to 6.3. The characteristic acid color is shown in (*a*), the characteristic basic color in (*b*). (Fundamental Photographs)

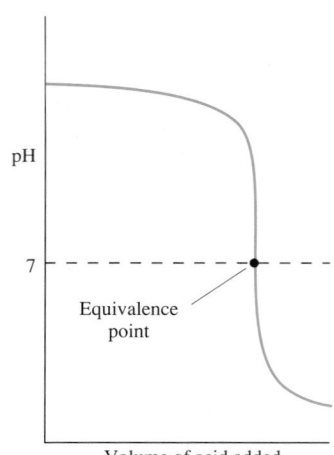

pH

7

Equivalence
point

Volume of acid added

FIGURE 17.5 The pH
curve for titration of a strong
base with a strong acid.

The Addition of a Strong Base to a Weak Acid

The titration of a weak acid by a strong base is slightly more complicated than the titration of a strong acid by a strong base: The conjugate base of a weak acid will undergo hydrolysis, which will affect the pH of the solution. Thus, we need to consider the stoichiometric reaction between the acid and the base *and* the equilibrium reactions of the species that remain.

Consider a solution formed by mixing acetic acid, $HC_2H_3O_2$, with the strong base NaOH. The net ionic equation for the reaction that occurs is

$$HC_2H_3O_2(aq) + OH^-(aq) \longrightarrow C_2H_3O_2^-(aq) + H_2O(l) \quad [17.3]$$

The reaction between a weak acid and a strong base (or between a weak base and a strong acid) proceeds essentially to completion. Thus, in Equation 17.3, each mole of OH^- ions consumes one mole of $HC_2H_3O_2$ and produces one mole of $C_2H_3O_2^-$ ions. If the number of moles of $HC_2H_3O_2$ exceeds the number of moles of NaOH, there will be unreacted $HC_2H_3O_2$ left after all the OH^- reacts according to Equation 17.3. To calculate the pH of the resultant solution, we will need to consider the proton transfer that occurs between the remaining $HC_2H_3O_2$ and H_2O, generating $C_2H_3O_2^-$ and H_3O^+:

$$HC_2H_3O_2(aq) + H_2O(l) \rightleftharpoons C_2H_3O_2^-(aq) + H_3O^+(aq) \quad [17.4]$$

For example, consider a 1.0-L solution that initially contains 0.20 mol of $HC_2H_3O_2$ and 0.10 mol of NaOH. The neutralization reaction (Equation 17.3) consumes all of the OH^- and 0.10 mol of $HC_2H_3O_2$, producing 0.10 mol of $C_2H_3O_2^-$ and leaving 0.10 mol of unreacted $HC_2H_3O_2$:

$$HC_2H_3O_2(aq) + OH^-(aq) \longrightarrow C_2H_3O_2^-(aq) + H_2O(l)$$

	$HC_2H_3O_2(aq)$	$OH^-(aq)$	$C_2H_3O_2^-(aq)$	$H_2O(l)$
Before rxn	0.20 mol	0.10 mol	0	—
Change	−0.10 mol	−0.10 mol	+0.10 mol	—
After rxn	0.10 mol	0	0.10 mol	—

The resulting solution is 0.10 M in $C_2H_3O_2^-$ and 0.10 M in $HC_2H_3O_2$, which is identical to a solution produced by mixing 0.10 mol of $NaC_2H_3O_2$ and 0.10 mol of $HC_2H_3O_2$ to form 1.0 L of solution. To obtain the pH of this solution, we use Equation 17.4, just as we did in Sample Exercise 17.1. In that exercise, we saw that the pH of a solution that contains equal molar quantities of $HC_2H_3O_2$ and $C_2H_3O_2^-$ is 4.74.

This example suggests a general two-step procedure for calculating pH whenever a strong base is added to a weak acid:

1. *Stoichiometric calculation:* We allow the strong base to react to completion with the weak acid, producing a solution that contains the weak acid and its conjugate base.
2. *Equilibrium calculation:* We use the value of K_a and the equilibrium expression to calculate the equilibrium concentrations of the weak acid, its conjugate base, and H^+ (or H_3O^+).

This general procedure is diagramed in Figure 17.6. The procedure for the addition of a strong acid to a weak base is analogous.

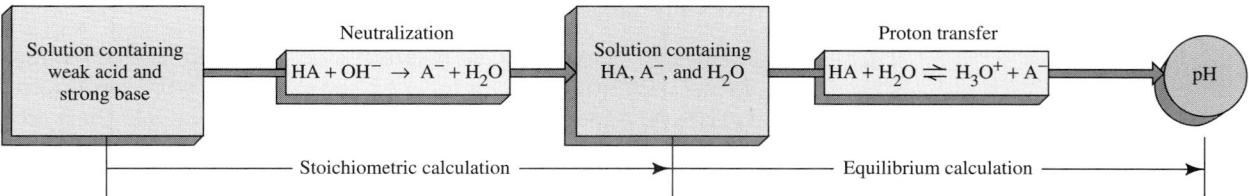

Neutralization — $HA + OH^- \longrightarrow A^- + H_2O$

Proton transfer — $HA + H_2O \rightleftharpoons H_3O^+ + A^-$

Solution containing weak acid and strong base

Solution containing HA, A⁻, and H₂O

pH

Stoichiometric calculation ———————————→ Equilibrium calculation ———————————→

FIGURE 17.6 Outline of the procedure used to calculate the pH of a mixture in which a weak acid has been partially neutralized by strong base. An analogous procedure can be used for the addition of strong acid to a weak base.

We will use the procedures described above for calculating the pH as we titrate a weak acid with a strong base (or a weak base with a strong acid), as illustrated in Sample Exercise 17.4.

 Figure 17.6

SAMPLE EXERCISE 17.4

Calculate the pH in the titration of acetic acid by NaOH after 30.0 mL of 0.100 M NaOH has been added to 50.0 mL of 0.100 M acetic acid.

SOLUTION *Stoichiometric calculation:* The number of moles of $HC_2H_3O_2$ originally in the solution is

$$\left(\frac{0.100 \text{ mol } HC_2H_3O_2}{1 \text{ L soln}}\right)(0.0500 \text{ L soln}) = 5.00 \times 10^{-3} \text{ mol } HC_2H_3O_2$$

Similarly, 30.0 mL of 0.100 M NaOH solution contains 3.00×10^{-3} mol of OH^-. During the titration, this OH^- reacts with the acetic acid:

	$OH^-(aq)$ +	$HC_2H_3O_2(aq)$ $\longrightarrow$	$C_2H_3O_2^-(aq)$ +	$H_2O(l)$
Before rxn	3.00×10^{-3} mol	5.00×10^{-3} mol	0	—
Change	-3.00×10^{-3} mol	-3.00×10^{-3} mol	$+3.00 \times 10^{-3}$ mol	—
After rxn	0	2.00×10^{-3} mol	3.00×10^{-3} mol	—

The total volume of the solution is 30.0 mL + 50.0 mL = 80.0 mL. The resulting molarities are thus

$$[HC_2H_3O_2] = \frac{2.00 \times 10^{-3} \text{ mol } HC_2H_3O_2}{0.0800 \text{ L}} = 0.0250 \ M$$

$$[C_2H_3O_2^-] = \frac{3.00 \times 10^{-3} \text{ mol } C_2H_3O_2^-}{0.0800 \text{ L}} = 0.0375 \ M$$

Equilibrium calculation:
For the weak-acid dissociation equilibrium of $HC_2H_3O_2(aq)$, we have

$$K_a = \frac{[H^+][C_2H_3O_2^-]}{[HC_2H_3O_2]} = 1.8 \times 10^{-5}$$

$$[H^+] = K_a \frac{[HC_2H_3O_2]}{[C_2H_3O_2^-]} = (1.8 \times 10^{-5})\left(\frac{0.0250}{0.0375}\right) = 1.2 \times 10^{-5} \ M$$

$$pH = -\log(1.2 \times 10^{-5}) = 4.92$$

PRACTICE EXERCISE

Calculate the pH in the titration of ammonia by hydrochloric acid after 15.0 mL of 0.100 M HCl has been added to 25.0 mL of 0.100 M $NH_3(aq)$ solution.
Answer: 9.08

17.2 Acid-Base Titrations **623**

Titration Curves for Weak Acids or Weak Bases

Titration of a weak acid by a strong base results in pH curves similar to those for strong acid–strong base titrations. Figure 17.7 shows the pH curve produced when 50.0 mL of 0.100 M acetic acid is titrated with 0.100 M NaOH. There are three noteworthy differences between this curve and that for a strong acid–strong base titration (Figure 17.2):

1. The solution of the weak acid has a higher initial pH than a solution of a strong acid of the same concentration.
2. The pH rises more rapidly in the early part of the titration but more slowly near the equivalence point.
3. The pH at the equivalence point is *not* 7.00.

To illustrate these differences further, consider the family of titration curves shown in Figure 17.8. As expected, the initial pH of the weak-acid solutions is always higher than that of the strong-acid solution of the same concentration. Notice also that the pH change near the equivalence point becomes less marked as the acid becomes weaker (that is, as K_a becomes smaller). Finally, the pH at the equivalence point steadily increases as K_a decreases. Remember that the pH at the equivalence point in any acid-base titration is the pH of the resultant salt solution. For example, in the titration illustrated in Figure 17.7, the solution contains 0.050 M NaC$_2$H$_3$O$_2$ at the equivalence point. We can calculate the pH of salt solutions using methods developed in Chapter 16 (see, for example, Sample Exercise 16.15). The pH of a 0.050 M NaC$_2$H$_3$O$_2$ solution is 8.71.

Before the equivalence point is reached, the neutralization reaction results in a solution containing a mixture of the weak acid and its salt. We considered the calculation of the pH of these solutions in Sample Exercise 17.4. At the equivalence point, the solution contains only the salt. For the salt of a weak acid and strong base, the solution will be weakly basic because of the

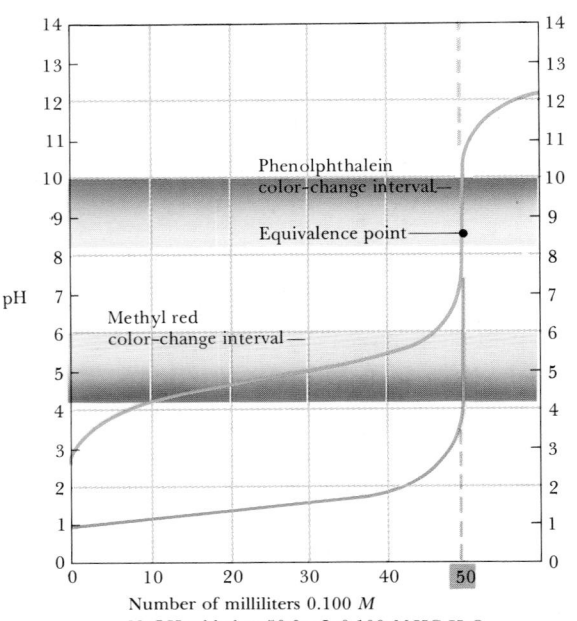

FIGURE 17.7 The green line shows the variation in pH as 0.100 M NaOH solution is added in the titration of 0.100 M acetic acid solution. The blue line segment shows the graph of pH versus added base for the titration of 0.100 M HCl.

Figure 17.7

FIGURE 17.8 Influence of acid strength on the shape of the curve for titration with NaOH. Each curve represents titration of 50.0 mL of 0.10 M acid with 0.10 M NaOH.

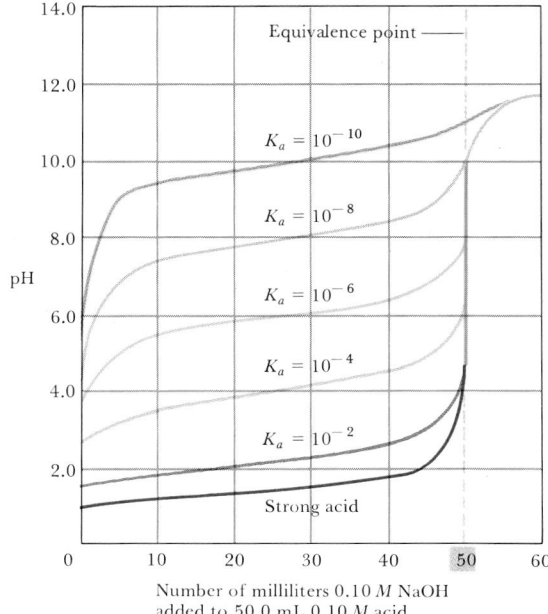

Equivalence point ──

$K_a = 10^{-10}$

$K_a = 10^{-8}$

$K_a = 10^{-6}$

$K_a = 10^{-4}$

$K_a = 10^{-2}$

Strong acid

Number of milliliters 0.10 M NaOH added to 50.0 mL 0.10 M acid

Figure 17.8

hydrolysis of the anion. After the equivalence point, the solution contains a mixture of the salt and the excess strong base; the pH of such solutions is controlled mainly by the concentration of the excess base. The calculation of this pH is the same as that for points after the equivalence point in the titration of a strong acid with a strong base.

SAMPLE EXERCISE 17.5

Calculate the pH when the following quantities of 0.0500 M KOH solution have been added to 50.0 mL of a 0.0250 M solution of benzoic acid, $HC_7H_5O_2$ ($K_a = 6.5 \times 10^{-5}$): **(a)** 20.0 mL; **(b)** 25.0 mL; **(c)** 30.0 mL.

SOLUTION **(a)** In this case, we have not added enough KOH solution to reach the equivalence point. Thus, we must calculate the pH by using a procedure similar to that used in Sample Exercise 17.4. First, we perform the *stoichiometric calculation:* The number of moles of $HC_7H_5O_2$ initially present in the solution is (0.0250 mol/L)(0.0500 L) = 1.25×10^{-3} mol. To this solution we are adding (0.0500 mol/L)(0.0200 L) = 1.00×10^{-3} mol of KOH. Thus, after the neutralization reaction, we are left with 70.0 mL of solution that contains both $HC_7H_5O_2$ and benzoate ions, $C_7H_5O_2^-$. The concentrations of these species will be

$$[HC_7H_5O_2] = \frac{1.25 \times 10^{-3} \text{ mol} - 1.00 \times 10^{-3} \text{ mol}}{0.0700 \text{ L}} = 3.57 \times 10^{-3} \, M$$

$$[C_7H_5O_2^-] = \frac{1.00 \times 10^{-3} \text{ mol}}{0.0700 \text{ L}} = 1.43 \times 10^{-2} \, M$$

We next perform the *equilibrium calculation* to determine the pH:

$$K_a = \frac{[H^+][C_7H_5O_2^-]}{[HC_7H_5O_2]} = 6.5 \times 10^{-5}$$

$$[H^+] = K_a \frac{[HC_7H_5O_2]}{[C_7H_5O_2^-]} = (6.5 \times 10^{-5})\left(\frac{0.00357}{0.0143}\right) = 1.6 \times 10^{-5} \, M$$

$$pH = -\log(1.6 \times 10^{-5}) = 4.80$$

Notice that $[H^+]$ is much smaller than both $[HC_7H_5O_2]$ and $[C_7H_5O_2^-]$, which allows us to simplify the equilibrium calculation; we did not have to consider the ionization of additional benzoic acid or the further hydrolysis of the benzoate ions.

(b) Because the number of moles of KOH added equals the number of moles of benzoic acid originally present, we have reached the equivalence point of the titration. The solution is thus identical to one that contains 1.25×10^{-3} mol $KC_7H_5O_2$ in a volume of 75.0 mL, corresponding to a 0.0167 M solution. By using the procedures described in Section 16.7, the pH of a 0.0167 M solution of $KC_7H_5O_2$ is 8.20.

(c) Past the equivalence point, there is no longer any benzoic acid to neutralize the additional KOH. Thus, the pH of the solution will be governed by the amount of excess KOH. The total volume of solution is 80.0 mL, and we have added 5.0 mL of 0.050 M KOH solution beyond the equivalence point. The concentration of OH^- in this solution and the resulting pH are:

$$[OH^-] = \frac{\text{mol } OH^- \text{ past equiv. pt.}}{\text{volume of soln}} = \frac{(0.050 \text{ mol/L})(0.0050 \text{ L})}{0.0800 \text{ L}} = 3.1 \times 10^{-3} M$$

$$pH = 14.00 - pOH = 14.00 - [-\log(3.1 \times 10^{-3})] = 14.00 - 2.51 = 11.49$$

Notice that we have used three different ways of calculating the pH during a titration: one when the equivalence point has not yet been reached, one when the equivalence point is reached, and one when we have added titrant beyond the equivalence point.

PRACTICE EXERCISE

A 0.030 M solution of benzoic acid of volume 0.050 L is titrated with 0.015 M NaOH solution. Calculate the pH after the addition of (a) 0.050 L of NaOH solution; (b) 0.100 L of NaOH solution. *Answers:* (a) 4.19; (b) 8.09

It is important to note that the pH at the equivalence point in the titration of the weak acid is considerably higher than it is in the titration of the strong acid. This observation is especially important when using an indicator to signal the equivalence point. We saw earlier that in titrating 0.100 M HCl with 0.100 M NaOH, either phenolphthalein or methyl red could be used as indicator. Although the pH of color change does not correspond precisely to the equivalence point for either indicator, both were close enough that no significant error would be introduced by using either of them (Figure 17.2). In a titration of acetic acid with NaOH, phenolphthalein is an ideal indicator because it changes color just at the pH of the equivalence point. However, methyl red is not a good choice. The pH at the midrange of its color change is 5.2. At this pH we are still far short of the equivalence point, as shown in Figure 17.7.

Titration of a weak base (for example, 0.10 M NH_3) with a strong acid solution (such as 0.10 M HCl) leads to the titration curve shown in Figure 17.9. In this particular example, the equivalence point occurs at pH 5.3. Thus, methyl red would be an ideal indicator, but phenolphthalein would be a poor choice.

Point of Emphasis: In general, the best indicator for an acid-base titration is one that changes color at the same pH as that of the equivalence point.

Titrations of Polyprotic Acids

In the case of weak acids containing more than one ionizable proton, reaction with OH^- occurs in a series of steps. An important example of the kind of equilibria that occur are those involving carbonic acid, H_2CO_3. We saw in Sample Exercise 16.13 that in an aqueous solution of CO_2 the relative concentrations of the species involved are $[H_2CO_3] \gg [HCO_3^-] \gg [CO_3^{2-}]$. Neutralization of H_2CO_3 proceeds in two stages:

$$H_2CO_3(aq) + OH^-(aq) \longrightarrow HCO_3^-(aq) + H_2O(l) \qquad [17.5]$$

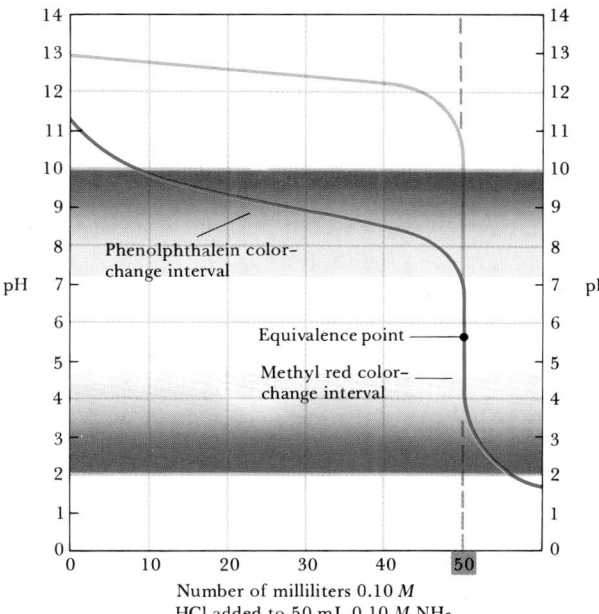

FIGURE 17.9 The red line shows pH versus volume of added HCl in the titration of 0.10 M ammonia with 0.10 M HCl. The orange line segment shows the graph of pH versus added acid for the titration of 0.10 M NaOH.

Figure 17.9

$$HCO_3^-(aq) + OH^-(aq) \longrightarrow CO_3^{2-}(aq) + H_2O(l) \qquad [17.6]$$

When the neutralization steps of a polyprotic acid or polybasic base are sufficiently separated, the substance exhibits a titration curve with multiple equivalence points. Figure 17.10 shows the titration curve for the H_2CO_3–HCO_3^-–CO_3^{2-} system. Notice that there are two distinct equivalence points along the titration curve.

FIGURE 17.10 Titration curve for the reaction of 25.0 mL of 0.10 M Na_2CO_3 with 0.10 M HCl.

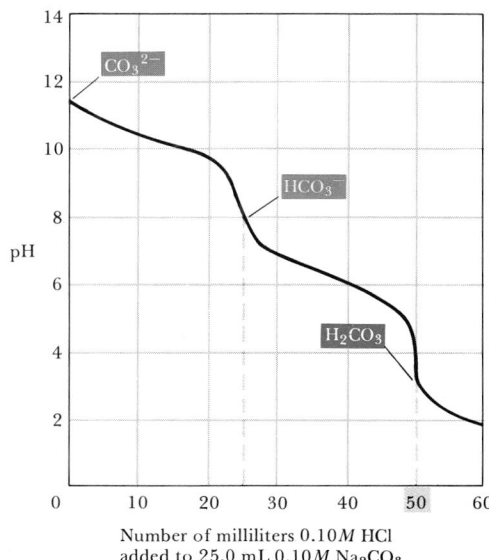

Figure 17.10

17.3 Buffered Solutions

The titration curve for titrating 0.100 M acetic acid with 0.100 M NaOH shown in Figure 17.7 reveals an important feature: a large region in which the pH changes little with the addition of titrant. For example, after 40 mL of NaOH has been added the pH is only about 1 pH unit higher than it is after 10 mL of NaOH has been added. In this portion of the titration curve, the solution seems to resist changes in pH. Solutions that resist a change in pH upon addition of small amounts of acid or base are called **buffered solutions** (or merely **buffers**). Human blood is an important example of a complex aqueous medium with a pH buffered at about 7.4 (see the Chemistry and Life box at the end of this section). Much of the chemical behavior of seawater is determined by its pH, buffered at about 8.1 to 8.3 near the surface. Buffered solutions find many important applications in the laboratory and in medicine (Figure 17.11).

Charles L. Bering, "A Good Idea Leads to a Better Buffer," *J. Chem. Educ.* 1987, 64, 803.

Composition and Action of Buffered Solutions

Learning Goal 5: Describe how a buffer solution of a particular pH is made and the reactions that allow it to control pH.

Point of Emphasis: Recall that $NH_3(aq)$ participates in an equilibrium: $NH_3(aq) + H_2O(l) \rightleftharpoons NH_4^+(aq) + OH^-(aq)$.

Buffers resist changes in pH because they contain both an acidic species to neutralize OH^- ions and a basic one to neutralize H^+ ions. It is necessary, of course, that these acidic and basic species not consume each other through a neutralization reaction. These requirements are fulfilled by a weak acid-base conjugate pair such as $HC_2H_3O_2 - C_2H_3O_2^-$ or $NH_4^+ - NH_3$. Thus, buffers are often prepared by mixing a weak acid or a weak base with a salt of that acid or base. For example, the $HC_2H_3O_2 - C_2H_3O_2^-$ buffer can be prepared by adding $NaC_2H_3O_2$ to a solution of $HC_2H_3O_2$; the $NH_4^+ - NH_3$ buffer can be prepared by adding NH_4Cl to a solution of NH_3. By choosing appropriate components and adjusting their relative concentrations, we can buffer a solution at virtually any pH.

FIGURE 17.11 Prepackaged buffer solutions and ingredients for forming buffer solutions of predetermined pH. (Donald Clegg and Roxy Wilson)

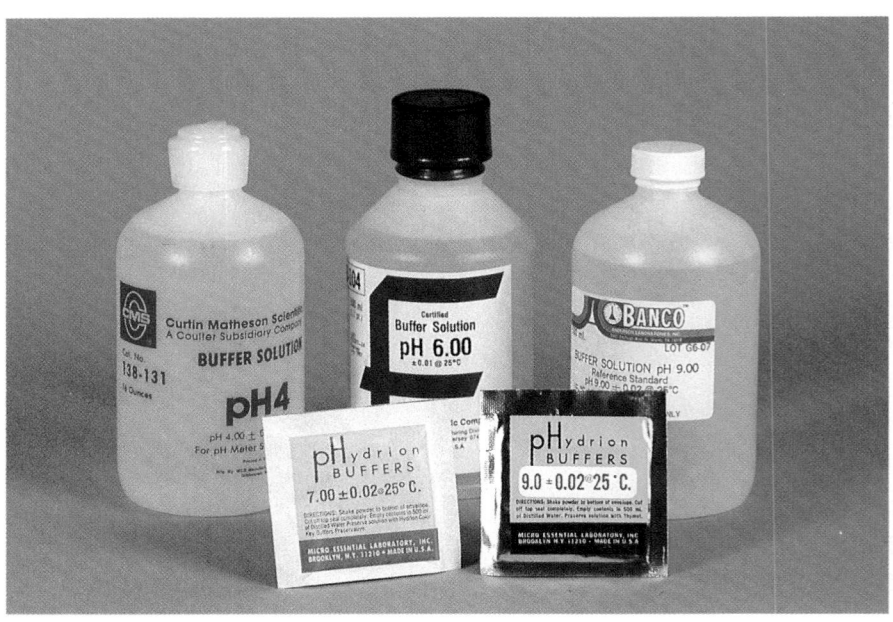

To understand better how a buffer works, consider a buffer composed of a weak acid (HX) and one of its salts (MX, where M^+ could be Na^+, K^+, or other cations). The acid-dissociation equilibrium in this buffered solution involves both the acid and its conjugate base:

$$HX(aq) \rightleftharpoons H^+(aq) + X^-(aq) \qquad [17.7]$$

The corresponding acid-dissociation-constant expression is

$$K_a = \frac{[H^+][X^-]}{[HX]} \qquad [17.8]$$

Solving this expression for $[H^+]$, we have

$$[H^+] = K_a \frac{[HX]}{[X^-]} \qquad [17.9]$$

We see from this expression that $[H^+]$, and thus the pH, is determined by two factors: the value of K_a for the weak-acid component of the buffer, and the ratio of the concentrations of the conjugate acid-base pair, $[HX]/[X^-]$.

If OH^- ions are added to the buffered solution, they react with the acid component of the buffer:

$$OH^-(aq) + HX(aq) \longrightarrow H_2O(l) + X^-(aq) \qquad [17.10]$$

This reaction causes $[HX]$ to decrease and $[X^-]$ to increase. However, as long as the amounts of HX and X^- in the buffer are large compared to the amount of OH^- added, the ratio $[HX]/[X^-]$ doesn't change much, and thus the change in pH is small.

If H^+ ions are added, they react with the base component of the buffer:

$$H^+(aq) + X^-(aq) \longrightarrow HX(aq) \qquad [17.11]$$

In this case, $[HX]$ increases and $[X^-]$ decreases. Once again, as long as the change in the ratio $[HX]/[X^-]$ is small, the change in pH will be small.

Buffers most effectively resist a change in pH in *either* direction when the concentrations of HX and X^- are about the same. Notice that under these conditions $[H^+]$ is approximately equal to K_a. For this reason, we usually try to select a buffer whose acid form has a pK_a close to the desired pH.

Buffer Capacity and pH

Two important characteristics of a buffer are its capacity and its pH. **Buffer capacity** is the amount of acid or base the buffer can neutralize before the pH begins to change to an appreciable degree. This capacity depends on the amount of acid and base from which the buffer is made. The pH of the buffer depends on K_a for the acid and on the relative concentrations of the acid and base that comprise the buffer. For example, we can see from Equation 17.9 that $[H^+]$ for a 1-L solution that is 1 M in $HC_2H_3O_2$ and 1 M in $NaC_2H_3O_2$ will be the same as for a 1-L solution that is 0.1 M in $HC_2H_3O_2$ and 0.1 M in $NaC_2H_3O_2$. However, the first solution has a greater buffering capacity because

Teaching Note: The point at which $[HX] = [X^-]$ is often called the *half-equivalence point*. At this point, the titration curve has the smallest slope.

Point of Emphasis: *Buffer capacity* is an expression of how much acid or base the buffer can accept without an appreciable change in pH.

it contains more $HC_2H_3O_2$ and $C_2H_3O_2^-$. The greater the amounts of the conjugate acid-base pair, the more resistant the ratio of their concentrations, and hence the pH, is to change.

Teaching Note: Buffers represent a special case of the common-ion effect.

Because conjugate acid-base pairs share a common ion, we can use exactly the same procedures to calculate the pH of a buffer that we used in treating the common-ion effect (see Sample Exercise 17.1). However, an alternate approach is sometimes taken that is based on an equation derived from Equation 17.9. Taking the negative log of both sides of Equation 17.9, we have

$$-\log[H^+] = -\log\left(K_a \frac{[HX]}{[X^-]}\right) = -\log K_a - \log \frac{[HX]}{[X^-]}$$

Because $-\log[H^+] = \text{pH}$ and $-\log K_a = \text{p}K_a$, we have

$$\text{pH} = \text{p}K_a - \log \frac{[HX]}{[X^-]} = \text{p}K_a + \log \frac{[X^-]}{[HX]} \qquad [17.12]$$

In general,

$$\text{pH} = \text{p}K_a + \log \frac{[\text{base}]}{[\text{acid}]} \qquad [17.13]$$

Teaching Note: From Equation 17.13 it follows that if [base] = [acid], then pH = $\text{p}K_a$.

where [acid] and [base] refer to the equilibrium concentrations of the conjugate acid-base pair. Note that when [base] = [acid], pH = $\text{p}K_a$.

This relationship is known as the **Henderson-Hasselbalch equation.** Biologists, biochemists, and others who work frequently with buffers often use this equation to calculate the pH of buffers. What makes the Henderson-Hasselbalch equation particularly convenient is that we can normally neglect the amounts of the acid and base of the buffer that ionize. Therefore, we can use the *starting* concentrations of the acid and base components of the buffer directly in Equation 17.13.

SAMPLE EXERCISE 17.6

What is the pH of a buffer that is 0.12 *M* in lactic acid, $HC_3H_5O_3$, and 0.10 *M* in sodium lactate? For lactic acid, $K_a = 1.4 \times 10^{-4}$.

SOLUTION We will first determine the pH using the method described in Section 17.1. The major species in solution are $HC_3H_5O_3$, Na^+, $C_3H_5O_3^-$, and H_2O. The Na^+ ion is neither acidic nor basic; H_2O is a much weaker acid than $HC_3H_5O_3$ and a weaker base than $C_3H_5O_3^-$. Therefore, the pH will be controlled by the acid-dissociation equilibrium of lactic acid shown below. The initial and equilibrium concentrations of the species involved in this equilibrium are

$$HC_3H_5O_3(aq) \rightleftharpoons H^+(aq) + C_3H_5O_3^-(aq)$$

Initial	0.12 *M*	0	0.10 *M*
Change	$-x$ *M*	$+x$ *M*	$+x$ *M*
Equilibrium	$(0.12 - x)$ *M*	x *M*	$(0.10 + x)$ *M*

The equilibrium concentrations are governed by the equilibrium expression:

$$K_a = 1.4 \times 10^{-4} = \frac{[H^+][C_3H_5O_3^-]}{[HC_3H_5O_3]} = \frac{x(0.10 + x)}{0.12 - x}$$

Because of the small K_a and the presence of the common ion, we expect x to be small relative to 0.12 or 0.10 M. Thus, our equation can be simplified to give

$$K_a = 1.4 \times 10^{-4} = \frac{x(0.10)}{0.12}$$

Solving for x gives a value that justifies our approximation:

$$x = \left(\frac{0.12}{0.10}\right)(1.4 \times 10^{-4}) = 1.7 \times 10^{-4} \ M$$

$$pH = -\log(1.7 \times 10^{-4}) = 3.77$$

Alternatively, we could have used the Henderson-Hasselbalch equation to calculate pH directly:

$$pH = pK_a + \log\left(\frac{[base]}{[acid]}\right) = 3.85 + \log\left(\frac{0.10}{0.12}\right)$$

$$= 3.85 + (-0.08) = 3.77$$

PRACTICE EXERCISE

Calculate the pH of a buffer composed of 0.12 M benzoic acid and 0.20 M sodium benzoate. (Refer to Appendix D.)　　*Answer:* 4.41

SAMPLE EXERCISE 17.7

How many moles of NH_4Cl must be added to 2.0 L of 0.10 M NH_3 to form a buffer whose pH is 9.00? (Assume that the addition of NH_4Cl does not change the volume of the solution.)

SOLUTION　The major species in the solution will be NH_4^+, Cl^-, NH_3, and H_2O. Of these, the Cl^- ion is a spectator (it is the conjugate base of a strong acid), and H_2O is a very weak acid or base. Thus, the NH_4^+–NH_3 conjugate acid-base pair will determine the pH of the buffer solution. The equilibrium relationship between NH_4^+ and NH_3 is given by the base-dissociation constant for NH_3:

$$NH_3(aq) + H_2O(l) \rightleftharpoons NH_4^+(aq) + OH^-(aq) \qquad K_b = \frac{[NH_4^+][OH^-]}{[NH_3]}$$

$$= 1.8 \times 10^{-5}$$

Because K_b is small and the common ion NH_4^+ is present, the equilibrium concentration of NH_3 will essentially equal its initial concentration:

$$[NH_3] = 0.10 \ M$$

We obtain $[OH^-]$ from the pH:

$$pOH = 14.00 - pH = 14.00 - 9.00 = 5.00$$

and so

$$[OH^-] = 1.00 \times 10^{-5} \ M$$

We now solve the expression for K_b to obtain $[NH_4^+]$:

$$[NH_4^+] = K_b \frac{[NH_3]}{[OH^-]} = 1.8 \times 10^{-5} \frac{0.10 \ M}{1.00 \times 10^{-5} \ M} = 0.18 \ M$$

Thus, in order for the solution to have pH = 9.00, $[NH_4^+]$ must equal 0.18 M. The number of moles of NH_4Cl needed is given by the product of the volume of the solution and its molarity:

$$(2.0 \text{ L})(0.18 \text{ mol/L } NH_4Cl) = 0.36 \text{ mol } NH_4Cl$$

Because NH_4^+ and NH_3 comprise a conjugate acid-base pair, we could use the Henderson-Hasselbalch equation (Equation 17.13) to solve this problem. To do so requires first using Equation 16.36 to calculate pK_a for NH_4^+ from the value of pK_b for NH_3. We suggest you try this approach to convince yourself that you can use the Henderson-Hasselbalch equation for buffers for which you are given K_b for the conjugate base rather than K_a for the conjugate acid.

PRACTICE EXERCISE

Calculate the concentration of sodium benzoate that must be present in a 0.20 M solution of benzoic acid, $HC_7H_5O_2$, to produce a pH of 4.00.   *Answer:* 0.13 M

Addition of Strong Acids or Bases to Buffers

Let us now consider in a more quantitative way the response of a buffered solution to the addition of a strong acid or base. In solving these problems, it is important to recall that the reactions between strong acids and weak bases proceed essentially to completion, as do those between strong bases and weak acids. Thus, as long as we do not exceed the buffering capacity of the buffer, we can assume that the strong acid or strong base is completely consumed by these reactions. We can then consider the equilibria between the remaining ions in the solution.

Our general strategy is outlined in Figure 17.12, in which we consider a buffer that contains a weak acid HA and its conjugate base A^-. When a strong acid is added to this solution, the H^+ reacts with A^- to produce HA; thus, [HA] increases and $[A^-]$ decreases. When a strong base is added to the buffer, the OH^- reacts with HA to produce A^-; in this case, [HA] decreases and $[A^-]$ increases. We first use the stoichiometry of the acid-base neutralization reac-

FIGURE 17.12   Outline of the procedure used to calculate the pH of a buffer after the addition of strong acid or strong base. As long as the amount of added acid or base does not exceed the buffer capacity, the Henderson-Hasselbalch equation, Equation 17.13, can be used for the equilibrium calculation.

Figure 17.12

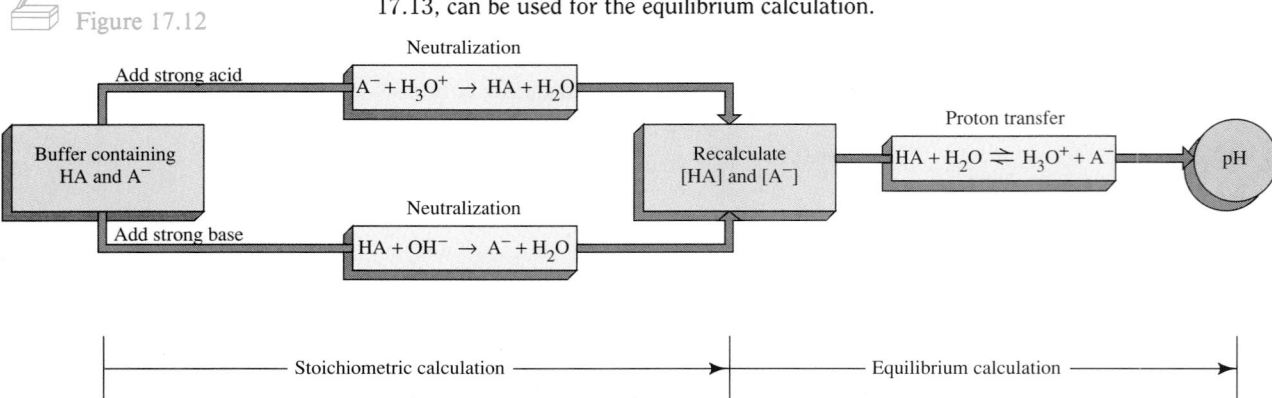

tion to calculate [HA] and [A⁻] after the addition of the strong acid or base. We can then recalculate the pH of the solution by a standard equilibrium calculation, as illustrated in Sample Exercise 17.8.

SAMPLE EXERCISE 17.8

A buffer is made by adding 0.300 mol $HC_2H_3O_2$ and 0.300 mol $NaC_2H_3O_2$ to enough water to make 1.00 L of solution. The pH of the buffer is 4.74 (Sample Exercise 17.1). Calculate the pH of this solution **(a)** after 0.020 mol of NaOH is added (neglect any volume changes); **(b)** after 0.020 mol of HCl is added (again, neglect volume changes).

SOLUTION   (a) Solving this problem involves the same types of calculations used for acid-base titrations (for example, Sample Exercise 17.4). As before, we use the two steps outlined in Figure 17.6.

Stoichiometric calculation: The OH⁻ provided by NaOH reacts with the weak-acid component of the buffer, $HC_2H_3O_2$. The following table summarizes the concentrations before and after the neutralization reaction:

$$HC_2H_3O_2(aq) + OH^-(aq) \rightleftharpoons H_2O(l) + C_2H_3O_2^-(aq)$$

Before rxn	0.300 M	0.020 M	—	0.300 M
Change	−0.020 M	−0.020 M	—	+0.020 M
After rxn	0.280 M	0.0 M	—	0.320 M

Equilibrium calculation: The solution after neutralization contains the $HC_2H_3O_2$–$C_2H_3O_2^-$ conjugate acid-base pair. We next consider the proton-transfer equilibrium in order to determine the pH of the solution:

$$HC_2H_3O_2(aq) + H_2O(l) \rightleftharpoons H_3O^+(aq) + C_2H_3O_2^-(aq)$$

Initial	0.280 M	—	0	0.320 M
Change	$-x$ M	—	$+x$ M	$+x$ M
Equilibrium	$(0.280 - x)$ M	—	x M	$(0.320 + x)$ M

$$K_a = \frac{[H_3O^+][C_2H_3O_2^-]}{[HC_2H_3O_2]} = \frac{(x)(0.320 + x)}{0.280 - x} \approx \frac{(x)(0.320)}{0.280} = 1.8 \times 10^{-5}$$

$$x = [H_3O^+] = \frac{(0.280)(1.8 \times 10^{-5})}{0.320} = 1.6 \times 10^{-5}\ M$$

$$pH = -\log(1.6 \times 10^{-5}) = 4.80$$

We could have obtained this answer directly by applying the Henderson-Hasselbalch equation, but until you are sure you have a thorough understanding of the important equilibria in these types of problems, it is best to set the problem up in full.

(b) *Stoichiometric calculation:* The H^+ (or H_3O^+) provided by HCl reacts completely with the weak-base component of the buffer, $C_2H_3O_2^-$:

$$C_2H_3O_2^-(aq) + H_3O^+(aq) \rightleftharpoons HC_2H_3O_2(aq) + H_2O(l)$$

After this reaction is completed, $[C_2H_3O_2^-] = (0.300 - 0.020)\ M = 0.280\ M$ and $[HC_2H_3O_2] = (0.300 + 0.020)\ M = 0.320\ M$.

Equilibrium calculation: As in part (a), we determine the pH by considering the equilibrium between $HC_2H_3O_2$ and $C_2H_3O_2^-$:

$$HC_2H_3O_2(aq) + H_2O(l) \rightleftharpoons H_3O^+(aq) + C_2H_3O_2^-(aq)$$

	$HC_2H_3O_2$	H_2O	H_3O^+	$C_2H_3O_2^-$
Initial	0.320 M	—	0	0.280 M
Change	$-x\ M$	—	$+x\ M$	$+x\ M$
Equilibrium	$(0.320 - x)\ M$	—	$x\ M$	$(0.280 + x)\ M$

Solving as above:

$$x = [H_3O^+] = \frac{(0.320)K_a}{0.280} = 2.1 \times 10^{-5}$$

$$pH = -\log(2.1 \times 10^{-5}) = 4.70$$

The pH decreases, as expected for addition of a strong acid to a solution. However, the magnitude of the decrease is small because the buffer capacity is great enough to absorb the added acid.

PRACTICE EXERCISE

Consider a 1.00-L buffer made by adding 0.140 mol cyanic acid, HCNO, and 0.110 mol potassium cyanate, KCNO, to sufficient water. Calculate the pH of the buffer **(a)** before any acid or base is added; **(b)** after the addition of 0.015 mol of HNO_3; **(c)** after the addition of 0.015 mol KOH. In parts (b) and (c), assume the volume does not change. *Answers:* **(a)** 3.03; **(b)** 2.92; **(c)** 3.13

[handwritten: 3.53]

To appreciate more fully the buffer action of the solution of acetic acid and sodium acetate that we've just considered, let's compare its behavior with the action of a solution that is not a buffer. We saw in Sample Exercise 17.1 that the pH of a solution that is 0.30 M in acetic acid and 0.30 M in sodium acetate is 4.74. A solution of this same pH is obtained by addition of 1.8×10^{-5} mol of HCl to a liter of water. Now suppose that 2.0 mL of 10 M HCl solution — that is, 0.020 mol of HCl — is added to a liter of each of these two solutions, as shown in Figure 17.13. As we've seen in Sample Exercise 17.8(b), the pH of the buffer will decrease to 4.70, a change of 0.04 pH unit. In contrast, the pH of the unbuffered solution will decrease to 1.70, a change of 3.04 pH units.

We might have chosen to add 0.020 mol of hydroxide ion to the solutions illustrated in Figure 17.13. This addition would have caused the pH of the dilute HCl solution to go from 4.74 to 12.3 (you should be able to explain why this is so), whereas the pH of the buffer solution would have increased by only 0.06 pH unit. Thus, a buffer solution responds to approximately the same degree, but in the opposite direction, to acid or base addition.

Teaching Note: Because each pH unit corresponds to a factor of 10 change in $[H^+]$, a 3 pH unit change is a 1000-fold change in $[H^+]$!

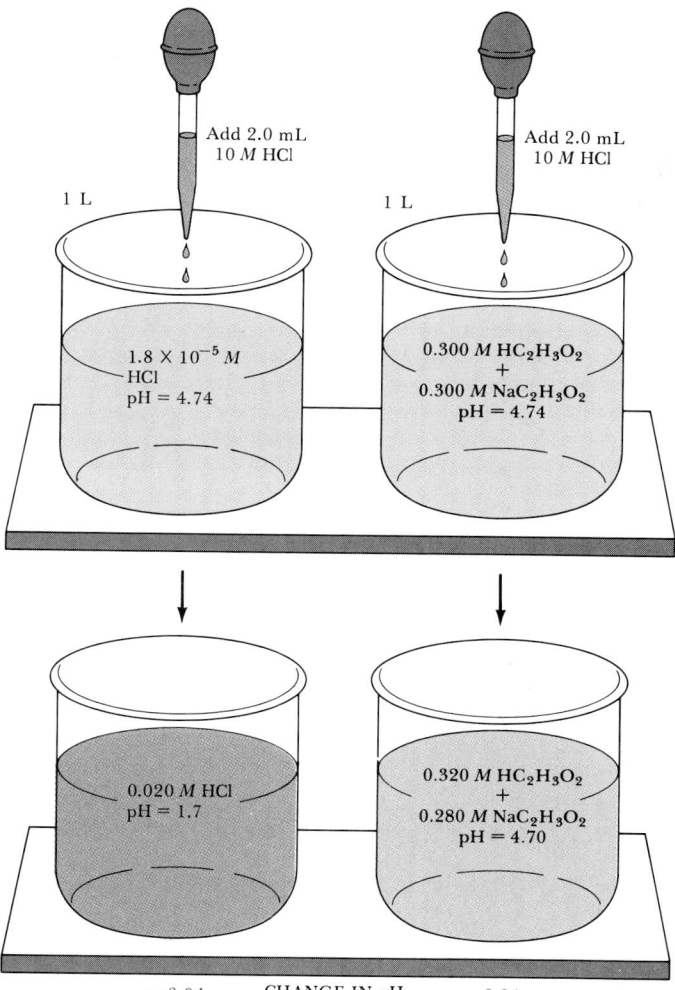

FIGURE 17.13 The effect of added acid on a buffer solution of pH 4.74 compared with the effect on an HCl solution of pH 4.74.

Add 2.0 mL
10 M HCl

Add 2.0 mL
10 M HCl

1 L

1 L

$1.8 \times 10^{-5} M$ HCl
pH = 4.74

$0.300 M \ HC_2H_3O_2$
+
$0.300 M \ NaC_2H_3O_2$
pH = 4.74

$0.020 M$ HCl
pH = 1.7

$0.320 M \ HC_2H_3O_2$
+
$0.280 M \ NaC_2H_3O_2$
pH = 4.70

− 3.04   CHANGE IN pH   0.04

What would happen if we continued to add strong acid to the buffer solution? Eventually, nearly all of the A^- in the buffer would be converted to HA, leaving us with essentially a solution of HA. Because the solution would not be able to neutralize any additional strong acid, it would therefore no longer serve as a buffer, and the pH would decrease rapidly. Likewise, the continued addition of strong base would deplete the HA in the solution, and the pH would eventually rise rapidly. In each of these cases, the continual addition of strong acid or strong base would eventually exceed the buffer capacity of the solution.

In Section 17.2, we saw that the addition of a strong base to a weak acid produces a solution that contains a weak acid and its conjugate base (as long as the weak acid remains in excess). We now see that such a solution will be a buffer. In the laboratory, buffers are often prepared by adding a carefully measured quantity of strong base to a solution of a weak acid or by adding strong acid to a solution of a weak base.

CHEMISTRY AND LIFE

Blood as a Buffered Solution

Many of the chemical reactions that occur in living systems are extremely sensitive to pH. For example, many of the enzymes that catalyze important biochemical reactions are effective only within a narrow pH range. For this reason, the human body maintains a remarkably intricate system of buffers, both within tissue cells and in the fluids that transport cells. Blood, the fluid that transports oxygen to all parts of the body (Figure 17.14), is one of the most prominent examples of the importance of buffers in living beings.

Human blood is slightly basic with a normal pH of 7.35 to 7.45. Any deviation from this normal pH range can have extremely disruptive effects on the stability of cell membranes, the structures of proteins, and the activities of enzymes. Death may result if the blood pH falls below 6.8 or rises above 7.8. When the pH falls below 7.35, the condition is called *acidosis*; when it rises above 7.45, the condition is called *alkalosis*. Acidosis is the more common tendency because ordinary metabolism generates several acids within the body.

The major buffer system used to control the pH of blood is the *carbonic acid–bicarbonate buffer system*. Carbonic acid, H_2CO_3, and bicarbonate ion, HCO_3^-, form a conjugate acid-base pair. In addition, carbonic acid can decompose into carbon dioxide gas and water. The important equilibria in this buffer system are

$$H^+(aq) + HCO_3^-(aq) \rightleftharpoons H_2CO_3(aq) \rightleftharpoons$$
$$H_2O(l) + CO_2(g) \quad [17.14]$$

Several aspects of these equilibria are notable. First, although carbonic acid is a diprotic acid, the carbonate ion, CO_3^{2-}, is not important in this system. Second, one of the components of this equilibrium, CO_2, is a gas, which provides a mechanism for the body to adjust the equilibria. Removal of CO_2 via exhalation shifts the equilibria to the right, consuming H^+ ions. Third, the buffer system in blood operates at a pH of 7.4, which is fairly far removed from the pK_{a1} value of H_2CO_3 (6.1 at physiological temperatures). In order for the buffer to have a pH of 7.4, the ratio [base]/[acid] must have a value of about 20. In normal blood plasma, the concentrations of HCO_3^- and H_2CO_3 are about 0.024 M and 0.0012 M, respectively. As a consequence, the buffer has a high capacity to neutralize additional acid, but only a low capacity with respect to additional base.

The principal organs that regulate the pH of the carbonic acid–bicarbonate buffer system are the lungs and kidneys. Some of the receptors in the brain are sensitive to the concentrations of H^+ and CO_2 in bodily fluids. When the concentration of CO_2 rises, the equilibria in Equation 17.14 shift to the left, which leads to the formation of more H^+. The receptors trigger a reflex to breathe faster and deeper, which increases the rate of elimination of CO_2 from the lungs and shifts the equilibria back to the right. The kidneys serve to absorb or

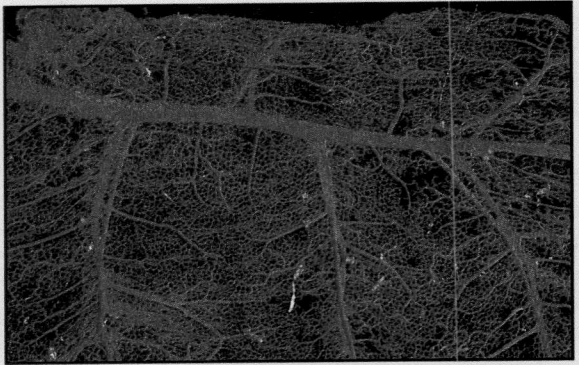

FIGURE 17.14 Blood vessels; blood is a buffered solution whose pH is maintained at 7.4. (Biophoto Associates, Science Source/Photo Researchers)

release H^+ and HCO_3^-; much of the excess acid leaves the body in urine, which normally has a pH of 5.0 to 7.0.

The regulation of the pH of blood plasma relates directly to the effective transport of O_2 to bodily tissues. Oxygen is carried by the protein hemoglobin, which is found in red blood cells. Hemoglobin (Hb) reversibly binds both H^+ and O_2. These two substances compete for the Hb, which can be represented approximately by the following equilibrium:

$$HbH^+ + O_2 \rightleftharpoons HbO_2 + H^+ \quad [17.15]$$

Oxygen enters the body through the lungs, where it passes into the red blood cells and binds to Hb. When the blood reaches tissue in which the concentration of O_2 is low, the equilibrium in Equation 17.15 shifts to the left, and O_2 is released. An increase in H^+ ion concentration (decrease in blood pH) also shifts this equilibrium to the left, as does increasing temperature.

During periods of strenuous exertion, three factors work together to ensure the delivery of O_2 to active tissues: (1) As O_2 is consumed, the equilibrium in Equation 17.15 shifts to the left according to Le Châtelier's principle. (2) Exertion raises the temperature of the body, also shifting the equilibrium to the left. (3) Large amounts of CO_2 are produced by metabolism, which shifts the equilibrium in Equation 17.14 to the left, thus decreasing the pH. Other acids, such as lactic acid, are also produced during strenuous exertion as tissues become starved for oxygen. The decrease in pH shifts the hemoglobin equilibrium to the left, leading to the delivery of more O_2. In addition, the decrease in pH stimulates an increase in the rate of breathing, which furnishes more O_2 and eliminates CO_2. Without this elaborate arrangement, the O_2 in tissues would be rapidly depleted, making further activity impossible.

17.4 Solubility Equilibria

The equilibria that we have considered thus far in this chapter have involved acids and bases. Furthermore, they have been homogeneous; that is, all the species have been in the same phase. In this section we will consider the equilibria involved in another important type of solution reaction: the dissolution or precipitation of ionic compounds. These reactions are heterogeneous.

The dissolving and precipitating of compounds are phenomena that occur both within us and around us. For example, the dissolving of tooth enamel in acidic solutions causes tooth decay. The precipitation of certain salts in our kidneys produces kidney stones. The waters of the earth contain salts dissolved as water passes over and through the ground. Precipitation of $CaCO_3$ from groundwater is responsible for the formation of stalactites and stalagmites within limestone caves (Figure 4.1).

We discussed precipitation reactions briefly in Section 4.5. In that discussion, we considered some general rules for predicting the solubility of common salts in water. These rules give us a qualitative sense of whether a compound will have a low or high solubility in water. By considering solubility equilibria, in contrast, we can make quantitative predictions about the amount of a given compound that will dissolve.

The Solubility-Product Constant, K_{sp}

Learning Goal 7: Set up the expression for the solubility-product constant for a salt.

Recall that a *saturated solution* is one in which the solution is in contact with undissolved solute. ∞ (Sec. 13.3) As an example, consider a saturated aqueous solution of $BaSO_4$ that is in contact with solid $BaSO_4$. Because the solid is an ionic compound, it is a strong electrolyte, which yields $Ba^{2+}(aq)$ and $SO_4^{2-}(aq)$ ions upon dissolving. An equilibrium exists between the undissolved solid and hydrated ions in solution:

$$BaSO_4(s) \rightleftharpoons Ba^{2+}(aq) + SO_4^{2-}(aq) \qquad [17.16]$$

Equation 17.16 is another example of a *dynamic equilibrium* (Section 11.5): The Ba^{2+} and SO_4^{2-} ions are continually moving between the undissolved solid and the solution, as shown in Figure 17.15.

The left side of Equation 17.16 contains a pure solid substance. For heterogeneous equilibria, we ignore the concentration of pure solids and liquids. ∞ (Sec. 15.3) Therefore, the equilibrium expression will depend only on the molar concentrations of the species in solution. Because the equilibrium expresses the degree to which the solid is soluble in water, the equilibrium constant is called a **solubility-product constant** (or simply a **solubility product**) and is denoted K_{sp}. For the equilibrium in Equation 17.16, the expression for K_{sp} is

$$K_{sp} = [Ba^{2+}][SO_4^{2-}] \qquad [17.17]$$

Remember that some undissolved $BaSO_4(s)$ must be present in order for the system to be at equilibrium.

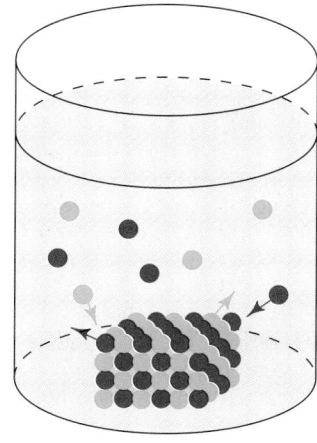

FIGURE 17.15 A system consisting of a saturated solution of an ionic solid in contact with undissolved solid exists in a dynamic equilibrium: The cations (red spheres) and anions (blue spheres) continually move between the solution and the undissolved solid.

Point of Emphasis: $K_{sp} = K_c[BaSO_4(s)] = [Ba^{2+}(aq)][SO_4^{2-}(aq)]$. Solids have constant concentrations.

The numerical values of K_{sp} at 25°C for many ionic solids are tabulated in Appendix D. The value of K_{sp} for $BaSO_4$ is 1.1×10^{-10}, a very small number. Only a very small amount of the solid will dissolve in water.

The rules for writing the solubility-product expression are the same as those for writing any other equilibrium expression: *The solubility product is equal to the product of the concentrations of the ions involved in the equilibrium, each raised to the power of its coefficient in the equilibrium equation.*

SAMPLE EXERCISE 17.9

Write the expression for the solubility-product constant for $Ca_3(PO_4)_2$.

SOLUTION We first write the equation for the solubility equilibrium:

$$Ca_3(PO_4)_2(s) \rightleftharpoons 3Ca^{2+}(aq) + 2PO_4^{3-}(aq)$$

Following the rule stated above, the power to which the Ca^{2+} concentration is raised is 3 and the power to which the PO_4^{3-} concentration is raised is 2. The resulting expression for K_{sp} is

$$K_{sp} = [Ca^{2+}]^3[PO_4^{3-}]^2$$

In Appendix D, we see that this K_{sp} has a value of 2.0×10^{-29}.

PRACTICE EXERCISE

Give the solubility-product expressions and the values of the solubility-product constants (from Appendix D) for the following: **(a)** cadmium sulfide; **(b)** chromium(III) hydroxide. **Answers: (a)** $K_{sp} = [Cd^{2+}][S^{2-}] = 8.0 \times 10^{-27}$; **(b)** $K_{sp} = [Cr^{3+}][OH^-]^3 = 6.3 \times 10^{-31}$

Solubility and K_{sp}

Lee R. Summerlin, Christie L. Borgford, and Julie B. Ealy, "Silver Ion Solubilities: Red and White Precipitates," *Chemical Demonstrations, A Sourcebook for Teachers, Volume 2* (Washington: American Chemical Society, 1987), pp. 124–25.

It is important to distinguish carefully between solubility and solubility product. The *solubility* of a substance is the quantity that dissolves to form a saturated solution. ∞ (Sec. 13.3) Solubility is often expressed as grams of solute per liter of solution (g/L). The *molar solubility* is the number of moles of the solute that dissolve in forming a liter of a saturated solution of the solute (mol/L). The solubility product (K_{sp}) is the equilibrium constant for the equilibrium between an ionic solid and its saturated solution.

Point of Emphasis: Molar solubility is calculated by dividing the solubility, in grams per liter, by the solute's molar mass.

The solubility of a substance changes as the concentrations of other solutes change. For example, the solubility of $Mg(OH)_2$ changes as the pH of the solution changes. In contrast, the solubility product has only one value for a given solute at any specific temperature.*

Learning Goal 8: Calculate K_{sp} from solubility data, and solubility from the value of K_{sp}.

In studying solubility equilibria, it is important to be able to interconvert solubility and K_{sp}. Sample Exercise 17.10 shows the calculation of K_{sp} from solubility data when the slightly soluble salt is the only solute present. Sample Exercise 17.11 similarly shows the calculation of solubility from K_{sp}. Figure 17.16 summarizes these procedures.

---

* This is strictly true only for very dilute solutions. The values of equilibrium constants are somewhat altered when the total concentration of ionic substances in water is increased. However, we shall ignore these effects, which are taken into consideration only for very accurate work.

FIGURE 17.16 Outline of steps involved in interconverting solubility and K_{sp}.

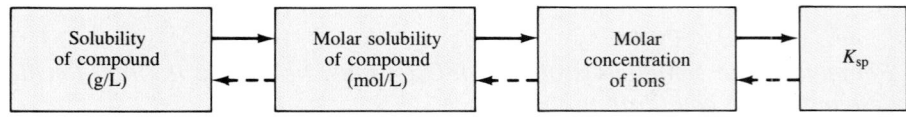

SAMPLE EXERCISE 17.10

Solid silver chloride is added to pure water at 25°C. Some of the solid remains undissolved at the bottom of the flask. The mixture is stirred for several days to ensure that equilibrium is achieved between the undissolved $AgCl(s)$ and the solution. Analysis of the equilibrated solution shows that its silver-ion concentration is 1.34×10^{-5} M. What is K_{sp} for AgCl?

SOLUTION The description of the experiment indicates that a saturated solution of AgCl is in contact with undissolved solid. The equilibrium equation and the expression for K_{sp} are

$$AgCl(s) \rightleftharpoons Ag^+(aq) + Cl^-(aq) \qquad K_{sp} = [Ag^+][Cl^-]$$

At equilibrium, $[Ag^+] = 1.34 \times 10^{-5}$ M. All the Ag^+ and Cl^- ions come from the AgCl that dissolves, and, from the stoichiometry, there must be one Cl^- in solution for each Ag^+ in solution. Consequently, $[Cl^-] = [Ag^+] = 1.34 \times 10^{-5}$ M. We can now calculate the value of K_{sp}:

$$K_{sp} = [Ag^+][Cl^-] = (1.34 \times 10^{-5})(1.34 \times 10^{-5}) = 1.80 \times 10^{-10}$$

This value agrees with the one given in Appendix D.

PRACTICE EXERCISE

A saturated solution of MgF_2 in contact with undissolved solid is prepared at 27°C. The concentration of Mg^{2+} ions in the solution is found to be 1.2×10^{-3} M. What is the value of K_{sp} for MgF_2 at this temperature? (Notice that the salt produces unequal numbers of cations and anions when it dissolves.)   ***Answer:*** 6.9×10^{-9}

SAMPLE EXERCISE 17.11

The K_{sp} for CaF_2 is 3.9×10^{-11} at 25°C. What is the solubility of CaF_2 in water in grams per liter?

SOLUTION Recall that the *solubility* of a substance is the quantity that can dissolve in solvent, whereas the *solubility product* is an equilibrium constant. We can approach this problem by using our standard techniques for solving equilibrium problems. Assume initially that none of the salt has dissolved and then allow x moles/liter of CaF_2 to dissolve as equilibrium is achieved:

$$CaF_2(s) \rightleftharpoons Ca^{2+}(aq) + 2F^-(aq)$$

		Ca^{2+}	F^-
Initial	—	0	0
Change	—	$+x$ M	$+2x$ M
Equilibrium	—	x M	$2x$ M

Notice that the stoichiometry of the equilibrium dictates that $2x$ moles/liter of F^- are produced for each x moles/liter of CaF_2 that dissolves.

We now use the expression for K_{sp} and substitute the equilibrium concentrations to solve for the value of x:

$$K_{sp} = [Ca^{2+}][F^-]^2 = (x)(2x)^2 = 4x^3 = 3.9 \times 10^{-11}$$

$$x = \sqrt[3]{\frac{3.9 \times 10^{-11}}{4}} = 2.1 \times 10^{-4} \text{ M}$$

(Remember that $\sqrt[3]{y} = y^{1/3}$; to calculate the cube root of a number, you can use the y^x function on your calculator, with $x = \frac{1}{3}$.) Thus, the molar solubility of CaF_2 is 2.1×10^{-4} mol/L. The mass of CaF_2 that dissolves in water to form a liter of solution is

$$\left(\frac{2.1 \times 10^{-4} \text{ mol } CaF_2}{1 \text{ L soln}}\right)\left(\frac{78.1 \text{ g } CaF_2}{1 \text{ mol } CaF_2}\right) = 1.6 \times 10^{-2} \text{ g } CaF_2/\text{L soln}$$

PRACTICE EXERCISE

The K_{sp} for $Cu(N_3)_2$ is 6.3×10^{-10}. What is the solubility of $Cu(N_3)_2$ in water in grams per liter?   *Answer:* 0.080 g/L

The Common-Ion Effect

Learning Goal 9:   Calculate the effect of an added common ion on the solubility of a slightly soluble salt.

In the sample exercises above, we considered the dissolving of ionic compounds in pure water. The presence of other solutes, however, can affect the solubility of a substance. For example, the presence of either $Ca(NO_3)_2$ or NaF will decrease the solubility of CaF_2. Le Châtelier's principle explains this observation. The additional Ca^{2+} or F^- ions shift the solubility equilibrium of CaF_2 to the left, thereby reducing the quantity of CaF_2 that dissolves:

$$CaF_2(s) \rightleftharpoons Ca^{2+}(aq) + 2F^-(aq)$$

Addition of Ca^{2+} or F^- shifts
equilibrium, reducing solubility

In general, the solubility of a salt decreases when a solute is added that contains a common cation or anion. This reduction in solubility is another application of the common-ion effect.   ∞ (Sec. 17.1)   The procedures used in treating this effect quantitatively are illustrated in Sample Exercise 17.12.

17.5 Criteria for Precipitation or Dissolution

Equilibrium can be achieved starting with the substances on either side of the chemical equation. The equilibrium among $BaSO_4(s)$, $Ba^{2+}(aq)$, and $SO_4^{2-}(aq)$ (Equation 17.16) can be achieved starting with solid $BaSO_4$. It can also be achieved starting with solutions of salts containing Ba^{2+} and SO_4^{2-}, say $BaCl_2$ and Na_2SO_4. When these two solutions are mixed, $BaSO_4$ will precipitate if the product of ion concentrations, $Q = [Ba^{2+}][SO_4^{2-}]$, is greater than K_{sp}.

Learning Goal 10:   Predict whether a precipitate will form when two solutions are mixed, given appropriate K_{sp} values.

The use of the reaction quotient, Q, to determine the direction in which a reaction must proceed to reach equilibrium was discussed earlier.   ∞ (Sec. 15.5)   In the present case, the equilibrium expression contains no denominator and therefore is really not a quotient. Thus, Q is often referred to simply as the *ion product*. The possible relationships between Q and K_{sp} are summarized as follows:

Point of Emphasis: The value of Q in this context is interpreted in the same way as it was in Section 15.5.

If $Q > K_{sp}$, precipitation occurs until $Q = K_{sp}$.
If $Q = K_{sp}$, equilibrium exists (saturated solution).
If $Q < K_{sp}$, solid dissolves until $Q = K_{sp}$.

SAMPLE EXERCISE 17.12

Calculate the molar solubility of CaF_2 at 25°C in a solution containing (a) 0.010 M $Ca(NO_3)_2$; (b) 0.010 M NaF.

A CLOSER LOOK

Limitations of Solubility Products

The concentrations of ions calculated from K_{sp} sometimes deviate appreciably from those found experimentally. In part, these deviations are due to electrostatic interactions between ions in solution, which can lead to *ion pairs*. (See the Closer Look box on colligative properties of electrolyte solutions in Section 13.5.) These interactions increase in magnitude as the concentrations of ions in solution increase, and they tend to cause salts to have somewhat higher solubilities than calculated. Chemists have developed procedures for correcting for these "ionic-strength" or "ionic-activity" effects.

Another common source of error in calculating ion concentrations is ignoring other equilibria that occur simultaneously in the solution. For example, we have assumed that *all* the salt that dissolves is present in solu-

tion as ions. This assumption is not always valid. For example, when MgF_2 dissolves, it yields not only Mg^{2+} and F^- ions but also a very small but not always negligible concentration of MgF^+ ions in solution. Simultaneous solubility and acid-base or complex-ion equilibria are also sometimes overlooked. In particular, both basic anions and cations with high charge-to-size ratios undergo hydrolysis reactions that can measurably increase the solubilities of their salts. For example, if we ignore the hydrolysis of the PO_4^{3-} ion ($K_b = 2.4 \times 10^{-2}$) when we consider the solubility of Li_3PO_4 ($K_{sp} = 3.2 \times 10^{-9}$), we calculate a molar solubility of 3.3×10^{-3} M. Hydrolysis of PO_4^{3-} causes the solubility to increase to 3.5×10^{-3} M. We consider briefly the effect of acid-base equilibria on solubility in Section 17.5.

SOLUTION   As in Sample Exercise 17.11, the solubility product at 25°C is

$$K_{sp} = [Ca^{2+}][F^-]^2 = 3.9 \times 10^{-11}$$

The value of K_{sp} is unchanged by the presence of additional solutes. Because of the common-ion effect, however, the solubility of the salt will decrease in the presence of common ions.

(a) We can again use our standard equilibrium techniques. In this instance, however, the initial concentration of Ca^{2+} is 0.010 M from the dissolved $Ca(NO_3)_2$:

	$CaF_2(s)$	$\rightleftharpoons$	$Ca^{2+}(aq)$	+	$2F^-(aq)$
Initial	—		0.010 M		0
Change	—		$+x$ M		$+2x$ M
Equilibrium	—		$(0.010 + x)$ M		$2x$ M

Substituting into the solubility-product expression gives

$$K_{sp} = 3.9 \times 10^{-11} = [Ca^{2+}][F^-]^2 = (0.010 + x)(2x)^2$$

This would be a messy problem to solve exactly, but fortunately it is possible to simplify matters greatly. Even without the common-ion effect, the solubility of CaF_2 is very small. Assume that the 0.010 M concentration of Ca^{2+} from $Ca(NO_3)_2$ is very much greater than the small additional concentration resulting from the solubility of CaF_2. That is, x is small compared to 0.010 M, and $0.010 + x \approx 0.010$. We then have

$$3.9 \times 10^{-11} = (0.010)(2x)^2$$

$$x^2 = \frac{3.9 \times 10^{-11}}{4(0.010)} = 9.8 \times 10^{-10}$$

$$x = \sqrt{9.8 \times 10^{-10}} = 3.1 \times 10^{-5} \ M$$

The very small value for x validates the simplifying assumption we have made. Our calculation indicates that 3.1×10^{-5} mol of solid CaF_2 dissolves per liter of the 0.010 M $Ca(NO_3)_2$ solution.

(b) In this case the common ion is F⁻, and at equilibrium we have

$$[Ca^{2+}] = x \quad \text{and} \quad [F^-] = 0.010 + 2x$$

Assuming that $2x$ is small compared to 0.010 M (that is, $0.010 + 2x \approx 0.010$), we have

$$3.9 \times 10^{-11} = x(0.010)^2$$

$$x = \frac{3.9 \times 10^{-11}}{(0.010)^2} = 3.9 \times 10^{-7} M$$

Thus, 3.9×10^{-7} mol of solid CaF_2 dissolves per liter of 0.010 M NaF solution.

PRACTICE EXERCISE

The value of K_{sp} for cerium hydroxide, $Ce(OH)_3$, is 1.5×10^{-20}. What is the molar solubility of $Ce(OH)_3$ in a solution that contains 0.10 M NaOH?   *Answer:* $1.5 \times 10^{-17} M$

SAMPLE EXERCISE 17.13

Will a precipitate form when 0.100 L of 3.0×10^{-3} M $Pb(NO_3)_2$ is added to 0.400 L of 5.0×10^{-3} M Na_2SO_4?

SOLUTION   The possible metathesis products are $PbSO_4$ and $NaNO_3$. Sodium salts are quite soluble; however, $PbSO_4$ has a K_{sp} of 1.6×10^{-8} (Appendix D). To determine whether the $PbSO_4$ precipitates, we must calculate $Q = [Pb^{2+}][SO_4^{2-}]$ and compare it with K_{sp}.

When the two solutions are mixed, the total volume becomes 0.100 L + 0.400 L = 0.500 L. The number of moles of Pb^{2+} in 0.100 L of 3.0×10^{-3} M $Pb(NO_3)_2$ is

$$(0.100 \text{ L}) \left(3.0 \times 10^{-3} \frac{\text{mol}}{\text{L}} \right) = 3.0 \times 10^{-4} \text{ mol}$$

The concentration of Pb^{2+} in the 0.500-L mixture is therefore

$$[Pb^{2+}] = \frac{3.0 \times 10^{-4} \text{ mol}}{0.500 \text{ L}} = 6.0 \times 10^{-4} M$$

The number of moles of SO_4^{2-} is

$$(0.400 \text{ L}) \left(5.0 \times 10^{-3} \frac{\text{mol}}{\text{L}} \right) = 2.0 \times 10^{-3} \text{ mol}$$

Therefore, $[SO_4^{2-}]$ in the 0.500-L mixture is

$$[SO_4^{2-}] = \frac{2.0 \times 10^{-3} \text{ mol}}{0.500 \text{ L}} = 4.0 \times 10^{-3} M$$

We then have

$$Q = [Pb^{2+}][SO_4^{2-}] = (6.0 \times 10^{-4})(4.0 \times 10^{-3})$$
$$= 2.4 \times 10^{-6}$$

Because $Q > K_{sp}$, precipitation of $PbSO_4$ will occur.

PRACTICE EXERCISE

Assume that 0.10 M NaF solution is added slowly, with stirring, to a solution that contains 0.10 M $Cr(NO_3)_3$ and 0.10 M $Ca(NO_3)_2$. Which salt—CrF_3 or CaF_2—precipitates first? (K_{sp} for CaF_2 is 5.3×10^{-9}; for CrF_3 it is 6.6×10^{-11}). *Answer:* CaF_2

SAMPLE EXERCISE 17.14

What concentration of OH^- must be exceeded in a 0.010 M solution of $Ni(NO_3)_2$ in order to precipitate $Ni(OH)_2$? (Assume that the added OH^- does not change the concentration of Ni^{2+}.)

SOLUTION From Appendix D we have $K_{sp} = 1.6 \times 10^{-14}$ for $Ni(OH)_2$. Any OH^- in excess of that in a saturated solution of $Ni(OH)_2$ will cause some $Ni(OH)_2$ to precipitate. For a saturated solution we have

$$K_{sp} = [Ni^{2+}][OH^-]^2 = 1.6 \times 10^{-14}$$

Thus, if $Q = [Ni^{2+}][OH^-]^2 > 1.6 \times 10^{-14}$, precipitation will occur. Letting $[OH^-] = x$ and using $[Ni^{2+}] = 0.010\ M$, we have

$$(0.010)x^2 > 1.6 \times 10^{-14}$$

$$x^2 > \frac{1.6 \times 10^{-14}}{0.010} = 1.6 \times 10^{-12}$$

$$x > \sqrt{1.6 \times 10^{-12}} = 1.3 \times 10^{-6}\ M$$

Thus, $Ni(OH)_2$ will precipitate if $[OH^-]$ exceeds $1.3 \times 10^{-6}\ M$.

This concentration of OH^- corresponds to a solution pH of 8.11 (pH = 14.00 − pOH = 14.00 − 5.89 = 8.11). Thus, $Ni(OH)_2$ will precipitate when the solution pH is 8.11 or higher.

PRACTICE EXERCISE

The solubility product for gadolinium hydroxide, $Gd(OH)_3$, is 1.8×10^{-23}. If a solution is 0.010 M in Gd^{3+} ion and the pH of the solution is slowly increased, at what pH will $Gd(OH)_3$ begin to precipitate? **Answer:** 7.08

Solubility and pH

The solubility of any substance whose anion is basic will be affected to some extent by the pH of the solution. For example, consider $Mg(OH)_2$, for which the solubility equilibrium is

$$Mg(OH)_2(s) \rightleftharpoons Mg^{2+}(aq) + 2OH^-(aq) \qquad [17.18]$$

The value of K_{sp} for $Mg(OH)_2$ is 1.8×10^{-11}. Suppose that solid $Mg(OH)_2$ is equilibrated with a solution buffered at a pH of 9.0. Then pOH is 5.0; that is, $[OH^-] = 1.0 \times 10^{-5}$. Inserting this value for $[OH^-]$ into the solubility-product expression, we have

$$K_{sp} = [Mg^{2+}][OH^-]^2 = 1.8 \times 10^{-11}$$

$$[Mg^{2+}][1.0 \times 10^{-5}]^2 = 1.8 \times 10^{-11}$$

$$[Mg^{2+}] = 0.18\ M$$

Thus, $Mg(OH)_2$ is quite soluble in a buffered, slightly basic medium. If the solution were made more acidic, the solubility of $Mg(OH)_2$ would increase because the OH^- concentration decreases with increasing acidity. The Mg^{2+} concentration would thus increase to maintain the equilibrium condition (Figure 17.17).

The solubility of almost any salt is affected if the solution is made sufficiently acidic or basic. The effects are very noticeable, however, only when one

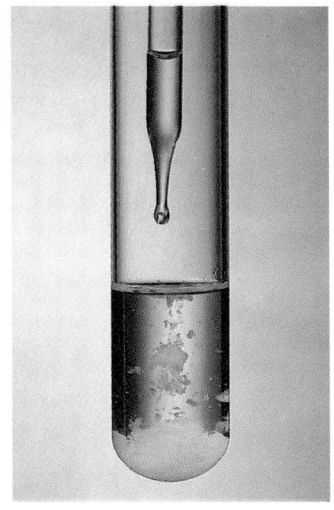

(a)

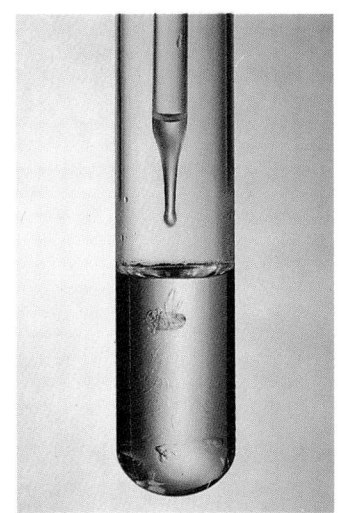

(b)

FIGURE 17.17 (a) A precipitate of $Mg(OH)_2$ (s). (b) The precipitate dissolves upon addition of acid. (© Richard Megna/Fundamental Photographs)

or both ions involved are moderately acidic or basic. The metal hydroxides we've just discussed are good examples of compounds with a strong base, the hydroxide ion. As an additional example, the fluoride ion of CaF_2 is a weak base; it is the conjugate base of the weak acid HF. As a result, CaF_2 is more soluble in acidic solutions than in neutral or basic ones because of the reaction of F^- with H^+ to form HF. The solution process can be considered as two consecutive reactions:

$$CaF_2(s) \rightleftharpoons Ca^{2+}(aq) + 2F^-(aq) \qquad [17.19]$$

$$F^-(aq) + H^+(aq) \rightleftharpoons HF(aq) \qquad [17.20]$$

The equation for the overall process is

$$CaF_2(s) + 2H^+(aq) \rightleftharpoons Ca^{2+}(aq) + 2HF(aq) \qquad [17.21]$$

Qualitatively, we can understand what occurs in terms of Le Châtelier's principle: The solubility equilibrium is driven to the right because the free F^- concentration is reduced by reaction with H^+. The reduction of $[F^-]$ causes Q to be reduced so that it becomes smaller than K_{sp}. Thus, more CaF_2 dissolves.

These examples illustrate a general rule: *The solubility of slightly soluble salts containing basic anions increases as $[H^+]$ increases (as pH is lowered).* Salts with anions of negligible basicity (the anions of strong acids) are largely unaffected by pH.

SAMPLE EXERCISE 17.15

Which of the following substances will be more soluble in acidic solution than in basic solution: **(a)** $Ni(OH)_2(s)$; **(b)** $CaCO_3(s)$; **(c)** $BaSO_4(s)$; **(d)** $AgCl(s)$?

SOLUTION (a) We can conclude that $Ni(OH)_2(s)$ will be more soluble in acidic solution because of the basicity of OH^-; the H^+ ion reacts with the OH^- ion, forming water:

$$Ni(OH)_2(s) \rightleftharpoons Ni^{2+}(aq) + 2OH^-(aq)$$
$$\underline{2OH^-(aq) + 2H^+(aq) \rightleftharpoons 2H_2O(l)}$$
$$\text{Overall:} \quad Ni(OH)_2(s) + 2H^+(aq) \rightleftharpoons Ni^{2+}(aq) + 2H_2O(l)$$

(b) Similarly, $CaCO_3(s)$ dissolves in acid solutions because CO_3^{2-} is a basic anion:

$$CaCO_3(s) \rightleftharpoons Ca^{2+}(aq) + CO_3^{2-}(aq)$$
$$CO_3^{2-}(aq) + 2H^+(aq) \rightleftharpoons H_2CO_3(aq)$$
$$\underline{H_2CO_3(aq) \longrightarrow CO_2(g) + H_2O(l)}$$
$$\text{Overall:} \quad CaCO_3(s) + 2H^+(aq) \longrightarrow Ca^{2+}(aq) + CO_2(g) + H_2O(l)$$

(c) The solubility of $BaSO_4$ is largely unaffected by changes in solution pH because SO_4^{2-} is a rather weak base and thus has little tendency to combine with a proton. However, $BaSO_4$ is slightly more soluble in strongly acidic solutions.

(d) The solubility of AgCl is unaffected by changes in pH because Cl^- is the anion of a strong acid and therefore has negligible basicity.

PRACTICE EXERCISE

Write the net ionic equation for the reaction of the following copper(II) compounds with acid: **(a)** $CuCrO_4$; **(b)** $Cu(N_3)_2$. **Answers: (a)** $CuCrO_4(s) + H^+(aq) \rightleftharpoons Cu^{2+}(aq) + HCrO_4^-(aq)$; **(b)** $Cu(N_3)_2(s) + 2H^+(aq) \rightleftharpoons Cu^{2+}(aq) + 2HN_3(aq)$

CHEMISTRY AND LIFE

Tooth Decay and Fluoridation

Tooth enamel consists mainly of a mineral called hydroxyapatite, $Ca_{10}(PO_4)_6(OH)_2$. It is the hardest substance in the body. Tooth cavities are caused by the dissolving action of acids on tooth enamel:

$$Ca_{10}(PO_4)_6(OH)_2(s) + 8H^+(aq) \longrightarrow$$
$$10Ca^{2+}(aq) + 6HPO_4^{2-}(aq) + 2H_2O(l)$$

The resultant Ca^{2+} and HPO_4^{2-} ions diffuse out of the tooth enamel and are washed away by saliva. The acids that attack the hydroxyapatite are formed by the action of specific bacteria on sugars and other carbohydrates present in the plaque adhering to the teeth.

Fluoride ion, present in drinking water, toothpaste, or other sources, can react with hydroxyapatite to form fluoroapatite, $Ca_{10}(PO_4)_6F_2$. This mineral, in which F^- has replaced OH^-, is much more resistant to attack by acids because the fluoride ion is a much weaker Brønsted-Lowry base than the hydroxide ion.

Because the fluoride ion is so effective in preventing cavities, it is added to the public water supply in many places to give a concentration of 1 mg/L (that is, 1 ppm). The compound added may be NaF or Na_2SiF_6. The latter compound reacts with water to release fluoride ion by the following reaction:

$$SiF_6^{2-}(aq) + 2H_2O(l) \longrightarrow$$
$$6F^-(aq) + 4H^+(aq) + SiO_2(s)$$

About 80 percent of all toothpastes now sold in the United States contain fluoride compounds, usually at the level of 0.1 percent fluoride by weight. The most common compounds in toothpastes are stannous fluoride, SnF_2, sodium monofluorophosphate, Na_2PO_3F, and sodium fluoride, NaF.

Selective Precipitation of Ions

Ions can be separated from each other on the basis of the solubilities of their salts. Take, for example, a solution containing both Ag^+ and Cu^{2+}. If HCl is added to the solution, AgCl ($K_{sp} = 1.8 \times 10^{-10}$) precipitates, while Cu^{2+} remains in solution because $CuCl_2$ is soluble. Separation of ions in an aqueous solution by using a reagent that forms a precipitate with one or a few of the ions is called *selective precipitation.*

Sulfide ion is often used to separate metal ions because the solubilities of sulfide salts span a wide range and $[S^{2-}]$ can be regulated using pH. For example, suppose a solution contains both Cu^{2+} and Zn^{2+}. These ions can be separated by bubbling H_2S gas through a properly acidified solution. Because CuS ($K_{sp} = 6.3 \times 10^{-36}$) is less soluble than ZnS ($K_{sp} = 1.1 \times 10^{-21}$), $[S^{2-}]$ can be adjusted so that CuS precipitates while ZnS does not (Figure 17.18). To understand this separation further, let's consider the equilibria involved.

When H_2S is bubbled through an aqueous solution at 25°C and 1 atm, a saturated solution of H_2S forms that is approximately 0.1 M in H_2S. H_2S is a weak diprotic acid:

$$H_2S(aq) \rightleftharpoons H^+(aq) + HS^-(aq) \qquad K_{a1} = 5.7 \times 10^{-8} \qquad [17.22]$$
$$HS^-(aq) \rightleftharpoons H^+(aq) + S^{2-}(aq) \qquad K_{a2} = 1.3 \times 10^{-13} \qquad [17.23]$$

These equations can be combined to give an equation for the overall dissociation of H_2S into S^{2-}:

$$H_2S(aq) \rightleftharpoons 2H^+(aq) + S^{2-}(aq)$$

(a)   (b)   (c)

FIGURE 17.18 (a) Solution containing $Zn^{2+}(aq)$ and $Cu^{2+}(aq)$. (b) When H_2S is added to a solution whose pH exceeds 0.6, CuS precipitates. (c) After CuS is removed, pH is increased, allowing ZnS to precipitate. (© Richard Megna/Fundamental Photographs)

The equilibrium expression for this overall dissociation process is

$$K = \frac{[H^+]^2[S^{2-}]}{[H_2S]} = K_{a1} \times K_{a2} = 7.4 \times 10^{-21} \qquad [17.24]$$

Substituting the solubility of H_2S, 0.1 M, into this expression gives

$$\frac{[H^+]^2[S^{2-}]}{0.1} = 7.4 \times 10^{-21}$$

$$[H^+]^2[S^{2-}] = (0.1)(7.4 \times 10^{-21}) = 7 \times 10^{-22} \qquad [17.25]$$

Equation 17.25 can be used to calculate the concentration of S^{2-} in saturated solutions of H_2S at various pH values.

Now consider how we can calculate the pH that will allow us to prevent precipitation of ZnS while precipitating CuS from a solution that is 0.10 M in Zn^{2+}, 0.10 M in Cu^{2+}, and saturated with H_2S. The maximum concentration of S^{2-} that can be present in the solution before precipitation of ZnS occurs can be calculated from the solubility-product expression for this substance:

$$[Zn^{2+}][S^{2-}] = K_{sp} = 1.1 \times 10^{-21}$$

$$[S^{2-}] = \frac{1.1 \times 10^{-21}}{[Zn^{2+}]} = \frac{1.1 \times 10^{-21}}{0.10} = 1.1 \times 10^{-20} \ M$$

The concentration of hydrogen ions necessary to give $[S^{2-}] = 1.1 \times 10^{-20}\ M$ can be calculated using Equation 17.25:

$$[H^+]^2[S^{2-}] = 7 \times 10^{-22}$$

$$[H^+]^2 = \frac{7 \times 10^{-22}}{[S^{2-}]} = \frac{7 \times 10^{-22}}{1.1 \times 10^{-20}} = 6 \times 10^{-2}$$

$$[H^+] = \sqrt{6 \times 10^{-2}} = 0.24\ M$$

$$pH = -\log(2.4 \times 10^{-1}) = 0.6$$

Thus, ZnS will not precipitate if the pH is 0.6 or lower. However, at pH 0.6, where $[S^{2-}] = 1.1 \times 10^{-20}$, the ion product for a 0.10 M Cu^{2+} solution would be

$$Q = [Cu^{2+}][S^{2-}] = (0.10)(1.1 \times 10^{-20}) = 1.1 \times 10^{-21}$$

Because Q exceeds the K_{sp} of CuS (that is, 6.3×10^{-36}), CuS will precipitate under these conditions. Indeed, because $[Cu^{2+}] = 0.10\ M$, $[S^{2-}]$ must be less than $6.3 \times 10^{-35}\ M$ to prevent the precipitation of CuS from this solution. Even under strongly acidic conditions, $[S^{2-}]$ will be high enough to cause precipitation of CuS. Thus, a fairly broad range of sulfide concentration will allow for effective separation of Cu^{2+} (as CuS) from Zn^{2+}.

Effect of Complex Formation on Solubility

A characteristic property of metal ions is their ability to act as Lewis acids, or electron-pair acceptors, toward water molecules, which act as Lewis bases, or electron-pair donors. ∞ (Sec. 16.10) Lewis bases other than water can also interact with metal ions, particularly with transition-metal ions. Such interactions can have a dramatic effect on the solubility of a metal salt. For example, AgCl, whose $K_{sp} = 1.82 \times 10^{-10}$, will dissolve in the presence of aqueous ammonia because of the interaction between Ag^+ and the Lewis base NH_3, as shown in Figure 17.19. This process can be viewed as the sum of two reactions, the solubility equilibrium of AgCl and the Lewis acid-base interaction between Ag^+ and NH_3:

$$
\begin{array}{llr}
& AgCl(s) \rightleftharpoons Ag^+(aq) + Cl^-(aq) & [17.26] \\
& Ag^+(aq) + 2NH_3(aq) \rightleftharpoons Ag(NH_3)_2{}^+(aq) & [17.27] \\
\hline
\text{Overall:} & AgCl(s) + 2NH_3(aq) \rightleftharpoons Ag(NH_3)_2{}^+(aq) + Cl^-(aq) & [17.28]
\end{array}
$$

The presence of NH_3 drives the top reaction, the solubility equilibrium of AgCl, to the right as $Ag^+(aq)$ is removed to form $Ag(NH_3)_2{}^+$.

For a Lewis base such as NH_3 to increase the solubility of a metal salt, it must be able to interact more strongly with the metal ion than water does. The NH_3 must displace solvating H_2O molecules (Sections 13.1 and 16.10) in order to form $Ag(NH_3)_2{}^+$:

$$Ag^+(aq) + 2NH_3(aq) \rightleftharpoons Ag(NH_3)_2{}^+(aq) \qquad [17.29]$$

Learning Goal 12: Formulate the equilibrium between a metal ion and a Lewis base to form a complex ion of a metal.

Learning Goal 13: Describe how complex formation can affect the solubility of a slightly soluble salt.

FIGURE 17.19 (*a*) A precipitate of AgCl(*s*). (*b*) The precipitate dissolves upon addition of concentrated NH₃(*aq*). (Fundamental Photographs)

(*a*)   (*b*)

Point of Emphasis: Metal complexes are formed by the Lewis bases sharing their non-bonded electron pairs with vacant orbitals on the metal atom. The attached Lewis bases are called *ligands,* which are discussed in Chapter 25.

An assembly of a metal ion and the Lewis bases bonded to it, such as $Ag(NH_3)_2^+$, is called a **complex ion.** The stability of a complex ion in aqueous solution can be judged by the size of the equilibrium constant for its formation from the hydrated metal ion. For example, the equilibrium constant for formation of $Ag(NH_3)_2^+$ (Equation 17.29) is 1.7×10^7:

$$K_f = \frac{[Ag(NH_3)_2^+]}{[Ag^+][NH_3]^2} = 1.7 \times 10^7 \qquad [17.30]$$

Learning Goal 14: Calculate the concentration of a metal ion in equilibrium with a Lewis base with which it forms a soluble complex ion, from a knowledge of initial concentrations and K_f.

Such an equilibrium constant is called a **formation constant, K_f.** The formation constants for several complex ions are shown in Table 17.2.

TABLE 17.2 △ Formation Constants for Some Metal Complex Ions in Water at 25°C

Complex ion	K_f	Equilibrium equation
$Ag(NH_3)_2^+$	1.7×10^7	$Ag^+(aq) + 2NH_3(aq) \rightleftharpoons Ag(NH_3)_2^+(aq)$
$Ag(CN)_2^-$	1×10^{21}	$Ag^+(aq) + 2CN^-(aq) \rightleftharpoons Ag(CN)_2^-(aq)$
$Ag(S_2O_3)_2^{3-}$	2.9×10^{13}	$Ag^+(aq) + 2S_2O_3^{2-}(aq) \rightleftharpoons Ag(S_2O_3)_2^{3-}(aq)$
$CdBr_4^{2-}$	5×10^3	$Cd^{2+}(aq) + 4Br^-(aq) \rightleftharpoons CdBr_4^{2-}(aq)$
$Cr(OH)_4^-$	8×10^{29}	$Cr^{3+}(aq) + 4OH^-(aq) \rightleftharpoons Cr(OH)_4^-(aq)$
$Co(SCN)_4^{2-}$	1×10^3	$Co^{2+}(aq) + 4SCN^-(aq) \rightleftharpoons Co(SCN)_4^{2-}(aq)$
$Cu(NH_3)_4^{2+}$	5×10^{12}	$Cu^{2+}(aq) + 4NH_3(aq) \rightleftharpoons Cu(NH_3)_4^{2+}(aq)$
$Cu(CN)_4^{2-}$	1×10^{25}	$Cu^{2+}(aq) + 4CN^-(aq) \rightleftharpoons Cu(CN)_4^{2-}(aq)$
$Ni(NH_3)_6^{2+}$	5.5×10^8	$Ni^{2+}(aq) + 6NH_3(aq) \rightleftharpoons Ni(NH_3)_6^{2+}(aq)$
$Fe(CN)_6^{4-}$	1×10^{35}	$Fe^{2+}(aq) + 6CN^-(aq) \rightleftharpoons Fe(CN)_6^{4-}(aq)$
$Fe(CN)_6^{3-}$	1×10^{42}	$Fe^{3+}(aq) + 6CN^-(aq) \rightleftharpoons Fe(CN)_6^{3-}(aq)$

SAMPLE EXERCISE 17.16

Calculate the concentration of Ag^+ present in solution at equilibrium when concentrated ammonia is added to a 0.010 M solution of $AgNO_3$ to give an equilibrium concentration of $[NH_3] = 0.20$ M. Neglect the small volume change that occurs on addition of NH_3.

SOLUTION Because K_f is quite large, we begin with the assumption that essentially all of the Ag^+ is converted to $Ag(NH_3)_2^+$, in accordance with Equation 17.29. Thus, $[Ag^+]$ will be small at equilibrium. If $[Ag^+]$ was 0.010 M initially, then $[Ag(NH_3)_2^+]$ will be 0.010 M following addition of the NH_3. Let the concentration of Ag^+ at equilibrium be x. Then, at equilibrium

$$\underset{x\ M}{Ag^+(aq)} + \underset{0.20\ M}{2NH_3(aq)} \rightleftharpoons \underset{(0.010 - x)\ M}{Ag(NH_3)_2^+(aq)}$$

Because the concentration of Ag^+ is very small, we can ignore x in comparison with 0.010. Thus, $0.010 - x \approx 0.010$ M. Substituting these values into the equilibrium expression, Equation 17.29, we obtain

$$\frac{[Ag(NH_3)_2^+]}{[Ag^+][NH_3]^2} = \frac{0.010}{(x)(0.20)^2} = 1.7 \times 10^7$$

Solving for x, we obtain $x = 1.5 \times 10^{-8}$ $M = [Ag^+]$. It is evident that formation of the $Ag(NH_3)_2^+$ complex drastically reduces the concentration of free Ag^+ ion in solution.

PRACTICE EXERCISE

Calculate the concentration of free Cr^{3+} ion when 0.010 mol of $Cr(NO_3)_3$ is dissolved in a liter of solution buffered at pH 10.0.　　***Answer:*** $[Cr^{3+}] = 1.2 \times 10^{-16}$ M

The general rule is that metal salts will dissolve in the presence of a suitable Lewis base, such as NH_3, CN^-, or OH^-, if the metal forms a sufficiently stable complex with the base. The ability of metal ions to form complexes is an extremely important aspect of their chemistry. In Chapter 25, we will take a much closer look at complex ions. In that chapter and others, we shall see applications of complex ions to areas such as biochemistry, metallurgy, and photography.

Point of Emphasis: The list of Lewis bases that form complexes with various metals is quite long. See Chapter 25.

Lee R. Summerlin, Christie L. Borgford, and Julie B. Ealy, "The Colors of Some Chromium and Manganese Ions," *Chemical Demonstrations, A Sourcebook for Teachers, Volume 2* (Washington: American Chemical Society, 1987), pp. 82–83.

Amphoterism

Many metal hydroxides and oxides that are relatively insoluble in neutral water dissolve in strongly acidic *and* strongly basic media. These substances are soluble in strong acids and bases because they themselves are capable of behaving as either an acid or a base; they are *amphoteric.*　∞ (Sec. 16.2)　Examples of amphoteric substances include the hydroxides and oxides of Al^{3+}, Cr^{3+}, Zn^{2+}, and Sn^{2+} (see the Closer Look box in Section 8.10).

The dissolution of these species in acidic solutions should be anticipated based on the earlier discussions in this section. We have seen that acids promote the dissolving of compounds with basic anions. What makes amphoteric oxides and hydroxides special is that they also dissolve in strongly basic solutions (Figure 17.20). This behavior results from the formation of complex anions containing several (typically four) hydroxides bound to the metal ion:

Learning Goal 15: Explain the origin of amphoteric behavior, and write equations describing the dissolution of an amphoteric metal hydroxide in either an acidic or a basic medium.

$$Al(OH)_3(s) + OH^-(aq) \rightleftharpoons Al(OH)_4^-(aq) \qquad [17.31]$$

Amphoterism is often interpreted in terms of the behavior of the water molecules that surround the metal ion and that are bonded to it by Lewis

FIGURE 17.20 As NaOH is added to a solution of Al^{3+} (a), a precipitate of $Al(OH)_3$ forms (b). As more NaOH is added, the $Al(OH)_3$ dissolves (c), demonstrating the amphoterism of the $Al(OH)_3$. (Richard Megna/Fundamental Photographs)

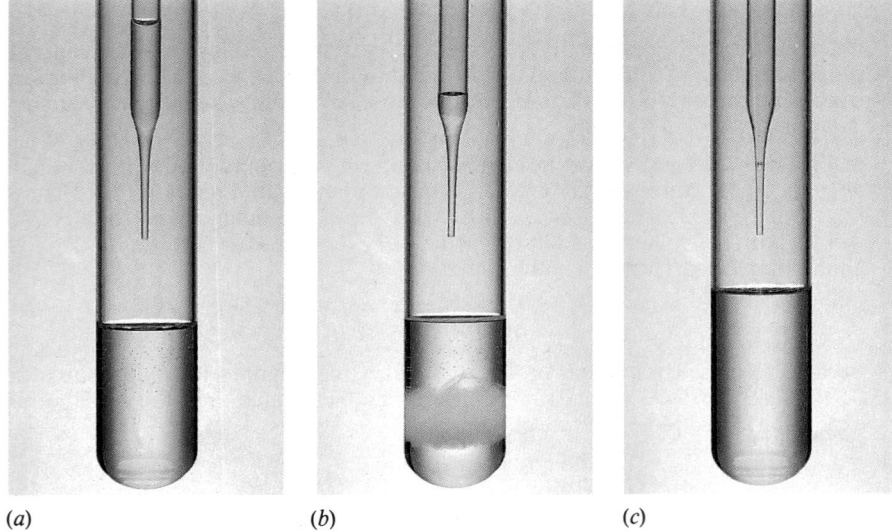

(a)　　　　　　　(b)　　　　　　　(c)

acid-base interactions. ∞ (Sec. 16.10) For example, $Al^{3+}(aq)$ is more accurately represented as $Al(H_2O)_6^{3+}(aq)$; six water molecules are bonded to the Al^{3+} in aqueous solution. As discussed in Section 16.10, this hydrated ion is a weak acid. As a strong base is added, $Al(H_2O)_6^{3+}$ loses protons in a stepwise fashion, eventually forming neutral and water-insoluble $Al(H_2O)_3(OH)_3$. This substance then dissolves upon removal of an additional proton to form the anion $Al(H_2O)_2(OH)_4^-$. The reactions that occur are as follows:

$$Al(H_2O)_6^{3+}(aq) + OH^-(aq) \rightleftharpoons Al(H_2O)_5(OH)^{2+}(aq) + H_2O(l)$$

$$Al(H_2O)_5(OH)^{2+}(aq) + OH^-(aq) \rightleftharpoons Al(H_2O)_4(OH)_2^+(aq) + H_2O(l)$$

$$Al(H_2O)_4(OH)_2^+(aq) + OH^-(aq) \rightleftharpoons Al(H_2O)_3(OH)_3(s) + H_2O(l)$$

$$Al(H_2O)_3(OH)_3(s) + OH^-(aq) \rightleftharpoons Al(H_2O)_2(OH)_4^-(aq) + H_2O(l)$$

Further proton removals are possible, but each successive reaction occurs less readily than the one before. As the charge on the ion becomes more negative, it becomes increasingly difficult to remove a positively charged proton. Addition of an acid reverses these reactions. The proton adds in a stepwise fashion to convert the OH^- groups to H_2O, eventually reforming $Al(H_2O)_6^{3+}$. The common practice is to simplify the equations for these reactions by excluding the bound H_2O molecules. Thus, we usually write Al^{3+} instead of $Al(H_2O)_6^{3+}$, $Al(OH)_3$ instead of $Al(H_2O)_3(OH)_3$, $Al(OH)_4^-$ instead of $Al(H_2O)_2(OH)_4^-$, and so forth.

The extent to which an insoluble metal hydroxide reacts with either acid or base varies with the particular metal ion involved. Many metal hydroxides —for example, $Ca(OH)_2$, $Fe(OH)_2$, and $Fe(OH)_3$—are capable of dissolving in acidic solution but do not react with excess base. These hydroxides are not amphoteric.

The purification of aluminum ore in the manufacture of aluminum metal provides an interesting application of the property of amphoterism. As we have seen, $Al(OH)_3$ is amphoteric, whereas $Fe(OH)_3$ is not. Aluminum occurs in large quantities as the ore *bauxite,* which is essentially Al_2O_3 with additional

Point of Emphasis: Determining whether a substance is a hydroxide or a hydrated oxide is important in understanding its reactivity but is not important in looking at stoichiometry.

water molecules. The ore is contaminated with Fe_2O_3 as an impurity. When bauxite is added to a strongly basic solution, the Al_2O_3 dissolves because the aluminum forms complex ions, such as $Al(OH)_4^-$. The Fe_2O_3 impurity, however, is not amphoteric and remains as a solid. The solution is filtered, getting rid of the iron impurity. Aluminum hydroxide is then precipitated by addition of acid. The purified hydroxide receives further treatment and eventually yields aluminum metal.

SAMPLE EXERCISE 17.17

Write the balanced net ionic equation for the reaction between $Al_2O_3(s)$ and aqueous solutions of NaOH that causes the $Al_2O_3(s)$ to dissolve. (H_2O is also present as a reactant.)

SOLUTION   The NaOH is a strong electrolyte that provides the necessary OH^- ions. The reaction product can be taken to be $Al(OH)_4^-$, an assembly of Al^{3+} and four OH^- ions. The unbalanced equation is

$$Al_2O_3(s) + OH^-(aq) \rightleftharpoons Al(OH)_4^-(aq)$$

Two Al are needed among the products:

$$Al_2O_3(s) + OH^-(aq) \rightleftharpoons 2Al(OH)_4^-(aq)$$

To balance the charge on both sides of the equation requires $2OH^-$. Sufficient H_2O is then added to balance the O and H counts. The balanced equation is

$$Al_2O_3(s) + 2OH^-(aq) + 3H_2O(l) \rightleftharpoons 2Al(OH)_4^-(aq)$$

PRACTICE EXERCISE

Write balanced net ionic equations for the dissolution of **(a)** $Zn(OH)_2(s)$ and **(b)** $ZnO(s)$ in excess base.   ***Answers:*** **(a)** $Zn(OH)_2(s) + 2OH^-(aq) \rightleftharpoons Zn(OH)_4^{2-}(aq)$; **(b)** $ZnO(s) + H_2O(l) + 2OH^-(aq) \rightleftharpoons Zn(OH)_4^{2-}(aq)$

17.6 Qualitative Analyses for Metallic Elements

In this chapter, we have seen several examples of equilibria involving metal ions in aqueous solution. In this final section, we look briefly at how solubility equilibria and complex formation can be used to detect the presence of particular metal ions in solution. Before the development of modern analytical instrumentation, it was necessary to analyze mixtures of metals in a sample by so-called wet chemical methods. For example, a metallic sample that might contain several metallic elements was dissolved in a concentrated acid solution. This solution was then tested in a systematic way for the presence of various metallic ions.

Dale D. Clyde, "Swimming Pools, Hot Rods, and Qualitative Analysis," *J. Chem. Educ.* **1988,** *65,* 911.

Qualitative analysis determines only the presence or absence of a particular metal ion. It should be distinguished from **quantitative analysis,** which determines how much of a given substance is present. Wet methods of qualitative analysis have become less important as a means of analysis. However, they are frequently used in general chemistry laboratory programs to illustrate equilibria, teach the properties of common metal ions in solution, and develop laboratory skills. Typically, such analyses proceed in three stages. (1) The ions are separated into broad groups on the basis of solubility properties. (2) The individual ions within each group are then separated by selectively dissolving members in the group. (3) The ions are then identified by means of specific tests.

Point of Emphasis: *Qualitative analysis* uses relative solubilities (and some color changes) to identify ions in a sample.

Learning Goal 16: Explain the general principles that apply to the groupings of metal ions in the qualitative analysis of an aqueous mixture.

Bassam Z. Shakhashiri, "Precipitates and Complexes of Copper(II)," *Chemical Demonstrations: A Handbook for Teachers of Chemistry, Volume 1* (Madison: The University of Wisconsin Press, 1983), pp. 318–23.

A scheme in common use divides the common cations into five groups, as shown in Figure 17.21. The order of addition of reagents is important. The most selective separations—that is, those that involve the smallest number of ions—are carried out first. The reactions that are used must proceed so far toward completion that any concentration of cations remaining in the solution is too small to interfere with subsequent tests. Let's take a closer look at each of these five groups of cations, examining briefly the logic used in this qualitative analysis scheme.

1. *Insoluble chlorides:* Of the common metal ions, only Ag^+, Hg_2^{2+}, and Pb^{2+} form insoluble chlorides. Therefore, when dilute HCl is added to a mixture of cations, only $AgCl$, Hg_2Cl_2, and $PbCl_2$ will precipitate, leaving the other cations in solution. The absence of a precipitate indicates that the starting solution contains no Ag^+, Hg_2^{2+}, or Pb^{2+}.

2. *Acid-insoluble sulfides:* After any insoluble chlorides have been removed, the remaining solution, now acidic, is treated with H_2S. As we saw in Section 17.5, the dissociation of H_2S is repressed in acidic solutions so that the concentration of free S^{2-} is very low. Consequently, only the most insoluble metal sulfides, CuS, Bi_2S_3, CdS, PbS, HgS, As_2S_3, Sb_2S_3, and SnS_2, can precipitate. (Note the very small values of K_{sp} for some of these sulfides in Appendix D.) Those metal ions whose sulfides are somewhat more soluble—for example, ZnS or NiS—remain in solution.

3. *Base-insoluble sulfides:* After the solution is filtered to remove any acid-insoluble sulfides, the remaining solution is made slightly basic, and $(NH_4)_2S$ is added. In basic solutions, the concentration of S^{2-} is higher than in acidic solutions. Thus, the ion products for many of the more soluble sulfides are caused to exceed their K_{sp} values and precipitation occurs. The metal ions precipitated at this stage are Al^{3+}, Cr^{3+}, Fe^{3+}, Zn^{2+}, Ni^{2+}, Co^{2+}, and Mn^{2+}. (Actually, the Al^{3+}, Fe^{3+}, and Cr^{3+} ions do not form insoluble sulfides; instead they are precipitated as insoluble hydroxides at the same time.)

4. *Insoluble phosphates:* At this point, the solution contains only metal ions from periodic table groups 1A and 2A. Addition of $(NH_4)_2HPO_4$ to a basic solution causes precipitation of the group 2A elements Mg^{2+}, Ca^{2+}, Sn^{2+}, and Ba^{2+}, because these metals form insoluble phosphates.

5. *The alkali metal ions and NH_4^+:* The ions that remain after removal of the insoluble phosphates form a small group. We can test for each ion individually. For example, the flame test is useful to show the presence of K^+ because the flame turns a characteristic violet color if K^+ is present.

Additional separation and testing is necessary to determine which ions are present within each of the groups. As an example, consider the ions of the insoluble chloride group. The precipitate containing the metal chlorides is boiled in water. It happens that $PbCl_2$ is relatively soluble in hot water, whereas $AgCl$ and Hg_2Cl_2 are not. The hot solution is filtered, and a solution of Na_2CrO_4 added to the filtrate. If Pb^{2+} is present, a yellow precipitate of $PbCrO_4$ forms. The test for Ag^+ consists of treating the metal chloride precipitate with dilute

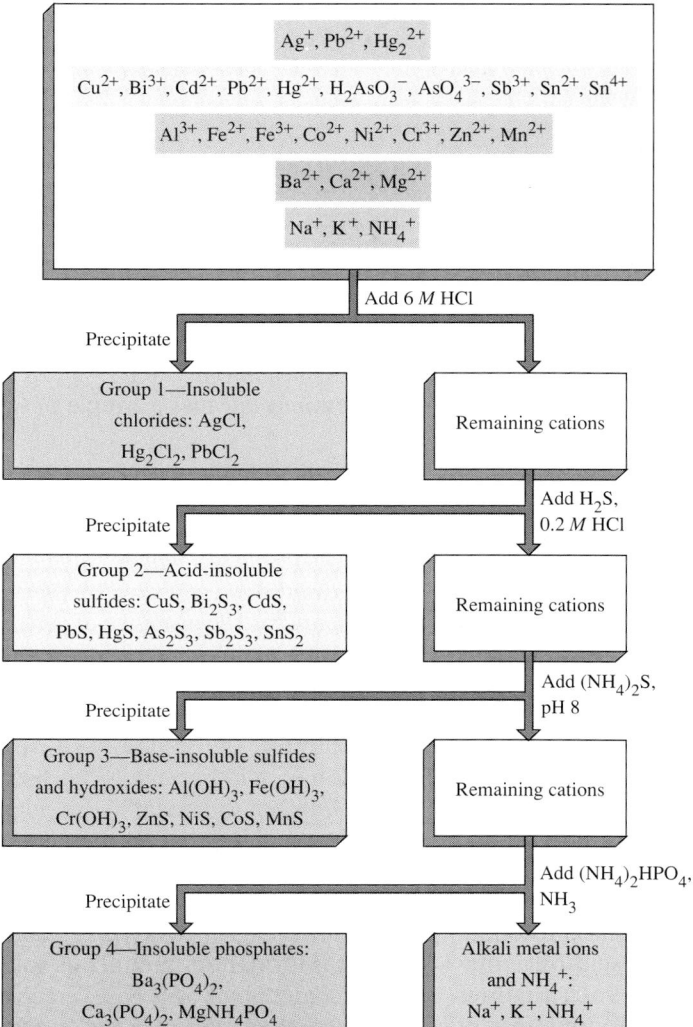

FIGURE 17.21 Qualitative analysis scheme for separating cations into groups.

Figure 17.21

ammonia. Only Ag^+ forms an ammonia complex. If AgCl is present in the precipitate, it will dissolve in the ammonia solution:

$$AgCl(s) + 2NH_3(aq) \rightleftharpoons Ag(NH_3)_2^+(aq) + Cl^-(aq) \qquad [17.32]$$

After treatment with ammonia, the solution is filtered and the filtrate made acidic by adding nitric acid. The nitric acid removes ammonia from solution by forming NH_4^+, thus releasing Ag^+, which should re-form the AgCl precipitate:

$$Ag(NH_3)_2^+(aq) + Cl^-(aq) + 2H^+(aq) \rightleftharpoons AgCl(s) + 2NH_4^+(aq) \qquad [17.33]$$

The analyses for individual ions in the acid-insoluble and base-insoluble sulfides are a bit more complex, but the same general principles are involved. The detailed procedures for carrying out such analyses are given in laboratory manuals.

For Review

Summary

In this chapter we've considered several types of important equilibria that occur in aqueous solution. Our primary emphasis has been on acid-base equilibria in solutions containing two or more solutes and on solubility equilibria. We observed that the dissociation of a weak acid or weak base is repressed by the presence of a strong electrolyte that provides an ion common to the equilibrium. This phenomenon is called the common-ion effect.

The plot of the pH of an acid (or base) as a function of the volume of added base (or acid) is called a titration curve. Titration curves aid in selecting a proper pH indicator for an acid-base titration. The titration curve of a strong acid–strong base titration exhibits a large change in pH in the immediate vicinity of the equivalence point; at the equivalence point for this titration, pH = 7. For strong acid–weak base or weak acid–strong base titrations, the pH change in the vicinity of the equivalence point is not as large. Furthermore, the pH at the equivalence point is not 7 in either of these cases. Rather, it is the pH of the salt solution that results from the neutralization reaction.

A particularly important type of acid-base mixture is a weak conjugate acid-base pair. Such mixtures function as buffers. Addition of small amounts of additional acid or base to a buffered solution causes only small changes in pH because the buffer reacts with the added acid or base. (Recall that strong acid–strong base, strong acid–weak base, and weak acid–strong base reactions proceed essentially to completion.) Buffer solutions are usually prepared from a weak acid and a salt of that acid or from a weak base and a salt of that base. Two important characteristics of a buffer solution are its buffering capacity and its pH.

The equilibrium between a solid salt and its ions in solution provides an example of heterogeneous equilibrium. The solubility-product constant, K_{sp}, is an equilibrium constant that expresses quantitatively the extent to which the salt dissolves. Addition to the solution of an ion common to a solubility equilibrium causes the solubility of the salt to decrease. This phenomenon is another example of the common-ion effect.

Comparison of the ion product, Q, with the value of K_{sp} can be used to judge whether a precipitate will form when solutions are mixed or whether a slightly soluble salt will dissolve under various conditions. Solubility is affected by the common-ion effect, by pH, and by the presence of certain Lewis bases that react with metal ions to form stable complex ions. Solubility is affected by pH when one or more of the ions in the solubility equilibrium is an acid or base. For example, the solubility of MnS is increased on addition of acid because S^{2-} is basic.

Amphoteric metal hydroxides are those slightly soluble metal hydroxides that dissolve on addition of either acid or base. The reactions that give rise to the amphoterism are acid-base reactions involving the OH^- or H_2O groups bound to the metal ions. Complex-ion formation in aqueous solution involves the displacement by Lewis bases (such as NH_3 and CN^-) of water molecules attached to the metal ion. The extent to which such complex formation occurs is expressed quantitatively by the formation constant for the complex ion.

The fact that the ions of different metallic elements vary a great deal in the solubilities of their salts, in their acid-base behavior, and in their tendencies to form complexes can be used to separate and detect the presence of metal ions in mixtures. Qualitative analysis determines the presence or absence of a metal ion in a mixture of metal ions in solution. The analysis usually proceeds by separating the ions into groups on the basis of precipitation reactions and then analyzing each group for individual metal ions.

Key Terms

common-ion effect (Sec. 17.1)
titration curve (Sec. 17.2)

buffered solutions (buffers) (Sec. 17.3)
buffer capacity (Sec. 17.3)

Henderson-Hasselbalch equation (Sec. 17.3)
solubility-product constant (solubility product) (Sec. 17.4)
complex ion (Sec. 17.5)

formation constant (Sec. 17.5)
qualitative analysis (Sec. 17.6)
quantitative analysis (Sec. 17.6)

Exercises

Common-Ion Effect

17.1. **(a)** What is the common-ion effect? **(b)** Give an example of a salt that can decrease the ionization of HOCl in solution. **(c)** Explain why the ionization of a weak base is suppressed by the presence of its conjugate acid.

17.2. **(a)** Consider the equilibrium $HA(aq) \rightleftharpoons H^+(aq) + A^-(aq)$. In terms of Le Châtelier's principle, explain the effect of the presence of a salt of A^- on the ionization of HA. **(b)** Give an example of a salt that can decrease the ionization of NH_3 in solution. **(c)** Explain why the ionization of a weak acid is suppressed by the presence of its conjugate base.

17.3. Describe the effect on pH (increase, decrease, or no change) that results from each of the following additions: **(a)** sodium formate, $NaCHO_2$, to a solution of formic acid, $HCHO_2$; **(b)** ammonium perchlorate, NH_4ClO_4, to a solution of ammonia, NH_3; **(c)** potassium bromide to a solution of potassium nitrite, KNO_2; **(d)** hydrochloric acid, HCl, to a solution of sodium acetate, $NaC_2H_3O_2$.

17.4. Describe the effect on pH (increase, decrease, or no change) that results from each of the following additions: **(a)** ammonia to a solution of HCl; **(b)** ammonium chloride to a solution of HCl; **(c)** sodium cyanide, NaCN, to a solution of HBr; **(d)** pyridinium nitrate, $C_5H_5NHNO_3$, to a solution of pyridine, C_5H_5N.

17.5. Using equilibrium constants from Appendix D, calculate the pH of the following solutions: **(a)** 0.080 M in potassium propionate, $KC_3H_5O_2$, and 0.16 M in propionic acid, $HC_3H_5O_2$; **(b)** 0.15 M in trimethylamine, $(CH_3)_3N$, and 0.12 M in trimethylammonium chloride, $(CH_3)_3NHCl$.

17.6. Calculate the pH of the following solutions: **(a)** 0.100 M in sodium formate, $NaCHO_2$, and 0.180 M in formic acid, $HCHO_2$; **(b)** 0.0750 M in pyridine, C_5H_5N, and 0.0500 M in pyridinium chloride, C_5H_5NHCl.

Acid-Base Titrations

17.7. How many milliliters of 0.0350 M NaOH are required to titrate each of the following solutions to the equivalence point: **(a)** 40.0 mL of 0.0350 M HNO_3; **(b)** 65.0 mL of 0.0620 M HBr; **(c)** 80.0 mL of a solution that contains 1.65 g of HCl per liter?

17.8. How many milliliters of 0.0750 M HCl are needed to titrate each of the following solutions to the equivalence point: **(a)** 50.0 mL of 1.50 M NaOH; **(b)** 43.5 mL of 0.0320 M KOH; **(c)** 27.0 mL of 0.0600 M $Ca(OH)_2$?

17.9. Three 20.0-mL samples of different HBr solutions were titrated with 0.100 M NaOH solution. The volumes of base required to reach the equivalence point in each case were **(a)** 27.5 mL; **(b)** 21.8 mL; **(c)** 48.9 mL. Calculate the concentrations of the three HBr solutions.

17.10. Three 40.0-mL samples of different KOH solutions are titrated with 0.0750 M HNO_3 solution. The volumes of acid needed to reach the equivalence point for each sample are **(a)** 39.1 mL; **(b)** 20.7 mL; **(c)** 48.5 mL. What was the original pH of each of the KOH solutions?

17.11. A 20.0-mL sample of 0.200 M HBr solution is titrated with 0.200 M NaOH solution. Calculate the pH of the solution after the following volumes of base have been added: **(a)** 15.0 mL; **(b)** 19.9 mL; **(c)** 20.0 mL; **(d)** 20.1 mL; **(e)** 35.0 mL.

17.12. A 30.0-mL sample of 0.200 M KOH is titrated with 0.150 M $HClO_4$ solution. Calculate the pH after the following volumes of acid have been added: **(a)** 30.0 mL; **(b)** 39.5 mL; **(c)** 39.9 mL; **(d)** 40.0 mL; **(e)** 40.1 mL.

17.13. How does titration of a strong acid with a strong base differ from titration of a weak acid with a strong base with respect to the following points: **(a)** quantity of base required to reach the equivalence point; **(b)** pH at the beginning of the titration; **(c)** pH at the equivalence point; **(d)** pH after addition of a slight excess of base; **(e)** choice of indicator for determining the equivalence point?

17.14. Assume that 30.0 mL of a 0.10 M solution of a weak base B that accepts one proton is titrated with a 0.10 M solution of the monoprotic strong acid HX. **(a)** How many moles of HX have been added at the equivalence point? **(b)** What is the predominant form of B at the equivalence point? **(c)** What factor determines the pH at the equivalence point? **(d)** Which indicator, phenolphthalein or methyl red, is likely to be the better choice for this titration?

17.15. A 50.0-mL sample of 0.150 M acetic acid, $HC_2H_3O_2$, is titrated with 0.150 M NaOH solution. Calculate the pH after the following volumes of base have been added: **(a)** 0 mL; **(b)** 25.0 mL; **(c)** 49.0 mL; **(d)** 50.0 mL; **(e)** 51.0 mL; **(f)** 75.0 mL.

17.16. Consider the titration of 60.0 mL of 0.100 M NH_3 with 0.150 M HCl. Calculate the pH after the following volumes of titrant have been added: **(a)** 0 mL; **(b)** 20.0 mL; **(c)** 39.5 mL; **(d)** 40.0 mL; **(e)** 40.5 mL; **(f)** 60.0 mL.

17.17. Calculate the pH at the equivalence point for titrating 0.200 M solutions of each of the following bases with

0.200 M HBr: **(a)** sodium hydroxide, NaOH; **(b)** hydroxylamine, NH_2OH; **(c)** aniline, $C_6H_5NH_2$.

17.18. Calculate the pH at the equivalence point in titrating 0.100 M solutions of each of the following with 0.080 M NaOH: **(a)** hydrobromic acid, HBr; **(b)** lactic acid, $HC_3H_5O_3$; **(c)** sodium hydrogen chromate, $NaHCrO_4$.

Buffers

17.19. Explain why a mixture of HCl and KCl does not function as a buffer, whereas a mixture of $HC_2H_3O_2$ and $NaC_2H_3O_2$ does.

17.20. What factors determine **(a)** the pH, and **(b)** the capacity of a buffer solution?

17.21. A buffer is prepared by adding 20.0 g of acetic acid, $HC_2H_3O_2$, and 20.0 g of sodium acetate, $NaC_2H_3O_2$, to enough water to form 2.00 L of solution. **(a)** Determine the pH of the buffer. **(b)** Write the complete ionic equation for the reaction that occurs when a few drops of hydrochloric acid are added to the buffer. **(c)** Write the complete ionic equation for the reaction that occurs when a few drops of sodium hydroxide solution are added to the buffer.

17.22. A buffer is prepared by adding 5.0 g of ammonia, NH_3, and 20.0 g of ammonium chloride, NH_4Cl, to enough water to form 2.50 L of solution. **(a)** What is the pH of this buffer? **(b)** Write the complete ionic equation for the reaction that occurs when a few drops of nitric acid are added to the buffer. **(c)** Write the complete ionic equation for the reaction that occurs when a few drops of potassium hydroxide solution are added to the buffer.

17.23. **(a)** Write the net ionic equation for the reaction that occurs when a solution of perchloric acid, $HClO_4$, is mixed with a solution of sodium nitrite, $NaNO_2$. **(b)** Calculate the equilibrium constant for this reaction. **(c)** Calculate the concentrations of Na^+, ClO_4^-, H^+, NO_2^-, and HNO_2 when 50.0 mL of 0.15 M $HClO_4$ is mixed with 50.0 mL of 0.15 M $NaNO_2$.

17.24. **(a)** Write the net ionic equation for the reaction that occurs when a solution of NaOH is mixed with a solution of methylammonium bromide, CH_3NH_3Br. **(b)** Calculate the equilibrium constant for this reaction. **(c)** Calculate the concentrations of Na^+, Br^-, H^+, $CH_3NH_3^+$, and

CH_3NH_2 when 0.250 L of 0.300 M NaOH is mixed with 0.400 L of 0.100 M CH_3NH_3Br.

17.25. How many moles of sodium hypobromite, NaBrO, should be added to 1.00 L of 0.200 M hypobromous acid, HBrO, to form a buffer solution of pH 8.80? Assume that no volume change occurs when the NaBrO is added.

17.26. How many grams of sodium lactate, $NaC_3H_5O_3$, should be added to 1.00 L of 0.0150 M lactic acid, $HC_3H_5O_3$, to form a buffer solution with pH 3.90? Assume that no volume change occurs when the $NaC_3H_5O_3$ is added.

17.27. A buffer is prepared by adding 1.00 g of acetic acid, $HC_2H_3O_2$, and 1.50 g of sodium acetate, $NaC_2H_3O_2$, to enough water to form 0.100 L of solution. **(a)** What is the pH of this buffer? **(b)** What is the pH after the addition of 1.00 mL of 1.00 M HNO_3 solution? **(c)** What is the pH after the addition of 1.00 mL of 1.00 M KOH solution?

17.28. A buffer solution contains 0.120 mol of propionic acid, $HC_3H_5O_2$, and 0.105 mol of sodium propionate, $NaC_3H_5O_2$, and has a total volume of 1.00 L. **(a)** What is the pH of this buffer? **(b)** What is the pH after the addition of 10 mL of 1.50 M HCl solution? **(c)** What is the pH after the addition of 50 mL of 0.400 M NaOH solution?

17.29. **(a)** What is the ratio of HCO_3^- to H_2CO_3 in blood of pH 7.4? **(b)** What is the ratio of HCO_3^- to H_2CO_3 in an exhausted marathon runner whose blood pH is 7.1?

17.30. A phosphate buffer, consisting of $H_2PO_4^-$ and HPO_4^{2-}, helps control the pH of physiological fluids. Many carbonated soft drinks also use this buffer system. What is the pH of a soft drink in which the major buffer ingredients are 6.5 g of NaH_2PO_4 and 8.0 g of Na_2HPO_4 per 355 mL of solution?

Solubility Equilibria

17.31. **(a)** Why is the concentration of undissolved solid not explicitly included in the expression for the solubility-product constant? **(b)** Write the expression for the solubility-product constant for each of the following strong electrolytes: AgI, $BaCO_3$, Cu_2S, CeF_3, and $Ca_3(PO_4)_2$.

17.32. **(a)** Explain the difference between *solubility* and *solubility-product constant*. **(b)** Write the expression for the

solubility-product constant for each of the following ionic compounds: CuS, NiC_2O_4, Ag_2SO_4, $Co(OH)_3$, and $Fe_3(AsO_4)_2$.

17.33. **(a)** If the molar solubility of CaF_2 at 35°C is 1.24×10^{-3} mol/L, what is K_{sp} at this temperature? **(b)** It is found that 1.1×10^{-2} g of SrF_2 dissolves per 100 mL of aqueous solution at 25°C. Calculate the solubility product for SrF_2. (c) The K_{sp} of $Ba(IO_3)_2$ at 25°C is 6.0×10^{-10}. What is the molar solubility of $Ba(IO_3)_2$?

17.34. (a) The molar solubility of $PbBr_2$ at 25°C is 1.0×10^{-2} mol/L. Calculate K_{sp}. (b) If 0.0490 g of $AgIO_3$ dissolves per liter of solution, calculate the solubility product. (c) Using the appropriate K_{sp} value from Appendix D, calculate the solubility of $Cu(OH)_2$ in grams per liter of solution.

17.35. Using Appendix D, calculate the molar solubility of AgBr in (a) pure water; (b) 3.0×10^{-2} M $AgNO_3$ solution; (c) 0.50 M NaBr solution.

17.36. Calculate the solubility of CaF_2 in grams per liter in (a) pure water; (b) 0.15 M KF solution; (c) 0.080 M $Ca(NO_3)_2$ solution.

17.37. Calculate the molar solubility of $Cu(OH)_2$ (a) at pH 7.0; (b) at pH 9.0; (c) at pH 11.0.

17.38. Calculate the solubility of $Mn(OH)_2$ in grams per liter (a) at pH 7.0; (b) at pH 9.5; (c) at pH 11.8.

17.39. A 0.010 M solution of NaF is shaken with a mixture of solid CaF_2 and BaF_2. At equilibrium, what is the ratio of the concentration of $Ca^{2+}(aq)$ to that of $Ba^{2+}(aq)$?

17.40. What is the ratio of $[Ca^{2+}]$ to $[Fe^{2+}]$ in a lake in which the water is in equilibrium with deposits of both $CaCO_3$ and $FeCO_3$?

17.41. The solubility-product constant for barium permanganate, $Ba(MnO_4)_2$, is 2.5×10^{-10}. Suppose that solid $Ba(MnO_4)_2$ is in equilibrium with a solution of $KMnO_4$. What concentration of $KMnO_4$ is required to establish a concentration of 2.0×10^{-8} M for the Ba^{2+} ion in solution?

17.42. (a) The K_{sp} for cerium iodate, $Ce(IO_3)_3$, is 3.2×10^{-10}. Calculate the molar solubility of $Ce(IO_3)_3$ in pure water. (b) What concentration of $NaIO_3$ in solution would be necessary to reduce the Ce^{3+} concentration in a saturated solution of $Ce(IO_3)_3$ by a factor of 10 below that calculated in part (a)?

Precipitation; Dissolution

17.43. (a) Will $Mn(OH)_2$ precipitate from solution if the pH of a 0.050 M solution of $MnCl_2$ is adjusted to 8.0? (b) Will Ag_2SO_4 precipitate when 100 mL of 0.010 M $AgNO_3$ is mixed with 20 mL of 5.0×10^{-2} M H_2SO_4 solution?

17.44. (a) Will $Co(OH)_2$ precipitate from solution if the pH of a 0.020 M solution of $Co(NO_3)_2$ is adjusted to 8.5? (b) Will $AgIO_3$ precipitate when 100 mL of 0.010 M $AgNO_3$ is mixed with 10 mL of 0.015 M $NaIO_3$? (K_{sp} of $AgIO_3$ is 3.0×10^{-8}.)

17.45. Calculate the minimum pH needed to precipitate $Ni(OH)_2$ so completely that the concentration of Ni^{2+} is less than 1 μg per liter [that is, 1 part per billion (ppb)].

17.46. Suppose that a 50-mL sample of a solution is to be tested for Cl^- ion by addition of 1 drop (0.2 mL) of 0.10 M $AgNO_3$. What is the minimum number of grams of Cl^- that must be present in order for $AgCl(s)$ to form?

17.47. For each of the following slightly soluble salts, write the net ionic equation, if any, for reaction with acid: (a) MnS; (b) PbF_2; (c) $AuCl_3$; (d) $Hg_2C_2O_4$; (e) CuBr.

17.48. Which of the following salts will be substantially more soluble in acidic solution than in pure water: (a) $ZnCO_3$; (b) LaF_3; (c) BiI_3; (d) AgCN; (e) $Ba_3(PO_4)_2$?

17.49. A solution contains 2.0×10^{-4} M Ag^+ and 1.5×10^{-3} M Pb^{2+}. If NaI is added, will AgI ($K_{sp} = 8.3 \times 10^{-17}$) or PbI_2 ($K_{sp} = 1.4 \times 10^{-8}$) precipitate first? Specify the concentration of I^- needed to begin precipitation.

17.50. A solution of Na_2SO_4 is added dropwise to a solution that is 0.010 M in Ba^{2+} and 0.010 M in Sr^{2+}. (a) What concentration of SO_4^{2-} is necessary to begin precipitation? (Neglect volume changes; $BaSO_4$: $K_{sp} = 1.1 \times 10^{-10}$; $SrSO_4$: $K_{sp} = 2.8 \times 10^{-7}$) (b) Which cation precipitates

first? (c) What is the concentration of SO_4^{2-} when the second cation begins to precipitate?

17.51. Calculate the molar solubility of PbS in a 0.10 M solution of H_2S in which the pH is 1.80.

17.52. Calculate the solubility of ZnS (in grams per liter) in a 0.10 M solution of H_2S in which the pH is 2.40.

17.53. Complete and balance each of the following reactions. In each case indicate which species in the reaction can be considered a Lewis base and which a Lewis acid:
(a) $Zn(OH)_2(s) + H^+(aq) \longrightarrow$
(b) $Cd(CN)_2(s) + CN^-(aq) \longrightarrow$
(c) $CrF_3(s) + OH^-(aq) \longrightarrow$

17.54. Complete and balance each of the following reactions. In each case indicate which species in the reaction can be considered a Lewis base and which a Lewis acid:
(a) $Cu^{2+}(aq) + CN^-(aq) \longrightarrow$
(b) $AgCl(s) + S_2O_3^{2-}(aq) \longrightarrow$
(c) $Cu(OH)_2(s) + NH_3(aq) \longrightarrow$

17.55. From the value for K_f listed in Table 17.2 calculate the concentration of Cu^{2+} in 1 L of a solution that contains a total of 1×10^{-3} mol of copper(II) ion and that is 0.10 M in NH_3.

17.56. To what final concentration of NH_3 must a solution be adjusted to just dissolve 0.020 mol of NiC_2O_4 in 1 L of solution? (Hint: You can neglect the hydrolysis of $C_2O_4^{2-}$, because the solution will be quite basic.)

17.57. By using the values of K_{sp} for AgI and K_f for $Ag(CN)_2^-$, calculate the equilibrium constant for the following reaction:

$$AgI(s) + 2CN^-(aq) \rightleftharpoons Ag(CN)_2^-(aq) + I^-(aq)$$

17.58. Using the value of K_{sp} for Ag_2S, K_{a1} and K_{a2} for H_2S, and $K_f = 1.1 \times 10^5$ for $AgCl_2^-$, calculate the equilibrium constant for the following reaction:

$$Ag_2S(s) + 4Cl^-(aq) + 2H^+(aq) \rightleftharpoons$$
$$2AgCl_2^-(aq) + H_2S(aq)$$

Qualitative Analysis

17.59. A solution containing an unknown number of metal ions is treated with dilute HCl; no precipitate forms. The pH is adjusted to about 1, and H_2S is bubbled through. Again no precipitate forms. The pH of the solution is then adjusted to about 8. Again H_2S is bubbled through. This time a precipitate forms. The filtrate from this solution is treated with $(NH_4)_2HPO_4$. No precipitate forms. Which metal ions discussed in Section 17.6 are possibly present? Which are definitely absent within the limits of these tests?

17.60. An unknown solid is entirely soluble in water. On addition of dilute HCl, a precipitate forms. After the precipitate is filtered off, the pH is adjusted to about 1 and H_2S is bubbled in; a precipitate again forms. After filtering off this precipitate, the pH is adjusted to 8 and H_2S is again added; no precipitate forms. No precipitate forms upon addition of $(NH_4)_2HPO_4$. The remaining solution shows a yellow color in a flame test (see Exercise 6.64). Based on these observations, which of the following compounds might be present, which are definitely present, and which are definitely absent: CdS, $Pb(NO_3)_2$, HgO, $ZnSO_4$, $Cd(NO_3)_2$, and Na_2SO_4?

17.61. In the course of various qualitative analysis procedures, the following mixtures are encountered: **(a)** Zn^{2+} and Cd^{2+}; **(b)** $Cr(OH)_3$ and $Fe(OH)_3$; **(c)** Mg^{2+} and K^+; **(d)** Ag^+ and Mn^{2+}. Suggest how each mixture might be separated.

17.62. Suggest how the cations in each of the following solution mixtures can be separated: **(a)** Na^+ and Cd^{2+}; **(b)** Cu^{2+} and Mg^{2+}; **(c)** Pb^{2+} and Al^{3+}; **(d)** Ag^+ and Hg^{2+}.

17.63. **(a)** Precipitation of the group 4 cations (Figure 17.21) requires a basic medium. Why is this so? **(b)** What is the most significant difference between the sulfides precipitated in group 2 and those precipitated in group 3? **(c)** Suggest a procedure that would serve to redissolve all of the group 3 cations following their precipitation and separation.

17.64. A student who is in a great hurry to finish his laboratory work decides that his qualitative analysis unknown contains a metal ion from the insoluble phosphate group, group 4 (Figure 17.21). He therefore tests his sample directly with $(NH_4)_2HPO_4$, skipping earlier tests for the metal ions in groups 1 through 3. He observes a precipitate and concludes that a metal ion from group 4 is indeed present. Why is this possibly an erroneous conclusion?

Additional Exercises

17.65. Furoic acid, $HC_5H_3O_3$, has a K_a value of 6.76×10^{-4} at 25°C. Calculate the pH at 25°C of **(a)** a solution formed by adding 35.0 g of furoic acid and 30.0 g of sodium furoate, $NaC_5H_3O_3$, to enough water to form 0.250 L of solution; **(b)** a solution formed by mixing 30.0 mL of 0.250 M $HC_5H_3O_3$ and 20.0 mL of 0.22 M $NaC_5H_3O_3$ and diluting the total volume to 125 mL; **(c)** a solution prepared by adding 50.0 mL of 1.65 M NaOH solution to 0.500 L of 0.0850 M $HC_5H_3O_3$.

17.66. A certain organic compound that is used as an indicator for acid-base reactions exists in aqueous solution as equal concentrations of the acid form, HB, and the base form, B^-, at a pH of 7.80. What is pK_a for the acid form of this indicator, HB?

17.67. The acid-base indicator bromcresol green is a weak acid. The yellow acid and blue base forms of the indicator are present in equal concentrations in a solution when the pH is 4.68. What is pK_a for bromcresol green?

17.68. A sample of 0.1355 g of an unknown monoprotic acid was dissolved in 25.0 mL of water and titrated with 0.0950 M NaOH. The acid required 19.3 mL of base to reach the equivalence point. **(a)** What is the molar mass of the acid? **(b)** After 12.0 mL of base had been added in the titration, the pH was found to be 5.10. What is the K_a for the unknown acid?

17.69. Potassium hydrogen phthalate, often abbreviated KHP, can be obtained in high purity and is used to determine the concentrations of solutions of strong bases. Strong bases react with the hydrogen phthalate ion as follows:

$$HP^-(aq) + OH^-(aq) \longrightarrow H_2O(l) + P^{2-}(aq)$$

The molar mass of KHP is 204.2 g/mol and K_a for the HP^- ion is 3.1×10^{-6}. **(a)** If a titration experiment begins with 0.4885 g of KHP and has a final volume of about 100 mL, which indicator from Figure 16.7 would be most appropriate? **(b)** If the titration required 38.55 mL of NaOH solution to reach the endpoint, what is the concentration of the NaOH solution?

17.70. Use the answers you obtained for Exercise 17.16 to produce a titration curve for the titration of 0.100 M NH_3 with 0.150 M HCl.

17.71. If 50.00 mL of 0.100 M Na_2SO_3 is titrated with 0.100 M HCl, calculate **(a)** the pH at the start of the titration; **(b)** the volume of HCl required to reach the first equivalence point, and the predominant species present at this point; **(c)** the volume of HCl required to reach the second equivalence point and the pH at the second equivalence point.

17.72. Equal quantities of 0.10 M solutions of an acid HA and a base B are mixed. The pH of the resulting solution is 8.8. **(a)** Write the equilibrium equation and equilibrium expression for the reaction between HA and B. **(b)** If K_a for HA is 5.0×10^{-6}, what is the value of the equilibrium constant for the reaction between HA and B? **(c)** What is the value of K_b for B?

17.73. Consider a buffer solution prepared from Na_2CO_3 and $NaHCO_3$. Write chemical equations for the reactions by which this buffer neutralizes H^+ and OH^-.

17.74. A hypothetical weak acid, HA, was combined with NaOH in the following proportions: 0.20 mol of HA, 0.080 mol of NaOH. The mixture was diluted to a total volume of 1 L, and the pH measured. **(a)** If pH = 4.80, what is the pK_a of the acid? **(b)** How many additional moles of NaOH should be added to the solution to increase the pH to 5.00?

17.75. Two buffers are prepared by adding an equal number of moles of formic acid, $HCHO_2$, and sodium formate, $NaCHO_2$, to enough water to form 1.00 L of solution. Buffer A is prepared using 1.00 mol each of formic acid and sodium formate. Buffer B is prepared by using 0.010 mol of each. **(a)** Calculate the pH of each buffer, and explain why they are equal. **(b)** Which buffer will have the greater capacity? Explain. **(c)** Calculate the change in pH for each buffer upon the addition of 1 mL of 1.00 M HCl. **(d)** Calculate the change in pH for each buffer upon the addition of 10 mL of 1.00 M HCl. **(e)** Discuss your answers for parts (c) and (d) in light of your response to part (b).

17.76. Suppose you need to prepare a buffer at pH 10.6. Using Appendix D, select at least two different acid-base pairs that would be appropriate. Describe the composition of the buffers.

[17.77]. What is the pH of a solution made by mixing 0.30 mol NaOH, 0.25 mol Na_2HPO_4, and 0.20 mol H_3PO_4 with water and diluting to 1.00 L?

[17.78]. Suppose you want to do a physiological experiment that calls for a pH 6.5 buffer. You find that the organism with which you are working is not sensitive to a certain weak acid (H_2X: $K_{a1} = 2 \times 10^{-2}$; $K_{a2} = 5.0 \times 10^{-7}$) and its sodium salts. You have available a 1.0 M solution of this acid and a 1.0 M solution of NaOH. How much of the NaOH solution should be added to 1.0 L of the acid to give a buffer at pH 6.50? (Ignore any volume change.)

17.79. You have 1.0 M solutions of H_3PO_4 and NaOH. Describe how you would prepare a buffer solution of pH 7.20 with the highest possible buffering capacity from these reagents. Describe the composition of the buffer solution.

17.80. A biochemist needs 750 mL of an acetic acid–sodium acetate buffer with pH 4.50. Solid sodium acetate, $NaC_2H_3O_2$, and glacial acetic acid, $HC_2H_3O_2$, are available. Glacial acetic acid is 99 percent $HC_2H_3O_2$ by mass and has a density of 1.05 g/mL. If the buffer is to be 0.30 M in $HC_2H_3O_2$, how many grams of $NaC_2H_3O_2$ and how many milliliters of glacial acetic acid must be used?

[17.81]. How many microliters of 1.000 M NaOH solution must be added to 50.00 mL of a 0.1000 M solution of lactic acid, $HC_3H_5O_3$, to produce a buffer with pH = 3.50?

17.82. Calculate the pH of a saturated solution of $Mn(OH)_2$ at 25°C.

17.83. For each pair of compounds, use K_{sp} values to determine which has the greater molar solubility: **(a)** CdS or CuS; **(b)** $PbCO_3$ or $BaCrO_4$; **(c)** $Hg(OH)_2$ or $Fe(OH)_3$; **(d)** $Ba_3(PO_4)_2$ or NiC_2O_4.

[17.84]. The solubility products of $PbSO_4$ and $SrSO_4$ are 1.6×10^{-8} and 2.8×10^{-7}, respectively. What are the values of $[SO_4^{2-}]$, $[Pb^{2+}]$, and $[Sr^{2+}]$ in a solution at equilibrium with both substances?

[17.85]. Fluoridation of drinking water is employed in many places to aid in the prevention of dental caries. Typically the F^- ion concentration is adjusted to about 1 ppb. Some water supplies are also "hard"; that is, they contain certain cations such as Ca^{2+} that interfere with the action of soap. Consider a case where the concentration of Ca^{2+} is 8 ppb. Could a precipitate of CaF_2 form under these conditions? (Make any necessary approximations.)

[17.86]. What should be the pH of a buffer solution that will result in a Mg^{2+} concentration of 3.0×10^{-2} M in equilibrium with solid magnesium oxalate?

[17.87]. Calculate the solubility of $CuCO_3$ in a strongly buffered solution of pH 7.5.

17.88. What concentration of Pb^{2+} remains in a solution after $PbCl_2$ has been precipitated from a solution that is 0.1 M in Cl^- at 25°C? Will PbS form if the filtrate from the $PbCl_2$ precipitate is saturated with H_2S at pH 1?

[17.89]. The value of K_{sp} for $Mg_3(AsO_4)_2$ is 2.1×10^{-20}. The AsO_4^{3-} ion is derived from the weak acid H_3AsO_4 ($pK_{a1} = 2.22$; $pK_{a2} = 6.98$; $pK_{a3} = 11.50$). When asked to calculate the molar solubility of $Mg_3(AsO_4)_2$ in water, a student used the K_{sp} expression and assumed that $[Mg^{2+}] = 1.5[AsO_4^{3-}]$. Why was this a mistake?

17.90. The pH of a solution that is 0.020 M in Hg^{2+}, 0.020 M in Ni^{2+}, and 0.020 M in Pb^{2+} is adjusted to 2.0 and then saturated with H_2S gas. Which metal ions, if any, will precipitate?

[17.91]. A solution is 0.010 M in Hg^{2+} and 0.010 M in Fe^{2+}. What pH range will allow the selective precipitation of one of the ions after saturation with H_2S?

17.92. Calculate the solubility of $Fe(OH)_3$ in grams per liter in **(a)** a solution buffered at pH 4; **(b)** a solution buffered at pH 10.

[17.93]. Calculate the molar solubility of $Cr(OH)_3$ in **(a)** a solution buffered at pH 7; **(b)** pure water. (This problem is not as simple as it might first appear; consider carefully the concentration of OH^-.)

[17.94]. In the process known as *cyanidation,* gold metal from low-grade ores is oxidized to Au^+ by air and dissolved in solutions of the cyanide ion, CN^-. The Au^+ ion forms a complex with the cyanide ion:

$$Au^+(aq) + 2CN^-(aq) \rightleftharpoons Au(CN)_2^-(aq)$$

The formation constant for this equilibrium is $K_f = 2.0 \times 10^{38}$. Calculate the number of moles of $AuCl(s)$ that will dissolve in 1.0 L of 0.080 M NaCN solution.

[17.95]. The solubility product for $Zn(OH)_2$ is 1.2×10^{-17}. The formation constant for the hydroxo complex, $Zn(OH)_4^{2-}$, is 4.6×10^{17}. What concentration of OH^- is required to dissolve 0.010 mol of $Zn(OH)_2$ in a liter of solution?

Chemistry of the Environment 18

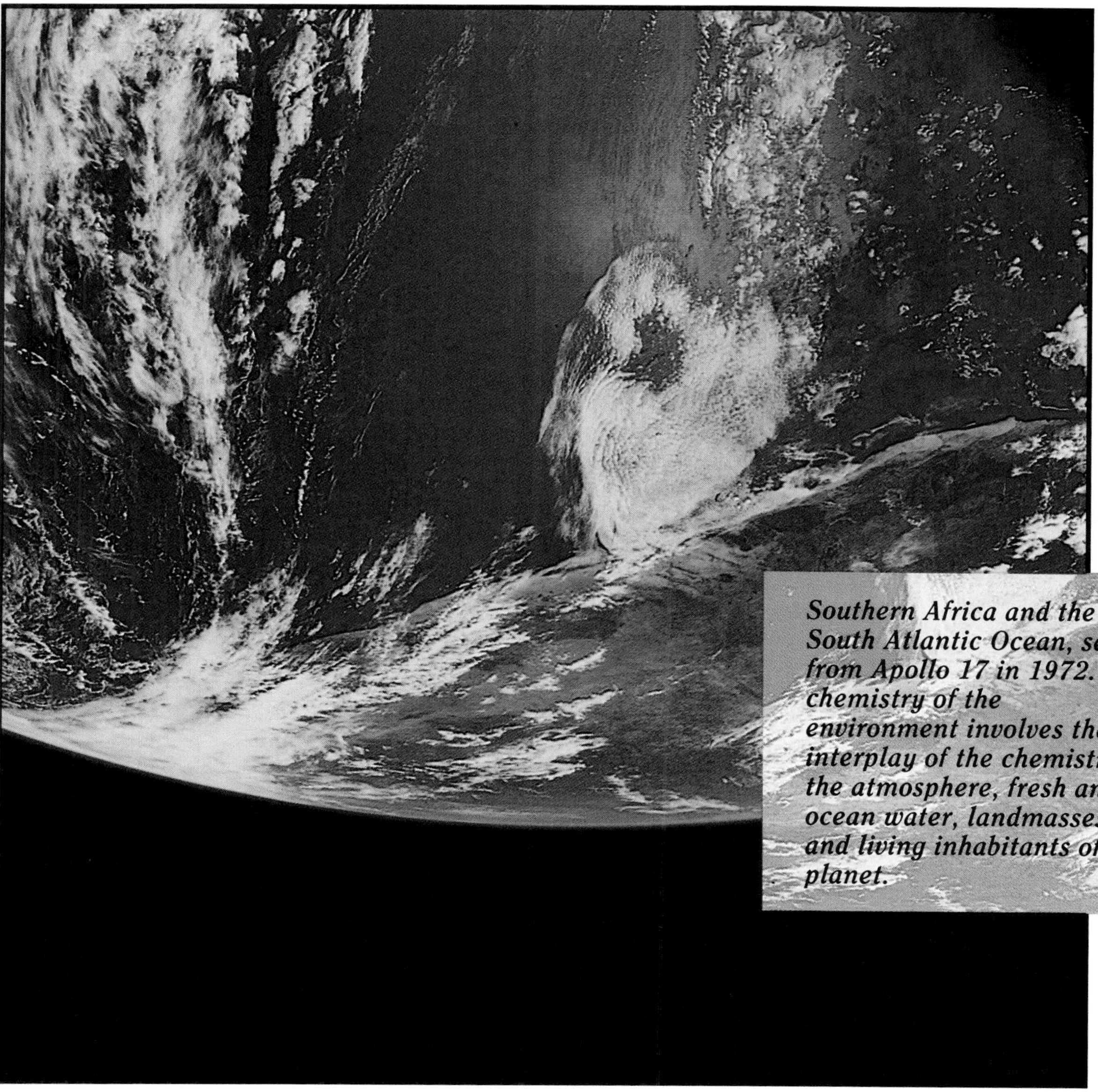

Southern Africa and the South Atlantic Ocean, seen from Apollo 17 in 1972. The chemistry of the environment involves the interplay of the chemistry of the atmosphere, fresh and ocean water, landmasses, and living inhabitants of our planet.

CONTENTS

Point of Emphasis: The *hydrosphere,* which consists of the lower atmosphere and the upper crust of the earth, contains water and is where known life occurs.

Learning Goal 1: Sketch the manner in which atmospheric temperature varies with altitude, and list the various regions of the atmosphere and the boundaries between them.

Point of Emphasis: The divisions among the regions of the atmosphere are gradual and somewhat arbitrary.

Learning Goal 2: Sketch the manner in which atmospheric pressure decreases with elevation, and explain in general terms the reason for the decrease.

In June 1992, representatives of 172 countries met in Rio de Janeiro, Brazil, for the United Nations Conference on Environment and Development—a conference that became known as the Earth Summit. The Earth Summit brought together the largest number of heads of state that had ever gathered in one place. Their principal focus was one of the most important aspects of modern chemistry: the effects of human activities on our environment. The economic growth of both developed and underdeveloped nations depends critically on chemical processes, some of which are harmful to the environment. We are now in a position to apply the principles we have learned in earlier chapters to an understanding of these processes. In this chapter, we consider some aspects of the chemistry of our environment, focusing on the earth's *atmosphere* and on the aqueous environment, called the *hydrosphere.*

Both the atmosphere and hydrosphere of our planet make life as we know it possible. Thus, management of the environment so as to maintain and enhance the quality of life is one of the most important concerns of our time. Our daily decisions as consumers mirror those of the leaders at the Earth Summit: We must weigh the costs versus the benefits of our actions. Unfortunately, the environmental impacts of our decisions are often very subtle and not immediately evident. Our intent in this chapter is to provide an introduction to the nature of the earth's atmosphere and hydrosphere and to indicate some of the ways in which our actions have altered their chemical behavior.

18.1 Earth's Atmosphere

Because most of us have never been very far from the earth's surface, we tend to take for granted the many ways in which the atmosphere determines the environment in which we live. In this section, we will examine some of the important characteristics of our planet's atmosphere.

The temperature of the atmosphere varies in a complex manner as a function of altitude, as shown in Figure 18.1. The atmosphere is divided into four regions based on this temperature profile. Just above the surface, in the **troposphere,** the temperature normally decreases with increasing altitude, reaching a minimum of about 215 K at about 12 km. Nearly all of us live out

FIGURE 18.1 Temperature variations in the atmosphere at altitudes below 110 km.

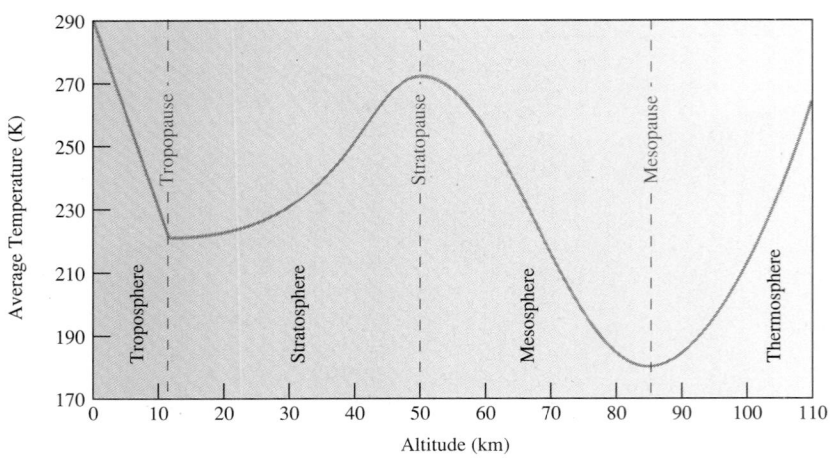

Figure 18.1

our entire lives in the troposphere. Howling winds and soft breezes, rain, sunny skies—all that we normally think of as "weather"—occur in this region. Commercial jet aircraft typically fly about 9 km (30,000 ft) above earth, an altitude that approaches the upper limit of the troposphere, which we call the *tropopause.*

Above the tropopause, the temperature increases with altitude, reaching a maximum of about 275 K at about 50 km. This region is called the **stratosphere.** Beyond the stratosphere are the *mesosphere* and the *thermosphere.* Notice in Figure 18.1 that the temperature extremes that are the boundaries for each region are denoted by the suffix *-pause.* The boundaries are important because mixing of gases across the boundaries is relatively slow. For example, pollutant gases generated in the troposphere find their way into the stratosphere only very slowly.

In contrast to the temperature changes that occur in the atmosphere, the pressure of the atmosphere decreases in a regular way with increasing elevation, as shown in Figure 18.2. We see that atmospheric pressure drops off much more rapidly at lower elevations than at higher ones. The explanation for this characteristic of the atmosphere lies in its compressibility. As a result of the atmosphere's compressibility, the pressure decreases from an average value of 760 torr at sea level to 2.3×10^{-3} torr at 100 km, to only 1.0×10^{-6} torr at 200 km. The troposphere and stratosphere together account for 99.9 percent of the mass of the atmosphere, with 75 percent of the mass in the troposphere.

Composition of the Atmosphere

The atmosphere is an extremely complex system. Its temperature and pressure change over a wide range with altitude, as we have just seen. The atmosphere is subjected to bombardment by radiation and energetic particles from the sun and by cosmic radiation from outer space. This barrage of energy has profound chemical effects, especially on the outer reaches of the atmosphere (Figure 18.3). In addition, because of the earth's gravitational field, lighter atoms and molecules tend to rise to the top. As a result of all these factors, the composition of the atmosphere is not uniform.

Table 18.1 shows the composition by mole fraction of dry air near sea level. Although traces of many substances are present, N_2 and O_2 make up

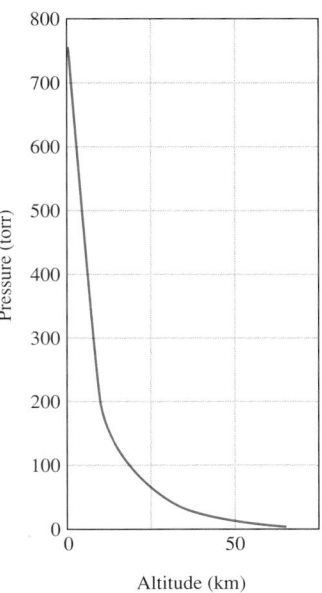

FIGURE 18.2 Variations in atmospheric pressure with altitude.

Figure 18.2

FIGURE 18.3 The aurora borealis, or northern lights. This luminous display in the northern sky is produced by collisions of high-speed electrons and protons from the sun with air molecules. The charged particles are channeled toward the polar regions by the earth's magnetic field. (Jack Finch/Science Photo Library/Science Source/Photo Researchers)

TABLE 18.1 △ Composition of Dry Air Near Sea Level

Component[a]	Content (mole fraction)	Molecular weight
Nitrogen	0.78084	28.013
Oxygen	0.20948	31.998
Argon	0.00934	39.948
Carbon dioxide	0.000355	44.0099
Neon	0.00001818	20.183
Helium	0.00000524	4.003
Methane	0.000002	16.043
Krypton	0.00000114	83.80
Hydrogen	0.0000005	2.0159
Nitrous oxide	0.0000005	44.0128
Xenon	0.000000087	131.30

[a] Ozone, sulfur dioxide, nitrogen dioxide, ammonia, and carbon monoxide are present as trace gases in variable amounts.

Table 18.1

about 99 percent of the entire atmosphere. The noble gases and CO_2 make up most of the remainder.

> **SAMPLE EXERCISE 18.1**
>
> What is the partial pressure of CO_2 in dry air when the total dry air pressure, P_t, is 735 torr?
>
> **SOLUTION** The partial pressure of a given component in the atmosphere is given by the product of its mole fraction and the total atmospheric pressure. ∞ (Sec. 10.6) Referring to Table 18.1, we see that the mole fraction of CO_2 is 3.55×10^{-4}. Thus, we have
>
> $$P_{CO_2} = X_{CO_2}P_t = (3.55 \times 10^{-4})(735 \text{ torr}) = 0.261 \text{ torr}$$
>
> **PRACTICE EXERCISE**
>
> What is the partial pressure of argon in dry air when the total pressure is 750 torr?
> *Answer:* 7.0 torr

In speaking of trace constituents of substances, we commonly use *parts per million* (ppm) as the unit of concentration. When applied to substances in solution, parts per million refers to grams of the substance per million grams of solution. ∞ (Sec. 13.2) However, in dealing with gases, one part per million refers to one part by *volume* in 1 million volume units of the whole. Because of the properties of gases, volume fraction and mole fraction are the same. Thus, 1 ppm of a trace constituent of the atmosphere amounts to 1 mol of that constituent in 1 million moles of total gas; that is, the concentration in ppm is equal to the mole fraction times 10^6. Note that Table 18.1 lists the mole fraction of CO_2 in the atmosphere as 0.000355. Its concentration in ppm is $0.000355 \times 10^6 = 355$ ppm.

Before we consider the chemical processes that occur in the atmosphere, let's review some of the important chemical properties of the two major components of the atmosphere, N_2 and O_2. We saw in Chapter 8 that the N_2 molecule possesses a triple bond between the nitrogen atoms. This very strong bond is largely responsible for the very low reactivity of N_2, which undergoes reaction only under extreme conditions. The $O—O$ bond energy in O_2 is much lower than that for N_2 (Table 8.4), and O_2 is therefore much more reactive than N_2. Oxygen reacts with many substances to form oxides. ∞ (Sec. 7.8) The oxides of nonmetals—for example SO_2—usually form acidic solutions when dissolved in water. The oxides of active metals and other metals in low oxidation states—for example CaO—form basic solutions when dissolved in water.

18.2 The Outer Regions of the Atmosphere

Although the outer portion of the atmosphere, beyond the stratosphere, contains only a small fraction of the atmospheric mass, it plays an important role in determining the conditions of life at the earth's surface. This upper layer forms the outer bastion of defense against the hail of radiation and high-energy particles that continually bombard the planet. As this occurs, the molecules and atoms of the upper atmosphere undergo chemical changes.

Photodissociation

The sun emits radiant energy over a wide range of wavelengths. The shorter-wavelength, higher-energy radiations in the ultraviolet range of the spectrum are sufficiently energetic to cause chemical changes. Recall that electromagnetic radiation can be pictured as a stream of photons. ∞ (Sec. 6.2) The energy of each photon is given by the relationship $E = h\nu$, where h is Planck's constant and ν is the frequency of the radiation. For a chemical change to occur when radiation falls on the earth's atmosphere, two conditions must be met. First, there must be photons with energy sufficient to accomplish whatever chemical process is being considered. Second, molecules must absorb these photons. When these requirements are met, the energy of the photons is converted into some other form of energy within the molecule.

The rupture of a chemical bond resulting from absorption of a photon by a molecule is called **photodissociation.** One of the most important processes occurring in the upper atmosphere above about 120 km elevation is the photodissociation of the oxygen molecule:

$$O_2(g) + h\nu \longrightarrow 2O(g) \qquad\qquad [18.1]$$

The minimum energy required to cause this change is determined by the dissociation energy of O_2, 495 kJ/mol. In Sample Exercise 18.2, we calculate the longest-wavelength photon having sufficient energy to dissociate the O_2 molecule.

SAMPLE EXERCISE 18.2

What is the maximum wavelength of light that has enough energy per photon to dissociate the O_2 molecule?

SOLUTION As stated above, the dissociation energy of O_2 is 495 kJ/mol. We first calculate the amount of energy needed to break the bond in a single O_2 molecule:

$$\left(495 \times 10^3\ \frac{J}{mol}\right)\left(\frac{1\ mol}{6.022 \times 10^{23}\ molecules}\right) = 8.22 \times 10^{-19}\ \frac{J}{molecule}$$

We next use the Planck relation, $E = h\nu$, to calculate the frequency, ν, at which a photon will have this amount of energy:

$$\nu = \frac{E}{h} = \frac{8.22 \times 10^{-19}\ J}{6.625 \times 10^{-34}\ \text{J-s}} = 1.24 \times 10^{15}\ s^{-1}$$

Finally, we use the relationship between the frequency and wavelength of light (Section 6.1) to calculate the wavelength of the light:

$$\lambda = \frac{c}{\nu} = \left(\frac{3.00 \times 10^8\ m/s}{1.24 \times 10^{15}\ /s}\right)\left(\frac{10^9\ nm}{1\ m}\right) = 242\ nm$$

Thus, ultraviolet light of wavelength 242 nm has sufficient energy per photon to photodissociate an O_2 molecule. Because photon energy increases as wavelength *decreases,* any photon of wavelength *shorter* than 242 nm will have sufficient energy to dissociate O_2.

PRACTICE EXERCISE

The bond energy in N_2 is 941 kJ/mol (Table 8.4). What is the longest-wavelength photon that has sufficient energy to dissociate N_2? *Answer:* 127 nm

The second condition that must be met before dissociation actually occurs is that the photon must be absorbed by O_2. Fortunately for us, O_2 absorbs much of the high-energy, short-wavelength radiation from the solar spectrum before it reaches the lower atmosphere. As it does, atomic oxygen, O, is formed. At higher elevations, the dissociation of O_2 is very extensive. At 400 km, only 1 percent of the oxygen is in the form of O_2; the other 99 percent is in the form of atomic oxygen. At 130 km, O_2 and O are just about equally abundant. Below this elevation, O_2 is more abundant than O.

Teaching Note: The equilibrium $2O \rightleftharpoons O_2$ has not changed and still lies to the right. The reason O atoms are so abundant is that the input photochemical energy drives the system to the left side of the equilibrium.

The bond-dissociation energy of N_2 is very high (Table 8.4). As shown in Practice Exercise 18.2, only photons of very short wavelength possess sufficient energy to cause dissociation of this molecule. Furthermore, N_2 does not readily absorb photons, even when they do possess sufficient energy. The overall result is that very little atomic nitrogen is formed in the upper atmosphere by dissociation of N_2.

Photoionization

Learning Goal 5: Explain what is meant by *photoionization,* and relate the energy requirement for photoionization to the ionization potential for the species undergoing ionization.

In 1901, Guglielmo Marconi carried out a sensational experiment. He received in St. John's, Newfoundland, a radio signal transmitted from Land's End, England, some 2900 km away. Because radio waves were thought to travel in straight lines, it had been assumed that radio communication over large distances on earth would be impossible. Marconi's successful experiment suggested that the earth's atmosphere in some way substantially affects radio-wave propagation. His discovery led to intensive study of the upper atmosphere. In about 1924, the existence of electrons in the upper atmosphere was established by experimental studies.

Point of Emphasis: *Photoionization* generally involves the loss of a valence electron through the absorption of high-energy photons by a molecule.

For each electron present in the upper atmosphere, there is a corresponding positively charged ion. The electrons in the upper atmosphere result mainly from the **photoionization** of molecules, caused by solar radiation. For photoionization to occur, a photon must be absorbed by the molecule, and this photon must have enough energy to remove the highest-energy electron. Some of the more important ionization processes occurring in the upper atmosphere above about 90 km appear in Table 18.2, together with the ionization energies and λ_{max}, the maximum wavelength of a photon capable of causing ionization. Photons with energies sufficient to cause ionization have wavelengths in the high-energy region of the ultraviolet. These wavelengths are completely filtered out of the radiation reaching earth as a result of their absorption by the upper atmosphere.

TABLE 18.2 △ Ionization Processes, Ionization Energies, and Maximum Wavelengths Capable of Causing Ionization

Process		Ionization energy (kJ/mol)	λ_{max} (nm)
$N_2 + h\nu \longrightarrow$	$N_2^+ + e^-$	1495	80.1
$O_2 + h\nu \longrightarrow$	$O_2^+ + e^-$	1205	99.3
$O + h\nu \longrightarrow$	$O^+ + e^-$	1313	91.2
$NO + h\nu \longrightarrow$	$NO^+ + e^-$	890	134.5

Table 18.2

18.3 Ozone in the Upper Atmosphere

In contrast to N_2, O_2, and O, which absorb photons with wavelengths shorter than 240 nm, ozone is the key absorber of photons with wavelengths of 240 to 310 nm. Let's consider how ozone forms in the upper atmosphere and how it absorbs photons.

Below 90 km, most of the short-wavelength radiation capable of photoionization has been absorbed. Radiation capable of dissociating the O_2 molecule is sufficiently intense, however, for photodissociation of O_2 (Equation 18.1) to remain important down to 30 km. The chemical processes that occur in the region below about 90 km following photodissociation of O_2 are very different from processes that occur at higher elevations.

In the mesosphere and stratosphere, the concentration of O_2 is much greater than that of atomic oxygen. Therefore, the O atoms that form in the mesosphere and stratosphere undergo frequent collisions with O_2 molecules. These collisions lead to formation of ozone, O_3:

$$O(g) + O_2(g) \longrightarrow O_3{}^*(g) \qquad \text{[18.2]}$$

The asterisk over the O_3 denotes that the ozone molecule contains an excess of energy. Reaction of O with O_2 to form O_3 results in release of 105 kJ/mol. This energy must be gotten rid of by the O_3 molecule in a very short time, or else it will simply fly apart again into O_2 and O. This decomposition is the reverse of the process by which O_3 is formed. An energy-rich O_3 molecule can get rid of its excess energy by colliding with another atom or molecule and transferring some of the excess energy to it. Let us represent the atom or molecule with which O_3 collides as M. (Usually M is N_2 or O_2 because these are the most abundant molecules.) The formation of O_3 and the transfer of excess energy to M are summarized by the following equations:

$$O(g) + O_2(g) \rightleftharpoons O_3{}^*(g) \qquad \text{[18.3]}$$
$$\underline{O_3{}^*(g) + M(g) \longrightarrow O_3(g) + M^*(g) \qquad \text{[18.4]}}$$
$$O(g) + O_2(g) + M(g) \longrightarrow O_3(g) + M^*(g) \quad \text{(net)} \qquad \text{[18.5]}$$

The rate at which O_3 forms according to Equations 18.3 and 18.4 depends on two factors that vary in opposite directions with increasing altitude. First, the formation of $O_3{}^*$ according to Equation 18.3 depends on the presence of O atoms. At low altitudes, most of the radiation energetic enough to dissociate O_2 has been absorbed; thus, the formation of O is favored at higher altitudes. However, both Equations 18.3 and 18.4 depend on molecular collisions. Because the concentration of molecules is greater at low altitudes, the frequency of collisions between O and O_2 (Equation 18.3) and between $O_3{}^*$ and M (Equation 18.4) are both greater at lower altitudes. Because of the opposite altitude dependence of these processes, the highest rate of O_3 formation occurs in a band at an altitude of about 50 km, near the stratopause (Figure 18.1).

Once formed, the ozone molecule does not last long. Ozone is capable of absorbing solar radiation, which results in its decomposition into O_2 and O. Because only 105 kJ/mol is required for this process, photons of wavelength shorter than 1140 nm are sufficiently energetic to photodissociate O_3. The strongest and most important absorptions, however, are of photons from 200 to 310 nm. If it were not for the layer of ozone in the stratosphere, these high-energy photons would penetrate to the earth's surface. Plant and animal life as we know it could not survive in the presence of this high-energy radiation. The "ozone shield" is therefore essential for our continued well-being. It should be noted, however, that the ozone molecules that form this essential shield against radiation represent only a tiny fraction of the oxygen atoms present in the stratosphere. This is because the ozone molecules are continually destroyed even as they are formed.

The photodecomposition of ozone reverses the reaction leading to its formation. We thus have a cyclic process of ozone formation and decomposition, summarized as follows:

$$O_2(g) + h\nu \longrightarrow O(g) + O(g)$$

$$O(g) + O_2(g) + M(g) \longrightarrow O_3(g) + M^*(g) \qquad \text{(heat released)}$$

$$O_3(g) + h\nu \longrightarrow O_2(g) + O(g)$$

$$O(g) + O(g) + M(g) \longrightarrow O_2(g) + M^*(g) \qquad \text{(heat released)}$$

The first and third processes are photochemical; they use a solar photon to initiate a chemical reaction. The second and fourth processes are exothermic chemical reactions. The net result of all four processes is a cycle in which solar radiant energy is converted into thermal energy. The ozone cycle in the stratosphere is responsible for the temperature rise that reaches its maximum at the stratopause, as illustrated in Figure 18.1.

The scheme described above for the life and death of ozone molecules accounts for some but not all of the known facts about the ozone layer. Many chemical reactions occur that involve substances other than just oxygen. In addition, the effects of turbulence and winds that mix up the stratosphere must be considered. A very complicated picture results. The overall result of ozone formation and removal reactions, coupled with atmospheric turbulence and other factors, is to produce an ozone profile in the upper atmosphere as shown in Figure 18.4.

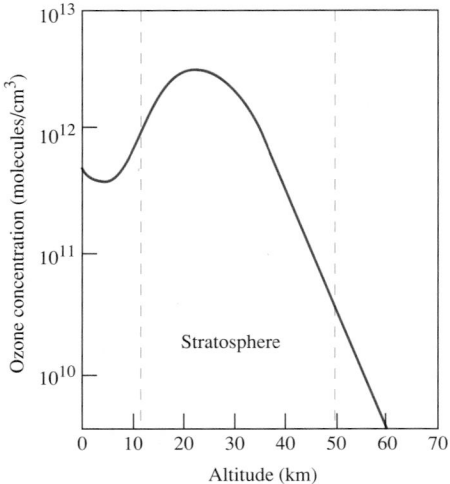

Figure 18.4

Depletion of the Ozone Layer

In 1974, F. Sherwood Rowland and Mario Molina of the University of California, Irvine, proposed that chlorine from **chlorofluorocarbons** (CFCs) may deplete the ozone layer. These substances, principally $CFCl_3$ (Freon-11) and CF_2Cl_2 (Freon-12), have been widely used as propellants in spray cans, as refrigerant and air-conditioner gases, and as foaming agents for plastics. They are virtually unreactive in the lower atmosphere. Furthermore, they are relatively insoluble in water and are therefore not removed from the atmosphere by rainfall or by dissolution in the oceans. Unfortunately, the lack of reactivity that makes them commercially useful also allows them to survive in the atmosphere and to diffuse eventually into the stratosphere. It is estimated that several million tons of chlorofluorocarbons are present in the atmosphere.

As CFCs diffuse into the stratosphere, they are exposed to high-energy radiation, which can cause photodissociation. The C—Cl bonds are considerably weaker that the C—F bonds (Table 8.4). As a result, free chlorine atoms are formed readily in the presence of light with wavelengths in the range 190 to 225 nm, as shown below for Freon-12:

$$CF_2Cl_2(g) + h\nu \longrightarrow CF_2Cl(g) + Cl(g) \qquad [18.6]$$

Calculations suggest that chlorine atom formation occurs at the greatest rate at an altitude of about 30 km.

Atomic chlorine reacts rapidly with ozone to form chlorine oxide, ClO, and molecular oxygen, O_2:

$$Cl(g) + O_3(g) \longrightarrow ClO(g) + O_2(g) \qquad [18.7]$$

Equation 18.7 follows a second-order rate law with a very large rate constant:

$$\text{Rate} = -\frac{\Delta[O_3]}{\Delta t} = k[Cl][O_3] \qquad k = 7.2 \times 10^9 \ M^{-1} \ s^{-1} \text{ at 298 K} \quad [18.8]$$

Under certain conditions, the ClO generated in Equation 18.7 can react to regenerate free Cl atoms (see the Closer Look box):

$$2ClO(g) \longrightarrow O_2(g) + 2Cl(g) \qquad [18.9]$$

The Cl atoms generated in Equation 18.9 can react with more O_3, according to Equation 18.7. These two equations form a cycle for the Cl-atom-catalyzed decomposition of O_3 to O_2:

$$\text{Net:} \qquad 2O_3(g) \xrightarrow{\ Cl\ } 3O_2(g) \qquad [18.10]$$

Because the rate of Equation 18.7 increases linearly with [Cl], the rate at which ozone is destroyed increases as the quantity of Cl atoms increases. Thus, the greater the amount of CFCs that diffuse into the stratosphere, the faster the destruction of the ozone layer. Rates of diffusion of molecules from the troposphere into the stratosphere are slow. Nevertheless, a thinning of the ozone layer over the South Pole has already been observed, particularly during the month of October (Figure 18.5). Scientists are now finding evidence that the North Pole

Teaching Note: Refrigerants that do not contain Freon are beginning to appear on the market. Aerosol propellants without Freon have been available for several years, although they do not function well in all applications.

Teaching Note: Chlorine atoms are a catalyst for the decomposition of ozone. A *catalyst* is a substance that alters the rate of a reaction without being consumed. See Chapter 14.

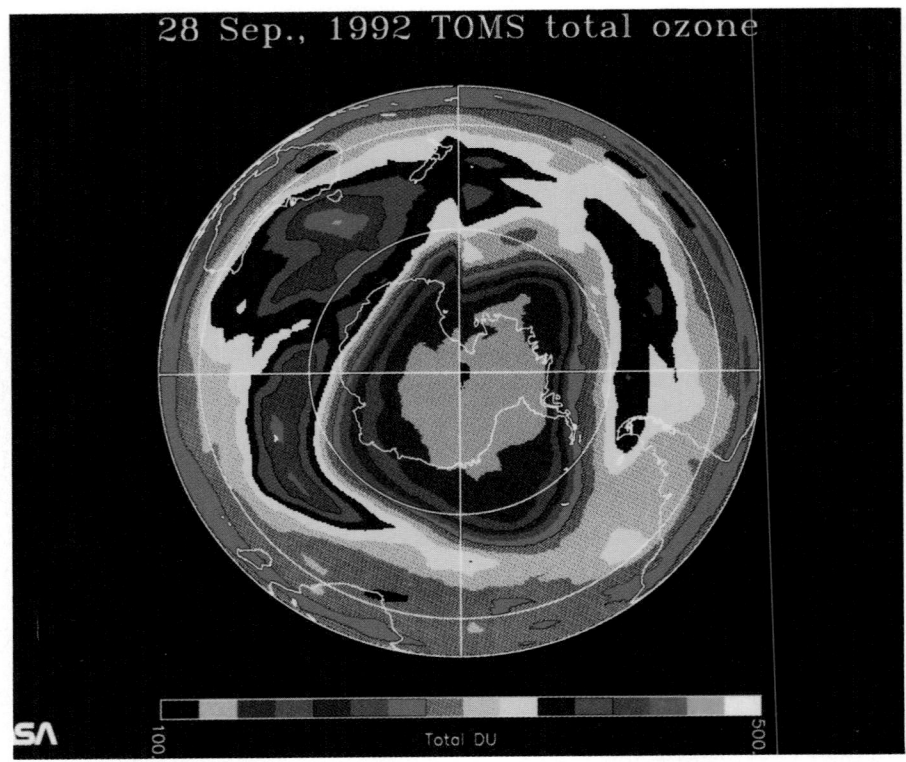

FIGURE 18.5 Map of the total ozone present in the Southern Hemisphere, taken in September 1992 from an orbiting satellite. The scale on the right indicates ozone levels as measured in Dobson units (DU): The lower the DU, the lower the ozone level. (NASA/Goddard Space Flight Center)

suffers a similar but less pronounced ozone loss during late winter. There is also increasing evidence of some depletion at lower altitudes.

Because of the environmental problems associated with continued CFC production, the 1990 Clean Air Act mandated that CFC production in the United States cease by the year 2000. In February 1992, increasing evidence of stratospheric ozone depletion prompted President George Bush to move this deadline to 1995. Nevertheless, because CFCs are so unreactive and because they diffuse so slowly into the stratosphere, scientists estimate that ozone depletion over both the Arctic and Antarctic will continue until at least the year 2000.

18.4 Chemistry of the Troposphere

Point of Emphasis: Most gas-phase photochemical reactions occur in the stratosphere, and nonphotochemical reactions generally occur in the troposphere.

Learning Goal 7: List the names and chemical formulas of the more important pollutant substances present in the troposphere in urban atmospheres.

The troposphere consists primarily of N_2 and O_2, which together comprise 99 percent of the earth's atmosphere at sea level (Table 18.1). Other gases, although present only at very low concentrations, can have major effects on our environment. Table 18.3 lists the major sources and typical concentrations of some of the important minor constituents of the troposphere. Many of these substances occur to only a slight extent in the natural environment but exhibit much higher concentrations in certain areas as a result of human activities. Indeed, in some areas the concentrations of these substances have increased considerably during the last 50 years. In this section, we will discuss the most important characteristics of a few of these substances and their chemical role as air pollutants. As we will see, most form as either a direct or indirect result of our widespread use of combustion reactions.

A CLOSER LOOK

Stratospheric Clouds and Ozone Depletion

Since the mid-1970s, chemists and atmospheric scientists have extensively studied the depletion of ozone in the stratosphere above Antarctica. One of the puzzling aspects of the ozone depletion is that it maximizes in September and October, the beginning of the Antarctic spring. About 70 percent of the ozone above Antarctica is lost during these months, with most of the loss occurring at altitudes between 12 and 30 km.

The most recent theories about the formation of the ozone hole describe a fascinating interplay of chemical and physical effects that occur in the Antarctic stratosphere. As indicated in Equation 18.7, the release of free chlorine atoms (from CFCs and other sources) leads to the destruction of ozone and the formation of ClO. Both $Cl(g)$ and $ClO(g)$ undergo reactions with other constituents of the atmosphere, such as CH_4 and NO_2, to form hydrogen chloride, HCl, and chlorine nitrate, $ClONO_2$:

$$Cl(g) + CH_4(g) \longrightarrow HCl(g) + CH_3(g) \quad [18.11]$$

$$ClO(g) + NO_2(g) \longrightarrow ClONO_2(g) \quad [18.12]$$

Neither HCl nor $ClONO_2$ reacts directly with ozone. Consequently, once Cl and ClO are tied up in this so-called chlorine reservoir of HCl and $ClONO_2$, they no longer lead to the destruction of ozone. For this reason, early models predicted that CFCs would not have a sizable effect on the stratospheric ozone concentration.

The seasonal change in the size of the ozone hole provided a clue as to why ozone depletion by Cl is more extensive than was originally proposed. The current model, proposed in the mid-1980s, suggests that *polar stratospheric clouds* (PSCs) accelerate the destruction of ozone. Clouds in the stratosphere are thought to be uncommon, in large part because so little water vapor is found in the stratosphere. During the dark Antarctic winter, however, the temperatures are low enough (<195 K) for clouds to form, typically at an altitude of about 20 km (Figure 18.6). The formation of clouds removes NO_2 from the atmosphere, which stops the removal of ClO (Equation 18.12). The crystallite surfaces in the clouds also catalyze the reaction between the two components of the chlorine reservoir, HCl and $ClONO_2$, which leads to the formation of Cl_2:

$$HCl + ClONO_2 \xrightarrow{PSC} Cl_2 + HNO_3 \quad [18.13]$$

In September, when sunlight returns to the Antarctic region, the Cl_2 is photodissociated into Cl atoms, which react with ozone to form ClO and O_2 (Equation 18.7). Because so little NO_2 is present in the atmosphere, the ClO that is produced is not tied up in the chlorine reservoir. Instead, ClO reacts with itself to form Cl_2O_2, a molecule that photodissociates into O_2 and free Cl

FIGURE 18.6 Polar stratospheric clouds (PSCs) form over Antarctica during its cold winter months. (Courtesy of Dr. Susan Solomon, NOAA)

atoms:

$$ClO + ClO \longrightarrow Cl_2O_2$$

$$Cl_2O_2 + h\nu \longrightarrow O_2 + 2Cl$$

The Cl atoms react with more ozone, and the cycle begins anew. Thus, the PSCs make free chlorine atoms more readily available for the destruction of ozone; a single chlorine atom may destroy thousands of ozone molecules before it is deactivated by a hydrocarbon or NO_2.

As the Antarctic spring progresses into November, warming temperatures and changing wind currents break up the PSCs, ending the period of massive ozone destruction. The ozone-depleted air spreads outward from the Antarctic, leading to a decrease of stratospheric ozone levels throughout the Southern Hemisphere. The long-term effect of this global ozone depletion promises to be of major concern to both the chemistry and the health science communities well into the next century.

TABLE 18.3 △ Sources and Typical Concentrations of Some Minor Atmospheric Constituents

Minor constituent	Sources	Typical concentrations
Carbon dioxide, CO_2	Decomposition of organic matter; release from the oceans; fossil-fuel combustion	355 ppm throughout troposphere
Carbon monoxide, CO	Decomposition of organic matter; industrial processes; fuel combustion	0.05 ppm in nonpolluted air; 1 to 50 ppm in urban traffic areas
Methane, CH_4	Decomposition of organic matter; natural-gas seepage	1 to 2 ppm throughout troposphere
Nitric oxide, NO	Electrical discharges; internal-combustion engines; combustion of organic matter	0.01 ppm in nonpolluted air; 0.2 ppm in smog atmospheres
Ozone, O_3	Electrical discharges; diffusion from stratosphere; photochemical smog	0 to 0.01 ppm in nonpolluted air; 0.5 ppm in photochemical smog
Sulfur dioxide, SO_2	Volcanic gases; forest fires; bacterial action; fossil-fuel combustion; industrial processes (roasting of ores, and so on)	0 to 0.01 ppm in nonpolluted air; 0.1 to 2 ppm in polluted urban environment

Sulfur Compounds and Acid Rain

Sulfur-containing compounds are present to some extent in the natural, unpolluted atmosphere. They originate in the bacterial decay of organic matter, in volcanic gases, and from other sources listed in Table 18.3. The concentration of sulfur-containing compounds in the atmosphere resulting from natural sources is very small in comparison with the concentrations built up in urban and industrial environments as a result of human activities. Sulfur compounds, chiefly sulfur dioxide, SO_2, are among the most unpleasant and harmful of the common pollutant gases. Table 18.4 shows the concentrations of several pollutant gases in a *typical* urban environment (not one that is particularly affected by smog). According to these data, the level of sulfur dioxide is 0.08 ppm or higher about half the time. This concentration is considerably lower than that of other pollutants, notably carbon monoxide. Nevertheless, sulfur dioxide is regarded as the most serious health hazard among the pollutants shown, especially for people with respiratory difficulties. Studies of the medical case histories of large population segments in urban environments have shown clearly that those living in the most heavily polluted parts of cities have higher levels of respiratory disease and shorter life expectancies.

Combustion of coal and oil accounts for about 80 percent of the total SO_2 released in the United States. The extent to which SO_2 emissions are a problem

Point of Emphasis: Sulfur emissions and acid rain originate mainly from the combustion of coal.

TABLE 18.4 △ Median Concentrations of Atmospheric Pollutants in a Typical Urban Atmosphere

Pollutant	Concentration (ppm)
Carbon monoxide	10
Hydrocarbons	3
Sulfur dioxide	0.08
Nitrogen oxides	0.05
Total oxidants (ozone and others)	0.02

in the burning of coal and oil depends on the level of their sulfur concentration. Some oil, known as *sweet crude oil,* is relatively low in sulfur. High-sulfur oil, such as that from Venezuela, is called *sour crude.* Because of concern about SO_2 pollution, low-sulfur oil, such as that from the Middle East, is in greater demand and is consequently more expensive.

Learning Goal 8: List the major sources of sulfur dioxide as an atmospheric pollutant.

Coals vary considerably in their sulfur content. Much of the coal lying in beds east of the Mississippi is relatively high in sulfur content, up to 6 percent by mass. Much of the coal lying in the western states has a lower sulfur content. This coal, however, also has a lower heat content per unit mass of coal, so that the difference in sulfur content on the basis of a unit amount of heat produced is not as large as is often assumed.

More than 30 million tons of SO_2 is released into the atmosphere in the United States each year. (By comparison, the 1982 eruption of the El Chichón volcano in Mexico spewed about 5 million tons of sulfur compounds.) This material causes severe damage to both property and human health. Sulfur dioxide itself is harmful; furthermore, atmospheric SO_2 can be oxidized to SO_3 by any of several different pathways (such as the reaction with O_2 or O_3). Once SO_3 is formed, it dissolves in water droplets, producing sulfuric acid, H_2SO_4:

$$SO_3(g) + H_2O(l) \longrightarrow H_2SO_4(aq)$$

The presence of sulfuric acid in rain is largely responsible for the phenomenon of **acid rain.** (Nitrogen oxides, which form nitric acid, also contribute.) About 200 years ago, rain had a pH between 6 and 7. Today it is common in many regions for rain to have a pH between 4 and 4.5. In Los Angeles, the pH of fog has actually fallen to 2, about the acidity of lemon juice. Acid rain has affected many lakes in northern Europe, the northern United States, and Canada. The acidity has dramatically reduced fish populations and has measurably affected other parts of the ecological network within the lakes and surrounding forests.

The pH of most productive natural waters is between 6.5 and 8.5. At pH levels below 4.0, all vertebrates, most invertebrates, and many microorganisms are destroyed. The lakes that are most susceptible to damage are those with low concentrations of basic ions like HCO_3^- that buffer them against changes in pH. Over 300 lakes in New York State contain no fish, and 140 lakes in Ontario, Canada, are devoid of life. The acid rain that appears to have killed these lakes originates hundreds of kilometers downwind in the Ohio Valley and Great Lakes regions.

Acid rain also corrodes many metals and building materials. For example, marble and limestone, whose major constituent is $CaCO_3$, are readily attacked by acid rain (Figure 18.7). Billions of dollars each year are lost as a result of corrosion due to SO_2 pollution.

Obviously, we all want to reduce the quantity of this noxious gas that is released into the environment. One way to do this is to remove sulfur from coal and oil before it is burned. This is presently too difficult and expensive to be technologically feasible. However, several methods have been developed for removing SO_2 from the gases formed when coal and oil are combusted. For example, powdered limestone, $CaCO_3$, may be blown into the combustion chamber. The limestone is decomposed into lime, CaO, and carbon dioxide:

$$CaCO_3(s) \longrightarrow CaO(s) + CO_2(g)$$

FIGURE 18.7 The erosion of historical statues and other objects, such as this statuary at Notre Dame Cathedral in France, is largely the result of the reaction of acidic rainfall with limestone. (Richard Megna/Fundamental Photographs)

The lime then reacts with SO_2 to form calcium sulfite:

$$CaO(s) + SO_2(g) \longrightarrow CaSO_3(s)$$

Only about half the SO_2 is removed by contact with the dry solid. The furnace gas must then be "scrubbed" with an aqueous suspension of lime to remove the $CaSO_3$ and any unreacted SO_2. This process, which is illustrated in Figure 18.8, is difficult to engineer, reduces the heat effectiveness of the fuel, and leaves an enormous solid-waste disposal problem. An electric power plant serving the needs of a population of about 150,000 people would produce about 160,000 tons per year of solid waste if it were equipped with the purification system just described. This is three times the normal fly-ash waste from a plant of this size. Various schemes may be employed to recover elemental sulfur or some other

Teaching Note: A major controversy surrounding the acid rain problem involves methods of reducing sulfur emissions and their costs.

FIGURE 18.8 Common method for removing SO_2 from combusted fuel. Powdered limestone decomposes into CaO, which reacts with SO_2 to form $CaSO_3$. The $CaSO_3$ and any unreacted SO_2 enter a purification chamber, where a shower of CaO and water converts the remaining SO_2 into $CaSO_3$ and precipitates the $CaSO_3$ into a watery residue called a *slurry*.

Figure 18.8

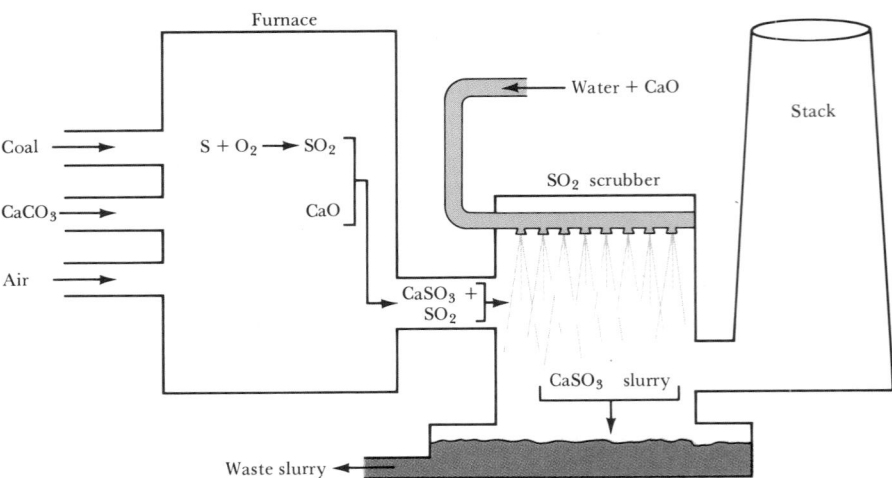

industrially useful chemical from the SO_2, but as yet no process has been found sufficiently attractive from an economic point of view to warrant large-scale development. Pollution by sulfur dioxide will probably remain a major problem for some time.

Carbon Monoxide

Carbon monoxide is formed by the incomplete combustion of carbon-containing materials—for example, fossil fuels. In terms of total mass, CO is the most abundant of all the pollutant gases. The level of CO present in unpolluted air is low, probably on the order of 0.05 ppm. The estimated total amount of CO in the atmosphere is about 5.2×10^{14} g. In the United States alone, roughly 1×10^{14} g of CO is produced each year, about two-thirds of which comes from automobiles.

Learning Goal 9: Explain why carbon monoxide constitutes a health hazard.

Carbon monoxide is a relatively unreactive molecule and consequently poses no direct threat to vegetation or materials. It does affect humans, however. It has the unusual ability to bind very strongly to **hemoglobin,** the iron-containing protein responsible for oxygen transport in the blood. Hemoglobin consists of four protein chains loosely held together in a cluster. Each chain has within its folds a heme molecule. The structure of heme is shown in Figure 18.9. Note that iron is situated in the center of a plane of four nitrogen atoms. A hemoglobin molecule in the lungs picks up an O_2 molecule, which reacts with the iron atom to form a species called *oxyhemoglobin.* As the blood circulates, the oxygen molecule is released in tissues as needed for cell metabolism, that is, for the chemical processes occurring in the cell. (See the Chemistry and Life box on blood as a buffered solution in Section 17.3.)

Point of Emphasis: We frequently hear stories of injuries and deaths due to carbon monoxide. This attests to the extreme toxicity of CO, which binds to hemoglobin 210 times more strongly than does oxygen.

Like O_2, CO also binds very strongly to the iron in hemoglobin. The complex is called *carboxyhemoglobin* and is represented as COHb. The affinity of human hemoglobin for CO is about 210 times greater than for O_2. As a result, a relatively small quantity of CO can inactivate a substantial fraction of the hemoglobin in the blood for oxygen transport. For example, a person breathing air that contains only 0.1 percent of CO takes in enough CO after a few hours of breathing to convert up to 60 percent of the hemoglobin into COHb, thus reducing the blood's normal oxygen-carrying capacity by 60 percent.

Under normal conditions, a nonsmoker breathing unpolluted air has about 0.3 to 0.5 percent COHb in the bloodstream. This amount arises mainly

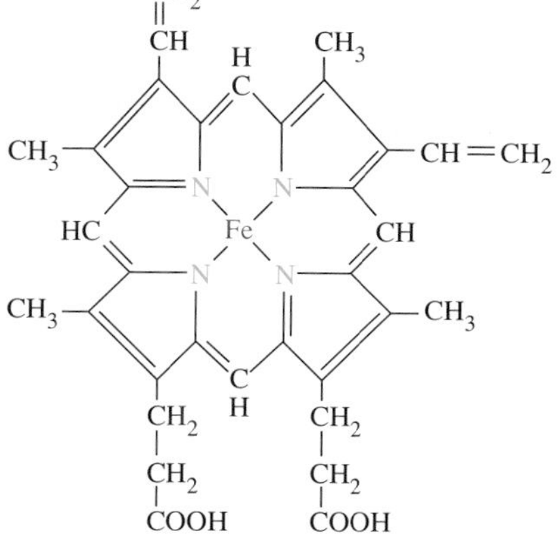

FIGURE 18.9 Structure of the heme molecule.

Figure 18.9

from the production of small quantities of CO in the course of normal body chemistry and from the small amount of CO present in clean air. Exposure to higher concentrations of CO causes the COHb level to increase, which in turn leaves fewer Hb sites to which O_2 can bind. If the level of COHb becomes too high, oxygen transport is effectively shut down, and death occurs. Because CO is colorless and odorless, CO poisoning occurs with very little warning. Improperly ventilated combustion devices, such as kerosene lanterns and stoves, thus pose a potential health hazard (Figure 18.10).

Teaching Note: Victims of CO poisoning often become sleepy from the lack of oxygen.

Nitrogen Oxides and Photochemical Smog

Learning Goal 10: List the more important reactions of nitrogen oxides and ozone that occur in smog formation.

The atmospheric chemistry of nitrogen oxides is interesting because these substances are primary components of smog, a phenomenon with which city dwellers are all too familiar. The term *smog* refers to a particularly unpleasant condition of pollution in certain urban environments that occurs when weather conditions produce a relatively stagnant air mass. The smog made famous by Los Angeles, but now common in many other urban areas as well, is more accurately described as **photochemical smog,** because photochemical processes play a major role in its formation (Figure 18.11).

Nitric oxide, NO, forms in small quantities in the cylinders of internal-combustion engines by the direct combination of nitrogen and oxygen:

$$N_2(g) + O_2(g) \rightleftharpoons 2NO(g) \qquad \Delta H = 180.8 \text{ kJ} \qquad [18.14]$$

Point of Emphasis: Nitrogen oxide emissions and smog originate with the high-temperature combustion of petroleum fuels.

As noted in the Chemistry at Work box in Section 15.6, the equilibrium constant, K_p, for this reaction increases from about 10^{-15} at 300 K (near room temperature) to about 0.05 at 2400 K (approximately the temperature in the cylinder of an engine during combustion). Thus, the reaction is more favorable at higher temperatures. Before the installation of pollution-control devices, typical emission levels of NO_x were 4 g/mi. (The x is either 1 or 2; both NO and NO_2 are formed, although NO predominates.) Present auto emission standards call for NO_x emission levels of less than 1 g/mi.

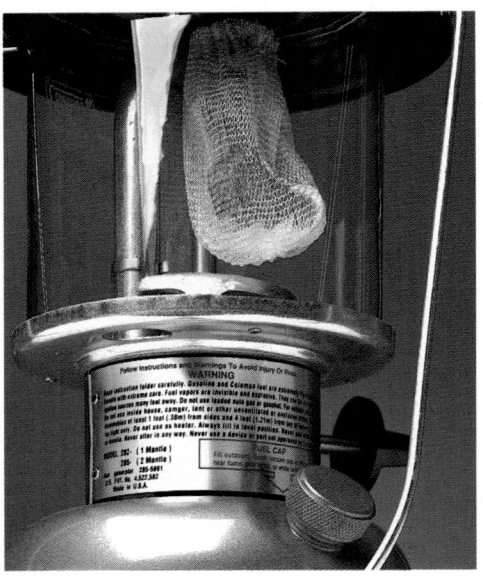

FIGURE 18.10 Kerosene lamps and stoves have warning labels concerning use in enclosed spaces, such as an indoor room. Incomplete combustion can produce colorless, odorless carbon monoxide, CO, which is toxic. (Richard Megna/Fundamental Photographs)

In air, NO is rapidly oxidized to nitrogen dioxide, NO_2:

$$2NO(g) + O_2(g) \rightleftharpoons 2NO_2(g) \qquad \Delta H = -113.1 \text{ kJ} \qquad [18.15]$$

The equilibrium constant for this reaction decreases from about 10^{12} at 300 K to about 10^{-5} at 2400 K. The photodissociation of NO_2 initiates the reactions associated with photochemical smog. The dissociation of NO_2 into NO and O requires 304 kJ/mol, which corresponds to a photon wavelength of 393 nm. In sunlight, therefore, NO_2 undergoes dissociation to NO and O:

$$NO_2(g) + h\nu \longrightarrow NO(g) + O(g) \qquad [18.16]$$

The atomic oxygen formed undergoes several possible reactions, one of which forms ozone, as described earlier:

$$O(g) + O_2 + M(g) \longrightarrow O_3(g) + M^*(g) \qquad [18.17]$$

Ozone is a key component of photochemical smog. Although it is an essential UV screen in the upper atmosphere, it is an undesirable pollutant in the troposphere. It is extremely reactive and toxic, and breathing air that contains appreciable amounts of ozone can be especially dangerous for asthma sufferers, exercisers, and the elderly. We therefore have two ozone problems: excessive amounts in many urban environments, where it is harmful, and depletion in the stratosphere, where it is vital.

In addition to nitrogen oxides and carbon monoxide, an automobile engine also emits as pollutants unburned *hydrocarbons*. These organic compounds, which are composed entirely of carbon and hydrogen, are the principal components of gasoline (Section 26.1). A typical engine without effective emission controls emits about 10 to 15 g of these compounds per mile. Current standards require that hydrocarbon emissions be less than 0.4 g/mi.

Reduction or elimination of smog requires that the essential ingredients for its formation be removed from automobile exhaust. Catalytic converters are designed to reduce drastically the levels of two of the major ingredients of smog: NO_x and hydrocarbons (see the Chemistry at Work box in Section 14.6). However, emission-control systems are notably unsuccessful in poorly maintained automobiles.

Water Vapor, Carbon Dioxide, and Climate

We have seen how the atmosphere makes life as we know it possible on earth by screening out harmful short-wavelength radiation. In addition, the atmosphere is essential in maintaining a reasonably uniform and moderate temperature on the surface of the planet. The two atmospheric components of major importance in maintaining the earth's surface temperature are carbon dioxide and water.

The earth is in overall thermal balance with its surroundings. This means that the planet radiates energy into space at a rate equal to the rate at which it absorbs energy from the sun. The sun has a temperature of about 6000 K. As seen from outer space, the earth is relatively cold, with a temperature of about 254 K. The distribution of wavelengths in the radiation emitted from an object is determined by its temperature. Why does the earth, viewed from outside its

FIGURE 18.11 Photochemical smog over Los Angeles. Smog is produced largely by the action of sunlight on automobile exhaust gases. (Bill Ross/West Light)

Point of Emphasis: Although ozone is a desirable component of the upper atmosphere, in the troposphere it causes a variety of health and pollution problems. For example, ozone is largely responsible for the aging and cracking of plastic and rubber.

Teaching Note: The vapor boots around gas station nozzles are designed to minimize the contribution of evaporated fuel to air pollution.

Learning Goal 11: Explain why the concentration of carbon dioxide in the troposphere has an effect on the average temperature at the earth's surface.

atmosphere, appear so much colder than the temperature we usually experience at its surface? The troposphere, transparent to visible light, is not transparent to infrared radiation. Figure 18.12 shows the distribution of radiation from the earth's surface and the wavelengths absorbed by atmospheric water vapor and carbon dioxide. Clearly, these atmospheric gases absorb much of the outgoing radiation from the earth's surface. It is indeed fortunate for us that they do so; they serve to maintain a livably uniform temperature at the surface by holding in, as it were, the infrared radiation from the surface, which we feel as heat. The influence of water and carbon dioxide on the earth's climate is often called the *greenhouse effect*. (See the Chemistry at Work box in Section 3.6.)

The partial pressure of water vapor in the atmosphere varies greatly from place to place and time to time, but, in general, it is highest near the surface and drops off very sharply with increased elevation. Because water vapor absorbs infrared radiation so strongly, it plays the major role in maintaining the atmospheric temperature at night, when the surface is emitting radiation into space and not receiving energy from the sun. In very dry desert climates, where the water-vapor concentration is unusually low, it may be extremely hot during the day but very cold at night. In the absence of an extensive layer of water vapor to absorb and then radiate back to the earth part of the infrared radiation, the surface loses this radiation into space and cools off very rapidly.

Carbon dioxide plays a secondary, but very important, role in maintaining the surface temperature. The worldwide combustion of fossil fuels, principally coal and oil, on a prodigious scale in the modern era has materially increased the carbon dioxide level of the atmosphere. Measurements carried out over several decades show clearly that the CO_2 concentration in the atmosphere is steadily increasing (Figure 18.13). On the basis of present and expected future rates of fossil-fuel use, the atmospheric CO_2 level is expected to increase about 100 percent by 2050. From a knowledge of the infrared-absorbing characteristics of CO_2 and water, and using a theoretical model for the atmosphere, scientists have estimated that doubling the concentration of CO_2 from its present level would cause the average surface temperature of the planet to increase by 3°C. Major changes in global climate could result from a temperature change of this or even a smaller magnitude. Because so many factors go into determining climate, we cannot predict with certainty what changes will

Teaching Note: Volcanic activity is a major natural source of CO_2 in the atmosphere, although it is not responsible for the increase in CO_2 concentration seen over the last 140 years.

FIGURE 18.12 Long-wavelength radiation from earth compared with the absorption of infrared radiation by carbon dioxide and water.

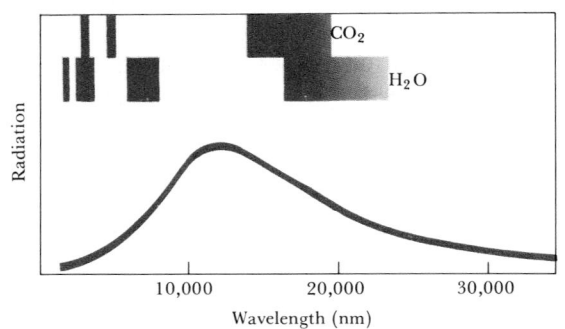

Figure 18.12

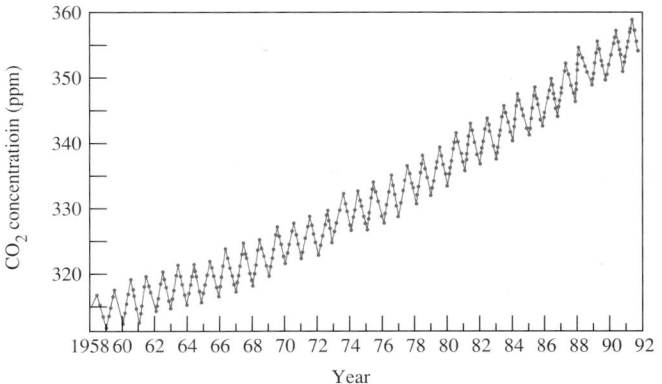

FIGURE 18.13 The concentration of atmospheric CO_2 has risen more than 10 percent since the late 1950s. These data were recorded at the Mauna Loa Observatory in Hawaii by monitoring the absorption of infrared radiation. The sawtoothed shape of the graph is due to regular seasonal variations in CO_2 concentration for each year.

Figure 18.13

occur. Clearly, however, humanity has acquired the potential, by changing the CO_2 concentration in the atmosphere, to alter substantially the climate of the planet.

18.5 The World Ocean

Water is the most common liquid on earth. It covers 72 percent of the earth's surface and is essential to life. Our bodies are about 65 percent water by mass. We have learned that water has many exceptional properties. Because of extensive hydrogen bonding, water has high melting and boiling points and a high heat capacity. ∞ (Sec. 11.2) Its highly polar character is responsible for its exceptional ability to dissolve a wide range of ionic and polar-covalent substances. Many reactions occur in water, including reactions in which H_2O itself is a reactant. For example, we have seen that H_2O can participate in acid-base reactions as either a proton donor or a proton acceptor. ∞ (Sec. 16.2) In Chapter 20 we will see that H_2O can also participate in oxidation-reduction reactions as either a source or a receptor of electrons. All these properties play a role in our environment.

Seawater

The vast layer of salty water that covers so much of the earth is connected and is generally constant in composition. For this reason, oceanographers speak of a world ocean rather than of the separate oceans we learn about in geography books. The world ocean is indeed huge. Its volume is 1.35×10^9 km^3. Almost all the water on earth, 97.2 percent, is in the world ocean. Of the remainder, 2.1 percent is in the form of ice caps and glaciers. All the fresh water—in lakes, rivers, and groundwater—amounts to only 0.6 percent. Most of the remaining 0.1 percent is in brackish (salty) water, such as that in the Great Salt Lake in Utah.

Seawater is often referred to as saline water. The **salinity** of seawater is defined as the mass in grams of dry salts present in 1 kg of seawater. In the world ocean, the salinity varies from 33 to 37, with an average of about 35. To put it another way, seawater contains about 3.5 percent dissolved salts by mass. The list of elements present in seawater is very long. Most, however, are present only in very low concentrations. Table 18.5 lists the 11 ionic species that are most abundant in seawater.

The sea is so vast that if a substance is present in seawater to the extent of only 1 part per billion (ppb, that is, 1×10^{-6} g per kilogram of water), there is still 5×10^9 kg of it in the world ocean. Nevertheless, the ocean is not used very much as a source of raw materials because the cost of extracting the desired substances from the water is too high. Only three substances are recovered from seawater in commercially important amounts: sodium chloride, bromine, and magnesium.

Desalination

Because of its high salt content, seawater is unfit for human consumption and indeed for most of the uses to which we put water. In the United States, the salt content of municipal water supplies is restricted by health codes to no more than about 500 ppm. This amount is much lower than the 3.5 percent dissolved salts present in seawater and the 0.5 percent or so present in brackish water found underground in some regions. The removal of salts from seawater or brackish water to make the water usable is called **desalination.**

Water can be separated from dissolved salts by *distillation* (described in the Closer Look box in Section 13.5) because water is a volatile substance and the salts are nonvolatile. The principle of distillation is simple enough, but carrying out the process on a large scale presents many problems. For example, as water is distilled from a vessel containing seawater, the salts become more and more concentrated and eventually precipitate out.

Seawater can also be desalinated using **reverse osmosis.** Recall that osmosis is the net movement of solvent molecules, but not solute molecules, through a semipermeable membrane. ∞ (Sec. 13.5) In osmosis, solvent passes from the more dilute solution into the more concentrated one. However, if sufficient external pressure is applied, osmosis can be stopped and, at still higher pressures, reversed. When this occurs, solvent passes from the more concentrated into the more dilute solution. In a modern reverse-osmosis facility, tiny hollow fibers are used as the semipermeable membrane. Water is introduced under pressure into the fibers, and desalinated water is recovered on the outside, as illustrated in Figure 18.14.

TABLE 18.5 △ Ionic Constituents of Seawater Present in Concentrations Greater Than 0.001 g/kg (1 ppm)

Ionic constituent	g/kg seawater	Concentration (M)
Chloride, Cl^-	19.35	0.55
Sodium, Na^+	10.76	0.47
Sulfate, SO_4^{2-}	2.71	0.028
Magnesium, Mg^{2+}	1.29	0.054
Calcium, Ca^{2+}	0.412	0.010
Potassium, K^+	0.40	0.010
Carbon dioxide[a]	0.106	2.3×10^{-3}
Bromide, Br^-	0.067	8.3×10^{-4}
Boric acid, H_3BO_3	0.027	4.3×10^{-4}
Strontium, Sr^{2+}	0.0079	9.1×10^{-5}
Fluoride, F^-	0.001	7×10^{-5}

Table 18.5

[a] CO_2 is present in seawater as HCO_3^- and CO_3^{2-}.

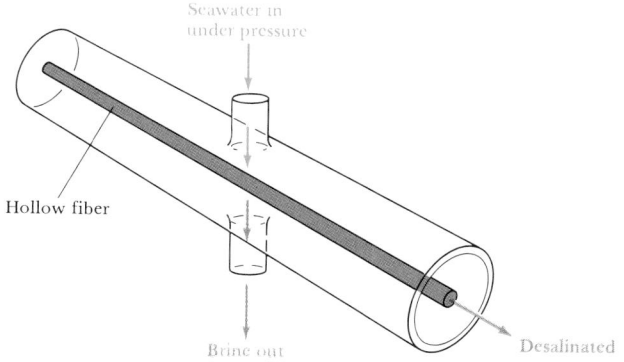

FIGURE 18.14 Schematic view of a hollow-fiber reverse-osmosis unit. Water is introduced under pressure around the hollow fibers. Desalinated water is recovered from the inside of the fiber. In practice each unit contains more than 3 million fibers, each of which has about the diameter of a human hair. The fibers are bundled together in units such as those shown in Figure 18.15(*b*).

Figure 18.14

The island of Malta, located in the Mediterranean Sea, is formed from limestone, and there is little underground fresh water. Part of the island's water supply is obtained from a reverse-osmosis desalination plant (Figure 18.15) that produces 5.3 million gallons per day of desalinated water. The salt content is reduced from 36,000 ppm of dissolved salts to less than 500 ppm, within the acceptable limits for drinkable water.

(*a*)

FIGURE 18.15 (*a*) Seawater reverse-osmosis desalination plant at Ghar Lapsi on the island of Malta, in the Mediterranean Sea. (*b*) A permeator room at Ghar Lapsi. Each of the cylinders shown contains several million tiny hollow fibers. When seawater is introduced under pressure into the cylinder, water passes through the fiber wall to the desalinated, or largely salt-free, side. (Courtesy Polymetrics, Inc. and DuPont)

(*b*)

Ocean Pollution

Many countries exploit the oceans, but no country is legally responsible for their well-being. For this reason, the oceans are all the more difficult to safeguard. From the discharge of sewage and industrial wastes, the runoff of agricultural fertilizers, and oil spills, the oceans have been assaulted with a heavy burden of pollutants. In the past, the oceans have demonstrated a remarkable ability to cleanse themselves, but now they may be perilously close to their capacity to absorb civilization's wastes. The most obvious damage has been to coastal zones, where fouled waters and littered beaches are costing the fishing and resort industries billions of dollars. Major oil spills, such as the disaster in 1989 involving the *Exxon Valdez* oil tanker, lead to the fouling of coastal waters and the destruction of wildlife (Figure 18.16). The longer we use the oceans as a giant garbage dump, the more difficult and costly the cleanup will be.

Some of the pollution problems of the oceans also affect our lakes and rivers. Principal among these are the problems of oxygen depletion due to the decomposition of oxygen-demanding wastes, the effects of plant nutrients that stimulate algal growth, and the accumulation of toxic substances. We examine some of these pollution problems in the next section.

18.6 Fresh Water

Water is essential to support life. An adult person needs about 1.5 L/day for drinking. In the United States, our daily use of water per person far exceeds this subsistence level. We use about 7 L per person for cooking and drinking, about 110 L for cleaning (bathing, laundering, and housecleaning), 80 L for flushing toilets, and 80 L for lawns. We use far greater quantities indirectly in agriculture and industry to produce food and other items. For example, about 1×10^5 L of

FIGURE 18.16 Accidents involving oil supertankers can pollute the ocean with huge amounts of crude petroleum. Because petroleum is less dense than ocean water, it forms a large oceanic oil slick. If the oil slick washes ashore, it can have disastrous effects on the coastal ecology. (Reuters/Bettmann)

water is used in the manufacture of 1000 kg of steel, about the quantity of steel in an average automobile.

We've seen that the total amount of fresh water on earth is not a very large fraction of the total water present. Indeed, fresh water is one of our most precious resources. Fresh water forms by evaporation from the oceans and the land. The water vapor that accumulates in the atmosphere is transported by global atmospheric circulation, eventually returning to earth as rain and snow.

As rain falls and as water runs off the land on its way to the oceans, it dissolves numerous substances. Fresh water contains a variety of cations (mainly Na^+, K^+, Mg^{2+}, Ca^{2+}, and Fe^{2+}), anions (mainly Cl^-, SO_4^{2-}, and HCO_3^-), and dissolved gases (principally O_2, N_2, and CO_2). As we use water, it becomes laden with additional dissolved material, including the wastes of human society. As our population and output of environmental pollutants increase, we find that we must spend ever-increasing amounts of money and resources to guarantee a supply of fresh water.

Dissolved Oxygen and Water Quality

The amount of dissolved O_2 in water is an important indicator of the quality of water. Water fully saturated with air at 1 atm and 20°C contains about 9 ppm of O_2. Oxygen is necessary for fish and much other aquatic life. Cold-water fish require about 5 ppm of dissolved oxygen for survival. Aerobic bacteria consume dissolved oxygen in order to oxidize organic materials and so meet their energy requirements. The organic material that the bacteria are able to oxidize is said to be **biodegradable.** This oxidation occurs by a complex set of chemical reactions, and the organic material disappears gradually.

Excessive quantities of biodegradable organic materials in water are detrimental because they deplete the water of the oxygen necessary to sustain normal animal life. Indeed, these biodegradable materials are called *oxygen-demanding wastes.* Typical sources of oxygen-demanding wastes include sewage, industrial wastes from food-processing plants and paper mills, and effluent (liquid waste) from meat-packing plants.

In the presence of oxygen, the carbon, hydrogen, nitrogen, sulfur, and phosphorus in biodegradable material end up mainly as CO_2, HCO_3^-, H_2O, NO_3^-, SO_4^{2-}, and phosphates. These oxidation reactions sometimes reduce the amount of dissolved oxygen to the point where aerobic bacteria can no longer survive. Anaerobic bacteria then take over the decomposition process, forming CH_4, NH_3, H_2S, PH_3, and other products that contribute to the offensive odors of some polluted waters.

Plant nutrients, particularly nitrogen and phosphorus, contribute to water pollution by stimulating excessive growth of aquatic plants. The most visible results of excessive plant growth are floating algae and murky water. More significantly, however, as plant growth becomes excessive, the amount of dead and decaying plant matter increases rapidly, a process called *eutrophication* (Figure 18.17). Decaying plants consume O_2 as they are biodegraded, leading to the depletion of oxygen in the water. Without sufficient supplies of oxygen, the water in turn cannot sustain any form of animal life. The most important sources of nitrogen and phosphorus compounds in water are domestic sewage (phosphate-containing detergents and nitrogen-containing body wastes), runoff from agricultural land (fertilizers containing both nitrogen and phosphorus), and runoff from livestock areas (animal wastes containing nitrogen).

FIGURE 18.17 The algae growth in this lake in New Jersey is due to runoff of agricultural wastes, particularly those that contain phosphates. The wastes feed the growth of the algae, which depletes the oxygen in the water, a process called *eutrophication*. A eutrophic lake cannot support fish or other animal life. (S. R. Maglione/Photo Researchers)

Treatment of Municipal Water Supplies

Learning Goal 14: List and explain the various stages of treatment that are used to treat freshwater sources and waste water.

The water needed for domestic uses, agriculture, and industrial processes is taken from naturally occurring lakes, rivers, and underground sources or from reservoirs. Much of the water that finds its way into municipal water systems is "used" water; it has already passed through one or more sewage systems or industrial plants. Consequently, this water must be treated before it is distributed to our faucets. Municipal water treatment usually involves five steps: coarse filtration, sedimentation, sand filtration, aeration, and sterilization. Figure 18.18 shows a typical treatment process.

Figure 18.18

FIGURE 18.18 Common steps in treating water for a public water system.

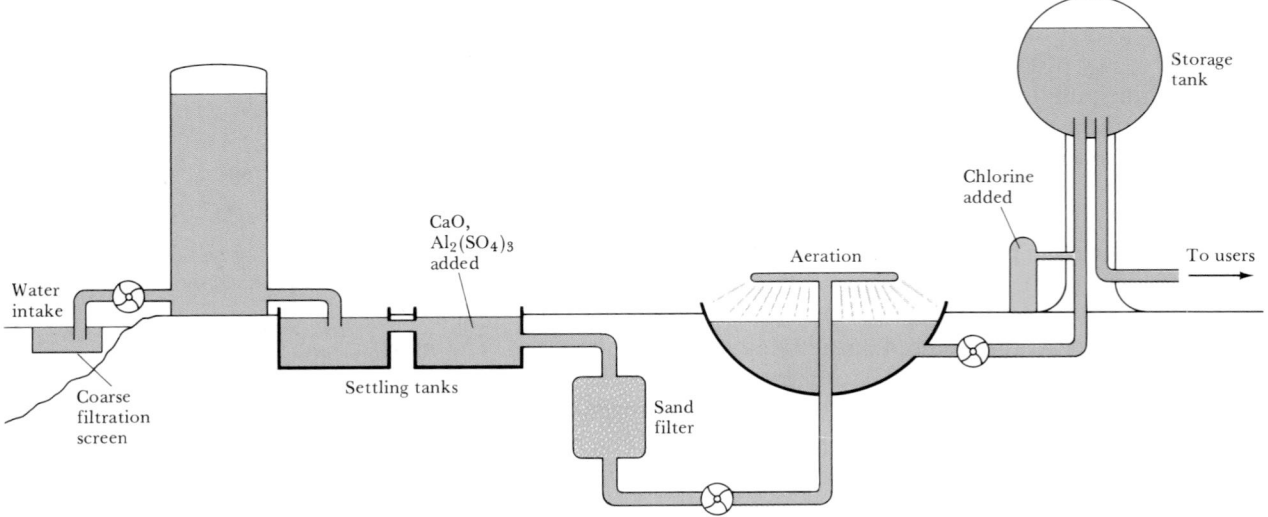

A CLOSER LOOK

Water Softening

Water containing Ca^{2+} and Mg^{2+} is called **hard water.** The presence of these ions makes water unsuitable for some household and industrial uses. For example, these ions react with soaps to form an insoluble soap scum. Although they do not form precipitates with detergents, they adversely affect the performance of such cleaning agents. In addition, mineral deposits may form when water containing these ions is heated. When water containing Ca^{2+} and bicarbonate ions is heated, some carbon dioxide is driven off. As a result, the solution becomes less acidic, and insoluble calcium carbonate forms:

$$Ca^{2+}(aq) + 2HCO_3^-(aq) \xrightarrow{\text{heat}}$$
$$CaCO_3(s) + CO_2(g) + H_2O(l)$$

The solid $CaCO_3$ coats the surface of hot-water systems and the insides of teakettles, thereby reducing heating efficiency. These deposits, called *scale,* can be especially serious in boilers in which water is heated under pressure in pipes running through a furnace. Formation of scale reduces the efficiency of heat transfer and may cause the pipes to melt.

Not all municipal water supplies require water softening. In those that do, the water is generally taken from underground sources in which it has had considerable contact with limestone, $CaCO_3$, and other minerals containing Ca^{2+}, Mg^{2+}, and Fe^{2+}. The **lime-soda process** is used for large-scale municipal water-softening operations. The water is treated with lime, CaO [or slaked lime, $Ca(OH)_2$], and soda ash, Na_2CO_3. These chemicals cause precipitation of calcium as $CaCO_3$ ($K_{sp} = 2.8 \times$

10^{-9}) and of magnesium as $Mg(OH)_2$ ($K_{sp} = 1.8 \times 10^{-11}$):

$$Ca^{2+}(aq) + CO_3^{2-}(aq) \longrightarrow CaCO_3(s)$$
$$Mg^{2+}(aq) + 2OH^-(aq) \longrightarrow Mg(OH)_2(s)$$

The role of Na_2CO_3 is to provide a source of CO_3^{2-}, if needed. If the water already contains a high concentration of bicarbonate ion, calcium can be removed as $CaCO_3$ simply by adding $Ca(OH)_2$:

$$Ca^{2+}(aq) + 2HCO_3^-(aq) + [Ca^{2+}(aq) + 2OH^-(aq)]$$
$$\longrightarrow 2CaCO_3(s) + 2H_2O(l)$$

Lime is used only to the extent that bicarbonate is present: 1 mol of $Ca(OH)_2$ for each 2 mol of HCO_3^-. When bicarbonate is not present, addition of Na_2CO_3 causes removal of Ca^{2+} as $CaCO_3$. The carbonate ion also serves to cause precipitation of $Mg(OH)_2$:

$$Mg^{2+}(aq) + 2CO_3^{2-}(aq) + 2H_2O(l) \longrightarrow$$
$$2HCO_3^-(aq) + Mg(OH)_2(s)$$

There are two problems with the lime-soda process. First, $CaCO_3$ and $Mg(OH)_2$ may form as very fine particles that do not settle out very well. Second, the solution that results after removal of the precipitates is too strongly basic for subsequent uses. To resolve the first problem, alum, $Al_2(SO_4)_3$, is added to aid the settling of the precipitates. In the basic solution, Al^{3+} from the alum forms a gelatinous precipitate of $Al(OH)_3$, which carries the finely divided $CaCO_3$ and $Mg(OH)_2$ particles with it as it settles out of solution. The basicity of the solution is then decreased by bubbling CO_2 through the water.

After coarse filtration through a screen, the water is allowed to stand in large settling tanks in which finely divided sand and other minute particles can settle out. To aid in removal of very small particles, the water may first be made slightly basic by adding CaO. Then $Al_2(SO_4)_3$ is added. The aluminum sulfate reacts with OH^- ions to form a spongy, gelatinous precipitate of $Al(OH)_3$ ($K_{sp} = 3.7 \times 10^{-15}$). This precipitate settles slowly, carrying suspended particles down with it, thereby removing nearly all finely divided matter and most bacteria. The water is then filtered through a sand bed. Following filtration, the water may be sprayed into the air to hasten the oxidation of dissolved organic substances.

The final stage of the operation normally involves treating the water with a chemical agent to ensure the destruction of bacteria. Ozone is most effective, but it must be generated at the place where it is used. Chlorine, Cl_2, is therefore more convenient. Chlorine can be shipped in tanks as a liquefied gas and

Learning Goal 15: Describe the chemical principles involved in the lime-soda process for reducing water hardness.

John E. Fulkrod, "The Water Softener—A Relevant, Unifying Example of Many Common Chemical Principles and Calculations," *J. Chem.Educ.* **1985,** *62,* 529.

dispensed from the tanks through a metering device directly into the water supply. The amount used depends on the presence of other substances with which the chlorine might react and on the concentrations of bacteria and viruses to be removed. The sterilizing action of chlorine is probably due not to Cl_2 itself but to hypochlorous acid, which forms when chlorine reacts with water:

$$Cl_2(aq) + H_2O(l) \longrightarrow HClO(aq) + H^+(aq) + Cl^-(aq) \qquad [18.18]$$

 # For Review

Summary

In this chapter we have examined the physical and chemical properties of the earth's atmosphere. The complex temperature variations in the atmosphere give rise to several regions, each with characteristic properties. The lowest of these regions, the troposphere, extends from the surface to about 12 km. Above the troposphere, in order of increasing altitude, are the stratosphere, mesosphere, and thermosphere. In the upper reaches of the atmosphere, only the simplest chemical species can survive the bombardment of highly energetic particles and radiation from the sun. The average molecular weight of the atmosphere at high elevations is lower than at the earth's surface, because the lightest atoms and molecules diffuse upward and because of photodissociation. Absorption of radiation may also lead to photoionization.

Ozone is produced in the mesosphere and stratosphere as a result of the reaction of atomic oxygen with O_2. Ozone is itself decomposed by absorption of a photon or by reaction with an active species such as NO. Human activities could result in addition to the stratosphere of atomic chlorine, which is capable of reacting with ozone in a catalytic cycle to convert ozone to O_2. A marked reduction in the ozone level in the upper atmosphere would have serious adverse consequences, because the ozone layer filters out certain wavelengths of ultraviolet light that are not taken out by any other atmospheric component.

In the troposphere, the chemistry of trace atmospheric components is of major importance. Many of these minor components are pollutants; sulfur dioxide is one of the more noxious and prevalent. It is oxidized in air to form sulfur trioxide, which upon dissolving in water forms sulfuric acid. One method of preventing SO_2 from escaping from industrial operations involves reacting the SO_2 with CaO to form calcium sulfite, $CaSO_3$.

Carbon monoxide is found in high concentrations in the exhaust of automobile engines and in cigarette smoke. This compound is a health hazard because of its ability to form a strong bond with hemoglobin and thus reduce the capacity of blood for oxygen transfer from the lungs.

Photochemical smog is a complex mixture of components in which both nitrogen oxides and ozone play important roles. Smog components are generated mainly in automobile engines, and smog control consists largely of controlling auto emissions.

Carbon dioxide and water vapor are the only major components of the atmosphere that strongly absorb infrared radiation. The level of carbon dioxide in the atmosphere is thus important in determining worldwide climate. As a result of the extensive combustion of fossil fuels (coal, oil, and natural gas), the carbon dioxide level of the atmosphere is steadily increasing.

Seawater contains about 3.5 percent by mass of dissolved salts. Because most of the world's water is in the oceans, humankind may eventually look to the seas for fresh water. Desalination is the removal of dissolved salts from seawater, brine, or brackish water to make it fit for human consumption. Among the means by which desalination may be accomplished are distillation and reverse osmosis.

Fresh water contains many dissolved substances, including dissolved oxygen, which is necessary for fish and other aquatic life. Substances that are decomposed by bacteria are said to be biodegradable. Because the oxidation of biodegradable substances by aerobic bacteria consumes dissolved oxygen, these substances are called oxygen-demanding wastes. The presence of an excess amount of oxygen-demanding wastes in water can deplete the dissolved oxygen sufficiently to kill fish and produce offensive odors. Plant nutrients can contribute to the problem by stimulat-ing the growth of plants that become oxygen-demanding wastes when they die.

The water available from freshwater sources may require treatment before it can be used domestically. The several steps usually used in municipal water treatment include coarse filtration, sedimentation, sand filtration, aeration, sterilization, and water softening.

Key Terms

troposphere (Sec. 18.1)
stratosphere (Sec. 18.1)
photodissociation (Sec. 18.2)
photoionization (Sec. 18.2)
chlorofluorocarbons (Sec. 18.3)
acid rain (Sec. 18.4)
hemoglobin (Sec. 18.4)

photochemical smog (Sec. 18.4)
salinity (Sec. 18.5)
desalination (Sec. 18.5)
reverse osmosis (Sec. 18.5)
biodegradable (Sec. 18.6)
hard water (Sec. 18.6)
lime-soda process (Sec. 18.6)

Exercises

Earth's Atmosphere

18.1. (a) What is the primary basis for the division of the atmosphere into different regions? (b) Name the regions of the atmosphere, indicating the altitude interval for each one.

18.2. (a) What is the difference between the troposphere and the tropopause? (b) Is the pressure of the atmosphere greater in the mesosphere or in the thermosphere? Explain.

18.3. From the data in Table 18.1, calculate the partial pressures of argon and neon when the total atmospheric pressure is 765 torr.

18.4. From the data in Table 18.1, calculate the number of xenon atoms in 1.0 L of air at a pressure of 0.94 atm and a temperature of 300 K.

18.5. The dissociation energy of a carbon-bromine bond is typically about 210 kJ/mol. What is the maximum wavelength of photons that can cause C—Br bond dissociation?

18.6. In CF_3Cl, the C—Cl bond-dissociation energy is 339 kJ/mol. In CCl_4, the C—Cl bond-dissociation energy is 293 kJ/mol. What is the range of wavelengths of photons that can cause C—Cl bond rupture in one molecule but not in the other?

18.7. Give two reasons why photodissociation of N_2 is a relatively unimportant process compared to photodissociation of O_2.

18.8. In terms of the energy requirements, explain why photodissociation of oxygen is more important than photoionization of oxygen at altitudes below about 90 km.

Chemistry of the Stratosphere

18.9. (a) Why do oxygen atoms exist longer at a 120-km altitude than at a 50-km altitude? (b) What is the biological significance of the stratospheric ozone layer at the earth's surface?

18.10. (a) Why is the temperature of the stratosphere higher near the stratopause than near the tropopause? (b) Explain how ozone is formed in the stratosphere.

18.11. Using the thermodynamic data in Appendix C, calculate the overall enthalpy change in each step in the following cycle that converts O_3 to O_2:

$$NO(g) + O_3(g) \longrightarrow NO_2(g) + O_2(g)$$

$$NO_2(g) + O(g) \longrightarrow O_2(g) + NO(g)$$

18.12. The standard enthalpies of formation of ClO and ClO_2 are 101 and 102 kJ/mol, respectively. Using these data and the thermodynamic data in Appendix C, calculate the overall enthalpy change for each step in the following catalytic cycle:

$$ClO(g) + O_3(g) \longrightarrow ClO_2(g) + O_2(g)$$

$$ClO_2(g) + O(g) \longrightarrow ClO(g) + O_2(g)$$

On the basis of your results indicate whether the ClO/ClO_2

pair is at least a possible catalyst for decomposition of ozone in the atmosphere.

18.13. **(a)** What substances comprise the chlorine reservoir of the stratosphere? **(b)** What is the role of the chlorine reservoir in regulating the rate of ozone depletion in the stratosphere?

18.14. The reaction between hydrogen chloride, $HCl(g)$, and chlorine nitrate, $ClONO_2(g)$, is extremely slow in the absence of a crystalline surface. The reaction occurs quite rapidly in the presence of ice crystals. How does this observation relate to the current theory about the role of polar stratospheric clouds in ozone depletion?

Chemistry of the Troposphere

18.15. What are the major health effects of each of the following pollutants: **(a)** CO; **(b)** SO_2; **(c)** O_3?

18.16. Both CO and SO_2 can be oxidized to compounds that contain one more oxygen atom. Do these conversions alleviate the potential harm to the environment?

18.17. Compare typical concentrations of CO, SO_2, and NO in nonpolluted air (Table 18.3) and urban air (Table 18.4), and indicate in each case at least one possible source of the higher values in Table 18.4.

18.18. For each of the following gases, make a list of known or possible naturally occurring sources: **(a)** CH_4; **(b)** SO_2; **(c)** NO; **(d)** CO.

18.19. In a particular urban environment, the ozone concentration is 0.31 ppm. Assuming a temperature of 16°C and an atmospheric pressure of 745 torr, calculate the partial pressure of ozone and the number of O_3 molecules per cubic meter.

18.20. In a particular urban environment the NO concentration is 0.45 ppm. If the atmospheric pressure is 730 torr and the temperature is 18°C, calculate the partial pressure of NO and the number of NO molecules per cubic meter.

18.21. Why is rainwater naturally acidic, even in the absence of polluting gases such as SO_3?

18.22. Write chemical reactions that illustrate the attack of acid rain on **(a)** iron metal; **(b)** limestone, $CaCO_3$.

18.23. Assuming an overall efficiency of about 30 percent, how much calcium carbonate would be required to remove the SO_2 formed in burning a ton of coal containing 2.7 percent sulfur by mass?

18.24. In 1986 Georgia Power Company's electrical power plant in Taylorsville, Georgia, burned 8,376,726 tons of coal and produced 21,170,999 megawatts of electricity, a national record at that time. **(a)** Assuming that the coal was 83 percent carbon and 2.5 percent sulfur and that combustion was complete, calculate the number of tons of carbon dioxide and sulfur dioxide produced by the plant during the year. **(b)** If 55 percent of the SO_2 could be removed by reaction with powdered CaO to form $CaSO_3$, how many tons of $CaSO_3$ would be produced?

18.25. An important reaction in the formation of photochemical smog is the photodissociation of NO_2:

$$NO_2 + hv \longrightarrow NO + O$$

The maximum wavelength of light that can cause this reaction is 420 nm. **(a)** In what part of the electromagnetic spectrum is light with this wavelength found? **(b)** What is the maximum strength of a bond, in kJ/mol, that can be broken by absorption of a photon of 420 nm light?

18.26. Alcohol-based fuels for automobiles lead to the production of formaldehyde, CH_2O, in exhaust gases. Formaldehyde undergoes photodissociation, which contributes to photochemical smog:

$$CH_2O + hv \longrightarrow CHO + H$$

The maximum wavelength of light that can cause this reaction is 335 nm. **(a)** In what part of the electromagnetic spectrum is light with this wavelength found? **(b)** What is the maximum strength of a bond, in kJ/mol, that can be broken by absorption of a photon of 335 nm light? **(c)** Compare your answer from part (b) to the appropriate value from Table 8.4. What do you conclude about the C—H bond energy in formaldehyde?

[18.27]. Assume that an equilibrium of N_2, O_2, and NO is achieved at a temperature of 2400 K:

$$N_2(g) + O_2(g) \Longrightarrow 2NO(g) \qquad K_p = 0.05$$

If the original reaction mixture consists of air at sea level and at 1.0 atm in a 1.0-L vessel, what is the partial pressure of NO at equilibrium? What is the concentration of NO in ppm?

[18.28]. A 1.0-L sample of air at 1.5 atm and 900°C is composed of 78 percent N_2, 21 percent O_2, and 3200 ppm NO. The gas sample is brought to equilibrium using a heterogeneous catalyst:

$$N_2(g) + O_2(g) \Longrightarrow 2NO(g) \qquad K_p = 1.0 \times 10^{-5}$$

What are the equilibrium concentrations of N_2, O_2, and NO?

The World Ocean

18.29. What is the molarity of Na^+ in a solution of NaCl whose salinity is 5 if the solution has a density of 1.0 g/mL?

18.30. Phosphorus is present in seawater to the extent of 0.07 ppm by weight. If the phosphorus is present as phos-

phate, PO_4^{3-}, calculate the corresponding molar concentration of phosphate.

18.31. Assuming a 10 percent efficiency of recovery, how many liters of seawater must be processed to obtain 10^8 kg of bromine in a commercial production process, assuming the bromide ion concentration listed in Table 18.5?

18.32. A first stage in the recovery of magnesium from seawater is precipitation of $Mg(OH)_2$ by the use of CaO:

$$Mg^{2+}(aq) + CaO(s) + H_2O(l) \longrightarrow$$
$$Mg(OH)_2(s) + Ca^{2+}(aq)$$

What mass of CaO is needed to precipitate 4.0×10^7 g of $Mg(OH)_2$?

Fresh Water

18.33. Explain why the concentration of dissolved oxygen in fresh water is an important indicator of the quality of the water.

18.34. What forms of decomposition occur when dissolved oxygen levels in water drop below the levels at which aerobic bacteria can survive? Give examples of the decomposition products that form.

18.35. The following organic anion is found in most detergents:

$$H_3C-(CH_2)_9-\overset{\overset{\displaystyle H}{|}}{\underset{\underset{\displaystyle CH_3}{|}}{C}}-\bigcirc-SO_3^-$$

Assume that the anion undergoes aerobic decomposition in the following manner:

$$2C_{18}H_{29}O_3S^-(aq) + 51O_2(aq) \longrightarrow$$
$$36CO_2(aq) + 28H_2O(l) + 2H^+(aq) + 2SO_4^{2-}(aq)$$

What is the total mass of O_2 required to biodegrade 1.0 g of this substance?

18.36. The average daily mass of O_2 taken up by sewage discharged in the United States is 59 g per person. How many liters of water at 9 ppm O_2 are totally depleted of oxygen in 1 day by a population of 50,000 people?

18.37. Write a balanced chemical equation to describe what occurs when hard water is heated.

18.38. Write a balanced chemical equation to describe how magnesium ion is removed in water treatment by the addition of slaked lime, $Ca(OH)_2$.

18.39. How many moles of $Ca(OH)_2$ and of Na_2CO_3 should be added to soften 10^3 L of water in which $[Ca^{2+}] = 5.0 \times 10^{-4}$ M and $[HCO_3^-] = 7.0 \times 10^{-4}$ M?

18.40. The concentration of Ca^{2+} in a particular water supply is 5.7×10^{-3}. The concentration of bicarbonate ion, HCO_3^-, in the same water is 1.7×10^{-3}. What masses of $Ca(OH)_2$ and Na_2CO_3 must be added to 5.0×10^7 L of this water to reduce the level of Ca^{2+} to 20 percent of its original level?

18.41. The precipitation of $Al(OH)_3$ $(K_{sp} = 3.7 \times 10^{-15})$ is sometimes used to purify water. (a) At what pH will precipitation of $Al(OH)_3$ begin if 2.0 lb of $Al_2(SO_4)_3$ is added to 1000 gal of water? (b) Approximately how many pounds of CaO must be added to the water to achieve this pH?

18.42. (a) Explain why $Mg(OH)_2$ precipitates when CO_3^{2-} ion is added to a solution containing Mg^{2+}. (b) Will $Mg(OH)_2$ precipitate when 5.0 g of Na_2CO_3 is added to 1.00 L of a solution containing 150 ppm of Mg^{2+}?

Additional Exercises

18.43. A friend of yours has seen each of the following terms in newspaper articles and would like an explanation: (a) acid rain; (b) greenhouse effect; (c) photochemical smog; (d) ozone hole. Give a brief explanation of each term and identify one or two of the chemicals associated with each.

18.44. Suppose that on another planet the atmosphere consists of 20 percent Ar, 35 percent CH_4, and 45 percent O_2. What is the average molecular weight at the surface? What is the average molecular weight at an altitude at which all the O_2 is photodissociated?

18.45. Experiments have been performed in which a metal such as sodium or barium has been released into the atmosphere at an altitude of about 120 km. Assuming that the metal is present in the atomic form, what reactions would you expect to occur with the ionic species present? Explain.

18.46. Explain why the stratosphere, which extends from 12 km to about 50 km, contains a smaller total atmospheric mass than the troposphere, which extends from the surface to 12 km.

[18.47]. A reaction that contributes to the depletion of ozone in the stratosphere is the direct reaction of oxygen atoms with ozone:

$$O(g) + O_3(g) \longrightarrow 2O_2(g)$$

At 298 K, the rate constant for this reaction is 4.8×10^5 M^{-1} s^{-1}. (a) Based on the units of the rate constant, write the likely rate law for this reaction. (b) Would you expect this reaction to occur via a single elementary process? Explain why or why not. (c) From the magnitude of the rate constant, would you expect the activation energy of this reaction to be large or small? Explain. (d) Use ΔH_f° values from Appendix C to estimate the enthalpy change for this reaction. Would this reaction raise or lower the temperature of the stratosphere?

18.48. *Halons* are fluorocarbons that contain bromine, such as $CBrF_3$. They are used extensively as foaming agents for fighting fires. Like CFCs, halons are very unreactive and ultimately can diffuse into the stratosphere. (a) Based on the data in Table 8.4, would you expect photodissociation of Br atoms to occur in the stratosphere? (b) Propose a mechanism by which the presence of halons in the stratosphere could lead to the depletion of stratospheric ozone.

[18.49]. The *hydroxyl radical,* OH, is formed at low altitudes via the reaction of excited oxygen atoms with water:

$$O^* + H_2O \longrightarrow 2\ OH$$

Once produced, the hydroxyl radical is very reactive. Explain why each of the following series of reactions has an effect on the pollution in the troposphere:

(a) $OH + NO_2 \longrightarrow HNO_3$
(b) $OH + CO + O_2 \longrightarrow CO_2 + OOH$
  $OOH + NO \longrightarrow OH + NO_2$
(c) $OH + CH_4 \longrightarrow H_2O + CH_3$
  $CH_3 + O_2 \longrightarrow OOCH_3$
  $OOCH_3 + NO \longrightarrow OCH_3 + NO_2$

18.50. *Anthracite* is a clean-burning, low-sulfur coal. Over half of the anthracite originally present in the western United States has been mined. By comparison, *bituminous* coal is relatively high in sulfur (2 to 3 percent). Bituminous coal is still mined extensively in the Appalachian and north central states of the United States. (a) Which would you expect to be more expensive, anthracite or bituminous coal? Explain. (b) Explain how the combustion of bituminous coal in Ohio and Pennsylvania could have a harmful effect on lakes in eastern Canada.

18.51. Why is NO rather than NO_2 the principal nitrogen oxide formed during combustion reactions?

18.52. Explain, using Le Châtelier's principle, why the equilibrium constant for the formation of NO from N_2 and O_2 increases with increasing temperature, whereas the equilibrium constant for the formation of NO_2 from NO and O_2 decreases with increasing temperature.

18.53. If an urban environment contains 10.5 ppm CO at an atmospheric pressure of 745 torr and a temperature of 18°C, how many CO molecules will be present in a room that measures 12 ft × 14 ft × 8 ft?

18.54. We have noted that the affinity of carbon monoxide for hemoglobin is about 210 times that of O_2. Assume that a person is inhaling air that contains 86 ppm of CO. If all the hemoglobin leaving the lungs carries either oxygen or CO, calculate the fraction in the form of carboxyhemoglobin.

18.55. Natural gas consists primarily of methane, $CH_4(g)$. (a) Write a balanced chemical equation for the complete combustion of methane to produce $CO_2(g)$ as the only carbon-containing product. (b) Write a balanced chemical equation for the incomplete combustion of methane to produce $CO(g)$ as the only carbon-containing product. (c) At 25°C and 1.0 atm pressure, what is the minimum quantity of dry air needed to combust 1.0 L of $CH_4(g)$ completely to $CO_2(g)$? (d) What are the health consequences of running a home natural-gas furnace with a mixture of air and natural

gas that is too "rich," that is, with a natural-gas concentration that is too high?

18.56. One of the possible consequences of global warming is an increase in the temperature of ocean water. The oceans serve as a "sink" for CO_2 by dissolving a large amount of the substance. (a) How would the solubility of CO_2 in the oceans be affected by an increase in the temperature of the water? (b) Discuss the implications of your answer to part (a) for the problem of global warming.

18.57. The Henry's law constant for CO_2 in water at 25°C is 3.1×10^{-2} *M*/atm. (a) What is the solubility of CO_2 in water at this temperature if the solution is in contact with air at normal atmospheric pressure. (b) Assume that all of this CO_2 is in the form of H_2CO_3 produced by the reaction between CO_2 and H_2O:

$$CO_2(aq) + H_2O(l) \longrightarrow H_2CO_3(aq)$$

What is the pH of this solution?

18.58. Write balanced chemical equations for each of the following verbal descriptions. (a) The nitric oxide molecule undergoes photodissociation in the upper atmosphere. (b) The nitric oxide molecule undergoes photoionization in the upper atmosphere. (c) Nitric oxide undergoes oxidation by ozone in the stratosphere. (d) Nitrogen dioxide dissolves in water to form nitric acid and nitric oxide.

18.59. Suppose that seawater to be processed in a reverse-osmosis plant has the concentrations of dissolved salts listed in Table 18.5. If the concentration of salts on the pure desalinated water side is taken as zero, what osmotic pressure must be applied before water begins to flow from the seawater through the semipermeable membrane to the desalinated water side? (Refer to Section 13.5.)

18.60. (a) In Figure 18.18, what is the purpose of the aeration step? (b) Why is chlorine, Cl_2, rather than ozone, O_3, generally used as an antibacterial agent for municipal water supplies? (c) In 1993, the municipal water supply in Milwaukee was infected with parasitic protozoa called *Cryptosporidium.* The parasite, which presumably entered the water supply from fecal material from farm animals, causes diarrhea in many humans. According to medical guides, *Cryptosporidium* "is resistent to most disinfectants, to chlorine concentrations generally present in municipal water supplies, and to temperatures between −20°C and 60°C." What advice do you think was given to residents of Milwaukee while the parasite was present?

18.61. Write balanced chemical equations for each of the following verbal descriptions: (a) Hypochlorous acid is formed when chlorine is added to water. (b) A sample of water containing Ca^{2+} and bicarbonate ion forms a precipitate when heated.

[18.62]. It has recently been pointed out that there may be increased amounts of NO in the troposphere as compared with the past because of massive use of nitrogen-containing compounds in fertilizers. Assuming that NO can eventually diffuse into the stratosphere, what role might it play in affecting the conditions of life on earth? Using the index to this text, look up the chemistry of nitrogen oxides. What chemical pathways might NO in the troposphere follow?

Chemical Thermodynamics 19

The rusting of iron is an example of a spontaneous reaction. In thermodynamics, the tendencies toward lower energy and greater disorder serve as the criteria for spontaneous change.

CONTENTS

In several of the preceding chapters, we have asked two important questions that are at the heart of designing and understanding chemical reactions: How rapidly does the reaction progress? How far toward completion does the reaction proceed? We derive the answer to the first question from a study of the reaction rate, and the answer to the second question from a knowledge of the equilibrium constant. Let's briefly review these concepts.

In Chapter 14, we learned that reaction rates are principally controlled by *energy,* namely, the activation energy of the reaction. The lower the activation energy, the faster a reaction proceeds. ∞ (Sec. 14.4) When we discussed chemical equilibrium in Chapter 15, we defined it from a kinetic point of view: Equilibrium occurs when opposing reactions occur at equal rates. ∞ (Sec. 15.1) Because reaction rates are intimately tied to energy, it seems logical that chemical equilibrium also depends in some way on energy.

How do we relate chemical equilibrium to the energies of the reactants and the products? What kind of energy is important in determining whether a reaction will occur? Questions such as these are the focus of *chemical thermodynamics,* the area of chemistry dealing with energy relationships. We first encountered thermodynamics in Chapter 5, where we discussed the nature of energy, the first law of thermodynamics, the concept of enthalpy, and the enthalpies of reactions. We might be tempted to presume that the enthalpy change of a reaction determines whether the reaction proceeds. After all, an exothermic reaction is "downhill" in enthalpy, so we might expect reactants to be readily converted into products. However, we also know of endothermic processes that proceed readily. For example, ice at room temperature (22°C) melts to liquid water even though the process is endothermic. Ammonium nitrate readily dissolves in water even though ΔH_{soln} is positive. ∞ (Sec. 13.1) Clearly, the sign of the enthalpy changes alone is not enough to tell us whether a reaction will proceed.

In this chapter, we shall address several additional aspects of chemical thermodynamics that were not discussed in Chapter 5, including the second and third laws of thermodynamics. We shall see that, in addition to enthalpy, the change in the *randomness* or *disorder* of a chemical system (a notion to which we alluded in Section 13.1) is extremely important in determining whether equilibrium favors reactants or products. Finally, we shall learn how to combine the enthalpy change of a reaction with the change in randomness to define a new type of energy that relates directly to equilibrium.

19.1 Spontaneous Processes

Thermodynamics is based on several fundamental laws that summarize our experience with energy changes. The first law of thermodynamics, which we discussed at length in Chapter 5, states that energy is conserved. By this we mean that energy is neither created nor destroyed in any process, such as the falling of a brick, the melting of an ice cube, or the reacting of chemicals. Energy flows from one part of nature to another or is converted from one form to another, but the total remains constant. We saw in Chapter 5 that we could express the first law in the form $\Delta E = q + w$, where ΔE is the change in energy of a system, q is the heat absorbed by the system from its surroundings, and w is the work done on the system by its surroundings.

Once we specify a particular process or change, the first law helps us to balance the books, so to speak, on the heat released, work done, and so forth. However, it says nothing about whether the process or change we specify can in fact occur. That question is encompassed in the second law of thermodynamics.

The **second law of thermodynamics** expresses the notion that there is an inherent direction in which any system moves if it is not at equilibrium. For example, if you drop a brick, it falls to the floor. Water placed in a freezer compartment turns into ice. A shiny nail left outdoors eventually rusts. Every one of these processes occurs without outside intervention; such processes are said to be **spontaneous.**

For every spontaneous process, we can imagine a reverse process. For example, we can imagine a brick moving from the floor into your hand, ice cubes melting at $-10°C$, or a rusty iron nail being transformed into a shiny one. It is inconceivable that any of these occurrences is spontaneous. If we saw a movie in which these things happened, we would conclude that it was being run backward. Our years of observing nature at work have impressed us with a simple rule: *Processes that are spontaneous in one direction are not spontaneous in the reverse direction.* This fact is illustrated by the example shown in Figure 19.1.

Consider the reaction used in the Haber process (Section 15.1):

$$N_2(g) + 3H_2(g) \rightleftharpoons 2NH_3(g) \qquad [19.1]$$

When we mix N_2 and H_2 at a particular temperature, say 472°C, the reaction proceeds in the forward direction; this process is spontaneous. However, if we place a mixture of 1.00 mol of N_2, 3.00 mol of H_2, and 1.00 mol of NH_3 in a 1-L container at 472°C, it is not immediately obvious whether the formation of more NH_3 should be spontaneous. Nevertheless, if we know the equilibrium constant, which at this temperature happens to be $K_c = 0.105$, we can predict the direction in which the reaction proceeds to reach equilibrium. In this case

$$Q = \frac{[NH_3]^2}{[N_2][H_2]^3} = \frac{(1.00)^2}{(1.00)(3.00)^3} = 0.0370$$

Because the reaction quotient, Q, is smaller than K_c, the system moves spontaneously toward equilibrium by formation of NH_3. ∞ (Sec. 15.5) The opposite process, conversion of NH_3 into N_2 and H_2, is not spontaneous for this particular reaction mixture at 472°C.

The fact that a process is spontaneous does not mean that it will occur at an observable rate. A spontaneous reaction may be very fast, as in the case of an acid-base neutralization, or very slow, as in the case of rusting of iron. Thermodynamics can tell us the *direction* and *extent* of a reaction, but it can say nothing about its *speed.* Reaction rates are the subject of chemical kinetics.

What factors make a process spontaneous? In Chapter 5, we saw that the enthalpy change for a process is an important factor in determining whether the process is favorable. Processes in which the enthalpy of the system decreases (exothermic processes) tend to occur spontaneously. However, we shall see that considering only the enthalpy change of a process is not enough. The spontaneity of a process also depends on how the disorder of the system changes during the process. In the next section, we consider these factors, especially the matter of disorder, in greater detail.

FIGURE 19.1 Processes that are spontaneous in one direction, like the rusting of an iron nail, are not spontaneous in the opposite direction. (Richard Megna/Fundamental Photographs)

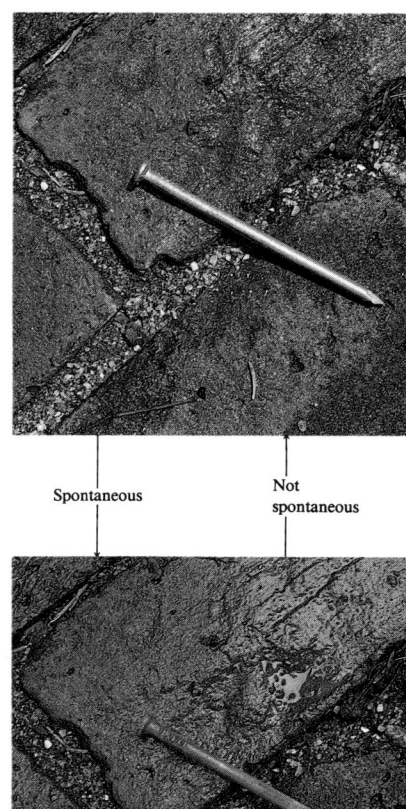

Spontaneous   Not spontaneous

19.2 Spontaneity, Enthalpy, and Entropy

The spontaneous motion of a brick released from your hand is toward the ground. As the brick falls, it loses potential energy. This potential energy is first converted into kinetic energy, the energy of motion of the brick. When the brick hits the floor, its kinetic energy is converted into heat. The overall result of the brick's fall is thus a conversion of the potential energy of the brick into heat in its surroundings. Our experience with other simple mechanical systems is similar: objects fall, clocks run down, stretched rubber bands contract. All of these phenomena can be summarized by saying that such systems seek a resting place of minimum energy.

The tendency for a system to achieve the lowest possible energy is one of the driving forces that determine the behavior of molecular systems. For example, just as a brick possesses potential energy because of its position relative to the floor, so also does a chemical substance possess potential energy relative to other substances because of the arrangements of nuclei and electrons. When these arrangements change, energy may be released. For example, the combustion of propane (bottled gas), which is clearly a spontaneous process, is strongly exothermic:

$$C_3H_8(g) + 5O_2(g) \longrightarrow 3CO_2(g) + 4H_2O(l) \qquad \Delta H° = -2202 \text{ kJ} \qquad [19.2]$$

The rearrangements in space of nuclei and electrons in going from propane and oxygen to carbon dioxide and water lead to a lower chemical potential energy, and so heat is evolved. Reactions that are highly exothermic are generally spontaneous. However, the tendency toward minimum enthalpy is not the only factor that determines spontaneity in molecular processes. It is instructive to consider some spontaneous processes that are not exothermic.

Spontaneity and Entropy Change

We can think of several processes that are spontaneous even though they are not exothermic. For example, consider an ideal gas confined at 1 atm pressure to a 1-L flask, as shown in Figure 19.2. The flask is connected by a closed stopcock to another 1-L flask, which is evacuated, and the two flasks are kept at a constant temperature. Now suppose the stopcock is opened. Is there any doubt about what would happen? We intuitively recognize that the gas would expand into the second flask until the pressure is equally distributed in both flasks, at 0.5 atm. In the course of expanding from the 1-L flask into the larger volume, the ideal gas neither absorbs nor emits heat. Nevertheless, the process is spontaneous. The reverse process, in which the gas that is evenly distributed between the two flasks suddenly moves entirely into one of the flasks, leaving the other vacant, is inconceivable. Yet this process would also involve no emission or absorption of heat. Evidently, some factor other than heat emitted or absorbed is important in making the process of gas expansion spontaneous.

As another example, consider the melting of ice cubes at room temperature. The process

$$H_2O(s) \longrightarrow H_2O(l) \qquad [19.3]$$

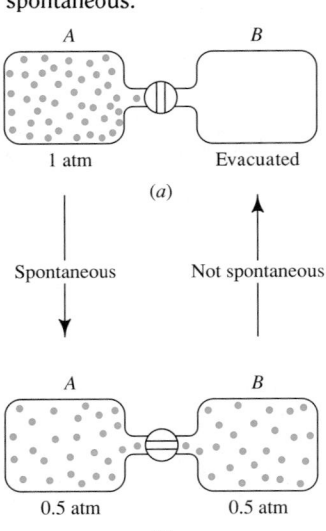

FIGURE 19.2 Expansion of an ideal gas into an evacuated space is spontaneous. In (a), flask A holds an ideal gas at 1 atm pressure and flask B is evacuated. In (b), the stopcock connecting the flasks has been opened. The ideal gas expands to occupy both flasks A and B at a pressure of 0.5 atm. The reverse process is not spontaneous.

is highly spontaneous at 22°C, yet it is an endothermic change. The melting of ice above 0°C thus represents an example of a spontaneous endothermic process.

A similar type of process, discussed in Section 13.1, is the endothermic dissolving of many salts in water. If we add solid potassium chloride, KCl, to a glass of water at room temperature, we can feel the solution growing colder as the salt dissolves. The process is endothermic and yet spontaneous.

The three processes just described have something in common that accounts for their being spontaneous. In each instance, the products of the process are in a more random or disordered state than the reactants. Let's consider each case in turn.

L. Glasser, "Order, Chaos, and All That!" *J. Chem. Educ.* **1989,** *66,* 997.

When we have a gas confined to a 1-L volume, as in Figure 19.2(*a*), we can specify the location of every gas molecule as being in that liter of space. After the gas has expanded, we can't be sure which gas molecules are still in container A at any one instant and which are in container B. We must say that the location of every gas molecule is specified as being in the entire 2-L space. In other words, the gas molecules, because they can be anywhere within a 2-L space, are more randomized than when they are confined to a 1-L space.

The molecules of water that make up an ice crystal are held rigidly in place in the ice crystal lattice (Figure 19.3). When the ice melts, the water molecules are free to move about with respect to one another and to tumble around. Thus, in liquid water the individual water molecules are more randomly distributed than in the solid. The highly ordered solid structure is replaced by the much more disordered liquid structure.

A similar situation applies when KCl dissolves in water, although here we must be a little careful not to take too much for granted. In solid KCl, the K^+ and Cl^- are in a highly ordered, crystalline state. When the solid dissolves, the ions are free to move about in the water. They are obviously in a much more random and disordered state than before. At the same time, though, water molecules are held around the ions as water of hydration as shown in Figure 19.4. ⚭ (Sec. 13.1)   These water molecules are in a *more* ordered state than

FIGURE 19.3   Structure of ice, a regular ordered system.

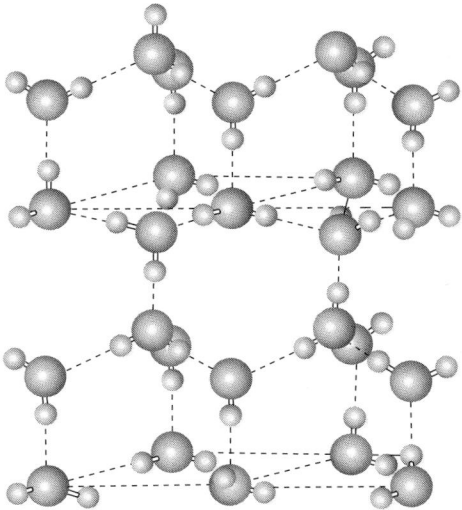

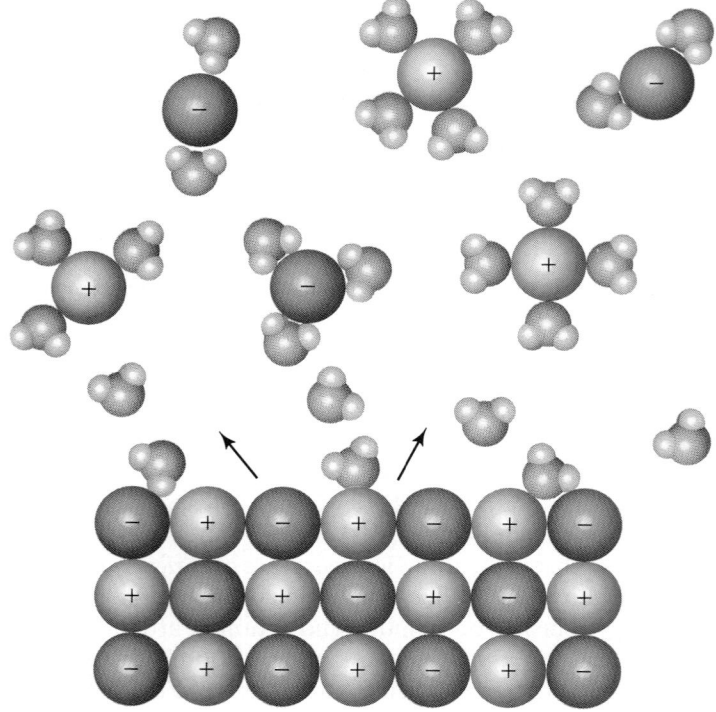

FIGURE 19.4 Changes in degree of order in the ions and solvent molecules on dissolving an ionic solid in water. The ions themselves become more randomized, but the water molecules that hydrate the ions become less randomized.

Figure 19.4

before because they are confined to the immediate environment of the ions. Therefore, the dissolving of a salt involves both ordering and disordering processes. It happens that the disordering processes are usually dominant, and so the overall effect is an increase in disorder upon dissolving most salts in water.

As these examples illustrate, spontaneity is associated with an increase in randomness or disorder of a system. The randomness is expressed by a thermodynamic quantity called **entropy,** given the symbol S. *The more disordered a system, the larger its entropy.* Like enthalpy, entropy is a state function. ∞ (Sec. 5.2) The change in entropy of a system, $\Delta S = S_{final} - S_{initial}$, depends only on the initial and final states of the system and not on the particular pathway by which the system changes. Like other thermodynamic quantities, ΔS has three parts, a number and unit giving the magnitude of the change and a sign giving its direction. A positive ΔS indicates an increase in randomness or disorder. A negative ΔS indicates a decrease in randomness or disorder.

SAMPLE EXERCISE 19.1

By considering the relative extents of randomness or disorder in the reactants and products, predict whether ΔS is positive or negative for each of the following processes:

(a) $H_2O(l) \longrightarrow H_2O(g)$
(b) $Ag^+(aq) + Cl^-(aq) \longrightarrow AgCl(s)$
(c) $4Fe(s) + 3O_2(g) \longrightarrow 2Fe_2O_3(s)$

SOLUTION (a) The evaporation of a liquid is accompanied by a large increase in volume. One mole of water (18 g) occupies about 18 mL as a liquid and 22.4 L as a gas at STP. Because the molecules are distributed throughout a much larger volume in the gaseous state than in the liquid state, an increase in disorder accompanies vaporization. Therefore, ΔS is positive.

(b) In this process the ions that are free to move about in the larger volume of the solution form a solid in which the ions are confined to highly ordered positions. Thus, there is a decrease in disorder, and ΔS is negative.

(c) The particles of a solid are much more highly ordered and confined to specific locations than are the molecules of a gas. Because a gas is converted into part of a solid product, disorder decreases and ΔS is negative.

PRACTICE EXERCISE

Indicate whether each of the following reactions produces an increase or decrease in the entropy of the system:
(a) $CO_2(s) \longrightarrow CO_2(g)$
(b) $CaO(s) + CO_2(g) \longrightarrow CaCO_3(s)$.
Answers: **(a)** increase; **(b)** decrease

The Second Law of Thermodynamics

Our introduction of the concept of entropy allows us to reexamine the second law of thermodynamics and its implications. In the discussion of spontaneity in Section 19.1, we noted that the second law concerns the direction in which processes move; it is associated with the idea that processes that are spontaneous in one direction are not spontaneous in the opposite direction.

There are many ways to state the second law. In chemical contexts it is usually expressed in terms of entropy. To develop such a statement, we must think in terms of an **isolated system,** one that doesn't exchange energy or matter with its surroundings. When a process occurs spontaneously in an isolated system, the system always ends up in a more random state. For example, when a gas expands under the conditions shown in Figure 19.2, there is no exchange of heat, work, or matter with the surroundings; this is an isolated system. The spontaneous expansion corresponds to an increase in entropy.

In the real world, we rarely deal with isolated systems. We are usually concerned with systems that exchange energy with their surroundings in the form of heat or work. If we consider the entire universe as a giant isolated system, however, we can state the second law as follows: *In any spontaneous process, there is always an increase in the entropy of the universe.* Thus, even if the entropy of a particular system decreases in a spontaneous process, the *total* change in the entropy of the universe (that is, the system and *all* its surroundings) must be positive.

To examine the implications of the second law, let's consider the oxidation of iron to $Fe_2O_3(s)$:

$$4Fe(s) + 3O_2(g) \longrightarrow 2Fe_2O_3(s) \qquad [19.4]$$

As discussed in Sample Exercise 19.1, this spontaneous process results in a decrease in the entropy of the system; that is, ΔS for the system is negative. But as the reaction occurs, the surroundings are also affected. Because the reaction is exothermic, heat is evolved, which increases the entropy of the surroundings by increasing the thermal motion of surrounding molecules. The second law tells us that the increase in the entropy of the surroundings *must* be greater than the decrease in the entropy of the system, so that the *total* entropy increases:

$$\Delta S_{universe} = \Delta S_{system} + \Delta S_{surroundings} > 0 \qquad [19.5]$$

Learning Goal 3: State the second law of thermodynamics.

Point of Emphasis: In any spontaneous process, the entropy of the universe will increase.

Entropy and Life

The second law of thermodynamics has profound implications concerning our existence as humans. We are very complex, highly organized, and well-ordered systems. As a result, our entropy content is much lower than it would be if we were completely decomposed into carbon dioxide, water, and several other simple chemicals. Does this mean that our existence is a violation of the second law? The answer is no because the thousands of chemical reactions necessary to produce and maintain a human life have caused a very large increase in the entropy of the rest of the universe. Thus, as the second law requires, the overall entropy change during the lifetime of a human, or for that matter any other living system, is positive.

We humans are masters of producing order in the world around us. We build impressive, highly ordered structures and buildings (Figure 19.5). We use tremendous quantities of raw materials to produce highly ordered materials—copper metal from copper ore, silicon for computer chips from sand, paper from wood pulp, and so forth. In so doing, we must expend a great deal of energy to, in essence, "fight" the second law of thermodynamics; for every bit of order we produce in our world, we produce an even greater amount of disorder. Coal and oil are burned to form CO_2 and H_2O. Sulfide ores are roasted (Section 24.2), producing SO_2 that spreads throughout the atmosphere. Waste products are scattered in various forms throughout the environment.

Modern human society is, in effect, using up its storehouse of energy-rich materials in its headlong rush to create order and exploit technology. We must eventually learn to live within the limits of the energy supply that reaches the earth daily from the sun, before we exhaust the supplies of readily available energy of other kinds.

FIGURE 19.5 In both ancient and modern times, humans have constructed highly ordered structures based on the pyramid. The Great Pyramid of Cheops (left) was built in Egypt around 2600 B.C. The Transamerica Building in San Francisco (right) is a modern skyscraper built in 1972. From the second law of thermodynamics, the introduction of order into these structures requires that an even greater amount of disorder be imparted to the universe. (a, © Michael Dalton/ Fundamental Photographs; b, © Peter Saloutos/The Stock Market)

No process that produces order (a decrease in entropy) in a system can proceed without producing an even larger disorder (an increase in entropy) in its surroundings. Thus, while the energy of the universe is conserved (the first law), the entropy of the universe continues to increase (the second law).

Throughout the remainder of this chapter, we will focus mainly on the systems that we encounter, rather than on their surroundings. To simplify the notation, we will usually refer to the entropy change of the system merely as ΔS rather than explicitly indicating ΔS_{system}.

Learning Goal 4: Predict whether the entropy change in a given process is positive, negative, or near zero.

19.3 A Molecular Interpretation of Entropy

It is useful to develop a qualitative sense of how changes in entropy within a system depend on changes in structure, physical state, and so forth. In Section 19.2, we considered some examples of spontaneous, endothermic processes. We saw, for example, that the increase in volume that occurs when a gas expands results in an increase in the randomness of the system (positive ΔS). In a similar fashion, the distribution of a liquid or solid solute in a solution is accompanied by an increase in entropy. For example, ΔS is positive when KCl dissolves in water. However, the dissolving of a gas, such as CO_2 in H_2O, causes the gas molecules to move in a much smaller volume; consequently, for this process the entropy of the system decreases (negative ΔS). Similarly, a decrease in the number of gaseous particles as the result of a reaction causes a decrease in entropy (negative ΔS). For example, ΔS for the following reaction is negative because 3 molecules react to form 2 molecules:

$$2NO(g) + O_2(g) \longrightarrow 2NO_2(g) \qquad [19.6]$$

Entropy changes can also be associated with molecular motions within a substance. A molecule consisting of more than one atom can engage in several types of motion. The entire molecule can move in one direction, as in the movements of gas molecules. We call such movement **translational motion.** The atoms within a molecule may also undergo **vibrational motion,** in which they move periodically toward and away from one another, much as a tuning fork vibrates about its equilibrium shape. Figure 19.6 shows the vibrational motions possible for the water molecule. In addition, molecules may possess **rotational motion,** as though they were spinning like a top. One of the rotational motions of the water molecule is also illustrated in Figure 19.6. These forms of motion are ways that the molecule has of storing energy. *As the temperature of a system increases, the amounts of energy stored in these forms of motion increase.*

To see what this has to do with entropy, let's imagine that we begin with a pure substance that forms a perfect crystalline lattice at the lowest temperature possible, absolute zero. The individual atoms and molecules are as well defined in position and in terms of energy as they can ever be. The **third law of thermodynamics** states that *the entropy of a pure crystalline substance at absolute zero is zero:* $S(0\ K) = 0$. As the temperature is raised, the units of the solid lattice begin to acquire energy. In a crystalline solid, the molecules or atoms that occupy the lattice sites are constrained to remain essentially in place. Nevertheless, they may store energy in the form of vibrational motion about their lattice positions. Instead of all the molecules necessarily being in the lowest possible energy state, the number of possible energies that the lattice atoms or molecules

Figure 19.6

FIGURE 19.6 Examples of vibrational and rotational motion, illustrated for the water molecule. Vibrational motions involve periodic displacements of the atoms with respect to one another, a phenomenon similar to the vibrations of the arms of a tuning fork. Rotational motions involve the spinning of a molecule about an axis.

Vibrations

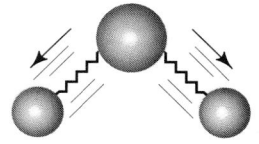

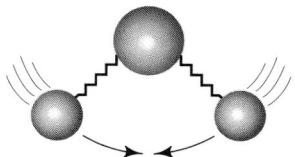

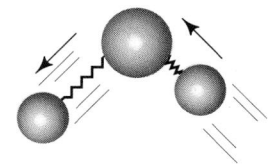

Rotation

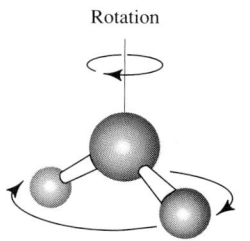

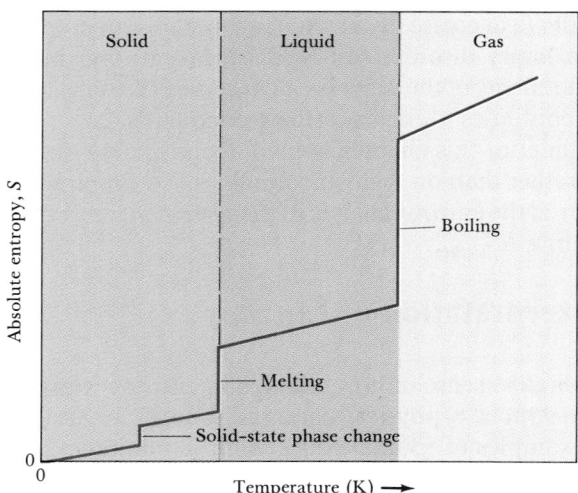

Figure 19.7

may have expands. This increase in possible energy states is not unlike the expansion of the gas illustrated in Figure 19.2. The entropy of the gas increases on expansion because the volume through which the gas molecules move is larger. The entropy of the lattice increases with temperature because the num-ber of possible energy states in which the molecules or atoms are distributed is larger.

It is instructive to follow what happens to the entropy of the substance as we continue to heat it. Let's suppose that at some temperature a solid-state phase change occurs, converting the substance from one solid form to another. This means that the arrangement of the lattice units changes in some way, possibly so that the lattice is less regular. This type of phase change occurs sharply at one temperature, just as other types of phase changes do (for exam-ple, the change from a solid to a liquid). When the phase change occurs, entropy changes because the two lattice arrangements do not have precisely the same degree of randomness. Not all substances undergo such solid-state phase changes. One that does is tin. Below 13°C, a solid form called gray tin is stable, whereas above this temperature, another solid form called white tin is stable. When heated, gray tin converts at 13°C to white tin, which has a higher entropy.

Figure 19.7 shows the variation in entropy with temperature for the sample. Note that the change in S with temperature is gradual up to the solid-state phase change and that there is then a sharp increase in S at that tempera-ture. At temperatures above the phase change, the entropy increases with in-creasing temperature up to the melting point of the solid.

When the solid melts, the units of the lattice are no longer confined to specific locations relative to other units but are free to move about the entire volume of the substance. This added freedom of motion for the individual molecules adds greatly to the entropy content of the substance. At the tempera-ture of melting, we therefore see a large increase in entropy content. After all the solid has melted, the temperature again increases, and with it the entropy.

SAMPLE EXERCISE 19.2

Figure 19.7 shows that the entropy of a liquid increases as its temperature increases. What factors are responsible for the increase in entropy?

SOLUTION   The average kinetic energy of the molecules in a liquid increases with temperature. As temperature increases, more molecules at any given instant possess higher energies. This "expansion" in the energies that the molecules possess is measured by the increase in entropy. The increase in S with increasing temperature results from increased energy of motion of all kinds within the liquid.

PRACTICE EXERCISE

Based on Figure 19.7, what general relationship exists among the magnitudes of the entropies of the gas, liquid, and solid phases of a substance?
Answer: $S_{gas} > S_{liquid} > S_{solid}$

At the boiling point of the liquid, another big increase in entropy occurs. The increase in this case results largely from the increased volume in which the molecules may be found. This is intuitively in line with our earlier ideas about entropy, because an increase in volume means an increase in randomness.

As the gas is heated, the entropy increases steadily because more and more energy is being stored in the gas molecules. The distribution of molecular speeds is spread out toward higher values, as illustrated in Figure 10.13. Again, the idea of an expansion in the range of energies in which molecules may be found helps us remember that increased average energy means increased entropy.

SAMPLE EXERCISE 19.3

Choose the substance with greater entropy in each pair and explain your choice: (a) 1 mol of NaCl(s) and 1 mol of HCl(g) at 25°C; (b) 2 mol of HCl(g) and 1 mol of HCl(g) at 25°C; (c) 1 mol of HCl(g) and 1 mol of Ar(g) at 25°C; (d) 1 mol of N_2(s) at 24 K and 1 mol of N_2(g) at 298 K.

SOLUTION   (a) Gaseous HCl has the higher entropy because it has acquired a high degree of randomness as a result of being in the gaseous state. (b) The sample containing 2 mol of HCl has twice the entropy of the sample containing 1 mol. (c) The HCl sample has the higher entropy because the HCl molecule is capable of storing energy in more ways than is Ar. It can rotate, and the H—Cl distance can change periodically in a vibrational motion. (d) The gaseous N_2 sample has the higher entropy because gases are more disordered than solids.

PRACTICE EXERCISE

Choose the substance with the greater entropy in each case: (a) 1 mol of H_2(g) at STP or 1 mol of H_2(g) at 100°C and 0.5 atm; (b) 1 mol of H_2O(s) at 0°C or 1 mol of H_2O(l) at 25°C; (c) 1 mol of H_2(g) at STP or 1 mol of SO_2(g) at STP: (d) 1 mol of N_2O_4(g) at STP or 2 mol of NO_2(g) at STP.   *Answers:* (a) 1 mol of H_2(g) at 100°C and 0.5 atm; (b) 1 mol of H_2O(l) at 25°C; (c) 1 mol of SO_2(g) at STP; (d) 2 mol of NO_2(g) at STP

In general, entropy *increases* are expected to accompany processes in which

1. Liquids or solutions are formed from solids.
2. Gases are formed from either solids or liquids.
3. The number of molecules of gas increases during a chemical reaction.
4. The temperature of a substance is increased.

Point of Emphasis: Overall, an increase in entropy is associated with a net increase in *mobility* of the substances in a reaction.

A CLOSER LOOK

Entropy, Randomness, and Ludwig Boltzmann

The entropy of a system is related to its randomness or disorder. The fact that we can assign a definite value to the entropy of a system implies that disorder can be quantified in some sense. The quantitative correspondence between entropy and randomness was first advanced by the Austrian physicist Ludwig Boltzmann (1844–1906). Boltzmann reasoned that the randomness of a particular state of a system, and thus its entropy, is related to the number of possible arrangements of molecules in the state.

We can illustrate Boltzmann's idea by using the poker hands shown in Table 19.1. The probability that a poker hand will contain five *specific* cards is the same, regardless of which five cards are specified. Thus, there is an equal probability of dealing either of the specific hands shown in Table 19.1. However, the first hand, a royal flush (the ten through ace of a single suit), strikes us as much more highly ordered than the second hand, a "nothing." The reason for this is clear if we compare the number of arrangements of five cards that correspond to a royal flush to the number corresponding to a nothing. There are only 4 poker hands that are in the "state" of a royal flush; in contrast, there are over 1.3 million nothing hands. The nothing state has a higher degree of disorder than the royal-flush state because there are so many more arrangements of cards that correspond to the nothing state.

We can use the same reasoning for chemical systems. For example, consider the two states for the gas molecules represented in Figure 19.2. In Figure 19.2(a), the atoms are confined to one flask. When the stopcock

is opened, as in Figure 19.2(b), the volume available to the atoms is doubled. There are more possible arrangements of the atoms in Figure 19.2(b) than in Figure 19.2(a); thus, the randomness of the former is greater than that of the latter. Likewise, there are more possible arrangements of water molecules in liquid water than there are in ice (Figure 19.3). Hence, liquid water is more disordered than ice.

Boltzmann showed that the entropy of a system equals a constant times the natural logarithm of the number of possible arrangements of atoms or molecules in the system:

$$S = k \ln W \qquad [19.7]$$

In Equation 19.7, W is the number of possible arrangements in the system, and k is a constant known as *Boltzmann's constant*. Boltzmann's constant is the "atomic equivalent" of the gas constant R. It equals the gas constant (usually expressed in joules) divided by Avogadro's number:

$$k = \frac{R}{N} = \frac{8.31 \text{ J/mol-K}}{6.02 \times 10^{23} \text{ mol}^{-1}} = 1.38 \times 10^{-23} \text{ J/K}$$

A pure crystalline substance at absolute zero is assumed to have only one arrangement of atoms or molecules; that is, $W = 1$. Thus, Equation 19.7 is consistent with the third law of thermodynamics: If $W = 1$, then $S = k \ln 1 = 0$. At any temperature above absolute zero, the atoms acquire energy, more arrangements become possible, and so $W > 1$ and $S > 0$.

TABLE 19.1 △ A Comparison of the Number of Combinations That Can Lead to a Royal Flush and to a "Nothing" Hand in Poker

Hand	State	Number of hands that lead to this state[a]
	Royal flush	4
	"Nothing"	1,302,540

[a] There are 2,598,960 total possible five-card poker hands.

Boltzmann made many other significant contributions to science, particularly in the area of *statistical mechanics*, which is the derivation of bulk thermodynamic properties for large collections of atoms or molecules by using the laws of probability. For example, the molecular speed distributions shown in Figure 10.14 are derived by using statistical mechanics; such plots are known as *Maxwell-Boltzmann distributions*. Unfortunately, Boltzmann's life had a tragic ending. He strongly believed in the existence of atoms, which, as strange as it seems to us now, was an unpopular viewpoint in physics at the beginning of the twentieth century. In poor health and unable to endure continual intellectual attacks on his beliefs, Boltzmann committed suicide on September 5, 1906. Ironically, it was only a few years later that the work of Thomson, Millikan, and Rutherford led to acceptance of the nuclear atom model. ⚭ (Sec. 2.2) Although Boltzmann made many contributions to science, the connection between entropy and randomness described in Equation 19.7 is arguably his greatest. This equation is so significant that it is inscribed on his gravestone (Figure 19.8).

FIGURE 19.8 Ludwig Boltzmann's gravestone in Vienna is inscribed with his famous relationship between the entropy of a state and the number of arrangements available in the state (in Boltzmann's time, "log" was used to represent the natural logarithm). (Institut für Theoretische Physik der Universität Wien)

P. G. Nelson, "Derivation of the Second Law of Thermodynamics from Boltzmann's Distribution Law," *J. Chem. Educ.* **1989,** *65,* 390.

SAMPLE EXERCISE 19.4

Predict whether the entropy change of the system in each of the following reactions is positive or negative.
(a) $CaCO_3(s) \longrightarrow CaO(s) + CO_2(g)$
(b) $N_2(g) + 3H_2(g) \longrightarrow 2NH_3(g)$
(c) $N_2(g) + O_2(g) \longrightarrow 2NO(g)$

SOLUTION (a) The entropy change here is positive because a solid is converted into a solid and a gas. Gaseous substances generally possess more entropy than solids, and so whenever the products contain more moles of gas than the reactants, the entropy change is probably positive.

(b) The entropy change in formation of ammonia from nitrogen and hydrogen is negative because there are fewer moles of gas in the product than in the reactants.

(c) This represents a case in which the entropy change will be small because the same number of moles of gas is involved in the reactants and in the product. The sign of ΔS is impossible to predict based on our discussions thus far, but we can predict that ΔS will be small.

PRACTICE EXERCISE

Predict whether ΔS is positive or negative in each of the following processes:
(a) $HCl(g) + NH_3(g) \longrightarrow NH_4Cl(s)$
(b) $2SO_2(g) + O_2(g) \longrightarrow 2SO_3(g)$
(c) cooling of nitrogen gas from $20°C$ to $-50°C$.
Answers: (a) negative; (b) negative; (c) negative

TABLE 19.2 △
Standard Entropies of Selected Substances at 298 K

Substance	$S°$, J/mol-K
Gases	
$H_2(g)$	130.6
$H_2O(g)$	188.7
$N_2(g)$	191.5
$NH_3(g)$	192.5
$C_6H_6(g)$	269.2
Liquids	
$H_2O(l)$	70.0
$C_6H_6(l)$	172.8
Solids	
$Fe(s)$	27.2
$Ca(OH)_2(s)$	83.4

Learning Goal 7: Calculate $\Delta S°$ for any reaction from tabulated absolute entropy values, $S°$.

Point of Emphasis: The calculation of $\Delta S°$ is analogous to the calculation of $\Delta H°$ in Chapter 5.

19.4 Calculation of Entropy Changes

In Section 5.5, we discussed how calorimetry can be used to measure ΔH for chemical reactions. No comparable, easy means exists for measuring ΔS for a reaction. By using experimental measurements of the variation of heat capacity with temperature, however, we can determine the absolute entropy, S, for many substances at any temperature. (The theory and the methods used for these measurements and calculations are beyond the scope of this text.) These entropies are based on the reference point of zero entropy for perfect crystalline solids at 0 K (the third law). Entropies are usually tabulated in units of joules per mole per Kelvin: J/mol-K.

The entropy values of substances in their standard states are known as *standard entropies* and are denoted $S°$. For a substance, the standard state is the pure substance at 1 atm pressure.* Table 19.2 lists the values of $S°$ for several substances at 298 K; Appendix C gives a more extensive list. Notice that the standard entropies of gases are greater than those of liquids and solids and that the standard entropy increases with increasing molecular complexity. Notice also that the standard entropies of elements are not zero.

The entropy change in a chemical reaction is given by the sum of the entropies of the products less the sum of the entropies of the reactants:

$$\Delta S° = \sum nS°(\text{products}) - \sum mS°(\text{reactants}) \qquad [19.8]$$

As in Equation 5.18, the coefficients n and m are the coefficients in the chemical equation. In other words, we sum the standard entropies of all the products, multiplying each by its coefficient in the balanced equation, and then subtract the sum of the entropies of the reactants, multiplied by their coefficients.

SAMPLE EXERCISE 19.5

Calculate $\Delta S°$ for the synthesis of ammonia from $N_2(g)$ and $H_2(g)$:

$$N_2(g) + 3H_2(g) \longrightarrow 2NH_3(g)$$

SOLUTION Using Equation 19.8, we have

$$\Delta S° = 2S°(NH_3) - [S°(N_2) + 3S°(H_2)]$$

Substituting the appropriate $S°$ values from Table 19.2 yields

$$\Delta S° =$$

$$(2\text{ mol})\left(192.5\,\frac{J}{\text{mol-K}}\right) - \left[(1\text{ mol})\left(191.5\,\frac{J}{\text{mol-K}}\right) + (3\text{ mol})\left(130.6\,\frac{J}{\text{mol-K}}\right)\right]$$

$$= -198.3\text{ J/K}$$

The value for $\Delta S°$ is negative, as we predicted in Sample Exercise 19.4(b).

PRACTICE EXERCISE

Using the standard entropies in Appendix C, calculate the standard entropy change, $\Delta S°$, for the following reaction at 298 K:
$Al_2O_3(s) + 3H_2(g) \longrightarrow 2Al(s) + 3H_2O(g)$. ***Answer:*** 179.9 J/K

---

* The standard pressure used in thermodynamics is actually no longer 1 atm but is now based on the SI unit for pressure, the pascal (Pa). The standard pressure is 10^5 Pa, a quantity known as a *bar:* 1 bar = 10^5 Pa. Because 1 bar differs from 1 atm by only 1.3 percent, we will continue to refer to the standard pressure as 1 atm.

19.5 Gibbs Free Energy

We have seen that the spontaneity of a reaction involves two thermodynamic concepts, enthalpy and entropy. Now that we can assign a quantitative value to the entropy change during a reaction, is there a way to use ΔH and ΔS to predict whether a given reaction will be spontaneous? The means for incorporating both ΔH and ΔS into a new quantity that tells us whether a reaction will be spontaneous was first developed by the American mathematician J. Willard Gibbs (1839–1903). Gibbs (Figure 19.9) proposed a new state function, now called the **Gibbs free energy** (or just **free energy**). The Gibbs free energy, G, of a state is defined as

$$G = H - TS \qquad [19.9]$$

where T is the absolute temperature.

For a process occurring at constant temperature, the change in free energy is given by the expression

$$\Delta G = \Delta H - T\,\Delta S \qquad [19.10]$$

Thus, a process that is driven spontaneously toward equilibrium both by decreasing energy (negative ΔH) and increasing randomness (positive ΔS) will have a negative ΔG. Indeed, there is a simple relationship between the sign of ΔG for a reaction and the spontaneity of that reaction operated at constant temperature and pressure:

1. If ΔG is negative, the reaction is spontaneous in the forward direction.
2. If ΔG is zero, the reaction is at equilibrium; there is no driving force tending to make the reaction go in either direction.
3. If ΔG is positive, the reaction in the forward direction is nonspontaneous; work must be supplied from the surroundings to make it occur. However, the reverse reaction will be spontaneous.

An analogy is often drawn between the free-energy change in a spontaneous reaction and the potential-energy change in a boulder rolling down a hill. Potential energy in a gravitational field "drives" the boulder until it reaches a state of minimum potential energy in the valley [Figure 19.10(a)]. Similarly, the free energy of a chemical system decreases (negative ΔG) until it reaches a minimum value [Figure 19.10(b)]. When this minimum is reached, a state of equilibrium exists. In any spontaneous process at constant temperature and pressure, the free energy always decreases. As shown in Figure 19.10(b), the equilibrium condition can be approached by a spontaneous change from either direction, from the product side or the reactant side.

As an example of these ideas, let's return to the synthesis of ammonia from nitrogen and hydrogen. Imagine that we have a certain number of moles of nitrogen and three times that number of moles of hydrogen in a reaction vessel that permits us to maintain a constant temperature and pressure. We know from our earlier discussions that the formation of ammonia will not be complete; an equilibrium will be reached in which the reaction vessel contains some mixture of N_2, H_2, and NH_3. The free energy of the system decreases

FIGURE 19.9 Josiah Willard Gibbs (1839–1903) was the first person to be awarded a Ph.D. in science from an American university (Yale, 1863). From 1871 until his death he held the chair of mathematical physics at Yale. Gibbs developed much of the theoretical foundation that led to the development of chemical thermodynamics. (Culver Pictures)

Learning Goal 8: Define free energy in terms of enthalpy and entropy.

Learning Goal 9: Explain the relationship between the sign of the free-energy change, ΔG, and whether a process is spontaneous in the forward direction.

Point of Emphasis: If $\Delta G° < 0$ then the forward reaction will be spontaneous. If $\Delta G° > 0$ then the reverse reaction will be spontaneous. If $\Delta G° = 0$ then the system is at equilibrium and no net reaction will occur.

Teaching Note: When $\Delta G°$ is negative, reactions are said to be *exergonic;* when $\Delta G°$ is positive, reactions are said to be *endergonic.*

FIGURE 19.10 Analogy between the potential-energy change of a boulder rolling down a hill (a) and the free-energy change in a spontaneous reaction (b). The equilibrium position in (a) is given by the minimum potential energy available to the system. The equilibrium position in (b) is given by the minimum free energy available to the system.

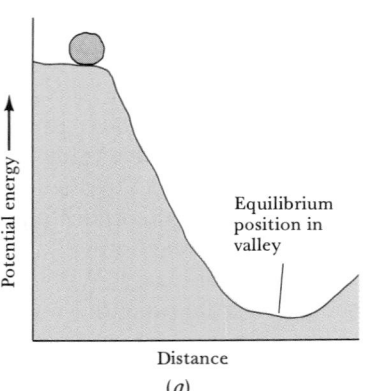

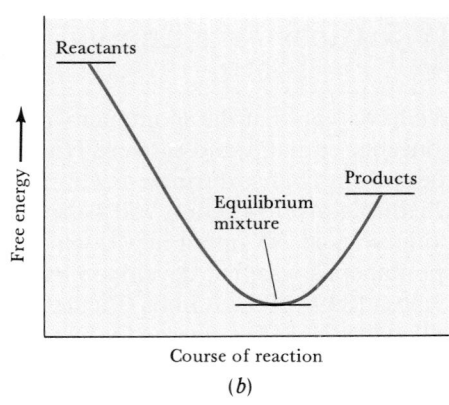

Distance
(a)

Course of reaction
(b)

Zheng Xianmin, "The Free Energy Prediction and the Principle of Le Châtelier," *J. Chem. Educ.* **1989**, *66*, 401.

Teaching Note: Observing that an equilibrium mixture can be approached from both the product and reactant sides is a valuable method to verify the position of the equilibrium.

Lee R. Summerlin, Christie L. Borgford, and Julie B. Ealy, "A Chemical Hand Warmer," *Chemical Demonstrations, a Sourcebook for Teachers, Volume 2* (Washington: American Chemical Society, 1987), pp. 99–100.

Point of Emphasis: As with enthalpy, free energy is a *relative* quantity, not an absolute quantity. Therefore, we choose the pure elements in their standard states as our basis and tabulate ΔG_f for substances.

Learning Goal 10: List the usual conventions regarding standard states in setting the *values* for standard free energies.

(negative ΔG) until this equilibrium is attained. Once the equilibrium has been reached, there is no further spontaneous net formation of NH_3. The equilibrium condition is the one in which the free energy of the system is at a minimum at this temperature and pressure. To form more NH_3 from N_2 and H_2 after equilibrium has been reached requires an increase in free energy (positive ΔG).

It is not necessary that we reach equilibrium beginning only with N_2 and H_2. We could reach the same equilibrium by beginning with an appropriate amount of NH_3. Ammonia held at a constant temperature and pressure will decompose to form N_2 and H_2 until an equilibrium is attained. This process is also spontaneous, involving a decrease in free energy as the system approaches equilibrium. The equilibrium can be reached from either the reactant side or the product side, as indicated in a general fashion in Figure 19.10(b).

Standard Free-Energy Changes

We have noted that free energy is a state function. This means that it is possible to tabulate **standard free energies of formation** for substances, just as it is possible to tabulate standard enthalpies of formation. It is important to remember that standard values for these functions imply a particular set of conditions, or standard states. ⟳ (Sec. 5.7) The standard state for gaseous substances is 1 atm pressure. For solid substances, the standard state is the pure solid; for liquids, the pure liquid. For substances in solution, the standard state is normally a concentration of 1 *M*. (In accurate work, it may be necessary to make certain corrections, but we need not worry about these.) The temperature usually chosen for purposes of tabulating data is 25°C, but we will calculate $\Delta G°$ at other temperatures as well. Just as for the standard heats of formation, the free energies of elements in their standard states are arbitrarily set to zero. This arbitrary choice of a reference point has no effect on the quantity in which we are really interested, namely, the *difference* in free energy between reactants and products. The rules about standard states are summarized in Table 19.3. A listing of standard free energies of formation, denoted $\Delta G_f°$, appears in Appendix C.

The standard free energies of formation for substances are useful in calculating the *standard free-energy change* in a chemical process. The general procedure is analogous to the calculation of $\Delta H°$ (Equation 5.18) and $\Delta S°$ (Equation 19.8):

CHEMISTRY AT WORK

Learning Goal 11: Describe the relationship between ΔG and the maximum work that can be derived from a spontaneous process, or the minimum work required to accomplish a nonspontaneous process.

Free Energy and Work

One of the important ways we use chemical reactions is to produce energy for performing work. Naturally, we want to accomplish the work as efficiently and economically as possible. Any process that occurs spontaneously can be utilized to perform work, at least in principle. For example, the burning of gasoline in the cylinders of a car produces the work accomplished in moving the car. How much work is extracted from a particular process depends on how it is carried out. For example, we might burn gasoline in an open container and extract no useful work at all. In an automobile engine, less than 20 percent of the released energy is used to accomplish work. If the gasoline were burned under more favorable conditions, we could extract more work. However, there is a theoretical limit to the amount of work we can obtain from a spontaneous process. In practice, we always obtain less than this maximum possible amount. Nevertheless, it is useful to know the maximum for a process so that we can measure our success in extracting work from it.

Thermodynamics tells us that *the change in free energy for a process, ΔG, equals the maximum useful work that can be done by the system on its surroundings in a spontaneous process occurring at constant temperature and pressure:*

$$w_{max} = \Delta G \qquad [19.11]$$

This relationship explains why ΔG is called the *free* energy. It is the portion of the energy change of a spontaneous reaction that is free to do useful work. The remainder of the energy enters the environment as heat.

For processes that are not spontaneous ($\Delta G > 0$), the free-energy change is a measure of the *minimum* amount of work that must be done to cause the process to occur. In actual cases, we always need to do more than this theoretical minimum amount because of the inefficiencies in the way the changes occur.

$$\Delta G^\circ = \sum n\Delta G_f^\circ(\text{products}) - \sum m\Delta G_f^\circ(\text{reactants}) \qquad [19.12]$$

Stated verbally, the standard free-energy change for a reaction equals the sum of the standard free-energy values per mole of each product, each multiplied by the corresponding coefficient in the balanced equation, less the corresponding sum for the reactants.

What use can be made of this standard free-energy change for a chemical reaction? The quantity ΔG° tells us whether a mixture of reactants and products, each present under standard conditions, would spontaneously react in the forward direction to produce more products (ΔG° negative) or in the reverse direction to form more reactants (ΔG° positive). Because standard free-energy values are readily available for a large number of substances, the standard free-energy change is easy to calculate for many reaction systems of interest.

TABLE 19.3 △ Conventions Used in Establishing Standard Free-Energy Values

State of matter	Standard state
Solid	Pure solid
Liquid	Pure liquid
Gas	1 atm pressure
Solution	1 M concentration
Elements	Standard free energy of formation of an element in its normal state is defined as zero

SAMPLE EXERCISE 19.6

Determine the standard free-energy change for the following reaction at 298 K:

$$N_2(g) + 3H_2(g) \longrightarrow 2NH_3(g)$$

SOLUTION Using Appendix C, we find that the standard free energies for the three substances of interest are as follows: $N_2(g)$, $\Delta G_f^\circ = 0.0$; $H_2(g)$, $\Delta G_f^\circ = 0.0$; $NH_3(g)$, $\Delta G_f^\circ = -16.66$ kJ/mol.

The standard free-energy change for the reaction of interest is

$$\Delta G^\circ = 2\Delta G_f^\circ(NH_3) - [3\Delta G_f^\circ(H_2) + \Delta G_f^\circ(N_2)]$$

Inserting numerical quantities, we obtain

$$\Delta G^\circ = -33.32 \text{ kJ}$$

The fact that ΔG° is negative tells us that a mixture of H_2, N_2, and NH_3 at 25 °C, each present at a pressure of 1 atm, would react spontaneously to form more ammonia. (Remember, however, that this says nothing about the rate at which the reaction occurs.)

PRACTICE EXERCISE

Using the standard free energies of formation tabulated in Appendix C, calculate ΔG° for the following reaction at 298 K: $2CH_3OH(l) + 3O_2(g) \longrightarrow 2CO_2(g) + 4H_2O(g)$. **Answer:** -1370.8 kJ

19.6 Free Energy and Temperature

The values of ΔG° are tabulated at 25 °C, but we are often interested in examining reactions at other temperatures. How is the free-energy change affected by temperature? Let's examine again Equation 19.10:

$$\Delta G = \Delta H - T\,\Delta S$$

Were it not for entropy effects, all exothermic reactions—those in which ΔH is negative—would be spontaneous. The entropy contribution, represented by the quantity $-T\,\Delta S$, may increase or decrease the tendency of the reaction to proceed spontaneously. When ΔS is positive, meaning that the final state is more random or disordered than the initial state, the term $-T\,\Delta S$ makes ΔG less positive (or more negative), increasing the tendency of the reaction to occur spontaneously. When ΔS is negative, however, the term $-T\,\Delta S$ decreases the tendency of the reaction to occur spontaneously.

When ΔH and $-T\,\Delta S$ are of opposite sign, the relative importance of the two terms determines whether ΔG is negative or positive. In these instances, temperature is an important consideration. Generally, both ΔH and ΔS change very little with temperature. The only term in the equation $\Delta G = \Delta H - T\,\Delta S$ that changes markedly with temperature is $-T\,\Delta S$. Thus, at high temperatures the $-T\,\Delta S$ term becomes relatively more important in determining the sign and magnitude of ΔG.

Various possible situations for the relative signs of ΔH and ΔS are shown in Table 19.4, with examples of each. By applying the concepts we have developed for predicting entropy changes, we may often predict how ΔG will change with change in temperature.

TABLE 19.4 △ Effect of Temperature on Reaction Spontaneity

ΔH	ΔS	ΔG	Reaction characteristics	Example
−	+	Always negative	Reaction is spontaneous at all temperatures; reverse reaction is always non-spontaneous	$2O_3(g) \longrightarrow 3O_2(g)$
+	−	Always positive	Reaction is nonspontaneous at all temperatures; reverse reaction is spontaneous	$3O_2(g) \longrightarrow 2O_3(g)$
−	−	Negative at low temperatures; positive at high temperatures	Reaction is spontaneous at low temperatures but becomes nonspontaneous at high temperatures	$CaO(s) + CO_2(g) \longrightarrow CaCO_3(s)$
+	+	Positive at low temperatures; negative at high temperatures	Reaction is nonspontaneous at low temperatures but becomes spontaneous as temperature is raised	$CaCO_3(s) \longrightarrow CaO(s) + CO_2(g)$

SAMPLE EXERCISE 19.7

(a) Predict the direction in which $\Delta G°$ for the equilibrium

$$N_2(g) + 3H_2(g) \rightleftharpoons 2NH_3(g)$$

will change with increase in temperature. (b) Calculate $\Delta G°$ at 500°C, assuming that $\Delta H°$ and $\Delta S°$ do not change with temperature.

Table 19.4

Learning Goal 14: Estimate $\Delta G°$ at any temperature given $\Delta S°_{298}$ and $\Delta H°_{298}$.

SOLUTION (a) In Sample Exercise 19.5, we saw that the change in $\Delta S°$ for the equilibrium of interest is negative. This means that the term $-T\Delta S°$ is positive and grows larger with increasing temperature. The standard free-energy change, $\Delta G°$, is the sum of the negative quantity $\Delta H°$ and the positive quantity $-T\Delta S°$. Because only the latter grows larger with increasing temperature, $\Delta G°$ grows less negative. Thus, the driving force for the reaction becomes smaller with increasing temperature, indicating less conversion to products.

(b) The $\Delta H_f°$ and $S°$ values necessary to calculate $\Delta H°$ and $\Delta S°$ for this reaction can be taken from Appendix C. We have previously performed the enthalpy calculation in Sample Exercise 15.14 (Section 15.6) and the entropy calculation in Sample Exercise 19.5, giving $\Delta H° = -92.38$ kJ and $\Delta S° = -198.3$ J/K. To calculate $\Delta G°$ given $\Delta H°$ and $\Delta S°$, we use the following relationship:

$$\Delta G° = \Delta H° - T\Delta S°$$

(Recall that the superscript ° indicates that the process is operated under standard conditions.) Assuming that $\Delta H°$ and $\Delta S°$ do not change with temperature, and using $T = 500 + 273 = 773$ K, we have

$$\Delta G° = -92.38 \text{ kJ} - (773 \text{ K})\left(-198.3 \frac{\text{J}}{\text{K}}\right)\left(\frac{1 \text{ kJ}}{10^3 \text{ J}}\right)$$

$$= -92.38 \text{ kJ} + 153.29 \text{ kJ} = 60.91 \text{ kJ}$$

Notice that we changed $T\Delta S°$ from units of joules to kilojoules so it could be added to $\Delta H°$, which is in units of kilojoules.

In Sample Exercise 19.6, we calculated $\Delta G°$ for this reaction at 298 K: $\Delta G°_{298} = -33.32$ kJ. Thus, we see that increasing the temperature from 298 K to 773 K changes $\Delta G°$ from -33.32 kJ to $+60.91$ kJ. Of course, the result at 773 K is not as accurate as that at 298 K because $\Delta H°$ and $\Delta S°$ do change slightly with temperature. Nevertheless, the result should be a reasonable approximation. The positive increase in $\Delta G°$ with increasing temperature is in agreement with the qualitative prediction made in part (a) of this exercise. Our result indicates that a mixture of $N_2(g)$, $H_2(g)$, and $NH_3(g)$, each at 1 atm pressure (standard conditions), will react spontaneously at 298 K to form more $NH_3(g)$; however, this same reaction is not spontaneous at 773 K. In fact, at 773 K the reaction will proceed in the opposite direction, to form more $N_2(g)$ and $H_2(g)$.

PRACTICE EXERCISE

(a) Using the standard enthalpies of formation and standard entropies in Appendix C, calculate $\Delta H°$ and $\Delta S°$ at 298 K for the following reaction: $2SO_2(g) + O_2(g) \longrightarrow 2SO_3(g)$. (b) Using the values for $\Delta H°$ and $\Delta S°$ from part (a), estimate $\Delta G°$ at 400 K. *Answers:* (a) $\Delta H° = -196.6$ kJ, $\Delta S° = -189.6$ J/K; (b) $\Delta G° = -120.8$ kJ

19.7 Free Energy and the Equilibrium Constant

Although it is useful to have a ready means of determining $\Delta G°$ for a reaction from tabulated values, we usually want to know about the direction of spontaneous change for systems that are not at standard conditions. For any chemical process, the general relationship between the free-energy change under standard conditions, $\Delta G°$, and the free-energy change under any other conditions, ΔG, is given by the following expression.

$$\Delta G = \Delta G° + RT \ln Q \qquad [19.13]$$

In this expression, R is the ideal-gas constant, 8.314 J/mol-K; T is the absolute temperature; and Q is the reaction quotient (Section 15.5) that corresponds to the chemical reaction and particular reaction mixture of interest.

SAMPLE EXERCISE 19.8

Calculate ΔG at 298 K for the following reaction if the reaction mixture consists of 1.0 atm N_2, 3.0 atm H_2, and 1.0 atm NH_3:

$$N_2(g) + 3H_2(g) \longrightarrow 2NH_3(g)$$

SOLUTION For the balanced equation and set of concentrations given, the reaction quotient Q is

$$Q = \frac{P_{NH_3}^2}{P_{N_2}P_{H_2}^3} = \frac{(1.0)^2}{(1.0)(3.0)^3} = 3.7 \times 10^{-2}$$

$\Delta G_{298}°$ was calculated in Sample Exercise 19.6: $\Delta G_{298}° = -33.32$ kJ. Therefore, for 1 mol N_2 reacting with 3 mol H_2, we have

$$\Delta G = \Delta G° + RT \ln Q$$

$$= (-33.32 \text{ kJ}) + \left(8.314 \frac{J}{K}\right)(298 \text{ K})\left(\frac{1 \text{ kJ}}{10^3 \text{ J}}\right)\ln (3.7 \times 10^{-2})$$

$$= -33.32 \text{ kJ} + (-8.17 \text{ kJ})$$

$$= -41.49 \text{ kJ}$$

The free-energy change becomes more negative, changing from -33.32 kJ to -41.49 kJ, as the pressures of N_2, H_2, and NH_3 are changed from 1.0 atm each (standard conditions, $\Delta G°$) to 1.0 atm, 3.0 atm, and 1.0 atm, respectively. The larger negative value for ΔG when the pressure of H_2 is increased from 1.0 atm to 3.0 atm indicates a larger "driving force" to produce NH_3. This result bears out the prediction of Le Châtelier's principle, which indicates that increasing P_{H_2} should shift the reaction more to the product side, thereby forming more NH_3.

PRACTICE EXERCISE

Calculate ΔG at 298 K for the reaction of nitrogen and hydrogen to form ammonia if the reaction mixture consists of 3.0 atm NH_3, 1.0 atm N_2, and 0.50 atm H_2. *Answer:* -22.72 kJ

When a system is at equilibrium, ΔG must be zero, and the reaction quotient Q must by definition equal K. ∞ (Sec. 15.5) Thus, for a system at equilibrium (when $\Delta G = 0$ and $Q = K$), Equation 19.13 transforms as follows:

$$\Delta G = \Delta G° + RT \ln Q$$

$$0 = \Delta G° + RT \ln K$$

$$\Delta G° = -RT \ln K \qquad [19.14]$$

From Equation 19.14 we can readily see that if $\Delta G°$ is negative, $\ln K$ must be positive. A positive value for $\ln K$ means that $K > 1$. Therefore, the more negative $\Delta G°$ is, the larger the equilibrium constant, K. Conversely, if $\Delta G°$ is positive, $\ln K$ is negative, which means that $K < 1$. To summarize:

$\Delta G°$ negative:	$K > 1$
$\Delta G°$ zero:	$K = 1$
$\Delta G°$ positive:	$K < 1$

It is possible from a knowledge of $\Delta G°$ for a reaction to calculate the value for the equilibrium constant, using Equation 19.14. Some care is necessary, however, in the matter of units. When dealing with gases, the concentrations of reactants should be expressed in units of atmospheres. The concentrations of pure solids and liquids are 1. For substances in solution, concentrations in moles per liter are appropriate.

SAMPLE EXERCISE 19.9

From standard free energies of formation, calculate the equilibrium constant for the reaction

$$N_2(g) + 3H_2(g) \rightleftharpoons 2NH_3(g)$$

at 25°C.

SOLUTION The equilibrium constant for this reaction is written as

$$K_p = \frac{P_{NH_3}^2}{P_{N_2}P_{H_2}^3}$$

where the gas concentrations are expressed in atmospheres pressure. The standard free-energy change for the reaction was determined in Sample Exercise 19.6 to be -33.32 kJ. Inserting this into Equation 19.14, we obtain

$$-33,320 \text{ J} = -(8.314 \text{ J/K})(298 \text{ K})(\ln K_p)$$

$$\ln K_p = 13.45$$

Thus, K_p is given by

$$K_p = e^{13.45} = 6.9 \times 10^5$$

Driving Nonspontaneous Reactions

Free-energy considerations are very important in thinking about many nonspontaneous reactions that we might wish to carry out for our own purposes or that occur in nature. For example, we might wish to extract a metal from an ore. If we look at a reaction such as

$$Cu_2S(s) \longrightarrow 2Cu(s) + S(s) \quad \Delta G° = +86.2 \text{ kJ} \quad [19.15]$$

we find that it is highly nonspontaneous. Clearly, then, we cannot hope to obtain copper metal from Cu_2S merely by trying to catalyze the reaction shown in Equation 19.15. Instead, we must "do work" on the reaction in some way in order to force it to occur as we wish. We might do this by coupling the reaction we've written with another reaction so that we arrive at an overall reaction that *is* spontaneous. Consider, for example, the reaction

$$S(s) + O_2(g) \longrightarrow SO_2(g) \quad \Delta G° = -300.1 \text{ kJ} \quad [19.16]$$

This is a spontaneous reaction. Adding Equations 19.15 and 19.16, we obtain

$$\Delta G° =$$

$Cu_2S(s) \longrightarrow 2Cu(s) + S(s)$	$+86.2$ kJ
$S(s) + O_2(g) \longrightarrow SO_2(g)$	-300.1 kJ
$Cu_2S(s) + O_2(g) \longrightarrow 2Cu(s) + SO_2(g)$	-213.9 kJ

The free-energy change for the overall reaction is the sum of the free-energy changes of the two reactions. Because the negative free-energy change for the second reaction is much larger than the positive free-energy change for the first, the overall reaction has a large, negative standard free-energy change.

The coupling of two or more reactions to cause a nonspontaneous chemical process to occur is very important in biochemical systems. Many of the reactions that are essential to the maintenance of life do not occur spontaneously within the human body. These necessary reactions are made to occur, however, by coupling them with reactions that are spontaneous and release energy. The energy releases that accompany the metabolism of foodstuffs provide the primary source of necessary free energy. For example, the compound glucose, $C_6H_{12}O_6$, is oxidized in the body, and a substantial amount of free energy is released.

$$C_6H_{12}O_6(s) + 6O_2(g) \longrightarrow 6CO_2(g) + 6H_2O(l)$$
$$\Delta G° = -2880 \text{ kJ} \quad [19.17]$$

This energy "does work" in the body. However, some means is necessary to couple, or connect, the energy released by glucose oxidation to the reactions that require energy. One means of accomplishing this is shown in Figure 19.11. Adenosine triphosphate (ATP) is a high-energy molecule. When ATP is converted to a lower-energy molecule, adenosine diphosphate (ADP), the energy to drive other chemical reactions becomes available. The energy released in glucose oxidation is used in part to reconvert ADP back to ATP. The ATP-ADP interconversions thus act to store energy and release it to drive needed reactions. The coupling of reactions so that the free energy released in one may be used in another way requires particular enzymes as catalysts.

FIGURE 19.11 Schematic representation of part of the free-energy changes that occur in cell metabolism. The oxidation of glucose to CO_2 and H_2O produces free energy. This released free energy is used to convert ADP into the more energetic ATP. The ATP is then used, as needed, as an energy source to convert simple molecules into more complex cell constituents. When ATP releases its free energy, it is converted to ADP.

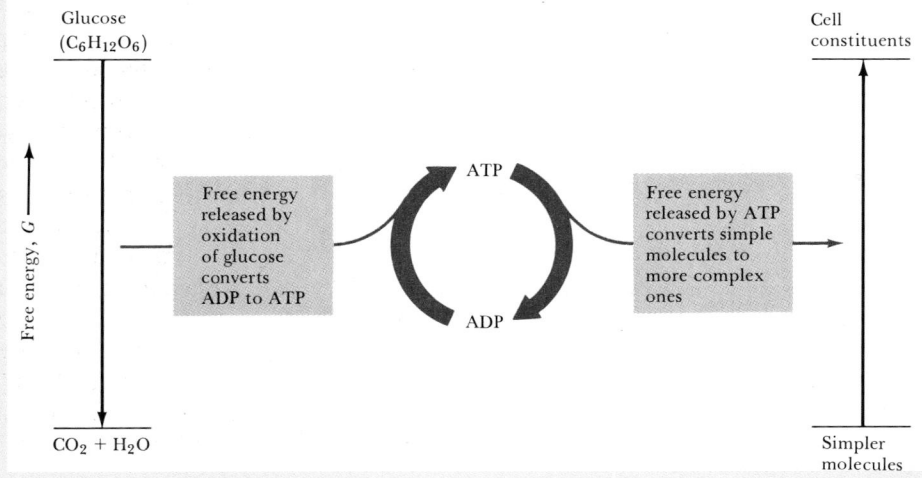

This is a large equilibrium constant. Compare its magnitude with the equilibrium constants at higher temperature, as listed in Table 15.4. If a catalyst could be found that would permit reasonably rapid reaction of N_2 with H_2 at room temperature, high pressures would not be required to force the equilibrium toward NH_3.

PRACTICE EXERCISE

Using data given in Appendix C, calculate first the standard free-energy change, $\Delta G°$, and then the equilibrium constant at 298 K for the following reaction: $2H_2(g) + O_2(g) \longrightarrow 2H_2O(g)$. *Answers:* −457.2 kJ; 1.4×10^{80}

For Review

Summary

In this chapter, we have examined the concepts of spontaneity and equilibrium from a thermodynamic point of view. The enthalpy change of a system, ΔH, is a measure of the potential-energy change in a process. Exothermic processes ($\Delta H < 0$) tend to occur spontaneously. The spontaneous character of a reaction is also determined by the change in randomness or disorder of the system, measured by the entropy, S. Processes that produce an increase in randomness or disorder of the system ($\Delta S > 0$) tend to occur spontaneously.

Entropy changes in a system are associated with an increase in the number of ways the particles of the system can be distributed among possible energy states or spatial arrangements. For example, an increase in volume, in translational energy, or in number of particles leads to an increase in entropy. In any process, the total entropy change is the sum of the entropy change of the system and the surroundings. The second law of thermodynamics tells us that in any spontaneous process the entropy of the universe increases. That is,

$$\Delta S_{system} + \Delta S_{surroundings} > 0$$

The standard entropy change in a system, $\Delta S°$, can be calculated from tabulated standard entropy values, $S°$. Entropies are determined with the aid of the third law of thermodynamics, which states that the entropy of a pure crystalline solid at 0 K is zero.

The Gibbs free energy, G, is a thermodynamic state function that combines the two state functions enthalpy and entropy: $G = H - TS$. For processes that occur at constant temperature, $\Delta G = \Delta H - T\Delta S$. The free-energy change for a process occurring at constant temperature and pressure relates directly to reaction spontaneity. For all spontaneous processes, ΔG is negative, whereas a positive value for ΔG indicates a nonspontaneous process (one that is spontaneous in the reverse direction). At equilibrium, ΔG is zero. The free energy also is a measure of the maximum useful work that can be performed by a system in a spontaneous process. In practice, this amount of useful work is never realized because processes in the real world have inherent inefficiencies.

The standard free-energy change, $\Delta G°$, for any process can be calculated from tabulated standard free energies of formation, $\Delta G_f°$; it can also be calculated from standard enthalpy and entropy changes: $\Delta G° = \Delta H° - T\Delta S°$. Temperature changes will change the value of ΔG and can also change its sign.

The free-energy change under nonstandard conditions is related to the standard free-energy change; $\Delta G = \Delta G° + RT\ln Q$. At equilibrium ($\Delta G = 0$, $Q = K$), $\Delta G° = -RT\ln K$. Thus, the standard free-energy change is related to the equilibrium constant. Consequently, we can understand the position of a chemical equilibrium in terms of the $\Delta H°$ and $T \Delta S°$ functions of which $\Delta G°$ is composed.

Key Terms

second law of thermodynamics (Sec. 19.1)
spontaneous (Sec. 19.1)
entropy (Sec. 19.2)
isolated system (Sec. 19.2)
translational motion (Sec. 19.3)

vibrational motion (Sec. 19.3)
rotational motion (Sec. 19.3)
third law of thermodynamics (Sec. 19.3)
Gibbs free energy (free energy) (Sec. 19.5)
standard free energy of formation (Sec. 19.5)

Exercises

Spontaneity and Entropy

19.1. Which of the following processes are spontaneous and which are nonspontaneous: **(a)** spreading of the fragrance of perfume through a room; **(b)** separation of N_2 and O_2 molecules in air from each other; **(c)** mending a broken clock; **(d)** the reaction of sodium metal with chlorine gas to form sodium chloride; **(e)** the dissolution of HCl(g) in water to form concentrated hydrochloric acid?

19.2. Which of the following processes are spontaneous and which are nonspontaneous: **(a)** the melting of ice cubes at $-5°C$ and 1 atm pressure; **(b)** dissolution of sugar in a cup of hot coffee; **(c)** the reaction of nitrogen atoms to form N_2 molecules at 25°C and 1 atm; **(d)** alignment of iron filings in a magnetic field; **(e)** formation of CH_4 and O_2 molecules from CO_2 and H_2O at room temperature and 1 atm pressure?

19.3. A nineteenth-century chemist, Marcellin Berthelot, suggested that all chemical processes that proceed spontaneously are exothermic. Is this correct? If you think not, offer some counterexamples.

19.4. The freezing of water to ice is an exothermic process. **(a)** In what temperature range is it a spontaneous process? **(b)** In what temperature range is it a nonspontaneous process? **(c)** Why isn't this exothermic process *always* spontaneous?

19.5. When steam condenses to water at 90°C, the entropy of the system decreases. What must be true if the second law of thermodynamics is to be satisfied?

19.6. In a living cell, large molecules are assembled from smaller ones. Is this process consistent with the second law of thermodynamics?

19.7. How does the entropy of the system change when the following processes occur: **(a)** a solid is melted; **(b)** a liquid is vaporized; **(c)** a solid is dissolved in water; **(d)** a gas is liquefied?

19.8. Why is the increase in entropy of the system greater for the vaporization of a substance than for its melting?

19.9. For each of the following pairs, choose the substance with the higher entropy (per mole) at a given temperature:

(a) $O_2(g)$ at 5 atm or $O_2(g)$ at 0.5 atm; **(b)** $Br_2(l)$ or $Br_2(g)$; **(c)** 1 mol of $N_2(g)$ in 22.4 L or 1 mol of $N_2(g)$ in 2.24 L; **(d)** $CO_2(g)$ or $CO_2(aq)$.

19.10. For each of the following pairs, indicate which substance you would expect to possess the larger standard entropy: **(a)** 1 mol of $Cl_2(g)$ at 273 K, 1 atm pressure, or 1 mol of $Cl_2(g)$ at 373 K, 1 atm pressure; **(b)** 1 mol of $H_2O(g)$ at 100°C, 1 atm pressure, or 1 mol of $H_2O(l)$ at 100°C; **(c)** 1 mol of $O_2(g)$ at 300 K, 30.0 L volume, or 2 mol of $O(g)$ at 300 K, 60.0 L volume; **(d)** 1 mol of $KNO_3(s)$ at 40°C, or 1 mol of $KNO_3(aq)$ at 40°C.

19.11. Using Appendix C, compare the standard entropies at 298 K for the substances in the following pairs: **(a)** $CCl_4(l)$ and $CCl_4(g)$; **(b)** C(diamond) and C(graphite); **(c)** 1 mol of $N_2O_4(g)$ and 2 mol of $NO_2(g)$; **(d)** $KClO_3(s)$ and $KClO_3(aq)$. Explain the origin of the difference in entropy values in each case.

19.12. Using Appendix C, compare the standard entropies at 298 K for the substances in the following pairs: **(a)** $Si(g)$ and $Si(s)$; **(b)** 1 mol of $C_6H_{12}O_6(s)$ and 6 mol C(graphite) plus 6 mol $H_2O(l)$; **(c)** 2 mol $P_2(g)$ and 1 mol $P_4(g)$; **(d)** NaOH(s) and NaOH(aq).

19.13. Predict the sign of ΔS for the system in each of the following processes: **(a)** freezing of 1 mol of $H_2O(l)$; **(b)** evaporation of 1 mol of $Br_2(l)$; **(c)** precipitation of $BaSO_4$ upon mixing $Ba(NO_3)_2(aq)$ and $H_2SO_4(aq)$; **(d)** oxidation of magnesium metal: $2Mg(s) + O_2(g) \longrightarrow 2MgO(s)$.

19.14. For each of the following processes, predict whether the entropy change in the system is positive or negative:
(a) $2C(s) + O_2(g) \longrightarrow 2CO(g)$
(b) $2K(s) + Br_2(l) \longrightarrow 2KBr(s)$
(c) $2MnO_2(s) \longrightarrow 2MnO(s) + O_2(g)$
(d) $O(g) + O_2(g) \longrightarrow O_3(g)$

19.15. Using tabulated $S°$ values from Appendix C, calculate $\Delta S°$ for each of the following reactions:
(a) $2HBr(g) + F_2(g) \longrightarrow 2HF(g) + Br_2(g)$
(b) $2NO(g) + O_2(g) \longrightarrow 2NO_2(g)$

(c) $2CH_3OH(g) + 3O_2(g) \longrightarrow 2CO_2(g) + 4H_2O(g)$
(d) $4FeO(s) + O_2(g) \longrightarrow 2Fe_2O_3(s)$
In each case, account for the sign of $\Delta S°$.

19.16. Using standard entropies tabulated in Appendix C, calculate $\Delta S°$ for each of the following processes:

(a) $2O_3(g) \longrightarrow 3O_2(g)$
(b) $SiCl_4(l) + 2H_2O(l) \longrightarrow SiO_2(s) + 4HCl(g)$
(c) $3C_2H_2(g) \longrightarrow C_6H_6(g)$
(d) $H_2(g) + Cl_2(g) \longrightarrow 2HCl(g)$

Gibbs Free Energy

19.17. (a) For a process that occurs at constant temperature, express the change in Gibbs free energy in terms of the changes in the enthalpy and entropy of the system. (b) What is the relationship between ΔG for a process and the speed at which it occurs?

19.18. (a) What is the significance of $\Delta G = 0$ for any process in a system? (b) What is the meaning of the *standard* free-energy change in a process, $\Delta G°$, as contrasted with simply the free-energy change, ΔG?

19.19. Calculate $\Delta G°_{298}$ for

$$H_2O_2(g) \longrightarrow H_2O(g) + \tfrac{1}{2}O_2(g)$$

given that $\Delta H°_{298} = -106$ kJ and $\Delta S°_{298} = +58$ J/K for this process. Would you expect $H_2O_2(g)$ to be very stable at 298 K? Explain briefly.

19.20. Using the data in Appendix C, calculate $\Delta H°$, $\Delta S°$, and $\Delta G°$ at 25°C for each of the following reactions. In each case, show that $\Delta G° = \Delta H° - T \Delta S°$.
(a) $BaO(s) + CO_2(g) \longrightarrow BaCO_3(s)$
(b) $2KClO_3(s) \longrightarrow 2KCl(s) + 3O_2(g)$
(c) $2CH_3OH(l) + 3O_2(g) \longrightarrow 2CO_2(g) + 4H_2O(g)$
(d) $NOCl(g) + Cl(g) \longrightarrow NO(g) + Cl_2(g)$

19.21. Using the data from Appendix C, calculate $\Delta G°$ for each of the following processes. In each case, indicate whether the reaction is spontaneous under standard conditions.
(a) $H_2(g) + Cl_2(g) \longrightarrow 2HCl(g)$
(b) $MgCl_2(s) + H_2O(l) \longrightarrow MgO(s) + 2HCl(g)$
(c) $2NH_3(g) \longrightarrow N_2H_4(g) + H_2(g)$
(d) $2NOCl(g) \longrightarrow 2NO(g) + Cl_2(g)$

19.22. Using the data from Appendix C, calculate the change in Gibbs free energy for each of the following processes. In each case, indicate whether the reaction is spontaneous under standard conditions.
(a) $2SO_2(g) + O_2(g) \longrightarrow 2SO_3(g)$
(b) $NO_2(g) + N_2O(g) \longrightarrow 3NO(g)$
(c) $6Cl_2(g) + 2Fe_2O_3(s) \longrightarrow 4FeCl_3(s) + 3O_2(g)$
(d) $SO_2(g) + 2H_2(g) \longrightarrow S(s) + 2H_2O(g)$

19.23. Classify each of the following reactions as belonging to one of the four possible types summarized in Table 19.4:
(a) $N_2(g) + 3F_2(g) \longrightarrow 2NF_3(g)$
$\Delta H° = -249$ kJ; $\Delta S° = -278$ J/K
(b) $N_2(g) + 3Cl_2(g) \longrightarrow 2NCl_3(g)$
$\Delta H° = 460$ kJ; $\Delta S° = -275$ J/K
(c) $N_2F_4(g) \longrightarrow 2NF_2(g)$
$\Delta H° = 85$ kJ; $\Delta S° = 198$ J/K

(d) $2H_2O(l) \longrightarrow 2H_2(g) + O_2(g)$
$\Delta H° = 572$ kJ; $\Delta S° = 329$ J/K

19.24. From the values given for $\Delta H°$ and $\Delta S°$, calculate $\Delta G°$ for each of the following reactions at 298 K. If the reaction is not spontaneous under standard conditions at 298 K, at what temperature (if any) would the reaction become spontaneous?
(a) $2PbS(s) + 3O_2(g) \longrightarrow 2PbO(s) + 2SO_2(g)$
$\Delta H° = -844$ kJ; $\Delta S° = -0.165$ kJ/K
(b) $2POCl_3(g) \longrightarrow 2PCl_3(g) + O_2(g)$
$\Delta H° = 572$ kJ; $\Delta S° = 179$ J/K

19.25. A certain reaction is nonspontaneous at 298 K. The entropy change during the reaction is 121 J/K. (a) Is the reaction endothermic or exothermic? (b) What is the minimum value of ΔH for the reaction?

19.26. A certain reaction is spontaneous at 85°C. The reaction is endothermic by 34 kJ. What is the minimum value of ΔS for the reaction?

19.27. For a certain process, $\Delta H = 178$ kJ, and $\Delta S = 160$ J/K. What is the minimum temperature at which the process will be spontaneous? (You may assume that ΔH and ΔS do not vary with temperature.)

19.28. Reactions in which a substance decomposes by losing CO_2 are called *decarboxylation* reactions. The decarboxylation of acetic acid proceeds as follows:

$$CH_3COOH(l) \longrightarrow CH_4(g) + CO_2(g)$$

By using data from Appendix C, calculate the minimum temperature at which this process will be spontaneous under standard conditions. (You may assume that $\Delta H°$ and $\Delta S°$ do not vary with temperature.)

19.29. (a) Using the data in Appendix C, predict how $\Delta G°$ for the following process will change with increasing temperature:

$$P_4(g) \longrightarrow 2P_2(g)$$

(b) Calculate $\Delta G°$ at 900 K, assuming that $\Delta H°$ and $\Delta S°$ do not change with temperature.

19.30. (a) Using the data in Appendix C, predict how $\Delta G°$ for the following process will change with increasing temperature:

$$SO_3(g) + H_2(g) \longrightarrow SO_2(g) + H_2O(g)$$

(b) Calculate $\Delta G°$ at 600 K, assuming that $\Delta H°$ and $\Delta S°$ do not change with variation in temperature.

19.31. Natural gas consists primarily of methane, CH_4. (a) How much heat is produced in burning a mole of CH_4 under standard conditions if reactants and products are brought to 298 K and $H_2O(l)$ is formed? (b) What is the maximum amount of useful work that can be accomplished under standard conditions by this system?

19.32. Acetylene gas, $C_2H_2(g)$, is used in welding. (a) How much heat is produced in burning a mole of C_2H_2 under standard conditions if both reactants and products are brought to 298 K and $H_2O(l)$ is formed? (b) What is the maximum amount of useful work that can be accomplished under standard conditions by this system?

Free Energy and Equilibrium

19.33. Explain qualitatively how ΔG changes for each of the following reactions as the partial pressure of N_2 is increased:
(a) $N_2H_4(g) \longrightarrow N_2(g) + 2H_2(g)$
(b) $N_2(g) + 3F_2(g) \longrightarrow 2NF_3(g)$
(c) $NH_4NO_2(s) \longrightarrow N_2(g) + 2H_2O(g)$

19.34. Indicate whether ΔG increases, decreases, or does not change when the partial pressure of H_2 is increased in each of the following reactions:
(a) $N_2(g) + 3H_2(g) \longrightarrow 2NH_3(g)$
(b) $2HBr(g) \longrightarrow H_2(g) + Br_2(g)$

19.35. Consider the reaction $2NO_2(g) \longrightarrow N_2O_4(g)$. (a) Using data from Appendix C, calculate $\Delta G°$ at 298 K for this reaction. (b) Calculate ΔG at 298 K if the partial pressures of NO_2 and N_2O_4 are 2.00 atm and 0.10 atm, respectively.

19.36. Consider the reaction

$$2CO(g) + O_2(g) \longrightarrow 2CO_2(g)$$

(a) Using data from Appendix C, calculate $\Delta G°$ for this reaction at 298 K. (b) Calculate ΔG at 298 K if the reaction mixture consists of 6.0 atm of CO, 300 atm of O_2, and 0.10 atm of CO_2.

19.37. By using data from Appendix C, calculate K_p at 298 K for each of the following reactions:
(a) $H_2(g) + Cl_2(g) \rightleftharpoons 2HCl(g)$
(b) $3C_2H_2(g) \rightleftharpoons C_6H_6(g)$
(c) $N_2O(g) + NO_2(g) \rightleftharpoons 3NO(g)$

19.38. Write the equilibrium expression and calculate the magnitude of the equilibrium constant for each of the fol-

lowing reactions at 298 K, using data from Appendix C:
(a) $NaHCO_3(s) \rightleftharpoons NaOH(s) + CO_2(g)$
(b) $2HBr(g) + Cl_2(g) \rightleftharpoons 2HCl(g) + Br_2(g)$
(c) $2SO_2(g) + O_2(g) \rightleftharpoons 2SO_3(g)$

[19.39]. Consider the decarboxylation of calcium carbonate:

$$CaCO_3(s) \rightleftharpoons CaO(s) + CO_2(g)$$

By using data from Appendix C, calculate the equilibrium pressure of CO_2 at (a) 298 K and (b) 800 K.

[19.40]. Consider the following reaction:

$$PbCO_3(s) \longrightarrow PbO(s) + CO_2(g)$$

Using data in Appendix C, calculate the equilibrium pressure of CO_2 in the system at (a) 25°C and (b) 500°C.

19.41. (a) Given K_a for benzoic acid at 298 K (Appendix D), calculate $\Delta G°$ for the dissociation of this substance in aqueous solution. (b) What is the value of ΔG at equilibrium? (c) What is the value of ΔG when $[H^+] = 3.0 \times 10^{-3}$ M, $[C_7H_5O_2^-] = 2.0 \times 10^{-5}$ M, and $[HC_7H_5O_2] = 0.10$ M?

19.42. (a) Given K_b for ammonia at 298 K (Appendix D), calculate $\Delta G°$ for the following reaction:

$$NH_3(aq) + H_2O(l) \longrightarrow NH_4^+(aq) + OH^-(aq)$$

(b) What is the value of ΔG at equilibrium? (c) What is the value of ΔG when $[NH_3] = 0.10$ M, $[NH_4^+] = 0.10$ M and $[OH^-] = 0.050$ M?

Additional Exercises

19.43. Indicate whether each of the following statements is true or false. If it is false, correct it. (a) The feasibility of manufacturing NH_3 from N_2 and H_2 depends entirely on the value of ΔH for the process $N_2(g) + 3H_2(g) \longrightarrow 2NH_3(g)$. (b) The reaction of $H_2(g)$ with $Cl_2(g)$ to form $HCl(g)$ is an example of a spontaneous process. (c) A spontaneous process is one that occurs rapidly. (d) A process that is nonspontaneous in one direction is spontaneous in the opposite direction. (e) Spontaneous processes are those that are exothermic and that lead to a higher degree of order in the system.

19.44. For each of the following processes, indicate whether the signs of ΔS and ΔH are expected to be positive, negative, or about zero. (a) A solid sublimes. (b) The temperature of a solid is lowered by 25°C. (c) Ethyl alcohol

evaporates from a beaker. (d) A diatomic molecule dissociates into atoms. (e) A piece of charcoal is combusted to form $CO_2(g)$ and $H_2O(g)$.

19.45. The reaction $2Mg(s) + O_2(g) \longrightarrow 2$ $MgO(s)$ has associated with it a negative value for $\Delta S°$, and it is a highly spontaneous process. The second law of thermodynamics states that in any spontaneous process there is always an increase in the entropy of the universe. Is there an inconsistency between the second law and what we know about the oxidation of magnesium? Explain.

19.46. The melting and boiling points of HCl are $-115°C$ and $-84°C$, respectively. Using this information and the value of $S°$ listed in Appendix C, draw a rough sketch of $S°$ for HCl from absolute zero to 298 K.

19.47. (a) Calculate $\Delta H°$, $\Delta S°$, and $\Delta G°$ for each of the following reactions at 25°C, using the data in Appendix C:
(i) $2RbCl(s) + 3O_2(g) \longrightarrow 2RbClO_3(s)$
(ii) $2CH_4(g) \longrightarrow C_2H_6(g) + H_2(g)$
(iii) $C_2H_2(g) + 4Cl_2(g) \longrightarrow 2CCl_4(l) + H_2(g)$
(b) Which of these processes are spontaneous under standard conditions at 25°C? (c) For each of these processes, predict the manner in which the change in free energy varies with an increase in temperature.

[19.48]. (a) Listed below are the normal boiling points for several substances and their enthalpies of vaporization at those temperatures. From these data calculate ΔS of vaporization for each substance. (Hint: The gaseous and liquid states are in equilibrium: What does this imply about ΔG?)

Substance	Normal boiling point (°C)	Enthalpy of vaporization (kJ/mol)
Acetone, $(CH_3)_2CO$	56.2	30.3
Benzene, C_6H_6	80.1	30.7
Ammonia, NH_3	−33.4	23.4
Water, H_2O	100.0	40.6

(b) What significance can be attached to the variations in ΔS_{vap} among these compounds? Explain.

19.49. Using the data in Appendix C and given the pressures listed, calculate ΔG for each of the following reactions:
(a) $N_2(g) + 3H_2(g) \longrightarrow 2NH_3(g)$
$P_{N_2} = 8.5$ atm, $P_{H_2} = 2.4$ atm, $P_{NH_3} = 4.7$ atm
(b) $2N_2H_4(g) + 2NO_2(g) \longrightarrow 3N_2(g) + 4H_2O(g)$
$P_{N_2H_4} = P_{NO_2} = 1.0 \times 10^{-3}$ atm, $P_{N_2} = 2.5$ atm,
$P_{H_2O} = 1.2$ atm
(c) $N_2H_4(g) \longrightarrow N_2(g) + 2H_2(g)$
$P_{N_2H_4} = 6.0$ atm, $P_{N_2} = 1 \times 10^{-3}$ atm,
$P_{H_2} = 2 \times 10^{-4}$ atm

19.50. For the following equilibria, calculate $\Delta G°$ at the temperature indicated:
(a) $H_2(g) + I_2(g) \longrightarrow 2HI(g)$ $K_p = 50.2$ at 445°C
(b) $2SO_2(g) + O_2(g) \longrightarrow 2SO_3(g)$
$K_p = 9.1 \times 10^2$ at 800°C

19.51. (a) In each of the following reactions, predict the sign of $\Delta H°$ and $\Delta S°$ and discuss briefly how these factors determine the magnitude of K. (b) Based on your general chemical knowledge, predict which of these reactions will have $K > 1$. (c) In each case, indicate whether K should increase or decrease with increasing temperature.
(i) $2Mg(s) + O_2(g) \rightleftharpoons 2MgO(s)$
(ii) $2KI(l) \rightleftharpoons 2K(g) + I_2(g)$
(iii) $Na_2(g) \rightleftharpoons 2Na(g)$
(iv) $V_2O_5(s) \rightleftharpoons 2V(s) + \frac{5}{2}O_2(g)$

[19.52]. The relationship between the temperature of a reaction, its standard enthalpy change, and the equilibrium constant at that temperature can be expressed in terms of the following linear equation:

$$\ln K = \frac{-\Delta H°}{RT} + \text{constant}$$

(a) Explain how this equation can be used to determine $\Delta H°$ experimentally from the equilibrium constants at several different temperatures. (b) Derive the equation above using relationships given in this chapter. What is the constant equal to?

[19.53]. The conversion of natural gas, which is mostly methane, into products that contain two or more carbon atoms, such as ethane, C_2H_6, is a very important industrial chemical process. In principle, methane can be converted into ethane and hydrogen:

$$2CH_4(g) \longrightarrow C_2H_6(g) + H_2(g)$$

In practice, this reaction is carried out in the presence of oxygen:

$$2CH_4(g) + \tfrac{1}{2}O_2(g) \longrightarrow C_2H_6(g) + H_2O(g)$$

(a) Using the data in Appendix C, calculate K_p for the above reactions at 25°C and 500°C. (b) Is the difference in $\Delta G°$ for the two reactions primarily enthalpic (due to ΔH) or entropic (due to ΔS)? (c) Explain how a comparison of the above reactions is an example of driving a nonspontaneous reaction, as discussed in the Chemistry at Work box in Section 19.7. (d) The reaction of CH_4 and O_2 to form C_2H_6 and H_2O must be carried out very carefully to avoid a competing reaction. What is the most likely competing reaction?

[19.54]. The potassium-ion concentration in blood plasma is about 5.0×10^{-3} M, whereas the concentration in muscle-cell fluid is much greater, 0.15 M. The plasma and intracellular fluid are separated by the cell membrane, which we assume is permeable only to K^+. (a) What is ΔG for the transfer of 1 mol of K^+ from blood plasma to the cellular fluid at body temperature, 37°C? (b) What is the minimum amount of work that must be used to transfer this K^+?

19.55. Acetic acid can be manufactured by reacting methanol with carbon monoxide, an example of a *carbonylation* reaction:

$$CH_3OH(l) + CO(g) \longrightarrow CH_3COOH(l)$$

(a) Calculate the equilibrium constant for the reaction at 25°C. (b) Industrially, this reaction is run at temperatures above 25°C. Will an increase in temperature produce an increase or decrease in the mole fraction of acetic acid in an equilibrium mixture? Why are elevated temperatures used for the reaction? (c) At what temperature will this reaction have an equilibrium constant equal to 1? (You may assume that $\Delta H°$ and $\Delta S°$ are temperature-independent, and you may ignore any phase changes that might occur.)

19.56. The oxidation of glucose, $C_6H_{12}O_6$, in body tissue produces CO_2 and H_2O. In contrast, anaerobic decomposition, which occurs during fermentation, produces ethyl alcohol, C_2H_5OH, and CO_2. (a) By using data given in Appendix C, compare the equilibrium constants for the following reactions:

$$C_6H_{12}O_6(s) + 6O_2(g) \rightleftharpoons 6CO_2(g) + 6H_2O(l)$$
$$C_6H_{12}O_6(s) \rightleftharpoons 2C_2H_5OH(l) + 2CO_2(g)$$

(b) Compare the maximum amounts of work that can be obtained from these two processes under standard conditions.

[19.57]. Consider the apparatus shown in Figure 19.12, which is much like that shown in Figure 19.2. $N_2(g)$ is initially confined in flask A, of 1 L volume, at 2.0 atm pressure. Chamber B, of volume 1 L, is evacuated. When the stopcock is opened, N_2 expands to both sides. **(a)** Assuming that N_2 behaves as an ideal gas, what is ΔH for this process? **(b)** Describe the process by which the gas can be returned to its original condition. What change in ΔH occurs in the system in this process? **(c)** What are the changes in ΔG and ΔH of the system for the overall processes of expansion followed by compression to the original condition state? **(d)** In this overall process, is work done by the system on the surroundings or by the surroundings on the system? Explain. **(e)** Describe how this example illustrates the second law of thermodynamics.

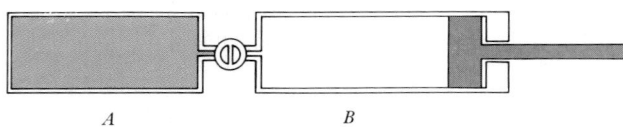

A B

FIGURE 19.12

[19.58]. The reaction
$$SO_2(g) + 2H_2S(g) \rightleftharpoons 3S(s) + 2H_2O(g)$$
is the basis of a suggested method for removal of SO_2 from power-plant stack gases. The standard free energy of each substance is given in Appendix C. **(a)** What is the equilibrium constant for the reaction at 298 K? **(b)** In principle, is this reaction a feasible method of removing SO_2? **(c)** If $P_{SO_2} = P_{H_2S}$ and the vapor pressure of water is 25 torr, calculate the equilibrium SO_2 pressure in the system at 298 K. **(d)** Would you expect the process to be more or less effective at higher temperatures?

[19.59]. Cells use the hydrolysis of adenosine triphosphate, ATP, as a source of energy (Figure 19.11). The conversion of ATP to ADP has a standard free-energy change of -30.5 kJ/mol. If all the free energy from the metabolism of glucose,
$$C_6H_{12}O_6(s) + 6O_2(g) \longrightarrow 6CO_2(g) + 6H_2O(l)$$
goes into the conversion of ADP to ATP, how many moles of ATP can be produced for each mole of glucose?

[19.60]. Consider the following equilibrium:
$$N_2O_4(g) \rightleftharpoons 2NO_2(g)$$
Thermodynamic data on these gases are given in Appendix C. You may assume that $\Delta H°$ and $\Delta S°$ do not vary with temperature. **(a)** At what temperature will an equilibrium mixture contain equal amounts of the two gases? **(b)** At what temperature will an equilibrium mixture of 1 atm total pressure contain twice as much NO_2 as N_2O_4? **(c)** At what temperature will an equilibrium mixture of 10 atm total pressure contain twice as much NO_2 as N_2O_4? **(d)** Rationalize the results from parts (b) and (c) by using Le Châtelier's principle.

[19.61]. The number of ways of arranging n ideal-gas particles in a volume V is proportional to the volume raised to the n power:
$$W \propto V^n$$

(a) By using this relationship and Boltzmann's relationship between entropy and number of arrangements (Equation 19.7), show that the entropy change for the compression or expansion of 1 mol of an ideal gas is given by
$$\Delta S = R \ln \left(\frac{V_2}{V_1} \right)$$
where R is the gas constant and V_1 and V_2 are the initial and final volumes of the gas. **(b)** Calculate the entropy change accompanying the gas expansion shown in Figure 19.12, assuming the two flasks are of equal volume. **(c)** Assuming $\Delta H = 0$ and $T = 298$ K, calculate the change in free energy accompanying the gas expansion shown in Figure 19.12.

Electrochemistry 20

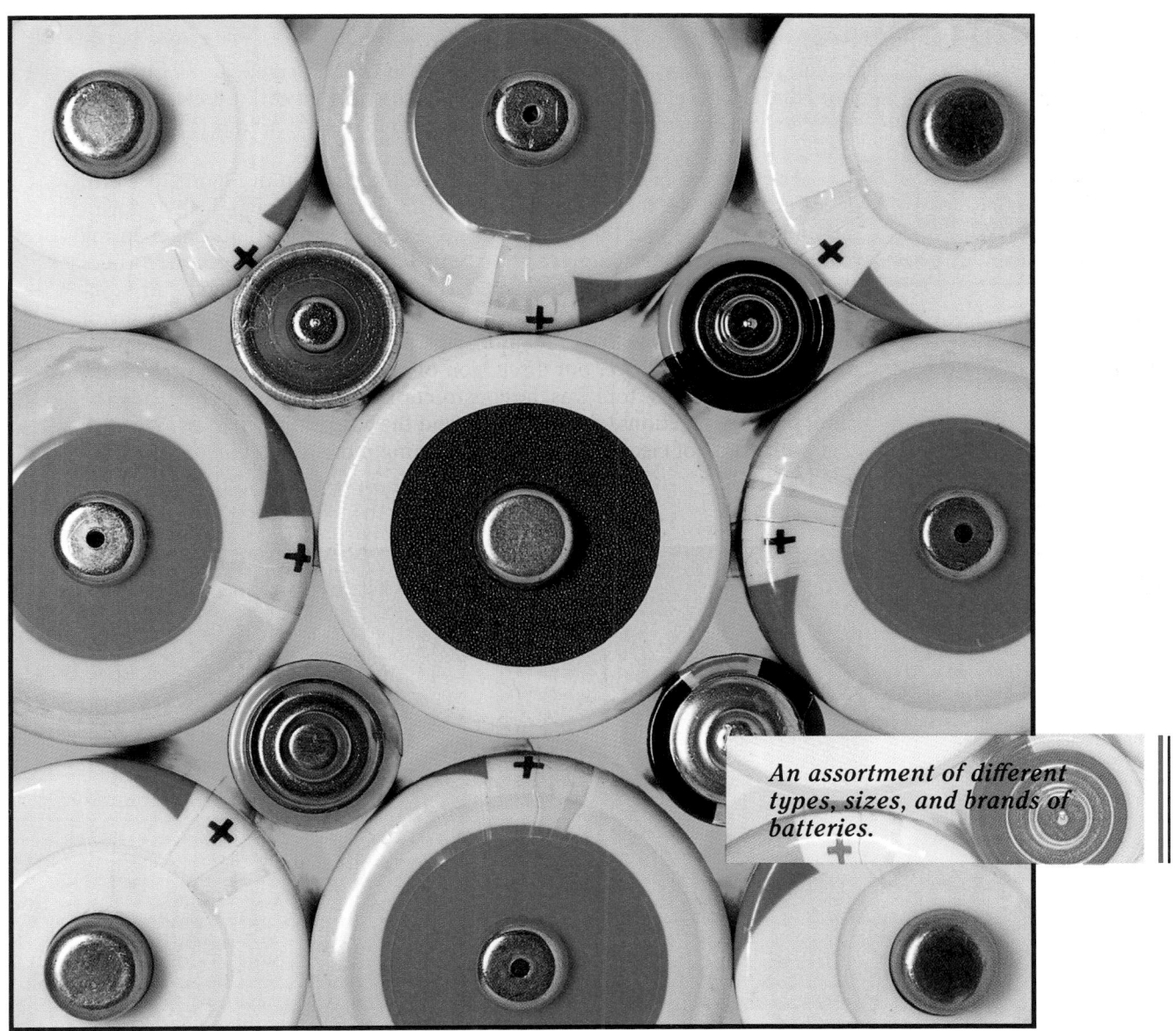

An assortment of different types, sizes, and brands of batteries.

CONTENTS

Teaching Note: Many authors have suggested mnemonics for oxidation and reduction. Perhaps the most common is *"LEO goes GER,"* for lose electrons = oxidation and gain electrons = reduction.

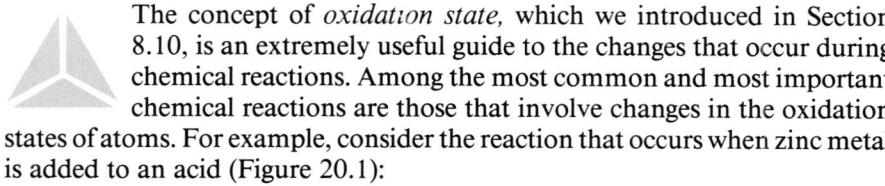

The concept of *oxidation state,* which we introduced in Section 8.10, is an extremely useful guide to the changes that occur during chemical reactions. Among the most common and most important chemical reactions are those that involve changes in the oxidation states of atoms. For example, consider the reaction that occurs when zinc metal is added to an acid (Figure 20.1):

$$\text{Zn}(s) + 2\text{H}^+(aq) \longrightarrow \text{Zn}^{2+}(aq) + \text{H}_2(g) \qquad [20.1]$$

During this reaction, the oxidation state of zinc increases from 0 in $\text{Zn}(s)$ to $+2$ in $\text{Zn}^{2+}(aq)$, whereas that of hydrogen decreases from $+1$ to 0. Chemical reactions in which the oxidation state of one or more substances changes are called **oxidation-reduction reactions** (or *redox* reactions).

As we discussed earlier, *oxidation* refers to the loss of electrons. Conversely, *reduction* refers to the gain of electrons. ∞ (Sec. 4.6) We can view oxidation-reduction reactions as involving the transfer of electrons from the atom that is oxidized to the atom that is reduced. In Equation 20.1, electrons are transferred from zinc atoms (zinc is oxidized) to hydrogen ions (hydrogen is reduced).

The transfer of electrons that occurs in the reaction in Figure 20.1 produces energy in the form of heat; the reaction is thermodynamically "downhill" and proceeds spontaneously. The transfer of electrons that occurs during oxidation-reduction reactions can also be used to produce energy in the form of electricity. In other instances, we use electrical energy to make certain nonspontaneous chemical processes occur. **Electrochemistry** is the branch of chemistry that deals with the relationships between electricity and chemical reactions. As we shall see, our discussion of electrochemistry will provide insight into such diverse topics as the construction and operation of batteries, the spontaneity of reactions, electroplating, and the corrosion of metals. We shall begin our study of electrochemistry by learning more about oxidation-reduction reactions.

FIGURE 20.1 The addition of zinc metal to hydrochloric acid leads to a spontaneous oxidation-reduction reaction: Zinc metal is oxidized to $\text{Zn}^{2+}(aq)$, and $\text{H}^+(aq)$ is reduced to $\text{H}_2(g)$, which produces the vigorous bubbling. (© Richard Megna/Fundamental Photographs)

20.1 Oxidation-Reduction Reactions

How do we determine whether a given chemical reaction is an oxidation-reduction reaction? We can do so by keeping track of the oxidation numbers of all the elements involved in the reaction. This procedure tells us which elements (if any) are changing oxidation state. For example, the reaction in Equation 20.1 can be written

Point of Emphasis: Assigning oxidation numbers follows from the question, *"If this were an ionic compound, what would the ion charges be?"*

$$Zn(s) + 2H^+(aq) \longrightarrow Zn^{2+}(aq) + H_2(g) \qquad [20.2]$$

with oxidation numbers: Zn is 0, H^+ is $+1$, Zn^{2+} is $+2$, H_2 is 0.

By writing the oxidation number of each element under the equation, we can easily see the oxidation state changes that occur: The oxidation state of Zn changes from 0 to $+2$, and that of H changes from $+1$ to 0.

In an oxidation-reduction reaction such as Equation 20.2, a clear transfer of electrons occurs. Zinc must lose electrons as the $Zn(s)$ is converted to $Zn^{2+}(aq)$. Likewise, hydrogen must gain electrons as $H^+(aq)$ is turned into $H_2(g)$. In other reactions, changes occur in the oxidation states, but we can't say that any substance literally gains or loses electrons. For example, consider the combustion of hydrogen gas:

$$2H_2(g) + O_2(g) \longrightarrow 2H_2O(g) \qquad [20.3]$$

with oxidation numbers: H_2 is 0, O_2 is 0, H is $+1$, O is -2.

Hydrogen has been oxidized from the 0 to the $+1$ oxidation state, and oxygen has been reduced from the 0 to the -2 oxidation state. Therefore, Equation 20.3 is an oxidation-reduction reaction. However, because water is not an ionic substance, there is not a complete transfer of electrons from hydrogen to oxygen as water is formed. It is important to remember that using oxidation numbers is a convenient form of "bookkeeping." In general, you should not equate the oxidation state of an atom with its actual charge in a chemical compound.

In any oxidation-reduction reaction, both oxidation and reduction must occur. In other words, if one substance is oxidized, then another must be reduced. The substance that makes it possible for another substance to be oxidized is called the **oxidizing agent,** or **oxidant.** The oxidizing agent removes electrons from another substance by acquiring them itself; in oxidizing another substance, the oxidizing agent is itself reduced. Similarly, a **reducing agent,** or **reductant,** is a substance that gives up electrons, thereby causing another substance to be reduced. The reducing agent is oxidized in the process. In Equation 20.2, $H^+(aq)$ is the oxidizing agent, and $Zn(s)$ is the reducing agent.

Point of Emphasis: In every redox reaction, the oxidation of one species must be accompanied by the reduction of another.

Learning Goal 1: Identify the oxidant and reductant in an oxidation-reduction reaction.

SAMPLE EXERCISE 20.1

The nickel-cadmium (nicad) battery, a popular rechargeable "dry cell" used in battery-operated tools, uses the following redox reaction to generate electricity:

$$Cd(s) + NiO_2(s) + 2H_2O(l) \longrightarrow Cd(OH)_2(s) + Ni(OH)_2(s)$$

Identify the substances that are oxidized and reduced and indicate which are oxidizing agents and which are reducing agents.

SOLUTION *First,* we assign oxidation numbers to all the atoms in the reaction:

$$Cd(s) + NiO_2(s) + 2H_2O(l) \longrightarrow Cd(OH)_2(s) + Ni(OH)_2(s)$$

0   +4 −2   +1 −2   +2 −2 +1   +2 −2 +1

Second, we identify the elements that are changing oxidation numbers. We see that Cd undergoes an increase in oxidation number from 0 to +2 and that Ni undergoes a decrease from +4 to +2.

Third, we apply the definitions of oxidation and reduction. The substance oxidized is the one that contains the atom that loses electrons (increases oxidation number), Cd. The substance that is reduced is the one that contains the atom that gains electrons (decreases oxidation number), NiO_2. (A common mnemonic for remembering oxidation and reduction is "LEO the lion says GER": *l*osing *e*lectrons is *o*xidation; *g*aining *e*lectrons is *r*eduction.) Because Cd is oxidized, it is the reducing agent (that is, it causes NiO_2 to be reduced). Similarly, because NiO_2 is reduced, it is the oxidizing agent (that is, it causes Cd to be oxidized).

PRACTICE EXERCISE

Identify the oxidizing and reducing agents in the following oxidation-reduction equation:

$$2H_2O(l) + Al(s) + MnO_4^-(aq) \longrightarrow Al(OH)_4^-(aq) + MnO_2(s)$$

Answer: Al is the reducing agent; $MnO_4^-(aq)$ is the oxidizing agent

20.2 Balancing Oxidation-Reduction Equations

We know that whenever we balance a chemical reaction, we must obey the law of conservation of mass: The amount of each element must be the same on both sides of the equation. When we balance an oxidation-reduction reaction, we have an additional requirement: The gains and losses of electrons must be balanced. In other words, if a substance loses a certain number of electrons during a reaction, then another substance must gain that same number of electrons. In many simple chemical reactions, such as Equation 20.2, this balance of electrons is handled "automatically"; we can balance the equation without explicitly considering the transfer of electrons. However, many redox reactions are more complex than Equation 20.2 and cannot be balanced easily without taking into account the number of electrons lost and gained in the course of the reaction. In this section, we examine a systematic procedure for balancing oxidation-reduction equations.

Half-Reactions

Although oxidation and reduction must take place simultaneously, it is often convenient to consider them as separate processes. For example, the oxidation of Sn^{2+} by Fe^{3+}

$$Sn^{2+}(aq) + 2Fe^{3+}(aq) \longrightarrow Sn^{4+}(aq) + 2Fe^{2+}(aq)$$

can be considered to consist of two processes: (1) the oxidation of Sn^{2+} (Equation 20.4) and (2) the reduction of Fe^{3+} (Equation 20.5).

| Oxidation: | $Sn^{2+}(aq) \longrightarrow Sn^{4+}(aq) + 2e^-$ | [20.4] |
| Reduction: | $2Fe^{3+}(aq) + 2e^- \longrightarrow 2Fe^{2+}(aq)$ | [20.5] |

Notice that in the oxidation process, electrons are shown as products; in the reduction process, electrons are shown on the reactant side of the equation.

Equations that show either oxidation or reduction alone, as in Equations 20.4 and 20.5, are called **half-reactions.** In the overall redox reaction, the number of electrons lost in the oxidation half-reaction must equal the number of electrons gained in the reduction half-reaction. When this condition is met and each half-reaction is balanced, the electrons on each side cancel when the two half-reactions are added to give the overall balanced oxidation-reduction equation.

Point of Emphasis: Half-reactions cannot occur by themselves. For one to occur, it must be accompanied by another.

Point of Emphasis: The half-reactions must be balanced *and the numbers of electrons made equal* before the half-reactions can be added.

Learning Goal 2: Balance simple oxidation-reduction reactions by the method of half-reactions.

Balancing Equations by the Method of Half-Reactions

The use of half-reactions provides a general method for balancing oxidation-reduction equations. As an example, let's consider the reaction that occurs between permanganate ion, MnO_4^-, and oxalate ion, $C_2O_4^{2-}$, in acidic aqueous solutions. When MnO_4^- is added to an acidified solution of $C_2O_4^{2-}$, the deep purple color of the MnO_4^- ion fades, as illustrated in Figure 20.2. Bubbles of CO_2 form, and the solution takes on the pale pink color of Mn^{2+}. We can therefore write the unbalanced equation as follows:

$$MnO_4^-(aq) + C_2O_4^{2-}(aq) \longrightarrow Mn^{2+}(aq) + CO_2(g) \qquad [20.6]$$

Experiments also show that H^+ is consumed and H_2O produced in the reaction. We shall see that these facts can be deduced in the course of balancing the equation.

To complete and balance Equation 20.6 by the method of half-reactions, we begin with the unbalanced reaction and write two incomplete half-reactions,

(a)

(b)

(c)

FIGURE 20.2 (*a*) Titration of an acidic solution of oxalic acid, which contains oxalate ions, $C_2O_4^{2-}$, with an aqueous permanganate solution (deep purple). As the reaction proceeds, MnO_4^- is reduced to $Mn^{2+}(aq)$, which has a pink color too pale to be clearly seen. The reaction is rapid, and no MnO_4^- persists in solution until all the $C_2O_4^{2-}$ has been consumed. (*b*) When the reaction is complete, the purple color of unreacted MnO_4^- is visible in the solution. The endpoint of the titration corresponds to the faintest discernible purple color in the solution. (*c*) Beyond the endpoint the purple MnO_4^- is clearly evident. (© Richard Megna/ Fundamental Photographs)

one involving the oxidant and the other involving the reductant.

$$MnO_4^-(aq) \longrightarrow Mn^{2+}(aq)$$
$$C_2O_4^{2-} \longrightarrow CO_2(g)$$

At this point, we have not explicitly stated which substance is oxidized and which is reduced. As we shall see, this information emerges as we balance the half-reactions.

We can now complete and balance the half-reactions separately. This means that the number of atoms of each element appearing in the half-reaction must be the same on both sides of the equation. First, the atoms undergoing oxidation or reduction are balanced by adding coefficients on one side or the other as necessary. Then, the remaining elements are balanced in the same way. If the reaction occurs in acidic aqueous solution, H^+ and H_2O can be added either to reactants or to products to balance hydrogen and oxygen. Similarly, in basic solution the equation can be completed using OH^- and H_2O. These species are in large supply in the respective solutions, and their formation as products or their use as reactants can easily go undetected experimentally. In the permanganate half-reaction, we already have one manganese atom on each side of the equation. However, we have four oxygens on the left and none on the right side; four H_2O molecules are needed among the products to balance the four oxygen atoms in MnO_4^-:

$$MnO_4^-(aq) \longrightarrow Mn^{2+}(aq) + 4H_2O(l)$$

The eight hydrogen atoms that this introduces among the products can then be balanced by adding $8H^+$ to the reactants:

$$8H^+(aq) + MnO_4^-(aq) \longrightarrow Mn^{2+}(aq) + 4H_2O(l)$$

At this stage there are equal numbers of each type of atom on both sides of the equation, but the charge still needs to be balanced. The total charge of the reactants is $+8 - 1 = +7$, and that of the products is $+2 + 4(0) = +2$. To balance the charge, five electrons are added to the reactant side.*

$$5e^- + 8H^-(aq) + MnO_4^-(aq) \longrightarrow Mn^{2+}(aq) + 4H_2O(l)$$

Proceeding similarly with the oxalate half-reaction, we first realize that mass balance requires the production of two CO_2 molecules for each oxalate ion that reacts:

$$C_2O_4^{2-}(aq) \longrightarrow 2CO_2(g)$$

Charge is balanced by adding two electrons among the products, giving a balanced half-reaction:

$$C_2O_4^{2-}(aq) \longrightarrow 2CO_2(g) + 2e^-$$

---

* Although the oxidation numbers of the elements need not be used in balancing a half-reaction by this method, oxidation numbers can be used as a check. In this example MnO_4^- contains manganese in a $+7$ oxidation state. Because manganese changes from a $+7$ to a $+2$ oxidation state, it must gain five electrons, just as we have already concluded.

Now that we have two balanced half-reactions, we need to multiply each by an appropriate factor so that the number of electrons gained in one half-reaction equals the number of electrons lost in the other. The half-reactions are then added to give the overall balanced equation. In our example, the MnO_4^- half-reaction must be multiplied by 2, and the $C_2O_4^{2-}$ half-reaction must be multiplied by 5 in order for the same number of electrons (10) to appear on both sides of the equation:

$$10e^- + 16H^+(aq) + 2MnO_4^-(aq) \longrightarrow 2Mn^{2+}(aq) + 8H_2O(l)$$
$$\underline{5C_2O_4^{2-}(aq) \longrightarrow 10CO_2(g) + 10e^-}$$
$$16H^+(aq) + 2MnO_4^-(aq) + 5C_2O_4^{2-}(aq) \longrightarrow 2Mn^{2+}(aq) + 8H_2O(l) + 10CO_2(g)$$

The balanced equation is the sum of the balanced half-reactions. Note that the electrons on the reactant and product sides of the equation cancel each other.

Finally, the balanced equation is checked by counting atoms and charges: There are 16 H, 2 Mn, 28 O, 10 C, and a net charge of $4+$ on both sides of the equation, confirming that the equation is correctly balanced.

The following steps summarize the procedure that we use to balance an oxidation-reduction equation by the method of half-reactions when the reaction occurs in acid solution:

1. Divide the equation into two incomplete half-reactions, one for oxidation and the other for reduction.
2. Balance each half-reaction.
   a. First, balance the elements other than H and O.
   b. Next, balance the O atoms by adding H_2O.
   c. Then, balance the H atoms by adding H^+.
   d. Finally, balance the charge by adding e^- to the side with the greater positive charge.
3. Multiply each half-reaction by an integer so that the number of electrons lost in one half-reaction equals the number gained in the other.
4. Add the two half-reactions and simplify where possible by canceling species appearing on both sides of the equation.
5. Check the equation to make sure that there are the same number of atoms of each kind and the same total charge on both sides.

SAMPLE EXERCISE 20.2

Complete and balance the following equation by the method of half-reactions:

$$Cr_2O_7^{2-}(aq) + Cl^-(aq) \longrightarrow Cr^{3+}(aq) + Cl_2(g) \quad \text{(acidic solution)}$$

SOLUTION *First,* we divide the equation into two half-reactions:

$$Cr_2O_7^{2-}(aq) \longrightarrow Cr^{3+}(aq)$$
$$Cl^-(aq) \longrightarrow Cl_2(g)$$

Second, we balance each half-reaction. In the first half-reaction the presence of $Cr_2O_7^{2-}$ among the reactants requires two Cr^{3+} among the products. The 7 oxygen atoms in $Cr_2O_7^{2-}$ are balanced by adding $7H_2O$ to the products. The 14 hydrogen atoms in $7H_2O$ are then balanced by adding $14H^+$ to the reactants:

$$14H^+(aq) + Cr_2O_7^{2-}(aq) \longrightarrow 2Cr^{3+}(aq) + 7H_2O(l)$$

Charge is balanced by adding electrons to the left side of the equation so that the total charge is the same on both sides:

$$6e^- + 14H^+(aq) + Cr_2O_7^{2-}(aq) \longrightarrow 2Cr^{3+}(aq) + 7H_2O(l)$$

In the second half-reaction, two Cl^- are required to balance one Cl_2:

$$2Cl^-(aq) \longrightarrow Cl_2(g)$$

We add two electrons to the right side to attain charge balance:

$$2Cl^-(aq) \longrightarrow Cl_2(g) + 2e^-$$

Third, we equalize the number of electrons transferred in the two half-reactions. To do so, we multiply the second half-reaction by 3 so that the 6 electrons gained in the first half-reaction equal the number lost in the second, allowing the electrons to cancel when the reactions are added.

Fourth, the equations are added to give the balanced equation:

$$14H^+(aq) + Cr_2O_7^{2-}(aq) + 6Cl^-(aq) \longrightarrow 2Cr^{3+}(aq) + 7H_2O(l) + 3Cl_2(g)$$

Fifth, a check of the final equation indicates that there are equal numbers of atoms of each kind on both sides of the equation: 14 H, 2 Cr, 7 O, 6 Cl. In addition, the charge is the same on both sides, 6+. Thus, the equation is correctly balanced.

PRACTICE EXERCISE

Complete and balance the following oxidation-reduction equations using the method of half-reactions. Both reactions occur in acidic solution.
(a) $Cu(s) + NO_3^-(aq) \longrightarrow Cu^{2+}(aq) + NO_2(g)$
(b) $Mn^{2+}(aq) + NaBiO_3(s) \longrightarrow Bi^{3+}(aq) + MnO_4^-(aq)$
Answers:
(a) $Cu(s) + 4H^+(aq) + 2NO_3^-(aq) \longrightarrow Cu^{2+}(aq) + 2NO_2(g) + 2H_2O(l)$
(b) $2Mn^{2+}(aq) + 5NaBiO_3(s) + 14H^+(aq) \longrightarrow$
$2MnO_4^-(aq) + 5Bi^{3+}(aq) + 5Na^+(aq) + 7H_2O(l)$

Balancing Equations for Reactions Occurring in Basic Solution

Point of Emphasis: Balancing a reaction in basic solution is much easier if the reaction is first balanced as if it were in acidic medium, after which any H^+ ions are neutralized by adding OH^-.

If an oxidation-reduction equation occurs in basic solution, the equation must be completed by using OH^- and H_2O rather than H^+ and H_2O. The half-reactions can nevertheless be balanced initially as if they occurred in acidic solution. The H^+ ions can then be "neutralized" by adding an equal number of OH^- ions to both sides of the equation. This procedure is shown in Sample Exercise 20.3.

SAMPLE EXERCISE 20.3

Complete and balance the following equation:

$$CN^-(aq) + MnO_4^-(aq) \longrightarrow CNO^-(aq) + MnO_2(s) \quad \text{(basic solution)}$$

SOLUTION *First,* we write the incomplete and unbalanced half-reactions:

$$CN^-(aq) \longrightarrow CNO^-(aq)$$

$$MnO_4^-(aq) \longrightarrow MnO_2(s)$$

Second, we initially balance each half-reaction as if it took place in acidic solution. The resultant balanced half-reactions are

$$CN^-(aq) + H_2O(l) \longrightarrow CNO^-(aq) + 2H^+(aq) + 2e^-$$

$$3e^- + 4H^+(aq) + MnO_4^-(aq) \longrightarrow MnO_2(s) + 2H_2O(l)$$

Third, because H^+ cannot exist in any appreciable concentration in basic solution, we remove it from the equation by adding an appropriate amount of OH^-. In the CN^- half-reaction, 2 OH^- is added to both sides of the equation to neutralize the 2 H^+. The 2 OH^- and 2 H^+ form 2 H_2O:

$$2OH^-(aq) + H_2O(l) + CN^-(aq) \longrightarrow CNO^-(aq) + 2H_2O(l) + 2e^-$$

The half-reaction can be simplified because H_2O occurs on both sides of the equation. The simplified equation is

$$2OH^-(aq) + CN^-(aq) \longrightarrow CNO^-(aq) + H_2O(l) + 2e^-$$

For the MnO_4^- half-reaction, 4 $OH^-(aq)$ is added to both sides of the equation:

$$3e^- + 4H_2O(l) + MnO_4^-(aq) \longrightarrow MnO_2(s) + 2H_2O(l) + 4OH^-(aq)$$

Simplifying gives

$$3e^- + 2H_2O(l) + MnO_4^-(aq) \longrightarrow MnO_2(s) + 4OH^-(aq)$$

Fourth, we multiply the top equation by 3 and the bottom one by 2 to equalize electron loss and gain in the two half-reactions. The half-reactions are then added and simplified:

$$6OH^-(aq) + 3CN^-(aq) \longrightarrow 3CNO^-(aq) + 3H_2O(l) + 6e^-$$
$$\underline{6e^- + 4H_2O(l) + 2MnO_4^-(aq) \longrightarrow 2MnO_2(s) + 8OH^-(aq)}$$
$$6OH^-(aq) + 3CN^-(aq) + 4H_2O(l) + 2MnO_4^-(aq) \longrightarrow$$
$$3CNO^-(aq) + 3H_2O(l) + 2MnO_2(s) + 8OH^-(aq)$$

The overall equation can be simplified because H_2O and OH^- occur on both sides. The simplified equation is

$$3CN^-(aq) + H_2O(l) + 2MnO_4^-(aq) \longrightarrow 3CNO^-(aq) + 2MnO_2(s) + 2OH^-(aq)$$

Fifth, the result is checked by counting atoms and charges: There are 3 C, 3 N, 2 H, 9 O, 2 Mn, and 5− on both sides of the equation.

PRACTICE EXERCISE

Complete and balance the following equations for oxidation-reduction reactions that occur in basic solution:
(a) $NO_2^-(aq) + Al(s) \longrightarrow NH_3(aq) + Al(OH)_4^-(aq)$
(b) $Cr(OH)_3(s) + ClO^-(aq) \longrightarrow CrO_4^{2-}(aq) + Cl_2(g)$
Answers:
(a) $NO_2^-(aq) + 2Al(s) + 5H_2O(l) + OH^-(aq) \longrightarrow NH_3(aq) + 2Al(OH)_4^-(aq)$
(b) $2Cr(OH)_3(s) + 6ClO^-(aq) \longrightarrow 2CrO_4^{2-}(aq) + 3Cl_2(g) + 2OH^-(aq) + 2H_2O(l)$

20.3 Voltaic Cells

In principle, the energy released in any spontaneous redox reaction can be directly harnessed to perform electrical work. This task is accomplished through a **voltaic (or galvanic) cell,** which is merely a device in which electron transfer is forced to take place through an external pathway rather than directly between reactants.

One such spontaneous reaction occurs when a piece of zinc is placed in contact with a solution containing Cu^{2+}. As the reaction proceeds, the blue color that is characteristic of $Cu^{2+}(aq)$ ions fades, and copper metal begins to deposit on the zinc. At the same time, the zinc begins to dissolve. These transformations are shown in Figure 20.3 and are summarized by Equation 20.7:

$$Zn(s) + Cu^{2+}(aq) \longrightarrow Zn^{2+}(aq) + Cu(s) \qquad [20.7]$$

Figure 20.4 shows a voltaic cell that uses the oxidation-reduction reaction between Zn and Cu^{2+} expressed in Equation 20.7. Although the experimental

Learning Goal 3: Diagram simple voltaic and electrolytic cells, labeling the anode, the cathode, the directions of ion and electron movement, and the signs of the electrodes.

Lee R. Summerlin, Christie L. Borgford, and Julie B. Ealy, "Visible Oxidation-Reduction in Electrochemical Cells," *Chemical Demonstrations, A Sourcebook for Teachers, Volume 2* (Washington: American Chemical Society, 1987), pp. 202–3.

FIGURE 20.3 (*a*) A strip of zinc is placed in a solution of copper(II) sulfate. (*b*) Electrons are transferred from the zinc to the Cu^{2+} ion, forming Zn^{2+} ions and copper. Thus, as the reaction proceeds, the zinc dissolves, the blue color due to $Cu^{2+}(aq)$ fades, and copper (seen here as the dark material on the zinc strip and on the bottom of the beaker) deposits. (Fundamental Photographs)

(*a*)   (*b*)

design shown in Figure 20.4 is more complex than that in Figure 20.3, it is important to recognize that the chemical reaction is the same in both cases. The major difference between the two arrangements is that in Figure 20.4 the zinc metal and $Cu^{2+}(aq)$ are no longer in direct contact. Consequently, reduction of the Cu^{2+} can occur only by a flow of electrons through the wire that connects Zn and Cu (the external circuit).

The two solid metals that are connected by the external circuit are called *electrodes*. By definition, the electrode at which oxidation occurs is called the **anode;** the electrode at which reduction occurs is called the **cathode.*** We can think of the voltaic cell as two "half-cells," one corresponding to the oxidation

---

* To help remember these definitions, note that anode and oxidation both begin with a vowel, and cathode and reduction both begin with a consonant.

FIGURE 20.4 An electrochemical cell based on the reaction shown in Equation 20.7. The compartment on the left contains 1 M CuSO$_4$ and a copper electrode. The one on the right contains 1 M ZnSO$_4$ and a zinc electrode. The solutions are connected electrically through the bridge, which has a porous glass disc that permits contact of the solutions in the two compartments. The metal electrodes are connected through a digital voltmeter, which reads the standard potential of the cell, 1.10 V. (© Richard Megna/Fundamental Photographs)

half-reaction and one corresponding to the reduction half-reaction. In our present example, Zn is oxidized and Cu^{2+} is reduced:

Anode (oxidation half-reaction): $Zn(s) \longrightarrow Zn^{2+}(aq) + 2e^-$

Cathode (reduction half-reaction): $Cu^{2+}(aq) + 2e^- \longrightarrow Cu(s)$

Electrons become available as zinc metal is oxidized at the anode. They flow through the external circuit to the cathode, where they are consumed as $Cu^{2+}(aq)$ is reduced. Because $Zn(s)$ is oxidized in the cell, the zinc electrode loses mass, and the concentration of the Zn^{2+} solution increases as the cell operates. Similarly, the Cu electrode gains mass, and the Cu^{2+} solution becomes less concentrated as Cu^{2+} is reduced to $Cu(s)$.

We must be careful about the signs we attach to the electrodes in a voltaic cell. We have seen that electrons are released at the anode as the zinc is oxidized. Electrons are thus flowing out of the anode and into the external circuit, as illustrated in Figure 20.5. Because the electrons are negatively charged, we assign a negative sign to the anode. Conversely, electrons flow into the cathode, where they are consumed in the reduction of copper. A positive sign is thus assigned to the cathode because it appears to attract the negative electrons.

As the cell pictured in Figure 20.4 operates, oxidation of Zn introduces additional Zn^{2+} ions into the anode compartment. Unless a means is provided to neutralize this positive charge, no further oxidation can take place. Similarly, the reduction of Cu^{2+} at the cathode leaves an excess of negative charge in solution in that compartment. Electrical neutrality is maintained by a migration of ions through the porous glass disc separating the two compartments, or through a *salt bridge,* as illustrated in Figure 20.5. A salt bridge consists of a U-shaped tube that contains an electrolyte solution, such as $NaNO_3(aq)$, whose ions will not react with other ions in the cell or with the electrode materials. The ends of the U-tube may be loosely plugged with glass wool, or the electrolyte may be incorporated into a gel so that the electrolyte solution does not run out when the U-tube is inverted. As oxidation and reduction proceed at the electrodes, ions from the salt bridge migrate to neutralize charge in the anode and

P. J. Moran and E. Gileadi, "Alleviating the Common Confusion Caused by Polarity in Electrochemistry," *J. Chem. Educ.* **1989,** *66,* 912.

Point of Emphasis: In a voltaic cell, the anode has a *negative* charge, and the cathode has a *positive* charge.

Teaching Note: An aid to remembering the signs of the electrodes in a voltaic cell is that the "an" in anode stands for "*a n*egative electrode."

FIGURE 20.5 Voltaic cell using a salt bridge to complete the electrical circuit.

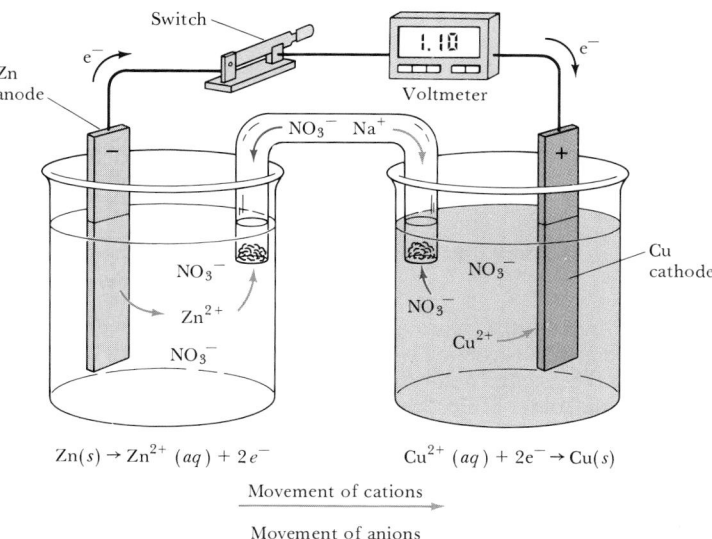

Movement of cations

Movement of anions

Figure 20.5

FIGURE 20.6 A summary of the terminology used in describing voltaic cells. The oxidation process is the source of electrons and occurs at the anode; the electrons are used in the reduction process, which occurs at the cathode. The electrons flow spontaneously from the negative to the positive electrode (that is, from the anode to the cathode). The electrical circuit is completed by the movement of ions in solution. Anions move toward the anode, whereas cations move toward the cathode. The compartments of the cell can be separated by either a porous glass barrier (as in Figure 20.4) or by a salt bridge (as in Figure 20.5).

Figure 20.6

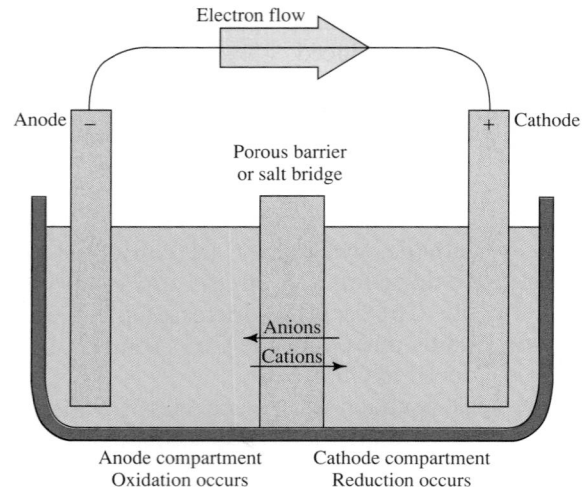

cathode compartments. Anions migrate toward the anode, and cations toward the cathode. In fact, no measurable electron flow will occur through the external circuit unless a means is provided for ions to migrate through the solution from one electrode compartment to another, thereby completing the circuit.

Figure 20.6 summarizes the relationships among the anode, the cathode, the chemical process occurring in a voltaic cell, the signs of the electrodes, the direction of migration of ions in solution, and the motion of electrons in the external circuit.

SAMPLE EXERCISE 20.4

The following oxidation-reduction reaction is spontaneous:

$$Cr_2O_7^{2-}(aq) + 14H^+(aq) + 6I^-(aq) \longrightarrow 2Cr^{3+}(aq) + 3I_2(s) + 7H_2O(l)$$

A solution containing $K_2Cr_2O_7$ and H_2SO_4 is poured into one beaker, and a solution of KI is poured into another. A salt bridge is used to join the beakers. A metallic conductor that will not react with either solution (such as platinum foil) is suspended in each solution, and the two conductors are connected with wires through a voltmeter or some other device to detect an electric current. The resultant voltaic cell generates an electric current. Indicate the reaction occurring at the anode, the reaction at the cathode, the direction of electron and ion migrations, and the signs of the electrodes.

SOLUTION The first step in answering this question is to divide the chemical equation into half-reactions so that we can identify the oxidation and the reduction processes:

$$Cr_2O_7^{2-}(aq) + 14H^+(aq) + 6e^- \longrightarrow 2Cr^{3+}(aq) + 7H_2O(l)$$

$$6I^-(aq) \longrightarrow 3I_2(s) + 6e^-$$

Now we can use the information summarized in Figure 20.6 to describe the voltaic cell. The first half-reaction is the reduction process, which by definition occurs at the cathode. The second half-reaction is an oxidation, which occurs at the anode. The I^- ions are the source of electrons, and the $Cr_2O_7^{2-}$ ions are the receptors. Consequently, the electrons flow through the external circuit from the electrode immersed in the KI solution (the anode) to the electrode immersed in the $K_2Cr_2O_7 - H_2SO_4$ solution (the cathode). The electrodes themselves do not react in any way; they merely provide a means of transferring electrons from or to the solutions. The cations move through the solutions toward the cathode, and the anions move toward the anode. The anode (from which the electrons move) is the negative electrode, and the cathode (toward which the electrons move) is the positive one.

PRACTICE EXERCISE

The two half-reactions in a voltaic cell are

$$Zn(s) \longrightarrow Zn^{2+}(aq) + 2e^-$$

$$ClO_3^-(aq) + 6H^+(aq) + 6e^- \longrightarrow Cl^-(aq) + 3H_2O(l)$$

(a) Indicate which reaction occurs at the anode and which at the cathode. **(b)** Which electrode is consumed in the cell reaction? **(c)** Which electrode is positive? *Answers:* **(a)** The first reaction occurs at the anode, the second reaction at the cathode. **(b)** The anode (Zn) is consumed in the cell reaction. **(c)** The cathode is positive.

20.4 Cell EMF

As we have been discussing voltaic cells, you may have wondered why electrons flow spontaneously through the external circuit. In the cell shown in Figure 20.5, for example, what causes the electrons to leave the Zn electrode, pass through the external circuit, and enter the Cu electrode? Like all chemical processes that occur spontaneously, the answer involves energy: *It is energetically favorable for electrons to flow from the anode to the cathode of a voltaic cell.*

In each half-cell of a voltaic cell, the electrons have a different potential energy. For example, Figure 20.7 illustrates the difference in potential energy of the electrons in the two electrodes of the voltaic cell in Figure 20.5. The potential energy of electrons is higher in the Zn electrode than in the Cu electrode. If the electrodes are connected by an external circuit, the electrons can lower their potential energy by flowing from the zinc to the copper electrode. The *potential difference* (the difference in potential energy per electrical charge) between two electrodes is measured in units of volts. One volt (V) is the potential difference required to impart 1 J of energy to a charge of 1 coulomb (C):

$$1\ V = 1\ \frac{J}{C}$$

In the Zn/Cu voltaic cell in Figure 20.5, the potential difference is 1.10 V.

We can view the potential difference between two electrodes of a voltaic cell as a "driving force" or "electrical pressure" that pushes electrons through the external circuit. Therefore, we call the potential difference between the electrodes of a cell the **electromotive force** (abbreviated **emf**), or **cell potential**. The emf of a cell, denoted E_{cell}, is also referred to as the *cell voltage* because it is measured in volts.

The emf of the Zn/Cu voltaic cell is 1.10 V when operated under standard conditions. You will recall from Section 19.5 that standard conditions include 1 M concentrations for reactants and products in solution and 1 atm pressure for those that are gases (Table 19.3). In the present example, the cell would be operated with both [Cu^{2+}] and [Zn^{2+}] at 1 M. Under standard conditions, the emf is called the **standard emf** or the **standard cell potential, E°_{cell}**:

$$Zn(s) + Cu^{2+}(aq, 1\ M) \longrightarrow Zn^{2+}(aq, 1\ M) + Cu(s) \qquad E^\circ_{cell} = 1.10\ V$$

(We often drop the subscript "cell" when it is clear that we are discussing the emf of a cell.) The emf of any voltaic cell depends on the chemical reaction

Learning Goal 4: Given appropriate electrode potentials, calculate the emf generated by a voltaic cell.

FIGURE 20.7 A schematic comparison of the potential energy of electrons in the two electrodes in Figure 20.5. The potential energy of electrons is lower in the Cu electrode than in the Zn electrode, and so electrons flow through the external circuit in order to become lower in energy. The *potential difference* between the electrodes is 1.10 V.

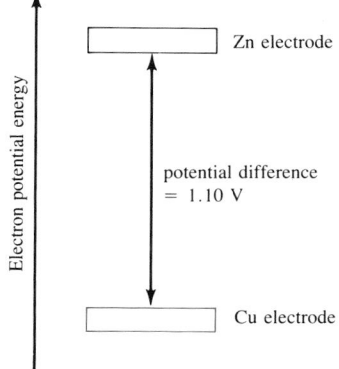

taking place in the cell, the concentrations of reactants and products, and the temperature of the cell, which we shall take to be 25°C unless otherwise noted. Recall that the superscript degree sign (°) indicates standard-state conditions. ⊂⊃ (Sec. 5.7)

Standard Electrode Potentials

Just as we can think of an overall cell reaction as the sum of two half-reactions, we can think of the emf of a cell, E_{cell}, as the sum of two half-cell potentials. The half-cell potential due to the loss of electrons at the anode is called the *oxidation potential, E_{ox}*, and that due to electron gain at the cathode is called the *reduction potential, E_{red}*:

$$E_{cell} = E_{ox} + E_{red}$$

If all reagents are under standard conditions, the half-cell potentials are called the **standard oxidation potential, E_{ox}°**, and the **standard reduction potential, E_{red}°**; the sum of these equals the standard emf:

$$E_{cell}^{\circ} = E_{ox}^{\circ} + E_{red}^{\circ}$$

We cannot directly measure an isolated oxidation or reduction potential. However, if we assign a standard half-cell potential to a certain half-reaction, we can then determine the standard potentials of other half-reactions relative to that reference. The reference half-reaction is the reduction of H^+ to H_2, which is assigned a standard reduction potential of exactly 0 V:

$$2H^+(aq, 1\ M) + 2e^- \longrightarrow H_2(g, 1\ atm) \qquad E_{red}^{\circ} = 0\ V$$

Point of Emphasis: The potential of the standard hydrogen electrode (SHE) is arbitrarily assigned the value of exactly 0 V.

An electrode designed to produce this half-reaction is called a **standard hydrogen electrode**; it is one of the electrodes illustrated in Figure 20.8. A standard hydrogen electrode consists of a platinum wire and a piece of platinum foil covered with finely divided platinum that serves as an inert surface for the

FIGURE 20.8 Voltaic cell using a standard hydrogen electrode.

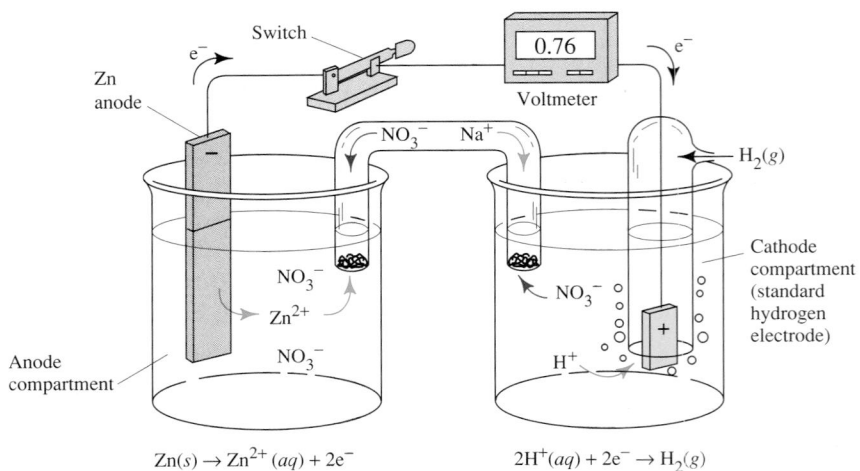

$$Zn(s) \rightarrow Zn^{2+}(aq) + 2e^- \qquad\qquad 2H^+(aq) + 2e^- \rightarrow H_2(g)$$

cathode reaction. The electrode is encased in a glass tube so that hydrogen gas can bubble over the platinum.

Figure 20.8 shows a voltaic cell constructed to use the following redox reaction between Zn and H^+, the reaction shown in Figure 20.1:

$$Zn(s) + 2H^+(aq) \longrightarrow Zn^{2+}(aq) + H_2(g)$$

Oxidation of zinc occurs in the anode compartment, and reduction of H^+ occurs in the cathode compartment, which is a standard hydrogen electrode. This voltaic cell generates a standard emf (E°_{cell}) of 0.76 V. By using the defined standard reduction potential of H^+ ($E^\circ_{red} = 0$), we can calculate the standard oxidation potential of Zn:

$$E^\circ_{cell} = E^\circ_{ox} + E^\circ_{red}$$
$$0.76 \text{ V} = E^\circ_{ox} + 0$$

Thus, a standard oxidation potential of 0.76 V can be assigned to Zn:

$$Zn(s) \longrightarrow Zn^{2+}(aq, 1 \text{ } M) + 2e^- \qquad E^\circ_{ox} = 0.76 \text{ V} \qquad \text{[20.8]}$$

The standard potentials for other half-reactions can be established from other cell emfs in a similar fashion.

By convention, half-cell potentials are tabulated as standard *reduction* potentials. For the Zn half-reaction, we therefore want to calculate the potential for the reduction of Zn^{2+} to Zn, which is the reverse of Equation 20.8. As with energy-related quantities, such as ΔH and ΔG, reversing a reaction changes the sign of E°. Thus, *the half-cell potential for a reduction is equal in magnitude but opposite in sign to the half-cell potential for the same reaction written as an oxidation:*

$$E^\circ_{red} = -E^\circ_{ox} \qquad \text{[20.9]}$$

For the Zn half-reaction, we can therefore write

$$Zn^{2+}(aq, 1 \text{ } M) + 2e^- \longrightarrow Zn(s) \qquad E^\circ_{red} = -0.76 \text{ V}$$

Changing the stoichiometric coefficient in a half-reaction does not affect the value of the electrode potential because *electrode potentials are intensive properties;* they do not depend on the quantities of reactants and products but only on their concentrations. Therefore, E°_{red} for 2 mol of Zn^{2+} is the same as for 1 mol of Zn^{2+} because the standard concentration is 1 M in either case:

$$2Zn^{2+}(aq, 1 \text{ } M) + 4e^- \longrightarrow 2Zn(s) \qquad E^\circ_{red} = -0.76 \text{ V}$$

Table 20.1 lists some standard reduction potentials, also called **standard electrode potentials.** A more complete list of standard electrode potentials is found in Appendix E. These standard electrode potentials can be combined to calculate the standard emfs of a large variety of voltaic cells.

TABLE 20.1 △ Standard Electrode Potentials in Water at 25°C

Standard potential (V)	Reduction half-reaction
2.87	$F_2(g) + 2e^- \longrightarrow 2F^-(aq)$
1.51	$MnO_4^-(aq) + 8H^+(aq) + 5e^- \longrightarrow Mn^{2+}(aq) + 4H_2O(l)$
1.36	$Cl_2(g) + 2e^- \longrightarrow 2Cl^-(aq)$
1.33	$Cr_2O_7^{2-}(aq) + 14H^+(aq) + 6e^- \longrightarrow 2Cr^{3+}(aq) + 7H_2O(l)$
1.23	$O_2(g) + 4H^+(aq) + 4e^- \longrightarrow 2H_2O(l)$
1.06	$Br_2(l) + 2e^- \longrightarrow 2Br^-(aq)$
0.96	$NO_3^-(aq) + 4H^+(aq) + 3e^- \longrightarrow NO(g) + 2H_2O(l)$
0.80	$Ag^+(aq) + e^- \longrightarrow Ag(s)$
0.77	$Fe^{3+}(aq) + e^- \longrightarrow Fe^{2+}(aq)$
0.68	$O_2(g) + 2H^+(aq) + 2e^- \longrightarrow H_2O_2(aq)$
0.59	$MnO_4^-(aq) + 2H_2O(l) + 3e^- \longrightarrow MnO_2(s) + 4OH^-(aq)$
0.54	$I_2(s) + 2e^- \longrightarrow 2I^-(aq)$
0.40	$O_2(g) + 2H_2O(l) + 4e^- \longrightarrow 4OH^-(aq)$
0.34	$Cu^{2+}(aq) + 2e^- \longrightarrow Cu(s)$
0	$2H^+(aq) + 2e^- \longrightarrow H_2(g)$
-0.28	$Ni^{2+}(aq) + 2e^- \longrightarrow Ni(s)$
-0.44	$Fe^{2+}(aq) + 2e^- \longrightarrow Fe(s)$
-0.76	$Zn^{2+}(aq) + 2e^- \longrightarrow Zn(s)$
-0.83	$2H_2O(l) + 2e^- \longrightarrow H_2(g) + 2OH^-(aq)$
-1.66	$Al^{3+}(aq) + 3e^- \longrightarrow Al(s)$
-2.71	$Na^+(aq) + e^- \longrightarrow Na(s)$
-3.05	$Li^+(aq) + e^- \longrightarrow Li(s)$

SAMPLE EXERCISE 20.5

Given that E_{cell}° is 1.10 V for the Zn–Cu^{2+} cell shown in Figure 20.5, and that E_{ox}° is 0.76 V for the oxidation of zinc (Equation 20.8), calculate E_{red}° for the reduction of Cu^{2+} to Cu:

$$Cu^{2+}(aq) + 2e^- \longrightarrow Cu(s)$$

SOLUTION

$$E_{cell}^\circ = E_{ox}^\circ + E_{red}^\circ$$
$$1.10 \text{ V} = 0.76 \text{ V} + E_{red}^\circ$$
$$E_{red}^\circ = 1.10 \text{ V} - 0.76 \text{ V} = 0.34 \text{ V}$$

PRACTICE EXERCISE

A voltaic cell employs the following half-reactions:

$$In^+(aq) \longrightarrow In^{3+}(aq) + 2e^-$$
$$Br_2(l) + 2e^-(aq) \longrightarrow 2Br^-(aq)$$

The standard cell potential for this cell is 1.46 V. Using the data in Table 20.1, calculate E_{ox}° for the first half-cell reaction.   *Answer:* +0.40 V

SAMPLE EXERCISE 20.6

Using the standard electrode potentials listed in Table 20.1, calculate the standard emf for the cell described in Sample Exercise 20.4:

$$Cr_2O_7^{2-}(aq) + 14H^+(aq) + 6I^-(aq) \longrightarrow 2Cr^{3+}(aq) + 3I_2(s) + 7H_2O(l)$$

SOLUTION The standard emf of the cell, E_{cell}°, is the sum of the standard oxidation and reduction potentials for the appropriate half-reactions:

$$E_{cell}^\circ = E_{ox}^\circ + E_{red}^\circ$$

The half-reactions and their potentials are as follows:

$$Cr_2O_7^{2-}(aq) + 14H^+(aq) + 6e^- \longrightarrow 2Cr^{3+}(aq) + 7H_2O(l) \qquad E_{red}^\circ = 1.33 \text{ V}$$
$$\underline{\phantom{Cr_2O_7^{2-}(aq) + 14H^+(aq)} 6I^-(aq) \longrightarrow 3I_2(s) + 6e^- E_{ox}^\circ = -0.54 \text{ V}}$$
$$Cr_2O_7^{2-}(aq) + 14H^+(aq) + 6I^-(aq) \longrightarrow$$
$$2Cr^{3+}(aq) + 7H_2O(l) + 3I_2(s) \qquad E_{cell}^\circ = 0.79 \text{ V}$$

Notice that E_{ox}° for I^- has a sign opposite that of the reduction potential of I_2 listed in Table 20.1. Also notice that even though the iodide half-reaction must be multiplied by 3 in order to obtain a balanced equation for the reaction, the half-cell potential is *not* multiplied by 3. As we have noted, the standard potential is an intensive property; it does not depend on the quantities of reactants and products but only on their concentrations.

Just as the sum of the half-reactions gives the chemical equation for the overall cell reaction, the sum of the corresponding oxidation and reduction potentials gives the cell emf. In this case, $E_{cell}^\circ = 0.79$ V; a positive emf is characteristic of all voltaic cells.

PRACTICE EXERCISE

Using Table 20.1, calculate the standard emf for a cell that employs the following overall cell reaction:

$$2Al(s) + 3I_2(s) \longrightarrow 2Al^{3+}(aq) + 6I^-(aq)$$

Answer: 2.20 V

Oxidizing and Reducing Agents

The half-cell potential provides us with a tool for quantitatively expressing the ease with which a species is oxidized or reduced. *The more positive the $E°$ value for a half-reaction, the greater the tendency for that reaction to occur as written.* A negative reduction potential indicates that the species is more difficult to reduce than $H^+(aq)$, whereas a negative oxidation potential indicates that the species is more difficult to oxidize than H_2. Examination of the half-reactions in Table 20.1 shows that F_2 is the most easily reduced species and is consequently the strongest oxidizing agent listed:

$$F_2(g) + 2e^- \longrightarrow 2F^-(aq) \qquad E_{red}^\circ = 2.87 \text{ V}$$

Lithium ion, Li^+, is the most difficult to reduce and is therefore the poorest oxidizing agent:

$$Li^+(aq) + e^- \longrightarrow Li(s) \qquad E_{red}^\circ = -3.05 \text{ V}$$

Among the most frequently encountered oxidizing agents are the halogens, oxygen, and oxyanions such as MnO_4^-, $Cr_2O_7^{2-}$, and NO_3^-, whose central atoms have high positive oxidation states. Metal ions in high positive oxidation states—such as Ce^{4+}, which is readily reduced to Ce^{3+}—are also employed as oxidizing agents.

Equation 20.9 tells us that a half-reaction with a very negative E_{red}° will have a very positive E_{ox}°. Thus, among the substances listed in Table 20.1, $Li(s)$

is the most easily oxidized and is consequently the strongest reducing agent:

$$Li(s) \longrightarrow Li^+(aq) + e^- \qquad E^\circ_{ox} = 3.05 \text{ V}$$

Fluoride ion, F^-, is the most difficult to oxidize and is therefore the poorest reducing agent:

$$2F^-(aq) \longrightarrow F_2(g) + 2e^- \qquad E^\circ_{ox} = -2.87 \text{ V}$$

Commonly used reducing agents include H_2 and a variety of metals having positive oxidation potentials (such as Zn and Fe). Some metal ions in low oxidation states — such as Sn^{2+}, which is oxidized to Sn^{4+} — also function as reducing agents. Solutions of reducing agents are difficult to store for extended periods because of the ubiquitous presence of O_2, a good oxidizing agent. For example, developer solutions used in photography are mild reducing agents; they have only a limited shelf life because they are readily oxidized by O_2 from the air.

SAMPLE EXERCISE 20.7

Using Table 20.1, determine which of the following species is the strongest oxidizing agent: MnO_4^- (in acid solution), $I_2(s)$, $Zn^{2+}(aq)$.

SOLUTION   The strongest oxidizing agent will be the species that is most readily reduced. Therefore, we should compare reduction potentials. From Table 20.1 we have

$$MnO_4^-(aq) + 8H^+(aq) + 5e^- \longrightarrow Mn^{2+}(aq) + 4H_2O(l) \qquad E^\circ_{red} = 1.51 \text{ V}$$
$$I_2(s) + 2e^- \longrightarrow 2I^-(aq) \qquad E^\circ_{red} = 0.54 \text{ V}$$
$$Zn^{2+}(aq) + 2e^- \longrightarrow Zn(s) \qquad E^\circ_{red} = -0.76 \text{ V}$$

Because the reduction of MnO_4^- has the highest positive potential, MnO_4^- is the strongest oxidizing agent of the three.

PRACTICE EXERCISE

Using Table 20.1, determine which of the following species is the strongest reducing agent: $F^-(aq)$, $Zn(s)$, $I^-(aq)$.   *Answer:* $Zn(s)$

20.5 Spontaneity of Redox Reactions

Learning Goal 5: Use electrode potentials to predict whether a reaction will be spontaneous.

Teaching Note: A negative emf indicates that a reaction will be spontaneous in the reverse direction, i.e., from right to left.

We have observed that voltaic cells use redox reactions that proceed spontaneously. Conversely, any reaction that can occur in a voltaic cell to produce a positive emf must be spontaneous. Consequently, it is possible to decide whether a redox reaction will be spontaneous by using half-cell potentials to calculate the emf associated with it: *A positive emf indicates a spontaneous process, and a negative emf indicates a nonspontaneous one.*

SAMPLE EXERCISE 20.8

Using the standard electrode potentials listed in Table 20.1, determine whether the following reactions are spontaneous under standard conditions:
(a) $Cu(s) + 2H^+(aq) \longrightarrow Cu^{2+}(aq) + H_2(g)$
(b) $Cl_2(g) + 2I^-(aq) \longrightarrow 2Cl^-(aq) + I_2(s)$

Chapter 20   Electrochemistry

SOLUTION (a) We use Table 20.1 to obtain the necessary half-cell potentials. Because the overall reaction converts Cu to Cu^{2+}, we use the standard oxidation potential for Cu. Because the overall reaction converts H^+ to H_2, we use the reduction potential for H^+. Adding these, we obtain the standard emf for the overall reaction:

$$
\begin{array}{lll}
Cu(s) \longrightarrow Cu^{2+}(aq) + 2e^- & E^\circ_{ox} = -0.34\ V \\
2e^- + 2H^+(aq) \longrightarrow H_2(g) & E^\circ_{red} = \quad 0 \quad V \\
\hline
Cu(s) + 2H^+(aq) \longrightarrow Cu^{2+}(aq) + H_2(g) & E^\circ = -0.34\ V
\end{array}
$$

Because the standard emf is negative, the reaction is not spontaneous in the direction written. Copper does not react with acids in this fashion. However, the reverse reaction is spontaneous: Cu^{2+} can be reduced by H_2.

(b) We write equations to obtain the standard emf for the overall reaction:

$$
\begin{array}{lll}
2e^- + Cl_2(g) \longrightarrow 2Cl^-(aq) & E^\circ_{red} = \quad 1.36\ V \\
2I^-(aq) \longrightarrow I_2(s) + 2e^- & E^\circ_{ox} = -0.54\ V \\
\hline
Cl_2(g) + 2I^-(aq) \longrightarrow 2Cl^-(aq) + I_2(s) & E^\circ = \quad 0.82\ V
\end{array}
$$

Because E° is positive, this reaction is spontaneous and could be used to build a voltaic cell. It is often used as a qualitative test for the presence of I^- in aqueous solution. The solution is treated with a solution of Cl_2. If I^- is present, I_2 forms. If CCl_4 is added, the I_2 dissolves in the CCl_4, imparting a characteristic violet color to the solution (see Figure 23.2).

PRACTICE EXERCISE

Using the standard electrode potentials listed in Appendix E, determine which of the following reactions are spontaneous under standard conditions:
(a) $I_2(s) + 5Cu^{2+}(aq) + 6H_2O(l) \longrightarrow 2IO_3^-(aq) + 5Cu(s) + 12H^+(aq)$
(b) $Hg^{2+}(aq) + 2I^-(aq) \longrightarrow Hg(l) + I_2(s)$
(c) $H_2SO_3(aq) + 2Mn(s) + 4H^+(aq) \longrightarrow S(s) + 2Mn^{2+}(aq) + 3H_2O(l)$
Answer: Reactions (b) and (c) are spontaneous.

We can use standard electrode potentials to understand the activity series of metals. ∞ (Sec. 4.6) Recall the main rule concerning the activity series: Any metal in the series is able to displace the elements below it from their compounds. We can now recognize the origin of this rule on the basis of standard electrode potentials. The activity series is simply the oxidation half-reactions of the metals ordered from highest to lowest E°_{ox} (see Table 4.5). For example, iron lies above silver in the activity series. We therefore expect iron to displace silver according to the net reaction.

Teaching Note: With this topic in mind, review the activity series, Section 4.6.

$$Fe(s) + 2Ag^+(aq) \longrightarrow Fe^{2+}(aq) + 2Ag(s) \qquad [20.10]$$

By using the data in Table 20.1, we have:

$$
\begin{array}{lll}
Fe(s) \longrightarrow Fe^{2+}(aq) + 2e^- & E^\circ_{ox} = 0.44\ V \\
2Ag^+(aq) + 2e^- \longrightarrow 2Ag(s) & E^\circ_{red} = 0.80\ V \\
\hline
Fe(s) + 2Ag^+(aq) \longrightarrow Fe^{2+}(aq) + 2Ag(s) & E^\circ = 1.24\ V
\end{array}
$$

The positive value of E° indicates that Equation 20.10 should occur spontaneously.

Point of Emphasis: Note that, even though the silver half-reaction has been multiplied by 2, the E° is *not* multiplied.

Emf and Free-Energy Change

We have seen that the free-energy change, ΔG, accompanying a chemical process is a measure of its spontaneity (Chapter 19). Because the cell emf indicates whether a redox reaction is spontaneous, we might expect some rela-

Learning Goal 6: Interconvert E°, ΔG°, and K for oxidation-reduction reactions.

FIGURE 20.9 Michael Faraday (1791–1867) was born in England, 1 of 10 children of a poor blacksmith. At the age of 14, he was apprenticed to a bookbinder who gave the young man time to read and to attend lectures. In 1812, he became an assistant in Humphry Davy's laboratory at the Royal Institution. He eventually succeeded Davy as the most famous and influential scientist in England. During his scientific career he made an amazing number of important discoveries. He developed methods for liquefying gases, discovered benzene, and formulated the quantitative relationships between electrical current and the extent of chemical reaction in electrochemical cells. He also worked out the design of the first electric generator and laid the theoretical foundations for the development of our modern theory of electricity. (Bettmann)

Common Misconception: In the expression $\Delta G = -nFE$, n is *not* the sum of the number of electrons used in oxidation and the number of electrons used in reduction. The electrons used in oxidation *are the same electrons* used in reduction, and n is the number of electrons transferred.

tionship to exist between the cell emf and the free-energy change. Indeed, this is the case; the emf, E, and the free-energy change, ΔG, are related by Equation 20.11:

$$\Delta G = -nFE \qquad [20.11]$$

In this equation, n is the number of moles of electrons transferred in the reaction and F is Faraday's constant, named after Michael Faraday (Figure 20.9). Faraday's constant is the electrical charge on 1 mol of electrons. This quantity of charge is called a **faraday:**

$$1\ F = 96{,}500\ \frac{C}{\text{mol e}^-} = 96{,}500\ \frac{J}{\text{V-mol e}^-}$$

Notice that, because n and F are both positive quantities, a positive value of E in Equation 20.11 leads to a negative value of ΔG. Remember: A positive value of E and a negative value of ΔG both indicate that a reaction is spontaneous.

When both the reactants and products are in their standard states, Equation 20.11 can be modified to relate $\Delta G°$ and $E°$:

$$\Delta G° = -nFE° \qquad [20.12]$$

SAMPLE EXERCISE 20.9

Use the standard electrode potentials given in Table 20.1 to calculate the standard free-energy change, $\Delta G°$, for the following reaction:

$$2Br^-(aq) + F_2(g) \longrightarrow Br_2(l) + 2F^-(aq)$$

SOLUTION

$2Br^-(aq) \longrightarrow Br_2(l) + 2e^-$	$E°_{ox} = -1.06$ V
$F_2(g) + 2e^- \longrightarrow 2F^-(aq)$	$E°_{red} = 2.87$ V
$2Br^-(aq) + F_2(g) \longrightarrow Br_2(l) + 2F^-(aq)$	$E° = 1.81$ V

Notice that two electrons are transferred in the reaction, and so $n = 2$.

$$\Delta G° = -nFE°$$

$$= -(2 \text{ mol e}^-)\left(96{,}500 \; \frac{\text{J}}{\text{V-mol e}^-}\right)(1.81 \text{ V})$$

$$= -3.49 \times 10^5 \text{ J} = -349 \text{ kJ}$$

PRACTICE EXERCISE

Use the standard electrode potentials given in Appendix E to calculate the free-energy change for the following reaction:

$$I_2(s) + 5Cu^{2+}(aq) + 6H_2O(l) \longrightarrow 2IO_3^-(aq) + 5Cu(s) + 12H^+(aq)$$

Answer: $+828$ kJ

20.6 Effect of Concentration on Cell EMF

As a voltaic cell is discharged, its emf falls until $E = 0$, at which point we say that the cell is "dead." Studies reveal that the emf depends on the concentrations of the reactants and products in the cell reaction. When reactant concentrations increase, the emf increases. On the other hand, when product concentrations increase, the emf decreases. The emf generated under nonstandard conditions can be calculated using an equation first derived by Walther Hermann Nernst (1864–1941), a German chemist who established many of the theoretical foundations of electrochemistry.

Teaching Note: The response of cell emf to increasing product or reactant concentrations can be explained by Le Châtelier's principle.

The Nernst Equation

The dependence of the cell emf on concentration can be obtained directly from the dependence of the free-energy change on concentration. ∞ (Sec. 19.7) Recall that the free-energy change, ΔG, is related to the standard free-energy change, $\Delta G°$:

Learning Goal 7: Use the Nernst equation to calculate an emf under nonstandard conditions.

$$\Delta G = \Delta G° + RT \ln Q \qquad [20.13]$$

The quantity Q is the reaction quotient, which has the form of the equilibrium expression except that the concentrations are those that exist in the reaction mixture at a given moment.

Substituting $\Delta G = -nFE$ (Equation 20.11) into Equation 20.13 gives

$$-nFE = -nFE° + RT \ln Q$$

Solving this equation for E gives the **Nernst equation:**

Teaching Note: Walther Nernst was awarded the 1920 Nobel Prize in Chemistry for his work in electrochemistry.

$$E = E° - \frac{RT}{nF} \ln Q \qquad [20.14]$$

This equation is customarily expressed in terms of common (base 10) logarithms:

$$E = E° - \frac{2.30 \; RT}{nF} \log Q \qquad [20.15]$$

At 298 K, the quantity $2.30RT/F$ equals 0.0592 V-mol, and so the equation can be written in a simplified form:

$$E = E° - \frac{0.0592}{n} \log Q \qquad (T = 298 \text{ K}) \qquad [20.16]$$

This equation allows us to find the emf produced by a cell under nonstandard conditions, or to find the concentration of a reactant or product by measuring the emf of the cell.

As an example of how Equation 20.16 might be used, consider the following reaction:

$$Zn(s) + Cu^{2+}(aq) \longrightarrow Zn^{2+}(aq) + Cu(s)$$

In this case, $n = 2$ (two electrons are transferred from Zn to Cu^{2+}), and at 298 K the Nernst equation gives

$$E = 1.10 \text{ V} - \frac{0.0592 \text{ V}}{2} \log \frac{[Zn^{2+}]}{[Cu^{2+}]} \qquad [20.17]$$

Recall that Q includes expressions for species in solution but not for solids. ∞ (Sec. 15.5) From Equation 20.17, it is evident that the emf of a cell based on this chemical reaction increases as $[Cu^{2+}]$ increases and as $[Zn^{2+}]$ decreases. For example, when $[Cu^{2+}]$ is 5.0 M and $[Zn^{2+}]$ is 0.050 M, we have

$$E = 1.10 \text{ V} - \frac{0.0592 \text{ V}}{2} \log \left(\frac{0.050}{5.0} \right)$$

$$= 1.10 \text{ V} - \frac{0.0592 \text{ V}}{2} (-2.00) = 1.16 \text{ V}$$

The fact that E (1.16 V) is greater than $E°$ (1.10 V) indicates that, at these concentrations, the driving force for the reaction is greater than under standard conditions. We could have anticipated this result by applying Le Châtelier's principle. ∞ (Sec. 15.6) If the concentrations of reactants increase relative to the concentrations of products, the cell reaction becomes more highly spontaneous, and the emf increases. Conversely, if the concentrations of products increase relative to reactants, emf decreases. As a cell operates, reactants are consumed and products form. The decreases in reactant concentrations and increases in product concentrations cause the emf to decrease.

Point of Emphasis: The fact that cell emf drops as reactant concentrations decrease and product concentrations increase is important in viewing the approach to equilibrium and leads to the known observation that $E = 0$ at equilibrium.

SAMPLE EXERCISE 20.10

Calculate the emf generated by the cell described in Sample Exercise 20.4 when $[Cr_2O_7^{2-}] = 2.0$ M, $[H^+] = 1.0$ M, $[I^-] = 1.0$ M, and $[Cr^{3+}] = 1.0 \times 10^{-5}$ M:

$$Cr_2O_7^{2-}(aq) + 14H^+(aq) + 6I^-(aq) \longrightarrow 2Cr^{3+}(aq) + 3I_2(s) + 7H_2O(l)$$

SOLUTION   The standard emf for this reaction was calculated in Sample Exercise 20.6: $E° = 0.79$ V. As you will see if you refer back to that exercise, $n = 6$. The reaction quotient, Q, is

$$Q = \frac{[Cr^{3+}]^2}{[Cr_2O_7^{2-}][H^+]^{14}[I^-]^6} = \frac{(1.0 \times 10^{-5})^2}{(2.0)(1.0)^{14}(1.0)^6} = 5.0 \times 10^{-11}$$

Using Equation 20.16, we have

$$E = 0.79 \text{ V} - \frac{0.0592 \text{ V}}{6} \log (5.0 \times 10^{-11})$$

$$= 0.79 \text{ V} - \frac{0.0592 \text{ V}}{6} (-10.30)$$

$$= 0.79 \text{ V} + 0.10 \text{ V}$$

$$= 0.89 \text{ V}$$

This result is qualitatively what we expect: Because the concentration of $Cr_2O_7^{2-}$ (a reactant) is above 1 M and the concentration of Cr^{3+} (a product) is below 1 M, the emf is greater than $E°$.

PRACTICE EXERCISE

Calculate the emf generated by the cell described in the practice exercise accompanying Sample Exercise 20.6 when $[Al^{3+}] = 4.0 \times 10^{-3} M$ and $[I^-] = 0.010 M$.
Answer: $E = 2.36$ V

SAMPLE EXERCISE 20.11

If the measured voltage in a Zn–H^+ cell (such as that shown in Figure 20.8) is 0.45 V at 25°C when $[Zn^{2+}]$ is 1 M and P_{H_2} is 1 atm, what is the concentration of H^+?

Learning Goal 8: Use the Nernst equation to calculate the concentration of an ion, given E, $E°$, and the concentrations of the remaining ions.

SOLUTION The cell reaction is

$$Zn(s) + 2H^+(aq) \longrightarrow Zn^{2+}(aq) + H_2(g)$$

The standard emf is $E° = 0.76$ V. Applying Equation 20.16 with $n = 2$ gives

$$0.45 = 0.76 - \frac{0.0592}{2} \log \frac{[Zn^{2+}]P_{H_2}}{[H^+]^2}$$

$$= 0.76 - \frac{0.0592}{2} \log \frac{1}{[H^+]^2}$$

Because

$$\log \frac{1}{x^2} = -\log x^2 = -2 \log x$$

we can write

$$0.45 = 0.76 - \frac{0.0592}{2} (-2 \log [H^+])$$

Solving for $\log [H^+]$ gives

$$\log [H^+] = \frac{0.45 - 0.76}{0.0592} = -5.25$$

$$[H^+] = 10^{-5.25} = 5.6 \times 10^{-6} M$$

This example shows how a voltaic cell whose cell reaction involves H^+ can be used to measure $[H^+]$ or pH. A pH meter (Section 16.3) is merely a specially designed voltaic cell with a voltmeter calibrated to read pH directly.

PRACTICE EXERCISE

What is the pH of the solution in the cathode compartment of the cell pictured in Figure 20.8 when $P_{H_2} = 1$ atm, $[Zn^{2+}]$ in the anode compartment is 0.10 M, and cell emf is 0.542 V?   *Answer:* pH = 4.19

Equilibrium Constants for Redox Equations

Recall that when $\Delta G = 0$, a system is at equilibrium. ⟳ (Sec. 19.7) Because $\Delta G = -nFE$ (Equation 20.11), an emf of zero means that no net reaction is

Heartbeats and Electrocardiography

The human heart is a marvel of efficiency and dependability. In a typical day, an adult's heart pumps more than 7000 L of blood through the circulatory system, usually with no maintenance required beyond a sensible diet and lifestyle. We generally think of the heart as a mechanical device, a muscle that circulates blood via regularly spaced muscular contractions. However, more than 2 centuries ago, two pioneers in electricity, Luigi Galvani (1729–1787) and Alessandro Volta (1745–1827), discovered that the contractions of the heart are controlled by electrical phenomena, as are nerve impulses throughout the body. The pulses of electricity that cause the heart to beat result from a remarkable combination of electrochemistry and the properties of semipermeable membranes. ∞ (Sec. 13.5)

Cell walls are membranes with variable permeability with respect to a number of physiologically important ions (especially Na^+, K^+, and Ca^{2+}). The concentrations of these ions are different for the fluids inside the cells (the *intracellular fluid*, or ICF) and outside the cells (the *extracellular fluid*, or ECF). For example, in cardiac muscle cells, the concentrations of K^+ in the ICF and ECF are typically about 135 millimolar (mM) and 4 mM, respectively. Importantly, for Na^+ the concentration difference between the ICF and ECF is opposite that for K^+; typically, $[Na^+]_{ICF} = 10$ mM and $[Na^+]_{ECF} = 145$ mM.

The cell membrane is initially permeable to K^+ ions, but much less so to Na^+ and Ca^{2+}. The difference in concentration of K^+ ions between the ICF and ECF generates a concentration cell: Even though the same ions are present on both sides of the membrane, there is a potential difference between the two fluids that we can calculate using the Nernst equation with $E^\circ = 0$. At the physiological temperature of 37°C, the potential in millivolts for moving K^+ from the ECF to the ICF is

$$E = E^\circ - \frac{2.30RT}{nF} \log \frac{[K^+]_{ICF}}{[K^+]_{ECF}}$$

$$= 0 - (6.15 \text{ mV}) \log\left(\frac{135 \text{ m}M}{4 \text{ m}M}\right) = -94 \text{ mV}$$

In essence, the interior of the cell and the ECF together serve as a voltaic cell. The negative sign for the potential indicates that work is required to move K^+ into the intracellular fluid.

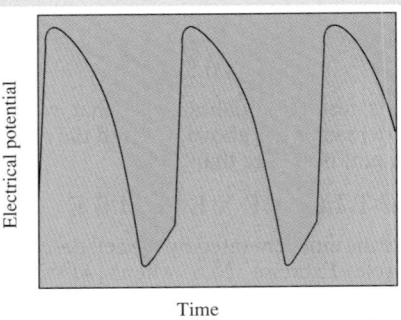

FIGURE 20.10 Variation of the electrical potential caused by changes of ion concentrations in the pacemaker cells of the heart.

Changes in the relative concentrations of the ions in the ECF and ICF lead to changes in the emf of the voltaic cell. The cells of the heart that govern the rate of heart contraction are called the *pacemaker cells*. The membranes of the cells regulate the concentrations of ions in the ICF, allowing them to change in a systematic way. The concentration changes cause the emf to change in a cyclic fashion, as shown in Figure 20.10. The emf cycle determines the rate at which the heart beats. If the pacemaker cells malfunction because of disease or injury, an artificial pacemaker can be surgically installed. The artificial pacemaker is a small battery that generates the electrical pulses needed to trigger the contractions of the heart.

In the late 1800s, scientists discovered that the electrical impulses that cause the contraction of the heart muscle are strong enough to be detected at the surface of the body. This observation formed the basis for *electrocardiography*, noninvasive monitoring of the heart by using a complex array of electrodes on the skin to measure voltage changes during heartbeats. A typical electrocardiogram is shown in Figure 20.11. It is quite striking that, although the heart's major function is the *mechanical* pumping of blood, it is most easily monitored by using the *electrical* impulses generated by tiny voltaic cells.

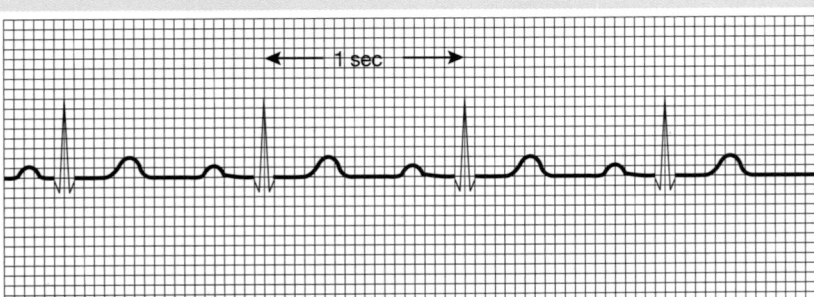

FIGURE 20.11 An electrocardiogram (ECG) printout is a strip of graph paper with the record of the electrical events monitored by electrodes attached to the body surface. The vertical displacement is the emf.

occurring within a voltaic cell, indicating that the cell reaction has reached equilibrium. That is, when $E = 0$, the reaction quotient equals the equilibrium constant for the reaction, $Q = K$. Substituting $E = 0$ and $Q = K$ into the Nernst equation at 298 K gives

$$0 = E^\circ - \frac{0.0592}{n} \log K$$

Rearranging this equation gives

$$\log K = \frac{nE^\circ}{0.0592} \qquad [20.18]$$

This useful equation tells us that the equilibrium constant for a redox reaction can be obtained from the value of the standard emf for the reaction.

SAMPLE EXERCISE 20.12

Using standard electrode potentials listed in Appendix E, calculate the equilibrium constant at 25°C for the reaction

$$O_2(g) + 4H^+(aq) + 4Fe^{2+}(aq) \longrightarrow 4Fe^{3+}(aq) + 2H_2O(l)$$

SOLUTION

$O_2(g) + 4H^+(aq) + 4e^- \longrightarrow 2H_2O(l)$	$E^\circ_{red} = 1.23$ V
$4Fe^{2+}(aq) \longrightarrow 4Fe^{3+}(aq) + 4e^-$	$E^\circ_{ox} = -0.77$ V
$O_2(g) + 4H^+(aq) + 4Fe^{2+}(aq) \longrightarrow 4Fe^{3+}(aq) + 2H_2O(l)$	$E^\circ = 0.46$ V

From the half-reactions given above we see that $n = 4$. Using Equation 20.18, we have

$$\log K = \frac{nE^\circ}{0.0592 \text{ V}} = \frac{4(0.46 \text{ V})}{0.0592 \text{ V}} = 31.1$$

$$K = 10^{31.1} = 1 \times 10^{31}$$

Thus, Fe^{2+} ions are stable in acidic solutions only in the absence of O_2 (unless a suitable reducing agent is present).

PRACTICE EXERCISE

Using standard electrode potentials (Appendix E), calculate the equilibrium constant at 25°C for the reaction

$$2IO_3^-(aq) + 5Cu(s) + 12H^+(aq) \longrightarrow I_2(s) + 5Cu^{2+}(aq) + 6H_2O(l)$$

Answer: $K = 1 \times 10^{145}$

20.7 Commercial Voltaic Cells

Voltaic cells are widely used as convenient energy sources whose primary virtue is portability. Although any spontaneous redox reaction can serve as the basis of a voltaic cell, making a commercial cell that utilizes a particular redox reaction can require considerable ingenuity. The salt-bridge cells that we have been discussing provide us with considerable insight into the operation of voltaic cells. However, these cells are generally unsuitable for commercial use because they have high internal resistances. This means that the flow of current within

John D. Worley and James Fournier, "A Home-made Lemon Battery," *J. Chem. Educ.* **1988**, *65*, 158.

Lee R. Summerlin, Christie L. Borgford, and Julie B. Ealy, "Making a Simple Battery: The *Gerber Cell*," *Chemical Demonstrations, A Sourcebook for Teachers, Volume 2* (Washington: American Chemical Society, 1987), pp. 115–16.

Point of Emphasis: The emf of two or more cells connected in series is the *sum* of the individual cell emfs.

Learning Goal 9: Describe the lead storage battery, the dry cell, and the nickel-cadmium cell.

Teaching Note: Automobile batteries are very heavy due to the large amount of lead they contain.

the cell, due to movement of the ions within the cell compartments and the electrolyte bridge, is restricted. Because the flow is restricted, there is resistance. As a result, if we attempt to draw a large current, voltage drops sharply. Furthermore, the cells that we have pictured so far lack the compactness and ruggedness required for portability.

Voltaic cells cannot yet compete with other common energy sources on the basis of cost alone. The cost of electricity from a common flashlight battery is on the order of $80 per kilowatt-hour. By comparison, electrical energy from power plants normally costs the consumer less than 10¢ per kilowatt-hour.

In this section, we shall consider some common batteries (Figure 20.12). A *battery* consists of one or more voltaic cells. When the cells are connected in series (that is, with the positive terminal of one attached to the negative terminal of another), the battery produces an emf that is the sum of the emfs of the individual cells.

Lead Storage Battery

One of the most common batteries is the lead storage battery used in automobiles. A 12-V lead storage battery consists of six cells, each producing 2 V. The anode of each cell is composed of lead; the cathode is composed of lead dioxide, PbO_2, packed on a metal grid. Both electrodes are immersed in sulfuric acid. The electrode reactions that occur during discharge are as follows:

Anode: $\quad Pb(s) + SO_4^{2-}(aq) \longrightarrow PbSO_4(s) + 2e^- \qquad E° = +0.356\ V$

Cathode: $\quad PbO_2(s) + SO_4^{2-}(aq) + 4H^+(aq) + 2e^- \longrightarrow$
$$PbSO_4(s) + 2H_2O(l) \qquad E° = +1.685\ V$$

$$Pb(s) + PbO_2(s) + 4H^+(aq) + 2SO_4^{2-}(aq) \longrightarrow$$
$$2PbSO_4(s) + 2H_2O(l) \qquad E° = +2.041\ V$$
$$[20.19]$$

FIGURE 20.12 Batteries are voltaic cells that serve as portable sources of electricity. Batteries vary markedly in size and in the electrochemical reaction used to generate electricity. The large battery in back is a lead-based automobile battery. Those in front are, from left to right, rechargeable nickel-cadmium batteries, alkaline cells, and a conventional zinc-graphite dry cell. (© Richard Megna/Fundamental Photographs)

The reactants Pb and PbO_2, between which electron transfer occurs, serve as the electrodes. Because the reactants are solids, there is no need to separate the cell into anode and cathode compartments; the Pb and PbO_2 cannot come into direct physical contact unless one electrode plate touches another. To keep the electrodes from touching, wood or glass-fiber spacers are placed between them. To increase the current output, each cell contains a number of anode and cathode plates, as shown in Figure 20.13.

Using a reaction whose reactants and products contain solids has another benefit. Because solids are excluded from the reaction quotient for a reaction, Q, the relative amounts of Pb(s), PbO_2(s), and $PbSO_4$(s) have no effect on the emf of the lead storage battery, helping the battery maintain a relatively constant emf during discharge. The emf does vary somewhat with use because the concentration of H_2SO_4 varies with the extent of cell discharge. As Equation 20.19 indicates, H_2SO_4 is consumed during the discharge.

One advantage of a lead storage battery is that it can be recharged. During recharging, an external source of energy is used to reverse the direction of the spontaneous redox reaction, Equation 20.19. Thus, the overall process during charging is as follows:

$$2PbSO_4(s) + 2H_2O(l) \longrightarrow Pb(s) + PbO_2(s) + 4H^+(aq) + 2SO_4^{2-}(aq)$$

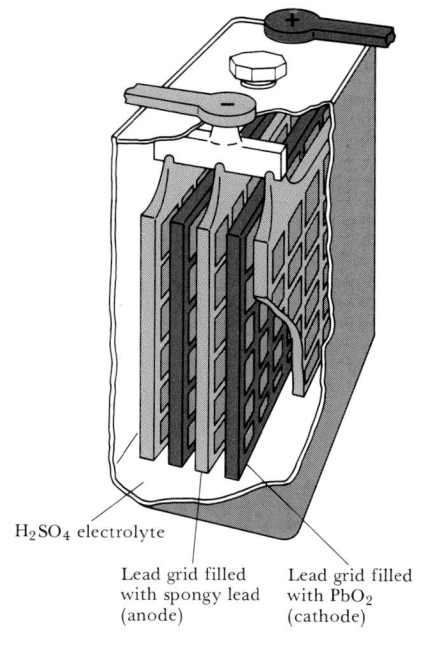

H_2SO_4 electrolyte

Lead grid filled with spongy lead (anode)   Lead grid filled with PbO_2 (cathode)

The energy necessary for recharging the battery is provided in an automobile by a generator driven by the engine. Recharging is possible because $PbSO_4$ formed during discharge adheres to the electrodes. Thus, as the external source forces electrons from one electrode to another, the $PbSO_4$ is converted to Pb at one electrode and to PbO_2 at the other; these, of course, are the materials of a fully charged cell.

A problem can arise if the battery is charged too rapidly: Water may be decomposed into H_2 and O_2. Besides the explosive potential of H_2–O_2 mixtures, this secondary reaction can shorten the lifetime of the battery. The evolution of these gases can dislodge Pb, PbO_2, or $PbSO_4$ from the plates. These solids can then accumulate as a sludge at the bottom of the battery. In time, they may form a short circuit that renders the cell useless.

These problems can be substantially reduced by adding calcium (about 0.07 percent by mass) to the lead in forming the electrodes. The presence of the calcium reduces the extent to which water is decomposed during the charging cycle. In newer batteries, electrolysis of water is sufficiently low so that the battery is "sealed"; that is, no provision is made for addition of water and escape of gases, as was necessary in the older designs.

Dry Cell

The common dry cell is widely used in flashlights, portable radios, and the like. In fact, a dry cell is often called a flashlight battery. It is also known as the Leclanché cell after its inventor, who patented it in 1866. In the acid version, the anode consists of a zinc can in contact with a paste of MnO_2, NH_4Cl, and carbon. An inert cathode, consisting of a graphite rod, is immersed in the center of the paste, as shown in Figure 20.14. The cell has an exterior layer of cardboard or metal to seal it against the atmosphere. The electrode reactions are complex, and the cathode reaction appears to vary with the rate of discharge.

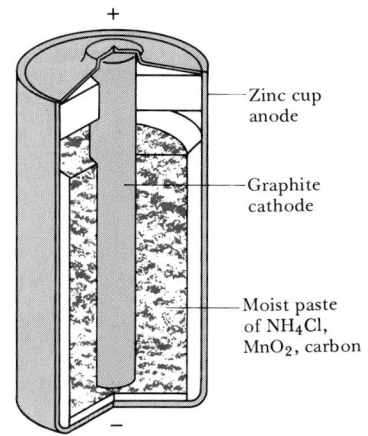

Zinc cup anode

Graphite cathode

Moist paste of NH_4Cl, MnO_2, carbon

The reactions at the electrodes are generally represented as shown below:

Anode: $$Zn(s) \longrightarrow Zn^{2+}(aq) + 2e^-$$

Cathode: $$2NH_4^+(aq) + 2MnO_2(s) + 2e^- \longrightarrow Mn_2O_3(s) + 2NH_3(aq) + H_2O(l)$$

Only a fraction of the cathode material, that near the electrode, is electrochemically active because of the limited mobility of the chemicals in the cell.

In the alkaline version of a dry cell, NH_4Cl is replaced by KOH, which is basic (alkaline). The anode reaction still involves oxidation of Zn, but the zinc is present as a powder, mixed with the electrolyte in a gel formulation. As in a common dry cell, the cathode reaction involves reduction of MnO_2. Figure 20.15 shows a cutaway view of a miniature alkaline cell of the type used in camera exposure controls, calculators, and some watches. Although more costly than the common dry cell, alkaline cells provide improved performance. They maintain usable voltage over a longer fraction of consumption of anode and cathode materials, and they provide up to 50 percent more total energy than a common dry cell of the same size.

Nickel-Cadmium Batteries

Because dry cells are not rechargeable, they have to be replaced frequently. For this reason, a rechargeable cell, the nickel-cadmium battery, has become increasingly popular, especially for use in battery-operated tools and calculators. Cadmium metal acts as the anode, and $NiO_2(s)$, which is reduced to $Ni(OH)_2(s)$, serves as the cathode. The following electrode reactions occur within this cell during discharge:

Anode: $$Cd(s) + 2OH^-(aq) \longrightarrow Cd(OH)_2(s) + 2e^-$$

Cathode: $$NiO_2(s) + 2H_2O(l) + 2e^- \longrightarrow Ni(OH)_2(s) + 2OH^-(aq)$$

As in the lead storage cell, the solid reaction products adhere to the electrodes. This permits the reactions to be readily reversed during charging. Because no gases are produced during either charging or discharging, the battery can be sealed.

Fuel Cells

Teaching Note: The H_2-O_2 fuel cells are currently being used in the U.S. space-shuttle fleet.

Many substances are used as fuels. The thermal energy released by combustion is often converted to electrical energy. The heat may convert water to steam,

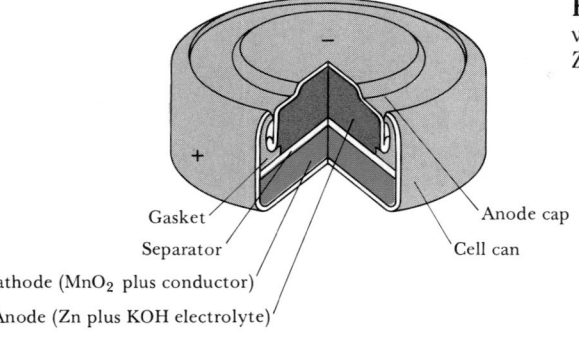

FIGURE 20.15 Cutaway view of a miniature alkaline Zn–MnO_2 dry cell.

Gasket
Separator
Cathode (MnO_2 plus conductor)
Anode (Zn plus KOH electrolyte)
Anode cap
Cell can

which drives a turbine that in turn drives the generator. Typically a maximum of only 40 percent of the energy from combustion is converted to electricity; the remainder is lost as heat. The *direct* production of electricity from fuels by a voltaic cell could, in principle, yield a higher rate of conversion of the chemical energy of the reaction. Voltaic cells that perform this conversion using conventional fuels, such as H_2 and CH_4, are called **fuel cells.**

A great deal of research has gone into attempts to develop practical fuel cells. One of the problems encountered is the high operating temperature of most cells, which not only siphons off energy but also accelerates corrosion of cell parts. A low-temperature cell has been developed that uses H_2, but the present cost of the cell makes it too expensive for large-scale use. However, it has been used in special situations, such as in space vehicles. For example, a $H_2 - O_2$ fuel cell was used as the primary source of electrical energy on the *Apollo* moon flights. The weight of a fuel cell sufficient for 11 days in space was approximately 500 lb. This may be compared to the several tons that would have been required for an engine-generator set.

The electrode reactions in the $H_2 - O_2$ fuel cell are as follows:

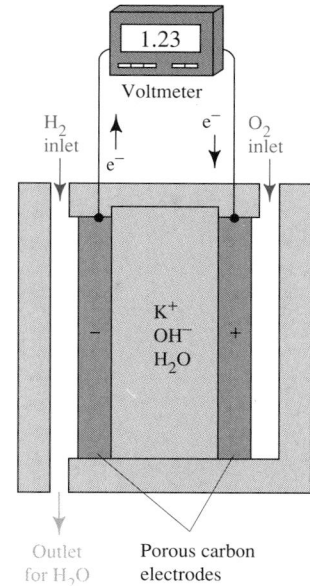

FIGURE 20.16 Cross section of a $H_2 - O_2$ fuel cell.

Anode: $\quad 2H_2(g) + 4OH^-(aq) \longrightarrow 4H_2O(l) + 4e^-$

Cathode: $\quad \underline{4e^- + O_2(g) + 2H_2O(l) \longrightarrow 4OH^-(aq)}$

$$2H_2(g) + O_2(g) \longrightarrow 2H_2O(l)$$

The cell is illustrated in Figure 20.16. The electrodes are composed of hollow tubes of porous, compressed carbon impregnated with catalyst; the electrolyte is KOH.

20.8 Electrolysis

We have seen that spontaneous oxidation-reduction reactions are used as the basis for voltaic cells. Conversely, it is possible to use electrical energy to cause nonspontaneous oxidation-reduction reactions to occur. For example, electricity can be used to decompose molten sodium chloride into its component elements:

$$2NaCl(l) \longrightarrow 2Na(l) + Cl_2(g)$$

Such processes, which are driven by an outside source of electrical energy, are called **electrolysis reactions** and take place in **electrolytic cells.**

An electrolytic cell consists of two electrodes in a molten salt or solution. The cell is driven by a battery or some other source of direct electrical current. The battery acts as an electron pump, pushing electrons into one electrode and pulling them from the other. Withdrawing electrons from an electrode gives it a positive charge, and adding electrons to an electrode makes it negative. In the electrolysis of molten NaCl, shown in Figure 20.17, Na^+ ions pick up electrons at the negative electrode and are thereby reduced. As the Na^+ ions in the vicinity of this electrode are depleted, additional Na^+ ions migrate in. In a related fashion, there is a net movement of Cl^- ions to the positive electrode, where they give up electrons and are thereby oxidized. Just as in voltaic cells, the

Point of Emphasis: In electrolytic cells, as in voltaic cells, oxidation occurs at the anode, and reduction occurs at the cathode. The signs of the electrodes are reversed, however; in electrolytic cells the cathode is negative, and the anode is positive.

FIGURE 20.17 Electrolysis of molten sodium chloride.

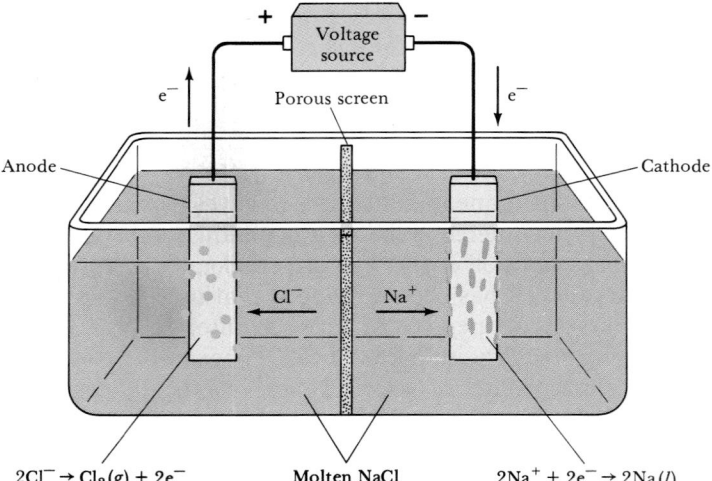

Figure 20.17

$2Cl^- \rightarrow Cl_2(g) + 2e^-$ Molten NaCl $2Na^+ + 2e^- \rightarrow 2Na(l)$

electrode at which reduction occurs is called the cathode, and the electrode at which oxidation occurs is called the anode.

Anode:	$2Cl^-(l) \longrightarrow Cl_2(g) + 2e^-$
Cathode:	$2Na^+(l) + 2e^- \longrightarrow 2Na(l)$

$$2Na^+(l) + 2Cl^-(l) \longrightarrow 2Na(l) + Cl_2(g)$$

Notice that the sign convention for the electrodes in an electrolytic cell is just the opposite of that for a voltaic cell. The cathode in the electrolytic cell is negative because electrons are being forced onto it by the external voltage source. The anode is positive because electrons are being withdrawn by the external source.

Electrolyses of molten salts and molten-salt solutions for the production of active metals such as sodium and aluminum are important industrial processes. We shall have more to say about them in Chapter 24, when we discuss processes for obtaining metals.

Electrolysis of Aqueous Solutions

When an aqueous solution is used in an electrolytic cell, we must consider whether it is the water or the solute that is oxidized or reduced. Water can be both oxidized (to form O_2) and reduced (to form H_2). For example, sodium cannot be prepared by electrolysis of aqueous solutions of NaCl because water is more easily reduced than $Na^+(aq)$, as we see from the following electrode potentials:

$$2H_2O(l) + 2e^- \longrightarrow H_2(g) + 2OH^-(aq) \qquad E^\circ_{red} = -0.83 \text{ V}$$
$$Na^+(aq) + e^- \longrightarrow Na(s) \qquad E^\circ_{red} = -2.71 \text{ V}$$

Recall that the more positive (or less negative) the E° for a half-reaction, the more readily that reaction occurs. Consequently, H_2 rather than Na is produced at the cathode.

The possible anode reactions are the oxidation of Cl^- and of H_2O:

$$2Cl^-(aq) \longrightarrow Cl_2(g) + 2e^- \qquad E^\circ_{ox} = -1.36 \text{ V}$$

$$2H_2O(l) \longrightarrow 4H^+(aq) + O_2(g) + 4e^- \qquad E^\circ_{ox} = -1.23 \text{ V}$$

These standard oxidation potentials are not greatly different, but they do suggest that H_2O should be oxidized more readily than Cl^-. However, the actual voltage required for a reaction is sometimes much greater than the theoretical voltage based on the electrode potentials. The additional voltage required to cause electrolysis is called the *overvoltage*. The overvoltage is believed to be caused by slow reaction rates at the electrodes. Overvoltages for the deposition of metals are low, but those required for the liberation of hydrogen gas or oxygen gas are usually high. The overvoltage for O_2 formation usually is sufficiently high to favor oxidation of Cl^- rather than H_2O. Consequently, electrolysis of aqueous solutions of NaCl, known as brines, normally produces H_2 and Cl_2 unless the concentration of Cl^- is quite low:

Anode: $2Cl^-(aq) \longrightarrow Cl_2(g) + 2e^-$

Cathode: $\underline{2H_2O(l) + 2e^- \longrightarrow H_2(g) + 2OH^-(aq)}$

$2Cl^-(aq) + 2H_2O(l) \longrightarrow Cl_2(g) + H_2(g) + 2OH^-(aq)$

The Na^+ ion is merely a spectator ion (Section 4.4) in the electrolysis. This process is used commercially because all the products (H_2, Cl_2, and NaOH) are commercially important chemicals.

Electrode potentials can be used to determine the minimum emf required for an electrolysis. In the case of the formation of H_2 and Cl_2 from a brine solution under standard conditions, a minimum emf of 2.19 V is required:

$$E^\circ = E^\circ_{ox}(Cl^-) + E^\circ_{red}(H_2O)$$
$$= -1.36 \text{ V} + (-0.83 \text{ V}) = -2.19 \text{ V}$$

The emf calculated above is negative, reminding us that the process is not spontaneous but must be driven by an outside source of energy.

SAMPLE EXERCISE 20.13

Explain why the electrolysis of an aqueous solution of $CuCl_2$ produces Cu(s) and $Cl_2(g)$. What is the minimum emf required for this process under standard conditions?

SOLUTION At the cathode we can envision reduction of either Cu^{2+} or H_2O:

$$Cu^{2+}(aq) + 2e^- \longrightarrow Cu(s) \qquad E^\circ_{red} = 0.34 \text{ V}$$
$$2H_2O(l) + 2e^- \longrightarrow H_2(g) + 2OH^-(aq) \qquad E^\circ_{red} = -0.83 \text{ V}$$

The electrode potentials indicate that reduction of Cu^{2+} occurs more readily. Reduction of H_2O is made even more difficult because of the overvoltage for H_2 formation.

At the anode, we can envision the oxidation of either Cl^- or H_2O. As in the case of NaCl solutions, Cl_2 is usually produced because of the overvoltage for O_2 formation.

The minimum emf required for this electrolysis under standard conditions is 1.02 V:

$$E° = E°_{red}(Cu^{2+}) + E°_{ox}(Cl^-)$$
$$= 0.34\ V + (-1.36\ V) = -1.02\ V$$

PRACTICE EXERCISE

(a) What are the expected products of electrolysis of a 1.0 *M* aqueous HBr solution?
(b) What is the minimum emf required to produce these products?
Answers: **(a)** at the cathode, $H_2(g)$; at the anode, $Br_2(l)$; **(b)** -1.06 V

Electrolysis with Active Electrodes

In our discussion of the electrolysis of molten NaCl and of NaCl solutions, we considered the electrodes to be inert. Consequently, they did not undergo reaction but merely served as the surface at which oxidation and reduction of solvent or solute occurred. However, the electrodes themselves often participate in the electrolysis process.

When aqueous solutions are electrolyzed using metal electrodes, an electrode will be oxidized if its oxidation potential is more positive than that for water. For example, nickel is oxidized more readily than water:

$$Ni(s) \longrightarrow Ni^{2+}(aq) + 2e^- \qquad\qquad E°_{ox} = +0.28\ V$$
$$2H_2O(l) \longrightarrow 4H^+(aq) + O_2(g) + 4e^- \qquad E°_{ox} = -1.23\ V$$

If nickel is made the anode in an electrolytic cell, nickel metal is oxidized as the anode reaction. If Ni^{2+} *(aq)* is present in the solution, it is reduced at the cathode in preference to reduction of water. An electrolytic cell of this kind is illustrated in Figure 20.18. As current flows, nickel dissolves from the anode and deposits on the cathode:

Anode: $\qquad\qquad\qquad\qquad Ni(s) \longrightarrow Ni^{2+}(aq) + 2e^-$

Cathode: $\qquad\qquad Ni^{2+}(aq) + 2e^- \longrightarrow Ni(s)$

Electrolytic processes involving active metal electrodes — that is, in which the metal electrodes participate in the cell reaction — have several important applications. We will see in Chapter 24 that electrolysis affords a means of

FIGURE 20.18 Electrolytic cell with an active metal electrode. Nickel dissolves from the anode to form $Ni^{2+}(aq)$. At the cathode, $Ni^{2+}(aq)$ is reduced and forms a nickel "plate."

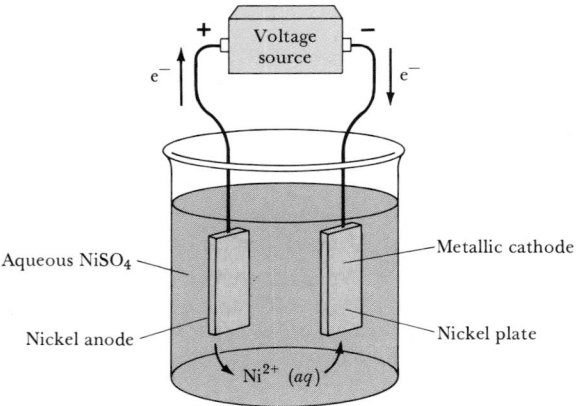

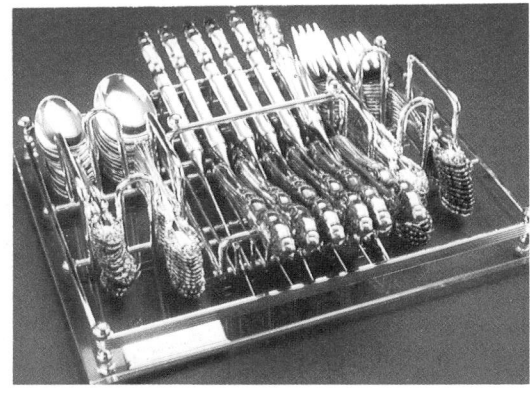

(a)   (b)

FIGURE 20.19 Electroplating of silverware. (a) The silverware is being withdrawn from the electroplating bath. (b) The polished final product. (Courtesy Oneida Silversmiths)

purifying crude metals such as copper, zinc, cobalt, and nickel. An additional important application is in *electroplating,* in which one metal is "plated," or deposited, on another. Electroplating is used to protect objects against corrosion and to improve their appearance. For example, fine dinnerware is silver-plated electrochemically by making the dinnerware utensils the cathode in an electrolytic plating bath (Figure 20.19).

20.9 Quantitative Aspects of Electrolysis

The stoichiometry of a half-reaction tells us how many electrons are needed to achieve an electrolytic process. For example, the reduction of Na^+ to Na is a one-electron process:

$$Na^+ + e^- \longrightarrow Na$$

Thus, 1 mol of electrons will plate out 1 mol of Na metal, 2 mol of electrons will plate out 2 mol of Na metal, and so forth. Similarly, 2 mol of electrons are required to produce 1 mol of copper from Cu^{2+}, and 3 mol of electrons are required to produce 1 mol of aluminum from Al^{3+}:

$$Cu^{2+} + 2e^- \longrightarrow Cu$$
$$Al^{3+} + 3e^- \longrightarrow Al$$

For any half-reaction, the amount of a substance that is reduced or oxidized in an electrolytic cell is directly proportional to the number of electrons passed into the cell.

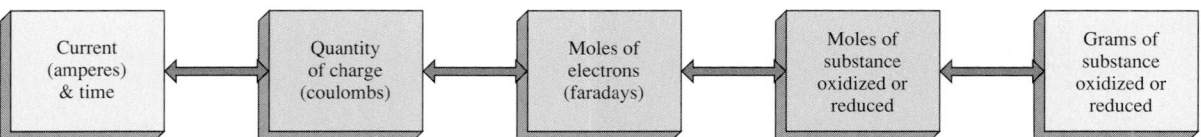

| Current (amperes) & time | Quantity of charge (coulombs) | Moles of electrons (faradays) | Moles of substance oxidized or reduced | Grams of substance oxidized or reduced |

FIGURE 20.20   The steps relating the quantity of electrical charge used in electrolysis to the amounts of substances oxidized or reduced.

The quantity of charge passing through an electrical circuit, such as that in an electrolytic cell, is generally measured in *coulombs*. As noted in Section 20.5, the charge on 1 mol of electrons is 96,500 C (1 faraday):

$$\text{Charge of 1 mol of electrons} = 96{,}500\ C = 1F$$

In terms of other, perhaps more familiar electrical units, a coulomb is the quantity of electrical charge passing a point in a circuit in 1 s when the current is 1 ampere (A).* Therefore, the number of coulombs passing through a cell can be obtained by multiplying the amperage and the elapsed time in seconds:

$$\text{Coulombs} = \text{amperes} \times \text{seconds} \qquad [20.20]$$

Figure 20.20 shows how the quantities of substances produced or consumed in electrolysis are related to the quantity of electrical charge that is used. The steps shown are used in Sample Exercise 20.14. Although the exercise involves electrolytic cells, the same relationships can also be applied to voltaic cells.

Learning Goal 11: Interrelate time, current, and the amount of substance produced or consumed in an electrolysis reaction; given two of the three quantities, you should be able to calculate the third.

SAMPLE EXERCISE 20.14

Calculate the mass of aluminum produced in 1.00 hr by the electrolysis of molten $AlCl_3$ if the electrical current is 10.0 A.

SOLUTION   *First,* we use Equation 20.20 to calculate the coulombs of electrical charge that are passed into the electrolytic cell:

$$\text{Coulombs} = \text{amperes} \times \text{seconds}$$

$$= (10.0\ A)(1.00\ hr)\left(\frac{3600\ s}{1\ hr}\right)\left(\frac{1\ C}{1\ A\text{-}s}\right) = 3.60 \times 10^4\ C$$

Second, we calculate the number of moles of electrons (that is, the number of faradays of electrical charge) that pass into the cell:

$$\text{Moles e}^- = (3.60 \times 10^4\ C)\left(\frac{1\ \text{mol e}^-}{96{,}500\ C}\right) = 0.373\ \text{mol e}^-$$

Third, we relate the number of moles of electrons to the number of moles of aluminum being formed. The half-reaction for the reduction of Al^{3+} is

$$Al^{3+} + 3e^- \longrightarrow Al$$

---

* Conversely, current is the rate of flow of electricity. An ampere (often referred to merely as an amp) is the current associated with the flow of 1 C past a point each second.

Thus, 3 mol of electrons (that is, 3 F of electrical charge) are required to form 1 mol of Al:

$$\text{Moles Al} = (0.373 \text{ mol e}^-)\left(\frac{1 \text{ mol Al}}{3 \text{ mol e}^-}\right) = 0.124 \text{ mol Al}$$

Finally, we convert moles to grams

$$\text{Grams Al} = (0.124 \text{ mol Al})\left(\frac{27.0 \text{ g Al}}{1 \text{ mol Al}}\right) = 3.36 \text{ g Al}$$

Because each step involves a multiplication by a new factor, the steps can be combined into a single sequence of factors:

$$\text{Grams Al} = (3.60 \times 10^4 \text{ C})\left(\frac{1 \text{ mol e}^-}{96,500 \text{ C}}\right)\left(\frac{1 \text{ mol Al}}{3 \text{ mol e}^-}\right)\left(\frac{27.0 \text{ g Al}}{1 \text{ mol Al}}\right) = 3.36 \text{ g}$$

PRACTICE EXERCISE

The half-reaction for formation of magnesium metal upon electrolysis of molten $MgCl_2$ is $Mg^{2+} + 2e^- \longrightarrow Mg$. Calculate the mass of magnesium formed upon passage of a current of 60.0 A for a period of 4.00×10^3 s.   *Answer:* 30.2 g of Mg

Electrical Work

This is a good point at which to consider the relationship between electrochemical processes and work. We have already seen that a positive value for E is associated with a negative value for the free-energy change and thus with a spontaneous process. We also know that for any spontaneous process, ΔG is a measure of the maximum useful work, w_{max}, that can be extracted from the process: $\Delta G = w_{max}$. ∞ (Sec. 19.5)   Because $\Delta G = -nFE$, the maximum useful electrical work obtainable from a voltaic cell should be simply

$$w_{max} = -nFE \qquad [20.21]$$

A word about sign conventions is in order here. Remember that work done *by* the system *on* its surroundings is indicated by a negative sign for w. ∞ (Sec. 5.2)   Therefore, a negative value for w_{max} corresponds to a spontaneous process, for which E is positive.

Notice that the maximum work obtainable is proportional to the cell potential E. We can think of E as a kind of pressure, a measure of the driving force for the process. Recall from Section 20.4 that the units of E are J/C; w_{max} is also proportional to the number of coulombs that flow, measured by nF. When we put these quantities together, we can see how the units cancel to leave us with units of energy:

$$w_{max} = -n \times F \times E$$

$$\text{J} = \text{mol} \times \frac{\text{C}}{\text{mol}} \times \frac{\text{J}}{\text{C}}$$

In an electrolytic cell, we employ an external source of energy to bring about a nonspontaneous electrochemical process. In this case, ΔG for the cell process is positive, and the cell potential is negative. The *minimum* amount of work done on the system to cause the nonspontaneous cell reaction to occur, w_{min}, is given by

$$w_{min} = -nFE$$

Learning Goal 12: Calculate the maximum electrical work performed by a voltaic cell and the minimum electrical work required of an electrolytic process.

Point of Emphasis: When work has a negative value, work is performed *by* the system.

where E is the calculated cell potential. In practice, we always need to expend more than this minimum amount of work because of inefficiencies in the process. In addition, a higher potential E' may be required to cause the cell reaction to occur, because of overvoltage. In this case, the minimum work required is given by

$$w_{min} = -nFE' \quad\quad\quad [20.22]$$

Electrical work is usually expressed in energy units of watts times time. The *watt* is a unit of electrical power, that is, the rate of energy expenditure:

$$1 \text{ watt (W)} = 1 \text{ J/s}$$

Therefore, a watt-second is a joule. The unit employed by electric utilities is the kilowatt-hour (kWh), which works out to be 3.6×10^6 J:

$$1 \text{ kWh} = (1000 \text{ W})(1 \text{ hr})\left(\frac{3600 \text{ s}}{1 \text{ hr}}\right)\left(\frac{1 \text{ J/s}}{1 \text{ W}}\right) = 3.6 \times 10^6 \text{ J} \quad [20.23]$$

Using these considerations, we can calculate the maximum work obtainable from voltaic cells and the minimum work required to bring about desired electrolysis reactions.

SAMPLE EXERCISE 20.15

Calculate the minimum number of kilowatt-hours of electricity required to produce 1000 kg of aluminum by electrolysis of Al^{3+} if the required emf is 4.50 V.

SOLUTION We need to employ Equation 20.22 to calculate w_{min} for an applied potential of 4.50 V. First we need to calculate nF, the number of coulombs required.

$$\text{Coulombs} = (1000 \text{ kg Al})\left(\frac{1000 \text{ g Al}}{1 \text{ kg Al}}\right)\left(\frac{1 \text{ mol Al}}{27.0 \text{ g Al}}\right)\left(\frac{3 \text{ } F}{1 \text{ mol Al}}\right)\left(\frac{96,500 \text{ C}}{1 \text{ } F}\right)$$

$$= 1.07 \times 10^{10} \text{ C}$$

We can now employ Equation 20.22 to calculate w_{min}. In doing so, we must apply the unit conversion factor of Equation 20.23:

$$\text{Kilowatt-hours} = (1.07 \times 10^{10} \text{ C})(4.50 \text{ V})\left(\frac{1 \text{ J}}{1 \text{ C-V}}\right)\left(\frac{1 \text{ kWh}}{3.6 \times 10^6 \text{ J}}\right)$$

$$= 1.34 \times 10^4 \text{ kWh}$$

(The negative sign on the right in Equation 20.22 is canceled by the negative sign for E' because it is a voltage applied to make the cell reaction occur.)

This quantity of energy does not include the energy used to mine, transport, and process the aluminum ore, and to keep the electrolysis bath molten during electrolysis. A typical electrolytic cell used to reduce aluminum is only 40 percent efficient, 60 percent of the electrical energy being dissipated as heat. It therefore requires on the order of 33 kWh of electricity to produce 1 kg of aluminum. The aluminum industry consumes about 2 percent of the electrical energy generated in the United States. Because this is used mainly for reduction of aluminum, recycling this metal saves large quantities of energy.

PRACTICE EXERCISE

Calculate the minimum number of kilowatt-hours of electricity required to produce 1.00 kg of Mg from electrolysis of molten $MgCl_2$ if the applied emf is 5.00 V.
Answer: 11.0 kWh

SAMPLE EXERCISE 20.16

A 12-V lead storage battery contains 410 g of lead in its anode plates and a stoichiometrically equivalent amount of PbO_2 in the cathodes. **(a)** What is the maximum number of coulombs of electrical charge it can deliver without being recharged? **(b)** For how many hours could the battery deliver a steady current of 1.0 A assuming that the current does not fall during discharge? **(c)** What is the maximum electrical work that the battery can accomplish in kilowatt-hours?

SOLUTION   (a) The lead anode undergoes a two-electron oxidation:

$$Pb \longrightarrow Pb^{2+} + 2e^-$$

Consequently, $2\ F \simeq 1$ mol Pb. Using this relationship, we have

$$\text{Coulombs} = (410\ \text{g Pb}) \left(\frac{1\ \text{mol Pb}}{207\ \text{g Pb}} \right) \left(\frac{2\ F}{1\ \text{mol Pb}} \right) \left(\frac{96,500\ \text{C}}{1\ F} \right)$$

$$= 3.82 \times 10^5\ \text{C}$$

Although the emf of a cell is independent of the masses of the solid reactants involved in the cell, the total electrical charge the cell can deliver depends on these quantities. The size and surface area further affect the *rate* at which electrical charge can be delivered.

(b) We calculate the number of hours of operation at a current level of 1.0 A by recalling that a coulomb corresponds to a current of 1 A flowing for 1 s:

$$\text{Hours} = (3.8 \times 10^5\ \text{C}) \left(\frac{1\ \text{A-s}}{1\ \text{C}} \right) \left(\frac{1\ \text{hr}}{3600\ \text{s}} \right) \left(\frac{1}{1.0\ \text{A}} \right) = 1.1 \times 10^2\ \text{hr}$$

This battery might be described as a 110 A-hr battery.

(c) The maximum work is given by the product $-nFE$, Equation 20.22:

$$\text{Kilowatt-hours} = -(3.82 \times 10^5\ \text{C})(12\ \text{V}) \left(\frac{1\ \text{J}}{1\ \text{C-V}} \right) \left(\frac{1\ \text{kWh}}{3.6 \times 10^6\ \text{J}} \right)$$

$$= -1.3\ \text{kWh}$$

(The negative sign indicates that the system does work on its surroundings.)

PRACTICE EXERCISE

A "deep discharge" lead-acid battery for marine use is advertised as having an 80-A-hr capacity. What amount of Pb would be oxidized if this battery were discharged so as to consume 80 percent of its capacity?   ***Answer:*** 247 g of Pb

20.10 Corrosion

Before we close our discussion of electrochemistry, we should apply some of what we have learned to a very important problem, the **corrosion** of metals. Corrosion reactions are redox reactions in which a metal is attacked by some substance in its environment and converted to an unwanted compound.

All metals except gold and platinum are thermodynamically capable of undergoing oxidation in air at room temperature. When the oxidation process is not inhibited in some way, it can be very destructive. However, oxidation can result in the formation of an insulating, protective oxide layer that prevents further reaction of the underlying metal. For example, on the basis of the standard oxidation potential for aluminum ($E^\circ_{ox} = 1.66$ V), we would expect aluminum to be very readily oxidized. The many aluminum soft-drink and beer cans that litter the environment are ample evidence, however, that aluminum undergoes only very slow chemical corrosion. The exceptional stability of this active metal in air is due to the formation of a thin, protective coat of

Learning Goal 13: Describe corrosion in terms of the electrochemistry involved, and explain the principles that underlie cathodic protection.

Point of Emphasis: Although only gold and platinum are *thermodynamically* stable toward oxidation, the process is too slow to detect for certain other metals, such as iridium and rhodium.

A. I. Onuchukwu, "Evaluation of Corrosion Susceptibility of a Metal: Student Corrosion Experiment II," *J. Chem. Educ.* **1988,** *65,* 934.

oxide — a hydrated form of Al_2O_3 — on the surface of the metal. The oxide coat is impermeable to the passage of O_2 or H_2O and so protects the underlying metal from further corrosion. Magnesium, which also has a high oxidation potential, is similarly protected. Some metal alloys, such as stainless steel, also form protective, impervious oxide coats.

Corrosion of Iron

One of the most familiar corrosion processes is the rusting of iron (Figure 20.21). From an economic standpoint, this is a significant process. It is estimated that up to 20 percent of the iron produced annually in this country is used to replace iron objects that have been discarded because of rust damage.

The rusting of iron is known to require oxygen; iron does not rust in water unless O_2 is present. Rusting also requires water; iron does not rust in oil, even if it contains O_2, unless H_2O is also present. Other factors — such as the pH of the solution, the presence of salts, contact with metals more difficult to oxidize than iron, and stress on the iron — can accelerate rusting.

The corrosion of iron is generally believed to be electrochemical in nature. A region on the surface of the iron serves as an anode at which the iron undergoes oxidation:

$$Fe(s) \longrightarrow Fe^{2+}(aq) + 2e^- \qquad E^\circ_{ox} = 0.44 \text{ V}$$

The electrons so produced migrate through the metal to another portion of the surface that serves as the cathode. Here oxygen can be reduced:

$$O_2(g) + 4H^+(aq) + 4e^- \longrightarrow 2H_2O(l) \qquad E^\circ_{red} = 1.23 \text{ V}$$

Notice that H^+ takes part in the reduction of O_2. As the concentration of H^+ is lowered (that is, as pH is increased), the reduction of O_2 becomes less favorable. It is observed that iron in contact with a solution whose pH is above 9 does not corrode. In the course of the corrosion, the Fe^{2+} formed at the anode is further oxidized to Fe^{3+}. The Fe^{3+} forms the hydrated iron(III) oxide known as rust.*

$$4Fe^{2+}(aq) + O_2(g) + 4H_2O(l) + 2xH_2O(l) \longrightarrow 2Fe_2O_3 \cdot xH_2O(s) + 8H^+(aq)$$

---

* Frequently, metal compounds obtained from aqueous solution have water associated with them. For example, copper(II) sulfate crystallizes from water with 5 mol of water per mole of $CuSO_4$. We represent this formula as $CuSO_4 \cdot 5H_2O$. Such compounds are called hydrates (Section 13.1). Rust is a hydrate of iron(III) oxide with a variable amount of water of hydration. We represent the variable water content by writing the formula as $Fe_2O_3 \cdot xH_2O$.

FIGURE 20.21 Corrosion of iron in a shipyard. The corrosion of iron is an electrochemical process of great economic importance. The annual cost of metallic corrosion in the United States is estimated to be $70 billion. (Bonnie McGrath/Rainbow)

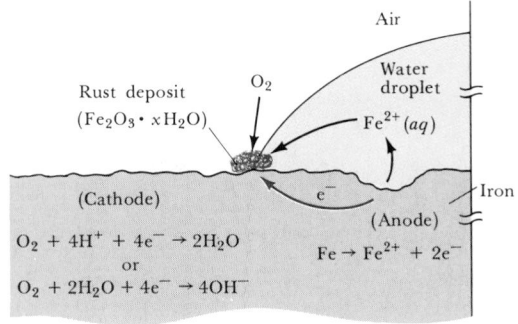

FIGURE 20.22 Corrosion of iron in contact with water.

Figure 20.22

Rust deposit
($Fe_2O_3 \cdot xH_2O$)

Air

O_2

Water droplet

$Fe^{2+}(aq)$

(Cathode)

e^-

Iron

(Anode)

$O_2 + 4H^+ + 4e^- \rightarrow 2H_2O$
or
$O_2 + 2H_2O + 4e^- \rightarrow 4OH^-$

$Fe \rightarrow Fe^{2+} + 2e^-$

Because the cathode is generally the area having the largest supply of O_2, rust often deposits there. If you look closely at a shovel after it has stood outside in the moist air with wet dirt adhered to its blade, you may notice that pitting has occurred under the dirt but that rust has formed elsewhere, where O_2 is more readily available. The corrosion process is summarized in Figure 20.22.

The enhanced corrosion caused by the presence of salts is usually evident on autos in areas where heavy salting of roads occurs during winter. The effect of salts is readily explained by the voltaic mechanism: The ions of a salt provide the electrolyte necessary for completion of the electrical circuit.

Prevention of Corrosion

Iron is often covered with a coat of paint or another metal such as tin, zinc, or chromium to protect its surface against corrosion. Sheet steel used in beverage and food cans can be coated by dipping the sheets in molten tin or by depositing a thin coat (1 to 20 μm) of tin electrochemically. The tin protects the iron only as long as the protective layer remains intact. Once it is broken and the iron exposed to air and water, tin actually promotes the corrosion of the iron by serving as the cathode in the electrochemical corrosion. As shown by the following half-cell potentials, iron is more readily oxidized than tin:

$$Fe(s) \longrightarrow Fe^{2+}(aq) + 2e^- \qquad E_{ox}^\circ = 0.44 \text{ V}$$
$$Sn(s) \longrightarrow Sn^{2+}(aq) + 2e^- \qquad E_{ox}^\circ = 0.14 \text{ V}$$

The iron therefore serves as the anode and is oxidized, as shown in Figure 20.23.

Galvanized iron is produced by coating iron with a thin layer of zinc. The zinc protects the iron against corrosion even after the surface coat is broken. In

Point of Emphasis: *Galvanized iron* is iron coated with a thin film of zinc.

FIGURE 20.23 Corrosion of iron in contact with tin.

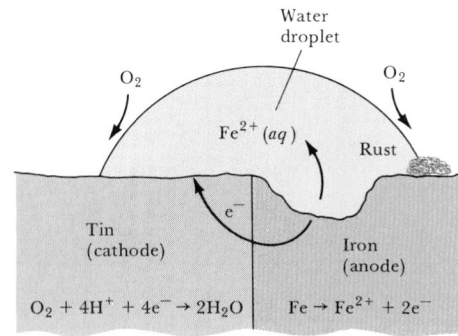

Water droplet

O_2

$Fe^{2+}(aq)$

O_2

Rust

e^-

Tin (cathode)

Iron (anode)

$O_2 + 4H^+ + 4e^- \rightarrow 2H_2O$

$Fe \rightarrow Fe^{2+} + 2e^-$

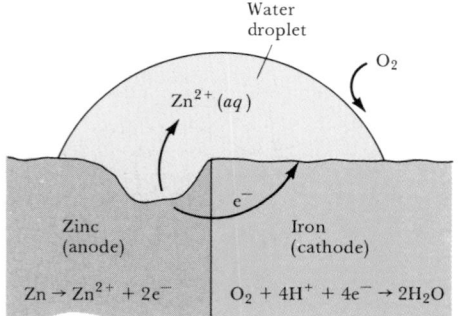

FIGURE 20.24 Cathodic protection of iron in contact with zinc.

this case, the iron serves as the cathode in the electrochemical corrosion because zinc is oxidized more easily than iron:

$$Zn(s) \longrightarrow Zn^{2+}(aq) + 2e^- \qquad E^\circ_{ox} = 0.76 \text{ V}$$

The zinc therefore serves as the anode and is corroded instead of the iron, as shown in Figure 20.24. Protection of a metal by making it the cathode in an electrochemical cell is known as **cathodic protection.** The metal that oxidizes while protecting the cathode is called the *sacrificial anode.* Underground pipelines are often protected against corrosion by making the pipeline the cathode of a voltaic cell. Pieces of an active metal such as magnesium are buried along the pipeline and connected to it by wire, as shown in Figure 20.25. In moist soil, where corrosion can occur, the active metal serves as the anode, and the pipe experiences cathodic protection.

FIGURE 20.25 Cathodic protection of an iron water pipe. The magnesium anode is surrounded by a mixture of gypsum, sodium sulfate, and clay to promote conductivity of ions. The pipe, in effect, is the cathode of a voltaic cell.

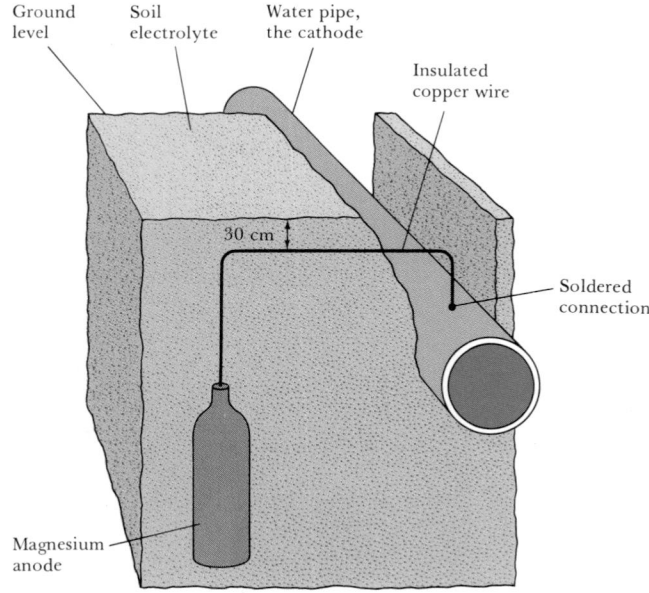

SAMPLE EXERCISE 20.17

Predict the nature of the corrosion that would take place if an iron gutter were nailed to a house using aluminum nails.

SOLUTION   A voltaic cell can be formed at the point of contact of the two metals. The metal that is more easily oxidized will serve as the anode, and the other metal will serve as the cathode. By comparing standard oxidation potentials of Al and Fe, we see that Al will be the anode:

$$Al(s) \longrightarrow Al^{3+}(aq) + 3e^- \qquad E_{ox}^\circ = 1.66 \text{ V}$$

$$Fe(s) \longrightarrow Fe^{2+}(aq) + 2e^- \qquad E_{ox}^\circ = 0.44 \text{ V}$$

The gutter will thus be protected against corrosion in the vicinity of the nail because the iron serves as the cathode. However, the nail will quickly corrode, leaving the gutter on the ground.

  What do you think would happen if aluminum siding were nailed to a house using iron nails?

PRACTICE EXERCISE

From an examination of Table 20.1, indicate which of the following metals could provide cathodic protection to iron: Al, Cu, Ni, Zn.   *Answer:* Al, Zn

For Review

Summary

Oxidation-reduction reactions are reactions that involve a change in the oxidation state of one or more elements. In every oxidation-reduction reaction, one substance is oxidized; that is, it undergoes an increase in oxidation state. This substance is referred to as a reducing agent, or reductant, because it causes the reduction of some other substance. Similarly, a substance that undergoes reduction (decrease in oxidation state) is referred to as an oxidizing agent, or oxidant, because it causes the oxidation of some other substance.

  In one approach to balancing oxidation-reduction reactions, called the method of half-reactions, the overall process is divided into two half-reactions, one for oxidation, the other for reduction. Each half-reaction is balanced separately, and the two are brought together with proper coefficients to produce a balance of electrons gained and lost.

  Spontaneous oxidation-reduction reactions can be used to generate electricity in voltaic cells. Conversely, electricity can be used to bring about nonspontaneous reactions in electrolytic cells. In either type of cell, the electrode at which oxidation occurs is called the anode, and the electrode at which reduction occurs is called the cathode.

  A voltaic cell may be thought to possess a "driving force" that moves the electrons through the external circuit, from anode to cathode. This driving force is called the electromotive force (emf) and is measured in volts. The emf of a cell can be regarded as being composed of two parts: that due to oxidation at the anode and that due to reduction at the cathode $(E_{cell} = E_{ox} + E_{red})$.

  Oxidation potentials (E_{ox}) and reduction potentials (E_{red}) can be assigned to half-reactions by defining the standard hydrogen electrode as a reference:

$$2H^+(1\ M) + 2e^- \longrightarrow H_2(1 \text{ atm}) \qquad E^\circ = 0 \text{ V}$$

Standard reduction potentials are referred to as standard electrode potentials and are tabulated for a great variety of reduction half-reactions. The oxidation potential for an oxidation half-reaction will be of the same magnitude as, but opposite in sign to, the electrode potential for the reverse reduction process. The more positive the potential associated with a half-reaction, the greater the tendency for that reaction to occur as written. Electrode potentials can be used to determine the maximum voltages generated by voltaic cells or the minimum voltages required in electrolytic cells. They can also be used to predict whether certain redox reactions are spontaneous (positive E). The emf is related to free-energy changes: $\Delta G = -nFE$, where F is a unit called the faraday. The faraday is the amount of charge on 1 mol of electrons: $1\ F = 96{,}500$ C/mol e$^-$ = 96,500 J/V-mol e$^-$.

The emf of a cell varies in magnitude with temperature and with the concentrations of reactants and products. The Nernst equation relates emf under nonstandard conditions to the standard emf:

$$E = E^\circ - \frac{2.30RT}{nF} \log Q$$

At equilibrium, $Q = K$ and $E = 0$, so that

$$E^\circ = \frac{2.30RT}{nF} \log K$$

Thus, standard emfs are related to equilibrium constants.

The maximum electrical work that can be obtained from a voltaic cell is the product of the total charge it delivers, nF, and its emf, E: $w_{max} = -nFE$. The principles involved in voltaic cells were illustrated by simple cells utilizing salt bridges. Commercial cells need to be more rugged. Four common batteries were discussed: the lead storage battery, the nickel-cadmium battery, the common dry cell, and the alkaline dry cell. The first two are rechargeable; the latter two are not. Fuel cells, still largely experimental, are voltaic cells that utilize redox reactions involving conventional fuels, such as H_2 and CH_4.

In an electrolytic cell, an external source of electricity is used to "pump" electrons from the anode to the cathode. The current-carrying medium within the cell may be either a molten salt or an electrolyte solution. The products of electrolysis can generally be predicted by comparing electrode potentials associated with possible oxidation and reduction processes. However, because of the overvoltage phenomenon, some reactions (such as those that generate H_2 or O_2) occur less readily than electrode potentials would suggest. The quantity of electrical charge that passes into a cell can be used to calculate the amount of substance formed at an electrode.

Our knowledge of electrochemistry allows us to design batteries and to bring about desirable redox reactions, such as those used in electroplating and in the reduction and refining of metals. Electrochemical principles also help us to understand and combat corrosion. Corrosion of a metal such as iron is electrochemical in origin. A metal can be protected against corrosion by putting it in contact with another metal that more readily undergoes oxidation. This process is known as cathodic protection.

Key Terms

oxidation-reduction reaction
electrochemistry
oxidizing agent (oxidant) (Sec. 20.1)
reducing agent (reductant) (Sec. 20.1)
half-reaction (Sec. 20.2)
voltaic (galvanic) cell (Sec. 20.3)
anode (Sec. 20.3)
cathode (Sec. 20.3)
electromotive force (emf) (Sec. 20.4)
cell potential (Sec. 20.4)
standard emf (Sec. 20.4)
standard cell potential (E°_{cell}) (Sec. 20.4)

standard oxidation potential (E°_{ox}) (Sec. 20.4)
standard reduction potential (E°_{red}) (Sec. 20.4)
standard hydrogen electrode (Sec. 20.4)
standard electrode potential (Sec. 20.4)
faraday (Sec. 20.5)
Nernst equation (Sec. 20.6)
fuel cell (Sec. 20.7)
electrolysis (Sec. 20.8)
electrolytic cell (Sec. 20.8)
corrosion (Sec. 20.10)
cathodic protection (Sec. 20.10)

Exercises

Oxidation-Reduction Reactions

20.1. In each of the following balanced oxidation-reduction equations, identify those elements that undergo changes in oxidation number and indicate the magnitude of the change in each case.
(a) $I_2O_5(s) + 5CO(g) \longrightarrow I_2(s) + 5CO_2(g)$
(b) $2Hg^{2+}(aq) + N_2H_4(aq) \longrightarrow$
$$2Hg(l) + N_2(g) + 4H^+(aq)$$
(c) $3H_2S(aq) + 2H^+(aq) + 2NO_3^-(aq) \longrightarrow$
$$3S(s) + 2NO(g) + 4H_2O(l)$$
(d) $Ba^{2+}(aq) + 2OH^-(aq) + H_2O_2(aq) + 2ClO_2(aq) \longrightarrow$
$$Ba(ClO_2)_2(s) + 2H_2O(l) + O_2(g)$$

20.2. Indicate whether the following balanced equations involve oxidation-reduction. If they do, identify the elements that undergo changes in oxidation number.
(a) $2OH^-(aq) + Cr_2O_7^{2-}(aq) \longrightarrow$
$$2CrO_4^{2-}(aq) + 2H_2O(l)$$
(b) $3NO_2(g) + H_2O(l) \longrightarrow 2HNO_3(aq) + NO(g)$
(c) $PBr_3(l) + 3H_2O(l) \longrightarrow H_3PO_3(aq) + 3HBr(aq)$
(d) $2H_2SO_4(aq) + 2NaBr(s) \longrightarrow$
$$Br_2(l) + SO_2(g) + Na_2SO_4(aq) + 2H_2O(l)$$

20.3. Hydrazine, N_2H_4, and dinitrogen tetroxide, N_2O_4, form a self-igniting mixture that has been used as a rocket propellant. The reaction products are N_2 and H_2O. (a) Write a balanced chemical equation for this reaction. (b) Which substance serves as reducing agent and which as oxidizing agent?

20.4. Solid lead(II) sulfide reacts at elevated temperatures with oxygen in the air to form lead(II) oxide and sulfur dioxide. (a) Write a balanced chemical equation for this reaction. (b) Which substances are reductants, and which are oxidants?

20.5. Complete and balance the following half-reactions. In each case, indicate whether oxidation or reduction occurs.
(a) $H_2O_2(aq) \longrightarrow H_2O(l)$ (acidic solution)
(b) $Cl_2(g) \longrightarrow ClO_3^-(aq)$ (acidic solution)
(c) $OH^-(aq) \longrightarrow O_2(g)$ (basic solution)
(d) $CrO_4^{2-}(aq) \longrightarrow Cr(OH)_3(s)$ (basic solution)

20.6. Complete and balance the following half-reactions. In each case, indicate whether oxidation or reduction occurs.
(a) $NO_3^-(aq) \longrightarrow NO(g)$ (acidic solution)
(b) $H_2O_2(aq) \longrightarrow O_2(g)$ (acidic solution)
(c) $SO_3^{2-}(aq) \longrightarrow SO_4^{2-}(aq)$ (basic solution)
(d) $ClO^-(aq) \longrightarrow Cl^-(aq)$ (basic solution)

20.7. Complete and balance the following equations:
(a) $Pb(OH)_4^{2-}(aq) + ClO^-(aq) \longrightarrow$
$$PbO_2(s) + Cl^-(aq)$$ (basic solution)
(b) $Tl_2O_3(s) + NH_2OH(aq) \longrightarrow$
$$TlOH(s) + N_2(g)$$ (basic solution)
(c) $Cr_2O_7^{2-}(aq) + CH_3OH(aq) \longrightarrow$
$$HCO_2H(aq) + Cr^{3+}(aq)$$ (acidic solution)
(d) $MnO_4^-(aq) + Cl^-(aq) \longrightarrow$
$$Mn^{2+}(aq) + Cl_2(aq)$$ (acidic solution)
(e) $H_2O_2(aq) + ClO_2(aq) \longrightarrow$
$$ClO_2^-(aq) + O_2(g)$$ (basic solution)
(f) $NO_2^-(aq) + Cr_2O_7^{2-}(aq) \longrightarrow$
$$Cr^{3+}(aq) + NO_3^-(aq)$$ (acidic solution)

20.8. Complete and balance the following equations:
(a) $Cr_2O_7^{2-}(aq) + I^-(aq) \longrightarrow$
$$Cr^{3+}(aq) + IO_3^-(aq)$$ (acidic solution)
(b) $MnO_4^-(aq) + CH_3OH(aq) \longrightarrow$
$$Mn^{2+}(aq) + HCO_2H(aq)$$ (acidic solution)
(c) $As(s) + ClO_3^-(aq) \longrightarrow$
$$H_3AsO_3(aq) + HClO(aq)$$ (acidic solution)
(d) $As_2O_3(s) + NO_3^-(aq) \longrightarrow$
$$H_3AsO_4(aq) + N_2O_3(aq)$$ (acidic solution)
(e) $MnO_4^-(aq) + Br^-(aq) \longrightarrow$
$$MnO_2(s) + BrO_3^-(aq)$$ (basic solution)
(f) $H_2O_2(aq) + Cl_2O_7(aq) \longrightarrow$
$$ClO_2^-(aq) + O_2(g)$$ (basic solution)

Voltaic Cells; Emf

20.9. What is the role of the salt bridge in the voltaic cell diagramed in Figure 20.5?

20.10. Why are Na^+ ions drawn into the cathode compartment as the voltaic cell shown in Figure 20.5 operates?

20.11. A voltaic cell similar to that shown in Figure 20.5 is constructed. One electrode compartment consists of a zinc strip placed in a solution of $Zn(NO_3)_2$, and the other has a nickel strip placed in a solution of $NiCl_2$. The overall cell reaction is
$$Zn(s) + Ni^{2+}(aq) \longrightarrow Zn^{2+}(aq) + Ni(s)$$

(a) Write the half-reactions that occur in the two electrode compartments. (b) Which electrode is the anode, and which is the cathode? (c) Indicate the signs of the electrodes. (d) Do electrons flow from the zinc electrode to the nickel electrode or from the nickel to the zinc? (e) In which directions do the cations and anions migrate through the solution?

20.12. A voltaic cell similar to that shown in Figure 20.5 is constructed. One electrode compartment consists of a silver strip placed in a solution of $AgNO_3$, and the other has a nickel strip placed in a solution of $NiCl_2$. The overall cell reaction is

$$2Ag^+(aq) + Ni(s) \longrightarrow 2Ag(s) + Ni^{2+}(aq)$$

(a) Write the half-reactions that occur in the two electrode compartments. (b) Which electrode is the anode, and which is the cathode? (c) Indicate the signs of the electrodes. (d) Do electrons flow from the silver electrode to the nickel electrode or from nickel to silver? (e) In which directions do the cations and anions migrate through the solution?

20.13. A voltaic cell that uses the reaction

$$Tl^{3+}(aq) + 2Cr^{2+}(aq) \longrightarrow Tl^+(aq) + 2Cr^{3+}(aq)$$

has a measured emf of 1.19 V under standard conditions. (a) What is $E°$ for the half-cell reaction $Tl^{3+}(aq) + 2e^- \longrightarrow Tl^+(aq)$? (b) What is meant by the expression "under standard conditions"? (c) Sketch the voltaic cell, label the anode and cathode, and indicate the direction of electron flow.

20.14. A voltaic cell that uses the reaction

$$PdCl_4^{2-}(aq) + Cd(s) \longrightarrow Pd(s) + 4Cl^-(aq) + Cd^{2+}(aq)$$

has a measured emf under standard conditions of 1.03 V. (a) Write the two half-cell reactions. (b) From the known value of $E°$ for the half-cell involving Cd (Appendix E), determine the half-cell potential for the reaction involving Pd. (c) Sketch the cell, label the anode and cathode, and indicate the direction of electron flow.

20.15. Using a table of standard electrode potentials, calculate the standard emf for each of the following reactions:
(a) $Cu^{2+}(aq) + Fe(s) \longrightarrow Cu(s) + Fe^{2+}(aq)$
(b) $2Fe^{3+}(aq) + 2I^-(aq) \longrightarrow 2Fe^{2+}(aq) + I_2(s)$

20.16. Using a table of standard electrode potentials, calculate the standard emf for the following reactions:

(a) $Al(s) + Cr^{3+}(aq) \longrightarrow Al^{3+}(aq) + Cr(s)$
(b) $2Fe^{2+}(aq) + Cl_2(g) \longrightarrow 2Fe^{3+}(aq) + 2Cl^-(aq)$

20.17. Given the following half-reactions and associated standard electrode potentials:

$$AuBr_4^-(aq) + 3e^- \longrightarrow Au(s) + 4Br^-(aq)$$
$$E° = -0.858 \text{ V}$$

$$Eu^{3+}(aq) + e^- \longrightarrow Eu^{2+}(aq) \quad E° = -0.43 \text{ V}$$

$$IO^-(aq) + H_2O(l) + 2e^- \longrightarrow I^-(aq) + 2OH^-(aq)$$
$$E° = 0.49 \text{ V}$$

$$Sn^{2+}(aq) + 2e^- \longrightarrow Sn(s) \quad E° = -0.14 \text{ V}$$

(a) Write the cell reaction for the combination of these half-cell reactions that leads to the largest cell emf and calculate the value. (b) Write the cell reaction for the combination of half-cell reactions that leads to the smallest cell emf and calculate that value.

20.18. The standard electrode potentials of the following half-reactions are given in Appendix E:

$$Mn^{2+}(aq) + 2e^- \longrightarrow Mn(s)$$
$$Hg^{2+}(aq) + 2e^- \longrightarrow Hg(l)$$
$$Co^{2+}(aq) + 2e^- \longrightarrow Co(s)$$
$$Cu^+(aq) + e^- \longrightarrow Cu(s)$$

(a) Write the cell reaction for the combination of these half-cell reactions that leads to the largest cell emf and calculate the value. (b) Write the cell reaction for the combination of half-cell reactions that leads to the smallest cell emf and calculate the value.

Ease of Oxidation or Reduction; Spontaneity

20.19. The two half-reactions in a voltaic cell are the following (or their reverse):

$$Fe^{3+}(aq) + e^- \longrightarrow Fe^{2+}(aq)$$
$$H_2O_2(aq) + 2H^+(aq) + 2e^- \longrightarrow 2H_2O(l)$$

(a) By referring to Appendix E, select the reduction process that occurs more readily. (b) In a voltaic cell, which reaction occurs at the cathode? (c) What reaction occurs at the anode? (d) What is the standard cell potential?

20.20. A voltaic cell similar to that shown in Figure 20.8 is constructed. One electrode compartment has an aluminum strip in contact with a solution of $Al(NO_3)_3$, and the other is a standard hydrogen electrode. (a) By referring to Table 20.1 or Appendix E, write the half-reactions involved and determine which electrode is the anode and which is the cathode. (b) Will the aluminum strip gain or lose mass as the cell operates? (c) What is the standard emf of the cell?

20.21. A 1 M solution of $Cu(NO_3)_2$ is placed in a beaker with a strip of Cu metal. A 1 M solution of $SnSO_4$ is placed in a second beaker with a strip of Sn metal. The two beakers are connected by a salt bridge, and the two metal electrodes

are linked by wires to a voltmeter. (a) Which electrode serves as the anode, and which as the cathode? (b) Which electrode gains mass and which loses mass as the cell reaction proceeds? (c) Write the chemical equation for the overall cell reaction. (d) What is the emf generated by the cell under standard conditions?

20.22. A voltaic cell consists of a strip of lead metal in a solution of $Pb(NO_3)_2$ in one beaker, and in the other beaker a platinum electrode immersed in an NaCl solution, with Cl_2 gas bubbled around the electrode. The two beakers are connected with a salt bridge. (a) Which electrode serves as the anode, and which as the cathode? (b) Which electrode gains mass and which loses mass as the cell reaction proceeds? (c) Write the chemical equation for the overall cell reaction. (d) What is the emf generated by the cell under standard conditions?

20.23. (a) Assuming standard conditions, arrange the following species in order of increasing strength as oxidizing agents in acidic solution: $Cr_2O_7^{2-}$, H_2O_2, Cu^{2+}, Cl_2, O_2. (b) Arrange the following species in order of increasing strength as reducing agents in acidic solution: Zn, I^-, Sn^{2+}, H_2O_2, Al.

20.24. Based on the data in Appendix E, **(a)** which of the following is the strongest oxidizing agent and which is the weakest in acidic solution: Ce^{4+}, Br_2, H_2O_2, Zn? **(b)** Which of the following is the strongest reducing agent and which is the weakest in acidic solution: F^-, Zn, $N_2H_5^+$, I_2, NO?

20.25. Using Table 20.1, suggest one or more agents capable of reducing $Eu^{3+}(aq)$ to $Eu^{2+}(aq)$ under standard conditions ($E^\circ = -0.43$ V).

20.26. Based on Table 20.1, suggest one or more agents capable of oxidizing $RuO_4^{2-}(aq)$ to $RuO_4^-(aq)$ under standard conditions. [E° for the reaction $RuO_4^{2-}(aq) \longrightarrow RuO_4^-(aq) + e^-$ is -0.59 V.]

20.27. Which of the following reactions are spontaneous under standard conditions?
(a) $Hg_2^{2+}(aq) + Zn(s) \longrightarrow 2Hg(l) + Zn^{2+}(aq)$
(b) $2Ag(s) + I_2(s) \longrightarrow 2AgI(s)$
(c) $2CO_2(g) + Cl_2(g) + 2H_2O(l) \longrightarrow$
$ H_2C_2O_4(aq) + 2HClO(aq)$

20.28. Write a balanced equation for each of the following reactions and determine whether the reaction is spontaneous under standard conditions: **(a)** Aqueous iodide ion is oxidized to $I_2(s)$ by $Hg_2^{2+}(aq)$. **(b)** In acidic solution, copper(I) ion is oxidized to copper(II) ion by nitrate ion. **(c)** In basic solution, $Cr(OH)_3(s)$ is oxidized to $CrO_4^{2-}(aq)$ by $ClO^-(aq)$.

20.29. From the standard emfs, calculate ΔG° at 298 K for each of the reactions listed in Exercise 20.27.

20.30. Given the following half-cell potentials:
$$Fe^{2+}(aq) \longrightarrow Fe^{3+}(aq) + e^-$$
$$E^\circ = -0.771 \text{ V}$$
$$S_2O_6^{2-}(aq) + 4H^+(aq) + 2e^- \longrightarrow 2H_2SO_3(aq)$$
$$E^\circ = 0.60 \text{ V}$$
$$N_2O(aq) + 2H^+(aq) + 2e^- \longrightarrow N_2(g) + H_2O(l)$$
$$E^\circ = -1.77 \text{ V}$$
$$VO_2^+(aq) + 2H^+(aq) + e^- \longrightarrow VO^{2+}(aq) + H_2O(l)$$
$$E^\circ = 1.00 \text{ V}$$

(a) Write balanced chemical equations for the oxidation of $Fe^{2+}(aq)$ by the other three reagents for which the half-cell reaction is given. **(b)** Calculate ΔG° for each reaction at 298 K.

Nernst Equation; K

20.31. A voltaic cell utilizes the following reaction:
$$Al(s) + 3Ag^+(aq) \longrightarrow Al^{3+}(aq) + 3Ag(s)$$
What is the effect on the cell emf of each of the following changes? **(a)** Some $Al(NO_3)_3$ is added to the anode compartment, increasing the concentration of Al^{3+} ions. **(b)** The size of the aluminum electrode is increased. **(c)** Additional water is added to the cathode compartment. **(d)** A solution of $AgNO_3$ is added to the cathode compartment, increasing the quantity of Ag^+ but not changing its concentration.

20.32. What is the effect on the emf of the cell shown in Figure 20.8 of each of the following changes? **(a)** The pressure of the H_2 gas is decreased. **(b)** The area of the anode is doubled. **(c)** Sulfuric acid is added to the cathode compartment, increasing $[H^+]$. **(d)** Sodium nitrate is added to the anode compartment.

20.33. A voltaic cell is constructed that uses the following reaction and operates at 298 K:
$$2Al(s) + 3Mn^{2+}(aq) \longrightarrow 2Al^{3+}(aq) + 3Mn(s)$$
(a) What is the emf of this cell under standard conditions? **(b)** What is the emf of this cell when $[Mn^{2+}] = 0.10$ M and $[Al^{3+}] = 1.5$ M?

20.34. A voltaic cell utilizes the following reaction and operates at 298 K:
$$3Ce^{4+}(aq) + Cr(s) \longrightarrow 3Ce^{3+}(aq) + Cr^{3+}(aq)$$
(a) What is the emf of this cell under standard conditions? **(b)** What is the emf of this cell when $[Ce^{4+}] = 1.5$ M; $[Ce^{3+}] = 0.010$ M; and $[Cr^{3+}] = 0.010$ M?

20.35. A voltaic cell utilizes the following reaction and operates at 298 K:

$$4Fe^{2+}(aq) + O_2(g) + 4H^+(aq) \longrightarrow 4Fe^{3+}(aq) + 2H_2O(l)$$
(a) What is the emf of this cell under standard conditions? **(b)** What is the emf of this cell when $[Fe^{2+}] = 2.0$ M, $[Fe^{3+}] = 0.0010$ M, $P_{O_2} = 0.50$ atm, and the pH of the solution in the cathode compartment is 3.00?

20.36. A voltaic cell utilizes the following reaction and operates at 20°C:
$$2Fe^{3+}(aq) + H_2(g) \longrightarrow 2Fe^{2+}(aq) + 2H^+(aq)$$
(a) What is the emf of this cell under standard conditions? **(b)** What is the emf of this cell when $[Fe^{3+}] = 0.50$ M, $P_{H_2} = 0.25$ atm, $[Fe^{2+}] = 0.010$ M, and the pH in both compartments is 4.00.

20.37. The cell in Figure 20.8 could be used to provide a measure of the pH in the cathode compartment. Calculate the pH of the cathode compartment solution if the cell emf is measured to be 0.720 V when $[Zn^{2+}] = 0.10$ M and $P_{H_2} = 1.0$ atm.

20.38. A voltaic cell is constructed that is based on the following reaction:
$$Sn^{2+}(aq) + Pb(s) \longrightarrow Pb^{2+}(aq) + Sn(s)$$
If the concentration of Sn^{2+} in the cathode compartment is 1.00 M and the cell generates an emf of 0.22 V, what is the concentration of Pb^{2+} in the anode compartment? If the anode compartment contains $[SO_4^{2-}] = 1.00$ M in equilibrium with $PbSO_4(s)$, what is the K_{sp} of the $PbSO_4$?

20.39. Using the standard half-cell potentials listed in Appendix E, calculate the equilibrium constant for each of the following reactions at 298 K:
(a) $Zn(s) + Sn^{2+}(aq) \longrightarrow Zn^{2+}(aq) + Sn(s)$
(b) $Co(s) + 2H^+(aq) \longrightarrow Co^{2+}(aq) + H_2(g)$

(c) $10Br^-(aq) + 2MnO_4^-(aq) + 16H^+(aq) \longrightarrow$
$$2Mn^{2+}(aq) + 8H_2O(l) + 5Br_2(l)$$

20.40. Using the standard half-cell potentials listed in Appendix E, calculate the equilibrium constant for each of the following reactions at 298 K:
(a) $2VO_2^+(aq) + 4H^+(aq) + Ni(s) \longrightarrow$
$$2VO^{2+}(aq) + 2H_2O(l) + Ni^{2+}(aq)$$
(b) $3Ce^{4+}(aq) + Bi(s) + H_2O(l) \longrightarrow$
$$3Ce^{3+}(aq) + BiO^+(aq) + 2H^+(aq)$$

(c) $N_2H_5^+(aq) + 4Fe(CN)_6^{3-}(aq) \longrightarrow$
$$N_2(g) + 5H^+(aq) + 4Fe(CN)_6^{4-}(aq)$$

20.41. A cell exhibits a standard emf of 0.35 V at 298 K. What is the value of the equilibrium constant for the cell reaction (a) if $n = 1$? (b) if $n = 2$? (c) if $n = 3$?

20.42. At 298 K, a cell reaction exhibits a standard emf of 0.21 V. The equilibrium constant for the cell reaction is 1.31×10^7. What is the value of n for the cell reaction?

Commercial Voltaic Cells

20.43. If 120 g of zinc is employed in the casing of a particular Leclanché dry cell, and if all of this is consumed in the cell reaction, how many grams of MnO_2 undergo reaction?

20.44. During a period of discharge of a lead-acid battery, 600 g of Pb from the anode is converted into $PbSO_4(s)$. What mass of $PbO_2(s)$ is reduced at the cathode during this same period?

20.45. (a) Write the reactions for discharge and charge of a nickel-cadmium rechargeable cell. (b) Given the following half-cell potentials, calculate the standard emf of the cell:

$$Cd(OH)_2(s) + 2e^- \longrightarrow Cd(s) + 2OH^-(aq)$$
$$E° = -0.76 \text{ V}$$
$$NiO_2(s) + 2H_2O(l) + 2e^- \longrightarrow Ni(OH)_2(s) + 2OH^-(aq)$$
$$E° = +0.49 \text{ V}$$

20.46. Mercuric oxide dry-cell batteries are often used where a high energy density is required, for example, in hearing aids, watches, cameras, and electronic systems. The

two half-cell reactions that occur in the battery are as follows:

$$HgO(s) + H_2O(l) + 2e^- \longrightarrow Hg(l) + 2OH^-(aq)$$
$$Zn(s) + 2OH^-(aq) \longrightarrow ZnO(s) + H_2O(l) + 2e^-$$

(a) Write the overall cell reaction. (b) The value of $E°$ for the reduction half-reaction written above is 0.098 V. The measured potential for a fresh mercury dry cell is 1.35 V. Assuming that both half-cells are operating under standard conditions, what is the standard potential for the oxidation half-cell reaction? Why is this potential different from that for oxidation of Zn in aqueous acidic medium?

20.47. Suppose that an alkaline dry cell were manufactured using cadmium metal rather than zinc. What effect would this have on the cell emf?

20.48. The most promising experimental batteries that might someday find their way into commercial use employ lithium or sodium as the anodic metal. What advantages might be realized by using these metals rather than zinc, cadmium, lead, or nickel?

Electrolysis

20.49. (a) Why are different products obtained when molten $MgCl_2$ and aqueous $MgCl_2$ are electrolyzed with inert electrodes? (b) Predict the products in each case. (c) What is the minimum emf required in each case?

20.50. (a) What are the expected half-reactions at each electrode upon electrolysis of molten $AlBr_3$ using inert electrodes? (b) What are the expected half-reactions upon electrolyzing aqueous $AlBr_3$? (c) What is the minimum emf required in each case?

20.51. Sketch a cell for electrolysis of a $NiCl_2$ solution using inert electrodes. Indicate the directions in which the ions and electrons move. Give the electrode reactions and label the anode and cathode, indicating which is positive and which is negative.

20.52. Sketch a cell for the electrolysis of aqueous HCl using copper electrodes. Give the electrode reactions, labeling the anode and cathode. Calculate the minimum applied voltage required to cause electrolysis to occur, assuming standard conditions.

20.53. (a) A $Cr^{3+}(aq)$ solution is electrolyzed using a current of 1.50 A. What mass of $Cr(s)$ is plated out after 24

hr? (b) What amperage is required to plate out 2.85 g of Cr from a Cr^{3+} solution in a period of 2.50 hr?

20.54. Metallic magnesium can be made by the electrolysis of molten $MgCl_2$. (a) What mass of Mg is formed by passing a current of 3.50 A through molten $MgCl_2$ for a period of 550 min? (b) How many seconds are required to plate out 2.00 g Mg from molten $MgCl_2$ using 5.00 A current?

20.55. (a) In the electrolysis of aqueous NaCl, how many liters of $Cl_2(g)$ (measured at STP) are generated by a current of 7.50 A for a period of 100 min? (b) How many moles of $NaOH(aq)$ have formed in the solution in this period?

20.56. If 0.500 L of a 0.600 M $SnSO_4(aq)$ solution is electrolyzed for a period of 30.0 min using a current of 4.60 A, and if inert electrodes are used, what is the final concentration of each ion remaining in the solution? (Assume that the volume of the solution does not change.)

Electrical Work

20.57. Indicate whether each of the following statements is true or false. Correct those that are false. **(a)** The theoretical maximum work obtainable from a voltaic cell is exactly equal to the theoretical minimum work required to drive the cell reaction in the opposite direction under the same conditions. **(b)** For a given cell reaction the maximum work obtainable is proportional to the total mass of reactants that form products. **(c)** The minimum work required to cause an electrolytic cell reaction to proceed is often less than the theoretical value because of overvoltage.

20.58. Provide a simple, direct argument to support the statement that the maximum work obtainable from a given voltaic cell is a state function; that is, it depends only on the initial and final states of the cell. Is this true also of the *actual* work obtainable from the cell? Give examples to illustrate your answer.

20.59. Under standard conditions, what is the maximum electrical work, in joules, that a cell employing the cell reaction

$$Cd(s) + 2H^+(aq) \longrightarrow Cd^{2+}(aq) + H_2(g)$$

can accomplish if 0.870 mol of Cd is consumed?

20.60. Under standard conditions, what is the maximum electrical work, in joules, that a cell employing the cell reaction

$$Sn(s) + I_2(s) \longrightarrow Sn^{2+}(aq) + 2I^-(aq)$$

can accomplish if 0.360 mol of Sn is consumed?

20.61. **(a)** Calculate the mass of magnesium produced at a large facility by electrolysis of molten $MgCl_2$ by a current of 90,000 A flowing for 16 hr. Assume that the cell is 50 percent efficient. **(b)** What is the total energy requirement for this electrolysis if the applied emf is 4.20 V?

20.62. **(a)** Calculate the mass of Li formed by electrolysis of molten LiCl by a current of 6.6×10^4 A flowing for a period of 12 hr. Assume the cell is 85 percent efficient. **(b)** What is the energy requirement for this electrolysis per mole of Li formed if the applied emf is 5.50 V?

Corrosion

20.63. An iron object is plated with a coating of cobalt to protect against corrosion. Does the cobalt protect iron by cathodic protection? Explain.

20.64. When an iron object is plated with tin, does the tin act as a sacrificial anode in protecting against corrosion? Explain.

20.65. *Amines* are compounds related to ammonia. One of their characteristics is their ability to function as Brønsted-Lowry bases (Section 16.2). Suggest how they act as corrosion inhibitors when added to antifreeze.

20.66. The following quotation is taken from an article dealing with corrosion of electronic materials: "Sulfur dioxide, its acidic oxidation products, and moisture are well established as the principal causes of outdoor corrosion of many metals." Using Ni as an example, explain why the factors cited affect the rate of corrosion. Write chemical equations to illustrate your points. Note that $NiO(s)$ is soluble in acidic solution (Figure 4.10).

Additional Exercises

20.67. Complete and balance the following equations:
(a) $Fe^{2+}(aq) + HBrO_3(aq) \longrightarrow Fe^{3+}(aq) + Br_2(l)$
(acidic solution)
(b) $Cu(s) + NO_3^-(aq) \longrightarrow Cu^{2+}(aq) + NO(g)$
(acidic solution)
(c) $IO_3^-(aq) + I^-(aq) \longrightarrow I_3^-(aq)$ (basic solution)

20.68. A *disproportionation reaction* is an oxidation-reduction reaction in which the same substance is oxidized and reduced. Complete and balance the following disproportionation reactions:
(a) $MnO_4^{2-}(aq) \longrightarrow MnO_4^-(aq) + MnO_2(s)$
(acidic solution)
(b) $H_2SO_3(aq) \longrightarrow S(s) + HSO_4^-(aq)$ (acidic solution)
(c) $Cl_2(aq) \longrightarrow Cl^-(aq) + ClO^-(aq)$ (basic solution)

20.69. The following oxidation-reduction reaction is spontaneous:

$$5Fe^{2+}(aq) + MnO_4^-(aq) + 8H^+(aq) \longrightarrow$$
$$5Fe^{3+}(aq) + Mn^{2+}(aq) + 4H_2O(l)$$

A solution containing $KMnO_4$ and H_2SO_4 is poured into one beaker, and a solution of $FeSO_4$ is poured into another. A salt bridge is used to join the beakers. A platinum foil is placed in each solution, and the two solutions are connected by a wire that passes through a voltmeter. **(a)** Indicate the reactions occurring at the anode and at the cathode, the direction of electron movement though the external circuit, the direction of ion migrations through the solutions, and the signs of the electrodes. **(b)** Calculate the emf of the cell under standard conditions.

20.70. A common shorthand way to represent a voltaic cell is to list its components as follows:

anode|anode solution||cathode solution|cathode

A double vertical line represents a salt bridge or porous barrier. A single vertical line represents a change in phase, such as from solid to solution. **(a)** Write the half-reactions and overall cell reaction represented by Fe|Fe²⁺||Ag⁺|Ag; sketch the cell. **(b)** Write the half-reactions and overall cell reaction represented by Zn|Zn²⁺||H⁺|H₂; sketch the cell. **(c)** Using the notation just described, represent a cell based on the following reaction.

$$\text{ClO}_3^-(aq) + \text{Cu}(s) + 6\text{H}^+(aq) \longrightarrow$$
$$\text{Cl}^-(aq) + \text{Cu}^{2+}(aq) + 3\text{H}_2\text{O}(l)$$

Pt is used as an inert electrode in contact with the ClO_3^- and Cl^-. Sketch the cell.

20.71. A voltaic cell is constructed from two half-cells. The first contains a Cd(s) electrode immersed in $1\ M$ $\text{Cd}^{2+}(aq)$ solution. The other contains a Rh(s) electrode in $1\ M$ $\text{Rh}^{3+}(aq)$ solution. The overall cell potential is $+1.20$ V, and, as the cell operates, the concentration of the $\text{Rh}^{3+}(aq)$ solution decreases, and the mass of the Rh electrode increases. **(a)** Write a balanced equation for the overall cell reaction. **(b)** Which electrode is the anode, and which is the cathode? **(c)** What is the standard reduction potential for the reduction of $\text{Rh}^{3+}(aq)$ to Rh(s)? **(d)** What is the value of $\Delta G°$ for the cell reaction?

20.72. The zinc–silver oxide cell used in hearing aids and electrical watches is based on the following half-reactions:

$$\text{Zn}^{2+}(aq) + 2\text{e}^- \longrightarrow \text{Zn}(s) \qquad E° = -0.763 \text{ V}$$
$$\text{Ag}_2\text{O}(s) + \text{H}_2\text{O}(l) + 2\text{e}^- \longrightarrow 2\text{Ag}(s) + 2\text{OH}^-(aq)$$
$$E° = 0.344 \text{ V}$$

(a) Which substance is oxidized and which is reduced in the cell during discharge? **(b)** Which is the positive electrode, and which is the negative electrode? **(c)** What emf does this cell generate under standard conditions?

20.73. Predict whether the following reactions will be spontaneous in acidic solution under standard conditions: **(a)** oxidation of Sn to Sn^{2+} by I_2 (to form I^-); **(b)** reduction of Ni^{2+} to Ni by I^- (to form I_2); **(c)** reduction of Ce^{4+} to Ce^{3+} by Br^- (to form Br_2); **(d)** reduction of Ag^+ to Ag by H_2O_2.

20.74. Cytochrome, a complicated molecule that we shall represent as CyFe^{2+}, reacts with the air we breathe to supply energy required to synthesize adenosine triphosphate, ATP. The body uses ATP as an energy source to drive other reactions (Section 19.7). At pH 7 the following electrode potentials pertain to this oxidation of CyFe^{2+}:

$$\text{O}_2(g) + 4\text{H}^+(aq) + 4\text{e}^- \longrightarrow 2\text{H}_2\text{O}(l) \qquad E = 0.82 \text{ V}$$
$$\text{CyFe}^{3+}(aq) + \text{e}^- \longrightarrow \text{CyFe}^{2+}(aq) \qquad E = 0.22 \text{ V}$$

(a) What is ΔG for the oxidation of CyFe^{2+} by air? **(b)** If the synthesis of 1 mol of ATP from adenosine diphosphate, ADP, requires a ΔG of 37.7 kJ, how many moles of ATP are synthesized per mole of O_2?

20.75. A *concentration cell* is a voltaic cell that contains the same substances in both the anode and cathode compartments, but at different concentrations. Calculate the emf of a cell containing $0.040\ M\ \text{Cr}^{3+}(aq)$ in one compartment and $2.0\ M\ \text{Cr}^{3+}(aq)$ in the other if Cr electrodes are used in both. Which is the anode compartment?

[20.76]. Gold exists in two common positive oxidation states, $+1$ and $+3$. The standard reduction potentials for these oxidation states are

$$\text{Au}^+(aq) + \text{e}^- \longrightarrow \text{Au}(s) \qquad E° = +1.69 \text{ V}$$
$$\text{Au}^{3+}(aq) + 3\text{e}^- \longrightarrow \text{Au}(s) \qquad E° = +1.50 \text{ V}$$

(a) Can you use these data to explain why gold does not tarnish in the air? **(b)** Suggest several substances that should be strong enough oxidizing agents to oxidize gold metal. **(c)** Would $\text{Au}^+(aq)$ disproportionate (see Exercise 20.68) spontaneously into $\text{Au}^{3+}(aq)$ and Au(s)? **(d)** Based on your answers to parts (b) and (c), predict the result of reacting gold metal with fluorine gas.

[20.77]. A voltaic cell is constructed that uses the following half-cell reactions:

$$\text{Cu}^+(aq) + \text{e}^- \longrightarrow \text{Cu}(s)$$
$$\text{I}_2(s) + 2\text{e}^- \longrightarrow 2\text{I}^-(aq)$$

The cell is operated at 298 K with $[\text{Cu}^+] = 2.1\ M$ and $[\text{I}^-] = 3.2\ M$. **(a)** Determine E for the cell at these concentrations. **(b)** Which electrode is the anode of the cell? **(c)** Is the answer to part (b) the same as it would be if the cell were operated under standard conditions? **(d)** If $[\text{Cu}^+]$ were equal to $1.4\ M$, at what concentration of I^- would the cell have a zero potential?

[20.78]. The standard electrode potential for the reduction of AgSCN(s) is 0.0895 V:

$$\text{AgSCN}(s) + \text{e}^- \longrightarrow \text{Ag}(s) + \text{SCN}^-(aq)$$

Using this value and the electrode potential for $\text{Ag}^+(aq)$, calculate the K_{sp} for AgSCN.

[20.79]. The K_{sp} value for PbS(s) is 8.0×10^{-28}. By using this value together with an electrode potential from Appendix E, determine the value of the standard electrode potential for the reaction

$$\text{PbS}(s) + 2\text{e}^- \longrightarrow \text{Pb}(s) + \text{S}^{2-}(aq)$$

20.80. By using the standard electrode potentials in Appendix E, calculate the equilibrium constant for the disproportionation of copper(I) ion:

$$2\text{Cu}^+(aq) \longrightarrow \text{Cu}(s) + \text{Cu}^{2+}(aq)$$

20.81. **(a)** How many coulombs are required to plate a layer of chromium metal 0.23 mm thick on an auto bumper with a total area of 0.32 m² from a solution containing CrO_4^{2-}? The density of chromium metal is 7.20 g/cm³. **(b)** What current flow is required for this electroplate if the bumper is to be plated in 6.0 s?

20.82. The element indium is to be obtained by electrolysis of a molten halide of the element. Passage of a current of

3.20 A for a period of 40.0 min results in formation of 4.57 g of In. What is the oxidation state of indium in the halide melt?

20.83. An electrolytic cell is set up for the production of aluminum by the Hall process (Chapter 24), which involves the reduction of Al^{3+} to Al. The external source passes a current of 11.2 A through the cell with an emf of 6.0 V. **(a)** How long does it take for the cell to produce 1.0 lb of aluminum metal? **(b)** If the cell has an efficiency of 40 percent, how much electrical power is expended to produce 1.0 lb of aluminum?

20.84. Explain why electrolysis of an aqueous solution of Na_2SO_4 containing litmus develops a blue color at the cathode and a red color at the anode.

20.85. Peroxyborate bleaches, such as those found in Borateem, have replaced older "chlorine" bleaches in many bleaching agents. Sodium peroxyborate, $NaBO_3$, can be prepared by electrolytic oxidation of borax ($Na_2B_4O_7$) solutions:

$$Na_2B_4O_7(aq) + 10NaOH(aq) \longrightarrow$$
$$4NaBO_3(aq) + 5H_2O(l) + 8Na^+(aq) + 8e^-$$

How many grams of $NaBO_3$ can be prepared in 24.0 hr if the current is 20.0 A?

20.86. **(a)** Calculate the minimum applied voltage required to cause the following electrolysis reaction to occur, assuming that the anode is platinum and the cathode is nickel:

$$Ni^{2+}(aq) + 2Br^-(aq) \longrightarrow Ni(s) + Br_2(l)$$

(b) In practice, a larger voltage than this calculated minimum is required to produce the electrode reactions. Why is this so?

20.87. **(a)** What is the maximum amount of work that a 6-V golf-cart lead storage battery can accomplish if it is rated at 300 A-h? **(b)** List some of the reasons why this amount of work is never realized.

20.88. The type of lead storage cell used in automobiles does not tolerate deep discharge (in which the cell reaction is allowed to proceed to near completion) very well. Typically, the battery fails after 20 to 30 such cycles. **(a)** Why does deep discharge lead to battery failure? **(b)** How is deep discharge avoided during normal auto use?

20.89. If you were going to apply a small potential to a steel ship resting in the water as a means of inhibiting corrosion, would you apply a negative or a positive charge? Explain.

[20.90]. Several years ago, a unique proposal was made to raise the *Titanic*. The plan involved placing pontoons within the ship using a surface-controlled submarine-type vessel. The pontoons would contain cathodes and would be filled with hydrogen gas formed by the electrolysis of water. It has been estimated that it would require about 7×10^8 mol of H_2 to provide the buoyancy to lift the ship [*Journal of Chemical Education*, **50**, 61, (1973)]. **(a)** How many coulombs of electrical charge would be required? **(b)** What is the minimum voltage required to generate H_2 and O_2 if the pressure on the gases at the depth of the wreckage (2 mi) is 300 atm? **(c)** What is the minimum electrical energy required to raise the *Titanic* by electrolysis? **(d)** What is the minimum cost of the electrical energy required to generate the necessary H_2 if the electricity costs 23¢ per kilowatt-hour?

[20.91]. Edison's invention of the light bulb and its public demonstration in December 1879 generated considerable demand for the distribution of electricity to homes. One problem was how to measure the amount of electricity consumed by each household. Edison invented a coulometer [described in the *Journal of Chemical Education*, **49**, 627, (1972)] that could be used with alternating current. Zinc plated out at the cathode of the coulometer. Every month the cathode was removed and weighed to determine the quantity of electricity used. If the cathode increased in mass by 1.62 g and the coulometer drew 0.35 percent of the current entering the home, how many coulombs of electricity were used in that month?

21 Nuclear Chemistry

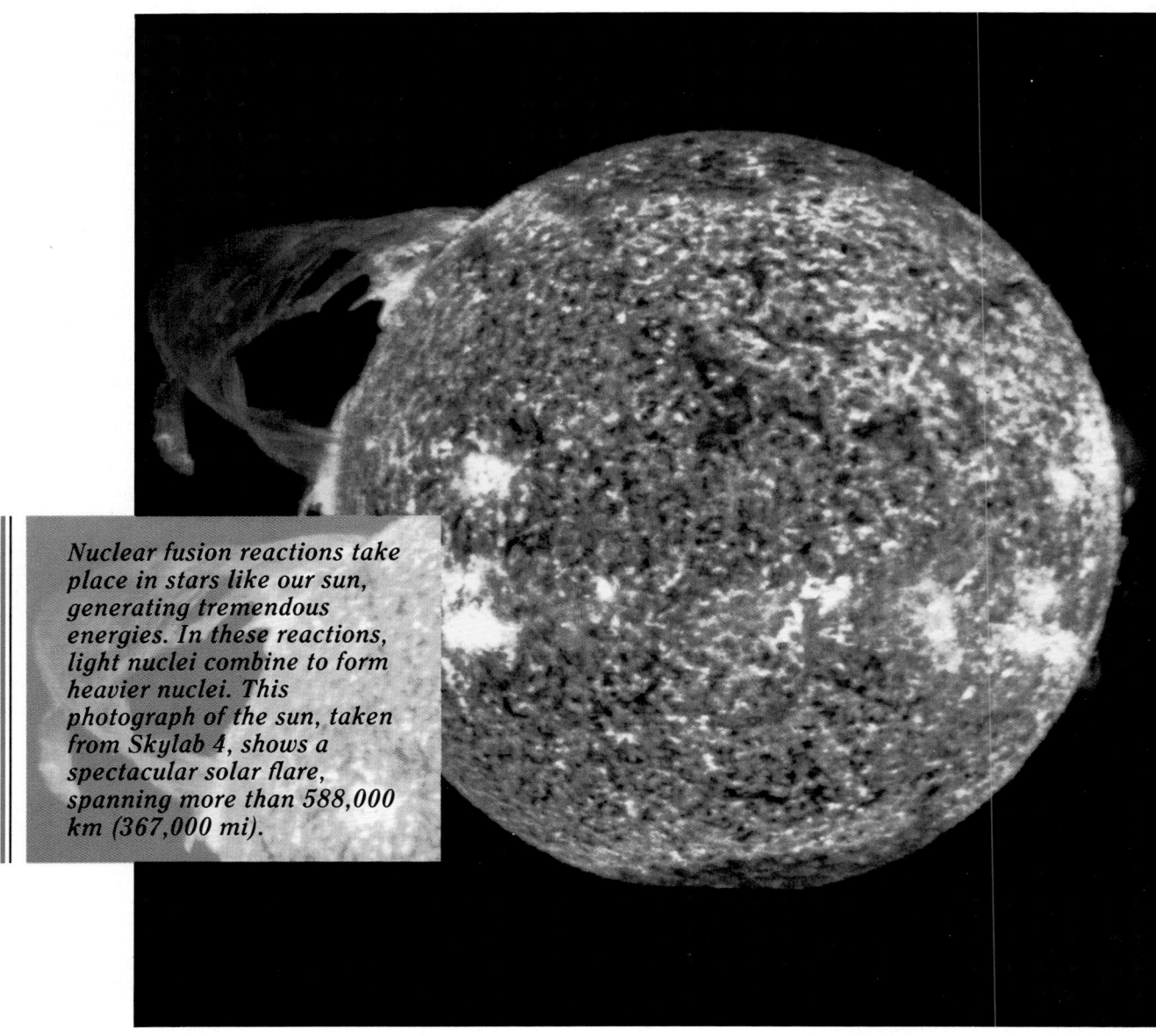

Nuclear fusion reactions take place in stars like our sun, generating tremendous energies. In these reactions, light nuclei combine to form heavier nuclei. This photograph of the sun, taken from Skylab 4, shows a spectacular solar flare, spanning more than 588,000 km (367,000 mi).

As we have progressed through this text, our focus has been on chemical reactions, specifically reactions in which electrons play a dominant role. In this chapter, we consider *nuclear reactions,* changes in matter originating in the nucleus of an atom. When nuclei change spontaneously, emitting radiation, they are said to be **radioactive.** As we shall see, there are other kinds of nuclear reactions as well. *Nuclear chemistry* is the study of nuclear reactions and their uses in chemistry.

Nuclear chemistry affects our lives in a variety of ways. Radioactive elements are widely used in medicine as diagnostic tools and as a means of treatment, especially for cancer (Figure 21.1). They are also used to help determine the mechanisms of chemical reactions, to trace the movement of atoms in biological systems, and to date important historical artifacts. Nuclear reactions are used both to generate electricity and to create weapons of massive destruction.

Although the growth of commercial nuclear power has slowed in the United States, it still accounts for almost 20 percent of the total electricity generated. The use of nuclear energy and the disposal of nuclear wastes, however, are extremely controversial social and political issues. Because these topics evoke such a strong emotional reaction, it is often difficult to sift fact from opinion and make rational decisions. It is imperative, therefore, that educated people of our time have some understanding of nuclear reactions and the uses of radioactive substances.

21.1 Radioactivity

In order to understand nuclear reactions, we need to review and develop some ideas introduced in Section 2.3. First, recall that two subatomic particles reside in the nucleus, the *proton* and the *neutron.* We shall refer to these particles as **nucleons.** Recall also that all atoms of a given element have the same number of

Learning Goal 1: Write the nuclear symbols for protons, neutrons, electrons, alpha particles, and positrons.

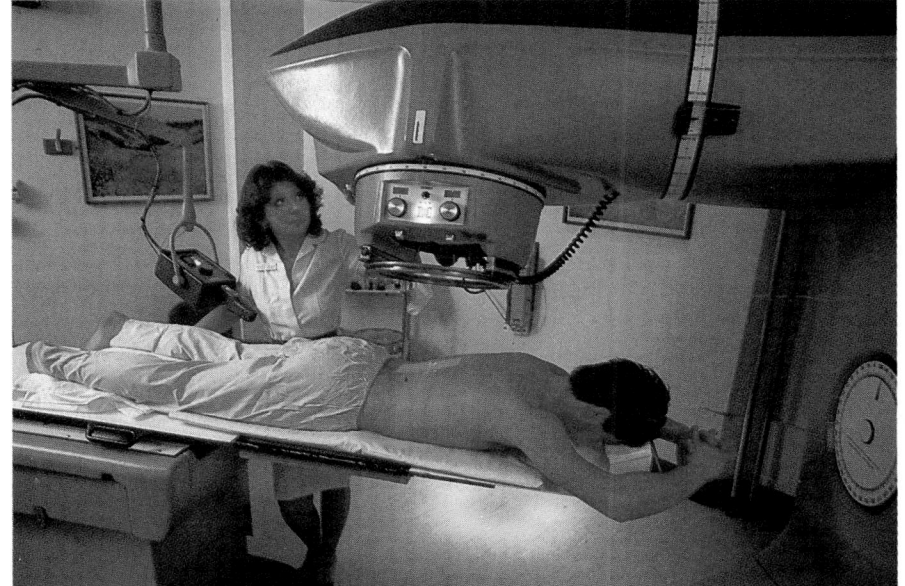

FIGURE 21.1 Radioactive isotopes, such as ^{60}Co, are used in the treatment of cancer. (Martin Dohan, Science Photo Library, Science Source Photo Researchers)

protons; this number is known as the element's *atomic number.* However, the atoms of a given element can have different numbers of neutrons and therefore different *mass numbers;* the mass number is the total number of nucleons in the nucleus. Atoms with the same atomic number but different mass numbers are known as *isotopes.*

The different isotopes of an element are distinguished by citing their mass numbers. For example, the three naturally occurring isotopes of uranium are identified as uranium-233, uranium-235, and uranium-238, where the numerical suffixes represent the mass numbers. These isotopes are also labeled, using chemical symbols, as $^{233}_{92}\text{U}$, $^{235}_{92}\text{U}$, and $^{238}_{92}\text{U}$. The superscript is the mass number; the subscript is the atomic number.

Different isotopes have different natural abundances. For example, 99.3 percent of naturally occurring uranium is uranium-238, 0.7 percent is uranium-235, and only a trace is uranium-233. Different nuclei also have different stabilities. Indeed, the nuclear properties of an atom depend on the number of protons and neutrons in its nucleus. Recall that the term *nuclide* applies to a nucleus with a specified number of protons and neutrons. ∞ (Sec. 2.3) Nuclei that are radioactive are called **radionuclides,** and atoms containing these nuclei are called **radioisotopes.**

Nuclear Equations

Radionuclides are unstable and spontaneously emit particles and electromagnetic radiation. Emission of radiation is one of the ways in which an unstable nucleus is transformed into a more stable one with less energy. The emitted radiation is the carrier of the excess energy. For example, uranium-238 is radioactive, undergoing a nuclear reaction in which helium-4 nuclei are spontaneously emitted. The helium-4 particles are known as **alpha particles,** and a stream of these particles is called *alpha radiation.* When a uranium-238 nucleus loses an alpha particle, the remaining fragment has an atomic number of 90 and a mass number of 234. It is therefore a thorium-234 nucleus. We represent this reaction by the following nuclear equation:

$$^{238}_{92}\text{U} \longrightarrow {}^{234}_{90}\text{Th} + {}^{4}_{2}\text{He} \qquad [21.1]$$

When a nucleus spontaneously decomposes in this way, it is said to have decayed, or undergone *radioactive decay.* Because an alpha particle is involved in this reaction, scientists also describe the process as alpha decay.

Notice in Equation 21.1 that the sum of the mass numbers is the same on both sides of the equation ($238 = 234 + 4$). Likewise, the sum of the atomic numbers on both sides of the equation is equal ($92 = 90 + 2$). Mass numbers and atomic numbers are similarly balanced in all nuclear equations. The radioactive properties of the nucleus are essentially independent of the state of chemical combination of the atom. Thus, in writing nuclear equations, we are not concerned with the chemical form of the atom in which the nucleus resides. It makes no difference whether we are dealing with the atom in the form of an element or of one of its compounds.

SAMPLE EXERCISE 21.1

What product is formed when radium-226 undergoes alpha decay?

SOLUTION The periodic table or a list of elements shows that radium has an atomic number of 88. The complete chemical symbol for radium-226 is therefore $^{226}_{88}\text{Ra}$. An alpha particle is a helium-4 nucleus, and so its symbol is $^{4}_{2}\text{He}$ (which is sometimes written as $^{4}_{2}\alpha$). The alpha particle is a product of the nuclear reaction, and so the equation is of the form

$$^{226}_{88}\text{Ra} \longrightarrow ^{A}_{Z}\text{X} + ^{4}_{2}\text{He}$$

where A is the mass number of the product nucleus and Z is its atomic number. We need $226 = A + 4$ and $88 = Z + 2$. Hence, $A = 222$ and $Z = 86$. Again from the periodic table, we see that the element with $Z = 86$ is radon (Rn). Hence the product is $^{222}_{86}\text{Rn}$, and the nuclear equation is

$$^{226}_{88}\text{Ra} \longrightarrow ^{222}_{86}\text{Rn} + ^{4}_{2}\text{He}$$

PRACTICE EXERCISE

What element undergoes alpha decay to form lead-208?   *Answer:* $^{212}_{84}\text{Po}$

Types of Radioactive Decay

The three most common kinds of radioactive decay are alpha (α), beta (β), and gamma (γ) radiation. Table 21.1 summarizes some of the important properties of these kinds of radiation. Alpha radiation consists of a stream of helium-4 nuclei known as alpha particles.

Beta radiation consists of streams of **beta particles,** which are high-speed electrons emitted by an unstable nucleus. Beta particles are represented in nuclear equations by the symbol $^{0}_{-1}\text{e}$ or sometimes $^{0}_{-1}\beta$. The superscript zero indicates that the mass of the electron is exceedingly small in comparison to the mass of a nucleon. The subscript -1 represents the negative charge of the particle, which is opposite that of the proton. Iodine-131 is an example of an isotope that undergoes decay by beta emission:

$$^{131}_{53}\text{I} \longrightarrow ^{131}_{54}\text{Xe} + ^{0}_{-1}\text{e} \qquad [21.2]$$

Notice in Equation 21.2 that beta decay results in increasing the atomic number of the nucleus from 53 to 54. Beta emission is equivalent to the conversion of a neutron ($^{1}_{0}\text{n}$) to a proton ($^{1}_{1}\text{p}$), thereby increasing the atomic number by 1:

$$^{1}_{0}\text{n} \longrightarrow ^{1}_{1}\text{p} + ^{0}_{-1}\text{e} \qquad [21.3]$$

However, just because an electron is ejected from the nucleus, we need not think that the nucleus is composed of these particles, any more than we consider

Point of Emphasis: Beta particles originate in the nucleus; they are *not* orbital electrons.

TABLE 21.1 △ Summary of the Properties of Alpha, Beta, and Gamma Radiation

Property	Type of radiation		
	α	β	γ
Charge	$2+$	$1-$	0
Mass	6.64×10^{-24} g	9.11×10^{-28} g	0
Relative penetrating power	1	100	1000
Nature of radiation	$^{4}_{2}\text{He}$ nuclei	Electrons	High-energy photons

Robert L. Wolke, "Marie Curie's Doctoral Thesis: Prelude to a Nobel Prize," *J. Chem. Educ.* **1988**, *65*, 561.

Point of Emphasis: Gamma rays are more energetic (shorter wavelength) than X-rays.

Point of Emphasis: *Inner-shell* means an orbital electron with a small value of *n*.

a match to be composed of sparks simply because it gives them off when struck. The electron comes into being only when the nucleus undergoes a nuclear reaction.

Gamma radiation (or gamma rays) consists of high-energy photons, that is, electromagnetic radiation of very short wavelength. Gamma radiation changes neither the atomic number nor the mass number of a nucleus and is represented as $^0_0\gamma$, or merely γ. It almost always accompanies other radioactive emission because it represents the energy lost when the remaining nucleons reorganize into more stable arrangements. Generally, we will not show the gamma photons when writing nuclear equations.

Two other types of radioactive decay that occur are positron emission and electron capture. A **positron** is a particle that has the same mass as an electron but an opposite charge.* The positron is represented as ^0_1e. Carbon-11 is an example of an isotope that decays by positron emission:

$$^{11}_{6}C \longrightarrow ^{11}_{5}B + ^{0}_{1}e \qquad [21.4]$$

Notice that positron emission causes the atomic number to decrease from 6 to 5. The emission of a positron has the effect of converting a proton to a neutron, thereby decreasing the atomic number of the nucleus by 1:

$$^{1}_{1}p \longrightarrow ^{1}_{0}n + ^{0}_{1}e \qquad [21.5]$$

Electron capture is the capture by the nucleus of an inner-shell electron from the electron cloud surrounding the nucleus. Rubidium-81 undergoes decay in this fashion, as shown in Equation 21.6:

$$^{81}_{37}Rb + ^{0}_{-1}e \text{ (orbital electron)} \longrightarrow ^{81}_{36}Kr \qquad [21.6]$$

Because the electron is consumed rather than formed in the process, it is shown on the reactant side of the equation. Electron capture has the effect of converting a proton to a neutron:

$$^{1}_{1}p + ^{0}_{-1}e \longrightarrow ^{1}_{0}n \qquad [21.7]$$

Table 21.2 summarizes the symbols used to represent the various elementary particles commonly encountered in nuclear reactions.

TABLE 21.2 △ Particles Common in Radioactive Decay and Nuclear Transformations

Particle	Symbol
Neutron	^1_0n
Proton	^1_1p or ^1_1H
Electron	$^0_{-1}e$
Alpha particle	$^4_2\alpha$ or ^4_2He
Beta particle	$^0_{-1}\beta$ or $^0_{-1}e$
Positron	^0_1e

Point of Emphasis: Both positron emission and electron capture decrease the number of protons and increase the number of neutrons by $^1_1p \longrightarrow ^1_0n + ^0_1e$ and $^1_1p + ^0_{-1}e \longrightarrow ^1_0n$, respectively.

S A M P L E   E X E R C I S E   2 1 . 2

Write nuclear equations for the following processes: **(a)** Mercury-201 undergoes electron capture; **(b)** thorium-231 decays to form protactinium-231.

SOLUTION   **(a)** The information given in the question can be summarized as

$$^{201}_{80}Hg + ^{0}_{-1}e \longrightarrow ^{A}_{Z}X$$

Because the mass numbers must have the same sum on both sides of the equation, $201 + 0 = A$. Thus, the product nucleus must have an atomic mass of 201. Similarly, balancing the atomic numbers gives $80 - 1 = Z$. Thus, the atomic number of the product nucleus must be 79, which identifies it as gold (Au):

$$^{201}_{80}Hg + ^{0}_{-1}e \longrightarrow ^{201}_{79}Au$$

---

* The positron has a very short life because it is annihilated when it collides with an electron, producing gamma rays: $^0_1e + ^0_{-1}e \longrightarrow 2^0_0\gamma$.

(b) In this case, we must determine what type of particle is emitted in the course of the radioactive decay:

$$^{231}_{90}\text{Th} \longrightarrow {}^{231}_{91}\text{Pa} + {}^{A}_{Z}\text{X}$$

From $231 = 231 + A$ and $90 = 91 + Z$, we deduce that $A = 0$ and $Z = -1$. As seen in Table 21.2, the particle with these characteristics is the beta particle (electron). We therefore write the following:

$$^{231}_{90}\text{Th} \longrightarrow {}^{231}_{91}\text{Pa} + {}^{0}_{-1}\text{e}$$

PRACTICE EXERCISE

Write a balanced nuclear equation for the reaction in which oxygen-15 undergoes positron emission. *Answer:* $^{15}_{8}\text{O} \longrightarrow {}^{15}_{7}\text{N} + {}^{0}_{1}\text{e}$

21.2 Patterns of Nuclear Stability

The stability of a particular nucleus depends on a variety of factors, and no single rule allows us to predict whether a particular nucleus is radioactive and how it might decay. There are, however, several empirical observations that are helpful in making predictions.

Neutron-to-Proton Ratio

Because like charges repel each other, it may seem surprising that a large number of protons can reside within the small volume of the nucleus. At close distances, however, a strong force of attraction, called the *strong nuclear force,* exists between nucleons. Neutrons are intimately involved in this attractive force. All nuclei with two or more protons contain neutrons. The more protons packed in the nucleus, the more neutrons are needed to bind the nucleus together. Stable nuclei with low atomic numbers (up to about 20) have approximately equal numbers of neutrons and protons. For nuclei with higher atomic numbers, the number of neutrons exceeds the number of protons. Indeed, the number of neutrons necessary to create a stable nucleus increases more rapidly than the number of protons, as shown in Figure 21.2. Thus, the neutron-to-proton ratios of stable nuclei increase with increasing atomic number.

The colored band in Figure 21.2 is the area within which all stable nuclei are found and is known as the *belt of stability.* The belt of stability ends at element 83 (bismuth). *All nuclei with 84 or more protons (atomic number ≥ 84) are radioactive.* For example, all isotopes of uranium, atomic number 92, are radioactive.

The type of radioactive decay that a particular radionuclide undergoes depends to a large extent on its neutron-to-proton ratio compared to those of nearby nuclei within the belt of stability. We can envision three general situations:

1. *Nuclei above the belt of stability (high neutron-to-proton ratios):* These nuclei can lower their ratio and move toward the belt of stability by emitting a beta particle. Beta emission decreases the number of neutrons and increases the number of protons in a nucleus, as shown in Equation 21.3.

2. *Nuclei below the belt of stability (low neutron-to-proton ratios):* These nuclei can increase their ratio by either positron emission or electron

Learning Goal 2: Determine the effect of different types of decay on the proton-neutron ratio, and predict the type of decay that a nucleus will undergo based on its position relative to the belt of stability.

Point of Emphasis: The issue of nuclear stability is very complex. The belt of stability is meant to serve only as a general guide to predicting nuclear stability.

21.2 Patterns of Nuclear Stability **773**

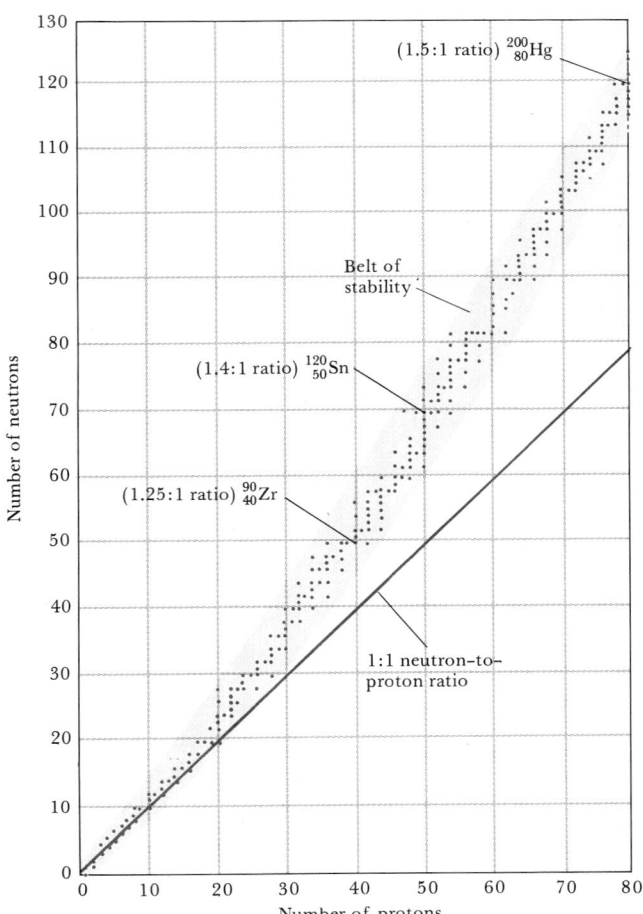

FIGURE 21.2 Plot of the number of neutrons versus the number of protons in stable nuclei. As the atomic number increases, the neutron-to-proton ratio of the stable nuclei increases. The stable nuclei are located in the shaded area of the graph known as the belt of stability. The majority of radioactive nuclei occur outside this belt.

capture. Both kinds of decay increase the number of neutrons and decrease the number of protons, as shown in Equations 21.5 and 21.7. Positron emission is more common than electron capture among the lighter nuclei; however, electron capture becomes increasingly common as nuclear charge increases.

3. *Nuclei with atomic numbers ≥ 84:* These nuclei, which lie beyond the upper right edge of the band of stability, tend to undergo alpha emission. Emission of an alpha particle decreases both the number of neutrons and the number of protons by 2, moving the nucleus diagonally toward the belt of stability.

These three situations are summarized in Figure 21.3.

FIGURE 21.3 Results of alpha emission ($^4_2$He), beta emission ($^0_{-1}$e), positron emission ($^0_1$e), and electron capture on the number of protons and neutrons in a nucleus. The squares represent unstable nuclei, and the circle represents a stable one. Moving from left to right or from bottom to top, each tick mark represents an additional proton or neutron, respectively. Moving in the reverse direction indicates the loss of a proton or neutron.

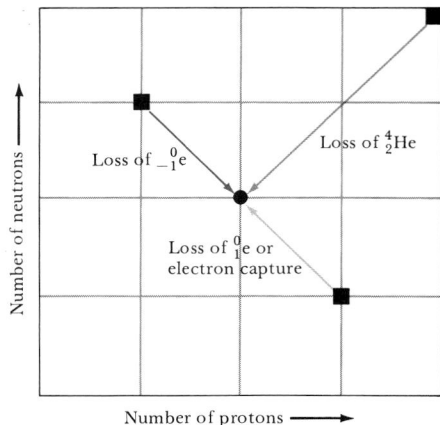

Figure 21.3

SAMPLE EXERCISE 21.3

Predict the mode of decay of **(a)** carbon-14; **(b)** xenon-118.

SOLUTION **(a)** Carbon has an atomic number of 6. Thus carbon-14 has 6 protons and $14 - 6 = 8$ neutrons, giving it a neutron-to-proton ratio of $\frac{8}{6} = 1.3$. Elements with low atomic numbers normally have stable nuclei with approximately equal numbers of neutrons and protons. Thus, carbon-14 has a high neutron-to-proton ratio, and we expect that it will decay by emitting a beta particle:

$$^{14}_6C \longrightarrow {}^0_{-1}e + {}^{14}_7N$$

This is indeed the mode of decay observed for carbon-14.

   (b) Xenon has an atomic number of 54. Thus, xenon-118 has 54 protons and $118 - 54 = 64$ neutrons, giving it a neutron-to-proton ratio of $\frac{64}{54} = 1.2$. By examining Figure 21.2, we see that stable nuclei in this region of the belt of stability have higher neutron-to-proton ratios. The nucleus can increase this ratio by either positron emission or electron capture:

$$^{118}_{54}Xe \longrightarrow {}^0_1e + {}^{118}_{53}I$$
$$^{118}_{54}Xe + {}^0_{-1}e \longrightarrow {}^{118}_{53}I$$

In this case, both modes of decay are observed.

PRACTICE EXERCISE

Predict the mode of decay for **(a)** plutonium-239; **(b)** indium-120.
Answers: **(a)** α decay; **(b)** β decay

At this point we should note that our guidelines don't always work. For example, thorium-233, $^{233}_{90}$Th, which we might expect to undergo alpha decay, actually undergoes beta decay. Furthermore, a few radioactive nuclei actually lie within the belt of stability. For example, both $^{146}_{60}$Nd and $^{148}_{60}$Nd are stable and lie in the belt of stability; however, $^{147}_{60}$Nd, which lies between them, is radioactive.

Radioactive Series

Some nuclei, like uranium-238, cannot gain stability by a single emission. Consequently, a series of successive emissions occurs. As shown in Figure 21.4,

FIGURE 21.4 Nuclear disintegration series for uranium-238. The $^{238}_{92}$U nucleus decays to $^{234}_{90}$Th. Subsequent decay processes eventually form the stable $^{206}_{82}$Pb nucleus. Each blue arrow corresponds to the loss of an alpha particle; each red arrow corresponds to the loss of a beta particle.

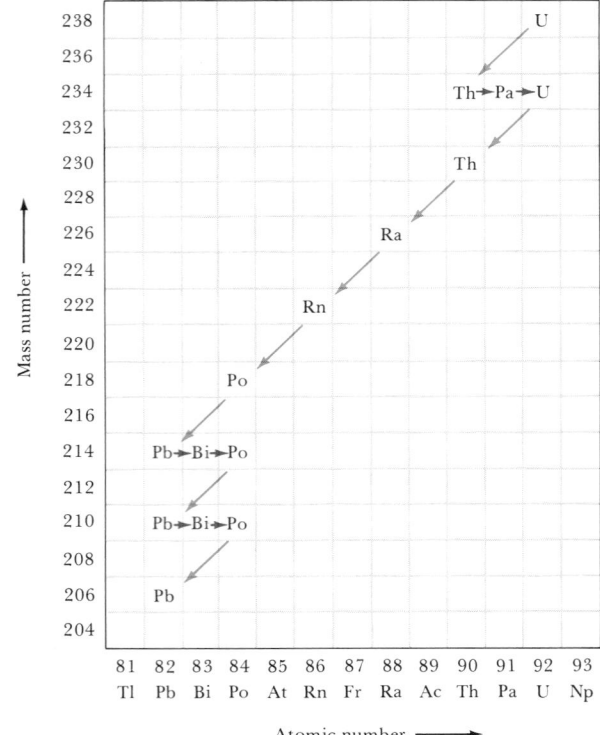

Figure 21.4

Teaching Note: The nuclei resulting from radioactive decay of other nuclei are called *daughter nuclei.*

uranium-238 decays to thorium-234, which is radioactive and decays to protactinium-234. This nucleus is also unstable and subsequently decays. Such successive reactions continue until a stable nucleus, lead-206, is formed. A series of nuclear reactions that begins with an unstable nucleus and terminates with a stable one is known as a **radioactive series** or a **nuclear disintegration series.** Three such series occur in nature. In addition to the series that begins with uranium-238 and terminates with lead-206, there is one that begins with uranium-235 and ends with lead-207. The third series begins with thorium-232 and ends with lead-208.

Further Observations

Two further observations are useful in predicting nuclear stability:

- Nuclei with 2, 8, 20, 28, 50, or 82 protons or 2, 8, 20, 28, 50, 82, or 126 neutrons are generally more stable than nuclei that do not contain these numbers of nucleons. These numbers of protons and neutrons are called **magic numbers.**
- Nuclei with even numbers of both protons and neutrons are generally more stable than those with odd numbers of nucleons, as shown in Table 21.3.

These observations can be understood in terms of the *shell model of the nucleus,* in which nucleons are described as residing in shells analogous to the shell structure for electrons in the atom. Just as certain numbers of electrons (2,

TABLE 21.3 △ **The Number of Stable Isotopes with Even and Odd Numbers of Protons and Neutrons**

Number of stable isotopes	Protons	Neutrons
157	Even	Even
52	Even	Odd
50	Odd	Even
5	Odd	Odd

8, 18, 36, 54, and 86) correspond to stable closed-shell electron configurations, so also the magic numbers of nucleons represent closed shells in nuclei. As an example of the stability of nuclei with magic numbers of nucleons, note that the radioactive series depicted in Figure 21.4 ends with formation of the stable $^{206}_{82}$Pb nucleus, which has a magic number of protons (82).

Evidence also suggests that pairs of protons and pairs of neutrons have a special stability, analogous to the pairs of electrons in molecules. Thus, stable nuclei with an even number of protons and an even number of neutrons are far more numerous that those with odd numbers (Table 21.3).

SAMPLE EXERCISE 21.4

Which of the following nuclei are especially stable: $^{4}_{2}$He, $^{40}_{20}$Ca, $^{98}_{43}$Tc?

SOLUTION The $^{4}_{2}$He nucleus (the alpha particle) has a magic number of both protons (2) and neutrons (2) and is very stable.

The $^{40}_{20}$Ca nucleus also has a magic number of both protons (20) and neutrons (20) and is especially stable.

The $^{98}_{43}$Tc nucleus does not have a magic number of either protons or neutrons. In fact, it has an odd number of both protons (43) and neutrons (55). There are very few stable nuclei with odd numbers of both protons and neutrons. Indeed, technetium-98 is radioactive.

PRACTICE EXERCISE

Which of the following nuclei would you expect to exhibit a special stability? $^{118}_{50}$Sn, $^{210}_{85}$At, $^{208}_{82}$Pb   *Answer:* $^{118}_{50}$Sn, $^{208}_{82}$Pb

21.3 Nuclear Transmutations

Thus far we have examined nuclear reactions in which a nucleus spontaneously decays. Another way a nucleus can change identity is to be struck by a neutron or by another nucleus. Nuclear reactions that are induced in this way are known as **nuclear transmutations.**

The first conversion of one nucleus into another was performed in 1919 by Ernest Rutherford. He succeeded in converting nitrogen-14 into oxygen-17 using the high-velocity alpha particles emitted by radium. The reaction is

$$^{14}_{7}\text{N} + {}^{4}_{2}\text{He} \longrightarrow {}^{17}_{8}\text{O} + {}^{1}_{1}\text{H} \qquad [21.8]$$

(The symbols $^{1}_{1}$H and $^{1}_{1}$p are equivalent; both represent a proton.) This reaction demonstrated that nuclear reactions can be induced by striking nuclei with particles such as alpha particles. Such reactions have permitted synthesis of hundreds of radioisotopes in the laboratory.

Nuclear transmutations are commonly represented by listing, in order, the target nucleus, the bombarding particle, the ejected particle, and the product nucleus. Written in this fashion, Equation 21.8 is $^{14}_{7}$N$(\alpha, \text{p})^{17}_{8}$O. The alpha particle, proton, and neutron are abbreviated as α, p, and n, respectively.

Learning Goal 3: Complete and balance nuclear equations, having been given all but one of the particles involved.

Learning Goal 4: Write the shorthand notation for a nuclear reaction, or, given the shorthand notation, write the nuclear reaction.

Point of Emphasis: The notation $^{14}_{7}$N$(\alpha, \text{p})^{17}_{8}$O seems awkward at first, but it is a commonly used shorthand notation for nuclear reactions.

SAMPLE EXERCISE 21.5

Write the balanced nuclear equation for the process summarized as $^{27}_{13}$Al(n, $\alpha)^{24}_{11}$Na.

SOLUTION The n is the abbreviation for a neutron, and α represents an alpha particle. The neutron is the bombarding particle, and the alpha particle is a product. Therefore, the nuclear equation is

$$^{27}_{13}Al + ^1_0n \longrightarrow ^{24}_{11}Na + ^4_2He$$

PRACTICE EXERCISE

Write the nuclear reaction

$$^{16}_8O + ^1_1H \longrightarrow ^{13}_7N + ^4_2He$$

in a shorthand notation. *Answer:* $^{16}_8O(p, \alpha)^{13}_7N$

Using Charged Particles

Charged particles, such as alpha particles, must be moving very fast in order to overcome the electrostatic repulsion between them and the target nucleus. The higher the nuclear charge on either the projectile or the target, the faster the projectile must be moving to bring about a nuclear reaction. Many methods have been devised to accelerate charged particles using strong magnetic and electrostatic fields. These **particle accelerators,** popularly called "atom smashers," bear such names as *cyclotron* and *synchrotron.* The cyclotron is illustrated in Figure 21.5. The hollow D-shaped electrodes are called "dees." The projectile particles are introduced into a vacuum chamber within the cyclotron. The particles are then accelerated by making the dees alternately positively and negatively charged. Magnets placed above and below the dees keep the particles moving in a spiral path until they are finally deflected out of the cyclotron and emerge to strike a target substance. Particle accelerators have been used mainly to synthesize heavy elements and to investigate the fundamental structure of matter. Figure 21.6 shows an aerial view of Fermilab, the National Accelerator Laboratory near Chicago. An even larger and higher-energy accelerator, the Superconducting Supercollider (SSC), is currently under construction in Texas. Completion of the SSC will require more than \$10 billion. At this writing, it is not certain that the U.S. government will provide the funds to finish the project. If completed, this accelerator will have a circumference of 105 km (65 mi).

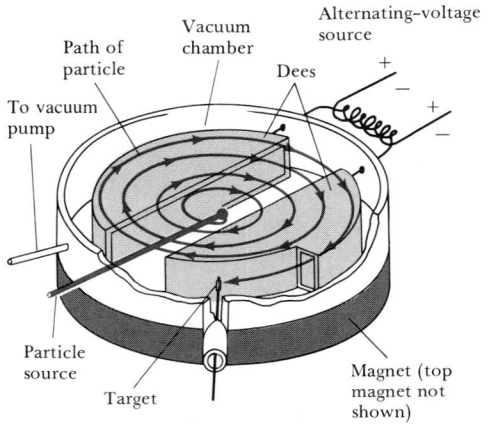

FIGURE 21.5 Schematic drawing of a cyclotron. Charged particles are accelerated around the ring by the application of alternating voltage to the dees.

FIGURE 21.6 An aerial view of the Fermi National Accelerator Laboratory at Batavia, Illinois. Particles are accelerated to very high energies by circulating them through magnets in the ring, which has a circumference of 6.3 km. (Fermilab Photo Dept.)

Using Neutrons

Most synthetic isotopes used in quantity in medicine and scientific research are made using neutrons as projectiles. Because neutrons are neutral, they are not repelled by the nucleus; consequently, they do not need to be accelerated, as do charged particles, in order to cause nuclear reactions (indeed, they cannot be so accelerated). The necessary neutrons are produced by the reactions that occur in nuclear reactors. For example, cobalt-60, used in radiation therapy for cancer, is produced by neutron capture. Iron-58 is placed in a nuclear reactor, where it is bombarded by neutrons. The following sequence of reactions takes place:

$$^{58}_{26}\text{Fe} + ^{1}_{0}\text{n} \longrightarrow ^{59}_{26}\text{Fe} \qquad [21.9]$$

$$^{59}_{26}\text{Fe} \longrightarrow ^{59}_{27}\text{Co} + ^{0}_{-1}\text{e} \qquad [21.10]$$

$$^{59}_{27}\text{Co} + ^{1}_{0}\text{n} \longrightarrow ^{60}_{27}\text{Co} \qquad [21.11]$$

Transuranium Elements

Artificial transmutations have been used to produce the elements from atomic number 93 to 109. These are known as the **transuranium elements** because they occur immediately following uranium in the periodic table. Elements 93 (neptunium) and 94 (plutonium) were first discovered in 1940. They were produced by bombarding uranium-238 with neutrons, as shown below:

$$^{238}_{92}\text{U} + ^{1}_{0}\text{n} \longrightarrow ^{239}_{92}\text{U} \longrightarrow ^{239}_{93}\text{Np} + ^{0}_{-1}\text{e} \qquad [21.12]$$

$$^{239}_{93}\text{Np} \longrightarrow ^{239}_{94}\text{Pu} + ^{0}_{-1}\text{e} \qquad [21.13]$$

Elements with larger atomic numbers are normally formed in small quantities in particle accelerators. For example, curium-242 is formed when a plutonium-239 target is struck with accelerated alpha particles:

$$^{239}_{94}\text{Pu} + ^{4}_{2}\text{He} \longrightarrow ^{242}_{96}\text{Cm} + ^{1}_{0}\text{n}$$ [21.14]

21.4 Rates of Radioactive Decay

Learning Goal 5: Use the half-life of a substance to predict the amount of radioisotope present after a given period of time.

Our discussions to this point may have raised some questions in your mind. For example, why are some radioisotopes, such as uranium-238, found in nature, whereas others are not and must be synthesized? The key to answering this question is to realize that different nuclei undergo radioactive decay at different rates. Many radioisotopes decay essentially completely in a matter of seconds; obviously, we do not find such nuclei in nature. In contrast, uranium-238 decays very slowly; therefore despite its instability, we can still observe this isotope in nature. An important characteristic of a radioisotope is its rate of radioactive decay.

Point of Emphasis: Radioactive decay processes are invariably first-order and therefore obey the rate law $\ln N_t/N_0 = -kt$ and the half-life expression $t_{1/2} = 0.693/k$, where k is the characteristic rate constant. See Chapter 14.

Radioactive decay is a first-order process. ∞ (Sec. 14.3) Recall that a first-order process has a characteristic **half-life,** which is the time required for half of any given quantity of a substance to react. ∞ (Sec. 14.3) The rates of decay of nuclei are commonly discussed in terms of their half-lives.

Each isotope has its own characteristic half-life. For example, the half-life of strontium-90 is 29 yr. If we started with 10.0 g of strontium-90, only 5.0 g of that isotope would remain after 29 yr, 2.5 g would remain after another 29 yr, and so on. Strontium-90 decays to yttrium-90, as shown in Equation 21.15:

$$^{90}_{38}\text{Sr} \longrightarrow ^{90}_{39}\text{Y} + ^{0}_{-1}\text{e}$$ [21.15]

The loss of strontium-90 as a function of time is shown in Figure 21.7.

Half-lives as short as millionths of a second and as long as billions of years are observed. The half-lives of some radioisotopes are listed in Table 21.4. One important feature of half-lives for nuclear decay is that they are unaffected by external conditions such as temperature, pressure, or state of chemical combination. Therefore, unlike toxic chemicals, radioactive atoms cannot be rendered harmless by chemical reaction or by any other practical treatment. At this

Point of Emphasis: The kinetics of nuclear reactions, unlike those of chemical reactions, are unaffected by temperature, pressure, or the chemical or physical state of the reactants.

FIGURE 21.7 Decay of a 10.0-g sample of $^{90}_{38}$Sr ($t_{1/2} =$ 28.8 yr).

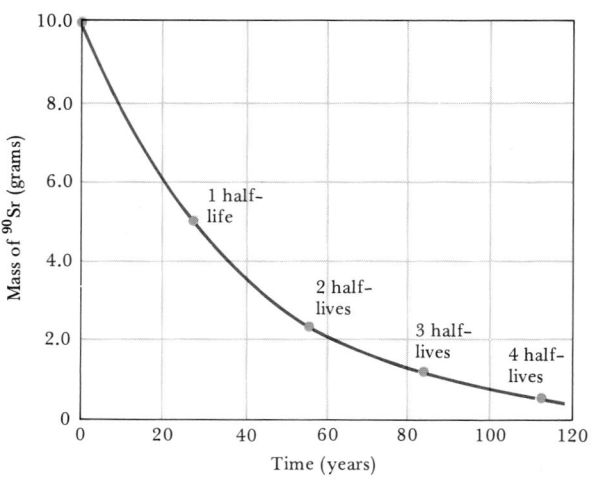

TABLE 21.4 △ The Half-Lives and Type of Decay for Several Radioisotopes

	Isotope	Half-life (yr)	Type of decay
Natural radioisotopes	$^{238}_{92}U$	4.5×10^9	Alpha
	$^{235}_{92}U$	7.1×10^8	Alpha
	$^{232}_{90}Th$	1.4×10^{10}	Alpha
	$^{40}_{19}K$	1.3×10^9	Beta
	$^{14}_{6}C$	5,730	Beta
Synthetic radioisotopes	$^{239}_{94}Pu$	24,000	Alpha
	$^{137}_{55}Cs$	30	Beta
	$^{90}_{38}Sr$	28.8	Beta
	$^{131}_{53}I$	0.022	Beta

point, we can do nothing but allow these nuclei to lose radioactivity at their characteristic rates. In the meantime, of course, we must take precautions to isolate the radioisotopes because of the damage radiation can cause.

SAMPLE EXERCISE 21.6

The half-life of cobalt-60 is 5.3 yr. How much of a 1.000-mg sample of cobalt-60 is left after a 15.9-yr period?

SOLUTION A period of 15.9 yr is three half-lives for cobalt-60. At the end of one half-life 0.500 mg of cobalt-60 remains, 0.250 mg at the end of two half-lives, and 0.125 mg at the end of three half-lives.

PRACTICE EXERCISE

Carbon-11, used in medical imaging, has a half-life of 20.4 min. The carbon-11 nuclides are formed and then incorporated into a desired compound. The resulting sample is injected into a patient, and the medical image is obtained. The entire process lasts five half-lives. What percentage of the original carbon-11 activity remains at this time? *Answer:* 3.1 percent

Dating

Because the half-life of any particular nuclide is constant, the half-life can serve as a molecular clock to determine the ages of different objects. For example, carbon-14 has been used to determine the age of organic materials (Figure 21.8). The procedure is based on the formation of carbon-14 by neutron capture in the upper atmosphere:

$$^{14}_{7}N + ^{1}_{0}n \longrightarrow ^{14}_{6}C + ^{1}_{1}p \qquad [21.16]$$

This reaction provides a small but reasonably constant source of carbon-14. The carbon-14 is radioactive, undergoing beta decay with a half-life of 5730 yr:

$$^{14}_{6}C \longrightarrow ^{14}_{7}N + ^{0}_{-1}e \qquad [21.17]$$

In using radiocarbon dating, we generally assume that the ratio of carbon-14 to carbon-12 in the atmosphere has been constant for at least 50,000 yr. The

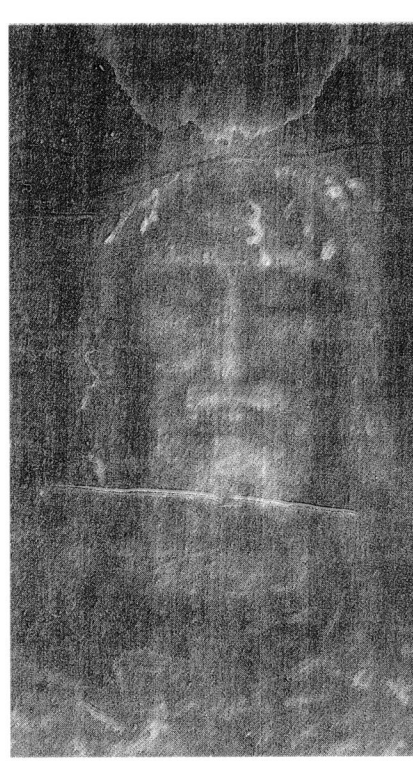

FIGURE 21.8 The Shroud of Turin, a linen cloth over 4 m long, bears a faint image of a man, seen here in a photographic negative of the image. The shroud had been alleged to have been the burial shroud of Jesus Christ. Numerous tests have been performed on fragments of the cloth in recent years to determine its origin and age. Scientists who used radiocarbon dating to determine the age of the cloth concluded that the linen was made between A.D. 1260 and 1390. (© Vernon Miller/Brooks Institute)

carbon-14 is incorporated into carbon dioxide, which is in turn incorporated, through photosynthesis, into more complex carbon-containing molecules within plants. When the plants are eaten by animals, the carbon-14 becomes incorporated within them. Because a living plant or animal has a constant intake of carbon compounds, it is able to maintain a ratio of carbon-14 to carbon-12 that is identical with that of the atmosphere. However, once the organism dies, it no longer ingests carbon compounds to replenish the carbon-14 that is lost through radioactive decay. The ratio of carbon-14 to carbon-12 therefore decreases. By calculating this ratio and contrasting it to that of the atmosphere, we can estimate the age of an object. For example, if the ratio diminishes to half that of the atmosphere, we can conclude that the object is one half-life, or 5730 yr, old. This method cannot be used to date objects older than about 20,000 to 50,000 yr. After this length of time, the radioactivity is too low to be measured accurately.

The radiocarbon-dating technique has been checked by comparing the ages of trees determined by counting their rings and by radiocarbon analysis. As a tree grows, it adds a ring each year. In the old growth, the carbon-14 decays, while the concentration of carbon-12 remains constant. The two dating methods agree to within about 10 percent. Most of the wood used in these tests was from California bristle-cone pines, which reach ages up to 2000 yr. By using trees that died at a known time thousands of years ago, it is possible to make comparisons back to about 5000 B.C.

Other isotopes can be similarly used to date other types of objects. For example, it takes 4.5×10^9 yr for half of a sample of uranium-238 to decay to lead-206. The age of rocks containing uranium can therefore be determined by measuring the ratio of lead-206 to uranium-238. If the lead-206 had somehow become incorporated into the rock by normal chemical processes instead of by radioactive decay, the rock would also contain large amounts of the more abundant isotope lead-208. In the absence of large amounts of this "geonormal" isotope of lead, it is assumed that all of the lead-206 was at one time uranium-238.

The oldest rocks found on the earth are approximately 3×10^9 yr old. This age indicates that the crust of the earth has been solid for at least this length of time. Scientists estimate that it required 1 to 1.5×10^9 yr for the earth to cool and its surface to become solid. This places the age of the earth at 4.0 to 4.5 $\times 10^9$ (about 4.5 billion) yr.

Calculations Based on Half-Life

So far our discussion has been mainly qualitative. We now consider the topic of half-lives from a more quantitative point of view. This approach enables us to answer questions of the following types: How do we determine the half-life of uranium-238? Similarly, how do we determine quantitatively the age of an object?

The rate of radioactive decay of any radioisotope is first-order. It can therefore be described by Equation 21.18:

$$\text{Rate} = kN \qquad [21.18]$$

where N is the number of nuclei of a particular radioisotope, and k is the first-order rate constant. This equation can be transformed into Equation 21.19. (Note that the equations that follow are the same as those we encountered in Section 14.3 in dealing with first-order chemical processes.)

$$\ln \frac{N_t}{N_0} = -kt \qquad \ln N_t - \ln N_0 = -kt \qquad [21.19]$$

In this equation, t is the time interval of decay, k is the rate constant, N_0 is the initial number of nuclei (at zero time), and N_t is the number remaining after the time interval. The relationship between the rate constant, k, and half-life, $t_{1/2}$, is given by Equation 21.20:

$$k = \frac{0.693}{t_{1/2}} \qquad [21.20]$$

SAMPLE EXERCISE 21.7

A rock contains 0.257 mg of lead-206 for every milligram of uranium-238. The half-life for the decay of uranium-238 to lead-206 is 4.5×10^9 yr. How old is the rock?

SOLUTION Let us assume that the rock contains 1.000 mg of uranium-238 at present. The amount of uranium-238 in the rock when it was first formed therefore equals 1.000 mg plus the quantity that decayed to lead-206. We obtain the latter quantity by multiplying the present mass of lead-206 by the ratio of the atomic mass of uranium to that of lead, into which it has decayed. The total original $^{238}_{92}U$ was thus

$$\text{Original } ^{238}_{92}U = 1.000 \text{ mg} + \frac{238}{206}(0.257 \text{ mg})$$

$$= 1.297 \text{ mg}$$

Using Equation 21.20, we can calculate the rate constant for the process from its half-life:

$$k = \frac{0.693}{4.5 \times 10^9 \text{ yr}} = 1.5 \times 10^{-10} \text{ yr}^{-1}$$

Rearranging Equation 21.19 to solve for time, t, and substituting known quantities gives

$$t = -\frac{1}{k} \ln \frac{N_t}{N_0} = -\frac{1}{1.5 \times 10^{-10} \text{ yr}^{-1}} \ln \frac{1.000}{1.297} = 1.7 \times 10^9 \text{ yr}$$

PRACTICE EXERCISE

A wooden object from an archeological site is subjected to radiocarbon dating. The radioactivity of the sample due to ^{14}C is measured to be 12.4 disintegrations per second. The radioactivity of a carbon sample of equal mass from fresh wood is 19.5 disintegrations per second. The half-life of ^{14}C is 5730 yr. What is the age of the archeological sample?   *Answer:* 3740 yr

SAMPLE EXERCISE 21.8

If we start with 1.000 g of strontium-90, 0.953 g will remain after 2.00 yr. **(a)** What is the half-life of strontium-90? **(b)** How much strontium-90 will remain after 5.00 yr?

SOLUTION **(a)** Equation 21.19 is solved for the rate constant, k, and then Equation 21.20 is used to calculate half-life, $t_{1/2}$:

$$k = -\frac{1}{t} \ln \frac{N_t}{N_0} = -\frac{1}{2.00 \text{ yr}} \ln \frac{0.953 \text{ g}}{1.000 \text{ g}}$$

$$= -\frac{1}{2.00 \text{ yr}} (-0.0481) = 0.0241 \text{ yr}^{-1}$$

$$t_{1/2} = \frac{0.693}{k} = \frac{0.693}{0.0241 \text{ yr}^{-1}} = 28.8 \text{ yr}$$

(b) Again using Equation 21.19, with $k = 0.0241 \text{ yr}^{-1}$, we have

$$\ln \frac{N_t}{N_0} = -kt = -(0.0241 \text{ yr}^{-1})(5.00 \text{ yr}) = -0.120$$

Calculation of N_t/N_0 from $\ln (N_t/N_0) = -0.120$ is readily accomplished using the e^x or INV LN function of a calculator:

$$\frac{N_t}{N_0} = e^{-0.120} = 0.887$$

Because $N_0 = 1.000$ g, we have

$$N_t = (0.887) N_0 = (0.887)(1.000 \text{ g}) = 0.887 \text{ g}$$

PRACTICE EXERCISE

A sample to be used for medical imaging is labeled with ^{18}F, which has a half-life of 110 min. What percentage of the original activity in the sample remains after 300 min?   *Answer:* 15.1 percent

21.5 Detection of Radioactivity

A variety of methods have been devised to detect emissions from radioactive substances. Becquerel discovered radioactivity because of the effect of radiation on photographic plates. Photographic plates and film have long been used to detect radioactivity. The radiation affects photographic film in much the same way as x-rays do. With care, film can be used to give a quantitative measure of activity. The greater the extent of exposure to radiation, the darker the area of the developed negative. People who work with radioactive substances carry film badges to record the extent of their exposure to radiation (Figure 21.9).

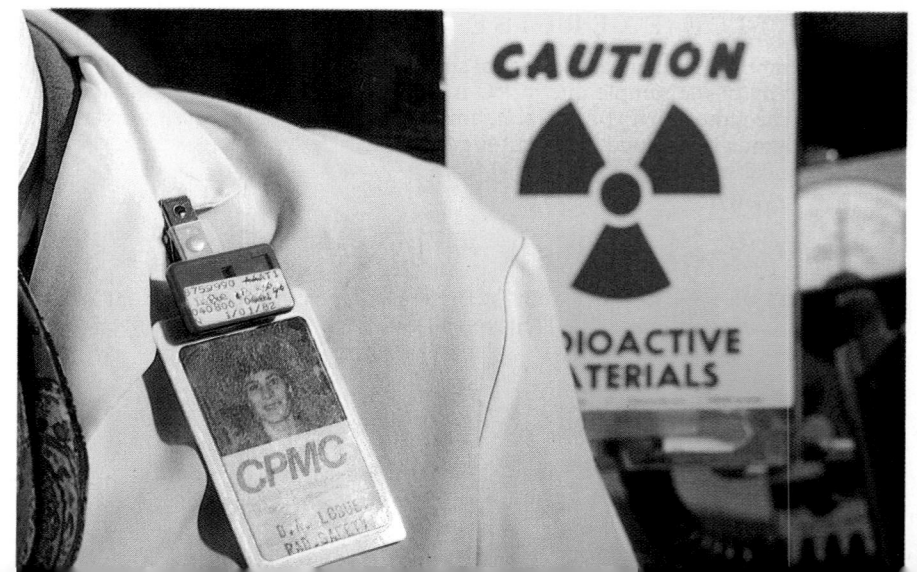

FIGURE 21.9 Badge dosimeter. Badges such as the one on this worker's lapel are used to monitor the extent to which the individual has been exposed to high-energy radiation. The radiation dose is determined from the extent of fogging of the film in the dosimeter. Monitoring the radiation in this way helps prevent overexposure for people whose jobs require them to use radioactive materials or X-rays. (© Yoav Levy/Phototake NYC)

Radioactivity can also be detected and measured using a device known as a **Geiger counter.** The operation of a Geiger counter is based on the ionization of matter caused by radiation. The ions and electrons produced by the ionizing radiation permit conduction of an electrical current. The basic design of a Geiger counter is shown in Figure 21.10. It consists of a metal tube filled with gas. The cylinder has a "window" made of material that can be penetrated by alpha, beta, or gamma rays. In the center of the tube is a wire. The wire is connected to one terminal of a source of direct current, and the metal cylinder is attached to the other terminal. Current flows between the wire and metal cylinder whenever ions are produced by entering radiation. The current pulse created when radiation enters the tube is amplified; each pulse is counted as a measure of the amount of radiation.

Teaching Note: Ionizing radiation produces ions by displacing electrons from molecules in high-energy collisions.

Certain substances that are electronically excited by radiation can also be used to detect and measure radiation. For example, some substances excited by radiation give off light as electrons return to their lower-energy states. These substances are called *phosphors.* Different substances respond to different particles. For example, zinc sulfide responds to alpha particles. In the past, dials of luminous watches were painted with a mixture of ZnS and a tiny quantity of $RaSO_4$ (Figure 21.11). The ZnS emits visible light when struck by alpha particles from the radioactive decay of the radium, causing the dial to glow in the dark.

An instrument called a **scintillation counter** is used to detect and measure radiation based on the tiny flashes of light produced when radiation strikes a suitable phosphor. The flashes are magnified electronically and counted to measure the amount of radiation.

Radiotracers

Because radioisotopes can be detected so readily, they can be used to follow an element through its chemical reactions. For example, the incorporation of carbon atoms from CO_2 into glucose in photosynthesis has been studied using CO_2 containing carbon-14:

$$6\ ^{14}CO_2 + 6H_2O \xrightarrow[\text{chlorophyll}]{\text{sunlight}} {}^{14}C_6H_{12}O_6 + 6O_2 \qquad [21.21]$$

Teaching Note: Reactions with radiotracers are often written to emphasize the presence of the radioisotope, such as $^{12}CO_2$ or $^{14}CO_2$ in the example here.

The CO_2 is said to be labeled with the carbon-14. Detection devices such as scintillation counters follow the carbon-14 as it moves from the CO_2 through the various intermediate compounds to glucose.

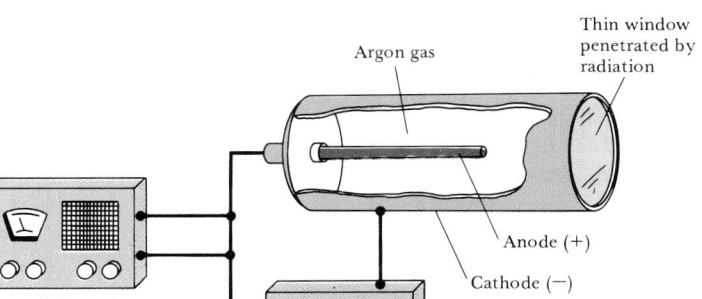

Argon gas

Thin window penetrated by radiation

Anode (+)

Cathode (−)

Amplifier and counter

High voltage

FIGURE 21.10 Schematic representation of a Geiger counter.

Such use of radioisotopes is possible because all isotopes of an element have essentially identical chemical properties. When a small quantity of a radioisotope is mixed with the naturally occurring stable isotopes of the same element, all the isotopes go through the same reactions together. The element's path is revealed by the radioactivity of the radioisotope. Because the radioisotope can be used to trace the path of the element, it is called a **radiotracer.**

21.6 Energy Changes in Nuclear Reactions

So far we have said little about the energies associated with nuclear reactions. These energies can be considered with the aid of Einstein's famous equation relating mass and energy:

$$E = mc^2 \qquad [21.22]$$

In this equation, E stands for energy, m for mass, and c for the speed of light, 3.00×10^8 m/s. This equation states that the mass and energy of an object are proportional. If a system loses mass, it loses energy (exothermic); if it gains mass, it gains energy (endothermic). Because the proportionality constant in the equation, c^2, is such a large number, even small changes in mass are accompanied by large changes in energy.

The mass changes in chemical reactions are too small to detect easily. For example, the mass change associated with the combustion of a mole of CH_4 (an exothermic process) is -9.9×10^{-9} g. Because the mass change is so small, it is possible to speak of the conservation of mass in chemical reactions.

The mass changes and the associated energy changes in nuclear reactions are much greater than those in chemical reactions. For example, the mass change accompanying the radioactive decay of a mole of uranium-238 is 50,000 times greater than that for the combustion of a mole of CH_4. Let's examine the energy change for this nuclear reaction:

$$^{238}_{92}\text{U} \longrightarrow {}^{234}_{90}\text{Th} + {}^{4}_{2}\text{He}$$

Medical Applications of Radiotracers

Radiotracers have found wide use as a diagnostic tool in medicine. Table 21.5 lists some of the radiotracers and their uses. These radioisotopes are incorporated into a compound that is administered to the patient, usually by an intravenous route. The diagnostic use of these isotopes is based upon the ability of the radioactive compound to localize and concentrate in the organ or tissue under investigation. For example, iodine-131 has been used to test the activity of the thyroid gland. This gland is the only important user of iodine in the body. The patient drinks a solution of NaI containing iodine-131. Only a very small amount is used so that the patient does not receive a harmful dose of radioactivity. A Geiger counter placed close to the thyroid, in the neck region, determines the ability of the thyroid to take up the iodine. A normal thyroid will absorb about 12 percent of the iodine within a few hours.

TABLE 21.5 △ Some Radionuclides Used as Radiotracers

Nuclide	Half-life	Area of the body studied
Iodine-131	8.1 days	Thyroid
Iron-59	45.1 days	Red blood cells
Phosphorus-32	14.3 days	Eyes, liver, tumors
Technetium-99	6.0 hours	Heart, bones, liver, and lungs
Sodium-23	14.8 hours	Circulatory system

The medical applications of radiotracers are further illustrated by another technique, positron emission tomography (PET). PET is a promising tool for clinical diagnosis of many diseases. In this method, compounds containing radionuclides that decay by positron emission are injected into a patient. These compounds are chosen to enable researchers to monitor blood flow, oxygen and glucose metabolic rates, and other biological functions. Some of the most interesting work involves the study of the brain, which depends on glucose for most of its energy. Changes in how this sugar is metabolized or used by the brain may signal a disease such as cancer, epilepsy, Parkinson's disease, or schizophrenia.

The compound to be detected in the patient must be labeled with a radionuclide that is a positron emitter. The most widely used nuclides are carbon-11 (half-life 20.4 min), fluorine-18 (half-life 110 min), oxygen-15 (half-life 2 min), and nitrogen-13 (half-life 10 min). As an example, glucose can be labeled with ^{11}C. Because the half-lives of positron emitters are so short, the chemist must quickly incorporate the radionuclide into the sugar (or other appropriate) molecule and inject the compound immediately. The patient is placed in an elaborate instrument [Figure 21.12(a)] that measures the positron emission and constructs a computer-based image of the organ in which the emitting compound is localized. The nature of this image [Figure 21.12(b)] provides clues as to the presence of disease or other abnormality and helps medical researchers understand how a particular disease affects the functioning of the brain.

FIGURE 21.12 (a) In positron emission tomography (PET), a patient is injected with a solution of radiolabeled compound that quickly moves to the brain. Radioactive nuclei within the compound emit positrons. The PET instrument measures the positron emissions and develops a three-dimensional image of the brain. (b) PET images of human brains. The red line in the figure at the lower right shows the view of the brain that appears in the images. The brain of a normal person and those of patients suffering from schizophrenia and manic depression show different image patterns. (Brookhaven National Laboratory and New York University Medical Center)

(a)

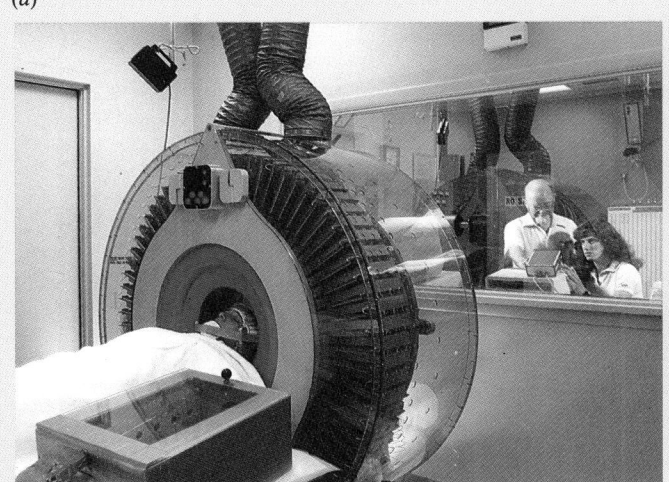

(b)

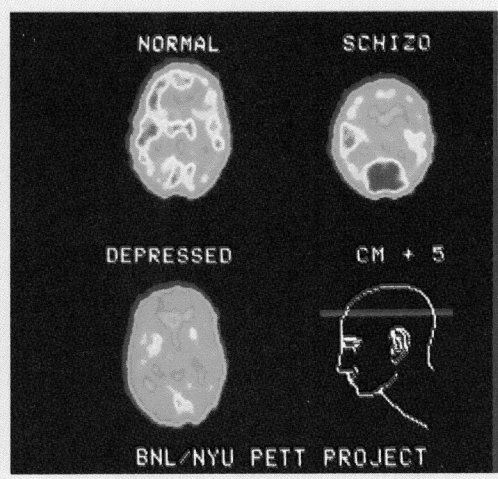

The nuclei in this reaction have the following masses: $^{238}_{92}U$, 238.0003 amu; $^{234}_{90}Th$, 233.9942 amu; and ^4_2He, 4.0015 amu. The mass change, Δm, is defined as the total mass of the products minus the total mass of the reactants. The mass change for decay of a mole of uranium-238 is

$$233.9942 \text{ g} + 4.0015 \text{ g} - 238.0003 \text{ g} = -0.0046 \text{ g}$$

The fact that the system has lost mass indicates that the process is exothermic. All spontaneous nuclear reactions are exothermic.

The energy change per mole associated with this reaction can be calculated using Einstein's equations:

$$\Delta E = \Delta(mc^2) = c^2 \, \Delta m$$

$$= (3.00 \times 10^8 \text{ m/s})^2 (-0.0046 \text{ g}) \left(\frac{1 \text{ kg}}{1000 \text{ g}} \right)$$

$$= -4.1 \times 10^{11} \, \frac{\text{kg-m}^2}{\text{s}^2} = -4.1 \times 10^{11} \text{ J}$$

In calculating the mass change in a nuclear reaction, it is usually acceptable to employ the masses of the atoms containing the nuclei of interest, because the number of electrons in the reactants and products is usually the same. Thus, the difference in atomic masses is usually the same as the difference in nuclear masses.

SAMPLE EXERCISE 21.9

How much energy is lost or gained when a mole of cobalt-60 undergoes beta decay: $^{60}_{27}Co \longrightarrow \, _{-1}^{0}e + \, ^{60}_{28}Ni$? The mass of the $^{60}_{27}Co$ atom is 59.9338 amu, and that of a $^{60}_{28}Ni$ atom is 59.9308 amu.

SOLUTION A $^{60}_{27}Co$ atom has 27 electrons, which are unaffected by the beta decay. The products are a beta particle and a Ni nucleus surrounded by 27 electrons (that is, a $^{60}_{28}Ni^+$ ion). Thus, the total mass of the products is just the mass of the neutral $^{60}_{28}Ni$ atom. The mass change in the reaction, therefore, is given by

$$\Delta m = \text{mass of } ^{60}_{28}Ni \text{ atom} - \text{mass of } ^{60}_{27}Co \text{ atom}$$
$$= 59.9308 \text{ amu} - 59.9338 \text{ amu}$$
$$= -0.0030 \text{ amu}$$

Because the mass decreases ($\Delta m < 0$), energy is released when cobalt-60 decays. For a mole of cobalt-60, $\Delta m = -0.0030$ g. The energy produced per mole by the reaction can be calculated from this mass:

$$\Delta E = c^2 \, \Delta m$$

$$= (3.00 \times 10^8 \text{ m/s})^2 (-0.0030 \text{ g}) \left(\frac{1 \text{ kg}}{1000 \text{ g}} \right)$$

$$= -2.7 \times 10^{11} \, \frac{\text{kg-m}^2}{\text{s}^2} = -2.7 \times 10^{11} \text{ J}$$

PRACTICE EXERCISE

Positron emission from ^{11}C,

$$^{11}_6C \longrightarrow \, ^{11}_5B + \, ^0_1e$$

occurs with release of 2.87×10^{11} J per mole of ^{11}C. What is the mass change per mole of ^{11}C in this nuclear reaction?   ***Answer:*** -3.19×10^{-3} g

Nuclear Binding Energies

Scientists discovered in the 1930s that the masses of nuclei are always less than the masses of the individual nucleons of which they are composed. For example, the helium-4 nucleus has a mass of 4.00150 amu. The mass of a proton is 1.00728 amu, and that of a neutron is 1.00867 amu. Consequently, two protons and two neutrons have a total mass of 4.03190 amu:

Learning Goal 10: Calculate the binding energies of nuclei, having been given their masses and the masses of protons and neutrons.

$$\text{Mass of two protons} = 2(1.00728 \text{ amu}) = 2.01456 \text{ amu}$$
$$\text{Mass of two neutrons} = 2(1.00867 \text{ amu}) = \underline{2.01734 \text{ amu}}$$
$$\text{Total mass} \qquad\qquad = 4.03190 \text{ amu}$$

The mass of the individual nucleons is 0.03040 amu greater than that of the helium-4 nucleus:

$$\text{Mass of two protons and two neutrons} = 4.03190 \text{ amu}$$
$$\text{Mass of } {}^{4}_{2}\text{He nucleus} = \underline{4.00150 \text{ amu}}$$
$$\text{Mass difference} = 0.03040 \text{ amu}$$

The mass difference between a nucleus and its constituent nucleons is called the **mass defect.** The origin of the mass difference is readily understood if we consider that energy must be added to a nucleus in order to break it into separated protons and neutrons:

$$\text{Energy} + {}^{4}_{2}\text{He} \longrightarrow 2{}^{1}_{1}\text{p} + 2{}^{1}_{0}\text{n} \qquad\qquad [21.23]$$

The addition of energy to a system must be accompanied by a proportional increase in mass. The mass change for the conversion of helium-4 into separated nucleons is $\Delta m = 0.03040$ amu, as shown in the calculations above. The energy required for this process is readily calculated:

$$\Delta E = c^2 \Delta m =$$
$$(3.00 \times 10^8 \text{ m/s})^2 (0.0304 \text{ amu}) \left(\frac{1.00 \text{ g}}{6.02 \times 10^{23} \text{ amu}} \right) \left(\frac{1 \text{ kg}}{1000 \text{ g}} \right)$$
$$= 4.54 \times 10^{-12} \text{ J}$$

The energy required to separate a nucleus into its individual nucleons is called the **nuclear binding energy.** The larger the binding energy, the more stable the nucleus toward decomposition. The nuclear binding energies of helium-4 and two other nuclei (iron-56 and uranium-238) are compared in Table 21.6.

TABLE 21.6 △ Mass Differences and Binding Energies for Three Nuclei

Nucleus	Mass of nucleus (amu)	Mass of individual nucleons (amu)	Mass difference (amu)	Binding energy (J)	Binding energy per nucleon (J)
${}^{4}_{2}\text{He}$	4.00150	4.03190	0.03040	4.54×10^{-12}	1.14×10^{-12}
${}^{56}_{26}\text{Fe}$	55.92066	56.44938	0.52872	7.90×10^{-11}	1.41×10^{-12}
${}^{238}_{92}\text{U}$	238.0003	239.9356	1.9353	2.89×10^{-10}	1.22×10^{-12}

FIGURE 21.13 The average binding energy per nucleon increases to a maximum at a mass number of 50 to 60 and decreases slowly thereafter. As a result of these trends, fusion of light nuclei and fission of heavy nuclei are exothermic processes.

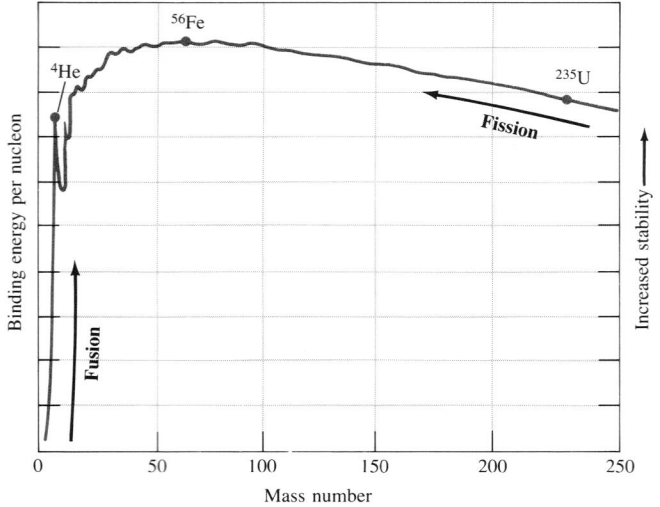

The binding energies per nucleon (that is, the binding energy of each nucleus divided by the total number of nucleons in that nucleus) are also compared in the table.

The binding energies per nucleon are helpful in comparing the stabilities of different combinations of nucleons (such as 2 protons and 2 neutrons arranged either as $_2^4He$ or 2_1^2H). Figure 21.13 shows the binding energy per nucleon plotted against mass number. The binding energy per nucleon at first increases in magnitude as the mass number increases, reaching about 1.4×10^{-12} J for nuclei whose mass numbers are in the vicinity of iron-56. It then decreases slowly to about 1.2×10^{-12} J for very heavy nuclei. This trend indicates that nuclei of intermediate mass numbers are more tightly bound (and therefore more stable) than those with either smaller or larger mass numbers. This trend has two significant consequences: First, heavy nuclei gain stability and therefore give off energy if they are fragmented into two mid-sized nuclei. This process, known as **fission,** is used to generate energy in nuclear power plants. Second, even greater amounts of energy are released if very light nuclei are combined or fused together to give more massive nuclei. This **fusion** process is the essential energy-producing process in the sun. We shall look more closely at fission and fusion in Sections 21.7 and 21.8.

Point of Emphasis: The higher binding energies per nucleon of the elements with atomic masses near ~56 amu results in these being the most stable nuclei.

Learning Goal 11: Define *fission* and *fusion,* and state which types of nuclei produce energy when undergoing these processes.

21.7 Nuclear Fission

Our discussion of the energy changes in nuclear reactions (Section 21.6) revealed an important observation: Both the splitting of heavy nuclei (fission) and the union of light nuclei (fusion) are exothermic processes. Commercial nuclear power plants and the most common forms of nuclear weaponry depend on the process of nuclear fission for their operation. The first nuclear fission to be discovered was that of uranium-235. This nucleus, as well as those of uranium-233 and plutonium-239, undergoes fission when struck by a slow-moving neu-

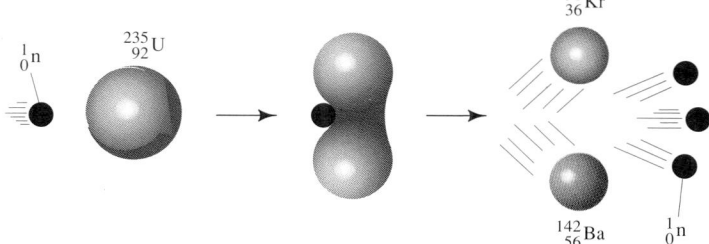

FIGURE 21.14   Schematic representation of the fission of uranium-235 showing one of its many fission patterns. In this process, 3.5×10^{-11} J of energy is produced per ^{235}U nucleus.

tron.* This induced fission process is illustrated in Figure 21.14. A heavy nucleus can split in many different ways. Two different ways that the uranium-235 nucleus splits are shown in Equations 21.24 and 21.25:

$$^{1}_{0}\text{n} + ^{235}_{92}\text{U} \begin{cases} \longrightarrow ^{137}_{52}\text{Te} + ^{97}_{40}\text{Zr} + 2^{1}_{0}\text{n} & \text{[21.24]} \\ \longrightarrow ^{142}_{56}\text{Ba} + ^{91}_{36}\text{Kr} + 3^{1}_{0}\text{n} & \text{[21.25]} \end{cases}$$

More than 200 different isotopes of 35 different elements have been found among the fission products of uranium-235. Most of them are radioactive.

On the average, 2.4 neutrons are produced by every fission of uranium-235. If one fission produces 2 neutrons, these 2 neutrons can cause two fissions. The 4 neutrons thereby released can produce four fissions, and so forth, as shown in Figure 21.15. The number of fissions and the energy released quickly escalate, and, if the process is unchecked, the result is a violent explosion. Reactions that multiply in this fashion are called **chain reactions.**

In order for a fission chain reaction to occur, the sample of fissionable material must have a certain minimum mass. Otherwise, neutrons escape from the sample before they have the opportunity to strike another nucleus and cause additional fission. The chain stops if enough neutrons are lost. The amount of fissionable material large enough to maintain the chain reaction with a constant rate of fission is called the **critical mass.** When a critical mass of material is present, only one neutron from each fission is subsequently effective in pro-

---

* Other heavy nuclei can be induced to undergo fission. However, these three are the only ones of practical importance.

Teaching Note: Slow-moving neutrons are required because the fission process involves initial absorption of the neutron by the nucleus. The resulting heavier nucleus is often unstable and spontaneously undergoes fission. Fast neutrons tend to bounce off the nucleus, and little fission occurs.

Ruth Lewin Sime, "Lise Meitner and the Discovery of Fission," *J. Chem. Educ.* **1989,** 66, 373. This issue of *J. Chem. Educ.* includes several papers on radiochemistry.

Teaching Note: For samples of roughly spherical shape, as the sample size increases, the mass increases faster than the surface area. Critical mass is attained when the number of neutrons lost through the surface of the uranium becomes sufficiently small in comparison to its total mass.

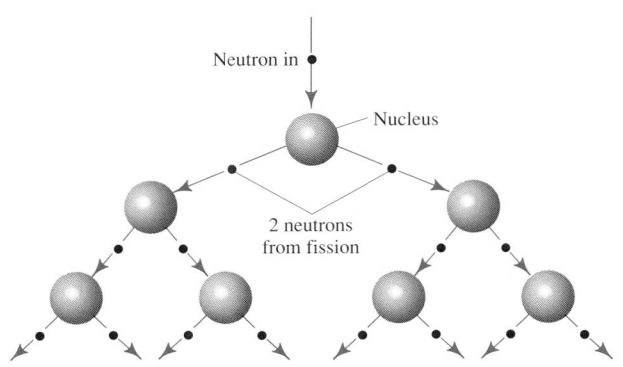

FIGURE 21.15   Chain fission reaction in which each fission produces two neutrons. The process leads to an accelerating rate of fission, with the number of fissions doubling at each stage.

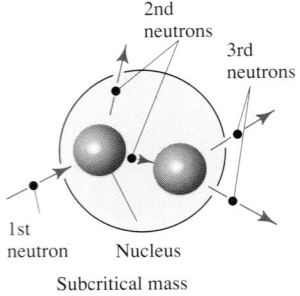

2nd
neutrons

3rd
neutrons

1st
neutron   Nucleus

Subcritical mass
(chain reaction stops)

FIGURE 21.16 The chain reaction in a subcritical mass soon stops because neutrons are lost from the mass without causing fission. As the size of the mass increases, fewer neutrons are able to escape. In a supercritical mass, the chain reaction is able to expand.

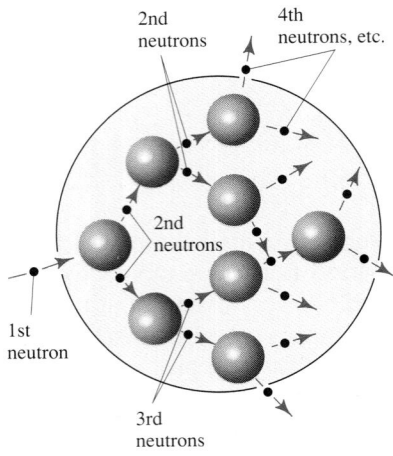

2nd
neutrons

4th
neutrons, etc.

2nd
neutrons

1st
neutron

3rd
neutrons

Supercritical mass
(chain reaction accelerates)

ducing another fission. The critical mass of uranium-235 is about 1 kg. If more than a critical mass of fissionable material is present, very few neutrons escape. The chain reaction thus multiplies the number of fissions, which can lead to a nuclear explosion. A mass in excess of a critical mass is referred to as a **supercritical mass.** The effect of mass on a fission reaction is illustrated in Figure 21.16.

Figure 21.17 shows a schematic diagram of the first atomic bomb used in warfare, the "Little Boy" bomb that was dropped on Hiroshima, Japan, on August 6, 1945. To trigger the fission reaction, two subcritical masses of uranium-235 are slammed together using chemical explosives. The combined masses of the uranium form a supercritical mass, which leads to a rapid, uncontrolled chain reaction and, ultimately, a nuclear explosion. The energy released

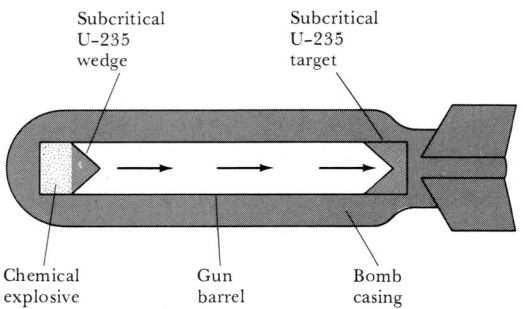

Subcritical
U-235
wedge

Subcritical
U-235
target

Chemical
explosive

Gun
barrel

Bomb
casing

FIGURE 21.17 One design used in atomic bombs. A conventional explosive is used to bring two subcritical masses together to form a supercritical mass.

The Dawning of the Nuclear Age

The fission of uranium-235 was first achieved in the late 1930s by Enrico Fermi and his colleagues in Rome, and shortly thereafter by Otto Hahn and his co-workers in Berlin. Both groups were trying to produce transuranium elements. In 1938, Hahn identified barium among his reaction products. He was puzzled by this observation and questioned the identification because the presence of barium was so unexpected. He sent a detailed letter describing his experiments to Lise Meitner, a former co-worker. Meitner had been forced to leave Germany because of the anti-Semitism of the Third Reich and had settled in Sweden. She surmised that Hahn's experiment indicated a new nuclear process was occurring in which the uranium-235 split. She called this process *nuclear fission.*

Meitner passed word of this discovery to her nephew, Otto Frisch, a physicist working at Niels Bohr's institute in Copenhagen. He repeated the experiment, verifying Hahn's observations and finding that tremendous energies were involved. In January 1939, Meitner and Frisch published a short article describing this new reaction. In March 1939, Leo Szilard and Walter Zinn at Columbia University discovered that more neutrons are produced than were used in each fission. As we have seen, this allows a chain reaction process to occur.

News of these discoveries and an awareness of their potential use in explosive devices spread rapidly within the scientific community. Several scientists finally persuaded Albert Einstein, the most famous physicist of the time, to write a letter to President Roosevelt outlining the implications of these discoveries. Einstein's letter, written in August 1939, outlined the possible military applications of nuclear fission and emphasized the danger that weapons based on fission would pose if they were to be developed by the Nazis. Roosevelt judged it imperative that the United States investigate the possibility of such weapons. Late in 1941, the decision was made to build a bomb based on the fission reaction. An enormous research project, known as the "Manhattan Project," began.

On December 2, 1942, the first artificial self-sustaining nuclear fission chain reaction was achieved in an abandoned squash court at the University of Chicago (Figure 21.18). This accomplishment led to the development of the first atomic bomb at Los Alamos National Laboratory in New Mexico in July 1945. In August 1945, the United States dropped atomic bombs on two Japanese cities, Hiroshima and Nagasaki. The nuclear age had arrived.

FIGURE 21.18 The first self-sustaining nuclear fission reactor was built on a squash court at the University of Chicago. The painting depicts the scene in which the scientists witnessed the reactor as it became self-sustaining on December 2, 1942. (Argonne National Laboratory)

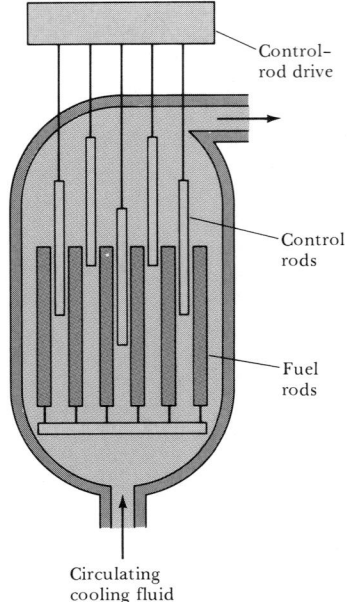

FIGURE 21.19 Reactor core showing fuel elements, control rods, and cooling fluid.

by the bomb dropped on Hiroshima was equivalent to that of 40,000 lb of TNT (it therefore is called a *20-kiloton* bomb). Unfortunately, the basic design of a fission-based atomic bomb is quite simple. The fissionable materials are potentially available to any nation with a nuclear reactor. This simplicity has resulted in the proliferation of atomic weapons.

Nuclear Reactors

Nuclear fission produces the energy generated by nuclear power plants. The "fuel" of the nuclear reactor is a fissionable substance, such as uranium-235. Typically, uranium is enriched to about 3 percent uranium-235 and then used in the form of UO_2 pellets. These enriched uranium pellets are encased in zirconium or stainless-steel tubes. Rods composed of materials such as cadmium or boron control the fission process by absorbing neutrons. These *control rods* regulate the flux of neutrons to keep the reaction chain self-sustaining, while preventing the reactor core from overheating.*

The reactor is started by a neutron-emitting source; it is stopped by inserting the control rods more deeply into the reactor core, the site of the fission (Figure 21.19). The reactor core also contains a *moderator,* which acts to slow down neutrons so that they can be captured more readily by the fuel. A *cooling liquid* circulates through the reactor core to carry off the heat generated by the nuclear fission. The cooling liquid can also serve as the neutron moderator.

The design of a nuclear power plant is basically the same as that of a power plant that burns fossil fuel (except that the burner is replaced by a reactor core). In both instances, steam is used to drive a turbine connected to an electrical generator. The steam must be condensed, and so additional cooling water, generally obtained from a large source such as a river or lake, is needed. The nuclear power plant design shown in Figure 21.20 is currently the most popular. The primary coolant, which passes through the core, is in a closed system. Other coolants never pass through the reactor core at all. This lessens the chance that radioactive products could escape the core. Additionally, the reactor is surrounded by a concrete shell to shield personnel and nearby residents from radiation.

Fission products accumulate as the reactor operates. These products decrease the efficiency of the reactor by capturing neutrons. The reactor must be stopped periodically so that the nuclear fuel can be replaced or reprocessed. When the fuel rods are removed from the reactor, they are initially very radioactive. It was originally intended that they be stored for several months in pools at the reactor site to allow decay of short-lived radioactive nuclei. They were then to be transported in shielded containers to reprocessing plants, where the fuel would be separated from the fission products. However, reprocessing plants have been plagued with operational difficulties, and there is intense opposition to the transport of nuclear wastes on the nation's highways. Even if the transportation difficulties could be overcome, the high radioactivity of the spent fuel makes reprocessing a hazardous operation. At present, the spent fuel rods are simply being kept in storage at reactor sites.

---

* The reactor core cannot reach supercritical levels and explode with the violence of an atomic bomb because the concentration of uranium-235 is too low. However, if the core overheats, sufficient damage might be done to release radioactive materials into the environment.

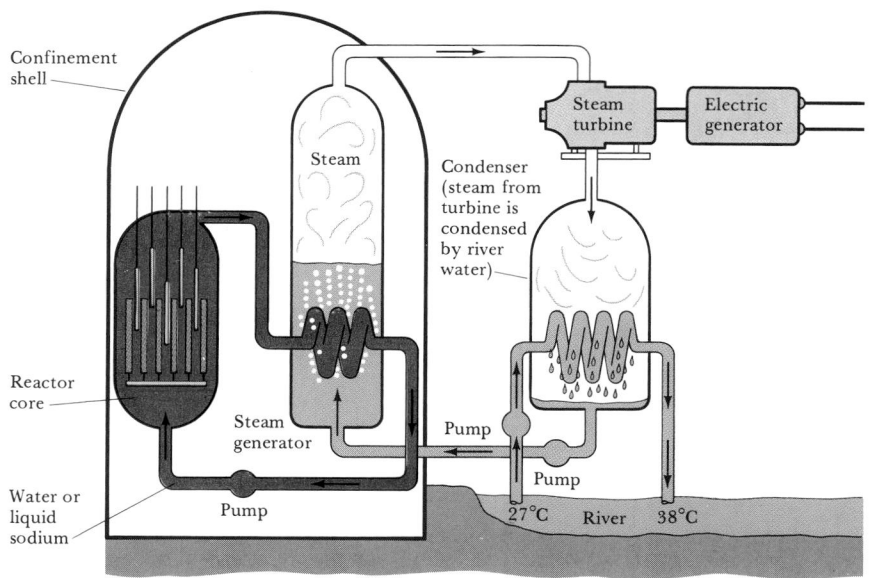

FIGURE 21.20 Basic design of a nuclear power plant. Heat produced by the reactor core is carried by a cooling fluid such as water or liquid sodium to a steam generator. The steam so produced is used to drive an electrical generator.

Figure 21.20

Teaching Note: In addition to being dangerously radioactive, many radioactive waste products, such as plutonium, are chemically toxic.

Storage poses a major problem because the fission products are extremely radioactive. It is estimated that 20 half-lives are required for their radioactivity to reach levels acceptable for biological exposure. Based on the 28.8-yr half-life of strontium-90, one of the longer-lived and most dangerous of the products, the wastes must be stored for 600 yr. If plutonium-239 is not removed, storage must be for longer periods; plutonium-239 has a half-life of 24,000 yr. It is advantageous, however, to remove plutonium-239 because it can be used as a fissionable fuel.

A considerable amount of research has been and will continue to be devoted to disposal of radiaoactive wastes. At present, the most attractive possibilities appear to be formation of glass, ceramic, or synthetic rock from the wastes, as a means of immobilizing them (Figure 21.21). These solid materials would then be placed in containers of high corrosion resistance and durability and buried deep underground. The United States is currently investigating Yucca Mountain in Nevada as the disposal site. Because the radioactivity will persist for a long time, there must be assurances that the solids and their containers will not crack from the heat generated by nuclear decay and allow radioactivity to find its way into underground water supplies.

FIGURE 21.21 One method of immobilizing nuclear waste is to make a glass or ceramic material from it. Here molten glass containing nuclear waste is poured into a steel bar mold. (© D.O.E./Science Source/ Photo Researchers)

21.8 Nuclear Fusion

As shown in Section 21.6, energy is produced when light nuclei are fused to form heavier ones. Reactions of this type are responsible for the energy produced by the sun. Spectroscopic studies indicate that the sun is composed of 73 percent H, 26 percent He, and only 1 percent of all other elements, by mass. Among the several fusion processes that are believed to occur are the following:

$$\ce{_1^1H + _1^1H -> _1^2H + _1^0e} \qquad [21.26]$$

$$\ce{_1^1H + _1^2H -> _2^3He} \qquad [21.27]$$

$$\,^3_2\text{He} + \,^3_2\text{He} \longrightarrow \,^4_2\text{He} + 2\,^1_1\text{H} \qquad \text{[21.28]}$$

$$\,^3_2\text{He} + \,^1_1\text{H} \longrightarrow \,^4_2\text{He} + \,^0_1\text{e} \qquad \text{[21.29]}$$

Theories have been proposed for the generation of the other elements through fusion processes.

Fusion is appealing as an energy source because of the availability of light isotopes and because fusion products are generally not radioactive. Despite this fact, fusion is not presently used to generate energy. The problem is that high energies are needed to overcome the repulsion between nuclei. The required energies are achieved by high temperatures. Fusion reactions are therefore also known as **thermonuclear reactions.** The lowest temperature required for any fusion is that needed to fuse ^2_1H and ^3_1H, shown in Equation 21.30. This reaction requires a temperature of about 40,000,000 K:

$$\,^2_1\text{H} + \,^3_1\text{H} \longrightarrow \,^4_2\text{He} + \,^1_0\text{n} \qquad \text{[21.30]}$$

Such high temperatures have been achieved by using an atomic bomb to initiate the fusion process. This is done in the thermonuclear, or hydrogen, bomb. Clearly, this approach is unacceptable for controlled power generation.

Numerous problems must be overcome before fusion becomes a practical energy source. In addition to the high temperatures necessary to initiate the reaction, there is the problem of confining the reaction. No known structural material is able to withstand the enormous temperatures necessary for fusion. Research has centered on the use of an apparatus called a *tokamak*, which uses strong magnetic fields to contain and heat the reaction (Figure 21.22). Temperatures of nearly 3,000,000 K have been achieved in a tokamak, but this is not yet hot enough to initiate continuous fusion. Much research has also been directed at the use of powerful lasers to generate the necessary temperatures.

Point of Emphasis: Use of fusion as an energy source is very appealing for a number of reasons. The fuel, hydrogen, can be obtained in virtually limitless supply from sea water, and the waste is non-toxic and is not radioactive.

FIGURE 21.22 The tokamak fusion test reactor at Princeton University. A tokamak is essentially a magnetic "bottle" for confining and heating nuclei in an effort to cause them to fuse. (Princeton Plasma Physics Laboratory/Princeton University)

21.9 Biological Effects of Radiation

The increased pace of synthesis and use of radioisotopes has led to increased concern about the effects of radiation on matter, particularly in biological systems. Alpha, beta, and gamma rays (as well as X-rays) possess energies far in excess of ordinary bond energies and ionization energies. Consequently, these forms of radiation are able to fragment and ionize molecules, generating unstable, highly reactive particles as they pass through matter. For example, gamma rays are able to ionize water molecules, forming unstable H_2O^+ ions. An H_2O^+ ion can react with another water molecule to form an H_3O^+ ion and a neutral OH molecule:

$$H_2O^+ + H_2O \longrightarrow H_3O^+ + OH \qquad\qquad [21.31]$$

The unstable and highly reactive OH molecule is an example of a **free radical,** a substance with one or more unpaired electrons. In cells and tissues, such particles can attack a host of other compounds to produce new free radicals, which in turn attack yet other compounds. Thus, the formation of a single free radical can initiate a large number of chemical reactions that are ultimately able to disrupt the normal operations of cells.

The resultant radiation damage to living systems can be classified as either somatic or genetic. **Somatic damage** affects the organism during its own lifetime. **Genetic damage,** as the term implies, has a genetic effect; it harms offspring through damage to genes and chromosomes, the body's reproductive material. Genetic effects are more difficult to study than somatic ones because they may not become apparent for several generations. Somatic damage includes "burns," molecular disruptions similar to those produced by high temperatures. It also includes cancer. Cancer is brought about by damage to the growth-regulation mechanism of cells, which causes them to reproduce in an uncontrolled manner. In general, the tissues that show the greatest damage from radiation are those that reproduce at a rapid rate, such as bone marrow, blood-forming tissues, and lymph nodes. Leukemia, which is characterized by excessive growth of white blood cells, is probably the major cancer problem associated with radiation.

The clinical symptoms of acute (short-term) exposure to radiation include a decrease in the number of white blood cells, fatigue, nausea, and diarrhea. Sufficient exposure can result in death from blood disorders, gastrointestinal failure, and damage to the central nervous system. In light of these effects, we must determine whether any levels of exposure to radiation are actually safe. What are the maximum levels of radiation that we should permit from various human activities? Unfortunately, we are hampered in our attempts to set realistic standards by our lack of understanding of the effects of chronic (long-term) exposure to radiation.

Scientists concerned with setting health standards for exposure to radiation have used the hypothesis that the effects of radiation are proportional to exposure, even down to low doses. Any amount of radiation is assumed to cause some finite risk of injury, and the effects of high dosage rates are extrapolated to those of lower ones. Other scientists, however, believe that there is a threshold below which there are no radiation risks. Indeed, numerous studies indicate that there are low levels below which harmful effects cannot be discerned. Furthermore, studies in molecular biology give us reason to believe that biolog-

Learning Goal 13: Explain the roles played by the chemical behavior of an isotope and its mode of radioactivity in determining its ability to damage biological systems.

Learning Goal 14: Describe various sources of radiation to which the general population is exposed, and indicate the relative contributions of each.

Teaching Note: There has been much controversy in the last few years about the effects of low exposures to radiation.

ical systems have repair mechanisms that counter the effects of very low levels of radiation. Nevertheless, until scientific evidence enables us to settle the matter with some confidence, it is safer to assume that even low levels of radiation represent some danger.

Radiation Doses

Learning Goal 15: Define the units used to describe the level of radioactivity *(curie)* and to measure the effects of radiation on biological systems *(rem* and *rad)*.

The SI unit of radioactivity is called the **becquerel,** after Henri Becquerel. A becquerel is defined as one nuclear disintegration per second. The older and more widely used unit of activity is the **curie** (Ci), after Marie Curie. ∞ (Sec. 2.2) A curie is 3.7×10^{10} disintegrations per second, the number of nuclear disintegrations per second from 1 g of radium. For example, a 5.0-mCi sample of cobalt-60 undergoes $(5.0 \times 10^{-3})(3.7 \times 10^{10}) = 1.8 \times 10^8$ disintegrations per second.

The damage produced by radiation outside the body depends not only on the nuclear activity but also on the energy and penetrating power of the radiation. Gamma rays are particularly dangerous because they penetrate human tissue very effectively, just as X-rays do. Consequently, their damage is not limited to the skin. In contrast, most alpha rays are stopped by skin, and beta rays are able to penetrate only about 1 cm beyond the surface of the skin. Hence, neither is as dangerous as gamma rays unless the radiation source somehow enters the body. Within the body, alpha rays are particularly dangerous because they leave a very dense trail of damaged molecules as they move through matter.

Two units, the rad and rem, are commonly used to measure radiation doses. (A third unit, the roentgen, is essentially the same as the rad.) A **rad** (radiation *a*bsorbed *d*ose) is the amount of radiation that deposits 1×10^{-2} J of energy per kilogram of tissue. A rad of alpha rays can produce more damage than a rad of beta rays. Consequently, the rad is often multiplied by a factor that measures the relative biological damage caused by the radiation. This factor is known as the *relative biological effectiveness* of the radiation, abbreviated **RBE.** The RBE is approximately 1 for beta and gamma rays, and 10 for alpha rays. The exact value of the RBE varies with dose rate, total dose, and type of tissue affected. The product of the number of rads and the RBE of the radiation gives the effective dosage in **rems** (*r*oentgen *e*quivalent for *m*an):

$$\text{Number of rems} = (\text{number of rads})(\text{RBE}) \qquad [21.32]$$

Teaching Note: The Chernobyl disaster was discussed in the Chemistry at Work box in Section 2.4.

The effects of some short-term exposures to radiation appear in Table 21.7. An exposure to 600 rem is fatal to most humans. To put this number in perspective, a typical dental X-ray entails an exposure of about 0.5 mrem. The disaster at Chernobyl (see the Chemistry at Work box in Section 2.4) led to some truly large radiation exposures. It is estimated that the total radiation released at Chernobyl was 50 to 100 MCi. The service personnel and firefighters at the plant received more than 100 rem of radiation. By comparison, the accident at Three Mile Island in Pennsylvania released 20 Ci of radiation, and no individual was exposed to more than 0.1 rem.

Radon

Over the long term, we are all exposed to potentially damaging radiation from both natural sources and human activity. Since the mid-1980s, concern has

TABLE 21.7 △ Effects of Short-Time Exposures to Radiation

Dose (rem)	Effect
0 to 25	No detectable clinical effects
25 to 50	Slight, temporary decrease in white blood cell counts
100 to 200	Nausea; marked decrease in white blood cells
500	Death of half the exposed population within 30 days after exposure

grown over radiation exposure due to radon, the radioactive noble gas with atomic number 86. As Figure 21.23 indicates, radon exposure is estimated to account for more than half the 360-mrem average annual exposure to radiation. Radon-222 is a decay product in the nuclear disintegration series of uranium-238 (Figure 21.4) and is therefore continually generated as uranium decays.

It is interesting to consider the interplay between the chemical and nuclear properties of radon that make it a health hazard. Being a noble gas, radon is extremely unreactive and is therefore free to bubble up out of the ground without becoming trapped chemically along the way. It is readily inhaled and exhaled with no direct chemical effects. However, the half-life of ^{222}Rn is a short 3.82 days. It decays through alpha-particle loss into a radioisotope of polonium:

$$^{222}_{86}\text{Rn} \longrightarrow {}^{218}_{84}\text{Po} + {}^{4}_{2}\text{He} \qquad [21.33]$$

Because radon has such a short half-life and alpha particles have a high RBE, inhaled radon is considered a probable cause of lung cancer. Even worse, however, is the fact that the decay product polonium-218 is an alpha-emitting solid that has even a shorter half-life (3.11 min) than radon-222:

$$^{218}_{84}\text{Po} \longrightarrow {}^{214}_{82}\text{Pb} + {}^{4}_{2}\text{He} \qquad [21.34]$$

The atoms of polonium-218 can become trapped in the lungs, where they continually bathe the delicate tissue with harmful alpha radiation.

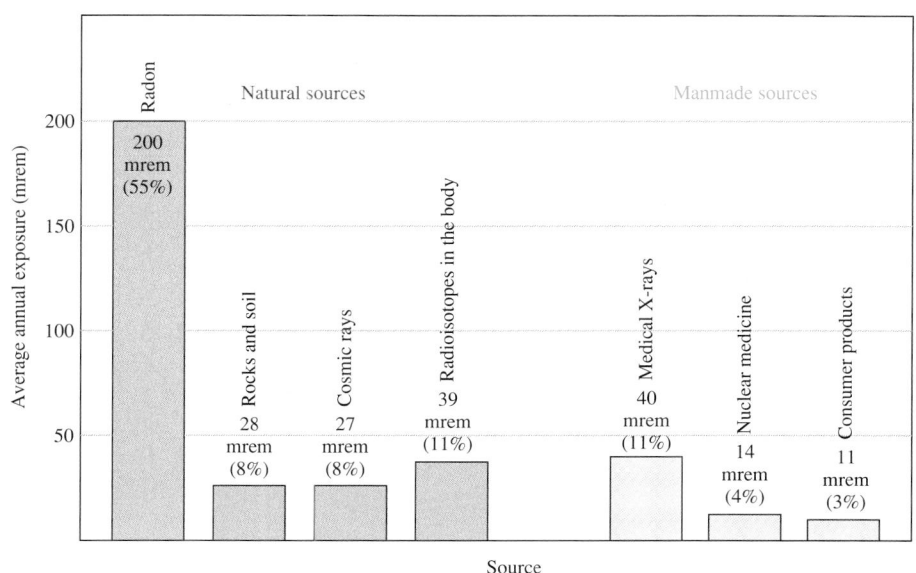

FIGURE 21.23 A graph of the sources of the average annual exposure of the U.S. population to high-energy radiation. The total average annual exposure is 360 mrem.

Figure 21.23

Radiation Therapy

High-energy radiation poses a health hazard because of the damage it does to cells. Healthy cells are either destroyed or damaged by radiation, leading to physiological disorders. However, radiation can also destroy *unhealthy* cells, including cancerous cells. All cancers are characterized by the runaway growth of abnormal cells. This growth can produce masses of abnormal tissue, called *malignant tumors*. Malignant tumors can be caused by the exposure of healthy cells to high-energy radiation. However, somewhat paradoxically, malignant tumors can be destroyed by exposing them to the same radiation. In fact, cancerous cells are more susceptible to destruction by radiation than are healthy ones, allowing radiation to be used effectively in the treatment of cancer. As early as 1904, physicians attempted to use the radiation emitted by radioactive substances to treat tumors by destroying the mass of unhealthy tissue. The treatment of disease by high-energy radiation is called *radiation therapy*.

Many different radionuclides are currently used in radiation therapy. Some of the more commonly used ones are listed in Table 21.8, along with their half-lives. You will note that most of the half-lives are quite short, meaning that these radioisotopes emit a great deal of radiation in a short period of time (Figure 21.24).

The radiation source used in radiation therapy may be inside or outside the body. In almost all cases, radiation therapy is designed to use the high-energy gamma radiation emitted by radioisotopes. Alpha and beta radiation, which are not as penetrating as gamma radiation, can be blocked by appropriate packaging. For example, ^{192}Ir is often administered as "seeds" consisting of a core of radioactive isotope coated with 0.1 mm of platinum metal. The platinum coating stops the alpha and beta rays, but the gamma rays penetrate it readily. The radioactive seeds can be surgically implanted in a tumor. In other cases, human physiology allows the radioisotope to be ingested. For example, most of the iodine in the human body ends up in the thyroid gland (see the Chemistry and Life box in Section 21.5), a fact that allows thyroid cancer to be treated by using large doses of ^{131}I. Radiation therapy on deep organs, where a surgical implant is impractical, often uses a ^{60}Co "gun" outside the body to shoot a beam of gamma rays at the tumor.

Particle accelerators are also used as an external source of high-energy radiation for radiation therapy.

Because gamma radiation is so strongly penetrating, it is nearly impossible to avoid damaging healthy cells during radiation therapy. Most cancer patients undergoing radiation treatments experience unpleasant and dangerous side effects such as fatigue, nausea, hair loss, a weakened immune system, and even death. Thus, in many cases, radiation therapy is used only if other cancer treatments such as *chemotherapy* (the treatment of cancer with powerful drugs) are unsuccessful. Nevertheless, radiation therapy is one of the major weapons we have in the fight against cancer.

FIGURE 21.24 A sample of a salt of cesium-137, which is used in radiation therapy. The blue glow is from the radioactivity of the cesium. In Goiânia, Brazil, in 1987, a cylinder containing cesium-137 was left in an abandoned medical clinic. It was discovered by unsuspecting townspeople, who were fascinated by the strange blue glow. The results were tragic: Four people died from radiation exposure, and 249 others were contaminated. (Earl Roberge, Science Source/Photo Researchers)

TABLE 21.8 △ Some Radioisotopes Used in Radiation Therapy

Isotope	Half-life	Isotope	Half-life
^{32}P	14.3 days	^{137}Cs	30 yr
^{60}Co	5.26 yr	^{192}Ir	74.2 days
^{90}Sr	28.8 yr	^{198}Au	2.7 days
^{125}I	60.25 days	^{222}Ra	3.82 days
^{131}I	8.06 days	^{226}Rn	1,622 yr

FIGURE 21.25 Radon home-testing kit. Kits such as this are available for measuring radon levels in the home. (Richard Megna/Fundamental Photographs)

The U.S. Environmental Protection Agency (EPA) has recommended that ^{222}Rn levels in the home not exceed 4 pCi per liter of air. We are aware today, however, that houses that are built on foundations naturally rich in uranium ore or that are improperly sealed can have levels much greater than that. Public awareness of the potential health risk of radon has grown rapidly, and home radon-testing kits have become common household items in many parts of the country (Figure 21.25).

Equations 21.33 and 21.34 give an indication of the complex nuclear reactions that affect our health. As with many other aspects of human activity, the question at issue is one of risk versus benefit. In order to make intelligent decisions concerning radiation health hazards, we must have a deeper understanding of the risks than we do at present.

Charles H. Atwood, "How Much Radon Is Too Much?" *J. Chem. Educ.* **1992,** *69,* 351.

For Review

Summary

Certain nuclei are radioactive. Most of these nuclei gain stability by emitting alpha particles ($^{4}_{2}$He), beta particles ($^{0}_{-1}$e), and gamma radiation ($^{0}_{0}\gamma$). Some nuclei undergo decay by positron ($^{0}_{1}$e) emission or by electron capture. The neutron-to-proton ratio is one factor determining nuclear stability. The presence of magic numbers of nucleons and an even number of protons and neutrons is also important. Nuclear transmutations can be induced by bombarding nuclei with charged particles using particle accelerators or with neutrons in a nuclear reactor.

Radioisotopes have characteristic rates of decay. These rates are generally expressed in terms of half-lives. The constant half-lives of nuclides permit their use in dating objects. The ease of detection of radioisotopes also permits their use as tracers, to follow elements through their reactions. Three methods of detection are photographic film, scintillation counters, and Geiger counters.

The energy produced in nuclear reactions is accompanied by measurable losses of mass in accordance with Einstein's relationship, $\Delta E = c^2 \Delta m$. The difference in mass between nuclei and the nucleons of which they are composed is known as the mass defect. The mass defect of a nuclide allows calculation of its nuclear binding energy, the energy required to separate the nucleus into individual nucleons. Examination of binding energies per nucleon reveals that energy is produced when heavy nuclei split (fission) and when light nuclei fuse (fusion).

Uranium-235, uranium-233, and plutonium-239 undergo fission when they capture a neutron. The resulting nuclear reaction is a chain reaction. A reaction that maintains a constant rate is said to be critical. In nuclear reactors, the fission is controlled to generate a constant power. The reactor core consists of fissionable fuel, control rods, a moderator, and cooling fluid. The nuclear power plant resembles a conventional power plant except that the core replaces the fuel burner. There is growing concern regarding the safety with which nuclear power plants can be operated. In addition, the reprocessing of spent fuel rods and disposal of highly radioactive nuclear wastes are unsolved problems.

Nuclear fusion requires high temperatures because nuclei must have large kinetic energies to overcome their mutual repulsions. It is not yet possible to generate a controlled fusion process.

The SI unit of radioactivity is the becquerel, defined as one nuclear disintegration per second. Radioactivity is more often measured in curies. One curie corresponds to 3.7×10^{10} disintegrations per second. The amount of energy deposited in biological tissue by radiation is measured in terms of the rad; one rad corresponds to 1×10^{-2} J per kilogram of tissue. The rem is a more useful measure of the biological damage created by the deposited energy. We receive radiation from both naturally occurring and human sources in roughly equal amounts for the general population. The effects of long-term exposure to low levels of radiation are not completely understood, but it is often assumed that the extent of biological damage varies in direct proportion to the level of exposure.

Key Terms

radioactive
nucleon (Sec. 21.1)
radionuclide (Sec. 21.1)
radioisotope (Sec. 21.1)
alpha particles (Sec. 21.1)
beta particles (Sec. 21.1)
gamma radiation (Sec. 21.1)
positron (Sec. 21.1)
electron capture (Sec. 21.1)
magic numbers (Sec. 21.2)
radioactive series (Sec. 21.2)
nuclear disintegration series (Sec. 21.2)
nuclear transmutations (Sec. 21.3)
particle accelerators (Sec. 21.3)
transuranium elements (Sec. 21.3)
half-life (Sec. 21.4)
Geiger counter (Sec. 21.5)
scintillation counter (Sec. 21.5)

radiotracer (Sec. 21.5)
mass defect (Sec. 21.6)
nuclear binding energy (Sec. 21.6)
fission (Sec. 21.6)
fusion (Sec. 21.6)
chain reactions (Sec. 21.7)
critical mass (Sec. 21.7)
supercritical mass (Sec. 21.7)
thermonuclear reactions (Sec. 21.8)
free radical (Sec. 21.9)
somatic damage (Sec. 21.9)
genetic damage (Sec. 21.9)
becquerel (Sec. 21.9)
curie (Sec. 21.9)
rad (Sec. 21.9)
RBE (Sec. 21.9)
rems (Sec. 21.9)

Exercises

Radioactivity

21.1. Indicate the number of protons and neutrons in the following nuclei: **(a)** $^{56}_{26}$Fe; **(b)** ^{88}Sr; **(c)** phosphorus-31.

21.2. Indicate the number of protons and neutrons in the following nuclei: **(a)** $^{75}_{33}$As; **(b)** ^{101}Ru; **(c)** rubidium-85.

21.3. Give the symbol for each of the following particles: **(a)** electron; **(b)** positron; **(c)** neutron.

21.4. Give the symbol for each of the following particles: **(a)** proton; **(b)** alpha particle; **(c)** beta particle.

21.5. Write balanced nuclear equations for the following transformations: **(a)** iodine-131 undergoes beta decay; **(b)** thorium-230 decays to a radium isotope; **(c)** tungsten-181 undergoes electron capture; **(d)** nitrogen-13 decays by positron emission.

21.6. Write nuclear equations for the following processes: **(a)** bismuth-214 undergoes beta decay; **(b)** gold-195 undergoes electron capture; **(c)** potassium-38 undergoes positron emission; **(d)** plutonium-242 emits alpha radiation.

21.7. The naturally occurring radioactive decay series that begins with $^{235}_{92}$U stops with formation of the stable $^{207}_{82}$Pb. The decays proceed through a series of alpha particle and beta particle emissions. How many of each type of emission are involved in this series?

21.8. A radioactive decay series that begins with $^{237}_{93}$Np ends with formation of the stable nuclide $^{209}_{83}$Bi. How many alpha particle emissions and how many beta particle emissions are involved in the sequence of radioactive decays?

Nuclear Stability

21.9. Predict the type of radioactive decay process for the following radionuclides: **(a)** $^{8}_{5}$B; **(b)** $^{68}_{29}$Cu; **(c)** neptunium-241; **(d)** chlorine-39.

21.10. Each of the following nuclei undergoes either beta or positron emission. Predict the type of emission for each: **(a)** $^{66}_{32}$Ge; **(b)** $^{105}_{45}$Rh; **(c)** iodine-137; **(d)** cerium-133.

21.11. Indicate whether each of the following nuclides lies within the belt of stability in Figure 21.2: **(a)** $^{108}_{49}$In; **(b)** $^{102}_{47}$Ag; **(c)** $^{17}_{7}$N; **(d)** $^{210}_{86}$Rn. For any that do not, describe a nuclear decay process that would alter the neutron-to-proton ratio in the direction of increased stability.

21.12. Indicate whether each of the following nuclides lies within the belt of stability in Figure 21.2: **(a)** $^{70}_{33}$As; **(b)** $^{34}_{15}$P; **(c)** $^{74}_{32}$Ge; **(d)** $^{248}_{98}$Cf. For any that do not, describe a nuclear decay process that would alter the neutron-to-proton ratio in the direction of increased stability.

21.13. One of the nuclides in each of the following pairs is radioactive. Predict which is radioactive and which is stable: **(a)** $^{39}_{19}$K and $^{40}_{19}$K; **(b)** ^{209}Bi and ^{208}Bi; **(c)** magnesium-25 and neon-24. Explain.

21.14. In each of the following pairs, which nuclide would you expect to be the more abundant in nature: **(a)** $^{19}_{9}$F or $^{18}_{9}$F; **(b)** $^{80}_{34}$Se or $^{81}_{34}$Se; **(c)** $^{56}_{26}$Fe or $^{57}_{26}$Fe; **(d)** $^{118}_{50}$Sn or $^{118}_{51}$Sb? Justify your choices.

21.15. Give three examples of nuclides that have a magic number of both protons and neutrons.

21.16. Explain the following statement: There is an analogy between the stability of the nucleus of ^{208}Pb and the lack of reactivity of argon gas.

21.17. Which of the following nuclides would you expect to be radioactive: **(a)** $^{17}_{8}$O; **(b)** $^{176}_{74}$W; **(c)** $^{108}_{50}$Sn; **(d)** $^{92}_{40}$Zr; **(e)** $^{238}_{94}$Pu? Justify your choices.

21.18. Which of the following nuclides of group 6A elements would you expect to be radioactive: $^{14}_{8}$O, $^{32}_{16}$S, $^{78}_{34}$Se, $^{84}_{34}$Se, $^{115}_{52}$Te, $^{208}_{84}$Po? Justify your choices.

Nuclear Transmutations

21.19. Why are nuclear transmutations involving neutrons generally easier than those involving protons or alpha particles?

21.20. Rutherford was able to carry out the first nuclear transmutation reactions by bombarding nitrogen-14 nuclei with alpha particles. However, in the famous experiment on scattering of alpha particles by gold foil (Section 2.2), a nuclear transmutation reaction did not occur. What is the difference between the two experiments? What would one need to do to carry out a successful nuclear transmutation reaction involving gold nuclei and alpha particles?

21.21. Complete and balance the following nuclear equations by supplying the missing particle:

(a) $^{32}_{16}$S + $^{1}_{0}$n $\longrightarrow$ $^{1}_{1}$p + ?

(b) $^{7}_{4}$Be + $^{0}_{-1}$e (orbital electron) $\longrightarrow$?

(c) ? $\longrightarrow$ $^{187}_{76}$Os + $^{0}_{-1}$e

(d) $^{98}_{42}$Mo + $^{2}_{1}$H $\longrightarrow$ $^{1}_{0}$n + ?

(e) $^{235}_{92}$U + $^{1}_{0}$n $\longrightarrow$ $^{135}_{54}$Xe + 2^{1}_{0}n + ?

21.22. Complete and balance the following nuclear equations by supplying the missing particle:

(a) $^{252}_{98}$Cf + $^{10}_{5}$B $\longrightarrow$ 3^{1}_{0}n + ?

(b) $^{2}_{1}$H + $^{3}_{2}$He $\longrightarrow$ $^{4}_{2}$He + ?

(c) $^{1}_{1}$H + $^{11}_{5}$B $\longrightarrow$ 3?

(d) $^{122}_{53}$I $\longrightarrow$ $^{122}_{54}$Xe + ?

(e) $^{59}_{26}$Fe $\longrightarrow$ $^{0}_{-1}$e + ?

21.23. Write balanced equations for: **(a)** $^{238}_{92}U(n, \gamma)^{239}_{92}U$; **(b)** $^{14}_{7}N(p, \alpha)^{11}_{6}C$; **(c)** $^{18}_{8}O(n, \beta)^{19}_{9}F$.

21.24. Write balanced equations for each of the following nuclear reactions: **(a)** $^{14}_{7}N(p, \alpha)^{11}_{6}C$; **(b)** $^{14}_{7}N(\alpha, p)^{17}_{8}O$; **(c)** $^{59}_{26}Fe(\alpha, \beta)^{63}_{29}Cu$.

Half-life; Dating

21.25. It has been suggested that strontium-90 (derived from nuclear testing) deposited in the hot desert will undergo radioactive decay more rapidly because it will be exposed to much higher average temperatures. Is this a reasonable suggestion?

21.26. Harmful chemicals are often destroyed by chemical treatment. For example, an acid can be neutralized by a base. Why can't chemical treatment be applied to destroy the radioactive products produced in a nuclear reactor?

21.27. Gallium-68 decays by positron emission, with a half-life of 68.3 min. Write the equation for the nuclear reaction. How much ^{68}Ga remains from a 10.0-mg sample after 683 min?

21.28. The half-life of tritium (hydrogen-3) is 12.3 yr. If 48.0 mg of tritium is released from a nuclear power plant during the course of an accident, what mass of this nuclide will remain after 12.3 yr? After 49.2 yr?

21.29. A sample of the synthetic nuclide curium-243 was prepared. After 1.00 yr, the radioactivity of the sample had declined from 3012 disintegrations per second to 2921 disintegrations per second. What is the half-life of the decay process?

21.30. A sample of a radioactive nuclide exhibits 8540 disintegrations per second. After 350.0 min, the number of disintegrations per second is 1250. What is the half-life of the radionuclide?

21.31. An experiment was designed to determine whether an aquatic plant absorbed iodide ion from water. Iodine-131 ($t_{1/2} = 8.1$ days) was added as a tracer, in the form of iodide ion, to a tank containing the plants. The initial activity of a 1.00-μL sample of the water was 89 counts per

minute. After 32 days the level of activity in a 1.00-μL sample was 5.7 counts per minute. Did the plants absorb iodide from the water?

21.32. A sample of strontium-89 has an initial activity of 4600 counts per minute on a device that measures the level of radioactivity. After exactly 30 days the activity has declined to 3130 counts per minute. What is the half-life for decay of strontium-89?

[21.33]. Radium-226, which undergoes alpha decay, has a half-life of 1622 yr. How many alpha particles are emitted in 1.0 min from a 5.0-mg sample of ^{226}Ra?

[21.34]. Cobalt-60, which undergoes beta decay, has a half-life of 5.26 yr. How many beta particles are emitted in 10.0 s from a 650-μg sample of ^{60}Co?

21.35. A wooden artifact from a Chinese temple has a ^{14}C activity of 25.8 counts per minute as compared with an activity of 31.7 counts per minute for a standard of zero age. From the half-life for ^{14}C decay, 5.73×10^3 yr, determine the age of the artifact.

21.36. An ancient wooden object is found to have an activity of 9.6 disintegrations per minute per gram of carbon. By contrast, the carbon in a living tree undergoes 18.4 disintegrations per minute per gram of carbon. Based on the activity of carbon-14 (with a half-life of 5.73×10^3 yr) in the object, calculate its age.

21.37. The half-life for the process $^{238}U \longrightarrow {}^{206}Pb$ is 4.5×10^9 yr. A mineral sample contains 50.0 mg of ^{238}U and 14.0 mg of ^{206}Pb. What is the age of the mineral?

21.38. Potassium-40 decays to argon-40 with a half-life of 1.27×10^9 yr. What is the age of a rock in which the mass ratio of ^{40}Ar to ^{40}K is 3.6?

Energy Changes

21.39. How much energy must be supplied to break a single $^9_4$Be nucleus into separated protons and neutrons if the nucleus has a mass of 9.00999 amu? What is the energy for 1 mol of $^9_4$B nuclei?

21.40. How much energy must be supplied to break a single $^{16}_8$O nucleus into separated protons and neutrons if the nucleus has a mass of 15.99052 amu? How much energy is required per mole of this nucleus?

21.41. Calculate the binding energy per nucleon for the following nuclei: **(a)** $^{12}_6$C (atomic mass, 12.00000 amu); **(b)** $^{59}_{27}$Co (atomic mass, 58.9332 amu); **(c)** $^{206}_{82}$Pb (atomic mass, 205.97447 amu).

21.42. Calculate the binding energy per nucleon for the following nuclei: **(a)** $^7_3$Li (atomic mass, 7.01600 amu); **(b)** $^{64}_{30}$Zn (atomic mass, 63.92914 amu); **(c)** $^{232}_{90}$Th (atomic mass, 232.0382 amu).

21.43. The solar radiation falling on earth amounts to 1.07×10^{16} kJ/min. What is the mass equivalence of the solar energy falling on earth in a 24-hr period? If the energy released in the reaction

$$^{235}_{92}U + {}^1_0n \longrightarrow {}^{141}_{56}Ba + {}^{92}_{36}Kr + 3{}^1_0n$$

(^{235}U atomic mass, 235.0439 amu; ^{141}Ba atomic mass, 140.9140 amu; ^{92}Kr atomic mass, 91.9218 amu)

is taken as typical of that occurring in a nuclear reactor, what mass of uranium-235 is required to equal 0.10 percent of the solar energy that falls on the earth in 1 day?

21.44. Based on the following atomic mass values—$^1_1$H, 1.00782 amu; $^2_1$H, 2.01410 amu; $^3_1$H, 3.01605 amu; $^3_2$He, 3.01603 amu; $^4_2$He, 4.00260 amu—and the mass of the neutron given in the text, calculate the energy released per mole in each of the following nuclear reactions, all of which are possibilities for a controlled fusion process:

(a) $_1^2H + _1^3H \longrightarrow _2^4He + _0^1n$

(b) $_1^2H + _1^2H \longrightarrow _1^3H + _0^1n$

(c) $_1^2H + _2^3He \longrightarrow _2^4He + _1^1H$

21.45. Which of the following nuclei is likely to have the largest mass defect per nucleon: (a) $_{27}^{59}Co$; (b) $_5^{11}B$; (c) $_{50}^{118}Sn$; (d) $_{96}^{243}Cm$? Explain your answer.

21.46. Based on Figure 21.13, explain why we should expect energy to be released in the course of the fission of heavy nuclei.

Effects and Uses of Radioisotopes

21.47. Complete and balance the nuclear equations for the following fission reactions:

(a) $_{92}^{235}U + _0^1n \longrightarrow _{62}^{160}Sm + _{30}^{72}Zn +$ ____ $_0^1n$

(b) $_{94}^{239}Pu + _0^1n \longrightarrow _{58}^{144}Ce +$ ____ $+ 2_0^1n$

21.48. Complete and balance the nuclear equation for the following fission or fusion reactions:

(a) $_1^2H + _1^1H \longrightarrow _2^3He +$ ____

(b) $_{92}^{233}U + _0^1n \longrightarrow _{51}^{133}Sb + _{41}^{98}Nb +$ ____ $_0^1n$

21.49. Explain how you might use radioactive ^{59}Fe (a beta emitter with $t_{1/2} = 46$ days) to determine the extent to which rabbits are able to convert a particular iron compound in their diet into blood hemoglobin, which contains an iron atom.

21.50. Chlorine-36 is a convenient radiotracer. It is a weak beta emitter, with $t_{1/2} = 3 \times 10^5$ yr. Describe how you would use this radiotracer to carry out each of the following experiments. (a) Determine whether trichloroacetic acid, CCl_3COOH, undergoes any ionization of its chlorines as chloride ion in aqueous solution. (b) Demonstrate that the equilibrium between dissolved $BaCl_2$ and solid $BaCl_2$ in a saturated solution is a dynamic process. (c) Determine the effects of soil pH on the uptake of chloride ion from the soil by soybeans.

21.51. A portion of the sun's energy comes from the reaction

$$4_1^1H \longrightarrow _2^4He + 2_1^0e$$

This reaction requires a temperature of about 10^6 to 10^7 K. Why is such a high temperature required?

21.52. What are the advantages of a fusion reactor over a fission reactor? What practical difficulties must be overcome to develop a fusion reactor?

21.53. Explain the function of the following components of a nuclear reactor: (a) control rods; (b) moderator.

21.54. Explain the following terms that apply to fission reactions: (a) chain reaction; (b) critical mass.

21.55. What SI unit equals 1 disintegration per second? What other common unit is used for the activity of a radioactive sample?

21.56. Distinguish between the two common units for radiation doses, the rad and the rem.

Additional Exercises

21.57. Polonium is a radioactive element discovered in uranium ores by Marie Curie and named after her native country, Poland. Polonium-210 decays by emitting a single alpha particle. Write the nuclear equation for this process.

21.58. Figure 21.4 shows the stepwise decay of uranium-238 to form the stable lead-206 nucleus. Write balanced nuclear equations for the steps in this sequence.

21.59. A free neutron is unstable and decays into a proton with a half-life of 10.4 min. What other particle forms in this process?

21.60. Why doesn't $_2^2He$ exist?

21.61. The 13 known nuclides of zinc range from $_{30}^{60}Zn$ to $_{30}^{72}Zn$. The naturally occurring nuclides have mass numbers 64, 66, 67, 68, and 70. What mode or modes of decay would you expect for the least massive radioactive nuclides of zinc? What mode for the most massive nuclides?

21.62. Chlorine has two stable nuclides, ^{35}Cl and ^{37}Cl. In contrast, ^{36}Cl is a radioactive nuclide that decays by beta emission. (a) Predict the product of decay of ^{36}Cl. (b) Based on the empirical rules about nuclear stability, explain why the nucleus of ^{36}Cl is less stable than either ^{35}Cl or ^{37}Cl.

21.63. During the past 30 years, nuclear scientists have synthesized approximately 1600 nuclei not known in nature. Many more might be discovered by using heavy-ion bombardment, which is possible only if high-energy instruments are used to accelerate the ions. Complete and balance the following reactions, which involve heavy-ion bombardments:

(a) $_3^6Li + _{28}^{56}Ni \longrightarrow$?

(b) $_{20}^{40}Ca + _{96}^{248}Cm \longrightarrow$?

(c) $_{38}^{88}Sr + _{36}^{84}Kr \longrightarrow _{46}^{116}Pd +$?

(d) $_{20}^{40}Ca + _{92}^{238}U \longrightarrow _{30}^{70}Zn + 4_0^1n + 2?$

21.64. Cobalt-60 has a half-life of 5.26 yr. The cobalt-60 in a certain radiation therapy unit must be replaced whenever its radioactivity falls to 80 percent of the original sample. If the original sample was purchased in November 1993, when will it be necessary to replace the cobalt-60?

[21.65]. The energies of gamma rays are commonly expressed in units of millions of electron volts (MeV). (a) By using conversion factors on the back inside cover of this book, determine the energy in kilojoules of a 1.0-MeV gamma ray. (b) Cesium-137 emits gamma rays of energy 0.662 MeV. The half-life of ^{137}Cs is 30 yr. Determine the energy in kilojoules emitted in 30 min by a 10.0-mg sample of $^{137}CsCl$. **(c)** Ultraviolet radiation of wavelength 300 nm can cause skin burn. Calculate the ratio of the energy of a 0.662-MeV gamma-ray photon to that of a 300-nm ultraviolet photon. What does your answer tell you about the potential health risk of exposure to gamma rays?

21.66. Plutonium-239 emits alpha particles that possess energies of about 5×10^8 kJ/mol. The half-life for the decay is about 24,000 yr. It has been said that the main danger from plutonium is inhalation of plutonium-containing dust. Why is inhalation, rather than mere exposure to plutonium in the environment, the major concern?

[21.67]. The synthetic radioisotope technetium-99, which decays by beta emission, is the most widely used isotope in nuclear medicine. The following data were collected on a sample of ^{99}Tc:

Disintegrations per minute	Time (hr)
180	0
130	2.5
104	5.0
77	7.5
59	10.0
46	12.5
24	17.5

Make a graph of these data similar to Figure 21.7 and determine the half-life. (You may wish to make a graph of the natural log of the disintegration rate versus time; a little rearranging of Equation 21.19 will produce an equation for a linear relation between $\ln N_t$ and t; from the slope you can obtain k.)

[21.68]. According to current regulations, the maximum permissible dose of strontium-90 in the body of an adult is 1 μCi (1×10^{-6} Ci). Using the relationship

$$\text{Rate} = kN$$

calculate the number of atoms of strontium-90 to which this corresponds. To what mass of strontium-90 does this correspond ($t_{1/2}$ for strontium-90 is 28.8 yr)?

[21.69]. Suppose you had a detection device that could count every decay from a radioactive sample of plutonium-239 ($t_{1/2}$ is 24,000 yr). How many counts per second would

you obtain from a sample containing 0.500 g of plutonium-239? (Hint: Look at Equations 21.19 and 21.20.)

21.70. A cobalt-60 source used for radiation treatment for cancer has an activity of 1.25 Ci. **(a)** What is the activity of this source in becquerels? **(b)** What will its activity be after 2.0 yr if its half-life is 5.26 yr?

21.71. How many alpha particles per second are emitted by a 0.0010-g sample of uranium-238? Assume that each decay emits a single alpha particle. The half-life of uranium-238 is 4.5×10^9 yr.

21.72. Consider the following statement: A radioisotope with a short half-life is a lesser health hazard than one with a long half-life. Do you agree or disagree with this statement?

[21.73]. A 26.00-g sample of water containing tritium, ^3_1H, emits 1.50×10^3 beta particles per second. Tritium is a weak beta emitter, with a half-life of 12.26 yr. What fraction of all the hydrogen in the water sample is tritium? (Hint: Use Equations 21.19 and 21.20.)

[21.74]. When a positron is annihilated by combination with an electron, two photons of equal energy result. What is the wavelength of these photons? Are they gamma-ray photons?

21.75. The nuclear masses of ^7Be, ^9Be, and ^{10}Be are 7.0147, 9.0100, and 10.0113 amu, respectively. Which of these nuclei has the largest binding energy per nucleon?

21.76. The sun radiates energy into space at the rate of 3.9×10^{26} J/s. Calculate the rate of mass loss from the sun.

[21.77]. The average energy released in the fission of a single uranium-235 nucleus is about 3×10^{-11} J. If the conversion of this energy to electricity in a nuclear power plant is 40 percent efficient, what mass of uranium-235 undergoes fission in a year in a plant that produces 1000 MW? Recall that a watt is 1 J/s.

[21.78]. Tests on human subjects in Boston in 1965 and 1966, following the era of atomic bomb testing, revealed average quantities of about 2 pCi of plutonium radioactivity in the average person. How many disintegrations per second does this level of activity imply? If each alpha particle deposits 8×10^{-13} J of energy and if the average person weighs 75 kg, calculate the number of rads of radiation dose in 1 yr from such a level of plutonium, and also calculate the number of rems.

Chemistry of Hydrogen, Oxygen, Nitrogen, and Carbon

22

Lightning storm. During lightning flashes, N_2 combines with O_2 to form NO.

CONTENTS

Point of Emphasis: Many chemical phenomena can be rationalized, and often predicted, using periodic trends.

Learning Goal 1: Identify an element as a metal, semimetal, or nonmetal on the basis of its position in the periodic table or its properties.

Learning Goal 2: Predict the relative electronegativities and metallic character of any two members of a periodic family or a horizontal row of the periodic table.

FIGURE 22.1 Trends in key properties of the elements as a function of position in the periodic table.

The previous chapters of this book have primarily involved chemical principles, such as rules for bonding, the laws of thermodynamics, the factors influencing reaction rates, and so forth. In the course of explaining these principles, we have described the chemical and physical properties of many substances. However, we have done little to examine systematically the chemical elements and the compounds they form. This aspect of chemistry, often referred to as *descriptive chemistry,* is the subject of the next several chapters.

In this chapter, we examine four important nonmetals: hydrogen, oxygen, nitrogen, and carbon. These nonmetals form many commercially important compounds and are the primary elements in biological systems. In fact, 99 percent of the atoms required by living cells are atoms of these four elements. In Chapter 23, we will examine the remaining nonmetals on a group-by-group basis.

In studying descriptive chemistry, it is important to look for trends and general types of behavior, rather than trying to memorize all the facts presented. The periodic table is, of course, an invaluable tool in this task. Before we begin our examination of particular nonmetals, it is useful to review briefly some general periodic trends.

22.1 Periodic Trends

Figure 22.1 summarizes the way in which several important properties of elements vary in relation to the periodic chart. One of the most useful features shown is the division of elements into the broad categories of metals and nonmetals. We discussed this division in Section 7.6 and examined the other trends elsewhere in Chapters 7 and 8.

As shown in Figure 22.1, electronegativity decreases as we move down a given group and increases from left to right across the table. As a result, nonmetals have higher electronegativities than do metals. Consequently, compounds formed between strongly metallic and strongly nonmetallic elements tend to be ionic (for example, metal fluorides and metal oxides). These substances are solids at room temperature. In contrast, compounds formed between nonmetals are molecular substances. Molecular substances with low

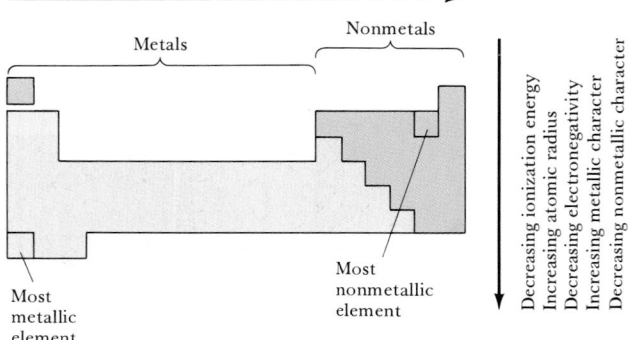

Increasing ionization energy
Decreasing atomic radius
Increasing nonmetallic character and electronegativity
Decreasing metallic character

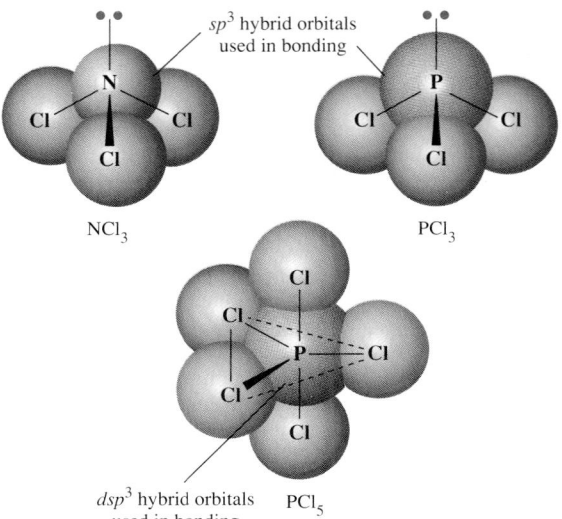

FIGURE 22.2 Comparison of NCl_3, PCl_3, and PCl_5. Nitrogen is unable to form NCl_5 because it does not have *d* orbitals available for bonding.

sp^3 hybrid orbitals used in bonding

NCl_3

PCl_3

dsp^3 hybrid orbitals used in bonding

PCl_5

Figure 22.2

molecular weight tend to be gases, liquids, or volatile solids at room temperature.

Among the nonmetals, the chemistry of the first member of each family often differs in several important ways from that of subsequent members. The differences are due in part to the smaller size and greater electronegativity of the first member. In addition, the first member is restricted to forming a maximum of four bonds because it has only the 2*s* and the three 2*p* orbitals for bonding. Subsequent members of the family are able to use *d* orbitals in bonding in addition to *s* and *p* orbitals; they can therefore form more than four bonds. ⊃ (Sec. 8.8) As an example, consider the chlorides of nitrogen and phosphorus, the first two members of group 5A. Nitrogen forms a maximum of three bonds with chlorine, NCl_3. Although phosphorus can form the trichloride compound, PCl_3, it is also able to form five bonds with chlorine, PCl_5. These compounds are shown in Figure 22.2. Because hydrogen has only the 1*s* orbitals available for bonding, it is restricted to forming one bond.

Another difference between the first member of any family and subsequent members of the same family is the greater ability of the former to form π bonds. We can understand this, in part, in terms of atomic size. As atoms increase in size, the sideways overlap of *p* orbitals, which form the strongest type of π bond, becomes less effective. This is shown in Figure 22.3. As an illustration of this effect, consider two differences in the chemistry of carbon and silicon, the first two members of group 4A. Carbon has three crystalline allotropes, diamond, graphite, and buckminsterfullerene. In diamond there are σ

Learning Goal 3: Give examples of how the first member in each family of nonmetallic elements differs from the other elements of the same family, and account for these differences.

FIGURE 22.3 Comparison of π-bond formation by sideways overlap of *p* orbitals between two carbon atoms and between two silicon atoms. The distance between nuclei increases as we move from carbon to silicon. The *p* orbitals do not overlap as effectively between two silicon atoms because of this greater separation.

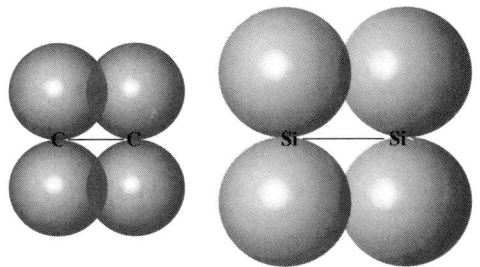

Figure 22.3

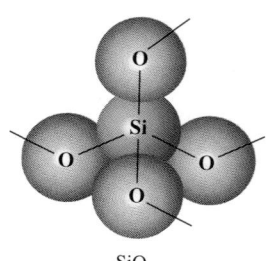

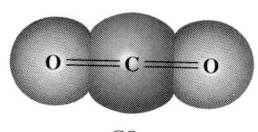

CO_2

FIGURE 22.4 Comparison of the structures of CO_2 and SiO_2; CO_2 has double bonds, whereas SiO_2 has only single bonds.

bonds between carbon atoms but no π bonds. In graphite and buckminsterfullerene, π bonds result from sideways overlap of p orbitals. ∞ (Sec. 11.8) Silicon occurs only in the diamondlike crystal form. Silicon does not exhibit a graphitelike structure because of the low stability of π bonds between silicon atoms.

We see the same type of difference in the dioxides of these elements (Figure 22.4). In CO_2, carbon forms double bonds to oxygen, thereby achieving an octet by π bonding. In contrast, SiO_2 contains no double bonds. Instead, four oxygens are bonded to each silicon, forming an extended structure.*

SAMPLE EXERCISE 22.1

Sulfur forms a fluoride compound, SF_6, that has six sulfur-fluorine bonds. In contrast, oxygen is able to form at most two bonds to fluorine, OF_2. **(a)** Rationalize this difference. **(b)** Predict the molecular geometry of each compound and describe the hybridization employed by S and O.

SOLUTION **(a)** The electron configuration of oxygen is $[He]2s^2 2p^4$. The next-highest-energy orbitals available for bonding are in the third shell. Thus, oxygen uses only the $2s$ and $2p$ orbitals in bonding. These orbitals can accommodate only eight electrons. In OF_2, oxygen already has eight electrons, six of its own and one from each fluorine atom:

$$:\ddot{F}—\ddot{O}—\ddot{F}:$$

Consequently, it is unable to accommodate additional fluorine atoms.

The electron configuration of sulfur is $[Ar]3s^2 3p^4$. In this case, the $3d$ orbitals are available for bonding. Therefore, sulfur is able to expand its octet to accommodate more than eight electrons:

$$F—\underset{F}{\overset{F}{\underset{|}{\overset{F}{S}}}}—F$$

(b) According to the VSEPR theory, the four electron pairs around oxygen are disposed at the corners of a tetrahedron. ∞ (Sec. 9.1) The four electron pairs are accommodated in sp^3 hybrid orbitals. ∞ (Sec. 9.4) The geometric arrangement of atoms with two bonded pairs and two nonbonded pairs is nonlinear.

In the case of SF_6, the six electron pairs around sulfur are disposed at the corners of an octahedron. The associated hybridization is $sp^3 d^2$. Because all six electrons are bonded pairs, the geometric arrangement of atoms is also octahedral.

PRACTICE EXERCISE

Consider the following list of elements: Li, K, N, P, Ne. From this list, select the element that **(a)** is most electronegative; **(b)** has the greatest metallic character; **(c)** can bond to more than four surrounding atoms in a molecule; **(d)** forms π bonds most readily. ***Answers:*** **(a)** N; **(b)** K; **(c)** P; **(d)** N

22.2 Chemical Reactions

Throughout this chapter and subsequent ones, you will find a large number of chemical reactions presented. To remember all of them is an overwhelming task. However, you will probably need to remember some, especially those of a

---

* The formula SiO_2 is consistent with this structure because each oxygen is shared by two silicon atoms (not shown in Figure 22.4). For bookkeeping purposes, we may therefore count a half of each of the four oxygens that are bound to a given silicon atom as belonging to that silicon. We shall consider silicon-oxygen compounds in some detail in Chapter 23.

more general nature. In earlier discussions, we have encountered several general categories of reactions: combustion reactions (Section 3.2), metathesis reactions (Section 4.5), Brønsted-Lowry acid-base (proton-transfer) reactions (Section 16.2), Lewis acid-base reactions (Section 16.10), and redox reactions (Section 20.1). Because O_2 and H_2O are abundant and widespread in our environment, it is particularly important to consider the possible reactions of these substances with other compounds. About one-third of the reactions discussed in this chapter involve either O_2 (oxidation or combustion reactions) or H_2O (especially proton-transfer reactions).

In oxidation reactions with O_2, hydrogen-containing compounds produce H_2O. Carbon-containing ones produce CO_2 (unless the amount of O_2 is insufficient, in which case CO or even C can form). Nitrogen-containing compounds tend to form N_2, although NO can form in special cases. The following reactions illustrate these generalizations:

$$2CH_3OH(l) + 3O_2(g) \longrightarrow 2CO_2(g) + 4H_2O(l) \qquad [22.1]$$

$$4CH_3NH_2(g) + 9O_2(g) \longrightarrow 4CO_2(g) + 10H_2O(l) + 2N_2(g) \quad [22.2]$$

The formation of H_2O, CO_2, and N_2 reflects the high thermodynamic stabilities of these substances, which are indicated by the large bond energies for the O—H, C=O, and N≡N bonds that they contain (463, 799, and 941 kJ/mol, respectively). ∞ (Sec. 8.9) The formation of the stable H_2O and CO_2 molecules also occurs when H_2 and C are used to reduce metal oxides:

$$NiO(s) + H_2(g) \longrightarrow Ni(s) + H_2O(l) \qquad [22.3]$$

$$2CuO(s) + C(s) \longrightarrow 2Cu(s) + CO_2(g) \qquad [22.4]$$

In dealing with proton-transfer reactions, remember that the weaker a Brønsted-Lowry acid, the stronger its conjugate base. ∞ (Sec. 16.2) For example, H_2, OH^-, NH_3, CH_4, and C_2H_2, which we encounter in this chapter, are exceedingly weak proton donors. In fact, they have *no* tendency to act as acids in water. Thus, species formed from them by removing one or more protons (such as H^-, O^{2-}, NH_2^-, N^{3-}, CH_3^-, C^{4-}, and C_2^{2-}) are extremely strong bases. All react readily with water, removing protons from H_2O to form OH^-. The following reactions are illustrative:

$$CH_3^-(aq) + H_2O(l) \longrightarrow CH_4(g) + OH^-(aq) \qquad [22.5]$$

$$N^{3-}(aq) + 3H_2O(l) \longrightarrow NH_3(aq) + 3OH^-(aq) \qquad [22.6]$$

Of course, substances that are stronger proton donors than H_2O, such as HCl, H_2SO_4, $HC_2H_3O_2$, and other acids, also react readily with basic anions.

SAMPLE EXERCISE 22.2

Predict the products formed in each of the following reactions and write a balanced chemical equation:
(a) $CH_3NHNH_2(g) + O_2(g) \longrightarrow$
(b) $Mg_3P_2(s) + H_2O(l) \longrightarrow$
(c) $NaCN(s) + HCl(aq) \longrightarrow$

SOLUTION (a) This combustion reaction should produce CO_2, H_2O, and N_2:

$$2CH_3NHNH_2(g) + 5O_2(g) \longrightarrow 2CO_2(g) + 6H_2O(l) + 2N_2(g)$$

(b) The Mg_3P_2 consists of Mg^{2+} and P^{3-} ions. The P^{3-} ion, like N^{3-}, has a strong affinity for protons and reacts with H_2O to form OH^- and PH_3 (PH^{2-}, PH_2^-, and PH_3 are all exceedingly weak proton donors):

$$Mg_3P_2(s) + 6H_2O(l) \longrightarrow 2PH_3(g) + 3Mg(OH)_2(aq)$$

The $Mg(OH)_2$ is of low solubility in water and may precipitate.
  (c) The NaCN consists of Na^+ and CN^- ions. The CN^- ion is basic (HCN is a weak acid). Thus CN^- reacts with protons to form its conjugate acid:

$$NaCN(s) + HCl(aq) \longrightarrow HCN(aq) + NaCl(aq)$$

The HCN has limited solubility in water and readily escapes as a gas. HCN is *extremely* toxic; in fact, this reaction is used to produce the lethal gas in gas chambers.

P R A C T I C E   E X E R C I S E

Write a balanced chemical equation for the reaction of solid sodium hydride with water.   ***Answer:*** $NaH(s) + H_2O(l) \longrightarrow NaOH(aq) + H_2(g)$

22.3 Hydrogen

The English chemist Henry Cavendish (1731–1810) first isolated pure hydrogen and distinguished it from other gases. Because the element produces water when burned in air, the French chemist Lavoisier gave it the name *hydrogen,* which means "water producer" (Greek: *hydro,* water; *gennao,* to produce).
  Hydrogen is the most abundant element in the universe. It is the nuclear fuel consumed by our sun and other stars to produce energy. ∞ (Sec. 21.8) Although about 70 percent of the universe is composed of hydrogen, it constitutes only 0.87 percent of the earth's mass. Most of the hydrogen on our planet is found associated with oxygen. Water, which is 11 percent hydrogen by mass, is the most abundant hydrogen compound. Hydrogen is also an important part of petroleum, cellulose, starch, fats, alcohols, acids, and a wide variety of other materials.

Isotopes of Hydrogen

The most common isotope of hydrogen, $_1^1H$, has a nucleus consisting of a single proton. This isotope, sometimes referred to as **protium,*** comprises 99.9844 percent of naturally occurring hydrogen.
  Two other isotopes are known: $_1^2H$, whose nucleus contains a proton and a neutron, and $_1^3H$, whose nucleus contains a proton and two neutrons. The $_1^2H$ isotope, called **deuterium,** comprises 0.0156 percent of naturally occurring hydrogen. It is not radioactive. In writing the chemical formulas of compounds containing deuterium, that isotope is often given the symbol D. For example, D_2O, which is called deuterium oxide or *heavy water,* can be obtained by electrolysis of ordinary water. The heavier D_2O undergoes electrolysis at a slower rate than does the lighter H_2O and therefore becomes concentrated during the electrolysis. Some of the physical properties of H_2O and D_2O are compared in Table 22.1. Notice the small but discernible differences.

---

* Giving unique names to isotopes is limited to hydrogen. Because of the proportionally large differences in their masses, the isotopes of H show appreciably more differences in their chemical and physical properties than do isotopes of heavier elements.

Learning Goal 4: Cite the most common occurrences of hydrogen and how it is obtained in its elemental form.

Teaching Note: Fusion of hydrogen is the energy source in the sun.

Learning Goal 5: Describe and name the three isotopes of hydrogen.

Teaching Note: During World War II, scientists sought methods to isolate D_2O because it plays an important role in nuclear reactions.

TABLE 22.1 △ Comparison of Properties of H_2O and D_2O

Property	H_2O	D_2O
Melting point (°C)	0.00	3.81
Boiling point (°C)	100.00	101.42
Density at 25°C (g/mL)	0.997	1.104
Heat of fusion (kJ/mol)	6.008	6.276
Heat of vaporization (kJ/mol)	40.67	41.61
Ion product (K_w) at 25°C	1.01×10^{-14}	1.95×10^{-15}

The third isotope, ^3_1H, is known as **tritium**. It is radioactive, with a half-life of 12.3 yr:

$$^3_1H \longrightarrow \, ^3_2He + \, _{-1}^0e \qquad t_{1/2} = 12.3 \text{ yr} \qquad [22.7]$$

Tritium is formed continuously in the upper atmosphere in nuclear reactions induced by cosmic rays; however, because of its short half-life, only trace quantities exist naturally. The isotope can be synthesized in nuclear reactors by neutron bombardment of lithium-6:

$$^6_3Li + \, ^1_0n \longrightarrow \, ^3_1H + \, ^4_2He \qquad [22.8]$$

Each isotope of hydrogen contains a single electron and consequently undergoes the same chemical reactions. However, the heavier deuterium and tritium generally undergo reactions at a somewhat slower rate than protium.

Deuterium and tritium have proved valuable in studying the reactions of compounds containing hydrogen. A compound can be "labeled" by replacing one or more ordinary hydrogen atoms at specific locations within a molecule with deuterium or tritium. By comparing the location of the heavy hydrogen label in the reactants with that in the products, the mechanism of the reaction can often be inferred. As an example of the chemical insight that can be gained by using deuterium, consider what happens when methyl alcohol, CH_3OH, is placed in D_2O. The H atom of the O—H bond exchanges rapidly with the D atoms in D_2O, forming CH_3OD. The H atoms of the CH_3 group do not exchange. This experiment demonstrates the kinetic stability of C—H bonds and reveals the speed at which the O—H bond in the molecule breaks and reforms.

Properties of Hydrogen

Hydrogen is the only element that is not a member of any family in the periodic table. Because of its $1s^1$ electron configuration, it is generally placed above lithium in the periodic table. However, it is definitely not an alkali metal. It forms a positive ion much less readily than any alkali metal; the ionization energy of the hydrogen atom is 1310 kJ/mol, whereas that of lithium is 517 kJ/mol. Furthermore, the hydrogen atom has no electrons below its valence shell; the H^+ ion is just a bare proton. The simple H^+ ion is not known to exist in any compound. Its small size gives it a strong attraction for electrons; either it strips electrons from surrounding matter (forming hydrogen atoms that combine to form H_2), or it shares electron pairs, forming covalent bonds with other atoms. Although we may represent the aquated hydrogen ion as $H^+(aq)$, the proton is bonded to one or more water molecules and is thus often represented as $H_3O^+(aq)$. ∞ (Sec. 16.1)

Point of Emphasis: Recall the discussions of half-life in Chapters 14 and 21.

Teaching Note: The similar chemical behaviors of different isotopes of the same element make them difficult to separate by chemical means. This is one reason why "isotopically pure" compounds are expensive.

Teaching Note: Such an experiment is called an "isotope labeling" experiment.

Hydrogen is also sometimes placed above the halogens in the periodic table because the hydrogen atom can pick up one electron to form the *hydride ion,* H^-, which has a noble-gas electron configuration. However, the electron affinity of hydrogen, $E = -73$ kJ/mol, is not as large as that of any halogen; the electron affinity of fluorine is -332 kJ/mol, and that of iodine is -295 kJ/mol. In general, hydrogen shows no closer resemblance to the halogens than it does to the alkali metals.

In its elemental form, hydrogen exists at room temperature as a colorless, odorless, tasteless gas composed of diatomic molecules, H_2. We can call H_2 dihydrogen, but it is more commonly referred to as molecular hydrogen or merely hydrogen. Because H_2 is nonpolar and has only two electrons, attractive forces between molecules are extremely weak. Consequently, the melting point ($-259°C$) and boiling point ($-253°C$) of H_2 are very low.

The $H—H$ bond-dissociation energy (436 kJ/mol) is high for a single bond (Table 8.4). By comparison, the $Cl—Cl$ bond-dissociation energy is only 242 kJ/mol. Because H_2 has a strong bond, most reactions of H_2 are slow at room temperature. However, the molecule is readily activated by heating, irradiation, or catalysis. The activation process generally produces hydrogen atoms, which are very reactive. The activation of H_2 by finely divided nickel, palladium, and platinum was considered briefly in our earlier discussions of heterogeneous catalysis. ∞ (Sec. 14.6) Once H_2 is activated, it reacts rapidly and exothermically with a wide variety of substances.

Hydrogen forms strong covalent bonds with many elements, including oxygen; the $O—H$ bond-dissociation energy is 463 kJ/mol. The strong $O—H$ bond makes hydrogen an effective reducing agent for many metal oxides. For example, when H_2 is passed over heated CuO, copper is produced:

$$CuO(s) + H_2(g) \longrightarrow Cu(s) + H_2O(g) \qquad [22.9]$$

When H_2 is ignited in air, a vigorous reaction occurs, forming H_2O:

$$2H_2(g) + O_2(g) \longrightarrow 2H_2O(l) \qquad \Delta H = -571.7 \text{ kJ} \qquad [22.10]$$

Air containing as little as 4 percent H_2 (by volume) is potentially explosive. The disastrous burning of the hydrogen-filled airship *Hindenburg* in 1937 (Figure 22.5) dramatically demonstrated the high flammability of H_2.

FIGURE 22.5 Burning of the airship *Hindenburg* while landing at Lakehurst, New Jersey, on May 6, 1937. This picture was taken only 22 seconds after the first explosion occurred. (UPI/Bettmann Newsphotos)

Preparation of Hydrogen

When a small quantity of H_2 is needed in the laboratory, it is usually obtained by the reaction between an active metal such as zinc and a dilute strong acid such as HCl or H_2SO_4:

$$Zn(s) + 2H^+(aq) \longrightarrow Zn^{2+}(aq) + H_2(g) \qquad [22.11]$$

Lee R. Summerlin, Christie L. Borgford, and Julie B. Ealy, "Making Hydrogen Gas from an Acid and a Base," *Chemical Demonstrations, a Sourcebook for Teachers, Volume 2* (Washington: American Chemical Society, 1987), pp. 33–34.

Because H_2 has an extremely low solubility in water, it can be collected by displacement of water, as shown in Figure 22.6.

When commercial quantities of H_2 are needed, the raw materials are usually hydrocarbons (from either natural gas or petroleum) or water. Hydrocarbons are substances that consist of carbon and hydrogen, such as CH_4 and C_8H_{18}. Much hydrogen is presently obtained in the course of refining petroleum. In the refining process, large hydrocarbons are catalytically broken into smaller molecules with the accompanying production of H_2 as a by-product.

The method used to produce the largest quantities of H_2 is the reaction of methane, CH_4 (the principal component of natural gas), with steam at 1100°C:

$$CH_4(g) + H_2O(g) \longrightarrow CO(g) + 3H_2(g) \qquad [22.12]$$

$$CO(g) + H_2O(g) \longrightarrow CO_2(g) + H_2(g) \qquad [22.13]$$

Teaching Note: Water gas was also the original piped-in gas for homes and led to the popularity of keeping canaries as pets, because these birds die from carbon monoxide gas more easily than do humans.

When heated to about 1000°C, carbon also reacts with steam to produce a mixture of H_2 and CO gases:

$$C(s) + H_2O(g) \longrightarrow H_2(g) + CO(g) \qquad [22.14]$$

This mixture, known as **water gas,** is used as an industrial fuel.

Simple electrolysis of water consumes too much energy and is consequently too costly to be used commercially to produce H_2. However, H_2 is produced as a by-product in the electrolysis of brine (NaCl) solutions in the

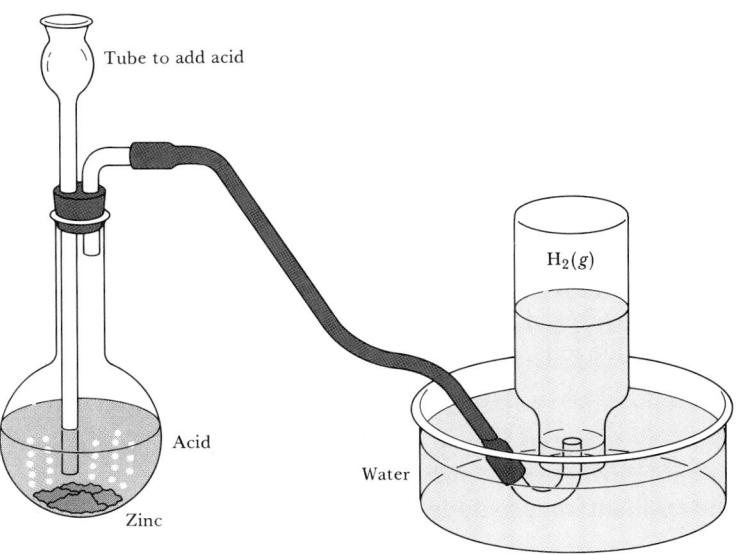

Tube to add acid

$H_2(g)$

Acid

Water

Zinc

FIGURE 22.6 Apparatus commonly used in the laboratory for preparation of hydrogen.

course of Cl$_2$ and NaOH manufacture:

$$2NaCl(aq) + 2H_2O(l) \xrightarrow{\text{electrolysis}} H_2(g) + Cl_2(g) + 2NaOH(aq) \qquad [22.15]$$

Uses of Hydrogen

Learning Goal 6: Cite at least two uses for hydrogen.

Hydrogen is a commercially important substance: About 2×10^8 kg (200,000 tons) is produced annually in the United States. Over two-thirds of the annual production is consumed in the synthesis of ammonia by the Haber process. ∞ (Sec. 15.1) Hydrogen is also used to manufacture methanol, CH$_3$OH. As shown in Equation 22.16, the synthesis involves the catalytic combination of CO and H$_2$ at high pressure and temperature:

Alton Banks, "What's the Use? Hydrogen," *J. Chem. Educ.* **1989**, *66*, 801.

$$CO(g) + 2H_2(g) \longrightarrow CH_3OH(l) \qquad [22.16]$$

Hydrogenation of vegetable oils in the manufacture of margarine and vegetable shortening is another important use. In this process, H$_2$ is added to carbon-carbon double bonds in the oil. A simple example of hydrogenation occurs in the conversion of ethylene to ethane:

Teaching Note: The term "partially hydrogenated vegetable oil" is frequently seen in the ingredient list of processed foods.

$$\underset{\text{Ethylene}}{\overset{\text{H}\;\;\;\;\;\;\text{H}}{\underset{\text{H}\;\;\;\;\;\;\text{H}}{\text{C}=\text{C}}}} + H_2 \xrightarrow{\text{catalyst}} \underset{\text{Ethane}}{\overset{\text{H}\;\;\text{H}}{\underset{\text{H}\;\;\text{H}}{\text{H}-\text{C}-\text{C}-\text{H}}}} \qquad [22.17]$$

Because organic compounds with double bonds have the ability to add additional hydrogen atoms, they are said to be *unsaturated*. The term *polyunsaturated,* which often appears in food advertisements, refers to molecules that have several (poly) double bonds between carbon atoms. The following molecule is a polyunsaturated hydrocarbon:

$$\overset{\text{H}}{\underset{\text{H}_3\text{C}}{}}\text{C}=\text{C}\overset{\text{CH}_2-\text{CH}_2}{\underset{\text{H}}{}}\text{C}=\text{C}\overset{\text{H}}{\underset{\text{H}}{}}$$

Binary Hydrogen Compounds

Learning Goal 7: Distinguish among ionic, metallic, and molecular hydrides.

Hydrogen reacts with other elements to form compounds of three general types: (1) ionic hydrides, (2) metallic hydrides, and (3) molecular hydrides.

The **ionic hydrides** are formed by the alkali metals and by the heavier alkaline earths (Ca, Sr, and Ba). These active metals are much less electronegative than hydrogen. Consequently, hydrogen acquires electrons from them to form hydride ions, H$^-$, as shown below:

$$2Li(s) + H_2(g) \longrightarrow 2LiH(s) \qquad [22.18]$$

$$Ca(s) + H_2(g) \longrightarrow CaH_2(s) \qquad [22.19]$$

The resultant ionic hydrides are solids with high melting points (LiH melts at 680°C).

The hydride ion is very basic and reacts readily with compounds having even weakly acidic protons to form H_2. For example, H^- reacts readily with H_2O:

$$H^-(aq) + H_2O(l) \rightarrow H_2(g) + OH^-(aq) \qquad [22.20]$$

Ionic hydrides can therefore be used as convenient (although expensive) sources of H_2. Calcium hydride, CaH_2, is sold in commercial quantities and is used for inflation of life rafts, weather balloons, and the like, where a simple, compact means of H_2 generation is desired. It is also used to remove H_2O from organic liquids. The reaction of CaH_2 with H_2O is shown in Figure 22.7.

The reaction between H^- and H_2O (Equation 22.20) is not only an acid-base reaction but a redox reaction as well. The H^- ion can be viewed not only as a good base but also as a good reducing agent. In fact, hydrides are able to reduce O_2 to H_2O:

Point of Emphasis: The H^- ion is oxidized by two electrons to H^+.

$$2NaH(s) + O_2(g) \longrightarrow Na_2O(s) + H_2O(l) \qquad [22.21]$$

Thus, hydrides are normally stored in an environment that is free of both moisture and air.

Metallic hydrides are formed when hydrogen reacts with transition metals. These compounds are so named because they retain their metallic conductivity and other metallic properties. In many metallic hydrides the ratio of metal atoms to hydrogen atoms is not a ratio of small whole numbers, nor is it a fixed ratio. The composition can vary within a range, depending on the conditions of synthesis. For example, although TiH_2 can be produced, preparations usually yield substances with about 10 percent less hydrogen than this, $TiH_{1.8}$. These nonstoichiometric metallic hydrides are sometimes called **interstitial hydrides.** They may be considered to be solutions of hydrogen atoms in the metal, with the hydrogen atoms occupying the holes or interstices between metal atoms in the solid lattice. However, this description is an oversimplification; there is evidence for chemical interaction between metal and hydrogen.

Teaching Note: The interstitial hydrides are the primary examples of nonstoichiometric compounds seen in general chemistry.

FIGURE 22.7 Reaction of CaH_2 with water in the presence of phenolphthalein. The red color of the phenolphthalein is due to the presence of OH^- ions. The gas bubbles are H_2. (Richard Megna/ Fundamental Photographs)

Using Metal Hydrides

The ready absorption of H_2 by palladium metal has been used to separate H_2 from other gases and in purifying H_2 on an industrial scale. At 300 to 400 K, H_2 dissociates into atomic hydrogen on the Pd surface. The H atoms dissolve in the Pd, and under H_2 pressure they diffuse through, recombining to form H_2 on the opposite surface. Because no other molecules exhibit this property, absolutely pure H_2 results.

Research is in progress investigating metallic hydrides as storage media for hydrogen. In the case of many metals, hydride formation occurs directly upon contact between the metal and H_2. Furthermore, the reaction is often readily reversible so that H_2 can be obtained from the hydride by reducing the pressure of the hydrogen gas above the metal. Metals accommodate an extremely high density of hydrogen because the hydrogen atoms are closely packed into the interstitial sites between metal atoms. Indeed, the number of hydrogen atoms per unit volume is greater in some metallic hydrides than in liquid H_2. In some hydrides, the metal can accommodate two or three times as many hydrogen atoms as there are metal atoms; that is, the stoichiometry approaches MH_3 (where M is the metal).

The absorption of hydrogen by metals also has detrimental effects. The hydrides tend to be more brittle than the metal. Thus, absorption of hydrogen can weaken and embrittle steel and other structural metals (Figure 22.8).

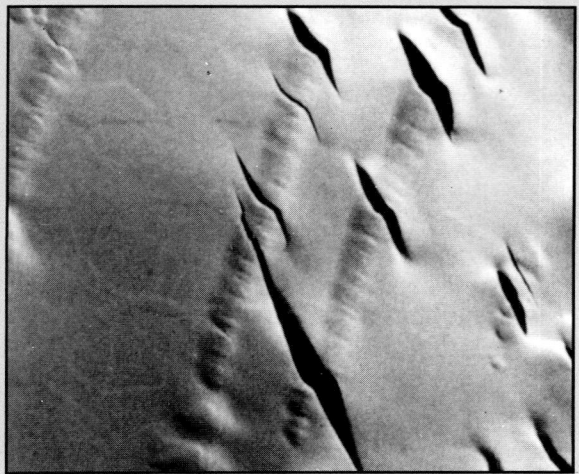

FIGURE 22.8 Cracking in niobium metal due to hydride formation when the metal is stressed under a 1 percent H_2 atmosphere. The raised lines running nearly vertically are due to formation of NbH at certain planes within the metal. The cracks begin in these regions because NbH is very brittle. (Photo courtesy of Professor Howard Birnbaum, University of Illinois; electron microscope photo, about 200× magnification. Reprinted with permission from *Acta Metallurgica*, vol. 25, M. L. Grossbeck and H. K. Birnbaum, "Low Temperature Hydrogen Embrittlement of Niobium II — Microscopic Observations," copyright 1977, Pergamon Press Ltd.)

FIGURE 22.9 Standard free energies of formation (kJ/mol) of molecular hydrides.

4A	5A	6A	7A
$CH_4(g)$ −50.8	$NH_3(g)$ −16.7	$H_2O(l)$ −237	$HF(g)$ −271
$SiH_4(g)$ +56.9	$PH_3(g)$ +18.2	$H_2S(g)$ −33.0	$HCl(g)$ −95.3
$GeH_4(g)$ +117	$AsH_3(g)$ +111	$H_2Se(g)$ +71	$HBr(g)$ −53.2
	$SbH_3(g)$ +187	$H_2Te(g)$ +138	$HI(g)$ +1.30

The **molecular hydrides,** formed by nonmetals and semimetals, are either gases or liquids under standard conditions. The simple molecular hydrides are listed in Figure 22.9, together with their standard free energies of formation, ΔG_f°. In each family, the thermal stability (measured by ΔG_f°) decreases as we move down the family. (Recall that the more stable a compound with respect to its elements under standard conditions, the more negative ΔG_f° is.) We will discuss the molecular hydrides further in the course of examining the other nonmetallic elements.

22.4 Oxygen

By the middle of the seventeenth century, scientists recognized that air contained a component associated with burning and breathing. That component was not isolated until 1774, however, when Joseph Priestley discovered oxygen

(Figure 22.10). Lavoisier subsequently named the element *oxygen,* meaning "acid former."

Oxygen plays an important role in the chemistries of most other elements and is found in combination with other elements in a great variety of compounds. Indeed, oxygen is the most abundant element by mass both in the earth's crust and in the human body. It constitutes 89 percent of water by mass and 20.9 percent of air by volume (23 percent by mass). It also comprises 50 percent by mass of the sand, clay, limestone, and igneous rocks that make up the bulk of the earth's crust.

Learning Goal 8: Cite the most common occurrences of oxygen and how it is obtained in its elemental form.

Properties of Oxygen

Oxygen has two allotropes, O_2 and O_3. When we speak of elemental or molecular oxygen, it is usually understood that we are speaking of dioxygen, O_2, the normal form of the element; O_3 is called *ozone.*

Learning Goal 9: Describe the allotropes of oxygen.

Dioxygen exists at room temperature as a colorless, odorless, and tasteless gas. It condenses to a liquid at $-183°C$ and freezes to a solid at $-218°C$. It is only slightly soluble in water, but its presence in water is essential to marine life.

Michael Laing, "The Three Forms of Molecular Oxygen," *J. Chem. Educ.* **1989,** *66,* 453.

The electron configuration of the oxygen atom is $[He]2s^2 2p^4$. Thus, oxygen can complete its octet of electrons either by picking up two electrons to form the oxide ion, O^{2-}, or by sharing two electrons. In its covalent compounds it tends to form two bonds: either two single bonds, as in H_2O, or a double bond, as in formaldehyde, $H_2C=O$. The O_2 molecule itself contains a double bond.

The bond in O_2 is very strong (the bond-dissociation energy is 495 kJ/mol). Oxygen also forms strong bonds with many other elements. Consequently, many oxygen-containing compounds are thermodynamically more stable than O_2. However, in the absence of a catalyst, most reactions of O_2 have high activation energies and thus require high temperatures to proceed at a suitable rate. Once a sufficiently exothermic reaction begins, however, it may accelerate rapidly, producing a reaction of explosive violence.

FIGURE 22.10 Joseph Priestley (1733–1804). Priestley became interested in chemistry at the age of 39, perhaps through his personal acquaintance with Benjamin Franklin. Because Priestley lived next door to a brewery from which he could obtain carbon dioxide, his studies focused on this gas first and were later extended to other gases. Because he was suspected of sympathizing with the American and French Revolutions, his church, home, and laboratory in Birmingham, England, were burned by a mob in 1791. Priestley had to flee in disguise. He eventually emigrated to the United States in 1794, where he lived his remaining years in relative seclusion in Pennsylvania. (The Granger Collection)

Preparation of Oxygen

Oxygen can be obtained either from air or from certain oxygen-containing compounds. Nearly all commercial oxygen is obtained by fractional distillation of liquefied air. The normal boiling point of O_2 is $-183\,^\circ$C, whereas that of N_2, the other principal component of air, is $-196\,^\circ$C. Thus, when liquefied air is warmed, the N_2 boils off, leaving liquid O_2 contaminated mainly with small amounts of N_2 and Ar.

A common laboratory preparation of O_2 is the thermal decomposition of potassium chlorate, $KClO_3$, with manganese dioxide, MnO_2, added as a catalyst:

$$2KClO_3(s) \xrightarrow{\text{MnO}_2} 2KCl(s) + 3O_2(g) \qquad [22.22]$$

Like H_2, O_2 can be collected by displacement of water because of its relatively low solubility.

Uses of Oxygen

Learning Goal 10: Cite at least two uses for oxygen.

Bassam Z. Shakhashiri, "Combining Volume of Oxygen with Sulfur," *Chemical Demonstrations: A Handbook for Teachers of Chemistry, Volume 2* (Madison: The University of Wisconsin Press, 1985), pp. 190–92.

Oxygen is one of the most widely used industrial chemicals. In 1992, it ranked behind only sulfuric acid, H_2SO_4, and nitrogen, N_2. About 1.9×10^{10} kg (21 million tons) of O_2 is used annually in the United States. Oxygen can be shipped and stored either as liquid or in steel containers as compressed gas. However, about 70 percent of O_2 output is generated at the site where it is needed.

Oxygen is by far the most widely used oxidizing agent. Over half of the O_2 produced is used in the steel industry, mainly to remove impurities from steel. It is also used to bleach pulp and paper. (Oxidation of intensely colored compounds often gives colorless products.) In medicine, oxygen eases breathing difficulties. It is also used together with acetylene, C_2H_2, in oxyacetylene welding (Figure 22.11). The reaction between C_2H_2 and O_2 is highly exothermic,

FIGURE 22.11 Welding with an oxyacetylene torch. The heat of combustion of acetylene is exceptionally high, thus giving rise to a very high flame temperature when acetylene is combusted in oxygen. (Leonard L. T. Rhodes/The Image Bank)

producing temperatures in excess of 3000°C:

$$2C_2H_2(g) + 5O_2(g) \longrightarrow 4CO_2(g) + 2H_2O(g) \quad \Delta H° = -2510 \text{ kJ} \quad [22.23]$$

Ozone

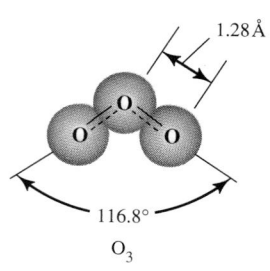

FIGURE 22.12 Structure of the ozone molecule.

Ozone is a pale-blue gas with a sharp, irritating odor. It is poisonous, although no human deaths have been attributed to it. Most people can detect about 0.01 ppm in air. Exposure to 0.1 to 1 ppm produces headaches, burning of the eyes, and irritation to the respiratory passages.

The structure of the O_3 molecule is shown in Figure 22.12. The molecule possesses a π bond that is delocalized over the three oxygen atoms. The molecule dissociates readily, forming reactive oxygen atoms:

$$O_3(g) \longrightarrow O_2(g) + O(g) \qquad \Delta H° = 107 \text{ kJ} \qquad [22.24]$$

Teaching Note: Bleaching is defined as the removal of color from a material. Although commercial household bleach is an aqueous solution of sodium hypochlorite (NaOCl), any compound that removes color can be used as a bleach.

Not surprisingly, ozone is a stronger oxidizing agent than dioxygen. One measure of this oxidizing power is the high reduction potential of O_3, compared to that of O_2:

$$O_3(g) + 2H^+(aq) + 2e^- \longrightarrow O_2(g) + H_2O(l) \qquad E° = 2.07 \text{ V} \qquad [22.25]$$
$$O_2(g) + 4H^+(aq) + 4e^- \longrightarrow 2H_2O(l) \qquad E° = 1.23 \text{ V} \qquad [22.26]$$

Ozone forms oxides with many elements under conditions where O_2 will not react; indeed, it oxidizes all of the common metals except gold and platinum.

Ozone can be prepared by passing electricity through dry O_2:

$$3O_2(g) \xrightarrow{\text{electricity}} 2O_3(g) \qquad \Delta H° = 285 \text{ kJ} \qquad [22.27]$$

Teaching Note: The pungent odor of ozone gas can sometimes be detected when a spark jumps during short circuits in electrical equipment or near lightning strikes in thunderstorms.

The preparation of O_3 may be accomplished in an apparatus such as that shown in Figure 22.13. The gas cannot be stored for long except at low temperature because it readily decomposes to O_2. The decomposition is catalyzed by certain metals, such as Ag, Pt, and Pd, and by many transition-metal oxides.

FIGURE 22.13 Apparatus for producing ozone from O_2.

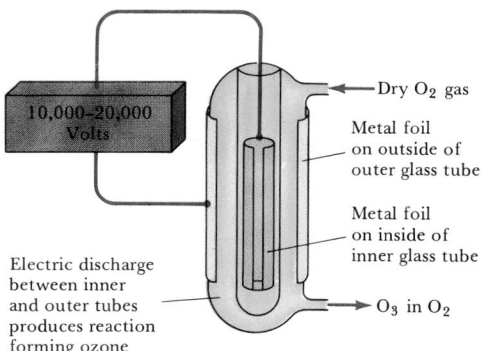

SAMPLE EXERCISE 22.3

Using ΔG_f° for ozone from Appendix C, calculate the equilibrium constant, K_p, for Equation 22.27 at 298.0 K.

SOLUTION From Appendix C we have $\Delta G_f^\circ(O_3) = 163.4$ kJ/mol. Thus, for Equation 22.27, $\Delta G^\circ = (2 \text{ mol } O_3)(163.4 \text{ kJ/mol } O_3) = 326.8$ kJ. From Equation 19.14, we have $\Delta G^\circ = -RT \ln K$. Thus,

$$\ln K = \frac{-\Delta G^\circ}{RT} = \frac{-326.8 \times 10^3 \text{ J}}{(8.314 \text{ J/K-mol})(298.0 \text{ K})} = -131.9$$

$$K = 5 \times 10^{-58}$$

In spite of the unfavorable equilibrium constant, ozone can be prepared from O_2 as described in the text above. The unfavorable free energy of formation is overcome by energy from the electrical discharge, and O_3 is removed before the reverse reaction can occur, so a nonequilibrium mixture results.

PRACTICE EXERCISE

Using the data in Appendix C, calculate ΔG° and the equilibrium constant, K_p, for Equation 22.24 at 298.0 K.   *Answer:* $\Delta G^\circ = 66.7$ kJ; $K_p = 2 \times 10^{-12}$

At the present time, uses of ozone as an industrial chemical are relatively limited. Ozone is sometimes used in treatment of domestic water in place of chlorine. Like Cl_2, it serves to kill bacteria and oxidize organic compounds. The largest use of ozone, however, is in the preparation of pharmaceuticals, synthetic lubricants, and other commercially useful organic compounds, where O_3 is used to sever carbon-carbon double bonds.

Ozone is an important component of the upper atmosphere, where it serves to screen out ultraviolet radiation. In this way, ozone protects the earth from the effects of these high-energy rays. For this reason, depletion of stratospheric ozone is a major scientific concern. ∞ (Sec. 18.3) However, in the lower atmosphere ozone is considered an air pollutant. It is a major constituent of smog. ∞ (Sec. 18.4) Because of its oxidizing power, it causes damage to living systems and structural materials, especially rubber.

Oxides

The electronegativity of oxygen is second only to that of fluorine. Consequently, oxygen exhibits negative oxidation states in all compounds except those with fluorine, OF_2 and O_2F_2. The -2 oxidation state is by far the most common. As we have seen, compounds in this oxidation state are called *oxides*.

Nonmetals form covalent oxides. Most of these oxides are simple molecules with low melting and boiling points. However, SiO_2 and B_2O_3 have polymeric structures (Sections 23.5 and 23.6). Most nonmetal oxides combine with water to give oxyacids. For example, sulfur dioxide, SO_2, dissolves in water to give sulfurous acid, H_2SO_3:

$$SO_2(g) + H_2O(l) \longrightarrow H_2SO_3(aq) \qquad [22.28]$$

This reaction and that of SO_3 with water to form H_2SO_4 are largely responsible for acid rain. ∞ (Sec. 18.4) The analogous reaction of CO_2 with water to form carbonic acid, H_2CO_3, accounts for the acidity of carbonated water.

Oxides that react with water to form acids are called **acidic anhydrides** (anhydride means "without water") or **acidic oxides.** A few nonmetal oxides,

Point of Emphasis: Oxides don't have to be ionic compounds. Covalent oxides, such as CO, CO_2, and B_2O_3, are common.

especially ones with the nonmetal in a low oxidation state—such as N_2O, NO, and CO—are not acidic anhydrides. These oxides do not react with water.

Most metal oxides are ionic compounds. Those ionic oxides that dissolve in water form hydroxides and are consequently called **basic anhydrides** or **basic oxides.** For example, barium oxide, BaO, dissolves in water to form barium hydroxide, $Ba(OH)_2$:

$$BaO(s) + H_2O(l) \longrightarrow Ba(OH)_2(aq) \qquad [22.29]$$

This reaction is shown in Figure 22.14. Such reactions can be attributed to the high basicity of the O^{2-} ion and consequently its virtually complete hydrolysis in water:

$$O^{2-}(aq) + H_2O(l) \longrightarrow 2OH^-(aq) \qquad [22.30]$$

Even those ionic oxides that are water-insoluble tend to dissolve in acids. Iron(III) oxide, for example, dissolves in acids:

$$Fe_2O_3(s) + 6H^+(aq) \longrightarrow 2Fe^{3+}(aq) + 3H_2O(l) \qquad [22.31]$$

This reaction is used to remove rust, $Fe_2O_3 \cdot nH_2O$, from iron or steel before application of a protective coat of zinc or tin.

Oxides that can exhibit both acidic and basic characters are said to be *amphoteric.* ∞ (Sec. 16.2) If a metal forms more than one oxide, the basic character of the oxide decreases as the oxidation state of the metal increases:

Compound	Oxidation state of Cr	Nature of oxide
CrO	+2	Basic
Cr_2O_3	+3	Amphoteric
CrO_3	+6	Acidic

FIGURE 22.14 Barium oxide, BaO, the white solid at the bottom of the container, reacts with water to produce barium hydroxide, $Ba(OH)_2$. The red color of the solution is caused by phenolphthalein and indicates the presence of OH^- ions in solution. (Donald Clegg and Roxy Wilson)

Point of Emphasis: As the oxidation state of the central atom increases, acidic character increases, and basic character decreases.

Peroxides and Superoxides

Compounds containing O—O bonds and oxygen in an oxidation state of -1 are called *peroxides.* Oxygen has an oxidation state of $-\frac{1}{2}$ in O_2^-, which is called the *superoxide* ion. The most active metals (Cs, Rb, and K) react with O_2 to give superoxides (CsO_2, RbO_2, and KO_2). Their active neighbors in the periodic table (Na, Ca, Sr, and Ba) react with O_2, producing peroxides (Na_2O_2, CaO_2, SrO_2, and BaO_2). Less active metals and nonmetals produce normal oxides. ∞ (Sec. 7.7)

When superoxides dissolve in water, O_2 is produced:

$$2KO_2(s) + 2H_2O(l) \longrightarrow 2K^+(aq) + 2OH^-(aq) + O_2(g) + H_2O_2(aq) \quad [22.32]$$

Because of this reaction, potassium superoxide, KO_2, is used as an oxygen source in masks worn for rescue work. Moisture in the breath causes the compound to decompose to form O_2 and KOH. The KOH so formed serves to remove CO_2 from the exhaled breath:

$$2OH^-(aq) + CO_2(g) \longrightarrow H_2O(l) + CO_3^{2-}(aq) \qquad [22.33]$$

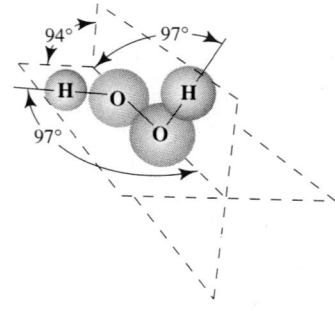

Hydrogen peroxide, H_2O_2, is the most familiar and commercially important peroxide. The structure of H_2O_2 is shown in Figure 22.15. The peroxide linkage (—O—O—) exists in species other than H_2O_2 and O_2^{2-} ion. For example, the peroxydisulfate ion, $S_2O_8^{2-}$ or $O_3SOOSO_3^{2-}$, contains this linkage.

Pure hydrogen peroxide is a clear, syrupy liquid, density 1.47 g/cm^3 at 0°C. It melts at −0.4°C, and its normal boiling point is 151°C. These properties are characteristic of a highly polar, strongly hydrogen-bonded liquid such as water. Concentrated hydrogen peroxide is a dangerously reactive substance because the decomposition to form water and oxygen gas is very exothermic:

$$2H_2O_2(l) \longrightarrow 2H_2O(l) + O_2(g) \qquad \Delta H° = -196.0 \text{ kJ} \qquad [22.34]$$

Teaching Note: There are also peroxycarboxylic acids and peroxyalcohols.

The decomposition can occur with explosive violence if concentrated hydrogen peroxide comes in contact with substances that can catalyze the reaction. Hydrogen peroxide is marketed as a chemical reagent in aqueous solutions of up to about 30 percent by mass. A solution containing about 3 percent by mass H_2O_2 is commonly used as a mild antiseptic; somewhat more concentrated solutions are employed to bleach fabrics such as cotton, wool, and silk.

Learning Goal 11: Describe the chemical and physical properties of hydrogen peroxide and its method of preparation.

The peroxide ion is also important in biochemistry. It is a by-product of metabolism that results from the reduction of molecular oxygen, O_2. The body disposes of this reactive species with enzymes with such names as peroxidase and catalase. The fizzing that occurs when a dilute H_2O_2 solution is applied to an open wound is due to decomposition of the H_2O_2 into O_2 and H_2O, a reaction catalyzed by the enzymes.

Hydrogen peroxide can act as either an oxidizing or a reducing agent. Equations 22.35 and 22.36 show the half-reactions for acid solution.

$$2H^+(aq) + H_2O_2(aq) + 2e^- \longrightarrow 2H_2O(l) \qquad E° = 1.77 \text{ V} \quad [22.35]$$

$$H_2O_2(aq) \longrightarrow O_2(g) + 2H^+(aq) + 2e^- \qquad E° = -0.67 \text{ V} \quad [22.36]$$

The Oxygen Cycle

Oxygen accounts for about one-fourth of the atoms in living matter. The number of oxygen atoms is fixed; as O_2 is removed from air through respiration and other processes, it is replenished. The major nonliving sources of oxygen other than O_2 are CO_2 and H_2O. A simplified picture of the movement of oxygen in our environment is shown in Figure 22.16. This figure points out both how O_2 is removed from the atmosphere and how it is replenished. Oxygen, O_2, is reformed mainly from CO_2 through the process of photosynthesis. Energy is produced when O_2 is converted to CO_2; energy must therefore be supplied to reform O_2 from CO_2. This energy is provided by the sun. Thus, life on earth depends on chemical recycling made possible by solar energy.

22.5 Nitrogen

Nitrogen was discovered in 1772 by the Scottish botanist Daniel Rutherford. He found that when a mouse was enclosed in a sealed jar, the animal quickly consumed the life-sustaining component of air (oxygen) and died. When the

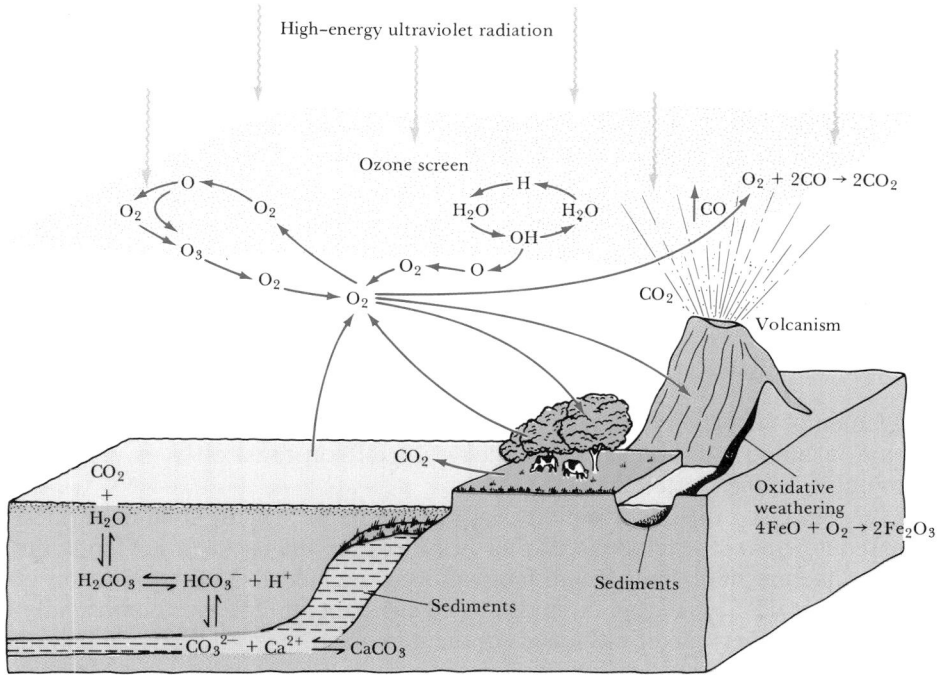

High–energy ultraviolet radiation

Ozone screen

O_2

O

O_2

O_3

O_2

$O_2 \leftarrow O$

O_2

$H \leftarrow$

H_2O H_2O

OH

CO

$O_2 + 2CO \rightarrow 2CO_2$

CO_2

Volcanism

CO_2

Oxidative
weathering
$4FeO + O_2 \rightarrow 2Fe_2O_3$

CO_2
+
H_2O

$H_2CO_3 \rightleftharpoons HCO_3^- + H^+$

Sediments

Sediments

$CO_3^{2-} + Ca^{2+} \rightleftharpoons CaCO_3$

FIGURE 22.16 Simplified view of the oxygen cycle. The atmosphere, which contains O_2, is one of the primary sources of the element. Some O_2 is produced by radiation-induced dissociation of H_2O in the upper atmosphere. Some O_2 is produced by green plants from H_2O and CO_2 in the course of photosynthesis. Atmospheric CO_2, in turn, results from combustion reactions, animal respiration, and the dissociation of bicarbonate in water. The O_2 is used to produce ozone in the upper atmosphere, in oxidative weathering of rocks, in animal respiration, and in combustion reactions.

Figure 22.16

"fixed air" (CO_2) in the container was removed, a "noxious air" remained that would not sustain combustion or life. That gas is known to us now as nitrogen.

Nitrogen constitutes 78 percent by volume of the earth's atmosphere, where it occurs as N_2 molecules. Although nitrogen is a key element in living creatures, compounds of nitrogen are not abundant in the earth's crust. The major natural deposits of nitrogen compounds are those of KNO_3 (saltpeter) in India and $NaNO_3$ (Chile saltpeter) in Chile and other desert regions of South America.

Learning Goal 12: Cite the most common occurrences of nitrogen and how it is obtained in its elemental form.

Properties of Nitrogen

Nitrogen is a colorless, odorless, and tasteless gas composed of N_2 molecules. Its melting point is $-210°C$, and its normal boiling point is $-196°C$.

The N_2 molecule is very unreactive because of the strong triple bond between nitrogen atoms (the $N{\equiv}N$ bond-dissociation energy is 941 kJ/mol, nearly twice that for the bond in O_2; see Table 8.4). When substances burn in air they normally react with O_2 but not with N_2. However, when magnesium burns in air, reaction with N_2 also occurs to form magnesium nitride, Mg_3N_2. A similar reaction occurs with lithium:

$$3Mg(s) + N_2(g) \longrightarrow Mg_3N_2(s) \qquad [22.37]$$

$$6Li(s) + N_2(g) \longrightarrow 2Li_3N(s) \qquad [22.38]$$

Teaching Note: Lithium is so reactive that lithium nitride is formed by exposing lithium metal to nitrogen gas at room temperature.

The nitride ion is a strong Brønsted-Lowry base. It reacts with water to form ammonia, NH_3:

$$Mg_3N_2(s) + 6H_2O(l) \longrightarrow 2NH_3(aq) + 3Mg(OH)_2(s) \qquad [22.39]$$

TABLE 22.2 △ **Oxidation States of Nitrogen**

Oxidation state	Examples
+5	N_2O_5, HNO_3, NO_3^-
+4	NO_2, N_2O_4
+3	HNO_2, NO_2^-, NF_3
+2	NO
+1	N_2O, $H_2N_2O_2$, $N_2O_2^{2-}$, HNF_2
0	N_2
−1	NH_2OH, NH_2F
−2	N_2H_4
−3	NH_3, NH_4^+, NH_2^-

Learning Goal 13: Cite at least one example of a nitrogen compound for each of nitrogen's oxidation states from −3 to +5, and be able to name them.

Learning Goal 14: Cite at least two uses for nitrogen.

Teaching Note: Argon is also used as an inert atmosphere to exclude O_2. However, it is more costly than N_2 and is normally used only in situations where N_2 reacts.

Teaching Note: Ammonia is also called a *choking gas* because the lungs cease to function when exposed to any but a very low concentration of it.

The electron configuration of the nitrogen atom is $[He]2s^22p^3$. The element exhibits all formal oxidation states from +5 to −3, as shown in Table 22.2. The +5, 0, and −3 oxidation states are the most common and generally the most stable of these. Because nitrogen is the fourth most electronegative element after fluorine, oxygen, and chlorine, it exhibits positive oxidation states only in combination with these three elements.

Figure 22.17 summarizes the standard electrode potentials for interconversion of several common nitrogen species. The potentials in the diagram are large and positive, which indicates that the nitrogen oxides and oxyanions shown are strong oxidizing agents.

Preparation and Uses of Nitrogen

Elemental nitrogen is obtained in commercial quantities by fractional distillation of liquid air. About 2.7×10^{10} kg (29 million tons) of N_2 is produced annually in the United States.

Because of its low reactivity, large quantities of N_2 are used as an inert gaseous blanket to exclude O_2 during the processing and packaging of foods, the manufacture of chemicals, the fabrication of metals, and the production of electronic devices. Liquid N_2 is employed as a coolant to freeze foods rapidly.

The largest use of nitrogen is in the manufacture of nitrogen-containing chemicals. The formation of nitrogen compounds from N_2 is known as *nitrogen fixation.* The demand for fixed nitrogen is high because the element is required in maintaining soil fertility. Although we are immersed in an ocean of air that contains abundant N_2, our supply of food is limited more by the availability of fixed nitrogen than by that of any other plant nutrient. Thus, N_2 is used primarily for the manufacture of nitrogen-containing fertilizers. It is also used to manufacture explosives, plastics, and many important chemicals.

The chain of conversion of N_2 into a variety of useful, simple nitrogen-containing species is given in Figure 22.18. The processes shown are discussed in more detail in later portions of the section.

Hydrogen Compounds of Nitrogen

Ammonia is one of the most important compounds of nitrogen. It is a colorless, toxic gas that has a characteristic, irritating odor. As we have noted in previous discussions, the NH_3 molecule is basic ($K_b = 1.8 \times 10^{-5}$). (Sec. 16.6)

In the laboratory, NH_3 is prepared by the action of NaOH on an ammonium salt. The NH_4^+ ion, which is the conjugate acid of NH_3, transfers a proton

FIGURE 22.17 Standard electrode potentials in acid solution for reduction of some common nitrogen-containing compounds in various oxidation states. For example, reduction of NO_3^- to NO_2 in acid solution has a standard electrode potential of 0.79 V (leftmost entry). You should be able to write the complete, balanced half-reaction for this reduction using the techniques discussed in Section 20.2.

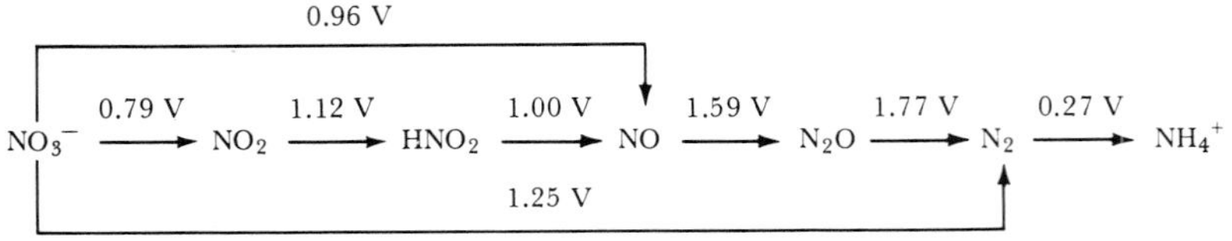

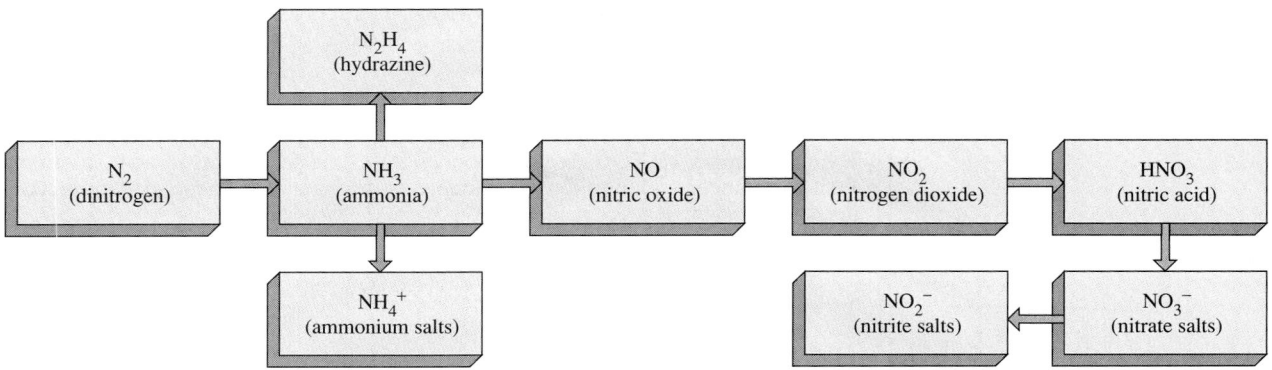

FIGURE 22.18 Conversion of N_2 into common nitrogen compounds.

to OH^-. The resultant NH_3 is volatile and is driven from the solution by mild heating:

$$NH_4Cl(aq) + NaOH(aq) \longrightarrow NH_3(g) + H_2O(l) + NaCl(aq) \quad [22.40]$$

Commercial production of NH_3 is achieved by the *Haber process* (Section 15.1), in which N_2 and H_2 are catalytically combined at high pressure and high temperature:

$$N_2(g) + 3H_2(g) \longrightarrow 2NH_3(g) \quad [22.41]$$

About 1.6×10^{10} kg (18 million tons) of ammonia is produced annually in the United States. About 75 percent is used for fertilizer.

Hydrazine, N_2H_4, bears the same relationship to ammonia that hydrogen peroxide does to water. As shown in Figure 22.19, the hydrazine molecule contains an N—N single bond. Hydrazine is quite poisonous. It can be prepared by the reaction of ammonia with hypochlorite ion, OCl^-, in aqueous solution:

$$2NH_3(aq) + OCl^-(aq) \longrightarrow N_2H_4(aq) + Cl^-(aq) + H_2O(l) \quad [22.42]$$

The reaction is complex, involving several intermediates including chloramine, NH_2Cl. The poisonous NH_2Cl bubbles out of solution when household ammonia and chlorine bleach (which contains OCl^-) are mixed. This reaction is one reason for the frequently cited warning not to mix household cleansing agents.

Pure hydrazine is an oily, colorless liquid that explodes on heating. It is a highly reactive reducing agent. Hydrazine is normally employed in aqueous solution, where it can be handled safely. The substance is weakly basic, and salts of $N_2H_5^+$ can be formed:

$$N_2H_4(aq) + H_2O(l) \rightleftharpoons N_2H_5^+(aq) + OH^-(aq) \quad K_b = 1.3 \times 10^{-6} \quad [22.43]$$

The combustion of hydrazine is highly exothermic:

$$N_2H_4(l) + O_2(g) \longrightarrow N_2(g) + 2H_2O(g) \quad \Delta H° = -534 \text{ kJ} \quad [22.44]$$

FIGURE 22.19 Lewis structures of hydrazine, N_2H_4, and monomethylhydrazine, CH_3NHNH_2.

$$H - \overset{\cdot\cdot}{\underset{H}{N}} - \overset{\cdot\cdot}{\underset{H}{N}} - H$$

Hydrazine

$$H - \overset{\cdot\cdot}{\underset{H}{N}} - \overset{\cdot\cdot}{\underset{H}{N}} - \overset{H}{\underset{H}{C}} - H$$

Monomethyl hydrazine

Hydrazine and compounds derived from it, such as monomethylhydrazine (Figure 22.19), are used as rocket fuels.

SAMPLE EXERCISE 22.4

Hydroxylamine, NH_2OH, reduces copper(II) to the free metal in acid solutions. Write a balanced equation for the reaction, assuming that N_2 is the oxidation product.

SOLUTION   The unbalanced and incomplete half-reactions are

$$Cu^{2+}(aq) \longrightarrow Cu(s)$$

$$NH_2OH(aq) \longrightarrow N_2(g)$$

Balancing these equations as described in Section 20.2 gives

$$Cu^{2+}(aq) + 2e^- \longrightarrow Cu(s)$$

$$2NH_2OH(aq) \longrightarrow N_2(g) + 2H_2O(l) + 2H^+(aq) + 2e^-$$

Adding these half-reactions gives the balanced equation:

$$Cu^{2+}(aq) + 2NH_2OH(aq) \longrightarrow Cu(s) + N_2(g) + 2H_2O(l) + 2H^+(aq)$$

PRACTICE EXERCISE

(a) In power plants hydrazine is used to prevent corrosion of the metal parts of steam boilers by the O_2 dissolved in the water. The hydrazine reacts with O_2 in water to give N_2 and H_2O. Write a balanced chemical equation for this reaction. (b) Monomethylhydrazine, $N_2H_3CH_3(l)$, is used with the oxidizer dinitrogen tetroxide, $N_2O_4(l)$, to power the steering rockets of the space shuttle orbiter. The reaction of these two substances produces N_2, CO_2, and H_2O. Write a balanced chemical equation for this reaction.
Answers: (a) $N_2H_4(aq) + O_2(aq) \longrightarrow N_2(g) + 2H_2O(l)$

(b) $5N_2O_4(l) + 4N_2H_3CH_3(l) \longrightarrow 9N_2(g) + 4CO_2(g) + 12H_2O(g)$

Oxides and Oxyacids of Nitrogen

Nitrogen forms three common oxides: N_2O (nitrous oxide), NO (nitric oxide), and NO_2 (nitrogen dioxide). It also forms two unstable oxides that we will not discuss, N_2O_3 (dinitrogen trioxide) and N_2O_5 (dinitrogen pentoxide).

Nitrous oxide, N_2O, is also known as laughing gas because a person becomes somewhat giddy after inhaling only a small amount of it. This colorless gas was the first substance used as a general anesthetic. It is used as the compressed gas propellant in several aerosols and foams, such as in whipped cream. It can be prepared in the laboratory by carefully heating ammonium nitrate to about 200°C:

$$NH_4NO_3(s) \xrightarrow{\Delta} N_2O(g) + 2H_2O(g) \qquad [22.45]$$

Nitric oxide, NO, is also a colorless gas, but unlike N_2O it is slightly toxic. It can be prepared in the laboratory by reduction of dilute nitric acid, using copper or iron as a reducing agent, as shown in Figure 22.20.

$$Cu(s) + 2NO_3^-(aq) + 8H^+(aq) \longrightarrow 3Cu^{2+}(aq) + 2NO(g) + 4H_2O(l) \quad [22.46]$$

It is also produced by direct combination of N_2 and O_2 at elevated temperatures. This reaction is a significant source of nitrogen oxide air pollutants, which form

(a)   (b)   (c)

FIGURE 22.20 (a) Nitric oxide, NO, can be prepared by reacting copper with 6 M nitric acid. In this photo, a jar containing 6 M HNO$_3$ has been inverted over some pieces of copper. Colorless NO, which is only slightly soluble in water, is collected in the jar. The blue color of the solution is due to the presence of Cu^{2+} ions. (b) Colorless NO gas, collected as shown on the left. (c) When the stopper is removed from the jar of NO, the NO reacts with oxygen in the air to form yellow-brown NO$_2$. (Donald Clegg and Roxy Wilson)

during combustion reactions in air. ∞ (Sec. 18.4) However, the direct combination of N$_2$ and O$_2$ is not presently used for commercial production of NO because the yield is low; the equilibrium constant K_c at 2400 K is only 0.05.

The commercial route to NO (and hence to other oxygen-containing compounds of nitrogen) is by means of the catalytic oxidation of NH$_3$ (Figure 22.21):

$$4NH_3(g) + 5O_2(g) \xrightarrow[850°C]{Pt\ catalyst} 4NO(g) + 6H_2O(g) \qquad [22.47]$$

The catalytic conversion of NH$_3$ to NO is the first step in a three-step process known as the **Ostwald process,** by which NH$_3$ is converted commercially into nitric acid, HNO$_3$ (Figure 22.22). Nitric oxide reacts readily with O$_2$,

FIGURE 22.21 The oxidation of ammonia during the production of nitric acid is undertaken on a large industrial scale. The reaction is carried out in the presence of a platinum-rhodium catalyst, which is usually in the form of a woven gauze. Here new catalyst gauzes are being installed in an ammonia oxidation plant. (Johnson-Matthey Metals Limited)

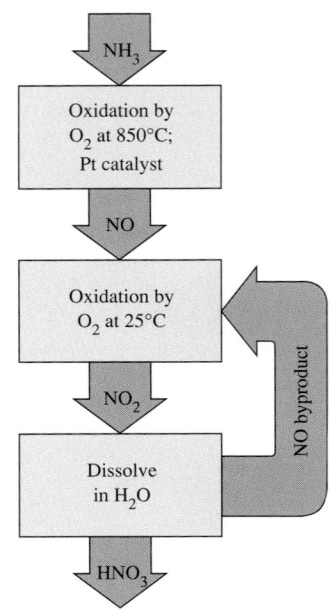

FIGURE 22.22 The Ostwald process for converting NH_3 to HNO_3.

Teaching Note: Despite its toxicity, NO is an important neurotransmitter molecule in the human body.

forming NO_2 when exposed to air (see Figure 22.20):

$$2NO(g) + O_2(g) \longrightarrow 2NO_2(g) \qquad [22.48]$$

When dissolved in water, NO_2 forms nitric acid:

$$3NO_2(g) + H_2O(l) \longrightarrow 2H^+(aq) + 2NO_3^-(aq) + NO(g) \quad [22.49]$$

Note that nitrogen is both oxidized and reduced in this reaction. The NO_2 is said to have undergone **disproportionation.** The reduction product NO can be converted back into NO_2 by exposure to air and thereafter dissolved in water to prepare more HNO_3.

Recently, NO has been found to be an important neurotransmitter in the human body. It causes the muscles that line blood vessels to relax, thus allowing an increased passage of blood.

Nitrogen dioxide is a yellow-brown gas. Like NO, it is a major constituent of smog. ∞ (Sec. 18.4) It is poisonous and has a choking odor. Below room temperature two NO_2 molecules combine to form the colorless N_2O_4 (Figure 15.1):

$$2NO_2(g) \longrightarrow N_2O_4(g) \qquad \Delta H° = -58 \text{ kJ} \qquad [22.50]$$

The two common oxyacids of nitrogen are nitric acid, HNO_3, and nitrous acid, HNO_2 (Figure 22.23). *Nitric acid* is a colorless, corrosive liquid. Nitric acid solutions often take on a slightly yellow color (Figure 22.24) as a result of small amounts of NO_2 formed by photochemical decomposition:

$$4HNO_3(aq) \xrightarrow{h\nu} 4NO_2(g) + O_2(g) + 2H_2O(l) \qquad [22.51]$$

Nitric acid is a strong acid. It is also a powerful oxidizing agent, as the following electrode potentials indicate:

$$NO_3^-(aq) + 2H^+(aq) + e^- \longrightarrow NO_2(g) + H_2O(l) \quad E° = 0.79 \text{ V} \quad [22.52]$$
$$NO_3^-(aq) + 4H^+(aq) + 3e^- \longrightarrow NO(g) + 2H_2O(l) \quad E° = 0.96 \text{ V} \quad [22.53]$$

Concentrated nitric acid will attack and oxidize most metals, except Au, Pt, Rh, and Ir.

FIGURE 22.23 Structures of nitric acid and nitrous acid.

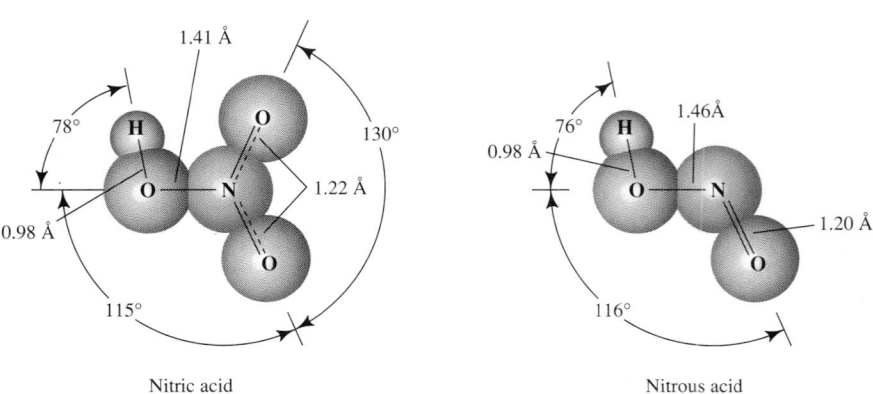

Nitric acid

Nitrous acid

FIGURE 22.24 Colorless nitric acid solution (left) becomes yellow upon standing in sunlight (right). (Fundamental Photographs)

About 7.3×10^9 kg (8 million tons) of nitric acid is produced annually in the United States. The largest use of nitric acid is in the manufacture of NH_4NO_3 for fertilizers, which accounts for about 80 percent of that produced. The acid is also used in the production of plastics, drugs, and explosives.

The development of the Haber and Ostwald processes in Germany just before World War I permitted Germany to make munitions even though naval blockades prevented access to traditional sources of nitrates. Among the explosives made from nitric acid are nitroglycerin, trinitrotoluene (TNT), and nitro-cellulose. The reaction of nitric acid with glycerin to form nitroglycerin is shown in Equation 22.54:

$$
\begin{array}{l}
\quad\ \ \text{H} \qquad\qquad\qquad\quad\ \text{H} \\
\quad\ \ | \qquad\qquad\qquad\quad\ \ | \\
\text{H—C—OH} \qquad\qquad \text{H—CONO}_2 \\
\quad\ \ | \qquad\qquad\qquad\quad\ \ | \\
\text{H—C—OH} + 3\text{HNO}_3 \longrightarrow \text{H—CONO}_2 + 3\text{H}_2\text{O} \qquad [22.54] \\
\quad\ \ | \qquad\qquad\qquad\quad\ \ | \\
\text{H—C—OH} \qquad\qquad \text{H—CONO}_2 \\
\quad\ \ | \qquad\qquad\qquad\quad\ \ | \\
\quad\ \ \text{H} \qquad\qquad\qquad\quad\ \text{H}
\end{array}
$$

When nitroglycerin explodes, the reaction summarized in Equation 22.55 occurs:

$$4C_3H_5N_3O_9(l) \longrightarrow 6N_2(g) + 12CO_2(g) + 10H_2O(g) + O_2(g) \quad [22.55]$$

All the products of this reaction contain very strong bonds. As a result, the reaction is very exothermic. Furthermore, a considerable amount of gaseous products form from the liquid. The sudden formation of these gases, together with their expansion resulting from the heat generated by the reaction, produces the explosion. (See the Chemistry at Work box in Section 8.9.)

Nitrous acid, HNO_2 (Figure 22.23) is considerably less stable than HNO_3 and tends to disproportionate into NO and HNO_3. It is normally made by

Teaching Note: The explosive force of nitroglycerin results from the formation of 29 moles of gas from only 4 moles of liquid. The rapid volume expansion *is* the explosion. See the Chemistry at Work box in Chapter 8, p. 274.

Nitrites in Food

Sodium nitrite is used as a food additive in cured meats such as frankfurters, ham, and cold cuts. The NO_2^- serves two functions. It inhibits growth of bacteria, especially *Clostridium botulinum,* which produces the potentially fatal food poisoning known as *botulism.* It also preserves the red color of the meat and thereby its appetizing appearance. Debate over the continued use of nitrites in cured meat products arises because HNO_2 can react with certain organic compounds to form compounds known as *nitrosoamines.* These reactions occur at high temperatures, as during frying. These are compounds of the type given in Figure 22.25. These organic compounds have been shown to produce cancer in laboratory animals, which has caused the U.S. Food and Drug Administration to reduce the limits of allowable concentrations of NO_2^- in foods.

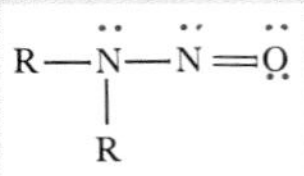

Nitrosoamine

FIGURE 22.25   General formula for a nitrosoamine (R = groups such as CH_3).

action of a strong acid such as H_2SO_4 on a cold solution of a nitrite salt such as $NaNO_2$. Nitrous acid is a weak acid ($K_a = 4.5 \times 10^{-4}$).

The Nitrogen Cycle in Nature

Teaching Note: Nitrogen fixation is performed by the bacteria living in the roots of the plants. Both the plant and bacteria benefit from this symbiotic relationship. The plants do not initially possess the bacteria. Rather, they need to be inoculated with the bacteria or acquire the bacteria from the soil.

Two primary routes for nitrogen fixation exist in nature: Lightning causes the formation of NO from N_2 and O_2 in air, and the root nodules of certain leguminous plants, such as peas, beans, peanuts, and alfalfa, contain nitrogen-fixing bacteria. Both iron and molybdenum are part of the enzyme system responsible for the nitrogen fixation in these root nodules. It is of interest to understand this process and to develop catalysts that, like enzymes, fix nitrogen at ambient pressure and temperature (and hence potentially at an energy savings over the Haber process).

Nitrogen is found in many compounds that are vital to life, including proteins, enzymes, nucleic acids, vitamins, and hormones. Plants employ very simple compounds as starting materials from which such complex, biologically necessary compounds are formed. Plants are able to use several forms of nitrogen, especially NH_3, NH_4^+, and NO_3^-. Liquid ammonia, ammonium nitrate, NH_4NO_3, and urea, $(NH_2)_2CO$, are among the most commonly applied nitrogen fertilizers. Urea is made by the reaction of ammonia and carbon dioxide:

$$2NH_3(aq) + CO_2(aq) \rightleftharpoons \overset{\overset{\displaystyle O}{\|}}{H_2NCNH_2}(aq) + H_2O(l) \qquad [22.56]$$

Urea

NH_3 is slowly released as the urea reacts with water in the soil.

Animals are unable to synthesize the complex nitrogen compounds they require from the simple substances used by plants. Instead, they rely on more complicated precursors present in foods. Those nitrogen compounds not needed by the animal are excreted as nitrogenous waste. Certain microorganisms are able to convert this waste back into N_2. Nitrogen is recycled in this fashion. As in the case of the cycling of oxygen, energy from the sun is required. A simplified picture of the nitrogen cycle is shown in Figure 22.26.

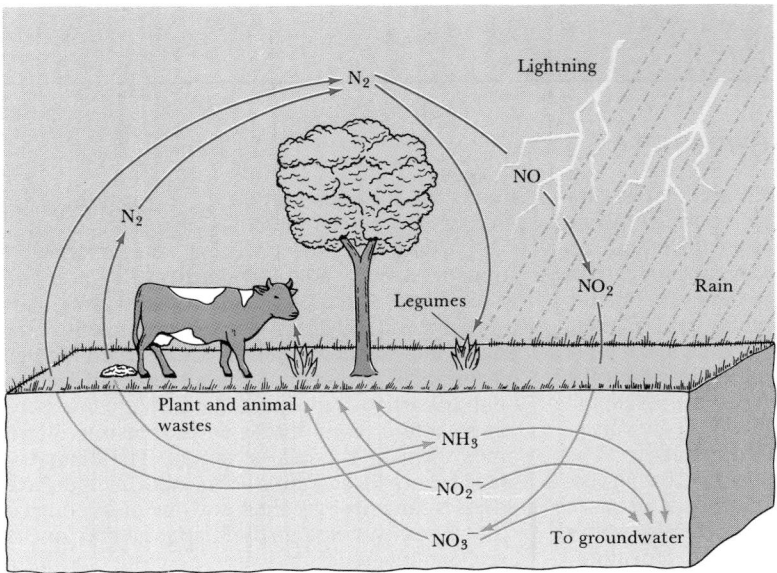

Figure 22.26

Learning Goal 16: Cite the most common occurrences of carbon and how it is obtained in its elemental form.

Learning Goal 17: Cite at least two uses for carbon.

22.6 Carbon

Carbon is not an abundant element; it constitutes only 0.027 percent of the earth's crust. Although some carbon occurs in elemental form as graphite and diamond, most is found in combined form. Over half occurs in carbonate compounds, such as $CaCO_3$. Carbon is also found in coal, petroleum, and natural gas. The importance of the element stems in large part from its occurrence in all living organisms: Life as we know it is based on carbon compounds. About 150 years ago, scientists believed that these life-sustaining compounds could be made only within living systems. They were consequently called *organic compounds*. It is now known that organic compounds can be synthesized in the laboratory from simple inorganic (nonorganic) substances. Although the name *organic chemistry* persists, it is now used to describe the portion of chemistry that focuses on hydrocarbons and compounds derived from them by substituting other atoms for some hydrogen atoms. In this section, we will take a brief look at carbon and its most common inorganic compounds. We will discuss organic chemistry in Chapter 26.

Elemental Forms of Carbon

We have seen that carbon exists in three crystalline forms: graphite, diamond, and buckminsterfullerene. ∞ (Sec. 11.8) *Graphite* is a soft, black, slippery solid that has a metallic luster and conducts electricity. It consists of parallel sheets of carbon atoms held together by London forces [Figure 11.40(*b*)].

Diamond is a clear, hard solid in which the carbon atoms form a covalent network [Figure 11.40(a)]. Diamond is denser than graphite ($d = 2.25$ g/cm^3 for graphite; $d = 3.51$ g/cm^3 for diamond). At very high pressures and temperatures (on the order of 100,000 atm at 3000°C), graphite converts to diamond (Figure 22.27). About 3×10^4 kg of industrial-grade diamonds are synthesized each year, mainly for use in cutting, grinding, and polishing tools.

FIGURE 22.27 Graphite and synthetic diamond prepared from graphite. Most synthetic diamonds lack the size, color, and clarity of natural diamonds and are therefore not used in jewelry. (General Electric Research and Development Center)

Carbon Fibers and Composites

The properties of graphite are anisotropic (that is, they differ in different directions through the solid). Along the carbon planes, graphite possesses great strength because of the number and strength of the carbon-carbon bonds in this direction. In contrast, we have seen that the bonds between planes are relatively weak, making graphite weak in that direction.

Fibers of graphite can be prepared in which the carbon planes are aligned to varying extents parallel to the fiber axis. These fibers are also lightweight (density of about 2 g/cm³) and chemically quite unreactive. The oriented fibers are made by first slowly pyrolyzing (decomposing by action of heat) organic fibers at about 150°C to 300°C. These fibers are then heated to about 2500°C to graphitize them (that is, to convert amorphous carbon to graphite). Stretching the fiber during pyrolysis helps orient the graphite planes parallel to the fiber axis. More amorphous carbon fibers are formed by pyrolysis of organic fibers at lower temperatures, 1200°C to 1400°C. These amorphous materials, commonly called *carbon fibers,* are the type most commonly used in commercial materials [Figure 22.28(a)].

Composite materials that take advantage of the strength, stability, and low density of carbon fibers are widely used. Composites are combinations of two or more materials. These materials are present as separate phases and are combined to form structures that take advantage of certain desirable properties of each component. In carbon composites, the graphite fibers are often woven into a fabric that is embedded in a matrix that binds them into a solid structure. The fibers transmit loads evenly throughout the matrix. The finished composite is thus stronger than any one of its components.

Epoxy systems are useful matrices because of their excellent adherence, but they are costly and limited to service temperatures below 150°C. More heat-resistant resins are required for many aerospace applications, where carbon composites find wide use. Some parts of high-performance aircraft are now made out of such carbon composites [Figure 22.28(b)].

FIGURE 22.28 (a) Carbon fibers used to make composite materials. (Courtesy American Cyanamid Co.) (b) Extensive use has been made of carbon composites in the construction of the B-2 "stealth" bomber. (Mark Warmkessel; Department of Defense, U.S. Air Force)

(a)

(b)

Buckminsterfullerene is a molecular form of carbon that was discovered in the mid-1980s (see A Closer Look in Section 11.8). This form of carbon consists of C_{60} molecules that resemble soccer balls (Figure 11.42). Because buckminsterfullerene is such a recently discovered molecule, its chemical properties are currently being explored by numerous research groups around the world.

Carbon also exists in three common microcrystalline or amorphous forms of graphite. *Carbon black* is formed when hydrocarbons are heated in a very limited supply of oxygen:

$$CH_4(g) + O_2(g) \longrightarrow C(s) + 2H_2O(g) \qquad [22.57]$$

It is used as a pigment in black inks; large amounts are also used in making automobile tires. **Charcoal** is formed when wood is heated strongly in the absence of air. Charcoal has a very open structure, giving it an enormous surface area per unit mass. Activated charcoal, a pulverized form whose surface is cleaned by heating with steam, is widely used to adsorb molecules. It is used in filters to remove offensive odors from air and colored or bad-tasting impurities from water. **Coke** is an impure form of carbon formed when coal is heated strongly in the absence of air. It is widely used as a reducing agent in metallurgical operations (Chapter 24).

Oxides of Carbon

Carbon forms two principal oxides: carbon monoxide, CO, and carbon dioxide, CO_2. *Carbon monoxide* is formed when carbon or hydrocarbons are burned in a limited supply of oxygen:

$$2C(s) + O_2(g) \longrightarrow 2CO(g) \qquad [22.58]$$

It is a colorless, odorless, and tasteless gas (m.p. $= -199°C$; b.p. $= -192°C$). It is toxic because of its ability to bind to hemoglobin and thus interfere with oxygen transport. ∞ (Sec. 18.4) Low-level poisoning results in headaches and drowsiness; high-level poisoning can cause death. Carbon monoxide is produced in large quantities by automobile engines, and it is a major air pollutant.

Carbon monoxide is an unusual carbon compound because it has a lone pair of electrons on carbon: $:C≡O:$. One might imagine that CO would be unreactive, like the isoelectronic N_2 molecule. Both substances have high bond energies (1072 kJ/mol for C≡O and 941 kJ/mol for N≡N). However, because of the lower nuclear charge on carbon (compared with either N or O), the lone pair on carbon is not held as strongly as that on N or O. Consequently, CO is better able to function as an electron-pair donor (Lewis base) than is N_2. It is therefore able to form a wide variety of covalent compounds, known as metal carbonyls, with transition metals. An example of such a compound is $Ni(CO)_4$, a volatile, very toxic compound that is formed by simply warming metallic nickel in the presence of CO. The formation of such metal carbonyls is the first step in the transition-metal catalysis of a variety of reactions of CO.

Carbon monoxide has several commercial uses. Because it burns readily, forming CO_2, it is employed as a fuel:

$$2CO(g) + O_2(g) \longrightarrow 2CO_2(g) \qquad \Delta H = -566 \text{ kJ} \qquad [22.59]$$

22.6 Carbon   **835**

It is also an important reducing agent, widely used in metallurgical operations to reduce metal oxides. For example, it is the most important reducing agent in the blast furnace reduction of iron oxides:

$$Fe_3O_4(s) + 4CO(g) \longrightarrow 3Fe(s) + 4CO_2(g) \qquad [22.60]$$

This reaction is discussed in greater detail in Section 24.2. Carbon monoxide is also used in the preparation of several organic compounds. In Section 22.3 we saw that it can be combined catalytically with H_2 to manufacture methanol, CH_3OH (Equation 22.16).

Carbon dioxide is produced when carbon-containing substances are burned in excess oxygen:

$$C(s) + O_2(g) \longrightarrow CO_2(g) \qquad [22.61]$$

$$CH_4(g) + 2O_2(g) \longrightarrow CO_2(g) + 2H_2O(l) \qquad [22.62]$$

$$C_2H_5OH(l) + 3O_2(g) \longrightarrow 2CO_2(g) + 3H_2O(l) \qquad [22.63]$$

It is also produced when many carbonates are heated:

$$CaCO_3(s) \longrightarrow CaO(s) + CO_2(g) \qquad [22.64]$$

Large quantities are also obtained as a by-product of the fermentation of sugar during the production of alcohol:

$$C_6H_{12}O_6(aq) \xrightarrow{\text{yeast}} 2C_2H_5OH(aq) + 2CO_2(g) \qquad [22.65]$$

Glucose   Ethanol

In the laboratory, CO_2 is normally produced by the action of acids on carbonates, as shown in Figure 22.29:

$$CO_3^{2-}(aq) + 2H^+(aq) \longrightarrow CO_2(g) + H_2O(l) \qquad [22.66]$$

Carbon dioxide is a colorless and odorless gas. It is a minor component of the earth's atmosphere but a major contributor to the so-called greenhouse effect (see the Chemistry at Work box in Section 3.6). Although it is not toxic, high concentrations increase respiration rate and can cause suffocation. It is readily liquefied by compression. However, when cooled at atmospheric pressure, it condenses as a solid rather than as a liquid. The solid sublimes at atmospheric pressure at $-78°C$. This property makes solid CO_2 valuable as a refrigerant that is always free of the liquid form. Solid CO_2 is known as *Dry Ice*. About half of the CO_2 consumed annually is used for refrigeration. The other major use is in the production of carbonated beverages. Large quantities are also used to manufacture *washing soda*, $Na_2CO_3 \cdot 10H_2O$, and *baking soda*, $NaHCO_3$. Baking soda is so named because the following reaction occurs in baking:

$$NaHCO_3(s) + H^+(aq) \longrightarrow Na^+(aq) + CO_2(g) + H_2O(l) \qquad [22.67]$$

The $H^+(aq)$ is provided by vinegar, sour milk, or hydrolysis of certain salts. The bubbles of CO_2 that form are trapped in the dough, causing it to rise. Washing

Teaching Note: CO_2 is a respiratory byproduct of virtually every living organism on earth.

FIGURE 22.29 Solid $CaCO_3$ reacts with a solution of hydrochloric acid to produce CO_2 gas, seen here as the bubbles in the test tube. (Paul Silverman/Fundamental Photographs)

soda is used to precipitate metal ions that interfere with the cleansing action of soap.

Teaching Note: Yeast in dough also liberates CO_2, causing the dough to rise.

Carbonic Acid and Carbonates

Carbon dioxide is moderately soluble in H_2O at atmospheric pressure. The resultant solutions are moderately acidic as a result of the formation of carbonic acid, H_2CO_3:

$$CO_2(aq) + H_2O(l) \rightleftharpoons H_2CO_3(aq) \qquad [22.68]$$

Carbonic acid is a weak diprotic acid. Its acidic character causes carbonated beverages to have a sharp, slightly acidic taste.

Although carbonic acid cannot be isolated as a pure compound, two types of salts can be obtained by neutralization of carbonic acid solutions: hydrogen carbonates (bicarbonates) and carbonates. Partial neutralization produces HCO_3^-, and complete neutralization gives CO_3^{2-}.

The HCO_3^- ion is a stronger base than acid ($K_a = 5.6 \times 10^{-11}$; $K_b = 2.3 \times 10^{-8}$). Consequently, aqueous solutions of HCO_3^- are weakly alkaline:

$$HCO_3^-(aq) + H_2O(l) \rightleftharpoons H_2CO_3(aq) + OH^-(aq) \qquad [22.69]$$

The carbonate ion is much more strongly basic ($K_b = 1.8 \times 10^{-4}$):

$$CO_3^{2-}(aq) + H_2O(l) \rightleftharpoons HCO_3^-(aq) + OH^-(aq) \qquad [22.70]$$

Minerals containing the carbonate ion are plentiful.* The principal carbonate minerals are calcite, $CaCO_3$, magnesite, $MgCO_3$, dolomite, $MgCa(CO_3)_2$, and siderite, $FeCO_3$. Calcite is the principal mineral in limestone rock, large deposits of which occur in many parts of the world. It is also the main constituent of marble, chalk, pearls, coral reefs, and the shells of marine animals such as clams and oysters. Although $CaCO_3$ has low solubility in pure water, it dissolves readily in acidic solutions with evolution of CO_2:

$$CaCO_3(s) + 2H^+(aq) \rightleftharpoons Ca^{2+}(aq) + H_2O(l) + CO_2(g) \qquad [22.71]$$

Because water containing CO_2 is slightly acidic (Equation 22.68), $CaCO_3$ dissolves slowly in this medium:

$$CaCO_3(s) + H_2O(l) + CO_2(g) \longrightarrow Ca^{2+}(aq) + 2HCO_3^-(aq) \qquad [22.72]$$

This reaction occurs when surface waters move underground through limestone deposits. It is the principal way that Ca^{2+} enters groundwater, producing "hard water." ∞ (Sec. 18.6) If the dissolving limestone underlies a comparatively thin layer of earth, sinkholes, such as that shown in Figure 22.30, are produced. If the limestone deposit is deep enough underground, the dissolution of the limestone produces a cave. Two well-known limestone caves are the

---

* *Minerals* are solid substances that occur in nature. They are usually known by their common names rather than by their chemical names. What we know as *rock* is merely an aggregate of different kinds of minerals.

FIGURE 22.30 A sinkhole. Ground on the surface may collapse suddenly after sufficient limestone has dissolved from underground deposits. (M. Timothy O'Keefe/Tom Stack & Associates)

Mammoth Cave in Kentucky and the Carlsbad Caverns in New Mexico (Figure 22.31).

One of the most important reactions of $CaCO_3$ is its decomposition into CaO and CO_2 at elevated temperatures, given earlier in Equation 22.64. Over 1.5×10^{10} kg (17 million tons) of calcium oxide, known as lime or quicklime, is used in the United States each year. Because calcium oxide reacts with water to form $Ca(OH)_2$, it is an important commercial base. It is also important in making mortar, which is a mixture of sand, water, and CaO used in construction to bind bricks, blocks, and rocks together. Calcium oxide reacts with water and CO_2 to form $CaCO_3$, which binds the sand in the mortar:

$$CaO(s) + H_2O(l) \rightleftharpoons Ca^{2+}(aq) + 2OH^-(aq) \quad [22.73]$$

$$Ca^{2+}(aq) + 2OH^-(aq) + CO_2(aq) \longrightarrow CaCO_3(s) + H_2O(l) \quad [22.74]$$

FIGURE 22.31 Carlsbad Caverns, New Mexico. (Chad Ehlers/Allstock)

Carbides

The binary compounds of carbon with metals, metalloids, and certain nonmetals are called carbides. There are three types: ionic, interstitial, and covalent. The ionic, or saltlike, carbides are formed by the more active metals. The most common ionic carbides contain C_2^{2-} ions, $[:C \equiv C:]^{2-}$. This ion hydrolyzes to form acetylene:

Learning Goal 19: Distinguish among ionic, interstitial, and covalent carbides.

$$CaC_2(s) + 2H_2O(l) \longrightarrow Ca(OH)_2(aq) + C_2H_2(g) \qquad [22.75]$$

Carbides containing C_2^{2-} are thus called *acetylides*. The most important ionic carbide is calcium carbide, CaC_2, which is produced industrially by the reduction of CaO with carbon at high temperature:

Teaching Note: The reaction of CaC_2 with water is also sometimes used in helmet-mounted lanterns used by spelunkers (cave explorers).

$$2CaO(s) + 5C(s) \longrightarrow 2CaC_2(s) + CO_2(g) \qquad [22.76]$$

The CaC_2 is used to prepare acetylene, which is used in welding.

Interstitial carbides are formed by many transition metals. The carbon atoms occupy open spaces (interstices) between metal atoms in a manner analogous to the interstitial hydrides. (Sec. 22.3) An example is tungsten carbide, WC, which is very hard and heat-resistant and consequently is used in making cutting tools.

Covalent carbides are formed by boron and silicon. Silicon carbide, SiC, is known as *Carborundum*. It is made by heating SiO_2 (sand) and carbon to high temperatures:

$$SiO_2(s) + 3C(s) \longrightarrow SiC(s) + 2CO(g) \qquad [22.77]$$

SiC has the same structure as diamond except that silicon atoms alternate with carbon atoms. Like industrial diamond, Carborundum is very hard and is thus used as an abrasive and in cutting tools.

Other Inorganic Compounds of Carbon

Hydrogen cyanide, HCN (Figure 22.32), is an extremely toxic gas that has the odor of bitter almonds. In the laboratory it is made by the reaction of a cyanide salt, such as NaCN, with an acid [see Sample Exercise 22.2(c)].

Aqueous solutions of HCN are known as hydrocyanic acid. Neutralization with a base, such as NaOH, produces cyanide salts, such as NaCN. Cyanides find use in the manufacture of several well-known plastics, including nylon and Orlon. The CN^- ion forms very stable complexes with most transition metals. (Sec. 17.5) The toxic action of CN^- is caused by its combination with iron(III) in cytochrome oxidase, a key enzyme that is involved in respiration.

Carbon disulfide, CS_2 (Figure 22.32), is an important industrial solvent for waxes, greases, celluloses, and other nonpolar substances. It is a colorless, volatile liquid (b.p. 46.3°C). The vapor is very poisonous and highly flammable. The compound is formed by direct reaction of carbon and sulfur at high temperature.

FIGURE 22.32 Structures of hydrogen cyanide and carbon disulfide.

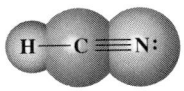

Hydrogen cyanide

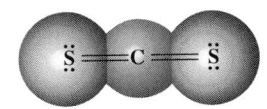

Carbon disulfide

For Review

Summary

The periodic table is useful in organizing and remembering the descriptive chemistry of the elements: Among elements of a given family, size increases with increasing atomic number. Correspondingly, electronegativity and ionization energy decrease. Nonmetallic character parallels electronegativity trends. Among the nonmetallic elements, the first member of each family differs dramatically from the other members; it forms a maximum of four bonds to other atoms (that is, it is confined to an octet of valence shell electrons). Also, it exhibits a much greater tendency to form π bonds than do the heavier elements in its family.

Hydrogen has three isotopes: protium (^1_1H), deuterium (^2_1H), and tritium (^3_1H). Hydrogen is not a member of any periodic family, although it is usually placed above lithium. The hydrogen atom can either lose an electron, forming H^+, or gain one, forming H^-, the hydride ion. Because the H—H bond is relatively strong, H_2 is fairly unreactive unless activated by heat, irradiation, or catalysis. Industrially, H_2O and hydrocarbons are used as sources of hydrogen; in the lab, H_2 is usually obtained by the action of acids on active metals, such as Zn. The binary compounds of hydrogen are of three general types: ionic hydrides (formed by active metals), metallic hydrides (formed by transition metals), and molecular hydrides (formed by nonmetals).

Oxygen exhibits two allotropes, O_2 and O_3 (ozone). O_2 is separated from air; small amounts can be obtained by heating $KClO_3$. Ozone is obtained by passing an electrical discharge through O_2. Both O_2 and O_3 are good oxidizing agents, but O_3 is the stronger. Oxygen normally exhibits an oxidation state of -2 in compounds (oxides). The soluble oxides of nonmetals generally produce acidic aqueous solutions; they are called acidic anhydrides. In contrast, soluble metal oxides produce basic solutions and are called basic anhydrides. Peroxides contain O—O bonds and oxygen in the -1 oxidation state. In superoxides, which contain the O_2^- ion, oxygen has an oxidation state of $-\frac{1}{2}$.

The primary source of nitrogen is the atmosphere, where it occurs as N_2 molecules. Molecular nitrogen is chemically very stable because of the strong $N{\equiv}N$ bond. In its compounds nitrogen exhibits oxidation states ranging from -3 to $+5$. The most important process for converting N_2 into compounds is the Haber process, used to prepare ammonia. Another commercially important process is the Ostwald process, which is the preparation of HNO_3 beginning with the catalytic oxidation of NH_3. Nitrogen has three common oxides: N_2O (nitrous oxide), NO (nitric oxide), and NO_2 (nitrogen dioxide). It has two common oxyacids, HNO_2 (nitrous acid) and HNO_3 (nitric acid). Nitric acid is both a strong acid and a good oxidizing agent. Other important nitrogen compounds include hydrazine, N_2H_4, and hydrogen azide, HN_3. Nitrogen compounds are important fertilizers.

Carbon exhibits three allotropes: diamond, graphite, and buckminsterfullerene. Amorphous forms of graphite include charcoal, carbon black, and coke. Carbon exhibits two common oxides, CO and CO_2. Aqueous solutions of CO_2 produce carbonic acid, H_2CO_3, which is the parent acid of carbonate salts. Binary compounds of carbon are called carbides. Carbides may be ionic, interstitial, or covalent. Calcium carbide, CaC_2, is used to prepare acetylene. Carbon also forms a vast number of organic compounds, discussed in a later chapter.

Key Terms

protium (Sec. 22.3)
deuterium (Sec. 22.3)
tritium (Sec. 22.3)
water gas (Sec. 22.3)
ionic hydrides (Sec. 22.3)

metallic hydrides (Sec. 22.3)
interstitial hydrides (Sec. 22.3)
molecular hydrides (Sec. 22.3)
acidic anhydrides (Sec. 22.4)
acidic oxides (Sec. 22.4)

basic anhydrides (Sec. 22.4)
basic oxides (Sec. 22.4)
Ostwald process (Sec. 22.5)

disproportionation (Sec. 22.5)
charcoal (Sec. 22.6)
coke (Sec. 22.6)

Exercises

Periodic Trends and Chemical Reactions

22.1. Identify each of the following elements as a metal, nonmetal, or metalloid: (a) antimony; (b) strontium; (c) cerium; (d) selenium; (e) rhodium; (f) krypton.

22.2. Identify each of the following elements as a metal, nonmetal, or metalloid: (a) germanium; (b) zirconium; (c) xenon; (d) indium; (e) cesium; (f) bromine.

22.3. List two chemical and two physical properties that help us distinguish metals from nonmetals.

22.4. State two important ways in which the first member of each family of nonmetals differs from subsequent members.

22.5. Which element of group 5A would you expect to have the most metallic character? Describe two properties of the elements in the group that should relate to this degree of metallic character.

22.6. Which element of group 3A would you expect to have the most nonmetallic character? Describe two properties of the elements that should demonstrate the greater nonmetallic character of this element compared to the others in the group.

22.7. Consider the following list of elements: Li, K, Cl, C, Ne, Ar. From this list select the element that (a) is most electronegative; (b) has the greatest metallic character; (c) most readily forms a positive ion; (d) has the smallest atomic radius; (e) forms π bonds most readily.

22.8. Consider the following list of elements: O, Ba, Co, Be, Br, Se. From this list select the element that (a) is most electronegative; (b) exhibits a maximum oxidation state of $+7$; (c) loses an electron most readily; (d) forms π bonds most readily; (e) is a transition metal.

22.9. In each of the following pairs of substances, select the one that has the more polar bonds: (a) NF_3 and IF_3; (b)
N_2O_3 and B_2O_3; (c) BN and BF_3; (d) H_2O and H_2Se. Explain your choice in each case.

22.10. In each of the following pairs of substances, select the one that has the more polar bonds: (a) CO_2 and SnO_2; (b) P_2O_3 and V_2O_3; (c) SiO_2 and SO_2; (d) CCl_4 and CBr_4. Explain your choice in each case.

22.11. Explain the following observations: (a) The highest fluoride compound formed by nitrogen is NF_3, whereas phosphorus readily forms PF_5. (b) Although CO is a well-known compound, SiO doesn't exist under ordinary conditions. (c) AsH_3 is a stronger reducing agent than NH_3.

22.12. Explain the following observations: (a) HNO_3 is a stronger oxidizing agent than H_3PO_4. (b) Silicon is able to form an ion with six fluorides, $SiF_6{}^{2-}$, whereas carbon is able to bond to a maximum of four, CF_4. (c) There are three compounds formed by carbon and hydrogen that contain two carbon atoms each (C_2H_2, C_2H_4, and C_2H_6), whereas silicon forms only one analogous compound (Si_2H_6).

22.13. Complete and balance the following equations:
(a) $NaNH_2(s) + H_2O(l) \longrightarrow$
(b) $C_3H_7OH(l) + O_2(g) \longrightarrow$
(c) $NiO(s) + C(s) \longrightarrow$
(d) $AlP(s) + H_2O(l) \longrightarrow$
(e) $Na_2S(s) + HCl(aq) \longrightarrow$

22.14. Complete and balance the following equations:
(a) $NaOCH_3(s) + H_2O(l) \longrightarrow$
(b) $Na_2O(s) + HC_2H_3O_2(aq) \longrightarrow$
(c) $WO_3(s) + H_2(g) \longrightarrow$
(d) $NH_2OH(l) + O_2(g) \longrightarrow$
(e) $Al_4C_3(s) + H_2O(l) \longrightarrow$

Hydrogen

22.15. Give the names and chemical symbols for the three isotopes of hydrogen.

22.16. Which isotope of hydrogen is radioactive? Write the nuclear equation for the radioactive decay of this isotope.

22.17. Why is hydrogen placed in either group 1A or 7A of the periodic table?

22.18. Why are the properties of hydrogen different from those of either the group 1A or 7A elements?

22.19. Give a balanced chemical equation for the preparation of H_2 using (a) Mg and an acid; (b) carbon and steam; (c) methane and steam.

22.20. List (a) three commercial means of producing H_2; (b) three industrial uses of H_2.

22.21. Identify the following hydrides as ionic, metallic, or molecular: (a) BaH_2; (b) H_2Te; (c) $TiH_{1.7}$.

22.22. Identify the following hydrides as ionic, metallic, or molecular: (a) B_2H_6; (b) RbH; (c) $Th_4H_{1.5}$.

22.23. Complete and balance the following equations:
(a) $NaH(s) + H_2O(l) \longrightarrow$
(b) $Fe(s) + H_2SO_4(aq) \longrightarrow$
(c) $H_2(g) + Br_2(g) \longrightarrow$
(d) $Na(l) + H_2(g) \longrightarrow$
(e) $PbO(s) + H_2(g) \longrightarrow$

22.24. Write balanced chemical equations for each of the following reactions (some of these are analogous to reactions shown in the chapter). **(a)** Aluminum metal reacts with acids to form hydrogen gas. **(b)** Steam reacts with magnesium metal to give magnesium oxide and hydrogen. **(c)** Manganese(IV) oxide is reduced to manganese(II) oxide by hydrogen gas. **(d)** Calcium hydride reacts with water to generate hydrogen gas.

22.25. About 1.6×10^{10} kg of ethylene, C_2H_4, is produced annually in the United States by the pyrolysis of ethane, C_2H_6: $C_2H_6(g) \longrightarrow C_2H_4(g) + H_2(g)$. How many kilograms of H_2 are produced as a by-product?

22.26. Hydrogen gas has a higher fuel value than natural gas on a mass basis but not on a volume basis. Thus hydrogen is not competitive with natural gas as a fuel transported long distance through pipelines. Calculate the heat of combustion of H_2 and of CH_4 (the principal component of natural gas) **(a)** per mole of each; **(b)** per gram of each; **(c)** per cubic meter of each at STP. Assume $H_2O(l)$ as a product.

Oxygen

22.27. List three industrial uses of O_2.

22.28. List two industrial uses of O_3.

22.29. Give the structure of ozone. Explain why the O—O bond length in ozone (1.28 Å) is longer than that in O_2 (1.21 Å).

22.30. How is O_2 normally prepared in the laboratory?

22.31. Complete and balance the following equations:
(a) $CaO(s) + H_2O(l) \longrightarrow$
(b) $Al_2O_3(s) + H^+(aq) \longrightarrow$
(c) $Na_2O_2(s) + H_2O(l) \longrightarrow$
(d) $N_2O_3(g) + H_2O(l) \longrightarrow$
(e) $KO_2(s) + H_2O(l) \longrightarrow$
(f) $NO(g) + O_3(g) \longrightarrow$

22.32. Write the balanced chemical equations for each of the following reactions. **(a)** When mercury(II) oxide is heated, it decomposes to form O_2 and mercury metal. **(b)** When copper(II) nitrate is heated strongly, it decomposes to form copper(II) oxide, nitrogen dioxide, and oxygen. **(c)** Lead(II) sulfide, $PbS(s)$, reacts with ozone to form $PbSO_4(s)$

and $O_2(g)$. **(d)** When heated in air, $ZnS(s)$ is converted to ZnO. **(e)** Potassium peroxide reacts with $CO_2(g)$ to give the carbonate ion and O_2. **(f)** Although silver does not react with oxygen at room temperature, it reacts with ozone, forming Ag_2O.

22.33. Predict whether each of the following oxides is acidic, basic, amphoteric, or neutral: **(a)** CO; **(b)** CO_2; **(c)** CaO; **(d)** Al_2O_3.

22.34. Select the more acidic member of each of the following pairs: **(a)** Mn_2O_7 and MnO_2; **(b)** SnO and SnO_2; **(c)** SO_2 and SO_3; **(d)** SiO_2 and SO_2; **(e)** Ga_2O_3 and In_2O_3; **(f)** SO_2 and SeO_2.

22.35. Hydrogen peroxide is capable of oxidizing **(a)** K_2S to S; **(b)** SO_2 to SO_4^{2-}; **(c)** NO_2^- to NO_3^-; **(d)** As_2O_3 to AsO_4^{3-}; **(e)** Fe^{2+} to Fe^{3+}. Write a balanced net ionic equation for each of these oxidations.

22.36. Hydrogen peroxide reduces **(a)** MnO_4^- to Mn^{2+}; **(b)** Cl_2 to Cl^-; **(c)** Ce^{4+} to Ce^{3+}; **(d)** O_3 to H_2O. Write a balanced net ionic equation for each of these reductions.

Nitrogen

22.37. List three industrial uses for N_2.

22.38. What is meant by the term *nitrogen fixation?* Why is the N_2 molecule so unreactive?

22.39. Write the chemical formula for each of the following compounds and indicate the oxidation state of nitrogen in each: **(a)** nitrous acid; **(b)** hydrazine; **(c)** potassium cyanide; **(d)** sodium nitrate; **(e)** ammonium chloride; **(f)** lithium nitride.

22.40. Write the chemical formula for each of the following compounds and indicate the oxidation state of nitrogen in each: **(a)** sodium nitrite; **(b)** ammonia; **(c)** nitrous oxide; **(d)** sodium cyanide; **(e)** nitric acid; **(f)** nitrogen dioxide.

22.41. Write the Lewis structure for each of the following species and describe its molecular geometry: **(a)** NH_4^+; **(b)** HNO_3; **(c)** N_2O; **(d)** NO_2.

22.42. Write the Lewis structure for each of the following species and describe its molecular geometry: **(a)** HNO_2; **(b)** N_3^-; **(c)** $N_2H_5^+$; **(d)** NO_3^-.

22.43. Complete and balance the following equations:
(a) $Mg_3N_2(s) + H_2O(l) \longrightarrow$
(b) $NO(g) + O_2(g) \longrightarrow$

(c) $NH_3(g) + O_2(g) \xrightarrow{\Delta}$ (no catalyst)
(d) $NaNH_2(s) + H_2O(l) \longrightarrow$

22.44. Complete and balance the following equations:
(a) $N_2O_5(g) + H_2O(l) \longrightarrow$
(b) $Li_3N(s) + H_2O(l) \longrightarrow$
(c) $NH_3(aq) + H^+(aq) \longrightarrow$
(d) $N_2H_4(l) + O_2(g) \longrightarrow$

22.45. Write balanced net ionic equations for each of the following reactions. **(a)** Dilute nitric acid reacts with zinc metal with formation of nitrous oxide. **(b)** Concentrated nitric acid reacts with sulfur with formation of nitrogen dioxide. **(c)** Concentrated nitric acid oxidizes sulfur dioxide with formation of nitric oxide. **(d)** Urea reacts with water to form ammonia and carbon dioxide.

22.46. Write balanced net ionic equations for each of the following reactions. **(a)** Hydrazine is burned in excess fluorine gas, forming NF_3. **(b)** Hydrazine reduces CrO_4^{2-} to $Cr(OH)_4^-$ (hydrazine is oxidized to N_2). **(c)** Hydroxylamine is oxidized to N_2 by Cu^{2+} in aqueous solutions (Cu^{2+} is reduced to copper metal). **(d)** Aqueous azide ion, N_3^-, reacts with Cl_2, forming N_2.

22.47. Write complete balanced half-reactions for **(a)** reduction of nitrate ion to N_2 in acidic solution; **(b)** oxidation of NH_4^+ to N_2 in acidic solution. What is the standard electrode potential in each case? (See Figure 22.17.)

22.48. Write complete balanced half-reactions for **(a)** reduction of nitrate ion to NO in acidic solution; **(b)** oxidation of HNO_2 to NO_2 in acidic solution. What is the standard electrode potential in each case? (See Figure 22.17.)

22.49. It is estimated that 95 percent of the ammonia production in the United States uses H_2 obtained from natural gas (Equations 22.12 and 22.13). If 50 percent of the CH_4 used to manufacture H_2 is burned to maintain proper temperature for ammonia synthesis, how many kilograms of CH_4 are consumed in supplying the 1.6×10^{10} kg of NH_3 produced annually?

22.50. From the thermodynamic data in Appendix C, calculate $\Delta H°$ and $\Delta G°$ at 25°C for the oxidation of NH_3 in the following reactions:

$$4NH_3(g) + 5O_2(g) \longrightarrow 4NO(g) + 6H_2O(g)$$
$$4NH_3(g) + 3O_2(g) \longrightarrow 2N_2(g) + 6H_2O(g)$$

Carbon

22.51. Give three industrial uses of carbon dioxide.

22.52. Give three industrial uses of carbon monoxide.

22.53. Give the chemical formulas for **(a)** hydrocyanic acid; **(b)** Carborundum; **(c)** calcium carbonate; **(d)** calcium acetylide.

22.54. Give the chemical formulas for **(a)** carbonic acid; **(b)** sodium cyanide; **(c)** potassium hydrogen carbonate; **(d)** acetylene.

22.55. Write the Lewis structure of each of the following species: **(a)** CN^-; **(b)** CO; **(c)** C_2^{2-}; **(d)** CS_2; **(e)** CO_2; **(f)** CO_3^{2-}.

22.56. Indicate the geometry and the type of hybrid orbitals used by each carbon atom in the following species: **(a)** $CH_3C\equiv CH$; **(b)** NaCN; **(c)** CS_2; **(d)** C_2H_6.

22.57. Complete and balance the following equations:

(a) $ZnCO_3(s) \xrightarrow{\Delta}$
(b) $BaC_2(s) + H_2O(l) \longrightarrow$
(c) $C_2H_4(g) + O_2(g) \longrightarrow$
(d) $CH_3OH(l) + O_2(g) \longrightarrow$
(e) $NaCN(s) + HCl(aq) \longrightarrow$

22.58. Complete and balance the following equations:

(a) $CO_2(g) + OH^-(aq) \longrightarrow$
(b) $NaHCO_3(s) + H^+(aq) \longrightarrow$
(c) $CaO(s) + C(s) \xrightarrow{\Delta}$
(d) $C(s) + H_2O(g) \xrightarrow{\Delta}$
(e) $CuO(s) + CO(g) \longrightarrow$

22.59. Write a balanced chemical equation for each of the following reactions. **(a)** Burning magnesium metal in a carbon dioxide atmosphere reduces the CO_2 to carbon. **(b)** In photosynthesis, solar energy is used to produce glucose, $C_6H_{12}O_6$, and O_2 out of carbon dioxide and water. **(c)** When carbonate salts dissolve in water, they produce basic solutions.

22.60. Write a balanced chemical equation for each of the following reactions. **(a)** Hydrogen cyanide is formed commercially by passing a mixture of methane, ammonia, and air over a catalyst at 800°C. Water is a by-product of the reaction. **(b)** Baking soda reacts with acids to produce carbon dioxide gas. **(c)** When barium carbonate reacts in air with sulfur dioxide, barium sulfate and carbon dioxide form.

22.61. What volume of dry acetylene, measured at 27°C and 720 torr, is formed when 10.0 g of calcium carbide is placed in water?

22.62. A certain carbide of magnesium is reacted with water to form $Mg^{2+}(aq)$ and a volatile hydrocarbon. Hydrolysis of 0.3052 g of the carbide produces 0.1443 g of the hydrocarbon. The hydrocarbon consists of 90.0 percent C and 10.0 percent H. The density of the hydrocarbon gas at 25°C and 742 torr is 1.60 g/L. What is the formula for the carbide, and what is the molecular formula for the hydrocarbon?

Additional Exercises

22.63. The annual production of H_2, N_2, and O_2 in the United States is generally reported in cubic feet, measured at STP. If 2.2×10^8 kg of H_2, 2.4×10^{10} kg of N_2, and 1.7×10^{10} kg of O_2 are produced in a particular year, how many cubic feet are produced of **(a)** H_2; **(b)** N_2; **(c)** O_2?

22.64. **(a)** How many grams of H_2 can be stored in 1.00 kg of the alloy FeTi if the hydride $FeTiH_2$ is formed? **(b)** What volume does this quantity of H_2 occupy at STP?

22.65. Starting with D_2O, suggest preparations of **(a)** ND_3; **(b)** D_2SO_4; **(c)** NaOD; **(d)** DNO_3; **(e)** C_2D_2; **(f)** DCN.

22.66. A student had three tubes containing colorless gases. One tube held H_2, one O_2, and one CO_2. A glowing splint was inserted into each tube. In tube A, the splint was extinguished; in tube B, a sharp pop was produced; in tube C, the splint burst into flames. Which tube contained which gas?

22.67. Which of the following substances will burn in oxygen: SiH_4; SiO_2; CO; CO_2; Mg; CaO? Why won't some of these substances burn in oxygen?

22.68. Write a balanced chemical equation for the reaction of each of the following compounds with water: (a) $SO_2(g)$; (b) $Cl_2O(g)$; (c) $Na_2O(s)$; (d) $BaC_2(s)$; (e) $RbO_2(s)$; (f) $Mg_3N_2(s)$; (g) $Na_2O_2(s)$; (h) $NaH(s)$.

22.69. What is the anhydride for each of the following acids: (a) H_2SO_4; (b) $HClO_3$; (c) HNO_2; (d) H_2CO_3; (e) H_3PO_4?

22.70. Write a series of chemical equations that describes how Na_2CO_3 could be prepared starting with only H_2O, $NaCl$, and $CaCO_3$ as raw materials.

22.71. Hydrogen peroxide can be prepared in the laboratory by air oxidation of barium metal followed by treatment of the resultant product with dilute sulfuric acid. Write balanced chemical equations for the two reactions that take place.

22.72. Both dimethylhydrazine, $(CH_3)_2NNH_2$, and monomethylhydrazine, CH_3HNNH_2, have been used as rocket fuels. When dinitrogen tetraoxide, N_2O_4, is used as the oxidizer, the products are H_2O, CO_2, and N_2. If the thrust of the rocket depends on the volume of the products produced, which of the substituted hydrazines produces a greater thrust per gram total mass of oxidizer plus fuel? [Assume that both fuels generate the same temperature and that $H_2O(g)$ is formed.]

22.73. (a) What is the oxidation state of P in PO_4^{3-} and of N in NO_3^-? (b) Why doesn't N form a stable NO_4^{3-} ion analogous to P?

22.74. Suggest why each of the following compounds is either unstable or does not exist: (a) NCl_5; (b) $(CH_3)_2Si=O$; (c) P_2O; (d) H_3.

22.75. Each of the following compounds is used as a nitrogen fertilizer: $(NH_2)_2CO$ (urea), NH_3, $(NH_4)_2SO_4$, and $NaNO_3$. Calculate the percentage of nitrogen by mass in each compound.

22.76. Hydrazine has been employed as a reducing agent for metals. Using standard electrode potentials, predict whether the following metals can be reduced to the metallic state by hydrazine under standard conditions in acidic solution: (a) Fe^{2+}; (b) Sn^{2+}; (c) Cu^{2+}; (d) Ag^+; (e) Cr^{3+}.

[22.77]. Thermodynamic data for $HNO_3(aq)$ at $25°C$ follow: $\Delta H_f^\circ = -207.3$ kJ/mol; $\Delta G_f^\circ = -111.3$ kJ/mol. Calculate $\Delta H°$ and $\Delta G°$ for the reaction

$$N_2(g) + H_2O(g) + \tfrac{5}{2}O_2(g) \longrightarrow 2HNO_3(aq)$$

It has been suggested that if a suitable catalyst were present, atmospheric gases could react to make the oceans a dilute nitric acid solution. In thermodynamic terms, is this a possible process?

22.78. The Haber process is carried out at high temperatures, even though the equilibrium constant for the reaction decreases with increasing temperature. Explain why a high temperature is necessary.

22.79. If the lunar lander on the Apollo moon missions used 4.0 tons of dimethylhydrazine, $(CH_3)_2NNH_2$, as fuel, how many tons of N_2O_4 oxidizer were required to react with it? (The reaction produces N_2, CO_2, and H_2O.)

[22.80]. The dissolved oxygen present in any highly pressurized, high-temperature steam boiler can be extremely corrosive to its metal parts. Hydrazine, which is completely miscible with water, can be added to remove oxygen by reacting with it to form nitrogen and water. (a) Write the balanced chemical equation for the reaction between dissolved hydrazine and oxygen. (b) Calculate the enthalpy change accompanying this reaction. (c) Oxygen in air dissolves in water to the extent of 9.1 ppm at $20°C$ at sea level. How many grams of hydrazine are required to react with all of the oxygen in 3.0×10^4 L (the volume of a small swimming pool) under these conditions?

22.81. Complete and balance the following equations:
(a) $Li_3N(s) + H_2O(l) \longrightarrow$
(b) $NH_3(aq) + H_2O(l) \longrightarrow$
(c) $NO_2(g) + H_2O(l) \longrightarrow$
(d) $2NO_2(g) \longrightarrow$

(e) $NH_3(g) + O_2(g) \xrightarrow{\text{catalyst}}$
(f) $CO(g) + O_2(g) \longrightarrow$

(g) $H_2CO_3(aq) \xrightarrow{\Delta}$
(h) $Ni(s) + CO(g) \longrightarrow$
(i) $CS_2(g) + O_2(g) \longrightarrow$
(j) $CaO(s) + SO_2(g) \longrightarrow$
(k) $Na(s) + H_2O(l) \longrightarrow$

(l) $CH_4(g) + H_2O(g) \xrightarrow{\Delta}$
(m) $LiH(s) + H_2O(l) \longrightarrow$
(n) $Fe_2O_3(s) + 3H_2(g) \longrightarrow$

22.82. Complete and balance the following equations:
(a) $MnO_4^-(aq) + H_2O_2(aq) + H^+(aq) \longrightarrow$
(b) $Fe^{2+}(aq) + H_2O_2(aq) \longrightarrow$
(c) $I^-(aq) + H_2O_2(aq) + H^+(aq) \longrightarrow$
(d) $MnO_2(s) + H_2O_2(aq) + H^+(aq) \longrightarrow$
(e) $I^-(aq) + O_3(g) \longrightarrow I_2(s) + O_2(g) + OH^-(aq)$

[22.83]. Using this chapter and material elsewhere in the text (use the index), compile a list of physical and chemical properties of the elements oxygen and zinc. How do these properties justify the classification of one as a nonmetal and the other as a metal?

[22.84]. The electronegativity of a given element can be regarded as varying with its oxidation state. How would you expect the electronegativity to change as a function of oxidation state? Although manganese (Mn) is completely different from chlorine in properties as an element, the characteristics of MnO_4^- rather closely resemble those of ClO_4^-. Cite at least two instances of this similarity (you may need to look in a handbook; think in terms of acid-base properties, oxidation-reduction behavior, solubility, and so on). Discuss your observations in terms of the oxidation states, electron configurations, and electronegativities of the central atoms.

Chemistry of Other Nonmetallic Elements

23

Crystals of amethyst, a purplish silicate mineral used as a gemstone. Over 90 percent of the earth's crust consists of silicates.

CONTENTS

In Chapter 22, we discussed the chemistry of four important non-metals: hydrogen, oxygen, nitrogen, and carbon. In this chapter, we take a more panoramic view of nonmetals. We begin with the noble gases and then move, group by group, from right to left through the periodic table. We will, of course, have little to say about those elements discussed in Chapter 22. Of the remaining nonmetals, the most important are the halogens, sulfur, phosphorus, and silicon.

23.1 The Noble-Gas Elements

We have mentioned at several points in the text that the elements of group 8A are chemically unreactive. Indeed, most of our references to these elements have been in relation to their physical properties, as when we discussed inter-molecular forces. ∞(Sec. 11.2)   According to the Lewis theory of chemical bonding, the relative inertness of these elements is due to the presence of a completed octet of valence-shell electrons. The stability of such an arrangement is reflected in the high ionization energies of the group 8A elements. ∞(Sec. 7.4)

The group 8A elements are all gases at room temperature. They are components of the earth's atmosphere, except for radon, which exists only as a short-lived radioisotope. Only argon is relatively abundant (Table 18.1). Neon, argon, krypton, and xenon are recovered from liquid air by distillation. Argon is used as a blanketing atmosphere in electric light bulbs. The gas conducts heat away from the filament but does not react with it. It is also used as a protective atmosphere to prevent oxidation in welding and certain high-temperature met-allurgical processes. Neon is used in electric signs; the gas is caused to radiate by passing an electric discharge through the tube. Krypton, xenon, and radon are not commercially important.

Helium is, in many ways, the most important of the noble gases. Liquid helium is used as a coolant to conduct experiments at very low temperatures. Helium boils at 4.2 K under 1 atm pressure, the lowest boiling point of any substance. Until recently, liquid helium was an essential coolant for all super-conducting devices. ∞(Sec. 12.3)   Because helium has such a low abun-dance in the atmosphere and boils at such a low temperature, recovery of the gas from the atmosphere would require an immense expenditure of energy. Fortu-nately, helium is found in relatively high concentrations in many natural-gas wells. Some of this helium is separated to meet current demands, and a little is kept for later use. Unfortunately, however, most of the helium escapes.

Noble-Gas Compounds

Because the noble gases are exceedingly stable, they will undergo reaction only under rigorous conditions. Furthermore, we might expect that the heavier noble gases would be most likely to form compounds because their ionization energies are lower (Figure 7.7). A lower ionization energy suggests the possibil-ity of sharing an electron with another atom, leading to a chemical bond. In addition, because the group 8A elements (except helium) already contain eight electrons in their valence shell, formation of covalent bonds will require an expanded valence shell. Valence-shell expansion occurs most readily with larger atoms. ∞ (Sec. 8.8)

8A

2
He
10
Ne
18
Ar
36
Kr
54
Xe
86
Rn

Learning Goal 1: Cite the most common occurrence of each of the noble gases.

Point of Emphasis: From Table 18.1, the natural abun-dances of the noble gases ex-pressed as mole fractions are: argon, $9.34 \times 10.^{-3}$; neon, 1.818×10^{-5}; helium, 5.24×10^{-6}; krypton, 1.14×10^{-6}; and xenon, 8.7×10^{-8}.

TABLE 23.1 △ Properties of Xenon Compounds

Compound	Oxidation state of Xe	Melting point (°C)	ΔH_f° (kJ/mol)[a]
XeF_2	+2	129	−109(g)
XeF_4	+4	117	−218(g)
XeF_6	+6	49	−298(g)
$XeOF_4$	+6	−41 to −28	+146(l)
XeO_3	+6	—[b]	+402(s)
XeO_2F_2	+6	31	+145(s)
XeO_4	+8	—[c]	—

[a] At 25°C, for the compound in the state indicated.
[b] A solid; decomposes at 40°C.
[c] A solid; decomposes at −40°C.

The first noble-gas compound was prepared in 1962 by Neil Bartlett while he was on the faculty of the University of British Columbia. His work caused a sensation because it undercut the belief that the noble-gas elements were truly chemically inert. Bartlett initially worked with xenon in combination with fluorine, the element we would expect to be most reactive. Since that time, chemists have prepared several xenon compounds of fluorine and oxygen. Some properties of these substances are listed in Table 23.1. The three fluorides XeF_2, XeF_4, and XeF_6 are made by direct reaction of the elements. By varying the ratio of reactants and altering reaction conditions, one or the other of the three compounds can be obtained. Figure 7.25 (p. 243) shows crystals of XeF_4. The oxygen-containing compounds are formed when the fluorides are reacted with water, as in Equations 23.1 and 23.2

$$XeF_6(s) + H_2O(l) \longrightarrow XeOF_4(l) + 2HF(g) \qquad [23.1]$$

$$XeF_6(s) + 3H_2O(l) \longrightarrow XeO_3(aq) + 6HF(aq) \qquad [23.2]$$

SAMPLE EXERCISE 23.1

Predict the structure of XeF_4.

SOLUTION To predict the structure, we must first write the Lewis structure for the molecule. The total number of valence-shell electrons involved is 36 (8 from xenon and 7 from each of the four fluorines). This leads to the Lewis structure shown in Figure 23.1(a). We see that Xe has 12 electrons in its valence shell. We thus expect an octahedral disposition of 6 electron pairs. Two of these are nonbonded pairs. Because nonbonded pairs have a larger volume requirement than bonded pairs (Section 9.1), it is reasonable to expect these nonbonded pairs to be opposite one another. The expected structure is square planar, as shown in Figure 23.1(b). The experimentally determined structure agrees with this prediction.

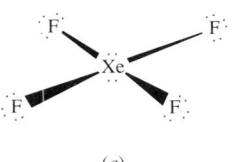
(a)

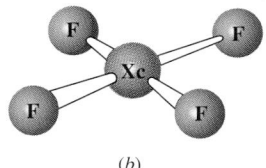
(b)

FIGURE 23.1
Lewis and geometrical structures of XeF_4.

PRACTICE EXERCISE

Describe the electron-pair geometry and the molecular geometry of XeF_2.
Answer: trigonal bipyramidal; linear

The enthalpies of formation of the xenon fluorides are negative (Table 23.1), which suggests that these compounds should be reasonably stable. This is indeed found to be the case. They are, however, powerful fluorinating agents and must be handled in containers that do not readily react to form fluorides. Notice that the enthalpies of formation of the oxyfluorides and oxides of xenon are positive; these compounds are quite unstable.

As we might expect, formation of compounds by the other noble-gas elements occurs much less readily than in the case of xenon. Only one binary krypton compound, KrF_2, is known with certainty; it decomposes to the elements at $-10°C$.

23.2 The Halogens

9 F
17 Cl
35 Br
53 I
85 At

The elements of group 7A, the halogens, have played an important part in the development of chemistry. Chlorine was first prepared by the Swedish chemist Karl Wilhelm Scheele in 1774, but not until 1810 did the English chemist Humphry Davy identify it as an element. Iodine was discovered in 1811, and bromine in 1825. Compounds of fluorine were known for a long time, but not until 1886 did the French chemist Henri Moissan succeed in preparing the very reactive free element.

The general valence-electron configuration of the halogens is ns^2np^5, where n may have values ranging from 2 through 6. The halogens have large electron affinities, and they most often achieve a noble-gas configuration by gaining an electron, which results in a -1 oxidation state. Fluorine, being the most electronegative element, exists in compounds only in the -1 state. The other halogens also exhibit positive oxidation states up to $+7$ by sharing valence electrons with a more electronegative atom such as O. In the positive oxidation states, the halogens tend to be good oxidizing agents (that is, they readily gain electrons).

Occurrences of the Halogens

Table 23.2 summarizes the occurrences of the halogens in nature. Although fluorine and chlorine are fairly abundant, they are quite differently distributed. This happens because the salts of chlorine are generally soluble, whereas some of those of fluorine are not. Bromine is much less abundant than chlorine or fluorine, and iodine is much rarer still.

Chlorine, bromine, and iodine occur as the halides in seawater and in salt deposits. The concentration of iodine in these sources is generally very small. However, it is concentrated by certain seaweeds. When they are harvested, dried, and burned, iodine can be extracted from the ashes. The element is also extracted commercially from oil-well brines in California. Fluorine occurs in the minerals fluorspar, CaF_2, cryolite, Na_3AlF_6, and fluoroapatite, $Ca_5(PO_4)_3F$. Only the first of these is an important commercial source of fluorine for the chemical industry.

All isotopes of astatine are radioactive. The longest-lived isotope is astatine-210, which has a half-life of 8.3 hr and decays mainly by electron capture. Astatine was first synthesized by bombarding bismuth-209 with high-energy

Learning Goal 5: Predict the maximum and minimum oxidation state of each halogen discussed in this chapter. Give an example of a compound containing the element in each of these oxidation states.

Robert C. Hansen, "An Overhead Demonstration of Some Descriptive Chemistry of the Halogens and Le Châtelier's Principle," *J. Chem. Educ.* **1988**, *65*, 264.

Point of Emphasis: Common oxidation states for the halogens (other than fluorine) are -1, $+1$, $+3$, $+5$, and $+7$, although by far the most common is -1.

Learning Goal 6: Cite the most common occurrences of each halogen discussed in this chapter.

TABLE 23.2 △ Occurrences of the Halogens

Element	Occurrences
Fluorine	Fluorspar, CaF_2; fluoroapatite, $Ca_5(PO_4)_3F$; cryolite, Na_3AlF_6 Biologically: teeth, bones
Chlorine	Seawater ($0.55\ M$); salt beds, salt lakes (for example, Dead Sea, Great Salt Lake); NaCl deposits Biologically: gastric juice [as $HCl(aq)$], tissue fluids
Bromine	Seawater ($8.3 \times 10^{-4}\ M$); underground brines; salt beds, salt lakes Biologically: minor concentrations of bromide along with chloride
Iodine	Seawater ($4 \times 10^{-7}\ M$); seaweeds; $NaIO_3$ in minor amounts in nitrate deposits; oil-well brines Biologically: in human thyroid gland

alpha particles, as shown in Equation 23.3:

$$^{209}_{83}Bi + {}^{4}_{2}He \longrightarrow {}^{211}_{85}At + 2{}^{1}_{0}n \qquad [23.3]$$

A cyclotron must be used to synthesize astatine, which makes it very expensive and limits its application and study.

Properties and Preparation of the Halogens

Some of the properties of the halogens are summarized in Table 23.3. These properties vary in a regular fashion as a function of atomic number. Within each horizontal row of the periodic table, each halogen has a high ionization energy, second only to the noble-gas element adjacent to it. Each halogen has the highest electronegativity of all the elements in its row. Within the halogen family, atomic and ionic radii increase with increasing atomic number. Correspondingly, the ionization energy and electronegativity steadily decrease as we go down the family, from fluorine to iodine.

Under ordinary conditions, the halogens exist as diatomic molecules. The molecules are held together in the solid and liquid states by London dispersion forces. ∞ (Sec. 11.2) Because I_2 is the largest and most polarizable of the halogen molecules, it is not surprising that the intermolecular forces between I_2 molecules are the strongest. Thus, I_2 has the highest melting point and boiling

TABLE 23.3 △ Some Properties of the Halogen Atoms

Property	F	Cl	Br	I
Atomic radius (Å)	0.72	0.99	1.14	1.33
Ionic radius, X^- (Å)	1.33	1.84	1.96	2.20
First ionization energy (kJ/mol)	1681	1256	1143	1009
Electron affinity (kJ/mol)	-332	-349	-325	-295
Electronegativity	4.0	3.2	3.0	2.7
X—X single-bond energy (kJ/mol)	155	242	193	151
Reduction potential (V): $\frac{1}{2}X_2(aq) + e^- \longrightarrow X^-(aq)$	2.87	1.36	1.07	0.54

point. At room temperature and 1 atm pressure, I_2 is a solid, Br_2 is a liquid, and Cl_2 and F_2 are gases. Chlorine readily liquefies upon compression at room temperature and is normally stored and handled in liquid form in steel containers.

The comparatively low bond energy in F_2 (155 kJ/mol) accounts in part for the extreme reactivity of elemental fluorine. Because of its high reactivity, F_2 is very difficult to work with. Certain metals, such as copper and nickel, can be used to contain F_2 because their surfaces form a protective coating of metal fluoride. Chlorine and the heavier halogens are also reactive, although less so than fluorine. They combine directly with most elements except the rare gases.

Because of their high electronegativities compared with those of other elements, the halogens tend to gain electrons from other substances and thereby serve as oxidizing agents. The oxidizing ability of the halogens, which is indicated by their reduction potentials, decreases going down the group. As a result, we find that a given halogen is able to oxidize the anions of the halogens below it in the family. For example, Cl_2 will oxidize Br^- and I^-, but not F^-, as seen in Figure 23.2.

Teaching Note: As discussed in Chapter 19, many metals are protected from corrosion or oxidation by formation of an impenetrable layer of oxidized material on the surface.

SAMPLE EXERCISE 23.2

Write the balanced chemical equation for the reaction, if any, that occurs between **(a)** $I^-(aq)$ and $Br_2(l)$; **(b)** $Cl^-(aq)$ and $I_2(s)$.

SOLUTION **(a)** Br_2 is able to oxidize (remove electrons from) the anions of the halogens below it in the periodic table. Thus, it will oxidize I^-:

$$2I^-(aq) + Br_2(l) \longrightarrow I_2(s) + 2Br^-(aq)$$

(b) Cl^- is the anion of a halogen above iodine in the periodic table. Thus, I_2 cannot oxidize Cl^-; there is no reaction.

PRACTICE EXERCISE

Write the balanced chemical equation for the reaction that occurs between $Br^-(aq)$ and $Cl_2(aq)$.   ***Answer:*** $2Br^-(aq) + Cl_2(aq) \longrightarrow Br_2(l) + 2Cl^-(aq)$

FIGURE 23.2 Aqueous solutions of NaF, NaBr, and NaI (from left to right) to which Cl_2 has been added. Each solution is in contact with carbon tetrachloride, CCl_4, which forms the lower layer in each container. The halogens are more soluble in CCl_4. The F^- ion in the NaF solution (left) does not react with Cl_2, and thus both the aqueous and CCl_4 layers remain colorless. The Br^- ion (center) is oxidized by Cl_2 to form Br_2, producing a yellow color in the water layer and an orange color in the CCl_4 layer. The I^- ion (right) is oxidized to I_2, producing an amber color in the water layer and a violet color in the CCl_4 layer. (Donald Clegg and Roxy Wilson)

Notice from Table 23.3 that the reduction potential of F_2 is exceptionally high. Fluorine gas readily oxidizes water:

$$F_2(aq) + H_2O(l) \longrightarrow 2HF(aq) + \tfrac{1}{2}O_2(g) \qquad E° = +1.64 \text{ V} \qquad [23.4]$$

Fluorine cannot be prepared by electrolytic oxidation of aqueous solutions of fluoride salts because water itself is oxidized more readily than F^-. In practice, the element is formed by electrolytic oxidation of a solution of KF in anhydrous HF. The KF reacts with HF to form a salt, $K^+ HF_2^-$, which acts as the current carrier in the liquid. (The HF_2^- ion is stable because of very strong hydrogen bonding, as described in Section 11.2.) The overall cell reaction is

Learning Goal 7: Write balanced chemical equations describing at least one means of preparation of each halogen from naturally occurring sources.

$$2KHF_2(l) \longrightarrow H_2(g) + F_2(g) + 2KF(l) \qquad [23.5]$$

Chlorine is produced mainly by electrolysis of either molten or aqueous sodium chloride, as described in Sections 20.8 and 24.4. Both bromine and iodine are obtained commercially from brines containing the halide ions by oxidation with Cl_2.

Uses of the Halogens

Fluorine has become an important industrial chemical. It is used, for example, to prepare fluorocarbons, very stable carbon-fluorine compounds. An example is CF_2Cl_2, known as Freon 12, which is used as a refrigerant and as a propellant for aerosol cans. These substances deplete ozone in the stratosphere, and consequently their use is being phased out. ∞ (Sec. 18.3) Fluorocarbons are also used as lubricants and in plastics. Teflon (Figure 23.3) is a polymeric fluorocarbon noted for its high thermal stability and lack of chemical reactivity (see the Chemistry at Work box in Section 26.2).

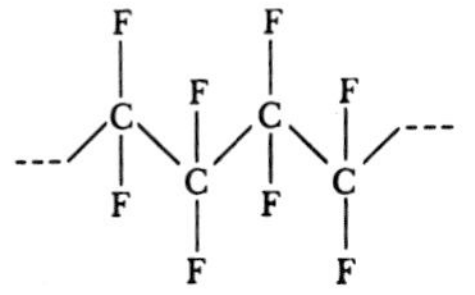

Chlorine is by far the most commercially important halogen. About 1.0×10^{10} kg (11.1 million tons) of Cl_2 is produced in the United States each year. In addition, hydrogen chloride production is about 2.6×10^9 kg (2.9 million tons) annually. About half of this inorganic chlorine finds its way eventually into vinyl chloride, C_2H_3Cl, used in polyvinyl chloride (PVC) plastics manufacture; ethylene dichloride, $C_2H_2Cl_2$, an organic solvent; and other chlorine-containing organic compounds. Much of the remainder of the chlorine is used as a bleach in the paper and textile industries. When Cl_2 dissolves in cold dilute base it disproportionates into Cl^- and the hypochlorite ion, ClO^-:

$$2OH^-(aq) + Cl_2(aq) \rightleftharpoons Cl^-(aq) + ClO^-(aq) + H_2O(l) \qquad [23.6]$$

Sodium hypochlorite, NaClO, is the active ingredient in many liquid bleaches. Chlorine is also used in water treatment to oxidize and thereby destroy bacteria. ∞ (Sec.18.6)

Neither bromine nor iodine is as widely used as fluorine and chlorine. One familiar application of bromine is in the production of silver bromide used in photographic film. A common use of iodine is its addition, as KI, to table salt to form iodized table salt. Iodized salt (Figure 23.4) provides the small amount of iodine necessary in our diets; it is essential for the formation of thyroxin, a hormone secreted by the thyroid gland. Lack of iodine in the diet results in an enlarged thyroid gland, a condition called *goiter.*

FIGURE 23.3 Structure of Teflon, a fluorocarbon polymer.

Learning Goal 8: Describe at least one important use of each halogen element.

Lee R. Summerlin and James L. Ealy, Jr., "Preparation of Chlorine Gas from Laundry Bleach," *Chemical Demonstrations, A Sourcebook for Teachers* (Washington: American Chemical Society, 1985), p. 13.

FIGURE 23.4 Iodized salt contains about 0.02% KI by mass. (© Paul Silverman/Fundamental Photographs)

The Hydrogen Halides

All of the halogens form stable diatomic molecules with hydrogen. These are very important compounds, in part because aqueous solutions of the hydrogen halides other than HF are strongly acidic. Table 23.4 lists some of the more important properties of the hydrogen halides. Notice that the boiling point of HF is abnormally high as compared with those of the other hydrogen halides. The cause of this unusual behavior is the strong hydrogen bonding that exists between HF molecules in the liquid state. ∞ (Sec. 11.2)

Learning Goal 9: Write a balanced chemical equation describing the preparation of each of the hydrogen halides.

The hydrogen halides can be formed by direct reaction of the elements. However, the most important means of preparing hydrogen halides is through reaction of a salt of the halide with a strong nonvolatile acid. Hydrogen fluoride and hydrogen chloride are prepared in this manner by reaction of an inexpensive, readily available salt with concentrated sulfuric acid:

$$CaF_2(s) + H_2SO_4(l) \xrightarrow{\Delta} 2HF(g) + CaSO_4(s) \qquad [23.7]$$

$$NaCl(s) + H_2SO_4(l) \xrightarrow{\Delta} HCl(g) + NaHSO_4(s) \qquad [23.8]$$

Because the hydrogen halide is the only volatile component in the mixture, it can be easily removed. It is usually absorbed in water and marketed as the corresponding acid.

Neither hydrogen bromide nor hydrogen iodide can be prepared by analogous reactions of salts with H_2SO_4 because Br^- and I^- undergo oxidation by

TABLE 23.4 △ Properties of the Hydrogen Halides

Property	HF	HCl	HBr	HI
Molecular weight	20.01	36.45	80.92	127.91
Melting point (°C)	−83	−115	−89	−51
Boiling point (°C)	19.5	−84.2	−67.1	−35.1
Bond-dissociation energy (kJ/mol)	567	431	366	299
H—X bond length (Å)	0.92	1.27	1.41	1.61
Solubility in H_2O (g/100 g H_2O, 10°C)	∞	78	210	234

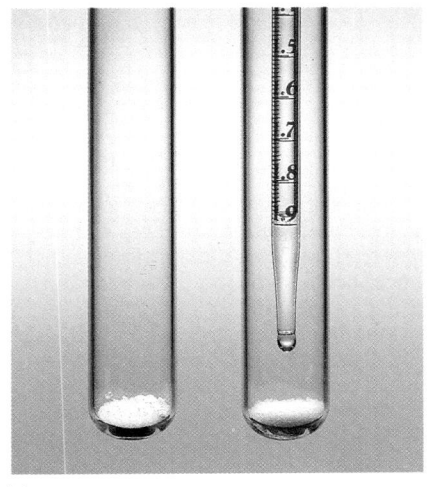

(a)

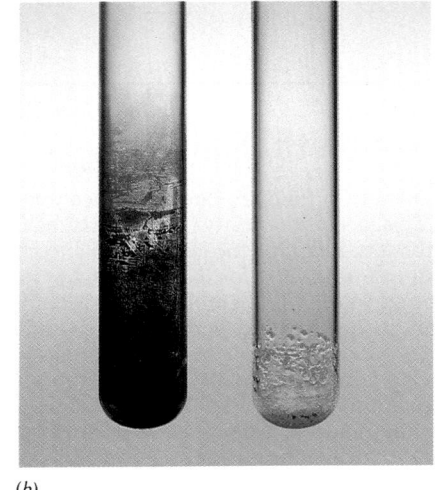

(b)

FIGURE 23.5 (a) Sodium iodide in the left test tube, and sodium bromide on the right. Sulfuric acid is in the pipet. (b) Addition of sulfuric acid to the test tubes oxidizes sodium iodide to form the dark-colored iodine on the left. Sodium bromide is oxidized to the yellow-brown bromine on the right. When more concentrated, bromine has a reddish-brown color. (Richard Megna/Fundamental Photographs)

H_2SO_4 (Figure 23.5). The overall reactions are described by Equations 23.9 and 23.10:

$$2NaBr(s) + 2H_2SO_4(l) \longrightarrow Br_2(g) + SO_2(g) + Na_2SO_4(s) + 2H_2O(g) \qquad [23.9]$$

$$8NaI(s) + 9H_2SO_4(l) \longrightarrow 8NaHSO_4(s) + H_2S(g) + 4I_2(g) + 4H_2O(g) \qquad [23.10]$$

Notice that in the case of the bromide, part of the H_2SO_4 is reduced to SO_2, in which sulfur is in the $+4$ oxidation state. In the reaction with iodide, sulfur is reduced all the way to H_2S, in which sulfur is in the -2 oxidation state. This difference in products reflects the greater ease of oxidation of the iodide. The difficulties associated with use of H_2SO_4 can be avoided by using a nonvolatile acid that is a poorer oxidizing agent than H_2SO_4; concentrated phosphoric acid, H_3PO_4, serves well.

The hydrogen halides are also formed when certain molecular halides are hydrolyzed, as in the following examples (Figure 23.6):

$$PCl_3(l) + 3H_2O(l) \longrightarrow H_3PO_3(s) + 3HCl(g) \qquad [23.11]$$

$$SeBr_4(s) + 3H_2O(l) \longrightarrow H_2SeO_3(s) + 4HBr(g) \qquad [23.12]$$

FIGURE 23.6 Phosphorus trichloride is added to water containing methyl orange indicator. As the PCl_3 hydrolyzes to form H_3PO_3 and HCl, the indicator turns red, its color in acid solutions. (© Richard Megna/Fundamental Photographs)

SAMPLE EXERCISE 23.3

Write a balanced chemical equation for the formation of hydrogen bromide gas from the reaction of solid sodium bromide with phosphoric acid.

SOLUTION   The chemical formulas of sodium bromide and phosphoric acid are NaBr and H_3PO_4, respectively. Let us assume that only one of the hydrogens of H_3PO_4 undergoes reaction. (The actual number depends on the reaction conditions.) The balanced equation is then

$$NaBr(s) + H_3PO_4(l) \longrightarrow NaH_2PO_4(s) + HBr(g)$$

PRACTICE EXERCISE

Write the balanced chemical equation for the preparation of HI from NaI and H_3PO_4.   *Answer:* $NaI(s) + H_3PO_4(l) \longrightarrow NaH_2PO_4(s) + HI(g)$

A CLOSER LOOK

The Hydrolysis of Nonmetal Halides

Some nonmetal halides, such as NF_3, CCl_4, and SF_6, are quite unreactive toward water. This lack of reactivity is not due to thermodynamic factors but rather to the kinetic features of the reaction. For example, $\Delta G°$ for the hydrolysis of CCl_4 is highly negative, -377 kJ/mol, which implies that the reaction should proceed very nearly to completion. ∞ (Sec. 19.7) However, no low-energy reaction mechanism is available; the hydrolysis reaction has a very high activation barrier.

Generally, a molecular halide is unreactive when the central atom is unable to expand further the number of electrons in its valence shell (that is, the central atom has its maximum stable coordination number). For example, carbon can accommodate a maximum of eight electrons in its valence shell. Silicon, on the other hand, can accommodate a greater number of electrons by using d orbitals in bonding. The hydrolysis of $SiCl_4$ is believed to occur by attack at the silicon atom by the H_2O molecule, which expands the coordination number of Si. This attack is followed by loss of H^+ and Cl^- ions, as shown in Figure 23.7. This reaction pathway is not available to CCl_4.

FIGURE 23.7 Proposed mechanism for the first stage of the reaction between $SiCl_4$ and H_2O. After the H_2O forms an adduct with $SiCl_4$, that adduct loses H^+ and Cl^- ions. The process of H_2O attack is then repeated three additional times, with $Si(OH)_4$ ultimately formed.

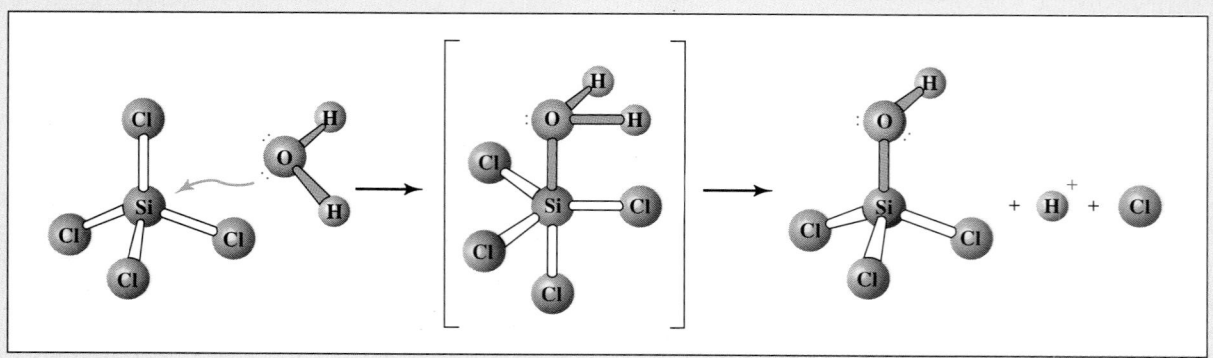

Figure 23.7

SAMPLE EXERCISE 23.4

Write the balanced chemical equation for the reaction between $SiCl_4$ and H_2O.

SOLUTION The oxidation state of Si in $SiCl_4$ is $+4$. Because the hydrolysis of non-metal chlorides is not an oxidation-reduction reaction, the product acid must also have Si in the $+4$ oxidation state. That acid is H_4SiO_4, which we can also write as $Si(OH)_4$. Thus, the equation is

$$SiCl_4(l) + 4H_2O(l) \longrightarrow Si(OH)_4(s) + 4HCl(g)$$

Because $Si(OH)_4$ readily undergoes loss of water to form SiO_2, the reaction is also written in the following way:

$$SiCl_4(l) + 2H_2O(l) \longrightarrow SiO_2(s) + 4HCl(g)$$

PRACTICE EXERCISE

What is the oxidation state of P in PCl_5? What is the chemical formula of the oxyacid of P in this oxidation state? Write the balanced chemical equation for the reaction of solid PCl_5 with water. *Answer:* $+5$; H_3PO_4; $PCl_5(s) + 4H_2O(l) \longrightarrow H_3PO_4(aq) + 5HCl(aq)$

The hydrogen halides form hydrohalic acid solutions when dissolved in water. These solutions exhibit the characteristic properties of acids, such as reactions with active metals to produce hydrogen gas. ∞ (Sec. 4.6) Hydrofluoric acid also reacts readily with silica, SiO_2, and with various silicates to form hexafluorosilicic acid, H_2SiF_6, as in these examples:

$$SiO_2(s) + 6HF(aq) \longrightarrow H_2SiF_6(aq) + 2H_2O(l) \qquad [23.13]$$

$$CaSiO_3(s) + 8HF(aq) \longrightarrow H_2SiF_6(aq) + CaF_2(s) + 3H_2O(l) \quad [23.14]$$

Glass consists mostly of silicate structures (Section 23.5), and these reactions allow HF to etch or frost glass (Figure 23.8). It is also the reason that HF is stored in wax or plastic containers rather than glass.

Interhalogen Compounds

Because the halogens form diatomic molecules in their most stable state at ordinary temperatures and pressures, it is not surprising to discover that diatomic molecules consisting of two different halogen atoms exist. These compounds are the simplest examples of **interhalogens,** that is, compounds formed between two different halogen elements. Some properties of the diatomic interhalogens are listed in Table 23.5.

Unlike the diatomic halogen elements, the oxidation states in the diatomic interhalogen compounds are not zero. We always assign an oxidation state of -1 to the more electronegative halogen. For example, in ClF we assign oxidation states of $+1$ and -1 to Cl and F, respectively.

The higher interhalogen compounds have formulas of the form XF_3, XF_5, or XF_7, where X is Cl, Br, or I. The oxidation state of the central halogen

FIGURE 23.8 Etched or frosted glass. Designs such as this are produced by first coating the glass with wax. The wax is then removed in the areas to be etched. When treated with hydrofluoric acid, the exposed areas of the glass are attacked, producing the etching effect. The hydrofluoric acid is then washed from the surface and the remaining wax is removed. (Richard Megna/Fundamental Photographs)

TABLE 23.5 △ Properties of Interhalogen Compounds, XX′

Compound	ClF	BrF	BrCl	IF	ICl	IBr
Molecular weight	54.6	98.9	115.4	145.9	162.4	206.8
Melting point (°C)	−156	−33	−66	a	27	41
Boiling point (°C)	−100	20	5	a	98	116
Bond distance (Å)	1.63	1.76	2.14	1.91	2.32	2.49
Dipole moment (D)	0.9	1.3	0.6	a	0.7	1.21
Bond-dissociation energy (kJ/mol)	253	237	218	278	208	175

[a] Property cannot be measured because of sample decomposition.

atom in XF_3, XF_5, and XF_7 compounds is $+3$, $+5$, and $+7$ respectively. The compound ICl_3, in which iodine is in the $+3$ oxidation state, is also known.

The central atom in these higher interhalogen compounds has valence-shell d orbitals available for bonding. Thus, the valence shell can be expanded beyond the octet. The central atom in all cases is relatively large compared to the atoms grouped around it. Because fluorine is small and forms very strong bonds, it is ideally suited as the X′ atom. Only when the central atom is very large, as in the case of iodine, can the larger chlorine atom form an interhalogen, as in ICl_3. The importance of size is also seen in the fact that iodine is capable of forming IF_7, but with bromine a maximum of five fluorines can be fitted around the central atom, in BrF_5. Chlorine and fluorine can form the ClF_5 molecule, but only with great difficulty. As illustrated in the following Sample Exercise, the geometries of these compounds can be predicted by using the VSEPR model. ∞ (Sec. 9.1) We can also describe the bonding about the central atom in terms of a hybrid orbital description. ∞ (Sec. 9.4)

SAMPLE EXERCISE 23.5

Account for the valence-shell electron distribution and geometrical structure in BrF_3. What hybrid orbital description is most suitable for the central atom in this molecule?

SOLUTION Bromine has seven valence-shell electrons. When the Br atom is singly bonded to three fluorine atoms, there are three additional electrons from this source. According to the VSEPR model, these ten electrons are disposed as five electron pairs about the central atom at the vertices of a trigonal bipyramid (Table 9.3). Three of the electron pairs are used in bonding to fluorine; the other two are unshared electron pairs. These unshared pairs require a larger space, so they are placed in the equatorial plane of the trigonal bipyramid:

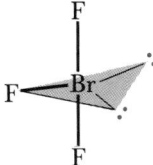

Because the unshared pairs push the bonding pairs back a little, the molecule should have the shape of a bent T. In terms of a hybridization description, we need to employ one of the bromine valence-shell d orbitals (the $4d$) in addition to the $4s$ and three $4p$ orbitals to provide the five atomic orbitals to contain the five electron pairs in the valence shell. Thus the appropriate hybrid orbital description is sp^3d, which results in orbitals directed toward the vertices of a trigonal bipyramid.

PRACTICE EXERCISE

Predict the molecular geometry and hybridization of the orbitals of iodine in IF_5.
Answer: square pyramidal; sp^3d^2

Because the interhalogen compounds contain a halogen atom in a positive oxidation state, they are exceedingly reactive. They invariably are powerful oxidizing agents. When the compound acts as an oxidant, the oxidation state of the central halogen atom is decreased to a more preferable value (usually 0 or -1). They are also very active fluorinating agents, as in these examples:

$$2CoCl_2(s) + 2ClF_3(g) \longrightarrow 2CoF_3(s) + 3Cl_2(g) \qquad [23.15]$$

$$Se(s) + 3BrF_5(l) \longrightarrow SeF_6(l) + 3BrF_3(l) \qquad [23.16]$$

The *polyhalide ions* are closely related to the interhalogens. Many of these ions are relatively stable as salts of the alkali metal ions—for example, KI_3, $CsIBr_2$, $KICl_4$, and $KBrF_4$. Some of them, notably I_3^-, are also stable in aqueous solution.

Oxyacids and Oxyanions

Table 23.6 summarizes the formulas of the known oxyacids of the halogens and the way they are named.* ∞ (Sec. 2.6)   The oxyacids are rather unstable; they generally decompose (sometimes explosively) on attempts to isolate them. All of the oxyacids are strong oxidizing agents. The oxyanions, formed on removal of a proton from the oxyacids, are generally more stable than the oxyacids themselves. Hypochlorite salts are used as bleaches and disinfectants because of the powerful oxidizing capabilities of the hypochlorite ion. Sodium chlorite, which can be isolated as the trihydrate, $NaClO_2 \cdot 3H_2O$, is used as a bleaching agent. Chlorate salts are similarly very reactive. For example, a mixture of potassium chlorate and sulfur may explode when struck. Potassium chlorate is used in making matches and fireworks.

Perchloric acid and its salts are the most stable of the oxyacids and oxyanions. Dilute perchloric acid solutions are quite safe, and most perchlorate salts are stable except when heated with organic materials. When heated, perchlorates can become vigorous, even violent oxidizers. Therefore, considerable caution should be exercised when handling these substances, and it is crucial to avoid contact between perchlorates and readily oxidized materials such as

Learning Goal 11:   Name and give the formulas of the oxyacids and oxyanions of the halogens.

---

* Fluorine forms one oxyacid, HFO. Because the electronegativity of fluorine is greater than that of oxygen, we must consider fluorine to be in a -1 oxidation state and oxygen to be in the 0 oxidation state.

TABLE 23.6 △ The Oxyacids of the Halogens

Oxidation state of halogen	Formula of acid			Name
	Cl	Br	I	
$+1$	HClO	HBrO	HIO	*Hypo*hal*ous* acid
$+3$	$HClO_2$	—	—	Hal*ous* acid
$+5$	$HClO_3$	$HBrO_3$	HIO_3	Hal*ic* acid
$+7$	$HClO_4$	$HBrO_4$	HIO_4, H_5IO_6	*Per*hal*ic* acid

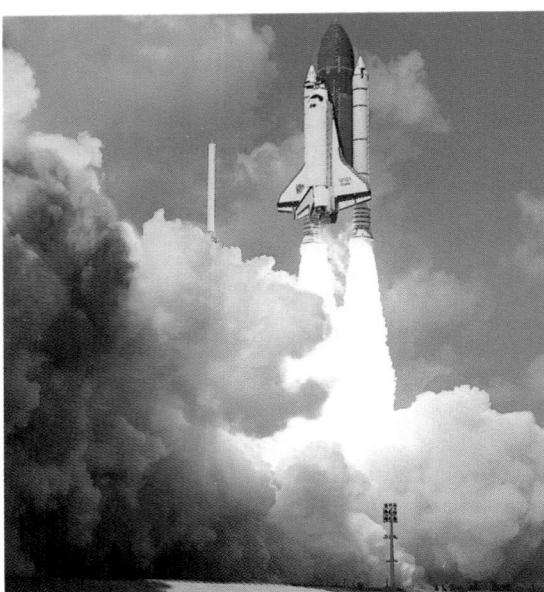

FIGURE 23.9 Launch of the space shuttle *Atlantis,* October 18, 1989. (NASA, Johnson Space Center)

Teaching Note: A dramatic example of the explosive danger of perchlorate compounds was seen in May 1988 when one of the factories that produced NH_4ClO_4 for the space shuttle boosters was completely destroyed by an explosion. Such unpredictable explosions are common with perchlorate salts, especially those of the heavier metals.

active metals and combustible organic compounds. The use of ammonium perchlorate as the oxidizer in the solid booster rockets for the space shuttle demonstrates the oxidizing power of perchlorates. The solid propellent contains a mixture of NH_4ClO_4 and powdered aluminum, the reducing agent. Each shuttle launch requires about 6×10^5 kg (700 tons) of NH_4ClO_4 (Figure 23.9).

There are two oxyacids that have iodine in the +7 oxidation state. These periodic acids are HIO_4 (called metaperiodic acid) and H_5IO_6 (called paraperiodic acid). The two forms exist in equilibrium in aqueous solution:

$$H_5IO_6(aq) \rightleftharpoons H^+(aq) + IO_4^-(aq) + 2H_2O(l) \qquad K = 0.015 \quad [23.17]$$

FIGURE 23.10 Paraperiodic acid, H_5IO_6.

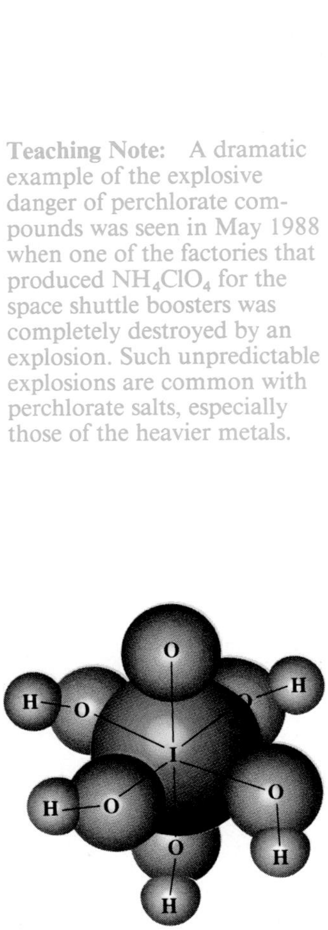

HIO_4 is a strong acid, and H_5IO_6 is a weak one; the first two acid-dissociation constants for H_5IO_6 are $K_{a1} = 2.8 \times 10^{-2}$ and $K_{a2} = 4.9 \times 10^{-9}$. Crystalline H_5IO_6 is obtained when periodic acid solutions are evaporated at low temperatures. Mild heating of H_5IO_6 under vacuum produces HIO_4. The structure of H_5IO_6 is given in Figure 23.10. The large size of the iodine atom allows it to accommodate six surrounding oxygen atoms. The smaller halogens do not form acids of this type.

The acid strengths of the oxyacids increase with increasing oxidation state of the central atom. ∞ (Sec. 16.9) The stability of the oxyacids and of the corresponding oxyanions toward reduction increases with increasing oxidation state of the central halogen atom. Because the halogens are relatively electronegative elements, compounds in which the halogen has an increasingly positive oxidation number would be expected to be *less* stable. The origins of this unexpected trend are rather complicated and beyond the scope of our survey.

Learning Goal 12: Describe the variation in acid strength and oxidizing strength of the oxyacids of chlorine.

23.3 The Group 6A Elements

The elements of group 6A are oxygen, sulfur, selenium, tellurium, and polonium. We have already discussed oxygen in Section 22.4. In this section, we will examine the group as a whole and then look at sulfur, selenium, and tellurium, focusing on sulfur. We will not say much about polonium, an element produced by radioactive decay of radium. There are no stable isotopes of this element, and it is found only in minute quantities in radium-containing minerals.

General Characteristics of the Group 6A Elements

The group 6A elements possess the general outer-electron configuration ns^2np^4, where n may have values ranging from 2 through 6. These elements thus may attain a noble-gas electron configuration by the addition of two electrons, which results in a -2 oxidation state. Because the group 6A elements are nonmetals, this is a common oxidation state. Except for oxygen, however, the group 6A elements are also commonly found in positive oxidation states up to $+6$, which corresponds to the sharing of all six valence-shell electrons with atoms of a more electronegative element. Sulfur, selenium, and tellurium also differ from oxygen in being able to use d orbitals in bonding. Thus, compounds with expanded valence shells such as SF_6, SeF_6, and TeF_6 occur.

Table 23.7 summarizes some of the more important properties of the atoms of the group 6A elements. The energy of the X—X single bond is estimated from data for the elements, except for oxygen. In this case, because the O—O bond in O_2 is not a single bond (Section 9.7), the estimated O—O bond energy in hydrogen peroxide is employed. The reduction potential listed in the last line of the table refers to the reduction of the element in its standard state to form $H_2X(aq)$ in acidic solution. In most of the properties listed in Table 23.7, we see a regular variation as a function of atomic number. Atomic and ionic radii increase and ionization energies decrease, as expected, as we move down the family.

The electron affinities listed apply to the process shown in Equation 23.18:

$$X(g) + e^- \longrightarrow X^-(g) \qquad [23.18]$$

This, of course, does not produce the commonly observed stable ion of these elements, X^{2-}, but it is the first step in its formation. It is interesting to note that the addition of an electron to oxygen is less exothermic than the addition of an electron to any other group 6A element. This effect is due to the relatively small

TABLE 23.7 △ Some Properties of the Atoms of the Group 6A Elements

Property	O	S	Se	Te
Atomic radius (Å)	0.73	1.03	1.40	1.60
X^{2-} ionic radius (Å)	1.40	1.84	1.98	2.21
First ionization energy (kJ/mol)	1314	999	941	869
Electron affinity (kJ/mol)	-141	-201	-195	-186
Electronegativity	3.5	2.5	2.4	2.1
X—X single-bond energy (kJ/mol)	146[a]	266	172	126
Reduction potential to H_2X in acidic solution (V)	1.23	0.14	-0.40	-0.72

[a] Based on O—O bond energy in H_2O_2.

size of the oxygen atom. Addition of a single extra electron to the smaller atom results in larger electron-electron repulsions, offsetting the gain in stability that results from the closer approach of the electron to the nucleus.

Note that the ease of reduction of the free element to form H_2X varies greatly throughout the series. Whereas oxygen is very readily reduced to the -2 oxidation state, the potential for reduction of tellurium is strongly negative. These observations indicate an increasingly metallic character in the group 6A elements as atomic number increases. The physical properties of the elements are also consistent with an increasing metallic character. At the top of the family we have oxygen, a diatomic molecule, and sulfur, a nonconducting solid that melts at $113°C$. Near the bottom we have tellurium, whose stable form has a bright luster, low electrical conductivity, and a melting point of $452°C$.

Point of Emphasis: Recall that the more negative the reduction potential, the more difficult the reduction. See Chapter 20.

Occurrences and Preparation of Sulfur, Selenium, and Tellurium

Learning Goal 14: Cite the most common occurrences of each group 6A element discussed in this chapter.

Large underground deposits are the principal source of elemental sulfur. The *Frasch process,* illustrated in Figure 23.11, is used to obtain the element from these deposits. The method is based on the low melting point and low density of sulfur. Superheated water is forced into the deposit, where it melts the sulfur. Compressed air then forces the molten sulfur up a pipe that is concentric with the ones that introduce the hot water and compressed air into the deposit.

Sulfur also occurs widely as sulfide and sulfate minerals. Its presence as a minor component of coal and petroleum poses a major problem. Combustion of these "unclean" fuels leads to serious sulfur oxide pollution. ∞ (Sec. 18.4) Also, operations that use sulfide minerals as sources of metals liberate sulfur oxides. Much effort has been directed at removing this sulfur, and these efforts have increased the availability of sulfur. The sale of this sulfur helps

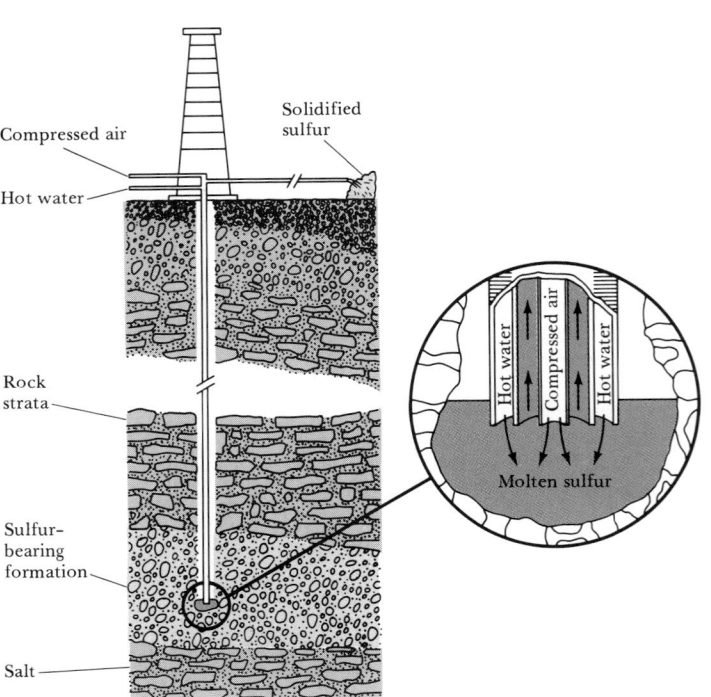

FIGURE 23.11 Mining of sulfur by the Frasch process. The process is named after Herman Frasch, who invented it in the early 1890s. The process is particularly useful for recovering sulfur from deposits located under quicksand or water.

partially to offset the costs of the desulfurizing processes and equipment. About half the sulfur used in the United States each year is produced by means other than the Frasch process.

Selenium and tellurium occur in rare minerals such as Cu_2Se, $PbSe$, Ag_2Se, Cu_2Te, $PbTe$, Ag_2Te, and Au_2Te. They also occur as minor constituents in sulfide ores of copper, iron, nickel, and lead. However, these elements are not very important commercially, so we will not consider the details of how they are obtained.

Properties and Uses of Sulfur, Selenium, and Tellurium

As we normally encounter it, sulfur is yellow, tasteless, and nearly odorless. It is insoluble in water and exists in several allotropic forms. The thermodynamically stable form at room temperature is rhombic sulfur, which consists of puckered S_8 rings, as shown in Figure 23.12. When heated above its melting point (113°C), sulfur undergoes a variety of changes. The molten sulfur first contains S_8 molecules and is fluid because the rings readily slip over one another. Further heating of this straw-colored liquid causes rings to break, the fragments joining to form very long molecules that can become entangled. The sulfur consequently becomes highly viscous. This change is marked by a color change to dark reddish brown (Figure 23.13). Further heating breaks the chains, and the viscosity again decreases.

Most of the 1.3×10^{10} kg (14 million tons) of sulfur produced in the United States each year is used in the manufacture of sulfuric acid. Sulfur is also used in vulcanizing rubber, a process that toughens rubber by introducing crosslinking between polymer chains. ∞ (Sec. 12.2)

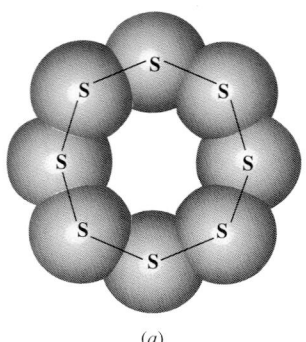

(a)

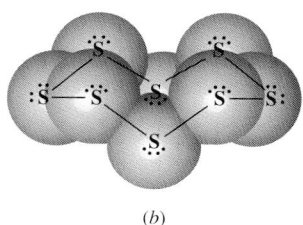

(b)

FIGURE 23.12 Top view (a) and side view (b) of the S_8 molecule in rhombic sulfur.

Learning Goal 15: Cite the most common form of each group 6A element discussed in this chapter.

Lee R. Summerlin, Christie L. Borgford, and Julie B. Ealy, "Plastic Sulfur," *Chemical Demonstrations, A Sourcebook for Teachers, Volume 2* (Washington: American Chemical Society, 1987), p. 53.

FIGURE 23.13 When sulfur is heated above its melting point, 113°C, it becomes dark and viscous. Here the liquid is shown falling into cold water, where it again solidifies. (Lawrence Migdale, Science Source/Photo Researchers)

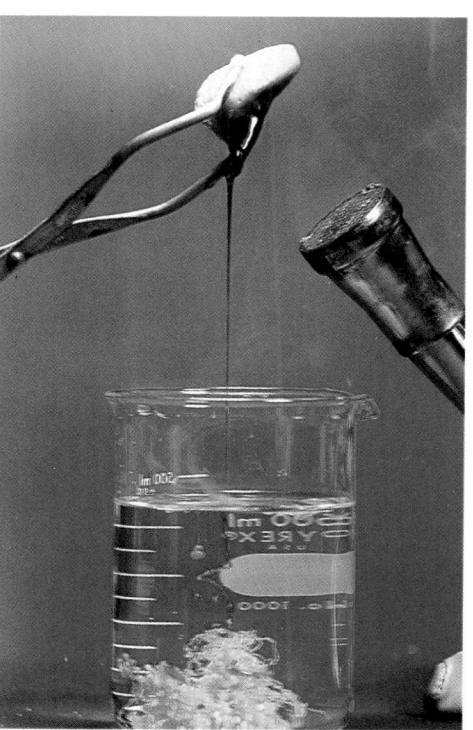

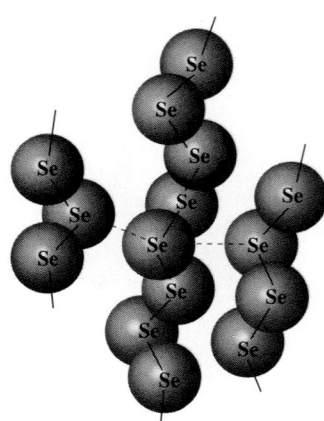

FIGURE 23.14 Portion of the structure of crystalline selenium. The dashed lines represent weak bonding interactions between atoms in adjacent chains. Tellurium has the same structure.

The most stable allotropes of both selenium and tellurium are crystalline substances containing helical chains of atoms, as illustrated in Figure 23.14. Each atom of the chain is close to atoms in adjacent chains, and it appears that some sharing of electron pairs between these atoms occurs, as indicated by the dashed lines in Figure 23.14.

The electrical conductivity of selenium is very low in the dark but increases greatly upon exposure to light. This property of the element is utilized in photoelectric cells and light meters. Photocopiers also depend on the photoconductivity of selenium. Photocopy machines contain a belt or drum coated with a film of selenium. This drum is electrostatically charged and then exposed to light reflected from the image being photocopied. The electric charge drains from the selenium where the selenium is made conductive by exposure to light. A black powder (the "toner") sticks only to the areas that remain charged. The photocopy is made when the toner is transferred to a sheet of plain paper, which is heated to fuse the toner to the paper.

Sulfur is widely distributed in biological systems. It is present in most proteins, as a component of the amino acids cysteine and methionine. In contrast, selenium is rare in biological systems. Only recently has the human nutritional requirement for the element been established. Selenium is present in minute quantities in most vegetables, especially spinach. The amount of selenium required for adequate nutrition is very small. In quantities much larger than this small nutritional requirement, the element becomes toxic. Tellurium does not have a known role in human nutrition. Its compounds are poisonous and, if they are volatile, usually have highly offensive odors.

Oxides, Oxyacids, and Oxyanions of Sulfur

Sulfur dioxide was first discovered by Joseph Priestley in 1774, when he heated mercury with concentrated sulfuric acid:

$$Hg(l) + 2H_2SO_4(l) \longrightarrow HgSO_4(s) + SO_2(g) + 2H_2O(l) \quad [23.19]$$

In the laboratory, SO_2 is prepared by the action of aqueous acid on a sulfite salt:

$$2H^+(aq) + SO_3^{2-}(aq) \longrightarrow SO_2(g) + H_2O(l) \quad [23.20]$$

Sulfur dioxide is formed when sulfur is combusted in air; it has a choking odor and is poisonous. The gas is particularly toxic to lower organisms, such as fungi, and is consequently used for sterilizing dried fruit. At 1 atm pressure and room temperature, SO_2 dissolves in water to the extent of 45 volumes of gas per volume of water, to produce a solution of about 1.6 M concentration. The solution is acidic, and we describe it as sulfurous acid, $H_2SO_3(aq)$. Sulfurous acid is a diprotic acid that ionizes according to Equations 23.21 and 23.22:

$$H_2SO_3(aq) \rightleftharpoons H^+(aq) + HSO_3^-(aq) \qquad K_{a1} = 1.7 \times 10^{-2}\ (25°C) \quad [23.21]$$

$$HSO_3^-(aq) \rightleftharpoons H^+(aq) + SO_3^{2-}(aq) \qquad K_{a2} = 6.4 \times 10^{-8}\ (25°C) \quad [23.22]$$

Although H_2SO_3 cannot be isolated, salts of SO_3^{2-} (sulfites) and HSO_3^- (hydrogen sulfites or bisulfites) are well known. Small quantities of Na_2SO_3 or $NaHSO_3$ are used as food additives to prevent bacterial spoilage. Because some people are extremely allergic to sulfites, all products with sulfites must now carry a warning disclosing their presence (Figure 23.15).

FIGURE 23.15 The presence of sulfites in foods and beverages is indicated on their labels. (© Richard Megna/ Fundamental Photographs)

As we have seen, combustion of sulfur in air produces mainly SO_2, but small amounts of SO_3 are also formed. The reaction produces mainly SO_2 because the activation-energy barrier for further oxidation to SO_3 is very high unless the reaction is catalyzed. Sulfur trioxide is of great commercial importance because it is the anhydride of sulfuric acid. In the manufacture of sulfuric acid, SO_2 is first obtained by burning sulfur. The SO_2 is then oxidized to SO_3 using a catalyst such as V_2O_5 or platinum. The SO_3 is dissolved in H_2SO_4 because it does not dissolve quickly in water (Equation 23.23). The $H_2S_2O_7$ formed in this reaction, called pyrosulfuric acid, is then added to water to form H_2SO_4, as shown in Equation 23.24:

Learning Goal 17: Write balanced chemical equations for the formation of sulfuric acid from sulfur, and describe the important properties of the acid.

$$SO_3(g) + H_2SO_4(l) \longrightarrow H_2S_2O_7(l) \qquad [23.23]$$

$$H_2S_2O_7(l) + H_2O(l) \longrightarrow 2H_2SO_4(l) \qquad [23.24]$$

Commercial sulfuric acid is generally 98 percent H_2SO_4. It is a dense, colorless, oily liquid that boils at 340°C. Sulfuric acid has many useful properties: it is a strong acid, a good dehydrating agent,* and a moderately good oxidizing agent. Its dehydrating ability is demonstrated in Figure 23.16.

Year after year, the production of sulfuric acid is the largest of any chemical produced in the United States. In 1992, about 4.0×10^{10} kg (44 million tons) were produced in this country. Sulfuric acid is employed in some way in almost all manufacturing. Consequently, its consumption is considered a standard measure of industrial activity.

Sulfuric acid is classified as a strong acid. However, only the first proton in sulfuric acid is completely ionized in aqueous solution. The second proton ionizes only partially:

$$H_2SO_4(aq) \longrightarrow H^+(aq) + HSO_4^-(aq)$$

$$HSO_4^-(aq) \rightleftharpoons H^+(aq) + SO_4^{2-}(aq) \qquad K_a = 1.1 \times 10^{-2}$$

---

*Considerable heat is given off when sulfuric acid is diluted with water. Consequently, dilution must always be done carefully by pouring the acid into water to distribute the heat as uniformly as possible and to avoid spattering of the acid.

FIGURE 23.16 The reaction between sucrose, $C_{12}H_{22}O_{11}$, and concentrated sulfuric acid. Sucrose is a carbohydrate, containing two H atoms for each O atom. Sulfuric acid, which is an excellent dehydrating agent, removes H_2O from the sucrose to form carbon, the black mass remaining at the end of the reaction. (Kristen Brochman/ Fundamental Photographs)

FIGURE 23.17 Comparison of the structures of the sulfate, SO_4^{2-}, and thiosulfate, $S_2O_3^{2-}$, ions.

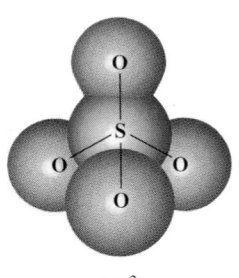

SO_4^{2-}

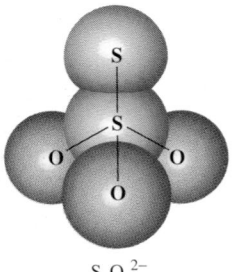

$S_2O_3^{2-}$

Consequently, sulfuric acid forms two series of compounds: sulfates and bisulfates (or hydrogen sulfates). Bisulfate salts are common components of the "dry acids" used for adjusting the pH of swimming pools and hot tubs; they are also components of many toilet bowl cleaners.

Related to the sulfate ion is the thiosulfate ion, $S_2O_3^{2-}$, formed by boiling an alkaline solution of SO_3^{2-} with elemental sulfur:

$$8SO_3^{2-}(aq) + S_8(s) \longrightarrow 8S_2O_3^{2-}(aq) \qquad [23.25]$$

The term *thio* indicates substitution of sulfur for oxygen. The structures of the sulfate and thiosulfate ions are compared in Figure 23.17. When acidified, the thiosulfate ion decomposes to form sulfur and H_2SO_3.

The pentahydrated salt of sodium thiosulfate, $Na_2S_2O_3 \cdot 5H_2O$, known as "hypo," is used in photography. Photographic film consists of a suspension of microcrystals of AgBr in gelatin. When exposed to light, some AgBr decomposes, forming very small grains of silver. When the film is treated with a mild reducing agent (the "developer"), Ag^+ ions in AgBr near the silver grains are reduced, forming an image of black, metallic silver. The film is then treated with sodium thiosulfate solution to remove the unexposed AgBr. The thiosulfate ion reacts with AgBr to form a soluble silver thiosulfate complex:

$$AgBr(s) + 2S_2O_3^{2-}(aq) \rightleftharpoons Ag(S_2O_3)_2^{3-}(aq) + Br^-(aq) \qquad [23.26]$$

This step in the process is called "fixing." Thiosulfate ion is also used in quantitative analysis as a reducing agent for iodine:

$$2S_2O_3{}^{2-}(aq) + I_2(s) \longrightarrow 2I^-(aq) + S_4O_6{}^{2-}(aq) \qquad [23.27]$$

Oxides, Oxyacids, and Oxyanions of Se and Te

Selenium and tellurium form acidic dioxides and trioxides. Selenium dioxide, SeO_2, dissolves in water producing selenous acid, H_2SeO_3, a weak diprotic acid. Tellurium dioxide, TeO_2, is insoluble in water, but tellurite salts such as $NaHTeO_3$ and Na_2TeO_3 form when TeO_2 is dissolved in an aqueous base.

Oxidation of H_2SeO_3 with hydrogen peroxide produces selenic acid, H_2SeO_4, a strong diprotic acid that resembles sulfuric acid:

$$H_2SeO_3(aq) + H_2O_2(aq) \longrightarrow HSeO_4{}^-(aq) + H_2O(l) + H^+(aq) \qquad [23.28]$$

Telluric acid (also called orthotelluric acid) forms when TeO_2 is treated with various aqueous oxidizing agents. We might expect the formula for this acid to be H_2TeO_4 by analogy with the corresponding acids of sulfur and selenium. However, orthotelluric acid is H_6TeO_6, which can be viewed as the result of adding two molecules of H_2O to H_2TeO_4. [The formula can also be written $Te(OH)_6$.] As in H_5IO_6 (Figure 23.10), the central atom in H_6TeO_6 is surrounded by six O atoms. The large sizes of Te and I permit them to bond to six surrounding O atoms. Orthotelluric acid is a weak acid, capable of dissociating two protons in aqueous solution (at 25°C, $K_{a1} = 2.4 \times 10^{-8}$, $K_{a2} = 1.0 \times 10^{-11}$).

Sulfides, Selenides, and Tellurides

Sulfur forms compounds by direct combination with many elements. When the element is less electronegative than sulfur, *sulfides,* which contain S^{2-}, form. For example, iron(II) sulfide, FeS, forms by direct combination of iron and sulfur. Many metallic elements are found in the form of sulfide ores, for example, PbS (galena) and HgS (cinnabar). A series of related ores containing the disulfide ion, $S_2{}^{2-}$ (analogous to the peroxide ion), are known as *pyrites.* Iron pyrite, FeS_2, occurs as golden-yellow cubic crystals (Figure 23.18). Because it has been occasionally mistaken for gold by overeager miners, it is often called "fool's gold."

One of the most important sulfides is hydrogen sulfide, H_2S. This substance is not normally produced by direct union of the elements because it is unstable at elevated temperature and decomposes into the elements. It is normally prepared by action of dilute sulfuric acid on iron(II) sulfide:

$$FeS(s) + 2H^+(aq) \longrightarrow H_2S(aq) + Fe^{2+}(aq) \qquad [23.29]$$

Hydrogen sulfide is often used in the laboratory for qualitative analysis of certain metal ions. ⇨ (Sec. 17.6)

One of hydrogen sulfide's most readily recognized properties is its odor; H_2S is largely responsible for the offensive odor of rotten eggs. Hydrogen sulfide is actually quite toxic; it has about the same level of toxicity as hydrogen cyanide, the gas that has been used in gas chambers. Fortunately, our noses are able to detect H_2S in extremely low, nontoxic concentrations. Sulfur-contain-

Learning Goal 18: Compare the chemical behaviors of selenium and tellurium with that of sulfur, with respect to common oxidation states and formulas of oxides and oxyacids.

FIGURE 23.18 Iron pyrite, FeS_2, is also known as fool's gold because its color has fooled people into thinking it was gold. Gold is much more dense and much softer than iron pyrite. (Charles R. Belinky/ Photo Researchers)

23.3 The Group 6A Elements **865**

Point of Emphasis: If not for sulfur-containing additives such as methyl mercaptan, CH_3SH, natural gas would be nearly odorless, and gas leaks would be difficult to detect.

Teaching Note: The smells associated with skunks, garlic, and onions are other examples of the odors caused by sulfur-containing compounds.

ing organic molecules, which are similarly odoriferous, are added to natural gas to give it a detectable odor.

The volatile hydrides H_2Se and H_2Te are similar to H_2S in many respects. Both compounds possess very offensive, lingering odors and are toxic. In aqueous solutions the acid strength increases in the order $H_2S < H_2Se < H_2Te$.

23.4 The Group 5A Elements

The elements of group 5A are nitrogen, phosphorus, arsenic, antimony, and bismuth. We have already discussed the chemistry of nitrogen. ∞ (Sec. 22.5) In our present discussion we will find it convenient to examine the general characteristics of the group, to consider phosphorus, and finally to comment briefly on the heavier elements of the group.

General Characteristics of the Group 5A Elements

7
N

15
P

33
As

51
Sb

83
Bi

The group 5A elements possess the outer-electron configuration ns^2np^3, where n may have values ranging from 2 to 6. A noble-gas configuration results from the addition of three electrons to form the -3 oxidation state. Ionic compounds containing X^{3-} ions are not common, however, except for salts of the more active metals, for example, Na_3N. More commonly, the group 5A element acquires an octet of electrons via covalent bonding. The oxidation number may range from -3 to $+5$, depending on the nature and number of the atoms to which the group 5A element is bonded.

Because of its lower electronegativity, phosphorus is found more frequently in positive oxidation states than is nitrogen. Furthermore, compounds in which phosphorus has the $+5$ oxidation state are not as strongly oxidizing as the corresponding compounds of nitrogen. Conversely, compounds in which phosphorus has a -3 oxidation state are much stronger reducing agents than are corresponding compounds of nitrogen.

Some of the important properties of the atoms of the group 5A elements are listed in Table 23.8. The general pattern that emerges from these data is similar to what we have seen before with other groups: size and metallic character increase as atomic number increases within the group.

The variation in properties among the elements of group 5A is more striking than that seen in groups 6A and 7A. Nitrogen at the one extreme exists

Learning Goal 19: Predict the maximum and minimum oxidation state of each group 5A element discussed in the chapter. Give an example of a compound containing the element in each of those oxidation states.

Point of Emphasis: Common oxidation states of the group 5A elements are -3, -1, $+1$, $+3$, $+5$.

TABLE 23.8 △ Properties of the Atoms of the Group 5A Elements

Property	N	P	As	Sb	Bi
Atomic radius (Å)	0.70	1.10	1.20	1.40	1.50
First ionization energy (kJ/mol)	1402	1012	947	834	703
Electron affinity (kJ/mol)	$+6.8$	-72	-77	-101	-106
Electronegativity	3.0	2.1	2.0	1.9	1.9
X—X single-bond energy (kJ/mol)[a]	163	200	150	120	—
X≡X triple-bond energy (kJ/mol)	941	490	380	295	192

[a] Approximate values only.

as a gaseous diatomic molecule; it is clearly nonmetallic in character. At the other extreme, bismuth is a reddish-white, metallic-looking substance that has most of the characteristics of a metal.

The values listed for X—X single-bond energies are not very reliable because it is difficult to obtain such data from thermochemical experiments. However, there is no doubt about the general trend: a low value for the N—N single bond, an increase at phosphorus, and then a gradual decline to arsenic and antimony. From observations of the group 5A elements in the gas phase, it is possible to estimate the X≡X triple-bond energy, as listed in Table 23.8. Here we see a trend that is different than that for the X—X single bond. Nitrogen forms a much stronger bond than do the other elements, and there is a steady decline in the triple-bond energy down through the group. These data help us to appreciate why nitrogen alone of the group 5A elements exists as a diatomic molecule in its stable state at 25°C. All the other elements exist in structural forms with single bonds between the atoms.

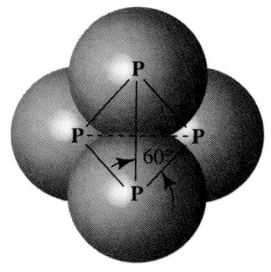

P_4

FIGURE 23.19 Tetrahedral structure of the P_4 molecule of white phosphorus.

Occurrence, Isolation, and Properties of Phosphorus

Phosphorus occurs mainly in the form of phosphate minerals. The principal source of phosphorus is phosphate rock, which contains phosphate mainly as $Ca_3(PO_4)_2$. Deposits of phosphate rock occur mostly in Florida, the western United States, North Africa, and parts of Russia. The element is produced commercially by reduction of phosphate with coke in the presence of SiO_2:

$$2Ca_3(PO_4)_2(s) + 6SiO_2(s) + 10C(s) \xrightarrow{1500°C} P_4(g) + 6CaSiO_3(l) + 10CO(g)$$
$$[23.30]$$

The phosphorus produced in this fashion is the allotrope known as white phosphorus. This form distills from the reaction mixture as the reaction proceeds.

White phosphorus consists of P_4 tetrahedra, as shown in Figure 23.19. The 60° bond angles in P_4 are unusually small for molecules. There must consequently be much strain in the bonding, a fact that is consistent with the high reactivity of white phosphorus. This allotrope bursts spontaneously into flames if exposed to air. It is a white, waxlike solid that melts at 44.2°C and boils at 280°C. When heated in the absence of air to about 400°C, it is converted to a more stable allotrope known as red phosphorus. This form does not ignite on contact with air. It is also considerably less poisonous than the white form. Both allotropes are shown in Figure 23.20.

FIGURE 23.20 White and red allotropes of phosphorus, both stored under water. White phosphorus is very reactive and is normally stored under water to protect it from oxygen. The yellowish cast on the white phosphorus in this photo is due to reactions with air. Red phosphorus is much less reactive than white phosphorus, and it is not necessary to store it under water. (Donald Clegg and Roxy Wilson)

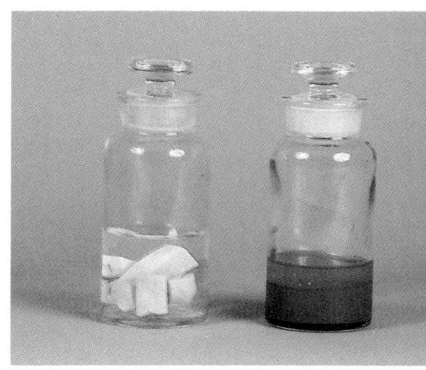

Phosphorus Halides

Phosphorus forms a wide range of compounds with the halogens, the most important of which are the trihalides and pentahalides. Phosphorus trichloride, PCl_3, is commercially the most significant of these compounds and is used to prepare a wide variety of products, including soaps, detergents, plastics, and insecticides.

Phosphorus chlorides, bromides, and iodides can be made by the direct oxidation of elemental phosphorus with the elemental halogen. For example,

PCl_3, which is a liquid at room temperature, is made by passing a stream of dry chlorine gas over white or red phosphorus:

$$2P(s) + 3Cl_2(g) \longrightarrow 2PCl_3(l) \qquad [23.31]$$

If excess chlorine gas is present, an equilibrium is established between PCl_3 and PCl_5:

$$PCl_3(l) + Cl_2(g) \rightleftharpoons PCl_5(s) \qquad [23.32]$$

A similar equilibrium exists between PBr_3 and PBr_5. Phosphorus pentaiodide, PI_5, which was first prepared only in 1978, is made by reacting PCl_5 with I^- in an appropriate solvent.

Because F_2 is such a strong oxidant, the direct reaction of phosphorus with F_2 usually produces the gas PF_5, in which phosphorus is in its most positive oxidation state:

$$2P(s) + 5F_2(g) \longrightarrow 2PF_5(g) \qquad [23.33]$$

Phosphorus trifluoride, PF_3, is most conveniently prepared from PCl_3 via a halogen-exchange reaction with another fluorine-containing compound:

$$PCl_3(l) + AsF_3(l) \longrightarrow PF_3(g) + AsCl_3(l) \qquad [23.34]$$

The driving force for this reaction is the greater strength of the phosphorus-fluorine bond as compared with the other bond energies (490 kJ/mol for P—F as compared with 406 kJ/mol for As—F, 326 kJ/mol for P—Cl, and 322 kJ/mol for As—Cl).

In the trihalides, the central phosphorus atom has three bonding electron pairs and one nonbonding pair in its valence shell, giving rise to a pyramidal structure. ∞ (Sec. 9.1)   In the pentahalides, the phosphorus is surrounded by 10 valence-shell electrons. Therefore, we would expect these molecules to have trigonal-bipyramidal structures. In fact, PF_5 has this structure in both the vapor and solid phases. In contrast, PCl_5 has this structure in the vapor, but the solid consists of $[PCl_4]^+$ tetrahedra and $[PCl_6]^-$ octahedra. Solid PBr_5, which dissociates into PBr_3 and Br_2 when vaporized, consists of $[PBr_4]^+$ tetrahedra and Br^- ions.

The phosphorus halides hydrolyze on contact with water. The reactions occur readily, and most of the phosphorus halides fume in air as a result of reaction with water vapor. In the presence of excess water, the products are the corresponding phosphorus oxyacid and hydrogen halide, as in the following examples:

$$PF_3(g) + 3H_2O(l) \longrightarrow H_3PO_3(aq) + 3HF(aq) \qquad [23.35]$$

$$PCl_5(l) + 4H_2O(l) \longrightarrow H_3PO_4(aq) + 5HCl(aq) \qquad [23.36]$$

Oxy Compounds of Phosphorus

Probably the most significant compounds of phosphorus are those in which the element is combined in some way with oxygen. Phosphorus(III) oxide, P_4O_6, is obtained by allowing white phosphorus to oxidize in a limited supply of oxygen. When oxidation takes place in the presence of excess oxygen, phosphorus(V) oxide, P_4O_{10}, forms. This compound is also readily formed by oxidation of P_4O_6. These two oxides represent the two most common oxidation states for phosphorus, $+3$ and $+5$. The structural relationship between P_4O_6 and P_4O_{10} is shown in Figure 23.21. Notice the resemblance these molecules have to the P_4 molecule, Figure 23.19; all three substances have a P_4 core.

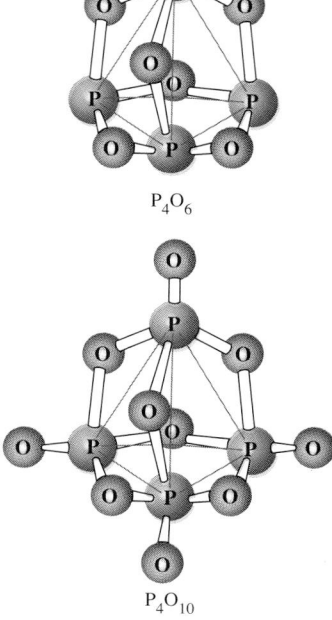

P_4O_6

P_4O_{10}

FIGURE 23.21 Structures of P_4O_6 and P_4O_{10}.

SAMPLE EXERCISE 23.6

The reactive chemicals on the tip of a "strike anywhere" match are usually P_4S_3 and an oxidizing agent such as $KClO_3$. When the match is struck on a rough surface, the heat generated by the friction ignites the P_4S_3, and the oxidizing agent brings about rapid combustion. The products of the combustion are P_4O_{10} and SO_2. Calculate the standard enthalpy for the combustion of P_4S_3 in air, given the following standard enthalpies of formation: P_4S_3 (-154.4 kJ/mol); P_4O_{10} (-2940 kJ/mol); SO_2 (-296.9 kJ/mol).

SOLUTION The chemical equation for the combustion is

$$P_4S_3(s) + 8O_2(g) \longrightarrow P_4O_{10}(s) + 3SO_2(g)$$

Recalling that the standard enthalpy of formation of any element in its standard state is zero, we have $\Delta H_f^\circ(O_2) = 0$. Thus we can write

$$\Delta H^\circ = \Delta H_f^\circ(P_4O_{10}) + 3\Delta H_f^\circ(SO_2) - \Delta H_f^\circ(P_4S_3)$$
$$= -2940 \text{ kJ} + 3(-296.9) \text{ kJ} - (-154.4 \text{ kJ})$$
$$= -3616 \text{ kJ}$$

The reaction is strongly exothermic, making it evident why P_4S_3 is used on match tips.

FIGURE 23.22 Structures of H_3PO_4 and H_3PO_3.

PRACTICE EXERCISE

Write the balanced equation for the reaction of P_4O_{10} with water and calculate ΔH° for this reaction using data from Appendix D.
Answer: $P_4O_{10}(s) + 6H_2O(l) \longrightarrow 4H_3PO_4(aq)$; -498.0 kJ

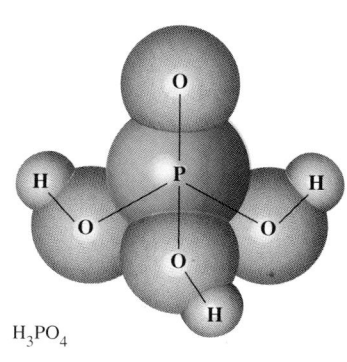

H_3PO_4

Phosphorus(V) oxide is the anhydride of phosphoric acid, H_3PO_4, a weak triprotic acid. In fact, P_4O_{10} has a very high affinity for water and is consequently used as a drying agent. Phosphorus(III) oxide is the anhydride of phosphorous acid, H_3PO_3, a weak diprotic acid.* The structures of H_3PO_4 and H_3PO_3 are shown in Figure 23.22. The hydrogen atom that is attached directly to phosphorus in H_3PO_3 is not acidic.

One characteristic of phosphoric and phosphorus acids is their tendency to undergo condensation reactions when heated. A *condensation reaction* is one in which two or more molecules combine to form a larger molecule by eliminating a small molecule, for example, H_2O. ∞ (Sec. 12.2) The reaction in which two H_3PO_4 molecules are joined by the elimination of one H_2O molecule to form $H_4P_2O_7$ is represented in Equation 23.37.

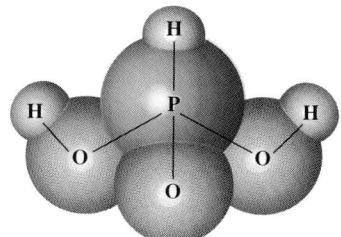

H_3PO_3

---

* Note that the element phosphor*us* (FOS·for·us) has an -*us* suffix, whereas phosphor*ous* (fos·FOR·us) acid has an -*ous* suffix.

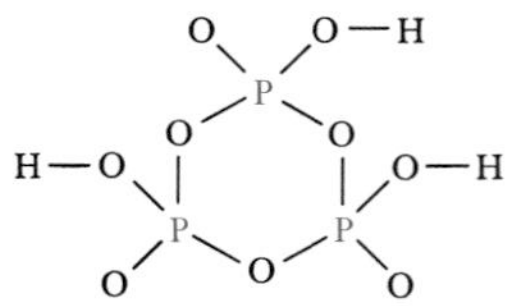

(HPO₃)₃
Trimetaphosphoric acid

Repeating unit from which empirical formula is obtained

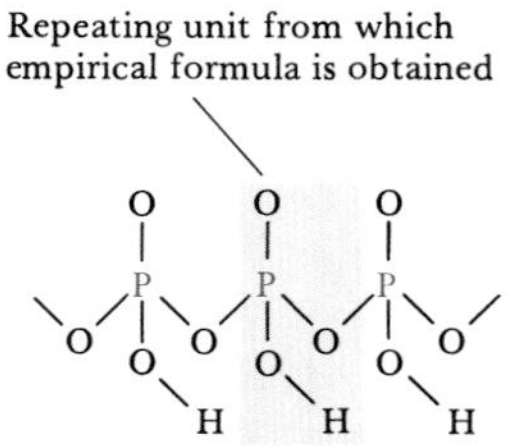

(HPO₃)ₙ
Polymetaphosphoric acid

FIGURE 23.23 Structures of trimetaphosphoric acid and polymetaphosphoric acid.

Learning Goal 25: Describe a condensation reaction, and give examples involving compounds of phosphorus.

Teaching Note: Phosphoric acid is also an ingredient in cola soft drinks.

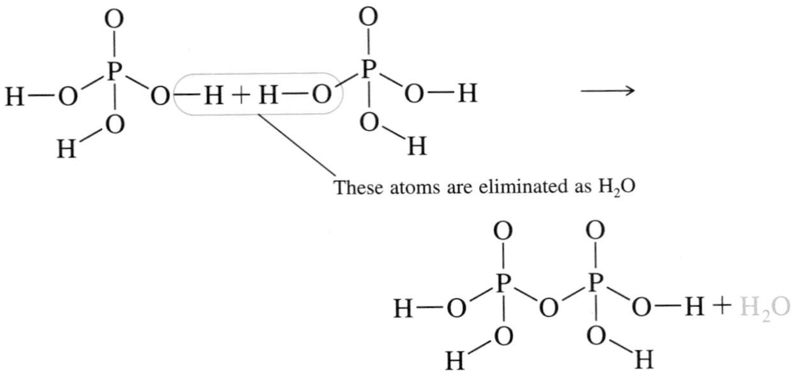

These atoms are eliminated as H₂O

$$H-O-\overset{O}{\underset{H}{\overset{|}{P}}}-O-\overset{O}{\underset{H}{\overset{|}{P}}}-O-H + H_2O \qquad [23.37]$$

Further condensation produces phosphates having an empirical formula of HPO_3.

$$nH_3PO_4 \longrightarrow (HPO_3)_n + nH_2O \qquad [23.38]$$

Two phosphates having this empirical formula, one cyclic and the other polymeric, are shown in Figure 23.23. The three acids H_3PO_4, $H_4P_2O_7$, and $(HPO_3)_n$ all contain phosphorus in its $+5$ oxidation state, and all are therefore called phosphoric acids. To differentiate them, the prefixes *ortho-*, *pyro-*, and *meta-* are used: H_3PO_4 is orthophosphoric acid, $H_4P_2O_7$ is pyrophosphoric acid, and HPO_3 is metaphosphoric acid.

Phosphoric acid and its salts find their most important uses in detergents and fertilizers. The phosphates in detergents are often in the form of sodium tripolyphosphate, $Na_5P_3O_{10}$ (Section 25.2). A typical detergent formulation contains 47 percent phosphate, 16 percent bleaches, perfumes, and abrasives, and 37 percent linear alkylsulfonate (LAS) surfactant (shown as follows):

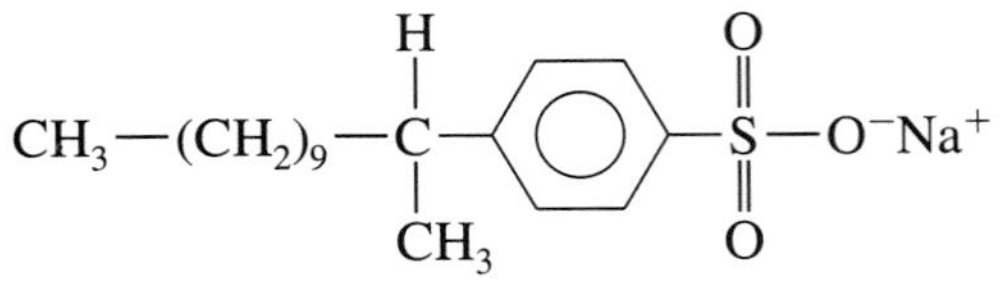

(We have used the notation for the benzene ring described in Section 9.5.) The phosphate ions form bonds with metal ions that contribute to the hardness of water. This keeps the metal ions from interfering with the action of the surfactant. The phosphates also keep the pH above 7 and thus prevent the surfactant molecules from becoming protonated (gaining an H^+ ion).

Most mined phosphate rock is converted to fertilizers. The $Ca_3(PO_4)_2$ in phosphate rock is insoluble ($K_{sp} = 2.0 \times 10^{-29}$). It is converted to a soluble form for use in fertilizers by treating the concentrated phosphate rock with sulfuric or phosphoric acid:

$$Ca_3(PO_4)_2(s) + 4H^+(aq) + 3SO_4^{2-}(aq) \longrightarrow$$
$$3CaSO_4(s) + 2H_2PO_4^-(aq) \qquad [23.39]$$

$$Ca_3(PO_4)_2(s) + 4H^+(aq) \longrightarrow 3Ca^{2+}(aq) + 2H_2PO_4^-(aq) \qquad [23.40]$$

The mixture formed when ground phosphate rock is treated with sulfuric acid and then dried and pulverized is known as superphosphate. The $CaSO_4$ formed in this process is of little use in soil except when deficiencies in calcium or sulfur exist. It also dilutes the phosphorus, which is the nutrient of interest. If the phosphate rock is treated with phosphoric acid, the product contains no $CaSO_4$ and has a higher percentage of phosphorus. This product is known as triple superphosphate. Although the solubility of $Ca(H_2PO_4)_2$ allows it to be assimilated by plants, it also allows it to be washed from the soil and into water bodies, thereby contributing to water pollution. ∞(Sec. 18.6)

Phosphorus compounds are important in biological systems. The element occurs, for example, in phosphate groups in RNA and DNA, the molecules responsible for control of protein biosynthesis and transmission of genetic information (Section 26.7). It also occurs in adenosine triphosphate (ATP), which stores energy within biological cells:

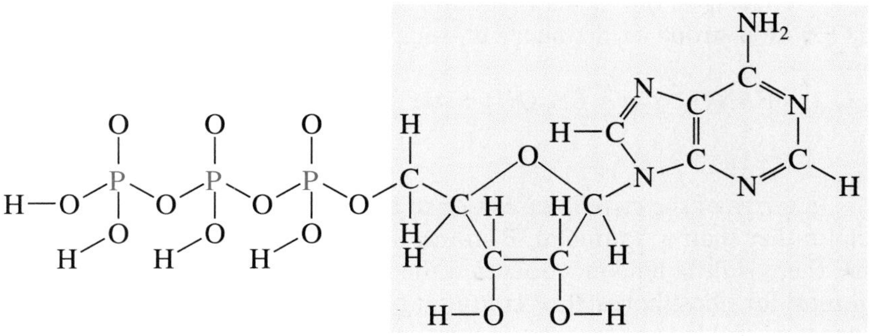

Adenosine

The P—O—P bond of the end phosphate group is broken by hydrolysis with water, forming adenosine diphosphate (ADP). This reaction produces 33 kJ of energy:

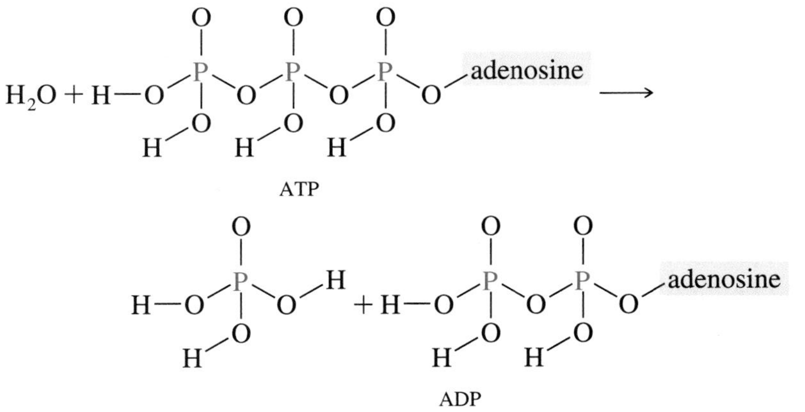

ATP

ADP [23.41]

This energy is used to perform the mechanical work in muscle contraction and in many other biochemical reactions (Figure 19.11).

Arsenic, Antimony, and Bismuth

Arsenic, antimony, and bismuth occur in nature in the form of sulfide minerals, such as As_2S_3, Sb_2S_3, and Bi_2S_3. In addition, the elements are found as minor components in ores of various metals, such as Cu, Pb, Ag, and Hg. Arsenic and antimony exhibit allotropy similar to that of phosphorus. Both elements can be prepared as soft, yellow, nonmetallic solids by quickly cooling the high-temperature vapor of the element. In this allotropic form, the elements are present as As_4 or Sb_4 tetrahedra, analogous to the white allotrope of phosphorus. Heating or the action of light converts the substances into the gray, more metallic forms containing sheets of atoms. In its common form, bismuth has a reddish-white, rather metallic appearance. The element forms alloys with many metallic elements. Alloys of lead, bismuth, and tin are used in the construction of low-melting plugs in fire-sprinkler systems. Water is discharged when the metal plug melts.

Arsenic and antimony resemble phosphorus in much of their chemical behavior. For example, the oxy compounds of these two elements are rather similar to those of phosphorus, except that the higher oxidation state is not so easily attained. Thus, the product of burning arsenic in oxygen is As_4O_6, not As_4O_{10}. Arsenic in the higher oxidation state can be obtained by oxidation of As_4O_6 with a strong oxidizing agent, such as nitric acid:

$$As_4O_6(s) + 4NO_3^-(aq) + 6H_2O(l) + 4H^+(aq) \longrightarrow$$
$$4H_3AsO_4(aq) + 4HNO_2(aq) \quad [23.42]$$

In terms of the criteria discussed in Section 7.6, bismuth is considered a metal rather than a nonmetal. Bismuth usually appears in the $+3$ oxidation state; there is little tendency to attain the higher $+5$ oxidation state that is so common for phosphorus. The common oxide of bismuth is Bi_2O_3. This substance is insoluble in water or basic solution but is soluble in acidic solution. It is therefore classified as a basic anhydride. As we have seen, the oxides of metals characteristically behave as basic anhydrides. ∞ (Sec. 22.4)

23.5 The Group 4A Elements

6
C

14
Si

32
Ge

50
Sn

82
Pb

The elements of group 4A are carbon, silicon, germanium, tin, and lead. The general trend from nonmetallic to metallic as we go down a family is strikingly evident in group 4A. Carbon is strictly nonmetallic; silicon is essentially nonmetallic, although it does exhibit some characteristics of a metalloid, particularly in its electrical and physical properties; germanium is a metalloid; tin and lead are both metallic. We discussed the chemistry of carbon in Section 22.6. In the present discussion we will consider a few general characteristics of group 4A and then look more thoroughly at silicon.

General Characteristics of the Group 4A Elements

Some properties of the group 4A elements are given in Table 23.9. The elements possess the outer-electron configuration ns^2np^2. The electronegativities of the elements are generally low; carbides that formally contain C^{4-} ions are observed only in the case of a very few compounds of carbon with very active metals. Formation of 4+ ions by electron loss is not observed for any of these elements; the ionization energies are too high. However, the 2+ state is found in the chemistry of germanium, tin, and lead; it is the principal oxidation state for lead. The vast majority of the compounds of the group 4A elements are covalently bonded. Carbon forms a maximum of four bonds. The other members of the family are able to form higher coordination numbers because of the availability of d orbitals for bonding.

TABLE 23.9 △ Some Properties of the Group 4A Elements

Property	C	Si	Ge	Sn	Pb
Atomic radius (Å)	0.77	1.18	1.22	1.41	1.46
First ionization energy (kJ/mol)	1086	786	761	708	715
Electronegativity	2.5	1.8	1.8	1.8	1.9
X—X single-bond energy (kJ/mol)	348	226	188	151	—

Carbon differs from the other group 4A elements in its pronounced ability to form multiple bonds both with itself and with other nonmetals, especially N, O, and S. The origin of this behavior was considered earlier. ∞(Sec. 22.1)

Table 23.9 shows that the strength of a bond between two atoms of a given element decreases as we go down group 4A. Carbon-carbon bonds are quite strong. As a consequence, carbon has a striking ability to form compounds in which carbon atoms are bonded to one another. This property permits the formation of extended chains and rings of carbon atoms and accounts for the large number of organic compounds that exist. Other elements, especially those in the vicinity of carbon in the periodic table, can also form chains and rings. However, such self-linkage is far less important in the chemistries of these other elements. For example, the Si—Si bond strength (226 kJ/mol) is far smaller than the Si—O bond strength (368 kJ/mol). As a result, the chemistry of silicon is dominated by the formation of Si—O bonds, and Si—Si bonds play a rather minor role.

Occurrence and Preparation of Silicon

Silicon is the second most abundant element, after oxygen, in the earth's crust. It occurs in SiO_2 and in an enormous variety of silicate minerals. The element is obtained by the reduction of molten silicon dioxide with carbon at high temperature:

$$SiO_2(l) + 2C(s) \longrightarrow Si(l) + 2CO(g) \qquad [23.43]$$

Learning Goal 26: Cite the most common occurrences of silicon and the most common form of elemental silicon.

Elemental silicon has a diamond-type structure [see Figure 11.40(a)]. Crystalline silicon is a gray, metallic-looking solid that melts at 1410°C (Figure 23.24). The element is a semiconductor (Section 24.5) and is thus used in making transistors and solar cells. To be used as a semiconductor, it must be extremely pure. One method of purification is to treat the element with Cl_2 to form $SiCl_4$. The $SiCl_4$ is a volatile liquid that is purified by fractional distillation and then converted back to elemental silicon by reduction with H_2:

$$SiCl_4(g) + 2H_2(g) \longrightarrow Si(s) + 4HCl(g) \qquad [23.44]$$

The element can be further purified by the process of zone refining. In the zone-refining process, a heated coil is passed slowly along a silicon rod, as shown in Figure 23.25. A narrow band of the element is thereby melted. As the molten area is swept slowly along the length of the rod, the impurities concentrate in the molten region, following it to the end of the rod. The end in which the impurities are collected is cut off and recycled through the purification process starting with the formation of $SiCl_4$. The purified top portion of the rod is retained for manufacture of electronic devices.

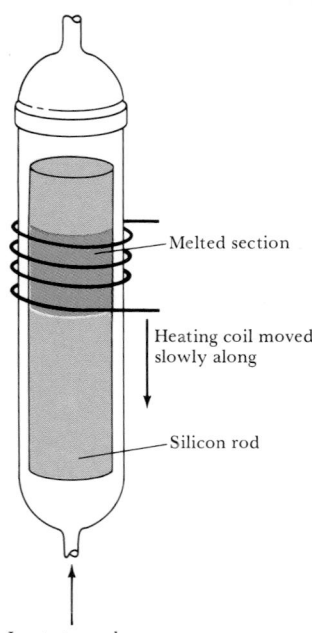

FIGURE 23.24 Elemental silicon. To prepare electronic devices, silicon (powder, left) is melted, drawn into a single crystal, and purified by zone refining. Wafers of silicon, cut from the crystal, are subsequently treated by a series of elegant techniques to produce various electronic devices. (Courtesy of Texas Instruments)

FIGURE 23.25 Zone-refining apparatus.

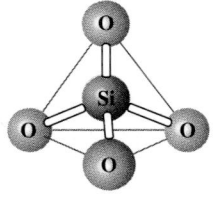

FIGURE 23.26 Structure of the SiO₄ tetrahedron of the SiO_4^{4-} ion. This ion is found in several minerals, such as zircon, $ZrSiO_4$.

Silicates

Silicon dioxide and other compounds that contain silicon and oxygen comprise over 90 percent of the earth's crust. **Silicates** are compounds in which a silicon atom is surrounded in a tetrahedral fashion by four oxygens, as shown in Figure 23.26. In silicates, silicon is found in its most common oxidation state, $+4$. The simple SiO_4^{4-} ion, which is known as the orthosilicate ion, is found in very few silicate minerals. Usually, silicate tetrahedra share oxygen atoms to build up more complex structures containing Si—O—Si linkages. When two tetrahedra share a single oxygen, the $Si_2O_7^{6-}$ ion shown in Figure 23.27 results.

It is possible to form a chain of SiO_4 tetrahedra by sharing oxygens at two corners of each tetrahedron, as shown in Figure 23.28. The simplest formula

FIGURE 23.27 Geometrical structure of the $Si_2O_7^{6-}$ ion, which is formed by the sharing of an oxygen atom by two silicon atoms. This ion occurs in several minerals, such as hardystonite, $Ca_2Zn(Si_2O_7)$.

 Figure 23.28

FIGURE 23.28 Schematic representation of a single-strand silicate chain. This chain has an empirical formula of SiO_3^{2-}, as in the mineral enstatite, $MgSiO_3$.

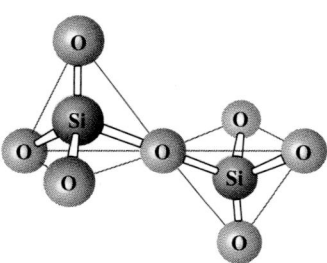

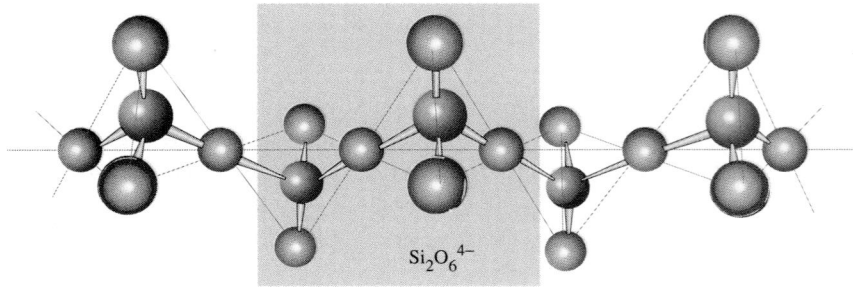

$Si_2O_6^{4-}$

Repeating unit of chain

The Asbestos Minerals

Asbestos is a general term applied to a group of fibrous silicate minerals. These minerals possess chainlike arrangements of the silicate tetrahedra, or sheet structures in which the sheets are formed into rolls. The result is that the minerals have a fibrous character, as shown in Figure 23.29. Asbestos has been widely used as thermal insulation material, especially in high-temperature applications where the high chemical stability of the silicate structure serves well. Until the last decade, asbestos was extensively used as a thermal insulator in buildings. However, in recent years there has been a growing awareness that certain forms of asbestos pose a health hazard. Tiny fibers readily penetrate the tissues of the lungs and digestive tract, and they remain there over a long period of time. Eventually, they may cause lesions, including cancers, within the body.

FIGURE 23.29   (*a*) Serpentine asbestos; note the fibrous character of this mineral. (*b*) Fibers of amosite, an asbestos mineral, viewed under a polarizing microscope. (Bureau of Mines, U.S. Department of the Interior: Don Thomson/Science Photo Library/Photo Researchers)

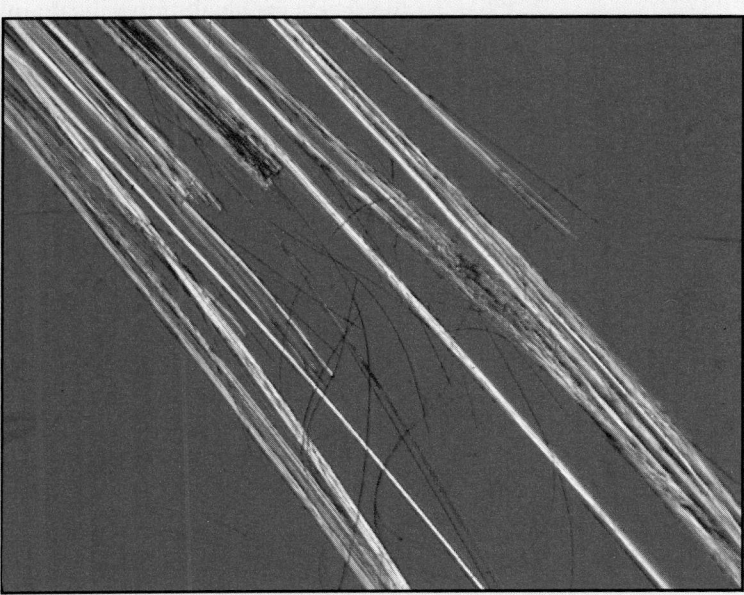

(*a*)   (*b*)

associated with this single-chain silicate anion is SiO_3^{2-}. This anion occurs, for example, in the mineral enstatite, $MgSiO_3$, which consists of silicate chains with Mg^{2+} ions between strands to balance charge.

Other, more complex, structures are also found in silicates. For example, it is possible for each tetrahedron to share three corners, giving rise to sheet structures. Such an arrangement results in a simplest formula $Si_2O_5^{2-}$ as in talc, $Mg_3(Si_2O_5)_2(OH)_2$. When all four oxygens of each SiO_4 unit have Si—O—Si linkages, the structure extends in all three dimensions in space, forming quartz,

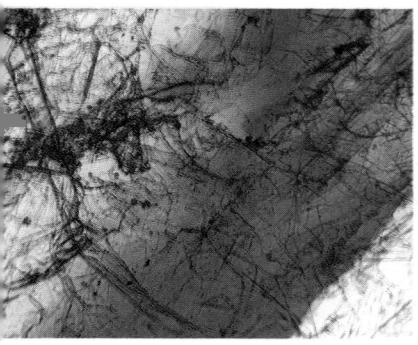

FIGURE 23.30 A thin sheet of mica viewed under polarized light through a microscope. (Paul Silverman/ Fundamental Photographs)

SiO_2. Because the structure is locked together in a three-dimensional array much like diamond, quartz is harder than the strand or sheet-type silicates.

Aluminosilicates

In many silicate minerals, Si^{4+} ions are replaced by Al^{3+} ions within the silicate tetrahedra. This replacement produces **aluminosilicates.** In order to maintain charge balance, an extra cation, such as K^+, must accompany each of these substitutions. Muscovite, $KAl_2(AlSi_3O_{10})(OH)_2$,* a mica mineral, is an aluminosilicate.

Replacement of a quarter of the silicon atoms in a sheet silicate, $Si_4O_{10}^{4-}$, with aluminum produces the $AlSi_3O_{10}^{5-}$ sheets found in muscovite. In both the silicate-sheet and aluminosilicate-sheet minerals, cations are located between sheets to balance the charge. The electrostatic attraction between these cations and the charges in the sheets is greater for the aluminosilicate than for the corresponding silicate because there are higher charges in the aluminosilicates. Thus, the sheets in the silicate mineral talc slide readily over one another, but the sheets in the aluminosilicate mica do not. Nevertheless, mica does cleave readily into thin sheets, as illustrated in Figure 23.30.

When aluminum replaces up to half of the silicon atoms in SiO_2, the *feldspar* minerals result. Orthoclase, $KAlSi_3O_8$, is a common feldspar mineral. The cations that compensate for the extra negative charge accompanying this replacement are usually Na^+, K^+ or Ca^{2+} ions. The feldspars are the most abundant rock-forming silicates, comprising about 50 percent of the minerals in the earth's crust.

SAMPLE EXERCISE 23.7

The mineral anorthite is a feldspar mineral formed by replacing half of the silicon atoms in SiO_2 with aluminum and maintaining charge balance with Ca^{2+} ions. What is the simplest formula for this mineral?

SOLUTION If we write SiO_2 as Si_2O_4, the replacement of half of the Si^{4+} with Al^{3+} produces $AlSiO_4^-$. One Ca^{2+} therefore requires two $AlSiO_4^-$ units to maintain charge balance, and the empirical formula of the mineral is $CaAl_2Si_2O_8$.

PRACTICE EXERCISE

The mineral albite may be considered to form by replacement of one-fourth of the Si atoms of SiO_2 with Al and maintaining charge balance with Na^+ ions. What is the chemical formula of this mineral? ***Answer:*** $NaAlSi_3O_8$

The **clay minerals** are hydrated aluminosilicates having sheet-type structures. An example is kaolinite, $Al_2Si_2O_5(OH)_4$. These minerals have small particle size and correspondingly large surface areas. They have the ability to adsorb cations on their surfaces. Often the metal ions displace H^+ ions from the OH groups on the surfaces of the clay particle:

$$M^+(aq) + H—O—clay \rightleftharpoons H^+(aq) + M—O—clay \qquad [23.45]$$

---

* Aluminum is found in this mineral in two different environments. The first two Al^{3+} ions are located between the aluminosilicate sheets. The aluminum that is shown in parentheses is located within the sheets. It has replaced a silicon and is therefore located in an AlO_4 tetrahedron.

This situation gives rise to pH-dependent equilibria. Notice that the higher the concentration of $H^+(aq)$, the more the equilibrium is shifted to the left. If the soil is basic, the equilibrium lies to the right, and $M^+(aq)$ is not available to plants. Thus, the pH of the soil plays an important role in determining the soil's fertility (that is, its ability to supply plants with essential nutrients).

Glass

Quartz melts at approximately $1600°C$, forming a tacky liquid. In the course of melting, many silicon-oxygen bonds are broken. When the liquid is rapidly cooled, silicon-oxygen bonds are re-formed before the atoms are able to arrange themselves in a regular fashion. An amorphous solid, known as quartz glass or silica glass, results (see Figure 11.27). Many different substances can be added to SiO_2 to cause it to melt at a lower temperature. The common **glass** used in windows and bottles is known as soda-lime glass. It contains CaO and Na_2O in addition to SiO_2 from sand. The CaO and Na_2O are produced by heating two inexpensive chemicals: limestone, $CaCO_3$, and soda ash, Na_2CO_3. These carbonates decompose at elevated temperatures:

Learning Goal 31: Describe the composition and manufacture of soda-lime glass.

$$CaCO_3(s) \longrightarrow CaO(s) + CO_2(g) \qquad [23.46]$$

$$Na_2CO_3(s) \longrightarrow Na_2O(s) + CO_2(g) \qquad [23.47]$$

Other substances can be added to soda-lime glass to produce color or to change the properties of the glass in various ways. For example, addition of CoO produces the deep blue color of "cobalt glass." Replacement of Na_2O by K_2O results in a harder glass that has a higher melting point. Replacement of CaO by PbO results in a denser glass with a higher refractive index. Addition of non-metal oxides, such as B_2O_3 and P_2O_5, which form network structures related to the silicates, also causes a change in properties of the glass. Addition of B_2O_3 creates a glass with a higher melting point and a greater ability to withstand temperature changes. Such glasses, sold commercially under trade names such as Pyrex and Kimax, are used where resistance to thermal shock is important, for example, in laboratory glassware or coffee makers. Table 23.10 lists the formulations and properties of several representative types of glass.

Teaching Note: The addition of PbO to glass produces the beautiful "lead crystal" glass used in decorative glassware. The higher refractive index of this glass gives these objects a particularly sparkling appearance.

TABLE 23.10 △ Compositions, Properties, and Uses of Various Types of Glass

Type of glass	Composition by mass	Properties and uses
Soda-lime	12% Na_2O, 12% CaO, 76% SiO_2	Window glass, bottles
Aluminosilicate	5% B_2O_3, 10% MgO, 10% CaO, 20% Al_2O_3, 55% SiO_2	High melting—used in cooking ware
Lead alkali	10% Na_2O, 20% PbO, 70% SiO_2	High refractive index—used in lenses, decorative glass
Borosilicate	5% Na_2O, 3% CaO, 16% B_2O_3, 76% SiO_2	Low coefficient of thermal expansion—used in laboratory ware, cooking utensils
Bioglass	24% Na_2O, 24% CaO, 6% P_2O_5, 46% SiO_2	Compatible with bone—used as coating on surgical implants

CHEMISTRY AT WORK

Optical Fibers

Optical fibers (Figure 23.31) represent a high-technology application of glassmaking. An optical fiber is a glass thread that conducts light, just as a copper wire conducts electrons. Optical fibers transmit information, using the light waves that pass through the fiber. Optical fibers are capable of carrying much more information for a given cross section of fiber than can be transmitted via the conventional coaxial cable.

The key to long-distance transmission of signals via optical fibers is glass purity. Impurities, such as Fe^{2+},

cause absorption of the light waves, with resulting signal loss. Today it is possible to obtain optical fibers that undergo a loss of only about 1 percent of signal over a distance of 1 km. To achieve that level of performance, impurities must be reduced to the level of 1 ppb. This ultrahigh purity is achieved by distilling high-purity liquid glass to separate it from any remaining impurities.

FIGURE 23.31 The optical fiber on the right has the same information-carrying capacity as the much larger copper cable on the left. (Corning, Inc.)

Silicones

Silicones consist of O—Si—O chains in which the remaining bonding positions on each silicon are occupied by organic groups such as CH_3:

$$\cdots \overset{\displaystyle H_3C \quad CH_3}{\underset{O}{Si}} \overset{\displaystyle H_3C \quad CH_3}{\underset{O}{Si}} \overset{\displaystyle H_3C \quad CH_3}{\underset{O}{Si}} \cdots$$

Depending on the length of the chain and the degree of crosslinking between chains, silicones can be either oils or rubberlike materials. Silicones are nontoxic and have good stability toward heat, light, oxygen, and water. They are used commercially in a wide variety of products, including lubricants, car polishes, sealants, and gaskets. They are also used for waterproofing fabrics. When applied to a fabric, the oxygen atoms form hydrogen bonds with the molecules on the surface of the fabric. The hydrophobic (water-repelling) organic groups of the silicone are then left pointing away from the surface as a barrier.

23.6 Boron

At this point there is only one additional element to consider in our survey of nonmetallic elements: boron. Boron is the only element of group 3A that can be considered nonmetallic. The element has an extended network structure. Its melting point, 2300°C, is intermediate between that of carbon, 3550°C, and that of silicon, 1410°C. The electronic configuration of boron is $[He]2s^2 2p^1$.

Numerous molecules contain only boron and hydrogen, a family of compounds called **boranes**. The simplest borane is BH_3. This molecule contains only six valence electrons and is therefore an exception to the octet rule. ∞ (Sec. 8.8) As a result, BH_3 reacts with itself to form *diborane,* B_2H_6. This reaction can be viewed as a Lewis acid-base reaction (Section 16.10), in which one B-H bonding pair of electrons in each BH_3 molecule is donated to the other. As a result, diborane is an unusual molecule in which hydrogen atoms appear to form two bonds (Figure 23.32).

The sharing of hydrogen atoms between the two boron atoms compensates somewhat for the deficiency in valence electrons around each boron. Nevertheless, diborane is an extremely reactive molecule that is spontaneously flammable in air. The reaction of B_2H_6 with O_2 is extremely exothermic:

$$B_2H_6(g) + 3O_2(g) \longrightarrow B_2O_3(s) + 3H_2O(g) \quad \Delta H = -2030 \text{ kJ} \quad [23.48]$$

Other boranes, such as pentaborane(9), B_5H_9, are also very reactive. Decaborane, $B_{10}H_{14}$, is stable in air at room temperature, but it undergoes a very exothermic reaction with O_2 at higher temperatures. Boranes have been explored as solid fuels for rockets.

Boron and hydrogen also form a series of anions, called *borane anions.* Salts of the borohydride ion, BH_4^-, are widely used as reducing agents. This ion is isoelectronic to CH_4 and NH_4^+. The lower charge of the central atom in BH_4^- means that the hydrogens of the BH_4^- are "hydridic"; that is, they carry a partial negative charge. Thus, it is not surprising that borohydrides are good reducing agents, as illustrated by the reaction in Equation 23.49:

$$3BH_4^-(aq) + 4IO_3^-(aq) \longrightarrow 4I^-(aq) + 3H_2BO_3^-(aq) + 3H_2O(l) \quad [23.49]$$

The only important oxide of boron is boric oxide, B_2O_3. This substance is the anhydride of boric acid, which we may write as H_3BO_3 or $B(OH)_3$. Boric acid is so weak an acid that solutions of H_3BO_3 are used as an eyewash. Upon heating, orthoboric acid loses water by a condensation reaction similar to that described for phosphorus in Section 23.4:

$$4H_3BO_3(s) \longrightarrow H_2B_4O_7(s) + 5H_2O(g) \quad [23.50]$$

5	B
13	Al
31	Ga
49	In
81	Tl

FIGURE 23.32 The structure of diborane, B_2H_6. Two of the hydrogen atoms bridge between the two B atoms, giving a planar B_2H_2 core to the molecule. Two of the remaining H atoms lie on either side of the B_2H_2 core, giving a nearly tetrahedral bonding environment about the B atoms.

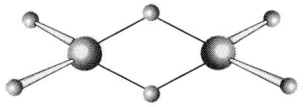

Diborane, B_2H_6

Learning Goal 32: Cite the most common occurrence of boron.

Learning Goal 33: Describe the structure of diborane, and explain its unusual feature.

Learning Goal 34: Describe a condensation reaction involving compounds of boron.

The diprotic acid $H_2B_4O_7$ is called tetraboric acid. The sodium salt, $Na_2B_4O_7 \cdot 10H_2O$, called borax, occurs in dry lake deposits in California and can also be readily prepared from other borate minerals. Solutions of borax are alkaline, and the substance is used in various laundry and cleaning products.

 # For Review

Summary

The noble-gas elements exhibit a very limited chemical behavior because of the exceptional stability of their electronic configurations. The xenon fluorides and oxides and KrF_2 are the best established examples of chemical reactivity among these elements.

The halogens occur as diatomic molecules. These elements possess the highest electronegativities of the elements in each row of the periodic table. All except fluorine exhibit oxidation states varying from -1 to $+7$. Fluorine, being the most electronegative element, is restricted to the oxidation states 0 and -1. The tendency to form the -1 oxidation state from the free element (that is, the oxidizing power of the element) decreases with increasing atomic number. The halogens form compounds with one another, called interhalogens. In the higher interhalogens—XX'_n—the element X may be Cl, Br, or I, and X$'$ is nearly always F; n may have the value 3, 5, or 7.

The group 6A elements range from the very abundant and strongly nonmetallic oxygen to the rare and rather metallic tellurium. Sulfur occurs widely in the form of sulfide ores and in elemental sulfur beds. The element has several allotropic forms; the most stable one consists of S_8 rings. The most important compound of the element is sulfuric acid, a strong acid that is a good dehydrating agent and has a high boiling point. Selenium and tellurium are chemically rather similar to sulfur, especially with respect to formation of oxides and oxyanions.

The group 5A elements exhibit a wide range of behavior, from strongly nonmetallic in the case of nitrogen to distinctly metallic in the case of bismuth.

Phosphorus occurs in nature in certain phosphate minerals. The element exhibits several allotropes, including one known as white phosphorus, a reactive form consisting of P_4 tetrahedra. Phosphorus forms compounds of formula PX_3 and PX_5 with the halogens. These undergo hydrolysis in water to produce the corresponding oxyacid of phosphorus and HX. Phosphorus forms two oxides, P_4O_6 and P_4O_{10}. Their corresponding acids, phosphorous acid and phosphoric acid, show a strong tendency to undergo condensation reactions when heated. Compounds of phosphorus are important components of fertilizers.

The group 4A elements show great diversity in physical and chemical properties. Carbon excels in being able to form multiple bonds and in forming chains of C—C bonds. Silicon is noteworthy as a semiconductor and for its tendency to form Si—O bonds. Silicon is the second most abundant element, and it occurs in a wide variety of silicates. Silicates are composed of SiO_4 tetrahedra, which, by sharing oxygen atoms, are able to link together to form chains, sheets, and three-dimensional arrays. In many minerals, Si^{4+} ions are replaced by Al^{3+} ions, thus forming aluminosilicates. Silicates are important components of glass. Silicones contain O—Si—O chains with organic groups bonded to the Si atoms.

Boranes are compounds that contain only boron and hydrogen. Boron commonly exhibits an oxidation state of $+3$, as in boric oxide, B_2O_3, and boric acid, H_3BO_3. The acid readily undergoes condensation reaction.

Key Terms

interhalogens (Sec. 23.2)

silicates (Sec. 23.5)

aluminosilicates (Sec. 23.5)

clay minerals (Sec. 23.5)

glass (Sec. 23.5)

boranes (Sec. 23.6)

Exercises

23.1. Write the chemical formula for each of the following compounds and indicate the oxidation state of the halogen or noble-gas atom in each: (a) iodate ion; (b) bromic acid; (c) bromine trifluoride; (d) sodium hypochlorite; (e) iodous acid; (f) xenon trioxide.

23.2. Write the chemical formula for each of the following compounds and indicate the oxidation state of the halogen or noble-gas atom in each: (a) calcium bromide; (b) perchloric acid; (c) xenon oxytetrafluoride; (d) chlorite ion; (e) hypobromous acid; (f) iodine pentafluoride.

23.3. Name the following compounds: (a) $KClO_3$; (b) $Ca(IO_3)_2$; (c) $AlCl_3$; (d) $HBrO_3$; (e) H_5IO_6; (f) XeF_4.

23.4. Name the following compounds: (a) $Fe(ClO_4)_2$; (b) $HClO_2$; (c) XeF_2; (d) IF_5; (e) XeO_3; (f) HBr (named as an acid).

23.5. Predict the geometrical structures of the following: (a) I_3^-; (b) ICl_4^-; (c) ClO_3^-; (d) H_5IO_6; (e) XeF_4.

23.6. The interhalogen compound $BrF_3(l)$ reacts with antimony(V) fluoride to form the salt $(BrF_2^+)(SbF_6^-)$. Write the Lewis structure for both the cation and anion in this substance and describe the likely geometrical structure of each.

23.7. What are the major factors responsible for the fact that xenon forms stable compounds with fluorine, whereas argon does not?

23.8. Why were the noble gases the last family of elements to be discovered?

23.9. Explain each of the following observations. (a) At room temperature, I_2 is a solid, Br_2 is a liquid, and Cl_2 and F_2 are both gases. (b) F_2 cannot be prepared by electrolytic oxidation of aqueous F^- solutions. (c) The boiling point of HF is much higher than those of the other hydrogen halides. (d) The halogens decrease in oxidizing power in the order $F_2 > Cl_2 > Br_2 > I_2$.

23.10. Explain the following observations: (a) For a given oxidation state, the acid strength of the oxyacid in aqueous solution decreases in the order chlorine > bromine > iodine. (b) Hydrofluoric acid cannot be stored in glass bottles. (c) HI cannot be prepared by treating NaI with sulfuric acid. (d) The interhalogen ICl_3 is known, but $BrCl_3$ is not. (e) I_2 is more soluble in aqueous solutions of I^- than in pure water.

23.11. List one commercial use of each of the halogens.

23.12. Write a balanced chemical equation for the commercial preparation of each halogen element.

23.13. Write balanced net ionic equations for the reaction of each of the following substances with water: (a) PBr_5; (b) IF_5; (c) $SiBr_4$; (d) F_2; (e) ClO_2 (chloric acid is a product); (f) $HI(g)$.

23.14. Write a balanced chemical equation that describes a suitable means of preparing each of the following substances: (a) HF; (b) I_2; (c) XeF_4; (d) $Ca(OCl)Cl$; (e) SF_6; (f) NaClO.

23.15. Write balanced chemical equations for each of the following reactions (some of which are analogous but not identical to reactions shown in this chapter). (a) Bromine forms hypobromite ion on addition to aqueous base. (b) Chlorine reacts with an aqueous solution of sodium bromide. (c) Bromine reacts with an aqueous solution of hydrogen peroxide, liberating O_2.

23.16. Write balanced chemical equations for each of the following reactions (some of which are analogous but not identical to reactions shown in this chapter). (a) Hydrogen bromide is produced upon heating calcium bromide with phosphoric acid. (b) Hydrogen bromide is formed upon hydrolysis of aluminum bromide. (c) Aqueous hydrogen fluoride reacts with solid calcium carbonate, forming water-insoluble calcium fluoride.

23.17. (a) Write the balanced net ionic equation for the reduction of ClO_3^- to Cl_2 by Fe^{2+} in acidic aqueous solution. (b) Calculate the standard emf for this reaction.

23.18. Chloride ion is oxidized in aqueous solution to $Cl_2(aq)$ by each of the following reagents: (a) $MnO_2(s)$; (b) $MnO_4^-(aq)$; (c) $Cr_2O_7^{2-}(aq)$. In each case, write a complete, balanced net ionic equation.

[23.19]. Using the thermochemical data in Table 23.1 and Appendix C, calculate the average Xe—F bond energies in XeF_2, XeF_4, and XeF_6, respectively. What is the significance of the trend in these quantities?

[23.20]. The solubility of Cl_2 in 100 g of water at STP is 310 cm^3. Assume that this quantity of Cl_2 is dissolved and equilibrated as follows:

$$Cl_2(aq) + H_2O(l) \rightleftharpoons Cl^-(aq) + HClO(aq) + H^+(aq)$$

If the equilibrium constant for this reaction is 4.7×10^{-4}, calculate the equilibrium concentration of HClO formed.

Group 6A

23.21. Write the chemical formula for each of the following compounds and indicate the oxidation state of the group 6A element in each: (a) selenous acid; (b) potassium hydrogen sulfite; (c) hydrogen telluride; (d) carbon disulfide; (e) calcium sulfate; (f) sodium thiosulfate.

23.22. Write the chemical formula for each of the following compounds and indicate the oxidation state of the group 6A element in each: (a) selenium trioxide; (b) orthotelluric acid; (c) zinc selenate; (d) sulfur tetrafluoride; (e) hydrogen sulfide; (f) sulfurous acid.

23.23. Name each of the following compounds: (a) $K_2S_2O_3$; (b) Al_2S_3; (c) $NaHSeO_3$; (d) SeF_6.

23.24. Name each of the following compounds: (a) H_2Se; (b) FeS_2; (c) $NaHSO_4$; (d) Na_2SeO_4.

23.25. Write the Lewis structure for each of the following species and indicate the geometrical structure of each: (a) SeO_4^{2-}; (b) H_6TeO_6; (c) $TeO_2(g)$; (d) S_2Cl_2; (e) chlorosulfonic acid, HSO_3Cl (chlorine is bonded to sulfur).

23.26. The SF_5^- ion is formed when $SF_4(g)$ reacts with fluoride salts containing large cations, such as $CsF(s)$. Draw the Lewis structures for SF_4 and SF_5^- and predict the molecular structure of each.

23.27. Write a balanced chemical equation for each of the following reactions. (a) Selenium dioxide dissolves in water. (b) Solid zinc sulfide reacts with hydrochloric acid. (c) Elemental sulfur reacts with sulfite ion to form thiosulfate. (d) Elemental selenium is heated with sulfuric acid. (e) Sulfur trioxide is dissolved in sulfuric acid. (f) Selenous acid is oxidized by hydrogen peroxide.

23.28. Write a balanced chemical equation for each of the following reactions. (You may have to guess at one or more of the reaction products, but you should be able to make a reasonable guess based on your study of this chapter.) (a) Selenous acid is reduced by hydrazine in aqueous solution to yield elemental selenium (see p. 827 for a discussion of hydrazine). (b) Heating orthotelluric acid to temperatures over 200°C yields the acid anhydride. (c) Hydrogen selenide can be prepared by reaction of aqueous acid solution on aluminum selenide. (d) Sodium thiosulfate is used to remove excess Cl_2 from chlorine-bleached fabrics. The thiosulfate ion forms SO_4^{2-} and elemental sulfur while Cl_2 is reduced to Cl^-.

23.29. An aqueous solution of SO_2 acts as a reducing agent to reduce (a) aqueous $KMnO_4$ to $MnSO_4(s)$; (b) acidic aqueous $K_2Cr_2O_7$ to aqueous Cr^{3+}; (c) aqueous $Hg_2(NO_3)_2$ to mercury metal. Write balanced chemical equations for these reactions.

23.30. In aqueous solution, hydrogen sulfide reduces (a) Fe^{3+} to Fe^{2+}; (b) Br_2 to Br^-; (c) MnO_4^- to Mn^{2+}; (d) HNO_3 to NO_2. In all cases, under appropriate conditions, the product is elemental sulfur. Write a balanced net ionic equation for each reaction.

[23.31]. Explain why telluric acid is a weak acid whereas sulfuric acid and selenic acid are strong acids.

[23.32]. SF_4 is very reactive; for example, it reacts readily with water to produce HF and SO_2. By contrast, SF_6 is very stable. It has even been used, with O_2, for X-ray examination of the lungs. (a) What features of the molecules make attack of sulfur by Lewis bases much more likely for SF_4 than for SF_6? (b) What feature of SF_4 makes attack of sulfur by Lewis acids possible? (c) Why is SF_4 subject to oxidation, whereas SF_6 is not?

Group 5A

23.33. Write formulas for the following compounds and indicate the oxidation state of the group 5A element in each: (a) orthophosphoric acid; (b) arsenous acid; (c) antimony(III) sulfide; (d) calcium dihydrogen phosphate; (e) potassium phosphide.

23.34. Write formulas for the following compounds and indicate the oxidation state of the group 5A element in each: (a) phosphorous acid; (b) pyrophosphoric acid; (c) antimony trichloride; (d) magnesium arsenate; (e) diphosphorus pentoxide.

23.35. Name each of the following compounds: (a) Na_3P; (b) H_3AsO_4; (c) P_4O_{10}; (d) AsF_5.

23.36. Name each of the following compounds: (a) K_3As; (b) PBr_3; (c) Sb_2O_3; (d) NaH_2AsO_4.

23.37. Phosphorus pentachloride exists in one form in the solid state as an ionic lattice of PCl_4^+ and PCl_6^- ions. (a) Draw the Lewis structures of these ions and predict their geometries. (b) What set of hybrid orbitals is employed by phosphorus in each case? (c) Why should PCl_5 exist as an ionic substance in the solid state, whereas it is stable as the neutral molecule in the gas phase?

23.38. Sodium trimetaphosphate, $Na_3P_3O_9$, and sodium tetrametaphosphate, $Na_4P_4O_{12}$, are used as water-softening agents. They contain cyclic $P_3O_9^{3-}$ and $P_4O_{12}^{4-}$ ions, respectively. Propose reasonable structures for these ions.

23.39. Account for the following observations. (a) H_3PO_3 is a diprotic acid. (b) Nitric acid is a strong acid, whereas phosphoric acid is weak. (c) Phosphate rock is not effective as a phosphate fertilizer. (d) Phosphorus does not exist at room temperature as diatomic molecules, but nitrogen does. (e) Solutions of Na_3PO_4 are quite basic.

23.40. Account for the following observations. (a) Phosphorus forms a pentachloride, but nitrogen does not. (b) H_3PO_2 is a monoprotic acid. (c) Phosphonium salts, such as PH_4Cl, can be formed under anhydrous conditions, but they can't be made in aqueous solution. (d) Whereas PCl_3 hydrolyzes readily in water to form H_3PO_3, $SbCl_3$ hydrolyzes only in part, forming $SbOCl$. (e) White phosphorus is extremely reactive.

23.41. Write a balanced chemical equation for each of the following reactions: (a) preparation of white phosphorus from calcium phosphate; (b) hydrolysis of PCl_3; (c) preparation of PCl_3 from P_4; (d) reaction of P_4O_{10} with water.

23.42. Write a balanced chemical equation for each of the following reactions: (a) Preparation of PF_5 from PCl_5 using AsF_3; (b) reaction of As_2O_3 with water; (c) dehydration of orthophosphoric acid to form pyrophosphoric acid; (d) reaction of elemental arsenic with dilute nitric acid to form NO and arsenous acid, H_3AsO_3.

Group 4A and Boron

23.43. Write the formulas for the following compounds and indicate the oxidation state of the group 4A element or of boron in each: (a) silicon dioxide; (b) germanium tetrachloride; (c) sodium borohydride; (d) stannous chloride; (e) diborane.

23.44. Write the formulas for the following compounds and indicate the oxidation state of the group 4A element or of boron in each: (a) boric acid; (b) silicon tetrabromide; (c) lead chloride; (d) sodium tetraborate decahydrate (borax); (e) boric oxide.

23.45. Covalent silicon-hydrogen compounds are called silanes. The silane Si_2H_6, known as disilane, exists, but Si_2H_4 and Si_2H_2 are not known. In contrast, carbon forms C_2H_6, C_2H_4, and C_2H_2. Explain why silicon doesn't form Si_2H_4 and Si_2H_2.

23.46. Suggest some reasons why carbon is more suitable than silicon as the major structural element in living systems.

23.47. Select the member of group 4A that best fits each of the following descriptions: (a) forms the most acidic oxide; (b) is most commonly found in the $+2$ oxidation state; (c) is a component of sand.

23.48. Select the member of group 4A that best fits each of the following descriptions: (a) forms chains to the greatest extent; (b) forms the most basic oxide; (c) is a metalloid that can form $+2$ ions.

23.49. Both $GeCl_4$ and $SiCl_4$ fume in moist air because of hydrolysis to GeO_2 and SiO_2. Write balanced equations for these reactions.

23.50. Germanium differs markedly from silicon in that the 2+ halides are fairly stable. These halides can be prepared by the reduction of the tetrahalide with germanium metal. (a) Write the balanced chemical equation for the formation of $GeCl_2$. (b) Predict the geometrical structure of the gaseous $GeCl_2$ molecule.

23.51. The mineral orthoclase is a feldspar mineral formed by replacing a quarter of the Si^{4+} ions in SiO_2 with Al^{3+} and maintaining charge balance with K^+ ions. What is the empirical formula for this mineral?

23.52. How is the mica mineral $KMg_3(AlSi_3O_{10})(OH)_2$ related structurally to the mica mineral muscovite mentioned in the text?

23.53. What empirical formula and unit charge are associated with each of the following structural types: (a) isolated SiO_4 tetrahedra; (b) a chain structure of SiO_4 tetrahedra joined at corners to adjacent units; (c) a structure consisting of tetrahedra joined at corners to form a six-membered ring of alternating Si and O atoms?

23.54. Propose a reasonable description of the structure of each of the following minerals: (a) albite, $NaAlSi_3O_8$; (b) leucite, $KAlSi_2O_6$; (c) zircon, $ZrSiO_4$; (d) sphene, $CaTiSiO_5$.

Additional Exercises

23.55. Name each of the following compounds: (a) $H_2B_4O_7$; (b) SiC; (c) HPO_3; (d) XeF_2; (e) Na_2S; (f) $KClO_3$; (g) $B_{10}H_{14}$.

23.56. Explain each of the following observations. (a) H_2S is a better reducing agent than H_2O. (b) H_2SO_4 is a stronger acid than H_2SeO_4. (c) Astatine is generally not considered in any detail in the discussion of halogens. (d) White phosphorus is quite volatile, whereas red phosphorus is not. (e) Xenon hexafluoride is a stable compound, whereas krypton hexafluoride is unknown. (f) Addition of SF_4 to water results in an acidic solution. (g) Silicate-sheet minerals are softer than aluminosilicate-sheet ones. (h) Sulfur occurs naturally as sulfates, but not as sulfites.

23.57. Xenon trioxide disproportionates in strongly alkaline solution to form the thermally stable perxenate ion, XeO_6^{4-}. Predict the geometry of this ion. Describe the bonding in terms of the hybridization of xenon valence-shell orbitals.

23.58. What pressure of gas is formed when 0.654 g of XeO_3 decomposes completely to the free elements at 48 °C in a 0.452-L volume?

23.59. Write balanced chemical equations to account for the following observations. (There may not be closely similar reactions shown in the chapter; however, you should be able to make reasonable guesses at the likely products.) (a) When burning sodium metal is immersed in a pure HCl atmosphere, it continues to burn. (b) Bubbling SO_2 gas through liquid bromine that is covered with a layer of water results in formation of a strongly acidic solution; upon distillation, an aqueous HBr solution is collected. The remaining liquid is still strongly acidic. (c) When bromine is added to a basic solution containing potassium hypochlorite, insoluble potassium bromate is formed. (d) When bromic acid is reacted with SO_2, $Br_2(aq)$ is formed. (e) Uranium(VI) fluoride is formed by the action of ClF_3 on uranium(IV) chloride.

23.60. The cyano group behaves in some ways like a halogen. Thus, cyanogen gas, $(CN)_2$, has been called a pseudohalogen, and the cyanide ion, CN^-, a pseudohalide. Cyanogen reacts with an aqueous solution of NaOH in a fashion analogous to Cl_2. (a) Write a balanced chemical equation for this reaction. (b) Write the Lewis structure for $(CN)_2$ and describe its geometrical structure.

23.61. Although the ClO_4^- and IO_4^- ions have been known for a long time, BrO_4^- was not synthesized until 1965. The ion was synthesized by oxidizing the bromate ion with xenon difluoride, producing xenon, hydrofluoric acid, and the perbromate ion. Write the balanced chemical equation for this reaction.

23.62. List the halogens in order of increasing $X-X$ halogen bond energies. Suggest a reason for the low $F-F$ bond energy.

23.63. What structural feature do the molecules P_4, P_4O_6, and P_4O_{10} have in common? What is the common structural feature of all of the acids containing phosphorus(V)?

23.64. Elemental sulfur is capable of reacting under suitable conditions with Fe, F_2, O_2, or H_2. Write balanced chemical equations to describe these reactions. In which reactions is sulfur acting as a reducing agent and in which as an oxidizing agent?

23.65. Sodium sulfide is used in the leather industry to remove hair from hides. It can be synthesized by reducing sodium sulfate with carbon. (Carbon monoxide forms together with the sodium sulfide.) Write a balanced chemical equation for this reaction.

23.66. Sulfur and the group 6A elements below it in the periodic chart exhibit oxidation states ranging from -2 to $+6$. What factors control the lowest and highest oxidation states? Explain.

23.67. Draw the Lewis structures for the following species and predict the relative $S-O$ bond lengths in each: SO_2, SO_3, SO_4^{2-}.

23.68. One method proposed for removal of SO_2 from the flue gases of power plants involves reaction with aqueous H_2S. Elemental sulfur is the product. **(a)** Write a balanced chemical equation for the reaction. **(b)** What volume of H_2S at $27°C$ and 740 torr would be required to remove the SO_2 formed by burning 1.0 ton of coal containing 3.5 percent S by mass? **(c)** What mass of elemental sulfur is produced? Assume that all reactions are 100 percent efficient.

23.69. Although H_2Se is toxic, no deaths have been attributed to it. One reason is its vile odor, which serves as a sensitive warning of its presence. In addition, H_2Se is readily oxidized by O_2 in air to nontoxic elemental red selenium before harmful amounts of H_2Se can enter the body. **(a)** Write a balanced chemical equation for this oxidation. **(b)** Calculate $\Delta G°$ and the equilibrium constant (at 298 K) for the reaction.

23.70. A sulfuric acid plant produces a considerable amount of heat. This heat is used to generate electricity, which helps reduce operating costs. The synthesis of H_2SO_4 consists of three main chemical processes: (1) oxidation of S to SO_2; (2) oxidation of SO_2 to SO_3; (3) the dissolving of SO_3 in H_2SO_4 and its reaction with water to form H_2SO_4. If the third process produces 130 kJ/mol, how much heat is produced in preparing a mole of H_2SO_4 from a mole of S? How much heat is produced in preparing a ton of H_2SO_4?

23.71. Ultrapure germanium, like silicon, is used in semiconductors. Germanium of "ordinary" purity is prepared by the high-temperature reduction of GeO_2 with carbon. The Ge is converted to $GeCl_4$ by treatment with Cl_2 and then purified by distillation; $GeCl_4$ is then hydrolyzed in water to GeO_2 and reduced to the elemental form with H_2. The element is then zone-refined. Write a balanced chemical equation for each of the chemical transformations in the course of forming ultrapure Ge from GeO_2.

23.72. Describe the fundamental structural unit present in all silicate minerals. How is this unit modified in aluminosilicates?

23.73. Draw the Lewis structure for the cyclic $Si_3O_9^{6-}$ ion.

[23.74]. The maximum allowable concentration of $H_2S(g)$ in air is 20 mg per kilogram of air (20 ppm by mass). How many grams of FeS would be required to react with hydrochloric acid to produce this concentration in an average room measuring 2.7 m $\times$ 4.3 m $\times$ 4.3 m?

[23.75]. The standard heats of formation of $H_2O(g)$, $H_2S(g)$, $H_2Se(g)$, and $H_2Te(g)$ are -241.8, -20.17, $+29.7$, and $+99.6$ kJ/mol, respectively. The enthalpies necessary to convert the elements in their standard states to 1 mol of gaseous atoms are 248, 277, 227, and 197 kJ/mol of atoms for O, S, Se, and Te, respectively. The enthalpy for dissociation of H_2 is 436 kJ/mol. Calculate the average $H-O$, $H-S$, $H-Se$, and $H-Te$ bond energies and comment on their trend.

[23.76]. **(a)** Calculate the $P-P$ bond distance in both P_4O_6 and P_4O_{10} from the following data: the $P-O-P$ bond angle for P_4O_6 is $127.5°$, while that for P_4O_{10} is $124.5°$. The $P-O$ distance (to bridging oxygens) is 1.65 Å in P_4O_6 and 1.60 Å in P_4O_{10}. **(b)** Rationalize the relative $P-P$ bond distances in the two compounds.

[23.77]. The $N-X$ bond distances in the nitrosyl halides, NOX, are 1.52, 1.98, and 2.14 Å for NOF, NOCl, and NOBr, respectively. Compare the distances with the atomic radii for the halogens (Table 23.3). Is the variation in $N-X$ distance what you expect from these covalent radii? If not, account for the deviations.

[23.78]. Considering the chemical formulas and structures of clay minerals, suggest an explanation for why they can be molded and then become hard and brittle when heated.

[23.79]. Boron nitride has a graphitelike structure with $B-N$ bond distances of 1.45 Å within sheets and a separation of 3.30 Å between sheets. At high temperatures, the BN assumes a diamondlike form that is harder than diamond. Rationalize the similarity between BN and elemental carbon.

Metals and Metallurgy 24

The production of lightweight, high-tech metallic materials, such as these bicycle frames, depends on the processing and alloying of metals.

CONTENTS

In Chapters 22 and 23, we examined the chemistry of nonmetallic elements. In this chapter, we turn our attention to metals. Metals have played a major role in the development of civilization. Early history is often divided into the Stone Age, the Bronze Age, and the Iron Age, based on the compositions of the tools used in each era. Modern societies rely on a large variety of metals for making tools, machines, and other items. Chemists and other scientists have found uses for even the least abundant metals as they search for materials to meet evolving technological needs. To illustrate this point, Figure 24.1 shows the approximate composition of a high-performance jet engine. Notice that iron, long the dominant metal of technology, is not even present to a significant extent.

In this chapter, we shall consider the chemical forms in which metallic elements occur in nature and the means by which we obtain metals from these sources. We shall also examine the bonding in solids and see how metals and mixtures of metals, called alloys, are employed in modern technology. Finally, we shall look specifically at the properties of transition metals. As we shall see, metals have a varied and interesting chemistry.

24.1 Occurrence and Distribution of Metals

Teaching Note: Refer to Chapter 18 for a more complete description of the earth's zones.

The portion of our environment that constitutes the solid earth beneath our feet is called the **lithosphere.** The lithosphere provides most of the materials we use to feed, clothe, shelter, support, and entertain ourselves. Although the bulk of the earth is solid, we have access to only a small region near the surface. The deepest well ever drilled is only about 8 km deep, and the deepest mine extends between 3 and 4 km into the earth. In comparison, the earth has a radius of 6370 km.

Many of the metals that are most useful to us are not especially abundant in that portion of the lithosphere to which we have ready access. Consequently, the occurrence and distribution of *concentrated* deposits of these elements often play a role in international politics as nations compete for access to these materials. Deposits that contain metals in economically exploitable quantities

FIGURE 24.1 Metallic elements employed in construction of a jet engine.

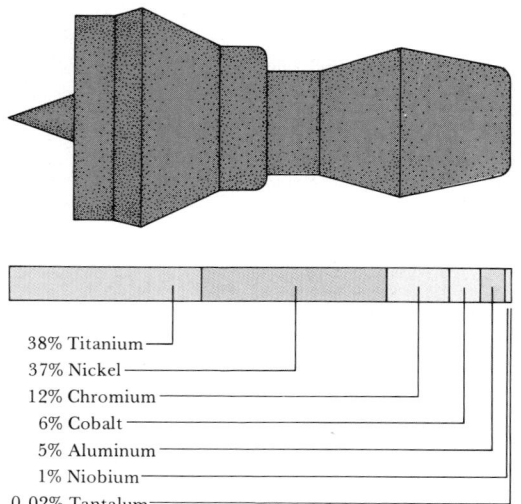

38% Titanium
37% Nickel
12% Chromium
6% Cobalt
5% Aluminum
1% Niobium
0.02% Tantalum

FIGURE 24.2 Large open-pit mining operation. (Georg Gerster/Photo Researchers)

are known as **ores.** Usually, the compounds or elements that we desire must be separated from a large quantity of unwanted material and then chemically processed to be rendered useful. By processing large quantities of substances, we have literally changed the surface of our planet (Figure 24.2). About 2.3×10^4 kg (25 tons) of materials are extracted from the lithosphere and processed annually to support each person in our country. Because the richest sources of many substances are becoming exhausted, it will be necessary in the future to process larger volumes of lower-quality raw materials. Consequently, extraction of the compounds and elements we need will cost more in terms of both energy and environmental impact.

Minerals

With the exception of gold and the platinum-group metals (Ru, Rh, Pd, Os, Ir, and Pt), most metallic elements are found in nature in solid inorganic compounds called **minerals.** Table 24.1 lists the principal mineral sources of several

Point of Emphasis: According to *The American Heritage Dictionary,* an ore is a mineral or aggregate of minerals from which a valuable constituent, especially a metal, can be profitably mined or extracted.

Learning Goal 1: Describe what is meant by the term *mineral,* and provide a few examples of common minerals.

Teaching Note: Gold and the platinum metals (Pd, Pt, Ru, Rh, Os, Ir) are relatively inert and can be found, often together, in metallic form in nature.

TABLE 24.1 △ Principal Mineral Sources of Some Common Metals

Metal	Mineral	Composition
Aluminum	Bauxite	Al_2O_3
Chromium	Chromite	$FeCr_2O_4$
Copper	Chalcocite	Cu_2S
	Chalcopyrite	$CuFeS_2$
	Malachite	$Cu_2CO_3(OH)_2$
Iron	Hematite	Fe_2O_3
	Magnetite	Fe_3O_4
Lead	Galena	PbS
Manganese	Pyrolusite	MnO_2
Mercury	Cinnabar	HgS
Molybdenum	Molybdenite	MoS_2
Tin	Cassiterite	SnO_2
Titanium	Rutile	TiO_2
	Ilmenite	$FeTiO_3$
Zinc	Sphalerite	ZnS

common metals, two of which are shown in Figure 24.3. Notice that minerals are identified by common names rather than by chemical names. Names of minerals are usually based on the locations where they were discovered, the person who discovered them, or some characteristic such as color. For example, the name *malachite* comes from the Greek word *malache,* the name of a type of tree whose leaves are the color of the mineral.

Commercially, the most important sources of metals are oxide, sulfide, and carbonate minerals. Silicate minerals (Section 23.5) are very abundant, but they are generally difficult to concentrate and reduce. Therefore, most silicates are not economical sources of metals.

Metallurgy

Daniel Bartet and Eugenia Aguila, "Teaching the Concepts of Metallurgy through the Use of Postage Stamps," *J. Chem. Educ.* 1987, *64,* 526.

Learning Goal 2: Define various terms employed in discussions of metallurgy, notably *gangue, calcination, roasting, smelting, refining,* and *leaching.*

Teaching Note: Because of the continuing search for materials with novel properties, metallurgy is a growing field of study and employment.

Metallurgy is the science and technology of extracting metals from their natural sources and preparing them for practical use. It usually involves several steps: (1) mining, (2) concentrating the ore or otherwise preparing it for further treatment, (3) reducing the ore to obtain the free metal, (4) refining or purifying the metal, and (5) alloying the metal, if necessary. (An **alloy** is a metallic material that is composed of two or more elements; see Section 24.6.)

After being mined, an ore is usually crushed and ground and then treated to concentrate the desired metal. The concentration stage relies on differences in the properties of the mineral and the undesired material that accompanies it, which is called **gangue** (pronounced "gang"). For example, miners who panned for gold (Figure 24.5) used a pan to rinse away the gangue from the denser gold nuggets. In another example, magnetite, a mineral of iron, can be concentrated by moving finely ground ore on a conveyor belt past a series of magnets. The

FIGURE 24.3 Two common minerals: (*a*) beryl, (*b*) tourmaline. Note the different colors and shapes. (Roberto De Gugliemo/Science Photo Library/Photo Researchers; © Karl Hartmann/Sachs/Phototake NYC)

Metals as Strategic Materials

A modern, high-technology society depends on the availability of many metallic elements. Dependable access to the mineral sources from which these essential metals are derived is critical to the economic and military security of a highly industralized nation. In recent years, this access has become a matter of deep concern in the United States, because this country has no domestic sources of many of the most critical elements. Figure 24.4 shows the extent of our dependence on imports in terms of percentages of annual consumption that are imported. Note that all the elements listed in Figure 24.1 as important components of a modern jet engine are on this list. Furthermore, the most important sources of some of the metals are nations that are not highly developed and have uncertain relations with the United States.

In response to this situation, the United States has developed a strategic minerals policy. Part of this policy establishes stockpiles of the most critical metals, so that if all foreign sources were cut off, the United States could function for an extended time by drawing on the reserves. Intensive efforts to develop new reserves within the United States and to recycle old metal have also been initiated.

FIGURE 24.4 Dependence of the United States on imports of strategic metals.

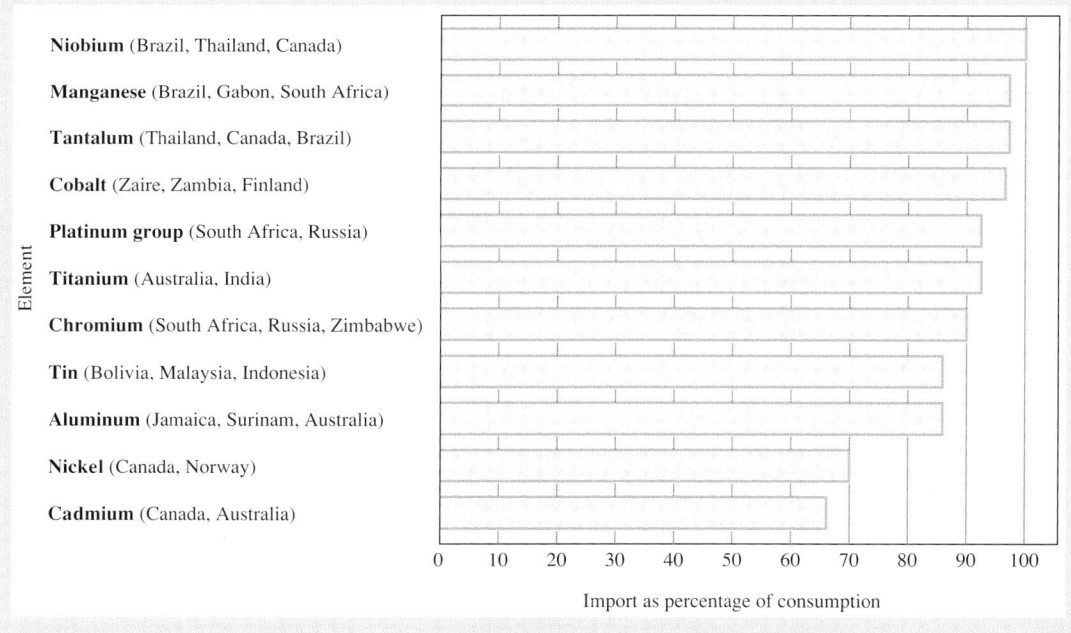

iron mineral is magnetic (attracted to a magnet), whereas the accompanying gangue is not.

After an ore is concentrated, a variety of chemical processes are used to obtain the metal in suitable purity. In the next three sections, we shall examine some of the most common metallurgical processes. You will see that these techniques depend on many of the basic concepts that were discussed earlier in the text.

FIGURE 24.5 Panning for gold relies on the different densities of gold and its accompanying gangue. (The Bettman Archive)

24.2 Pyrometallurgy

A large number of metallurgical processes utilize high temperatures to alter the mineral chemically and ultimately to reduce it to the free metal. The use of heat to alter or reduce the mineral is called **pyrometallurgy**. (*Pyro* means "at high temperature.")

Calcination is the heating of an ore to bring about its decomposition and the elimination of a volatile product. The volatile product could be, for example, CO_2 or H_2O. Carbonates are often calcined to drive off CO_2, forming the metal oxide. For example,

$$PbCO_3(s) \longrightarrow PbO(s) + CO_2(g) \qquad [24.1]$$

Most carbonates decompose reasonably rapidly at temperatures in the range of 400 to 500°C, although $CaCO_3$ requires a temperature of about 1000°C. Most hydrated minerals lose H_2O at temperatures on the order of 100 to 300°C.

Roasting is a thermal treatment that causes chemical reactions between the ore and the furnace atmosphere. Roasting may lead to oxidation or reduction and may be accompanied by calcination. An important roasting process is the oxidation of sulfide ores, in which the metal is converted to the oxide, as in the following examples:

$$2ZnS(s) + 3O_2(g) \longrightarrow 2ZnO(s) + 2SO_2(g) \qquad [24.2]$$

$$2MoS_2(s) + 7O_2(g) \longrightarrow 2MoO_3(s) + 4SO_2(g) \qquad [24.3]$$

The sulfide ore of a less active metal, such as mercury, can be roasted to the free metal:

$$HgS(s) + O_2(g) \longrightarrow Hg(g) + SO_2(g) \qquad [24.4]$$

The free metal can also be produced when a reducing atmosphere is present during the roast. Carbon monoxide, CO, provides such an atmosphere:

$$PbO(s) + CO(g) \longrightarrow Pb(l) + CO_2(g) \qquad [24.5]$$

Roasting is not always a feasible method of reduction. Some metals that are difficult to obtain as the free metal by roasting are best converted to the metal halide, which can then be reduced. To obtain the metal halide, the metal oxide or another compound, such as metal carbide, is roasted in an atmosphere of the halogen, usually chlorine. For example,

$$TiC(s) + 4Cl_2(g) \longrightarrow TiCl_4(g) + CCl_4(g) \qquad [24.6]$$

Smelting is a melting process in which the materials formed in the course of chemical reactions separate into two or more layers. Smelting often involves a roasting stage in the same furnace. Two of the important types of layers formed in smelters are molten metal and slag. The molten metal may consist almost entirely of a single metal, or it may be a solution of two or more metals.

Slag consists mainly of molten silicate minerals, with aluminates, phosphates, fluorides, and other ionic compounds as constituents. A slag is formed when a basic metal oxide such as CaO reacts at high temperatures with molten silica, SiO_2:

$$CaO(l) + SiO_2(l) \longrightarrow CaSiO_3(l) \qquad [24.7]$$

Pyrometallurgical operations may involve not only the concentration and reduction of a mineral, but the refining of the metal as well. **Refining** is the treatment of a crude, relatively impure metal product from a metallurgical process to improve its purity and to define its composition better. Sometimes the goal of the refining process is to obtain the metal itself in pure form. However, the goal may also be to produce a mixture with a well-defined composition, as in the production of steels from crude iron, which we now examine.

The Pyrometallurgy of Iron

The most important pyrometallurgical operation is the reduction of iron. Iron occurs in many different minerals, but the most important sources are the iron oxide minerals, hematite, Fe_2O_3, and magnetite, Fe_3O_4. The reduction of these oxides occurs in a *blast furnace,* such as the one illustrated in Figure 24.6. A blast furnace is essentially a huge chemical reactor capable of continuous operation. The largest furnaces are over 60 m high and 14 m wide. When operating at full capacity, they produce up to 10,000 tons of iron per day. The blast furnace is charged at the top with a mixture of iron ore, coke, and limestone. Coke is coal that has been heated in the absence of air to drive off volatile components. It is about 85 to 90 percent carbon. Coke serves as the fuel, producing heat as it is burned in the lower part of the furnace. It is also the source of the reducing gases CO and H_2. Limestone, $CaCO_3$, serves as the source of basic oxide in slag formation. Air, which enters the blast furnace at the bottom after preheating, is also an important raw material; it is required for combustion of the coke. Production of 1 kg of crude iron, called *pig iron,* requires about 2 kg of ore, 1 kg of coke, 0.3 kg of limestone, and 1.5 kg of air.

FIGURE 24.6 Blast furnace used for reduction of iron ore. Notice the approximate temperatures in the varioius regions of the furnace.

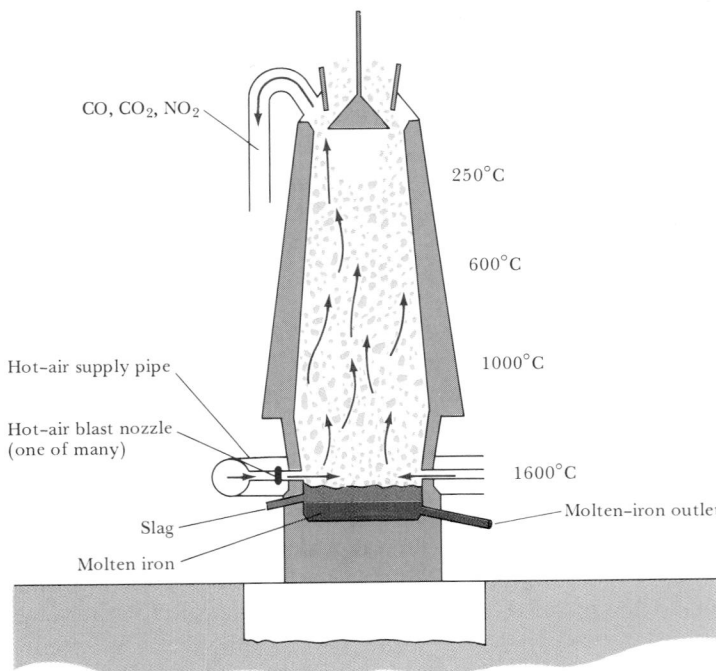

Figure 24.6

In the furnace, oxygen reacts with the carbon in the coke to form carbon monoxide:

$$2C(s) + O_2(g) \longrightarrow 2CO(g) \qquad \Delta H = -110 \text{ kJ} \qquad [24.8]$$

Water vapor present in the air also reacts with carbon:

$$C(s) + H_2O(g) \longrightarrow CO(g) + H_2(g) \qquad \Delta H = +113 \text{ kJ} \qquad [24.9]$$

Note that the reaction of coke with oxygen is exothermic and provides heat for furnace operation, but that its reaction with water vapor is endothermic. Addition of water vapor to the air thus provides a means of controlling furnace temperature.

In the upper part of the furnace limestone is calcined (Equation 22.64). Here also the iron oxides are reduced by CO and H_2. For example, the important reactions for Fe_3O_4 are

$$Fe_3O_4(s) + 4CO(g) \longrightarrow 3Fe(s) + 4CO_2(g) \qquad \Delta H = -19 \text{ kJ} \qquad [24.10]$$
$$Fe_3O_4(s) + 4H_2(g) \longrightarrow 3Fe(s) + 4H_2O(g) \qquad \Delta H = +149 \text{ kJ} \qquad [24.11]$$

Reduction of other elements present in the ore also occurs in the hottest parts of the furnace, where carbon is the major reducing agent.

Molten iron collects at the base of the furnace, as shown in Figure 24.6. It is overlaid with a layer of molten slag formed by the reaction of CaO with the silica present in the ore, as described by Equation 24.7. The layer of slag over the molten iron helps to protect it from reaction with the incoming air. Periodically, the furnace is tapped to drain off slag and molten iron. The iron produced in the furnace may be cast into solid ingots. However, most is used directly in the manufacture of steel. For this purpose, it is transported, while still liquid, to the steel-making shop (Figure 24.7).

Formation of Steel

Steel is an alloy of iron. The production of iron from its ore is a chemical reduction process that results in a crude iron containing many undesired impurities. Iron from a blast furnace typically contains 0.6 to 1.2 percent silicon, about 0.2 percent phosphorus, 0.4 to 2.0 percent manganese, and about 0.03 percent sulfur. In addition, there is considerable dissolved carbon. In the production of steel, these impurity elements are removed by oxidation in a vessel called a *converter*. In modern steel making, the oxidizing agent is either pure O_2 or O_2 diluted with argon. Air cannot be used directly as the source of O_2 because N_2 reacts with the molten iron, forming iron nitride that causes the steel to become brittle.

Teaching Note: The converter was invented by Henry Bessemer and is often called a *Bessemer converter.*

A cross-sectional view of one converter design appears in Figure 24.8. In this converter, O_2, diluted with argon, is blown directly into the molten metal. The oxygen reacts exothermically with carbon, silicon, and metal impurities, reducing the concentrations of these elements in the iron. Carbon and sulfur are expelled as CO and SO_2 gases, respectively. Silicon is oxidized to SiO_2 and adds to whatever slag may have been present initially in the melt. Metal oxides react with the SiO_2 to form silicates. The presence of a basic slag is important for removal of phosphorus:

$$3CaO(l) + P_2O_5(l) \longrightarrow Ca_3(PO_4)_2(l) \qquad [24.12]$$

Nearly all of the O_2 blown into the converter is consumed in the oxidation reactions. By monitoring the O_2 concentration in the gas coming from the converter, it is possible to tell when the oxidation is essentially complete. Oxidation of the impurities present in the iron normally requires only about 20

FIGURE 24.7 Molten iron being poured into a basic oxygen furnace. Steel makers convert iron to steel by adding other metals as alloying agents and by blowing $O_2(g)$ through the molten mixture to oxidize impurities. (Steve Dunwell/The Image Bank)

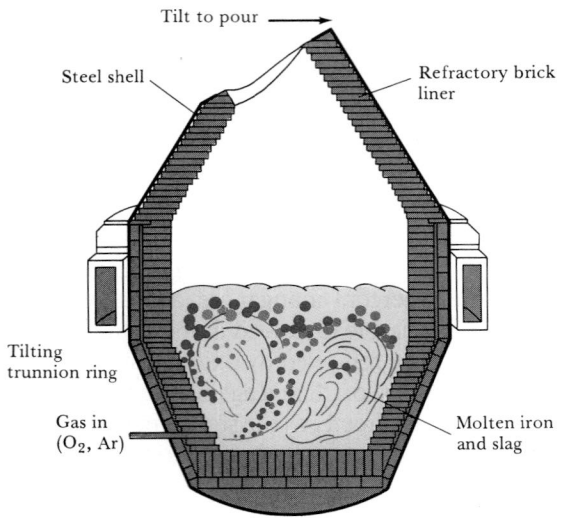

FIGURE 24.8 Converter for refining of iron. A mixture of oxygen and argon is blown through the molten iron and slag. The heat of oxidation of impurities maintains the mixture in a molten state. When the desired composition is attained, the converter is tilted to pour.

Tilt to pour

Steel shell

Refractory brick liner

Tilting trunnion ring

Gas in (O_2, Ar)

Molten iron and slag

min. When the desired composition is attained, the contents of the converter are dumped into a large ladle. To produce steels with various kinds of properties, alloying elements are added as the ladle is being filled. The still-molten mixture is then poured into molds, where it solidifies.

24.3 Hydrometallurgy

Pyrometallurgical operations require large quantities of energy and are often a source of atmospheric pollution, especially by sulfur dioxide. In the last 100 years, new techniques have been developed in which metals are extracted from their ores by use of aqueous reactions. These processes are called **hydrometallurgy** (*hydro* means "water").

The most important hydrometallurgical process is **leaching,** in which the desired metal-containing compound is selectively dissolved. If the compound is water-soluble, water by itself is a suitable leaching agent. More commonly the agent is an aqueous solution of an acid, a base, or a salt. Often the dissolving process involves formation of a complex ion. ∞ (Sec. 17.5) An example of this process is the leaching of gold.

As we discussed in the Closer Look box in Section 4.6, gold metal is often found relatively pure in nature. As concentrated deposits of elemental gold have been depleted, lower-grade sources have become more important. Gold from low-grade ores is often concentrated by the process of *cyanidation.* The crushed ore is placed on large concrete slabs, and a solution of NaCN is sprayed over it. In the presence of CN^- and air, the gold is oxidized and dissolves, forming the stable $Au(CN)_2^-$ ion:

$$4Au(s) + 8CN^-(aq) + O_2(g) + 2H_2O(l) \longrightarrow$$
$$4Au(CN)_2^-(aq) + 4OH^-(aq) \quad [24.13]$$

After a metal ion is selectively leached from the ore, it is precipitated from solution as the free metal or as an insoluble ionic compound. For example, gold is obtained from its cyanide complex by reduction with zinc powder.

$$2Au(CN)_2^-(aq) + Zn(s) \longrightarrow Zn(CN)_4^{2-}(aq) + 2Au(s) \qquad [24.14]$$

The Hydrometallurgy of Aluminum

Among metals, aluminum is second only to iron in commercial use. World production of the metal is about 1.5×10^{10} kg (16 million tons) per year. The most useful ore of aluminum is *bauxite,* in which Al is present as hydrated oxides, $Al_2O_3 \cdot xH_2O$. The value of x varies, depending on the particular mineral present. Because bauxite deposits in the United States are very limited, the nation imports most of the ore used in the production of aluminum (Fig. 24.4).

The major impurities found in bauxite are silica, SiO_2, and iron(III) oxide, Fe_2O_3. It is essential to separate alumina, Al_2O_3, from these impurities before the metal is recovered by electrochemical reduction, as described in Section 24.4. The process used to purify bauxite, called the **Bayer process,** is a hydrometallurgical procedure. The ore is first crushed and ground, then digested in a concentrated aqueous NaOH solution, about 30 percent NaOH by mass, at a temperature in the range 150 to 230°C. Sufficient pressure, between 4 and 30 atm, is maintained to prevent boiling. The reaction leads to a complex aluminate anion of the form $Al(H_2O)_2(OH)_4^-$. ∞ (Sec. 17.5) For example,

$$Al_2O_3 \cdot H_2O(s) + 6H_2O(l) + 2OH^- \longrightarrow 2Al(H_2O)_2(OH)_4^-(aq) \qquad [24.15]$$

Unlike Al^{3+}, Fe^{3+} is not amphoteric. Thus, iron(III) oxides are not soluble in the strongly basic solution, and filtration of the aluminate solution separates the aluminum from iron-containing impurities. After filtration the pH is lowered, which leads to the precipitation of a highly hydrated aluminum hydroxide.

After the aluminum hydroxide precipitate has been filtered, it is calcined in preparation for electroreduction of the ore to the metal. The solution recovered from the filtration is reconcentrated so that it can be used again. This is accomplished by heating to evaporate water from the solution. The energy requirements of this evaporative stage are high, and it is the most costly part of the process.

24.4 Electrometallurgy

Electrolysis methods are often used either to reduce a metal compound to obtain the free metal or to refine the metal. Collectively, these processes are referred to as **electrometallurgy.** The principles of electrolysis were discussed in Section 20.7, which you should review if necessary.

Electrometallurgical procedures can be broadly differentiated according to whether they involve electrolysis of a molten salt or of an aqueous solution. Electrolytic methods are very important as a means of obtaining the more active metals, such as sodium, magnesium, and aluminum, in the free state. These metals cannot be reduced in aqueous solution because water is more

Learning Goal 7: Describe the Bayer process for purifying bauxite, including balanced chemical equations.

Point of Emphasis: Electrometallurgy is the process of obtaining and purifying metals through electrolysis.

easily reduced than the metal ions. The standard potentials for reduction of water under both acidic and basic conditions are more positive than the standard potentials for reduction of such active metals as Na ($E° = -2.71$ V), Mg ($E° = -2.37$ V), and Al ($E° = -1.66$ V):

$$2H^+(aq) + 2e^- \longrightarrow H_2(g) \qquad\qquad E° = 0.00 \text{ V} \qquad [24.16]$$
$$H_2O(l) + 2e^- \longrightarrow H_2(g) + 2OH^-(aq) \qquad E° = -0.83 \text{ V} \quad [24.17]$$

To form such metals by electrochemical reduction, therefore, we must employ a molten-salt medium in which the metal ion of interest is the most readily reduced species.

Electrometallurgy of Sodium

Learning Goal 8: Describe the process by which sodium metal is obtained from NaCl, including balanced chemical equations for the electrode processes.

In the commercial preparation of sodium, molten NaCl is electrolyzed in a specially designed cell called the **Downs cell,** illustrated in Figure 24.9. The electrolyte medium through which current flows is molten NaCl. Calcium chloride, $CaCl_2$, is added to lower the melting point of the cell medium from the normal melting point of NaCl, 804°C, to around 600°C. The Na(l) and $Cl_2(g)$ produced in the electrolysis are kept from coming in contact and reforming NaCl. In addition, the Na must be prevented from contact with oxygen, because the metal would quickly oxidize under the high-temperature conditions of the cell reaction.

Electrometallurgy of Aluminum

Learning Goal 9: Describe the Hall process for obtaining aluminum, including balanced chemical equations for the electrode processes.

In Section 24.3, we discussed the Bayer process, in which bauxite is concentrated to produce aluminum hydroxide. When this concentrate is calcined at temperatures in excess of 1000°C, anhydrous aluminum oxide, Al_2O_3, is formed. Anhydrous aluminum oxide melts at over 2000°C. This is too high to

FIGURE 24.9 Downs cell used in the commercial production of sodium.

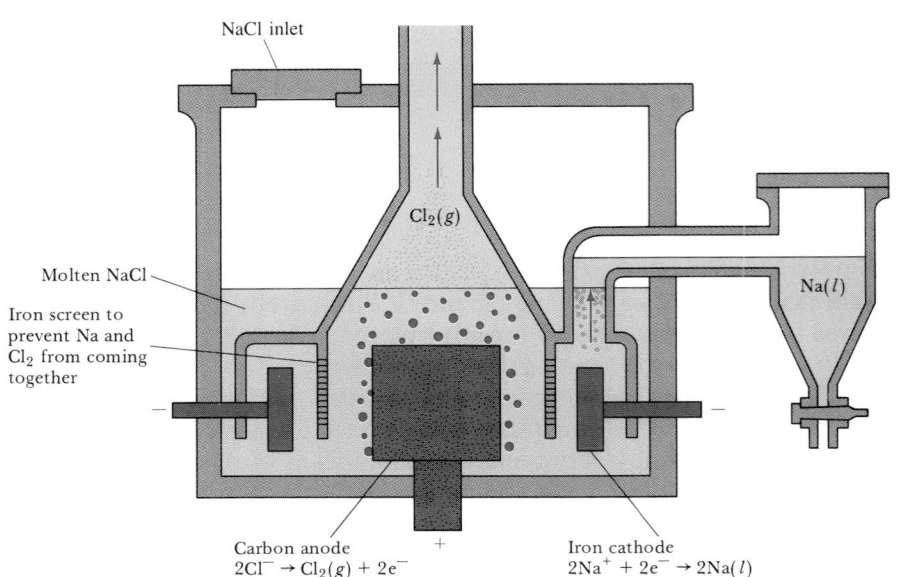

NaCl inlet

$Cl_2(g)$

Molten NaCl

Iron screen to prevent Na and Cl_2 from coming together

Na(l)

Carbon anode
$2Cl^- \rightarrow Cl_2(g) + 2e^-$

Iron cathode
$2Na^+ + 2e^- \rightarrow 2Na(l)$

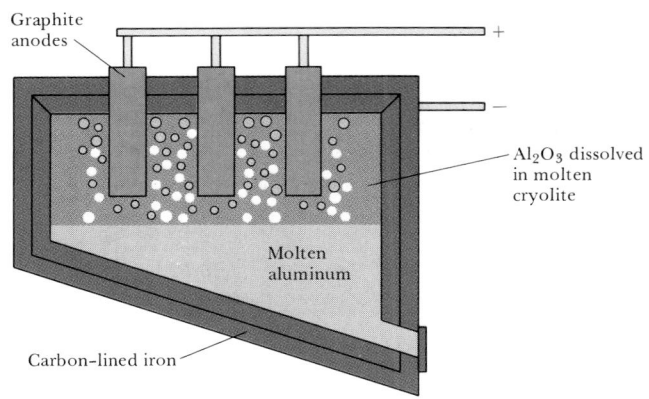

Figure 24.10

FIGURE 24.10 Typical Hall process electrolysis cell used to reduce aluminum. Because molten aluminum is more dense than the molten mixture of Na_3AlF_6 and Al_2O_3, the metal collects at the bottom of the cell.

permit its use as a molten medium for electrolytic formation of free aluminum. The electrolytic process used commercially to produce aluminum is known as the **Hall process,** named after its inventor, Charles M. Hall (see the Closer Look box in this section). The purified Al_2O_3 is dissolved in molten cryolite, Na_3AlF_6, which has a melting point of 1012°C and is an effective conductor of electric current. A schematic diagram of the electrolysis cell is shown in Figure 24.10. Graphite rods are employed as anodes and are consumed in the electrolysis process. The electrode reactions are given in Equations 24.18 and 24.19.

$$\text{Anode:} \quad C(s) + 2O^{2-}(l) \longrightarrow CO_2(g) + 4e^- \quad [24.18]$$

$$\text{Cathode:} \quad 3e^- + Al^{3+}(l) \longrightarrow Al(l) \quad [24.19]$$

The amounts of raw materials and energy required to produce 1000 kg of aluminum metal from bauxite by this procedure are summarized in Figure 24.11.

Electrorefining of Copper

Copper is widely used to make electrical wiring and in other applications that utilize its high electrical conductivity. Crude copper, which is usually obtained

Learning Goal 10: Describe the electrometallurgical purification of copper, including balanced chemical equations for electrode processes.

FIGURE 24.11 The quantities of bauxite, cryolite, graphite, and energy required to produce 1000 kg of aluminum.

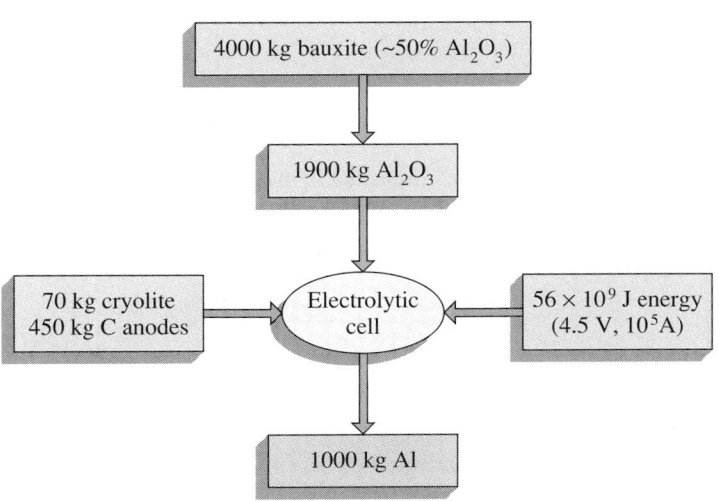

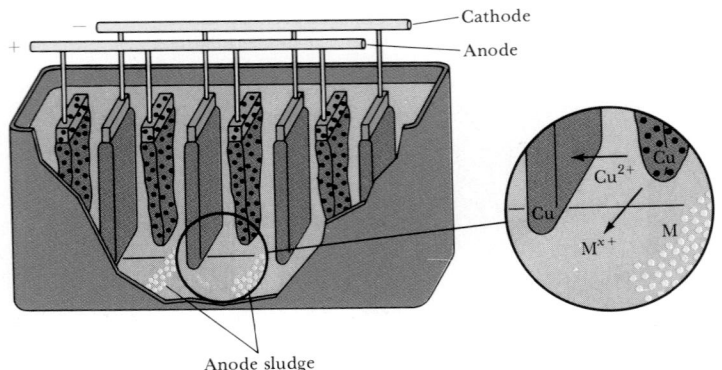

FIGURE 24.12 Electrolysis cell for refining of copper. Notice that as the anodes dissolve away, the cathodes on which the pure metal is deposited grow in size.

Point of Emphasis: Recall from Chapter 20 that an overvoltage must be applied in order for the electrolysis to occur, but that the quantity of copper produced is related to the current and the time.

by pyrometallurgical methods, is not suitable to serve in electrical applications because impurities greatly reduce the metal's conductivity.

Purification of copper is achieved by electrolysis, as illustrated in Figure 24.12. Large slabs of crude copper serve as the anodes in the cell, and thin sheets of pure copper serve as the cathodes. The electrolyte consists of an acidic solution of $CuSO_4$. Application of a suitable voltage to the electrodes causes oxidation of copper metal at the anode and reduction of Cu^{2+} to form copper metal at the cathode. This strategy can be used because copper is oxidized more readily than water:

$$Cu(s) \longrightarrow Cu^{2+}(aq) + 2e^- \qquad E° = -0.34 \text{ V} \qquad [24.20]$$

$$2H_2O(l) \longrightarrow 4H^+(aq) + O_2(g) + 4e^- \qquad E° = -1.23 \text{ V} \qquad [24.21]$$

The impurities in the copper anode include lead, zinc, nickel, arsenic, selenium, tellurium, and several precious metals including gold and silver. Metallic impurities that are more active than copper are readily oxidized at the anode but do not plate out at the cathode because their reduction potentials are more negative than that for copper. However, less active metals are not oxidized at the anode. Instead, they collect below the anode as a sludge that is collected and processed to recover the valuable metals. The anode sludges from copper refining cells provide one-fourth of U.S. silver production and about one-eighth of U.S. gold production.

SAMPLE EXERCISE 24.1

Nickel is one of the chief impurities in the crude copper that is subjected to electrorefining. What happens to this nickel in the course of the electrolytic process?

SOLUTION The standard potential for oxidation of nickel is more positive than that for copper:

$$Ni(s) \longrightarrow Ni^{2+}(aq) + 2e^- \qquad E° = 0.28 \text{ V}$$

$$Cu(s) \longrightarrow Cu^{2+}(aq) + 2e^- \qquad E° = -0.34 \text{ V}$$

Nickel will thus be more readily oxidized than copper at the anode, assuming standard conditions. Of course, we do not have standard conditions in the electrolytic cell. The crude copper anode is nearly all copper, and so we can assume that the activity, or effective concentration, of copper in the anode is essentially the same as that for pure metal. However, the nickel is present as a highly dilute impurity in the

▲ A CLOSER LOOK

Teaching Note: Hall's story is a classic example of a major discovery made by a college chemistry student. Hall was a student at Oberlin College, a small school in Ohio.

Charles M. Hall

Charles M. Hall (Figure 24.13) began to work on the problem of reducing aluminum in about 1885, after he had learned from a professor of the difficulty of reducing ores of very active metals. Prior to the development of his electrolytic process, aluminum was obtained by a chemical reduction using sodium or potassium as the reducing agent. The procedure was very costly; as late as 1852 the cost of aluminum was $545 per pound. During the Paris Exposition in 1855, aluminum was exhibited as a rare metal in spite of the fact that it is the third most abundant element in the earth's crust. Hall, who was 21 years old when he began his research, utilized handmade and borrowed equipment in his studies, and used a woodshed near his home as his laboratory. In about a year's time, he was able to solve the problem of reducing aluminum. His solution consisted of finding an ionic compound that could be melted to form a conducting medium that would dissolve Al_2O_3 but would not interfere in the electrolysis reactions. The relatively rare mineral cryolite, Na_3AlF_6, found in Greenland, met these criteria. Ironically, Paul Héroult, who was the same age as Hall, made the same discovery in France at about the same time. As a result of the research of Hall and Héroult, large-scale production of aluminum became commercially feasible, and aluminum became a common and familiar metal.

FIGURE 24.13 Charles M. Hall (1863–1914) as a young man. (Courtesy of ALCOA)

copper. Thus the activity, or effective concentration, of nickel in the anode is much lower than it would be if we had a pure nickel anode. Nonetheless, the nickel is preferentially oxidized at the anode. The reduction of Ni^{2+}, which is just the reverse of the oxidation process, occurs less readily than the reduction of Cu^{2+}. The Ni^{2+} thus accumulates in the electrolyte solution, while the Cu^{2+} is reduced at the cathode. After a time it is necessary to recycle the electrolyte solution to remove the accumulated metal ion impurities, such as Ni^{2+}

PRACTICE EXERCISE

Zinc is another common impurity in copper. Using electrode potentials, determine whether zinc will accumulate in the anode sludge or in the electrolytic solution during the electrorefining of copper.   *Answer:* electrolytic solution

24.5 Metallic Bonding

In our discussion of metallurgy, we have so far confined ourselves to discussing the methods employed for obtaining metals in pure form. Metallurgy is also concerned with understanding the properties of metals and with developing useful new materials. As with any branch of science and engineering, our ability to make advances is coupled to our understanding of the fundamental properties of the systems with which we work. At several places in the text, we have referred to the differences between metals and nonmetals with regard to both physical and chemical behavior. Let us now consider the distinctive properties of metals and then relate these properties to a model for metallic bonding.

Physical Properties of Metals

You have no doubt at some time held a length of copper wire or an iron bolt. Perhaps you have had occasion to observe the surface of a freshly cut piece of sodium metal. These substances, although distinct from one another, share certain similarities that enable us to classify them as metallic. A fresh metal surface has a characteristic luster. In addition, metals that we can handle with bare hands have a characteristic cold feeling related to their high heat conductivity. Metals also have high electrical conductivities; electrical current flows easily through them. Current flow occurs without any displacement of atoms within the metal structure and is due to the flow of electrons within the metal. The heat conductivity of a metal usually parallels its electrical conductivity. For example, silver and copper, which possess the highest electrical conductivities, also possess the highest heat conductivities. This observation suggests that the two types of conductivity have the same origin in metals, which we shall soon discuss.

Most metals are *malleable,* which means that they can be hammered into thin sheets, and *ductile,* which means that they can be drawn into wires (Figure 24.14). These properties indicate that the atoms are capable of slipping with respect to one another. Ionic solids or crystals of most covalent compounds do not exhibit such behavior. These types of solids are typically brittle and fracture easily. Consider, for example, the difference between dropping an ice cube and a block of aluminum metal onto a concrete floor.

Metals form solid structures in which the atoms are arranged as close-packed spheres or in a similar packing arrangement. For example, copper possesses a cubic close-packed structure (Section 11.7) in which each copper atom is in contact with 12 other copper atoms. The number of valence-shell electrons available for bond formation is insufficient for a copper atom to form an electron-pair bond to each of its neighbors. If each atom is to share its bonding electrons with all its neighbors, these electrons must be able to move from one bonding region to another.

FIGURE 24.14 Gold leaf (left) and copper wire (right) demonstrate the characteristic malleability and ductility of metals. (Richard Megna/Fundamental Photographs)

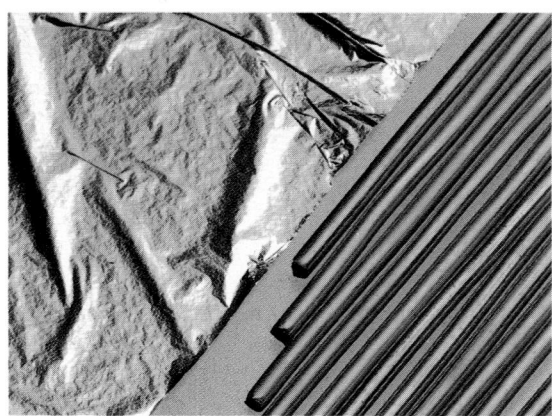

Electron-Sea Model for Metallic Bonding

One very simple model that accounts for some of the most important characteristics of metals is the *electron-sea model*. In this model, the metal is pictured as an array of metal cations in a "sea" of electrons, as illustrated in Figure 24.15. The electrons are confined to the metal by electrostatic attractions to the cations, and they are uniformly distributed throughout the structure. However, the electrons are mobile, and no individual electron is confined to any particular metal ion. When a metal wire is connected to the terminals of a battery, electrons flow through the metal toward the positive terminal and into the metal from the battery at the negative terminal. The high heat conductivity of metals is also accounted for by the mobility of the electrons, which permits ready transfer of kinetic energy throughout the solid. The ability of metals to deform (their malleability and ductility) can be explained by the fact that metal atoms can move without any specific bonds being broken; the change in the positions of the atoms brought about in reshaping the metal is readily accommodated by a redistribution of electrons.

The electron-sea model explains some properties of metals, but does not adequately explain others. For example, the strength of bonding between metal atoms should increase as the number of valence electrons increases. This should result in higher melting points as the number of valence electrons increases. However, the group 6B metals (Cr, Mo, W), which are in the center of the transition metals, have the highest melting points in their respective periods. The melting points on either side of the center are lower (Table 24.2), which implies that the strength of metallic bonding first increases with increasing number of electrons and then decreases. Similar trends are seen in other physical properties of the metals, such as the heat of fusion, hardness, and boiling point.

In order to explain some of the physical properties of metals, we need a more refined model than the electron-sea model to describe metallic bonding. We obtain a better model by applying the concepts of molecular-orbital theory to metals.

Molecular-Orbital Model for Metals

In considering the structures of molecules such as benzene, we saw that in some cases electrons are delocalized, or distributed, over several atoms. ∞ (Sec. 9.5)   This happens when the atomic orbitals on one atom are able to interact with atomic orbitals on several neighboring atoms. In graphite the electrons are delocalized over an entire plane. ∞ (Sec. 11.8)   It is useful to think of the

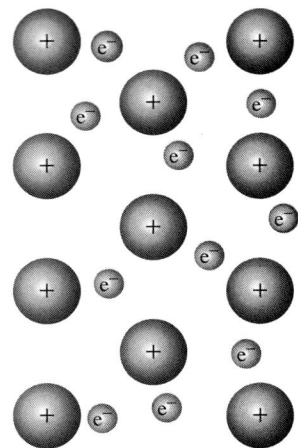

FIGURE 24.15   Schematic illustration of the electron-sea model of the electronic structure of metals.

Learning Goal 11: Describe the simple electron-sea model for metals, and indicate how it accounts for certain important properties of metals.

Frank Rioux, "An Ionic Model for Metallic Bonding," *J. Chem. Educ.* **1985,** *62,* 383.

Analogy: Consider a "Chinese Checkers" board. The marbles are placed in very shallow depressions but, as any player has experienced, the slightest motion of the board causes the marbles to leave their depressions and roll to others. In a similar way, the electrons in metallic solids are very weakly held; a very slight input of energy causes the electrons to move fairly freely.

Learning Goal 12: Describe the molecular-orbital model for metals, including the idea of bands of allowed energies. You should also be able to distinguish between metals and insulators in terms of this model.

TABLE 24.2 △ Melting Points of Selected Transition Metals

	Group 3B	Group 6B	Group 8B
Metal	Sc	Cr	Ni
Melting point (°C)	1541	1857	1455
Metal	Y	Mo	Pd
Melting point (°C)	1522	2617	1554
Metal	La	W	Pt
Melting point (°C)	918	3410	1772

bonding in metals in a similar way. The valence atomic orbitals on one metal atom overlap with those on several nearest neighbors, which in turn overlap with atomic orbitals on still other atoms.

Point of Emphasis: The number of molecular orbitals formed equals the number of atomic orbitals used. See Chapter 9.

We saw in Section 9.6 that the overlap of atomic orbitals can lead to the formation of molecular orbitals. The number of molecular orbitals is equal to the number of atomic orbitals that overlap. In a metal, the number of atomic orbitals that interact or overlap is very large. Thus, the number of molecular orbitals is also very large. Figure 24.16 shows schematically what happens as increasing numbers of metal atoms come together to form molecular orbitals. As overlap of atomic orbitals occurs, bonding and antibonding molecular-orbital combinations are formed. The energies of these molecular orbitals lie at closely spaced intervals in the energy range between the highest- and lowest-energy orbitals. Consequently, interaction of all the valence atomic orbitals of each metal atom with the orbitals of adjacent metal atoms gives rise to a huge number of very closely spaced molecular orbitals that extend over the entire metal structure. The energy separations between these metal orbitals are so tiny that for all practical purposes we may think of the orbitals as forming a continuous *band* of allowed energy states, referred to as an *energy band,* as shown in Figure 24.16.

The electrons available for metallic bonding do not completely fill the available molecular orbitals; we can think of the energy band as a partially filled container for electrons. The incomplete filling of the energy band gives rise to characteristic metallic properties. The electrons in orbitals near the top of the occupied levels require very little energy input to be "promoted" to still higher energy orbitals, which are unoccupied. Under the influence of any source of excitation, such as an applied electrical potential or an input of thermal energy, electrons move into previously vacant levels and are thus freed to move through the lattice, giving rise to electrical and thermal conductivity.

Learning Goal 13: Describe how the extent of metallic bonding among the first transition elements varies with the number of valence electrons.

Trends in properties of transition metals, such as the melting point (Table 24.2), can be readily explained by the molecular-orbital model. Recall the molecular-orbital description of second-period diatomic molecules. ∞ (Sec. 9.7)   Half of the molecular orbitals were bonding, and half were antibonding. As we proceed across the period, the bond order generally increases until N_2, at which point it begins to decrease. This trend occurs because N_2 possesses the right number of electrons to completely fill the bonding molecular orbitals while leaving the high-energy antibonding molecular orbitals empty.

FIGURE 24.16 Schematic illustration of the interactions of metal atomic orbitals to form the delocalized orbitals of the metal lattice. As the number of interacting orbitals increases, the number of molecular orbitals increases, and the spacing between them decreases, eventually forming a nearly continuous "band" of molecular orbitals. The number of electrons available does not completely fill these orbitals.

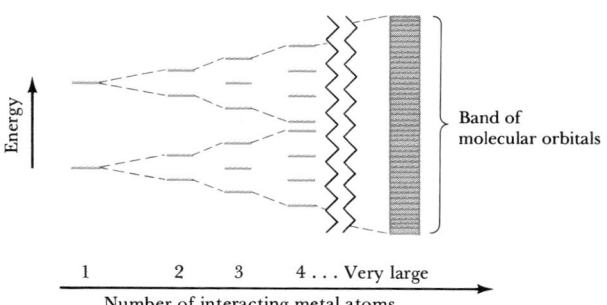

Insulators and Semiconductors

A solid exhibits metallic character because it has a partially filled energy band, as shown in Figure 24.17(a); there are more molecular orbitals in the band than are needed to accommodate all the bonding electrons of the structure. Thus, an excited electron may easily move to the nearby higher orbital. In some solids, however, the electrons completely fill the allowed levels in a band. Such a situation applies, for example, to diamond. When we apply molecular-orbital theory to this solid, we find that the bands of allowed energies are as shown in Figure 24.17(b). The carbon $2s$ and $2p$ atomic orbitals combine to form two energy bands, each of which accommodates four electrons per carbon atom. One of these is completely filled with electrons. The other is completely empty. There is a large energy gap between the two bands. Because there is no readily available vacant orbital into which the highest-energy electrons can move under the influence of an applied electrical potential, diamond is not a good electrical conductor. Solids in which the energy bands are either completely filled or completely empty are electrical *insulators.*

Silicon and germanium have electronic structures like diamond. However, the energy gap between the filled and empty bands becomes smaller as we move from carbon (diamond) to silicon to germanium, as seen in Table 24.3. For silicon and germanium, the energy gap is small enough that at ordinary temperatures a few electrons have sufficient energy to jump from the filled band (called the *valence band*) to the empty band (called the *conduction band*). As a result, there are some empty orbitals in the valence band, permitting electrical conductivity; the electrons in the upper energy band also serve as carriers of electrical current. Therefore, silicon and germanium are *semiconductors,* solids with electrical conductivities between those of metals and those of

TABLE 24.3 △ Energy Gaps in Diamond, Silicon, and Germanium

Element	Energy gap (kJ/mol)
C	502
Si	100
Ge	67

insulators. Other substances, for example GaAs, also behave as semiconductors.

The electrical conductivity of a semiconductor or insulator can be modified by adding small amounts of other substances. This process, called *doping,* causes the solid to have either too few or too many electrons to fill the valence band. Consider what happens to silicon when a small amount of phosphorus or another element from group 5A is added. The phosphorus atoms substitute for silicon atoms at random sites in the structure. Phosphorus, however, possesses five valence-shell electrons per atom, as compared to four for silicon. There is no room for these extra electrons in the valence band. They must therefore occupy the conduction band, as illustrated in Figure 24.18. These higher-energy electrons have access to many vacant orbitals within the energy band they occupy and serve as carriers of electri-

FIGURE 24.18 Effect of doping on the occupancy of the allowed energy levels in silicon. (*a*) Pure silicon. The valence-shell electrons just fill the lower-energy allowed energy levels. (*b*) Silicon doped with phosphorus. Excess electrons occupy the lowest-energy orbitals in the higher-energy band of allowed energies. These electrons are capable of conducting current. (*c*) Silicon doped with gallium. There are not quite enough electrons to fully occupy the orbitals of the lower-energy allowed band. The presence of vacant orbitals in this band permits current flow.

FIGURE 24.17 Metallic conductors have partly filled energy bands, as shown in (*a*). Insulators have filled and empty energy bands, as in (*b*).

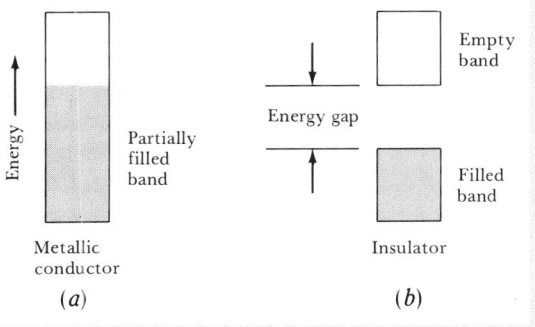

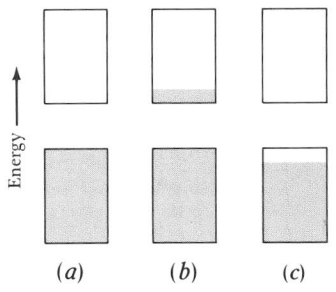

cal current [Figure 24.18(b)]. Silicon doped with phosphorus in this manner is called an *n-type* semiconductor, because this doping introduces extra *n*egative charges (electrons) into the system.

If the silicon is doped instead with a group 3A element, such as gallium, the atoms that substitute for silicon have one electron too few to meet their bonding requirements to the four neighboring silicon atoms. The valence band is thus not completely filled, as illustrated in Figure 24.18(c). Under the influence of an applied field, electrons can move from occupied molecular orbitals to the few that are vacant in the valence band. A semiconductor formed by doping silicon with a group 3A element is called a *p-type* semiconductor because this doping creates electron vacancies that can be thought of as *p*ositive holes in the system. The modern electronics industry is based on integrated circuitry formed from silicon or germanium doped with various elements to create the desired electronic characteristics (Figure 24.19).

FIGURE 24.19
Semiconductors permit tremendous miniaturization of electronic devices, as in this central processing unit (CPU) chip used in personal computers.
(Photo courtesy of Intel)

Teaching Note: The energy gap between adjacent bands (Figs. 24.17 and 24.18) is commonly referred to as the *band gap* of the material.

The energy states that lead to the band for transition metals can likewise be divided roughly into two types: lower-energy states that result from metal-metal bonding interactions, and those at higher energy that result from metal-metal antibonding interactions. The group 6B metals (Cr, Mo, W) possess the correct number of electrons to fill the portion of the energy band that results from metal-metal bonding interactions and to leave most of the metal-metal antibonding states empty. Metals with a smaller number of electrons than the group 6B metals have fewer metal-metal bonding states occupied. Metals with a greater number of electrons than the group 6B metals have more metal-metal antibonding states occupied. In each case, the metal-metal bonding should be weaker than that of the group 6B metals, consistent with the trends in melting point and other properties. Of course, factors other than the number of electrons (such as atomic radius, nuclear charge, and the particular packing structure of the metal) also play a role in determining the properties of metals.

Teaching Note: The electron-sea model is essentially a qualitative molecular-orbital view of metallic bonding.

The *molecular-orbital model* (or *band theory,* as it is also called) is not so different in some respects from the electron-sea model. In both models, the electrons are free to move about in the solid. However, the molecular-orbital model is more quantitative than the simple electron-sea model. Although we cannot go into the details here, many properties of metals can be accounted for by quantum-mechanical calculations using molecular-orbital theory.

904   Chapter 24   Metals and Metallurgy

24.6 Alloys

An *alloy* is a material that contains more than one element and has the characteristic properties of metals. The alloying of metals is of great importance because it is one of the primary ways of modifying the properties of pure metallic elements. For example, nearly all the common uses of iron involve alloy compositions. As another example, pure gold is too soft to be used in jewelry, whereas alloys of gold and copper are quite hard. Pure gold is termed 24 karat; the common alloy used in jewelry is 14 karat, meaning that it is 58 percent gold ($\frac{14}{24} \times 100$). A gold alloy of this composition has suitable hardness to be used in jewelry. The alloy can be either yellow or white, depending on the elements added. Some further examples of alloys are given in Table 24.4.

Alloys can be classified as solution alloys, heterogeneous alloys, and intermetallic compounds. **Solution alloys** are homogeneous mixtures in which the components are dispersed randomly and uniformly. Atoms of the solute can take positions normally occupied by a solvent atom, thereby forming a *substitutional alloy,* or they can occupy interstitial positions, thereby forming an *interstitial alloy.* These types are diagramed in Figure 24.20.

Substitutional alloys are formed when the two metallic components have similar atomic radii and chemical-bonding characteristics. For example, silver and gold form such an alloy over the entire range of possible compositions. When two metals differ in radii by more than about 15 percent, solubility is more limited.

For an interstitial alloy to form, the component present in the interstitial positions between the solvent atoms must have a much smaller covalent radius than the solvent atoms. Typically, an interstitial element is a nonmetal that participates in bonding to neighboring atoms. The presence of the extra bonds provided by the interstitial component causes the metal lattice to become harder, stronger, and less ductile. For example, iron containing up to 3 percent carbon is much harder and stronger than pure iron. *Mild steels* contain less than 0.2 percent carbon; they are malleable and ductile and are used to make cables, nails, and chains. *Medium steels* contain 0.2 to 0.6 percent carbon; they are tougher than mild steels and are used to make girders and rails. *High-carbon steel,* used in cutlery, tools, and springs, contains 0.6 to 1.5 percent carbon. In all these cases, other elements may be added to form *alloy steels.* Vanadium and

Learning Goal 14: Name the important types of alloys, and distinguish between them.

TABLE 24.4 △ Some Common Alloys

Primary element	Name of alloy	Composition by mass	Properties	Uses
Bismuth	Wood's metal	50% Bi, 25% Pb, 12.5% Sn, 12.5% Cd	Low melting point (70°C)	Fuse plugs, automatic sprinklers
Copper	Yellow brass	67% Cu, 33% Zn	Ductile, takes polish	Hardware items
Iron	Stainless steel	80.6% Fe, 0.4% C, 18% Cr, 1% Ni	Resists corrosion	Tableware
Lead	Plumber's solder	67% Pb, 33% Sn	Low melting point (275°C)	Soldering joints
Silver	Sterling silver	92.5% Ag, 7.5% Cu	Bright surface	Tableware
	Dental amalgam	70% Ag, 18% Sn, 10% Cu, 2% Hg	Easily worked	Dental fillings

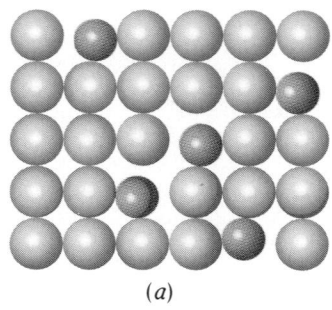

(a)

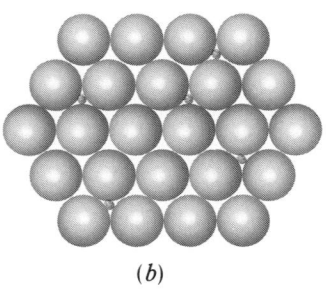

(b)

FIGURE 24.20
(a) Substitutional and (b) interstitial alloys. The gray spheres are host metal; the purple spheres are the other component of the alloy.

chromium may be added to impart strength and to increase resistance to fatigue and corrosion. For example, a rail steel used in Sweden on lines bearing heavy ore carriers contains 0.7 percent carbon, 1 percent chromium, and 0.1 percent vanadium.

One of the most important iron alloys is stainless steel, which contains 0.4 percent carbon, 18 percent chromium, and 1 percent nickel. The chromium is obtained by carbon reduction of chromite, $FeCr_2O_4$, in an electric furnace. The product of the reduction is *ferrochrome,* $FeCr_2$, which is then added in the appropriate amount to molten iron that comes from the converter to achieve the desired steel composition. The ratio of elements present in the steel may vary over a wide range, imparting a variety of specific physical and chemical properties to the materials.

In **heterogeneous alloys,** the components are not dispersed uniformly. For example, in the form of steel known as pearlite, two distinct phases—essentially pure iron and the compound Fe_3C, known as cementite—are present in alternating layers. In general, the properties of heterogeneous alloys depend not only on the composition but also on the manner in which the solid is formed from the molten mixture. Rapid cooling leads to distinctly different properties than does slow cooling.

Intermetallic Compounds

Intermetallic compounds are homogeneous alloys that have definite properties and composition. For example, copper and aluminum form a compound, $CuAl_2$, known as duraluminum. Intermetallic compounds play many important roles in modern society. The intermetallic compound Ni_3Al is a major component of jet aircraft engines because of its strength and low density. Razor blades are often coated with Cr_3Pt, which adds hardness, allowing the blade to stay sharp longer. The compound Co_5Sm is used in the permanent magnets in lightweight headsets (Figure 24.21) because of its high magnetic strength per unit weight.

These examples illustrate some unusual ratios of combining elements. Nothing we have yet discussed in this text would lead us to predict such compositions. Among the many fundamental problems that remain unresolved in chemistry is the problem of developing a good theoretical model to predict the stoichiometries of intermetallic compounds.

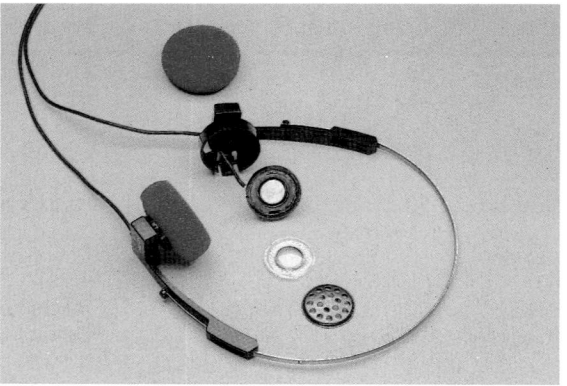

FIGURE 24.21 Interior of a lightweight audio headset. The assembly can be made small because of the very strong magnetism of the Co_5Sm alloy used. (Fundamental Photographs)

24.7 Transition Metals

Many of the most important metals of modern society are transition metals. Transition metals, which occupy the *d* block of the periodic table (Figure 24.22), include such familiar elements as chromium, iron, nickel, and copper. They also include less familiar elements that have come to play important roles in modern technology, such as those in the high-performance jet engine pictured in Figure 24.1. In this section and those that follow, we consider some of the physical and chemical properties of transition metals.

Learning Goal 16: Identify the transition elements in a periodic table.

Physical Properties

Some of the physical properties of the elements of the first transition series are listed in Table 24.5. Some of the properties, such as ionization energy and atomic radius, are characteristic of isolated atoms of the elements. Others, including density and melting point, are characteristic of the bulk solid metal.

The properties of individual atoms show a relatively smooth and rather small variation across each series. For example, notice that the atomic radii of the transition metals shown in Figure 24.23 exhibit a slight decrease in size in moving across the first part of each series. This trend can be understood in terms of the concept of increasing effective nuclear charge. ∞ (Sec. 6.7) For example, as we move across the first series, electrons are being added to the 3*d* orbitals. The 3*d* electrons effectively shield the outer 4*s* electrons from the increasing nuclear charge. Thus, the effective nuclear charge experienced by the outer 4*s* electrons increases only slowly, leading to a small decrease in radius across the series. The slight increase in radius at groups 1B and 2B is due to increasing electron-electron repulsions as the 3*d* subshell is completed.

The incomplete screening of the nuclear charge by added electrons produces a very interesting and important effect in the third transition-metal series. In general, atomic size tends to increase going down a family because of the increasing principal quantum number of the outer-shell electrons. ∞ (Sec. 7.3) Notice that the radii of the 3B elements follow the expected trend, Sc <

Learning Goal 17: Describe the manner in which atomic properties such as ionization energy and atomic radius vary within each transition element series and within each vertical group of transition elements.

FIGURE 24.22 Transition metals are those elements that occupy the *d* block of the periodic table.

	3B	4B	5B	6B	7B	8B	8B	8B	1B	2B
	21 Sc	22 Ti	23 V	24 Cr	25 Mn	26 Fe	27 Co	28 Ni	29 Cu	30 Zn
	39 Y	40 Zr	41 Nb	42 Mo	43 Tc	44 Ru	45 Rh	46 Pd	47 Ag	48 Cd
	57 La	72 Hf	73 Ta	74 W	75 Re	76 Os	77 Ir	78 Pt	79 Au	80 Hg

TABLE 24.5 △ Properties of the First Transition-Series Element

Group:	3B	4B	5B	6B	7B	8B			1B	2B
Element:	Sc	Ti	V	Cr	Mn	Fe	Co	Ni	Cu	Zn
Electron configuration	$3d^14s^2$	$3d^24s^2$	$3d^34s^2$	$3d^54s^1$	$3d^54s^2$	$3d^64s^2$	$3d^74s^2$	$3d^84s^2$	$3d^{10}4s^1$	$3d^{10}4s^2$
First ionization energy (kJ/mol)	631	658	650	653	717	759	758	737	745	906
Atomic radius (Å)	1.44	1.32	1.22	1.17	1.17	1.16	1.16	1.15	1.17	1.24
Density (g/cm³)	3.0	4.5	6.1	7.9	7.2	7.9	8.7	8.9	8.9	7.1
Melting point (°C)	1541	1660	1917	1857	1244	1537	1494	1455	1084	420

Y < La. In group 4B, we would similarly expect the radius to increase in the order Ti < Zr < Hf. However, Hf has virtually the same radius as Zr. This effect has its origin in the lanthanide series, the elements with atomic numbers 58 through 71, which occur between La and Hf. The filling of $4f$ orbitals through the lanthanide elements causes a steady increase in the effective nuclear charge, producing a contraction in size called the **lanthanide contraction.** This contraction just offsets the increase we would expect as we go from the second to the third series. You can see from Figure 24.23 that the second- and third-series transition metals in each group have about the same radii all the way across the series. As a consequence, the second- and third-series metals in a given group have great similarity in their chemical properties. For example, the chemical properties of zirconium and hafnium are remarkably similar. They always occur together in nature, and they are very difficult to separate.

FIGURE 24.23 Variation in covalent radius of transition elements as a function of the periodic table group number.

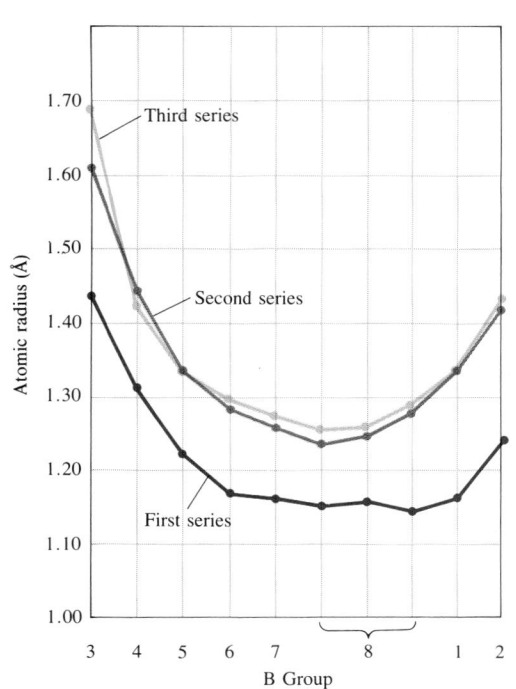

908 Chapter 24 Metals and Metallurgy

Electron Configurations and Oxidation States

Transition metals owe their location in the periodic table to the filling of the d subshells. When these metals are oxidized, however, they lose their outer s electrons before they lose electrons from the d subshell. ∞ (Sec. 8.2) For example, the electron configuration of Fe is $[Ar]3d^64s^2$, whereas that of Fe^{2+} is $[Ar]3d^6$. Formation of Fe^{3+} requires loss of one $3d$ electron, giving $[Ar]3d^5$. Most transition-metal ions contain partially occupied d subshells. The existence of these d electrons is partially responsible for several characteristics of transition metals:

Learning Goal 19: Write the electron configurations for the transition metals.

1. They often exhibit more than one stable oxidation state.
2. Many of their compounds are colored (see Figure 24.24). We shall discuss the origin of these colors in Chapter 25.
3. Transition metals and their compounds exhibit interesting magnetic properties.

Figure 24.25 summarizes the common nonzero oxidation states for transition metals. The ones shown as large circles are those most frequently encountered either in solution or in solid compounds. The ones shown as small circles are less common, but several well-known examples exist for each of these. For example, manganese is commonly found in solution in the $+2$ (Mn^{2+}) and $+7$ (MnO_4^-) oxidation states. In the solid state the $+4$ oxidation state (as in MnO_2) is common. The $+3$, $+5$, and $+6$ oxidation states are less common species in solution and in the solid state. The figure does not give a complete listing of all the oxidation states observed.

Learning Goal 20: Describe the general manner in which the maximum observed oxidation state varies as a function of group number among the transition elements, and account for the observed variation.

Inspection of Figure 24.25 and further study of transition metals reveal some interesting periodic trends in the occurrences and stabilities of oxidation states.

FIGURE 24.24 Salts of transition-metal ions and their solutions. From left to right: Mn^{2+}, Fe^{2+}, Co^{2+}, Ni^{2+}, Cu^{2+}, and Zn^{2+}. (Donald Clegg and Roxy Wilson)

FIGURE 24.25 Nonzero oxidation states of transition elements. The most common oxidation states are indicated by the larger circles.

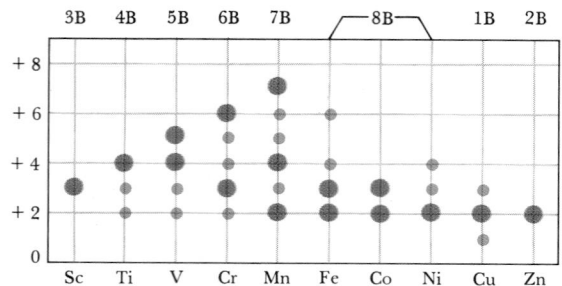

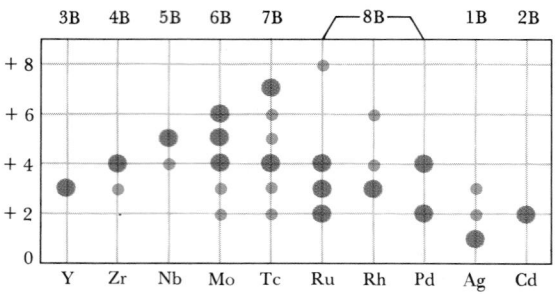

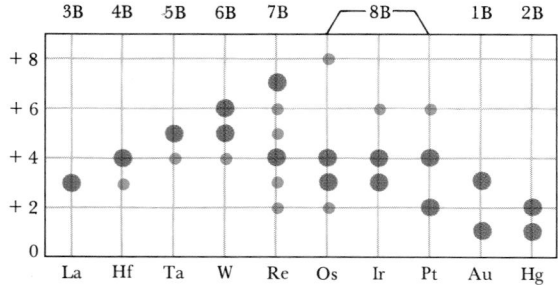

1. Oxidation states of $+2$ and $+3$ are more frequently observed in the first transition series than in the second and third. For example, in group 6B, the $+3$ oxidation state is common for Cr, occasionally observed for Mo, and only rarely found for W. Indeed, *as we go down a group of transition metals, the higher oxidation states become increasingly more stable relative to the $+2$ and $+3$ states.*

2. From Sc through Mn, the *maximum* oxidation state increases from $+3$ to $+7$, equaling in each case the total number of $4s$ plus $3d$ electrons in the atom. In the second and third series, the maximum is $+8$, an oxidation state found in RuO_4 and OsO_4. As we move to the right beyond Mn, Ru, and Os, the maximum observed oxidation state decreases. In general, the highest oxidation states are found only when the metals are combined with the most electronegative elements: O, F, and possibly Cl.

SAMPLE EXERCISE 24.2

The manganate ion, MnO_4^{2-}, is stable only in strongly basic solution. In acidic solution, it decomposes to form the permanganate ion and solid MnO_2. Write a balanced chemical equation to show this reaction.

SOLUTION In this reaction, the same species is both the oxidizing and the reducing agent. Such reactions are known as *disproportionation reactions.* Here, manganese in the $+6$ oxidation state is oxidized to $+7$ and reduced to $+4$. Because there is a change in oxidation state of $+1$ for the oxidation and -2 for the reduction, there must be twice as much MnO_4^- produced as MnO_2. The two half-reactions and overall reaction are:

$$2[MnO_4^{2-}(aq) \longrightarrow MnO_4^-(aq) + e^-]$$
$$\underline{MnO_4^{2-}(aq) + 2e^- + 4H^+(aq) \longrightarrow MnO_2(s) + 2H_2O(l)}$$
$$3MnO_4^{2-}(aq) + 4H^+(aq) \longrightarrow 2MnO_4^-(aq) + MnO_2(s) + 2H_2O(l)$$

PRACTICE EXERCISE

Which of the following do you expect to be the stronger oxidizing agent, MnO_4^- or ReO_4^-? **Answer:** MnO_4^-

Magnetism

The magnetic properties of transition metals and their compounds are both interesting and important. Measurements of magnetic properties provide information about chemical bonding. In addition, many important uses are made of magnetic properties in modern technology.

An electron possesses a "spin" that gives it a magnetic moment; that is, it behaves like a tiny magnet. ∞ (Sec. 6.7) When all the electrons in an atom or ion are paired, the magnetic moments of the electrons effectively cancel each other, and the substance is *diamagnetic.* ∞ (Sec. 9.7) When a diamagnetic substance is placed in a magnetic field, the motions of the electrons are affected in such a way that the substance is very weakly repelled by the magnet. Figure 24.26(*a*) represents a diamagnetic solid, one in which all the electrons in the solid are paired.

When an atom or ion possesses one or more unpaired electrons, the substance is *paramagnetic.* ∞ (Sec. 9.7) In a paramagnetic solid, the unpaired electrons on the atoms or ions of the solid are not influenced by the electrons on adjacent atoms or ions. The magnetic moments on the individual ions are randomly oriented, as shown in Figure 24.26(*b*). When placed in a magnetic field, however, the magnetic moments become aligned roughly parallel to one another, producing a net attractive interaction with the magnet. Thus, a paramagnetic substance is drawn into a magnetic field.

Learning Goal 21: Name and describe the types of magnetic behavior discussed in this chapter: diamagnetism, paramagnetism, ferromagnetism.

Learning Goal 22: Provide an explanation of each type of magnetic behavior in terms of the arrangements in the lattice of metal ions with unpaired spins, and their interactions with one another.

Learning Goal 23: Describe an experimental method for determining the magnetic moment of a solid sample.

 Figure 24.26

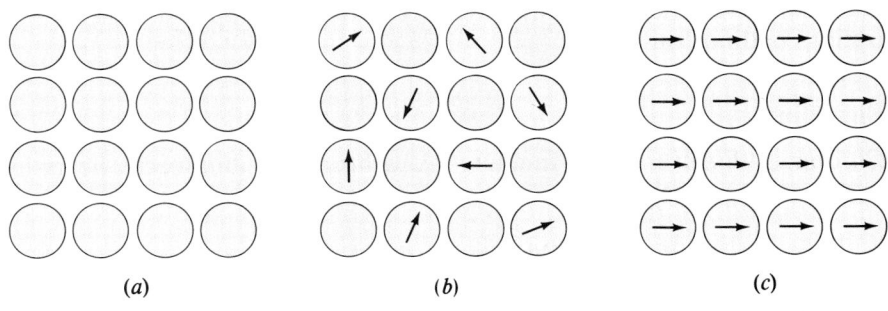

(a) (b) (c)

FIGURE 24.26 Types of magnetic behavior. (*a*) Diamagnetic; no centers (atoms or ions) with magnetic moments. (*b*) Simple paramagnetic; centers with magnetic moments are not aligned unless the substance is in a magnetic field. (*c*) Ferromagnetic; coupled centers aligned in a common direction.

FIGURE 24.27 Permanent magnets are made from ferromagnetic materials. (© Richard Megna/Fundamental Photographs)

FIGURE 24.28 The tube on the left shows the reaction of chromium metal with 6 *M* sulfuric acid in the absence of air. If air had not been excluded, the solution would have taken on a violet cast. The tube on the right shows the reaction of chromium metal with 6 *M* hydrochloric acid in the presence of air. (Donald Clegg and Roxy Wilson)

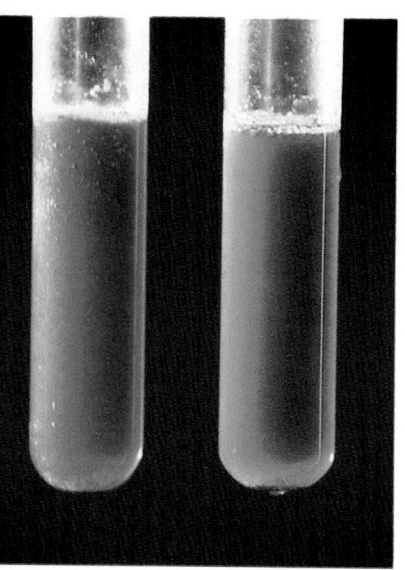

You are probably much more familiar with the magnetic behavior of simple iron magnets (Figure 24.27), a much stronger form of magnetism called **ferromagnetism**. Ferromagnetism arises when the unpaired electrons of the atoms or ions in a solid are influenced by the orientations of the electrons of their neighbors. The most stable (lowest-energy) arrangement results when the spins of electrons on adjacent atoms or ions are aligned in the same direction, as shown in Figure 24.26(*c*). When a ferromagnetic solid is placed in a magnetic field, the electrons tend to align strongly along the magnetic field. The attraction for the magnetic field that results may be as much as 1 million times stronger than that for a simple paramagnetic substance. When the external magnetic field is removed, the interactions between the electrons cause the solid as a whole to maintain a magnetic moment. We then refer to it as a *permanent magnet*. The most common examples of ferromagnetic solids are the elements Fe, Co, and Ni. Many alloys exhibit greater ferromagnetism than do the pure metals themselves. Some metal oxides (for example, CrO_2 and Fe_3O_4) are also ferromagnetic. Several ferromagnetic oxides are used in magnetic recording tape and computer disks.

24.8 Chemistry of Selected Transition Metals

Let's now consider briefly some of the chemistry of three common elements from the first transition series: chromium, iron, and copper. As you read this material, you should look for evidence of the trends that illustrate the generalizations outlined earlier.

Chromium

Chromium dissolves slowly in dilute hydrochloric or sulfuric acid, liberating hydrogen and forming a blue solution of chromous ion (Figure 24.28, left):

$$Cr(s) + 2H^+(aq) \longrightarrow Cr^{2+}(aq) + H_2(g) \qquad [24.22]$$

Normally, however, you do not observe this blue color because the chromium(II) ion is rapidly oxidized in air to the violet-colored chromium(III) ion:

$$4Cr^{2+}(aq) + O_2(g) + 4H^+(aq) \longrightarrow 4Cr^{3+}(aq) + 2H_2O(l) \quad [24.23]$$

Learning Goal 24: Write a balanced chemical equation corresponding to the simple aqueous solution chemistry of chromium, iron, and copper, and account for the variations in chemical properties observed among these elements in terms of the characteristics of the elements themselves.

When hydrochloric acid solution is used, the solution appears green as a result of the formation of complex ions containing chloride coordinated to chromium, for example, $Cr(H_2O)_4Cl_2^+$ (Figure 24.28, right).

Chromium is frequently encountered in aqueous solution in the $+6$ oxidation state. In basic solution, the yellow chromate ion, CrO_4^{2-}, is the most stable. In acidic solution, the dichromate ion, $Cr_2O_7^{2-}$, is formed:

$$CrO_4^{2-}(aq) + H^+(aq) \rightleftharpoons HCrO_4^-(aq) \quad [24.24]$$

$$2HCrO_4^-(aq) \rightleftharpoons Cr_2O_7^{2-}(aq) + H_2O(l) \quad [24.25]$$

You might recognize the second of these reactions as a condensation reaction in which water is split out from between two $HCrO_4^-$ ions. Similar reactions occur among the oxyanions of other elements, such as phosphorus. ∞ (Sec. 23.4)   The equilibrium between the dichromate and chromate ions is readily observable because CrO_4^{2-} is bright yellow and $Cr_2O_7^{2-}$ is deep orange, as seen in Figure 24.29. The dichromate ion in acidic solution is a strong oxidizing agent, as evidenced by its large, positive reduction potential. By contrast, chromate ion in basic solution is not a particularly strong oxidizing agent.

Iron

We have already discussed the metallurgy of iron in considerable detail in Section 24.2. Let's consider here some of the important aqueous solution chemistry of the metal. Iron exists in aqueous solution in either the $+2$ (ferrous) or $+3$ (ferric) oxidation state. It often appears in natural waters because of contact of these waters with deposits of $FeCO_3$ ($K_{sp} = 3.2 \times 10^{-11}$). Dissolved CO_2 in the water can lead to dissolution of the mineral:

$$FeCO_3(s) + CO_2(aq) + H_2O(l) \longrightarrow Fe^{2+}(aq) + 2HCO_3^-(aq) \quad [24.26]$$

The dissolved Fe^{2+}, together with Ca^{2+} and Mg^{2+}, contributes to water hardness. ∞ (Sec. 18.6)

FIGURE 24.29 Lead chromate, $PbCrO_4$ (on the left), and potassium dichromate, $K_2Cr_2O_7$ (on the right), illustrate the difference in color of the chromate and dichromate ions. (Richard Megna/Fundamental Photographs)

FIGURE 24.30 Stain in a sink caused by iron in water, which is oxidized to Fe^{3+} and precipitated as Fe_2O_3. (Page Poore)

Point of Emphasis: Most metal ions (M^{n+}) form complex ions of the type $M(H_2O)_6^{n+}$ in aqueous solution. See Chapter 25.

FIGURE 24.31 Addition of an NaOH solution to an aqueous solution of Fe^{3+} causes $Fe(OH)_3$ to precipitate. (Donald Clegg and Roxy Wilson)

The standard reduction potentials in Appendix E tell us much about the kind of chemical behavior we should expect to observe for iron. The potential for reduction from the $+2$ state to the metal is negative; however, the reduction from the $+3$ to the $+2$ state is positive. This tells us that iron should react with nonoxidizing acids such as dilute sulfuric acid or acetic acid to form $Fe^{2+}(aq)$, as indeed occurs. However, in the presence of air, $Fe^{2+}(aq)$ tends to oxidize to $Fe^{3+}(aq)$, as evidenced by the positive standard voltage for Equation 24.27:

$$4Fe^{2+}(aq) + O_2(g) + 4H^+(aq) \longrightarrow$$
$$4Fe^{3+}(aq) + 2H_2O(l) \qquad E° = +0.46 \text{ V} \quad [24.27]$$

You may have seen instances in which water dripping from a faucet has left a brown stain in a sink (see Figure 24.30). The brown color is due to insoluble iron(III) oxide, formed by oxidation of iron(II) present in the water:

$$4Fe^{2+}(aq) + 8HCO_3^-(aq) + O_2(g) \longrightarrow$$
$$2Fe_2O_3(s) + 8CO_2(g) + 4H_2O(l) \quad [24.28]$$

When iron metal reacts with an oxidizing acid such as warm, dilute nitric acid, $Fe^{3+}(aq)$ is formed directly:

$$Fe(s) + NO_3^-(aq) + 4H^+(aq) \longrightarrow Fe^{3+}(aq) + NO(g) + 2H_2O(l) \quad [24.29]$$

In the $+3$ oxidation state, iron is soluble in acidic solution as the hydrated ion, $Fe(H_2O)_6^{3+}$. However, this ion hydrolyzes readily (Section 16.10):

$$Fe(H_2O)_6^{3+}(aq) \rightleftharpoons Fe(H_2O)_5(OH)^{2+}(aq) + H^+(aq) \quad [24.30]$$

As an acidic solution of iron(III) is made more basic, a gelatinous red-brown precipitate, most accurately described as a hydrous oxide, $Fe_2O_3 \cdot nH_2O$, is formed (Figure 24.31). In this formulation, n represents an indefinite number of water molecules, depending on the precise conditions of the precipitation. Usually, the precipitate that forms is represented merely as $Fe(OH)_3$. The solubility of $Fe(OH)_3$ is very low ($K_{sp} = 4 \times 10^{-38}$). It dissolves in strongly acidic solution but not in basic solution. The fact that it does *not* dissolve in basic solution is the basis of the Bayer process, in which aluminum is separated from impurities, primarily iron(III). ∞ (Sec. 24.3)

Copper

In its aqueous-solution chemistry, copper exhibits two oxidation states, $+1$ (cuprous) and $+2$ (cupric). Note that in the $+1$ oxidation state copper possesses a d^{10} electron configuration. Salts of Cu^+ are often water-insoluble and are mostly white in color. In solution, the Cu^+ ion readily disproportionates:

$$2Cu^+(aq) \longrightarrow Cu^{2+}(aq) + Cu(s) \qquad K_c = 1.2 \times 10^6 \quad [24.31]$$

FIGURE 24.32 Crystals of copper(II) sulfate pentahydrate, $CuSO_4 \cdot 5H_2O$. (Fundamental Photographs)

Because of this reaction, and because copper(I) is readily oxidized to copper(II) under most solution conditions, the $+2$ oxidation state is by far the more common.

Many salts of Cu^{2+}, including $Cu(NO_3)_2$, $CuSO_4$, and $CuCl_2$, are water-soluble. Copper sulfate pentahydrate, $CuSO_4 \cdot 5H_2O$, a widely used salt, has four water molecules bound to the copper ion, and a fifth held to the SO_4^{2-} ion by hydrogen bonding. The salt is blue (it is called *blue vitriol;* see Figure 24.32). Aqueous solutions of Cu^{2+}, in which the copper ion is coordinated by water molecules, are also blue. Among the insoluble compounds of copper(II) is $Cu(OH)_2$, which is formed when NaOH is added to an aqueous Cu^{2+} solution (Figure 24.33). This blue compound readily loses water on heating to form black copper(II) oxide:

$$Cu(OH)_2(s) \longrightarrow CuO(s) + H_2O(l) \qquad [24.32]$$

CuS is one of the least soluble copper(II) compounds ($K_{sp} = 6.3 \times 10^{-36}$). This black substance does not dissolve in NaOH, NH_3, or in nonoxidizing acids such as HCl. However, it does dissolve in HNO_3, which oxidizes the sulfide to sulfur:

$$3CuS(s) + 8H^+(aq) + 2NO_3^-(aq) \longrightarrow$$
$$3Cu^{2+}(aq) + 3S(s) + 2NO(g) + 4H_2O(l) \qquad [24.33]$$

$CuSO_4$ is often added to water to stop algae or fungal growth, and other copper preparations are used to spray or dust plants to protect them from lower organisms and insects. Copper compounds are not generally toxic to human beings, except in massive quantities. Our daily diet normally includes from 2 to 5 mg of copper.

Lee R. Summerlin, Christie L. Borgford, and Julie B. Ealy, "The Copper Mirror," *Chemical Demonstrations, A Sourcebook for Teachers, Volume 2* (Washington: American Chemical Society, 1987), p. 184.

FIGURE 24.33 Addition of an NaOH solution to an aqueous solution of Cu^{2+} causes $Cu(OH)_2$ to precipitate. (Donald Clegg and Roxy Wilson)

For Review

Summary

Metallic elements occur in nature in minerals, which are solid inorganic substances found in various deposits or ores. Metallurgy is concerned with obtaining metals from these sources and with understanding and modifying the properties of metals.

Pyrometallurgy is the use of heat to bring about chemical reactions that convert an ore from one chemical form to another. One such process is calcination, in which an ore is heated to drive off a volatile substance, as in heating a carbonate ore to drive off CO_2. In roasting, the ore is heated under conditions that bring about reaction with the furnace atmosphere. For example, sulfide ores might be heated to cause oxidation of sulfur to SO_2. In a smelting operation, two or more layers of mutually insoluble materials form in the furnace. One layer consists of molten metal, and the other layer (slag) is composed of molten silicate minerals and other ionic materials such as phosphates.

Iron, the most important metal in modern society, is obtained from its oxide ores by reduction in a blast furnace. The reducing agent is carbon, in the form of coke. Limestone, $CaCO_3$, is added to react with the silicates present in the crude ore to form slag. The raw iron from the blast furnace, called pig iron, is usually taken directly to a converter, in which it is refined to form various kinds of steel. In the converter, the molten iron is reacted with pure oxygen to oxidize impurity elements.

Hydrometallurgy is the use of chemical processes occurring in aqueous solution to effect separation of a mineral from its ore or of one particular element from others. In leaching, an ore is treated with an aqueous reagent to dissolve a component selectively. In the Bayer process, aluminum is selectively dissolved from bauxite by treatment with concentrated NaOH solution.

Electrometallurgy is the use of electrolytic methods for the preparation or purification of a metallic element. Sodium is prepared by electrolysis of molten NaCl in a Downs cell. Aluminum is obtained in the Hall process by electrolysis of Al_2O_3 in molten cryolite, Na_3AlF_6. Copper is purified by electrolysis of aqueous copper sulfate solution using anodes composed of impure copper.

The properties of metals can be accounted for in a general way by the electron-sea model, in which the electrons are free to move throughout the metal structure. In the molecular-orbital model, the valence atomic orbitals of the metal atoms interact to form an energy band, which is not completely filled by valence electrons. The orbitals that comprise the energy band are delocalized over the atoms of the metal, and their energies are closely spaced. Because the energy differences between orbitals in the band are so small, promotion of electrons to higher-energy orbitals requires very little energy, giving rise to high electrical and thermal conductivity, as well as other characteristic metallic properties. In contrast, in an insulator, all the orbitals of the band are completely filled.

Alloys are materials that possess characteristic metallic properties and are composed of more than one element. Usually, one or more metallic elements are major components. Solution alloys are homogeneous alloys in which the components are distributed uniformly throughout. In heterogeneous alloys, the components are not distributed uniformly; instead, two or more distinct phases with characteristic compositions are present. Intermetallic compounds are homogeneous alloys that have definite properties and compositions.

Transition metals are characterized by incomplete filling of the d orbitals. The presence of d electrons in transition elements leads to the existence of multiple oxidation states. As we proceed through a given series of transition metals (horizontal row), the effective nuclear charge for the valence electrons increases slowly. As a result, the later transition elements in a given row tend to adopt lower oxidation states and have slightly smaller ionic radii. In comparing the elements of a given group (vertical column), we find that the first-series metals tend to adopt lower oxidation states. Although the atomic and ionic radii increase in the second series as compared to the first, the elements of the second and third series are similar with respect to these properties. This similarity is due to the lanthanide contraction. Lanthanide elements, atomic numbers 58 through 71, display an increase in effective nuclear charge that compensates for the increase in major quantum number in the third series.

The presence of unpaired electrons in valence orbitals leads to interesting magnetic behavior in transition metals and their compounds. In ferromagnetic substances, the unpaired electron spins on atoms in a solid are affected by those on neighboring atoms. In a magnetic field, the spins become aligned along the direction of the magnetic field. When the magnetic field is removed, this orientation remains, giving the solid a magnetic moment as observed in permanent magnets.

In this chapter, we also briefly considered some chemistry of three of the common transition metals: chromium, iron, and copper.

Key Terms

lithosphere (Sec. 24.1)
ore (Sec. 24.1)
mineral (Sec. 24.1)
metallurgy (Sec. 24.1)
alloy (Sec. 24.1)
gangue (Sec. 24.1)
pyrometallurgy (Sec. 24.2)
calcination (Sec. 24.2)
roasting (Sec. 24.2)
smelting (Sec. 24.2)
slag (Sec. 24.2)
refining (Sec. 24.2)

hydrometallurgy (Sec. 24.3)
leaching (Sec. 24.3)
Bayer process (Sec. 24.3)
electrometallurgy (Sec. 24.4)
Downs cell (Sec. 24.4)
Hall process (Sec. 24.4)
solution alloy (Sec. 24.6)
heterogeneous alloy (Sec. 24.6)
intermetallic compound (Sec. 24.6)
lanthanide contraction (Sec. 24.7)
ferromagnetism (Sec. 24.7)

Exercises

Metallurgy

24.1. Two of the most heavily utilized metals are aluminum and iron. What are the most important natural sources of these elements? In what oxidation state is each metal found in nature?

24.2. Sphalerite is a common zinc-containing mineral. What is the chemical formula of this mineral? What is the oxidation state of zinc in sphalerite?

24.3. Complete and balance each of the following equations:
(a) $ZnCO_3(s) \xrightarrow{\Delta}$
(b) $MnO(s) + CO(g) \longrightarrow$
(c) $Al(OH)_3(s) + OH^-(aq) \longrightarrow$
(d) $TiCl_4(g) + K(l) \longrightarrow$
(e) $CaO(l) + P_2O_5(l) \longrightarrow$

24.4. Complete and balance each of the following equations:
(a) $PbS(s) + O_2(g) \longrightarrow$
(b) $PbCO_3(s) \xrightarrow{\Delta}$
(c) $WO_3(s) + H_2(g) \longrightarrow$
(d) $ZnO(s) + CO(g) \longrightarrow$
(e) $ZrC(s) + Cl_2(g) \longrightarrow$

24.5. Write balanced chemical equations for the reductions of FeO and Fe_2O_3 by H_2 or CO.

24.6. What is the major reducing agent in the reduction of iron ore in a blast furnace? Write a balanced chemical equation for the reduction process.

24.7. A sample containing $PbSO_4$ is to be refined to Pb metal via calcination followed by roasting. (a) What volatile product would you expect to be produced by calcination? (b) Propose an appropriate atmosphere to accompany the roasting. (c) Write balanced chemical equations for the two steps.

24.8. Suppose a metallurgist wanted to use nickel(II) hydroxide as a source of nickel metal. (a) What products would you expect from calcination of this substance? (b) Under what conditions might roasting produce Ni metal? (c) Write balanced chemical equations for the processes discussed in parts (a) and (b).

24.9. A charge of 2.0×10^4 kg of material containing 32 percent Cu_2S and 7 percent FeS is added to a converter and oxidized. What mass of $SO_2(g)$ is formed?

24.10. A charge of 1.2×10^4 kg of concentrate from a partial roast of a chalcopyrite ore, containing 26 percent FeO, is added to a furnace. Then SiO_2 is added to form a slag with FeO. Write the balanced equation for the reaction leading to slag formation and calculate the mass of SiO_2 required to react with the FeO to form slag.

24.11. What role does each of the following materials play in the chemical processes that occur in a blast furnace: (a) air; (b) limestone; (c) coke; (d) water? Write balanced chemical equations to illustrate your answers.

24.12. In terms of the concepts discussed in Chapter 13, indicate why the molten metal and slag phases formed in the blast furnace shown in Figure 24.6 are immiscible.

24.13. Describe how electrometallurgy could be employed to purify crude cobalt metal. Describe the compositions of the electrodes and electrolyte and write out all electrode reactions.

24.14. The element tin is generally recovered from deposits of the ore cassiterite, SnO_2. The oxide is reduced with carbon, and the crude metal is purified by electrolysis. Write balanced chemical equations for the reduction process and the electrode reactions in the electrolysis, assuming that an acidic solution of $SnSO_4$ is employed as an electrolyte.

24.15. In an electrolytic process nickel sulfide is oxidized in a two-step reaction:

$$Ni_3S_2(s) \longrightarrow Ni^{2+}(aq) + 2NiS(s) + 2e^-$$
$$NiS(s) \longrightarrow Ni^{2+}(aq) + S(s) + 2e^-$$

What mass of Ni^{2+} is produced in solution by passage of a current of 66 A for a period of 8.0 hr, assuming the cell to be 100 percent efficient?

24.16. What mass of copper is deposited in an electrolytic refining cell by a passage of 240 A current for a period of 10 hr, assuming 80 percent current efficiency?

[24.17]. Using the data in Appendix C, estimate the free-energy change for each of the following reactions at 1200°C:
(a) $PbO(s) + CO(g) \longrightarrow Pb(s) + CO_2(g)$
(b) $Si(s) + 2MnO(s) \longrightarrow SiO_2(s) + 2Mn(s)$
(c) $FeO(s) + H_2(g) \longrightarrow Fe(s) + H_2O(g)$

[24.18]. In terms of thermodynamic functions, particularly free energies of formation, what conditions must be operative for refining iron in the converter shown in Figure 24.8 to be a workable process?

Metals and Alloys

24.19. Sodium is a highly malleable substance, whereas sodium chloride is not. Explain this difference in properties.

24.20. Elemental silicon (Figure 7.15) has a metallic luster. Propose two different tests you could perform on a sample of elemental silicon to determine whether it is a metal.

24.21. Silver has the highest electrical and thermal conductivities of any metal. How does the electron-sea model account for these conductivities?

24.22. As illustrated in Figure 24.14, copper can be drawn into thin wires. **(a)** What is this property of metals called? **(b)** How is this property explained on the basis of the electron-sea model?

24.23. Moving across the fourth period of the periodic table, hardness increases at first, reaching a maximum at Cr; the hardness then decreases as we move from Cr to Zn. Explain this trend.

24.24. The densities of the elements K, Ca, Sc, and Ti are 0.86, 1.5, 3.2, and 4.5 g/cm³, respectively. What factors are likely to be of major importance in determining this variation?

24.25. According to band theory, how do insulators differ from conductors? How do semiconductors differ from conductors?

24.26. Which would you expect to be a better conductor of electricity, germanium or germanium doped with arsenic? Explain using the molecular-orbital model.

24.27. Tin exists in two allotropic forms; gray tin has a diamond structure, and white tin has a close-packed structure. Which of these allotropic forms would you expect to be more metallic in character? Explain why the electrical conductivity of white tin is much greater than that of gray tin. Which form would you expect to have the longer Sn—Sn bond distance?

24.28. The interatomic distance in silver metal, 2.88 Å, is much greater than the calculated Ag—Ag single-bond distance, 1.34 Å. Nevertheless, the melting point of silver, 906°C, and its high boiling point, 2164°C, suggest that there is strong bonding between silver atoms in the metal. Describe a model for the structure of silver metal that is consistent with these observed properties.

24.29. Define the term *alloy*. Distinguish among solution alloys, heterogeneous alloys, and intermetallic compounds.

24.30. Distinguish between substitutional and interstitial alloys. What conditions favor formation of substitutional alloys?

Transition Metals

24.31. Which of the following properties are better considered characteristic of the free isolated atoms, and which are characteristic of the bulk metal: **(a)** electrical conductivity; **(b)** first ionization energy; **(c)** atomic radius; **(d)** melting point?

24.32. Which of the following properties are better considered characteristic of bulk metals, and which are characteristic of the free isolated atoms: **(a)** heat of fusion; **(b)**

malleability; **(c)** hardness; **(d)** electrode potential for $M^{2+}(aq) + 2e^- \longrightarrow M(s)$?

24.33. What is meant by the term *lanthanide contraction*? What properties of the transition elements are affected by the lanthanide contraction?

24.34. Zirconium and hafnium are the group 4B elements in the second and third transition series. The atomic radii of these elements are virtually the same (Figure 24.23). How does the lanthanide contraction account for this similarity in atomic radius?

24.35. Write the formula for the chloride corresponding to the highest expected oxidation state for each of the following elements: **(a)** Nb; **(b)** W; **(c)** Co; **(d)** Cd; **(e)** Re.

24.36. Write the formula for the oxide corresponding to the highest expected oxidation state for each of the following elements: **(a)** Cr; **(b)** Zn; **(c)** Hf; **(d)** Os; **(e)** Sc.

24.37. What accounts for the fact that chromium exhibits several oxidation states in its compounds, whereas aluminum exhibits only the +3 oxidation state?

24.38. Account for the fact that zinc exhibits only the +2 oxidation state in its compounds, whereas copper exhibits both the +1 and +2 oxidation states.

24.39. Write the expected electron configuration for each of the following ions: **(a)** Cr^{3+}; **(b)** Au^{3+}; **(c)** Ru^{2+}; **(d)** Cu^{+}; **(e)** Mn^{4+}; **(f)** Ir^{3+}.

24.40. What is the expected electron configuration for each of the following ions: **(a)** Fe^{2+}; **(b)** Sc^{2+}; **(c)** Ag^{+}; **(d)** Mo^{4+}; **(e)** Nb^{3+}; **(f)** Rh^{3+}?

24.41. Which would you expect to be more easily oxidized, Ti^{2+} or Ni^{2+}?

24.42. Which would you expect to be the stronger reducing agent, Cr^{2+} or Fe^{2+}?

24.43. Which would you expect to be the better oxidizing agent, MnO_4^- or TcO_4^-?

24.44. Which would you expect to be harder to reduce, CrO_3 or WO_3?

24.45. What are the two most common oxidation states of gold? Which of these is the more likely to be found in a solution of a strongly oxidizing acid?

24.46. Copper(I) is an uncommon oxidation state in aqueous acidic solution because it disproportionates into Cu^{2+} and Cu. Use data from Appendix E to calculate the equilibrium constant for the reaction $2Cu^{+}(aq) \longrightarrow Cu^{2+}(aq) + Cu(s)$.

24.47. Give the chemical formulas and colors of the chromate and dichromate ions. Which of these is more stable in acidic solution?

24.48. How does the presence of air affect the relative stabilities of ferrous and ferric ions?

24.49. Write balanced chemical equations for the reaction between iron and **(a)** hydrochloric acid; **(b)** nitric acid.

24.50. Write balanced chemical equations for the reaction of **(a)** $Fe^{3+}(aq)$ and sodium hydroxide solution; **(b)** $FeCO_3(s)$ and hydrochloric acid solution.

24.51. What, on an atomic level, distinguishes a paramagnetic material from a diamagnetic one? How does each behave in a magnetic field?

24.52. What characteristics of a ferromagnetic material distinguish it from one that is paramagnetic? What type of interaction must occur in the solid to bring about ferromagnetic behavior?

Additional Exercises

24.53. Write a balanced chemical equation to correspond to each of the following verbal descriptions. **(a)** $NiO(s)$ can be solubilized by leaching with aqueous sulfuric acid. **(b)** After concentration, an ore containing the mineral carrollite, $CuCo_2S_4$, is leached with aqueous sulfuric acid to produce a solution containing copper and cobalt ions. **(c)** Titanium dioxide is treated with chlorine in the presence of carbon as reducing agent to form $TiCl_4$. **(d)** Under oxygen pressure, $ZnS(s)$ reacts at 150°C with aqueous sulfuric acid to form soluble zinc sulfate, with deposition of elemental sulfur.

24.54. Write a balanced chemical equation for each of the following verbal descriptions. **(a)** Vanadium(V) oxide is formed by thermal decomposition of ammonium metavanadate, NH_4VO_3. **(b)** Vanadium(V) oxide is reduced to vanadium(IV) oxide by thermal reduction with gaseous SO_2. **(c)** Vanadium(V) oxide is reduced by magnesium in hydrochloric acid to give a green solution of vanadium(III). **(d)** Niobium(V) chloride reacts with water to yield crystals of niobic acid, $HNbO_3$.

24.55. In the early days of iron mining in the United States, the iron oxide mined in the Lake Superior region was reduced to pig iron in blast furnaces located near the mines. The furnaces used charcoal made from hardwood as the reducing agent (transportation savings prompted this procedure). What mass of pig iron containing 2.5 percent carbon was produced from each kilogram of iron ore, assuming that it is mined as magnetite, Fe_3O_4, of 70 percent purity?

24.56. The reduction of metal oxides is often accomplished using carbon monoxide as a reducing agent. Carbon (coke) and carbon dioxide are usually present, leading to the following reactions:

$$C(s) + CO_2(g) \rightleftharpoons 2CO(g)$$

Using data from Appendix C, calculate the equilibrium constant for this reaction at 289 K and at 2000 K, assuming that the enthalpies and entropies do not depend upon temperature.

24.57. Magnesium is obtained by electrolysis of molten $MgCl_2$. Several cells are connected in parallel by very large copper buses that convey current to the cells. Assuming that the cells are 96 percent efficient in producing the desired products in electrolysis, what mass of Mg is formed by passage of a current of 97,000 A for a period of 24 hr?

24.58. Hafnium metal is often refined using the *Kroll process,* a process in which the chloride of the metal is reduced with sodium metal. Write balanced chemical equations for the production of hafnium metal from HfC via the Kroll process.

24.59. The galvanizing of iron sheet can be carried out electrolytically using a bath containing a zinc sulfate solution. The sheet is made the cathode, and a graphite anode is used. Calculate the cost of the electricity required to deposit a 0.30-mm layer of zinc on both sides of an iron sheet 1.0 m wide and 50 m long if the current is 30 A, the voltage is 3.5 V, and the energy efficiency of the process is 90 percent. Assume the cost of electricity is \$0.080 per kilowatt hour. The density of zinc is 7.1 g/cm^3.

24.60. The crude copper that is subjected to electrorefining contains selenium and tellurium as impurities. Describe the probable fate of these elements during electrorefining and relate your answer to the positions of these elements in the periodic table.

[24.61]. Silver is found as Ag_2S in the ore *argentite.* **(a)** By using data in Table 17.2 and Appendix D.3, determine the equilibrium constant for the cyanidation of Ag_2S to $Ag(CN)_2^-$. **(b)** Based on your answer to part (a), would you consider cyanidation to be a practical means of leaching silver from argentite ore? **(c)** Silver is also found as AgCl in the ore *horn silver.* Would it be feasible to use cyanidation as a leaching process for this ore?

[24.62]. In the electrolytic purification of nickel, some iron may be present in the crude metal. It is found that as iron accumulates in the electrolyte solution, the current efficiency of the electrolysis cell decreases when the contents of the cathode cell compartment are not isolated from the air. Write reactions involving iron species that could account for the loss in current efficiency. (Hint: Recall that iron can exist in solution in more than one oxidation state.)

[24.63]. Write balanced chemical equations that correspond to the steps in the following brief account of the metallurgy of molybdenum: Molybdenum occurs primarily as the sulfide, MoS_2. On boiling with concentrated nitric acid, a white residue of MoO_3 is obtained. This is an acidic oxide; from a solution of hot, excess concentrated ammonia, ammonium molybdate crystallizes on cooling. On heating ammonium molybdate, white MoO_3 is obtained. On heating to 1200°C in hydrogen, a gray powder of metallic molybdenum is obtained.

24.64. A nugget of gold weighing 1 troy ounce (31.1 g) can be hammered into a sheet of area 300 ft². **(a)** What property of metals is demonstrated by this observation? **(b)** The density of gold is 19.31 g/cm^3. Calculate the thickness of the sheet in millimeters, assuming it has uniform thickness.

[24.65]. Indicate whether each of the following is likely to be an insulator, a metallic conductor, an *n*-type semiconductor, or a *p*-type semiconductor: **(a)** germanium doped with Ga; **(b)** pure $CuAl_2$; **(c)** pure boron; **(d)** silicon doped with As; **(e)** pure Nb; **(f)** pure MgO.

24.66. Distinguish between **(a)** a substitutional and an interstitial alloy; **(b)** an intermetallic compound and a heterogeneous alloy; **(c)** a metal and an insulator; **(d)** the bonding in $Na_2(g)$ and in $Na(s)$.

24.67. Pure silicon is a very poor conductor of electricity. Titanium, which also possesses four valence-shell electrons, is a metallic conductor. Explain the difference.

[24.68]. The stabilities of the three complexes $Zn(H_2O)_4^{2+}$, $Zn(NH_3)_4^{2+}$, and $Zn(CN)_4^{2-}$ increase from the H_2O to the NH_3 to the CN^- complex. How do you expect the electrode potentials of these three complexes to compare to that of the processes in which $Zn^{2+}(aq)$ is reduced to Zn metal?

[24.69]. Associated with every ferromagnetic solid is a temperature known as its *Curie temperature.* When heated above its Curie temperature, the substance no longer exhibits ferromagnetism but rather becomes paramagnetic. Explain this observation in terms of the kinetic-molecular theory of solids. ∞ (Sec. 11.1)

[24.70]. Based on the chemistry seen in this chapter and others, propose balanced chemical equations for the following sequence of reactions involving nickel: **(a)** The ore *millerite,* which contains NiS, is roasted in an atmosphere of oxygen to produce an oxide; **(b)** the oxide is reduced to the metal using coke; **(c)** dissolving the metal in hydrochloric acid produces a green solution; **(d)** addition of excess sodium hydroxide to the solution causes the precipitation of a gelatinous green material; **(e)** upon heating, the green material loses water and yields a green powder.

Chemistry of Coordination Compounds

25

The colors in the glass panels that make up this window are obtained by addition of oxides, usually of the transition metals, to the molten glass before the glass sheet is formed.

CONTENTS

Point of Emphasis: The term *coordination* comes from the fact that ligands form coordinate bonds with the metal. That is, both bonding electrons come from one of the atoms of the ligand. Chemists also use the term *dative* to describe the bonding of a ligand to a metal center.

Point of Emphasis: Ligands bind to metal ions through unshared pairs of electrons (lone pairs) on the donor atom.

Point of Emphasis: Metal-ligand bonds have some covalent character in addition to ionic character.

 In earlier chapters, we noted that metallic elements tend to lose electrons in chemical reactions. For this reason, positively charged metal ions play a primary role in the chemical behavior of metals. Of course, metal ions do not exist in isolation. In the first place, they are accompanied by anions whose negative charge balances the positive charge of the metal ions, producing neutral compounds. In addition, metal ions act as Lewis acids. ∞ (Sec. 16.10) Anions or molecules with unshared pairs of electrons can act as Lewis bases and bind to the metal center. On several occasions, we have discussed compounds in which a metal ion is surrounded by a group of anions or neutral molecules. Some examples are $[Au(CN)_2]^-$, discussed in connection with metallurgy in Section 24.3; hemoglobin, discussed in connection with the oxygen-carrying capacity of the blood in Section 18.4; and $[Fe(H_2O)_6]^{3+}$ and $[Ag(NH_3)_2]^+$, encountered in our discussion of equilibria in Sections 16.10 and 17.5. Such species are known as **complex ions,** or merely **complexes.** Compounds containing them are called **coordination compounds.**

25.1 The Structure of Complexes

The molecules or ions that surround a metal ion in a complex are known as *complexing agents* or **ligands** (from the Latin word *ligare,* meaning "to bind"). Ligands are normally either anions or polar molecules. Furthermore, they have at least one unshared pair of valence electrons, as illustrated in the following examples:

$$\ddot{\text{O}}-\text{H} \qquad :\!\text{N}-\text{H} \qquad :\!\ddot{\text{Cl}}:^- \qquad :\text{C}\!\equiv\!\text{N}:^-$$
$$\underset{\text{H}}{|} \qquad\quad \underset{\text{H}}{\overset{\text{H}}{|}}$$

In many cases, we can think of the bonding between a metal ion and its ligands as an electrostatic interaction between the positive cation and the surrounding negative ions, or dipoles oriented with their negative ends toward the metal ion. We would expect the ability of metal ions to bind ligands to increase as the positive charge of the cation increases and its size decreases. The weakest complexes are formed by the alkali metal ions, such as Na^+ and K^+. Conversely, the $2+$ and $3+$ ions of the transition elements show a great tendency to form complexes. In fact, many of the transition-metal ions form complexes more readily than their charge and size would suggest. For example, on the basis of size alone we might expect that the Al^{3+} ion (radius $= 0.45$ Å) would form complexes more readily than the larger Cr^{3+} ion (radius $= 0.62$ Å). However, with most ligands, Cr^{3+} forms much more stable complexes than does Al^{3+}. Indeed, the bonding in most transition-metal ions cannot be explained entirely on the basis of electrostatic attractions, and we must assume some degree of covalent character in the metal-ligand bond.

Because metal ions have empty valence orbitals, they can act as Lewis acids (electron-pair acceptors). Because ligands have unshared pairs of electrons, they can function as Lewis bases (electron-pair donors). We can picture the bond between metal and ligand as the result of their sharing a pair of electrons that was initially on the ligand:

$$\text{Ag}^+(aq) + 2 \ :\!\!\begin{array}{c} \text{H} \\ | \\ \text{N}\!-\!\text{H} \\ | \\ \text{H} \end{array}\!\!(aq) \longrightarrow \left[\begin{array}{cc} \text{H} & \text{H} \\ | & | \\ \text{H}\!-\!\text{N} : \text{Ag} : \text{N}\!-\!\text{H} \\ | & | \\ \text{H} & \text{H} \end{array} \right]^{+} (aq) \quad [25.1]$$

We shall examine the bonding in complexes more closely in Section 25.7.

In forming a complex, the ligands are said to *coordinate* to the metal or to *complex* the metal. The central metal and the ligands bound to it constitute the **coordination sphere.** In writing the chemical formula for a coordination compound, we use square brackets to set off the groups within the coordination sphere from other parts of the compound. For example, the formula $[\text{Cu(NH}_3)_4]\text{SO}_4$ represents a coordination compound consisting of the $[\text{Cu(NH}_3)_4]^{2+}$ complex ion and the SO_4^{2-} ion. The four ammonia ligands in the compound are bound directly to the copper(II) ion.

A metal complex is a distinct chemical species with its own characteristic physical and chemical properties. Thus, it has different properties than the metal ion or the ligands from which it is formed. For example, complexes may have colors that differ markedly from those of their component metal ions and ligands. Figure 25.1 shows the color change that occurs when aqueous solutions of SCN^- and Fe^{3+} are mixed, forming $[\text{Fe(H}_2\text{O})_5\text{SCN}]^{2+}$.

Complex formation can also dramatically change other properties of metal ions such as their ease of oxidation or reduction. For example, Ag^+ is readily reduced in water:

$$\text{Ag}^+(aq) + \text{e}^- \longrightarrow \text{Ag}(s) \qquad E° = +0.799 \text{ V} \qquad [25.2]$$

In contrast, the $[\text{Ag(CN)}_2]^-$ ion is not at all readily reduced, because complexation by CN^- ions stabilizes silver in the $+1$ oxidation state:

$$[\text{Ag(CN)}_2]^-(aq) + \text{e}^- \longrightarrow \text{Ag}(s) + 2\text{CN}^-(aq) \qquad E° = -0.31 \text{ V} \quad [25.3]$$

Of course, aquated metal ions are themselves complex ions in which the ligand is water. Thus, $\text{Fe}^{3+}(aq)$ consists largely of $[\text{Fe(H}_2\text{O})_6]^{3+}$. ∞ (Sec. 16.10) When we speak of complex formation in aqueous solutions, we are actually considering reactions in which ligands such as SCN^- and CN^- replace H_2O molecules in the coordination sphere of the metal ion.

Charges, Coordination Numbers, and Geometries

The charge of a complex is the sum of the charges on the central metal and on its surrounding ligands. In $[\text{Cu(NH}_3)_4]\text{SO}_4$, we can deduce the charge on the complex if we first recognize SO_4 as representing the sulfate ion and therefore having a $2-$ charge. Because the compound is neutral, the complex ion must have a $2+$ charge, $[\text{Cu(NH}_3)_4]^{2+}$. We can then use the charge of the complex ion to deduce the oxidation number of copper. Because the NH_3 ligands are neutral, the oxidation number of copper must be $+2$:

$$\underset{[\text{Cu(NH}_3)_4]^{2+}}{+2 + 4(0) = +2}$$

Point of Emphasis: The square brackets denote the metal ion and the ligands within the coordination sphere.

FIGURE 25.1 When an aqueous solution of NH_4SCN is added to an aqueous solution of Fe^{3+}, the intensely colored $[\text{Fe(H}_2\text{O})_5\text{SCN}]^{2+}$ ion is formed. (Richard Megna/Fundamental Photographs)

(a)

(b)

SAMPLE EXERCISE 25.1

What is the oxidation number of the central metal in $[Co(NH_3)_5Cl](NO_3)_2$?

SOLUTION The NO_3 group is the nitrate anion and has a 1− charge, NO_3^-. The NH_3 ligands are neutral; the Cl is a coordinated chloride ion and therefore has a 1− charge. The sum of all the charges must be zero:

$$x + 5(0) + (-1) + 2(-1) = 0$$
$$[Co(NH_3)_5Cl](NO_3)_2$$

The oxidation number of the cobalt, x, must therefore be +3.

PRACTICE EXERCISE

What is the charge of the complex formed by a platinum(II) metal ion surrounded by two ammonia molecules and two bromide ions?   **Answer:** zero

SAMPLE EXERCISE 25.2

Given that a complex ion contains a chromium(III) bound to four water molecules and two chloride ions, write its formula.

SOLUTION The metal has a +3 oxidation number, water is neutral, and chloride has a 1− charge:

$$+3 + 4(0) + 2(-1) = +1$$
$$Cr(H_2O)_4Cl_2$$

Therefore, the charge on the ion is 1+, $[Cr(H_2O)_4Cl_2]^+$.

PRACTICE EXERCISE

Write the formula for the complex ion described in the Practice Exercise accompanying Sample Exercise 25.1.   **Answer:** $[Pt(NH_3)_2Br_2]$

The atom of the ligand bound directly to the metal is called the **donor atom.** For example, nitrogen is the donor atom in the $[Ag(NH_3)_2]^+$ complex shown in Equation 25.1. The number of donor atoms attached to a metal is known as the **coordination number** of the metal. In $[Ag(NH_3)_2]^+$, silver has a coordination number of 2; in $[Cr(H_2O)_4Cl_2]^+$, chromium has a coordination number of 6.

Some metal ions exhibit constant coordination numbers. For example, the coordination number of chromium(III) and cobalt(III) is invariably 6, and that of platinum(II) is always 4. However, the coordination numbers of most metal ions vary with the ligand. The most common coordination numbers are 4 and 6.

The coordination number of a metal ion is often influenced by the relative sizes of the metal ion and the surrounding ligands. As the ligand gets larger, fewer can coordinate to the metal. This helps explain why iron(III) is able to coordinate to six fluorides in $[FeF_6]^{3-}$, but to only four chlorides in $[FeCl_4]^-$. Ligands that transfer substantial negative charge to the metal also produce reduced coordination numbers. For example, six neutral ammonia molecules can coordinate to nickel(II), forming $[Ni(NH_3)_6]^{2+}$; however, only four negatively charged cyanide ions coordinate, forming $[Ni(CN)_4]^{2-}$.

Four-coordinate complexes have two common geometries—tetrahedral and square planar—as shown in Figure 25.2. The tetrahedral geometry is the

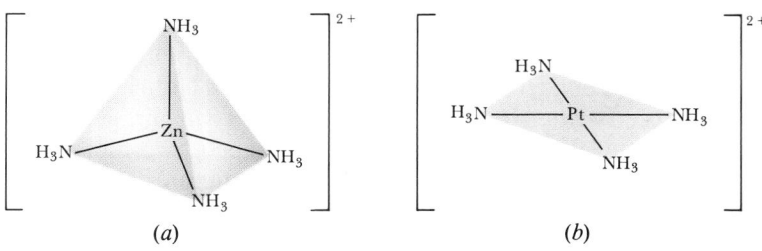

FIGURE 25.2 Structures of (*a*) [Zn(NH₃)₄]²⁺ and (*b*) [Pt(NH₃)₄]²⁺, illustrating the tetrahedral and square-planar geometries, respectively. These are the two common geometries for complexes in which the metal ion has a coordination number of 4. The shaded surfaces shown in the figure are not bonds; they are included merely to assist in visualizing the shape of the metal complex.

more common of the two and is especially common among nontransition metals. Square-planar geometry is characteristic of transition-metal ions with eight *d* electrons in the valence shell, for example, platinum(II) and gold(III); it is also found in some copper(II) complexes.

The vast majority of 6-coordinate complexes have an octahedral geometry, as shown in Figure 25.3(*a*). The octahedron is often represented as a planar square with ligands above and below the plane, as in Figure 25.3(*b*). Recall, however, that all positions on an octahedron are geometrically equivalent. ∞ (Sec. 9.1)

Figure 25.2

Learning Goal 2: Describe, with the aid of drawings, the common geometries of complexes. (You will need to recognize whether the common ligands are functioning as monodentate or polydentate ligands.)

25.2 Chelates

The ligands that we have discussed so far, such as NH₃ and Cl⁻, are called **monodentate ligands** (from the Latin meaning "one-toothed"). These ligands possess a single donor atom and are able to occupy only one site in a coordination sphere. Some ligands have two or more donor atoms that can simultaneously coordinate to a metal ion, thereby occupying two or more coordination sites. They are called **polydentate ligands** ("many-toothed" ligands.) Because they appear to grasp the metal between two or more donor atoms, polydentate ligands are also known as **chelating agents** (from the Greek word *chele*, "claw"). One such ligand is *ethylenediamine:*

$$\underset{..}{H_2N}\diagup\overset{\displaystyle CH_2-CH_2}{}\diagdown\underset{..}{NH_2}$$

This ligand, which is abbreviated en, has two nitrogen atoms (shown in color) that have unshared pairs of electrons. These donor atoms are sufficiently far apart that the ligand can wrap around a metal ion with the two nitrogen atoms

Teaching Note: The geometries found in metal complexes are analogous to the geometries discussed in VSEPR theory. See Chapter 9.

Figure 25.3

FIGURE 25.3 Two representations of an octahedral coordination sphere, the common geometric arrangement for complexes in which the metal ion has a coordination number of 6.

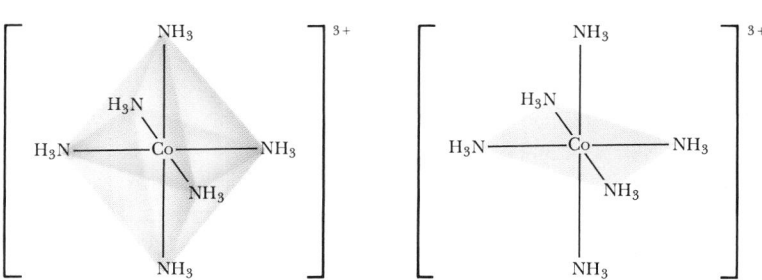

FIGURE 25.4 [Co(en)₃]³⁺ ion, showing how each bidentate ethylenediamine ligand is able to occupy two positions in the coordination sphere.

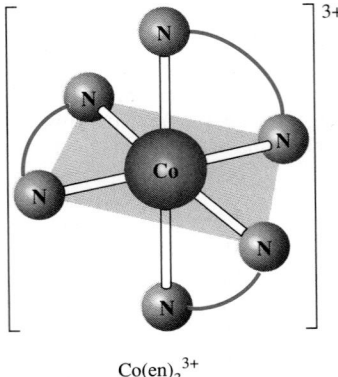

$Co(en)_3{}^{3+}$

simultaneously complexing to the metal in adjacent positions. The [Co(en)₃]³⁺ ion, which contains three ethylenediamine ligands in the octahedral coordination sphere of cobalt(III), is shown in Figure 25.4. Notice that the ethylenediamine has been written in a shorthand notation as two nitrogen atoms connected by a line. Ethylenediamine is a **bidentate ligand** ("two-toothed" ligand), one that can occupy two coordination sites. The structures of several other bidentate ligands are shown in Figure 25.5.

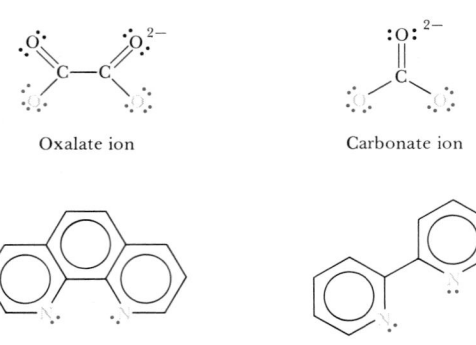

Oxalate ion   Carbonate ion

FIGURE 25.5 Structures of some bidentate ligands. The coordinating atoms are shown in blue.

Ortho-phenanthroline (*o*-phen)

Bipyridine (bipy)

The ethylenediaminetetraacetate ion is another important polydentate ligand:

[EDTA]⁴⁻

Teaching Note: The chelate effect is largely entropic in origin. See "A Closer Look: The Stability of Chelates."

FIGURE 25.6 The [CoEDTA]⁻ ion, showing how the ethylenediaminetetraacetate ion is able to wrap around a metal ion, occupying six positions in the coordination sphere.

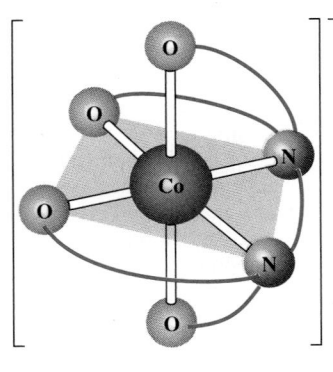

CoEDTA⁻

This ion, abbreviated EDTA⁴⁻, has six donor atoms. It can wrap around a metal ion using all six of these donor atoms, as shown in Figure 25.6.

In general, chelating agents form more stable complexes than do related monodentate ligands. This is illustrated by the formation constants for [Ni(NH₃)₆]²⁺ and [Ni(en)₃]²⁺, shown in Equations 25.4 and 25.5.

$$[Ni(H_2O)_6]^{2+}(aq) + 6NH_3(aq) \rightleftharpoons$$
$$[Ni(NH_3)_6]^{2+}(aq) + 6H_2O(l) \qquad K_f = 4 \times 10^8 \quad [25.4]$$

$$[Ni(H_2O)_6]^{2+}(aq) + 3en(aq) \rightleftharpoons$$
$$[Ni(en)_3]^{2+}(aq) + 6H_2O(l) \qquad K_f = 2 \times 10^{18} \quad [25.5]$$

Although the donor atom is nitrogen in both instances, [Ni(en)₃]²⁺ has a formation constant nearly 10¹⁰ times larger than that of [Ni(NH₃)₆]²⁺. The generally larger formation constants for polydentate ligands as compared with the corresponding monodentate ligands is known as the **chelate effect.**

The Stability of Chelates

Thermochemical studies of complex formation in aqueous solution show that in nearly all cases *the chelate effect is due to a more favorable entropy change for complex formation involving polydentate ligands.* As an example, let's compare the thermodynamic data at 25°C for formation of two closely related complexes of Cd^{2+}:

$$Cd^{2+}(aq) + 4CH_3NH_2(aq) \rightleftharpoons [Cd(CH_3NH_2)_4]^{2+}(aq)$$
$$\Delta G° = -37.2 \text{ kJ}; \Delta H° = -57.3 \text{ kJ}; \Delta S° = -67.3 \text{ J/K}$$

$$Cd^{2+}(aq) + 2H_2NCH_2CH_2NH_2(aq) \rightleftharpoons$$
$$[Cd(H_2NCH_2CH_2NH_2)_2]^{2+}(aq)$$
$$\Delta G° = -60.7 \text{ kJ}; \Delta H° = -56.5 \text{ kJ}; \Delta S° = +14.1 \text{ J/K}$$

Recall that a large negative value for $\Delta G°$ corresponds to a large equilibrium constant for the forward reaction. ∞ (Sec. 19.7) The equilibrium constant for complex formation is thus much greater for the second reaction, with en as ligand. Although the enthalpy changes in the two reactions are nearly the same, the entropy change is much more positive for the second reaction. The more positive $\Delta S°$ accounts for the more negative value for $\Delta G°$ for the second reaction.

The more positive entropy change associated with reactions involving polydentate ligands is related to some of the ideas regarding entropy discussed in Section 19.3. Ligands bound to the metal ion are constrained to remain with that metal ion; they are not free to move about the solution independently. Therefore, coordination of ligands leads to a reduction in entropy. In the first reaction above, four CH_3NH_2 molecules become bound to the metal ion, and four water molecules are freed to move about the solution. Although it might seem at first that this should lead to a net entropy change of zero, differences in the hydrogen-bonding ability of H_2O as compared with the CH_3NH_2 molecules, and the tighter binding of CH_3NH_2 to the Cd^{2+} ion as compared with water, lead to a net negative entropy change. However, when two ethylenediamine molecules bind to Cd^{2+}, four H_2O molecules are released to move about freely in the solution. There is a net increase in the number of species that move about independently in the solution. The system has become more disordered, and the entropy change is accordingly more positive.

Chelating agents are often used to prevent one or more of the customary reactions of a metal ion without actually removing it from solution. For example, a metal ion that interferes with a chemical analysis can often be complexed and its interference thereby removed. In a sense, the chelating agent hides the metal ion. For this reason, scientists sometimes refer to these ligands as *sequestering agents.* Phosphates such as sodium tripolyphosphate, shown below, are used to complex or sequester metal ions in hard water (Section 18.6) so these ions cannot interfere with the action of soap or detergents:

$$Na_5 \begin{bmatrix} O & O & O \\ \parallel & \parallel & \parallel \\ O-P-O-P-O-P-O \\ | & | & | \\ O & O & O \end{bmatrix}$$

Chelating agents such as EDTA are often used in consumer products, including many prepared foods such as salad dressings and frozen desserts, to complex trace metal ions that catalyze decomposition reactions. Chelating agents are used in medicine to remove metal ions such as Hg^{2+}, Pb^{2+}, and Cd^{2+}, which are detrimental to health. One method of treating lead poisoning is to administer $Na_2[CaEDTA]$. The EDTA chelates the lead, allowing its removal from the body in urine. Chelating agents are also quite common in nature. Mosses and lichens secrete chelating agents to capture metal ions from the rocks they inhabit.

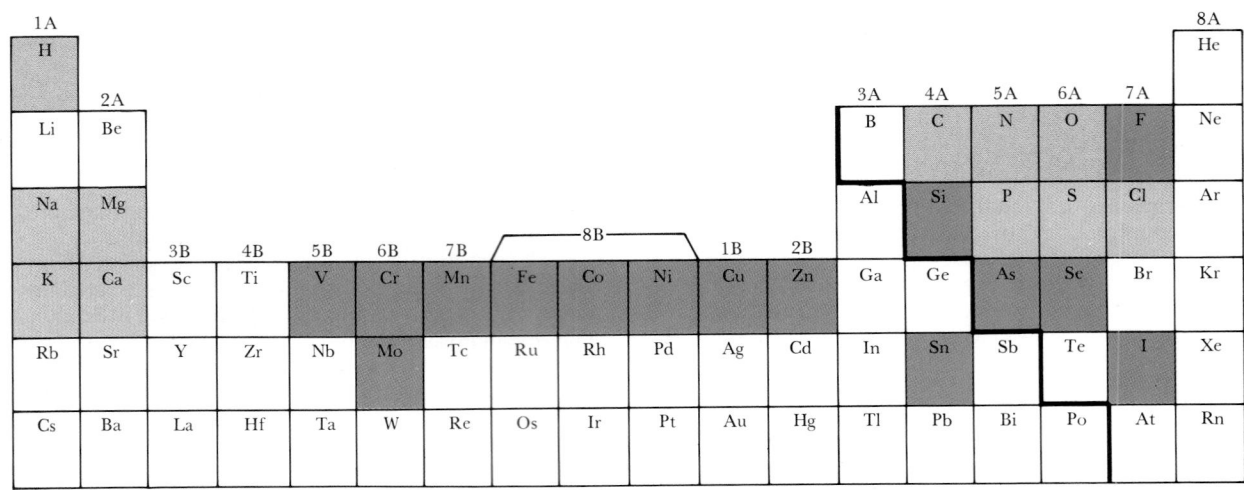

FIGURE 25.7 The elements that are essential for life are indicated by colors. The red denotes the four most abundant elements in living systems (hydrogen, carbon, nitrogen, and oxygen). The orange indicates the seven next most abundant elements. The green indicates the elements needed in only trace amounts.

Metals and Chelates in Living Systems

Living systems consist mainly of hydrogen, oxygen, carbon, and nitrogen. Nevertheless, many other elements are known to be essential for life (Figure 25.7). Nine of the essential elements are transition metals—vanadium, chromium, iron, copper, zinc, manganese, cobalt, nickel, and molybdenum. These elements owe their roles in living systems mainly to their ability to form complexes with a variety of donor groups present in biological systems. Many enzymes, the body's catalysts, require metal ions to function.

Although our bodies require only small quantities of metals, deficiencies can lead to serious illness. For example, a deficiency of manganese in the diet can lead to convulsive disorders. Some epilepsy patients have been helped by the addition of manganese to their diets.

Among the most important chelating agents in nature are those derived from the *porphine* molecule, which is shown in Figure 25.8. This molecule can coordinate to a metal using the four nitrogen atoms as donors. Upon coordination to a metal, the two H^+ shown bonded to nitrogen are displaced. Complexes derived from porphine are called **porphyrins.** Different porphyrins contain different metals and have different substituent groups attached to the carbon atoms at the ligand's periphery. Two of the most important porphyrin or porphyrinlike compounds are heme, which contains iron(II), and chlorophyll, which contains magnesium(II).

Figure 25.9 shows schematically the structure of myoglobin, a protein whose molecular weight is about 18,000 amu and that contains one heme group. Myoglobin is an example of a globular protein, one that folds into a compact, roughly spherical shape. Globular proteins are generally soluble in water and are mobile within cells. Myoglobin is found in the cells of skeletal muscle, particularly in seals, whales, and porpoises. It serves to store oxygen in cells until it is needed for metabolic activities. Hemoglobin, the protein that

FIGURE 25.8 Structure of the porphine molecule. This molecule forms a tetradentate ligand with the loss of the two protons bound to nitrogen atoms. Porphine is the basic component of porphyrins, compounds whose complexes play a variety of important roles in nature.

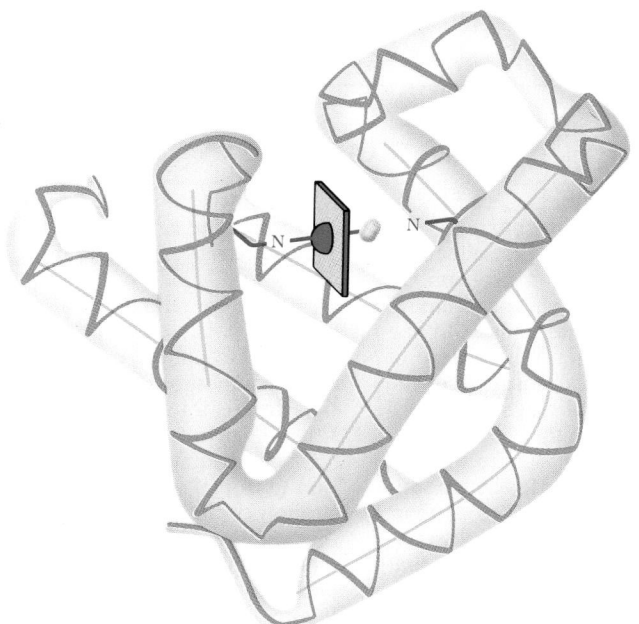

FIGURE 25.9 The structure of myoglobin, a protein that acts to store oxygen in cells. This protein contains one heme unit, symbolized by the red sphere and surrounding square. The heme unit is bound to the protein through a nitrogen-containing ligand, represented by the red N on the left. In the oxygenated form, an O_2 molecule is coordinated to the heme group, as shown. The protein chain is represented by the continuous orange ribbon. The helical sections are denoted by the green lines. The protein wraps around to make a kind of pocket for the heme group.

transports oxygen in human blood, is made up of four subunits, each of which is very similar to myoglobin.

The coordination environment of the iron in myoglobin and hemoglobin is illustrated in Figure 25.10. The iron is coordinated to the four nitrogen atoms of the porphyrin and also to a nitrogen atom from the protein. The sixth position around the iron is occupied either by O_2 (in oxyhemoglobin, the bright red form) or by water (in deoxyhemoglobin, the purplish-red form). The oxy form is shown in Figure 25.10. As noted in Section 18.4, some substances, such as CO, act as poisons because they bind to iron more strongly than O_2 can.

A metal complex is also at the heart of **photosynthesis,** the major means for conversion of solar energy into forms that can be used by living organisms. The photosynthetic reaction that occurs in the leaves of plants is conversion of carbon dioxide and water to carbohydrate, with release of oxygen:

$$6CO_2 + 6H_2O \xrightarrow{48\ hv} C_6H_{12}O_6 + 6O_2 \qquad\qquad [25.6]$$

Note that formation of a mole of sugar, $C_6H_{12}O_6$, requires the absorption and utilization of 48 mol of photons. This needed radiant energy comes from the

FIGURE 25.10 Schematic representation of oxymyoglobin or oxyhemoglobin. The iron is bound to four nitrogen atoms of the porphyrin, to a nitrogen from the surrounding protein, and to an O_2 molecule.

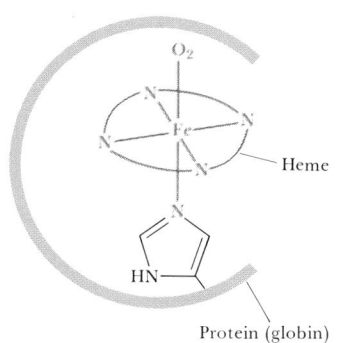

The Battle for Iron in Living Systems

Although iron is the fourth most abundant element in the earth's crust, living systems have difficulty in assimilating enough iron to satisfy their needs. Consequently, iron-deficiency anemia is a common problem in humans. In plants, chlorosis, an iron deficiency that results in yellowing of leaves, is also commonplace. Living systems have difficulty in assimilating iron because of changes that occurred in the earth's atmosphere in the course of geological time. The earliest living systems had a plentiful supply of soluble iron(II) in the oceans. However, when oxygen appeared in the atmosphere, vast deposits of insoluble iron(III) oxide formed. The amount of dissolved iron remaining was too small to support life. Microorganisms adapted to this problem by secreting an iron-binding compound, called *siderophore,* that forms an extremely stable, water-soluble complex with iron(III). This complex is called *ferrichrome;* its structure is shown in Figure 25.11. The iron-binding strength of siderophore is so great that it can extract iron from Pyrex glassware, and it readily solubilizes the iron in iron oxides.

The overall charge of ferrichrome is zero, which makes it possible for the complex to pass through the rather hydrophobic membrane walls of cells. When a dilute solution of ferrichrome is added to a cell suspension, iron is found entirely within the cells in an hour. When ferrichrome enters the cell, the iron is removed through an enzyme-catalyzed reaction that reduces the iron to iron(II). Iron in the lower oxidation state is not strongly complexed by the siderophore. Microorganisms thus acquire iron by excreting siderophore into their immediate environment, then taking the ferrichrome complex into the cell. The overall process is illustrated in Figure 25.12.

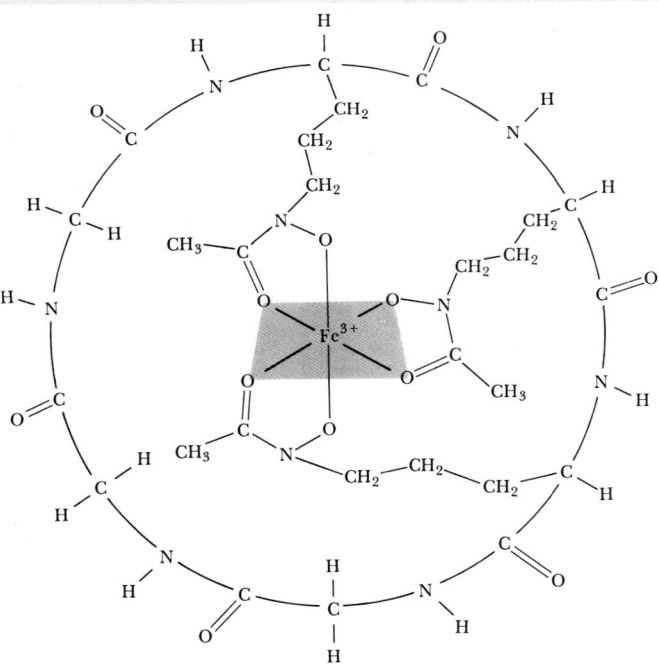

FIGURE 25.12 The iron-transport system of a bacterial cell. The iron-binding ligand, called siderophore, is synthesized inside the cell and excreted into the surrounding medium. It reacts with Fe^{3+} ion to form ferrichrome, which is then absorbed by the cell. Inside the cell the ferrichrome is reduced, forming Fe^{2+}, which is not tightly bound by the siderophore. Having released the iron for use in the cell, the siderophore may be recycled back into the medium.

FIGURE 25.11 The structure of ferrichrome. In this complex an Fe^{3+} ion is coordinated by six oxygen atoms. The complex is very stable; it has a formation constant of about 10^{30}. The overall charge of the complex is zero.

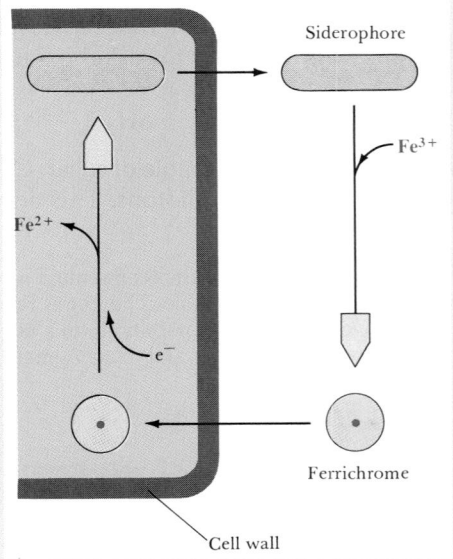

In humans, iron is assimilated from food in the intestine. A protein called *transferrin* binds iron and transports it across the intestinal wall to distribute it to other tissues in the body. The normal adult human carries a total of about 4 g of iron. At any one time, about 3 g, or 75 percent, of the iron is in the blood, mostly in the form of hemoglobin. Most of the remainder is carried by transferrin.

A bacterium that infects the blood requires a source of iron if it is to grow and reproduce. The bacterium excretes siderophore into the blood to compete with transferrin for the iron it holds. The formation constants for iron binding are about the same for transferrin and siderophore. The more iron available to the bacterium, the more rapidly it can reproduce, and thus the more harm it can do. Several years ago, New Zealand clinics regularly gave iron supplements to infants soon after birth. However, the incidence of certain bacterial infections was eight times higher in treated than in un-treated infants. Presumably, the presence in the blood of more iron than absolutely necessary makes it easier for bacteria to obtain the iron necessary for growth and reproduction.

In the United States, it is common medical practice to supplement infant formula with iron sometime during the first year of life. This practice is based on the fact that human milk is virtually devoid of iron. Given what is now known about iron metabolism by bacteria, many research workers in nutrition believe that iron supplementation is not generally justified or wise.

For bacteria to continue to multiply in the bloodstream, they must synthesize new supplies of siderophore. It has been discovered that synthesis of siderophore in bacteria slows as the temperature is increased above the normal body temperature of 37°C, and it stops completely at 40°C. This suggests that fever in the presence of an invading microbe is a mechanism used by the body to deprive bacteria of iron.

---

visible region of the spectrum (Figure 6.3). The photons are absorbed by photosynthetic pigments in the leaves of plants. The key pigments are the **chlorophylls.** The structure of the most abundant chlorophyll, called chlorophyll *a,* is shown in Figure 25.13.

Chlorophyll is a coordination compound; it contains a Mg^{2+} ion bound to four nitrogen atoms arranged around the metal in a planar array. The nitrogen atoms are part of a porphinelike ring (Figure 25.8). Notice that a series of alternating double bonds in the ring surrounds the metal ion. This system of alternating, or conjugated, double bonds gives rise to the strong absorptions of chlorophyll in the visible region of the spectrum. Figure 25.14 shows the absorption spectrum of chlorophyll as compared with the distribution of solar energy at the earth's surface. Chlorophyll is green in color because it absorbs red light (maximum absorption at 655 nm) and blue light (maximum absorption at 430 nm) and transmits green light.

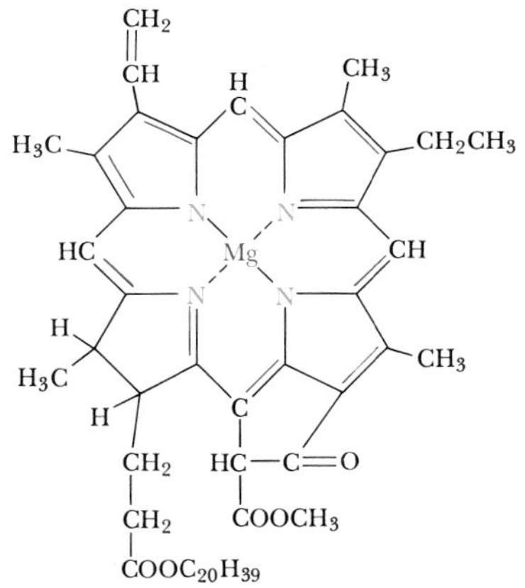

FIGURE 25.13 Structure of chlorophyll *a.* All chlorophyll molecules are essentially alike; they differ only in details of the side chains.

FIGURE 25.14 Absorption spectrum of chlorophyll (green curve), in comparison with the solar radiation at ground level (red curve).

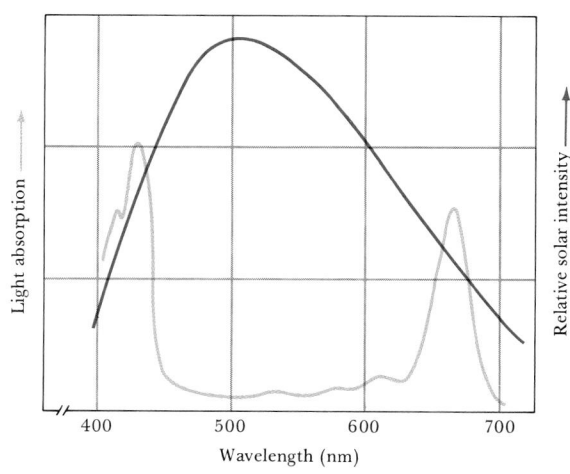

The solar energy absorbed by chlorophyll is converted by a complex series of steps into chemical energy. This stored energy is then used to drive the reaction in Equation 25.6 to the right, a direction in which it is highly endothermic. Plant photosynthesis is nature's solar-energy-conversion machine; all living systems on earth are dependent on it for continued existence (Figure 25.15).

25.3 Nomenclature

When complexes were first discovered and few were known, they were named after the chemist who originally prepared them. A few of these names persist; for example, $NH_4[Cr(NH_3)_2(NCS)_4]$ is known as Reinecke's salt. As the number of known complexes grew, chemists began to give them names based on their color. For example, $[Co(NH_3)_5Cl]Cl_2$, whose formula was then written $CoCl_3 \cdot 5NH_3$, was known as purpureocobaltic chloride after its purple color. Once the structures of complexes were more fully understood, it became possible to name them in a more systematic manner. Let's consider two examples:

FIGURE 25.15 The absorption and conversion of solar energy that occurs in the maple leaf provides the energy necessary to drive all the living processes of the tree, including growth. (Calvin Larsen/Photo Researchers)

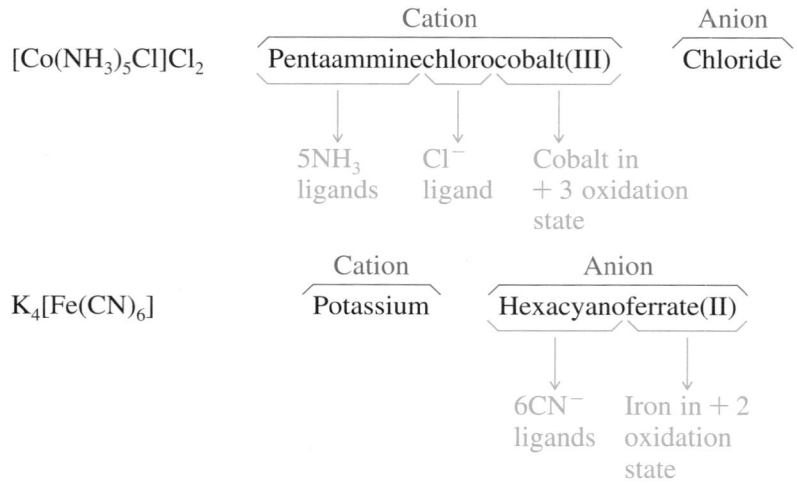

The rules of nomenclature are as follows*:

1. *In naming salts, the name of the cation is given before the name of the anion.* Thus, in $[Co(NH_3)_5Cl]Cl_2$ we name the $[Co(NH_3)_5Cl]^{2+}$ and then Cl^-.

2. *Within a complex ion or molecule, the ligands are named before the metal. Ligands are listed in alphabetical order, regardless of charge on the ligand. Prefixes that give the number of ligands are not considered part of the ligand name in determining alphabetical order.* Thus, in the $[Co(NH_3)_5Cl]^{2+}$ ion, we name the ammonia ligands first, then the chlo-

---

* The rules of nomenclature are approved by the International Union of Pure and Applied Chemistry and are subject to periodic revision. Some rules are more important than others. For example, the order in which ligands are named (rule 2) is not as important as assigning each ligand its correct name.

ride, then the metal: pentaamminechlorocobalt(III). Note, however, that in writing the formula the metal is listed first.

3. *Anionic ligands end in the letter o, whereas neutral ones ordinarily bear the name of the molecule.* Some common ligands and their names are listed in Table 25.1. Special names are given to H_2O (aqua) and NH_3 (ammine). For example, the terms *chloro* and *ammine* occur in the name for $[Co(NH_3)_5Cl]Cl_2$.

4. *A Greek prefix (for example, di-, tri-, tetra-, penta-, and hexa-) is used to indicate the number of each kind of ligand when more than one is present.* Therefore, in the name for $[Co(NH_3)_5Cl]^{2+}$ we have pentaammine, indicating five NH_3 ligands. *If the name of the ligand itself contains a Greek prefix, such as mono- or di-, the name of the ligand is enclosed in parentheses, and alternate prefixes (bis-, tris-, tetrakis-, pentakis-, and hexakis-) are used.* For example, the name for $[Co(en)_3]Cl_3$ is tris(ethylenediamine)cobalt(III) chloride.

5. *If the complex is an anion, its name ends in -ate.* For example, in $K_4[Fe(CN)_6]$ the anion is called the hexacyanoferrate(II) ion. The suffix *-ate* is often added to the Latin stem, as in this example.

6. *The oxidation number of the metal is given in parentheses in Roman numerals following the name of the metal.* For example, the Roman numeral III is used to indicate the +3 oxidation state of cobalt in $[Co(NH_3)_5Cl]^{2+}$.

Point of Emphasis: *Aqua* for water and *ammine* for ammonia are among the few special ligand names used in naming metal complexes. Older sources may use the name *aquo* for coordinated water.

Point of Emphasis: If the metal's symbol is derived from a Latin root, the name of the metal in an anionic complex reverts to that root, for example: cuprate, ferrate, or aurate.

We apply these rules to the compounds listed below on the left to derive the names given on the right:

$[Ni(C_5H_5N)_6]Br_2$ hexapyridinenickel(II) bromide
$[Co(NH_3)_4(H_2O)CN]Cl_2$ tetraammineaquacyanocobalt(III) chloride
$Na_2[MoOCl_4]$ sodium tetrachlorooxomolybdate(IV)
$Na[Al(OH)_4]$ sodium tetrahydroxoaluminate

In the last example, the oxidation state of the metal is not mentioned in the name because aluminum in complexes is always in the +3 oxidation state.

TABLE 25.1 △ Some Common Ligands

Ligand	Ligand name
Azide, N_3^-	Azido
Bromide, Br^-	Bromo
Chloride, Cl^-	Chloro
Cyanide, CN^-	Cyano
Hydroxide, OH^-	Hydroxo
Carbonate, CO_3^{2-}	Carbonato
Oxalate, $C_2O_4^{2-}$	Oxalato
Ammonia, NH_3	Ammine
Ethylenediamine, en	Ethylenediamine
Pyridine, C_5H_5N	Pyridine
Water, H_2O	Aqua

SAMPLE EXERCISE 25.3

Give the name of the following compounds: (a) $[Cr(H_2O)_4Cl_2]Cl$; (b) $K_4[Ni(CN)_4]$.

SOLUTION (a) We begin with the four water molecules, which are indicated as tetraaqua. Then there are two chloride ions, indicated as dichloro. The oxidation state of Cr is $+3$.

$$+3 + 4(0) + 2(-1) + (-1) = 0$$
$$[Cr(H_2O)_4Cl_2]Cl$$

Thus, we have chromium(III). Finally, the anion is chloride. Putting these parts together, we have the compound's name: tetraaquadichlorochromium(III) chloride.

(b) The complex has four CN^-, which we indicate as tetracyano. The oxidation state of the nickel is zero:

$$4(+1) + 0 + 4(-1) = 0$$
$$K_4[Ni(CN)_4]$$

Because the complex is an anion, the metal is indicated as nickelate(0). Putting these parts together and naming the cation first, we have: potassium tetracyanonickelate(0).

PRACTICE EXERCISE

Name the following compounds: (a) $[Mo(NH_3)_3Br_3]NO_3$; (b) $(NH_4)_2[CuBr_4]$.
Answers: (a) triamminetribromomolybdenum(IV) nitrate; (b) ammonium tetrabromocuprate(II)

SAMPLE EXERCISE 25.4

Write the formula for bis(ethylenediamine)difluorocobalt(III) perchlorate.

SOLUTION The complex cation contains two fluorides, two ethylenediamines, and a cobalt with a $+3$ oxidation number. Knowing this, we can determine the charge on the complex:

$$+3 + 2(0) + 2(-1) = +1$$
$$[Co(en)_2F_2]$$

The perchlorate anion has a single negative charge, ClO_4^-. Therefore, only one is needed to balance the charge on the complex cation. The formula is thus $[Co(en)_2F_2]ClO_4$.

PRACTICE EXERCISE

Write the formula for sodium diaquabis(oxalato)ruthenate(III).
Answer: $Na[Ru(H_2O)_2(C_2O_4)_2]$

25.4 Isomerism

Learning Goal 4: Describe the common types of isomerism, and distinguish between structural isomerism and stereoisomerism.

When two or more compounds have the same composition but a different arrangement of atoms, we call them **isomers**. Isomerism—the existence of isomers—is a characteristic feature of coordination compounds. Although isomers are composed of the same collection of atoms, they differ in one or

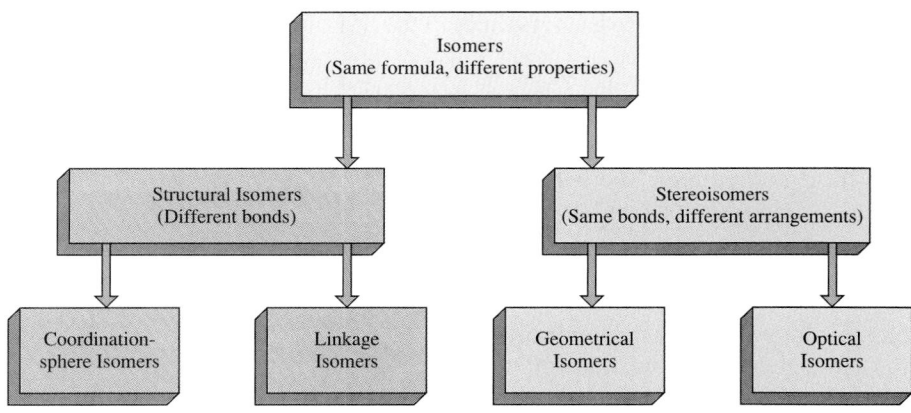

FIGURE 25.16   Forms of isomerism in coordination compounds.

Figure 25.16

more physical or chemical properties such as color, solubility, or rate of reaction with some reagent. We will consider two main kinds of isomers: **structural isomers** (which have different bonds) and **stereoisomers** (which have the same bonds but different spatial arrangements of the bonds). Each of these classes also has subclasses, which we now consider (see Figure 25.16).

Teaching Note: Structural isomers have different connectivity of atoms. Stereoisomers have the same connectivity but different spatial arrangements of the atoms.

Structural Isomerism

Many different types of structural isomerism are known in coordination chemistry. Figure 25.16 gives two examples: linkage isomerism and coordination-sphere isomerism. **Linkage isomerism** is a relatively rare but interesting type that arises when a particular ligand is capable of coordinating to a metal in two different ways. For example, the nitrite ion, NO_2^-, can coordinate through either a nitrogen or an oxygen atom, as shown in Figure 25.17. When it coordinates through the nitrogen atom, the NO_2^- ligand is called *nitro;* when it coordinates through the oxygen atom, it is called *nitrito* and is generally written ONO^-. The isomers shown in Figure 25.17 differ in their chemical and physical properties. For example, the N-bonded isomer is yellow, whereas the O-bonded isomer is red. Another ligand capable of coordinating through either of two donor atoms is thiocyanate, SCN^-, whose potential donor atoms are N and S.

FIGURE 25.17   (*a*) Yellow N-bound and (*b*) red O-bound isomers of $[Co(NH_3)_5NO_2]^{2+}$.

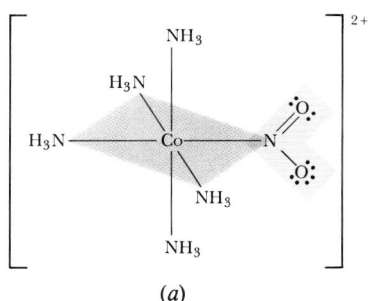

(*a*)

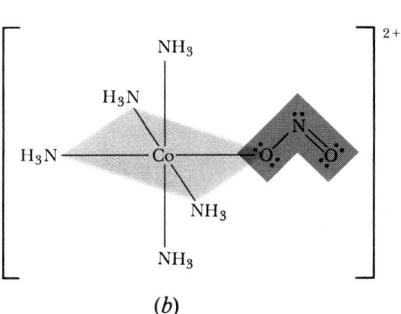

(*b*)

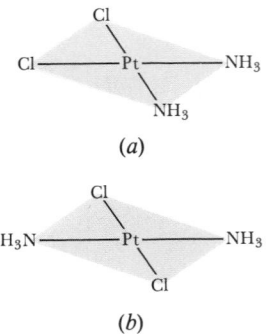

(a)

(b)

FIGURE 25.18 (a) Cis and (b) trans geometric isomers of the square-planar [Pt(NH₃)₂Cl₂].

Learning Goal 5: Determine the possible number of stereo-isomers for a complex, having been given its composition.

FIGURE 25.19 (a) Cis and (b) trans geometric iso-mers of the octahedral [Co(NH₃)₄Cl₂]⁺ ion. (The symbol N represents the coordinated NH₃ group.)

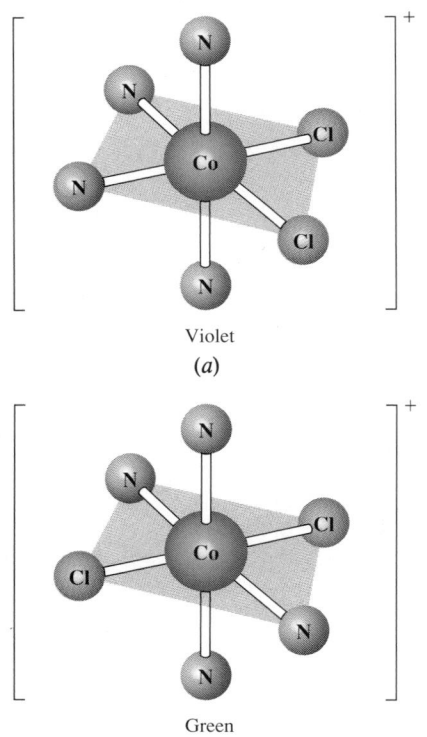

Violet

(a)

Green

(b)

Coordination-sphere isomers differ in the ligands that are directly bonded to the metal, as opposed to being outside the coordination sphere in the solid lattice. For example, $CrCl_3(H_2O)_6$ exists in three common forms: $[Cr(H_2O)_6]Cl_3$ (a violet compound), $[Cr(H_2O)_5Cl]Cl_2 \cdot H_2O$ (a green compound), and $[Cr(H_2O)_4Cl_2]Cl \cdot 2H_2O$ (also a green compound). In the second and third compounds, the water has been displaced from the coordination sphere by chloride ions and occupies a site in the solid lattice.

Stereoisomerism

Stereoisomerism is the most important form of isomerism. Stereoisomers have the same chemical bonds but different spatial arrangements. For example, in $[Pt(NH_3)_2Cl_2]$ the chloro ligands can be either adjacent to or opposite each other, as illustrated in Figure 25.18. This particular form of isomerism, in which the arrangement of the constituent atoms is different though the same bonds are present, is called **geometrical isomerism.** Isomer (a), with like groups in adjacent positions, is called the *cis* isomer. Isomer (b), with like ligands across from one another, is called the *trans* isomer. The cis isomer is used as a chemotherapy agent in treating cancer and carries the name *cisplatin.*

Geometrical isomerism is possible also in octahedral complexes when two or more different ligands are present. The cis and trans isomers of tetraammine-dichlorocobalt(III) ion are shown in Figure 25.19. Note that these two isomers have different colors. Their salts also possess different solubilities in water. In general, geometrical isomers possess distinct physical and chemical properties.

Because all of the corners of a tetrahedron are adjacent to one another, cis-trans isomerism is not observed in tetrahedral complexes.

SAMPLE EXERCISE 25.5

How many geometrical isomers are there for $[Cr(H_2O)_2Br_4]^-$?

SOLUTION This complex has a coordination number of 6 and therefore presumably has an octahedral geometry. Like $[Co(NH_3)_4Cl_2]^+$ (Figure 25.19), it has four ligands of one type and two of another. Consequently, it possesses two isomers: one with H_2O ligands across the metal from each other (the trans isomer) and one with H_2O ligands adjacent (the cis isomer).

In general, the number of isomers of a complex can be determined by making a series of drawings of the structure with ligands in different locations. It is easy to overestimate the number of geometrical isomers. Sometimes different orientations of a single isomer are incorrectly thought to be different isomers. Therefore, you should keep in mind that if two structures can be rotated so that they are equivalent, they are not isomers of each other. The problem of identifying isomers is compounded by the difficulty we often have in visualizing three-dimensional molecules from their two-dimensional representations. It is easier to determine the number of isomers if we are working with three-dimensional models.

PRACTICE EXERCISE

How many isomers exist for square-planar $[Pt(NH_3)_2ClBr]$? ***Answer:*** two

A second type of stereoisomerism is known as **optical isomerism.** Optical isomers are mirror images that cannot be superimposed on each other. Such isomers are called **enantiomers.** They bear the same resemblance to each other

A CLOSER LOOK

Alfred Werner and the Structures of Coordination Compounds

In 1893, Alfred Werner, a 26-year-old Swiss chemist, proposed a theory that successfully accounted for the known properties of coordination compounds and became the basis for our subsequent understanding of their structures. Although many coordination compounds had been prepared by that time, it was not clear how the atoms within them were connected. Werner postulated that metals exhibit both primary and secondary valences. Today we refer to these valences as the metal's oxidation state and coordination number, respectively. For cobalt(III), for example, Werner postulated a primary valence of 3 and a secondary valence of 6. He therefore rewrote the formula $CoCl_3 \cdot 5NH_3$ as $[Co(NH_3)_5Cl]Cl_2$. The ligands within the brackets satisfy the metal's secondary valence of 6; the three chlorides satisfy the primary valence of 3.

Werner proposed that the ligands within the coordination sphere (that is, directly bound to the metal ion) are so tightly held that they remain with the metal ion and do not undergo reaction. When dissolved in solu-

tion, the complex separates into a $Co(NH_3)_5Cl^{2+}$ and two Cl^- ions. It thus has an electrical conductivity in solution similar to that for a salt such as $CaCl_2$. If a solution containing $AgNO_3$ is added to the solution, only the two free Cl^- ions react with Ag^+ to form $AgCl(s)$, in agreement with Werner's model.

Werner also sought to deduce the arrangement of ligands about the central metal. He postulated that cobalt(III) complexes exhibit an octahedral geometry. He sought to test this hypothesis by comparing the number of observed isomers with the number expected for various geometries. For example, the ion $Co(NH_3)_4Cl_2^+$ should exist as cis and trans isomers if the complex is octahedral, as illustrated in Figure 25.19. At the time of Werner's work only one isomer, colored green, was known. After considerable effort, in 1907, a second isomer, colored violet, was prepared. Werner was awarded the Nobel Prize in Chemistry in 1913 for his outstanding research in the field of coordination chemistry.

that our left hand bears to our right hand. If you look at your left hand in a mirror, the image is identical to your right hand. Furthermore, your two hands are not superimposable on one another. A good example of a complex that exhibits this type of isomerism is the $[Co(en)_3]^{3+}$ ion. Figure 25.20 shows the two enantiomers of $[Co(en)_3]^{3+}$ and their mirror-image relationship to each other. Just as there is no way that we can twist or turn our right hand to make it look identical to our left, so also there is no way to rotate one of these enantiomers to make it identical to the other. Molecules or ions that have enan-

 Figure 25.20

FIGURE 25.20 Just as our hands are nonsuper-imposable mirror images of each other (*a*), so too are optical isomers such as the two optical isomers of $[Co(en)_3]^{3+}$ (*b*).

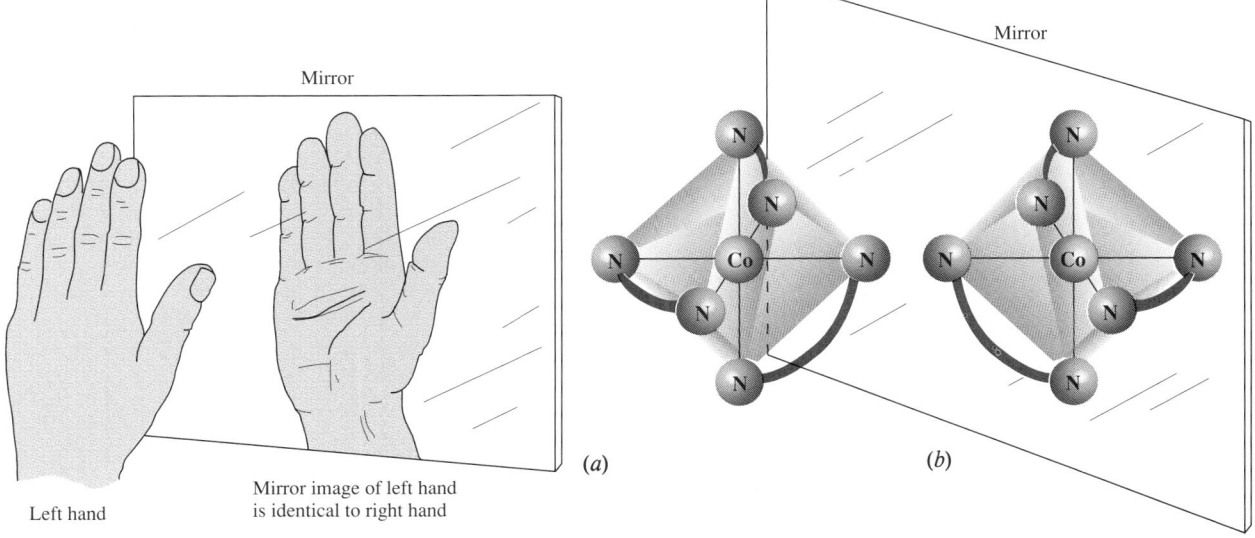

Left hand

Mirror image of left hand is identical to right hand

(*a*)

(*b*)

tiomers are said to be **chiral** (pronounced KY-rul). Enzymes are among the most highly chiral molecules known. As noted in Section 25.2, many enzymes contain complexed metal ions. However, a molecule need not contain a metallic atom to be chiral.

SAMPLE EXERCISE 25.6

Does either *cis-* or *trans-*$[Co(en)_2Cl_2]^+$ have optical isomers?

SOLUTION   To answer this question you should draw out both the cis and trans isomers of $[Co(en)_2Cl_2]^+$, then their mirror images. Note that the mirror image of the trans isomer is identical to the original. Consequently *trans-*$[Co(en)_2Cl_2]^+$ has no optical isomer. However, the mirror image of *cis-*$[Co(en)_2Cl_2]^+$ is not identical to the original. Consequently, there are optical isomers (enantiomers) for this complex.

PRACTICE EXERCISE

Does the square-planar complex ion $[Pt(NH_3)(N_3)ClBr]^-$ have optical isomers?
Answer: no

Most of the physical and chemical properties of optical isomers are identical. The properties of two optical isomers differ only if they are in a chiral environment — that is, one in which there is a sense of right- and left-handedness. For example, in the presence of a chiral enzyme, the reaction of one optical isomer might be catalyzed, whereas the other isomer would remain totally unreacted. Consequently, one optical isomer may produce a specific physiological effect within the body, whereas its mirror image produces a different effect or none at all.

Optical isomers are usually distinguished from each other by their interaction with plane-polarized light. If light is polarized — for example, by passage through a sheet of Polaroid film — the light waves are vibrating in a single plane, as shown in Figure 25.21. If the polarized light is passed through a solution containing one optical isomer, the plane of polarization is rotated either to the

FIGURE 25.21   Effect of an optically active solution on the plane of polarization of plane-polarized light. The unpolarized light is passed through a polarizer. The resultant polarized light thereafter passes through a solution containing a dextrorotatory optical isomer. As a result, the plane of polarization of the light is rotated to the right relative to an observer looking toward the light source.

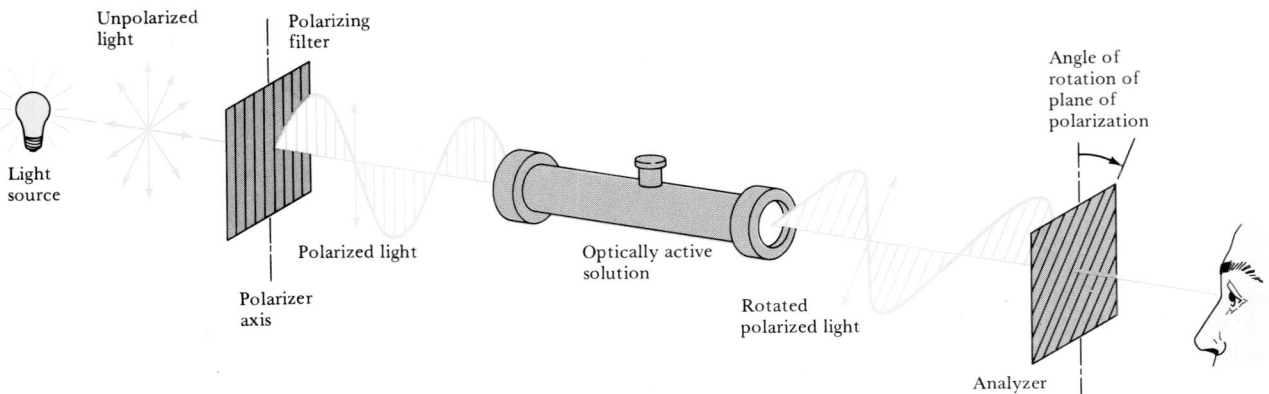

right (clockwise) or to the left (counterclockwise). The isomer that rotates the plane of polarization to the right is said to be **dextrorotatory**; it is labeled the dextro, or *d*, isomer (Latin *dexter*, "right"). Its mirror image rotates the plane of polarization to the left; it is said to be **levorotatory** and is labeled the levo, or *l*, isomer (Latin *laevus*, "left"). Because of their effect on plane-polarized light, chiral molecules are said to be **optically active.**

When a substance with optical isomers is prepared in the laboratory, the chemical environment during the synthesis is not usually chiral. Consequently, equal amounts of the two isomers are obtained; the mixture is said to be **racemic.** A racemic mixture will not rotate polarized light because the rotatory effects of the two isomers cancel each other. In order to separate the isomers from the racemic mixture, the isomers must be placed in a chiral environment. For example, one optical isomer of the chiral tartrate anion,* $C_4H_4O_6^{2-}$, can be used to separate a racemic mixture of $[Co(en)_3]Cl_3$. If *d*-tartrate is added to an aqueous solution of $[Co(en)_3]Cl_3$, *d*-$[Co(en)_3](d$-$C_4H_4O_6)Cl$ will precipitate, leaving *l*-$[Co(en)_3]^{3+}$ in solution.

Teaching Note: The terms *dextrorotatory* and *levorotatory* refer only to the direction of rotation of polarized light. These terms and the direction of rotation of polarized light are unrelated to whether the molecule is considered to be right- or left-handed.

25.5 Ligand-Exchange Rates

Many complexes are prepared by simply mixing solutions of the metal ion with the appropriate ligand. For example, addition of ammonia to an aqueous solution of $CuSO_4$ produces an essentially instantaneous color change as the pale-blue $[Cu(H_2O)_4]^{2+}$ ion is converted to the deep-blue $[Cu(NH_3)_4]^{2+}$ ion (Figure 25.22). When this solution is acidified, the pale-blue color is regenerated at a rapid rate:

$$[Cu(NH_3)_4]^{2+}(aq) + 4H_2O(l) + 4H^+(aq) \longrightarrow$$
$$[Cu(H_2O)_4]^{2+}(aq) + 4NH_4^+(aq) \quad [25.7]$$

Reactions in which one ligand replaces another in the coordination sphere of a metal ion are called *ligand-exchange reactions* or *substitution reactions.* Although many ligand-exchange reactions are very rapid, others are slow. For example, $[Co(NH_3)_6]^{3+}$ is more difficult to prepare than $[Cu(NH_3)_4]^{2+}$. However, once it has been formed and placed in an acidic solution, the reaction to form NH_4^+ takes several days. This tells us that the coordinated NH_3 groups are not readily removed from the metal.

Complexes like $[Cu(NH_3)_4]^{2+}$ that undergo rapid ligand exchange are called **labile complexes;** those like $[Co(NH_3)_6]^{3+}$ that undergo slow ligand exchange are called **inert complexes.** The distinction between labile and inert complexes applies to how rapidly equilibrium is attained and not to the position of the equilibrium. For example, although $[Co(NH_3)_6]^{3+}$ is inert in acidified

Bassam Z. Shakhashiri, "Precipitates and Complexes of Copper (II)" *Chemical Demonstrations: A Handbook for Teachers of Chemistry, Volume 1* (Madison: The University of Wisconsin Press, 1983), pp. 318-23.

Learning Goal 6: Distinguish between inert and labile complexes.

---

* When sodium ammonium tartrate, $NaNH_4C_4H_4O_6$, is crystallized from solution, the two isomers form separate crystals whose shapes are mirror images of each other. In 1848, Louis Pasteur achieved the first separation of a racemic mixture into optical isomers; using a microscope he picked the "right-handed" crystals of this compound from the "left-handed" ones.

FIGURE 25.22 An aqueous solution of $CuSO_4$ is pale blue because of $Cu(H_2O)_4^{2+}$ (left). When $NH_3(aq)$ is added (middle and right), the deep-blue $Cu(NH_3)_4^{2+}$ ion forms. (© Richard Megna/Photo Researchers)

Teaching Note: The distinction between *labile* and *inert* is somewhat arbitrary. Some authors suggest that inert complexes are those for which the half-life of a substitution reaction, using 0.1 M concentrations, is greater than 1 minute.

R. Bruce Martin, "A Stability Ruler for Metal Ion Complexes," *J. Chem. Educ.* **1987,** *64,* 402.

Gregory M. Williams, John Olmstead III, and Andrew P. Breksa III, "Coordination Complexes of Cobalt: Inorganic Synthesis in the General Chemistry Laboratory," *J. Chem. Educ.* **1989,** *66,* 1043.

Learning Goal 7: Explain how the conductivity, precipitation reactions, and isomerism of complexes are used to infer their structures.

aqueous solutions, the equilibrium constant indicates that the complex is not thermodynamically stable under these conditions:

$$[Co(NH_3)_6]^{3+}(aq) + 6H_2O(l) + 6H^+(aq) \rightleftharpoons$$
$$[Co(H_2O)_6]^{3+}(aq) + 6NH_4^+(aq) \qquad K_f \simeq 10^{20} \quad [25.8]$$

The kinetic inertness of $[Co(NH_3)_6]^{3+}$ can be attributed to a high activation energy for the reaction.

Cobalt(III) is one of a few metal ions that consistently forms inert complexes; others include chromium(III), platinum(IV), and platinum(II). Complexes of these ions maintain their identity in solution long enough to permit study of their structures and properties. They were therefore among the first complexes studied. Much of our understanding of structure and isomerism comes from studies of these complexes. (See the Closer Look box in Section 25.4.)

25.6 Color and Magnetism

Studies of the colors and magnetic properties of transition-metal complexes have played an important role in the development of modern models for metal-ligand bonding. We have discussed the various types of magnetic behavior in Section 24.7; we also discussed the interaction of radiant energy with matter in Section 6.3. Let's briefly examine the significance of these two properties for transition-metal complexes before we try to develop a model for metal-ligand bonding.

Color

One of the striking features of transition-metal compounds is that they are often intensely colored. We have seen photos of some colored complexes and have noted the colors of others. In general, the colors depend on the particular metal, on its oxidation state, and on the particular ligands bound to the metal. The presence of a partly filled d subshell on the metal ion is usually necessary. Metal ions that have completely empty d subshells (such as Al^{3+} and Ti^{4+}) or completely filled d subshells (such as Zn^{2+}, $3d^{10}$) are colorless.

We consider the relationship between electron configuration and color in Section 25.7. First, however, we need to review our earlier discussion of light and to introduce a few additional concepts. Recall first that visible light consists of electromagnetic radiation whose wavelength, λ, ranges from 400 nm to 700 nm (Figure 6.3). The energy of this radiation is inversely proportional to its wavelength: ∞ (Sec. 6.2)

$$E = h\nu = h(c/\lambda) \qquad [25.9]$$

The visible spectrum is shown in Figure 25.23.

When a sample absorbs light, what we see is the sum of the remaining colors that strike our eyes. If a sample absorbs all wavelengths of visible light, none reaches our eyes from that sample. Consequently, it appears black. If the sample absorbs no visible light, it is white or colorless. If it absorbs all but orange, the sample appears orange. Each of these situations is shown in Figure 25.24. That figure shows one further situation; we also perceive an orange color when visible light of all colors except blue strikes our eyes. In a complementary fashion, if the sample absorbed only orange, it would appear blue; blue and orange are said to be **complementary colors**. Complementary colors can be determined with the aid of the artist's color wheel, shown in Figure 25.25. Complementary colors, like orange and blue, are across the wheel from each other.

Learning Goal 8: Explain how the colors of substances are related to their absorption and reflection of incident light.

Point of Emphasis: Generally, a partially filled d subshell is required for a complex to show visible color. Ions with filled (d^{10}) or empty (d^0) subshells are usually colorless. Some d^0 metal oxide ions, such as MnO_4^- and CrO_4^{2-}, are exceptions to this rule.

Laurence Poncini and Franz L. Wimmer, "Color Classification of Coordination Compounds," *J. Chem. Educ.* 1987, *64*, 1001.

SAMPLE EXERCISE 25.7

The complex ion *trans*-[Co(NH$_3$)$_4$Cl$_2$]$^+$ absorbs light primarily in the red region of the visible spectrum (the most intense absorption is at 680 nm). What is the color of the complex?

SOLUTION Because the complex absorbs red light, its color will be complementary to red. From Figure 25.25, we see that this is green.

PRACTICE EXERCISE

The [Cr(H$_2$O)$_6$]$^{2+}$ ion has an absorption band at about 630 nm. Which of the following colors—sky blue, yellow, green, or deep red—is most likely to describe this ion? *Answer:* sky blue

FIGURE 25.23 Visible spectrum showing the relation between color and wavelength.

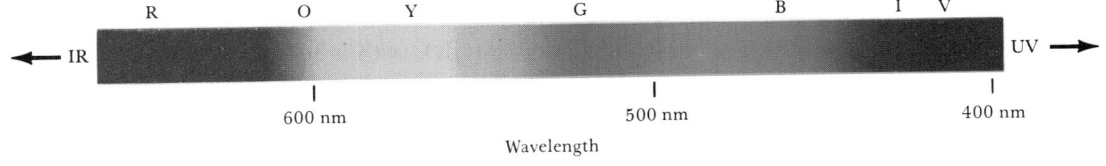

FIGURE 25.24 (*a*) An object is black if it absorbs all colors of light. (*b*) An object is white if it reflects all colors of light. (*c*) An object is orange if it reflects only this color and absorbs all others. (*d*) An object is also orange if it reflects all colors except blue, the complementary color of orange.

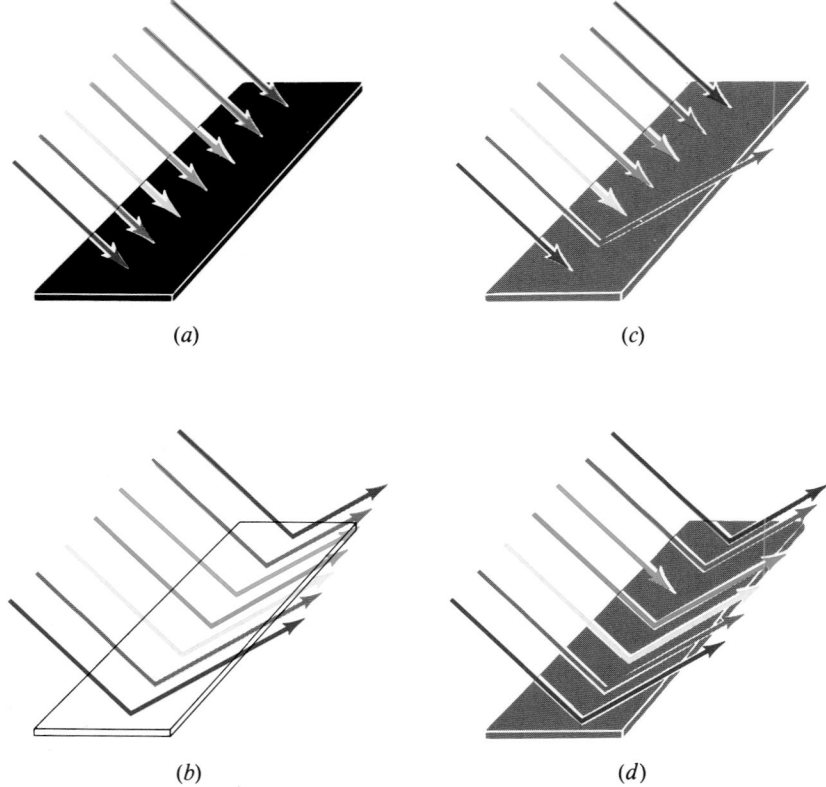

(*a*)

(*c*)

(*b*)

(*d*)

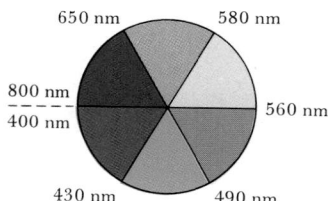

FIGURE 25.25 Artist's color wheel, showing the colors that are complementary to one another and the wavelength range of each color.

Learning Goal 9: Explain how the magnetic properties of a compound can be measured and used to infer the number of unpaired electrons.

The amount of light absorbed by a sample as a function of wavelength is known as its **absorption spectrum.** The visible absorption spectrum of a transparent sample, such as a solution of *trans*-[Co(NH$_3$)$_4$Cl$_2$]$^+$, can be determined as shown in Figure 25.26. The spectrum of [Ti(H$_2$O)$_6$]$^{3+}$, which we shall discuss in the next section, is shown in Figure 25.27. The absorption maximum of [Ti(H$_2$O)$_6$]$^{3+}$ is at 510 nm. Because the sample absorbs most strongly in the green and yellow regions of the visible spectrum, it appears purple.

Magnetism

Many transition-metal complexes exhibit simple paramagnetism, as described in Section 9.7. In such compounds, the individual metal ions possess some number of unpaired electrons. It is possible to determine the number of unpaired electrons per metal ion from the degree of paramagnetism. The experiments reveal some interesting comparisons. For example, compounds of the complex ion [Co(NH$_3$)$_6$]$^{3+}$ have no unpaired electrons, but compounds of the [CoF$_6$]$^{3-}$ ion have four per metal ion. Both complexes contain Co(III) with a $3d^6$ electron configuration. Clearly, there is a major difference in the ways in which the electrons are arranged in the metal orbitals in these two cases, even though both are complexes of cobalt(III), with a $3d^6$ electron configuration. Any successful bonding theory must explain this and other related observations.

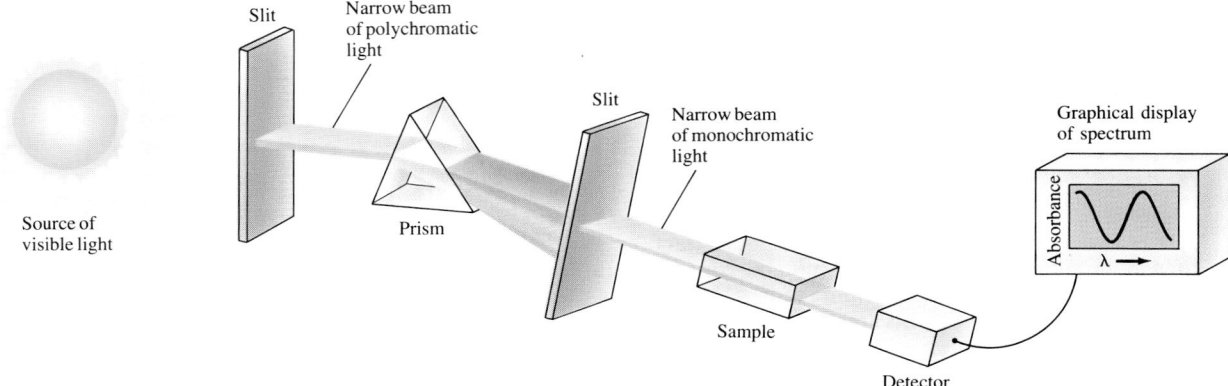

FIGURE 25.26 Experimental determination of the absorption spectrum of a solution. The prism is rotated so that different wavelengths of light pass through the sample. The detector measures the amount of light reaching it, and this information can be displayed as the absorption at each wavelength.

25.7 Crystal-Field Theory

Although the ability to form complexes is common to all metal ions, the most numerous and interesting complexes are formed by the transition elements. Scientists have long recognized that the magnetic properties and colors of transition-metal complexes are related to the presence of d electrons in metal orbitals. In this section, we shall consider a model for bonding in transition-metal complexes, called the **crystal-field theory,** that accounts for many of the observed properties of these substances.*

We have already noted that the ability of a metal ion to attract ligands such as water around itself can be viewed as a Lewis acid-base interaction. ∞(Sec. 16.10) The base — that is, the ligand — can be considered to donate a pair of electrons into a suitable empty orbital on the metal, as shown in Figure 25.28. However, we can assume that much of the attractive interaction between

---

* The name *crystal field* arose because the theory was first developed to explain the properties of solid, crystalline materials, such as ruby. The same theoretical model applies to complexes in solution.

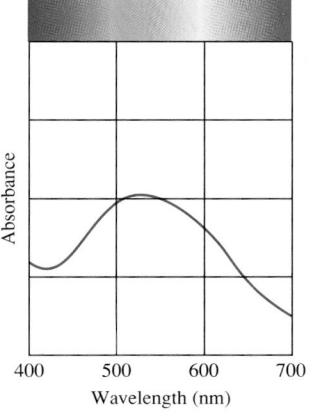

FIGURE 25.27 Visible absorption spectrum of the $[Ti(H_2O)_6]^{3+}$ ion.

Learning Goal 10: Explain how the electrostatic interaction between ligands and metal d orbitals in an octahedral complex results in a splitting of energy levels.

FIGURE 25.28 Representation of the metal-ligand bond in a complex as a Lewis acid-base interaction. The ligand, which acts as a Lewis base, donates charge to the metal via a metal hybrid orbital. The bond that results is strongly polar, with some covalent character. For many purposes it is sufficient to assume that the metal-ligand interaction is entirely electrostatic in character, as is done in the crystal-field model.

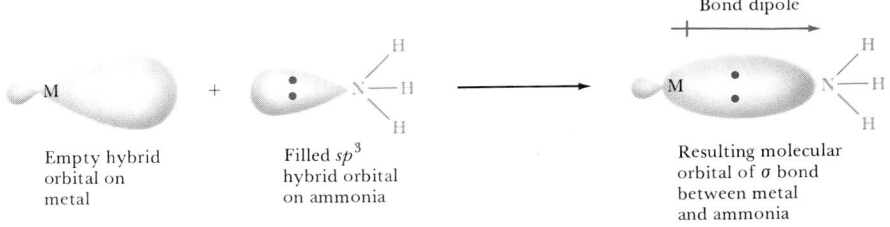

Empty hybrid orbital on metal

Filled sp^3 hybrid orbital on ammonia

Bond dipole

Resulting molecular orbital of σ bond between metal and ammonia

▲ A CLOSER LOOK

Gemstones

Gemstones (Figure 25.29) such as ruby and emerald owe their color to the presence of trace amounts of transition-metal ions. For example, replacement of a fraction of the aluminum in the colorless mineral corundum, Al_2O_3, produces several different gems: chromium forms ruby, manganese forms amethyst, and iron forms topaz. Sapphire, which occurs in a variety of colors but is most often blue, contains titanium and cobalt. Several other gems are produced by replacing a trace of aluminum in the colorless mineral beryl, $Be_3Al_2Si_6O_{18}$, with transition-metal ions. For example, emerald contains chromium, and aquamarine contains iron.

FIGURE 25.29 A selection of gemstones, some mounted in rings: (*a*) aquamarine, (*b*) emerald, (*c*) amethyst, (*d*) blue sapphire, (*e*) ruby (an example of an uncut mineral sample), and (*f*) citrine quartz. In all these cases the colors are due to transition-metal ions present as minor components in the parent mineral, such as quartz, alumina, or beryl. (Gem Media, a Division of the Gemological Institute of America)

(*a*)   (*b*)   (*c*)

(*d*)   (*e*)   (*f*)

Teaching Note: The bonding in complexes is also often described using *ligand-field theory*. For our purposes here, the two are indistinguishable, and the conclusions reached by the two are essentially the same.

the metal ion and the surrounding ligands is due to the electrostatic forces between the positive charge on the metal and negative charges on the ligands. If the ligand is ionic, as in the case of Cl^- or SCN^-, the electrostatic interaction occurs between the positive charge on the metal center and the negative charge on the ligand. When the ligand is neutral, as in the case of H_2O or NH_3, the negative ends of these polar molecules, containing an unshared electron pair, are directed toward the metal. In this case, the attractive interaction is of the ion-dipole type. ∞ (Sec. 11.2) In either case, the result is the same; the ligands are attracted strongly toward the metal center. The assembly of metal ion and ligands is lower in energy than the fully separated charges, as illustrated on the left side of Figure 25.30.

In a 6-coordinate octahedral complex, we can envision the ligands approaching along the x, y, and z axes, as shown in Figure 25.31. Using the physical arrangement of ligands and metal ion shown in this figure as our starting point, let us consider what happens to the energies of electrons in the metal d orbitals as the ligands approach the metal ion. Keep in mind that the d electrons are the outermost electrons of the metal ion. We know that the overall energy of the metal ion plus ligands will be lower (that is, more stable) when the ligands are drawn toward the metal center. At the same time, however, there is a repulsive interaction between the outermost electrons on the metal and the negative charges on the ligands. This interaction is called the *crystal field*. The crystal field causes the energies of the d electrons on the metal ion to increase, as shown in Figure 25.30. The d orbitals of the metal ion, however, do not all

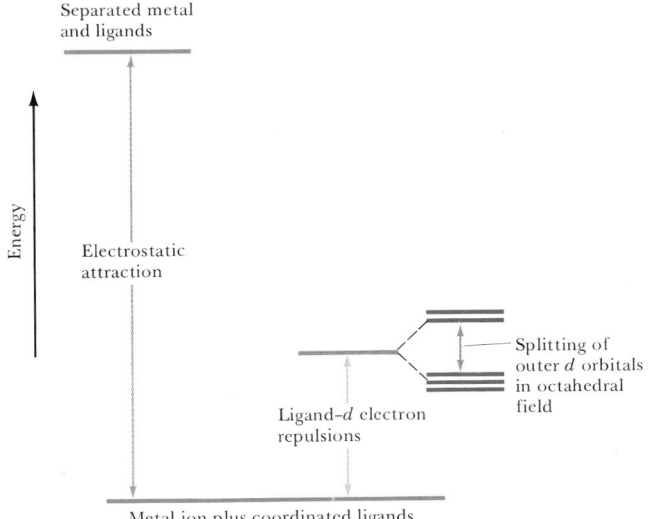

FIGURE 25.30 In the crystal-field model, the bonding between metal ion and donor atoms is considered to be largely electrostatic. The energy of the metal ion plus coordinated ligands is lower than that of the separated metal ion plus ligands because of the electrostatic attraction. At the same time, the energies of the metal d electrons are increased by the repulsive interaction between these electrons and the electrons of the ligands. These repulsive interactions give rise to the splitting of the metal d-orbital energies.

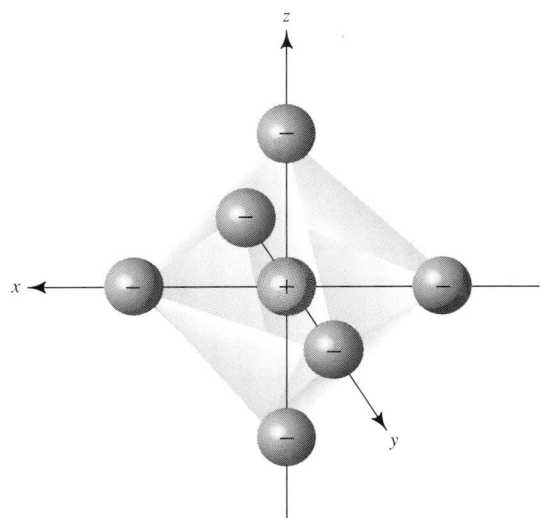

FIGURE 25.31 Octahedral array of negative charges surrounding a positive charge.

behave in the same way under the influence of the crystal field. To see why this is so, recall the shapes of the five d orbitals, illustrated in Figure 6.21. In the isolated metal ion, these five orbitals are equivalent in energy. However, as the ligands approach the metal ion, the $d_{x^2-y^2}$ and d_{z^2} orbitals, which are directed *along* the x, y, and z axes, are more strongly repelled by the ligands than the d_{xy}, d_{xz}, and d_{yz} orbitals. These latter are directed *between* the axes along which the ligands approach. Thus, an energy separation, or *splitting,* occurs. The $d_{x^2-y^2}$ and d_{z^2} orbitals are raised in energy more than d_{xz}, d_{yz}, and d_{xy} orbitals are. This energy splitting is illustrated on the right side of Figure 25.30. In the material that follows, we shall concentrate only on the splitting of the d orbital energies by the crystal field. This process is illustrated in a slightly different form in Figure 25.32.

Let's examine how the crystal-field model accounts for the observed colors in transition-metal complexes. The energy gap between the d orbitals, labeled Δ, is of the same order of magnitude as the energy of a photon of visible light. (The energy gap, Δ, is sometimes referred to as the *crystal-field splitting energy.*) It is therefore possible for a transition-metal complex to absorb visible light, which thereby excites an electron from the lower-energy d orbitals into the higher-energy ones. The $[Ti(H_2O)_6]^{3+}$ ion provides a simple example, because titanium(III) has only one $3d$ electron. As shown in Figure 25.27, $[Ti(H_2O)_6]^{3+}$ has a single absorption peak in the visible region of the spectrum. The maximum absorption is at 510 nm (235 kJ/mol). Light of this wavelength causes the d electron to move from the lower-energy set of d orbitals into the higher-energy set, as shown in Figure 25.33. The absorption of 510-nm radiation that produces this transition causes substances containing the $Ti(H_2O)_6^{3+}$ ion to appear purple.

The magnitude of the energy gap, Δ — and consequently the color of a complex — depend on both the metal and the surrounding ligands. For example, $[Fe(H_2O)_6]^{3+}$ is light violet, $[Cr(H_2O)_6]^{3+}$ is violet, and $[Cr(NH_3)_6]^{3+}$ is yellow. Ligands can be arranged in order of their abilities to increase the energy gap, Δ. The following is an abbreviated list of common ligands arranged in order of increasing Δ:

Learning Goal 11: Explain the significance of the spectrochemical series.

$$\xrightarrow{\text{increasing }\Delta}$$
$$Cl^- < F^- < H_2O < NH_3 < en < NO_2^- \text{ (N-bonded)} < CN^-$$

This list is known as the **spectrochemical series.**

Ligands that lie on the low end of the spectrochemical series are termed *weak-field ligands;* those on the high end are termed *strong-field ligands.* Figure

FIGURE 25.32 Energies of the d orbitals in an octahedral crystal field.

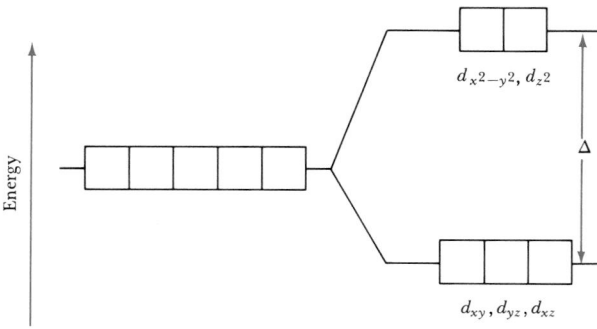

Figure 25.32

FIGURE 25.33 The 3d electron of $[Ti(H_2O)_6]^{3+}$ is excited from the lower-energy d orbitals to the higher-energy ones when irradiated with light of 510-nm wavelength.

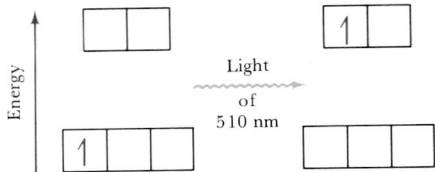

25.34 shows schematically what happens to the crystal-field splitting when the ligand is varied in a series of chromium(III) complexes. [This is a good place to remind you that when a transition metal is ionized, the valence s electrons are removed first. ∞ (Sec. 8.2) Therefore, the outer electron configuration for chromium is $[Ar]3d^54s^1$; that for Cr^{3+} is $[Ar]3d^3$.] Notice that as the field exerted by the six surrounding ligands increases, the splitting of the metal d orbitals increases. Because the absorption spectrum is related to this energy separation, these complexes vary in color.

SAMPLE EXERCISE 25.8

Which of the following complexes of Ti^{3+} exhibits the shortest wavelength absorption in the visible spectrum: $[Ti(H_2O)_6]^{3+}$; $[Ti(en)_3]^{3+}$; $[TiCl_6]^{3-}$?

SOLUTION The wavelength of the absorption is determined by the magnitude of the splitting between the d-orbital energies in the field of the surrounding ligands. The larger the splitting, the shorter the wavelength of the absorption corresponding to the transition of the electron from the lower- to the higher-energy orbital. The splitting will be largest for ethylenediamine, en, the ligand that is highest in the spectrochemical series. Thus, the complex with the shortest wavelength absorption is $[Ti(en)_3]^{3+}$.

PRACTICE EXERCISE

The absorption spectrum of $[Ti(NCS)_6]^{3-}$ shows a band that lies intermediate in wavelength between those for $[TiCl_6]^{3-}$ and $[TiF_6]^{3-}$. What can we conclude about the place of NCS^- in the spectrochemical series? **Answer:** It lies between Cl^- and F^-; that is, $Cl^- < NCS^- < F^-$

FIGURE 25.34 Crystal-field splitting in a series of octahedral chromium(III) complexes.

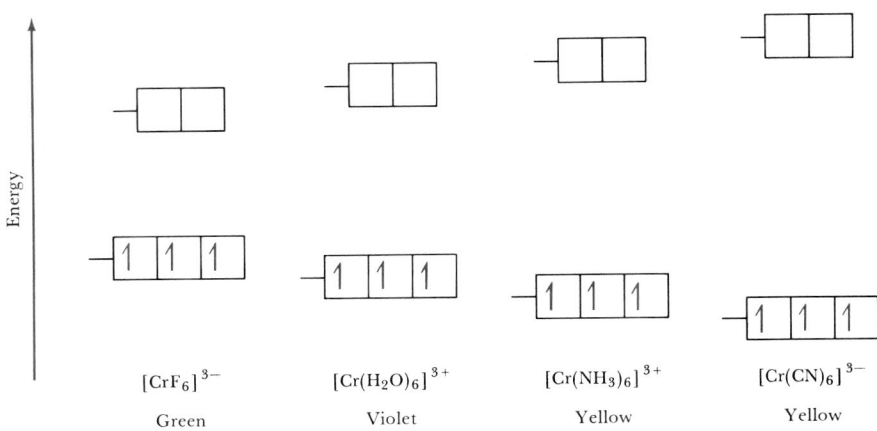

Electron Configurations in Octahedral Complexes

The crystal-field model helps us understand the magnetic properties and some important chemical properties of transition-metal ions. From our earlier discussion of electronic structure in atoms, we expect that electrons will always occupy the lowest-energy vacant orbitals first and that they will occupy a set of degenerate orbitals one at a time with their spins parallel (Hund's rule). ∞ (Sec. 6.8) Thus, if we have one, two, or three electrons to add to the *d* orbitals in an octahedral complex ion, the electrons will go into the lower-energy set of orbitals, with their spins parallel, as shown in Figure 25.35. When we wish to add a fourth electron, a problem arises. If the electron is added to the lower-energy orbital, an energy gain of magnitude Δ is realized, as compared with placing the electron in the higher-energy orbital. However, there is a penalty for doing this, because the electron must now be paired up with the electron already occupying the orbital. The energy required to do this, relative to putting it in another orbital with parallel spin, is called the **spin-pairing energy.** The spin-pairing energy arises from the greater electrostatic repulsion of electrons that share an orbital as compared with two that are in different orbitals.

Teaching Note: Cobalt(III) is a d^6 cation.

The ligands that surround the metal ion, and the charge on the metal, often play major roles in determining which of the two electronic arrangements arises. Consider the $[CoF_6]^{3-}$ and $[Co(CN)_6]^{3-}$ ions. In both cases the ligands have a 1− charge. However, the F^- ion, on the low end of the spectrochemical series, is a weak-field ligand. The CN^- ion, on the high end of the spectrochemical series, is a strong-field ligand. It produces a larger energy gap than does the F^- ion. The splittings of the *d*-orbital energies in the complexes are compared in Figure 25.36.

A count of the electrons in cobalt(III) tells us that we have six electrons to place in the 3*d* orbitals. Let us imagine that we add these electrons one at a time to the *d* orbitals of the CoF_6^{3-} ion. The first three will, of course, go into the lower-energy orbitals with spins parallel. The fourth electron could go into a lower-energy orbital, pairing up with one of those already present. This would result in an energy gain of Δ as compared with putting it in one of the higher-energy orbitals. However, it would cost energy in an amount equal to the spin-pairing energy. Because F^- is a weak-field ligand, Δ is small, and the more stable arrangement is the one in which the electron is placed in the higher-energy orbital. Similarly, the fifth electron we add goes into a higher-energy orbital. With all of the orbitals containing at least one electron, the sixth must be paired up, and it goes into a lower-energy orbital. In the case of the $[Co(CN)_6]^{3-}$ complex, the crystal-field splitting is much larger. The spin-pairing energy is smaller than Δ, so electrons are paired in the lower-energy orbitals, as illustrated in Figure 25.36.

Learning Goal 12: Account for the tendency of electrons to pair in strong-field, low-spin complexes.

The $[CoF_6]^{3-}$ complex is referred to as a **high-spin complex;** that is, the electrons are arranged so that they remain unpaired as much as possible. On the other hand, the $[Co(CN)_6]^{3-}$ ion is referred to as a **low-spin complex.** These two

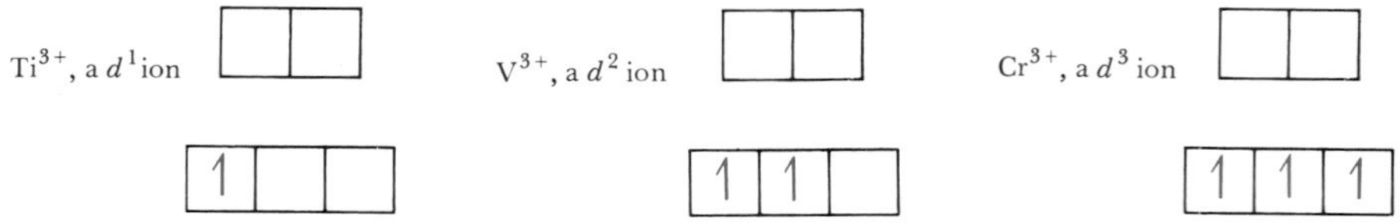

FIGURE 25.35 Electron configurations associated with one, two, and three electrons in the 3*d* orbitals in octahedral complexes.

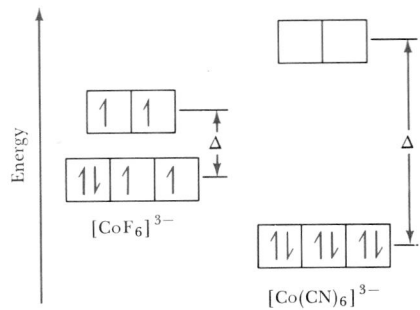

FIGURE 25.36 Population of *d* orbitals in the high-spin $[CoF_6]^{3-}$ ion (small Δ) and low-spin $[Co(CN)_6]^{3-}$ ion (large Δ).

different electronic arrangements can be readily distinguished by measuring the magnetic properties of the complex, as described earlier. The absorption spectrum also shows characteristic features that indicate the electronic arrangement.

Point of Emphasis: The terms *high spin* and *weak field* can be used interchangeably, as can the terms *low spin* and *strong field*.

SAMPLE EXERCISE 25.9

Predict the number of unpaired electrons in 6-coordinate high-spin and low-spin complexes of Fe^{3+}.

SOLUTION The Fe^{3+} ion possesses five $3d$ electrons. In a high-spin complex, these are all unpaired. In a low-spin complex the electrons are confined to the lower-energy set of *d* orbitals, with the result that there is one unpaired electron:

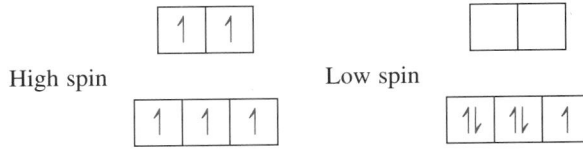

High spin   Low spin

For which *d* electron configurations does the possibility of a distinction between high-spin and low-spin arrangements exist in octahedral complexes?
Answer: d^4, d^5, d^6, d^7

Learning Goal 13: Sketch a representation of the *d* orbital energy levels in a tetrahedral complex, and explain the reason for smaller crystal-field splitting in this geometry as compared to the octahedral complexes.

Tetrahedral and Square-Planar Complexes

Thus far, we have considered the crystal-field model only for the complexes of octahedral geometry. When there are only four ligands about the metal, the geometry is tetrahedral, except for the special case of metal ions with a d^8 electron configuration, which we will discuss in a moment. The crystal-field splitting of the metal *d* orbitals in tetrahedral complexes differs from that in octahedral complexes. Four equivalent ligands can interact with a central metal ion most effectively by approaching along the vertices of a tetrahedron. It turns out—and this is not easy to explain in just a few sentences—that the splitting of the metal *d* orbitals in a tetrahedral crystal is just the opposite of that for the octahedral case. That is, three of the metal *d* orbitals are raised in energy, and the other two are lowered, as illustrated in Figure 25.37. Because there are only four ligands instead of six, as in the octahedral case, the crystal-field splitting is much smaller for tetrahedral complexes. Calculations show that for the same metal ion and ligand set, the crystal-field splitting for a tetrahedral complex is

 Figure 25.37

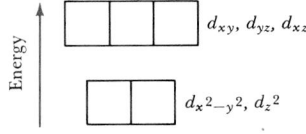

FIGURE 25.37 Energies of the *d* orbitals in a tetrahedral crystal field.

FIGURE 25.38 Effect on the relative energies of the d orbitals caused by removing the two negative charges from the z axis of an octahedral complex. When the charges are completely removed, the square-planar geometry results.

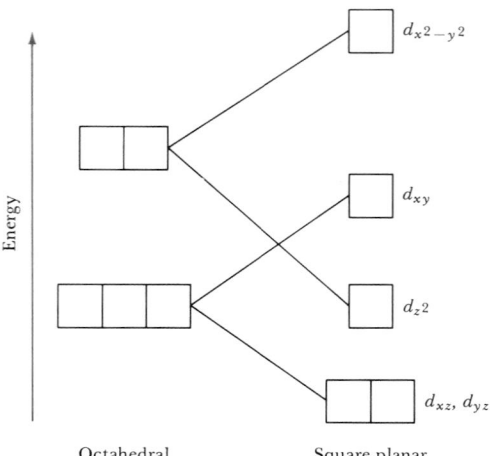

Figure 25.38

Octahedral   Square planar

only four-ninths as large as for the octahedral complex. For this reason, all tetrahedral complexes are high spin; the crystal field is never large enough to overcome the spin-pairing energies.

Square-planar complexes, in which four ligands are arranged about the metal ion in a plane, represent a common geometric form. You can envision the square-planar complex as formed by removing two ligands from along the vertical z axis of the octahedral complex. As this happens, the four ligands in the plane are drawn in more tightly. The changes that occur in the energy levels of the d orbitals are illustrated in Figure 25.38.

Square-planar complexes are characteristic of metal ions with a d^8 electron configuration. They are nearly always low spin; that is, the eight d electrons are spin-paired to form a diamagnetic complex. Such an electronic arrangement is particularly common among the ions of heavier metals, such as Pd^{2+}, Pt^{2+}, Ir^+, and Au^{3+}.

Learning Goal 14: Sketch the d orbital energy levels in a square-planar complex.

SAMPLE EXERCISE 25.10

Four-coordinate nickel(II) complexes exhibit both square-planar and tetrahedral geometries. The tetrahedral ones, such as $[NiCl_4]^{2-}$, are paramagnetic; the square-planar ones, such as $[Ni(CN)_4]^{2-}$, are diamagnetic. Show how the d electrons of nickel(II) populate the d orbitals in the appropriate crystal-field splitting diagram in each case.

SOLUTION Nickel(II) has an electron configuration of $[Ar]3d^8$. The population of the d electrons in the two geometries is given below:

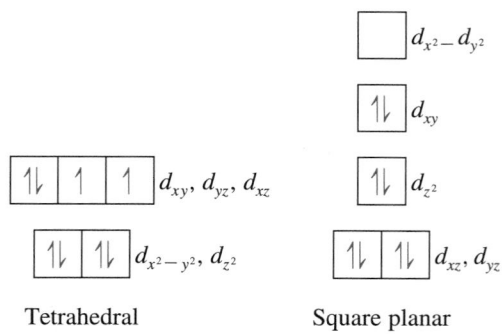

Tetrahedral   Square planar

We have seen that the crystal-field model provides a basis for explaining many features of transition-metal complexes. In fact, it can be used to explain many observations in addition to those we have discussed. However, many lines of evidence show that the bonding between transition-metal ions and ligands must have some covalent character. Molecular orbital theory (Sections 9.6 and 9.7) can also be used to describe the bonding in complexes. However, the application of molecular-orbital theory to coordination compounds is beyond the scope of our discussion. The crystal-field model, although not entirely accurate in all details, provides an adequate and useful description.

 # For Review

Summary

Coordination compounds or complexes contain metal ions bonded to several surrounding anions or molecules known as ligands. The metal ion and its ligands comprise the coordination sphere of the complex. The atom of the ligand that bonds to the metal ion is known as the donor atom. The number of donor atoms attached to the metal ion is known as the coordination number of the metal ion. The most common coordination numbers are 4 and 6; the most common coordination geometries are tetrahedral, square planar, and octahedral.

If a ligand has several donor atoms that can coordinate simultaneously to the metal, it is said to be polydentate and is referred to as a chelating agent. Two common examples are ethylenediamine (en), which is potentially bidentate, and ethylenediamine-tetraacetate ($EDTA^{4-}$), which has six potential donor atoms. Many biologically important molecules, such as the porphyrins, are complexes of chelating agents.

Isomerism is common among coordination compounds. Structural isomerism involves differences in the bonding arrangements of the ligands. One simple form of structural isomerism, known as linkage isomerism, occurs when a ligand is capable of coordinating to a metal through either of two donor atoms. Coordination-sphere isomerism occurs when two compounds with the same overall formula contain different ligands in the coordination sphere.

Stereoisomerism involves complexes with the same chemical bonding arrangements but with differing spatial arrangements of ligands. The most common forms are geometrical and optical isomerism. Geometrical isomers differ from one another in the relative locations of donor atoms in the coordination sphere; the most common are cis-trans isomers. Optical isomers differ from one another in that they are nonsuperimposable mirror images of one another. Geometrical isomers differ from one another in their chemical and physical properties; however, optical isomers differ only in the presence of a chiral environment. Optical isomers can be distinguished from one another by their interactions with plane-polarized light; solutions of one isomer rotate the plane of polarization to the right (dextrorotatory), and solutions of its mirror image rotate the plane to the left (levorotatory). Chiral molecules are said to be optically active. A 50-50 mixture of two optical isomers does not rotate plane-polarized light and is said to be racemic.

Many of the early studies that served as a basis for our current understanding of complexes focused on complexes of chromium(III), cobalt(III), platinum(II), and platinum(IV). Complexes of these metal ions are inert, in that they undergo ligand exchange at a slow rate. Complexes undergoing rapid exchange are said to be labile.

Studies of the magnetic properties and colors of transition-metal complexes have played an important role in formulation of bonding theories for these compounds. The crystal-field theory successfully accounts for many properties of coordination compounds. In this model, the interaction between metal ion and ligand is viewed as electrostatic. The ligands produce an electric field that causes a splitting in the energies of the metal d orbitals. In the spectrochemical series, the ligands are listed in order of their ability to split the d-orbital energies in octahedral complexes.

In strong-field complexes, the splitting of d-orbital energies is large enough to overcome spin-pairing energies, and d electrons preferentially pair up in the lower-energy orbitals. Such complexes are low spin. When the ligands exert a relatively weak crystal field, the electrons occupy the higher-energy d orbitals in preference to pairing up in the lower-energy set, and the complexes are high spin.

The crystal-field model is applicable also to tetrahedral and square-planar complexes. However, the ordering of the d-orbital energies is different than in octahedral complexes.

Key Terms

complex ion
complex
coordination compound
ligand (Sec. 25.1)
coordination sphere (Sec. 25.1)
donor atom (Sec. 25.1)
coordination number (Sec. 25.1)
monodentate ligand (Sec. 25.2)
polydentate ligand (Sec. 25.2)
chelating agent (Sec. 25.2)
bidentate ligand (Sec. 25.2)
chelate effect (Sec. 25.2)
porphyrin (Sec. 25.2)
photosynthesis (Sec. 25.2)
chlorophyll (Sec. 25.2)
isomer (Sec. 25.4)
structural isomer (Sec. 25.4)
stereoisomer (Sec. 25.4)
linkage isomerism (Sec. 25.4)

coordination-sphere isomer (Sec. 25.4)
geometrical isomerism (Sec. 25.4)
optical isomerism (Sec. 25.4)
enantiomer (Sec. 25.4)
chiral (Sec. 25.4)
dextrorotatory (Sec. 25.4)
levorotatory (Sec. 25.4)
optically active (Sec. 25.4)
racemic (Sec. 25.4)
labile complex (Sec. 25.5)
inert complex (Sec. 25.5)
complementary colors (Sec. 25.6)
absorption spectrum (Sec. 25.6)
crystal-field theory (Sec. 25.7)
spectrochemical series (Sec. 25.7)
spin-pairing energy (Sec. 25.7)
high-spin complex (Sec. 25.7)
low-spin complex (Sec. 25.7)

Exercises

Structure and Nomenclature

25.1. Indicate the coordination number about the metal and the oxidation number of the metal in each of the following complexes:
(a) $[Zn(en)_2]Br_2$
(b) $[Co(NH_3)_4Cl_2]Cl$
(c) $K[Co(C_2O_4)_2(NH_3)_2]$
(d) $K_2[MoOCl_4]$
(e) $K_3[Au(CN)_4]$

25.2. Indicate the coordination number about the metal and the oxidation number of the metal in each of the following complexes:
(a) $K_3[V(C_2O_4)_3]$
(b) $K_3[Fe(CN)_6]$
(c) $[Pd(NH_3)_2Cl_2]$
(d) $[Cr(en)_2F_2]NO_3$
(e) $K_2[HgCl_4]$

25.3. Sketch the structure of each of the following complexes:
(a) $[AlCl_4]^-$
(b) $[Ag(CN)_2]^-$
(c) $[PtCl_4(en)]$
(d) $trans$-$[Cr(NH_3)_4(H_2O)_2]^{3+}$

25.4. Sketch the structure of each of the following complexes:
(a) $[Zn(NH_3)_4]^{2+}$
(b) $[Ru(H_2O)Cl_5]^{2-}$
(c) cis-$[Co(en)_2(NO_2)_2]^+$
(d) $trans$-$[Pt(NH_3)_2H(Br)]$

25.5. Name each of the complexes listed in Exercises 25.3 and 25.4.

25.6. Name each of the following complexes:
(a) $[Cr(NH_3)_4Br_2]$
(b) $[Co(en)(NH_3)_2Br_2]Cl$

(c) $K_3[Fe(C_2O_4)_3]$ (d) $Cs[Cr(C_2O_4)_2Cl_2]$
(e) $K_3[IrCl_5(S_2O_3)]$ (f) $[Pd(en)_2][Cr(NH_3)_2Br_4]_2$

25.7. Write the formula for each of the following compounds, being sure to use brackets to indicate the coordination sphere:
(a) hexaamminechromium(III) nitrate
(b) tetraamminecarbonatocobalt(III) sulfate
(c) dichlorobis(ethylenediamine)platinum(IV) bromide
(d) potassium diaquatetrabromovanadate(III)
(e) bis(ethylenediamine)zinc(II) tetraiodomercurate(II)

25.8. Write the formula for each of the following compounds, being sure to use brackets to indicate the coordination sphere:
(a) pentaaquabromomanganese(III) sulfate
(b) tris(bipyridyl)ruthenium(II) nitrate

Isomerism

25.11. By writing formulas or drawing structures related to any one of the following complexes, illustrate (a) geometrical isomerism; (b) linkage isomerism; (c) optical isomerism; (d) coordination-sphere isomerism. The complexes are: $[Co(NH_3)_4Br_2]Cl$; $[Pd(NH_3)_2(ONO)_2]$; and cis-$[V(en)_2Cl_2]^+$.

25.12. (a) Draw the two linkage isomers of $[Co(NH_3)_5SCN]^{2+}$. (b) Draw the two geometrical isomers of $[Co(NH_3)_3Cl_3]$. (c) Two compounds with the formula $Co(NH_3)_5ClBr$ can be prepared. Use structural formulas to show how they differ. What kind of isomerism does this illustrate?

25.13. Draw the four geometrical isomers of $[Co(en)(NH_3)_2BrCl]^+$. Two of these geometrical isomers have optical isomers. Identify them and draw the structures of their enantiomers.

25.14. Sketch all the possible stereoisomers of each of the following complexes:

Color; Magnetism; Crystal-Field Theory

25.17. Indicate which of the following compounds you would expect to have color, and explain briefly:
(a) ZnO; (b) CrO_2; (c) $[Ni(NH_3)_6]Cl_2$; (d) $NaAlCl_4$; (e) $[Cd(NH_3)_4](NO_3)_2$; (f) $[Fe(SO_4)(H_2O)_4]$.

25.18. Which of the following compounds would you expect to yield a colored solution on dissolution in water?
(a) $ScBr_3$; (b) $NiSO_4$; (c) $SrBr_2 \cdot 6H_2O$; (d) VBr_3; (e) $Rh(bipy)_3Cl_3$; (f) $Pb(NO_3)_2$

25.19. Give the number of d electrons associated with the central metal ion in each of the following complexes:
(a) $K_2[Fe(CN)_6]$; (b) $[Co(H_2O)_6](NO_3)_2$; (c) $Na_2[Ni(CN)_4]$; (d) $Na[Au(CN)_4]$; (e) [MoEDTA].

25.20. Give the number of d electrons associated with the central metal ion in each of the following complexes: (a) $[Ru(en)_3]Cl_3$; (b) $K_2[Cu(CN)_4]$; (c) $Na_3[Co(NO_2)_6]$; (d) $[MoEDTA]ClO_4$; (e) $K_3[ReCl_6]$.

25.21. What is the observed color of a coordination compound that absorbs radiation of wavelength 580 nm?

(c) dichlorobis(ortho-phenanthroline)iron(III) perchlorate
(d) sodium tetrabromo(ethylenediamine)cobaltate(III)
(e) hexaamminenickel(II) tris(oxalato)chromate(III)

25.9. Polydentate ligands can vary in the number of coordination positions they occupy. In each of the following, identify the polydentate ligand present, and indicate the probable number of coordination positions it occupies:
(a) $[Co(NH_3)_4(o\text{-phen})]Cl_3$ (b) $[Cr(C_2O_4)(H_2O)_4]Br$
(c) $[CrEDTA(H_2O)]^-$ (d) $[Zn(en)_2](ClO_4)_2$

25.10. Indicate the likely coordination number of the metal in each of the following complexes:
(a) $[Cd(en)_2]Br_2$ (b) $K_2[HgBr_4]$
(c) $Na[Co(o\text{-phen})Cl_4]$ (d) [CeEDTA]

(a) square-planar $[Pt(en)(CN)_2]$
(b) tetrahedral $[Cd(en)Cl(SCN)]$
(c) octahedral $[Fe(o\text{-phen})_2Cl_2]Cl$
(d) octahedral $[Ce(CO_3)Cl_2(en)]$

25.15. The compound $Co(NH_3)_5(SO_4)Br$ exists in two forms, one red and one violet. Both forms dissociate in solution to form two ions. Solutions of the red compound form a precipitate of AgBr on addition of $AgNO_3$ solution, but no precipitate of $BaSO_4$ on addition of $BaCl_2$ solution. For the violet compound, just the reverse occurs. From this evidence, indicate the structures of the complex ions in each case, and give the correct name of each compound.

25.16. Write the formula for, and properly name, the most probable crystalline Ce(IV) coordination compound with formula $Ce(SO_4)_2 \cdot 4H_2O$. Suggest one or more possible coordination sphere isomers, assuming that water molecules may exist in the solid lattice outside the coordination sphere.

25.22. A coordination compound is bright blue in color. Assuming that this color is due to a single absorption band, what is the approximate wavelength of the absorption?

25.23. Explain why the d_{xy}, d_{xz}, and d_{yz} orbitals lie lower in energy than the $d_{x^2-y^2}$ and d_{z^2} orbitals in the presence of an octahedral arrangement of ligands about the central metal ion.

25.24. What properties of the ligand determine the size of the splitting of the d-orbital energies in the presence of an octahedral arrangement of ligands about a central transition-metal ion? Explain.

25.25. Explain why many cyano complexes of divalent transition-metal ions are yellow, whereas many aqua complexes of these ions are blue or green.

25.26. The $[Ni(H_2O)_6]^{2+}$ ion is green, whereas the $[Ni(NH_3)_6]^{2+}$ ion is purple. Predict the predominant color of light absorbed by each ion. Which ion absorbs light with the shorter wavelength? Do your conclusions agree with the spectrochemical series?

25.27. For each of the following metals, write the electronic configuration of the metal atom and the 3+ ion: **(a)** Rh; **(b)** Mn; **(c)** Pd. Draw the crystal-field energy-level diagram for the d orbitals of an octahedral complex, and show the placement of the d electrons in each case, assuming a strong-field complex.

25.28. For each of the following metals, write the electronic configuration of the metal atom and the 2+ ion: **(a)** Ni; **(b)** Tc; **(c)** Cr. Draw the crystal-field energy-level diagram for the d electrons of an octahedral complex, and show the placement of the d electrons in each case, assuming a weak-field complex of the 2+ ion.

25.29. Draw the crystal-field energy-level diagrams, and show the placement of d electrons for each of the follow-

ing: **(a)** $[Cr(H_2O)_6]^{2+}$ (four unpaired electrons); **(b)** $[Mn(H_2O)_6]^{2+}$ (high spin); **(c)** $[Ru(NH_3)_5H_2O]^{2+}$ (low spin); **(d)** $[IrCl_6]^{2-}$ (low spin); **(e)** $[Cr(en)_3]^{3+}$; **(f)** $[NiF_6]^{4-}$.

25.30. Draw the crystal-field energy-level diagrams, and show the placement of electrons for the following complexes: **(a)** $[ZrCl_6]^{2-}$; **(b)** $[MnF_6]^{3-}$ (a high-spin complex); **(c)** $[Rh(NH_3)_6]^{3+}$ (a low-spin complex); **(d)** $[NiCl_4]^{2-}$ (tetrahedral); **(e)** $[PtBr_4]^{2-}$ (square planar); **(f)** $[Cu(en)_3]^{2+}$.

25.31. The complex $[Mn(NH_3)_6]^{2+}$ contains five unpaired electrons. Sketch the energy-level diagram for the d orbitals, and indicate the placement of electrons for this complex ion. Is the ion a high-spin or a low-spin complex?

25.32. Explain why the ion $[Fe(CN)_6]^{3-}$ has one unpaired electron, whereas $[Fe(NCS)_6]^{3-}$ has five unpaired electrons.

Additional Exercises

25.33. Give one or more examples of each of the following:
(a) An octahedral complex containing one bidentate and four monodentate ligands.
(b) A complex with coordination number 4.
(c) A high-spin and a low-spin complex of the same metal ion.
(d) A ligand that is capable of linkage isomerism.
(e) A complex ion that can exhibit both geometrical and optical isomerism.
(f) An inert complex of a transition-metal ion.

25.34. Based on the molar conductance values listed below for the series of platinum(IV) complexes, write the formula for each complex so as to show which ligands are in the coordination sphere of the metal. All of the Pt complexes are kinetically inert. By way of example, the molar conductances of NaCl and BaCl$_2$ are 107 ohm^{-1} and 197 ohm^{-1}, respectively.

Complex	Molar conductance (ohm^{-1})[a] of 0.05 M solution
Pt(NH$_3$)$_6$Cl$_4$	523
Pt(NH$_3$)$_4$Cl$_4$	228
Pt(NH$_3$)$_3$Cl$_4$	97
Pt(NH$_3$)$_2$Cl$_4$	0
KPt(NH$_3$)Cl$_5$	108

[a] The ohm is a unit of resistance; conductance is the inverse of resistance.

25.35. In Werner's early studies, he observed that when the complex $[Co(NH_3)_4Br_2]Br$ was placed in water, the electrical conductivity of a 0.05 M solution changed from an initial value of 191 ohm^{-1} to a final value of 374 ohm^{-1} over a period of an hour or so. Suggest an explanation of the observed results. Write a balanced chemical equation to describe the reaction.

25.36. A palladium complex formed from a solution containing bromide ion and pyridine, C$_5$H$_5$N (a good electron-

pair donor), is found on elemental analysis to contain 37.6 percent bromine, 28.3 percent carbon, 6.60 percent nitrogen, and 2.37 percent hydrogen. The compound is slightly soluble in several organic solvents; its solutions in water or alcohol do not conduct electricity. It is found experimentally to have a zero dipole moment. Write the chemical formula, and indicate its probable structure. Name the compound.

25.37. A manganese complex formed from a solution containing potassium bromide and oxalate ion is purified and analyzed. It contains 10.0 percent Mn, 28.6 percent potassium, 8.8 percent carbon, and 29.2 percent bromine. The remainder of the compound is oxygen. An aqueous solution of the complex has about the same electrical conductivity as an equimolar solution of K$_4$[Fe(CN)$_6$]. Write the formula of the compound, using brackets to denote the manganese and its coordination sphere. Name the compound.

25.38. Draw the geometrical structure of each of the following complexes:
(a) $[Pt(en)_2]^{2+}$
(b) *cis*-diaquabis(oxalato)ferrate(III) ion
(c) *trans*-$[Pt(bipy)_2Cl_2]Cl_2$
(d) tetraiodomercurate(II) ion
(e) $[Mo(en)_3]^{3+}$
(f) pentaamminechlorovanadium(II) ion
(g) *cis*-diamminebis(thiocyanato)palladium(II)

25.39. Acetylacetone forms very stable complexes with many metallic ions. It acts as a bidentate ligand, coordinating to the metal at two adjacent positions. Suppose that one of the CH$_3$ groups of the ligand is replaced by a CF$_3$ group, as shown:

Trifluoromethyl acetylacetonate (tfac)

Sketch all possible isomers for the complex with three tfac ligands on cobalt(III). (You can use the symbol ● ○ to represent the ligand.)

25.40. Many trace metal ions exist in the bloodstream as complexes with amino acids or small peptides. The anion of the amino acid glycine,

$$H_2NCH_2C\overset{\displaystyle O}{\overset{\displaystyle \|}{}}-O^-$$

symbol gly, is capable of acting as a bidentate ligand, coordinating to the metal through nitrogen and $-O^-$ atoms. How many isomers are possible for (a) $[Zn(gly)_2]$ (tetrahedral); (b) $[Pt(gly)_2]$ (square planar); (c) $[Co(gly)_3]$ (octahedral)? Sketch all possible isomers. Use N O to represent the ligand.

25.41. Write balanced chemical equations to represent the following observations. (In some instances, the complex involved has been discussed previously at some point in the text.) (a) Solid silver chloride dissolves in an excess of aqueous ammonia. (b) The green complex $[Cr(en)_2Cl_2]Cl$, on treatment with water over a long time, converts to a brown-orange complex. Reaction of $AgNO_3$ with 1 L of 1 *M* solution of the product results in precipitation of 3 mol of AgCl. (Write *two* chemical equations.) (c) Insoluble zinc hydroxide dissolves in excess aqueous ammonia. (d) A pink solution of $Co(NO_3)_2$ turns deep blue on addition of concentrated hydrochloric acid.

25.42. What changes would you expect in the absorption spectrum of complexes of V(III) as the ligand is varied in the order F^-, NH_3, NO_2^-?

25.43. Solutions containing the $[Co(H_2O)_6]^{2+}$ ion absorb at about 520 nm; those containing the $[CoCl_4]^{2-}$ ion absorb at about 690 nm. What colors do you expect for the solutions?

25.44. Oxyhemoglobin, with an O_2 bound to iron, is a low-spin Fe(II) complex; deoxyhemoglobin, without the O_2 molecule, is a high-spin complex. How many unpaired electrons are centered on the metal ion in each case? Explain in a general way why the two forms of hemoglobin have different colors, hemoglobin being red and deoxyhemoglobin having a bluish cast.

25.45. Sketch the *d*-orbital energy-level diagram for each of the following complexes, and indicate the most likely placement of *d* electrons: (a) $[Au(CN)_4]^-$; (b) $[Ni(C_2O_4)_3]^{4-}$; (c) $[PtF_6]$; (d) $[Rh(CN)_6]^{3-}$.

25.46. Indicate whether each of the following statements is true or false. If it is false, modify it to make it true. (a) Spin-pairing energy is larger than Δ in low-spin complexes. (b) Δ is larger for complexes of Mn^{3+} with a given ligand than for complexes of Mn^{2+}. (c) $[NiCl_4]^{2-}$ is more likely to be square planar than is $[Ni(CN)_4]^{2-}$.

25.47. The value of Δ for the $[CrF_6]^{3-}$ complex is 182 kJ/mol. Calculate the expected wavelength of the absorption corresponding to promotion of an electron from the lower-energy to the higher-energy *d*-orbital set in this complex. Should the complex absorb in the visible range? (You may need to review Sample Exercise 6.2; remember to divide by Avogadro's number.)

25.48. In each of the following pairs of complexes, which would you expect to absorb at the longer wavelength: (a) $[CoF_6]^{4-}$ or $[Co(CN)_6]^{4-}$; (b) $[V(H_2O)_6]^{2+}$ or $[V(H_2O)_6]^{3+}$; (c) $[Mn(CN)_6]^{3-}$ or $[MnCl_4]^-$? Explain your reasoning in each case.

[25.49]. The red color of ruby is due to the presence of Cr(III) ions at octahedral sites in the close-packed oxide lattice of Al_2O_3. Draw the crystal-field splitting diagram for Cr(III) in this environment. Suppose that the ruby crystal is subjected to high pressure. What do you predict for the variation in the wavelength of absorption of the ruby as a function of pressure? Explain.

[25.50]. The d^3 and d^6 electronic configurations are favorable for octahedral coordination, but not for tetrahedral. Explain why this is so in terms of crystal-field theory.

[25.51]. Suppose that a transition-metal ion were in a lattice in which it was in contact with just two nearby anions, located on opposite sides of the metal. Diagram the splitting of the metal *d* orbitals that would result from such a crystal field. Assuming a strong field, how many unpaired electrons would you expect for a metal ion with six *d* electrons? (Hint: Consider the linear axis to be the *z* axis.)

[25.52]. A Cu electrode is immersed in a solution that is 1.00 *M* in $[Cu(NH_3)_4]^{2+}$ and 1.00 *M* in NH_3. When the cathode is a standard hydrogen electrode, the emf of the cell is found to be $+0.08$ V. What is the formation constant for $[Cu(NH_3)_4]^{2+}$?

26 The Chemistry of Life: Organic and Biological Chemistry

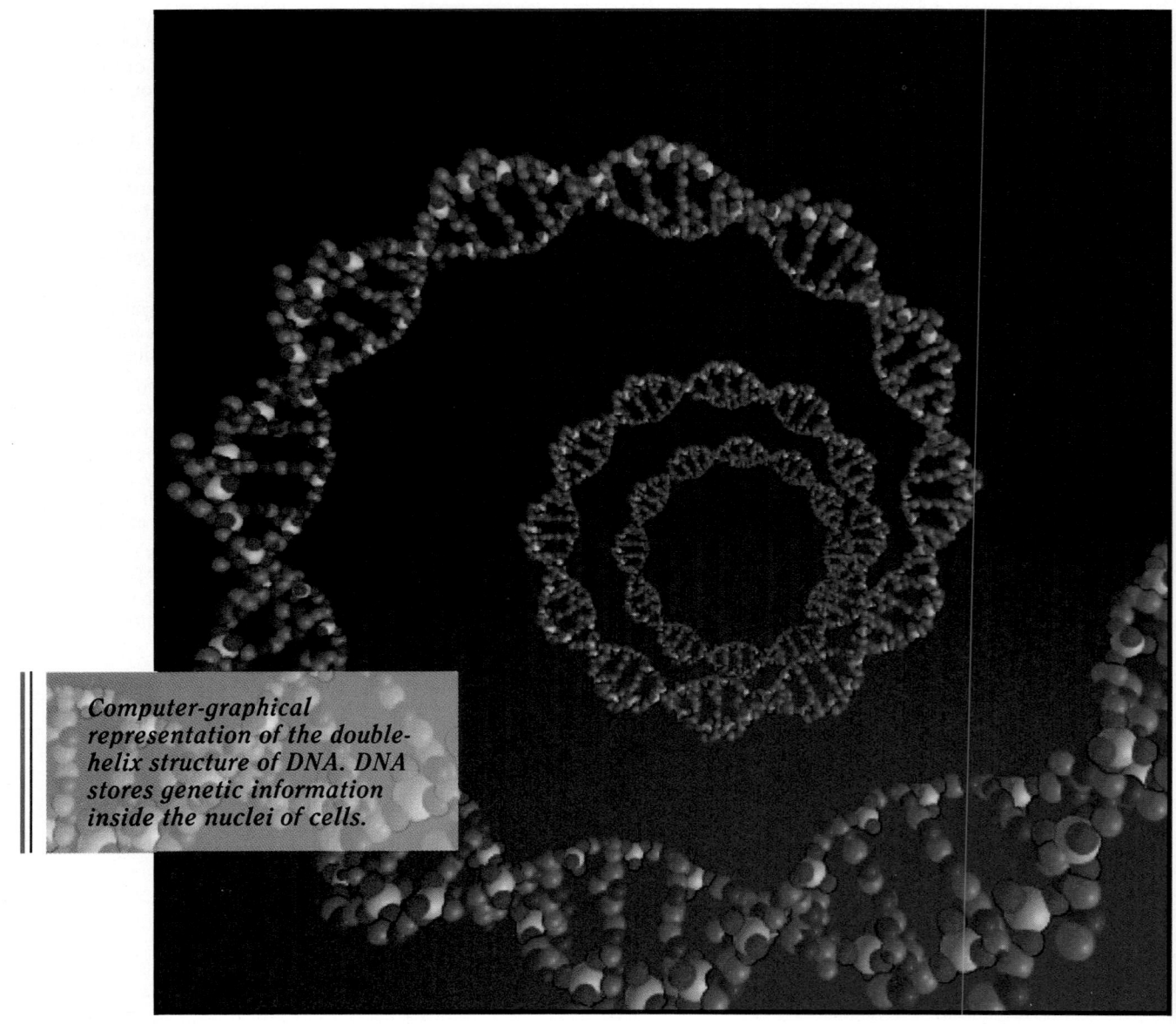

Computer-graphical representation of the double-helix structure of DNA. DNA stores genetic information inside the nuclei of cells.

The element carbon forms a vast number of compounds. Over 7 million carbon-containing compounds are known, and about 90 percent of the new compounds synthesized each year contain carbon. The study of compounds of carbon constitutes a separate branch of chemistry known as **organic chemistry.** This term arose from the eighteenth-century belief that organic compounds could be formed only by living systems. This idea was disproved in 1828 by the German chemist Friedrich Wöhler, who synthesized urea, H_2NCONH_2, an organic substance found in the urine of mammals, from inorganic starting materials.

The notion that organic chemicals and living organisms are connected is certainly true in one sense: Life as we know it could not exist without a vast array of complex, biologically important organic molecules. The study of the chemistry of living species is called *biological chemistry,* or **biochemistry.**

In this final chapter, we present a brief view of some of the elementary aspects of organic chemistry and biochemistry. Many of you will study these subjects in greater detail by taking additional courses devoted entirely to these topics. As you read the material presented here, you will notice that many of the basic concepts that we developed earlier in this text are important in understanding the fundamentals of organic chemistry and biochemistry.

Because the compounds of carbon are so numerous, it is convenient to organize them into families that exhibit structural similarities. The simplest class of organic compounds is the *hydrocarbons,* compounds composed only of carbon and hydrogen. We shall see that organic compounds containing other elements can be considered derivatives of hydrocarbons.

The key structural feature of hydrocarbons, and for that matter of most other organic substances, is the presence of stable carbon-carbon bonds. Carbon is the only element capable of forming stable, extended chains of atoms bonded through single, double, or triple bonds. Hydrocarbons can be divided into four general types, depending on the kinds of carbon-carbon bonds in their molecules. Figure 26.1 shows an example of each of the four types: alkanes, alkenes, alkynes, and aromatic hydrocarbons.

Alkanes are hydrocarbons that contain only single bonds, as in ethane, C_2H_6. Because alkanes contain the largest possible number of hydrogen atoms per carbon atom, they are called *saturated hydrocarbons.* **Alkenes,** also known as olefins, are hydrocarbons with one or more carbon-carbon double bonds, as in ethylene, C_2H_4. **Alkynes** contain at least one carbon-carbon triple bond, as in acetylene, C_2H_2. In **aromatic hydrocarbons,** the carbon atoms are connected in a planar ring structure, joined by both σ and π bonds between carbon atoms. Benzene, C_6H_6, is the best-known example of an aromatic hydrocarbon. Alkenes, alkynes, and aromatic hydrocarbons are called *unsaturated hydrocarbons* because they contain less hydrogen than an alkane having the same number of carbon atoms.

The members of these different classes of hydrocarbons exhibit different chemical behaviors, as we shall see shortly. However, they are similar in many ways. Because carbon and hydrogen do not differ greatly in electronegativity (2.5 for carbon, 2.1 for hydrogen), hydrocarbon molecules are relatively nonpolar. Thus, they are almost completely insoluble in water, but they dissolve readily in other nonpolar solvents. Furthermore, they tend to become less volatile with increasing molar mass because of London dispersion forces. ∞ (Sec. 11.2)

CONTENTS

Teaching Note: The distinction between organic and inorganic molecules is somewhat vague. As a rule of thumb, inorganic carbon is carbon that is *not* bound to hydrogen, for example, H_2CO_3. Often, the species is completely devoid of hydrogen, such as in CN^- and CO_2.

Teaching Note: Carbon is the only element that forms extensive *extended* structures with itself. The observation is the basis of the speculation that life cannot be based on another element.

Learning Goal 1: List the four groups of hydrocarbons, and draw the structural formula from each group.

The Chemistry of Life: Organic and Biological Chemistry **957**

FIGURE 26.1 Names, geometrical structures, and molecular formulas for examples of each type of hydrocarbon.

Figure 26.1

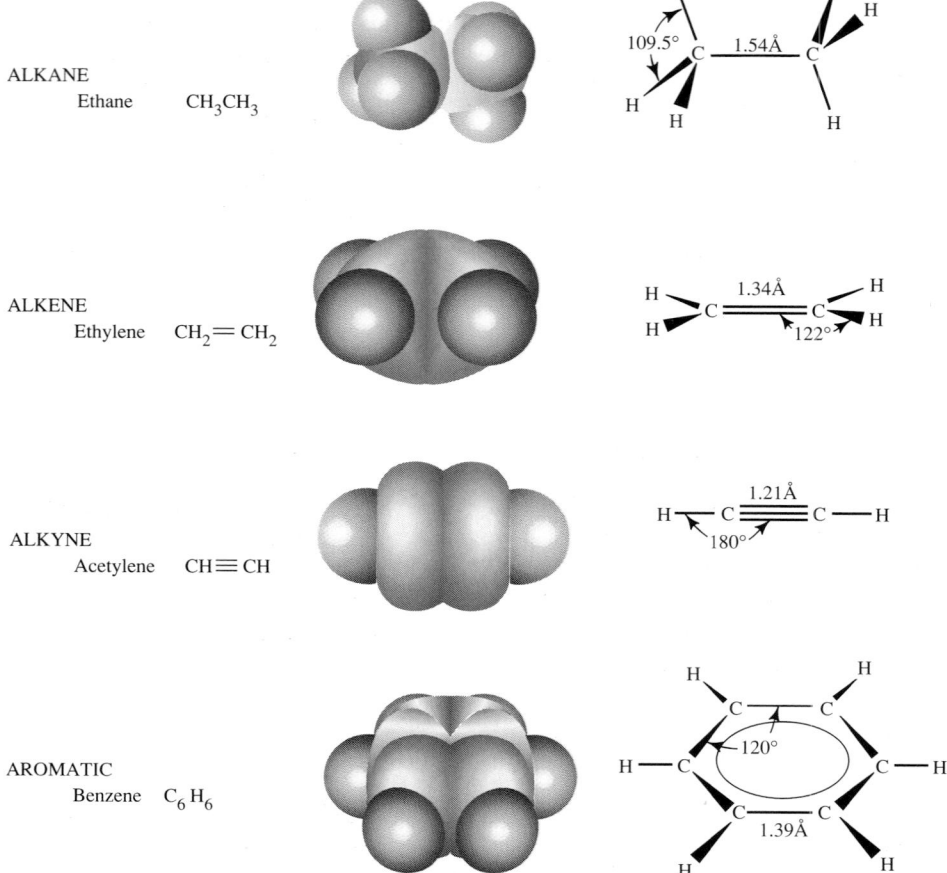

ALKANE
Ethane CH_3CH_3

ALKENE
Ethylene $CH_2 = CH_2$

ALKYNE
Acetylene $CH \equiv CH$

AROMATIC
Benzene C_6H_6

26.1 Alkanes

Table 26.1 lists several of the simplest alkanes. Many of these substances are familiar because of their widespread use. Methane is a major component of natural gas and is used for home heating and in gas stoves and hot-water heaters.

TABLE 26.1 △ First Several Members of the Straight-Chain Alkane Series

Molecular formula	Condensed structural formula	Name	Boiling point (°C)
CH_4	CH_4	Methane	−161
C_2H_6	CH_3CH_3	Ethane	−89
C_3H_8	$CH_3CH_2CH_3$	Propane	−44
C_4H_{10}	$CH_3CH_2CH_2CH_3$	Butane	−0.5
C_5H_{12}	$CH_3CH_2CH_2CH_2CH_3$	Pentane	36
C_6H_{14}	$CH_3CH_2CH_2CH_2CH_2CH_3$	Hexane	68
C_7H_{16}	$CH_3CH_2CH_2CH_2CH_2CH_2CH_3$	Heptane	98
C_8H_{18}	$CH_3CH_2CH_2CH_2CH_2CH_2CH_2CH_3$	Octane	125
C_9H_{20}	$CH_3CH_2CH_2CH_2CH_2CH_2CH_2CH_2CH_3$	Nonane	151
$C_{10}H_{22}$	$CH_3CH_2CH_2CH_2CH_2CH_2CH_2CH_2CH_2CH_3$	Decane	174

Propane is the major component of bottled, or LP, gas used for home heating and cooking in areas where natural gas is not available. Butane is used in disposable lighters and in fuel cannisters for gas camping stoves and lanterns. Alkanes with from 5 to 12 carbon atoms per molecule are found in gasoline.

The formulas for the alkanes given in Table 26.1 are written in a notation called the *condensed structural formula*. This notation reveals the way in which atoms are bonded to one another but does not require drawing in all the bonds. For example, the Lewis structure and the condensed structural formula for butane, C_4H_{10}, are

Learning Goal 2: Write the formulas and names of the first ten members of the alkane series.

$$H-\underset{\underset{H}{|}}{\overset{\overset{H}{|}}{C}}-\underset{\underset{H}{|}}{\overset{\overset{H}{|}}{C}}-\underset{\underset{H}{|}}{\overset{\overset{H}{|}}{C}}-\underset{\underset{H}{|}}{\overset{\overset{H}{|}}{C}}-H \qquad\qquad CH_3CH_2CH_2CH_3$$

Lewis structure   Condensed structural formula

We shall frequently use either Lewis structures or condensed structural formulas to represent organic compounds. You should practice drawing the structural formulas from the condensed ones. Notice that each carbon atom in an alkane has four single bonds, whereas each hydrogen atom forms one single bond. Notice also that each succeeding compound in the series listed in Table 26.1 has an additional CH_2 unit.

Structures of Alkanes

The Lewis structures and condensed structural formulas for alkanes do not tell us anything about the three-dimensional structures of these substances. As we would predict from the VSEPR model, the geometry about each carbon atom in an alkane is tetrahedral; that is, the four groups attached to each carbon are located at the vertices of a tetrahedron. ∞ (Sec. 9.1) The three-dimensional structures can be represented as shown for methane in Figure 26.2. The bonding may be described as involving sp^3 hybridized orbitals on the carbon. ∞ (Sec. 9.4)

Point of Emphasis: Carbon cannot exceed an octet in a stable compound.

Rotation about the carbon-carbon single bond is relatively easy. You might imagine grasping the top left methyl group in Figure 26.3, which shows the structure of propane, and twisting it relative to the rest of the structure. Motion of this sort occurs very rapidly in alkanes at room temperature. Conse-

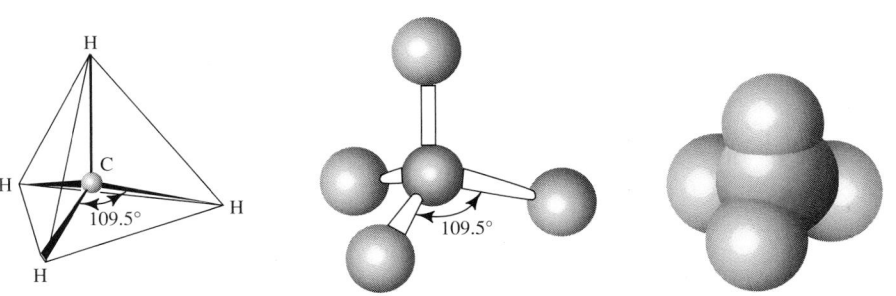

FIGURE 26.2 Representations of the three-dimensional arrangement of bonds about carbon in methane.

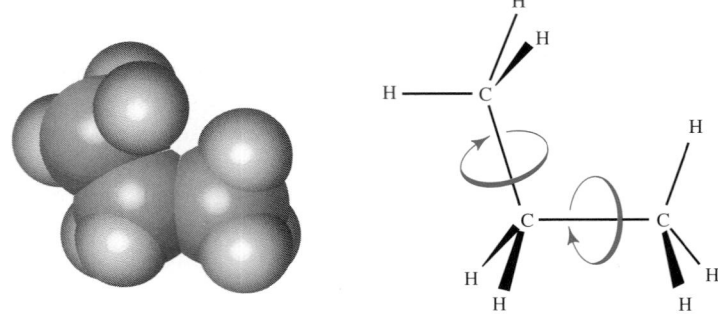

Teaching Note: Some energy is required for atoms to rotate about a single bond, but sufficient energy for this process exists at room temperature.

Common Misconception: Students often interpret the term *straight-chain* to mean geometrically linear. Straight-chain hydrocarbons are actually bent at each carbon atom, as predicted by the VSEPR model.

Learning Goals 3: Give an example of structural isomerism in alkanes.

quently, a long-chain alkane is constantly undergoing motions that cause it to change its shape, something like a length of chain that is being shaken.

Structural Isomers

The alkanes listed in Table 26.1 are called *straight-chain hydrocarbons* because all the carbon atoms are joined in a continuous chain. Alkanes consisting of four or more carbon atoms can also form branched chains; hydrocarbons with branched chains are called *branched hydrocarbons*. Figure 26.4 shows the condensed formulas and space-filling models for all the possible structures of alkanes containing four and five carbon atoms. Notice that there are two ways that four carbon atoms can be joined to give C_4H_{10}—as a straight chain (left) or a branched chain (right). For alkanes with five carbon atoms, C_5H_{12}, there are three different arrangements.

Compounds with the same molecular formula but with different bonding arrangements and hence different structures are called **structural isomers.** The structural isomers of a given alkane differ slightly from one another in physical properties. Note the melting and boiling points of the isomers of butane and pentane, given in Figure 26.4. The number of possible isomers increases rapidly with the number of carbon atoms in the alkane. For example, there are 18 possible isomers of octane, C_8H_{18}, and 75 possible isomers of decane, $C_{10}H_{22}$.

Nomenclature of Alkanes

The first names given to the structural isomers shown in Figure 26.4 are the so-called common names. The straight-chain isomer is called the normal isomer, abbreviated by the prefix *n-*. The isomer in which one CH_3 group is branched off the major chain is labeled the iso- isomer (for example, isobutane). However, as the number of isomers grows, it becomes impossible to find a suitable prefix to denote each isomer. The need for a systematic means of naming organic compounds was recognized early in the history of organic chemistry. In 1892, an organization called the International Union of Chemistry met in Geneva, Switzerland, to formulate rules for systematic naming of organic substances. Since that time, the task of keeping the rules for naming compounds up-to-date has fallen to the International Union of Pure and Applied Chemistry (IUPAC). It is interesting to note that through two devastating world wars and major social upheavals, the work of IUPAC has continued. Chemists everywhere, regardless of their nationality or political affiliation, subscribe to a common system for naming compounds.

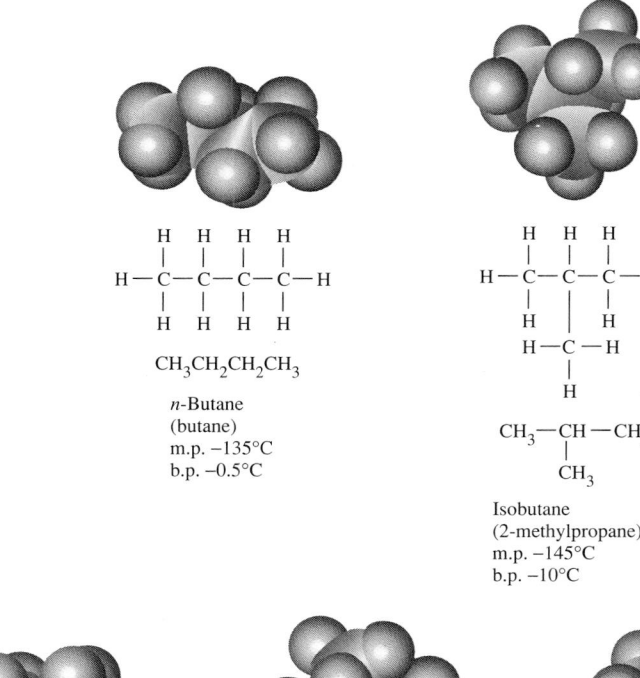

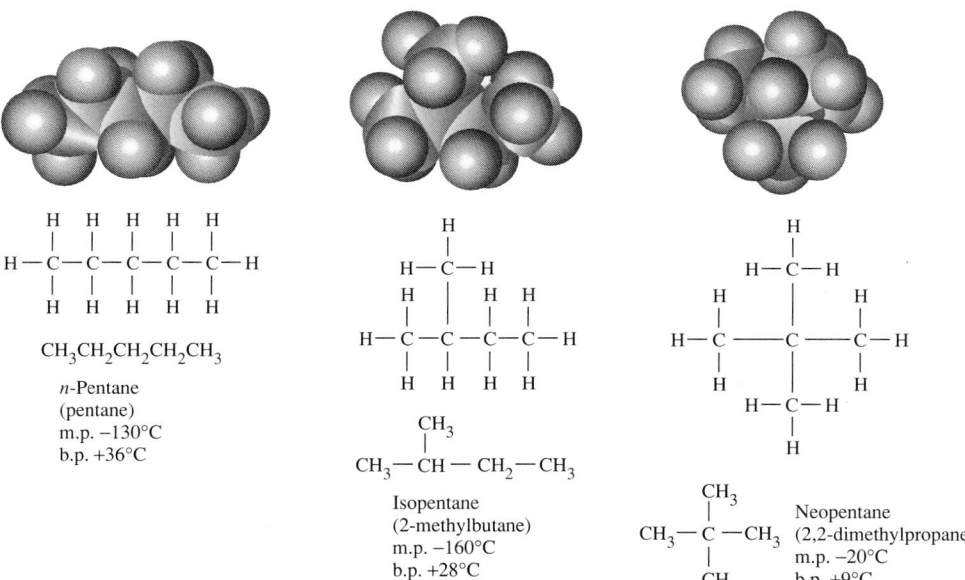

The IUPAC names for the isomers of butane and pentane are the ones given in parentheses for each compound in Figure 26.4. The following rules summarize the procedures used to arrive at these names. We shall see that a similar approach is taken in writing the names for other organic compounds.

Learning Goals 4: Write the structural formula of an alkane given its systematic (IUPAC) name.

Learning Goal 5: Name an alkane, given its structural formula.

1. Each compound is named for the longest continuous chain of carbon atoms present. For example, the longest chain of carbon atoms in isobutane is three (Figure 26.4). Consequently, this compound is named as a derivative of propane, which has three carbon atoms; in the IUPAC system it is called 2-methylpropane.

TABLE 26.2 △ Condensed Structural Formulas and Common Names for Several Alkyl Groups

Group	Name
CH_3-	Methyl
CH_3CH_2-	Ethyl
$CH_3CH_2CH_2-$	n-Propyl
$CH_3CH_2CH_2CH_2-$	n-Butyl
CH_3 | $HC-$ | CH_3	Isopropyl
CH_3 | CH_3-C- | CH_3	t-Butyl

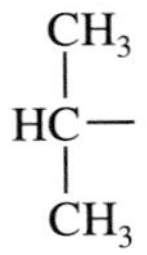

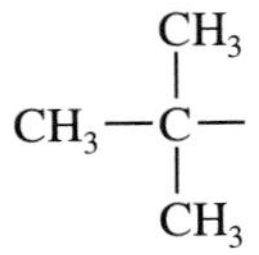

2. In general, a group that is formed by removing a hydrogen atom from an alkane is called an **alkyl group.** The names for alkyl groups are derived by dropping the -*ane* ending from the name of the parent alkane and adding -*yl*. For example, the methyl group, CH_3, is derived from methane, CH_4; likewise, the ethyl group, C_2H_5, is derived from ethane, C_2H_6. Table 26.2 lists several of the more common alkyl groups.

3. The location of an alkyl group along a carbon-atom chain is indicated by numbering the carbon atoms along the chain. Thus, the name 2-methylpropane indicates the presence of a methyl, CH_3, group on the second carbon atom of a propane (three-carbon) chain. In general, the chain is numbered from the end that gives the lowest numbers for the alkyl positions.

4. If there is more than one substituent group of a certain type along the chain, the number of groups of that type is indicated by a prefix: *di-* (two), *tri-* (three), *tetra-* (four), *penta-* (five), and so forth. Therefore, the IUPAC name for neopentane (Figure 26.4) is 2,2-dimethylpropane. Dimethyl indicates the presence of two methyl groups; the 2,2- prefix indicates that both are on the second carbon atom of the propane chain.

SAMPLE EXERCISE 26.1

Name the following alkane:

$$CH_3-CH-CH_3$$
$$CH_3-CH-CH_2$$
$$CH_3$$

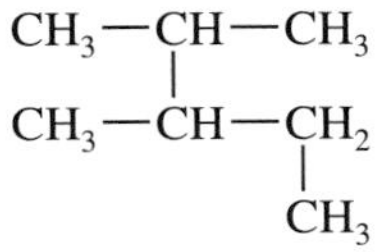

SOLUTION To name this compound properly, you must first find the longest continuous chain of carbon atoms. This chain, extending from the upper left CH_3 group to the lower right CH_3 group, is five carbon atoms long:

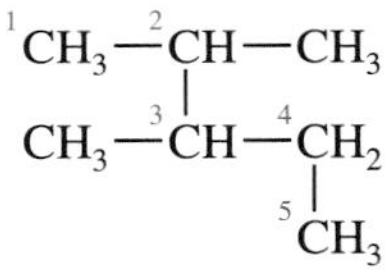

$$^1CH_3-^2CH-CH_3$$
$$CH_3-^3CH-^4CH_2$$
$$^5CH_3$$

The compound is thus named as a derivative of pentane. We could number the carbon atoms starting from either end. However, IUPAC rules state that the numbering should be done so that the numbers of carbons bearing side chains are as low as possible. This means that we should start numbering with the upper carbon. There is a methyl group on carbon 2, and one on carbon 3. The compound is thus called 2,3-dimethylpentane.

PRACTICE EXERCISE

Name the following alkane:

$$CH_3-CH-CH_3$$
$$CH_3-CH-CH_2$$
$$CH_3$$

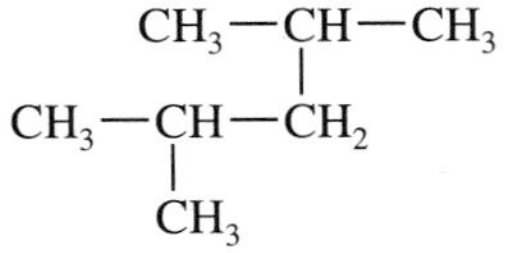

Answer: 2,4-dimethylpentane

SAMPLE EXERCISE 26.2

Write the condensed structural formula for 2-methyl-3-ethylpentane.

SOLUTION The longest continuous chain of carbon atoms in this compound is five. We can therefore begin by writing out a string of five C atoms:

$$C-C-C-C-C$$

We next place a methyl group on the second carbon, and an ethyl group on the middle carbon atom of the chain. Hydrogens are then added to all the other carbon atoms to make the four bonds to each carbon. Thus, the structural formula is

$$CH_3-\underset{\underset{CH_2CH_3}{|}}{\overset{\overset{CH_3}{|}}{CH}}-CH-CH_2-CH_3$$

The formula can be written more concisely as $CH_3CH(CH_3)CH(C_2H_5)CH_2CH_3$.

PRACTICE EXERCISE

Write the condensed structural formula for 2,3-dimethylhexane.

Answer:

$$CH_3\underset{\overset{|}{CH_3}}{CH}-\underset{\overset{|}{CH_3}}{CH}CH_2CH_2CH_3 \quad \text{or} \quad CH_3CH(CH_3)CH(CH_3)CH_2CH_2CH_3$$

Cycloalkanes

Alkanes can form not only branched chains, but rings or cycles as well. Alkanes with this form of structure are called **cycloalkanes.** Figure 26.5 illustrates a few examples of cycloalkanes. Cycloalkane structures are sometimes drawn as simple polygons in which each corner of the polygon represents a CH_2 group. This method of representation is similar to that used for benzene rings. ∞ (Sec. 9.5) In the case of aromatic structures, each corner represents a CH group.

Carbon rings containing fewer than five carbon atoms are strained because the C—C—C bond angle in the smaller rings must be less than the 109.5° tetrahedral angle. The amount of strain increases as the rings get smaller. In cyclopropane, which has the shape of an equilateral triangle, the angle is only 60°; this molecule is therefore much more reactive than either propane, its straight-chain analog, or cyclohexane, which has no ring strain.

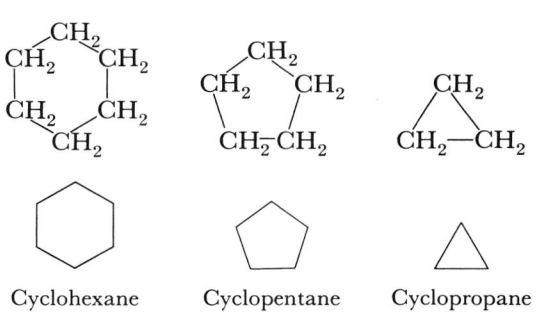

Cyclohexane   Cyclopentane   Cyclopropane

FIGURE 26.5 Condensed structural formulas for three cycloalkanes.

Figure 26.5

Gasoline

Petroleum, or crude oil, is a complex mixture of organic compounds, mainly hydrocarbons, with smaller quantities of other organic compounds containing nitrogen, oxygen, or sulfur. The tremendous demand for petroleum to meet the world's energy needs has led to the tapping of oil wells in such forbidding places as the North Sea and northern Alaska.

The usual first step in the *refining,* or processing, of petroleum is to separate it into fractions on the basis of boiling point. The fractions commonly taken are shown in Table 26.3. Because gasoline is the most commercially important of these fractions, various processes are used to maximize its yield.

Gasoline is a mixture of volatile hydrocarbons containing varying amounts of aromatic hydrocarbons in addition to alkanes. In an automobile engine, a mixture of air and gasoline vapor is compressed by a piston and then ignited by a spark plug. The burning of the gasoline should create a strong, smooth expansion of gas, forcing the piston outward and imparting force along the driveshaft of the engine. If the gas burns too rapidly, the piston receives a single hard slam rather than a strong, smooth push. The result is a "knocking" or "pinging" sound and a reduction in the efficiency with which energy produced by the combustion is converted to work.

The *octane number* of a gasoline is a measure of its resistance to knock. Gasolines with high octane num-

FIGURE 26.6 The octane rating of gasoline measures its resistance to knocking when burned in an engine. The octane rating of this gasoline is 93, as shown on the face of the pump. (Marmel Studios/The Stock Market)

TABLE 26.3 △ Hydrocarbon Fractions from Petroleum

Fraction	Size range of molecules	Boiling-point range (°C)	Uses
Gas	C_1 to C_5	−160 to 30	Gaseous fuel, production of H_2
Straight-run gasoline	C_5 to C_{12}	30 to 200	Motor fuel
Kerosene, fuel oil	C_{12} to C_{18}	180 to 400	Diesel fuel, furnace fuel, cracking
Lubricants	C_{16} and up	350 and up	Lubricants
Paraffins	C_{20} and up	Low-melting solids	Candles, matches
Asphalt	C_{36} and up	Gummy residues	Surfacing roads, fuel

Reactions of Alkanes

Alkanes are relatively unreactive. For example, at room temperature they do not react with acids, bases, or strong oxidizing agents, and they are not even attacked by boiling nitric acid. One reason for their low chemical reactivity is the strength of the C—C and C—H bonds.

bers burn more smoothly and are thus more effective fuels (Figure 26.6). The more highly branched alkanes have higher octane numbers than the straight-chain alkanes. The octane number of gasoline is obtained by comparing its knocking characteristics with those of "isooctane" (2,2,4-trimethylpentane) and heptane. Isooctane is assigned an octane number of 100, whereas heptane is assigned 0. Gasoline with the same knocking characteristics as a mixture of 90 percent isooctane and 10 percent heptane is rated as 90 octane.

The gasoline obtained directly from fractionation of petroleum (called *straight-run* gasoline) contains mainly straight-chain hydrocarbons and has an octane number around 50. It is therefore subjected to a process called *cracking,* which converts the straight-chain alkanes into more desirable branched-chain ones (Figure 26.7). Cracking is also used to convert some of the less volatile kerosene and fuel-oil fraction into compounds with lower molecular weights that are suitable for use as automobile fuel. In the cracking process, the hydrocarbons are mixed with a catalyst and heated to 400 to 500°C. The catalysts used are naturally occurring clay minerals or synthetic $Al_2O_3 - SiO_2$ mixtures. In addition to forming molecules more suitable for gasoline, cracking results in the formation of hydrocarbons of lower molecular weight, such as ethylene and propene. These substances are used in a variety of processes to form plastics and other chemicals.

The octane rating of gasoline is further improved by adding certain compounds called *antiknock agents.* Until the mid-1970s, the principal antiknock agent was tetraethyllead, $(C_2H_5)_4Pb$. Its use has been drastically curtailed because of the environmental hazards of lead and because it poisons catalytic converters (see the Chemistry at Work box in Section 14.6). Oxygenated hydrocarbons are now generally used as antiknock agents. One of the most cost-effective is methyl *t*-butyl ether (MTBE):

$$CH_3-\overset{\overset{\displaystyle CH_3}{|}}{\underset{\underset{\displaystyle CH_3}{|}}{C}}-O-CH_3$$

FIGURE 26.7 Petroleum is separated into fractions by distillation and is subjected to catalytic cracking in a refinery, as shown here. (Jim Zuckerman/Westlight)

Alkanes are not completely inert, however. One of their most commercially important reactions is *combustion* in air, which is the basis of their use as fuels. ∞ (Sec. 3.2) For example, the complete combustion of ethane proceeds as follows:

$$2C_2H_6(g) + 7O_2(g) \longrightarrow 4CO_2(g) + 6H_2O(g) \qquad \Delta H = -1888 \text{ kJ}$$

Teaching Note: Hydrocarbon fuels such as gasoline and kerosene are largely composed of alkanes.

In the following sections, we will see two ways in which hydrocarbons can be modified to impart greater reactivity: the introduction of unsaturation into the carbon-carbon framework, and the attachment of reactive groups to the hydrocarbon backbone.

26.2 Unsaturated Hydrocarbons

The presence of one or more multiple bonds makes unsaturated hydrocarbons significantly different from alkanes both in terms of their structure and their reactivity.

Alkenes

Teaching Note: *Ethene* and *propene* are IUPAC names; *ethylene* and *propylene* are historical or trivial names.

Alkenes are unsaturated hydrocarbons that contain one or more $C{=}C$ bonds. The simplest alkene is $CH_2{=}CH_2$, called ethene or ethylene. The next member of the series is $CH_3{-}CH{=}CH_2$, called propene or propylene. For alkenes with four or more carbon atoms, several isomers exist for each molecular formula. For example, there are four isomers of C_4H_8, as shown in Figure 26.8. Notice both their structures and their names.

The names of alkenes are based on the longest continuous chain of carbon atoms that contains the double bond. The name given to the chain is obtained from the name of the corresponding alkane (Table 26.1) by changing the ending from *-ane* to *-ene*. For example, the compound on the left in Figure 26.8 has a three-carbon chain; thus, the parent alkene is considered to be propene.

Learning Goal 6: Give an example of structural and geometric isomerism in alkenes and alkynes.

The location of the double bond along an alkene chain is indicated by a prefix number that designates the number of the carbon atom that is part of the double bond and is nearest an end of the chain. The chain is always numbered from the end that brings us to the double bond sooner and hence gives the smallest number prefix. In propene, the only possible location for the double bond is between the first and second carbons; thus, a prefix indicating its location is unnecessary. For the compound on the left in Figure 26.8, numbering the carbon chain from the end closer to the double bond places a methyl group on the second carbon. Thus, the name of the isomer is 2-methylpropene. For the other compounds in Figure 26.8, the longest carbon chain contains four carbons, and there are two possible positions for the double bond, either after the first carbon (1-butene) or after the second carbon (2-butene).

Learning Goal 7: Write the structural formula of an alkene or alkyne, given its systematic (IUPAC) name. Name an alkene or alkyne, given its structural formula.

If a substance contains two or more double bonds, each is located by a numerical prefix. Furthermore, the ending of the name is altered to identify the number of double bonds: diene (two), triene (three), and so forth. For example, $CH_2{=}CH{-}CH_2{-}CH{=}CH_2$ is 1,4-pentadiene.

Notice that the two isomers on the right in Figure 26.8 differ in the relative locations of their terminal methyl groups. These two compounds are examples of **geometrical isomers,** compounds that have the same molecular formula and

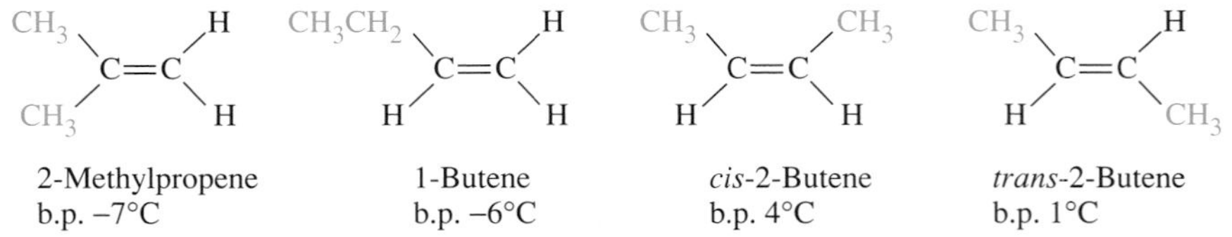

FIGURE 26.8 Structures, names, and boiling points of alkenes with molecular formula C_4H_8.

2-Methylpropene
b.p. −7°C

1-Butene
b.p. −6°C

cis-2-Butene
b.p. 4°C

trans-2-Butene
b.p. 1°C

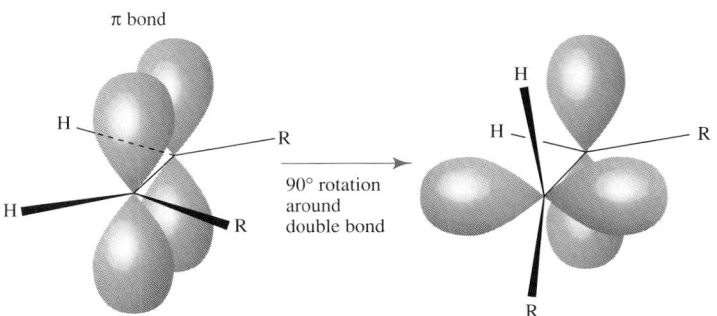

π bond

90° rotation around double bond

FIGURE 26.9 Schematic illustration of rotation about a carbon-carbon double bond in an alkene. The overlap of the *p* orbitals that form the π bond is lost in the rotation. For this reason, rotation about carbon-carbon double bonds does not occur readily.

the same groups bonded to one another but differ in the spatial arrangement of these groups. ∞ (Sec. 25.4)   In the *cis* isomer, the two methyl groups are on the same side of the double bond, whereas in the *trans* isomer, they are on opposite sides. Geometrical isomers possess distinct physical properties and may even differ significantly in their chemical behavior.

Geometrical isomerism in alkenes arises because unlike the C—C bond, the C=C bond is resistant to twisting. Recall that the double bond between two carbon atoms consists of a σ and a π part. ∞ (Sec. 9.5)   Figure 26.9 shows a cis alkene. The carbon-carbon bond axis and the bonds to the hydrogen atoms and to the alkyl groups (designated R), are all in a plane. The *p* orbitals that overlap sideways to form the π bond are perpendicular to the molecular plane. As Figure 26.9 shows, rotation around the carbon-carbon double bond requires the π bond to be broken, a process that requires considerable energy (about 250 kJ/mol).

Point of Emphasis: As with transition-metal complexes, you can remember the geometrical isomers by simply recalling that *trans* means "across."

Teaching Note: The cis and trans isomers of most alkenes are nearly identical in stability. Therefore, the resistance to twisting is a large activation energy resulting from breaking the π bond in the transition state.

SAMPLE EXERCISE 26.3

Name the following compound:

$$CH_3CH_2CH_2 - \underset{H}{\overset{CH_3}{\underset{|}{CH}}} \underset{H}{\overset{}{C}} = \underset{H}{\overset{CH_3}{C}}$$

SOLUTION   Because this compound possesses a double bond, it is an alkene. The longest continuous chain of carbons that contains the double bond is seven in length. The parent compound is therefore considered a heptene. The double bond begins at carbon 2 (numbering from the end closest to the double bond); thus the parent hydrocarbon chain is named 2-heptene. Continuing the numbering along the chain, a methyl group is bound at carbon atom 4. Thus the compound is 4-methyl-2-heptene. Finally, we note that the geometrical configuration at the double bond is cis; that is, the alkyl groups are bonded to the double bond on the same side. For this reason, the full name is 4-methyl-*cis*-2-heptene.

PRACTICE EXERCISE

Draw the structural formula for the compound *trans*-1,3-hexadiene.

Answer:
$$CH_2=CH \underset{H}{\overset{}{C}} = \underset{CH_2CH_3}{\overset{H}{C}}$$

Alkynes

Alkynes are unsaturated hydrocarbons containing one or more C≡C bonds. The simplest alkyne is acetylene, C_2H_2, a highly reactive molecule. When

Teaching Note: The IUPAC name of acetylene is *ethyne*.

acetylene is burned in a stream of oxygen in an oxyacetylene torch, the flame reaches a very high temperature, about 3200 K. The oxyacetylene torch is widely used in welding, which requires high temperatures. Alkynes in general are highly reactive molecules. Because of their higher reactivity, they are not as widely distributed in nature as alkenes; however, they are important intermediates in many industrial processes.

Alkynes are named by identifying the longest continuous chain in the molecule containing the triple bond and modifying the ending of the name as listed in Table 26.1 from -*ane* to -*yne*, as shown in Sample Exercise 26.4.

SAMPLE EXERCISE 26.4

Name the following compounds:

(a) $CH_3CH_2CH_2-C\equiv C-CH_3$
(b) $CH_3CH_2CH_2CH-C\equiv CH$
$\qquad\qquad\quad |$
$\qquad\qquad CH_2CH_2CH_3$

SOLUTION   In (a) the longest chain of carbon atoms is six. There are no side chains. The triple bond begins at carbon 2 (remember, we always arrange the numbering so that the smallest possible number is assigned to the carbon containing the multiple bond). Thus, the name is 2-hexyne.

In (b) the longest continuous chain of carbon atoms is seven; but because this chain does not contain the triple bond we do not count it as derived from heptane. The longest chain containing the triple bond is six, and so this compound is named as a derivative of hexyne, 3-propyl-1-hexyne.

PRACTICE EXERCISE

Draw the condensed structural formula for 4-methyl-2-pentyne.

Answer: $CH_3-C\equiv C-CH-CH_3$
$\qquad\qquad\qquad\quad |$
$\qquad\qquad\qquad CH_3$

Addition Reactions of Alkenes and Alkynes

Learning Goal 8: Give examples of addition reactions of alkenes and alkynes, showing the structural formulas of reactants and products.

The presence of carbon-carbon double or triple bonds in hydrocarbons markedly increases their chemical reactivity. The most characteristic reactions of alkenes and alkynes are **addition reactions,** in which a reactant is added to the two atoms that form the multiple bond. A simple example is the addition of a halogen such as Br_2 to ethene:

$$H_2C=CH_2 + Br_2 \longrightarrow H_2C-CH_2 \qquad\qquad [26.1]$$
$$\qquad\qquad\qquad\qquad\qquad | \quad |$$
$$\qquad\qquad\qquad\qquad\quad Br \;\; Br$$

The pair of electrons that form the π bond in ethylene is uncoupled and is used to form two new bonds to the two bromine atoms. The σ bond between the carbon atoms remains.

Addition of H_2 to an alkene converts it to an alkane:

$$CH_3CH=CHCH_3 + H_2 \xrightarrow{\text{Ni, 500°C}} CH_3CH_2CH_2CH_3 \qquad [26.2]$$

This reaction, referred to as *hydrogenation,* does not occur readily under ordinary temperature and pressure conditions. One reason for the lack of reactivity of H_2 toward alkenes is the high bond energy of the H_2 bond. To promote the reaction, it is necessary to use a catalyst that assists in rupturing the H—H bond. The most widely used catalysts are finely divided metals on which H_2 is adsorbed. ∞ (Sec. 14.6)

Hydrogen halides and water can also add to the double bond of alkenes, as illustrated by the following reactions of ethene:

$$CH_2=CH_2 + HBr \longrightarrow CH_3CH_2Br \qquad [26.3]$$

$$CH_2=CH_2 + H_2O \xrightarrow{H_2SO_4} CH_3CH_2OH \qquad [26.4]$$

The addition of water is catalyzed by a strong acid such as H_2SO_4.

The addition reactions of alkynes resemble those of alkenes, as shown in the following examples:

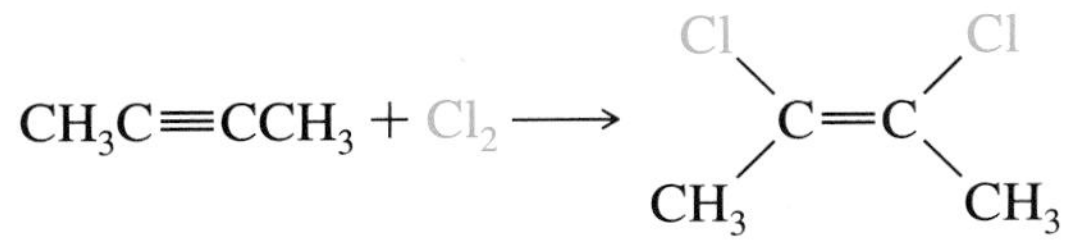

$$CH_3C\equiv CCH_3 + Cl_2 \longrightarrow \underset{\substack{\text{} \\ \textit{cis}\text{-1,2-Dichloro-2-butene}}}{\overset{\substack{Cl \qquad\quad Cl \\ \diagdown \qquad\quad \diagup \\ C=C \\ \diagup \qquad\quad \diagdown \\ CH_3 \qquad\quad CH_3}}{}} \qquad [26.5]$$

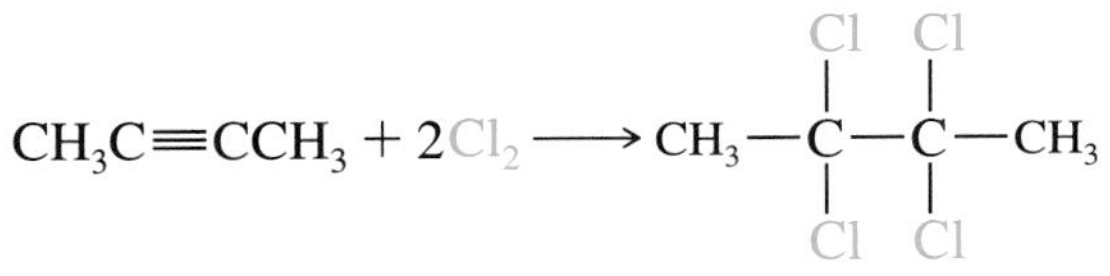

2-Butyne

$$CH_3C\equiv CCH_3 + 2Cl_2 \longrightarrow \underset{\substack{\text{} \\ \text{2,2,3,3-Tetrachlorobutane}}}{\overset{\substack{Cl \quad Cl \\ | \quad\; | \\ CH_3-C-C-CH_3 \\ | \quad\; | \\ Cl \quad Cl}}{}} \qquad [26.6]$$

2-Butyne

SAMPLE EXERCISE 26.5

Predict the product of the hydrogenation of 3-methyl-1-pentene.

SOLUTION The name of the starting compound tells us that we have a chain of five carbon atoms with a double bond at one end (position 1) and a methyl group on the third carbon from that end (position 3):

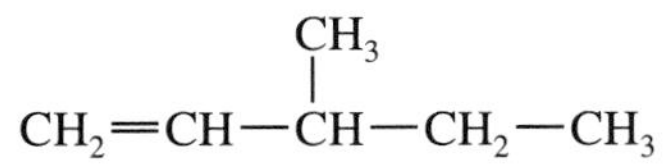

$$\overset{\displaystyle CH_3}{\underset{\displaystyle |}{CH_2=CH-CH-CH_2-CH_3}}$$

The addition of H_2 across the double bond leads to the following alkane:

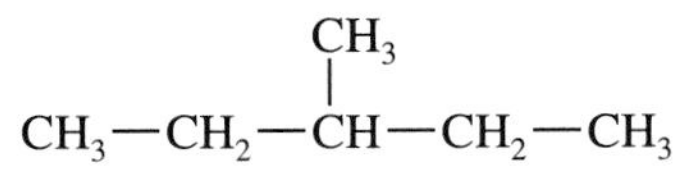

$$\overset{\displaystyle CH_3}{\underset{\displaystyle |}{CH_3-CH_2-CH-CH_2-CH_3}}$$

The longest chain in this alkane has five carbon atoms; its name is therefore 3-methylpentane.

PRACTICE EXERCISE

Addition of HCl to an alkene leads to the formation of 2-chloropropane. What is the alkene?   *Answer:* propene

The Accidental Discovery of Teflon

A *polymer* is a material with a high molecular weight that is formed from simple molecules called monomers. (Sec. 12.2)   Polymers may be either natural or synthetic in origin. Later in this chapter, we shall see several examples of natural polymers, such as proteins and starch. In Section 12.2, we saw several examples of synthetic polymers, such as polyethylene and nylon. Another synthetic polymer, with which you are probably familiar, is Teflon. This substance was discovered quite by accident.

In 1938, a scientist at Du Pont named Roy J. Plunkett made a rather curious observation: A tank of the gaseous compound *tetrafluoroethylene,* $CF_2{=}CF_2$, that was supposed to be full seemed to have no gas in it. Rather than discarding the tank, Plunkett decided to explore further by cutting the tank open. He found that the inside of the tank was coated with a waxy white substance that was remarkably unreactive toward even the most corrosive chemical reagents. The compound was formed by the *addition polymerization* (Section

12.2) of tetrafluoroethylene:

$$nCF_2{=}CF_2 \xrightarrow{\text{polymerization}} -\!\!(CF_2{-}CF_2)_n\!\!-$$

As it turned out, the properties of Teflon were ideal for an immediate and important application in the development of the first atomic bomb. Uranium hexafluoride, UF_6, which was used to separate fissionable ^{235}U by gaseous diffusion (see the Chemistry at Work box in Section 10.9), is an extremely corrosive material. Teflon was used as a gasket material in the gaseous diffusion plant. It is now used in a variety of applications, from nonstick cookware to space suits.

Plunkett's desire to know more about something that just didn't seem right is a wonderful example of how natural scientific curiosity can lead to remarkable discoveries. If you wish to read about more such accidental discoveries, we recommend Royston M. Roberts, *Serendipity: Accidental Discoveries in Science,* John Wiley and Sons, 1989.

Aromatic Hydrocarbons

Teaching Note: The English language definition of aromatic is "of or having an aroma; smelling sweet or spicy; fragrant or pungent." Historically, aromatic compounds were identified as such by their characteristic odor. The modern chemical definition of aromatic has to do with the cyclic delocalized bonding in a molecule rather than its odor.

Aromatic hydrocarbons are members of a large and important class of hydrocarbons. The simplest member of the series is benzene (see Figure 26.1), with molecular formula C_6H_6. As we have already noted, benzene is a planar, highly symmetrical molecule. The molecular formula for benzene suggests a high degree of unsaturation. You might therefore expect benzene to resemble the unsaturated hydrocarbons and to be highly reactive. In fact, however, benzene is not at all similar to alkenes or alkynes in chemical behavior. The great stability of benzene and the other aromatic hydrocarbons as compared with alkenes and alkynes is due to stabilization of the π electrons through delocalization in the π orbitals.   (Sec. 9.5)

There is no widely used systematic nomenclature for naming aromatic rings. Each ring system is given a common name; several aromatic compounds are shown in Figure 26.10. The aromatic rings are represented by hexagons with a circle inscribed inside to denote aromatic character. Each corner represents a

FIGURE 26.10 Structures and names of several aromatic compounds.

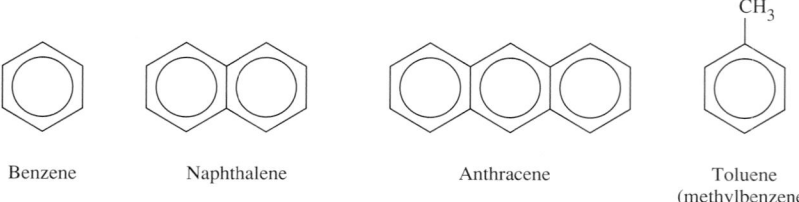

| Benzene | Naphthalene | Anthracene | Toluene (methylbenzene) |

carbon atom. Each carbon is bound to three other atoms—either three carbons or two carbons and a hydrogen. The hydrogen atoms are not shown.

Although aromatic hydrocarbons are unsaturated, they do not readily undergo addition reactions. The delocalized π bonding causes aromatic compounds to behave quite differently from alkenes and alkynes. For example, benzene does not add Cl_2 or Br_2 to its double bonds under ordinary conditions. In contrast, aromatic hydrocarbons undergo **substitution reactions** relatively easily. In a substitution reaction, one atom of a molecule is removed and replaced (substituted) by another atom or group of atoms. For example, when benzene is warmed in a mixture of nitric and sulfuric acids, hydrogen is replaced by the nitro group, NO_2:

Learning Goal 9: Explain why aromatic hydrocarbons do not readily undergo addition reactions.

Learning Goal 10: Give two or three examples of substitution reactions of aromatic hydrocarbons.

$$\text{\Large$\bigcirc$} + HNO_3 \xrightarrow{H_2SO_4} \text{\Large$\bigcirc$}^{NO_2} + H_2O \qquad [26.7]$$

More vigorous treatment results in substitution of a second nitro group into the molecule:

$$\text{\Large$\bigcirc$}^{NO_2} + HNO_3 \xrightarrow{H_2SO_4} \text{\Large$\bigcirc$}^{NO_2}_{NO_2} + H_2O \qquad [26.8]$$

There are three possible isomers of benzene with two nitro groups attached. These three isomers are named *ortho-, meta-,* and *para*-dinitrobenzene:

ortho-Dinitrobenzene
m.p. 118°C

meta-Dinitrobenzene
m.p. 90°C

para-Dinitrobenzene
m.p. 174°C

Only the meta isomer is formed in the reaction of nitric acid with nitrobenzene.

Another example of a substitution reaction is the bromination of benzene, which is carried out using $FeBr_3$ as a catalyst:

$$\text{\Large$\bigcirc$} + Br_2 \xrightarrow{FeBr_3} \text{\Large$\bigcirc$}^{Br} + HBr \qquad [26.9]$$

In a similar reaction, called the *Friedel-Crafts reaction*, alkyl groups can be substituted onto an aromatic ring by reaction of an alkyl halide with an aromatic compound in the presence of $AlCl_3$ as a catalyst:

$$\text{\Large$\bigcirc$} + CH_3CH_2Cl \xrightarrow{AlCl_3} \text{\Large$\bigcirc$}^{CH_2CH_3} + HCl \qquad [26.10]$$

Aromatic Stabilization

We can obtain an estimate of the stabilization of the π electrons in benzene by comparing the energy required to add hydrogen to benzene to form a saturated compound with the energy required to hydrogenate simple alkenes. The hydrogenation of benzene to form cyclohexane can be represented as

$$\Delta H^\circ = -208 \text{ kJ/mol}$$

The enthalpy change in this reaction is -208 kJ/mol. The heat of hydrogenation of the cyclic alkene cyclohexene is -120 kJ/mol:

Cyclohexene

$$\Delta H^\circ = -120 \text{ kJ/mol}$$

Similarly, the heat released on hydrogenating 1,4-cyclohexadiene is -232 kJ/mol:

1,4-Cyclohexadiene

$$\Delta H^\circ = -232 \text{ kJ/mol}$$

From these last two reactions, it appears that the heat of hydrogenating each double bond is roughly 116 kJ/mol for each bond. There is the equivalent of three double bonds in benzene. Therefore, we might expect that the heat of hydrogenating benzene would be about three times -116, or -348 kJ/mol, if benzene behaved as though it were "cyclohexatriene"; that is, if it behaved as though it had three double bonds in a ring. Instead, the heat released is much less than this, indicating that benzene is more stable than would be expected for three double bonds. The difference of 140 kJ/mol between -348 kJ/mol and the observed heat of hydrogenation, -208 kJ/mol, can be ascribed to stabilization of the π electrons through delocalization in the π orbitals that extend around the ring.

26.3 Hydrocarbon Derivatives

Learning Goal 11: Identify the groups or arrangement of atoms in a molecule that correspond to the following functional groups: alcohols; ethers; aldehydes and ketones; carboxylic acids; esters; amines and amides.

Because double and triple carbon-carbon bonds impart reactivity not seen in simple alkanes, they are examples of **functional groups.** A functional group is a group of atoms that alters the reactivity of organic molecules. In addition to multiple carbon-carbon bonds, certain other groups of atoms impart characteristic behavior to an organic molecule. These other functional groups contain elements other than carbon and hydrogen, most often oxygen, nitrogen, or a halogen. Compounds in which one or more hydrogen atoms have been replaced by these functional groups are *hydrocarbon derivatives.*

In describing hydrocarbon derivatives, it is convenient to use the designation R to represent any alkyl group—methyl, ethyl, propyl, and so on. For example, alkanes are often represented as R—H. Hydrocarbon derivatives often consist of an alkyl group, which is usually relatively unreactive, attached to a functional group that gives the compound a particular type of reactivity. If two different alkyl groups are present, we will designate them as R and R'. In this section we shall consider the structure and chemical properties of several of the most common functional groups.

Robert C. Mebane and Thomas R. Rybolt, "Chemistry in the Dyeing of Eggs," *J. Chem. Educ.* **1987,** *64,* 291.

Alcohols (R—OH)

Alcohols are hydrocarbon derivatives in which one or more hydrogens of a parent hydrocarbon have been replaced by a *hydroxyl* or *alcohol* functional group, OH. Figure 26.11 shows the structural formulas and names of several alcohols. Note that the accepted name for an alcohol ends in *-ol*. The simple alcohols are named by changing the last letter in the name of the corresponding alkane to *-ol*—for example, ethan*e* becomes ethan*ol*. Where necessary, the location of the OH group is designated by an appropriate prefix numeral that indicates the number of the carbon atom bearing the OH group, as shown in the examples in Figure 26.11.

Because the O—H bond is polar, alcohols are much more soluble in polar solvents such as water than are hydrocarbons. The OH functional group can participate in hydrogen bonding. As a result, the boiling points of alcohols are much higher than those of their parent alkanes.

Figure 26.12 shows several familiar commercial products that consist entirely or in major part of an organic alcohol. Let's consider how some of the more important alcohols are formed and used.

The simplest alcohol, methanol, has many important industrial uses and is produced on a large scale. Carbon monoxide and hydrogen are heated together under pressure in the presence of a metal oxide catalyst:

$$CO(g) + 2H_2(g) \xrightarrow[400°C]{200-300 \text{ atm}} CH_3OH(g) \qquad [26.11]$$

Because methanol has a very high octane rating as an automobile fuel, it is used as a gasoline additive and as a fuel in its own right.

Ethanol, C_2H_5OH, is a product of the fermentation of carbohydrates such as sugar and starch. In the absence of air, yeast converts carbohydrates into a

> **Point of Emphasis:** Even though alcohols contain the —OH group, they are *not* hydroxides. The —OH is *covalently* bound to the carbon.

FIGURE 26.11 Structural formulas of several important alcohols. Their common names are given in parentheses.

Figure 26.11

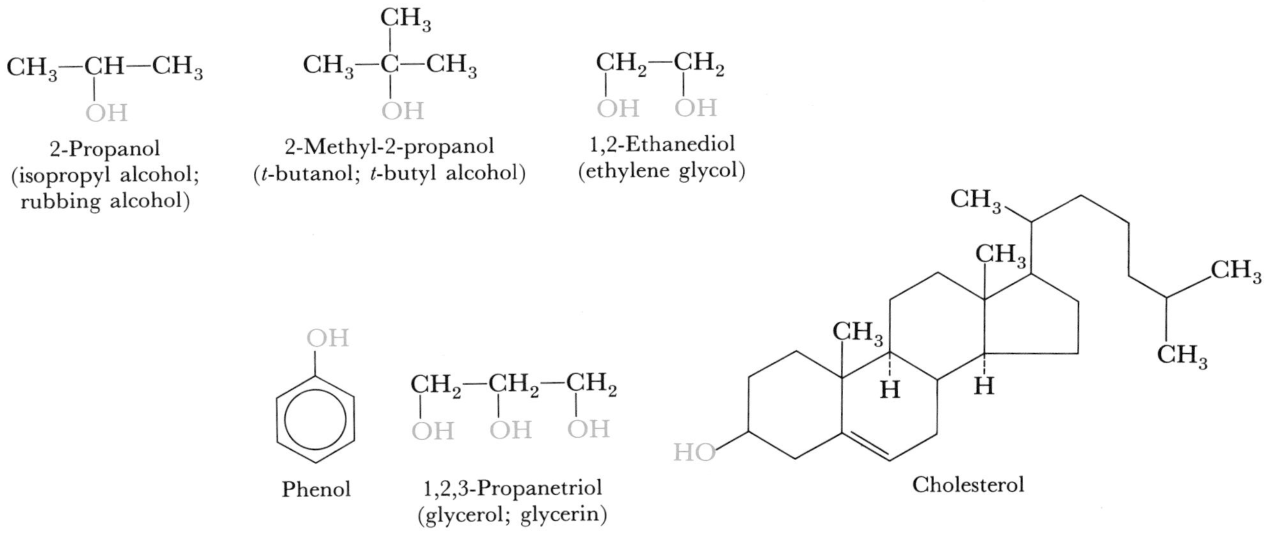

2-Propanol
(isopropyl alcohol; rubbing alcohol)

2-Methyl-2-propanol
(*t*-butanol; *t*-butyl alcohol)

1,2-Ethanediol
(ethylene glycol)

Phenol

1,2,3-Propanetriol
(glycerol; glycerin)

Cholesterol

FIGURE 26.12 Some commercial products that are composed entirely or mainly of alcohols. (Donald Clegg and Roxy Wilson)

mixture of ethanol and CO_2, as shown in Equation 26.12. In the process, yeast derives energy necessary for growth:

$$C_6H_{12}O_6(aq) \xrightarrow{\text{yeast}} 2C_2H_5OH(aq) + 2CO_2(g) \qquad [26.12]$$

This reaction is carried out under carefully controlled conditions to produce beer, wine, and other beverages in which ethanol is the active ingredient. It is often said that ethanol is the least toxic of the straight-chain alcohols. Although this is true in the strictest sense, the combination of ethanol and automobile driving produces more human fatalities each year than any other chemical agent.

Many polyhydroxyl alcohols (those containing more than one OH group) are known. The simplest of these is 1,2-ethanediol (ethylene glycol), $HOCH_2CH_2OH$. This substance is the major ingredient in automobile antifreeze. Another common polyhydroxyl alcohol is 1,2,3-propanetriol (glycerol), $HOCH_2CH(OH)CH_2OH$. It is a viscous liquid that dissolves readily in water and is widely used as a skin softener in cosmetic preparations. It is also used in foods and candies to keep them moist.

Phenol is the simplest example of a compound with an OH group attached to an aromatic ring. One of the most striking effects of the aromatic group is the greatly increased acidity of the proton. Phenol is about 1 million times more acidic in water than a typical nonaromatic alcohol such as ethanol. Even so, it is not a very strong acid ($K_a = 1.3 \times 10^{-10}$). Phenol is used industrially in the making of several kinds of plastics and in the preparation of dyes. It is also used as a topical anesthetic in many sore throat sprays.

Cholesterol, shown in Figure 26.11, is an example of a biochemically important alcohol. Notice that the OH group forms only a small component of this rather large molecule. As a result, cholesterol is not very soluble in water (0.26 g per 100 mL of H_2O). Cholesterol is a normal component of our bodies.

Teaching Note: Ethanol is used as an antiknock component in gasolines. Gasoline with a major component of ethanol is often called "gasohol" and is available in many parts of the country.

Point of Emphasis: Polyhydroxyl alcohols are also referred to as *polyols*.

However, when present in excessive amounts it may precipitate from solution. It precipitates in the gallbladder to form crystalline lumps called *gallstones*. It may also precipitate against the walls of veins and arteries and thus contribute to high blood pressure and other cardiovascular problems. The amount of cholesterol in our blood is determined not only by how much cholesterol we eat but also by total dietary intake. There is evidence that excessive caloric intake leads the body to synthesize excessive cholesterol.

Teaching Note: Because most of the body's cholesterol content is synthesized in the body, dietary restriction of cholesterol-containing foods alone cannot sufficiently lower the blood concentration in most people for whom it is a problem.

Ethers (R—O—R′)

Compounds in which two hydrocarbon groups are bonded to one oxygen are called **ethers**. Ethers can be formed from two molecules of alcohol by splitting out a molecule of water. The reaction is thus a dehydration process; it is catalyzed by sulfuric acid, which takes up water to remove it from the system:

$$CH_3CH_2—OH + H—OCH_2CH_3 \xrightarrow{H_2SO_4}$$
$$CH_3CH_2—O—CH_2CH_3 + H_2O \quad [26.13]$$

A reaction in which water is split out from two substances is called a *condensation reaction*.

Ethers are used as solvents; both diethyl ether and the cyclic ether tetrahydrofuran are common solvents for organic reactions.

Learning Goal 12: Give examples of the condensation reactions of alcohols to form ethers, of alcohols and carboxylic acids to form esters, and of amines and carboxylic acids to form amides.

Teaching Note: Diethyl ether is a very sweet-smelling and flammable liquid that once was used as an anesthetic.

$$CH_3CH_2—O—CH_2CH_3$$

$$\begin{array}{cc} CH_2—CH_2 \\ | \quad\quad | \\ CH_2 \quad CH_2 \\ \diagdown O \diagup \end{array}$$

Diethyl ether   Tetrahydrofuran (THF)

Aldehydes (R—Ö—H) and Ketones (R—Ö—R′)

Several classes of organic compounds contain the **carbonyl group:**

$$\diagup\hspace{-0.3em}C{=}O$$

In **aldehydes,** the carbonyl group has at least one hydrogen atom attached, as in the following examples:

$$\underset{\text{Formaldehyde}}{H\overset{O}{\overset{||}{C}}H} \qquad \underset{\text{Acetaldehyde}}{CH_3\overset{O}{\overset{||}{C}}H}$$

In **ketones,** the carbonyl group occurs at the interior of a carbon chain and is therefore flanked by carbon atoms:

$$\underset{\text{Acetone}}{CH_3{-}\overset{O}{\overset{||}{C}}{-}CH_3} \qquad \underset{\text{Methyl ethyl ketone}}{CH_3{-}\overset{O}{\overset{||}{C}}{-}CH_2CH_3}$$

26.3 Hydrocarbon Derivatives   **975**

Lee R. Summerlin, Christie L. Borgford, and Julie B. Ealy, "A Variation of the Starch-Iodine Clock Reaction," *Chemical Demonstrations, A Sourcebook for Teachers, Volume 2* (Washington: American Chemical Society, 1987), pp. 147–48.

Lee R. Summerlin and James L. Ealy, Jr., "Oxidation of Alcohol by Mn₂O₇," *Chemical Demonstrations, A Sourcebook for Teachers* (Washington: American Chemical Society, 1985), pp. 103–4.

Aldehydes and ketones can be prepared by careful oxidation of alcohols. It is fairly easy to oxidize alcohols. Complete oxidation results in formation of CO_2 and H_2O, as in the burning of methanol:

$$CH_3OH(g) + \tfrac{3}{2}O_2(g) \longrightarrow CO_2(g) + 2H_2O(g)$$

Controlled partial oxidation to form other organic substances, such as aldehydes and ketones, is carried out by using various oxidizing agents such as air, hydrogen peroxide, H_2O_2, ozone, O_3, and potassium dichromate, $K_2Cr_2O_7$.

Ketones are less reactive than aldehydes and are used extensively as solvents. Acetone, which boils at 56°C, is the most widely used ketone. The carbonyl functional group imparts polarity to the solvent. Acetone is completely miscible with water, yet it dissolves a wide range of organic substances. Methyl ethyl ketone, $CH_3COCH_2CH_3$, which boils at 80°C, is also used industrially as a solvent.

Teaching Note: Among its many uses, acetone is commercially used as paint thinner and nail polish remover.

Carboxylic Acids (R—C(=O)—OH)

We first discussed carboxylic acids in Section 16.9. Carboxylic acids contain the *carboxyl* functional group, which is often written as COOH. These weak acids are widely distributed in nature and are commonly used in consumer products [Figure 26.13(a)]. They are also important in the manufacture of polymers used to make fibers, films, and paints. Figure 26.14 shows the structural formulas of

FIGURE 26.13 Carboxylic acids and esters are components of many household items: (a) Spinach and some cleaners contain oxalic acid; vinegar contains acetic acid; vitamin C is ascorbic acid; citrus fruits contain citric acid; and aspirin is acetylsalicylic acid (also an ester). (b) Many sunburn lotions contain benzocaine (an ester); some nail-polish remover is ethyl acetate; vegetable oils, polyester thread, and aspirin are also esters. (© Richard Megna/Fundamental Photographs)

(a)

(b)

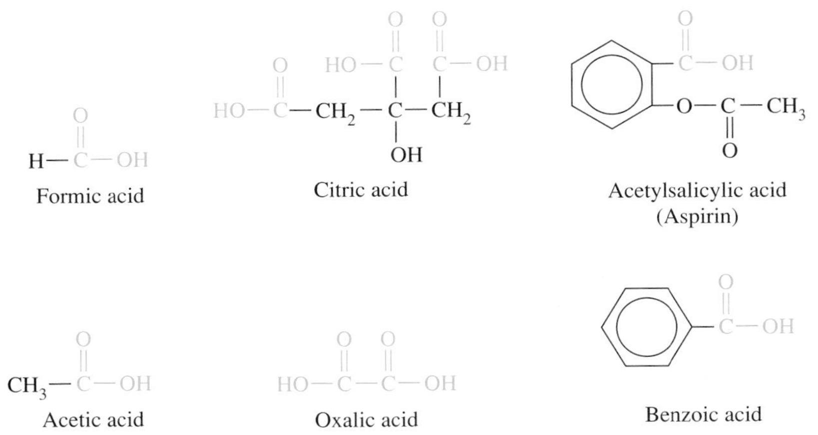

FIGURE 26.14 Structural formulas of several common carboxylic acids.

several carboxylic acids. Notice that oxalic acid and citric acid contain two and three carboxyl groups, respectively. The names of many carboxylic acids are based on their historical origins. For example, formic acid was first prepared by extraction from ants; its name is derived from the Latin word *formica,* meaning "ant."

Carboxylic acids can be produced by oxidation of alcohols in which the OH group is attached to a CH_2 group, such as ethanol or *n*-propanol. Under appropriate conditions, the corresponding aldehyde may be the first product of oxidation. These transformations are shown for ethanol in the following equations, in which (O) represents an oxidant that can provide oxygen atoms (such as H_2O_2):

$$CH_3CH_2OH + (O) \longrightarrow CH_3CH + H_2O \qquad [26.14]$$

Ethanol   Acetaldehyde

$$CH_3CH + (O) \longrightarrow CH_3COH \qquad [26.15]$$

Acetaldehyde   Acetic acid

The air-oxidation of ethanol to acetic acid is responsible for causing wines to turn sour, producing vinegar.

Acetic acid can also be produced by the reaction of methanol with carbon monoxide in the presence of a rhodium catalyst:

$$CH_3OH + CO \xrightarrow{\text{catalyst}} CH_3-\overset{O}{\overset{\|}{C}}-OH \qquad [26.16]$$

Notice that this reaction involves, in effect, the insertion of a carbon monoxide molecule between the CH_3 and OH groups. A reaction of this kind is called **carbonylation.**

Teaching Note: Carbonylation reactions, when catalyzed by a transition-metal complex, are often called *insertion reactions,* because it *appears* that the C = O has been inserted into a bond of the organic molecule.

Esters (R—C(=O)—O—R′)

Carboxylic acids can undergo condensation reactions with alcohols to form **esters:**

$$CH_3-\overset{\overset{\displaystyle O}{\|}}{C}-OH + HO-CH_2CH_3 \longrightarrow$$

Acetic acid   Ethanol

$$CH_3-\overset{\overset{\displaystyle O}{\|}}{C}-O-CH_2CH_3 + H_2O \quad [26.17]$$

Ethyl acetate

As seen in this example, esters are compounds in which the H atom of a carboxylic acid is replaced by a hydrocarbon group:

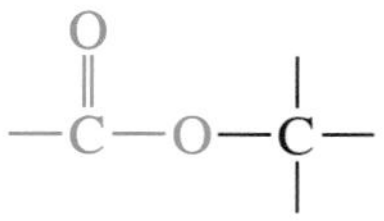

$$-\overset{\overset{\displaystyle O}{\|}}{C}-O-\overset{\overset{\displaystyle |}{}}{\underset{|}{C}}-$$

Esters are named by using first the group from which the alcohol is derived and then the group from which the acid is derived. Figure 26.13(*b*) shows some common esters.

SAMPLE EXERCISE 26.6

Name the following esters:

(a) 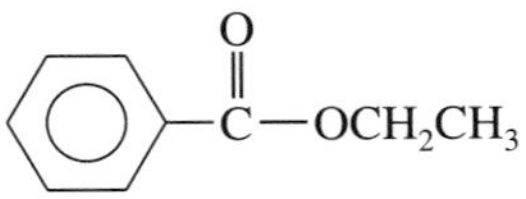 C₆H₅—C(=O)—OCH₂CH₃

(b) 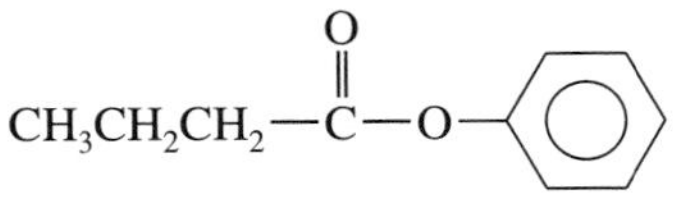 $CH_3CH_2CH_2-\overset{\overset{\displaystyle O}{\|}}{C}-O-$ C₆H₅

SOLUTION In **(a)** the ester is derived from ethanol and benzoic acid. Its name is therefore ethyl benzoate. In **(b)** the ester is derived from phenol and butyric acid. The residue from the phenol, C_6H_5, is called the phenyl group. The ester is therefore named phenyl butyrate.

PRACTICE EXERCISE

Draw the structural formula for the compound propyl propionate.

Answer:

$$CH_3CH_2\overset{\overset{\displaystyle O}{\|}}{C}-O-CH_2CH_2CH_3$$

Esters generally have very pleasant odors. They are largely responsible for the pleasant aromas of fruit. For example, one of the esters responsible for the odor of bananas is pentyl acetate, $CH_3COOCH_2CH_2CH_2CH_2CH_3$.

When esters are treated with an acid or a base in aqueous solution, they are hydrolyzed; that is, the molecule is split into its alcohol and acid components:

$$CH_3CH_2 - \overset{\displaystyle O}{\overset{\|}{C}} - O - CH_3 + Na^+ + OH^- \longrightarrow$$
Methyl propionate

$$CH_3CH_2 - \overset{\displaystyle O}{\overset{\|}{C}} - O^- + Na^+ + CH_3OH \quad [26.18]$$
Sodium propionate   Methanol

In this example, the hydrolysis was carried out in basic medium. The products of the reaction are the sodium salt of the carboxylic acid and the alcohol.

The hydrolysis of an ester in the presence of a base is called **saponification,** a term that comes from the Latin word for soap (*sapon*). Naturally occurring esters include fats and oils. In the soap-making process, an animal fat or a vegetable oil is boiled with a strong base, usually NaOH. The resultant soap consists of a mixture of sodium salts of long-chain carboxylic acids (called fatty acids) which form during the saponification reaction (Figure 26.15).

Amines and Amides

Amines are organic bases. ∞ (Sec. 16.6) They have the general formula R_3N, where R may be H or a hydrocarbon group, as in the following examples:

$$CH_3CH_2NH_2 \qquad (CH_3)_3N$$

Ethylamine   Trimethylamine   Aniline

Teaching Note: Amines are among the most noxious-smelling of all organic compounds.

FIGURE 26.15 Saponification of fats and oils has long been used to make soap. This etching shows soap manufacture in France during the mid-nineteenth century. (The Bettman Archive)

Amines containing a proton can undergo condensation reactions with carboxylic acids to form **amides:**

$$CH_3\overset{\displaystyle O}{\overset{\|}{C}}-OH + H-N(CH_3)_2 \longrightarrow CH_3\overset{\displaystyle O}{\overset{\|}{C}}-N(CH_3)_2 + H_2O \quad [26.19]$$

We may consider the amide functional group to be derived from a carboxylic acid with an NR_2 group replacing the OH of the acid, as in these additional examples:

$$CH_3\overset{\displaystyle O}{\overset{\|}{C}}-NH_2 \qquad \bigcirc-\overset{\displaystyle O}{\overset{\|}{C}}-NH_2$$

Acetamide   Benzamide

The amide linkage,

$$R-\overset{\displaystyle O}{\overset{\|}{C}}-\underset{\underset{\displaystyle H}{|}}{N}-R'$$

where R and R′ are organic groups, is the key functional group in the structures of proteins, as we shall see shortly.

26.4 Introduction to Biochemistry

Sheldon J. Kopperl, "Icie Macy Hoobler: Pioneer Woman Biochemist," *J. Chem. Educ.* **1988,** *65,* 97.

The several types of organic functional groups discussed in the preceding section generate a vast array of molecules with very specific chemical reactivities. Nowhere is this specificity more apparent than in biochemistry, the chemistry of living organisms. Ponder for a moment the fortunate circumstances that allow life to exist on the earth. The part of our earth in which living organisms are formed and live is called the **biosphere.** The biosphere includes the influences on life of the atmosphere, natural waters, and the solid earth. Living organisms require a supply of available energy to grow and to sustain themselves. They also require an adequate supply of water because organisms are composed largely of water and use it for exchange of materials with their environment.

Gil Downs, "Why Teach Biochemistry?" *J. Chem. Educ.* **1987,** *64,* 339.

Before we discuss specific biochemical molecules, we can make some general observations. As we shall see, many biologically important molecules are quite large. The synthesis of these molecules is a remarkable aspect of biochemistry, one that places large demands on the chemical systems in living organisms. Organisms build biomolecules from much smaller and simpler substances that are readily available in the biosphere. The synthesis of large molecules requires energy because most of the reactions are endothermic. The ultimate source of this energy is the sun. Mammals and other animals have essentially no capacity for using solar energy directly; rather they depend on plant photosynthesis to supply the bulk of their energy needs. ∞ (Sec. 25.2)

Learning Goal 13: Describe two distinct reasons why energy is required by living organisms.

In addition to requiring large amounts of energy, living organisms are highly organized. The complexity of all the substances that make up even the simplest single-cell organisms and the relationships among all the many chemical processes that occur are truly amazing. In thermodynamic terms, living systems are very low in entropy as compared to the raw materials from which they are formed. Thus, the chemistry of living systems must continually resist the tendency toward increased entropy that is required by the second law of thermodynamics (see the Chemistry and Life box in Section 19.2). Maintaining a high degree of order places additional energetic requirements on organisms.

We have introduced you to some important biochemical applications of fundamental chemical ideas in the Chemistry and Life essays that appear throughout this text; a complete summary of the topics covered and their locations in the text are included in the table of contents. The remainder of this chapter will serve as only a brief introduction to other aspects of biochemistry. Nevertheless, you will see some patterns emerging. For example, we will see that hydrogen bonding (Section 11.2) is critical to the function of many biochemical systems and that the geometry of molecules can govern their biological importance and activity. Many of the large molecules in living systems are polymers (Section 12.2) of much smaller molecules. These **biopolymers** can be classified into three broad categories: proteins, carbohydrates, and nucleic acids. We discuss these classes of biopolymers in the next three sections.

26.5 Proteins

Proteins are macromolecular substances present in all living cells. About 50 percent of your body's dry weight is protein. Proteins serve as the major structural components in animal tissues; they are a key part of skin, nails, cartilage, and muscles. Other proteins catalyze reactions, transport oxygen, serve as hormones to regulate specific body processes, and perform other tasks. Whatever their function, all proteins are chemically similar, being composed of the same basic building blocks, called **amino acids.**

Learning Goal 14: List the several functions of proteins in living systems.

Amino Acids

The building blocks of all proteins are α-amino acids, which are substances in which the amino group is located on the carbon atom immediately adjacent to the carboxylic acid group. The general formula for an α-amino acid is represented in the following ways:

$$H_2N-\underset{\underset{R}{|}}{\overset{\overset{H}{|}}{C}}-\overset{\overset{O}{\parallel}}{C}-OH \quad \text{or} \quad {}^{+}H_3N-\underset{\underset{R}{|}}{\overset{\overset{H}{|}}{C}}-\overset{\overset{O}{\parallel}}{C}-O^{-}$$

The doubly ionized form predominates in the near-neutral pH of biological systems. This form results from the transfer of a proton from the carboxylic acid group to the basic amine group (see the Chemistry and Life box in Section 16.9).

Amino acids differ from one another in the nature of their R groups. Figure 26.16 shows the structural formulas of several of the 20 amino acids found in most proteins. Our bodies can synthesize 10 of these in sufficient

Teaching Note: These molecules in which the carboxylic proton has been transferred to the amine, resulting in molecules with both cationic and anionic sites, are called *zwitterions.*

FIGURE 26.16 Condensed structural formulas for several amino acids, with the three-letter abbreviation for each acid.

Figure 26.16

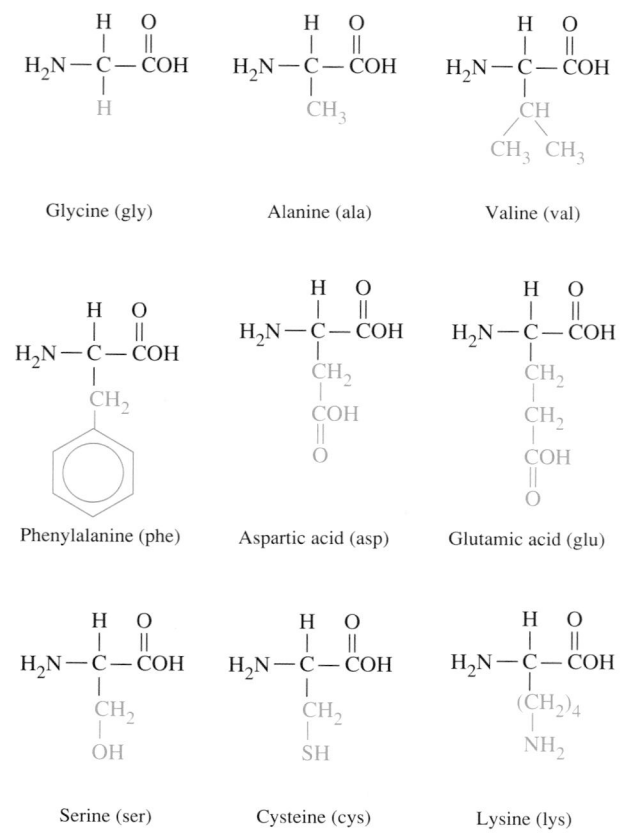

amounts for our needs. The other 10 must be ingested and are called *essential amino acids* because they are necessary components of our diet.

You can see from the structural formulas of amino acids that the α-carbon atom, which bears both the amine and carboxylic acid groups, has four different groups attached to it.* *Any molecule containing a carbon with four different attached groups is chiral.* A **chiral** molecule is capable of existing as isomers that are nonsuperimposable mirror images of each other. ∞ (Sec. 25.4)

Learning Goal 15: Define the terms *chiral* and *enantiomer,* and draw the enantiomer of a given chiral molecule.

The mirror-image isomers of a chiral substance are called **enantiomers.** The two enantiomers of a mirror-image pair are sometimes distinguished by using the labels D- (from the Latin *dexter,* "right") and L- (from the Latin *laevus,* "left"). The enantiomers of a chiral substance possess the same physical properties, such as solubility, melting point, and so forth. Their chemical behavior toward ordinary chemical reagents is also the same. However, they differ in chemical reactivity toward other chiral molecules. It is a striking fact that all the amino acids normally found in proteins are of the L- configuration at the carbon center (except glycine, which is not chiral). Only amino acids with this specific configuration at the chiral carbon center are biologically effective in

---

* The sole exception is glycine, for which R = H. For this amino acid, there are two H atoms on the α-carbon atom.

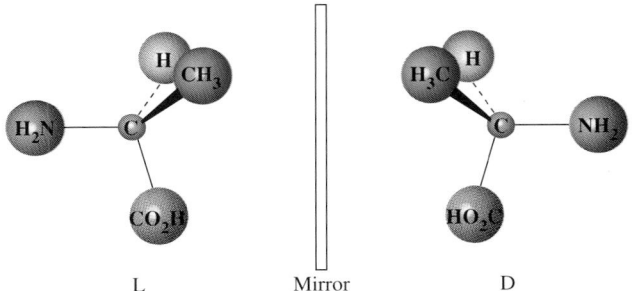

FIGURE 26.17 Alanine is chiral and therefore has two enantiomers, which are nonsuperimposable mirror images of each other.

L   Mirror   D

forming proteins in most organisms. Figure 26.17 shows the two enantiomers of the amino acid alanine.

Polypeptides and Proteins

In proteins, amino acids are linked by amide groups, one of the functional groups introduced in Section 26.3:

$$
R-\underset{\displaystyle}{\overset{\displaystyle O}{\overset{\displaystyle \|}{C}}}-\underset{\displaystyle H}{\overset{\displaystyle |}{N}}-R
$$

Each of these amide groups is called a **peptide** bond when it is formed by amino acids. A peptide bond is formed by a condensation reaction between the carboxyl group of one amino acid and the amino group of another amino acid. For example, alanine and glycine can be caused to react to form the dipeptide glycylalanine:

Learning Goal 16: Write the reaction for the formation of a peptide bond between two amino acids.

$$
\underset{\text{Glycine}}{H_2N-\overset{\overset{\displaystyle H}{|}}{\underset{\underset{\displaystyle H}{|}}{C}}-\overset{\overset{\displaystyle O}{\|}}{C}-OH} + \underset{\text{Alanine}}{HN-\overset{\overset{\displaystyle H}{|}}{\underset{\underset{\displaystyle CH_3}{|}}{C}}-\overset{\overset{\displaystyle O}{\|}}{C}-OH} \longrightarrow
$$

$$
\underset{\text{Glycylalanine}}{H_2N-\overset{\overset{\displaystyle H}{|}}{\underset{\underset{\displaystyle H}{|}}{C}}-\overset{\overset{\displaystyle O}{\|}}{C}-N-\overset{\overset{\displaystyle H}{|}}{\underset{\underset{\displaystyle CH_3}{|}}{C}}-\overset{\overset{\displaystyle O}{\|}}{C}-OH} + H_2O \quad [26.20]
$$

Notice that the acid that furnishes the carboxyl group for peptide-bond formation is named first, with a -*yl* ending; then the amino acid furnishing the amino group is named. Based on the three-letter codes for the amino acids from Figure 26.16, glycylalanine can be abbreviated gly-ala. In this notation, it is understood that the unreacted amino group is on the left and the unreacted carboxyl

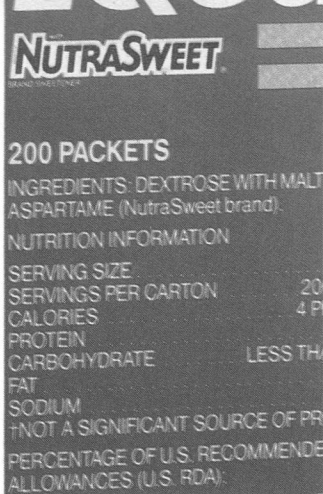

FIGURE 26.18 The
artificial sweetener aspartame is
the methyl ester of a dipeptide.
(© Richard Megna/Fundamental
Photographs)

group on the right. The artificial sweetener *aspartame* (Figure 26.18) is the
methyl ester of the dipeptide of aspartic acid and phenylalanine:

SAMPLE EXERCISE 26.7

Draw the structural formula for alanylglycylserine.

SOLUTION The name of this substance suggests that three amino acids—alanine,
glycine, and serine—have been linked together, forming a *tripeptide*. Note that the
ending *-yl* has been added to each amino acid except for the last one, serine. We can
view this tripeptide as three "building blocks" connected by peptide bonds:

Amino group ⟶ Carboxyl group

By convention, the first-named amino acid (alanine in this case) has a free amino
group, and the last-named one (serine) has a free carboxyl group. We can abbreviate
this tripeptide as ala-gly-ser.

PRACTICE EXERCISE

Name the dipeptide that has this structure and give its abbreviation:

Answer: serylaspartic acid; ser-asp

Polypeptides are formed when a large number of amino acids are linked
together by peptide bonds. Proteins are polypeptide molecules with molecular
weights ranging from about 6000 to over 50 million amu. Because 20 different
amino acids are present in proteins and because proteins consist of hundreds of
amino acids, the number of possible arrangements of amino acids within proteins is virtually limitless.

Protein Structure

The arrangement, or sequence, of amino acids along a protein chain is called its **primary structure.** The primary structure gives the protein its unique identity. A change in even one amino acid can alter the biochemical characteristics of the protein. For example, sickle-cell anemia is a genetic disorder resulting from a single misplacement in a protein chain in hemoglobin. The chain that is affected contains 146 amino acids. The substitution of a single amino acid with a hydrocarbon side chain for one that has an acidic functional group in the side chain alters the solubility properties of the hemoglobin, and normal blood flow is impeded (see the Chemistry and Life box in Section 13.6).

Proteins in living organisms are not simply long, flexible chains with random shapes. Rather, the chains coil or stretch in particular ways. The **secondary structure** of a protein refers to how segments of the protein chain are oriented in a regular pattern.

One of the most important and common secondary structure arrangements is the **α-helix,** first proposed by Linus Pauling and R. B. Corey. The helix arrangement is shown in schematic form in Figure 26.19. Imagine winding a long protein chain in a helical fashion around a long cylinder. The helix is held in position by hydrogen-bond interactions between N—H bonds and the oxygens of nearby carbonyl groups. The pitch of the helix and the diameter of the cylinder must be such that (1) no bond angles are strained and (2) the N—H and C=O functional groups on adjacent turns are in proper position for hydrogen bonding. An arrangement of this kind is possible for some amino acids along the chain, but not for others. Large protein molecules may contain segments of chain that have the α-helical arrangement interspersed with sections in which the chain is in a random coil.

The overall shape of a protein, determined by all the bends, kinks, and sections of rodlike α-helical structure, is called the **tertiary structure.** Figure 25.9 shows the tertiary structure of myoglobin, a protein whose molecular weight is about 18,000 amu and which contains one heme group. ∞ (Sec. 25.2) Notice the helical sections of the protein.

Myoglobin is an example of a *globular protein,* one that folds into a compact, roughly spherical shape. Globular proteins are generally soluble in water and are mobile within cells. They have nonstructural functions, such as combating the invasion of foreign objects, transporting and storing oxygen, and acting as catalysts. In *fibrous proteins,* the long coils align themselves in a more-or-less parallel fashion to form long, water-insoluble fibers. Fibrous proteins provide structural integrity and strength to many kinds of tissue and are the main components of muscle, tendons, and hair.

The tertiary structure of a protein is maintained by many different interactions. Certain foldings of the protein chain lead to lower-energy (more stable) arrangements than do other folding patterns. For example, a globular protein dissolved in aqueous solution folds in such a way that the nonpolar hydrocarbon portions are tucked within the molecule, away from the polar water molecules. The more polar acidic and basic side chains, however, project into the solution where they can interact with water molecules through ion-dipole, dipole-dipole, or hydrogen-bonding interactions.

One of the most important classes of proteins are the *enzymes,* large protein molecules that serve as catalysts. ∞ (Sec. 14.6) Enzymes are usually

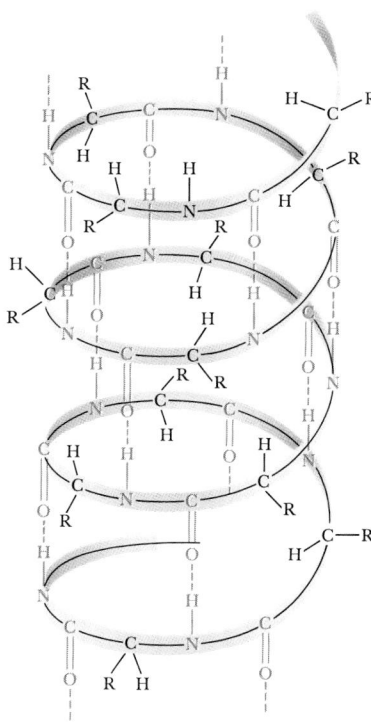

FIGURE 26.19 α-Helix structure for a protein. The symbol R represents any one of the several side chains shown in Figure 26.16.

Figure 26.19

Learning Goal 17: Explain the primary, secondary, and tertiary structures of proteins.

C. M. Drain and Barry B. Corden, "Reversible Oxygenation of Oxygen Transport Proteins," *J. Chem. Educ.* **1987,** *64,* 441.

FIGURE 26.20 A computer-generated structure of an enzyme (red), with a substrate (blue) at its active site. The white ribbon shows how the protein chain of the enzyme folds. (From R. Bott, E. Subramanian, and D. R. Davies: "Three-Dimensional Structure of the Complex of the *Rhizopus chinensis* Carboxyl Proteinase and Pepstatin at 2.5-Å Resolution." *Biochemistry* (1982), *21*, 6956. Courtesy of Dr. Christine Humblett/Parke-Davis.)

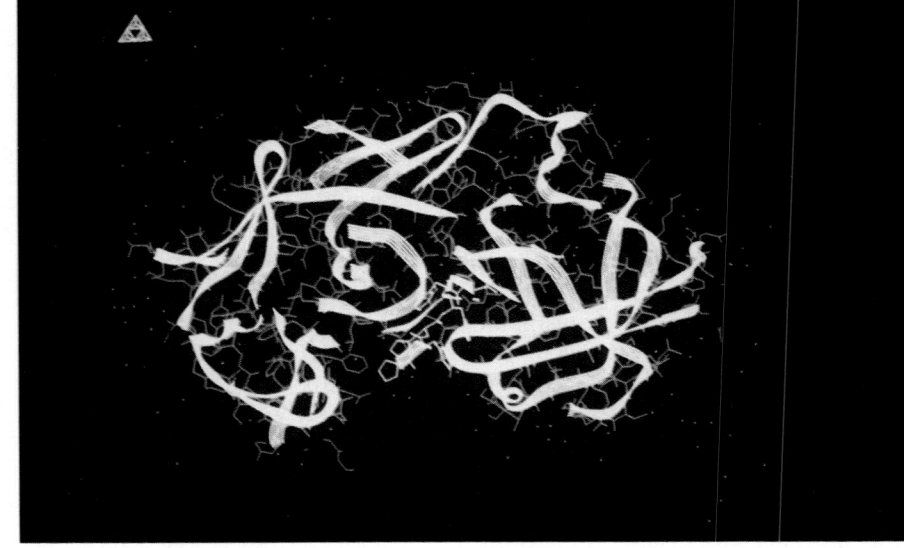

Bassam Z. Shakhashiri, "Dehydration of Sugar by Sulfuric Acid," *Chemical Demonstrations: A Handbook for Teachers of Chemistry, Volume 1* (Madison: The University of Wisconsin Press, 1983), pp. 77–78.

Learning Goal 18: Describe the formation of cyclic structures for sugars from their open-chain forms, and distinguish between the α and β forms of the cyclic structure of glucose.

FIGURE 26.21 Linear structures of glucose and fructose.

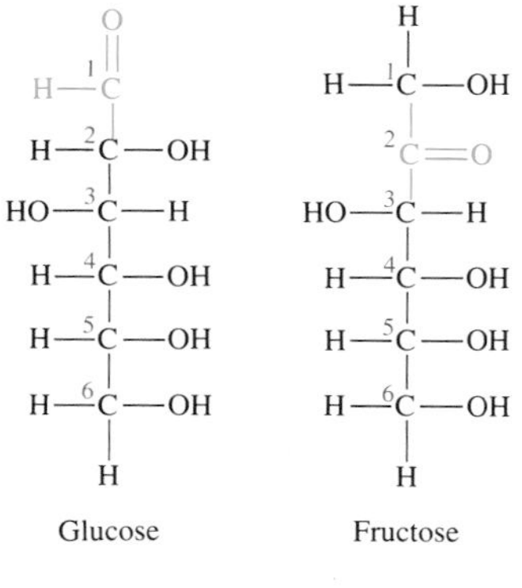

Glucose

Fructose

very specific with respect to the reactions they catalyze. Their tertiary structure generally dictates that only a certain substrate molecule can interact with the active site of the enzyme (Figure 26.20).

26.6 Carbohydrates

Carbohydrates are an important class of naturally occurring substances found in both plant and animal matter. The name **carbohydrate** (hydrate of carbon) comes from the empirical formulas for most substances in this class; they can be written as $C_x(H_2O)_y$. For example, **glucose,** the most abundant carbohydrate, has the molecular formula $C_6H_{12}O_6$, or $C_6(H_2O)_6$. Carbohydrates are not really hydrates of carbon; rather, they are polyhydroxy aldehydes and ketones. For example, glucose is a six-carbon aldehyde sugar, whereas *fructose,* the sugar that occurs widely in fruit, is a six-carbon ketone sugar (Figure 26.21).

Glucose, having both alcohol and aldehyde functional groups and having a reasonably long and flexible backbone, can react with itself to form a six-member-ring structure, as shown in Figure 26.22. Indeed, only a small percentage of the glucose molecules are in the open-chain form in aqueous solution. Although the ring is often drawn in a planar form, the molecules are actually nonplanar.

During formation of the ring structure of glucose, the OH group on carbon 1 can be on the same side of the ring as the OH group of carbon 2 (giving the cyclic α form of glucose) or on the opposite side (giving the cyclic β form). Another way to distinguish these two forms is to notice that in the α form the OH group on carbon 1 and the CH_2OH group on carbon 5 point in opposite directions. In the β form, the OH on carbon 1 and the CH_2OH on carbon 5 point in the same direction. Although the difference between the α and β forms might seem small, it has enormous biological consequences. As we shall soon see, this one small change in structure accounts for the vast difference between starch and cellulose.

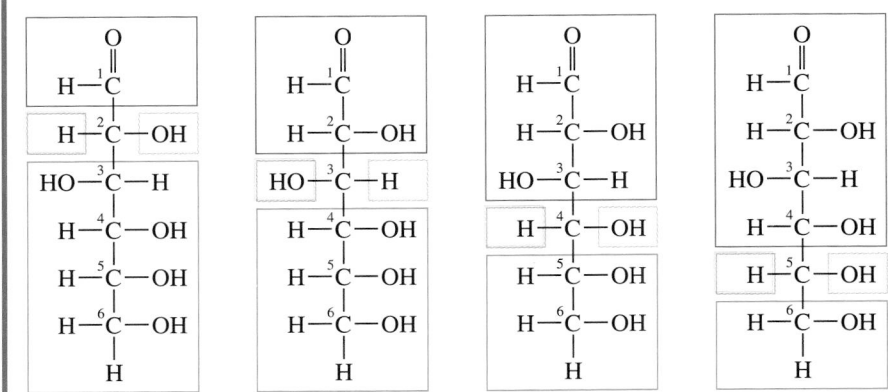

FIGURE 26.22 Glucose reacts with itself to form two six-member-ring structures, designated α and β.

Figure 26.22

α-Glucose

β-Glucose

Fructose can cyclize to form either five- or six-member rings. The five-member ring forms when the OH group on carbon 5 reacts with the carbonyl group on carbon 2:

Charles L. Bering, "The Biochemistry of Brewing," *J. Chem. Educ.* **1988,** *65,* 519.

[26.21]

The six-member ring results from the reaction between the OH group on carbon 6 and the carbonyl group on carbon 2.

SAMPLE EXERCISE 26.8

How many chiral carbon atoms are in the open-chain form of glucose (Figure 26.21)?

SOLUTION Notice that the carbon atoms numbered 2, 3, 4, and 5 each have four different groups attached to them, as indicated below:

Carbon atoms 1 and 6 have only three different substituents on them. Thus, there are four chiral carbon atoms in the glucose molecule.

PRACTICE EXERCISE

How many chiral carbon atoms are in the open-chain form of fructose (Figure 26.21)? **Answer:** three

Disaccharides

Learning Goal 19: Describe the manner in which monosaccharides are joined together to form polysaccharides.

Both glucose and fructose are examples of **monosaccharides** (mah-no-SACK-uh-rides), simple sugars that can't be broken into smaller molecules by hydrolysis with aqueous acids. Two monosaccharide units can be linked together by a condensation reaction to form a *disaccharide*. The structures of three common disaccharides — *sucrose* (table sugar), *maltose* (malt sugar), and *lactose* (milk sugar) — are shown in Figure 26.23.

The word *sugar* makes us think of sweetness. All sugars are sweet, but they differ in the degree of sweetness we perceive when we taste them. Sucrose is about six times sweeter than lactose, slightly sweeter than glucose, but only about half as sweet as fructose. Disaccharides can be hydrolyzed; that is, they can be reacted with water in the presence of an acid catalyst to form monosaccharides. When sucrose is hydrolyzed, the mixture of glucose and fructose that

FIGURE 26.23 The structures of three disaccharides. Note that in each case the sugar units are joined by a linkage that is termed the α form.

Figure 26.23

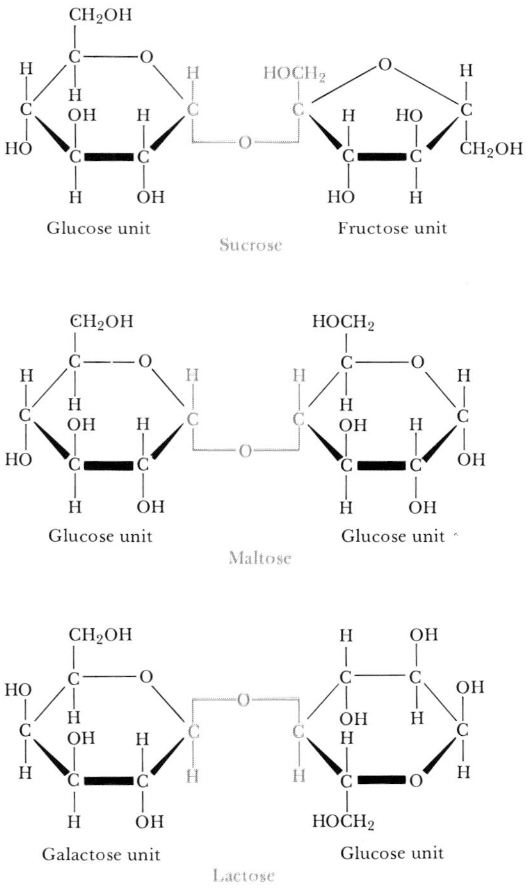

forms, called *invert sugar,** is sweeter to the taste than the original sucrose. The sweet syrup present in canned fruits and candies is largely invert sugar formed from hydrolysis of added sucrose.

Polysaccharides

Polysaccharides are made up of several monosaccharide units joined together by a bonding arrangement similar to those shown for disaccharides in Figure 26.23. The most important polysaccharides are starch, glycogen, and cellulose, which are formed from repeating glucose units.

Learning Goal 20:   Enumerate the major groups of polysaccharides, and indicate their sources and general functions.

Starch is not a pure substance. The term refers to a group of polysaccharides found in plants. Starches serve as a major method of food storage in plant seeds and tubers. Corn, potatoes, wheat, and rice all contain substantial amounts of starch. These plant products serve as major sources of needed food energy for humans. Enzymes within the digestive system catalyze the hydrolysis of starch to glucose.

Some starch molecules are unbranched chains, whereas others are branched. Figure 26.24 illustrates an unbranched starch structure. It is particularly important to note that the glucose units that are linked together are in the α form. (Notice that the bridging oxygen atom is opposite the CH_2OH groups.)

Glycogen is a starchlike substance synthesized in the body. Glycogen molecules vary in molecular weight from about 5000 to more than 5 million amu. Glycogen acts as a kind of energy bank in the body. It is concentrated in the muscles and liver. In muscles, it serves as an immediate source of energy; in the liver, it serves as a storage place for glucose and helps to maintain a constant glucose level in the blood.

Cellulose forms the major structural unit of plants. Wood is about 50 percent cellulose; cotton fibers are almost entirely cellulose. Cellulose consists of a straight chain of glucose units, with molecular weights averaging more than 500,000 amu. The structure of cellulose is shown in Figure 26.25. At first glance, this structure looks very similar to that of starch. However, the differences in the arrangements of bonds that join the glucose units are important. Notice that glucose in cellulose is in the β form.

---

* The term *invert sugar* comes from the fact that rotation of the plane of polarized light by the glucose-fructose mixture is in the opposite direction, or inverted, from that of the sucrose solution.

FIGURE 26.24   Structure of a starch molecule. The molecule consists of many units of the kind enclosed in brackets, joined by linkages of the α form. (You can identify this form by noting that the C—O bonds on the linking carbons are on the opposite side of the ring from the CH_2OH groups.)

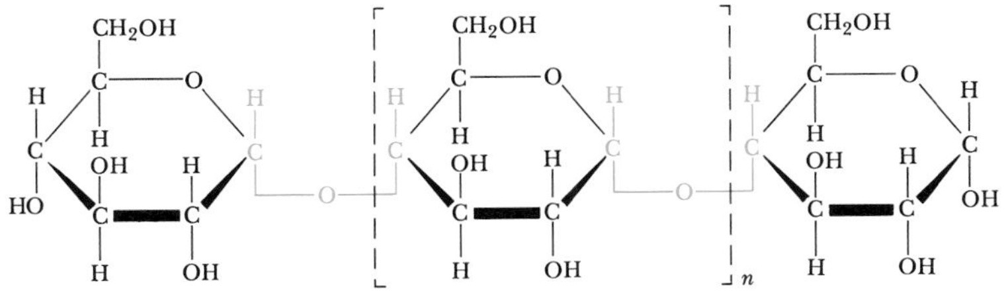

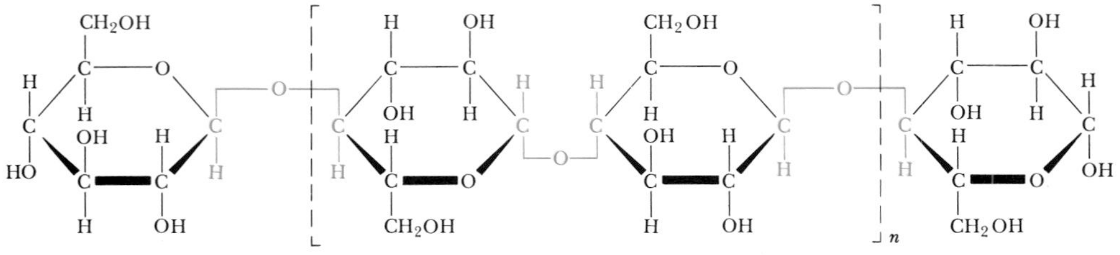

FIGURE 26.25 Structure of cellulose. Like starch, cellulose is a polymer. The repeating unit is shown between brackets. The linkage in cellulose is of the β form, different from that in starch (see Figure 26.24).

The distinction between starch and cellulose is made clearer when we examine their structures in a more realistic three-dimensional representation, as shown in Figure 26.26. You can see that the individual glucose units have different relationships to one another in the two structures. Enzymes that readily hydrolyze starches do not hydrolyze cellulose. Thus, you might eat a pound of cellulose and receive no caloric value from it whatsoever, even though the heat of combustion per unit weight is essentially the same for both cellulose and starch. A pound of starch, on the other hand, would represent a substantial caloric intake. The difference is that the starch is hydrolyzed to glucose, which is eventually oxidized with release of energy. Cellulose, however, is not hydrolyzed by any enzymes present in the body, and so it passes through the digestive system unchanged. Many bacteria contain enzymes, called cellulases, that hydrolyze cellulose. These bacteria are present in the digestive systems of grazing animals, such as cattle, that use cellulose for food.

Figure 26.26

FIGURE 26.26 Structures of starch (*a*) and cellulose (*b*). These representations show the geometrical arrangements of bonds about each carbon atom. It is easy to see that the glucose rings are oriented differently with respect to one another in the two structures.

(*a*)

(*b*)

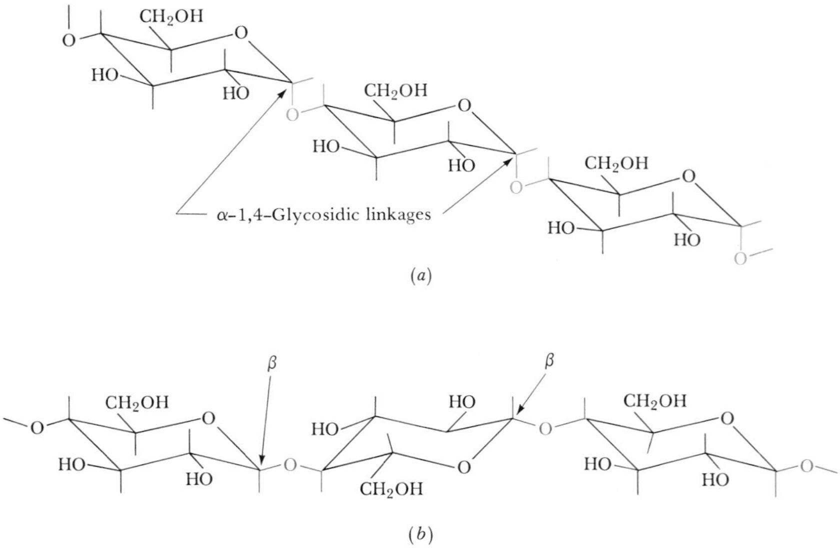

26.7 Nucleic Acids

Nucleic acids are a class of biopolymers that are the chemical carriers of an organism's genetic information. **Deoxyribonucleic acids (DNA)** are huge molecules (Figure 26.27) whose molecular weights may range from 6 to 16 million amu. **Ribonucleic acids (RNA)** are smaller molecules, with molecular weights in the range of 20,000 to 40,000 amu. Whereas DNA is found primarily in the nucleus of the cell, RNA is found mostly outside the nucleus in the surrounding fluid called the *cytoplasm.* The DNA stores the genetic information of the cell and controls the production of proteins. The RNA carries the information stored by DNA out of the nucleus of the cell into the cytoplasm, where the information can be used in protein synthesis.

The monomers of nucleic acids, called **nucleotides,** consist of three parts:

1. A phosphoric acid molecule, H_3PO_4
2. A five-carbon sugar
3. A nitrogen-containing organic base.

The sugar component of RNA is *ribose,* whereas that in DNA is *deoxyribose:*

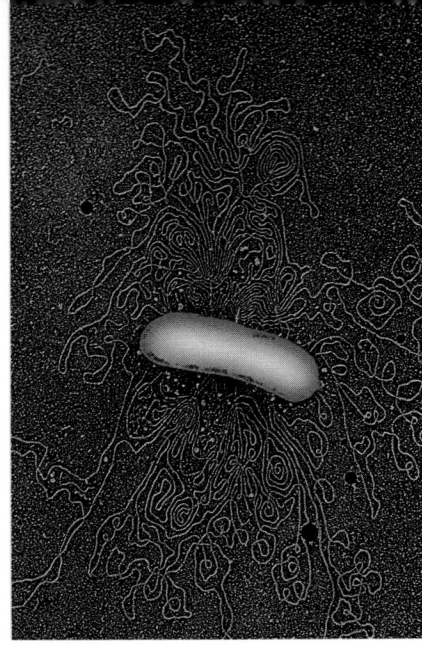

FIGURE 26.27 The DNA molecule is very large. In this micrograph, a DNA molecule is seen to spill out of the damaged cell wall of a bacterium. (© Dr. Gopal Murti, Science Photo Library, Science Source/Photo Researchers)

Ribose

Deoxyribose

Learning Goal 21: Draw the structures of the nucleotides that make up DNA.

Notice that *deoxy*ribose differs from ribose only in having one less oxygen atom (at carbon 2). The following nitrogen bases are the only ones found in DNA and RNA:

Adenine (A)
DNA
RNA

Guanine (G)
DNA
RNA

Cytosine (C)
DNA
RNA

Thymine (T)
DNA

Uracil (U)
RNA

The base is attached to a ribose or deoxyribose molecule through a bond to the nitrogen atom shown in color. An example of a nucleotide in which the base is adenine and the sugar is deoxyribose is shown in Figure 26.28.

Nucleic acids are polynucleotides formed by condensation reactions between an OH group of the phosphoric acid on one nucleotide and an OH group of the sugar of another nucleotide. Figure 26.29 shows a portion of the polymeric chain of a DNA molecule.

Learning Goal 22: Describe the way in which nucleotides polymerize to form polynucleotides.

Figure 26.28

FIGURE 26.28 Structure of deoxyadenylic acid, a nucleotide formed from phosphoric acid, deoxyribose, and an organic base, adenine.

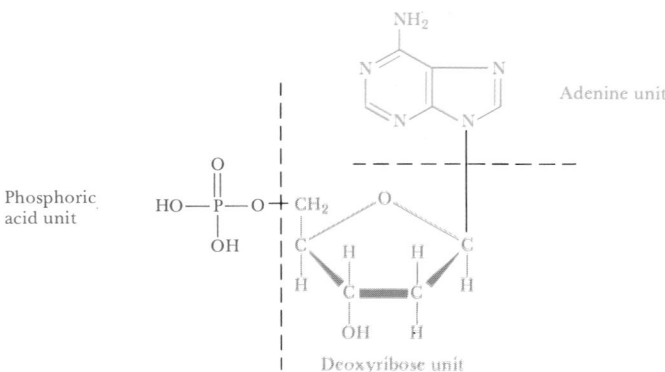

Adenine unit

Phosphoric acid unit

Deoxyribose unit

Learning Goal 23: Describe the double-stranded structure of DNA, and explain the principle that determines the relationship between bases in the two strands.

Figure 26.29

FIGURE 26.29 Structure of a polynucleotide. Because the sugar in each nucleotide is deoxyribose, this polynucleotide is of the form found in DNA.

DNA molecules consist of two deoxyribonucleic acid chains or strands that are wound together in the form of a **double helix,** as shown in Figure 26.30. The determination of the double-helical structure of DNA was a major feat in X-ray crystallography (see the Closer Look box in Section 11.7). The drawing on the right [Figure 26.30(b)] has been simplified to show the essential features of the structure. The sugar and phosphate groups, which form the backbone of each strand, are represented as —S— and —P—, respectively. The bases (represented by the letters T, A, C, and G) are attached to the sugars. The two strands are held together by hydrogen bonding between bases on the two strands. As shown in Figure 26.31, the structures of thymine (T) and adenine

Figure 26.30

FIGURE 26.30 (*a*) A computer-generated model of a DNA double helix. The blue and white atoms represent the sugar-phosphate chains that wrap around the outside. Inside the chains are the bases, shown in red and yellow. (*b*) A schematic illustration of the double helix showing the hydrogen-bond interactions between complementary base pairs (green symbols). (Richard Feldman/National Institutes of Health)

(*a*)

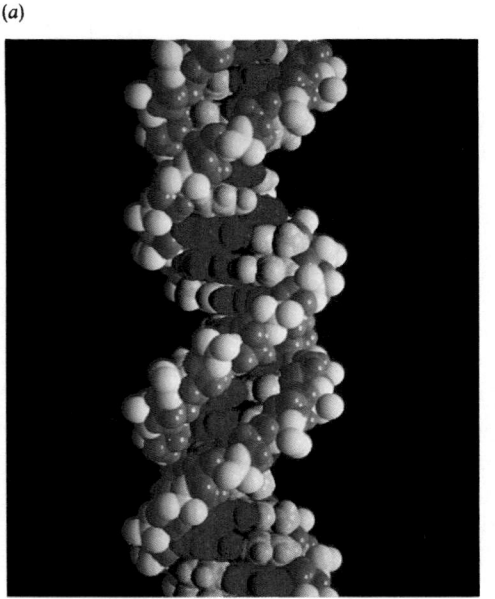

(*b*)

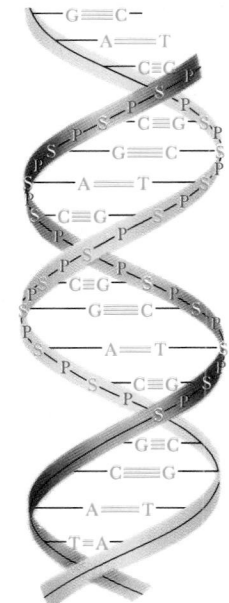

CH₃

Thymine — Adenine

T=A

Cytosine — Guanine

C≡G

FIGURE 26.31 Hydrogen bonding between complementary base pairs. The hydrogen bonds shown here are responsible for formation of the double-stranded helical structure for DNA, as shown in Figure 26.30(*b*).

Figure 26.31

(A) make them perfect partners for hydrogen bonding. Likewise, cytosine (C) and guanine (G) form ideal hydrogen-bonding partners. In the double-helix structure, each thymine on one strand is always opposite an adenine on the other strand. Likewise, each cytosine is always opposite a guanine. The double-helical structure with complementary bases on the two strands is the key to understanding the functioning of DNA.

The two strands of DNA unwind during cell division and new complementary strands are constructed on the unraveling strands (Figure 26.32). This process results in two identical double-helix DNA structures, each containing one strand from the original structure and one newly synthesized strand. This replication process allows for the transmission of genetic information when cells divide. The structure of DNA is also the key to understanding protein synthesis, the means by which viruses infect cells, and many other problems of central importance to modern biology. These themes are beyond the scope of this book. However, if you take courses in the life sciences, you will learn a good deal about such matters.

Michael D. Jones and Jeffrey T. Fayerman, "Industrial Applications of Recombinant DNA Technology," *J. Chem. Educ.* **1987**, *64*, 337.

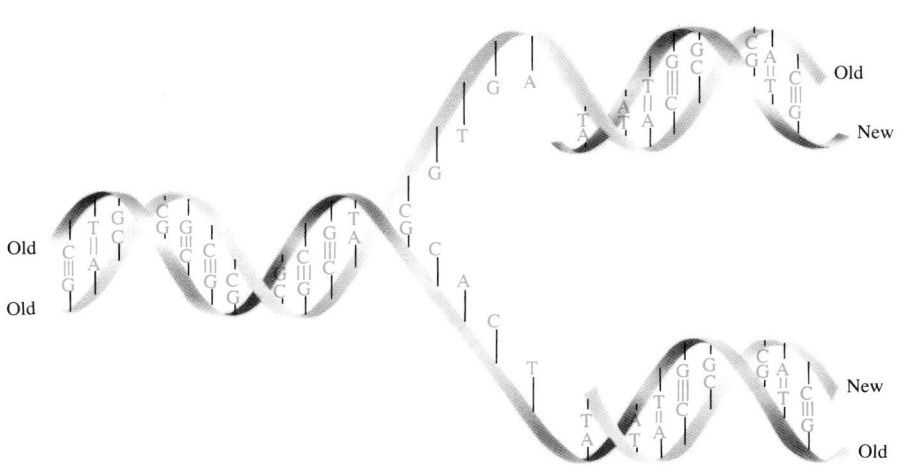

Figure 26.32

FIGURE 26.32 A schematic representation of DNA replication. The original DNA double helix partially unwinds, and new nucleotides line up on each strand in complementary fashion. When the new nucleotides are joined by condensation reactions, two identical double-helix DNA molecules result.

STRATEGIES IN CHEMISTRY

What Now?

If you are reading this box, you have made it to the end of our text. We congratulate you on the tenacity and dedication that you have exhibited to make it this far!

As an epilogue, we offer the ultimate study strategy in the form of a question: What do you plan to do with the knowledge of chemistry that you have gained thus far in your studies? Many of you will enroll in additional courses in chemistry as part of your required curriculum. For others, this will be the last formal course in chemistry that you will take. Regardless of the career path you plan to take—be it chemistry, one of the biomedical fields, engineering, the liberal arts, or whatever—we hope that this text has increased your appreciation of the chemistry in the world around you. If you pay attention, you will be aware of encounters with chemistry on a daily basis, from food and pharmaceutical labels to gasoline pumps to sports equipment to news reports.

We have also tried to give you a sense of the dynamic nature of chemistry. Chemistry is constantly changing. Research chemists synthesize new compounds, develop new reactions, uncover chemical properties that were previously not known, find new applications for known compounds, and refine theories. You may wish to participate in the fascinating venture of chemical research by taking part in an undergraduate research program. Given all of the answers that chemists seem to have, you may be surprised at the large number of questions that they still find to ask.

Finally, we hope you have enjoyed using this textbook. We certainly enjoyed putting so many of our thoughts about chemistry on paper. We truly believe it to be the central science, one that benefits all who learn about it and from it.

For Review

Summary

Organic compounds are carbon-containing compounds that include both hydrocarbons and derivatives of hydrocarbons. There are four major kinds of hydrocarbons: alkanes, alkenes, alkynes, and aromatic hydrocarbons. Alkanes are composed of only C—H and C—C single bonds. Alkenes contain one or more carbon-carbon double bonds. Alkynes contain one or more carbon-carbon triple bonds. Aromatic hydrocarbons contain cyclic arrangements of carbon atoms bonded through both σ and delocalized π bonds. Alkanes are saturated hydrocarbons; the others are unsaturated. Hydrocarbons may form straight-chain, branched-chain, and cyclic arrangements.

Isomers are substances that possess the same molecular formula but differ in the arrangements of atoms. In structural isomers, the bonding arrangements of the atoms differ. In geometrical isomers, the bonds are the same, but the molecules have different geometries. Geometrical (cis-trans) isomerism is possible in alkenes because of restricted rotation about the C=C double bond.

The naming of hydrocarbons is based on the longest continuous chain of carbon atoms in the structure. The locations of alkyl side groups, which branch off the chain, are specified by numbering along the carbon chain. In naming alkenes and alkynes, the continuous chain must contain the multiple bond, and its location is also specified by a numerical prefix.

Combustion of hydrocarbons is a highly exothermic process. The chief use of hydrocarbons is as sources of heat energy produced by combustion. Alkenes and alkynes readily undergo addition reactions to the carbon-carbon multiple bonds. Addition reactions are difficult to carry out with aromatic hydrocarbons, but substitution reactions are easily accomplished in the presence of catalysts.

The chemistry of hydrocarbon derivatives is often dominated by the nature of their functional groups. The functional groups we have considered are summarized here:

$$R-O-H \qquad R-\overset{\overset{\displaystyle O}{\|}}{C}-H \qquad \diagup\!\!\!C=C\!\!\!\diagdown$$

Alcohol   Aldehyde   Alkene

$$-C\equiv C- \qquad R-\overset{\overset{\displaystyle O}{\|}}{C}-N\diagup^{} \qquad R-\overset{\overset{\displaystyle R'\,(or\,H)}{|}}{N}-R''\,(or\,H)$$

Alkyne   Amide   Amine

$$R\ \overset{\overset{\displaystyle O}{\|}}{C}-O-H \qquad R-\overset{\overset{\displaystyle O}{\|}}{C}-O-R'$$

Carboxylic   Ester
acid

$$R-O-R' \qquad R-\overset{\overset{\displaystyle O}{\|}}{C}-R'$$

Ether   Ketone

(Remember that R, R', and R'' represent some hydrocarbon groups—for example, methyl, CH_3, or phenyl, C_6H_5.)

Alcohols are hydrocarbon derivatives containing one or more OH groups. Ethers are related compounds formed by a condensation reaction of two molecules of alcohol, with water splitting out. Oxidation of certain alcohols can lead to formation of aldehydes; further oxidation of the aldehydes produces carboxylic acids. Oxidation of other alcohols leads to formation of ketones.

Carboxylic acids can form esters by a condensation reaction with alcohols, or they can form amides by a condensation reaction with amines. Esters undergo hydrolysis (saponification) in the presence of strong bases.

Proteins are polymers of amino acids. They are the major structural materials in animal systems. All naturally occurring proteins are formed from 20 amino acids. Amino acids are chiral substances; that is, they are capable of existing as nonsuperimposable mirror-image isomers called enantiomers. Usually, only one of the enantiomers is found to be biologically active. Protein structure is determined by the sequence of amino acids in the chain, the coiling or stretching of the chain, and the overall shape of the complete molecule. All these aspects of protein structure are important in determining its biological activity.

Carbohydrates, which are formed from polyhydroxy aldehydes and ketones, are the major structural constituent of plants and are a source of energy in both plants and animals. The three most important groups of carbohydrates are starch, which is found in plants, glycogen, which is found in mammals, and cellulose, which is also found in plants. All are polysaccharides; that is, they are polymers of a simple sugar, glucose.

Nucleic acids are biopolymers of high molecular weight that carry the genetic information necessary for cell reproduction. In addition, nucleic acids control cell development through control of protein synthesis. Nucleic acids consist of a polymeric backbone of alternating phosphate and ribose sugar groups, with organic bases attached to the sugar molecules. The DNA polymer is a double-stranded helix held together by hydrogen bonding between matching organic bases situated across from one another on the two strands.

Key Terms

organic chemistry
biochemistry
alkanes
alkenes
alkynes
aromatic hydrocarbons
structural isomer (Sec. 26.1)
alkyl group (Sec. 26.1)
cycloalkane (Sec. 26.1)

geometrical isomers (Sec. 26.2)
addition reaction (Sec. 26.2)
substitution reaction (Sec. 26.2)
functional group (Sec. 26.3)
alcohol (Sec. 26.3)
ether (Sec. 26.3)
carbonyl group (Sec. 26.3)
aldehyde (Sec. 26.3)
ketone (Sec. 26.3)

Exercises

Hydrocarbon Structures and Nomenclature

26.1. Give the molecular formula of a hydrocarbon containing five carbon atoms that is **(a)** an alkane; **(b)** a cycloalkane; **(c)** an alkene; **(d)** an alkyne. Which are saturated and which are unsaturated hydrocarbons?

26.2. Give the molecular formula of an alkane, an alkene, an alkyne, and an aromatic hydrocarbon that in each case contains six carbon atoms. Which are saturated and which are unsaturated hydrocarbons?

26.3. Draw the five structural isomers of hexane, C_6H_{14}. Name each compound.

26.4. Write the condensed structural formulas for as many alkanes, alkenes, and alkynes as you can think of that have the molecular formula **(a)** C_5H_8; **(b)** C_5H_{10}.

26.5. Write the Lewis structural formula for each of the following hydrocarbons:
(a) $CH_3CH(CH_3)CH_2CH_3$ (b) $CH_3C{\equiv}CCH_3$
(c) $CH_2{=}CHCH_3$

26.6. Write the Lewis structural formula for each of the following hydrocarbons:

(a) 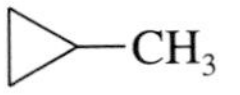 ▷—CH_3 (b) $CH_2{=}CHCH_2CH{=}CH_2$

(c) $(CH_3)_2CHCH_3$

26.7. What are the characteristic bond angles **(a)** about carbon in an alkane; **(b)** about the carbon-carbon double bond in an alkene; **(c)** about the carbon-carbon triple bond in an alkyne?

26.8. What are the characteristic hybrid orbitals employed by **(a)** carbon in an alkane; **(b)** carbon in a double bond in an alkene; **(c)** carbon in the benzene ring; **(d)** carbon in a triple bond in an alkyne?

26.9. Write the condensed structural formula for each of the following compounds:

(a) 5-methyl-*trans*-2-heptene
(b) 3-chloropropyne
(c) *ortho*-dichlorobenzene
(d) 2,2,4,4-tetramethylpentane
(e) 2-methyl-3-ethylhexane
(f) 2-methyl-6-chloro-3-heptyne
(g) 1,5-dimethylnaphthalene
(h) 1,6-heptadiene

26.10. Write the condensed structural formula for each of the following compounds:
(a) 2,2-dimethylpentane   (b) 2,3-dimethylhexane
(c) *cis*-2-hexene   (d) methylcyclopentane
(e) 2-chlorobutane   (f) 1,2-dibromobenzene
(g) methylcyclobutane   (h) 4-methyl-2-pentyne

26.11. Name the following compounds:

(a) 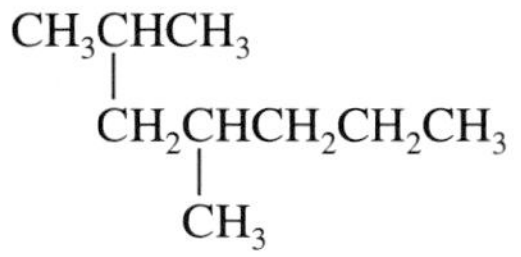 CH_3CHCH_3
          |
      $CH_2CHCH_2CH_2CH_3$
          |
         CH_3

(b) 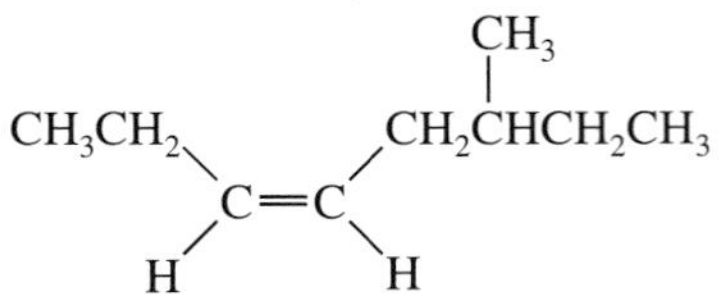 CH_3CH_2 CH_3
                                     |
                \ $CH_2CHCH_2CH_3$
                 $C{=}C$
                /   \
              H H

(c)   Br
      ⬡
      Br

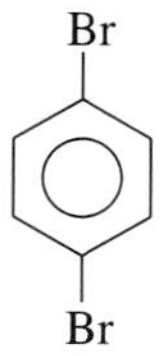

(d) $HC \equiv CCH_2\underset{\underset{CH_3}{|}}{\overset{\overset{CH_2CH_3}{|}}{C}}CH_3$

(e) —CH_3

26.12. Name the following compounds:

(a) $CH_3\underset{\underset{Br}{|}}{C}HCH_2\underset{\underset{Br}{|}}{C}HCH_3$

(b) $CH_3CH = CHCH_2CH = CHCH_2CH_3$

(c) $CH_3\underset{\underset{Cl}{|}}{C}HCH\underset{}{C}H_2\underset{\underset{Cl}{|}}{C}HCH_3$

(d) $CH_3—CH—CH_2Cl$

(e) $\underset{\underset{H}{}}{\overset{\overset{Cl}{}}{}}C = C\underset{\underset{Cl}{}}{\overset{\overset{H}{}}{}}$

26.13. Using butene as an example, distinguish between structural and geometrical isomers.

26.14. Why is structural isomerism possible for alkenes but not for alkanes and alkynes?

26.15. Draw all the structural and geometrical isomers of dichloropropene.

26.16. Indicate whether each of the following molecules is capable of geometrical (cis-trans) isomerism. For those that are, draw the structures of the isomers: **(a)** 2,3-dichlorobutane; **(b)** 2,3-dichloro-2-butene; **(c)** 1,3-dimethylbenzene; **(d)** 4,4-dimethyl-2-pentyne.

26.17. What is the octane number of a mixture of 30 percent *n*-heptane and 70 percent isooctane?

26.18. Describe two ways in which the octane number of a gasoline consisting of alkanes can be increased.

Reactions of Hydrocarbons

26.19. Give an example, in the form of a balanced equation, of each of the following chemical reactions: **(a)** combustion of an alkane; **(b)** addition reaction of an alkyne; **(c)** substitution reaction of an aromatic hydrocarbon.

26.20. Using condensed structural formulas, write a balanced chemical equation for each of the following reactions: **(a)** hydrogenation of 1-butene; **(b)** addition of H_2O to *cis*-3-hexene using H_2SO_4 as a catalyst; **(c)** chlorination of benzene in the presence of $FeCl_3$.

26.21. When cyclopropane is treated with HI, 1-iodopropane is formed. A similar type of reaction does not occur with cyclopentane or cyclohexane. How do you account for the activity of cyclopropane?

26.22. Why do addition reactions occur more readily with alkenes and alkynes than with aromatic hydrocarbons?

26.23. Suggest a method of preparing ethylbenzene, starting with benzene and ethylene as the only organic reagents.

26.24. Write a series of reactions leading to *para*-bromoethylbenzene, beginning with benzene and using other reagents as needed.

26.25. The heat of combustion of decahydronaphthalene, $C_{10}H_{18}$, is -6286 kJ/mol. The heat of combustion of naphthalene, $C_{10}H_8$, is -5157 kJ/mol. (In both cases, $CO_2(g)$ and $H_2O(l)$ are the products.) Using these data and data in Appendix C, calculate the heat of hydrogenation of naphthalene. Does this value provide any evidence for aromatic character in naphthalene?

26.26. The molar heat of combustion of cyclopropane is 2089 kJ/mol; that for cyclopentane is 3317 kJ/mol. Calculate the heat of combustion per CH_2 group in the two cases and account for the difference.

Hydrocarbon Derivatives

26.27. Identify the functional groups in each of the following compounds:

(a) $CH_3\underset{\underset{O}{\|}}{C}CH_2CH_3$

(b) $CH_3C = O$
     $|$
     OH

(c) $\underset{\underset{OH}{|}}{C}H_2CH_2CH_3$

(d) $CH_3O\underset{\underset{O}{\|}}{C}CH_2CH_3$

(e) $H_2N\underset{\underset{O}{\|}}{C}CH_3$

(f) $CH_3CH_2NH(CH_3)$

26.28. Identify the functional groups in each of the following compounds:

(a)

(b) $CH_2=CH-CH_2OH$

(c)
$$CH_3\overset{\overset{\displaystyle O}{\|}}{C}-NHCH_3$$

(d)
$$CH_3\overset{\overset{\displaystyle CH_3}{|}}{C}=O$$

(e) $HCCH_2CH_3$
$$\overset{\overset{\displaystyle O}{\|}}{}$$

(f) $HC\equiv C-CH_2OH$

26.29. Give the structural formula for an aldehyde that is an isomer of acetone.

26.30. Give the structural formula for an ether that is an isomer of ethanol.

26.31. Predict the bond angles around each carbon atom in acetone:

$$CH_3\overset{\overset{\displaystyle O}{\|}}{C}CH_3$$

26.32. Identify the carbon atom(s) in the following structure that has each of the following hybridizations: (a) sp^3; (b) sp; (c) sp^2.

$$HC\equiv C-\overset{\overset{\displaystyle O}{\|}}{C}-O-CH_3$$

26.33. Draw the structures of the esters formed from (a) acetic acid and 2-propanol; (b) acetic acid and 1-propanol; (c) formic acid and ethanol. Name the compound in each case.

26.34. Draw the structures of the compounds formed by condensation reactions between (a) benzoic acid and ethanol; (b) propionic acid and methylamine; (c) acetic acid and phenol. Name the compound in each case.

Proteins

26.41. (a) What is an α-amino acid? (b) How do amino acids react to form proteins?

26.42. How do the side chains (R groups) of amino acids affect their behavior?

26.43. Draw the dipeptides formed by a condensation reaction between glycine and valine.

26.44. Write a chemical equation for the formation of aspartylcysteine from the constituent amino acids.

26.45. Draw the structure of the tripeptide ala-glu-lys.

26.46. What amino acids would be obtained by hydrolysis of the following tripeptide?

26.35. Write a balanced chemical equation for the saponification of ethyl formate.

26.36. Write a balanced chemical equation for the saponification of methyl acetate.

26.37. Write the structural formula for each of the following compounds: (a) 2-butanol; (b) 1,2-ethanediol; (c) methyl formate; (d) diethyl ketone; (e) diethyl ether.

26.38. Write the structural formula for each of the following compounds: (a) 3-chloropropionaldehyde; (b) methyl isopropyl ketone; (c) *meta*-chlorobenzaldehyde; (d) methyl-*cis*-2-butenyl ether; (e) N,N-diethylpropionamide.

26.39. The IUPAC name for a carboxylic acid is based on the name of the hydrocarbon with the same number of carbon atoms. The ending -*oic* is appended, as in ethanoic acid, which is the IUPAC name for acetic acid,

$$CH_3\overset{\overset{\displaystyle O}{\|}}{C}OH$$

Give the IUPAC name for each of the following acids:

(a) $HCOH$
$$\overset{\overset{\displaystyle O}{\|}}{}$$

(b) $CH_3CH_2CH_2\overset{\overset{\displaystyle O}{\|}}{C}OH$

(c)
$$CH_3CH_2\overset{\overset{\displaystyle }{\underset{\underset{\displaystyle CH_3}{|}}{C}}}HCH_2\overset{\overset{\displaystyle O}{\|}}{C}OH$$

26.40. Aldehydes and ketones can be named in a systematic way by counting the number of carbon atoms (including the carbonyl carbon) that they contain. The name of the aldehyde or ketone is based on the hydrocarbon with the same number of carbon atoms. The ending -*al*, for aldehyde, or -*one*, for ketone, is added as appropriate. Draw the structural formulas for the following aldehydes or ketones: (a) propanal; (b) 2-pentanone; (c) 3-methyl-2-butanone; (d) 2-methylbutanal.

26.47. How many different tripeptides can be made from the two amino acids serine and phenylalanine? Give the abbreviations for each of these tripeptides using the three-letter codes for amino acids.

26.48. How many different tripeptides can be made from the amino acids glycine, valine, and alanine? Give the abbreviation for each of these tripeptides using the three-letter codes for amino acids.

26.49. Describe the primary, secondary, and tertiary structures of proteins.

26.50. Describe the role of hydrogen bonding in determining the α-helix structure of a protein.

Carbohydrates

26.51. What is the difference between α-glucose and β-glucose? Show the condensation of two glucose molecules to form a disaccharide with α linkages; with β linkages.

26.52. Identify each of the following as an α or a β form of a sugar:

(a)

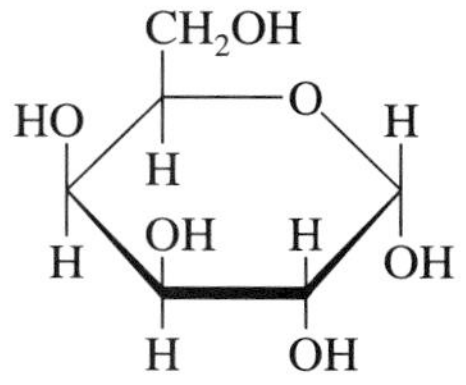

(b)

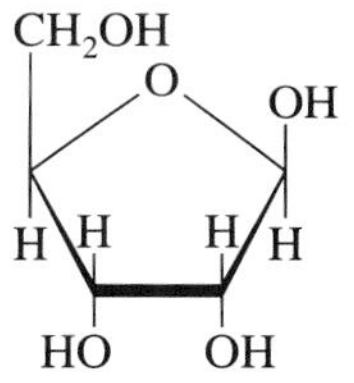

(c)

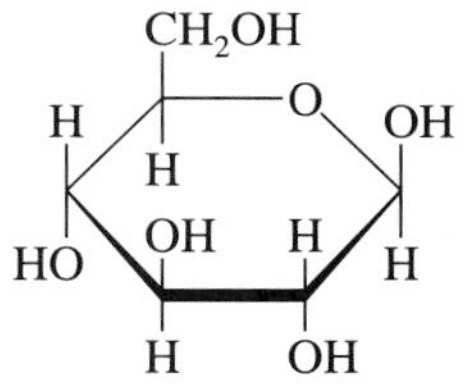

26.53. The structural formula for the linear form of galactose is shown here. Draw the structure of the six-member-ring form of this sugar.

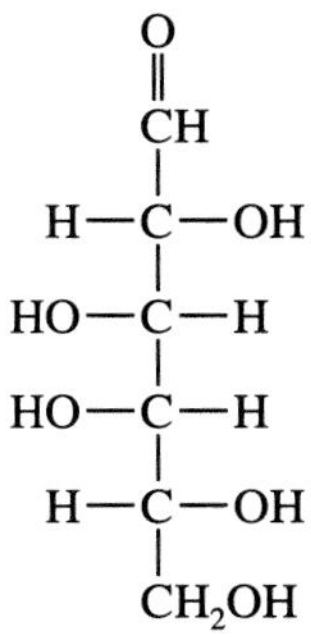

26.54. The structural formula for the linear form of L-sorbose is shown here. Draw the structure of the five-member-ring form of this sugar.

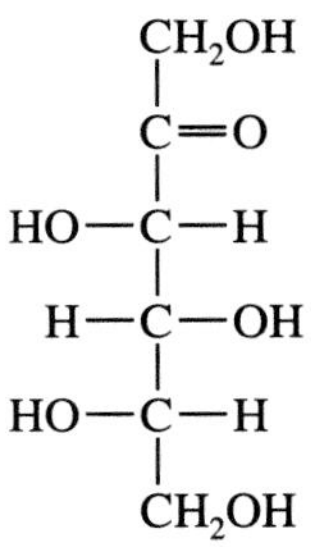

26.55. Which carbon atoms in galactose (see Exercise 26.53) are chiral?

26.56. Which carbon atoms in sorbose (see Exercise 26.54) are chiral?

Nucleic Acids

26.57. Describe a nucleotide. Draw the structural formula for deoxycytidine monophosphate in which cytosine is the organic base.

26.58. A nucleoside consists of an organic base of the kind shown in Section 26.7, bound to ribose or deoxyribose. Draw the structure for thymidine, formed from thymine and deoxyribose.

26.59. Write a balanced chemical equation for the condensation reaction between a mole of deoxyribose and a mole of phosphoric acid.

26.60. An unknown substance undergoes hydrolysis under neutral conditions to yield 1 mol of phosphoric acid and an organic product. The same starting material undergoes hydrolysis under acidic conditions to yield guanine and ribose-monophosphate. Draw the structure of the unknown substance.

26.61. Imagine a single DNA strand containing a section with the following base sequence: A, C, T, C, G, A. What is the base sequence of the complementary strand?

26.62. When samples of double-stranded DNA are analyzed, the quantity of adenine present equals that of thymine. Similarly, the quantity of guanine equals that of cytosine. Explain the significance of these observations.

Additional Exercises

26.63. Draw the structural formulas for two molecules with the formula C_4H_6.

26.64. Unbranched hydrocarbons are often called straight-chain hydrocarbons. Does this mean that the carbon atoms have a linear arrangement? Explain.

26.65. Draw the Lewis structures for the cis and trans isomers of 2-pentene. Can cyclopentene exhibit cis-trans isomerism? Explain.

26.66. Give the IUPAC name for each of the following molecules:

(a) CH_3CHCH_3 with OH

(b) CH_3OCH_3

(c) $CH_2=CHCH_2CH_2OH$

(d) $CH_3C=CHCH_2CH_3$ with CH_2CH_3

(e) $CH_3C\equiv C-CH$ with CH_3 and CH_3

26.67. Write the formulas for all of the structural isomers of C_3H_8O.

26.68. Explain why *trans*-1,2-dichloroethene has no dipole moment, whereas *cis*-1,2-dichloroethene has a dipole moment.

26.69. Would you expect cyclohexyne to be a stable compound? Explain.

26.70. Identify all of the functional groups in each of the following molecules:

(a) $CH_2=CH-O-CH=CH_2$ (an anesthetic)

(b) (acetylsalicylic acid, aspirin)

(c) (testosterone, a male sex hormone)

26.71. Write the structural formula for each of the following: **(a)** an ether with the formula C_3H_8O; **(b)** an aldehyde with the formula C_3H_6O; **(c)** a ketone with the formula C_3H_6O; **(d)** a carboxylic acid with the formula $C_3H_6O_2$; **(e)** an ester with the formula $C_3H_6O_2$.

26.72. Give the condensed formulas for the carboxylic acid and the alcohol from which each of the following esters is formed:

(a) (b)

26.73. In each of the following pairs, indicate which molecule is the more reactive and give a reason for the greater reactivity: **(a)** butane and cyclobutane; **(b)** cyclohexane and cyclohexene; **(c)** benzene and 1-hexene; **(d)** 2-hexyne and 2-hexene.

[26.74]. An unknown organic compound is found on analysis to have the empirical formula $C_5H_{12}O$. It is slightly soluble in water. Upon careful oxidation it is converted into a compound of empirical formula $C_5H_{10}O$, which behaves chemically like a ketone. Indicate two or more reasonable structures for the unknown.

[26.75]. An unknown substance is found to contain only carbon and hydrogen. It is a liquid that boils at 49°C at 1 atm pressure. Upon analysis it is found to contain 85.7 percent carbon and 14.3 percent hydrogen by mass. At 100°C and 735 torr, the vapor of this unknown has a density of 2.21 g/L. When it is dissolved in hexane solution and bromine water added, no reaction occurs. Suggest the identity of the unknown compound.

26.76. Name at least four processes occurring in an organism (such as yourself) that require energy. These may occur at the molecular level, or they may involve the complete organism.

26.77. In each of the following substances, locate the chiral carbon atoms, if any:

(a) $HOCH_2CH_2CCH_2OH$ with O double bonded

(b) $HOCH_2CHCCH_2OH$ with OH and O double bonded

(c) $HOCCHCHC_2H_5$ with O, CH_3, and NH_2

26.78. Draw the condensed structural formula of each of the following tripeptides: **(a)** val-gly-asp; **(b)** phe-ser-ala.

26.79. Glutathione is a tripeptide found in most living cells. Partial hydrolysis yields cys-gly and glu-cys. What structures are possible for glutathione?

26.80. The standard free energy of formation of solid glycine is -369 kJ/mol, whereas that of solid glycylglycine is -488 kJ/mol. What is $\Delta G°$ for condensation of glycine to form glycylglycine?

26.81. Give a specific example of each of the following: **(a)** a disaccharide; **(b)** a sugar present in nucleic acids; **(c)** a sugar present in human blood serum; **(d)** a polysaccharide.

26.82. The standard free energy of formation for aqueous solutions of glucose is -917.2 kJ/mol, whereas that of glycogen is -662.3 kJ/mol of glucose units. Derive a general expression for ΔG° for the formation of a glycogen molecule that contains n units of glucose.

26.83. Write a complementary nucleic acid strand for the following strand, using the concept of complementary base pairing: TATGCA.

[26.84]. The monoanion of adenosine monophosphate (AMP) is an intermediate in phosphate metabolism:

$$A-O-\underset{\underset{O}{\|}}{\overset{\overset{O^-}{|}}{P}}-OH = AMP-OH^-$$

where A = adenosine. If the pK_a for this anion is 7.21, what is the ratio of [AMP—OH$^-$] to [AMP—O^{2-}] in blood at pH 7.40?

Mathematical Operations

A

A.1 Exponential Notation

The numbers used in chemistry are often either extremely large or extremely small. Such numbers are conveniently expressed in the form

$$N \times 10^n$$

where N is a number between 1 and 10, and n is the exponent. Some examples of this *exponential notation*, which is also called *scientific notation*, follow:

1,200,000 is 1.2×10^6 (read "one point two times ten to the sixth power")

0.000604 is 6.04×10^{-4} (read "six point zero four times ten to the negative fourth power")

A positive exponent, as in the first example, tells us how many times a number must be multiplied by 10 to give the long form of the number:

$$1.2 \times 10^6 = 1.2 \times 10 \times 10 \times 10 \times 10 \times 10 \times 10 \quad \text{(six tens)}$$
$$= 1,200,000$$

It is also convenient to think of the positive exponent as the number of places the decimal point must be moved to the *left* to obtain a number greater than 1 and less than 10: If we begin with 3450 and move the decimal point three places to the left, we end up with 3.45×10^3.

In a related fashion, a negative exponent tells us how many times we must divide a number by 10 to give the long form of the number:

$$6.04 \times 10^{-4} = \frac{6.04}{10 \times 10 \times 10 \times 10} = 0.000604$$

It is convenient to think of the negative exponent as the number of places the decimal point must be moved to the *right* to obtain a number greater than 1 but less than 10: If we begin with 0.0048 and move the decimal point three places to the right, we end up with 4.8×10^{-3}.

In the system of exponential notation, with each shift of the decimal point one place to the right, the exponent *decreases* by 1:

$$4.8 \times 10^{-3} = 48 \times 10^{-4}$$

Similarly, with each shift of the decimal point one place to the left, the exponent *increases* by 1:

$$4.8 \times 10^{-3} = 0.48 \times 10^{-2}$$

Most scientific calculators have a key labeled EXP or EE, which is used to enter numbers in exponential notation. To enter the number 5.8×10^3, the key sequence is

$$\boxed{5}\ \boxed{\cdot}\ \boxed{8}\ \boxed{\text{EXP}}\ (\text{or}\ \boxed{\text{EE}}\ )\ \boxed{3}$$

On some calculators the display will show 5.8, then a space, followed by 03, the exponent. On other calculators, a small 10 is shown with an exponent 3.

To enter a negative exponent, use the key labeled $+/-$. For example, to enter the number 8.6×10^{-5}, the key sequence is

$$\boxed{8}\ \boxed{\cdot}\ \boxed{6}\ \boxed{\text{EXP}}\ \boxed{+/-}\ \boxed{5}$$

When entering a number in exponential notation, do not key in the 10.

In working with exponents, it is important to recall that $10^0 = 1$. The following rules are useful for carrying exponents through calculations.

1. **Addition and Subtraction**   In order to add or subtract numbers expressed in exponential notation, the powers of 10 must be the same:

$$
\begin{aligned}
(5.22 \times 10^4) + (3.21 \times 10^2) &= (522 \times 10^2) + (3.21 \times 10^2) \\
&= 525 \times 10^2 \quad \text{(3 significant figures)} \\
&= 5.25 \times 10^4
\end{aligned}
$$

$$
\begin{aligned}
(6.25 \times 10^{-2}) - (5.77 \times 10^{-3}) &= (6.25 \times 10^{-2}) - (0.577 \times 10^{-2}) \\
&= 5.67 \times 10^{-2} \quad \text{(3 significant figures)}
\end{aligned}
$$

When you use a calculator to add or subtract, you need not be concerned with having numbers with the same exponents because the calculator automatically takes care of this matter.

2. **Multiplication and Division**   When numbers expressed in exponential notation are multiplied, the exponents are added; when numbers expressed in exponential notation are divided, the exponent of the denominator is subtracted from the exponent of the numerator:

$$
\begin{aligned}
(5.4 \times 10^2)(2.1 \times 10^3) &= (5.4)(2.1) \times 10^{2+3} \\
&= 11 \times 10^5 \\
&= 1.1 \times 10^6
\end{aligned}
$$

$$(1.2 \times 10^5)(3.22 \times 10^{-3}) = (1.2)(3.22) \times 10^{5-3} = 3.9 \times 10^2$$

$$\frac{3.2 \times 10^5}{6.5 \times 10^2} = \frac{3.2}{6.5} \times 10^{5-2} = 0.49 \times 10^3 = 4.9 \times 10^2$$

$$\frac{5.7 \times 10^7}{8.5 \times 10^{-2}} = \frac{5.7}{8.5} \times 10^{7-(-2)} = 0.67 \times 10^9 = 6.7 \times 10^8$$

3. **Powers and Roots** When numbers expressed in exponential notation are raised to a power, the exponents are multiplied by the power; when the roots of numbers expressed in exponential notation are taken, the exponents are divided by the root:

$$(1.2 \times 10^5)^3 = (1.2)^3 \times 10^{5 \times 3}$$
$$= 1.7 \times 10^{15}$$
$$\sqrt[3]{2.5 \times 10^6} = \sqrt[3]{2.5} \times 10^{6/3}$$
$$= 1.3 \times 10^2$$

Scientific calculators usually have keys labeled x^2 and $\sqrt{x}$ for squaring and taking the square root of a number, respectively. To take higher powers or roots, many calculators have y^x and $\sqrt[x]{y}$ (or INV y^x) keys. For example, to perform the operation $\sqrt[3]{7.5 \times 10^{-4}}$ on such a calculator, you would key in 7.5×10^{-4}, press the $\sqrt[x]{y}$ key (or the INV and then the y^x keys), enter the root, 3, and finally press =. The result is 9.1×10^{-2}.

SAMPLE EXERCISE 1

Perform each of the following operations, using your calculator where possible:
(a) Write the number 0.0054 in standard exponential notation;
(b) $(5.0 \times 10^{-2}) + (4.7 \times 10^{-3})$;
(c) $(5.98 \times 10^{12})(2.77 \times 10^{-5})$;
(d) $\sqrt[4]{1.75 \times 10^{-12}}$.

SOLUTION (a) Because we move the decimal three places to the right to convert 0.0054 to 5.4, the exponent is -3:

$$5.4 \times 10^{-3}$$

Scientific calculators are generally able to convert numbers to exponential notation using one or two keystrokes. Consult your instruction manual to see how this operation is accomplished on your calculator.

(b) To add these numbers longhand, we must convert them to the same exponent:

$$(5.0 \times 10^{-2}) + (0.47 \times 10^{-2}) = (5.0 + 0.47) \times 10^{-2} = 5.5 \times 10^{-2}$$

(Note that the result has only two significant figures.) To perform this operation on a calculator, we enter the first number, strike the + key, then enter the second number and strike the = key.

(c) Performing this operation longhand, we have

$$(5.98 \times 2.77) \times 10^{12-5} = 16.6 \times 10^7 = 1.66 \times 10^8$$

On a scientific calculator, we enter 5.98×10^{12}, press the $\times$ key, enter 2.77×10^{-5}, and press the = key.

(d) To perform this operation on a calculator, we enter the number, press the $\sqrt[x]{y}$ key (or the INV and y^x keys), enter 4, and press the = key. The result is 1.15×10^{-3}.

PRACTICE EXERCISE

Perform the following operations: (a) Write 67,000 in exponential notation, showing two significant figures; (b) $(3.378 \times 10^{-3}) - (4.97 \times 10^{-5})$; (c) $(1.84 \times 10^{15})/(7.45 \times 10^{-2})$; (d) $(6.67 \times 10^{-8})^3$. *Answers:* (a) 6.7×10^4; (b) 3.328×10^{-3}; (c) 2.47×10^{16}; (d) 2.97×10^{-22}

A.2 Logarithms

Common Logarithms

The common, or base-10, logarithm (abbreviated log) of any number is the power to which 10 must be raised to equal the number. For example, the common logarithm of 1000 (written log 1000) is 3 because raising 10 to the third power gives 1000:

$$10^3 = 1000, \text{ therefore, } \log 1000 = 3$$

Futher examples are

$$\log 10^5 = 5$$
$$\log 1 = 0 \quad (\text{Remember that } 10^0 = 1)$$
$$\log 10^{-2} = -2$$

In these examples, the common logarithm can be obtained by inspection. However, it is not possible to obtain the logarithm of a number such as 31.25 by inspection. The logarithm of 31.25 is the number x that satisfies

$$10^x = 31.25$$

Most electronic calculators have a key labeled LOG that can be used to obtain logarithms. For example, we can obtain the value of log 31.25 by entering 31.25 and pressing the LOG key. We obtain the following result:

$$\log 31.25 = 1.4949$$

Notice that 31.25 is greater than 10 (10^1) and less than 100 (10^2). The value for log 31.25 is accordingly between log 10 and log 100, that is, between 1 and 2.

Significant Figures and Common Logarithms

For the common logarithm of a measured quantity, the number of digits after the decimal point equals the number of significant figures in the original number. For example, if 23.5 is a measured quantity (three significant figures), then log 23.5 = 1.371 (three significant figures after the decimal point).

Antilogarithms

The process of determining the number that corresponds to a certain logarithm is known as obtaining an *antilogarithm.* It is the reverse of taking a logarithm. For example, we saw above that log 23.5 = 1.371. This means that the antilogarithm of 1.371 equals 23.5:

$$\log 23.5 = 1.371$$

$$\text{antilog } 1.371 = 23.5$$

The process of taking the antilog of a number is the same as raising 10 to a power equal to that number:

$$\text{antilog } 1.371 = 10^{1.371} = 23.5$$

Many calculators have a key labeled 10^x that allows you to obtain antilogs directly. On others, it will be necessary to press a key labeled INV (for *inverse*), followed by the LOG key.

Natural Logarithms

Logarithms based on the number e are called natural, or base e, logarithms (abbreviated ln). The natural log of a number is the power to which e (which has the value 2.71828...) must be raised to equal the number. For example, the natural log of 10 equals 2.303:

$$e^{2.303} = 10, \text{ therefore } \ln 10 = 2.303$$

Your calculator probably has a key labeled LN that allows you to obtain natural logarithms. For example, to obtain the natural log of 46.8, you enter 46.8 and press the LN key:

$$\ln 46.8 = 3.846$$

The natural antilog of a number is e raised to a power equal to that number. If your calculator can calculate natural logs, it will also be able to calculate natural antilogs. On some calculators, there is a key labeled e^x that allows you to calculate natural antilogs directly; on others, it will be necessary to first press the INV key followed by the LN key. For example, the natural antilog of 1.679 is given by

$$\text{Natural antilog } 1.679 = e^{1.679} = 5.36$$

The relation between common and natural logarithms is as follows:

$$\ln a = 2.303 \log a$$

Notice that the factor relating the two, 2.303, is the natural log of 10, which we calculated above.

Mathematical Operations Using Logarithms

Because logarithms are exponents, mathematical operations involving logarithms follow the rules for the use of exponents. For example, the product of z^a and z^b (where z is any number) is given by

$$z^a \cdot z^b = z^{(a+b)}$$

Similarly, the logarithm (either common or natural) of a product equals the *sum* of the logs of the individual numbers:

$$\log ab = \log a + \log b \qquad \ln ab = \ln a + \ln b$$

For the log of a quotient:

$$\log (a/b) = \log a - \log b \qquad \ln (a/b) = \ln a - \ln b$$

Using the properties of exponents, we can also derive the rules for the logarithm of a number raised to a certain power:

$$\log a^n = n \log a \qquad \ln a^n = n \ln a$$

$$\log a^{1/n} = (1/n) \log a \qquad \ln a^{1/n} = (1/n) \ln a$$

pH Problems

One of the most frequent uses for common logarithms in general chemistry is in working pH problems. The pH is defined as $-\log [H^+]$, where $[H^+]$ is the hydrogen ion concentration of a solution (Section 16.3). The following sample exercise illustrates this application.

SAMPLE EXERCISE 2

(a) What is the pH of a solution whose hydrogen ion concentration is 0.015 *M*?
(b) If the pH of a solution is 3.80, what is its hydrogen ion concentration?

SOLUTION   (a) We are given the value of $[H^+]$. We use the LOG key of our calculator to calculate the value of $\log [H^+]$. The pH is obtained by changing the sign of the value obtained. (Be sure to change the sign *after* taking the logarithm.):

$$[H^+] = 0.015$$
$$\log [H^+] = -1.82 \qquad \text{(2 significant figures)}$$
$$pH = -(-1.82) = 1.82$$

(b) To obtain the hydrogen ion concentration when given the pH, we must take the antilog of $-pH$:

$$pH = -\log [H^+] = 3.80$$
$$\log [H^+] = -3.80$$
$$[H^+] = \text{antilog}(-3.80) = 10^{-3.80} = 1.6 \times 10^{-4} \ M$$

PRACTICE EXERCISE

Perform the following operations: (a) $\log (2.5 \times 10^{-5})$; (b) $\ln 32.7$; (c) antilog -3.47; (d) $e^{-1.89}$.   *Answers:* (a) -4.60; (b) 3.487; (c) 3.4×10^{-4}; (d) 1.5×10^{-1}

A.3 Quadratic Equations

An algebraic equation of the form $ax^2 + bx + c = 0$ is called a *quadratic equation*. The two solutions to such an equation are given by the quadratic formula:

$$x = \frac{-b \pm \sqrt{b^2 - 4ac}}{2a}$$

SAMPLE EXERCISE 3

Find the values of x that satisfy the equation $2x^2 + 4x = 1$.

SOLUTION To solve the given equation for x, we must first put it in the form

$$ax^2 + bx + c = 0$$

and then use the quadratic formula. If

$$2x^2 + 4x = 1$$

then

$$2x^2 + 4x - 1 = 0$$

Using the quadratic formula, where $a = 2$, $b = 4$, and $c = -1$, we have

$$x = \frac{-4 \pm \sqrt{(4)(4) - 4(2)(-1)}}{2(2)}$$

$$= \frac{-4 \pm \sqrt{16 + 8}}{4} = \frac{-4 \pm \sqrt{24}}{4} = \frac{-4 \pm 4.899}{4}$$

The two solutions are

$$x = \frac{0.899}{4} = 0.225 \quad \text{and} \quad x = \frac{-8.899}{4} = -2.225$$

Often in chemical problems the negative solution has no physical meaning, and only the positive answer is used.

A.4 Graphs

Often the clearest way to represent the interrelationship between two variables is to graph them. Usually, the variable that is being experimentally varied, called the *independent variable,* is shown along the horizontal axis (x axis). The variable that responds to the change in the independent variable, called the *dependent variable,* is then shown along the vertical axis (y axis). For example, consider an experiment in which we vary the temperature of an enclosed gas and measure its pressure. The independent variable is temperature, and the dependent variable is pressure. The data shown in Table 1 can be obtained by means of this experiment. These data are shown graphically in Figure 1. The relationship between temperature and pressure is linear. The equation for any straight-line graph has the form

$$y = mx + b$$

where m is the slope of the line, and b is the intercept with the y axis. In the case of Figure 1, we could say that the relationship between temperature and pressure takes the form

$$P = mT + b$$

where P is pressure in atm and T is temperature in °C. As shown in Figure 1, the slope is 4.10×10^{-4} atm/°C, and the intercept—the point where the line crosses the y axis—is 0.112 atm. Therefore, the equation for the line is

$$P = \left(4.10 \times 10^{-4}\,\frac{\text{atm}}{°\text{C}}\right) T + 0.112 \text{ atm}$$

TABLE 1 △ Interrelation Between Pressure and Temperature

Temperature (°C)	Pressure (atm)
20.0	0.120
30.0	0.124
40.0	0.128
50.0	0.132

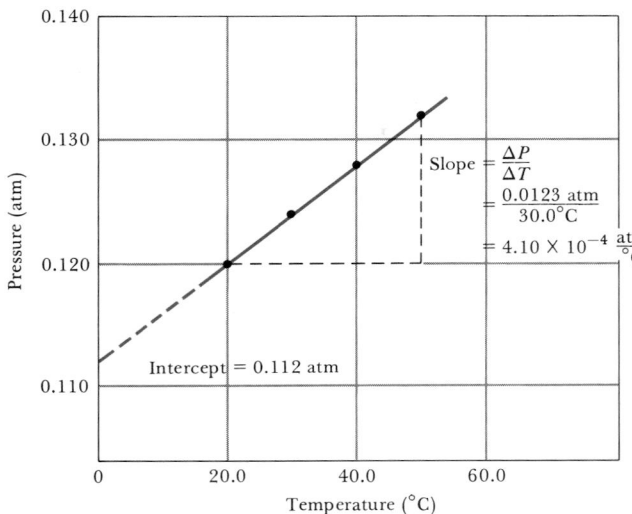

FIGURE 1

Properties of Water

B

Density:	0.99987 g/mL at 0°C
	1.00000 g/mL at 4°C
	0.99707 g/mL at 25°C
	0.95838 g/mL at 100°C
Heat of fusion:	6.008 kJ/mol at 0°C
Heat of vaporization:	44.94 kJ/mol at 0°C
	44.02 kJ/mol at 25°C
	40.67 kJ/mol at 100°C
Ion-product constant, K_w:	1.14×10^{-15} at 0°C
	1.01×10^{-14} at 25°C
	5.47×10^{-14} at 50°C
Specific heat:	Ice $(-3°C)$ — 2.092 J/g-K
	Water at 14.5°C — 4.184 J/g-K
	Steam (100°C) — 1.841 J/g-K

Vapor pressure (torr):

$T(°C)$	P	$T(°C)$	P	$T(°C)$	P	$T(°C)$	P
0	4.58	21	18.65	35	42.2	92	567.0
5	6.54	22	19.83	40	55.3	94	610.9
10	9.21	23	21.07	45	71.9	96	657.6
12	10.52	24	22.38	50	92.5	98	707.3
14	11.99	25	23.76	55	118.0	100	760.0
16	13.63	26	25.21	60	149.4	102	815.9
17	14.53	27	26.74	65	187.5	104	875.1
18	15.48	28	28.35	70	233.7	106	937.9
19	16.48	29	30.04	80	355.1	108	1004.4
20	17.54	30	31.82	90	525.8	110	1074.6

C Thermodynamic Quantities for Selected Substances at 298.15 K (25°C)

Substance	ΔH_f° (kJ/mol)	ΔG_f° (kJ/mol)	S° (J/mol-K)	Substance	ΔH_f° (kJ/mol)	ΔG_f° (kJ/mol)	S° (J/mol-K)
Aluminum				**Carbon**			
Al(s)	0	0	28.32	C(g)	718.4	672.9	158.0
$AlCl_3(s)$	−705.6	−630.0	109.3	C(s, diamond)	1.88	2.84	2.43
$Al_2O_3(s)$	−1669.8	−1576.5	51.00	C(s, graphite)	0	0	5.69
				$CCl_4(g)$	−106.7	−64.0	309.4
Barium				$CCl_4(l)$	−139.3	−68.6	214.4
Ba(s)	0	0	63.2				
$BaCO_3(s)$	−1216.3	−1137.6	112.1	$CF_4(g)$	−679.9	−635.1	262.3
BaO(s)	−553.5	−525.1	70.42	$CH_4(g)$	−74.8	−50.8	186.3
				$C_2H_2(g)$	226.7	209.2	200.8
Beryllium				$C_2H_4(g)$	52.30	68.11	219.4
Be(s)	0	0	9.44	$C_2H_6(g)$	−84.68	−32.89	229.5
BeO(s)	−608.4	−579.1	13.77				
$Be(OH)_2(s)$	−905.8	−817.9	50.21	$C_3H_8(g)$	−103.85	−23.47	269.9
				$C_4H_{10}(g)$	−124.73	−15.71	310.0
Bromine				$C_4H_{10}(l)$	−147.6	−15.0	231.0
Br(g)	111.8	82.38	174.9	$C_6H_6(g)$	82.9	129.7	269.2
$Br^-(aq)$	−120.9	−102.8	80.71	$C_6H_6(l)$	49.0	124.5	172.8
$Br_2(g)$	30.71	3.14	245.3				
$Br_2(l)$	0	0	152.3	$CH_3OH(g)$	−201.2	−161.9	237.6
HBr(g)	−36.23	−53.22	198.49	$CH_3OH(l)$	−238.6	−166.23	126.8
				$C_2H_5OH(g)$	−235.1	−168.5	282.7
Calcium				$C_2H_5OH(l)$	−277.7	−174.76	160.7
Ca(g)	179.3	145.5	154.8	$C_6H_{12}O_6(s)$	−1273.02	−910.4	212.1
Ca(s)	0	0	41.4				
$CaCO_3$ (s, calcite)	−1207.1	−1128.76	92.88	CO(g)	−110.5	−137.2	197.9
$CaCl_2(s)$	−795.8	−748.1	104.6	$CO_2(g)$	−393.5	−394.4	213.6
$CaF_2(s)$	−1219.6	−1167.3	68.87	$HC_2H_3O_2(l)$	−487.0	−392.4	159.8
CaO(s)	−635.5	−604.17	39.75	**Cesium**			
$Ca(OH)_2(s)$	−986.2	−898.5	83.4	Cs(g)	76.50	49.53	175.6
$CaSO_4(s)$	−1434.0	−1321.8	106.7	Cs(s)	0	0	85.15
				CsCl(s)	−442.8	−414.4	101.2

Substance	ΔH_f° (kJ/mol)	ΔG_f° (kJ/mol)	S° (J/mol-K)	Substance	ΔH_f° (kJ/mol)	ΔG_f° (kJ/mol)	S° (J/mol-K)
Chlorine				**Lead**			
$Cl(g)$	121.7	105.7	165.2	$Pb(s)$	0	0	68.85
$Cl^-(aq)$	−167.2	−131.2	56.5	$PbBr_2(s)$	−277.4	−260.7	161
$Cl_2(g)$	0	0	222.96	$PbCO_3(s)$	−699.1	−625.5	131.0
$HCl(aq)$	−167.2	−131.2	56.5	$Pb(NO_3)_2(aq)$	−421.3	−246.9	303.3
$HCl(g)$	−92.30	−95.27	186.69	$Pb(NO_3)_2(s)$	−451.9	—	—
				$PbO(s)$	−217.3	−187.9	68.70
Chromium							
$Cr(g)$	397.5	352.6	174.2	**Lithium**			
$Cr(s)$	0	0	23.6	$Li(g)$	159.3	126.6	138.8
$Cr_2O_3(s)$	−1139.7	−1058.1	81.2	$Li(s)$	0	0	29.09
				$Li^+(g)$	685.7	648.5	133.0
Cobalt				$LiCl(s)$	−408.3	−384.0	59.30
$Co(g)$	439	393	179				
$Co(s)$	0	0	28.4	**Magnesium**			
				$Mg(g)$	147.1	112.5	148.6
Copper				$Mg(s)$	0	0	32.51
$Cu(g)$	338.4	298.6	166.3	$MgCl_2(s)$	−641.6	−592.1	89.6
$Cu(s)$	0	0	33.30	$MgO(s)$	−601.8	−569.6	26.8
$CuCl_2(s)$	−205.9	−161.7	108.1	$Mg(OH)_2(s)$	−924.7	−833.7	63.24
$CuO(s)$	−156.1	−128.3	42.59				
$Cu_2O(s)$	−170.7	−147.9	92.36	**Manganese**			
				$Mn(g)$	280.7	238.5	173.6
Fluorine				$Mn(s)$	0	0	32.0
$F(g)$	80.0	61.9	158.7	$MnO(s)$	−385.2	−362.9	59.7
$F^-(aq)$	−332.6	−278.8	−13.8	$MnO_2(s)$	−519.6	−464.8	53.14
$F_2(g)$	0	0	202.7	$MnO_4^-(aq)$	−541.4	−447.2	191.2
$HF(g)$	−268.61	−270.70	173.51				
				Mercury			
Hydrogen				$Hg(g)$	60.83	31.76	174.89
$H(g)$	217.94	203.26	114.60	$Hg(l)$	0	0	77.40
$H^+(aq)$	0	0	0	$HgCl_2(s)$	−230.1	−184.0	144.5
$H^+(g)$	1536.2	1517.0	108.9	$Hg_2Cl_2(s)$	−264.9	−210.5	192.5
$H_2(g)$	0	0	130.58				
				Nickel			
Iodine				$Ni(g)$	429.7	384.5	182.1
$I(g)$	106.60	70.16	180.66	$Ni(s)$	0	0	29.9
$I^-(aq)$	−55.19	−51.57	111.3	$NiCl_2(s)$	−305.3	−259.0	97.65
$I_2(g)$	62.25	19.37	260.57	$NiO(s)$	−239.7	−211.7	37.99
$I_2(s)$	0	0	116.73				
$HI(g)$	25.94	1.30	206.3	**Nitrogen**			
				$N(g)$	472.7	455.5	153.3
Iron				$N_2(g)$	0	0	191.50
$Fe(g)$	415.5	369.8	180.5	$NH_3(aq)$	−80.29	−26.50	111.3
$Fe(s)^{\cdot}$	0	0	27.15	$NH_3(g)$	−46.19	−16.66	192.5
$Fe^{2+}(aq)$	−87.86	−84.93	113.4	$NH_4^+(aq)$	−132.5	−79.31	113.4
$Fe^{3+}(aq)$	−47.69	−10.54	293.3				
$FeCl_2(s)$	−341.8	−302.3	117.9	$N_2H_4(g)$	95.40	159.4	238.5
$FeCl_3(s)$	−400	−334	142.3	$NH_4CN(s)$	0.0	—	—
$FeO(s)$	−271.9	−255.2	60.75	$NH_4Cl(s)$	−314.4	−203.0	94.6
$Fe_2O_3(s)$	−822.16	−740.98	89.96	$NH_4NO_3(s)$	−365.6	−184.0	151
$Fe_3O_4(s)$	−1117.1	−1014.2	146.4	$NO(g)$	90.37	86.71	210.62
$FeS_2(s)$	−171.5	−160.1	52.92				

Substance	ΔH_f° (kJ/mol)	ΔG_f° (kJ/mol)	S° (J/mol-K)	Substance	ΔH_f° (kJ/mol)	ΔG_f° (kJ/mol)	S° (J/mol-K)
$NO_2(g)$	33.84	51.84	240.45	Scandium			
$N_2O(g)$	81.6	103.59	220.0	$Sc(g)$	377.8	336.1	174.7
$N_2O_4(g)$	9.66	98.28	304.3	$Sc(s)$	0	0	34.6
$NOCl(g)$	52.6	66.3	264				
$HNO_3(aq)$	-206.6	-110.5	146	Selenium			
$HNO_3(g)$	-134.3	-73.94	266.4	$H_2Se(g)$	29.7	15.9	219.0
Oxygen							
$O(g)$	247.5	230.1	161.0	Silicon			
$O_2(g)$	0	0	205.0	$Si(g)$	368.2	323.9	167.8
$O_3(g)$	142.3	163.4	237.6	$Si(s)$	0	0	18.7
$OH^-(aq)$	-230.0	-157.3	-10.7	$SiC(s)$	-73.22	-70.85	16.61
$H_2O(g)$	-241.8	-228.61	188.7	$SiCl_4(l)$	-640.1	-572.8	239.3
$H_2O(l)$	-285.85	-236.81	69.96	$SiO_2(s, quartz)$	-910.9	-856.5	41.84
$H_2O_2(g)$	-136.10	-105.48	232.9				
$H_2O_2(l)$	-187.8	-120.4	109.6	Silver			
				$Ag(s)$	0	0	42.55
Phosphorus				$Ag^+(aq)$	105.90	77.11	73.93
$P(g)$	316.4	280.0	163.2	$AgCl(s)$	-127.0	-109.70	96.11
$P_2(g)$	144.3	103.7	218.1	$Ag_2O(s)$	-31.05	-11.20	121.3
$P_4(g)$	58.9	24.4	280	$AgNO_3(s)$	-124.4	-33.41	140.9
$P_4(s, red)$	-17.46	-12.03	22.85				
$P_4(s, white)$	0	0	41.08	Sodium			
				$Na(g)$	107.7	77.3	153.7
$PCl_3(g)$	-288.07	-269.6	311.7	$Na(s)$	0	0	51.45
$PCl_3(l)$	-319.6	-272.4	217	$Na^+(aq)$	-240.1	-261.9	59.0
$PF_5(g)$	-1594.4	-1520.7	300.8	$Na^+(g)$	609.3	574.3	148.0
$PH_3(g)$	5.4	13.4	210.2	$NaBr(aq)$	-360.6	-364.7	141
$P_4O_6(s)$	-1640.1	—	—				
				$NaBr(s)$	-361.4	-349.3	86.82
$P_4O_{10}(s)$	-2940.1	-2675.2	228.9	$Na_2CO_3(s)$	-1130.9	-1047.7	136.0
$POCl_3(g)$	-542.2	-502.5	325	$NaCl(aq)$	-407.1	-393.0	115.5
$POCl_3(l)$	-597.0	-520.9	222	$NaCl(g)$	-181.4	-201.3	229.8
$H_3PO_4(aq)$	-1288.3	-1142.6	158.2	$NaCl(s)$	-410.9	-384.0	72.33
Potassium				$NaHCO_3(s)$	-947.7	-851.8	102.1
$K(g)$	89.99	61.17	160.2	$NaNO_3(aq)$	-446.2	-372.4	207
$K(s)$	0	0	64.67	$NaNO_3(s)$	-467.9	-367.0	116.5
$KCl(s)$	-435.9	-408.3	82.7	$NaOH(aq)$	-469.6	-419.2	49.8
$KClO_3(s)$	-391.2	-289.9	143.0	$NaOH(s)$	-425.6	-379.5	64.46
$KClO_3(aq)$	-349.5	-284.9	265.7				
				Strontium			
$KNO_3(s)$	-492.70	-393.13	288.1	$SrO(s)$	-592.0	-561.9	54.9
$K_2O(s)$	-363.2	-322.1	94.14	$Sr(g)$	164.4	110.0	164.6
$KO_2(s)$	-284.5	-240.6	122.5				
$K_2O_2(s)$	-495.8	-429.8	113.0	Sulfur			
$KOH(s)$	-424.7	-378.9	78.91	$S(s, rhombic)$	0	0	31.88
$KOH(aq)$	-482.4	-440.5	91.6	$SO_2(g)$	-296.9	-300.4	248.5
				$SO_3(g)$	-395.2	-370.4	256.2
Rubidium				$SO_4^{2-}(aq)$	-909.3	-744.5	20.1
$Rb(g)$	85.8	55.8	170.0	$SOCl_2(l)$	-245.6	—	—
$Rb(s)$	0	0	76.78				
$RbCl(s)$	-430.5	-412.0	92				
$RbClO_3(s)$	-392.4	-292.0	152				

Substance	ΔH_f° (kJ/mol)	ΔG_f° (kJ/mol)	S° (J/mol-K)	Substance	ΔH_f° (kJ/mol)	ΔG_f° (kJ/mol)	S° (J/mol-K)
$H_2S(g)$	−20.17	−33.01	205.6	Vanadium			
$H_2SO_4(aq)$	−909.3	−744.5	20.1	$V(g)$	514.2	453.1	182.2
$H_2SO_4(l)$	−814.0	−689.9	156.1	$V(s)$	0	0	28.9
Titanium							
$Ti(g)$	468	422	180.3	Zinc			
$Ti(s)$	0	0	30.76	$Zn(g)$	130.7	95.2	160.9
$TiCl_4(g)$	−763.2	−726.8	354.9	$Zn(s)$	0	0	41.63
$TiCl_4(l)$	−804.2	−728.1	221.9	$ZnCl_2(s)$	−415.1	−369.4	111.5
$TiO_2(s)$	−944.7	−889.4	50.29	$ZnO(s)$	−348.0	−318.2	43.9

D Aqueous-Equilibrium Constants

TABLE D.1 △ Dissociation Constants for Acids at 25°C

Name	Formula	K_{a1}	K_{a2}	K_{a3}
Acetic	$HC_2H_3O_2$	1.8×10^{-5}		
Arsenic	H_3AsO_4	5.6×10^{-3}	1.0×10^{-7}	3.0×10^{-12}
Arsenous	H_3AsO_3	$6 \ \times 10^{-10}$		
Ascorbic	$HC_6H_7O_6$	8.0×10^{-5}	1.6×10^{-12}	
Benzoic	$HC_7H_5O_2$	6.5×10^{-5}		
Boric	H_3BO_3	5.8×10^{-10}		
Carbonic	H_2CO_3	4.3×10^{-7}	5.6×10^{-11}	
Chloroacetic	$HC_2H_2O_2Cl$	1.4×10^{-3}		
Citric	$H_3C_6H_5O_7$	7.4×10^{-4}	1.7×10^{-5}	4.0×10^{-7}
Cyanic	$HCNO$	3.5×10^{-4}		
Formic	$HCHO_2$	1.8×10^{-4}		
Hydroazoic	HN_3	1.9×10^{-5}		
Hydrocyanic	HCN	4.9×10^{-10}		
Hydrofluoric	HF	6.8×10^{-4}		
Hydrogen chromate ion	$HCrO_4^-$	3.0×10^{-7}		
Hydrogen peroxide	H_2O_2	2.4×10^{-12}		
Hydrogen selenate ion	$HSeO_4^-$	2.2×10^{-2}		
Hydrogen sulfide	H_2S	5.7×10^{-8}	1.3×10^{-13}	
Hypobromous	$HBrO$	$2 \ \times 10^{-9}$		
Hypochlorous	$HClO$	3.0×10^{-8}		
Hypoiodous	HIO	$2 \ \times 10^{-11}$		
Iodic	HIO_3	1.7×10^{-1}		
Lactic	$HC_3H_5O_3$	1.4×10^{-4}		
Malonic	$H_2C_3H_2O_4$	1.5×10^{-3}	2.0×10^{-6}	
Nitrous	HNO_2	4.5×10^{-4}		
Oxalic	$H_2C_2O_4$	5.9×10^{-2}	6.4×10^{-5}	
Paraperiodic	H_5IO_6	2.8×10^{-2}	5.3×10^{-9}	
Phenol	HC_6H_5O	1.3×10^{-10}		
Phosphoric	H_3PO_4	7.5×10^{-3}	6.2×10^{-8}	4.2×10^{-13}
Propionic	$HC_3H_5O_2$	1.3×10^{-5}		
Pyrophosphoric	$H_4P_2O_7$	3.0×10^{-2}	4.4×10^{-3}	
Selenous	H_2SeO_3	2.3×10^{-3}	5.3×10^{-9}	
Sulfuric	H_2SO_4	Strong acid	1.2×10^{-2}	
Sulfurous	H_2SO_3	1.7×10^{-2}	6.4×10^{-8}	
Tartaric	$H_2C_4H_4O_6$	1.0×10^{-3}	4.6×10^{-5}	

TABLE D.2 △ Dissociation Constants for Bases at 25°C

Name	Formula	K_b
Ammonia	NH_3	1.8×10^{-5}
Aniline	$C_6H_5NH_2$	4.3×10^{-10}
Dimethylamine	$(CH_3)_2NH$	5.4×10^{-4}
Ethylamine	$C_2H_5NH_2$	6.4×10^{-4}
Hydrazine	H_2NNH_2	1.3×10^{-6}
Hydroxylamine	$HONH_2$	1.1×10^{-8}
Methylamine	CH_3NH_2	4.4×10^{-4}
Pyridine	C_5H_5N	1.7×10^{-9}
Trimethylamine	$(CH_3)_3N$	6.4×10^{-5}

TABLE D.3 △ Solubility-Product Constants for Compounds at 25°C

Name	Formula	K_{sp}	Name	Formula	K_{sp}
Barium carbonate	$BaCO_3$	5.1×10^{-9}	Lead chloride	$PbCl_2$	1.6×10^{-5}
Barium chromate	$BaCrO_4$	1.2×10^{-10}	Lead chromate	$PbCrO_4$	2.8×10^{-13}
Barium fluoride	BaF_2	1.0×10^{-6}	Lead fluoride	PbF_2	2.7×10^{-8}
Barium hydroxide	$Ba(OH)_2$	5×10^{-3}	Lead hydroxide	$Pb(OH)_2$	1.2×10^{-15}
Barium oxalate	BaC_2O_4	1.6×10^{-7}	Lead sulfate	$PbSO_4$	1.6×10^{-8}
Barium phosphate	$Ba_3(PO_4)_2$	3.4×10^{-23}	Lead sulfide	PbS	8.0×10^{-28}
Barium sulfate	$BaSO_4$	1.1×10^{-10}	Magnesium hydroxide	$Mg(OH)_2$	1.8×10^{-11}
Cadmium carbonate	$CdCO_3$	5.2×10^{-12}	Magnesium oxalate	MgC_2O_4	8.6×10^{-5}
Cadmium hydroxide	$Cd(OH)_2$	2.5×10^{-14}	Manganese carbonate	$MnCO_3$	1.8×10^{-11}
Cadmium sulfide	CdS	8.0×10^{-27}	Manganese hydroxide	$Mn(OH)_2$	1.9×10^{-13}
Calcium carbonate	$CaCO_3$	2.8×10^{-9}	Manganese(II) sulfide	MnS	1.0×10^{-13}
Calcium chromate	$CaCrO_4$	7.1×10^{-4}	Mercury(I) chloride	Hg_2Cl_2	1.3×10^{-18}
Calcium fluoride	CaF_2	3.9×10^{-11}	Mercury(I) oxalate	$Hg_2C_2O_4$	2.0×10^{-13}
Calcium hydroxide	$Ca(OH)_2$	5.5×10^{-6}	Mercury(I) sulfide	Hg_2S	1.0×10^{-47}
Calcium phosphate	$Ca_3(PO_4)_2$	2.0×10^{-29}	Mercury(II) hydroxide	$Hg(OH)_2$	3.0×10^{-26}
Calcium sulfate	$CaSO_4$	9.1×10^{-6}	Mercury(II) sulfide	HgS	4×10^{-53}
Cerium(III) fluoride	CeF_3	8×10^{-16}	Nickel carbonate	$NiCO_3$	6.6×10^{-9}
Chromium(III) fluoride	CrF_3	6.6×10^{-11}	Nickel hydroxide	$Ni(OH)_2$	1.6×10^{-14}
Chromium(III) hydroxide	$Cr(OH)_3$	6.3×10^{-31}	Nickel oxalate	NiC_2O_4	4×10^{-10}
Cobalt(II) carbonate	$CoCO_3$	1.4×10^{-13}	α-Nickel sulfide[a]	NiS	3.2×10^{-19}
Cobalt(II) hydroxide	$Co(OH)_2$	1.6×10^{-15}	Silver arsenate	Ag_3AsO_4	1.0×10^{-22}
Cobalt(III) hydroxide	$Co(OH)_3$	1.6×10^{-44}	Silver bromide	$AgBr$	5.0×10^{-13}
α-Cobalt(II) sulfide[a]	CoS	4.0×10^{-21}	Silver carbonate	Ag_2CO_3	8.1×10^{-12}
Copper(I) bromide	$CuBr$	5.3×10^{-9}	Silver chloride	$AgCl$	1.8×10^{-10}
Copper(I) chloride	$CuCl$	1.2×10^{-6}	Silver chromate	Ag_2CrO_4	1.1×10^{-12}
Copper(I) sulfide	Cu_2S	2.5×10^{-48}	Silver cyanide	$AgCN$	1.2×10^{-16}
Copper(II) carbonate	$CuCO_3$	1.4×10^{-10}	Silver iodide	AgI	8.3×10^{-17}
Copper(II) chromate	$CuCrO_4$	3.6×10^{-6}	Silver sulfate	Ag_2SO_4	1.4×10^{-5}
Copper(II) hydroxide	$Cu(OH)_2$	2.2×10^{-20}	Silver sulfide	Ag_2S	6.3×10^{-50}
Copper(II) phosphate	$Cu_3(PO_4)_2$	1.3×10^{-37}	Strontium carbonate	$SrCO_3$	1.1×10^{-10}
Copper(II) sulfide	CuS	6.3×10^{-36}	Tin(II) hydroxide	$Sn(OH)_2$	1.4×10^{-28}
Gold(I) chloride	$AuCl$	2.0×10^{-13}	Tin(II) sulfide	SnS	1.0×10^{-25}
Gold(III) chloride	$AuCl_3$	3.2×10^{-25}	Zinc carbonate	$ZnCO_3$	1.4×10^{-11}
Iron(II) carbonate	$FeCO_3$	3.2×10^{-11}	Zinc hydroxide	$Zn(OH)_2$	1.2×10^{-17}
Iron(II) hydroxide	$Fe(OH)_2$	8.0×10^{-16}	Zinc oxalate	ZnC_2O_4	2.7×10^{-8}
Iron(II) sulfide	FeS	6.3×10^{-18}	α-Zinc sulfide[a]	ZnS	1.1×10^{-21}
Iron(III) hydroxide	$Fe(OH)_3$	4×10^{-38}			
Lanthanum fluoride	LaF_3	4×10^{-17}			
Lanthanum iodate	$La(IO_3)_3$	6.1×10^{-12}			
Lead carbonate	$PbCO_3$	7.4×10^{-14}			

[a] Some substances exist in more than one crystalline form; the prefix indicates the particular form for which K_{sp} is listed.

E Standard Electrode Potentials at 25°C

Half-reaction	$E°$ (V)
$Ag^+(aq) + e^- \rightleftharpoons Ag(s)$	$+0.799$
$AgBr(s) + e^- \rightleftharpoons Ag(s) + Br^-(aq)$	$+0.095$
$AgCl(s) + e^- \rightleftharpoons Ag(s) + Cl^-(aq)$	$+0.222$
$Ag(CN)_2^-(aq) + e^- \rightleftharpoons Ag(s) + 2CN^-(aq)$	-0.31
$Ag_2CrO_4(s) + 2e^- \rightleftharpoons 2Ag(s) + CrO_4^{2-}(aq)$	$+0.446$
$AgI(s) + e^- \rightleftharpoons Ag(s) + I^-(aq)$	-0.151
$Ag(S_2O_3)_2^{3-} + e^- \rightleftharpoons Ag(s) + 2S_2O_3^{2-}(aq)$	$+0.01$
$Al^{3+}(aq) + 3e^- \rightleftharpoons Al(s)$	-1.66
$H_3AsO_4(aq) + 2H^+(aq) + 2e^- \rightleftharpoons H_3AsO_3(aq) + H_2O(l)$	$+0.559$
$Ba^{2+}(aq) + 2e^- \rightleftharpoons Ba(s)$	-2.90
$BiO^+(aq) + 2H^+(aq) + 3e^- \rightleftharpoons Bi(s) + H_2O(l)$	$+0.32$
$Br_2(l) + 2e^- \rightleftharpoons 2Br^-(aq)$	$+1.065$
$BrO_3^-(aq) + 6H^+(aq) + 5e^- \rightleftharpoons \frac{1}{2}Br_2(l) + 3H_2O(l)$	$+1.52$
$2CO_2(g) + 2H^+(aq) + 2e^- \rightleftharpoons H_2C_2O_4(aq)$	-0.49
$Ca^{2+}(aq) + 2e^- \rightleftharpoons Ca(s)$	-2.87
$Cd^{2+}(aq) + 2e^- \rightleftharpoons Cd(s)$	-0.403
$Ce^{4+}(aq) + e^- \rightleftharpoons Ce^{3+}(aq)$	$+1.61$
$Cl_2(g) + 2e^- \rightleftharpoons 2Cl^-(aq)$	$+1.359$
$HClO(aq) + H^+(aq) + e^- \rightleftharpoons \frac{1}{2}Cl_2(g) + H_2O(l)$	$+1.63$
$ClO^-(aq) + H_2O(l) + 2e^- \rightleftharpoons Cl^-(aq) + 2OH^-(aq)$	$+0.89$
$ClO_3^-(aq) + 6H^+(aq) + 5e^- \rightleftharpoons \frac{1}{2}Cl_2(g) + 3H_2O(l)$	$+1.47$
$Co^{2+}(aq) + 2e^- \rightleftharpoons Co(s)$	-0.277
$Co^{3+}(aq) + e^- \rightleftharpoons Co^{2+}(aq)$	$+1.842$
$Cr^{3+}(aq) + 3e^- \rightleftharpoons Cr(s)$	-0.74
$Cr^{3+}(aq) + e^- \rightleftharpoons Cr^{2+}(aq)$	-0.41
$Cr_2O_7^{2-}(aq) + 14H^+(aq) + 6e^- \rightleftharpoons 2Cr^{3+}(aq) + 7H_2O(l)$	$+1.33$
$CrO_4^{2-}(aq) + 4H_2O(l) + 3e^- \rightleftharpoons Cr(OH)_3(s) + 5OH^-(aq)$	-0.13
$Cu^{2+}(aq) + 2e^- \rightleftharpoons Cu(s)$	$+0.337$
$Cu^{2+}(aq) + e^- \rightleftharpoons Cu^+(aq)$	$+0.153$
$Cu^+(aq) + e^- \rightleftharpoons Cu(s)$	$+0.521$
$CuI(s) + e^- \rightleftharpoons Cu(s) + I^-(aq)$	-0.185
$F_2(g) + 2e^- \rightleftharpoons 2F^-(aq)$	$+2.87$
$Fe^{2+}(aq) + 2e^- \rightleftharpoons Fe(s)$	-0.440
$Fe^{3+}(aq) + e^- \rightleftharpoons Fe^{2+}(aq)$	$+0.771$
$Fe(CN)_6^{3-}(aq) + e^- \rightleftharpoons Fe(CN)_6^{4-}(aq)$	$+0.36$

Half-reaction	$E°$ (V)
$2H^+(aq) + 2e^- \rightleftharpoons H_2(g)$	0.000
$2H_2O(l) + 2e^- \rightleftharpoons H_2(g) + 2OH^-(aq)$	-0.83
$HO_2^-(aq) + H_2O(l) + 2e^- \rightleftharpoons 3OH^-(aq)$	$+0.88$
$H_2O_2(aq) + 2H^+(aq) + 2e^- \rightleftharpoons 2H_2O(l)$	$+1.776$
$Hg_2^{2+}(aq) + 2e^- \rightleftharpoons 2Hg(l)$	$+0.789$
$2Hg^{2+}(aq) + 2e^- \rightleftharpoons Hg_2^{2+}(aq)$	$+0.920$
$Hg^{2+}(aq) + 2e^- \rightleftharpoons Hg(l)$	$+0.854$
$I_2(s) + 2e^- \rightleftharpoons 2I^-(aq)$	$+0.536$
$IO_3^-(aq) + 6H^+(aq) + 5e^- \rightleftharpoons \frac{1}{2}I_2(s) + 3H_2O(l)$	$+1.195$
$K^+(aq) + e^- \rightleftharpoons K(s)$	-2.925
$Li^+(aq) + e^- \rightleftharpoons Li(s)$	-3.05
$Mg^{2+}(aq) + 2e^- \rightleftharpoons Mg(s)$	-2.37
$Mn^{2+}(aq) + 2e^- \rightleftharpoons Mn(s)$	-1.18
$MnO_2(s) + 4H^+(aq) + 2e^- \rightleftharpoons Mn^{2+}(aq) + 2H_2O(l)$	$+1.23$
$MnO_4^-(aq) + 8H^+(aq) + 5e^- \rightleftharpoons Mn^{2+}(aq) + 4H_2O(l)$	$+1.51$
$MnO_4^-(aq) + 2H_2O(l) + 3e^- \rightleftharpoons MnO_2(s) + 4OH^-(aq)$	$+0.59$
$HNO_2(aq) + H^+(aq) + e^- \rightleftharpoons NO(g) + H_2O(l)$	$+1.00$
$N_2(g) + 4H_2O(l) + 4e^- \rightleftharpoons 4OH^-(aq) + N_2H_4(aq)$	-1.16
$N_2(g) + 5H^+(aq) + 4e^- \rightleftharpoons N_2H_5^+(aq)$	-0.23
$NO_3^-(aq) + 4H^+(aq) + 3e^- \rightleftharpoons NO(g) + 2H_2O(l)$	$+0.96$
$Na^+(aq) + e^- \rightleftharpoons Na(s)$	-2.71
$Ni^{2+}(aq) + 2e^- \rightleftharpoons Ni(s)$	-0.28
$O_2(g) + 4H^+(aq) + 4e^- \rightleftharpoons 2H_2O(l)$	$+1.23$
$O_2(g) + 2H_2O(l) + 4e^- \rightleftharpoons 4OH^-(aq)$	$+0.40$
$O_2(g) + 2H^+(aq) + 2e^- \rightleftharpoons H_2O_2(aq)$	$+0.68$
$O_3(g) + 2H^+(aq) + 2e^- \rightleftharpoons O_2(g) + H_2O(l)$	$+2.07$
$Pb^{2+}(aq) + 2e^- \rightleftharpoons Pb(s)$	-0.126
$PbO_2(s) + HSO_4^-(aq) + 3H^+(aq) + 2e^- \rightleftharpoons PbSO_4(s) + 2H_2O(l)$	$+1.685$
$PbSO_4(s) + H^+(aq) + 2e^- \rightleftharpoons Pb(s) + HSO_4^-(aq)$	-0.356
$PtCl_4^{2-}(aq) + 2e^- \rightleftharpoons Pt(s) + 4Cl^-(aq)$	$+0.73$
$S(s) + 2H^+(aq) + 2e^- \rightleftharpoons H_2S(g)$	$+0.141$
$H_2SO_3(aq) + 4H^+(aq) + 4e^- \rightleftharpoons S(s) + 3H_2O(l)$	$+0.45$
$HSO_4^-(aq) + 3H^+(aq) + 2e^- \rightleftharpoons H_2SO_3(aq) + H_2O(l)$	$+0.17$
$Sn^{2+}(aq) + 2e^- \rightleftharpoons Sn(s)$	-0.136
$Sn^{4+}(aq) + 2e^- \rightleftharpoons Sn^{2+}(aq)$	$+0.154$
$VO_2^+(aq) + 2H^+(aq) + e^- \rightleftharpoons VO^{2+}(aq) + H_2O(l)$	$+1.00$
$Zn^{2+}(aq) + 2e^- \rightleftharpoons Zn(s)$	-0.763

Answers to Selected Exercises

Chapter 1

1.1 (a) Liquid; (b) solid; (c) gas; (d) gas. **1.3** (a) Chemical; (b) physical; (c) chemical; (d) physical. **1.5** Physical properties: silvery white; lustrous; melting point = 649°C; boiling point = 1105°C; density at 20°C = 1.738 g/cm³; pounded into sheets; drawn into wires; good conductor. Chemical properties: burns in air; reacts with Cl_2. **1.7** (a) Heterogeneous mixture; (b) pure substance; (c) homogeneous mixture; (d) pure substance. **1.9** (a) C; (b) Na; (c) Fe; (d) P; (e) K; (f) Cl; (g) N; (h) Ag. **1.11** The classification of a pure substance as an element was determined by whether it could be broken down into component elements. If the results of all attempted decompositions were negative, the substance was considered an element. **1.13** (a) Meters; (b) (meters)²; (c) (meters)³; (d) kilograms; (e) meters/second; (f) kelvins. **1.15** (a) 1×10^{-1}; (b) 1×10^{-2}; (c) 1×10^{-15}; (d) 1×10^{-6}; (e) 1×10^{6}; (f) 1×10^{3}; (g) 1×10^{-9}; (h) 1×10^{-3}; (i) 1×10^{-12}. **1.17** (a) Volume; (b) area; (c) volume; (d) density; (e) time; (f) length; (g) temperature. **1.19** (a) 0.454 g; (b) 5.0×10^{1} nm; (c) 76 μL; (d) 1.55 g/L. **1.21** (a) 1.49 g/mL; (b) 1.17×10^{3} g; (c) 101 cm³. **1.23** (a) 20°C; (b) -34.1°F; (c) 258 K; (d) 288°F; (e) 1088.7 K. **1.25** Exact: (a), (d), (e), (f). **1.27** (a) 3; (b) 4; (c) 3; (d) 4; (e) 5. **1.29** (a) 1.235×10^{7}; (b) 2.355; (c) 4.565×10^{5}; (d) 3.218×10^{3}; (e) 6.570×10^{-4}; (f) 1.005×10^{5}. **1.31** (a) 69.040; (b) -476; (c) 1.09×10^{4}; (d) 3917.0. **1.33** (a) 5.79×10^{3} m; (b) 1.73×10^{5} s; (c) \$0.515/L; (d) 5.0×10^{-6} m/s; (e) 37.99 m/s; (f) 9.444×10^{5} cm³. **1.35** (a) 45 L; (b) 7.6 mi/hr; (c) 5.24 L. **1.37** 3.6×10^{2} kg. **1.39** 2.54 L. **1.41** 3.8×10^{10} mL. **1.43** Behavior when pressure is applied, or density, or boiling point. **1.45** Physical properties: reddish-brown liquid at room temperature; vaporizes readily; red vapor; boiling point = 58.8°C; freezing point = -7.2°C; density (g) = 7.59 g/L; density (l) = 3.12 g/mL (at 20°C). Chemical properties: reacts readily with many metals including iron and aluminum. **1.48** (a) m/s²; (b) kg-m/s²; (c) kg-m²/s²; (d) kg/m-s²; (e) kg-m²/s³. **1.50** 4.3 K; -452.0°F. **1.52** (a) 1.106×10^{13} g; (b) 5.194×10^{-3} km³. **1.55** (a) 3.9×10^{11} mm; (b) 0.58 Ms. **1.57** (a) 0.16¢/L; (b) \$1000/yr. **1.59** (a) 1.91×10^{4} cm³; (b) 0.56 m³; (c) 7.6×10^{3} kg H_2O. **1.61** (a) 61.5%; (b) 15-karat gold.

Chapter 2

2.1 (a) In nitrogen dioxide, the nitrogen and oxygen atoms have chemically combined to form molecules, the relative number of nitrogen and oxygen atoms is the same in each molecule, and the molecules cannot be broken down by physical means into elemental nitrogen and oxygen. (b) In air, nitrogen and oxygen molecules exist independently; the properties of this mixture are an average of the properties of the components. The mixture can be separated by physical means, such as selective condensation, into the component elements. **2.3** (a) A: 2.37 g fluorine/1 g sulfur; B: 0.59 g fluorine/1 g sulfur; C: 3.55 g fluorine/1 g sulfur; (b) The masses in part (a) are in the ratio of small whole numbers (4 : 1 : 6) and, therefore, obey the law of multiple proportions. **2.5** The total mass of the products of a reaction must equal the total mass of the reactants. Therefore, 11.0 g carbon dioxide is produced. **2.7** (1) Electric and magnetic fields deflected the rays in the same way they would deflect negatively charged particles. (2) A metal plate exposed to cathode rays acquired a negative charge. **2.9** 2.02×10^{13} electrons. **2.11** The diffuse positive charge in the "plum pudding" model would not produce a repulsion strong enough to deflect alpha particles at the large angles observed in the experiment. In Rutherford's model, the positive charge in an atom is concentrated in the small nucleus. If an alpha particle strikes a gold nucleus directly, it is deflected at a large angle. **2.13** (a) 0.47 nm; (b) 2.1×10^{7} Cs atoms. **2.15** (a) ^{20}Ne: 10 p, 10 n, 10 e; (b) ^{39}K: 19 p, 20 n, 19 e; (c) ^{48}Ti: 22 p, 26 n, 22 e; (d) ^{80}Br: 35 p, 45 n, 35 e; (e) ^{109}Ag: 47 p, 62 n, 47 e; (f) ^{137}Ba: 56 p, 81 n, 56 e.

2.17

Symbol	^{19}F	^{74}As	^{137}Ba	^{122}Sb	^{196}Pt
Protons	9	33	**56**	51	78
Neutrons	10	41	**81**	71	118
Electrons	9	33	56	**51**	**78**
Mass no.	19	74	137	122	**196**

2.19 (a) $^{23}_{11}$Na; (b) $^{51}_{23}$V; (c) $^{4}_{2}$He; (d) $^{37}_{17}$Cl; (e) $^{24}_{12}$Mg. **2.21** (a) Mn (metal); (b) P (nonmetal); (c) Al (metal); (d) Ar (nonmetal); (e) I (nonmetal); (f) Cr (metal); (g) Ge (metalloid). **2.23** (a) Cl, halogens (nonmetal); (b) Xe, noble gases (nonmetal); (c) Li, alkali metals (metal); (d) Ba, alkaline earth metals (metal); (e) S, chalcogens (nonmetal). **2.25** The molecular formula conveys more information because it indicates *both* the combining ratio of elements in the compound and the exact number of atoms of each element in a molecule of the compound. **2.27** (a) NO_2; (b) CH_2; (c) C_2HO_2; (d) P_2O_5; (e) CH_2O; (f) SO_3.

2.29

Symbol	$^{37}Cl^-$	$^{88}Sr^{2+}$	$^{44}Sc^{3+}$	$^{59}Ni^{2+}$	$^{31}P^{3-}$
Protons	17	38	**21**	**28**	15
Neutrons	20	50	**23**	**31**	**16**
Electrons	18	36	18	**26**	18
Net charge	1−	2+	**3+**	**2+**	**3−**

2.31 (a) Mg^{2+}; (b) S^{2-}; (c) Al^{3+}; (d) K^+; (e) Br^-; (f) Y^{3+}. **2.33** (a) $CaBr_2$; (b) NH_4Cl; (c) $Al(C_2H_3O_2)_3$; (d) K_2SO_4; (e) $Mg_3(PO_4)_2$; (f) $Ba(OH)_2$. **2.35** Molecular: (a) NO_2, (b) BF_3, (f) PF_5, (g) NF_3. Ionic: (c) Li_2O, (d) Sc_2O_3, (e) $CsBr$, (h) LaP. **2.37** Sulfate, SO_4^{2-}. Sulfite, SO_3^{2-}; sulfite has one less oxygen atom. Sulfide, S^{2-}; sulfide has no oxygen atoms. Hydrogen sulfate, HSO_4^-; H^+ added to SO_4^{2-} increases the net charge by 1+. **2.39** (a) Zinc chloride; (b) calcium cyanide; (c) copper(II) hydroxide; (d) barium nitrate; (e) potassium phosphate; (f) mercury(I) sulfide; (g) ammonium sulfate; (h) iron(III) fluoride; (i) sodium chromate; (j) chromium(III) carbonate. **2.41** (a) Ca_3N_2; (b) FeS; (c) $Cr_2(SO_4)_3$; (d) $Cu(C_2H_3O_2)_2$; (e) $Ca(HCO_3)_2$; (f) $KClO$. **2.43** (a) HNO_3; (b) HI; (c) H_2SO_3; (d) chlorous acid; (e) phosphoric acid; (f) carbonic acid. **2.45** (a) Dinitrogen pentoxide; (b) iodine heptafluoride; (c) xenon trioxide; (d) $SiCl_4$; (e) H_2Se; (f) P_4O_6. **2.47** (a) $ZnCO_3$, ZnO, CO_2; (b) HF, SiO_2, SiF_4, H_2O; (c) SO_2, H_2O, H_2SO_3; (d) H_3P (or PH_3); (e) $HClO_4$, Cd, $Cd(ClO_4)_2$; (f) VBr_3. **2.50** (a) Five significant figures; (b) 0.05444%. **2.53** Ca. **2.56** (a) NH_4^+, SO_4^{2-}, $(NH_4)_2SO_4$, ammonium sulfate; (b) Ca^{2+}, HCO_3^-, $Ca(HCO_3)_2$, calcium hydrogen carbonate (or calcium bicarbonate); (c) Al^{3+}, HSO_4^-, $Al(HSO_4)_3$, aluminum hydrogen sulfate (or aluminum bisulfate); (d) K^+, CrO_4^{2-}, K_2CrO_4, potassium chromate; (e) Na^+, $C_2H_3O_2^-$, $NaC_2H_3O_2$, sodium acetate; (f) Ag^+, S^{2-}, Ag_2S, silver sulfide; (g) Be^{2+}, Br^-, $BeBr_2$, beryllium bromide; (h) K^+, Te^{2-}, K_2Te, potassium telluride. **2.59** (a) CaS, $Ca(HS)_2$; (b) HBr, $HBrO_3$; (c) AlN, $Al(NO_2)_3$; (d) FeO, Fe_2O_3; (e) NH_3, NH_4^+; (f) K_2SO_3, $KHSO_3$; (g) Hg_2Cl_2, $HgCl_2$; (h) $HClO_3$, $HClO_4$.

Chapter 3

3.1 (a) Conservation of mass; (b) (g), (l) (s), (aq); (c) P_4, four phosphorus atoms bound together into a single molecule; 4P, four separate phosphorus atoms. **3.3** (a) $N_2O_5(g) + H_2O(l) \longrightarrow 2HNO_3(aq)$; (b) $(NH_4)_2Cr_2O_7(s) \longrightarrow N_2(g) + Cr_2O_3(s) + 4H_2O(l)$; (c) $PCl_3(l) + 3H_2O(l) \longrightarrow H_3PO_3(aq) + 3HCl(aq)$; (d) $Mg_3N_2(s) + 8HCl(aq) \longrightarrow 3MgCl_2(aq) + 2NH_4Cl(aq)$; (e) $2C_6H_6(l) + 15O_2(g) \longrightarrow 12CO_2(g) + 6H_2O(l)$; (f) $4C_3H_5NO(g) + 19O_2(g) \longrightarrow 12CO_2(g) + 4NO_2(g) + 10H_2O(l)$. **3.5** (a) $SO_3(g) + H_2O(l) \longrightarrow H_2SO_4(aq)$; (b) $B_2S_3(s) + 6H_2O(l) \longrightarrow 2H_3BO_3(aq) + 3H_2S(g)$; (c) $4PH_3(g) + 8O_2(g) \longrightarrow 6H_2O(g) + P_4O_{10}(s)$; (d) $2Hg(NO_3)_2(s) \longrightarrow 2HgO(s) + 4NO_2(g) + O_2(g)$; (e) $3H_2S(g) + 2Fe(OH)_3(s) \longrightarrow Fe_2S_3(s) + 6H_2O(g)$. **3.7** (a) $C_7H_{16}(l) + 11O_2(g) \longrightarrow 7CO_2(g) + 8H_2O(l)$; (b) $2CH_3OC_2H_5(l) + 9O_2(g) \longrightarrow 6CO_2(g) + 8H_2O(l)$; (c) $2Rb(s) + 2H_2O(l) \longrightarrow 2RbOH(aq) + H_2(g)$; (d)

$Mg(s) + Cl_2(g) \longrightarrow MgCl_2(s)$. **3.9** (a) $2KClO_3(s) \longrightarrow 2KCl(s) + 3O_2(g)$, decomposition; (b) $C_7H_8O_2(l) + 8O_2(g) \longrightarrow 7CO_2(g) + 4H_2O(l)$, combustion; (c) $2Cr(s) + 3Cl_2(g) \longrightarrow 2CrCl_3(s)$, combination; (d) $2SO_3(g) \longrightarrow 2SO_2(g) + O_2(g)$, decomposition. **3.11** (a) $2K(s) + 2NH_3(l) \longrightarrow 2KNH_2(solv) + H_2(g)$; (b) $4CH_3NO_2(g) + 7O_2(g) \longrightarrow 4NO_2(g) + 4CO_2(g) + 6H_2O(l)$; (c) $CH_4(g) + 4F_2(g) \longrightarrow CF_4(g) + 4HF(g)$. **3.13** (a) $^{12}_6C$. (b) An atomic mass unit is exactly 1/12 of the mass of one atom of ^{12}C, 1.66054×10^{-24} g. **3.15** 10.81 amu. **3.17** 93.05 (arbitrary units). **3.19** (a) 80.1 amu; (b) 138.0 amu; (c) 252.0 amu; (d) 142.3 amu; (e) 60.0 amu. **3.21** (a) 40.1% S, 59.9% O; (b) 7.79% C, 92.2% Cl; (c) 37.5% C, 12.5% H, 50.0% O; (d) 24.4% Ca, 17.1% N, 58.5% O; (e) 21.2% N, 6.06% H, 24.3% S, 48.4% O. **3.23** (a) 3; (b) 2.01566 amu, 3.02194 amu, 4.02822 amu; the mass ratios are 1: 1.5: 2; (c) ^1H—^1H (2.02 amu) is the largest. ^2H—^2H (4.03 amu) is the smallest. **3.25** (a) A *mole* is the amount of matter that contains as many objects as the number of atoms in exactly 12 g of ^{12}C. (b) 6.022×10^{23}. (c) The formula weight of a substance in amu has the same numerical value as the molar mass expressed in grams. **3.27** (a) 4.0×10^{22} H atoms; (b) 3.3×10^{21} $C_6H_{12}O_6$ molecules; (c) 5.5×10^{-3} mol; (d) 0.99 g $C_6H_{12}O_6$. **3.29** (a) 187.57 g; (b) 60.0 g $Cu(NO_3)_2$; (c) 2.77×10^{-2} mol; (d) 3.37×10^{19} N atoms. **3.31** (a) 0.416 g SO_2; (b) 3.04 g Ar; (c) 4.03×10^{-2} g $C_8H_{10}N_4O_2$. **3.33** (a) 2.11×10^{23} C_2H_4 molecules; (b) 1.71×10^{21} $C_6H_8O_6$ molecules; (c) 1.7×10^{18} H_2O molecules. **3.35** 3.28×10^{-8} mol C_2H_3Cl; 1.97×10^{16} molecules C_2H_3Cl. **3.37** An *empirical formula* gives the relative number and kind of each atom in a compound, but a *molecular formula* gives the actual number of each kind of atom in the molecule. **3.39** (a) C_3H_8; (b) SnF_4; (c) NH_2. **3.41** (a) $CSCl_2$; (b) C_3OF_6. **3.43** (a) Empirical and molecular formulas are $C_9H_{13}O_3N$; (b) empirical formula: C_5H_7N; molecular formula: $C_{10}H_{14}N_2$. **3.45** CH_2. **3.47** $x = 7$; $MgSO_4 \cdot 7H_2O$. **3.49** Molar mass of fungal laccase is approximately 6.5×10^4 g. **3.51** The mole ratios implicit in the coefficients of a balanced chemical equation are essential for solving stoichiometry problems. If the equation is not balanced, the mole ratios will be incorrect and lead to erroneous calculated amounts of reactants and products. **3.53** (a) 10.0 mol CO_2; (b) 9.55 g CO_2. **3.55** (a) 12.0 mol HF; (b) 31.5 g NaF; (c) 2.29 g Na_2SiO_3. **3.57** 4.36 kg NH_4ClO_4. **3.59** (a) $Al(OH)_3(s) + 3HCl(aq) \longrightarrow AlCl_3(aq) + 3H_2O(l)$; (b) 3.51 g HCl. **3.61** (a) The *limiting reagent* is the reactant that regulates the amount of products produced during a chemical reaction. The *excess reagent* is the other reactant or reactants. (b) The limiting reagent regulates the amount of products because it is completely used up during the reaction; no more product can be made when one of the reactants is unavailable. **3.63** (a) 2675 bicycles; (b) 458 frames leftover, 110 handlebars leftover; (c) the wheels. **3.65** (a) 3.34 g SiC; (b) 3.00 g C; (c) 1.67 g SiC. (d) SiO_2 is the limiting reactant and C is present in excess. (e) 1.00 g C remains. **3.67** 1.80 g Na_2S. **3.69** (a) C_6H_6 is the limiting reagent, and the theoretical yield is 60.3 g C_6H_5Br.

(b) 94.0% yield. **3.71** (a) $PBr_5(l) + 4H_2O(l) \longrightarrow$ $H_3PO_4(aq) + 5HBr(aq)$; (b) $Li_3N(s) + 3H_2O(l) \longrightarrow$ $NH_3(g) + 3LiOH(aq)$; (c) $C_4H_9OH(l) + 6O_2(g) \longrightarrow$ $4O_2(g) + 5H_2O(l)$. **3.74** (a) $^{69}_{31}Ga$: 31 p, 38 n; $^{71}_{31}Ga$: 31 p, 40 n; (b) 60.3% $^{69}_{31}Ga$ and 39.7% $^{71}_{31}Ga$. **3.77** (a) 5.2×10^{20} C_5H_5N molecules; (b) 71 ZnO units: 1 C_5H_5N molecule; (c) 46 $Å^2/C_5H_5N$ molecule. **3.80** 14.010 (calculated) vs. 14.007 (accepted value). **3.82** $C_8H_8O_3$. **3.84** 4.85% Cl; 34.21% Br. **3.86** 2.2 kg H_2O. **3.88** 5.0 mol H_2; 3.0 mol N_2. **3.90** 10.2 g $KClO_3$; 20.0 g $KHCO_3$; 13.8 g K_2CO_3; 56.0 g KCl. **3.92** (a) $2C_2H_2(g) + 5O_2(g) \longrightarrow 4CO_2(g) + 2H_2O(g)$; (b) O_2 limits; (c) 0.0 g O_2; 6.74 g C_2H_2; 11.0 g CO_2; 2.25 g H_2O.

Chapter 4

4.1 Intensive; the *ratio* of amount of solute to total amount of solution is the same, regardless of how much solution is present. **4.3** 17.5 g solute. **4.5** (a) 0.144 M NH_4Cl; (b) 0.123 mol HNO_3; (c) 167 mL of 1.50 M KOH. **4.7** (a) 2.98 g KBr; (b) 2.13 g Na_2SO_4; (c) 2.09 g $KBrO_3$; (d) 15.3 g $C_6H_{12}O_6$. **4.9** Add 12.8 g $C_{12}H_{22}O_{11}$ to a 250-mL volumetric flask, dissolve in a small volume of water, and add water to the mark on the neck of the flask. Agitate thoroughly to ensure total mixing. **4.11** Thoroughly clean, rinse, and fill a 50-mL buret with the 1.50 M $C_{12}H_{22}O_{11}$. Dispense 33.3 mL of this solution into a 500-mL volumetric flask, add water to the mark, and mix thoroughly. **4.13** 1.747 M $HC_2H_3O_2$. **4.15** Tap water contains enough dissolved electrolytes to complete a circuit between an electrical appliance and our body, producing a shock. **4.17** (a) HBrO, weak electrolyte; (b) HNO_3, strong electrolyte; (c) KOH, strong electrolyte; (d) $CoSO_4$, strong electrolyte; (e) $C_{12}H_{22}O_{11}$, nonelectrolyte; (f) O_2, nonelectrolyte. **4.19** (a) 0.14 M Na^+, 0.14 M OH^-, 0.28 M total; (b) 0.25 M Ca^{2+}, 0.50 M Br^-, 0.75 M total; (c) 0.25 M CH_3OH; (d) 0.13 M K^+, 0.13 M ClO_3^-, 0.13 M Na^+, 0.067 M SO_4^{2-}, 0.46 M total. **4.21** 0.15 M $K_2Cr_2O_7$. **4.23** H_3PO_3. **4.25** (a) A *monoprotic acid* has one ionizable (acidic) H, whereas a *diprotic acid* has two. (b) A *strong acid* is completely ionized in aqueous solution, whereas only a fraction of *weak acid* molecules are ionized. (c) An *acid* is a H^+ donor, and a *base* is a H^+ acceptor. **4.27** The single arrow indicates that HNO_3 is completely dissociated into H^+ and NO_3^- in aqueous solution. The double arrow indicates that HCN is only partially ionized and exists as a mixture of H^+, CN^-, and undissociated HCN molecules in solution. **4.29** (a) $Ba(OH)_2(s) + 2HNO_3(aq) \longrightarrow Ba(NO_3)_2(aq) + 2H_2O(l)$; (b) $H_3PO_4(aq) + 3KOH(aq) \longrightarrow K_3PO_4(aq) + 3H_2O(l)$; (c) $2Y(OH)_3(s) + 3H_2SO_4(aq) \longrightarrow Y_2(SO_4)_3(aq) + 6H_2O(l)$. **4.31** (a) $Pb^{2+}(aq) + SO_4^{2-}(aq) \longrightarrow PbSO_4(s)$; spectators: Na^+, NO_3^-; (b) $Zn(s) + 2H^+(aq) \longrightarrow$ $Zn^{2+}(aq) + H_2(g)$; spectator: Cl^-; (c) $FeO(s) +$ $2H^+(aq) \longrightarrow H_2O(l) + Fe^{2+}(aq)$; spectator: ClO_4^-. **4.33** The driving force in a metathesis reaction is the formation of a product that removes ions from solution.

Driving forces in Exercise 4.32: (a) $H_2O(l)$, nonelectrolyte; (b) $H_2O(l)$, nonelectrolyte; $CO_2(g)$, gas; (c) $Cu(OH)_2(s)$, precipitate. **4.35** (a) Insoluble; (b) soluble; (c) soluble; (d) insoluble; (e) soluble. **4.37** Ba^{2+}. **4.39** (a) $ZnS(s) + 2H^+(aq) \longrightarrow H_2S(g) + Zn^{2+}(aq)$; (b) $Ba^{2+}(aq) + CO_3^{2-}(aq) \longrightarrow BaCO_3(s)$; (c) $3H^+(aq) +$ $PO_4^{3-}(aq) \longrightarrow H_3PO_4(aq)$; (d) $H^+(aq) + OH^-(aq) \longrightarrow$ $H_2O(l)$; (e) $Sr^{2+}(aq) + SO_4^{2-}(aq) \longrightarrow SrSO_4(s)$; (f) $SO_3^{2-}(aq) + 2H^+(aq) \longrightarrow H_2SO_3(aq) \longrightarrow H_2O(l) +$ $SO_2(g)$; (g) $Pb^{2+}(aq) + H_2S(aq) \longrightarrow PbS(s) + 2H^+(aq)$; (h) $Fe(OH)_3(s) + 3H^+(aq) \longrightarrow Fe^{3+}(aq) + 3H_2O(l)$. **4.41** The most easily oxidized metals are near the bottom of groups on the left side of the chart, especially groups 1A and 2A. The least easily oxidized metals are on the lower right of the transition metals, particularly those near the bottom of groups 8B and 1B. **4.43** (a) $2HCl(aq) + Ni(s) \longrightarrow NiCl_2(aq) + H_2(g)$; $Ni(s) +$ $2H^+(aq) \longrightarrow Ni^{2+}(aq) + H_2(g)$; (b) $H_2SO_4(aq) +$ $Fe(s) \longrightarrow FeSO_4(aq) + H_2(g)$; $Fe(s) + 2H^+(aq) \longrightarrow$ $Fe^{2+}(aq) + H_2(g)$; (c) $2HBr(aq) + Zn(s) \longrightarrow$ $ZnBr_2(aq) + H_2(g)$; $Zn(s) + 2H^+(aq) \longrightarrow Zn^{2+}(aq) +$ $H_2(g)$; (d) $2HC_2H_3O_2(aq) + Mg(s) \longrightarrow$ $Mg(C_2H_3O_2)_2(aq) + H_2(g)$; $Mg(s) + 2HC_2H_3O_2(aq) \longrightarrow$ $Mg^{2+}(aq) + 2C_2H_3O_2^-(aq) + H_2(g)$. **4.45** (a) $2Al(s) +$ $3NiCl_2(aq) \longrightarrow 2AlCl_3(aq) + 3Ni(s)$; (b) no reaction; (c) $2Cr(s) + 3NiSO_4(aq) \longrightarrow Cr_2(SO_4)_3(aq) + 3Ni(s)$; (d) $Mn(s) + 2HBr(aq) \longrightarrow MnBr_2(aq) + H_2(g)$; (e) $H_2(g) + CuCl_2(aq) \longrightarrow Cu(s) + 2HCl(aq)$; (f) $Ba(s) +$ $2H_2O(l) \longrightarrow Ba(OH)_2(aq) + H_2(g)$. **4.47** (a) (i) $Zn(s) + Cd^{2+}(aq) \longrightarrow Cd(s) + Zn^{2+}(aq)$; (ii) $Cd(s) +$ $Ni^{2+}(aq) \longrightarrow Ni(s) + Cd^{2+}(aq)$. (b) Cd is between Zn and Ni in the activity series. (c) Place an iron strip in $CdCl_2(aq)$. If $Cd(s)$ is deposited, Cd is less active than Fe; if there is no reaction, Cd is more active than Fe. Do the same test with Co if Cd is less active than Fe or with Cr if Cd is more active than Fe. **4.49** In a mixture of the two acids, NO_3^- initiates the oxidation of Au to Au^{3+}, and Cl^- stabilizes the Au^{3+} as $AuCl_4^-$ anion. The stability of $AuCl_4^-$ is the driving force for the oxidation of gold in aqua regia. **4.51** (a) 41.7 mL of 0.105 M $HClO_4$; (b) 623 mL of 0.158 M HCl; (c) 0.465 M $AgNO_3$; (d) 0.235 g KOH. **4.53** 25 g $NaHCO_3$. **4.55** 1.22×10^{-2} M $Ca(OH)_2$ solution; the solubility of $Ca(OH)_2$ is 0.0904 g in 100 mL soln. **4.58** 1.60 M HCl. **4.61** (a) $Al(OH)_3(s) + 3H^+(aq) \longrightarrow Al^{3+}(aq) +$ $3H_2O(l)$; (b) $Mg(OH)_2(s) + 2H^+(aq) \longrightarrow Mg^{2+}(aq) +$ $2H_2O(l)$; (c) $MgCO_3(s) + 2H^+(aq) \longrightarrow Mg^{2+}(aq) +$ $H_2O(l) + CO_2(g)$; (d) $NaAl(CO_3)(OH)_2(s) +$ $4H^+(aq) \longrightarrow Na^+(aq) + Al^{3+}(aq) + 3H_2O(l) + CO_2(g)$; (e) $CaCO_3(s) + 2H^+(aq) \longrightarrow Ca^{2+}(aq) + H_2O(l) +$ $CO_2(g)$. **4.64** (a) No reaction; (b) $Zn^{2+}(aq) + Pb^0(s)$; (c) no reaction; (d) $Zn^{2+}(aq) + Fe^0(s)$; (e) $Zn^{2+}(aq) +$ $Cu^0(s)$; (f) no reaction. **4.67** $H_2C_4H_4O_6 +$ $2OH^-(aq) \longrightarrow C_4H_4O_6^{2-}(aq) + 2H_2O(l)$; 0.05655 M $H_2C_4H_4O_6$ soln.

Chapter 5

5.1 (a) *Work* is a force applied over a distance. (b) The amount of work done is the magnitude of the force times the distance over which it is applied: $w = F \times d$. **5.3** (a) Electrostatic repulsion; no work is done because the particles are held stationary. (b) Gravity; work is done because the force of gravity is opposed and the paper clip is lifted. **5.5** (a) 84 J; (b) 20 cal. (c) As the ball hits the tree, its speed (hence its kinetic energy) drops to zero. Most of the kinetic energy is transferred to the potential energy of a slightly deformed golf ball, and some is absorbed by the tree. As the ball bounces off the tree, the potential energy is reconverted to kinetic energy. **5.7** 1 Btu = 1054 J. **5.9** (a) Energy can be neither created nor destroyed, but it can be changed in form. (b) The system is the part of the universe whose energy changes are being described. (c) The energy change of a system is equal in magnitude and opposite in sign to that of its surroundings. **5.11** (a) $\Delta E = -22$ J, decreased; (b) $\Delta E = -2.3$ kJ, decreased; (c) $\Delta E = +15$ J, increased. **5.13** (a) A *state function* is a property that depends only on the physical state (pressure, temperature, etc.) of the system, not on the route used to get to the current state. (b) Internal energy *is* a state function; work *is not* a state function. (c) Temperature is a state function; regardless of how hot or cold the sample has been, the temperature depends only on its present condition. **5.15** (a) Exothermic; (b) $-\Delta H$; (c) $\Delta H = q$. **5.17** (a) Exothermic; (b) endothermic; (c) exothermic; (d) exothermic; (e) endothermic. **5.19** $\Delta H = -135$ kJ, $\Delta E = -198$ kJ. **5.21** (a) $CH_3OH(l) + 2O_2(g) \longrightarrow 2H_2O(l) + CO_2(g)$, $\Delta H = -726.7$ kJ (b)

$$CH_3OH(l) + 2O_2(g)$$
$$\Delta H = \boxed{-726.7 \text{ kJ}}$$
$$2H_2O(l) + CO_2(g)$$

5.23 (a) Endothermic; (b) $+18.5$ kJ of heat transferred, ΔH_{sys} increases; (c) 0.343 g N_2; (d) 27.8 kJ of heat produced, ΔH_{sys} decreases. **5.25** (a) -13.1 kJ; (b) -1.14 kJ; (c) $+22.9$ kJ. **5.27** Enthalpy of $H_2O(s) < H_2O(l) < H_2O(g)$. Heat must be added to convert solid to liquid to gas. **5.29** (a) 4.18 J/g-K; (b) 1.46×10^3 J/K; (c) 355 kJ. **5.31** 7.60×10^3 J. **5.33** $\Delta H = -44.4$ kJ/mol NaOH. **5.35** $\Delta H = -48.1$ kJ/g C_8H_{18} or -5.49×10^3 kJ/mol C_8H_{18}. **5.37** (a) Heat capacity of the complete calorimeter = 8.67 kJ/°C; (b) heat capacity of the empty calorimeter = 2.39 kJ/°C; (c) $\Delta T = 4.82$°C. **5.39** If a reaction can be described as a series of steps, ΔH for the reaction is the sum of the enthalpy changes for each step. As long as we can describe a route where ΔH for each step is known, ΔH for any process can be calculated. **5.41** $\Delta H_{rxn} = +297$ kJ. **5.43** $\Delta H_{rxn} = -2.49 \times 10^3$ kJ. **5.45** (a) $\frac{1}{2}N_2(g) + \frac{3}{2}H_2(g) \longrightarrow NH_3(g)$, $\Delta H_f = -46.19$ kJ; (b) $\frac{1}{2}N_2(g) + \frac{1}{2}O_2(g) + \frac{1}{2}Cl_2(g) \longrightarrow NOCl(g)$, $\Delta H_f = +52.6$ kJ; (c) $C(s) + 2H_2(g) + \frac{1}{2}O_2(g) \longrightarrow CH_3OH(l)$, $\Delta H_f = -238.6$ kJ; (d) $K(s) + \frac{1}{2}Cl_2(g) + \frac{3}{2}O_2(g) \longrightarrow KClO_3(s)$, $\Delta H_f = -391.2$ kJ. **5.47** $\Delta H_{rxn}^\circ = -847.6$ kJ. **5.49** (a) $\Delta H_{rxn}^\circ = -38.9$ kJ; (b) $\Delta H_{rxn}^\circ = -36.4$ kJ; (c) $\Delta H_{rxn}^\circ = -1300.0$ kJ; (d) $\Delta H_{rxn}^\circ = -876.9$ kJ. **5.51** ΔH_f° for

$CaC_2(s) = -60.6$ kJ. **5.53** ΔH_f° for $Mg(OH)_2(s) = -924.8$ kJ. **5.55** 1.6×10^2 Cal. **5.57** 59.7 Cal. **5.59** $\Delta H_{comb} = -1849.5$ kJ/mol C_3H_4, -1926.3 kJ/mol C_3H_6, -2043.9 kJ/mol C_3H_8; (b) $\Delta H_{comb} = 4.6162 \times 10^4$ kJ/kg C_3H_4, 4.5777×10^4 kJ/kg C_3H_6; 4.6351×10^4 kJ/kg C_3H_8; (c) These three substances yield nearly identical quantities of heat per unit mass, but propane is marginally higher than the other two. **5.61** Since the temperature of the system decreases when water freezes, heat is removed, ΔH_{sys} is negative, and the process is exothermic. Melting is the opposite of freezing; heat is gained by the system, and the process endothermic. **5.63** $w = -0.23$ kJ. The negative sign for w indicates that work is done by the system on the surroundings. **5.66** 1.0×10^4 or 10,000 bricks. **5.68** $\Delta H = -52$ kJ. **5.70** The heat of combustion of pure $C_7O_3H_6 = 3.00 \times 10^3$ kJ/mol. The heat of combustion of the sample = 1.35×10^3 kJ/ 138.1 g. The sample yields 45.0% of the expected heat; the mass percent of boric oxide impurity is 55.0%. **5.72** ΔH_f° for $TiO_2(s) = -939.7$ kJ/mol. **5.75** (a) $\Delta H_{rxn}^\circ = -631.1$ kJ. (b) Since the reaction is exothermic, the product, 1 mol of $C_6H_6(l)$, has less enthalpy than the reactants, 3 mol of $C_2H_2(g)$. (c) The fuel value of C_2H_2 is 50 kJ/g. The fuel value of C_6H_6 is 42 kJ/g.

Chapter 6

6.1 (a) Meters; (b) 1/second; (c) meters/second. **6.3** Wavelength of (a) gamma rays < (d) yellow (visible) light < (e) red (visible) light < (b) 93.1-MHz FM (radio) waves < (c) 680-kHz or 0.680-MHz AM (radio) waves. **6.5** (a) $\lambda = 481$ nm; (b) $\nu = 8.45 \times 10^{13}$ s^{-1}. (c) The radiation in part (a) is visible; the radiation in part (b) is not visible. (d) 4.50×10^{10} m. **6.7** $\nu = 4.87 \times 10^{14}$ s^{-1}; the color is orange. **6.9** *Quantization* means that energy can be absorbed or emitted only in specific amounts or multiples of this amount. This minimum amount of energy is equal to a constant times the frequency of the radiation absorbed or emitted, $E = h\nu$. **6.11** (a) $E = 4.91 \times 10^{-19}$ J; (b) $E = 4.2 \times 10^{-20}$ J; (c) $\lambda = 7.03 \times 10^{-7}$ m. **6.13** $\lambda = 1.54$ Å, $E = 1.29 \times 10^{-15}$ J; $\nu = 5.87 \times 10^{10}$ s^{-1}, $E = 3.89 \times 10^{-23}$ J. $E_{micro} < E_{X-ray}$. **6.15** 1.46×10^{22} photons. **6.17** Maximum $\lambda = 242$ nm; this is ultraviolet radiation. **6.19** (a) $E_{min} = 3.69 \times 10^{-19}$ J; (b) $\lambda = 539$ nm; (c) visible; (d) $E_{510} = 3.90 \times 10^{-19}$ J. The difference between these energy values is the maximum possible kinetic energy of the electron. $E_k = 2.1 \times 10^{-20}$ J/electron. **6.21** A *continuous spectrum* contains light of all wavelengths; a *line spectrum* contains only a few specific wavelengths. **6.23** (a) Emitted; (b) absorbed; (c) absorbed. **6.25** (a) $\Delta E = 1.94 \times 10^{-18}$ J absorbed, $\nu = 2.92 \times 10^{15}$ s^{-1}, $\lambda = 1.03 \times 10^{-7}$ m; (b) $\Delta E = 4.58 \times 10^{-19}$ J absorbed, $\nu = 6.91 \times 10^{14}$ s^{-1}, $\lambda = 4.34 \times 10^{-7}$ m; (c) $\Delta E = 1.61 \times 10^{-20}$ J absorbed, $\nu = 2.43 \times 10^{13}$ s^{-1}, $\lambda = 1.24 \times 10^{-5}$ m. **6.27** $\lambda = 434$ nm. This is the "blue" line in the visible portion of the emission spectrum of hydrogen shown in Figure 6.12(a). **6.29** (a) $\lambda = 4.7 \times 10^{-37}$ m; (b) $\lambda = 3.3 \times 10^{-35}$ m; (c) $\lambda = 8.9 \times 10^{-14}$ m. **6.31** $\nu = 4.5 \times 10^3$ m/s. **6.33** The quantity ψ^2, at a given point in space, is the probability of locating an electron within a small volume element

around that point at any given instant. **6.35** (a) $n = 5$, $l = 4, 3, 2, 1, 0$; (b) $l = 2$, $m_l = -2, -1, 0, 1, 2$.
6.37 (a) $4, 2, -2$; $4, 2, -1$; $4, 2, 0$; $4, 2, 1$; $4, 2, 2$; (b) $3, 0, 0$; $3, 1, -1$; $3, 1, 0$; $3, 1, 1$; $3, 2, -2$; $3, 2, -1$; $3, 2, 0$; $3, 2, 1$; $3, 2, 2$. **6.39** (a) Permissible, $2p$; (b) not permissible; (c) permissible, $4d$; (d) not permissible.
6.41 $3d$, $6p$, $3s$ are permissible.
6.43

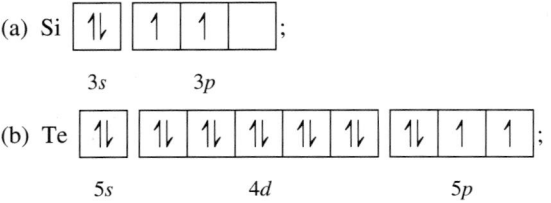

(a)   (b)

(c)

6.45 (a) The $2s$ and $3s$ orbitals have the same overall spherical shape, but the $3s$ orbital has a larger radial extension and one more node than the $2s$ orbital. (b) The shapes of the $2s$ and $2p_x$ are different (spherical vs. dumbbell), while the average distance from the nucleus of an electron occupying either orbital is similar. (c) In the hydrogen atom, $2s$ and $2p_x$ have the same energy and $3s$ is at a higher energy. **6.47** (a) The principal quantum number, n; (b) both the principal and azimuthal quantum numbers, n and l. **6.49** A $3s$ electron has a greater probability of being close to the nucleus than does a $3d$ electron, and so it is less effectively shielded from the nuclear charge by the inner electrons ($1s$, $2s$, $2p$) than is a $3d$ electron. **6.51** The $3s$ electron in Mg experiences a total nuclear charge ($Z = 12$) that is 1 higher than that in Na ($Z = 11$). This added unit of nuclear charge is partially but not totally canceled by the presence of a second $3s$ electron. The overall effect is an increase in the effective nuclear charge for Mg. **6.53** (a) 10; (b) 2; (c) 6; (d) 14. **6.55** Li: $1s^2 2s^1$. $1s$ electrons: $1, 0, 0, \frac{1}{2}$; $1, 0, 0, -\frac{1}{2}$. $2s$ electron: $2, 0, 0, \frac{1}{2}$ or $2, 0, 0, -\frac{1}{2}$. **6.57** (a) Ca, [Ar]$4s^2$; (b) Ge, [Ar]$4s^2 3d^{10} 4p^2$; (c) Br, [Ar]$4s^2 3d^{10} 4p^5$; (d) Co, [Ar]$4s^2 3d^7$; (e) Eu, [Xe]$6s^2 4f^7$; (f) Hf, [Xe]$6s^2 4f^{14} 5d^2$.
6.59

(a) Si [diagram] $3s$ $3p$;

(b) Te [diagram] $5s$ $4d$ $5p$;

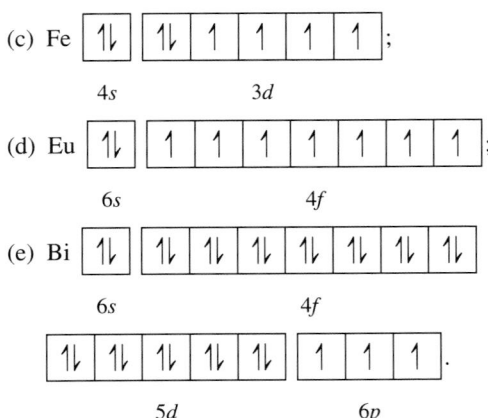

(c) Fe [diagram] $4s$ $3d$;

(d) Eu [diagram] $6s$ $4f$;

(e) Bi [diagram] $6s$ $4f$ [diagram] $5d$ $6p$.

(a) two unpaired electrons; (b) two unpaired electrons; (c) four unpaired electrons; (d) seven unpaired electrons; (e) three unpaired electrons.
6.61 (a) O; (b) Cl; (c) K; (d) Cr. **6.63** (a) $\lambda_A = 6.0 \times 10^{-7}$ m, $\lambda_B = 12 \times 10^{-7}$ m; (b) $\nu_A = 5.0 \times 10^{-14}$ s^{-1}, $\nu_B = 2.5 \times 10^{14}$ s^{-1}; (c) A—visible, B—infrared.
6.65 4.20 hr. **6.67** 78.9 kJ/mol is absorbed by the system. **6.70** $\Delta H_{rxn} = 105.2$ kJ/mol O_3; $\Delta H_{rxn} = 1.747 \times 10^{-19}$ J/O_3 atom; maximum $\lambda = 1.137 \times 10^{-6}$ m; radiation with this wavelength is in the infrared portion of the spectrum. **6.73** 2.18×10^{-18} J/atom, 1.31×10^3 kJ/mol.
6.76 (a) $2s$; (b) $4d$; (c) $5p$; (d) $3d$; (e) $4f$. **6.78** In a Cl atom, the $3p$ electrons experience the smallest effective nuclear charge because they are shielded by all the core electrons and to some extent by the $3s$ electrons. The $1s$ electrons experience the greatest effective nuclear charge because they are not shielded by inner electrons.
6.81 (a) Cd: $1s^2 2s^2 2p^6 3s^2 3p^6 4s^2 3d^{10} 4p^6 5s^2 4d^{10}$; (b) As: $1s^2 2s^2 2p^6 3s^2 3p^6 4s^2 3d^{10} 4p^3$; (c) La: $1s^2 2s^2 2p^6 3s^2 3p^6 4s^2 3d^{10} 4p^6 5s^2 4d^{10} 5p^6 6s^2 5d^1$; (d) Pd: $1s^2 2s^2 2p^6 3s^2 3p^6 4s^2 3d^{10} 4p^6 5s^2 4d^8$; (e) S: $1s^2 2s^2 2p^6 3s^2 3p^4$. **6.84** (a) O, excited; (b) Br, ground; (c) P, excited; (d) In, ground.

Chapter 7

7.1 (a) Mendeleev noted that certain chemical and physical properties recur periodically. He arranged the known elements by increasing atomic weight so that elements with similar properties were in the same family or vertical column. (b) Mosely proposed that each element be assigned an integer or atomic number which corresponded to the charge on the nucleus of the atom. If the elements are arranged by increasing atomic number, a few seeming contradictions in the Mendeleev table are eliminated.
7.3 On a plot of the radial electron density of an atom, there are certain distances from the nucleus where there are high electron densities. The number of these maxima corresponds to the number of *electron shells* or principal quantum levels in the atom. **7.5** Rh < Ti < K < P < Mg. **7.7** The quantum-mechanical description of the atom does not specify the exact location of electrons;

electron density decreases gradually as the distance from the nucleus increases. There is no quantum-mechanical "edge" of an atom. **7.9** $r_{Cl} = 0.995$ Å, $r_P = 1.05$ Å. **7.11** (a) Decrease; (b) increase; (c) B < Si < Al < Ge. **7.13** $Z = 2$ for He and $Z = 1$ for H. The electrons in H and He are in the $n = 1$ shell; those in He experience a greater nuclear charge and are drawn closer to the nucleus. Valence electrons in Ne are in the $n = 2$ shell and those of He are in the $n = 1$ shell. He is smaller because the valence electrons are closer to the nucleus and are not shielded from the full nuclear charge. **7.15** $Sc^+ \longrightarrow Sc^{2+} + 1e^-$; $Sc^{2+} \longrightarrow Sc^{3+} + 1e^-$. **7.17** Much more energy is required to remove a $1s$ core electron close to the nucleus of Li^+ than to remove a $2s$ valence electron farther from the nucleus of Be^+. **7.19** (a) F; (b) N; (c) Hf; (d) O; (e) Ge. **7.21** First ionization energies increase going from K to Ar, and atomic sizes decrease. As valence electrons are drawn closer to the nucleus (atom size decreases), more energy is required to completely remove them from the atom (first ionization energy increases). **7.23** The effective nuclear charge in Si^{3+} is greater. According to Table 7.2, I_4 for Si is greater than I_3 for Al; more energy is required to remove a valence electron from Si^{3+} than from Al^{2+}. **7.25** In Cl, the additional electron experiences some nuclear attraction (it is not completely shielded from the nucleus by the other five $3p$ electrons), and it completes a stable octet of valence electrons. In Ar, the stable octet already exists. The added electron occupies a $4s$ orbital and is almost completely shielded from the attraction of the nucleus. This electronic arrangement is not lower in energy than that in Ar atoms. **7.27** Metals are good conductors, and nonmetals are poor ones. Metallic character increases going from right to left across a row and from top to bottom in a column. The order of increasing metallic character and electrical conductivity is S < Si < Ge < Ca. **7.29** (a) Li; (b) Na; (c) Sn; (d) Al. **7.31** Ionic: Na_2O, CaO, Fe_2O_3; molecular: N_2O, CO, P_2O_5, Cl_2O_7. Ionic compounds are formed by combining a metal and a nonmetal; covalent compounds are formed by two or more nonmetals. **7.33** An acidic oxide dissolved in water produces an acidic solution; oxides of nonmetals, such as SO_3, are acidic. A basic oxide dissolved in water produces a basic solution; oxides of metals, such as CaO, are basic. **7.35** (a) $Na_2O(s) + H_2O(l) \longrightarrow 2NaOH(aq)$; (b) $CuO(s) + 2HNO_3(aq) \longrightarrow Cu(NO_3)_2(aq) + H_2O(l)$; (c) $SO_3(g) + H_2O(l) \longrightarrow H_2SO_4(aq)$; (d) $SeO_2(s) + 2NaOH(aq) \longrightarrow Na_2SeO_3(aq) + H_2O(l)$. **7.37** (a) Na, $[Ne]3s^1$; Mg, $[Ne]3s^2$. (b) When forming ions, both adopt the stable configuration of Ne, but Na loses 1 electron and Mg loses two electrons. (c) The effective nuclear charge of Mg is greater, so its ionization energy is greater. (d) Mg is less reactive because it has a filled subshell and a higher ionization energy. (e) The atomic radius of Mg is smaller because the effective nuclear charge is greater. **7.39** (a) The valence electrons in Sr are less tightly held (greater n value) than those of Be, so Sr is more easily oxidized. (b) Na reacts with O_2 to form Na_2O_2, sodium *peroxide*, instead of the expected metal oxide, Na_2O. **7.41** (a) $2K(s) + 2H_2O(l) \longrightarrow$

$2KOH(aq) + H_2(g)$; (b) $Ba(s) + 2H_2O(l) \longrightarrow Ba(OH)_2(aq) + H_2(g)$; (c) $6Li(s) + N_2(g) \longrightarrow 2Li_3N(s)$; (d) $2Mg(s) + O_2(g) \longrightarrow 2MgO(s)$. **7.43** H, $1s^1$; Li, $[He]2s^1$; F, $[He]2s^22p^5$. Like Li, H has only one valence electron, and its most common oxidation number is $+1$. Like F, H needs only one electron to adopt the stable electron configuration of the nearest noble gas; both H and F can exist in the -1 oxidation state. **7.45** (a) O, $[He]2s^22p^4$; F, $[He]2s^22p^5$. (b) When forming ions, O atoms gain 2 electrons and F atoms gain 1 electron to form the stable electron configuration of Ne. (c) The ionization energy of F is greater because its valence electrons experience a greater Z_{eff}. (d) O_2 is unreactive toward H_2O, whereas F_2 reacts with H_2O to form HF. (e) Both elements react with H_2, forming H_2O and HF, respectively. (f) Electronic repulsions in the small $2p$ orbitals of F counterbalance its larger Z_{eff}, and the two elements have approximately equal atomic radii. (Fluorine is slightly smaller.) **7.47** Both Xe and Kr were found to react with substances with a strong tendency to remove electrons, such as F_2. Thus, the term *inert* no longer described all the group 8A elements. **7.49** (a) $S_8(s) + 16Li(s) \longrightarrow 8Li_2S(s)$; (b) $2O_3(g) \longrightarrow 3O_2(g)$; (c) $2KBr(aq) + 2H_2O(l) \longrightarrow 2KOH(aq) + H_2(g) + Br_2(aq)$; (d) $Cl_2(g) + Ca(s) \longrightarrow CaCl_2(s)$. **7.51** (a) Te has more metallic character and is a better electrical conductor. (b) At room temperature, oxygen molecules are diatomic and exist in the gas phase. Sulfur molecules are eight-membered rings and exist in the solid state. (c) Chlorine is generally more reactive than bromine because Cl atoms have a more exothermic electron affinity than Br atoms. **7.53** Exceptions to Mendeleev's periodic law: Ar and K; Co and Ni; Te and I; Th and Pa; U and Np; Pu and Am; (possibly Cm and Bk). If placed in order of increasing atomic weight, these elements would not fall in the group with which they share similar properties. **7.56** (a) Increasing ionization energy: Si < Se < C < O < F. (b) Increasing atomic radius: F < O < C < Si ≈ Se. **7.58** In order to form Na^{2+} or Mg^{3+}, an electron would have to be removed from the completed second shell, a stable octet. This is energetically very unfavorable and unlikely. **7.60** (a) Zn has a significantly greater Z and Z_{eff} than Ca and thus a smaller atomic radius. (b) In the 2+ ions, both elements have lost their $4s$ electrons, the outermost electrons in Ca are in the $3p$ sublevel, and those in Zn are in the $3d$ sublevel, significantly shielded by core electrons. Thus, the electron clouds in the two ions are more similar in size than in the neutral atoms. **7.63** (a) F and O^- have the same electron configuration; they are isoelectronic. (b) In the first process, an electron is added to a neutral F atom, whereas in the second an electron is added to a negative O^- ion. Also, F has a larger Z_{eff} than does O^-. (c) Following the same trend, $N^{2-}(g)$ will have a less exothermic electron affinity than O^-. **7.65** The electron affinity of Na^+ is the reverse of the ionization energy of Na. EA of $Na^+ = -$ IE of Na $= -496$ kJ/mol. **7.68** Because Xe reacts with F_2 and O_2 has approximately the same ionization energy as Xe, O_2 will probably react with F_2. Possible products would be O_2F_2, analogous to XeF_2, or OF_2.

Chapter 8

8.1 (a) Valence electrons are those that take part in chemical bonding. This usually means the electrons beyond the core noble-gas configuration of the atom, although it is sometimes only the outer shell electrons. (b) N has five valence electrons.

8.3 (a) ·Si· (b) Na· (c) :Se· (d) ·Al·

8.5 Li· + ·F: ⟶ Li⁺ + [:F:]⁻

8.7 (a) AlF_3; (b) K_2S; (c) Mg_3N; (d) BaO. **8.9** (a) I⁻, $[Kr]5s^24d^{10}5p^6 = [Xe]$, noble-gas configuration; (b) Se²⁻, $[Ar]5s^25p^6 = [Kr]$, noble-gas configuration; (c) Sr²⁺, [Kr], noble-gas configuration; (d) Ni²⁺, $[Ar]3d^8$; (e) Pb²⁺, $[Xe]6s^24f^{14}5d^{10}$. **8.11** (a) Lattice energy is the energy required to totally separate 1 mol of solid ionic compound into its gaseous ions. (b) The magnitude of the lattice energy depends on the magnitudes of the charges of the ions, their radii, and the arrangement of ions in the lattice. **8.13** The large attractive energy between oppositely charged Ca²⁺ and O²⁻ more than compensates for the energy required to form Ca²⁺ and O²⁻ from the neutral atoms. **8.15** In MgH_2, twice the positive charge is manifested over a smaller distance, so the lattice energy is more than twice as large as that of LiH. **8.17** The lattice energy of RbCl(s) is +692 kJ/mol. This value is smaller than the lattice energy for NaCl because Rb⁺ has a larger ionic radius than Na⁺ and therefore cannot approach Cl⁻ as closely as Na⁺ can.
8.19 (a) As Z stays constant and the number of electrons in the particle increases, the electron-electron repulsions increase, and the size of the particle increases. (b) Going down a family, the increased distance of the electrons from the nucleus and increased shielding by inner electrons outweigh the increase in Z and cause the size of particles with like charges to increase. (c) Removing one electron from Fe²⁺ to form Fe³⁺ significantly reduces electron-electron repulsion, and so Fe³⁺ is smaller.
8.21 (a) In an isoelectronic series, the number of electrons and the electron configurations of the particles are the same, but the values of Z are different. (b) Cl⁻, Ar; Se²⁻, Kr; Mg²⁺, Ne. **8.23** Since the electron configurations in an isoelectronic series are the same, repulsion and shielding effects do not vary for the different particles. As Z increases, the valence electrons are more strongly attracted to the nucleus and the size of the particle decreases. **8.25** (a) Li⁺ < K⁺ < Rb⁺; (b) Mg²⁺ < Na⁺ < Br⁻; (c) K⁺ < Ar < Cl⁻ < S²⁻; (d) Ar < Cl < Cl⁻.

8.27 H· + H· + ·S: ⟶ H—S: with H above
     |
     H

8.29 (a) O=C=O; (b) :N≡N: or :C≡O:.

8.31 (a) *Electronegativity* is the ability of an atom in a molecule to attract electrons to itself. (b) Fluorine is the most electronegative element. **8.33** (a) P < S < O; (b) Mg < Al < Si; (c) S < Br < Cl; (d) Si < C < N.
8.35 All except (b) are polar to some extent. The more electronegative element in each polar bond is: (a) O; (c) Br; (d) N; (e) F.

8.37 (a) H—P—H with H below; (b) [:O—Br—O: with :O: below]⁻

(c) :C≡O:; (d) :O—Cl—O—H; (e) :Cl—Se—Cl:.

8.39 (a) three resonance structures of sulfite/sulfur trioxide with S central and three O atoms

(b) three resonance structures of $C_2O_4^{2-}$ (oxalate) anion, 2− charge

Nonbonded pairs on terminal O atoms have been omitted on all but the first form.

(c) three resonance structures with N central, O and OH groups

The third form is not a significant contributor because of the nonzero formal charges on all three O atoms.

(d) :O—Cl—O: ⟷ :O—Cl—O: ⟷ :O—Cl—O: ⟷ :O—Cl—O·

8.41 The more pairs of electrons shared by two atoms, the shorter the bond between the atoms. Therefore, the order of increasing bond length is CO < CO_2 < CO_3^{2-}. **8.43** (a) +1; (b) −1; (c) +1 (assuming the odd electron is on N); (d) 0; (e) +3. **8.45** The most common exceptions to the octet rule are molecules with more than eight electrons around one or more atoms.

8.47 (a) O=N—O: ⟷ :O—N=O

The odd-electron molecule violates the octet rule. The odd electron is probably on N because it is less electronegative than O.

(b) :F—Ge—F: with F above and F below (central Ge bonded to four F)

(c) :F—Te—F: with F above and F below (central Te)

10 electrons around Te;

(d) $: \ddot{C}l - B - \ddot{C}l :$
$\quad\quad\quad |$
$\quad\quad : \ddot{C}l :$

(e) $: \ddot{F} - \ddot{X}e - \ddot{F} :$ (with F above and below)
$\quad\quad\quad : \ddot{F} :$

6 electrons around B;   12 electrons around Xe.

8.49

(a) $: \ddot{C}l - Be - \ddot{C}l :$; this structure violates the octet rule.

(b) $\overset{0}{\ddot{C}l} = \overset{0}{Be} = \overset{0}{\ddot{C}l} \longleftrightarrow : \ddot{C}l - Be \equiv Cl : \longleftrightarrow : Cl \equiv Be - \ddot{C}l :$
$\quad +1 \quad -2 \quad +1 \quad\quad\quad 0 \quad -2 \quad +2 \quad\quad\quad +2 \quad -2 \quad 0$

(c) Since formal charges are minimized on the structure that violates the octet rule, this form is probably most important. **8.51** (a) $\Delta H = -15$ kJ. **8.53** (a) $\Delta H = -213$ kJ. **8.55** The average Ti—Cl bond energy is 430 kJ/mol. **8.57** (a) P, 0; (b) As, +3; (c) C, +4; (d) P, +5; (e) N, +3; (f) Br, +3; (g) O, −1; (h) Pb, +2. **8.59** (a) N: +5, −3; (b) Se: +6, −2; (c) Ca: +2, 0; (d) Mn: +7, 0. **8.61** (a) FeF_3; (b) MoO_3; (c) $AsBr_5$; (d) vanadium(III) oxide; (e) cobalt(III) fluoride; (f) manganese(II) sulfide. **8.63** (a) Xe: 0 to +4, F: 0 to −1; (b) Cu: +2 to +1, I: −1 to 0; (c) N: −3 to +3, Cl: 0 to −1; (d) I: 0 to −1, S: +4 to +6; (e) S: −2 to +4, O: 0 to −2. **8.65** (a) Group 4A or 4B; (b) group 2A; (c) group 5A or 5B. **8.68** Each elemental transition metal has two ns electrons in its outer shell that will be lost before $(n-1)d$ electrons upon ionization. Thus the +2 oxidation state will be stable, regardless of further ionization involving the $(n-1)d$ electrons. **8.70** (a) 2.64×10^3 kJ/mol; (b) 471 kJ/mol. **8.72** The "second electron affinity" of oxygen is +893 kJ/mol.

8.75 $: N \equiv N - \ddot{O} : \longleftrightarrow : \ddot{N} - N \equiv O : \longleftrightarrow : \ddot{N} = N = \ddot{O} :$
$\quad\quad 0 \quad 1 \quad -1 \quad\quad\quad -2 \quad 1 \quad 1 \quad\quad\quad -1 \quad 1 \quad 0$

The structures on the left and right both minimize formal charge to the same extent, but the one on the left is slightly preferred because the negative formal charge is on the more electronegative O atom. **8.78** (a) Exothermic. (b) The ΔH calculated from bond energies (−97 kJ) is slightly more exothermic (more negative) than that obtained using ΔH_f° values (−92.4 kJ). **8.80** $H_2(g) \longrightarrow H(g) + H(g)$, $\Delta H = +436$ kJ; $H_2(g) \longrightarrow H^+(g) + H^-(g)$, $\Delta H = 1675$ kJ. The first reaction requires a much smaller energy input than the second, and so it would be the preferred pathway for bond cleavage. **8.82** (a) $\Delta H = +40$ kJ; ethanol has the lower enthalpy. (b) $\Delta H = -83$ kJ; acetaldehyde has the lower enthalpy. (c) $\Delta H = +82$ kJ; cyclopentene has the lower enthalpy. (d) $\Delta H = -55$ kJ; acetonitrile has the lower enthalpy. **8.85** SeO_2 and N_2O_3 can be ruled out because both are low-melting covalent compounds. SrO is not likely to react with NaOH, and so it is most likely that the compound in question is GeO_2.

Chapter 9

9.1 (a) Trigonal planar; (b) tetrahedral; (c) trigonal bipyramidal; (d) octahedral. **9.3** The electron-pair geom- etry describes the locations of electron pairs as predicted by VSEPR. The molecular geometry indicates the positions of the atoms in the molecule. In H_2O, there are four pairs of electrons around oxygen, and so the electron-pair geometry is tetrahedral. Because there are two bonding and two nonbonding pairs, the molecular geometry (the arrangement of the three atoms) is bent. **9.5** (a) Tetrahedral, bent; (b) linear, linear; (c) trigonal planar, trigonal planar; (d) tetrahedral, trigonal pyramidal; (e) tetrahedral, tetrahedral; (f) trigonal bipyramidal, seesaw. **9.7** NF_3, trigonal pyramidal; BF_3, trigonal planar; ClF_3, T-shaped. The molecular geometries or shapes differ because there is a different number of nonbonding pairs of electrons around each central atom. **9.9** Going from NO_2^+ to NO_2 to NO_2^-, the number of nonbonding electrons in the valence shell of N increases from 0 to 1 to 2, and the bond angle decreases correspondingly. **9.11** (a) 1—109°, 2—120°; (b) 3—109°, 4—120°; (c) 5—109°, 6—109°; (d) 7—180°, 8—109°. **9.13** (a) Polar; (b) polar; (c) nonpolar; (d) polar; (e) nonpolar; (f) polar. **9.15** In $BeCl_2$ there are just two electron pairs around Be. The structure is linear, and the individual bond dipoles cancel. In SCl_2, there are four electron pairs around S, and the structure is bent. The bond dipoles *do not* cancel. **9.17** The middle isomer has a zero net dipole moment. **9.19** (a) The charge on H and Br is 1.9×10^{-20} C. (b) 12%. **9.21** (a) *Orbital overlap* occurs when valence atomic orbitals on two adjacent atoms share the same region of space. (b) In valence bond theory, orbital overlap allows two bonding electrons to mutually occupy the space between the bonded nuclei. (c) Valence bond theory is a combination of the atomic orbital concept and the Lewis model of electron-pair bonding. **9.23** (a) sp^2, 120° angles; (b) sp^3d, 90°, 120°, and 180° angles; (c) sp^3d^2, 90° and 180° angles.

9.25 $\left[: \ddot{O} - \ddot{C}l - \ddot{O} : \right]^{-}$ with $: \ddot{O} :$ below Cl. The electron-pair geometry is tetrahedral, and the molecular shape is trigonal pyramidal. Each Cl—O bond is formed by the overlap of an sp^3 hybrid orbital on Cl with an atomic or hybrid orbital on O.

9.27 (a) sp^2; (b) sp^3; (c) sp^3; (d) sp^3d; (e) sp^3d^2. **9.29** A sigma (σ) bond is formed by the end-to-end overlap of two orbitals pointing along the internuclear axis. It has electron density symmetrically distributed along a line connecting the two bonding atoms. A pi (π) bond is formed by the side-to-side overlap of two p orbitals oriented perpendicular to the internuclear axis. There are two regions of overlap, but no electron density along the internuclear axis. Sigma bonds are generally stronger than pi bonds. **9.31** A single valence p orbital remains, and one π bond can form. **9.33** (a) $\sim 109°$ about the leftmost C, sp^3; $\sim 120°$ about the right-hand C, sp^2. (b) The doubly bonded O can be viewed as sp^2, and the other as sp^3; the nitrogen is sp^3 with approximately 109° bond angles. (c) nine σ bonds, one π bond. **9.35** In a localized π bond, the electron density is concentrated between the two atoms forming the bond. In a delocalized π bond, the electron density is spread over all the atoms that contribute p orbitals to the π network. **9.37** (a) The two resonance forms for O_3, each with one single and one double bond, indicate that the O—O bonds are neither single nor double, but some intermediate between the two. (b) If there is delocalized π bonding in O_3, the O—O distance must be shorter than an O—O single bond to facilitate π overlap, but longer than an isolated O—O double bond because the π electron density is delocalized. **9.39** (a) Bonding MOs are lower in energy than the starting atomic orbitals, and antibonding MOs are higher. (b) The electron density is concentrated between the nuclei in a bonding MO and away from the nuclei in an antibonding MO. **9.41** (a) *Bond order* is the net number of bonding electron pairs in a molecule [$\frac{1}{2}$(bonding e$^-$ − antibonding e$^-$)]. (b) *Paramagnetism* is the magnetic behavior of molecules with unpaired electrons. (c) An *energy-level diagram* shows the interacting atomic orbitals in the left and right columns and the resulting molecular orbitals and their relative energies in the center column. **9.43** (a) BO = 3.0, diamagnetic; (b) BO = 2.0, paramagnetic; (c) BO = 3.0, diamagnetic; (d) BO = 1.5, paramagnetic. **9.45** In order of increasing bond length: $O_2^+ < O_2 < O_2^- < O_2^{2-}$. **9.47** (a) When two atomic orbitals interact, the resulting bonding molecular orbital is always lower in energy because it concentrates electron density between the two bonding nuclei, while the antibonding orbital channels electrons away from the nuclei. (b) The σ_{1s}^* orbital is higher in energy than the H $1s$ atomic orbitals because an electron in this orbital is repelled from the area between the H nuclei and is actually farther from a single H nucleus than in the isolated H atom. (c) The Li $2s$ orbitals are larger than the $1s$, the area of overlap is greater, and the energy separation of the resulting σ_{2s} and σ_{2s}^* orbitals is larger than that between σ_{1s} and σ_{1s}^*. **9.49** (a) Trigonal pyramidal; (b) linear; (c) trigonal planar; (d) linear. **9.52** (a) Two sigma, two pi; (b) two sigma, two pi; (c) four sigma, zero pi; (e) four sigma, one pi. **9.54** (a) The bond dipoles in H_2O lie along the O—H bonds with the positive end at H and the negative end at O. The dipole moment vector of the H_2O molecule bisects the H—O—H angle and has a magnitude of 1.85 D with the negative end pointing toward O. (b) The magnitude of the O—H bond dipole is 1.51 D. **9.57** (b) The electron-pair geometry around each N is trigonal planar with bond angles of $\sim 120°$; because of the geometric requirements of the π bond, the entire molecule must be planar. (c) Each N atom will use sp^2 hybrid orbitals for σ bonding and pure p orbitals for the π bond. (e) The two N—H bonds must be on opposite sides of the molecule to produce a dipole moment of zero. If the two N—H bonds were on one side of the molecule and the two nonbonding electron pairs on the other side, the molecule would have a net dipole moment. **9.60** The number of electron pairs shared by the two N atoms increases in the series, and there is a corresponding decrease in the N—N distance. **9.62** From bond dissociation energies, $\Delta H = 5364$ kJ; according to Hess's law, $\Delta H° = 5535$ kJ. The difference in the two results, 171 kJ, is due to the resonance stabilization in benzene. The amount of energy actually required to decompose 1 mol of $C_6H_6(g)$ is greater

than the sum of the localized bond energies. **9.66** (a) The order of increasing bond strength is $He_2 < H_2^-$, He_2^+, $H_2^+ < H_2$, with small distinctions between the three ions with equal bond orders. (b) The order of increasing bond length is $H_2 < H_2^+$, He_2^+, $H_2^- < He_2$. **9.69** (a) $\sigma_{2s}^2 \, \sigma_{2s}^{*2} \, \pi_{2p}^4 \, \sigma_{2p}^2 \, \pi_{2p}^{*1}$. (b) Paramagnetic. (c) The electron that is lost is in an antibonding molecular orbital, increasing the bond order from 2.5 in NO to 3.0 in NO$^+$. (d) NO$^- <$ NO $<$ NO$^+$. (e) NO$^+$ is isoelectronic with N_2, and NO$^-$ is isoelectronic with O_2.

Chapter 10

10.1 In $Cl_2(g)$, the molecules are very far apart; most of the 1.0-L volume occupied by 2.90 g of Cl_2 molecules in the gas phase is empty space. In $Br_2(l)$, the molecules are touching; 3.19 g of Br_2 molecules in the liquid phase occupies almost all of the 1.0-cm^3 volume. **10.3** (a) $F = m \times a$. The forces they exert on the floor are exactly equal. (b) $P = F/A$. The person standing on one foot applies this force over a smaller area and thus exerts a greater pressure on the floor. **10.5** (a) 10.3 m; (b) $P_{total} = P_{atm} + P_{H_2O} = 1.74$ atm. **10.7** (a) 66.9 kPa; (b) 0.457 atm; (c) 1.09 atm; (d) 697 torr. **10.9** (a) $P = 773.4$ torr. (b) The pressure in Chicago is greater than standard atmospheric pressure, and so it makes sense to classify this weather system as a "high-pressure system." **10.11** 1.8×10^3 kPa. **10.13** (a) It is *not* necessary to know the atmospheric pressure to use a closed-end manometer. The gas on one side of the Hg is working against a vacuum on the other side of the Hg. (b) It *is* necessary to know the atmospheric pressure to use an open-end manometer. In an open-end manometer the pressure of the sample is balanced against the atmospheric pressure. **10.15** (a) If X and Y are *directly proportional,* a change in X will cause a proportional change in Y in the *same* direction. If X and Y are *inversely proportional,* a change in X will cause a proportional change in $1/Y$. (b) Volume is inversely proportional to pressure, directly proportional to absolute temperature, and directly proportional to quantity of gas. **10.17** (a) $V = 7.22$ L; (b) $P = 494$ torr. **10.19** (a) If equal volumes of gases at the same temperature and pressure contain equal numbers of molecules and molecules react in the ratios of small whole numbers, it follows that the volumes of reacting gases are in the ratios of small whole numbers. (b) Since the two gases are at the same temperature and pressure, the ratio of the numbers of atoms is the same as the ratio of volumes. There are 1.5 times as many Xe atoms as Ne atoms. **10.21** An *ideal gas* exhibits pressure, volume, and temperature relationships described by the equation $PV = nRT$. (b) $PV = nRT$; P in atmospheres, V in liters, n in moles, T in kelvins. **10.23** (a) $P = 4.53$ atm; (b) $n = 0.278$ mol; (c) $V = 61$ L; (d) $T = 19.2$ K. **10.25** 2.42×10^{22} gas molecules. **10.27** (a) $V = 2.59$ L; (b) $V = 0.530$ L. **10.29** (a) 9.83×10^3 g O_2; (b) 6.88×10^3 L at STP. **10.31** (a) $n = 2 \times 10^{-4}$ mol O_2; (b) The roach needs 8×10^{-3} mol O_2 in 48 hr, more than 100% of the O_2 in the jar. **10.33** (a) $d = 1.82$ g/L; (b) $\mathcal{M} = 44.0$ g/mol.

10.35 The molecular formula of cyanogen is C_2N_2.
10.37 $\mathcal{M} = 89.4$ g/mol. **10.39** (a) The total pressure of a mixture of gases is equal to the sum of the pressures the individual gases would exert if they were present in the same container alone. (b) Partial pressure is the pressure exerted by a single component of a gaseous mixture at the same temperature and volume as the mixture.
10.41 (a) P of He = 1.51 atm, P of Ne = 1.25 atm, P of Ar = 0.360 atm; (b) $P_t = 3.12$ atm. **10.43** P of N_2 = 0.74 atm; P of O_2 = 0.41 atm; P of CO_2 = 0.16 atm.
10.45 (a) The partial pressure of gas A is not affected by the addition of gas C. (b) The total pressure in the vessel increases when gas C is added. (c) The mole fraction of gas B decreases when gas C is added. **10.47** P of N_2 = 0.451 atm; P of O_2 = 1.71 atm; $P_t = 2.16$ atm.
10.49 10.0 L = 0.401 mol H_2; 8.44 g CaH_2. **10.51** V = 4.25 L CO_2. **10.53** 0.00470 mol H_2 collected; 0.307 g Zn consumed. **10.55** (a) They have the same number of molecules. (b) SF_6 is more dense. (c) The average kinetic energies are equal. (d) N_2 will effuse faster.
10.57 (a) False; the average kinetic energy per molecule in a collection of gas molecules is the same for all gases at the same temperature. (b) True. (c) False; the molecules in a gas sample at a given temperature exhibit a distribution of kinetic energies. (d) True. **10.59** (a) In order of increasing speed: SF_6 < HI < Cl_2 < H_2S < CO. (b) $u_{CO} = 515$ m/s. **10.61** The order of increasing rate of effusion is: $^2H^{37}Cl$ < $^1H^{37}Cl$ < $^2H^{35}Cl$ < $^1H^{35}Cl$.
10.63 $\mathcal{M} = 210$ g/mol. **10.65** (a) Nonideal-gas behavior is observed at very high pressures and low temperatures. (b) The real volumes of gas molecules and attractive intermolecular forces between molecules cause gases to behave nonideally. **10.67** According to the ideal-gas law, the ratio PV/RT should be constant for a given gas sample at all combinations of pressure, volume, and temperature. If this ratio changes with increasing pressure, the gas sample is not behaving ideally. **10.69** Ar ($a = 1.34$, $b = 0.0322$) will behave more like an ideal gas than CO_2 ($a = 3.59$, $b = 0.0427$) at high pressures. **10.71** (a) P = 0.918 atm; (b) P = 0.896 atm. **10.74** 1.6×10^4 kg H_2.
10.77 $T = 405$ K or 132°C. **10.80** 2.1×10^{-3} g $Ni(CO)_4$. **10.83** Oxygen is 70.1 mole percent of the mixture. **10.85** Neon is 43.7 mole percent of the mixture. **10.90** (a) P(ideal) = 134.2 atm; (b) P(van der Waals) = 139.8 atm; (c) The correction for the real volume of molecules dominates.

Chapter 11

11.1 The solid state is characterized by a high degree of order. The units of the solid, ions or molecules, are arranged in a regular array. In a liquid, molecules are still in close contact, but their orientations with respect to near neighbors are not regular. Liquids are fluid and take the shape of their container. Solids have their own volume and do not flow. **11.3** Gases are compressible because there are large distances between particles. Particles in the solid and liquid states are close together and relatively incompressible. **11.5** As the temperature of a substance is increased, the average kinetic energy of the particles increases. As the average kinetic energy increases,

more particles are able to overcome intermolecular attractive forces and move to a less ordered state, from solid to liquid to gas. **11.7** (a) *Dipole-dipole forces* are the attractions between the positive end of a neutral polar molecule and the negative end of another. Example: interactions between acetone, CH_3COCH_3, molecules. (b) *Ion-dipole forces* are attractions between one end of the dipole in a polar molecule and an oppositely charged ion. Example: the attraction of Cu^{2+} to the negative end of a H_2O molecule. (c) *London dispersion forces* are the attractive forces between nonpolar molecules or neutral atoms produced by transient dipoles due to the mobile electron clouds of the molecules or atoms. Example: interactions between I_2 molecules. (d) *Van der Waals forces* are any dipole-dipole or London dispersion forces. Example: interactions between slightly polar molecules such as CH_2Cl_2. (e) A *hydrogen bond* is the attraction between the H atom in a polar bond and a nonbonded pair of electrons on an adjacent electronegative atom, primarily F, N, or O. Example: interactions between HF molecules. **11.9** (a) Ion-ion forces (ionic bonds); (b) London dispersion forces; (c) ion-dipole forces; (d) hydrogen bonds. **11.11** (a) HCl; (b) HI. **11.13** (a) *Polarizability* is the ease with which the charge distribution in a molecule can be distorted to produce a transient dipole. (b) Te is most polarizable because its valence electrons are farthest from the nucleus and least tightly held. (c) In order of increasing polarizability: CH_4 < SiH_4 < $SiCl_4$ < $GeCl_4$ < $GeBr_4$. **11.15** (a) O_2; higher molecular weight. (b) SiH_4; higher molecular weight. (c) NaCl; ion-ion forces are stronger than dipole-dipole forces. (d) C_2H_5OH; hydrogen bonding is stronger than dipole-dipole forces. **11.17** Surface tension, high boiling point, high heat capacity per gram. **11.19** Viscosities and surface tensions of liquids both increase as intermolecular forces become stronger. **11.21** (a) The stronger hydrogen-bonding interactions between ethanol molecules make the liquid more resistant to flow, more viscous. (b) Polar water molecules have strong cohesive intermolecular interactions relative to the weak adhesive forces between polar water molecules and nonpolar polyethylene molecules in the capillary, and so the meniscus is concave downward. **11.23** Endothermic: melting, vaporization, sublimation; exothermic: condensation, freezing, deposition. **11.25** 4.4×10^2 g H_2O. **11.27** 2.59 kJ. **11.29** (a) The *critical temperature* is the highest temperature at which a gas can be liquefied, regardless of pressure. (b) The *critical pressure* is the pressure required to cause liquefaction at the critical temperature. **11.31** The *boiling point* is the temperature at which the vapor pressure of the liquid equals the external pressure acting on the liquid; the lower the external pressure, the lower the boiling point. The *melting point* is the temperature at which the solid and liquid phases are in equilibrium; neither solids nor liquids are significantly affected by pressure because neither is very compressible. **11.33** CBr_4 < $CHBr_3$ < CH_2Br_2 < CH_2Cl_2 < CH_3Cl < CH_4. The order of increasing volatility is the order of decreasing molar mass and decreasing strength of dispersion forces. **11.35** The temperature of the water in the two pans is the same. **11.37** (a) Approximately 48°C; (b) approxi-

mately 14°C. **11.39** 97°C. **11.41** The liquid-gas line of a phase diagram ends at the critical point, the temperature and pressure beyond which the gas and liquid phases are indistinguishable. **11.43** (a) $H_2O(g)$ will condense to $H_2O(s)$ at approximately 4 mm Hg; at a higher pressure, perhaps 5 atm or so, $H_2O(s)$ will melt to form $H_2O(l)$. (b) $H_2O(s)$ will melt at just above 0°C to form $H_2O(l)$. Just below 70°C, the vapor pressure of $H_2O(l)$ reaches 0.3 atm, and $H_2O(l)$ boils to form $H_2O(g)$.
11.45 (a)

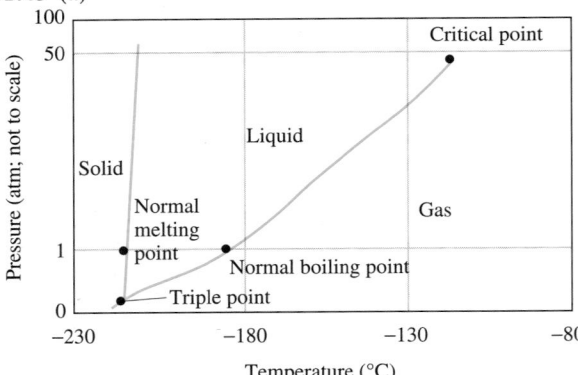

(b) $O_2(s)$ is denser than $O_2(l)$ because the solid-liquid line on the phase diagram is normal. (c) O_2 will melt when heated at a pressure of 1 atm. **11.47** (a) In a crystalline solid, the component particles are arranged in an ordered repeating pattern. In an amorphous solid, there is no orderly structure. **11.49** The unit cell is the building block of the crystal lattice. When repeated in three dimensions, it produces the crystal lattice. It is a parallelepiped with the characteristic distances and angles, a, b, c, α, β, and γ. Unit cells can be primitive or centered. **11.51** (a) 4; (b) 12; (c) $a = 4.07$ Å; (d) density = 10.6 g/cm³. **11.53** (a) 12; (b) 6; (c) 8. **11.55** density = 6.79 g/cm³. **11.57** Atomic weight = 55.7 g/mol. **11.59** (a) Hydrogen bonding, dipole-dipole forces, London Dispersion forces; (b) covalent chemical bonds; (c) ionic bonds; (d) metallic bonds. **11.61** Graphite (carbon) and quartz (SiO_2). **11.63** (a) KBr, ion-ion vs. dispersion; (b) SiO_2, (network) covalent vs. dispersion; (c) Se, (network) covalent vs. dispersion; (d) MgF_2, higher charges, stronger electrostatic forces in the solid. **11.65** According to Table 11.6, the solid could be either ionic with low water solubility or network covalent. Because of the extremely high sublimation temperature, it is probably *network covalent.* **11.67** (a) $a = 6.50$ Å. (b) The Ag^+-to-1^- distance is 2.81 Å. **11.71** (a) The cis isomer has stronger dipole-dipole forces and the higher boiling point. (b) Since the nonpolar trans isomer with weaker intermolecular forces has the higher melting point, it must pack more efficiently in the solid state. **11.75** Propylamine experiences hydrogen-bonding interactions, while trimethylamine does not. Also, the rodlike shape of propylamine leads to stronger dispersion forces than in trimethylamine. The stronger intermolecular forces in propylamine lead to the lower vapor pressure. **11.77** 2.60 kJ. **11.80** (a) A plot of ln (VP) vs. $1/T$ is linear; the slope is -4.29×10^3 and $\Delta H_v = 35.7$ kJ/mol.

(b) From the graph, the boiling point is 354 K. **11.83** From the graph of ln (VP) vs. $1/T$, the slope is -5.91×10^3 and $\Delta H_s = 49.1$ kJ/mol. **11.86** (a) There are 90 bonds in the C_{60} molecule; (b) 30 double bonds.

Chapter 12

12.1 A liquid is clear and fluid, while a liquid crystal is cloudy and often viscous. A crystal is rigid and has its own well-defined volume, while a liquid crystal is fluid. **12.3** Reinitzer observed that cholesteryl benzoate has a phase that exhibits properties intermediate between those of the solid and liquid phases. This liquid-crystalline phase is opaque, is defined by sharp transition temperatures, and becomes clear as the temperature is increased. **12.5** Long, rodlike molecules. **12.7** *Nematic* and *smetic* phases are formed by rodlike molecules aligned with their long axes parallel; smetic phases have some additional ordering. In *cholesteric* phases the molecules are stacked in layers and are often twisted with respect to molecules in adjacent layers. **12.9** The presence of a second substance creates new solute–liquid crystal intermolecular forces which disrupt the orienting forces present in the pure liquid-crystalline phase. A single solute–liquid crystal interaction reduces the long-range order, and very few of these disruptions can be tolerated before the stability of the liquid-crystalline phase is destroyed. **12.11** *Polymers* are substances with high molecular mass formed by joining together many *monomers,* small molecules with lower molecular mass.
12.13
$$n CH_2{=}CH{-}\underset{\underset{Cl}{|}}{C}{=}CH_2 \longrightarrow \left[CH_2{-}CH{=}\underset{\underset{Cl}{|}}{C}{-}CH_2 \right]_n$$
12.15 In a *condensation* reaction two molecules are combined to form a larger molecule by elimination of a small molecule such as H_2O. Polymers are formed when condensation occurs at both ends of the reacting molecules (monomers).

12.17 n HO—⟨CH₃ / CH₃⟩—OH ⟶

$$\left[O{-}\text{⟨CH}_3\text{/CH}_3\text{⟩}{-}O{-}\text{⟨CH}_3\text{/CH}_3\text{⟩}{-}O \right]_n + n H_2O$$

12.19 (a) Increases hardness; (b) increases hardness; (c) decreases hardness; (d) increases hardness; (e) decreases hardness. **12.21** (a) An *elastomer* is a polymer material that recovers its shape when released from a distorting force. (b) A *thermoplastic polymer* can be shaped and reshaped on application of heat and/or pressure. (c) A *thermosetting plastic* cannot easily be reshaped once set because of the presence of chemical bonds that crosslink the polymer chains. **12.23** Engineering ceramics are more resistant to heat than are plastics, are significantly less dense than metals, are resistant to corrosion and wear, and are not easily deformed by stress. **12.25** Each Si is bound to four C atoms, and each C is bound to four Si atoms in a tetrahedral arrangement, producing an extended three-dimensional network. The extended three-dimensional nature of the structure produces the exceptional hardness, and the covalent character of the bonding network provides the great thermal stability. **12.27** Ceramic materials typically have rigid three-dimensional lattices; movements of atoms with respect to one another require the breaking of chemical bonds. As bonds in a ceramic are broken under stress, the break tends to propagate itself by applying stress to adjacent atoms and bonds. **12.29** If we begin with solid metal hydroxide and add the appropriate solvents, we have little control over the particle size of the suspended solid or the uniformity of the sol. These characteristics of the sol are very important in determining the ultimate purity, particle size, and fracture resistance of the ceramic produced. **12.31** A *composite* is a material in which ceramic fibers have been embedded in a host ceramic matrix; the composite will be much more fracture-resistant than the pure host ceramic. **12.33** (a) Limited electrical conductivity that changes reproducibly with temperature; (b) hardness and fracture resistance due to fiber reinforcement; (c) structural stability and electrical insulation; (d) heat resistance and low density. **12.35** A *superconducting* material exhibits no resistance to the flow of an electrical current. A related property, known as the Meissner effect, is that all magnetic field lines are excluded from the volume of the material. **12.37** A *thin film* is a very thin (0.1- to 300-μm) coating of a material deposited on a substrate. **12.39** A tantalum carbide thin film on a cutting tool should be heat- and fracture-resistant, adhere well to the metal substrate of the tool, have a uniform thickness, be of precisely known composition, and be free of imperfections or dislocations. **12.41** Vacuum deposition, sputtering, and chemical vapor deposition. **12.43** In order to show liquid-crystalline behavior, a substance must be ordered in one or more directions. Molecules with strictly C—C backbones have so much flexibility that long-range ordering is unlikely, even in one direction. **12.46** Because hydrogen bonding is a much stronger intermolecular interaction than London dispersion forces, nylon has stronger interactions between polymer chains and is a harder material than polyethylene. **12.49** (a) Polymer; (b) ceramic; (c) ceramic; (d) polymer; (e) liquid crystal.

12.53 (a)

(b) $2NbBr_5(g) + 5H_2(g) \longrightarrow 2Nb(s) + 10HBr(g)$
(c) $SiCl_4(l) + C_2H_5OH(l) \longrightarrow Si(OC_2H_5)_4(s) + 4HCl(g)$

(d)

12.56 These compounds cannot be vaporized without destroying their chemical identities. Under the conditions of vacuum deposition, anions with names ending in *ite* or *ate* tend to chemically decompose to form gaseous nonmetal oxides.

Chapter 13

13.1 The solubility of a solute in a particular solvent depends on the strength of the "new" solute-solvent interactions relative to the strengths of "old" solute-solute and solvent-solvent interactions. **13.3** (a) Ion-dipole; (b) London dispersion; (c) hydrogen bonding; (d) dipole-dipole. **13.5** A solute is more likely to dissolve in a solvent if the strengths of the solute-solute, solvent-solvent, and solute-solvent interactions are similar. **13.7** (a) There are no solute-solvent interactions between ionic KCl and nonpolar covalent C_6H_6 strong enough to compete with the ionic lattice forces in KCl. (b) Because the molar masses of CCl_4 and Br_2 are very similar, the London dispersion forces in Br_2 are more similar to those in CCl_4. **13.9** (a) Since the solute and solvent in this case experience very similar London dispersion forces, the energy required to separate them individually and the energy released when they are mixed are approximately equal. $\Delta H_1 + \Delta H_2 \approx -\Delta H_3$. Thus, ΔH_{soln} is nearly zero. (b) Since no strong intermolecular forces prevent the molecules from mixing, they do so spontaneously because of the increase in disorder. **13.11** (a) 5.66% Na_2SO_4 by mass; (b) 5.5 ppm Au. **13.13** (a) $X_{CH_3OH} = 6.98 \times 10^{-3}$; (b) $X_{CH_3OH} = 0.290$. **13.15** (a) 0.513 M NaCl; (b) 2.03 M $LiClO_4 \cdot 3H_2O$; (c) 0.120 M HNO_3. **13.17** (a) 9.79 m C_6H_6; (b) 0.402 m NaCl. **13.19** (a) $X_{CH_3OH} = 0.205$; (b) 6.28 m CH_3OH; (c) 4.12 M CH_3OH. **13.21** (a) 41.1% H_2O by mass; (b) $X_{H_2O} = 0.691$; (c) 38.6 m H_2O; (d) 21.1 M H_2O. **13.23** 16 M HNO_3. **13.25** (a) 2.61×10^{-2} mol $MgCl_2$; (b) 7.00×10^{-6} mol HCl; (c) 7.10×10^{-3} mol $(NH_4)_2CrO_4$. **13.27** (a) Weigh 2.50 g KBr, dissolve in water, dilute with stirring to 1.40 L. (b) Weigh 11.4 g KBr, dissolve in 238.6 g H_2O to make 250 g of solution. (c) Weigh 198 g KBr, dissolve in 1452 g H_2O to make 1.50 L of solution. (d) Weigh 13.3 g KBr, dissolve in a small amount of H_2O, dilute to 0.560 L. **13.29** (a) 0.282 N; (b) 0.0675 M H_3PO_4. **13.31** (a) A *saturated* solution is one that is in equilibrium with undissolved solute. (b) A *supersaturated* solution contains more dissolved solute than is needed to form a saturated solution. (c) A supersaturated solution can be prepared by saturating a solution at high temperature and then carefully cooling it. **13.33** (a) Not saturated; (b) saturated; (c) saturated; (d) not saturated. **13.35** The aqueous solubility of most ionic solids increases with increasing temperature, and the solubility of most gases decreases with increasing temperature. **13.37** 9.2×10^{-4} M He, $1.5 \times$

10^{-3} M N_2. **13.39** The total number, or concentration, of particles in a solution. **13.41** For a solution with a nonvolatile solute, the vapor pressure of the solution is equal to the mole fraction of the *solvent* times the vapor pressure of the pure solvent. Nonvolatile solute molecules inhibit escape of solvent molecules to the vapor phase, reducing the vapor pressure above the solution. **13.43** (a) 119 g $C_2H_6O_2$; (b) 125 g KBr. **13.45** (a) $X_{eth} = 0.281$; (b) $P_{soln} = 238$ torr; (c) X_{eth} in vapor = 0.471. **13.47** (a) $T_f = -115.5°C$, $T_b = 79.0°$; (b) $T_f = -65.1°C$, $T_b = 62.5°C$; (c) $T_f = -1.4°C$, $T_b = 100.4°C$. **13.49** 0.03 m glycerin < 0.03 m benzoic acid < 0.02 m KBr. **13.51** $T_b = 102.5°C$. **13.53** $\pi = 4.40$ atm. **13.55** $M = 1.8 \times 10^2$ g/mol adrenaline. **13.57** $M = 1.39 \times 10^4$ g/mol lysozyme. **13.59** (a) $i = 2.75$. (b) As the solution becomes more concentrated, the value of i decreases. **13.61** A *solution* has very small dispersed solute particles, does not scatter light, and is transparent. A *colloid* has much larger dispersed particles, scatters light, and is usually cloudy. White vinegar is a solution; milk is a colloid. **13.63** (a) Hydrophobic; (b) hydrophilic; (c) hydrophobic. **13.65** Colloids do not coalesce because of electrostatic repulsions between groups at the surface of the dispersed particles. Hydrophilic colloids can be coagulated by adding electrolytes, and some colloids can be coagulated by heating. **13.67** For ionic solids, the exothermic part of the solution process is ΔH_3, the enthalpy released when solute and solvent particles interact. In hydrated salts, the ions are already interacting with water molecules; therefore, less enthalpy is released during solvation, and the overall enthalpy of solution is more positive. **13.69** (a) 1.90 m NaCl; (b) 1.83 M NaCl. **13.71** 2.72×10^3 g $CuSO_4 \cdot 5H_2O$, 1.36 M $CuSO_4$. **13.75** (a) The solution is saturated. (b) 3.60 m $SmCl_3$. **13.79** 7.4 kg C_2H_5OH. **13.81** (a) $T_f = -0.558°C$; (b) $T_f = -0.432°C$. **13.84** (a) $K_b = 2.3°C/m$; (b) $M = 2.5 \times 10^2$ g/mol. **13.88** The nonelectrolyte beaker contains 18.2 mL; the NaCl(aq) beaker holds 21.8 mL.

Chapter 14

14.1 (a) $-\Delta[H_2O]/2\Delta t = \Delta[H_2]/2\Delta t = \Delta[O_2]\Delta t$; (b) $-\Delta[CO]/\Delta t = -\Delta[H_2]/2\Delta t = \Delta[CH_3OH]/\Delta t$; (c) $-\Delta[S_2O_8^{2-}]\Delta t = -\Delta[I^-]/2\Delta t = [SO_4^{2-}]/2\Delta t = \Delta[I_2]/\Delta t$. **14.3** (a) $-\Delta[O_2]/\Delta t = 2.3$ mol/s; $\Delta[H_2O]/\Delta t = 4.6$ mol/s; (b) $\Delta P_T/\Delta t = -15$ torr/min.

14.5

Time (min)	Time interval (min)	Concentration (M)	ΔM	Rate (M/min)
0		1.85		
	79		0.18	2.3×10^{-3}
79		1.67		
	79		0.15	1.9×10^{-3}
158		1.52		
	158		0.22	1.4×10^{-3}
316		1.30		
	316		0.30	0.95×10^{-3}
632		1.00		

14.7 From the slopes of the tangents to the graph, the rates are: $t = 100$ min, 1.9×10^{-3} M/min; $t = 500$ min, 9.4×10^{-4} M/min. **14.9** (a) Rate = $k[N_2O_5]$; (b) rate = 6.08×10^{-5} M/s. (c) When the concentration of N_2O_5 doubles, the rate of the reaction doubles. **14.11** (a, b) $k = 2.8 \times 10^2$ $M^{-1}s^{-1}$. (c) If $[OH^-]$ is tripled, the rate triples. **14.13** (a) Rate = $k[A]$; (b) rate = $[A][B]^2$. **14.15** Rate = $k[NO]^2[O_2]$; $k = 7.11 \times 10^3$ $M^{-2}s^{-1}$. **14.17** (a) Rate = $k[NO]^2[Br_2]$; (b) $k = 1.2 \times 10^4$ $M^{-2}s^{-1}$; (c) $\Delta[NOBr]/2\Delta t = -\Delta[Br_2]/\Delta t$; (d) $\Delta[NOBr]/\Delta t = 68$ M/s; (e) $-\Delta[Br_2]/\Delta t = 6.2$ M/s. **14.19** *Half-life* is the time required to reduce the concentration of a reactant to one-half of its initial value. For first-order reactions, half-life depends only on the value of the rate constant, k. **14.21** $t_{1/2} = 1.4 \times 10^3$ s. **14.23** (a) 0.162 mol N_2O_5; (b) 5.63 min; (c) $t_{1/2} = 102$ s = 1.69 min. **14.25** Plot ln $P_{SO_2Cl_2}$ vs. time, slope = $k = 2.19 \times 10^{-5}$ s^{-1}. **14.27** (a) The reaction is first-order in N_2O_5; (b) $k = 6.0 \times 10^{-4}$ s^{-1}. **14.29** The kinetic energies of the colliding particles and their orientation determines whether a collision leads to a chemical reaction.

14.31 (a)

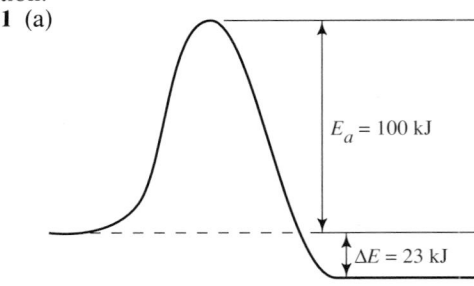

$E_a = 100$ kJ

$\Delta E = 23$ kJ

(b) +123 kJ/mol. **14.33** Reaction (a) is fastest, and reaction (c) is slowest. **14.35** No. The value of A, related to frequency and effectiveness of collisions, is different for each reaction, and k is proportional to A. **14.37** (a) k at $600°C = 1.19 \times 10^{-4}$ M/s; (b) k at $800°C = 1.28 \times 10^{-2}$ M/s. **14.39** A plot of ln k vs. $1/T$ has a slope of -5.6×10^3; $E_a = -R$(slope) = 47 kJ/mol. **14.41** $E_a = 53.6$ kJ/mol. **14.43** A *unimolecular process* has one reactant molecule, a *bimolecular process* has two reactant molecules, and a *termolecular process* has three reactant molecules. Termolecular processes are rare because it is highly unlikely that three molecules will collide effectively to form an activated complex. **14.45** (a) Bimolecular, rate = $k[N_2O][Cl]$; (b) unimolecular, rate = $k[Cl_2]$; (c) bimolecular, rate = $k[NO][Cl_2]$. **14.47** (b) First step: $-\Delta[NO]/\Delta t = k[NO]^2$; second step: $-\Delta[H_2]/\Delta t = k[H_2][N_2O_2]$. (c) N_2O_2 is the intermediate. (d) The second step is slow relative to the first. **14.49** Both (b) and (d) are consistent with the observed rate law. **14.51** A catalyst increases the rate of reaction by decreasing the activation energy, E_a, or increasing the frequency factor, A. **14.53** A *homogeneous catalyst* is in the same physical state as the reactants, while a *heterogeneous catalyst* is in a different state. **14.55** (a) $2N_2O(g) \longrightarrow 2N_2(g) + O_2(g)$. (b) A catalyst is present when a reaction sequence begins and after the last step is completed. In this reaction, NO is the catalyst and NO_2 is the intermediate. (c) homogeneous; (d) rate = $k[N_2O][NO]$. **14.57** Finely ground iron filings would be a more effective catalyst because they would have a greater surface area and provide a greater number of active sites. **14.59** As illustrated in Figure 14.18 the two C—H bonds that exist on each carbon atom of the ethylene molecule before adsorption are retained in the process in which a single D atom is added to each C (assuming we use D_2 rather than H_2). To put two D atoms on a single carbon, it is necessary that one of the already existing C—H bonds in ethylene be broken while the molecule is adsorbed, so that the H atom moves off as an adsorbed atom and is replaced by a D atom. This requires a larger activation energy than simply adsorbing C_2H_4 and adding one D atom to each carbon. **14.61** An *enzyme* is a large biomolecule that acts as a catalyst for a specific reaction by distorting the molecular structure or electron distribution of the reacting molecule. The *active site* is the specific location on the enzyme where the reactant is bound. **14.63** The body fluids at the surface of the wound contain an enzyme that catalyzes the decomposition of hydrogen peroxide. **14.66** $\Delta[Cl^-]/\Delta t = 7.8 \times 10^{-7}$ M/s. **14.68** (a) Rate $= k[HgCl_2][C_2O_4^{2-}]^2$; (b) $k = 7.5 \times 10^{-3}$ $M^{-2}s^{-1}$; (c) rate $= 6.0 \times 10^{-6}$ M/s. **14.70** (a) The reaction is first-order; $k = 1.49 \times 10^{-3}$ s^{-1}; (b) $t_{1/2} = 465$ s. **14.73** A plot of k vs. $1/T$ is linear with a slope of -7.8×10^3. $E_a = -R$ (slope) $= 65$ kJ/mol. **14.75** (a) Rate $= k[H_2O_2][I^-]$; (b) $2H_2O_2(aq) \longrightarrow 2H_2O(l) + O_2(g)$; (c) IO^- is the intermediate. **14.78** The enzyme must lower E_a by approximately 10 kJ/mol for the reaction to be viable in the body. **14.80** Enzyme, carbonic anhydrase; substrate, carbonic acid (H_2CO_3); turnover number, 1×10^7 molecules/s.

Chapter 15

15.1 (a) At equilibrium, the forward and reverse reactions proceed at equal rates. (b) At equilibrium, the net concentrations of reactants and products are *constant* but not necessarily equal. **15.3** $K = 1.3 \times 10^3$. **15.5** (a) $K_c = [HCl]^2/[H_2][Cl_2]$, homogeneous; (b) $K_c = [NO_2]^2[O_2]/[N_2O_5]^2$, homogeneous; (c) $K_c = [CS_2][H_2]^4/[CH_4][H_2S]^2$, homogeneous; (d) $K_c = [CO]^2/[CO_2]$, heterogeneous; (e) $K_c = [H_2O]/[H_2]$, heterogeneous. **15.7** (a) $K_c = 4.2 \times 10^2$. (b) The equilibrium favors SO_3 at this temperature. **15.9** $K_c = 1.84 \times 10^{-2}$. **15.11** (a) $[H_2] = 0.012$ M, $[N_2] = 0.019$ M, $[H_2O] = 0.138$ M; (b) $K_c = 6.5 \times 10^2$. **15.13** (a) $K_p = 0.133$; (b) $K_c = 0.11$. **15.15** (a) $K_p = 66.8$. (b) The equilibrium favors products. **15.17** (a) At equilibrium, $P_{NO_2} = 0.30$ atm. (b) $K_p = 0.15$. **15.19** (a) $Q = 2.19 \times 10^{-10}$; the mixture is at equilibrium. (b) $Q = 1.03 \times 10^{-8}$; the reaction will proceed to the left. (c) $Q = 1.68 \times 10^{-12}$; the reaction will proceed to the right. **15.21** $[NO] = 2.8 \times 10^{-3}$ M. **15.23** $[Br_2] = 7.67 \times 10^{-3}$ M, $[Br] = 2.82 \times 10^{-3}$ M, 0.0451 g Br. **15.25** $P_{CO_2} = 1.49 \times 10^{-3}$ atm. **15.27** $[H_2S] = [NH_3] = 1.1 \times 10^{-2}$ M. **15.29** $[I_2] = [Br_2] = 0.0267$ M, $[IBr] = 0.447$ M. **15.31** (a) Increase; (b) increase; (c) decrease; (d) no effect; (e) no effect; (f) no effect. **15.33** (a) No effect; (b) no effect; (c) increase equilibrium constant; (d) no effect. **15.35** (a) $K = 1.5 \times 10^{-39}$. (b) Reactants are much more plentiful than products at equilibrium.

15.38 $K_c = 4.4 \times 10^{-4}$. **15.41** (a) 1.46 g N_2; 0.317 g H_2; (b) 2.53 g NH_3; (c) $P_t = 11.93$ atm. **15.44** (a) $K_c' = 7.0 \times 10^{-5}$; (b) $[PH_3] = 1.6 \times 10^{-3}$ M. **15.47** $K_c = 4.4 \times 10^{-2}$, $K_p = 4.0$. **15.50** (a) Left; (b) right; (c) left; (d) right; (e) left. **15.53** (a) $K_c = 0.013$; (b) 26% of the CCl_4 reacted; (c) $P_{Cl_2} = 1.06$ atm, $P_{CCl_4} = 1.47$ atm. **15.56** $[H_2] = [I_2] = 2.46 \times 10^{-2}$ M; $[HI] = 0.170$ M.

Chapter 16

16.1 Solutions of HCl and H_2SO_4 conduct electricity, taste sour, turn litmus paper red (are acidic), neutralize solutions of bases, and react with active metals to form $H_2(g)$. HCl and H_2SO_4 solutions have these properties in common because both compounds are strong acids. That is, they both dissociate completely in H_2O to form $H^+(aq)$ and an anion. (HSO_4^- is not completely dissociated, but the first dissociation step for H_2SO_4 is complete.) The presence of ions enables the solutions to conduct electricity; the presence of $H^+(aq)$ in excess of 1×10^{-7} M accounts for all other properties listed. **16.3** (a) *Autoionization* is the dissociation of a neutral molecule into an anion and a cation. The equilibrium expression for the autoionization of water is $H_2O(l) \rightleftharpoons H^+(aq) + OH^-(aq)$. (b) Pure water is a poor conductor of electricity because it contains very few ions. (c) If a solution is *acidic,* it contains more H^+ than OH^-. **16.5** (a) Acidic; (b) basic; (c) basic; (d) neutral; (e) basic. **16.7** (a) $[OH^-] = 2.0 \times 10^{-12}$ M; (b) $[OH^-] = 7.7 \times 10^{-6}$ M; (c) $[OH^-] = 1.0 \times 10^{-6}$ M. **16.9** (a) The Arrhenius definition of an acid is confined to aqueous solution; the Brønsted-Lowry definition applies to any physical state. (b) HCl is the Brønsted-Lowry acid; NH_3 is the Brønsted-Lowry base. **16.11** (a) HS^-; (b) NO_3^-; (c) ClO^-; (d) CO_3^{2-}; (e) NH_3. **16.13** (a) Acid, H_2O; conjugate base, OH^-; base, NH_2^-; conjugate acid, NH_3. (b) Acid, $H_2C_2O_4$; conjugate base, $HC_2O_4^-$; base, H_2O; conjugate acid, H_3O^+. (c) Acid, H^+; conjugate base, H_2O; base, HPO_4^{2-}; conjugate acid, $H_2PO_4^-$. **16.15** (a) H_2O; NH_3 is a well-known base in aqueous solution. (b) $HClO_4$; $HClO_4$ is one of the six acids which completely dissociate in water. **16.17** (a) A substance is *amphoteric* if it can act as either an acid or a base. (b) $H_2O(l) + H_2O(l) \rightleftharpoons H_3O^+(aq) + OH^-$. **16.19** (a) Acidic; (b) basic; (c) neutral. **16.21** (a) pH = 2.44; (b) pH = 1.33; (c) pH 8.67; (d) pH = 12.83. **16.23** (a) $[H^+] = 1.66 \times 10^{-5}$ M; (b) $[H^+] = 4.79 \times 10^{-13}$ M; (c) $[H^+] = 4.68$ M; (d) $[H^+] = 7.94 \times 10^{-8}$ M. **16.25** $[H^+] = [OH^-] = 1.5 \times 10^{-7}$ M; pH = pOH = 6.81. **16.27** (a) $[H^+]$ changes by a factor of 100. (b) $[H^+]$ changes by a factor of 3.2. **16.29** (a) A *strong* acid is completely dissociated into ions in aqueous solution. (b) $[H^+] = 0.500$ M; (c) HCl, HBr, HI. **16.31** (a) $[H^+] = 0.025$ M, pH = 1.60; (b) $[H^+] = 0.0164$ M, pH = 1.785; (c) $[H^+] = 0.075$ M, pH = 1.12; (d) $[H^+] = 0.0125$ M, pH = 1.90. **16.33** (a) $[OH^-] = 0.050$ M, pH = 12.70; (b) $[OH^-] = 0.116$ M, pH = 13.066; (c) $[OH^-] = 6.00 \times 10^{-3}$ M, pH = 11.778; (d) $[OH^-] = 0.0125$ M, pH = 12.10. **16.35** $[OH^-] = 0.223$ M, pH = 13.348. **16.37** Strongest, $HClO_4$; weakest, HClO.

16.39 $K_a = 1.4 \times 10^{-4}$. **16.41** (a) $[H^+] = 1.8 \times 10^{-3}$ M, pH = 2.74; (b) $[H^+] = 7.2 \times 10^{-4}$ M, pH = 3.14; (c) $[OH^-] = 5.3 \times 10^{-3}$ M, pH = 11.73. **16.43** From the quadratic formula, $[H^+] = 0.018$ M, pH = 1.74. **16.45** (a) $[H^+] = 2.8 \times 10^{-3}$ M, 0.70% ionization; (b) $[H^+] = 1.4 \times 10^{-3}$ M, 1.4% ionization; (c) $[H^+] = 8.7 \times 10^{-4}$ M, 2.2% ionization. **16.47** $[H^+] = [X^-] = 0.019$ M, $[HX] = 0.181$ M, $K_a = 2.0 \times 10^{-3}$. **16.49** $HX(aq) \rightleftharpoons H^+(aq) + X^-(aq)$; $K_a = [H^+][X^-]/[HX]$. Assume that the percent of acid that dissociates (ionizes) is small. Let $[H^+] = [X^-] = y$. $K_a = y^2/[HX]$; $y = K_a^{1/2}[HX]^{1/2}$. Percent ionization = $(y/[HX]) \times 100$. Substituting for y, percent ionization = $100 \, K_a^{1/2}[HX]^{1/2}/[HX]$ or $100 \, K_a^{1/2}/[HX]^{1/2}$. That is, percent ionization varies inversely as the square root of the concentration of HX. **16.51** $[H^+] = 5.7 \times 10^{-3}$ M, pH = 2.24. The approximation that the first dissociation is less than 5% of the total acid concentration is not valid; the quadratic equation must be solved. The $[H^+]$ produced from the second and third dissociations is small with respect to that present from the first step; the second and third ionizations can be neglected when calculating the $[H^+]$ and pH. **16.53** (a) $C_3H_7NH_2(aq) + H_2O(l) \rightleftharpoons C_3H_7NH_3^+(aq) + OH^-(aq)$; $K_b = [C_3H_7NH_3^+][OH^-]/[C_3H_7NH_2]$. (b) $CN^-(aq) + H_2O(l) \rightleftharpoons HCN(aq) + OH^-(aq)$; $K_b = [HCN][OH^-]/[CN]$. (c) $CHO_2^-(aq) + H_2O(l) \rightleftharpoons HCHO_2(aq) + OH^-(aq)$; $K_b = [HCHO_2][OH^-]/[CHO_2^-]$. **16.55** (a) Ionization of HCN $[HCN(aq) \rightleftharpoons H^+(aq) + CN^-(aq)]$ + hydrolysis of CN^- $[CN^-(aq) + H_2O(l) \rightleftharpoons HCN(aq) + OH^-(aq)]$ = autoionization of H_2O $[H_2O(l) \rightleftharpoons H^+(aq) + OH^-(aq)]$. (b) $K_a \times K_b = [H^+][CN^-]/[HCN] \times [OH^-][HCN]/[CN^-] = [H^+][OH^-] = K_w$. **16.57** (a) $K_b = 2.2 \times 10^{-11}$; (b) $K_b = 5.3 \times 10^{-10}$; (c) $K_b = 1.6 \times 10^{-7}$; (d) $K_b = 5.6 \times 10^{-11}$. **16.59** (a) $[OH^-] = 1.4 \times 10^{-3}$ M, pH = 11.15; (b) $[OH^-] = 3.8 \times 10^{-3}$ M, pH = 11.58; (c) $[NO_2^-] = 0.50$ M, $[OH^-] = 3.3 \times 10^{-6}$ M, pH = 8.52. **16.61** (a) Basic; (b) basic; (c) acidic; (d) basic. **16.63** $[OH^-] = 6.6 \times 10^{-6}$ M, pH = 8.82. **16.65** (a) As the electronegativity of the central atom (X) increases, the strength of the oxyacid increases. (b) As the number of nonprotonated oxygen atoms in the molecule increases, the strength of the oxyacid increases. **16.67** (a) H_2SO_3; (b) H_3PO_4; (c) H_2SO_3. **16.69** (a) True. (b) False. In a series of acids that have the same central atom, acid strength increases with the number of nonprotonated oxygen atoms bonded to the central atom. (c) False. H_2Te is a stronger acid than H_2S because the H—Te bond is longer, weaker, and more easily dissociated than the H—S bond.

16.71

Theory	Acid	Base
Arrhenius	Forms H^+ ions in water	Produces OH^- in water
Brønsted-Lowry	Proton (H^+) donor	Proton acceptor
Lewis	Electron-pair acceptor	Electron-pair donor

The Brønsted-Lowry theory is more general than Arrhenius's definition because it is based on a unified model for the processes responsible for acidic or basic character, and it shows the relationships between these processes. The Lewis theory is more general still because it does not restrict the acidic species to compounds having ionizable hydrogen. Any substance that can be viewed as an electron-pair acceptor is defined as a Lewis acid. **16.73** (a) Acid, $Fe(ClO_4)_3$ or Fe^{3+}; base, H_2O. (b) Acid, H_2O; base, CN^-. (c) Acid, BF_3; base, $(CH_3)_3N$. (d) Acid, HIO; base, NH_2^-. **16.75** (a) CdI_2; (b) $Fe(NO_3)_3$; (c) $CrCl_3$. **16.77** (a) $[H^+] = 8 \times 10^{-7}$ M, acidic; (b) $[H^+] = 8 \times 10^{-3}$ M, acidic; (c) $[H^+] = 4 \times 10^{-2}$ M, acidic; (d) $[H^+] = 1 \times 10^{-12}$ M, basic. **16.80** The equilibrium shifts to the right, and the NaOH solution is blue. **16.83** pH = 6.34. **16.87** $[H^+] = 2.4 \times 10^{-2}$ M, $[H_2PO_4] = 2.4 \times 10^{-2}$ M, $[HPO_4^-] = 6.2 \times 10^{-8}$ M, $[PO_4^{3-}] = 1.1 \times 10^{-18}$ M. **16.90** (a) $K_i = 5.6 \times 10^3$, $K_{ii} = 10$. (b) Both (i) and (ii) have $K > 1$, although $K = 10$ is not *much* greater than 1. Both could be written with a single arrow. **16.92** (a) There is 2% dissociation. (b) $K_a = 4 \times 10^{-4}$.

Chapter 17

17.1 (a) The extent of dissociation of a weak electrolyte is decreased when a strong electrolyte containing an ion in common with the weak electrolyte is added to it. (b) NaOCl. (c) If an external source of BH^+ such as BH^+Cl^- is added to a solution of B(aq), the equilibrium shifts so that $[OH^-]$ decreases and [B] increases, effectively suppressing the ionization of B. **17.3** (a) Increase; (b) decrease; (c) no change; (d) decrease. **17.5** (a) pH = 4.59; (b) pH = 9.90. **17.7** (a) 40.0 mL NaOH solution; (b) 115 mL NaOH solution; (c) 104 mL NaOH solution. **17.9** (a) 0.137 M HBr; (b) 0.109 M HBr; (c) 0.244 M HBr. **17.11** (a) pH = 1.54; (b) pH = 3.30; (c) pH = 7.00; (d) pH = 10.70; (e) pH = 12.74. **17.13** (a) The quantity of base required to reach the equivalence point is the same in the two titrations. (b) The pH is higher initially in the titration of a weak acid. (c) The pH is higher at the equivalence point in the titration of a weak acid. (d) The pH in excess base is essentially the same for the two cases. (e) In titrating a weak acid, one needs an indicator that changes at a higher pH than for the strong acid titration. **17.15** (a) pH = 2.78; (b) pH = 4.74; (c) pH = 6.44; (d) pH = 8.81; (e) pH = 11.17; (f) pH = 12.48. **17.17** (a) pH = 7.00; (b) $[HONH_3^+] = 0.100$ M, pH = 3.52; (c) $[C_6H_5NH_3^+] = 0.100$ M, pH = 2.82. **17.19** In a mixture of $HC_2H_3O_2$ and $NaC_2H_3O_2$, $HC_2H_3O_2$ reacts with added base, and $C_2H_3O_2^-$ combines with added acid, leaving $[H^+]$ relatively unchanged. Although HCl and KCl are a conjugate acid–base pair, Cl^- has no tendency to combine with added acid to form undissociated HCl. Any added acid simply increases $[H^+]$ in an HCl-KCl mixture. **17.21** (a) pH = 4.60; (b) $Na^+(aq) + C_2H_3O_2^-(aq) + H^+(aq) + Cl^-(aq) \longrightarrow HC_2H_3O_2(aq) + Na^+(aq) + Cl^-(aq)$; (c) $HC_2H_3O_2(aq) + Na^+(aq) + OH^-(aq) \longrightarrow C_2H_3O_2^-(aq) + H_2O(l) + Na^+(aq)$.

17.23 (a) $H^+(aq) + NO_2^-(aq) \rightleftharpoons HNO_2(aq)$;
(b) $K = 2.2 \times 10^3$; (c) $[Na^+] = [ClO_4^-] = 0.075\ M$,
$[HNO_2] = 0.069\ M$, $[H^+] = [NO_2^-] = 0.0056\ M$.
17.25 0.25 mol NaBrO. **17.27** (a) pH = 4.78; (b)
pH = 4.73; (c) pH = 4.83. **17.29** (a) $[HCO_3^-]/$
$[H_2CO_3] = 11$; (b) $[HCO_3^-]/[H_2CO_3] = 5.4$. **17.31** (a)
The concentration of undissolved solid does not appear
in the solubility product expression because it is constant
as long as there is solid present. (b) $K_{sp} = [Ag^+][I^-]$;
$K_{sp} = [Ba^{2+}][CO_3^{2-}]$; $K_{sp} = [Cu^+]^2[S^{2-}]$; $K_{sp} =$
$[Ce^{3+}][F^-]^3$; $K_{sp} = [Ca^{2+}]^3[PO_4^{3-}]^2$. **17.33** (a) $K_{sp} =$
7.63×10^{-9}; (b) $K_{sp} = 2.7 \times 10^{-9}$; (c) 5.3×10^{-4} mol
$Ba(IO_3)_2/L$. **17.35** (a) 7.1×10^{-7} mol AgBr/L; (b)
1.7×10^{-11} mol AgBr/L; (c) 1.0×10^{-12} mol AgBr/L.
17.37 (a) 2.2×10^{-6} mol $Cu(OH)_2/L$; (b) 2.2×10^{-10}
mol $Cu(OH)_2/L$; (c) 2.2×10^{-14} mol $Cu(OH)_2/L$.
17.39 $[Ca^{2+}]/[Ba^{2+}] = 3.9 \times 10^{-9}/1.0 \times 10^{-4} = 3.9 \times$
10^{-5}. **17.41** $[KMnO_4] = 0.11\ M$. **17.43** (a) $Q < K_{sp}$;
no $Mn(OH)_2$ precipitates. (b) $Q < K_{sp}$; no Ag_2SO_4 precipitates. **17.45** $[OH^-] = 9.7 \times 10^{-4}\ M$, pH = 10.99.
17.47 (a) $MnS(s) + 2H^+(aq) \longrightarrow H_2S(aq) + Mn^{2+}(aq)$;
(b) $PbF_2(s) + 2H^+(aq) \longrightarrow 2HF(aq) + Pb^{2+}(aq)$; (c)
$AuCl_3(s) + H^+(aq) \longrightarrow$ no reaction; (d) $Hg_2C_2O_4(s) +$
$2H^+(aq) \longrightarrow H_2C_2O_4(aq) + Hg_2^{2+}(aq)$; (e) $CuBr(s) +$
$H^+(aq) \longrightarrow$ no reaction. **17.49** AgI will precipitate first,
at $[I^-] = 4.2 \times 10^{-13}\ M$. **17.51** 3×10^{-10} mol PbS/L.
17.53 (a) $Zn(OH)_2(s) + 2H^+(aq) \longrightarrow Zn^{2+}(aq) +$
$2H_2O(l)$; Lewis base: OH^-; Lewis acid: H^+. (b)
$Cd(CN)_2(s) + 2CN^-(aq) \longrightarrow [Cd(CN)_4]^{2-}(aq)$; Lewis
base: CN^-; Lewis acid: Cd^{2+}. (c) $CrF_3(s) +$
$3OH^-(aq) \longrightarrow Cr(OH)_3(s) + 3F^-(aq)$; Lewis base: OH^-;
Lewis acid: Cr^{3+}. **17.55** $[Cu^{2+}] = 2 \times 10^{-12}\ M$.
17.57 $K = K_{sp} \times K_f = 8 \times 10^4$. **17.59** The first two experiments eliminate group 1 and 2 ions (Figure 17.21).
The absence of insoluble carbonate precipitates in the filtrate from the third experiment rules out group 4 ions.
The ions that might be in the sample are those from
group 3, Al^{3+}, Fe^{2+}, Zn^{2+}, Cr^{3+}, Ni^{2+}, Co^{2+}, or Mn^{2+}, and
from group 5, NH_4^+, Na^+, or K^+. **17.61** (a) Make the
solution acidic with 0.5 M HCl; saturate with H_2S. CdS
will precipitate; ZnS will not. (b) Add excess base;
$Fe(OH)_3(s)$ precipitates, but Cr^{3+} forms the soluble complex $Cr(OH)_4^-$. (c) Add $(NH_4)_2HPO_4$; Mg^{2+} precipitates
as $MgNH_4PO_4$; K^+ remains soluble. (d) Add 6 M HCl;
precipitate Ag^+ as $AgCl(s)$. **17.63** (a) Base is required to
increase $[PO_4^{3-}]$ so that the solubility product of the
metal phosphates of interest is exceeded and the phosphate salts precipitate. (b) K_{sp} for the cations in group 3
is much larger, and so to exceed K_{sp} a higher $[S^{2-}]$ is required. (c) They should all redissolve in strongly acidic
solution. **17.66** $pK_a = 7.80$. **17.69** (a) The pH at the
equivalence point is 8.94; either phenolphthalein or thy-
mol blue is appropriate. Phenolphthalein is usually chosen because the colorless-to-pink endpoint is easier to
see. (b) 0.06206 M NaOH. **17.74** (a) $pK_a = 4.98$; (b)
0.024 mol NaOH. **17.78** 0.39 mol HX^-, 0.61 mol X^{2-};
1.6 L of 1.0 M NaOH. **17.81** 1.5×10^3 μL of 1.0 M
NaOH. **17.85** $[Ca^{2+}] = 2 \times 10^{-7}\ M$, $[F^-] = 5 \times 10^{-8}\ M$;
$Q < K_{sp}$, and no CaF_2 will precipitate. **17.88** $[Pb^{2+}]$ in
solution is $1.6 \times 10^{-3}\ M$. At pH = 1, $Q = 1 \times 10^{-22}$ and
$Q > K_{sp}$. PbS will precipitate from the solution.

17.92 (a) 4×10^{-6} g $Fe(OH)_3/L$; (b) 4×10^{-24} g
$Fe(OH)_3/L$.

Chapter 18

18.1 (a) Its temperature profile. (b) Troposphere, 0 to
12 km; stratosphere, 12 to 50 km; mesosphere, 50 to
85 km; thermosphere, 85 to 110 km. **18.3** $P_{Ar} = 7.15$
torr; $P_{Ne} = 0.0139$ torr. **18.5** 569 nm. **18.7** Photons
with a wavelength short enough to photodissociate N_2 are
scarce, and N_2 does not readily absorb these photons.
18.9 (a) Oxygen atoms exist longer at 120 km because
there are fewer particles and thus fewer collisions and
subsequent reactions that consume O atoms. (b) Stratospheric ozone is the primary absorber of high-energy ultraviolet radiation from the sun. Without it, plants and
animals at the earth's surface would be seriously and adversely affected. **18.11** First step, $\Delta H = -198.9$ kJ; second step, $\Delta H = -190.9$ kJ. **18.13** (a) HCl(g),
$ClONO_2(g)$. (b) The chlorine tied up in the "chlorine
reservoir" does not participate in the destruction of
ozone; the larger the chlorine reservoir, the slower the
rate of ozone depletion. **18.15** (a) CO binds with hemoglobin in the blood to block O_2 transport to the cells; people with CO poisoning suffocate from lack of O_2. (b)
SO_2 is very corrosive to tissue and contributes to respiratory disease, especially for people with other respiratory
problems. It is also a major source of acid rain, which
damages forests and wildlife in natural waters. (c) O_3 is
extremely reactive and toxic because of its strong oxidizing ability. The products of its reactions with other atmospheric pollutants cause eye irritation and breathing difficulties. **18.17** CO in unpolluted air is typically 0.05
ppm, about 10 ppm in urban air. A major source is automobile exhaust. SO_2 is less than 0.01 ppm in unpolluted
air, about 0.08 ppm in urban air. Major sources are coal
and oil-burning power plants. NO is about 0.01 ppm in
unpolluted air, about 0.05 ppm in urban air. It comes
mainly from auto exhausts. **18.19** $P = 2.3 \times 10^{-4}$ torr;
7.7×10^{18} O_3 molecules/m^3. **18.21** Naturally occurring
sulfur oxides and carbon dioxide dissolve in atmospheric
moisture and cause unpolluted rainwater to be acidic.
18.23 2.6×10^5 g $CaCO_3$. **18.25** (a) Visible; (b) 285
kJ/mol. **18.27** $P_{NO} = 0.08$ atm $= 8 \times 10^4$ ppm.
18.29 0.09 M Na^+. **18.31** 1.5×10^{13} L H_2O. **18.33** A
high concentration of dissolved O_2 supports biodegrada-
tion of organic matter by aerobic bacteria. Lack of O_2 indicates pollution by organic and other materials that have
depleted O_2. **18.35** 2.5 g O_2. **18.37** $Ca^{2+}(aq) +$
$2HCO_3^-(aq) \longrightarrow CaCO_3(s) + CO_2(g) + H_2O(l)$.
18.39 0.35 mol $Ca(OH)_2$, 0.15 mol Na_2CO_3. **18.41** (a)
$[OH^-] = 1.4 \times 10^{-4}\ M$, pH = 10.14; (b) 0.53 mol OH^-
needed, 0.033 lb CaO. **18.43** (a) Acid rain is rain with a
larger $[H^+]$ and thus a lower pH than normal precipitation. The additional H^+ is produced by the dissolution of
sulfur and nitrogen oxides in rain droplets to form sulfuric and nitric acids. **18.46** Atmospheric pressure drops
rapidly with increasing elevation. The number of molecules per unit volume is thus much lower in the stratosphere. **18.50** (a) Anthracite coal would be more expen-

sive than bituminous coal because the supply is lower and the demand is higher. (b) In the troposphere, $SO_2(g)$ and $SO_3(g)$ from the combustion of coal can be carried from their point of origin to other parts of the country or the world. The gases dissolve in atmospheric moisture, and when water droplets collect, acid rain falls at a point far from the power plant that released the combustion products. **18.54** 7.9 percent of the blood is in the form of carboxyhemoglobin. **18.57** (a) $1.1 \times 10^{-5}\ M$; (b) by solving the quadratic formula, $[H^+] = 2.0 \times 10^{-6}\ M$, pH = 5.71. **18.61** (a) $Cl_2(g) + H_2O(l) \longrightarrow HOCl(aq) + H^+(aq) + Cl^-(aq)$; (b) $Ca^{2+}(aq) + 2HCO_3^-(aq) \xrightarrow{\Delta} CaCO_3(s) + CO_2(g) + H_2O(l)$.

Chapter 19

19.1 Spontaneous: (a), (d), (e); nonspontaneous: (b), (c). **19.3** Berthelot's suggestion is incorrect. Some nonexothermic spontaneous processes are the expansion of certain pressurized gases, the dissolving of one liquid in another, and the dissolving of many salts in water. **19.5** For a process to be spontaneous, $\Delta S_{universe}$ must be positive. When steam condenses at 90°C, there must be an increase in the entropy of the surroundings, and it must be greater than the decrease in the entropy of the system. **19.7** S increases in (a), (b), and (c); S decreases in (d). **19.9** (a) $O_2(g)$ at 0.5 atm; (b) $Br_2(g)$; (c) 1 mol of $N_2(g)$ in 22.4 L; (d) $CO_2(g)$. **19.11** (a) $CCl_4(l)$, 214.4 J/K-mol; $CCl_4(g)$, 309.4 J/K-mol. In general, the gas phase of a substance has a larger $S°$ than the liquid phase because of the greater volume and motional freedom of the gas. (b) C(diamond), 2.43 J/K-mol; C(graphite), 5.69 J/K-mol. The internal entropy in graphite is greater because there is translational freedom among the planar sheets of C atoms, but there is very little freedom within the network covalent diamond lattice. (c) 1 mol of $N_2O_4(g)$, 304.3 J/K; 2 mol of $NO_2(g)$, 480.9 J/K; 2 mol of $NO_2(g)$ occupies a larger volume and has greater motional freedom than 1 mol of $N_2O_4(g)$. (d) 1 mol of $KClO_3(s)$, 143.0 J/K; 1 mol of $KClO_3(aq)$, 265.7 J/K. Ions in solution have greater motional freedom than ions in a solid lattice. **19.13** (a) $-\Delta S$; (b) $+\Delta S$; (c) $-\Delta S$; (d) $-\Delta S$. **19.15** (a) $\Delta S° = -7.4$ J/K-mol. The value is near zero because the number of moles and the kinds of molecules are the same on both sides of the equation. The reason for the slightly negative value cannot be determined from the equation alone. (b) $\Delta S° = -145.3$ J/K-mol. The value is negative because the number of moles of gas is lower in the products. (c) $\Delta S° = +91.8$ J/K-mol. The value is positive because there are more moles of gas in the products. (d) $\Delta S° = -268.2$ J/K-mol. The value is negative because a gaseous reactant is converted to a solid product. **19.17** (a) $\Delta G = \Delta H - T\Delta S$. (b) There is no relationship between ΔG and rate of reaction. **19.19** $\Delta G° = -1.23 \times 10^5$ J. The process is highly spontaneous, so we would not expect that $H_2O_2(g)$ would be stable in the gas phase at 298 K. **19.21** (a) $\Delta G° = -190.5$ kJ, spontaneous; (b) $\Delta G° = +68.8$ kJ, nonspontaneous; (c) $\Delta G° = +192.7$ kJ, nonspontaneous; (d) $\Delta G° = +40.8$ kJ, nonspontaneous.

19.23 (a) The reaction proceeds spontaneously in the forward direction but spontaneously reverses at higher temperatures. (b) The reaction is nonspontaneous in the forward direction at all temperatures. (c) The reaction will proceed spontaneously in the forward direction at high temperatures but is spontaneous in the reverse direction at lower temperatures. (d) The reaction becomes spontaneous in the forward direction at some very high temperature. **19.25** (a) Endothermic; (b) $\Delta H > +36.1$ kJ. **19.27** The process will become spontaneous above 1112 K or 839°C. **19.29** (a) $\Delta H = +229.7$ kJ; $\Delta S° = +156$ J/K. The reaction is nonspontaneous at low temperatures and will become spontaneous at some very high temperature. (b) $\Delta G°(900\ K) = +89$ kJ. **19.31** (a) -890.4 kJ of heat produced/mol CH_4 burned; (b) $w_{max} = -817.2$ kJ/mol CH_4. **19.33** (a) ΔG becomes more positive; (b) ΔG becomes more negative; (c) ΔG becomes more positive. **19.35** (a) $\Delta G° = -5.40$ kJ; (b) $\Delta G = -14.54$ kJ. **19.37** (a) $\Delta G° = -190.5$ kJ, $K_p = 2.4 \times 10^{33}$; (b) $\Delta G° = -497.9$ kJ, $K_p = 1.8 \times 10^{87}$; (c) $\Delta G° = +104.70$ kJ, $K_p = 4.45 \times 10^{-19}$. **19.39** $\Delta H° = +176.1$ kJ, $\Delta S° = +0.1605$ kJ/K; (a) $P_{CO_2} = 3.3 \times 10^{-23}$ atm; (b) $P_{CO_2} = 4.6 \times 10^{-9}$ atm. **19.41** (a) $\Delta G° = +23.9$ kJ. (b) By definition, $\Delta G = 0$ when the system is at equilibrium. (c) $\Delta G = -11.6$ kJ. **19.44** (a) $+\Delta H$, $+\Delta S$; (b) $-\Delta H$, $-\Delta S$; (c) $+\Delta H$, $+\Delta S$; (d) $+\Delta H$, $+\Delta S$; (e) $-\Delta H$, $+\Delta S$. **19.47** (a) (i) $\Delta H° = +76.2$ kJ, $\Delta S° = -0.495$ kJ/K, $\Delta G° = +240.0$ kJ; (ii) $\Delta H° = +64.9$ kJ, $\Delta S° = -0.0125$ kJ/K, $\Delta G° = +68.71$ kJ; (iii) $\Delta H° = -505.3$ kJ, $\Delta S° = -0.533$ kJ/K, $\Delta G° = -346.4$ kJ. (b) (i) nonspontaneous; (ii) nonspontaneous; (iii) spontaneous. (c) All three reactions have $-\Delta S$, and so $\Delta G°$ will become more positive with increasing temperature. There is little effect for reaction (ii) because the magnitude of $\Delta S°$ is so small. **19.50** (a) $\Delta G°(718\ K) = -23.4$ kJ; (b) $\Delta G°(1073\ K) = -60.8$ kJ. **19.54** (a) For the aqueous equilibrium $K^+(plasma) \rightleftharpoons K^+(muscle)$, $K = 1$ and $\Delta G° = 0$. Therefore, $\Delta G = +8.77$ kJ. (b) The minimum amount of work required to transfer 1 mol of K^+ is 8.77 kJ, although in practice more than minimum work is required. **19.56** (a) For the first reaction, $\Delta G° = -2875$ kJ, $K = 3 \times 10^{504}$; for the second, $\Delta G° = -226$ kJ, $K = 4 \times 10^{39}$. (b) Considerably more work can in principle be obtained from the first reaction because $\Delta G°$ is more negative. **19.59** $\Delta G° = -2876.9$ kJ, 94.3 mol ATP/mol glucose.

Chapter 20

20.1 (a) I, $+5$ to 0; C, $+2$ to $+4$; (b) Hg, $+2$ to 0; N, -2 to 0; (c) N, $+5$ to $+2$; S, -2 to 0; (d) Cl, $+4$ to $+3$; O, -1 to 0. **20.3** (a) $2N_2H_4(g) + N_2O_4(g) \longrightarrow 3N_2(g) + 4H_2O(l)$; (b) N_2O_4, oxidizing agent; N_2H_4, reducing agent. **20.5** (a) $H_2O_2(aq) + 2H^+(aq) + 2e^- \longrightarrow 2H_2O(l)$, reduction; (b) $Cl_2(g) + 6H_2O(l) \longrightarrow 2ClO_3^-(aq) + 12H^+(aq) + 10e^-$, oxidation; (c) $4OH^-(aq) \longrightarrow O_2(g) + 2H_2O(l) + 4e^-$, oxidation; (d) $CrO_4^{2-}(aq) + 4H_2O(l) + 3e^- \longrightarrow Cr(OH)_3(s) + 5OH^-(aq)$, reduction. **20.7** (a) $Pb(OH)_4^{2-}(aq) + ClO^-(aq) \longrightarrow PbO_2(s) + Cl^-(aq) + 2OH^-(aq) + H_2O(l)$;

(b) $Tl_2O_3(s) + 4NH_2OH(aq) \longrightarrow 2TlOH(s) + 2N_2(g) + 5H_2O(l)$; (c) $2Cr_2O_7^{2-}(aq) + 3CH_3OH(aq) + 16H^+(aq) \longrightarrow 4Cr^{3+}(aq) + 3HCO_2H(aq) + 11H_2O(l)$; (d) $2MnO_4^-(aq) + 10Cl^-(aq) + 16H^+(aq) \longrightarrow 2Mn^{2+}(aq) + 5Cl_2(g) + 8H_2O(l)$; (e) $H_2O_2(aq) + 2ClO_2(aq) + 2OH^-(aq) \longrightarrow O_2(g) + 2ClO_2^-(aq) + 2H_2O(l)$; (f) $3NO_2^-(aq) + Cr_2O_7^{2-}(aq) + 8H^+(aq) \longrightarrow 3NO_3^-(aq) + 2Cr^{3+}(aq) + 4H_2O(l)$. **20.9** The salt bridge provides a mechanism by which ions not directly involved in the redox reaction can migrate into the anode and cathode compartments to maintain charge neutrality of the solutions. **20.11** (a) $Zn(s) \longrightarrow Zn^{2+}(aq) + 2e^-$; $Ni^{2+}(aq) + 2e^- \longrightarrow Ni(s)$. (b) Anode, $Zn(s)$; cathode, $Ni(s)$. (c) $Zn(s)(-)$, $Ni(s)(+)$. (d) Electrons flow from the $Zn(-)$ electrode toward the $Ni(+)$ electrode. (e) Cations migrate toward the $Ni(s)$ cathode; anions migrate toward the $Zn(s)$ anode. **20.13** (a) $E° = 0.78$ V. (b) "Under standard conditions" refers to solutions that are $1\ M$ in concentration with all gases at 1 atm pressure. (c) Both electrodes are inert metals, probably $Pt(s)$. $Cr^{2+}(aq)/Cr^{3+}(aq)$ are in the anode compartment, $Tl^+(aq)/Tl^{3+}(aq)$ in the cathode compartment. Electrons flow from the anode to the cathode.

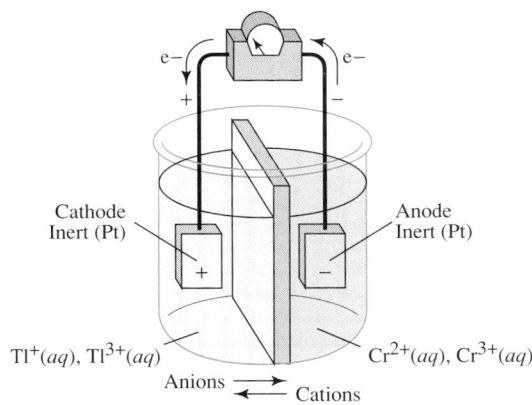

Cathode Inert (Pt)

Anode Inert (Pt)

$Tl^+(aq), Tl^{3+}(aq)$

$Cr^{2+}(aq), Cr^{3+}(aq)$

Anions ⟶ ⟵ Cations

20.15 (a) $E° = 0.777$ V; (b) $E° = 0.235$ V. **20.17** (a) $2Au(s) + 8Br^-(aq) + 3IO^-(aq) + 3H_2O(l) \longrightarrow 2AuBr_4^-(aq) + 3I^-(aq) + 6OH^-(aq)$, $E° = 1.35$ V; (b) $2Eu^{2+}(aq) + Sn^{2+}(aq) \longrightarrow 2Eu^{3+}(aq) + Sn(s)$, $E° = 0.29$ V. **20.19** (a) $H_2O_2(aq) + 2H^+(aq) + 2e^- \longrightarrow 2H_2O(l)$ occurs more readily. (b) Cathode reaction: $H_2O_2(aq) + 2H^+(aq) + 2e^- \longrightarrow 2H_2O(l)$. (c) Anode reaction: $Fe^{2+}(aq) \longrightarrow Fe^{3+}(aq) + 1e^-$. (d) $E°_{cell} = 1.005$ V. **20.21** (a) Anode, $Sn(s)$; cathode, $Cu(s)$. (b) The copper electrode gains mass as Cu is plated out, and the tin electrode loses mass as Sn is oxidized. (c) $Cu^{2+}(aq) + Sn(s) \longrightarrow Cu(s) + Sn^{2+}(aq)$. (d) $E° = 0.473$ V. **20.23** (a) Oxidizing strength: $Cu^{2+}(aq) < O_2(g) < Cr_2O_7^{2-}(aq) < Cl_2(g) < H_2O_2(aq)$. (b) Reducing strength: $H_2O_2(aq) < I^-(aq) < Sn^{2+}(aq) < Zn(s) < Al(s)$. **20.25** Any *reduced* species in Table 20.1 for which the oxidation potential is more positive than $+0.43$ V; these include $Zn(s)$, $H_2(g)$, etc. $[Fe(s)$ is questionable.] **20.27** (a) $E° = +1.552$ V, spontaneous; (b) $E° = 0.687$ V, spontaneous; (c) $E° = -2.12$ V, nonspontaneous. **20.29** (a) $\Delta G° = -299.5$ kJ; (b) $\Delta G° = -133$ kJ; (c) $\Delta G° = +409$ kJ. **20.31** (a) Decreases E;

(b) no effect; (c) decreases E; (d) no effect. **20.33** (a) $E° = 0.48$ V; (b) $E = 0.45$ V. **20.35** (a) $E° = 0.46$ V; (b) $E = 0.47$ V. **20.37** $E° = 0.763$ V, pH = 1.23. **20.39** (a) $E° = 0.627$ V, $K = 2 \times 10^{21}$; (b) $E° = +0.277$ V, $K = 2 \times 10^9$; (c) $E° = +0.44$ V, $K = 1 \times 10^{74}$. **20.41** (a) $K = 8.4 \times 10^5$; (b) $K = 7.0 \times 10^{11}$; (c) $K = 5.8 \times 10^{17}$. **20.43** 319 g MnO_2. **20.45** (a) Discharge: $Cd(s) + NiO_2(s) + 2H_2O(l) \rightleftharpoons Cd(OH)_2(s) + Ni(OH)_2(s)$; in charging, the reverse reaction occurs. (b) $E° = 1.25$ V. **20.47** $E°$ for the half-reaction $Cd(s) \longrightarrow Cd^{2+}(aq) + 2e^-$ is $+0.40$ V, smaller than the value of $+0.76$ V for the corresponding oxidation of Zn. Thus, the overall cell emf will be reduced. **20.49** (a) The products are different because in aqueous electrolysis water is reduced in preference to Mg^{2+}. (b) $MgCl_2(l) \longrightarrow Mg(l) + Cl_2(g); 2Cl^-(aq) + 2H_2O(l) \longrightarrow Cl_2(g) + H_2(g) + OH^-(aq)$. (c) Mg^{2+} is reduced, $E° = -3.73$ V; H_2O is reduced, $E° = -2.19$ V. **20.51** Chlorine is oxidized in preference to water because of the large overvoltage for the formation of $O_2(g)$.

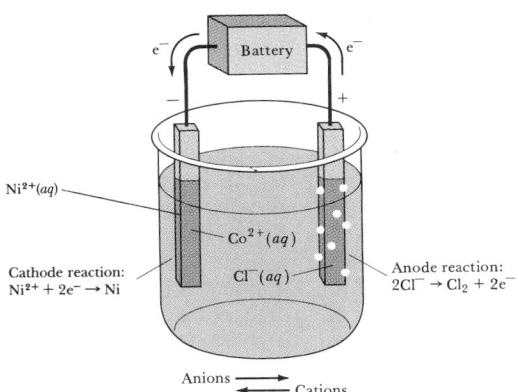

Battery

$Ni^{2+}(aq)$

$Co^{2+}(aq)$

$Cl^-(aq)$

Cathode reaction: $Ni^{2+} + 2e^- \rightarrow Ni$

Anode reaction: $2Cl^- \rightarrow Cl_2 + 2e^-$

Anions ⟶ ⟵ Cations

20.53 (a) 13 g $Cr(s)$; (b) 1.02 amps. **20.55** (a) 3.83 L $Cl_2(g)$; (b) 0.342 mol $NaOH(aq)$. **20.57** (a) True. (b) True. (c) False. Overvoltage requires a higher applied potential than calculated theoretically. Thus, more energy than the minimum is expended in driving the cell reaction. **20.59** $w_{max} = -60.7$ kJ [The $(-)$ sign means work is done *by* the cell.] **20.61** (a) 3.2×10^5 g Mg; (b) 6.1×10^3 kWh. **20.63** No. The potential for oxidation of cobalt to Co^{2+}, $+0.28$ V, is lower than that for oxidation of iron to Fe^{2+}, $+0.44$ V. To provide cathodic protection, a metal must be more readily oxidized than iron. **20.65** The added amines, acting as Brønsted bases, keep the $[H^+]$ in the antifreeze solution low. This makes the reduction of O_2 less favorable (Section 20.10), and corrosion therefore slows down. **20.67** (a) $10Fe^{2+}(aq) + 2HBrO_3(aq) + 10H^+(aq) \longrightarrow 10Fe^{3+}(aq) + Br_2(l) + 6H_2O(l)$; (b) $3Cu(s) + 2NO_3^-(aq) + 8H^+(aq) \longrightarrow 3Cu^{2+}(aq) + 2NO(g) + 4H_2O(l)$; (c) $IO_3^-(aq) + 8I^-(aq) + 3H_2O(l) \longrightarrow 3I_3^-(aq) + 6OH^-(aq)$. **20.69** (a) Anode reaction: $5Fe^{2+}(aq) \longrightarrow 5Fe^{3+}(aq) + 5e^-$. Cathode reaction: $8H^+(aq) + MnO_4^-(aq) + 5e^- \longrightarrow Mn^{2+}(aq) + 4H_2O(l)$. Electrons move from the Pt electrode in the $Fe^{2+}(aq)$ solution to the Pt electrode in the $MnO_4^-(aq)$ solution. Anions migrate through the salt bridge from the cathode beaker to the anode beaker;

cations migrate in the opposite direction. The electrode in the iron-containing beaker has a negative sign; that in the MnO_4^- beaker has a positive sign. (b) $E° = 0.74$ V. **20.71** (a) $2Rh^{3+}(aq) + 3Cd(s) \longrightarrow 2Rh(s) + 3Cd^{2+}(aq)$; (b) anode, $Cd(s)$; cathode, $Rh(s)$; (c) $E°_{cathode} = +0.80$ V; (d) $\Delta G°_{cell} = -695$ kJ. **20.73** (a) Spontaneous; (b) nonspontaneous; (c) spontaneous; (d) nonspontaneous. **20.75** $E_{cell} = 0.033$ V; the anode is in the compartment containing the dilute (0.040 M) $Cr^{3+}(aq)$ solution. **20.78** $K_{sp} = 9.69 \times 10^{-13}$. **20.81** (a) 10 mol $Cr(s)$ deposited, 5.9×10^6 C required; (b) 9.8×10^5 amps. **20.83** (a) 1.2×10^2 hr; (b) 20 kWh. **20.85** 732 g $NaBO_3$. **20.87** (a) $w_{max} \approx 2$ kWh; (b) This maximum amount of work is never realized because of internal resistance of the battery; because the cell voltage does not remain constant; because the vehicle is not capable of completely converting electrical energy into work. **20.89** The ship's hull should be made negative. The ship, as a negatively charged "electrode," becomes the site of reduction, rather than oxidation, in an electrolytic process.

Chapter 21

21.1 (a) 26 protons, 30 neutrons; (b) 38 protons, 50 neutrons; (c) 15 protons, 16 neutrons. **21.3** (a) $_{-1}^{0}e$; (b) $_{1}^{0}e$; (c) $_{0}^{1}n$. **21.5** (a) $_{53}^{131}I \longrightarrow _{54}^{131}Xe + _{-1}^{0}e$; (b) $_{90}^{230}Th \longrightarrow _{88}^{226}Ra + _{2}^{4}He$; (c) $_{74}^{181}W \longrightarrow _{73}^{181}Ta$; (d) $_{7}^{13}N \longrightarrow _{6}^{13}C + _{1}^{0}e$. **21.7** 7 alpha emissions, 4 beta emissions. **21.9** (a) Positron emission (for low atomic numbers, positron emission is more common than electron capture); (b) beta emission; (c) beta emission; (d) beta emission. **21.11** (a) No (low neutron/proton ratio, should be a positron emitter); (b) no (low neutron/proton ratio, should be a positron emitter or possibly undergo orbital electron capture); (c) no (high neutron/proton ratio, should be a beta emitter); (d) no (high atomic number, should be an alpha emitter). **21.13** (a) Stable: $_{19}^{39}K$, 20 neutrons is a magic number; (b) stable: $_{83}^{209}Bi$, 126 neutrons is a magic number; (c) stable: $_{12}^{25}Mg$, $_{10}^{24}Ne$ has a much higher neutron/proton ratio. **21.15** $_{2}^{4}He$, $_{8}^{16}O$, $_{20}^{40}Ca$. **21.17** Radioactive: (b), low neutron/proton ratio, (c), low neutron/proton ratio, and (e), atomic number greater than 83. Stable: (a) and (d). **21.19** Protons and alpha particles are positively charged and must be moving very fast to overcome electrostatic repulsions that would repel them from the target nucleus. Neutrons are electrically neutral and more easily captured by a target nucleus. **21.21** (a) $_{15}^{32}P$; (b) $_{3}^{7}Li$; (c) $_{75}^{187}Re$; (d) $_{43}^{99}Tc$; (e) $_{38}^{90}Sr$. **21.23** (a) $_{92}^{238}U + _{0}^{1}n \longrightarrow _{92}^{239}U + _{0}^{0}\gamma$; (b) $_{7}^{14}N + _{1}^{1}H \longrightarrow _{6}^{11}C + _{2}^{4}He$; (c) $_{8}^{18}O + _{0}^{1}n \longrightarrow _{9}^{19}F + _{-1}^{0}e$. **21.25** The suggestion is not reasonable. The energies of nuclear states are very large relative to ordinary temperatures. Merely changing the temperature by less than 100 K would not significantly affect the behavior of nuclei with regard to nuclear decay rates. **21.27** $_{31}^{68}Ga \longrightarrow _{30}^{68}Zn + _{1}^{0}e$; 9.78×10^{-6} g ^{68}Ga remain. **21.29** $k = 0.0307$ yr^{-1}, $t_{1/2} = 22.6$ yr. **21.31** Taking only the spontaneous radioactive decay of ^{131}I into account, the activity after 32 days should be 5.7

counts/min, which is the observed activity. The plants do not absorb iodide. **21.33** 4.0×10^{-12} g ^{226}Ra decays in 1.0 min, 1.1×10^{10} alpha particles emitted. **21.35** $k = 1.21 \times 10^{-4}$ yr^{-1}; 1.70×10^3 yr. **21.37** $k = 1.5 \times 10^{-10}$ yr^{-1}; the original rock contained 66.2 mg ^{238}U and is 1.9×10^9 yr old. **21.39** 9.317×10^{-12} J/nucleus; 5.611×10^{12} J/mol. **21.41** (a) $\Delta m = 8.25 \times 10^{-3}$ amu/nucleon; $\Delta E = 1.23 \times 10^{-12}$ J/nucleon; (b) $\Delta m = 9.41 \times 10^{-3}$ amu/nucleon; $\Delta E = 1.41 \times 10^{-12}$ J/nucleon; (c) $\Delta m = 8.46 \times 10^{-3}$ amu/nucleon; $\Delta m = 1.26 \times 10^{-12}$ J/nucleon. **21.43** 1.71×10^5 kg/day; 2.10×10^8 g ^{235}U. **21.45** (a) ^{59}Co; it has the largest binding energy per nucleon, and binding energy gives rise to mass defect. **21.47** (a) $4 _{0}^{1}n$; (b) $_{36}^{94}Kr$. **21.49** The ^{59}Fe is incorporated into the diet component and fed to the rabbits. Blood samples are removed from the animals, the red blood cells separated, and the radioactivity of the sample measured. If the iron in the dietary compounds has been incorporated into blood hemoglobin, the blood cell sample should show beta emission. Samples can be taken at various times to determine the rate of iron uptake, rate of loss of iron from the blood, and so forth. **21.51** The extremely high temperature is required to overcome the electrostatic charge repulsions between the nuclei so that they can come together to react. **21.53** (a) *Control rods* control neutron flux so that there are enough neutrons to sustain the chain reaction but not so many that the core overheats. (b) A *moderator* slows neutrons so that they are more easily captured by fissioning nuclei. **21.55** The becquerel; the curie (Ci). **21.57** $_{84}^{210}Po \longrightarrow _{82}^{206}Pb + _{2}^{4}He$. **21.59** An electron. **21.62** (a) $_{17}^{36}Cl \longrightarrow _{18}^{36}Ar + _{-1}^{0}e$. (b) ^{36}Cl has an odd number of protons and neutrons (17p, 19n), and so it is less stable than the other two isotopes. **21.64** The source will last 1.69 yr; it needs to be replaced in early July 1995. **21.68** 3.7×10^4 disintegrations/s; 4.8×10^{13} ^{90}Sr nuclei or 7.2×10^{-9} g ^{90}Sr. **21.71** 12 alpha particles (disintegrations)/s. **21.73** The mole fraction of $_{1}^{3}H$ atoms in the sample is 4.82×10^{-13}. **21.75** ^7Be, 8.63×10^{-13} J/nucleon; ^9Be, 1.04×10^{-12} J/nucleon; ^{10}Be, 1.04×10^{-12} J/nucleon. The binding energies per nucleon for ^9Be and ^{10}Be are very similar; the value for ^{10}Be is slightly higher.

Chapter 22

22.1 Metals: Sr, Ce, Rh; nonmetals: Se, Kr; metalloid: Sb. **22.3** Metals have high melting points and large thermal and electrical conductivity, whereas nonmetals have much lower melting points and are poor conductors. Metals react with nonmetals to produce ionic solids that melt at high temperatures; nonmetals react with other nonmetals to form covalent compounds that can be solids, liquids, or gases. Oxides of metals produce basic aqueous solutions, whereas oxides of nonmetals produce acidic aqueous solutions. **22.5** Bismuth should be the most metallic. It has a metallic luster and a relatively low ionization energy. Bi_2O_3 is soluble in acid but not in base, characteristic of the basic properties of the oxide of a metal rather than of the oxide of a nonmetal. **22.7** (a)

N; (b) K; (c) K in the gas phase (lowest ionization energy), Li in aqueous solution (most positive $E°$ value); (d) N has the smallest *covalent* radius; Ne is difficult to compare because it doesn't form compounds. (e) N. **22.9** (a) IF_3; (b) B_2O_3; (c) BF_3; (d) H_2O. **22.11** (a) N is too small a central atom to fit five fluorine atoms, and it does not have available d orbitals, which can help accommodate more than eight electrons. (b) Si does not readily form π bonds, which are necessary to satisfy the octet rule for both atoms in the molecule. (c) As has a lower electronegativity than N; that is, it more readily gives up electrons to an acceptor and is more easily oxidized. **22.13** (a) $NaNH_2(s) + H_2O(l) \longrightarrow NH_3(aq) + Na^+(aq) + OH^-(aq)$; (b) $2C_3H_7OH(l) + 9O_2(g) \longrightarrow 6CO_2(g) + 8H_2O(l)$; (c) $NiO(s) + C(s) \longrightarrow CO(g) + Ni(s)$ or $2NiO(s) + C(s) \longrightarrow CO_2(g) + 2Ni(s)$; (d) $AlP(s) + 3H_2O(l) \longrightarrow PH_3(g) + Al(OH)_3(s)$; (e) $Na_2S(s) + 2HCl(aq) \longrightarrow H_2S(g) + 2Na^+(aq) + 2Cl^-(aq)$. **22.15** ^1_1H, protium; ^2_1H, deuterium; ^3_1H, tritium. **22.17** Like other elements in group 1A, hydrogen has only one valence electron. Like other elements in group 7A, hydrogen needs only one electron to complete its valence shell. **22.19** (a) $Mg(s) + 2H^+(aq) \longrightarrow Mg^{2+}(aq) + H_2(g)$; (b) $C(s) + H_2O(g) \xrightarrow{1000°C} CO(g) + H_2(g)$; (c) $CH_4(g) + H_2O(g) \xrightarrow{1100°C} CO(g) + 3H_2(g)$. **22.21** (a) Ionic; (b) molecular; (c) metallic. **22.23** (a) $NaH(s) + H_2O(l) \longrightarrow NaOH(g) + H_2(g)$; (b) $Fe(s) + H_2SO_4(aq) \longrightarrow Fe^{2+}(aq) + H_2(g) + SO_4^{2-}(aq)$; (c) $H_2(g) + Br_2(g) \longrightarrow 2HBr(g)$; (d) $Na(l) + H_2(g) \longrightarrow 2NaH(s)$; (e) $PbO(s) + H_2(g) \xrightarrow{\Delta} Pb(s) + H_2O(g)$. **22.25** 7.9×10^8 kg H_2. **22.27** As an oxdizing agent in steel making; to bleach pulp and paper; in oxyacetylene torches; in medicine to assist in breathing.

22.29

Ozone has two resonance forms; the molecular structure is bent, with an O—O—O bond angle of approximately 120°. The π bond in ozone is delocalized over the entire molecule; neither individual O—O bond is a full double bond, and so the observed O—O distance of 1.28 Å is greater than the 1.21 Å distance in O_2, which has a full O—O double bond. **22.31** (a) $CaO(s) + H_2O(l) \longrightarrow Ca^{2+}(aq) + 2OH^-(aq)$; (b) $Al_2O_3(s) + 6H^+(aq) \longrightarrow 2Al^{3+}(aq) + 3H_2O(l)$; (c) $Na_2O_2(s) + 2H_2O(l) \longrightarrow 2Na^+(aq) + 2OH^-(aq) + H_2O_2(aq)$; (d) $N_2O_3(g) + H_2O(l) \longrightarrow 2HNO_2(aq)$; (e) $2KO_2(s) + 2H_2O(l) \longrightarrow 2K^+(aq) + 2OH^-(aq) + O_2(g) + H_2O_2(aq)$; (f) $NO(g) + O_3(g) \longrightarrow NO_2(g) + O_2(g)$. **22.33** (a) Neutral; (b) acidic; (c) basic; (d) amphoteric. **22.35** Assuming that the reactions occur in basic solution: (a) $H_2O_2(aq) + S^{2-}(aq) \longrightarrow 2OH^-(aq) + S(s)$. (b) $SO_2(g) + 2OH^-(aq) + H_2O_2(aq) \longrightarrow SO_4^{2-}(aq) + H_2O(l)$. (c) $NO_2^-(aq) + H_2O_2(aq) \longrightarrow NO_3^-(aq) + H_2O(l)$. (d) $As_2O_3(s) + 2H_2O_2(aq) + 6OH^-(aq) \longrightarrow 2AsO_4^{3-}(aq) + 5H_2O(l)$. (e) This reaction must be occurring in acidic solution, because $Fe(OH)_3$ would form if the solution were basic. $2Fe^{2+}(aq) + H_2O_2(aq) + 2H^+(aq) \longrightarrow 2Fe^{3+}(aq) + 2H_2O(l)$. **22.37** Formation of ammonia, NH_3, and fertilizers; as an inert gas in manufacturing

processes; as a coolant in liquid form. **22.39** (a) HNO_2, $+3$; (b) N_2H_4, -2; (c) KCN, -3; (d) $NaNO_3$, $+5$; (e) NH_4Cl, -3; (f) Li_3N, -3.

22.41 (a)

Tetrahedral

(b)

The molecular geometry around nitrogen is trigonal planar, but the hydrogen atom is not required to lie in this plane. (There is a third resonance form, which makes a smaller contribution to the observed structure.) (c)

The molecular geometry is linear. (There are two other possible resonance forms involving triple bonds.) (d)

The molecule is bent. **22.43** (a) $Mg_3N_2(s) + 6H_2O(l) \longrightarrow 3Mg(OH)_2(s) + 2NH_3(aq)$; (b) $2NO(g) + O_2(g) \longrightarrow 2NO_2(g)$; (c) $4NH_3(g) + 3O_2(g) \longrightarrow 2N_2(g) + 6H_2O(g)$; (d) $NaNH_2(s) + H_2O(l) \longrightarrow Na^+(aq) + OH^-(aq) + NH_3(aq)$. **22.45** (a) $4Zn(s) + 2NO_3^-(aq) + 10H^+(aq) \longrightarrow 4Zn^{2+}(aq) + N_2O(g) + 5H_2O(l)$; (b) $4NO_3^-(aq) + S(s) + 4H^+(aq) \longrightarrow 4NO_2(g) + SO_2(g) + 2H_2O(l)$ or $6NO_3^-(aq) + S(s) + 4H^+(aq) \longrightarrow 6NO_2(g) + SO_4^{2-}(aq) + 2H_2O(l)$; (c) $2NO_3^-(aq) + 3SO_2(g) + 2H_2O(l) \longrightarrow 2NO(g) + 3SO_4^{2-}(aq) + 4H^+(aq)$; (d) $CO(NH_2)_2(aq) + H_2O(l) \longrightarrow 2NH_3(aq) + CO_2(g)$. **22.47** (a) $2NO_3^-(aq) + 12H^+(aq) + 10e^- \longrightarrow N_2(g) + 6H_2O(l)$, $E° = +1.25$ V; (b) $2NH_4^+(aq) \longrightarrow N_2(g) + 8H^+(aq) + 6e^-$, $E° = -0.27$ V. **22.49** 1.1×10^{10} kg CH_4 is required to produce the NH_3. **22.51** In fire extinguishers; as a coolant (dry ice); in the manufacture of $Na_2CO_3 \cdot 10H_2O$; in the carbonation of beverages. **22.53** (a) HCN; (b) SiC; (c) $CaCO_3$; (d) CaC_2. **22.55** (a) $[:C\equiv N:]^-$; (b) $:C\equiv O:$; (c) $[:C\equiv C:]^{2-}$; (d) $\overset{..}{S}=C=\overset{..}{S}$; (e) $\overset{..}{O}=C=\overset{..}{O}$;

(f)

; one of three equivalent resonance structures

22.57 (a) $ZnCO_3 \xrightarrow{\Delta} ZnO(s) + CO_2(g)$; (b) $BaC_2(s) + 2H_2O(l) \longrightarrow Ba^{2+}(aq) + 2OH^-(aq) + C_2H_2(g)$; (c) $C_2H_4(g) + 3O_2(g) \longrightarrow 2CO_2(g) + 2H_2O(g)$; (d) $2CH_3OH(l) + 3O_2(g) \longrightarrow 2CO_2(g) + 4H_2O(g)$; (e) $NaCN(s) + H^+(aq) \longrightarrow Na^+(aq) + HCN(g)$. **22.59** (a) $2Mg(s) + CO_2(g) \longrightarrow 2MgO(s) + C(s)$; (b) $6CO_2(g) + 6H_2O(l) \xrightarrow{hv} C_6H_{12}O_6(aq) + 6O_2(g)$; (c) $CO_3^{2-}(aq) + H_2O(l) \longrightarrow HCO_3^-(aq) + OH^-(aq)$. **22.61** 4.06 L $C_2H_2(g)$. **22.63** 1 $ft^3 = 28.3$ L; at STP,

1 ft³ = 1.26 mol gas; (a) 7.9×10^{10} ft³ of H_2; (b) 3.1×10^{11} ft³ of N_2; (c) 3.5×10^{11} ft³ of O_2. **22.66** A, CO_2; B, H_2; C, O_2. **22.69** (a) SO_3; (b) Cl_2O_5; (c) N_2O_3; (d) CO_2; (e) P_2O_5. **22.72** $(CH_3)_2NNH_2$: 9 mol gaseous products/244 g reactants = 0.0369 mol gas/1 g reactants; $(CH_3)HNNH_2$: 6.25 mol gaseous products/161 g reactants = 0.0388 mol gas/1 g reactants; $(CH_3)HNNH_2$ has greater thrust. **22.75** $(NH_2)_2CO$ is 46.6% N by mass; NH_3 is 82.3% N by mass; $(NH_4)_2SO_4$ is 21.2% N by mass; $NaNO_3$ is 16.5% N by mass. **22.78** For this reaction, the temperature dependence of the equilibrium constant and the reaction rate are opposing effects. At ambient temperatures, the rate of the reaction is extremely slow, and equilibrium is not established in an economically viable length of time. To establish a reasonable rate, the reaction must be carried out at high temperature. **22.81** (a) $Li_3N(s) + H_2O(l) \longrightarrow 3Li^+(aq) + 3OH^-(aq) + NH_3(aq)$; (c) $3NO_2(g) + H_2O(l) \longrightarrow NO(g) + 2H^+(aq) + 2NO_3^-(aq)$; (e) $4NH_3(g) + 5O_2(g) \xrightarrow{catalyst} 4NO(g) + 6H_2O(g)$; (g)$H_2CO_3(aq) \xrightarrow{\Delta} H_2O(g) + CO_2(g)$; (i) $CS_2(g) + O_2(g) \longrightarrow CO_2(g) + S_2(g)$; (k) $Na(s) + H_2O(l) \longrightarrow NaOH(aq) + H_2(g)$; (m) $LiH(s) + H_2O(l) \longrightarrow LiOH(aq) + H_2(g)$.

Chapter 23

23.1 (a) IO_3^-, +5; (c) BrF_3; Br, +3; F, −1; (e) HIO_2, +3. **23.3** (a) Potassium chlorate; (c) aluminum chloride; (e) paraperiodic acid. **23.5** (a) Linear; (c) trigonal pyramid; (e) square planar. **23.7** Xenon has a lower ionization energy than argon; because the valence electrons are not as strongly attracted to the nucleus, they are more readily promoted to a state in which the atom can form bonds with fluorine. Also, Xe is larger and can more easily accommodate an expanded octet of electrons. **23.9** (a) Van der Waals intermolecular attractive forces increase with increasing number of electrons in the atoms. (b) F_2 reacts with water: $F_2(g) + H_2O(l) \longrightarrow 2HF(g) + O_2(g)$. That is, fluorine is too strong an oxidizing agent to exist in water. (c) HF has extensive hydrogen bonding. (d) Oxidizing power is related to electronegativity. Electronegativity decreases in the order given. **23.11** *Fluorine* is used to prepare fluorocarbons such as Teflon, used as a lubricant. *Chlorine* is used to prepare vinyl chloride, C_2H_3Cl, for plastics, and in bleach containing ClO^-. *Bromine* is used to produce silver bromide, AgBr, used in photographic film. *Iodine* is used in the form of KI as an additive to table salt. **23.13** (a) $PBr_5(l) + 4H_2O(l) \longrightarrow H_3PO_4(aq) + 5H^+(aq) + 5Br^-(aq)$; (b) $IF_5(l) + 3H_2O(l) \longrightarrow H^+(aq) + IO_3^-(aq) + 5HF(aq)$; (c) $SiBr_4(l) + 4H_2O(l) \longrightarrow Si(OH)_4(s) + 4H^+(aq) + 4Br^-(aq)$. **23.15** (a) $Br_2(l) + 2OH^-(aq) \longrightarrow BrO^-(aq) + Br^-(aq) + H_2O(l)$; (b) $Cl_2(g) + 2Br^-(aq) \longrightarrow Br_2(l) + 2Cl^-(aq)$; (c) $Br_2(l) + H_2O_2(aq) \longrightarrow 2Br^-(aq) + O_2(g) + 2H^+(aq)$. **23.17** (a) $2ClO_3^-(aq) + 10Fe^{2+}(aq) + 12H^+(aq) \longrightarrow Cl_2(g) + 10Fe^{3+}(aq) + 6H_2O(l)$; (b) $E° = +0.70$ V. **23.19** The average Xe—F bond enthalpies in the three compounds:

XeF_2, 134 kJ; XeF_4, 134 kJ; XeF_6, 130 kJ. They are remarkably constant in the series. **23.21** (a) H_2SeO_3, +4; (c) H_2Te, −2; (e) $CaSO_4$, +6. **23.23** (a) Potassium thiosulfate; (b) aluminum sulfide; (c) sodium hydrogen selenite; (d) selenium hexafluoride.

23.25 (a) 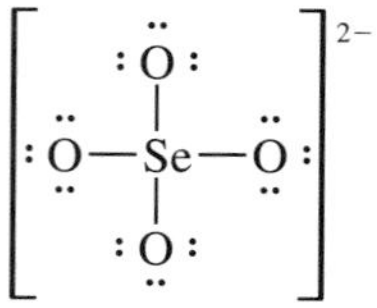 (b)

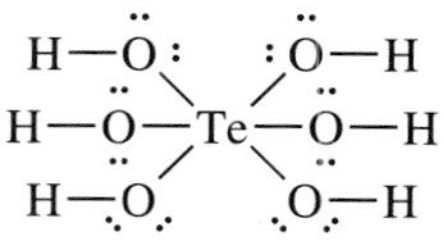

Tetrahedral   Octahedral

23.27 (a) $SeO_2(s) + H_2O(l) \longrightarrow H_2SeO_3(aq) \rightleftharpoons H^+(aq) + HSeO_3^-(aq)$; (c) $8SO_3^{2-}(aq) + S_8(s) \longrightarrow 8S_2O_3^{2-}(aq)$; (e) $SO_3(g) + H_2SO_4(l) \longrightarrow H_2S_2O_7(l)$. **23.29** (b) $Cr_2O_7^{2-}(aq) + 3H_2SO_3(aq) + 2H^+(aq) \longrightarrow 2Cr^{3+}(aq) + 3SO_4^{2-}(aq) + 4H_2O(l)$. **23.31** Te is less electronegative than Se or S, and so it withdraws less charge from the oxygens, making the O—H bonds less polar and less likely to ionize as H^+. Also, Te is larger than Se or S and in aqueous solution is likely to be coordinated by solvent water molecules. This interaction increases the electron density on the central tellurium and further reduces the withdrawal of charge from the O—H bonds in H_2TeO_4. **23.33** (a) H_3PO_4, +5; (b) H_3AsO_3, +3; (c) Sb_2S_3, +3; (d) $Ca(H_2PO_4)_2$, +5; (e) K_3P, −3. **23.35** (a) Arsenic acid; (c) tetraphosphorus decaoxide. **23.37** (a) PCl_4^+ is tetrahedral; PCl_6^- is octahedral. (b) PCl_4^+, sp^3; PCl_6^-, sp^3d^2. (c) The ionic form is stabilized in the solid state by the lattice energy gained from forming the ions. **23.39** (a) Only two of the hydrogen atoms in H_3PO_3 are bound to oxygen. The third is attached directly to phosphorus and is not readily ionized because the H—P bond is not very polar. (c) Phosphate rock consists of $Ca_3(PO_4)_2$, which is only slightly soluble in water. The phosphorus is unavailable for plant use. (e) In solution, Na_3PO_4 is completely dissociated into Na^+ and PO_4^{3-}. PO_4^{3-}, the conjugate base of the very weak acid HPO_4^{2-}, has a K_b of 2.4×10^{-2} and produces a considerable amount of OH^- by hydrolysis of H_2O. **23.41** (a) $2Ca_3(PO_4)_2(s) + 6SiO_2(s) + 10C(s) \longrightarrow P_4(g) + 6CaSiO_3(l) + 10CO_2(g)$; (b) $3H_2O(l) + PCl_3(l) \longrightarrow H_3PO_3(aq) + 3H^+(aq) + 3Cl^-(aq)$. **23.43** (a) SiO_2, +4; (b) $GeCl_4$, +4; (c) $NaBH_4$, +3; (d) $SnCl_2$, +2; (e) B_2H_6, −3. **23.45** In C_2H_4 and C_2H_2 the carbon atoms are joined by π bonds as well as σ bonds. Silicon does not form Si—Si π bonds of great strength, and so Si compounds involving such bonds are unstable relative to other bonding configurations. **23.47** (a) Carbon; (b) lead; (c) silicon. **23.49** $GeCl_4(g) + 2H_2O(l) \longrightarrow GeO_2(s) + 4HCl(g)$; $SiCl_4(g) + 2H_2O(l) \longrightarrow SiO_2(s) + 4HCl(g)$. **23.51** KSi_3AlO_8. **23.53** (a) SiO_4^{4-}; (b) SiO_3^{2-}; (c) SiO_3^{2-}. **23.56** (a) Sulfur is a less electronegative element than oxygen and can be expected to more readily give up its electrons in the course of being oxidized. (c) Astatine is radioactive and not present in nature to a significant extent. (e) The ionization energy of Xe is lower, so it has a greater tendency to form bonds with F; the larger Xe atom can more easily accommodate six bound F atoms.

(g) In aluminosilicate sheets the overall charge is more negative than in silicates because of replacement of Si^{4+} by Al^{3+}. More cations are present between layers, increasing electrostatic interactions between the cations and the sheets and the rigidity of the structure. **23.58** 0.533 atm. **23.61** $BrO_3^-(aq) + XeF_2(aq) + H_2O(l) \longrightarrow$ $Xe(g) + 2HF(aq) + BrO_4^-(aq)$. **23.64** $8Fe(s) +$ $S_8(s) \longrightarrow 8FeS(s); S_8(s) + 16F_2(g) \longrightarrow 8SF_4(g)$ or $S_8(s) + 24F_2(g) \longrightarrow 8SF_6(g); S_8(s) + 8O_2(g) \longrightarrow$ $8SO_2(g); S_8(s) + 8H_2(g) \longrightarrow 8H_2S(g)$. **23.66** The valence-shell electron arrangement controls the upper and lower limits of oxidation state. For group 6A the configuration is ns^2np^4. Addition of two electrons or loss of six electrons produces a closed shell. Thus, the oxidation state limits are -2 to $+6$. **23.69** (a) $2H_2Se(g) +$ $O_2(g) \longrightarrow 2H_2O(g) + 2Se(s)$; (b) $\Delta G° = -489.0$ kJ; $\Delta G° = -RT \ln K, K = 5 \times 10^{85}$. **23.71** $GeO_2(s) +$ $C(s) \xrightarrow{\Delta} Ge(l) + CO_2(g); Ge(l) + 2Cl_2(g) \longrightarrow$ $GeCl_4(l); GeCl_4(l) + 2H_2O(l) \longrightarrow GeO_2(s) + 4HCl(g);$ $GeO_2(s) + 2H_2(g) \longrightarrow Ge(s) + 2H_2O(l)$. **23.74** $2.0 \times$ 10^3 mol air in the room (average molecular weight of air = 29.0 g/mol); 4.0×10^{-2} mol H_2S allowable; 3.5 g FeS required. **23.77** The atomic radii calculated for N in the three compounds are: NOF, 0.80 Å; NOCl, 0.98 Å; NOBr, 0.99Å. The possible resonance forms are $X—N{=}O \longleftrightarrow X{=}N—O$. Because fluorine is a second-row element, we expect that π-bond formation is more important than for Cl or Br. The π character of the X—N bond in the second structure suggests that this form will be more important in NOF than NOCl or NOBr and that the N—F bond should be shorter than otherwise expected.

Chapter 24

24.1 Iron: hematite, Fe_2O_3; magnetite, Fe_3O_4. Aluminum: bauxite, $Al_2O_3 \cdot xH_2O$. In ores, iron is present as the $+3$ ion or as both the $+2$ and $+3$ ions as in magnetite. Aluminum is always present in the $+3$ oxidation state. **24.3** (a) $ZnCO_3(s) \xrightarrow{\Delta} ZnO(s) + CO_2(g)$; (b) $MnO(s) + CO(g) \longrightarrow Mn(l) + CO_2(g)$; (c) $Al(OH)_3(s) + OH^-(aq) \longrightarrow [Al(OH)_4]^-(aq)$; (d) $TiCl_4(g) + K(l) \longrightarrow Ti(s) + 4KCl(s)$; (e) $3CaO(l) +$ $P_2O_5(l) \longrightarrow Ca_3(PO_4)_2(l)$. **24.5** $FeO(s) + H_2(g) \longrightarrow$ $Fe(l) + H_2O(g); Fe_2O_3(s) + 3H_2(g) \longrightarrow 2Fe(l) +$ $3H_2O(g); FeO(s) + CO(g) \longrightarrow Fe(l) + CO_2(g);$ $Fe_2O_3(s) + 3CO(g) \longrightarrow 2Fe(l) + 3CO_2(g)$. **24.7** (a) $SO_3(g)$. (b) $CO(g)$ provides a reducing environment for the transformation of Pb^{2+} to Pb^0. (c) $PbSO_4(s) \longrightarrow$ $PbO(s) + SO_3(g); PbO(s) + CO(g) \longrightarrow Pb(s) + CO_2(g)$. **24.9** 3.6×10^3 kg SO_2 (or, to one significant figure, 4×10^3 kg SO_2). **24.11** (a) Air serves mainly to oxidize coke to CO; this exothermic reaction also provides heat for the furnace: $2C(s) + O_2(g) \longrightarrow 2CO(g), \Delta H = -110$ kJ. (b) Limestone, $CaCO_3$, is the source of basic oxide for slag formation: $CaCO_3(s) \xrightarrow{\Delta} CaO(s) + CO_2(g);$ $CaO(l) + SiO_2(l) \longrightarrow CaSiO_3(l)$. **24.13** To purify electrochemically, use a soluble cobalt salt such as

$CoSO_4 \cdot 7H_2O$ as electrolyte. Reduction of H_2O does not occur because of overvoltage. Anode reaction: $Co(s) \longrightarrow Co^{2+}(aq) + 2e^-$; cathode reaction: $Co^{2+}(aq) +$ $2e^- \longrightarrow Co(s)$. **24.15** 5.8×10^2 g $Ni^{2+}(aq)$. **24.17** (c) $\Delta G = \Delta H - T \Delta S; \Delta H° = +30.1$ kJ; $\Delta S° = +24.5$ J/K; $\Delta G° = -6.0$ kJ. **24.19** Sodium is metallic; each atom is bonded to many others. When the metal lattice is distorted, many bonds remain intact. In NaCl the ionic forces are strong, and the ions are arranged in very regular arrays. The ionic forces tend to be broken along certain cleavage planes in the solid, and the substance does not tolerate much distortion before cleaving. **24.21** In the electron-sea model the electrons move about in the metallic lattice, while the silver atoms remain more-or-less fixed in position. Under the influence of an applied potential, the electrons are free to move throughout the structure, giving rise to thermal and electrical conductivity. **24.23** According to the molecular-orbital or band theory of metallic bonding, the maximum bond order and highest bond strength occur in metals with six to eight valence electrons. Assuming that hardness is directly related to the bond strength between metal atoms, Cr, with six valence electrons, should have the highest bond strength and greatest hardness in the fourth row. **24.25** According to band theory, an *insulator* has energy bands that are either completely filled or completely empty, with a large energy gap between the full and empty bands. A *conductor* has partially filled energy bands. A *semiconductor* has a filled or partially filled energy band separated by a small energy gap from an empty or nearly empty band. **24.27** White tin is more metallic in character; it has a higher conductivity and a larger Sn—Sn distance (3.02 Å) than gray tin (2.81 Å). **24.29** An *alloy* contains atoms of more than one element and has the properties of a metal. In a *solution alloy* the components are randomly dispersed. In a *heterogeneous alloy* the components are not evenly dispersed and can be distinguished at a macroscopic level. In an *intermetallic compound* the components have interacted to form a compound substance, as in Cu_3As. **24.31** Isolated atoms: (b), (c); bulk metal: (a), (d). **24.33** The *lanthanide contraction* is the name given to the decrease in atomic size due to the buildup in effective nuclear charge as we move through the lanthanides (elements 58 to 71) and beyond them. The lanthanide contraction affects size-related properties such as ionization energy, electron affinity, and density. **24.35** See Figure 24.25. (a) $NbCl_5$; (b) WCl_6. **24.37** Chromium, $[Ar] 3d^54s^1$, has six valence electrons, some or all of which can be involved in bonding, leading to multiple stable oxidation states. Al, $[Ne]3s^23p^1$, has only three valence electrons, which are all lost or shared during bonding, producing the $+3$ state exclusively. **24.39** (a) $Cr^{3+}, [Ar]3d^3$; (b) $Au^{3+}, [Xe]4f^{14}5d^8$; (c) $Ru^{2+}, [Kr]4d^6$; (d) $Cu^+,$ $[Ar]3d^{10}$; (e) $Mn^{4+}, [Ar]3d^3$; (f) $Ir^{3+}, [Xe]4f^{14}5d^6$. **24.41** Ti^{2+}. **24.43** MnO_4^-. **24.45** Au(I) and Au(III); Au(III) would be present in a solution of a strongly oxidizing acid. **24.47** Chromate ion, CrO_4^{2-}, is bright yellow. Dichromate, $Cr_2O_7^{2-}$, is orange and more stable in acid solution than CrO_4^{2-} because of the equilibrium $2CrO_4^{2-}(aq) + 2H^+(aq) \rightleftharpoons Cr_2O_7^{2-}(aq) + H_2O(l)$.

24.49 (a) $Fe(s) + 2HCl(aq) \longrightarrow FeCl_2(aq) + H_2(g)$; (b) $Fe(s) + 4HNO_3(g) \longrightarrow Fe(NO_3)_3(aq) + NO(g) + 2H_2O(l)$. **24.51** The unpaired electrons in a paramagnetic material cause it to be weakly attracted into a magnetic field. A diamagnetic material, where all electrons are paired, is very weakly repelled by a magnetic field. **24.55** 493 g pig iron. **24.59** 3.4×10^2 kWh; \$27. **24.63** $5MoS_2(s) + 14H^+(aq) + 14NO_3^-(aq) \longrightarrow 5MoO_3(s) + 10SO_2(g) + 7N_2(g) + 7H_2O(l)$; $MoO_3(s) + 2NH_3(aq) + H_2O(l) \longrightarrow (NH_4)_2MoO_4(s)$; $(NH_4)_2MoO_4(s) \longrightarrow 2NH_3(g) + H_2O(l) + MoO_3(s)$; $MoO_3(s) + H_2(g) \longrightarrow Mo(s) + 3H_2O(g)$. **24.67** In Si, the 4 valence electrons are localized between the central Si and its 4 nearest neighbors. In the closest-packed Ti lattice, there are 12 nearest neighbors for each Ti atom and the valence electrons cannot be localized; they are delocalized and free to move throughout the lattice. **24.70** (a) $2NiS(s) + 3O_2(g) \longrightarrow 2NiO(s) + 2SO_2(g)$; (b) $2C(s) + O_2(g) \longrightarrow 2CO(g)$; $C(s) + H_2O(g) \longrightarrow CO(g) + H_2(g)$; $NiO(s) + CO(g) \longrightarrow Ni(s) + CO_2(g)$; $NiO(s) + H_2(g) \longrightarrow Ni(s) + H_2O(g)$; (c) $Ni(s) + 2HCl(aq) \longrightarrow NiCl_2(aq) + H_2(g)$; (d) $NiCl_2(aq) + 2NaOH(aq) \longrightarrow Ni(OH)_2(s) + 2NaCl(aq)$; (e) $Ni(OH)_2(s) \longrightarrow NiO(s) + H_2O(g)$.

Chapter 25

25.1 (a) Coordination number = 4, oxidation number = +2; (c) coordination number = 6, oxidation number = +3.

25.3 (a)

$$\begin{array}{c} Cl \\ | \\ Cl \diagup \overset{\displaystyle Al}{\underset{\displaystyle Cl}{\big|}} \diagdown Cl \end{array}$$

Tetrahedral

(b) $[:N\equiv C\!-\!Ag\!-\!C\equiv N:]^-$, linear. **25.5** [25.3] (a) Tetrachloroaluminate(III); (b) dicyanoargentate(I); (c) dichloroethylenediamineplatinum(II); (d) *trans*-tetraamminediaquachromium(III). [25.4] (a) Tetraamminezinc(II); (b) aquapentachlororuthenate(III); (c) *trans*-bis(ethylenediamine)dinitrocobalt(III); (d) *cis*-diamminebromohydridoplatinum(II). **25.7** (a) $[Cr(NH_3)_6](NO_3)_3$; (b) $[Co(NH_3)_4CO_3]_2SO_4$; (d) $K[V(H_2O)_2Br_4]$. **25.9** (a) *Ortho*-phenanthroline (*o*-phen) is bidentate; (b) oxalate, $C_2O_4^{2-}$, is bidentate; (c) ethylenediaminetetraacetate, EDTA, is hexadentate; (d) ethylenediamine (en) is bidentate.

25.11 (a)

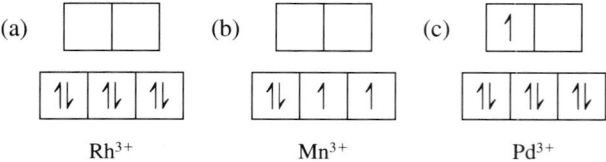

cis   trans

(b) $[Pd(NH_3)_2(ONO)_2]$, $[Pd(NH_3)_2(NO_2)_2]$

(c)

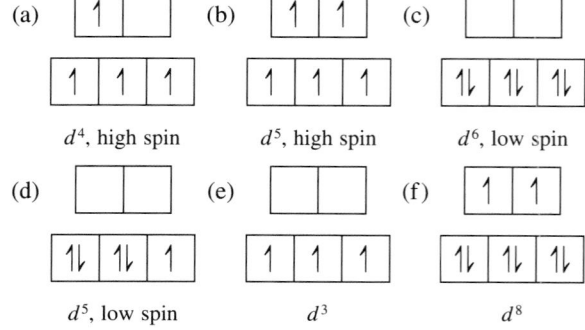

(d) $[Co(NH_3)_4Br_2]Cl$, $[Co(NH_3)_4BrCl]Br$.

25.13

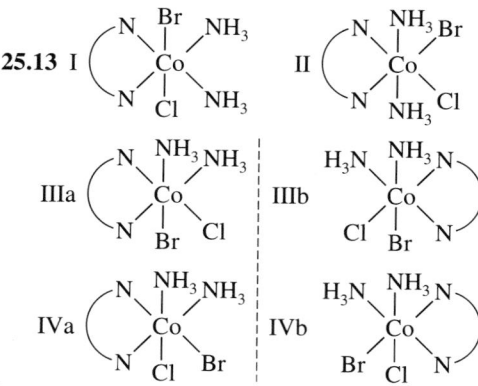

I, II, IIIa, and IVa are geometric isomers; IIIa/IIIb and IVa/IVb are the pairs of optical isomers. **25.15** Cobalt(III) complexes are generally inert. Thus, the ions that form precipitates are outside the coordination sphere. The red complex is $[Co(NH_3)_5SO_4]Br$, pentaamminesulfatocobalt(III) bromide; the violet complex is $[Co(NH_3)_5Br]SO_4$, pentaamminebromocobalt(III) sulfate. **25.17** Colored compounds: (b), (c), (f). **25.19** (a) Fe^{4+}, d^4; (b) Co^{2+}, d^7; (c) Ni^{2+}, d^8; (d) Au^{3+}, d^8; (e) Mo^{4+}, d^2. **25.21** Blue to blue-violet. **25.23** The $d_{x^2-y^2}$ and d_{z^2} metal orbitals point directly toward the six ligands in an octahedron. Electrons in these metal orbitals experience greater electrostatic repulsion by the negative charge or dipole of the ligands than electrons in the d_{xy}, d_{xz}, and d_{yz} orbitals. Thus, the d_{xy}, d_{xz}, and d_{yz} orbitals are lower in energy. **25.25** A yellow color is due to absorption of light around 400 to 430 nm, a blue color to absorption near 620 nm. The shorter wavelength corresponds to a higher-energy electron transition and larger Δ value. Cyanide is a stronger field ligand, and its complexes are expected to have larger Δ values than aqua complexes. **25.27** (a) $[Kr]4d^85s^1$, $[Kr]4d^6$ (b) $[Ar]3d^54s^2$, $[Ar]3d^4$ (c) $[Kr]5s^24d^8$, $[Kr]4d^7$

(a) [ ][ ][ ]
[↿⇂][↿⇂][↿⇂]
Rh^{3+}

(b) [ ][ ][ ]
[↿⇂][↿][↿]
Mn^{3+}

(c) [↿][ ][ ]
[↿⇂][↿⇂][↿⇂]
Pd^{3+}

25.29 All complexes in this exercise are 6-coordinate octahedral.

(a) [↿][ ][ ]
[↿][↿][↿]
d^4, high spin

(b) [↿][↿][ ]
[↿][↿][↿]
d^5, high spin

(c) [ ][ ][ ]
[↿⇂][↿⇂][↿⇂]
d^6, low spin

(d) [ ][ ][ ]
[↿⇂][↿⇂][↿]
d^5, low spin

(e) [ ][ ][ ]
[↿][↿][↿]
d^3

(f) [↿][↿][ ]
[↿⇂][↿⇂][↿⇂]
d^8

25.31 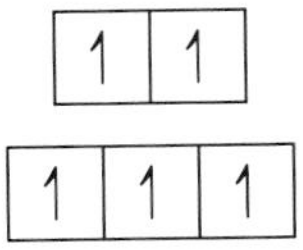

High spin

25.33 (a) $K_2[Ni(en)Cl_4]$; (b) $K_2[Ni(CN)_4]$; (c) $[CoF_6]^{3-}$, high spin; $[Co(NH_3)_6]^{3+}$, low spin; (d) thiocyanate, SCN^- or NCS^-; (e) $[Co(en)_2Cl_2]Cl$; (f) $[Co(en)_3]Cl_3$. **25.36** $[Pd(NC_5H_5)_2Br_2]$; square planar, trans isomer; *trans*-dibromodipyridinepalladium(II).

25.38 (a) 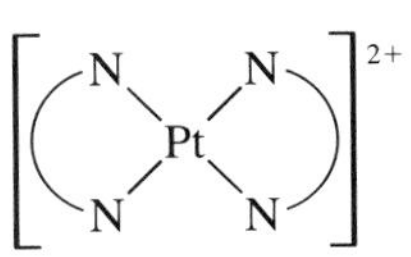 (b) 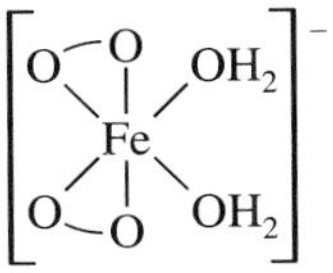

(c) 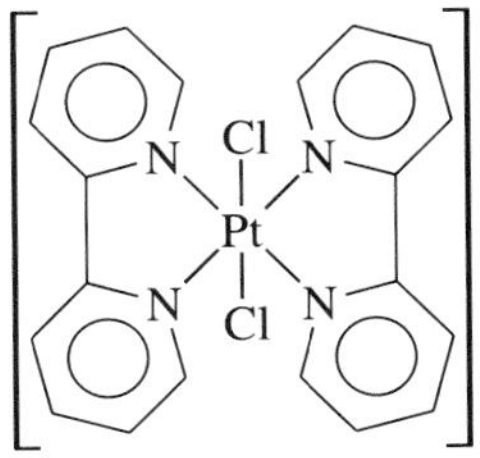

(d) Hg^{2+} is d^{10}, and so the complex is probably tetrahedral.

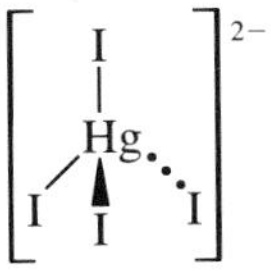

(e) 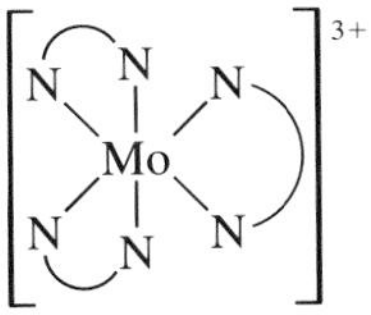 (f) 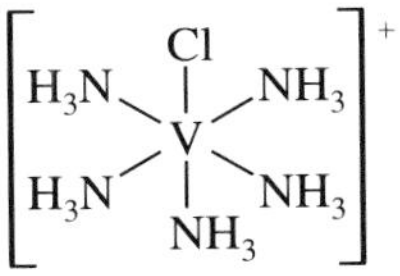

(g) 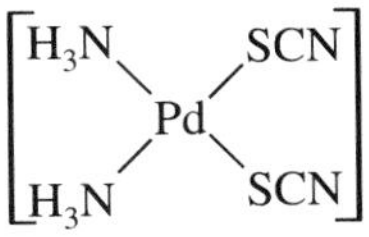

25.40 (a) 1; (b) 2; (c) 4. **25.43** $[Co(H_2O)_6]^{2+}$, pink or rose-colored; $[CoCl_4]^{2-}$, green or blue-green.

25.45 (a) 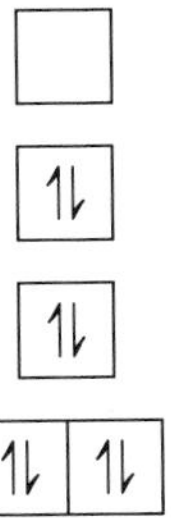 (b) 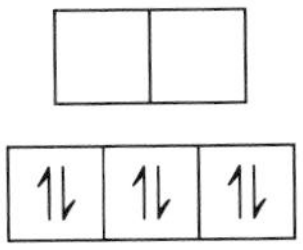

(c) 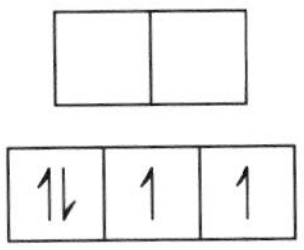 (d) 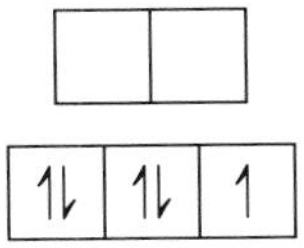

25.47 The complex will absorb in the visible range at around 660 nm and appear green.

25.49 Application of pressure would increase ligand-electron repulsions, causing a larger crystal field splitting and a shorter wavelength of absorption.

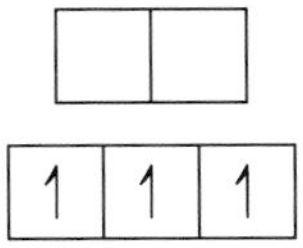

Chapter 26

26.1 (a) C_5H_{12}; (b) C_5H_{10}; (c) C_5H_{10}; (d) C_5H_8; saturated: (a), (b), unsaturated: (c), (d). **26.3** There are five isomers. Their carbon skeletons are as follows:

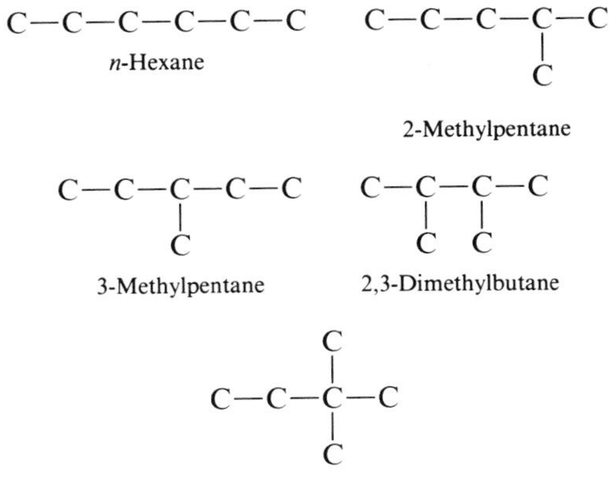
n-Hexane
2-Methylpentane
3-Methylpentane
2,3-Dimethylbutane
2,2-Dimethylbutane

26.5 (a) 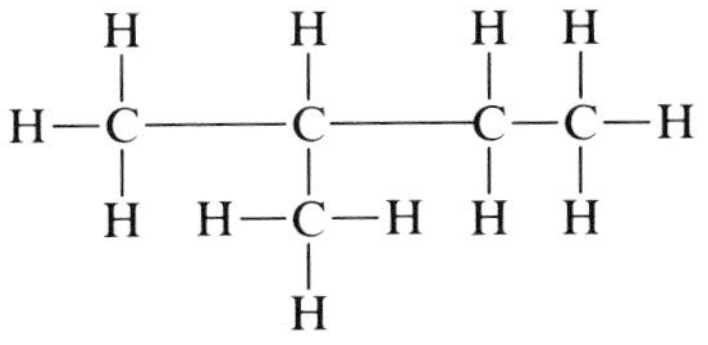

(c) 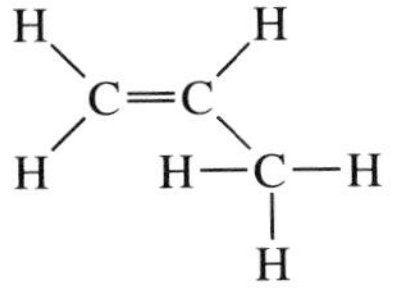

26.7 (a) 109°; (b) 120°; (c) 180°.

26.9 (a) 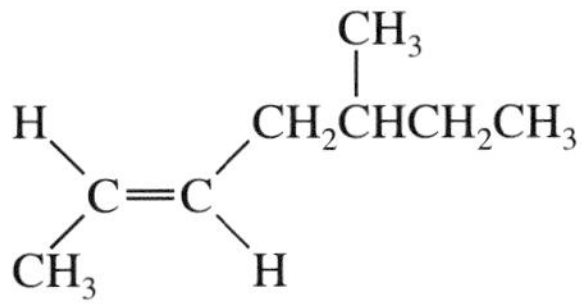 (b) $HC{\equiv}C{-}CH_2Cl$

(c) 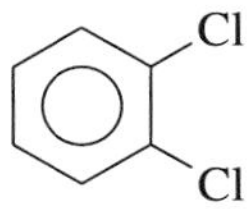

26.11 (b) *cis*-6-methyl-3-octene; (c) *para*-dibromobenzene. **26.13** There are two possible placements for the double bond in butene; these compounds are structural isomers: $CH_2=CHCH_2CH_3$ (1-butene) and $CH_3CH=CHCH_3$ (2-butene). For 2-butene, there are two arrangements of the carbon skeleton with respect to the double bond; these compounds are geometric isomers:

cis-2-Butene   *trans*-2-Butene

26.15

I   II

III   IV

V

II and III are geometric isomers, and the others are structural isomers (different placement of the Cl atoms).
26.17 70. **26.19** (a) $CH_3CH_2CH_3(g) + 5O_2(g) \longrightarrow 3CO_2(g) + 4H_2O(g)$; (b) $CH_3CH_2C\equiv CH + Br_2 \longrightarrow CH_3CH_2CBr=CHBr$; (c) $C_6H_6 + Br_2 \xrightarrow{FeBr_3} C_6H_5Br + HBr$. **26.21** The $60°$ C—C—C angles in the cyclopropane ring cause strain that provides a driving force for reactions that result in ring opening. There is no comparable strain in the five- or six-membered rings.
26.23 $C_2H_4(g) + HBr(g) \longrightarrow CH_3CH_2Br(l)$; $C_6H_6(l) + CH_3CH_2Br(l) \xrightarrow{AlCl_3} C_6H_5CH_2CH_3(l) + HBr(g)$.
26.25 Heat of hydrogenation of naphthalene $= -300$ kJ/mol; for $C_2H_4 = -137$ kJ/mol. The second value applies to one double bond, and so for five double bonds we would expect about -685 kJ. Since hydrogenation of naphthalene produces only -300 kJ, we can conclude that there is some special stability associated with the aromatic system in this molecule. **26.27** (a) Ketone; (b) carboxylic acid; (c) alcohol; (d) ester; (e) amide; (f) amine.

26.29 Propionaldehyde (or propanal):

26.31 About each methyl (CH_3) carbon, $109°$; about the carbonyl carbon, $120°$, planar.

26.33 (a)

2-Propylacetate

(b)

1-Propylacetate

(c)

Ethylformate

26.35

26.37 (b) $HOCH_2CH_2OH$; (d) $CH_3CH_2\overset{\displaystyle O}{\overset{\|}{C}}CH_2CH_3$; (e) $CH_3CH_2OCH_2CH_3$. **26.39** (a) Methanoic acid; (b) butanoic acid; (c) 3-methylpentanoic acid. **26.41** (a) An α amino acid contains an NH_2 function on the carbon adjacent to the carboxylic acid function. (b) In protein formation, amino acids undergo a condensation reaction between the amino group of one molecule and the carboxylic acid group of another to form the amide linkage. **26.43** Two peptides are possible: $H_2NCH_2CONHCH(CH(CH_3)_2)COOH$ (glycylvaline) and $H_2NCH(CH(CH_3)_2)CONHCH_2COOH$ (valylglycine).

26.45

26.47 Eight: ser-ser-ser; ser-phe-ser; phe-ser-ser; ser-phe-phe; phe-ser-phe; phe-phe-ser; phe-phe-phe. **26.49** The *primary structure* of a protein refers to the sequence of amino acids in the chain. The *secondary structure* is the configuration (helical, folded, open) of the protein chain. The *tertiary structure* is the overall shape of the protein, determined by the way the segments come together or pack. **26.51** When the glucose chain closes to form the hemiacetal (Figure 26.22), α-glucose has the "new" OH group on carbon 1 on the same side of the six-membered ring as the OH group on the adjacent carbon 2, while the β form has the OH groups on carbon 1 and carbon 2 on opposite sides of the ring.

α Linkage

β Linkage

26.53 Both the β form (shown here) and the α form (OH on carbon 1 on same side of ring as OH on carbon 2) are possible.

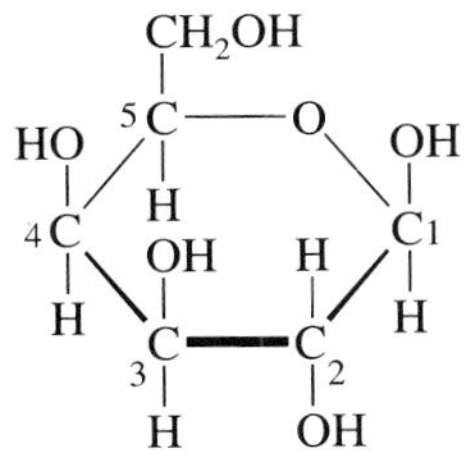

Galactose

26.55 In the six-membered-ring form, carbon atoms 1, 2, 3, 4, and 5 are chiral because there are four different groups on each. **26.57** A nucleotide consists of a nitrogen-containing aromatic compound, a sugar in the furanose (five-membered) ring form, and a phosphoric acid molecule. The structure of deoxycytidine monophosphate is:

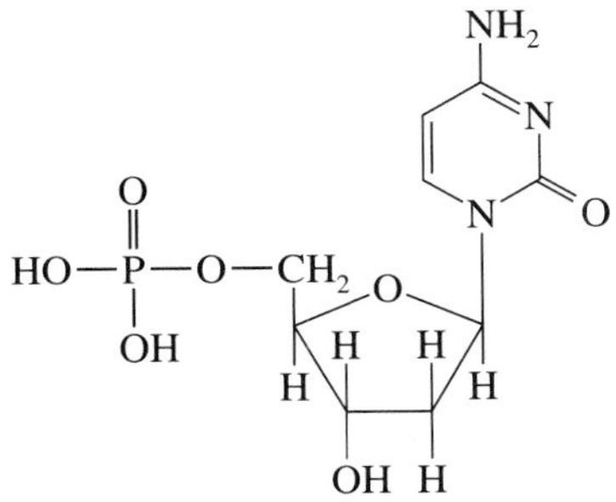

26.59 $C_4H_7CH_2OH + H_3PO_4 \longrightarrow$
$C_4H_7CH_2-O-PO_3H_2 + H_2O.$

26.61
```
—A—C—T—C—G—A—
  |  |  |  |  |  |
  T—G—A—G—C—T—  ←— Complementary strand
```
26.63 $HC\equiv C-CH_2CH_3$; $CH_3-C\equiv C-CH_3$;
$HC=CH$; $CH_2=CH-CH=CH_2$.
```
   |      |
 H_2C—CH_2
```

26.67 $CH_3CH_2CH_2$ (OH); CH_3CHCH_3 (OH);
$CH_3-O-CH_2CH_3$. **26.69** Because of the strain in bond angles about the ring, cyclohexyne would not be stable. The alkyne carbon atoms preferentially have a 180° bond angle, but there are not enough carbon atoms in the ring to make this possible without gross distortions of other bond lengths and angles.
26.70 (a) $C-O-C$, ether; $-CH=CH_2$, alkene.
(b) $-\overset{O}{\underset{\|}{C}}-OH$, carboxylic acid; $CH_3\overset{O}{\underset{\|}{C}}-O-$, ester.
26.73 (a) *Cyclobutane*. There is strain in the four-membered ring because the $C-C-C$ angles must be less than the desired 109°. (c) *1-Hexene*. The alkene readily undergoes addition, whereas the aromatic hydrocarbon is extremely stable, due to resonance. **26.70** Hydrolysis of the ester or amide linkages under strong base conditions. **26.75** Cyclopentane. **26.79** Glu-cys-gly is the only possible structure.
26.83
```
—T—A—T—G—C—A—
  |  |  |  |  |  |
—A—T—A—C—G—T—  ←— Complementary strand
```

Glossary

absorption spectrum The amount of light absorbed by a sample as a function of wavelength. (Section 25.6)

accuracy A measure of how closely individual measurements agree with the correct value. (Section 1.4)

acid A substance that is able to donate a H^+ ion (a proton) and hence increases the concentration of H^+ (aq) when it dissolves in water. (Section 4.3)

acid-dissociation constant (K_a) An equilibrium constant that expresses the extent to which an acid transfers a proton to solvent water. (Section 16.5)

acidic anhydride (acidic oxide) An oxide that forms an acid when added to water; soluble nonmetal oxides are acidic anhydrides. (Section 22.4)

acidic oxide (acidic anhydride) An oxide that either reacts with a base to form a salt or reacts with water to form an acid. (Section 22.4)

acid rain Rainwater that has become excessively acidic because of absorption of pollutant oxides, notably SO_3, produced by human activities. (Section 18.4)

actinide element Element in which the $5f$ orbitals are only partially occupied. (Section 6.8)

activated complex (transition state) The particular arrangement of atoms found at the top of the potential-energy barrier as a reaction proceeds from reactants to products. (Section 14.4)

activation energy (E_a) The minimum energy needed for reaction: the height of the energy barrier to formation of products. (Section 14.4)

active site Specific site on a heterogeneous catalyst or an enzyme where catalysis occurs. (Section 14.6)

activity series A list of metals in order of decreasing ease of oxidation. (Section 4.6)

addition polymerization Polymerization that occurs through coupling of monomers with one another, with no other products formed in the reaction. (Section 12.2)

addition reaction A reaction in which a reagent adds to the two carbon atoms of a carbon-carbon multiple bond. (Section 26.2)

adsorption The binding of molecules to a surface. (Section 14.6)

alcohol An organic compound obtained by substituting a hydroxyl group (—OH) for a hydrogen on a hydrocarbon. (Section 26.3)

aldehyde An organic compound that contains a carbonyl group to which at least one hydrogen atom is attached. (Section 26.3)

alkali metals Members of group 1A in the periodic table. (Section 7.7)

alkaline earth metals Members of group 2A in the periodic table. (Section 7.7)

alkanes Compounds of carbon and hydrogen containing only carbon-carbon single bonds. (Chapter 26: Introduction)

alkenes Hydrocarbons containing one or more carbon-carbon double bonds. (Chapter 26: Introduction)

alkyl group A group that is formed by removing a hydrogen atom from an alkane. (Section 26.1)

alkynes Hydrocarbons containing one or more carbon-carbon triple bonds. (Chapter 26: Introduction)

allotropes Different chemical forms of the same element existing in the same physical state. (Section 7.8)

alloy A substance that has the characteristic properties of a metal and contains more than one element. Often there is one principal metallic component, with other elements present in smaller amounts. Alloys may be homogeneous or heterogeneous in nature. (Section 24.1)

alpha (α) helix A protein structure in which the protein is coiled in the form of a helix, with hydrogen bonds between C=O and N—H groups on adjacent turns. (Section 26.5)

alpha particles Particles that are identical to helium-4 nuclei, consisting of two protons and two neutrons, symbol ^4_2He or $^4_2\alpha$. (Section 21.1)

aluminosilicates Compounds that are structurally related to silicates and in which some Si^{4+} ions are replaced by Al^{3+} ions. (Section 23.5)

amide An organic compound that has an NR_2 group attached to a carbonyl. (Section 26.3)

amine A compound that has the general formula R_3N, where R may be H or a hydrocarbon group. (Sections 16.6 and 26.3)

amino acid A carboxylic acid that contains an amino (—NH_2) group attached to the carbon atom adjacent to the carboxylic acid (COOH) functional group. (Section 26.4)

amorphous solid A solid whose molecular arrangement lacks a regular, long-range pattern. (Section 11.7)

amphoteric Capable of behaving as either an acid or a base. (Section 16.2)

angstrom A common non-SI unit of length, denoted Å, that is used to measure atomic dimensions: $1 \text{ Å} = 10^{-10}$ m. (Section 2.3)

anion A negatively charged ion. (Section 2.5)

anode An electrode at which oxidation occurs. (Section 20.3)

antibonding molecular orbital A molecular orbital in which electron density is concentrated outside the region between the two nuclei of bonded atoms. Such orbitals, designated as σ^* or π^*, are less stable (of higher energy) than bonding molecular orbitals. (Section 9.6)

aqueous solution A solution in which water is the solvent. (Chapter 4: Introduction)

aromatic hydrocarbons Hydrocarbon compounds that contain a planar, cyclic arrangement of carbon atoms linked by both σ and delocalized π bonds. (Chapter 26: Introduction)

Arrhenius equation An equation that relates the rate constant for a reaction to the frequency factor, A, the activation energy, E_a, and the temperature, T: $k = Ae^{-E_a/RT}$. In its logarithmic form, it is written: $\ln k = -E_a/RT + \ln A$. (Section 14.4)

atmosphere (atm) A unit of pressure equal to 760 torr; 1 atm = 101.325 kPa. (Section 10.2)

atom The smallest representative particle of an element. (Chapter 2: Introduction)

atomic mass unit (amu) A unit based on the value of exactly 12 amu for the mass of the isotope of carbon that has six protons and six neutrons in the nucleus. (Section 3.3)

atomic number The number of protons in the nucleus of an atom of an element. (Section 2.3)

atomic radius An estimate of the size of an atom, in which it is assumed to be a spherical object. (Section 7.3)

atomic weight (average atomic mass) The average mass of the atoms of an element in atomic mass units (amu); it is numerically equal to the mass in grams of 1 mol of the element. (Section 3.3)

autoionization The process whereby water spontaneously forms low concentrations of $H^+(aq)$ and $OH^-(aq)$ ions by proton transfer from one water molecule to another. (Section 16.1)

Avogadro's hypothesis A statement that equal volumes of gases at the same temperature and pressure contain equal numbers of molecules. (Section 10.3)

Avogadro's law A statement that the volume of a gas maintained at constant temperature and pressure is directly proportional to the quantity of the gas. (Section 10.3)

Avogadro's number The number of ^{12}C atoms in exactly 12 g of ^{12}C; it equals 6.022×10^{23}. (Section 3.4)

base A substance that is a H^+ acceptor; a base produces an excess of $OH^-(aq)$ ions when it dissolves in water. (Section 4.3)

base-dissociation constant (K_b) An equilibrium constant that expresses the extent to which a base reacts with solvent water, accepting a proton and forming $OH^-(aq)$. (Section 16.6)

basic anhydride (basic oxide) An oxide that forms a base when added to water; soluble metal oxides are basic anhydrides. (Section 22.4)

basic oxide (basic anhydride) An oxide that either reacts with water to form a base or reacts with an acid to form a salt and water. (Section 22.4)

Bayer process A hydrometallurgical procedure for purifying *bauxite* in the recovery of aluminum from bauxite-containing ores. (Section 24.3)

becquerel The SI unit of radioactivity. It corresponds to one nuclear disintegration per second. (Section 21.9)

beta particles Energetic electrons emitted from the nucleus, symbol $_{-1}^{0}e$. (Section 21.1)

bidentate ligand A ligand in which two coordinating atoms are bound to a metal. (Section 25.2)

bimolecular reaction An elementary reaction that involves two molecules. (Section 14.5)

biochemistry The study of the chemistry of living systems. (Chapter 26: Introduction)

biodegradable Organic material that bacteria are able to oxidize. (Section 18.6)

biopolymer A polymeric molecule of high molecular weight found in living systems. The three major classes of biopolymer are proteins, carbohydrates, and nucleic acids. (Section 26.4)

biosphere The part of the earth in which living organisms can exist and live out their life cycles. (Section 26.4)

body-centered cubic cell A cubic unit cell in which the lattice points occur at the corners and at the center. (Section 11.7)

bomb calorimeter A device for measuring the heat evolved in the combustion of a substance under constant-volume conditions. (Section 5.5)

bond angles The angles made by the lines joining the nuclei of the atoms in a molecule. (Section 9.1)

bond-dissociation energy The enthalpy change, ΔH, required to break a particular bond in a mole of gaseous substance; also called **bond energy**. (Section 8.9)

bond energy The enthalpy change, ΔH, required to break a particular bond when the substance is in the gas phase; also called **bond-dissociation energy**. (Section 8.8)

bonding molecular orbital A molecular orbital in which the electron density is concentrated in the internuclear region. The energy of a bonding molecular orbital is lower than the energy of the separate atomic orbitals from which it forms. (Section 9.6)

bonding pair In a Lewis structure, a pair of electrons that is shared by two atoms. (Section 9.1)

bond order The number of bonding electron pairs shared between two atoms, less the number of antibonding electron pairs: bond order = $\frac{1}{2}$ (number of bonding electrons − number of antibonding electrons). (Section 9.6)

bond polarity A measure of how equally the electrons are shared between the two atoms in a chemical bond. (Section 8.5)

boranes Covalent hydrides of boron. (Section 23.6)

Born-Haber cycle A thermodynamic cycle based on Hess's law that relates the lattice energy of an ionic substance to its enthalpy of formation and to other measurable quantities. (Section 8.2)

Boyle's law A law stating that at constant temperature, the product of the volume and pressure of a given amount of gas is a constant. (Section 10.3)

Brønsted-Lowry acid A substance that acts as a proton donor. (Section 16.2)

Brønsted-Lowry base Any substance that acts as a proton acceptor. (Section 16.2)

buffered solution (buffer) A solution that undergoes a limited change in pH upon addition of a small amount of acid or base. (Section 17.3)

buffering capacity The amount of acid or base a buffer can neutralize before the pH begins to change appreciably. (Section 17.3)

calcination The heating of an ore to bring about its decomposition and the elimination of a volatile product. For example, a carbonate ore might be calcined to drive off CO_2. (Section 24.2)

calorie A unit of energy, it is the amount of energy needed to raise the temperature of 1 g of water by $1\,°C$, from $14.5\,°C$ to $15.5\,°C$. A related unit is the joule: 1 cal = 4.184 J. (Section 5.1)

calorimeter An apparatus that measures the evolution of heat. (Section 5.5)

calorimetry The experimental measurement of heat produced in chemical and physical processes. (Section 5.5)

capillary action The process by which a liquid rises in a tube because of a combination of adhesion to the walls of the tube and cohesion between liquid particles. (Section 11.3)

carbohydrates A class of substances formed from polyhydroxy aldehydes or ketones. (Section 26.6)

carbonylation A reaction in which the carbonyl functional group is introduced into a molecule. (Section 26.3)

carbonyl group The $C=O$ double bond, a characteristic feature of several organic functional groups, such as ketones and aldehydes. (Section 26.3)

carboxylic acid A compound that contains the —COOH functional group. (Sections 16.9 and 26.3)

catalyst A substance that changes the speed of a chemical reaction without itself undergoing a permanent chemical change in the process. (Section 14.6)

cathode An electrode at which reduction occurs. (Section 20.3)

cathode rays Streams of electrons that are produced when a high voltage is applied to electrodes in an evacuated tube. (Section 2.2)

cathodic protection A means of protecting a metal against corrosion by making it the cathode in a voltaic cell. This can be achieved by attaching a more easily oxidized metal, which serves as an anode, to the metal to be protected. (Section 20.10)

cation A positively charged ion. (Section 2.5)

cell potential A measure of the driving force, or "electrical pressure," for the completion of an electrochemical reaction; it is measured in volts: 1 V = 1 J/C. Also called **electromotive force.** (Section 20.4)

cellulose A polysaccharide of glucose; it is the major structural element in plant matter. (Section 26.6)

Celsius scale A temperature scale on which water freezes at $0°$ and boils at $100°$ at sea level. (Section 1.3)

ceramic A solid inorganic material, either crystalline (oxides, carbides, silicates) or amorphous (glasses). Most ceramics melt at high temperatures. (Section 12.3)

chain reaction A series of reactions in which one reaction initiates the next. (Section 21.7)

changes of state Transformations of matter from one state to a different one, for example, from a gas to a liquid. (Section 1.1)

charcoal A form of carbon produced when wood is heated strongly in a deficiency of air. (Section 22.6)

Charles's law A law stating that at constant pressure, the volume of a given quantity of gas is proportional to absolute temperature. (Section 10.3)

chelate effect The generally larger formation constants for polydentate ligands as compared with the corresponding monodentate ligands. (Section 25.2)

chelating agent A polydentate ligand that is capable of occupying two or more sites in the coordination sphere. (Section 25.2)

chemical changes Processes in which one or more substances are converted into other substances; also called **chemical reactions.** (Section 1.1)

chemical equation A representation of a chemical reaction using the chemical formulas of the reactants and products; a **balanced chemical equation** contains equal numbers of atoms of each element on both sides of the equation. (Section 3.1)

chemical equilibrium A state of dynamic balance in which the rate of formation of the products of a reaction from the reactants equals the rate of formation of the reactants from the products; at equilibrium, the concentrations of the reactants and products remain constant. (Section 4.2, Chapter 15: Introduction.)

chemical formula A notation that uses atomic symbols with numerical subscripts to convey the relative proportions of atoms of the different elements in a substance. (Section 2.5)

chemical kinetics The area of chemistry concerned with the speeds, or rates, at which chemical reactions occur. (Chapter 14: Introduction)

chemical properties Properties that describe a substance's composition and its reactivity; how the substance reacts, or changes into other substances. (Section 1.1)

chemical reactions Processes in which one or more substances are converted into other substances; also called **chemical changes.** (Section 1.1)

chemical-vapor deposition A method for forming thin films in which a substance is deposited on a surface and then undergoes some form of chemical reaction to form the film. (Section 12.4)

chemistry The scientific discipline that treats the composition, properties, and transformations of matter. (Chapter 1: Introduction)

chiral A term describing a molecule or an ion that cannot be superimposed on its mirror image. (Sections 25.4 and 26.4)

chlorofluorocarbons Compounds composed entirely of chlorine, fluorine, and carbon. (Section 18.3)

chlorophyll A plant pigment that plays a major role in conversion of solar energy to chemical energy in photosynthesis. (Section 25.2)

cholesteric liquid crystal A liquid crystal formed from flat, disc-shaped molecules that align through a stacking of the molecular discs. (Section 12.1)

clay minerals A class of hydrated aluminosilicates. (Section 23.5)

coal A naturally occurring solid containing hydrocarbons of high molecular weight, as well as compounds containing sulfur, oxygen, and nitrogen. (Section 5.8)

coke An impure form of carbon formed when coal is heated strongly in the absence of air. (Section 22.6)

colligative properties Those properties of a solvent (vapor-pressure lowering, freezing-point lowering, boiling-point elevation, osmotic pressure) that depend on the total concentration of solute particles present. (Section 13.5)

collision model A theory based on the idea that molecules must collide to react; it explains the factors influencing reaction rates in terms of the frequency of collisions, the number of collisions with energies exceeding the activation energy, and the probability that the collisions occur with suitable orientations. (Section 14.4)

colloidal dispersions (colloids) Mixtures containing particles larger than normal solutes but small enough to remain suspended in the dispersing medium. (Section 13.6)

combination reaction A chemical reaction in which two or more substances combine to form a single product. (Section 3.2)

combustion reaction A chemical reaction that proceeds with evolution of heat and usually also a flame; most combustion involves reaction with oxygen, as in the burning of a match. (Section 3.2)

common-ion effect A shift of an equilibrium induced by an ion common to the equilibrium. For example, added Na_2SO_4 decreases the solubility of the slightly soluble salt $BaSO_4$, or added $NaC_2H_3O_2$ decreases the percent ionization of $HC_2H_3O_2$. (Section 17.1)

complementary colors Colors that, when mixed in proper proportions, appear white or colorless. (Section 25.6)

complex ion (complex) An assembly of a metal ion and the Lewis bases (ligands) bonded to it. (Section 17.5; Chapter 25: Introduction)

composite A complex solid mixture of two or more components. One component is usually present in much greater quantity than the others and acts as the primary host matrix for the other components. (Section 12.3)

compound A substance composed of two or more elements united chemically in definite proportions. (Section 1.2)

concentration The quantity of solute present in a given quantity of solvent or solution. (Section 4.1)

condensation polymerization Polymerization in which

molecules are joined together through condensation reactions. (Section 12.2)

condensation reaction A chemical reaction in which a small molecule (such as a molecule of water) is split out from between two reacting molecules, as for example between an organic acid and an amine function:

$$-\underset{\underset{O}{\|}}{C}-O-H + H-\underset{\underset{H}{|}}{N}- \longrightarrow -\underset{\underset{O}{\|}}{C}-\underset{\underset{H}{|}}{N}- + H_2O$$

(Section 12.2)

conjugate acid A substance formed by addition of a proton to a Brønsted-Lowry base. (Section 16.2)

conjugate acid-base pair An acid and a base, such as H_2O and OH^-, that differ only in the presence or absence of a proton. (Section 16.2)

conjugate base A substance formed by the loss of a proton from a Brønsted-Lowry acid. (Section 16.2)

continuous spectrum A spectrum that contains radiation distributed over all wavelengths. (Section 6.3)

conversion factor A ratio relating the same quantity in two systems of units that is used to convert the units of measurement. (Section 1.5)

coordination compound A compound containing a complex ion. (Chapter 25: Introduction)

coordination number The number of adjacent atoms to which an atom is directly bonded. In a complex, the coordination number of the metal ion is the number of donor atoms to which it is bonded. (Sections 11.7 and 25.1)

coordination sphere The metal ion and its surrounding ligands. (Section 25.1)

coordination-sphere isomers Structural isomers of coordination compounds in which the ligands within the coordination sphere differ. (Section 25.4)

core electrons The electrons that are not in the outermost shell of an atom. (Section 6.8)

corrosion The process by which a metal is oxidized by substances in its environment. (Section 20.10)

covalent bond A bond formed between two or more atoms by a sharing of electrons. (Section 8.4)

covalent (network) solids Solids in which the units that make up the three-dimensional network are joined by covalent bonds. (Section 11.8)

critical mass The amount of fissionable material necessary to maintain a chain reaction. (Section 21.7)

critical pressure The pressure at which a gas at its critical temperature is converted to a liquid state. (Section 11.4)

critical temperature The highest temperature at which it is possible to convert the gaseous form of a substance to a liquid. The critical temperature increases with an increase in the magnitude of intermolecular forces. (Section 11.4)

crosslinking The formation of bonds between polymer chains. (Section 12.2)

crystal-field theory A theory that accounts for the colors and the magnetic and other properties of transition-metal complexes in terms of the splitting of the energies of metal ion *d* orbitals by the electrostatic interaction with the ligands. (Section 25.7)

crystal lattice An imaginary network of points on which the repeating unit of the structure of a solid (the contents of the unit cell) may be imagined to be laid down so that the structure of the crystal is obtained. Each point represents an identical environment in the crystal. (Section 11.7)

crystalline solid (crystal) A solid whose internal arrangement of atoms, molecules, or ions shows a regular repetition in any direction through the solid. (Section 11.7)

crystallization The process in which a dissolved solute comes out of solution and forms a crystalline solid. (Section 13.3)

cubic close packing A close-packing arrangement in which the atoms of the third layer of a solid are not directly over those in the first layer. (Section 11.7)

curie A measure of radioactivity: 1 curie = 3.7×10^{10} nuclear disintegrations per second. (Section 21.9)

cycloalkanes Saturated hydrocarbons of general formula C_nH_{2n} in which the carbon atoms form a closed ring. (Section 26.1)

Dalton's law of partial pressures A law stating that the total pressure of a mixture of gases is the sum of the pressures that each gas would exert if it were present alone. (Section 10.6)

decomposition reaction A chemical reaction in which a single compound reacts to give two or more products. (Section 3.2)

degenerate orbitals Orbitals that have the same energy. (Section 6.7)

delocalized electrons Electrons that are spread over a number of atoms in a molecule rather than localized between a pair of atoms. (Section 9.5)

density The ratio of an object's mass to its volume. (Section 1.3)

deoxyribonucleic acid (DNA) A polynucleotide in which the sugar component is deoxyribose. (Section 26.7)

desalination The removal of salts from seawater, brine, or brackish water to make it fit for human consumption. (Section 18.5)

deuterium The isotope of hydrogen whose nucleus contains a proton and a neutron: ^2_1H. (Section 22.3)

dextrorotatory, or merely **dextro** or *d* A term used to label a chiral molecule that rotates the plane of polarization of plane-polarized light to the right (clockwise). (Section 25.4)

diamagnetism A type of magnetism that causes a substance with no unpaired electrons to be weakly repelled from a magnetic field. (Section 9.7)

diffusion The spreading of one substance through another. (Section 10.9)

dilution The process of preparing a less concentrated solution from a more concentrated one by adding solvent. (Section 4.1)

dimensional analysis A method of problem solving in which units are carried through all calculations. Dimensional analysis ensures that the final answer of a calculation has the desired units. (Section 1.5)

dipole A molecule with one end having a slight negative charge and the other end having a slight positive charge; a polar molecule. (Section 9.2)

dipole-dipole force The force that exists between polar molecules. (Section 11.2)

dipole moment A measure of the separation between the positive and negative charges in polar molecules. (Section 9.2)

disproportionation A reaction in which a species undergoes simultaneous oxidation and reduction [as in $N_2O_3(g) \rightarrow NO(g) + NO_2(g)$]. (Section 22.5)

donor atom The atom of a ligand that bonds to the metal. (Section 25.1)

double bond A covalent bond involving two electron pairs. (Section 8.4)

double helix The structure for DNA that involves the winding of two DNA polynucleotide chains together in a helical arrangement. The two strands of the double helix are complementary in that the organic bases on the two strands are paired for optimal hydrogen bond interaction. (Section 26.7)

Downs cell A cell used to obtain sodium metal by electrolysis of molten NaCl. (Section 24.4)

dynamic equilibrium A state of balance in which opposing processes occur at the same rate. (Section 11.5)

effective nuclear charge The net positive charge experienced by an electron in a many-electron atom; this charge is not the full nuclear charge because there is some shielding of the nucleus by the other electrons in the atom. (Section 6.7)

effusion The escape of a gas through an orifice or hole. (Section 10.9)

elastomer A material that can undergo a substantial change in shape via stretching, bending, or compression and return to its original shape upon release of the distorting force. (Section 12.2)

electrochemistry The branch of chemistry that deals with the relationships between electricity and chemical reactions. (Chapter 20: Introduction)

electrolysis reaction A reaction in which a nonspontaneous redox reaction is brought about by the passage of current under a sufficient external electrical potential. The devices in which electrolysis reactions occur are called **electrolytic cells.** (Section 20.8)

electrolyte A solute that produces ions in solution; an electrolytic solution conducts an electric current. (Section 4.2)

electrolytic cell A device in which a nonspontaneous redox reaction is caused to occur by passage of current under a sufficient external electrical potential. (Section 20.8)

electromagnetic radiation (radiant energy) A form of energy that has wave characteristics and that propagates through a vacuum at the characteristic speed of 3.00×10^8 m/s. (Section 6.1)

electrometallurgy The use of electrolysis to reduce or refine metals. (Section 24.4)

electromotive force (emf) A measure of the driving force, or "electrical pressure," for the completion of an electrochemical reaction. Electromotive force is measured in volts: $1\ V = 1\ J/C$. Also called the **cell potential**. (Section 20.4)

electron A negatively charged subatomic particle found outside the atomic nucleus; it is a part of all atoms. An electron has a mass 1/1836 times that of a proton. (Section 2.3)

electron affinity The energy change that occurs when an electron is added to a gaseous atom or ion. (Section 7.5)

electron capture A mode of radioactive decay in which an inner-shell orbital electron is captured by the nucleus. (Section 21.1)

electron configuration A particular arrangement of electrons in the orbitals of an atom. (Section 6.8)

electron density The probability of finding an electron at any particular point in an atom; this probability is equal to ψ^2, the square of the wave function. (Section 6.5)

electron-dot symbol (Lewis symbol) The chemical symbol for an element with a dot for each valence electron. (Section 8.1)

electronegativity A measure of the ability of an atom that is bonded to another atom to attract electrons to itself. (Section 8.5)

electronic charge The negative charge carried by an electron; it has a magnitude of 1.602×10^{-19} C. (Section 2.3)

electronic structure The arrangement of electrons of an atom or molecule. (Chapter 6: Introduction)

electron-pair geometry The three-dimensional arrangement of the electron pairs around an atom according to the VSEPR model. (Section 9.1)

electron shell A collection of orbitals that have the same value of n. For example, the orbitals with $n = 3$ (the $3s$, $3p$, and $3d$ orbitals) comprise the third shell. (Section 6.5)

electron spin A property of the electron that makes it behave as though it were a tiny magnet. The electron behaves as if it were spinning on its axis; electron spin is quantized. (Section 6.7)

electron spin quantum number (m_s) A quantum number associated with the electron spin; it may have values of $+\frac{1}{2}$ or $-\frac{1}{2}$. (Section 6.7)

element A substance that cannot be separated into simpler substances by chemical means. (Section 1.2)

elementary steps (elementary processes) Processes in a chemical reaction that occur in a single event or step. (Section 14.5)

empirical formula (simplest formula) A chemical formula that shows the kinds of atoms and their relative numbers in a substance. (Section 2.5)

enantiomers Two mirror-image molecules of a chiral substance. The enantiomers are nonsuperimposable. (Sections 25.4 and 26.4)

endothermic process A process in which a system absorbs heat from its surroundings. (Section 5.2)

energy The ability to do work or to transfer heat. (Section 5.1)

energy-level diagram A diagram that shows the energies of molecular orbitals relative to the atomic orbitals from which they are derived. Also called a **molecular orbital diagram**. (Section 9.6)

enthalpy A quantity defined by the relationship $H = E + PV$; the enthalpy change, ΔH, for a reaction that occurs at constant pressure is the heat evolved or absorbed in the reaction: $\Delta H = q_p$. (Section 5.3)

enthalpy (heat) of formation The enthalpy change that accompanies the formation of a substance from the most stable forms of its component elements. (Section 5.7)

entropy A thermodynamic function associated with the number of different, equivalent energy states or spatial arrangements in which a system may be found. It is a thermodynamic state function, which means that once we specify the conditions for a system — that is, the temperature, pressure, and so on — the entropy is defined. (Section 19.2)

enzyme A protein molecule that acts to catalyze specific biochemical reactions. (Section 14.6)

equilibrium constant The numerical value of the equilibrium expression for a system at equilibrium. The equilibrium constant is denoted by K. When the concentrations are expressed in moles/liter, the constant is denoted K_c; when concentrations are expressed in atmospheres, the constant is denoted K_p. (Section 15.2)

equilibrium expression The expression that describes the relationship among the concentrations (or partial pressures) of the substances present in a system at equilibrium. The numerator is obtained by multiplying the concentrations of the substances on the product side of the equation, each raised to a power equal to its coefficient in the chemical equation. The denominator similarly contains the concentrations of the substances on the reactant side of the equation. (Section 15.2)

equivalence point The point in a titration at which the added solute reacts completely with the solute present in the solution. (Section 4.7)

ester An organic compound that has an OR group attached to a carbonyl; it is the product of a reaction between a carboxylic acid and an alcohol. (Section 26.3)

ether A compound in which two hydrocarbon groups are bonded to one oxygen. (Section 26.3)

excited state A higher energy state than the ground state. (Section 6.3)

exothermic process A process in which a system releases heat to its surroundings. (Section 5.2)

extensive property A property that depends on the amount of material considered; for example, mass or volume. (Section 1.3)

face-centered cubic cell A cubic unit cell that has lattice points at each corner as well as at the center of each face. (Section 11.7)

family (group) Elements that are in the same column of the periodic table; elements within the same family exhibit similarities in their chemical behavior. (Section 2.4)

faraday A unit of charge that equals the total charge of 1 mol of electrons: $1\ F = 96,500$ C. (Section 20.5)

f-block metals Lanthanide and actinide elements, in which the $4f$ or $5f$ orbitals are partially occupied. (Section 6.9)

ferromagnetism The ability of some substances to become permanently magnetized. (Section 24.7)

first law of thermodynamics A statement of our experience that energy is conserved in any process. We can express the first law in many ways. One of the more useful expressions is that the change in internal energy, ΔE, of a system in any process is equal to the heat, q, added *to* the system, plus the work, w, done *on* the system by its surroundings: $\Delta E = q + w$. (Section 5.2)

first-order reaction A reaction in which the reaction rate is proportional to the concentration of a single reactant, raised to the first power. (Section 14.2)

fission The splitting of a large nucleus into two smaller ones. (Section 21.6)

force A push or a pull. (Section 5.1)

formal charge The number of valence electrons in an isolated atom minus the number of electrons assigned to the atom in the Lewis structure. (Section 8.7)

formation constant For a metal ion complex, the equilibrium constant for formation of the complex from the metal ion and base species present in solution. It is a measure of the tendency of the complex to form. (Section 17.5)

formula weight The mass of the collection of atoms represented by a chemical formula. For example, the formula weight of NO_2 (46.0 amu) is the sum of the masses of one nitrogen atom and two oxygen atoms. (Section 3.3)

fossil fuels Coal, oil, and natural gas, which are presently our major sources of energy. (Section 5.8)

free energy (Gibbs free energy, G) A thermodynamic state function that gives a criterion for spontaneous change in terms of enthalpy and entropy: $G = H - TS$. (Section 19.5)

free radical A substance with one or more unpaired electrons. (Section 21.9)

frequency The number of times per second that one complete wavelength passes a given point. (Section 6.1)

frequency factor (A) A term in the Arrhenius equation that is related to the frequency of collision and the probability that the collisions are favorably oriented for reaction. (Section 14.4)

fuel cell A voltaic cell that utilizes the oxidation of a conventional fuel, such as H_2 or CH_4, in the cell reaction. (Section 20.7)

fuel value The energy released when 1 g of a substance is combusted. (Section 5.8)

functional group An atom or group of atoms that imparts characteristic chemical properties to an organic compound. (Section 26.3)

fusion The joining of two light nuclei to form a more massive one. (Section 21.6)

gamma radiation Energetic electromagnetic radiation emanating from the nucleus of a radioactive atom. (Section 21.1)

gangue Material of little or no value that accompanies the desired mineral in most raw ores. (Section 24.1)

gas Matter that has no fixed volume or shape; it conforms to the volume and shape of its container. (Section 1.1)

gas constant (R) The constant of proportionality in the ideal-gas equation. (Section 10.4)

Geiger counter A device that can detect and measure radioactivity. (Section 21.5)

gel A semisolid suspension of a material of high molecular mass in a liquid solvent. (Section 12.3)

genetic damage Damage to genes and chromosomes that may have consequences in subsequent generations. (Section 21.9)

geometrical isomers Compounds with the same type and number of atoms and the same chemical bonds but different spatial arrangements of these atoms and bonds. (Sections 25.4 and 26.2)

Gibbs free energy A thermodynamic state function that combines enthalpy and entropy, in the form $G = H - TS$. For a change occurring at constant temperature and pressure, the change in free energy is $\Delta G = \Delta H - T\Delta S$. (Section 19.5)

glass An amorphous solid formed by fusion of SiO_2, CaO, and Na_2O. Other oxides may also be used to form glasses with differing characteristics. (Section 23.5)

glucose A polyhydroxy aldehyde whose formula is $CH_2OH(CHOH)_4CHO$; it is the most important of the monosaccharides. (Section 26.6)

glycogen The general name given to a group of polysaccharides of glucose that are synthesized in mammals and used to store energy from carbohydrates. (Section 26.6)

Graham's law A law stating that the rate of effusion of a gas is inversely proportional to the square root of its molecular weight. (Section 10.9)

ground state The lowest-energy, or most stable, state. (Section 6.3)

Haber process The catalyst system and conditions of temperature and pressure developed by Fritz Haber and co-workers for the formation of NH_3 from H_2 and N_2. (Section 15.1)

half-life The time required for the concentration of a reactant substance to decrease to half its initial value; the time required for half of a sample of a particular radioisotope to decay. (Sections 14.3 and 21.4)

half-reaction An equation for either an oxidation or a reduction that explicitly shows the electrons involved [for example, $Zn^{2+}(aq) + 2e^- \rightarrow Zn(s)$]. (Section 20.2)

Hall process A process used to obtain aluminum by electrolysis of Al_2O_3 dissolved in molten cryolite, Na_3AlF_6. (Section 24.4)

halogens Members of group 7A in the periodic table. (Section 7.8)

hard water Water that contains appreciable concentrations of Ca^{2+} and Mg^{2+}; these ions react with soaps to form an insoluble material. (Section 18.6)

heat The flow of energy from a body at higher temperature to one at lower temperature when they are placed in thermal contact. (Section 5.1)

heat capacity The quantity of heat required to raise the temperature of a sample of matter by 1°C (or 1 K). (Section 5.5)

heat of fusion The enthalpy change, ΔH, for melting a solid. (Section 11.4)

heat of vaporization The enthalpy change, ΔH, for vaporizing a liquid. (Section 11.4)

hemoglobin An iron-containing protein responsible for oxygen transport in the blood. (Section 18.4)

Henderson-Hasselbalch equation The relationship among the pH, pK_a, and the concentrations of acid and conjugate base in an aqueous solution:

$$pH = pK_a = \log \frac{[\text{base}]}{[\text{acid}]}.$$ (Section 17.3)

Henry's law A law stating that the concentration of a gas in a solution, C_g, is proportional to the pressure of gas over the solution: $C_g = kP_g$. (Section 13.4)

Hess's law The heat evolved in a given process can be expressed as the sum of the heats of several processes that, when added, yield the process of interest. (Section 5.6)

heterogeneous alloy An alloy in which the components are not distributed uniformly; instead, two or more distinct phases with characteristic compositions are present. (Section 24.6)

heterogeneous catalyst A catalyst that is in a different phase from that of the reactant substances. (Section 14.6)

heterogeneous equilibrium The equilibrium established between substances in two or more different phases, for example, between a gas and a solid or between a solid and a liquid. (Section 15.4)

hexagonal close packing A close-packing arrangement in which the atoms of the third layer of a solid lie directly over those in the first layer. (Section 11.7)

high-spin complex A complex whose electrons populate the d orbitals to give the maximum number of unpaired electrons. (Section 25.7)

homogeneous catalyst A catalyst that is in the same phase as the reactant substances. (Section 14.6)

homogeneous equilibrium The equilibrium established between reactant and product substances that are all in the same phase. (Section 15.4)

Hund's rule A rule stating that electrons occupy degenerate orbitals in such a way as to maximize the number of electrons with the same spin. In other words, each orbital has one electron placed in it before pairing of electrons in orbitals occurs. Note that this rule applies only to orbitals that are *degenerate,* which means that they have the same energy. (Section 6.8)

hybridization The mixing of different types of atomic orbitals to produce a set of equivalent hybrid orbitals. (Section 9.4)

hybrid orbital An orbital that results from the mixing of different kinds of atomic orbitals on the same atom. For example, an sp^3 hybrid results from the mixing, or hybridizing, of one s orbital and three p orbitals. (Section 9.4)

hydration Solvation when the solvent is water. (Section 13.1)

hydride ion An ion formed by the addition of an electron to a hydrogen atom: H^-. (Section 7.7)

hydrogen bonding Bonding that results from intermolec-

ular attractions between molecules containing hydrogen bonded to an electronegative element. The most important examples involve oxygen, nitrogen, or fluorine. (Section 11.2)

hydrolysis A reaction with water. When a cation or anion reacts with water, it changes the pH. (Section 16.8)

hydrometallurgy Aqueous chemical processes for recovery of a metal from an ore. (Section 24.3)

hydronium ion (H_3O^+) The predominant form of the proton in aqueous solution. (Section 16.1)

hydrophilic Water-attracting. (Section 13.6)

hydrophobic Water-repelling. (Section 13.6)

hypothesis A tentative explanation of a series of observations or of a natural law. (Section 1.1)

ideal gas A hypothetical gas whose pressure, volume, and temperature behavior is completely described by the ideal-gas equation. (Section 10.4)

ideal-gas equation An equation of state for gases that embodies Boyle's law, Charles's law, and Avogadro's hypothesis in the form $PV = nRT$. (Section 10.4)

ideal solution A solution that obeys Raoult's law. (Section 13.5)

immiscible liquids Liquids that do not mix. (Section 13.4)

indicator A substance added to a solution to indicate by a color change the point at which the added solute has just reacted with all the solute present in solution. (Section 4.7)

inert complex A complex that exchanges ligands at a slow rate. (Section 25.5)

instantaneous rate The reaction rate at a particular time as opposed to the average rate over an interval of time. (Section 14.1)

intensive property A property that is independent of the amount of material considered; for example, density. (Section 1.3)

interhalogens Compounds formed between two different halogen elements. Examples include IBr and BrF_3. (Section 23.2)

intermediate A substance formed in one elementary step of a multistep mechanism and consumed in another; it is neither a reactant nor an ultimate product of the overall reaction. (Section 14.5)

intermetallic compound A homogeneous alloy with definite properties and composition. Intermetallic compounds are stoichiometric compounds, but their compositions are not readily explained in terms of ordinary chemical bonding theory. (Section 24.6)

intermolecular forces The short-range attractive forces operating between the particles that make up the units of a liquid or solid substance. These same forces also cause gases to liquefy or solidify at low temperatures and high pressures. (Chapter 11: Introduction)

internal energy The total energy possessed by a system. When a system undergoes a change, the change in internal energy, ΔE, is defined as the heat, q, added to the system, plus the work, w, done on the system by its surroundings: $\Delta E = q + w$. (Section 5.2)

interstitial hydrides Nonstoichiometric metallic hydrides in which the ratio of metal atoms to hydrogen atoms is neither a ratio of small whole numbers, nor a fixed ratio. (Section 22.3)

ion Electrically charged atom or group of atoms (polyatomic ion); ions can be positively or negatively charged, depending on whether electrons are lost (positive) or gained (negative) by the atoms. (Section 2.5)

ion-dipole force The force that exists between an ion and a neutral polar molecule that possesses a permanent dipole moment. (Section 11.2)

ionic bond A bond formed on the basis of the electrostatic forces that exist between oppositely charged ions. The ions are formed from atoms by transfer of one or more electrons. (Chapter 8: Introduction)

ionic compound A compound composed of cations and anions. (Section 2.5)

ionic hydrides Compounds formed when hydrogen reacts with alkali metals and also the heavier alkaline earths (Ca, Sr, and Ba); these compounds contain the hydride ion, H^-. (Section 22.3)

ionic solids Solids that are composed of ions. (Section 11.8)

ionization energy The energy required to remove an electron from a gaseous atom when the atom is in its ground state. (Section 7.4)

ion pair A combination of a single cation and a single anion. (Section 13.5)

ion-product constant For water, K_w is the product of the aquated hydrogen ion and hydroxide ion concentrations: $[H^+][OH^-] = K_w = 1.0 \times 10^{-14}$ at $25°C$. (Section 16.1)

isoelectronic series A series of atoms, ions, or molecules having the same number of electrons. (Section 8.3)

isolated system A system that does not exchange energy or matter with its surroundings. (Section 19.2)

isomers Compounds whose molecules have the same overall composition but different structures. (Section 25.4)

isotopes Atoms of the same element containing different numbers of neutrons and therefore having different masses. (Section 2.3)

joule (J) The SI unit of energy, 1 kg-m^2/s^2. A related unit is the calorie: 4.184 J = 1 cal. (Section 5.1)

Kelvin scale The absolute temperature scale; the SI unit for temperature is the kelvin. Zero on the Kelvin scale corresponds to $-273.15°C$; therefore, K = °C + 273.15. (Section 1.3)

ketone A compound in which the carbonyl group occurs at the interior of a carbon chain and is therefore flanked by carbon atoms. (Section 26.3)

kinetic energy The energy that an object possesses by virtue of its motion. (Section 5.1)

kinetic-molecular theory A set of assumptions about the nature of gases. These assumptions, when translated into mathematical form, yield the ideal-gas equation. (Section 10.8)

labile complex A complex that exchanges ligands at a rapid rate. (Section 25.5)

lanthanide contraction The gradual decrease in atomic

and ionic radii with increasing atomic number among the lanthanide elements, atomic numbers 58 through 71. The decrease arises because of a gradual increase in effective nuclear charge through the lanthanide series. (Section 24.7)

lattice energy The energy required to separate completely the ions in an ionic solid. (Section 8.2)

law of conservation of mass A scientific law stating that the total mass of the products of a chemical reaction is the same as the total mass of the reactants, so that mass remains constant during the reaction. (Chapter 2: Introduction)

law of constant composition A law that states that the elemental composition of a pure compound is always the same, regardless of its source; also called the **law of definite proportions.** (Section 1.2)

law of definite proportions A law that states that the elemental composition of a pure substance is always the same, regardless of its source; also called the **law of constant composition.** (Section 1.2)

law of mass action The rules according to which the equilibrium constant is expressed in terms of the concentrations of reactants and products, in accordance with the balanced chemical equation for the reaction. (Section 15.2)

leaching The selective dissolution of a desired mineral by passing an aqueous reagent solution through an ore. (Section 24.3)

Le Châtelier's principle A principle stating that when we disturb a system at chemical equilibrium, the relative concentrations of reactants and products shift so as to undo partially the effects of the disturbance. (Section 15.6)

levorotatory, or merely **levo** or **l** A term used to label a chiral molecule that rotates the plane of polarization of plane-polarized light to the left (counterclockwise). (Section 25.4)

Lewis acid An electron-pair acceptor. (Section 16.10)

Lewis base An electron-pair donor. (Section 16.10)

Lewis structure A representation of covalent bonding in a molecule that is drawn using Lewis symbols. Shared electron pairs are shown as lines, and unshared electron pairs are shown as pairs of dots. Only the valence-shell electrons are shown. (Section 8.4)

ligand An ion or molecule that coordinates to a metal atom or to a metal ion to form a complex. (Section 25.1)

lime-soda process A method for removal of Mg^{2+} and Ca^{2+} ions from water to reduce water hardness. The substances added to the water are "lime," CaO [or "slaked lime," $Ca(OH)_2$], and "soda ash," Na_2CO_3, in amounts determined by the concentrations of the undesired ions. (Section 18.6)

limiting reactant (limiting reagent) The reactant present in the smallest stoichiometric quantity in a mixture of reactants; the amount of product that can form is limited by the complete consumption of the limiting reactant. (Section 3.5)

line spectrum A spectrum that contains radiation at only certain specific wavelengths. (Section 6.3)

linkage isomers Structural isomers of coordination compounds in which a ligand differs in its mode of attachment to a metal ion. (Section 25.4)

liquid Matter that has a distinct volume but no specific shape. (Section 1.1)

liquid crystal A substance that exhibits one or more partially ordered liquid phases above the melting point of the solid form. By contrast, in nonliquid crystalline substances the liquid phase that forms upon melting is completely unordered. (Section 12.1)

lithosphere That portion of our environment consisting of the solid earth. (Section 24.1)

lock-and-key model A model of enzyme action in which the substrate molecule is pictured as fitting rather specifically into the active site on the enzyme. It is assumed that in being bound to the active site the substrate is somehow activated for reaction. (Section 14.6)

London dispersion forces Intermolecular forces resulting from attractions between induced dipoles. (Section 11.2)

low-spin complex A complex that has the lowest possible number of unpaired electrons. (Section 25.7)

magic numbers Total numbers of protons and neutrons that result in very stable nuclei. (Section 21.2)

mass A measure of the amount of material in an object. It measures the resistance of an object to being moved. In SI units, mass is measured in kilograms. (Section 1.3)

mass defect The difference between the mass of a nucleus and the total masses of the individual nucleons that it contains. (Section 21.6)

mass number The sum of the number of protons and neutrons in the nucleus of a particular atom. (Section 2.3)

mass percentage The number of grams of solute in each 100 g of solution. (Section 13.1)

mass spectrometer An instrument used to measure the precise masses and relative amounts of atomic and molecular ions. (Section 3.3)

matter Anything that occupies space and has mass; the physical material of the universe. (Section 1.1)

matter waves The term used to describe the wave characteristics of a particle. (Section 6.4)

mean free path The average distance traveled by a gas molecule between collisions. (Section 10.9)

metallic bond Bonding in which the bonding electrons are relatively free to move throughout the three-dimensional structure. (Chapter 8: Introduction)

metallic character The extent to which an element exhibits the physical and chemical properties characteristic of metals, for example, luster, malleability, ductility, and good thermal and electrical conductivity. (Section 7.6)

metallic elements (metals) Elements that are usually solids at room temperature, exhibit high electrical and heat conductivity, and appear lustrous. Most of the elements in the periodic table are metals. (Section 2.4)

metallic hydrides Compounds formed when hydrogen reacts with transition metals; these compounds contain the hydride ion, H^-. (Section 22.3)

metallic solids Solids that are composed of metal atoms. (Section 11.8)

metalloids Elements that lie along the diagonal line separating the metals from the nonmetals in the periodic table; the properties of metalloids are intermediate between those of metals and nonmetals. (Section 2.4)

metallurgy The science of extracting metals from their natural sources by a combination of chemical and physical processes. It is also concerned with the properties and structures of metals and alloys. (Section 24.1)

metathesis reaction A reaction in which two substances react through an exchange of their component ions: $AX + BY \rightarrow AY + BX$; also called a **double displacement reaction**. Precipitation and acid-base neutralization reactions are examples of metathesis reactions. (Section 4.5)

metric system A system of measurement used in science and in most countries. The meter and the gram are examples of metric units. (Section 1.3)

mineral A solid, inorganic substance occurring in nature, such as calcium carbonate, which occurs as calcite. (Section 24.1)

miscible Liquids that mix in all proportions. (Section 13.4)

mixture A combination of two or more substances in which each substance retains its own chemical identity. (Section 1.1)

molal boiling-point-elevation constant (K_b) A constant characteristic of a particular solvent that gives the change in boiling point as a function of solution molality: $\Delta T_b = K_b m$. (Section 13.5)

molal freezing-point-depression constant (K_f) A constant characteristic of a particular solvent that gives the change in freezing point as a function of solution molality: $\Delta T_f = K_f m$. (Section 13.5)

molality The concentration of a solution expressed as moles of solute per kilogram of solvent; abbreviated m. (Section 13.2)

molar heat capacity The heat required to raise the temperature of 1 mol of a substance by $1°C$. (Section 5.7)

molarity The concentration of a solution expressed as moles of solute per liter of solution; abbreviated M. (Section 4.1)

molar mass The mass of 1 mol of a substance in grams; it is numerically equal to the formula weight in atomic mass units. (Section 3.4)

mole A collection of Avogadro's number (6.022×10^{23}) of objects; for example, a mole of H_2O is 6.022×10^{23} H_2O molecules. (Section 3.4)

molecular equation A chemical equation in which the formula for each substance is written without regard for whether it is an electrolyte or a nonelectrolyte. (Section 4.4)

molecular formula A chemical formula that indicates the actual number of atoms of each element in one molecule of a substance. (Section 2.5)

molecular geometry The arrangement in space of the atoms of a molecule. (Section 9.1)

molecular hydrides Compounds formed when hydrogen reacts with nonmetals and metalloids. (Section 22.3)

molecularity The number of molecules that participate as reactants in an elementary reaction. (Section 14.5)

molecular orbital An allowed state for an electron in a

molecule. According to **molecular orbital theory,** a molecular orbital is entirely analogous to an atomic orbital, which is an allowed state for an electron in an atom. A molecular orbital may be classified as σ or π, depending on the disposition of electron density with respect to the internuclear axis. (Section 9.6)

molecular orbital diagram A diagram that shows the energies of molecular orbitals relative to the atomic orbitals from which they are derived; also called an **energy-level diagram.** (Section 9.6)

molecular orbital theory A theory that accounts for the allowed states for electrons in molecules. (Section 9.6)

molecular solids Solids that are composed of molecules. (Section 11.8)

molecular weight The mass of the collection of atoms represented by the chemical formula for a molecule. (Section 3.3)

molecule A chemical combination of two or more atoms. (Section 2.5)

mole fraction The ratio of the number of moles of one component of a mixture to the total moles of all components; abbreviated X, with a subscript to identify the component. (Section 10.6)

momentum The product of the mass, m, and velocity, v, of a particle. (Section 6.4)

monodentate ligand A ligand that binds to the metal ion via a single donor atom. It occupies one position in the coordination sphere. (Section 25.2)

monomers Molecules with low molecular weights, which can be joined together (polymerized) to form a polymer. (Section 12.2)

monosaccharide A simple sugar, most commonly containing six carbon atoms. The joining together of monosaccharide units by condensation reactions results in formation of polysaccharides. (Section 26.6)

multiple bonding Bonding involving two or more electron pairs. (Section 8.4)

natural gas A naturally occurring mixture of gaseous hydrocarbons, compounds composed of hydrogen and carbon. (Section 5.8)

nematic liquid crystal A liquid crystal in which the molecules are aligned in the same general direction, along their long axes, but in which the ends of the molecules are not aligned. (Section 12.1)

Nernst equation An equation that relates the cell emf, E, to the standard emf, $E°$, and the reaction quotient, Q: $E = E° - 2.30RT/n\text{F} \log Q$. (Section 20.6)

net ionic equation A chemical equation for a solution reaction in which soluble strong electrolytes are written as ions and spectator ions are omitted. (Section 4.4)

neutralization reaction A reaction in which an acid and a base react in stoichiometrically equivalent amounts; the neutralization reaction between an acid and a metal hydroxide produces water and a salt. (Section 4.3)

neutron An electrically neutral particle found in the nucleus of an atom; it has approximately the same mass as a proton. (Section 2.3)

noble gases Members of group 8A in the periodic table. (Section 7.8)

nodal surface (node) A locus of points in an atom at which the electron density is zero. For example, the node in a $2s$ orbital (Figure 6.18) is a spherical surface. (Section 6.6)

nonbonding pair In a Lewis structure, a pair of electrons assigned completely to one atom; also called a *lone pair.* (Section 9.1)

nonelectrolyte A substance that does not ionize in water and consequently gives a nonconducting solution. (Section 4.2)

nonmetallic elements (nonmetals) Elements in the upper-right corner of the periodic table; nonmetals differ from metals in their physical and chemical properties. (Section 2.4)

nonpolar bond A covalent bond in which the electrons are shared equally. (Section 8.5)

normal boiling point The temperature at which a liquid boils when the external pressure is 1 atm (that is, the temperature at which the vapor pressure of the liquid is 1 atm). (Section 11.5)

normal melting point The melting point at 1 atm pressure. (Section 11.6)

nuclear binding energy The energy required to decompose an atomic nucleus into its component protons and neutrons. (Section 21.6)

nuclear disintegration series A series of nuclear reactions that begins with an unstable nucleus and terminates with a stable one. Also called a **radioactive series.** (Section 21.2)

nuclear transmutation A conversion of one kind of nucleus to another. (Section 21.3)

nucleic acids Polymers of high molecular weights that carry genetic information and control protein synthesis. (Section 26.7)

nucleon A particle found in the nucleus of an atom. (Section 21.1)

nucleotide Compounds formed from a molecule of phosphoric acid, a sugar molecule, and an organic nitrogen base. Nucleotides form linear polymers called DNA and RNA, which are involved in protein synthesis and cell reproduction. (Section 26.7)

nucleus The very small, very dense, positively charged portion of an atom; it is composed of protons and neutrons. (Section 2.2)

nuclide A nucleus of a specific isotope of an element. (Section 2.3)

octet rule A rule stating that bonded atoms tend to possess or share a total of eight valence-shell electrons. (Section 8.1)

optical isomers Stereoisomers in which the two forms of the compound are nonsuperimposable mirror images. (Section 25.4)

optically active Possessing the ability to rotate the plane of polarized light. (Section 25.4)

orbital An allowed energy state of an electron in the quantum-mechanical model of the atom; the term *orbital* is also used to describe the spatial distribution of the electron. An

orbital is defined by the values of three quantum numbers: n, l, and m_l. (Section 6.5)

orbital diagram A representation of an electron configuration in which each orbital is represented by a box and each electron by a half-arrow. (Section 6.8)

ore A source of a desired element or mineral, usually accompanied by large quantities of other materials such as sand and clay. (Section 24.1)

organic chemistry The study of carbon-containing compounds, typically containing carbon-carbon bonds. (Chapter 26: Introduction)

osmosis The net movement of solvent through a semipermeable membrane toward the solution with greater solute concentration. (Section 13.5)

osmotic pressure The pressure that must be applied to a solution to stop osmosis from pure solvent into the solution. (Section 13.5)

Ostwald process An industrial process used to make nitric acid from ammonia. The NH_3 is catalytically oxidized by O_2 to form NO; NO in air is oxidized to NO_2; HNO_3 is formed in a disproportionation reaction when NO_2 dissolves in water. (Section 22.5)

overall reaction order The sum of the reaction orders of all the reactants appearing in the rate expression. (Section 14.2)

overlap The extent to which atomic orbitals on different atoms share the same region of space. When the overlap between two orbitals is large, a strong bond may be formed. (Section 9.3)

oxidation A process in which a substance loses one or more electrons. (Section 4.6)

oxidation number (oxidation state) A positive or negative whole number assigned to an element in a molecule or ion on the basis of a set of formal rules; to some degree it reflects the positive or negative character of that atom. (Section 8.10)

oxidation-reduction reaction A chemical reaction in which the oxidation states of certain atoms change. (Chapter 20: Introduction)

oxidizing agent or **oxidant** The substance that is reduced and thereby causes the oxidation of some other substance in an oxidation-reduction reaction. (Section 20.1)

oxyacid A compound in which one or more OH groups, and possibly additional oxygen atoms, are bonded to a central atom. (Section 16.9)

oxyanion A polyatomic ion that contains one or more oxygen atoms. (Section 2.6)

ozone The name given to O_3, an allotrope of oxygen. (Section 7.8)

paramagnetism A property that a substance possesses if it contains one or more unpaired electrons. A paramagnetic substance is drawn into a magnetic field. (Section 9.7)

partial pressure The pressure exerted by a particular gas in a mixture. (Section 10.6)

particle accelerator A device that uses strong magnetic and electrostatic fields to accelerate charged particles. (Section 21.3)

parts per million (ppm) The concentration of a solution in grams of solute per 10^6 (million) grams of solution; equals milligrams of solute per liter of solution for aqueous solutions. (Section 13.2)

pascal The SI unit of pressure: $1 \text{ Pa} = 1 \text{ N/m}^2$. (Section 10.2)

Pauli exclusion principle A rule stating that no two electrons in an atom may have the same four quantum numbers (n, l, m_l, and m_s). As a consequence of this principle, there can be no more than two electrons in any one atomic orbital. (Section 6.7)

peptide A substance composed of two or more amino acids. (Section 26.4)

percent yield The ratio of the actual (experimental) yield of a product to its theoretical (calculated) yield, multiplied by 100. (Section 3.5)

periodic table The arrangement of elements in order of increasing atomic number, with elements having similar properties placed in vertical columns. (Section 2.4)

petroleum A naturally occurring combustible liquid composed of hundreds of hydrocarbons and other organic compounds. (Section 5.8)

pH The negative log in base 10 of the aquated hydrogen ion concentration: $pH = -\log[H^+]$. (Section 16.3)

phase change The conversion of a substance from one state of matter to another. The phase changes we consider are *melting* and *freezing* (solid ↔ liquid), *sublimation* and *deposition* (solid ↔ gas), and *vaporization* and *condensation* (liquid ↔ gas). (Section 11.4)

phase diagram A graphic representation of the equilibria among the solid, liquid, and gaseous phases of a substance as a function of temperature and pressure. (Section 11.6)

photochemical smog A complex mixture of undesirable substances produced by the action of sunlight on an urban atmosphere polluted with automobile emissions. The major starting ingredients are nitrogen oxides and organic substances, notably olefins and aldehydes. (Section 18.4)

photodissociation The breaking of a molecule into two or more neutral fragments as a result of absorption of light. (Section 18.2)

photoionization The removal of an electron from an atom or molecule by absorption of light. (Section 18.2)

photon The smallest increment (a *quantum*) of radiant energy; a photon of light with frequency v has an energy equal to hv. (Section 6.2)

photosynthesis The process that occurs in plant leaves by which light energy is used to convert CO_2 and water to carbohydrates and oxygen. (Section 25.2)

physical changes Changes (such as a phase change) that occur with no change in chemical composition. (Section 1.1)

physical properties Properties that can be measured without changing the composition of a substance, for example, color and freezing point. (Section 1.1)

pi (π) bond A covalent bond in which electron density is concentrated above and below the line joining the bonded atoms. (Section 9.3)

piezoelectric material   A crystalline substance that generates an electric potential along its length when subjected to a mechanical stress. Quartz is a well-known piezoelectric material. (Section 12.3)

pi (π) molecular orbital   A molecular orbital that concentrates the electron density on opposite sides of a line that passes through the nuclei. (Section 9.7)

plastic   A material that can be formed into particular shapes by application of heat and pressure. (Section 12.2)

plasticizers   Organic molecules added to a polymer to reduce the intermolecular interactions between polymer chains. The effect of the plasticizer is to make the material more pliable. (Section 12.2)

polar covalent bond   A covalent bond in which the electrons are not shared equally. (Section 8.5)

polarizability   The ease with which the electron cloud of an atom or a molecule is distorted by an outside influence, thereby inducing a dipole moment. (Section 11.2)

polar molecule   A molecule that possesses a nonzero dipole moment. (Section 9.2)

polyatomic ion   An electrically charged group of two or more atoms. (Section 2.5)

polydentate ligand   A ligand in which two or more donor atoms can coordinate to the same metal ion. (Section 25.2)

polymer   A large molecule of high molecular mass, formed by the joining together, or *polymerization,* of a large number of molecules of low molecular mass. The individual molecules forming the polymer are called *monomers.* (Section 12.2)

polypeptide   A polymer of amino acids that has a molecular weight of less than 10,000. (Section 26.4)

polyprotic acid   A substance capable of ionizing more than one proton in water; H_2SO_4 is an example. (Section 16.5)

polysaccharide   A substance made up of several monosaccharide units joined together. (Section 26.6)

porphyrin   A complex derived from the porphine molecule. (Section 25.2)

positron   A particle with the same mass as an electron but with a positive charge, symbol $^0_1 e$. (Section 21.1)

potential energy   The energy that an object possesses as a result of its composition or its position with respect to another object. (Section 5.1)

precipitate   An insoluble substance that forms in, and separates from, a solution. (Section 4.5)

precipitation reaction   A reaction that occurs between substances in solution in which one of the products is insoluble. (Section 4.5)

precision   The closeness of agreement among several measurements of the same quantity; the reproducibility of a measurement. (Section 1.4)

pressure   A measure of the force exerted on a unit area. In chemistry, pressure is often expressed in units of atmospheres (atm) or torr: 760 torr = 1 atm; in SI units, pressure is expressed in pascals (Pa). (Section 10.2)

primary structure   The sequence of amino acids along a protein chain. (Section 26.4)

primitive cubic cell   A cubic unit cell in which the lattice points are at the corners only. (Section 11.7)

probability density (ψ^2)   A value that represents the probability that an electron will be found at a given point in space. (Section 6.5)

product   A substance produced in a chemical reaction; it appears to the right of the arrow in a chemical equation. (Section 3.1)

protein   A biopolymer formed from amino acids. (Section 26.4)

protium   The most common isotope of hydrogen: $^1_1 H$. (Section 22.3)

proton   A positively charged subatomic particle found in the nucleus of an atom. (Section 2.3)

pure substance   Matter that has a fixed composition and distinct properties. (Section 1.1)

pyrometallurgy   A process in which heat converts a mineral in an ore from one chemical form to another and eventually to the free metal. (Section 24.2)

qualitative analysis   The determination of the presence or absence of a particular substance in a mixture. (Section 17.6)

quantitative analysis   The determination of the amount of a given substance that is present in a sample. (Section 17.6)

quantum   The smallest increment of radiant energy that may be absorbed or emitted; the magnitude of radiant energy is $h\nu$. (Section 6.2)

racemic mixture   A mixture of equal amounts of the dextrorotatory and levorotatory forms of a chiral molecule. A racemic mixture will not rotate polarized light. (Section 25.4)

rad   A measure of the energy absorbed from radiation by tissue or other biological material; 1 rad = transfer of 1×10^{-2} J of energy per kilogram of material. (Section 21.9)

radioactive series   A series of nuclear reactions that begins with an unstable nucleus and terminates with a stable one. Also called **nuclear disintegration series.** (Section 21.2)

radioactivity   The spontaneous disintegration of an unstable atomic nucleus with accompanying emission of radiation. (Section 2.21; Chapter 21: Introduction)

radioisotope   An isotope that is radioactive; that is, it is undergoing nuclear changes with emission of radiation. (Section 21.1)

radionuclide   A radioactive nuclide. (Section 21.1)

radiotracer   A radioisotope that can be used to trace the path of an element. (Section 21.5)

Raoult's law   A law stating that the partial pressure of a solvent over a solution, P_A, is given by the vapor pressure of the pure solvent, P_A°, times the mole fraction of solvent in the solution, $X_A: P_A = X_A P_A^\circ$. (Section 13.5)

rare-earth (lanthanide) element   Element in which the $4f$ subshell is only partially occupied. (Section 6.8)

rate constant   A constant of proportionality between the reaction rate and the concentrations of reactants that appear in the rate law. (Section 14.2)

rate-determining step The slowest elementary step in a reaction mechanism. (Section 14.5)

rate law An equation that relates the reaction rate to the concentrations of reactants (and sometimes of products also). (Section 14.2)

reactant A starting substance in a chemical reaction; it appears to the left of the arrow in a chemical equation. (Section 3.1)

reaction mechanism A detailed picture, or model, of how the reaction occurs; that is, the order in which bonds are broken and formed, and the changes in relative positions of the atoms as the reaction proceeds. (Section 14.5)

reaction order The power to which the concentration of a reactant is raised in a rate law. (Section 14.2)

reaction quotient (Q) The value that is obtained when concentrations of reactants and products are inserted into the equilibrium expression. If the concentrations are equilibrium concentrations, $Q = K$; otherwise $Q \neq K$. (Section 15.5)

reaction rate The decrease in concentration of a reactant or the increase in concentration of a product with time. (Section 14.1)

reducing agent or **reductant** The substance that is oxidized and thereby causes the reduction of some other substance in an oxidation-reduction reaction. (Section 20.1)

reduction A process in which a substance gains one or more electrons. (Section 4.6)

refining The process of converting an impure form of a metal into a more usable substance of well-defined composition. For example, crude pig iron from the blast furnace is refined in a converter to produce steels of desired compositions. (Section 24.2)

relative biological effectiveness (RBE) An adjustment factor used to convert rads to rems; it accounts for differences in biological effects of different particles having the same energy. (Section 21.9)

rem A measure of the biological damage caused by radiation; rems = rads × RBE. (Section 21.9)

representative (main-group) element Element in which the *s* and *p* orbitals are partially occupied. (Section 6.9)

resonance structures (resonance forms) Individual Lewis structures in cases where two or more Lewis structures are equally good descriptions of a single molecule. The resonance structures in such an instance are "averaged" to give a correct description of the real molecule. (Section 8.7)

reverse osmosis The process by which water molecules move under high pressure through a semipermeable membrane from the more concentrated to the less concentrated solution. (Section 18.5)

ribonucleic acid (RNA) A polynucleotide in which ribose is the sugar component. (Section 26.7)

roasting Thermal treatment of an ore to bring about chemical reactions involving the furnace atmosphere. For example, a sulfide ore might be roasted in air to form a metal oxide and SO_2. (Section 24.2)

root-mean-square (rms) speed (u) The square root of the average of the squared speeds of the gas molecules in a gas sample. (Section 10.8)

rotational motion Movement of a molecule as though it is spinning like a top. (Section 19.3)

salinity A measure of the salt content of seawater, brine, or brackish water. It is equal to the mass in grams of dissolved salts present in 1 kg of seawater. (Section 18.5)

salt An ionic compound formed by replacing one or more H^+ of an acid by other cations. (Section 4.3)

saponification Hydrolysis of an ester in the presence of a base. (Section 26.3)

saturated solution A solution in which undissolved solute and dissolved solute are in equilibrium. (Section 13.3)

scientific law A concise verbal statement or a mathematical equation that summarizes a broad variety of observations and experiences. (Section 1.1)

scientific method The general process of advancing scientific knowledge by making experimental observations and by formulating laws, hypotheses, and theories. (Section 1.1)

scintillation counter An instrument that is used to detect and measure radiation by the fluorescence it produces in a fluorescing medium. (Section 21.5)

screening effect The effect of inner electrons in decreasing the nuclear charge experienced by outer electrons. (Section 6.7)

secondary structure The manner in which a protein is coiled or stretched. (Section 26.4)

second law of thermodynamics A statement of our experience that there is a direction to the way events occur in nature. When a process occurs spontaneously in one direction, it is nonspontaneous in the reverse direction. It is possible to state the second law in many different forms, but they all relate back to the same idea about spontaneity. One of the most common statements found in chemical contexts is that in any spontaneous process the entropy of the universe increases. (Section 19.1)

second-order reaction A reaction in which the overall reaction order (the sum of the concentration-term exponents) in the rate law is 2. (Section 14.3)

sigma (σ) bond A covalent bond in which electron density is concentrated along the internuclear axis. (Section 9.5)

sigma (σ) molecular orbital A molecular orbital that centers the electron density about an imaginary line passing through two nuclei. (Section 9.6)

significant figures The digits that indicate the precision with which a measurement is made; all digits of a measured quantity are significant, including the last digit, which is uncertain. (Section 1.4)

silicates Compounds containing silicon and oxygen, structurally based on SiO_4 tetrahedra. (Section 23.5)

single bond A covalent bond involving one electron pair. (Section 8.4)

SI units The preferred metric units for use in science. (Section 1.3)

slag A mixture of molten silicate minerals. Slags may be acidic or basic, according to the acidity or basicity of the oxide added to silica. (Section 24.2)

smectic liquid crystal A liquid crystal in which the molecules are aligned along their long axes and arranged in sheets, with the ends of the molecules aligned. There are several different kinds of smectic phases. (Section 12.1)

smelting A melting process in which the materials formed in the course of the chemical reactions that occur separate into two or more layers. For example, the layers might be slag and molten metal. (Section 24.2)

sol-gel process A process in which extremely small particles (0.003 to 0.1 μm in diameter) of uniform size are produced in a series of chemical steps followed by controlled heating. (Section 12.3)

solid Matter that has both a definite shape and a definite volume. (Section 1.1)

solubility The amount of a substance that dissolves in a given quantity of solvent at a given temperature to form a saturated solution. (Sections 4.5, 13.3)

solubility-product constant (K_{sp}) An equilibrium constant related to the equilibrium between a solid salt and its ions in solution. It provides a quantitative measure of the solubility of a slightly soluble salt. (Section 17.4)

solute A substance dissolved in a solvent to form a solution; it is normally the component of a solution present in the smaller amount. (Section 4.1)

solution A mixture of substances that has a uniform composition; a homogeneous mixture. (Section 1.1)

solution alloy A homogeneous alloy, with the components distributed uniformly throughout. (Section 24.6)

solvation The clustering of solvent molecules around a solute particle. (Section 13.1)

solvent The dissolving medium of a solution; it is normally the component of a solution present in the greater amount. (Section 4.1)

somatic damage Damage to living systems that affects an organism during its own lifetime. (Section 21.9)

specific heat (specific heat capacity) The heat capacity of 1 g of a substance; the heat required to raise the temperature of 1 g of a substance by 1°C. (Section 5.5)

spectator ions Ions that go through a reaction unchanged and that appear on both sides of the complete ionic equation. (Section 4.4)

spectrochemical series A list of ligands arranged in order of their abilities to split the d-orbital energies (using the terminology of the crystal-field model). (Section 25.7)

spectrum The distribution among various wavelengths of the radiant energy emitted or absorbed by an object. (Section 6.2)

spin-pairing energy The energy required to pair an electron with another electron occupying an orbital. (Section 25.7)

spontaneous process A process that is capable of proceeding in a given direction, as written or described, without needing to be driven by an outside source of energy. A process may be spontaneous even though it is very slow. (Section 19.1)

sputtering A method for forming thin films in which the material that is to form the film is made the cathode in a high-voltage gaseous discharge of an inert gas. (Section 12.4)

standard atmospheric pressure Defined as 760 torr or, in SI units, 101.325 kPa. (Section 10.2)

standard electrode potential $(E°)$ The reduction potential of a half-reaction with all solution species at 1 M concentration and all gaseous species at 1 atm pressure. Standard electrode potentials are measured relative to the standard hydrogen electrode, for which $E° = 0$ V. (Section 20.4)

standard emf, also called the **standard cell potential** $(E°)$ The emf of a cell when all reagents are at standard conditions at 25°C. (Section 20.4)

standard enthalpy of formation $(\Delta H_f°)$ The change in enthalpy that accompanies the formation of 1 mol of a substance from its elements, with all substances in their standard states. (Section 5.7)

standard free energy of formation $(\Delta G_f°)$ The change in free energy associated with the formation of a substance from its elements under standard conditions. (Section 19.5)

standard hydrogen electrode An electrode based on the half-reaction $2H^+$ $(1 M) + 2e^- \rightarrow H_2$ (1 atm). The standard electrode potential of the standard hydrogen electrode is defined as 0 V. (Section 20.4)

standard oxidation potential $(E_{ox}°)$ The potential of an oxidation half-reaction under standard conditions, measured relative to the standard hydrogen electrode. (Section 20.4)

standard reduction potential $(E_{red}°)$ The potential of a reduction half-reaction under standard conditions, measured relative to the standard hydrogen electrode. A standard reduction potential is also called a **standard electrode potential.** (Section 20.4)

standard solution A solution of known concentration. (Section 4.7)

standard state Pure material in the physical state (gas, liquid, or solid) most stable at the temperature in question (usually 25°C) and under 1 atm pressure. (Section 5.7)

standard temperature and pressure (STP) Defined as 0°C and 1 atm pressure; frequently used as reference conditions for a gas. (Section 10.4)

starch The general name given to a group of polysaccharides that act as energy-storage substances in plants. (Section 26.6)

state function A property of a system that is determined by the state or condition of the system and not by how it got to that state; its value is fixed when temperature, pressure, composition, and physical form are specified; P, V, T, E, and H are state functions. (Section 5.2)

stereoisomers Compounds possessing the same formula and bonding arrangement but differing in the spatial arrangements of the atoms. (Section 25.4)

stoichiometry The relationships among the quantities of reactants and products involved in chemical reactions. (Chapter 3: Introduction)

stratosphere The region of the atmosphere directly above the troposphere. (Section 18.1)

strong acid An acid that ionizes completely in water. (Section 4.3)

strong base A base that ionizes completely in water. (Section 4.3)

strong electrolyte A substance that is completely ionized in solution, for example, strong acids, strong bases, and most salts. (Section 4.2)

structural formula A formula that shows not only the number and kind of atoms in the molecule but also the arrangement of the atoms. (Section 2.5)

structural isomers Compounds possessing the same formula but differing in the bonding arrangements of the atoms. (Sections 25.4 and 26.1)

subshell One or more orbitals with the same set of quantum numbers n and l. For example, we speak of the $2p$ subshell ($n = 2$, $l = 1$), which is composed of three orbitals ($2p_x$, $2p_y$, and $2p_z$). (Section 6.5)

substrate A substance that undergoes a reaction at the active site in an enzyme. (Section 14.6)

superconducting ceramic A complex metal oxide that undergoes a transition to a superconducting state at a low temperature. (Section 12.3)

superconducting transition temperature (T_c) The temperature below which a substance exhibits superconductivity. (Section 12.3)

superconductivity The "frictionless" flow of electrons that occurs when a substance loses all resistance to the flow of electrical current. (Section 12.3)

supercritical mass An amount of fissionable material larger than the critical mass. (Section 21.7)

supersaturated solutions Solutions containing more solute than a saturated solution. (Section 13.3)

surface tension The intermolecular, cohesive attraction that causes a liquid to minimize its surface area. (Section 11.3)

surroundings In thermodynamics, everything that lies outside the system that we study. (Section 5.1)

syngas A mixture of gases, mainly H_2 and CO, that results from heating coal in the presence of steam; the mixture can be used as a fuel or for synthesis of other substances. (Section 5.8)

system In thermodynamics, the portion of the universe that we single out for study: We must be careful to state exactly what the system contains and what transfers of energy it may have with its surroundings. (Section 5.1)

termolecular reaction An elementary reaction that involves three molecules. (Section 14.5)

tertiary structure The overall shape of a large protein, specifically, the manner in which sections of the protein fold back upon themselves or intertwine. (Section 26.5)

theoretical yield The quantity of product that is calculated to form when all of the limiting reagent reacts. (Section 3.5)

theory A tested model or explanation of the general principles of certain phenomena. (Section 1.1)

thermistor A ceramic material whose electric resistance decreases in a regular, reproducible manner with increasing temperature. (Section 12.3)

thermochemistry The relationship between chemical reactions and energy changes. (Chapter 5: Introduction)

thermodynamics The study of energy and its transformation. (Chapter 5: Introduction)

thermonuclear reaction Another name for fusion reactions, reactions in which two light nuclei are joined to form a more massive one. (Section 21.8)

thermoplastic A polymeric material that can be readily reshaped by application of heat and pressure. (Section 12.2)

thermosetting plastic A plastic that, once formed in a particular mold, is not readily reshaped by application of heat and pressure. (Section 12.2)

thin film A film deposited on an underlying substrate to provide decoration or protection from chemical attack or to enhance a desirable property, such as reflectivity, electrical conductivity, color, or hardness. (Section 12.4)

third law of thermodynamics A law stating that the entropy of a pure, crystalline solid at absolute zero temperature is zero: $S(0\ \mathrm{K}) = 0$. (Section 19.3)

titration The process of reacting a solution of unknown concentration with one of known concentration (a standard solution). (Section 4.7)

titration curve A graph of pH as a function of added titrant. (Section 17.2)

torr A unit of pressure (1 torr = 1 mm Hg). (Section 10.2)

transition metals Elements in which the d orbitals are partially occupied; also called **transition elements.** (Section 6.9)

transition state (activated complex) The particular arrangement of reactant and product molecules at the point of maximum energy in the rate-determining step of a reaction. (Section 14.4)

translational motion Movement in which an entire molecule moves in a definite direction. (Section 19.3)

transuranium elements Elements that follow uranium in the periodic table. (Section 21.3)

triple bond A covalent bond involving three electron pairs. (Section 8.4)

triple point The temperature at which solid, liquid, and gas phases coexist in equilibrium. (Section 11.6)

tritium The isotope of hydrogen whose nucleus contains a proton and two neutrons: ${}_1^3\mathrm{H}$. (Section 22.3)

troposphere The region of earth's atmosphere extending from the surface to about 12 km altitude. (Section 18.1)

Tyndall effect The scattering of a beam of visible light by the particles in a colloidal dispersion. (Section 13.6)

uncertainty principle A principle stating there is an inherent uncertainty in the precision with which we can simultaneously specify the position and momentum of a particle. This uncertainty is significant only for extremely small particles, such as electrons. (Section 6.4)

unimolecular reaction An elementary reaction that involves a single molecule. (Section 14.5)

unit cell The smallest portion of a crystal that reproduces the structure of the entire crystal when repeated in different directions in space. It is the repeating unit or "building block" of the crystal lattice. (Section 11.7)

unsaturated solutions Solutions containing less solute than a saturated solution. (Section 13.3)

vacuum deposition A method of forming thin films in which a substance is sublimed at high temperature without decomposition and then deposited on the object to be coated. (Section 12.4)

valence bond theory A model of chemical bonding in which an electron-pair bond is formed between two atoms by the overlap of orbitals on the two atoms. (Section 9.3)

valence electrons The outermost electrons of an atom; these are the ones the atom uses in bonding. (Sections 6.8 and 8.1)

valence orbitals Orbitals that contain the outer-shell electrons of an atom. (Chapter 7: Introduction)

valence-shell electron-pair repulsion (VSEPR) model A model that accounts for the geometric arrangements of shared and unshared electron pairs around a central atom in terms of the repulsions between electron pairs. (Section 9.1)

van der Waals equation An equation of state for nonideal gases that is based on adding corrections to the ideal-gas equation. The correction terms account for intermolecular forces of attraction and for the volumes occupied by the gas molecules themselves. (Section 10.10)

vapor Gaseous state of any substance that normally exists as a liquid or solid. (Section 10.1)

vapor pressure The pressure exerted by a vapor in equilibrium with its liquid or solid phase. (Section 11.5)

vibrational motion Movement of the atoms within a molecule in which they move periodically toward and away from one another. (Section 19.3)

viscosity A measure of the resistance of fluids to flow. (Section 11.3)

volatile Tending to evaporate readily. (Section 11.5)

voltaic (galvanic) cell A device in which a spontaneous oxidation-reduction reaction occurs with the passage of electrons through an external circuit. (Section 20.3)

water gas A mixture of H_2 and CO produced by passing steam through a bed of hot carbon. (Section 22.3)

wave function A mathematical description of an allowed energy state (an *orbital*) for an electron in the quantum-mechanical model of the atom; it is usually symbolized by the Greek letter ψ. (Section 6.5)

wavelength The distance between identical points on successive waves. (Section 6.1)

weak acid An acid that only partly ionizes in water. (Section 4.3)

weak base A base that only partly ionizes in water. (Section 4.3)

weak electrolyte A substance that only partly ionizes in solution. (Section 4.2)

work The movement of an object against some force. (Section 5.1)

X-ray diffraction The scattering of X-rays by the units of a regular crystalline solid. The scattering patterns obtained can be used to deduce the arrangements of particles in the crystal. (Section 11.7)

Index

Length, 13
   bond, 273–75, 298
Leukemia, 797
Levorotatory isomer, 939
Lewis, Gilbert N., 218, 251, 259, 605
Lewis acids and bases, 603–7, 647
   hydrolysis of metal ions, 606–7
   metal ions as, 647–49
Lewis structures, 259–60, 263–65, 286
   formal charge and, 266
Lewis symbols, 251
Life, entropy and, 698
Ligand(s). *See also* Complex ions (complexes)
   bidentate, 926
   chelates, 925–32
      metals and, 928–32
      stability of, 927
   common, 933
   defined, 922
   iron-binding, 930
   ligand-exchange rates, 939–40
   monodentate, 925
   polydentate, 925, 926
   strong-field, 946
   weak-field, 946
Light
   absorption of, 323
   wave nature of, 175–78
Lime, 4
Lime-soda process, 685
Limestone, 74, 673–74, 837–38, 891, 892
Linear geometry, 291, 294
Line spectrum, 184
Linkage isomerism, 935
Liquid(s)
   characteristic properties of, 372
   defined, 3–5
   kinetic-molecular description of, 372–73
   state changes, 383–87
   surface tension of, 382–83
   vapor pressure, 387–91
      boiling point and, 389–91
      molecular level explanation of, 388–89
      volatility, temperature and, 389
   viscosity of, 382
Liquid-crystal displays (LCDs), 420
Liquid crystals, 415–21
Liter (L), 15
Lithium
   electron configuration of, 201, 202
   molecular orbitals for, 318–19
Lithosphere, 886
Litmus, 115, 578
Living systems, 928–32
   iron in, 929, 930–31
Lock-and-key model, 522, 523
Logarithm, negative, 575, 577
London, Fritz, 375
London dispersion forces, 375–77, 381, 451
Lone pairs, 288
Los Alamos National Laboratory, 793
Low-density polyethylene (LDPE), 426
Lowest unoccupied molecular orbital (LUMO), 323
Lowry, Thomas, 571

Low-spin complex, 948–49
Lysine, 604

Macromolecules, 425
Macroscopic world, 33
Magic numbers, 776
Magnesium, 236, 756
Magnesium metal, oxidation of, 125
Magnetic field, diatomic molecules' behavior in, 321–25
Magnetic quantum number, 190
Magnetic resonance imaging (MRI), 200–201
Magnetism, 911–12, 942
Main-group (representative) elements, 205
Malachite, 888
Malignant tumors, 800
Malleability, 900
Maltose, 988
Mammoth Cave, Kentucky, 838
Manhattan Project, 793
Manometers, 335–37
Many-electron atoms, 195–99
Marconi, Guglielmo, 666
Marsden, Ernest, 39
Mass, 13
   average atomic, 76
   conservation of, 35, 68
   critical, 791–92
   of electron, 37
   energy and, 789–90
   interconverting moles to, 82–84
   molar, 80–82, 475–76
   supercritical, 792–94
Mass action, law of, 538
Mass defect (difference), 786–88
Mass number, 43, 770
Mass percentage, 454
Mass spectrometer, 78
Mass spectrum, 78
Matter, 2–9
   atomic theory of, 33–35
   classification of, 9
   conservation of, 35, 68
   defined, 3
   mixtures, 6–9
   physical and chemical changes, 5–6
   physical and chemical properties of, 5
   states of, 3, 391–93
   substances, 5
Matter waves, 187
Mauveine, 323
Maxwell-Boltzmann distributions, 703
Mean free path, 358–59
Measurement
   uncertainty in, 19–23
      precision and accuracy, 19–20
      significant figures, 20–23
   uncertainty principle and, 188
   units of, 11–19
      density, 16
      derived SI units, 15
      intensive and extensive properties, 19
      length and mass, 13
      SI units, 11–13
      temperature, 13–14
      volume, 15
Medical applications of radiotracers, 787

Medium steels, 905
Meissner effect, 435
Meitner, Lise, 793
Melamine, 430
Melting, 384
Melting points, 229–30, 374, 392
Mendeleev, Dmitri, 217–18
Meniscus, 383
Mercury, mass spectrum of, 78
Mesosphere, 663
Metabolism, 91
Metal(s), 45, 46, 227–29. *See also* Transition metals
   active, 127, 232–37
      hydrogen reaction with, 238
   activity series of, 737
   alkali, 46, 205
   alkaline earth, 46, 205
   alloys, 129, 885, 888, 905–6
   chelates and, 928–32
   f-block, 205–6
   occurrence and distribution of, 886–89
   oxidation state of, 937
   physical properties of, 900
   qualitative analysis for, 651–54
   reactions of, 124–28
      activity series and, 126–28, 737
      oxidation and reduction, 124–25
      oxidation of metals by acids and salts, 125–26
   as strategic materials, 889
Metal hydrides, 600
Metal ions, 922. *See also* Complex ions (complexes)
   alkali, 652
   as Lewis acids, 647–49
Metallic bonds, 250, 251, 899–904
   electron-sea model for, 901
   molecular-orbital model (band theory) for, 901–4
Metallic character, 231–32
Metallic elements. *See* Metal(s)
Metallic hydrides, 817, 818
Metallic solids, 405–6
Metalloids, 45, 46
Metallurgy
   defined, 888–89
   electrometallurgy, 895–99
      of aluminum, 896–97
      electrorefining of copper, 897–98
      of sodium, 896
   hydrometallurgy, 894–95
   metallic bonding, 250, 251, 899–904
      electron-sea model for, 901
      molecular-orbital model (band theory) for, 901–4
   pyrometallurgy, 890–94
      of iron, 891–93
      steel formation, 893–94
Metal oxides, 18, 228–29, 278, 522, 823
   ionic, 580
Metaperiodic acid, 858
Metathesis reactions, 117–24
   precipitation reactions, 118
   solubility rules, 118–20
   in which gas forms, 121–24
   in which weak electrolyte or nonelectrolyte forms, 120–21

PHYSICAL AND CHEMICAL CONSTANTS

Atomic mass unit	$1\ \text{amu} = 1.6605402 \times 10^{-27}\ \text{kg}$
	$6.0221367 \times 10^{23}\ \text{amu} = 1\ \text{g}$
Avogadro's number	$N = 6.0221367 \times 10^{23}/\text{mol}$
Boltzmann's constant	$k = 1.38066 \times 10^{-23}\ \text{J/K}$
Electron rest mass	$m_e = 5.485799 \times 10^{-4}\ \text{amu}$
	$= 9.1093897 \times 10^{-28}\ \text{g}$
Electronic charge	$e = 1.60217733 \times 10^{-19}\ \text{C}$
Faraday's constant	$\mathcal{F} = Ne = 9.6485309 \times 10^4\ \text{C/mol}$
Gas constant	$R = Nk = 8.3145\ \text{J/K-mol}$
	$= 0.082058\ \text{L-atm/K-mol}$
Neutron rest mass	$m_n = 1.00866\ \text{amu}$
	$= 1.67495 \times 10^{-24}\ \text{g}$
Pi	$\pi = 3.1415926536$
Planck's constant	$h = 6.6260755 \times 10^{-34}\ \text{J-s}$
Proton rest mass	$m_p = 1.0072765\ \text{amu}$
	$= 1.672623 \times 10^{-24}\ \text{g}$
Speed of light (in vacuum)	$c = 2.997925 \times 10^8\ \text{m/s}$

COMMON IONS

Positive ions (Cations)

1+

Ammonium (NH_4^+)
Cesium (Cs^+)
Copper (I) or cuprous (Cu^+)
Hydrogen (H^+)
Lithium (Li^+)
Potassium (K^+)
Silver (Ag^+)
Sodium (Na^+)

2+

Barium (Ba^{2+})
Cadmium (Cd^{2+})
Calcium (Ca^{2+})
Chromium(II) or chromous (Cr^{2+})
Cobalt(II) or cobaltous (Co^{2+})
Copper(II) or cupric (Cu^{2+})
Iron(II) or ferrous (Fe^{2+})
Lead(II) or plumbous (Pb^{2+})
Magnesium (Mg^{2+})
Manganese(II) or manganous (Mn^{2+})
Mercury(I) or mercurous (Hg_2^{2+})
Mercury(II) or mercuric (Hg^{2+})
Strontium (Sr^{2+})
Nickel (Ni^{2+})
Tin(II) or stannous (Sn^{2+})
Zinc (Zn^{2+})

3+

Aluminum (Al^{3+})
Chromium(III) or chromic (Cr^{3+})
Iron(III) or ferric (Fe^{3+})

Negative ions (Anions)

1–

Acetate ($C_2H_3O_2^-$)
Bromide (Br^-)
Chlorate (ClO_3^-)
Chloride (Cl^-)
Cyanide (CN^-)
Dihydrogen phosphate ($H_2PO_4^-$)
Fluoride (F^-)
Hydride (H^-)
Hydrogen carbonate or bicarbonate (HCO_3^-)
Hydrogen sulfite or bisulfite (HSO_3^-)
Hydroxide (OH^-)
Iodide (I^-)
Nitrate (NO_3^-)
Nitrite (NO_2^-)
Perchlorate (ClO_4^-)
Permanganate (MnO_4^-)
Thiocyanate (SCN^-)

2–

Carbonate (CO_3^{2-})
Chromate (CrO_4^{2-})
Dichromate ($Cr_2O_7^{2-}$)
Hydrogen phosphate (HPO_4^{2-})
Oxide (O^{2-})
Peroxide (O_2^{2-})
Sulfate (SO_4^{2-})
Sulfide (S^{2-})
Sulfite (SO_3^{2-})

3–

Arsenate (AsO_4^{3-})
Phosphate (PO_4^{3-})